The Hotel Guide 2007

CLASSIC
BRITISH HOTELS

Save up to 40%
off two-night breaks

Stay at any one of over 50 quality, independent 3, 4 & 5 star Classic British Hotels throughout the UK. Most of our hotels have AA rosettes for fine dining. Save as much as 40% with our best available prices. (These may change daily depending on demand.) What's more, as a 2007 AA Guide owner, you will receive an additional 10% off the best available price. You can add anything from champagne to a round of golf or an invigorating massage when making your booking.

To book go to
www.classicbritishhotels.com,
enter your unique code AA07 in the
'Sign In' box and click 'Go'

Or call our Reservations Centre on 0870 241 8732 and quote AA07. To qualify you must show a 2007 AA Guide on check-in at the hotel .

1) Prices are based on 2 people sharing a double/twin room for a minimum of 2 nights. **2)** Offer applies to new bookings only on the best available price to the general public and cannot be used in conjunction with any other offer including Hot Classic Offers or packages. **3)** Offer excludes Valentine's, Bank Holiday weekends, Christmas & New Year and is subject to availability. **4)** Offer is valid until 21st December 2007. **5)** Must show a 2007 AA Guide on check-in. **6)** This offer is only valid on bookings made via www.classicbritishhotels.com or the Classic Reservations Centre (Open from 8 am – 8 pm Monday – Friday, 9 am - 5 pm Saturday and 10 am – 4 pm Sunday).

40th edition September 2006 First published by the Automobile Association as the Hotel and Restaurant Guide, 1967
© Automobile Association Developments Limited 2006.

The AA strives to ensure accuracy of the information in this guide at the time of printing. Due to the constantly evolving nature of the subject matter the information is subject to change. The AA will gratefully receive any advice from our readers of any necessary updated information. Please contact:

Advertising Sales Department: advertisingsales@theAA.com
Editorial Department: lifestyleguides@theAA.com
AA Hotel Scheme Enquiries: 01256 844455

Cover photographs courtesy of: Hand Picked Hotels
(Norton House Hotel & Restaurant)
Letter and tafiff on page 16 reproduced courtesy of
Netherwood Hotel, Grange-over-Sands
Typeset/Repro: Servis Filmsetting Ltd, Manchester
Printed and bound in Spain by Printer Industria Grafica S.A., Barcelona
Directory compiled by the AA Hotel Services Department and generated from the AA establishment database.
www.theAA.com
Published by AA Publishing, a trading name of Automobile Association Developments Limited, whose registered office is Fanum House, Basing View, Basingstoke, Hampshire RG21 4EA. Registered number 1878835
A CIP catalogue record for this book is available from the British Library
ISBN-10: 0-7495-4919-X
ISBN-13: 978-0-7495-4919-0
A02826

Contents

④

❶ **BEDFORD**　　　　　　　　　**MAP 12 TL04**

❷
❸ ★★★70% ◉◉ **HOTEL**

❺ ## Woodlands Manor
❼ Green Ln, Clapham MK41 6EP
☎ 01234 363281 📠 01234 272390
e-mail: admin@woodlandsmanorhotel.com
web: www.signaturegroup.co.uk

 ❻

❽ *dir:* A6 towards Kettering. Clapham 1st village N of town centre. On entering village 1st right into Green Lane, Manor 200mtrs

❾

❿ Sitting in acres of well-tended grounds, this Victorian manor offers a warm welcome. Bedrooms are spacious and provide a variety of thoughtful extras. Traditional public areas include a cosy bar and a smart restaurant, where award-winning food is served.

⓫ **Rooms** 29 en suite 3 annexe en suite (4 fmly) (9 GF) S £75-£140;
⓬ D £85-£150 (incl. bkfst) **Facilities** STV Wi-fi available Xmas **Conf** Thtr 80
Class 40 Board 40 from £135 **Parking** 100 **Notes** LB ⊗ in restaurant
⓭ Civ Wed 86
⓮

❶ **Location** Town listed alphabetically within county

❷ **Grading** Hotels are listed in star rating and merit score order within each location
★ Star rating (see page 8),
% Merit score (see page 6),
◉ Rosette award (see page 9).

❸ **Type of Hotel** (see page 9)

❹ **Map reference** Map page number followed by a 2-figure National Grid reference (see page 7)

❺ **Hotel Name** Where the name appears in italic type the information that follows has not been confirmed by the establishment for 2007

❻ **Hotel logo** If a symbol appears here it represents a hotel group or consortium (See pages 29-37)

❼ **Address and contact details**

❽ **Directions** Brief details of how to find the hotel

❾ **Picture** Optional photograph supplied by establishment

❿ **Description** Written by the AA inspector at the time of visit

⓫ **Rooms** Number of rooms and prices (see page 6)

⓬ **Facilities** Additional facilities including those for children and for leisure

⓭ **Conference** Conference facilities as available (see page 7)

⓮ **Notes** Additional information (see pages 5-7)

Key to Symbols
and abbreviations

★	Black stars (see page 8)
★	Red stars – indicate AA Inspectors' Choice (see page 9)
◉	AA Rosettes – indicate an AA award for food (see page 9)
%	Inspector's Merit score (see page 6)
A	Associate Hotels (see page 9)
○	Hotel due to open during the currency of the guide
U	Star rating not confirmed
Fmly	Number of family rooms available
GF	Ground floors rooms available
⊗	No smoking in area indicated
S	Single room
D	Double room
fr	From
incl. bkfst	Breakfast included in the price
FTV	Freeview
STV	Satellite television
Wi-fi	Wireless network connection
Air con	Air conditioning
🏊	Indoor swimming pool
🏊	Heated indoor swimming pool
🏊	Outdoor swimming pool
🏊	Heated outdoor swimming pool
🎵	Entertainment
ch fac	Children's facilities (see page 6)
Xmas	Special programme for Christmas/New Year
🎾	Tennis court
🏏	Croquet lawn
⛳	Golf course
CONF	Conference facilities
BC	Business centre available
Thtr	Number of theatre style seats
Class	Number of classroom style seats
Board	Number of boardroom style seats
⊗	No dogs allowed in bedrooms (guide dogs for the blind and assist dogs may be allowed)
No children	Children cannot be accommodated
RS	Restricted opening time (e.g. RS Jan–Mar, closed Xmas/New Year)
Civ Wed	Establishment licensed for civil weddings (+ maximum number of guests at ceremony)
LB	Special leisure breaks available

AA Assessment

In collaboration with VisitBritain, Visit Scotland and the Wales Tourist Board, the AA has developed new Common Quality Standards for inspecting and rating acommodation. These standards and rating categories are now applied throughout the British Isles.

Any hotel applying for AA recognition receives an unannounced visit to check standards. The hotels with full entries in this guide have all paid an annual fee for AA inspection, recognition and rating.

AA inspectors pay as a guest for their inspection visit, they do not accept free hospitality of any kind. Although AA inspectors do not stay overnight at Budget Hotels or Associate Hotels (see page 9) they do carry out regular visits to verify standards and procedures.

Merit Score (%)

AA inspectors supplement their reports with an additional quality assessment of everything the hotel provides, including hospitality, based on their findings as a 'mystery guest'. This wider ranging quality assessment results in an overall Merit Score which is shown as a pecentage beside the hotel name. When making your selection of hotel accommodation this enables you to see at a glance that a three star hotel with a percentage score of 79% offers a higher standard overall than one in the same star classification but with a percentage score of 69%.

To gain AA recognition, a hotel must achieve a minimum quality score of 50%.

AA Awards

Every year the AA present a range of awards to the finest AA-inspected and rated hotels from England, Scotland, Wales and the Republic of Ireland. The Hotel of the Year is our ultimate accolade and is awarded to those hotels that are recognised as outstanding examples in their field. Often innovative, the winning hotels always set high standards in hotel keeping. The winners for 2007 are listed on page 12-13.

Rooms

The entries show the number of en suite letting bedrooms available. This may also be shown as the total number of letting bedrooms followed by the number with en suite facilities or family rooms.

Bedrooms in an annexe or extension are only noted if they are at least equivalent in quality to those in the main building, but facilities and prices may differ. In some hotels all bedrooms are in an annexe or extension.

Colour television is provided in all bedrooms unless otherwise stated.

Prices

Prices are per room per night and are provided by the hoteliers in good faith. These prices are indications and not firm quotations.

Payment

As most hotels now accept credit or debit cards we only indicate if an establishment does not accept any cards for payment. Credit cards may be subject to a surcharge – check when booking if this is how you intend to pay. Not all hotels accept travellers' cheques.

Children (ch fac)

These facilities may include baby intercom, baby sitting service, playroom, playground, laundry, drying/ironing facilities, cots, high chairs or special meals. In some hotels children can sleep in parents' rooms at no extra cost – check when booking.

If 'No children' is indicated a minimum age may be also given e.g. No children 4yrs would mean no children under 4 years of age would be accepted.

Some hotels, although accepting children, may not have any special facilities for them so it is well worth checking before booking.

Leisure breaks (LB)

Some hotels offer special leisure breaks and the prices may differ from those quoted in this guide.

Parking

We indicate the number of parking spaces available for guests. These may include covered and/or charged spaces.

Civil Weddings (Civ Wed)

Indicates that the establishment holds a civil wedding licence, and we indicate the number of guests that can be accommodated at the ceremony

Conference Facilities

We include three types of meeting layouts – Theatre, Classroom and Boardroom style and include the maximum number of delegates for each. The price shown is the maximum rate per delegate per day. We also show if a hotel has a Business Centre and if Wi-fi connectivity is available.

Dogs

Although many hotels allow dogs, they may be excluded from some areas of the hotel and some breeds may be forbidden altogether. However, guide dogs for the blind and assist dogs should be accepted, but please check the hotel's policy when making your booking.

Entertainment (♫)

This indicates that live entertainment should be available at least once a week all year. Some hotels provide live entertainment only in summer or on special occasions – check when booking.

Hotel logos

If an establishment belongs to a hotel group or consortium their logo is included in their entry and these are all listed on pages 29-35.

Map references

Each town is given a map reference – the map page number and a two-figure map reference based on the National Grid.

For example: **Map 05 SU 48:**

05 refers to the page number of the map section at the back of the guide

SU is the National Grid lettered square (represents 100,000sq metres) in which the location will be found

4 is the figure reading across the top or bottom of the map page

8 is the figure reading down at each side of the map page.

Restricted Service (RS)

Some hotels have restricted service during quieter months, and at this time some of the listed facilities will not be available.

Smoking regulations

We have tried to obtain accurate information on smoking restrictions within establishments, but the situation may change during the currency of this guide. If the freedom to smoke or to be in a non-smoking atmosphere is important to you, please check when you book.

AA Star Classification

Hotels recognised by the AA should:

- have high standards of cleanliness
- keep proper records of booking
- give prompt and professional service to guests, assist with luggage on request, accept and deliver messages
- provide a designated area for breakfast and dinner, with drinks available in a bar or lounge
- provide an early morning call on request
- have good quality furniture and fittings
- provide adequate heating and lighting
- undertake proper maintenance

A guide to some of the general expectations for each star classification is as follows:

★ One Star

Polite, courteous staff providing a relatively informal yet competent style of service, available during the day and evening to receive guests

- At least one designated eating area open to residents for breakfast
- If dinner is offered it should be on at least five days a week, with last orders no later than 6.30pm
- Television in lounge or bedroom
- Majority of rooms en suite, bath or shower room available at all times

★★ Two Star

As for one star, plus

- At least one restaurant or dining room open to residents for breakfast (and for dinner at least five days a week)
- Last orders for dinner no earlier than 7pm
- Television in bedroom
- En suite or private bath or shower and WC

★★★ Three Star

- Management and staff smartly and professionally presented and usually uniformed
- A dedicated receptionist on duty at peak times
- At least one restaurant or dining room open to residents and non-residents for breakfast and dinner whenever the hotel is open

- Last orders for dinner no earlier than 8pm
- Remote-control television, direct-dial telephone
- En suite bath or shower and WC.

★★★★ Four Star

- A formal, professional staffing structure with smartly presented, uniformed staff anticipating and responding to your needs or requests. Usually spacious, well-appointed public areas
- Reception staffed 24 hours by well-trained staff
- Express checkout facilities where appropriate
- Porterage available on request
- Night porter available
- At least one restaurant open to residents and non-residents for breakfast and dinner seven days per week, and lunch to be available in a designated eating area
- Last orders for dinner no earlier than 9pm
- En suite bath with fixed overhead shower and WC

★★★★★ Five Star

- Luxurious accommodation and public areas with a range of extra facilities. First time guests shown to their bedroom
- Multilingual service
- Guest accounts well explained and presented
- Porterage offered
- Guests greeted at hotel entrance, full concierge service provided
- At least one restaurant open to residents and non-residents for all meals seven days per week

Continued

- Last orders for dinner no earlier than 10pm
- High-quality menu and wine list
- Evening service to turn down the beds. Remote-control television, direct-dial telephone at bedside and desk, a range of luxury toiletries, bath sheets and robes. En suite bathroom incorporating fixed overhead shower and WC

★ Inspectors' Choice

Each year we select the best hotels in each rating. These hotels stand out as the very best in the British Isles, regardless of style. The selected Inspectors' Choice hotels are identified by red stars. (see page 20)

Types of hotel

The majority of establishments in this guide come under the category of Hotel; other categories are listed below:

Town House Hotel

A small, individual city or town centre property, which provides a high degree or personal service and privacy

Country House Hotel

These are quietly located in a rural area

Small Hotel

Has less than 20 bedrooms and is owner managed

Metro Hotel

A hotel in an urban location that does not offer an evening meal

Budget Hotel

These are usually purpose built modern properties offering inexpensive accommodation. Often located near motorways and in town or city centres

Restaurant with Rooms

This category of accommodation is now assessed under the AA's B&B scheme, therefore, although they continue to have an entry in this guide, we do not

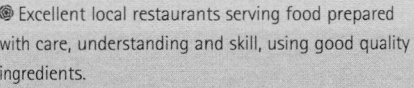

AA Rosette Awards

Out of the many thousands of restaurants in the UK, the AA identifies some 1,800 as the best. The following is an outline of what to expect from restaurants with AA Rosette Awards. For a more detailed explanation of Rosette criteria please see www.theAA.com

◉ Excellent local restaurants serving food prepared with care, understanding and skill, using good quality ingredients.

◉◉ The best local restaurants, which aim for and achieve higher standards, better consistency and where a greater precision is apparent in the cooking. There will be obvious attention to the selection of quality ingredients.

◉◉◉ Outstanding restaurants that demand recognition well beyond their local area.

◉◉◉◉ Amongst the very best restaurants in the British Isles, where the cooking demands national recognition.

◉◉◉◉◉ The finest restaurants in the British Isles, where the cooking stands comparison with the best in the world.

include their star rating. Most Restaurants with Rooms have been awarded AA rosettes for their food and the rooms will meet the required AA standard. For more detailed information about any restaurant with rooms please consult The AA Bed and Breakfast Guide or see www.theAA.com

U A small number of hotels in the guide have this symbol because their star classification was not confirmed at the time of going to press.

A These are establishments that have been inspected and rated by the national bodies in Britain and Northern Ireland. Associate Hotels have paid to belong to the AA Associate Hotel Scheme and therefore receive a limited entry in the guide. Descriptions of these hotels can be found on the AA website.*

O These hotels were not open at the time of going to press, but will open in late 2006, or in 2007.

* Check the AA Website **www.theAA.com** for current information and ratings

Additional Information

Hints on booking your stay

It's always worth booking as early as possible, particularly for the peak holiday period from the beginning of June to the end of September. Bear in mind that Easter and other public holidays may be busy too and in some parts of Scotland, the ski season is a peak holiday period.

Some hotels will ask for a deposit or full payment in advance, especially for one-night bookings. And some hotels charge half-board (bed, breakfast and dinner) whether you require the meals or not, while others may only accept full-board bookings. Not all hotels will accept advance bookings for bed and breakfast, overnight or short stays. Some will not take reservations from mid week.

Once a booking is confirmed, let the hotel know at once if you are unable to keep your reservation. If the hotel cannot re-let your room you may be liable to pay about two-thirds of the room price (a deposit will count towards this payment). In Britain a legally binding contract is made when you accept an offer of accommodation, either in writing or by telephone, and illness is not accepted as a release from this contract. You are advised to take out insurance against possible cancellation, for example AA Single Trip Insurance (telephone 0800 085 7240 or consult the AA website www.theAA.com for details).

Booking online

Booking a place to stay can be a time-consuming process, but you can search quickly and easily online for a place that best suits your needs. Simply visit www.theAA.com/hotels to search from around 8,000 quality rated hotels and B&Bs in Great Britain and Ireland. Then either check availability and book online by clicking on the 'Booking' button, or contact the establishment for further information.

Prices

The AA encourages the use of the Hotel Industry Voluntary Code of Booking Practice, which aims to ensure that guests know how much they will have to pay and what services and facilities are included, before entering a financially binding agreement. If the price has not previously been confirmed in writing, guests should be given a card stipulating the total obligatory charge when they register at reception.

The Tourism (Sleeping Accommodation Price Display) Order of 1977 compels hotels, travel accommodation, guest houses, farmhouses, inns and self-catering accommodation with four or more letting bedrooms, to display in entrance halls the minimum and maximum price for one or two persons but they may vary without warning.

Facilities for disabled guests

The final stage (Part III) of the Disability Discrimination Act (access to Goods and Services) came into force in October 2004. This means that service providers may have to make permanent adjustments to their premises. For further information, see the government website www.disability.gov.uk/dda.

Please note: AA inspectors are not accredited to make inspections under the National Accessibility Scheme. We indicate in entries if an establishment has ground floor rooms; and if a hotel tells us that they have disabled facilities this is included in the description.

The establishments in this guide should all be aware of their responsibilities under the Act. We recommend that you always telephone in advance to ensure that the establishment you have chosen has appropriate facilities.

Useful Websites
www.disability.gov.uk/disabledpeople/fs/en
www.holidaycare.org.uk
www.dptac.gov.uk/door-to-door

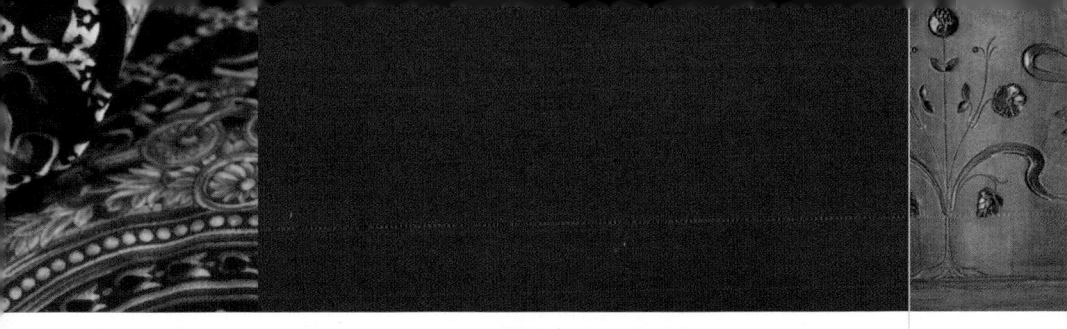

Licensing Laws

Licensing laws differ in England, Wales, Scotland, the Republic of Ireland, the Isle of Man, the Isles of Scilly and the Channel Islands. Public houses are generally open from mid morning to early afternoon, and from about 6 or 7pm until 11pm, although closing times may be earlier or later and some pubs are open all afternoon. Unless otherwise stated, establishments listed are licensed. Hotel residents can obtain alcoholic drinks at all times, if the licensee is prepared to serve them. Non-residents eating at the hotel restaurant can have drinks with meals. Children under 14 may be excluded from bars where no food is served. Those under 18 may not purchase or consume alcoholic drinks. Club license means that drinks are served to club members only, 48 hours must lapse between joining and ordering.

The Fire Precautions Act does not apply to the Channel Islands, Republic of Ireland, or the Isle of Man, which have their own rules. As far as we are aware, all hotels listed in Great Britain have applied for and not been refused a fire certificate.

For information on Ireland see page 946

Website Addresses

Website addresses are included where they have been supplied and specified by the respective establishment. Such Websites are not under the control of The Automobile Association Developments Limited and as such the AA has no control over them and will not accept any responsibility or liability in respect of any and all matters whatsoever relating to such Websites including access, content, material and functionality. By including the addresses of third party Websites the AA does not intend to solicit business or offer any security to any person in any country, directly or indirectly.

Bank and Public Holidays 2007

New Year's Day	1st January
New Year's Holiday	2nd January (Scotland)
Good Friday	6th April
Easter Monday	9th April
May Day Bank Holiday	7th May
Spring Bank Holiday	28th May
August Holiday	1st August (Scotland)
Late Summer Holiday	27th August
Christmas Day	25th December
Boxing Day	26th December

AA Hotel of the Year

Hotel of the Year is the AA's most prestigious award. One hotel from each country is chosen as a winner.

Winner for
England

Baglioni Hotel

London SW7

★★★★★ ⑱⑱

Page 446

Winner for
Scotland

Marcliffe Hotel & Spa

Aberdeen

★★★★ ⑱

Page 776

 **∧∧ Hotel Group of the Year**
Malmaison

hotels that dare to be different — This award reflects the hotel group which demonstrated an outstanding commitment to improving and developing their portfolio of hotels, whilst maintaining a high level of consistency throughout the group.

Winner for
Wales

Park Plaza Cardiff

Cardiff
★★★★ ❀
Page 890

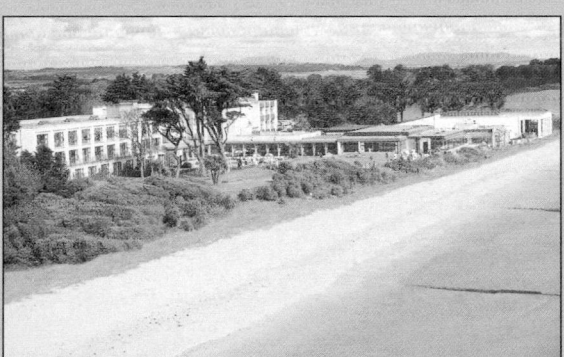

Winner for
Republic of
Ireland

Kelly's Resort Hotel

Rosslare
County Wexford
★★★★ ❀❀
Page 1002

Forty years ago

Denise Laing

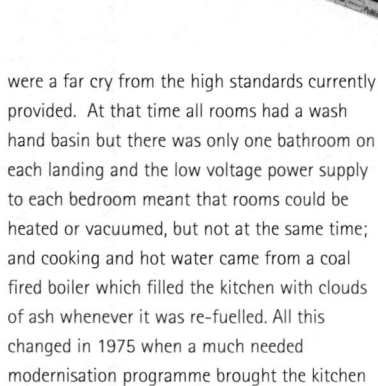

It was the year that England brought home the World Cup, *The Sound of Music* won an Oscar, the Beatles gave their last ever concert, and John Lennon claimed that they were more popular than Jesus.

The year was 1966, and the AA made publishing history by producing the first edition of a combined guide to hotels and restaurants. Since those early days the first title has spawned two offspring; The Hotel Guide and The Restaurant Guide. These continue to be leaders in their field, and each is prized for providing clear and objective guidance for consumers.

Despite appearances and the modern comforts boasted by many hotels in 1966, it is clear that we were a hardier lot 40 years ago. Central heating was a luxury not commonly available, though in its absence gas or electric fires were sometimes provided to take away the chill in colder weather. The Hotel and Restaurants Guide circa 1966 points out in its introduction that "Some hotels which are indicated as having central heating often do not have it operating – especially in bedrooms – during cold weather which may prevail outside the normally recognised winter months".

The bare necessities

En suite or private bathroom facilities were the luxurious exception in most hotels and found at only 10% of three-star bedrooms, and 20% at four star hotels. In contrast the requirement now is 100% en suite bathrooms in all hotels by 2008. The majority of visitors had to share bathrooms and toilets, which at least were required to be located on the same floor as the bedrooms. Queues in draughty corridors were presumably unavoidable.

One of the AA's top hotels, Farlam Hall in Brampton, Cumbria, recalls that in 1963 facilities

were a far cry from the high standards currently provided. At that time all rooms had a wash hand basin but there was only one bathroom on each landing and the low voltage power supply to each bedroom meant that rooms could be heated or vacuumed, but not at the same time; and cooking and hot water came from a coal fired boiler which filled the kitchen with clouds of ash whenever it was re-fuelled. All this changed in 1975 when a much needed modernisation programme brought the kitchen and power supply up-to-date and needless to say there have been many more changes and improvements since then.

Recollections from our more mature AA hotel inspectors have provided a first-hand insight into the standards of hotel management at the time. One inspector recalls going into a vast, unattended kitchen on the third floor of a sea-side hotel where, because every window was open, the bubbling stockpot in the middle on the cooking range was surrounded by hopeful pigeons and seagulls. Other inspectors have remembered mattresses that sagged so badly in the middle they made getting out of bed an uphill struggle, and lights so dim that they could barely see across the room.

Kettles in bedrooms were unheard of, and the water from a bathroom tap wasn't usually suit-able for drinking so where room service was not available there was no option but down to the lounge for a nice cup of tea.

Visitors to the Castle Venlaw Hotel in Peebles once had to hire the bath plug from the owners if they wanted a bath. But while facilities may

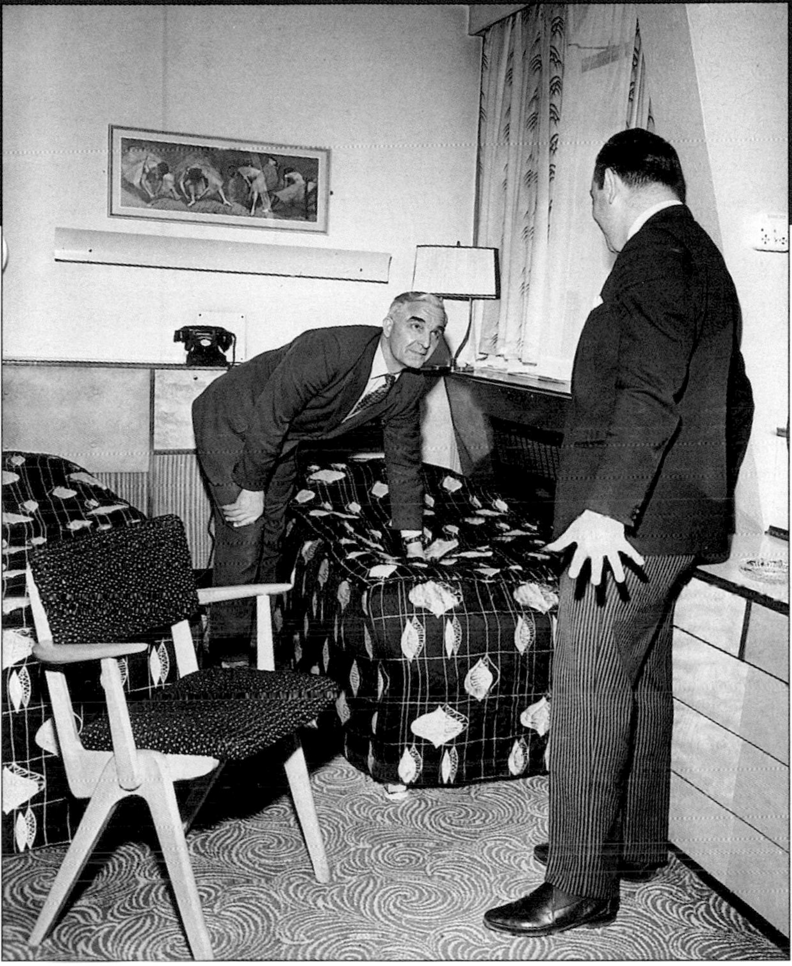

Mattress inspection

seem sparten in this day and age, the service was more often than not cheerfully and willingly performed. A case in point was a story that came to us from the Belmont Hotel in Thorne, South Yorkshire, where on one memorable occasion staff visited a bedroom hourly to change the TV channel so that a dog, left alone by its owners, was kept suitably entertained.

The provision of television in the 60s was usually relegated to a television room separate from the main lounge, and a personal television in a bedroom was an unheard of luxury – a far cry from the state-of-the-art entertainment and communication systems and connections provided by many hotels today.

Decades of loyalty

Despite these early privations, suffered on both sides of the green baize door, hotels have attracted an extraordinary loyalty from both customers and staff. In our search for tales and recollections of the 60s we learned of many staff members who are still employed by the same hotel after 40 years. The Bear Hotel in Woodstock has a member of staff from the West of Ireland who in the mid-sixties planned to train as a nurse, but ended up at The Bear where she remains today. A shy girl who disliked the very grand Bear Hotel when she first arrived, especially the pomp and ceremony of meals served by waiters in tails.

15

NETHERWOOD HOTEL
GRANGE-OVER-SANDS
LANCS.

TELEPHONES:
OFFICE 2552.
RESIDENTS 2530.

Mr. J. H. Summerfield,
Croydon,
Surrey.

31st. May. 1966

Dear Mr. Summerfield,

I thank you for your letter of the 27th. May and am
pleased to be able to offer you a front-facing, first floor twin-bedded room
large enough to accommodate your wife and self and daughter, or a
twin-bedded room and a single room if you preferred your daughter to have
separate accommodation, for the week commencing Saturday 13th. to the 20th.
The terms are 50/-d. per person per day full inclusive
terms or 35/-d. per person per day bed and breakfast if you could let us
know which terms you prefer on confirmation.
We look forward to hearing from you again in the near
future assuring you of our personal attention at all times.

Yours faithfully,

J.D.&.J.K.Fallowfield.

Netherwood Hotel
GRANGE-OVER-SANDS
Telephone 2552

Tariff

SUMMER TERMS

(1st April — 31st October)

Inclusive (3 day minimum)	...	50/-
Bed & Breakfast	...	35/-

(Single rooms 2/6d. per day extra)

WINTER TERMS

(1st November — 31st March)

Inclusive (3 day minimum)	...	40/-
Bed & Breakfast ...	...	30/-

Children 5 years and under		½ terms
Children 6 years to 10 years	...	¾ terms

Children occupying Adult accommodation or
separate rooms will be charged full terms.

Bank Holidays (4 day minimum)	...	55/-
Christmas (4 day minimum)	...	60/-

Breakfast 7/-	Luncheon 9/6
Afternoon Tea 4/-	Dinner 13/6

Dogs are welcomed subject to being under
proper control, but are **NOT** allowed in the
Dining Room.   Charge 3/- per day.

Covered Garage 2/6 per night.

Ample free Parking Space.

Prices Subject to alteration without notice.

Above: Booking a room at the
Netherwood Hotel
Left: An AA sign in the 1960s

The very formal restaurant régime demanded
carving meat at tables and making flambées
under the gaze of diners and the critical scrutiny
of the head waiter, a daunting experience for a
shy young girl. Forty years on she is comfortable
with royalty and Hollywood stars alike – she's
had plenty of time to get used to them as The
Bear is a mecca for the rich and famous visiting
Oxford from all over the world.

Another long-timer began working as a
chambermaid at the Kingswood Hotel in
Sidmouth in 1965. Over 40 years later she is still
there. She remembers the early morning routine
of climbing several flights of stairs with trays of
tea, a necessary exercise before the lift was
installed. Hotel work was very hard in the mid
Sixties, and an afternoon spent in exhausted
sleep was very common. Later, when working in
the dining room, her day was charted by other
people's meals – breakfast, morning coffee,
lunch, afternoon tea and finally dinner in a
never-ending cycle. But, like all the hotel
employees we spoke to, she quickly got used to
the work and came to love both it and the hotel.
Now aged 70, she still works in the dining room
every evening supervising staff and serving
coffee. She particularly enjoys welcoming back
guests who first came in the Sixties, and now

return with their grandchildren.

The Athenaeum Hotel in London has enjoyed the benefits of the same concierge for 40 years. A man eenowned for his ability to satisfy the needs of the guests, no matter how difficult their demands. Tickets for sold-out shows or tables at fully-booked restaurants pose no problem for the ever resourceful concierge, who has even been known to locate an elephant for an American purchaser.

Hotel kitchens were very different in the sixties

Dressing down, looking up

One of the key changes from the Sixties has been the relaxing of rigid standards. In many hotels there is now a more informal relationship between staff and guests. This has been a welcome development for hotel workers, but former AA Inspector Fred Chrystal and his colleagues found this difficult to deal with at first. In the Sixties it was unheard of for hotel managers to go without a tie, and staff always wore uniforms. But the relaxing of dress and other rigid social codes did not lead to a lowering of standards as he feared, and Fred proudly acknowledges that "standards have gone through the roof in recent years," and most hotels are pretty impressive. "The AA used to almost wage war on the hotel industry, trying to force positive changes, but now we are all on the same side of the fence and working together."

Forty years on

The AA's Chief Hotel Inspector, Peter Birnie confirms these positive changes, describing the AA's approach as more advisory and less policing than 40 years ago. "We are still robust about standards of cleaning and maintenance, but the lack of a second chair in a bedroom, for example, would no longer preclude entry to a higher star rating. We are in partnership with hotels today, and our job is to steer them towards trends that reflect consumer expectations. We encourage rather than dictate."

This 40th anniversary is shared by the Chewton Glen Hotel in the New Forest. Graded by the AA since the 1960s, Chewton Glen (five red stars, three rosettes) has grown from an 8-bedroom property to a luxury hotel and spa with 58 bedrooms and 205 staff. Managing director Andrew Stembridge values this long connection. "The AA inspectors have helped us to focus on industry standards and have made an invaluable contribution to the success of Chewton Glen."

Best Western has over 300 independently owned hotels throughout Great Britai each with a charm and character all of their own. Many offering a fantastic range leisure facilities. Best Western also has more AA Rosettes for fine dining than a other hotel group. So whether you're looking for a break in the bright lights of the ci along one of Britain's picturesque coastlines or at a relaxing countryside retreat, yo simply can't go wrong with a Best Western Getaway Break.

For more information, to make a booking or request brochure call now on:

08457 74 74 74

or visit our website at www.bestwestern.co.uk

EVERY ONE IS UNIQUE 300 individual hotels to choose fro

Inspectors' Choice
Hotel Index

Assessed and announced annually, the AA's Inspectors' Choice Awards recognise the very best hotels in Britain and Ireland. These hotels offer consistently outstanding levels of quality, comfort, cleanliness and customer care.

AA

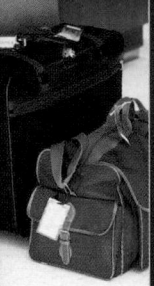

Inspectors' Choice
Hotel Index

The number shown against each hotel in the index corresponds with the number given on the Inspectors' Choice map on page 26. Hotels are listed in county order, showing their star classification, rosettes and telephone number.

ENGLAND

BERKSHIRE

#	Location	Hotel
1	Maidenhead	**Fredrick's Hotel**
	★★★★ ⊛⊛⊛	☎ 01628 581000
2	Newbury	**The Vineyard at Stockcross**
	★★★★★ ⊛⊛⊛⊛	☎ 01635 528770

BUCKINGHAMSHIRE

#	Location	Hotel
3	Aylesbury	**Hartwell House**
	★★★★ ⊛⊛⊛	☎ 01296 747444
4	Taplow	**Cliveden**
	★★★★★ ⊛⊛⊛	☎ 01628 668561

CHESHIRE

#	Location	Hotel
5	Chester	**The Chester Grosvenor & Spa**
	★★★★★ ⊛⊛⊛	☎ 01244 324024
6	Sandiway	**Nunsmere Hall**
	★★★★ ⊛⊛	☎ 01606 889100

CORNWALL & ISLES OF SCILLY

#	Location	Hotel
7	Bryher	**Hell Bay Hotel**
	★★★ ⊛⊛	☎ 01720 422947
8	Fowey	**Marina Hotel**
	★★ ⊛⊛	☎ 01726 833315
9	Portscatho	**Driftwood**
	★★★ ⊛⊛⊛	☎ 01872 580644
10	St Martin's	**St Martin's on the Isle**
	★★★ ⊛⊛⊛	☎ 01720 422090
11	Tresco	**The Island Hotel**
	★★★ ⊛⊛	☎ 01720 422883

CUMBRIA

#	Location	Hotel
12	Brampton	**Farlam Hall Hotel**
	★★★ ⊛⊛	☎ 016977 46234
13	Grange-over-Sands	**Clare House**
	★ ⊛	☎ 015395 33026
14	Grasmere	**White Moss House**
	★★ ⊛	☎ 015394 35295
15	Howtown	**Sharrow Bay Country House Hotel**
	★★★ ⊛⊛	☎ 017684 86301
16	Keswick	**Swinside Lodge**
	★★ ⊛⊛	☎ 017687 72948
17	Watermillock	**Rampsbeck Country House Hotel**
	★★★ ⊛⊛⊛	☎ 017684 86442
18	Windermere	**Gilpin Lodge Country House Hotel**
	★★★★ ⊛⊛⊛	☎ 015394 88818
19	Windermere	**Holbeck Ghyll Country House Hotel**
	★★★★ ⊛⊛⊛	☎ 015394 32375
20	Windermere	**Lindeth Fell Country House Hotel**
	★★ ⊛	☎ 015394 43286
21	Windermere	**Linthwaite House Hotel**
	★★★ ⊛⊛	☎ 015394 88600
22	Windermere	**Miller Howe***
	★★★	☎ 015394 42536
23	Windermere	**The Samling**
	★★★ ⊛⊛⊛	☎ 015394 31922

DERBYSHIRE

#	Location	Hotel
24	Baslow	**Fischer's Baslow Hall**
	★★★ ⊛⊛⊛⊛	☎ 01246 583259

DEVON

#	Location	Hotel
25	Ashwater	**Blagdon Manor Hotel & Restaurant**
	★★★ ⊛⊛	☎ 01409 211224
26	Burrington	**Northcote Manor**
	★★★ ⊛⊛	☎ 01769 560501
27	Chagford	**Gidleigh Park**
	★★★ ⊛⊛⊛⊛	☎ 01647 432367
28	Chagford	**Mill End Hotel**
	★★ ⊛⊛	☎ 01647 432282
29	Honiton	**Combe House Hotel & Restaurant – Gittisham**
	★★★ ⊛⊛	☎ 01404 540400
30	Kingsbridge	**Buckland-Tout-Saints**
	★★★ ⊛⊛	☎ 01548 853055
31	Lewdown	**Lewtrenchard Manor**
	★★★ ⊛⊛⊛	☎ 01566 783256
32	Torquay	**Orestone Manor Hotel**
	★★★ ⊛⊛	☎ 01803 328098

Hotels marked with an asterisk* had not had their Rosette rating confirmed at the time of going to press. See the AA website www.theAA.com for current information

DORSET

| 33 | Evershot | **Summer Lodge Country House Hotel** |
| ★★★★ | @@@ | ☎ 01935 482000 |

| 34 | Gillingham | **Stock Hill Country House** |
| ★★★ | @@@ | ☎ 01747 823626 |

| 35 | Poole | **Best Western Mansion House Hotel** |
| ★★★ | @@ | ☎ 01202 685666 |

CO DURHAM

| 36 | Romaldkirk | **Rose & Crown Hotel** |
| ★★ | @@ | ☎ 01833 650213 |

| 37 | Seaham | **Seaham Hall Hotel** |
| ★★★★★ | @@@ | ☎ 0191 516 1400 |

ESSEX

| 38 | Dedham | **Maison Talbooth** |
| ★★★ | @@ | ☎ 01206 322367 |

GLOUCESTERSHIRE

| 39 | Buckland | **Buckland Manor** |
| ★★★ | @@@ | ☎ 01386 852626 |

| 40 | Cheltenham | **Hotel on the Park** |
| ★★★ | @@ | ☎ 01242 518898 |

| 41 | Chipping Campden | **Cotswold House** |
| ★★★★ | @@@ | ☎ 01386 840330 |

| 42 | Corse Lawn | **Corse Lawn House Hotel** |
| ★★★ | @@ | ☎ 01452 780479 |

| 43 | Lower Slaughter | **Lower Slaughter Manor** |
| ★★★ | @@ | ☎ 01451 820456 |

| 44 | Tetbury | **Calcot Manor** |
| ★★★★ | @@ | ☎ 01666 890391 |

| 45 | Thornbury | **Thornbury Castle** |
| ★★★ | @@ | ☎ 01454 281182 |

| 46 | Upper Slaughter | **Lords of the Manor** |
| ★★★ | @@@ | ☎ 01451 820243 |

HAMPSHIRE

| 47 | Beaulieu | **Montagu Arms Hotel** |
| ★★★ | @@ | ☎ 01590 612324 |

| 48 | Brockenhurst | **Rhinefield House** |
| ★★★★ | @@ | ☎ 01590 622922 |

| 49 | Milford on Sea | **Westover Hall Hotel** |
| ★★★ | @@@ | ☎ 01590 643044 |

| 50 | New Milton | **Chewton Glen Hotel** |
| ★★★★★ | @@@ | ☎ 01425 275341 |

| 51 | Rotherwick | **Tylney Hall Hotel** |
| ★★★★ | @ | ☎ 01256 764881 |

| 52 | Winchester | **Lainston House Hotel** |
| ★★★★ | @@@ | ☎ 01962 863588 |

HEREFORDSHIRE

| 53 | Hereford | **Castle House Hotel** |
| ★★★ | @@@ | ☎ 01432 356321 |

ISLE OF WIGHT

| 54 | Yarmouth | **George Hotel** |
| ★★★ | @@@ | ☎ 01983 760331 |

KENT

| 55 | Ashford | **Eastwell Manor** |
| ★★★★ | @@ | ☎ 01233 213000 |

| 56 | Lenham | **Chilston Park** |
| ★★★★ | @@ | ☎ 01622 859803 |

LEICESTERSHIRE

| 57 | Melton Mowbray | **Stapleford Park** |
| ★★★★ | @@ | ☎ 01572 787522 |

LINCOLNSHIRE

| 58 | Winteringham | **Winteringham Fields** |
| ★★★ | @@@@ | ☎ 01724 733096 |

LONDON

| 59 | London E14 | **Four Seasons Hotel Canary Wharf** |
| ★★★★★ | @ | ☎ 020 7510 1999 |

| 60 | London NW1 | **The Landmark London** |
| ★★★★★ | @@ | ☎ 020 7631 8000 |

| 61 | London SW1 | **The Berkeley** |
| ★★★★★ | @@@@@ | ☎ 020 7235 6000 |

| 62 | London SW1 | **The Goring** |
| ★★★★★ | @@ | ☎ 020 7396 9000 |

| 63 | London SW1 | **The Halkin Hotel** |
| ★★★★★ | @@@ | ☎ 020 7333 1000 |

| 64 | London SW1 | **Jumeirah Carlton Tower Hotel** |
| ★★★★★ | @@ | ☎ 020 7235 1234 |

| 65 | London SW1 | **The Lanesborough** |
| ★★★★★ | @@ | ☎ 020 7259 5599 |

| 66 | London SW1 | **Mandarin Oriental Hyde Park** |
| ★★★★★ | @@@@@ | ☎ 020 7235 2000 |

| 67 | London SW1 | **No 41** |
| ★★★★★ | | ☎ 020 7300 0041 |

| 68 | London SW1 | **The Stafford** |
| ★★★★ | @@ | ☎ 020 7493 0111 |

| 69 | London SW3 | **The Capital** |
| ★★★★★ | @@@@ | ☎ 020 7589 5171 |

| 70 | London SW7 | **Baglioni Hotel** |
| ★★★★★ | @@ | ☎ 020 7368 5700 |

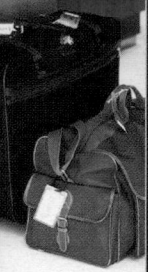

Inspectors' Choice
Hotel Index Continued

71	London W1	Athenaeum
★★★★★ ⊚	☎ 020 7499 3464	
72	London W1	Claridge's
★★★★★ ⊚⊚⊚	☎ 020 7629 8860	
73	London W1	The Connaught
★★★★★ ⊚⊚⊚	☎ 020 7499 7070	
74	London W1	The Dorchester
★★★★★ ⊚⊚	☎ 020 7629 8888	
75	London W1	Four Seasons Hotel London
★★★★★ ⊚	☎ 020 7499 0888	
76	London W1	The Ritz
★★★★★ ⊚⊚	☎ 020 7493 8181	
77	London W8	Royal Garden Hotel
★★★★★ ⊚⊚⊚	☎ 020 7937 8000	
78	London W8	Milestone Hotel
★★★★★ ⊚	☎ 020 7917 1000	
79	London WC2	One Aldwych
★★★★★ ⊚⊚	☎ 020 7300 1000	

NORFOLK

80	Blakeney	Morston Hall
★★★ ⊚⊚⊚	☎ 01263 741041	
81	Grimston	Congham Hall Country House Hotel
★★★ ⊚⊚	☎ 01485 600250	
82	North Walsham	Beechwood Hotel
★★★ ⊚⊚	☎ 01692 403231	
83	Norwich	The Old Rectory
★★ ⊚⊚	☎ 01603 700772	

NORTHAMPTONSHIRE

| 84 | Daventry | Fawsley Hall |
| ★★★★ ⊚⊚⊚ | ☎ 01327 892000 | |

NOTTINGHAMSHIRE

| 85 | Nottingham | Restaurant Sat Bains with Rooms |
| ★★★ ⊚⊚⊚⊚ | ☎ 0115 986 6566 | |

OXFORDSHIRE

| 86 | Great Milton | Le Manoir Aux Quat' Saisons |
| ★★★★★ ⊚⊚⊚⊚⊚ | ☎ 01844 278881 | |

RUTLAND

| 87 | Oakham | Hambleton Hall |
| ★★★★ ⊚⊚⊚⊚ | ☎ 01572 756991 | |

SHROPSHIRE

| 88 | Worfield | Old Vicarage Hotel |
| ★★★ ⊚⊚⊚ | ☎ 01746 716497 | |

SOMERSET

89	Bath	The Bath Priory Hotel
★★★★ ⊚⊚⊚	☎ 01225 331922	
90	Bath	The Queensberry Hotel
★★★ ⊚⊚	☎ 01225 447928	
91	Porlock	The Oaks Hotel
★★★ ⊚	☎ 01643 862265	
92	Shepton Mallet	Charlton House*
★★★★	☎ 01749 342008	
93	Wellington	Bindon Country House Hotel & Restaurant
★★★ ⊚⊚	☎ 01823 400070	

STAFFORDSHIRE

| 94 | Lichfield | Swinfen Hall Hotel |
| ★★★★ ⊚⊚ | ☎ 01543 481494 | |

SUFFOLK

| 95 | Hintlesham | Hintlesham Hall Hotel |
| ★★★★ ⊚⊚⊚ | ☎ 01473 652334 | |

SURREY

| 96 | Bagshot | Pennyhill Park Hotel & The Spa |
| ★★★★★ ⊚⊚⊚ | ☎ 01276 471774 | |

SUSSEX, EAST

97	Forest Row	Ashdown Park Hotel and Country Club
★★★★ ⊚⊚	☎ 01342 824988	
98	Newick	Newick Park Hotel & Country Estate
★★★ ⊚⊚	☎ 01825 723633	
99	Uckfield	Horsted Place
★★★ ⊚⊚	☎ 01825 750581	

SUSSEX, WEST

100	Cuckfield	Ockenden Manor
★★★ ⊚⊚⊚	☎ 01444 416111	
101	East Grinstead	Gravetye Manor Hotel
★★★ ⊚⊚⊚	☎ 01342 810567	
102	Gatwick Airport	Langshott Manor
★★★ ⊚⊚	☎ 01293 786680	
103	Lower Beeding	South Lodge Hotel
★★★★ ⊚⊚⊚	☎ 01403 891711	
104	Turners Hill	Alexander House Hotel
★★★★ ⊚⊚	☎ 01342 714914	

Hotels marked with an asterisk* had not had their Rosette rating confirmed at the time of going to press. See the AA website www.theAA.com for current information

Hotels marked with an asterisk* had not had their Rosette rating confirmed at the time of going to press.
See the AA website www.theAA.com for current information

Inspectors' Choice
Hotel Index Continued

Hotels marked with an asterisk ***** *had not had their Rosette rating confirmed at the time of going to press.*
See the AA website www.theAA.com for current information

170 Portmarnock		Portmarnock Hotel
		& Golf Links
★★★★	⑳⑳	☎ 01 8460611

Co GALWAY

171 Cashel		Cashel House Hotel
★★★	⑳⑳	☎ 095 31001

172 Recess		Lough Inagh Lodge Hotel
★★★	⑳	☎ 095 34706

Co KERRY

173 Kenmare		Sheen Falls Lodge
★★★★	⑳⑳⑳	☎ 064 41600

174 Killarney		Aghadoe Heights Hotel
★★★★	⑳	☎ 064 31766

175 Killarney		Killarney Park Hotel
★★★★	⑳⑳	☎ 064 35555

Co KILDARE

176 Straffan		The K Club
★★★★★	⑳⑳⑳	☎ 01 6017200

Co KILKENNY

177 Thomastown		Mount Juliet Conrad Hotel
★★★★	⑳⑳	☎ 056 777 3000

Co WATERFORD

178 Waterford		Waterford Castle Hotel
★★★★	⑳⑳	☎ 051 878203

Co WEXFORD

179 Gorey		Marlfield House Hotel
★★★	⑳⑳	☎ 055 21124

180 Rosslare		Kelly's Resort Hotel
★★★★	⑳⑳	☎ 053 32114

Premier Collection Restaurant with Rooms

These establishments are now inspected under the AA's Bed & Breakfast scheme. They have been awarded the highest accommodation rating under this scheme.

ENGLAND

CORNWALL

181 Fowey	The Old Quay House Hotel
⑳⑳	☎ 01726 833302

182 Padstow	St Ervan Manor
⑳⑳⑳	☎ 01841 540 255

OXFORDSHIRE

183 Stadhampton	The Crazy Bear Hotel
⑳⑳	☎ 01865 890714

SOMERSET

184 Yeovil	Little Barwick House
⑳⑳⑳	☎ 01935 423902

SUSSEX, WEST

185 Chichester	West Stoke House
⑳⑳	☎ 01243 575226

WILTSHIRE

186 Whitley	The Pear Tree Inn
⑳⑳	☎ 01225 709131

YORKSHIRE, NORTH

187 Ramsgill	Yorke Arms
⑳⑳⑳	☎ 01423 755243

SCOTLAND

CITY OF EDINBURGH

188 Edinburgh	The Witchery by the Castle
⑳	☎ 0131 225 5613

HIGHLAND

189 Colbost	The Three Chimneys & The
	House Over-By
⑳⑳⑳	☎ 01470 511258

190 Kingussie	The Cross at Kingussie
⑳⑳⑳	☎ 01540 661166

STIRLING

191 Strathyre	Creagan House
⑳⑳	☎ 01877 384638

WALES

MONMOUTHSHIRE

192 Skenfrith	The Bell at Skenfrith
⑳⑳	☎ 01600 750235

193 Whitebrook	The Crown at Whitebrook
⑳⑳	☎ 01600 860254

POWYS

194 Builth Wells	The Drawing Room
⑳⑳	☎ 01982 552493

Central London

Location	Number
Regent's Park	60
BLOOMSBURY	
MARYLEBONE	
MAYFAIR	73, 72, 74, 76, 75, 71, 68
STRAND	79
Hyde Park	77, 70, 66, 65, 59
KNIGHTS BRIDGE	61, 63, 64, 62
WESTMINSTER	78, 69, 67
LAMBETH	
Thames	

Inverness — 140, 142, 144, 145, 141, *189*, 190, 123

Aberdeen

Fort William — 143, 139, 126, 127, 125, 148, 149, 124
Perth — *191*, 147, 134, 135,136,137, 133

Glasgow — 138, 128, Edinburgh, 129,130,*188*, 150
Ayr — 146, 153, 154, 152, 151, 131, 132
Stranraer

Belfast

Carlisle — 12, 16, 17, 15, 36, 37
Newcastle upon Tyne
Middlesbrough — 115, 112
Kendal — 14, 18,19,20,21, 22,23, 13, *187*, 114, 116,117
York — 111, 113, 118
Leeds
Kingston upon Hull

Galway — 172, 171, 162, 163
Limerick
Dublin — 168,169, 170, 176, 179
Holyhead

Liverpool — 156,157,158, 159, 6, 5
Manchester
Sheffield — 24
Lincoln — 58

Rosslare — 177, 178, 180
Cork — 174,175, 173, 167, 166, 164, 165

Aberystwyth — 155, *194*, 160
Nottingham — 57, 87, 85
Norwich — 81, 80, 82, 83, 95, 38
Colchester

Carmarthen — 161
Cardiff — 192, *193*, 45, 44, 109, 108, 107, 186, 89,90
Gloucester — 53, 42, 39, 41, 46, 43, 40
Birmingham — 88, 94, 110, 105, 106, 84
Cambridge
Oxford — 3, *183*, 86, 4
LONDON — 1, 96, 102, 101, 97, 99, 98
Guildford — 2, 51, 52, 104, 103, 100
Maidstone — 55, 56
Dover

Barnstaple — 91, 26, 93, 184, 34, 48, 33, 35, 50, 49, 54, 185
Bristol — 92
Southampton — 47
Brighton

Exeter — 25, 29
Weymouth
182, 31, 27,28, 32, 30, 8,*181*, 9
Plymouth
Penzance

Isles of Scilly — 11, 7, 10

The Channel Islands — 119,120, 121,122

● 54 Hotel
●*184* Restaurant with rooms

© Automobile Association Developments Limited 2006

ARISTEL HOTELS

From city chic to country charm, all our hotels have one thing in common...Us!

Aristel Group operate seven individual high quality hotels in the UK. Our experience, dedication and professionalism ensure that every hotel exceeds the highest standards of it's class!

RAMADA CREWE – BEST WESTERN MOSTYN HOTEL, MARBLE ARCH – BEST WESTERN CORONA HOTEL, VICTORIA – BEST WESTERN FRENSHAM POND HOTEL, FARNHAM – BEST WESTERN DONNINGTON MANOR HOTEL, SEVENOAKS – BEST WESTERN CARLTON HOTEL, BLACKPOOL – CHATSWORTH HOTEL, HASTINGS

www.aristelhotels.co.uk

time for a relaxing break

leisure times

Hotel Groups Information

The following hotel groups have at least four hotels and 400 rooms or are part of an internationally significant company with a central reservations number

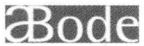

Abode A small expanding group currently represented by four hotels in key city centre locations.
www.abodehotels.co.uk

Apex Hotels A small group of predominately four star hotels based primarily in Edinburgh, with one hotel in Dundee and their latest hotel, the Apex City in London.
0845 365 0000 www.apexhotels.co.uk

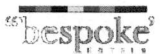

Bespoke A small group of personally managed three and four star hotels in leisure locations.
0870 890 3740 (Head Office) www.bespokehotels.com

Best Western Britain's largest consortia group has around 300 independently owned and managed hotels, modern and traditional, in the two, three and four star range. Many have leisure facilities and rosette awards.
08457 737373 www.bestwestern.co.uk

PREMIER

Best Western Premier Best Western Premier Hotels are selected for their beautiful settings, range of facilities and enhanced levels of service. There are currently four Best Western Great Britain hotels that have achieved Premier status. These join over 45 Best Western Premier accredited hotels across Europe and Asia.
08457 737373 www.bestwestern.co.uk

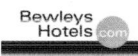

Bewley's Hotels A privately owned group of high quality, contemporary three star hotels in key locations in the UK and Ireland.
01293 5000 www.BewleysHotels.com

Brend A privately owned group of 11 three and four star hotels in Devon and Cornwall.
01271 344 496 www.brendhotels.co.uk

Crerar Hotels
A division of North British Trust Group, with five hotels in Scotland.
08700 554 433 www.crerarhotels.com

Campanile A French owned company, Campanile has 16 properties in the UK offering modern accommodation in budget hotels.
020 8326 1500 www.envergure.fr

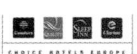

Choice Choice has four different brands in the UK: Clarion and Quality Hotels are three star hotels, Comfort Inns are two star hotels and Sleep Inns are budget hotels.
0800 44 44 44 www.choicehotelseurope.com

Classic British A consortium of independent hotels at the four star and high-quality three star level, categorised by quality and style, and marketed under the Classic British Hotels hallmark.
0845 070 7090 www.classicbritishhotels.com

COPTHORNE

Copthorne Part of the Millennium and Copthorne group, with 11 four star hotels in primary provincial locations as well as London.
0800 41 47 41 www.millenniumhotels.com

Corus A large group of three star hotels ranging from rural to city centre locations across the UK.
0845 602 6787 www.corushotels.com

great hotels
great locations
great facilities

From country locations to historic towns, beautiful cities to popular tourist spots, our range of hotels offer stylish accommodation, superb leisure facilities and excellent bars and restaurants.

Come on give us a call.

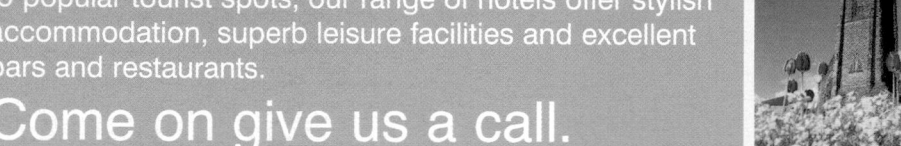

Holiday Inn Bolton Centre	0870 4420901
Holiday Inn Doncaster A1(M) Jct 36	0870 4428761
Holiday Inn Harrogate	0870 4431761
Holiday Inn London-Elstree M25 Jct 23	0870 4431271
Holiday Inn London-Shepperton	0870 2258701
Holiday Inn Luton South M1 Jct 9	0870 4431781
Holiday Inn Manchester Airport	0870 4436961
Holiday Inn Newcastle-upon-Tyne	0870 7873291
Holiday Inn Peterborough West	0870 7879861
Holiday Inn Plymouth	0870 2250301
Holiday Inn Solihull	0870 2255401
Holiday Inn Stratford-upon-Avon	0870 2254701
Crowne Plaza Chester	0870 4421081
Crowne Plaza Glasgow	0870 4431691
Crowne Plaza Nottingham	0870 7875161
Best Western Gatwick Moat House	0870 4431671
Best Western Reading Moat House	0870 2250601
Best Western Stoke-on-Trent Moat House	0870 2254601
Cambridge Garden House	0870 4420971
Oakley Court Hotel, Windsor	0870 7879061

QMH

Hotel Groups
Information Continued

Courtyard by Marriott There are 11 hotels in this group in the UK, part of an international brand of modern three star hotels.
0800 1927 1927 www.marriott.co.uk

Crowne Plaza Four star hotels predominately found in key city centre locations.
0870 400 9670 www.crowneplaza.co.uk

Days Inn Good quality modern budget accommodation at motorway services.
www.welcomebreak.co.uk

De Vere De Vere comprises 21 four and five star hotels, which specialise in leisure, golf and conference facilities.
0870 111 0516 www.devere.co.uk

Exclusive A small privately owned group of luxury five and four star hotels, all located in the South of England.
01276 471 774 www.exclusivehotels.co.uk

Folio Hotels A newly developed small group of three and four star hotels.
0208 940 2247 www.foliohotels.co.uk

Forestdale Hotels A privately owned group of 18 three star hotels located across the UK.
0808 144 9494 www.forestdale.com

Four Pillars Hotels A group of six three and four star hotels in the Oxfordshire area.
0800 374692 www.four-pillars.co.uk

Grange Hotels A collection of privately owned hotels, seven located in central London and one in Bracknell, Berkshire.
0845 450 4400 www.grangehotels.co.uk

Gresham Hotels Part of the Ryan Hotels group, Gresham is a collection of four star hotels, located in city centre locations in the Republic of Ireland.
00 353 1 8797 966 www.greshamhotels.com

Handpicked Hotels A group of 15 predominately four star, high quality country house hotels, with a real emphasis on quality food.
0845 458 0901 www.handpicked.co.uk

Holiday Inn
A major international group with many hotels across the UK.
0870 400 9670 www.holiday-inn.co.uk

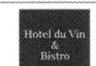
Hotel du Vin A small expanding group of high quality four star hotels with seven properties, including the latest addition in Henley.
01962 850676 www.hotelduvin.com

Ibis Ibis is a growing chain of modern budget hotels with properties across the UK.
0870 609 0963 www.ibishotel.com

Independents A consortium of independently owned, mainly two and three star hotels across Britain.
0800 88 55 44 www.iha.uk.com

DAYS INN

The Best Value Under The Sun™

NOW AA MEMBERS
CAN SAVE 10%
WHEN BOOKING
YOUR HOTEL WITH US

Great locations across the UK & Ireland

Abington	London North
Belfast	London South Mimms
Birmingham	London South Ruislip
Bradford	London Stansted
Bristol	London Waterloo
Cardiff	London Westminster
Clacton-on-Sea	Luton
Derby	Manchester City
Donington	Membury
Dublin City Rathmines	Michaelwood
Dublin City Talbot Street	Nuneaton
Dundee	Oxford
Ferrybridge South A1	Sedgemoor
Fleet	Sheffield South
Galway City	Stratford-upon-Avon
Gretna Green	Telford Ironbridge
Leicester Central	Tullamore
Leicester Forest East	Wakefield
London Hyde Park	Warwick South

Tel: 0800 0280 400

www.daysinn.co.uk

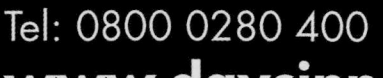

Hotel Groups
Information Continued

Innkeeper's Lodge A growing collection of lodges located adjacent to a pub restaurant and featuring comfortable rooms and complimentary breakfast.
.0870 243 0500 www.innkeeperslodge.com

INTER-CONTINENTAL.
HOTELS AND RESORTS
Inter-Continental This internationally renowned group has two five star hotels in central London.
0800 0289 387

Ireland's Blue Book An association of owner-managed establishments across Ireland.
00 353 1 0462 3416

IRISH COUNTRY
HOTELS
Irish Country Hotels Friendly and informal in style, Irish Country Hotels is a collection of 30 individual family owned and run hotels, located throughout the country.
00 353 1 295 8900 www.irishcountryhotels.com

JURYS DOYLE
HOTELS
Jury's Doyle This Irish company has a range of three and four star hotels in the UK and the Republic of Ireland.
0870 907 2222 (Group Information) www.jurysdoyle.com

Leisureplex
Leisureplex A group of 16 two star hotels located in many popular seaside resorts
08451 305 666 (Head Office) www.alfatravel.co.uk

MACDONALD
HOTELS & RESORTS
Macdonald A large group of predominately four star hotels, both traditional and modern in style and located across the UK.
0870 830 4812 www.macdonald hotels.co.uk

hotels that dare to be different
Malmaison A growing brand of modern, three star city centre hotels including new hotels in Oxford and Liverpool.
0845 365 4247 www.malmaison.com

MANOR
HOUSE
Manor House Located throughout Northern and Southern Ireland, Manor House Hotels is an independent group that includes castles, Georgian manors, country houses, shooting lodges and four star guest houses.
00 353 1 295 8900 FH 1820S and 700 www.manorhousehotels.com

Marriott.
HOTELS & RESORTS
Marriott This international brand has four star hotels in primary locations. Most are modern and have leisure facilities such as a focus on golf.
00800 1927 1927 www.marriott.co.uk

MarstonHotels
Marston A quality independent group of four star hotels with leisure facilities in primary locations across England.
0845 1300 700 www.marstonhotels.com

MAYBOURNE
HOTEL
GROUP
Maybourne Hotels Newly formed hotel group representing the prestigious London five star hotels, The Berkeley, Claridge's and The Connaught.
020 7107 8830 (Head Office) www.maybourne.com

MILLENNIUM
HOTELS AND RESORTS
Millennium Part of the Millennium and Copthorne group with six high-quality four star hotels, mainly in central London.
0800 41 47 41 www.millenniumhotels.com

MORAN
HOTELS
Moran Hotels A small family owned hotel group with four hotels in Dublin, Cork and two in London.
+353 0 1459 3650 www.moranhotels.com

NOVOTEL
Accor
Novotel Part of French group Accor, Novotel provides mainly modern three star hotels and new generation four star hotels in key locations throughout the UK.
0870 609 0962 www.novotel.com

Revolutionary thinking.

Book a hotel the same way you book a flight.

1,000,000 rooms at £26.

Travelodge has a revolutionary pricing system based on first come, lowest prices. Rooms start at £26 and you can now book them up to 12 months in advance online.

Before you go anywhere, go to www.travelodge.co.uk

Hotel Groups
Information Continued

Old English Inns A large collection of former coaching inns that are mainly graded two and three star.
0800 917 3085 www.oldenglish.co.uk

Paramount A group of predominately four star hotels, many with leisure facilities.
0870 1688833 www.paramount-hotels.co.uk

Park Plaza Hotels A European based group increasing its presence within the UK with quality four star hotels in primary locations.
0800 1696128 www.parkplaza.com

Peel Hotels A group of mainly three star hotels located across the UK.
0207 2661100 www.peelhotel.com

Premier Travel Inn The largest budget hotel group in the UK offering high quality, modern accommodation in key locations throughout the UK. Every Premier Travel Inn is located adjacent to a family restaurant and bar.
0870 242 8000 www.premiertravelinn.com

Pride of Britain A consortium of privately owned British hotels, often in the country house style.
0800 0893929 www.prideofbritainhotels.com

Principal A small group of four star hotels currently represented by five hotels situated in prime city centre locations.
0870 242/474 www.principal-hotels.com

QHotels A newly formed hotel group currently with eight four star hotels across the UK.
0845 0740060 www.qhotels.co.uk

Queens Moat House A group of 18 hotels including various well known names in the three and four star range of hotels.
(01708 730522) www.moathousehotels.com

Radisson Edwardian This high-quality London-based group offers mainly four star hotels in key locations throughout the capital.
020 8757 7900 www.radissonedwardian.com

Radisson SAS A recognised international brand increasing its hotels in the UK and offering high-quality four star hotels in key locations.
0800 374411 www.radisson.com

Ramada A large hotel group with many properties throughout the UK and three brands - Ramada Plaza, Ramada and Ramada Hotel & Resort .
08457 30 30 40 www.ramadajarvis.co.uk

Red Carnation A unique collection of prestigious four and five star central London hotels, providing luxurious surroundings and attentive service.
0845 634 2665 www.redcarnationhotels.com

Relais et Chateaux An international consortium of rural, privately owned hotels, mainly in the country house style.
00 800 2000 00 02 www.relaischateaux.com

Renaissance One of the Marriott brands, Renaissance is a collection of individual hotels offering comfortable guest rooms, quality cuisine and good levels of service.
00800 1927 1927 www.marriott.co.uk

Don't just break your journey...
Welcome Break
your journey

With Welcome Break offering both Days Inn and Welcome Lodge Hotels across the UK, located right on Britain's motorway network, the break in your journey has never been so convenient. All Welcome Break hotels offer free parking, 24 hour reception and all rooms feature complimentary **SKY** channels and hot drinks tray - we'll even throw in a hot chocolate and a biscuit to aid a peaceful sleep!

All hotels are **AA** pet friendly.
We don't charge any extra for your furry four legged family member.

AA members get 10% off the published rate on production of their **AA** membership card at reception.

Promotional rates from £35 for a family room at many locations - search the website for your ideal location at www.welcomebreak.co.uk then either book on line or call your chosen hotel direct and quote ref **AA**10% to obtain the discount.
To order a brochure call 01908 299705.

Welcome Break

Welcome Lodge

DAYS INN®

Your next night's stay is just a click away...
www.welcomebreak.co.uk

Hotel Groups
Information Continued

Rocco Forte Hotels A small group of luxury hotels spread across Europe. Owned by Sir Rocco Forte, there are four hotels in the UK, all situated in major city locations.
0870 4584040 www.roccofortehotels.com

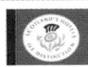
Scotland's Hotels of Distinction A consortium of independent Scottish hotels in the three and four star range.
01333 360 888 www.hotels-of-distinction.com

Sheraton Represented in the UK by a small number of four and five star hotels in London and Scotland.
0800 35 35 35 www.starwoodhotels.com

Shire A small group of mostly four star hotels many of which many feature spa facilities.
01282 414141 (Head Office) www.shirehotels.com

Small Luxury Hotels of the World Part of an international consortium of mainly privately owned hotels, often in the country house style.
00800 525 48000 www.slh.com

Stop Inn A new brand from Choice Hotels with a small group of hotels in the Midlands and Northern England.
0800 44 44 44 www.choicehotelseurope.com

Swallow Hotels One of the UK's largest hotel groups with over 130 hotels across the UK.
0870 600 4666 www.swallowhotels.com

The Circle A consortium of independently-owned mainly two and three star hotels across Britain.
(0845 345 1965) www.circlehotels.co.uk

Thistle A large group of approximately 50 hotels across the UK with a number of hotels in London.
0870 414 1516 www.thistlehotels.com

Travelodge Good-quality, modern, budget accommodation found across the UK. Almost every lodge has an adjacent family restaurant, often a Little Chef, Harry Ramsden's or Burger King.
08700 850 950 www.travelodge.co.uk

Tulip Inn With over 90 properties across Europe, this group now has hotels in in Manchester and Glasgow.

Von Essen A privately owned collection of country house hotels, all individual in style and found predominately in the south of England.
01761 240121 www.vonessenhotels.co.uk

Welcome Break Good-quality, modern, budget accommodation at motorway services.
www.welcomebreak.co.uk

Wrens Hotels A small group of individual character hotels, located in countryside settings and in the historic towns of Windsor and Eton.
01753 838859 (Head Office) www.wrensgroup.com

3 nights for the price of 2

Stay Friday and Saturday night and get Sunday night **FREE**!

FREE Breakfast!

Breaks available from **£39.95** per room per night!

At Innkeepers Lodge all the extra's come as standard

- Fresh food available all day every day
- All rooms en-suite with shower
- Phone/modem points in every room
- SKY TV**
- Prices per room not per person
- Family rooms available at most locations

- FREE BREAKFAST
- Complimentary Shampoo/Shower Gel
- Tea/Coffee making facilities

**Except Maidstone and South Queensferry

experience the difference

room reservations: 0870 243 0500
www.innkeeperslodge.com

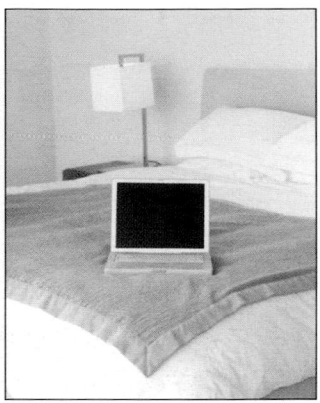

NEW!

Real-time, online booking at

www.theAA.com

Take the hassle out of booking accommodation online

We are delighted to announce that it is now possible
to book many AA establishments on the website

How do I find the perfect place?

THAANKS.

VOTED AA HOTEL GROUP OF THE YEAR 2006 BY THE AUTOMOBILE ASSOCIATION.

Mal life. Thaanks a million. We've been down this road now for over ten years. It's nice to know when someone pulls you over and admires your slinky interior, your unusual bodywork or your blistering performance. We must be giving all the right signals. With nine luxurious locations the length of the UK and many more stops planned in the future, we are talking a totally different kind of service here. Think divine dining, a bar serving astounding vino and rivers of daring cocktails. Imagine a hotel with a GTI badge at a diesel price. Are we nearly there yet? (The AA seems to think so.) **That's Mal life.**

Malmaison

hotels that dare to be different

Book online at malmaison.com or call bookings central 0845 365 4247

Edinburgh | Glasgow | Leeds | Manchester | Newcastle | Birmingham | London | Belfast | Oxford | Liverpool | Reading

England

Folkstone Harbour,
Kent

England

BEDFORDSHIRE

ASPLEY GUISE   MAP 11 SP93

★★★ 70% **HOTEL**

Best Western Moore Place
The Square MK17 8DW

☎ 01908 282000 ▣ 01908 281888
e-mail: manager@mooreplace.com
web: www.mooreplace.co.uk

dir: *M1 junct 13, take A507 signed Aspley Guise & Woburn Sands. Hotel on left side of village square*

This impressive Georgian house, set in delightful gardens in the village centre, is very conveniently located for the M1. Bedrooms do vary in size, but consideration has been given to guest comfort, with many thoughtful extras provided. There is a wide range of meeting rooms and private dining options.

Rooms 35 en suite 27 annexe en suite (16 GF) ⊛ in 43 bedrooms
S £55-£125; D £85-£145 (incl. bkfst) **Facilities** Wi-fi available Xmas
Conf Thtr 40 Class 24 Board 20 Del from £145 **Parking** 70 **Notes LB**
⊛ in restaurant Closed 3 days btwn Xmas & New Yr Civ Wed 80

BEDFORD   MAP 12 TL04

★★★ 73% **HOTEL**

The Barns Hotel
Cardington Rd MK44 3SA

folio Hotels

☎ 0870 609 6108 ▣ 01234 273102

dir: *From M1 junct 13, A421, approx 10m to A603 Sandy/Bedford exit, hotel on right at 2nd rdbt*

A tranquil location on the outskirts of Bedford, friendly staff and well-equipped bedrooms are the main attractions here. Cosy day rooms and two informal bars add to the appeal, while large windows in the restaurant make the most of the view over the river. The original barn now houses the conference and function suite.

Rooms 48 en suite (18 GF) ⊛ in 28 bedrooms S £99; D £99
Facilities STV Free use of local leisure centre (1m) **Conf** Thtr 120
Class 40 Board 40 Del from £100 **Parking** 90 **Notes LB** ⊛ in restaurant
Civ Wed 90

★★★ 70% ◉◉ **HOTEL**

Woodlands Manor
Green Ln, Clapham MK41 6EP
☎ 01234 363281 ▣ 01234 272390
e-mail: admin@woodlandsmanorhotel.com
web: www.signaturegroup.co.uk

dir: *A6 towards Kettering. Clapham 1st village N of town centre. On entering village 1st right into Green Lane, Manor 200mtrs on right*

Sitting in acres of well-tended grounds, this Victorian manor offers a warm welcome. Bedrooms are spacious and provide a variety of thoughtful extras. Traditional public areas include a cosy bar and a smart restaurant, where award-winning food is served.

Rooms 29 en suite 3 annexe en suite (4 fmly) (9 GF) S £75-£140;
D £85-£150 (incl. bkfst) **Facilities** STV Wi-fi available Xmas **Conf** Thtr 80
Class 40 Board 40 Del from £135 **Parking** 100 **Notes LB** ⊛ in
restaurant Civ Wed 86

BUDGET HOTEL

Innkeeper's Lodge Bedford
403 Goldington Rd MK41 0DS
☎ 01234 272707 ▣ 01234 343926
web: www.innkeeperslodge.com

Innkeeper's Lodge

dir: *on A428*

Smart, en suite accommodation ideal for both business & leisure guests. Bedrooms are very well equipped, including Sky TV, telephone, modem points, tea & coffee making facilities, (family rooms in most locations). Complimentary breakfast. The adjacent Pub Restaurant; a Harvester, Vintage Inn, Toby Carvery, Ember Inn, Sizzling Pubco or Pub & Carvery offers an all day menu. See Hotel Groups pages for further details.

Rooms 47 en suite S £45-£49.95; D £45-£49.95 **Conf** Thtr 25 Class 25
Board 20

BUDGET HOTEL

Premier Travel Inn Bedford
Priory Country Park, Barkers Ln MK41 9DJ

premier travel inn

☎ 08701 977030 ▣ 01234 325697
web: www.premiertravelinn.com

dir: *M1 junct 13/A421/A6 towards Bedford then A428 signed Cambridge. Cross River Ouse & right at next rdbt, follow signs for Priory Country Park*

High quality, modern budget accommodation ideal for both families and business travellers. Spacious, en suite bedrooms feature bath and shower, satellite TV and many have telephones and modem points. The adjacent family restaurant features a wide and varied menu. For further details consult the Hotel Groups page.

Rooms 32 en suite

BUDGET HOTEL

Travelodge Bedford

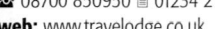

Saturn Heights, Brickhill Dr MK41 7PH
☎ 08700 850950 📠 01234 270908
web: www.travelodge.co.uk

dir: *From M1 into Bedford via A421 and A6. Follow the A5141 to Manton Lane.*

Travelodge offers good quality, good value, modern accommodation. Ideal for families, the spacious en suite bedrooms include remote-control TV, tea and coffee-making facilities and comfortable beds. Meals can be taken at the nearby family restaurant. See Hotel Groups pages for further details.

Rooms 51 en suite S fr £26; D fr £26

Travelodge Bedford Wyboston

Black Cat Roundabout MK44 3BE
☎ 08700 850 950

dir: *A1 N'bound at Black Cat rndbt at junct with A421*
Rooms 40 en suite S fr £26; D fr £26

DUNSTABLE   MAP 11 TL02

★★★ 72% HOTEL

Old Palace Lodge

Church St LU5 4RT
☎ 01582 662201 📠 01582 696422
e-mail: reservations@mgmhotels.co.uk
web: www.oldpalacelodge.com

dir: *M1 junct 11 take A505. Hotel 2m on right opposite Priory church*

Situated close to the town centre and major road networks this hotel is steeped in history and has many original features. The spacious bedrooms are smartly decorated with co ordinated fabrics and have many thoughtful touches. Public rooms include a large lounge bar with plush sofas and an intimate restaurant.

Rooms 68 en suite (12 fmly) (21 GF) ⊘ in 33 bedrooms S £70-£160; D £70-£160 **Facilities** STV Wi-fi in bedrooms Full leisure facilities provided off site with local fitness centre Xmas **Conf** BC Thtr 60 Class 40 Board 40 Del from £90 **Services** Lift **Parking** 50 **Notes** Civ Wed 70

★★ 61% HOTEL

Highwayman

OLD ENGLISH INNS

London Rd LU6 3DX
☎ 01582 601122 📠 01582 603812
e-mail: 6466@greeneking.co.uk
web: www.oldenglish.co.uk

dir: *Northbound, exit M1 junct 9, take A5, 6m on the right. Southbound, exit M1 junct 11, take A505 then left on A5 to London, on the left.*

This hotel continues to be popular with business people, partly due to its convenient location just south of the town, and to the ample car parking. The accommodation is comfortable, well equipped and cheerfully decorated. The public areas include a large public bar in which bar meals are available.

Rooms 52 en suite (3 fmly) (24 GF) ⊘ in all bedrooms S £45-£49; D £50-£65 (incl. bkfst) **Facilities** ♬ **Parking** 76 **Notes** ⊗ ⊘ in restaurant

---

BUDGET HOTEL

Premier Travel Inn Dunstable/Luton

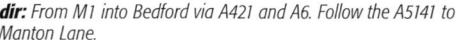

350 Luton Rd LU5 4LL
☎ 08701 977083 📠 01582 664114
web: www.premiertravelinn.com

dir: *on A505. From M1 junct 11 follow signs to Dunstable. At first rdbt turn right. Inn on left*

High quality, modern budget accommodation ideal for both families and business travellers. Spacious, en suite bedrooms feature bath and shower, satellite TV and many have telephones and modem points. The adjacent family restaurant features a wide and varied menu. For further details consult the Hotel Groups page.

Rooms 42 en suite

Premier Travel Inn Dunstable South

Watling St, Kensworth LU6 3QP
☎ 08701 977082 📠 01582 842811

dir: *M1 junct 9 towards Dunstable on A5. Inn on right past Packhorse pub*
Rooms 40 en suite

BUDGET HOTEL

Travelodge Dunstable Hockliffe

Watling St LU7 9LZ
☎ 08700 850 950 📠 01525 211177
web: www.travelodge.co.uk

dir: *M1 junct 12, take A5120 to Toddington. Then 1st right through Tebworth, right onto A5*

Travelodge offers good quality, good value, modern accommodation. Ideal for families, the spacious en suite bedrooms include remote-control TV, tea and coffee-making facilities and comfortable beds. Meals can be taken at the nearby family restaurant. See Hotel Groups pages for further details.

Rooms 28 en suite S fr £26; D fr £26

LUTON   MAP 06 TL02

★★★ 73% HOTEL

Thistle Luton

THISTLE HOTELS

Arndale Centre LU1 2TR
☎ 0870 333 9138 📠 0870 333 9238
e-mail: Luton@Thistle.co.uk

dir: *From M1 Junct 10a towards Luton town centre, adjacent to Arndale Centre car park.*

Situated in the town centre with adjacent parking this hotel is convenient for the shopping areas, and many guests stay here prior to flights from the nearby airport. There is a range of bedroom options - all are well equipped. In addition there are good leisure and treatment facilities, and impressive function and conference rooms. There is a contemporary restaurant and the New York deli-style, CoMotion.

Rooms 152 en suite ⊘ in 87 bedrooms **Facilities** STV 🏊 supervised Sauna Solarium Gym Jacuzzi **Conf** Thtr 250 Class 120 Board 80 **Services** Lift **Parking** 30 **Notes** LB ⊗ ⊘ in restaurant Civ Wed 200

LUTON *continued*

★★★ 72% **HOTEL**

Hotel St Lawrence

40A Guildford St LU1 2PA

☎ 01582 482119 📠 01582 482818

e-mail: reservations@hotelstlawrence.co.uk

web: www.hotelstlawrence.co.uk

dir: M1 junct 10a & follow signs to town centre, after university take left fork at mini rdbt. Hotel 70yds on right

Ideally situated in a central location close to both the town centre and railway station. The smart public areas include a modern restaurant, a welcoming bar and a stylish lounge/lobby with leather chairs. Bedrooms come in a variety of styles; each one is pleasantly decorated and thoughtfully equipped. Parking is available in the multi-storey opposite.

Rooms 28 en suite ⊛ in 4 bedrooms S £72-£82; D £82-£92 (incl. bkfst) **Facilities** Wi-fi in bedrooms Use of local fitness centre & snooker club **Notes LB** ⊛ ⊛ in restaurant RS 25 Dec-1 Jan

Ⓤ

Swallow Chiltern

Waller Av LU4 9RU

SWALLOW

☎ 01582 575911 📠 01582 581859

web: www.swallowhotels.com

dir: M1 junct 11 take A505 to Luton past 2 sets of lights. Over rdbt, left at lights, hotel on right

At the time of going to press, the star classification for this hotel was not confirmed. Please refer to the AA internet site www.theAA.com for current information.

Rooms 91 en suite

BUDGET HOTEL

Days Hotel Luton

Regent St LU1 5FA

☎ 0870 429 9540 📠 0870 429 9541

e-mail: luton@kewgreen.co.uk

web: www.welcomebreak.co.uk

This modern building offers accommodation in smart, spacious and well-equipped bedrooms, suitable for families and business travellers, and all with en suite bathrooms. Continental breakfast is available and other refreshments may be taken at the nearby family restaurant. For further details see the Hotel Groups page.

Rooms 120 en suite **Conf** BC Thtr 50 Class 15 Board 20

LUTON AIRPORT   MAP 06 TL12

BUDGET HOTEL

Hotel Ibis Luton

Spittlesea Rd LU2 9NH

☎ 01582 424488 📠 01582 455511

e-mail: H1040@accor-hotels.com

web: www.ibishotel.com

dir: from M1 junct 10 follow signs to Luton Airport signs. Hotel 600mtrs from airport

Modern, budget hotel offering comfortable accommodation in bright and practical bedrooms. Breakfast is self-service and dinner is available in the restaurant. For further details, consult the Hotel Groups page.

Rooms 98 en suite **Conf** Thtr 114 Class 64 Board 80

BUDGET HOTEL

Premier Travel Inn Luton Airport

premier travel inn

Osbourne Rd LU1 3HJ

☎ 08701 977166 📠 01582 421900

web: www.premiertravelinn.com

dir: M1 junct 10 follow signs for Luton on A1081, at 3rd rdbt turn left onto Gypsy Lane, turn left at next rdbt

High quality, modern budget accommodation ideal for both families and business travellers. Spacious, en suite bedrooms feature bath and shower, satellite TV and many have telephones and modem points. The adjacent family restaurant features a wide and varied menu. For further details consult the Hotel Groups page.

Rooms 129 en suite **Conf** Thtr 70 Board 50

MARSTON MORETAINE   MAP 11 SP94

BUDGET HOTEL

Travelodge Bedford Marston Morstaine

Travelodge

Beancroft Rd Junction MK43 0PZ

☎ 08700 850 950 📠 01234 766755

web: www.travelodge.co.uk

dir: on A421, northbound

Travelodge offers good quality, good value, modern accommodation. Ideal for families, the spacious en suite bedrooms include remote-control TV, tea and coffee-making facilities and comfortable beds. Meals can be taken at the nearby family restaurant. See Hotel Groups pages for further details.

Rooms 54 en suite S fr £26; D fr £26

MILTON ERNEST   MAP 11 TL05

★★ 69% **HOTEL**

Queens Head

OLD ENGLISH INNS

2 Rushden Rd MK44 1RU

☎ 01234 822412

web: www.oldenglish.co.uk

This character Inn provides newly refurbished bedrooms together with a wide range of dishes from the imaginative menu, and real ales from the cosy bar. Staff are friendly and polite.

Rooms 13 en suite (4 GF)

TODDINGTON MOTORWAY SERVICE AREA (M1)　MAP 11 TL02

BUDGET HOTEL

Travelodge Toddington (M1 Southbound)

LU5 6HR

☎ 08700 850 950 🖷 01525 878452

web: www.travelodge.co.uk

dir: M1 between juncts 11 & 12

Travelodge offers good quality, good value, modern accommodation. Ideal for families, the spacious en suite bedrooms include remote-control TV, tea and coffee-making facilities and comfortable beds. Meals can be taken at the nearby family restaurant. See Hotel Groups pages for further details.

Rooms 66 en suite S fr £26; D fr £26

WOBURN　MAP 11 SP93

★★★ 79% ⊛ **HOTEL**

The Inn at Woburn

George St MK17 9PX

☎ 01525 290441 🖷 01525 290432

e-mail: enquiries@theinnatwoburn.com

dir: M1 junct 13, left to Woburn, at Woburn left at T-junct, hotel in village

This inn has been substantially refurbished and provides a high standard of accommodation. Bedrooms are divided between the original house, a modern extension and some stunning cottage suites. Public areas include the beamed, club-style Tavistock Bar, a range of meeting rooms and an attractive restaurant with interesting dishes on offer.

Rooms 50 en suite 7 annexe en suite (4 fmly) (21 GF) ⊘ in 49 bedrooms **Facilities** STV ♨ 54 Access to Woburn Safari Park and Woburn Abbey **Conf** Thtr 60 Class 40 Board 40 **Parking** 80 **Notes LB** No children ⊘ in restaurant

★★ 63% **HOTEL**

Bell Hotel & Inn

OLD ENGLISH INNS

21 Bedford St MK17 9QB

☎ 01525 290280 🖷 01525 290017

e-mail: bell.woburn@oldenglishinns.co.uk

web: www.oldenglish.co.uk

dir: Exit M1 junct 13, take A507 to Woburn Sands. Take 1st left, then next left. At T-junct turn right

One part of this hotel, that houses most of the bedrooms, a lounge, residents' bar and breakfast room, is located in a Georgian building on

continued

one side of Bedford Street. Directly opposite is the other part of the hotel with the bar and a more formal restaurant. Ample parking is provided behind both buildings.

Rooms 24 en suite (4 GF) ⊘ in all bedrooms S £65; D £85-£95 (incl. bkfst) **Facilities** Xmas **Parking** 50 **Notes** ⊗ ⊘ in restaurant

BERKSHIRE

ASCOT　MAP 06 SU96

★★★★ 79% ⊛ **HOTEL**

Macdonald Berystede Hotel & Spa

MACDONALD
HOTELS & RESORTS

Bagshot Rd, Sunninghill SL5 9JH

☎ 0870 400 8111 🖷 01344 872301

e-mail: general.berystede@macdonald-hotels.co.uk

web: www.macdonald-hotels.co.uk

dir: A30/B3020 (Windmill Pub). Continue 1.25m to hotel on left just before junct with A330

This impressive Victorian mansion, close to Ascot Racecourse, has undergone a stylish refurbishment. New executive bedrooms are spacious, comfortable and particularly well equipped. Public rooms include a cosy bar and an elegant restaurant in which creative dishes are served. An impressive self-contained conference centre and brand new spa facility appeal to both conference and leisure guests.

Rooms 126 en suite (61 fmly) (33 GF) ⊘ in all bedrooms S fr £99; D fr £148 (incl. bkfst) **Facilities** Spa STV 🖼 supervised Sauna ♨ Putt green Wi-fi in bedrooms Leisure complex Xmas **Conf** BC Thtr 150 Class 90 Board 70 Del from £90 **Services** Lift **Parking** 250 **Notes LB** ⊗ in restaurant Civ Wed 140

★★★★ 76% **HOTEL**

The Royal Berkshire Ramada Plaza

⊛RAMADA.
PLAZA

London Rd, Sunninghill SL5 0PP

☎ 01344 623322 🖷 01344 627100

e-mail: sales.royalberkshire@ramadajarvis.co.uk

web: www.ramadajarvis.co.uk

dir: A30 towards Bagshot, right opposite Wentworth Club onto A329, continue for 2m, hotel entrance on right

Once occupied by the Churchill family, this delightful Queen Anne house is set in 14 acres of attractive gardens on the edge of Ascot. Public areas include a comfortable lounge bar, an attractive restaurant that overlooks the rear gardens and extensive conference facilities. The main house has been skilfully extended to offer smart, well-equipped bedrooms.

continued on page 48

England

ASCOT *continued*

Rooms 63 en suite (2 fmly) (8 GF) ⊘ in 25 bedrooms S £70-£225; D £70-£225 **Facilities** STV 🔲 ♨ Sauna Gym ⌣ Putt green Wi-fi in bedrooms Xmas **Conf** Thtr 100 Class 60 Board 45 Del £265 **Parking** 150 **Notes LB** ⊘ in restaurant Civ Wed 90

★★ 68% HOTEL

Highclere

19 Kings Rd, Sunninghill SL5 9AD

☎ 01344 625220 📠 01344 872528

e-mail: info@highclerehotel.com

web: www.highclerehotel.com

dir: opp Sunninghill Post Office

This privately owned establishment is situated in a quiet residential area, close to the racecourse, Windsor and the M3. Modest bedrooms are attractively decorated and well equipped. A cosy bar is available adjacent to the comfortable conservatory lounge. A short dinner menu is available with a number of restaurants within walking distance.

Rooms 11 en suite (1 fmly) (2 GF) ⊘ in 7 bedrooms S £60-£75; D £75-£90 (incl. bkfst) **Facilities** Wi-fi in bedrooms **Conf** Thtr 15 Class 15 **Parking** 11 **Notes** ⊗ ⊘ in restaurant

★★ 67% HOTEL

Brockenhurst

Brockenhurst Rd SL5 9HA

☎ 01344 621912 📠 01344 873252

e-mail: info@brockenhurst.com

dir: on A330

Located within easy reach of the famous racecourse, Windsor Castle and other local attractions, this attractive Edwardian house offers comfortable accommodation. Bedrooms are mostly spacious with a range of thoughtful extras. Relaxed and friendly service is provided in the cosy bar and restaurant, both of which overlook the charming grounds.

Rooms 12 en suite 5 annexe en suite (2 fmly) (2 GF) S fr £89; D fr £89 **Facilities** STV Wi-fi in bedrooms **Conf** Thtr 50 Class 25 Board 30 **Parking** 32 **Notes** ⊗ ⊘ in restaurant

BINFIELD   MAP 05 SU87

BUDGET HOTEL

Travelodge Bracknell

London Rd RG12 4AA

☎ 08700 850 950 📠 01344 485940

web: www.travelodge.co.uk

dir: M4 junct 10 (Bracknell) take 1st exit towards Binfield B3408

Travelodge offers good quality, good value, modern accommodation. Ideal for families, the spacious en suite bedrooms include remote-control TV, tea and coffee-making facilities and comfortable beds. Meals can be taken at the nearby family restaurant. See Hotel Groups pages for further details.

Rooms 35 en suite S fr £26; D fr £26

BRACKNELL   MAP 05 SU86
See also Crowthorne

★★★★ 77% ⓦ ⓦ HOTEL

Coppid Beech

John Nike Way RG12 8TF

☎ 01344 303333 📠 01344 301200

e-mail: welcome@coppid-beech-hotel.co.uk

web: www.coppidbeech.com

dir: M4 junct 10 take Wokingham/Bracknell onto A329. In 2m take B3408 to Binfield at rdbt. Hotel 200yds on right

This chalet designed hotel offers extensive facilities and includes a ski-slope, ice rink, nightclub, health club and Bier Keller. Bedrooms range from suites to standard rooms - all are impressively equipped. A choice of dining is offered; there's a full bistro menu available in the Keller and for more formal dining, Rowan's restaurant provides award-winning cuisine.

Rooms 205 en suite (6 fmly) ⊘ in 138 bedrooms **Facilities** Spa STV 🔲 supervised Sauna Solarium Gym Jacuzzi Dry ski slope, Ice rink 🎵 Xmas **Conf** BC Thtr 400 Class 240 Board 24 **Services** Lift **Parking** 350 **Notes** Civ Wed 120

★★★★ 75% HOTEL

Grange Bracknell

Charles Square RG12 1DF

☎ 01344 474000 📠 01344 474125

e-mail: bracknell@grangehotels.com

web: www.grangehotels.co.uk

dir: M4/A329 follow Bracknell town centre signs , hotel on left

Lighting is used to impressive effect both inside and outside this former office building to create a modern environment that is both comfortable and stylish. Public rooms include the Callela Bar, Ascot Green Restaurant, a small fitness suite and a range of interconnecting conference and banqueting rooms. Air-conditioned bedrooms are spacious and are equipped with a host of extras.

Rooms 120 en suite (6 fmly) ⊘ in 60 bedrooms S £175-£230; D £175-£230 **Facilities** STV Gym Wi-fi in bedrooms Xmas **Conf** Thtr 200 Class 120 Board 80 Del £220 **Services** Lift air con **Parking** 111 **Notes LB** ⊗

★★★ 78% HOTEL

Stirrups Country House

Maidens Green RG42 6LD

☎ 01344 882284 📠 01344 882300

e-mail: reception@stirrupshotel.co.uk

web: www.stirrupshotel.co.uk

dir: 3m N on B3022 towards Windsor

Situated in a peaceful location between Maidenhead, Bracknell and Windsor, this hotel has high standards of comfort in the bedrooms, with some rooms boasting a small sitting room area. There is a popular bar, a restaurant, function rooms and delightful grounds.

Rooms 30 en suite (4 fmly) (2 GF) ⊘ in 20 bedrooms **Facilities** STV Wi-fi in bedrooms **Conf** Thtr 100 Class 50 Board 40 Del £150 **Services** Lift **Parking** 100 **Notes** ⊘ in restaurant Civ Wed 100

England

BUDGET HOTEL

Premier Travel Inn Bracknell
Arlington Square, Wokingham Rd RG42 1NA
☎ 08701 977036 ▤ 01344 319526
web: www.premiertravelinn.com

dir: *M4 (J10) A329(M) Bracknell to lights. 1st left, 3rd exit rdbt by Safeway to town centre. Left at rdbt, left at next rdbt. Inn on left.*

High quality, modern budget accommodation ideal for both families and business travellers. Spacious, en suite bedrooms feature bath and shower, satellite TV and many have telephones and modem points. The adjacent family restaurant features a wide and varied menu. For further details consult the Hotel Groups page.

Rooms 60 en suite

BRAY   MAP 06 SU97

★★★★ 69% ◉ **HOTEL**

Monkey Island
Old Mill Ln SL6 2EE
☎ 01628 623400 ▤ 01628 784732
e-mail: info@monkeyisland.co.uk

dir: *M4 junct 8/9/A308 signed Windsor. 1st left into Bray, 1st right into Old Mill Lane, opp Crown pub*

This hotel is charmingly set on an island in the Thames, yet is within easy reach of major routes. Access is by footbridge or boat, but there is a large car park nearby. The hotel comprises two buildings, one for accommodation and the other for dining and drinking. Ample grounds are beautifully maintained and provide a peaceful haven for wildlife.

Rooms 26 en suite (1 fmly) (12 GF) **Facilities** STV Fishing ⚓ Boating ⅝ **Conf** Thtr 120 Class 70 Board 50 **Parking** 100 **Notes** ⊗ ⊛ in restaurant Civ Wed

---

CHIEVELEY   MAP 05 SU47

◎◎ **RESTAURANT WITH ROOMS**

The Crab at Chieveley
Wantage Rd RG20 8UE
☎ 01635 247550 ▤ 01635 247440
e-mail: info@crabatchieveley.com

dir: *M4 junct 13 N A34 to Oxford, 1st left to Chieveley after Red Lion. Left at school road 1.5m. At T-junct turn right. Hotel at top of hill*

The individually themed bedrooms at this former pub have been appointed to a very high standard and include a full range of modern amenities. Ground-floor rooms have a small private patio area complete with a hot tub. The restaurant is divided into a modern Fishbar brasserie area and a more formal dining area. Both offer an extensive and award-winning range of fish and seafood dishes.

Rooms 13 en suite (8 GF) ⊛ in all bedrooms S £100-£130; D £150-£170 (incl. bkfst) (Sun only incl. bkfst & dinner) **Facilities** STV Sauna Gym Jacuzzi Hot tub **Conf** Thtr 40 Class 40 Board 20 Del from £50 **Parking** 80 **Notes LB** Civ Wed 120

COOKHAM DEAN

◎◎ **RESTAURANT WITH ROOMS**

The Inn on the Green
The Old Cricket Common SL6 9NZ
☎ 01628 482638 ▤ 01628 487474
e-mail: reception@theinnonthegreen.com

dir: *A404 towards Marlow High St. Cross suspension bridge towards Bisham. 1st left into Quarry Wood Rd, right Hills Ln, right at Memorial Cross*

A traditional English country inn set in rural Berkshire. Bedrooms are spacious and comfortable, with antique furnishings adding to the character. The building retains many traditional features including a wood panelled dining room and Old English bar with log fire. Food is imaginative and noteworthy and can be enjoyed outside in the garden or terrace in warmer months.

Rooms 9 en suite (4 GF) S £90-£130; D £110-£160 (inc. bkfst) **Facilities** STV FTV **Conf** BC Thtr 30 Class 30 Board 30 Del from £185 **Parking** 50 **Notes LB** ⊗ RS Sun Civ Wed 100

CROWTHORNE   MAP 05 SU86

★★★ 70% **HOTEL**

The Waterloo Hotel
Duke's Ride RG45 6DW
☎ 0870 609 6111 ▤ 01344 778913

***folio** Hotels*

dir: *M3 junct 4, A331 to Camberley, follow signs to Sandhurst/Crowthorne A3095, left B3348, hotel past 2nd rdbt*

Situated in a quiet location but convenient for both the M3 and M4, this hotel attracts a high proportion of business guests. The modern bedrooms, which include interconnecting pairs of rooms, are attractively appointed and well maintained. Public areas include a pleasant brasserie-style restaurant and a bar area.

Rooms 79 en suite ⊛ in 43 bedrooms S fr £120; D fr £120 **Facilities** STV Wi-fi available Discounts at local leisure facilities Xmas **Conf** Thtr 50 Class 20 Board 24 Del from £150 **Parking** 96 **Notes LB** ⊛ in restaurant Civ Wed 40

England

HUNGERFORD
MAP 05 SU36

★★★ 70% **HOTEL**

Three Swans
117 High St RG17 0LZ
☎ 01488 682721 ▤ 01488 681708
e-mail: info@threeswans.net

dir: M4 junct 14 follow signs to Hungerford. Hotel half way along High St on left. Through archway to car park.

Centrally located in this bustling market town the Three Swans is a charming establishment renovated in a fresh and airy style. Choose between the wood-panelled bar, spacious lounge or attractive rear garden to relax and sample the local ales or a fresh cream tea. The informal restaurant is enhanced by selection of work from local artists. Bedrooms are well appointed and comfortable.

Rooms 15 en suite (1 fmly) ⊛ in 11 bedrooms S £75-£120; D £80-£125 (incl. bkfst) **Facilities** Access to local private gym. Xmas **Conf** Thtr 55 Class 40 Board 30 **Parking** 30 **Notes LB** ⊛ in restaurant

HURLEY
MAP 05 SU88

⊛⊛ **RESTAURANT WITH ROOMS**

Black Boys Inn
Henley Rd SL6 5NQ
☎ 01628 824212
e-mail: info@blackboysinn.co.uk
web: www.blackboysinn.co.uk

dir: 1m W of Hurley on A4130

This 16th-century inn has been restored to provide stylish contemporary accommodation with modern en suites. Extra facilities include DVD players and complimentary internet access. Imaginative food and interesting wines are served in the bar-restaurant, where local produce and fresh fish are prominent.

Rooms 8 annexe en suite (5 GF) ⊛ in all bedrooms D £65-£75 **Conf** Board 10 **Parking** 40 **Notes** ⊛ No children 12yrs ⊛ in restaurant Closed 24 Dec-9 Jan

KNOWL HILL
MAP 05 SU87

★★★ Ⓐ

Bird In Hand Country Inn
Bath Rd RG10 9UP
☎ 01628 826622 & 822781 ▤ 01628 826748
e-mail: sthebirdinhand@aol.com
web: www.birdinhand.co.uk

dir: on A4 between Maidenhead & Reading

Rooms 15 en suite (1 fmly) (6 GF) **Conf** Thtr 50 Class 40 Board 50 Del from £150 **Parking** 80 **Notes** ⊛ in restaurant

If the freedom to smoke or be in a non-smoking atmosphere is important to you, check the rules when you book

MAIDENHEAD
MAP 06 SU88
See also Bray

INSPECTORS' CHOICE

★★★★ ⊛⊛⊛ **HOTEL**

Fredrick's Hotel Restaurant Spa
Shoppenhangers Rd SL6 2PZ
☎ 01628 581000 ▤ 01628 771054
e-mail: reservations@fredricks-hotel.co.uk
web: www.fredricks-hotel.co.uk

dir: M4 junct 8/9 onto A404(M) to Maidenhead West & Henley. 1st exit 9a to White Waltham. Left into Shoppenhangers Road to Maidenhead, hotel on right

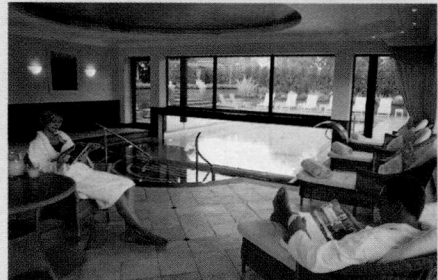

Just 30 minutes from London, this delightful hotel enjoys a peaceful location yet is within easy reach of the M4 and only 20 minutes' drive from Wentworth and Sunningdale golf courses. The spacious bedrooms are comfortably furnished and very well equipped. An enthusiastic team of staff ensure friendly and efficient service. The imaginative cuisine is a highlight, as is the newly completed luxurious spa offering the ultimate in relaxation and wellbeing.

Rooms 34 en suite (11 GF) S £215-£235; D £295-£320 (incl. bkfst) **Facilities** Spa STV 🏊 ⚡ supervised Sauna Gym Jacuzzi Wi-fi in bedrooms Treatment, hydrotherapy, Oriental steam & Dead Sea flotation room Rasul Suite **Conf** BC Thtr 120 Class 80 Board 60 Del from £295 **Services** air con **Parking** 90 **Notes LB** ⊛ ⊛ in restaurant Closed 24 Dec-3 Jan Civ Wed 120

★★★ Ⓐ

The Thames Hotel
Raymead Rd SL6 8NR
☎ 01628 628721 ▤ 01628 773921
e-mail: reservations@thameshotel.co.uk

Rooms 35 en suite (3 fmly) ⊛ in 18 bedrooms S £45-£80; D £60-£95 (incl. bkfst) **Facilities** STV Wi-fi in bedrooms **Conf** Thtr 50 Class 35 Board 25 Del from £125 **Parking** 38 **Notes** ⊛ ⊛ in restaurant Closed 23-31 Dec

★★ 72% HOTEL

Elva Lodge

Castle Hill SL6 4AD
☎ 01628 622948 📠 01628 778954
e-mail: reservations@elvalodgehotel.co.uk
web: www.elvalodgehotel.co.uk
dir: A4 from Maidenhead towards Reading. Hotel at top of hill on left

Within easy reach of the town centre, this family-run hotel offers a warm welcome and friendly service. Bedrooms are pleasantly decorated, continually maintained and equipped with thoughtful extras. Spacious public areas include a smart, stylish lounge, a bar, and the Lion's Brasserie, which offers a wide range of popular dishes.

Rooms 26 rms (23 en suite) (1 fmly) (5 GF) ✆ in 6 bedrooms S £55-£90; D £70-£108 (incl. dinner) **Facilities** FTV Wi-fi in bedrooms Reduced rates at local Leisure Centre **Conf** Thtr 50 Class 30 Board 30 **Parking** 32 **Notes** ✆ in restaurant Closed 24-30 Dec Civ Wed 60

MEMBURY MOTORWAY SERVICE AREA (M4)   MAP 05 SU37

BUDGET HOTEL

Days Inn Membury

Membury Service Area RG17 7TZ
☎ 01488 72336 📠 01488 72336
e-mail: membury.hotel@welcomebreak.co.uk
web: www.welcomebreak.co.uk
dir: M4 between junct 14 & 15

This modern building offers accommodation in smart, spacious and well-equipped bedrooms, suitable for families and business travellers, and all with en suite bathrooms. Continental breakfast is available and other refreshments may be taken at the nearby family restaurant. For further details see the Hotel Groups page.

Rooms 38 en suite **Conf** BC Board 10

NEWBURY   MAP 05 SU46
See also Andover (Hampshire)

INSPECTORS' CHOICE

★★★★★ ◉◉◉◉ HOTEL

The Vineyard at Stockcross

Stockcross RG20 8JU
☎ 01635 528770 📠 01635 528398
e-mail: general@the-vineyard.co.uk
web: www.the-vineyard.co.uk
dir: from M4 take A34 towards Newbury, exit at 3rd junct for Speen. Right at rdbt then right again at 2nd rdbt.

A haven of style in the Berkshire countryside, this hotel prides itself on a superb art collection, which can be seen throughout the building. Bedrooms come in a variety of styles - many split-level suites that are exceptionally well equipped. Comfortable lounges lead into the stylish restaurant, which serves award-winning, imaginative and precise cooking, complemented by an equally impressive selection of wines from California and around the world. The welcome is warm and sincere, the service professional yet relaxed.

Rooms 49 en suite (15 GF) ✆ in 10 bedrooms S fr £200, D £420-£617 **Facilities** Spa STV 🔲 Sauna Gym Jacuzzi Wi-fi in bedrooms Treatment rooms 🎵 Xmas **Conf** BC Thtr 100 Class 50 Board 30 Del from £340 **Services** Lift air con **Parking** 100 **Notes LB** ✆ ✆ in restaurant Civ Wed 100

★★★★ 83% ◉◉ HOTEL

Donnington Valley Hotel & Spa   CLASSIC

Old Oxford Rd, Donnington RG14 3AG
☎ 01635 551199 📠 01635 551123
e-mail: general@donningtonvalley.co.uk
web: www.donningtonvalley.co.uk
dir: M4 junct 13, take A34 southbound, take exit signed 'Donnington Hotels' towards Donnington. Hotel 2m

This friendly hotel stands on its own 18-hole golf course and provides stylish and exceedingly high quality accommodation. The striking building houses well-equipped meeting rooms and public areas with views over the countryside. The WinePress restaurant offers imaginative food and a comprehensive choice of wines in comfortable surroundings; service is attentive and friendly.

continued on page 52

Some hotels, although accepting children, may not have any special facilities for them so it is well worth checking before booking

NEWBURY *continued*

Donnington Valley Hotel & Spa

Rooms 111 en suite (20 fmly) (36 GF) ⊛ in 107 bedrooms S £170-£250;
D £210-£250 **Facilities Spa** STV 🔦 ♨ 18 Sauna Gym Putt green Jacuzzi
Wi-fi in bedrooms health club, spa, dance studio, aromatherapy room ♫
Xmas **Conf** BC Thtr 140 Class 60 Board 40 Del from £145 **Services** Lift
Parking 160 **Notes LB** ⊗ Civ Wed 90

★★★★ 79% ⊛ **HOTEL**

Regency Park Hotel
Bowling Green Rd, Thatcham RG18 3RP
☎ 01635 871555 📠 01635 871571
e-mail: info@regencyparkhotel.co.uk
web: www.regencyparkhotel.co.uk

dir: *from Newbury take A4 signed Thatcham & Reading. 2nd
rdbt exit signed Cold Ash. Hotel 1m on left*

This smart, stylish hotel has benefited from major investment over the
last few years and is ideal for both business and leisure guests.
Spacious, well-equipped bedrooms include a number of
contemporary, tasteful executive rooms. Smart airy public areas
include a state-of-the-art spa and leisure club and the Watermark
restaurant, offering imaginative, award-winning cuisine.

Rooms 109 en suite (7 fmly) (9 GF) ⊛ in 84 bedrooms S £95-£175;
D £95-£175 **Facilities Spa** STV FTV 🔦 Sauna Solarium Gym Jacuzzi
Wi-fi in bedrooms 4 Health & Beauty treatment rooms Xmas **Conf** BC
Thtr 200 Class 80 Board 70 Del from £165 **Services** Lift **Parking** 160
Notes LB ⊗ ⊛ in restaurant Civ Wed 100

See advert on opposite page

★★★ 77% **COUNTRY HOUSE HOTEL**

Ramada Hotel & Resort Elcot Park
RG20 8NJ
☎ 01488 658100 📠 01488 658288
e-mail: sales.elcotpark@ramadajarvis.co.uk
web: www.ramadahotelandresortelcotpark.co.uk

dir: *Take A4 towards Hungerford, hotel is on right after The
Halfway Inn.*

Enjoying a peaceful location yet within easy access to both the A4 and
M4, this country-house hotel is set in 16 acres of gardens and
woodland. Bedrooms are comfortably appointed and include some
located in an adjacent Mews. Public areas include the Orangery
restaurant, which enjoys views over the Kennet Valley, a leisure club
and a range of conference rooms.

continued

Rooms 55 en suite 17 annexe en suite (1 fmly) (26 GF) ⊛ in
64 bedrooms S £50-£150; D £60-£150 (incl. bkfst) **Facilities Spa** STV
🔦 supervised ♨ Sauna Solarium Gym ♨ Putt green Wi-fi in bedrooms
Xmas **Conf** Thtr 110 Class 45 Board 35 Del from £110 **Parking** 120
Notes ⊛ in restaurant Civ Wed 120

★★★ 74% **HOTEL**

West Grange
Cox's Ln, Bath Rd, Midgham RG7 5UP
☎ 01635 273074 📠 01635 862351
e-mail: reservations@westgrangehotel.co.uk

This former farmhouse has been turned into a smart and modern
hotel and is set in well-managed grounds only a short drive away
from Thatcham and Newbury. Bedrooms offer a quiet and
comfortable stay and guests can relax in the large bar lounge and
attractive restaurant. There is also a patio for warmer months.

Rooms 45 en suite (3 fmly) (12 GF) ⊛ in all bedrooms S fr £75;
D fr £95 (incl. bkfst) **Conf** BC Thtr 50 Class 25 Board 30 **Services** Lift
Parking 70 **Notes** ⊗ ⊛ in restaurant

★★★ 71% **HOTEL**

Newbury Manor Hotel
London Rd RG14 2BY
☎ 01635 528838 📠 01635 523406
e-mail: enquiries@newbury-manor-hotel.co.uk

dir: *from Newbury follow A4 towards Thatcham. 300yds after
rdbt for Newbury Business Park. Hotel on right*

Now under new ownership. A former Georgian watermill, which
features the original millrace and the River Kennet which flows
through the well tended grounds. The character bedrooms offer a
variety of styles and sizes whilst diners can choose between the river
bar in the grounds and the more formal hotel restaurant in the main
building.

Rooms 33 en suite (22 fmly) (12 GF) ⊛ in all bedrooms S £120-£165;
D £130-£175 (incl. bkfst) **Facilities** STV Fishing Wi-fi in bedrooms
Conf Thtr 230 Class 96 Board 170 Del from £155 **Parking** 150
Notes LB ⊗ ⊛ in restaurant Civ Wed 85

U

Swallow Chequers
SWALLOW
6-8 Oxford St RG14 1JB
☎ 01635 38000 📠 01635 37170
e-mail: reservations.newbury@swallowhotels.com
web: www.swallowhotels.com

dir: *Exit M4 junct 13 and take A34 S then A339 to Newbury. At
2nd rdbt turn right to town centre. At clock tower rdbt turn right,
hotel on right*

At the time of going to press, the star classification for this hotel was
not confirmed. Please refer to the AA internet site www.theAA.com for
current information.

Rooms 45 en suite 11 annexe en suite (3 fmly) (7 GF) ⊛ in
39 bedrooms S £89-£122; D £89-£135 (incl. bkfst) **Facilities** Xmas
Conf Thtr 120 Class 50 Board 40 Del from £102 **Parking** 60 **Notes LB**
⊗ ⊛ in restaurant Civ Wed 100

England

BUDGET HOTEL

Premier Travel Inn Newbury
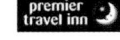
Bath Rd, Midgham RG7 5UX
☎ 0870 9906556 🗎 0870 9906557
web: www.premiertravelinn.com
dir: Exit M4 junct 12, A4 towards Newbury. Inn 7m on right

High quality, modern budget accommodation ideal for both families and business travellers. Spacious, en suite bedrooms feature bath and shower, satellite TV and many have telephones and modem points. The adjacent family restaurant features a wide and varied menu. For further details consult the Hotel Groups page.

Rooms 49 en suite **Conf** Thtr 10 Board 10

BUDGET HOTEL

Travelodge Newbury Chieveley (M4)
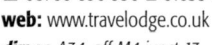
Chieveley, Oxford Rd RG18 9XX
☎ 08700 850 950 🗎 01635 247886
web: www.travelodge.co.uk
dir: on A34, off M4 junct 13

Travelodge offers good quality, good value, modern accommodation. Ideal for families, the spacious en suite bedrooms include remote-control TV, tea and coffee-making facilities and comfortable beds. Meals can be taken at the nearby family restaurant. See Hotel Groups pages for further details.

Rooms 127 en suite S fr £26; D fr £26

Travelodge Newbury Tot Hill
Tot Hill Services (A34), Newbury by-pass RG20 9ED
☎ 08700 850 950 🗎 01635 278169
dir: Tot Hill Services on A34
Rooms 52 en suite S fr £26; D fr £26

PANGBOURNE MAP 05 SU67
★★★ 66% HOTEL

Best Western George Hotel Pangbourne
The Square RG8 7AJ
☎ 0118 984 2237 🗎 0118 984 4354
e-mail: info@georgehotelpangbourne.co.uk
dir: M4 junct 12, follow sign for A340. On entering the village turn right.

Occupying a site where an inn has stood since 1295, The George offers modern facilities. Bedrooms are thoughtfully appointed and comfortable, a number are specifically equipped for families. The Kidsden rooms have computers and Playstations, and considering the hotel's location, just 30 minutes from Legoland, this is a popular venue for families. Dinner with an Italian theme is available in Mia Bene Restaurant.

Rooms 24 en suite (2 fmly) ⊗ in all bedrooms S £69-£100; D £75-£110 **Facilities** STV Wi-fi in bedrooms **Conf** Thtr 60 Class 25 Board 20 **Parking** 30

READING MAP 05 SU77
See also Swallowfield

★★★★ 81% ⚜⚜ HOTEL

Millennium Madejski Hotel Reading
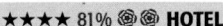
Madejski Stadium RG2 0FL
☎ 0118 925 3500 🗎 0118 925 3501
e-mail: sales.reading@mill-cop.com
web: www.millenniumhotels.com
dir: M4 junct 11 onto A33, follow signs for Madejski Stadium Complex

A stylish hotel, that features an atrium lobby with specially commissioned water sculpture, is part of the Madejski stadium complex, home to both Reading Football and London Irish Rugby teams. Bedrooms are appointed with spacious workstations and plenty of amenities; there is also a choice of suites and a club floor with its own lounge. The hotel also has an award-winning, fine dining restaurant.

Rooms 140 en suite (4 fmly) ⊗ in 92 bedrooms S £75-£200; D £95-£200 **Facilities** Spa STV ⌨ supervised Sauna Solarium Gym Jacuzzi Wi-fi available **Conf** Board 12 Del from £199 **Services** Lift air con **Parking** 150 **Notes** LB ⊗ in restaurant RS Xmas & New Yr

England

READING *continued*

★★★★ 72% HOTEL

Renaissance Hotel Reading

Oxford Rd RG1 7RH

☎ 0118 958 6222 📠 0118 959 7842

e-mail: rhi.lhrlr.dos@renaissancehotels.com

web: www.marriott.co.uk/lhrlr

dir: M4 junct 11 follow A33 into Reading and signs for Broad Street Mall car park

Situated in the heart of the town, this long-established hotel is well positioned for both business travellers and shoppers. Air-conditioned bedrooms feature a host of extras especially for the business guest including high-speed internet access. Public areas include a leisure area, a variety of meeting rooms and a business centre. Free parking is available in the adjoining multi-storey.

Rooms 196 en suite (67 fmly) ⊘ in 160 bedrooms S £145-£170; D £145-£170 **Facilities** STV ⬚ supervised Sauna Solarium Gym Jacuzzi **Conf** BC Thtr 220 Class 130 Board 60 Del from £120 **Services** Lift air con **Parking** 20 **Notes LB** ⊗ ⊘ in restaurant Civ Wed 140

★★★ 74% HOTEL

Courtyard by Marriott Reading

Bath Rd, Padworth RG7 5HT

☎ 0870 400 7234 📠 0870 400 7334

web: www.kewgreen.co.uk

dir: M4 junct 12 onto A4 towards Newbury. Hotel 3.5m on left, after petrol station

This purpose-built hotel combines the benefits of a peaceful rural location with the accessibility afforded by good road links. Modern comforts include air-conditioned bedrooms and rooms with easy access for less mobile guests. A feature of the hotel is its pretty courtyard garden, which can be seen from the restaurant.

Rooms 50 en suite (25 GF) ⊘ in 45 bedrooms **Facilities** STV Gym Fitness room **Conf** Thtr 200 Class 70 Board 80 **Services** air con **Parking** 200 **Notes LB** ⊘ in restaurant Civ Wed 100

★★★ 73% HOTEL

Copthorne Hotel Reading

COPTHORNE

Pingewood RG30 3UN

☎ 0118 950 0885 📠 0118 939 1996

dir: A33 towards Basingstoke. At Three Mile Cross rdbt right signed Burghfield. After 300mtrs 2nd right, over M4, through lights, hotel on left

Enjoying a secluded and rural setting and yet just a few minutes south of Reading, this modern hotel been built around a man-made lake which is occasionally used for water sports. Bedrooms are generally spacious with good facilities, and most have balconies overlooking the lake and wildlife. Public areas include Brasserie 209 and a well-equipped leisure centre.

Rooms 81 en suite (23 fmly) ⊘ in all bedrooms S £59-£171; D £59-£171 **Facilities** Spa STV ⬚ ♨ Squash Snooker Sauna Solarium Gym Jacuzzi Watersports Team building Xmas **Conf** BC Thtr 110 Class 60 Board 60 Del from £135 **Services** Lift **Parking** 6 **Notes LB** ⊗ ⊘ in restaurant Civ Wed 80

★★★ 71% HOTEL

Quality Hotel Reading

648-654 Oxford Rd RG30 1EH

☎ 0118 950 0541 📠 0118 956 7220

e-mail: info@qualityreading.co.uk

dir: M4 junct 11, A33 bypass towards town centre, then A329 towards Pangbourne, follow Oxford Road signs

Close to the city centre this modern, purpose-built hotel is a popular choice with business guests. Bedrooms are generally spacious and offer a good range of facilities. Guests have a choice of eating lighter meals and snacks in the bar lounge or a more formal menu is offered in the spacious restaurant. The hotel benefits from conference facilities and ample parking.

Rooms 96 en suite (15 fmly) ⊘ in 39 bedrooms **Facilities** STV **Conf** BC Thtr 100 Class 50 Board 40 **Services** Lift **Parking** 60 **Notes LB** ⊗ ⊘ in restaurant

★★★ 70% HOTEL

Best Western Calcot Hotel

98 Bath Rd, Calcot RG31 7QN

☎ 0118 941 6423 📠 0118 945 1223

e-mail: enquiries@calcothotel.co.uk

web: www.calcothotel.co.uk

dir: M4 junct 12 onto A4 towards Reading, hotel in 0.5m on N side of A4

This hotel is conveniently located in a residential area just off the motorway. Bedrooms are well equipped with good business facilities, such as data ports and good workspace. There are attractive public rooms and function suites and the informal restaurant offers enjoyable food in welcoming surroundings.

Rooms 78 en suite (2 fmly) ⊘ in 60 bedrooms S £55-£130; D £68-£140 **Facilities** STV FTV Wi-fi in bedrooms ♪ **Conf** Thtr 120 Class 35 Board 35 Del from £140 **Parking** 130 **Notes** ⊗ ⊘ in restaurant Closed 25-27 Dec Civ Wed 60

★★ 74% HOTEL

The Mill House

THE INDEPENDENTS

Old Basingstoke Rd, Swallowfield RG7 1PY

☎ 0118 988 3124 📠 0118 988 5550

e-mail: info@themillhousehotel.co.uk

(For full entry see Swallowfield)

continued

★★ 67% HOTEL

Comfort Hotel Padworth Reading

Bath Rd, Padworth RG7 5HT

☎ 0118 971 3282 📠 0118 971 4238

e-mail: gm@comfortreading.co.uk

dir: M4 junct 12. Onto A4 Bath Road signed Newbury. Hotel approx 2m on left.

This modern and homely hotel enjoys a convenient location close to the motorway network and Reading. Smart open plan public areas include a lounge bar and dining area whilst bedrooms are geared to the needs of the business and holiday guest alike and include some family rooms.

Rooms 33 en suite (1 fmly) (21 GF) ❷ in 20 bedrooms **Facilities** STV Wi-fi in bedrooms **Conf** Thtr 120 Class 70 Board 40 **Parking** 40 **Notes LB** ❷ ❷ in restaurant

★★ 67% HOTEL

The Wee Waif

OLD ENGLISH INNS

Old Bath Rd, Charvil RG10 9RJ

☎ 0118 944 0066 & 0800 917 3085 📠 0118 969 1525

e-mail: weewaif.charvil@newbridgeinns.co.uk

web: www.oldenglish.co.uk

This friendly and modern hotel is conveniently located on the outskirts of Reading and close to the main road network. The popular bar and restaurant are atmospheric and open for most of the day. The comfortable and spacious bedrooms are situated in lodge accommodation in an adjoining wing.

Rooms 42 en suite (28 fmly) (21 GF) ❷ in 36 bedrooms S £65-£80; D £65-£80 (incl. bkfst) **Facilities** STV Xmas **Parking** 50 **Notes LB** ❷ ❷ in restaurant

BUDGET HOTEL

Premier Travel Inn Reading South

Grazeley Green Rd RG7 1LS

☎ 0870 9906454 📠 0870 9906455

web: www.premiertravelinn.com

dir: Exit M4 junct 11 signed A33 towards Basingstoke. At rdbt take exit towards Burghfield & Mortimer. 3rd right into Grazeley Green. Under rail bridge turn left. Inn on left

High quality, modern budget accommodation ideal for both families and business travellers. Spacious, en suite bedrooms feature bath and shower, satellite TV and many have telephones and modem points. The adjacent family restaurant features a wide and varied menu. For further details consult the Hotel Groups page.

Rooms 32 en suite **Conf** Class 8 Board 8

BUDGET HOTEL

Travelodge Reading Central

Oxford Rd RG1 7LT

☎ 08700 850 950 📠 0118 950 3257

web: www.travelodge.co.uk

dir: M4 junct 11, A33 towards Reading, follow signs for A329 (Oxford road)

Travelodge offers good quality, good value, modern accommodation. Ideal for families, the spacious en suite bedrooms include remote-

control TV, tea and coffee-making facilities and comfortable beds. Meals can be taken at the nearby family restaurant. See Hotel Groups pages for further details.

Rooms 80 en suite S fr £26; D fr £26

Travelodge Reading (M4 Eastbound)

Burghfield RG30 3UQ

☎ 08700 850 950 📠 0118 959 2045

Rooms 86 en suite S fr £26; D fr £26 **Conf** Thtr 20 Class 20 Board 20

Travelodge Reading (M4 Westbound)

Burghfield RG30 3UQ

☎ 08700 850 950 📠 0118 958 2350

dir: M4 between junct 11 & 12 westbound

Rooms 102 en suite S fr £26; D fr £26

Travelodge Reading Whitley

387 Basingstoke Rd RG2 0JE

☎ 08700 850 950 📠 0118 975 1303

dir: M4 junct 11, onto A33 to Reading, right onto B3031, 1m on right

Rooms 36 en suite S fr £26; D fr £26

SLOUGH

MAP 06 SU97

★★★★ 76% ❀ HOTEL

The Pinewood Hotel

"bespoke"

Uxbridge Rd, George Green SL3 6AP

☎ 01753 824848 📠 01753 824282

e-mail: info@pinewoodhotel.co.uk

web: www.bespokehotels.com

dir: A4 N from Slough onto A412 towards Uxbridge. Hotel 3m on left

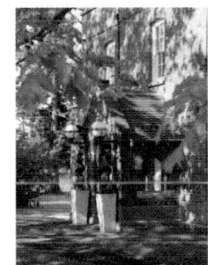

This is a small luxury hotel on the outskirts of Slough. Excellent design is at the forefront throughout, together with good levels of comfort. The Eden brasserie specialises in quality produce, carefully prepared, including dishes cooked on the wood-burning stove. Service is friendly and attentive.

Rooms 33 en suite 16 annexe en suite (4 fmly) (12 GF) ❷ in 4 bedrooms **Facilities** STV Wi-fi available Xmas **Conf** Thtr 36 Class 46 Board 40 Del from £185 **Services** Lift air con **Parking** 40 **Notes** ❷ ❷ in restaurant Civ Wed 3

continued

England

SLOUGH *continued*

★★★★ 75% HOTEL

Copthorne Hotel Slough-Windsor

COPTHORNE

400 Cippenham Ln SL1 2YE
☎ 01753 516222 ▤ 01753 516237
e-mail: sales.slough@mill-cop.com
web: www.copthorne.com
dir: M4 junct 6 & follow A355 to Slough at next rdbt turn left &
left again for hotel entrance

Conveniently located for the motorway and for Heathrow Airport, this
modern hotel offers visitors a wide range of facilities including indoor
leisure and a choice of dining options. The hotel also offers
discounted entrance fee to some of the attractions in the area. Air-
conditioned bedrooms provide a useful range of extras including
satellite TV and trouser press.

Rooms 219 en suite (47 fmly) ⊗ in 148 bedrooms **Facilities** STV FTV
▣ Sauna Gym Wi-fi in bedrooms **Conf** Thtr 250 Class 160 Board 60
Del from £150 **Services** Lift **Parking** 300 **Notes** ⊛ ⊗ in restaurant
Civ Wed 100

★★★ 79% HOTEL

Courtyard by Marriott Slough/ Windsor

Church St SL1 2NH
☎ 0870 400 7215 & 07153 551551 ▤ 0870 400 7315
web: www.kewgreen.co.uk
dir: M4 junct 6, follow A355 to rdbt, turn right, hotel approx
50yds on right

With Heathrow Airport and the motorway networks easily accessible
by car this modern hotel is in an ideal location. Spacious bedrooms
feature a comprehensive range of facilities. The public areas are lively,
modern and have an informal atmosphere.

Rooms 150 en suite (65 fmly) (6 GF) ⊗ in 113 bedrooms S £60-£129;
D £60-£129 **Facilities** STV Gym Wi-fi available Xmas **Conf** Thtr 40
Class 16 Board 20 Del from £110 **Services** Lift air con **Parking** 130
Notes LB ⊛ ⊗ in restaurant

★★★ 67% HOTEL

Quality Hotel Heathrow

QUALITY

London Rd, Brands Hill SL3 8QB
☎ 01753 684001 ▤ 01753 685767
e-mail: info@qualityheathrow.com
dir: M4 junct 5, follow signs for Colnbrook. Hotel approx
250mtrs on right

This stylish, modern hotel is ideally located for Heathrow Airport, and
for commercial visitors to Slough. Bedrooms have good facilities,
benefit from all-day room service and are smartly furnished. There is a
bright and airy open-plan restaurant, bar and lounge. Transfers are
available to and from the airport.

Rooms 128 en suite (23 fmly) (5 GF) ⊗ in 60 bedrooms S £45-£129;
D £45-£149 **Facilities** STV Gym Wi-fi in bedrooms **Conf** Thtr 120 Class 50
Board 40 Del from £99 **Services** Lift **Parking** 100 **Notes** LB ⊛

BUDGET HOTEL

Innkeeper's Lodge Slough/ Windsor

399 London Rd, Langley SL3 8PS
☎ 01753 591212 ▤ 01753 211362
web: www.innkeeperslodge.com
dir: M4 junct 5 onto London Rd, 100yds on right

Smart, en suite accommodation ideal for both business & leisure
guests. Bedrooms are very well equipped, including Sky TV,
telephone, modem points, tea & coffee making facilities, (family
rooms in most locations). Complimentary breakfast. The adjacent Pub
Restaurant; a Harvester, Vintage Inn, Toby Carvery, Ember Inn, Sizzling
Pubco or Pub & Carvery offers an all day menu. See Hotel Groups
pages for further details.

Rooms 57 en suite S £49.95-£69.95; D £49.95-£69.95 **Conf** Board 15

BUDGET HOTEL

Premier Travel Inn Slough

76 Uxbridge Rd SL1 1SU
☎ 0870 9906500 ▤ 0870 9906501
web: www.premiertravelinn.com
dir: 2m from M4 junct 5, 3m from junct 6. Just off A4

High quality, modern budget accommodation ideal for both families
and business travellers. Spacious, en suite bedrooms feature bath and
shower, satellite TV and many have telephones and modem points.
The adjacent family restaurant features a wide and varied menu. For
further details consult the Hotel Groups page.

Rooms 84 en suite

BUDGET HOTEL

Travelodge Slough

Landmark Place SL1 1BZ
☎ 08700 850 950 ▤ 01753 516897
web: www.travelodge.co.uk

Travelodge offers good quality, good value, modern accommodation.
Ideal for families, the spacious en suite bedrooms include remote-
control TV, tea and coffee-making facilities and comfortable beds.
Meals can be taken at the nearby family restaurant. See Hotel Groups
pages for further details.

Rooms 157 en suite S fr £26; D fr £26

SONNING

MAP 05 SU77

★★★ 78% ◉◉ HOTEL

French Horn

RG4 6TN
☎ 0118 969 2204 ▤ 0118 944 2210
e-mail: info@thefrenchhorn.co.uk
dir: From A4 into Sonning, follow B478 through village over
bridge, hotel on right, car park on left

This long established Thames-side establishment has a lovely village
setting and retains the traditions of classic hotel keeping. The
restaurant is a particular attraction and provides attentive service.
Bedrooms are spacious and comfortable, many offering stunning
views over the river and include four cottage suites. A private
boardroom is available for corporate guests.

continued

Rooms 13 en suite 8 annexe en suite (4 GF) S £120-£165; D £150-£205 (incl. bkfst) **Facilities** STV FTV Fishing Wi-fi in bedrooms **Conf** Board 16 Del from £245 **Services** air con **Parking** 40 **Notes** ⊗ Closed 26 Dec-30 Jan RS 1 Jan

STREATLEY
MAP 05 SU58

★★★★ 72% ⍟⍟ **HOTEL**

The Swan at Streatley
High St RG8 9HR
☎ 01491 878800 ▤ 01491 872554
e-mail: sales@swan-at-streatley.co.uk

dir: *from S right at lights in Streatley, hotel on left before bridge*

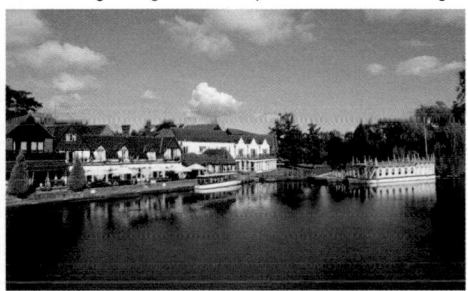

A stunning location set beside the Thames, ideal for an English summer's day. Many bedrooms enjoy the views and rooms are well appointed. The hotel offers a range of facilities including meeting rooms and leisure, the 'Streatley Belle' is moored beside the hotel and is a perfect, yet unusual meeting venue. Cuisine is accomplished and dining here should not be missed.

Rooms 45 en suite (13 GF) ⊘ in 9 bedrooms S £110-£120; D £138-£150 (incl. bkfst) **Facilities Spa** STV ⏃ Fishing Sauna Solarium Gym ⛱ Jacuzzi Wi-fi in bedrooms Electric motor launches for hire Xmas **Conf** BC Thtr 140 Class 60 Board 40 Del £230 **Parking** 170 **Notes** ⊘ in restaurant Civ Wed 130

SWALLOWFIELD
MAP 05 SU76

★★ 74% **HOTEL**

The Mill House
THE INDEPENDENTS

Old Basingstoke Rd, Swallowfield RG7 1PY
☎ 0118 988 3124 ▤ 0118 988 5550
e-mail: info@themillhousehotel.co.uk

dir: *M4 junct 11, S on A33, left at 1st rdbt onto B3349. Approx 1m after sign for Three Mile Cross & Spencer's Wood, hotel on right*

This smart Georgian house hotel enjoys a tranquil setting in its own delightful gardens, making it a popular wedding venue. Guests can enjoy fine dining in the conservatory-style restaurant or lighter meals in the cosy bar. Well-equipped bedrooms vary in size and style and include a number of spacious, well-appointed executive rooms.

Rooms 12 en suite (2 fmly) ⊘ in 3 bedrooms S £77.50-£97.50; D £100-£120 (incl. bkfst) **Facilities** ⛱ Wi-fi in bedrooms **Conf** Thtr 250 Class 100 Board 60 Del from £150 **Parking** 60 **Notes** ⊘ in restaurant RS Sun evenings Civ Wed 125

WINDSOR
MAP 06 SU97

★★★★ 79% **HOTEL**

Oakley Court
QMH
UK LIMITED

Windsor Rd, Water Oakley SL4 5UR
☎ 01753 609988 ▤ 01753 609942
e-mail: reservations.oakleycourt@moathousehotels.com

dir: *M4 junct 6, towards Windsor, then right onto A308 Maidenhead. Pass racecourse & hotel is 2.5m on right.*

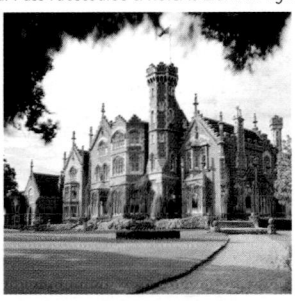

Built in 1859 this splendid Victorian Gothic mansion is enviably situated in extensive grounds that lead down to The Thames. All rooms are spacious, beautifully furnished and many enjoy river views. Extensive public areas include a range of comfortable lounges and the Oakleaf restaurant.

Rooms 69 en suite 49 annexe en suite (15 fmly) (43 GF) S £119-£190; D £129-£200 (incl. bkfst) **Facilities Spa** STV ⏃ supervised ⛱ ⛱ ⛱ Fishing Snooker Sauna Gym Putt green Jacuzzi Boating **Conf** BC Thtr 170 Class 90 Board 50 Del from £240 **Services** air con **Parking** 120 **Notes** ⊗ Civ Wed 120

★★★★ 75% ⍟⍟ **HOTEL**

Sir Christopher Wren's House Hotel & Spa
WREN'S HOTELS
— *The unique hotel collection* —

Thames St SL4 1PX
☎ 01753 861354 ▤ 01753 860172
e-mail: reservations@wrensgroup.com
web: www.wrensgroup.com

dir: *M4 junct 6, 1st exit from relief road, follow signs to Windsor, 1st major exit on left, turn left at lights*

This hotel has an enviable location right on the edge of the River Thames overlooking Eton Bridge. Diners in Strok's, the award-winning restaurant, enjoy the best views. A variety of well-appointed bedrooms are available, including several in adjacent annexes. There is also a luxury health and leisure spa.

continued on page 58

WINDSOR *continued*

Rooms 57 en suite 33 annexe en suite (11 fmly) (3 GF) ⊗ in 22 bedrooms S fr £165; D fr £220 **Facilities Spa** STV Sauna Solarium Gym Jacuzzi Health & beauty club ♫ Xmas **Conf** Thtr 90 Class 80 Board 50 Del from £195 **Parking** 15 **Notes LB** ⊗ ⊗ in restaurant Civ Wed 90

★★★ 81% METRO HOTEL

Christopher Hotel

110 High St, Eton SL4 6AN

☎ 01753 852359 📠 01753 830914

e-mail: sales@thechristopher.co.uk

web: www.wrensgroup.com

WREN'S HOTELS
— The unique hotel collection —

dir: *M4 junct 5 (Slough E), Colnbrook Datchet Eton (B470). At rdbt 2nd exit for Datchet. Right at mini rdbt (Eton), left into Eton Rd (3rd rdbt). Left, hotel on right*

Centrally located on Eton High Street, this former coaching inn has now undergone a massive makeover. It boasts modern bedrooms with muted colour schemes and a contemporary feel. Public areas are not extensive, but there is a popular bar and parking is a bonus.

continued

Christopher Hotel

Rooms 11 en suite 22 annexe en suite (17 GF) ⊗ in all bedrooms S £80-£100; D £100-£130 **Facilities** STV Wi-fi available Use of Health & beauty centre at nearby sister hotel 3 mins walk **Parking** 23 **Notes LB** ⊗ ⊗ in restaurant

★★★ 79% ◉◉ HOTEL

Macdonald Castle

18 High St SL4 1LJ

☎ 0870 400 8300 📠 01753 586930 & 01753 841149

e-mail: castle@macdonald-hotels.co.uk

web: www.macdonald-hotels.co.uk

MACDONALD HOTELS & RESORTS

dir: *M4 junct 6/M25 junct 15 - follow signs to Windsor town centre & Castle. Hotel at top of hill by Castle opposite Guildhall*

This is one of the oldest hotels in Windsor, beginning life as a coaching inn in the 16th century. Located opposite Windsor Castle, it

continued on page 60

England

WINDSOR *continued*

is an ideal base from which to explore the town. Stylish bedrooms are thoughtfully equipped and include four-poster and executive rooms. Public areas were, at the time of inspection, about to benefit from a major stylish refurbishment programme; this will include the lounge and the fine-dining restaurant.

Rooms 38 en suite 70 annexe en suite (18 fmly) ⊘ in 97 bedrooms
S £110-£210; D £140-£240 (incl. bkfst) **Facilities** STV Wi-fi available Xmas **Conf** BC Thtr 400 Class 130 Board 80 Del from £195 **Services** Lift air con **Parking** 110 **Notes LB** ⊗ ⊘ in restaurant Civ Wed 60

See advert on page 59

★★★ 74% **HOTEL**

Royal Adelaide

46 Kings Rd SL4 2AG
☎ 01753 863916 ▤ 01753 830682
e-mail: royaladelaide@meridianleisure.com
web: www.meridianleisure.com
dir: *M4 junct 6, A322 to Windsor. 1st left off rdbt into Clarence Rd. At 4th lights right into Sheet St and into Kings Rd. Hotel on right*

This attractive Georgian-style hotel enjoys a quiet location yet is only a short walk from the town centre; it also benefits from its own private car park. Bedrooms vary in size but all are smartly furnished and well equipped. Public areas are tastefully appointed and include a range of meeting rooms, a bar and an elegant restaurant.

Rooms 38 en suite 4 annexe en suite (5 fmly) (8 GF) ⊘ in 30 bedrooms **Facilities** STV 25% discount for residents at Windsor leisure centre **Conf** Thtr 120 Class 80 Board 60 **Services** air con **Parking** 22 **Notes LB** ⊘ in restaurant Civ Wed 120

See advert on page 59

[U]

Harte & Garter

High St SL4 1PH
☎ 01753 863426 ▤ 01753 830527
e-mail: res.harteandgarter@foliohotels.com
web: www.foliohotels.com/harteandgarter

folio Hotels

dir: *In town centre opposite front entrance to Windsor Castle*

At the time of going to press, the star classification for this hotel was not confirmed. Please refer to the AA internet site www.theAA.com for current information.

Rooms 39 en suite 19 annexe en suite (6 fmly) ⊘ in 30 bedrooms
S £70-£110; D £140-£190 **Facilities** STV Wi-fi in bedrooms **Conf** Thtr 300 Class 150 Board 80 Del from £150 **Services** Lift **Notes LB** ⊗ ⊘ in restaurant Civ Wed 180

See advert on page 59

BUDGET HOTEL

Innkeeper's Lodge Old Windsor

14 Straight Rd, Old Windsor SL4 2RR
☎ 01753 860769 ▤ 01753 851649
web: www.innkeeperslodge.com

Smart, en suite accommodation ideal for both business & leisure guests. Bedrooms are very well equipped, including Sky TV, telephone, modem points, tea & coffee making facilities, (family rooms in most locations). Complimentary breakfast. The adjacent Pub Restaurant; a Harvester, Vintage Inn, Toby Carvery, Ember Inn, Sizzling Pubco or Pub & Carvery offers an all day menu. See Hotel Groups pages for further details.

Rooms 15 en suite S £55-£79.95; D £55-£79.95

WOKINGHAM   MAP 05 SU86

★★★★ 75% **HOTEL**

Best Western Reading Moat House

Mill Ln, Sindlesham RG41 5DF
☎ 0118 949 9988 ▤ 0118 935 1646
dir: *towards Reading on the A329(M), take first exit to Winnersh. Follow Lower Earley Way North. Hotel is on left*

Located just off the M4 on the outskirts of Reading, this smart, modern hotel has been sympathetically built around the 18th-century Sindlesham mill house. Bedrooms are stylish and have a contemporary feel to them. Spacious public areas include good conference rooms, a spacious bar and restaurant as well as a business centre and a small fitness area.

Rooms 99 en suite (10 fmly) (22 GF) ⊘ in 87 bedrooms S £54-£139; D £54-£139 **Facilities** STV Fishing Gym ♫ **Conf** Thtr 80 Class 40 Board 40 **Services** Lift air con **Parking** 250 **Notes LB** ⊗ ⊘ in restaurant Civ Wed 80

YATTENDON   MAP 05 SU57

★★ 72% ⊛⊛ **HOTEL**

Royal Oak

The Square RG18 0UG
☎ 01635 201325 ▤ 01635 201926
e-mail: info@royaloakyattendon.com
dir: *M4 junct 13, N on A34, 1st slip road right to Hermitage, left at T-junct, 2nd right signed Yattendon*

This smart country inn dates back to the 16th century and is located in a charming Berkshire village within easy reach of the M4. Bedrooms are equipped to a high standard and bathrooms are well appointed.

continued

The kitchen offers interesting dishes, available in the bar or the more formal restaurant.

Rooms 5 en suite ⊘ in all bedrooms S £85-£110; D £110-£130 (incl. bkfst) **Facilities** Wi-fi in bedrooms Xmas **Conf** Thtr 30 Class 18 Board 22 Del from £190 **Notes LB** No children ⊘ in restaurant

BRISTOL

BRISTOL
MAP 04 ST57

★★★★ 80% HOTEL

Bristol Marriott Royal Hotel
Marriott
HOTELS & RESORTS

College Green BS1 5TA
☎ 0117 925 5100 📠 0117 925 1515
e-mail: bristol.royal@marriotthotels.co.uk
web: www.marriott.co.uk
dir: next to cathedral

A truly stunning hotel located in the centre of the city, next to the cathedral. Public areas are particularly impressive with luxurious lounges and a leisure club. Dining options include the more informal Terrace and the more formal restaurant, adjacent to the champagne bar. The spacious bedrooms have the benefit of air conditioning, comfortable armchairs and marbled bathrooms.

Rooms 242 en suite ⊘ in 163 bedrooms **Facilities** STV 🏊 Sauna Solarium Gym Jacuzzi **Conf** BC Thtr 300 Class 80 Board 84 **Services** Lift air con **Parking** 200 **Notes LB** ⊗ ⊘ in restaurant Civ Wed 200

★★★★ 78% HOTEL

Bristol Marriott City Centre
Marriott
HOTELS & RESORTS

Lower Castle St BS1 3AD
☎ 0870 400 7210 📠 0870 400 7310
web: www.marriott.co.uk
dir: M32 follow signs to Broadmead, take slip road to large rdbt, take 3rd exit. Hotel on right

Situated at the foot of the picturesque Castle Park, this mainly business-orientated hotel is well placed for the city centre. Executive and de-luxe bedrooms have high speed internet access. In addition to a coffee bar and lounge menu, the Mediterrano restaurant offers an interesting selection of well-prepared dishes.

Rooms 301 en suite (135 fmly) ⊘ in 232 bedrooms S £135-£165; D £135-£165 **Facilities Spa** STV 🏊 supervised Sauna Solarium Gym Jacuzzi Steam room **Conf** BC Thtr 600 Class 280 Board 40 **Services** Lift air con **Notes LB** ⊗ ⊘ in restaurant Civ Wed

★★★★ 77% ⊛ TOWN HOUSE HOTEL

Hotel du Vin & Bistro

The Sugar House, Narrow Lewins Mead BS1 2NU
☎ 0117 925 5577 📠 0117 925 1199
e-mail: info@bristol.hotelduvin.com
web: www.hotelduvin.com
dir: A4 follow city centre signs. After 400yds pass Rupert St NCP on right. Hotel on opposite carriageway.

This hotel is one of Britain's most innovative and expanding hotel groups that extends the high standards of hospitality and accommodation. Housed in a Grade II listed, converted 18th-century sugar refinery, the hotel provides great facilities with a modern, minimalist feel. The bedrooms are exceptionally well designed and the bistro offers an excellent menu.

Rooms 40 en suite ⊘ in all bedrooms S £130-£135; D £135-£140 **Facilities** STV Snooker Wi-fi in bedrooms Xmas **Conf** Thtr 72 Class 36 Board 34 Del from £190 **Services** Lift **Parking** 28 **Notes** ⊘ in restaurant

★★★★ 76% ⊛ HOTEL

Aztec Hotel & Spa
SHIRE HOTELS

Aztec West Business Park, Almondsbury BS32 4TS
☎ 01454 201090 📠 01454 201593
e-mail: aztec@shirehotels.com
web: www.shirehotels.com
dir: access via M5 junct 16 & M4

Situated close to Cribbs Causeway shopping centre and major motorway links, this stylish hotel offers comfortable, very well-equipped bedrooms. Built in a Nordic style, public rooms boast log fires and vaulted ceilings. Leisure facilities include a popular gym and good size pool. The new-look Quarterjacks restaurant offers relaxed informal dining with a focus on simply prepared, quality regional foods.

Rooms 128 en suite (6 fmly) (29 GF) ⊘ in 84 bedrooms S £93-£169; D £136-£194 (incl. bkfst) **Facilities** STV 🏊 Sauna Solarium Gym Jacuzzi Wi-fi in bedrooms Steam room, Health & beauty, Childrens splash pool, Activity Studio Xmas **Conf** BC Thtr 200 Class 120 Board 36 Del £184 **Services** Lift air con **Parking** 240 **Notes LB** ⊗ ⊘ in restaurant Civ Wed 120

★★★★ 74% HOTEL

Ramada Plaza Bristol
RAMADA PLAZA

Redcliffe Way BS1 6NJ
☎ 0117 926 0041 📠 0117 925 5054
e-mail: sales.plazabristol@ramadajarvis.co.uk
web: www.ramadajarvis.co.uk
dir: adjacent to St Mary Redcliffe church and 400yds from Temple Meads BR station

This large modern hotel is situated in the heart of the city centre and offers spacious public areas and ample parking. Bedrooms are well equipped for both business and leisure guests. Dining options include a relaxed bar and a unique kiln restaurant where a good selection of freshly prepared dishes is available.

Rooms 201 en suite (4 fmly) ⊘ in 173 bedrooms S £80-£140; D £90-£150 **Facilities** STV 🏊 supervised Sauna Gym Wi-fi available Steam room Xmas **Conf** Thtr 437 Class 332 Board 213 Del from £135 **Services** Lift air con **Parking** 150 **Notes LB** ⊗ ⊘ in restaurant Civ Wed 250

BRISTOL *continued*

★★★★ 73% HOTEL

The Brigstow

5-7 Welsh Back BS1 4SP
☎ 0117 929 1030 📠 0117 929 2030
e-mail: brigstow@fullers.co.uk
dir: *Follow signs to City Centre. Turn left into Baldwin St, 2nd right into Queen Charlotte St. NCP on left*

In a prime position on the river this handsome purpose-built hotel is designed and finished with care. The shopping centre and theatres are within easy walking distance. The stylish bedrooms are extremely well equipped, including plasma TV screens in the bathrooms. There is an integrated state-of-the-art conference and meeting centre, and a smart restaurant and bar overlooking the harbour. Guests have complimentary use of a squash and health club, plus free internet access.

Rooms 116 en suite ⊘ in 78 bedrooms S £99-£175; D £99-£175 (incl. bkfst at weekend) **Facilities** STV Wi-fi available Complimentary access to squash & health club nearby **Conf** BC Thtr 60 Class 30 Board 36 Del from £175 **Services** Lift air con **Notes LB** ⊗ RS 24 Dec-5 Jan Civ Wed 50

★★★★ 72% HOTEL

Jurys Bristol Hotel

⦿JURYS DOYLE
HOTELS

Prince St BS1 4QF
☎ 0117 923 0333 📠 0117 923 0300
e-mail: bristol@jurysdoyle.com
web: www.jurysdoyle.com
dir: *from Temple Meads at 1st rdbt into Victoria St. At Bristol Bridge lights left into Baldwin St, 2nd left into Marsh St, straight ahead at rdbt*

This modern hotel enjoys an excellent location near Bristol's Millennium project. Bedrooms vary in size and are well appointed with a range of facilities. There is a choice of eating options, including a Quayside restaurant and adjoining inn. Extensive conference facilities are also available.

Rooms 192 en suite (17 fmly) ⊘ in 163 bedrooms S £69-£155; D £69-£155 **Facilities** STV Wi-fi available Complimentary use of local gym 2mins walk from hotel. ♫ Xmas **Conf** Thtr 400 Class 160 Board 80 Del from £149 **Services** Lift **Parking** 400 **Notes LB** ⊗ ⊘ in restaurant

★★★★ 71% HOTEL

Novotel Bristol Centre

NOVOTEL
ACCOR
Hotels

Victoria St BS1 6HY
☎ 0117 976 9988 📠 0117 925 5040
e-mail: h5622@accor.com
web: www.novotel.com
dir: *at end of M32 follow signs for Temple Meads station to rdbt. Final exit, hotel immediately on right*

This city centre hotel provides smart, contemporary style accommodation. Most of the bedrooms demonstrate the latest Novotel 'Novation' style with unique swivel desk, air-conditioning and a host of extras. The hotel is convenient for the mainline railway station and also has its own car park.

Rooms 131 en suite (20 fmly) ⊘ in 119 bedrooms **Facilities** STV Solarium Gym **Conf** Thtr 230 Class 70 Board 35 **Services** Lift **Parking** 120 **Notes LB** ⊘ in restaurant

★★★★ 71% HOTEL

Thistle Bristol

THISTLE HOTELS

Broad St BS1 2EL
☎ 0870 333 9130 📠 0870 333 9230
e-mail: bristol@thistle.co.uk
dir: *Hotel is located in city centre.*

This large hotel is situated in the heart of the city, and benefits from having its own secure parking. Bedrooms are well equipped and comfortably appointed, there are a number of Premium Executive rooms, which provide spacious and superior aspects. The public areas offer leisure and therapy treatment rooms and there is an impressive range of conference and banqueting facilities.

Rooms 182 en suite (9 fmly) ⊘ in 90 bedrooms **Facilities Spa** STV supervised Sauna Solarium Gym ⤙ Jacuzzi **Conf** Thtr 600 Class 250 Board 40 **Services** Lift air con **Parking** 150 **Notes** ⊗ Civ Wed 200

★★★ 77% HOTEL

Berkeley Square

CLASSIC
BRITISH HOTELS

15 Berkeley Square, Clifton BS8 1HB
☎ 0117 925 4000 📠 0117 925 2970
e-mail: berkeley@cliftonhotels.com
web: www.cliftonhotels.com/chg.html
dir: *M32 follow Clifton signs. 1st left at traffic lights by Nills Memorial Tower (University) into Berkeley Sq*

Set in a pleasant square close to the university, art gallery and Clifton Village, this smart, elegant Georgian hotel has modern, stylishly decorated bedrooms that feature many welcome extras. There is a cosy lounge and stylish restaurant on the ground floor and a smart, contemporary bar in the basement. A small garden is also available at the rear of the hotel.

Rooms 43 en suite (4 GF) ⊘ in 30 bedrooms **Facilities** STV use of local gym and swimming pool £5 day pass **Services** Lift **Parking** 20 **Notes LB** ⊘ in restaurant

England

★★★ 75% ☺ HOTEL

Arno's Manor

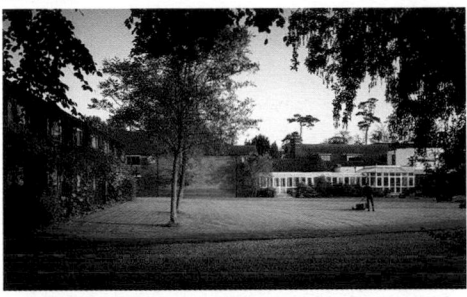
Forestdale Hotels

470 Bath Rd, Arno's Vale BS4 3HQ
☎ 0117 971 1461 🖹 0117 971 5507
e-mail: arnos.manor@forestdale.com
web: www.forestdale.com

dir: From end of M32 follow signs for Bath hotel on right side of A4 after 2m. Next to ITV West television studio

Once the home of a wealthy merchant, this historic 18th-century building is now a comfortable hotel and offers spacious, well-appointed bedrooms with plenty of workspace. The lounge was once the chapel and has many original features, while meals are taken in the atmospheric, conservatory-style restaurant.

Rooms 73 en suite (5 fmly) (7 GF) ⊗ in 50 bedrooms S £90-£100; D £120-£130 (incl. bkfst) **Facilities** STV Wi-fi in bedrooms Pool table Xmas **Conf** Thtr 150 Class 40 Board 40 Del from £100 **Services** Lift **Parking** 200 **Notes LB** ⊗ in restaurant Civ Wed 100

★★★ 75% HOTEL

Ramada Grange

® RAMADA.

Northwoods, Winterbourne BS36 1RP
☎ 01454 777333 🖹 01454 777447
e-mail: sales.grange@ramadajarvis.co.uk
web: www.ramadajarvis.co.uk

dir: Take A38 towards Filton/Bristol. At rdbt take 1st exit into Bradlet Stoke Way, at lights take 1st left into Woodlands Lane, at 2nd rdbt turn left into Tench Lane. After 1m turn left at T junct, hotel is 200yds on left.

Situated in 18 acres of attractive grounds, this pleasant hotel is only a short drive from the city centre. Bedrooms are spacious and well equipped; there is a leisure centre and pool, which are currently being refurbished, and a range of meeting facilities

Rooms 68 en suite (6 fmly) (22 GF) ⊗ in 51 bedrooms **Facilities** Spa STV ◻ supervised Sauna Solarium Gym ⊌ Jacuzzi Xmas **Conf** Thtr 245 Class 120 Board 134 Del from £140 **Parking** 150 **Notes** ⊌ in restaurant

★★★ 74% ☺ HOTEL

City Inn Bristol

Temple Way BS1 6BF
☎ 0117 925 1001 🖹 0117 907 4116
e-mail: bristol.reservations@cityinn.com

This popular hotel offers spacious, contemporary public areas and bedrooms, and is situated within walking distance of the city centre and railway station. The young team of staff are well motivated and friendly. The City Café offers an interesting selection of carefully prepared, quality ingredients and the adjacent bar serves coffee and tea throughout the day.

Rooms 167 en suite (3 GF) ⊗ in 134 bedrooms **Facilities** STV Gym **Conf** Thtr 45 Class 22 Board 24 **Services** Lift air con **Parking** 45 **Notes LB** ⊗ ⊗ in restaurant

★★★ 70% HOTEL

Redwood Hotel & Country Club

folio Hotels

Beggar Bush Ln, Failand BS8 3TG
☎ 0870 609 6144 🖹 01275 392104

dir: M5 junct 19, A369 for 3m then right at traffic lights. Hotel 1m on left

Situated close to the suspension bridge, this popular hotel offers guests a peaceful location combined with excellent leisure facilities, including a cinema, gym, squash, badminton and tennis courts, plus indoor and outdoor pools. Bedrooms have plenty of amenities and are well suited to the business guest.

Rooms 112 en suite (1 fmly) (52 GF) ⊗ in 81 bedrooms **Facilities** STV ◻ ⊀ ⊌ Squash Sauna Solarium Gym 175 seater Cinema, Aerobics/Dance studios, Badminton courts **Conf** BC Thtr 175 Class 80 Board 40 **Parking** 1000 **Notes LB** ⊗ ⊗ in restaurant Civ Wed 200

England

BRISTOL continued

★★★ 66% HOTEL

The Avon Gorge

PEEL HOTELS

Sion Hill, Clifton BS8 4LD

☎ 0117 973 8955 & 906 4655 📠 0117 923 8125

e-mail: info@avongorge-hotel-bristol.com

web: www.peelhotel.com

dir: *M5 junct 19, follow signs for Clifton Toll, over suspension bridge, 1st right into Sion Hill*

Overlooking Avon Gorge and Brunel's famous suspension bridge, this popular hotel offers many rooms with splendid views. Bedrooms are very well equipped and have extras such as ceiling fans. Public areas include a newly refurbished, light and airy café/restaurant; an extensive choice is offered on the dinner menu and afternoon tea features home made scones and cakes. Adjoining this is a large outdoor terraced area, ideal for sipping an aperitif in warmer weather.

Rooms 76 en suite (9 fmly) ❷ in 53 bedrooms S £50-£120; D £70-£140 **Facilities** STV Wi-fi available Xmas **Conf** Thtr 100 Class 50 Board 30 Del from £120 **Services** Lift **Notes** ❸ ❷ in restaurant Civ Wed 100

★★★ 66% HOTEL

Henbury Lodge

Station Rd, Henbury BS10 7QQ

☎ 0117 950 2615 📠 0117 950 9532

e-mail: contactus@henburylodgehotel.com

web: www.henburylodgehotel.com

dir: *M5 junct 17/A4018 towards city centre, 3rd rdbt right into Crow Ln. At end turn right & hotel 200mtrs on right*

This comfortable 18th-century country house has a delightful home-from-home atmosphere and is conveniently situated with easy access to the M5 and the city centre. Bedrooms are available both within the main house and in the adjacent converted stables; all are attractively

continued

decorated and well equipped. The pleasant dining room offers a selection of carefully prepared dishes using fresh ingredients.

Rooms 12 en suite 9 annexe en suite (4 fmly) (6 GF) ❷ in all bedrooms S £40-£112; D £60-£112 (incl. bkfst) **Facilities** STV Sauna Solarium **Conf** Thtr 32 Class 20 Board 20 Del from £150 **Parking** 24 **Notes LB** ❷ in restaurant

★★ 79% HOTEL

Best Western Victoria Square

Best Western

Victoria Square, Clifton BS8 4EW

☎ 0117 973 9058 📠 0117 970 6929

e-mail: victoriasquare@btinternet.com

web: www.vicsquare.com

dir: *M5 junct 19, follow Clifton signs. Over suspension bridge, right into Clifton Down Rd. Left at mini rdbt into Merchants Rd then into Victoria Sq*

Situated with convenient access to the heart of Clifton and the city centre, these two former Victorian houses offer bedrooms that are generally spacious and well equipped with a range of useful extras such as modem points for internet access. A pleasant conference room and small rear car park are also on hand.

Rooms 21 en suite 19 annexe en suite (3 fmly) (2 GF) ❷ in all bedrooms S £79-£99; D £89-£109 (incl. bkfst) **Facilities** STV Wi-fi in bedrooms **Conf** Thtr 25 Class 15 Board 20 **Parking** 14 **Notes LB** ❸ ❷ in restaurant Closed 22 Dec-2 Jan

★★ 72% HOTEL

Clifton

St Pauls Rd, Clifton BS8 1LX

☎ 0117 973 6882 📠 0117 974 1082

e-mail: clifton@cliftonhotels.com

web: www.cliftonhotels.com/clifton

dir: *M32 follow Bristol/Clifton signs, along Park St. Left at lights into St Pauls Rd*

This popular hotel offers very well equipped bedrooms and relaxed, friendly service. There is a welcoming lounge by the reception, and in summer months drinks and meals can be enjoyed on the terrace. Racks Bar and Restaurant offers an interesting selection of modern dishes in informal surroundings. Some street parking is possible, although for a small charge secure garage parking is available.

Rooms 59 en suite (2 fmly) ❷ in 28 bedrooms **Facilities** STV **Services** Lift **Parking** 20

England

★★ 71% **HOTEL**

Rodney Hotel

4 Rodney Place, Clifton BS8 4HY
☎ 0117 973 5422 🖷 0117 946 7092
e-mail: rodney@cliftonhotels.com
dir: off Clifton Down Rd

With easy access from the M5, this attractive, listed building in Clifton is conveniently close to the city centre. The individually decorated bedrooms provide a useful range of extra facilities for the business traveller and the public areas include a smart bar and restaurant. A pleasant rear garden provides additional seating in the summer months.

Rooms 31 en suite (2 GF) ⊗ in 10 bedrooms S fr £87; D £99 (incl. bkfst) **Facilities** STV Wi-fi in bedrooms **Conf** Thtr 30 Class 20 Board 20 **Parking** 10 **Notes** ⊗ in restaurant Closed 22 Dec-3 Jan RS Sun

★★ 68% **HOTEL**

The Bowl Inn

16 Church Rd, Lower Almondsbury BS32 4DT
☎ 01454 612757 🖷 01454 619910
e-mail: reception@thebowlinn.co.uk
web: www.thebowlinn.co.uk
dir: M5 junct 16 onto Gloucester road, N for 500yds. Left into Over Lane, right by garden centre. Hotel next to church on right

With easy access to the motorway network, this popular 16th-century village inn offers all the comforts of modern life. Each bedroom has been individually furnished to complement the many original features. Dining options include an extensive bar menu with cask ales, and a more intimate restaurant.

Rooms 11 rms (2 en suite) 2 annexe en suite (1 GF) ⊗ in 4 bedrooms S £48.50-£87.50; D £76-£97.50 **Facilities** STV **Conf** Thtr 30 Class 20 Board 24 **Parking** 30 **Notes LB** ⊗ in restaurant RS 25-Dec

★★ 60% **HOTEL**

Westbourne

THE INDEPENDENTS

40-44 St Pauls Rd, Clifton BS8 1LR
☎ 0117 973 4214 🖷 0117 974 3552
e-mail: westbournehotel@bristol8.fsworld.co.uk
web: www.westbournehotel-bristol.co.uk
dir: M32/A4018 along Park St to Triangle, then Whiteladies Rd. Turn left at 1st lights opp the BBC onto St Pauls Rd. Hotel 200yds on right

This privately owned hotel is situated in the heart of Clifton and is popular with business guests during the week. It offers comfortable, well-equipped bedrooms. Freddie's Bar and Restaurant provide a

continued

choice of eating options, and in the summer guests can enjoy a drink on the terrace.

Westbourne

Rooms 29 en suite (7 fmly) (1 GF) ⊗ in 1 bedroom S £75; D £89 (incl. bkfst) **Parking** 9 **Notes** ⊗

Ⓤ

Swallow Wheatsheaf

SWALLOW
HOTELS

41 High St, Winterbourne BS36 1JG
☎ 01454 777937 🖷 01454 773752
web: www.swallowhotels.com

At the time of going to press, the star classification for this hotel was not confirmed. Please refer to the AA internet site www.theAA.com for current information.

Rooms 12 en suite

BUDGET HOTEL

Premier Travel Inn Bristol City Centre

premier travel inn

Haymarket BS1 3LR
☎ 0870 238 3307 🖷 0117 9100619
web: www.premiertravelinn.com
dir: M4 junct 19/M32 towards city centre. Through 2 sets of lights, at 3rd set, turn right. To rdbt, take 2nd exit. Inn on left.

High quality, modern budget accommodation ideal for both families and business travellers. Spacious, en suite bedrooms feature bath and shower, satellite TV and many have telephones and modem points. The adjacent family restaurant features a wide and varied menu. For further details consult the Hotel Groups page.

Rooms 224 en suite

Premier Travel Inn Bristol East

200/202 Westerleigh Rd, Emersons Green BS16 7AN
☎ 08701 977042 🖷 0117 956 4644
dir: From M4 (junct 19) onto M32 (junct 1), turn left onto A4174 (Avon Ring Rd). Inn on 3rd rdbt
Rooms 40 en suite **Conf** Thtr 26 Board 17

Premier Travel Inn Bristol (Filton)

Shield Retail Park, Gloucester Rd North, Filton BS34 7BR
☎ 0870 9906456 🖷 0870 9906457
dir: Exit M5 junct 16, towards A38 signed Filton/Pathway. Pass airport & Royal Mail on right. Left at 2nd rdbt, then 1st left into retail park
Rooms 60 en suite **Conf** Board 12

BRISTOL *continued*

Premier Travel Inn Bristol (King Street)

Llandoger Trow, Kings St BS1 4ER

☎ 0870 9906424 🖹 0870 9906425

dir: *A38 into city centre. Left onto B4053 Baldwin St. Right into Queen Charlotte St, follow one-way system, bear right at river. Inn on right*

Rooms 60 en suite

Premier Travel Inn Bristol North West

Cribbs Causeway, Catbrain Ln BS10 7TQ

☎ 0870 9906570 🖹 0870 9906571

dir: *Exit M5 junct 17 onto A4018. 1st left at rdbt into Lysander Rd. Right into Catbrain Hill which leads into Catbrain Ln*

Rooms 106 en suite

Premier Travel Inn Bristol South

Hengrove Leisure Park, Hengrove Way BS14 0HR

☎ 08701 977043 🖹 01275 834721

dir: *From city centre take A37 to Wells & Shepton Mallet. Right onto A4174. Inn at 3rd traffic lights*

Rooms 40 en suite

Travelodge Bristol Central

Anchor Rd, Harbourside BS1 5TT

☎ 08700 850 950 🖹 0117 9255149

web: www.travelodge.co.uk

dir: *on Anchor Road (A4) on left*

Travelodge offers good quality, good value, modern accommodation. Ideal for families, the spacious en suite bedrooms include remote-control TV, tea and coffee-making facilities and comfortable beds. Meals can be taken at the nearby family restaurant. See Hotel Groups pages for further details.

Rooms 119 en suite S fr £26; D fr £26

Travelodge Bristol Cribbs Causeway

Cribbs Causeway BS10 7TL

☎ 08700 850 950 🖹 0117 950 1530

dir: *A4018, off M5 junct 17*

Rooms 56 en suite S fr £26; D fr £26

BUCKINGHAMSHIRE

AMERSHAM   MAP 06 SU99

★★★ 72% **HOTEL**

The Crown

High St HP7 0DH

☎ 01494 721 541 🖹 01494 431283

e-mail: crownres@dhillonhotels.co.uk

dir: *A413 (London road) into Old Amersham. Left into High St. Hotel ahead on left*

A 16th-century coaching inn with a wealth of original charm and character. One claim to fame is that the hotel was featured in the film *'Four Weddings and a Funeral'*. Bedrooms are noteworthy as all are

continued

individually styled and some feature original hand-painted murals. Public rooms include a welcoming bar and a smart restaurant.

Rooms 19 en suite 18 annexe en suite (5 fmly) (12 GF) ⊘ in 21 bedrooms S £110-£135; D £130-£155 (incl. bkfst) **Facilities** STV Wi-fi in bedrooms Xmas **Conf** Thtr 30 Board 18 Del from £150 **Parking** 30 **Notes LB** ⊘ in restaurant Civ Wed 100

ASTON CLINTON   MAP 05 SP81

Innkeeper's Lodge Aylesbury East

London Rd HP22 5HP

☎ 01296 632777 🖹 01296 632685

web: www.innkeeperslodge.com

dir: *on A41 in Aston Clinton, between Aylesbury & Tring*

Smart, en suite accommodation ideal for both business & leisure guests. Bedrooms are very well equipped, including Sky TV, telephone, modem points, tea & coffee making facilities, (family rooms in most locations). Complimentary breakfast. The adjacent Pub Restaurant; a Harvester, Vintage Inn, Toby Carvery, Ember Inn, Sizzling Pubco or Pub & Carvery offers an all day menu. See Hotel Groups pages for further details.

Rooms 11 en suite S £55-£75; D £55-£75

AYLESBURY   MAP 11 SP81

INSPECTORS' CHOICE

★★★★ ◉◉◉ **HOTEL**

Hartwell House Hotel, Restaurant & Spa

Oxford Rd HP17 8NL

☎ 01296 747444 🖹 01296 747450

e-mail: info@hartwell-house.com

web: www.hartwell-house.com

dir: *from S - M40 junct 7, A329 to Thame, then A418 towards Aylesbury. After 6m, through Stone, hotel on left. From N - M40 junct 9 for Bicester. A41 to Aylesbury, A418 to Oxford for 2m. Hotel on right*

This beautiful, historic house is set in 90 acres of unspoilt parkland. The grand public rooms are truly magnificent, and feature many fine works of art. The service standards are very high, being attentive and traditional without stuffiness. There is an elegant, award-winning restaurant, where carefully prepared dishes use the best local produce. Bedrooms are spacious, elegant and very comfortable. Most are in the main house, but some, including suites, are in the nearby, renovated coachhouse, which also houses a fine spa.   *continued*

Rooms 30 en suite 16 annexe en suite (10 GF) ⊗ in 12 bedrooms
S fr £155; D fr £280 **Facilities Spa** STV ⌧ supervised ☌ Sauna
Solarium Gym ☙ Jacuzzi Wi-fi in bedrooms Treatment
rooms & Steam rooms ♫ Xmas **Conf** BC Thtr 100 Class 40
Board 40 Del from £265 **Services** Lift **Parking** 91 **Notes LB**
No children 6yrs ⊗ in restaurant Civ Wed 60

BUDGET HOTEL

Innkeeper's Lodge Aylesbury South
40 Main St, Weston Turville HP22 5RW
☎ 01296 613131 & 0870 243 0500 ▤ 01296 616902
web: www.innkeeperslodge.com

dir: M25 junct 20/A41 (Hemel Hempstead). Continue for 12m to
Aston Clinton. Left onto B4544 to Weston Turville, lodge on left

Smart, en suite accommodation ideal for both business & leisure
guests. Bedrooms are very well equipped, including Sky TV,
telephone, modem points, tea & coffee making facilities, (family
rooms in most locations). Complimentary breakfast. The adjacent Pub
Restaurant, a Harvester, Vintage Inn, Toby Carvery, Ember Inn, Sizzling
Pubco or Pub & Carvery offers an all day menu. See Hotel Groups
pages for further details.

Rooms 16 en suite S £49.95-£62; D £49.95-£62

BUDGET HOTEL

Premier Travel Inn Aylesbury
Buckingham Rd HP19 9QL
☎ 08701 977019 ▤ 01206 330432
web: www.premiertravelinn.com

dir: N from Aylesbury centre on A413, Inn 1m on left, adjacent to
rdbt

High quality, modern budget accommodation ideal for both families
and business travellers. Spacious, en suite bedrooms feature bath and
shower, satellite TV and many have telephones and modem points.
The adjacent family restaurant features a wide and varied menu. For
further details consult the Hotel Groups page.

Rooms 64 en suite

BEACONSFIELD   MAP 06 SU99

BUDGET HOTEL

Innkeeper's Lodge Beaconsfield
Aylesbury End HP9 1LW
☎ 01494 671211 ▤ 01494 685042
web: www.innkeeperslodge.com

dir: M40 junct 2 turn left at next two rdbts. Pub on rdbt

Smart, en suite accommodation ideal for both business & leisure
guests. Bedrooms are very well equipped, including Sky TV,
telephone, modem points, tea & coffee making facilities, (family
rooms in most locations). Complimentary breakfast. The adjacent Pub
Restaurant; a Harvester, Vintage Inn, Toby Carvery, Ember Inn, Sizzling
Pubco or Pub & Carvery offers an all day menu. See Hotel Groups
pages for further details.

Rooms 32 en suite S £49.95-£79.95; D £49.95-£79.95

BUCKINGHAM   MAP 11 SP63

★★★★ 73% ⊛⊛ **HOTEL**

Villiers
3 Castle St MK18 1BS
☎ 01280 822444 ▤ 01280 822113
e-mail: buckingham@villiershotels.com
web: www.villiershotels.com

dir: M1 junct 13 (N) or 15 (S) follow signs to Buckingham.
Castle St by Town Hall.

Guests can enjoy a town centre location with a high degree of comfort
at this 400-year-old former coaching inn. Relaxing public areas feature
flagstone floors, oak panelling and real fires whilst bedrooms are
modern, spacious and equipped to a high level. Diners can unwind in
the atmospheric bar before taking dinner in the award-winning and
newly refurbished restaurant.

Rooms 46 en suite (43 fmly) ⊗ in 40 bedrooms S £105-£135;
D £120-£150 (incl. bkfst) **Facilities** STV Wi-fi available Xmas **Conf** BC
Thtr 250 Class 120 Board 80 Del from £140 **Services** Lift **Parking** 40
Notes LB ⊛ ⊗ in restaurant Civ Wed 180

★★★ 68% **HOTEL**

Best Western Buckingham Beales
Buckingham Ring Rd MK18 1RY
☎ 01280 822622 ▤ 01280 823074
e-mail: buckingham@bealeshotels.co.uk

dir: M1 junct 13/14 follow signs to Buckingham A422/A421. M40
exit junct 9/10 follow signs Buckingham. Hotel on ring road

A purpose-built hotel, which offers spacious rooms with well-designed
working spaces for business travellers. There are also extensive
conference facilities. The open-plan restaurant and bar offer a good
range of dishes, and the well-equipped leisure suite is popular with
guests.

Rooms 70 en suite (6 fmly) (32 GF) ⊗ in 55 bedrooms S £69-£99;
D £80-£118 **Facilities** STV ⌧ Sauna Solarium Gym Jacuzzi Wi-fi in
bedrooms Beauty treatment Massage Xmas **Conf** BC Thtr 160 Class 90
Board 30 Del from £144 **Parking** 120 **Notes LB** ⊗ in restaurant
Civ Wed 120

Some hotels have restricted service during
quieter months, and at this time some of the
facilities will not be available

England

BUCKINGHAM *continued*

BUDGET HOTEL

Travelodge Buckingham

A421 Bypass MK18 1SH

☎ 08700 850950 📠 01280 815 136

web: www.travelodge.co.uk

dir: *M1 junct 38/39. Travelodge on northbound and southbound carriageways of the M1.*

Travelodge offers good quality, good value, modern accommodation. Ideal for families, the spacious en suite bedrooms include remote-control TV, tea and coffee-making facilities and comfortable beds. Meals can be taken at the nearby family restaurant. See Hotel Groups pages for further details.

Rooms 45 en suite S fr £26; D fr £26

BURNHAM   MAP 06 SU98

★★★ 73% HOTEL

Grovefield

Taplow Common Rd SL1 8LP

☎ 01628 603131 📠 01628 668078

e-mail: gm.grovefield@classiclodges.co.uk

dir: *From M4 left on A4 towards Maidenhead. Next rdbt turn right under railway bridge. Straight over mini rdbt, garage on right. Continue for 1.5m, hotel on right*

Set in its own spacious grounds, the Grovefield is conveniently located for Heathrow Airport as well as the industrial centres of Slough and Maidenhead. Accommodation is spacious and well presented and most rooms have views over the attractive gardens. Public areas include a range of meeting rooms, comfortable bar/lounge area and Hamilton's restaurant.

Rooms 40 en suite (5 fmly) (7 GF) ⊛ in 24 bedrooms S £80-£147; D £95-£167 (incl. bkfst) **Facilities** STV Fishing ⬛ Putt green Wi-fi available Xmas **Conf** Thtr 180 Class 80 Board 80 Del from £145 **Services** Lift **Parking** 155 **Notes LB** ⊛ in restaurant Civ Wed 200

★★★ 72% HOTEL

Burnham Beeches Hotel

Grove Rd SL1 8DP

☎ 0870 609 6124 📠 01628 603994

e-mail: burnhambeeches@corushotels.com

web: www.corushotels.com

dir: *A355 towards Slough. Left at 2 mini-rdbts, left at next mini-rdbt. Grove Rd 1st on right*

Set in attractive mature grounds on the fringes of woodland, this
continued

extended Georgian manor house has spacious and comfortable well-equipped bedrooms. Public rooms include a cosy lounge/bar offering all-day snacks and an elegant wood-panelled restaurant that serves interesting cuisine; there are also conference facilities, a fitness centre and pool.

Burnham Beeches Hotel

Rooms 82 en suite (19 fmly) (9 GF) ⊛ in 68 bedrooms S £55-£125; D £110-£132 (incl. bkfst) **Facilities Spa** STV 🎱 🏊 Snooker Sauna Gym ⬛ Jacuzzi Wi-fi available Xmas **Conf** Thtr 180 Class 100 Board 60 Del from £145 **Services** Lift **Parking** 200 **Notes LB** ⊛ ⊛ in restaurant Civ Wed 120

CHENIES   MAP 06 TQ09

★★★ 75% HOTEL

The Bedford Arms Hotel

WD3 6EQ

☎ 01923 283301 📠 01923 284825

e-mail: contact@bedfordarms.co.uk

web: www.bedfordarms.co.uk

dir: *M25 junct 18, then A404, follow signs for Amersham, approx 2.5m*

This attractive, 19th-century country inn enjoys a peaceful rural setting. Comfortable bedrooms are decorated in traditional style and feature a range of thoughtful extras. Each room is named after a relation of the Duke of Bedford, whose family has an historic association with the hotel. There are two bars, a lounge and a cosy, wood-panelled restaurant.

Rooms 10 en suite 8 annexe en suite (2 fmly) (8 GF) ⊛ in 6 bedrooms S £60-£120; D £95-£120 (incl. bkfst) **Facilities** STV Wi-fi in bedrooms **Conf** Thtr 50 Class 16 Board 24 Del from £150 **Parking** 60 **Notes** ⊛ in restaurant Civ Wed 55

FORD   MAP 05 SP70

★ 75% HOTEL

Dinton Hermit

Water Ln HP17 8XH

☎ 01296 747473

web: www.dinton-hermit.co.uk

dir: *A418 (Aylesbury to Thame) turn left signed Dinton, drive through Dinton village, straight across x-rds, hotel 0.3m on left.*

A restored 400-year-old, Grade II listed property that now provides a smart restaurant and atmospheric bedrooms in both the old inn and in the 200-year-old wychet barn. Bedrooms are well equipped and comfortable and the restaurant is popular with locals.

continued

Dinton Hermit

Rooms 7 en suite 6 annexe en suite (11 GF) ☺ in all bedrooms
Facilities ⚑ **Parking** 35 **Notes LB** ⊗ No children ☺ in restaurant
Closed Xmas

GERRARDS CROSS   MAP 06 TQ08

★★ 71% HOTEL

Ethorpe

Packhouse Rd SL9 8HY
☎ 01753 882039 📠 01753 887012
e-mail: ethorpe.hotel@thespiritgroup.com
web: www.ethorpehotel.com

dir: M40 junct 2 for Beaconsfield. At island right onto A40 to
Gerrards Cross. At lights left into Packhouse Rd. Hotel at end on
left

This attractive hotel is located in the centre of town, within easy reach
of the motorway network and Heathrow Airport. Stylish bedrooms are
particularly thoughtfully equipped and all boast spacious well-
appointed en suite bathrooms. Meals are served all day in the popular
informal 'Chef and Brewer' restaurant and bar.

Rooms 32 en suite (3 fmly) (11 GF) ☺ in 25 bedrooms **Facilities** STV
Conf Thtr 40 Class 30 Board 22 **Services** air con **Parking** 80 **Notes** ⊗

HIGH WYCOMBE   MAP 05 SU89
See also Stokenchurch

★★★ 67% HOTEL

Ambassador Court

145 West Wycombe Rd HP12 3AB
☎ 01494 461818 📠 01494 461919
e-mail: ach@fardellhotels.com
web: www.fardellhotels.com/ambassadorcourt

dir: M4 junct 4/A404 to A40 west towards Aylesbury. Hotel 0.5m
on left next to petrol station

A small privately owned hotel situated midway between London and
Oxford, and handily placed for access to the M40. Bedrooms are
pleasantly decorated and equipped with both business and leisure
guests in mind. Public rooms are contemporary in style and include a
lounge with leather sofas, a cosy bar and Fusions restaurant.

Rooms 18 en suite (2 fmly) (1 GF) ☺ in all bedrooms S £55-£109;
D £65-£119 (incl. bkfst) **Facilities** STV Free access to local gym Xmas
Conf Thtr 32 Class 18 Board 16 Del from £150 **Parking** 18 **Notes LB** ⊗
☺ in restaurant

Premier Travel Inn High Wycombe

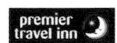

Thanestead Farm, London Rd, Loudwater HP10 9YL
☎ 08701 977135 📠 01494 446855
web: www.premiertravelinn.com

dir: from M40 (West), take J2. Follow signs to High Wycombe
via Beaconsfield

High quality, modern budget accommodation ideal for both families
and business travellers. Spacious, en suite bedrooms feature bath and
shower, satellite TV and many have telephones and modem points.
The adjacent family restaurant features a wide and varied menu. For
further details consult the Hotel Groups page.

Rooms 81 en suite **Conf** Class 24 Board 24

MARLOW   MAP 05 SU88

★★★★ 85% ⦿⦿⦿ HOTEL

Danesfield House Hotel & Spa

Henley Rd SL7 2EY
☎ 01628 891010 📠 01628 890408
e-mail: reservations@danesfieldhouse.co.uk
web: www.danesfieldhouse.co.uk

dir: 2m from Marlow on A4155 towards Henley

Set in 65 acres of elevated grounds just 45 minutes from central
London and 30 minutes from Heathrow, this hotel enjoys spectacular

continued on page 70

MARLOW continued

views across the River Thames. Impressive public rooms include the cathedral-like Great Hall, the panelled Oak Room Restaurant and The Orangery, a less formal option for dining. Some bedrooms have balconies and stunning views. Staff are committed and nothing is too much trouble.

Danesfield House Hotel & Spa

Rooms 87 en suite (3 fmly) (27 GF) ⊗ in 5 bedrooms S £215; D £260-£355 (incl. bkfst) **Facilities Spa** STV ⟲ ☃ Snooker Sauna Solarium Gym ❧ Putt green Jacuzzi Wi-fi in bedrooms Jogging trail, Steam room, Hydrotherapy room, Treatment rooms Xmas **Conf** Thtr 100 Class 60 Board 50 Del from £275 **Services** Lift **Parking** 100 **Notes LB** ⊛ ⊘ in restaurant Civ Wed 100

See advert on page 69

★★★★ 80% ❀❀❀ **HOTEL**

Macdonald Compleat Angler

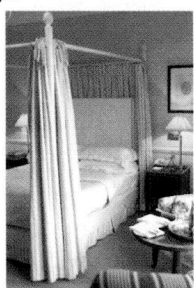

Marlow Bridge SL7 1RG
☎ 0870 400 8100 ▤ 01628 486388
e-mail: general.compleatangler@macdonald-hotels.co.uk
web: www.macdonald-hotels.co.uk
dir: M4 junct 8/9, A404 to rdbt, Bisham exit, 1m to Marlow Bridge, hotel on right

This well-established hotel enjoys a wonderful setting overlooking the River Thames and the Marlow weir. Bedrooms, which differ in size and style, are all individually decorated and comfortable. Dining choices include a cosy bar, informal brasserie-style restaurant and the award-winning Riverside restaurant.

Rooms 64 en suite (6 GF) ⊗ in 22 bedrooms **Facilities** STV Fishing ❧ Boating, Fly fishing and course fishing ♫ **Conf** Thtr 120 Class 65 Board 36 **Services** Lift **Parking** 60 **Notes LB** ⊘ in restaurant Civ Wed 120

See advert on opposite page

MILTON KEYNES
See also Aspley Guise (Bedfordshire)

MAP 11 SP83

★★★ 83% ❀❀ **HOTEL**

Macdonald Parkside

Newport Rd, Woughton on the Green MK6 3LR
☎ 0870 194 2128 ▤ 01908 676186
e-mail: parkside@macdonald-hotels.co.uk
web: www.macdonald-hotels.co.uk

Situated in five acres of landscaped grounds in a peaceful village setting, this hotel is only five minutes' drive from the centre of town. Bedrooms are divided between executive rooms in the main house and standard rooms in the adjacent coach house. Public rooms include a range of meeting rooms, Lanes restaurant and Strollers bar.

Rooms 49 rms (38 en suite) (1 fmly) (19 GF) ⊗ in 15 bedrooms **Facilities** STV Wi-fi in bedrooms Discounted entry to local health & fitness club Xmas **Conf** Thtr 150 Class 60 Board 50 Del from £145 **Parking** 75 **Notes** ⊘ in restaurant Civ Wed 120

★★★ 78% **HOTEL**

Courtyard by Marriott Milton Keynes

London Rd, Newport Pagnell MK16 0JA
☎ 01908 613688 ▤ 01908 617335
e-mail: events.mkcourtyard@kewgreen.co.uk
web: www.kewgreen.co.uk
dir: M1 junct 14, A509 (Newport Pagnell), hotel 0.5m on right

Ideally situated for access to the M1 motorway, town centre and local attractions, this former Georgian coach house enjoys a pleasant and

continued

peaceful rural location. The bedrooms are comfortable and well appointed. Public rooms include a small fitness room, modern bar and conservatory restaurant overlooking the courtyard.

Rooms 53 en suite (9 fmly) (22 GF) ⊗ in 36 bedrooms **Facilities** STV Gym **Conf** Thtr 200 Class 90 Board 50 **Parking** 160 **Notes LB** ⊗ ⊗ in restaurant Civ Wed 120

★★★ 73% **HOTEL**

Novotel Milton Keynes

Saxon St, Layburn Court, Heelands MK13 7RA
☎ 01908 322212 🖹 01908 322235
e-mail: H3272@accor-hotels.com
web: www.novotel.com

dir: *M1 junct 14, follow Childsway signs towards city centre. Right into Saxon Way, straight across all rdbts hotel on left*

Contemporary in style, this purpose-built hotel is situated on the outskirts of the town, just a few minutes' drive from the centre and mainline railway station. Bedrooms provide ample workspace and a good range of facilities for the modern traveller, and public rooms include a children's play area and indoor leisure centre.

Rooms 124 en suite (40 fmly) (40 GF) ⊗ in 105 bedrooms S £49-£135; D £49 £135 **Facilities** STV FTV 🏊 Sauna Gym Steam bath **Conf** Thtr 120 Class 75 Board 40 Del from £159 **Services** Lift **Parking** 130 **Notes LB** Civ Wed 100

★★★ 70% **HOTEL**

Quality Hotel & Suites MiltonKeynes

Monks Way, Two Mile Ash MK8 8LY
☎ 01908 561666 🖹 01908 568303
e-mail: enquiries@hotels milton-keynes.com
web: www.choicehotelseurope.com

dir: *junct of A5/A422*

Bedrooms at this purpose-built hotel are particularly well-equipped, many including air conditioning. There are also a number of suites with fax machines and kitchenettes. Eating options include an all-day room and lounge service in addition to the restaurant.

Rooms 88 en suite (15 fmly) ⊗ in 44 bedrooms S £45-£124; D £55-£128 **Facilities** 🏊 supervised Sauna Solarium Gym Jacuzzi Steam room, Whirlpool spa Wi fi available **Conf** BC Thtr 120 Class 50 Board 50 Del from £84 **Services** air con **Parking** 200 **Notes** ⊗ ⊗ in restaurant Civ Wed 100

★★ 76% **HOTEL**

Different Drummer

94 High St, Stony Stratford MK11 1AH
☎ 01908 564733 🖹 01908 260646
e-mail: info@hoteldifferentdrummer.co.uk
web: www.hoteldifferentdrummer.co.uk

This attractive hotel located on the high street in historic Stony Stratford offers a genuine welcome to its guests. The oak-panelled restaurant is a popular dining venue and offers an Italian-style menu. Bedrooms are generally spacious and well equipped. A contemporary bar has now been added, and provides a further dining option.

continued

Different Drummer

Rooms 19 en suite 4 annexe en suite (1 fmly) (3 GF) ⊗ in 15 bedrooms **Facilities** STV **Parking** 4 **Notes** ⊗

★★ 72% **HOTEL**

Swan Revived

THE INDEPENDENTS

High St, Newport Pagnell MK16 8AR
☎ 01908 610565 🖹 01908 210995
e-mail: info@swanrevived.co.uk
web: www.swanrevived.co.uk

dir: *M1 junct 14 onto A509 then B526 into Newport Pagnell for 2m. Hotel on High St*

Once a coaching inn, this hotel dates from the 17th century, occupying a prime location in the centre of town. Well-appointed bedrooms are mostly spacious, individually styled and have good levels of comfort.

continued on page 72

England

MILTON KEYNES *continued*

Public areas include a popular bar and a restaurant offering a variety of freshly prepared dishes.

Swan Revived

Rooms 42 en suite (2 fmly) S £58-£85; D £74-£95 (incl. bkfst)
Facilities STV **Conf** Thtr 70 Class 30 Board 28 Del from £120
Services Lift **Parking** 18 **Notes LB** ⊘ in restaurant RS 25 Dec-1 Jan Civ Wed 75

★★ 67% **HOTEL**

Broughton

OLD ENGLISH INNS

Broughton Village MK10 9AA
☎ 01908 667726 📠 01908 604844
e-mail: broughtonhotel@greeneking.co.uk
web: www.oldenglish.co.uk
dir: *Exit M1 junct 14, at 1st rdbt take A5130 signed Woburn 600yds. Turn right for Broughton village, located on left*

This establishment is located within easy reach of road networks on the periphery of Milton Keynes and offers modern accommodation. Day rooms are dominated by an open-plan lounge bar and food operation - the Hungry Horse concept that proves particularly popular with young families.

Rooms 30 en suite (2 fmly) (14 GF) ⊘ in all bedrooms S £39.95-£69.95; D £69.95 **Facilities** STV **Conf** Thtr 80 Class 30 Board 30 **Parking** 120 **Notes LB** ⊗

★★ 63% **HOTEL**

The Cock Hotel

OLD ENGLISH INNS

72 High St, Stony Stratford MK11 1AH
☎ 01908 567733 📠 01908 562109
e-mail: cock.stonystratford@oldenglishinns.co.uk
web: www.oldenglish.co.uk
dir: *Exit M1 junct 15 signed for Stony Stratford on A508. Hotel along High St*

This Grade II listed coaching inn dates from 1742. The bar is the dominant area, but there is also a brasserie-style restaurant. Bedrooms are at present being refurbished and offer a variety of styles. Some are located in the main house while others are around the colourful courtyard.

Rooms 18 en suite 13 annexe en suite (3 fmly) (7 GF) ⊘ in 20 bedrooms S £55-£85; D £75-£110 (incl. bkfst) **Facilities** Xmas **Conf** Thtr 120 Class 50 Board 60 Del from £125 **Parking** 30 **Notes** ⊘ in restaurant Civ Wed 120

BUDGET HOTEL

Campanile

40 Penn Rd, Fenny Stratford, Bletchley MK2 2AU
☎ 01908 649819 📠 01908 649818
e-mail: mk@campanile-hotels.com
web: www.envergure.fr
dir: *M1 junct 14, follow A4146 to A5. Southbound on A5. 4th exit at 1st rdbt to Fenny Stratford. Hotel 500yds on left*

This modern building offers accommodation in smart, well-equipped bedrooms, all with en suite bathrooms. Refreshments may be taken at the informal Bistro. For further details consult the Hotel Groups page.

Rooms 80 en suite **Conf** Thtr 40 Class 30 Board 30 Del from £70

BUDGET HOTEL

Innkeeper's Lodge Milton Keynes

Burchard Crescent, Shenley Church End MK5 6HQ
☎ 01908 505467
web: www.innkeeperslodge.com

Smart, en suite accommodation ideal for both business & leisure guests. Bedrooms are very well equipped, including Sky TV, telephone, modem points, tea & coffee making facilities, (family rooms in most locations). Complimentary breakfast. The adjacent Pub Restaurant; a Harvester, Vintage Inn, Toby Carvery, Ember Inn, Sizzling Pubco or Pub & Carvery offers an all day menu. See Hotel Groups pages for further details.

Rooms 50 en suite S £45-£69.95; D £45-£69.95 **Conf** Thtr 100 Class 40 Board 60

BUDGET HOTEL

Premier Travel Inn Milton Keynes Central

premier travel inn

Secklow Gate West MK9 3BZ
☎ 08701 977184 📠 01908 607481
web: www.premiertravelinn.com
dir: *from M1 junct 14 follow H6 route over 6 rdbts, at 7th (called Sth Secklow) turn right, Inn on left*

High quality, modern budget accommodation ideal for both families and business travellers. Spacious, en suite bedrooms feature bath and shower, satellite TV and many have telephones and modem points. The adjacent family restaurant features a wide and varied menu. For further details consult the Hotel Groups page.

Rooms 38 en suite **Conf** Thtr 16

Premier Travel Inn Milton Keynes Central (SW)

Shirwell Crescent, Furzton MK4 1GA

☎ 0870 9906396 📠 0870 9906397

dir: Exit M1 junct 14 take A509 to Milton Keynes. Straight over 8 rdbts, at 9th (North Grafton) turn left onto V6. Right at next onto H7. Over The Bowl rdbt and hotel on left

Rooms 120 en suite **Conf** Thtr 10 Class 10 Board 10

Premier Travel Inn Milton Keynes East

Willen Lake, Brickhill St MK15 9HQ

☎ 08701 977185 📠 01908 678561

dir: M1 junct 14 follow H6 Childsway. Turn right at 3rd rdbt into Brickhill St. Right at 1st mini rdbt, Inn 1st left

Rooms 41 en suite

Premier Travel Inn Milton Keynes South

Bletcham Way, Caldecotte MK7 8HP

☎ 0870 9906558 📠 0870 9906559

dir: Exit M1 junct 14. Right towards Milton Keynes on H6 Childs Way. Straight over 2 rdbts. Left at 3rd onto V10 Brickhill St. Straight over 5 rdbts, at 6th turn right onto H10 Bletcham Way

Rooms 40 en suite **Conf** Board 10

BUDGET HOTEL

Travelodge Milton Keynes Central

109 Grafton Gate MK9 1AL

☎ 08700 850 950 📠 01908 241737

web: www.travelodge.co.uk

dir: M1 junct 14 to city centre, H6 Childs Ways to junct V6 Grafton Gate, on right after rail station

Travelodge offers good quality, good value, modern accommodation. Ideal for families, the spacious en suite bedrooms include remote-control TV, tea and coffee-making facilities and comfortable beds. Meals can be taken at the nearby family restaurant. See Hotel Groups pages for further details.

Rooms 80 en suite S fr £26; D fr £26

Travelodge Milton Keynes Old Stratford

Old Stratford Roundabout MK19 6AQ

☎ 08700 850 950 📠 01908 260802

Rooms 33 en suite S fr £26; D fr £26

NEWPORT PAGNELL   MAP 11 SP84
MOTORWAY SERVICE AREA (M1)

BUDGET HOTEL

Welcome Lodge Newport Pagnell

Newport Pagnell MK16 8DS

☎ 01908 610878 📠 01908 216539

e-mail: newport.hotel@welcomebreak.co.uk

web: www.welcomebreak.co.uk

dir: M1 junct 14-15. In service area - follow signs to Barrier Lodge

This modern building offers accommodation in smart, spacious and well-equipped bedrooms, suitable for families and business travellers, and all with en suite bathrooms. Refreshments may be taken at the

continued

nearby family restaurant. For further details consult the Hotel Groups page.

Rooms 90 en suite S £45-£60; D £45-£60 **Conf** Thtr 40 Class 12 Board 16 Del from £60

STOKENCHURCH   MAP 05 SU79

★★★ 68% **HOTEL**

Best Western Kings Hotel

Oxford Rd HP14 3TA

☎ 01494 609090 📠 01494 484582

e-mail: jobeer@dhillonhotels.co.uk

Located on the village green, this hotel blends traditional elegance with contemporary design. Rooms are attractively decorated and well equipped, particularly for the business guest. Public areas include a busy bar and a relaxed, informal restaurant serving a wide range of dishes throughout the day. The smart conference rooms are air conditioned.

Rooms 43 en suite (3 fmly) ⊛ in 20 bedrooms S £99-£109; D £109-£129 (incl. bkfst) **Facilities** STV Gym Jacuzzi Wi-fi in bedrooms Xmas **Conf** BC Thtr 150 Class 90 Board 50 **Services** Lift air con **Parking** 100 **Notes** ⊗ ⊛ in restaurant Civ Wed

---

TAPLOW   MAP 06 SU98

INSPECTORS' CHOICE

★★★★★ ⧆⧆⧆ **COUNTRY HOUSE HOTEL**

Cliveden

SL6 0JF

☎ 01628 668561 📠 01628 661837

e-mail: reservations@clivedenhouse.co.uk

web: www.vonessenhotels.co.uk

dir: M4 junct 7, follow A4 towards Maidenhead for 1.5m, turn onto B476 towards Taplow, 2.5m, hotel on left

This wonderful stately home stands at the top of a gravelled boulevard. Visitors are treated as house-guests and staff recapture the tradition of fine hospitality. Bedrooms have individual quality and style, and reception rooms retain a timeless elegance. Both restaurants here are awarded AA rosettes - The Terrace with its delightful views has two rosettes, and Waldo's, offering innovative menus in discreet, luxurious surroundings, has three. Exceptional leisure facilities include cruises along Cliveden Reach and massages in the Pavilion.

Rooms 39 en suite (8 GF) ⊛ in 12 bedrooms D £335-£950 (incl. bkfst) **Facilities Spa** STV 🎱 ⚲ 🏊 Squash Snooker Sauna Gym 🏌 Jacuzzi Wi-fi available Full range of beauty treatments at the Pavilion Spa, 3 vintage launches ♫ Xmas **Conf** Thtr 40 Board 24 Del £355 **Services** Lift **Parking** 60 **Notes LB** ⊛ in restaurant Civ Wed 60

England

★★★ 77% ◉◉ **HOTEL**

Taplow House Hotel

Berry Hill SL6 0DA

WREN'S HOTELS
The unique hotel collection

☎ 01628 670056 🖷 01628 773625

e-mail: reception@taplow.wrensgroup.com

web: www.wrensgroup.com

dir: *off A4 onto Berry Hill, hotel 0.5m on right*

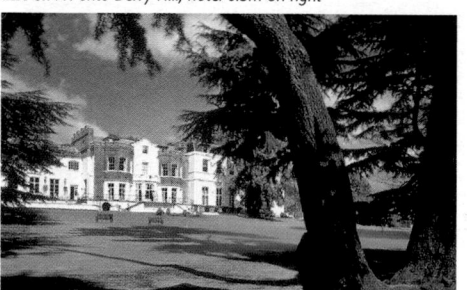

This elegant Georgian manor is set amid beautiful gardens and has been skilfully restored. Character public rooms are pleasing and include a number of air-conditioned conference rooms and an elegant restaurant. Comfortable bedrooms are individually decorated and furnished to a high standard.

Rooms 32 en suite (4 fmly) ⊗ in all bedrooms S £80–£200; D £80–£200 (incl. bkfst) **Facilities** FTV ⚑ Putt green Wi-fi in bedrooms Xmas **Conf** Thtr 100 Class 45 Board 40 Del from £210 **Parking** 100 **Notes LB** ⊗ ⊘ in restaurant Civ Wed 100

WOOBURN COMMON   MAP 06 SU98

★★★ 72% ◉ **HOTEL**

Chequers Inn

Kiln Ln, Wooburn HP10 0JQ

☎ 01628 529575 🖷 01628 850124

e-mail: info@chequers-inn.com

web: www.thechequersatwooburncommon.co.uk

dir: *M40 junct 2 take A40 through Beaconsfield Old Town towards High Wycombe. 2m from town turn left into Broad Lane. Hotel 2.5m*

This 17th-century inn enjoys a peaceful, rural location beside the common. Bedrooms feature stripped-pine furniture, co-ordinated fabrics and an excellent range of extra facilities. The bar, with its massive oak post, beams and flagstone floor, and the restaurant that

overlooks a pretty patio, are very much the focus of this establishment.

Rooms 17 en suite (8 GF) S £99.50; D £107.50 (incl. bkfst) **Facilities** STV Wi-fi in bedrooms **Conf** Thtr 50 Class 30 Board 20 Del £150 **Parking** 60 **Notes LB** ⊗ ⊘ in restaurant

CAMBRIDGESHIRE

BOXWORTH   MAP 12 TL36

BUDGET HOTEL

Sleep Inn Cambridge

Cambridge Services A14 CB3 8WU

SLEEP INN

☎ 01954 268400 🖷 01954 268419

e-mail: enquiries@hotels-cambridge.com

web: www.hotels-cambridge.com

dir: *A14 junct 28 6m N of Cambridge. 8m S of Huntington*

This modern, purpose built accommodation offers smartly appointed, well-equipped bedrooms, with good power showers. There is a choice of adjacent food outlets where guests may enjoy breakfast, snacks and meals.

Rooms 82 en suite S £58–£64; D £58–£64

BRAMPTON   MAP 12 TL27

★★ 74% ◉◉ **HOTEL**

The Grange

115 High St PE28 4RA

☎ 01480 459516 🖷 01480 459391

e-mail: nsteiger@grangehotelbrampton.com

web: www.grangehotelbrampton.co.uk

dir: *A1(M)/A14 towards Cambridge. After 0.5m take B1514 (racecourse) towards Huntingdon. After mini rdbt turn right into Grove Ln, hotel opp T-junct at bottom of road*

Located on the high street in the quiet village of Brampton, this historic building offers smart bedrooms. Imaginative cuisine is served in both the light and airy restaurant and in the more informal and inviting bar area. Guests have access to a comfortable lounge and service is both friendly and attentive.

Rooms 7 en suite ⊘ in all bedrooms S £65–£90; D £85–£110 (incl. bkfst) **Conf** Thtr 30 Class 15 Board 36 **Parking** 20 **Notes** ⊗ ⊘ in restaurant RS 29 Dec–5 Jan Civ Wed 40

continued

England

BUDGET HOTEL

Premier Travel Inn Huntingdon
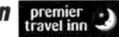

Brampton Hut PE28 4NQ

☎ 08701 977139 🖺 01480 811298

web: www.premiertravelinn.com

dir: *junct of A1/A14. (From north do not use junct 14 but take next main exit for Huntingdon & Brampton). Access via services*

High quality, modern budget accommodation ideal for both families and business travellers. Spacious, en suite bedrooms feature bath and shower, satellite TV and many have telephones and modem points. The adjacent family restaurant features a wide and varied menu. For further details consult the Hotel Groups page.

Rooms 80 en suite **Conf** Thtr 25

CAMBOURNE   MAP 12 TL35

★★★★ 81% ◉ **HOTEL**

The Cambridge Belfry
MarstonHotels

Back St CB3 6BW

☎ 01954 714600 🖺 01954 714610

e-mail: cambridge@marstonhotels.com

web: www.marstonhotels.com

dir: *M11 junct 13 take A428 towards Bedford, follow signs to Cambourne. Leave at Cambourne keeping left. Left at rdbt. Hotel on the left.*

One of the new hotels within the Marston Hotels portfolio, this exciting hotel is located at the gateway to Cambourne Village & Business Park. Contemporary in style throughout, the hotel boasts two eating options, state-of-the-art leisure facilities and extensive conference and banqueting rooms. Original artwork within the public areas takes guests on a guided tour of Cambridge, along the River Cam.

Rooms 120 en suite (30 GF) ⊘ in 105 bedrooms S fr £149; D fr £178 (incl. bkfst) **Facilities** Spa STV ⛹ ♨ Sauna Solarium Gym Jacuzzi Beauty treatments Wi-fi available Xmas **Conf** Thtr 258 Class 104 Board 72 Del from £219 **Services** Lift **Parking** 260 **Notes LB** ⊗ ⊘ in restaurant Civ Wed 160

See advert on page 77

CAMBRIDGE   MAP 12 TL45

★★★★ 80% ◉◉ **HOTEL**

Hotel Felix

Whitehouse Ln CB3 0LX

☎ 01223 277977 🖺 01223 277973

e-mail: help@hotelfelix.co.uk **web:** www.hotelfelix.co.uk

dir: *N on A1307 right at The Travellers Rest*

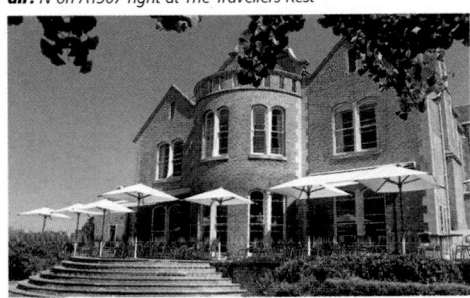

A beautiful Victorian mansion set amidst three acres of landscaped gardens, this property was originally built in 1852 for a surgeon from the famous Addenbrookes Hospital. The contemporary-style bedrooms have carefully chosen furniture and many thoughtful touches, whilst public rooms feature an open-plan bar, the adjacent Graffiti restaurant and a small quiet lounge.

Rooms 52 en suite (5 fmly) (26 GF) ⊘ in 33 bedrooms S £136-£186; D £168-£275 **Facilities** STV Wi-fi in bedrooms Xmas **Conf** Thtr 60 Class 36 Board 34 Del from £190 **Services** Lift **Parking** 90 **Notes LB** ⊘ in restaurant Civ Wed 70

★★★★ 74% **HOTEL**

Cambridge Garden House
QMH
UK LIMITED

Granta Place, Mill Ln CB2 1RT

☎ 01223 259988 🖺 01223 316605

dir: *M11 junct 12 follow road into Cambridge. Take left turn into Mill Ln, hotel at bottom of Mill Ln.*

A modern purpose-built hotel now totally refurbished. The property is situated in its own peaceful grounds overlooking the River Cam. The air conditioned bedrooms are well equipped with modern amenities. Public areas include a stylish restaurant and a well-equipped leisure club.

Rooms 122 en suite (8 fmly) (7 GF) ⊘ in 110 bedrooms S £100-£304; D £110-£314 (incl. bkfst) **Facilities** Spa STV ⛹ supervised Sauna Solarium Gym Jacuzzi Beauty salon Steam room Xmas **Conf** BC Thtr 150 Class 80 Board 50 Del from £166.50 **Services** Lift air con **Parking** 170 **Notes LB** ⊗ ⊘ in restaurant Civ Wed 150

England

CAMBRIDGE *continued*

★★★★ 73%

De Vere University Arms

Regent St CB2 1AD
☎ 01223 351241 ▤ 01223 273037
e-mail: dua.sales@devere-hotels.com
web: www.devere.co.uk

dir: M11 junct 11, follow city centre signs for 3m. Right at 2nd mini rdbt, left at lights into Regent St. Hotel 600yds on right

Built as a post house in 1834, the University Arms has an enviable position in the very heart of the city, overlooking Parker's Piece. Public rooms include an elegant domed lounge, a smart restaurant, a bar and lounge overlooking the park. Conference and banqueting rooms are extensive, many with oak panelling. Given the hotel's central location parking is a bonus.

Rooms 120 en suite (2 fmly) ⊘ in 83 bedrooms S £99-£159; D £99-£159 (incl. bkfst) **Facilities** STV Wi-fi available Reduced rate at local fitness centre Play Stations and pay movies in all rooms Xmas **Conf** Thtr 300 Class 150 Board 80 Del from £120 **Services** Lift **Parking** 88 **Notes LB** ⊘ in restaurant Civ Wed 250

★★★ 79% HOTEL

Arundel House

Chesterton Rd CB4 3AN
☎ 01223 367701 ▤ 01223 367721
e-mail: info@arundelhousehotels.co.uk
web: www.arundelhousehotels.co.uk
dir: city centre on A1303

Overlooking the River Cam and enjoying views over open parkland, this popular smart hotel was originally a row of Victorian townhouses. Bedrooms are attractive and have a special character. The smart public areas feature a conservatory for informal snacks, a spacious bar and an elegant restaurant for serious dining.

Rooms 81 en suite 22 annexe en suite (7 fmly) (14 GF) ⊘ in all bedrooms S £75-£95; D £95-£120 **Conf** Thtr 50 Class 34 Board 32 Del from £125 **Parking** 70 **Notes LB** ⊛ ⊘ in restaurant Closed 25-26 Dec

See advert on opposite page

★★★ 79% ⊛ HOTEL

Best Western Cambridge Quy Mill Hotel

Church Rd Stow-cum-Quy CB5 9AF
☎ 01223 293383 ▤ 01223 293770
e-mail: cambridgequy@bestwestern.co.uk
dir: off A14 at junct E of Cambridge onto B1102 for 50yds.

Set in open countryside, this 19th-century former watermill is convenient for Cambridge. Bedroom styles differ, yet each room is smartly appointed and brightly decorated; superior spacious courtyard rooms are noteworthy. Well-designed public areas include several spacious bar/lounges, with a choice of casual and formal eating areas; service is both friendly and helpful. A smart leisure club with state-of-the-art equipment is an impressive addition to the hotel.

Rooms 23 en suite 26 annexe en suite (2 fmly) (26 GF) ⊘ in 26 bedrooms S £90-£140; D £98-£180 **Facilities** STV ⌗ supervised Sauna Gym Jacuzzi Wi-fi in bedrooms Clay pigeon shooting by prior booking subject to availability **Conf** Thtr 80 Class 30 Board 24 Del from £165 **Parking** 90 **Notes LB** ⊛ Closed 24-30 Dec RS 31-Dec Civ Wed 80

★★★ 77% HOTEL

Best Western The Gonville

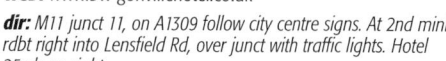

Gonville Place CB1 1LY
☎ 01223 366611 & 221111 ▤ 01223 315470
e-mail: all@gonvillehotel.co.uk
web: www.bw-gonvillehotel.co.uk

dir: M11 junct 11, on A1309 follow city centre signs. At 2nd mini rdbt right into Lensfield Rd, over junct with traffic lights. Hotel 25yds on right

This hotel is situated on the inner ring road, a short walk across the green from the city centre. Well-established, with regular guests and very experienced staff, the Gonville is popular for its relaxing, informal atmosphere. The air-conditioned public areas are cheerfully furnished, and include a lounge bar and brasserie; bedrooms are well appointed and appealing, offering a good range of facilities for both corporate and leisure guests.

Rooms 103 en suite (1 fmly) (5 GF) ⊘ in 38 bedrooms S £89-£150; D £99-£170 **Facilities** Wi-fi available **Conf** BC Thtr 200 Class 100 Board 50 Del from £129 **Services** Lift Arrangement with gym/swimming pool **Parking** 80 **Notes LB** ⊘ in restaurant Civ Wed 100 RS 24-29 Dec

England

★★★ 73% **METRO HOTEL**

Lensfield

53-57 Lensfield Rd CB2 1EN
☎ 01223 355017 ▤ 01223 312022
e-mail: reservations@lensfield.co.uk
web: www.lensfieldhotel.co.uk

dir: M11 junct 11/12/13, follow signs to City Centre, approach hotel via Silver St, Trumpington St (turning left into Lensfield Rd).

Located close to all attractions, this constantly improving hotel provides a range of attractive bedrooms, equipped with thoughtful extras. Comprehensive breakfasts are taken in an elegant dining room and a comfortable bar and cosy foyer lounge are also available.

Rooms 28 en suite (4 fmly) (4 GF) ⊘ in 27 bedrooms S £65-£95; D £98-£110 (incl. bkfst) **Facilities** STV **Parking** 5 **Notes LB** ⊗ Closed last 2 wks in Dec-4 Jan

★★★ 73% **HOTEL**

Royal Cambridge

Trumpington St CB2 1PY
☎ 01223 351631 ▤ 01223 352972
e-mail: royal.cambridge@forestdale.com
web: www.forestdale.com

dir: M11 junct 11, signed city centre. 1st mini rdbt left into Fen Causeway. Hotel 1st right

This impressive Georgian hotel enjoys a central location. Bedrooms are well equipped and comfortable, and include superior

continued on page 78

AA★★★★

The hotel offers 120 bedrooms including 19 executive rooms and two suites on the ground, first and second floors. The third floor is dedicated to six penthouse suites. The public areas are all on the ground floor based around the classic courtyard or overlooking the hotel's small lake.

THE CAMBRIDGE BELFRY

Cambourne Cambridge CB3 6BW **t:** 01954 714600
f: 01954 714610 cambridge@marstonhotels.com

www.marstonhotels.com

★★★ *Arundel House Hotel*

Occupies one of the finest sites in the City of Cambridge overlooking the river Cam and open parkland, close to the city centre and historic University colleges.

Our Restaurant has achieved a reputation for providing some of the best food in the area, in elegant, relaxed and welcoming surroundings at very modest prices. Alternatively you might like to try our magnificent all day Conservatory Brasserie which offers light snacks, cooked meals and cream teas, overlooking our tranquil and secluded garden.

If you have never visited Arundel House Hotel before we think you will be delighted when you see for yourself the facilities and menus we offer.

Visit our website for more details
Chesterton Road, Cambridge CB4 3AN
Tel: 01223 367701. Fax: 01223 367721

www.arundelhousehotels.co.uk   email:info@arundelhousehotels.co.uk

CAMBRIDGE *continued*

bedrooms/apartments. Public areas are traditionally decorated to a good standard; the elegant restaurant is a popular choice and the lounge/bar serves evening snacks. Parking and conferencing are added benefits.

Rooms 57 en suite (9 fmly) ⊘ in 28 bedrooms S £120; D £155 (incl. bkfst) **Facilities** STV Wi-fi in bedrooms Xmas **Conf** Thtr 120 Class 40 Board 40 **Services** Lift **Parking** 80 **Notes LB** ⊘ in restaurant Civ Wed 100

★★★ 72% HOTEL

Sorrento

THE INDEPENDENTS

190-196 Cherry Hinton Rd CB1 7AN
☎ 01223 243533 ▤ 01223 213463
e-mail: info@sorrentohotel.com
web: www.sorrentohotel.com

dir: *M11 junct 11 towards Cambridge on B1309, 2nd set lights right into Long Road. 1st set lights left into Hills Road. 1st set lights right into Cherry Hinton Rd*

Friendly, family run hotel situated close to the city centre. Although the bedrooms vary in size and style, they are all pleasantly decorated and equipped with many thoughtful extras. Public rooms have an Italian feel with superb marble flooring throughout; they include a smart lounge bar, attractive restaurant and a huge conservatory.

Rooms 30 en suite (4 fmly) (8 GF) ⊘ in 20 bedrooms S £69.50-£95; D £99-£139.50 (incl. bkfst) **Facilities** STV Wi-fi in bedrooms Xmas **Conf** Thtr 60 Class 35 Board 35 **Parking** 40 **Notes LB** ⊘ in restaurant

★★ 75% METRO HOTEL

Helen Hotel

167-169 Hills Rd CB2 2RJ
☎ 01223 246465 ▤ 01223 214406
e-mail: enquiries@helenhotel.co.uk

dir: *On A1307 1.25m from City Centre (S side). Cherry-Hinton Rd junct, opposite Homerton College.*

This extremely well maintained privately owned hotel is situated close to the city centre and a range of popular eateries. Public areas include a smart lounge bar with plush sofas and a cosy breakfast room. Bedrooms are pleasantly decorated with co-ordinated fabrics and have many thoughtful touches.

Rooms 19 en suite (2 fmly) (2 GF) ⊘ in 16 bedrooms S £55-£65; D £75 (incl. bkfst) **Facilities** STV **Parking** 12 **Notes** ⊗ ⊘ in restaurant Closed Xmas & New Year

★★ 74% HOTEL

Centennial

63-71 Hills Rd CB2 1PG
☎ 01223 314652 ▤ 01223 315443
e-mail: reception@centennialhotel.co.uk

dir: *M11 junct 11 take A1309 to Cambridge. Right onto Brooklands Ave to end. Left, hotel 100yds on right*

This friendly hotel is convenient for the railway station and town centre. Well-presented public areas include a welcoming lounge, and a relaxing bar and restaurant on the lower-ground level. Bedrooms are generally spacious, well maintained and thoughtfully equipped with a good range of facilities; several rooms are available on the ground floor.

continued

Rooms 39 en suite (1 fmly) (7 GF) ⊘ in 26 bedrooms S £70-£80; D £88-£96 (incl. bkfst) **Conf** Thtr 25 Class 25 Board 25 **Parking** 30 **Notes LB** ⊗ ⊘ in restaurant Closed 23 Dec-1 Jan

See advert on opposite page

BUDGET HOTEL

Travelodge Cambridge Central

Cambridge Leisure Park, Clifton Way CB1 7DY
☎ 01223 241066
web: www.travelodge.co.uk

Travelodge

Travelodge offers good quality, good value, modern accommodation. Ideal for families, the spacious en suite bedrooms include remote-control TV, tea and coffee-making facilities and comfortable beds. Meals can be taken at the nearby family restaurant. See Hotel Groups pages for further details.

Rooms 120 rms S fr £26; D fr £26

Travelodge Cambridge Fourwentways

Fourwentways CB1 6AP
☎ 08700 850 950 ▤ 01223 839479

dir: *adjacent to Little Chef at junct A11/A1307, 5m S of Cambridge*

Rooms 40 en suite S fr £26; D fr £26

DUXFORD
MAP 12 TL44

★★★ 75% ⊛⊛ HOTEL

Duxford Lodge

Ickleton Rd CB2 4RT
☎ 01223 836444 ▤ 01223 832271
e-mail: admin@duxfordlodgehotel.co.uk
web: www.duxfordlodgehotel.co.uk

dir: *M11 junct 10, onto A505 to Duxford. 1st right at T- junct. Hotel on left*

A warm welcome is assured at this attractive red-brick hotel in the heart of a delightful village. Public areas include a cosy relaxing bar, separate lounge, and an attractive restaurant, where an excellent and imaginative menu is offered. The bedrooms are well appointed, comfortable and smartly furnished.

Rooms 11 en suite 4 annexe en suite (2 fmly) (4 GF) ⊘ in all bedrooms S £76-£86; D £106-£116 (incl. bkfst) **Facilities** Wi-fi in bedrooms ch fac Xmas **Conf** Thtr 30 Class 20 Board 20 **Parking** 34 **Notes LB** ⊘ in restaurant Closed 26-30 Dec Civ Wed 50

See advert on opposite page

ELY

MAP 12 TL58

★★★ 72% HOTEL

Lamb

OLD ENGLISH INNS

2 Lynn Rd CB7 4EJ

☎ 01353 663574 01353 662023

e-mail: lamb.ely@oldenglishinns.co.uk

web: www.oldenglish.co.uk

dir: from A10 into Ely, hotel in town centre

This 15th-century former coaching inn is situated in the heart of this popular market town. The hotel offers a combination of light, modern and traditional public rooms, whilst the bedrooms provide contemporary standards of accommodation. Food is available throughout the hotel - the same menu provided in the bar and restaurant areas.

Rooms 31 en suite (6 fmly) ⊘ in 24 bedrooms **Facilities** STV
Conf Thtr 100 Class 40 Board 70 **Parking** 20 **Notes LB** ⊘ in restaurant

BUDGET HOTEL

Travelodge Ely

Witchford Rd CB6 3NN

☎ 08700 850 950 01353 668499

web: www.travelodge.co.uk

dir: at rdbt A10/A142

Travelodge offers good quality, good value, modern accommodation. Ideal for families, the spacious en suite bedrooms include remote-control TV, tea and coffee-making facilities and comfortable beds. Meals can be taken at the nearby family restaurant. See Hotel Groups pages for further details.

Rooms 39 en suite S fr £26; D fr £26

FENSTANTON

MAP 12 TL36

BUDGET HOTEL

Travelodge Huntingdon Fenstanton

Travelodge

PE18 9LP

☎ 08700 850 950 01954 230919

web: www.travelodge.co.uk

dir: 4m SE of Huntingdon, on A14 eastbound

Travelodge offers good quality, good value, modern accommodation. Ideal for families, the spacious en suite bedrooms include remote-control TV, tea and coffee-making facilities and comfortable beds. Meals can be taken at the nearby family restaurant. See Hotel Groups pages for further details.

Rooms 40 en suite S fr £26; D fr £26

HOLYWELL

MAP 12 TL37

★★ 63% HOTEL

The Old Ferryboat Inn

OLD ENGLISH INNS

Back Ln PE27 4TG

☎ 01480 463227 01480 463245

e-mail: 8638@greeneking.co.uk

web: www.oldenglish.co.uk

This delightful thatched inn sits in a tranquil setting beside the Great Ouse river, on the periphery of the village of Holywell. Said to be the

continued on page 80

HOLYWELL *continued*

oldest inn in England, with foundations dating back to 560AD, the inn retains much original character and charm. Bedrooms are soundly appointed and open plan public rooms have a pleasing relaxed atmosphere: the extensive gardens, with views of the river, are a popular attraction in the summer months.

Rooms 7 en suite ⊛ in all bedrooms S £50; D £60–£70 (incl. bkfst) **Conf** Thtr 60 Class 50 Board 35 **Parking** 70 **Notes** ⊗

HUNTINGDON   MAP 12 TL27

★★★★ 75% **HOTEL**

Huntingdon Marriott Hotel

Marriott
HOTELS & RESORTS

Kingfisher Way, Hinchingbrooke Business Park PE29 6FL

☎ 01480 446000 ▧ 01480 451111
e-mail: reservations.huntingdon@marriotthotels.com
web: www.marriott.com/cbghd

dir: *1m from Huntington centre on A14, close to Brampton racecourse*

With its excellent road links, this modern, purpose-built hotel is a popular venue for conferences and business meetings, and is convenient for Huntingdon, Cambridge and racing at Newmarket. Bedrooms are spacious and offer every modern comfort, including air conditioning. Leisure facilities are also impressive.

Rooms 150 en suite (45 GF) ⊛ in 60 bedrooms S £67–£120; D £94–£180 **Facilities Spa** STV ⌕ supervised Sauna Solarium Gym Jacuzzi Wi-fi available Dinner disco most Sat eve. Salsa 2nd and last Fri ♫ Xmas **Conf** Thtr 300 Class 150 Board 100 **Del from** £149 **Services** Lift air con **Parking** 200 **Notes LB** ⊛ in restaurant Civ Wed 300

★★★ 80% ⊛⊛ **HOTEL**

The Old Bridge

1 High St PE29 3TQ

☎ 01480 424300 ▧ 01480 411017
e-mail: oldbridge@huntsbridge.co.uk
web: www.huntsbridge.com

dir: *from A14 or A1 follow Huntingdon signs. Hotel visible from inner ring road*

An imposing 18th-century building on the ring road, close to shops and amenities. This charming hotel offers superb accommodation in stylish and individually decorated bedrooms that include many useful extras. Guests can choose from the same menu whether dining in the open-plan terrace, or the more formal restaurant with its bold colour scheme (now with a good fixed-price option). There is a particularly good business centre with secretarial services.

Rooms 24 en suite (2 fmly) (2 GF) S £95–£125; D fr £125 (incl. bkfst) **Facilities** STV Fishing Wi-fi available Private mooring for boats Xmas **Conf** BC **Del from** £175 **Services** air con **Parking** 50 **Notes LB** ⊛ in restaurant Civ Wed

---

Ⓤ

George

OLD ENGLISH INNS

George St PE29 3AB

☎ 01480 432444 ▧ 01480 453130
e-mail: george.huntingdon@oldenglishinns.co.uk
web: www.oldenglish.co.uk

dir: *Leave A14 at Huntingdon racecourse exit. Then 3m to junct with ring road. Hotel opposite*

At the time of going to press, the star classification for this hotel was not confirmed. Please refer to the AA internet site www.theAA.com for current information.

Rooms 24 en suite (3 fmly) ⊛ in all bedrooms S £60–£80; D £80–£90 (incl. bkfst) **Facilities** ♫ Xmas **Conf** Thtr 80 Class 60 Board 60 **Del** £120 **Parking** 55 **Notes LB** ⊛ in restaurant Civ Wed 120

LOLWORTH   MAP 12 TL36

BUDGET HOTEL

Travelodge Cambridge Lolworth

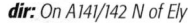
Travelodge

Huntingdon Rd CB3 8DR

☎ 08700 850 950 ▧ 01954 781335
web: www.travelodge.co.uk

dir: *on A14 northbound, 3m N of M11 junct 14*

Travelodge offers good quality, good value, modern accommodation. Ideal for families, the spacious en suite bedrooms include remote-control TV, tea and coffee-making facilities and comfortable beds. Meals can be taken at the nearby family restaurant. See Hotel Groups pages for further details.

Rooms 36 en suite S fr £26; D fr £26

MARCH   MAP 12 TL49

★★ 61% **HOTEL**

Olde Griffin

High St PE15 9JS

☎ 01354 652517 ▧ 01354 650086
e-mail: griffhotel@aol.com

dir: *On A141/142 N of Ely*

Overlooking the town square, this former coaching inn (now under new ownership) dates back to the 16th century, and retains many period features. Bedrooms vary in size and style and all are appropriately equipped and furnished. Meals are available in the lounge and bar areas, and there is a restaurant for more formal dining on a Friday and Saturday.

continued

England

Rooms 21 rms (20 en suite) (1 fmly) ⊘ in all bedrooms S from £45; D from £59.50 (incl. bkfst) **Conf** Thtr 100 Class 50 Board 36 **Parking** 50 **Notes** ⊘ in restaurant

---

PETERBOROUGH   MAP 12 TL19

★★★★ 71% HOTEL

Peterborough Marriott

Marriott
HOTELS & RESORTS

Peterborough Business Park, Lynchwood
PE2 6GB
☎ 01733 371111 📠 01733 236725
e-mail: reservations.peterborough@marriotthotels.co.uk
web: www.marriott.com/xvhpb
dir: *opp East of England Showground. From A1 off at Alwalton Showground, Chesterton. Left at T-junct. Hotel on left at next rdbt*

This modern hotel is opposite the East of England Showground, and a just few minutes' drive from the heart of the city. Alwalton is famous for being the birthplace of Sir Frederick Henry Royce, one of the founders of the Rolls-Royce company. Air-conditioned bedrooms are spacious and well designed for business use. Public rooms include the Garden Lounge, cocktail bar, Laurels Restaurant and a leisure club.

Rooms 163 en suite (8 fmly) (74 GF) ⊘ in 125 bedrooms S fr £115; D fr £115 **Facilities** Spa STV ⤵ Sauna Solarium Gym Jacuzzi Wi-fi available Beauty therapist Hairdressing Xmas **Conf** Thtr 300 Class 160 Board 45 Del from £129 **Services** air con **Parking** 175 **Notes LB** ⊘ in restaurant Civ Wed 80

★★★ 78% ⊛ HOTEL

Best Western Orton Hall

Best
Western

Orton Longueville PE2 7DN
☎ 01733 391111 📠 01733 231912
e-mail: reception@ortonhall.co.uk
dir: *off A605 E opposite Orton Mere*

Impressive country house hotel set amidst 20 acres of woodland on the outskirts of town. The spacious and relaxing public areas have
continued

---

many original features that include The Great Room and 17th-century oak panelling in the Huntly Restaurant. The Ramblewood Inn offers an alternative informal dining and bar option.

Rooms 65 en suite (2 fmly) (15 GF) ⊘ in 42 bedrooms S £70-£140; D £90-£160 **Facilities** STV FTV Wi-fi available Three quarter size snooker table Xmas **Conf** Thtr 120 Class 48 Board 42 Del from £135 **Parking** 200 **Notes LB** ⊘ in restaurant Civ Wed 90

★★★ 77% ⊛ HOTEL

Bell Inn

Great North Rd PE7 3RA
☎ 01733 241066 & 242626 📠 01733 245173
e-mail: reception@thebellstilton.co.uk
web: www.thebellstilton.co.uk
(For full entry see Stilton)

★★★ 75% HOTEL

Holiday Inn
Peterborough West

Holiday Inn
HOTELS · RESORTS

Thorpe Wood PE3 6SG
☎ 0870 7879 861 & 01733 289988 📠 01733 262737
e-mail: hipeterborough@qmh-hotels.com
dir: *Exit A1 S at Peterborough sign onto A1139. Follow city centre signs at junct 3 & 33. Take route marked Thorpe Wood, hotel on right.*

Situated just over two miles from the city centre, with ample parking and easy access to road networks, this hotel is located opposite a challenging 10 hole golf course and a short distance to the River Nene. Popular for both the extensive conference and banqueting facilities and the modern leisure club. The refurbished accommodation offers well equipped rooms; air-conditioning is a real plus.

Rooms 133 en suite (10 fmly) (27 GF) ⊘ in 111 bedrooms S £48-£94; D £48-£94 **Facilities** Spa STV ⤵ supervised Sauna Solarium Gym Jacuzzi Steam room Beauty salon Pool table Xmas **Conf** BC Thtr 400 Class 150 Board 100 Del from £120 **Services** Lift **Parking** 250 **Notes LB** ⊛ ⊘ in restaurant Civ Wed 180

England

PETERBOROUGH *continued*

★★★ 74% HOTEL

Bull
Westgate PE1 1RB
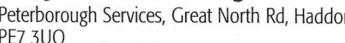
☎ 01733 561364 🖹 01733 557304
e-mail: info@bull-hotel-peterborough.com
web: www.peelhotel.com

dir: off A1, follow city centre signs. Hotel opp Queensgate
shopping centre. Car park on Broadway next to Library

This pleasant city-centre hotel offers well-equipped, modern
accommodation, which includes several wings of deluxe bedrooms.
Public rooms include a popular bar and a brasserie-style restaurant
serving a flexible range of dishes, with further informal dining
available in the lounge. There is a good range of meeting rooms and
conference facilities.

Rooms 118 en suite (3 fmly) ⊛ in 40 bedrooms S £70-£109; D £90-£119
Facilities STV Wi-fi available Xmas **Conf** Thtr 200 Class 80 Board 60
Parking 100 **Notes** LB ⊗ ⊛ in restaurant Civ Wed 200

BUDGET HOTEL

Premier Travel Inn
Peterborough (Ferry Meadow)
Ham Ln, Orton Meadows, Nene Park PE2 5UU
☎ 08701 977205 🖹 01733 391055
web: www.premiertravelinn.com

dir: From south A1(M) junct 16, then A15 through Yaxley. Left at
rdbt. From north A1 junct 17, A1139 junct 3 right to Yaxley. Right
at 2nd rdbt

High quality, modern budget accommodation ideal for both families
and business travellers. Spacious, en suite bedrooms feature bath and
shower, satellite TV and many have telephones and modem points.
The adjacent family restaurant features a wide and varied menu. For
further details consult the Hotel Groups page.

Rooms 40 en suite **Conf** Thtr 24 Board 24

Premier Travel Inn Peterborough
(Hampton)
4 Ashbourne Rd, Off London Rd, Hampton PE7 8BT
☎ 08701 977206 🖹 01733 391055

dir: From south: A1(M) junct 16, follow A15 through Yaxley. Inn
on left at 1st rdbt. From north: A1(M) junct 17 follow A1139, 2nd
exit junct 3 follow signs for Yaxley. Inn is on right at 2nd rdbt
Rooms 80 en suite

BUDGET HOTEL

Sleep Inn Peterborough
Peterborough Services, Great North Rd, Haddon
PE7 3UQ
☎ 01733 396850 🖹 01733 396869
e-mail: enquiries@hotels-peterborough.co.uk
web: www.hotels-peterborough.co.uk

dir: A1(M) junct 17 take A605 towards Northampton. Inn
100mtrs on left

This modern, purpose built accommodation offers smartly appointed,
well-equipped bedrooms, with good power showers. There is a choice
of adjacent food outlets where guests may enjoy breakfast, snacks and
meals.

Rooms 82 en suite S £53.10-£59; D £53.10-£64

BUDGET HOTEL

Travelodge Peterborough
Alwalton
Great North Rd, Alwalton PE7 3UR
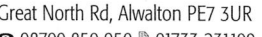
☎ 08700 850 950 🖹 01733 231109
web: www.travelodge.co.uk

dir: on A1, southbound

Travelodge offers good quality, good value, modern accommodation.
Ideal for families, the spacious en suite bedrooms include remote-
control TV, tea and coffee-making facilities and comfortable beds.
Meals can be taken at the nearby family restaurant. See Hotel Groups
pages for further details.

Rooms 32 en suite S fr £26; D fr £26

Travelodge Peterborough Eye Green
Crowlands Rd PE6 7SZ
☎ 08700 850 950 🖹 01733 223199
dir: junct of A47/A1073
Rooms 42 en suite S fr £26; D fr £26

ST IVES   MAP 12 TL37

★★★ 70% HOTEL

Olivers Lodge
Needingworth Rd PE27 5JP
☎ 01480 463252 🖹 01480 461150
e-mail: reception@oliverslodge.co.uk
web: www.oliverslodge.co.uk

dir: follow A14 towards Huntingdon/Cambridge, take B1040 to
St Ives. Cross 1st rdbt, left at 2nd then 1st right. Hotel 500mtrs on
right

Expect a warm welcome at this well run hotel situated in a quiet
residential area on the outskirts of the town. Bedrooms are situated in
the main house and adjoining wing, each room is pleasantly
decorated and thoughtfully equipped. Public rooms include a
conservatory restaurant, a cosy lounge bar and function/meeting
rooms are available.

continued

Olivers Lodge

Rooms 12 en suite 5 annexe en suite (3 fmly) (5 GF) ⊗ in 16 bedrooms S £65-£78; D £75-£100 (incl. bkfst) **Facilities** STV Free use of local health club **Conf** BC Thtr 65 Class 35 Board 28 Del from £118.70 **Parking** 30 **Notes LB** ⊗ in restaurant Civ Wed 85

★★★ 70% HOTEL

Slepe Hall
Ramsey Rd PE27 5RB
☎ 01480 463122 ▤ 01480 300706
e-mail: mail@slepehall.co.uk
web: www.slepehall.co.uk
dir: *from A14 on A1096 & follow by-pass signed Huntingdon towards St Ives, left into Ramsey Rd at lights by Toyota garage, hotel on left*

A welcoming and friendly atmosphere can be found at Slepe Hall, which is located close to the town centre. Bedroom types vary with both traditional and modern styles available. A choice of dining options is provided with light meals served in the lounge and bar, and more formal eating options in the restaurant.

Rooms 16 en suite (1 fmly) ⊗ in all bedrooms S £60-£80; D £80-£99 (incl. bkfst) **Facilities** STV ch fac **Conf** Thtr 200 Class 80 Board 60 Del £110 **Parking** 70 **Notes LB** ⊗ in restaurant Closed 24-26 Dec & 1 Jan Civ Wed 60

★★★ 68% HOTEL

Dolphin
London Rd PE27 5EP
☎ 01480 466966 ▤ 01480 495597
e-mail: enquiries@dolphinhotelcambs.co.uk
dir: *from A14 between Huntingdon & Cambridge onto A1096 towards St Ives. Left at 1st rdbt & immediately right. Hotel on left after 0.5m*

This modern hotel sits by delightful water meadows on the banks of the River Ouse. Open-plan public rooms include a choice of bars and
continued

a pleasant restaurant offering fine river views. The bedrooms are modern and varied in style; some are in the hotel while others occupy an adjacent wing. All are comfortable and spacious. Conference and function suites are available.

Rooms 30 en suite 37 annexe en suite (4 fmly) (22 GF) ⊗ in 36 bedrooms S £80-£100; D £100-£120 (incl. bkfst) **Facilities** STV Fishing Sauna Gym **Conf** Thtr 150 Class 50 Board 50 Del from £100 **Parking** 400 **Notes LB** ⊛ ⊗ in restaurant RS 24 Dec-2 Jan Civ Wed 80

ST NEOTS   MAP 12 TL16

★★★ 77% HOTEL

The George Hotel & Brasserie
High St, Buckden PE19 5XA
☎ 01480 812300 ▤ 01480 813920
e-mail: mail@thegeorgebuckden.com
web: www.thegeorgebuckden.com
dir: *Just off A1 at Buckden 2m S of A1/A14 interchange.*

Ideally situated in the heart of this historic town centre just a short drive from the A1. Public rooms feature a bustling ground floor brasserie, which offers casual dining throughout the day and evening; there is also an informal lounge bar with an open fire and comfy seating. Bedrooms are stylish, tastefully appointed and thoughtfully equipped.

Rooms 12 en suite ⊗ in all bedrooms S £80-£130; D £100-£130 (incl. bkfst) **Facilities** STV Membership at local leisure centre Xmas **Conf** Thtr 20 Class 10 Board 10 Del from £150 **Services** Lift **Parking** 25 **Notes LB** ⊗ in restaurant

BUDGET HOTEL

Premier Travel Inn St Neots (Colmworth Park)
Colmworth Business Park PE19 8YH
☎ 08701 977238 ▤ 01480 408541
web: www.premiertravelinn.com
dir: *from A1 at southern St Neots junct. Inn at 1st rdbt (A428/B1428)*

High quality, modern budget accommodation ideal for both families and business travellers. Spacious, en suite bedrooms feature bath and shower, satellite TV and many have telephones and modem points. The adjacent family restaurant features a wide and varied menu. For further details consult the Hotel Groups page.

Rooms 41 en suite

England

ST NEOTS continued

Premier Travel Inn St Neots (Eaton Socon)

Great North Rd, Eaton Socon PE19 8EN
☎ 0870 9906314 📠 0870 9906315
dir: Just off A1 at rdbt of A428 & B1428 before St.Neots, 1m from St.Neots rail station
Rooms 63 en suite

SIX MILE BOTTOM   MAP 12 TL55

★★★ 80% ◉ HOTEL

Swynford Paddocks

CB8 0UE
☎ 01638 570234 📠 01638 570283
e-mail: info@swynfordpaddocks.com
web: www.swynfordpaddocks.com
dir: M11 junct 9, take A11 towards Newmarket, then onto A1304 to Newmarket, hotel 0.75m on left

This smart country house is set in attractive grounds, within easy reach of Newmarket. Bedrooms are comfortably appointed, thoughtfully equipped and include some delightful four-poster rooms. Imaginative, carefully prepared food is served in the elegant restaurant; service is friendly and attentive. Meeting and conference facilities are available.

Rooms 15 en suite (1 fmly) S £110-£140; D £135-£195 (incl. bkfst)
Facilities STV ⌣ **Conf** Thtr 60 Class 40 Board 40 Del from £170
Parking 180 **Notes LB** ⊘ in restaurant Civ Wed 100

STILTON   MAP 12 TL18

★★★ 77% ◉ HOTEL

Bell Inn

Great North Rd PE7 3RA
☎ 01733 241066 & 242626 📠 01733 245173
e-mail: reception@thebellstilton.co.uk
web: www.thebellstilton.co.uk
dir: A1(M) junct 16, follow Stilton signs. Hotel in village centre

This delightful inn is steeped in history and retains many original features, with imaginative food served in both the character village bar/brasserie and the elegant beamed first-floor restaurant; refreshments can be enjoyed in the attractive courtyard and rear gardens when weather permits. Individually designed bedrooms are stylish and equipped to a high standard.

continued

Rooms 19 en suite 3 annexe en suite (1 fmly) (3 GF) ⊘ in all bedrooms S £72.50-£79.50; D £99.50-£129.50 (incl. bkfst) **Facilities** STV FTV Wi-fi available **Conf** Thtr 100 Class 46 Board 50 Del £129.50 **Parking** 30 **Notes** ⊗ ⊘ in restaurant Closed 25-Dec pm RS 26-Dec pm Civ Wed 100

SWAVESEY   MAP 12 TL36

BUDGET HOTEL

Travelodge Cambridge Swavesey

Cambridge Rd CB4 5QR
☎ 08700 850 950 📠 01954 789113
web: www.travelodge.co.uk
dir: on eastbound carriageway of A14

Travelodge offers good quality, good value, modern accommodation. Ideal for families, the spacious en suite bedrooms include remote-control TV, tea and coffee-making facilities and comfortable beds. Meals can be taken at the nearby family restaurant. See Hotel Groups pages for further details.

Rooms 36 en suite S fr £26; D fr £26

WANSFORD   MAP 12 TL09

★★★ 87% ◉◉ HOTEL

The Haycock

PE8 6JA
☎ 01780 782223 📠 01780 783508
e-mail: sales@thehaycock.co.uk
dir: from A1 follow Wansford signs, hotel on right

Charming 17th-century coaching inn set amidst attractive landscaped grounds in a peaceful village location. The smartly decorated bedrooms are tastefully furnished and thoughtfully equipped. Public rooms include a choice of restaurants, a lounge bar, a cocktail bar and a stylish lounge. The hotel has a staffed business centre and banqueting facilities are also available.

Rooms 48 en suite (5 fmly) (14 GF) ⊘ in all bedrooms S £85-£183; D £120-£195 (incl. bkfst) **Facilities** STV Fishing Shooting Xmas **Conf** BC Thtr 300 Class 100 Board 45 Del from £160 **Parking** 200 **Notes LB** ⊘ in restaurant Civ Wed 150

WISBECH   MAP 12 TF40

★★★ 77% ◉ HOTEL

Crown Lodge

THE INDEPENDENTS

Downham Rd, Outwell PE14 8SE
☎ 01945 773391 & 772206 📠 01945 772668
e-mail: office@thecrownlodgehotel.co.uk
web: www.thecrownlodgehotel.co.uk
dir: on A1122/A1101 approx 5m from Wisbech

Friendly, privately owned hotel situated in a peaceful location on the banks of Well Creek a short drive from Wisbech. The bedrooms are pleasantly decorated, have co-ordinated fabrics and modern facilities. The public areas are very stylish, and include a lounge bar, brasserie restaurant and a large seating area with plush leather sofas.

continued

England

Crown Lodge

Rooms 10 en suite (10 GF) ⊗ in 8 bedrooms S fr £60; D fr £80 (incl. bkfst) **Facilities** Squash Solarium Wi-fi available **Conf** BC Thtr 80 Class 60 Board 40 **Services** air con **Parking** 57 **Notes LB** ⊗ in restaurant

★★★ 73% **HOTEL**

Elme Hall

Elm High Rd PE14 0DQ

☎ 01945 475566 ▤ 01945 475666

e-mail: elme@paktel.co.uk

web: www.paktel.co.uk

dir: off A47 onto A1101 towards Wisbech. Hotel on right

An imposing Georgian-style property conveniently situated on the outskirts of the town centre just off the A47. Individually decorated bedrooms are tastefully furnished with quality reproduction pieces and equipped to a high standard. Public rooms include a choice of attractive lounges, as well as two bars, meeting rooms and a banqueting suite.

Rooms 7 en suite (3 fmly) ⊗ in all bedrooms S fr £48; D £68-£220 (incl. bkfst) **Facilities** FTV Wi-fi in bedrooms ♫ **Conf** Thtr 350 Class 200 Board 20 **Parking** 200 **Notes** ⊗ in restaurant Civ Wed 350

CHESHIRE

ALDERLEY EDGE   MAP 16 SJ87

★★★ 83% ⊛⊛ **HOTEL**

Alderley Edge

Macclesfield Rd SK9 7BJ

☎ 01625 583033 ▤ 01625 586343

e-mail: sales@alderleyedgehotel.com

web: www.alderleyedgehotel.com

dir: off A34 in Alderley Edge onto B5087 towards Macclesfield. Hotel 200yds on right

This well-furnished hotel, with its charming grounds, was originally a country house built for one of the region's cotton kings. The bedrooms and suites are attractively furnished, offering excellent quality and comfort. The welcoming bar and adjacent lounge lead into the split-level conservatory restaurant; imaginative, memorable food and friendly attentive service are highlights of any visit.

continued

Alderley Edge

Rooms 52 en suite (6 GF) ⊗ in 19 bedrooms **Facilities** STV Wi-fi in bedrooms ♫ ch fac Xmas **Conf** Thtr 90 Class 40 Board 30 Del £165 **Services** Lift **Parking** 90 **Notes** ⊛ ⊗ in restaurant Civ Wed 90

BUDGET HOTEL

Innkeeper's Lodge
Alderley Edge

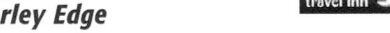

5-9 Wilmslow Rd SK9 7NZ

☎ 01625 599959 ▤ 01625 599432

web: www.innkeeperslodge.com

dir: M56 junct 6, S on A538. Right at traffic lights towards Alderley Edge. Lodge on left, after 2nd rdbt

Smart, en suite accommodation ideal for both business & leisure guests. Bedrooms are very well equipped, including Sky TV, telephone, modem points, tea & coffee making facilities. (family rooms in most locations). Complimentary breakfast. The adjacent Pub Restaurant; a Harvester, Vintage Inn, Toby Carvery, Ember Inn, Sizzling Pubco or Pub & Carvery offers an all day menu. See Hotel Groups pages for further details.

Rooms 10 en suite S £65-£95; D £65-£95

BUDGET HOTEL

Premier Travel Inn
Alderley Edge

Congleton Rd, Alderley Edge SK9 7AA

☎ 0870 9906498 ▤ 0870 9906499

web: www.premiertravelinn.com

dir: From N, exit M56 junct 6 onto A538 towards Wilmslow or from S, exit M6 junct 17, follow A534 to Congleton. Then take A34 to Alderley Edge

High quality, modern budget accommodation ideal for both families and business travellers. Spacious, en suite bedrooms feature bath and shower, satellite TV and many have telephones and modem points. The adjacent family restaurant features a wide and varied menu. For further details consult the Hotel Groups page.

Rooms 37 en suite **Conf** Thtr 20

Some hotels, although accepting children, may not have any special facilities for them so it is well worth checking before booking

ALSAGER
MAP 15 SJ75

★★★ 82% ◉ **HOTEL**

Best Western Manor House
Audley Rd ST7 2QQ
☎ 01270 884000 📠 01270 882483
e-mail: mhres@compasshotels.co.uk
web: www.compasshotels.co.uk

dir: M6 junct 16/A500 toward Stoke. After 0.5m take 1st slip road to Alsager. Left at top & continue, hotel on left approaching village

Developed around an old farmhouse, the original oak beams are still very much a feature in the hotel bars and restaurant. Modernised and extended over the years, the hotel today is well geared towards the needs of the modern traveller. Some of the main features include a range of conference rooms, a lovely patio garden and an indoor swimming pool.

Rooms 57 en suite (4 fmly) (21 GF) ⊘ in 31 bedrooms S £70-£98; D £90-£145 (incl. bkfst) **Facilities** STV FTV ⌕ supervised Jacuzzi Wi-fi in bedrooms **Conf** Thtr 200 Class 108 Board 82 Del from £105 **Parking** 150 **Notes LB** ⊗ ⊘ in restaurant RS Sat & Sun Civ Wed 150

BROXTON
MAP 15 SJ45

★★★★ 84% **HOTEL**

De Vere Carden Park
Carden Park CH3 9DQ
☎ 01829 731000 📠 01829 731599
e-mail: reservations.carden@devere-hotels.com
web: www.devere.co.uk

dir: M56 junct 15/M53 Chester. Take A41 for Whitchurch for approx 8m. At Broxton rdbt right onto A534 Wrexham. Hotel 1.5m on left

This impressive Cheshire estate dates back to the 17th-century and consists of 750 acres of mature parkland. The hotel offers a choice of dining options along with superb leisure facilities that include golf courses, a fully equipped gym, a swimming pool and popular spa. Spacious, thoughtfully equipped bedrooms have undergone a quality refurbishment which includes excellent business and in-room entertainment facilities.

Rooms 113 en suite 83 annexe en suite (24 fmly) ⊘ in 138 bedrooms **Facilities** Spa STV ⌕ supervised ♨ 45 ⌕ Snooker Sauna Solarium Gym ⛳ Putt green Jacuzzi Archery, Quadbikes, Off road driving, Mountain biking, Walking trails Xmas **Conf** BC Thtr 400 Class 240 Board 125 **Services** Lift **Parking** 500 **Notes** ⊗ ⊘ in restaurant Civ Wed 375

If the freedom to smoke or be in a non-smoking atmosphere is important to you, check the rules when you book

BURWARDSLEY
MAP 15 SJ55

★★ 81% ◉ **HOTEL**

Pheasant Inn
Higher Burwardsley CH3 9PF
☎ 01829 770434 📠 01829 771097
e-mail: info@thepheasantinn.co.uk
web: www.thepheasantinn.co.uk

dir: from A41, left to Tattenhall, right at 1st junct and left at 2nd to Higher Burwardsley. At post office left, hotel signed

This delightful 300-year-old inn sits high on the Peckforton Hills and enjoys spectacular views over the Cheshire Plain. Well-equipped, comfortable bedrooms are housed in an adjacent converted barn. Creative dishes are served either in the stylish restaurant or in the traditional, beamed bar. Real fires are lit in the winter months.

Rooms 2 en suite 10 annexe en suite (2 fmly) (5 GF) ⊘ in all bedrooms S £65-£90; D £80-£130 (incl. bkfst) **Facilities** Fishing Wi-fi in bedrooms **Conf** Thtr 15 Board 10 Del from £105 **Parking** 80 **Notes LB** ⊘ in restaurant

CHESTER
MAP 15 SJ46
See also Puddington

INSPECTORS' CHOICE

★★★★★ ◉◉◉ **HOTEL**

The Chester Grosvenor & Spa
Eastgate CH1 1LT
☎ 01244 324024 📠 01244 313246
e-mail: hotel@chestergrosvenor.com

dir: off M56 for M53, then A56. Follow signs for city centre hotels

Located within the Roman walls of the city, this Grade II listed, half-timbered building is the essence of Englishness. Furnished with fine fabrics and queen or king-size beds, the suites and bedrooms are of the highest standard, each designed with guest comfort as a priority. The art deco La Brasserie (awarded one AA rosette) is bustling, and the fine-dining restaurant, The Arkle (awarded three AA rosettes), offers creative cuisine with flair and style. A luxury spa & small fitness centre are also available.

Rooms 80 en suite (7 fmly) ⊘ in all bedrooms D £190-£600 **Facilities** Spa STV Sauna Solarium Gym Membership of nearby Country Club ♬ **Conf** BC Thtr 250 Class 120 Board 48 Del from £195 **Services** Lift air con **Notes LB** ⊗ ⊘ in restaurant Closed 25-26 Dec RS 27-30 Dec & 1-20 Jan Civ Wed 100

★★★★ 80% ☸ **HOTEL**

Rowton Hall Country House Hotel

Whitchurch Rd, Rowton CH3 6AD
☎ 01244 335262 📠 01244 335464
e-mail: rowtonhall@rowtonhall.co.uk
web: www.rowtonhallhotel.co.uk
dir: *2m SE of Chester at Rowton off A41 towards Whitchurch*

This delightful Georgian manor house set in mature grounds retains many original features such as a superb carved staircase and several eye-catching fireplaces. Bedrooms vary in style and all have been stylishly fitted and have impressive en suites. Public areas include a smart leisure centre, extensive function facilities and a striking restaurant that serves imaginative dishes.

Rooms 38 en suite (4 fmly) (8 GF) S £135-£500; D fr £135 **Facilities Spa** STV 🏊 ♨ Sauna Solarium Gym 🛁 Jacuzzi Wi-fi in bedrooms ch fac Xmas **Conf** Thtr 170 Class 48 Board 50 Del from £165 **Parking** 90 **Notes LB** ⊗ ⊘ in restaurant Civ Wed 120

★★★★ 77% **HOTEL**

Crowne Plaza Chester

Trinity St CH1 2BD
☎ 0870 442 1081 📠 01244 316118
e-mail: cpchester@qmh-hotels.com
dir: *M53 junct 12 to A56 onto St Martins Way, under foot bridge, left at lights then 1st right, hotel on right.*

Conveniently located in the heart of the city, this modern hotel has undergone a complete refurbishment. Spacious public areas include the Silks restaurant, a leisure club and a range of meeting rooms. Smart air-conditioned bedrooms are comfortably appointed and particularly well equipped. The hotel's own car park is a further plus for guests.

Rooms 160 en suite (4 fmly) ⊘ in 142 bedrooms S £149-£228; D £159-£238 (incl. bkfst) **Facilities Spa** STV 🏊 supervised Sauna Solarium Gym **Conf** BC Thtr 600 Class 250 Board 100 Del from £117 **Services** Lift **Parking** 80 **Notes LB** ⊗ ⊘ in restaurant Civ Wed 150

★★★★ 73% **HOTEL**

Best Western The Queen Hotel

City Rd CH1 3AH
☎ 01244 305000 📠 01244 318483
e-mail: queenhotel@feathers.uk.com
web: www.feathers.uk.com
dir: *follow signs for railway station, hotel opposite*

This hotel is ideally located opposite the railway station and just a couple minutes' walk from the city. Public areas include a restaurant, small gym, waiting room bar, separate lounge and Roman-themed gardens. Bedrooms are generally spacious and reflect the hotel's Victorian heritage.

Rooms 129 en suite (6 fmly) (10 GF) ⊘ in 59 bedrooms S fr £95; D fr £129 (incl. bkfst) **Facilities** STV Gym Wi-fi available Xmas **Conf** BC Thtr 400 Class 150 Board 60 Del from £145 **Services** Lift **Parking** 100 **Notes LB** ⊗ ⊘ in restaurant Civ Wed 250

★★★★ 73% ☸ **HOTEL**

Mollington Hotel & Spa

Parkgate Rd CH1 6NN
☎ 01244 851471 📠 01244 851165
e-mail: info@mollingtonhotel.co.uk
dir: *M56 junct 16 then left follow signs for North Wales. At next rdbt turn left to Chester on A540. Hotel 2m on right*

Set in its own attractive grounds, this hotel remains popular with both the business and the leisure markets. The bedrooms, which come in various styles, are well equipped and comfortable. Stylish, open plan public areas include a comfortable bar and lounge, the Garden Room restaurant and a comprehensive leisure club.

Rooms 63 en suite (7 fmly) (16 GF) ⊘ in 40 bedrooms S £105-£110; D £131-£151 (incl. bkfst) **Facilities Spa** STV 🏊 Squash Sauna Solarium Gym Jacuzzi Wi-fi available Hairdressing Health & beauty salon 🎵 Xmas **Conf** BC Thtr 200 Class 60 Board 50 Del from £125 **Services** Lift **Parking** 200 **Notes LB** ⊘ in restaurant Civ Wed 150

★★★★ 73% **HOTEL**

Ramada Chester

Whitchurch Rd, Christleton CH3 5QL
☎ 01244 332121 📠 01244 335287
e-mail: sales.chester@ramadajarvis.co.uk
web: www.ramadajarvis.co.uk
dir: *Take A41 towards Newport, through Whitchurch, hotel is on left, 1.5m from city*

This smart, modern hotel is located just a short drive from the city centre; with extensive meeting and function facilities, a well-equipped leisure club and ample parking, it is a popular conference venue. Bedrooms vary in size and style but all are well equipped for both business and leisure guests. Food is served in both the airy restaurant and in the large open-plan bar lounge.

Rooms 126 en suite (6 fmly) (58 GF) ⊘ in 95 bedrooms S £59-£160; D £59-£160 **Facilities** STV 🏊 Sauna Gym Jacuzzi Wi-fi in bedrooms Xmas **Conf** Class 230 Board 140 Del from £100 **Services** Lift **Parking** 160 **Notes LB** ⊗ ⊘ in restaurant Civ Wed 180

England

CHESTER *continued*

★★★ 80% **HOTEL**

Best Western Westminster

City Rd CH1 3AF
☎ 01244 317341 🖹 01244 325369
e-mail: westminsterhotel@feathers.uk.com
web: www.feathers.uk.com

dir: A56, 3m to city centre, left signed rail station. Hotel opposite station, on right

Situated close to the railway station and city centre, the Westminster is an old, established hotel. It has an attractive Tudor-style exterior, while bedrooms are brightly decorated with a modern theme. No smoking bedrooms and family rooms are both available. There is a choice of bars and lounges, and the dining room serves a good range of dishes.

Rooms 75 en suite (5 fmly) (6 GF) ⊘ in 35 bedrooms S £49.95-£89.95; D £69.95-£129.95 (incl. bkfst) **Facilities** STV Wi-fi in bedrooms Free gym facilities at sister hotel Xmas **Conf** Thtr 150 Class 60 Board 40 Del from £99.95 **Services** Lift **Notes LB** ⊗ ⊘ in restaurant Civ Wed 100

★★★ 80% **HOTEL**

Grosvenor Pulford

Wrexham Rd, Pulford CH4 9DG
☎ 01244 570560 🖹 01244 570809
e-mail: reservations@grosvenorpulfordhotel.co.uk
web: www.grosvenorpulfordhotel.co.uk

dir: M53/A55 at junct signed A483 Chester/Wrexham & North Wales. Left onto B5445, hotel 2m on right

Set in rural surroundings, this modern, stylish hotel features a magnificent leisure club with a large Roman-style swimming pool. Among the bedrooms are several executive suites, and others that have spiral staircases leading to the bedroom sections. A smart brasserie restaurant and bar provide a wide range of imaginative dishes in a relaxed atmosphere.

Rooms 73 en suite (6 fmly) (21 GF) ⊘ in 43 bedrooms S £90-£105; D £120-£135 (incl. bkfst) **Facilities Spa** STV 🎾 ⛲ Snooker Sauna Solarium Gym Jacuzzi Wi-fi available Hairdressing & Beauty salon, coffee bar Xmas **Conf** Thtr 200 Class 100 Board 50 Del from £110 **Parking** 200 **Notes LB** ⊘ in restaurant Civ Wed 120

See advert on opposite page

★★★ 79% **HOTEL**

Mill

Milton St CH1 3NF
☎ 01244 350035 🖹 01244 345635
e-mail: reservations@millhotel.com
web: www.millhotel.com

dir: M53 junct 12, onto A56, left at 2nd rdt (A5268), then 1st left and 2nd left

This hotel is a stylish conversion of an old corn mill and enjoys an idyllic canalside location next to the inner ring road and close to the city centre. The bedrooms offer varying styles, and public rooms are spacious and comfortable. There are several dining options and dinner is often served on a large boat that cruises Chester's canal system between courses. A well-equipped leisure centre is also provided.

Rooms 80 en suite 49 annexe en suite (57 fmly) ⊘ in 51 bedrooms **Facilities Spa** STV 🖂 supervised Sauna Solarium Gym Jacuzzi Steam room, hairdressing, nails, beauty treatments, fitness classes 🎵 **Conf** Thtr 40 Class 27 Board 28 **Services** Lift **Parking** 120 **Notes** ⊗

★★★ 71% **HOTEL**

Hoole Hall Hotel

Warrington Rd, Hoole Village CH2 3PD
☎ 0870 609 6126 01244 408800 🖹 01244 320251
e-mail: hoolehall@corushotels.com
web: www.corushotels.com

dir: M53 junct 12, A56 for 0.5m towards city centre, hotel 500yds on left

Situated in extensive gardens on the outskirts of the city, part of this hotel dates back to the 18th century. The newly refurbished reception lounge now offers BT Openzone. Meetings, banquets and conferences are well catered for and ample parking space is available.

Rooms 97 en suite (4 fmly) (33 GF) ⊘ in 78 bedrooms S £85-£110; D £85-£110 **Facilities** STV Xmas **Conf** Thtr 160 Class 40 Board 50 Del from £99 **Services** Lift **Parking** 200 **Notes LB** ⊘ in restaurant Civ Wed 140

★★★ 71% HOTEL

Macdonald Blossoms

St John St CH1 1HL

☎ 0870 400 8108 🖹 01244 346433

e-mail: general.blossoms@macdonald hotels.co.uk

web: www.macdonald-hotels.co.uk

dir: in city centre, follow signs for Eastgate and City Centre Hotels, continue through pedestrianised zone, hotel on the left

For those seeking to explore this charming, medieval walled city, the central location of this elegant hotel is ideal. The public areas retain much of their Victorian charm. Occasionally, piano music at dinner adds to the intimate atmosphere.

Rooms 64 en suite (3 fmly) ⊛ in all bedrooms **Facilities** Free use of local health club **Conf** Thtr 80 Class 60 Board 60 **Services** Lift **Notes** ⊛ in restaurant

★★ 82% HOTEL

The Gateway To Wales

Welsh Rd, Sealand, Deeside CH5 2HX

☎ 01244 830332 🖹 01244 836190

e-mail: enquires@gatewaytowaleshotel.co.uk

web: www.gatewaytowaleshotel.co.uk

dir: 5m NW of Chester at junct of A548 & A550

This modern hotel enjoys an ideal location offering easy access to Chester, the Wirral and North Wales. Bedrooms are stylish and comfortably appointed, as is the Louis XVI lounge bar. Meals are served in either the bar or elegant restaurant and a well equipped leisure club is also available.

Rooms 40 en suite (18 GF) ⊛ in 20 bedrooms S £65-£75; D £75-£85 (incl. bkfst) **Facilities** STV 🔄 Sauna Solarium Gym Jacuzzi Wi fi in bedrooms Use of nearby Indoor Snooker Club **Conf** Thtr 100 Class 50 Board 50 Del from £85 **Services** Lift **Parking** 60 **Notes LB** ⊗ ⊛ in restaurant

★★ 76% HOTEL

Curzon

52/54 Hough Green CH4 8JQ

☎ 01244 678581 🖹 01244 680866

e-mail: curzon.chester@virgin.net

web: www.curzonhotel.co.uk

dir: at junct of A55/A483 follow sign for Chester, 3rd rdbt, 2nd exit (A5104). Hotel 500yds on right

This smart period property is located in a residential suburb, close to the racecourse and just a short walk from the city centre. Spacious bedrooms are comfortable, well equipped and include family and four-poster rooms. The atmosphere is friendly, and the dinner menu offers a creative choice of freshly prepared dishes.

continued on page 90

THE GROSVENOR PULFORD HOTEL

Wrexham Road, Pulford, Chester CH4 9DG
Tel: 01244 570560   Fax: 01244 570809
Email: enquiries@grosvenorpulfordhotel.co.uk
www.grosvenorpulfordhotel.co.uk

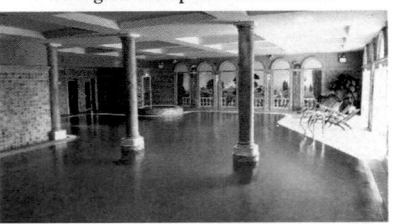

18 metre Swimming Pool – Whirlpool – Aromatherapy Steam Room – Sauna – Solarium – Fully equipped Gymnasium – Hair and Beauty Salon – Snooker Room – Tennis Court. 73 en-suite bedrooms with all the modern conveniences. Award winning restaurant Ciro's Brasserie open daily serving Mediterranean style cuisine. All day coffee bar overlooking courtyard. Bar snacks and Sunday Carvery luncheon. Conference and Banqueting facilities for between 10 and 250 delegates – Wedding receptions our speciality. Leisure break packages available Golf course adjacent to hotel
Ideally located only five minutes from Chester city centre

The Beaufort Park Hotel and Conference Centre

Mold, Flintshire CH7 6RQ Wales

Tel: 01352 758646 Fax: 01352 757132

accommodation@beaufortparkhotel.co.uk

Located near the town of Mold in the delightful North Wales Borderlands, ideally located for both the business and leisure traveller, the Beaufort Park is convenient for both Chester North Wales and Snowdonia, with excellent access to Liverpool, Manchester, the Irish ferries and the motorway network.
Why not enjoy freshly prepared meals and snacks in our informal Arches Mediterranean Bar. Its exciting decor adds to the warm & friendly ambience. Friday there is an International Buffet serving food from around the world and entertainment every Saturday.

CHESTER continued

Curzon

Rooms 16 en suite (7 fmly) (1 GF) ⊘ in all bedrooms S £65-£75; D £85-£110 (incl. bkfst) **Parking** 20 **Notes LB** ⊗ ⊘ in restaurant Closed 20 Dec-6 Jan

See advert on opposite page

★★ 74% HOTEL

Dene
95 Hoole Rd CH2 3ND
☎ 01244 321165 📠 01244 350277
e-mail: info@denehotel.com
web: www.denehotel.com

dir: *M53 junct 12 take A56 towards Chester. Hotel 1m from M53 next to Alexander Park*

This friendly hotel is now part of a small privately owned group and is located close to both the city centre and M53. The bedrooms are very well equipped and many are on ground floor level. Family rooms and interconnecting rooms are also available. In addition to bar meals, an interesting choice of dishes is offered in the welcoming Castra Brasserie, which is also very popular with locals.

Rooms 44 en suite 8 annexe en suite (5 fmly) (20 GF) ⊘ in 16 bedrooms S £45-£95; D £65-£125 (incl. bkfst) **Facilities** FTV Wi-fi in bedrooms **Conf** Thtr 30 Class 12 Board 16 Del from £80 **Parking** 55 **Notes LB** ⊘ in restaurant

See advert on opposite page

★★ 67% HOTEL

Brookside
Brook Ln CH2 2AN
☎ 01244 381943 & 01244 390898 📠 01244 651910
e-mail: info@brookside-hotel.co.uk
web: www.brookside-hotel.co.uk

dir: *from city centre take A5116 towards Birkenhead/Ellesmere Port. Right at mini-rdbt into Brook Lane. Hotel 200yds on left. From M53 take A56 then A41, left into Plas Newton Lane, right into Brook Lane, hotel on right*

This hotel is conveniently located in a residential area just north of the city centre. The attractive public areas consist of a foyer lounge, a small bar and a split-level restaurant. Homely bedrooms are thoughtfully furnished and some feature four-poster beds.

continued

Brookside

Rooms 26 en suite (9 fmly) (4 GF) ⊘ in all bedrooms S £45-£60; D £70-£80 (incl. bkfst) **Conf** Class 20 Board 12 Del from £26.90 **Parking** 20 **Notes LB** ⊗ ⊘ in restaurant Closed 20 Dec-3 Jan

Ⓤ

Oaklands
93 Hoole Rd CH2 3NB
☎ 01244 345528 📠 01244 322156
e-mail: 7878@greeneking.co.uk
web: www.oldenglish.co.uk

OLD ENGLISH INNS

dir: *A56 into Chester, Hoole Rd, hotel 0.5m on left*

At the time of going to press, the star classification for this hotel was not confirmed. Please refer to the AA internet site www.theAA.com for current information.

Rooms 14 rms (12 en suite) (1 fmly) (4 GF) ⊘ in all bedrooms S £25-£40; D £55 **Facilities** ♫ **Conf** Board 18 **Parking** 40 **Notes LB** ⊗

Ⓤ

Swallow Crabwall Manor
Parkgate Rd, Mollington CH1 6NE
☎ 01244 851666 📠 01244 851400
e-mail: swallow.crabwall@londoninns.com
web: www.swallowhotels.com

SWALLOW HOTELS

dir: *Exit M56 signed for Queensferry onto A5117 0.5m. At rdbt turn left onto A540, 2m. Follow road to the right, hotel on right set back from road*

At the time of going to press, the star classification for this hotel was not confirmed. Please refer to the AA internet site www.theAA.com for current information.

Rooms 48 en suite (19 GF) ⊘ in 27 bedrooms S £95-£120; D £120-£170 (incl. bkfst & dinner) **Facilities** Spa 🏊 supervised Snooker Sauna Gym ⛹ Jacuzzi Xmas **Conf** Thtr 100 Class 60 Board 40 Del from £135 **Parking** 120 **Notes LB** ⊗ ⊘ in restaurant Civ Wed

BUDGET HOTEL

Innkeeper's Lodge Chester
Whitchurch Rd CH3 6AE
☎ 01244 332200 📠 01244 336415
web: www.innkeeperslodge.com

Innkeeper's Lodge

dir: *on A41. 1m outside Chester towards Whitchurch*

Smart, en suite accommodation ideal for both business & leisure guests. Bedrooms are very well equipped, including Sky TV, telephone, modem points, tea & coffee making facilities, (family rooms in most locations). Complimentary breakfast. The adjacent Pub

continued

England

Restaurant; a Harvester, Vintage Inn, Toby Carvery, Ember Inn, Sizzling Pubco or Pub & Carvery offers an all day menu. See Hotel Groups pages for further details.

Rooms 5 en suite 9 annexe en suite S £55-£58; D £55-£58

Innkeeper's Lodge Chester Northeast

Warrington Rd, Mickle Trafford CH2 4EX

☎ 01244 301391 📠 01244 302002

dir: M53 junct 12, onto A56 signed Helsby, hotel 0.25m on right

Rooms 36 en suite S £49.95-£55; D £49.95-£55 **Conf** Thtr 20 Class 12 Board 20

BUDGET HOTEL

Premier Travel Inn Chester Central

Caldy Valley Rd CH3 5QJ

☎ 08701 977058 📠 01244 403687

web: www.premiertravelinn.com

dir: Exit M53 junct 12 and at rdbt 3rd exit onto A56 (signed Chester). At rdt take 1st exit onto A41 (signed Whitchurch) then at 2nd rdbt take 3rd exit onto Caldy Valley Rd (signed Huntingdon) for Inn on right.

High quality, modern budget accommodation ideal for both families and business travellers. Spacious, en suite bedrooms feature bath and shower, satellite TV and many have telephones and modem points. The adjacent family restaurant features a wide and varied menu. For further details consult the Hotel Groups page.

Rooms 70 en suite **Conf** Class 20

Premier Travel Inn Chester Central (North)

76 Liverpool Rd CH2 1AU

☎ 0870 9906470 📠 0870 9906471

dir: Exit M53 junct 12. At 1st rdbt right for A56. At 2nd rdbt right signed A41 to Chester Zoo. At 1st lights left into Heath Rd leading into Mill Ln. Under small rail bridge. Inn at end on right

Rooms 31 en suite **Conf** Class 17

CHESTER MOTORWAY SERVICE AREA (M56)

MAP 15 SJ47

BUDGET HOTEL

Premier Travel Inn Chester East

Junction 14 M56, Chester East Service Area, Elton CH2 4QZ

☎ 08701 977059 📠 01928 726721

web: www.premiertravelinn.com

dir: M56 junct 14/A5117 interchange

High quality, modern budget accommodation ideal for both families and business travellers. Spacious, en suite bedrooms feature bath and shower, satellite TV and many have telephones and modem points. The adjacent family restaurant features a wide and varied menu. For further details consult the Hotel Groups page.

Rooms 40 en suite **Conf** Thtr 20

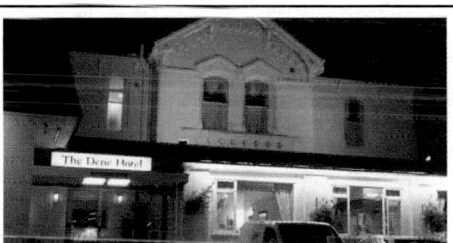

England

CHILDER THORNTON MAP 15 SJ37

BUDGET HOTEL

Premier Travel Inn Wirral Childer Thornton

New Chester Rd CH66 1QW
☎ 08701 977275 📠 0151 347 1401
web: www.premiertravelinn.com

dir: *M53 junct 5, on A41 towards Chester. Inn is on the right, same entrance as Burleydam Garden Centre*

High quality, modern budget accommodation ideal for both families and business travellers. Spacious, en suite bedrooms feature bath and shower, satellite TV and many have telephones and modem points. The adjacent family restaurant features a wide and varied menu. For further details consult the Hotel Groups page.

Rooms 31 en suite **Conf** Thtr 20

CREWE MAP 15 SJ75

★★★★ 80% ⊛ HOTEL

Crewe Hall

Weston Rd CW1 6UZ
☎ 01270 253333 📠 01270 253322
e-mail: crewehall@marstonhotels.com
web: www.marstonhotels.com

dir: *M6 junct 16 follow A500 to Crewe. Last exit at rdbt onto A5020. 1st exit next rdbt to Crewe. Crewe Hall 150yds on right*

Standing in 500 acres of mature grounds, this historic hall dates back to the 17th century. It retains an elaborate interior with Victorian-style architecture. Bedrooms are spacious, well equipped and comfortable with traditionally styled rooms in the main hall and modern suites in the west wing. Guests have a choice of formal dining in the elegant Ranulph restaurant or the more relaxed atmosphere of the modern brasserie.

Rooms 26 en suite 39 annexe en suite (5 fmly) (17 GF) ⊛ in 40 bedrooms S fr £154.50; D fr £194 (incl. bkfst) **Facilities** STV ⬚ Full size football pitch Xmas **Conf** Thtr 260 Class 110 Board 100 Del from £130 **Services** Lift **Parking** 140 **Notes LB** ⊗ ⊛ in restaurant Civ Wed 200

★★★ 78% ⊛ HOTEL

Hunters Lodge

Sydney Rd, Sydney CW1 5LU
☎ 01270 583440 📠 01270 500553
e-mail: info@hunterslodge.co.uk
web: www.hunterslodge.co.uk
dir: *1m from Crewe station, off A534*

Dating back to the 18th century, this family-run hotel has been extended and modernised. Accommodation, mainly located in adjacent well-equipped bedroom wings, includes family and four-poster rooms. Imaginative dishes are served in the spacious restaurant, and the popular bar also offers a choice of tempting meals. Service throughout is friendly and efficient.

Rooms 57 en suite (4 fmly) (31 GF) ⊛ in 31 bedrooms S fr £71.50; D fr £94 (incl. bkfst) **Facilities** STV Gym **Conf** Thtr 160 Class 100 Board 80 Del from £123.70 **Parking** 240 **Notes** ⊗ ⊛ in restaurant RS Sunday Civ Wed 130

★★★ 74% HOTEL

Crewe Arms

Nantwich Rd CW2 6DN
☎ 01270 213204 📠 01270 588615
e-mail: reservations@crewearmshotel.com
web: www.crewearmshotel.com
dir: *From M6 junct 6 towards Crewe. At 1st rdbt take 3rd exit, at 2nd rdbt 1st exit. Hotel at end, opposite rail station*

Close to Crewe station this popular, busy commercial hotel has now been refurbished and offers attractive, well-equipped accommodation. Meals are served in the comfortable Carriages lounge bar and the more formal Sophia's restaurant. There is also a selection of conference and meeting rooms.

Rooms 59 en suite (4 fmly) (1 GF) S £50-£90; D £50-£120 (incl. bkfst) **Facilities** Gym Fitness Room **Conf** Thtr 100 Class 60 Board 60 Del from £80 **Parking** 120 **Notes LB** ⊗ ⊛ in restaurant Civ Wed 60

★★ 63% HOTEL

White Lion

Weston CW2 5NA
☎ 01270 587011 & 500303 📠 01270 500303
e-mail: whitelion.inn@landmarkinns.co.uk
dir: *M6 junct 16, A500 signed Crewe/Nantwich/ Chester. 2nd rdbt right into Weston village. Hotel in centre on left*

Once a Tudor farmhouse, this hotel (now under new ownership) provides comfortable, modern accommodation, yet retains much of its old charm. Dining choices include The White Lion Restaurant and its adjoining cocktail lounge; a selection of bar snacks is available in the oak-beamed lounge bar.

Rooms 16 en suite (2 fmly) (7 GF) **Facilities** Crown Green bowling **Conf** Thtr 50 Class 28 Board 20 **Parking** 100 **Notes LB** ⊛ in restaurant Civ Wed 65

England

Premier Travel Inn Crewe

Coppenhall Ln, Woolstanwood CW2 8SD

☎ 08701 977068 ▤ 01270 256316

web: www.premiertravelinn.com

dir: *at junct of A530 & A532, 9m from M6 junct 16 N'bound*

High quality, modern budget accommodation ideal for both families and business travellers. Spacious, en suite bedrooms feature bath and shower, satellite TV and many have telephones and modem points. The adjacent family restaurant features a wide and varied menu. For further details consult the Hotel Groups page.

Rooms 41 en suite

Travelodge Crewe

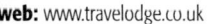

Crewe Green Rd, A534 CW1 2BJ

☎ 0870 0850 950 ▤ 01270 253 518

web: www.travelodge.co.uk

dir: *M6 junct 6 A500 to town centre(A2534)*

Travelodge offers good quality, good value, modern accommodation. Ideal for families, the spacious en suite bedrooms include remote-control TV, tea and coffee-making facilities and comfortable beds. Meals can be taken at the nearby family restaurant. See Hotel Groups pages for further details.

Rooms 56 en suite S fr £26; D fr £26

Travelodge Crewe Barthomley

Alsager Rd, Barthomley CW2 5PT

☎ 08700 850 950 ▤ 01270 883157

dir: *M6 junct 16, A500 between Nantwich & Stoke-on-Trent*

Rooms 42 en suite S fr £26; D fr £26

DISLEY
MAP 16 SJ98

★★★ 75% **HOTEL**

Best Western Moorside Grange Hotel & Spa

Mudhurst Ln, Higher Disley SK12 2AP

☎ 01663 764151 ▤ 01663 762794

dir: *Leave A6 at Rams Head, Disley continue along Buxton Old Rd for 1m, turn right onto Mudhurst Lane, hotel on left*

Spectacular views of the moors above Higher Disley are one of the attractions of this large complex. The extensive grounds include a 9-hole golf course and two tennis courts; there are excellent conference and function facilities and a well equipped leisure centre. Suites, and bedrooms with four-poster beds are available.

Rooms 98 en suite (3 fmly) ❷ in 87 bedrooms S £70-£120; D £70-£120 (incl. bkfst) **Facilities Spa** STV ⚐ supervised ☺ Squash Sauna Solarium Gym Putt green Jacuzzi Wi-fi in bedrooms Xmas **Conf** Thtr 280 Class 140 Board 100 Del from £115 **Services** Lift **Parking** 200 **Notes LB** ❸ ❷ in restaurant Civ Wed 160

ELLESMERE PORT
MAP 15 SJ47

★★★ 73% **HOTEL**

Quality Hotel Chester

Berwick Rd, Little Sutton CH66 4PS

☎ 0151 339 5121 ▤ 0151 339 3214

e-mail: enquiries@quality-hotels-chester.com

web: www.choicehotelseurope.com

dir: *M53 junct 5 left at rdbt. At 2nd lights right onto A550 over hump-back bridge, left into Berwick Rd. Hotel immediately on left*

This modern hotel is conveniently located for access to Chester, the M53 and the many attractions of the area. The well-equipped accommodation includes bedrooms on ground-floor level and no-smoking rooms, and facilities include a leisure complex and versatile banqueting and conference suites. Staff are friendly and keen to please.

Rooms 75 en suite (10 fmly) (23 GF) ❷ in 30 bedrooms **Facilities** STV ⚐ Sauna Gym Wi-fi available Steam room Exercise equipment ♫ Xmas **Conf** Thtr 300 Class 150 Board 50 Del from £99 **Parking** 150 **Notes** ❷ in restaurant Civ Wed 200

★★ 69% **HOTEL**

Woodcote Hotel & Restaurant

3 Hooton Rd CH66 1QU

☎ 0151 327 1542 ▤ 0151 328 1328

e-mail: thewoodcotehotel@lineone.net

web: www.thewoodcotehotel.co.uk

dir: *M53 junct 5, take A41 towards Chester, 1st lights right to Willaston. Hotel 300yds on left*

This popular commercial hotel offers generally spacious bedrooms; some are located in a separate building adjacent to the pretty garden. Public areas include a bar and restaurant serving a range of popular, reasonably priced dishes and a separate breakfast room. Staff are friendly and helpful

Rooms 10 en suite 11 annexe en suite (1 fmly) (6 GF) S £50-£45; D £50-£60 **Facilities** ♫ **Conf** Thtr 90 Class 50 Board 48 **Parking** 35 **Notes** ❸ RS Sun

FRODSHAM
MAP 15 SJ57

★★★ 77% **HOTEL**

Forest Hill Hotel & Leisure Complex

Overton Hill WA6 6HH

☎ 01928 735255 ▤ 01928 735517

e-mail: info@foresthillshotel.com

dir: *at Frodsham turn onto B5151. After 1m right into Manley Rd, right into Simons Ln after 0.5m. Hotel 0.5m past Frodsham golf course*

This modern, purpose-built hotel is set high up on Overton Hill, so offering panoramic views. There is a range of spacious, well-equipped bedrooms, including executive rooms. Guests have a choice of bars and there is a tasteful split-level restaurant, as well as conference facilities and a very well equipped leisure suite and gym.

Rooms 58 en suite (4 fmly) ❷ in 39 bedrooms S £55-£120; D £70-£160 **Facilities** STV ⚐ Snooker Sauna Solarium Gym Jacuzzi Wi-fi in bedrooms Nightclub, Dance studio, Aerobics/pilates ♫ Xmas **Conf** Thtr 200 Class 80 Board 70 Del from £90 **Parking** 350 **Notes LB** ❷ in restaurant Civ Wed 200

GLAZEBROOK
MAP 15 SJ69

★★★ 75% **HOTEL**

Rhinewood Country House
Glazebrook Ln, Glazebrook WA3 5BB
☎ 0161 775 5555 ▤ 0161 775 7965
e-mail: info@therhinewoodhotel.co.uk
web: www.therhinewoodhotel.co.uk
dir: M6 Junct 21, follow A57 towards Irlam. Turn left at Glazebrook sign, hotel 0.25m on left

A warm welcome and attentive service are assured at this privately owned and personally run hotel. It stands in spacious grounds and gardens and is located between Warrington and Manchester. Facilities here include conference and function rooms and the hotel is also licensed for civil wedding ceremonies.

Rooms 32 en suite (4 fmly) (16 GF) ⊗ in 8 bedrooms S £50-£85; D £75-£115 (incl. bkfst) **Facilities** STV Complimentary membership to nearby health spa Xmas **Conf** Thtr 120 Class 60 Board 50 Del from £100 **Parking** 120 **Notes LB** ⊗ in restaurant Civ Wed 120

HANDFORTH
See **Manchester Airport (Greater Manchester)**

HOLMES CHAPEL
MAP 15 SJ76

★★★ 71% **HOTEL**

Ye Olde Vicarage
Knutsford Rd CW4 8EF
☎ 01477 532041 ▤ 01477 535728
e-mail: yeoldevicarage@harlequinhotels.co.uk
web: www.cheshire-hotels.com
dir: on A50, 1m from M6 junct 18

Now refurbished, this attractive hotel is located just to the north of the village and is situated in picturesque countryside. Bedrooms are very well equipped and are furnished in several styles. Public rooms are comfortable, and the attractive restaurant offers a good choice of dishes.

Rooms 31 en suite (3 fmly) (12 GF) ⊗ in 29 bedrooms S £55-£80; D £65-£100 (incl. bkfst) **Facilities** STV Wi-fi in bedrooms Xmas **Conf** Thtr 36 Class 10 Board 30 Del £140 **Parking** 52 **Notes LB** ⊗ ⊗ in restaurant Civ Wed 80

HYDE
MAP 16 SJ99

BUDGET HOTEL

Premier Travel Inn Manchester (Mottram)
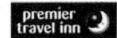
Stockport Rd, Mottram SK14 3AU
☎ 0870 9906334 ▤ 0870 9906335
web: www.premiertravelinn.com
dir: At end of M67 between A57 & A560

High quality, modern budget accommodation ideal for both families and business travellers. Spacious, en suite bedrooms feature bath and shower, satellite TV and many have telephones and modem points. The adjacent family restaurant features a wide and varied menu. For further details consult the Hotel Groups page.

Rooms 83 en suite

KNUTSFORD
MAP 15 SJ77

★★★★ 78% **HOTEL**

Cottons Hotel & Spa
SHIRE HOTELS
Manchester Rd WA16 0SU
☎ 01565 650333 ▤ 01565 755351
e-mail: cottons@shirehotels.com
web: www.shirehotels.com
dir: on A50 1m from M6 junct 19

The superb leisure facilities and quiet location are great attractions at this hotel, which is just a short distance from Manchester Airport. Bedrooms are smartly appointed in various styles and executive rooms have very good working areas. The hotel has spacious lounge areas and an improved leisure centre.

Rooms 109 en suite (14 fmly) (38 GF) ⊗ in 80 bedrooms S £93-£155; D £136-£175 (incl. bkfst) **Facilities** Spa STV 🎱 ᧕ Sauna Solarium Gym Jacuzzi Wi-fi in bedrooms Spa treatment, Steam room, Activity studio for Exercise classes Xmas **Conf** BC Thtr 200 Class 100 Board 36 Del £175 **Services** Lift **Parking** 180 **Notes LB** ⊗ ⊗ in restaurant Civ Wed 120

★★★★ 78% **HOTEL**

Mere Court Hotel & Conference Centre
Warrington Rd, Mere WA16 0RW
☎ 01565 831000 ▤ 01565 831001
e-mail: sales@merecourt.co.uk
web: www.merecourt.co.uk
dir: A50, 1m W of junct with A556, on right

This is a smart and attractive hotel, set in extensive, well-tended gardens. The elegant and spacious bedrooms are all individually styled

continued

nd offer a host of thoughtful extras. Conference facilities are articularly impressive and there is a large, self contained, onservatory function suite. Dining is available in the fine dining rboreum Restaurant.

ooms 34 en suite (24 fmly) (12 GF) ⊘ in 5 bedrooms S £120-£155; £135-£175 **Facilities** STV Wi-fi in bedrooms **Conf** Thtr 100 Class 60 ard 35 Del from £139 **Services** Lift **Parking** 150 **Notes** ⊗ ⊘ in staurant Civ Wed 120

See advert on this page

★★★ 73% HOTEL

ottage Restaurant & Lodge

ondon Rd, Allostock WA16 9LU
☎ 01565 722470 ▤ 01565 722749
-**mail:** reception@thecottageknutsford.co.uk
eb: www.thecottageknutsford.co.uk
ir: M6 junct 18/19 onto A50. Hotel between Holmes Chapel & nutsford

his well presented family run hotel enjoys a peaceful location. Smart, acious lodge-style bedrooms complement an attractive open-plan staurant and bar lounge. Bedrooms are thoughtfully equipped and fer good levels of comfort. Conference and meeting facilities as well ample parking are available.

ooms 12 en suite (6 GF) ⊘ in 8 bedrooms S £45-£69; D £60-£85 (incl kfst) **Facilities** STV **Conf** Thtr 40 Class 20 Board 24 Del from £65 **arking** 40 **Notes** ⊗ ⊘ in restaurant Closed New Years Day

★★ 76% HOTEL

he Longview Hotel & Restaurant

5 Manchester Rd WA16 0LX
☎ 01565 632119 ▤ 01565 652402
-**mail:** enquiries@longviewhotel.com
eb: www.longviewhotel.com
ir: M6 junct 19 take A556 W towards Chester. Left at lights onto 5033, 1.5m to rdbt then left. Hotel 200yds on right

his Victorian hotel offers high standards of hospitality and service. tractive public areas include a cellar bar and foyer lounge area. edrooms, some in a superb renovation of nearby houses, are dividually styled and offer a good range of thoughtful amenities, cluding broadband internet access. The restaurant offers imaginative shes.

ooms 13 en suite 19 annexe en suite (1 fmly) (5 GF) S £60-£129; £82-£149 (incl. bkfst) **Facilities** Wi-fi in bedrooms **Parking** 20 **otes** LB ⊘ in restaurant

BUDGET HOTEL

remier Travel Inn nutsford North

premier travel inn

ucklow Hill WA16 6RD
☎ 0870 9906428 ▤ 0870 9906429
eb: www.premiertravelinn.com
ir: Exit M6 junct 19 onto A556 towards Manchester irport/Stockport

igh quality, modern budget accommodation ideal for both families nd business travellers. Spacious, en suite bedrooms feature bath and hower, satellite TV and many have telephones and modem points. he adjacent family restaurant features a wide and varied menu. For rther details consult the Hotel Groups page.

ooms 66 en suite **Conf** Thtr 60 Board 30

Premier Travel Inn Knutsford North West

Warrington Rd, Hoo Green, Mere WA16 0PZ
☎ 0870 9906482 ▤ 0870 9906483
dir: Exit M6 junct 19, follow A556 to Manchester signs. At 1st lights left onto A50 towards Warrington. Hotel 1m on right
Rooms 28 en suite

BUDGET HOTEL

Travelodge Knutsford Tabley

Travelodge

Chester Rd, Tabley WA16 0PP
☎ 08700 850 950 ▤ 01565 652187
web: www.travelodge.co.uk
dir: on A556, N'bound just E M6 junct 19

Travelodge offers good quality, good value, modern accommodation. Ideal for families, the spacious en suite bedrooms include remote-control TV, tea and coffee-making facilities and comfortable beds. Meals can be taken at the nearby family restaurant. See Hotel Groups pages for further details.

Rooms 32 en suite S fr £26; D fr £26

England

KNUTSFORD MOTORWAY SERVICE AREA (M6) — MAP 15 SJ77

BUDGET HOTEL

Travelodge Knutsford (M6)

Granada Services, M6 junct 18/19 WA16 0TL

☎ 08700 850 950

web: www.travelodge.co.uk

dir: between junct 18 & 19 of M6 northbound

Travelodge offers good quality, good value, modern accommodation. Ideal for families, the spacious en suite bedrooms include remote-control TV, tea and coffee-making facilities and comfortable beds. Meals can be taken at the nearby family restaurant. See Hotel Groups pages for further details.

Rooms 54 en suite S fr £26; D fr £26

LYMM — MAP 15 SJ68

★★★ 72% **HOTEL**

The Lymm Hotel

MACDONALD HOTELS & RESORTS

Whitbarrow Rd WA13 9AQ

☎ 0870 1942121 🖹 01925 756035

e-mail: general.lymm@macdonald-hotels.co.uk

web: www.macdonald-hotels.co.uk

dir: take M6 to B5158 to Lymm. Left at junct, first right, left at mini rdbt, into Brookfield Rd and 3rd left into Whitbarrow Rd

Situated in a peaceful residential area, this hotel benefits from both the quiet setting and convenient access to local motorway networks. The hotel offers comfortable bedrooms equipped for both the business and leisure guest. Public areas include an attractive bar and an elegant restaurant. There is extensive parking.

Rooms 14 en suite 48 annexe en suite (5 fmly) (4 GF) ⊛ in 56 bedrooms S £69-£85; D £75-£105 (incl. bkfst) **Facilities** STV Xmas **Conf** BC Thtr 220 Class 140 Board 100 Del from £138 **Parking** 120 **Notes LB** ⊛ in restaurant Civ Wed 120

BUDGET HOTEL

Travelodge Warrington Lymm Services

Granada Services A50, Cliffe Ln WA13 0SP

☎ 08700 850 950 🖹 01925 759341

web: www.travelodge.co.uk

dir: A50, intersection of M6 junct 20 & M56 junct 9

Travelodge offers good quality, good value, modern accommodation. Ideal for families, the spacious en suite bedrooms include remote-control TV, tea and coffee-making facilities and comfortable beds.

continued

Meals can be taken at the nearby family restaurant. See Hotel Groups pages for further details.

Rooms 61 en suite S fr £26; D fr £26

MACCLESFIELD — MAP 16 SJ97

★★★★ 74% **HOTEL**

Paramount Shrigley Hall

PARAMOUNT
GROUP OF HOTELS

Shrigley Park, Pott Shrigley SK10 5SB

☎ 01625 575757 🖹 01625 573323

e-mail: shrigleyhall@paramount-hotels.co.uk

web: www.paramount-hotels.co.uk

dir: off A523 at Legh Arms towards Pott Shrigley. Hotel 2m on left before village

Originally built in 1825, Shrigley Hall is an impressive hotel set in 262 acres of mature parkland and provides stunning views of the countryside. Features include a championship golf course. There is a wide choice of bedroom size and style. The public areas are spacious, combining traditional and contemporary decor, and include a well-equipped gym.

Rooms 150 en suite (8 fmly) ⊛ in 28 bedrooms S fr £69; D fr £118 (incl. bkfst) **Facilities** STV ⊠ supervised ⚐ 18 ⚐ Fishing Sauna Solarium Gym Putt green Jacuzzi Wi-fi in bedrooms Beauty salon Hydro centre ♫ Xmas **Conf** BC Thtr 280 Class 140 Board 50 Del £185 **Services** Lift **Parking** 300 **Notes LB** ⊛ in restaurant Civ Wed 150

★★★ 75% **HOTEL**

Best Western Hollin Hall

Best Western

Jackson Ln, Kerridge, Bollington SK10 5BG

☎ 01625 573246 🖹 01625 574791

e-mail: sales@hollinhallhotel.com

dir: off A523, 2m along B5090

Set in the peaceful Cheshire countryside, this hotel is convenient for Manchester Airport (courtesy transport available). The main building has an impressive carved staircase, high ceilings and a bar lounge. Modern cooking is provided in the Orangey conservatory, and both a gym and sauna are available. Attractively furnished accommodation is situated in a modern extension.

Rooms 54 en suite (2 fmly) ⊛ in 36 bedrooms **Facilities** STV Sauna Gym Free use neighbouring Leisure Club & Golf Course **Conf** Thtr 120 Class 50 Board 50 **Parking** 200 **Notes** ⊗ ⊛ in restaurant Civ Wed 100

BUDGET HOTEL

Premier Travel Inn Macclesfield North

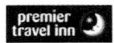
premier travel inn

Tytherington Business Park, Springwood Way, Tytherington SK10 2XA

☎ 08701 977167 📠 01625 422874

web: www.premiertravelinn.com

dir: on A523 Tytherington Business Park

High quality, modern budget accommodation ideal for both families and business travellers. Spacious, en suite bedrooms feature bath and shower, satellite TV and many have telephones and modem points. The adjacent family restaurant features a wide and varied menu. For further details consult the Hotel Groups page.

Rooms 40 en suite **Conf** Thtr 20

Premier Travel Inn Macclesfield South West

Congleton Rd, Gawsworth SK11 7XD

☎ 0870 9906412 📠 0870 9906413

dir: 2m from Macclesfield. Exit M6 junct 17. Follow A534 to Congleton, then A536 towards Macclesfield to Gawsworth. Hotel on left

Rooms 28 en suite **Conf** Thtr 10 Board 10

BUDGET HOTEL

Travelodge Macclesfield Adlington

Travelodge

London Rd South SK10 4NG

☎ 08700 850 950 📠 01625 875292

web: www.travelodge.co.uk

dir: on A523

Travelodge offers good quality, good value, modern accommodation. Ideal for families, the spacious en suite bedrooms include remote-control TV, tea and coffee-making facilities and comfortable beds. Meals can be taken at the nearby family restaurant. See Hotel Groups pages for further details.

Rooms 32 en suite S fr £26; D fr £26

MIDDLEWICH   MAP 15 SJ76

BUDGET HOTEL

Travelodge Middlewich

Travelodge

CW10 0JB

☎ 08700 850 950 📠 01606 738229

web: www.travelodge.co.uk

dir: A54 westbound off M6 junct 18

Travelodge offers good quality, good value, modern accommodation. Ideal for families, the spacious en suite bedrooms include remote-control TV, tea and coffee-making facilities and comfortable beds. Meals can be taken at the nearby family restaurant. See Hotel Groups pages for further details.

Rooms 32 en suite S fr £26; D fr £26

NANTWICH   MAP 15 SJ65

★★★★ 84% ◉◉ **HOTEL**

Rookery Hall

Hand PICKED HOTELS

Main Rd, Worleston CW5 6DQ

☎ 01270 610016 📠 01270 626027

e-mail: rookeryhall-cro@handpicked.co.uk

web: www.handpicked.co.uk

dir: B5074 off 4th rdbt, on Nantwich by-pass. Hotel 1.5m on right

This fine 19th-century mansion is set in 38 acres of gardens, pasture and parkland. Bedrooms, are spacious and appointed to a high standard. The public areas are particularly stylish and include a salon with enormous sofas and a mahogany-panelled dining room. Many of the bedrooms provide a dazzling array of extras such as wide-screen plasma TVs and DVD players.

Rooms 30 en suite 16 annexe en suite (6 GF) S fr £150; D fr £180 **Facilities** STV Fishing ⌁ Wi-fi available Xmas **Conf** Thtr 90 Class 40 Board 40 Del from £180 **Services** Lift **Parking** 100 **Notes LB** ⊗ in restaurant Civ Wed 66

★★ 71% **HOTEL**

Best Western Crown

Best Western

High St CW5 5AS

☎ 01270 625283 📠 01270 628047

e-mail: info@crownhotelnantwich.com

web: www.crownhotelnantwich.com

dir: A52 to Nantwich, hotel in centre of town

Ideally set in the heart of this historic and delightful market town, The Crown has been offering hospitality for centuries. It has an abundance of original features and the well-equipped bedrooms retain an old world charm. There is also a bar with live entertainment throughout the week and diners can enjoy Italian food in the atmospheric brasserie.

Rooms 18 en suite (2 fmly) ⊗ in 2 bedrooms S fr £72; D fr £82 **Facilities** Putt green Wi-fi in bedrooms ♫ **Conf** Thtr 200 Class 150 Board 70 **Parking** 18 **Notes LB** Civ Wed 140

BUDGET HOTEL

Premier Travel Inn Nantwich

premier travel inn

221 Crewe Rd CW5 6NE

☎ 0870 9906418 📠 0870 9906419

web: www.premiertravelinn.com

dir: Exit M6 junct 16, A500 signed Nantwich & Chester. At 1st rdbt take 2nd exit, approx 4m. At 3rd rdbt, take 3rd exit signed A500 to Chester, at 4th left onto A534 towards Nantwich. Inn approx 100yds on right

High quality, modern budget accommodation ideal for both families and business travellers. Spacious, en suite bedrooms feature bath and shower, satellite TV and many have telephones and modem points. The adjacent family restaurant features a wide and varied menu. For further details consult the Hotel Groups page.

Rooms 37 en suite

England

NORTHWICH
MAP 15 SJ67

★★★ 64% **HOTEL**

The Floatel, Northwich
London Rd CW9 5HD
☎ 01606 44443 📠 01606 42596
e-mail: enquiries@hotels-northwich.com
web: www.hotels-northwich.com
dir: M6 junct 19, follow A556 for 4m, take right turn & follow signs for town centre

A first in the UK, this floating hotel has been built on the River Weaver in the town centre and is proving a very successful concept. The bedrooms are modern and well equipped, and there is a pleasant restaurant that overlooks the river.

Rooms 60 en suite (2 fmly) ⊘ in 30 bedrooms S £35-£81; D £40-£91 **Facilities** STV Wi-fi available Xmas **Conf** Thtr 80 Class 40 Board 30 Del from £50 **Services** Lift **Parking** 110 **Notes LB** ⊘ in restaurant Civ Wed 80

BUDGET HOTEL

Premier Travel Inn Northwich

520 Chester Rd, Sandiway CW8 2DN
☎ 0870 9906494 📠 0870 9906495
web: www.premiertravelinn.com
dir: 11m from M6 junct 19, on A556 towards Chester

High quality, modern budget accommodation ideal for both families and business travellers. Spacious, en suite bedrooms feature bath and shower, satellite TV and many have telephones and modem points. The adjacent family restaurant features a wide and varied menu. For further details consult the Hotel Groups page.

Rooms 52 en suite **Conf** Thtr 65

Premier Travel Inn Northwich South
London Rd, Leftwich CW9 8EG
☎ 0870 9906362 📠 0870 9906363
dir: Just off M6 junct 19 follow A556 to Chester. Right at sign for Northwich & Davenham
Rooms 32 en suite **Conf** Thtr 15 Class 15 Board 15

PRESTBURY
MAP 16 SJ87

★★★ 75% **HOTEL**

Bridge
The Village SK10 4DQ
☎ 01625 829326 📠 01625 827557
e-mail: reception@bridge-hotel.co.uk
web: www.bridge-hotel.co.uk
dir: off A538 through village. Hotel next to church

Dating in parts from the 17th century, this delightful, stylish hotel stands between the River Bollin and the ancient church. The cocktail bar is the ideal place to relax before enjoying a meal in the Bridge Restaurant. A wide range of bedroom styles is available in both the original building and the modern extension.

continued

Bridge

Rooms 23 en suite (1 fmly) ⊘ in all bedrooms S fr £50; D fr £88 **Facilities** FTV Wi-fi in bedrooms ♫ **Conf** Thtr 100 Class 56 Board 48 Del from £125 **Parking** 52 **Notes LB** ⊗ ⊘ in restaurant Civ Wed 100

PUDDINGTON
MAP 15 SJ37

★★★★ 76% ⊛ **HOTEL**

Macdonald Craxton Wood
[MACDONALD HOTELS & RESORTS]
Parkgate Rd, Ledsham CH66 9PB
☎ 0870 1942118 📠 0151 347 4040
e-mail: craxton@macdonald-hotels.co.uk
web: www.macdonald-hotels.co.uk
dir: from M6 take M56 towards N Wales, then A5117 then A540 to Hoylake. Hotel 200yds past lights

Set in extensive grounds, this hotel offers a variety of bedroom styles; the modern rooms are particularly comfortable. The nicely furnished restaurant overlooks the grounds and offers a wide choice of dishes, whilst full leisure facilities and a choice of function suites completes the package.

Rooms 72 en suite (8 fmly) (30 GF) ⊘ in all bedrooms **Facilities** STV 🖳 Sauna Solarium Gym Beauty spa **Conf** Thtr 400 Class 200 Board 160 **Services** Lift **Parking** 220 **Notes LB** ⊘ in restaurant Civ Wed 350

BUDGET HOTEL

Premier Travel Inn Wirral (Two Mills)
[premier travel inn]
Parkgate Rd, Two Mills CH66 9PD
☎ 0870 9906564 📠 0870 9906565
web: www.premiertravelinn.com
dir: 5m from M56 junct 16 & M53 junct 5. On x-rds of A550 & A540

High quality, modern budget accommodation ideal for both families and business travellers. Spacious, en suite bedrooms feature bath and shower, satellite TV and many have telephones and modem points. The adjacent family restaurant features a wide and varied menu. For further details consult the Hotel Groups page.

Rooms 31 en suite

RUNCORN
MAP 15 SJ58

★★★ 75% **HOTEL**

Lawson House Hotel & Conference Centre

Moughland Centre WA7 4SQ

☎ 01928 593300 ▤ 01928 593355

e-mail: reception@lawsonhouse.co.uk

dir: M56 junct 12/A557 Widnes. Exit at Rocksavage Weston Village sign, right at Heath mini rdbt. After church right into Cavendish Farm Rd, left at lights, hotel 200yds on left

This hotel, conveniently located for the motorway network, road and air links, offers comfortable well-equipped accommodation. Rooms are split between the original house and a modern extension. Extensive conference and function rooms are available which are ideal for weddings or corporate entertaining. The Harewood dining room offers interesting cuisine.

Rooms 30 en suite **Facilities** Gym **Conf** Thtr 150 Class 80 Board 50 **Parking** 70 **Notes** ⊘ in restaurant Civ Wed 80

BUDGET HOTEL

Campanile

Lowlands Rd WA7 5TP

☎ 01928 581771 ▤ 01928 581730

e-mail: runcorn@envergure.co.uk

web: www.envergure.fr

dir: M56 junct 12, take A557, then follow signs for Runcorn rail station/Runcorn College

This modern building offers accommodation in smart, well-equipped bedrooms, all with en suite bathrooms. Refreshments may be taken at the informal Bistro. For further details consult the Hotel Groups page.

Rooms 53 en suite **Conf** Thtr 35 Class 24 Board 24

BUDGET HOTEL

Premier Travel Inn Runcorn

Chester Rd, Preston Brook WA7 3BB

☎ 08701 977224 ▤ 01928 719852

web: www.premiertravelinn.com

dir: 1m from M56 junct 11, at Preston Brook

High quality, modern budget accommodation ideal for both families and business travellers. Spacious, en suite bedrooms feature bath and shower, satellite TV and many have telephones and modem points. The adjacent family restaurant features a wide and varied menu. For further details consult the Hotel Groups page.

Rooms 40 en suite **Conf** Thtr 40

SANDBACH
MAP 15 SJ76

★★★ 70% **HOTEL**

The Chimney House Hotel

Congleton Rd CW11 4ST

☎ 0870 609 6164 ▤ 01270 768916

folio Hotels

dir: on A534, 1m from M6 junct 17 towards Congleton

This conveniently positioned Tudor-style building benefits from ease of access to major motorway networks. The hotel is ideal for business meetings and functions. Bedrooms are well planned and equipped. Relax in the spacious lounge areas, or enjoy a meal in the patio restaurant overlooking the hotel gardens.

Rooms 48 en suite (16 fmly) (18 GF) ⊘ in 32 bedrooms S fr £85; D fr £85 **Facilities** STV Sauna Putt green Wi-fi in bedrooms Xmas **Conf** Thtr 120 Class 40 Board 40 Del from £90 **Parking** 110 **Notes LB** ⊗ ⊘ in restaurant RS Bank Holidays Civ Wed 100

BUDGET HOTEL

Innkeeper's Lodge Sandbach

Brereton Green CW11 1RS

☎ 01477 544732

web: www.innkeeperslodge.com

dir: M6, junct 17, at rdbt bear left towards Holmes Chapel, follow road until Brereton, lodge on left at Brereton Green

Smart, en suite accommodation ideal for both business & leisure guests. Bedrooms are very well equipped, including Sky TV, telephone, modem points, tea & coffee making facilities, (family rooms in most locations). Complimentary breakfast. The adjacent Pub Restaurant; a Harvester, Vintage Inn, Toby Carvery, Ember Inn, Sizzling Pubco or Pub & Carvery offers an all day menu. See Hotel Groups pages for further details.

Rooms 25 en suite S £55-£75; D £55-£75

Some hotels have restricted service during quieter months, and at this time some of the facilities will not be available

England

SANDIWAY
MAP 15 SJ67

INSPECTORS' CHOICE

★★★★ ◉ ◉ **HOTEL**

Nunsmere Hall Country House Hotel
Tarporley Rd CW8 2ES
☎ 01606 889100 ▤ 01606 889055
e-mail: reservations@nunsmere.co.uk

dir: *A54 to Chester, at x-rds with A49, turn right towards Warrington, hotel 2m on right*

In an idyllic and peaceful setting of well-kept grounds, including a 60-acre lake, this delightful house dates back to 1900. Spacious bedrooms are individually styled, thoughtfully equipped and tastefully appointed to a very high standard. Guests can relax in a choice of elegant lounges, the library or the oak-panelled bar. Dining in the Crystal Restaurant is a highlight, and both a traditional carte and gourmet menu are offered.

Rooms 36 en suite (2 GF) ⊛ in 10 bedrooms S £145-£167; D £200-£360 (incl. bkfst) **Facilities** Fishing Snooker ⌣ Wi-fi available Archery air rifle Clay pigeon shooting Falconry Xmas **Conf** Thtr 50 Class 32 Board 26 Del from £217.50 **Services** Lift **Parking** 80 **Notes LB** ⊗ ⊛ in restaurant RS Sunday Civ Wed 120

TARPORLEY
MAP 15 SJ56

★★★ 78% **HOTEL**

Willington Hall
Willington CW6 0NB
☎ 01829 752321 ▤ 01829 752596
e-mail: enquiries@willingtonhall.co.uk
web: www.willingtonhall.co.uk

dir: *3m NW off unclass road linking A51 & A54, at Clotton turn off A51 at Bulls Head, then follow signs*

Situated in 17 acres of parkland and built in 1829, this attractively furnished country-house hotel offers spacious bedrooms, many with views over open countryside. Service is courteous and friendly, and freshly prepared meals are offered in the dining room or in the adjacent bar and drawing room. A smart function suite confirms the popularity of this hotel as a premier venue for weddings and conferences.

Rooms 10 en suite S £70-£80; D £110-£120 (incl. bkfst) **Facilities** STV Fishing Riding ⌣ **Conf** Thtr 160 Class 80 Board 50 Del £120 **Parking** 60 **Notes LB** ⊛ in restaurant Closed 25 & 26 Dec Civ Wed 130

★★★ 72% **HOTEL**

The Wild Boar
Whitchurch Rd, Beeston CW6 9NW
☎ 01829 260309 ▤ 01829 261081
e-mail: enquiries@wildboarhotel.com

dir: *turn off A51 (Nantwich/Chester road) onto A49 to Whitchurch at Red Fox pub lights, hotel on left at brow of hill after 1.5m*

This 17th-century, half-timbered former hunting lodge has been extended over the years to create a smart, spacious hotel with comfortable bedrooms and stylish public areas. Guests can choose between the elegant Tower Restaurant or the more informal Stables Grill. The hotel is a popular venue for meetings, functions and weddings, and offers impressive conference facilities.

Rooms 37 en suite (20 fmly) (11 GF) ⊛ in 23 bedrooms S £65.11-£88.13; D £94-£105.75 (incl. bkfst) **Facilities** FTV ↧ 18 Putt green Xmas **Conf** Thtr 100 Class 40 Board 40 Del from £109 **Parking** 70 **Notes LB** ⊛ in restaurant Civ Wed 100

WARRINGTON
MAP 15 SJ68
See also Glazebrook

★★★★ 77% **HOTEL**

De Vere Daresbury Park
Chester Rd, Daresbury WA4 4BB
☎ 01925 267331 ▤ 01925 265615
e-mail: reservations.daresbury@devere-hotels.com
web: www.devere.co.uk

dir: *M56 junct 11, take 'Daresbury Park' exit at rdbt. Hotel 100mtrs*

Its proximity to the motorway makes this modern, purpose-built hotel an excellent base for visiting the cities of Liverpool, Manchester and Chester. Parts of the hotel have an 'Alice in Wonderland' theme, as its author, Lewis Caroll was born in nearby village of Daresbury. There are a number of spacious bedrooms, including 12 well-appointed suites. Public rooms include a bright and airy foyer serving informal snacks and drinks, a large bar and restaurant and an indoor leisure centre.

Rooms 183 en suite (12 fmly) (62 GF) ⊛ in 128 bedrooms S £79-£129; D £89-£139 (incl. bkfst) **Facilities** Spa STV ⏐ supervised Squash Solarium Gym Jacuzzi Wi-fi available Steam Room, Beauty salon Xmas **Conf** BC Thtr 300 Class 200 Board 80 Del from £130 **Services** Lift **Parking** 400 **Notes LB** Civ Wed 220

★★★★ 77% **HOTEL**

The Park Royal Hotel
Stretton Rd, Stretton WA4 4NS
☎ 01925 730706 ▤ 01925 730740
e-mail: parkroyalreservations@qhotels.co.uk
web: www.qhotels.co.uk

dir: *M56 junct 10, A49 to Warrington, at lights turn right to Appleton Thorn, hotel 200yds on right*

This modern hotel enjoys a peaceful setting, yet is conveniently located minutes from the M56. Comfortable bedrooms are smartly appointed and thoughtfully equipped. Spacious, attractive public areas include extensive conference and function facilities, and a comprehensive leisure centre complete with outdoor tennis courts and an impressive beauty centre.

Rooms 144 en suite (2 fmly) (34 GF) ⊛ in all bedrooms S £125-£200; D £135-£210 (incl. bkfst) **Facilities** Spa STV ⏐ ⌣ Wi-fi in bedrooms Sauna Solarium Gym Jacuzzi Dance Studio **Conf** Thtr 400 Class 200 Board 90 Del £160 **Services** Lift **Parking** 400 **Notes LB** ⊗ ⊛ in restaurant Civ Wed 300

★★★ 77% **HOTEL**

Best Western Fir Grove

Knutsford Old Rd WA4 2LD

☎ 01925 267471 ▤ 01925 601092

e-mail: firgrove@bestwestern.co.uk

web: www.bw-firgrovehotel.co.uk

dir: M6 junct 20, follow signs for A50 to Warrington for 2.4m, before swing bridge over canal, turn right, and right again

Situated in a quiet residential area, this hotel is convenient for both the town centre and the motorway network. Comfortable, smart bedrooms, including spacious executive rooms, offer some excellent extra facilities such as PlayStations and CD players. Public areas include a smart lounge/bar, a neatly appointed restaurant and excellent function and meeting facilities.

Rooms 52 en suite (3 fmly) (20 GF) ⊘ in 20 bedrooms **Facilities** STV **Conf** BC Thtr 200 Class 150 Board 50 **Parking** 100 **Notes** ⊘ in restaurant Civ Wed 200

★★ 71% **HOTEL**

Paddington House

THE INDEPENDENTS

514 Old Manchester Rd WA1 3TZ

☎ 01925 816767 ▤ 01925 816651

e-mail: hotel@paddingtonhouse.co.uk

web: www.paddingtonhouse.co.uk

dir: 1m from M6 junct 21, off A57, 2m from town centre

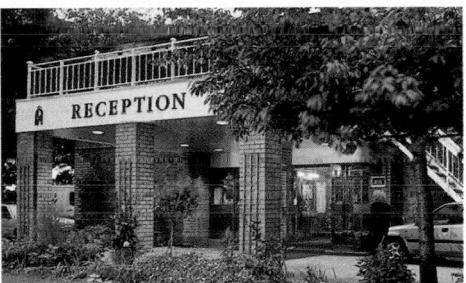

This busy, friendly hotel is conveniently situated just over a mile from the M6. Bedrooms are attractively furnished, and include four-poster and ground-floor rooms. Guests can dine in the wood-panelled Padgate restaurant or in the cosy bar. Conference and function facilities are available.

Rooms 37 en suite (9 fmly) (6 GF) ⊘ in 17 bedrooms S £50-£80; D £60-£90 **Facilities** FTV Wi-fi in bedrooms **Conf** Thtr 180 Class 100 Board 40 Del from £90 **Services** Lift **Parking** 50 **Notes** LB ⊘ in restaurant Civ Wed 150

BUDGET HOTEL

Innkeeper's Lodge Warrington Haydock

Inn keeper's Lodge

322 Newton Rd, Lowton Village WA3 1HD

☎ 01942 671421 ▤ 01942 269692

web: www.innkeeperslodge.com

dir: A580 via M56 junct 23 towards Manchester, follow signs for Toby Carvery

Smart, en suite accommodation ideal for both business & leisure guests. Bedrooms are very well equipped, including Sky TV, telephone, modem points, tea & coffee making facilities, (family rooms in most locations). Complimentary breakfast. The adjacent Pub Restaurant; a Harvester, Vintage Inn, Toby Carvery, Ember Inn, Sizzling Pubco or Pub & Carvery offers an all day menu. See Hotel Groups pages for further details.

Rooms 58 en suite S £45; D £45

BUDGET HOTEL

Premier Travel Inn Warrington Centre (South)

 premier travel inn

1430 Centre Park, Park Boulevard WA1 1QR

☎ 08701 977259 ▤ 01925 244259

web: www.premiertravelinn.com

dir: at Bridgefoot junct of A49/A50/A56 in centre of Warrington

High quality, modern budget accommodation ideal for both families and business travellers. Spacious, en suite bedrooms feature bath and shower, satellite TV and many have telephones and modem points. The adjacent family restaurant features a wide and varied menu. For further details consult the Hotel Groups page.

Rooms 42 en suite

Premier Travel Inn Warrington East

Manchester Rd, Woolston WA1 4GB

☎ 0870 9906524 ▤ 0870 9906525

dir: Just off M6 junct 21 on A57 to Warrington

Rooms 105 en suite

Premier Travel Inn Warrington North East

Golborne Rd, Winwick WA2 8LF

☎ 0870 9906600 ▤ 0870 9906601

dir: Exit M6 junct 22. Follow signs for A573 towards Newton-le-Willows. Dual carriageway to end, take 3rd exit at rdbt. (Church opp). Inn to right of church

Rooms 42 en suite **Conf** Thtr 30 Class 20 Board 25

Premier Travel Inn Warrington North West

Woburn Rd WA2 8RN

☎ 08701 977260 ▤ 01925 414544

dir: M62 junct 9 towards Warrington, 100yds from junct

Rooms 40 en suite

Premier Travel Inn Warrington South

Tarporley Rd, Stretton WA4 4NB

☎ 0870 9906526 ▤ 0870 9906527

dir: Just off M56 junct 10. Follow A49 to Warrington, left at 1st lights

Rooms 29 en suite

Packed in a hurry?
Ironing facilities should be available at all star
levels, either in the rooms or on request

England

WARRINGTON *continued*

BUDGET HOTEL

Travelodge Warrington

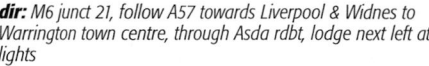

Kendrick/Leigh St WA1 1UZ
☎ 08700 850 950 📠 01925 639432
web: www.travelodge.co.uk

dir: M6 junct 21, follow A57 towards Liverpool & Widnes to
Warrington town centre, through Asda rdbt, lodge next left at
lights

Travelodge offers good quality, good value, modern accommodation.
Ideal for families, the spacious en suite bedrooms include remote-
control TV, tea and coffee-making facilities and comfortable beds.
Meals can be taken at the nearby family restaurant. See Hotel Groups
pages for further details.

Rooms 63 en suite S fr £26; D fr £26

WIDNES   MAP 15 SJ58

★★★ 67% HOTEL

The Hillcrest Hotel

75 Cronton Ln WA8 9AR
☎ 0870 609 6174 📠 0151 495 1348
e-mail: thehillcrest@corushotels.com
web: www.corushotels.com

dir: Exit M62, junction 6, take A5080 to Cronton for 2m, across
at lights, hotel 1m on left

This comfortable hotel is located within easy reach of the motorway
network. All bedrooms are comfortable and well equipped, particularly
the executive rooms. Suites with four-poster or canopy beds, and spa
baths are also available. Public areas include extensive conference
facilities, Palms restaurant and bar, as well as Nelsons public bar.

Rooms 50 en suite (5 fmly) ⊘ in 22 bedrooms S £49-£59; D £59-£79
Facilities STV ♫ Xmas **Conf** Thtr 140 Class 80 Board 40 Del from £89
Services Lift **Parking** 150 **Notes LB** ⊘ in restaurant Civ Wed 100

BUDGET HOTEL

Travelodge Widnes

Fiddlers Ferry Rd WA8 0HA
☎ 08700 850 950 📠 0151 424 8930
web: www.travelodge.co.uk

dir: on A562, 3m south of Widnes

Travelodge offers good quality, good value, modern accommodation.
Ideal for families, the spacious en suite bedrooms include remote-
control TV, tea and coffee-making facilities and comfortable beds.

continued

Meals can be taken at the nearby family restaurant. See Hotel Groups
pages for further details.

Rooms 32 en suite S fr £26; D fr £26

WILMSLOW   MAP 16 SJ88

See also Manchester Airport (Greater Manchester)

★★★★ 80% HOTEL

De Vere Mottram Hall

Wilmslow Rd, Mottram St Andrew, Prestbury
SK10 4QT
☎ 01625 828135 📠 01625 828950
e-mail: dmh.sales@devere-hotels.com
web: www.devere.co.uk

dir: M6 junct 18 from S, M6 junct 20 from N, M56 junct 6, A538
Prestbury

Set in 272 acres of some of Cheshire's most beautiful parkland, this
18th-century Georgian house is certainly an idyllic retreat. The hotel
boasts extensive leisure facilities, including a championship golf
course, swimming pool, gym and spa. Bedrooms are well equipped
and elegantly furnished, and include a number of four-poster rooms
and suites.

Rooms 131 en suite (44 GF) ⊘ in all bedrooms S £85-£230; D £95-£240
(incl. bkfst) **Facilities** STV ⃗ supervised ⅃ 18 ⅃ Squash Snooker
Sauna Solarium Gym Putt green Jacuzzi Wi-fi available Childrens play
ground, Football pitch, Beauty treatments Xmas **Conf** Thtr 275 Class 140
Board 60 Del from £120 **Services** Lift **Parking** 300 **Notes LB** ⊛ ⊘ in
restaurant Civ Wed 160

★★ 79% HOTEL

Wilmslow Lodge

Alderley Rd SK9 1PA
☎ 01625 532300 📠 01625 418150
e-mail: relax@wilmslowlodge.com

Close to the centre of the thriving town of Wilmslow this
establishment offers luxurious, comfortable accommodation in a
modern style. Breakfast and wide selection of meals are served in the
Coach and Four which is open all day.

Rooms 36 en suite (4 fmly) (11 GF) ⊘ in all bedrooms S £49.95-£52.95;
D £49.95-£52.95 **Facilities** FTV Xmas **Conf** Thtr 50 Class 20 Board 30
Del £75 **Services** Lift air con **Parking** 53 **Notes** ⊛

CORNWALL & ISLES OF SCILLY

BODMIN
MAP 02 SX06

★★ 76% ⊛ HOTEL

Trehellas House Hotel & Restaurant
Washaway PL30 3AD
☎ 01208 72700 & 74499 ▤ 01208 73336
e-mail: enquiries@trehellashouse.co.uk
web: www.trehellashouse.co.uk

dir: take A389 from Bodmin towards Wadebridge. Hotel on right. 0.5m beyond road to Camelford

This 18th-century former posting inn retains many original features and provides comfortable accommodation. Bedrooms are located in both the main house and adjacent coach house - all provide the same high standards. An interesting choice of cuisine, with an emphasis on locally-sourced ingredients, is offered in the impressive slate-floored restaurant.

Rooms 4 en suite 7 annexe en suite (2 fmly) (5 GF) ⊘ in all bedrooms S £70-£78; D £78-£170 (incl. bkfst) **Facilities** ↘ Wi-fi in bedrooms **Conf** Thtr 12 Board 12 **Parking** 30 **Notes** LB ⊘ in restaurant Closed 24-31 Dec

★★ 76% HOTEL

Westberry
Rhind St PL31 2EL
☎ 01208 72772 ▤ 01208 72212
e-mail: westberry@btconnect.com
web: www.westberryhotel.net

dir: on ring road off A30 & A38. St Petroc's Church on right, at mini rdbt turn right. Hotel on right

This popular hotel is conveniently located for both Bodmin town centre and the A30. The bedrooms, now refurbished, are attractive and well equipped. A spacious bar lounge and a billiard room are also provided. The restaurant serves a variety of dishes, ranging from bar snacks to a more extensive carte menu.

Rooms 12 en suite 8 annexe en suite (1 fmly) (6 GF) ⊘ in 16 bedrooms S £58-£68; D £68-£78 (incl. bkfst) **Facilities** STV Snooker Gym Full sized snooker table **Conf** BC Thtr 100 Class 80 Board 80 Del from £90 **Parking** 30 **Notes** LB ⊘ in restaurant

---

BUDGET HOTEL

Premier Travel Inn Bodmin
premier travel inn

Launceston Rd PL31 2AR
☎ 08701 977107 ▤ 08701 977705
web: www.premiertravelinn.com

dir: 1m N of town on A389. From A30 S/bound exit onto A389, Inn 0.5m on right. N/bound exit onto A38, follow A389 signs. At T-junct turn left

High quality, modern budget accommodation ideal for both families and business travellers. Spacious, en suite bedrooms feature bath and shower, satellite TV and many have telephones and modem points. The adjacent family restaurant features a wide and varied menu. For further details consult the Hotel Groups page.

Rooms 44 en suite

BOSCASTLE
MAP 02 SX09

★★ 81% ⊛⊛ SMALL HOTEL

The Bottreaux Hotel and Restaurant
PL35 0BG
☎ 01840 250231 ▤ 01840 250170
e-mail: info@boscastlecornwall.co.uk
web: www.boscastlecornwall.co.uk

Built some 200 years ago, this hotel is just a short walk from the picturesque harbour. This is a stylish establishment where guests are genuinely welcomed. Bedrooms are light and airy - the doubles have wonderful six-foot teak beds. The bar is a convivial venue for a drink, and perusal of the imaginative menu that makes good use of local produce.

Rooms 9 en suite ⊘ in all bedrooms **Facilities** Xmas **Parking** 10 **Notes** ⊛ No children 10yrs ⊘ in restaurant

★★ 81% ⊛⊛ HOTEL

The Wellington Hotel
The Harbour PL35 0AQ
☎ 01840 250202 ▤ 01840 250621
e-mail: info@boscastle-wellington.com
web: www.boscastle-wellington.com

dir: A30/A395, right at Davidstow, signed to Boscastle

Following the disastrous flood of 2004, this 16th-century coaching inn has been totally restored to its former glory. The Long Bar is popular with visitors and locals alike and features a delightful galleried area. Bedrooms come in varying sizes, including the spacious Tower rooms; all are comfy and suitably equipped. There is a bar menu and, in the elegant restaurant, a daily-changing carte.

Rooms 15 en suite (2 fmly) S £40-£45; D £80-£90 (incl. bkfst) **Facilities** Wi-fi in bedrooms ♫ Xmas **Conf** Thtr 40 Class 6 Board 24 Del from £65 **Parking** 20 **Notes** LB ⊛ ⊘ in restaurant

BUDE

MAP 02 SS20

★★★ 77% **HOTEL**

Falcon

Breakwater Rd EX23 8SD
☎ 01288 352005 📄 01288 356359
e-mail: reception@falconhotel.com
web: www.falconhotel.com
dir: off A39 into Bude, follow road to Widemouth Bay. Hotel on right over canal bridge

Dating back to 1798, this long-established hotel boasts delightful walled gardens, ideal for afternoon teas. Bedrooms all offer high standards of comfort and quality, with a four-poster room available complete with spa bath. A choice of menus is offered in the elegant restaurant or the friendly bar, and there is an impressive function room.

Rooms 29 en suite (7 fmly) ⊘ in all bedrooms S fr £55 D fr £110 (incl. bkfst) **Facilities** STV ⤴ Mini gym Wi-fi in bedrooms **services** Lift **Conf** BC Thtr 200 Class 50 Board 50 **Parking** 40 **Notes LB** ⊗ ⊘ in restaurant RS 25-Dec Civ Wed 160

★★★ 74% **HOTEL**

Camelot

Downs View EX23 8RE
☎ 01288 352361 📄 01288 355470
e-mail: stay@camelot-hotel.co.uk
web: www.camelot-hotel.co.uk
dir: off A39 into Bude town centre, join one-way system, left lane, bottom of hill on left

This friendly and welcoming Edwardian property offers a range of facilities including a smart and comfortable conservatory bar and lounge, a games room and Hawkers restaurant, which offers skilful cooking using much local produce. Bedrooms are light and airy, with high standards of housekeeping and maintenance.

continued

Rooms 24 en suite (2 fmly) (7 GF) ⊘ in 21 bedrooms S £49-£69; D £98 (incl. bkfst) **Facilities** Darts Pool table Table tennis **Parking** 21 **Notes LB** ⊘ in restaurant

★★★ 74% **HOTEL**

Hartland

Hartland Ter EX23 8JY
☎ 01288 355661 📄 01288 355664
e-mail: hartlandhotel@aol.com
dir: off A39 to Bude, follow town centre signs. Left into Hartland Terrace opp Boots chemist. Hotel at seaward end of road

Enjoying a pleasantly quiet yet convenient location, the Hartland has excellent sea views. A popular stay for those wishing to tour the area and also with families, this hotel offers entertainment on many evenings throughout the year. Bedrooms are comfortable and offer a range of sizes. The public areas are smart, and in the dining room a pleasant fixed-price menu is available.

Rooms 28 en suite (2 fmly) ⊘ in 11 bedrooms S £50-£62; D £90-£100 (incl. bkfst) **Facilities** ᐁ ♫ Xmas **Services** Lift **Parking** 30 **Notes LB** ⊘ in restaurant Closed mid Nov-Etr (ex Xmas & New Year) No credit cards accepted

★★ 74% **SMALL HOTEL**

Penarvor

Crooklets Beach EX23 8NE
☎ 01288 352036 📄 01288 355027
e-mail: hotel.penarvor@boltblue.com
dir: From A39 towards Bude for 1.5m. At 2nd rdbt right, pass shops. Top of hill left signed Crooklets Beach

Adjacent to the golf course and overlooking Crooklets Beach, this family owned hotel benefits from a relaxed and friendly atmosphere. Bedrooms vary in size and are all equipped to a similar standard. An interesting selection of dishes, using fresh local produce, is available in the restaurant; bar meals are also provided.

Rooms 16 en suite (6 fmly) ⊘ in all bedrooms S £32-£45; D £64-£90 (incl. bkfst) **Parking** 20 **Notes LB** ⊘ in restaurant

BUDE *continued*

★★ 71% **SMALL HOTEL**

Atlantic House
Summerleaze Crescent EX23 8HJ
☎ 01288 352451 ▤ 01288 356666
e-mail: enq@atlantichousehotel.com
dir: *M5 junct 31, follow A30 to by-pass in Okehampton. Follow signs to Bude via Halwill & Holsworthy*

This pleasant hotel has splendid views of the coast and offers a peaceful and relaxing environment. The resident proprietors and staff are friendly and attentive. Bedrooms are comfortable and well appointed, and some rooms have sea views. Cuisine offers freshly prepared and appetising dishes served in the spacious dining room.

Rooms 16 rms (15 en suite) (5 fmly) ⊗ in all bedrooms S £28-£30; D £56-£76 (incl. bkfst) **Facilities** Instructor-led outdoor pursuits. Games room with pool table, darts Xmas **Parking** 7 **Notes LB** ⊗ ⊗ in restaurant

CAMBORNE   MAP 02 SW64

★★★ 71% **HOTEL**

Tyacks
27 Commercial St TR14 8LD
☎ 01209 612424 ▤ 01209 612435
e-mail: tyacks@smallandfriendy.co.uk
dir: *W on A30 past A3047 junct & turn off at Camborne West junct. Left & left again at rdbt, follow town centre signs. Hotel on left*

This 18th-century former coaching inn has spacious, well-furnished public areas which include a smart lounge and bar, the popular Coach Bar and a restaurant serving fixed-price and carte menus. The comfortable bedrooms are attractively decorated and well equipped; two have separate sitting areas.

Rooms 15 en suite (2 fmly) ⊗ in all bedrooms S fr £49.50; D fr £75 (incl. bkfst) **Facilities** STV 6x6 sports entertainment screen Xmas **Conf** Class 35 Del from £67.50 **Parking** 27 **Notes LB** ⊗ in restaurant

CAMELFORD   MAP 02 SX18

★★★ 72% **HOTEL**

Bowood Park Hotel & Golf Course
Lanteglos PL32 9RF
☎ 01840 213017 ▤ 01840 212622
e-mail: golf@bowoodpark.com
web: www.bowoodpark.com
dir: *A39 W through Camelford, 0.5m, turn right for Tintagel/Boscastle, 1st left after garage*

Situated in wonderfully picturesque countryside, this hotel provides much for golfers and non-golfers alike. Spacious bedrooms are comfortable and some have private patios and wonderful views over the course. Salmon and trout fishing is available on the River Camel and the hotel's treatment room is just the place for a relaxing massage or beauty treatment.

Rooms 31 en suite (3 fmly) ⊗ in 12 bedrooms **Facilities** ⌁ 18 Fishing Putt green Massage, Sports therapy **Conf** BC Thtr 130 Class 100 Board 100 **Parking** 100 **Notes LB** ⊗ ⊗ in restaurant
See advertisement on page 105

CARBIS BAY
See **St Ives**

CONSTANTINE BAY   MAP 02 SW87

★★★★ 74% ❀ **HOTEL**

Treglos
PL28 8JH
☎ 01841 520727 ▤ 01841 521163
e-mail: stay@tregloshotel.com
web: www.tregloshotel.com
dir: *At St Merryn x-rds take B3276 towards Newquay. 500m right to Constantine Bay, follow brown signs*

Owned by the Barlow family for over 30 years, this hotel has a tradition of high standards. The genuine welcome, choice of comfortable lounges, indoor-pool and children's play facilities entice guests back year after year. Bedrooms vary in size; those with sea views are always popular. The restaurant continues to provide imaginative menus incorporating seasonal local produce.

Rooms 42 en suite (12 fmly) (1 GF) ⊗ in all bedrooms **Facilities** Spa FTV ⌁ ⌁ 18 Snooker ❦ Putt green Jacuzzi Wi-fi available Converted 'boat house' for table tennis **Services** Lift **Parking** 58 **Notes** ⊗ in restaurant Closed 30 Nov-1 Mar

CRANTOCK   MAP 02 SW76

★★★ 75% **HOTEL**

Crantock Bay
West Pentire TR8 5SE
☎ 01637 830229 ▤ 01637 831111
e-mail: stay@crantockbayhotel.co.uk
web: www.crantockbayhotel.co.uk
dir: *at Newquay A3075 to Redruth. After 500yds right towards Crantock, follow signs to West Pentire*

This family-run hotel has spectacular sea views and a tradition of friendly and attentive service. With direct access to the beach from its four acres of grounds, and its extensive leisure facilities, the hotel is a great place for family guests. There are separate lounges, a spacious bar and enjoyable cuisine is served in the dining room.

Rooms 32 en suite (3 fmly) (10 GF) S £59-£99; D £118-£198 (incl. bkfst & dinner) **Facilities** ⌁ ⌁ Sauna Gym ❦ Putt green Jacuzzi Wi-fi in bedrooms Spa Children's games room Xmas **Conf** Thtr 60 Class 12 Board 12 Del from £105 **Parking** 40 **Notes LB** ⊗ in restaurant Closed 2 wks Nov & Jan RS Dec & Feb

★★ 75% SMALL HOTEL

Fairbank

West Pentire Rd TR8 5SA
☎ 01637 830424 📄 01637 830424
e-mail: enquiries@fairbankhotel.co.uk
web: www.fairbankhotel.co.uk
dir: Signed from A3075

This hotel, which has undergone an extensive renovation, offers spectacular views over Crantock Bay from most of the bedrooms, the dining room and the conservatory. Guests receive a warm welcome from the resident owners who create a relaxed and friendly atmosphere. Honest home cooking is served.

Rooms 14 en suite (3 fmly) ⊗ in all bedrooms S £32-£35; D £64-£80 (incl. bkfst) **Conf** Thtr 32 Class 22 Board 22 Del from £70 **Parking** 16 **Notes LB** ⊗ in restaurant Closed Xmas & 3 Jan-31 Jan RS End Feb/early Mar

---

FALMOUTH — MAP 02 SW83
See also Mawnan Smith

★★★★ 78% ⊛⊛ HOTEL

Royal Duchy

Cliff Rd TR11 4NX
☎ 01326 313042 📄 01326 319420
e-mail: info@royalduchy.com
web: www.brend-hotels.co.uk
dir: on Cliff Rd, along Falmouth seafront

Looking out over the sea and towards Pendennis Castle, this hotel provides a friendly environment. The comfortable lounge and cocktail bar are well appointed, and leisure facilities and meeting rooms are also available. The restaurant serves carefully prepared dishes and bedrooms vary in size and aspect, with many rooms having sea views.

Rooms 43 en suite (6 fmly) (1 GF) S fr £75; D fr £150 (incl. bkfst) **Facilities Spa** STV ⦾ Sauna Table tennis ♬ ch fac Xmas **Conf** Thtr 50 Class 50 Board 50 **Services** Lift **Parking** 50 **Notes LB** ⊗ ⊗ in restaurant Civ Wed 100

See advert on this page

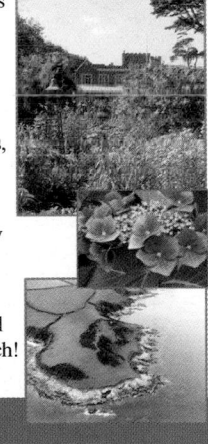
Hairdryers in all rooms three stars and above

England

FALMOUTH *continued*

★★★ 78% HOTEL

Best Western Falmouth Beach Resort Hotel

Gyllyngvase Beach, Seafront TR11 4NA
☎ 01326 310500 ▤ 01326 319147
e-mail: info@falmouthbeachhotel.co.uk
web: www.falmouthbeachhotel.co.uk

dir: *A39 to Falmouth, follow seafront signs.*

Enjoying wonderful views, this popular hotel is situated opposite the beach and within easy walking distance of Falmouth's attractions and port. A friendly atmosphere is maintained and guests have a good choice of leisure and fitness, entertainment and dining options. Bedrooms, many with balconies and sea views, are well equipped and comfortable.

Rooms 116 en suite 7 annexe en suite (20 fmly) (4 GF) ⊘ in 94 bedrooms S £57-£70; D £114-£140 (incl. bkfst) **Facilities Spa** STV ⃝ supervised ⌁ Sauna Solarium Gym Jacuzzi Wi-fi in bedrooms Steam room Hair & beauty salon ♫ Xmas **Conf** Thtr 300 Class 200 Board 250 Del £90 **Services** Lift **Parking** 88 **Notes LB** ⊘ in restaurant Civ Wed 220

See advert on opposite page

★★★ 77% ⊛ HOTEL

The Greenbank

Harbourside TR11 2SR
☎ 01326 312440 ▤ 01326 211362
e-mail: sales@greenbank-hotel.com
web: www.greenbank-hotel.com

dir: *500yds past Falmouth Marina on Penryn River*

Located by the marina, and with its own private quay dating from the 17th century, this smart hotel has a strong maritime theme throughout. Set at the water's edge, the lounge, restaurant and many bedrooms all benefit from having harbour views. The restaurant provides a choice of interesting and enjoyable dishes.

Rooms 60 en suite (6 fmly) ⊘ in all bedrooms S £70-£100; D £105-£150 (incl. bkfst) **Facilities** Private beach ch fac **Conf** Thtr 60 Class 45 Board 20 Del from £100 **Services** Lift **Parking** 68 **Notes LB** ⊗ ⊘ in restaurant Civ Wed 90

★★★ 75% HOTEL

Best Western Penmere Manor

Mongleath Rd TR11 4PN
☎ 01326 211411 & 214525 ▤ 01326 317588
e-mail: reservations@penmere.co.uk
web: www.penmere.co.uk

dir: *right off A39 at Hillhead rdbt, over double mini rdbt. After 0.75m left into Mongleath Rd*

Set in five acres on the outskirts of Falmouth, this family-owned hotel provides friendly service and a range of facilities. A choice of freshly prepared dishes is served in either the bar or in the more formal Bolitho's Restaurant. A wide range of bedrooms is available - the spacious garden-wing rooms are furnished and equipped to a particularly high standard.

Rooms 37 en suite (12 fmly) (13 GF) ⊘ in all bedrooms S £59-£129; D £110-£160 (incl. bkfst) **Facilities Spa** FTV ⃝ ⃕ Sauna Gym ⌁ Jacuzzi Wi-fi available ch fac **Conf** Thtr 60 Class 20 Board 30 **Parking** 50 **Notes LB** ⊗ ⊘ in restaurant Closed 24-27 Dec Civ Wed 80

See advert on opposite page

★★★ 75% ⊛ HOTEL

Falmouth

Castle Beach TR11 4NZ
☎ 01326 312671 & 0800 0193121 ▤ 01326 319533
e-mail: info@falmouthhotel.com

dir: *take A30 to Truro then A390 to Falmouth. Follow signs for beaches, hotel on seafront near Pendennis Castle*

Please note that this establishment has recently changed hands. This spectacular beach front Victorian property affords wonderful sea views from many of its comfortable bedrooms, some of which have their own balconies. Spacious public areas include a number of inviting lounges, beautiful leafy grounds, a choice of dining options and an impressive range of leisure facilities.

Rooms 69 en suite 35 annexe en suite (13 fmly) ⊘ in 50 bedrooms S £94-£125; D £64-£210 (incl. bkfst & dinner) **Facilities** STV ⃝

continued

supervised Snooker Sauna Solarium Gym Putt green Jacuzzi Beauty Salon & Therapeutic Rooms ch fac Xmas **Conf** Thtr 250 Class 150 Board 100 Del from £79 **Services** Lift **Parking** 175 **Notes LB** ⊗ in restaurant Civ Wed 250

See advert on this page

★★★ 75% **HOTEL**

Green Lawns

THE INDEPENDENTS

Western Ter TR11 4QJ

☎ 01326 312734 📠 01326 211427

e-mail: info@greenlawnshotel.com

web: www.greenlawnshotel.com

dir: on A39

This attractive property enjoys a convenient location close to the town centre and within easy reach of the sea. Spacious public areas include

continued on page 110

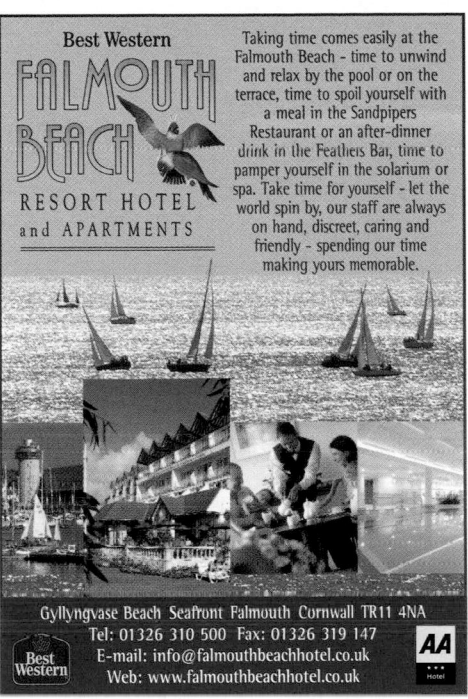

Best Western

FALMOUTH BEACH

RESORT HOTEL and APARTMENTS

Taking time comes easily at the Falmouth Beach - time to unwind and relax by the pool or on the terrace, time to spoil yourself with a meal in the Sandpipers Restaurant or an after-dinner drink in the Feathers Bar, time to pamper yourself in the solarium or spa. Take time for yourself - let the world spin by, our staff are always on hand, discreet, caring and friendly - spending our time making yours memorable.

Gyllyngvase Beach Seafront Falmouth Cornwall TR11 4NA
Tel: 01326 310 500 Fax: 01326 319 147
E-mail: info@falmouthbeachhotel.co.uk
Web: www.falmouthbeachhotel.co.uk

Best Western

AA ★★★ Hotel

The Falmouth Hotel **AA** ★★★

The Falmouth Hotel commands an unrivalled seafront location with 100 quality rooms, serviced apartments and self-catering cottages with optional balcony and Jacuzzi.
Enjoy delightful views from ambient restaurants, bars and lounge. The Oasis leisure complex includes an indoor pool, sauna, Jacuzzi, solarium and gym.
The perfect venue for weddings, conferences and all functions.

CASTLE BEACH ROAD, FALMOUTH, CORNWALL TR11 4NZ

Please call for a brochure and tariffs.
FREEPHONE: 0800 019 3121   Fax: 01326 319533
Email: info@falmouthhotel.com   www.falmouthhotel.com

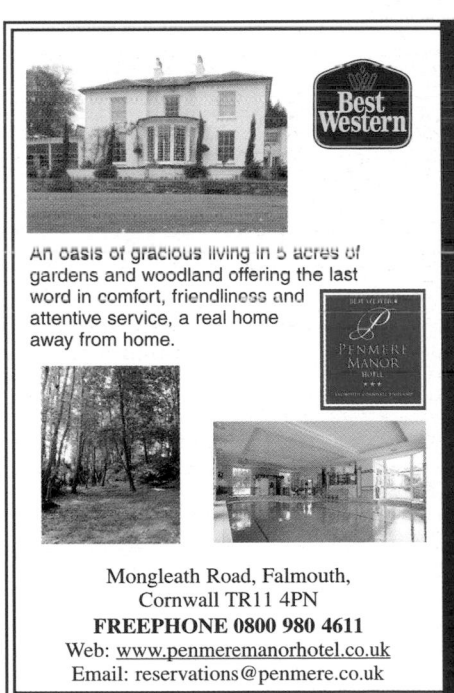

Best Western

An oasis of gracious living in 5 acres of gardens and woodland offering the last word in comfort, friendliness and attentive service, a real home away from home.

PENMERE MANOR HOTEL

Mongleath Road, Falmouth, Cornwall TR11 4PN
FREEPHONE 0800 980 4611
Web: www.penmeremanorhotel.co.uk
Email: reservations@penmere.co.uk

FALMOUTH continued

inviting lounges, an elegant restaurant, conference and meeting facilities and a leisure centre. Bedrooms vary in size and style but all are well equipped and comfortable. The friendly service is particularly noteworthy.

Rooms 39 en suite (8 fmly) (11 GF) ⊗ in 24 bedrooms S £60-£115; D £110-£180 (incl. bkfst) **Facilities** 🎾 🏊 Squash Sauna Solarium Gym Jacuzzi Swimming pool cameras **Conf** Thtr 200 Class 80 Board 100 Del from £95 **Parking** 69 **Notes LB** ⊗ in restaurant Closed 24-30 Dec Civ Wed 50

★★★ 75% ⊛ **HOTEL**

St Michael's Hotel and Spa

Gyllyngvase Beach, Seafront TR11 4NB

☎ 01326 312707 🖥 01326 211772

e-mail: info@stmichaelshotel.co.uk

dir: A39 into Falmouth, follow beach signs, at 2nd mini-rdbt into Pennance Rd. Take 2nd left & 2nd left again

Overlooking the bay, this establishment is in an excellent location. The contemporary public areas have bags of style with superb views out to sea. There are excellent leisure facilities and the attractive gardens also provide a place to relax and unwind. The Flying Fish restaurant and has a great atmosphere and buzz. The light and bright bedrooms, some with balconies, are well equipped.

Rooms 54 en suite 8 annexe en suite (7 fmly) (12 GF) ⊗ in 15 bedrooms **Facilities** 🎾 Sauna Solarium Gym 🌊 Jacuzzi **Conf** Thtr 200 Class 150 Board 50 **Parking** 30 **Notes LB** ⊗ ⊗ in restaurant Civ Wed 80

See advert on opposite page

★★★ 71% **HOTEL**

Penmorvah Manor

Budock Water TR11 5ED

☎ 01326 250277 🖥 01326 250509

e-mail: reception@penmorvah.co.uk

web: www.penmorvah.co.uk

dir: A39 to Hillhead rdbt, take 2nd exit. Right at Falmouth Football Club, through Budock and hotel opposite Penjerrick Gardens

Situated within two miles of central Falmouth, this extended Victorian manor house is a peaceful hideaway, set in six acres of private woodland and gardens. Penmorvah is well positioned for visiting the local gardens, and offers many garden-tour breaks. Dinner features locally sourced, quality ingredients such as Cornish cheeses, meat, fish and game.

continued

Penmorvah Manor

Rooms 27 en suite (1 fmly) (10 GF) ⊗ in all bedrooms S fr £65; D fr £100 (incl. bkfst) **Facilities** Wi-fi available Xmas **Conf** Thtr 250 Class 100 Board 56 Del from £100 **Parking** 150 **Notes LB** ⊗ in restaurant Civ Wed 120

★★ 79% **HOTEL**

Crill Manor

Maen Valley, Budock Water TR11 5BL

☎ 01326 211880 🖥 01326 211229

e-mail: info@crillmanor.com

dir: A39 Truro towards Falmouth, right for Mawnan Smith/ Budock Water. Over double mini rdbt. Through village to 40mph sign then left

Set in a secluded Area of Outstanding Natural Beauty, between Falmouth and the Helford River, this delightful hotel offers friendly and attentive service. Bedrooms are well equipped and attractively decorated. The open-plan, split-level lounge and bar area overlooks the gardens. Dining here is a treat with the restaurant offering a daily-changing menu with an emphasis upon locally-sourced fish and meats.

Rooms 14 en suite (2 GF) ⊗ in all bedrooms S £49-£69; D £98-£138 (incl. bkfst & dinner) **Facilities** Xmas **Parking** 20 **Notes LB** ⊗ No children 14yrs ⊗ in restaurant Closed 1 Nov-1 Feb RS 22-29 Dec

---

★★ 75% **HOTEL**

Hotel Anacapri

Gyllyngvase Rd TR11 4DJ

☎ 01326 311454 🖥 01326 311454

e-mail: anacapri@btconnect.com

web: www.hotelanacapri.co.uk

dir: A39 (Truro to Falmouth), straight on at lights, straight on at 2 rdbts. 5th right into Gyllyngvase Rd, hotel on right

In an elevated position, overlooking Gyllyngvase Beach and Falmouth Bay beyond, this family run establishment extends a warm welcome

continued

to all. Bedrooms all share similar standards of comfort and quality and the majority have sea views. Public areas include a convivial bar, a lounge and the smart restaurant, where carefully prepared and very enjoyable cuisine is on offer.

Rooms 15 en suite (1 fmly) ⊛ in 16 bedrooms S £30-£60; D £60-£85 **Parking** 20 **Notes LB** ⊛ No children 8yrs ⊛ in restaurant Closed 10 Dec-29 Dec RS Except Xmas 20-28 Dec

---

★★ 71% **HOTEL**

Park Grove

THE INDEPENDENTS

Kimberley Park Rd TR11 2DD
☎ 01326 313276 📠 01326 211926
e-mail: reception@parkgrovehotel.com
web: www.parkgrovehotel.com

dir: off A39 at lights by Riders Garage towards harbour. Hotel 400yds on left opposite park

Within walking distance of the town centre, this friendly family-run hotel is situated in a pleasant residential area opposite Kimberley Park. Comfortable accommodation is provided and public areas include a relaxing and stylish lounge and a well-spaced dining room and bar. Bedrooms are also comfortable and well equipped.

Rooms 17 en suite (6 fmly) **Parking** 25 **Notes LB** ⊛ ⊛ in restaurant Closed Dec-Feb

---

★★ 69% **SMALL HOTEL**

Broadmead

THE CIRCLE
Selected Bed & Island Hotels
GREAT BRITAIN

66/68 Kimberley Park Rd TR11 2DD
☎ 01326 315704 📠 01326 311048
e-mail: mail@broadmeadhotel.fsnet.co.uk

dir: A39 from Truro to Falmouth, at lights turn left into Kimberley Park Rd, hotel 200yds on left

Conveniently located, with views across the park and within easy walking distance of the beaches and town centre, this pleasant hotel has smart and comfortable accommodation. Bedrooms are well equipped and attractively decorated. A choice of lounges is available and, in the dining room, menus offer freshly prepared home-cooked dishes.

Rooms 12 en suite (2 fmly) (2 GF) ⊛ in all bedrooms S £33-£37; D £64-£74 (incl. bkfst) **Parking** 8 **Notes LB** ⊛ ⊛ in restaurant

---

★★ 69% **HOTEL**

Rosslyn

110 Kimberley Park Rd TR11 2JJ
☎ 01326 312699 & 315373 📠 01326 312699
e-mail: mail@rosslynhotel.co.uk
web: www.rosslynhotel.co.uk

dir: on A39 towards Falmouth, to Hillend rdbt, turn right and over next mini rdbt. At 2nd mini rdbt left into Trescobeas Rd. Hotel on left past hospital

A relaxed and friendly atmosphere is maintained at this family-run hotel. Situated on the northern edge of Falmouth, the Rosslyn is easily located and is suitable for both business and leisure guests. A comfortable lounge overlooks the well-tended garden, and enjoyable freshly prepared dinners are offered in the restaurant.

Rooms 27 en suite (3 fmly) (6 GF) ⊛ in all bedrooms S £25-£40; D £50-£70 (incl. bkfst) **Facilities** Table tennis Pool table Computer in lounge Internet access Xmas **Conf** BC Class 60 Board 20 **Parking** 22 **Notes LB** ⊛ in restaurant

---

★★ 67% **HOTEL**

Madeira Hotel

Leisureplex

Cliff Rd TR11 4NY
☎ 01326 313531 📠 01326 319143
e-mail: madeira.falmouth@alfatravel.co.uk
web: www.alfatravel.co.uk

dir: A39 (Truro to Falmouth), follow tourist signs 'Hotels' to seafront

This popular hotel offers splendid sea views and a pleasant, convenient location, which is close to the town. Extensive sun lounges are popular haunts in which to enjoy the views, while additional facilities include an oak panelled cocktail bar. Bedrooms, many with sea views, are available in a range of sizes.

Rooms 50 en suite (8 fmly) (7 GF) ⊛ in all bedrooms S £34-£46; D £56-£80 (incl. bkfst) **Facilities** ♫ Xmas **Services** Lift **Parking** 11 **Notes LB** ⊛ ⊛ in restaurant Closed Dec-Feb RS Nov & Mar

We have indicated only the hotels that do not accept credit or debit cards

Relax. Pamper. Indulge. Enjoy.

Stunning sea and tropical garden views, opposite sandy beach.

Award winning food.

Spa with large heated pool, sauna, Jacuzzi, steam, gym and full range of treatments.

Simply, one of the finest contemporary hotels in the South West.

Call 01326 312707 for more info, or visit our website at stmichaelshotel.co.uk

St Michael's Hotel & Spa
Gyllyngvase Beach, Falmouth, Cornwall TR11 4NB

FALMOUTH continued

★★ 65% HOTEL

Membly Hall
Sea Front, Cliff Rd TR11 4NT
☎ 01326 312869 & 311115 📠 01326 211751
e-mail: memblyhallhotel@btopenworld.com
dir: A39 to Falmouth. Follow seafront and beaches sign.

Located conveniently on the seafront and enjoying splendid views, this family-run hotel offers friendly service. Bedrooms are pleasantly spacious and well equipped. Carefully prepared and enjoyable meals are served in the spacious dining room. Live entertainment is provided on some evenings and there is also a spa/sauna and pool table.

Rooms 37 en suite (3 fmly) **Facilities Spa** STV Riding Sauna Putt green Indoor short bowls, Table tennis, Pool table ♬ **Conf** Thtr 150 Class 130 Board 60 **Services** Lift **Parking** 30 **Notes LB** ⊗ ⊘ in restaurant Closed Xmas week RS Dec-Jan No credit cards accepted

---

FOWEY   MAP 02 SX15

★★★ 80% ⊛⊛ HOTEL

Fowey Hall
Hanson Dr PL23 1ET
☎ 01726 833866 📠 01726 834100
e-mail: info@foweyhallhotel.co.uk
dir: In Fowey, over mini rdbt into town centre. Pass school on right, 400mtrs right into Hanson Drive

Built in 1899, this listed mansion looks out to the English Channel. The imaginatively designed bedrooms offer charm, individuality and sumptuous comfort, and the new Garden Wing rooms add a further dimension. The beautifully appointed public rooms include the wood-panelled dining room where accomplished cuisine is served. With

continued

glorious views as a backdrop, the well-kept grounds have a covered pool and sunbathing area for guest relaxation.

Rooms 28 en suite 8 annexe en suite (30 fmly) (8 GF) S £120-£360; D £170-£430 (incl. bkfst & dinner) **Facilities** STV 🖎 supervised ⚑ Wi-fi in bedrooms Childrens play area Table tennis Basketball Xmas **Conf** Thtr 30 Class 20 Board 20 Del from £150 **Parking** 40

See advert on opposite page

★★★ 80% ⊛⊛ HOTEL

The Fowey Hotel
The Esplanade PL23 1HX
☎ 01726 832551 📠 01726 832125
e-mail: fowey@richardsonhotels.co.uk
web: www.thefoweyhotel.co.uk
dir: A30 to Okehampton, continue to Bodmin. Then B3269 to Fowey for 1m, on right bend left junct then right into Dagands Rd. Hotel 200mtrs on left

This attractive hotel stands proudly above the estuary, with marvellous views of the river from the public areas and the majority of the bedrooms. High standards are evident throughout, augmented by a relaxed and welcoming atmosphere. There is a spacious bar, elegant restaurant and smart drawing room. Imaginative dinners make good use of quality local ingredients.

Rooms 37 en suite (1 fmly) ⚑ in 8 bedrooms S £94-£143; D £108-£164 (incl. bkfst) **Facilities** Fishing ⚑ Xmas **Conf** Thtr 100 Class 60 Board 20 Del from £125 **Services** Lift **Parking** 18 **Notes LB** ⊘ in restaurant

INSPECTORS' CHOICE

★★ ⊛⊛ HOTEL

Marina
Esplanade PL23 1HY
☎ 01726 833315 📠 01726 832779
e-mail: marina.hotel@dial.pipex.com
web: www.themarinahotel.co.uk
dir: into town down Lostwithiel St, near bottom of hill, right into Esplanade

Built in 1815 as a seaside retreat, the Marina has much style, and from its setting on the water's edge has glorious views of the river and the sea. Bedrooms, some with balconies, are spacious and comfortable - not forgetting the addition of a host of thoughtful touches that are provided. Skilled cuisine, using the freshest local produce, including fish landed nearby, is the hallmark of the waterside restaurant.

continued

Marina

Rooms 13 en suite (1 fmly) ⊗ in all bedrooms S £70-£150; D £100-£200 (incl. bkfst) **Facilities** Fishing Sailing Xmas **Parking** 13 **Notes LB** ⊗ in restaurant Civ Wed 55

◎◎ **RESTAURANT WITH ROOMS**

The Old Quay House Hotel

28 Fore St PL23 1AQ

☎ 01726 833302 🖹 01726 833668

e-mail: info@theoldquayhouse.com

web: www.theoldquayhouse.com

dir: M5 junct 31 onto A30 to Bodmin. Then A389 through town and take B3269 to Fowey

Looking out across Fowey's busy waterway, situated at the end of steep and winding streets so typical of Cornwall, this hotel offers very comfortable, stylish bedrooms; some have harbour views. The old quay itself is where guests can either dine or take drinks - the cuisine is accomplished, and breakfast is also noteworthy.

Rooms 12 en suite ⊗ in all bedrooms S £130 £210; D £160-£210 **Facilities** STV **Notes LB** ⊛ No children 12yrs Civ Wed 100

FRADDON   MAP 02 SW95

BUDGET HOTEL

Premier Travel Inn Newquay

Penhale TR9 6NA

☎ 08701 977194 🖹 01726 860641

web: www.premiertravelinn.com

dir: on A30 2m S of Indian Queens

High quality, modern budget accommodation ideal for both families and business travellers. Spacious, en suite bedrooms feature bath and shower, satellite TV and many have telephones and modem points. The adjacent family restaurant features a wide and varied menu. For further details consult the Hotel Groups page.

Rooms 40 en suite

HAYLE   MAP 02 SW53

BUDGET HOTEL

Premier Travel Inn Hayle

Carwin Rise TR27 4PN

☎ 08701 977133 🖹 01736 759514

web: www.premiertravelinn.com

dir: on A30 at Loggans Moor rdbt, take 1st exit on left, Carwin Rise, Inn on right

High quality, modern budget accommodation ideal for both families and business travellers. Spacious, en suite bedrooms feature bath and shower, satellite TV and many have telephones and modem points. The adjacent family restaurant features a wide and varied menu. For further details consult the Hotel Groups page.

Rooms 40 en suite

BUDGET HOTEL

Travelodge Hayle

Carwin Roundabout TR27 5DG

☎ 08700 850 950

web: www.travelodge.co.uk

dir: Leave the M5 at J30 and take A312.After 2m turn right onto A244 (Hounslow road)

Travelodge offers good quality, good value, modern accommodation. Ideal for families, the spacious en suite bedrooms include remote-control TV, tea and coffee-making facilities and comfortable beds. Meals can be taken at the nearby family restaurant. See Hotel Groups pages for further details.

Rooms 39 en suite S fr £26; D fr £26

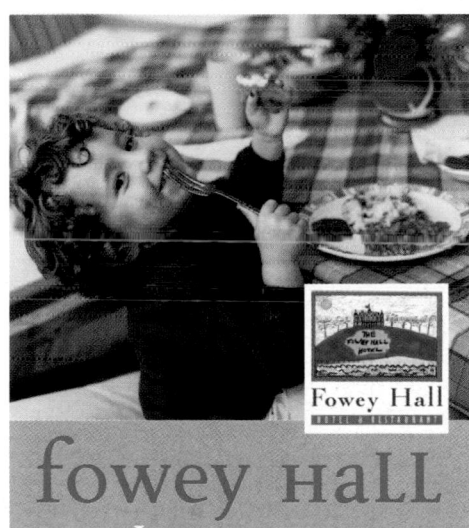

England

HELSTON MAP 02 SW62

★★ 72% **HOTEL**

The Gwealdues

THE INDEPENDENTS

Falmouth Rd TR13 8JX
☎ 01326 572808 🖹 01326 561388
e-mail: gwealdueshotel@btinternet.com
dir: *from Truro/Falmouth on A394 towards Helston. Through Trenennack, right at next rdbt onto B3297 towards Helston/Redruth. Hotel in 100mtrs*

The family-run Gwealdues is a friendly establishment located just outside Helston. Bedrooms are comfortable and well maintained, some with the added bonus of balconies. A major attraction here is the Thai restaurant (although European dishes are also available) which has a great local following. For a relaxing drink, there is the convivial bar, conservatory or attractive water garden.

Rooms 18 en suite (2 fmly) (1 GF) ⊘ in 5 bedrooms S £45-£50; D £65-£70 (incl. bkfst) **Facilities** Wi-fi available Sailing on hotel yacht Xmas **Conf** Thtr 70 Class 50 Board 50 **Parking** 50 **Notes LB** ⊘ in restaurant

ISLES OF SCILLY

See **Scilly, Isles of**

LAND'S END MAP 02 SW32

See also **Sennen**

★★★ 64% **HOTEL**

The Land's End Hotel

TR19 7AA
☎ 01736 871844 🖹 01736 871599
e-mail: rescrvations@landsendhotel.wanadoo.co.uk
web: www.landsendhotel.co.uk
dir: *from Penzance take A30 and follow Land's End signs. After Sennen 1m to Land's End*

This famous location provides a very impressive setting for this well-established hotel. Bedrooms, many with stunning views of the Atlantic, are pleasantly decorated and comfortable. A relaxing lounge and attractive bar are provided. The Longships restaurant with far reaching sea views offers fresh local produce, and fish dishes are a speciality.

Rooms 33 en suite (2 fmly) **Facilities** STV Free entry Lands End visitor centre Xmas **Conf** BC Thtr 200 Class 100 Board 50 **Parking** 1000 **Notes** ⊘ in restaurant Civ Wed 110

LAUNCESTON MAP 03 SX38

See also **Lifton (Devon)**

★★ 69% **SMALL HOTEL**

Eagle House

Castle St PL15 8BA
☎ 01566 772036 🖹 01566 772036
e-mail: eaglehousehotel@aol.com
dir: *from Launceston on Holsworthy Rd follow brown signs for hotel*

Next to the castle, this elegant Georgian house dates back to 1767 and is within walking distance of all the local amienties. Many of the bedrooms have wonderful views over the Cornish countryside. A short carte is served each evening in the restaurant.

Rooms 14 en suite (1 fmly) S fr £36; D fr £62 (incl. bkfst) **Facilities** STV **Conf** Thtr 190 Class 190 Board 190 **Parking** 100 **Notes LB** ⊗ ⊘ in restaurant Civ Wed 190

LISKEARD MAP 02 SX26

★★ 84% **HOTEL**

Well House

St Keyne PL14 4RN
☎ 01579 342001 🖹 01579 343891
e-mail: enquiries@wellhouse.co.uk
dir: *from Liskeard on A38 take B3254 to St Keyne (3m). At church fork left and hotel 0.5m*

Tucked away in an attractive valley and set in impressive grounds, Well House enjoys a tranquil setting. Friendly staff provide attentive yet relaxed service and add to the elegant atmosphere of the house. The comfortable lounge offers deep cushioned sofas and an open fire and in the intimate bar an extensive choice of wines and drinks is available. As we went to press the rosette award for this hotel had not been confirmed due to a change of ownership.

Rooms 9 en suite (1 fmly) S £80-£95; D £125-£180 (incl. bkfst) **Facilities** ⚲ ♨ ↵ Xmas **Parking** 30 **Notes LB** ⊘ in restaurant Closed 2 wks in Jan

LIZARD, THE MAP 02 SW71

★★★ 67% **HOTEL**

Housel Bay

Housel Cove TR12 7PG
☎ 01326 290417 & 290917 🖹 01326 290359
e-mail: info@houselbay.com
web: www.houselbay.com
dir: *A39 or A394 to Helston, then A3083. At Lizard sign turn left, left at school, down lane to hotel*

This long-established hotel has stunning views across the Western Approaches, equally enjoyable from the lounge and many of the bedrooms. Enjoyable cuisine is available in the stylish dining room, after which guests might enjoy a stroll to the end of the garden, which leads directly onto the Cornwall coastal path.

Rooms 20 en suite (1 fmly) ⊘ in 10 bedrooms **Facilities** STV **Conf** Thtr 20 Class 16 Board 12 **Services** Lift **Parking** 37 **Notes LB** ⊗ ⊘ in restaurant RS Winter

LOOE
See also Portwrinkle

MAP 02 SX25

★★★ 64% **HOTEL**

Hannafore Point

THE INDEPENDENTS

Marine Dr, West Looe PL13 2DG
☎ 01503 263273 ▤ 01503 263272
e-mail: stay@hannaforepointhotel.com

dir: A38, left onto A385 to Looe. Over bridge left. Hotel 0.5m on left

With panoramic coastal views of St George's Island around to Rame Head, this popular hotel provides a warm welcome. The wonderful view is certainly a feature of the spacious restaurant and bar, providing a scenic backdrop for dinners and breakfasts. Additional facilities include a heated indoor pool, squash court and gym.

Rooms 37 en suite (5 fmly) S £48-£66; D £96-£132 (incl. bkfst)
Facilities Spa FTV ⬥ Squash Sauna Solarium Gym Jacuzzi Tennis/bowls 200yds away ♫ Xmas **Conf** BC Thtr 120 Class 80 Board 40 Del from £80 **Services** Lift **Parking** 32 **Notes LB** ⊘ in restaurant Civ Wed 150

See advert on this page

★★ 76% **HOTEL**

Fieldhead

THE INDEPENDENTS

Portuan Rd, Hannafore PL13 2DR
☎ 01503 262689 ▤ 01503 264114
e-mail: enquiries@fieldheadhotel.co.uk
web: www.fieldheadhotel.co.uk

dir: Exit A38 at Trerulefoot rdbt, follow signs to Looe (approx 8m). In Looe pass Texaco garage, cross bridge, left to Hannafore. At Tom Sawyer turn right, right again into Portuan Rd. Hotel on left

Overlooking the bay, this engaging hotel has a relaxing atmosphere. Bedrooms are furnished with care and many have sea views. Smartly presented public areas include a convivial bar and restaurant, and outside there is a palm-filled garden with a secluded patio and swimming pool. The fixed-price menu changes daily and features quality local produce.

Rooms 16 en suite (2 fmly) (2 GF) S £36-£49; D £73-£150 (incl. bkfst)
Facilities ⬥ Wi-fi in bedrooms Xmas **Parking** 15 **Notes LB** ⊘ in restaurant Closed Xmas

See advert on this page

England

LOOE *continued*

★★ 65% HOTEL

Rivercroft Hotel

Station Rd PL13 1HL

☎ 01503 262251 🖹 01503 265494

e-mail: rivercroft.hotel@virgin.net

web: www.rivercrofthotel.co.uk

dir: from A38 take B387 to Looe. Hotel on left near bridge

Standing high above the river, this family-run hotel is conveniently located, just a short walk from the town centre and beach. Bedrooms are comfortably furnished and well equipped, and many enjoy wonderful views. A carte menu is offered in the Croft Restaurant, or alternatively, meals can be enjoyed in the convivial atmosphere of the bar.

Rooms 15 en suite (8 fmly) **Notes LB** ⊗ ⊘ in restaurant

LOSTWITHIEL   MAP 02 SX15

★★★ 73% HOTEL

Best Western Restormel Lodge

Castle Hill PL22 0DD

☎ 01208 872223 🖹 01208 873568

e-mail: restlodge@aol.com

web: www.restormelhotel.co.uk

dir: on A390 in Lostwithiel

A short drive from the Eden Project, this popular hotel offers a friendly welcome to all visitors and is ideally situated for exploring the area. The original building houses the bar, restaurant and lounges, with some features adding to the character. Bedrooms are comfortably furnished, with a number overlooking the secluded outdoor pool.

Rooms 24 en suite 12 annexe en suite (2 fmly) (9 GF) ⊘ in 32 bedrooms S £75; D £100-£140 (incl. bkfst) **Facilities** ⁕ Wi-fi available Xmas **Conf** Thtr 12 Class 12 Board 12 **Parking** 40 **Notes LB** ⊘ in restaurant

★★★ 66% HOTEL

Lostwithiel Hotel Golf & Country Club

Lower Polscoe PL22 0HQ

☎ 01208 873550 🖹 01208 873479

e-mail: info@golf-hotel.co.uk

web: www.golf-hotel.co.uk

dir: off A38 at Dobwalls onto A390. In Lostwithiel right and hotel signed

This rural hotel is based around its own golf club and other leisure activities. The main building offers guests a choice of eating options, *continued*

including all-day snacks in the popular Sports Bar. The bedroom accommodation, designed to incorporate beamed ceilings, has been developed from old Cornish barns that are set around a courtyard.

Lostwithiel Hotel Golf & Country Club

Rooms 27 en suite (2 fmly) (17 GF) ⊘ in 16 bedrooms S £34-£53 D £68-£106 (incl. bkfst) **Facilities** ⁕ ↕ 18 ⚐ Fishing Snooker Gym Putt green Undercover floodlit driving range, Indoor golf simulator **Conf** Thtr 120 Class 60 Board 40 **Parking** 120 **Notes LB** ⊘ in restaurant Civ Wed 120

MARAZION   MAP 02 SW53

★★ 84% ⚜ HOTEL

Mount Haven Hotel & St Michaels Restaurant

Turnpike Rd TR17 0DQ

☎ 01736 710249 🖹 01736 711658

e-mail: reception@mounthaven.co.uk

web: www.mounthaven.co.uk

dir: From A30 towards Penzance. At rdbt take exit for Helston onto A394. Next rdbt right into Marazion, hotel on left

A stylish and delightfully located hotel where exceptional views can be enjoyed - sunsets and sunrises can be particularly splendid. Bedrooms, many with balconies, are comfortably appointed. Fresh seafood and local produce are simply treated to produce interesting menus and enjoyable dining. A range of holistic therapies is available. Service is attentive and friendly

Rooms 18 en suite (2 fmly) (6 GF) ⊘ in all bedrooms S £60-£80; D £84-£160 (incl. bkfst) **Facilities Spa** FTV Aromatherapy reflexology, massage & reiki, hot rocks **Parking** 30 **Notes LB** ⊗ ⊘ in restaurant Closed 20 Dec-5 Feb

★★ 72% SMALL HOTEL

Godolphin Arms

TR17 0EN

☎ 01736 710202 🖥 01736 710171

e-mail: enquiries@godolphinarms.co.uk

web: www.godolphinarms.co.uk

dir: *from A30 follow Marazion signs for 1m to hotel. At end of causeway to St Michael's Mount*

This 170-year-old waterside hotel is in a prime location where the stunning views of St Michael's Mount provide a backdrop for the restaurant and lounge bar. Bedrooms are colourful, comfortable and spacious. A choice of menu is offered in the main restaurant and the Gig Bar, all with an emphasis on local seafood.

Rooms 10 en suite (2 fmly) (2 GF) ⊛ in all bedrooms S £64-£90; D £90-£140 (incl. bkfst) **Facilities** STV Direct access to large beach **Parking** 48 **Notes** LB ⊛ in restaurant Closed 24 & 25 Dec

★★ 69% SMALL HOTEL

Marazion

The Square TR17 0AP

☎ 01736 710334

e-mail: stephanie@marazionhotel.co.uk

dir: *Town centre*

Within 50 yards of one of Cornwall's safest beaches, this family-run hotel, offers a relaxed atmosphere with friendly service. The individually furnished and decorated bedrooms are comfortable, and many enjoy stunning views across to St Michaels' Mount. The hotel incorporates the Cutty Sark public bar and restaurant which offers a wide range of meals to suit all palates and budgets.

Rooms 10 en suite

MAWGAN PORTH   MAP 02 SW86

★★★★ 75% ⊛ HOTEL

Bedruthan Steps Hotel

TR8 4BU

☎ 01637 860555 & 860860 🖥 01637 860714

e-mail: office@bedruthan.com

dir: *from A39/A30 follow signs to Newquay Airport. Right at T-junct, past airport, to Mawgan Porth. Hotel on left at top of hill*

With stunning views over Mawgan Porth Bay from the public rooms and the majority of the bedrooms, this is child-friendly hotel. Children's clubs for various ages are provided in addition to children's

continued

dining areas and appropriate meals and times. A homage to architecture of the 1970s, with a modern, comfortable, contemporary feel, this hotel is adding conference facilities. In the spacious restaurants, an imaginative fixed-price menu is offered and a short carte from Tuesday-Saturday.

Bedruthan Steps Hotel

Rooms 90 en suite 9 annexe en suite (60 fmly) (1 GF) ⊛ in all bedrooms **Facilities Spa** 🖐 ⤳ ♨ Snooker Sauna Gym Jacuzzi Jungle tumble ball pool ♬ ch fac **Conf** BC Thtr 200 Class 100 Board 40 **Services** Lift **Parking** 100 **Notes** LB ⊗ ⊛ in restaurant Civ Wed 150

MAWNAN SMITH   MAP 02 SW72

★★★ 85% ⊛ COUNTRY HOUSE HOTEL

Meudon

TR11 5HT

☎ 01326 250541 🖥 01326 250543

e-mail: wecare@meudon.co.uk

web: www.meudon.co.uk

dir: *from Truro A39 towards Falmouth at Hillhead (anchor & cannons) rdbt, follow signs to Maenporth Beach. Hotel on left 1m after beach*

This charming late Victorian mansion is a relaxing place to stay, with its friendly hospitality and attentive service. It sits in impressive nine-acre gardens that lead down to a private beach. The spacious and comfortable bedrooms are situated in a more modern building than the main house. The cuisine features the best of local Cornish produce and is served in the conservatory restaurant.

Rooms 29 en suite (2 fmly) (15 GF) S £70-£120; D £140-£240 (incl. bkfst & dinner) **Facilities** FTV Fishing Riding Wi-fi available Private beach, Hair salon, Yacht for skippered charter, sub-tropical gardens ch fac Xmas **Conf** Thtr 30 Class 20 Board 15 Del from £85 **Services** Lift **Parking** 52 **Notes** LB ⊛ in restaurant Closed Jan

See advert on page 107

England

MAWNAN SMITH *continued*

★★★★ 79% ⊛ **COUNTRY HOUSE HOTEL**

Budock Vean-The Hotel on the River
TR11 5LG
☎ 01326 252100 & 0800 833927 📠 01326 250892
e-mail: relax@budockvean.co.uk
web: www.budockvean.co.uk
dir: *from A39 follow tourist signs to Trebah Gardens. 0.5m to hotel*

Set in 65 acres of attractive, well-tended grounds, this peaceful hotel offers an impressive range of facilities. Convenient for visiting the Helford River Estuary and many local gardens, or simply as a tranquil setting for a leisure break. Bedrooms are spacious and offer a choice of styles; some overlook the grounds and golf course.

Rooms 57 en suite (2 fmly) ⊛ in 6 bedrooms S £70-£116; D £140-£232 (incl. bkfst & dinner) **Facilities** 🎾 ♨9 ♨ Fishing Snooker Sauna 🏌 Putt green Hot tub Natural health spa, private motor boat & foreshore 🎣 ch fac Xmas **Conf** Thtr 60 Class 40 Board 30 Del from £100 **Services** Lift **Parking** 100 **Notes LB** ⊛ in restaurant Closed 3 wks Jan Civ Wed 65

★★★ 77% ⊛ **HOTEL**

Trelawne
TR11 5HS
☎ 01326 250226 📠 01326 250909
e-mail: info@trelawnehotel.co.uk
dir: *A39 to Falmouth, right at Hillhead rdbt signed Maenporth. Past beach, up hill and hotel on left*

This hotel is surrounded by attractive lawns and gardens, and enjoys superb coastal views. An informal atmosphere prevails, and many guests return year after year. Bedrooms, many with sea views, are of

continued

varying sizes, but all are well equipped. Dinner features quality local produce used in imaginative dishes.

Rooms 14 en suite (2 fmly) (4 GF) S £70-£97; D £140-£194 (incl. bkfst & dinner) **Parking** 20 **Notes LB** ⊛ in restaurant Closed 23 Dec-12 Feb

See advert on opposite page

MEVAGISSEY   MAP 02 SX04

★★ 72% **HOTEL**

Tremarne
Polkirt PL26 6UL
☎ 01726 842213 📠 01726 843420
e-mail: info@tremarne-hotel.co.uk
web: www.tremarne-hotel.co.uk
dir: *from A390 at St Austell take B3273 to Mevagissey. Follow Portmellon signs through Mevagissey, at top of Polkirt Hill bear right*

A relaxing, family-run hotel ideal for those exploring this beautiful area or visiting the nearby Eden Project. Many of the bedrooms have views across the countryside to the sea beyond. The friendly team of staff makes every effort to ensure a comfortable and enjoyable stay. Public areas include a bar, a well-appointed restaurant and a comfortable lounge.

Rooms 13 en suite (2 fmly) ⊛ in all bedrooms S £40-£55; D £60-£120 (incl. bkfst) **Facilities** 🎾 **Parking** 13 **Notes LB** ⊛ No children 5yrs ⊛ in restaurant Closed Dec-Jan

MOUSEHOLE   MAP 02 SW42

★★ 79% ⊛ **HOTEL**

Old Coastguard Hotel
The Parade TR19 6PR
☎ 01736 731222 📠 01736 731720
e-mail: bookings@oldcoastguardhotel.co.uk
web: www.oldcoastguardhotel.co.uk
dir: *A30 to Penzance, coast road to Newlyn then Mousehole. 1st building on left on entering village*

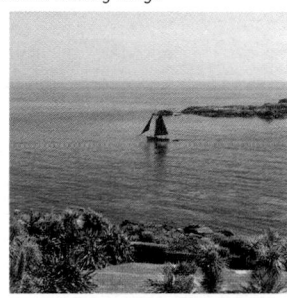

This truly is a wonderful place to unwind with superb views across Mounts Bay providing a stunning backdrop. The atmosphere is convivial and relaxing thanks to friendly staff who are keen to help. Bedrooms are bright and stylish, most have sea views and some have balconies. The impressive food features the best of the catch from Newlyn market which can be enjoyed either in the restaurant, or in summer months, alfresco on the terrace.

Rooms 14 en suite 7 annexe en suite (2 fmly) S £40-£100; D £80-£160 (incl. bkfst) **Facilities** FTV Wi-fi available Sub-tropical garden Xmas **Parking** 12 **Notes LB** ⊛ ⊛ in restaurant

◎◎ RESTAURANT WITH ROOMS

The Cornish Range Restaurant with Rooms

6 Chapel St TR19 6BD

☎ 01736 731488

e-mail: info@cornishrange.co.uk

dir: Follow coast road through Newlyn into Mousehole. Along harbour past Ship Inn, turn sharp right, then left, located on right

This charming restaurant with rooms is a memorable place to eat and stay. Comfortable, stylish rooms, with delightful Cornish handmade furnishings, and attentive, friendly service create a relaxing environment. Interesting and accurate cuisine relies heavily on local freshly landed fish and shellfish, as well as local meat and poultry and the freshest fruit and vegetables.

Rooms 3 en suite **Notes** Closed 26 Dec & 1 Jan, Mon & Tue in winter

---

MULLION   MAP 02 SW61

★★★ 74% HOTEL

Mullion Cove Hotel

TR12 7EP

☎ 01326 240328 ▤ 01326 240998

e-mail: mullion.cove@btinternet.com

web: www.mullioncove.com

dir: from Helston follow signs to The Lizard, right at Mullion Holiday Park. Through village, left for Cove. Then right and hotel on top of hill

Built at the turn of the last century and set high above the working harbour of Mullion, this hotel has spectacular views of the rugged coastline; seaward facing rooms are always popular. The stylish restaurant offers some carefully prepared dishes using local produce; an alternative option is to eat less formally in the bar. After dinner guests might like to relax in one of the elegant lounges.

Rooms 30 en suite (7 fmly) (3 GF) ⊗ in all bedrooms S £85.50-£221.50; D £104-£300 (incl. bkfst & dinner) **Facilities** ᳤ Sauna Solarium Beauty treatments Xmas **Parking** 60 **Notes LB** ⊗ in restaurant

★★★ 71% HOTEL

Polurrian

TR12 7EN

☎ 01326 240421 ▤ 01326 240083

e-mail: relax@polurrianhotel.com

web: www.polurrianhotel.com

dir: A30 onto A3076 to Truro. Follow signs for Helston on A39 then A394 to The Lizard and Mullion

This long-established hotel (now under new ownership) is set in 12 acres of landscaped gardens, 300 feet above the sea. The spectacular views over Polurrian Cove will remain long in the memory, along with the wonderful sunsets. Public areas are spacious and comfortable, and the bedrooms are individually styled. There is a well-equipped leisure centre.

Rooms 39 en suite (22 fmly) (8 GF) ⊗ in 20 bedrooms S £53-£127.50; D £106-£170 (incl. bkfst & dinner) **Facilities** STV ᳤ ᳤ ᳤ Squash Snooker Sauna Solarium Gym Putt green Jacuzzi ch fac Xmas **Conf** Thtr 100 Class 60 Board 30 Del from £85 **Parking** 80 **Notes LB** ⊗ in restaurant Civ Wed 100

England

NEWQUAY

MAP 02 SW86

★★★★ 77% ⊛ **HOTEL**

Headland

Fistral Beach TR7 1EW

☎ 01637 872211 🖹 01637 872212

e-mail: office@headlandhotel.co.uk

web: www.headlandhotel.co.uk

dir: *off A30 onto A392 at Indian Queens, approaching Newquay follow signs for Fistral Beach, hotel adjacent*

This Victorian hotel enjoys a stunning location overlooking the sea on three sides - views can be enjoyed from most of the windows. Bedrooms are comfortable and spacious. Grand public areas, with impressive floral displays, include various lounges and in addition to the formal dining room, Sands Brasserie offers a relaxed alternative. A unique collection of self-catering cottages is available, using hotel facilities, including bars and eating options.

Rooms 104 en suite (40 fmly) S £80-£130; D £90-£320 (incl. bkfst) **Facilities Spa** STV 🔽 🔽 ⚓ 9 🟤 Snooker Sauna 🟤 Putt green Children's outdoor play area, Harry Potter playroom, Surf school 🎵 ch fac Xmas **Conf** Thtr 250 Class 120 Board 40 Del from £135 **Services** Lift **Parking** 400 **Notes LB** ⊘ in restaurant Closed 24-27 Dec Civ Wed 200

★★★ 77% **HOTEL**

Best Western Hotel Bristol

Narrowcliff TR7 2PQ

☎ 01637 875181 🖹 01637 879347

e-mail: info@hotelbristol.co.uk

web: www.hotelbristol.co.uk

dir: *off A30 onto A392, then onto A3058. Hotel 2.5m on left*

This hotel is conveniently situated and many of the bedrooms enjoy fine sea views. Staff are friendly and provide a professional and attentive service. There is a range of comfortable lounges, ideal for

continued

relaxing prior to eating in the elegant dining room. There are also leisure and conference facilities.

Rooms 74 en suite (23 fmly) ⊘ in 41 bedrooms S £75-£120; D £120-£170 (incl. bkfst) **Facilities** STV 🔽 Snooker Sauna Solarium Wi-fi available Table tennis ch fac Xmas **Conf** Thtr 200 Class 80 Board 20 Del from £122 **Services** Lift **Parking** 105 **Notes LB** ⊘ in restaurant

See advert on opposite page

★★★ 75% **HOTEL**

Esplanade Hotel

Esplanade Rd, Pentire TR7 1PS

☎ 01637 873333 🖹 01637 851413

e-mail: info@newquay-hotels.co.uk

web: www.newquay-hotels.co.uk

dir: *from A30 take A392 at Indian Queens towards Newquay, follow to rdbt and take left to Pentire, then right fork to beach*

Overlooking the rolling breakers at Fistral Beach, this family-owned hotel offers a friendly welcome. There is a choice of bedroom sizes; all have modern facilities and the most popular rooms benefit from stunning sea views. There are a number of bars, a continental-style coffee shop and the more formal Ocean View Restaurant.

Rooms 92 en suite (44 fmly) ⊘ in 5 bedrooms **Facilities Spa** STV 🔽 🔽 Sauna Solarium Jacuzzi Table tennis 🎵 ch fac **Conf** Thtr 300 Class 180 Board 150 **Services** Lift **Parking** 40 **Notes LB** ⊘ in restaurant

★★★ 75% **HOTEL**

Trebarwith

Trebarwith Crescent TR7 1BZ

☎ 01637 872288 🖹 01637 875431

e-mail: trebahotel@aol.com

web: www.trebarwith-hotel.co.uk

dir: *from A3058 to Mount Wise Rd. 3rd right down Marcus Hill, across East St into Trebarwith Cres. Hotel at end*

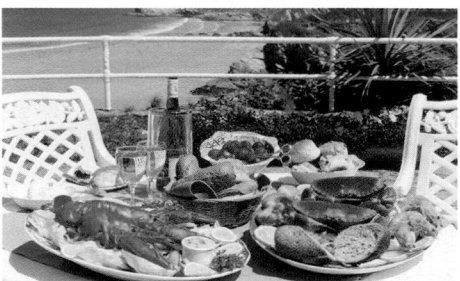

With breathtaking views of the rugged coastline and a path leading to the beach, this friendly, family-run hotel is set in its own grounds close to the town centre. The public rooms include a lounge, ballroom, restaurant and cinema. The comfortable bedrooms include four-poster and family rooms, and many benefit from the sea views.

Rooms 41 en suite (8 fmly) (1 GF) S £35-£72; D £70-£144 (incl. bkfst & dinner) **Facilities Spa** FTV 🔽 Fishing Snooker Sauna Solarium Jacuzzi Video theatre Games room Surf lessons 🎵 ch fac **Conf** Thtr 45 **Parking** 41 **Notes LB** 🚫 ⊘ in restaurant Closed Nov-5 Apr

See advert on opposite page

★★★ 73% **HOTEL**

Porth Veor Manor

Porth Way, Porth TR7 3LW
☎ 01637 873274 & 860280 📠 01637 879572
e-mail: enquiries@porthveormanor.com
web: www.porthveormanor.com

dir: From A3058 turn right at main rdbt onto B3276, hotel 0.5m on left

Overlooking Porth Beach, this hotel has undergone extensive renovation. A relaxed and friendly atmosphere is maintained at this pleasant, professionally run hotel, which is set is a quiet area. Bedrooms are pleasantly spacious, many with views over the beach. A daily-changing set price menu is served in the dining room.

Rooms 19 en suite (6 fmly) ⊗ in all bedrooms S £35-£59; D £70-£118 (incl. bkfst) **Facilities** STV FTV 🏌 Putt green **Parking** 26 **Notes LB** ⊗ ⊗ in restaurant Closed Nov-Mar

★★★ 72% **HOTEL**

Barrowfield

Hilgrove Rd TR7 2QY
☎ 01637 878878 📠 01637 879490
e-mail: booking@barrowfield.prestel.co.uk
web: www.cranstar.co.uk

dir: A3058 to Newquay towards Quintrell Downs. Right at rdbt into town, left at Texaco rdbt

Offering a pleasant range of facilities and spacious public rooms, this popular hotel is ideally situated just 200 yards from the seafront, and offers friendly and attentive service. Bedrooms, some with sea views and balconies, are well appointed and comfortable. Public areas include an elegant restaurant, spacious foyer lounge, a coffee shop and an intimate piano bar.

Rooms 81 en suite (18 fmly) ⊗ in 12 bedrooms S £35-£76; D £70-£152 (incl. bkfst & dinner) **Facilities** Spa STV 🎾 🏓 Snooker Sauna Jacuzzi Pool room, Snooker room 🎵 Xmas **Conf** Thtr 250 Class 150 Board 90 **Services** Lift **Parking** 37 **Notes LB** ⊗ in restaurant Civ Wed 60

★★★ 70% **HOTEL**

Hotel Victoria

East St TR7 1DB
☎ 01637 872255 📠 01637 859295
e-mail: bookings@hotel-victoria.co.uk

Standing on the cliffs, overlooking Newquay Bay, this hotel is situated at the centre of this vibrant town. The spacious lounges and bar areas all benefit from glorious views. Varied menus, using the best of local produce, are offered in the restaurant. Bedrooms vary from spacious

continued on page 122

England

NEWQUAY *continued*

superior rooms and suites to standard inland-facing rooms. Berties pub, a nightclub and indoor leisure facilities are available.

Rooms 70 en suite (26 fmly) (18 GF) ⊘ in all bedrooms S fr £65; D £95 (incl. bkfst) **Facilities Spa** STV ⊋ supervised Snooker Sauna Solarium Gym Jacuzzi Xmas **Conf** BC **Services** Lift air con **Parking** 50 **Notes** ⊗ ⊘ in restaurant Civ Wed

★★★ 68% **HOTEL**

Hotel California

Pentire Crescent TR7 1PU
☎ 01637 879292 & 872798 🗎 01637 875611
e-mail: info@hotel-california.co.uk
web: www.hotel-california.co.uk

dir: A392 to Newquay, follow signs for Pentire Hotels & Guest Houses

This hotel is tucked away in a delightful location, close to Fistral Beach and adjacent to the River Gannel. Many rooms have views across the river towards the sea, and some have balconies. There is an impressive range of leisure facilities, including indoor and outdoor pools, and ten-pin bowling. Cuisine is enjoyable and menus offer a range of interesting dishes.

Rooms 70 en suite (27 fmly) (13 GF) S £39.50-£65; D £80-£136 (incl. bkfst) **Facilities Spa** ⊋ ⊋ Squash Snooker Sauna Solarium 10 pin bowling alley ♫ Xmas **Conf** Thtr 100 Class 100 Board 30 Del from £45 **Services** Lift **Parking** 66 **Notes LB** ⊘ in restaurant Civ Wed 150

★★★ 68% **HOTEL**

Hotel Riviera

Lusty Glaze Rd TR7 3AA
☎ 01637 874251 🗎 01637 850823
e-mail: hotelriviera@btconnect.com

dir: approaching Newquay from Porth right at The Barrowfields. Hotel on right

This popular cliff-top hotel enjoys panoramic views across the gardens to the sea beyond. Bedrooms vary in size and style, and many have sea views. Comfortable lounges are provided for rest and relaxation; the more energetic may wish to use the squash court or heated outdoor pool. There is also a range of conference and function facilities.

Rooms 48 en suite (6 fmly) S £50-£55; D £100-£110 (incl. bkfst) **Facilities** ⊋ Squash Sauna ♫ Xmas **Conf** Thtr 200 Class 150 Board 50 Del from £78.95 **Services** Lift **Parking** 80 **Notes** ⊗ ⊘ in restaurant Civ Wed 150

See advert on opposite page

★★★ 66% **HOTEL**

Kilbirnie

Narrowcliff TR7 2RS
☎ 01637 875155 🗎 01637 850769
e-mail: info@kilbirniehotel.co.uk
web: www.kilbirniehotel.co.uk

dir: on A392

With delightful views over the Barrowfields and the sea, this privately run hotel offers an impressive range of facilities. The reception rooms are spacious and comfortable, and during summer months feature a programme of entertainment. Bedrooms vary in size and style, and some enjoy fine sea views.

Rooms 66 en suite (3 fmly) (8 GF) S £30-£50; D £60-£100 (incl. bkfst) **Facilities** ⊋ ⊋ Snooker Sauna Solarium Gym Jacuzzi Wi-fi available Fitness room, hair salon Xmas **Conf** BC Thtr 100 Class 50 Board 50 **Services** Lift air con **Parking** 48 **Notes LB** ⊗ ⊘ in restaurant

See advert on opposite page

★★ 76% **HOTEL**

Whipsiderry

Trevelgue Rd, Porth TR7 3LY
☎ 01637 874777 & 876066 🗎 01637 874777
e-mail: info@whipsiderry.co.uk

dir: right onto Padstow road (B3276) out of Newquay, in 0.5m right at Trevelgue Rd

Quietly located, overlooking Porth Beach, this friendly hotel offers bedrooms in a variety of sizes and styles, many with superb views. A daily-changing menu offers interesting and well-cooked dishes with the emphasis on fresh, local produce. An outdoor pool is available, and at dusk guests may be able to watch badgers in the attractive grounds.

Rooms 20 rms (19 en suite) (5 fmly) (3 GF) ⊘ in 15 bedrooms S £53-£65; D £106-£130 (incl. bkfst & dinner) **Facilities** ⊋ Sauna American Pool room ♫ ch fac Xmas **Parking** 30 **Notes LB** ⊘ in restaurant Closed Nov-Etr (ex Xmas)

★★ 65% **HOTEL**

Eliot

Edgcumbe Av TR7 2NH
☎ 01637 878177 🗎 01637 852053
e-mail: eliot.newquay@alfatravel.co.uk
web: www.alfatravel.co.uk

Leisureplex

dir: A30 onto A392 towards Quintrell Downs. Right at rdbt onto A3058. 4m to Newquay, left at amusements onto Edgcumbe Av. Hotel on left

Located in a quiet residential area just a short walk from the beaches and the varied attractions of the town, this long-established hotel offers comfortable accommodation. Entertainment is provided most nights throughout the season and guests can relax in the spacious public areas.

Rooms 76 en suite (10 fmly) ⊘ in all bedrooms S £24-£29; D £48-£58 (incl. bkfst) **Facilities** ⊋ Sauna Pool table, Table tennis ♫ Xmas **Services** Lift **Parking** 20 **Notes LB** ⊗ ⊘ in restaurant Closed Dec-Jan RS Nov & Feb-Mar

[U]

Sandy Lodge

6-12 Hilgrove Rd TR7 2QY

☎ 01637 872851 📠 01637 872851

e-mail: info@sandylodgehotel.co.uk

At the time of going to press, the star classification for this hotel was not confirmed. Please refer to the AA internet site www.theAA.com for current information.

Rooms 81 en suite (8 fmly) (12 GF) S £26-£39; D £52-£78 (incl. bkfst) **Facilities** ⊠ ⊰ Sauna Gym Jacuzzi 🎜 Xmas **Conf** Thtr 100 Class 50 Board 30 Del from £47 **Services** Lift **Notes** ⊗ ⊘ in restaurant Closed 5 Jan-23 Jan RS Jan

---

PADSTOW   MAP 02 SW97

See also Constantine Bay

★★★ 77% ⊛ **HOTEL**

The Metropole

Station Rd PL28 8DB

☎ 01841 532486 📠 01841 532867

e-mail: info@the-metropole.co.uk

web: www.the-metropole.co.uk

dir: M5/A30 pass Launceston, turn off & follow signs for Wadebridge & N Cornwall. Take A39 & follow signs for Padstow

This long-established hotel first opened its doors to guests back in 1904 and there is still an air of the sophistication and elegance of a

continued on page 124

PADSTOW *continued*

bygone age. Bedrooms are soundly appointed and well-equipped and dining options include the informal Met Café Bar and the main restaurant, with enjoyable cuisine and wonderful views over the Camel estuary.

The Metropole

Rooms 50 en suite (3 fmly) (2 GF) ⊗ in 10 bedrooms S £84-£100; D £118-£150 (incl. bkfst) **Facilities** FTV ⚲ Wi-fi in bedrooms Swimming pool open Jul & Aug only Xmas **Services** Lift **Parking** 36 **Notes LB** ⊗ in restaurant

★★★ 70% HOTEL

Old Custom House Inn

South Quay PL28 8BL

☎ 01841 532359 📄 01841 533372

e-mail: oldcustomhouse@smallandfriendly.co.uk

dir: A359 from Wadebridge, take 2nd right. In Padstow follow road round bend to bottom of hill. Hotel on left

Situated by the harbour, this charming inn continues to be a popular choice for locals and visitors alike. The lively bar serves real ales and good bar meals. Pescadou's restaurant provides a stylish and convivial venue for imaginative dishes that place the emphasis on locally caught fish. A wide selection of beauty treatments is available in the hotel's Lavender Room.

Rooms 24 en suite (8 fmly) ⊗ in all bedrooms **Facilities** STV **Notes LB** ⊛ ⊗ in restaurant

★★ 84% ⊛ SMALL HOTEL

St Petroc's Hotel and Bisto

4 New St PL28 8EA

☎ 01841 532700 📄 01841 532942

e-mail: reservations@rickstein.com

dir: A39 onto A389, follow signs to Padstow town centre. Follow one-way system

One of the oldest buildings in town, this charming establishment is just up the hill from the picturesque harbour. Style, comfort and individuality are all great strengths here, particularly so in the impressively equipped bedrooms. Breakfast, lunch and dinner all reflect a serious approach to cuisine, and the popular restaurant has a relaxed bistro style. Comfortable lounges, a reading room and lovely gardens complete the picture.

Rooms 10 en suite (3 fmly) D £120-£190 (incl. bkfst) **Facilities** STV Cookery school **Parking** 10 **Notes LB** ⊗ in restaurant Closed 1 May & 24-26 Dec

★★ 72% HOTEL

The Old Ship Hotel

Mill Square PL28 8AE

☎ 01841 532357 📄 01841 533211

e-mail: stay@oldshiphotel-padstow.co.uk

web: www.oldshiphotel-padstow.co.uk

dir: from M5 take A30 to Bodmin then A389 to Padstow, follow brown tourist signs to car park

This attractive inn is situated in the heart of the old town's quaint and winding streets, just a short walk from the harbour. A warm welcome is assured, accommodation is pleasant and comfortable, and public areas offer plenty of character. Freshly caught fish features on both the bar and restaurant menus. On site parking is a bonus.

Rooms 14 en suite (4 fmly) ⊗ in all bedrooms S £35-£49; D £70-£98 (incl. bkfst) **Facilities** STV Wi-fi in bedrooms ♫ Xmas **Parking** 20 **Notes LB** ⊗ in restaurant

◉◉◉ RESTAURANT WITH ROOMS

St Ervan Manor

The Old Rectory, St Ervan PL27 7TA

☎ 01841 540255

e-mail: info@stervanmanor.co.uk

dir: 4m S of Padstow. A39 onto B3274 for Padstow, 2.5m left & signs to St Ervan Manor

The proprietors of this former Victorian rectory are at the cutting edge for providing good food and relaxed accommodation. They provide a pleasant Cornish welcome, a tranquil environment and professional service. Cuisine is very much to the fore, heavily reliant on fresh and local produce; there's a choice of tasting menus and an impressive wine selection too. The Garden Suite cottage has a bedroom, bathroom and a lounge.

Rooms 5 rms (4 en suite) 1 annexe en suite ⊗ in all bedrooms S £100-£185; D £140-£245 **Parking** 16 **Notes** ⊛ No children 14yrs ⊗ in restaurant Closed 19 Dec-19 Jan

◉◉◉◉ 𝗨

The Seafood Restaurant

Riverside PL28 8BY

☎ 01841 532700 📄 01841 532942

e-mail: reservations@rickstein.com

dir: A38 towards Newquay, then A389 towards Padstow. After 3m, right at T-junct, follow signs for Padstow town centre. Restaurant on left

At the time of going to press Rick Stein's famous establishment on the quayside in Padstow had not received confirmation of its AA classification. Please refer to the AA internet site www.theAA.com for current information.

Rooms 14 en suite 6 annexe en suite (6 fmly) (3 GF) ⊗ in all bedrooms D £120-£250 **Facilities** STV **Parking** 12 **Notes LB** No children 3yrs RS May & Dec

PENZANCE

MAP 02 SW43

★★★ 82% ◉◉ **HOTEL**

Hotel Penzance

Britons Hill TR18 3AE

☎ 01736 363117 📠 01736 350970

e-mail: enquiries@hotelpenzance.com

web: www.hotelpenzance.com

dir: from A30 pass heliport on right, left at next rdbt for town centre. 3rd right and hotel on right

This Edwardian house has been tastefully redesigned, particularly in the contemporary Bay Restaurant. The focus on style is not only limited to the decor, but is also apparent in the award-winning cuisine that is based upon fresh Cornish produce. Bedrooms have been appointed to modern standards and are particularly well equipped; many have views across Mounts Bay.

Rooms 24 en suite (2 GF) ⊗ in all bedrooms S £55-£74; D £100-£132 (incl. bkfst) **Facilities** STV ⊱ Wi-fi available Xmas **Conf** Thtr 80 Class 50 Board 25 Del from £98 **Parking** 14 **Notes LB** ⊗ in restaurant RS Nov-Apr

★★★ 71% **HOTEL**

Queen's

The Promenade TR18 4HG

☎ 01736 362371 📠 01736 350033

e-mail: enquiries@queens-hotel.com

web: www.queens-hotel.com

dir: A30 to Penzance, follow signs for seafront pass harbour and into promenade, hotel 0.5m on right

With views across Mounts Bay towards Newlyn, this impressive Victorian hotel has a long and distinguished history. Comfortable public areas are filled with interesting pictures and artefacts, and in the dining room guests can choose from the daily-changing menu. Bedrooms, many with sea views, are of varying style and size.

Rooms 70 en suite (10 fmly) S fr £62; D fr £62 (incl. bkfst)
Facilities STV Yoga weekends Xmas **Conf** Thtr 200 Class 100 Board 80
Services Lift **Parking** 50 **Notes LB** ⊗ in restaurant Civ Wed 250

See advert on this page

★★ 74% **HOTEL**

Tarbert

11-12 Clarence St TR18 2NU

☎ 01736 363758 & 331336 📠 01736 331336

e-mail: reception@anicelittlehotel.com

dir: take Land's End turn at town approach. At 3rd rdbt, turn left signed to hospital, over mini rdbt. After 100yds right into Clarence St

Located close to the town centre, this hotel has undergone complete refurbishment. The restaurant is fresh, light and airy. There is a bar/lounge area in which to relax or enjoy an aperitif. A small sun terrace is available at the rear of the hotel.

Rooms 12 en suite (4 fmly) ⊗ in all bedrooms **Facilities** STV **Parking** 4
Notes LB ⊗ in restaurant

See advert on this page

England

POLPERRO
MAP 02 SX25

★★★ 83% ◎◎◎ COUNTRY HOUSE HOTEL

Talland Bay
PL13 2JB
☎ 01503 272667 ▤ 01503 272940
e-mail: reception@tallandbayhotel.co.uk
web: www.tallandbayhotel.co.uk
dir: signed from x-rds on A387 Looe to Polperro road

This hotel has the benefit of a wonderful location, being sited in its own extensive gardens that run down almost to the cliff's edge. The atmosphere is warm and friendly throughout, and some of the bedrooms, available in number of styles, have sea views and balconies. Accomplished cooking remains a key feature here; the talented kitchen team make excellent use of the abundance of quality local produce.

Rooms 20 en suite 3 annexe en suite (4 fmly) (6 GF) ⊘ in all bedrooms S £85-£215; D £95-£225 (incl. bkfst) **Facilities** ⚡ ⚓ Putt green Xmas **Parking** 23 **Notes LB** ⊘ in restaurant

POLZEATH
MAP 02 SW97

★★ 🅰

Seascape
Dunder Hill PL27 6SX
☎ 01208 863638 & 07968 010644 ▤ 01208 862940
e-mail: information@seascapehotel.co.uk
web: www.seascapehotel.co.uk
dir: M5 from Exeter/A30 towards Launceston. Onto A395 & A39. From A39 take B3314 to Polzeath & follow signs to hotel

Rooms 12 en suite 3 annexe en suite (9 GF) ⊘ in 2 bedrooms S £48-£95; D £76-£140 (incl. bkfst) **Conf** BC **Parking** 20 **Notes** No children 12yrs ⊘ in restaurant Closed Nov-Feb

PORT GAVERNE
MAP 02 SX08

★★ 74% HOTEL

Port Gaverne
PL29 3SQ
☎ 01208 880244 ▤ 01208 880151
dir: signed from B3314

In a quiet seaside port half a mile from the old fishing village of Port Isaac, this hotel has a romantic feel, retaining its flagged floors, beamed ceilings and steep stairways. Bedrooms are available in a range of sizes. Local produce features on the hotel's restaurant menus; bar meals always have a popular following here.

Rooms 14 en suite (4 fmly) S £50-£60; D £80-£100 (incl. bkfst) **Parking** 30 **Notes LB** ⊘ in restaurant

PORTSCATHO
MAP 02 SW83

INSPECTORS' CHOICE

★★★ ◎◎◎ HOTEL

Driftwood
Rosevine TR2 5EW
☎ 01872 580644 ▤ 01872 580801
e-mail: info@driftwoodhotel.co.uk
dir: A390 towards St Mawes. On A3078 turn left to Rosevine at Trewithian

Poised on the cliffside with panoramic views, this contemporary hotel has a peaceful and secluded location. A warm welcome is guaranteed here, where professional standards of service are provided in an effortless and relaxed manner. Cuisine is a feature of any stay with quality local produce used in a sympathetic and highly skilled manner. The extremely comfortable and elegant bedrooms are decorated in soft shades reminiscent of the seashore. The style is uncluttered. There is a sheltered terraced garden that has a large deck with steamer chairs for sunbathing.

Rooms 14 en suite 1 annexe en suite (3 fmly) (1 GF) ⊘ in all bedrooms S £127.50-£157.50; D £170-£210 (incl. bkfst) **Facilities** Wi-fi in bedrooms Private Beach **Parking** 30 **Notes** ⊗ ⊘ in restaurant Closed 11 Dec-8 Feb

★★★ 80% ◎ COUNTRY HOUSE HOTEL

Rosevine
TR2 5EW
☎ 01872 580206 ▤ 01872 580230
e-mail: info@rosevinehotels.co.uk
web: www.rosevine.co.uk
dir: from St Austell take A390 for Truro. Left onto B3287 to Tregony. Then A3078 through Ruan High Lanes. Hotel 3rd left

Located on the coast, this family run hotel benefits from magnificent sea views and has beautifully tended gardens. The hotel also boasts its own beach at the head of the Roseland peninsula. The spacious bedrooms feature traditional decor and welcoming extras such as fresh fruit and mineral water; most have sea views and some have balconies. Public rooms include a cosy bar, spacious lounges and a large restaurant featuring fresh seafood dishes.

Rooms 11 en suite 6 annexe en suite (7 fmly) (3 GF) S £86-£171; D £172-£276 (incl. bkfst) **Facilities** ⚡ Jacuzzi Wi-fi available Outdoor table tennis & play area ♫ ch fac **Parking** 20 **Notes LB** ⊘ in restaurant Closed 28 Dec-4 Feb

PORTWRINKLE
See also Looe

MAP 03 SX35

★★★ 74% ⊛ HOTEL

Whitsand Bay Hotel & Golf Club
PL11 3BU

☎ 01503 230276 📠 01503 230329

e-mail: whitsandbayhotel@btconnect.com

web: www.whitsandbayhotel.co.uk

dir: A38 from Exeter over River Tamar, left at Trerulefoot rdbt
onto A374 to Crafthole/Portwrinkle. Follow hotel signs

An imposing Victorian stone building with oak panelling, stained-glass
windows and a sweeping staircase. Bedrooms include family rooms
and a suite with a balcony, many have superb sea views. Facilities
include an 18-hole cliff-top golf course and indoor swimming pool.
The fixed-price menu offers an interesting selection of dishes.

Rooms 32 en suite (7 fmly) ⊗ in 10 bedrooms S £95; D £150-£160
(incl. bkfst & dinner) **Facilities** 🏹 ♨ 18 Sauna Solarium Gym Putt green
Games room, Lounge with wide screen TV ♫ Xmas **Conf** BC **Parking** 60
Notes LB ⊗ in restaurant

REDRUTH

MAP 02 SW64

★★★ 77% HOTEL

Penventon Park
TR15 1TE

☎ 01209 203000 📠 01209 203001

e-mail: hello@penventon.com

web: www.penventon.com

dir: off A30 at Redruth. Follow signs for Redruth West, hotel 1m S

Set in attractive parkland, this Georgian mansion is ideal for either the
business or leisure guest. Bedrooms include 20 Garden Suites. Cuisine
offers a wide choice and specialises in British, Cornish, Italian and

continued

French dishes. Leisure facilities include a fitness suite and health spa
as well as function rooms and bars.

Rooms 68 en suite (3 fmly) (25 GF) ⊗ in 6 bedrooms S £35-£100;
D £64-£138 (incl. bkfst) **Facilities Spa** FTV 🏹 supervised Sauna
Solarium Gym Jacuzzi Leisure spa Masseuse Steam bath Pool table,
beautician ♫ Xmas **Conf** Thtr 200 Class 100 Board 60 Del from £86
Services Lift **Parking** 100 **Notes LB** ⊗ in restaurant Civ Wed 150

★★ 74% COUNTRY HOUSE HOTEL

Aviary Court
Mary's Well, Illogan TR16 4QZ

☎ 01209 842256 📠 01209 843744

e-mail: info@aviarycourthotel.co.uk

web: www.aviarycourthotel.co.uk

dir: off A30 at A3047 Camborne, Pool and Portreath sign. Follow
Portreath & Illogan signs for 2m to Alexandra Rd

This tranquil hotel is set in well-tended gardens on the edge of Illogan
Woods. There is a tennis court for guest use (free of charge during the
day). Bedrooms are well equipped and include many thoughtful
extras. Dinner features home cooked dishes.

Rooms 6 en suite (1 fmly) **Facilities** ♨ **Parking** 25 **Notes** ⊗
No children 3yrs ⊗ in restaurant

★★ 67% HOTEL

Crossroads Lodge
Scorrier TR16 5BP

THE INDEPENDENTS

☎ 01209 820551 📠 01209 820392

e-mail: crossroads@hotelstruro.com

web: www.hotelstruro.com/crossroads

dir: turn off A30 onto A3047 towards Scorrier

Situated on an historic stanary site and conveniently located just off
the A30, Crossroads Lodge has a smart appearance with attractive
flower baskets. Bedrooms are soundly furnished and include executive
and family rooms. Public areas include an attractive dining room, a
quiet lounge and a lively bar. Conference, banqueting and business
facilities are also available.

Rooms 36 en suite (2 fmly) (8 GF) ⊗ in 8 bedrooms **Facilities** STV
Conf BC Thtr 150 Class 80 Board 60 **Services** Lift **Parking** 140
Notes LB ⊗ in restaurant

RUAN HIGH LANES

MAP 02 SW93

★★ 79% COUNTRY HOUSE HOTEL

Hundred House
TR2 5JR

☎ 01872 501336 📠 01872 501151

e-mail: enquiries@hundredhousehotel.co.uk

dir: from B3287 at Tregony, left onto A3078 to St Mawes, hotel
4m on right

This Edwardian house is set in attractive gardens and has good access
to the Roseland Peninsula, which makes it an ideal base for a relaxing
break or for touring the area. Bedrooms are well equipped and the
lounge and bar offer a good level of comfort. Service is attentive and
the staff are very much focussed on their guests' needs. Both dinner
and breakfast offer freshly cooked and appetising dishes.

Rooms 10 en suite (1 GF) ⊗ in all bedrooms S £66.15-£90;
D £132.30-£180 (incl. dinner) **Facilities** ⚘ Xmas **Parking** 15 **Notes LB**
⊗ No children 14yrs ⊗ in restaurant

England

ST AGNES MAP 02 SW75

★★★ 77% **COUNTRY HOUSE HOTEL**

Rose in Vale Country House

Mithian TR5 0QD

☎ 01872 552202 & 0845 1235527 📠 01872 552700

e-mail: reception@roseinvalehotel.co.uk

web: www.roseinvalehotel.co.uk

dir: A30 through Cornwall, right onto B3277 signed St Agnes. In 500yds follow hotel signs

Peacefully located in a wooded valley this Georgian manor house has a wonderfully relaxed atmosphere and abundant charm and where guests are assured of a warm welcome. Accommodation varies in size and style; several rooms are situated on the ground floor. An imaginative fixed-price menu featuring local produce is served in the spacious restaurant.

Rooms 18 en suite (3 fmly) (3 GF) ⊗ in all bedrooms S £68-£135; D £120-£180 (incl. bkfst) **Facilities** ₹ Sauna ⅍ games room, table tennis, garden badminton Xmas **Conf** Thtr 75 Class 50 Board 40 Del from £90 **Parking** 40 **Notes LB** ⊗ in restaurant Closed Jan Civ Wed 75

★★★ 70% **HOTEL**

Rosemundy House

Rosemundy Hill TR5 0UF

☎ 01872 552101 📠 01872 554000

e-mail: info@rosemundy.co.uk

dir: off A30 to St Agnes continue for approx 3m. On entering village take 1st right signed Rosemundy, hotel at foot of hill

This elegant Queen Anne house has been carefully restored and extended to provide comfortable bedrooms and spacious, inviting public areas. The hotel is set in well-maintained gardens complete with an outdoor pool for warmer months. There is a choice of relaxing lounges and a cosy bar.

Rooms 46 en suite (3 fmly) (9 GF) ⊗ in 10 bedrooms S £31-£63; D £62-£126 (incl. bkfst) **Facilities** ₹ ⅍ Putt green ♫ Xmas **Conf** Board 80 **Parking** 50 **Notes LB** ⊛ No children 5yrs ⊗ in restaurant

★★ 78% **COUNTRY HOUSE HOTEL**

Beacon Country House Hotel

Goonvrea Rd TR5 0NW

☎ 01872 552318 📠 01872 552318

e-mail: info@beaconhotel.co.uk

web: www.beaconhotel.co.uk

dir: from A30 take B3277 to St Agnes. At rdbt left onto Goonvrea Rd. Hotel 0.75m on right

Set in a quiet and attractive area away from the busy village, this friendly, relaxed hotel has splendid views over the countryside towards the sea. Guests are assured of a friendly welcome, and many return for another stay. Now totally upgraded the public areas and bedrooms are comfortable and well equipped; many benefit from the glorious views.

Rooms 11 en suite (1 fmly) (2 GF) ⊗ in all bedrooms S £37-£66; D £74-£92 (incl. bkfst) **Parking** 16 **Notes LB** ⊗ in restaurant

ST AUSTELL MAP 02 SX05

★★★★ 80% ® **HOTEL**

Carlyon Bay

Brend Hotels

Sea Rd, Carlyon Bay PL25 3RD

☎ 01726 812304 📠 01726 814938

e-mail: reservations@carlyonbay.com

web: www.brend-hotels.co.uk

dir: from St Austell, follow signs for Charlestown. Carlyon Bay signed on left, hotel at end of Sea Road

Originally built in the 1920s, this long-established hotel lies on the cliff top in 250 acres of grounds, which include indoor and outdoor pools and a golf course. Bedrooms are well maintained, many with marvellous views across St Austell Bay. A good choice of comfortable

continued

lounges is available, whilst facilities for families include kids' clubs and entertainment.

Rooms 87 en suite (14 fmly) ⊗ in 14 bedrooms S £75-£100; D £145-£270 **Facilities Spa** STV ⏣ ⏣ ⏣ 18 ⏣ Snooker Sauna Solarium Putt green Table tennis 9-hole approach course, Health and beauty salon ♫ ch fac Xmas **Services** Lift **Parking** 100 **Notes LB** ⊛ ⊗ in restaurant Civ Wed 100

See advert on this page

★★★ 77% HOTEL

Porth Avallen

Sea Rd, Carlyon Bay PL25 3SG
☎ 01726 812802 ▤ 01726 817097
e-mail: info@porthavallen.co.uk
web: www.porthavallen.co.uk

dir: A30 onto A391 to St Austell. Right onto A390. Left at lights, left at rdbt, right into Sea Road

This traditional hotel boasts panoramic views over the rugged Cornish coastline. It offers smartly appointed public areas and well-presented bedrooms, many with sea views. There is an oak-panelled lounge and conservatory, both are ideal for relaxation. Extensive dining options, including the stylish Apple Tree Restaurant, let guests choose from fixed-price, carte and all-day brasserie menus.

Rooms 28 en suite (3 fmly) ⊗ in all bedrooms S fr £59; D fr £108 (incl. bkfst) **Facilities** FTV Wi-fi in bedrooms Xmas **Cont** 1hr 100 Class 40 Board 40 Del from £108 **Parking** 50 **Notes LB** ⊛ ⊗ in restaurant Civ Wed 70

See advert on this page

★★★ 72% HOTEL

Cliff Head

Sea Rd, Carlyon Bay PL25 3RB
☎ 01726 812345 ▤ 01726 815511
e-mail: into@cliffheadhotel.com

dir: 2m E off A390

Set in extensive grounds and conveniently located for visiting the Eden Project, this hotel faces south and enjoys views over Carlyon Bay. A choice of lounges is provided, together with a swimming pool and solarium. Expressions restaurant offers a range of menus that feature an interesting selection of dishes.

Rooms 57 en suite (6 fmly) (11 GF) ⊗ in all bedrooms S £60-£70; D £110-£130 (incl. bkfst) **Facilities** ⏣ Sauna Xmas **Conf** Thtr 150 Class 130 Board 70 Del from £65 **Parking** 60 **Notes LB** ⊛ ⊗ in restaurant Civ Wed 120

England

ST AUSTELL *continued*

★★ 82% HOTEL

Boscundle Manor Country House
Tregrehan PL25 3RL
☎ 01726 813557 📠 01726 814997
e-mail: stay@boscundlemanor.co.uk
dir: 2m E on A390, 200yds on road signed Tregrehan

Set in beautifully maintained gardens and grounds, this handsome 18th-century stone manor house is a short distance from the Eden Project. Quality and comfort are apparent in the public areas and spacious, well-equipped bedrooms. A choice of eating options is available, with both fine dining and brasserie alternatives. Equally suitable for leisure and business guests, the hotel has both indoor and outdoor pools.

Rooms 11 en suite 3 annexe en suite (4 fmly) (4 GF) ⊘ in all bedrooms **Facilities** ⤵ ⤴ ⤹ ch fac **Conf** Thtr 40 Class 20 Board 20 **Parking** 15 **Notes** ⊘ in restaurant Closed 2 Jan-13 Feb Civ Wed 60

★★ 76% HOTEL

Pier House
Harbour Front, Charlestown PL25 3NJ
☎ 01726 67955 📠 01726 69246
e-mail: pierhouse@btconnect.com
dir: follow A390 to St Austell, at Mt Charles rdbt left down Charlestown Rd

This genuinely friendly hotel boasts a wonderful harbour location. The unspoilt working port has been the setting for many film and television productions. Most bedrooms have sea views, and the hotel's convivial Harbourside Inn is popular with locals and tourists alike. Locally caught fish features on the varied and interesting restaurant menu.

Rooms 28 en suite (4 fmly) (2 GF) ⊘ in all bedrooms S £55-£80; D £90-£120 (incl. bkfst) **Facilities** FTV **Parking** 50 **Notes LB** ⊗ ⊘ in restaurant

★★ 74% HOTEL

Victoria Inn & Lodge
Victoria, Roche PL26 8LQ
☎ 01726 890207 📠 01726 891233
e-mail: victoriainn@smallandfriendly.co.uk
dir: 6m W of Bodmin on A30. 1st left after garage, Victoria Inn approx 500yds on right

Situated midway between Bodmin and Newquay, this is a convenient choice for both the business and leisure traveller. The lodge-style

continued

bedrooms are purpose built and offer spacious, comfortable and well-equipped accommodation. A wide choice of meals is available in the convivial surroundings of the inn.

Rooms 42 en suite (11 fmly) (20 GF) ⊘ in all bedrooms S £48; D £48 **Facilities** FTV Wi-fi available ch fac Xmas **Conf** Thtr 30 Class 12 Board 14 **Parking** 100 **Notes LB** ⊗ ⊘ in restaurant

★★ 74% HOTEL

White Hart
Church St PL25 4AT
☎ 01726 72100 📠 01726 74705
e-mail: whitehart@smallandfriendly.co.uk

Situated in the town centre, this 18th-century, stone-built inn offers bedrooms with high standards of comfort and public areas are stylish and contemporary. The light and airy restaurant is the venue for a modern menu that makes good use of local produce.

Rooms 17 en suite (2 fmly) ⊘ in all bedrooms S fr £50; D fr £80 (incl. bkfst) **Facilities** Wi-fi in bedrooms 🎵 Xmas **Conf** Thtr 50 Board 20 **Parking** 13 **Notes LB** ⊗ ⊘ in restaurant

BUDGET HOTEL

Travelodge St Austell
Trevanion Rd PL25 5DR
☎ 08700 850950
web: www.travelodge.co.uk

Travelodge

dir: Take A391 into St Austell. At Mont Charles rbt take the 2nd exit onto Polmear rd A390. At next rbt take 1st exit onto Pentewan rd, B3273.

Travelodge offers good quality, good value, modern accommodation. Ideal for families, the spacious en suite bedrooms include remote-control TV, tea and coffee-making facilities and comfortable beds. Meals can be taken at the nearby family restaurant. See Hotel Groups pages for further details.

Rooms 67 en suite S fr £26; D fr £26

ST IVES MAP 02 SW54

★★★ 79% SMALL HOTEL

Boskerris
Boskerris Rd, Carbis Bay TR26 2NQ
☎ 01736 795295 📠 01736 798632
e-mail: boskerris.hotel@btinternet.com

dir: From Exeter take A30 until A3074 towards St Ives. On entering Carbis Bay take 3rd on right

This hotel enjoys a peaceful location and superb views, particularly from the terraced area, which looks out over Carbis Bay and St Ives harbour. The accommodation is stylish, light and airy and some bedrooms have a sea view. Freshly prepared dishes are offered on the dinner menu and service is friendly and relaxed. There is a comfortable guest lounge, a cosy bar and attractive gardens.

Rooms 15 en suite (2 fmly) (2 GF) ⊘ in all bedrooms S £75-£142.50; D £100-£190 (incl. bkfst) **Facilities** Wi-fi in bedrooms **Parking** 20 **Notes LB** ⊗ ⊘ in restaurant

England

★★★ 78% ® HOTEL

Carbis Bay

Carbis Bay TR26 2NP

☎ 01736 795311 ▤ 01736 797677

e-mail: carbisbayhotel@talk21.com

web: www.carbisbayhotel.co.uk

dir: M5 junct 31, take A30 then A3074. After 2m through Lelant, pass garage on right. Take next right (Porthreptor Rd), continue to sea

In a peaceful location with access to its own white-sand beach, this hotel offers comfortable accommodation. Attractive public areas feature a smart bar and lounge, and a sun lounge overlooking the sea. Bedrooms, many with fine views, are well equipped. Interesting cuisine and particularly enjoyable breakfasts are offered. A small, new complex of luxury, self-catering apartments is available.

Rooms 40 en suite (16 fmly) ⊛ in 6 bedrooms **Facilities** ⚓ Fishing Snooker Private beach ♫ **Conf** Thtr 120 Class 80 Board 60 **Parking** 200 **Notes LB** ⊛ ⊘ in restaurant Closed Xmas Civ Wed 140

See advert on this page

★★★ 77% HOTEL

Porthminster

The Terrace TR26 2BN

☎ 01736 795221 ▤ 01736 797043

e-mail: reception@porthminster-hotel.co.uk

web: www.porthminster-hotel.co.uk

dir: on A3074

This friendly hotel enjoys an enviable location with spectacular views of St Ives Bay. Extensive leisure facilities, a versatile function suite and a number of lounges are available. The majority of bedrooms have been totally refurbished to a very high standard, and many rooms have spectacular sea views. Two suites are available.

Rooms 43 en suite (9 fmly) ⊛ in 26 bedrooms S £50-£125; D £100-£250 (incl. bkfst) **Facilities Spa** ⚓ ⚓ ⚓ Sauna Solarium Gym Xmas **Conf** Thtr 130 Class 20 Board 35 **Services** Lift **Parking** 43 **Notes LB** ⊘ in restaurant Closed 2-12 Jan Civ Wed 130

See advert on this page

England

ST IVES *continued*

★★★ 73% ⊛ HOTEL

Garrack

Burthallan Ln, Higher Ayr TR26 3AA
☎ 01736 796199 📄 01736 798955
e-mail: aa@garrack.com

dir: turn off A30 for St Ives. Follow yellow holiday route signs on B3311. In St Ives, hotel is signed from 1st mini rdbt

Enjoying a peaceful, elevated position with splendid views across the harbour and Porthmeor Beach, the Garrack sits in its own delightful grounds and gardens. Bedrooms are comfortable and many have sea views. Public areas include a small leisure suite, a choice of lounges and an attractive restaurant, where locally sourced ingredients are used in the dishes.

Rooms 16 en suite 2 annexe en suite (2 fmly) S £87-£110; D £144-£150 (incl. bkfst) **Facilities** 🏊 Sauna Solarium Gym Wi-fi in bedrooms Xmas **Conf** Thtr 20 Board 10 **Parking** 30 **Notes LB** ⊗ in restaurant

★★★ 71% HOTEL

Tregenna Castle Hotel

TR26 2DE
☎ 01736 795254 📄 01736 796066
e-mail: hotel@tregenna-castle.co.uk

dir: A30 from Exeter to Penzance, at Lelant (W of Hayle) take A3074 to St Ives, through Carbis Bay, entrance signed on left

Sitting at the top of town in beautiful landscaped gardens, this popular hotel boasts spectacular views of St Ives. Many leisure facilities are available, including indoor and outdoor pools, a gym and a sauna. Families are particularly welcome. Bedrooms are generally spacious. A carte menu or carvery buffet are offered in the restaurant, during the summer months, the Castle Bar and Brasserie provide lighter options.

Rooms 81 en suite (12 fmly) (16 GF) ⊗ in 49 bedrooms S £45-£65; D £90-£130 (incl. bkfst) **Facilities** STV 🏊 🛥 supervised ♨ 14 ⚲ Squash Sauna Solarium Gym ☘ Putt green Jacuzzi Health spa Steam room ch fac Xmas **Conf** Thtr 250 Class 150 Board 30 Del from £85 **Services** Lift **Parking** 200 **Notes** ⊗ ⊗ in restaurant Civ Wed 160

★★★ 70% HOTEL

Chy-an-Albany

Albany Ter TR26 2BS
☎ 01736 796759 📄 01736 795584
e-mail: info@chyanalbanyhotel.com

dir: A30 onto A3074 signed St Ives, hotel on left before junct

Conveniently located, this pleasant hotel enjoys splendid sea views. The comfortable bedrooms come in a variety of sizes; some featuring balconies and sea views. Friendly staff and the relaxing environment mean that guests return on a regular basis. Freshly prepared and appetising cuisine is served in the dining room and a bar menu is also available.

Rooms 39 en suite (11 fmly) ⊗ in all bedrooms **Facilities** STV 🎵 Xmas **Conf** Thtr 80 Class 40 Board 30 **Services** Lift **Parking** 33 **Notes** ⊗ ⊗ in restaurant Civ Wed 80

★★ 76% HOTEL

Pedn-Olva

West Porthminster Beach TR26 2EA
☎ 01736 796222 📄 01736 797710
e-mail: pednolva@smallandfriendly.co.uk

dir: A30 to Hayle, then A3074 to St Ives. In St Ives turn sharp right at bus station into railway station car park, down steps to hotel

Perched on the water's edge, this hotel is the closest thing to being aboard a ship, and the stylish public areas complement the unique location. Bedrooms combine comfort with quality; many have spectacular views across the bay. An imaginative, fixed-price menu is offered in the restaurant; during the summer, lighter meals are served on the terraces.

Rooms 31 en suite (5 fmly) ⊗ in all bedrooms S fr £73; D fr £156 (incl. bkfst) **Facilities** STV FTV 🛥 **Notes** ⊗ ⊗ in restaurant Civ Wed 60

★★ 68% HOTEL

Cottage Hotel

Boskerris Rd, Carbis Bay TR26 2PE
☎ 01736 795252 📄 01736 798636
e-mail: cottage.stives@alfatravel.co.uk
web: www.alfatravel.co.uk

Leisureplex

dir: from A30 take A3074 to Carbis Bay. Right into Porthreptor Rd. Just before railway bridge, left through railway car park and into hotel car park

Set in quiet, lush gardens, this pleasant hotel offers friendly and attentive service. Smart bedrooms are pleasantly spacious and many rooms enjoy splendid views. Public areas are varied and include a snooker room, a comfortable lounge and a spacious dining room with sea views over the beach and Carbis Bay.

Rooms 80 en suite (7 fmly) (2 GF) ⊗ in all bedrooms S £31-£41; D £50-£70 (incl. bkfst) **Facilities** 🛥 Snooker Sauna Gym 🎵 Xmas **Services** Lift **Parking** 20 **Notes LB** ⊗ ⊗ in restaurant Closed Dec-Feb (ex Xmas) RS Nov & Mar

★★ 67% **HOTEL**

Hotel St Eia

Trelyon Av TR26 2AA

☎ 01736 795531 🖹 01736 793591

e-mail: hotelsteia@tinyonline.co.uk

dir: off A30 onto A3074, follow signs to St Ives, approaching town, hotel on right

This smart hotel is conveniently located and enjoys spectacular views over St Ives, the harbour and Porthminster Beach. The friendly proprietors provide a relaxing environment. Bedrooms are comfortable and well equipped; some have sea views. The spacious lounge bar has a well-stocked bar and views can be enjoyed from the rooftop terrace.

Rooms 18 en suite (3 fmly) ⊘ in all bedrooms S £28.50-£45; D £57-£90 (incl. bkfst) **Parking** 16 **Notes LB** ⊗ ⊘ in restaurant Closed Dec-Jan

ST MAWES   MAP 02 SW83

★★★ 86% ◉◉ **HOTEL**

Idle Rocks

Harbour Side TR2 5AN

☎ 01326 270771 🖹 01326 270062

e-mail: reception@idlerocks.co.uk

web: www.idlerocks.co.uk

dir: off A390 onto A3078, 14m to St Mawes. Hotel on left

This hotel has splendid sea views overlooking the attractive fishing port. The lounge and bar also benefit from the views and in warmer months service is available on the terrace. Bedrooms are individually styled and tastefully furnished to a high standard. The daily-changing menu served in the restaurant features fresh, local produce in imaginative cuisine.

Rooms 23 en suite 10 annexe en suite (7 fmly) (2 GF) S £118.50-£238.50; D £158-£318 (incl. bkfst & dinner) **Facilities** Xmas **Parking** 6 **Notes LB** ⊘ in restaurant

★★★ 80% ◉ **COUNTRY HOUSE HOTEL**

Rosevine

TR2 5EW

☎ 01872 580206 🖹 01872 580230

e-mail: info@rosevinehotels.co.uk

web: www.rosevine.co.uk

(For full entry see Portscatho)

★★ 78% ◉ **HOTEL**

Rising Sun

TR2 5DJ

☎ 01326 270233 🖹 01326 270198

e-mail: info@risingsunstmawes.com

dir: from A39 take A3078 signed St Mawes, hotel in village centre

Looking out across the harbour and the Fal estuary, this smart hotel is a popular venue. Bedrooms are stylish and many rooms have sea views. Menus feature seafood and local produce; the bar, which has a large selection of ales, quality wines and malt whiskies, offers a good range of dishes. More casual dining is available in the brasserie.

Rooms 8 en suite (1 fmly) **Parking** 6 **Notes** ⊘ in restaurant

ST MELLION   MAP 03 SX36

★★★ 72% **HOTEL**

St Mellion International

PL12 6SD

☎ 01579 351351 🖹 01579 350537

e-mail: itmellion@crown-golf.uk.com

web: www.st-mellion.co.uk

dir: from M5/A38 towards Plymouth & Saltash. St Mellion off A38 on A388 towards Callington & Launceston

This purpose-built hotel, golfing and leisure complex is surrounded by over 450 acres of land with two highly regarded 18-hole golf courses. The bedrooms generally have views over the courses and public areas include a choice of bars and eating options. Function suites are also available.

Rooms 39 annexe en suite (15 fmly) (8 GF) **Facilities** Spa 🏂 supervised ♨ 36 ♨ Squash Snooker Sauna Solarium Gym Putt green Jacuzzi Steam room Skincare **Conf** 1hr 350 Class 140 Board 80 **Services** Lift **Parking** 400 **Notes LB** ⊗ ⊘ in restaurant Civ Wed 120

SALTASH   MAP 03 SX45

★★★ 67% **HOTEL**

China Fleet Country Club

PL12 6LJ

☎ 01752 848668 🖹 01752 848456

e-mail: sales@china-fleet.co.uk

web: www.china-fleet.co.uk

dir: A38 towards Plymouth/Saltash. Cross Tamar Bridge, take slip road before tunnel. Right at lights, 1st left follow signs, 0.5m

In a convenient, quiet location, ideal for access to Plymouth and the countryside, this hotel offers an extensive range of leisure facilities including an impressive golf course. Bedrooms are all located in
continued on page 134

England

SALTASH continued

annexe buildings; each is equipped with its own kitchen. There is a range of dining options, and the restaurant offers interesting and imaginative choices.

Rooms 40 en suite (21 GF) ⊘ in all bedrooms S £66-£82; D £73.50-£84.50 (incl. bkfst) **Facilities Spa** STV ⊡ supervised ⌗ 18 ⌕ Squash Sauna Solarium Gym Putt green Jacuzzi Wi-fi available 28 bay Floodlit driving range Health & beauty suite Hairdressers **Conf** Thtr 80 Class 30 Board 34 **Services** Lift **Parking** 400 **Notes** ⊗ ⊘ in restaurant Civ Wed 80

BUDGET HOTEL

Travelodge Saltash

Callington Rd, Carkeel PL12 6LF
☎ 08700 850 950 🖷 01752 841079
web: www.travelodge.co.uk

dir: on A38 Saltash bypass - 1m from Tamar Bridge

Travelodge offers good quality, good value, modern accommodation. Ideal for families, the spacious en suite bedrooms include remote-control TV, tea and coffee-making facilities and comfortable beds. Meals can be taken at the nearby family restaurant. See Hotel Groups pages for further details.

Rooms 53 en suite S fr £26; D fr £26 **Conf** Thtr 25 Class 15 Board 12

SCILLY, ISLES OF

BRYHER   MAP 02 SV81

INSPECTORS' CHOICE

★★★ ⊛⊛ **HOTEL**

Hell Bay

TR23 0PR
☎ 01720 422947 🖷 01720 423004
e-mail: contactus@hellbay.co.uk
web: www.hellbay.co.uk

dir: Island location means it is only accessible by helicopter or ship from Penzance or plane from Southampton, Bristol, Exeter, Newquay or Land's End

Located on the smallest of the inhabited of the Scilly Isles on the edge of the Atlantic, this hotel makes a really special destination. The owners have filled the hotel with original works of art by artists who have connections with the islands, and the interior is decorated in cool blues and greens creating an extremely restful environment. The contemporary bedrooms are equally stylish and many have garden access and stunning sea views. Eating here is a delight, and naturally seafood features strongly on the award-winning, daily-changing menus.

continued

Rooms 25 annexe en suite (3 fmly) (15 GF) ⊘ in all bedrooms S £150-£237.50; D £240-£380 (incl. bkfst & dinner) **Facilities** STV ⌇ ⌗ Sauna Gym ⌣ Jacuzzi Boules Par 3 golf ch fac Xmas **Conf** Thtr 36 Class 36 Board 36 **Notes LB** ⊘ in restaurant Closed Jan-Feb Civ Wed 50

ST MARTIN'S   MAP 02 SV91

INSPECTORS' CHOICE

★★★ ⊛⊛⊛ **HOTEL**

St Martin's on the Isle

Lower Town TR25 0QW
☎ 01720 422090 & 422092 🖷 01720 422298
e-mail: stay@stmartinshotel.co.uk
web: www.stmartinshotel.co.uk

dir: 20-minute helicopter flight to St Mary's, then 10-minute launch to St Martin's

This attractive hotel, complete with its own sandy beach, enjoys an idyllic position on the waterfront overlooking Tresco and Tean. Bedrooms are brightly appointed, comfortably furnished and overlook the sea or the well-tended gardens. There is an elegant, award-winning restaurant and a split-level lounge bar where guests can relax and enjoy the memorable view. Locally caught fish features significantly on the daily-changing menus.

Rooms 30 en suite (10 fmly) (14 GF) S £143-£170; D £260-£340 **Facilities** ⌇ ⌕ Snooker Clay pigeon shooting Boating Bikes Diving Snorkelling **Conf** Thtr 50 Class 50 Board 50 **Notes LB** ⊘ in restaurant Closed Nov-Feb Civ Wed 100

ST MARY'S   MAP 02 SV91

★★★ 80% ⊛ **HOTEL**

St Mary's Hall Hotel

Church St, Hugh Town TR21 0JR
☎ 01720 422316 🖷 01720 422252
e-mail: recep@stmaryshallhotel.co.uk

Hospitality, service and cuisine are all strengths at this elegant townhouse, which was originally built by Count Leon de Ferrari, after whom the smart restaurant is named. The brasserie bar is smartly metropolitan in style while the elegant wood-panelled foyer and two separate comfortable lounges are more traditional. Two distinct bedroom styles are offered, the refurbished 'Count Leon' rooms offering slightly more comforts.

Rooms 20 en suite (3 fmly) (4 GF) ⊘ in all bedrooms **Facilities** STV Sauna **Notes LB** ⊗ ⊘ in restaurant

England

★★★ 74% **HOTEL**

Tregarthens

Hugh Town TR21 0PP

☎ 01720 422540 📠 01720 422089

e-mail: reception@tregarthens-hotel.co.uk

dir: 100yds from quay

Opened in 1848 by Captain Tregarthen this is now a well-established hotel. The impressive public areas provide wonderful views overlooking St Mary's harbour and some of the many islands, including Tresco and Bryher. Bedrooms are well equipped and neatly furnished. Traditional cuisine is served in the restaurant.

Rooms 31 en suite 1 annexe en suite (5 fmly) ⊗ in all bedrooms S £95-£130; D £174-£244 (incl. bkfst & dinner) **Notes LB** ⊗ ⊗ in restaurant Closed late Oct-mid Mar

---

TRESCO   **MAP 02 SV81**

INSPECTORS' CHOICE

★★★ ⊛⊛ **HOTEL**

The Island

TR24 0PU

☎ 01720 422883 📠 01720 423008

e-mail: islandhotel@tresco.co.uk

web: www.tresco.co.uk/holidays/island_hotel.asp

dir: helicopter service Penzance to Tresco, hotel on NE of island

This delightful colonial-style hotel enjoys a waterside location in its own attractive gardens. The spacious, comfortable lounges, airy restaurant and many of the bedrooms enjoy stunning sea views. All of the rooms are brightly furnished and many benefit from lounge areas, balconies or terraces. Carefully prepared, imaginative cuisine makes good use of locally caught fish.

Rooms 48 en suite (27 fmly) S £125-£165; D £260-£440 (incl. bkfst & dinner) **Facilities** STV ⤳ ⤴ Fishing ⤴ Boating Table tennis Bowls Boutique **Conf** BC Thtr 80 Class 80 Board 80 **Notes LB** ⊗ ⊗ in restaurant Closed Nov-Feb

---

★★ 78% ⊛⊛ **HOTEL**

New Inn

TR24 0QQ

☎ 01720 422844 423006 📠 01720 423200

e-mail: newinn@tresco.co.uk

web: www.tresco.co.uk/holidays/new_inn.asp

dir: by New Grimsby Quay

This friendly, popular inn enjoys a central location and offers bright, attractive, well-equipped bedrooms, many with splendid sea views. The popular bar offering real ales, serves an interesting range of snacks and meals. In addition guests may choose to dine in the airy bistro-style Pavilion or the elegant restaurant complete with its own bar.

Rooms 16 en suite (2 GF) **Facilities** ⤳ ⤴ Sea fishing, Bird watching, Walking **Notes LB** ⊗ ⊗ in restaurant

---

SENNEN   **MAP 02 SW32**

★★ 69% **HOTEL**

Old Success Inn

Sennen Cove TR19 7DG

☎ 01736 871232 📠 01736 871457

e-mail: oldsuccess@sennencove.fsbusiness.co.uk

dir: turn right off A30 approx 1m before Land's End, signed Sennen Cove. Hotel on left at bottom of hill

This inn is romantically located at the water's edge, with spectacular views of the cove and the Atlantic Ocean. Popular with locals and visitors alike, the inn offers friendly service and a choice of dining in either the restaurant and bar; there is always a selection of fresh fish dishes.

Rooms 12 en suite (1 fmly) **Facilities** ⤴ **Parking** 12 **Notes LB** ⊗ in restaurant

---

TINTAGEL   **MAP 02 SX08**

★★ 72% **SMALL HOTEL**

Atlantic View

Treknow PL34 0EJ

☎ 01840 770221 📠 01840 770995

e-mail: atlantic.view@eclipse.co.uk

web: www.holidayscornwall.com

dir: B3263 to Tregatta, turn left into Treknow, hotel on road to Trebarwith Strand Beach

Conveniently located for all the attractions of Tintagel, this family-run hotel has a wonderfully relaxed and welcoming atmosphere. Public areas include a bar, comfortable lounge, TV/games room and heated swimming pool. Bedrooms are generally spacious and some have the added advantage of distant sea views.

Rooms 9 en suite (1 fmly) ⊗ in all bedrooms **Facilities** ⊠ Indoor pool heated Apr-Oct **Parking** 10 **Notes LB** ⊗ ⊗ in restaurant Closed Nov-Jan RS Feb-Mar

England

TINTAGEL *continued*

★★ 67% HOTEL

Bossiney House

Bossiney PL34 0AX

☎ 01840 770240 🖷 01840 770501

e-mail: bossineyhh@eclipse.co.uk

web: www.bossineyhouse.co.uk

dir: *from A39 take B3263 into Tintagel, then Boscastle Rd, 0.5m to hotel on left*

This personally run, friendly hotel is located on the outskirts of the picturesque coastal village. An attractive Scandinavian-style log cabin houses the majority of the leisure facilities, including a swimming pool. Public areas include a comfortable lounge and the convivial bar, which is a popular venue for pre-dinner drinks and a chat.

Rooms 19 en suite (2 fmly) (8 GF) ⊘ in all bedrooms S fr £38; D £56-£76 (incl. bkfst) **Facilities** 🏊 Sauna Solarium Putt green Wi-fi available **Conf** BC **Parking** 30 **Notes LB** ⊘ in restaurant Closed 25-26 Dec, 2-31 Jan

TRURO   MAP 02 SW84

★★★ 81% ◉◉ HOTEL

Alverton Manor

Tregolls Rd TR1 1ZQ

☎ 01872 276633 🖷 01872 222989

e-mail: reception@alvertonmanor.co.uk

dir: *from at Carland Cross take A39 to Truro*

Formerly a convent, this impressive sandstone property stands in six acres of grounds, within walking distance of the city centre. It has a wide range of smart bedrooms, combining comfort with character. Stylish public areas include the library and the former chapel, now a striking function room. An interesting range of dishes, using the very best of local produce (organic whenever possible) is offered in the elegant restaurant.

continued

Rooms 32 en suite (3 GF) ⊘ in 10 bedrooms S £80-£135; D £135-£180 (incl. bkfst) **Facilities** STV ⌿ 18 Xmas **Conf** Thtr 80 Class 60 Board 40 Del from £150 **Services** Lift **Parking** 120 **Notes LB** ⊘ in restaurant Closed 28 Dec RS 4 Jan Civ Wed 80

★★★ 75% HOTEL

Royal

Lemon St TR1 2QB

☎ 01872 270345 🖷 01872 242453

e-mail: reception@royalhotelcornwall.co.uk

web: www.royalhotelcornwall.co.uk

dir: *A30 to Carland Cross then Truro. Follow brown signs to hotel in city centre*

This popular hotel is located in the heart of Truro and has an engaging blend of traditional and contemporary. Public areas offer a stylish atmosphere with the bar and restaurant proving popular with locals and residents alike. Bedrooms are pleasantly appointed. A wide selection of appetising dishes of ethnic, classical and vegetarian choices, as well as daily specials, is offered.

Rooms 35 en suite 9 annexe en suite (4 fmly) (3 GF) ⊘ in 31 bedrooms S fr £69; D £90-£130 (incl. bkfst) **Facilities** STV Wi-fi available **Conf** Thtr 25 Class 25 Board 20 **Parking** 44 **Notes LB** ⊗ ⊘ in restaurant Closed 25 & 26 Dec

See advert on opposite page

★★★ 66% HOTEL

Brookdale

THE INDEPENDENTS

Tregolls Rd TR1 1JZ

☎ 01872 273513 🖷 01872 272400

e-mail: brookdale@hotelstruro.com

dir: *from A30 onto A39, at A390 junct turn right into city centre. Hotel 600mtrs down hill*

Pleasantly situated in an elevated position close to the city centre, the Brookdale provides a range of accommodation options; all rooms are pleasantly spacious and well equipped, with some located in an adjacent annexe. Meals can be served in guests' rooms, and in the dining room a pleasant selection of dishes is available.

Rooms 30 en suite (2 fmly) ⊘ in 22 bedrooms S £55-£69.80; D fr £87.50 (incl. bkfst) **Facilities** STV Wi-fi available Xmas **Conf** Thtr 100 Class 65 Board 30 Del from £78 **Parking** 30 **Notes LB** ⊘ in restaurant

★★ 71% HOTEL

Carlton

Falmouth Rd TR1 2HL

☎ 01872 272450 🖷 01872 223938

e-mail: reception@carltonhotel.co.uk

dir: *on A39 straight across 1st & 2nd rdbts onto bypass (Morlaix Avenue). At top of sweeping bend/hill turn right at mini rdbt into Falmouth Rd. Hotel is 100mtrs on right*

This family-run hotel is pleasantly located a short stroll from the city centre. A friendly welcome is assured and both business and leisure guests choose the Carlton on a regular basis. A smart, comfortable lounge is available, along with leisure facilities. A wide selection of home-cooked dishes is offered in the dining room.

continued

Carlton

Rooms 29 en suite (4 fmly) (4 GF) ⊘ in 23 bedrooms S £42.50-£50; D £60-£70 (incl. bkfst) **Facilities** STV Sauna Jacuzzi **Conf** Thtr 60 Class 24 Board 36 Del from £66.95 **Parking** 31 **Notes** Closed 22 Dec to 6 Jan

BUDGET HOTEL

Premier Travel Inn Truro
Old Carnon Hill, Carnon Downs TR3 6JT
☎ 08701 977255 📠 01872 865620
web: www.premiertravelinn.com
dir: on A39 (Truro to Falmouth road), 3m SW of Truro

High quality, modern budget accommodation ideal for both families and business travellers. Spacious, en suite bedrooms feature bath and shower, satellite TV and many have telephones and modem points. The adjacent family restaurant features a wide and varied menu. For further details consult the Hotel Groups page.

Rooms 40 en suite

TYWARDREATH   MAP 02 SX05

★★★ 80% ❀ COUNTRY HOUSE HOTEL

Trenython Manor
Castle Dore Rd PL24 2TS
☎ 01726 814797 📠 01726 817030
e-mail: nick.waddington@clublacosta.com
web: www.trenython.co.uk
dir: A390/B3269 towards Fowey, after 2m right into Castledore. Hotel 100mtrs on left

Dating from the 1800s, there is something distinctly different about Trenython, an English manor house designed by an Italian architect. Peacefully situated in extensive grounds, public areas have grace and elegance with original features, and many of the bedrooms have wonderful views. The splendour of the panelled restaurant is the venue for contemporary cuisine.

Rooms 24 en suite (2 fmly) ⊘ in all bedrooms S £105-£195; D £125-£225 (incl. bkfst) **Facilities** Spa ☒ supervised ⌘ Sauna Solarium Gym ⌘ Jacuzzi Woodland walks, health & beauty centre Xmas **Conf** BC Thtr 40 Class 20 Board 30 Del from £125 **Parking** 50 **Notes** LB ⊗ ⊘ in restaurant Civ Wed 85

England

VERYAN
MAP 02 SW93

★★★★ 82% ⊛ **COUNTRY HOUSE HOTEL**

Nare
Carne Beach TR2 5PF
☎ 01872 501111 ▤ 01872 501856
e-mail: office@narehotel.co.uk
web: www.narehotel.co.uk
dir: *from Tregony follow A3078 for approx 1.5m. Left at Veryan sign, through village towards sea & hotel*

This delightful hotel offers a relaxed, country-house atmosphere in a spectacular coastal setting. Many of the bedrooms have balconies, and fresh flowers, carefully chosen artwork and antiques all contribute to the engaging individuality. A choice of dining options is available, from light snacks to superb local seafood.

Rooms 38 en suite (4 fmly) (6 GF) S £95-£195; D £180-£360 (incl. bkfst) **Facilities** Spa STV ⬚ ⤳ ⬭ Snooker Sauna Gym ⬛ Jacuzzi Health & Beauty clinic Hotel Boat Shooting, steam room Xmas **Services** Lift **Parking** 80 **Notes LB** ⊘ in restaurant

WATERGATE BAY
MAP 02 SW86

★★★ 73% ⊛ **HOTEL**

The Hotel and Extreme Academy Watergate Bay
TR8 4AA
☎ 01637 860543 ▤ 01637 860333
e-mail: hotel@watergatebay.co.uk
web: www.watergatebay.co.uk
dir: *A30 onto A3059. Follow airport/Watergate Bay signs.*

With its own private beach, which is home to the 'Extreme Academy' of beach and watersports activities, this hotel boasts a truly a spectacular location. The style here is relaxed with a genuine welcome for all the family. Public areas are stylish and contemporary. Many bedrooms share the breathtaking outlook and a number have balconies. Several dining options are on offer, including the Beach Hut, Brasserie and Jamie Oliver's restaurant, Fifteen Cornwall.

Rooms 54 en suite 17 annexe en suite (36 fmly) S £135; D £270 (incl. bkfst & dinner) **Facilities** Spa STV ⬚ ⤳ ⬭ Squash Snooker Jacuzzi Wi-fi available Surfing, Badminton, Table Tennis, Billiards, Mountain Boarding, Wave ski-ing ♫ ch fac Xmas **Conf** BC Thtr 150 Class 40 Board 20 **Services** Lift **Parking** 72 **Notes LB** ⊘ in restaurant Civ Wed 40

See advert on page 137

★ 70% **HOTEL**

Tregurrian
TR8 4AB
☎ 01637 860280 ▤ 01637 851690
e-mail: enquiries@tregurrianhotel.com
web: www.tregurrianhotel.com
dir: *Leave A30 onto A3059 towards airport, 2nd exit at rdbt, right onto B3276, left to Watergate Bay*

Located almost on the beach at this increasingly popular destination, the Tregurrian is a friendly and convenient place to stay. Bedrooms are comfortable and attractively presented, and some have sea views. In the dining room, both breakfast and dinner are served buffet-style with good use of fresh ingredients.

Rooms 26 en suite (8 fmly) ⊘ in all bedrooms **Facilities** ⤳ Sauna Jacuzzi Games room **Parking** 26 **Notes LB** ⊗ ⊘ in restaurant Closed Dec-Feb

CUMBRIA

ALSTON
MAP 18 NY74

★★★ 74% ⊛ **HOTEL**

Lovelady Shield Country House
CA9 3LF
☎ 01434 381203 & 381305 ▤ 01434 381515
e-mail: enquiries@lovelady.co.uk
dir: *2m E, signed off A689 at junct with B6294*

Located in the heart of the Pennines close to England's highest market town, this delightful country house is set in three acres of landscaped gardens. Accommodation is provided in stylish, thoughtfully equipped bedrooms. Carefully prepared meals are served in the elegant dining room and there is a choice of appealing lounges with log fires in the cooler months.

Rooms 10 en suite (1 fmly) **Conf** Class 12 Board 12 **Parking** 20 **Notes LB** ⊘ in restaurant Civ Wed 100

★★ 76% **HOTEL**

Nent Hall Country House Hotel
CA9 3LQ
☎ 01434 381584 ▤ 01434 382668
web: www.nenthall.com
dir: *from main street turn left at top onto A689. Hotel is 2m on right*

This delightful old house stands in well-kept gardens. Warm and friendly hospitality is provided, with well-appointed and comfortable accommodation, some rooms being on the ground floor and others being suitable for families. There are two comfortable lounges and a pleasant bar serving bar meals and light snacks as well as a more formal dining room.

Rooms 18 en suite (2 fmly) (9 GF) ⊘ in all bedrooms **Conf** Thtr 50 Class 50 Board 50 **Parking** 100 **Notes LB** ⊗ ⊘ in restaurant Civ Wed 200

AMBLESIDE
MAP 18 NY30
See also Elterwater

★★★★ 74% TOWN HOUSE HOTEL

Waterhead
Lake Rd LA22 0ER
☎ 015394 32566 ▤ 015394 31255
e-mail: waterhead@elhmail.co.uk
web: www.elh.co.uk/hotels/waterhead.htm
dir: A591 into Ambleside, hotel opposite Waterhead Pier

With an enviable location opposite the bay, this well-established hotel offers contemporary and comfortable accommodation with some innovative features, including CD/DVD players, plasma screens and internet access. There is a bar with a garden terrace overlooking the lake and a stylish restaurant serving classical cuisine with a modern twist. Staff are very attentive and friendly. Guests can enjoy full use of the Low Wood Hotel leisure facilities nearby.

Rooms 41 en suite (3 fmly) (7 GF) ⊗ in 35 bedrooms S £85-£130; D £170-£230 (incl. bkfst) **Facilities** STV Wi fi available Xmas **Conf** Thtr 40 Class 30 Board 26 Del from £135 **Parking** 43 **Notes LB** ⊗ in restaurant

See advertisement under WINDERMERE

★★★ 82% ⊛ HOTEL

Rothay Manor
Rothay Bridge LA22 0EH
☎ 015394 33605 ▤ 015394 33607
e-mail: hotel@rothaymanor.co.uk
web: www.rothaymanor.co.uk/aa
dir: In Ambleside follow signs for Coniston (A593). Hotel 0.25 mile SW of Ambleside opposite rugby pitch

A long-established hotel, this attractive listed building built in Regency style, is a short walk from both the town centre and Lake Windermere. Spacious bedrooms, including suites, family rooms and rooms with balconies, are comfortably equipped and furnished to a very high standard. Public areas include a choice of lounges, a spacious restaurant and conference facilities.

Rooms 17 en suite 2 annexe en suite (7 fmly) (3 GF) ⊗ in all bedrooms S £85-£130; D £135-£210 (incl. bkfst) **Facilities** Nearby leisure centre free to guests, free fishing permit available ch fac Xmas **Conf** Thtr 22 Board 18 Del from £150 **Parking** 45 **Notes LB** ⊛ ⊗ in restaurant Closed 3-26 Jan

See advert on this page

★★★ 80% HOTEL

Best Western Ambleside Salutation Hotel
Lake Rd LA22 9BX
☎ 015394 32244 ▤ 015394 34157
e-mail: enquiries@hotelambleside.uk.com
web: www.hotelslakedistrict.com
dir: A591 to Ambleside, onto one-way system down Wansfell Rd into Compston Rd. Right at lights back into village

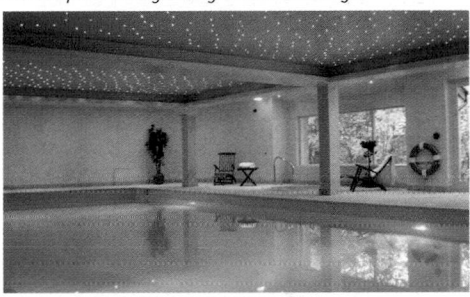

A former coaching inn, this hotel lies in the centre of the town. Bedrooms are tastefully appointed and thoughtfully equipped; many boast balconies and fine views. Inviting public areas include an attractive re-furbished restaurant and a choice of comfortable lounges

continued on page 140

AMBLESIDE *continued*

for relaxing and for the more energetic there is a swimming pool and a small gym.

Rooms 38 en suite 4 annexe en suite (4 fmly) ⊗ in 19 bedrooms S £74.50-£106; D £99-£142 (incl. bkfst) **Facilities** STV ⛱ Sauna Gym Jacuzzi Use of pool at sister hotel Xmas **Conf** Thtr 100 Class 40 Board 16 Del from £103 **Parking** 50 **Notes LB** ⊗ in restaurant

See advert on opposite page

★★★ 80% ® HOTEL

Regent

Waterhead Bay LA22 0ES
☎ 015394 32254 📠 015394 31474
e-mail: info@regentlakes.co.uk
dir: 1m S on A591

This attractive holiday hotel, situated close to Waterhead Bay, offers a warm welcome. Bedrooms come in a variety of styles, including three suites and five bedrooms in the garden wing. There is a modern swimming pool and the restaurant offers a fine dining experience in a tasteful contemporary setting.

Rooms 30 en suite (7 fmly) ⊗ in all bedrooms S £65-£135; D £114-£144 (incl. bkfst) **Facilities** ⛱ Xmas **Parking** 39 **Notes LB** ⊗ in restaurant Closed 19-27 Dec

★★★ 75% HOTEL

Skelwith Bridge

Skelwith Bridge LA22 9NJ
☎ 015394 32115 📠 015394 34254
e-mail: skelwithbr@aol.com
web: www.skelwithbridgehotel.co.uk
dir: 2.5m W on A593 at junct with B5343 to Langdale

This 17th-century inn is now a well-appointed tourist hotel located at the heart of the Lake District National Park and renowned for its friendly and attentive service. Bedrooms include two rooms with four-poster beds. Spacious public areas include a choice of lounges and bars and an attractive restaurant overlooking the gardens to the bridge from which the hotel takes its name.

Rooms 22 en suite 6 annexe en suite (2 fmly) (1 GF) ⊗ in 22 bedrooms S fr £55; D fr £100 (incl. bkfst) **Facilities** Xmas **Parking** 60 **Notes LB** ⊗ in restaurant

★★ 68% HOTEL

Queens

Market Place LA22 9BU
☎ 015394 32206 📠 015394 32721
e-mail: enquiries@queenshotelambleside.com
web: www.queenshotelambleside.com
dir: A591 to Ambleside, follow town centre signs on one way system. Right lane at traffic lights, hotel on right.

Situated in the heart of the village, this traditional Lakeland stone-clad hotel offers good tourist facilities. The bar meal operation, along with a good range of real ales, makes this a popular venue throughout the year. Bedrooms vary in size and have all the expected features.

Rooms 26 en suite (4 fmly) S £34-£47; D £68-£94 (incl. bkfst) **Facilities** STV Xmas **Parking** 6 **Notes** ⊗ ⊗ in restaurant

APPLEBY-IN-WESTMORLAND MAP 18 NY62

★★★ 85% ® HOTEL

BW Appleby Manor Country House

Roman Rd CA16 6JB
☎ 017683 51571 📠 017683 52888
e-mail: reception@applebymanor.co.uk
web: www.applebymanor.co.uk
dir: M6 junct 40/A66 towards Brough. Take Appleby turn, then immediately right. Continue for 0.5m

This imposing country mansion is set in extensive grounds amid stunning Cumbrian scenery. The Dunbobbin family and their experienced staff ensure a warm welcome and attentive service. The thoughtfully equipped bedrooms vary in style and include the impressive Heelis suite; some rooms also have patio areas. The bar offers a wide range of malt whiskies and the restaurant serves carefully prepared meals. This hotel is totally non-smoking.

Rooms 23 en suite 7 annexe en suite (9 fmly) (10 GF) ⊗ in all bedrooms S £87-£97; D £134-£220 (incl. bkfst) **Facilities** STV ⛱ Sauna Solarium Putt green Jacuzzi Wi-fi in bedrooms Steam room, Table tennis, Pool table ch fac **Conf** Thtr 38 Class 25 Board 28 Del £119.50 **Parking** 53 **Notes LB** ⊗ ⊗ in restaurant Closed 24-26 Dec

BARROW-IN-FURNESS   MAP 18 SD26

★★★ 77% ® HOTEL

Clarence House Country Hotel & Restaurant

Skelgate LA15 8BQ
☎ 01229 462508 📠 01229 467177
e-mail: clarencehsehotel@aol.com
web: www.clarencehouse-hotel.co.uk

This hotel is peacefully located in its own ornamental grounds with unrestricted countryside views. Bedrooms are individually themed with
continued

...hose in the main hotel being particularly stylish and comfortable. The public rooms are spacious and also furnished to a high standard. The popular conservatory restaurant offers well-prepared dishes from extensive menus. There is a delightful barn conversion that is ideal for weddings.

Rooms 7 en suite 12 annexe en suite (1 fmly) (5 GF) ⊘ in 11 bedrooms £79-£100; D £105-£130 (incl. bkfst) **Facilities** STV Jacuzzi ♫ ch fac Xmas **Conf** Thtr 100 Class 40 Board 15 Del from £120 **Parking** 40 **Notes LB** ⊘ in restaurant Civ Wed 100

★★★ 75% HOTEL

Abbey House
Abbey Rd LA13 0PA
☎ 01229 838282 ▤ 01229 820403
e-mail: enquiries@abbeyhousehotel.com

Dir: A590 follow signs for Furness general hospital & Furness Abbey. Hotel approx 100yds on left

Set in its own gardens, this smart hotel provides stylish public areas, as well as extensive function and conference facilities. The well-equipped bedrooms vary in style, the more traditional rooms in the main house and a more contemporary style in the extension. Service is friendly and obliging.

Rooms 57 en suite (6 fmly) (2 GF) ⊘ in 15 bedrooms S £65-£91, D £102.50-£111 (incl. bkfst) **Facilities** STV Wi-fi in bedrooms Xmas **Conf** Thtr 280 Class 120 Board 80 Del from £115 **Services** Lift **Parking** 100 **Notes LB** ⊘ in restaurant Civ Wed 120

See advert on this page

★★★ 74% HOTEL

Clarke's Hotel & Brasserie
Rampside LA13 0PX
☎ 01229 820303 ▤ 01229 430954
e-mail: bookings@clarkeshotel.co.uk

Dir: A590 to Ulverston then A5087, take coastal road for 8m, turn left at rdbt into Rampside

This smart, well-maintained hotel enjoys a peaceful location on the south Cumbrian coastline, overlooking Morecambe Bay. The tastefully appointed bedrooms come in a variety of sizes and are thoughtfully equipped especially for the business guest. Inviting public areas include an open-plan bar and brasserie offering freshly prepared food throughout the day.

Rooms 14 en suite (1 fmly) ⊘ in 7 bedrooms S £45-£75; D £69-£85 incl. bkfst) **Facilities** STV FTV **Parking** 50 **Notes LB** ⊘ in restaurant

★★ 64% HOTEL

Lisdoonie
307/309 Abbey Rd LA14 5LF
☎ 01229 827312 ▤ 01229 820944
e-mail: lisdoonie@aol.com

Dir: on A590, at 1st set of lights in town (Strawberry pub on left) continue for 100yds, hotel on right

This friendly hotel is conveniently located for access to the centre of the town and is popular with commercial visitors. The comfortable bedrooms are well equipped, and vary in size and style. There are two comfortable lounges, one with a bar and restaurant adjacent. There is also a large function suite.

Rooms 12 en suite (2 fmly) **Conf** Class 255 **Parking** 30 **Notes** Closed Xmas & New Year

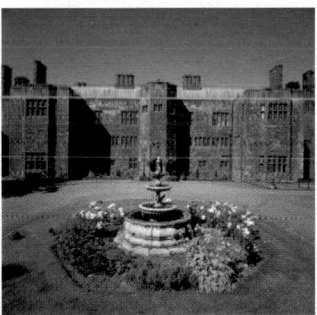

BARROW-IN-FURNESS *continued*

BUDGET HOTEL

Travelodge Barrow-in-Furness

Cockden Villas, Walney Rd LA14 5UG

☎ 08700 850950 📠 01229 827129

web: www.travelodge.co.uk

dir: *Just off A590, south of Hawcoat*

Travelodge offers good quality, good value, modern accommodation. Ideal for families, the spacious en suite bedrooms include remote-control TV, tea and coffee-making facilities and comfortable beds. Meals can be taken at the nearby family restaurant. See Hotel Groups pages for further details.

Rooms 40 en suite S fr £26; D fr £26

BASSENTHWAITE   MAP 18 NY23

★★★★ 80% ⊛ HOTEL

Armathwaite Hall

CA12 4RE

☎ 017687 76551 📠 017687 76220

e-mail: reservations@armathwaite-hall.com

web: www.armathwaite-hall.com

dir: *M6 junct 40/A66 to Keswick rdbt then A591 signed Carlisle. 8m to Castle Inn junct, turn left. Hotel 300yds*

Enjoying fine views over Bassenthwaite Lake, this impressive mansion, dating from the 17th century, is peacefully situated amid 400 acres of deer park. Comfortably furnished bedrooms are complemented by a choice of public rooms featuring splendid wood panelling and roaring log fires in the cooler months.

Rooms 42 en suite (4 fmly) (8 GF) S £125-£155; D £200-£350 (incl. bkfst) **Facilities Spa** STV ☒ supervised ♨ Fishing Snooker Sauna Solarium Gym ♨ Putt green Jacuzzi Wi-fi available Archery, Beauty salon, Clayshooting, Quad bikes, Falconry, Mountain Bikes ch fac Xmas **Conf** Thtr 80 Class 50 Board 60 Del from £145 **Services** Lift **Parking** 100 **Notes LB** ⊗ in restaurant Civ Wed 80

See advertisment under KESWICK

★★★ 79% ⊛ HOTEL

The Pheasant

CA13 9YE

☎ 017687 76234 📠 017687 76002

e-mail: info@the-pheasant.co.uk

web: www.the-pheasant.co.uk

dir: *Midway between Keswick & Cockermouth, signed from A66*

Enjoying a rural setting, within well-tended gardens, on the western

continued

---

side of Bassenthwaite Lake, this 500-year-old, friendly inn is steeped tradition. The attractive oak panelled bar has seen few changes over the years and features log fires and a great selection of malt whiskies The individually decorated bedrooms are stylish and thoughtfully equipped.

The Pheasa

Rooms 13 en suite 2 annexe en suite (2 GF) ⊗ in all bedrooms S £85-£95; D £150-£190 (incl. bkfst) **Parking** 40 **Notes LB** No children 12yrs ⊗ in restaurant Closed 25-Dec

---

Ⓤ

Castle Inn

CA12 4RG

☎ 017687 76401 📠 017687 76604

e-mail: gm@castleinncumbria.co.uk

web: www.castleinncumbria.co.uk

dir: *A591 to Carlisle, pass Bassenthwaite village on right & hote is on left side of T-junct.*

At the time of going to press, the star classification for this hotel was not confirmed. Please refer to the AA internet site www.theAA.com fo current information.

Rooms 48 en suite (8 fmly) (4 GF) ⊗ in 25 bedrooms S £53-£70; D £75-£110 (incl. bkfst) **Facilities Spa** STV ☒ supervised ♨ Sauna Solarium Gym Putt green Jacuzzi Table tennis Pool table Xmas **Conf** BC Thtr 120 Class 60 Board 60 Del £98 **Parking** 80 **Notes LB** ⊗ in restaurant Civ Wed 180

BORROWDALE   MAP 18 NY2

See also Keswick & Rosthwaite

★★★ 80% ⊛ HOTEL

Borrowdale Gates Country House

CA12 5UQ

☎ 017687 77204 📠 017687 77254

e-mail: hotel@borrowdale-gates.com

web: www.borrowdale-gates.com

dir: *From A66 follow B5289 for approx 4m. Turn right over bridge, hotel 0.25m beyond village.*

An attractive, well maintained and friendly hotel enjoys an idyllic, peaceful, woodland location in the middle of the Borrowdale Valley. Inviting public rooms include a choice of lounges and a smart restaurant, enjoying stunning views. Bedrooms come in a variety of styles and sizes, including superior rooms that are particularly thoughtfully equipped.

continue

Borrowdale Gates Country House

Rooms 27 en suite (10 GF) S £80-£85; D £160-£190 (incl. bkfst & dinner) **Facilities** STV Xmas **Parking** 29 **Notes LB** ⊗ ⊘ in restaurant

See advertisment under KESWICK

★★★ 80% **HOTEL**

Lodore Falls Hotel

CA12 5UX

☎ 017687 77285 🖻 017687 77343

e-mail: info@lodorefallshotel.co.uk

dir: M6 junct 40 take A66 to Keswick, then B5289 to Borrowdale. Hotel on left

This impressive hotel has an enviable location overlooking Derwentwater. Bedrooms, many with lake or fell views, are comfortably equipped and tastefully styled. The dining room, bar and lounge areas are appointed to a very high standard. The Elemis Spa as one treatment that actually incorporates using the Lodore Waterfall.

Rooms 71 en suite (11 fmly) ⊘ in 14 bedrooms S £95-£101; D £160-£170 incl. bkfst and dinner) **Facilities Spa** STV FTV 🏊 ✦ supervised 🐾 shing Squash Sauna Solarium Gym Wi-fi in bedrooms ♬ ch fac Xmas **Conf** Thtr 200 Class 90 Board 45 **Services** Lift **Parking** 91 **Notes LB** ⊘ in restaurant Civ Wed 130

See advertisement under KESWICK

★★★ 79% ❀ **HOTEL**

Leathes Head

CA12 5UY

☎ 017687 77247 & 77650 🖻 017687 77363

e-mail: enq@leatheshead.co.uk

web: www.leatheshead.co.uk

dir: 3.5m out of Keswick on Borrowdale road (B5289) hotel on left 0.25m before Grange Bridge.

Located within well-tended gardens in the picturesque Borrowdale Valley, this personally run hotel offers a haven of calm and tranquillity.

continued

There are three comfortable lounge areas and an elegant restaurant serving interesting meals. The well appointed bedrooms are mostly spacious with many enjoying splendid views of towering fells and rolling countryside.

Leathes Head

Rooms 12 en suite (2 fmly) (3 GF) ⊘ in all bedrooms **Facilities** Xmas **Parking** 16 **Notes** ⊗ No children 9yrs ⊘ in restaurant Closed mid Nov-Xmas & 3 Jan-mid Feb

★★★ 73% **HOTEL**

Borrowdale

CA12 5UY

☎ 017687 77224 🖻 017687 77338

e-mail: theborrowdalehotel@yahoo.com

dir: 3 miles from Keswick, on B5289 at S end of Lake Derwentwater

Situated in the beautiful Borrowdale Valley overlooking Derwentwater, this traditionally styled hotel has been family-run for over 30 years. Extensive public areas include a choice of lounges, a stylish dining room, and a lounge bar, plus a popular conservatory. There is a wide variety of bedroom sizes and styles; some rooms are rather spacious, including two that are particularly suitable for less able guests.

Rooms 34 en suite 2 annexe en suite (9 fmly) (2 GF) S £60-£78; D £120-£190 (incl. bkfst & dinner) **Facilities** ch fac Xmas **Parking** 100 **Notes LB** ⊘ in restaurant

★ 68% **HOTEL**

Royal Oak

CA12 5XB

☎ 017687 77214 🖻 017687 77214

e-mail: info@royaloakhotel.co.uk

web: www.royaloakhotel.co.uk

dir: 6m S of Keswick on B5289 in centre of Rosthwaite

Set in a village in one of Lakeland's most picturesque valleys, this family-run hotel offers friendly and obliging service. There is a variety of accommodation styles, with particularly impressive rooms being located in a converted barn across the courtyard and backed by a stream. Family rooms are available. The cosy bar is for residents and diners only. A set home-cooked dinner is served at 7pm.

Rooms 11 rms (8 en suite) 4 annexe en suite (6 fmly) (4 GF) ⊘ in all bedrooms S £38-£56; D £68-£108 (incl. bkfst & dinner) **Facilities** no TV in bdrms **Parking** 15 **Notes LB** ⊘ in restaurant Closed 5-19 Jan & 7-27 Dec

BOWNESS ON WINDERMERE

See Windermere

England

BRAITHWAITE
MAP 18 NY22

★★ 76% ◉ **HOTEL**

The Cottage in the Wood
Whinlatter Pass CA12 5TW
☎ 017687 78409 ▤ 017687 78064
e-mail: info@thecottageinthewood.co.uk

dir: A66 for Cockermouth & Keswick. After Keswick, turn off for Braithwaite & Lorton via Whinlatter Pass (B5292). Hotel at top of Whinlatter Pass

This charming hotel sits amid wooded hills with striking views of Skiddaw, and is in a convenient location for Keswick. The professional owners provide excellent hospitality in a relaxed manner and offer a freshly prepared dinner from a set menu that includes a vegetarian choice. There is a cosy lounge and a small bar. The bedrooms are individually decorated, and the superior rooms include many useful extras.

Rooms 10 en suite (1 fmly) (1 GF) ◎ in all bedrooms **Parking** 15
Notes LB ⊗ No children 7yrs ◎ in restaurant Closed Jan-mid Feb RS Mon eve

BRAMPTON
MAP 21 NY56
See also Castle Carrock

INSPECTORS' CHOICE

★★★ ◎◎ **HOTEL**

Farlam Hall
CA8 2NG
☎ 016977 46234 ▤ 016977 46683
e-mail: farlam@relaischateaux.com
web: www.farlamhall.co.uk

dir: On A689 (Brampton to Alston). Hotel 2m on left (not in Farlam village)

This delightful family-run country house dates back to 1428. Steeped in history, the hotel is set in beautifully landscaped Victorian gardens complete with an ornamental lake and stream. Lovingly restored over many years, it now provides the highest standards of comfort and hospitality. Gracious public rooms invite relaxation, whilst every thought has gone into the beautiful bedrooms, many of which are simply stunning.

Rooms 11 en suite 1 annexe en suite (2 GF) ◎ in all bedrooms S £147-£167; D £275-£315 (incl. bkfst & dinner) **Facilities** FTV ✆ **Conf** Thtr 24 Class 24 Board 12 **Parking** 35 **Notes LB** No children 5yrs ◎ in restaurant Closed 24-30 Dec

BURTON MOTORWAY SERVICE AREA (M6)
MAP 18 SD57

BUDGET HOTEL

Travelodge Burton (M6 Northbound)
Burton in Kendal LA6 1JF
☎ 08700 850 950 ▤ 01524 784014
web: www.travelodge.co.uk

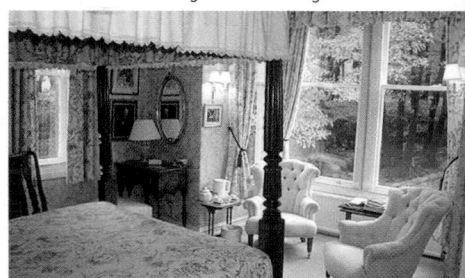

dir: between M6 junct 35 & 36 northbound

Travelodge offers good quality, good value, modern accommodation. Ideal for families, the spacious en suite bedrooms include remote-control TV, tea and coffee-making facilities and comfortable beds. Meals can be taken at the nearby family restaurant. See Hotel Groups pages for further details.

Rooms 47 en suite S fr £26; D fr £26

BUTTERMERE
MAP 18 NY11

★★★ 75% **HOTEL**

Bridge
CA13 9UZ
☎ 017687 70252 ▤ 70215
e-mail: enquiries@bridge-hotel.com
web: www.bridge-hotel.com

dir: A66 around town centre, exit at Braithwaite. Over Newlands Pass. Follow Buttermere signs. Hotel in village

Enjoying a tranquil setting in a dramatic valley close to Buttermere, this long-established hotel offers bedrooms that are tastefully appointed with stylish bathrooms. The comfortable public areas include a delightful lounge, attractive dining room and lively bar popular with walkers.

Rooms 21 en suite ◎ in all bedrooms S £75-£95; D £150-£190 (incl. bkfst & dinner) **Facilities** no TV in bdrms Xmas **Conf** Board 10 **Parking** 40 **Notes LB** ⊗ ◎ in restaurant

CARLISLE

MAP 18 NY35

★★★ 77% HOTEL

Crown

Wetheral CA4 8ES

☎ 01228 561888 📠 01228 561637 & 564184

e-mail: info@crownhotelwetheral.co.uk

web: www.crownhotelwetheral.co.uk

dir: M6 junct 42 take B6263 to Wetheral, right at village shop,
car park at rear of hotel

Set in the attractive village of Wetheral and with landscaped gardens
to the rear, this hotel is well suited to both business and leisure
guests. Rooms vary in size and style and include two apartments in an
adjacent house that is ideal for long stays. A choice of dining options
is available, with the popular Waltons Bar an informal alternative to
the main restaurant.

Rooms 49 en suite 2 annexe en suite (10 fmly) (3 GF) ⊘ in
30 bedrooms **Facilities Spa** STV ℞ supervised Squash Sauna Solarium
Gym Jacuzzi Wi-fi available Children's splash pool Steam room Beauty
facilities Xmas **Conf** BC Thtr 175 Class 90 Board 50 Del from £115
Parking 80 **Notes** ⊘ in restaurant Civ Wed 120

★★★ 73% HOTEL

Best Western Cumbria Park

32 Scotland Rd, Stanwix CA3 9DG

☎ 01228 522887 📠 01228 514796

e-mail: enquiries@cumbriaparkhotel.co.uk

web: www.cumbriaparkhotel.co.uk

dir: M6 junct 44, 1.5 miles on main road into Carlisle on left

Just minutes from the M6, this privately owned hotel, with its own
feature garden, is also convenient for the city centre. Well-equipped
bedrooms come in a variety of sizes, and several have four-poster
beds and whirlpool baths. Functions, conferences and weddings are all
well catered for with a wide choice of rooms. The whole hotel is now
equipped with Wi-fi internet access.

Rooms 47 en suite (3 fmly) (7 GF) ⊘ in 13 bedrooms S £76-£90;
D £99-£125 (incl. bkfst) **Facilities** STV Sauna Solarium Gym Jacuzzi
Steam room **Conf** Thtr 120 Class 50 Board 35 Del £105 **Services** Lift
Parking 51 **Notes LB** ⊗ Closed 25-26 Dec

★★★ 70% HOTEL

Lakes Court

Court Square CA1 1QY

☎ 01228 531951 📠 01228 547799

e-mail: reservations@lakescourthotel.co.uk

dir: M6 junct 43, to city centre, then follow road to left & railway
station

This Victorian building is located in the heart of the city centre,
adjacent to the railway station. The bedrooms, including a four-poster
room, are modern in style and mostly spacious. There are extensive
conference facilities and a secure car park. A comfortable bar serves
light meals and a wide range of drinks.

Rooms 70 en suite (3 fmly) ⊘ in 19 bedrooms **Facilities** STV Xmas
Conf BC Thtr 175 Class 60 Board 60 **Services** Lift **Parking** 20
Notes ⊘ in restaurant Civ Wed 170

★★★ 64% HOTEL

The Crown & Mitre

4 English St CA3 8HZ

☎ 01228 525491 📠 01228 514553

e-mail: info@crownandmitre-hotel-carlisle.com

web: www.peelhotel.com

PEEL HOTELS

dir: A6 to city centre, pass station & Woolworths on left. Right
into Blackfriars St. Rear entrance at end

Located in the heart of the city, this Edwardian hotel is close to the
cathedral and a few minutes' walk from the castle. Bedrooms vary in
size and style, from small executive rooms to more functional
standard rooms. Public rooms include a comfortable lounge area and
the lovely bar with its feature stained-glass windows.

Rooms 74 en suite 20 annexe en suite (4 fmly) ⊘ in 10 bedrooms
S £69-£110; D £89-£120 (incl. bkfst) **Facilities** STV ℞ Jacuzzi Xmas
Conf Thtr 400 Class 250 Board 50 Del from £110 **Services** Lift
Parking 42 **Notes LB** Civ Wed 100

★★★ Ⓐ

Dalston Hall

CA5 7JX

☎ 01228 710271 📠 01228 711273

e-mail: info@dalston-hall-hotel.co.uk

dir: M6 junct 42 and follow signs to Dalston 3m from Carlisle
centre on B5299.

Rooms 13 en suite ⊘ in all bedrooms S £85-£115; D £125-£190 (incl.
bkfst) **Facilities** Fishing Xmas **Parking** 80 **Notes** ⊗ ⊘ in restaurant

Ⓤ

Swallow Hilltop

London Rd CA1 2NS

☎ 01228 529255 📠 01228 525238

web: www.swallowhotels.com

SWALLOW HOTELS

At the time of going to press, the star classification for this hotel was
not confirmed. Please refer to the AA internet site www.theAA.com for
current information.

Rooms 92 en suite

England

CARLISLE *continued*

Hotel Ibis Carlisle

Portlands, Botchergate CA1 1RP
☎ 01228 518000 ▤ 01228 518010
e-mail: H3443@accor-hotels.com
web: www.ibishotels.com

dir: *M6 junct 42/43 follow signs for city centre. Hotel on Botchergate*

Modern, budget hotel offering comfortable accommodation in bright and practical bedrooms. Breakfast is self-service and dinner is available in the restaurant. For further details, consult the Hotel Groups page.

Rooms 102 en suite S £45-£50; D £45-£50

Premier Travel Inn Carlisle (Central)

Warwick Rd CA1 2WF
☎ 08701 977053 ▤ 01228 534096
web: www.premiertravelinn.com

dir: *M6 junct 43, on A69*

High quality, modern budget accommodation ideal for both families and business travellers. Spacious, en suite bedrooms feature bath and shower, satellite TV and many have telephones and modem points. The adjacent family restaurant features a wide and varied menu. For further details consult the Hotel Groups page.

Rooms 44 en suite

Premier Travel Inn Carlisle North

Kingstown Rd CA3 0AT
☎ 0870 9906502 ▤ 0870 9906503
dir: *1m from M6 junct 44, on A7 towards Carlisle, on left*
Rooms 49 en suite **Conf** Board 12

Premier Travel Inn Carlisle South

Carleton CA4 0AD
☎ 08701 977054 ▤ 01228 633313
dir: *just off M6 junct 42, south of Carlisle*
Rooms 40 en suite **Conf** Thtr 50 Class 50

Travelodge Carlisle Todhills

A74 Southbound, Todhills CA6 4HA
☎ 08700 850 950 ▤ 01228 674335
web: www.travelodge.co.uk

dir: *S'bound carriageway of A74 (M)*

Travelodge offers good quality, good value, modern accommodation. Ideal for families, the spacious en suite bedrooms include remote-control TV, tea and coffee-making facilities and comfortable beds. Meals can be taken at the nearby family restaurant. See Hotel Groups pages for further details.

Rooms 40 en suite S fr £26; D fr £26

CARTMEL   MAP 18 SD37

★★ 78% ◉ **HOTEL**

Aynsome Manor

LA11 6HH
☎ 015395 36653 ▤ 015395 36016
e-mail: info@aynsomemanorhotel.co.uk

dir: *M6 junct 36, A590 signed Barrow-in-Furness towards Cartmel. Left at end of road, hotel before village*

Dating back, in part, to the early 16th century, this manor house overlooks the fells and the nearby priory. Spacious bedrooms, including some courtyard rooms, are comfortably furnished. Dinner in the elegant restaurant features local produce whenever possible, and there is a choice of lounges to relax in afterwards.

Rooms 10 en suite 2 annexe en suite (2 fmly) S £85-£92; D £120-£162
(incl. bkfst & dinner) **Parking** 20 **Notes LB** ⊗ in restaurant Closed 2-31 Jan RS Sun

CASTLE CARROCK   MAP 18 NY55

◉ **RESTAURANT WITH ROOMS**

The Weary at Castle Carrock

Castle Carrock CA8 9LU
☎ 01228 670230 & 670089 ▤ 01228 670089
e-mail: relax@theweary.com
web: www.theweary.com

dir: *A69 onto B6143 immediate left. Continue for 4m, at T-junct turn left. Hotel 1m on right in centre of village*

Dating back to 1740 but transformed over the past four years into a stylish & contemporary restaurant with rooms. Bedrooms & bathrooms are features in themselves brimming with modern gadgets - the bathrooms have TVs built into the bath/shower areas. The restaurant is light and airy and opens up into the walled garden area in the summer months. Hospitality is noteworthy.

Rooms 5 en suite ⊗ in all bedrooms S £65-£85; D £95-£135
Facilities STV **Parking** 8 **Notes LB** ⊗

CLEATOR
MAP 18 NY01

★★★ 77% **HOTEL**

Swallow Ennerdale Country House

SWALLOW HOTELS

CA23 3DT

☎ 01946 813907 ▤ 01946 815260

dir: *M6 junct 40, A66 to Cockermouth. A5086 from Cockermouth to Egremont, hotel 12m on left in village*

This fine Grade II listed building (now under new ownership) lies on the edge of the village and is backed by landscaped gardens. Impressive bedrooms, including split-level suites and four-poster rooms, are richly furnished, smartly decorated and offer an amazing array of facilities. Attractive public areas include an elegant restaurant, an inviting lounge and an American themed bar, which offers a good range of bar meals.

Rooms 30 en suite (4 fmly) ⊛ in 24 bedrooms S £69-£109; D £79-£149 (incl. bkfst) **Facilities** STV Xmas **Conf** BC Thtr 150 Class 100 Board 40 Del from £99 **Parking** 65 **Notes LB** ⊗ ⊛ in restaurant Civ Wed 120

COCKERMOUTH
MAP 18 NY13

★★★ 77% ⚫ **HOTEL**

The Trout

Crown St CA13 0EJ

☎ 01900 823591 ▤ 01900 827514

e-mail: enquiries@trouthotel.co.uk

web: www.trouthotel.co.uk

dir: *next to Wordsworth House*

Dating back to 1670, this privately owned hotel has an enviable setting on the banks of the River Derwent. The well-equipped bedrooms, some contained in a wing overlooking the river, are mostly spacious and comfortable. The Terrace Bar and Bistro, serving food all day, has a sheltered patio area. There is also a cosy bar, a choice of lounge areas and an attractive, traditional-style dining room that offers a good choice of set-price dishes.

Rooms 47 en suite (4 fmly) (15 GF) ⊛ in 12 bedrooms S £59.95-£89.95, D £109-£159 (incl. bkfst) **Facilities** STV Fishing Wi-fi in bedrooms Xmas **Conf** Thtr 25 Class 20 Board 20 Del from £150 **Parking** 40 **Notes LB** ⊛ in restaurant Civ Wed 60

★★★ 70% **HOTEL**

Shepherds Hotel

Lakeland Sheep & Wool Centre, Egremont Rd CA13 0QX

☎ 01900 822673 ▤ 01900 822673

e-mail: reception@shepherdshotel.co.uk

web: www.shepherdshotel.co.uk

dir: *at junct of A66 & A5086 S of Cockermouth, entrance off A5086, 200mtrs off rdbt*

This hotel is modern in style and offers thoughtfully equipped accommodation. The property also houses the Lakeland Sheep and Wool Centre, with live sheep shows from Easter to mid November. A restaurant serving a wide variety of meals and snacks is open all day.

Rooms 26 en suite (4 fmly) (13 GF) ⊛ in 13 bedrooms S £49-£60; D £49-£60 (incl. bkfst) **Facilities** FTV Pool table, Small childs play area **Conf** BC **Services** Lift **Parking** 100 **Notes** Closed 4-14 Jan, 25 Dec

CROOKLANDS
MAP 18 SD58

★★★ 70% **HOTEL**

Crooklands

LA7 7NW

☎ 015395 67432 ▤ 015395 67525

e-mail: reception@crooklands.com

web: www.crooklands.com

dir: *M6 junct 36 onto A65. Left at rdbt. Hotel 1.5m on right past garage*

Although only a stone's throw from the M6, this hotel enjoys a peaceful rural location. Housed in a converted 200-year-old farmhouse, the restaurant retains many original features such as beams and stone walls. Bedrooms are a mix of modern and traditional and vary in size. The hotel is a popular stop for both leisure and corporate guests travelling between England and Scotland.

Rooms 30 en suite (3 fmly) (14 GF) ⊛ in 29 bedrooms S £60; D £72 (incl. bkfst) **Facilities** FTV **Conf** Thtr 80 Class 50 Board 40 Del from £110 **Parking** 80 **Notes LB** ⊗ ⊛ in restaurant Closed 24-26 Dec

CROSTHWAITE
MAP 18 SD49

★★★ 68% **HOTEL**

Damson Dene

LA8 8JE

☎ 015395 68676 ▤ 015395 68227

e-mail: info@damsondene.co.uk

web: www.bestlakesbreaks.co.uk

dir: *M6 junct 36, A590 signed Barrow-in-Furness. 5m right onto A5074. Hotel on right in 5m*

A short drive from Lake Windermere, this hotel enjoys a tranquil and scenic setting. Bedrooms include a number with four-poster beds and jacuzzi baths. The spacious restaurant serves a daily-changing menu, with some of the produce originating from the hotel's own kitchen garden. Real fires warm the lounge in the cooler months and leisure facilities are available.

Rooms 37 en suite (4 fmly) (9 GF) ⊛ in 29 bedrooms S £54-£74; D £78-£118 (incl. bkfst) **Facilities** Spa 🟅 Squash Sauna Solarium Gym Jacuzzi Beauty salon Xmas **Conf** Thtr 140 Class 60 Board 40 Del from £95 **Parking** 45 **Notes LB** ⊛ in restaurant Civ Wed 120

England

ELTERWATER   MAP 18 NY30

★★★ 81% **HOTEL**

Langdale Hotel & Country Club
LA22 9JD
☎ 015394 37302 📠 015394 37694
e-mail: info@langdale.co.uk
web: www.langdale.co.uk/accomm/frhotel.htm
dir: into Langdale, hotel part of private estate on left

Founded on the site of an abandoned 19th-century gunpowder works, this modern hotel is set in 35 acres of woodland and waterways. Comfortable bedrooms, many with spa baths, vary in size. Extensive public areas include a choice of stylish restaurants, conference and leisure facilities and an elegant bar with an interesting selection of snuff. There is also a traditional pub run by the hotel just along the main road.

Rooms 5 en suite 52 annexe en suite (8 fmly) (17 GF) ⊘ in all bedrooms S £65-£110; D £80-£170 (incl. bkfst) **Facilities Spa** STV Wi-fi available 🏊 supervised ⌣ Fishing Squash Sauna Solarium Gym Jacuzzi Steam room Hair & beauty salon Cycle hire Xmas **Conf** Thtr 80 Class 40 Board 35 **Parking** 65 **Notes LB** ⊗ ⊘ in restaurant

★★ 72% **HOTEL**

New Dungeon Ghyll
Langdale LA22 9JX
☎ 015394 37213 📠 015394 37666
e-mail: enquiries@dungeon-ghyll.com
web: www.dungeon-ghyll.com
dir: from Ambleside follow A593 towards Coniston for 3m, at Skelwith Bridge right onto B5343 towards 'The Langdales'

This friendly hotel enjoys a tranquil, idyllic position at the head of the valley, set among the impressive peaks of Langdale. Bedrooms vary in size and style and are brightly decorated with smart furnishings. Bar meals are served all day, and dinner can be enjoyed in the restaurant overlooking the landscaped gardens; there is also a cosy lounge/bar.

Rooms 20 en suite (1 fmly) (3 GF) ⊘ in all bedrooms **Facilities** Xmas **Parking** 30 **Notes** ⊘ in restaurant

ESKDALE GREEN   MAP 18 NY10

★★ 72% **HOTEL**

Bower House Inn
CA19 1TD
☎ 019467 23244 📠 019467 23308
e-mail: Info@bowerhouseinn.freeserve.co.uk
web: www.bowerhouseinn.co.uk
dir: 4m off A595 0.5m W of Eskdale Green

This former farmhouse enjoys a countryside location with delightful mountain views and offers true peace and relaxation. The traditional bar and formal restaurant, where a good range of dishes is served, reflect the coaching inn origins of the house. There are ten attractive

continued

bedrooms situated in a converted barn, plus those in both the original house and the Garden Cottage.

Bower House Inn

Rooms 10 en suite 19 annexe en suite (2 fmly) (9 GF) **Facilities** STV **Conf** Thtr 40 Class 20 Board 30 **Parking** 60 **Notes LB** ⊘ in restaurant Civ Wed 40

GLENRIDDING   MAP 18 NY31

★★★ 77% **HOTEL**

The Inn on the Lake
Lake Ullswater, Glenridding CA11 0PE
☎ 017684 82444 📠 017684 82303
e-mail: info@innonthelakeullswater.co.uk
web: www.innonthelakeullswater.com
dir: M6 junct 40, then A66 to Keswick. At rdbt take A592 to Ullswater Lake. Along lake to Glenridding. Hotel on left on entering village

In a picturesque lakeside setting, this restored Victorian hotel is a popular leisure destination as well as catering for weddings and conferences. Superb views may be enjoyed from the bedrooms and from the garden terrace where afternoon teas are served during warmer months. There is a popular pub in the grounds, and moorings for yachts are available to guests. Sailing tuition can be arranged.

Rooms 46 en suite (6 fmly) (2 GF) ⊘ in 15 bedrooms S fr £75; D £67-£97 (incl. bkfst) **Facilities** STV ⅃ 9 ⌣ Fishing Sauna Solarium Gym ⌣ Putt green Jacuzzi Wi-fi in bedrooms Sailing, 9 hole pitch and putt, Bowls, Lake Bathing Xmas **Conf** BC Thtr 120 Class 60 Board 40 Del from £110 **Services** Lift **Parking** 200 **Notes LB** ⊘ in restaurant Civ Wed 100

See advertisement under PENRITH

★★★ 73% **HOTEL**

Best Western Glenridding Hotel

CA11 0PB

☎ 01768 482228 📠 01768 482555

e-mail: glenridding@bestwestern.co.uk

dir: Northbound M6 exit 36, A591 Windermere then A592 14m. Southbound M6 exit 40, A592 for 13m

This friendly hotel benefits from a picturesque location in the village centre, and many of the bedrooms have fine views of the lake and fells. Public areas are extensive and include a choice of restaurants and bars, a coffee shop including a cyber café, and smart leisure facilities. The Garden Room has now been refurbished and is an ideal venue for weddings and functions.

Rooms 36 en suite (9 fmly) ⊛ in all bedrooms S £60-£85; D £120-£155 (incl. bkfst) **Facilities** STV ☒ ☻ Sauna Jacuzzi Wi-fi in bedrooms Billiards 3/4 Snooker table Table tennis Xmas **Conf** Thtr 30 Class 30 Board 20 Del from £110 **Services** Lift **Parking** 38 **Notes LB** ⊛ in restaurant Civ Wed 100

GRANGE-OVER-SANDS   **MAP 18 SD47**

★★★ 80% **HOTEL**

Netherwood

Lindale Rd LA11 6ET

☎ 015395 32552 📠 34121

e-mail: enquiries@netherwood-hotel

dir: on B5277 before station

This imposing hotel stands in terraced grounds and enjoys fine views of Morecambe Bay. Though a popular conference and wedding venue, good levels of hospitality and service ensure all guests are well looked after. Bedrooms vary in size but all are well furnished and decorated & have smart modern bathrooms. Magnificent woodwork is a feature of the public areas.

Rooms 32 en suite (5 fmly) ⊛ in 18 bedrooms S £105-£115; D £170-£190 (incl. bkfst) **Facilities** Spa ☒ supervised Solarium Gym ☻ Jacuzzi Beauty salon, Steam room ch fac **Conf** BC Thtr 150 Class 30 Board 40 Del from £135 **Services** Lift **Parking** 100 **Notes LB** ⊛ in restaurant Civ Wed 180

★★★ 71% **HOTEL**

Cumbria Grand

LA11 6EN

☎ 015395 32331 📠 015395 34534

e-mail: salescumbria@strathmorehotels.com

dir: M6 junct 36, A590 & follow Grange-over-Sands signs

Set within extensive grounds, this large hotel offers fine views over Morecambe Bay and caters well for a mixed market. Public areas are pure nostalgia, and include a grand dining room and fine ballroom.

continued

At the time of inspection nearly all the bedrooms and the public areas had been refurbished. Good value is provided.

Cumbria Grand

Rooms 122 en suite (10 fmly) **Facilities** STV ☻ Snooker Putt green Pool table Putting Table tennis Darts ♫ **Services** Lift **Parking** 75 **Notes** ⊛ in restaurant

---

★★★ 67% **HOTEL**

Graythwaite Manor

Fernhill Rd LA11 7JE

☎ 015395 32001 & 33755 📠 015395 35549

e-mail: enquiries@graythwaitemanor.co.uk

dir: B5277 through Grange, Fernhill Rd opposite fire station behind small traffic island, hotel 1st left

This well established hotel is set in very well tended gardens, complete with sub-tropical plants, and offers a delightful outlook over Morecambe Bay. Public areas include an Orangery, a number of comfortable lounges and an elegant restaurant. The comfortable bedrooms, which vary in size, are traditional in style.

Rooms 24 en suite S £58-£65.50 (incl. bkfst) **Facilities** Snooker ☻ Bowling green Xmas **Services** Lift **Parking** 34 **Notes LB** ⊛ in restaurant Civ Wed

---

★★ 72% **HOTEL**

Hampsfell House

Hampsfell Rd LA11 6BG

☎ 015395 32567 📠 015395 35995

e-mail: hampsfellhotel@msn.com

dir: M6 junct 36 take A590 signed Barrow-in-Furness. At junct with B5277, follow to Grange-over-Sands signs. Left at rdbt into Main St, 2nd rdbt right and right at x-rds. At Hampsfell Rd left

Dating back to 1800, this owner managed hotel is peacefully set in two acres of private grounds yet is just a comfortable walk from the town centre. Bedrooms are smartly decorated and well maintained. The two cosy and comfortable lounges, where guests can enjoy pre-dinner drinks, share a central bar. Comprehensive and imaginative dinners are taken in an attractive dining room.

Rooms 9 en suite (1 GF) ⊛ in all bedrooms S £54-£85; D £78-£150 (incl. bkfst) **Conf** Thtr 20 Class 10 Board 15 Del from £70 **Parking** 20 **Notes LB** ⊛ No children ⊛ in restaurant Closed 3-31 Jan

England

GRANGE-OVER-SANDS *continued*

INSPECTORS' CHOICE

★ ⑧ **HOTEL**

Clare House

Park Rd LA11 7HQ

☎ 015395 33026 & 34253 🖷 015395 34310

e-mail: info@clarehousehotel.co.uk

web: www.clarehousehotel.co.uk

dir: *off A590 onto B5277, through Lindale into Grange, keep left, hotel 0.5m on left past Crown Hill and St Paul's Church*

A warm and genuine welcome awaits guests at this delightful family-run hotel. Sitting in its own secluded gardens, it provides a relaxed haven in which to enjoy the panoramic views across Morecambe Bay. Bedrooms and public areas are comfortable and attractively furnished. Skilfully prepared dinners and hearty breakfasts are served in the elegant dining room.

Rooms 19 rms (18 en suite) (1 fmly) (4 GF) S £68; D £136 (incl. bkfst & dinner) **Facilities** ⋓ Putt green **Parking** 18 **Notes LB** ⊗ ⊘ in restaurant Closed Dec-Mar RS 10-30 Nov

---

GRASMERE   MAP 18 NY30

★★★★ 77% ⑧⑧ **HOTEL**

Wordsworth

LA22 9SW

☎ 015394 35592 🖷 015394 35765

e-mail: enquiry@thewordsworthhotel.couk

web: www.thewordsworthhotel.co.uk

dir: *centre of village adjacent to St Oswald's Church*

This traditional hotel, named after the famous poet who is buried in the adjacent churchyard, is set in well-tended gardens against a backdrop of towering fells. Bedrooms, varying in size and style, are

continued

complemented by a choice of comfortable lounge areas. To complete the package there are comprehensive leisure facilities, and diners have a choice between the popular pub and the more formal Prelude restaurant.

Rooms 37 en suite (3 fmly) S £70-£100; D £140-£180 (incl. bkfst) **Facilities** 🏋 Sauna Solarium Gym ⋓ Jacuzzi Wi-fi in bedrooms 🎵 ch fac Xmas **Conf** BC Thtr 100 Class 50 Board 40 Del from £130 **Services** Lift **Parking** 60 **Notes LB** ⊗ ⊘ in restaurant Civ Wed 100

See advert on opposite page

★★★ 78% **HOTEL**

Best Western Grasmere Red Lion

Red Lion Square LA22 9SS

☎ 015394 35456 🖷 015394 35579

e-mail: enquiries@hotelgrasmere.uk.com

web: www.hotelslakedistrict.com

dir: *off A591, signed Grasmere Village, hotel in centre of village*

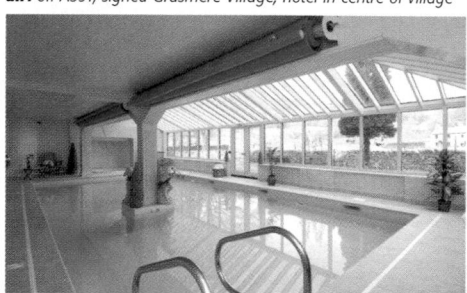

This modernised and extended 18th-century coaching inn, located in the heart of the village, offers spacious well-equipped rooms and a number of meeting and conference facilities. The Lamb Inn offers a range of pub meals to complement the more formal Courtyard restaurant. The spacious and comfortable lounge area is ideal for relaxing, and for the more energetic there is a pool and gym.

Rooms 47 en suite (4 fmly) ⊘ in 22 bedrooms S £49.50-£63.50; D £100-£128 (incl. bkfst) **Facilities** STV 🏋 Sauna Gym Jacuzzi Hairdressing Guests may borrow a permit to fish the local angling assoc. waters Xmas **Conf** Thtr 60 Class 30 Board 30 **Services** Lift **Parking** 38 **Notes** ⊘ in restaurant

---

★★★ 78% **COUNTRY HOUSE HOTEL**

Gold Rill Country House

Red Bank Rd LA22 9PU

☎ 015394 35486 🖷 015394 35486

e-mail: reception@gold-rill.com

web: www.goldrill.co.uk

dir: *turn off A591 into village centre, turn into road opposite St Oswald's Church. Hotel 300yds on left*

This popular hotel enjoys a fine location on the edge of the village with spectacular views of the lake and surrounding fells. Attractive bedrooms, some with balconies, are tastefully decorated and many have separate, comfortable seating areas. The hotel boasts a private pier, an outdoor heated pool and a putting green. Public areas include a well-appointed restaurant and choice of lounges.

Rooms 25 en suite 6 annexe en suite (2 fmly) S £54-£76; D £108-£152 (incl. bkfst & dinner) **Facilities** STV 🏋 Putt green Xmas **Parking** 35 **Notes LB** ⊗ ⊘ in restaurant Closed mid Dec-mid Jan (open New Year)

★★★ 77% **HOTEL**

Macdonald Swan

LA22 9RF

☎ 0870 400 8132 ▤ 015394 35741

e-mail: swangrasmere@macdonald-hotels.co.uk

web: www.macdonald-hotels.co.uk

dir: M6 junct 36, A591 towards Kendal, A590 to Keswick through Ambleside. The Swan on right on entering the village

Close to Dove Cottage and occupying a prominent position on the edge of the village, this 300-year-old inn is mentioned in Wordsworth's poem '*The Waggoner*'. Attractive public areas are spacious and comfortable, and bedrooms are equally stylish - some have CD players. A good range of bar meals is available, while the elegant restaurant offers more formal dining.

Rooms 38 en suite (1 fmly) (28 GF) ⊛ in 14 bedrooms S £90-£115; D £120-£200 (incl. bkfst) **Facilities** Xmas **Conf** Thtr 30 Class 24 Board 16 Del from £125 **Parking** 45 **Notes** LB ⊛ in restaurant Civ Wed 58

★★★ 73% ◉◉ **HOTEL**

Rothay Garden

Broadgate LA22 9RJ

☎ 015394 35334 ▤ 015394 35723

e-mail: stay@rothay-garden.com

web: www.rothay-garden.com

dir: off A591, opposite Swan Hotel, into Grasmere, 300yds on left

Located on the northern approach to this unspoilt Cumbrian village, this hotel offers comfortable bedrooms, including some with four-posters and whirlpool baths. There is a choice of relaxing lounges, a cosy cocktail bar and an attractive conservatory restaurant, that looks out across the garden towards the fells.

Rooms 25 en suite (2 fmly) (6 GF) ⊛ in 6 bedrooms S fr £75; D fr £150 (incl. bkfst & dinner) **Facilities** STV FTV Fishing Jacuzzi use of local leisure club ch fac Xmas **Parking** 38 **Notes** LB ⊛ in restaurant

See advert on this page

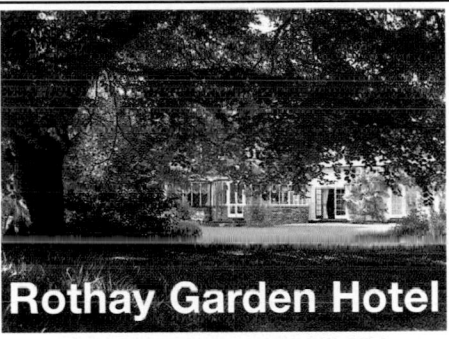
England

GRASMERE *continued*

★★★ 70% HOTEL

Waterside Hotel

Keswick Rd LA22 9PR

☎ 0870 333 9135 🖷 0870 333 9235

e-mail: mark@watersidegrasmere.com

dir: *M6 junct 36 then A591, past Windermere & Ambleside. Hotel on left on entering Grasmere.*

This large hotel stands in its own gardens leading to the lake, and many of the bedrooms have fine views over the surrounding fells. Bedrooms are comfortably furnished and include a stylish suite, complete with a four-poster bed. Service is friendly and the choice of meals, from a selection of restaurant and bar menus, should suit most tastes.

Rooms 71 en suite (8 fmly) ⊘ in 58 bedrooms S £54-£88; D £64-£160 (incl. bkfst) **Facilities** STV Fishing Wi-fi available Xmas **Conf** Thtr 110 Class 60 Board 40 **Parking** 60 **Notes LB** ⊘ in restaurant Civ Wed 120

INSPECTORS' CHOICE

★★ ◉ HOTEL

White Moss House

Rydal Water LA22 9SE

☎ 015394 35295 🖷 015394 35516

e-mail: sue@whitemoss.com

web: www.whitemoss.com

dir: *on A591, 1m S of Grasmere*

This traditional Lakeland house was once bought by Wordsworth for his son. It benefits from a central location and has a loyal following. The individually styled bedrooms are comfortable and thoughtfully equipped. There is also a two-room suite in a cottage on the hillside above the hotel. The five-course set dinner makes

continued

---

good use of the quality local ingredients, and afternoon tea and pre-dinner drinks are served in the inviting lounge.

Rooms 5 en suite 2 annexe en suite S fr £99; D £170-£218 (incl. bkfst & dinner) **Facilities** Free use local leisure club, Free fishing at local waters, walking **Parking** 10 **Notes LB** ⊗ ⊘ in restaurant Closed Dec-Jan RS Sun

★★ 76% ◉ HOTEL

Grasmere

Broadgate LA22 9TA

☎ 015394 35277 🖷 015394 35277

e-mail: enquiries@grasmerehotel.co.uk

web: www.grasmerehotel.co.uk

dir: *A591 north from Ambleside, 2nd left into Grasmere town centre. Follow road over humpback bridge, past playing field. Hotel on left*

Attentive and hospitable service contribute to the atmosphere at this family-run hotel, set in secluded gardens by the River Rothay. There are two inviting lounges (one with residents' bar) and an attractive dining room looking onto the garden. The thoughtfully prepared dinner menu makes good use of fresh ingredients. Pine furniture is featured in most bedrooms, along with welcome personal touches.

Rooms 13 en suite (2 GF) ⊘ in all bedrooms S £60-£75; D £110-£150 (incl. bkfst & dinner) **Facilities** Full leisure facilities at nearby country club, Free fishing permit available Xmas **Parking** 14 **Notes LB** No children 10yrs ⊘ in restaurant Closed 3 Jan-early Feb

★★ 74% HOTEL

Oak Bank

Broadgate LA22 9TA

☎ 015394 35217 🖷 015394 35685

e-mail: info@lakedistricthotel.co.uk

dir: *on right in village centre*

This privately owned and personally run hotel provides well-equipped accommodation, including a bedroom on ground-floor level and a four-poster room. Public areas include a choice of comfortable lounges with welcoming log fires when the weather is cold. There is a pleasant bar and an attractive restaurant with a conservatory extension overlooking the garden.

Rooms 15 en suite (1 fmly) (1 GF) ⊘ in all bedrooms S £80-£85; D £120-£140 (incl. bkfst & dinner) **Facilities** Jacuzzi Xmas **Parking** 11 **Notes LB** ⊘ in restaurant Closed 6-20 Jan

HAWKSHEAD (NEAR AMBLESIDE)

MAP 18 SD39

★★ 71% ⊛ HOTEL

Queen's Head

Main St LA22 0NS

☎ 015394 36271 ⊟ 015394 36722

e-mail: enquiries@queensheadhotel.co.uk

web: www.queenshead.co.uk

dir: M6 junct 36, then A590 to Newby Bridge. Over rdbt, 1st right for 8m into Hawkshead

This 16th century inn features a wood-panelled bar with low, oak-beamed ceilings and an open log fire. Substantial, carefully prepared meals are served in the bar and in the pretty dining room. The bedrooms, three of which are in an adjacent cottage, are attractively furnished and include some four-poster rooms.

Rooms 11 rms (9 en suite) 3 annexe en suite (2 fmly) (2 GF) ⊛ in all bedrooms S £50-£60; D £75-£90 (incl. bkfst) **Facilities** Xmas **Notes LB** ⊛ ⊘ in restaurant

See advert on this page

HOWTOWN (NEAR POOLEY BRIDGE)

MAP 18 NY41

INSPECTORS' CHOICE

★★★ ⊛⊛ HOTEL

Sharrow Bay Country House

Sharrow Bay CA10 2LZ

☎ 017684 86301 & 86483 ⊟ 017684 86349

e-mail: info@sharrowbay.co.uk

web: www.vonessenhotels.co.uk

dir: at Pooley Bridge right fork by church to Howtown. At x-rds right and follow Lakeside Rd for 2m

Enjoying breathtaking views and an idyllic location on the shores
continued

of Lake Ullswater, Sharrow Bay is often described as the first country-house hotel. Individually styled bedrooms, all with a host of thoughtful extras, are situated either in the main house, in delightful buildings in the grounds or at Bank House - an Elizabethan farmhouse complete with lounges and breakfast room. Opulently furnished public areas include a choice of inviting lounges and two elegant dining rooms.

Rooms 8 en suite 14 annexe en suite (5 GF) **Conf** Thtr 30 Class 15 Board 20 **Parking** 35 **Notes LB** ⊛ No children 13yrs ⊘ in restaurant Civ Wed 30

KENDAL

MAP 18 SD59

See also Crooklands

★★★ 81% ⊛⊛ HOTEL

The Castle Green Hotel in Kendal

LA9 6BH

Best Western

☎ 01539 734000 ⊟ 01539 735522

e-mail: reception@castlegreen.co.uk

web: www.castlegreen.co.uk

dir: M6 junct 36, towards Kendal. Right at 1st lights, left at rdbt to "K" Village then right for 0.75m to hotel at T- junct

This smart, modern hotel enjoys a peaceful location and is conveniently situated for access to both the town centre and the M6. Stylish bedrooms are thoughtfully equipped for both the business and leisure guest. The Greenhouse Restaurant provides imaginative dishes from its theatre-style kitchen; alternatively Alexander's pub serves food

continued on page 154

England

KENDAL *continued*

all day. The hotel has a fully equipped business centre and leisure club.

Rooms 100 en suite (3 fmly) (25 GF) ⊗ in 79 bedrooms S £79-£129; D £88-£158 (incl. bkfst) **Facilities** STV ⊠ Solarium Gym Wi-fi available Steam Room, Aerobics, Yoga, Beauty Salon ♫ Xmas **Conf** BC Thtr 350 Class 120 Board 100 Del £145 **Services** Lift **Parking** 200 **Notes LB** ⊗ ⊗ in restaurant Civ Wed 250

★★★ 70% **HOTEL**

Riverside Hotel Kendal

Beezon Rd, Stramongate Bridge LA9 6EL
☎ 01539 734861 ▤ 01539 734863
e-mail: info@riversidekendal.co.uk
web: www.bestlakesbreaks.co.uk
dir: M6 junct 36 Sedburgh, Kendal 7m, left at end of Ann St, 1st right onto Beezon Rd, hotel on left

Centrally located in this market town, and enjoying a peaceful riverside location, this 17th-century former tannery provides a suitable base for both business travellers and tourists. The comfortable bedrooms are well equipped, and open-plan day rooms include the attractive restaurant and bar. Conference facilities are available, and the leisure club proves popular.

Rooms 47 en suite (18 fmly) (10 GF) ⊗ in 20 bedrooms **Facilities Spa** STV ⊠ supervised Sauna Gym Jacuzzi Beauty Salon Xmas **Conf** Thtr 200 Class 200 Board 90 Del from £85 **Services** Lift **Parking** 60 **Notes** ⊗ in restaurant Civ Wed 120

See advert on opposite page

KESWICK   MAP 18 NY22

★★★ 78% ◉ ◉ **COUNTRY HOUSE HOTEL**

Dale Head Hall Lakeside

Lake Thirlmere CA12 4TN
☎ 017687 72478 ▤ 017687 71070
e-mail: onthelakeside@daleheadhall.co.uk
web: www.daleheadhall.co.uk
dir: between Keswick & grasmere. Off A591 onto private drive

Set in attractive grounds, this historic lakeside residence dates from the 16th century. Comfortable and inviting public areas include a choice of lounges (no bar) and an atmospheric beamed restaurant featuring a short but daily-changing menu. Most bedrooms are very spacious, with most having lake views.

continued

Dale Head Hall Lakeside

Rooms 12 en suite (1 fmly) (2 GF) ⊗ in all bedrooms S £127.50-£135; D £205-£260 (incl. bkfst & dinner) **Facilities** no TV in bdrms ⊗ ⊌ Fishing permit available Boating ch fac Xmas **Parking** 32 **Notes LB** ⊗ ⊗ in restaurant Closed 3 Jan-26 Jan

See advert on page 157

★★★ 77% **HOTEL**

Derwentwater

Portinscale CA12 5RE
☎ 017687 72538 ▤ 017687 71002
e-mail: info@derwentwater-hotel.co.uk
web: www.derwentwater-hotel.co.uk
dir: off A66 turn into Portinscale and through village then as road turns right take left turn as signed

This is a popular and friendly holiday hotel with gardens that stretch down to the shores of Derwentwater. It offers a wide range of bedrooms, all thoughtfully equipped and some with good views of the lake. Inviting public areas include a conservatory lounge and shop.

Rooms 46 en suite (1 fmly) (2 GF) S £75-£95; D £150-£210 (incl. bkfst) **Facilities** Fishing ⊌ Putt green Access to local leisure facilities ♫ Xmas **Conf** Thtr 20 Class 10 Board 14 **Services** Lift **Parking** 60 **Notes LB** ⊗ in restaurant

See advert on page 157

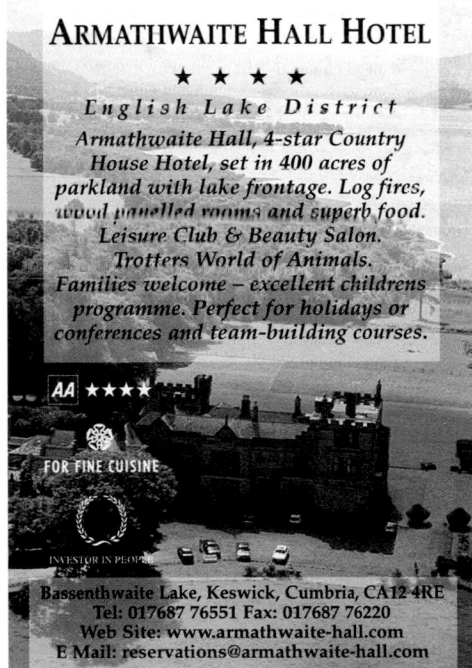

KESWICK *continued*

★★★ 73% HOTEL

Skiddaw
Main St CA12 5BN
☎ 017687 72071 📠 017687 74850
e-mail: info@skiddawhotel.co.uk
web: www.skiddawhotel.co.uk
dir: *A66 to Keswick, follow town centre signs. Hotel in market square*

Occupying a central position overlooking Market Square, this hotel provides smartly furnished bedrooms that include some family suites and a room with a four-poster bed. In addition to the restaurant, food is served all day in the bar. There is also a quiet residents' lounge and two conference rooms.

Rooms 40 en suite (7 fmly) ⊘ in 10 bedrooms S £40-£146; D £80-£146 (incl. bkfst) **Facilities** STV Sauna Xmas **Conf** Thtr 70 Class 60 Board 40 Del from £90 **Services** Lift **Parking** 22 **Notes LB** ⊗ ⊘ in restaurant Civ Wed 90

See advert on opposite page

★★★ 67% HOTEL

Keswick Country House
Station Rd CA12 4NQ
☎ 0845 458 4333 📠 01253 754222
e-mail: reservations@choice-hotels.co.uk
web: www.thekeswickhotel.co.uk
dir: *M6 junct 40/A66 , 1st slip road into Keswick, then follow signs for leisure pool.*

This impressive Victorian hotel is set amid attractive gardens close to the town centre. Eight superior bedrooms are available in the Station Wing which is accessed through a Victorian conservatory. Main house rooms are comfortably modern in style and offer a good range of amenities. Public areas include a well-stocked bar, a spacious and relaxing lounge, and an attractive restaurant serving interesting dinners.

Rooms 74 en suite (6 fmly) (4 GF) **Facilities** STV Snooker ✤ Putt green Leisure facilities close by. **Conf** Thtr 110 Class 70 Board 60 Del from £95 **Services** Lift **Parking** 70 **Notes** ⊗ ⊘ in restaurant Civ Wed 100

★★ ⊛⊛ HOTEL

Swinside Lodge
Grange Rd, Newlands CA12 5UE
☎ 017687 72948 📠 017687 73312
e-mail: info@swinsidelodge-hotel.co.uk
web: www.swinsidelodge-hotel.co.uk
dir: *off A66 left at Portinscale. Follow road to Grange for 2m ignoring signs to Swinside & Newlands Valley*

No visit to the Lake District is complete without a stay at this delightful country house. Superb hospitality and attentive services are the key to this popular hotel. Bedrooms are cosy, comfortable and thoughtfully equipped, and the elegantly furnished lounges are an ideal place to relax before dinner. The four-course set dinner menu is creative, well prepared and provides superb value for money.

Rooms 8 rms (7 en suite) ⊘ in all bedrooms S fr £98; D £156-£196 (incl. bkfst & dinner) **Facilities** Wi-fi in bedrooms Table Tennis Xmas **Conf** BC **Parking** 12 **Notes LB** ⊗ No children 12yrs ⊘ in restaurant

★★ 82% ⊛⊛ HOTEL

Highfield
The Heads CA12 5ER
☎ 017687 72508 📠 017687 80634
e-mail: info@highfieldkeswick.co.uk
web: www.highfieldkeswick.co.uk
dir: *M6 junct 40, take A66 2nd exit at rdbt. Left following road to T- junct. Left again and right at mini rdbt. Then turn 4th right*

This friendly hotel close to the centre of town offers stunning views of Skiddaw, Cats Bells and Derwent Water. Elegant bedrooms, many of them spacious, are thoughtfully equipped. Public areas include a choice of comfortable lounges and a traditional restaurant, where imaginative, modern cuisine is served.

Rooms 18 en suite (2 fmly) (2 GF) ⊘ in all bedrooms S £65-£75; D £110-£170 (incl. bkfst & dinner) **Facilities** Xmas **Conf** BC **Parking** 20 **Notes LB** ⊗ ⊘ in restaurant Closed Jan

The Skiddaw Hotel

★★★

Keswick, The Lake District

Situated in the centre of picturesque Keswick, family owned & run, warm welcome, 40 comfortable bedrooms, cosy lounge bar & superb restaurant.

Main Street, Keswick, Cumbria CA12 5BN
Tel: 017687 72071 Fax: 017687 74850
www.skiddawhotel.co.uk

The Derwentwater Hotel

Privately owned, on the shore of Derwentwater one mile from Keswick.

48 bedrooms many with Lake and Borrowdale Valley view. 16 acres of conservation gardens and grounds down to the Lake.
Magnificent Garden Room/Conservatory with views over putting green to the Lake.

Excellent 'Deer's Leap' restaurant with friendly staff, serving a wide variety of locally produced fare, all prepared with care by our Head Chef.

Guests have temporary membership of luxury health club and spa (no children under 16) at nearby Oxley's Health Club.

Well mannered dogs welcome, and full disabled facilities in two ground floor rooms.

Telephone 017687 72538
www.derwentwater-hotel.co.uk

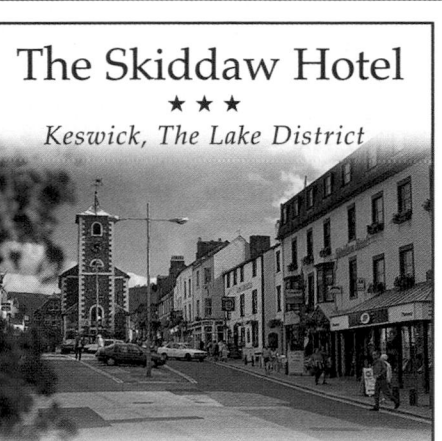

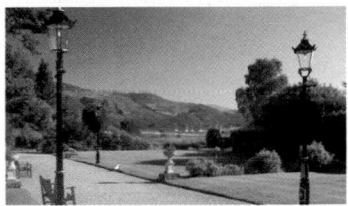

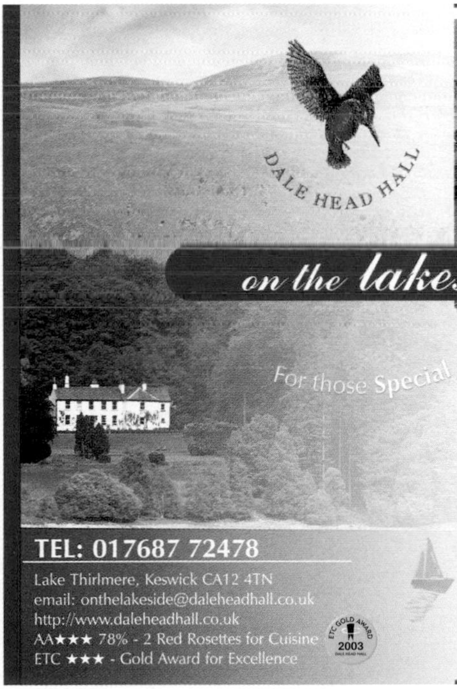

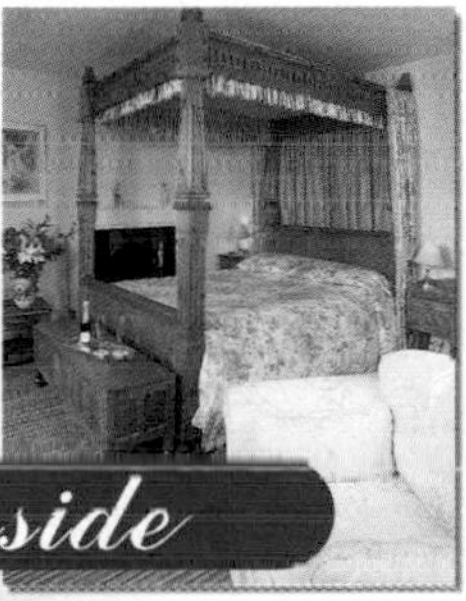

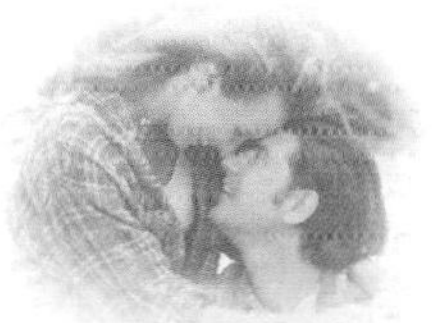

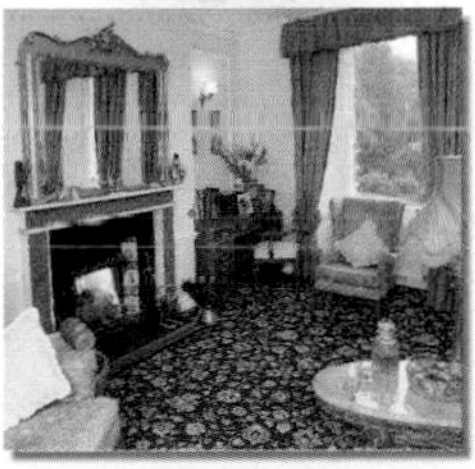

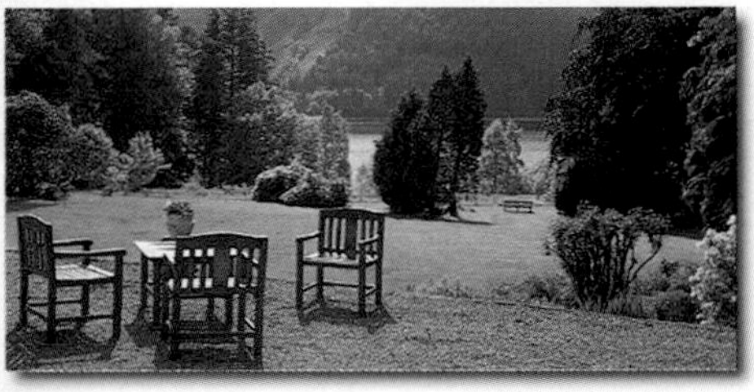

RECOMMENDED BY LEADING HOTEL GUIDES

England

KESWICK *continued*

★★ 79% ⊛ **HOTEL**

Lyzzick Hall Country House

Under Skiddaw CA12 4PY
☎ 017687 72277 🖷 017687 72278
e-mail: lyzzickhall@btconnect.com
web: www.lyzzickhall.co.uk

dir: M6 junct 40 onto A66 to Keswick. Do not enter town, keep on Keswick by-pass. At rdbt 3rd exit onto A591 to Carlisle. Hotel 1.5m on right

This delightful privately-owned and personally run hotel stands in lovely landscaped gardens in the foothills of Skiddaw and enjoys fabulous views across the valley. Bedrooms are smartly appointed and thoughtfully equipped. Public areas include two spacious lounges, a small bar and an attractive restaurant offering a wide range of international cuisine. Staff are delightful and nothing is too much trouble.

Rooms 30 en suite 1 annexe en suite (3 fmly) **Facilities** 🖫 Sauna Jacuzzi ch fac **Conf** Board 15 **Parking** 40 **Notes LB** ⊗ ⊘ in restaurant Closed 24-26 Dec & mid Jan-mid Feb

★★ 78% **HOTEL**

Lairbeck

Vicarage Hill CA12 5QB
☎ 017687 73373 🖷 017687 73144
e-mail: aa@lairbeckhotel-keswick.co.uk
web: www.lairbeckhotel-keswick.co.uk

dir: A66 to rdbt with A591. Left then right onto Vicarage Hill, hotel 150yds on right

This impeccably maintained Victorian country house is situated close to the town in peacefully secluded, attractive gardens. There is a welcoming residents' bar and a formal dining room where a range of freshly prepared dishes are served each day. Bedrooms, which include rooms at ground-floor level, are individually styled and well equipped.

Rooms 14 en suite (1 fmly) (2 GF) ⊘ in all bedrooms S £42-£48; D £84-£96 (incl. bkfst) **Parking** 15 **Notes LB** ⊗ No children 5yrs ⊘ in restaurant Closed Mid Nov-Mid Mar

KILLINGTON LAKE   MAP 18 SD59 MOTORWAY SERVICE AREA (M6)

BUDGET HOTEL

Premier Travel Inn Kendal (Killington Lake)

Killington Lake, Motorway Service Area, Killington LA8 0NW
☎ 08701 977145 🖷 01539 621660
web: www.premiertravelinn.com

dir: From M6 southbound, Inn is 1m S of junct 37. From M6 northbound, exit junct 37 and rejoin southbound. Take access road to Inn

High quality, modern budget accommodation ideal for both families and business travellers. Spacious, en suite bedrooms feature bath and shower, satellite TV and many have telephones and modem points. The adjacent family restaurant features a wide and varied menu. For further details consult the Hotel Groups page.

Rooms 36 en suite **Conf** Thtr 10

KIRKBY LONSDALE   MAP 18 SD67

★★ 72% ⊛ **HOTEL**

The Whoop Hall

Burrow with Burrow LA6 2HP
☎ 015242 71284 🖷 015242 72154
e-mail: info@whoophall.co.uk
dir: on A65 1m SE of Kirkby Lonsdale

This popular inn combines traditional charm with modern facilities, that include a very well-equipped leisure complex. Bedrooms, some with four-poster beds, and some housed in converted barns, are appointed to a smart stylish standard. A fire warms the bar on chillier days, and an interesting choice of dishes is available in the bar and galleried restaurant throughout the day and evening.

Rooms 24 rms (23 en suite) (4 fmly) (2 GF) S £69.50-£80; D £87.50-£120 (incl. bkfst) **Facilities Spa** 🖫 supervised Sauna Solarium Gym Jacuzzi Beauty salon Pool Table ♫ Xmas **Conf** Thtr 169 Class 72 Board 56 **Parking** 100 **Notes LB** ⊗ ⊘ in restaurant Civ Wed 120

England

LITTLE LANGDALE   MAP 18 NY30

★★ 71% HOTEL

Three Shires Inn

LA22 9NZ

☎ 015394 37215 📄 015394 37127

e-mail: enquiry@threeshiresinn.co.uk

web: www.threeshiresinn.co.uk

dir: *off A593, 2.5m from Ambleside at 2nd junct signed Langdales & Wrynose Pass. 1st left after 0.5m, hotel in 1m*

Enjoying an outstanding rural location, this family-run inn was built in 1872. The brightly decorated bedrooms are individual in style and many offer panoramic views. The attractive lounge features a roaring fire in the cooler months and there is a traditional style bar with a great selection of local ales. Meals can be taken in either the bar or cosy restaurant.

Rooms 10 en suite (1 fmly) ⊘ in all bedrooms S £40-£70; D £74-£100 (incl. bkfst) **Facilities** Wi-fi available **Parking** 21 **Notes LB** ⊗ ⊘ in restaurant Closed Xmas **RS** Dec & Jan

LOWESWATER   MAP 18 NY12

★★ 69% HOTEL

Grange Country House

CA13 0SU

☎ 01946 861211 & 861570

e-mail: gchloweswater@hotmail.com

dir: *left off A5086 for Mockerkin, through village. After 2m left for Loweswater Lake. Hotel at bottom of hill on left*

This delightful country hotel is set in a quiet valley at the north-western end of Loweswater and continues to prove popular with guests seeking peace and quiet. It has a friendly and relaxed atmosphere, and the cosy public areas include a small bar, a residents' lounge and an attractive dining room. The bedrooms are well equipped and comfortable.

Rooms 8 en suite (2 fmly) (1 GF) ⊘ in 4 bedrooms S £40-£50, D £76-£100 (incl. bkfst) **Facilities** Wi-fi in bedrooms National Trust boats & fishing Xmas **Conf** Thtr 25 Class 25 Board 25 **Parking** 22 **Notes** ⊘ in restaurant RS Jan-Feb No credit cards accepted

NETHER WASDALE   MAP 18 NY10

★★ 74% ⊛ HOTEL

Low Wood Hall Hotel & Restaurant

CA20 1ET

☎ 019467 26100 📄 019467 26111

e-mail: enquiries@lowwoodhall.co.uk

web: www.lowwoodhall.co.uk

dir: *A590/A595 towards Barrow-Whitehaven, through village of Gosforth, follow signs for Nether Wasdale*

This delightful country hotel is peacefully set in five acres of wooded gardens overlooking the village and valley. There is a comfortable lounge and a cosy bar/reception lounge, both of which are stocked with plenty to read and have roaring fires in season. Stylish interior designs blend well with the classical architecture. The carefully prepared meals are a highlight.

Rooms 7 en suite 6 annexe en suite (4 GF) ⊘ in all bedrooms S £35-£90; D £70-£110 (incl. bkfst) **Facilities** STV **Conf** BC Thtr 30 Class 30 Board 20 **Parking** 15 **Notes** ⊗ No children 12yrs ⊘ in restaurant Civ Wed 40

NEWBY BRIDGE   MAP 18 SD38

★★★★ 84% ⊛⊛ HOTEL

Lakeside Hotel Lake Windermere

Lakeside LA12 8AT

☎ 015395 30001 📄 015395 31699

e-mail: sales@lakesidehotel.co.uk

web: www.lakesidehotel.co.uk

dir: *M6 junct 36 join A590 to Barrow, take signs to Newby Bridge. Right over bridge, hotel 1m on right or follow Lakeside Steamers signs from junct 36*

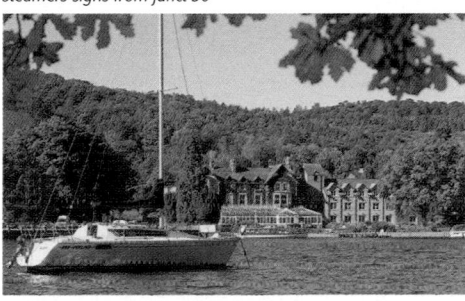

This impressive hotel enjoys an enviable location on the southern edge of Lake Windermere and has easy access to the Lakeside Steam Railway and Ferry terminal. Bedrooms are individually styled and many enjoy delightful views of the lake. Spacious lounges and a choice of restaurants are available for those who enjoy a range of dining styles. The state-of-the-art spa is exclusive to residents and provides a range of treatment suites and a pool suitable for young children. Staff throughout are friendly and nothing is too much trouble.

Rooms 76 en suite (7 fmly) (8 GF) ⊘ in all bedrooms S £145-£345; D £195-£565 (incl. bkfst) **Facilities Spa** STV ㉑ Fishing Sauna Gym 🏊 Jacuzzi Private jetty, Rowing boats ♫ Xmas **Conf** Thtr 100 Class 50 Board 40 Del from £140 **Services** Lift **Parking** 200 **Notes LB** ⊗ ⊘ in restaurant Civ Wed 80

★★★★ 81% ⊛ HOTEL

Swan

LA12 8NB

☎ 015395 31681 📄 015395 31917

e-mail: enquiries@swanhotel.com

web: www.swanhotel.com

dir: *M6 junct 36 follow A590 signed Barrow for 16m. Hotel on right of old 5-arch bridge, at Newby Bridge*

Set among 14 acres of gardens and lakeside pathways with mooring for 80 boats, this hotel stands on the River Leven at the south end of
continued on page 160

England

NEWBY BRIDGE *continued*

Lake Windermere. Bedrooms are comfortable, spacious and thoughtfully equipped. Public areas include a choice of lounges and restaurants, a traditional bar and impressive spa facilities.

Rooms 55 en suite (4 fmly) (14 GF) ⊘ in 32 bedrooms **Facilities** STV ⚑ supervised Fishing Sauna Solarium Gym Jacuzzi Wi-fi in bedrooms Steam Room Xmas **Conf** Thtr 120 Class 40 Board 40 Del from £135 **Services** Lift **Parking** 100 **Notes** ⊗ ⊘ in restaurant Civ Wed 80

★★★ 73% HOTEL

Whitewater

The Lakeland Village LA12 8PX
☎ 015395 31133 ▤ 015395 31881
e-mail: enquiries@whitewater-hotel.co.uk
web: www.whitewater-hotel.co.uk
dir: *M6 junct 36 follow signs for A590 Barrow, 1m through Newby Bridge. Right at sign for Lakeland Village, hotel on left*

This tasteful conversion of an old mill on the River Leven is close to the southern end of Lake Windermere. Bedrooms, many with lovely river views, are spacious and comfortable. Public areas include a luxurious, well-equipped spa, squash courts, and a choice of dining options. Mountain bikes are available. The Fisherman's bar hosts regular jazz nights that are popular with locals.

Rooms 35 en suite (10 fmly) (2 GF) ⊘ in 10 bedrooms S £85-£105; D £135-£195 (incl. bkfst) **Facilities Spa** STV ⚑ supervised ◓ Squash Sauna Solarium Gym Putt green Jacuzzi Beauty treatment Table tennis Steam room Golf driving range Xmas **Conf** Thtr 80 Class 32 Board 40 Del from £120 **Services** Lift **Parking** 50 **Notes LB** ⊗ ⊘ in restaurant Civ Wed 110

PATTERDALE MAP 18 NY31

★★ 68% HOTEL

Patterdale

CA11 0NN
☎ 0845 458 4333 & 01768 482231 ▤ 01253 754222
e-mail: reservations@choice-hotels.co.uk
dir: *M6 junct 40, take A592 towards Ullswater, then 10m on Lakeside Rd to Patterdale*

Patterdale is a real tourist destination and this hotel enjoys delightful views of the valley and fells, being located at the southern end of Ullswater. Bedrooms vary in style, some are brightly decorated with a modern feel. In busier periods accommodation is let for a minimum period of two nights.

Rooms 57 en suite (16 fmly) S £35-£65; D £60-£100 (incl. bkfst & dinner) **Facilities** ◓ Fishing ◔ Free bike hire ♫ ch fac Xmas **Services** Lift **Parking** 30 **Notes LB** ⊗ ⊘ in restaurant

PENRITH MAP 18 NY53
See also Shap

★★★★ 78% HOTEL

North Lakes Hotel & Spa

Ullswater Rd CA11 8QT
☎ 01768 868111 ▤ 01768 868291
e-mail: nlakes@shirehotels.com
web: www.shirehotels.com
dir: *M6 junct 40 at junct with A66*

SHIRE HOTELS

With a great location, it's no wonder that this modern hotel is perpetually busy. Amenities include a good range of meeting and function rooms and excellent health and leisure facilities including a full spa. Themed public areas have a contemporary, Scandinavian country style and offer plenty of space and comfort. High standards of service are provided by a friendly team of staff.

Rooms 84 en suite (6 fmly) (22 GF) ⊘ in 62 bedrooms S £90-£132; D £130-£179 (incl. bkfst) **Facilities Spa** STV ⚑ Sauna Solarium Gym Putt green Jacuzzi Wi-fi in bedrooms Children's splash pool, Steam & 6 treatment rooms, Activity & Wellness Studios ch fac Xmas **Conf** BC Thtr 200 Class 140 Board 24 Del £155 **Services** Lift **Parking** 150 **Notes LB** ⊗ ⊘ in restaurant Civ Wed 200

★★★ 83% ⍟⍟ HOTEL

Temple Sowerby House Hotel & Restaurant

CA10 1RZ
☎ 017683 61578 ▤ 017683 61958
e-mail: stay@templesowerby.com
web: www.templesowerby.com
(For full entry see Temple Sowerby)

★★★ 79% ⍟ HOTEL

Westmorland Hotel

Westmorland Place, Orton CA10 3SB
☎ 015396 24351 ▤ 015396 24354
e-mail: reservations@westmorlandhotel.com
web: www.westmorlandhotel.com
(For full entry see Tebay)

★★★ 74% HOTEL

The George

Devonshire St CA11 7SU
☎ 01768 862696 ▤ 01768 868223
e-mail: info@georgehotelpenrith.co.uk
web: www.georgehotelpenrith.co.uk
dir: *M6 junct 40, 1m to town centre. From A6/A66 to Penrith*

This inviting and popular, long-standing hotel can trace its history back some 300 years. The spacious public areas retain a timeless sense of charm and include a choice of lounge areas where morning coffees and afternoon teas can be enjoyed. Bedrooms & bathrooms are of a very good standard.

Rooms 32 en suite (3 fmly) ⊘ in 24 bedrooms S £55-£71; D £96-£116 (incl. bkfst) **Facilities** STV FTV Wi-fi available Free use of local pool & gym Xmas **Conf** Thtr 120 Class 60 Board 40 Del from £80 **Parking** 34 **Notes LB** ⊗ ⊘ in restaurant Civ Wed 120

See advert on opposite page

★★ 67% **HOTEL**

Brantwood Country Hotel

Stainton CA11 0EP
☎ 01768 862748 📠 01768 890164
e-mail: brantwood2@aol.com

dir: M6 junct 40, A66. Left in 0.5m then right signed Stainton. Left at x-roads. Hotel on left

Located in a peaceful village this family-run hotel enjoys an open outlook to the rear. The traditional and cheerfully decorated bedrooms are individual in design and have all the expected facilities. Hearty meals are served in both the bar and restaurant, and there is a separate conservatory-style residents' lounge

Rooms 7 en suite (3 fmly) ⊛ in 5 bedrooms S £48-£53; D fr £72 (incl. bkfst) **Facilities** ch fac Xmas **Conf** Thtr 60 Class 30 Board 30 Del from £75 **Parking** 35 **Notes LB** ⊗ ⊛ in restaurant Closed 25-28 Dec

★★ 65% ⊛ **HOTEL**

Edenhall Country Hotel

Edenhall CA11 8SX
☎ 01768 881454 📠 01768 881266
e-mail: info@edenhallhotel.co.uk

dir: A686 from Penrith to Alston. Hotel signed on right in 3m

Located in a peaceful hamlet yet convenient for the M6, this hotel is popular with business guests. The comfortable lounge bar serves an attractive range of meals, and carefully prepared and well-presented dinners are served in the dining room that overlooks the well-tended gardens.

Rooms 17 en suite 8 annexe rms (7 en suite) (3 fmly) (7 GF) S £45-£65; D £65-£87.50 (incl. bkfst) **Facilities** STV ♨ Jacuzzi Xmas **Conf** Thtr 50 Class 30 Board 30 Del from £79.95 **Parking** 60 **Notes LB** ⊗ ⊛ in restaurant Civ Wed 60

BUDGET HOTEL

Travelodge Penrith

Redhills CA11 0DT
☎ 08700 850 950 📠 01768 866958
web: www.travelodge.co.uk

dir: on A66, 0.25m from M6 junct 40

Travelodge offers good quality, good value, modern accommodation. Ideal for families, the spacious en suite bedrooms include remote-control TV, tea and coffee-making facilities and comfortable beds. Meals can be taken at the nearby family restaurant. See Hotel Groups pages for further details.

Rooms 54 en suite S fr £26; D fr £26

England

England

RAVENSTONEDALE
MAP 18 NY70

★★ 67% HOTEL

The Fat Lamb
Crossbank CA17 4LL
☎ 015396 23242 ▤ 015396 23285
e-mail: fatlamb@cumbria.com
dir: on A683, between Kirkby Stephen and Sedbergh

Open fires and solid stone walls are a feature of this 17th-century inn, set on its own nature reserve. There is a choice of dining options with an extensive menu available in the traditional bar or a more formal dining experience in the restaurant. Bedrooms are bright and cheerful and include family rooms and easily accessible rooms for guests with limited mobility.

Rooms 12 en suite (4 fmly) (5 GF) ⊛ in all bedrooms S £46-£52; D £76-£84 (incl. bkfst) **Facilities** Fishing Private 5 acre nature reserve Xmas **Parking** 60 **Notes LB** ⊛ in restaurant

ROSTHWAITE
MAP 18 NY21
See also Borrowdale

★★ 69% HOTEL

Scafell
CA12 5XB
☎ 017687 77208 ▤ 017687 77280
e-mail: info@scafell.co.uk
dir: 6m S of Keswick on B5289

This friendly hotel has long been popular with walkers and enjoys a peaceful location. Bedrooms vary in style from traditional to modern, but are all well equipped and neatly decorated. Public areas include a residents' cocktail bar, lounge and spacious restaurant as well as the popular Riverside Inn pub, offering all-day eating in summer months.

Rooms 24 en suite (2 fmly) (8 GF) ⊛ in all bedrooms S £22.50-£50.75; D £45-£101.50 (incl. bkfst) **Facilities** FTV Wi-fi in bedrooms Guided walks Xmas **Parking** 50 **Notes LB** ⊛ in restaurant Civ Wed 75

SHAP
MAP 18 NY51

★★★ 73% HOTEL

Best Western Shap Wells
Nr: Penrith CA10 3QU
☎ 01931 716628 ▤ 01931 716377
e-mail: manager@shapwells.com
dir: between A6 and B6261, 4m S of Shap

This hotel occupies a wonderful secluded position amid trees and waterfalls. Extensive public areas include function and meeting rooms,

continued

a well-stocked bar, a choice of lounges and a spacious restaurant. Bedrooms vary in size and style and all are equipped with the expected facilities.

Rooms 91 en suite 7 annexe en suite (10 fmly) (10 GF) ⊛ in 20 bedrooms S £62; D £94 (incl. bkfst) **Facilities** STV FTV Snooker Wi-fi available Games room, walking in the 30 acre grounds Xmas **Conf** Thtr 170 Class 80 Board 40 Del from £75 **Services** Lift **Parking** 200 **Notes LB** ⊛ in restaurant Civ Wed 150

SILLOTH
MAP 18 NY15

★★ 68% HOTEL

Golf Hotel
Criffel St CA5 4AB
☎ 016973 31438 ▤ 016973 32582
e-mail: golf.hotel@virgin.net
web: www.golfhotelsilloth.co.uk
dir: off B5302, left in Silloth at T-junct

This friendly, family-run hotel occupies a prime position in the centre of the historic market town and is a popular meeting place for the local community. Bedrooms are mostly well proportioned, and are comfortably equipped. Public areas include a spacious lounge bar, the setting for a wide range of tasty meals featuring local produce.

Rooms 22 en suite (4 fmly) S £44-£62.50; D £53-£105 (incl. bkfst) **Facilities** Snooker **Conf** Thtr 100 Class 40 Board 40 **Notes LB** Closed 25-Dec

SOUTHWAITE MOTORWAY SERVICE AREA (M6)
MAP 18 NY44

BUDGET HOTEL

Travelodge Carlisle (M6)
Broadfield Site CA4 0NT
☎ 08700 850 950 ▤ 016974 75354
web: www.travelodge.co.uk
dir: M6 junct 41/42

Travelodge offers good quality, good value, modern accommodation. Ideal for families, the spacious en suite bedrooms include remote-control TV, tea and coffee-making facilities and comfortable beds. Meals can be taken at the nearby family restaurant. See Hotel Groups pages for further details.

Rooms 38 en suite S fr £26; D fr £26

TEBAY
MAP 18 NY60

★★★ 79% ⊛ HOTEL

Westmorland Hotel & Bretherdale Restaurant
Westmorland Place, Orton CA10 3SB
☎ 015396 24351 ▤ 015396 24354
e-mail: reservations@westmorlandhotel.com
web: www.westmorlandhotel.com
dir: at N'bound service area between juncts 38 & 39 on M6. Accessible from S'bound service area

With fine views over rugged moorland, this modern and friendly hotel is ideal for conferences and meetings. Bedrooms are spacious and comfortable, with the executive rooms particularly well equipped. Open-plan public areas provide a Tyrolean touch and include a split-level restaurant.

continued

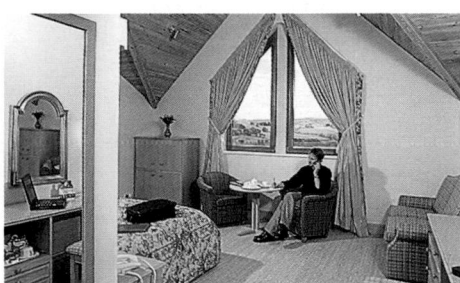

Westmorland Hotel & Bretherdale Restaurant

Rooms 50 en suite (18 fmly) (13 GF) ⊗ in 35 bedrooms S £65-£75;
D £83-£90 (incl. bkfst) **Facilities** STV Xmas **Conf** BC Thtr 75 Class 40
Board 30 Del from £115 **Services** Lift **Parking** 60 **Notes LB** ⊗ in
restaurant RS 1 Jan Civ Wed 80

See advert on this page

TEMPLE SOWERBY   MAP 18 NY62

★★★ 83% ◉◉ **HOTEL**

Temple Sowerby House Hotel & Restaurant

CA10 1RZ
☎ 017683 61578 🗎 017683 61958
e-mail: stay@templesowerby.com
web: www.templesowerby.com

dir: *midway between Penrith and Appleby, 7m from M6 junct 40*

Set in the heart of Eden Valley, this hotel is perfectly located to explore
both The Pennines and the Lake District. The original part of the
building dates back to the 16th century. Bedrooms are comfortable
and stylish, and some have four-poster beds and ultra modern
bathrooms. There is a choice of comfortable lounges and a
conservatory overlooks a beautiful walled garden. Staff throughout are
friendly and keen to please.

Rooms 8 en suite 4 annexe en suite (2 GF) ⊗ in all bedrooms
S £85-£100; D £115-£175 (incl. bkfst) **Facilities** ⅃ **Conf** Thtr 30 Class 20
Board 20 Del from £135 **Parking** 15 **Notes LB** No children 12yrs ⊗ in
restaurant Closed 23-28 Dec Civ Wed 40

TROUTBECK   MAP 18 NY40
(NEAR WINDERMERE)

★★ 72% **HOTEL**

Mortal Man

LA23 1PL
☎ 01539 433193 🗎 01539 431261
e-mail: themortalman@msn.com
web: www.themortalman.co.uk

dir: *2.5m N of A591/A592 junct. Left before church into village,
right at T-junct, hotel 800mtrs on right*

Dating from 1689, this traditional Lakeland inn enjoys a superb setting
with stunning views towards Windermere. The owners continue to
improve the hotel; the public areas include two bar areas and a cosy
lounge. A range of enjoyable meals is served in either the bars, with
real fires, outside on fine days, or in the formal restaurant. Bedrooms
are spacious and there is a four-poster room.

Rooms 12 en suite ⊗ in all bedrooms S £45-£65; D £60-£100 (incl.
bkfst) **Facilities** Fishing, Horse Riding, Sailing, Guided Walks, Water sports
Xmas **Conf** Thtr 30 **Parking** 20 **Notes LB** ⊗ in restaurant

---

ULLSWATER
See **Glenridding, Patterdale & Watermillock**

ULVERSTON   MAP 18 SD27

★★ 72% **HOTEL**

Lonsdale House Hotel

11 Daltongate LA12 7BD
☎ 01229 582598 🗎 01229 581260
e-mail: info@lonsdalehousehotel.co.uk
web: www.lonsdalehousehotel.co.uk

dir: *In Ulverston right at 2nd rdbt, follow one-way system to
mini-rdbt. Left pass zebra crossing then right & 1st right*

Enjoying a town centre location, this family-run hotel was once a
coaching inn. Bedrooms vary in style and size but all are extremely
well equipped and benefit from stylish furniture and soft furnishings.
Public areas include an attractive bar and restaurant, an inviting lounge
and a delightful rear garden.

Rooms 20 en suite (2 fmly) ⊗ in 16 bedrooms S £49.95-£75;
D £55-£110 (incl. bkfst) **Facilities** STV Xmas **Notes LB** ⊗ in restaurant
Civ Wed 20

WATERMILLOCK — MAP 18 NY42

★★★★ 76% ◉◉ **HOTEL**

Macdonald Leeming House

CA11 0JJ

☎ 0870 400 8131 ▤ 017684 86443

e-mail: leeminghouse@macdonald-hotels.co.uk

web: www.macdonald-hotels.co.uk

dir: *M6 junct 40, take A66 to Keswick. At rdbt take A592 (Ullswater). Continue for 5m to T-junct and turn right (A592). Hotel on left (3m)*

This hotel enjoys a superb location, being set in 20 acres of mature wooded gardens in the Lake District National Park, and overlooking Ullswater and the towering fells. Many rooms offer views of the lake and the rugged fells beyond, with more than half having their own balcony. Public rooms include three sumptuous lounges, a cosy bar and library.

Rooms 41 en suite (1 fmly) (10 GF) ⊗ in all bedrooms S £150-£185; D £260-£330 (incl. bkfst & dinner) **Facilities** STV Fishing ✎ Wi-fi in bedrooms Xmas **Conf** Thtr 24 Class 24 Board 24 Del from £140 **Parking** 50 **Notes LB** ⊗ in restaurant Civ Wed 65

INSPECTORS' CHOICE

★★★ ◉◉◉ **HOTEL**

Rampsbeck Country House

CA11 0LP

☎ 017684 86442 & 86688 ▤ 017684 86688

e-mail: enquiries@rampsbeck.fsnet.co.uk

web: www.rampsbeck.fsnet.co.uk

dir: *M6 junct 40, signs for A592 to Ullswater, at T-junct with lake in front, turn right, hotel is 1.5m along lake's edge*

This fine country house lies in 18 acres of parkland on the shores of Lake Ullswater and is furnished with many period and antique pieces. There are three delightful lounges, an elegant restaurant and a traditional bar. Bedrooms come in three grades; the most spacious rooms are spectacular and overlook the lake. Service is attentive and the cuisine is a real highlight of any stay.

Rooms 19 en suite (1 GF) ⊗ in 7 bedrooms S £75-£150; D £120-£250 (incl. bkfst) **Facilities** Fishing ✎ Wi-fi available Xmas **Conf** Board 15 Del from £130 **Parking** 30 **Notes LB** ⊗ in restaurant Closed early Jan-early Feb Civ Wed 65

WHITEHAVEN — MAP 18 NX91

BUDGET HOTEL

Premier Travel Inn Whitehaven

premier travel inn

Howgate CA28 6PL

☎ 08701 977268 ▤ 01946 590106

web: www.premiertravelinn.com

dir: *On outskirts of Whitehaven on A595 towards Workington*

High quality, modern budget accommodation ideal for both families and business travellers. Spacious, en suite bedrooms feature bath and shower, satellite TV and many have telephones and modem points. The adjacent family restaurant features a wide and varied menu. For further details consult the Hotel Groups page.

Rooms 38 en suite

WINDERMERE — MAP 18 SD49

INSPECTORS' CHOICE

★★★★ ◉◉◉ **HOTEL**

Gilpin Lodge Country House Hotel & Restaurant

RELAIS & CHATEAUX

Crook Rd LA23 3NE

☎ 015394 88818 ▤ 015394 88058

e-mail: hotel@gilpinlodge.co.uk

web: www.gilpinlodge.co.uk

dir: *M6 junct 36, take A590/A591 to rdbt north of Kendal, take B5284, hotel 5m on right*

This smart Victorian residence is set amidst delightful gardens leading to the fells, and is just a short drive from the lake. The individually styled bedrooms are elegant and a number benefit from private terraces; all are spacious and thoughtfully equipped. The welcoming atmosphere is notable and the attractive day rooms are perfect for relaxing, perhaps beside a real fire. Vibrant, exciting cuisine is served in one of five intimate dining rooms.

Rooms 14 en suite 6 annexe en suite (11 GF) ⊗ in all bedrooms S fr £175; D £240-£330 (incl. bkfst & dinner) **Facilities** ✎ Free membership at local Leisure Club Xmas **Parking** 30 **Notes LB** ⊗ No children 7yrs ⊗ in restaurant

★★★★ ◎◎◎ **COUNTRY HOUSE HOTEL**

Holbeck Ghyll Country House

Holbeck Ln LA23 1LU

☎ 015394 32375 📠 015394 34/43

e-mail: stay@holbeckghyll.com

dir: *3m N of Windermere on A591, right into Holbeck Lane (signed Troutbeck), hotel 0.5m on left*

With a peaceful setting in extensive grounds, this beautifully maintained hotel enjoys breathtaking views over Lake Windermere and the Langdale Fells. Public rooms include luxurious, comfortable lounges and two elegant dining rooms, where memorable meals are served. Bedrooms are individually styled, beautifully furnished and many have balconies or patios. Some in an adjacent, more private lodge are less traditional in design and have superb views. The professionalism and attentiveness of the staff is exemplary.

Rooms 14 en suite 6 annexe en suite (3 fmly) (3 GF) ⊘ in all bedrooms S £135-£175; D £220-£270 (incl. bkfst & dinner) **Facilities** Spa STV ⨝ Sauna Gym ⛳ Putt green Jacuzzi Wi-fi available Steam room, Treatment Rooms for Beauty and Massage Xmas **Conf** BC Thtr 45 Class 25 Board 25 Del from £165 **Parking** 28 **Notes LB** ⊘ in restaurant Civ Wed 65

★★★★ 75% ◎◎ **HOTEL**

Storrs Hall

Storrs Park LA23 3LG

☎ 015394 47111 📠 015394 47555

e-mail: storrshall@elhmail.co.uk

web: www.elh.co.uk/hotels/storrshall

dir: *on A592 2m S of Bowness, on Newby Bridge road*

Set in 17 acres of landscaped grounds by the lakeside, this imposing Georgian mansion is delightful. There are numerous lounges to relax in, furnished with fine art and antiques. Individually styled bedrooms are generally spacious and boast impressive bathrooms. Imaginative

continued

cuisine is served in the elegant restaurant, which offers fine views across the lawn to the lake and fells beyond.

Rooms 29 en suite ⊘ in 10 bedrooms S fr £110; D fr £170 (incl. bkfst) **Facilities** Fishing Use of nearby sports/beauty facilities. Xmas **Conf** Thtr 50 Class 35 Board 24 Del from £142.50 **Parking** 50 **Notes LB** No children 12yrs ⊘ in restaurant Civ Wed 94

★★★★ 75% **HOTEL**

Low Wood

LA23 1LP

☎ 015394 33338 & 0845 850 3502 📠 015394 34275

e-mail: lowwood@elhmail.co.uk

dir: *M6 junct 36, follow A590 then A591 to Windermere, then 3m towards Ambleside, hotel on right*

Benefiting from a lakeside location, this hotel offers an excellent range of leisure and conference facilities. Bedrooms, many with panoramic

continued on page 166

England

WINDERMERE *continued*

lake views, are attractively furnished, and include a number of larger executive rooms and suites. There is a choice of bars, a spacious restaurant and the more informal Café del Lago. The Poolside bar offers internet and e-mail access.

Rooms 111 en suite (13 fmly) ⊗ in 55 bedrooms S £105-£128; D £160-£206 (incl. bkfst) **Facilities Spa** STV [R] Fishing Squash Snooker Sauna Solarium Gym Jacuzzi Wi-fi in bedrooms Water skiing Canoeing, Beauty salon Bungy Trampoline Wall Climbing Marina Xmas **Conf** Thtr 340 Class 180 Board 150 Del from £103 **Services** Lift **Parking** 200 **Notes LB** ⊗ in restaurant Civ Wed 200

INSPECTORS' CHOICE

★★★ ⚙⚙ **COUNTRY HOUSE HOTEL**

Linthwaite House Hotel

Crook Rd LA23 3JA
☎ 015394 88600 🖨 015394 88601
e-mail: stay@linthwaite.com
web: www.linthwaite.com

dir: *A591 towards The Lakes for 8m to large rdbt, take 1st exit (B5284), 6m, hotel on left , 1m past Windermere golf club*

Linthwaite House is set in 14 acres of hilltop grounds and enjoys stunning views over Lake Windermere. Inviting public rooms include an attractive conservatory and adjoining lounge, a smokers' bar and an elegant restaurant. Bedrooms, which are individually decorated, combine contemporary furnishings with classical styles. All are thoughtfully equipped and include CD players. Service and hospitality are attentive and friendly.

Rooms 27 en suite (1 fmly) (7 GF) ⊗ in all bedrooms S £130-£160; D £170-£320 (incl. bkfst & dinner) **Facilities** STV Fishing ⛳ Putt green Wi-fi in bedrooms Xmas **Conf** BC Thtr 40 Class 19 Board 25 Del from £130 **Parking** 40 **Notes LB** ⊗ ⊗ in restaurant Civ Wed 54

See advert on opposite page

INSPECTORS' CHOICE

★★★ **HOTEL**

Miller Howe

Rayrigg Rd LA23 1EY
☎ 015394 42536 & 44522 🖨 015394 45664
e-mail: lakeview@millerhowe.com
web: www.millerhowe.com

dir: *on A592 between Bowness & Windermere*

This long established hotel of much character enjoys a lakeside setting amidst delightful landscaped gardens. Day rooms are
continued

bright and welcoming and include sumptuous lounges, a conservatory and an opulently decorated restaurant. Imaginative dinners make use of fresh, local produce where possible and there is an extensive, well-balanced wine list. Stylish bedrooms, many with fabulous lake views, include well-equipped cottage rooms and a number with whirlpool baths. At the time of going to press the Rosette award for this hotel had not been confirmed. For current information see the AA website www.theAA.com.

Miller Howe

Rooms 12 en suite 3 annexe en suite (1 GF) ⊗ in 2 bedrooms **Facilities** Wi-fi available ♫ Xmas **Parking** 40 **Notes** No children 8yrs ⊗ in restaurant Civ Wed 60

INSPECTORS' CHOICE

★★★ ⚙⚙⚙ **HOTEL**

The Samling

Ambleside Rd LA23 1LR
☎ 015394 31922 🖨 015394 30400
e-mail: info@thesamling.com
web: www.thesamling.com

dir: *turn right off A591, 300mtrs after Low Wood Hotel*

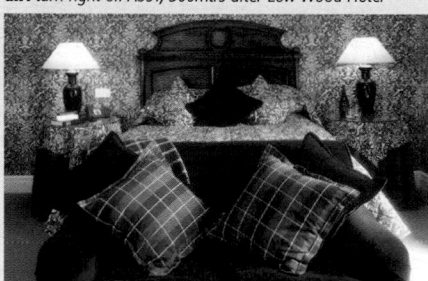

This stylish house built in the late 1700s, is situated in 67 acres of grounds and enjoys an elevated position overlooking Lake Windermere. The spacious, beautifully furnished bedrooms and suites, some in adjacent buildings, are thoughtfully equipped and have superb bathrooms. Public rooms include a sumptuous drawing room, a small library and an elegant dining room where imaginative, skilfully prepared food is served.

Rooms 5 en suite 6 annexe en suite S £195-£395; D £195-£395 (incl. bkfst) **Facilities** STV Jacuzzi Xmas **Conf** Thtr 60 Class 14 Board 14 Del £260 **Parking** 15 **Notes** ⊗ ⊗ in restaurant Civ Wed 100

★★★ 85% ⊛ **HOTEL**

Lindeth Howe Country House

CLASSIC
BRITISH HOTELS

Lindeth Dr, Longtail Hill LA23 3JF

☎ 015394 45759 📠 015394 46368

e-mail: hotel@lindeth-howc.co.uk

web: www.lindeth-howe.co.uk

dir: *turn off A592, 1m S of Bowness onto B5284 (Longtail Hill) signed Kendal & Lancaster, hotel last driveway on right*

Historic photographs commemorate the fact that this delightful house was once the family home of Beatrix Potter. Secluded in landscaped grounds, it enjoys views across the valley and Lake Windermere. Public rooms are plentiful and inviting, with the restaurant being the perfect setting for modern country-house cooking. Deluxe and superior bedrooms are spacious and smartly appointed.

Rooms 36 en suite (3 fmly) (2 GF) ⊛ in 33 bedrooms S £59-£84; D fr £118 (incl. bkfst) **Facilities** STV 🏊 Sauna Solarium Gym ch fac Xmas **Conf** Thtr 30 Class 20 Board 18 Del from £137 **Parking** 50 **Notes LB** ⊛ ⊛ in restaurant

★★★ 81% ⊛⊛ **HOTEL**

Best Western Beech Hill

Newby Bridge Rd LA23 3LR

☎ 015394 42137 📠 015394 43745

e-mail: reservations@beechhillhotel.co.uk

web: www.beechhillhotel.co.uk

dir: *A592 from Bowness to Newby Bridge, hotel 4m on right*

This stylish, terraced hotel is set on high ground leading to the shore of Lake Windermere and has a spacious, open-plan lounge which, like the restaurant, affords splendid views across the lake. The well equipped bedrooms come in a range of styles; some have four poster beds. Leisure facilities and a choice of conference rooms complete the package.

Rooms 59 en suite (4 fmly) (4 GF) ⊛ in 34 bedrooms **Facilities** 🏊 Sauna Solarium 🎵 Xmas **Parking** 70 **Notes** ⊛ in restaurant Civ Wed 130

See advert on this page

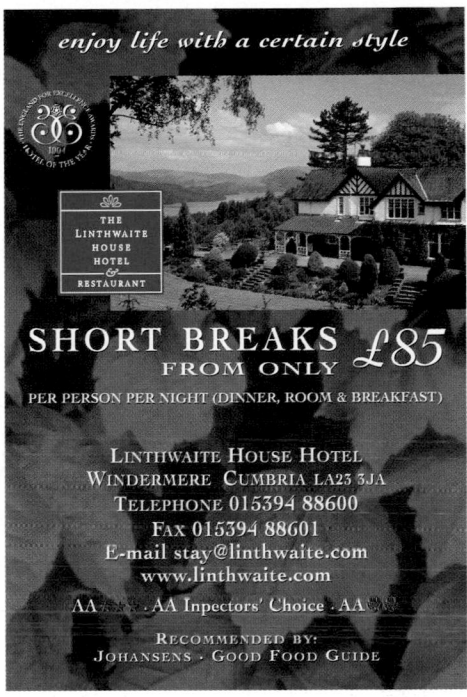

WINDERMERE *continued*

★★★ 79% @ @ HOTEL

Fayrer Garden Hotel

Lyth Valley Rd, Bowness on Windermere LA23 3JP
☎ 015394 88195 ▤ 015394 45986
e-mail: lakescene@fayrergarden.com
web: www.fayrergarden.com
dir: on A5074 1m from Bowness Bay

Sitting in lovely landscaped gardens, this elegant hotel enjoys
spectacular views over the lake. Bedrooms come in a variety of styles
and sizes, some with high spec bathrooms, and all are comfortably
appointed. There is a choice of lounges and a stylish, conservatory
restaurant. The attentive, hospitable staff ensure a relaxing stay.

Rooms 24 en suite 5 annexe en suite (10 GF) ⊘ in all bedrooms
S £75-£124; D £132-£268 (incl. bkfst & dinner) **Facilities** FTV Fishing
Free membership of leisure club Xmas **Parking** 40 **Notes LB** ⊗
No children 5yrs ⊘ in restaurant Civ Wed 60

★★★ 79% @ HOTEL

Langdale Chase

Langdale Chase LA23 1LW
☎ 015394 32201 ▤ 015394 32604
e-mail: sales@langdalechase.co.uk
web: www.langdalechase.co.uk
dir: 2m S of Ambleside and 3m N of Windermere, on A591

Enjoying unrivalled views of Lake Windermere, this imposing country
manor has been trading as a hotel for over 70 years. Public areas
feature carved fireplaces, oak panelling and a galleried staircase.
Bedrooms have stylish, spacious bathrooms and outstanding views.

Rooms 20 en suite 7 annexe en suite (2 fmly) (1 GF) ⊘ in all bedrooms
S £80-£114; D £90-£158 (incl. bkfst) **Facilities** Fishing ⚘ Putt green
Sailing boats Xmas **Conf** Thtr 30 Class 30 Board 28 Del from £120
Parking 50 **Notes LB** ⊘ in restaurant Civ Wed 100

★★★ 78% @ HOTEL

Best Western Burn How Garden House Hotel

Back Belsfield Rd, Bowness LA23 3HH
☎ 015394 46226 ▤ 015394 47000
e-mail: info@burnhow.co.uk
web: www.burnhow.co.uk

dir: Exit A591 at Windermere, following signs to Bowness. Pass
Lake Piers on right, take 1st left to hotel entrance

Set in its own leafy grounds, this hotel is only a few minutes' walk
from both the lakeside and the town centre. Attractive, spacious
rooms, some with four-poster beds, are situated in modern chalets or
in an adjacent Victorian house. Many have private patios or terraces.
Creative dinners can be enjoyed in the stylish dining room.

Rooms 28 annexe en suite (10 fmly) (6 GF) ⊘ in 18 bedrooms
S £55-£85; D £90-£130 (incl. bkfst) **Parking** 30 **Notes LB** ⊗ ⊘ in
restaurant

★★★ 78% HOTEL

Best Western Famous Wild Boar Hotel

Crook LA23 3NF
☎ 015394 45225 ▤ 015394 42498
e-mail: wildboar@elhmail.co.uk

dir: 2.5m S of Windermere on B5284. From Crook 3.5m, hotel
on right

This historic former coaching inn enjoys a peaceful rural location close
to Windermere. Public areas include a cosy bar where an extensive
range of wines is served by the glass, a character restaurant serving
wholesome food and a welcoming lounge. Bedrooms, some with
four-poster beds, vary in style and size.

Rooms 36 en suite (3 fmly) ⊘ in 6 bedrooms S £78-£88; D £106-£126
(incl. bkfst) **Facilities** STV Use of sports/beauty facilities at sister hotel
whilst in residence Xmas **Conf** Thtr 40 Class 20 Board 26 Del from £89
Parking 60 **Notes LB** ⊘ in restaurant

★★★ 72% HOTEL

Craig Manor

Lake Rd LA23 2JF
☎ 015394 88877 ▤ 015394 88878
e-mail: info@craigmanor.co.uk

dir: A590, then A591 into Windermere, left at Windermere Hotel,
through village, pass Magistrates' Court, hotel on left

There are fine views across the lake towards the surrounding fells from
this family-run hotel. Traditionally furnished bedrooms, including family

continued

rooms and some with four-poster beds, are complemented by spacious public areas. There is a choice of comfortable lounges and a wide selection of dishes is served in the restaurant that overlooks the lake.

Rooms 16 en suite **Facilities** Use of Parklands Leisure Club **Parking** 70 **Notes LB** ⊘ in restaurant

---

★★★ 70% HOTEL

The Belsfield Hotel

Kendal Rd, Bowness LA23 3EL

☎ 0870 609 6109 🖨 015394 46397

e-mail: belsfield@corushotels.com

web: www.corushotels.com

dir: In Bowness take 1st left after Royal Hotel

This hotel stands in six acres of gardens and has one of the best locations in the area. Bedrooms are generally spacious and well equipped, and come in a variety of styles. Views from public areas are outstanding. Main meals are taken in the spacious dining room overlooking the lake.

Rooms 64 en suite (6 fmly) (6 GF) ⊘ in 56 bedrooms S fr £110; D fr £110 **Facilities** ▣ Snooker Sauna Mini golf - Pitch & Putt 9 holes Xmas **Conf** Thtr 130 Class 60 Board 50 Del from £128 **Services** Lift **Parking** 64 **Notes LB** ⊗ ⊘ in restaurant Civ Wed 100

INSPECTORS' CHOICE

★★ ⊛ HOTEL

Lindeth Fell

Lyth Valley Rd, Bowness-on-Windermere LA23 3JP

☎ 015394 43286 & 44287 🖨 015394 47455

e-mail: kennedy@lindethfell.co.uk

web: www.lindethfell.co.uk

dir: 1m S of Bowness on A5074

Enjoying delightful views, this smart Edwardian residence stands in seven acres of glorious, landscaped gardens. Bedrooms, which vary in size and style, are comfortably equipped. Skilfully

continued

---

prepared dinners are served in the spacious dining room that commands fine views. The resident owners and their attentive, friendly staff provide high levels of hospitality and service.

Rooms 14 en suite (2 fmly) (1 GF) ⊘ in all bedrooms S £70-£90; D £140-£180 (incl. bkfst & dinner) **Facilities** STV Fishing ⇩ Putt green Wi-fi available Bowling Xmas **Conf** Board 12 Del from £75 **Parking** 20 **Notes LB** ⊗ ⊘ in restaurant Closed 6-31 Jan

---

★★ 78% HOTEL

Glenburn

New Rd LA23 2EE

☎ 015394 42649 🖨 015394 88998

e-mail: glen.burn@virgin.net

web: www.glenburn.uk.com

dir: M6 junct 36, A591, through Windermere, hotel 500yds on left

Tastefully furnished throughout and offering stylish, modern, fully equipped bedrooms, including one with four-poster, and impressive bathrooms. Public areas include an inviting, comfortable lounge/bar and attractive dining room. The restaurant menu changes frequently and features freshly prepared local ingredients.

Rooms 16 en suite (2 fmly) ⊘ in all bedrooms S £54-£75; D £68-£110 (incl. bkfst) **Facilities** Free use of nearby country club **Parking** 17 **Notes LB** ⊗ No children 4yrs ⊘ in restaurant Closed 14-28 Dec

---

★★ 76% HOTEL

Cedar Manor Hotel & Restaurant

Ambleside Rd LA23 1AX

☎ 015394 43192 🖨 015394 45970

e-mail: info@cedarmanor.co.uk

web: www.cedarmanor.co.uk

dir: 0.25m N on A591 by St Mary's Church

Built in 1854 as a country retreat this lovely old house enjoys a peaceful location that is within easy walking distance of the town centre. Bedrooms, some on the ground floor, are attractive and well equipped, with two bedrooms in the adjacent coach house. There is a comfortable lounge bar where guests can relax before enjoying a meal in the well-appointed dining room.

Rooms 9 en suite 2 annexe en suite (1 fmly) (2 GF) ⊘ in all bedrooms S £59-£70; D £84-£140 (incl. bkfst) **Facilities** Xmas **Parking** 15 **Notes** ⊘ in restaurant

---

★★ 72% HOTEL

The Hideaway

Phoenix Way LA23 1DB

☎ 015394 43070

e-mail: enquiries@hideaway-hotel.co.uk

web: www.hideaway-hotel.co.uk

dir: off A591 at Ravensworth Hotel. Hotel 100yds on right

Enjoying a secluded location, yet only a few minutes from the centre of town, hospitality is a real feature at this family-run hotel. Bedrooms, some housed in a separate building across the courtyard, are smartly appointed and individually furnished. Four-poster and family rooms are available. Dinner features tasty, home-made food and breakfasts are hearty.

Rooms 10 en suite 5 annexe en suite (2 fmly) S £60-£90; D £100-£180 (incl. bkfst & dinner) **Facilities** Free use of nearby leisure facilities Xmas **Parking** 16 **Notes LB** ⊗ ⊘ in restaurant Closed 3 Jan-9 Feb

England

WINDERMERE *continued*

★★ 67% **HOTEL**

Cranleigh

Kendal Rd, Bowness on Windermere LA23 3EW
☎ 015394 43293 ▤ 015394 47283
e-mail: mike@thecranleigh.com
web: www.thecranleigh.com
dir: *off Lake Rd opp St Martin's Church, 150 mtrs along Kendal Rd*

This friendly hotel is located just a short walk from the centre of town. Comfortable bedrooms, including a number with four-poster beds, vary in style. Guests have a choice of lounges, one with a real fire, a small bar that offers a wide range of drinks and an attractive dining room where freshly prepared meals are served.

Rooms 9 en suite 6 annexe en suite (3 fmly) (2 GF) ⊗ in 7 bedrooms S £43-£75; D £56-£120 (incl. bkfst) **Facilities** Free membership of leisure club **Parking** 15 **Notes LB** ⊛ ⊗ in restaurant

Ⓤ

Macdonald Old England

Church St, Bowness LA23 3DF
☎ 0870 400 8130 ▤ 015394 43432
e-mail: oldengland@macdonald-hotels.co.uk
web: www.macdonald-hotels.co.uk
dir: *Through Windermere to Bowness. Hotel behind church*

MACDONALD
HOTELS & RESORTS

At the time of going to press, the star classification for this hotel was not confirmed. Please refer to the AA internet site www.theAA.com for current information.

Rooms 56 en suite (3 fmly) ⊗ in 26 bedrooms S £135-£145; D £170-£190 (incl. bkfst) **Facilities** Wi-fi available Xmas **Conf** BC Thtr 80 Class 40 Board 30 Del from £129.25 **Services** Lift **Parking** 82 **Notes LB** ⊛ ⊗ in restaurant Civ Wed 80

WORKINGTON

MAP 18 NY02

★★★ 85% ⊛ **HOTEL**

Washington Central

Washington St CA14 3AY
☎ 01900 65772 ▤ 01900 68770
e-mail: kawildwchotel@aol.com
web: www.washingtoncentralhotelworkington.com
dir: *M6 junct 40 towards Keswick, follow signs to Workington. At lights at bottom of Ramsey Brow, turn right and follow signs for hotel*

Enjoying a prominent town centre location, this modern hotel boasts memorably hospitable staff. The well-maintained and comfortable bedrooms are equipped with a range of thoughtful extras. Public areas include numerous lounges, a spacious bar, Ceasars leisure club, a smart restaurant and a popular coffee shop. The comprehensive conference facilities are ideal for meetings and weddings.

Rooms 46 en suite (4 fmly) ⊗ in 37 bedrooms S £79.95; D £115.95 (incl. bkfst) **Facilities** STV ▣ supervised Sauna Solarium Gym Jacuzzi Free bike hire, Nightclub ♫ ch fac **Conf** BC Thtr 300 Class 250 Board 100 Del £125 **Services** Lift **Parking** 16 **Notes LB** ⊛ ⊗ in restaurant RS 25-Dec Civ Wed 300

★★★ 75% **HOTEL**

Hunday Manor Country House

Hunday, Winscales CA14 4JF
☎ 01900 61798 ▤ 01900 601202
e-mail: info@hunday-manor-hotel.co.uk
dir: *off A66 onto A595 towards Whitehaven, hotel is 3m on right, signed*

Delightfully situated and enjoying distant views of the Solway Firth, this charming hotel has well-furnished rooms with lots of extras. The open-plan bar and foyer lounge boast welcoming open fires, and the attractive restaurant overlooks the woodland gardens. The provision of a function suite makes the hotel an excellent wedding venue.

Rooms 24 en suite (1 fmly) ⊗ in all bedrooms S £55-£80; D £95-£125 (incl. bkfst) **Facilities** Wi-fi in bedrooms **Conf** BC Thtr 200 Class 200 Board 200 **Parking** 50 **Notes LB** ⊗ in restaurant Civ Wed 250

DERBYSHIRE

ALFRETON MAP 16 SK45

BUDGET HOTEL

Travelodge Alfreton
Old Swanwick Colliery Rd DE55 1HJ
☎ 08700 850 950 ▤ 01773 520040
web: www.travelodge.co.uk

dir: 3m from M1 junct 28, at A38 & A61 junct

Travelodge offers good quality, good value, modern accommodation. Ideal for families, the spacious en suite bedrooms include remote-control TV, tea and coffee-making facilities and comfortable beds. Meals can be taken at the nearby family restaurant. See Hotel Groups pages for further details.

Rooms 60 en suite S fr £26; D fr £26

ASHBOURNE MAP 10 SK14
See also Thorpe

★★★ 80% ◉◉ COUNTRY HOUSE HOTEL

Callow Hall
Mappleton Rd DE6 2AA
☎ 01335 300900 ▤ 01335 300512
e-mail: reservations@callowhall.demon.co.uk

dir: A515 through Ashbourne towards Buxton, left at Bowling Green pub, then 1st right

This delightful, creeper-clad, early Victorian house, set on a 44-acre estate, enjoys views over Bentley Brook and the Dove Valley. The atmosphere is relaxed and welcoming, and some of the spacious bedrooms in the main house have comfortable sitting areas. Public rooms feature high ceilings, ornate plasterwork and antique furniture. There is a good range of dishes offered on both the carte and the fixed-price, daily-changing menus.

Rooms 16 en suite (2 fmly) (2 GF) ⊗ in all bedrooms S £95-£120; D £140-£190 (incl. bkfst) **Facilities** Fishing Cycle hire nearby (Tissington Trail) Riding nearby Golf course within 2m **Conf** BC Thtr 30 Board 16 Del from £150 **Parking** 21 **Notes LB** ⊗ ⊗ in restaurant Closed 25-26 Dec RS Sun

See advert on this page

Good Food Guide Main Entry

AA ★★★ Hotel ◉◉ 80%

Mappleton, Ashbourne, Derbyshire DE6 2AA
Tel 01335 300900 Fax 01335 300512
e-mail enquiries@callowhall.co.uk www.callowhall.co.uk

THE IZAAK WALTON HOTEL
Dovedale, Ashbourne, Derbys DE6 2AY
Tel: +44 (0) 1335 350 555 Fax: +44 (0) 1335 350 539
Email: reception@izaakwaltonhotel.com
Website: www.izaakwaltonhotel.com

The Izaak Walton Hotel is a picturesque 17th century farmhouse nestled in the heart of the Derbyshire Peak District. We offer a warm welcome, comfort and tranquility with views of outstanding natural beauty. With cosy lounges and attractive country house décor we are able to offer a tailor-made conference service and we are also the perfect setting for weddings. Our 34 en-suite bedrooms mostly have breathtaking views of the Peaks. Savour the imaginative and classical cuisine in our Haddon Restaurant with its extensive menu and carefully selected wine list or relax in the informal surroundings of the Dovedale Bar. We are also able to offer excellent fishing on our own two-mile stretch of the River Dove.
See Thorpe for more details.

ASHBOURNE *continued*

★★ 68% HOTEL

The Dog & Partridge Country Inn

Swinscoe DE6 2HS
☎ 01335 343183 📠 01335 342742
e-mail: info@dogandpartridge.co.uk
web: www.dogandpartridge.co.uk
dir: A52 towards Leek, hotel 4m on left

This 17th-century inn is situated in the hamlet of Swinscoe, within easy reach of Alton Towers. Bedrooms, situated in the grounds, have their own direct access. Well-presented self-catering family suites are also available. Meals are served every evening until late and can be enjoyed either in the bar, the conservatory or on an outdoor terrace weather permitting.

Rooms 25 en suite (15 fmly) **Facilities** Fishing Xmas **Conf** Thtr 20 Class 15 Board 18 **Parking** 115 **Notes** ⊘ in restaurant

★★ 66% HOTEL

Beresford Arms Hotel

Station Rd DE6 1AA
☎ 01335 300035 📠 01335 300065
e-mail: reception@beresford-arms.demon.co.uk
web: www.beresford-arms.demon.co.uk

Steeped in history this traditional hotel is ideally located close to the centre of this well liked market town. Bedrooms are in the main spacious, well appointed and comfortable. The popular bar and restaurant are where hearty homemade fare is served.

Rooms 18 en suite (6 fmly) (6 GF) ⊘ in 12 bedrooms **Facilities** Xmas **Parking** 18 **Notes** ⊘ in restaurant

BAKEWELL   MAP 16 SK26

★★★ 70% ❀ HOTEL

Rutland Arms

The Square DE45 1BT
☎ 01629 812812 📠 01629 812309
e-mail: rutland@bakewell.demon.co.uk
dir: M1 junct 28 to Matlock, A6 to Bakewell. Hotel in town centre

This 19th-century hotel lies at the very centre of Bakewell and offers a wide range of quality accommodation. The friendly staff are attentive and welcoming, and The Four Seasons candlelit restaurant offers interesting fine dining in elegant surroundings.

Rooms 18 en suite 17 annexe en suite (2 fmly) ⊘ in 12 bedrooms **Facilities** FTV Wi-fi in bedrooms Xmas **Conf** Thtr 100 Class 60 Board 40 Del £119 **Parking** 25 **Notes** ⊘ in restaurant

★★ 75% HOTEL

Monsal Head Hotel

Monsal Head DE45 1NL
☎ 01629 640250 📠 01629 640815
e-mail: christine@monsalhead.com
web: www.monsalhead.com
dir: A6 from Bakewell to Buxton. After 2m turn into Ashford-in-the-Water, take B6465 for 1m

Popular with walkers, this friendly hotel commands one of the most splendid views in the Peak Park, overlooking Monsal Dale and the walking path along the disused railway line. Bedrooms are well equipped, and four have superb views down the valley. Imaginative food is served in either an attractive modern restaurant or separate original pub, which also offers a range of fine wines and real ales.

Rooms 7 en suite (1 fmly) S £45-£55; D £50-£70 (incl. bkfst)
Facilities Xmas **Conf** BC Thtr 20 Class 20 Board 20 Del from £100
Parking 20 **Notes LB** ⊘ in restaurant

BAMFORD   MAP 16 SK28

★★ 72% HOTEL

Yorkshire Bridge Inn

Ashopton Rd, Hope Valley S33 0AZ
☎ 01433 651361 📠 01433 651361
e-mail: enquiries@ybridge.force9.co.uk
web: www.yorkshire-bridge.co.uk
dir: A57 Sheffield/Glossop road, at Ladybower Reservoir take A6013 Bamford road, inn 1m on right

A well-established country inn, ideally located beside Ladybower Dam and within reach of the Peak District's many beauty spots. The hotel offers a wide range of excellent dishes in both the bar and dining area, along with a good selection of real ales. Bedrooms are attractively furnished, comfortable and well equipped.

Rooms 14 en suite (3 fmly) (4 GF) ⊘ in 10 bedrooms S fr £50; D £68-£94 (incl. bkfst) **Facilities** Xmas **Conf** Class 12 **Parking** 40 **Notes LB** ⊘ in restaurant

We have indicated only the hotels that do not accept credit or debit cards

BARLBOROUGH MAP 16 SK47

BUDGET HOTEL

Hotel Ibis Sheffield South

Tallys End, Chesterfield Rd S43 4TX

☎ 01246 813222 📠 01246 813444

e-mail: H3157@accor-hotels.com

web: www.ibishotel.com

dir: *M1 junct 30. Towards A619, right at rdbt towards Chesterfield. Hotel immediately left*

Modern, budget hotel offering comfortable accommodation in bright and practical bedrooms. Breakfast is self-service and dinner is available in the restaurant. For further details, consult the Hotel Groups page.

Rooms 86 en suite S £37.95-£44.95; D £37.95-£44.95 **Conf** Thtr 35 Class 20 Board 18

BASLOW
MAP 16 SK27

INSPECTORS' CHOICE

★★★ ◉◉◉◉ **HOTEL**

Fischer's Baslow Hall

Calver Rd DE45 1RR

☎ 01246 583259 ▤ 01246 583818

e-mail: m.s@fischers-baslowhall.co.uk

web: www.fischers-baslowhall.co.uk

dir: on A623 between Baslow & Calver

Located at the end of a chestnut tree-lined drive on the edge of the Chatsworth Estate, in marvellous gardens, this beautiful Derbyshire manor house offers sumptuous accommodation and facilities. Staff provide very friendly and personally attentive hospitality and service. There are two styles of bedroom available: traditional, individually-themed rooms in the main house and spacious, more contemporary-styled rooms with Italian marble bathrooms in the Garden House. The award-winning cuisine is extremely memorable and a highlight of any stay.

Rooms 6 en suite 5 annexe en suite (4 GF) ⊘ in all bedrooms S £100-£130; D £140-£180 (incl. bkfst) **Facilities** Wi-fi in bedrooms **Conf** Thtr 40 Board 18 Del from £160 **Parking** 40 **Notes LB** ⊘ ⊘ in restaurant Closed 25-26 Dec Civ Wed 40

★★★ 86% ◉◉ **HOTEL**

Cavendish

DE45 1SP

☎ 01246 582311 ▤ 01246 582312

e-mail: info@cavendish-hotel.net

web: www.cavendish-hotel.net

dir: M1 junct 29/A617 W to Chesterfield & A619 to Baslow. Hotel in village centre, off main road

This stylish property, dating back to the 18th century, is delightfully situated on the edge of the Chatsworth Estate. Elegantly appointed bedrooms offer a host of thoughtful amenities, while comfortable public areas are furnished with period pieces and paintings. Guests have a choice of dining in either the informal conservatory Garden Room or the elegant Gallery Restaurant.

Rooms 24 en suite (3 fmly) (2 GF) ⊘ in all bedrooms S £118.65-£153.30; D £152.25-£191.10 **Facilities** STV Fishing Putt green Xmas **Conf** Thtr 25 Class 8 Board 18 Del £190 **Parking** 50 **Notes LB** ⊘ ⊘ in restaurant Civ Wed 30

BELPER
MAP 11 SK34

★★★ 74% **HOTEL**

Makeney Hall Hotel

Makeney, Milford DE56 0RS

☎ 01332 842999 ▤ 01332 842777

e-mail: makeneyhall@foliohotels.co.uk

web: www.foliohotels.co.uk/makeneyhall

dir: off A6 at Milford, signed Makeney. Hotel 0.25m on left

This restored Victorian mansion stands in six acres of landscaped gardens and grounds above the River Derwent. Bedrooms, divided between the main house and the ground-floor courtyard, vary in style and are generally very spacious. Comfortable public rooms include a lounge, bar and spacious restaurant with views of the gardens.

Rooms 28 en suite 18 annexe en suite (8 fmly) (7 GF) ⊘ in 15 bedrooms S £65-£110; D £85-£110 **Facilities** STV Wi-fi in bedrooms Xmas **Conf** Thtr 180 Class 80 Board 50 Del from £130 **Services** Lift **Parking** 150 **Notes LB** ⊘ in restaurant Civ Wed 180

See advert on opposite page

★★★ 68% **HOTEL**

The Lion Hotel & Restaurant

Bridge St DE56 1AX

☎ 01773 824033 ▤ 01773 828393

e-mail: enquiries@lionhotel.uk.com

dir: 8m NW of Derby, hotel on A6

Situated in the centre of town and on the border of the Peak District, this 18th-century hotel provides an ideal base for exploring the many local attractions. The tastefully decorated bedrooms are well equipped and the public rooms include an attractive restaurant and two cosy bars; a modern function suite also proves popular.

Rooms 22 en suite (3 fmly) ⊘ in 7 bedrooms **Facilities** STV **Conf** Thtr 110 Class 60 Board 50 **Parking** 30 **Notes** ⊘ ⊘ in restaurant Civ Wed 90

BREADSALL
MAP 11 SK33

★★★★ 75% ◉ **HOTEL**

Marriott Breadsall Priory Hotel, Country Club

Moor Rd DE7 6DL

☎ 01332 832235 ▤ 01332 833509

web: www.marriott.co.uk

dir: A52 to Derby, then signs to Chesterfield. Right at 1st rdbt, left at next. Follow A608 to Heanor Rd, after 3m left then left again

This extended mansion house is set in 400 acres of parkland and well-tended gardens. The smart bedrooms are mostly contained in the

continued

modern wing. There is a vibrant café-bar, a more formal restaurant and a comprehensive room-service menu. There are extensive leisure facilities including two golf courses and a swimming pool. Dinner in the Priory Restaurant is a highlight of a stay.

Marriott Breadsall Priory Hotel, Country Club

Rooms 12 en suite 100 annexe en suite (35 fmly) ⊗ in 69 bedrooms **Facilities** STV ⚑ ⚓ 18 ♨ Sauna Solarium Gym ⚑ Putt green Jacuzzi Health, beauty & hair salon, dance studio **Conf** Thtr 120 Class 50 Board 30 **Services** Lift **Parking** 300 **Notes** ⊗ in restaurant Civ Wed 100

BUXTON   MAP 16 SK07

★★★★ 71% **HOTEL**

Palace Hotel
Palace Rd SK17 6AG

PARAMOUNT
GROUP OF HOTELS

☎ 01298 22001 ▤ 01298 72131
e-mail: palace@paramount-hotels.co.uk
web: www.paramount-hotels.co.uk

dir: *M6 junct 20, follow M56/M60 signs to Stockport then A6 to Buxton, hotel adjacent to railway station*

This impressive Victorian hotel is located on the hill overlooking the town. Public areas are traditional and elegant in style, including chandeliers and decorative ceilings. The bedrooms are spacious and equipped with modern facilities, and The Dovedale restaurant provides modern British cuisine. Good leisure facilities are available.

Rooms 122 en suite (18 fmly) ⊗ in 80 bedrooms S £94-£114; D £118-£128 (incl. bkfst) **Facilities** STV ⚑ supervised Sauna Solarium Gym Beauty facilities Xmas **Conf** BC Thtr 300 Class 125 Board 80 Del from £130 **Services** Lift **Parking** 180 **Notes LB** ⊗ in restaurant Civ Wed 100

★★★ 78% ⊛ **HOTEL**

Best Western Lee Wood
The Park SK17 6TQ

Best Western

☎ 01298 23002 ▤ 01298 23228
e-mail: leewoodhotel@btconnect.com
web: www.leewoodhotel.co.uk

dir: *NE on A5004, 300mtrs beyond Devonshire Royal Hospital*

This elegant Georgian hotel offers high standards of comfort and hospitality. Individually furnished bedrooms are generally spacious, with all of the expected modern conveniences. There is a choice of two comfortable lounges and a conservatory restaurant. Quality cooking, good service and fine hospitality are noteworthy.

Rooms 35 en suite 5 annexe en suite (4 fmly) ⊗ in 25 bedrooms S £69.50-£85; D £100-£150 (incl. bkfst) **Facilities** STV FTV Wi-fi in bedrooms Xmas **Conf** BC Thtr 120 Class 65 Board 40 Del from £110 **Services** Lift **Parking** 50 **Notes LB** ⊗ in restaurant Civ Wed 120

★★ 67% **HOTEL**

Portland Hotel & Park Restaurant
32 St John's Rd SK17 6XQ
☎ 01298 22462 ▤ 01298 27464
e-mail: portland.hotel@btinternet.com
dir: *on A53 opposite the Pavilion & Gardens*

This privately owned and personally run hotel is situated near the famous opera house and the Pavilion Gardens. Facilities include a comfortable lounge and an open-plan bar & restaurant area.

Rooms 22 en suite (3 fmly) ⊗ in 3 bedrooms **Conf** Thtr 50 Class 30 Board 25 **Parking** 18 **Notes** ⊗ in restaurant

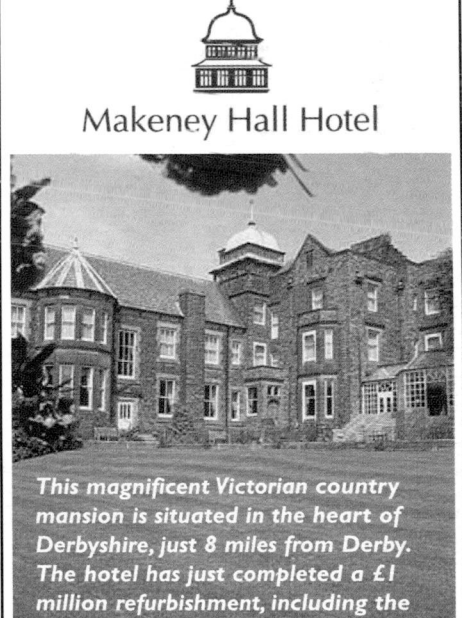

England

CASTLETON   MAP 16 SK18

BUDGET HOTEL

Innkeeper's Lodge Castleton
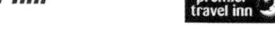
Castle St S33 8WG
☎ 01433 620578 ▤ 01433 622902
web: www.innkeeperslodge.com

dir: *on A6187, in the centre of the village*

Smart, en suite accommodation ideal for both business & leisure guests. Bedrooms are very well equipped, including Sky TV, telephone, modem points, tea & coffee making facilities, (family rooms in most locations). Complimentary breakfast. The adjacent Pub Restaurant; a Harvester, Vintage Inn, Toby Carvery, Ember Inn, Sizzling Pubco or Pub & Carvery offers an all day menu. See Hotel Groups pages for further details.

Rooms 6 en suite 6 annexe en suite S £59.95-£69.95; D £59.95-£69.95

CHESTERFIELD   MAP 16 SK37
See also Renishaw

★★★ 68% HOTEL

Sitwell Arms
Station Rd S21 3WF
☎ 01246 435226 & 01246 437327 ▤ 01246 433915
e-mail: sitwellarms@renishaw79.fsnet.co.uk

(For full entry see Renishaw)

★★★ 66% HOTEL

Sandpiper
THE INDEPENDENTS
Sheffield Rd, Sheepbridge S41 9EH
☎ 01246 450550 ▤ 01246 452805
e-mail: suedaykin@btconnect.com
web: www.sandpiperhotel.co.uk

dir: *M1 junct 29, A617 to Chesterfield then A61 to Sheffield. 1st exit take Dronfield/Unstone sign. Hotel 0.5m on left*

Conveniently situated for both the A61 and M1 and providing a good touring base, being just three miles from Chesterfield, this modern hotel offers comfortable and well-furnished bedrooms. Public areas are situated in a separate building across the car park, and include a cosy bar and open plan restaurant, serving a range of interesting and popular dishes.

Rooms 46 en suite (8 fmly) (16 GF) ⊘ in 32 bedrooms S £50; D £50-£55 **Facilities** STV Xmas **Conf** Thtr 100 Class 35 Board 35 Del from £90 **Services** Lift **Parking** 120 **Notes** LB ⊗ ⊘ in restaurant Civ Wed 90

BUDGET HOTEL

Hotel Ibis Chesterfield
ibis
Accor hotels
Lordsmill St S41 7RW
☎ 01246 221333 ▤ 01246 221444
e-mail: h3160@accor.com
web: www.ibishotel.com

dir: *M1 junct 29, take A617 to Chesterfield. 2nd exit at 1st rdbt. Hotel situated on right at 2nd rdbt.*

Modern, budget hotel offering comfortable accommodation in bright and practical bedrooms. Breakfast is self-service and dinner is
continued

available in the restaurant. For further details, consult the Hotel Groups page.

Rooms 86 en suite S £46.95-£50.95; D £46.95-£50.95 **Conf** Thtr 30 Board 20

BUDGET HOTEL

Premier Travel Inn Chesterfield

premier travel inn
Tapton Lock Hill, Off Rotherway S41 7NJ
☎ 08701 977060 ▤ 01246 560707
web: www.premiertravelinn.com

dir: *adjacent to Tesco, A61 and A619 rdbt, 1m N of city centre*

High quality, modern budget accommodation ideal for both families and business travellers. Spacious, en suite bedrooms feature bath and shower, satellite TV and many have telephones and modem points. The adjacent family restaurant features a wide and varied menu. For further details consult the Hotel Groups page.

Rooms 60 en suite **Conf** Thtr 25

BUDGET HOTEL

Travelodge Chesterfield
Travelodge
Brimmington Rd, Inner Ring Rd, Wittington Moor S41 9BE
☎ 08700 850 950 ▤ 01246 455411
web: www.travelodge.co.uk

dir: *on A61, N of town centre*

Travelodge offers good quality, good value, modern accommodation. Ideal for families, the spacious en suite bedrooms include remote-control TV, tea and coffee-making facilities and comfortable beds. Meals can be taken at the nearby family restaurant. See Hotel Groups pages for further details.

Rooms 20 en suite S fr £26; D fr £26

DERBY   MAP 11 SK33

★★★★ 84% HOTEL

Best Western Midland
Best Western
Midland Rd DE1 2SQ
☎ 01332 345894 ▤ 01332 293522
e-mail: sales@midland-derby.co.uk
web: www.midland-derby.co.uk

dir: *opposite Derby railway station*

This early Victorian hotel situated opposite Derby Midland Station provides very comfortable accommodation. The executive rooms are ideal for business travellers, equipped with writing desks and
continued

fax/computer points. Public rooms include a comfortable lounge and a popular restaurant. Service is skilled, attentive and friendly. Each bedroom is equipped with high-speed internet access, wired and wireless. There is also a walled garden and private parking.

Rooms 100 en suite ⊛ in 75 bedrooms S £66–£126; D £66–£136
Facilities FTV Wi-fi in bedrooms ♫ **Conf** Thtr 150 Class 50 Board 40 Del from £118 **Services** Lift **Parking** 90 **Notes LB** ⊛ ⊛ in restaurant Closed 24-26 Dec & 1 Jan Civ Wed 150

See advert on this page

★★★★ 75% ⊛ **HOTEL**

Marriott Breadsall Priory Hotel, Country Club

Marriott
HOTELS & RESORTS

Moor Rd DE7 6DL
☎ 01332 832235 ▤ 01332 833509
web: www.marriott.co.uk

(For full entry see Breadsall)

★★★ 73% **HOTEL**

Littleover Lodge

222 Rykneld Rd, Littleover DE23 7AN
☎ 01332 510161 ▤ 01332 514010
e-mail: enquiries@littleoverlodge.co.uk
web: www.littleoverlodge.co.uk

dir: A38 towards Derby approx 1m on left slip lane signed Littleover/Mickleover/Findon, take 2nd exit off island marked Littleover, 0.25m on right

Situated in a rural location this friendly hotel offers modern bedrooms with direct access from the car park. Two styles of dining are available - an informal carvery operation which is very popular locally, and a more formal restaurant experience at both lunch and dinner every day. Service is super with long serving staff being particularly friendly.

Rooms 16 en suite (3 fmly) (6 GF) S £55–£80; D £55–£90 (incl. bkfst)
Facilities STV ♫ Xmas **Parking** 75 **Notes LB** ⊛ in restaurant

See advert on this page

★★★ 67% **HOTEL**

International

288 Burton Rd DE23 6AD
☎ 01332 369321 ▤ 01332 294430
e-mail: internationalhotel.derby@virgin.net

dir: 0.5m from city centre on A5250

Within easy reach of the city centre, this hotel offers comfortable, modern public rooms. An extensive range of dishes is served in the pleasant restaurant. There is a wide range of bedroom sizes and styles, and each room is very well equipped; some spacious suites are also available. Parking is a bonus.

Rooms 41 en suite 21 annexe en suite (4 fmly) ⊛ in 28 bedrooms S fr £35; D fr £40 (incl. bkfst) **Facilities** STV ♫ Xmas **Conf** Thtr 100 Class 40 Board 40 Del from £101 **Services** Lift **Parking** 100 **Notes LB** Civ Wed 100

DERBY *continued*

U

Swallow Derby

SWALLOW HOTELS

Midland Rd DE1 2SL

☎ 01332 342716 📠 01332 293503

e-mail: reservations.derby@swallowhotels.co.uk

web: www.swallowhotels.com

dir: Opposite Derby Railway Station in city centre

At the time of going to press, the star classification for this hotel was not confirmed. Please refer to the AA internet site www.theAA.com for current information.

Rooms 55 en suite

BUDGET HOTEL

Days Hotel Derby

DAYS INN

Derbyshire C C Ground, Pentagon Roundabout, Nottingham Rd DE21 6DA

☎ 01332 363600 📠 01332 200630

e-mail: derby@kewgreen.co.uk

web: www.welcomebreak.co.uk

dir: M1 junct 25, take A52 towards Derby. At Pentagon rdbt take 4th exit and turn into cricket club

This modern building offers accommodation in smart, spacious and well-equipped bedrooms, suitable for families and business travellers, and all with en suite bathrooms. Continental breakfast is available and other refreshments may be taken at the nearby family restaurant. For further details see the Hotel Groups page.

Rooms 100 en suite **Conf** Thtr 50 Class 25 Board 18

BUDGET HOTEL

European Inn

Midland Rd DE1 2SL

☎ 01332 292000 📠 01332 293940

e-mail: admin@euro-derby.co.uk

web: www.euro-derby.co.uk

dir: City centre, 200yds from railway station

Excellent value accommodation is provided at this modern lodge. Bedrooms are well appointed and equipped with modern facilities. Shops form part of the complex and include a continental style restaurant. A good choice of English breakfast is served buffet-style in the breakfast room.

Rooms 88 en suite S fr £60.50; D fr £60.50 **Conf** Thtr 60 Class 25 Board 30 Del from £110

BUDGET HOTEL

Innkeeper's Lodge Derby

Inn keeper's Lodge

Nottingham Rd, Chaddesdon DE21 6LZ

☎ 01332 662504 & 01332 662504

📠 01332 673306

web: www.innkeeperslodge.com

dir: from M1 junct 25 take A52 towards Derby, take exit signed Spondon & Chaddesden, at rdbt take exit signed Chaddesden pass Asda store, 1m at lights right into car park

Smart, en suite accommodation ideal for both business & leisure guests. Bedrooms are very well equipped, including Sky TV,

continued

telephone, modem points, tea & coffee making facilities, (family rooms in most locations). Complimentary breakfast. The adjacent Pub Restaurant; a Harvester, Vintage Inn, Toby Carvery, Ember Inn, Sizzling Pubco or Pub & Carvery offers an all day menu. See Hotel Groups pages for further details.

Rooms 29 en suite S £48-£52; D £48-£52

BUDGET HOTEL

Premier Travel Inn Derby East

premier travel inn

The Wyvern Business Park, Chaddesden Sidings DE21 6BF

☎ 0870 238 3313 📠 01332 667827

web: www.premiertravelinn.com

dir: From M1 junct 25 follow A52 to Derby. After 6.5m take exit for Wyvern/Pride Park. 1st exit at rdbt (A52 Nottingham), straight over next rdbt. Inn on left

High quality, modern budget accommodation ideal for both families and business travellers. Spacious, en suite bedrooms feature bath and shower, satellite TV and many have telephones and modem points. The adjacent family restaurant features a wide and varied menu. For further details consult the Hotel Groups page.

Rooms 82 en suite

Premier Travel Inn Derby North West

95 Ashbourne Rd, Mackworth DE22 4LZ

☎ 0870 9906606 📠 0870 9906607

dir: Exit M1 junct 25 onto A52 towards Derby. At Pentagon Island straight ahead towards city centre. Follow A52/Ashbourne signs into Mackworth

Rooms 22 en suite

Premier Travel Inn Derby South

Foresters Leisure Park, Osmaston Park Rd DE23 8AG

☎ 0870 9906306 📠 0870 9906307

dir: On A5111 in Derby. Exit M1 junct 24 onto A6 to Derby. Left onto A5111 ring road for 2m

Rooms 27 en suite

Premier Travel Inn Derby West

Uttoxeter New Rd, Manor Park Way DE22 3HN

☎ 08701 977072 📠 01332 207506

dir: M1 junct 25 take A38W towards Burton-upon-Trent for approx. 15m. Left at island (city hospital), right at lights, 3rd exit at city hospital island

Rooms 43 en suite **Conf** Thtr 15

BUDGET HOTEL

Sleep Inn Derby

SLEEP INN

Prospect Place, Derwent Pde, Pride Park DE24 8HG

☎ 01332 611980 📠 01332 611999

e-mail: enquiries@hotels-derby.com

dir: A52 city centre, follow signs to Pride Park Stadium. Hotel on Millennium Way

This modern, purpose built accommodation offers smartly appointed, well-equipped bedrooms, with good power showers. There is a choice of adjacent food outlets where guests may enjoy breakfast, snacks and meals.

Rooms 84 en suite S £69-£79; D £69-£79 **Conf** Thtr 35 Class 35 Board 35 Del from £115

BUDGET HOTEL

Travelodge Derby

Kingsway, Rowditch DE22 3NN

☎ 08700 850 950 🖷 01332 367255

web: www.travelodge.co.uk

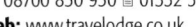

dir: A38 Derby north, exit at ringroad, A5111. Lodge 0.25m on left

Travelodge offers good quality, good value, modern accommodation. Ideal for families, the spacious en suite bedrooms include remote-control TV, tea and coffee-making facilities and comfortable beds. Meals can be taken at the nearby family restaurant. See Hotel Groups pages for further details.

Rooms 40 en suite S fr £26; D fr £26

DERBY SERVICE AREA (A50)   MAP 11 SK42

BUDGET HOTEL

Days Inn Donnington

Welcome Break Services, A50 Westbound DE72 2WA

☎ 01332 799666 🖷 01332 794166

e-mail: donnington.hotel@welcomebreak.co.uk

web: www.welcomebreak.co.uk

dir: M1 junct 24/24a, onto A50 towards Stoke/Derby. Hotel between juncts 1 & 2

This modern building offers accommodation in smart, spacious and well-equipped bedrooms, suitable for families and business travellers, and all with en suite bathrooms. Continental breakfast is available and other refreshments may be taken at the nearby family restaurant. For further details see the Hotel Groups page.

Rooms 47 en suite **Conf** Thtr 10 Class 10 Board 10

ETWALL   MAP 10 SK23

★★ 75% ⊛ **HOTEL**

Blenheim House

56-58 Main St DE65 6LP

☎ 01283 732254 🖷 01283 733860

e-mail: info@theblenheimhouse.com

web: www.theblenheimhouse.com

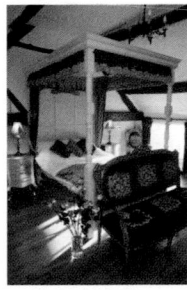

Located in the centre of the village and dating back, in parts, to the 1700s this popular hotel offers a well-furnished and individually designed bedrooms together with high standards of quality cooking.

Rooms 7 en suite 2 annexe en suite (2 fmly) (4 GF) ⊛ in all bedrooms S £65-£75; D £85-£135 (incl. bkfst) **Facilities** Blenheim House Beauty ♫ **Conf** Thtr 40 Class 25 Board 20 **Parking** 25 **Notes** LB ⊗ ⊛ in restaurant Closed 1 Jan RS 25-26 Dec

FENNY BENTLEY   MAP 16 SK14

★★ 69% **HOTEL**

Bentley Brook Inn

DE6 1LF

☎ 01335 350278 & 07976 614877 🖷 01335 350422

e-mail: all@bentleybrookinn.co.uk

dir: 2m N of Ashbourne at junct of A515 & B5056, entrance off B5056

This popular inn is located within the Peak District National Park, just north of Ashbourne. It is a charming building with an attractive terrace, sweeping lawns, and nursery gardens. A well-appointed family restaurant dominates the ground floor, where a wide range of dishes is available all day. The character bar serves beer from its own micro-brewery. Bedrooms vary in styles and sizes, but all are well equipped.

Rooms 8 en suite 4 annexe en suite (1 fmly) (1 GF) ⊛ in 5 bedrooms S fr £52; D fr £76 (incl. bkfst) **Facilities** Fishing ⅃ Xmas **Conf** Thtr 50 Class 30 Board 20 **Parking** 100 **Notes** LB ⊛ in restaurant Civ Wed 100

GLOSSOP   MAP 16 SK09

★★ 80% **HOTEL**

Wind in the Willows

Derbyshire Level SK13 7PI

☎ 01457 868001 🖷 01457 853354

e-mail: info@windinthewillows.co.uk

dir: 1m E of Glossop on A57, turn right opp Royal Oak, hotel 400yds on right

A warm and relaxed atmosphere prevails at this small and very comfortable hotel. The bedrooms are well furnished, each offering many thoughtful extras, and some executive rooms are available. Public areas include two comfortable lounges, a dining room, and a modern meeting room with views over the extensive grounds.

Rooms 12 en suite ⊛ in all bedrooms S £88-£105; D £125-£150 (incl. bkfst) **Facilities** Fishing Wi-fi in bedrooms **Conf** Thtr 40 Class 12 Board 16 Del from £140 **Parking** 16 **Notes** LB ⊗ No children 10yrs ⊛ in restaurant

England

HARTINGTON   MAP 16 SK16

★★ 🅰

Biggin Hall

SK17 0DH

☎ 01298 84451 📠 01298 84681

e-mail: enquiries@bigginhall.co.uk

web: www.bigginhall.co.uk

dir: 0.5m off A515 midway between Ashbourne and Buxton

Rooms 20 en suite (4 fmly) (4 GF) ⊘ in 3 bedrooms S £60-£110; D £70-£126 **Facilities** Xmas **Conf** Thtr 20 Class 20 Board 20 Del from £125 **Parking** 25 **Notes LB** No children 12yrs ⊘ in restaurant

See advert on opposite page

HATHERSAGE   MAP 16 SK28

★★★ 79% ◉ ◉ **HOTEL**

Best Western George at Hathersage

Main Rd S32 1BB

☎ 01433 650436 & 0845 456 0581 📠 01433 650099

e-mail: info@george-hotel.net

web: www.george-hotel.net

dir: in village centre on A6187 SW of Sheffield

The George is a relaxing 500-year-old hostelry in the heart of this picturesque town. The beamed bar lounge has great character and traditional comfort, and the restaurant is light, modern and spacious with original artworks. Upstairs the decor is simpler with lots of light hues; the split-level and four-poster rooms are especially appealing. Quality cooking is a key feature of the hotel.

Rooms 22 en suite (2 fmly) (2 GF) ⊘ in all bedrooms S £82-£124; D £114-£168 (incl. bkfst) **Facilities** Xmas **Conf** Thtr 80 Class 20 Board 36 Del £142 **Parking** 40 **Notes LB** ⊗ ⊘ in restaurant Civ Wed 50

HIGHAM   MAP 16 SK35

★★★ 72% ◉ **HOTEL**

Santo's Higham Farm Hotel

Main Rd DE55 6EH

☎ 01773 833812 📠 01773 520525

e-mail: reception@santoshighamfarm.demon.co.uk

web: www.santoshighamfarm.co.uk

dir: M1 junct 28, A38 towards Derby, then A61 towards Chesterfield. Onto B6013 towards Belper, hotel 300yds on right

With panoramic views across the rolling Amber Valley, this 15th-century crook barn and farmhouse has an Italian Wing and an

continued

International Wing of themed bedrooms. Freshly prepared dishes, especially fish, are available in Guiseppe's restaurant, and in summer barbecues are held in the Rose Garden. An ideal romantic hideaway.

Rooms 28 en suite (2 fmly) (7 GF) ⊘ in all bedrooms S £73-£113; D £104-£134 (incl. bkfst) **Facilities** STV Xmas **Conf** Thtr 100 Class 40 Board 34 Del from £100 **Parking** 100 **Notes LB** ⊗ ⊘ in restaurant Civ Wed 100

HOPE   MAP 16 SK18

★★★ 77% **HOTEL**

Losehill House

Edale Rd S33 6RF

☎ 01433 621219 📠 01433 622501

e-mail: peakretreat@btconnect.com

web: www.losehillhousehotel.com

dir: A6187 into Hope, take turn opposite church into Edale Road. 1m, left & follow signs to hotel

Standing in a peaceful location in the heart of the Hope Valley, this hotel offers very well equipped bedrooms together with a leisure pool and a comfortable lounge with spectacular views. Staff are friendly and helpful, and quality cooking is served in the pleasant restaurant.

Rooms 18 en suite 4 annexe en suite (2 fmly) (2 GF) ⊘ in all bedrooms S £65-£70; D £95-£120 (incl. bkfst) **Facilities** Spa 🏊 Sauna Outdoor Hot Tub Xmas **Conf** Thtr 25 Class 25 Board 16 Del from £110 **Services** Lift **Parking** 25 **Notes** ⊗ No children 12yrs ⊘ in restaurant Closed 31 Dec-10 Jan

LONG EATON   MAP 11 SK43

★★★ 67% **HOTEL**

Novotel Nottingham/Derby

Bostock Ln NG10 4EP

☎ 0115 946 5111 📠 0115 946 5900

e-mail: H0507@accor-hotels.com

web: www.novotel.com

dir: M1 junct 25 onto B6002 to Long Eaton. Hotel 400yds on left

In close proximity to the M1, this purpose-built hotel has much to offer. All bedrooms are spacious, have sofa beds and provide exceptional desk space. Public rooms include a bright brasserie, which is open all day and provides extended dining until midnight, and a comprehensive range of meeting rooms.

Rooms 108 en suite (40 fmly) (20 GF) ⊘ in 89 bedrooms S £49-£80; D £49-£80 **Facilities** STV 🏊 Wi-fi available **Conf** Thtr 250 Class 100 Board 100 Del from £115 **Services** Lift **Parking** 220

★★★ 67% **HOTEL**

Ramada Nottingham   ⓇRAMADA.

Bostock Ln NG10 4EP

☎ 0115 946 0000 📠 0115 946 0726

e-mail: sales.nottingham@ramadajarvis.co.uk

web: www.ramadajarvis.co.uk

dir: 0.25m from M1 junct 25

Conveniently located between Nottingham and Derby, this large modern hotel is set just off the M1. Bedrooms are comfortably appointed for both business and leisure guests and conference facilities are available.

Rooms 101 en suite (10 fmly) (40 GF) ⊘ in 70 bedrooms S £49.95-£99; D £49.95-£99 **Facilities** STV Wi-fi available Xmas **Conf** Thtr 85 Class 30 Board 20 Del from £99 **Parking** 200 **Notes LB** ⊗ ⊘ in restaurant

★★ 61% **HOTEL**

Europa
20-22 Derby Rd NG10 1LW
☎ 0115 972 8481 🗎 0115 849 6313
e-mail: k.riley3@ntlworld.com
dir: on A6005, in town centre. 1.5m from M1 junct 25 & A52

Convenient for the town centre and the M1, this commercial hotel offers suitably furnished bedrooms. In addition to the restaurant, where Chinese cooking is offered, light refreshments are available throughout the day in the conservatory.

Rooms 15 en suite (2 fmly) (3 GF) ⊘ in 3 bedrooms **Conf** Thtr 35 Class 35 Board 28 **Parking** 24 **Notes** ⊗ ⊘ in restaurant Closed 25-28 Dec

MATLOCK   MAP 16 SK35

★★★ 81% ◉◉ **COUNTRY HOUSE HOTEL**

Riber Hall
DE4 5JU
☎ 01629 582795 🗎 01629 580475
e-mail: info@riber-hall.co.uk
web: www.riber-hall.co.uk
dir: 1m off A615 at Tansley

This beautiful Elizabethan manor house enjoys an idyllic location in charming grounds overlooking Matlock. Beautifully furnished, thoughtfully equipped bedrooms, many with oak four-poster beds, are situated round a delightful courtyard with its own fountain. Tastefully appointed public rooms are furnished with period and antique pieces and an impressive wine list complements the imaginative, award-winning cuisine.

Rooms 3 en suite 11 annexe en suite (7 GF) ⊘ in 4 bedrooms S £98-£116; D £145-£188 (incl. bkfst) **Facilities** STV ⚓ ⚓ **Conf** Thtr 20 Class 20 Board 20 Del from £148 **Parking** 50 **Notes LB** No children 10yrs ⊘ in restaurant Closed 25-Dec Civ Wed 50

★★ 83% **HOTEL**

The Red House Country Hotel
Old Rd, Darley Dale DE4 2ER
☎ 01629 734854 🗎 01629 734885
e-mail: enquiries@theredhousecountryhotel.co.uk
web: www.theredhousecountryhotel.co.uk
dir: off A6 onto Old Rd signed Carriage Museum, 2.5m N of Matlock

A peaceful country hotel set in delightful Victorian gardens. Rich colour schemes are used to excellent effect throughout. The well-equipped bedrooms include three ground floor rooms in the adjacent coach house. A comfortable lounge with delightful rural views is available for refreshments and pre-dinner drinks; service is friendly and attentive.

Rooms 7 en suite 3 annexe en suite (3 GF) ⊘ in all bedrooms S £75; D £100 (incl. bkfst) **Conf** Thtr 10 Class 10 Board 10 Del from £130 **Parking** 12 **Notes LB** ⊗ No children 12yrs ⊘ in restaurant Closed 1-14 Jan

The vast majority of establishments in this guide accept credit and debit cards. We indicate only those that don't take any

England

MATLOCK *continued*

[U]

Swallow New Bath

SWALLOW HOTELS

New Bath Rd DE4 3PX
☎ 0870 400 8119 ▤ 01629 580268
e-mail: www.reservations.matlock@swallowhotels.com
web: www.swallowhotels.com

dir: M1 junct 28 follow A38, take A610 signed Ambergate. Turn
right onto A6 signed Matlock, hotel on left

At the time of going to press, the star classification for this hotel was
not confirmed. Please refer to the AA internet site www.theAA.com for
current information.

Rooms 55 en suite (17 fmly) (18 GF) ⊘ in 36 bedrooms S £60-£90;
D £120-£180 (incl. bkfst) **Facilities** STV ⬚ ⬚ supervised ⬚ Sauna
Solarium Xmas **Conf** Thtr 120 Class 80 Board 50 Del from £110
Parking 80 **Notes** ⊘ in restaurant Civ Wed 100

MORLEY

★★★★ 73% ⊛ **HOTEL**

The Morley Hayes Hotel

Main Rd DE7 6DG
☎ 01332 780480 ▤ 01332 781094
e-mail: hotel@morleyhayes.com
dir: 4m N of Derby on A608

Located in rolling countryside this modern golfing destination provides
an appealing mix of style and comfort. Stylish bedrooms offer much
comfort, wide-ranging facilities, plasma TVs, and state-of-the-art
bathrooms; the plush suites are particularly eye-catching. Creative
cuisine is offered in the Dovecote Restaurant, and both Roosters and
the Spikes sports bar provide an informal eating option.

Rooms 32 en suite (4 fmly) (15 GF) ⊘ in all bedrooms S £110-£235;
D £126-£249 (incl. bkfst) **Facilities** STV ⬚ 27 Putt green Wi-fi available
Golf driving range **Conf** Thtr 165 Class 130 Board 122 Del from £155
Services Lift air con **Parking** 245 **Notes** ⊗ ⊘ in restaurant Civ Wed 90

Packed in a hurry?
Ironing facilities should be available at all star
levels, either in the rooms or on request

RENISHAW   MAP 16 SK47

★★★ 68% **HOTEL**

Sitwell Arms

Station Rd S21 3WF
☎ 01246 435226 & 01246 437327 ▤ 01246 433915
e-mail: sitwellarms@renishaw79.fsnet.co.uk
dir: on A6135 to Sheffield, W of M1 junct 30

This stone-built hotel, parts of which date back to the 18th century, is
conveniently situated close to the M1. The hotel has an extensive gym
and hair and beauty salon, and offers good value accommodation.
Bedrooms are of a comfortable size and include modern facilities.
There are extensive bars and a restaurant serving a wide range of
meals and snacks.

Rooms 29 en suite (8 fmly) (9 GF) ⊘ in 10 bedrooms S £27-£37.95;
D £60-£80 (incl. bkfst) **Facilities** STV Gym Wi-fi available Fitness studio,
Hair & Beauty Salon Xmas **Conf** BC Thtr 160 Class 60 Board 60
Services Lift **Parking** 150 **Notes LB** ⊗ ⊘ in restaurant Civ Wed 150
See advertisement under SHEFFIELD, South Yorkshire

RIPLEY   MAP 16 SK35

★★ 65% **HOTEL**

Moss Cottage

Nottingham Rd DE5 3JT
☎ 01773 742555 ▤ 01773 741063
e-mail: mosshotel@aol.com
web: www.mosscottage.net
dir: M1 junct 26, A610 to Ripley. Hotel approx 4m from M1

This busy roadside inn is popular for its value-for-money food and
now has a modern bedroom block to the rear. Bedrooms are well
equipped and spacious and staff are friendly.

Rooms 14 en suite (4 fmly) (6 GF) ⊘ in 6 bedrooms **Facilities** cycling,
golf, outdoor pursuits. **Conf** BC Thtr 60 Class 40 Board 30 **Parking** 60
Notes ⊗ ⊘ in restaurant

RISLEY
MAP 11 SK43

[U]

Swallow Risley Hall

Derby Rd DE72 3SS

☎ 0115 939 9000 & 921 8523 ▤ 0115 939 7766

e-mail: sales.risleyhall@swallowhotels.com

web: www.swallowhotels.com

dir: M1 junct 25, Sandiacre exit into Bostock Lane. Left at x-roads, hotel 0.5m on left

At the time of going to press, the star classification for this hotel was not confirmed. Please refer to the AA internet site www.theAA.com for current information.

Rooms 16 en suite 19 annexe en suite (16 fmly) (8 GF) ⊗ in 12 bedrooms S £110-£145; D £125-£175 (incl. bkfst) **Facilities** Spa ⬚ Snooker Sauna ⬚ Jacuzzi **Conf** Thtr 100 Class 40 Board 22 Del from £165 **Services** Lift **Parking** 100 **Notes LB** ⊗ in restaurant Civ Wed 110

ROWSLEY
MAP 16 SK26

★★★ 80% ⊛ ⊛ **HOTEL**

East Lodge Country House

DE4 2EF

☎ 01629 734474 ▤ 01629 733949

e-mail: info@eastlodge.com

web: www.eastlodge.com

dir: A6, 3m from Bakewell, 5m from Matlock

The hotel enjoys a romantic setting in ten acres of landscaped grounds and gardens. The stylish bedrooms are equipped with many extras such as TVs with DVD players, and most have lovely garden views. The restaurant has a popular local following and offers much produce sourced from the area. The conservatory lounge, overlooking the gardens offers afternoon teas and light meals.

Rooms 12 en suite (2 fmly) (1 GF) ⊗ in all bedrooms S £110-£160; D £160-£233 (incl. bkfst) **Facilities** FTV ⬚ Wi-fi available Xmas **Conf** Thtr 75 Class 20 Board 22 Del £168 **Parking** 40 **Notes LB** ⊗ No children 7yrs ⊗ in restaurant Civ Wed 100

See advertisement under BAKEWELL

★★★ 85% ⊛ ⊛ **HOTEL**

The Peacock at Rowsley

Bakewell Rd DE4 2EB

☎ 01629 733518 ▤ 01629 732671

e-mail: reception@thepeacockatrowsley.com

web: www.thepeacockatrowsley.com

dir: A6, 3m before Bakewell, 6m from Matlock towards Bakewell

Owned by nearby Haddon Hall this hotel is now a smart contemporary destination, but still retains many original historic features and period pieces of furniture. The menus are well balanced and use local produce. Dry fly fishing is a great attraction here as the

continued

hotel owns fishing rights in the area. Staff are delightful and deliver high standards of service.

The Peacock at Rowsley

Rooms 16 en suite (5 fmly) ⊗ in 2 bedrooms S £75-£95; D £145-£185 (incl. bkfst) **Facilities** STV Fishing ⬚ Wi-fi in bedrooms Free use of Woodlands Fitness Centre ♫ **Conf** Thtr 16 Class 8 Board 16 Del from £170 **Parking** 27 **Notes** ⊗ in restaurant Civ Wed 20

SOUTH NORMANTON
MAP 16 SK45

★★★★ 75% **HOTEL**

Renaissance Derby/Nottingham Hotel

Carter Ln East DE55 2EH

☎ 01773 812000 & 0870 4007262

▤ 01773 580032 & 0870 4007362

e-mail: derby@renaissancehotels.co.uk

web: www.renaissancehotels.co.uk/emabr

dir: M1 junct 28, E on A38 to Mansfield

Ideally located on the M1 corridor, the hotel is only 20 minutes away from the major cities of Nottingham and Derby as well as numerous other places of interest. Air-conditioned bedrooms are tastefully decorated and equipped with a range of extras. Public areas include a smart leisure centre, conference facilities and Chatterley's Restaurant.

Rooms 158 en suite (7 fmly) (61 GF) ⊗ in 90 bedrooms **Facilities** STV ⬚ supervised Sauna Gym Jacuzzi Steam room, Whirlpool **Conf** BC Thtr 220 Class 100 Board 60 **Parking** 220 **Notes LB** ⊗ in restaurant Civ Wed 220

BUDGET HOTEL

Premier Travel Inn Mansfield

Carter Ln East DE55 2FH

☎ 08701 977180 ▤ 01773 861155

web: www.premiertravelinn.com

dir: just off M1 junct 28, on A38 signed Mansfield. Entrance 200yds on left

High quality, modern budget accommodation ideal for both families and business travellers. Spacious, en suite bedrooms feature bath and shower, satellite TV and many have telephones and modem points. The adjacent family restaurant features a wide and varied menu. For further details consult the Hotel Groups page.

Rooms 80 en suite

England

SUDBURY MAP 10 SK13

★★★ 73% HOTEL

The Boars Head

Lichfield Rd DE6 5GX

☎ 01283 820344 ▦ 01283 820075

e-mail: enquiries@boars-head-hotel.co.uk

web: www.boars-head-hotel.co.uk

dir: *off A50 onto A515 towards Lichfield, hotel 1m on right*

This well established and popular hotel offers comfortable accommodation in well-equipped bedrooms. There is a relaxed atmosphere in the public rooms, which consists of a several bars and dining options. The beamed lounge bar provides informal dining thanks to a popular carvery, while the restaurant and cocktail bar offer a more formal environment.

Rooms 22 en suite 1 annexe en suite (1 fmly) S £49.95-£59.95; D £59.95-£69.95 (incl. bkfst) **Facilities** STV Xmas **Parking** 85 **Notes LB** ⊗ in restaurant

See advert on page 571

SWANWICK

See **Alfreton**

THORPE (DOVEDALE) MAP 16 SK15

★★★ 78% ⊛ HOTEL

Izaak Walton

Dovedale DE6 2AY

☎ 01335 350555 ▦ 01335 350539

e-mail: reception@izaakwaltonhotel.com

web: www.izaakwaltonhotel.com

dir: *A515 on to B5054 to Thorpe village, continue straight over cattle grid & 2 small bridges, 1st right & sharp left*

This hotel is peacefully situated, with magnificent views over the valley of Dovedale to Thorpe Cloud. Many of the bedrooms have lovely

continued

views, and the executive rooms are particularly spacious. Meals are served in the bar area, with more formal dining in the Haddon Restaurant. Staff are friendly and efficient. Fishing on the River Dove can be arranged.

Rooms 34 en suite (6 fmly) (7 GF) ⊗ in 32 bedrooms S £100-£110; D £137-£177 (incl. bkfst) **Facilities** STV Fishing ⬙ Wi-fi in bedrooms Fly fishing on nearby River Dove ch fac Xmas **Conf** Thtr 50 Class 40 Board 50 Del from £150 **Parking** 80 **Notes LB** ⊗ in restaurant Civ Wed 80

See advertisement under ASHBOURNE

★★★ 70% HOTEL

The Peveril of the Peak

DE6 2AW

☎ 01335 350396 ▦ 01335 350507

e-mail: frontdesk@peverilofthepeak.com

web: www.peverilofthepeak.com

dir: *Ashbourne A515 towards Buxton, after 1m turn left to Thorpe, approx. 4m on right just before Thorpe village*

Dating back to the 1830s, the hotel takes its name from one of Sir Walter Scott's heroic novels. It is set in 11 acres of grounds and surrounded by the quintessentially English countryside of the Derbyshire Dales. Most rooms overlook the gardens and many have patios. There are lounges, meeting rooms, a cosy cocktail bar and a conservatory restaurant.

Rooms 46 en suite (16 fmly) (6 GF) ⊗ in all bedrooms S £85-£105; D £130-£160 (incl. bkfst) **Facilities** STV Xmas **Conf** Thtr 150 Class 150 Board 120 Del from £120 **Parking** 80 **Notes** ⊗ in restaurant Civ Wed 60

See advert under Ashbourne page 173

TIBSHELF MOTORWAY MAP 16 SK46
SERVICE AREA (M1)

BUDGET HOTEL

Premier Travel Inn Mansfield (Tibshelf)

premier travel inn

Tibshelf Motorway Service Area DE55 5TZ

☎ 08701 977181 ▦ 01773 876609

web: www.premiertravelinn.com

dir: *M1 northbound between junct 28/29, access available southbound*

High quality, modern budget accommodation ideal for both families and business travellers. Spacious, en suite bedrooms feature bath and shower, satellite TV and many have telephones and modem points. The adjacent family restaurant features a wide and varied menu. For further details consult the Hotel Groups page.

Rooms 40 en suite

DEVON

ASHBURTON

MAP 03 SX77

★★★ 79% ⊛ ⊛ **COUNTRY HOUSE HOTEL**

Holne Chase

Two Bridges Rd TQ13 7NS
☎ 01364 631471 📄 01364 631453
e-mail: info@holne-chase.co.uk
web: www.holne-chase.co.uk

dir: *3m N on unclass Two Bridges/Tavistock road*

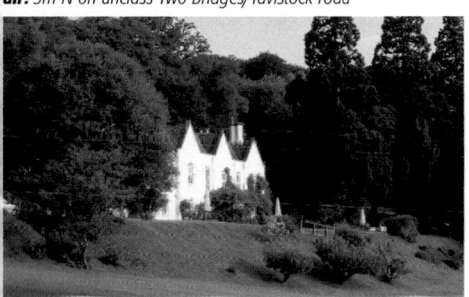

This former hunting lodge is peacefully situated in a secluded position, with sweeping lawns leading to the river and panoramic views of the moor. Bedrooms are attractively and individually furnished, and there are a number of split level suites available. Enjoyable dishes using local ingredients, some produced on the owners' farm, on featured on the daily-changing menu.

Rooms 10 en suite 7 annexe en suite (9 fmly) (1 GF) S £120-£130; D £160-£210 (incl. bkfst) **Facilities** Fishing Riding ⅏ Putt green Fly fishing, Riding, Beauty treatments dog grooming parlour Xmas **Conf** Thtr 40 Class 60 Board 60 **Parking** 40 **Notes LB** ⊘ in restaurant Civ Wed 75

★★ 63% **HOTEL**

Dartmoor Lodge

OLD ENGLISH INNS

Peartree Cross TQ13 7JW
☎ 01364 652232 📄 01364 653990
e-mail: dartmoor.ashburton@newbridgeinns.co.uk
web: www.oldenglish.co.uk

dir: *Exit A38 at 2nd exit for Ashburton, turn right across bridge, turn left at garage, hotel on right.*

Situated midway between Plymouth and Exeter, this popular hotel is close to the bustling town of Ashburton and ideally placed for exploring Dartmoor and the South Devon coast. Bedrooms, including two with four-poster beds, are well equipped, whilst public areas include the popular bar and smart restaurant where a range of dishes can be enjoyed.

Rooms 29 en suite (7 fmly) (9 GF) ⊘ in 11 bedrooms S £49.50-£60; D £59.50-£80 (incl. bkfst) **Facilities** STV Xmas **Conf** Thtr 90 Class 36 Board 36 Del £70 **Services** Lift **Parking** 100 **Notes LB** ⊘ in restaurant

ASHWATER

MAP 03 SX39

★★★ ⊛ ⊛ **HOTEL**

Blagdon Manor Hotel & Restaurant

EX21 5DF
☎ 01409 211224 📄 01409 211634
e-mail: stay@blagdon.com
web: www.blagdon.com

dir: *Take A388 N of Launceston towards Holsworthy. Approx 2m N of Chapman's Well take 2nd right for Ashwater. Next right beside Blagdon Lodge, hotel 0.25m*

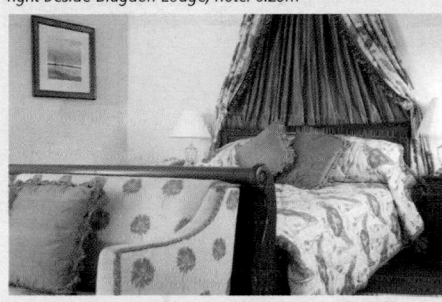

Located on the borders of Devon and Cornwall within easy reach of the coast and in its own beautifully kept yet natural gardens, this small and friendly hotel offers a charming home-from-home atmosphere. The tranquillity of the secluded setting, the character and charm of the house and its unhurried pace ensures calm and relaxation. High levels of service, personal touches and thoughtful extras are all part of a stay here. Stephen Morey cooks with passion and his dependence on only the finest of local ingredients speaks volumes.

Rooms 7 en suite ⊘ in all bedrooms S £85; D £120 (incl. bkfst) **Facilities** ⅏ Boules, giant chess/draughts **Parking** 11 **Notes** No children 12yrs ⊘ in restaurant Closed 2wks Jan/Feb & 2wks Oct/Nov

AXMINSTER

MAP 04 SY29

See also Colyford

★★★ 74% ⊛ ⊛ **HOTEL**

Fairwater Head Country House Hotel

Hawkchurch EX13 5TX
☎ 01297 678349 📄 01297 678459
e-mail: info@fairwaterheadhotel.co.uk
web: www.fairwaterheadhotel.co.uk

dir: *off B3165, Crewkerne to Lyme Regis road. Hotel signed to Hawkchurch*

Peacefully located in the countryside this charming hotel provides attractive gardens and stunning views. The proprietors and staff provide a friendly and attentive service in a relaxing environment. Bedrooms are individually decorated, spacious and comfortable. At lunch and dinner guests can enjoy best quality local ingredients cooked with great care.

Rooms 14 en suite 7 annexe en suite (9 GF) ⊘ in all bedrooms S £65-£100; D £100-£200 (incl. bkfst) **Facilities** ⅏ Wi-fi available ♫ Xmas **Conf** BC Thtr 30 Class 20 Board 20 Del from £120 **Parking** 25 **Notes LB** ⊘ in restaurant Closed 27 Dec-11 Feb

BABBACOMBE
See **Torquay**

BARNSTAPLE   MAP 03 SS53

★★★★ 79% HOTEL

The Imperial   *Brend Hotels*
Taw Vale Pde EX32 8NB
☎ 01271 345861 ▤ 01271 324448
e-mail: info@brend-imperial.co.uk
web: www.brend-hotels.co.uk

dir: *M5 junct 27/A361 to Barnstaple. Follow town centre signs, passing Tesco. Straight on at next 2 rdbts. Hotel on right*

This smart and attractive hotel is pleasantly located at the centre of Barnstaple and overlooks the river. The staff are friendly and offer attentive service. The comfortable bedrooms are in a range of sizes, some with balconies and many overlooking the river. Afternoon tea is available in the lounge, and the cuisine is appetising and freshly prepared.

Rooms 63 en suite (7 fmly) (4 GF) S £80-£160; D £90-£160 **Facilities** STV Wi-fi available leisure facilities at sister hotel ♫ Xmas **Conf** Thtr 60 Class 40 Board 30 **Services** Lift **Parking** 80 **Notes LB** ⊗ ⊘ in restaurant

See advert on opposite page

★★★ 80% HOTEL

Barnstaple Hotel   *Brend Hotels*
Braunton Rd EX31 1LE
☎ 01271 376221 ▤ 01271 324101
e-mail: info@barnstaplehotel.co.uk
web: www.brend-hotels.co.uk
dir: *outskirts of Barnstaple on A361*

This well-established hotel enjoys a convenient location on the edge of town. Bedrooms are spacious and well equipped, and many have access to a balcony overlooking the outdoor pool and garden. A wide choice is offered from various menus based on local produce, served in the Brasserie Restaurant. There is an extensive range of leisure and conference facilities.

Rooms 61 en suite (4 fmly) (17 GF) S £65-£100; D £70-£120 **Facilities Spa** STV ⊠ � Snooker Sauna Solarium Gym ch fac Xmas **Conf** BC Thtr 250 Class 100 Board 50 Del from £99.50 **Parking** 250 **Notes LB** ⊘ in restaurant Civ Wed 150

★★★ 77% HOTEL

Royal & Fortescue   *Brend Hotels*
Boutport St EX31 1HG
☎ 01271 342289 ▤ 01271 340102
e-mail: info@royalfortescue.co.uk
web: www.brend-hotels.co.uk

dir: *A361 along Barbican Rd signed town centre, turn right into Queen St & left onto Boutport St, hotel on left*

Formerly a coaching inn, this friendly and convivial hotel is conveniently located in the centre of town. Bedrooms vary in size but all are decorated and furnished to a consistently high standard. In addition to the formal restaurant, guests can take snacks in the popular coffee shop or dine more informally in The Bank, a bistro and café bar.

Rooms 49 en suite (4 fmly) (4 GF) S £60-£75; D £70-£85 **Facilities** STV ♫ Xmas **Conf** Thtr 25 Class 25 Board 25 **Services** Lift **Parking** 40 **Notes LB** ⊘ in restaurant

★★★ 72% HOTEL

Park   *Brend Hotels*
Taw Vale EX32 9AE
☎ 01271 372166 ▤ 01271 323157
e-mail: info@parkhotel.co.uk
web: www.brend-hotels.co.uk

dir: *opposite Rock Park, 0.5m from town centre*

Enjoying views across the park and in easy walking distance of the town centre, this modern hotel offers a choice of bedrooms in both the main building and the Garden Court, just across the car park. Public rooms are open-plan in style and the friendly staff offer attentive service in a relaxed atmosphere.

Rooms 23 en suite 17 annexe en suite (7 fmly) (5 GF) ⊘ in 11 bedrooms S £60-£75; D £70-£85 **Facilities** STV ♫ Xmas **Parking** 80 **Notes LB** ⊘ in restaurant Civ Wed 100

★★ 76% HOTEL

Cedars Lodge   OLD ENGLISH INNS
Bickington Rd EX31 2HP
☎ 01271 371784 ▤ 01271 325733
e-mail: cedars.barnstaple@oldenglishinns.co.uk
web: www.oldenglish.co.uk

Once a country house, this popular establishment stands in three acres of gardens and is situated just outside Barnstaple within easy reach of all major roads and the M5. Bedrooms are located in the adjacent lodge which is set around a courtyard facing the main house. All rooms offer generous levels of comfort and modern facilities. The conservatory restaurant has a popular following, serving a wide choice of dishes.

Rooms 2 en suite 32 annexe en suite (6 fmly) (14 GF) ⊘ in 24 bedrooms S £75-£95; D £90-£110 (incl. bkfst) **Facilities** STV Xmas **Conf** Thtr 200 Class 100 Board 100 Del from £80 **Parking** 150 **Notes LB** ⊗ ⊘ in restaurant Civ Wed 200

England

England

BUDGET HOTEL

Premier Travel Inn Barnstaple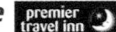

Eastern Av, Whiddon Dr EX32 8RY
☎ 08701 977025 📠 01271 377710
web: www.premiertravelinn.com

dir: *adjacent to North Devon Link Rd at junct with A39*

High quality, modern budget accommodation ideal for both families and business travellers. Spacious, en suite bedrooms feature bath and shower, satellite TV and many have telephones and modem points. The adjacent family restaurant features a wide and varied menu. For further details consult the Hotel Groups page.

Rooms 40 en suite

BIDEFORD   MAP 03 SS42

★★★ 75% HOTEL

Royal   (Brend Hotels)
Barnstaple St EX39 4AF
☎ 01237 472005 📠 01237 478957
e-mail: info@royalbideford.co.uk
web: www.brend-hotels.co.uk

dir: *at eastern end of Bideford Bridge*

A quiet and relaxing hotel, the Royal is set near the riverbank within five minutes' walk of the busy town centre and quay. Well-maintained public areas are bright and retain much of the charm and style of its 16th-century origins, particularly in the wood-panelled Kingsley Suite. Bedrooms are well equipped and comfortable.

Rooms 32 en suite (2 fmly) (2 GF) ❷ in 14 bedrooms S £65-£85; D £75-£105 **Facilities** STV ♫ Xmas **Conf** Thtr 100 Class 100 Board 100 **Services** Lift **Parking** 70 **Notes** LB ❷ in restaurant Civ Wed

★★ 79% ❸ HOTEL

Yeoldon Country House
Durrant Ln, Northam EX39 2RL
☎ 01237 474400 📠 01237 476618
e-mail: yeoldonhouse@aol.com
web: www.yeoldonhousehotel.co.uk

dir: *A39 from Barnstaple over River Torridge Bridge. At rdbt right onto A386 towards Northam, then 3rd right into Durrant Lane*

In a tranquil location with superb views over the River Torridge and attractive grounds, this is a charming Victorian house. The well-equipped bedrooms are individually decorated and some have balconies with breathtaking views. The public rooms are full of character with many interesting features and artefacts. The daily-

continued

changing dinner menu offers imaginative dishes that use fresh local produce.

Rooms 10 en suite ❷ in all bedrooms S £65-£75; D £100-£120 (incl. bkfst) **Parking** 20 **Notes** LB ❷ in restaurant Closed 24-27 Dec Civ Wed 100

BIGBURY-ON-SEA   MAP 03 SX64

★★ 76% SMALL HOTEL

Henley
TQ7 4AR
☎ 01548 810240 📠 01548 810240
e-mail: enquiries@thehenleyhotel.co.uk

dir: *through Bigbury, past Golf Centre into Bigbury-on-Sea. Hotel on left as road slopes towards shore*

Built in the Edwardian era, and complete with its own private cliff path to a sandy beach, this small hotel boasts stunning views from an elevated position. Family run, it is a perfect choice for guests wishing to escape the hurried pace of life to a peaceful retreat. Personal service, friendly hospitality and food cooked with care using local, fresh produce combine to make this a simple yet special place to stay.

Rooms 6 en suite (1 fmly) ❷ in all bedrooms S £50-£60; D £100-£120 (incl. bkfst) **Parking** 9 **Notes** LB No children ❷ in restaurant Closed Nov-Mar

BISHOPSTEIGNTON MAP 03 SX97

★★ 68% **HOTEL**

Cockhaven Manor Hotel

THE INDEPENDENTS

Cockhaven Rd TQ14 9RF
☎ 01626 775252 📠 01626 775572
e-mail: cockhaven.manor@virgin.net
web: www.cockhavenmanor.com

dir: M5/A380 towards Torquay, then A381 towards Teignmouth. Left at Metro Motors. Hotel 500yds on left

A friendly, family-run inn that dates back to the 16th century. Bedrooms are well equipped and many enjoy views across the beautiful Teign estuary. A choice of dining options is offered, and traditional and interesting dishes along with locally caught fish are popular with visitors and locals alike.

Rooms 12 en suite (2 fmly) ⊛ in 10 bedrooms S £42-£50; D £60-£72 (incl. bkfst) **Facilities** Wi-fi in bedrooms Petanque **Conf** BC Thtr 50 Class 50 Board 30 Del from £45 **Parking** 50 **Notes LB** ⊛ in restaurant RS 25-26 Dec

BOVEY TRACEY MAP 03 SX87

★★ 72% **HOTEL**

Coombe Cross

Coombe Ln TQ13 9EY
☎ 01626 832476 📠 01626 835298
e-mail: info@coombecross.co.uk
web: www.coombecross.co.uk

dir: A38 signed Bovey Tracey & town centre, along High St, up hill 400yds beyond Parish Church. Hotel on left

With delightful views over Dartmoor, this peaceful hotel is set in well-tended gardens on the edge of the town. Bedrooms are well equipped and offer ample comfort, whilst public areas include a choice of lounges and a range of leisure and fitness facilities. At dinner, carefully prepared dishes are served in the spacious dining room.

Rooms 23 en suite (1 fmly) (4 GF) ⊛ in all bedrooms S £45-£50; D £60-£70 (incl. bkfst) **Facilities** Spa 🏊 Sauna Solarium Gym Table tennis **Conf** Thtr 80 Class 30 Board 30 Del from £78.50 **Parking** 20 **Notes LB** ⊛ in restaurant Closed 24 Dec-1 Jan

BRANSCOMBE MAP 04 SY18

★★ 78% ⊛ **HOTEL**

The Masons Arms

EX12 3DJ
☎ 01297 680300 📠 01297 680500
e-mail: reception@masonsarms.co.uk

dir: off A3052 towards Branscombe, hotel in valley at bottom of hill

This delightful 14th-century village inn is just half a mile from the sea. Bedrooms in the thatched annexed cottages, that have their own patios with seating, tend to be more spacious; those in the inn reflect much period charm. In the bar, an extensive selection of dishes with many local specialities are available, and the restaurant offers an imaginative range of dishes.

Rooms 5 rms (3 en suite) 14 annexe en suite (1 fmly) ⊛ in 5 bedrooms S £60-£160; D £60-£160 (incl. bkfst) **Facilities** ch fac Xmas **Parking** 43 **Notes LB** ⊛ in restaurant

BRIXHAM MAP 03 SX95

★★★ 73% **HOTEL**

Quayside

41-49 King St TQ5 9TJ
☎ 01803 855751 📠 01803 882733
e-mail: reservations@quaysidehotel.co.uk
web: www.quaysidehotel.co.uk

dir: A380, at 2nd rdbt at Kinkerswell towards Brixham on A3022. Hotel overlooks harbour

With views over the harbour and bay, this hotel was converted from six cottages. The owners and their team of local staff provide friendly and attentive service. Public rooms retain a certain cosiness and intimacy, and include the lounge, residents' bar and Ernie Lister's public bar. Freshly landed fish features on menus in the well-appointed restaurant. Bar snacks are available in the public bar as a more informal eating alternative.

Rooms 29 en suite (2 fmly) ⊛ in 6 bedrooms S £57-£95; D £84-£120 (incl. bkfst) **Facilities** FTV Wi-fi in bedrooms Xmas **Conf** Thtr 25 Class 18 Board 18 **Parking** 30 **Notes LB** ⊛ in restaurant

★★★ 70% HOTEL

Berry Head

Berry Head Rd TQ5 9AJ

☎ 01803 853225 🖹 01803 882084

e-mail: stay@berryheadhotel.com

dir: From marina, 1m, hotel on left

THE INDEPENDENTS

From its stunning cliff-top location, this imposing property that dates back to 1809 has spectacular views across Torbay. Public areas include two comfortable lounges together with a bar serving a range of popular dishes. Many of the bedrooms enjoy splendid sea views.

Rooms 32 en suite (7 fmly) **Facilities Spa** 🔦 ⬏ Jacuzzi Petanque Sailing Deep sea fishing ♫ Xmas **Conf** BC Thtr 300 Class 250 Board 40 Del from £70 **Parking** 200 **Notes** ⊘ in restaurant Civ Wed 200

See advert on this page

★ 75% HOTEL

Smuggler's Haunt Hotel & Restaurant

Church Hill East TQ5 8HH

☎ 01803 853050 🖹 01803 858738

e-mail: enquiries@smugglershaunt-hotel-devon.co.uk

web: www.smugglershaunt-hotel-devon.co.uk

dir: end of A3022 turn left, hotel 200yds

This 300-year-old hotel, located near the harbour, is full of character. Bedrooms, some suitable for families, are comfortably equipped. A variety of freshly prepared food (including local fish and produce) is served in the family-friendly restaurant.

Rooms 14 en suite (2 fmly) **Notes** ⊘ in restaurant

The Berry Head Hotel

BERRY HEAD ROAD · BRIXHAM
SOUTH DEVON · TQ5 9AJ
Telephone 01803 853225/858583
Fax 01803 882084

| AA ★★★ | Email: stay@berryheadhotel.com www.berryheadhotel.com | ETC ★★★ |

Nestling on the waters edge with panoramic views of Torbay. Steeped in history, set in six acres of private grounds surrounded by National Trust land, a short walk from the picturesque fishing port. A warm, comfortable and friendly hotel with atmosphere and an indoor heated swimming pool. The ideal base for watersports, rambling, and exploring Devon.

BURRINGTON   MAP 03 SS61
(NEAR PORTSMOUTH ARMS STATION)

INSPECTORS' CHOICE

★★★ ◎◎ COUNTRY HOUSE HOTEL

Northcote Manor

EX37 9LZ

☎ 01769 560501 🖹 01769 560770

e-mail: rest@northcotemanor.co.uk

web: www.northcotemanor.co.uk

PRIDE OF BRITAIN HOTELS

dir: off A377 opposite Portsmouth Arms, into hotel drive. NB. Do not enter Burrington village

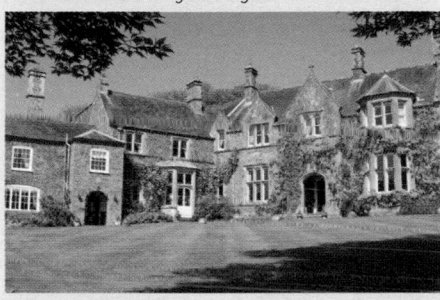

A warm and friendly welcome is assured at this beautiful country-house hotel. Built in 1716, the house sits in 20 acres of grounds and woodlands. Guests can enjoy wonderful views over the Taw River Valley whilst relaxing in the delightful environment created by the attentive staff. An elegant restaurant is a highlight of any stay with the finest of local produce used in well-prepared dishes. Bedrooms, including some suites, are individually styled, spacious and well appointed.

Rooms 11 en suite S £100-£170; D £150-£250 (incl. bkfst) **Facilities** STV ⬏ ⬏ Xmas **Conf** Thtr 80 Class 50 Board 30 Del from £155 **Parking** 30 **Notes** LB ⊘ in restaurant Civ Wed 100

Some hotels have restricted service during quieter months, and at this time some of the facilities will not be available

CHAGFORD MAP 03 SX78

INSPECTORS' CHOICE

★★★ ◎◎◎◎ **COUNTRY HOUSE HOTEL**

Gidleigh Park

TQ13 8HH
☎ 01647 432367 🖷 01647 432574
e-mail: gidleighpark@gidleigh.co.uk
web: www.gidleigh.com

dir: from Chagford, right at Lloyds Bank into Mill St. After
150yds fork right, follow lane 2m to end

Set in 45 acres of well-tended grounds and gardens this world-
renowned establishment is a delight. Individually styled bedrooms
are beautifully furnished some with separate seating areas and
many enjoying panoramic views of the grounds and countryside
beyond. Public areas are spacious featuring antique furniture and
beautiful flower arrangements. Facilities include a putting course,
bowling, croquet and tennis courts. The cuisine is a highlight of
any stay, with an accompanying wine list that is a testament to
the dedication the establishment has for everything being of the
highest quality.

Rooms 21 en suite 3 annexe en suite (4 fmly) (4 GF) ⊗ in all
bedrooms S £365-£525; D £440-£600 (incl. bkfst & dinner)
Facilities STV FTV ◢ Fishing ◥ Putt green Bowls Xmas
Conf Board 22 Del fr £300 **Parking** 30 **Notes LB** ⊗ in restaurant

INSPECTORS' CHOICE

★★ ◎◎ **HOTEL**

Mill End

Dartmoor National Park TQ13 8JN
☎ 0164/ 432282 🖷 01647 433106
e-mail: info@millendhotel.com
web: www.millendhotel.com

dir: from A30 at Whiddon Down follow A382 to
Moretonhampstead. After 3.5m humpback bridge at Sandy
Park, hotel on right

In an attractive location, Mill End, an 18th-century working water
mill sits by the River Teign that offers six miles of angling. The
atmosphere is akin to a family home where guests are
encouraged to relax and enjoy the peace and informality.
Bedrooms are available in a range of sizes and all are stylishly
decorated and thoughtfully equipped. Dining is certainly a
highlight of a stay here; the menus offer exciting dishes featuring
local produce.

continued

Mill End

Rooms 15 en suite (3 GF) ⊗ in all bedrooms S £80-£115;
D £110-£160 (incl. bkfst) **Facilities** Fishing ◥ Xmas **Conf** Thtr 40
Class 20 Board 30 **Parking** 29 **Notes LB** ⊗ in restaurant

★★ 69% **HOTEL**

Three Crowns Hotel

High St TQ13 8AJ
☎ 01647 433444 🖷 01647 433117
e-mail: threecrowns@msn.com
web: www.chagford-accom.co.uk

dir: exit A30 at Whiddon Down. Hotel in town centre opposite
church

This 13th-century inn is located in the heart of the village. Exposed
beams, mullioned windows and open fires are all part of the charm.
There is a range of bedrooms; all are comfortable and several have
four-poster beds. A choice of bars is available along with a pleasant
lounge and separate dining room.

Rooms 17 en suite (1 fmly) ⊗ in 8 bedrooms S £55-£80; D £60-£80
(incl. bkfst) **Facilities** STV Pool table in bar Xmas **Conf** Thtr 150
Board 150 Del £100 **Parking** 20 **Notes LB** ⊗ in restaurant Civ Wed 20●

CLOVELLY MAP 03 SS3

★★ 74% **HOTEL**

New Inn

High St EX39 5TQ
☎ 01237 431303 🖷 01237 431636
e-mail: newinn@clovelly.co.uk

dir: at Clovelly Cross, off A39 onto B3237. Follow down hill for
1.5m. Right at sign 'All vehicles for Clovelly'

Famed for its cobbled descent to the harbour, this fascinating fishing
village is a traffic-free zone. Consequently, luggage is conveyed by sledg

continue

or donkey to this much-photographed hotel. Bedrooms and public areas are smartly presented with quality, locally-made furnishings. Meals may be taken in the elegant restaurant or the popular Upalong bar.

New Inn

Rooms 8 en suite (2 fmly) **Notes LB** ⊗ ⊘ in restaurant

★★ 74% HOTEL

Red Lion Hotel

The Quay EX39 5TF

☎ 01237 431237 ▤ 01237 431044

e-mail: redlion@clovelly.co.uk

web: www.redlion-clovelly.co.uk/redlionindex.html

dir: turn off A39 at Clovelly Cross onto B3237. To bottom of hill and take 1st left by white rails to harbour

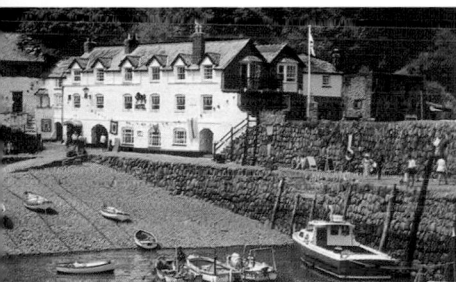

'Idyllic' is the only way to describe the harbour-side setting of this charming 16th century inn, where the historic fishing village forms a spectacular backdrop. Bedrooms are stylish and enjoy delightful views. The inn's relaxed atmosphere is conducive to switching off from the pressures of life, even if the harbour comes alive with the activities of the local fishermen during the day.

Rooms 11 en suite (2 fmly) ⊘ in all bedrooms **Facilities** Tennis can be arranged Xmas **Parking** 11 **Notes** ⊗ ⊘ in restaurant

See advert on this page

COLYFORD   MAP 04 SY29

★★ 81% ⊛ HOTEL

Swallows Eaves

EX24 6QJ

☎ 01297 553184 ▤ 01297 553574

e-mail: swallows_eaves@hotmail.com

web: www.lymeregis.com/swallowseaveshotel

dir: on A3052 between Lyme Regis & Sidmouth, in village centre, opposite post office store

This delightful hotel has gained a well-deserved reputation for

continued

excellent standards of service, food and hospitality; many guests return year after year. Bedrooms combine comfort with quality, each is individually styled and equipped with many thoughtful extras. The restaurant serves a daily-changing menu of carefully prepared dishes, that makes good use of fresh local ingredients. Safe, on-site parking is an added bonus.

Rooms 8 en suite (1 GF) ⊘ in all bedrooms S £55-£70; D £90-£110 (incl. bkfst) **Facilities** Free use of nearby Swimming Club **Parking** 10 **Notes LB** ⊗ No children 14yrs ⊘ in restaurant RS Nov-Easter

CULLOMPTON   MAP 03 ST00

★★★ 77% HOTEL

Padbrook Park

EX15 1RU

☎ 01884 836100 ▤ 01884 836101

e-mail: info@padbrookpark.co.uk

dir: 1m from M5 junct 28

This purpose built hotel is part of a golf and leisure complex located in the Culm Valley, just one mile from the M5. Set in 100 acres of parkland and golf course, Padbrook Park has a friendly, relaxed atmosphere and a contemporary feel. There are a variety of room types available including family, inter-connecting, superior and deluxe rooms.

Rooms 40 en suite (4 fmly) (11 GF) ⊘ in 26 bedrooms **Facilities** FTV ♨ ♪ Fishing Gym Putt green Wi-fi available 3 rink bowling centre ♬ Xmas **Conf** Thtr 200 Class 40 Board 30 **Services** Lift **Parking** 250 **Notes** ⊗ ⊘ in restaurant Civ Wed 200

England

DARTMOUTH   MAP 03 SX85

★★★ 82% ⍟ **HOTEL**

The Dart Marina

CLASSIC
BRITISH HOTELS

Sandquay Road TQ6 9PH

☎ 01803 832 580 📠 01803 835040

e-mail: info@dartmarinahotel.com

web: www.dartmarina.com

dir: *A3122 from Totnes to Dartmouth. Follow road which becomes College Way, before Higher Ferry. Hotel sharp left*

Boasting a stunning riverside location with its own marina, this is a truly special place to stay. Bedrooms, now refurbished, are varied in style but all have wonderful views; some have private balconies. Stylish public areas take full advantage of the waterside setting with opportunities to dine alfresco. The River Restaurant is the venue for accomplished cooking with much produce locally sourced. There is now a luxurious health spa and Wildfire Bar & Bistro.

Rooms 45 en suite 4 annexe en suite (4 fmly) (4 GF) ⊘ in all bedrooms **Facilities Spa** ⬚ Solarium Gym Jacuzzi Beauty treatments, Canoeing, Sailing **Services** Lift **Parking** 50 **Notes LB** ⊘ in restaurant Civ Wed 40

See advert on opposite page

★★★ 75% **HOTEL**

Royal Castle

11 The Quay TQ6 9PS

☎ 01803 833033 📠 01803 835445

e-mail: enquiry@royalcastle.co.uk

web: www.royalcastle.co.uk

dir: *in centre of town, overlooking Inner Harbour*

At the edge of the harbour, this imposing 17th-century former coaching inn is filled with charm and character. Bedrooms are well equipped and comfortable; many have harbour views. A choice of quiet seating areas is offered in addition to both the traditional and contemporary bars. A variety of eating options is available, including the main restaurant that offers accomplished cuisine.

Rooms 25 en suite (4 fmly) ⊘ in all bedrooms S £75-£95; D £125-£199 (incl. bkfst) **Facilities** STV Wi-fi in bedrooms ♫ Xmas **Conf** Thtr 70 Class 40 Board 40 **Parking** 17 **Notes LB** ⊘ in restaurant Civ Wed 60

★★★ 70% **HOTEL**

Stoke Lodge

Stoke Fleming TQ6 0RA

☎ 01803 770523 📠 01803 770851

e-mail: mail@stokelodge.co.uk

web: www.stokelodge.co.uk

dir: *2m S A379*

This family-run hotel continues to attract returning guests and is set in three acres of gardens and grounds with lovely views across to the sea. A range of leisure facilities is offered including both indoor and outdoor pools, along with a choice of comfortable lounges. Bedrooms are pleasantly appointed. The restaurant offers a choice of menus and an impressive wine list.

Rooms 25 en suite (5 fmly) S £62-£69; D £91-£120 (incl. bkfst) **Facilities Spa** ⬚ ⬚ ⬚ Snooker Sauna Putt green Table tennis Pool table Xmas **Conf** Thtr 80 Class 60 Board 30 Del from £77 **Parking** 50 **Notes LB** ⊘ in restaurant

DAWLISH   MAP 03 SX97

★★★ 77% **HOTEL**

Langstone Cliff

THE INDEPENDENTS

Dawlish Warren EX7 0NA

☎ 01626 868000 📠 01626 868006

e-mail: reception@langstone-hotel.co.uk

web: www.langstone-hotel.co.uk

dir: *1.5m NE off A379 Exeter road to Dawlish Warren*

A family owned and run hotel, the Langstone Cliff offers a range of leisure, conference and function facilities. Bedrooms, many with sea views and balconies, are spacious, comfortable and well equipped. There are a number of attractive lounges and a well stocked bar. Dinner is served, often carvery style, in the restaurant.

Rooms 62 en suite 4 annexe en suite (52 fmly) (10 GF) S £64-£79; D £108-£150 (incl. bkfst) **Facilities** STV FTV ⬚ ⬚ ⬚ Snooker Gym Wi-fi in bedrooms Table tennis, Golf practice area, Hair and beauty salon ♫ Xmas **Conf** Thtr 400 Class 200 Board 80 Del £95 **Services** Lift **Parking** 200 **Notes LB** ⊘ in restaurant Civ Wed 400

EXETER   MAP 03 SX99

★★★★ 75% **HOTEL**

Macdonald Southgate

MACDONALD
HOTELS & RESORTS

Southernhay East EX1 1QF

☎ 0870 400 8333 📠 01392 413549

e-mail: southgate@macdonald-hotels.co.uk

web: www.macdonald-hotels.co.uk

dir: *M5 junct 30, 3rd exit (Exeter), 2nd left towards city centre, 3rd exit at next rdbt, hotel 2m on right*

Centrally located and with excellent parking, The Southgate offers a diverse range of leisure and business facilities. Public areas are smart

continued

and spacious with comfortable seating in the bar and lounge; there is also a pleasant terrace. A range of bedroom sizes is available but all are well equipped with modern facilities.

Macdonald Southgate

Rooms 110 en suite (6 fmly) (13 GF) ⊘ in 85 bedrooms S £105-£155; D £130-£170 (incl. bkfst) **Facilities** STV ☒ supervised Sauna Solarium Jacuzzi Wi-fi in bedrooms Xmas **Conf** Thtr 150 Class 70 Board 50 Del £165 **Services** Lift **Parking** 115 **Notes LB** ⊗ ⊘ in restaurant RS Sat (restaurant closed for lunch) Civ Wed 80

★★★★ 72% ⊛ **TOWN HOUSE HOTEL**

Alias Hotel Barcelona

Magdalen St EX2 4HY
☎ 01392 281000 ▤ 01392 281001
e-mail: barcelona@aliashotels.com
web: www.aliasbarcelona.com

dir: from A30 Okehampton follow city centre signs. At Exe Bridges rdbt right for city centre, up hill, on at lights. Hotel on right

Situated within walking distance of the city centre, this hotel was once an eye hospital and was totally transformed to provide stylish accommodation in a glamorous setting. Public areas include Café Paradiso, an informal eatery with a varied menu, a night club, a range of meeting rooms and a delightful garden terrace ideal for alfresco dining.

Rooms 46 en suite (2 GF) ⊘ in 20 bedrooms S £90-£130; D £105-£130 **Facilities** STV Wi-fi available ♫ Xmas **Conf** Thtr 65 Class 18 Board 22 Del from £145 **Services** Lift **Parking** 35 **Notes LB** ⊘ in restaurant

See advert on this page

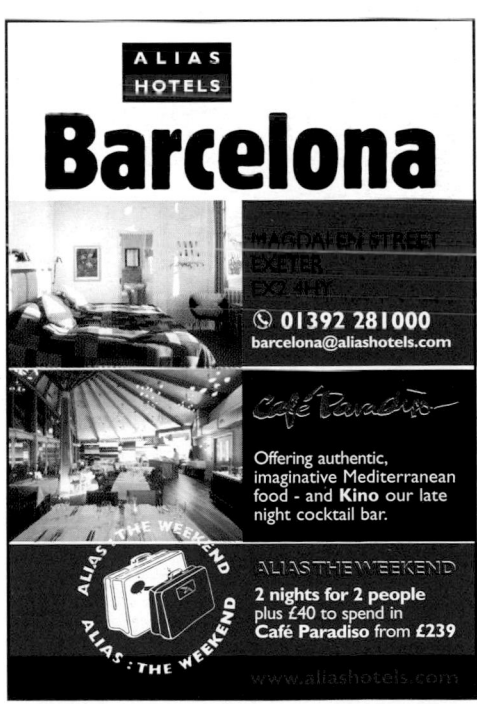

England

EXETER *continued*

★★★★ 68% ❀❀ **HOTEL**

Abode Hotel Exeter

Cathedral Yard EX1 1HD
☎ 01392 319955 📠 01392 439423
e-mail: reservationsexeter@abodehotels.co.uk
web: www.abodehotels.co.uk

dir: M5 junct 30 towards A379. Follow city centre signs. Hotel opposite cathedral behind High Street

Overlooking the cathedral, this hotel has an exciting contemporary style. Bedrooms are available in a range of comfort styles - all have handcrafted beds and modern facilities with internet access and CD players. The café bar here has a more informal style with live music most weekends and there is also a 'champagne bar'. The award winning Michael Caines restaurant delivers exciting cuisine from the finest local produce.

Rooms 53 en suite (4 fmly) ⊗ in all bedrooms **Facilities** STV Gym Beauty Therapy ♫ **Conf** BC Thtr 100 Class 50 Board 50 **Services** Lift air con **Parking** 15 **Notes LB** ⊗ ⊗ in restaurant Civ Wed 50

★★★ 75% **HOTEL**

Devon

Exeter Bypass, Matford EX2 8XU
☎ 01392 259268 📠 01392 413142
e-mail: info@devonhotel.co.uk
web: www.brend-hotels.co.uk

dir: M5 junct 30 follow Marsh Barton Industrial Estate signs on A379. Hotel on A38 rdbt

Within easy access of the city centre, the M5 and the city's business parks, this smart Georgian hotel offers modern, comfortable accommodation. The Carriages Bar and Brasserie is popular with guests and locals alike, offering a wide range of dishes as well as a carvery at both lunch and dinner. Service is friendly and attentive, and extensive meeting and business facilities are available.

Rooms 40 annexe en suite (3 fmly) (11 GF) ⊗ in 19 bedrooms S fr £68; D fr £78 **Facilities** STV Xmas **Conf** Thtr 150 Class 80 Board 40 Del from £110 **Parking** 250 **Notes LB** ⊗ in restaurant Civ Wed 100

★★★ 75% ❀❀ **HOTEL**

Lord Haldon

Dunchideock EX6 7YF
☎ 01392 832483 📠 01392 833765
e-mail: enquiries@lordhaldonhotel.co.uk

dir: M5 junct 31, 1st exit off A30 and follow signs through Ide to Dunchideock.

This is an attractive country house set in a peaceful rural location. Guests are assured of a warm welcome from the professional team of staff and the well-equipped bedrooms are comfortable, many with stunning views. The daily changing menu features skilfully cooked dishes with most of the produce sourced locally.

Rooms 23 en suite (3 fmly) ⊗ in 20 bedrooms S £65-£75; D £90-£110 (incl. bkfst) **Facilities** Wi-fi available Xmas **Conf** Thtr 250 Class 100 Board 40 Del from £115 **Parking** 120 **Notes LB** ⊗ in restaurant Civ Wed 120

See advert on opposite page

★★★ 73% **HOTEL**

Buckerell Lodge Hotel

folio Hotels

Topsham Rd EX2 4SQ
☎ 01392 221111 📠 01392 491111
e-mail: buckerelllodge@foliohotels.co.uk
web: www.foliohotels.co.uk/buckerelllodge

dir: M5 junct 30 follow city centre signs, hotel on Topsham Rd, 0.5m from Exeter

Although situated outside the city centre, this hotel is easily accessed by car or public transport. Bedrooms, all now refurbished in modern styles, are comfortable, fairly spacious and generally quiet. Public areas include a popular bar and restaurant and a variety of function rooms. The attractive and extensive gardens are a lovely feature and ideal for alfresco dining during warmer weather.

Rooms 54 en suite (2 fmly) ⊗ in all bedrooms S fr £105; D fr £125 **Facilities** STV Wi-fi in bedrooms **Conf** Thtr 80 Class 40 Board 40 **Parking** 60 **Notes LB** ⊗ ⊗ in restaurant Civ Wed 50

Some hotels, although accepting children, may not have any special facilities for them so it is well worth checking before booking

★★★ 73% ◉◉ **HOTEL**

St Olaves Court Restaurant & Hotel

Mary Arches St EX4 3AZ

☎ 01392 217736 🖹 01392 413054

e-mail: info@olaves.co.uk

web: www.olaves.co.uk

dir: *city centre, signed to Mary Arches Car Park. Hotel entrance opposite car park entrance*

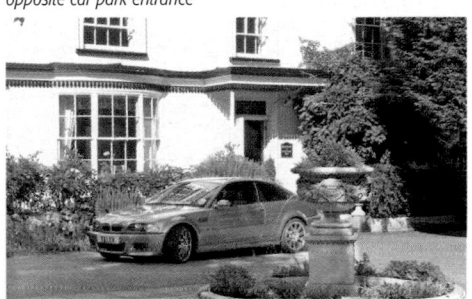

Only a short stroll from the cathedral and city centre and set in an attractive walled garden, St Olaves seems to be a country house in its almost hidden location. Bedrooms are comfortably furnished and full of character. The Treasury restaurant is the venue for enjoyable cooking with local produce very much in evidence.

Rooms 15 en suite (2 fmly) (1 GF) ⊛ in all bedrooms S £65-£95; D £95-£125 (incl. bkfst) **Facilities** Wi-fi available Xmas **Conf** Thtr 80 Class 60 Board 35 Del from £120 **Parking** 18 **Notes LB** ⊗ ⊘ in restaurant Civ Wed 65

★★★ 71% **HOTEL**

Thistle Exeter

Queen St EX4 3SP

THISTLE HOTELS

☎ 0870 333 9133 🖹 0870 333 9233

e-mail: cxeter@thistle.co.uk

dir: *From M5 junct 30 follow signs to services at 1st rdbt, then 1st left towards city centre. Once in city centre follow Museum & Central Station signs. Hotel opposite*

Centrally located, this elegant hotel is well situated for those visiting the city for business or pleasure. There is a charming old-fashioned atmosphere here, with traditional hospitality to the fore. All bedrooms offer high levels of comfort with a number of suites also available. A choice of bars is provided; either the convivial Drakes bar or the smart, formal cocktail bar.

Rooms 90 en suite ⊛ in all bedrooms **Facilities** STV **Conf** BC Thtr 300 Board 84 **Services** Lift air con **Parking** 31 **Notes LB** ⊗ ⊘ in restaurant Civ Wed

★★★ 70% ◉ **HOTEL**

Barton Cross Hotel & Restaurant

Huxham, Stoke Canon EX5 4EJ

☎ 01392 841245 🖹 01392 841942

e-mail: bartonxhuxham@aol.com

dir: *0.5m off A396 at Stoke Canon, 3m N of Exeter*

17th-century charm combined with 21st-century luxury perfectly sums up the appeal of this lovely country hotel. The bedrooms are spacious, tastefully decorated and well maintained. Public areas include the cosy first-floor lounge and the lounge/bar with its warming log fire. The *continued on page 196*

England

England

EXETER *continued*

restaurant offers a seasonally changing menu of consistently enjoyable cuisine.

Barton Cross Hotel & Restaurant

Rooms 9 en suite (2 fmly) (2 GF) ⊗ in 2 bedrooms **Facilities** STV **Conf** Thtr 20 Class 20 Board 20 **Parking** 35 **Notes LB** ⊗ in restaurant

See advert on page 195

★★★ 70% **HOTEL**

Queens Court

6-8 Bystock Ter EX4 4HY
☎ 01392 272709 ▤ 01392 491390
e-mail: enquiries@queenscourt-hotel.co.uk
web: www.queenscourt-hotel.co.uk
dir: Exit dual carriageway at junct 30 onto B5132 Topsham Rd towards city centre. Hotel 200yds from station

Quietly located within walking distance of the city centre, this privately owned hotel, now under new ownership, occupies listed, early Victorian premises and provides friendly hospitality. The smart public areas and bedrooms are tastefully furnished in contemporary style. Rooms are available for conferences, meetings and other functions. The bright and attractive Olive Tree restaurant offers an interesting selection of dishes.

Rooms 18 en suite (1 fmly) ⊗ in all bedrooms S £77-£87; D £101-£111 (incl. bkfst) **Conf** BC Thtr 60 Class 30 Board 30 Del £130 **Services** Lift **Notes LB** ⊗ ⊗ in restaurant RS Restaurant closed 25-30 Dec

★★★ 67% **HOTEL**

Best Western Gipsy Hill

Gipsy Hill Ln, Monkerton EX1 3RN
☎ 01392 465252 ▤ 01392 464302
e-mail: stay@gipsyhillhotel.co.uk
web: www.gipsyhillhotel.co.uk
dir: M5 junct 29 towards Exeter. Turn right at 1st rdbt and right again at next rdbt. Hotel 0.5m on right

Located on the edge of the city, with easy access to the M5 and the airport, this popular hotel is set in attractive, well-tended gardens and boasts far-reaching country views. The hotel offers a range of conference and function rooms, comfortable bedrooms and modern facilities. An intimate bar and lounge are next to the elegant restaurant.

Rooms 20 en suite 17 annexe en suite (4 fmly) (12 GF) ⊗ in 31 bedrooms S £50-£90; D £60-£120 (incl. bkfst) **Facilities** Wi-fi in bedrooms Xmas **Conf** Thtr 300 Class 80 Board 80 Del from £100 **Parking** 60 **Notes LB** ⊗ ⊗ in restaurant Civ Wed 130

BUDGET HOTEL

Innkeeper's Lodge Exeter East

Clyst St George EX3 0QJ
☎ 01392 876121 ▤ 01392 872022
web: www.innkeeperslodge.com
dir: M5 junct 30, A376 towards Exmouth. Right at 1st rdbt, straight over 2nd rdbt, at 3rd rdbt turn into Bridge Hill, lodge on right

Smart, en suite accommodation ideal for both business & leisure guests. Bedrooms are very well equipped, including Sky TV, telephone, modem points, tea & coffee making facilities, (family rooms in most locations). Complimentary breakfast. The adjacent Pub Restaurant; a Harvester, Vintage Inn, Toby Carvery, Ember Inn, Sizzling Pubco or Pub & Carvery offers an all day menu. See Hotel Groups pages for further details.

Rooms 13 en suite S £55-£57.50; D £55-£57.50 **Conf** Thtr 75 Class 45 Board 30

BUDGET HOTEL

Premier Travel Inn Exeter

398 Topsham Rd EX2 6HE
☎ 08701 977097 ▤ 01392 876174
web: www.premiertravelinn.com
dir: 2m from M5 junct 30/A30 junct 29. Follow signs for Exeter & Dawlish (A379). On dual carriageway take 2nd slip road on left at Countess Wear rdbt. Inn next to Beefeater

High quality, modern budget accommodation ideal for both families and business travellers. Spacious, en suite bedrooms feature bath and shower, satellite TV and many have telephones and modem points. The adjacent family restaurant features a wide and varied menu. For further details consult the Hotel Groups page.

Rooms 44 en suite

BUDGET HOTEL

Travelodge Exeter (M5)

Moor Ln, Sandygate EX2 7HF

☎ 08700 850 950 🖹 01392 410406

web: www.travelodge.co.uk

dir: *M5 junct 30*

Travelodge offers good quality, good value, modern accommodation. Ideal for families, the spacious en suite bedrooms include remote-control TV, tea and coffee-making facilities and comfortable beds. Meals can be taken at the nearby family restaurant. See Hotel Groups pages for further details.

Rooms 102 en suite S fr £26; D fr £26 **Conf** Thtr 80 Class 18 Board 25

EXMOUTH   MAP 03 SY08

★★★ 74% HOTEL

Royal Beacon

The Beacon EX8 2AF

☎ 01395 264886 🖹 01395 268890

e-mail: reception@royalbeaconhotel.co.uk

web: www.royalbeaconhotel.co.uk

dir: *From M5 take A376 and Marine Way. Follow seafront signs. On Imperial Rd turn left at T-junct then 1st right. Hotel 100yds on left*

This elegant Georgian property sits in an elevated position overlooking the town and has fine views of the estuary towards the sea. Bedrooms are individually styled and many have sea views. Public areas include a well stocked bar, a cosy lounge, an impressive function suite and a restaurant where freshly prepared and enjoyable cuisine is offered.

Rooms 60 en suite (2 fmly) ⊗ in 30 bedrooms S £60-£80; D £85-£110 (incl. bkfst) **Facilities** STV FTV Wi-fi in bedrooms ♫ Xmas **Conf** Thtr 160 Class 100 Board 60 **Services** Lift **Parking** 28 **Notes LB** ⊗ in restaurant Civ Wed 160

★★ 68% HOTEL

Manor Hotel

The Beacon EX8 2AG

☎ 01395 272549 & 274477 🖹 01395 225519

e-mail: post@manorexmouth.co.uk

dir: *M5 junct 30 take A376 to Exmouth. Hotel 300yds from seafront overlooking Manor Gardens*

Conveniently located for easy access to the town centre and with views overlooking the sea, this friendly hotel offers traditional values of

continued

hospitality and service, drawing guests back year after year. The well-equipped bedrooms vary in style and size; many have far-reaching views. The fixed price menu offers a varied selection of dishes.

Rooms 39 en suite (3 fmly) ⊗ in all bedrooms S £35-£40; D £30-£40 (incl. bkfst) **Facilities** Xmas **Conf** Thtr 100 Class 60 Board 60 Del from £50 **Services** Lift **Parking** 15 **Notes LB** ⊗ ⊗ in restaurant

---

★★ 62% HOTEL

Cavendish Hotel

11 Morton Crescent, The Esplanade EX8 1BE   **Leisureplex**

☎ 01395 272528 🖹 01395 269361

e-mail: cavendish.exmouth@alfatravel.co.uk

web: www.alfatravel.co.uk

dir: *follow seafront signs, hotel in centre of large crescent*

Situated on the seafront, this terraced hotel attracts many groups from around the country. With fine views out to sea, the hotel is within walking distance of the town centre. The bedrooms are neatly presented; front-facing rooms are always popular. Entertainment is provided on most evenings during the summer.

Rooms 76 en suite (3 fmly) (19 GF) ⊗ in all bedrooms S £33-£44; D £54-£76 (incl. bkfst) **Facilities** Snooker ♫ Xmas **Services** Lift **Parking** 25 **Notes LB** ⊗ ⊗ in restaurant Closed Dec-Jan ex Xmas RS Nov & Mar

---

GOODRINGTON See **Paignton**

GULWORTHY   MAP 03 SX47

★★★ 85% ❀❀❀ HOTEL

Horn of Plenty

PL19 8JD

☎ 01822 832528 🖹 01822 834390

e-mail: enquiries@thehornofplenty.co.uk

web: www.thehornofplenty.co.uk

dir: *from Tavistock take A390 W for 3m. Right at Gulworthy Cross. After 400yds turn left and after 400yds hotel on right*

With stunning views over the Tamar Valley, The Horn of Plenty maintains its reputation as one of Britain's best country-house hotels. The bedrooms are well equipped and have many thoughtful extras with the newly refurbished garden rooms offering impressive levels of comfort and quality. Cuisine here is also impressive and local produce provides interesting and memorable dining.

Rooms 4 en suite 6 annexe en suite (3 fmly) (4 GF) ⊗ in all bedrooms S £150-£220; D £160-£230 (incl. bkfst) **Facilities** Xmas **Conf** BC Thtr 28 Class 20 Board 16 **Parking** 25 **Notes LB** ⊗ in restaurant Closed 24-26 Dec Civ Wed 80

HAYTOR VALE   MAP 03 SX77

★★ 76% ⍟ **HOTEL**

Rock Inn

TQ13 9XP

☎ 01364 661305 & 661465 ▤ 01364 661242

e-mail: inn@rock-inn.co.uk

web: www.rock-inn.co.uk

dir: off A38 onto A382 to Bovey Tracey, after 0.5m turn left onto B3387 to Haytor

Dating back to the 1750s, this former coaching inn is in a pretty hamlet on the edge of Dartmoor. Each named after a Grand National winner, the individually decorated bedrooms have some nice extra touches. Bars are full of character, with flagstone floors and old beams and offer a wide range of dishes, cooked with imagination and flair.

Rooms 9 en suite (2 fmly) ⊘ in 2 bedrooms S fr £66.95; D £75.95-£106.95 (incl. bkfst) **Facilities** STV **Parking** 20 **Notes LB** ⊛ ⊘ in restaurant Closed 25-26 Dec

HOLSWORTHY   MAP 03 SS30

★★ 78% **COUNTRY HOUSE HOTEL**

Court Barn Country House

Clawton EX22 6PS

☎ 01409 271219 ▤ 01409 271309

e-mail: courtbarnhotel@talk21.com

web: www.hotels-devon.com

dir: 2.5m S of Holsworthy off A388 Tamerton Rd next to Clawton Church

This engaging, family-run Victorian country house is set in five acres of attractive grounds, including a 9-hole putting course and croquet lawn. Comfortable bedrooms are individually furnished, and there are two relaxing lounges. A four-course dinner featuring fresh, local produce is served in the spacious restaurant, and leisurely breakfasts are taken overlooking the garden.

Rooms 8 rms (7 en suite) (1 fmly) ⊘ in all bedrooms **Facilities** ⊰ ⌣ Putt green Badminton **Conf** BC Thtr 25 Board 8 **Parking** 13 **Notes LB** ⊘ in restaurant

HONITON   MAP 04 ST10

INSPECTORS' CHOICE

★★★ ⍟⍟ **HOTEL**

Combe House Hotel & Restaurant-Gittisham

Gittisham EX14 3AD

☎ 01404 540400 ▤ 01404 46004

e-mail: stay@thishotel.com

web: www.thishotel.com

dir: off A30 1m S of Honiton, follow Gittisham Heathpark signs

Standing proudly in an elevated position, this Elizabethan mansion enjoys uninterrupted views over acres of its own woodland, meadow and pasture. Bedrooms are a blend of comfort and quality creating a relaxing environment; the new Linen Room suite combines many original features with

continued

contemporary style. A range of atmospheric public rooms retain all the charm and history of the old house. Dining is equally impressive - a skilled kitchen brigade maximises the best of local and home-grown produce, augmented by excellent wines.

Combe House Hotel & Restaurant-Gittisham

Rooms 15 en suite (1 fmly) ⊘ in all bedrooms S £133-£158; D £164-£178 (incl. bkfst) **Facilities** ⌣ Wi-fi available **Conf** BC Thtr 50 Class 40 Board 26 Del from £225 **Parking** 39 **Notes LB** ⊘ in restaurant Civ Wed 80

★★ 78% ⍟ **SMALL HOTEL**

Home Farm Restaurant & Hotel

Wilmington EX14 9JR

☎ 01404 831278 ▤ 01404 831411

e-mail: info@thatchedhotel.co.uk

dir: 3m E of Honiton on A35 in village of Wilmington

Set in well-tended gardens, this thatched former farmhouse is now a comfortable hotel. Many of the original features have been retained with the cobbled courtyard. A range of interesting dishes is offered in the intimate restaurant, with bar meals available at lunchtime and most evenings except Saturday. Bedrooms, some with private gardens, are well equipped and comfortably furnished.

Rooms 7 en suite 5 annexe en suite (2 fmly) (6 GF) ⊘ in all bedrooms S £50-£70; D £84-£110 (incl. bkfst) **Facilities** FTV Wi-fi in bedrooms Xmas **Parking** 26 **Notes** ⊛ ⊘ in restaurant

★★ 64% **SMALL HOTEL**

Monkton Court

Monkton EX14 9QH

☎ 01404 42309 ▤ 01404 46861

e-mail: yeotelsmonkton@aol.com

dir: 2m E of Honiton on A30 towards Ilminster, opposite Monkton Church

Set in five acres of grounds, this attractive 17th-century manor house retains much of its historical character. Friendly staff provide attentive service, and many guests find that Monkton Court an ideal base for either business or leisure. A comfortable lounge and pleasant bar with crackling log fire are available. Cuisine includes a good choice of freshly cooked and imaginative dishes.

Rooms 6 en suite (1 fmly) S £45-£50; D £60-£75 (incl. bkfst) **Conf** Thtr 50 Class 25 Board 25 **Parking** 40 **Notes LB** ⊛ ⊘ in restaurant Closed Xmas & New Year

HOPE COVE
MAP 03 SX63

★★ 75% HOTEL

Lantern Lodge
TQ7 3HF

☎ 01548 561280 ▤ 01548 561736

e-mail: lanternlodge@hopecove.wanadoo.co.uk

web: www.lantern-lodge.co.uk

dir: *right off A381 Kingsbridge to Salcombe road. 1st right after passing Hope Cove sign then 1st left along Grand View Road*

This attractive hotel, close to the South Devon coastal path, benefits from a friendly team of loyal staff. Bedrooms are well furnished and some have balconies. An imaginative range of home cooked meals is available. There is a choice of lounges and a pretty garden with putting green. The indoor pool has large doors opening directly on to the garden.

Rooms 14 en suite (1 fmly) (1 GF) S £77-£98; D £114-£156 (incl. bkfst & dinner) **Facilities** ⬡ Sauna Putt green Multi-gym **Parking** 15 **Notes LB** ⊗ No children 12yrs ⊘ in restaurant Closed Dec-Feb

★★ 72% HOTEL

Cottage
TQ7 3HJ

☎ 01548 561555 ▤ 01548 561455

e-mail: info@hopecove.com

web: www.hopecove.com

dir: *from Kingsbridge on A381 to Salcombe. 2nd right at Marlborough, left for Inner Hope*

Glorious sunsets over the attractive bay can be seen from this popular hotel. Friendly and attentive service from the staff and management mean many guests return here. Bedrooms, many with sea views and some with balconies, are well equipped. The restaurant offers an enjoyable dining experience.

Rooms 35 rms (26 en suite) (5 fmly) (7 GF) S £55.50-£82.25; D £90-£144.50 (incl. bkfst & dinner) **Facilities** Wi-fi available Table Tennis Xmas **Conf** Thtr 50 Class 20 Board 24 Del from £66.95 **Parking** 50 **Notes LB** ⊘ in restaurant Closed early Jan-early Feb

HORNS CROSS
MAP 03 SS32

★★★ 71% ⊛ HOTEL

Hoops
THE INDEPENDENTS

The Hoops EX39 5DL

☎ 01237 451222 ▤ 01237 451247

e-mail: sales@hoopsinn.co.uk

web: www.hoopsinn.co.uk

dir: *M5 junct 27 follow Barnstaple signs. A39, by-passing Bideford, towards Bude. Hotel in dip just outside Horns Cross*

The Hoops with its whitewashed walls, thatched roof and real fires, has been welcoming guests for many centuries. Bedrooms offer plenty of character and include a number that have four-poster or half-tester beds. Guests have the private use of a quiet lounge and a pleasant seating area in the delightful rear garden. A fine selection of home-cooked meals can be taken in the bar or restaurant.

continued

Hoops

Rooms 4 en suite 9 annexe en suite (1 GF) ⊘ in 9 bedrooms S £65-£180; D £95-£190 (incl. bkfst) **Facilities** Wi-fi available Jacuzzi Falconry & flying golden eagle courses **Conf** BC **Parking** 101 **Notes LB** ⊘ in restaurant

ILFRACOMBE
MAP 03 SS54

★★ 74% HOTEL

Elmfield
Torrs Park EX34 8AZ

☎ 01271 863377 ▤ 01271 866828

e-mail: ann@elmfieldhotelilfracombe.co.uk

web: www.elmfieldhotelilfracombe.co.uk

dir: *A361 to Ilfracombe. Left at 1st lights, left at 2nd lights. After 10yds left, hotel near top of hill on left*

Set in attractive grounds and with good parking, this Victorian property
continued on page 200

England

ILFRACOMBE *continued*

maintains much of its charm and enjoys views over the town towards the sea. Bedrooms are well equipped and spacious. The friendly proprietor and staff provide attentive service and carefully prepared, home-cooked cuisine. Public areas include a cosy bar, a small games room and comfortable lounge.

Rooms 11 en suite 2 annexe en suite (3 GF) ⊗ in 5 bedrooms S £48-£52; D £96-£106 (incl. bkfst & dinner) **Facilities** 🕏 Sauna Solarium Gym Jacuzzi Pool table Xmas **Parking** 14 **Notes LB** ⊗ No children 8yrs ⊗ in restaurant Closed Nov-mid Mar (ex Xmas)

See advert on page 199

★★ 69% SMALL HOTEL

Darnley

3 Belmont Rd EX34 8DR

☎ 01271 863955 📠 01271 864076

e-mail: darnleyhotel@yahoo.co.uk

web: www.darnleyhotel.co.uk

dir: M5 junct 27 then A361 to Barnstaple/Ilfracombe. Left at Church Hill then first left into Belmont Rd.

This former Victorian gentleman's residence offers friendly, informal service. It stands in award-winning, mature gardens with a wooded path to the High Street and the beach - about a five minute' stroll away. The individually furnished and decorated bedrooms vary in size. Dinners feature honest home cooking, with 'old fashioned puddings' always proving popular.

Rooms 10 rms (7 en suite) (2 fmly) (2 GF) ⊗ in all bedrooms S £36-£40; D £56-£85 (incl. bkfst) **Facilities** Xmas **Parking** 10 **Notes LB** ⊗ in restaurant

★★ 68% HOTEL

Ilfracombe Carlton

Runnacleave Rd EX34 8AR

☎ 01271 862446 & 863711 📠 01271 865379

e-mail: enquiries@ilfracombecarlton.co.uk

dir: A361 to Ilfracombe, left at lights, left at lights. Follow signs Tunnel/Beaches

Situated in the town and just a short walk from the theatre and harbour, this well-maintained hotel has a loyal following. The public areas include two lounges and a bar with an entertainment area. The comfortable bedrooms are attractively decorated and well equipped. A short set-price menu is offered in the bright and airy dining room.

Rooms 47 en suite (8 fmly) (6 GF) ⊗ in all bedrooms S £30-£40, D £60-£80 (incl. bkfst) **Facilities** Xmas **Conf** Thtr 140 Class 50 Board 50 **Services** Lift **Parking** 20 **Notes LB** ⊗ ⊗ in restaurant

★★ 65% HOTEL

Imperial Hotel

Wilder Rd EX34 9AL

Leisureplex

☎ 01271 862536 📠 01271 862571

e-mail: imperial.ilfracombe@alfatravel.co.uk

web: www.alfatravel.co.uk

dir: opposite Landmark Theatre

This popular hotel is just a short walk from the shops and harbour, overlooking gardens and the sea. Public areas include the spacious

continued

sun lounge, where guests can relax and enjoy the excellent views. Comfortable bedrooms are well equipped, with several having the added bonus of sea views.

Rooms 104 en suite (6 fmly) ⊗ in all bedrooms S £31-£41; D £50-£70 (incl. bkfst) **Facilities** 🎵 Xmas **Services** Lift **Parking** 10 **Notes LB** ⊗ ⊗ in restaurant Closed Dec-Feb RS Mar & Nov

★★ 63% HOTEL

Palm Court

Wilder Rd EX34 9AS

☎ 01271 866644 📠 01271 863581

e-mail: holiday@palmcourt-hotel.co.uk

dir: A361 to Ilfracombe, then follow signs to seafront

This establishment is very popular with groups and is within level walking distance of the harbour. Bedrooms are neatly presented and all are of a similar standard. Entertainment is provided in the bar/ballroom on certain evenings during the season, and short-mat bowls can be played in another large area.

Rooms 50 en suite (20 fmly) (3 GF) ⊗ in all bedrooms S £41-£45; D £74-£80 (incl. bkfst & dinner) **Facilities** Pool table, Short mat bowls, Skittles 🎵 Xmas **Services** Lift **Parking** 16 **Notes LB** ⊗ No children 2yrs ⊗ in restaurant Closed 3-26 Jan

ILSINGTON

MAP 03 SX77

★★★ 85% ◉◉ HOTEL

Best Western Ilsington Country House

Ilsington Village TQ13 9RR

☎ 01364 661452 📠 01364 661307

e-mail: hotel@ilsington.co.uk

web: www.ilsington.co.uk

dir: M5 onto A38 to Plymouth. Exit at Bovey Tracey. 3rd exit from rdbt to 'Ilsington', then 1st right. Hotel 5m by Post Office

This friendly, family-owned hotel, offers tranquillity and far-reaching views from its elevated position on the southern slopes of Dartmoor. The stylish suites and bedrooms, some on the ground floor, are individually furnished. The newly refurbished restaurant provides a stunning venue for the innovative, daily-changing menus that are based on local fish, meat and game.

Rooms 25 en suite (4 fmly) (8 GF) ⊗ in all bedrooms S £92-£98; D £136-£144 (incl. bkfst) **Facilities** Spa 🕏 supervised 🏊 Sauna Gym Jacuzzi Wi-fi in bedrooms ch fac Xmas **Conf** Thtr 150 Class 60 Board 40 Del from £125 **Services** Lift **Parking** 100 **Notes LB** ⊗ in restaurant

INSTOW
MAP 03 SS43

★★★ 79% **HOTEL**

Commodore

Marine Pde EX39 4JN

☎ 01271 860347 🖷 01271 861233

e-mail: admin@commodore-instow.co.uk

web: www.commodore-instow.co.uk

dir: M5 junct 27 follow N Devon link road to Bideford. Right before bridge, hotel 3m from bridge

Maintaining its links with the local maritime and rural communities, The Commodore provides a comfortable and interesting place to stay. Situated at the mouth of the Tor and Torridge estuaries and overlooking the sandy beach, it offers well equipped bedrooms, many with balconies. There are five ground floor suites especially suited to less able visitors. Guests have the option of eating in the restaurant, less formally in the Quarterdeck bar, or on the terrace in the warmer months.

Rooms 20 en suite (5 GF) ⊗ in 25 bedrooms S £60-£80; D £110-£190 (incl. bkfst & dinner) **Facilities** FTV Xmas **Services** Lift **Parking** 200
Notes LB ⊗ ⊘ in restaurant

KINGSBRIDGE
MAP 03 SX74

INSPECTORS' CHOICE

★★★ ◉◉ **HOTEL**

Buckland-Tout-Saints

Goveton TQ7 2DS

☎ 01548 853055 🖷 01548 856261

e-mail: buckland@tout-saints.co.uk

dir: Turn off A381 to Goveton. Follow brown tourism signs to St Peter's Church. Hotel 2nd right after church

It's well worth navigating the winding country lanes to find this delightful Queen Anne manor house that has been host to many
continued

famous guests over the years. Set in 4.5 acres of gardens and grounds the hotel is a peaceful retreat. Bedrooms are tastefully furnished and attractively decorated; most enjoy views of the gardens. Local produce is used with care and imagination in the restaurant. The large function room opens onto the terrace and is a popular choice for weddings. The hotel is under new ownership.

Rooms 16 en suite (4 fmly) ⊗ in all bedrooms S £120-£180; D £140-£300 (incl. bkfst) **Facilities** STV ⥾ ch fac Xmas
Conf Thtr 80 Class 40 Board 26 Del from £140 **Parking** 40
Notes LB ⊗ ⊘ in restaurant Civ Wed 125

LEWDOWN
MAP 03 SX48

INSPECTORS' CHOICE

★★★ ◉◉◉ **HOTEL**

Lewtrenchard Manor

EX20 4PN

☎ 01566 783256 & 783222 🖷 01566 783332

e-mail: info@lewtrenchard.co.uk

web: www.vonessenhotels.co.uk

dir: A30 from Exeter to Plymouth/Tavistock road. At T-junct turn right, then left onto old A30 Lewdown road. After 6m left signed Lewtrenchard

This Jacobean mansion was built in the 1600s, with many interesting architectural features, and is surrounded by its own idyllic grounds in a quiet valley close to the northern edge of Dartmoor. Public rooms include a fine gallery, as well as magnificent carvings and oak panelling. Meals can be taken in the dining room where imaginative and carefully prepared dishes are served using the best of Devon produce. Bedrooms are comfortably furnished and spacious.

Rooms 14 en suite (2 fmly) (3 GF) ⊗ in all bedrooms S £85-£200; D £115-£250 (incl. bkfst) **Facilities** Fishing ⥾ Clay pigeon shooting Xmas **Conf** Thtr 50 Class 40 Board 20 Del £185 **Parking** 50
Notes LB ⊘ in restaurant Civ Wed 100

See advert on page 203

England

LIFTON
MAP 03 SX38

★★★ 81% ◎ ◎ **HOTEL**

Arundell Arms
PL16 0AA
☎ 01566 784666 ▤ 01566 784494
e-mail: reservations@arundellarms.com
dir: 1m off A30 in Lifton

This former coaching inn, boasting a long history, sits in the heart of a quiet Devon village. It is internationally famous for its country pursuits such as winter shooting and angling. The hotel has 20 miles of salmon and trout fishing & a 3 acre lake. bedrooms offer individual style and comfort. Public areas are full of character and present a relaxed atmosphere, particularly around the open log fire during colder evenings. Award-winning cuisine is a celebration of local produce.

Rooms 21 en suite (4 GF) S fr £99; D £155-£180 (incl. bkfst)
Facilities STV Skittle alley Winter shooting Fly fishing school
Conf Thtr 100 Class 30 Board 40 Del from £135 **Parking** 70 **Notes LB**
⊘ in restaurant Closed 3 days Xmas Civ Wed 80

◎ **RESTAURANT WITH ROOMS**

Tinhay Mill Guest House and Restaurant
Tinhay PL16 0AJ
☎ 01566 784201 ▤ 01566 784201
e-mail: tinhay.mill@talk21.com
web: www.tinhaymillrestaurant.co.uk
dir: A30/A388 on approach to Lifton, restaurant at bottom of village on right

Former mill cottages dating from the 15th century, this is now a delightful restaurant-with-rooms of much character and charm. Beams and open fireplaces set the scene, with everything geared to ensure a relaxed and comfortable stay. Bedrooms are spacious and well-equipped, with many thoughtful extras. Cuisine is taken seriously here, with the best of local produce used.

Rooms 3 en suite S fr £52.50; D £75-£80 **Parking** 18 **Notes LB** ⊗
No children 12yrs

LYNMOUTH
MAP 03 SS74
See also Lynton

★★★ 73% ◎ **HOTEL**

Tors
EX35 6NA
☎ 01598 753236 ▤ 01598 752544
e-mail: torshotel@torslynmouth.co.uk
web: www.torslynmouth.co.uk
dir: adjacent to A39 on Countisbury Hill just before entering Lynmouth from Minehead

In an elevated position overlooking Lynmouth Bay, this friendly hotel is set in five acres of woodland. The majority of the bedrooms benefit from the superb views, as do the public areas; which are generous and well presented. Both fixed-price and short carte menus are offered in the restaurant.

Rooms 31 en suite (6 fmly) ⊘ in 1 bedroom S £73-£185; D £106-£230 (incl. bkfst) **Facilities** ⊀ Table tennis, Pool table Xmas **Conf** Thtr 60 Class 40 Board 25 Del from £90 **Services** Lift **Parking** 40 **Notes LB** ⊘ in restaurant Closed 4-31 Jan Civ Wed 125

★★ 69% **HOTEL**

Bath
Sea Front EX35 6EL
☎ 01598 752238 ▤ 01598 753894
e-mail: bathhotel@torslynmouth.co.uk
dir: M5 junct 25, follow A39 to Minehead then Porlock and Lynmouth

This well-established, friendly hotel is situated near the harbour and offers lovely views from the attractive, sea-facing bedrooms and an excellent starting point for scenic walks. There are two lounges and a sun lounge. The restaurant menu is extensive and features daily changing specials, making good use of fresh produce and local fish.

Rooms 22 en suite (9 fmly) ⊘ in 1 bedroom S £35-£57; D £70-£130 (incl. bkfst) **Facilities** ch fac **Parking** 12 **Notes LB** ⊘ in restaurant Closed Jan & Dec RS Feb-Mar and Nov

★★ 69% ◎ ◎ **HOTEL**

Rising Sun
Harbourside EX35 6EG
☎ 01598 753223 ▤ 01598 753480
e-mail: reception@risingsunlynmouth.co.uk
web: www.risingsunlynmouth.co.uk
dir: M5 junct 23 to Minehead. A39 to Lynmouth, hotel on harbour

This delightful thatched inn, once a smugglers' inn, sits on the harbour front. Popular with locals and hotel guests alike, there is the option of eating in either the convivial bar or the restaurant; a comfortable,

continued on page 204

Lewtrenchard Manor

Lewdown, Okehampton, Devon EX20 4PN
Tel: 01566 783222 www.lewtrenchard.co.uk

A romantic Jacobean Manor tucked away in its own secret valley. Hidden away in a wooded hollow just beneath the wild tors of Dartmoor, Lewtrenchard is the most romantic luxury country house hotel; a most beautiful manor house virtually untouched by time.

Originally mentioned in the Domesday Book, today's impressive Jacobean dwelling, set in its own shrub-filled gardens and surrounded by peaceful parkland, dates from the early 1600s.

LYNMOUTH *continued*

quiet lounge is also available. Bedrooms, located in the inn and adjoining cottages, are individually designed and have modern facilities.

Rising Sun

Rooms 16 en suite (1 fmly) (1 GF) ⊗ in all bedrooms **Notes LB** ⊗ in restaurant

LYNTON
See also Lynmouth

MAP 03 SS74

★★★ 69% ⊛⊛ HOTEL

Lynton Cottage
Northwalk EX35 6ED
☎ 01598 752342 📠 01598 754016
e-mail: mail@lyntoncottage.co.uk
dir: M5 junct 23 to Bridgwater, then A39 to Minehead & follow signs to Lynton. 1st right after church and right again.

Boasting simply breathtaking views, this wonderfully relaxing and friendly hotel stands some 500 feet above the sea and provides a peaceful hideaway. Bedrooms are individual in style and size, with the added bonus of scenic views, whilst public areas have charm and character in equal measure. Accomplished cuisine is also on offer with taste-laden dishes constructed with care and considerable skill.

Rooms 16 en suite (1 fmly) (1 GF) ⊗ in all bedrooms **Parking** 20
Notes ⊗ in restaurant Closed 15 Dec-1 Feb

★★ 78% SMALL HOTEL

Seawood
North Walk EX35 6HJ
☎ 01598 752272
e-mail: seawoodhotel@aol.com
web: www.seawoodhotel.co.uk
dir: turn right at St. Mary's Church in Lynton High St for hotel, 2nd on left

Tucked away in a quiet area and spectacularly situated 400 feet above the seashore, the Seawood enjoys magnificent views, and is set in delightful grounds. Bedrooms, many with sea views and some with four-poster beds, are comfortable and well equipped. At dinner, the daily-changing menu provides freshly prepared and appetising dishes.

Rooms 12 en suite ⊗ in all bedrooms S £38-£45; D £68-£80 (incl. bkfst)
Facilities Xmas **Parking** 12 **Notes LB** No children 10yrs ⊗ in restaurant Closed Dec-Feb

★★ 70% HOTEL

Chough's Nest
North Walk EX35 6HJ
☎ 01598 753315 📠 01598 753315
e-mail: relax@choughsnesthotel.co.uk
dir: on Lynton High St. Turn at St. Marys Church, hotel 0.5m on left

Lying on the south-west coastal path, this charming hotel, now under new ownership, can claim to have one of the most spectacular views around. Bedrooms offer ample comfort and quality, the majority looking out to sea.

Rooms 9 en suite (2 fmly) ⊗ in all bedrooms S £52-£55; D £80-£100 (incl. bkfst) **Parking** 9 **Notes LB** ⊗ No children 12yrs ⊗ in restaurant Closed 15 Nov-10 Feb

MAIDENCOMBE
See **Torquay**

MARTINHOE
MAP 03 SS64

★★ 76% COUNTRY HOUSE HOTEL

Heddon's Gate Hotel
Heddon's Mouth EX31 4PZ
☎ 01598 763481
e-mail: hotel@heddonsgate.co.uk
web: www.heddonsgate.co.uk
dir: A39 towards Lynton, left after 4m towards Martinhoe, left towards Hunters Inn, over x-rds, 1st right after Mannacott

Superbly located on the slopes of the Heddon Valley, this hotel is hidden away at the end of 0.25m private drive. Guests are assured of a warm and friendly welcome, with a complimentary, traditional afternoon tea served daily between 4-5pm. The individually styled bedrooms are well equipped - the majority benefit from the superb views. Dinner each evening is described as 'an occasion', and features the best of local produce.

Rooms 11 en suite ⊗ in all bedrooms S £82-£101; D £156-£172 (incl. bkfst & dinner) **Facilities** ⚓ Xmas **Parking** 11 **Notes LB** No children 16yrs ⊗ in restaurant Closed Telephone for dates

★★ 75% ⊛ HOTEL

The Old Rectory
EX31 4QT
☎ 01598 763368 📠 01598 763567
e-mail: info@oldrectoryhotel.co.uk
dir: M5 junct 27, A361, right onto A399 Blackmoor Gate, right onto A39, bypass Parracombe. 2nd left, follow signs

Originally built in the 1800s for the local rector, this peaceful hideaway is an ideal base for exploring Exmoor and is just 500 yards from the
continued

coastal footpath. In addition to the comfortable lounges, guests can relax in the vinery, overlooking the delightful gardens. Interesting menus are served in the spacious dining room. The bedrooms are tastefully decorated and a self-catering cottage is also available.

Rooms 9 en suite (2 GF) ⊘ in all bedrooms S £65-£95; D £90-£150 (incl. bkfst) **Facilities** Wi-fi in bedrooms **Parking** 9 **Notes LB** No children 14yrs ⊘ in restaurant Closed Nov-Feb RS Mar

---

MORETONHAMPSTEAD
MAP 03 SX78

★★★ 74% HOTEL

The White Hart Hotel

The Square TQ13 8NF

☎ 01647 441340 📠 01647 441341

e-mail: whitehart1600@aol.com

dir: A30 towards Oakhampton. At Widdon Down take A382 for Moretonhampstead

Dating back to the 1700s, this former coaching inn is located on the edge of Dartmoor. A relaxed and friendly atmosphere prevails, with the young staff providing attentive service. Comfortable bedrooms have a blend of traditional and contemporary styles with lots of extras provided. Dining is in either the restaurant or more informally in the bar. Guest may use the Bovey Castle's golf and leisure facilities.

Rooms 29 en suite (2 fmly) (4 GF) ⊘ in all bedrooms S £60-£70; D £98-£120 (incl. bkfst) **Facilities Spa** Fishing Sauna Solarium Gym Jacuzzi Wi-fi available ♫ ch fac Xmas **Conf** Thtr 60 Class 40 Board 40 Del from £105 **Parking** 12 **Notes LB** ⊘ in restaurant Civ Wed 60

NEWTON ABBOT
MAP 03 SX87
See also Ilsington

★★★ 71% HOTEL

Passage House

Hackney Ln, Kingsteignton TQ12 3QH

☎ 01626 355515 📠 01626 363336

e-mail: hotel@passagehousegroup.co.uk

dir: leave A380 for A381 and follow racecourse signs

With memorable views of the Teign Estuary, this popular hotel provides spacious, well-equipped bedrooms. An impressive range of leisure and meeting facilities is offered and a conservatory provides a pleasant extension to the bar and lounge. A choice of eating options is available, either in the main restaurant, or the adjacent Passage House Inn for less formal dining.

Rooms 38 en suite (32 fmly) (6 GF) ⊘ in 20 bedrooms S £75-£85; D £87.50-£97.50 (incl. bkfst) **Facilities Spa** STV ⍐ supervised Sauna Solarium Gym **Conf** BC Thtr 120 Class 50 Board 40 Del £105 **Services** Lift **Parking** 300 **Notes LB** ⊗ ⊘ in restaurant RS 24-27 Dec

---

★★ 72% METRO HOTEL

Best Western Queens Hotel

Queen St TQ12 2EZ

☎ 01626 363133 📠 01626 354106

e-mail: reservations@queenshotel-southwest.co.uk

dir: M5 onto A380, follow signs for railway station. Hotel opposite station

Pleasantly and conveniently located close to the railway station and racecourse, this hotel continues to be a popular venue for both business people and tourists. Many of the bedrooms have now been upgraded but all are comfortable and spacious. Light snacks and sandwiches are available in the café/bar and lounge.

Rooms 26 en suite (3 fmly) ⊘ in all bedrooms S £65-£100; D £80-£120 (incl. bkfst) **Facilities** FTV Wi-fi in bedrooms **Conf** Thtr 40 Class 20 Board 20 Del from £90 **Parking** 6 **Notes LB** ⊗ ⊘ in restaurant RS 24 Dec-2 Jan

---

OKEHAMPTON
MAP 03 SX59

★★ 69% HOTEL

Ashbury

Higher Maddaford, Southcott EX20 4NL

☎ 01837 55453 📠 01837 55468

dir: off A30 at Sourton Cross onto A386. Left onto A3079 to Bude at Fowley Cross. After 1m right to Ashbury. Hotel 0.5m on right

Now boasting four courses and a clubhouse with lounge, bar and dining facilities, The Ashbury is a golfer's paradise. The majority of the well-equipped bedrooms are located in the farmhouse and courtyard-style development around the putting green. Guests can enjoy the many on-site leisure facilities or join the activities available at the adjacent sister hotel.

Rooms 69 en suite 30 annexe en suite (54 fmly) (29 GF) S £99-£162; D £190-£308 (incl. bkfst & dinner) (2 nights minimum stay) **Facilities** ⤏ ♨ 72 ♒ Fishing Snooker Sauna Putt green Jacuzzi Driving range, Indoor bowls, Ten-pin bowling, Outdoor chess, Golf simulator Xmas **Parking** 150 **Notes LB** ⊗ ⊘ in restaurant

---

★★ 69% HOTEL

Manor House Hotel

Fowley Cross EX20 4NA

☎ 01837 53053 📠 01837 55027

web: www.manorhousehotel.co.uk

dir: off A30 at Sourton Cross flyover, right onto A386. Hotel 1.5m on right

Enjoying views to Dartmoor in the distance, this hotel is set within 17 acres of grounds and is located close to the A30. An impressive range of facilities, including golf at the adjacent sister hotel, is available at this friendly establishment, which specialises in short breaks. Bedrooms, many located on the ground floor, are comfortable and well equipped.

Rooms 180 en suite (77 fmly) (96 GF) S £90-£163; D £172-£310 (incl. bkfst & dinner) (2 nights minimum stay) **Facilities Spa** ⤏ ♨ 72 ♒ Fishing Squash Snooker Sauna Gym ⤵ Putt green Jacuzzi Craft centre, Indoor bowls, Shooting range, Laser clay pigeon shooting, Aerobics Xmas **Parking** 200 **Notes LB** ⊗ ⊘ in restaurant

See advert on page 207

OKEHAMPTON *continued*

★★ 69% HOTEL

White Hart

Fore St EX20 1HD
☎ 01837 52730 & 54514 📠 01837 53979
e-mail: enquiry@thewhitehart-hotel.com
dir: in town centre, adjacent to lights, car park at rear of hotel

Dating back to the 17th century, the White Hart offers modern facilities. Bedrooms are well equipped and spacious and some have four-poster beds. A range of bar meals is offered or more relaxed dining may be taken in the Courtney restaurant. Guests can relax in the lounge or choice of bars, as well as a traditional skittles and games room.

Rooms 19 en suite (2 fmly) ⊘ in all bedrooms S fr £55; D fr £75 (incl. bkfst) **Facilities** Xmas **Conf** Thtr 100 Class 80 Board 40 **Parking** 20 **Notes LB** ⊘ in restaurant

BUDGET HOTEL

Travelodge Okehampton Whiddon Down

Whiddon Down EX20 2QT
☎ 08700 850 950 📠 01647 231626
web: www.travelodge.co.uk
dir: at Merrymeet rdbt on A30/A382

Travelodge offers good quality, good value, modern accommodation. Ideal for families, the spacious en suite bedrooms include remote-control TV, tea and coffee-making facilities and comfortable beds. Meals can be taken at the nearby family restaurant. See Hotel Groups pages for further details.

Rooms 40 en suite S fr £26; D fr £26

OTTERY ST MARY   MAP 03 SY19

★★ 74% SMALL HOTEL

Tumbling Weir Hotel

Canaan Way EX11 1AQ
☎ 01404 812752 📠 01404 812752
e-mail: reception@tumblingweirhotel.com
web: www.tumblingweir-hotel.co.uk
dir: off A30 take B3177 into Ottery St Mary, hotel signed off Mill St, access through old mill

Quietly located between the River Otter and its millstream and set in well-tended gardens, this family-run hotel offers friendly and attentive service. Bedrooms are attractively presented and equipped with

continued

modern comforts. In the dining room, where a selection of carefully prepared dishes makes up the carte menu, beams and subtle lighting help to create an intimate atmosphere.

Rooms 10 en suite (1 fmly) ⊘ in all bedrooms S £50-£58; D £80-£92 (incl. bkfst) **Facilities** ⛳ Wi-fi in bedrooms **Conf** Thtr 90 Class 60 Board 50 Del from £90 **Parking** 10 **Notes LB** ⊗ ⊘ in restaurant Closed 26 Dec-10 Jan Civ Wed 80

PAIGNTON   MAP 03 SX86

★★★ 75% HOTEL

Redcliffe

Marine Dr TQ3 2NL
☎ 01803 526397 📠 01803 528030
e-mail: redclfe@aol.com
dir: on seafront at Torquay end of Paignton Green

Set at the water's edge in three acres of well-tended grounds, this popular hotel enjoys uninterrupted views across Tor Bay. Offering a diverse range of facilities including a leisure complex, beauty treatments and lots of outdoor family activities in the summer. Bedrooms are pleasantly appointed and comfortably furnished, whilst public areas offer ample space for rest and relaxation.

Rooms 68 en suite (8 fmly) (3 GF) ⊘ in 12 bedrooms S £56-£62; D £112-£124 (incl. bkfst) **Facilities Spa** STV 🎱 supervised 🎣 Fishing Sauna Solarium Gym Putt green Jacuzzi Table tennis, Carpet Bowls Xmas **Conf** Thtr 150 Class 50 Board 50 Del £72 **Services** Lift **Parking** 80 **Notes LB** ⊗ ⊘ in restaurant Civ Wed 150

★★ 72% HOTEL

Dainton

95 Dartmouth Rd, Goodrington TQ4 6NA
☎ 01803 550067 📠 01803 666339
e-mail: enquiries@daintonhotel.com
web: www.daintonhotel.com
dir: on A379 at Goodrington. Pass zoo entrance, right onto Penwill Way. At bottom of road right into Dartmouth Rd. Hotel 0.25m on left

Located in a convenient position close to the beaches and Leisure Park, the Dainton provides a friendly and welcoming place to stay. Bedrooms are well equipped and brightly decorated. Service is attentive, particularly in Christie's restaurant, which has an extensive menu with vegetarian options.

Rooms 10 en suite (2 GF) ⊘ in all bedrooms S £35-£60; D £65-£100 (incl. bkfst) **Facilities** Xmas **Parking** 20 **Notes LB** ⊗ ⊘ in restaurant

★★ 69% HOTEL

Sea Verge Hotel

21 Marine Dr TQ3 2NJ
☎ 01803 557795
dir: on seafront

With the added benefit of dedicated owners, this family-run hotel is conveniently situated close to the seafront and Preston Green. Several of the light and airy bedrooms have balconies, with views over Torbay. Spacious public areas include a comfortable lounge with adjacent sunroom, a cosy bar and dining room.

Rooms 10 en suite (1 fmly) ⊘ in 4 bedrooms **Parking** 14 **Notes LB** ⊗ No children 9yrs ⊘ in restaurant Closed Dec-Feb No credit cards accepted

★★ 67% **HOTEL**

Torbay Holiday Motel

Totnes Rd TQ4 7PP
☎ 01803 558226 📠 01803 663375
e-mail: enquiries@thm.co.uk
dir: on A385 Totnes to Paignton road, 2.5m from Paignton

Situated between Paignton and Totnes, this small complex offers purpose built leisure facilities, self-catering apartments and motel accommodation. The spacious bedrooms are comfortable and well co-ordinated. There are two restaurants and traditional dining is offered throughout.

Rooms 16 en suite (16 fmly) (8 GF) S £37-£42; D £56-£66 (incl. bkfst)
Facilities STV ⬚ ⬚ Sauna Solarium Gym Putt green Crazy golf, Adventure playground **Parking** 150 **Notes LB** RS 24-31 Dec
See advert on this page

★★ 🅰

Summerhill

Braeside Rd TQ4 6BX
☎ 01803 558101 📠 01803 558101
e-mail: info@summerhillhotel.co.uk
web: www.summerhillhotel.co.uk
dir: with harbour on left, follow for 600yds

Rooms 26 en suite (9 fmly) (4 GF) ⊘ in all bedrooms S £39-£48; D £78-£86 (incl. bkfst) **Facilities** Wi-fi available ch fac Free membership to nearby leisure centre **Services** Lift **Parking** 40 **Notes LB** ⊗ ⊘ in restaurant

TORBAY HOLIDAY MOTEL
★★

The ideal centre for touring South Devon
Open all year

All rooms en suite with colour TV (inc SKY), radio, telephone and tea/coffee facilities

- Indoor and outdoor pools • Solarium • Sauna
- Mini-Gym • Launderette • Crazy golf
- Restaurant • Bar • Shop • Ample parking
- 35-acre picnic area •

Also studio apartments and family suites available

Brochure from: Dept AA, Torbay Holiday Motel Totnes Road, Paignton, Devon TQ4 7PP
Tel: 01803 558226 Website: www.thm.co.uk
E-mail: enquiries@thm.co.uk

England

PAIGNTON *continued*

★ 75% **HOTEL**

Britney

29 Esplanade Rd TQ4 6BL

☎ 01803 557820 📄 01803 551285

e-mail: stay@britneyhotel.com

dir: on seafront by pier

In an impressive location on the seafront, this pleasant hotel offers comfortable accommodation. The hotel is family run and the proprietors are friendly and attentive. Bedrooms, some sea facing and some with balconies, are available in a range of sizes. A lively bar is provided, as well as a quieter lounge and sun room.

Rooms 20 en suite (2 fmly) ⊗ in 3 bedrooms **Facilities** Xmas
Services Lift **Parking** 8 **Notes** ⊗ in restaurant Closed Oct-Etr RS Xmas

U

Redcliffe Lodge

1 Marine Dr TQ3 2NJ

☎ 01803 551394 📄 01803 551394

e-mail: holiday@redcliffelodge.co.uk

dir: Follow A3022 to Paignton seafront. Hotel is at the end of Marine Drive on the right adjacent to Paignton Green

At the time of going to press, the star classification for this hotel was not confirmed. Please refer to the AA internet site www.theAA.com for current information.

Rooms 17 en suite (2 fmly) (3 GF) ⊗ in 14 bedrooms S £18-£25;
D £36-£60 (incl. bkfst) **Conf** Class 40 Del from £40 **Parking** 16
Notes ⊗ ⊗ in restaurant

See advert on opposite page

PARKHAM   MAP 03 SS32

★★★ 74% ⊛ **COUNTRY HOUSE HOTEL**

Penhaven Country House

Rectory Ln EX39 5PL

☎ 01237 451388 & 451711 📄 01237 451878

e-mail: reservations@penhaven.co.uk

web: www.penhaven.co.uk

dir: off A39 at Horns Cross, follow signs to Parkham, 2nd left after church into Rectory Lane

The countryside is very much at the heart of this establishment and lucky guests can spot tame badgers most evenings in the lovely grounds. The tranquillity of the location and the friendliness of the staff combine to create a truly relaxing environment. Bedrooms are spacious and well equipped; some are located in the cottage annexe and two are on the ground floor. Dinner features fresh, local produce and vegetarians are especially welcome.

Rooms 12 en suite S £85; D £170-£190 (incl. bkfst & dinner)
Facilities 9 acres of woodland trail Xmas **Parking** 50 **Notes LB**
No children 10yrs ⊗ in restaurant

PLYMOUTH   MAP 03 SX45

See also St Mellion (Cornwall & Isles of Scilly)

★★★★ 77% **HOTEL**

Copthorne Hotel Plymouth

COPTHORNE

Armada Way PL1 1AR

☎ 01752 224161 📄 01752 670688

e-mail: sales.plymouth@mill-cop.com

web: www.copthorne.com

dir: from M5 follow A38 to Plymouth city centre. Follow ferryport signs over 2 rdbts. Hotel on 1st exit left before 4th rdbt

Located right in the city centre, this hotel possesses extensive conference facilities and parking. Suites, Connoisseur and Classic rooms are available; all are spacious and well equipped. Public areas are spread over two floors and include Bentley's brasserie, where the emphasis is firmly placed upon local produce, including excellent fish landed at the Barbican.

Rooms 135 en suite (29 fmly) ⊗ in 115 bedrooms S £125-£180;
D £125-£180 **Facilities** STV Wi-fi available Steam room **Conf** Thtr 140
Class 60 Board 60 Del from £125 **Services** Lift **Parking** 50 **Notes LB**
⊗ ⊗ in restaurant Civ Wed 65

★★★★ **A**

Kitley House Hotel

Kitley Estate, Yealmpton PL8 2NW

☎ 01752 881555 📄 01752 881667

e-mail: sales@kitleyhousehotel.com

web: www.kitleyhousehotel.com

dir: from Plymouth take A379 to Kingsbridge. Hotel on right after Brixton and before Yealmpton

Rooms 19 en suite (9 fmly) (1 GF) ⊗ in 12 bedrooms S £75-£95.50;
D £85-£125.50 (incl. bkfst) **Facilities** STV FTV Fishing ⤴ Wi-fi in bedrooms Beauty salon Xmas **Conf** BC Thtr 70 Class 40 Board 35 Del from £135 **Parking** 100 **Notes LB** ⊗ in restaurant

★★★ 79% ⊛ **COUNTRY HOUSE HOTEL**

Langdon Court

Down Thomas PL9 0DY

☎ 01752 862358 📄 01752 863428

e-mail: enquiries@langdoncourt.co.uk

dir: follow HMS Cambridge signs from Elburton and tourist signs on A379

This magnificent Grade II listed Tudor manor, set in seven acres of lush countryside, has a direct path leading to the beach at Wembury and coastal footpaths. Bedrooms all enjoy countryside views while

continued

public areas include a stylishly updated bar and brasserie restaurant, where the contemporary menu incorporates local produce with excellent seafood.

Rooms 18 en suite (4 fmly) ⊘ in all bedrooms **Conf** Thtr 60 Board 20 **Parking** 100 **Notes LB** ⊘ in restaurant Civ Wed 75

★★★ 75% ⊛ HOTEL

Best Western Duke of Cornwall

Millbay Rd PL1 3LG

☎ 01752 275850 ▤ 01752 275854

e-mail: info@thedukeofcornwallhotel.com

web: www.thedukeofcornwallhotel.com

dir: follow city centre, then Plymouth Pavilions Conference & Leisure Centre signs past hotel

An historic landmark, this city centre hotel is conveniently located. The spacious public areas include a popular bar, comfortable lounge and multi functional ballroom. Bedrooms, many with far reaching views, are individually styled and comfortably appointed. A range of dining options include bar meals, or the more formal atmosphere in the elegant dining room.

Rooms 71 en suite (6 fmly) ⊘ in 20 bedrooms **Facilities** STV ch fac **Conf** Thtr 300 Class 125 Board 84 **Services** Lift **Parking** 50 **Notes LB** ⊘ in restaurant Closed 24 Dec-1st Mon in Jan Civ Wed 300

★★★ 73% HOTEL

Elfordleigh Hotel Golf Leisure

Colebrook, Plympton PL7 5EB

☎ 01752 336428 ▤ 01752 344581

e-mail: reception@elfordleigh.co.uk

dir: Leave A38 at city centre exit, at Marsh Mills/Sainsbury's rdbt take Plympton road. At 4th lights left into Larkham Ln, at end right then left into Crossway. At end left into The Moors, hotel 1m

Located in the beautiful Plym Valley, this well-established hotel is set in attractive wooded countryside. Bedrooms, many with lovely views, are spacious and comfortable. There is an excellent range of leisure facilities including an 18-hole golf course. A choice of dining options is available, a friendly brasserie or the more formal restaurant.

Rooms 34 en suite (2 fmly) (7 GF) ⊘ in 9 bedrooms S £89-£95; D £95-£140 (incl. bkfst) **Facilities Spa** STV ⊠ supervised ⌔ 18 ⌗ Fishing Squash Sauna Solarium Gym ⌣ Putt green Jacuzzi Wi-fi in bedrooms Hairdresser, Beautician, Dance/Aerobics studio, 5-a-side football pitch (hard) Xmas **Conf** Thtr 200 Class 120 Board 50 Del from £120 **Services** Lift **Parking** 200 **Notes LB** ⊘ in restaurant Civ Wed 200

★★★ 71% HOTEL

New Continental

Millbay Rd PL1 3LD

☎ 01752 220782 ▤ 01752 227013

e-mail: newconti@tiscali.co.uk

web: www.newcontinental.co.uk

dir: A38, follow city centre signs for Continental Ferryport. Hotel before ferryport & next to Plymouth Pavilions Conference Centre

Within easy reach of the city centre and The Hoe, this privately owned hotel continues to offer high standards of service and hospitality. A variety of bedroom sizes and styles are available, all with the same levels of equipment and comfort. The hotel is a popular choice for conferences and functions.

Rooms 99 en suite (20 fmly) ⊘ in 28 bedrooms S £70-£98; D £85-£115 (incl bkfst) **Facilities** ⊠ supervised Sauna Solarium Gym Wi-fi available Steam Room, Beautician, Pool Table **Conf** Thtr 350 Class 100 Board 70 Del from £120 **Services** Lift **Parking** 100 **Notes LB** ⊛ Closed 24 Dec-2 Jan Civ Wed 110

We have indicated only the hotels that do not accept credit or debit cards

England

PLYMOUTH *continued*

★★★ 70% HOTEL

Novotel Plymouth

Marsh Mills PL6 8NH

☎ 01752 221422 📄 01752 223922

e-mail: h0508@accor.com
web: www.novotel.com

dir: Exit A38 at Marsh Mills, follow Plympton signs, hotel on left

Conveniently located on the outskirts of the city, close to Marsh Mills roundabout, this modern hotel offers good value accommodation. All rooms are spacious and designed with flexibility for family use. Public areas are open-plan with meals available throughout the day in either the Garden Brasserie, the bar, or from room service.

Rooms 100 en suite (17 fmly) (18 GF) ⊘ in 80 bedrooms S £50-£75; D £50-£85 **Facilities** STV ⚒ Xmas **Conf** Thtr 300 Class 120 Board 100 Del from £99 **Services** Lift **Parking** 140 **Notes LB** ⊘ in restaurant

★★★ 68% HOTEL

Invicta

11-12 Osborne Place, Lockyer St, The Hoe PL1 2PU

☎ 01752 664997 📄 01752 664994

e-mail: info@invictahotel.co.uk
web: www.invictahotel.co.uk

dir: A38 to Plymouth, follow city centre signs, then Hoe Park signs. Hotel opposite park entrance

Just a short stroll from the city centre, this elegant Victorian establishment stands opposite the famous bowling green. The atmosphere is relaxed and friendly and bedrooms are neatly presented, well-equipped and attractively decorated. Dining options include bar meals or the more formal setting of the dining room.

Rooms 23 en suite (6 fmly) (1 GF) S £55-£60; D £65-£80 (incl. bkfst) **Facilities** Wi-fi in bedrooms Xmas **Conf** BC Board 45 **Parking** 14 **Notes LB** ⊗ ⊘ in restaurant

★★ 74% HOTEL

Victoria Court

62/64 North Rd East PL4 6AL

☎ 01752 668133 📄 01752 668133

e-mail: victoria.court@btinternet.com
web: www.victoriacourthotel.co.uk

dir: from A38 follow city centre signs, past railway station. Follow North Road E for 200yds and hotel on left

Situated within walking distance of the city centre and railway station, this long-established, family-run hotel offers impeccably presented accommodation. The public areas retain the Victorian character of the building and include a comfortable lounge, bar and dining area. The attractively decorated bedrooms are well maintained with modern facilities.

Rooms 13 en suite (4 fmly) ⊘ in all bedrooms S £45-£52; D £65-£75 (incl. bkfst) **Parking** 6 **Notes LB** ⊗ ⊘ in restaurant Closed 22 Dec-1 Jan

★★ 71% HOTEL

Drake

1 & 2 Windsor Villas, Lockyer St, The Hoe
PL1 2QD

THE CIRCLE
Selected Individual Hotels
GREAT BRITAIN

☎ 01752 229730 📄 01752 255092

e-mail: reception@drakehotel.net

dir: follow city centre signs, left at Theatre Royal, last left and 1st right

Handily placed for access to the city centre and the historic Hoe, this popular hotel was originally two adjoining Victorian houses. Bedrooms are neatly presented, and public areas include a lounge, bar and elegant dining room. The convenient location, with its own parking, make this an ideal choice for business and leisure guests alike.

Rooms 35 rms (3 fmly) (1 GF) ⊘ in 20 bedrooms S £48-£54; D £62-£65 (incl. bkfst) **Parking** 26 **Notes LB** ⊗ ⊘ in restaurant Closed 24 Dec-3 Jan

★★ 68% HOTEL

The Moorland

Wotter, Shaugh Prior PL7 5HP

☎ 01752 839228 📄 01752 839153

e-mail: enquiries@moorlandhotel.com

dir: From A38 take Lee Mill exit. Through underpass turn right then left, 6m through Cornwood to Wotter

Situated on the southern slopes of the Dartmoor National Park, this hotel offers a warm welcome to visitors. Bedrooms are soundly appointed and most have pleasant views. The convivial bar is popular with both visitors and locals. A range of menus is available in either the bar or attractive restaurant.

Rooms 18 en suite (2 fmly) ⊘ in 4 bedrooms S £34.65-£48.50; D £54-£60 (incl. bkfst) **Facilities** Games room, secure field available for guests' horses. **Conf** BC Thtr 65 Class 22 Board 20 Del from £51.50 **Parking** 40 **Notes LB** ⊘ in restaurant

★★ 64% HOTEL

Camelot

5 Elliot St, The Hoe PL1 2PP

☎ 01752 221255 & 669667 📄 01752 603660

e-mail: camelot@hotelplymouth.fsnet.co.uk

dir: from A38 follow city centre signs, then signs to The Hoe. Into Citadel Road, then onto Elliot Street

Just a short walk from The Hoe, the Barbican and the city centre, this is a convenient choice for visitors to this historic naval city. The friendly, small hotel provides comfortable accommodation, with bedrooms varying in size and style. The bar proves popular as a

continued

meeting point, and additional facilities include a TV lounge and function room.

Rooms 18 en suite (5 fmly) ⊛ in 3 bedrooms S £30-£44; D £46-£56 (incl. bkfst) **Facilities** Wi-fi available **Notes LB** ⊛ in restaurant

Ⓤ

Holiday Inn Plymouth

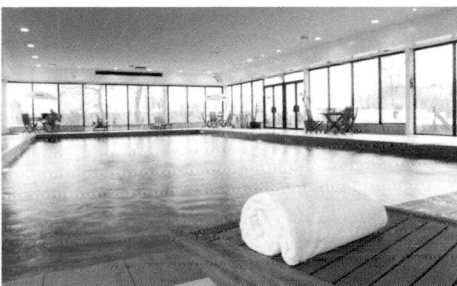

Armada Way PL1 2HJ

☎ 0870 225 0301 ▤ 01752 673816

e-mail: hiplymouth@qmh-hotels.com

dir: Exit A38 at Plymouth city centre & follow signs for Barbican/Hoe. On Notte St, turn left into Hoe Approach then right onto Citadel Rd. Hotel on right.

At the time of going to press, the star classification for this hotel was not confirmed. Please refer to the AA internet site www.theAA.com for current information.

Rooms 211 en suite (10 fmly) (12 GF) ⊛ in 150 bedrooms S £65-£135; D £65-£135 (incl. bkfst) **Facilities** STV ▤ supervised Sauna Solarium Gym Dance studio **Conf** Thtr 425 Class 260 Board 60 Del from £105 **Services** Lift air con **Parking** 125 **Notes LB** ⊛ ⊛ in restaurant Civ Wed 250

BUDGET HOTEL

Hotel Ibis

Marsh Mills, Longbridge Rd, Forder Valley PL6 8LD

☎ 01752 601087 ▤ 01752 223213

e-mail: H2093@accor-hotels.com

web: www.ibishotel.com

dir: A38 to Plymouth, 1st exit after flyover towards Estover, Leigham and Parkway Industrial Est. At rdbt, hotel on 4th exit

Modern, budget hotel offering comfortable accommodation in bright and practical bedrooms. Breakfast is self-service and dinner is available in the restaurant. For further details, consult the Hotel Groups page.

Rooms 52 en suite

BUDGET HOTEL

Innkeeper's Lodge Plymouth (Derriford)

8-9 Howeson Ln PL6 8BB

☎ 01752 783585

web: www.innkeeperslodge.com

Smart, en suite accommodation ideal for both business & leisure guests. Bedrooms are very well equipped, including Sky TV, telephone, modem points, tea & coffee making facilities, (family rooms in most locations). Complimentary breakfast. The adjacent Pub

Restaurant; a Harvester, Vintage Inn, Toby Carvery, Ember Inn, Sizzling Pubco or Pub & Carvery offers an all day menu. See Hotel Groups pages for further details.

Rooms 75 rms S £55-£57.50; D £55-£57.50

Innkeeper's Plymouth

399 Tavistock Rd PL6 7HB

☎ 01752 771527

Rooms 40 en suite S £55-£57.50; D £55-£57.50

BUDGET HOTEL

Premier Travel Inn Plymouth City Centre (Lockyers Quay)

Lockyers Quay, Coxside PL4 0DX

☎ 08701 977207 ▤ 01752 663872

web: www.premiertravelinn.com

dir: A38 Marsh Mills rdbt then A374 into Plymouth. Follow signs for Coxside & National Marine Aquarium

High quality, modern budget accommodation ideal for both families and business travellers. Spacious, en suite bedrooms feature bath and shower, satellite TV and many have telephones and modem points. The adjacent family restaurant features a wide and varied menu. For further details consult the Hotel Groups page.

Rooms 60 en suite **Conf** Thtr 25 Board 20

Premier Travel Inn Plymouth City Centre

Sutton Rd, Shepherds Wharf PL4 0HX

☎ 0870 9906458 ▤ 0870 9906459

dir: Follow signs for Plymouth city centre (A374) from Marsh Mills rdbt. After road splits, follow Barbican & Coxside signs. Pass Leisure Park, turn right at lights. Inn 50yds along Sutton Rd

Rooms 107 en suite **Conf** Thtr 20

Premier Travel Inn Plymouth East

300 Plymouth Rd, Crabtree, Marsh Mills PL3 6RW

☎ 08701 977208 ▤ 01752 600112

dir: From E: Exit A38 Marsh Mill junct. Straight across rdbt, exit slip road 100mtrs on left. From W: Plympton junct A38, at rdbt exit slip road next to A38 Liskeard

Rooms 40 en suite **Conf** Thtr 50 Board 30

BUDGET HOTEL

Travelodge Plymouth

Derry's Cross PL1 2SW

☎ 08700 850 950

web: www.travelodge.co.uk

Travelodge offers good quality, good value, modern accommodation. Ideal for families, the spacious en suite bedrooms include remote-control TV, tea and coffee-making facilities and comfortable beds. Meals can be taken at the nearby family restaurant. See Hotel Groups pages for further details.

Rooms 96 en suite S fr £26; D fr £26

continued

England

ROUSDON

MAP 04 SY29

★★ 72% ®® **HOTEL**

Dower House

Rousdon DT7 3RB

☎ 01297 21047 ▤ 01297 24748

e-mail: info@dhhotel.com

web: www.dhhotel.com

dir: *On A3052, 3m W of Lyme Regis*

Set in its own grounds, this hotel offers traditionally decorated bedrooms, each individually styled and well equipped with modern facilities. There is a more contemporary bar/lounge with a glowing stove on cold evenings. Both restaurants offer imaginative dishes - those in the bistro from a lighter menu and those in the fine dining restaurant having much creative flair.

Rooms 10 en suite (2 fmly) (1 GF) ⊗ in all bedrooms S £55; D £95-£150 (incl. bkfst) **Facilities** ₹ Xmas **Conf** Thtr 46 Class 30 Board 18 **Parking** 35 **Notes LB** ⊗ in restaurant Civ Wed 40

ST MARY CHURCH

See **Torquay**

SALCOMBE

MAP 03 SX73

See also **Hope Cove**

★★★★ 79% ® **HOTEL**

Thurlestone Hotel

TQ7 3NN

☎ 01548 560382 ▤ 01548 561069

e-mail: enquiries@thurlestone.co.uk

web: www.thurlestone.co.uk

(For full entry see Thurlestone)

★★★★ 78% ®® **HOTEL**

Soar Mill Cove

Soar Mill Cove, Malborough TQ7 3DS

☎ 01548 561566 ▤ 01548 561223

e-mail: info@soarmillcove.co.uk

web: www.soarmillcove.co.uk

dir: *3m W of town off A381 at Malborough. Follow 'Soar' signs*

Situated amid spectacular scenery with dramatic sea views, this hotel is ideal for a relaxing stay. Family-run, with a committed team, keen standards of hospitality and service are upheld. Bedrooms are well equipped and many rooms have private terraces. There are different seating areas where impressive cream teas are served, or, for the

continued

more active, a choice of swimming pools. Local produce and seafood is used to good effect in the restaurant.

Rooms 22 en suite (5 fmly) (21 GF) ⊗ in all bedrooms S £94-£150; D £150-£200 **Facilities** ᐁ ₹ ☼ Sauna Putt green Wi-fi available Table tennis, Games room, 9 hole Pitch n putt, Spa treatment suite ♫ Xmas **Conf** BC Thtr 100 Class 50 Board 50 Del from £150 **Parking** 30 **Notes LB** ⊗ in restaurant Closed 2 Jan-8 Feb

★★★ ®® **HOTEL**

Buckland-Tout-Saints

Goveton TQ7 2DS

☎ 01548 853055 ▤ 01548 856261

e-mail: buckland@tout-saints.co.uk

(For full entry see Kingsbridge)

★★★ 81% ® **HOTEL**

Tides Reach

South Sands TQ8 8LJ

☎ 01548 843466 ▤ 01548 843954

e-mail: enquire@tidesreach.com

web: www.tidesreach.com

dir: *off A38 at Buckfastleigh to Totnes. Then take A381 to Salcombe, follow signs to South Sands*

Superbly situated at the water's edge, this personally run, friendly hotel has splendid views of the estuary and beach. Bedrooms, many with balconies, are spacious and comfortable. In the bar and lounge, attentive service can be enjoyed along with the view, and the Garden Room restaurant serves appetising and accomplished cuisine.

Rooms 35 en suite (7 fmly) ⊗ in 14 bedrooms S £110-£137; D £190-£300 (incl. bkfst & dinner) **Facilities** ᐁ supervised Squash Snooker Sauna Solarium Gym Jacuzzi Wi-fi available Windsurfing, Sailing, Kayaking, Scuba diving, Hair & Beauty treatment ♫ **Services** Lift **Parking** 100 **Notes LB** No children 8yrs ⊗ in restaurant Closed Dec-early Feb

See advert on opposite page

SAMPFORD PEVERELL

MAP 03 ST01

★★ 65% **HOTEL**

Parkway House Country Hotel

32 Lowertown EX16 7BJ

☎ 01884 820255 & 07813 955274 ▤ 01884 820780

e-mail: p-way@m-way.freeserve.co.uk

dir: *M5 junct 27, follow signs for Tiverton Parkway Station. Hotel on right, on entering village*

An ideal choice for both business and leisure travellers, this hotel is located within a mile of the M5 and benefits from extensive views

continued

across the Culm Valley. The carvery is a popular choice at dinner in the conservatory style restaurant. Parkway House offers relaxed and welcoming hospitality and is well used for conferences and day meetings.

Rooms 10 en suite (2 fmly) ⊘ in 5 bedrooms **Conf** Thtr 120 Class 80 Board 40 **Parking** 80 **Notes** ⊘ in restaurant Civ Wed

BUDGET HOTEL

Travelodge Tiverton

Sampford Peverell Service Area EX16 7HD
☎ 08700 850 950 📠 01884 821087
web: www.travelodge.co.uk

dir: M5 junct 27

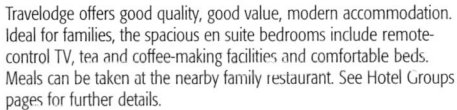

Travelodge offers good quality, good value, modern accommodation. Ideal for families, the spacious en suite bedrooms include remote-control TV, tea and coffee-making facilities and comfortable beds. Meals can be taken at the nearby family restaurant. See Hotel Groups pages for further details.

Rooms 40 en suite S fr £26; D fr £26

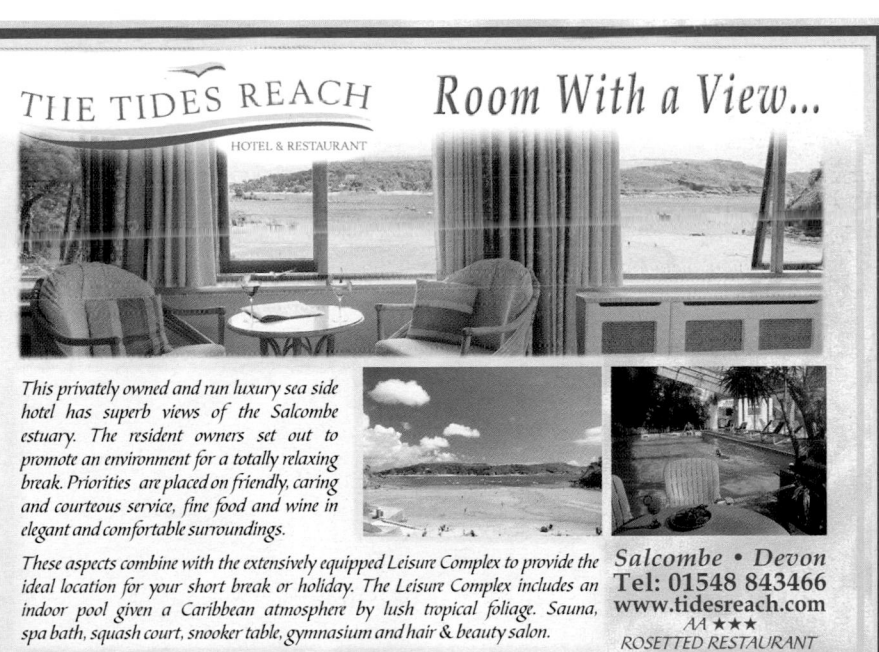

SAUNTON   MAP 03 SS43

★★★★ 79% ⊛ **HOTEL**

Saunton Sands   *Brend Hotels*

EX33 1LQ

☎ 01271 890212 📠 01271 890145

e-mail: reservations@sauntonsands.com

web: www.brend-hotels.co.uk

dir: off A361at Braunton, signed Croyde B3231, hotel 2m on left

Stunning sea views and direct access to five miles of sandy beach are just two of the highlights at this popular hotel. The majority of sea-facing rooms have balconies, and splendid views can be enjoyed from all of the public areas, which include comfortable lounges. The Sands café/bar is a successful innovation and provides an informal eating option.

Rooms 92 en suite (39 fmly) S £72-£109; D £144-£318 **Facilities** STV ⏏ ⏏ ⚘ Squash Snooker Sauna Solarium Gym Putt green Sun Shower, Health and beauty salon, ch fac OFSTED registered nursery ♫ Xmas **Conf** Thtr 200 Class 180 Board 50 Del from £125 **Services** Lift **Parking** 142 **Notes LB** ⊗ ⊘ in restaurant Civ Wed 200

See advert on page 213

SIDMOUTH   MAP 03 SY18

★★★★ 83% ⊛ **HOTEL**

Victoria   *Brend Hotels*

The Esplanade EX10 8RY

☎ 01395 512651 📠 01395 579154

e-mail: info@victoriahotel.co.uk

web: www.brend-hotels.co.uk

dir: on seafront

This imposing building, with manicured gardens, is situated overlooking the town. Wonderful sea views can be enjoyed from many of the comfortable bedrooms and elegant lounges. With indoor and outdoor leisure, the hotel caters to a year-round clientele.

continued

Carefully prepared meals are served in the refined atmosphere of the restaurant, with staff providing a professional and friendly service.

Rooms 61 en suite (18 fmly) S £90-£280; D £130-£280 **Facilities Spa** STV ⏏ ⏏ ⚘ Snooker Sauna Solarium Putt green ♫ ch fac Xmas **Conf** Thtr 60 **Services** Lift **Parking** 104 **Notes LB** ⊗ ⊘ in restaurant

See advert on opposite page

★★★★ 80% ⊛⊛ **HOTEL**

Riviera

The Esplanade EX10 8AY

☎ 01395 515201 📠 01395 577775

e-mail: enquiries@hotelriviera.co.uk

web: www.hotelriviera.co.uk

dir: M5 junct 30 & follow A3052

Overlooking the sea and close to the town centre, the Riviera is a fine example of Regency architecture. The large number of guests that become regular visitors here pay testament to the high standards of service and hospitality offered. The front-facing bedrooms benefit from wonderful sea views. The daily-changing menu places an emphasis on fresh, local produce.

Rooms 26 en suite (6 fmly) S £104-£156; D £208-£290 (incl. bkfst & dinner) **Facilities** STV Putt green ♫ Xmas **Conf** Thtr 85 Class 60 Board 30 **Services** Lift air con **Parking** 26 **Notes LB** ⊘ in restaurant

See advert on page 217

★★★★ 74% **HOTEL**

Belmont   *Brend Hotels*

The Esplanade EX10 8RX

☎ 01395 512555 📠 01395 579101

e-mail: reservations@belmont-hotel.co.uk

web: www.brend-hotels.co.uk

dir: on seafront

Prominently positioned on the seafront just a few minutes' walk from the town centre, this traditional hotel has a regular following. A choice

continued on page 216

The Victoria Hotel
AA ★★★★
Rosette ※ for cuisine

The Belmont Hotel
AA ★★★★

The most luxurious choice in East Devon

Perfectly positioned on Sidmouth's famous esplanade, the Victoria is one of the resorts finest and most picturesque hotels. It's extensive leisure facilities include indoor and outdoor pools, sauna, solarium, spa bath, hairdressing salon, putting green, tennis court and snooker room.

Telephone : 01395 512651

www.victoriahotel.co.uk Email: info@victoriahotel.co.uk

The Belmont too commands spectacular views from the famous esplanade. As inviting in January as July, the Belmont offers fine cusine and superlative service that brings guests back year after year. With the indoor and outdoor leisure facilities of the adjacent Victoria Hotel at your disposal, the Belmont provides the perfect location for your holiday.

Telephone: 01395 512555

www.belmont-hotel.co.uk Email: info@belmont-hotel.co.uk

Brend Hotels
The Westcountry's Leading Hotel Group

England

SIDMOUTH *continued*

of comfortable lounges provide ample space for relaxation, and the air-conditioned restaurant has a pianist most evenings. Bedrooms are attractively furnished and many have fine views over the esplanade. Leisure facilities are available at the adjacent sister hotel, the Victoria.

Rooms 50 en suite (4 fmly) (2 GF) S £80-£190; D £110-£190 **Facilities** STV Putt green ♫ ch fac Xmas **Conf** Thtr 50 **Services** Lift **Parking** 45 **Notes LB** ⊛ ⊘ in restaurant Civ Wed 110

See advert on page 215

★★★ 85% HOTEL

Westcliff

Manor Rd EX10 8RU
☎ 01395 513252 & 513091 📠 01395 578203
e-mail: stay@westcliffhotel.co.uk
web: www.westcliffhotel.co.uk
dir: *A3052 to seafront, right, hotel ahead*

This charming hotel, run by the same family for more than 38 years, is ideally located within walking distance of the promenade and beaches. Elegant lounges and the cocktail bar open onto a terrace, leading to the pool and croquet lawn. Bedrooms, several with balconies and glorious sea views, are spacious and comfortable, whilst the restaurant offers a choice of well-prepared dishes.

Rooms 40 en suite (4 fmly) (5 GF) ⊘ in 4 bedrooms S £66-£132; D £132-£236 (incl. bkfst & dinner) **Facilities** STV ⩗ Gym ⩘ Putt green Jacuzzi Mini tennis, Pool table, Table tennis **Services** Lift **Parking** 40 **Notes LB** ⊛ No children 6yrs ⊘ in restaurant Closed Mid Nov-Mid Mar

★★★ 🄰

Bedford

Esplanade EX10 8NR
☎ 01395 513047 📠 01395 578563
dir: *M5 junct 30, A3052 towards Sidmouth.*

continued

Rooms 37 en suite (8 fmly) (1 GF) ⊘ in all bedrooms S £55-£85; D £110-£170 (incl. bkfst & dinner) **Facilities** STV Xmas **Services** Lift **Parking** 6

★★ 78% HOTEL

Royal York & Faulkner

The Esplanade EX10 8AZ
☎ 01395 513043 & 0800 220714 📠 01395 577472
e-mail: stay@royalyorkhotel.co.uk
web: www.royalyorkhotel.co.uk
dir: *exit M5 junct 30 take A3052, 10m to Sidmouth, hotel in centre of Esplanade*

This seafront hotel, owned and run by the same family for generations, maintains its Regency charm and grandeur. The attractive bedrooms vary in size; many have balconies and sea views. Public rooms are spacious and traditional dining is offered plus the contemporary Blini's café-bar that serves coffees, lunch and afternoon teas. Newly developed spa facilities include a hydrotherapy pool, steam room, sauna and a variety of treatments.

Rooms 68 en suite 2 annexe en suite (8 fmly) (5 GF) ⊘ in 2 bedrooms S £50-£88.50; D £100-£177 (incl. bkfst & dinner) **Facilities Spa** STV ⬚ supervised Snooker Sauna Jacuzzi Free swim at local indoor pool, Steam Room & Treatment Rooms ♫ Xmas **Services** Lift **Parking** 20 **Notes LB** ⊘ in restaurant Closed Jan

★★ 76% HOTEL

Kingswood

The Esplanade EX10 8AX
☎ 01395 516367 📠 01395 513185
e-mail: kingswood@hotel-sidmouth.co.uk
web: www.hotel-sidmouth.co.uk
dir: *take Sidmouth road off A3052 towards seafront. Hotel in centre of Esplanade*

Super standards of hospitality are only surpassed by this hotel's prominent position on the esplanade. All bedrooms have modern facilities and some enjoy the stunning sea views. The two lounges offer comfort and space, and the attractive dining room serves good traditional cooking.

Rooms 26 rms (25 en suite) (7 fmly) (2 GF) ⊘ in all bedrooms S £39-£59; D £78-£118 (incl. bkfst) **Facilities** FTV guests receive vouchers for local swimming pool Xmas **Services** Lift **Parking** 17 **Notes LB** ⊘ in restaurant Closed 28 Dec-9 Feb

★★ 75% HOTEL

Mount Pleasant

Salcombe Rd EX10 8JA
☎ 01395 514694
dir: *exit A3052 at Sidford x-rds after 1.25m turn left into Salcombe Rd, opposite Radway Cinema. Hotel on right after bridge*

Quietly located in almost an acre of gardens, this modernised Georgian hotel is minutes from the town centre and seafront. Bedrooms and public areas offer good levels of comfort and high quality furnishings. Guests return on a regular basis to experience the friendly, relaxed atmosphere. The daily-changing menu offers a choice of imaginative, yet traditional, home-cooked dishes, which are enjoyed in the light and airy restaurant that overlooks the pleasant garden.

Rooms 17 en suite (1 fmly) (3 GF) ⊘ in all bedrooms S £51-£70; D £88-£140 (incl. bkfst & dinner) **Facilities** Putt green **Parking** 20 **Notes LB** ⊛ No children 8yrs ⊘ in restaurant Closed Dec-Feb

★★ 74% **HOTEL**

Hunters Moon

Sid Rd EX10 9AA

☎ 01395 513380 ▤ 01395 514270

e-mail: huntersmoon.hotel@virgin.net

dir: from Exeter on A3052 to Sidford. Right at lights into Simouth, 1.5m, at cinema turn left. Hotel in 0.25m

Set amid three acres of attractive and well-tended grounds, this friendly, family-run hotel is peacefully located in a quiet area within walking distance of the town and esplanade. Bedrooms, some located at ground floor level, are comfortable, well equipped and light and airy. There is a lounge and a cosy bar. Dining provides a choice of imaginative dishes and tea may be taken on the lawn.

Rooms 33 en suite (2 fmly) (12 GF) ⊘ in all bedrooms S £66-£70; D £114-£132 (incl. bkfst & dinner) **Facilities** Putt green Outdoor bowling green Putting green **Parking** 33 **Notes LB** No children 2yrs ⊘ in restaurant Closed Jan-12 Feb RS Dec & Feb

★★ 72% **HOTEL**

The Woodlands Hotel

Cotmaton Cross EX10 8HG

☎ 01395 513120 ▤ 01395 513548

e-mail: info@woodlands-hotel.com

web: www.woodlands-hotel.com

dir: follow signs for Sidmouth

Located in the heart of the town and ideally situated for exploring Devon and Dorset, this listed property has numerous character features. There is a spacious bar and a lounge where guests may relax. Freshly prepared dinners can be enjoyed in the smart dining room. Families with children are made very welcome and may dine early.

Rooms 20 en suite (4 fmly) (8 GF) ⊘ in all bedrooms S £70-£110; D £35-£55 (incl. bkfst) **Conf** Del from £75 **Parking** 20 **Notes LB** ⊘ in restaurant Closed 20 Dec-15 Jan Civ Wed 70

★★ 71% **HOTEL**

Devoran

Esplanade EX10 8AU

☎ 01395 513151 ▤ 01395 579929

e-mail: enquiries@devoran.com

dir: turn off B3052 at Bowd Inn follow Sidmouth sign for approx 2m turn left onto seafront, hotel 50yds at centre of Esplanade

Superbly situated, this family-run hotel, known locally as 'the pink hotel on the seafront' offers friendly, personal service. It has comfortable and attractively decorated bedrooms, some with their

continued on page 218

England

SIDMOUTH *continued*

own balconies that benefit from the wonderful sea views. Well-maintained public rooms include a large dining room, offering a five-course dinner, a comfortable lounge and cosy bar. Guests can use the leisure facilities at the sister hotel.

Devoran

Rooms 26 en suite (4 fmly) ⊗ in all bedrooms S £36-£64; D fr £72 **Facilities** Fishing Wi-fi available **Services** Lift **Parking** 8 **Notes LB** ⊗ in restaurant Closed mid Nov-late Feb RS Dec-Feb

SOURTON   MAP 03 SX59

★★ 76% **HOTEL**

Collaven Manor

EX20 4HH

☎ 01837 861522 📠 01837 861614

e-mail: collavenmanor@supanet.com

dir: off A30 onto A386 to Tavistock, hotel 2m on right

This delightful 15th-century manor house is quietly located in five acres of well-tended grounds. The friendly proprietors provide attentive service and ensure a relaxing environment. Charming public rooms have old oak beams and granite fireplaces, and provide a range of comfortable lounges and a well stocked bar. In the restaurant, a daily changing menu offers interesting dishes.

Rooms 9 en suite (1 fmly) S £61; D £98-£138 (incl. bkfst) **Facilities** 🏐 Bowls **Conf** Thtr 30 Class 20 Board 16 Del from £99 **Parking** 50 **Notes LB** ⊗ in restaurant Civ Wed 50

SOURTON CROSS   MAP 03 SX59

BUDGET HOTEL

Travelodge Okehampton Sourton Cross

EX20 4LY

☎ 08700 850 950 📠 0870 1911548

web: www.travelodge.co.uk

dir: 4m W, at junct of A30/A386

Travelodge offers good quality, good value, modern accommodation. Ideal for families, the spacious en suite bedrooms include remote-control TV, tea and coffee-making facilities and comfortable beds. Meals can be taken at the nearby family restaurant. See Hotel Groups pages for further details.

Rooms 42 en suite S fr £26; D fr £26

SOUTH BRENT   MAP 03 SX66

★★ 75% ⊛ **HOTEL**

Glazebrook House Hotel & Restaurant

TQ10 9JE

☎ 01364 73322 📠 01364 72350

e-mail: enquiries@glazebrookhouse.com

web: www.glazebrookhouse.com

dir: from Exeter take Marley Head exit to South Brent. 2nd turning on right after London Inn. From Plymouth take Woodpecker exit

Enjoying a tranquil and convenient location next to the Dartmoor National Park and set within four acres of gardens, this 18th-century former gentleman's residence offers comfortable and friendly accommodation. Bedrooms are well appointed and public areas are elegant and spacious. Cuisine offers interesting combinations of fresh, locally-sourced produce.

Rooms 10 en suite ⊗ in all bedrooms S £30-£55; D £60-£145 (incl. bkfst) **Facilities** Wi-fi in bedrooms **Conf** BC Thtr 80 Class 40 Board 40 Del from £75 **Parking** 40 **Notes LB** ⊗ ⊗ in restaurant Closed 1st 2 weeks in Jan Civ Wed 80

SOUTH MOLTON
MAP 03 SS72

★★ 69% **HOTEL**

The George Hotel

1 Broad St EX36 3AB

☎ 01769 572514 🖥 01769 579218

e-mail: info@georgehotelsouthmolton.co.uk

web: www.georgehotelsouthmolton.co.uk

dir: *off A361 at rdbt signed South Molton 1.5m to centre. Hotel in square*

Retaining many of its original features, this charming 17th-century hotel is situated in the centre of town. Providing comfortable accommodation, complemented by informal and friendly service, this hotel is an ideal base for touring the area. Regularly changing menus, featuring local produce, are offered in the both the restaurant and bar.

Rooms 9 en suite (3 fmly) ❷ in all bedrooms S fr £60; D fr £75 (incl. bkfst) **Facilities** FTV Wi-fi in bedrooms Local Gym facilities available nearby ♫ Xmas **Conf** Thtr 100 Class 30 Board 30 **Parking** 12 **Notes LB** ❸ ❷ in restaurant RS 1st wk Jan

SOUTH ZEAL
MAP 03 SX69

★★ 67% **HOTEL**

Oxenham Arms

EX20 2JT

☎ 01837 840244 & 840577 🖥 01837 840791

e-mail: theoxenhamarms@aol.com

dir: *off A30, 4m E of Okehampton in centre of village*

Dating back to the 12th century this attractive inn features original stonework, an ancient standing stone, aged beams, flagstone floors and interesting nooks and crannies. Equipped with modern facilities, the bedrooms are comfortable and spacious. A welcoming fire crackles in the lounge during colder months and dining options include bar meals and the relaxed dining room.

Rooms 8 rms (7 en suite) (3 fmly) S £40-£45; D £70 (incl. bkfst) **Facilities** Xmas **Parking** 5 **Notes** ❷ in restaurant

TAVISTOCK
MAP 03 SX47

★★★★ 🅰

Browns Hotel, Brasserie & Wine Bar

80 West St PL19 8AQ

☎ 01822 618686 🖥 01822 618646

e-mail: enquiries@brownsdevon.co.uk

web: www.brownsdevon.co.uk

dir: *200mtrs from Pannier Market & Church*

Rooms 16 en suite 4 annexe en suite (1 fmly) **Facilities** STV Gym **Services** Lift **Parking** 15 **Notes** ❸ ❷ in restaurant

★★★ 70% **HOTEL**

Bedford

THE INDEPENDENTS

1 Plymouth Rd PL19 8BB

☎ 01822 613221 🖥 01822 618034

e-mail: enquiries@bedford-hotel.co.uk

web: www.bedford-hotel.co.uk

dir: *M5 junct 31, A30 (Launceston/Okehampton). Then A386 to Tavistock, follow town centre signs. Hotel opposite church*

Built on the site of a Benedictine abbey, this impressive castellated
continued

building has been welcoming visitors for over 200 years. Very much a local landmark, the hotel offers comfortable and relaxing public areas, all reflecting charm and character throughout. Bedrooms are traditionally styled with contemporary comforts, whilst the Woburn Restaurant provides a refined setting for enjoyable cuisine.

Bedford

Rooms 29 en suite (2 fmly) (5 GF) ❷ in 11 bedrooms S fr £65; D £130-£140 (incl. bkfst) **Facilities** Xmas **Conf** Thtr 70 Class 45 Board 25 Del from £95 **Parking** 45 **Notes LB** ❷ in restaurant

THURLESTONE
MAP 03 SX64

★★★★ 79% ❀ **HOTEL**

Thurlestone

TQ7 3NN

☎ 01548 560382 🖥 01548 561069

e-mail: enquiries@thurlestone.co.uk

web: www.thurlestone.co.uk

dir: *A38 take A384 into Totnes, A381 towards Kingsbridge, onto A379 towards Churchstow, onto B3197 turn into lane signed to Thurlestone*

This popular hotel has been in the same family-ownership since 1896 and continues to go from strength to strength. A vast range of facilities are available for all the family. Bedrooms are equipped to ensure a comfortable stay and many have wonderful coastal views. Eating options include the local village inn or the elegant restaurant benefiting from the stunning views.

Rooms 64 en suite (23 fmly) **Facilities** Spa STV 🎱 ≒ supervised ⅃ 9 ⊐ Squash Snooker Sauna Solarium Gym ⇘ Putt green Jacuzzi Badminton courts, games room, toddler room. ♫ ch fac **Conf** Thtr 150 Class 100 Board 40 **Services** Lift **Parking** 121 **Notes LB** ❷ in restaurant Closed 1-2 wks Jan Civ Wed

TIVERTON
MAP 03 SS91

★★★ 72% **HOTEL**

Best Western Tiverton

Best Western

Blundells Rd EX16 4DB

☎ 01884 256120 🖥 01884 258101

e-mail: sales@tivertonhotel.co.uk

web: www.bw-tivertonhotel.co.uk

dir: *M5 junct 27, onto dual carriageway A361 Devon link road, Tiverton exit 7m W. Hotel on Blundells Rd next to business park*

Conveniently situated on the outskirts of the town, with easy access to the M5, this comfortable hotel has a relaxed atmosphere. The spacious bedrooms are well equipped and decorated in a contemporary style. A formal dining option is offered in the Gallery

continued on page 220

England

TIVERTON *continued*

Restaurant, and lighter snacks are served in the bar area. Room service is extensive, as is the range of conference facilities.

Rooms 69 en suite (4 fmly) ✆ in 53 bedrooms S £50-£96; D £70-£128 (incl. bkfst) **Facilities** STV Fishing Wi-fi in bedrooms Xmas **Conf** Thtr 300 Class 140 Board 70 Del from £90 **Parking** 130 **Notes LB** ✆ in restaurant Civ Wed 200

TORBAY
See under Brixham, Paignton & Torquay

TORQUAY   MAP 03 SX96

★★★★ 77% HOTEL

Palace
Babbacombe Rd TQ1 3TG
☎ 01803 200200 ▤ 01803 299899
e-mail: info@palacetorquay.co.uk
web: www.palacetorquay.co.uk

dir: *towards harbour, left by clocktower into Babbacombe Rd, hotel on right after 1m*

Set in 25 acres of stunning, beautifully tended wooded grounds, the Palace offers a tranquil environment. Suitable for business and leisure, the hotel boasts a huge range of well-presented indoor and outdoor facilities. Much of the original charm and grandeur has been maintained, particularly in the dining room. Many of the bedrooms enjoy views of the magnificent gardens.

Rooms 141 en suite (7 fmly) ✆ in 11 bedrooms S £65-£80; D £130-£288 (incl. bkfst) **Facilities** FTV ▤ ⬩ ♪9 ⬩ Squash Snooker Sauna Gym ⬩ Putt green Wi-fi available Xmas **Conf** Thtr 1000 Class 800 Board 40 Del £130 **Services** Lift **Parking** 140 **Notes LB** ⬩ ✆ in restaurant

See advert on opposite page

★★★★ 75% ⬩ HOTEL

Grand
Sea Front TQ2 6NT
☎ 01803 296677 ▤ 01803 213462
e-mail: reservations@grandtorquay.co.uk
web: www.richardsonhotels.co.uk

dir: *A380 to Torquay. At seafront turn right, then 1st right. Hotel on corner, entrance 1st on left*

Within level walking distance of the town, this large Edwardian hotel overlooks the bay and offers modern facilities. Many of the bedrooms,

continued

some with balconies, enjoy the best of the views; all are very well equipped. Boaters Bar also benefits from the hotel's stunning position and offers an informal alternative to the Gainsborough Restaurant.

Rooms 131 en suite (32 fmly) ✆ in 61 bedrooms S £60-£80; D £120-£160 (incl. bkfst) **Facilities Spa** STV ▤ ⬩ ⬩ Sauna Solarium Gym Jacuzzi Wi-fi available Hairdressers Beauty clinic ♪ Xmas **Conf** Thtr 250 Class 150 Board 60 Del from £120 **Services** Lift **Parking** 57 **Notes LB** ⬩ in restaurant Civ Wed 280

See advert on opposite page

INSPECTORS' CHOICE

★★★ ⬩⬩ HOTEL

Orestone Manor Hotel & Restaurant
Rockhouse Ln, Maidencombe TQ1 4SX
☎ 01803 328098 ▤ 01803 328336
e-mail: enquiries@orestone.co.uk

dir: *off A379 coast road, Torquay-Teignmouth road (formerly B3199)*

This country-house hotel is located on the fringe of Torbay and occupies a spectacular location overlooking Lyme Bay. There is a colonial theme throughout the public areas, making a charming and comfortable environment. Bedrooms are individually styled and spacious; some have balconies. The hotel's cuisine is highly regarded and dishes, based on local ingredients, are skilfully prepared.

Rooms 12 en suite (3 fmly) (1 GF) **Facilities** STV ⬩ **Conf** Thtr 30 Class 20 Board 15 **Parking** 40 **Notes LB** ⬩ in restaurant

★★★ 77% ⬩⬩⬩ HOTEL

Corbyn Head Hotel & Orchid Restaurant
Torquay Rd, Sea Front, Livermead TQ2 6RH
☎ 01803 213611 ▤ 01803 296152
e-mail: info@corbynhead.com
web: www.corbynhead.com

dir: *follow signs to Torquay seafront, turn right on seafront. Hotel on right with green canopies*

The Corbyn Head occupies a prime position overlooking Torbay. Well-equipped bedrooms, many with sea views and some with balconies, come in a range of sizes. Staff are friendly and attentive, and a well-stocked bar and comfortable lounge are available. Guests can enjoy

continued on page 222

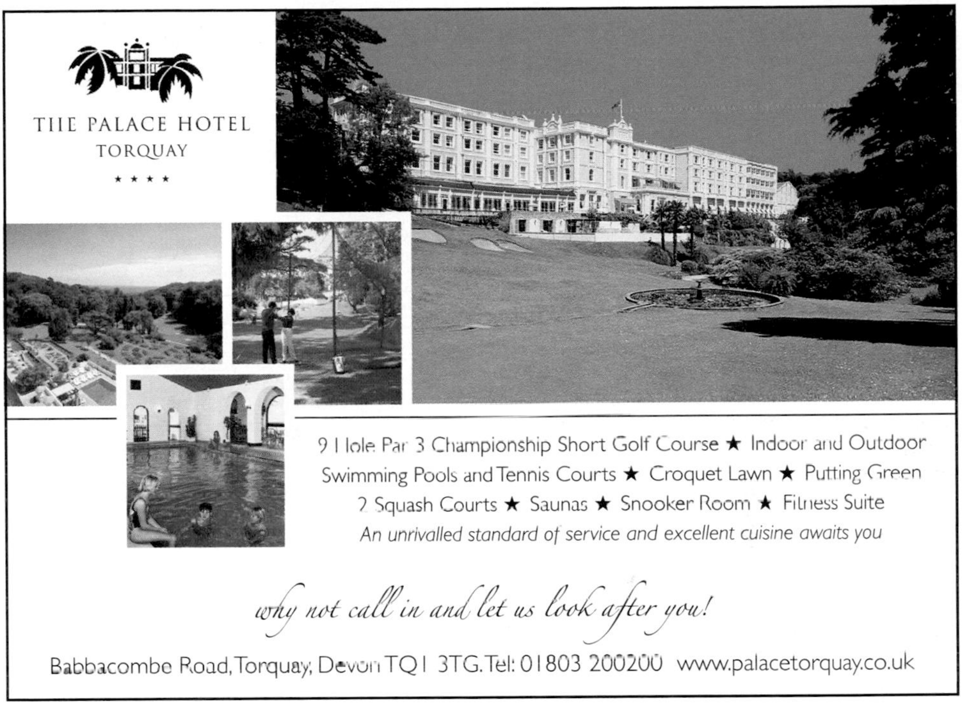

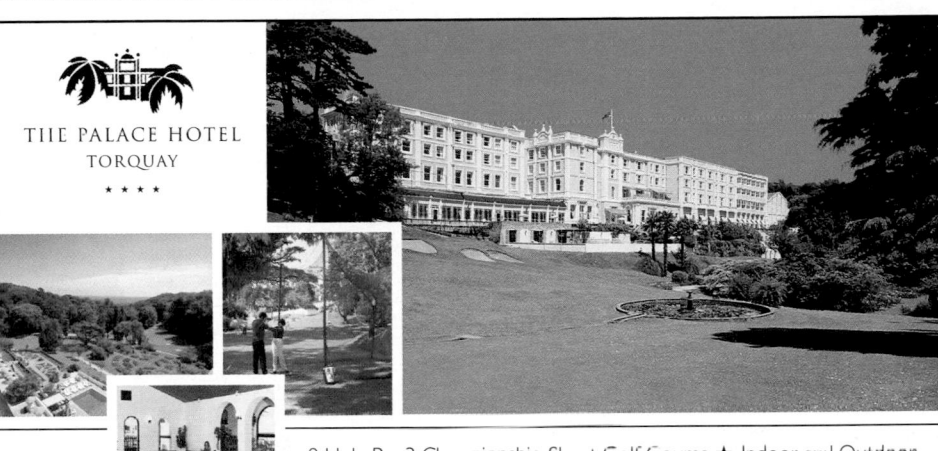

THE PALACE HOTEL
TORQUAY
★ ★ ★ ★
9 Hole Par 3 Championship Short Golf Course ★ Indoor and Outdoor Swimming Pools and Tennis Courts ★ Croquet Lawn ★ Putting Green
2 Squash Courts ★ Saunas ★ Snooker Room ★ Fitness Suite
An unrivalled standard of service and excellent cuisine awaits you
why not call in and let us look after you!
Babbacombe Road, Torquay, Devon TQ1 3TG. Tel: 01803 200200 www.palacetorquay.co.uk

Set in its own grounds with panoramic views over Torbay. Award winning cuisine, the finest indoor and outdoor swimming pools in the Bay, The Grand offers the best value for money in the South West for a short break or holiday – Winter through to Summer.
The Grand Hotel
★ ★ ★ ★
SEAFRONT
TORQUAY
75%
Freephone
0808 1002529
Fax 01803 213462
Website www.grandtorquay.co.uk
Email reservations@grandtorquay.co.uk

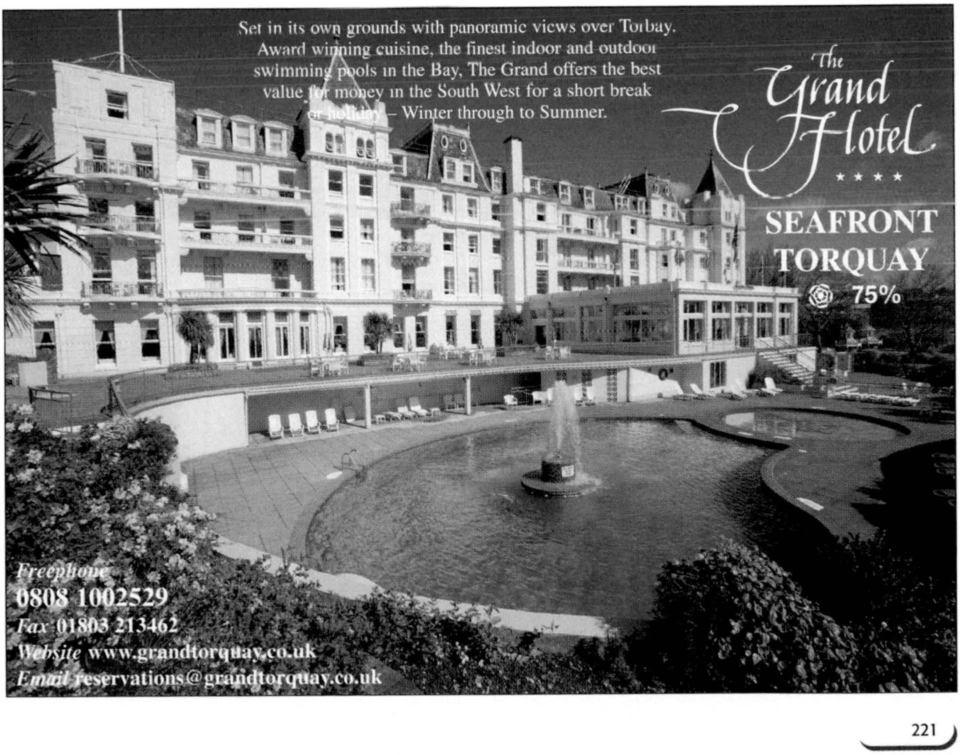

England

TORQUAY *continued*

fine dining in the award-winning Orchid Restaurant or more traditional dishes in the Harbour View restaurant.

Corbyn Head Hotel

Rooms 44 en suite (3 fmly) (9 GF) ⊘ in 15 bedrooms S £54-£160; D £108-£198 (incl. bkfst) **Facilities** ⚐ Squash Snooker Sauna Solarium Gym Wi-fi in bedrooms ♫ Xmas **Conf** Thtr 50 Class 30 Board 30 Del from £70 **Parking** 50 **Notes LB** ⊘ in restaurant

See advert on opposite page

★★★ **75% HOTEL**

Belgrave

Seafront TQ2 5HE

☎ 01803 296666 ▤ 01803 211308

e-mail: info@belgrave-hotel.co.uk

web: www.belgrave-hotel.co.uk

dir: on A380 into Torquay, continue to lights (Torre Station on right). Right into Avenue Road to Kings Drive. Left at seafront, hotel at lights

Enjoying an impressive position overlooking Torbay, the Belgrave offers a range of spacious and well-appointed public rooms, including comfortable lounges, the elegant restaurant and outdoor pool and patio areas. The Dickens bar is particularly stylish, and offers an innovative menu, featuring local produce. A variety of bedroom styles is available and many have the advantage of stunning sea views.

Rooms 72 en suite (20 fmly) (18 GF) ⊘ in 61 bedrooms S £55-£63; D £110-£126 (incl. bkfst) **Facilities** ⚐ Wi-fi in bedrooms ♫ Xmas **Conf** BC Thtr 430 Class 150 Board 170 Del from £80 **Services** Lift **Parking** 94 **Notes LB** ⊘ in restaurant

---

★★★ **72% HOTEL**

Best Western Livermead Cliff

Torbay Rd TQ2 6RQ

☎ 01803 299666 ▤ 01803 294496

e-mail: enquiries@livermeadcliff.co.uk

web: www.livermeadcliff.co.uk

dir: A379/A3022 to Torquay, through town centre, turn right for Paignton. Hotel 600yds on seaward side

Situated at the water's edge this long-established hotel offers friendly service. The splendid views can be enjoyed from the lounge, bar and dining room. Bedrooms, many with sea views and some with balconies, are comfortable and well equipped. A range of sizes is available.

Rooms 67 en suite (21 fmly) ⊘ in 56 bedrooms S £95; D £170 **Facilities** Wi-fi available ⚐ pool supervised Fishing Solarium ♫ Xmas **Conf** Thtr 80 Class 35 Board 35 Del from £50 **Services** Lift **Parking** 92 **Notes LB** ⊘ in restaurant

See advert on page 225

★★★ **72% HOTEL**

Lincombe Hall

Meadfoot Rd TQ1 2JX

☎ 01803 213361 ▤ 01803 211485

e-mail: lincombe.hall@lineone.net

web: www.lincombe-hall.co.uk

dir: From harbour into Torwood St, at traffic lights after 100yds, turn right into Meadfoot Rd. Hotel 200yds on left

With views over Torquay, this hotel is conveniently close to the town centre and is set in five acres of gardens and grounds. Facilities include both indoor and outdoor swimming pools. The tastefully furnished bedrooms vary in size, and the Sutherland rooms are most spacious. There are comfortable lounges and Harleys restaurant offers a comprehensive choice of dishes and wines.

Rooms 25 en suite 19 annexe en suite (7 fmly) (2 GF) **Facilities** STV ⚐ ⚐ ⚐ Putt green Child's play area Crazy golf Pool table Table Tennis **Conf** Thtr 30 Class 30 Board 30 **Parking** 44 **Notes LB** ⊘ in restaurant

★★★ 72% **HOTEL**

Livermead House

Torbay Rd TQ2 6QJ

☎ 01803 294361 & 291363 📄 01803 200758

e-mail: info@livermead.com

web: www.livermead.com

dir: *from seafront turn right, follow A379 towards Paignton & Livermead, hotel opposite Institute Beach*

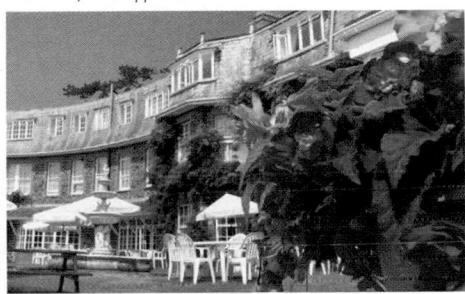

Having a splendid waterfront location, this hotel dates back to the 1820s and is where Charles Kingsley is said to have written *'The Water Babies'*. Bedrooms vary in size and style, excellent public rooms are popular for private parties and meetings and a range of leisure facilities

continued

is provided. Enjoyable cuisine is served in the impressively refurbished restaurant.

Rooms 67 en suite (6 fmly) (2 GF) ❷ in 12 bedrooms S £63-£73; D £126-£146 (incl. bkfst) **Facilities** ❀ Squash Snooker Sauna Solarium Gym Wi-fi available ♫ Xmas **Conf** Ihtr 320 Class 175 Board 80 Del from £55 **Services** Lift **Parking** 131 **Notes LB** ❷ in restaurant

See advert on page 227

★★★ 71% **HOTEL**

Toorak

Chestnut Av TQ2 5JS

☎ 01803 400400 📄 01803 400140

e-mail: toorak@tlh.co.uk

dir: *opposite Riviera Conference Centre*

Forming part of a much larger complex, this hotel offers excellent leisure facilities including indoor bowls, a cyber café and the magnificent Aztec Falls pool complex, gym and spa. Bedrooms have modern facilities, and both superior and standard rooms are available. The hotel also provides several relaxing lounges and conference rooms.

Rooms 92 en suite (29 fmly) (20 GF) ❷ in 40 bedrooms S £47-£89; D £94-£162 (incl. bkfst) **Facilities Spa** ❀ ❀ supervised ❄ Snooker Sauna Solarium Gym ❧ Jacuzzi Children's play area, Indoor Games Arena Internet Café ♫ ch fac Xmas **Conf** Thtr 220 Class 150 Board 60 Del from £28 **Services** Lift **Parking** 90 **Notes LB** ❀ ❷ in restaurant Civ Wed 120

TORQUAY *continued*

★★★ 66% **HOTEL**

The Grosvenor

Belgrave Rd TQ2 5HG

☎ 01803 294373 📄 01803 291032

e-mail: enquiries@grosvenorhoteltorquay.co.uk

web: www.grosvenorhoteltorquay.co.uk

dir: *follow signs to seafront, turn left, then 1st left into Belgrave Rd, hotel 1st on left*

Offering spacious and attractively furnished bedrooms, the Grosvenor is situated close to the seafront and the main attractions of the bay. Stylish public areas offer high levels of comfort, and guests can choose to dine in the restaurant, coffee shop or Mima's Italian Restaurant. A range of leisure facilities is available including indoor and outdoor pools, gym and sauna.

Rooms 44 en suite (8 fmly) ⊘ in 10 bedrooms **Facilities Spa** STV 🕄 ⤵ ⚓ Sauna Solarium Gym Jacuzzi Wi-fi available Mini snooker table, Library, Hair studio 🎵 Xmas **Conf** Thtr 150 Class 100 Board 40 **Parking** 50 **Notes** ⊗ ⊘ in restaurant Civ Wed 300

★★★ 66% **HOTEL**

Kistor Hotel

Belgrave Rd TQ2 5HF

☎ 01803 212632 📄 01803 212635

e-mail: stay@holidaytorquay.com

dir: *A380 to Torquay, hotel at junct of Belgrave Rd and promenade*

Being just a short stroll of Torquay's many amenities and the promenade, the Kistor is conveniently located. Popular with groups, the hotel offers a relaxing and informal base for guests. Most bedrooms have sea views. In the restaurant, a fixed-price menu offers good, straightforward cooking.

Rooms 57 en suite (4 fmly) ⊘ in all bedrooms S £26-£50; D £52-£100 (incl. bkfst) **Facilities Spa** 🕄 Sauna Putt green Jacuzzi Games room 🎵 Xmas **Conf** Thtr 60 Class 40 Board 30 **Services** Lift **Parking** 60 **Notes LB** ⊘ in restaurant

If the freedom to smoke or be in a non-smoking atmosphere is important to you, check the rules when you book

★★★ 60% **HOTEL**

Rainbow International

Belgrave Rd TQ2 5HJ

☎ 01803 213232

e-mail: gm@rainbow-hotel.co.uk

dir: *Close to harbour and marina*

Magnificent views can be enjoyed from this peaceful hideaway, which stands some 500 feet above the sea. Bedrooms vary in size and most have scenic views, whilst public areas, such as the cosy Victorian-style bar, provide a relaxing environment. Sanford's Restaurant offers a short carte of tempting dishes. The hotel is under new ownership.

Rooms 133 en suite 7 annexe en suite (70 fmly) S £68-£90; D £136-£180 (incl. bkfst & dinner) **Facilities** 🕄 ⤵ Gym 🎵 Xmas **Conf** Thtr 80 **Services** Lift **Parking** 100 **Notes LB** ⊗ ⊘ in restaurant

★★ 75% **HOTEL**

Torcroft

28-30 Croft Rd TQ2 5UE

☎ 01803 298292 📄 01803 291799

e-mail: enquiries@torcroft.co.uk

web: www.torcroft.co.uk

dir: *A390 onto A3022 to Avenue Rd. Follow seafront signs, turn left, cross lights, up Shedden Hill, 1st left into Croft Rd*

This elegant, Grade II listed Victorian property is pleasantly located in a quiet area, just a short stroll from the seafront. The delightful garden and patio are very popular with guests, ideal for a spot of sunbathing or relaxing with a good book. The comfortable bedrooms, two with balconies, are individually furnished. Pleasant, home-cooked meals are enthusiastically offered and make enjoyable dining.

Rooms 15 en suite (2 fmly) ⊘ in all bedrooms S £27-£37; D £54-£69 (incl. bkfst) **Facilities** Wi-fi available ch fac **Parking** 15 **Notes LB** ⊗ ⊘ in restaurant

★★ 74% HOTEL

Rawlyn House

Rawlyn Rd, Chelston TQ2 6PL
☎ 01803 605208 ▤ 01803 G07040
e-mail: shirley@rawlynhousehotel.co.uk
web: www.rawlynhousehotel.co.uk

dir: A3022 to Torquay, follow seafront signs, right at Halfords lights to Avenue Rd, at 2nd lights right to Walnut Rd, left to Old Mill Rd, Rawlyn Rd sharp right at top of hill

Quietly located close to Cockington village and within easy reach of the centre, this friendly family-run hotel is set in well-tended grounds. Bedrooms are individual in style and offer all the expected facilities, with two rooms located on the ground floor. Dinner features freshly cooked dishes and residents can take a snack lunch around the pool in the garden or in the bar

Rooms 12 rms (11 en suite) (1 fmly) (2 GF) ⊘ in all bedrooms
Facilities ⚡ Badminton Table tennis **Parking** 16 **Notes LB** ⊗ ⊘ in restaurant Closed Nov Apr

★★ 74% HOTEL

Seascape

8-10 Tor Church Rd TQ2 5UT
☎ 01803 292617 ▤ 01803 299260
e-mail: stay@seascapehoteltorquay.co.uk

dir: A380 Torquay, at Torre station turn right, left at 2nd lights. Through lights, hotel 100yds on right

Enjoying a convenient location, just a short stroll from the town centre, this friendly, family run hotel prides itself on genuine hospitality. Bedrooms are comfortable and well equipped; some have the added bonus of views across the bay. Public rooms include the convivial bar with regular live entertainment, and a sauna and solarium.

Rooms 60 en suite (10 fmly) (20 GF) ⊘ in 52 bedrooms S £25-£38; D £50-£75 **Facilities** Sauna Solarium ♫ Xmas **Services** Lift **Parking** 13 **Notes** ⊗ No children 12yrs ⊘ in restaurant

★★ 69% HOTEL

Anchorage Hotel

Cary Park, Aveland Rd TQ1 3PT
☎ 01803 326175 ▤ 01803 316439
e-mail: enquiries@anchoragehotel.co.uk

Quietly located in a residential area and providing a friendly welcome, this family-run establishment enjoys a great deal of repeat business. Bedrooms offer a range of sizes and all rooms are neatly presented.

continued on page 226

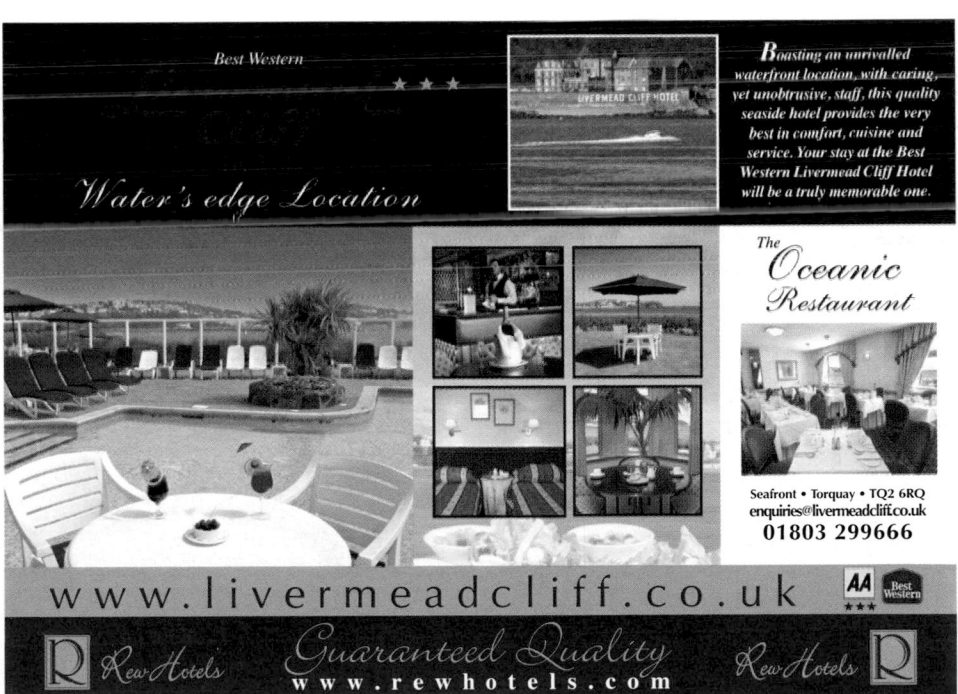

TORQUAY *continued*

Evening entertainment is provided regularly in the large and comfortable lounge.

Anchorage Hotel

Rooms 56 en suite (5 fmly) ⊘ in all bedrooms S £33.75-£45.75 (incl. bkfst & dinner) **Facilities** ⊰ ♫ Xmas **Services** Lift **Parking** 26 **Notes** LB ⊘ in restaurant

★★ 69% HOTEL

Hotel Balmoral

Meadfoot Sea Rd TQ1 2LQ
☎ 01803 293381 & 299224 🗎 01803 299224
e-mail: barry@hotel-balmoral.co.uk
dir: *at Torquay harbour left at clock tower towards Babbacombe. After 100yds right at lights. Follow to Meadfoot beach. Hotel on right*

Situated a short walk from the beach, this friendly, privately-owned hotel, now under new ownership, has modern, well-equipped bedrooms including family rooms and a room on ground floor level. The comfortable, spacious lounge has views over the well-tended gardens and the bar is an ideal venue for a drink before enjoying home-cooked dinners in the attractive dining room.

Rooms 24 en suite (4 fmly) (1 GF) **Parking** 18 **Notes** LB ⊘ in restaurant

★★ 69% HOTEL

Red House

Rousdown Rd, Chelston TQ2 6PB
☎ 01803 607811 & 200592 🗎 01803 200592
e-mail: stay@redhouse-hotel.co.uk
web: www.redhouse-hotel.co.uk
dir: *towards seafront/Chelston, turn into Avenue Rd, 1st lights turn right. Past shops & church, take next left. Hotel on right*

This friendly hotel enjoys pleasant views over Torbay in a quiet residential area of the town. Bedrooms vary in size but are generally spacious, comfortable and well appointed. Extensive leisure facilities are on offer including an outdoor and indoor pool, gym and beauty treatment rooms.

Rooms 9 en suite (3 fmly) **Facilities** Spa ⚡ ⊰ Sauna Solarium Gym Jacuzzi **Parking** 9 **Notes** ⊘ in restaurant

★★ 68% HOTEL

Albaston House

27 St Marychurch Rd TQ1 3JF
☎ 01803 296758 🗎 01803 211509
e-mail: albastonhousehotel@hotmail.com
dir: *A380 left at lights then B3199, follow signs for Plainmoor to Westhill Rd. Right at lights. Hotel 0.5m on left*

The Albaston is situated close to the town centre and is also convenient for the quieter attractions of Babbacombe. Public areas and bedrooms alike combine comfort and quality. Many guests return time after time to this hotel.

Rooms 13 en suite (2 fmly) ⊘ in 6 bedrooms S £36-£46; D fr £72 (incl. bkfst) **Facilities** Xmas **Parking** 6 **Notes** ⊗ ⊘ in restaurant

★★ 68% HOTEL

The Heritage Hotel

Seafront, Shedden Hill TQ2 5TY
☎ 01803 299332 01803 209191 🗎 01803 299332/209191
e-mail: enquiries@heritage.eclipse.co.uk
dir: *A380 to Torquay follow signs to seafront then left and Heritage Hotel is on left.*

In an elevated position overlooking Tor Abbey Sands this hotel is only a short walk from the harbour and the shops. The bedrooms are traditionally furnished and come in various sizes; all but one has a sea view. There is a variety of eating options available based on American food themes, and a large sun deck to relax on it summer. There is a ground-floor leisure complex.

Rooms 20 en suite 4 annexe en suite (24 fmly) (75 GF) **Facilities** STV ⚡ supervised Sauna Solarium Gym Jacuzzi **Services** Lift

★★ 67% HOTEL

Ashley Court

107 Abbey Rd TQ2 5NP
☎ 01803 292417 🗎 01803 215035
e-mail: reception@ashleycourt.co.uk
dir: *A380 to seafront, left to Shedden Hill to lights, hotel opposite*

Located close to the town centre and within easy strolling distance of the seafront, the Ashley Court offers a warm welcome to guests. Bedrooms are pleasantly appointed and some have sea views. The outdoor pool and patio are popular with guests wishing to soak up

continued

some sunshine. Live entertainment is provided every night throughout the season.

Ashley Court

Rooms 83 en suite (12 fmly) (8 GF) ⊗ in 29 bedrooms **Facilities** ⃗ Games Room / Garden ♫ Xmas **Services** Lift **Parking** 51 **Notes** ⊗ ⊗ in restaurant Closed 3 Jan-1 Feb

★★ 67% **HOTEL**

Coppice

Babbacombe Rd TQ1 2QJ

☎ 01803 297786 ▤ 01803 211085

e-mail: peter@coppicehotel.demon.co.uk

web: www.coppicehotel.co.uk

dir: From harbour left at clock tower for hotel 1m on left

A friendly, comfortable and well-established hotel, The Coppice is a popular choice and provides a convenient location within walking

continued

distance of the beaches and shops. In addition to the indoor and outdoor swimming pools, evening entertainment is often provided in the spacious bar. Bedrooms are bright and airy with modern amenities.

Rooms 39 en suite (16 fmly) (22 GF) ⊗ in all bedrooms S £26-£32.50; D £52-£65 (incl. bkfst) **Facilities Spa** ⃗ ⃗ Sauna Solarium Gym Putt green ♫ **Parking** 36 **Notes LB** ⊗ in restaurant Closed Dec-Jan

★★ 67% **HOTEL**

Elmington Hotel

St Agnes Ln, Chelston TQ2 6QE

☎ 01803 605192 ▤ 01803 690488

e-mail: mail@elmington.co.uk

web: www.elmington.co.uk

dir: to the rear of Torquay Station

Set in sub-tropical gardens with views over the bay, this splendid Victorian villa has been lovingly restored. The comfortable bedrooms are brightly decorated and vary in size and style. There is a spacious lounge, bar and dining room. Diners can choose from a menu of British dishes and from an oriental buffet.

Rooms 22 rms (19 en suite) (5 fmly) (2 GF) S £25-£33; D £50-£66 (incl. bkfst) ⊗ in all bedrooms **Facilities** ⃗ ⃝ Pool table Xmas **Conf** Thtr 40 Class 40 Board 30 **Parking** 22 **Notes** ⊗ ⊗ in restaurant

TORQUAY *continued*

★★ 67% **HOTEL**

Gresham Court

Babbacombe Rd TQ1 1HG

☎ 01803 293007 📠 01803 215951

e-mail: stay@gresham-court-hotel.co.uk

web: www.gresham-court-hotel.co.uk

dir: along seafront, left at clock tower, passing museum on left. Hotel immediately on left on corner of Braddons Hill Road West and Babbacombe Road

This privately owned and personally run hotel is soundly maintained and provides modern accommodation, including bedrooms on the ground floor. There is a bright and pleasant dining room, a lounge bar where live entertainment is provided, a non-smoking lounge and a games room with pool table. The hotel is a popular venue for coach tour parties.

Rooms 30 en suite (6 fmly) (5 GF) S £40-£45; D £60-£70 (incl. bkfst) **Facilities** Snooker ♫ Xmas **Services** Lift **Parking** 4 **Notes LB** ⊗ ⊘ in restaurant Civ Wed 75

★★ 67% **HOTEL**

Shelley Court

29 Croft Rd TQ2 5UD

☎ 01803 295642 📠 01803 215793

e-mail: shelleycourthotel@hotmail.com

dir: from B3199 up Shedden Hill Rd, 1st left into Croft Rd

This hotel, popular with groups is located in a pleasant, quiet area and overlooks the town towards Torbay. With a friendly team of staff, many guests return here time and again. Entertainment is provided most evenings in the season. Bedrooms come in a range of sizes and there is a large and comfortable lounge bar.

Rooms 27 en suite (2 fmly) (6 GF) S £32-£38; D £64-£76 **Facilities** ♨ ♫ Xmas **Conf** BC **Parking** 20 **Notes LB** ⊘ in restaurant Closed 5 Jan-12 Feb

★★ 65% **HOTEL**

Maycliffe

St Lukes Rd North TQ2 5DP

☎ 01803 294964 📠 01803 201167

e-mail: bob.west1@virgin.net

web: www.maycliffehotel.co.uk

dir: left from Kings Drive, along seafront keep left lane, next lights (Belgrave Rd) up Shedden Hill, 2nd right into St Lukes Rd then 1st left

Set in a quiet and elevated position which is convenient for the town centre and attractions, the Maycliffe is a popular venue for leisure breaks. Bedrooms are individually decorated and equipped with modern facilities, there are two rooms on the ground floor for less able guests. There is a quiet lounge to relax in and the bar is where a cabaret takes place on some nights during the season.

Rooms 28 en suite (1 fmly) (2 GF) ⊘ in 12 bedrooms **Facilities** ♫ **Services** Lift **Parking** 10 **Notes LB** ⊗ No children 4yrs ⊘ in restaurant Closed 2 Jan-12 Feb

★★ 65% **HOTEL**

Regina

Victoria Pde TQ1 2BE

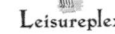
Leisureplex

☎ 01803 292904 📠 01803 290270

e-mail: regina.torquay@alfatravel.co.uk

web: www.alfatravel.co.uk

dir: into Torquay, follow harbour signs, hotel on outer corner of harbour

The Regina Hotel enjoys a pleasant and convenient location right on the harbour side, a short stroll from the town's attractions. Bedrooms, some with harbour views, vary in size. Entertainment is provided on most nights and there is a choice of bars.

Rooms 68 en suite (5 fmly) ⊘ in all bedrooms S £29-£37; D £48-£64 (incl. bkfst) **Facilities** ♫ Xmas **Services** Lift **Parking** 6 **Notes LB** ⊗ ⊘ in restaurant Closed Jan& part Feb RS Nov-Dec (ex Xmas) & Feb-Mar

★★ 63% **HOTEL**

Norcliffe

7 Babbacombe Downs Rd, Babbacombe TQ1 3LF

☎ 01803 328456 📠 01803 316851

e-mail: info@norcliffehotel.co.uk

dir: M5, take A380, after Sainsburys turn left at lights, across rdbt, next left at lights into Manor Rd, from Babbacombe Rd turn left

With marvellous views across Lyme Bay, the Norcliffe is conveniently situated on the Babbacombe Downs and ideally located for visitors to St Marychurch or nearby Oddicombe Beach. Public areas are relaxing, taking full advantage of the views. All bedrooms are comfortable, varying in style and size.

Rooms 26 en suite (3 fmly) (1 GF) ⊘ in all bedrooms **Facilities** ❧ Sauna Gym Games room ♫ **Services** Lift **Parking** 17 **Notes LB** ⊗ ⊘ in restaurant

★★ 61% **HOTEL**

Bute Court

Belgrave Rd TQ2 5HQ

☎ 01803 293771 & 213055 📠 01803 213429

e-mail: stay@butecourthotel.co.uk

web: www.butecourthotel.co.uk

dir: take A380 to Torquay, continue to lights, bear right past police station, straight across at lights, hotel 200yds on right

This popular hotel is only a short, level walk from the seafront and resort attractions. It still retains many of its Victorian features. Comfortable bedrooms offer modern facilities and many have far-reaching views. Public areas include a bar and lounges, while the attractive dining room looks across secluded gardens to the sea. Entertainment is offered during busier periods.

Rooms 44 en suite (10 fmly) (13 GF) ⊘ in all bedrooms **Facilities** ❧ Snooker Darts billiards ♫ **Services** Lift **Parking** 37 **Notes LB** ⊗ ⊘ in restaurant

The Imperial

PARAMOUNT
GROUP OF HOTELS

Park Hill Rd TQ1 2DG
☎ 01803 294301 🗎 01803 298293
e-mail: imperialtorquay@paramount-hotels.co.uk
web: www.paramount-hotels.co.uk

dir: A380 towards the seafront. Turn left and follow road to harbour, at clocktower turn right. Hotel 300yds on right

A substantial programme of refurbishment and standards review is starting at this hotel. During this period the star rating is suspended until we are able to undertake a full inspection on completion. Please refer to the AA internet site www.theAA.com for current information.

Rooms 151 en suite (7 fmly) ⊗ in 26 bedrooms **Facilities** STV ⊠ ⊼ supervised ⩍ Squash Snooker Sauna Solarium Gym Jacuzzi Beauty salon Hairdresser, Steam room ♫ Xmas **Conf** Thtr 350 Class 200 Board 30 **Services** Lift **Parking** 140 **Notes** ⊗ in restaurant Civ Wed 250

TWO BRIDGES   MAP 03 SX67

★★ 83% ⑱ **HOTEL**

Prince Hall

PL20 6SA
☎ 01822 890403 🗎 01822 890676
e-mail: info@princehall.co.uk
web: www.princehall.co.uk
dir: on B3357 1m E of Two Bridges road junct

Charm, peace and relaxed informality pervade at this small hotel, which has a stunning location at the heart of Dartmoor. Bedrooms, each named after a Dartmoor tor, have been equipped with thoughtful extras. The history of the house and its location are reflected throughout the public areas, which are very comfortable. Dogs are welcomed here as warmly as their owners. The accomplished cooking is memorable.

Rooms 8 en suite ⊗ in all bedrooms S £85-£95; D £185-£250 (incl. bkfst & dinner) **Facilities** Fishing Riding ⅌ Guided Dartmoor Walks, Fly fishing, Garden tours Xmas **Conf** Class 25 Board 20 Del from £220 **Parking** 13 **Notes LB** No children 10yrs ⊗ in restaurant Closed 2 Jan-2 Feb

---

★★ 76% **HOTEL**

Two Bridges Hotel

PL20 6SW
☎ 01822 890581 🗎 01822 892306
e-mail: enquiries@twobridges.co.uk
web: www.twobridges.co.uk
dir: junct of B3212 & B3357

This wonderfully relaxing hotel is set in the heart of the Dartmoor
continued

National Park, in a beautiful riverside location. Three standards of comfortable rooms provide every modern convenience. There is a choice of lounges and fine dining is available in the restaurant, with menus featuring seasonal produce including local game.

Rooms 33 en suite (2 fmly) (6 GF) ⊗ in 25 bedrooms S £65-£95; D £130-£180 (incl. bkfst) **Facilities** STV Fishing Xmas **Conf** Thtr 130 Class 60 Board 40 Del from £95 **Parking** 100 **Notes LB** ⊗ in restaurant Civ Wed 130

WOODBURY   MAP 03 SY08

★★★★ 75% ⑱ **HOTEL**

Woodbury Park Hotel Golf & Country Club

Woodbury Castle EX5 1JJ
☎ 01395 233382 🗎 01395 234701
e-mail: reservations@woodburypark.co.uk
web: www.woodburypark.co.uk
dir: M5 junct 30, A376 then A3052 towards Sidmouth, onto B3180, hotel signed

Situated in 500 acres of beautiful and unspoilt countryside, just a short drive from the M5, this hotel offers smart, well-equipped and immaculately presented accommodation together with a host of leisure, sporting and banqueting facilities. Re-live the thrills and drama of Nigel Mansell's career in 'The Nigel Mansell World of Racing', enjoy a game of golf on one of the two parkland courses, be pampered in the bodyzone beauty centre and enjoy creative dishes in the Atrium Restaurant.

Rooms 56 en suite (4 fmly) ⊗ in all bedrooms S £105-£125; D £150-£185 (incl. bkfst & dinner) **Facilities Spa** STV ⊠ ⤢ 27 ⩍ Fishing Squash Snooker Sauna Gym Putt green Jacuzzi Wi-fi in bedrooms beauty salon, football pitch, driving range, 2 golf courses, hydrotherapy spa Xmas **Conf** Thtr 250 Class 100 Board 50 Del from £145 **Services** Lift **Parking** 400 **Notes LB** ⊗ ⊗ in restaurant Civ Wed 150

WOODY BAY   MAP 03 SS64

★★ 67% **HOTEL**

Woody Bay Hotel

EX31 4QX
☎ 01598 763264 & 763563
e-mail: info@woodybayhotel.co.uk
dir: Signed off A39 between Blackmoor Gate & Lynton

Popular with walkers, this hotel is perfectly situated to enjoy sweeping views over Woody Bay. Bedrooms vary in style and size; the majority

continued on page 230

England

WOODY BAY *continued*

have stunning views. Similarly in the restaurant, where guests have a wide choice from the imaginative fixed-price menu.

Rooms 7 en suite (1 fmly) ⊗ in all bedrooms S £55; D £74-£84 (incl. bkfst) **Facilities** Wi-fi in bedrooms **Parking** 7 **Notes LB** ⊗ No children 5 yrs ⊗ in restaurant Closed Dec-Jan RS Nov -Feb

WOOLACOMBE   MAP 03 SS44

★★★ 88% ⊛ HOTEL

Watersmeet

Mortehoe EX34 7EB

☎ 01271 870333 ▤ 01271 870890

e-mail: info@watersmeethotel.co.uk

web: www.watersmeethotel.co.uk

dir: *follow B3343 into Woolacombe, turn right onto esplanade, hotel 0.75m on left*

With magnificent views and steps leading directly to the beach this popular hotel offers guests attentive service. Bedrooms benefit from these wonderful sea views and some have private balconies. Diners in the attractive tiered restaurant can admire the beautiful sunsets while enjoying innovative range of dishes offered on the fixed-price menu.

Rooms 25 en suite (4 fmly) (3 GF) S £72-£198; D £144-£236 (incl. bkfst & dinner) **Facilities Spa** STV ⊠ ⋨ ⋓ Jacuzzi Steam room, Hot tub ♫ Xmas **Parking** 38 **Notes LB** ⊗ ⊗ in restaurant Civ Wed 60

See advert on this page

★★★ 78% HOTEL

Woolacombe Bay

South St EX34 7BN

☎ 01271 870388 ▤ 01271 870613

e-mail: woolacombe.bayhotel@btinternet.com

web: www.woolacombe-bay-hotel.co.uk

dir: *from A361 take B3343 to Woolacombe. Hotel in centre on left*

This family-friendly hotel is adjacent to the beach and the village centre, and has a welcoming and friendly environment. The public areas are spacious and comfortable, and many of the well-equipped bedrooms have balconies with splendid views over the bay. In addition to the fixed-price menu served in the stylish restaurant, Maxwell's bistro offers an informal alternative.

Rooms 63 en suite (27 fmly) (2 GF) ⊗ in all bedrooms S £55-£147; D £110-£294 (incl. bkfst & dinner) **Facilities Spa** STV ⊠ ⋨ ⋨ 9 ⋓ Squash Snooker Sauna Solarium Gym Jacuzzi Beauty salon, Creche, Children's club, Table Tennis, Hairdresser ♫ ch fac Xmas **Conf** Thtr 200 Class 150 Board 150 Del from £69 **Services** Lift **Parking** 150 **Notes LB** ⊗ ⊗ in restaurant Closed 3 Jan-mid Feb

YELVERTON   MAP 03 SX56

★★★ 74% ⊛ HOTEL

Moorland Links

PL20 6DA

Forestdale Hotels

☎ 01822 852245 ▤ 01822 855004

e-mail: moorland.links@forestdale.com

web: www.forestdale.com

dir: *A38 from Exeter to Plymouth, then A386 towards Tavistock. 5m onto moorland, hotel 1m on left*

Set on Dartmoor National Park, in nine acres of well-tended grounds, this hotel has spectacular views from many of the rooms across open moorland and the Tamar Valley. Bedrooms are well equipped and comfortably furnished, and some rooms have open balconies. This is a popular venue for weddings, and a number of spacious meeting rooms are available.

Rooms 44 en suite (4 fmly) (17 GF) ⊗ in 20 bedrooms S £75-£110; D £120-£140 (incl. bkfst) **Facilities** STV ⋓ Wi-fi available ♫ Xmas **Conf** Thtr 120 Class 60 Board 40 Del from £115 **Parking** 120 **Notes LB** ⊗ in restaurant Civ Wed 80

DORSET

BEAMINSTER
MAP 04 ST40

★★★ 74% ⊛⊛ **HOTEL**

Bridge House

3 Prout Bridge DT8 3AY
☎ 01308 862200 📠 01308 863700
e-mail: enquiries@bridge-house.co.uk
web: www.bridge-house.co.uk
dir: off A3066, 100yds from Town Square

Dating back to the 13th century, this property offers friendly and attentive service. Bedrooms are tastefully furnished and decorated; those in the main house are generally more spacious than those in the adjacent coach house. Smartly presented public areas include the Georgian dining room, cosy bar and adjacent lounge, together with a breakfast room overlooking the attractive garden.

Rooms 9 en suite 5 annexe en suite (1 fmly) (5 GF) ⊛ in all bedrooms S £50-£126, D £110-£174 (incl bkfst) **Facilities** Wi-fi in bedrooms Xmas **Conf** BC Thtr 24 Class 14 Board 10 Del from £150 **Parking** 20 **Notes** LB ⊛ in restaurant Civ Wed 50

BLANDFORD FORUM
MAP 04 ST80

★★★ 72% **HOTEL**

Best Western Crown

West St DT11 7AJ
☎ 01258 456626 📠 01258 451084
e-mail: crownhotel.blandford@hall-woodhouse.co.uk
dir: 100mtrs from town bridge

Retaining much of its Georgian charm, this former coaching inn provides a friendly welcome allied with efficient service. The well-equipped, stylish bedrooms are furnished to high standards, combining comfort with practicality. A choice of menus is offered in the panelled dining room, whilst in the bar an extensive range of meals is served in a less formal atmosphere.

Rooms 32 en suite (2 fmly) ⊛ in 27 bedrooms S £78; D £96-£125 (incl. bkfst) **Facilities** FTV Wi-fi in bedrooms **Conf** BC Thtr 250 Class 200 Board 60 Del from £110 **Services** Lift **Parking** 144 **Notes** LB ⊛ in restaurant Closed 25-28 Dec Civ Wed 150

BOURNEMOUTH
MAP 05 SZ19
See also Christchurch & Ferndown

★★★★ 78% **HOTEL**

Bournemouth Highcliff Marriott

Marriott
HOTELS & RESORTS

St Michaels Rd, West Cliff BH2 5DU
☎ 0870 4007211 📠 0870 4007311
e-mail: reservations.bournemouth@marriotthotels.co.uk
web: www.marriott.co.uk
dir: A338 through Bournemouth. Follow BIC signs to West Cliff Rd. 2nd right into St Michaels Rd. Hotel at end of road on left

Originally built as a row of coastguard cottages, this establishment has expanded over the years into a very elegant and charming hotel. Impeccably maintained throughout, many of the bedrooms have sea views. An excellent range of leisure, business and conference facilities is offered, as well as private dining and banqueting rooms. The hotel also has direct access to the Bournemouth International Centre.

Rooms 141 en suite 19 annexe en suite (22 fmly) ⊛ in 109 bedrooms S £88-£140; D £126-£170 (incl. bkfst) **Facilities** STV 🏊 supervised ⚓ ☆ Sauna Solarium Gym 🏌 Putt green Jacuzzi Wi fi in bedrooms Beautician **Conf** Thtr 350 Class 180 Board 90 Del from £150 **Services** Lift air con **Parking** 92 **Notes** LB ⊛ ⊛ in restaurant Civ Wed 250

★★★★ 75% ⊛ **HOTEL**

De Vere Royal Bath

De Vere
HOTELS & RESORTS

Bath Rd BH1 2EW
☎ 01202 555555 📠 01202 554158
e-mail: royalbath@devere-hotels.com
web: www.devere.co.uk
dir: A338 follow signs for pier & beaches. Hotel on Bath Rd just before Lansdowne rdbt and pier

Overlooking the bay, this well-established seafront hotel is surrounded by beautifully kept gardens. Public rooms, which include lounges, a choice of restaurants and indoor leisure facilities, are of a scale and style befitting the golden era in which the hotel was built. Local attractions include the motor museum at Beaulieu and the Oceanarium. Valet parking is provided for a small charge.

Rooms 140 en suite (16 fmly) (5 GF) S £95-£180; D £105-£190 (incl. bkfst) **Facilities** Spa STV 🏊 supervised Sauna Gym Jacuzzi Beauty salon, Hairdressing Xmas **Conf** Thtr 400 Class 220 Board 100 **Services** Lift **Parking** 70 **Notes** LB ⊛ ⊛ in restaurant Civ Wed 200

BOURNEMOUTH *continued*

★★★ 80%  HOTEL

Best Western Chine Hotel

Boscombe Spa Rd BH5 1AX

☎ 01202 396234 🖹 01202 391737

e-mail: reservations@chinehotel.co.uk

web: www.chinehotel.co.uk

dir: *Follow BIC signs, A338/Wessex Way to St Pauls rdbt. 1st exit - St Pauls Rd to next rdbt, 2nd exit signed Eastcliff/Boscombe/Southbourne. Next rdbt, 1st exit into Christchurch Rd. After 2nd lights, right into Boscombe Spa Rd*

Benefiting from superb views this popular hotel is set in delightful gardens with private access to the seafront and beach. The excellent range of facilities includes an indoor and outdoor pool, a small leisure centre and a selection of meeting rooms. The spacious bedrooms, some with balconies, are well appointed and thoughtfully equipped.

Rooms 65 en suite 22 annexe en suite (13 fmly) ⊘ in 14 bedrooms S £70-£95; D £140-£180 (incl. bkfst) **Facilities Spa** STV FTV 🟥 🟥 pool supervised Sauna Solarium Gym 🟥 Putt green Jacuzzi Wi-fi in bedrooms Games room, Outdoor & indoor children's play area ch fac Xmas **Conf** Thtr 140 Class 70 Board 40 Del from £120 **Services** Lift **Parking** 50 **Notes LB** ⊘ in restaurant Civ Wed 120

See advert on opposite page

★★★ 80% **HOTEL**

Hermitage

Exeter Rd BH2 5AH

☎ 01202 557363 🖹 01202 559173

e-mail: info@hermitage-hotel.co.uk

web: www.hermitage-hotel.co.uk

dir: *A338 Ringwood, left at St. Pauls rdbt, follow signs for BIC and pier. Across bridge. Hotel entrance on right*

Occupying an impressive position overlooking the seafront, at the heart of the town centre, the Hermitage offers friendly and attentive service. The majority of the smart bedrooms are comfortably appointed and all are very well equipped; many rooms have sea views. The wood-panelled lounge provides an elegant and tranquil area, as does the restaurant where well-prepared and interesting dishes are served.

Rooms 63 en suite 11 annexe en suite (9 fmly) (7 GF) ⊘ in all bedrooms **Conf** Thtr 180 Class 60 Board 60 **Services** Lift **Parking** 58 **Notes LB** ⊗ ⊘ in restaurant

★★★ 80% **HOTEL**

Hotel Miramar

East Overcliff Dr, East Cliff BH1 3AL

☎ 01202 556581 🖹 01202 291242

e-mail: sales@miramar-bournemouth.com

web: www.miramar-bournemouth.com

dir: *Wessex Way rdbt turn into St Pauls Rd, right at next rdbt. 3rd exit at next rdbt, 2nd exit at next rdbt into Grove Rd. Hotel car park on right*

Conveniently located on the East Cliff, this Edwardian hotel enjoys glorious sea views. The Miramar was a favoured destination of Tolkien, who often stayed here. Friendly staff and a relaxing environment are keynotes, and the bedrooms are comfortable and well equipped. Spacious public areas and a choice of lounges complete the experience.

Rooms 43 rms (6 fmly) ⊘ in 23 bedrooms S £37-£73; D £75-£185 (incl. bkfst & dinner) **Facilities** FTV 🟥 Xmas **Conf** Thtr 200 Class 50 Board 50 Del from £75 **Services** Lift **Parking** 80 **Notes LB** ⊘ in restaurant Civ Wed 110

★★★ 78% **HOTEL**

Durley Hall Hotel & Spa

Durley Chine Rd, West Cliff BH2 5JS

☎ 01202 751000 🖹 01202 757585

e-mail: Sales@durleyhall.co.uk

web: www.durleyhall.co.uk

dir: *A338 follow signs to West Cliff & BIC*

This attractive, conveniently situated hotel offers a friendly atmosphere and attentive service. In addition to a diverse range of business and conference facilities, guests have access to extensive leisure, beauty and therapy treatments. The smart bedrooms are well designed, comfortable and suited to business and leisure guests alike. The hotel offers a variety of seasonal entertainment.

Rooms 66 en suite 11 annexe en suite (27 fmly) ⊘ in 57 bedrooms S £45-£95; D £90-£190 (incl. bkfst & dinner) **Facilities Spa** STV 🟥 supervised Sauna Gym Jacuzzi Wi-fi available Beauty therapist, aromatherapy, Steam room, Icezone, aromatherapy cave 🟥 Xmas **Conf** Thtr 200 Class 80 Board 35 Del from £76 **Services** Lift **Parking** 150 **Notes LB** ⊗ ⊘ in restaurant Civ Wed 200

★★★ 78%  HOTEL

Langtry Manor - Lovenest of a King

Derby Rd, East Cliff BH1 3QB

☎ 01202 553887 🖹 01202 290115

e-mail: lillie@langtrymanor.com

web: www.langtrymanor.co.uk

dir: *A31/A338, 1st rdbt by rail station turn left. Over next rdbt, 1st left into Knyveton Rd. Hotel opposite*

Retaining a stately air, this property was originally built in 1877 by Edward VII for his mistress, Lillie Langtry. The individually furnished and decorated bedrooms include several with four-poster beds. Enjoyable cuisine is served in the magnificent dining hall, complete with several large Tudor tapestries. There is an Edwardian banquet on Saturday evenings.

Rooms 12 en suite 8 annexe en suite (2 fmly) (3 GF) ⊘ in 4 bedrooms S £79-£99; D £98-£198 (incl. bkfst) **Facilities** STV Wi-fi in bedrooms Free use of local health club 🟥 Xmas **Conf** Thtr 100 Class 60 Board 40 Del from £110 **Parking** 30 **Notes LB** ⊘ in restaurant Civ Wed 100

★★★ 77% HOTEL

Elstead

Knyveton Rd BH1 3QP
☎ 01202 293071 📠 01202 293827
e-mail: info@the-elstead.co.uk
web: www.the-elstead.co.uk

dir: A338 Wessex Way to St Pauls rdbt, left & left again

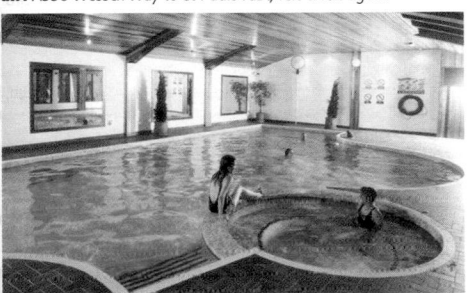

Ideal as a base for both business and leisure travellers, this popular hotel is conveniently located for the town centre, seafront and BIC. An impressive range of facilities is offered, including meeting rooms, an

continued

indoor leisure centre and comfortable lounges. Most bedrooms have been refurbished to a high standard.

Rooms 50 en suite (15 fmly) ⊘ in all bedrooms S £90; D £120 (incl. bkfst & dinner) **Facilities Spa** STV 🔄 supervised Snooker Sauna Gym Steam room, Pool Table, ♫ ch fac Xmas **Conf** BC Thtr 80 Class 60 Board 40 Del from £85 **Services** Lift **Parking** 40 **Notes LB** ⊘ in restaurant

★★★ 75% HOTEL

Carrington House

31 Knyveton Rd BH1 3QQ
☎ 01202 369988 📠 01202 292221
e-mail: carrington.house@forestdale.com
web: www.forestdale.com

dir: A338 at St Paul's rdbt, continue 200mtrs & turn left into Knyveton Rd. Hotel 400mtrs on right

Carrington House occupies a prominent position on a tree-lined avenue and a short walk from the seafront. Bedrooms are generally spacious, comfortable and usefully equipped. In addition to the hotel's bar and restaurant there are extensive conference facilities and a leisure complex.

Rooms 145 en suite (42 fmly) ⊘ in 40 bedrooms **Facilities** STV 🔄 Snooker Purpose built childrens play area Xmas **Conf** Thtr 500 Class 260 Board 80 **Services** Lift **Parking** 85 **Notes** ⊘ in restaurant Civ Wed 60

BOURNEMOUTH *continued*

★★★ 75% **HOTEL**

Hotel Collingwood

11 Priory Rd, West Cliff BH2 5DF
☎ 01202 557575 📠 01202 293219
e-mail: info@hotel-collingwood.co.uk
web: www.hotel-collingwood.co.uk

dir: A338 left at West Cliff sign, over 1st rdbt and left at 2nd rdbt. Hotel 500yds on left

This privately owned and managed hotel is situated close to the BIC. Bedrooms are airy, with the emphasis on comfort. An excellent range of leisure facilities is available and the public areas are spacious and welcoming. Pinks Restaurant offers carefully prepared cuisine and a fixed-price, five-course dinner.

Rooms 53 en suite (16 fmly) (6 GF) ⊘ in 6 bedrooms S £64-£73; D £128-£146 (incl. bkfst & dinner) **Facilities** STV ⟲ supervised Snooker Sauna Solarium Gym Jacuzzi Mini gym, Steam room, Games room ♫ ch fac Xmas **Services** Lift **Parking** 55 **Notes LB** ⊘ in restaurant Closed First 2 weeks of Jan.

★★★ 75% **HOTEL**

Royal Exeter

Exeter Rd BH2 5AG
☎ 01202 438000 📠 01202 789664
e-mail: enquiries@royalexeterhotel.com
web: www.royalexeterhotel.com

dir: opposite Bournemouth International Centre

Ideally located opposite the Bournemouth International Centre, and convenient for the beach and town centre, this busy hotel caters for both business and leisure guests. The public areas are smart, modern with an open-plan lounge bar and restaurant together with an exciting adjoining bar complex.

Rooms 54 en suite (13 fmly) S £50-£90; D £95-£160 (incl. bkfst) **Facilities Spa** STV Sauna Gym Wi-fi available Xmas **Conf** Thtr 100 Class 40 Board 40 Del from £75 **Services** Lift **Parking** 50 **Notes LB** ⊗ ⊘ in restaurant

See advert on opposite page

★★★ 74% **HOTEL**

Best Western Connaught Hotel

West Hill Rd, West Cliff BH2 5PH
☎ 01202 298020 📠 01202 298028
e-mail: sales@theconnaught.co.uk
web: www.theconnaught.co.uk

dir: Follow Town Centre West & BIC signs

Conveniently located on the West Cliff, close to the BIC, beaches and town centre, this privately-owned hotel offers well equipped, neatly decorated rooms, some with balconies. The hotel boasts a very well equipped leisure complex with a large pool and snooker table and

continued

gym. Breakfast and dinner offer imaginative dishes made with quality local ingredients.

Best Western Connaught Hotel

Rooms 56 en suite 33 annexe en suite (10 fmly) ⊘ in 46 bedrooms S £45-£70; D £90-£140 (incl. bkfst) **Facilities Spa** STV FTV ⟲ ⟲ supervised Snooker Sauna Solarium Gym Jacuzzi Wi-fi in bedrooms Xmas **Conf** Thtr 200 Class 60 Board 60 Del from £75 **Services** Lift **Parking** 72 **Notes LB** ⊗ ⊘ in restaurant Civ Wed

★★★ 74% **HOTEL**

The Montague Hotel

Durley Rd South, West Cliff BH2 5JH
☎ 01202 551074 📠 01202 553948
e-mail: enquiries@montaguehotel.co.uk
web: www.montaguehotel.co.uk

dir: A31/A338 to Bournemouth turn left into Cambridge Rd at Bournemouth West rdbt, take 2nd exit at next rdbt into Durley Chine Rd. Next rdbt take 2nd exit. Hotel on right

With its convenient location a short walk from the attractions of the town centre and beaches, this hotel has a busy leisure trade, especially at weekends. The well-equipped bedrooms are especially attractive with good levels of comfort and useful facilities. Guests can unwind by the outdoor pool or in the relaxing bar. The dinner menu offers an interesting selection of dishes.

Rooms 32 en suite (9 fmly) (10 GF) ⊘ in 6 bedrooms S £42-£60; D £64-£99 (incl. bkfst) **Facilities** ⟲ supervised Wi-fi available Xmas **Conf** Thtr 60 Class 12 Board 30 Del from £65 **Services** Lift **Parking** 30 **Notes LB** ⊗ ⊘ in restaurant

★★★ 74% **HOTEL**

Queens

Meyrick Rd, East Cliff BH1 3DL

☎ 01202 554415 ▤ 01202 294810

e-mail: queens@bluemermaidhotels.com

dir: A338 St Paul's rdbt take Holdenhurst Rd. 2nd exit at Lansdown rdbt onto Meyrick Rd

Please note that this establishment has now changed hands. This attractive hotel enjoys a good location near the seafront and is popular for conferences and functions. Public areas include a bar, lounge and a large restaurant. Leisure facilities include indoor pool and small gym. Bedrooms vary in size and style, many have sea views.

Rooms 109 en suite (15 fmly) ⊘ in 40 bedrooms S £39-£69; D £78-£138 (incl. bkfst) **Facilities Spa** ⚲ Snooker Sauna Solarium Gym Jacuzzi Wi-fi in bedrooms Beauty salon, Games Room, Snooker table ♫ ch fac Xmas **Conf** Thtr 220 Class 120 Board 50 Del from £89 **Services** Lift **Parking** 80 **Notes LB** ⊘ in restaurant Civ Wed 120

★★★ 74% **HOTEL**

Wessex

West Cliff Rd BH2 5EU

☎ 01202 551911 ▤ 01202 297354

e-mail: wessex@forestdale.com

web: www.forestdale.com

dir: Follow M27/A35 or A338 from Dorchester & A347 N. Hotel on West Cliff side of town

Centrally located and handy for the beach, the Wessex is a popular, relaxing hotel. Bedrooms vary in size and include premier rooms; all are comfortable, and equipped with a range of modern amenities. There are excellent leisure facilities, ample function rooms and an open-plan bar and lounge.

Rooms 109 en suite (32 fmly) (17 GF) ⊘ in 76 bedrooms S £35-£115; D £140-£310 (incl. bkfst) **Facilities** STV ⚲ ⚲ supervised Snooker Sauna Solarium Gym Wi-fi available Table tennis ch fac Xmas **Conf** Thtr 400 Class 160 Board 160 Del from £85 **Services** Lift **Parking** 160 **Notes LB** ⊘ in restaurant Civ Wed 200

★★★ 73% **HOTEL**

Best Western East Anglia

6 Poole Rd BH2 5QX

☎ 01202 765163 ▤ 01202 752949

e-mail: info@eastangliahotel.com

web: www.eastangliahotel.com

dir: A338 at Bournemouth West rdbt. Follow signs for BIC & West Cliff. At next rdbt right into Poole Rd. Hotel on right

This privately owned and well-managed hotel provides modern accommodation, including ground floor bedrooms. The friendly team of staff offers a warm welcome and attentive service. Public areas include a number of function and conference rooms, ample lounges and an air-conditioned restaurant. There is also an outdoor swimming pool.

Rooms 45 en suite 25 annexe en suite (18 fmly) (10 GF) ⊘ in 23 bedrooms S £60-£64; D £120-£128 (incl. bkfst) **Facilities Spa** STV ⚲ Sauna American Pool Room Xmas **Conf** Thtr 150 Class 75 Board 60 Del from £75 **Services** Lift **Parking** 70 **Notes LB** ⊗ ⊘ in restaurant

★★★ 73% **HOTEL**

Cliffeside

East Overcliff Dr BH1 3AQ

☎ 01202 555724 ▤ 01202 314534

e-mail: cliffeside@bluemermaidhotels.com

dir: M27/A338 approx 7m, then 1st rdbt left into East Cliff

Benefiting from an elevated position on the seafront and just a short walk to town, it is no wonder that this friendly hotel has many returning guests. Bedrooms, many with sea views, and the public areas are attractively appointed. The Atlantic Restaurant offers guests a fixed-price menu.

Rooms 62 en suite (10 fmly) **Facilities** ⚲ Table tennis **Conf** Thtr 180 Class 140 Board 60 **Services** Lift **Parking** 45 **Notes LB** ⊘ in restaurant

★★★ 73% **HOTEL**

The Riviera

Burnaby Rd, Alum Chine BH4 8JF

☎ 01202 763653 ▤ 01202 768422

e-mail: info@rivierabournemouth.co.uk

web: www.rivierabournemouth.co.uk

dir: A338, follow signs to Alum Chine

This hotel offers a range of comfortable, well-furnished bedrooms and bathrooms. Welcoming staff provide efficient service delivered in a friendly manner. In addition to a spacious lounge with regular

continued on page 236

England

BOURNEMOUTH *continued*

entertainment, there is an indoor and an outdoor pool, and all just a short walk from the beach.

Rooms 69 en suite 4 annexe en suite (25 fmly) (11 GF) S £30-£60; D £60-£120 (incl. bkfst) **Facilities** 🕄 ⤵ Sauna Jacuzzi Wi-fi in bedrooms Games room (seasonal) ♫ Xmas **Conf** Thtr 180 Class 120 Board 50 Del from £65 **Services** Lift **Parking** 45 **Notes LB** ⊘ in restaurant Civ Wed 160

★★★ 72% HOTEL

Marsham Court

Russell Cotes Rd, East Cliff BH1 3AB
☎ 01202 552111 📠 01202 294744
e-mail: reservations@marshamcourt.com
web: www.marshamcourt.com

dir: *From Wessex Way take Bournemouth East exit at St Pauls rdbt. Over station rdbt. Follow ringroad, over St Swithuns rdbt. Left with church on left over Meyrick rdbt. Left at St Peters rdbt. Hotel on left*

This hotel is set in attractive gardens with splendid views over the sea and town (as shown above), and is very accessible and convenient for the town and BIC. Bedrooms vary in size, are comfortably appointed and some have sea views. There is a well-stocked bar, lounge areas, terrace and pool, as well as impressive conference rooms.

Rooms 87 en suite (15 fmly) ⊘ in all bedrooms S £65-£100; D £102-£120 (incl. bkfst) **Facilities** STV ⤵ Wi-fi in bedrooms Pool table Xmas **Conf** Thtr 200 Class 100 Board 80 Del from £79 **Services** Lift **Parking** 100 **Notes LB** ⊛ ⊘ in restaurant Civ Wed 200

★★★ 72% HOTEL

Piccadilly

25 Bath Rd BH1 2NN
☎ 01202 552559 & 298024 📠 01202 298235
e-mail: enquiries@hotelpiccadilly.co.uk

dir: *From A338 take 1st exit rdbt, signed East Cliff. 3rd exit at next rdbt signed Lansdowne, 3rd exit at next rdbt into Bath Rd*

This hotel offers a friendly welcome to guests, many of whom return on a regular basis, particularly for the superb ballroom dancing

facilities and small breaks which are a feature here. Bedrooms are smartly decorated, well maintained and comfortable. Dining in the attractive restaurant is always popular and dishes are freshly prepared and appetising.

Rooms 45 en suite (2 fmly) (5 GF) S £85-£90; D £130-£135 (incl. dinner) **Facilities** Xmas **Services** Lift **Parking** 35 **Notes LB** ⊛ ⊘ in restaurant

★★★ 71% HOTEL

Suncliff

29 East Overcliff Dr BH1 3AG
☎ 01202 291711 📠 01202 293788
e-mail: info@suncliffbournemouth.co.uk

dir: *A338 to Bmouth. 1st left at rdbt into St Pauls Rd, follow signs East Cliff*

Enjoying splendid views from the East Cliff and catering mainly for leisure guests, this friendly hotel provides a range of facilities and services. The bedrooms are well equipped and comfortable, and many have sea views. Public areas include a large conservatory, an attractive bar and pleasant lounges. This hotel is under new ownership.

Rooms 94 en suite (29 fmly) (13 GF) **Facilities** 🕄 Squash Snooker Sauna Solarium Gym Jacuzzi Table tennis ♫ **Conf** Thtr 100 Class 70 Board 60 **Services** Lift **Parking** 60 **Notes LB** ⊘ in restaurant Civ Wed 100

★★★ 71% HOTEL

Trouville

Priory Rd BH2 5DH
☎ 01202 552262 📠 01202 293324
e-mail: trouville@younghotels.com

dir: *A338 onto A35, follow signs for BIC*

Located near Bournemouth International Centre, the seafront and the shops, this hotel has the advantage of indoor leisure facilities and a large car park. Bedrooms are generally a good size with comfortable furnishings; there are plenty of family rooms here. The air-conditioned restaurant offers a daily changing menu.

Rooms 77 en suite (21 fmly) S £49.50-£72.50; D £99-£145 (incl. bkfst) **Facilities** 🕄 Sauna Gym Jacuzzi ♫ Xmas **Conf** Thtr 100 Class 45 Board 50 **Services** Lift **Parking** 55 **Notes LB** ⊘ in restaurant

★★★ 70% HOTEL

Anglo Swiss

16 Gervis Rd BH1 3EQ
☎ 01202 554794 📠 01202 299615
e-mail: reservations@angloswisshotel.com

dir: *M27 junct 1, A31 onto A338 to Bournemouth follow signs for East Cliff and seafront. Over 2 rdbts into Gervis Rd. Hotel on right*

Located on the East Cliff, just a short walk from the seafront and local shops and amenities, this is a privately owned hotel. Public areas are contemporary in style and facilities and include a small health club

continued

and spacious function rooms. Bedrooms are comfortable and well furnished.

Anglo Swiss

Rooms 56 en suite 8 annexe en suite (22 fmly) (8 GF) ⊘ in 27 bedrooms S £39-£65; D £59-£120 (incl. bkfst) **Facilities** STV ⊠ supervised Sauna Gym Jacuzzi Wi-fi in bedrooms Xmas **Conf** Thtr 100 Class 60 Board 40 Del from £80 **Services** Lift **Parking** 80 **Notes** LB ⊛ ⊘ in restaurant Civ Wed 120

★★★ 70% **HOTEL**

Bay View Court

35 East Overcliff Dr BH1 3AH
☎ 01202 294449 ⧉ 01202 292883
e-mail: enquiry@bayviewcourt.co.uk
dir: on A338 left at St Pauls rdbt. Over St Swithuns rdbt. Bear left onto Manor Rd, 1st right, next right

This relaxed and friendly hotel enjoys far-reaching sea views from many of the public areas and bedrooms. Bedrooms vary in size and are attractively furnished. There is a choice of south facing lounges and, for the more energetic, an indoor swimming pool. Live entertainment is provided during the evenings.

Rooms 64 en suite (11 fmly) (5 GF) **Facilities** Spa STV ⊠ Snooker Jacuzzi Steam room ♨ **Conf** Thtr 170 Class 85 Board 50 **Services** Lift **Parking** 58 **Notes** LB ⊘ in restaurant

★★★ 70% **HOTEL**

Hinton Firs

Manor Rd, East Cliff BH1 3ET
☎ 01202 555409 ⧉ 01202 299607
e-mail: info@hintonfirshotel.co.uk
dir: A338 turn W at St Paul's rdbt, over next 2 rdbts then fork left to side of church. Hotel on next corner

This hotel is conveniently located on East Cliff, just a short stroll from the sea. Guests are offered leisure facilities including indoor pool and

continued

sauna. There is also a spacious lounge, bar and restaurant in which to relax. The well-appointed bedrooms are light and airy.

Rooms 46 en suite 6 annexe en suite (12 fmly) (6 GF) ⊘ in 26 bedrooms S £45-£64; D £90-£128 (incl. bkfst & dinner) **Facilities** Spa FTV ⊠ ♨ Sauna Games room ♨ ch fac Xmas **Conf** Thtr 50 Class 40 Board 30 Del from £64.50 **Services** Lift **Parking** 40 **Notes** LB ⊛ ⊘ in restaurant

★★★ 68% **HOTEL**

Belvedere

Bath Rd BH1 2EU
☎ 01202 297556 & 293336 ⧉ 01202 294699
e-mail: enquiries@belvedere-hotel.co.uk
web: www.belvedere-hotel.co.uk
dir: from A338 with railway station and Asda on left. At rdbt 1st left then 3rd exit at next 2 rdbts. Hotel on Bath Hill after 4th rdbt

Close to the town centre and the seafront, this friendly, family-run hotel has been extended and includes a small indoor leisure club with beauty treatments and a choice of bars and an attractive restaurant. There is a choice of meeting rooms, which provide an ideal location for conferences or functions.

Rooms 100 en suite (20 fmly) S £58; D from £56 (incl. bkfst) **Facilities** STV ⊠ Sauna Gym Jacuzzi Wi-fi available ♨ Xmas **Conf** Thtr 120 Class 60 Board 50 Del from £79 **Services** Lift **Parking** 90 **Notes** LB ⊛ ⊘ in restaurant

★★★ 68% **HOTEL**

Quality Hotel Bournemouth

47 Gervis Rd, East Cliff BH1 3DD
☎ 01202 316316 ⧉ 01202 316999
e-mail: reservations@qualityhotelbournemouth.com
web: www.qualityhotelbournemouth.com
dir: A338 left at rdbt, right at next rdbt. Take 2nd exit at next rdbt into Meyrick Rd. At next rdbt right into Gervis Rd. Hotel on left

Many years ago this hotel was run by the parents of British comic actor, Tony Hancock, and served as his childhood home. Situated just a short walk from the East Cliff, guests can enjoy the terrace, garden and the indoor heated swimming pool. A lounge menu is available through the day. Bedrooms are comfortable and well equipped.

Rooms 55 en suite (11 fmly) ⊘ in 22 bedrooms S £42-£57; D £84-£114 (incl. bkfst) **Facilities** ⊠ Sauna ch fac Xmas **Conf** Thtr 70 Class 60 Board 35 Del £84.50 **Services** Lift **Parking** 36 **Notes** LB ⊘ in restaurant

★★★ 67% **HOTEL**

Heathlands Hotel

12 Grove Rd, East Cliff BH1 3AY
☎ 01202 553336 ⧉ 01202 555937
e-mail: info@heathlandshotel.com
web: www.heathlandshotel.com
dir: A338 St Pauls rdbt 1st exit to East Cliff, 3rd exit at next rdbt to Holdenhurst Rd, 2nd exit off Lansdowne rdbt into Meyrick Rd. Left into Gervis Rd. Hotel on right

This is a large hotel on the East Cliff benefiting from an outdoor pool in summer and indoor fitness centre all year round. Heathlands is popular with many groups and conferences, public areas are bright

continued on page 238

England

BOURNEMOUTH *continued*

and spacious and the bedrooms offer a range of quality and comfort. Regular live entertainment is provided for guests.

Heathlands Hotel

Rooms 115 en suite (16 fmly) (11 GF) ⊘ in 15 bedrooms **Facilities** STV ✦ Sauna Gym Jacuzzi Health suite ♫ **Conf** Thtr 270 Class 102 Board 54 **Services** Lift **Parking** 100 **Notes** LB ⊘ in restaurant Civ Wed 90

★★★ 67% HOTEL

Ocean View Hotel

East Overcliff Dr BH1 3AR
☎ 01202 558057 ▤ 01202 556285
e-mail: enquiry@oceanview.uk.com

Splendid sea views can be enjoyed from all of the public rooms at this popular East Cliff hotel. Bedrooms vary in size, but all are light, airy and well equipped. A comfortable bar/lounge offers an informal alternative to the drawing room, whilst the spacious restaurant offers a fixed-price menu every evening.

Rooms 52 rms (51 en suite) (13 fmly) **Facilities** ✦ Indoor leisure suite at Bayview Court Hotel (sister hotel) ♫ ch fac **Conf** Thtr 120 Class 100 Board 30 **Services** Lift **Parking** 39 **Notes** LB ⊘ in restaurant Civ Wed 100

★★★ 64% HOTEL

Cumberland

East Overcliff Dr BH1 3AF
☎ 01202 290722 ▤ 01202 311394
e-mail: cumberland@bluemermaidhotels.com

Many of the well-equipped and attractively decorated bedrooms at this hotel benefit from sea views and balconies. The lounges and restaurant are spacious and comfortable. The restaurant offers a daily changing fixed price menu. Guests may use the leisure club at the sister hotel, The Queens.

Rooms 102 en suite (12 fmly) S £49-£79; D £98-£158 (incl. bkfst) **Facilities** ✦ Wi-fi in bedrooms Free membership of nearby Leisure Club in sister hotel ♫ Xmas **Conf** Thtr 120 Class 70 Board 45 Del from £85 **Services** Lift **Parking** 51 **Notes** LB ⊘ in restaurant Civ Wed 100

★★ 74% HOTEL

Maemar

91-95 Westhill Rd, Westcliff BH2 5PQ
☎ 01202 553167 ▤ 01202 297115
e-mail: enquiries@maemarhotel.co.uk

Centrally located and a short walk from the beach the Maemar Hotel offers well appointed comfortable accommodation. There are spacious

continued

lounges and meals are served in the attractive downstairs restaurant.
Rooms 40 en suite (16 fmly) (4 GF) ⊘ in 30 bedrooms **Services** Lift **Notes** ⊘ in restaurant

★★ 72% HOTEL

New Westcliff

27-29 Chine Crescent, West Cliff BH2 5LB
☎ 01202 551926 & 551062 ▤ 01202 315377
e-mail: reservations@newwestcliffhotel.co.uk

dir: off Wessex Way at signs for Westcliff and BIC. Over Poole Road rdbt, continue along Durley Chine Rd, hotel 0.5m right

A warm welcome awaits guests at this privately owned hotel. The bedrooms are of different sizes and are attractively decorated and well equipped. There is a lovely garden and a bowling green as well as three lounges. All-weather leisure facilities, including a small cinema, are a definite plus.

Rooms 55 en suite (16 fmly) (3 GF) ⊘ in 45 bedrooms **Facilities** ✦ Sauna Solarium Jacuzzi Cinema, Bowling Green, Ballroom ♫ **Services** Lift **Parking** 70 **Notes** LB ⊛ ⊘ in restaurant

★★ 71% HOTEL

Arlington

Exeter Park Rd BH2 5BD
☎ 01202 552879 & 553012 ▤ 01202 298317
e-mail: enquiries@arlingtonbournemouth.co.uk

dir: follow BIC signs through Priory Rd, onto rdbt and exit at Royal Exeter Hotel sign. Hotel along Exeter Park Rd

Well-equipped bedrooms and comfortable accommodation along with friendly hospitality are offered at this privately owned and run hotel, now under new ownership. Conveniently located, midway between the square and the pier and ideally situated for the BIC, the Arlington has direct access to the flower gardens, which are overlooked from the hotel's lounge and terrace bar.

Rooms 27 en suite 1 annexe en suite (6 fmly) **Facilities** STV Xmas **Services** Lift **Parking** 21 **Notes** ⊛ No children 2yrs ⊘ in restaurant Closed 4-15 Jan

★★ 71% HOTEL

Bourne Hall Hotel

14 Priory Rd, West Cliff BH2 5DN
☎ 01202 299715 ▤ 01202 552669
e-mail: info@bournehall.co.uk
web: www.bournehall.co.uk

dir: M27/A31 from Ringwood into Bournemouth on A338, Wessex Way. Follow signs to BIC, onto West Cliff. Hotel on right

This friendly, comfortable hotel is conveniently located close to the

continued

Bournemouth International Centre and the seafront. Bedrooms are well equipped, some located on the ground floor and some with sea views. In addition to the spacious lounge, there are two bars and a meeting room. A daily-changing menu is served in the dining room.

Rooms 48 en suite (9 fmly) (5 GF) ⊛ in all bedrooms S £35-£55; D £60-£95 (incl. bkfst) **Facilities** STV FTV Wi-fi available ♫ Xmas **Conf** Thtr 130 Class 60 Board 40 Del from £60 **Services** Lift **Parking** 35 **Notes LB** ⊛ in restaurant

★★ 71% HOTEL

Durley Grange

5 Durley Rd, West Cliff BH2 5JL
☎ 01202 554473 🖷 01202 293774
e-mail: reservations@durleygrange.com
dir: A338/St Michaels rdbt. Over next rdbt, 1st left into Sommerville Rd & right into Durley Rd

Located in a quiet area, with some parking, the town and beaches are all in walking distance of this welcoming and friendly hotel. Bedrooms are brightly decorated, comfortable and well equipped. There is an indoor pool and sauna for year-round use. Enjoyable meals are served in the newly decorated dining room.

Rooms 52 en suite (8 fmly) (4 GF) **Facilities Spa** ⌕ Sauna Jacuzzi ♫ Xmas **Services** Lift **Parking** 35 **Notes** ⊛ in restaurant

★★ 71% HOTEL

Whitehall

Exeter Park Rd BH2 5AX
☎ 01202 554682 🖷 01202 292637
e-mail: reservations@thewhitehallhotel.co.uk
web: www.thewhitehallhotel.co.uk
dir: follow BIC signs then turn into Exeter Park Rd off Exeter Rd

This friendly hotel enjoys an elevated position overlooking the park and is also close to the town centre and seafront. The spacious public areas include a choice of lounges, a cosy bar and a well-presented restaurant. The bedrooms are spread over three floors and are inviting and well equipped.

Rooms 46 en suite (5 fmly) (3 GF) ⊛ in 20 bedrooms **Facilities** ♫ **Conf** Thtr 70 Class 40 Board 32 **Services** Lift **Parking** 25 **Notes LB** ⊛ in restaurant

★★ 68% HOTEL

Ullswater

West Cliff Gardens BH2 5HW
☎ 01202 555181 🖷 01202 317896
e-mail: enquiries@ullswater.uk.com
web: www.ullswater.uk.com
dir: In Bournemouth follow signs to West Cliff. Hotel just off Westcliff Rd

Conveniently situated close to the city centre and seafront, this pleasant hotel enjoys comfortable accommodation and attracts a loyal following. Bedrooms are generously equipped and offer a range of sizes, and the lounge and dining room are spacious and smartly appointed. Cuisine offers a good choice from the daily-changing menu.

Rooms 42 en suite (8 fmly) (2 GF) S £32-£40; D £64-£80 (incl. bkfst) **Facilities** Snooker Wi-fi in bedrooms ♫ Xmas **Conf** Thtr 40 Class 30 Board 24 Del from £55 **Services** Lift **Parking** 10 **Notes LB** ⊛ in restaurant

★★ 65% HOTEL

Cliff Court

15 Westcliff Rd BH2 5EX
☎ 01202 555994 🖷 01202 780954
e-mail: info@cliffcourthotel.com
dir: A338 Wessex Way into Cambridge Rd. Follow Durley Chine Rd into West Cliff Rd

This friendly hotel enjoys easy access to the main approach roads and the seafront, which is only a few minutes' walk away. It is popular with tour groups, and boasts a spacious dining room, a bar and small lounge. The bedrooms, while not the most spacious, do make best use of the available space and are practically furnished.

Rooms 40 en suite (4 fmly) S £28-£48; D £56-£96 (incl. bkfst) **Facilities** STV ♫ Xmas **Services** Lift **Parking** 31 **Notes LB** ⊛ in restaurant

★★ 65% HOTEL

Devon Towers

58-62 St Michael's Rd, West Cliff BH2 5DD
Leisureplex
☎ 01202 553863 🖷 01202 315265
e-mail: devontowers.bournemouth@alfatravel.co.uk
web: www.alfatravel.co.uk
dir: A338 into Bournemouth, follow signs for BIC. Left into St. Michael's Rd at top of hill. Hotel 100mtrs on left

Located in a quiet road within walking distance of the West Cliff and central shops, this hotel appeals to the budget leisure market. The four-course menus offer plenty of choice and entertainment is featured on most evenings. The bar and lobby area provide plenty of space for relaxing.

Rooms 54 en suite (6 GF) ⊛ in all bedrooms S £29-£34; D £48-£58 (incl. bkfst) **Facilities** ♫ Xmas **Services** Lift **Parking** 6 **Notes LB** ⊗ ⊛ in restaurant Closed Jan-mid Feb ex Xmas RS Nov, Feb & Mar

England

BOURNEMOUTH *continued*

★★ 65% HOTEL

Mansfield

West Cliff Gardens, West Cliff BH2 5HL
☎ 01202 552659 ▤ 01202 297115
e-mail: mail@bournemouthhotel.net

dir: A338 to Bournemouth West rdbt, take 1st exit at next rdbt then 2nd exit signed BIC, at next rdbt take 2nd exit into West Cliff Gardens.

A friendly hotel located in a quiet crescent on the West Cliff. Only a short stroll away from the sandy beaches and the many shops and attractions, this is an ideal base for visitors. Perfect as a business base during the week, it will also suit people trying to get 'away from it all' at the weekend.

Rooms 30 en suite (7 fmly) (3 GF) ⊘ in 16 bedrooms S £35-£85; D £49-£99 (incl. bkfst) **Facilities** Xmas **Parking** 12 **Notes LB** ⊘ in restaurant

★★ 64% HOTEL

Aaron Croham Hurst

9 Durley Rd South, West Cliff BH2 5JH
☎ 01202 552353 ▤ 01202 311484
e-mail: crohamhurst.reception@aaron-hotels.com

This friendly hotel, now under new ownership, is popular with individuals and coach parties alike and is conveniently located for the beach and town centre. Bedrooms come in a variety of sizes and styles and all are well equipped. The lounge is also the venue for regular evening entertainment and the restaurant offers traditional home-cooked meals.

Rooms 41 en suite (11 fmly) (8 GF) **Facilities** STV Free use of indoor pool, sauna & jacuzzi at sister hotel, 5 mins walk away ♫ **Services** Lift **Parking** 28 **Notes LB** ⊗ ⊘ in restaurant

★★ Ⓐ

Tower House

West Cliff Gardens BH2 5HP
☎ 01202 290742 ▤ 01202 553305
e-mail: towerhouse.hotel@btconnect.com

dir: A31 onto A338 Wessex Way for 8m, across 1st rdbt, 1st exit 2nd rdbt (signed West Cliff), straight on at 3rd rdbt. At 4th rdbt take 2nd exit into West Cliff Gardens.

Rooms 32 en suite (13 fmly) (3 GF) S £32-£40; D £64-£80 (incl. bkfst) **Facilities** Xmas **Services** Lift **Parking** 32 **Notes LB** ⊘ in restaurant

Ⓤ

Swallow Bournemouth

SWALLOW HOTELS

28 West Cliff Rd BH2 5HE
☎ 01202 557711 ▤ 01202 292815
web: www.swallowhotels.com

At the time of going to press, the star classification for this hotel was not confirmed. Please refer to the AA internet site www.theAA.com for current information.

Rooms 122 en suite

BUDGET HOTEL

Innkeeper's Lodge Bournemouth

Cooper Dean Roundabout, Castle Ln East BH7 7DP
☎ 01202 390837 ▤ 01202 390378
web: www.innkeeperslodge.com

dir: A338 Bournemouth spur road, follow until exit signed Bournemouth Hospital. Hotel on corner next to hospital

Smart, en suite accommodation ideal for both business & leisure guests. Bedrooms are very well equipped, including Sky TV, telephone, modem points, tea & coffee making facilities, (family rooms in most locations). Complimentary breakfast. The adjacent Pub Restaurant; a Harvester, Vintage Inn, Toby Carvery, Ember Inn, Sizzling Pubco or Pub & Carvery offers an all day menu. See Hotel Groups pages for further details.

Rooms 28 en suite S £59.95; D £59.95 **Conf** Thtr 30 Class 22 Board 18

BUDGET HOTEL

Travelodge Bournemouth Central

43 Christchurch Rd BH1 3PA
☎ 08700 1911758
web: www.travelodge.co.uk

dir: Off A35, approaching town centre from Boscombe

Travelodge offers good quality, good value, modern accommodation. Ideal for families, the spacious en suite bedrooms include remote-control TV, tea and coffee-making facilities and comfortable beds. Meals can be taken at the nearby family restaurant. See Hotel Groups pages for further details.

Rooms 107 en suite S fr £26; D fr £26

BRANKSOME

See **Poole**

BRIDPORT   MAP 04 SY49

★★★ 68% HOTEL

Haddon House

West Bay DT6 4EL
☎ 01308 423626 & 425323 ▤ 01308 427348
dir: at Crown Inn rdbt take B3157 West Bay Rd, hotel 0.5m on right at mini-rdbt

This attractive, creeper-clad hotel offers good standards of accommodation and is situated a few minutes' walk from the seafront

continued

and the quay. A friendly and relaxed style of service is provided. An extensive range of dishes, from lighter bar snacks to main meals, is on offer in the Tudor-style restaurant.

Rooms 12 en suite (2 fmly) (1 GF) ⊛ in all bedrooms D £79-£105 (incl. bkfst) **Facilities** Wi-fi in bedrooms Xmas **Conf** Thtr 40 Class 20 Board 26 **Parking** 44 **Notes LB** ⊛ ⊘ in restaurant

★★ 67% HOTEL

Bridge House

THE INDEPENDENTS

115 East St DT6 3LB
☎ 01308 423371 ▤ 01308 459573
e-mail: info@bridgehousebridport.co.uk
dir: follow signs to town centre from A35 rdbt, hotel 200mtrs on right

A short stroll from the town centre, this 18th-century Grade II listed property offers well-equipped bedrooms that vary in size. In addition to the main lounge, there is a small bar-lounge and a separate breakfast room. An interesting range of home-cooked meals is provided in the restaurant.

Rooms 10 en suite (3 fmly) ⊛ in 5 bedrooms S £54-£73; D £79-£99 (incl. bkfst) **Parking** 13 **Notes** ⊘ in restaurant

CHRISTCHURCH   MAP 05 SZ19

★★★ 80% ❀ HOTEL

Best Western Waterford Lodge

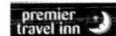

87 Burc Ln, Friars Cliff BH23 4DN
☎ 01425 272948 & 278801 ▤ 01425 279130
e-mail: waterford@bestwestern.co.uk
web: www.waterfordlodge.com
dir: A35 onto A337 towards Highcliffe. Turn right from rdbt signed Mudeford. Hotel 0.5m on left

Peacefully located within easy reach of Christchurch, this welcoming hotel is popular with business guests as well as holidaymakers. It offers attractive, spacious and well-equipped bedrooms, a comfortable bar lounge overlooking the gardens and a pleasant restaurant serving carefully prepared cuisine.

Rooms 18 en suite (2 fmly) (3 GF) ⊛ in 15 bedrooms S £65-£82; D £84-£114 (incl. bkfst) **Facilities** STV Wi-fi in bedrooms Xmas **Conf** Thtr 100 Class 48 Board 36 Del from £110 **Parking** 38 **Notes LB** ⊛ No children 7yrs ⊘ in restaurant

★★★ 77% ❀ HOTEL

The Avonmouth Hotel & Restaurant

95 Mudeford BH23 3NT
☎ 01202 483434 ▤ 01202 479004
e-mail: stay@theavonmouth.co.uk
web: www.theavonmouth.co.uk
dir: on A35 to Christchurch onto A337 to Highcliffe. Right at rdbt, hotel 1.5m on left

In a superb location alongside Mudeford Quay, this friendly hotel offers a variety of bedrooms including smart garden rooms with their own small patios. Several bedrooms in the main house overlook the quay and have private balconies. Modern facilities and decor enhance the overall comfort. Enjoyable cuisine is served in Quays Restaurant.

Rooms 26 en suite 14 annexe en suite (7 fmly) (14 GF) ⊛ in 20 bedrooms S £95-£110; D £138-£190 (incl. bkfst & dinner) **Facilities** STV FTV ✶ ➴ Wi-fi available Xmas **Conf** Thtr 70 Class 20 Board 24 Del from £110 **Parking** 80 **Notes LB** ⊛ ⊘ in restaurant Civ Wed 60

BUDGET HOTEL

Premier Travel Inn Christchurch East

premier travel inn

Somerford Rd BH23 3QG
☎ 08701 977062 ▤ 01202 474939
web: www.premiertravelinn.com
dir: from M27 take A337 to Lyndhurst, then A35 to Christchurch. On B3059 rdbt towards Somerford

High quality, modern budget accommodation ideal for both families and business travellers. Spacious, en suite bedrooms feature bath and shower, satellite TV and many have telephones and modem points. The adjacent family restaurant features a wide and varied menu. For further details consult the Hotel Groups page.

Rooms 70 en suite

Premier Travel Inn Christchurch West

Barrack Rd BH23 2BN
☎ 08701 977063 ▤ 01202 483453
dir: from A338 take A3060 towards Christchurch. Turn left onto A35 Inn on right
Rooms 42 en suite

England

CORFE CASTLE MAP 04 SY98

★★★ 85% ◎ ◎ **HOTEL**

Mortons House

49 East St BH20 5EE

☎ 01929 480988 📠 01929 480820

e-mail: stay@mortonshouse.co.uk

web: www.mortonshouse.co.uk

dir: on A351between Wareham & Swanage

Set in delightful gardens and grounds with excellent views of Corfe Castle, this impressive building dates back to Tudor times. The oak-panelled drawing room has a roaring log fire and an interesting range of enjoyable cuisine is available in the well-appointed dining room. Bedrooms, many with views of the castle, are comfortable and well equipped.

Rooms 14 en suite 7 annexe en suite (2 fmly) (7 GF) ⊘ in all bedrooms S £85-£140; D £129-£225 (incl. bkfst) **Facilities** Jacuzzi Wi-fi available Xmas **Conf** BC Thtr 45 Class 45 Board 20 Del from £119 **Parking** 40 **Notes LB** ⊗ ⊘ in restaurant Civ Wed 60

DORCHESTER MAP 04 SY69

★★★ 71% **HOTEL**

The Wessex Royale

THE INDEPENDENTS

High West St DT1 1UP

☎ 01305 262660 📠 01305 251941

e-mail: info@wessex-royale-hotel.com

web: www.wessex-royale-hotel.com

dir: from A35 turn right at rdbt signed Town Centre. Straight on and hotel at top of hill on left

This centrally situated Georgian townhouse dates from 1756 but has been sympathetically refurbished to combine its historic charm with modern comforts. Durberville's Restaurant is a relaxed location for enjoying innovative food, and the hotel offers the benefit of limited courtyard parking and a smart conservatory ideal for functions.

Rooms 25 en suite 2 annexe en suite (2 fmly) ⊘ in 10 bedrooms S £80-£100; D £100-£150 (incl. bkfst) **Facilities** STV Wi-fi in bedrooms **Conf** Thtr 80 Class 40 Board 40 **Parking** 12 **Notes** ⊗ ⊘ in restaurant Closed 23-30 Dec

★★★ 75% **HOTEL**

Best Western King's Arms

Best Western

30 High East St DT1 1HF

☎ 01305 265353 📠 01305 260269

e-mail: info@kingsarmsdorchester.com

web: www.kingsarmsdorchester.com

dir: In town centre half way along high street.

Previous guests at this 18th-century hotel, set in the very heart of

continued

Dorchester, have included Queen Victoria and John Lennon. Built in 1720, many Georgian features still remain, including beams in the cosy bar. Guests can dine in the bar, or the restaurant which offers a traditional English menu. Bedrooms have suitable facilities, including four with four-posters.

Rooms 35 en suite (4 fmly) (1 GF) ⊘ in all bedrooms S £69; D £69-£99 **Facilities** STV ᛝ **Conf** BC Thtr 100 Class 60 Board 40 Del from £69 **Services** Lift **Parking** 35 **Notes LB** ⊗ ⊘ in restaurant

EVERSHOT MAP 04 ST50

INSPECTORS' CHOICE

★★★★ ◎ ◎ ◎ **COUNTRY HOUSE HOTEL**

Summer Lodge Country House Hotel Restaurant & Spa

RELAIS & CHATEAUX

DT2 0JR

☎ 01935 482000 📠 01935 482040

e-mail: summer@relaischateaux.com

dir: 1m W of A37 halfway between Dorchester and Yeovil

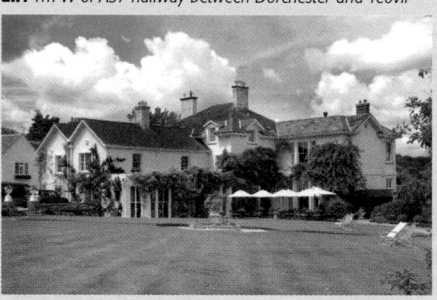

This picturesque hotel is situated in the heart of Dorset and is the ideal retreat for getting away from it all. Try to arrive for afternoon tea or try out the spa and swimming pool. Bedrooms are appointed to a very high standard; all are individually designed and come with a wealth of facilities. Delightful public areas include a sumptuous lounge complete with an open fire and the elegant restaurant where the award-winning cuisine continues to be a high point of any stay.

Rooms 10 en suite 14 annexe en suite (6 fmly) (2 GF) ⊘ in 10 bedrooms S £152.50-£305; D £185-£510 (incl. bkfst) **Facilities Spa** STV ⚄ ᛝ Sauna Solarium Gym ⚄ Jacuzzi Wi-fi in bedrooms spa bicycles Xmas **Conf** Thtr 24 Class 16 Board 16 Del from £265 **Services** air con **Parking** 41 **Notes LB** ⊘ in restaurant Civ Wed 30

FERNDOWN MAP 05 SU00

★★ 72% **HOTEL**

Bridge House

OLD ENGLISH INNS

2 Ringwood Rd, Longham BH22 9AN

☎ 01202 578828 📠 01202 572620

e-mail: 6416@greeneking.co.uk

web: www.oldenglish.co.uk

dir: on A348 towards Poole

The hotel enjoys a unique position overlooking the River Stour and surrounding countryside. In the spacious bar/lounge, a varied menu of popular dishes is offered, a range of lighter options is also available;

continued

the carvery is popular on Sundays. Bedrooms are on both ground and first floor levels, many offering wonderful views across the river.

Rooms 33 en suite (4 fmly) (1 GF) ⊛ in all bedrooms S £55-£65; D £65-£85 (incl. bkfst) **Facilities** Fishing ♫ Xmas **Conf** Thtr 120 Class 60 Board 50 Del from £74.95 **Parking** 300 **Notes LB** ⊛ ⊛ in restaurant Civ Wed 120

BUDGET HOTEL

Premier Travel Inn Bournemouth/Ferndown

premier travel inn ⤵

Ringwood Rd, Tricketts Cross BH22 9BB
☎ 08701 977102 🗎 01202 897794
web: www.premiertravelinn.com
dir: off A348 just before Tricketts Cross rdbt

High quality, modern budget accommodation ideal for both families and business travellers. Spacious, en suite bedrooms feature bath and shower, satellite TV and many have telephones and modem points. The adjacent family restaurant features a wide and varied menu. For further details consult the Hotel Groups page.

Rooms 32 en suite **Conf** Thtr 20

GILLINGHAM
MAP 04 ST82

INSPECTORS' CHOICE

★★★ ◉◉◉ **COUNTRY HOUSE HOTEL**

Stock Hill Country House Hotel & Restaurant

RELAIS & CHATEAUX

Stock Hill SP8 5NR
☎ 01747 823626 🗎 01747 825628
e-mail: reception@stockhillhouse.co.uk
web: www.stockhillhouse.co.uk
dir: 3m E on B3081, off A303

Set in eleven acres, Stock Hill House has an impressive beech-lined driveway and beautiful gardens. The luxurious bedrooms, tastefully furnished with antiques, combine high standards of comfort with modern facilities. Public rooms are delightful in every way with sumptuous fabrics and furnishings. The total tranquillity makes taking tea in front of fires a very enjoyable experience. Accomplished cooking based on top-quality local ingredients shows strong Austrian influences. Nita and Peter Hauser and their team are clearly dedicated to their guests' enjoyment of this lovely small hotel.

Rooms 6 en suite 3 annexe en suite (3 GF) S £145-£165; D £250-£300 (incl. bkfst & dinner) **Facilities** ॐ Sauna ☜ Bird watching, croquet Xmas **Conf** Thtr 12 **Parking** 20 **Notes LB** ⊛ No children 7yrs ⊛ in restaurant

LYME REGIS
MAP 04 SY39

★★★ 75% ◉ **HOTEL**

Alexandra

Pound St DT7 3HZ
☎ 01297 442010 🗎 01297 443229
e-mail: enquiries@hotelalexandra.co.uk
web: www.hotelalexandra.co.uk
dir: from A30, A35, then onto A358, A3052 to Lyme Regis

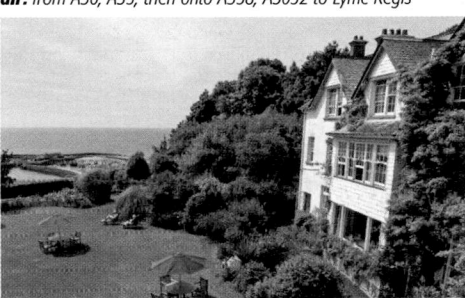

This welcoming, family-run hotel is Grade II listed and dates back to 1735. Public areas are spacious and comfortable, with ample seating areas to relax, unwind and enjoy the magnificent views. The elegant restaurant offers imaginative, innovative dishes. Bedrooms vary in size and shape, decorated with pretty chintz fabrics and attractive furniture.

Rooms 25 en suite 1 annexe en suite (8 fmly) (3 GF) S £60-£130; D £100-£145 (incl. bkfst) **Facilities** ch fac **Parking** 18 **Notes LB** ⊛ in restaurant Closed Xmas & Jan

★★ 81% ◉ **HOTEL**

Swallows Eaves

EX24 6QJ
☎ 01297 553184 🗎 01297 553574
e-mail: swallows_eaves@hotmail.com
web: www.lymeregis.com/swallowseaveshotel

(For full entry see Colyford, Devon)

★★ 74% ◉ **HOTEL**

Mariners Hotel

Silver St DT7 3HS
☎ 01297 442753 🗎 01297 442431
e-mail: marinershotel@btopenworld.com
dir: W of town on A3052, right on B3070

This small, friendly hotel has period character and charm and a relaxed atmosphere. The individually decorated bedrooms are comfortable; some rooms benefit from stunning views over the town to the sea. A beamed bar and choice of lounge is provided for guests, while in the restaurant carefully prepared meals use fresh ingredients, with locally caught fish a highlight on the menus.

Rooms 12 en suite ⊛ in all bedrooms S £40.50-£47; D £81-£94 (incl. bkfst) **Facilities** Xmas **Parking** 20 **Notes** No children 7yrs ⊛ in restaurant Closed 27 Dec-31 Jan

England

LYME REGIS *continued*

★★ 72% ◎◎ **HOTEL**

Dower House
Rousdon DT7 3RB
☎ 01297 21047 📠 01297 24748
e-mail: info@dhhotel.com
web: www.dhhotel.com

(For full entry see Rousdon, Devon)

★★ 65% **HOTEL**

Royal Lion
Broad St DT7 3QF
☎ 01297 445622 📠 01297 445859
e-mail: reception@royallionhotel.fsnet.co.uk
web: www.royallionhotel.com

dir: *From W on A35, take A3052 or from E take B3165 to Lyme Regis. Hotel in centre of town, opp The Fossil Shop. Car park at rear*

This 17th-century, former coaching inn is full of character and charm, and is situated a short walk from the seafront. Bedrooms vary in size; those in the newer wing are more spacious and some have balconies, sea views or a private terrace. In addition to the elegant dining room and guest lounges, many leisure facilities are available.

Rooms 29 en suite (11 fmly) ⊘ in 18 bedrooms **Facilities Spa** 🔲 Snooker Gym Jacuzzi Games room Pool table Table tennis **Conf** Thtr 50 Class 20 Board 20 **Parking** 30 **Notes LB** ⊘ in restaurant

MUDEFORD
See **Christchurch**

POOLE   MAP 04 SZ09

★★★★ 81% ◎◎ **HOTEL**

Harbour Heights
73 Haven Rd, Sandbanks BH13 7PS
☎ 01202 707272 📠 01202 708594
e-mail: enquiries@harbourheights.net
web: www.fjbhotels.co.uk

dir: *Follow signs for Sandbanks, hotel on left after Canford Cliffs*

The unassuming appearance of this hotel belies a wealth of innovation, quality and style. The contemporary bedrooms combine state-of-the-art facilities with traditional comforts. The smart public areas include the Harbar brasserie, popular bars and sitting areas where picture windows accentuate panoramic views of Poole Harbour.

continued

The sun deck is the perfect setting for watching the cross-channel ferries come and go.

Harbour Heights

Rooms 38 en suite (2 fmly) ⊘ in all bedrooms **Facilities** STV Wi-fi available Spa bath in all rooms Xmas **Conf** BC Thtr 70 Class 36 Board 22 Del £175 **Services** Lift air con **Parking** 50 **Notes** ⊗ ⊘ in restaurant Civ Wed 120

See advert on page 233

★★★★ 77% ◎ **HOTEL**

Sandbanks
15 Banks Rd, Sandbanks BH13 7PS
☎ 01202 707377 📠 01202 708885
e-mail: reservations@sandbankshotel.co.uk
web: www.sandbankshotel.co.uk

dir: *A338 from Bournemouth onto Wessex Way, to Liverpool Victoria rdbt. Left and take 2nd exit onto B3965. Hotel on left*

Set on the delightful Sandbanks Peninsula, this well loved hotel has direct access to the blue flag beach and stunning views across Poole Harbour. Most of the spacious bedrooms have sea view, some are air-conditioned. There is an extensive range of leisure facilities, which now include a state-of-the-art crèche.

Rooms 110 en suite (31 fmly) (4 GF) ⊘ in all bedrooms S £65-£121; D £130-£242 (incl. bkfst) **Facilities** STV FTV 🔲 supervised Sauna Solarium Gym Jacuzzi Wi-fi available Sailing, Mntn bikes, kids play area, massage room 🎵 ch fac Xmas **Conf** BC Thtr 150 Class 40 Board 25 Del from £110 **Services** Lift **Parking** 120 **Notes LB** ⊗ ⊘ in restaurant Civ Wed 70

See advert on page 233

★★★★ 73% ◉◉ **HOTEL**

Haven

Banks Rd, Sandbanks BH13 7QL
☎ 01202 707333 📠 01202 708796
e-mail: reservations@havenhotel.co.uk
web: www.havenhotel.co.uk

dir: *B3965 towards Poole Bay, left onto the Peninsula. Hotel 1.5m on left next to Swanage Toll Ferry point*

Enjoying an enviable location at the water's edge with views of Poole Bay, this well established hotel was also the home of radio pioneer, Guglielmo Marconi, during 1898. A friendly team of staff provide good levels of customer care through the range of stylish and comfortable lounge and bar areas. Bedrooms vary in size and style; many have balconies and wonderful sea views. Leisure facilities are noteworthy.

Rooms 78 en suite (4 fmly) S £80-£180; D £160-£360 (incl. bkfst)
Facilities Spa STV FTV 🎾 🏊 Sauna Solarium Gym Jacuzzi Wi-fi in bedrooms Steam room, Hair salon, Health & Beauty suite Xmas **Conf** BC Thtr 160 Class 70 Board 50 Del from £145 **Services** Lift **Parking** 160
Notes LB ⊗ ⊘ in restaurant Civ Wed 100

See advert on page 233

INSPECTORS' CHOICE

★★★ ◉◉ **HOTEL**

Best Western Mansion House

Thames St BH15 1JN
☎ 01202 685666 📠 01202 665709
e-mail: enquiries@themansionhouse.co.uk
web: www.themansionhouse.co.uk

dir: *A31 to Poole, follow channel ferry signs. Left at Poole bridge onto Poole Quay, 1st left into Thames St. Hotel opposite St James Church*

This sophisticated hotel offers friendly hospitality and award-winning cuisine, equalled only by its relaxing charm and elegance.
continued

The comfortably furnished bedrooms are very well equipped with many thoughtful touches. Ideal for business or pleasure, the Mansion House is tucked away off the Old Quay, with the added bonus of parking.

Rooms 32 en suite (2 fmly) (2 GF) ⊘ in 20 bedrooms S £75-£90; D £135-£150 (incl. bkfst) **Facilities** STV Wi-fi in bedrooms facilities available locally Water sports, use of local fitness club Xmas **Conf** Thtr 40 Class 18 Board 20 Del from £150 **Parking** 46
Notes LB ⊗ ⊘ in restaurant Civ Wed 35

★★★ 68% **HOTEL**

Arndale Court

62/66 Wimborne Rd BH15 2BY
☎ 01202 683746 📠 01202 668838
e-mail: info@arndalecourthotel.com
web: www.arndalecourthotel.com

dir: *on A349 close to town centre, opp Poole Stadium*

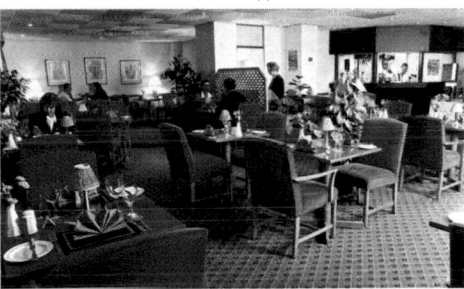

Ideally situated for the town centre and ferry terminal, this is a small, privately owned hotel. Bedrooms are well equipped, pleasantly spacious and comfortable. Particularly well suited to business guests, this hotel has a pleasant range of stylish public areas and good parking.

Rooms 39 en suite (7 fmly) (14 GF) ⊘ in 12 bedrooms S £69-£74; D £84-£89 (incl. bkfst) **Facilities** STV **Conf** Thtr 50 Class 35 Board 35 **Parking** 40 **Notes** ⊘ in restaurant

★★★ 67% **HOTEL**

Salterns

38 Salterns Way, Lilliput BH14 8JR
☎ 01202 707321 📠 01202 707488
e-mail: reception@salterns-hotel.co.uk
web: www.salterns-hotel.co.uk

dir: *in Poole follow B3369 Sandbanks road. 1m at Lilliput shops turn into Salterns Way by Barclays Bank*

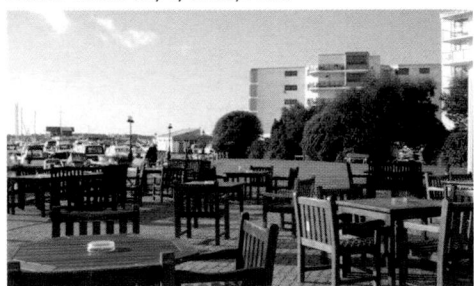

continued on page 246

England

POOLE *continued*

Located next to the marina with superb views across to Brownsea Island, this modernised hotel, now under new ownership, used to be the headquarters for the flying boats in WWII and was later a yacht club. Bedrooms are spacious and some have private balconies, whilst the busy bar and restaurant both share harbour views.

Rooms 20 en suite (4 fmly) ⊘ in 3 bedrooms S £70–£120; D £80–£130 (incl. bkfst & dinner) **Facilities** Xmas **Conf** Thtr 100 Class 50 Board 30 Del from £129.25 **Parking** 80 **Notes LB** ⊘ in restaurant Civ Wed 120

★★★ 64% **HOTEL**

Thistle Poole

THISTLE HOTELS

The Quay BH15 1HD
☎ 0870 333 9143 🖷 0870 333 9243
e-mail: poole@thistle.co.uk
dir: *next to Dolphin Marina.*

Situated on the quayside overlooking the harbour, this modern hotel is situated close to the ferry terminal and is also a good base for exploring the beautiful Dorset countryside. Many of the bedrooms have views of Poole harbour. There is a restaurant and two bars, plus two meeting rooms are available.

Rooms 70 en suite (24 GF) ⊘ in 48 bedrooms **Facilities** STV **Conf** Thtr 180 Class 50 Board 50 **Services** Lift **Parking** 120 **Notes LB** ⊘ in restaurant Civ Wed 80

★★ 65% **HOTEL**

Antelope Inn

OLD ENGLISH INNS

8 High St BH15 1BP
☎ 01202 672029 🖷 01202 678286
e-mail: 6603@greeneking.co.uk
web: www.oldenglish.co.uk

Close to Poole Quay, which is a one of the town's main attractions, this famous coaching inn is the oldest licensed premises in Poole, and has long been a popular meeting point. All rooms are furnished to a high standard with modern facilities, and include some feature rooms. Public areas include a bar, a restaurant, and a quiet area.

Rooms 21 en suite (2 fmly) ⊘ in all bedrooms S £60–£70; D £80–£90 (incl. bkfst) **Facilities** Xmas **Parking** 17 **Notes LB** ⊘ in restaurant

BUDGET HOTEL

Premier Travel Inn Poole Centre (Holes Bay)

Holes Bay Rd BH15 2BD
☎ 08701 977210 🖷 01202 661497
web: www.premiertravelinn.com
dir: *follow Poole Channel Ferry signs, hotel S of A35/A349 on A350 dual carriageway*

High quality, modern budget accommodation ideal for both families and business travellers. Spacious, en suite bedrooms feature bath and shower, satellite TV and many have telephones and modem points. The adjacent family restaurant features a wide and varied menu. For further details consult the Hotel Groups page.

Rooms 62 en suite

Premier Travel Inn Poole North

Cabot Ln BH17 7DA
☎ 0870 9906332 🖷 0870 6606333
dir: *Exit M3 follow signs for M27 (Southampton). M27 becomes A31 towards Bournemouth. Follow Poole/Channel Ferries signs. At Darby's Corner rdbt take 2nd exit. At 2nd lights turn right into Cabot Ln. Inn on right*

Rooms 126 en suite

ST LEONARDS

MAP 05 SU10

★★ 76% **HOTEL**

St Leonards

OLD ENGLISH INNS

Ringwood Rd BH24 2NP
☎ 01425 471220 🖷 01425 480274
e-mail: 9230@greeneking.co.uk
web: www.oldenglish.co.uk
dir: *At end of M27 continue to 1st rdbt. Take next slip road to the left.*

Close to Ringwood and Bournemouth, this hotel has an attractive bar and restaurant offering an extensive menu of popular dishes and children's menu. The spacious bedrooms are furnished to a high standard with modern facilities.

Rooms 35 en suite (5 fmly) (15 GF) ⊘ in all bedrooms S £65; D £80 (incl. bkfst) **Facilities** Xmas **Conf** Thtr 100 Class 40 Board 40 Del from £97.50 **Services** Lift **Parking** 50 **Notes LB** ⊘ in restaurant Civ Wed 60

SANDBANKS

See **Poole**

SHAFTESBURY

MAP 04 ST82

★★★ 72% ⊛ **HOTEL**

Best Western Royal Chase

Royal Chase Roundabout SP7 8DB
☎ 01747 853355 🖷 01747 851969
e-mail: royalchasehotel@btinternet.com
web: www.theroyalchasehotel.co.uk
dir: *A303 to A350 signed Blandford Forum. Avoid town centre, follow road to 3rd rdbt*

Equally suitable for both leisure and business guests, this well-known local landmark is situated close to the famous Gold Hill. Both Standard and Crown bedrooms offer good levels of comfort and quality. In addition to the fixed-price menu in the Byzant Restaurant, guests have the option of eating more informally in the convivial bar.

Rooms 33 en suite (13 fmly) (6 GF) ⊘ in 30 bedrooms S £95–£125; D £110–£185 **Facilities** Spa STV 🏊 Turkish steam bath Xmas **Conf** Thtr 180 Class 90 Board 50 Del from £112.50 **Parking** 100 **Notes LB** ⊘ in restaurant Civ Wed 76

Packed in a hurry?
Ironing facilities should be available at all star levels, either in the rooms or on request

⊛⊛ RESTAURANT WITH ROOMS

La Fleur de Lys Restaurant with Rooms

Bleke St SP7 8AW

☎ 01747 853717 🗎 01747 853130

e-mail: info@lafleurdelys.co.uk

dir: 0.25m off junct of A30 with A350 at Shaftesbury towards town centre

Located just a few minutes' walk from Gold Hill, this light and airy establishment combines efficient service in a relaxed and friendly atmosphere. Bedrooms, which are suitable for both business and leisure guests vary in size but all are well equipped, and deliver homely comfort. A relaxing guest lounge and courtyard are available for afternoon tea or pre-dinner drinks.

Rooms 7 en suite (2 fmly) (1 GF) ⊗ in all bedrooms S £65-£75; D £95-£110 **Facilities** STV **Conf** Board 10 **Parking** 7 **Notes** ⊗ ⊗ in restaurant

SHERBORNE   MAP 04 ST61

★★★ 78% HOTEL

The Grange at Oborne

Oborne DT9 4LA

☎ 01935 813463 🗎 01935 817464

e-mail: reception@thegrange.co.uk

dir: Turn off A30 & follow signs through village

Set in beautiful gardens in a quiet hamlet, this 200-year-old, family run, country-house hotel has a wealth of charm and character. It offers friendly hospitality together with attentive service. Bedrooms are comfortable and tastefully appointed. Public areas are elegantly furnished and the popular restaurant offers a good selection of dishes.

Rooms 18 en suite (3 fmly) (5 GF) ⊗ in all bedrooms S £85; D £100-£140 (incl. bkfst) **Facilities** Guests' own laundry Xmas **Conf** Thtr 80 Class 40 Board 30 **Parking** 45 **Notes LB** ⊗ ⊗ in restaurant Civ Wed 80

★★★ 73% ⊛⊛ HOTEL

Eastbury

Long St DT9 3BY

☎ 01935 813131 🗎 01935 817296

e-mail: enquiries@theeastburyhotel.co.uk

web: www.theeastburyhotel.co.uk

dir: From A30 westbound, left into North Rd, then St Swithins, left at bottom, hotel 800yds on right

Much of the original Georgian charm and elegance is maintained at this smart, comfortable hotel. Just five minutes' stroll from the abbey and close to the town centre, the Eastbury's friendly and attentive staff ensure a relaxed and enjoyable stay. Award-winning cuisine is served in the attractive dining room that overlooks the walled garden.

Rooms 21 en suite (1 fmly) (3 GF) ⊗ in 10 bedrooms **Facilities** STV ⊌ **Conf** Thtr 80 Class 40 Board 28 **Parking** 30 **Notes LB** ⊗ ⊗ in restaurant Civ Wed 80

★★ 65% HOTEL

The Sherborne Hotel

Horsecastles Ln DT9 6BB

☎ 01935 813191 🗎 01935 816493

e-mail: info@sherbornehotel.co.uk

dir: at junction of A30 & A352

This hotel has an attractive setting, within its own grounds, and provides a quiet location. Bedrooms are spacious and well equipped. The open plan lounge and bar area are comfortable, and satellite TV is available in this area. Cuisine offers a good range of choice and the dining room looks out to the garden.

Rooms 60 en suite (24 GF) ⊗ in 30 bedrooms S £45-£55; D from £98 (incl. bkfst) **Facilities** ⊌ Putt green Xmas **Conf** Thtr 80 Class 35 Board 30 Del from £70 **Parking** 100 **Notes LB** ⊗ ⊗ in restaurant

STUDLAND   MAP 05 SZ08

★★ 74% HOTEL

Manor House

BH19 3AU

☎ 01929 450288 🗎 01929 452255

e-mail: themanorhousehotel@lineone.net

web: www.themanorhousehotel.com

dir: A338 from Bournemouth, follow signs to Sandbanks ferry, cross on ferry, then 3m to Studland

Set in 20 acres of attractive grounds and with delightful views overlooking Studland Bay, this elegant hotel provides an impressive range of facilities. Bedrooms, many with excellent sea views, are all

continued on page 248

England

STUDLAND *continued*

well equipped and many retain many charming features of the original Gothic house. In the oak-panelled dining room, carefully prepared meals offer an interesting choice of dishes from the daily- changing menu.

Rooms 18 en suite 3 annexe en suite (9 fmly) (4 GF) S £82-£127 (incl. bkfst & dinner) **Facilities** ❣ ❧ Xmas **Parking** 80 **Notes LB** No children 5yrs ❷ in restaurant

SWANAGE   MAP 05 SZ07

★★★ 73% HOTEL

Purbeck House

91 High St BH19 2LZ

☎ 01929 422872 📠 01929 421194

e-mail: reservations@purbeckhousehotel.co.uk

web: www.purbeckhousehotel.co.uk

dir: A351 to Swanage via Wareham, right into Shore Road, then into Institute Road, right into High Street

Located close to the town centre, this former convent is set in well-tended grounds. The attractive bedrooms are located in the original building and also in an annexe. In addition to a very pleasant and spacious conservatory, the smartly presented public areas have some stunning features, such as painted ceilings, wood panelling and fine tiled floors.

Rooms 18 en suite 20 annexe en suite (5 fmly) (10 GF) ❷ in 10 bedrooms S £63-£72; D £114-£132 (incl. bkfst) **Facilities** STV ❧ Xmas **Conf** Thtr 100 Class 36 Board 25 Del £75 **Parking** 50 **Notes LB** ❽ ❷ in restaurant Civ Wed 100

See advert on opposite page

★★★ 72% HOTEL

Grand

Burlington Rd BH19 1LU

☎ 01929 423353 📠 01929 427068

e-mail: reservations@grandhotelswanage.com

Dating back to 1898, the Grand is located on the Isle of Purbeck and has spectacular views across Swanage Bay and Peveril Point. Bedrooms are individually decorated and well equipped; public rooms offer a number of choices from relaxing lounges to extensive leisure facilities. The hotel also has its own private beach.

Rooms 30 en suite (2 fmly) ❷ in 8 bedrooms **Facilities** STV ❧ supervised Fishing Sauna Solarium Gym Jacuzzi Table tennis Xmas **Conf** Thtr 120 Class 40 Board 40 **Services** Lift **Parking** 15 **Notes** ❽ ❷ in restaurant Closed 10 days in Jan (dates on application) Civ Wed

★★★ 71% HOTEL

The Pines

Burlington Rd BH19 1LT

☎ 01929 425211 📠 01929 422075

e-mail: reservations@pineshotel.co.uk

web: www.pineshotel.co.uk

dir: A351 to seafront, left then 2nd right. Hotel at end of road

Enjoying a peaceful location with spectacular views over the cliffs and sea, The Pines is a pleasant place to stay. Many of the comfortable bedrooms have sea views. Guests can take tea in the lounge, enjoy appetising bar snacks in the attractive bar and interesting and accomplished cuisine in the restaurant.

Rooms 49 en suite (26 fmly) (6 GF) S £58.50-£64.50; D £117-£141 (incl. bkfst) **Facilities** ♬ Xmas **Conf** Thtr 80 Class 80 Board 80 Del from £87.80 **Services** Lift **Parking** 60 **Notes LB** ❷ in restaurant

See advert on opposite page

WAREHAM   MAP 04 SY98

★★★ 72% HOTEL

Springfield Country Hotel & Leisure Club

Grange Rd BH20 5AL

☎ 01929 552177 📠 01929 551862

dir: from Wareham take Stoborough road then 1st right in village to join by-pass. Then left, and immediately right

Suitable for a touring base, this attractive hotel is well located in the heart of Purbeck in extensive grounds. Leisure facilities including both indoor and outdoor pools and conference and business facilities are well-patronised. Bedrooms are a good size.

Rooms 48 en suite (7 fmly) **Facilities** ❏ ⚲ ❣ Squash Snooker Sauna Gym Jacuzzi Steam room Table tennis Beauty treatment ch fac **Conf** Thtr 200 Class 50 Board 60 **Services** Lift **Parking** 150 **Notes LB** ❷ in restaurant

★★★ 70% HOTEL

Worgret Manor

Worgret Rd BH20 6AB

☎ 01929 552957 📠 01929 554804

e-mail: admin@worgretmanorhotel.co.uk

web: www.worgretmanorhotel.co.uk

dir: on A352 from Wareham to Wool, 0.5m from Wareham rdbt

On the edge of Wareham, with easy access to major routes, this privately owned Georgian manor house offers a friendly, cheerful

continued

ambience. The bedrooms come in a variety of sizes. Public rooms are well presented and comprise a popular bar, a quiet lounge and an airy restaurant.

Rooms 12 en suite (1 fmly) (3 GF) ⊗ in all bedrooms S £65; D £100-£110 (incl. bkfst) **Facilities** Free use of local sports centre **Conf** Thtr 50 **Parking** 25 **Notes LB** ⊗ in restaurant

---

★★ 72% ⊛ **COUNTRY HOUSE HOTEL**

Kemps Hotel

East Stoke BH20 6AL

☎ 01929 462563 📠 01929 405287

e-mail: kemps@hollybushhotels.co.uk

web: www.kempshotel.com

dir: midway between Wareham & Wool on A352

This relaxing hotel, now under new ownership, has views to the Purbeck Hills in the distance. Bedrooms, including modern garden rooms are spacious, and there are two comfortable lounges and an adjoining bar. An extensive choice is offered from the imaginative set-price and carte menus; bar meals are available at lunchtime.

Rooms 4 en suite 10 annexe en suite (4 fmly) (8 GF) ⊗ in all bedrooms S £69-£89; D £98-£150 (incl. bkfst) **Facilities** Xmas **Conf** Thtr 100 Class 50 Board 24 **Parking** 50 **Notes LB** ⊗ in restaurant

England

WEST BAY
See **Bridport**

WEST BEXINGTON   MAP 04 SY58

★★ 69% **HOTEL**

The Manor
Beach Rd DT2 9DF
☎ 01308 897616 📠 01308 897704
e-mail: themanorhotel@btconnect.com
dir: B3157 to Burton Bradstock, continue to The Bull public
house in Swire then turn immediately right to West Bexington.

This hotel is something special. Surrounded by scenic splendour and
just a short stroll from the magnificent sweep of Chesil Beach, the
atmosphere is relaxed and welcoming with snug lounges and crackling
wood fires. Bedrooms are individual in style, many with wonderful sea
views and the sound of waves in the background. With an abundance
of excellent local produce, dining here, in either the convivial Cellar
Bar, or the elegant dining room is highly recommended.

Rooms 13 en suite (2 fmly) ⊗ in 1 bedroom S £75-£95; D £120-£125
(incl. bkfst) **Facilities** Xmas **Conf** Thtr 40 Class 40 Board 40 **Parking** 80
Notes ⊗ in restaurant Civ Wed 65

WEST LULWORTH   MAP 04 SY88

★★ 74% **HOTEL**

Cromwell House
Lulworth Cove BH20 5RJ
☎ 01929 400253 & 400332 📠 01929 400566
e-mail: catriona@lulworthcove.co.uk
web: www.lulworthcove.co.uk
dir: 200yds beyond end of West Lulworth village, left onto high
slip road, hotel 100yds on left opposite beach car park

Built in 1881 by the Mayor of Weymouth, specifically as a guest house,
this family-run hotel now provides guests with an ideal base for
touring the area and for exploring the beaches and coast. Cromwell
House enjoys spectacular views across the sea and countryside.
Bedrooms, many with sea views, are comfortable and some have
been specifically designed for family use.

Rooms 17 en suite 3 annexe en suite (3 fmly) (1 GF) ⊗ in 17 bedrooms
S £48-£61.50; D £80-£92 (incl. bkfst) **Facilities** ⚓ Access to Dorset
Coastal footpath & Jurassic Coast **Parking** 17 **Notes LB** ⊗ in restaurant
Closed 22 Dec-3 Jan

WEYMOUTH   MAP 04 SY67

★★★ 75% ◉◉ **HOTEL**

Moonfleet Manor
Fleet DT3 4ED
☎ 01305 786948 📠 01305 774395
web: www.vonessenhotels.co.uk
dir: A354 to Weymouth, right on B3157 to Bridport. At Chickerell
left at mini rdbt to Fleet

This enchanting hideaway, peacefully located at the end of the village
of Fleet, enjoys a wonderful sea-facing position. Children are especially
welcomed throughout the hotel. Many of the well-equipped
bedrooms overlook Chesil Beach and the hotel is furnished with style
and panache, particularly the sumptuous lounges. Accomplished
cuisine is served in the beautiful restaurant.

Rooms 33 en suite 6 annexe en suite (26 fmly) S £128-£180;
D £160-£420 (incl. bkfst & dinner) **Facilities** STV 🏊 supervised ⌣
Squash Snooker Sauna Solarium 🏌 Wi-fi in bedrooms Childrens nursery
Xmas **Conf** Thtr 50 Class 18 Board 26 **Services** Lift **Parking** 50
Notes LB ⊗ in restaurant

★★★ 67% **HOTEL**

Best Western Hotel Prince Regent
139 The Esplanade DT4 7NR
☎ 01305 771313 📠 01305 778100
e-mail: regent@hollybushhotels.co.uk
dir: from A354 follow seafront signs. Left at Jubilee Clock, 0.25m
on seafront

Dating back to 1855, this welcoming resort hotel boasts splendid views
over Weymouth Bay from the majority of public rooms and front-
facing bedrooms. It is conveniently close to the town centre, harbour

continued

and opposite the beach. The restaurant offers a choice of menus, and entertainment is regularly provided in the ballroom during the season.

Rooms 70 en suite (14 fmly) (5 GF) ⊘ in 42 bedrooms S £49-£69; D £59-£135 (incl. bkfst) **Facilities** Wi-fi in bedrooms Use of leisure facilities at sister hotel ♫ Xmas **Conf** Thtr 180 Class 150 Board 150 Del from £99 **Services** Lift **Parking** 21 **Notes** LB ⊗ ⊘ in restaurant Civ Wed 200

★★★ 67% HOTEL

Hotel Rembrandt
12-18 Dorchester Rd DT4 7JU
☎ 01305 764000 ▤ 01305 764022
e-mail: reception@hotelrembrandt.co.uk
web: www.hotelrembrandt.co.uk
dir: 0.75m on left after Manor rdbt on A354 from Dorchester

Only a short distance from the seafront and town centre, this hotel is ideal for visiting local attractions. Facilities include indoor leisure, a bar and extensive meeting rooms. The hotel restaurant offers impressive carvery and carte menu choices and is popular with locals and residents alike.

Rooms 75 en suite (4 fmly) (7 GF) ⊘ in 65 bedrooms S £62.50-£85; D £75-£130 (incl. bkfst) **Facilities** STV ℝ Sauna Solarium Gym Wi-fi in bedrooms Steam room Xmas **Conf** Thtr 200 Class 100 Board 60 Del from £98.50 **Services** Lift **Parking** 80 **Notes** LB ⊘ in restaurant Civ Wed 100

★★★ 67% HOTEL

Hotel Rex
29 The Esplanade DT4 8DN
☎ 01305 760400 ▤ 01305 760500
e-mail: rex@kingshotels.co.uk
web: www.kingshotels.co.uk
dir: on seafront opp Alexandra Gardens

Originally built as the summer residence for the Duke of Clarence, this hotel benefits from a seafront location with stunning views across Weymouth Bay. Bedrooms, some facing the sea, are all well equipped. A wide range of imaginative dishes is served in the popular, vaulted restaurant.

Rooms 31 en suite (5 fmly) S £61-£64; D £80-£112 (incl. bkfst) **Facilities** STV **Conf** Thtr 40 Class 30 Board 25 Del from £80 **Services** Lift **Parking** 6 **Notes** LB ⊗ ⊘ in restaurant Closed Xmas

★★ 71% ⊛ HOTEL

Glenburn
42 Preston Rd DT3 6PZ
☎ 01305 832353 ▤ 01305 835610
e-mail: info@glenburnhotel.com
web: www.glenburnhotel.com
dir: on A353 1.5m E of town centre

This small family-run hotel is located close to the seafront. Offering good parking and attractive gardens, including a complimentary 'Hot Tub', the Glenburn is ideal for either business or leisure guests. Bedrooms are comfortable and well equipped. Good use is made of fresh local produce to create the dishes on the daily changing menu.

Rooms 13 en suite (2 fmly) ⊘ in 8 bedrooms S £35-£50; D £60-£85 (incl. bkfst) **Facilities** Jacuzzi **Conf** Thtr 20 Class 20 Board 15 Del from £75 **Parking** 15 **Notes** LB ⊗ ⊘ in restaurant

★★ 68% HOTEL

Acropolis
53-55 Dorchester Rd DT4 7JI
☎ 01305 784282 ▤ 01305 767172
e-mail: contact@acropolishotel.co.uk

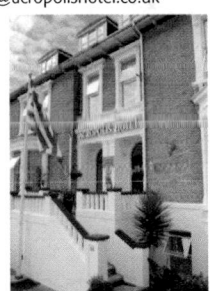

This friendly hotel offers comfortable, stylishly decorated and well-equipped rooms. A pleasant lounge and bar is provided and guests can relax around the pool in warmer months, where vines and olive trees create a reminder of the Mediterranean. Appetising authentic Greek cuisine and wines are served in the restaurant.

Rooms 10 en suite (3 fmly) ⊘ in all bedrooms S £50-£60; D £80-£90 (incl. bkfst) **Facilities** ℝ supervised **Parking** 14

England

WEYMOUTH *continued*

★★ 68% **HOTEL**

Russell
135-13 The Esplanade DT4 7NG
☎ 01305 786059 ▤ 01305 775723
e-mail: russell@hollybushhotels.co.uk
dir: *500yds from Clock Tower on Esplanade*

This hotel offers comfortable and spacious accommodation. It is situated on the seafront so many rooms benefit from magnificent views. With a sister hotel next door, banqueting facilities in a superb ballroom can be offered. Live music and entertainment are also provided.

Rooms 93 en suite (23 GF) ⊘ in 36 bedrooms S £33-£45; D £55-£89 (incl. bkfst) **Facilities** ♫ No ch 18 yrs Xmas **Services** Lift **Parking** 20 **Notes LB** ⊗ No children ⊘ in restaurant

★★ 63% **HOTEL**

Crown
51-53 St Thomas St DT4 8EQ
☎ 01305 760800 ▤ 01305 760300
e-mail: crown@kingshotels.co.uk
web: www.kingshotels.co.uk
dir: *From Dorchester, A354 to Weymouth. Follow Back Water on left & cross 2nd bridge*

This popular hotel is located adjacent to the old harbour and is ideally placed for shopping, the local attractions or transportation links, including the ferry. Public areas include an extensive bar, ballroom and comfortable residents' lounge on the first floor. Themed events, such as mock cruises, are a speciality.

Rooms 86 en suite (14 fmly) ⊘ in 56 bedrooms S £43-£47; D £80-£84 (incl. bkfst) **Facilities** Xmas **Conf** Class 140 Board 80 Del from £80 **Services** Lift **Parking** 14 **Notes LB** ⊗ ⊘ in restaurant Closed 25-26 Dec

BUDGET HOTEL

Premier Travel Inn Weymouth   premier travel inn ➤
Green Hill DT4 7SX
☎ 08701 977267 ▤ 01305 760589
web: www.premiertravelinn.com
dir: *Follow signs to Weymouth, then brown signs to Lodmoor Country Park*

High quality, modern budget accommodation ideal for both families and business travellers. Spacious, en suite bedrooms feature bath and shower, satellite TV and many have telephones and modem points. The adjacent family restaurant features a wide and varied menu. For further details consult the Hotel Groups page.

Rooms 40 en suite

WIMBORNE MINSTER   MAP 05 SZ06

★★ 71% **HOTEL**

Kings Head   OLD ENGLISH INNS
The Square BH21 1JG
☎ 01202 880101 ▤ 01202 881667
e-mail: 6474@greeneking.co.uk
web: www.oldenglish.co.uk
dir: *From A31 Dorchester take B3073 into Wimborne. Follow signs to town centre, hotel in square on left*

Situated in the town square this establishment offers 27 en suite rooms, one with a four poster and a family room. The restaurant specialises in seafood and there is also Laing's Bar that serves bar food and real ales. There are facilities for small meetings and wedding receptions.

Rooms 27 en suite (1 fmly) ⊘ in 20 bedrooms S £65-£75; D £95-£120 (incl. bkfst) **Facilities** Xmas **Conf** Thtr 25 Board 20 **Services** Lift **Parking** 20 **Notes LB** ⊘ in restaurant

CO DURHAM

BARNARD CASTLE   MAP 19 NZ01

★★★ 77% **HOTEL**

The Morritt Arms Hotel & Restaurant
Greta Bridge DL12 9SE
☎ 01833 627232 ▤ 01833 627392
e-mail: relax@themorritt.co.uk
web: www.themorritt.co.uk
dir: *turn off A1 at Scotch Corner onto A66 towards Penrith. Greta Bridge 9m on left*

Set off the main road at Greta Bridge, this 17th-century former coaching house provides comfortable public rooms full of character. The bar, with its interesting Dickensian mural, is very much focused on food, but in addition a fine-dining experience is offered in the oak-panelled restaurant. Bedrooms come in individual styles and varying sizes. The attentive service is noteworthy.

Rooms 27 en suite (3 fmly) (4 GF) ⊘ in 25 bedrooms S £85-£150; D £99-£150 (incl. bkfst) **Facilities** Xmas **Conf** Thtr 200 Class 60 Board 50 Del from £127.50 **Parking** 40 **Notes LB** ⊘ in restaurant Civ Wed 200

★★★ Ⓐ

Jersey Farm Country Hotel
Darlington Rd DL12 8TA
☎ 01833 638223 ▤ 01833 631988
e-mail: enquiries@jerseyfarm.co.uk
web: www.jerseyfarm.co.uk
dir: *On A67 1m E of Barnard Castle*

Rooms 20 rms (11 en suite) (6 fmly) (9 GF) S £61.20-£75; D £95-£120 (incl. bkfst) **Facilities** STV FTV Pool table Xmas **Conf** Thtr 200 Class 80 Board 60 **Parking** 202 **Notes LB** ⊘ in restaurant RS Mondays

BEAMISH   MAP 19 NZ25

★★★ 73% ⊛⊛ HOTEL

Beamish Park

Beamish Burn Rd NE16 5EG

☎ 01207 230666 📠 01207 281260

e-mail: reception@beamish-park-hotel.co.uk

web: www.beamish-park-hotel.co.uk

dir: A1(M)/A692 towards Consett, then A6076 towards Stanley. Hotel on left behind Causey Arch Inn

The Metro Centre, Beamish Museum and south Tyneside are all within striking distance of this modern hotel, set in open countryside alongside its own golf course and floodlit range. Bedrooms, some with their own patios, provide a diverse mix of styles and sizes. The conservatory bistro offers an interesting modern menu.

Rooms 47 en suite (7 fmly) ⊛ in 20 bedrooms S £47.50-£59; D £69.50-£85 **Facilities** STV ♨ 9 Putt green Wi-fi available 20 bay floodlit golf driving range. Golf tuition by PGA professional **Conf** Thtr 50 Class 20 Board 30 Del from £75 **Parking** 100

CHESTER-LE-STREET   MAP 19 NZ25

BUDGET HOTEL

Innkeeper's Lodge Durham North

Church Mouse, Great North Rd, Chester Moor DH2 3RJ

☎ 0191 389 2628

web: www.innkeeperslodge.com

dir: A1(M) junct 63, take A167 S Durham/Chester-Le-Street. Straight on at 3 rdbts, Inn on left

Smart, modern accommodation ideal for both business & leisure guests. Bedrooms are very well equipped, including Sky TV, telephone, modem points, tea & coffee making facilities, (family rooms in most locations). Complimentary breakfast. The adjacent Pub Restaurant, a Harvester, Vintage Inn, Toby Carvery, Ember Inn, Sizzling Pubco or Pub & Carvery offers an all day menu. See Hotel Groups pages for further details.

Rooms 21 en suite S £49.95-£57.95; D £49.95-£57.95

CONSETT   MAP 19 NZ15

Ⓤ

Swallow Derwent Manor

SWALLOW

Allensford DH8 9RR

☎ 01207 592000 📠 01207 502472

e-mail: info@derwent-manor-hotel.com

web: www.derwent-manor-hotel.com

dir: on A68 Darlington to Corbridge road

At the time of going to press, the star classification for this hotel was not confirmed. Please refer to the AA internet site www.theAA.com for current information.

Rooms 48 en suite (3 fmly) ⊛ in 26 bedrooms S £49-£99; D £59-£118 (incl. bkfst) **Facilities** STV ⊠ supervised Sauna Gym Jacuzzi Xmas **Conf** Thtr 300 Class 200 Board 80 Del from £75 **Services** Lift **Parking** 150 **Notes** LB ⊛ in restaurant Civ Wed 300

DARLINGTON   MAP 19 NZ21

★★★ 79% ⊛ HOTEL

Headlam Hall

Headlam, Gainford DL2 3HA

☎ 01325 730238 📠 01325 730790

e-mail: admin@headlamhall.co.uk

web: www.headlamhall.co.uk

dir: 2m N of A67 between Piercebridge and Gainford

This impressive Jacobean hall lies in farmland north-east of Piercebridge which includes a 9-hole golf course. The main house retains many historical features, including flagstone floors and a pillared hall. Bedrooms are well proportioned and traditionally styled. A converted coach house contains the more modern rooms, as well as a conference and leisure centre.

Rooms 19 en suite 15 annexe en suite (4 fmly) (10 GF) ⊛ in all bedrooms S £80-£120; D £100-£150 (incl. bkfst) **Facilities Spa** STV ⊠ ♨ 9 ⊇ Fishing Sauna Gym ⊁ Putt green Jacuzzi Wi-fi in bedrooms **Conf** Thtr 150 Class 40 Board 40 Del from £115 **Services** Lift **Parking** 60 **Notes LB** ⊛ ⊛ in restaurant Closed 24-25 Dec Civ Wed 150

★★★ 75% HOTEL

Walworth Castle Hotel

Walworth DL2 2LY

☎ 01325 485470 📠 01325 462257

e-mail: enquiries@walworthcastle.co.uk

web: www.walworthcastle.co.uk

dir: A1(M) junct 58 follow signs to Corbridge. Left at rdbt, left at The Dog pub. Hotel on left after 1m

This 12th-century castle is privately owned and has been tastefully converted. Accommodation is offered in a range of styles, including an impressive suite and more compact rooms in an adjoining wing. Dinner can be taken in the fine dining Hansards Restaurant or the more relaxed Farmer's Bar. This is a popular venue for conferences and weddings.

Rooms 20 en suite 14 annexe en suite (4 fmly) ⊛ in 6 bedrooms **Facilities** Xmas **Conf** BC Thtr 150 Class 100 Board 80 Del from £105 **Parking** 100 **Notes** ⊛ in restaurant

★★★ 74% HOTEL

Best Western Croft

Croft-on-Tees DL2 2ST

☎ 01325 720319 📠 01325 721252

e-mail: enquiries@croft-hotel.co.uk

web: www.croft-hotel.co.uk

dir: from Darlington take A167 Northallerton road. Hotel 3m S

Set in the village of Croft-on-Tees, this hotel offers smart well-equipped accommodation featuring a series of themed bedrooms reflecting different eras and countries around the world. The

continued on page 254

DARLINGTON *continued*

impressive Raffles Restaurant sports a colonial style and offers an interesting contemporary brasserie menu.

Best Western Croft

Rooms 20 en suite (2 fmly) ⊘ in all bedrooms D £100-£170 (incl. bkfst)
Facilities STV Snooker Sauna Gym Steam room **Conf** Thtr 200
Class 120 Board 50 **Parking** 60 Del £140 **Notes LB** ⊗ ⊘ in restaurant
Civ Wed 150

★★★ 73% ❀ HOTEL

Hall Garth Hotel, Golf and Country Club

*f*olio *Hotels*

Coatham Mundeville DL1 3LU
☎ 0870 6096131 🖺 01325 310083

dir: *A1(M) junct 59, A167 towards Darlington. After 600yds left at top of hill, hotel on right*

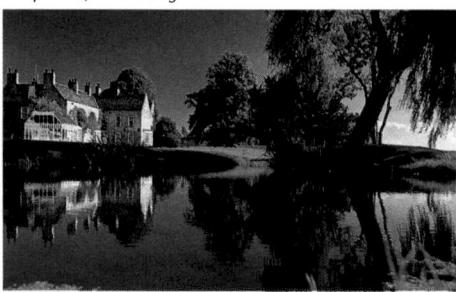

Peacefully situated in grounds that include a golf course, this hotel is just a few minutes from the motorway network. The well-equipped bedrooms come in various styles - its worth asking for the trendy, modern rooms. Public rooms include relaxing lounges, a fine-dining restaurant and a separate pub. The extensive leisure and conference facilities are an important focus here.

Rooms 40 en suite 11 annexe en suite (5 fmly) ⊘ in 31 bedrooms
Facilities STV ♖ ♪9 Sauna Solarium Gym Putt green Jacuzzi Steam room Beauty Salon ♬ **Conf** Thtr 300 Class 120 Board 80 **Parking** 150
Notes LB ⊘ in restaurant Civ Wed 170

★★★ 68% HOTEL

The Blackwell Grange Hotel

c⚬rus *hotels*

Blackwell Grange DL3 8QH
☎ 0870 609 6121 & 01325 509955
🖺 01325 380899
e-mail: blackwellgrange@corushotels.com
web: www.corushotels.com

dir: *on A167, 1.5m from central ring road*

A popular venue for the corporate and wedding market, this fine period mansion is peacefully situated in its own grounds yet convenient for the motorway network. The pick of the bedrooms are in a courtyard building or the impressive feature rooms in the original house. Standard rooms are practical and well equipped.

Rooms 99 en suite 11 annexe en suite (3 fmly) (36 GF) ⊘ in 51 bedrooms S £89-£109; D £89-£109 **Facilities Spa** STV ♖ ♨ Sauna Solarium Gym Jacuzzi Wi-fi in bedrooms Beauty room Xmas
Conf Thtr 300 Class 110 Board 50 Del from £125 **Services** Lift
Parking 250 **Notes LB** ⊘ in restaurant Civ Wed 200

BUDGET HOTEL

Premier Travel Inn Darlington

premier travel inn

Morton Park Way, Morton Park DL1 4PJ
☎ 08701 977300 🖺 01325 373341
web: www.premiertravelinn.com

High quality, modern budget accommodation ideal for both families and business travellers. Spacious, en suite bedrooms feature bath and shower, satellite TV and many have telephones and modem points. The adjacent family restaurant features a wide and varied menu. For further details consult the Hotel Groups page.

Rooms 58 en suite

DURHAM   MAP 19 NZ24

★★★★ 75% HOTEL

Durham Marriott Hotel, Royal County

Marriott HOTELS & RESORTS

Old Elvet DH1 3JN
☎ 0191 386 6821 🖺 0191 386 0704
e-mail: mhrs.xvudm.frontdesk@marriotthotels.com
web: www.marriott.co.ukxvudm

dir: *from A1(M) junct 62, then A690 to Durham, over 1st rdbt, left at 2nd rdbt left at lights, hotel on left*

In a wonderful position on the banks of the River Wear, the hotel's central location makes it ideal for visiting the attractions of this historic city. The building was developed from a series of Jacobean town houses (once owned by the Bowes-Lyon family, ancestors of the late

continued

Queen Mother). Today the hotel offers up-to-date, air-conditioned bedrooms, a choice of restaurants and lounge areas, a gym and swimming pool.

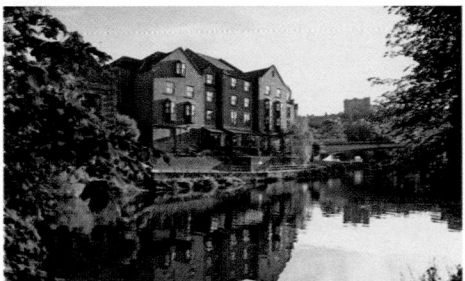

Durham Marriott Hotel, Royal County

Rooms 142 en suite 8 annexe en suite (10 fmly) (15 GF) ❀ in 111 bedrooms S £145-£150; D £155-£165 (incl. bkfst) **Facilities Spa** STV ITV 🔀 supervised Sauna Solarium Gym Jacuzzi Wi-fi available Turkish steam room Plunge pool, tropical fun shower **Conf** Thtr 120 Class 50 Board 50 Del from £145 **Services** Lift **Parking** 76 **Notes LB** ❀ in restaurant Civ Wed 70

★★★ 80% HOTEL

Ramside Hall
Carrville DH1 1TD
☎ 0191 386 5282 📠 0191 386 0399
e-mail: mail@ramsidehallhotel.co.uk
web: www.ramsidehallhotel.co.uk

dir: *from A1(M) junct 62 take A690 to Sunderland. Straight on at lights. 200mtrs after railway bridge turn right*

With its proximity to the motorway and delightful parkland setting, Ramside Hall combines the best of both worlds - convenience and tranquillity. The hotel boasts 27 holes of golf, a choice of lounges, two eating options and two bars. Bedrooms are furnished and decorated to a very high standard and include two very impressive presidential suites.

Rooms 80 en suite (10 fmly) (28 GF) ❀ in 36 bedrooms S £125-£195; D £145-£245 (incl. bkfst) **Facilities** STV ♨ 27 Snooker Sauna Putt green Wi-fi available Steam room Golf academy Driving Range ♬ ch fac **Conf** BC Thtr 400 Class 160 Board 40 Del from £160 **Services** Lift **Parking** 500 **Notes LB** ❀ in restaurant Civ Wed 400

See advert on this page

★★★ 77% HOTEL

BW Whitworth Hall Country Park
Mear DL16 7QX
☎ 01388 811772 📠 01388 818669
e-mail: enquiries@whitworthhall.co.uk

(For full entry see Spennymoor)

★★★ 73% HOTEL

Bowburn Hall
Bowburn DH6 5NH
☎ 0191 377 0311 📠 0191 377 3459
e-mail: info@bowburnhallhotel.co.uk

dir: *towards Bowburn. Right at Cooperage Pub, then 0.5m to junct signed Durham. Hotel on left*

A former country mansion, this hotel lies in five acres of grounds in a residential area, but within easy reach of the A1. The spacious lounge bar and conservatory overlook the gardens and are comfortable and popular venues for both bar and restaurant meals. Bedrooms are not large but are very smartly presented and well equipped.

Rooms 19 en suite **Facilities** STV **Conf** Thtr 150 Class 80 Board 30 Del from £85 **Parking** 100 **Notes** RS 24-26 Dec & 1 Jan Civ Wed 120

England

DURHAM *continued*

U

Swallow Three Tuns

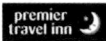

New Elvet DH1 3AQ

☎ 0191 386 4326 📠 0191 386 1406

web: www.swallowhotels.com

dir: A1(M) junct 62 follow city centre signs, over rdbt. Left at next rdbt, over bridge. Hotel past traffic lights on left

At the time of going to press, the star classification for this hotel was not confirmed. Please refer to the AA internet site www.theAA.com for current information.

Rooms 50 en suite

BUDGET HOTEL

Premier Travel Inn Durham East

Broomside Park, Belmont Industrial Estate DH1 1GG

☎ 08701 977084 📠 0191 370 6501

web: www.premiertravelinn.com

dir: from A1(M) junct 62 take A690 west towards Durham. 1st exit, after 1m turn left. Inn on left

High quality, modern budget accommodation ideal for both families and business travellers. Spacious, en suite bedrooms feature bath and shower, satellite TV and many have telephones and modem points. The adjacent family restaurant features a wide and varied menu. For further details consult the Hotel Groups page.

Rooms 40 en suite

Premier Travel Inn Durham North

Adj Arnison Retail Centre, Pity Me DH1 5GB

☎ 08701 977086 📠 0191 383 1166

dir: A1 junct 63, then A167 to Durham. Over 5 rbts and turn left at 6th rbt. Inn is on the right after 200yds

Rooms 60 en suite

BUDGET HOTEL

Travelodge Durham

Station Rd, Gilesgate DH1 1LJ

☎ 08700 850 950 📠 0191 386 5461

web: www.travelodge.co.uk

dir: A1(M) junct 62 onto A690 towards Durham, 1st rdbt, 1st left into Station Rd

Travelodge offers good quality, good value, modern accommodation. Ideal for families, the spacious en suite bedrooms include remote-control TV, tea and coffee-making facilities and comfortable beds. Meals can be taken at the nearby family restaurant. See Hotel Groups pages for further details.

Rooms 57 en suite S fr £26; D fr £26

DURHAM SERVICE AREA (A1(M))

MAP 19 NZ33

BUDGET HOTEL

Premier Travel Inn Durham South

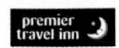

Motorway Service Area, Tursdale Rd, Bowburn DH6 5NP

☎ 08701 977087 📠 0191 377 8722

web: www.premiertravelinn.com

dir: A1(M) junct 61& A177 Bowburn junction

High quality, modern budget accommodation ideal for both families and business travellers. Spacious, en suite bedrooms feature bath and shower, satellite TV and many have telephones and modem points. The adjacent family restaurant features a wide and varied menu. For further details consult the Hotel Groups page.

Rooms 38 en suite **Conf** Thtr 1 Board 10

FIR TREE

MAP 19 NZ13

★★★ 68% **HOTEL**

Helme Park Hall Hotel

DL13 4NW

☎ 01388 730970 📠 01388 731799

e-mail: enquiries@helmeparkhotel.co.uk

web: www.helmeparkhotel.co.uk

dir: 1m N of A689/A68 rdbt between Darlington & Corbridge

Dating back to the 13th century, this welcoming hotel boasts superb panoramic views up the Wear Valley. The bedrooms are comfortably equipped and furnished. The cosy lounge bar is extremely popular for its comprehensive selection of bar meals, and the restaurant offers both table d'hote and carte menus.

Rooms 13 en suite (1 fmly) ⊛ in 5 bedrooms **Facilities** STV FTV Xmas **Conf** BC Thtr 150 Class 80 Board 80 **Parking** 70 **Notes** ⊛ in restaurant Civ Wed 100

HARTLEPOOL

MAP 19 NZ53

BUDGET HOTEL

Premier Travel Inn Hartlepool

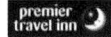

Maritme Av, Hartlepool Marina TS24 0XZ

☎ 08701 977127 📠 01429 233105

web: www.premiertravelinn.com

dir: approx 1m from A689/A179 link road on marina

High quality, modern budget accommodation ideal for both families and business travellers. Spacious, en suite bedrooms feature bath and shower, satellite TV and many have telephones and modem points. The adjacent family restaurant features a wide and varied menu. For further details consult the Hotel Groups page.

Rooms 40 en suite

MIDDLETON-IN-TEESDALE   MAP 18 NY92

★★ 65% **HOTEL**

The Teesdale Hotel

Market Place DL12 0QG

☎ 01833 640264 ▦ 01833 640651

e-mail: john@falconerO.wanadoo.co.uk

dir: *from Barnard Castle take B6278, follow signs for Middleton-in-Teesdale & Highforce. Hotel in town centre*

Located in the heart of the popular village, this family-run hotel offers a relaxed and friendly atmosphere. Bedrooms and bathrooms are well equipped and offer a good standard of quality and comfort. Public areas include a resident's lounge on the first floor, a lounge bar that is also popular with locals, and a spacious restaurant.

Rooms 14 en suite (1 fmly) ⊘ in all bedrooms S fr £42.50; D fr £70 (incl. bkfst) **Facilities** Xmas **Parking** 20 **Notes LB** ⊘ in restaurant

NEWTON AYCLIFFE   MAP 19 NZ22

BUDGET HOTEL

Premier Travel Inn Durham (Newton Aycliffe)

Great North Rd DL5 6JG

☎ 08701 977085 ▦ 01325 324910

web: www.premiertravelinn.com

dir: *on A167 east of Newton Aycliffe, 3 miles from A1 (M)*

High quality, modern budget accommodation ideal for both families and business travellers. Spacious, en suite bedrooms feature bath and shower, satellite TV and many have telephones and modem points. The adjacent family restaurant features a wide and varied menu. For further details consult the Hotel Groups page.

Rooms 44 en suite

PIERCEBRIDGE   MAP 19 NZ21

Ⓤ

Swallow George

SWALLOW
HOTELS

DL2 3SW

☎ 01325 374576 ▦ 01325 374652

e-mail: swallow.piercebridge@swallowhotels.com

web: www.swallowhotels.com

dir: *From A1 take B6275 for 4m, hotel on right.*

At the time of going to press, the star classification for this hotel was not confirmed. Please refer to the AA internet site www.theAA.com for current information.

Rooms 21 en suite 8 annexe en suite (6 fmly) (17 GF) ⊘ in 6 bedrooms S £30-£65; D £40-£90 (incl. bkfst) **Facilities** Fishing Xmas **Conf** Thtr 250 Class 100 Board 80 Del from £99 **Parking** 100 **Notes LB** ⊘ in restaurant Civ Wed 150

REDWORTH   MAP 19 NZ22

★★★★ 75% **HOTEL**

Redworth Hall Hotel

ⓅⓅ
PARAMOUNT
GROUP OF HOTELS

DL5 6NL

☎ 01388 770600 ▦ 01388 770654

e-mail: redworthhall@paramount-hotels.co.uk

web: www.paramount-hotels.co.uk

dir: *from A1(M) junct 58 take A68 signed Corbridge. Follow hotel signs*

This imposing Georgian building includes a health club with state-of-the-art equipment and impressive conference facilities making this a popular destination for business travellers. There are several spacious lounges and two restaurants: the relaxed Conservatory and the intimate 1744 fine-dining option.

Rooms 100 en suite (8 fmly) ⊘ in 45 bedrooms **Facilities** STV 🎱 ⌣ Sauna Solarium Gym 🏊 Jacuzzi Bodysense Health & Beauty Club 🎵 **Conf** Thtr 300 Class 150 Board 100 **Services** Lift **Parking** 300 **Notes LB** Civ Wed

England

ROMALDKIRK
MAP 19 NY92

★★ ◎◎ **HOTEL**

Rose & Crown
DL12 9EB
☎ 01833 650213 📠 01833 650828
e-mail: hotel@rose-and-crown.co.uk
web: www.rose-and-crown.co.uk
dir: 6m NW from Barnard Castle on B6277

This charming country inn is located in the heart of the village, overlooking fine fell scenery. Attractively furnished bedrooms, including suites, are split between the main house and the rear courtyard. There is a cosy bar, warmed by log fires, and a welcoming restaurant. Good local produce features extensively on the menu. Service is both friendly and attentive.

Rooms 7 en suite 5 annexe en suite (1 fmly) ⊗ in all bedrooms S £75; D £126-£140 (incl. bkfst) **Facilities** STV **Parking** 20 **Notes LB** ⊗ in restaurant Closed 24-26 Dec

RUSHYFORD
MAP 19 NZ22

Ⓤ

Swallow Eden Arms
SWALLOW
DL17 0LL
☎ 01388 720541 📠 01388 721871
e-mail: sales.rushyford@swallowhotels.com
web: www.swallowhotels.com
dir: A1(M) junct 60, follow A689 2m to Rushyford rdbt. Hotel clearly visable at 2nd exit

At the time of going to press, the star classification for this hotel was not confirmed. Please refer to the AA internet site www.theAA.com for current information.

Rooms 44 en suite (1 fmly) (5 GF) ⊗ in 24 bedrooms S £50-£90; D £60-£120 (incl. bkfst) **Facilities** Spa 🎿 supervised Sauna Gym Jacuzzi **Conf** Thtr 100 Class 50 Board 40 Del from £75 **Parking** 120 **Notes LB** ⊗ in restaurant Civ Wed 80

SEAHAM
MAP 19 NZ44

★★★★★ ◎◎◎ **HOTEL**

Seaham Hall Hotel
Lord Byron's Walk SR7 7AG
☎ 0191 516 1400 📠 0191 516 1410
e-mail: reservations@seaham-hall.com
web: www.seaham-hall.com
dir: from A19 take B1404 to Seaham. At lights straight over level crossing. Hotel approx 0.25m on right

This imposing house was the setting for Lord Byron's marriage to Annabella Milbanke in 1815. Now restored to its opulent glory, the hotel bedrooms, including some stunning suites, offer cutting edge technology, contemporary artwork and a real sense of style. Bathrooms are particularly lavish, with two-person baths a feature. Public rooms are equally impressive and accomplished cooking is a hallmark. The stunning Oriental Spa, accessed via an underground walkway, offers guests a wide range of treatments plus a Thai brasserie.

Rooms 19 en suite (4 GF) ⊗ in all bedrooms S £195-£575; D £195-£575 (incl. bkfst) **Facilities** Spa STV 🎱 Sauna Solarium Gym Jacuzzi Full spa Xmas **Conf** Thtr 120 Class 48 Board 40 Del from £255 **Services** Lift air con **Parking** 122 **Notes LB** ⊗ ⊗ in restaurant Civ Wed 100

See advert on opposite page

SEDGEFIELD
MAP 19 NZ32

★★★ 79% **HOTEL**

Best Western Hardwick Hall
TS21 2EH
☎ 01740 620253 📠 01740 622771
e-mail: info@hardwickhallhotel.co.uk
dir: off A1(M) junct 60 towards Sedgefield, left at 1st rdbt, hotel 400mtrs on left

Set in extensive parkland, this 18th-century house suits leisure and corporate guests very well. A top conference and function venue, which offers an impressive meeting and banqueting complex. There is a wing of stunning bedrooms to augment those in the original house, two of the main-house rooms have now been refurbished, and many have stunning views over the lake. The modern lounge bar and atmospheric Cellar Bar both offer a relaxed atmosphere.

Rooms 51 en suite (6 fmly) ⊗ in all bedrooms S fr £95; D fr £120 (incl. bkfst) **Facilities** STV Wi-fi in bedrooms **Conf** Thtr 700 Board 80 Del from £125 **Services** Lift **Parking** 200 **Notes** ⊗ ⊗ in restaurant Civ Wed 450

Sometimes hotel inspectors need a break.

Seaham Hall is dripping with so much style and taste, you'll never look back. Dine on incredible food and retire to unrivalled comfort. Connected to the hotel by an underground walkway is The Serenity Spa, a shrine to the Far Eastern principles of relaxation. This is a guide to just how good a hotel can be.

Lord Byron's Walk, Seaham, County Durham, SR7 7AG, United Kingdom.
Tel: +44 (0)191 516 1400 **Fax:** +44 (0)191 516 1410.
Email: reservations@seaham-hall.com **Web:** www.seaham-hall.com

SEAHAM HALL
HOTEL AND SERENITY SPA

★★★★★

England

SEDGEFIELD *continued*

Travelodge Sedgefield
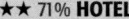
TS21 2JX
☎ 08700 850 950 ▤ 01740 623399
web: www.travelodge.co.uk

dir: on A689, 3m E of A1(M) junct 60

Travelodge offers good quality, good value, modern accommodation. Ideal for families, the spacious en suite bedrooms include remote-control TV, tea and coffee-making facilities and comfortable beds. Meals can be taken at the nearby family restaurant. See Hotel Groups pages for further details.

Rooms 40 en suite S fr £26; D fr £26

SPENNYMOOR   MAP 19 NZ23

★★★ 77% **HOTEL**

BW Whitworth Hall Country Park
Mear DL16 7QX
☎ 01388 811772 ▤ 01388 818669
e-mail: enquiries@whitworthhall.co.uk

dir: A690 to Crook, then follow brown signs

This hotel, peacefully situated in its own grounds in the centre of the deer park, offers comfortable accommodation. Spacious bedrooms, some with excellent views, offer stylish and elegant decor. Public areas include a choice of restaurants and bars, a bright conservatory and well-equipped function and conference rooms.

Rooms 29 en suite (3 fmly) (17 GF) ⊗ in 25 bedrooms S £65-£115; D £85-£135 (incl. bkfst) **Facilities** Fishing Hotel has own deer park ♫ Xmas **Conf** Thtr 100 Class 30 Board 30 Del £140 **Parking** 100 **Notes LB** ⊗ ⊘ in restaurant Civ Wed 120

STOCKTON-ON-TEES   MAP 19 NZ41

★★★ 79% **HOTEL**

Best Western Parkmore Hotel & Leisure Club
636 Yarm Rd, Eaglescliffe TS16 0DH
☎ 01642 786815 ▤ 01642 790485
e-mail: enquiries@parkmorehotel.co.uk
web: www.parkmorehotel.co.uk

dir: off A19 at Crathorne, follow A67 to Yarm. Through Yarm bear right onto A135 to Stockton. Hotel 1m on left

Set in its own gardens, this smart hotel has grown from its Victorian house origins to provide stylish public areas, as well as extensive leisure and conference facilities, including the addition of a hydrotherapy pool. The well-equipped bedrooms include studio rooms, whilst the restaurant offers a varied range of dishes. Service is friendly and obliging.

Rooms 55 en suite (8 fmly) (9 GF) ⊗ in 30 bedrooms S £68-£105; D £86-£118 **Facilities Spa** STV ⬆ supervised Sauna Solarium Gym Jacuzzi Wi-fi in bedrooms Beauty salon Badminton Aerobics studio Hydrotherapy spa **Conf** Thtr 140 Class 40 Board 40 Del from £85 **Parking** 90 **Notes LB** ⊘ in restaurant Civ Wed 150

★★ 71% **HOTEL**

Claireville
519 Yarm Rd, Eaglescliffe TS16 9BG
☎ 01642 780378 ▤ 01642 784109
e-mail: reception@clairevillehotel.com

dir: on A135 adjacent to Eaglescliffe Golf Course, between Stockton-on-Tees and Yarm

A family-run hotel with comfortable bedrooms. There is a cosy bar/lounge and an attractive dining room that offers good value meals. The conservatory to the rear provides a relaxing garden lounge area.

Rooms 18 en suite (2 fmly) ⊗ in 4 bedrooms **Facilities** STV **Conf** Thtr 40 Class 20 Board 25 **Parking** 30 **Notes** ⊘ in restaurant RS Xmas & New Year

Ⓤ

Swallow Stockton
John Walker Square TS18 1AQ
☎ 01642 679721 ▤ 01642 601714
e-mail: reservations.stockton@swallowhotels.com
web: www.swallowhotels.com

dir: From A19 take A66 then A1130, at rdbt take 3rd exit and 1st left into Tower St

At the time of going to press, the star classification for this hotel was not confirmed. Please refer to the AA internet site www.theAA.com for current information.

Rooms 125 en suite (9 fmly) ⊗ in 90 bedrooms S £60-£94; D £90-£124 (incl. bkfst) **Facilities Spa** FTV ⬆ supervised Sauna Solarium Gym Jacuzzi Steam room Xmas **Conf** Thtr 300 Class 200 Board 40 Del from £90 **Services** Lift **Parking** 400 **Notes LB** ⊘ in restaurant Civ Wed 150

Premier Travel Inn Stockton-on-Tees
Yarm Rd TS18 3RT
☎ 08701 977243 ▤ 01642 633339
web: www.premiertravelinn.com

dir: at junct A66/A135

High quality, modern budget accommodation ideal for both families and business travellers. Spacious, en suite bedrooms feature bath and shower, satellite TV and many have telephones and modem points. The adjacent family restaurant features a wide and varied menu. For further details consult the Hotel Groups page.

Rooms 40 en suite

Premier Travel Inn Stockton-on-Tees (Middlesbrough)
Whitewater Way, Thornaby TS17 6QB
☎ 08701 977244 ▤ 01642 671464

dir: A19 take A66 to Stockton/Darlington. Take 1st exit, Teeside Park/Teesdale. Right at lights over viaduct bridge rdbt & Tees Barrage

Rooms 62 en suite

WEST AUCKLAND

★★★ 73% HOTEL

The Manor House Hotel & Country Club

The Green DL14 9HW

☎ 01388 834834 ▤ 01388 833566

e-mail: enquiries@manorhousehotel.net

web: www.manorhousehotel.net

dir: A1(M) junct 58, then A68 to West Auckland. At T-junct turn left, hotel 150yds on right

This historic manor house, dating back to the 14th century, is full of character. Welcoming log fires await guests on cooler evenings. Comfortable bedrooms are individual in design, tastefully furnished and well equipped. The brasserie and Juniper's restaurant both offer an interesting selection of freshly prepared dishes. Well-equipped leisure facilities are available.

Rooms 24 en suite 11 annexe en suite (6 fmly) (2 GF) ⊛ in 20 bedrooms S £48.50-£65; D £77-£105 (incl. bkfst) **Facilities** FTV 🔾 Sauna Solarium Gym Jacuzzi Xmas **Conf** Thtr 100 Class 80 Board 50 **Parking** 200 **Notes LB** ⊛ in restaurant Civ Wed 120

ESSEX

BASILDON **MAP 06 TQ78**

★★★ 72% HOTEL

Chichester

Old London Rd, Wickford SS11 8UE

☎ 01268 560555 ▤ 01268 560580

e-mail: reception@chichester-hotel.com

web: www.chichester-hotel.com

dir: off A129

Set in landscaped gardens and surrounded by farmland, this friendly hotel has been owned and run by the same family for over 25 years. Spacious bedrooms are located around an attractive courtyard; each is pleasantly decorated and thoughtfully equipped. Public rooms include a cosy lounge bar and a smart restaurant.

Rooms 2 en suite 32 annexe en suite (4 fmly) (16 GF) ⊛ in 26 bedrooms S £49.95-£58.95; D £49.95-£67.95 **Facilities** STV Wi-fi in bedrooms **Parking** 150 **Notes LB** ⊛ ⊛ in restaurant

BUDGET HOTEL

Campanile

Pipps Hill, Southend Arterial Rd SS14 3AE

☎ 01268 530810 ▤ 01268 286710

e-mail: basildon@campanile-hotels.com

web: www.envergure.fr

dir: M25 junct 29 Basildon exit, back under A127, then left at rdbt

This modern building offers accommodation in smart, well-equipped bedrooms, all with en suite bathrooms. Refreshments may be taken at the informal Bistro. For further details consult the Hotel Groups page.

Rooms 97 annexe en suite S fr £48.50; D fr £48.50 **Conf** Thtr 35 Class 18 Board 24 Del from £92.25

BUDGET HOTEL

Premier Travel Inn Basildon (East Mayne)

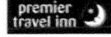

Felmores, East Mayne SS13 1BW

☎ 08701 977026 ▤ 01268 530092

web: www.premiertravelinn.com

dir: M25 junct 29/A127 towards Southend, then A132 towards Basildon

High quality, modern budget accommodation ideal for both families and business travellers. Spacious, en suite bedrooms feature bath and shower, satellite TV and many have telephones and modem points. The adjacent family restaurant features a wide and varied menu. For further details consult the Hotel Groups page.

Rooms 32 en suite

Premier Travel Inn Basildon (Festival Park)

Festival Leisure Park, Pipps Hill Rd South, off Cranes Farm Rd SS14 3WB

☎ 0870 9906598 ▤ 0870 9906599

dir: 9m from M25 junct 29. Follow A127 towards Basildon. Hotel 4m outside Basildon just off A1235

Rooms 64 en suite **Conf** Thtr 20 Class 20 Board 12

Premier Travel Inn Basildon South

High Rd, Fobbing, Stanford le Hope SS17 9NR

☎ 08701 977027 ▤ 01268 581752

dir: From M25 junct 30/31 take A13 towards Southend. Follow A13 for approx 10 miles then at the Five Bells rdbt turn right onto Fobbing High Rd for hotel on left

Rooms 60 en suite **Conf** Thtr 40

England

BASILDON *continued*

BUDGET HOTEL

Travelodge Basildon

Festival Leisure Park, Festival Way SS14 3WB
☎ 08700 850 950 🖷 01268 186559
web: www.travelodge.co.uk

dir: M25 junct 29, A127 follow signs Basildon town centre, onto A176 signed Festival Leisure Park

Travelodge offers good quality, good value, modern accommodation. Ideal for families; the spacious en suite bedrooms include remote-control TV, tea and coffee-making facilities and comfortable beds. Meals can be taken at the nearby family restaurant. See Hotel Groups pages for further details.

Rooms 60 en suite S fr £26; D fr £26

BIRCHANGER GREEN MOTORWAY SERVICE AREA (M11)
MAP 06 TL52

BUDGET HOTEL

Days Inn London Stansted

Birchanger Green, Bishop Stortford
CM23 5QZ
☎ 01279 656477 🖷 01279 656590
e-mail: birchanger.hotel@welcomebreak.co.uk
web: www.welcomebreak.co.uk

DAYS INN

dir: M11 junct 8

This modern building offers accommodation in smart, spacious and well-equipped bedrooms, suitable for families and business travellers, and all with en suite bathrooms. Continental breakfast is available and other refreshments may be taken at the nearby family restaurant. For further details see the Hotel Groups page.

Rooms 60 en suite

BRAINTREE
MAP 07 TL72

★★★ 72% **HOTEL**

White Hart

OLD ENGLISH INNS

Bocking End CM7 9AB
☎ 01376 321401 🖷 01376 552628
web: www.oldenglish.co.uk

dir: off A120 towards town centre. Hotel at junct B1256 & Bocking Causeway

This 18th-century former coaching inn is conveniently located in the heart of the bustling town centre. The smartly appointed public rooms include a large lounge bar, a restaurant and meeting rooms. The pleasantly decorated bedrooms have co-ordinated fabrics and many thoughtful touches.

Rooms 31 en suite (8 fmly) ⊗ in 21 bedrooms **Facilities** STV **Conf** Thtr 40 Class 16 Board 24 **Parking** 52 **Notes LB** ⊗ ⊗ in restaurant

---

BUDGET HOTEL

Premier Travel Inn Braintree

Cressing Rd, Galley's Corner CM7 8GG
☎ 08701 977039 🖷 01376 555087
web: www.premiertravelinn.com

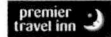

dir: on A120 bypass at Braintree junction of Cressing Rd & Galley's Corner

High quality, modern budget accommodation ideal for both families and business travellers. Spacious, en suite bedrooms feature bath and shower, satellite TV and many have telephones and modem points. The adjacent family restaurant features a wide and varied menu. For further details consult the Hotel Groups page.

Rooms 40 en suite

BRENTWOOD
MAP 06 TQ59

★★★★ 80% ◉ **HOTEL**

Marygreen Manor

London Rd CM14 4NR
☎ 01277 225252 🖷 01277 262809
e-mail: info@marygreenmanor.co.uk
web: www.marygreenmanor.co.uk

dir: M25 junct 28, onto A1023 over 2 sets of lights, hotel on left

A 16th-century house built in 1535 by Robert Wright, who named the house 'Manor of Mary Green' after his young bride. Public rooms exude character and have a wealth of original features that include exposed beams, carved panelling and the impressive Tudors restaurant. There are courtyard bedrooms overlooking the secluded garden and the original Tudor rooms that have four-poster or antique carved beds; plus Brampton Lodge offers further accommodation.

Rooms 4 en suite 52 annexe en suite (35 GF) ⊗ in 24 bedrooms S £135-£197; D £150-£240 **Facilities** STV **Conf** Thtr 50 Class 20 Board 25 Del from £205 **Parking** 100 **Notes** ⊗ ⊗ in restaurant Civ Wed 60

See advert on opposite page

★★★ 74% **HOTEL**

BW Weald Park Hotel, Golf & Country Club

Coxtie Green Rd, South Weald CM14 5RJ
☎ 01277 375101 🖷 01277 374888
e-mail: info@wealdpark.net

Best Western

dir: M25 junct 28 Brentwood, left at 1st traffic lights. Left at T-junct, follow winding road for 1.5m. 2nd turn on right , hotel is 1m on right

Expect a warm welcome at this family-run hotel situated in a peaceful rural location yet just a short drive from the M25 and M11. The spacious, tastefully appointed and well-equipped bedrooms are situated in attractive courtyard-style blocks adjacent to the main building. Public rooms include a first-floor function room, a lounge bar, a stylish restaurant and a conservatory.

Rooms 32 annexe en suite (2 fmly) (25 GF) **Facilities** ⌡ 18 Fishing Putt green **Conf** Thtr 80 Class 40 Board 20 **Parking** 180 **Notes LB** ⊗ ⊗ in restaurant

CHELMSFORD · MAP 06 TL70

★★★ 78% ⊛ HOTEL

Best Western Atlantic

New St CM1 1PP
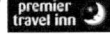
☎ 01245 268168 🖹 01245 268169
e-mail: info@atlantichotel.co.uk

dir: From Chelmsford rail station, left onto Victoria Rd, left at traffic lights into New St, hotel on right

Ideally situated just a short walk from the railway station with its quick links to London, this modern, purpose-built hotel has contemporary-style bedrooms equipped with modern facilities. The open-plan public areas include the popular New Street Brasserie, a lounge bar and a conservatory.

Rooms 59 en suite (3 fmly) (27 GF) ⊛ in 49 bedrooms S £60-£125; D £85-£140 (incl. bkfst) **Facilities** STV Sauna Solarium Gym Steam room ♫ **Conf** Thtr 15 Board 10 **Services** air con **Parking** 60 **Notes** ⊗ ⊛ in restaurant Closed 23 Dec-3 Jan

★★★ 75% HOTEL

County Hotel, Bar & Restaurant

Rainsford Rd CM1 2PZ
☎ 01245 455700 🖹 01245 492762
e-mail: kloftus@countyhotelgroup.co.uk
web: www.countyhotelgroup.co.uk

dir: from town centre, past rail and bus station. Hotel 300yds left beyond lights

Expect a friendly welcome at this popular hotel, which is ideally situated within easy walking distance of the railway station, bus depot and town centre. Public areas include a smart restaurant and the plushly furnished wine bar. The hotel also has a range of meeting rooms and banqueting facilities.

Rooms 54 en suite (2 fmly) (1 GF) ⊛ in 30 bedrooms S £50-£95, D £60-£130 (incl. bkfst) **Facilities** STV Xmas **Conf** Thtr 200 Class 84 Board 64 **Del** £140 **Services** Lift **Parking** 80 **Notes LB** ⊗ ⊛ in restaurant Closed 27-30 Dec Civ Wed 80

★★★ 75% HOTEL

Pontlands Park Country Hotel

West Hanningfield Rd, Great Baddow CM2 8HR
☎ 01245 476444 🖹 01245 478393
e-mail: sales@pontlandsparkhotel.co.uk
web: www.pontlandsparkhotel.co.uk

dir: A12/A130/A1114 to Chelmsford. 1st exit at rdbt, 1st slip road on left. Left towards Gt Baddow, 1st left into West Hanningfield Rd. Hotel 400yds on left

A Victorian country-house hotel situated in a peaceful rural location amidst attractive landscaped grounds. The stylishly furnished bedrooms are generally quite spacious; each is individually decorated and equipped with modern facilities. The elegant public rooms include a tastefully furnished sitting room, a cosy lounge bar, smart conservatory restaurant and an intimate dining room.

Rooms 36 en suite (10 fmly) (12 GF) ⊛ in 15 bedrooms S £105-£125; D £130-£170 **Facilities** Spa FTV ⤢ ⤳ Sauna Gym Jacuzzi Wi-fi in bedrooms Beauty Room **Conf** Thtr 100 Class 20 Board 22 **Del** from £150 **Parking** 100 **Notes LB** ⊗ ⊛ in restaurant Closed 24 Dec-3 Jan (ex 31 Dec) Civ Wed 100

★★★ 73% HOTEL

Best Western Ivy Hill

Writtle Rd, Margaretting CM4 0EH
☎ 01277 353040 🖹 01277 355038
e-mail: sales@ivyhillhotel.co.uk
web: www.ivyhillhotel.co.uk

dir: at top of slip road, off A12

A smartly appointed hotel ideally situated, just off the A12. The spacious bedrooms are tastefully decorated, have co-ordinated fabrics and all the usual facilities. Public rooms include a choice of lounges, a cosy bar, a smart conservatory and the Ivy restaurant, as well as a range of conference and banqueting facilities.

Rooms 33 en suite (5 fmly) (11 GF) ⊛ in 22 bedrooms S £95-£115; D £100-£170 **Facilities** FTV ⬉ Wi-fi in bedrooms **Conf** BC Thtr 80 Class 60 Board 20 **Del** from £130.50 **Parking** 60 **Notes** ⊗ ⊛ in restaurant Civ Wed 100

BUDGET HOTEL

Premier Travel Inn Chelmsford (Borehamwood)

Main Rd, Boreham CM3 3HJ
☎ 0870 9906394 🖹 0870 9906395
web: www.premiertravelinn.com

dir: From M25 junct 28, follow A12 to Colchester then B1137 to Boreham

High quality, modern budget accommodation ideal for both families and business travellers. Spacious, en suite bedrooms feature bath and

continued on page 264

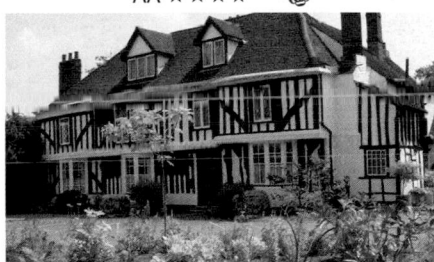

Marygreen Manor Hotel
Pantheon Hotels & Leisure Ltd
AA ★★★★   ⊛

In the warm and friendly atmosphere of this genuine Tudor House, you can enjoy the traditional comfort of open log fires in oak panelled lounges. Accommodation consists of 56 bedrooms including suites. Courtyard garden rooms face into an olde-worlde garden and The Tudor Rooms with authentic period furniture are in the original 16th Century House. Further rooms and suites are situated in a 'Country House' Style Lodge incorporating every modern facility - for the busy executive. The elegant restaurant offers imaginative fresh-produce menus. Twenty-four hour room service, afternoon teas and all day snack menu. You will find us just half a mile from the M25 Junction 28.

London Road, Brentwood, Essex CM14 4NR
Tel: 01277-225252   Fax: 01277-262809
www.marygreenmanor.co.uk

England

CHELMSFORD *continued*

shower, satellite TV and many have telephones and modem points. The adjacent family restaurant features a wide and varied menu. For further details consult the Hotel Groups page.

Rooms 78 en suite

Premier Travel Inn Chelmsford (Springfield)

Chelmsford Service Area, Colchester Rd, Springfield CM2 5PY
☎ 0870 238 3310 ▤ 01245 464010
dir: *on A12 junct 19, Chelmsford bypass, signed Chelmsford Service Area. 2nd service area from A12 on M25*
Rooms 61 en suite

CLACTON-ON-SEA MAP 07 TM11
See also Weeley

★★ 69% HOTEL

Esplanade Hotel

27-29 Marine Pde East CO15 1UU
☎ 01255 220450 ▤ 01255 221800
e-mail: mjs@esplanadehoteluk.com
web: www.esplanadehoteluk.com
dir: *from A133 to Clacton-on-Sea, follow seafront signs. At seafront turn right and hotel on right in 50yds*

Ideally situated on the seafront overlooking the pier and just a short walk from the town centre. Bedrooms vary in size and style: each one is pleasantly decorated and well equipped; some rooms have lovely sea views. Public rooms include a comfortable lounge bar and Coasters Restaurant.

Rooms 29 en suite (2 fmly) (3 GF) ⊘ in 2 bedrooms S £30-£40; D £55-£65 (incl. bkfst) **Facilities** STV Xmas **Conf** BC Thtr 80 Class 50 Board 50 **Parking** 13 **Notes LB** ⊗ ⊘ in restaurant Civ Wed 85

BUDGET HOTEL

Days Inn Clacton-on-Sea

8 Marine Pde West CO15 1RD
☎ 01255 422716 ▤ 01255 426354
e-mail: enquirires@daysinnclacton.com
web: www.welcomebreak.co.uk
dir: *from marine parade turn right at seafront. Hotel just after pier*

This modern building offers accommodation in smart, spacious and well-equipped bedrooms, suitable for families and business travellers, and all with en suite bathrooms. Continental breakfast is available and other refreshments may be taken at the nearby family restaurant. For further details see the Hotel Groups page.

Rooms 50 en suite **Conf** Thtr 250 Class 50 Board 50

COGGESHALL MAP 07 TL82

★★★ 73% HOTEL

White Hart

OLD ENGLISH INNS

Market End CO6 1NH
☎ 01376 561654 ▤ 01376 561789
e-mail: 6529@greeneking.co.uk
web: www.oldenglish.co.uk
dir: *from A12 through Kelvedon & onto B1024 to Coggeshall*

Delightful inn situated in the centre of this bustling market town. Bedrooms vary in size and style; each one offers good quality and comfort with extras such as CD players, fruit and mineral water. The heavily beamed public areas include a popular bar serving a varied menu, a large restaurant offering Italian cuisine and a cosy residents' lounge.

Rooms 18 en suite (1 fmly) **Facilities** STV ♫ ch fac **Conf** Thtr 30 Class 10 Board 22 **Parking** 47

COLCHESTER MAP 13 TL92
See also Earls Colne

★★★★ 77% ⊛⊛ HOTEL

Five Lakes Hotel, Golf, Country Club & Spa

Colchester Rd CM9 8HX
☎ 01621 868888 ▤ 01621 869696
e-mail: enquiries@fivelakes.co.uk
web: www.fivelakes.co.uk
(For full entry see Tolleshunt Knights)

★★★ 77% HOTEL

Best Western Stoke by Nayland Hotel, Golf & Spa

Best Western

Keepers Ln, Leavenheath CO6 4PZ
☎ 01206 262836 ▤ 01206 263356
e-mail: sales@stokebynaylandclub.co.uk
web: www.stokebynaylandclub.co.uk
dir: *off A134 at Leavenheath onto B1068, hotel 0.75m on right*

Situated on the edge of Dedham Vale, in 300 acres of undulating countryside with lakes and two golf courses. The spacious bedrooms

continued

are attractively decorated and equipped with modern facilities, including ISDN lines. Public rooms include the Spikes bar, a conservatory, a lounge, a smart restaurant, conference and banqueting suites and a superb leisure complex with treatment rooms.

Rooms 30 en suite (4 fmly) (15 GF) ⊗ in 22 bedrooms S £60-£109; D £80-£139 (incl. bkfst) **Facilities Spa** STV 🔲 supervised ♨ 36 Fishing Squash Snooker Sauna Solarium Gym Putt green Jacuzzi Wi-fi in bedrooms Health/beauty salon, Driving range Xmas **Conf** Thtr 500 Class 200 Board 60 Del from £125 **Services** Lift **Parking** 300 **Notes LB** ⊗ ⊘ in restaurant Civ Wed 200

★★★ 77% HOTEL

Best Western Rose & Crown

East St CO1 2TZ

☎ 01206 866677 📠 01206 866616

e-mail: info@rose-and-crown.com

web: www.rose-and-crown.com

dir: from A12 follow Rollerworld signs, hotel by level crossing

This delightful coaching inn is situated close to the shops and is full of charm. The character public areas feature a wealth of exposed beams and timbered walls, and The Oak Room restaurant offers an interesting concept - French and Indian fusion cuisine. Although the bedrooms vary in size and style all are pleasantly decorated and equipped with many thoughtful extras.

Rooms 38 en suite (3 fmly) (12 GF) ⊗ in 17 bedrooms S £62.50-£80; D £65-£105 **Facilities** STV Wi-fi in bedrooms Pay for Movie channels Internet/email each room **Conf** Thtr 100 Class 50 Board 45 Del from £140 **Parking** 50 **Notes** ⊗ ⊘ in restaurant Civ Wed 65

Ⓤ

Swallow George

116 High St CO1 1TD

SWALLOW ✦
HOTELS

☎ 01206 578494 📠 01206 761732

web: www.swallowhotels.com

dir: 200yds beyond Town Hall on High Street

At the time of going to press, the star classification for this hotel was not confirmed. Please refer to the AA internet site www.theAA.com for current information.

Rooms 47 en suite **Conf** Thtr 70 Class 30 Board 40

BUDGET HOTEL

Premier Travel Inn Colchester

premier travel inn 🌙

Ipswich Rd CO4 9WP

☎ 08701 977065 📠 01206 751327

web: www.premiertravelinn.com

dir: take A120 (A1232) junct off A12, follow A1232 towards Colchester, Travel Inn on right

High quality, modern budget accommodation ideal for both families and business travellers. Spacious, en suite bedrooms feature bath and shower, satellite TV and many have telephones and modem points. The adjacent family restaurant features a wide and varied menu. For further details consult the Hotel Groups page.

Rooms 40 en suite

DEDHAM   MAP 13 TM03

INSPECTORS' CHOICE

★★★ ◉◉ COUNTRY HOUSE HOTEL

Maison Talbooth

Stratford Rd CO7 6HN

PRIDE OF BRITAIN HOTELS

☎ 01206 322367 📠 01206 322752

e-mail: maison@milsomhotels.co.uk

web: www.milsomhotels.com

dir: A12 towards Ipswich, 1st turning signed Dedham, follow road until left bend, take right turn. Hotel 1m on right

Warm hospitality and quality service are to be expected at this Victorian country-house hotel, which is situated in a peaceful rural location amidst pretty landscaped grounds overlooking the Stour River Valley. Public areas include a comfortable drawing room where guests may take afternoon tea or snacks. Residents are chauffeured to the popular Le Talbooth Restaurant just a mile away for dinner. The spacious bedrooms are individually decorated, tastefully furnished, have lovely co-ordinated fabrics and many thoughtful touches.

Rooms 10 en suite (1 fmly) (5 GF) S £120-£250; D £170-£350 (incl. bkfst) **Facilities** STV ♨ Jacuzzi Garden chess, croquet Xmas **Conf** Thtr 30 Class 20 Board 16 Del from £175 **Parking** 20 **Notes LB** ⊗ ⊘ in restaurant Civ Wed 50

★★★ 73% ◉ HOTEL

milsoms

Stratford Rd, Dedham CO7 6HW

☎ 01206 322795 📠 01206 323689

e-mail: milsoms@milsomhotels.com

web: www.milsomhotels.com

dir: 6m N of Colchester off A12, turn off to Stratford St Mary/Dedham. Turn right over A12, hotel on left

Situated in the Dedham Vale, an Area of Outstanding Natural Beauty,

continued on page 266

England

DEDHAM *continued*

this is the perfect base to explore the countryside on the Essex/Suffolk border. Milsoms is styled along the lines of a contemporary gastro bar, combining good food served in an informal atmosphere, and also providing stylish and well-appointed accommodation.

Rooms 15 en suite (3 fmly) (4 GF) ⊘ in all bedrooms S £80–£100; D £100–£130 **Facilities** STV ♫ Xmas **Conf** Board 14 Del £150 **Parking** 70

EARLS COLNE   MAP 13 TL82
See also Colchester

★★★ 86% ◎◎ **HOTEL**

de Vere Arms
53 High St CO6 2PB
☎ 01787 223353 📄 01787 223365
e-mail: info@deverearms.com
web: www.deverearms.com

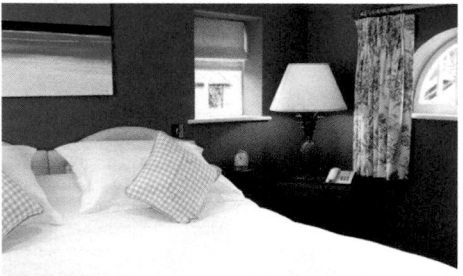

Centrally situated in Earls Colne, a village in the heart of the Colne Valley, this former inn has been transformed into a very stylish small hotel and fine dining restaurant. The open-plan reception/lounge and all the bedrooms have been decorated in vibrant, modern designs with hand-painted murals and original art. Guest comfort is paramount.

Rooms 9 en suite (1 fmly) (1 GF) ⊘ in all bedrooms S £65–£85; D £130–£220 (incl. bkfst) **Facilities** Xmas **Conf** Thtr 40 Board 20 **Parking** 12 **Notes** ⊗ ⊘ in restaurant

EAST HORNDON   MAP 06 TQ68
BUDGET HOTEL

Travelodge Brentwood East Horndon
CM13 3LL
☎ 08700 850 950 📄 01277 810819
web: www.travelodge.co.uk
dir: on A127, eastbound, 4m off M25 junct 29

Travelodge offers good quality, good value, modern accommodation. Ideal for families, the spacious en suite bedrooms include remote-control TV, tea and coffee-making facilities and comfortable beds. Meals can be taken at the nearby family restaurant. See Hotel Groups pages for further details.

Rooms 45 en suite S fr £26; D fr £26

FEERING   MAP 07 TL82
BUDGET HOTEL

Travelodge Colchester Feering
A12 London Rd Northbound CO5 9EL
☎ 08700 850 950 📄 01376 572848
web: www.travelodge.co.uk
dir: northbound carriageway of A12, 0.5m N of Kelvedon

Travelodge offers good quality, good value, modern accommodation. Ideal for families, the spacious en suite bedrooms include remote-control TV, tea and coffee-making facilities and comfortable beds. Meals can be taken at the nearby family restaurant. See Hotel Groups pages for further details.

Rooms 39 en suite S fr £26; D fr £26

GREAT CHESTERFORD   MAP 12 TL54
★★★ 73% ◎ **HOTEL**

The Crown House
CB10 1NY
☎ 01799 530515 📄 01799 530683
e-mail: stay@thecrownhouse.com
web: www.thecrownhousehotel.com
dir: from N exit M11 at junct 9, from S junct 10, follow signs for Saffron Walden & then Great Chesterford (B1383)

This Georgian coaching inn, situated in a peaceful village close to the M11, has been sympathetically restored and retains much original character. The bedrooms are well equipped and individually decorated; some rooms have delightful four-poster beds. Public rooms include an attractive lounge bar, an elegant oak-panelled restaurant and an airy conservatory.

Rooms 8 en suite 14 annexe en suite (2 fmly) (5 GF) S £69.50–£110; D £84.50–£145 (incl. bkfst) **Conf** Thtr 40 Class 12 Board 16 **Parking** 30 **Notes** LB ⊘ in restaurant Civ Wed 60 Closed 27-30 Dec

See advert on opposite page

GREAT DUNMOW   MAP 06 TL62
★★★ 83% ◎◎ **HOTEL**

Starr Restaurant with Rooms
Market Place CM6 1AX
☎ 01371 874321 📄 01371 876337
e-mail: starrrestaurant@btinternet.com
dir: M11 junct 8, onto A120. After 7m, left into Great Dunmow, then left. Hotel in town centre

A delightful 15th-century coaching inn situated in the heart of this bustling Essex village. This establishment is well known locally for its
continued

quality food, which is served in the elegantly appointed beamed restaurant and conservatory. The spacious individually decorated bedrooms are in a converted stable block adjacent to the main building.

Rooms 8 annexe en suite S £80-£95; D £120-£145 (incl. bkfst) **Conf** BC Thtr 36 Board 16 Del from £157.50 **Parking** 16 **Notes** ⊘ in restaurant Closed 26-31 Dec

HALSTEAD
MAP 13 TL83

★★ 69% **HOTEL**

Bull
OLD ENGLISH INNS

Bridge St CO9 1HU
☎ 01787 472144 🖹 01787 472496
e-mail: bull.halstead@oldenglishinns.co.uk
web: www.oldenglish.co.uk
dir: Off A131 at bottom of hill on High St

A charming inn situated in the heart of this bustling town centre between Sudbury and Braintree. Public areas include a large lounge bar, cosy restaurant and meeting rooms. Bedrooms are full of original character; each one is pleasantly decorated and equipped with modern facilities.

Rooms 10 en suite 6 annexe en suite ⊘ in 8 bedrooms S £55-£70; D £65-£85 (incl. bkfst) **Facilities** ᒫᒲ **Conf** Thtr 60 Class 25 Board 30 Del £85 **Parking** 25 **Notes** LB ⊗ ⊘ in restaurant Civ Wed 50

HARLOW
MAP 06 TL41

★★★ 64% **HOTEL**

The Green Man

Mulberry Green, Old Harlow CM17 0ET
☎ 0870 609 6146 🖹 01279 626113

dir: M11 junct 7 onto A414. Right at 4th rdbt then left into Mulberry Green, hotel on left

This popular coaching inn, dating back to the 14th century, is situated just a short drive from the town centre. The busy lounge bar proves popular, and there is also a brasserie-style restaurant offering both carte and daily changing menus. Modern, well-equipped bedrooms are located to the rear of the property.

Rooms 55 annexe en suite (14 GF) ⊘ in 27 bedrooms S £49-£94; D £49-£94 **Facilities** Wi-fi available Xmas **Conf** Thtr 60 Class 26 Board 30 Del from £99 **Parking** 75 **Notes** LB ⊘ in restaurant Civ Wed 100

[U]

Swallow Churchgate
SWALLOW

Churchgate St Village, Old Harlow CM17 0JT
☎ 01279 420246 🖹 01279 437720
e-mail: swallow.oldharlow@swallowhotels.com
web: www.swallowhotels.com

dir: Exit M11 junct 7 for Harlow. Right at 4th rdbt on B183, follow signs for Churchgate St. Right at junct and through village, hotel on right at bottom of hill

At the time of going to press, the star classification for this hotel was

continued on page 268

England

HARLOW *continued*

not confirmed. Please refer to the AA internet site www.theAA.com for current information.

Rooms 85 en suite (14 fmly) (40 GF) ⊘ in 60 bedrooms S £50-£110; D £84-£120 (incl. bkfst) **Facilities** STV ⊡ supervised Sauna Solarium Gym Jacuzzi Xmas **Conf** Thtr 150 Class 80 Board 45 Del from £115 **Parking** 80 **Notes** ⊗ ⊘ in restaurant Civ Wed 100

BUDGET HOTEL

Premier Travel Inn Harlow

Cambridge Rd CM20 2EP

☎ 08701 977125 📠 01279 452169

web: www.premiertravelinn.com

dir: *M11 junct 7, off A414 on Sawbridgeworth to Bishop's Stortford rd (A1184)*

High quality, modern budget accommodation ideal for both families and business travellers. Spacious, en suite bedrooms feature bath and shower, satellite TV and many have telephones and modem points. The adjacent family restaurant features a wide and varied menu. For further details consult the Hotel Groups page.

Rooms 61 en suite

BUDGET HOTEL

Travelodge Harlow

Burnt Mill CM20 2JE

☎ 08700 850950 📠 01279 437 349

web: www.travelodge.co.uk

dir: *From M11 junct 7 follow A414 E towards Hertford. The hotel is on the left.*

Travelodge offers good quality, good value, modern accommodation. Ideal for families, the spacious en suite bedrooms include remote-control TV, tea and coffee-making facilities and comfortable beds. Meals can be taken at the nearby family restaurant. See Hotel Groups pages for further details.

Rooms 90 en suite S fr £26; D fr £26

Travelodge Harlow North Weald

A414 Eastbound, Tylers Green, North Weald CM16 6BJ

☎ 08700 850 950 📠 01992 523276

dir: *M11 junct 7, take A414 towards Chelmsford, after 2nd rdbt on left*

Rooms 60 en suite S fr £26; D fr £26

HARWICH   MAP 13 TM23

★★★ 83% ⍟⍟ HOTEL

The Pier at Harwich

The Quay CO12 3HH

☎ 01255 241212 📠 01255 551922

e-mail: pier@milsomhotels.com

web: www.milsomhotels.co.uk

dir: *from A12, take A120 to Quay. Hotel opposite lifeboat station*

Situated on the quay, overlooking the ports of Harwich and Felixstowe. The bedrooms are tastefully decorated, thoughtfully equipped, and furnished in a contemporary style; many rooms have superb sea views. The newly refurbished public rooms include an informal bistro, the Harbour restaurant, a smart lounge bar and a plush residents' lounge.

continued

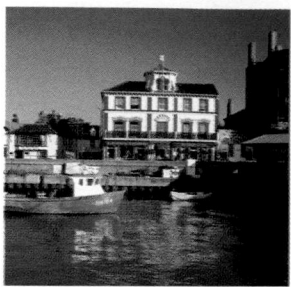

The Pier at Harwich

Rooms 7 en suite   7 annexe en suite (5 fmly) (1 GF) **Facilities** STV Xmas **Conf** Thtr 50 Class 50 Board 24 Del from £140 **Parking** 10 **Notes** ⊗ ⊘ in restaurant Civ Wed 50

★★ 72% HOTEL

Cliff

Marine Pde, Dovercourt CO12 3RE

☎ 01255 503345 & 507373 📠 01255 240358

e-mail: reception@cliffhotelharwich.fsnet.co.uk

web: www.thecliffhotelharwich.co.uk

dir: *A120 to Parkeston rdbt, take road to Dovercourt, on seafront after Dovercourt town centre*

Conveniently situated on the seafront close to the railway station and ferry terminal. Public rooms are smartly appointed and include the Shade Bar, a comfortable lounge, a restaurant and the Marine Bar with views of Dovercourt Bay. The pleasantly decorated bedrooms have co-ordinated soft furnishings and modern facilities; many have sea views.

Rooms 26 en suite (3 fmly) ⊘ in 1 bedroom S £55-£65; D £65-£80 (incl. bkfst) **Facilities** STV Jacuzzi ♫ **Conf** Thtr 200 Class 150 Board 40 Del from £74.75 **Parking** 50 **Notes** LB ⊗ RS Xmas & New Year

★★ 71% HOTEL

Hotel Continental

THE INDEPENDENTS

28/29 Marine Pde, Dovercourt CO12 3RG

☎ 01255 551298 📠 01255 551698

e-mail: hotconti@btconnect.com

web: www.hotelcontinental-harwich.co.uk

dir: *off A120 at Ramsay rdbt onto B1352 to pedestrian crossing and Co-op store on right, turn right into Fronks Rd*

Privately owned hotel situated on the seafront within easy reach of the ferry terminals and town centre. Bedrooms are pleasantly decorated, well equipped and have many innovative features; some rooms also have lovely sea views. Public rooms include a popular lounge bar, a restaurant and a non-smoking lounge.

continued

Rooms 14 en suite (2 fmly) ⊗ in 9 bedrooms S £40-£75; D £65-£95 (incl. bkfst) **Facilities** STV Jacuzzi **Parking** 4 **Notes** ⊗ ⊘ in restaurant

See advert on this page

BUDGET HOTEL

Premier Travel Inn Harwich

Stanton Euro Park CO12 4NX

☎ 0870 8500904 ▤ 0870 8500905

web: www.premiertravelinn.com

High quality, modern budget accommodation ideal for both families and business travellers. Spacious, en suite bedrooms feature bath and shower, satellite TV and many have telephones and modem points. The adjacent family restaurant features a wide and varied menu. For further details consult the Hotel Groups page.

MALDON   MAP 07 TL80

See also Tolleshunt Knights

★★ 72% HOTEL

Benbridge Hotel

Holloway Rd, The Square, Heybridge CM9 4LT

☎ 01621 857666 & 853667 ▤ 01621 841966

e-mail: enquiries@thebenbridgehotel.co.uk

Small privately owned hotel situated just a short walk from the town centre. The stylish public areas feature a large open plan lounge bar with plush seating and a cosy well appointed restaurant. The pleasantly decorated bedrooms are smartly furnished and equipped with modern facilities.

continued

Benbridge Hotel

Rooms 13 en suite (5 fmly) **Facilities** ♪ **Conf** BC **Notes LB** ⊗

PURFLEET   MAP 06 TQ57

BUDGET HOTEL

Premier Travel Inn

High St RM19 1QA

☎ 08701 977216 ▤ 01708 860852

web: www.premiertravelinn.com

dir: *from Dartford Tunnel follow signs Dagenham (A13), at rdbt take 1st exit to Purfleet (A1090)*

High quality, modern budget accommodation ideal for both families and business travellers. Spacious, en suite bedrooms feature bath and shower, satellite TV and many have telephones and modem points. The adjacent family restaurant features a wide and varied menu. For further details consult the Hotel Groups page.

Rooms 30 en suite

England

SOUTHEND-ON-SEA ★★★ 72% **HOTEL** MAP 07 TQ88

Roslin Hotel
Thorpe Esplanade SS1 3BG
☎ 01702 586375 ▤ 01702 586663
e-mail: info@roslinhotel.com
web: www.roslinhotel.com

dir: A127, follow Southend-on-Sea signs. Hotel between Walton Road & Clieveden Road on seafront

This friendly, family-run hotel is situated at the quiet end of the esplanade, overlooking the beach and sea. The spacious bedrooms are pleasantly decorated and thoughtfully equipped; some rooms have superb sea views. Public rooms include a large lounge bar, the Mulberry restaurant and a smart new conservatory that overlooks the sea.

Rooms 35 en suite (4 fmly) (7 GF) S £45-£77; D £68-£93 (incl. bkfst)
Facilities STV FTV Temp membership of local sports centre **Conf** Thtr 35 Class 24 Board 24 Del from £89 **Parking** 36 **Notes LB** ⊗ ⊘ in restaurant RS 26-Dec

See advert on page 269

★★★ 71% **HOTEL**

Westcliff
Westcliff Pde, Westcliff-on-Sea SS0 7QW
☎ 01702 345247 ▤ 01702 431814
e-mail: westcliff@zolahotels.com

dir: M25 junct 29, A127 towards Southend, follow signs for Cliffs Pavillion when approaching town centre

This impressive Grade II listed Victorian building is situated in an elevated position overlooking gardens and cliffs to the sea beyond. The spacious bedrooms are tastefully decorated and thoughtfully equipped; many have lovely sea views. Public rooms include a smart conservatory-style restaurant, a spacious lounge and a range of function rooms.

Rooms 55 rms (47 en suite) (2 fmly) ⊘ in all bedrooms S fr £65; D £75-£109 (incl. bkfst) **Facilities** FTV Jacuzzi ♫ Xmas **Conf** Thtr 225 Class 90 Board 64 Del from £99 **Services** Lift **Notes LB** ⊗ ⊘ in restaurant Civ Wed 60

We endeavour to be as accurate as possible, but changes to times and other information can occur after the guide has gone to press.

★★★ 68% **HOTEL**

Erlsmere
THE INDEPENDENTS
24/32 Pembury Rd, Westcliff-on-Sea SS0 8DS
☎ 0870 033 2020 ▤ 01702 337724
e-mail: erlsmerehotel@btconnect.com

dir: A127/A1158 to Westbourne Grove signed seafront. At next main junct (A13) straight ahead into Chalkwell Ave, under rail bridge, left, 4th turn right

Situated in a peaceful side road just a short walk from the seafront and shops. Bedrooms come in a variety of styles but each one is pleasantly decorated and well equipped. An interesting choice of dishes is served in the stylish 2432 restaurant, and guests also have the use of the Patio Bar as well as a cosy lounge.

Rooms 30 en suite 2 annexe en suite (2 fmly) S £42-£52; D £59.50-£79.50 (incl. bkfst) **Facilities** Wi-fi in bedrooms **Conf** Thtr 120 Class 40 Board 60 Del from £85 **Parking** 12 **Notes LB** ⊗

★★ 75% **HOTEL**

Balmoral
34 Valkyrie Rd, Westcliff-on-Sea SS0 8BU
☎ 01702 342497 ▤ 01702 337828
e-mail: enq@balmoralsouthend.com
web: www.balmoralsouthend.com
dir: off A13

Delightful property situated just a short walk from the main shopping centre, railway station and seafront. The attractively decorated bedrooms are tastefully furnished and equipped with many thoughtful touches. Public rooms feature a smart open-plan bar/lounge, a conservatory restaurant and a smart new terrace with a large wooden gazebo.

Rooms 34 rms en suite (4 fmly) (4 GF) ⊘ in 2 bedrooms S £49.95-£66; D £69-£150 (incl. bkfst) **Facilities** STV Wi-fi in bedrooms Arrangement with nearby healthclub **Parking** 32 **Notes** ⊘ in restaurant

BUDGET HOTEL

Premier Travel Inn Southend-on-Sea
premier travel inn
213 Eastern Esplanade SS1 3AD
☎ 0870 9906370 ▤ 0870 9906371
web: www.premiertravelinn.com

dir: A127 to Southend, follow signs for A1159 (A13) Shoebury onto dual carriageway. At rdbt follow signs for Thorpe Bay. At seafront turn right. Hotel on right

High quality, modern budget accommodation ideal for both families and business travellers. Spacious, en suite bedrooms feature bath and

continued

shower, satellite TV and many have telephones and modem points. The adjacent family restaurant features a wide and varied menu. For further details consult the Hotel Groups page.

Rooms 42 en suite

Premier Travel Inn Southend-on-Sea (West)

Thanet Grange SS2 6GB
☎ 08701 977235 ▤ 01702 430838
dir: *on A127 at junct with B1013*
Rooms 60 en suite

BUDGET HOTEL

Travelodge Southend-on-Sea

Maitland House, Warrior Square, Chichester Rd SS1 2JY

☎ 08700 850950 ▤ 01994 232957
web: www.travelodge.co.uk

dir: *in the town centre.*

Travelodge offers good quality, good value, modern accommodation. Ideal for families, the spacious en suite bedrooms include remote-control TV, tea and coffee making facilities and comfortable beds. Meals can be taken at the nearby family restaurant. See Hotel Groups pages for further details.

Rooms 107 en suite S fr £26; D fr £26

SOUTH WOODHAM FERRERS　　　　**MAP 07 TQ89**

★★ 69% HOTEL

The Oakland Hotel

2-6 Reeves Way CM3 5XF
☎ 01245 322811 ▤ 01245 329201
e-mail: info@theoaklandhotel.co.uk
web: www.theoaklandhotel.co.uk

Modern, purpose-built hotel situated in the centre of this bustling town. Bedrooms are generally quite spacious; each one is pleasantly decorated and equipped with modern facilities. The public areas include a large sports bar with Sky TV and an open-plan bar/restaurant with a selection of comfy sofas.

Rooms 34 en suite (4 fmly) ⊗ in 15 bedrooms S fr £49.50, D fr £59.50 (incl. bkfst) **Facilities** STV ♬ **Conf** Thtr 30 Class 20 Board 20 Del from £100 **Notes** ⊗ ⊘ in restaurant

---

STANSTED AIRPORT　　　　**MAP 06 TL52**
See also Birchanger Green Motorway Service Area (M11)

★★★ 72% HOTEL

Best Western Stansted Manor

Birchanger Ln CM23 5ST
☎ 01279 859800 ▤ 01279 467245
e-mail: info@stanstedmanor-hotel.co.uk
web: www.stanstedmanor-hotel.co.uk

dir: *M11 junct 8 onto A120 towards Bishop's Stortford. Right at next major rdbt. Hotel on left*

Modern purpose built hotel conveniently situated just off the M11 very close to Stansted Airport. The property is reached via a long drive and surrounded by landscaped grounds. Bedrooms feature modern decor, tasteful furnishings and a thoughtful range of extras, including broadband. Open-plan public rooms include a comfortable lobby lounge, a lounge/bar and a conservatory restaurant.

Best Western Stansted Manor

Rooms 70 en suite (8 fmly) (23 GF) ⊗ in 31 bedrooms S £70-£120; D £80-£120 **Facilities** FTV Wi-fi available **Conf** Thtr 35 Class 16 Board 20 Del from £135 **Services** Lift **Parking** 100 **Notes** ⊗ ⊘ in restaurant Civ Wed 60

U

Radisson SAS Hotel

Waltham Close, Stansted Airport CM24 1PP
☎ 01279 661012 ▤ 01279 661013
e-mail: info.stansted@radissonsas.com
web: www.radisson.com

dir: *directly linked to London Stansted Airport terminal by covered walkway*

At the time of going to press, the star classification for this hotel was not confirmed. Please refer to the AA internet site www.theAA.com for current information.

Rooms 500 en suite (42 fmly) ⊗ in 420 bedrooms S £89-£125; D £89-£125 (incl. bkfst) **Facilities** Spa STV ♦ Sauna Solarium Gym Wi-fi available ♬ Xmas **Conf** BC Thtr 400 Class 180 Board 36 Del £145 **Services** Lift air con **Parking** 220 **Notes** ⊗ Civ Wed 400

U

Swallow Whitehall

Church End CM6 2BZ
☎ 01279 850603 ▤ 01279 850385
e-mail: sales.whitehallhotel@swallowhotels.com
web: www.swallowhotels.com

dir: *M11 junct 8, follow signs to Stansted Airport, hotel on B1052 between Elsenham and Thaxted*

At the time of going to press, the star classification for this hotel was not confirmed. Please refer to the AA internet site www.theAA.com for current information.

Rooms 26 en suite (5 fmly) (11 GF) S £70-£100; D £85-£125 **Facilities** STV Xmas **Conf** Thtr 100 Class 45 Board 50 Del from £135 **Parking** 70 **Notes** ⊗ ⊘ in restaurant Civ Wed 75

continued

England

STOCK — MAP 06 TQ69

★★★★ 70% COUNTRY HOUSE HOTEL

Greenwoods Hotel Spa & Retreat

Stock Rd CM4 9BE

☎ 01277 829990 🖹 01277 829899

e-mail: info@greenwoodsestate.com

dir: *A12 junct 16 take B1007 signed Billericay. Hotel on right on entering village*

Grade II listed manor house situated in the picturesque village of Stock amid landscaped grounds and surrounded by open countryside. The stylish bedrooms are tastefully furnished and thoughtfully equipped; some rooms have lovely views of the gardens. Public rooms include a choice of elegant lounges, a smart restaurant, superb leisure facilities and conference rooms.

Rooms 39 en suite (6 GF) ⊛ in all bedrooms S £85-£219; D £105-£240 **Facilities Spa** STV 🔄 Sauna Solarium Gym Putt green Jacuzzi Therapy/relaxation rooms Xmas **Conf** Thtr 110 Class 60 Board 50 Del from £180 **Services** Lift **Parking** 100 **Notes LB** ⊗ No children 16yrs ⊛ in restaurant Closed 26 Dec-30 Dec Civ Wed 50

THAXTED — MAP 12 TL63

★★ 72% HOTEL

Swan

OLD ENGLISH INNS

Bullring, Watling St CM6 2PL

☎ 01371 830321 🖹 01371 831186

e-mail: swan.thaxted@greeneking.co.uk

web: www.oldenglish.co.uk

dir: *M11 junct 8, A120 to Great Dunmow, then B184 to Thaxted. Hotel is north end of High Street, opposite church.*

This popular village inn is situated in this busy town centre opposite the parish church. Public areas feature a large open plan beamed bar/restaurant serving real ales and a range of snacks. Bedrooms are located in the main building or more peaceful rear annexe; each one is pleasantly decorated and well equipped.

Rooms 13 en suite 6 annexe en suite (2 fmly) (3 GF) S £60; D £75 (incl. bkfst) **Facilities** Xmas **Parking** 15 **Notes** ⊛ in restaurant

★★ 72% HOTEL

Thaxted Hall

Walden Rd CM6 2RE

☎ 01371 830129 🖹 01371 830835

e-mail: reservations@thaxtedhall.co.uk

web: www.thaxtedhall.co.uk

dir: *B184/B1051 junct, 0.25m from town centre towards Saffron Walden*

Privately owned hotel set amidst two acres of attractive landscaped grounds and ideally placed just seven miles from Stansted Airport. Bedrooms are pleasantly decorated with co-ordinated soft furnishings and have many thoughtful touches. Public rooms include a smart lounge and a restaurant. The hotel offers 'park-and-fly' with free transfers to the airport.

Rooms 8 en suite (3 fmly) ⊛ in all bedrooms **Facilities** ch fac **Conf** BC Thtr 150 Class 70 Board 40 **Parking** 50 **Notes** ⊗ ⊛ in restaurant Civ Wed 150

TOLLESHUNT KNIGHTS — MAP 07 TL91

★★★★ 77% ⊛ ⊛ HOTEL

Five Lakes Hotel, Golf, Country Club & Spa

Colchester Rd CM9 8HX

☎ 01621 868888 🖹 01621 869696

e-mail: enquiries@fivelakes.co.uk

web: www.fivelakes.co.uk

dir: *exit A12 at Kelvedon, follow brown signs through Tiptree to hotel*

This hotel is set amidst 320 acres of open countryside, featuring two golf courses. The spacious bedrooms are furnished to a high standard and have excellent facilities. The public rooms offer a high degree of comfort and include five bars, two restaurants and a large lounge. The property also boasts extensive leisure facilities.

Rooms 114 en suite 80 annexe en suite (4 fmly) (40 GF) ⊛ in all bedrooms S fr £155; D fr £155 **Facilities Spa** STV 🔄 ♨ 36 ♨ Squash Snooker Sauna Solarium Gym Putt green Jacuzzi Wi-fi in bedrooms Steam room, Health & Beauty Spa, Badminton, Aerobics Studio, Hairdresser ♫ Xmas **Conf** Thtr 2000 Class 700 Board 60 Del from £152 **Services** Lift **Parking** 550 **Notes LB** ⊗ ⊛ in restaurant Civ Wed 250

WALTHAM ABBEY — MAP 06 TL30

★★★★ 78% HOTEL

Waltham Abbey Marriott

Marriott.
HOTELS & RESORTS

Old Shire Ln EN9 3LX

☎ 01992 717170 🖹 01992 711841

web: www.marriott.co.uk

dir: *M25 junct 26*

This hotel benefits from convenient access to London and the major road networks. Air-conditioned bedrooms are spacious, tastefully decorated and offer a range of facilities for the modern business traveller. The hotel also provides a range of meeting rooms, a substantial parking area and a well-equipped indoor leisure centre.

Rooms 162 en suite (16 fmly) (80 GF) ⊛ in 132 bedrooms S £70-£129; D £70-£129 **Facilities** STV 🔄 Sauna Solarium Gym Jacuzzi Wi-fi available Steam room Xmas **Conf** BC Thtr 280 Class 120 Board 50 Del from £129 **Services** air con **Parking** 250 **Notes LB** ⊗ ⊛ in restaurant Civ Wed 200

England

BUDGET HOTEL

Premier Travel Inn
Waltham Abbey

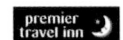

The Grange, Sewardstone Rd EN9 3QF
☎ 0870 9906568 ▤ 0870 9906569
web: www.premiertravelinn.com

dir: Exit M25 junct 26, A121 towards Waltham Abbey. Left onto A112, Inn 0.5m on left

High quality, modern budget accommodation ideal for both families and business travellers. Spacious, en suite bedrooms feature bath and shower, satellite TV and many have telephones and modem points. The adjacent family restaurant features a wide and varied menu. For further details consult the Hotel Groups page.

Rooms 93 en suite

WEELEY   MAP 07 TM12

BUDGET HOTEL

Premier Travel Inn
Clacton-on-Sea

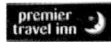

Crown Green Roundabout, Colchester Rd, Weeley CO16 9AA
☎ 08701 977064 ▤ 01255 833106
web: www.premiertravelinn.com

dir: take A120 off A12 towards Harwich. After 4m, A133 to Clacton-on-Sea. Located on Weeley rdbt

High quality, modern budget accommodation ideal for both families and business travellers. Spacious, en suite bedrooms feature bath and shower, satellite TV and many have telephones and modem points. The adjacent family restaurant features a wide and varied menu. For further details consult the Hotel Groups page.

Rooms 40 en suite

WEST THURROCK   MAP 06 TQ57

BUDGET HOTEL

Hotel Ibis London Thurrock

Weston Av RM20 3JQ
☎ 01708 686000 ▤ 01708 680525
e-mail: H2176@accor-hotels.com
web: www.ibishotel.com

dir: M25 junct 31 to West Thurrock Services, right at 1st and 2nd rdbts then left at 3rd rdbt. Hotel on right after 500yds

Modern, budget hotel offering comfortable accommodation in bright and practical bedrooms. Breakfast is self-service and dinner is available in the restaurant. For further details, consult the Hotel Groups page.

Rooms 102 en suite S £41.95-£51.95; D £41.95-£51.95

Some hotels, although accepting children, may not have any special facilities for them so it is well worth checking before booking

BUDGET HOTEL

Premier Travel Inn
Thurrock East

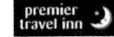

Fleming Rd, Unicorn Estate, Chafford Hundred RM16 6YJ
☎ 08701 977253 ▤ 01375 481876
web: www.premiertravelinn.com

dir: from A13 follow signs for Lakeside Shopping Centre. Turn right at 1st rdbt, straight over next rdbt then 1st slip road. Turn left at next rdbt

High quality, modern budget accommodation ideal for both families and business travellers. Spacious, en suite bedrooms feature bath and shower, satellite TV and many have telephones and modem points. The adjacent family restaurant features a wide and varied menu. For further details consult the Hotel Groups page.

Rooms 62 en suite

Premier Travel Inn Thurrock West

Stonehouse Ln RM19 1NS
☎ 0870 9906490 ▤ 0870 9906491

dir: From N, exit M25 junct 31 follow signs for A1090 to Purfleet. Do not cross Dartford Bridge or follow signs for Lakeside. From S, exit M25 junct 31. On approach to Dartford Tunnel, bear far left signed Dagenham. After tunnel, hotel at top of slip road

Rooms 161 en suite

BUDGET HOTEL

Travelodge Thurrock (M25)

Arterial Rd RM16 3BG
☎ 08700 850 950 & 0800 850950
▤ 01708 860971
web: www.travelodge.co.uk
dir: off A1306 (Arterial Rd)

Travelodge offers good quality, good value, modern accommodation. Ideal for families, the spacious en suite bedrooms include remote-control TV, tea and coffee-making facilities and comfortable beds. Meals can be taken at the nearby family restaurant. See Hotel Groups pages for further details.

Rooms 48 en suite S fr £26; D fr £26

WICKFORD   MAP 06 TQ79

BUDGET HOTEL

Innkeeper's Lodge Basildon/
Wickford

Runwell Rd SS11 7QJ
☎ 01268 769671 ▤ 01268 578012
web: www.innkeeperslodge.com

dir: M25 junct 29/A127 Southend, leave at Basildon/Wickford, left at rdbt towards Wickford. Straight over next 2 rdbts, at 3rd rdbt take 2nd exit

Smart, en suite accommodation ideal for both business & leisure guests. Bedrooms are very well equipped, including Sky TV, telephone, modem points, tea & coffee making facilities, (family rooms in most locations). Complimentary breakfast. The adjacent Pub Restaurant; a Harvester, Vintage Inn, Toby Carvery, Ember Inn, Sizzling Pubco or Pub & Carvery offers an all day menu. See Hotel Groups pages for further details.

Rooms 24 en suite S £48-£58; D £48-£58

England

WITHAM
MAP 07 TL81

★★★ 68% **HOTEL**

Rivenhall
Rivenhall End CM8 3HB
☎ 01376 516969 📠 01376 513674
e-mail: enquiries@rivenhallhotel.com
web: www.rivenhallhotel.com
dir: *M25 junct 28 towards Chelmsford on A12, take exit for Silver End/Great Braxted. At T-junct turn right, then 1st right, hotel directly ahead*

Please note that this establishment has recently changed hands. This modern hotel is ideally situated just off the main A12 between Chelmsford and Colchester. Bedrooms are pleasantly decorated and equipped with modern facilities. Public rooms include a large restaurant and a comfortable lounge bar; conference and leisure facilities are also available.

Rooms 18 en suite 37 annexe en suite (7 fmly) (42 GF) ⊘ in 41 bedrooms S £70–£90; D £80–£105 **Facilities** STV ⌨ Squash Sauna Solarium Gym Jacuzzi Steam Room **Conf** Thtr 180 Class 76 Board 45 Del from £121.50 **Parking** 150 **Notes** ⊗ ⊘ in restaurant Civ Wed 100

If the freedom to smoke or be in a non-smoking atmosphere is important to you, check the rules when you book

GLOUCESTERSHIRE

ALMONDSBURY
MAP 04 ST68

★★★★ 76% ⊛ **HOTEL**

Aztec Hotel & Spa
Aztec West Business Park, Almondsbury BS32 4TS
☎ 01454 201090 📠 01454 201593
e-mail: aztec@shirehotels.com
web: www.shirehotels.com

SHIRE HOTELS

(For full entry see Bristol)

★★ 68% **HOTEL**

The Bowl Inn
16 Church Rd, Lower Almondsbury BS32 4DT
☎ 01454 612757 📠 01454 619910
e-mail: reception@thebowlinn.co.uk
web: www.thebowlinn.co.uk

(For full entry see Bristol)

ALVESTON
MAP 04 ST68

★★★ 78% **HOTEL**

Alveston House
Davids Ln BS35 2LA
☎ 01454 415050 📠 01454 415425
e-mail: info@alvestonhousehotel.co.uk
web: www.alvestonhousehotel.co.uk
dir: *M5 junct 14 from N or junct 16 from S, on A38*

In a quiet area with easy access to the city and a short drive from both the M4 and M5, this smartly presented hotel provides an impressive combination of good service, friendly hospitality and a relaxed atmosphere. Bedrooms are well equipped and comfortable for both business or leisure use. The restaurant offers carefully prepared fresh food, and the pleasant bar and conservatory area is perfect for enjoying a pre-dinner drink.

Rooms 30 en suite (1 fmly) (6 GF) ⊘ in all bedrooms S £89.50–£99.50; D £99.50–£114.50 (incl. bkfst) **Facilities** STV **Conf** Thtr 85 Class 48 Board 50 Del from £135 **Parking** 75 **Notes LB** ⊘ in restaurant Civ Wed 75

See advertisement under BRISTOL page 63

BUDGET HOTEL

Premier Travel Inn Bristol (Alveston)

Thornbury Rd BS35 3LL
☎ 0870 9906496 📠 0870 9906497
web: www.premiertravelinn.com
dir: *Just off M5. From N, exit at junct 14 onto A38 towards Bristol. From S, exit at junct 16 take A38 towards Gloucester*

High quality, modern budget accommodation ideal for both families and business travellers. Spacious, en suite bedrooms feature bath and shower, satellite TV and many have telephones and modem points. The adjacent family restaurant features a wide and varied menu. For further details consult the Hotel Groups page.

Rooms 74 en suite **Conf** Thtr 70 Class 40 Board 40

BERKELEY ROAD   MAP 04 SO70

★★★ 68% **HOTEL**

Prince of Wales

GL13 9HD

☎ 01453 810474 🖺 01453 511370

e-mail: enquiries@theprinceofwaleshotel.com

dir: on A38, 6m S of M5 junct 13/6m N of junct 14

Handily placed, this smartly presented hotel is convenient for many major road networks. Bedrooms are generally a good size with a range of facilities. The public bar and lounge proves popular with both residents and locals alike, whilst the restaurant menu features a selection of Italian dishes. There's a pleasant garden and a large function room.

Rooms 43 en suite (2 fmly) (15 GF) ⊘ in 20 bedrooms S £60-£73; D £70-£83 (incl. bkfst) **Facilities** STV **Conf** Thtr 200 Class 60 Board 60 Del from £90 **Parking** 150 **Notes LB** ⊘ in restaurant Civ Wed 100

BIBURY   MAP 05 SP10

★★★ 73% ⊛⊛ **COUNTRY HOUSE HOTEL**

Bibury Court

GL7 5NT

☎ 01285 740337 🖺 01285 740660

e-mail: info@biburycourt.com

web: www.biburycourt.com

dir: on B4425 beside the River Coln, behind St Marys Church

Dating back to Tudor times, this elegant manor is the perfect antidote to the hustle and bustle of the modern world. Public areas have abundant charm and character. Bedrooms are spacious and offer traditional quality with modern comforts. A choice of interesting dishes is available in the conservatory at lunchtime, whereas dinner is served in the more formal restaurant. Staff are friendly and helpful.

Rooms 18 en suite (3 fmly) (1 GF) S £100-£125; D £125-£230 (incl. bkfst) **Facilities** Fishing ⚓ Wi-fi in bedrooms Billiards **Conf** Board 12 Del £200 **Parking** 100 **Notes LB** ⊘ in restaurant Civ Wed 32

★★★ 72% **HOTEL**

Swan

GL7 5NW

☎ 01285 740695 🖺 01285 740473

e-mail: info@swanhotel.co.uk

web: www.cotswold-inns-hotels.co.uk

dir: 9m S of Burford A40 on B4425, 6m N of Cirencester A4179 on B4425

The Swan, built in the 17th-century as a coaching inn, is set in peaceful, picturesque and beautiful surroundings. It now provides well-equipped and smartly presented accommodation, and public areas that are comfortable and elegant. There is a choice of dining options to suit all tastes.

Rooms 18 en suite (1 fmly) ⊘ in all bedrooms D £140-£180 (incl. bkfst) **Facilities** Spa Fishing Swan sanctuary, Beauty rooms Xmas **Conf** Thtr 48 Class 10 Board 20 Del from £130 **Services** Lift **Parking** 22 **Notes LB** ⊗ ⊘ in restaurant Civ Wed 90

BOURTON-ON-THE-WATER   MAP 10 SP12

★★ 65% **HOTEL**

Old Manse

OLD ENGLISH INNS

Victoria St GL54 2BX

☎ 01451 820082 🖺 01451 810381

e-mail: 6488@greeneking.co.uk

web: www.oldenglish.co.uk

dir: A429 Bourton turn off, hotel at far end of village high street next to Cotswold Motor Museum.

Originally built in 1748 for the local Baptist pastor, this welcoming hotel has the River Windrush flowing just a few feet from the front door. The lively bar is warmed by a real log fire and offers real ales, while the elegant restaurant is the place for table d'hote. Bedrooms are nicely decorated.

Rooms 12 en suite 3 annexe en suite ⊘ in all bedrooms S £65-£85; D £95-£140 (incl. bkfst) **Facilities** Xmas **Parking** 12 **Notes LB** ⊗ ⊘ in restaurant

★★ 🅰

The Old New Inn

Rissington Rd GL54 2AF

☎ 01451 820467 🖺 01451 810236

e-mail: reception@theoldnewinn.co.uk

dir: off A429, on the left at junct of High St and Rissington Rd

Rooms 8 en suite 1 annexe en suite S £38-£45; D £76 (incl. bkfst) **Parking** 21 **Notes LB** ⊗ No children 12yrs ⊘ in restaurant Closed Xmas & New Year

🅄

Chester House

Victoria St GL54 2BU

☎ 01451 820286 🖺 01451 820471

e-mail: info@chesterhousehotel.com

At the time of going to press, the star classification for this hotel was not confirmed. Please refer to the AA internet site www.theAA.com for current information.

Rooms 12 en suite 10 annexe en suite (8 fmly) (8 GF) ⊘ in all bedrooms S £80; D £80-£90 (incl. bkfst) **Facilities** Beauty therapist ch fac **Parking** 20 **Notes** ⊘ in restaurant

England

BUCKLAND (NEAR BROADWAY)   MAP 10 SP03

INSPECTORS' CHOICE

★★★ ◉◉◉ **HOTEL**

Buckland Manor

WR12 7LY
☎ 01386 852626 📠 01386 853557
e-mail: info@bucklandmanor.co.uk
web: www.vonessenhotels.co.uk
dir: off B4632 Broadway to Winchcombe Road

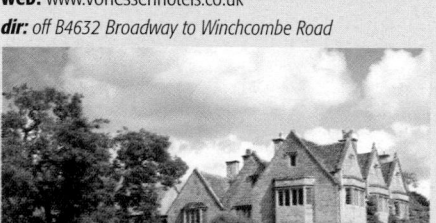

A grand 13th-century manor house surrounded by well-kept and beautiful gardens. Everything here is geared to encourage rest and relaxation. Spacious bedrooms and public areas are furnished with high quality pieces and decorated in keeping with the style of the manor; crackling log fires warm the wonderful lounges. The cuisine continues to impress, with high quality produce skilfully used.

Rooms 13 en suite (2 fmly) (4 GF) S £225-£410; D £250-£420 (incl. bkfst) **Facilities** STV ⌁ ⛳ Putt green Xmas **Parking** 30 **Notes LB** ⊗ No children 12yrs ⊘ in restaurant

CHARINGWORTH   MAP 10 SP13

★★★ 75% ◉◉ **COUNTRY HOUSE HOTEL**

Charingworth Manor

GL55 6NS
☎ 01386 593555 📠 01386 593353
e-mail: cmsales@englishrosehotels.co.uk
web: www.englishrosehotels.co.uk/hotels/charingworth/index.html
dir: on B4035 3m E of Chipping Campden

This 14th-century manor house retains many original features including flagstone floors, exposed beams and open fireplaces. The house has a beautiful setting in 50 acres of grounds and has been carefully extended to provide high quality accommodation and a delightful small leisure spa. Spacious bedrooms are furnished with period pieces and modern amenities.

Rooms 26 en suite (13 GF) S £125-£165; D £170 (incl. bkfst) **Facilities** ☈ ⌁ Sauna Solarium Gym ⛴ Steam room Xmas **Conf** Thtr 60 Class 30 Board 40 Del from £175 **Parking** 50 **Notes LB** ⊗ ⊘ in restaurant Civ Wed 60

CHELTENHAM   MAP 10 SO92

★★★★ 76% ◉ **HOTEL**

Macdonald Queen's

The Promenade GL50 1NN
☎ 0870 400 8107 📠 01242 224145
e-mail: general.queens@macdonald-hotels.co.uk
web: www.macdonald-hotels.co.uk
dir: follow town centre signs. Left at Montpellier Walk rdbt. Entrance 500mtrs right

With its spectacular position at the top of the main promenade, this landmark hotel is an ideal base from which to explore the charms of this Regency spa town and the Cotswolds. Bedrooms are very comfortable and include two beautiful four-poster rooms. Smart public rooms include the popular Gold Cup bar and a choice of dining options.

Rooms 79 en suite ⊘ in all bedrooms S £80-£140; D £105-£160 (incl. bkfst) **Facilities** STV Xmas **Conf** Thtr 100 Class 60 Board 40 Del from £150 **Services** Lift air con **Parking** 80 **Notes LB** ⊘ in restaurant Civ Wed 100

★★★★ 73% **HOTEL**

Paramount Cheltenham Park

Cirencester Rd, Charlton Kings GL53 8EA
☎ 01242 222021 📠 01242 254880
e-mail: cheltenhamparkreservations@paramount-hotels.co.uk
web: www.paramount-hotels.co.uk
dir: on A435, 2m SE of Cheltenham near Lilley Brook Golf Course

Located south of Cheltenham, this attractive Georgian hotel is set in its own landscaped gardens, adjacent to Lilley Brook Golf Course. All of the bedrooms are spacious and well equipped and the hotel has an impressive leisure club and extensive meeting facilities. The Lakeside restaurant serves carefully prepared cuisine.

Rooms 33 en suite 110 annexe en suite (2 fmly) ⊘ in 67 bedrooms **Facilities** STV ☈ Sauna Solarium Gym Jacuzzi Beauty treatment rooms **Conf** BC Thtr 350 Class 180 Board 110 **Parking** 170 **Notes LB** ⊘ in restaurant Civ Wed 100

England

Cheltenham and Gloucester Chase Hotel

 QHOTELS

Shurdington Rd, Brockworth GL3 4PB

☎ 01452 519988 📠 01452 519977

e-mail: cheltenham@qhotels.co.uk

web: www.qhotels.co.uk

dir: *M5 junct 11a onto A417 Cirencester. 1st exit A46 to Stroud, hotel 500yds on left.*

Conveniently positioned for Cheltenham, Gloucester, and the M5, this hotel is set in landscaped grounds with ample parking. Bedrooms are spacious with attractive colour schemes and excellent facilities; executive rooms and suites benefit from air-conditioning. Public areas include an open-plan bar/lounge, Coopers restaurant, extensive meeting and functions rooms and a well-equipped leisure club.

Rooms 120 en suite (19 fmly) (46 GF) ⊛ in 101 bedrooms S £70-£137; D £82-£147 (incl. bkfst) **Facilities** Spa STV ⚛ supervised Snooker Sauna Solarium Gym Jacuzzi Xmas **Conf** Thtr 350 Class 120 Board 60 Del from £105 **Services** Lift air con **Parking** 240 **Notes LB** ⊗ ⊛ in restaurant Civ Wed 200

Thistle Cheltenham

THISTLE HOTELS

Gloucester Rd GL51 0TS

☎ 0870 333 9131 📠 0870 333 9231

e-mail: Cheltenham@Thistle.co.uk

dir: *Leave M5 junct 11 onto A40 signed Cheltenham, at 1st rdbt take 2nd exit. Hotel is immediately on left.*

Conveniently located for easy access to the M5, this large hotel offers a good range of dining options in addition to extensive leisure facilities. Bedrooms and bathrooms are well equipped and offer good ease of use for either the business or leisure guest. Ample parking and a range of conference rooms are provided.

Rooms 122 en suite (8 fmly) (41 GF) ⊛ in 45 bedrooms **Facilities** Spa STV ⚛ ⚲ Sauna Solarium Gym Jacuzzi **Conf** BC Thtr 400 Class 200 Board 60 **Services** Lift air con **Parking** 200 **Notes LB** ⊛ in restaurant Civ Wed 240

Alias Hotel Kandinsky

Bayshill Rd, Montpellier GL50 3AS

☎ 01242 527788 📠 01242 226412

e-mail: info@aliaskandinsky.com

web: www.aliashotels.com

dir: *M5 junct 11, A40 to town centre. Right at 2nd rdbt. 2nd exit at 3rd rdbt into Bayshill Rd. Hotel on corner of Bayshill/Parabola Rds*

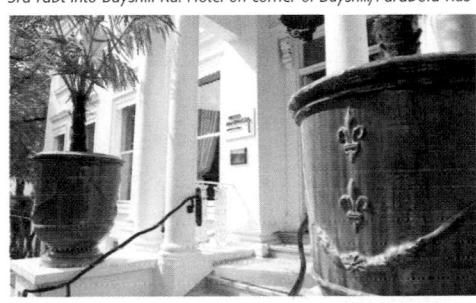

A large Regency villa successfully blending modern comfort with quirky eclectic decoration. Stylish bedrooms vary in size and have additional facilities such as CD/video players. There are several lounges, a conservatory, and the bright Café Paradiso restaurant. Hidden in the cellars is U-bahn, a wonderful 1950's style cocktail bar.

Rooms 48 en suite (3 fmly) (5 GF) ⊛ in 4 bedrooms S £75-£125, D £105-£130 **Facilities** STV Wi-fi in bedrooms Access to local pool & gym, free of charge to guests Xmas **Conf** Board 20 Del from £150 **Services** Lift **Parking** 32 **Notes LB** ⊗ ⊛ in restaurant

See advert on this page

England

CHELTENHAM *continued*

★★★ ◉ ◉ **SMALL HOTEL**

Hotel on the Park
38 Evesham Rd GL52 2AH
☎ 01242 518898 📠 01242 511526
e-mail: stay@hotelonthepark.com
web: www.hotelonthepark.com
dir: opposite Pittville Park. Join one-way system, off A435 towards Evesham

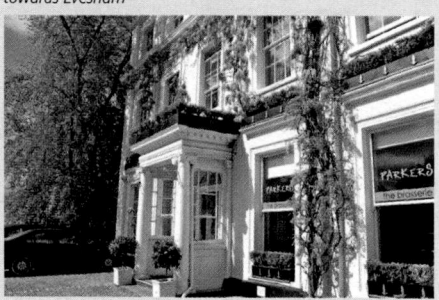

This establishment is a wonderfully different hotel with style, originality and flair throughout. Bedrooms have tremendous character and exceptional comfort, the bathrooms are exceptionally well appointed. Similar comments apply to public areas, comprising the elegant drawing room, library and Parkers, a modern brasserie, serving relaxed and enjoyable cuisine looking across the park.

Rooms 12 en suite ⊘ in all bedrooms S £86.50-£111; D £126-£186
Facilities STV Wi-fi in bedrooms **Parking** 8 **Notes LB** ⊗
No children 8yrs ⊘ in restaurant

★★★ 80% **HOTEL**

The Greenway
Shurdington GL51 4UG
☎ 01242 862352 📠 01242 862780
e-mail: info@thegreenway.co.uk
web: www.thegreenway.co.uk
dir: 2.5m SW on A46

This hotel, with a wealth of history, is peacefully located in a delightful setting close to the A46 and the M5. Within easy reach of the many attractions of the Cotswolds, as well as the interesting town of Cheltenham, The Greenway certainly offers something special. The attractive dining room overlooks the sunken garden and is the venue for exciting food, proudly served by dedicated and attentive staff. As we went to press the rosette award for this hotel had not been confirmed due to a change of chef.

Rooms 11 en suite 10 annexe en suite (1 fmly) (4 GF) ⊘ in
10 bedrooms S £99-£175; D £120-£290 (incl. bkfst) **Facilities** 🏌 Clay pigeon shooting, Horse riding, Mountain biking, Beauty treatment Xmas
Conf Thtr 40 Class 25 Board 18 Del from £145 **Parking** 50 **Notes LB**
⊘ in restaurant Civ Wed 45

★★★ 77% **HOTEL**

Charlton Kings
London Rd, Charlton Kings GL52 6UU
☎ 01242 231061 📠 01242 241900
e-mail: enquiries@charltonkingshotel.co.uk
web: www.charltonkingshotel.co.uk
dir: entering Cheltenham from Oxford on A40, 1st on left

Conveniently located on the outskirts of Cheltenham, the Charlton Kings is an attractive and friendly hotel providing comfortable, modern accommodation. The neatly presented bedrooms are well equipped with tasteful furnishings and contemporary comforts. The popular and stylish restaurant serves a variety of dishes to suit all tastes from a menu based on quality ingredients.

Rooms 13 en suite (1 fmly) (4 GF) ⊘ in 12 bedrooms S £65-£85;
D £98-£125 (incl. bkfst) **Facilities** STV Wi-fi in bedrooms **Parking** 26
Notes LB ⊘ in restaurant

★★★ 77% ◉ **HOTEL**

George Hotel
St Georges Rd GL50 3DZ
☎ 01242 235751 📠 01242 224359
e-mail: hotel@stayatthegeorge.co.uk
web: www.stayatthegeorge.co.uk
dir: M5 junct 11 follow town centre signs. At 1st lights left into Gloucester Rd, past rail station over mini-rdbt. At lights right into St Georges Rd. Hotel 0.75m on left

Just a short stroll from the town centre, this genuinely friendly hotel is privately owned and occupies part of an elegant Regency terrace. Standard and superior bedrooms are well equipped and tastefully furnished. There are two dining options - the modern and lively Monty's brasserie and the stylish and contemporary Seafood Restaurant. The chic designer bar in the basement is proving a popular venue for relaxation.

Rooms 38 en suite (1 GF) ⊘ in 30 bedrooms **Facilities** STV
Complimentary membership of local health club **Conf** Board 24
Parking 30 **Notes LB** ⊗ ⊘ in restaurant RS 24-26 Dec

★★★ 72% **HOTEL**

Royal George
Birdlip GL4 8JH
☎ 01452 862506 📠 01452 862277
e-mail: royalgeorge.birdlip@greeneking.co.uk
web: www.oldenglish.co.uk

OLD ENGLISH INNS

dir: M5 junct 11A take A417 towards Cirencester. At Air Balloon rdbt take 2nd exit then 1st right into Birdlip, hotel on right.

This attractive 18th-century Cotswold building has been sympathetically
continued

converted and extended into a pleasant hotel. Bedrooms are spacious and comfortably furnished with modern facilities. The public areas have been designed around a traditional English pub with the bar leading on to a terrace overlooking extensive lawns.

Rooms 34 en suite (4 fmly) (12 GF) @ in 19 bedrooms S fr £70; D fr £95 (incl. bkfst) **Facilities** STV ♬ Xmas **Conf** Thtr 90 Class 60 Board 40 Del from £85 **Notes LB** ⊛ ⊘ in restaurant Civ Wed 80

★★★ 71% HOTEL

Carlton
Parabola Rd GL50 3AQ
☎ 01242 514453 ▤ 01242 226487
e-mail: enquiries@thecarltonhotel.co.uk
web: www.thecarltonhotel.co.uk

dir: Follow signs to town centre, at Town Hall straight on through 2 sets of lights, turn left, then 1st right

This well-presented family owned and run Regency property is situated just a short walk from the town centre. Bedrooms are located both in the main hotel and also within an annexe building, where rooms are larger and more luxurious. Other features include a choice of bars, lounge and conference facilities.

Rooms 62 en suite 13 annexe en suite (2 fmly) (4 GF) ⊘ in 15 bedrooms S £45 £72.50; D £90-£106 (incl. bkfst) **Facilities** STV Xmas **Conf** Thtr 200 Class 150 Board 100 Del from £85 **Services** Lift **Parking** 85 **Notes LB** ⊘ in restaurant

★★★ 70% HOTEL

The Prestbury House Hotel
The Burgage, Prestbury GL52 3DN
☎ 01242 529533 ▤ 01242 227076
e-mail: enquiries@prestburyhouse.co.uk
web: www.prestburyhouse.co.uk

dir: 1m NE of Cheltenham. Follow all signs for racecourse. From racecourse follow Prestbury signs. Hotel 2nd left, 500mtrs from racecourse

This hotel retains much of its Georgian charm and is ideally situated for the town centre and racecourse. Well-equipped, spacious accommodation is offered in the main house and in the adjacent converted coach house. The owners also run a management training company, and team-building activities are sometimes held here.

Rooms 7 en suite 8 annexe en suite (3 GF) ⊘ in 16 bedrooms S £65-£79; D £70-£130 (incl. bkfst) **Facilities** STV Riding Gym ⍭ Wi-fi in bedrooms Archery, Bike hire, Trim Trail, Hill Walking, Petanque **Conf** BC Thtr 65 Class 30 Board 25 Del from £90 **Parking** 40 **Notes LB** ⊛ ⊘ in restaurant Civ Wed 60

★★★ 66% HOTEL

Hotel De La Bere
Southam GL52 3NH
☎ 0870 832 9903 ▤ 0870 8329904
e-mail: delabere@legacy-hotels.co.uk
web: www.legacy-hotels.co.uk

dir: M5 junct 11 take A40. On reaching Cheltenham turn right on to B4632, follow road through Prestbury. Hotel on left in 1m.

Set within its own grounds and with delightful surrounding gardens, this individual hotel offers much character and charm. Some bedrooms are located in the older 15th-century part of the hotel while others are in a more modern adjacent annexe. The panelled dining room and numerous large conference rooms offer a good sense of the historical feel of the hotel.

Rooms 33 en suite 24 annexe en suite (3 fmly) (10 GF) ⊘ in 21 bedrooms **Facilities** ⍭ ⌇ Squash Sauna Solarium Gym **Conf** Thtr 100 Class 60 Board 40 **Parking** 100 **Notes** ⊘ in restaurant Civ Wed 100

★★★ 60% HOTEL

Quality Hotel Cheltenham
Gloucester Rd GL51 0ST
☎ 01452 713226 ▤ 01452 857590
e-mail: info@qualitycheltenham.com

dir: M5 junct 11 onto A40 to Cheltenham. Left at rdbt, hotel 1m on left

This hotel, now under new ownership, is situated on the edge of town and provides comfortable and modern accommodation. The lounge bar and the restaurant are attractively presented and a number of function rooms are also available. Friendly service and helpful staff ensure a pleasant stay.

Rooms 49 en suite (4 fmly) ⊘ in 13 bedrooms **Facilities** Wi-fi available Bar games **Conf** Thtr 180 Class 80 Board 45 Del from £89 **Parking** 150 **Notes** ⊘ in restaurant RS 12-16 Mar & 10-12 Nov Civ Wed 150

★★ 71% HOTEL

Cotswold Grange
Pittville Circus Rd GL52 2QH
☎ 01242 515119 ▤ 01242 241537
e-mail: paul@cotswoldgrange.co.uk

dir: from town centre, follow Prestbury signs. Right at 1st rdbt, hotel 200yds on left

Built from Cotswold limestone, this attractive Georgian property retains many impressive architectural features. Situated conveniently close to the centre of Cheltenham, this long established, family-run hotel offers

continued on page 280

England

CHELTENHAM *continued*

well-equipped and comfortable accommodation. The convivial bar is a popular venue, and additional facilities include a spacious restaurant, cosy lounge, pleasant rear garden and ample parking.

Rooms 25 en suite (4 fmly) S £55-£65; D £80-£95 (incl. bkfst) **Facilities** Wi-fi in bedrooms ch fac **Conf** Thtr 12 Class 12 Board 12 Del from £100 **Parking** 20 **Notes** ⊗ in restaurant Closed 24 Dec-5 Jan RS Sat & Sun evening (food by arrangement)

★★ 71% HOTEL

North Hall

Pittville Circus Rd GL52 2PZ
☎ 01242 520589 ▤ 01242 261953
e-mail: northhallhotel@btinternet.com
web: www.northhallhotel.co.uk

dir: from Cheltenham town centre, follow Pittville signs. At Pittville Circus take 1st left into Pittville Circus Rd. Hotel on right

This three-storey Victorian house is conveniently located in a quiet residential area, within easy reach of the town centre and racecourse. Bedrooms are individually designed and offer ample comfort and quality with a range of extra facilities. A brasserie-style menu is served in the elegant surroundings of the restaurant, and there is also a bar/lounge with convivial atmosphere.

Rooms 20 en suite (2 fmly) ⊗ in 8 bedrooms S £55-£65; D £80-£100 (incl. bkfst) **Facilities** STV **Conf** Thtr 40 Class 25 Board 15 **Parking** 25 **Notes LB** ⊗ in restaurant

BUDGET HOTEL

Premier Travel Inn Cheltenham Central

374 Gloucester Rd GL51 7AY
☎ 08701 977056 ▤ 01242 260042
web: www.premiertravelinn.com

dir: M5 junct 11 onto A40 (Cheltenham). Follow dual carriageway to end, straight at 1st rdbt, turn right at 2nd

High quality, modern budget accommodation ideal for both families and business travellers. Spacious, en suite bedrooms feature bath and shower, satellite TV and many have telephones and modem points. The adjacent family restaurant features a wide and varied menu. For further details consult the Hotel Groups page.

Rooms 40 en suite

Premier Travel Inn Cheltenham West

Tewkesbury Rd, Uckington GL51 9SL
☎ 08701 977055 ▤ 01242 244887

dir: opposite Sainsbury's & Homebase on A4019, 2 miles from junct 10 (southbound exit only) and 3 miles from junct 11 (both exits) of M5

Rooms 40 en suite **Conf** Thtr 30 Class 30

BUDGET HOTEL

Travelodge Cheltenham

Golden Valley Roundabout, Hatherley Ln GL51 6PN
☎ 08700 850 950 ▤ 01242 241 748
web: www.travelodge.co.uk

dir: Exit junct 11 of M5 and follow signs for Cheltenham. Travelodge is at first rdbt.

Travelodge offers good quality, good value, modern accommodation. Ideal for families, the spacious en suite bedrooms include remote-control TV, tea and coffee-making facilities and comfortable beds. Meals can be taken at the nearby family restaurant. See Hotel Groups pages for further details.

Rooms 106 en suite S fr £26; D fr £26

CHIPPING CAMPDEN   MAP 10 SP13

INSPECTORS' CHOICE

★★★★ ⊛⊛⊛ HOTEL

Cotswold House

The Square GL55 6AN
☎ 01386 840330 ▤ 01386 840310
e-mail: reception@cotswoldhouse.com
web: www.cotswoldhouse.com

dir: A44 take B4081 to Chipping Campden. Right at T-junct into High St. House in The Square

This is at the cutting edge of hotel keeping and relaxation is inevitable at this mellow Cotswold stone house, set in the centre of the town. Bedrooms, including spacious suites in the courtyard, are impressively individual and offer a beguiling blend of style, quality and comfort. The restaurant provides a stunning venue to sample accomplished and imaginative cuisine, with local produce at the heart of dishes on offer here. Alternatively, Hicks Brasserie and Bar provides a more informal dining experience.

Rooms 29 en suite (1 fmly) (5 GF) ⊗ in 18 bedrooms S £140-£225; D fr £225 (incl. bkfst) **Facilities** STV Gym ♨ Wi-fi available Access to local Sports Centre Xmas **Conf** BC Thtr 90 Class 50 Board 30 Del from £225 **Parking** 28 **Notes LB** ⊗ in restaurant Civ Wed 100

★★★ 79% ◎ **HOTEL**

Three Ways House
Mickleton GL55 6SB
☎ 01386 438429 📠 01386 438118
e-mail: reception@puddingclub.com
web: www.puddingclub.com
dir: in centre of Mickleton, on B4632 Stratford-upon-Avon to Broadway road

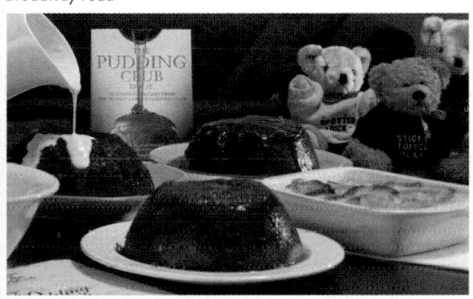

Built in 1870, this charming hotel has welcomed guests for over 100 years and is home to the world famous Pudding Club, formed in 1985 to promote traditional English puddings. Individuality is a hallmark here, as reflected in a number of bedrooms, which have been styled according to a pudding theme. Public areas are stylish and include the air-conditioned restaurant, lounges and meeting rooms.

Rooms 48 en suite (7 fmly) (14 GF) ⊛ in all bedrooms S £75-£90; D £125-£180 (incl. bkfst) **Facilities** Wi-fi available 🎵 Xmas **Conf** Thtr 100 Class 40 Board 35 Del £130 **Services** Lift **Parking** 37 **Notes LB** ⊛ in restaurant Civ Wed 100

★★★ 73% **HOTEL**

Noel Arms
High St GL55 6AT

CLASSIC
BRITISH HOTELS

☎ 01386 840317 📠 01386 841136
e-mail: reception@noelarmshotel.com
web: www.noelarmshotel.com
dir: off A44 onto B4081 to Chipping Campden, 1st right down hill into town. Hotel on right opposite Market Hall

This historic 14th-century hotel has a wealth of character and charm, and retains some of its original features. Bedrooms are very individual in style, and all have high levels of comfort and interesting interior design. Such distinctiveness is also evident throughout the public areas, which include the popular bar, conservatory lounge and attractive restaurant.

Rooms 26 en suite (1 fmly) (6 GF) S £90-£110; D £125-£175 (incl. bkfst) **Facilities** Wi-fi available Xmas **Conf** BC Thtr 60 Class 35 Board 35 Del from £135 **Parking** 26 **Notes LB** ⊛ in restaurant Civ Wed 50

CIRENCESTER   MAP 05 SP00

★★★ 79% **HOTEL**

Stratton House
Gloucester Rd GL7 2LE

Forestdale
Hotels

☎ 01285 651761 📠 01285 640024
e-mail: stratton.house@forestdale.com
web: www.forestdale.com
dir: M4 junct 15, A419 to Cirencester. Hotel on left on A417 or M5 junct 11 to Cheltenham onto B4070 to A417. Hotel on right

This attractive 17th-century manor house is quietly situated about half a mile from the town centre. Bedrooms are well presented, and spacious, stylish premier rooms are available. The comfortable drawing rooms and restaurant have views over well-tended gardens: the perfect place to enjoy pre-dinner drinks on a summer evening.

Rooms 39 en suite (9 GF) ⊛ in 19 bedrooms S £85-£110; D £125-£140 (incl. bkfst) **Facilities** Wi-fi in bedrooms Xmas **Conf** Thtr 150 Class 50 Board 40 Del from £100 **Parking** 100 **Notes LB** ⊛ in restaurant Civ Wed 100

★★★ 73% **HOTEL**

The Crown of Crucis
Ampney Crucis GL7 5RS
☎ 01285 851806 📠 01285 851735
e-mail: info@thecrownofcrucis.co.uk
web: www.thecrownofcrucis.co.uk
dir: A417 to Fairford, hotel 2.5m on left

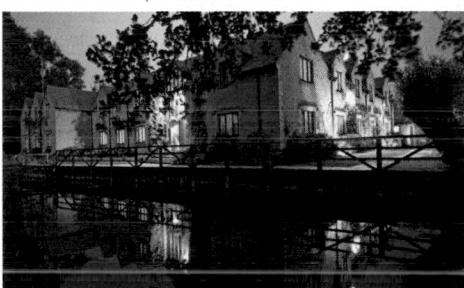

This delightful hotel consists of two buildings; one a 16th-century coaching inn, which now houses the bar and restaurant, and a more modern bedroom block which surrounds a courtyard. Rooms are attractively appointed and offer modern facilities; the restaurant serves a range of imaginative dishes.

Rooms 25 en suite (2 fmly) (13 GF) ⊛ in 21 bedrooms S fr £60; D fr £80 (incl. bkfst) **Facilities** Free membership of local leisure centre **Conf** Thtr 80 Class 40 Board 25 Del from £115 **Parking** 82 **Notes LB** ⊛ in restaurant RS 25-26 Dec & 1 Jan Civ Wed 50

England

CIRENCESTER *continued*

★★★ 70% **HOTEL**

Fleece Hotel

Market Place GL7 2NZ
☎ 01285 658507 🖨 01285 651017
e-mail: relax@fleecehotel.co.uk
web: www.fleecehotel.co.uk

dir: A417/A419 Burford road junct, follow signs for town centre. Right at lights into 'The Waterloo', car park 250yds on left

This old town centre coaching inn, which dates back to the Tudor period, retains many original features such as flagstone floors and oak beams. Well-equipped bedrooms vary in size and shape, but all offer good levels of comfort and have plenty of character. The bar lounge is a popular venue for morning coffee, and the stylish restaurant offers a range of dishes in an informal and convivial atmosphere.

Rooms 28 en suite (3 fmly) (4 GF) ⊗ in 20 bedrooms S £59-£115; D £79-£125 (incl. bkfst) **Facilities** Wi-fi available Local gym 100yds from hotel provides discount for hotel guests. Xmas **Parking** 10 **Notes LB** ⊗ in restaurant

★★ 🅰

Corinium Hotel

12 Gloucester St GL7 2DG
☎ 01285 659711 🖨 01285 885807
e-mail: info@coriniumhotel.co.uk
web: www.coriniumhotel.com

dir: from lights on A417 into Spitalgate Lane, hotel car park 50mtrs on right

Rooms 15 en suite (2 fmly) (2 GF) ⊗ in 12 bedrooms S £59-£69; D £84-£94 (incl. bkfst) **Facilities** Xmas **Parking** 30 **Notes LB** ⊗ in restaurant

BUDGET HOTEL

Travelodge Cirencester

Hare Bushes, Burford Rd GL7 5DS
☎ 08700 850 950 🖨 01285 655290
web: www.travelodge.co.uk

dir: M5 junct 12, take A417 to Swindon. Lodge a A417/A429 junct

Travelodge offers good quality, good value, modern accommodation. Ideal for families, the spacious en suite bedrooms include remote-control TV, tea and coffee-making facilities and comfortable beds. Meals can be taken at the nearby family restaurant. See Hotel Groups pages for further details.

Rooms 43 en suite S fr £26; D fr £26

CLEARWELL
MAP 04 SO50

★★★ 79% ◉◉ **HOTEL**

Tudor Farmhouse Hotel & Restaurant

High St GL16 8JS
☎ 01594 833046 🖨 01594 837093
e-mail: info@tudorfarmhousehotel.co.uk
web: www.tudorfarmhousehotel.co.uk

dir: off A4136 onto B4228, through Coleford, turn right into Clearwell, hotel on right just before War Memorial Cross

Dating from the 13th century, this idyllic former farmhouse retains a host of original features including exposed stonework, oak beams, wall panelling and wonderful inglenook fireplaces. Bedrooms have great individuality and style and are located either within the main house or in converted buildings in the grounds. Creative menus offer quality cuisine which is served in the intimate, candlelit restaurant.

Rooms 6 en suite 16 annexe en suite (2 fmly) (7 GF) ⊗ in 20 bedrooms S £55-£65; D £80-£150 (incl. bkfst) **Facilities** STV **Conf** Thtr 30 Class 20 Board 12 Del from £80 **Parking** 30 **Notes LB** ⊗ in restaurant Closed 24-27 Dec

CLEEVE HILL
MAP 10 SO92

★★ 76% **HOTEL**

Rising Sun

OLD ENGLISH INNS

GL52 3PX
☎ 01242 676281 🖨 01242 673069
web: www.oldenglish.co.uk

dir: On the B4632, 4m N of Cheltenham

This popular establishment offers commanding views across the Severn Vale to the Malvern Hills and beyond. There is a pleasant range of public rooms which include a large bar-bistro and a reception lounge. Bedrooms are well equipped and smartly presented with many boasting glorious views. A large garden is also available for summer drinking and dining.

Rooms 24 en suite (3 fmly) (6 GF) ⊗ in all bedrooms **Facilities** STV ♫ **Conf** Del from £95 **Parking** 70 **Notes** ⊗ ⊗ in restaurant

COLEFORD
MAP 04 SO51

★★★ 72% **HOTEL**

Best Western Speech House

GL16 7EL
☎ 01594 822607 🖨 01594 823658
e-mail: relax@thespeechhouse.co.uk
web: www.thespeechhouse.co.uk

dir: on B4226 between Cinderford and Coleford

Dating back to 1676, this former hunting lodge is tucked away in the

continued

Forest of Dean. Bedrooms, some with four-poster beds, combine modern amenities with period charm; they include some stylish, impressive rooms in the courtyard. The beamed restaurant serves good, imaginative food, whilst additional features include a mini gym, aqua spa and conference facilities.

Best Western Speech House

Rooms 15 en suite 22 annexe en suite (4 fmly) (12 GF) ⊘ in 6 bedrooms S £65-£100; D £90-£190 (incl. bkfst) **Facilities** Wi-fi available Beauty Salon Xmas **Conf** BC Thtr 50 Class 30 Board 20 Del from £120 **Parking** 70 **Notes LB** ⊘ in restaurant Civ Wed 70

★★ 64% **HOTEL**

The Angel Hotel

Market Place GL16 8AE

☎ 01594 833113 ▤ 01594 832413

dir: access to hotel via A48 or A40

This friendly 17th-century coaching inn is centrally located and provides an excellent base for exploring the area. All bedrooms are spacious, well equipped and suitable for both business and leisure guests. Additional features include a choice of bars, all with a relaxing atmosphere, a good range of real ales and wholesome cuisine.

Rooms 9 en suite (1 fmly) **Facilities** STV ♪↑ **Parking** 9

COLN ST ALDWYNS MAP 05 SP10

★★ 72% ◉◉ **HOTEL**

The New Inn At Coln

GL7 5AN

☎ 01285 750651 ▤ 01285 750657

e-mail: stay@new-inn.co.uk

web: www.new-inn.co.uk

dir: 8m E of Cirencester, between Bibury and Fairford

Set in the heart of the Coln Valley, this quintessential Cotswold inn has been welcoming weary travellers since the reign of Elizabeth I. The bedrooms are very cosy, while crackling log fires, flagstone floors, wooden beams and genuine hospitality make for a beguiling atmosphere. An excellent bar menu is available. Aperitifs can be enjoyed in the lounge, whilst perusing the interesting range of dishes on the restaurant menu.

Rooms 8 en suite 6 annexe en suite (1 GF) S £109-£119; D £126-£163 (incl. bkfst) **Facilities** Fishing Xmas **Conf** Thtr 20 Board 12 Del from £165 **Parking** 22 **Notes LB** No children 10yrs ⊘ in restaurant

CORSE LAWN MAP 10 SO83

INSPECTORS' CHOICE

★★★ ◉◉ **HOTEL**

Corse Lawn House

GL19 4LZ

☎ 01452 780479 & 780771 ▤ 01452 780840

e-mail: enquiries@corselawn.com

web: www.corselawn.com

dir: on B4211 5m SW of Tewkesbury

This gracious Grade II listed Queen Anne house has been home to the Hine family since 1978. Aided by an enthusiastic and committed team, the family still presides over all aspects, creating a relaxed and wonderfully comforting environment. Bedrooms offer a reassuring mix of comfort and quality. Impressive cuisine is based upon excellent produce, much of it locally sourced.

Rooms 19 en suite (2 fmly) (5 GF) S fr £90; D fr £140 (incl. bkfst) **Facilities** STV ⬚ ♫ ♨ Wi-fi available Badminton Croquet Table tennis **Conf** Thtr 50 Class 30 Board 25 Del from £140 **Parking** 62 **Notes LB** ⊘ in restaurant Closed 24-26 Dec Civ Wed 70

See advert under TEWKESBURY

DUMBLETON MAP 10 SP03

★★★ 73% **HOTEL**

Dumbleton Hall

WR11 7TS

☎ 01386 881240 ▤ 01386 882142

e-mail: dh@pofr.co.uk

dir: M5 junct 8 follow A46 for Evesham. 5m S of Evesham take right signed Dumbleton Hotel is set back at S end of village.

Originally constructed in the 16th century, and re-built in the mid-18th century this establishment is set in 19 acres of landscaped gardens

continued on page 264

DUMBLETON *continued*

and parkland. Spacious public rooms make this an ideal venue for weddings, conferences or a hideaway retreat - the location makes an ideal touring base. Panoramic views of the Vale of Evesham can be seen from every window.

Rooms 34 en suite (9 fmly) ⊗ in 25 bedrooms S fr £120; D £160-£260 (incl. bkfst) **Facilities** FTV ♨ **Conf** Thtr 100 Class 60 Board 60 Del from £145 **Services** Lift **Parking** 60 **Notes** LB ⊗ in restaurant Civ Wed 100

EWEN   MAP 04 SU09

★★ 68% **HOTEL**

Wild Duck Inn

Drakes Island GL7 6BY
☎ 01285 770310 📠 01285 770924
e-mail: wduckinn@aol.com
web: www.thewildduckinn.co.uk
dir: *from Cirencester take A429. At Kemble left to Ewen*

This bustling, ever-popular inn dates back to the early 16th century and is full of character. Bedrooms vary in style and are well equipped and tastefully furnished. Open fires, old beams and rustic pine tables add to the charm in the bar and restaurant, where the cooking has earned a loyal following.

Rooms 12 en suite (8 GF) S fr £70; D £95-£150 **Facilities** Discounted leisure facilities within 3m **Parking** 50 **Notes** ⊗ in restaurant RS 25 Dec

FAIRFORD   MAP 05 SP10

★★ 67% **HOTEL**

Bull Hotel

The Market Place GL7 4AA
☎ 01285 712535 & 712217 📠 01285 713782
e-mail: info@thebullhotelfairford.co.uk
dir: *on A417 in market square adjacent to post office*

Located in a picturesque Cotswold market town, the history of this family-run inn dates back to the 15th century, and it still retains much period character and charm. Bedrooms are individual in style with a number overlooking the square. A wide range of meals can be enjoyed in the popular bar or alternatively in the bistro restaurant.

Rooms 22 rms (20 en suite) 4 annexe en suite (4 fmly) ⊗ in 8 bedrooms S £50-£70; D £80-£100 (incl. bkfst) **Facilities** Fishing Cycle hire **Conf** Thtr 60 Class 40 Board 40 Del £92.50 **Parking** 10 **Notes** LB ⊗ in restaurant

See advert on opposite page

FALFIELD   MAP 04 ST69

★★★ 71% **HOTEL**

Bristol Inn

Bristol Rd GL12 8DL
☎ 01454 260502 📠 01454 261821
e-mail: info@bristolinn.co.uk
web: www.bristolinn.co.uk
dir: *M5 junct 14 follow sign to Dursley. Right at A38 junct, hotel 200yds on right*

Situated beside the A38, allowing easy access to the cities of Cheltenham, Gloucester, Bristol and also the M5, this modernised

continued

---

hotel offers comfortable, contemporary accommodation in a relaxed and informal atmosphere. There is also a range of meeting rooms.

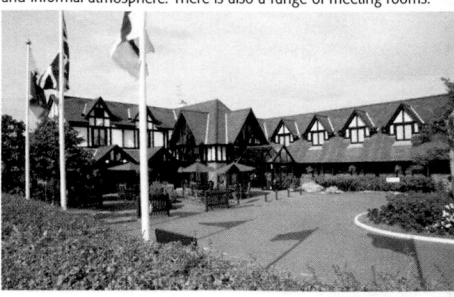

Bristol Inn

Rooms 46 en suite (18 GF) ⊗ in 40 bedrooms **Facilities** STV ♨ 18 Putt green **Conf** BC Thtr 200 Class 60 Board 50 **Parking** 107 **Notes** ⊗ ⊗ in restaurant Civ Wed 140

GLOUCESTER   MAP 10 SO81

★★★ 77% ⊛ **HOTEL**

Hatton Court

Upton Hill, Upton St Leonards GL4 8DE
☎ 01452 617412 📠 01452 612945
e-mail: res@hatton-court.co.uk
web: www.hatton-court.co.uk
dir: *leave Gloucester on B4073. Hotel at hill top on right*

Built in the style of a 17th-century Cotswold manor house, and set in seven acres of well-kept gardens this hotel is popular with both business and leisure guests. It commands truly spectacular views of the Severn Valley. Bedrooms are comfortable and tastefully furnished with many extra facilities. The elegant Carringtons Restaurant offers varied menus, and there is also a bar and foyer lounge.

Rooms 17 en suite 28 annexe en suite ⊗ in all bedrooms S £85-£90; D £100-£105 (incl. bkfst) **Facilities** Sauna Gym ♨ Jacuzzi Xmas **Conf** Thtr 60 Class 30 Board 30 Del from £135 **Parking** 80 **Notes** LB ⊗ in restaurant Civ Wed 75

★★★ 73% **HOTEL**

Ramada Bowden Hall   ⓡ RAMADA.

Bondend Ln, Upton St Leonards GL4 8ED
☎ 01452 614121 📠 01452 611885
e-mail: sales.bowdenhall@ramadajarvis.co.uk
web: www.ramadajarvis.co.uk
dir: *M5 junct 11, A40 towards Gloucester. At rdbt take A417. At next rdbt take A38/Gloucester. At next rdbt take 2nd exit. At 2nd lights left onto Abbeymead Ave. 1.5m, 3rd left onto Upton Lane, left into Bondend Rd. Hotel at end*

Conveniently located, a short distance from the M5, this country hotel is set in delightful grounds and is an ideal venue for weddings, banquets and meetings, or for a quiet country break. Bedrooms are spacious and well appointed and many have lovely views of the grounds. There is a treatment and leisure facility and guests can choose to dine in the restaurant or bar.

Rooms 72 en suite (21 fmly) ⊗ in 54 bedrooms S £62-£145; D £77-£145 **Facilities** STV ⓡ supervised Sauna Solarium Jacuzzi Trimnasium. Beauty Therapy Xmas **Conf** Thtr 120 Class 70 Board 70 Del from £105 **Parking** 150 **Notes** LB ⊗ ⊗ in restaurant Civ Wed 80

★★★ 70% HOTEL

Macdonald Hatherley Manor

Down Hatherley Ln GL2 9QA
☎ 0870 1942126 📠 01452 731032
e-mail: hatherleymanor@macdonaldhotels.co.uk
web: www.macdonald-hotels.co.uk
dir: off A38 into Down Hatherley Lane, signed. Hotel 600yds on left

Within easy striking distance of the M5, Gloucester, Cheltenham and the Cotswolds, this stylish 17th-century manor remains popular with both business and leisure guests. Bedrooms all offer contemporary comforts. A range of meeting and function rooms is available.

Rooms 52 en suite ⊛ in 41 bedrooms **Conf** Thtr 300 Class 90 Board 75
Parking 250 **Notes LB** ⊘ in restaurant Civ Wed 300

★★★ 68% HOTEL

Ramada Hotel & Resort Gloucester

RAMADA
HOTEL & RESORT

Matson Ln, Robinswood Hill GL4 6EA
☎ 01452 525653 📠 01452 307212
e-mail: sales.gloucester@ramadajarvis.co.uk
dir: A40 towards Gloucester onto A38. Take 1st exit at 4th rdbt (Painswick Rd) and turn right onto Matson Ln

Conveniently located close to the M5, this large hotel is set in 240 acres of grounds. Bedrooms are comfortably appointed for both business and leisure guests.

Rooms 97 en suite (7 fmly) (20 GF) ⊛ in 59 bedrooms D £54-£145
Facilities Spa ⊠ supervised ↓ 18 ⅀ Squash Snooker Sauna Solarium Gym Putt green Jacuzzi Dry ski slopes Xmas **Conf** Thtr 150 Class 80 Board 60 Del from £130 **Parking** 200 **Notes** ⊘ in restaurant Closed 24-26 Dec Civ Wed 140

U

Swallow New County

SWALLOW
HOTELS

44 Southgate St GL1 2DU
☎ 01452 307000 📠 01452 500487
e-mail: newcounty@swallowhotels.com
web: www.swallowhotels.com
dir: Follow City & Docks signs on A38, past docks. At lights take right lane onto one-way system, left at Black Swan Inn into Southgate St. Hotel 100yds on left

At the time of going to press, the star classification for this hotel was not confirmed. Please refer to the AA internet site www.theAA.com for current information.

Rooms 39 en suite (3 fmly) ⊘ in 12 bedrooms S £55-£65; D £70-£85 (incl. bkfst) **Conf** Thtr 100 Class 80 Board 40 Del from £105 **Notes LB** ⊗ ⊘ in restaurant RS 26-30 Dec, 1-7 Jan

BUDGET HOTEL

Premier Travel Inn Gloucester Business Park

premier
travel inn

Gloucester Business Park, Delta Way, Brockworth GL3 4EL
☎ 0870 8500347 📠 0870 8500342
web: www.premiertravelinn.com

High quality, modern budget accommodation ideal for both families and business travellers. Spacious, en suite bedrooms feature bath and shower, satellite TV and many have telephones and modem points. The adjacent family restaurant features a wide and varied menu. For further details consult the Hotel Groups page.

Rooms 48 en suite

Premier Travel Inn Gloucester East (Barnwood)

Barnwood GL4 3HR
☎ 0870 9906322 📠 0870 9906323
dir: Exit M5 junct 11 onto A40 towards Gloucester. At 1st rdbt take A417 towards Cirencester, at next rdbt take 4th exit
Rooms 83 en suite

Premier Travel Inn Gloucester (Longford)

Tewkesbury Rd, Longford GL2 9BE
☎ 08701 977115 📠 01452 300924
dir: from M5 junct 11, follow A40 to Gloucester, A40 to Ross. Inn on A38 to Gloucester
Rooms 60 en suite **Conf** Thtr 40

GLOUCESTER *continued*

Premier Travel Inn Gloucester North

Tewkesbury Rd, Twigworth GL2 9PG

☎ 0870 9906560 📠 0870 9906561

dir: *2m from Gloucester. Exit M5 junct 11, A40 towards Gloucester, then A38 towards Tewkesbury*

Rooms 52 en suite

Premier Travel Inn Gloucester (Witcombe)

Witcombe GL3 4SS

☎ 08701 977116 📠 01452 864926

dir: *M5 junct 11A follow A417 (Cirencester) at 1st exit turn right onto A46 towards Stroud/Witcombe. Left at next rdbt by Crosshands PH*

Rooms 39 en suite

LOWER SLAUGHTER   MAP 10 SP12

INSPECTORS' CHOICE

★★★ ◉◉ **HOTEL**

Lower Slaughter Manor

GL54 2HP

☎ 01451 820456 📠 01451 822150

e-mail: info@lowerslaughterter.co.uk

web: www.vonessenhotels.co.uk

dir: *off A429 signed "The Slaughters". Manor 0.5m on right on entering village*

There is a timeless elegance about this wonderful manor, which dates back to the 17th century. Its imposing presence makes it very much the centrepiece of this famous Cotswold village. Inside, the levels of comfort and quality are immediately evident, with crackling log fires warming the many sumptuous lounges. The hotel's dining room is an elegant creation that suitably complements the excellent cuisine on offer. Spacious and tastefully furnished bedrooms are either in the main building or in the adjacent coach house.

Rooms 11 en suite 5 annexe en suite (2 GF) S £155-£265; D £185-£295 (incl. bkfst) **Facilities** ☞ Xmas **Conf** Thtr 36 Class 20 Board 22 Del from £165 **Parking** 30 **Notes** No children 12yrs ⊘ in restaurant Civ Wed 60

★★★ 80% ◉◉ **HOTEL**

Washbourne Court

GL54 2HS

☎ 01451 822143 📠 01451 821045

e-mail: info@washbournecourt.co.uk

web: www.vonessenhotels.co.uk

dir: *off A429 at 'The Slaughters' signpost, between Stow-on-the-Wold and Bourton-on-the-Water. Hotel in centre of village*

Beamed ceilings, log fires and flagstone floors are some of the attractive features of this partly 17th-century built hotel, set in four acres of immaculate grounds beside the River Eye. There are smartly decorated bedrooms situated in the main house, plus self-contained cottages, many with lovely views. The riverside terrace is popular during summer months, whilst the elegant dining room serves an interesting menu and comprehensive wine list.

Rooms 15 en suite 13 annexe en suite (4 GF) ⊘ in all bedrooms S £90-£125; D £120-£190 (incl. bkfst & dinner) **Facilities** Xmas **Conf** Thtr 70 Class 40 Board 30 Del from £145 **Parking** 40 **Notes LB** ⊘ in restaurant Civ Wed 60

MICHAEL WOOD   MAP 04 ST79
MOTORWAY SERVICE AREA (M5)

BUDGET HOTEL

Days Inn Michaelwood

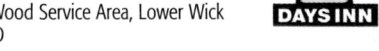

Michael Wood Service Area, Lower Wick
GL11 6DD

☎ 01454 261513 📠 01454 269150

e-mail: michaelwood.hotel@welcomebreak.co.uk

web: www.welcomebreak.co.uk

dir: *M5 northbound between junct 13 and 14*

This modern building offers accommodation in smart, spacious and well-equipped bedrooms, suitable for families and business travellers, and all with en suite bathrooms. Continental breakfast is available and other refreshments may be taken at the nearby family restaurant. For further details see the Hotel Groups page.

Rooms 38 en suite **Conf** Board 10

England

MORETON-IN-MARSH
MAP 10 SP23

★★★ 82% ◉◉ HOTEL

Manor House

CLASSIC
BRITISH HOTELS

High St GL56 0LJ
☎ 01608 650501 🖹 01608 651481
e-mail: info@manorhousehotel.info
web: www.costswold-inns-hotels.co.uk

dir: off A429 at south end of town. Take East St off High St, hotel car park 3rd on right

Dating back to the 16th century, this charming Cotswold coaching inn retains much of its original character with stone walls, impressive fireplaces and a relaxed, country-house atmosphere. Bedrooms vary in size and reflect the individuality of the building; all are well equipped and some are particularly opulent. Comfortable public areas include the popular bar and stylish Mulberry Restaurant - dinner should not be missed here.

Rooms 35 en suite 3 annexe en suite (3 fmly) ◉ in all bedrooms S £180; D £220 (incl. bkfst & dinner) **Facilities** FTV Xmas **Conf** Thtr 120 Class 48 Board 54 **Services** Lift **Parking** 24 **Notes LB** ⊗ ◉ in restaurant Civ Wed 120

★★★ 75% HOTEL

Redesdale Arms

High St GL56 0AW
☎ 01608 650308 🖹 01608 651843
e-mail: info@redesdalearms.co.uk

dir: on A429, 0.5m from rail station

This fine old inn has played a central role in this town for centuries. Traditional features combines successfully with contemporary comforts. Bedrooms are split between the main building and the former stables, but all have high standards of comfort; six new superior Courtyard bedrooms have been added. Guests can choose to dine either in the stylish restaurant or conservatory.

Rooms 8 en suite 10 annexe en suite (2 fmly) (5 GF) ◉ in all bedrooms S £50-£65; D £65-£120 (incl. bkfst) **Facilities** STV Xmas **Parking** 14 **Notes** ⊗ ◉ in restaurant

★★ 65% HOTEL

White Hart Royal

High St GL56 0BA
☎ 01608 650731 🖹 01608 650880

dir: on A429 in town centre

This Cotswold coaching inn dates back to the 17th century and once provided a hiding place for Charles I. Much of the original character has been retained with flagstone floors, a cobbled entrance hall and a feature fireplace. Bedrooms are brightly decorated and comfortably appointed.

Rooms 19 en suite (2 fmly) **Facilities** STV **Conf** Thtr 80 **Parking** 20 **Notes LB** ◉ in restaurant

NAILSWORTH
MAP 04 ST89

★★ 72% ◉ HOTEL

Egypt Mill

GL6 0AE
☎ 01453 833449 🖹 01453 839919
e-mail: reception@egyptmill.com

dir: on A46, midway between Cheltenham and Bath

Millstones and working waterwheels have been incorporated in the innovative design of this 17th-century former corn mill. Well-equipped bedrooms are located in two adjacent buildings and are tastefully furnished. Facilities include the stylish cellar bar and convivial bistro, where accomplished cuisine is proving very popular. During summer months the riverside patios and gardens are great places to enjoy a leisurely drink.

Rooms 10 en suite 18 annexe en suite (2 fmly) (2 GF) ◉ in all bedrooms S £65-£75; D £80-£95 (incl. bkfst) **Facilities** STV ⤴ Wi-fi in bedrooms Boules pitch Xmas **Conf** Thtr 100 Class 80 Board 80 Del from £100 **Parking** 80 **Notes LB** ⊗ ◉ in restaurant Civ Wed 120

NEWENT

◉◉ RESTAURANT WITH ROOMS

Three Choirs Vineyards

GL18 1LS
☎ 01531 890223 🖹 01531 890877
e-mail: info@threechoirs.com
web: www.threechoirs.com

dir: On B4215 north of Newent, follow brown tourist signs

This thriving vineyard continues to go from strength to strength and provides a wonderfully different place to stay. The restaurant, which overlooks the 100-acre estate, enjoys a popular following thanks to well-executed dishes that make good use of local produce. Spacious, high quality bedrooms are equipped with many extras and each opens onto a private patio area, from where wonderful views can be enjoyed.

Rooms 8 annexe en suite (2 fmly) (8 GF) ◉ in all bedrooms S £75-£115; D £95-£115 **Facilities** Wine tasting Vineyard Tours **Conf** Thtr 20 Class 15 Board 20 Del from £125 **Parking** 8 **Notes LB** ⊗ Closed 24 Dec-5 Jan Civ Wed 20

OLD SODBURY

★★ 74% HOTEL

Cross Hands

OLD ENGLISH INNS

BS37 6RJ

☎ 01454 313000 📠 01454 324409

e-mail: 6435@greeneking.co.uk

web: www.oldenglish.co.uk

dir: M4 junct 18 signed to Cirencester/Stroud on A46. After 1.5m hotel on left at 1st lights.

A former posting house dating back to the 14th century, conveniently located just off the main road, within easy reach of Bath and Bristol. Bedrooms are well equipped and some are at ground floor level. The public areas include a bar, comfortable seating area and a spacious split-level restaurant, which offers a selection of home cooked dishes. Alternatively, guests may choose to eat from the extensive menu in the bar area.

Rooms 21 en suite (1 fmly) (9 GF) ⊗ in 11 bedrooms S £70-£85; D £95-£115 (incl. bkfst) **Facilities** STV Xmas **Conf** Thtr 100 Class 40 Board 50 Del from £110 **Parking** 120 **Notes** ⊗ in restaurant Civ Wed 80

PAINSWICK

MAP 04 SO81

★★★ 78% ☺ ☺ HOTEL

Painswick Hotel and Restaurant

Kemps Ln GL6 6YB

☎ 01452 812160 📠 01452 814059

e-mail: reservations@painswickhotel.com

web: www.painswickhotel.com

dir: off A46 in village centre. Hotel off 2nd road behind church, off Tibbiwell Lane

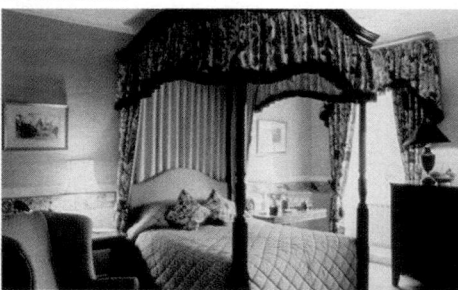

Dating back to 1790, this former rectory is situated in the heart of one of the Cotswolds' most enchanting villages. Attentive hospitality and service are key features. The day rooms house antiques and interesting artwork, contributing to a sense of timeless elegance. All bedrooms differ, yet reflect similar high standards. Accomplished cuisine and a serious choice of wine are served in the oak-panelled restaurant.

Rooms 19 en suite (2 fmly) (6 GF) ⊗ in all bedrooms S £135-£190; D £145-£200 (incl. bkfst) **Facilities** 🏊 Fishing ↳ Wi-fi in bedrooms Xmas **Conf** Thtr 50 Class 15 Board 26 **Parking** 20 **Notes LB** ⊗ in restaurant Civ Wed 80

RANGEWORTHY

MAP 04 ST68

★★ 69% HOTEL

Rangeworthy Court

Church Ln, Wotton Rd BS37 7ND

☎ 01454 228347 📠 01454 228945

e-mail: hotel@rangeworthy.demon.co.uk

web: www.rangeworthy.demon.co.uk

dir: signposted off B4058

This welcoming manor house hotel is peacefully located in its own grounds, and is within easy reach of the motorway network. The character bedrooms come in a variety of sizes and there is a choice of comfortable lounges to relax in. The candlelit restaurant offers a varied and interesting menu.

Rooms 13 en suite (4 fmly) ⊗ in 3 bedrooms S fr £82.25; D fr £99.87 (incl. bkfst) **Facilities** 🎾 ↳ Boules ch fac **Conf** BC Thtr 22 Class 14 Board 16 Del from £29.90 **Parking** 40 **Notes** ⊗ in restaurant

SEVERN VIEW MOTORWAY SERVICE AREA (M4)

MAP 04 ST58

BUDGET HOTEL

Travelodge Bristol Severn View (M48)

Severn Bridge BS35 4BH

☎ 08700 850 950 📠 01454 632482

web: www.travelodge.co.uk

dir: M48 junct 1

Travelodge offers good quality, good value, modern accommodation. Ideal for families, the spacious en suite bedrooms include remote-control TV, tea and coffee-making facilities and comfortable beds. Meals can be taken at the nearby family restaurant. See Hotel Groups pages for further details.

Rooms 50 en suite S fr £26; D fr £26

STONEHOUSE

MAP 04 SO80

Ⓤ

Stonehouse Court

GL10 3RA

☎ 0871 871 3240 📠 0871 871 3241

e-mail: info@stonehousecourt.co.uk

dir: M5 junct 13, off A419. Follow signs for Stonehouse, hotel on right 0.25m after 2nd rdbt

At the time of going to press, the star classification for this hotel was not confirmed. Please refer to the AA internet site www.theAA.com for current information.

Rooms 9 en suite 27 annexe en suite (2 fmly) (2 GF) ⊗ in 6 bedrooms **Facilities Spa** STV Gym ↳ 🎵 **Conf** Thtr 150 Class 75 Board 70 **Parking** 200 **Notes LB** ⊗ in restaurant Civ Wed 150

BUDGET HOTEL

Travelodge Stonehouse

A 419, Easington GL10 3SQ

☎ 08700 850 950 📠 01453 828590

web: www.travelodge.co.uk

dir: *M5 junct 13, onto A419*

Travelodge offers good quality, good value, modern accommodation. Ideal for families, the spacious en suite bedrooms include remote-control TV, tea and coffee-making facilities and comfortable beds. Meals can be taken at the nearby family restaurant. See Hotel Groups pages for further details.

Rooms 40 en suite S fr £26; D fr £26

STOW-ON-THE-WOLD   MAP 10 SP12

★★★★ 76% ◉ ◉ HOTEL

Wyck Hill House

Burford Rd GL54 1HY

☎ 01451 831936 📠 01451 832243

e-mail: enquiries@wyckhillhouse.com

dir: *turn off A429. Hotel 1m on right*

This charming 18th-century house enjoys superb views across the Windrush Valley and is ideally positioned for a relaxing weekend exploring the Cotswolds. The spacious and thoughtfully equipped bedrooms provide high standards of comfort and quality and are located both in the main house and the original coach house. Elegant public rooms include the cosy bar, library and the magnificent front hall with crackling log fire. The imaginative cuisine makes effective use of local produce.

Rooms 16 en suite 16 annexe en suite (1 fmly) (10 GF) **Facilities** STV ⛵ Archery Clay pigeon shooting Ballooning Honda pilots **Conf** BC Thtr 60 Class 30 Board 24 **Services** Lift **Parking** 100 **Notes LB** ⊛ in restaurant Civ Wed 80

★★★ 80% ◉ ◉ HOTEL

Fosse Manor

GL54 1JX

☎ 01451 830354 📠 01451 832486

e-mail: enquiries@fossemanor.co.uk

web: www.fossemanor.co.uk

dir: *1m S on A429, 300yds past junct with A424*

CLASSIC
BRITISH HOTELS

Deriving its name from the historic Roman Fosse Way, this popular hotel is ideally located for exploring the many delights of this

continued

picturesque area. Bedrooms, located both in the main building and the adjacent coach house, offer high standards of comfort and quality. Public areas include a comfortable lounge, elegant restaurant and convivial bar. Classy cuisine is on offer with quality produce used to create imaginative dishes.

Rooms 11 en suite 8 annexe en suite (3 fmly) (5 GF) ⊛ in all bedrooms S fr £95; D £130-£215 (incl. bkfst) **Facilities** STV ⛵ Xmas **Conf** Thtr 60 Class 20 Board 26 Del from £155 **Parking** 30 **Notes LB** ⊛ ⊛ in restaurant Civ Wed 60

★★★ 75% HOTEL

Stow Lodge

The Square GL54 1AB

☎ 01451 830485 📠 01451 831671

e-mail: enquiries@stowlodge.com

web: www.stowlodge.com

dir: *in town centre*

Situated in smart grounds, this non-smoking, family-run hotel has direct access to the market square and provides high standards of customer care. Bedrooms are offered both within the main building and in the converted coach house, all of which provide similar standards of homely comfort. Extensive menus and an interesting wine list make for an enjoyable dining experience.

Rooms 11 en suite 10 annexe en suite (1 fmly) ⊛ in all bedrooms S £65-£140; D £75-£160 (incl. bkfst) **Parking** 30 **Notes LB** ⊛ No children 5yrs ⊛ in restaurant Closed Xmas-end Jan

---

★★★ 75% HOTEL

The Unicorn

Sheep St GL54 1HQ

☎ 01451 830257 📠 01451 831090

e-mail: reception@birchhotels.co.uk

dir: *at junct of A429 & A436*

This attractive limestone hotel dates back to the 17th century. Individually designed bedrooms include some delightful four-poster rooms. Spacious public areas retain much character and include a choice of inviting lounges and a traditional bar offering a good selection of bar meals and ales. The newly refurbished restaurant provides a stylish venue for impressive cuisine.

Rooms 20 en suite ⊛ in all bedrooms **Facilities** ♬ Xmas **Conf** Thtr 50 Class 20 Board 28 **Parking** 40 **Notes** ⊛ in restaurant RS Dates Vary Civ Wed 45

England

STOW-ON-THE-WOLD *continued*

★★★ 74% ⊛ **HOTEL**

Best Western Grapevine

Sheep St GL54 1AU

☎ 01451 830344 📄 01451 832278

e-mail: enquiries@vines.co.uk

web: www.vines.co.uk

dir: on A436 towards Chipping Norton. 150yds on right, facing green

Situated in the heart of this unique market town, the Grapevine is a delightful 17th-century hotel with lots of charm and character. Original features abound, such as stone-flagged floors and aged beams. Individually styled bedrooms combine comfort and quality, and each is equipped with thoughtful extras. Canopied by an ancient vine, the Conservatory Restaurant is a lovely setting for accomplished cuisine. Alternatively, lighter meals can be enjoyed either in the popular bar or in La Vigna, the hotel's Mediterranean styled bistro.

Rooms 12 en suite 10 annexe en suite (2 fmly) (5 GF) ⊛ in all bedrooms S £85-£95; D £140-£160 (incl. bkfst) **Facilities** Putt green Wi-fi in bedrooms Xmas **Conf** Thtr 30 Class 18 Board 20 Del from £140 **Parking** 25 **Notes LB** ⊗ ⊛ in restaurant Civ Wed 85

See advert on opposite page

★★★ 73% ⊛⊛ **HOTEL**

The Royalist

Digbeth St GL54 1BN

☎ 01451 830670 📄 01451 870048

e-mail: info@theroyalisthotel.co.uk

dir: off A429 at lights in Stow, into Sheep Street , 2nd left into Digbeth Street

Verified as the oldest inn in England, this charming hotel has a wealth of history and character. Bedrooms and public areas have been stylishly and sympathetically decorated to ensure high levels of comfort at every turn. Some rooms are in an adjoining annexe. There are two eating options: the 947AD restaurant offering high-quality cooking, and the Eagle and Child, a more informal alternative.

Rooms 8 en suite (2 fmly) ⊛ in all bedrooms **Facilities** Jacuzzi Discounted rates at local gym **Conf** Thtr 46 Class 30 Board 20 **Parking** 8 **Notes** ⊗ in restaurant

★★ 71% **HOTEL**

Old Stocks

The Square GL54 1AF

☎ 01451 830666 📄 01451 870014

e-mail: aa@theoldstockshotel.co.uk

web: www.oldstockshotel.co.uk

dir: turn off A429 to town centre. Hotel facing village green

Overlooking the old market square, this Grade II listed, mellow Cotswold-stone building is a comfortable and friendly base from which to explore this picturesque area. There is a lot of character and atmosphere with bedrooms all offering individuality and charm. Facilities include a guest lounge, restaurant and bar, whilst outside, the patio is a popular summer venue for refreshing drinks and good food.

Rooms 15 en suite 3 annexe en suite (5 fmly) (4 GF) ⊛ in 14 bedrooms **Facilities** ch fac **Parking** 12 **Notes LB** ⊗ in restaurant

STROUD

MAP 04 SO80

★★★ 77% ⊛ **HOTEL**

Burleigh Court

Burleigh, Minchinhampton GL5 2PF

☎ 01453 883804 📄 01453 886870

e-mail: info@burleighcourthotel.co.uk

dir: From Stroud A419 towards Cirencester. Right after 2.5m signed Burleigh & Minchinhampton. Left after 500yds signed Burleigh Court. Hotel 300yds on right

Dating back to the 18th century, this former gentleman's manor house is in a secluded yet accessible elevated position with some wonderful countryside views. Public rooms are elegantly styled and include a wonderful oak-panelled bar for pre-dinner drinks beside a crackling fire. Combining comfort and quality, no two bedrooms are the same and some are in an adjoining coach house.

Rooms 18 en suite (2 fmly) (3 GF) ⊛ in 11 bedrooms S fr £85; D fr £125 (incl. bkfst) **Facilities** ◆ ◆ ch fac **Conf** Thtr 50 Class 30 Board 30 Del from £160 **Parking** 40 **Notes LB** ⊗ in restaurant Civ Wed 50

★★★ 73% ⊛ **HOTEL**

The Bear of Rodborough

CLASSIC
BRITISH HOTELS

Rodborough Common GL5 5DE

☎ 01453 878522 📄 01453 872523

e-mail: info@bearofrodborough.info

web: www.cotswold-inns-hotels.co.uk

dir: M5 junct 13, A419 to Stroud. Follow signs to Rodborough. Up hill, left at top at T-junct. Hotel on right.

This popular 17th-century coaching inn is situated high above Stroud in acres of National Trust parkland. Character abounds in the lounges, cocktail bar and Box Tree restaurant. Bedrooms offer equal measures of comfort and style with plenty of extra touches. There is also a traditional and well-patronised public bar. Cuisine, utilising much local produce, is a highlight.

Rooms 46 en suite (2 fmly) ⊛ in all bedrooms S £75; D £120-£140 (incl. bkfst) **Facilities** ◆ Putt green Wi-fi available Xmas **Conf** Thtr 60 Class 35 Board 30 Del from £120 **Parking** 70 **Notes LB** ⊗ in restaurant Civ Wed 70

BUDGET HOTEL

Premier Travel Inn Stroud

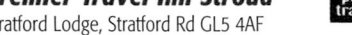

Stratford Lodge, Stratford Rd GL5 4AF
☎ 0870 9906378 🖷 0870 9906379
web: www.premiertravelinn.com

dir: Off M5 junct 13, follow A419 to town centre, then signs for leisure centre. Hotel is opposite, next to Tesco superstore

High quality, modern budget accommodation ideal for both families and business travellers. Spacious, en suite bedrooms feature bath and shower, satellite TV and many have telephones and modem points. The adjacent family restaurant features a wide and varied menu. For further details consult the Hotel Groups page.

Rooms 32 en suite

TETBURY   **MAP 04 ST89**

INSPECTORS' CHOICE

★★★★ ◉◉ **HOTEL**

Calcot Manor

Calcot GL8 8YJ
☎ 01666 890391 🖷 01666 890394
e-mail: reception@calcotmanor.co.uk
web: www.calcotmanor.co.uk

dir: 3m West of Tetbury at junct A4135/A46

Cistercian monks built the ancient barns and stables around which this lovely English farmhouse is set. No two rooms are identical, and each is beautifully decorated in a variety of styles and equipped with the contemporary comforts. Sumptuous sitting rooms, with crackling log fires in the winter, look out over immaculate gardens. There are two dining options: the elegant conservatory restaurant and the informal Gumstool Inn. There are also ample function rooms. A superb health and leisure spa includes an indoor pool, high-tech gym, massage tables, complementary therapies and much more. For children, a supervised crèche and 'playzone' are a great attraction.

Rooms 12 en suite 23 annexe en suite (10 fmly) D £195-£220 (incl. bkfst) **Facilities** Spa 🏸 ₹ ⚓ Sauna Solarium Gym 🏌 Jacuzzi Clay pigeon shooting ch fac Xmas **Conf** BC Thtr 100 Class 40 Board 35 Del from £215 **Parking** 120 **Notes** LB ⊗ ⊘ in restaurant Civ Wed 100

★★★ 77% **HOTEL**

Close

OLD ENGLISH INNS

8 Long St GL8 8AQ
☎ 01666 502272 🖷 01666 504401
e-mail: reception@theclosehotel.co.uk
web: www.oldenglish.co.uk

dir: From M4 junct 17 onto A429 to Malmesbury, then follow Tetbury signs. Or M5 junct 14 onto B4509 follow signs to Tetbury

Even with its town centre location, this charming hotel retains a country-house feel that has made it a favourite with many for years. Bedrooms are traditional and feature thoughtful touches such as home-made biscuits, fresh fruit and bottled water. The public rooms provide a choice of relaxing areas with log fires lit in the winter. In the summer, guests can enjoy the terrace in the attractive walled garden.

Rooms 15 en suite **Facilities** STV 🏌 **Conf** Thtr 50 Board 22 **Parking** 22 **Notes** LB ⊘ in restaurant Civ Wed 50

England

TETBURY *continued*

★★★ 72% HOTEL

Best Western Hare & Hounds

Westonbirt GL8 8QL

☎ 01666 880233 & 881000 📄 01666 880241

e-mail: enquiries@hareandhoundshotel.com

web: www.hareandhoundshotel.com

dir: 2.5m SW of Tetbury on A433

This popular hotel, set in extensive grounds, is situated close to Westonbirt Arboretum and has been run by the same family for 50 years. Genuine hospitality is a strength with staff keen to help. Public areas are charming, with polished parquet flooring, whilst bedrooms are traditional in style and located in both the main house and adjacent coach house. Leisure facilities include squash and tennis courts.

Rooms 24 en suite 7 annexe en suite (3 fmly) (5 GF) ⊗ in 12 bedrooms S £88-£93; D £112-£117 (incl. bkfst) **Facilities** STV ⬡ Squash ⬡ Putt green Half size snooker table Xmas **Conf** Thtr 120 Class 80 Board 40 Del £130 **Parking** 85 **Notes LB** ⊗ in restaurant Civ Wed 200

★★★ 72% HOTEL

The Priory Inn

London Rd GL8 8JJ

☎ 01666 502251 📄 01666 503534

e-mail: info@theprioryinn.co.uk

web: www.theprioryinn.co.uk

dir: on A433, Cirencester/Tetbury road 200yds from Market Square

A warm welcome is guaranteed at this attractive inn where friendly service is a high priority to the team. Public areas and bedrooms have a contemporary style that mixes well with more traditional features, such as an open fireplace in the cosy bar dining room. Cuisine uses locally sourced produce skilfully prepared. For those in need of a little pampering, the hotel also has a partnership with a beauty and well-being centre next door.

Rooms 14 en suite (1 fmly) (4 GF) ⊗ in 10 bedrooms S £69-£99; D £90-£109 (incl. bkfst) **Facilities** STV Wi-fi in bedrooms Health and Beauty Centre, Beauty Treatments etc. ♪ Xmas **Conf** Thtr 30 Class 28 Board 28 Del from £109 **Parking** 35 **Notes LB** ⊗ ⊗ in restaurant

★★★ 71% HOTEL

Snooty Fox

Market Place GL8 8DD

☎ 01666 502436 📄 01666 503479

e-mail: res@snooty-fox.co.uk

web: www.snooty-fox.co.uk

dir: in town centre

Centrally situated, the Snooty Fox is a popular venue for weekend breaks, and retains many of the historic features associated with a 16th-century coaching inn. The atmosphere is relaxed and friendly, the accommodation of a high standard, and the food offered in the bar and restaurant is another good reason why guests return.

Rooms 12 en suite ⊗ in all bedrooms S £72-£98; D £94-£205 (incl. bkfst) **Facilities** Xmas **Conf** Thtr 24 Class 12 Board 16 Del from £112 **Notes LB** ⊗ in restaurant

★★ 64% HOTEL

Hunters Hall

OLD ENGLISH INNS

Kingscote GL8 8XZ

☎ 01453 860393 📄 01453 860707

e-mail: huntershall.kingscote@greeneking.co.uk

web: www.oldenglish.co.uk

dir: M4 junct 18, take A46 towards Stroud. 10m turn left signed Kingscote, follow road to T-junct, turn left, hotel 0.5m on left.

A charming 16th century inn with much character. The modern bedrooms are situated in a separate building that was once the stables and blacksmiths' shop. Several bedrooms are on the ground floor and one room has been specially designed for disabled guests. The hotel has three bars and a restaurant offering home cooked traditional food. There is also a large garden for summer dining.

Rooms 12 annexe en suite (1 fmly) (8 GF) ⊗ in 8 bedrooms S £55-£60; D £90-£95 (incl. bkfst) **Facilities** Pool table ch fac Xmas **Conf** Thtr 30 Class 12 Board 20 Del from £75 **Parking** 100 **Notes LB** ⊗ in restaurant

TEWKESBURY

MAP 10 SO83

★★★ 71% HOTEL

Tewkesbury Park Hotel Golf & Country Club

folio Hotels

Lincoln Green Ln GL20 7DN

☎ 0870 609 6101 📄 01684 292386

dir: M5 junct 9/A438 through Tewkesbury, A38 (pass Abbey on left), right into Lincoln Green Lane

Only two miles from the M5, this extended 18th-century manor house boasts wonderful views across the Malvern Hills from its hilltop position. Bedrooms offer contemporary comforts and many have the

continued

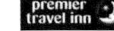

added bonus of countryside views. In addition to the well-established golf course, an indoor pool, gym, sauna, squash and tennis courts are also available.

Rooms 80 en suite (8 fmly) (21 GF) ⊘ in 58 bedrooms **Facilities** STV ℞ supervised ♨ 18 ♨ Squash Sauna Solarium Gym Putt green Jacuzzi Activity field, 6 hole pitch & put **Conf** Thtr 150 Class 100 Board 50 **Parking** 250 **Notes LB** ⊘ in restaurant Civ Wed 100

★★★ 62% HOTEL

Royal Hop Pole

Church St GL20 5RT

☎ 01684 293236 ▤ 01684 296680

e-mail: info@theroyalhoppolehotel.co.uk

web: www.theroyalhoppole.co.uk

dir: M5 junct 9 for Tewkesbury approx 1.5m. At War Memorial rdbt, straight across, hotel on right

This former coaching inn is within walking distance of historic Tewkesbury Abbey and has been offering a warm welcome to weary travellers since the 14th century. There is character in abundance here with many original features including age darkened beams and sloping floors. Bedrooms have great individuality some being in the main house, others in the more recent garden wing. Additional facilities include a popular bar, attractive restaurant and relaxing lounge.

Rooms 29 en suite (1 fmly) (5 GF) ⊘ in 20 bedrooms S £60-£75; D £100-£130 (incl. bkfst & dinner) **Facilities** Xmas **Conf** Board 34 Del from £100 **Parking** 35 **Notes** ⊘ in restaurant

---

★★ 60% HOTEL

Bell

OLD ENGLISH INNS

52 Church St GL20 5SA

☎ 01684 293296 ▤ 01684 295938

e-mail: 6408@greeneking.co.uk

web: www.oldenglish.co.uk

dir: M5 junct 9, follow brown tourist signs for Tewkesbury Abbey, hotel directly opposite Abbey.

This 14th-century former coaching house is situated on the edge of the town, opposite the Norman abbey. The bar and lounge are the focal point of this atmospheric and friendly establishment, with a large open fire providing warmth. Bedrooms offer good levels of comfort and quality with many extra facilities provided, such as CD players.

Rooms 24 en suite (1 fmly) (4 GF) ⊘ in 7 bedrooms S £65; D £85 (incl. bkfst) **Facilities** Xmas **Conf** Thtr 60 Class 16 Board 24 Del £100 **Parking** 20 **Notes LB** ⊘ in restaurant

---

Premier Travel Inn Tewkesbury Central

premier travel inn

Shannon Way, Ashchurch GL20 8RD

☎ 08708 501845

web: www.premiertravelinn.com

High quality, modern budget accommodation ideal for both families and business travellers. Spacious, en suite bedrooms feature bath and shower, satellite TV and many have telephones and modem points. The adjacent family restaurant features a wide and varied menu. For further details consult the Hotel Groups page.

Rooms 40 en suite

Sleep Inn Tewkesbury

SLEEP INN

Off Shannon Way, Ashchurch GL20 8BL

☎ 01684 853090 & 853097 ▤ 01684 853099

e-mail: enquiries@hotels-tewkesbury.com

dir: M5 junct 9, A438 to Tewkesbury. Right at 1st lights into Shannon Way, then 1st right

This modern, purpose built accommodation offers smartly appointed, well-equipped bedrooms, with good power showers. There is a choice of adjacent food outlets where guests may enjoy breakfast, snacks and meals.

Rooms 71 en suite **Conf** Thtr 40 Class 16 Board 12

THORNBURY   MAP 04 ST69

INSPECTORS' CHOICE

★★★ ◎◎ **HOTEL**

Thornbury Castle

Castle St BS35 1HH

☎ 01454 281182 📠 01454 416188

e-mail: info@thornburycastle.co.uk

web: www.vonessenhotels.co.uk

dir: *on A38 N'bound from Bristol take 1st turn to Thornbury. At end of High St left into Castle St, follow brown sign, entrance to Castle on left behind St Marys Church*

Henry VIII ordered the first owner of this castle to be beheaded! Guests today have the opportunity of sleeping in historical surroundings fitted out with all modern amenities. Most rooms have four-poster or coronet beds and real fires. Tranquil lounges enjoy views over the gardens, while elegant, wood-panelled dining rooms make a memorable setting for a leisurely award-winning meal.

Rooms 25 en suite (3 fmly) (3 GF) S £90-£110; D £150-£199 (incl. bkfst) **Facilities** STV Snooker ⛳ Wi-fi available Hot air ballooning, archery, helicopter ride, clay pigeon shooting Xmas **Conf** Thtr 70 Class 40 Board 30 Del £250 **Parking** 40 **Notes LB** ⊘ in restaurant Civ Wed 70

★★ 68% **HOTEL**

Thornbury Golf Lodge

Bristol Rd BS35 3XL

☎ 01454 281144 📠 01454 281177

e-mail: info@thornburygc.co.uk

web: www.thornburygc.co.uk

dir: *M5 junct 16 take A38 Thornbury. At traffic lights (Berkeley Vale Motors) take left. Entrance 1m on left*

The old farmhouse exterior of Thornbury Golf Lodge disguises an

continued

interior with spacious, well equipped and comfortable bedrooms. Many have pleasant views over the centre's two golf courses or towards the Severn Estuary. Meals are taken in the adjacent clubhouse which features a full bar and serves a range of hot and cold food all day.

Rooms 11 en suite (7 GF) S £45-£51.95; D £45-£64.95 **Facilities** STV ⛳ 18 Putt green **Conf** Thtr 100 Class 40 Board 40 **Parking** 150 **Notes LB** ⊗ No children 5yrs Closed 25 Dec

TORMARTON   MAP 04 ST77

★★ 78% **HOTEL**

Best Western Compass Inn

GL9 1JB

☎ 01454 218242 & 218577 📠 01454 218741

e-mail: info@compass-inn.co.uk

web: www.compass-inn.co.uk

dir: *0.5m from M4 junct 18*

Originally a coaching inn dating from the 18th century, this hostelry has grown considerably over the years. Bedrooms are spacious and well equipped, whilst public areas include a choice of bars and varied dining options. A range of conference rooms is also available, providing facilities for varied functions.

Rooms 26 en suite (5 fmly) (12 GF) ⊗ in 19 bedrooms S £88.50-£98.50; D £98.50-£108.50 **Facilities** Wi-fi in bedrooms French boules **Conf** Thtr 100 Class 30 Board 34 Del £114.50 **Parking** 160 **Notes LB** Closed 24-26 Dec Civ Wed 100

UPPER SLAUGHTER   MAP 10 SP12

INSPECTORS' CHOICE

★★★ ◎◎◎ **HOTEL**

Lords of the Manor

GL54 2JD

☎ 01451 820243 📠 01451 820696

e-mail: enquiries@lordsofthemanor.com

web: www.bespokehotels.com

dir: *2m W of A429. Turn off A40 onto A429, take 'The Slaughters' turn. Through Lower Slaughter for 1m to Upper Slaughter. Hotel on right*

This wonderfully welcoming 17th-century manor house hotel sits in eight acres of gardens and parkland surrounded by Cotswold countryside. A relaxed atmosphere, underpinned by professional and attentive service is the hallmark here, so that guests are often reluctant to leave. The public rooms are elegant and the restaurant is the venue for consistently impressive cuisine.

continued

Bedrooms have much character and charm, combined with the extra touches expected of a hotel of this stature.

Rooms 27 en suite (9 GF) S £110-£140; D fr £170 (incl. bkfst) **Facilities** STV Fishing ⏚ ch fac Xmas **Conf** Thtr 30 Class 20 Board 20 Del from £170 **Parking** 40 **Notes LB** ⊘ in restaurant Civ Wed 50

WINCHCOMBE

◉◉ RESTAURANT WITH ROOMS

Wesley House

High St GL54 5LJ

☎ 01242 602366 📠 01242 609046

e-mail: enquiries@wesleyhouse.co.uk

web: www.wesleyhouse.co.uk

dir: On B4632 between Cheltenham and Broadway

A 15th-century, half-timbered property named after John Wesley, founder of the Methodist Church, who stayed here while preaching in the town. In a complete refurbishment, a glass atrium has been added to cover the outside terrace. Bedrooms are comfortably appointed and offer much character and individuality. A unique lighting system changes colour to suit the mood required.

Rooms 6 en suite ⊘ in all bedrooms S £110-£120; D £150-£200 (incl. bkfst & dinner) **Notes LB** ⊗ Closed 25-26 Dec RS Sun nights Civ Wed 60

WOTTON-UNDER-EDGE   MAP 04 ST79

★★★★ 73% HOTEL

Tortworth Court Four Pillars

Tortworth GL12 8HH

☎ 0800 374 692 & 01454 263000 📠 01454 263001

e-mail: tortworth@four-pillars.co.uk

web: www.four-pillars.co.uk

dir: M5 junct 14, B4509 pass Tortworth Visitors Centre take next right, hotel 0.5m on right

Set within 30 acres of parkland, this Gothic mansion displays original features cleverly combined with contemporary additions. Elegant public rooms include a choice of dining options, one housed within the library, another in the atrium and the third in the orangery. Bedrooms are well equipped, and additional facilities include a host of conference rooms and a leisure centre.

Rooms 189 en suite (70 GF) ⊘ in 95 bedrooms S £79-£162; D £92-£209 (incl. bkfst) **Facilities** FTV ⏚ Sauna Gym Jacuzzi Wi-fi in bedrooms Beauty suite, Steam room Xmas **Conf** BC Thtr 400 Class 200 Board 80 Del £179 **Services** Lift **Parking** 350 **Notes LB** ⊗ ⊘ in restaurant Civ Wed 100

GREATER MANCHESTER

ALTRINCHAM   MAP 15 SJ78

★★★ 77% HOTEL

Best Western Cresta Court

Church St WA14 4DP

☎ 0161 927 7272 📠 0161 929 6548

e-mail: rooms@cresta-court.co.uk

web: www.cresta-court.co.uk

This modern hotel enjoys a prime location on the A56, close to the station and town centre shops and amenities. Bedrooms vary in style

continued

from spacious four-posters to smaller, traditionally furnished rooms. Public areas include a choice of bars, a small gym, beauty salon and extensive function and conference facilities.

Rooms 137 en suite (9 fmly) ⊘ in 126 bedrooms S £55-£89; D £65-£89 **Facilities** STV ⏚ Gym Wi-fi in bedrooms Running & Rowing Machine & Beauty Salon Xmas **Conf** BC Thtr 350 Class 200 Board 150 Del from £40 **Services** Lift **Parking** 200 **Notes LB** ⊘ in restaurant Civ Wed 300

See advert on this page

★★★ 72% HOTEL

Quality Hotel Altrincham

Langham Rd, Bowdon WA14 2HT

☎ 0161 928 7121 📠 0161 927 7560

e-mail: enquiries@hotels-altrincham.com

web: www.choicehotelseurope.com

dir: M6 junct 19 to airport, join A556, over M56 rdbt onto A56, right at traffic lights onto B5161. Hotel 1m on right

This popular hotel is located within easy reach of the motorways and airport. It provides comfortable and well-equipped bedrooms. The public areas consist of the modern Cafe Continental, the main restaurant which offers modern cuisine, and a leisure club. A range of conference rooms is also available.

Rooms 91 en suite (6 fmly) (13 GF) ⊘ in 53 bedrooms S £55-£105; D £65-£120 **Facilities** Spa STV ⏚ supervised Sauna Solarium Gym Wi-fi available Beauty treatments Xmas **Conf** Thtr 165 Class 60 Board 48 Del from £110 **Parking** 160 **Notes LB** ⊘ in restaurant Civ Wed 150

England

ALTRINCHAM *continued*

BUDGET HOTEL

Premier Travel Inn Altrincham North

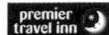

Manchester Rd WA14 4PH
☎ 0870 9906580 📄 0870 9906581
web: www.premiertravelinn.com
dir: *From N, exit M60 junct 7, follow A56 towards Altrincham. From S, exit M6 junct 19, take A556 then A56 towards Sale*

High quality, modern budget accommodation ideal for both families and business travellers. Spacious, en suite bedrooms feature bath and shower, satellite TV and many have telephones and modem points. The adjacent family restaurant features a wide and varied menu. For further details consult the Hotel Groups page.

Rooms 46 en suite

Premier Travel Inn Altrincham South

Manchester Rd, West Timperley WA14 5NH
☎ 0870 9906330 📄 0870 9906331
dir: *2m from Altrincham. From N, exit M60 junct 7, take A56 towards Altrincham. From S, exit M6 junct 19. Follow A556 then A56 towards Sale.*
Rooms 48 en suite **Conf** Thtr 50

BIRCH MOTORWAY SERVICE AREA (M62)   MAP 16 SD80

BUDGET HOTEL

Travelodge Manchester Birch (M62 Eastbound)

M62 Service Area East Bound OL10 2HQ
☎ 08700 850 950 📄 0161 655 3716
web: www.travelodge.co.uk
dir: *Between junct 18 & 19 on M62 eastbound*

Travelodge offers good quality, good value, modern accommodation. Ideal for families, the spacious en suite bedrooms include remote-control TV, tea and coffee-making facilities and comfortable beds. Meals can be taken at the nearby family restaurant. See Hotel Groups pages for further details.

Rooms 55 en suite S fr £26; D fr £26

Travelodge Manchester North (M62 Westbound)

M62 Service Area West Bound OL10 2HQ
☎ 08700 850 950 📄 0161 655 6422
dir: *Between junct 18 & 19 on M62 westbound*
Rooms 35 en suite S fr £26; D fr £26

BOLTON   MAP 15 SD70

★★★★ 76% HOTEL

Last Drop Village Hotel & Spa

Bromley Cross BL7 9PZ
☎ 0870 1942117 📄 01204 304122 & 598824
e-mail: lastdrop@macdonald-hotels.co.uk
web: www.macdonald-hotels.co.uk
dir: *3m N of Bolton off B5472*

Built along the lines of a small self-contained village, this resort complex includes a variety of shops, a pub, a steak house, a bakery and a tea room. Bedrooms are varied, including cottage-style accommodation set around a delightful courtyard. A dazzling, fully equipped spa and extensive conference facilities make this an ideal business and leisure destination.

Rooms 118 en suite 10 annexe en suite (29 fmly) (20 GF) ⊘ in 113 bedrooms S £77-£110; D £91-£130 (incl. bkfst) **Facilities Spa** STV ⬚ ⬚ supervised Solarium Gym Jacuzzi Craft shops, Thermal suite Rock sauna, steam room, bio sauna ♫ Xmas **Conf** Thtr 700 Class 300 Board 95 Del from £125 **Services** Lift **Parking** 400 **Notes LB** ⊘ in restaurant Civ Wed 500

★★★★ HOTEL

Holiday Inn Bolton Centre

1 Higher Bridge St BL1 2EW
☎ 01204 879988 & 0870 442 0901 📄 01204 879983
e-mail: reservations.hibolton@qmh-hotels.com
dir: *M61 junct 3 to A666, left at lights (Gordons Ford). Left at next lights, onto Higher Bridge St, hotel on right.*

Located close to Bolton town centre this modern hotel offers well-equipped accommodation. There is an attractive lounge bar, and

continued

England

breakfast and dinner both are available in Hardies Restaurant. There is also a spa and extensive conference facilities.

Rooms 132 en suite (2 fmly) ⊘ in 110 bedrooms S £64-£85; D £85 **Facilities** Spa STV ◨ supervised Sauna Solarium Gym **Conf** Thtr 340 Class 125 Board 80 Del £138 **Services** Lift air con **Parking** 100 **Notes** ⊗ ⊘ in restaurant Civ Wed 150

★★★ 78% HOTEL

Ramada Bolton
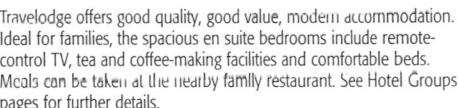

Manchester Rd, Blackrod BL6 5RU
☎ 01942 814598 📠 01942 816026
e-mail: sales.bolton@ramadajarvis.co.uk
web: www.ramadajarvis.co.uk

dir: Exit M61 junct 6, follow Blackrod A6027 signs. 200yds turn right onto A6 signed Chorley. Hotel 0.5m on right

This modern hotel enjoys easy access to the M61, M62, M60 and M6. Bedrooms are comfortably appointed for both business and leisure guests and there is a well-equipped leisure club.

Rooms 91 en suite (7 fmly) (8 GF) ⊘ in 80 bedrooms S £109; D £119 (incl. bkfst) **Facilities** STV ◨ supervised Snooker Sauna Solarium Gym Jacuzzi Wi-fi available Steam room hairdressing salon, reflexology sports injury Xmas **Conf** Thtr 700 Class 334 Board 274 Del from £105 **Services** Lift **Parking** 350 **Notes** LB ⊘ in restaurant Civ Wed 100

★★★ 72% HOTEL

Egerton House

Blackburn Rd, Egerton BL7 9SB
☎ 01204 307171 📠 01204 593030
e-mail: reservation@egertonhouse-hotel.co.uk
web: www.egertonhouse-hotel.co.uk

dir: from M61 take A666 (Bolton Rd), pass Asda on right. Hotel 500yds on right

Peace and relaxation come as standard at this popular, privately owned hotel, nestling in acres of well-tended woodland gardens. Public rooms are stylishly appointed and have an inviting, relaxing feel to them. Many of the individually styled, attractive guest bedrooms enjoy delightful garden views. Conferences and meetings are well catered for.

Rooms 32 en suite (7 fmly) ⊘ in 20 bedrooms S £69-£100; D £79-£120 (incl. bkfst) **Facilities** STV Xmas **Conf** Thtr 150 Class 90 Board 60 Del from £120 **Parking** 120 **Notes** ⊗ ⊘ in restaurant Civ Wed 200

BUDGET HOTEL

Premier Travel Inn Bolton

premier travel inn

991 Chorley New Rd, Horwich BL6 4BA
☎ 08701 977282 📠 01204 692585
web: www.premiertravelinn.com

dir: M61 junct 6 follow dual carriageway to Bolton/Horwich with Reebok Stadium on left, continue & Inn on the 2nd rdbt

High quality, modern budget accommodation ideal for both families and business travellers. Spacious, en suite bedrooms feature bath and shower, satellite TV and many have telephones and modem points. The adjacent family restaurant features a wide and varied menu. For further details consult the Hotel Groups page.

Rooms 40 en suite

BUDGET HOTEL

Travelodge Bolton West (M61 Southbound)

Travelodge

Bolton West Service Area, Horwich BL6 5UZ
☎ 08700 850 950 📠 01204 668585
web: www.travelodge.co.uk

dir: between junct 6 & 7 of M61

Travelodge offers good quality, good value, modern accommodation. Ideal for families, the spacious en suite bedrooms include remote-control TV, tea and coffee-making facilities and comfortable beds. Meals can be taken at the nearby family restaurant. See Hotel Groups pages for further details.

Rooms 32 en suite S fr £26; D fr £26 **Conf** Thtr 60 Class 60 Board 30

BURY   **MAP 15 SD81**

★★★ 72% HOTEL

Best Western Bolholt Country Park

Best Western

Walshaw Rd BL8 1PU
☎ 0161 762 4000 📠 0161 762 4100
e-mail: reservations@bolholt.co.uk

dir: M60 junct 17 for Whitefield, A56 to Bury for 4m. Follow signs for A58 to Bolton. Take 3rd lane at car showroom signed Tottington. Left at pub, left again

This former mill owner's house is located in attractive parkland and secluded gardens just a short walk from the town centre. Bedrooms are comfortable and modern, whilst an impressive leisure club boasts two swimming pools, extensive fitness facilities and a fashionable café-bar. Wide ranging conference and banqueting facilities are available and the setting is ideal for weddings.

Rooms 65 en suite (13 fmly) (16 GF) ⊘ in 29 bedrooms S £89; D £104 (incl. bkfst) **Facilities** STV ◨ supervised Fishing Squash Sauna Solarium Gym Jacuzzi Fitness & leisure centre Xmas **Conf** Thtr 300 Class 120 Board 40 Del from £75 **Parking** 300 **Notes** ⊘ in restaurant Civ Wed 200

England

BURY *continued*

BUDGET HOTEL

Travelodge Bury

Little 66, Route 66 Leisure Park, Pilsworth Rd BL9 8RS

☎ 08700 850 950 🖷 0161 796 7547

web: www.travelodge.co.uk

dir: *Exit M66 junct 3 and turn left. At roundabout take right and 1st right onto Little 66.*

Travelodge offers good quality, good value, modern accommodation. Ideal for families, the spacious en suite bedrooms include remote-control TV, tea and coffee-making facilities and comfortable beds. Meals can be taken at the nearby family restaurant. See Hotel Groups pages for further details.

Rooms 54 en suite S fr £26; D fr £26

CHEADLE   MAP 16 SJ88

BUDGET HOTEL

Premier Travel Inn Manchester (Cheadle)

Royal Crescent SK8 3FE

☎ 08701 977172 🖷 0161 491 5886

web: www.premiertravelinn.com

dir: *off Cheadle Royal rdbt off A34 behind TGI Friday's*

High quality, modern budget accommodation ideal for both families and business travellers. Spacious, en suite bedrooms feature bath and shower, satellite TV and many have telephones and modem points. The adjacent family restaurant features a wide and varied menu. For further details consult the Hotel Groups page.

Rooms 40 en suite **Conf** Thtr 30

DIDSBURY   MAP 16 SJ89

BUDGET HOTEL

Travelodge Manchester Didsbury

Kingsway M20 5PG

☎ 08700 850 950 🖷 0161 448 0399

web: www.travelodge.co.uk

dir: *M60 junct 4, follow A34 towards Didsbury. Lodge at Parswood Leisure Park*

Travelodge offers good quality, good value, modern accommodation. Ideal for families, the spacious en suite bedrooms include remote-control TV, tea and coffee-making facilities and comfortable beds. Meals can be taken at the nearby family restaurant. See Hotel Groups pages for further details.

Rooms 62 en suite S fr £26; D fr £26

HORWICH   MAP 15 SD61

★★★★ 75% ◉◉ **HOTEL**

De Vere White's

De Havilland Way BL6 6SF

☎ 01204 667788 🖷 01204 673721

e-mail: whites@devere-hotels.com

web: www.devere.co.uk

dir: *M61 junct 6. 3rd right from slip road rdbt onto A6027 Mansell Way. Follow visitors car park A for hotel*

Fully integrated within the Reebok Stadium, home of Bolton Wanderers FC, this modern hotel is a popular venue for business and conferences. Bedrooms are contemporary in style and equipped with a range of extras; many offer views of the pitch. The hotel has two eating options - a fine dining restaurant and informal brasserie. It also boasts a fully equipped indoor leisure centre and spacious bar/lounge area.

Rooms 125 en suite (1 fmly) ✿ in 99 bedrooms S £67-£135; D £67-£145 (incl. bkfst) **Facilities** Spa STV 🏊 supervised Sauna Solarium Gym Jacuzzi Wi-fi in bedrooms Steam room, Beauty salon Xmas **Conf** Thtr 1500 Class 1080 Board 72 Del from £125 **Services** Lift **Parking** 2750 **Notes** LB ⊗ ✿ in restaurant Civ Wed 1000

MANCHESTER   MAP 16 SJ89

See also Manchester Airport & Sale

★★★★★ 84% ◉◉ **HOTEL**

The Lowry Hotel

50 Dearmans Place, Chapel Wharf, Salford M3 5LH

ROCCO FORTE
HOTELS

☎ 0161 827 4000 🖷 0161 827 4001

e-mail: enquiries@roccofortehotels.com

web: www.roccofortehotels.com

dir: *M6 junct 19, A556 & M56 follow signs for Manchester. A5103 for 4.5m. At rdbt take A57(M) to lights, turn right onto Water St. Left to New Quay St/Trinity Way. At 1st lights turn right onto Chapel St to hotel*

This modern, contemporary hotel, set beside the River Irwell in the centre of the city, offers spacious bedrooms equipped to meet the needs of business and leisure visitors alike. Many of the rooms look out over the river, as do the sumptuous suites. The River Room restaurant produces good brasserie cooking. Extensive business and function facilities are available, together with a spa to provide extra pampering.

Rooms 165 en suite (7 fmly) ✿ in 90 bedrooms S £120-£235; D £120-£270 **Facilities** Spa STV Sauna Gym Wi-fi in bedrooms Spa facilities & swimming available offsite 🎵 Xmas **Conf** BC Thtr 400 Class 250 Board 60 Del from £225 **Services** Lift air con **Parking** 100 **Notes** LB ⊗ Civ Wed 400

★★★★ 83% ◉◉ **HOTEL**

Midland

QHOTELS

Peter St M60 2DS

☎ 0161 236 3333 🖷 0161 932 4100

web: www.qhotels.co.uk

dir: *M602 junct 3, follow G-Mex signs. Hotel opposite G-Mex*

This popular centrally located, well-established Edwardian-style hotel has undergone a major transformation. Refurbished bedrooms are stylish, thoughtfully equipped and have a wonderful contemporary

continued

feel. Elegant public areas are now equally impressive and facilities include a health and leisure spa, extensive function and meeting rooms and a choice of bars and dining options that include the award-winning classical French restaurant.

Rooms 303 en suite (62 fmly) @ in 170 bedrooms **Facilities** STV 🔲 Squash Sauna Solarium Gym Jacuzzi Hair & beauty salon **Conf** BC Thtr 500 Class 300 Board 120 **Services** Lift air con **Notes** Civ Wed 500

★★★★ 79% **HOTEL**

Marriott Manchester Victoria & Albert Hotel

Water St M3 4JQ

☎ 0161 832 1188 📠 0161 834 2484

web: www.marriott.co.uk

dir: M602 to A57 through lights on Regent Rd. Pass Sainsbury's, left at lights onto ring road, right at lights into Water St.

This uniquely converted warehouse, with an interior featuring exposed brickwork and iron pillars, is located on the banks of the River Irwell, just a short stroll from the city centre. A major refurbishment programme has resulted in stylish, comfortable and well-equipped bedrooms together with attractive public areas. A large bar lounge leads onto an intimate restaurant, and extensive conference facilities are available.

Rooms 158 en suite (2 fmly) @ in 90 bedrooms **Facilities** STV Complimentary use of Livingwell Health Club **Conf** BC Thtr 250 Class 120 Board 72 **Services** Lift air con **Parking** 120 **Notes LB** ⊗ Civ Wed 200

★★★★ 77% **HOTEL**

Renaissance Manchester

Blackfriars St M3 2EQ

☎ 0161 831 6000 📠 0161 835 3077

e-mail: rhi.manbr.sales@renaissancehotels.com

web: www.renaissancehotels.com

dir: Follow signs to Deansgate, turn left onto Blackfriars St at 2nd set of lights after Kendals, hotel on right

This smart hotel enjoys a central location just off Deansgate, within easy walking distance of The Arena and the city's many shops and attractions. Stylish, well-equipped bedrooms are extremely comfortable and those on higher floors offer wonderful views. Public areas include an elegant bar and restaurant and an impressive smart conference and banqueting suite.

Rooms 203 en suite @ in 153 bedrooms **Facilities** STV Complimentary leisure facilities nearby **Conf** BC Thtr 400 Class 300 Board 100 **Services** Lift air con **Parking** 80 **Notes** ⊗ @ in restaurant Civ Wed 100

★★★★ 76% @ **HOTEL**

Copthorne Hotel Manchester

Clippers Quay, Salford Quays M50 3SN

☎ 0161 873 7321 📠 0161 877 8112

e-mail: roomsales.manchester@mill-cop.com

web: www.copthorne.com

dir: from M602 follow signs for Salford Quays & Trafford Park on A5063. Hotel 0.75m on right

This smart hotel enjoys a convenient location on the redeveloped Salford Quays close to Old Trafford, The Lowry Centre and The Imperial War Museum. Bedrooms are comfortably appointed and well

continued

equipped for both business and leisure guests. A choice of dining options includes Chandlers Restaurant that serves accomplished food.

Rooms 166 en suite (6 fmly) @ in 118 bedrooms S £165 **Facilities** STV Wi-fi available **Conf** Thtr 150 Class 70 Board 70 Del from £85 **Services** Lift **Parking** 120 **Notes LB** ⊗ @ in restaurant Civ Wed 60

★★★★ 74% **HOTEL**

The Palace

Oxford St M60 7HA

☎ 0161 288 1111 📠 0161 288 2222

web: www.principal-hotels.com

dir: opposite Oxford Rd railway station

Formerly the offices of the Refuge Life Assurance Company, this impressive neo-Gothic building occupies a central location. There is a vast lobby, spacious open-plan bar lounge and restaurant, and extensive conference and function facilities. Bedrooms vary in size and style but are all spacious and well equipped.

Rooms 252 en suite (59 fmly) @ in 30 bedrooms **Facilities** STV 🎵 **Conf** Thtr 1000 Class 450 Board 100 **Services** Lift **Notes** ⊗ @ in restaurant Civ Wed 100

★★★★ 69% **HOTEL**

Marriott Worsley Park Hotel & Country Club

Worsley Park, Worsley M28 2QT

☎ 0161 975 2000 📠 0161 799 6341

e-mail: mhrs.mangs-ebcnorthwest@marriotthotels.com

web: www.marriott.co.uk/mangs

dir: M60 junct 13, over 1st rdbt, A575. Hotel 400yds on left

This smart, modern hotel is set in impressive grounds with a championship golf course. Bedrooms are comfortably appointed and well equipped for both leisure and business guests. Public areas include extensive leisure and conference facilities, an all-day bistro and an elegant restaurant offering imaginative cuisine.

Rooms 158 en suite (5 fmly) (50 GF) @ in 116 bedrooms S fr £125; D fr £145 **Facilities** Spa STV 🔲 ♣ 18 Sauna Solarium Gym Putt green Jacuzzi Wi-fi available Steam room Health & Beauty salon Xmas **Conf** Thtr 250 Class 150 Board 100 Del from £155 **Services** Lift **Parking** 400 **Notes LB** ⊗ @ in restaurant Civ Wed 200

MANCHESTER *continued*

★★★★ 68% ⊛ TOWN HOUSE HOTEL

Hotel Rossetti

aBode

107 Piccadilly M1 2DB
☎ 0161 247 7744 📠 0161 247 7747
e-mail: reservationsmanchester@abodehotels.co.uk
web: www.hotelrossetti.co.uk
dir: *M62/M602 follow signs for city centre/Piccadilly*

Used as a textile headquarters in Victorian times, this impressive building has been transformed to offer stylish accommodation. Bedrooms feature CD/DVD players and combine modern comfort with quirky eclectic decor. Unique 50's style diners are situated on each floor affording complimentary beverages, fresh fruit and cereals. Café Paradiso offers fresh Mediterranean food, while the basement has an exclusive club environment. This hotel has been acquired by Abode Hotels and is to be launched as Abode Manchester in early 2007.

Rooms 61 en suite ⊘ in 47 bedrooms S £110-£119; D £110-£119 **Facilities** STV Wi-fi available Xmas **Conf** Thtr 50 Class 20 Board 20 Del from £175 **Services** Lift **Notes** ⊘ in restaurant

See advert on opposite page

★★★ 85% ⊛⊛ HOTEL

Malmaison

Malmaison
hotels that dare to be different

Piccadilly M1 3AQ
☎ 0161 278 1000 📠 0161 278 1002
e-mail: manchester@malmaison.com
web: www.malmaison.com
dir: *follow city centre signs, then signs to Piccadilly station. Hotel opposite station, at bottom of station approach*

Stylish and chic, Malmaison Manchester offers the very best of contemporary hotel keeping in a relaxed and comfortable environment. The hotel offers a range of bright meeting rooms, health spa with gym and treatment rooms, as well as the ever popular bar and French-style brasserie. Air-conditioned bedrooms combine style and comfort and provide a range of extras.
Malmaison AA Hotel Group of the Year 2006-7.

Rooms 167 en suite S £140-£160; D £140-£160 **Facilities** Spa STV FTV Sauna Solarium Gym Jacuzzi Xmas **Conf** Thtr 80 Class 48 Board 30 Del from £175 **Services** Lift air con **Notes** ⊘ in restaurant

★★★ 81% ⊛⊛ HOTEL

Golden Tulip Manchester

TULIP INN

Waters Reach, Trafford Park M17 1WS
☎ 0161 873 8899 📠 0161 822 6556
e-mail: info@goldentulipmanchester.co.uk
dir: *Opposite Old Trafford Football Stadium. Manchester United North Stand*

Situated opposite Old Trafford football stadium and within easy reach of the airport and motorway network, this modern establishment is the official hotel of Manchester United FC. The stylish rooms are spacious and comfortable and include mini-bars and CD players. The Waters Reach Restaurant and Bar is a fashionable and popular venue in which to enjoy modern British cooking.

Rooms 160 en suite (37 fmly) (8 GF) ⊘ in 124 bedrooms S fr £140; D fr £140 **Facilities** STV **Conf** BC Thtr 180 Class 60 Board 45 Del from £140 **Services** Lift **Parking** 135 **Notes LB** ⊗ ⊘ in restaurant

★★★ 80% HOTEL

Best Western Princess on Portland

Best Western

101 Portland St M1 6DF
☎ 0161 236 5122 📠 0161 236 4468
e-mail: reception@princessonportland.co.uk
web: www.princessonportland.co.uk
dir: *From Piccadilly Station, along Piccadilly. Left on Portland St, hotel at junct of Princess Street*

Ideally located in the heart of the city, this former Victorian silk warehouse offers stylish accommodation. The open-plan public areas are contemporary in style and include a split-level brasserie offering an interesting selection of freshly prepared dishes. Smartly presented bedrooms are comfortably furnished and have modern facilities. Staff are friendly and keen to please.

Rooms 85 en suite (7 fmly) ⊘ in 51 bedrooms **Facilities** STV FTV Wi-fi available **Conf** Thtr 20 Class 10 Board 15 Del from £130 **Services** Lift **Notes** ⊗ ⊘ in restaurant

See advert on opposite page

★★★ 77% HOTEL

Best Western Willow Bank

Best Western

340-342 Wilmslow Rd, Fallowfield M14 6AF
☎ 0161 224 0461 📠 0161 257 2561
e-mail: gm-willowbank@feathers.uk.com
web: www.feathers.uk.com
dir: *M60 junct 5, A5103, left onto B5093. Hotel 2.5m*

This popular hotel is conveniently located three miles from the city centre, close to the universities. Bedrooms vary in size and style and
continued

England

most have now been refurbished to an impressive high standard; all are well equipped and many rooms benefit from CD players and PlayStations. Spacious, elegant public areas include a bar, a restaurant and meeting rooms.

Rooms 117 en suite (4 fmly) ⊗ in 30 bedrooms S F59-F89; D £69-£99 (incl. bkfst) **Facilities** STV Xmas **Conf** BC Thtr 125 Class 60 Board 70 Del from £120 **Parking** 100 **Notes LB** ⊗ ⊗ in restaurant Civ Wed 125

★★★ 77% **HOTEL**

Thistle Manchester

THISTLE HOTELS

3/5 Portland St, Piccadilly Gardens M1 6DP

☎ 0870 333 9139 📠 0870 333 9239

e-mail: manchester@thistle.co.uk

dir: M6 junct 19 onto M56, then A5103 signed Manchester City Centre, straight over rdbt, right at 2nd lights, straight at next lights onto Portland St, hotel on right.

The hotel is located in the centre of Manchester close to the Piccadilly Gardens and five minutes' walk from the central and financial districts. Rooms are compact and well equipped and the Portland Bar and Restaurant offers a wide selection of meals, drinks and wines. There is also an Otrium Leisure Centre and conference facilities are available.

Rooms 205 en suite (1 fmly) ⊗ in 120 bedrooms **Facilities** STV ℝ supervised Sauna Solarium Gym Jacuzzi **Conf** Thtr 300 Class 140 Board 40 **Services** Lift **Notes LB** ⊗ Civ Wed 150

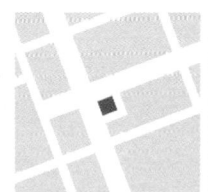

England

MANCHESTER *continued*

★★★ 77% **HOTEL**

Tulip Inn

TULIP INN

Old Park Ln M17 8PG
☎ 0161 755 3355 📠 0161 755 3344
e-mail: reservations@tulipinnmanchester.co.uk
web: www.goldentulip.co.uk

dir: *From Manchester M60 Orbital, take junct 10 towards the Trafford Centre*

This smart, modern hotel adjacent to the M60 and the Trafford Centre is easy to find and an ideal base from which to explore the city and local tourist attractions. Bedrooms are modern, stylish and well equipped. Day rooms include the Bibo bistro that serves creative dishes at dinner. Meeting rooms are also available.

Rooms 161 en suite (20 GF) ⊛ in 125 bedrooms S £54.50-£90; D £54.50-£90 **Facilities** STV **Conf** Thtr 40 Class 25 Board 25 **Services** Lift **Parking** 180 **Notes** ⊗ ⊛ in restaurant

★★★ 74% **HOTEL**

Jury's Inn Manchester
⁂ JURYS DOYLE
HOTELS

56 Great Bridgewater St M1 5LE
☎ 0161 953 8888 📠 0161 953 9090
e-mail: manchester_inn@jurysdoyle.com
web: www.jurysdoyle.com

dir: *In city centre next to G-Mex centre and Bridgewater Hall*

Enjoying a prime city centre location, Jury's Inn offers good-value, air-conditioned accommodation, ideal for both business travellers and families. Public areas include a smart, spacious lobby, the Inn Pub and the Infusion Restaurant. There are several convenient car parks with special rates available.

Rooms 265 en suite (11 fmly) (16 GF) ⊛ in 230 bedrooms S £65-£150; D £65-£150 **Facilities** STV Wi-fi available **Conf** Thtr 50 Class 25 Board 25 Del from £110 **Services** Lift air con **Notes** ⊗

★★★ 74% **HOTEL**

Quality Hotel Manchester - Central Park

QUALITY

888 Oldham Rd M40 2BS
☎ 0161 277 6910 📠 0161 277 6929
e-mail: enquiries@hotels-manchester-central-park.com
web: www.choicehotelseurope.com

dir: *M60 junct 22 onto A62. Hotel on A62.*

Located close to key transport links this new, stylish hotel provides a useful base for both the business or leisure guest. Bedrooms are spacious and comfortable and are equipped with modern facilities. A modern bistro and friendy bar ensure relaxation whilst secure parking provides peace of mind.

Rooms 83 en suite (16 fmly) (17 GF) ⊛ in 70 bedrooms S £55-£80; D £55-£80 **Facilities** STV Wi-fi available Xmas **Conf** BC Thtr 80 Class 50 Board 50 Del from £110 **Services** Lift **Parking** 48 **Notes** ⊗ ⊛ in restaurant

★★★ 73% **HOTEL**

Novotel Manchester Centre

NOVOTEL
ACCOR

21 Dickinson St Ml 4LX
☎ 0161 235220 📠 0161 2352210
e-mail: H3145@accor.com
web: www.novotel.com

dir: *from Oxford Street, into Portland Street, left into Dickinson Street. Hotel on right*

This smart, modern property enjoys a central location convenient for theatres, shops and Manchester's business district. Spacious bedrooms are thoughtfully equipped and brightly decorated. Open-plan, contemporary public areas include an all-day restaurant and a stylish bar. Extensive conference and meeting facilities are available.

Rooms 164 en suite (60 fmly) ⊛ in 123 bedrooms S £99-£115; D £99-£115 **Facilities** STV Sauna Gym Wi-fi in bedrooms Steam Room **Conf** BC Thtr 90 Class 50 Board 36 Del from £130 **Services** Lift air con

★★★ 73% **HOTEL**

Old Rectory Hotel

Meadow Ln, Haughton Green, Denton M34 7GD
☎ 0161 336 7516 📠 0161 320 3212
e-mail: reservations@oldrectoryhotelmanchester.co.uk

dir: *M60 junct 24, follow Denton signs*

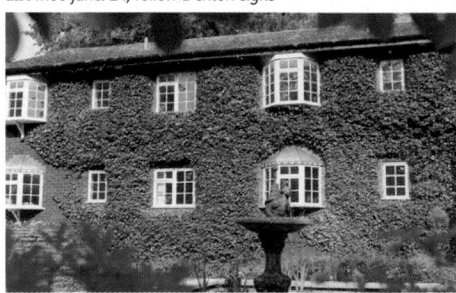

This former Victorian rectory, peacefully set around an enclosed garden, is only a short drive from Manchester's city centre. Modern bedrooms are generally spacious and well appointed. Public rooms include a bar, an attractive and popular restaurant and a mini-gym. Pleasant banqueting facilities make this a popular wedding venue.

Rooms 30 en suite 6 annexe en suite (1 fmly) (12 GF) ⊛ in 12 bedrooms S £50-£69; D £60-£79 (incl. bkfst) **Facilities** STV Gym Xmas **Conf** Thtr 100 Class 45 Board 50 **Parking** 50 **Notes** **LB** ⊛ in restaurant Civ Wed 90

★★★ 68% **HOTEL**

Novotel Manchester West

NOVOTEL
ACCOR

Worsley Brow M28 2YA
web: www.novotel.com

(For full entry see Worsley)

England

★★★ 67% HOTEL

Days Hotel Manchester City

Weston Building, Sackville St M1 3BB
☎ 0161 955 8400 📠 0161 955 8050
e-mail: weston@umist.ac.uk
web: www.welcomebreak.co.uk
dir: on Sackville St between Whitworth St & Mancunian Way

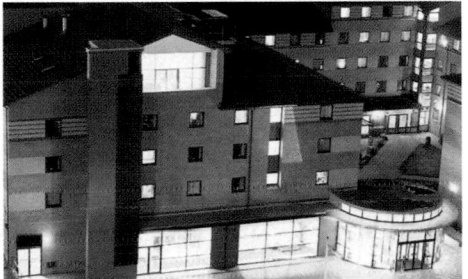

This state-of-the-art conference centre is conveniently located at the heart of the UMIST university buildings. Bedrooms are comfortable and equipped with a range of business-friendly facilities, including a high-speed internet connection. Public areas comprise a stylish bar and a spacious restaurant, as well as extensive conference and meeting room provision.

Rooms 117 en suite (2 fmly) ⊗ in 90 bedrooms **Facilities** STV **Conf** Thtr 300 Class 100 Board 40 **Services** Lift **Parking** 700 **Notes** ⊗ ⊗ in restaurant Closed 23 Dec-3 Jan

★★ 71% HOTEL

Diamond Lodge

Belle Vue, Hyde Rd, M18 7BA
☎ 0161 231 0770 📠 0161 231 0660
web: www.diamondlodge.co.uk
dir: On A57 Manchester E, 2.5m W of M60 junct 24, Manchester orbital

Offering very good value for money, this modern lodge provides comfortable accommodation near the city centre, motorway networks and football stadiums. Bright and airy, open-plan day rooms include a lounge and a brasserie-style dining room where complimentary continental breakfasts are served. An evening menu is also available.

Rooms 85 en suite S £46.95; D £46.95

See advert on this page

⊍

Jarvis Piccadilly

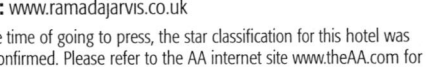

Piccadilly M60 1QR
☎ 0161 236 8414 📠 0161 228 1568
web: www.ramadajarvis.co.uk

At the time of going to press, the star classification for this hotel was not confirmed. Please refer to the AA internet site www.theAA.com for current information.

Rooms 272 en suite **Services** Lift **Parking** 80 **Notes** ⊗ in restaurant

⊍

Radisson Edwardian

Radisson
EDWARDIAN

Free Trade Hall, Peter St M2 5GP
☎ 0161 835 9929 📠 0161 835 9979
e-mail: resmanc@radisson.com
web: www.radissonedwardian.com
dir: From Deansgate, turn onto Peter St at Great Northern building. Hotel is 200yds on right.

At the time of going to press, the star classification for this hotel was not confirmed. Please refer to the AA internet site www.theAA.com for current information.

Rooms 263 en suite (5 fmly) ⊗ in 74 bedrooms **Facilities Spa** STV ⊡ supervised Sauna Gym Jacuzzi **Conf** BC Thtr 400 Class 220 Board 90 **Services** Lift air con **Notes** ⊗ ⊗ in restaurant Civ Wed 400

MANCHESTER *continued*

BUDGET HOTEL

Campanile

55 Ordsall Ln, Salford M5 4RS
☎ 0161 833 1845 ▤ 0161 833 1847
e-mail: manchester@campanile-hotels.com
web: www.envergure.fr

Campanile

dir: M602 to Manchester, then A57. After large rdbt with
Sainsbury's on left, left at next traffic lights. Hotel on right

This modern building offers accommodation in smart, well-equipped
bedrooms, all with en suite bathrooms. Refreshments may be taken at
the informal Bistro. For further details consult the Hotel Groups page.

Rooms 104 en suite S £51.95-£65; D £51.95-£65 **Conf** Thtr 50 Class 40
Board 30 Del from £95.70

BUDGET HOTEL

Hotel Ibis Manchester (Charles Street)

Charles St, Princess St M1 7DL
☎ 0161 272 5000 ▤ 0161 272 5010
e-mail: H3143@accor-hotels.com
web: www.ibishotel.com

ibis
Accor hotels

dir: M62, M602 towards Manchester Centre, follow signs to
UMIST(A34)

Modern, budget hotel offering comfortable accommodation in bright
and practical bedrooms. Breakfast is self-service and dinner is available
in the restaurant. For further details, consult the Hotel Groups page.

Rooms 126 en suite

Hotel Ibis Manchester City Centre

96 Portland St M1 4GY
☎ 0161 234 0600 ▤ 0161 234 0610
e-mail: H3142@accor-hotels.com

dir: In city centre, between Princess St & Oxford St. 10 min walk
from Piccadilly

Rooms 127 en suite S £56.95-£66.95; D £56.95-£66.95

BUDGET HOTEL

Premier Travel Inn Manchester City Centre

Portland St M1 4WB
☎ 0870 238 3315 ▤ 01823 322054
web: www.premiertravelinn.com

dir: M6 junct 19 take 3rd exit onto A556. Join M56, exit junct 3
(A5103) to Medlock St, turn right into Whitworth St, then left into
Oxford St & right into Portland St.

High quality, modern budget accommodation ideal for both families
and business travellers. Spacious, en suite bedrooms feature bath and
shower, satellite TV and many have telephones and modem points.
The adjacent family restaurant features a wide and varied menu. For
further details consult the Hotel Groups page.

Rooms 226 en suite

Premier Travel Inn Manchester City Centre (MEN Arena)

North Tower, Victoria Bridge St, Salford M3 5AS
☎ 0870 9906366 ▤ 0870 9906367

dir: Follow M602 to city centre, then A57(M) towards GMEX.
2nd exit, follow A56 city centre sign. Left before MEN arena onto
A6, 1st left

Rooms 170 en suite

Premier Travel Inn Manchester (Deansgate)

Gaythorne, River St M15 5FJ
☎ 0870 9906504 ▤ 0870 9906505

dir: Exit M60 junct 24 onto A57(M) Mancunian Way towards city
centre. Hotel adjacent A57(M) on A5103 Medlock St

Rooms 200 en suite

Premier Travel Inn Manchester (Denton)

Alphington Dr, Manchester Rd South, Denton M34 3SH
☎ 08701 977173 ▤ 0161 337 9652

dir: M60 junct 24 onto A57 signed Denton. 1st right at lights,
right at next lights, Inn on left

Rooms 40 en suite

Premier Travel Inn Manchester (GMEX)

Bishopsgate, 7-11 Lower Mosley St M2 3DW
☎ 0870 9906444 ▤ 0870 9906445

dir: Follow M56 to end, onto A5103 towards Manchester city.
Right at 2nd lights. At next lights left onto Oxford Rd, left at junct
of St Peters Sq. Hotel on left of Lower Mosley St

Rooms 147 en suite **Conf** Thtr 60

Premier Travel Inn Manchester (Heaton Park)

Middleton Rd, Crumpsall M8 4NB
☎ 08701 977174 ▤ 0161 740 9142

dir: off M60 junct 19, ring road east. Take A576 to Manchester
through 2 sets of traffic lights. Inn on left

Rooms 45 en suite **Conf** Thtr 15

Premier Travel Inn Manchester (Salford)

Basin 8 The Quays, Salford Quays M50 3SQ

☎ 08701 977176 🗎 0161 876 0094

dir: *From M602 junct 3 take A5063 on Salford Quays, 1m from Manchester United's stadium.*

Rooms 52 en suite

Premier Travel Inn Manchester (Trafford Cntr)

Wilderspool Wood, Trafford Centre, Urmston M17 8WW

☎ 08701 977307 🗎 0161 747 4763

dir: *M60 junct 10 on W side of Manchester*

Rooms 60 en suite **Conf** Thtr 12

Premier Travel Inn Manchester (West Didsbury)

Princess Parkway, Chorlton M21 7QS

☎ 08701 977 309 🗎 08701 977703

dir: *From M60 junct 5, to Manchester on A5103, Princess Parkway. Inn is approx 1m on left*

Rooms 78 en suite

BUDGET HOTEL

Travelodge Ashton Under Lyne

Lord Sheldon Way, Nr: Snipe Retail Park OL7 0DN

☎ 08700 850 950

web: www.travelodge.co.uk

dir: *From N - Follow M60 to junct 23, turn right onto A635, then 1st right onto Lord Sheldon Way. Travelodge entrance is on left.*

Travelodge offers good quality, good value, modern accommodation. Ideal for families, the spacious en suite bedrooms include remote-control TV, tea and coffee-making facilities and comfortable beds. Meals can be taken at the nearby family restaurant. See Hotel Groups pages for further details.

Rooms 62 en suite S fr £26; D fr £26

Travelodge Manchester Ancoats

22 Great Ancoats St, Ancoats M4 5AZ

☎ 08700 850950 🗎 0161 235 8631

dir: *M60 junct 11 to A57, take 5th exit off rdbt. Follow M60/M602 junct 3. Follow signs for A62 to lodge*

Rooms 117 en suite S fr £26; D fr £26

Travelodge Manchester Central

Townbury House, 11 Blackfriars St M3 5AL

☎ 08700 850 950 🗎 0161 839 5181

dir: *N on Deansgate, junct of Blackfriars St & St Mary Gate, turn left over bridge*

Rooms 181 en suite S fr £26; D fr £26

Travelodge Manchester Sportcity

Hyde Rd, Birch St, West Gorton M12 5NT

☎ 08700 850 950

dir: *M60 junct 24, follow A57 towards the city centre for 2 miles, hotel on right*

Rooms 90 en suite S fr £26; D fr £26 **Conf** Thtr 100 Class 50 Board 50

MANCHESTER AIRPORT　　MAP 15 SJ88

See also Altrincham

★★★★ 81% **HOTEL**

Manchester Airport Marriott

Marriott HOTELS & RESORTS

Hale Rd, Hale Barns WA15 8XW

☎ 0161 904 0301 🗎 0161 980 1787

e-mail: mhrs.manap.front.office@marriott.com

web: www.marriott.co.uk

dir: *M56 junct 6, then L, hotel on roundabout*

With good airport links and convenient access to the thriving city, this sprawling modern hotel is a popular destination. The hotel offers extensive leisure and business facilities, a choice of eating and drinking options and ample parking. Bedrooms are situated around a courtyard and offer a comprehensive range of facilities.

Rooms 215 en suite (22 fmly) ✷ in 160 bedrooms S fr £135; D fr £135 **Facilities** Spa STV 🏊 supervised Sauna Solarium Gym Jacuzzi Wi-fi available **Conf** BC Thtr 160 Class 70 Board 50 Del £175 **Services** Lift **Parking** 400 **Notes** LB ✷ ✷ in restaurant Civ Wed 110

★★★★ 81% ◎ **HOTEL**

Radisson SAS Hotel Manchester Airport

Radisson HOTELS & RESORTS

Chicago Av M90 3RA

☎ 0161 490 5000 🗎 0161 490 5100

e-mail: sales.airport.manchester@radissonsas.com

web: www.radisson.com

dir: *M56 junct 5, follow signs for Terminal 2. At rdbt 2nd left and follow signs for railway station. Hotel next to station*

All the airport terminals are quickly accessed from this modern hotel by covered, moving walkways. Facilities are excellent and include a well-equipped leisure club complete with indoor pool and extensive conference and banqueting facilities. Air-conditioned bedrooms are thoughtfully equipped and come in a variety of decorative themes. Super views of the runway can be enjoyed from the Phileas Fogg restaurant that offers creative international cuisine.

Rooms 360 en suite (27 fmly) ✷ in 280 bedrooms S £105-£155; D £105-£155 **Facilities** STV 🏊 Sauna Solarium Gym Wi-fi in bedrooms Health & beauty treatments **Conf** BC Thtr 350 Class 180 Board 50 Del from £165 **Services** Lift air con **Parking** 222 **Notes** LB ✷ Civ Wed 230

England

MANCHESTER AIRPORT *continued*

★★★★ 79% ◉◉ **HOTEL**

Stanneylands

Stanneylands Rd SK9 4EY

☎ 01625 525225 📠 01625 537282

e-mail: reservations@stanneylandshotel.co.uk

web: www.stanneylandshotel.co.uk

dir: from M56 for Airport turn off, follow signs to Wilmslow. Left
into Station Rd, onto Stanneylands Rd. Hotel on right

This traditional hotel offers well-equipped bedrooms and delightful,
comfortable day rooms. The cuisine in the restaurant is of a high
standard and ranges from traditional favourites to more imaginative
contemporary dishes. Staff throughout are friendly and obliging.

Rooms 54 en suite (2 fmly) (10 GF) ⊗ in all bedrooms S £68-£110;
D £90-£125 **Facilities** STV Wi-fi in bedrooms **Conf** BC Thtr 120 Class 50
Board 40 Del £140 **Services** Lift **Parking** 104 **Notes LB** ⊗ Civ Wed 100

See advert on opposite page

★★★ 77% ◉ **HOTEL**

Etrop Grange Hotel

Thorley Ln M90 4EG

☎ 0870 609 6123 📠 0161 499 0790

ſolio *Hotels*

dir: M56 junct 5 follow signs for Terminal 2, on slip road to rdbt
take 1st exit. Immediately left and hotel 400yds

This Georgian country-house style hotel is close to Terminal 2 but one
would never know once inside. Stylish, comfortable bedrooms provide
modern comforts and good business facilities. Comfortable, elegant
day rooms include the Coach House Restaurant that serves creative

continued

dishes. Complimentary chauffeured transport is available for guests
using the airport.

Rooms 64 en suite (10 GF) ⊗ in 46 bedrooms S £59-£149; D £69-£149
Facilities Wi-fi available **Conf** Thtr 80 Class 35 Board 35 Del from £125
Parking 80 **Notes LB** ⊗ ⊗ in restaurant RS 25-26 Dec Civ Wed 90

★★★ 75% **HOTEL**

Bewleys Hotel Manchester Airport

Bewleys
Hotels.com

Outwood Ln M90 4HL

☎ 0161 498 0333 📠 0161 498 0222

e-mail: man@bewleyshotels.com

web: www.bewleyshotels.com

dir: at Manchester Airport. Follow signs to Manchester Airport
Terminal 3. Hotel on left on Terminal 3 rdbt.

Located adjacent to the airport this modern, stylish hotel provides an
ideal stop-off for air travellers and business guests alike. All bedrooms
are spacious and well equipped and include a wing of superior rooms.
Spacious, open-plan day rooms are stylishly appointed and include a
large bar and restaurant along with a good range of meeting and
conference facilities.

Rooms 365 en suite (111 fmly) (30 GF) ⊗ in 307 bedrooms S fr £69;
D fr £69 **Facilities** STV Wi-fi in bedrooms ch fac **Conf** Thtr 72 Class 40
Board 40 Del from £129 **Services** Lift **Parking** 300 **Notes** ⊗ ⊗ in
restaurant

★★★ 74% **HOTEL**

Thistle Manchester Airport

THISTLE HOTELS

180 Wilmslow Rd, Handforth SK9 3LG

☎ 0870 333 9140 📠 0870 333 9240

e-mail: manchesterairport@thistle.co.uk

dir: M60 junct 3 follow A34 towards Wilmslow at 3rd rdbt turn
right following tourist signs. At end of dual carriageway turn left,
hotel on left.

Set in attractive gardens on the outskirts of Manchester and close to
the airport the hotel offers well-equipped, comfortable
accommodation. There are relaxing lounges and meals are taken in
either the Terrace Restaurant or bar. Extensive conference and
banqueting facilities are available.

Rooms 58 en suite (3 fmly) ⊗ in 42 bedrooms **Facilities** STV ⍾
Conf Thtr 150 Class 60 Board 50 **Services** Lift **Parking** 160 **Notes** ⊗ in
restaurant Civ Wed 150

★★★ 72% **HOTEL**

Best Western Belfry House

Stanley Rd SK9 3LD

☎ 0161 437 0511 🖹 0161 499 0597

e-mail: office@belfryhousehotel.co.uk

web: www.belfryhousehotel.co.uk

dir: off A34, 4m S of junct 3 M60

This popular hotel, set in its own grounds, enjoys a convenient position close to Manchester Airport and the motorway network. Extensive public areas include leisure and conference facilities and an elegant, contemporary restaurant. Bedrooms are traditionally furnished and overlook the attractive gardens.

Rooms 81 en suite (8 fmly) (12 GF) ⊗ in 69 bedrooms **Facilities** Spa STV 🏊 Sauna Solarium Gym Jacuzzi ♬ **Conf** Thtr 300 Class 120 Board 50 **Services** Lift **Parking** 150 **Notes** LB ⊗ Civ Wed 120

★★★ 72% **HOTEL**

Holiday Inn
Manchester Airport

Altrincham Rd SK9 4LR

☎ 0870 443 6961 🖹 01625 531876

e-mail: himanchester@qmh-hotels.com

dir: A538, follow road for approximtely 1m, hotel on left

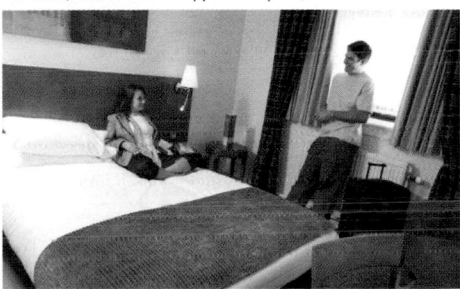

Just a short distance from Manchester Airport and the M56 motorway, this pleasant hotel offers spacious public areas, leisure and meeting facilities. The restaurant provides a good range of choice and guests can also dine in the bar. Bedrooms are air-conditioned and have a good range of facilities.

Rooms 126 en suite (6 fmly) (19 GF) ⊗ in 87 bedrooms S £68-£119; D £68-£119 **Facilities** 🏊 Squash Sauna Solarium Gym Jacuzzi Floatation room **Conf** Thtr 300 Class 150 Board 90 **Services** Lift air con **Parking** 529 **Notes** ⊗ ⊗ in restaurant RS 25-31 Dec Civ Wed 300

BUDGET HOTEL

Premier Travel Inn
Manchester Airport

Finney Ln, Heald Green SK8 3QH

☎ 08701 977178 🖹 0161 437 4910

web: www.premiertravelinn.com

dir: M56 junct 5 follow signs to Terminal 1, at rdbt take 2nd exit, at next rdbt follow signs for Cheadle. At traffic lights turn left, then right at next lights

High quality, modern budget accommodation ideal for both families and business travellers. Spacious, en suite bedrooms feature bath and shower, satellite TV and many have telephones and modem points.

continued

The adjacent family restaurant features a wide and varied menu. For further details consult the Hotel Groups page.

Rooms 66 en suite

Premier Travel Inn
Manchester Airport East

30 Wilmslow Rd SK9 3EW

☎ 0870 9906602 🖹 0870 9906603

dir: 4m from Manchester Airport. Exit M56 junct 6 follow A538 towards Wilmslow. At main junct into town centre, bear left. 2m, hotel at top of hill on right just after Wilmslow Garden Centre

Rooms 35 en suite

Premier Travel Inn
Manchester Airport South

Racecourse Rd SK9 5LR

☎ 0870 9906506 🖹 0870 9906507

dir: M6 junct 19 to Knutsford, follow Wilmslow signs. Left at 1st & 2nd lights towards Wilmslow. Through Mobberley, left just before Bird in Hand pub. At T-junct, right. Inn 150yds on right

Rooms 37 en suite

England

MANCHESTER AIRPORT *continued*

Travelodge Manchester Airport

Runger Ln WA15 8XW

web: www.travelodge.co.uk

Travelodge offers good quality, good value, modern accommodation. Ideal for families, the spacious en suite bedrooms include remote-control TV, tea and coffee-making facilities and comfortable beds. Meals can be taken at the nearby family restaurant. See Hotel Groups pages for further details.

Rooms S fr £26; D fr £26

MIDDLETON   **MAP 16 SD80**

BUDGET HOTEL

Premier Travel Inn Manchester (Middleton)

818 Manchester Old Rd, Rhodes M24 4RF

☎ 0870 9906406 📠 0870 9906407

web: www.premiertravelinn.com

dir: *At M60/M62 junct 18 follow Manchester/Middleton signs. Exit M60 junct 19 take A576 towards Middleton*

High quality, modern budget accommodation ideal for both families and business travellers. Spacious, en suite bedrooms feature bath and shower, satellite TV and many have telephones and modem points. The adjacent family restaurant features a wide and varied menu. For further details consult the Hotel Groups page.

Rooms 42 en suite **Conf** Thtr 60 Class 60

OLDHAM   **MAP 16 SD90**

★★★ 78% **HOTEL**

Hotel Smokies Park

Ashton Rd, Bardsley OL8 3HX

☎ 0161 785 5000 📠 0161 785 5010

e-mail: sales@smokies.co.uk

web: www.smokies.co.uk

dir: *on A627 between Oldham and Ashton-under-Lyne*

This modern, stylish hotel offers smart, comfortable bedrooms and suites. A wide range of Italian and English dishes is offered in the Mediterranean-style restaurant and there is a welcoming lounge bar with live entertainment at weekends. There is a small yet well equipped, residents' only fitness centre and guests can also gain free admission to the hotel's nightclub.

Rooms 73 en suite (2 fmly) (22 GF) ⊗ in 36 bedrooms S £68-£150; D £68-£150 (incl. bkfst) **Facilities** STV Sauna Solarium Gym Wi-fi in bedrooms Night club Cabaret lounge ♫ **Conf** BC Thtr 200 Class 100 Board 40 Del from £110 **Services** Lift **Parking** 120 **Notes LB** ⊗ ⊗ in restaurant RS 25 Dec-3 Jan Civ Wed 120

★★★ 70% **HOTEL**

La Pergola

THE INDEPENDENTS

Rochdale Rd, Denshaw OL3 5UE

☎ 01457 871040 📠 01457 873804

e-mail: reception@lapergola.freeserve.co.uk

web: www.hotel-restaurant-uk.com

dir: *M62 junct 21, right at rdbt onto A640, under motorway, left at Wagon & Horses public house. Hotel 500yds on left*

Situated in open moorland and convenient for the M62, this friendly, family-owned and run hotel offers comfortable and well-equipped bedrooms. There is a good range of food available either in the bar or restaurant, and a comfortable lounge in which to relax. Functions and conferences are well catered for.

Rooms 26 en suite (4 fmly) ⊗ in 14 bedrooms **Facilities** Xmas **Conf** Thtr 150 Board 25 Del £95 **Parking** 75 **Notes** ⊗ in restaurant Closed 26 Dec, 1 Jan & BH Mons

---

Ⓤ

Swallow Bower

SWALLOW

Hollinwood Av, Chadderton OL9 8DE

☎ 0161 682 7254 📠 0161 683 4605

e-mail: reservations.greatermanchester@swallowhotels.com

web: www.swallowhotels.com

dir: *Exit M60 junct 21, turn right at rdbt, right at lights and take left lane. Left onto Semple Way towards Morrison's, right at lights, hotel on left*

At the time of going to press, the star classification for this hotel was not confirmed. Please refer to the AA internet site www.theAA.com for current information.

Rooms 90 en suite (14 fmly) (32 GF) ⊗ in 65 bedrooms S £45-£135; D £65-£150 (incl. bkfst) **Facilities** Xmas **Conf** Thtr 200 Class 80 Board 60 Del from £95 **Parking** 100 **Notes LB** ⊗ in restaurant Civ Wed 150

BUDGET HOTEL

Innkeeper's Lodge Oldham

Burnley Ln, Chadderton OL1 2QS

☎ 0161 627 3883

web: www.innkeeperslodge.com

Smart, en suite accommodation ideal for both business & leisure guests. Bedrooms are very well equipped, including Sky TV, telephone, modem points, tea & coffee making facilities, (family rooms in most locations). Complimentary breakfast. The adjacent Pub Restaurant; a Harvester, Vintage Inn, Toby Carvery, Ember Inn, Sizzling Pubco or Pub & Carvery offers an all day menu. See Hotel Groups pages for further details.

Rooms 30 en suite S £45-£49.95; D £45-£49.95

England

BUDGET HOTEL

Premier Travel Inn Oldham Central

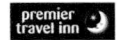

Westwood Park, Chadderton Way OL1 2PH

☎ 08701 977292 🗎 08701 977702

web: www.premiertravelinn.com

dir: From M62 junct 20, take A627 (M) to Oldham. Inn is on A627, opposite B&Q Depot

High quality, modern budget accommodation ideal for both families and business travellers. Spacious, en suite bedrooms feature bath and shower, satellite TV and many have telephones and modem points. The adjacent family restaurant features a wide and varied menu. For further details consult the Hotel Groups page.

Rooms 40 en suite

Premier Travel Inn Oldham (Chadderton)

The Broadway OL9 8DW

☎ 08701 977203 🗎 0161 682 7974

dir: M60 ringroad (anticlockwise) junct 21, signed Manchester City Centre. A663, 400yds on left

Rooms 40 en suite

BUDGET HOTEL

Travelodge Oldham

432 Broadway, Chadderton OL9 8AU

☎ 08700 850 950 🗎 0161 681 9021

web: www.travelodge.co.uk

Travelodge offers good quality, good value, modern accommodation. Ideal for families, the spacious en suite bedrooms include remote-control TV, tea and coffee-making facilities and comfortable beds. Meals can be taken at the nearby family restaurant. See Hotel Groups pages for further details.

Rooms 50 en suite S fr £26; D fr £26

PENDLEBURY   MAP 15 SD70

BUDGET HOTEL

Premier Travel Inn Manchester (Swinton)

219 Bolton Rd M27 8TG

☎ 0870 9906528 🗎 0870 9906529

web: www.premiertravelinn.com

dir: Exit M60 junct 13 towards A572, at rdbt take 3rd exit towards Swinton. At next take A572. After 2m right onto A580. After 2nd lights take A666 Kearsley, then 1st left at rdbt. Pass fire station on right, take 1st right

High quality, modern budget accommodation ideal for both families and business travellers. Spacious, en suite bedrooms feature bath and shower, satellite TV and many have telephones and modem points. The adjacent family restaurant features a wide and varied menu. For further details consult the Hotel Groups page.

Rooms 31 en suite

PRESTWICH   MAP 15 SD80

★★★ 70% **HOTEL**

Fairways Lodge & Leisure Club

George St, (Off Bury New Road) M25 9WS

☎ 0161 798 8905 🗎 0161 773 5562

e-mail: info@fairwayslodge.co.uk

dir: M60 junct 17, A56 for 1.5m, right into George Street (hotel in cul-de-sac)

This popular hotel is conveniently located within easy reach of the motorway network and just a short drive from both Manchester city centre and Bury. Smart bedrooms are thoughtfully equipped for both business guests and families. Public areas include an extensive leisure club with excellent squash facilities, conference and meeting rooms and a public bar and restaurant, both offering a wide range of dishes.

Rooms 40 en suite (2 fmly) (19 GF) ⊗ in 25 bedrooms S £60-£74; D £65-£79 (incl. bkfst) **Facilities** STV Squash Sauna Solarium Gym Jacuzzi ♬ ch fac Xmas **Conf** Thtr 100 Class 120 Del from £95 **Parking** 80 **Notes LB** ⊗ ⊘ in restaurant Civ Wed 50

BUDGET HOTEL

Premier Travel Inn Manchester (Prestwich)

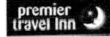

Bury New Rd M25 3AJ

☎ 08701 977175 🗎 0161 773 8099

web: www.premiertravelinn.com

dir: M60 junct 17, on A56

High quality, modern budget accommodation ideal for both families and business travellers. Spacious, en suite bedrooms feature bath and shower, satellite TV and many have telephones and modem points. The adjacent family restaurant features a wide and varied menu. For further details consult the Hotel Groups page.

Rooms 60 en suite

RAMSBOTTOM   MAP 15 SD71

★★★ 70% **HOTEL**

Old Mill

Springwood BL0 9DS

☎ 01706 822991 🗎 01706 822291

e-mail: reservations@oldmill-uk.com

dir: M66 junct 4, A56 towards Rawtenstall. 1st left into Bridge St. Over rail crossing, on at lights into Carr St. 2nd left into Springwood, to end of road, right to hotel

Extended from an original water mill, this friendly hotel enjoys fine views over the town and Rossendale Valley. Bedrooms have attractive floral furnishings and inter-connecting family rooms are available. In addition to a comfortable bar and beamed restaurant, a well-equipped leisure centre is available to guests during their stay.

Rooms 29 en suite (6 fmly) ⊗ in 9 bedrooms S £55-£65; D £69-£79 (incl. bkfst) **Facilities** STV 🏊 Sauna Solarium Gym Jacuzzi Steam Room **Conf** Thtr 70 Class 30 Board 20 Del £99 **Parking** 50 **Notes LB** ⊗ ⊘ in restaurant Civ Wed 60

England

ROCHDALE
MAP 16 SD81

★★★★ 76% HOTEL

Macdonald Norton Grange Hotel & Spa

Manchester Rd, Castleton OL11 2XZ

☎ 0870 1942119 🖺 01706 649313

e-mail: nortongrange@macdonald-hotels.co.uk

web: www.macdonald-hotels.co.uk/nortongrange

dir: M62 junct 20, follow signs for A664 Castleton. Right at next 2 rbts for hotel 0.5m on left

Standing in nine acres of grounds and mature gardens, this Victorian house provides comfort in elegant surroundings. The well-equipped bedrooms provide a host of extras for both the business and leisure guest. Public areas include the Pickwick bistro and bar and a smart restaurant, both offering a good choice of dishes. There is also now an impressive new leisure centre.

Rooms 81 en suite (17 fmly) (10 GF) ❷ in all bedrooms S £90-£125; D £100-£150 (incl. bkfst) **Facilities Spa** STV ❑ Sauna Solarium Gym Jacuzzi Wi-fi available Leisure centre Indoor/Outdoor Hydrotherapy Pool, Thermal suite, Rock Sauna Xmas **Conf** Thtr 220 Class 120 Board 70 Del from £120 **Services** Lift **Parking** 150 **Notes LB** ❷ in restaurant Civ Wed 150

BUDGET HOTEL

Premier Travel Inn Rochdale

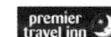

Newhey Rd, Milnrow OL16 4JF

☎ 08701 977219 🖺 01706 299074

web: www.premiertravelinn.com

dir: M62 junct 21 at rdbt, right towards Shaw, under motorway bridge & take 1st left

High quality, modern budget accommodation ideal for both families and business travellers. Spacious, en suite bedrooms feature bath and shower, satellite TV and many have telephones and modem points. The adjacent family restaurant features a wide and varied menu. For further details consult the Hotel Groups page.

Rooms 40 en suite **Conf** Thtr 25 Board 12

SALE
MAP 15 SJ79

★★★ 68% HOTEL

Amblehurst Hotel
44 Washway Rd M33 7QZ

☎ 0161 973 8800 🖺 0161 905 1697

e-mail: reception@theamblehurst.com

web: www.theamblehurst.co.uk

dir: M60 junct 7 onto A56 Washway Rd.

Now under new ownership this hotel is located in the centre of Sale and is a short distance from the centre of Manchester; it offers spacious accommodation. Meals are available in the formal dining room or in the popular lounge bar. There is also a small function room.

Rooms 66 en suite (4 fmly) (21 GF) ❷ in 43 bedrooms S £45-£60; D £55-£70 (incl. bkfst) **Facilities** Wi-fi in bedrooms ♫ ch fac Xmas **Conf** Thtr 80 Class 65 Board 30 **Parking** 58 **Notes LB** ❽ ❷ in restaurant

BUDGET HOTEL

Premier Travel Inn Manchester (Sale)

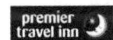

Carrington Ln, Ashton-Upon-Mersey M33 5BL

☎ 08701 977179 🖺 0161 905 1742

web: www.premiertravelinn.com

dir: M60 junct 8 take A6144(M) towards Carrington. Left at 1st lights, Inn on left

High quality, modern budget accommodation ideal for both families and business travellers. Spacious, en suite bedrooms feature bath and shower, satellite TV and many have telephones and modem points. The adjacent family restaurant features a wide and varied menu. For further details consult the Hotel Groups page.

Rooms 40 en suite **Conf** Thtr 25

STANDISH
MAP 15 SD51

BUDGET HOTEL

Premier Travel Inn Wigan North

Almond Brook Rd WN6 0SS

☎ 0870 9906474 🖺 0870 9906475

web: www.premiertravelinn.com

dir: Exit M6 junct 27 follow signs for Standish. Left at T-junct, then 1st right

High quality, modern budget accommodation ideal for both families and business travellers. Spacious, en suite bedrooms feature bath and shower, satellite TV and many have telephones and modem points. The adjacent family restaurant features a wide and varied menu. For further details consult the Hotel Groups page.

Rooms 36 en suite

STOCKPORT MAP 16 SJ89
See also Manchester Airport

★★★ 75% HOTEL

Alma Lodge Hotel
149 Buxton Rd SK2 6EL
☎ 0161 483 4431 ◳ 0161 483 1983
e-mail: reception@almalodgehotel.com
web: www.almalodgehotel.com

dir: M60 junct 1 at rdbt take 2nd exit under rail viaduct at lights opposite. At Debenhams turn right onto A6. Hotel approx 1.5m on left

A large hotel, located on the main road close to the town, offering modern and well-equipped bedrooms. It is family owned and run and serves a good range of quality Italian cooking in Luigi's restaurant. Good function rooms are also available.

Rooms 20 en suite 32 annexe en suite (2 fmly) ◈ in 22 bedrooms **Conf** Thtr 250 Class 100 Board 60 **Parking** 120 **Notes LB** ⊗ RS Bank Hols Civ Wed 100

★★★ 74% HOTEL

Bredbury Hall Hotel & Country Club
THE INDEPENDENTS
Goyt Valley SK6 2DH
☎ 0161 430 7421 ◳ 0161 430 5079
e-mail: reservations@bredburyhallhotel.co.uk

dir: M60 junct 25 signed Bredbury, right at lights, left onto Osbourne St, hotel 500mtrs on right

With views over open countryside, this large modern hotel is conveniently located for the M60. The stylish, well-equipped bedrooms offer space and comfort and the restaurant serves a very wide range of freshly prepared dishes. There is a popular nightclub next door to the hotel.

Rooms 150 en suite (2 fmly) (50 GF) S £59.50-£79.50; D £79.50-£94.50 **Facilities** STV FTV Fishing Snooker Jacuzzi Wi-fi in bedrooms Night club (Fri & Sat eve) La Cartis Restaurant, Casino 36 Stockport ♬ ch fac Xmas **Conf** Thtr 200 Class 120 Board 60 Del from £120 **Services** Lift **Parking** 400 **Notes LB** ⊗ Civ Wed 80

★★ 74% HOTEL

Wycliffe
74 Edgeley Rd, Edgeley SK3 9NQ
☎ 0161 477 5395 ◳ 0161 476 3219
e-mail: reception@wycliffe-hotel.com
web: www.wycliffe-hotel.com

dir: M60 junct 2 follow A560 for Stockport, at 1st lights turn right, hotel 0.5m on left

This family-run, welcoming hotel provides immaculately maintained and well-equipped bedrooms within main building, and more simply appointed rooms in two houses opposite. There is a well stocked bar and a popular restaurant where the menu has an Italian bias. There is ample, convenient parking.

Rooms 14 en suite ◈ in all bedrooms S £45-£65, D £65-£75 (incl. bkfst) **Facilities** FTV Wi-fi available **Conf** Thtr 30 Class 20 Board 20 Del from £100 **Parking** 46 **Notes** ⊗ ◈ in restaurant Closed 25-27 Dec RS BHs

BUDGET HOTEL

Innkeeper's Lodge Stockport
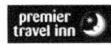
271 Wellington Rd, North Heaton Chapel SK4 5BP
☎ 0161 432 2753
web: www.innkeeperslodge.com

Smart, en suite accommodation ideal for both business & leisure guests. Bedrooms are very well equipped, including Sky TV, telephone, modem points, tea & coffee making facilities. (family rooms in most locations). Complimentary breakfast. The adjacent Pub Restaurant; a Harvester, Vintage Inn, Toby Carvery, Ember Inn, Sizzling Pubco or Pub & Carvery offers an all day menu. See Hotel Groups pages for further details.

Rooms 22 en suite S £45-£52; D £45-£52

BUDGET HOTEL

Premier Travel Inn Stockport East
premier travel inn
Churchgate SK1 1YG
☎ 0870 9906544 ◳ 0870 9906545
web: www.premiertravelinn.com

dir: Exit M60 junct 27, A626 towards Marple. Right at Spring Gardens.

High quality, modern budget accommodation ideal for both families and business travellers. Spacious, en suite bedrooms feature bath and shower, satellite TV and many have telephones and modem points.

continued on page 312

England

STOCKPORT *continued*

The adjacent family restaurant features a wide and varied menu. For further details consult the Hotel Groups page.

Rooms 46 en suite **Conf** Thtr 20 Board 20

Premier Travel Inn Stockport South

Buxton Rd SK2 6NB

☎ 08701 977242 📄 0161 477 8320

dir: on A6, 1.5m from town centre

Rooms 40 en suite

SWINTON   MAP 15 SD70

BUDGET HOTEL

Premier Travel Inn Manchester West

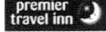

East Lancs Rd M27 0AA

☎ 0870 9906480 📄 0870 9906481

web: www.premiertravelinn.com

dir: Off M60 junct 13 (Swinton/Leigh) on A580.

High quality, modern budget accommodation ideal for both families and business travellers. Spacious, en suite bedrooms feature bath and shower, satellite TV and many have telephones and modem points. The adjacent family restaurant features a wide and varied menu. For further details consult the Hotel Groups page.

Rooms 27 en suite **Conf** Thtr 12 Board 12

URMSTON   MAP 15 SJ79

BUDGET HOTEL

Premier Travel Inn Manchester (Trafford Cntr)

Trafford Boulevard M41 7JE

☎ 0870 9906310 📄 0870 9906311

web: www.premiertravelinn.com

dir: Exit M6, onto M62 at junct 21a, towards Manchester. Exit M62 junct 1, M60 towards south. Exit M60 junct 10, take B5214. Hotel on left just before Ellesmere Circle

High quality, modern budget accommodation ideal for both families and business travellers. Spacious, en suite bedrooms feature bath and shower, satellite TV and many have telephones and modem points. The adjacent family restaurant features a wide and varied menu. For further details consult the Hotel Groups page.

Rooms 42 en suite

WIGAN   MAP 15 SD50

★★★★ 69% HOTEL

Macdonald Kilhey Court

Chorley Rd, Standish WN1 2XN

☎ 0870 1942122 📄 01257 422401

e-mail: events.kilheycourt@macdonald-hotels.co.uk

web: www.macdonald-hotels.co.uk

dir: M6 junct 27, A5209 Standish, over at lights, past church on right, left at T-junct, hotel on right 350yds. M61 junct 6, signed Wigan & Haigh Hall. 3m & right at T-junct. Hotel 0.5 m on right

This hotel is peacefully situated in its own grounds yet conveniently

continued

---

located for the motorway network. The accommodation is comfortable and the rooms are split between the original Victorian house and a modern extension. Public areas display many original features and the split-level restaurant has views over the Worthington Lakes. This hotel is an especially popular venue for weddings.

Rooms 62 en suite (3 fmly) (8 GF) ⊗ in 33 bedrooms S £65-£155; D £80-£170 **Facilities Spa** STV ⛱ Sauna Solarium Gym Jacuzzi Aerobics and yoga classes, private fishing arranged Xmas **Conf** BC Thtr 400 Class 180 Board 60 Del from £110 **Services** Lift **Parking** 200 **Notes LB** ⊗ ⊗ in restaurant Civ Wed 300

★★★ 78% HOTEL

BW Wrightington Hotel & Country Club

Moss Ln, Wrightington WN6 9PB

☎ 01257 425803 📄 01257 425830

e-mail: info@wrightingtonhotel.co.uk

dir: M6 junct 27, 0.25m W, hotel on right after church

Situated in open countryside close to the M6 motorway, this privately owned hotel offers friendly hospitality. Accommodation is well equipped and spacious and public areas include an extensive leisure complex complete with hair salon, boutique and sports injury lab. Blazers Restaurant, two bars and air-conditioned banqueting facilities appeal to a broad market.

Rooms 74 en suite (6 fmly) (36 GF) ⊗ in all bedrooms S £74-£100; D £84-£115 (incl. bkfst) **Facilities** STV ⛱ Squash Sauna Solarium Gym Jacuzzi Hairdressing salon Beauty spa Sports Injury clinic **Conf** Thtr 200 Class 120 Board 40 **Services** Lift **Parking** 240 **Notes LB** ⊗ in restaurant RS 24 Dec-3 Jan Civ Wed 100

★★★ 71% HOTEL

Quality Hotel Wigan

Riverway WN1 3SS

☎ 01942 826888 📄 01942 825800

e-mail: enquiries@hotels-wigan.com

web: www.choicehotelseurope.com

dir: from A49 take B5238 from rdbt, continue for 1.5m through lights, through 3 more sets of lights, right at 4th set, 1st left

Close to the centre of the town this modern hotel offers spacious and well-equipped bedrooms. The open plan public areas include a comfortable lounge bar adjacent to the popular restaurant, which serves a good range of dishes. Secure parking is a bonus.

Rooms 88 en suite (16 GF) ⊗ in 42 bedrooms S fr £90; D fr £100 **Facilities** STV Wi-fi available **Conf** Thtr 240 Class 90 Board 50 Del from £87.50 **Services** Lift **Parking** 100 **Notes LB** ⊗ in restaurant Civ Wed 60

England

★★ 65% HOTEL

Bel-Air
236 Wigan Ln WN1 2NU
☎ 01942 241410 🖷 01942 243967
e-mail: belair@hotelwigan.freeserve.co.uk
web: www.belairhotel.co.uk

dir: M6 junct 27, follow signs for Standish. In Standish turn right at lights towards A49. Hotel 1.5m on right, towards Wigan

This friendly, family-owned and run hotel is located just to the north of town. Accommodation varies in size and style but all rooms are well equipped. An extensive range of freshly prepared dishes is offered in the restaurant.

Rooms 11 en suite (1 fmly) S £35-£39.50; D £45-£49.50 (incl. bkfst) **Conf** Thtr 20 Board 8 **Parking** 10 **Notes** ⊗ in restaurant

BUDGET HOTEL

Premier Travel Inn Wigan South
53 Warrington Rd, Ashton-in-Makerfield WN4 9PI
☎ 0870 9906582 🖷 0870 9906583
web: www.premiertravelinn.com

dir: Just off M6 junct 23, A49 towards Wigan

High quality, modern budget accommodation ideal for both families and business travellers. Spacious, en suite bedrooms feature bath and shower, satellite TV and many have telephones and modem points. The adjacent family restaurant features a wide and varied menu. For further details consult the Hotel Groups page.

Rooms 28 en suite

Premier Travel Inn Wigan South (Marus Bridge)
Warrington Rd, Marus Bridge WN3 6XB
☎ 08701 977270 🖷 01942 498679

dir: M6 junct 25 (N'bound) slip road to rdbt turn left, Inn on left
Rooms 40 en suite

Premier Travel Inn Wigan West
Orrell Rd, Orrell WN5 0UQ
☎ 08701 977271 🖷 01942 215002

dir: From M6 junct 26 follow signs for Upholland and Orrell. At first set of lights turn left. Inn on right behind Priory Wood Beefeater
Rooms 40 en suite **Conf** Thtr 75 Board 40

WORSLEY · MAP 15 SD70

★★★ 68% HOTEL

Novotel Manchester West
Worsley Brow M28 2YA
web: www.novotel.com

dir: adjacent to M60 junct 13

Well placed for access to the Peak and Lake Districts, as well as the thriving City of Manchester, this modern hotel successfully caters for both families and business guests. The spacious bedrooms have sofa beds and a large work area; the hotel boasts an outdoor swimming pool and children's play area.

Rooms 119 en suite (4 fmly) (41 GF) ⊗ in 99 bedrooms **Facilities** STV ⚡ Wi-fi available **Conf** Thtr 230 Class 140 Board 20

HAMPSHIRE

ALDERSHOT · MAP 05 SU85

★★★ 71% HOTEL

Potters International
1 Fleet Rd GU11 2ET
☎ 01252 344000 🖷 01252 311611
e-mail: reservations@pottersinthotel.com

dir: access via A325 & A321 towards Fleet

This modern hotel is located within easy reach of Aldershot. Extensive air-conditioned public areas include ample lounge areas, a pub and a more formal restaurant; there are also conference rooms and a very good leisure club. Bedrooms, mostly spacious, are well equipped and have been attractively decorated and furnished.

Rooms 100 en suite (5 fmly) (7 GF) ⊗ in 83 bedrooms S fr £120; D fr £140 (incl. bkfst) **Facilities** STV ⚡ supervised Sauna Solarium Gym Jacuzzi **Conf** Thtr 400 Del from £165 **Services** Lift **Parking** 120 **Notes** ⊗ ⊗ in restaurant

BUDGET HOTEL

Premier Travel Inn Aldershot
7 Wellington Av GU11 1SQ
☎ 08701 977015 🖷 01252 344073
web: www.premiertravelinn.com

dir: Exit M3 junct 4. A331 then A325 through Farnborough, past airfield, over roundabout. Inn is ahead

High quality, modern budget accommodation ideal for both families and business travellers. Spacious, en suite bedrooms feature bath and shower, satellite TV and many have telephones and modem points. The adjacent family restaurant features a wide and varied menu. For further details consult the Hotel Groups page.

Rooms 60 en suite

ALTON · MAP 05 SU73

★★★ 72% ⊛⊛ HOTEL

Alton Grange
London Rd GU34 4EG
☎ 01420 86565 🖷 01420 541346
e-mail: info@altongrange.co.uk
web: www.altongrange.co.uk

dir: from A31 right at rdbt signed Alton/Holybourne/Bordon B3004. Hotel 300yds on left

A friendly family owned hotel, conveniently located on the outskirts of this market town and set in two acres of lovingly tended gardens. The

continued on page 314

England

ALTON *continued*

individually styled bedrooms, including three suites, are all thoughtfully equipped. Diners can choose between the more formal Truffles Restaurant or relaxed Muffins Brasserie. The attractive public areas include a function suite.

Rooms 26 en suite 4 annexe en suite (4 fmly) (7 GF) ⊘ in 6 bedrooms S fr £90; D fr £110 (incl. bkfst) **Facilities** STV Wi-fi in bedrooms Hot air ballooning **Conf** BC Thtr 80 Class 30 Board 40 Del from £150 **Parking** 48 **Notes** No children 3yrs ⊘ in restaurant Closed 24 Dec-2 Jan Civ Wed 100

★★★ 72% HOTEL

Alton House

Normandy St GU34 1DW

☎ 01420 80033 📠 01420 89222

e-mail: mail@altonhouse.com

web: www.altonhousehotel.com

dir: off A31, close to railway station

Conveniently located on the edge of the town, this popular hotel offers comfortably furnished and well-equipped bedrooms. The restaurant serves an extensive menu with daily specials with more informal meals served within the bar. Attractive rear gardens are a plus, along with an outdoor pool and tennis court.

Rooms 39 en suite (3 fmly) (3 GF) ⊘ in 2 bedrooms **Facilities** STV ⚘ ⛲ Snooker **Conf** BC Thtr 170 Class 80 Board 50 **Parking** 94 **Notes** LB ⊗ Closed 25-26 Dec RS 27-29 Dec Civ Wed 70

★★ 64% HOTEL

Swan

OLD ENGLISH INNS

High St GU34 1AT

☎ 01420 83777 📠 01420 87975

web: www.oldenglish.co.uk

dir: A31 to Alton follow signs to town centre. From north turn off M3 at Basingstoke then take A339 to Alton

This traditional High Street hotel is popular with locals and tourists alike, though it also caters for business guests. Bedrooms are well proportioned and have a range of useful facilities. Guests may enjoy the contemporary bustling bar for drinks and snacks or the attractive restaurant as a dining alternative. Parking is conveniently located to the rear of the hotel.

Rooms 36 en suite (2 fmly) ⊘ in 15 bedrooms **Conf** Thtr 150 Class 40 Board 60 **Parking** 70 **Notes** LB ⊘ in restaurant

ANDOVER   MAP 05 SU34

★★★ 78% ◎◎ HOTEL

Esseborne Manor

Hurstbourne Tarrant SP11 0ER

☎ 01264 736444 📠 01264 736725

e-mail: info@esseborne-manor.co.uk

web: www.esseborne-manor.co.uk

dir: halfway between Andover & Newbury on A343, just 1m N of Hurstbourne Tarrant

Set in two acres of well-tended gardens, this attractive manor house is surrounded by the open countryside of the North Wessex Downs. Bedrooms are delightfully individual and are split between the main

continued

house, an adjoining courtyard and separate garden cottage. A wonderfully relaxed atmosphere pervades throughout, with public rooms combining elegance with comfort.

Esseborne Manor

Rooms 11 en suite 9 annexe en suite (2 fmly) (6 GF) ⊘ in 6 bedrooms S £98-£130; D £125-£180 (incl. bkfst) **Facilities** STV ⛲ ⛲ Wi-fi in bedrooms **Conf** Thtr 60 Class 40 Board 30 Del from £140 **Parking** 50 **Notes LB** ⊘ in restaurant Civ Wed 100

★★★ 63% HOTEL

Quality Hotel Andover

Micheldever Rd SP11 6LA

☎ 01264 369111 📠 01264 369000

e-mail: andover@quality-hotels.co.uk

dir: off A303 at A3093. 1st rdbt take 1st exit, 2nd rdbt take 1st exit. Turn left immediately before BP petrol station, then left again

Located on the outskirts of the town, this hotel is popular with business guests. Bedrooms offer smart accommodation, and public areas consist of a cosy lounge, a bar and a traditional style restaurant serving a range of meals. There is also a large conference suite available.

Rooms 13 en suite 36 annexe en suite (13 GF) ⊘ in 21 bedrooms S £49-£72; D £59-£85 (incl. bkfst) **Facilities** STV Wi-fi in bedrooms Xmas **Conf** Thtr 180 Class 60 Board 60 Del from £80 **Parking** 100 **Notes LB** ⊗ ⊘ in restaurant Civ Wed 85

BARTON STACEY   MAP 05 SU44

BUDGET HOTEL

Travelodge Barton Stacey

SO21 3NP

☎ 08700 850 950 📠 01264 720260

web: www.travelodge.co.uk

dir: on A303 westbound

Travelodge offers good quality, good value, modern accommodation. Ideal for families, the spacious en suite bedrooms include remote-control TV, tea and coffee-making facilities and comfortable beds. Meals can be taken at the nearby family restaurant. See Hotel Groups pages for further details.

Rooms 20 en suite S fr £26; D fr £26

England

BASINGSTOKE   MAP 05 SU65
See also North Waltham, Odiham & Stratfield Turgis

★★★★ ⊛ **HOTEL**

Tylney Hall Hotel
RG27 9AZ
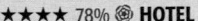
☎ 01256 764881 ▧ 01256 768141
e-mail: sales@tylneyhall.com
web: www.tylneyhall.com

(For full entry see Rotherwick)

★★★★ 78% ⊛ **HOTEL**

The Hampshire Centrecourt
MarstonHotels

Centre Dr, Chineham RG24 8FY
☎ 01256 319700 ▧ 01256 319730
e-mail: hampshirec@marstonhotels.com
web: www.marstonhotels.com

dir: off A33 (Reading road) behind Chineham Shopping Centre via Great Binfields Rd

This hotel boasts a range of smart, comfortable and stylish bedrooms and leisure facilities that are unrivalled locally. Facilities include indoor and outdoor tennis courts, two swimming pools, a gym and a number of treatment rooms.

Rooms 90 en suite (6 fmly) ⊛ in 25 bedrooms S fr £144; D fr £171 (incl. bkfst) **Facilities Spa** STV ⬚ ⬚ Sauna Solarium Gym Jacuzzi Wi-fi in bedrooms Steam room Beauty salon Xmas **Conf** Thtr 220 Class 130 Board 60 Del from £100 **Services** Lift Parking 200 **Notes LB** ⬚ ⬚ in restaurant Civ Wed 220

★★★★ 76% ⊛ **HOTEL**

Apollo
CLASSIC
BRITISH HOTELS

Aldermaston Roundabout RG24 9NU
☎ 01256 796700 ▧ 01256 796701
e-mail: admin@apollo-hotels.co.uk
web: www.apollohotels.com

dir: M3 junct 6. Follow ringroad N, exit A340 (Aldermaston). Hotel on rdbt, 5th exit into Popley Way for access

This modern hotel provides well-equipped accommodation and spacious public areas, appealing to both the leisure and business guest. Facilities include a smartly appointed leisure club, a business centre, along with a good choice of formal and informal eating in two restaurants - Vespers is the fine dining option.

Rooms 125 en suite ⊛ in 100 bedrooms **Facilities Spa** STV ⬚ supervised Sauna Solarium Gym Jacuzzi **Conf** BC Thtr 255 Class 196 Board 30 **Services** Lift air con **Parking** 200 **Notes LB** ⊛

★★★★ 74% **HOTEL**

Paramount Basingstoke Country Hotel
⟨P⟩ PARAMOUNT
GROUP OF HOTELS

Scures Hill, Nately Scures, Hook RG27 9JS
☎ 01256 764161 ▧ 01256 768341
e-mail: basingstokereception@paramount-hotels.co.uk
web: www.paramount-hotels.co.uk

dir: M3 junct 5, A287 towards Newnham. Left at lights. Hotel 200mtrs on right

This popular hotel is close to Basingstoke and its country location ensures a quiet stay. Bedrooms are available in a number of styles, and guests have a choice of dining in the formal restaurant, or for lighter meals and snacks there is a relaxed café and a smart bar. Extensive conference and leisure facilities complete the picture.

Rooms 100 en suite (14 fmly) (26 GF) ⊛ in 45 bedrooms S £140-£170; D £150-£180 **Facilities** STV ⬚ Sauna Solarium Gym Jacuzzi Wi-fi available BodySensual Beauty treatments Xmas **Conf** Thtr 220 Class 100 Board 80 Del from £150 **Services** Lift air con **Parking** 200 **Notes** ⊛ in restaurant RS 24 Dec-2 Jan Civ Wed 90

★★★ 72% **HOTEL**

Best Western Romans Country House
Best Western

Little London Rd RG7 2PN
☎ 0118 970 0421 ▧ 0118 970 0691
e-mail: romanhotel@hotmail.com

(For full entry see Silchester)

See advert on page 317

★★★ 68% **HOTEL**

Red Lion
Red Lion Ln RG21 7LX
☎ 01256 328525 ▧ 01256 844056
e-mail: mail@redlionhotelbasingstoke.com

dir: M3 junct 6 to Black Dam rdbt. 2nd exit onto Ringway East (A339). Take slip road signed town centre onto Churchill Way East (A3010). At rdbt take 1st exit onto Timberlake Rd, leads into New Rd. After pedestrian lights, right into Red Lion Lane

Centrally located in the town, the Red Lion is an ideal choice for business guests. Bedrooms are mostly spacious and include non-smoking rooms, interconnecting rooms and rooms with four-poster beds. Public areas comprise an attractive lounge and restaurant, and a popular bar.

Rooms 59 en suite (2 fmly) ⊛ in 16 bedrooms **Facilities** STV **Conf** Thtr 80 Class 40 Board 20 **Services** Lift **Parking** 62 **Notes LB** ⊛ in restaurant

England

BASINGSTOKE *continued*

BUDGET HOTEL

Premier Travel Inn Basingstoke Central

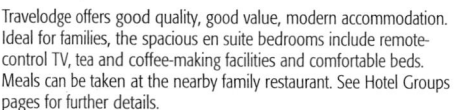

Basingstoke Leisure Park, Worting Rd RG22 6PG
☎ 08701 977028 ▤ 01256 819329
web: www.premiertravelinn.com
dir: M3 junct 6 follow signs for Leisure Park

High quality, modern budget accommodation ideal for both families and business travellers. Spacious, en suite bedrooms feature bath and shower, satellite TV and many have telephones and modem points. The adjacent family restaurant features a wide and varied menu. For further details consult the Hotel Groups page.

Rooms 71 en suite

BUDGET HOTEL

Travelodge Basingstoke

Stag and Hounds, Winchester Rd RG22 6HN
☎ 08700 850 950 ▤ 01256 843566
web: www.travelodge.co.uk
dir: off A30, S of town centre

Travelodge offers good quality, good value, modern accommodation. Ideal for families, the spacious en suite bedrooms include remote-control TV, tea and coffee-making facilities and comfortable beds. Meals can be taken at the nearby family restaurant. See Hotel Groups pages for further details.

Rooms 44 en suite S fr £26; D fr £26

BEAULIEU   MAP 05 SU30

INSPECTORS' CHOICE

★★★ ◉◉ HOTEL

Montagu Arms

Palace Ln SO42 7ZL
☎ 01590 612324 & 0845 123 5613 ▤ 01590 612188
e-mail: reservations@montaguarmshotel.co.uk
web: www.montaguarmshotel.co.uk
dir: M27 junct 2, turn left at rdbt, follow signs for Beaulieu. Continue to Dibden Purlieu, then right at rdbt. Hotel on left

Surrounded by the glorious scenery of the New Forest, this lovely hotel manages to achieve the impression of almost total seclusion, though it is within easy reach of the major towns and cities in the area. Bedrooms, each named after a species of tree,
continued

are individually decorated and come with a range of thoughtful extras. Public rooms include a cosy lounge, an adjoining conservatory and a choice of two dining options, the informal Monty's, or the stylish Terrace Restaurant.

Rooms 23 en suite (3 fmly) ✦ in all bedrooms S fr £130; D £185-£235 (incl. bkfst) **Facilities** ✦ Use of spa in Brockenhurst Xmas **Conf** Thtr 50 Class 16 Board 26 Del from £165 **Parking** 86 **Notes LB** ✦ ✦ in restaurant Civ Wed 50
See advert on opposite page

★★★ 78% ◉◉ HOTEL

Master Builders House Hotel

SO42 7XB
☎ 01590 616253 ▤ 01590 616297
e-mail: res@themasterbuilders.co.uk
web: www.themasterbuilders.co.uk
dir: M27 junct 2, follow Beaulieu signs. At T-junct left onto B3056, 1st left to Bucklers Hard. Hotel 2m on left before village entrance

The name of the hotel is a testament to master shipbuilder Henry Adams who once owned the property. A full list of the famous ships built in the village can be found in the Yachtsman's Bar. The Riverside Restaurant and many of the individually styled bedrooms enjoy views over the Beaulieu River. For guests wishing to travel to the Isle of Wight, the hotel has its own boat.

Rooms 8 en suite 17 annexe en suite (2 fmly) (8 GF) ✦ in 19 bedrooms S £99-£134; D £99-£180 (incl. bkfst) **Facilities** STV Sailing on Beaulieu River, mountain biking Xmas **Conf** Thtr 50 Class 18 Board 25 Del from £165 **Parking** 70 **Notes LB** Civ Wed 60

★★★ 73% ◉ HOTEL

Beaulieu

Beaulieu Rd SO42 7YQ
☎ 023 8029 3344 ▤ 023 8029 2729
e-mail: beaulieu@newforesthotels.co.uk
web: www.newforesthotels.co.uk
dir: M27 junct 1/A337 towards Lyndhurst. Left at lights in Lyndhurst, through village, right onto B3056, hotel in 3m.

Conveniently located in the heart of the New Forest and close to Beaulieu Road railway station, this popular, small hotel provides an ideal base for exploring the surrounding area. Facilities include an indoor swimming pool, an outdoor children's play area and an adjoining pub. A daily changing menu is offered in the restaurant.

Rooms 20 en suite 3 annexe en suite (2 fmly) (3 GF) S £77.50-£85; D £125-£140 (incl. bkfst) **Facilities** ✦ Steam room Xmas **Conf** Thtr 290 Class 100 Board 160 Del from £95 **Services** Lift **Parking** 60 **Notes** ✦ in restaurant Civ Wed 205

BOTLEY   MAP 05 SU51

★★★★ 77% **HOTEL**

Macdonald Botley Park, Golf & Country Club

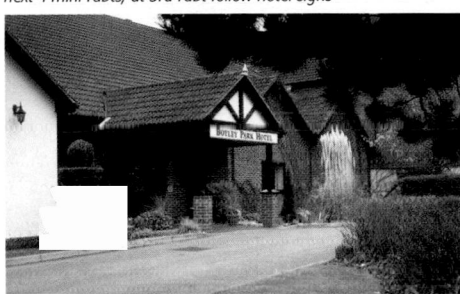

Winchester Rd, Boorley Green SO32 2UA

☎ 0870 1942132 📠 01489 789242

e-mail: botleypark@macdonald-hotels.co.uk

web: www.macdonald-hotels.co.uk

dir: A334 towards Botley, left at 1st rdbt past M&S, continue over next 4 mini-rdbts, at 3rd rdbt follow hotel signs

This modern and spacious hotel sits peacefully in the midst of its own 176 acres parkland golf course. Bedrooms are comfortably appointed with a good range of extras and an extensive range of leisure facilities

continued on page 318

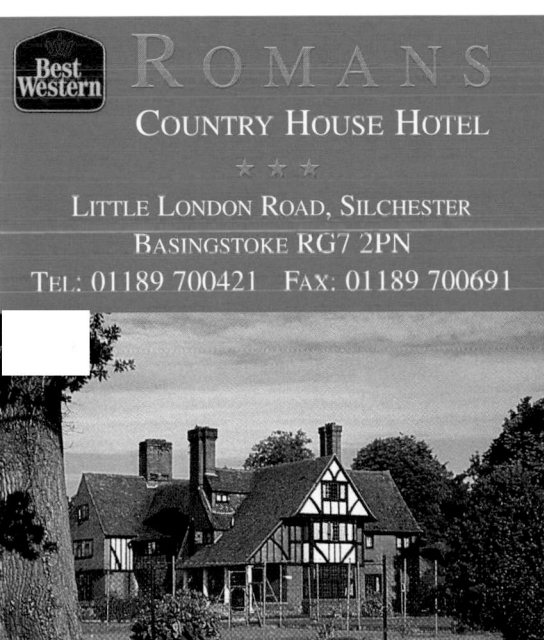

England

BOTLEY *continued*

is on offer. Attractive public areas include a relaxing restaurant and the more informal Swing and Divot Bar.

Rooms 100 en suite (34 GF) ⊘ in 52 bedrooms **Facilities** STV 🔁 ♨ 18 ♨ Squash Sauna Solarium Gym Jacuzzi Aerobics studio, Beauty salon, Golf driving range ch fac **Conf** Thtr 240 Class 100 Board 60 **Parking** 250 **Notes LB** ⊘ in restaurant Civ Wed 200

BROCKENHURST   MAP 05 SU30

INSPECTORS' CHOICE

★★★★ ֍֍ **HOTEL**

Rhinefield House   HandPICKED

Rhinefield Rd SO42 7QB

☎ 01590 622922 🖹 01590 622800

e-mail: rhinefieldhouse@handpicked.co.uk

web: www.handpicked.co.uk

dir: A35 towards Christchurch. 3m from Lyndhurst turn left to Rhinefield, 1.5m to hotel

This stunning 19th-century, mock-Elizabethan mansion is set in 40 acres of beautifully landscaped gardens and forest. Bedrooms are spacious and great consideration is given to guest comfort. The elegant and award-winning Armada Restaurant is richly furnished, and features a fireplace carving (nine years in the making) that is worth taking time to admire. If the weather permits, the delightful terrace is just the place for enjoying alfresco eating. A new spa opens in November 2006.

Rooms 34 en suite ⊘ in 30 bedrooms S £185-£285; D £230-£425 (incl. bkfst) **Facilities Spa** STV 🔁 ⤳ ♨ Sauna Solarium Gym ⤳ Jacuzzi Wi-fi in bedrooms indoor leisure facility ch fac Xmas **Conf** Thtr 120 Class 50 Board 35 **Del** from £175 **Parking** 100 **Notes LB** ֍ ⊘ in restaurant Civ Wed

★★★★ 75% ֍֍ **HOTEL**

Careys Manor

SO42 7RH

☎ 01590 623551 & 08707 512305 🖹 08707 512306

e-mail: stay@careysmanor.com

web: www.careysmanor.com

dir: M27 junct 3, then M271, then A35 to Lyndhurst. Then A337 towards Brockenhurst. Hotel on left after 30mph sign.

This smart property offers a host of facilities that include an Oriental-style spa and leisure suite with an excellent range of unusual treatments, and three very contrasting restaurants that offer a choice

continued

of Thai, French or modern British cuisine. Many of the spacious and well appointed bedrooms have balconies overlooking the gardens.

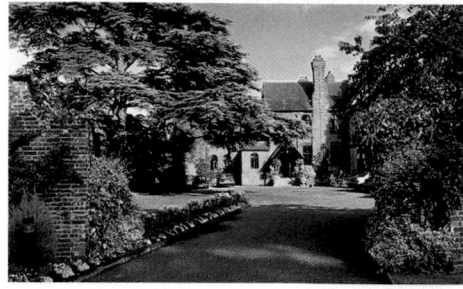

Careys Manor

Rooms 18 en suite 62 annexe en suite (32 GF) ⊘ in 28 bedrooms **Facilities Spa** STV 🔁 supervised Sauna Gym ⤳ Jacuzzi Wi-fi available Steam room, Beauty therapists, treatment rooms, hydrotherapy pool Xmas **Conf** Thtr 120 Class 70 Board 40 **Del** £170 **Services** Lift **Parking** 180 **Notes** ֍ ⊘ in restaurant Civ Wed 100

★★★ 85% ֍֍֍ **HOTEL**

Le Poussin @ Whitley Ridge Country House

Beaulieu Rd SO42 7QL

☎ 01590 622354 🖹 01590 622856

e-mail: whitleyridge@lepoussin.co.uk

web: www.whitleyridge.co.uk

dir: At Brockenhurst onto B3055 Beaulieu Road. 1m on left up private road.

This charming hotel enjoys a picturesque setting in the heart of the New Forest. Relaxing public areas, friendly and attentive staff and an intimate restaurant all help make this a truly memorable venue. Each bedroom has individual style and comfort whilst the award-winning Le Poussin restaurant is a highlight of any stay.

Rooms 14 en suite 4 annexe en suite (2 GF) ⊘ in all bedrooms **Facilities** ♨ **Conf** BC Thtr 35 Class 20 Board 20 **Parking** 40 **Notes LB** ⊘ in restaurant Civ Wed 50

★★★ 80% ֍ **HOTEL**

Balmer Lawn

Lyndhurst Rd SO42 7ZB

☎ 01590 623116 🖹 01590 623864

e-mail: info@balmerlawnhotel.com

dir: A337 towards Lymington, hotel on left

Situated in the heart of the New Forest, this imposing house provides comfortable public rooms and a wide range of bedrooms. A selection

continued

of carefully prepared and enjoyable dishes is offered in the spacious restaurant whilst extensive function and leisure facilities make this a popular conference venue.

Rooms 55 en suite (6 fmly) ⊗ in all bedrooms S £90-£99; D £135-£150 (incl. bkfst) **Facilities Spa** FTV ☒ ⇌ ♨ Squash Sauna Gym Jacuzzi Modems in bedrooms. Play stations in family rooms ♫ Xmas **Conf** BC Thtr 150 Class 76 Board 48 Del £165 **Services** Lift **Parking** 100 **Notes LB** ⊗ in restaurant Civ Wed 120

See advert on this page

★★★ 77% ⊛ **HOTEL**

New Park Manor

Lyndhurst Rd SO42 7QH
☎ 01590 623467 📠 01590 622268
e-mail: info@newparkmanorhotel.co.uk
web: www.vonessenhotels.co.uk

dir: M27 junct 1, A337 to Lyndhurst & Brockenhurst. Hotel 1.5m on right

Once the favoured hunting lodge of King Charles II, this well presented hotel enjoys a peaceful setting in the New Forest and comes complete with an equestrian centre. Bedrooms are divided between the old house and a purpose-built wing. Public areas include a range of lounges and an impressive spa.

Rooms 24 en suite (6 fmly) ⊗ in all bedrooms S £128-£148; D £155-£195 (incl. bkfst) **Facilities Spa** ☒ supervised ⇌ ♨ Riding Sauna Gym ⛳ Jacuzzi Mountain biking Xmas **Conf** Thtr 120 Class 52 Board 60 Del from £175 **Parking** 70 **Notes LB** ⊗ in restaurant Civ Wed 142

★★★ 72% **HOTEL**

Forest Park

Rhinefield Rd SO42 7ZG
☎ 01590 622844 📠 01590 623948
e-mail: forest.park@forestdale.com
web: www.forestdale.com

dir: A337 to Brockenhurst turn into Meerut Rd, follow road through Waters Green. Right at T-junct into Rhinefield Rd

A friendly hotel offering good facilities for both adults and children. A heated pool, riding, children's meal times and a quiet location in the forest are just a few of the advantages here. The well-equipped, comfortable bedrooms vary in size and style, and a choice of lounge and bar areas is available.

Rooms 38 en suite (2 fmly) (7 GF) ⊗ in 2 bedrooms **Facilities** ⇌ ♨ Riding Sauna Xmas **Conf** Thtr 50 Class 20 Board 24 **Parking** 80 **Notes** ⊗ in restaurant Civ Wed 50

★★ 76% **HOTEL**

Cloud

Meerut Rd SO42 7TD
☎ 01590 622165 📠 01590 622818
e-mail: enquiries@cloudhotel.co.uk
web: www.cloudhotel.co.uk

dir: 1st right off A337, follow tourist signs

This charming hotel enjoys a peaceful location on the edge of the village. The bedrooms are bright and comfortable with pine furnishings and smart en suite facilities. Public rooms include a selection of cosy lounges, a delightful rear garden with outdoor seating and a restaurant specialising in home-cooked wholesome English food.

Rooms 18 en suite (1 fmly) (2 GF) **Facilities** ⛳ **Conf** Thtr 40 Class 12 Board 12 **Parking** 20 **Notes LB** No children 8yrs ⊗ in restaurant Closed 28 Dec-10 Jan

★★ 65% **HOTEL**

Watersplash

The Rise SO42 7ZP
☎ 01590 622344 📠 01590 624047
e-mail: bookings@watersplash.co.uk
web: www.watersplash.co.uk

dir: M3 junct 13/M27 junct 1/A337 S through Lyndhurst to Brockenhurst. Through Brockenhurst, The Rise on left, hotel on left

This popular, welcoming Victorian hotel has been in the same family for 40 years. Bedrooms have co-ordinated decor and good facilities. The restaurant overlooks the neatly tended garden and there is also a comfortably furnished lounge, separate bar and an outdoor pool.

Rooms 23 en suite (6 fmly) (3 GF) ⊗ in all bedrooms S £51-£90; D £84-£138 (incl. bkfst) **Facilities** ⇌ ch fac Xmas **Conf** Thtr 80 Class 20 Board 20 Del from £90 **Parking** 29 **Notes LB** ⊗ in restaurant

England

BROOK (NEAR CADNAM)   MAP 05 SU21

★★★ 70% ⊛ **HOTEL**

Bell Inn

SO43 7HE

☎ 023 8081 2214 🖷 023 8081 3958

e-mail: bell@bramshaw.co.uk

web: www.bramshaw.co.uk

dir: M27 junct 1 onto B3079, hotel 1.5m on right

The inn is part of the Bramshaw Golf Club and has tailored its style to suit this market, but it is also an ideal base for visiting the New Forest. Bedrooms are comfortable and attractively furnished, and the public areas, particularly the welcoming bar, have a cosy and friendly atmosphere.

Rooms 25 en suite (8 GF) ⊛ in 11 bedrooms S £55-£85; D £130-£150 (incl. bkfst) **Facilities** FTV ♨ 54 Putt green ch fac Xmas **Conf** Thtr 50 Class 20 Board 30 Del from £85 **Parking** 150 **Notes LB** ⊗ ⊛ in restaurant

BURLEY   MAP 05 SU20

★★★ 74% **HOTEL**

Burley Manor

Ringwood Rd BH24 4BS

Forestdale Hotels

☎ 01425 403522 🖷 01425 403227

e-mail: burley.manor@forestdale.com

web: www.forestdale.com

dir: leave A31 at Burley sign, hotel 3m on left

Set in extensive grounds, this 18th-century mansion house enjoys a relaxed ambience and a peaceful setting. Half of the well-equipped, comfortable bedrooms, including several with four-posters, are located in the main house. The remainder, many of which have balconies, are in the adjacent converted stable block overlooking the outdoor pool. Cosy public rooms benefit from log fires in winter.

Rooms 21 en suite 17 annexe en suite (2 fmly) (17 GF) ⊛ in 10 bedrooms S £125-£145; D £135-£155 (incl. bkfst) **Facilities** ⊰ Riding Xmas **Conf** Thtr 60 Class 40 Board 40 **Parking** 60 **Notes LB** ⊛ in restaurant Civ Wed 70

★★★ 67% ⊛ **HOTEL**

Moorhill House

BH24 4AH

☎ 01425 403285 🖷 01425 403715

e-mail: moorhill@newforesthotels.co.uk

web: www.newforesthotels.co.uk

dir: M27, A31, follow signs to Burley village, through village, up hill, turn right opposite school and cricket grounds

Situated deep in the heart of the New Forest and formerly a grand gentleman's residence, this charming hotel offers a relaxed and friendly environment. Bedrooms, of varying sizes, are smartly decorated. A range of facilities is provided and guests can relax by walking around the extensive grounds. Both dinner and breakfast offer a choice of interesting and freshly prepared dishes.

Rooms 31 en suite (13 fmly) (3 GF) **Facilities** ⊠ Sauna Gym ⊱ Putt green badminton (Apr-Sep) **Conf** Thtr 120 Class 60 Board 65 **Parking** 50 **Notes LB** ⊛ in restaurant Civ Wed 80

CADNAM   MAP 05 SU31

★★★ 73% ⊛ **HOTEL**

Bartley Lodge

Lyndhurst Rd SO40 2NR

☎ 023 8081 2248 🖷 023 8081 2075

e-mail: bartley@newforesthotels.co.uk

web: www.newforesthotels.co.uk

dir: M27 junct 1 at 1st rdbt 1st exit, at 2nd rdbt 3rd exit onto A337. Hotel sign on left

This 18th-century former hunting lodge is very quietly situated, yet is just minutes from the M27. Bedrooms vary in size and all are well equipped. There is a selection of small lounge areas, a cosy bar and an indoor pool, together with a small fitness suite. The Crystal dining room offers a tempting choice of well prepared dishes.

Rooms 31 en suite (12 fmly) (2 GF) S £77.50-£85; D £125-£140 (incl. bkfst) **Facilities** ⊠ ⊱ Sauna Gym ⊱ Xmas **Conf** Thtr 120 Class 60 Board 60 Del from £95 **Parking** 60 **Notes LB** ⊛ in restaurant Civ Wed 80

See advert on opposite page

EASTLEIGH   MAP 05 SU41

★★★ 🅰

Concorde Club & Hotel
Stoneham Ln SO50 9HQ
☎ 023 8065 1478 & 8061 3989 📠 023 8065 1479
e-mail: hotel@theconcordeclub.com
web: www.theconcordeclub.com
dir: M27 junct 5, at rdbt follow Chandlers Ford signs, hotel 500yds on right

Rooms 35 en suite (18 GF) ⊘ in 26 bedrooms S £59.50-£100; D £65-£120 (incl. bkfst) **Facilities** STV Fishing Fishing available with prior notice & chargeable daily ♫ **Conf** Thtr 200 Class 50 Board 40 Del from £95 **Services** Lift air con **Parking** 250 **Notes** No children 18yrs ⊘ in restaurant Closed 24-26 Dec

BUDGET HOTEL

Premier Travel Inn Eastleigh

Leigh Rd SO50 9YX
☎ 08701 977090 📠 023 8062 9048
web: www.premiertravelinn.com
dir: adjacent to M3 junct 13, near Eastleigh on A335

High quality, modern budget accommodation ideal for both families and business travellers. Spacious, en suite bedrooms feature bath and shower, satellite TV and many have telephones and modem points. The adjacent family restaurant features a wide and varied menu. For further details consult the Hotel Groups page.

Rooms 60 en suite

BUDGET HOTEL

Travelodge Southampton Eastleigh
Twyford Rd SO50 4LF
☎ 08700 850 950 📠 023 8061 6813
web: www.travelodge.co.uk
dir: M3 junct 12 on A335 Eastleigh & Boyatt Wood to next rdbt, take 2nd exit signed Eastleigh town centre

Travelodge offers good quality, good value, modern accommodation. Ideal for families, the spacious en suite bedrooms include remote-control TV, tea and coffee-making facilities and comfortable beds. Meals can be taken at the nearby family restaurant. See Hotel Groups pages for further details.

Rooms 32 en suite S fr £26; D fr £26

EMSWORTH   MAP 05 SU70

★★★ 74% **HOTEL**

Brookfield
Havant Rd PO10 7LF
☎ 01243 373363 📠 01243 376342
e-mail: bookings@brookfieldhotel.co.uk
dir: From A27 onto A259 towards Emsworth. Hotel 0.5m on left

This well-established, family-run hotel has spacious public areas with popular conference and banqueting facilities. Bedrooms are modern in style and comfortably furnished. The popular Hermitage Restaurant offers a seasonally changing menu and an interesting wine list.

Rooms 40 en suite (4 fmly) (13 GF) ⊘ in 20 bedrooms S £69.50; D £90 (incl. bkfst) **Facilities** STV Wi-fi available **Conf** Thtr 100 Class 60 Board 40 Del £135.95 **Parking** 80 **Notes LB** ⊗ Closed 24 Dec-2 Jan

⊚⊚⊚ **RESTAURANT WITH ROOMS**

36 on the Quay
47 South St PO10 7EG
☎ 01243 375592 & 372257

Occupying a prime position with far reaching views over the estuary, this 16th-century house is the scene for some accomplished and exciting cuisine. As would be expected the elegant restaurant occupies centre stage with peaceful pastel shades, local art and crisp napery together with glimpses of the bustling harbour outside. The contemporary bedrooms offer style, comfort and thoughtful extras.

Rooms 5 en suite S £70-£90; D £95-£150 **Parking** 6 **Notes LB** ⊘ in restaurant Closed 3wks Jan, 1wk Oct

BUDGET HOTEL

Travelodge Chichester Emsworth
PO10 7RB
☎ 08700 850 950 📠 01243 370877
web: www.travelodge.co.uk
dir: eastbound carriageway of A27

Travelodge offers good quality, good value, modern accommodation. Ideal for families, the spacious en suite bedrooms include remote-control TV, tea and coffee-making facilities and comfortable beds. Meals can be taken at the nearby family restaurant. See Hotel Groups pages for further details.

Rooms 36 en suite S fr £26; D fr £26

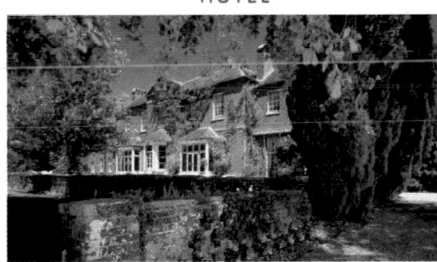

Grade II listed country house hotel set in 8 acres of grounds and beautifully landscaped gardens directly adjoining the New Forest.

31 delightfully furnished bedrooms including family, twin, double and single rooms, excellent cuisine, indoor leisure facilities with pool, sauna and fitness room. Two all weather surface tennis courts.

Cadnam, Nr. Southampton, Hampshire SO40 2NR
Tel: 023 8081 2248 Fax: 023 8081 2075
Email: bartley@newforesthotels.co.uk
Website: www.newforesthotels.co.uk

England

FAREHAM — MAP 05 SU50

★★★★ 77% ⊛ HOTEL

Solent
Rookery Av, Whiteley PO15 7AJ
☎ 01489 880000 🗎 01489 880007
e-mail: solent@shirehotels.com
web: www.shirehotels.com

SHIRE HOTELS

dir: M27 junct 9, hotel on Solent Business Park

Although close to the M27, this smart, purpose-built hotel enjoys a peaceful location. Bedrooms are very spacious and well appointed. There is a well-equipped leisure centre and spa, and the lounge, bar and restaurant feature beams and log fires throughout.

Rooms 111 en suite (9 fmly) (20 GF) ⊛ in 83 bedrooms S £91-£155; D £132-£180 (incl. bkfst) **Facilities** Spa STV 🎾 ♨ Sauna Solarium Gym Jacuzzi Wi-fi in bedrooms Steam room, Childrens splash pool, Activity studio, 8 Spa Treatment Rooms Xmas **Conf** BC Thtr 200 Class 120 Board 80 Del £175 **Services** Lift **Parking** 200 **Notes** LB ⊗ ⊘ in restaurant Civ Wed 160

★★★ 70% ⊛ HOTEL

Lysses House
51 High St PO16 7BQ
☎ 01329 822622 🗎 01329 822762
e-mail: lysses@lysses.co.uk
web: www.lysses.co.uk

dir: M27 junct 11, stay in left lane. At rdbt 3rd exit into East St & follow into High St. Hotel at top on right

This attractive Georgian hotel is situated on the edge of the town in a quiet location and provides spacious and well-equipped accommodation. There are conference facilities, and a lounge bar serving a range of snacks together with the Richmond Restaurant that serves accomplished and imaginative cuisine.

Rooms 21 en suite (7 GF) ⊛ in 17 bedrooms S £57.50-£82.50; D £85-£105 (incl. bkfst) **Facilities** Wi-fi in bedrooms **Conf** Thtr 95 Class 42 Board 28 Del from £124 **Services** Lift **Parking** 30 **Notes** ⊗ ⊘ in restaurant Closed 25 Dec-1 Jan RS 24 Dec & BHs Civ Wed 100

Ⓤ

Red Lion
East St PO16 0BP
☎ 01329 822640 🗎 01329 823579
e-mail: redlion.fareham@oldenglishinns.co.uk
web: www.oldenglish.co.uk

OLD ENGLISH INNS

dir: M27 junct 11, take A32 to Gosport. Avoid flyover & take 3rd exit from rdbt. Hotel on left

At the time of going to press, the star classification for this hotel was not confirmed. Please refer to the AA internet site www.theAA.com for current information.

Rooms 46 en suite (2 fmly) (11 GF) ⊛ in 31 bedrooms S £60-£80; D £70-£92 (incl. bkfst) **Facilities** Xmas **Conf** Thtr 100 Class 60 Board 40 Del £97.50 **Parking** 100 **Notes** LB ⊗ ⊘ in restaurant

BUDGET HOTEL

Premier Travel Inn Fareham
Southampton Rd, Park Gate SO31 6AF
☎ 08701 977100 🗎 01489 577238
web: www.premiertravelinn.com

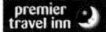

dir: on 2nd rdbt off M27 junct 9, signed A27 Fareham

High quality, modern budget accommodation ideal for both families and business travellers. Spacious, en suite bedrooms feature bath and shower, satellite TV and many have telephones and modem points. The adjacent family restaurant features a wide and varied menu. For further details consult the Hotel Groups page.

Rooms 41 en suite

FARNBOROUGH — MAP 05 SU85

★★★ 67% HOTEL

Falcon
68 Farnborough Rd GU14 6TH
☎ 01252 545378 🗎 01252 522539
e-mail: hotel@falconfarnborough.com
web: www.falconfarnborough.com

dir: A325 off M3, pass Farnborough Gate Retail Park. Left at next rdbt & straight at next 2 rdbts. Hotel on left at junct of aircraft esplanade & A325

This well-presented hotel is conveniently located for business guests. Modern bedrooms are practically furnished and equipped with a useful range of extras. Public areas include the conservatory restaurant offering a range of contemporary and traditional fare. Aircraft enthusiasts are well catered for as there is an aeronautical centre adjacent.

Rooms 30 en suite (1 fmly) (3 GF) ⊛ in 25 bedrooms S £55-£98; D £65-£112 (incl. bkfst) **Facilities** STV Wi-fi in bedrooms Xmas **Conf** Thtr 25 Class 8 Board 16 Del from £125 **Parking** 25 **Notes** ⊗ ⊘ in restaurant RS 23 Dec-4 Jan Civ Wed 50

BUDGET HOTEL

Premier Travel Inn Farnborough
Ively Rd, Southwood GU14 0JP
☎ 08701 977101 🗎 01252 546427
web: www.premiertravelinn.com

dir: From M3 junct 4a, onto A327 to Farnborough. Inn on left at 5th rbt (Monkey Puzzle roundabout)

High quality, modern budget accommodation ideal for both families and business travellers. Spacious, en suite bedrooms feature bath and shower, satellite TV and many have telephones and modem points. The adjacent family restaurant features a wide and varied menu. For further details consult the Hotel Groups page.

Rooms 62 en suite

FLEET
MAP 05 SU85

★★★ 74% HOTEL

Lismoyne
Church Rd GU51 4NE
☎ 01252 628555 🖩 01252 811761
e-mail: info@lismoynehotel.com
web: www.lismoynehotel.com

dir: M3 junct 4a. B3013, over railway bridge to town centre.
Through lights, take 4th right. Hotel 0.25m on left

Set in extensive grounds, this attractive hotel is located close to the
town centre. Public rooms include a comfortable lounge and pleasant
bar with a conservatory overlooking the garden, and a traditional
restaurant. Accommodation is divided between the bedrooms in the
original building and those in the modern extension; styles vary but all
rooms are well equipped.

Rooms 62 en suite (3 fmly) (19 GF) ⊗ in all bedrooms S £45-£124;
D £55-£159 **Facilities** STV Gym Wi-fi available Xmas **Conf** Thtr 170
Class 92 Board 80 Del from £148.95 **Parking** 150 **Notes LB** ⊗ ⊗ in
restaurant Civ Wed 170

BUDGET HOTEL

Innkeeper's Lodge Fleet
Cove Rd GU51 2SH
☎ 01252 774600
web: www.innkeeperslodge.com

dir: M3, junct 4a

Smart, en suite accommodation ideal for both business & leisure
guests. Bedrooms are very well equipped, including Sky TV,
telephone, modem points, tea & coffee making facilities, (family
rooms in most locations). Complimentary breakfast. The adjacent Pub
Restaurant; a Harvester, Vintage Inn, Toby Carvery, Ember Inn, Sizzling
Pubco or Pub & Carvery offers an all day menu. See Hotel Groups
pages for further details.

Rooms 40 en suite S £49.95-£69.95; D £49.95-£69.95

FLEET MOTORWAY SERVICE
AREA (M3)
MAP 05 SU75

BUDGET HOTEL

Days Inn Fleet
Fleet Services GU51 1AA
☎ 01252 815587 🖩 01252 815587
e-mail: fleethotel@welcomebreak.co.uk
web: www.welcomebreak.co.uk

dir: between junct 4a & 5 southbound on M3

This modern building offers accommodation in smart, spacious and
well-equipped bedrooms, suitable for families and business travellers,
and all with en suite bathrooms. Continental breakfast is available and
other refreshments may be taken at the nearby family restaurant. For
further details see the Hotel Groups page.

Rooms 58 en suite **Conf** Board 10

FOUR MARKS
MAP 05 SU63

BUDGET HOTEL

Travelodge Alton Four Marks
156 Winchester Rd GU34 5HZ
☎ 08700 850 950 🖩 01420 562659
web: www.travelodge.co.uk

dir: 5m S of Alton on A31 n'bound

Travelodge offers good quality, good value, modern accommodation.
Ideal for families, the spacious en suite bedrooms include remote-
control TV, tea and coffee-making facilities and comfortable beds.
Meals can be taken at the nearby family restaurant. See Hotel Groups
pages for further details.

Rooms 31 en suite S fr £26; D fr £26

HARTLEY WINTNEY
MAP 05 SU75

★★★ 78% HOTEL

Elvetham
RG27 8AR
☎ 01252 844871 🖩 01252 844161
e-mail: enq@theelvetham.co.uk
web: www.theelvetham.co.uk

dir: M3 junct 4a W, junct 5 E (or M4 junct 11, A33, B3011). Hotel
signed from A323 between Hartley Wintney & Fleet

A spectacular 19th century mansion set in 35 acres of grounds with an
arboretum. All bedrooms are individually styled and many have views
of the manicured gardens. A popular venue for weddings and
conferences, the hotel lends itself to team building events and
outdoor pursuits.

Rooms 41 en suite 29 annexe en suite (7 GF) S fr £110; D fr £135 (incl.
bkfst) **Facilities** STV ⌇ Squash Sauna Gym ≒ Putt green Jacuzzi Wi-fi
in bedrooms Volleyball, Badminton and Boules **Conf** BC Thtr 110
Class 80 Board 48 Del from £185 **Parking** 200 **Notes** ⊗ in restaurant
Closed 24 Dec-1 Jan Civ Wed 100

HAVANT
MAP 05 SU70

★★ 65% HOTEL

Bear
East St PO9 1AA
☎ 023 9248 6501 🖩 023 9247 0551
e-mail: 9110@greeneking.co.uk
web: www.oldenglish.co.uk

dir: From A27 turn off at Havant. Left at rdbt, right at 2nd lights.
Left at mini rdbt, 1st right and follow to end of road, car park
opposite.

This listed, former coaching inn is located in the heart of the town and
has informal public rooms, which include a small cocktail bar and the
Elizabethan public bar. The fully equipped bedrooms are well laid out
and equally suited to both the business and leisure guest.

Rooms 42 en suite (2 fmly) ⊗ in 20 bedrooms S £55-£75; D £65-£95
(incl. bkfst) **Facilities** STV ♫ Xmas **Conf** Thtr 100 Class 40 Board 40
Del from £75 **Parking** 80 **Notes** ⊗ in restaurant

England

HAVANT *continued*

Premier Travel Inn Havant, Portsmouth

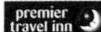

65 Bedhampton Hill, Bedhampton PO9 3JN
☎ 08701 977130 📄 023 9245 3471
web: www.premiertravelinn.com
dir: on rdbt just off A3(M) to Bedhampton

High quality, modern budget accommodation ideal for both families and business travellers. Spacious, en suite bedrooms feature bath and shower, satellite TV and many have telephones and modem points. The adjacent family restaurant features a wide and varied menu. For further details consult the Hotel Groups page.

Rooms 36 en suite

HIGHCLERE   MAP 05 SU45

U

The Furze Bush Inn

Hatt Common, Ball Hill RG20 0NQ
☎ 01635 253228 📄 01635 254883
e-mail: info@furzebushinn.co.uk
web: www.furzebushinn.co.uk

At the time of going to press, the star classification for this hotel was not confirmed. Please refer to the AA internet site www.theAA.com for current information.

Rooms 10 en suite (4 GF) ⊗ in all bedrooms S £54-£75; D £75-£100 (incl. bkfst) **Facilities** FTV Snooker **Conf** Board 1 Del from £100 **Parking** 60 **Notes LB** ⊗ ⊗ in restaurant RS 25 Dec

HOOK   MAP 05 SU75
See also Hartley Wintney

★★ 76% **HOTEL**

Raven   OLD ENGLISH INNS

Station Rd RG27 9HS
☎ 01256 762541 📄 01256 768677
e-mail: raven.hook@newbridgeinns.co.uk
web: www.oldenglish.co.uk

dir: Exit M3 junct 5 & take B3349 into Hook. Hotel 0.5m on right just over railway bridge

This well run hotel is informal and friendly. Situated in easy reach of the M3 and adjacent to the railway station it is a popular venue which does a brisk bar and restaurant trade. New refurbished bedrooms are modern, practical and well equipped for the business traveller.

Rooms 38 en suite (5 fmly) (14 GF) ⊗ in 29 bedrooms S £50-£82; D £55-£105 (incl. bkfst) **Facilities** ♫ Xmas **Conf** Thtr 100 Class 60 Board 70 Del £105 **Parking** 90 **Notes LB** ⊗ ⊗ in restaurant

★★ 74% **HOTEL**

Hook House

London Rd RG27 9EQ
☎ 01256 762630 📄 01256 760232
e-mail: reception@hookhousehotel.co.uk
dir: 1m E of Hook on A30

Several acres of landscaped grounds and a relaxing environment are provided at this friendly, small hotel. Bedrooms are well equipped, and some are located in an adjacent building. Public areas include two lounges and a dining room overlooking the gardens. The hotel is a popular wedding venue at weekends.

Rooms 13 en suite 9 annexe en suite (4 GF) S £69.50-£99.50; D £99.50 (incl. bkfst) **Facilities** Wi-fi available **Conf** Thtr 40 Class 20 Board 20 Del from £125 **Parking** 20 **Notes** ⊗ ⊗ in restaurant Closed Xmas Civ Wed 80

ISLE OF WIGHT
See **Wight, Isle of**

LIPHOOK   MAP 05 SU83

★★★ 79% ⊛⊛ **HOTEL**

Old Thorns Golf & Country Estate

Griggs Green GU30 7PE
☎ 01428 724555 📄 01428 725036
e-mail: info@oldthorns.com
web: www.oldthorns.com

dir: A3 Guildford to Portsmouth road. Griggs Green exit S of Liphook

This smartly presented hotel offers a range of leisure facilities, including a golf course, indoor pool, sauna and fitness room. The bedrooms are spacious, and equipped with good facilities. There is a choice of eating options: the Japanese Nippon Kan Restaurant or the Greenview, which enjoys views over the golf course.

Rooms 29 en suite 4 annexe rms (3 en suite) (2 fmly) (14 GF) ⊗ in all bedrooms S £130-£175; D £150-£195 (incl. bkfst) **Facilities** STV ⊠ ⅃ 18 ⊝ Sauna Solarium Gym Putt green Wi-fi in bedrooms Steam room, Beauty treatment rooms Xmas **Conf** Thtr 100 Class 50 Board 30 Del from £185 **Parking** 80 **Notes LB** Civ Wed 77

BUDGET HOTEL

Travelodge Liphook

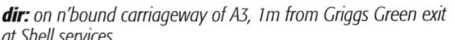

GU30 7TT

☎ 08700 850 950 📠 01428 727619

web: www.travelodge.co.uk

dir: on n'bound carriageway of A3, 1m from Griggs Green exit at Shell services

Travelodge offers good quality, good value, modern accommodation. Ideal for families, the spacious en suite bedrooms include remote-control TV, tea and coffee-making facilities and comfortable beds. Meals can be taken at the nearby family restaurant. See Hotel Groups pages for further details.

Rooms 40 en suite S fr £26; D fr £26

LYMINGTON   MAP 05 SZ39

★★★ 80% **HOTEL**

Passford House

Mount Pleasant Ln SO41 8LS

☎ 01590 682398 📠 01590 683494

e-mail: sales@passfordhousehotel.co.uk

web: www.passfordhousehotel.co.uk

dir: from A337 at Lymington over mini rdbt. 1st right at Tollhouse pub, then after 1m right into Mount Pleasant Lane

A peaceful hotel set in attractive grounds on the edge of town. Bedrooms vary in size but all are comfortably furnished and well equipped. Extensive public areas include lounges, a smartly appointed restaurant and bar plus leisure facilities. The friendly and well-motivated staff provide attentive service.

Rooms 49 en suite 2 annexe en suite (10 GF) ⊗ in 20 bedrooms S £75-£110; D £120-£200 (incl. bkfst) **Facilities** Spa 🏊 🏋 ♨ Sauna Gym 🏌 Putt green Petanque, Table tennis, Helipad, pool table Xmas **Conf** Thtr 80 Class 30 Board 30 Del from £98 **Parking** 100 **Notes LB** No children 8yrs ⊗ in restaurant

---

★★★ 77% ❀ **HOTEL**

Stanwell House

14-15 High St SO41 9AA

☎ 01590 677123 📠 01590 677756

e-mail: sales@stanwellhousehotel.co.uk

web: www.stanwellhousehotel.co.uk

dir: A337 to town centre, on right of High St

This stylish hotel enjoys a central location and offers friendly and attentive service. Bedrooms are comfortable and very well equipped; some rooms in the older part of the building are particularly interesting and some have four-poster beds. The award-winning cuisine provides interesting freshly prepared dishes.

Rooms 29 en suite (1 fmly) ⊗ in 10 bedrooms S fr £85; D fr £110 (incl. bkfst) **Facilities** FTV **Conf** Thtr 50 Class 30 Board 22 Del from £125 **Notes LB** ⊗ in restaurant Civ Wed 60

★★★ 75% **HOTEL**

Macdonald Elmers Court Hotel & Resort

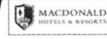

South Baddesley Rd SO41 5ZB

☎ 0870 1942131 📠 01590 679780

e-mail: elmerscourt@macdonald-hotels.co.uk

web: www.macdonald-hotels.co.uk

dir: M27 junct 1, through Lyndhurst, Brockenhurst & Lymington, hotel 200yds right after Lymington ferry terminal

Originally known as The Elms, this Tudor-gabled manor house dates back to the 1820s. Ideally located at the edge of the New Forest and overlooking The Solent with views towards the Isle of Wight, the hotel

continued on page 326

England

LYMINGTON *continued*

offers suites and self-catering accommodation, along with well-appointed leisure facilities.

Rooms 42 annexe en suite (8 fmly) (22 GF) ⊛ in 16 bedrooms
Facilities Spa ⚑ ⚐ supervised ⚐ Squash Sauna Solarium Gym ⚐ Putt green Jacuzzi Beauty treatment rooms,, Steam room, Aerobics classes ♫ **Conf** Thtr 100 Class 40 Board 40 **Parking** 100 **Notes** LB ⊗ ⊛ in restaurant Civ Wed 100

LYNDHURST   MAP 05 SU30

★★★ 75% HOTEL

Best Western Crown
High St SO43 7NF
☎ 023 8028 2922 📠 023 8028 2751
e-mail: reception@crownhotel-lyndhurst.co.uk
web: www.crownhotel-lyndhurst.co.uk

dir: in centre of village, opposite church

The Crown, with its stone mullioned windows, panelled rooms and elegant period decor evokes the style of an Edwardian English country house. Bedrooms are generally a good size and offer a useful range of facilities. Public areas have style and comfort and include a choice of function and meeting rooms. The pleasant garden and terrace are havens of peace and tranquillity.

Rooms 39 en suite (8 fmly) ⊛ in 23 bedrooms S £72.50-£97.50;
D £98-£157 (incl. bkfst) **Facilities** STV FTV Wi-fi in bedrooms Xmas
Conf Thtr 70 Class 30 Board 45 Del from £129 **Services** Lift **Parking** 60
Notes LB ⊛ in restaurant Civ Wed 70

★★★ 71% HOTEL

Lyndhurst Park
High St SO43 7NL
☎ 023 8028 3923 📠 023 8028 3019
e-mail: lyndhurst.park@forestdale.com
web: www.forestdale.com

dir: M27 junct 1-3 to A35 to Lyndhurst. Hotel at bottom of High Street

Although it is just by the High Street, the hotel is afforded seclusion from the town due to its five acres of mature grounds. The comfortable bedrooms include home-from-home touches such as ducks in the bath! The stunning bar offers a stylish setting for a snack whilst the restaurant provides a more formal dining venue.

Rooms 59 en suite (3 fmly) ⊛ in 10 bedrooms S £90; D £120 (incl. bkfst) **Facilities** STV ⚐ ⚐ Snooker Sauna Wi-fi in bedrooms Outdoor Games available at reception Xmas **Conf** Thtr 300 Class 120 Board 40 Del from £125 **Services** Lift **Parking** 100 **Notes** LB ⊛ in restaurant Civ Wed 120

★★★ 70% ⚙ HOTEL

Bell Inn
SO43 7HE
☎ 023 8081 2214 📠 023 8081 3958
e-mail: bell@bramshaw.co.uk
web: www.bramshaw.co.uk

(For full entry see Brook (Near Cadnam))

★★★ 70% HOTEL

Best Western Forest Lodge
Pikes Hill, Romsey Rd SO43 7AS
☎ 023 8028 3677 📠 023 8028 2940
e-mail: forest@newforesthotels.co.uk
web: www.newforesthotels.co.uk

dir: M27 junct 1, A337 towards Lyndhurst. In village, with police station & courts on right, take 1st right into Pikes Hill

Situated on the edge of Lyndhurst, this hotel is set well back from the main road. Bedrooms are on different floors and a number are well suited for family use. The indoor pool, with delightful murals, is a real bonus.

Rooms 28 en suite (7 fmly) (6 GF) ⊛ in 5 bedrooms **Facilities** ⚐ Sauna Gym **Conf** Thtr 120 Class 70 Board 60 **Parking** 50 **Notes** LB ⊛ in restaurant Civ Wed 60

★★ 74% HOTEL

Ormonde House
Southampton Rd SO43 7BT
☎ 023 8028 2806 📠 023 8028 2004
e-mail: enquiries@ormondehouse.co.uk
web: www.ormondehouse.co.uk

dir: 800yds E of Lyndhurst on A35 to Southampton

Set back from the main road on the edge of Lyndhurst, this welcoming hotel combines an efficient mix of relaxed hospitality and attentive service. Bedrooms, including some on the ground floor, are well furnished and equipped. Larger suites with kitchen facilities are also available. Home-cooked dinners offer a range of carefully presented fresh ingredients.

Rooms 19 en suite 4 annexe en suite (1 fmly) (6 GF) ⊛ in all bedrooms S £40-£90; D £75-£140 (incl. bkfst) **Facilities** Spa STV **Parking** 26 **Notes** LB ⊛ in restaurant Closed Xmas wk

---

★★ 64% HOTEL

Knightwood Lodge
Southampton Rd SO43 7BU
☎ 023 8028 2502 📠 023 8028 3730
e-mail: jackie4r@aol.com
web: www.knightwoodlodge.co.uk

dir: exit M27 junct 1 follow A337 to Lyndhurst. Left at lights in village onto A35 towards Southampton. Hotel 0.25m on left

This friendly, family-run hotel is situated on the outskirts of Lyndhurst. Comfortable bedrooms are modern in style and well equipped with many useful extras. The hotel offers an excellent range of facilities including a swimming pool, a jacuzzi and a small gym area. Two

continued

separate cottages are available for families or larger groups, and dogs are also welcome as guests in these.

Rooms 15 en suite 4 annexe en suite (2 fmly) (5 GF) S £47.50-£50; D £80-£100 (incl. bkfst) **Facilities** STV ☒ Sauna Gym Jacuzzi Steam room **Parking** 15 **Notes** LB ⊘ in restaurant

BUDGET HOTEL

Travelodge Stoney Cross Lyndhurst

A31 Westbound SO43 7GN

☎ 08700 850 950 ▤ 02380 811544

web: www.travelodge.co.uk

dir: M27 W'bound becomes A31, on left after Rufus Stone sign

Travelodge offers good quality, good value, modern accommodation. Ideal for families, the spacious en suite bedrooms include remote-control TV, tea and coffee-making facilities and comfortable beds. Meals can be taken at the nearby family restaurant. See Hotel Groups pages for further details.

Rooms 32 en suite S fr £26; D fr £26

MILFORD ON SEA   MAP 05 SZ29

INSPECTORS' CHOICE

★★★ ◉◉◉ HOTEL

Westover Hall

Park Ln SO41 0PT

☎ 01590 643044 ▤ 01590 644490

e-mail: info@westoverhallhotel.com

web: www.westoverhallhotel.com

dir: M3 & M27 W onto A337 to Lymington. Follow signs to Milford-on-Sea onto B3058. Hotel outside village centre towards cliff

Just a few moments' walk from the beach and boasting uninterrupted views across Christchurch Bay to the Isle of Wight in the distance, this late-Victorian mansion offers a relaxed, informal and friendly atmosphere together with efficient standards of hospitality and service. Each of the bedrooms has been decorated with flair and style. Architectural delights include dramatic stained-glass windows, extensive oak panelling and a galleried entrance hall. The award-winning cuisine is prepared with much care and attention to detail.

Rooms 12 en suite (1 fmly) ⊘ in all bedrooms S £95-£180; D £120-£260 (incl. bkfst) **Facilities** Beach Hut Xmas **Conf** Thtr 35 Class 20 Board 20 Del from £145 **Parking** 50 **Notes** LB ⊘ in restaurant Civ Wed 50

See advert under LYMINGTON

Ⓤ

Swallow South Lawn

SWALLOW HOTELS

Lymington Rd SO41 0RF

☎ 01590 643911 ▤ 01590 644820

e-mail: generalmanager.lymington@swallowhotels.com

web: www.swallowhotels.com

dir: Off A337 at Everton onto B3058 to Milford-on-Sea. Hotel 0.5m on left

At the time of going to press, the star classification for this hotel was not confirmed. Please refer to the AA internet site www.theAA.com for current information.

Rooms 24 en suite (2 fmly) (3 GF) ⊘ in all bedrooms S £140-£150; D £130-£160 (incl. bkfst) **Facilities** Xmas **Conf** Thtr 150 Class 50 Del £150 **Parking** 60 **Notes** ⊗ ⊘ in restaurant Civ Wed 150

NEW ALRESFORD   MAP 05 SU53

★★ 67% HOTEL

Swan

11 West St SO24 9AD

☎ 01962 732302 & 734427 ▤ 01962 735274

e-mail: swanhotel@btinternet.com

dir: off A31 onto B3047

This former coaching inn dates back to the 18th century and remains a busy and popular destination for travellers and locals. Bedrooms are in the main building and the more modern wing. The lounge bar and

continued on page 328

England

NEW ALRESFORD *continued*

adjacent restaurant are open all day; for more traditional dining there is another restaurant which overlooks the busy village street.

Rooms 11 rms (10 en suite) 12 annexe en suite (3 fmly) (5 GF) S £42.50-£47.50; D £70-£80 (incl. bkfst) **Conf** Thtr 90 Class 60 Board 40 Del from £75 **Parking** 25 **Notes** ⊛ in restaurant RS 25-26 Dec

See advert on page 327

NEW MILTON   MAP 05 SZ29

INSPECTORS' CHOICE

★★★★★ ⑧⑧⑧ **HOTEL**

Chewton Glen

Christchurch Rd BH25 5QS
☎ 01425 275341 🖹 01425 272310
e-mail: reservations@chewtonglen.com
web: www.chewtonglen.com

dir: A35 from Lyndhurst for 10m, left at staggered junct. Follow tourist sign for hotel through Walkford, take 2nd left

RELAIS & CHATEAUX

This outstanding hotel has been at the forefront of British hotel-keeping for many years. Once past the wrought iron entrance gates, guests are transported into a world of luxury. Log fires and afternoon tea are part of the tradition here, and lounges have fine views over the sweeping croquet lawns. Most bedrooms are very spacious, with their own private patios or balconies. Dining is a highlight, and the extensive wine lists are essential reading for the enthusiast. The spa and leisure facilities are among the best in the country.

Rooms 58 en suite (9 GF) **Facilities Spa** STV 🔲 🔾 ↓9 🏊 Snooker Sauna Gym ❧ Putt green Hydrotherapy spa, Hot tub, Dance studio, Cycling and jogging trail ♬ **Conf** BC Thtr 150 Class 70 Board 40 **Services** air con **Parking** 100 **Notes LB** ⊛ No children 5yrs ⊛ in restaurant Civ Wed 140

See advert on opposite page

NORTH WALTHAM   MAP 05 SU54

BUDGET HOTEL

Premier Travel Inn Basingstoke South

RG25 2BB
☎ 0870 9906476 🖹 0870 9906477
web: www.premiertravelinn.com

premier travel inn

dir: On A30 just off M3 junct 7. Turn left signed North Waltham, Popham & Kings Worthy. Inn 2m on right, before A303

High quality, modern budget accommodation ideal for both families

continued

and business travellers. Spacious, en suite bedrooms feature bath and shower, satellite TV and many have telephones and modem points. The adjacent family restaurant features a wide and varied menu. For further details consult the Hotel Groups page.

Rooms 28 en suite **Conf** Thtr 80 Class 30 Board 35

ODIHAM   MAP 05 SU75

★★★ 72% **HOTEL**

George

High St RG29 1LP
☎ 01256 702081 🖹 01256 704213
e-mail: reception@georgehotelodiham.com
web: www.georgehotelodiham.com

dir: M3 junct 5 follow Alton & Odiham signs. Through North Warnborough into Odiham left at top of hill, hotel on left

The George is over 450 years old and is a fine example of an old English inn. Bedrooms, many now refurbished, come in a number of styles; the older part of the property has beams and period features, whilst newer rooms have a contemporary feel. Guests can dine in the all-day bistro or the popular restaurant.

Rooms 19 en suite 9 annexe en suite (1 fmly) (6 GF) ⊛ in 14 bedrooms S £60-£85; D £80-£115 (incl. bkfst) **Facilities** STV Wi-fi in bedrooms **Conf** Thtr 30 Class 10 Board 26 Del from £135 **Parking** 20 **Notes LB** ⊛ in restaurant Closed 24-26 Dec

OWER   MAP 05 SU31

★★ 76% **HOTEL**

Mortimer Arms

Romsey Rd SO51 6AF
☎ 023 8081 4379 🖹 023 8081 2548
e-mail: info@mortimerarms.co.uk

dir: M27 junct 2 follow signs to Paultons Park. Hotel at entrance

Located at the entrance of Paultons Park, this is ideally situated for access to the M27 and to the New Forest, so will suit leisure guests and business travellers alike. Bedrooms are appointed to a high standard, and all have DVD players. Enjoyable meals are available in the relaxed, informal dining area.

Rooms 14 en suite (3 fmly) (2 GF) ⊛ in all bedrooms S fr £59.95; D fr £74.95 (incl. bkfst) **Facilities** STV Xmas **Conf** BC Thtr 80 Class 60 Board 50 **Parking** 64 **Notes LB** ⊛ ⊛ in restaurant

PURE INDULGENCE

'Probably the best combination of country house grandeur, food and spa facilities anywhere in the UK'

THE TIMES, LONDON

Chewton Glen

THE HOTEL, SPA AND COUNTRY CLUB

New Milton, Hampshire, England BH25 6QS. Telephone (01425) 275341 Fax (01425) 272310
reservations@chewtonglen.com   www.chewtonglen.com

★ ★ ★ ★ ★
AA

RELAIS &
CHATEAUX.

England

PETERSFIELD MAP 05 SU72

★★ 72% ⊛ **HOTEL**

Langrish House

Langrish GU32 1RN
☎ 01730 266941 ▤ 01730 260543
e-mail: frontdesk@langrishhouse.co.uk
web: www.langrishhouse.co.uk

dir: *A3 onto A272 towards Winchester. Hotel signed, 2.5m*

Located in an idyllic country location just outside Petersfield, this family home dates back to the 17th century. Rooms offer good levels of comfort with beautiful views over the countryside. The public areas consist of a small cosy restaurant, a bar in the vaults, and conference and banqueting rooms that are popular for weddings. Staff throughout are friendly and nothing is too much trouble.

Rooms 13 en suite (1 fmly) (3 GF) ⊗ in all bedrooms S fr £80;
D £105-£145 (incl. bkfst) **Facilities** Fishing Wi-fi available Xmas
Conf Thtr 60 Class 18 Board 25 Del from £130 **Parking** 80 **Notes LB**
⊗ in restaurant Civ Wed 60

PORTSMOUTH & SOUTHSEA MAP 05 SU60

★★★★ 71% **HOTEL**

Portsmouth Marriott Hotel **Marriott**
HOTELS & RESORTS

Southampton Rd PO6 4SH
☎ 0870 400 7285 ▤ 0870 400 7385
e-mail: london.regional.reservations@marriott.com
web: www.portsmouthmarriott.co.uk

dir: *M27 junct 12 keep left and hotel on left*

Close to the motorway and ferry port, this hotel is well suited to business trade. The comfortable and well laid-out bedrooms provide a comprehensive range of facilities including up-to-date workstations. The leisure club offers a pool, a gym, and a health and beauty salon.

Rooms 174 en suite (77 fmly) ⊗ in 149 bedrooms **Facilities** STV ⬚
supervised Sauna Solarium Gym Jacuzzi Wi-fi in bedrooms Exercise
studio, Beauty salon Xmas **Conf** Thtr 350 Class 180 Board 30
Services Lift air con **Parking** 250 **Notes** ⊗ in restaurant Civ Wed 100

★★★ 72% **HOTEL**

Best Western Royal Beach

South Pde, Southsea PO4 0RN
☎ 023 9273 1281 ▤ 023 9281 7572
e-mail: enquiries@royalbeachhotel.co.uk
web: www.royalbeachhotel.co.uk

dir: *M27 to M275, follow signs to seafront. Hotel on seafront*

This former Victorian seafront hotel is a smart and comfortable venue suitable for leisure and business guests alike. Bedrooms and public areas are well presented and generally spacious, and the smart Coast bar is an ideal venue for a relaxing drink.

Rooms 124 en suite (18 fmly) ⊗ in 72 bedrooms S £55-£95; D £65-£125
(incl. bkfst) **Facilities** STV Wi-fi available ♬ Xmas **Conf** Thtr 280
Class 180 Board 40 Del from £109.95 **Services** Lift **Parking** 50
Notes LB ⊗ in restaurant

See advert on opposite page

★★★ 72% **HOTEL**

Tulip Inn Portsmouth **TULIP INN**

Binnacle Way PO6 4FB
☎ 023 9237 3333 ▤ 023 9237 3335
e-mail: info@tulipinnportsmouth.co.uk

dir: *M27 junct 12, left at lights onto Southampton Rd. After 200mtrs turn left at lights onto Compass Rd. At mini-rdbt turn right onto Binnacle Way, hotel on right*

This hotel is well placed for many transport links and offers well appointed, air-conditioned bedrooms with en suite, walk-in power showers; some family rooms are available. The modern Bibo bar and bistro serves contemporary dishes in a relaxed atmosphere.

Rooms 108 en suite (16 fmly) (10 GF) ⊗ in 91 bedrooms S £62-£90;
D £62-£90 **Facilities** STV **Conf** Thtr 30 Board 20 Del from £119
Services Lift air con **Parking** 110 **Notes** ⊛ ⊗ in restaurant

★★★ 72% **HOTEL**

Westfield Hall

65 Festing Rd, Southsea PO4 0NQ
☎ 023 9282 6971 ▤ 023 9287 0200
e-mail: enquiries@whhotel.info
web: www.whhotel.info

dir: *Exit M275 & follow signs for Southsea seafront. Turn left onto Clarence Esplanade on South Parade Pier. Turn left onto St Helens Parade, hotel 150yds opposite.*

This hotel is situated in a quiet side road close to the seafront and town centre. The accommodation is split between two identical houses and all rooms are smartly appointed and well equipped.

continued

Public rooms are attractively decorated and include three lounges, a bar and a restaurant.

Rooms 15 en suite 11 annexe en suite (12 fmly) (6 GF) ⊘ in 15 bedrooms S £48-£56; D £68-£90 (incl. bkfst) **Facilities** STV **Parking** 16 **Notes LB** ⊗ ⊘ in restaurant

★★★ 71% **HOTEL**

The Farmhouse

OLD ENGLISH INNS

Burrfields Rd PO3 5HH
☎ 023 9265 0510 📠 023 9269 3458
e-mail: Innlodge@greeneking.co.uk
web: www.oldenglish.co.uk

dir: A3(M)/M27 onto A27. Take Southsea exit, follow A2030. 3rd lights right into Burrfields Road. Hotel car park on left

Located on the eastern fringe of the city, this purpose-built hotel is conveniently located for all major routes. The modern bedrooms are spacious and well equipped. Guests have two eating options: the contemporary styled 'Lounge' restaurant and the Farmhouse Inn. The hotel also boasts a large covered children's play area.

Rooms 74 en suite (6 fmly) (33 GF) ⊘ in 39 bedrooms **Facilities** STV Indoor fun factory & outdoor kids play area, Pool tables **Conf** BC Thtr 150 Class 64 Board 40 **Parking** 200 **Notes** ⊗ ⊘ in restaurant

★★ 74% **HOTEL**

Seacrest

THE INDEPENDENTS

11/12 South Pde, Southsea PO5 2JB
☎ 023 9273 3192 📠 023 9283 2523
e-mail: seacrest@boltblue.com
web: www.seacresthotel.co.uk

dir: from M27/M275 follow signs for seafront, Pyramids and Sea Life Centre. Hotel opposite Rock Gardens and Pyramids

In a premier seafront location, this smart hotel provides the ideal base for exploring the town. Bedrooms, many benefiting from sea views, are decorated to a high standard with good facilities. Guests can relax in either the south-facing lounge, furnished with large leather sofas, or the adjacent bar; there is also a cosy dining room popular with residents.

Rooms 28 en suite (3 fmly) ⊘ in 20 bedrooms **Facilities** STV **Services** Lift **Parking** 12 **Notes** ⊘ in restaurant

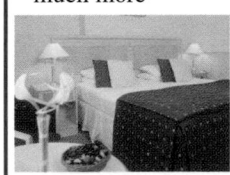
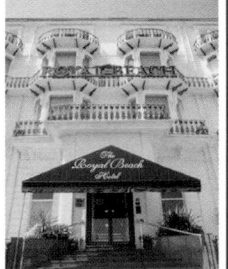

England

PORTSMOUTH & SOUTHSEA *continued*

★★ 72% HOTEL

The Beaufort Hotel

71 Festing Rd, Southsea PO4 0NQ
☎ 023 9282 3707 ▤ 023 9287 0270
e-mail: enq@beauforthotel.co.uk

dir: follow seafront signs. Left at South Parade Pier, then 4th on left

This intimate hotel is located within easy reach of the seafront and the city centre and is ideal for accessing both local attractions and amenities. Individually decorated bedrooms are generally spacious providing good levels of comfort. Public areas include a pleasant lounge and cosy bar.

Rooms 20 en suite (2 fmly) (7 GF) ⊘ in 7 bedrooms S £40-£60; D £50-£80 (incl. bkfst) **Facilities** STV **Parking** 7 **Notes** ⊗ ⊘ in restaurant

BUDGET HOTEL

Hotel Ibis

Winston Churchill Av PO1 2LX
☎ 023 9264 0000 ▤ 023 9264 1000
e-mail: h1461@accor.com
web: www.ibishotel.com

dir: M27 junct 12, M275. Follow city centre, Sealife Centre and then Guildhall. Right at rdbt into Winston Churchill Ave

Modern, budget hotel offering comfortable accommodation in bright and practical bedrooms. Breakfast is self-service and dinner is available in the restaurant. For further details, consult the Hotel Groups page.

Rooms 144 en suite S £54; D £54 **Conf** Thtr 30 Class 20 Board 20

BUDGET HOTEL

Innkeeper's Lodge Portsmouth

Copnor Rd, Hilsea PO3 5HS
☎ 023 9265 4645
web: www.innkeeperslodge.com

dir: From A27 take A2030. Right at lights, over 3 rdbts into Norway Road. Inn on A288

Smart, en suite accommodation ideal for both business & leisure guests. Bedrooms are very well equipped, including Sky TV, telephone, modem points, tea & coffee making facilities, (family rooms in most locations). Complimentary breakfast. The adjacent Pub Restaurant; a Harvester, Vintage Inn, Toby Carvery, Ember Inn, Sizzling Pubco or Pub & Carvery offers an all day menu. See Hotel Groups pages for further details.

Rooms 33 en suite S £55; D £55

BUDGET HOTEL

Premier Travel Inn Portsmouth

Southampton Rd, North Harbour, Cosham PO6 4SA
☎ 08701 977213 ▤ 023 9232 4895
web: www.premiertravelinn.com

dir: on A27, close to M27 junct 12

High quality, modern budget accommodation ideal for both families and business travellers. Spacious, en suite bedrooms feature bath and

continued

shower, satellite TV and many have telephones and modem points. The adjacent family restaurant features a wide and varied menu. For further details consult the Hotel Groups page.

Rooms 64 en suite **Conf** Thtr 25

Premier Travel Inn Southsea

Long Curtain Rd, Clarence Pier, Southsea PO5 3AA
☎ 08701 977236 ▤ 023 9273 3048

dir: Pier Rd leads to Clarence Pier. Inn next to amusement park and Isle of Wight hovercraft

Rooms 40 en suite

BUDGET HOTEL

Travelodge Portsmouth

Kingston Crescent, North End PO2 8AB
☎ 08700 850 950 ▤ 02392 639121
web: www.travelodge.co.uk

dir: M275 towards north end, Rudmore rdbt turn left into Kingston Crescent

Travelodge offers good quality, good value, modern accommodation. Ideal for families, the spacious en suite bedrooms include remote-control TV, tea and coffee-making facilities and comfortable beds. Meals can be taken at the nearby family restaurant. See Hotel Groups pages for further details.

Rooms 78 en suite S fr £26; D fr £26

RINGWOOD   MAP 05 SU10

★★★ 73% HOTEL

Tyrrells Ford Country House

Avon BH23 7BH
☎ 01425 672646 ▤ 01425 672262
e-mail: tyrrellsford@aol.com
web: www.tyrrellsfordhotel.com

dir: off A31 to Ringwood. B3347, hotel 3m S on left at Avon

Set in the New Forest, this delightful family-run hotel has much to offer. Most bedrooms have views over the open country. Diners may eat in the formal restaurant, or sample the wide range of bar meals, all prepared using fresh local produce. The Gallery lounge offers guests a peaceful area in which to relax.

Rooms 16 en suite ⊘ in all bedrooms S £50-£100 (incl. bkfst & dinner) **Facilities** arrangement with local David Lloyd Fitness Club. Xmas **Conf** Thtr 40 Class 20 Board 20 **Parking** 100 **Notes** LB ⊗ ⊘ in restaurant Civ Wed 60

BUDGET HOTEL

Travelodge Ringwood

St Leonards BH24 2NR
☎ 08700 850 950 ▤ 01425 475941
web: www.travelodge.co.uk

dir: Off A31 eastbound

Travelodge offers good quality, good value, modern accommodation. Ideal for families, the spacious en suite bedrooms include remote-control TV, tea and coffee-making facilities and comfortable beds. Meals can be taken at the nearby family restaurant. See Hotel Groups pages for further details.

Rooms S fr £26; D fr £26

England

ROMSEY   MAP 05 SU32

★★★ 72% **HOTEL**

Potters Heron Hotel

Winchester Rd, Ampfield SO51 9ZF

☎ 0870 609 6155 📄 023 8025 1359

e-mail: pottersheron.romsey@millhouseinns.co.uk

dir: M3 junct 12 follow Chandler's Ford signs. 2nd exit at 3rd rdbt follow Ampfield signs, over x-rds. Hotel on left in 1m

This distinctive thatched hotel retains many of its original features and is in convenient location for Winchester, Southampton and the M3. Modern accommodation and spacious public areas are offered. The pub and restaurant offer an interesting range of dishes that suit a variety of tastes.

Rooms 54 en suite (29 GF) ⊛ in all bedrooms S £40-£92; D £45-£92 **Facilities** STV Pool table Xmas **Conf** Thtr 120 Class 40 Board 40 Del from £99 **Services** Lift **Parking** 150 **Notes LB** ⊛ in restaurant Civ Wed 100

BUDGET HOTEL

Premier Travel Inn Southampton West

Romsey Rd, Ower SO51 6ZJ

☎ 0870 9906350 📄 0870 9906351

web: www.premiertravelinn.com

dir: Just off M27 junct 2. Take A36 towards Salisbury. Follow brown tourist signs 'Vine Inn'

High quality, modern budget accommodation ideal for both families and business travellers. Spacious, en suite bedrooms feature bath and shower, satellite TV and many have telephones and modem points. The adjacent family restaurant features a wide and varied menu. For further details consult the Hotel Groups page.

Rooms 67 en suite **Conf** Thtr 150 Class 80 Board 60

ROTHERWICK   MAP 05 SU75

INSPECTORS' CHOICE

★★★★ ⊛ **HOTEL**

Tylney Hall

RG27 9AZ

☎ 01256 764881 📄 01256 768141

e-mail: sales@tylneyhall.com

web: www.tylneyhall.com

dir: M3 junct 5, A287 to Basingstoke, over junct with A30, over railway bridge, towards Newnham. Right at Newnham Green. Hotel 1m on left

A grand Victorian country house set in 66 acres of beautiful parkland. The hotel offers high standards of comfort in relaxed yet elegant surroundings, featuring magnificently restored water gardens, originally laid out by the famous gardener, Gertrude Jekyll. Spacious public rooms include the Wedgwood drawing room and panelled Oak Room, which are filled with fresh flowers

continued

---

and warmed by log fires. The spacious bedrooms are traditionally furnished and offer a high degree of comfort.

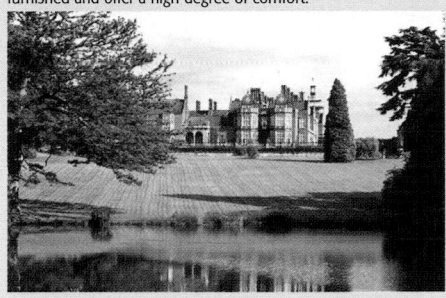

Tylney Hall

Rooms 35 en suite 77 annexe en suite (1 fmly) (21 GF) S £140-£430; D £170-£460 (incl. bkfst) **Facilities Spa** STV 🔲 ⇘ 💬 Snooker Sauna Solarium Gym ⇜ Wi-fi available Clay pigeon shooting, Archery, Falconry, Balloon rides, Laser shooting ♫ Xmas **Conf** BC Thtr 120 Class 70 Board 40 Del from £200 **Parking** 120 **Notes LB** ⊛ ⊛ in restaurant Civ Wed 100

ROWLAND'S CASTLE   MAP 05 SU71

BUDGET HOTEL

Innkeeper's Lodge Portsmouth North

Whichers Gate Rd PO9 6BB

☎ 02392 413761

web: www.innkeeperslodge.com

dir: M3 junct 2, at rdbt, right onto the B2149 (Rowlands Castle). After 2m, left onto B2148 Whichers Gate Rd, lodge on left

Smart, en suite accommodation ideal for both business & leisure guests. Bedrooms are very well equipped, including Sky TV, telephone, modem points, tea & coffee making facilities, (family rooms in most locations). Complimentary breakfast. The adjacent Pub Restaurant; a Harvester, Vintage Inn, Toby Carvery, Ember Inn, Sizzling Pubco or Pub & Carvery offers an all day menu. See Hotel Groups pages for further details.

Rooms 21 en suite S £49.95-£52.50; D £49.95-£52.50

ROWNHAMS MOTORWAY SERVICE AREA (M27)   MAP 05 SU31

BUDGET HOTEL

Premier Travel Inn Southampton (Rownhams)

Rownhams Service Area SO16 8AP

☎ 08701 977234 📄 023 8074 0204

web: www.premiertravelinn.com

dir: M27 Westbound - between junctions 3 & 4. No access from eastbound services

High quality, modern budget accommodation ideal for both families and business travellers. Spacious, en suite bedrooms feature bath and shower, satellite TV and many have telephones and modem points. The adjacent family restaurant features a wide and varied menu. For further details consult the Hotel Groups page.

Rooms 39 en suite

England

SHEDFIELD   MAP 05 SU51

★★★★ 73% **HOTEL**

Marriott Meon Valley Hotel & Country Club

Marriott
HOTELS & RESORTS

Sandy Ln SO32 2HQ

☎ 01329 833455 ▤ 01329 834411

web: www.marriott.co.uk

dir: *from W, M27 junct 7 take A334 then towards Wickham and Botley. Sandy Lane is on left 2m from Botley*

This modern, smartly appointed hotel and country club has extensive indoor and outdoor leisure facilities, including two golf courses. Bedrooms are spacious and well equipped, and guests have a choice of eating and drinking options. It is ideally suited for easy access to both Portsmouth and Southampton.

Rooms 113 en suite ⊗ in 80 bedrooms **Facilities** STV ⊠ ♣ 18 ⊜ Sauna Solarium Gym Putt green Jacuzzi Cardio-Vascular Aerobics Health & Beauty salon **Conf** Thtr 80 Class 50 Board 32 **Services** Lift **Parking** 320 **Notes** ⊗ ⊘ in restaurant Civ Wed 96

SILCHESTER   MAP 05 SU66

★★★ 72% **HOTEL**

Best Western Romans Country House

Best Western

Little London Rd RG7 2PN

☎ 0118 970 0421 ▤ 0118 970 0691

e-mail: romanhotel@hotmail.com

dir: *A340 (Basingstoke to Reading road), hotel is signed*

This Lutyens-style manor house is in a tranquil and attractive location. Bedrooms are smartly presented and well equipped, some located in an adjacent wing. The leisure club is beside an outdoor swimming pool, which is kept heated year round.

Rooms 11 en suite 14 annexe en suite (1 fmly) (11 GF) S £100-£110; D £110-£140 (incl. bkfst) ⊗ in 5 bedrooms **Facilities** STV ⊼ pool supervised ⊜ Sauna Gym Jacuzzi **Conf** Thtr 60 Class 30 Board 24 Del from £140 **Parking** 60 **Notes** ⊘ in restaurant Civ Wed 65

See advert on page 317

SOUTHAMPTON   MAP 05 SU41

See also Botley, Landford (Wilts) & Shedfield

★★★★★ 78% ◉◉ **HOTEL**

De Vere Grand Harbour

DeVere
HOTELS & RESORTS

West Quay Rd SO15 1AG

☎ 023 8063 3033 ▤ 023 8063 3066

e-mail: grandharbour@devere-hotels.com

web: www.devere.co.uk

dir: *M27 junct 3 follow Waterfront signs. Keep in left lane of dual carriageway, then follow Heritage & Waterfront signs onto West Quay Road*

Enjoying views of the harbour, this hotel stands alongside the medieval town walls and close to the West Quay centre. The modern design is impressive, with leisure facilities located in the dramatic glass pyramid. The spacious bedrooms are well appointed and thoughtfully equipped. For eating, guests can choose between two bars, as well as fine dining in Allertons Restaurant and the more informal No 5 Brasserie.

Rooms 173 en suite (22 fmly) ⊗ in 148 bedrooms S £119-£185; D £129-£195 (incl. bkfst) **Facilities** Spa STV ⊠ Sauna Solarium Gym Jacuzzi Wi-fi in bedrooms All new beauty suite serenity-4 treatment rooms, juice bar Xmas **Conf** BC Thtr 500 Class 200 Board 150 Del from £185 **Services** Lift **Parking** 190 **Notes LB** ⊗ ⊘ in restaurant Civ Wed 310

★★★★ 70% ◉◉ **HOTEL**

Best Western Botleigh Grange

Best Western

Hedge End SO30 2GA

☎ 01489 787700 ▤ 01489 788535

e-mail: enquiries@botleighgrangehotel.co.uk

dir: *from M27 junct 7 follow A334 to Botley, hotel is 0.5m on left*

This impressive mansion, situated close to the M27, displays good quality throughout. The bedrooms are spacious with a good range of facilities. Public areas include a large conference room and a pleasant terrace with views overlooking the gardens and lake. The restaurant offers interesting menus using fresh, local produce. An impressive leisure complex with pool, sauna, spa and treatments has now opened

Rooms 56 en suite (8 fmly) ⊗ in 17 bedrooms S fr £120; D fr £160 (incl bkfst) **Facilities Spa** STV ⊠ Fishing Sauna Gym Putt green Jacuzzi Three treatment rooms/ relaxation room Xmas **Conf** Thtr 500 Class 175 Board 60 Del £159 **Services** Lift **Parking** 200 **Notes LB** ⊗ ⊘ in restaurant Civ Wed 400

See advert on opposite page

★★★ 75% **HOTEL**

Chilworth Manor

SO16 7PT

CLASSIC
BRITISH HOTELS

☎ 023 8076 7333 📠 023 8070 1743

e-mail: sales@chilworth-manor.co.uk

web: www.chilworth-manor.co.uk

dir: 1m from M3/M27 junct on A27 Romsey Rd N from Southampton. Pass Clump Inn on left, 200mtrs further on turn left at Chilworth Science Park sign. Hotel immediately right

Set in 12 acres of delightful grounds, this attractive Edwardian manor house is conveniently located for the nearby City of Southampton and the New Forest, now designated a National Park. Bedrooms are located in both the main house and an adjoining wing. The hotel is particularly popular as both a conference and a wedding venue.

Rooms 95 en suite (6 fmly) ⊘ in 75 bedrooms S £55-£135; D £110-£150 (incl. bkfst) **Facilities** STV ⓢ ⓨ Wi-fi available Trim trail walking, Giant chess, Petanque **Conf** Thtr 130 Class 50 Board 50 Del from £135 **Services** Lift **Parking** 200 **Notes LB** ⊘ in restaurant Civ Wed 105

★★★ 75% ⓢ **HOTEL**

The Woodlands Lodge

Bartley Rd, Woodlands SO40 7GN

☎ 023 8029 2257 📠 023 8029 3090

e-mail: reception@woodlands-lodge.co.uk

web: www.woodlands-lodge.co.uk

dir: M27 junct 1, A336 towards Fawley. 2nd rdbt turn right, left after 0.25m by White Horse PH. In 1.5m cross cattle grid, hotel is 70yds on left

An 18th-century former hunting lodge, this hotel is set in four acres of impressive and well-tended grounds on the edge of the New Forest. Well-equipped bedrooms come in varying sizes and styles and all bathrooms have a jacuzzi bath. Public areas provide a pleasant lounge and intimate cocktail bar. The dining room, with its hand-painted ceiling, serves award-winning cuisine.

Rooms 16 en suite (1 fmly) (3 GF) ⊘ in 2 bedrooms S £72-£90; D £126-£142 (incl. bkfst) **Facilities** FTV ⓨ Wi-fi available Xmas **Conf** Thtr 55 Class 14 Board 20 Del from £140 **Parking** 30 **Notes LB** ⊘ in restaurant Civ Wed 90

★★★ 73% **HOTEL**

Jury's Inn Southampton

JURYSDOYLE
HOTELS

Charlotte Place SO14 0TB

☎ 023 8037 1111 📠 023 8037 1100

web: www.jurysdoyle.com

This is a stylish hotel in Southampton and is easily accessible from major road networks. Bedrooms provide good guest comfort and in-
continued

room facilities are suited to both leisure and business markets. Public areas include a number of meeting rooms, a popular bar and restaurant.

Rooms 270 en suite ⊘ in 206 bedrooms S £69-£150; D £69-£150 **Facilities** STV Wi-fi available Xmas **Conf** BC 1hr 120 Class 60 Board 48 Del from £124 **Services** Lift air con **Parking** 160 **Notes** ⊗ ⊘ in restaurant

★★★ 71% **HOTEL**

Novotel Southampton

1 West Quay Rd SO15 1RA

NOVOTEL
ACCOR

☎ 023 8033 0550 📠 023 8022 2158

e-mail: H1073@accor-hotels.com

web: www.novotel.com

dir: M27 junct 3 & signs for City Centre (A33). After 1m take right lane for West Quay & Dock Gates 4-10. Hotel entrance on left. Turn at lights by McDonalds, left at rdbt, hotel straight ahead

Modern purpose-built hotel situated close to the city centre, railway station, ferry terminal and major road networks. The brightly decorated bedrooms are ideal for families and business guests; four rooms have facilities for the less mobile. The open-plan public areas include the Garden brasserie, a bar and a leisure complex.

Rooms 121 en suite (50 fmly) ⊘ in 98 bedrooms **Facilities** STV ⓡ Sauna Gym **Conf** Thtr 450 Class 300 Board 150 **Services** Lift air con **Parking** 300 **Notes LB** ⊘ in restaurant Civ Wed 150

SOUTHAMPTON *continued*

★★★ 71% HOTEL

Southampton Park

Forestdale Hotels

Cumberland Place SO15 2WY
☎ 023 8034 3343 📠 023 8033 2538
e-mail: southampton.park@forestdale.com
web: www.forestdale.com
dir: at north end of Inner Ring Road

Located in the heart of the city opposite Watts Park, this modern hotel provides well-equipped, smartly appointed bedrooms with comfortable furnishings. The public areas include a good leisure centre, a spacious bar and lounge and the lively MJ's Brasserie. Parking is available in a multi-storey behind the hotel.

Rooms 72 en suite (10 fmly) ⊛ in 20 bedrooms S £40-£95; D £80-£125 (incl. bkfst) **Facilities Spa** STV 🎣 Sauna Solarium Gym Jacuzzi Wi-fi in bedrooms **Conf** Thtr 200 Class 60 Board 70 Del from £110 **Services** Lift **Notes LB** ⊛ in restaurant Closed 25 & 26 Dec nights

★★ 71% HOTEL

Elizabeth House

42-44 The Avenue SO17 1XP
☎ 023 8022 4327 📠 023 8022 4327
e-mail: enquiries@elizabethhousehotel.com
web: www.elizabethhousehotel.com
dir: on A33, towards city centre, after Southampton Common, before main lights on left

This hotel is conveniently situated close to the city centre, so provides an ideal base for both business and leisure guests. The bedrooms are well equipped and are attractively furnished with comfort in mind. There is also a cosy and atmospheric bistro in the cellar where evening meals are served.

Rooms 20 en suite 7 annexe en suite (9 fmly) (8 GF) S fr £57.50; D fr £67.50 (incl. bkfst) **Facilities** Wi-fi in bedrooms **Conf** Thtr 40 Class 24 Board 24 Del from £92 **Parking** 31 **Notes** ⊛ in restaurant

BUDGET HOTEL

Hotel Ibis

ibis
Accor hotels

West Quay Rd, Western Esplanade SO15 1RA
☎ 023 8063 4463 📠 023 8022 3273
e-mail: H1039@accor.com
web: www.ibishotel.com
dir: M27 junct 3/M271. Left to city centre (A35), follow Old Town Waterfront until 4th lights, left, then left again, hotel opposite station

Modern, budget hotel offering comfortable accommodation in bright and practical bedrooms. Breakfast is self-service and dinner is available in the restaurant. For further details, consult the Hotel Groups page.

Rooms 93 en suite S £55.95-£59.95; D £55.95-£59.95 **Facilities** FTV Wi-fi in bedrooms **Conf** Thtr 80 Class 50 Board 40 Del from £30

BUDGET HOTEL

Premier Travel Inn Southampton Airport

premier travel inn

Mitchell Way SO18 2XU
☎ 0870 9906436 📠 0870 9906437
web: www.premiertravelinn.com
dir: Exit M27 junct 5, A335 towards Eastleigh. Right at rdbt onto Wide Ln. 1st exit at next rdbt onto Mitchell Way

High quality, modern budget accommodation ideal for both families and business travellers. Spacious, en suite bedrooms feature bath and shower, satellite TV and many have telephones and modem points. The adjacent family restaurant features a wide and varied menu. For further details consult the Hotel Groups page.

Rooms 121 en suite

Premier Travel Inn Southampton City Centre

New Rd SO14 0AB
☎ 0870 238 3308 📠 023 8033 8395
dir: M27 junct 5/A335 towards city centre, at the Charlotte Place rdbt take 2nd left into East Park Terrace, then 1st left onto New Rd. Inn on right
Rooms 172 en suite

Premier Travel Inn Southampton North

Romsey Rd, Nursling SO16 0XJ
☎ 08701 977233 📠 023 8074 0947
dir: M27 junct 3 take M271 towards Romsey. At next rdbt take 3rd exit towards Southampton (A3057). Inn 1.5m on right
Rooms 32 en suite

BUDGET HOTEL

Travelodge Southampton

Travelodge

Lodge Rd SO14 6QR
☎ 08700 850 950 📠 023 8033 4569
web: www.travelodge.co.uk
dir: M3 junct 14, take A33 to Southampton, on left after 6th set of lights

Travelodge offers good quality, good value, modern accommodation. Ideal for families, the spacious en suite bedrooms include remote-control TV, tea and coffee-making facilities and comfortable beds. Meals can be taken at the nearby family restaurant. See Hotel Groups pages for further details.

Rooms 59 en suite S fr £26; D fr £26

STOCKBRIDGE   MAP 05 SU33

★★ 69% HOTEL

Grosvenor

OLD ENGLISH INNS

High St SO20 6EU
☎ 01264 810606 📠 01264 810747
e-mail: 9180@greeneking.co.uk
web: www.oldenglish.co.uk
dir: town centre

This 250-year-old coaching inn has retained lots of its historical charm. The area is popular with anglers, who come to fly fish in the nearby River Test. Dining options in the bright, airy interior include the Bank

continued

Side Bar which offers traditional country pub food, the elegant River Room Restaurant and No 23, the informal brasserie. The comfortable bedrooms are traditional in style, and offer all expected facilities.

Rooms 14 en suite 12 annexe en suite (1 fmly) (6 GF) ⊗ in 16 bedrooms S fr £85; D fr £99.50 (incl. bkfst) **Facilities** Fishing Riding Xmas **Conf** Thtr 100 Class 50 Board 35 **Parking** 26 **Notes LB** ⊗ in restaurant Civ Wed 70

STRATFIELD TURGIS   MAP 05 SU65

★★★ 70% **HOTEL**

Wellington Arms

RG27 0AS

☎ 01256 882214 ▤ 01256 882934

e-mail: Wellington.Arms@virgin.net

dir: A33 between Basingstoke & Reading

Situated at an entrance to the ancestral home of the Duke of Wellington. The majority of bedrooms are located in the modern Garden Wing, and those in the original building have a period feel and unusual furniture. Public rooms include a comfortable lounge bar with log fire and a brasserie.

Rooms 28 en suite (3 fmly) (11 GF) ⊗ in all bedrooms S £65-£120; D £75-£130 (incl. bkfst) **Conf** Thtr 160 Class 40 Board 50 Del from £152.50 **Parking** 150 **Notes LB** ⊗ in restaurant

SUTTON SCOTNEY   MAP 05 SU43

Ⓤ

Norton Manor

QHOTELS

Nr. Winchester SO21 3NE

☎ 0845 0740055 ▤ 01962 760860

e-mail: nortonmanor@qhotels.co.uk

web: www.qhotels.co.uk

dir: M3 Junct 8 onto A303, follow signs for Micheldever Station and Sutton Scotney. At next junct turn right, then left, follow signs for Sutton Scotney.

At the time of going to press, the star classification for this hotel was not confirmed. Please refer to the AA internet site www.theAA.com for current information.

Rooms (en ste) ⊗ in 65 bedrooms **Facilities** Spa ⊗ supervised ⌖ Snooker Sauna Gym ⊌ Jacuzzi **Services** Lift **Parking** 100 **Notes LB** ⊗ in restaurant Civ Wed 120

Travelodge Sutton Scotney (A34 Northbound)

SO21 3JY

☎ 08700 850 950 ▤ 01962 761096

web: www.travelodge.co.uk

dir: on A34 northbound

Travelodge offers good quality, good value, modern accommodation. Ideal for families, the spacious en suite bedrooms include remote-control TV, tea and coffee-making facilities and comfortable beds. Meals can be taken at the nearby family restaurant. See Hotel Groups pages for further details.

Rooms 30 en suite S fr £26; D fr £26

Travelodge Sutton Scotney (A34 Southbound)

SO21 3JY

☎ 08700 850 950 ▤ 01962 761096

dir: on A34 southbound

Rooms 40 en suite S fr £26; D fr £26

SWAY   MAP 05 SZ29

★★★ 72% **HOTEL**

Sway Manor Restaurant & Hotel

Station Rd SO41 6BA

☎ 01590 682754 ▤ 01590 682955

e-mail: info@swaymanor.com

web: www.swaymanor.com

dir: turn off B3055 Brockenhurst/New Milton road into Sway village centre

Built at the turn of the 20th century, this attractive mansion is set in its own grounds, and conveniently located in the village centre. Bedrooms are well appointed and generously equipped most have views over the gardens and pool. The bar and conservatory restaurant, both with views over the gardens, are popular with locals.

Rooms 15 en suite (3 fmly) ⊗ in 12 bedrooms S £55.50-£75.50; D £95-£111 (incl. bkfst) **Facilities** FTV ⌖ ch fac Xmas **Services** Lift **Parking** 40 **Notes LB** ⊗ in restaurant Civ Wed 50

WICKHAM   MAP 05 SU51

★★ 75% ◉◉ **HOTEL**

Old House Hotel & Restaurant

The Square PO17 5JG

☎ 01329 833049 ▤ 01329 833672

e-mail: oldhousehotel@aol.com

web: www.oldhousehotel.co.uk

dir: M27 junct 10, N on A32 for 2m towards Alton.

This creeper-clad former Georgian residence occupies a prime position in a charming square in the centre of town. The smart,

continued on page 338

England

England

WICKHAM *continued*

comfortable public areas include a choice of eating areas and an inviting bar and lounge. Bedrooms are well equipped although some are larger than others.

Old House Hotel & Restaurant

Rooms 8 en suite 4 annexe en suite (2 fmly) (4 GF) ⊘ in all bedrooms S £75-£120; D £85-£150 (incl. bkfst) **Facilities** STV FTV **Conf** Board 1 Del from £140 **Parking** 8 **Notes** ⊗ ⊘ in restaurant Closed 26-30 Dec & 1-4 Jan Civ Wed 70

WINCHESTER   MAP 05 SU42

INSPECTORS' CHOICE

★★★★ ◉◉◉ HOTEL

Lainston House

Sparsholt SO21 2LT
☎ 01962 863588 📠 01962 776672
e-mail: enquiries@lainstonhouse.com
web: www.exclusivehotels.co.uk
dir: 2m NW off B3049 towards Stockbridge

This graceful example of a William and Mary House enjoys a countryside location amidst mature grounds and gardens. Staff provide good levels of courtesy and care with a polished, professional service. Bedrooms are tastefully appointed and include some spectacular spacious rooms with stylish handmade beds and stunning bathrooms. Public rooms include a cocktail bar built entirely from a single cedar and stocked with an impressive range of rare drinks and cigars. The award winning cooking here is very accomplished and a highlight of any stay.

Rooms 50 en suite (6 fmly) (18 GF) S £75-£120; D £95-£298 **Facilities** STV ⊴ Fishing Gym ⬢ Putt green Wi-fi in bedrooms Archery, Clay pigeon shooting, Cycling, Hot Air Ballooning, Walking. ♫ Xmas **Conf** BC Thtr 166 Class 80 Board 40 Del from £255 **Parking** 150 **Notes LB** ⊘ in restaurant Civ Wed 200

★★★★ 75% ◉◉ TOWN HOUSE HOTEL

Hotel du Vin & Bistro

Southgate St SO23 9EF
☎ 01962 841414 📠 01962 842458
e-mail: info@winchester.hotelduvin.com
web: www.hotelduvin.com

dir: M3 junct 11 towards Winchester, follow signs. Hotel approx 2m from junct 11 on left side just past cinema

Continuing to set high standards, this inviting hotel is best known for its high profile bistro. The individually decorated bedrooms, each sponsored by a different wine house, show considerable originality of style, and are very well equipped including air conditioning. The bistro serves imaginative yet simply cooked dishes from a seasonal, daily-changing menu, by a very willing young team.

Rooms 24 en suite (4 GF) ⊘ in all bedrooms S £125-£135; D £125-£135 **Facilities** STV **Conf** Thtr 40 Class 30 Board 20 **Parking** 35 **Notes** Civ Wed 60

★★★★ 71% HOTEL

Macdonald Wessex

Paternoster Row SO23 9LQ
☎ 0870 400 8126 📠 01962 841503
e-mail: wessex@macdonald-hotels.co.uk
web: www.macdonald-hotels.co.uk

dir: M3, follow signs for town centre, at rdbt by King Alfred's statue past Guildhall, next left, hotel on right

A modern hotel occupying an enviably quiet location in the centre of this historic city and adjacent to the spectacular cathedral. Inside, the ambience is restful and welcoming, with many public areas and bedrooms enjoying unrivalled views of the hotel's centuries-old ecclesiastical neighbour.

Rooms 94 en suite (6 fmly) ⊘ in 61 bedrooms **Facilities** STV Solarium Gym Free use of local leisure centre, beauty therapy **Conf** Thtr 100 Class 60 Board 60 **Services** Lift **Parking** 60 **Notes LB** ⊗ ⊘ in restaurant Civ Wed 100

★★★ 77% HOTEL

The Winchester Royal

Saint Peter St SO23 8BS
☎ 01962 840840 📠 01962 841582
e-mail: winchester.royal@forestdale.com
web: www.forestdale.com

dir: M3 junct 9 to Winnall Trading Estate. Follow to city centre, cross river, left, 1st right. Onto one-way system, take 2nd right. Hotel immediately on right

Situated in the heart of the former capital of England, this friendly

continued

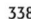

hotel dates back in parts to the 16th century. The bedrooms, in various styles, are split between the main original house and the modern annexe that overlooks the attractive gardens. This hotel is ideally located for both leisure and business guests.

Rooms 19 en suite 56 annexe en suite (1 fmly) (27 GF) ⊗ in 47 bedrooms S £100-£120; D £120-£145 (incl. bkfst) **Facilities** STV Wi-fi in bedrooms Xmas **Conf** Thtr 120 Class 40 Board 40 **Parking** 50 **Notes LB** ⊗ in restaurant Civ Wed 100

★★★ 71% HOTEL

Marwell

Thompsons Ln, Colden Common, Marwell
SO21 1JY

☎ 01962 777681 ▤ 01962 777625

e-mail: info@marwellhotel.co.uk

web: www.bespokehotels.com

dir: Follow brown signs for Marwell Zoological Park, hotel adjacent

Taking its theme from the adjacent zoo, this unusual hotel is based on the famous TreeTops safari lodge in Kenya. Bedrooms are well appointed and equipped, while the smart public areas include an airy lobby bar and an 'Out of Africa' style restaurant. There is also a selection of meeting and leisure facilities.

Rooms 66 en suite (10 fmly) (36 GF) ⊗ in 56 bedrooms S £79-£89; D £89-£99 (incl. bkfst) **Facilities Spa** STV ⚑ ♨ Sauna Gym Wi-fi available Xmas **Conf** Thtr 175 Class 60 Board 60 Del from £135 **Parking** 120 **Notes LB** ⊗ in restaurant Civ Wed 175

WINCHESTER MOTORWAY   MAP 05 SU53
SERVICE AREA (M3)

BUDGET HOTEL

Premier Travel Inn Winchester

SO21 1PP

☎ 08701 977272 ▤ 01962 791137

web: www.premiertravelinn.com

dir: M3 S'bound - between juncts 8 & 9. Note that distance to Inn from Winchester is approx 26m due to location on motorway

High quality, modern budget accommodation ideal for both families and business travellers. Spacious, en suite bedrooms feature bath and shower, satellite TV and many have telephones and modem points. The adjacent family restaurant features a wide and varied menu. For further details consult the Hotel Groups page.

Rooms 40 en suite

YATELEY   MAP 05 SU86

★★★ 70% HOTEL

Casa dei Cesari Restaurant & Hotel

Handford Ln GU46 6BT

☎ 01252 873275 ▤ 01252 870614

e-mail: reservations@casadeicesari.co.uk

dir: M3 junct 4a, follow signs for town centre. Hotel signed

This delightful hotel where a warm welcome is guaranteed is ideally located for transportation networks. It boasts rooms with quality and comfort, and the Italian-themed restaurant, which is very popular locally, serves an extensive, traditional menu

Rooms 44 en suite (2 fmly) (11 GF) ⊗ in 11 bedrooms S £70-£98.50; D £70-£120 (incl. bkfst) **Facilities** STV Riding Wi-fi available Xmas **Conf** Thtr 35 Class 30 Board 25 Del £139.95 **Parking** 80 **Notes LB** ⊗ ⊗ in restaurant Civ Wed 50

★★ 72% HOTEL

Ely

OLD ENGLISH INNS

London Rd GU17 9LJ

☎ 01252 860444 ▤ 01252 870265

e-mail: ely.yateley@newbridgeinns.co.uk

web: www.oldenglish.co.uk

dir: on A30

A purpose built lodge with adjacent bar and restaurant area just off the A30. Very popular location serving food through the day, with a garden and activities for children. Rooms are spacious and well equipped and staff are friendly and attentive.

Rooms 35 en suite (1 fmly) (18 GF) ⊗ in 20 bedrooms S £60; D £60 **Parking** 80 **Notes LB** ⊗ in restaurant RS 23 Dec-2 Jan

Some hotels, although accepting children, may
not have any special facilities for them so it is
well worth checking before booking

England

HEREFORDSHIRE

HEREFORD   **MAP 10 SO54**

See also Leominster & Much Birch

INSPECTORS' CHOICE

★★★ ◎◎◎ **HOTEL**

Castle House

Castle St HR1 2NW

☎ 01432 356321 📠 01432 365909

e-mail: info@castlehse.co.uk

web: www.castlehse.co.uk

dir: *city centre; near cathedral. Follow signs to City Centre East. At junct of Commercial Rd and Union St, follow Castle House hotel signs.*

Enjoying a prime city centre location and overlooking the castle moat, this delightful Victorian mansion is the epitome of elegance and sophistication. The character bedrooms are equipped with every luxury to ensure a memorable stay and are complemented perfectly by the well-proportioned and restful lounge and bar. The experience is completed by award-winning cuisine in the topiary style restaurant.

Rooms 15 en suite S £120; D £210-£258 (incl. bkfst) **Facilities** STV Xmas **Services** Lift **Parking** 15 **Notes LB** ⊗ in restaurant

See advert on opposite page

★★★ 72% **HOTEL**

Belmont Lodge & Golf Course

Belmont HR2 9SA

☎ 01432 352666 📠 01432 358090

e-mail: info@belmont-hereford.co.uk

web: www.belmont-hereford.co.uk

dir: *from Hereford towards Abergavenny on A465. Pass Tesco on right, straight on at rdbt. 0.25m turn right into Ruckhall Ln (signed Belmont Golf Course). Hotel on right in 0.5m*

Less than a 10-minute drive from the city centre, this impressive complex is surrounded by its own golf course and commands delightful views over the River Wye and surrounding countryside.

continued

Bedrooms, in a modern lodge, are comfortable and well equipped while the smart restaurant and bar, in the main house, offer an excellent choice of food.

Belmont Lodge & Golf Course

Rooms 30 en suite (4 fmly) (15 GF) ⊗ in 15 bedrooms S £57.50-£67.50; D £57.50-£67.50 **Facilities** ⌔ 18 ⌔ Fishing Putt green Wi-fi available Games room with pool table Xmas **Conf** Thtr 50 Class 25 Board 25 Del from £95 **Parking** 150 **Notes LB** ⊗ ⊗ in restaurant

★★★ 72% **HOTEL**

Three Counties Hotel

Belmont Rd HR2 7BP

☎ 01432 299955 📠 01432 275114

e-mail: enquiries@threecountieshotel.co.uk

web: www.threecountieshotel.co.uk

dir: *on A465 Abergavenny Rd*

A mile west of the city centre, this large, privately owned, modern complex has well-equipped, spacious bedrooms, many of which are located in separate single-storey buildings around the extensive car park. There is a spacious, comfortable lounge, a traditional bar and an attractive restaurant.

Rooms 28 en suite 32 annexe en suite (4 fmly) (14 GF) ⊗ in 23 bedrooms S £63-£83; D £84-£94 (incl. bkfst) **Facilities** STV **Conf** Thtr 350 Class 154 Board 80 Del from £83 **Parking** 250 **Notes LB** Civ Wed 250

See advert on opposite page

BUDGET HOTEL

Premier Travel Inn Hereford

premier travel inn

Holmer Rd, Holmer HR4 9RS

☎ 08701 977134 📠 01432 343003

web: www.premiertravelinn.com

dir: *from N M5 junct 7, follow A4103 to Worcester. M50 junct 4 take A49 Leominster road Inn 800yds on left*

High quality, modern budget accommodation ideal for both families and business travellers. Spacious, en suite bedrooms feature bath and shower, satellite TV and many have telephones and modem points. The adjacent family restaurant features a wide and varied menu. For further details consult the Hotel Groups page.

Rooms 60 en suite **Conf** Thtr 20 Board 24

KINGTON

MAP 09 SO25

★★★ 73% HOTEL

Burton

Mill St HR5 3BQ

☎ 01544 230323 📠 01544 239023

e-mail: burton@hotelherefordshire.co.uk

web: www.burtonhotel.co.uk

dir: *rdbt at A44/A411 junct take road signed Town Centre*

Situated in the town centre, this friendly, privately-owned hotel offers spacious, pleasantly proportioned and well equipped bedrooms. Smartly presented public areas include a lounge bar, swimming pool and leisure facilities. An attractive restaurant where carefully prepared cuisine can also be enjoyed. There are function and meeting facilities available in a purpose-built, modern wing.

Rooms 16 en suite (5 fmly) ⊗ in 2 bedrooms S £48-£58; D £88-£110 (incl. bkfst) **Facilities** 🖳 supervised Sauna Gym Wi-fi in bedrooms Steam Room, Jacuzzi, Therapy Rooms Xmas **Conf** BC 1htr 150 Class 100 Board 20 Del from £80 **Services** Lift **Parking** 50 **Notes LB** ⊗ in restaurant Civ Wed 120

England

LEDBURY

MAP 10 SO73

★★★ 79% @ **HOTEL**

Feathers

High St HR8 1DS

☎ 01531 635266 ▤ 01531 638955

e-mail: mary@feathers-ledbury.co.uk

web: www.feathers-ledbury.co.uk

dir: S from Worcester on A449, E from Hereford on A438, N from Gloucester on A417. Hotel in town centre

A wealth of old-fashioned charm greets guests at this historic timber-framed hostelry, set in the High Street in the middle of town. The comfortably equipped bedrooms are authentically and tastefully decorated while well-prepared meals can be taken in Fuggles Brasserie with its adjoining bar. Facilities include a leisure centre and a function suite.

Rooms 19 en suite (2 fmly) ⊘ in all bedrooms S £79.50-£95; D £110-£195 (incl. bkfst) **Facilities** STV ▣ Sauna Solarium Gym Jacuzzi Wi-fi in bedrooms Steam room **Conf** Thtr 140 Class 80 Board 40 Del from £130 **Parking** 30 **Notes** ⊘ in restaurant Civ Wed 100

★★ 82% @@ **HOTEL**

The Verzon

Hereford Rd, Trumpet HR8 2PZ

☎ 01531 670381 ▤ 01531 670830

e-mail: info@theverzon.co.uk

web: www.theverzon.co.uk

dir: 2m W of Ledbury on A438

Dating back to 1790 this elegant establishment stands in extensive gardens, from which far-reaching views over the Malvern Hills can be enjoyed. Bedrooms are very well appointed and spacious; one has a four-poster bed. Stylish public areas include the popular bar and the

continued

brasserie restaurant where a range of well executed and flavour packed dishes can be enjoyed.

Rooms 8 en suite (1 fmly) ⊘ in all bedrooms S £65-£98; D £75-£150 (incl. bkfst) **Facilities** Wi-fi available **Conf** Thtr 70 Class 30 Board 25 Del from £70 **Parking** 60 **Notes** ⊗ ⊘ in restaurant

@ **RESTAURANT WITH ROOMS**

Seven Ledbury

11 The Homend HR8 1BN

☎ 01531 631317 ▤ 01531 630168

e-mail: jasonkay@btconnect.com

dir: M50 junct 2 onto A417, follow Ledbury for approx 2m

Modern bistro dining hides behind the front of this traditional black and white timber-framed building in the town centre. The refurbished establishment offers friendly and efficient service, and the quality cuisine has more than a hint of the Mediterranean.

Rooms 3 en suite ⊘ in all bedrooms S £65; D £85 **Notes** ⊗ Closed 25 Dec

LEOMINSTER

MAP 10 SO45

★★★ 70% **HOTEL**

Best Western Talbot

West St HR6 8EP

☎ 01568 616347 ▤ 01568 614880

e-mail: talbot@bestwestern.co.uk

dir: from A49, A44 or A4112, hotel in centre of town

Best Western

This charming former coaching inn is located in the town centre and offers an ideal base from which to explore this delightful area. Public areas feature original beams and antique furniture, and include an atmospheric bar and elegant restaurant. Bedrooms vary in size but are comfortably furnished and equipped. Facilities are available for private functions and conferences.

Rooms 20 en suite (3 fmly) ⊘ in 15 bedrooms S £56-£68; D £78-£82 **Facilities** Xmas **Conf** Thtr 130 Class 25 Board 28 Del from £95 **Parking** 22 **Notes LB** ⊘ in restaurant RS 25 Dec

★★ 68% **HOTEL**

Royal Oak

South St HR6 8JA

☎ 01568 612610 ▤ 01568 612710

e-mail: reservations@theroyaloakhotel.net

web: www.theroyaloakhotel.net

dir: 0.25m from railway station

This privately owned hotel that was once a coaching inn, is conveniently located in the town centre. The charm and character of

continued

England

the traditional inn have been maintained in the public areas including the welcoming bar. Bedrooms are generally spacious and continue to undergo a complete refurbishment.

Rooms 17 en suite (1 fmly) **Conf** Thtr 140 Class 100 Board 70
Parking 15 **Notes LB** ⊘ in restaurant

MUCH BIRCH   MAP 10 SO53

★★★ 73% HOTEL

Pilgrim

THE INDEPENDENTS

Ross Rd HR2 8HJ
☎ 01981 540742 ▤ 01981 540620
e-mail: stay@pilgrimhotel.co.uk
web: www.pilgrimhotel.co.uk
dir: on A49 6m from Ross-on-Wye, 5m from Hereford

This much-extended former rectory is set back from the A49 and has sweeping views over the surrounding countryside. The extensive grounds contain a pitch and putt course. Privately owned and personally run, it provides accommodation that includes ground floor and four-poster rooms. Public areas include a restful lounge, a traditionally furnished restaurant and a pleasant bar.

Rooms 20 en suite (3 fmly) (8 GF) ⊘ in 17 bedrooms S fr £65;
D £85-£95 (incl. bkfst) **Facilities** ♪ 3 ᗌ ᗌ Wi-fi in bedrooms
Pitch & putt, Badminton Xmas **Conf** Thtr 45 Class 45 Board 25 Del £99
Parking 42 **Notes LB** ⊘ in restaurant Civ Wed 40

ROSS-ON-WYE   MAP 10 SO52

★★★ 80% HOTEL

Best Western Pengethley Manor

Best Western

Pengethley Park HR9 6LL
☎ 01989 730211 ▤ 01989 730238
e-mail: reservations@pengethleymanor.co.uk
web: www.pengethleymanor.co.uk
dir: 4m N on A49 Hereford road, from Ross-on-Wye

This fine Georgian mansion is set in extensive grounds with two vineyards and glorious views. The accommodation is tastefully appointed and offers a wide variety of bedroom styles, all similarly well equipped. The elegant public rooms are furnished in a style sympathetic to the character of the house. Dinner provides a range of enjoyable options and is served in the comfortable, spacious restaurant.

Rooms 11 en suite 14 annexe en suite (3 fmly) (4 GF) S £79-£115;
D £120-£160 (incl. bkfst) **Facilities** ♪ ♪ 9 ᗌ Wi-fi in bedrooms Golf
improvement course Xmas **Conf** Thtr 70 Class 25 Board 28 Del from
£115 **Parking** 70 **Notes LB** ⊘ in restaurant Civ Wed 90

★★★ 78% ⊛ HOTEL

Chase

CLASSIC
BRITISH HOTELS

Gloucester Rd HR9 5LH
☎ 01989 763161 & 760644 ▤ 01989 768550
e-mail: res@chasehotel.co.uk
web: www.chasehotel.co.uk
dir: M50 junct 4, 1st left exit towards rdbt, left at rdbt towards A40. Right at 2nd rdbt towards Ross-on-Wye town centre, hotel 0.5m on left

This attractive Georgian mansion sits in its own landscaped grounds and is only a short walk from the town centre. Bedrooms, including two four-poster rooms, vary in size and character. There is also a light and spacious bar and Harry's restaurant offering an excellent selection of enjoyable dishes

Rooms 36 en suite (1 fmly) ⊘ in all bedrooms S £79-£165; D £95-£179
(incl. bkfst) **Facilities** STV Wi-fi in bedrooms Xmas **Conf** Thtr 300
Class 100 Board 80 Del from £117.50 **Parking** 150 **Notes LB** ⊘ in
restaurant Closed 26-30 Dec Civ Wed 300

★★★ 75% ⊛⊛ HOTEL

Wilton Court Hotel

Wilton Ln HR9 6AQ
☎ 01989 562569 ▤ 01989 768460
e-mail: info@wiltoncourthotel.com
web: www.wiltoncourthotel.com
dir: M50 junct 4 onto A40 towards Monmouth at 3rd rdbt turn
left signed Ross then take 1st right, hotel on right facing river

Dating back to the 16th century, this hotel has great charm and a wealth of character. Standing on the banks of the River Wye and just a short walk from the town centre, there is a genuinely relaxed, friendly and unhurried atmosphere here. Bedrooms are tastefully furnished and well equipped, while public areas include a comfortable lounge,

continued on page 344

England

ROSS-ON-WYE *continued*

traditional bar and pleasant restaurant with a conservatory extension overlooking the garden.

Rooms 10 en suite (1 fmly) ⊛ in all bedrooms S £70-£110; D £90-£130 (incl. bkfst) **Facilities** Fishing Wi-fi in bedrooms Boule Xmas **Conf** Thtr 40 Class 25 Board 25 Del from £107.50 **Parking** 24 **Notes LB** ⊛ in restaurant

★★★ 70% COUNTRY HOUSE HOTEL

Pencraig Court Country House Hotel

Pencraig HR9 6HR
☎ 01989 770306 ◾ 01989 770040
e-mail: info@pencraig-court.co.uk
web: www.pencraig-court.co.uk
dir: off A40, into Pencraig 4m S of Ross-on-Wye

Impressive views of the River Wye to Ross-on-Wye beyond, set the scene for a relaxing stay at this former Georgian mansion. The proprietors are on hand to ensure personal attention and service, while the bedrooms evoke a traditional feel and include a room with a four-poster bed. The country-house ambience is carried through in the choice of lounges and the elegant restaurant.

Rooms 11 en suite (1 fmly) ⊛ in all bedrooms S £54-£56; D £88-£96 (incl. bkfst) **Facilities** ⇥ **Parking** 20 **Notes LB** ⊛ in restaurant

★★★ 64% HOTEL

The Royal   OLD ENGLISH INNS

Palace Pound HR9 5HZ
☎ 01989 565105 ◾ 01989 768058
e-mail: 6504@greeneking.co.uk
web: www.oldenglish.co.uk
dir: at end of M50 take A40 'Monmouth'. At 3rd rdbt, left to Ross, over bridge and take road signed 'The Royal Hotel' after left bend

Close to the town centre, this imposing hotel enjoys panoramic views from its prominent hilltop position. Reputedly visited by Charles Dickens in 1867, the establishment has been sympathetically furnished to combine the ambience of a bygone era with the comforts of today. In addition to the lounge and elegant restaurant, there are function rooms and an attractive garden.

Rooms 42 en suite (1 fmly) ⊛ in all bedrooms **Conf** Thtr 85 Class 20 Board 28 **Parking** 44 **Notes LB** ⊛ in restaurant Civ Wed 75

★★ 75% ⊛ COUNTRY HOUSE HOTEL

Glewstone Court

Glewstone HR9 6AW
☎ 01989 770367 ◾ 01989 770282
e-mail: glewstone@aol.com
web: www.glewstonecourt.com
dir: from Ross Market Place take A40/A49 Monmouth/Hereford, over Wilton Bridge to rdbt, turn left onto A40 to Monmouth, after 1m turn right for Glewstone

This charming hotel enjoys an elevated position with views over Ross-on-Wye, and is set in well-tended gardens. Informal service is delivered with great enthusiasm by Bill Reeve-Tucker, whilst the kitchen is the domain of Christine Reeve-Tucker who offers an

continued

extensive menu of well executed dishes. Bedrooms come in a variety of sizes and are tastefully furnished and well equipped.

Glewstone Court

Rooms 8 en suite (2 fmly) S £75-£95; D £110-£126 (incl. bkfst) **Facilities** ⇥ Wi-fi in bedrooms **Conf** Thtr 18 Board 12 Del £165 **Parking** 25 **Notes LB** ⊛ in restaurant Closed 25-27 Dec

★★ 72% HOTEL

Castle Lodge Hotel

Wilton HR9 6AD
☎ 01989 562234 ◾ 01989 768322
e-mail: info@castlelodge.co.uk
web: www.castlelodge.co.uk
dir: on rdbt at junct of A40/A49, 0.5m from Ross-on-Wye

This friendly hotel dates back to the 16th century and offers a convenient base on the outskirts of the town. Bedrooms are well equipped and comfortably furnished, while diners can choose between a good selection of bar meals and a varied restaurant menu, which features a wide range of fresh seafood.

Rooms 10 en suite (3 fmly) S fr £49.95; D fr £54.95 ⇲ **Conf** Thtr 100 Class 80 Board 60 **Parking** 40

★★ 69% SMALL HOTEL

Orles Barn   THE CIRCLE
                                               Selected Individual Hotels

Wilton HR9 6AE   GREAT BRITAIN
☎ 01989 562155 ◾ 01989 768470
e-mail: orles.barn@clara.net
web: www.orles.barn.clara.net
dir: off junct A40/A49

This privately owned and personally run hotel stands in extensive gardens. All of the bedrooms are well equipped, and during cold winter evenings guests can enjoy sitting beside an open fire in the cosy lounge and bar area. The owners' South African heritage is

continued

reflected in the interesting restaurant menu. Extra facilities include an outdoor heated swimming pool.

Rooms 8 en suite (1 fmly) ⊘ in 2 bedrooms **Facilities** ⇃ Fishing Golf chipping parctice facility **Conf** Board 16 **Parking** 20 **Notes LB** ⊗ ⊘ in restaurant RS Nov-Jan

★★ 67% SMALL HOTEL

Chasedale
Walford Rd HR9 5PQ
☎ 01989 562423 & 565801 📠 01989 567900
e-mail: chasedale@supanet.com
web: www.chasedale.co.uk
dir: from Ross-on-Wye town centre, S on B4234, hotel 0.5m on left

This large, mid-Victorian property is situated on the south-west outskirts of the town. Privately owned and personally run, it provides spacious, well-proportioned public areas and extensive grounds. The accommodation is well equipped and includes ground floor and family rooms, whilst the restaurant offers a wide selection of wholesome food.

Rooms 10 en suite (2 fmly) (1 GF) ⊘ in 1 bedroom S £39-£45; D £72-£78 (incl. bkfst) **Facilities** Xmas Wi-fi available **Conf** Thtr 40 Class 30 Board 25 **Parking** 14 **Notes LB** ⊘ in restaurant

★★ 67% HOTEL

King's Head
8 High St HR9 5HL
☎ 01989 763174 📠 01989 769578
e-mail: enquiries@kingshead.co.uk
web: www.kingshead.co.uk
dir: in town centre, turn right past Royal Hotel

Now in new ownership the King's Head dates back to the 14th century and has a wealth of charm and character. Bedrooms are well equipped and include both four-poster and family rooms. The restaurant doubles as a coffee shop during the day and is a popular venue with locals. There is also a very pleasant bar and comfortable lounge.

Rooms 15 en suite (1 fmly) ⊘ in 4 bedrooms S £53.50; D £90 (incl. bkfst) **Facilities** Xmas **Parking** 13 **Notes LB** ⊘ in restaurant

◉◉ RESTAURANT WITH ROOMS

Bridge House
Wilton HR9 6AA
☎ 01989 562655 📠 01989 567652
e-mail: info@bridge-house-hotel.com
web: www.bridge-house-hotel.com
dir: Off junct A40 & A49 into Ross, 300yds on left

Built about 1740, this elegant house is just a stroll across the bridge from delightful Ross-on-Wye. Standards here are impressive and bedrooms

continued

offer ample space, comfort and genuine quality. Period features in the public areas add to the stylish ambience, and the gardens run down to the river. The restaurant serves accomplished cuisine.

Rooms 9 en suite ⊘ in all bedrooms S £65; D £96-£110 **Facilities** Fishing **Parking** 20 **Notes LB** ⊗ No children 14yrs ⊘ in restaurant

BUDGET HOTEL

Premier Travel Inn Ross-on-Wye
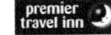
Ledbury Rd HR9 7QJ
☎ 08701 977221 📠 01989 566124
web: www.premiertravelinn.com
dir: 1m from town centre on M50 rdbt

High quality, modern budget accommodation ideal for both families and business travellers. Spacious, en suite bedrooms feature bath and shower, satellite TV and many have telephones and modem points. The adjacent family restaurant features a wide and varied menu. For further details consult the Hotel Groups page.

Rooms 43 en suite

WALTERSTONE   MAP 09 SO32

★★★ 72% COUNTRY HOUSE HOTEL

Allt-yr-Ynys Country House Hotel
HR2 0DU
☎ 01873 890307 📠 01873 890539
e-mail: allthotel@compuserve.com
(For full entry see Abergavenny, Monmouthshire, Wales)

WHITNEY-ON-WYE   MAP 09 SO24

★★ 74% SMALL HOTEL

The Rhydspence Inn
HR3 6EU
☎ 01497 831262 📠 01497 831751
e-mail: info@rhydspence-inn.co.uk
dir: 1m W of Whitney-on-Wye on A438 (Hereford to Brecon road)

With a history as an inn stretching back 600 years, this hotel offers the charm of yesteryear with the comforts of today and is personally run by the proprietors. Guests can expect well-equipped bedrooms and public areas with exposed beams and timber-framed walls. There is an extensive menu in the elegant restaurant and the atmospheric bar has a blackboard menu.

Rooms 7 en suite S £42.50-£85; D £85 (incl. bkfst) **Parking** 30 **Notes LB** ⊗ ⊘ in restaurant

HERTFORDSHIRE

BALDOCK   MAP 12 TL23

BUDGET HOTEL

Sleep Inn Baldock

Baldock Services (A1M/A507), Radwell SG7 5TR
☎ 01462 832900 ▤ 01462 832901
e-mail: enquiries@hotels-baldock.com
web: www.hotels-baldock.com

dir: 400yds E of A1(M) junct 10 & A507

This modern, purpose built accommodation offers smartly appointed, well-equipped bedrooms, with good power showers. There is a choice of adjacent food outlets where guests may enjoy breakfast, snacks and meals.

Rooms 62 en suite S £49.50-£56; D £49.50-£56

BUDGET HOTEL

Travelodge Baldock Hinxworth
Great North Rd, Hinxworth SG7 5EX
☎ 08700 850 950 ▤ 01462 835329
web: www.travelodge.co.uk

dir: on A1, southbound

Travelodge offers good quality, good value, modern accommodation. Ideal for families, the spacious en suite bedrooms include remote-control TV, tea and coffee-making facilities and comfortable beds. Meals can be taken at the nearby family restaurant. See Hotel Groups pages for further details.

Rooms 40 en suite S fr £26; D fr £26

BISHOP'S STORTFORD   MAP 06 TL42

★★★★ 75% ◉◉ **HOTEL**

Down Hall Country House
Hatfield Heath CM22 7AS
☎ 01279 731441 ▤ 01279 730416
e-mail: reservations@downhall.co.uk
web: www.downhall.co.uk

dir: A1060, at Hatfield Heath keep left. Turn right into lane opposite Hunters Meet restaurant & left at end, follow sign

This imposing Victorian country-house hotel, set amidst 100 acres of mature grounds, is handy for Stansted Airport. Bedrooms are generally quite spacious; each one is pleasantly decorated, tastefully furnished
continued

and equipped with modern facilities. Public rooms include a choice of restaurants, a cocktail bar, two lounges and leisure facilities.

Rooms 99 en suite (10 fmly) (20 GF) ⊘ in 81 bedrooms S £60-£90; D £75-£105 **Facilities** STV ◻ ◻ Snooker Sauna ⌣ Putt green Jacuzzi Wi-fi in bedrooms Giant chess, Whirlpool ch fac Xmas **Conf** BC Thtr 200 Class 140 Board 68 Del from £130 **Services** Lift **Parking** 150 **Notes LB** ⊘ in restaurant Civ Wed 120

BOREHAMWOOD   MAP 06 TQ19

★★★★ 71% **HOTEL**

Holiday Inn London - Elstree
Barnet Bypass WD6 5PU
☎ 0870 443 1271 & 020 8214 9988 ▤ 020 8207 6817
e-mail: res.hielstree@qmh-hotels.com

dir: M25 junct 23 take A1 S towards London. After 2m take B5135 towards Borehamwood. Hotel next to 1st rdbt

Ideally located for motorway links and easy travel into the city, this hotel boasts excellent conference and event facilities, secure parking and leisure and beauty treatment options. A range of bedroom sizes is available and all rooms are well equipped and have air conditioning. Dining is available in either the restaurant, which offers both carvery and carte choices, and also the bar, with a pleasant range of dishes.

Rooms 135 en suite (5 fmly) (25 GF) ⊘ in 102 bedrooms S fr £149 **Facilities Spa** STV ◻ Sauna Solarium Gym Wi-fi in bedrooms Xmas **Conf** BC Thtr 400 Class 150 Board 60 Del from £165 **Services** Lift air con **Parking** 350 **Notes** ⊗ ⊘ in restaurant Civ Wed 250

BUDGET HOTEL

Innkeeper's Lodge London Borehamwood
Studio Way WD6 5JY
☎ 020 8905 1455 ▤ 020 8236 9822
web: www.innkeeperslodge.com

dir: M25 junct 23/A1(M) signed to London. Follow signs to Borehamwood after double rdbt turn into Studio Way

Smart, en suite accommodation ideal for both business & leisure guests. Bedrooms are very well equipped, including Sky TV, telephone, modem points, tea & coffee making facilities, (family rooms in most locations). Complimentary breakfast. The adjacent Pub Restaurant; a Harvester, Vintage Inn, Toby Carvery, Ember Inn, Sizzling Pubco or Pub & Carvery offers an all day menu. See Hotel Groups pages for further details.

Rooms 55 en suite S £49.95-£59.95; D £49.95-£59.95 **Conf** Thtr 38 Class 20 Board 20

BUDGET HOTEL

Premier Travel Inn Elstree

Warwick Rd WD6 1US
☎ 0870 9906616 🖹 0870 9906617
web: www.premiertravelinn.com

High quality, modern budget accommodation ideal for both families and business travellers. Spacious, en suite bedrooms feature bath and shower, satellite TV and many have telephones and modem points. The adjacent family restaurant features a wide and varied menu. For further details consult the Hotel Groups page.

Rooms 120 en suite

CHESHUNT   MAP 06 TL30

★★★★ 76% HOTEL

Cheshunt Marriott

Marriott
HOTELS & RESORTS

Halfhide Ln, Turnford EN10 6NG
☎ 01992 451245 🖹 01992 440120
web: www.marriott.co.uk

dir: Exit A10 at Broxbourne, right and right again at rdbt, hotel on right at next rdbt.

This popular suburban hotel has an attractive courtyard garden, overlooked by many of the guest bedrooms. All rooms are spacious and air-conditioned. Public areas include a small, unsupervised leisure facility, along with the busy Washington Bar and Restaurant.

Rooms 143 en suite (37 fmly) (39 GF) ⊛ in 52 bedrooms S £134; D £134 **Facilities** STV 🏊 Gym Jacuzzi Xmas **Conf** BC Thtr 150 Class 72 Board 56 Del £169 **Services** Lift air con **Notes** ⊗ ⊛ in restaurant Civ Wed

CHIPPERFIELD   MAP 06 TL00

★★ 72% HOTEL

The Two Brewers

The Common WD4 9BS
☎ 01923 265266 🖹 01923 261884
e-mail: twobrewers.hotel@spiritgroup.com
web: www.twobrewers.com
dir: left in centre of village overlooking common

This 16th-century inn retains much old-world charm while providing modern comforts and amenities. The spacious, pleasantly decorated bedrooms are tastefully furnished and offer a comprehensive range of in-room facilities. The bar, popular with locals, is the focal point of the hotel, and serves enjoyable pub-style meals.

Rooms 20 en suite ⊛ in 10 bedrooms **Facilities** STV **Conf** Board 15 **Parking** 25 **Notes LB** ⊗

ELSTREE   MAP 06 TQ19

★★★ 73% ⊛ HOTEL

Corus hotel Elstree

corus
hotels

Barnet Ln WD6 3RE
☎ 0870 609 6151 🖹 020 8207 3668
e-mail: elstree@corushotels.com
web: www.corushotels.com

dir: M1 junct 5 follow A41 to Harrow, left onto A411 into Elstree. Through x-rds into Barnet Ln, hotel on right

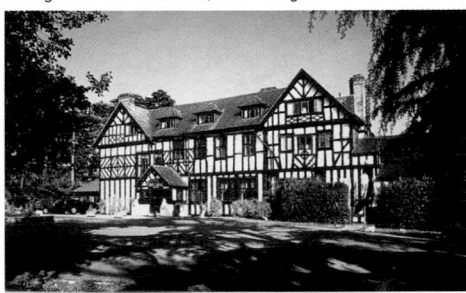

Sitting in ten acres of landscaped gardens this hotel is full of charm and character, with a Tudor-style façade and interiors of a traditional design. The oak-panelled bar, with two large fireplaces and the stately Cavendish restaurant enjoy wonderful views over the gardens and the city lights beyond.

Rooms 47 en suite (1 fmly) ⊛ in 43 bedrooms S fr £110; D fr £110 **Facilities** STV Xmas **Conf** Thtr 80 Class 35 Board 35 Del from £140 **Parking** 100 **Notes LB** ⊗ ⊛ in restaurant Civ Wed 150

HARPENDEN   MAP 06 TL11

★★★ 72% HOTEL

Harpenden House Hotel

ƒolio
Hotels

18 Southdown Rd AL5 1PE
☎ 01582 449955 🖹 01582 769858

dir: M1 junct 10 left at rdbt. Next rdbt right onto A1081 to Harpenden. Over mini rdbt, through town centre and over next mini rdbt. Next rdbt left, hotel 200yds on left

This attractive Grade II listed Georgian building overlooks East Common. The gardens are particularly attractive and the public areas are stylishly decorated, including the restaurant that has an impressively decorated ceiling. Some of the bedrooms and a large suite are located in the original house but most of the accommodation is in the annexe.

continued on page 348

England

HARPENDEN *continued*

Rooms 17 en suite 59 annexe en suite (13 fmly) (2 GF) ⊘ in 49 bedrooms S £50-£130; D £100-£130 **Facilities** STV Wi-fi available Complimentary use of local leisure centre **Conf** BC Thtr 150 Class 60 Board 60 Del from £125 **Parking** 80 **Notes LB** ⊛ ⊘ in restaurant RS wknds & BHs Civ Wed 120

HATFIELD   MAP 06 TL20

★★★★ 77% HOTEL

Beales

Comet Way AL10 9NG
☎ 01707 288500 📠 01707 256282
e-mail: hatfield@bealeshotels.co.uk
web: www.bealeshotels.co.uk
dir: *On A1001, follow signs for Galleria*

This establishment is a stunningly modern and contemporary property. Within easy access of the M25, its striking exterior incorporates giant glass panels and cedar wood slats. Bedrooms continue the contemporary feel with luxurious beds, flat screen TVs and smart bathrooms. Public areas include a small bar and attractive restaurant, which opens throughout the day. A selection of meeting rooms and ample parking are available.

Rooms 53 en suite (3 fmly) (21 GF) ⊘ in 46 bedrooms S fr £130 **Facilities** STV Wi-fi in bedrooms Use of nearby leisure club ♫ Xmas **Conf** Thtr 300 Class 80 Board 60 Del from £175 **Services** Lift **Parking** 126 **Notes LB** ⊛ ⊘ in restaurant Civ Wed 90

★★★ 75% ⑩⑩ HOTEL

Bush Hall

Mill Green AL9 5NT
☎ 01707 271251 📠 01707 272289
e-mail: enquiries@bush-hall.com
dir: *From A1(M) junct 4, 2nd left at rdbt onto A414 signed Hertford & Welwyn Garden City. Left at rdbt, A1000. Hotel on left*

Standing in delightful grounds with a river running through it, this hotel boasts extensive facilities. Outdoor enthusiasts can enjoy a range of activities including go-karting and clay pigeon shooting. Bedrooms and public areas are comfortable and tastefully decorated. Kipling's restaurant continues to offer a wide range freshly prepared dishes using quality produce; service is both professional and friendly.

continued

Bush Hall

Rooms 25 en suite (2 fmly) (8 GF) S £55-£79.50; D £90-£99.50 **Facilities** Wi-fi in bedrooms Clay pigeon shooting, archery, quad bikes and karting - pre booked only **Conf** Thtr 150 Class 70 Board 50 Del from £159 **Parking** 100 **Notes** ⊛ Closed 24 Dec-3 Jan Civ Wed 160

★★★ 75% HOTEL

Ramada Hatfield   ⑧RAMADA.

301 St Albans Rd West AL10 9RH
☎ 01707 265411 📠 01707 264019
e-mail: sales.hatfield@ramadajarvis.co.uk
web: www.ramadajarvis.co.uk
dir: *A1(M) junct 3, take 2nd exit at rdbt signed Hatfield. Hotel on left*

Conveniently located close to the A1(M) with great links to London, this large hotel is a themed art deco, Grade II listed building and retains many of its original 1930's features. Spacious bedrooms are comfortably appointed in a modern style and very well equipped. Public areas include a substantial range of conference rooms, a small gym and the popular Arts Bar & Grill.

Rooms 128 en suite (4 fmly) (53 GF) ⊘ in 100 bedrooms S £58-£149; D £58-£160 **Facilities** Gym **Conf** Thtr 120 Class 100 Board 60 Del from £110 **Parking** 150 **Notes LB** ⊘ in restaurant RS between Xmas & New Year Civ Wed 140

★★★ 72% HOTEL

Quality Hotel Hatfield

Roehyde Way AL10 9AF
☎ 01707 275701 📠 01707 266033
e-mail: enquiries@hotels-hatfield.com
web: www.choicehotelseurope.com
dir: *M25 junct 23 take A1(M) northbound to junct 2. At rdbt take exit left, hotel 0.5m on right*

The well-equipped rooms at this hotel feature extras such as trouser presses and modem access. Executive rooms are very spacious. Room service is 24 hour, or guests may dine in the bar or main restaurant, where service is informal and friendly.

Rooms 76 en suite (14 fmly) (39 GF) ⊘ in 39 bedrooms S £80-£110; D £90-£120 **Facilities** STV Wi-fi in bedrooms Xmas **Conf** Thtr 120 Class 60 Board 50 Del from £140 **Parking** 120 **Notes LB** ⊘ in restaurant

England

Premier Travel Inn Hatfield

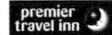

Comet Way, Lemsford Rd AL10 0DZ

☎ 08701 977129 📠 01707 256054

web: www.premiertravelinn.com

dir: From A1(M) junct 4, follow A1001 towards Hatfield. At next rbt take 2nd exit & 1st road on right

High quality, modern budget accommodation ideal for both families and business travellers. Spacious, en suite bedrooms feature bath and shower, satellite TV and many have telephones and modem points. The adjacent family restaurant features a wide and varied menu. For further details consult the Hotel Groups page.

Rooms 40 en suite

HEMEL HEMPSTEAD   MAP 06 TL00

★★★ 78% **HOTEL**

The Bobsleigh Inn

MACDONALD
HOTELS & RESORTS

Hempstead Rd, Bovingdon HP3 0DS

☎ 0870 194 2130 📠 01442 832471

e-mail: bobsleigh@macdonald-hotels.co.uk

web: www.macdonald-hotels.co.uk

dir: turn left after Hemel Hempstead station onto B4505 towards Chesham and follow into Bovingdon, hotel on left

Located just outside the town, the hotel enjoys a pleasant rural setting, yet is within easy reach of local transport links and the motorway network. Bedrooms vary in size, all are modern in style. There is an open-plan lobby and bar area and an attractive dining room with views over the garden.

Rooms 30 en suite 15 annexe en suite (8 fmly) (29 GF) ⊗ in 39 bedrooms S £65-£130; D £65-£130 **Facilities** STV Wi-fi in bedrooms Xmas **Conf** Thtr 150 Class 50 Board 40 Del from £120 **Parking** 60 **Notes LB** ⊗ in restaurant Civ Wed 100

★★★ 77% **HOTEL**

Ramada Hemel Hempstead

®RAMADA.

Hemel Hempstead Rd, Redbourn AL3 7AF

☎ 01582 792105 📠 01582 792001

e-mail: sales.hemel@ramadajarvis.co.uk

web: www.ramadajarvis.co.uk

dir: M1 junct 9 follow Hemel Hempstead & St Albans signs for 3m, straight across 2 rdbts onto B487 signed Hemel Hempstead. Hotel on right

With easy access to both the M1 and M25 motorways, this well presented hotel is set in six acres of landscaped gardens. Bedrooms

continued

are comfortably appointed for both business and leisure guests.

Rooms 137 en suite (4 fmly) (67 GF) ⊗ in 105 bedrooms S £60-£140; D £80-£160 (incl. bkfst) **Facilities** STV Wi-fi available Xmas **Conf** Thtr 100 Class 50 Board 40 Del from £110 **Services** Lift **Parking** 150 **Notes LB** ⊗ in restaurant

★★★ 74% **HOTEL**

Best Western Watermill

Best
Western

London Rd, Bourne End HP1 2RJ

☎ 01442 349955 📠 01442 866130

e-mail: info@hotelwatermill.co.uk

web: www.hotelwatermill.co.uk

dir: from M25 & M1 follow signs to Aylesbury on A41, then A4251 to Bourne End. Hotel 0.25m on right

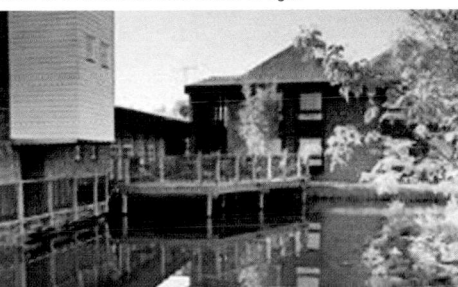

In the heart of the county this modern hotel has been built around an old flour mill situated on the banks of the River Bulbourne that has adjacent water meadows. The thoughtfully equipped, contemporary-style bedrooms are located in three annexes around the complex. A good range of air-conditioned conference and meeting rooms complement a lounge bar and restaurant.

Rooms 8 en suite 67 annexe en suite (9 fmly) (35 GF) ⊗ in 45 bedrooms S £65-£115; D £75-£125 **Facilities** STV Fishing Xmas **Conf** BC Thtr 100 Class 60 Board 50 Del from £135 **Parking** 100 **Notes LB** ⊗ ⊗ in restaurant Civ Wed 90

Premier Travel Inn Hemel Hempstead Central

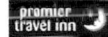

Moor End Rd HP1 1DI

☎ 0870 9906622 📠 0870 9906623

web: www.premiertravelinn.com

High quality, modern budget accommodation ideal for both families and business travellers. Spacious, en suite bedrooms feature bath and shower, satellite TV and many have telephones and modem points. The adjacent family restaurant features a wide and varied menu. For further details consult the Hotel Groups page.

Rooms 113 en suite

Premier Travel Inn Hemel Hempstead (West)

Stoney Ln, Bourne End Services HP1 2SB

☎ 0870 238 3309 📠 01442 879149

web: www.premiertravelinn.com

dir: from M25 junct 20 (A41) exit at services. From M1 junct 8, follow A414, then A41, exit at services

Rooms 61 en suite

England

HEMEL HEMPSTEAD *continued*

BUDGET HOTEL

Travelodge Hemel Hempstead

Wolsey House, Wolsey Rd HP2 4SS

☎ 08700 850 950 🖥 01442 266887

web: www.travelodge.co.uk

dir: M1 junct 8 into city centre, 5th rdbt turn back towards M1, take 1st left

Travelodge offers good quality, good value, modern accommodation. Ideal for families, the spacious en suite bedrooms include remote-control TV, tea and coffee-making facilities and comfortable beds. Meals can be taken at the nearby family restaurant. See Hotel Groups pages for further details.

Rooms 53 en suite S fr £26; D fr £26

HITCHIN   MAP 12 TL12

★★ 71% HOTEL

Firs

THE INDEPENDENTS

83 Bedford Rd SG5 2TY

☎ 01462 422322 🖥 01462 432051

e-mail: info@firshotel.co.uk

web: www.firshotel.co.uk

dir: Hotel on A600 in Hitchin, next to Shell petrol station

This family-run hotel is situated on the northern edge of town and caters for business as well as leisure guests. Well-equipped bedrooms vary in size and style, but are tastefully appointed with smart bathrooms. The restaurant offers a range of homemade Italian style dishes.

Rooms 29 en suite (3 fmly) (9 GF) ⊘ in 14 bedrooms S £55-£60; D £68-£80 (incl. bkfst) **Facilities** FTV Wi-fi available **Conf** Thtr 30 Class 24 Board 20 Del from £95 **Parking** 30 **Notes** ⊗ ⊘ in restaurant

---

★★ 67% HOTEL

Sun

OLD ENGLISH INNS

Sun St SG5 1AF

☎ 01462 432092 & 436411 🖥 01462 431488

e-mail: sun.hitchin@greeneking.co.uk

web: www.oldenglish.co.uk

This attractive 16th-century coaching inn is situated in the centre of town. Bedrooms are equipped with modern facilities and some retain their original character with exposed beams. Public areas offer an informal restaurant and a comfortably appointed bar; the rear car park is a bonus.

Rooms 32 en suite (6 GF) ⊘ in 26 bedrooms S £50-£75; D £65-£90 (incl. bkfst) **Facilities** STV **Conf** Thtr 100 **Parking** 24 **Notes LB** ⊗ ⊘ in restaurant Civ Wed 100

U

Thistle Stevenage/Hitchin

Blakemore End Rd, Little Wymondley SG4 7JJ THISTLE HOTELS

☎ 0870 333 9145 🖥 0870 333 9245

e-mail: stevenage@thistle.co.uk

dir: Exit A1(M) junct 8 through Little Wymondley, turn left at mini-rdbt, hotel is on left.

At the time of going to press, the star classification for this hotel was not confirmed. Please refer to the AA internet site www.theAA.com for current information.

Rooms 82 en suite (12 GF) ⊘ in 60 bedrooms **Facilities** STV ⤴ Putt green David Lloyd Leisure Club available to residents **Conf** Thtr 250 Class 80 Board 60 **Parking** 150 **Notes LB** ⊘ in restaurant Civ Wed 250

KINGS LANGLEY   MAP 06 TL00

BUDGET HOTEL

Premier Travel Inn Kings Langley

Hempstead Rd WD4 8BR

☎ 0870 9906372 🖥 0870 9906373

web: www.premiertravelinn.com

dir: 1m from M25 junct 20 on A4251 after Kings Langley

High quality, modern budget accommodation ideal for both families and business travellers. Spacious, en suite bedrooms feature bath and shower, satellite TV and many have telephones and modem points. The adjacent family restaurant features a wide and varied menu. For further details consult the Hotel Groups page.

Rooms 60 en suite

LONDON COLNEY   MAP 06 TL10

BUDGET HOTEL

Innkeeper's Lodge St Albans

1 Barnet Rd AL2 1BL

☎ 01727 823698 🖥 01727 820902

web: www.innkeeperslodge.com

dir: clockwise from Heathrow on M25 towards Harlow, exit at junct 22 (keep in left lane), at rdbt 1st left to London Colney. Straight over rdbt. Lodge 450yds on right

Smart, en suite accommodation ideal for both business & leisure guests. Bedrooms are very well equipped, including Sky TV, telephone, modem points, tea & coffee making facilities, (family rooms in most locations). Complimentary breakfast. The adjacent Pub Restaurant; a Harvester, Vintage Inn, Toby Carvery, Ember Inn, Sizzling Pubco or Pub & Carvery offers an all day menu. See Hotel Groups pages for further details.

Rooms S £49-£59; D £49-£59

POTTERS BAR · MAP 06 TL20

★★★★ 73% @ **HOTEL**

Ponsbourne Park Hotel

SG13 8QZ

☎ 01707 876191 & 879277 📠 01707 875190

e-mail: reservations@ponsbournepark.co.uk

web: www.ponsbournepark.co.uk

Set within 200 acres of quiet parkland, this 17th-century country house offers contemporary accommodation and public rooms, along with a flexible range of leisure and conference facilities. Smart modern bedrooms are located in the main house and adjacent annexe; each room is well equipped, but typically main house rooms are more spacious.

Rooms 23 en suite 28 annexe en suite (8 fmly) (10 GF) S £85-£182; D £85-£182 (incl. bkfst) **Facilities** ₹ ₺ 9 ₰ Gym Xmas **Conf** Thtr 100 Class 40 Board 40 Del £155 **Parking** 125 **Notes LB** ⊗ ⊘ in restaurant Civ Wed 94

RADLETT · MAP 06 TL10

BUDGET HOTEL

Premier Travel Inn
St Albans/Bricketwood

premier travel inn

Smug Oak Ln AL2 3PN

☎ 08701 977040 📠 01727 873289

web: www.premiertravelinn.com

dir: From M10 take A5183 towards Radlett. After bridge over M25 turn right. From M25 or M1, follow signs to Bricketwood then turn at The Gate pub into Smug Oak Lane

High quality, modern budget accommodation ideal for both families and business travellers. Spacious, en suite bedrooms feature bath and shower, satellite TV and many have telephones and modem points. The adjacent family restaurant features a wide and varied menu. For further details consult the Hotel Groups page.

Rooms 56 en suite

RICKMANSWORTH · MAP 06 TQ09

★★★★★ 89% @@@ **HOTEL**

The Grove

Chandler's Cross WD3 4TG

☎ 01923 807807 📠 01923 221008

e-mail: info@thegrove.co.uk

web: www.thegrove.co.uk

dir: From M25 follow A411 signs towards Watford. Hotel entrance on right. From M1 follow brown hotel signs

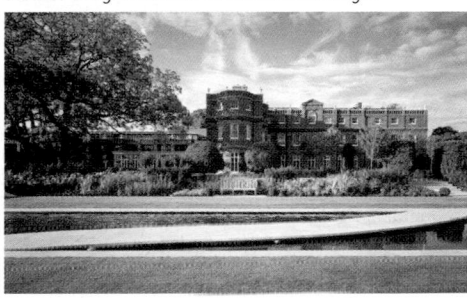

Set in 300 acres of rolling grounds, much of which is golf course, the hotel combines its historic character with cutting edge modern design. The spacious bedrooms feature the latest in temperature control, flat-screen TVs and lighting technology; many have balconies. Suites in the original mansion are particularly stunning. Championship golf, a world-class spa and three dining options are just a few of the treasures to sample here. The hotel also has extensive crèche facilities.

Rooms 227 en suite (31 fmly) (35 GF) ⊗ in 144 bedrooms S £294-£1175; D £294-£1175 **Facilities Spa** STV ₹ ₹ supervised ₺ 18 ₰ Fishing Sauna Solarium Gym ⚑ Putt green Jacuzzi Wi-fi available 12 Treatment rooms, Kids club, Jogging Trails, Golf Instruction ch fac Xmas **Conf** BC Thtr 450 Class 300 Board 78 Del from £230 **Services** Lift air con **Parking** 400 **Notes LB** ⊗ ⊘ in restaurant Civ Wed 450

★★ 67% **HOTEL**

Long Island

OLD ENGLISH INNS

2 Victoria Close WD3 4EQ

☎ 01923 779466 📠 01923 896248

e-mail: office@longisland.fsbusiness.co.uk

web: www.oldenglish.co.uk

dir: Exit M25 junct 18 onto A404 1.5m. Turn left at rdbt onto Nightingale Rd, 1st left

Located opposite Rickmansworth train station and 25 minutes from both Heathrow and Luton airports, this modern hotel provides comfortable accommodation for business or leisure guests. Evening meals and breakfasts are served in the American themed 'Exchange Bar & Grill'.

Rooms 50 en suite (3 fmly) (12 GF) ⊗ in 42 bedrooms S £25-£84; D £50-£84 (incl. bkfst) **Facilities** ♪ **Parking** 120 **Notes** ⊗ ⊘ in restaurant

England

ST ALBANS
MAP 06 TL10

★★★★ 72% ◉ **HOTEL**

Sopwell House
Cottonmill Ln, Sopwell AL1 2HQ
☎ 01727 864477 📄 01727 844741
e-mail: enquiries@sopwellhouse.co.uk
web: www.sopwellhouse.co.uk

dir: M25 junct 22, follow A1081 St Albans. At traffic lights, turn left into Mile House Lane, over mini-rdbt into Cottonmill Lane

This imposing Georgian house retains an exclusive ambience. Bedrooms vary in style and include a number of self-contained cottages within the Sopwell Mews. Meeting and function rooms are housed in a separate section and leisure and spa facilities are particularly impressive. Dining options include the brasserie and the fine-dining Magnolia restaurant.

Rooms 113 en suite 16 annexe en suite (12 fmly) (11 GF) ⊘ in 99 bedrooms S £99-£129; D £169-£185 **Facilities** Spa STV ➔ Sauna Solarium Gym Jacuzzi Wi-fi in bedrooms Health & Beauty Spa, Hairdressing salon, 12 spa treatment room ♫ Xmas **Conf** BC Thtr 400 Class 220 Board 120 Del from £235 **Services** Lift **Parking** 350 **Notes** LB ⊗ ⊘ in restaurant Civ Wed 250

★★★★ 72% **HOTEL**

Thistle St Albans
Watford Rd AL2 3DS
THISTLE HOTELS
☎ 0870 333 9144 📄 0870 333 9244
e-mail: Reservations.StAlbans@Thistle.co.uk

dir: M1 junct 6/M25 junct 21a follow sign for St. Albans, A405. Hotel 0.5m from M25 junct 21a

Conveniently located for access to both M1 and M25 motorways, this Victorian hotel is set within its own grounds with secure parking. Bedrooms are neatly appointed in a traditional style. Public areas include a choice of restaurants, The Noke or the more informal Oak and Avocado, and there is also a small modern leisure club.

Rooms 111 en suite ⊘ in 67 bedrooms **Facilities** STV ➔ supervised Sauna Solarium Gym **Conf** Thtr 60 Class 22 Board 24 **Parking** 150 **Notes** LB ⊘ in restaurant Civ Wed 150

★★★ 82% ◉◉ **HOTEL**

St Michael's Manor
Fishpool St AL3 4RY
☎ 01727 864444 📄 01727 848909
e-mail: reservations@stmichaelsmanor.com

dir: from St Albans Abbey follow Fishpool Street toward St Michael's village. Hotel 0.5m on left

Hidden from the street, adjacent to listed buildings, mills and ancient inns, this hotel is set in five acres of beautiful landscaped grounds. Inside there is a real sense of luxury, the high standard of décor and attentive service is complemented by award-winning food; the restaurant overlooks the immaculate gardens and the lake.

Rooms 30 rms (29 en suite) (1 fmly) (4 GF) ⊘ in 4 bedrooms S £145-£240; D £180-£320 (incl. bkfst) **Facilities** STV ➔ Wi-fi in bedrooms ch fac Xmas **Conf** Thtr 30 Class 20 Board 20 Del from £210 **Parking** 70 **Notes** LB ⊗ ⊘ in restaurant Civ Wed 70

★★★ 75% **HOTEL**

Holiday Inn Luton South
London Rd, Markyate AL3 8HH
Holiday Inn
HOTELS · RESORTS
☎ 0870 4431 781 & 01582 449988 📄 01582 449041
e-mail: hiluton@qmh-hotels.com

dir: M1 junct 9 N towards Dunstable/Whipsnade, hotel is 1m from motorway on right.

Situated a short drive from the M1 and Luton Airport, this hotel has a pleasant setting with country views. There is a health and fitness club and a good range of air-conditioned conference and meeting facilities. Bedrooms are well appointed, styled in contemporary fashion and have a good range of facilities including air conditioning.

Rooms 140 en suite (12 fmly) (44 GF) ⊘ in 108 bedrooms S £49-£149; D £49-£149 (incl. bkfst) **Facilities** Spa STV ➔ Sauna Solarium Gym Jacuzzi Beauty treatments **Conf** BC Thtr 200 Class 90 Board 50 Del from £99 **Services** Lift **Parking** 260 **Notes** LB ⊗ ⊘ in restaurant Civ Wed 80

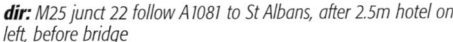

★★★ 71% HOTEL
Quality Hotel St Albans
232-236 London Rd AL1 1JQ
☎ 01727 857858 ▤ 01727 855666
e-mail: st.albans@quality-hotels.net

dir: M25 junct 22 follow A1081 to St Albans, after 2.5m hotel on left, before bridge

Newly refurbished to a smart modern standard, this hotel offers convenient access to the motorway network and the railway station in the town centre. Most of the bedrooms are appointed in a contemporary style, and each is suitably well equipped for the business guest. Public rooms now offer an open-plan lounge bar and brasserie restaurant. A new leisure complex has been created, along with air-conditioned meeting rooms.

Rooms 81 en suite (7 fmly) (13 GF) ⊛ in 51 bedrooms S £50-£90; D £70-£115 (incl. bkfst) **Facilities** STV ⊠ supervised Sauna Gym Wi-fi in bedrooms **Conf** Thtr 220 Class 40 Board 50 Del from £90 **Services** Lift **Parking** 80 **Notes** ⊛ ⊘ in restaurant

SAWBRIDGEWORTH — MAP 06 TL41

★★★ 78% HOTEL
Manor of Groves Hotel, Golf & Country Club
High Wych CM21 0JU
☎ 01279 600777 ▤ 01279 600374
e-mail: info@manorofgroves.co.uk
web: www.manorofgroves.com

dir: A1184 to Sawbridgeworth, left to High Wych, right at village green & hotel 200yds left

Delightful Georgian manor house set in 150 acres of secluded grounds and gardens, with its own 18-hole championship golf course and superb leisure facilities. Public rooms include an imposing open-plan glass atrium that features a bar, lounge area and modern restaurant. The spacious bedrooms are smartly decorated and equipped with modern facilities.

Rooms 80 en suite (2 fmly) (17 GF) ⊛ in 50 bedrooms S £85-£150; D £90-£155 (incl. bkfst) **Facilities** Spa STV FTV ⊠ supervised ⤱ 18 Sauna Solarium Gym Putt green Jacuzzi Wi-fi available Dance studio, beauty salon Xmas **Conf** Thtr 400 Class 250 Board 50 Del from £140 **Services** Lift **Parking** 350 **Notes** LB ⊛ ⊘ in restaurant RS 24 Dec-2 Jan **Civ Wed** 300

See advert on this page

SOUTH MIMMS SERVICE AREA (M25) — MAP 06 TL20

BUDGET HOTEL
Days Inn South Mimms
Bignells Corner EN6 3QQ
☎ 01707 665440 ▤ 01707 660189
e-mail: southmimmshotel@welcomebreak.co.uk
web: www.welcomebreak.co.uk

dir: M25 junct 23, at rdbt follow signs

This modern building offers accommodation in smart, spacious and well-equipped bedrooms, suitable for families and business travellers, and all with en suite bathrooms. Continental breakfast is available and other refreshments may be taken at the nearby family restaurant. For further details see the Hotel Groups page.

Rooms 74 en suite **Conf** Board 10

If the freedom to smoke or be in a non-smoking atmosphere is important to you, check the rules when you book

England

STEVENAGE   MAP 12 TL22

★★★ 71% **HOTEL**

Novotel Stevenage
Knebworth Park SG1 2AX
☎ 01438 346100 🗎 01438 723872
e-mail: H0992@accor.com
web: www.novotel.com

dir: A1(M) junct 7, at entrance to Knebworth Park

Ideally situated just off the A1(M) is this purpose built hotel, which is a popular business and conference venue. Bedrooms are pleasantly decorated and equipped with a good range of useful extras. Public rooms include a large open plan lounge bar serving a range of snacks, and a smartly appointed restaurant.

Rooms 101 en suite (20 fmly) (30 GF) ⊘ in 85 bedrooms **Facilities** STV ☆ Wi-fi in bedrooms Free use of local health club **Conf** BC Thtr 150 Class 80 Board 70 **Services** Lift **Parking** 120 **Notes** ⊘ in restaurant

★★★ 68% **HOTEL**

Best Western Roebuck Inn
London Rd, Broadwater SG2 8DS
☎ 01438 365445 🗎 01438 741308
e-mail: hotel@roebuckinn.com

dir: A1(M) junct 7, right towards Stevenage. At 2nd rdbt take 2nd exit signed Roebuck-London/Knebworth/B197. Hotel in 1.5m

Suitable for both the business and leisure traveller, this hotel provides spacious contemporary accommodation in well equipped bedrooms. The older part of the building, where there is a restaurant and a cosy public bar with log fire and real ales, dates back to the 15th century.

Rooms 54 en suite (8 fmly) ⊘ in 27 bedrooms S fr £69; D fr £69 **Facilities** Xmas **Conf** Thtr 50 Class 20 Board 30 Del from £6 **Parking** 70 **Notes LB** ⊗

★★★ 63% **HOTEL**

Corus hotel Stevenage
High St, Old Town SG1 3AZ
☎ 01438 779954 & 775859 🗎 01438 742169
e-mail: reception@cromwellhotelstevenage.co.uk

dir: A1(M) junct 8 signed Stevenage, over 2 rdbts. Join one-way system, 2nd exit. Hotel 200yds on left

Originally a farmhouse, this attractive hotel, now under new ownership, is located in the Old Town and is easily accessible from the nearby A1(M) and mainline railway. Bedrooms vary in style between modern and more traditional. Public areas include a cosy bar/lounge and a smart, modern business centre.

Rooms 76 en suite (7 fmly) (4 GF) ⊘ in 34 bedrooms S £95; D £115 **Facilities** STV Xmas **Conf** BC Thtr 180 Class 80 Board 56 Del £135 **Parking** 75 **Notes** ⊗ ⊘ in restaurant Civ Wed 140

BUDGET HOTEL

Hotel Ibis Stevenage
Danestrete SG1 1EJ
☎ 01438 779955 🗎 01438 741880
e-mail: H2497@accor-hotels.com
web: www.ibishotel.com

dir: in town centre adjacent to Tesco & Westgate Multi-Store

Modern, budget hotel offering comfortable accommodation in bright and practical bedrooms. Breakfast is self-service and dinner is available in the restaurant. For further details, consult the Hotel Groups page.

Rooms 98 en suite S £29.95-£39.95; D £29.95-£39.95

BUDGET HOTEL

Premier Travel Inn Stevenage Central

Six Hills Way, Horizon Technology Park SG1 2DA
☎ 0870 990 6628
web: www.premiertravelinn.com

dir: Exit A1(M) junct 7 onto A602 follow signs for Stevenage, until Horizon Technology Park

High quality, modern budget accommodation ideal for both families and business travellers. Spacious, en suite bedrooms feature bath and shower, satellite TV and many have telephones and modem points. The adjacent family restaurant features a wide and varied menu. For further details consult the Hotel Groups page.

Rooms 115 en suite

Premier Travel Inn Stevenage (North)
Corey's Mill Ln SG1 4AA
☎ 08701 977240 🗎 01438 721609

dir: A1(M) junct 8, at intersection of A602 Hitchin Rd & Corey's Mill Lane

Rooms 39 en suite

TRING   MAP 06 SP91

★★★★ 76% ⊛ **HOTEL**

Pendley Manor
Cow Ln HP23 5QY
☎ 01442 891891 🗎 01442 890687
e-mail: info@pendley-manor.co.uk
web: www.pendley-manor.co.uk

dir: M25 junct 20, A41 (Tring exit). At rdbt follow Berkhamsted/London signs. 1st left signed Tring Station & Pendley Manor

This impressive Victorian mansion is set in extensive and mature landscaped grounds where peacocks roam. The spacious bedrooms are situated in the manor house or in the wing, and offer a useful range of facilities. Public areas include a cosy bar, a conservatory lounge and an intimate restaurant as well as a leisure centre and spa.

Rooms 74 en suite (6 fmly) ⊘ in 21 bedrooms **Facilities** Spa STV ☆ supervised ⍣ Snooker Sauna Gym ⍩ Jacuzzi Steam room Dance Studio Beauty spa Xmas **Conf** BC Thtr 230 Class 100 Board 50 **Services** Lift **Parking** 250 **Notes** ⊘ in restaurant Civ Wed 200

See advert on opposite page

England

★★★ 68% **HOTEL**

The Rose & Crown

High St HP23 5AH

☎ 01442 824071 📄 01442 890735

dir: *off A41 between Aylesbury & Hempstead, in town centre*

This Tudor-style manor house in the centre of town, offers a great deal of charm. Bedrooms vary in size and style but all are generally well equipped. The restaurant and bar form the centre of the hotel and are popular with locals and residents

Rooms 27 en suite (3 fmly) ⊗ in 3 bedrooms **Facilities** STV Full indoor leisure facilities available at sister hotel Xmas **Conf** BC Thtr 80 Class 50 Board 30 **Parking** 60 **Notes** ⊗ Civ Wed 100

BUDGET HOTEL

Premier Travel Inn Tring

Tring Hill HP23 4LD

☎ 08701 977254 📄 01442 890787

web: www.premiertravelinn.com

dir: *M25 junct 20 take A41 towards Aylesbury, at end of Hemel Hempstead/Tring bypass straight over rdbt. Inn on the right in approx 100yds*

High quality, modern budget accommodation ideal for both families and business travellers. Spacious, en suite bedrooms feature bath and shower, satellite TV and many have telephones and modem points. The adjacent family restaurant features a wide and varied menu. For further details consult the Hotel Groups page.

Rooms 40 en suite

WARE　　　　　　　　　　　　　MAP 06 TL31

★★★★★ 82% ⊛⊛ **HOTEL**

Marriott Hanbury Manor Hotel & Country Club

Marriott.
HOTELS & RESORTS

SG12 0SD

☎ 01920 487722 & 0870 400 7222 📄 01920 487692

e-mail: guestrelations.hanburymanor@marriotthotels.com

web: www.marriott.co.uk

dir: *M25 junct 25, take A10 north for 12m, hotel is on the left*

Set in 200 acres of landscaped grounds, this impressive Jacobean-style mansion boasts an enviable range of leisure facilities, including an excellent health club and championship golf course. Bedrooms are traditionally and comfortably furnished in the country-house style and

continued

have lovely marbled bathrooms. There are a number of food and drink options, including the renowned Zodiac and Oakes restaurants.

Marriott Hanbury Manor Hotel & Country Club

Rooms 134 en suite 27 annexe en suite (3 GF) ⊗ in 96 bedrooms S £149-£159; D £149-£159 **Facilities Spa** STV ⊠ supervised ♨ 18 ⅃ Snooker Sauna Solarium Gym ⅃ Putt green Jacuzzi Wi-fi available Health & beauty treatments, Aerobics, Yoga Dance class Xmas **Conf** BC Thtr 120 Class 76 Board 36 Del from £199 **Services** Lift **Parking** 200 **Notes LB** Civ Wed 120

A luxurious country manor house hotel within easy reach of London, M25, M1, A41 and A5. The hotel has many original features and is set in its own magnificent 35 acre estate. Many of the bedrooms have four poster beds.

An extension was added in 1991 offering first class conference and banqueting amenities. The hotel is licensed for marriage services and various leisure activities can be arranged such as hot air balloon trips to complement the hotels own facilities - tennis, snooker, Clarins Beauty Spa, indoor swimming pool and gymnasium.

THE
PENDLEY MANOR
HOTEL

Cow Lane, Tring, Hertfordshire, HP23 5QY
Telephone: 01442 891891　Fax: 01442 890687
Email: info@pendley-manor.co.uk

 ★★★★

WARE *continued*

★★★ 70% HOTEL

Roebuck

Baldock St SG12 9DR
☎ 01920 409955 📠 01920 468016
e-mail: roebuck@forestdale.com
web: www.forestdale.com

dir: A10 onto B1001, left at rdbt, 1st left behind fire station

Close to the centre of this old market town, the hotel is convenient to major road networks connecting to major local towns and cities including Cambridge and Hertford; Stansted Airport is also a short drive away. The hotel has spacious bedrooms, a comfortable lounge, bar and conservatory restaurant. There is also a range of air-conditioned meeting rooms.

Rooms 50 en suite (1 fmly) (16 GF) ⊗ in 16 bedrooms S £60-£110; D £70-£120 (incl. bkfst) **Facilities** STV Wi-fi available **Conf** Thtr 200 Class 75 Board 60 Del from £100 **Services** Lift **Parking** 64 **Notes LB** ⊗ in restaurant Civ Wed 80

★★ 60% HOTEL

Feathers

OLD ENGLISH INNS

49 Cambridge Rd, Wadesmill SG12 0TN
☎ 01920 462606 📠 01920 469994
e-mail: feathers.wadesmill@newbridgeinns.co.uk
web: www.oldenglish.co.uk

dir: Exit A10 signed Ware, continue onto Cambridge Rd and down hill into Wadesmill. Over mini-rdbt, hotel on right

This coaching inn is situated beside the A10 on the Cambridge side of Ware. An adjacent modern accommodation annexe provides attractive cottage-style rooms, equipped with a good array of modern facilities. Meals are served in the adjacent inn, the dining room which provides a popular carvery and menu choices; the bars remain open all day.

Rooms 31 rms (30 en suite) (3 fmly) (16 GF) ⊗ in 16 bedrooms S £50; D £70-£85 (incl. bkfst) **Facilities** Xmas **Parking** 50 **Notes** ⊗ ⊗ in restaurant

WATFORD

MAP 06 TQ19

★★★ 77% HOTEL

Ramada Watford

⊗ RAMADA.

A41, Watford Bypass WD25 8JH
☎ 020 8901 0000 📠 020 8950 7809
e-mail: sales.watford@ramadajarvis.co.uk
web: www.ramadajarvis.co.uk

dir: M1 junct 5, A41 S to London. Straight on at island, hotel 1m on left

This large, modern hotel is conveniently located close to both the M1 and M25 and is a popular venue for conferences. Bedroom styles include stylish studio rooms with leather easy chairs. All bedrooms are well equipped and comfortably appointed for both business and leisure guests. A good choice of meals is served in the contemporary Arts Restaurant and Bar.

Rooms 218 en suite (6 fmly) (80 GF) ⊗ in 120 bedrooms S £69-£150; D £69-£150 **Facilities Spa** STV 🔲 🏊 Sauna Solarium Gym Jacuzzi Wi-fi in bedrooms Xmas **Conf** Thtr 728 Class 434 Board 310 Del from £110 **Services** Lift **Parking** 250 **Notes LB** ⊗ in restaurant Civ Wed 180

★★★ 71% HOTEL

Best Western White House

Best Western

Upton Rd WD18 0JF
☎ 01923 237316 📠 01923 233109
e-mail: info@whitehousehotel.co.uk
web: www.whitehousehotel.co.uk

dir: from main Watford centre ring road into Exchange Rd, Upton Rd left turn off, hotel on left

Ideally situated close to the town centre is this popular commercial hotel. Bedrooms are pleasantly decorated and offer a good range of in-room facilities that include interactive TV. The public areas are open plan in style; they include a lounge/bar and an attractive conservatory restaurant. Functions suites are also available.

Rooms 57 en suite (8 GF) ⊗ in 45 bedrooms S £89-£149; D £99-£164 (incl. bkfst) **Facilities** STV off site gym facilities **Conf** Thtr 200 Class 80 Board 50 Del from £135 **Services** Lift **Parking** 55 **Notes LB** ⊗ ⊗ in restaurant Civ Wed 120

BUDGET HOTEL

Premier Travel Inn Watford Centre (East)

premier travel inn

Timms Meadow, Water Ln WD17 2NJ
☎ 0870 9906620 📠 0870 9906621
web: www.premiertravelinn.com

dir: Exit M1 junct 5, A41 into town centre. At rdbt take 3rd exit, stay in left lane through lights. Take 1st left into Water Ln. Hotel on left

High quality, modern budget accommodation ideal for both families and business travellers. Spacious, en suite bedrooms feature bath and shower, satellite TV and many have telephones and modem points. The adjacent family restaurant features a wide and varied menu. For further details consult the Hotel Groups page.

Rooms 105 en suite

Premier Travel Inn Watford Centre West

2 Ascot Rd WD18 8AP
☎ 0870 8500328 📠 0870 850 0343
Rooms 120 en suite

Premier Travel Inn Watford North

859 St Albans Rd, Garston WD25 0LH
☎ 08701 977261 📠 01923 682164

dir: On A412 St Albans Rd, 200yds past the North Orbital (A405), 0.5m S of M1 junct 6

Rooms 45 en suite

England

WELWYN
MAP 06 TL21

★★★ 66% HOTEL

Quality Hotel Welwyn

The Link AL6 9XA

☎ 01438 716911 ▤ 01438 714065

e-mail: enquiries@hotels-welwyn.com

web: www.choicehotelseurope.com

dir: A1(M) junct 6 follow for A1000 Welwyn. Follow A1(M) Stevenage towards motorway again but at 3rd rdbt take first left and turn into hotel

The clock tower of this hotel is a local landmark, ensuring that it is easily located from the motorway. This hotel is particularly popular with business guests for the range of conference and meeting rooms provided. Bedrooms are suitably appointed and feature extras such as satellite TV and Playstation games.

Rooms 96 en suite (3 fmly) (28 GF) ⊛ in 60 bedrooms S fr £64; D fr £64 **Facilities** Wi-fi available Xmas **Conf** Thtr 250 Class 60 Board 50 Del £128 **Parking** 150 **Notes LB** ⊛ ⊛ in restaurant Civ Wed 100

WELWYN GARDEN CITY
MAP 06 TL21

★★★ 70% HOTEL

Best Western Homestead Court Hotel

Homestead Ln AL7 4LX

☎ 01707 324336 ▤ 01707 326447

e-mail: enquiries@homesteadcourt.co.uk

web: www.bw-homesteadcourt.co.uk

dir: off A1000, left at lights at Bushall Hotel. Right at rdbt into Howlands, 2nd left at Hollybush public house into Hollybush Lane. 2nd right at War Memorial into Homestead Lane

Friendly hotel ideally situated less than two miles from the city centre in a tranquil location, next to parkland. The property boasts stylish, brightly decorated public areas that include a smart lounge bar and a large restaurant. Bedrooms are pleasantly appointed and equipped with modern facilities. Conference rooms are also available.

Rooms 58 en suite 6 annexe en suite ⊛ in 46 bedrooms S £59.50-£120; D £79-£140 (incl. bkfst) **Facilities** STV Wi-fi in bedrooms Xmas **Conf** BC Thtr 200 Class 60 Board 60 Del from £110 **Services** Lift **Parking** 60 **Notes LB** ⊛ ⊛ in restaurant Civ Wed 110

BUDGET HOTEL

Premier Travel Inn Welwyn Garden City

Gosling Park AL8 6DQ

☎ 08701 977263 ▤ 01707 393789

web: www.premiertravelinn.com

dir: on A6129 off A1(M) junct 4

High quality, modern budget accommodation ideal for both families and business travellers. Spacious, en suite bedrooms feature bath and shower, satellite TV and many have telephones and modem points. The adjacent family restaurant features a wide and varied menu. For further details consult the Hotel Groups page.

Rooms 60 en suite

KENT

ASHFORD
MAP 07 TR04

INSPECTORS' CHOICE

★★★★ ⊛⊛ HOTEL

Eastwell Manor

Eastwell Park, Boughton Lees TN25 4HR

☎ 01233 213000 ▤ 01233 635530

e-mail: enquiries@eastwellmanor.co.uk

dir: on A251, 200yds on left when entering Boughton Aluph

Set in 62 acres of landscaped grounds, this lovely hotel dates back to the Norman Conquest and boasts a number of interesting features, including carved wood-panelled rooms and huge baronial stone fireplaces. Accommodation is divided between the manor house and the courtyard mews cottages. The luxury Pavilion Spa in the grounds has an all-day brasserie, whilst fine dining in the main restaurant is a highlight of any stay

Rooms 23 en suite 39 annexe en suite (2 fmly) ⊛ in 4 bedrooms S £110-£415; D £140-£445 (incl. bkfst) **Facilities** Spa STV ⊡ ⊡ ⊕ Sauna Solarium Gym ⊕ Putt green Jacuzzi Wi-fi in bedrooms Boules, & Beauty spa Xmas **Conf** Thtr 200 Class 60 Board 48 Del from £240 **Services** Lift **Parking** 200 **Notes LB** ⊛ in restaurant Civ Wed 250

★★★★ 76% HOTEL

Ashford International

Simone Weil Av TN24 8UX

☎ 01233 219988 ▤ 01233 647743

e-mail: info@ashfordinthotel.com

web: www.qhotels.co.uk

dir: off M20 junct 9, 3rd exit for Ashford/Canterbury. Take left at 1st rdbt, hotel 200m on left

Ideally situated just off the M20 with its links to the channel tunnel and ferry terminal. Public areas feature a superb mall housing a range of boutiques and eating places, including a popular brasserie, the Alhambra Restaurant and Florentine Bar. The spacious bedrooms are pleasantly furnished and equipped with modern facilities.

Rooms 177 en suite (4 fmly) ⊛ in 151 bedrooms S £80-£130; D £90-£130 **Facilities** ⊡ supervised Sauna Solarium Gym Jacuzzi Wi-fi in bedrooms Xmas **Conf** BC Thtr 400 Class 160 Del from £135 **Services** Lift **Parking** 400 **Notes LB** ⊛ in restaurant Closed 24-27 Dec Civ Wed 150

England

ASHFORD *continued*

Premier Travel Inn Ashford Central

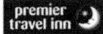

Hall Av, Orbital Park, Sevington TN24 0GN
☎ 08701 977305 📠 01233 500742
web: www.premiertravelinn.com

dir: *M20 junct 10. Southbound take 4th exit at rdbt. Northbound take 1st exit/ A2070 for Brenzett. Inn at next rdbt on right*

High quality, modern budget accommodation ideal for both families and business travellers. Spacious, en suite bedrooms feature bath and shower, satellite TV and many have telephones and modem points. The adjacent family restaurant features a wide and varied menu. For further details consult the Hotel Groups page.

Rooms 60 en suite

Premier Travel Inn Ashford North

Maidstone Rd, Hothfield Common TN26 1AP
☎ 08701 977018 📠 01233 713945

dir: *on A20, between Ashford & Charing, close to M20 junct 8/9*
Rooms 60 en suite

Travelodge Ashford

Eureka Leisure Park TN25 4BN
☎ 08700 850 950 📠 01233 622676
web: www.travelodge.co.uk

dir: *M20 junct 9, take 1st exit on left*

Travelodge offers good quality, good value, modern accommodation. Ideal for families, the spacious en suite bedrooms include remote-control TV, tea and coffee-making facilities and comfortable beds. Meals can be taken at the nearby family restaurant. See Hotel Groups pages for further details.

Rooms 67 en suite S fr £26; D fr £26

BRANDS HATCH MAP 06 TQ56

★★★★ 80% ◉◉ **HOTEL**

Brandshatch Place Hotel and Spa

 HANDPICKED

Brands Hatch Rd, Fawkham DA3 8NQ
☎ 01474 875000 📠 01474 879652
e-mail: brandshatchplace@handpicked.co.uk
web: www.handpicked.co.uk

dir: *M25 junct 3/A20 West Kingsdown. Left at paddock entrance/Fawkham Green sign. 3rd left signed Fawkham Rd. Hotel 500mtrs on right*

This charming 18th-century Georgian country house close to the famous racing circuit offers a range of stylish and elegant rooms. Bedrooms are appointed to a very high standard, with impressive facilities and levels of comfort and quality. The hotel also features a comprehensive leisure club with substantial crèche facilities.

Rooms 26 en suite 12 annexe en suite (1 fmly) ⊗ in 33 bedrooms S £99-£295; D £109-£330 (incl. bkfst) **Facilities** Spa STV Squash Snooker Sauna Solarium Gym Jacuzzi Wi-fi in bedrooms Use of health/leisure club Xmas **Conf** Thtr 120 Class 60 Board 50 Del

continued

---

from £135 **Services** Lift **Parking** 100 **Notes LB** ⊗ in restaurant Civ Wed 100

★★★★ 76% ◉ **HOTEL**

Thistle Brands Hatch

THISTLE HOTELS

DA3 8PE
☎ 0870 333 9128 📠 0870 333 9228
e-mail: BrandsHatch@Thistle.co.uk

dir: *Follow signs for Brands Hatch, hotel on left of racing circuit entrance.*

Ideally situated overlooking Brands Hatch race track and close to the major road networks (M20/M25). The open-plan public areas include a choice of bars, a large lounge, a restaurant, meeting rooms and superb leisure facilities. The bedrooms come in a variety of styles but each one is smartly decorated and well equipped.

Rooms 121 en suite (4 fmly) (43 GF) ⊗ in 59 bedrooms **Facilities** Spa STV Sauna Solarium Gym Jacuzzi Health & Beauty treatments & solarium available **Conf** Thtr 270 Class 120 Board 66 **Parking** 180 **Notes LB** ⊗ in restaurant Civ Wed 65

BROADSTAIRS MAP 07 TR36

★★★ 75% **HOTEL**

Royal Albion

Albion St CT10 1AN
☎ 01843 868071 📠 01843 861509
e-mail: enquiries@albionbroadstairs.co.uk
web: www.albionbroadstairs.co.uk

dir: *follow signs for seafront and town centre*

Situated on the seafront in the heart of this bustling town centre overlooking the beach. Bedrooms are smartly decorated and equipped with a good range of useful facilities; many rooms have superb views of the sea. Public areas include Ballards coffee lounge, a sun terrace, a lounge bar and a cosy restaurant.

Rooms 19 en suite (3 fmly) ⊗ in 4 bedrooms S £63-£75; D £83-£93 (incl. bkfst) **Facilities** STV **Conf** Thtr 30 Class 20 Board 20 Del from £110 **Parking** 21 **Notes LB** ⊗ ⊗ in restaurant

CANTERBURY MAP 07 TR15

★★★ 82% **HOTEL**

Best Western Abbots Barton

 Best Western

New Dover Rd CT1 3DU
☎ 01227 760341 📠 01227 785442
e-mail: sales@abbotsbartonhotel.com

dir: *Turn off A2 onto A2050 at bridge, S of Canterbury. Hotel is 0.75m past Old Gate Inn on left*

Delightful property with a country-house hotel feel set amid two acres of pretty landscaped gardens close to the city centre and major road networks. The spacious accommodation includes a range of stylish lounges, a smart bar and the Fountain Restaurant, which serves imaginative food. Conference and banqueting facilities are also available.

Rooms 50 en suite (2 fmly) (6 GF) ⊗ in 40 bedrooms S £75-£105; D £95-£180 (incl. bkfst) **Facilities** STV Wi-fi available Xmas **Conf** Thtr 150 Class 80 Board 60 Del from £130 **Services** Lift **Parking** 80 **Notes LB** ⊗ in restaurant Civ Wed 100

★★ 68% **HOTEL**

Victoria

59 London Rd CT2 8JY
☎ 01227 459333 📠 01227 781552
e-mail: manager@vichotel.fsnet.co.uk
dir: M2/A2 onto A2052, hotel on left off 1st rdbt

Ideally situated on the outskirts of the city centre yet just a short walk from the shops and within sight of the cathedral. Bedrooms vary in size and style; each one is pleasantly decorated and has a good range of useful facilities. Public areas include a busy bar and a carvery restaurant.

Rooms 34 en suite (12 fmly) ⊘ in 4 bedrooms **Conf** Thtr 20 Class 20 Board 20 **Parking** 70 **Notes LB** ⊛

Abode Canterbury

High St CT1 2RX
☎ 01227 766266 📠 01227 451512
e-mail: reservationscanterbury@abodehotels.co.uk

dir: M2 junct 7. Follow Canterbury signs onto ringroad. At Wincheap rdbt turn into city. Left into Rosemary Ln, into Stour St. Hotel at end

At the time of going to press, the star classification for this hotel was not confirmed. Please refer to the AA internet site www.theAA.com for current information.

Rooms 72 en suite (3 fmly) ⊘ in all bedrooms S £99-£140; D £99-£140 **Facilities** STV Gym & treatment room Xmas **Conf** Thtr 150 Class 60 Board 45 Del from £140 **Services** Lift air con **Parking** 22 **Notes** ⊛ ⊘ in restaurant Civ Wed 80

Swallow Chaucer

Ivy Ln CT1 1TU
☎ 01227 464427 📠 01227 450397
e-mail: swallow.chaucer@swallowhotels.com
web: www.swallowhotels.com

dir: Towards city on A2, exit at Harbledown. Right at 5th rdbt, then 1st left

At the time of going to press, the star classification for this hotel was not confirmed. Please refer to the AA internet site www.theAA.com for current information.

Rooms 42 en suite ⊘ in 34 bedrooms S £70-£93; D £90-£130 (incl. bkfst) **Conf** Thtr 100 Class 60 Board 40 Del from £130 **Parking** 42 **Notes** ⊛ ⊘ in restaurant Civ Wed 90

England

CANTERBURY *continued*

U

Swallow Falstaff

SWALLOW HOTELS

8-10 St Dunstan's St CT2 8AF
☎ 01227 462138 📠 01227 463525
web: www.swallowhotels.com

dir: In city take 2nd rdbt into St Peters Place, hotel is opposite Westgate, turn right then immediately left for car park

At the time of going to press, the star classification for this hotel was not confirmed. Please refer to the AA internet site www.theAA.com for current information.

U

Swallow Howfield

SWALLOW HOTELS

Chartham Hatch CT4 7HQ
☎ 01227 738294 📠 01227 731535
web: www.swallowhotels.com

dir: from A2, follow signs for Canterbury on slip road. Take 1st right signed Chartham Hatch, right at T-junct, follow winding road for 3m. Left at T-Junct, hotel 2m on left

At the time of going to press, the star classification for this hotel was not confirmed. Please refer to the AA internet site www.theAA.com for current information.

Rooms 15 en suite **Conf** Thtr 80 Class 45 Board 60

BUDGET HOTEL

Innkeeper's Lodge Canterbury

162 New Dover Rd CT1 3EL
☎ 01227 829951 📠 01227 829952
web: www.innkeeperslodge.com

dir: M2 junct 7, A2 left at junct for Rough Common onto A2050. At 2nd rdbt follow signs for Dover (A2), lodge on right

Smart, en suite accommodation ideal for both business & leisure guests. Bedrooms are very well equipped, including Sky TV, telephone, modem points, tea & coffee making facilities, (family rooms in most locations). Complimentary breakfast. The adjacent Pub Restaurant; a Harvester, Vintage Inn, Toby Carvery, Ember Inn, Sizzling Pubco or Pub & Carvery offers an all day menu. See Hotel Groups pages for further details.

Rooms 9 en suite S £55; D £55

BUDGET HOTEL

Travelodge Canterbury Dunkirk

Travelodge

A2 Gate Services, Dunkirk ME13 9LN
☎ 08700 850 950 📠 01227 752781
web: www.travelodge.co.uk

dir: 5m W on A2 northbound

Travelodge offers good quality, good value, modern accommodation. Ideal for families, the spacious en suite bedrooms include remote-control TV, tea and coffee-making facilities and comfortable beds. Meals can be taken at the nearby family restaurant. See Hotel Groups pages for further details.

Rooms 40 en suite S fr £26; D fr £26

CHATHAM   MAP 07 TQ76

★★★★ 74% ◎◎ **HOTEL**

Bridgewood Manor Hotel   Marston Hotels

Bridgewood Roundabout, Walderslade Woods ME5 9AX
☎ 01634 201333 📠 01634 201330
e-mail: bridgewoodmanor@marstonhotels.com
web: www.marstonhotels.com

dir: adjacent to Bridgewood rdbt on A229. Take 3rd exit signed Walderslade and Lordswood. Hotel 50mtrs on left

A modern, purpose-built hotel situated on the outskirts of Rochester. Bedrooms are pleasantly decorated, comfortably furnished and equipped with many thoughtful touches. The hotel has an excellent range of leisure and conference facilities. Guests can dine in the informal Terrace Bistro or experience fine dining in the more formal Squires restaurant, where the service is both attentive and friendly.

Rooms 100 en suite (12 fmly) (26 GF) ⊗ in 79 bedrooms S fr £132.50; D fr £171 (incl. bkfst) **Facilities Spa** STV 🏊 ♨ Snooker Sauna Solarium Gym Putt green Jacuzzi Wi-fi available Beauty treatments Xmas **Conf** Thtr 200 Class 110 Board 80 Del from £175 **Services** Lift **Parking** 170 **Notes LB** ⊗ ⊗ in restaurant Civ Wed 130

See advert under MAIDSTONE

CRANBROOK   MAP 07 TQ73

★★ 75% ◎ **HOTEL**

The George Hotel & Brasserie

Stone St TN17 3HE
☎ 01580 713348 📠 01580 715532
e-mail: reservations@thegeorgehotelkent.co.uk
web: www.thegeorgehotelkent.co.uk

dir: off A21 to Goudhurst & Cranbrook. At large rdbt, right into Cranbrook

This delightful 13th-century coaching inn is located in the heart of this bustling town centre. Bedrooms have a wealth of original features and include some with four-poster beds. Public rooms include a smart lounge bar, a cosy wine bar and a restaurant, where imaginative freshly prepared dishes are served.

Rooms 12 en suite (2 fmly) ⊗ in all bedrooms S £60-£80; D £75-£90 (incl. bkfst) **Facilities** STV Wi-fi available **Parking** 10 **Notes LB** ⊗ ⊗ in restaurant Closed 24-25 Dec

DARTFORD　　　　　　　　MAP 06 TQ57

★★★★ 80% ◎◎ **HOTEL**

Rowhill Grange Hotel & Spa

DA2 7QH

☎ 01322 615136 📠 01322 615137

e-mail: admin@rowhillgrange.co.uk

web: www.rowhillgrange.co.uk

dir: *M25 junct 3 take B2173 to Swanley, then B258 to Hextable*

Set within nine acres of mature woodland, including a Victorian walled garden, the hotel enjoys a tranquil setting, yet remains accessible to road networks. Bedrooms are stylishly and individually decorated, many have four-poster or sleigh beds. The hotel features a smart, conservatory restaurant and a more informal brasserie.

Rooms 38 en suite (3 fmly) (3 GF) ⊘ in all bedrooms S £165-£245; D £190-£350 (incl. bkfst) **Facilities Spa** STV ⟲ Sauna Solarium Gym ⭹ Jacuzzi Wi-fi in bedrooms Beauty treatment, Hair salon, Aerobic studio, Japanese Therapy pool Xmas **Conf** Thtr 160 Class 64 Board 34 **Services** Lift **Parking** 150 **Notes LB** ⊗ ⊘ in restaurant Civ Wed 150

BUDGET HOTEL

Campanile

1 Clipper Boulevard West, Crossways Business Park DA2 6QN

☎ 01322 278925 📠 01322 278948

e-mail: dartford@campanile-hotels.com

web: www.envergure.fr

dir: *follow signs for Ferry Terminal from Dartford Bridge*

This modern building offers accommodation in smart, well-equipped bedrooms, all with en suite bathrooms. Refreshments may be taken at the informal Bistro. For further details consult the Hotel Groups page.

Rooms 125 en suite S £51.95 **Conf** Thtr 40 Class 30 Board 30 Del from £75

BUDGET HOTEL

Travelodge Dartford

Charles St, Greenhithe DA9 9AP

☎ 08700 850 950 📠 01322 387854

web: www.travelodge.co.uk

dir: *M25 junct 1a, take A206 towards Gravesend*

Travelodge offers good quality, good value, modern accommodation. Ideal for families, the spacious en suite bedrooms include remote-control TV, tea and coffee-making facilities and comfortable beds. Meals can be taken at the nearby family restaurant. See Hotel Groups pages for further details.

Rooms 65 en suite S fr £26; D fr £26

DEAL　　　　　　　　　　MAP 07 TR35

★★★ 74% ◎◎ **HOTEL**

Dunkerleys Hotel & Restaurant

19 Beach St CT14 7AH

☎ 01304 375016 📠 01304 380187

e-mail: dunkerleysofdeal@btinternet.com

web: www.dunkerleys.co.uk

dir: *from M20 or M2 follow signs for A258 Deal.*

This hotel is situated on the seafront and is centrally located. Bedrooms are furnished to a high standard with a good range of amenities. The restaurant and bar offer a comfortable and attractive environment in which to relax and to enjoy the cuisine that makes the

continued on page 362

DEAL *continued*

best use of local ingredients. Service throughout is friendly and attentive.

Rooms 16 en suite (2 fmly) **Facilities** STV **Notes LB** ⊗ ⊘ in restaurant RS Mon morning

DOVER   MAP 07 TR34

★★★ 82% ◉◉ HOTEL

Wallett's Court Country House Hotel & Spa

West Cliffe, St Margarets-at-Cliffe CT15 6EW
☎ 01304 852424 & 0800 0351628 📠 01304 853430
e-mail: wc@wallettscourt.com

dir: *from Dover take A258 towards Deal. 1st right to St Margarets-at-Cliffe & West Cliffe, 1m on right opposite West Cliffe church*

A lovely Jacobean manor situated in a peaceful location on the outskirts of town. Bedrooms in the original house are traditionally furnished whereas the rooms in the courtyard buildings are more modern; all are equipped to a high standard. Public rooms include a smart bar, a lounge and a restaurant that utilises local organic produce. An impressive spa facility is housed in converted barn buildings in the grounds.

Rooms 3 en suite 13 annexe en suite (2 fmly) (7 GF) S £99-£119; D £119-£159 (incl. bkfst) **Facilities Spa** FTV 🏊 ♨ Sauna Solarium Gym ⛳ Putt green Jacuzzi Wi-fi available Treatment suite, aromatherapy massage, golf pitching range, beauty therapy **Conf** BC Thtr 25 Class 25 Board 16 Del from £169 **Parking** 30 **Notes LB** ⊗ ⊘ in restaurant Closed 24-26 Dec

★★★ 74% HOTEL

Ramada Hotel Dover   ⓦRAMADA.

Singledge Ln, Whitfield CT16 3EL
☎ 01304 821230 📠 01304 825576
e-mail: reservations@ramadadover.co.uk
web: www.ramadadover.co.uk

dir: *from M20 follow signs to A2 towards Canterbury. Turn right after Whitfield rdbt. From A2 towards Dover, turn left before Whitfield rdbt*

Modern purpose-built hotel situated in a quiet location between Dover and Canterbury, close to the ferry port and seaside. The open-plan public areas are contemporary in style and include a lounge, a bar and Bleriot's restaurant. The stylish bedrooms are simply decorated with co-ordinated soft furnishings and many thoughtful extras.

Rooms 68 en suite (19 fmly) (68 GF) ⊘ in 56 bedrooms S £56-£105; D £56-£105 **Facilities** STV Gym Wi-fi in bedrooms Xmas **Conf** BC Thtr 60 Class 18 Board 20 Del from £120 **Parking** 80 **Notes** ⊗ ⊘ in restaurant Civ Wed 45

★★★ 73% HOTEL

Best Western Churchill Hotel and Health Club

Dover Waterfront CT17 9BP
☎ 01304 203633 📠 01304 216320
e-mail: enquiries@churchill-hotel.com
web: www.bw-churchillhotel.co.uk

dir: *A20 follow signs for Hoverport, left onto seafront, hotel in 800yds*

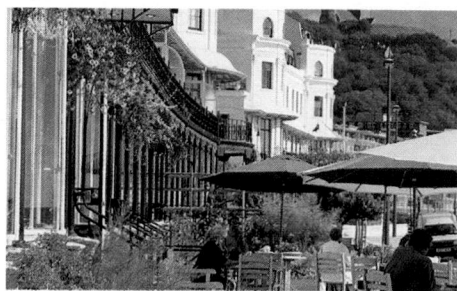

Attractive terraced waterfront hotel overlooking the harbour. The hotel offers a wide range of facilities including meeting rooms, health club, hairdressers and beauty treatments. Some of the tastefully decorated bedrooms have balconies, some have broadband access and many of the rooms have superb sea views. Public rooms include a large, open-plan lounge bar, and a smart Bistro restaurant.

Rooms 81 en suite (5 fmly) S fr £68; D £90 **Facilities** STV Sauna Solarium Gym Wi-fi available Health Club, Hair & Beauty Salons Xmas **Conf** Thtr 110 Class 60 Board 50 Del £91 **Services** Lift **Parking** 32 **Notes LB** ⊗ ⊘ in restaurant Civ Wed 100

★★★ 73% HOTEL

The Mildmay

78 Folkestone Rd CT17 9SF
☎ 01304 204278 📠 01304 215342
e-mail: themildmayhotel@btopenworld.com

dir: *on B2011 Dover to London road, 300yds from Dover Priory Railway Station*

This friendly, family-run hotel is ideally placed for the town centre, railway station and ferry terminal. The spacious bedrooms are pleasantly decorated and thoughtfully equipped with modern facilities. Public rooms include a large open-plan lounge bar with plush seating and a smartly appointed restaurant.

Rooms 21 en suite (3 fmly) (2 GF) ⊘ in 7 bedrooms **Parking** 20 **Notes** ⊗ ⊘ in restaurant

BUDGET HOTEL

Premier Travel Inn Dover Central   premier travel inn

Marine Court, Marine Pde CT16 1LW
☎ 0870 9906516 📠 0870 9906517
web: www.premiertravelinn.com

dir: *In town centre adjacent to ferry terminal. Exit M20 junct 13 onto A20 for 8.2m*

High quality, modern budget accommodation ideal for both families and business travellers. Spacious, en suite bedrooms feature bath and shower, satellite TV and many have telephones and modem points.

continued

The adjacent family restaurant features a wide and varied menu. For further details consult the Hotel Groups page.

Rooms 100 en suite

Premier Travel Inn Dover East

Jubilee Way, Guston Wood CT15 5FD

☎ 08701 977075 📠 01304 240614

dir: on rdbt of A2 & A258

Rooms 40 en suite

Premier Travel Inn Dover (West)

Folkestone Rd CT15 7AB

☎ 08701 977076 📠 01304 214504

dir: M20 then A20 to Dover. Through tunnel, take 2nd exit onto B2011. Take 1st left at rbt. Inn is on the left, after 1 mile

Rooms 64 en suite

EASTCHURCH   MAP 07 TQ97

Swallow Shurland

81 High St ME12 4EH   SWALLOW

☎ 01795 881100 📠 01795 880906

web: www.swallowhotels.com

At the time of going to press, the star classification for this hotel was not confirmed. Please refer to the AA internet site www.theAA.com for current information.

Rooms 17 en suite

FAVERSHAM   MAP 07 TR06

BUDGET HOTEL

Travelodge Canterbury Whitstable

Thanet Way ME13 9EL

☎ 08700 850 950 📠 01227 281135

web: www.travelodge.co.uk

dir: M2 from junct 7, A299 to Ramsgate. Lodge 4m on left

Travelodge offers good quality, good value, modern accommodation. Ideal for families, the spacious en suite bedrooms include remote-control TV, tea and coffee-making facilities and comfortable beds. Meals can be taken at the nearby family restaurant. See Hotel Groups pages for further details.

Rooms 40 en suite S fr £26; D fr £26

FOLKESTONE   MAP 07 TR23

★★★ 75% **HOTEL**

Best Western Clifton

The Leas CT20 2EB

☎ 01303 851231 📠 01303 223949

e-mail: reservations@thecliftonhotel.com

dir: M20 junct 13, 0.25m W of town centre on A259

This privately-owned Victorian-style hotel occupies a prime location, looking out across the English Channel. The bedrooms are comfortably appointed and most have views of the sea. Public areas include a comfortable, traditionally furnished lounge, a popular bar

continued

---

serving a good range of beers and several well-appointed conference rooms.

Rooms 80 en suite (5 fmly) ⊘ in 31 bedrooms S £60-£88; D £74-£97 **Facilities** STV FTV Wi-fi in bedrooms Games room Xmas **Conf** Thtr 80 Class 36 Board 32 Del from £105 **Services** Lift **Notes LB** ⊗ ⊘ in restaurant

★★★ 70% **HOTEL**

Quality Hotel Burlington

Earls Av CT20 2HR

☎ 01303 255301 📠 01303 251301

e-mail: sales@theburlingtonhotel.com

Situated close to the beach in a peaceful side road just a short walk from the town centre. The public rooms include a choice of lounges, the Bay Tree restaurant and a large cocktail bar. Bedrooms are pleasantly decorated and equipped with modern facilities; some rooms have superb sea views.

Rooms 50 en suite (6 fmly) (5 GF) ⊘ in 24 bedrooms S £63-£83; D £79-£99 **Facilities** Riding Putt green Jacuzzi Wi-fi available Xmas **Conf** Thtr 240 Class 100 Board 80 Del from £79 **Services** Lift **Parking** 20 **Notes LB** ⊘ in restaurant Civ Wed 100

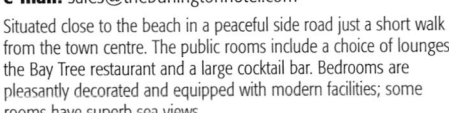

England

FOLKESTONE *continued*

U

The Southcliff

22-26 The Leas CT20 2DY
☎ 01303 850075 📄 01303 850070
e-mail: sales@thesouthcliff.co.uk
web: www.thesouthcliff.co.uk

At the time of going to press, the star classification for this hotel was not confirmed. Please refer to the AA internet site www.theAA.com for current information.

Rooms 68 en suite (2 fmly) S £27.50-£41.50; D £39.50-£69.50
Facilities ♬ Xmas **Conf** Thtr 200 Class 120 Del from £32 **Services** Lift
Parking 10 **Notes LB** ⊗ ⊘ in restaurant

BUDGET HOTEL

Premier Travel Inn Folkestone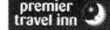

Cherry Garden Ln CT19 4AP
☎ 08701 977103 📄 01303 273641
web: www.premiertravelinn.com

dir: *M20 junct 13. At 1st rdbt turn right, at 2nd rdbt turn right signed Folkestone A20. At lights turn right, Inn on right*

High quality, modern budget accommodation ideal for both families and business travellers. Spacious, en suite bedrooms feature bath and shower, satellite TV and many have telephones and modem points. The adjacent family restaurant features a wide and varied menu. For further details consult the Hotel Groups page.

Rooms 79 en suite

GILLINGHAM   MAP 07 TQ76

BUDGET HOTEL

Premier Travel Inn Gillingham, Kent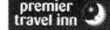

Will Adams Way ME8 6BY
☎ 08701 977105 📄 01634 261232
web: www.premiertravelinn.com

dir: *From M2 junct 4 turn left along A278 to A2. Turn left at Tesco & Inn is left at next rdbt*

High quality, modern budget accommodation ideal for both families and business travellers. Spacious, en suite bedrooms feature bath and shower, satellite TV and many have telephones and modem points. The adjacent family restaurant features a wide and varied menu. For further details consult the Hotel Groups page.

Rooms 45 en suite **Conf** Thtr 20

BUDGET HOTEL

Travelodge Medway (M2)

Medway Motorway Service Area, Rainham ME8 8PQ
☎ 08700 850 950 📄 01634 263187
web: www.travelodge.co.uk

dir: *between junct 4 & 5 of M2 westbound*

Travelodge offers good quality, good value, modern accommodation. Ideal for families, the spacious en suite bedrooms include remote-control TV, tea and coffee-making facilities and comfortable beds. Meals can be taken at the nearby family restaurant. See Hotel Groups pages for further details.

Rooms 58 en suite S fr £26; D fr £26

GRAVESEND   MAP 06 TQ67

★★★ 78% **HOTEL**

Best Western Manor Hotel

Hever Court Rd DA12 5UQ
☎ 01474 353100 📄 01474 354978
e-mail: manor@bestwestern.co.uk

dir: *at junct of A2 Gravesend East turn off*

Situated close to the major road networks with links to Dover, Channel Tunnel and Bluewater shopping village. The attractively decorated bedrooms are generally quite spacious and each one is equipped with many useful facilities. Public rooms include a bar and a smart restaurant as well as an impressive health club with swimming pool, sauna and gym.

Rooms 59 en suite (3 fmly) (20 GF) ⊘ in 50 bedrooms S £80-£99; D £89-£109 (incl. bkfst) **Facilities** STV ⊠ supervised Sauna Solarium Gym Wi-fi in bedrooms **Conf** BC Thtr 200 Class 100 Board 25 Del from £110 **Parking** 100 **Notes** ⊗ ⊘ in restaurant

BUDGET HOTEL

Premier Travel Inn Gravesend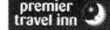

Wrotham Rd DA11 7LF
☎ 08701 977118 📄 01474 323776
web: www.premiertravelinn.com

dir: *1m from A2 on A227 towards Gravesend town centre*

High quality, modern budget accommodation ideal for both families and business travellers. Spacious, en suite bedrooms feature bath and shower, satellite TV and many have telephones and modem points. The adjacent family restaurant features a wide and varied menu. For further details consult the Hotel Groups page.

Rooms 36 en suite **Conf** Thtr 40 Board 20

Premier Travel Inn Gravesend South

Hevercourt Rd, Singlewell DA12 5UQ
☎ 0870 9906352 📄 0870 9906353

dir: *Just off A2 towards Rochester & Channel Tunnel. Turn off at Singlewell Services Rd*
Rooms 31 en suite

England

HOLLINGBOURNE MAP 07 TQ85

★★★ 73% **HOTEL**

Ramada Hotel & Resort Maidstone

RAMADA
HOTEL & RESORT

Ashford Rd ME17 1RE

☎ 01622 631163 📠 01622 735290

e-mail: sales.maidstone@ramadajarvis.co.uk

web: www.ramadajarvis.co.uk

dir: M20 junct 8, follow Leeds Castle signs, at 3rd rdbt turn right

A large purpose-built hotel ideally situated close to the M20 and the Channel Tunnel. Public areas include extensive conference facilities, a large open-plan bar/restaurant, a lounge and leisure facilities. Bedrooms come in a variety of styles; each one is pleasantly decorated and equipped with modern facilities.

Rooms 126 en suite (4 fmly) ⊘ in 86 bedrooms S £69-£99; D £79-£109 (incl. bkfst & dinner) **Facilities** 🏊 supervised ♨ Fishing Sauna Solarium Gym ♨ Jacuzzi Running track Clay pigeon shooting Archery Air rifle shooting ♪ Xmas **Conf** BC Thtr 650 Class 220 Board 60 Del from £115 **Services** Lift **Parking** 500 **Notes LB** ⊗ ⊘ in restaurant Civ Wed 150

HYTHE MAP 07 TR13

★★★★ 80% ⊛ **HOTEL**

The Hythe Imperial

MarstonHotels

Princes Pde CT21 6AE

☎ 01303 267441 📠 01303 264610

e-mail: hytheimperial@marstonhotels.com

web: www.marstonhotels.com

dir: M20, junct 11 onto A261. In Hythe follow Folkestone signs. Right into Twiss Rd to hotel

Enjoying a seafront setting in a historic town, this lovely hotel is surrounded by 50 acres of golf course and beautiful gardens. Well-kept bedrooms are spacious and many enjoy views of the grounds or sea. Guests have a whole host of facilities on hand, including indoor and outdoor leisure facilities, a beauty salon and a choice of dining.

Rooms 100 en suite (5 fmly) (6 GF) ⊘ in 38 bedrooms S fr £112; D fr £171 (incl. bkfst) **Facilities Spa** STV 🏊 ↓9 ♨ Squash Snooker Sauna Solarium Gym ♨ Putt green Jacuzzi Beauty salon, Fitness assessments Xmas **Conf** Thtr 220 Class 100 Board 50 Del from £185 **Services** Lift **Parking** 200 **Notes LB** ⊗ ⊘ in restaurant Civ Wed 220

See advert on pages 359 & 363

★★★ 73% **HOTEL**

Best Western Stade Court

Best Western

West Pde CT21 6DT

☎ 01303 268263 📠 01303 261803

e-mail: stadecourt@bestwestern.co.uk

dir: M20 junct 11 follow signs for Hythe town centre. Follow brown tourist sign for hotel

This privately owned hotel is built on the site of a landing place, or 'stade', and is located on the seafront in this historic Cinque Port. Many of its well-maintained bedrooms enjoy splendid sea views and some of these have additional seating areas. Guests can also enjoy the well-tended garden in warmer months and might like to sit and watch the world go by.

Rooms 42 en suite (5 fmly) ⊘ in 16 bedrooms S £39-£49; D £49-£89 (incl. bkfst) **Facilities** STV Fishing Wi-fi in bedrooms Xmas **Conf** BC Thtr 40 Class 20 Board 30 Del from £69 **Services** Lift **Parking** 11 **Notes LB** ⊘ in restaurant Civ Wed 60

KINGSGATE MAP 07 TR37

★★★ 75% **HOTEL**

The Fayreness

Marine Dr CT10 3LG

☎ 01843 868641 📠 01843 608750

e-mail: info@fayreness.co.uk

web: www.fayreness.co.uk

dir: A28 onto B2051 which becomes B2052. Pass Holy Trinity Church on right and '19th Hole' public house. Next left, down Kingsgate Ave, hotel at end on left

Situated on the cliff tops overlooking the English Channel, just a few steps from a sandy beach and adjacent to the North Foreland Golf Club. The spacious bedrooms are tastefully furnished with many thoughtful touches; some rooms have stunning sea views. Public rooms include a large open-plan lounge/bar, a function room, dining room and conservatory restaurant.

Rooms 29 en suite (3 fmly) (5 GF) ⊘ in 23 bedrooms S £54-£149; D £69-£159 (incl. bkfst) **Facilities** STV **Conf** Thtr 50 Class 28 Board 36 **Parking** 70 **Notes LB** ⊘ in restaurant Civ Wed 80

See advert on page 359

England

LENHAM
MAP 07 TQ85

INSPECTORS' CHOICE

★★★★ ◎ ◎ **HOTEL**

Chilston Park

Hand PICKED

Sandway ME17 2BE

☎ 01622 859803 📠 01622 858588

e-mail: chilstonpark@handpicked.co.uk

web: www.handpicked.co.uk

dir: *from A20 turn off to Lenham village, turn right onto High St, pass station on right, 1st left, over crossroads, hotel 0.25 mile on left*

This elegant Grade I listed country house is set in 23 acres of immaculately landscaped gardens and parkland. An impressive collection of original paintings and antiques creates a unique environment. The sunken Venetian-style restaurant serves modern British food with French influences. Bedrooms are individual in design, some have four-poster beds and many have garden views.

Rooms 30 en suite 23 annexe en suite (2 fmly) (3 GF) ⊗ in all bedrooms S £100-£130; D £100-£190 (incl. bkfst) **Facilities** STV ⚓ Fishing ⛵ Wi-fi available Xmas **Conf** Thtr 100 Class 60 Board 50 Del from £170 **Services** Lift **Parking** 100 **Notes LB** ⊗ in restaurant Civ Wed 90

LEYBOURNE
MAP 06 TQ65

BUDGET HOTEL

Premier Travel Inn Maidstone (Leybourne)

premier travel inn

Castle Way ME19 5TR

☎ 08701 977170 📠 01732 844474

web: www.premiertravelinn.com

dir: *M20 junct 4, take A228, Inn on left*

High quality, modern budget accommodation ideal for both families and business travellers. Spacious, en suite bedrooms feature bath and shower, satellite TV and many have telephones and modem points. The adjacent family restaurant features a wide and varied menu. For further details consult the Hotel Groups page.

Rooms 40 en suite

MAIDSTONE
MAP 07 TQ75

★★★★ 77% **HOTEL**

Marriott Tudor Park Hotel & Country Club

Marriott. HOTELS & RESORTS

Ashford Rd, Bearsted ME14 4NQ

☎ 01622 734334 📠 01622 735360

e-mail: salesadmin.tudorpark@marriotthotels.co.uk

web: www.marriott.co.uk

dir: *M20 junct 8 to Lenham. Right at rdbt towards Bearsted and Maidstone on A20. Hotel 1m on left*

Located on the outskirts of Maidstone in a wooded valley below Leeds Castle, this fine country hotel is set amidst 220 acres of parkland. Spacious bedrooms provide good levels of comfort and a comprehensive range of extras. Facilities include a championship golf course, a fully equipped gym, tennis courts, a beauty salon and two dining options.

Rooms 120 en suite (48 fmly) (60 GF) ⊗ in 65 bedrooms S £97-£122; D £115-£140 **Facilities Spa** STV ⚓ ⚓ 18 ⚓ Sauna Solarium Gym Putt green Wi-fi in bedrooms Driving range Beauty salon Steam room Xmas **Conf** Thtr 250 Class 100 Board 60 Del from £135 **Services** Lift **Parking** 250 **Notes** ⊗ ⊗ in restaurant Civ Wed

★★★ 77% **HOTEL**

Best Western Russell

Best Western

136 Boxley Rd ME14 2AE

☎ 01622 692221 📠 01622 762084

e-mail: res@therussellhotel.com

dir: *M20 junct 7 follow signs to Maidstone, A249. At 2nd rdbt take 2nd exit to Boxley. Turn left at 3rd rdbt, hotel on left at top of hill*

Since its days as a Carmelite convent, this Victorian building has been extended and modernised. Set in attractive grounds and offering a range of function rooms, the hotel is a popular venue for weddings and conferences. The well-maintained bedrooms are contemporary in style and equipped with modern facilities.

Rooms 42 en suite (4 fmly) ⊗ in 20 bedrooms S £65-£95; D £85-£125 (incl. bkfst) **Facilities** Wi-fi in bedrooms Free use of facilities at David Lloyd Health & Fitness Centre Xmas **Conf** Thtr 300 Class 100 Board 70 **Parking** 100 **Notes LB** ⊗ ⊗ in restaurant Civ Wed 250

★★ 74% **HOTEL**

Grange Moor

St Michael's Rd ME16 8BS

☎ 01622 677623 📠 01622 678246

e-mail: reservations@grangemoor.co.uk

dir: *Town centre, towards A26 Tonbridge Rd. Hotel 0.25m on left, just after church*

Expect a warm welcome at this friendly, privately owned hotel, which is ideally situated, within easy walking distance of the town centre. The smartly decorated bedrooms have co-ordinated soft fabrics and many thoughtful touches. Public areas include a popular bar, a cosy restaurant and a small residents' lounge.

Rooms 38 en suite 12 annexe en suite (6 fmly) (8 GF) ⊗ in 21 bedrooms S £45-£52; D £60-£62 (incl. bkfst) **Conf** Thtr 120 Class 60 Board 40 Del £85 **Parking** 60 **Notes LB** Closed 24-30 Dec Civ Wed 80

England

Swallow Larkfield Priory

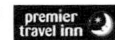

London Rd, Larkfield ME20 6HJ
☎ 01732 846858 ▤ 01732 846786
web: www.swallowhotels.com

dir: *M20 junct 4 take A228 to West Malling. At lights left signed to Maidstone on A20, after 1m hotel on left*

At the time of going to press, the star classification for this hotel was not confirmed. Please refer to the AA internet site www.theAA.com for current information.

Rooms 52 en suite (10 GF) ⊘ in 27 bedrooms S £55-£95; D £65-£105 (incl. bkfst) **Facilities** STV **Conf** Thtr 80 Class 38 Board 38 Del from £110 **Parking** 80 **Notes** ⊘ in restaurant

Swallow Stone Court

SWALLOW

28 Lower St ME15 6LX
☎ 01622 769769 ▤ 01622 769888
e-mail: swallow.stonecourt@swallowhotels.com
web: www.swallowhotels.com

At the time of going to press, the star classification for this hotel was not confirmed. Please refer to the AA internet site www.theAA.com for current information.

Rooms 16 en suite (2 fmly) ⊘ in all bedrooms S £70-£100; D £95-£110 (incl. bkfst) **Conf** Thtr 80 Class 30 Board 36 Del from £105 **Parking** 8 **Notes** ⊗ ⊘ in restaurant Civ Wed 60

BUDGET HOTEL

Innkeeper's Lodge Maidstone

Sandling Rd ME14 2RF
☎ 01622 692212 ▤ 01622 679265
web: www.innkeeperslodge.com

dir: *M20 junct 6, S onto A229 towards Maidstone. At 3rd rdbt, turn left and left again*

Smart, en suite accommodation ideal for both business & leisure guests. Bedrooms are very well equipped, including Sky TV, telephone, modem points, tea & coffee making facilities, (family rooms in most locations). Complimentary breakfast. The adjacent Pub Restaurant; a Harvester, Vintage Inn, Toby Carvery, Ember Inn, Sizzling Pubco or Pub & Carvery offers an all day menu. See Hotel Groups pages for further details.

Rooms 12 en suite S £57-£65; D £57-£65

BUDGET HOTEL

Premier Travel Inn Maidstone (Allington)

London Rd ME16 0HG
☎ 08701 977168 ▤ 01622 672469
web: www.premiertravelinn.com

dir: *M20 junct 5, 0.5m on London Rd towards Maidstone*

High quality, modern budget accommodation ideal for both families and business travellers. Spacious, en suite bedrooms feature bath and shower, satellite TV and many have telephones and modem points. The adjacent family restaurant features a wide and varied menu. For further details consult the Hotel Groups page.

Rooms 40 en suite **Conf** Thtr 45 Board 30

Premier Travel Inn Maidstone (Sandling)

Allington Lock, Sandling ME14 3AS
☎ 08701 977308 ▤ 01622 715159

dir: *M20 junct 6 follow sign for Museum of Kent Life*
Rooms 40 en suite

MAIDSTONE MOTORWAY SERVICE AREA (M20)   MAP 07 TQ85

BUDGET HOTEL

Premier Travel Inn Maidstone (Hollingbourne)

ME17 1SS
☎ 08701 977169 ▤ 01622 739535
web: www.premiertravelinn.com

dir: *M20 junct 8*

High quality, modern budget accommodation ideal for both families and business travellers. Spacious, en suite bedrooms feature bath and shower, satellite TV and many have telephones and modem points. The adjacent family restaurant features a wide and varied menu. For further details consult the Hotel Groups page.

Rooms 58 en suite **Conf** Thtr 30 Board 18

MARSTON HOTELS

AA★★★★

Situated on the edge of the historic city of Rochester, close to the ancient Pilgrims Way and near to many places of historic interest, Bridgewood Manor has 100 delightful bedrooms including twins, doubles, suites and inter-connecting rooms that are ideal for families.

BRIDGEWOOD MANOR

Bridgewood Roundabout Walderslade Woods Chatham
Kent ME5 9AX **t: 01634 201333** f: 01634 201330
bridgewoodmanor@marstonhotels.com

www.marstonhotels.com

England

MARGATE
MAP 07 TR37

★★★ A
Smiths Court
Eastern Esplanade, Cliftonville CT9 2HL
☎ 01843 222310 📠 01843 222312
e-mail: info@courthotels.com
dir: *from clocktower on seafront take left fork on A28 for approx 1m. Hotel on right Eastern Esplanade at junct with Godwin Rd.*
Rooms 40 en suite (6 fmly) (6 GF) ✆ in 10 bedrooms **Facilities** Gym
♫ ch fac **Conf** Thtr 80 Class 50 Board 80 **Services** Lift **Parking** 15
Notes LB ✆ in restaurant

U
Swallow Lonsdale Court
51-59 Norfolk Rd, Cliftonville CT9 2HX
☎ 01843 231027 📠 01843 229625
web: www.swallowhotels.com
At the time of going to press, the star classification for this hotel was not confirmed. Please refer to the AA internet site www.theAA.com for current information.
Rooms 63 en suite

BUDGET HOTEL
Premier Travel Inn Margate
Station Green, Marine Ter CT9 5AF
☎ 08701 977182 📠 01843 221101
web: www.premiertravelinn.com
dir: *M2 follow A299 then A28 to Margate seafront. Inn adjacent to Margate station, facing sea*
High quality, modern budget accommodation ideal for both families and business travellers. Spacious, en suite bedrooms feature bath and shower, satellite TV and many have telephones and modem points. The adjacent family restaurant features a wide and varied menu. For further details consult the Hotel Groups page.
Rooms 44 en suite

RAMSGATE
MAP 07 TR36

★★★ 66% HOTEL
Comfort Inn Ramsgate
Victoria Pde, East Cliff CT11 8DT
☎ 01843 592345 📠 01843 580157
e-mail: reservations@comfortinnramsgate.co.uk
dir: *From M2 take A299 signed Ramsgate, B2054 to Victoria Parade, follow sign to harbour*
This Victorian hotel stands on the seafront, close to the ferry and the town. Bedrooms, some with balconies, are generously sized and well equipped. Meals are served both in the bar lounge and in the restaurant, which serves a particularly wide choice of dishes ranging from traditional British cuisine to Indian favourites.
Rooms 44 en suite (5 fmly) ✆ in 22 bedrooms S £50-£80; D £80-£120
Facilities STV Wi-fi in bedrooms Xmas **Conf** Thtr 130 Class 30 Board 60
Del from £79 **Services** Lift **Parking** 10 **Notes LB** ✆ in restaurant

★★ 80% HOTEL
The Oak Hotel
66 Harbour Pde CT11 8LN
☎ 01843 583686 581582 📠 01843 581606
e-mail: reception@oakhotel.co.uk
The hotel enjoys spectacular views of the marina and harbourside from the Caffe Roma, the contemporary bar and some of the bedrooms. Located within easy reach of the railway station, the ferry terminal and the town centre's shops. All the bedrooms have now been refurbished and are well equipped.
Rooms 34 en suite (9 fmly) ✆ in all bedrooms S £48-£90; D £63.50-£100 (incl. bkfst) **Conf** Thtr 100 Class 60 Board 50 **Notes LB** ❋ ✆ in restaurant

U
Swallow Kent International
Harbour Pde CT11 8LZ
☎ 01843 588276 📠 01843 586866
web: www.swallowhotels.com
At the time of going to press, the star classification for this hotel was not confirmed. Please refer to the AA internet site www.theAA.com for current information.
Rooms 57 en suite

SANDWICH
MAP 07 TR35

★★★ 73% HOTEL
The Blazing Donkey Country Hotel & Restaurant
Hay Hill, Ham CT14 0ED
☎ 01304 617362 📠 01304 615264
e-mail: info@blazingdonkey.co.uk
web: www.blazingdonkey.co.uk
dir: *off A256 at Eastry into village, right at Five Bells public house, hotel 0.75m on left*
This former labourer's cottage and barn has been upgraded over the years and is now a distinctive inn of character. Set in the heart of peaceful Kentish farmland, the atmosphere is convivial and informal. Public rooms include an open-plan bar, a lounge and more formal dining area. Comfortably appointed bedrooms are spacious and arranged around a courtyard.
Rooms 19 en suite 3 annexe en suite (2 fmly) (19 GF) ✆ in 15 bedrooms **Facilities** STV ⛳ Putt green **Conf** BC Thtr 200 Class 200 Board 200 **Services** air con **Parking** 108 **Notes LB** ✆ in restaurant Civ Wed 250

SEVENOAKS
MAP 06 TQ55

★★★ 75% HOTEL
Best Western Donnington Manor
London Rd, Dunton Green TN13 2TD
☎ 01732 462681 📠 01732 458116
e-mail: reservations@donningtonmanorhotel.co.uk
web: www.donningtonmanorhotel.co.uk
dir: *M25 junct 4, follow signs for Bromley/Orpington to rdbt. Left onto A224 (Dunton Green), left at 2nd rdbt. Left at Rose & Crown, hotel 300yds on right*
An extended 15th-century manor house situated on the outskirts of

continued

Sevenoaks. Public rooms in the original part of the building have a wealth of character; they include an attractive oak-beamed restaurant, a comfortable lounge and a cosy bar. The purpose-built bedrooms are smartly decorated and well equipped. The hotel also has leisure facilities.

Best Western Donnington Manor

Rooms 60 en suite (2 fmly) (17 GF) ⊕ in 20 bedrooms S £75-£80; D £85-£90 (incl. bkfst) **Facilities** STV 🔄 supervised Squash Sauna Gym Jacuzzi Wi-fi available Xmas **Conf** Thtr 180 Class 60 Board 40 Del from £125 **Parking** 120 **Notes** LB ⊗ ⊕ in restaurant Civ Wed 70

See advertisement under DARTFORD

SITTINGBOURNE   MAP 07 TQ96

★★★ 74% ⊛ **HOTEL**

Hempstead House Country Hotel

London Rd, Bapchild ME9 9PP
☎ 01795 428020 📠 01795 436362
e-mail: info@hempsteadhouse.co.uk
web: www.hempsteadhouse.co.uk

dir: *1.5m from Sittingbourne town centre on A2 towards Canterbury*

Expect a warm welcome at this charming detached Victorian property, situated amidst three acres of mature landscaped gardens. Bedrooms are attractively decorated with lovely co-ordinated fabrics, tastefully furnished and equipped with many thoughtful touches. Public rooms feature a choice of beautifully furnished lounges as well as a superb conservatory dining room.

Rooms 27 en suite (7 fmly) (1 GF) ⊕ in all bedrooms S £80-£100; D £90-£130 (incl. bkfst) **Facilities** STV 🔄 ⛵ Wi-fi in bedrooms ch fac Xmas **Conf** BC Thtr 150 Class 150 Board 100 Del £135 **Parking** 100 **Notes** LB ⊕ in restaurant Civ Wed 150

Premier Travel Inn Sittingbourne, Kent

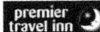

Bobbing Corner, Sheppy Way, Bobbing ME9 8PD
☎ 08701 977229 📠 01795 436748
web: www.premiertravelinn.com

dir: *M2 junct 5 take A249 towards Sheerness approx 2m, 1st slip road after A2 underpass. Inn on the left*

High quality, modern budget accommodation ideal for both families and business travellers. Spacious, en suite bedrooms feature bath and shower, satellite TV and many may have telephones and modem points. The adjacent family restaurant features a wide and varied menu. For further details consult the Hotel Groups page.

Rooms 40 en suite

TENTERDEN   MAP 07 TQ83

★★★ 77% **HOTEL**

Best Western London Beach Hotel & Golf Club

Ashford Rd TN30 6HX
☎ 01580 766279 📠 01580 763884
e-mail: enquiries@londonbeach.com
web: www.londonbeach.net

dir: *M20 junct 9, A28 follow signs to Tenterden (10m). Hotel on left*

Modern purpose-built hotel situated in mature grounds on the outskirts of Tenterden. The spacious bedrooms are smartly decorated, have co-ordinated soft furnishings and most rooms have balconies with superb views over the golf course. The open-plan public rooms feature a brasserie-style restaurant, where an interesting choice of dishes is served.

Rooms 26 en suite (2 fmly) ⊕ in 22 bedrooms S £65-£95; D £85-£150 (incl. bkfst) **Facilities** ⛳ 9 Fishing Putt green Driving range Pitch 'n' putt ♫ **Conf** Thtr 100 Class 75 Board 40 Del £135 **Services** Lift **Parking** 100 **Notes** LB ⊗ ⊕ in restaurant Civ Wed 100 RS 28-31 Dec

TONBRIDGE   MAP 06 TQ54

★★★ 70% **HOTEL**

Best Western Rose & Crown

125 High St TN9 1DD

☎ 01732 357966 🗏 01732 357194

e-mail: rose.crown@bestwestern.co.uk

dir: M25 junct 5 onto A21 to Hastings. At 2nd junct take B245 through Hildenborough. Continue to Tonbridge. At 1st lights right, over next set. Hotel on left

A 15th-century coaching inn situated in the heart of this bustling town centre. The hotel still retains much of its original character such as oak beams and Jacobean panelling. Bedrooms come in a variety of styles; each one is pleasantly decorated and well equipped. Guests can choose to dine in the bar or restaurant.

Rooms 54 en suite (2 fmly) (10 GF) ⊛ in 27 bedrooms **Facilities** STV **Conf** Thtr 80 Class 30 Board 35 **Parking** 39 **Notes** LB ⊗ ⊛ in restaurant Civ Wed 50

★★★ 68% **HOTEL**

The Langley

18-20 London Rd TN10 3DA

☎ 01732 353311 🗏 01732 771471

e-mail: thelangley@btconnect.com

dir: from Tonbridge towards Hildenborough N, hotel on Tonbridge/Hildenborough border

A privately owned hotel located just a short drive from the centre of Tonbridge and ideally situated for business and leisure guests alike. Bedrooms are generally quite spacious; each one is pleasantly decorated and equipped with modern facilities. The restaurant offers a varied menu of carefully prepared fresh produce, and there is a popular bar.

Rooms 39 en suite (3 fmly) (8 GF) ⊛ in 27 bedrooms S £65-£75; D £75-£95 (incl. bkfst) **Facilities** STV **Conf** Thtr 150 Class 50 Board 40 Del from £90 **Services** Lift **Parking** 60 **Notes** LB ⊗ ⊛ in restaurant Civ Wed 150

BUDGET HOTEL

Premier Travel Inn Tonbridge

Pembury Rd TN11 0NA

☎ 0870 9906552 🗏 0870 9906553

web: www.premiertravelinn.com

dir: 11m from M25 junct 5. Follow A21 towards Hastings, pass A26 (Tunbridge Wells) junct. Exit at next junct, 1st exit at rdbt

High quality, modern budget accommodation ideal for both families and business travellers. Spacious, en suite bedrooms feature bath and

continued

shower, satellite TV and many have telephones and modem points. The adjacent family restaurant features a wide and varied menu. For further details consult the Hotel Groups page.

Rooms 38 en suite **Conf** Class 14 Board 14

TUNBRIDGE WELLS (ROYAL) MAP 06 TQ53

★★★★ 74% ⊛ **HOTEL**

The Spa

Mount Ephraim TN4 8XJ

☎ 01892 520331 🗏 01892 510575

e-mail: info@spahotel.co.uk

web: www.spahotel.co.uk

dir: off A21 to A26, follow signs to A264 East Grinstead, hotel on right

This imposing 18th-century country house is set in 14 acres of attractive landscaped grounds, overlooking Royal Tunbridge Wells. The spacious bedrooms are individually decorated and are tastefully furnished and thoughtfully equipped; many rooms overlook the pretty gardens. Public rooms include a comfortable lounge, a large bar, the Chandelier restaurant and excellent leisure facilities.

Rooms 69 en suite (10 fmly) (2 GF) **Facilities** Spa STV ⊠ supervised ⊗ Riding Sauna Gym ⊌ Wi-fi in bedrooms Steam room Beauty Salon Jogging trail ♫ Xmas **Conf** BC Thtr 300 Class 93 Board 90 **Services** Lift **Parking** 120 **Notes** ⊗ ⊛ in restaurant Civ Wed 250

See advert on opposite page

★★★★ 73% ⊛⊛ **TOWN HOUSE HOTEL**

Hotel Du Vin & Bistro

Crescent Rd TN1 2LY

☎ 01892 526455 🗏 01892 512044

e-mail: reception@tunbridgewells.hotelduvin.com

web: www.hotelduvin.com

dir: follow town centre to main junct of Mount Pleasant Rd & Crescent Rd/Church Rd. Hotel 150yds on Crescent Rd on right just past Phillips House

This impressive Grade II listed building dates from 1762, and as a princess, Queen Victoria often stayed here. The spacious bedrooms are available in a range of sizes, beautifully and individually appointed, and equipped with a host of thoughtful extras. Public rooms include a bistro-style restaurant, two elegant lounges and a small bar.

Rooms 30 en suite 4 annexe en suite ⊛ in all bedrooms S £100-£295; D £100-£295 **Facilities** STV Snooker Wi-fi in bedrooms Boules court in garden **Conf** Thtr 40 Class 30 Board 25 Del £185 **Services** Lift **Parking** 30 **Notes** ⊛ in restaurant Civ Wed 84

★★★ 79% **HOTEL**

Ramada Tunbridge Wells

@RAMADA.

8 Tonbridge Rd, Pembury TN2 4QL
☎ 01892 823567 ▤ 01892 823931
e-mail: sales.tunwells@ramadajarvis.co.uk
web: www.ramadajarvis.co.uk

dir: *From M25 junct 5 follow A21 S. Turn left at 1st rdbt signed Pembury Hospital. Hotel on left, 400yds past hospital.*

Built in the style of a traditional Kentish oast house, this well presented hotel is conveniently located just off the A21 with easy access to the M25. Bedrooms are comfortably appointed for both business and leisure guests. Public areas include a leisure club and a range of meeting rooms.

Rooms 84 en suite (8 fmly) (40 GF) ⊘ in 64 bedrooms S £85-£110; D £85-£110 **Facilities Spa** STV ☒ Sauna Steam room Wi-fi available Xmas **Conf** Thtr 390 Class 150 Board 107 Del from £99 **Parking** 200 **Notes** ⊘ in restaurant Civ Wed 70

★★ 64% **METRO HOTEL**

Russell

THE INDEPENDENTS

80 London Rd TN1 1DZ
☎ 01892 544833 ▤ 01892 515846
e-mail: Sales@russell-hotel.com
web: www.russell-hotel.com

dir: *at junct A26/A264 uphill onto A26, hotel on right*

This detached Victorian property is situated just a short walk from the centre of town. The generously proportioned bedrooms in the main house are pleasantly decorated and well equipped. In addition, there are several smartly appointed self-contained suites in an adjacent building. The public rooms include a lounge and cosy bar.

Rooms 21 en suite 5 annexe en suite (5 fmly) (1 GF) ⊘ in 10 bedrooms S £55-£85; D £75-£99 (incl. bkfst) **Facilities** Wi-fi in bedrooms **Conf** BC Thtr 35 Class 35 Board 35 Del from £75 **Parking** 15 **Notes LB** ⊗ ⊘ in restaurant

BUDGET HOTEL

Innkeeper's Lodge Tunbridge Wells

Innkeeper's Lodge

21 London Rd, Southborough TN4 0RL
☎ 01892 529292 ▤ 01892 510620
web: www.innkeeperslodge.com

dir: *Off M25 onto A21, take A26 Tonbridge/Southborough turn off. Lodge in Southborough on A26, opposite cricket green*

Smart, en suite accommodation ideal for both business & leisure guests. Bedrooms are very well equipped, including Sky TV, telephone, modem points, tea & coffee making facilities, (family rooms in most locations). Complimentary breakfast. The adjacent Pub Restaurant; a Harvester, Vintage Inn, Toby Carvery, Ember Inn, Sizzling Pubco or Pub & Carvery offers an all day menu. See Hotel Groups pages for further details.

Rooms 15 en suite S £65-£95; D £65-£95

WATERINGBURY   MAP 06 TQ65

BUDGET HOTEL

Premier Travel Inn Maidstone (Wateringbury)

premier travel inn

103 Tonbridge Rd ME18 5NS
☎ 0870 9906346 ▤ 0870 9906347
web: www.premiertravelinn.com

dir: *Exit M25 junct 3 onto M20. Exit at junct 4 onto A228 towards West Malling. Follow A26 towards Maidstone for approx 3m*

High quality, modern budget accommodation ideal for both families and business travellers. Spacious, en suite bedrooms feature bath and shower, satellite TV and many have telephones and modem points. The adjacent family restaurant features a wide and varied menu. For further details consult the Hotel Groups page.

Rooms 40 en suite **Conf** Thtr 30

Some hotels have restricted service during quieter months, and at this time some of the facilities will not be available

England

England

WESTERHAM   MAP 06 TQ45

★★ 78% HOTEL

Kings Arms

OLD ENGLISH INNS

Market Square TN16 1AN
☎ 01959 562990 📠 01959 561240
e-mail: kingsarms.westerham@oldenglishinns.co.uk
web: www.oldenglish.co.uk

dir: *M25 junct 6 take A25 through Oxted to Westerham. Hotel in Market Square on right.*

Delightful Georgian coaching inn situated in the heart of this bustling town centre. Public areas include a large lounge bar, a restaurant and a conservatory where breakfast is served. The bedrooms are generally quite spacious; each one is smartly decorated, has co-ordinated fabrics and many thoughtful touches.

Rooms 16 en suite (1 fmly) ⊛ in 10 bedrooms S £80-£90; D £100-£115 (incl. bkfst) **Facilities** ♫ Xmas **Conf** Thtr 60 Class 30 Board 30 Del £100 **Parking** 26 **Notes LB** ⊛ in restaurant Civ Wed 60

WHITSTABLE   MAP 07 TR16

BUDGET HOTEL

Premier Travel Inn Whitstable

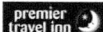

Thanet Way CT5 3DB
☎ 08701 977269 📠 01227 263151
web: www.premiertravelinn.com

dir: *2m W of town centre on B2205*

High quality, modern budget accommodation ideal for both families and business travellers. Spacious, en suite bedrooms feature bath and shower, satellite TV and many have telephones and modem points. The adjacent family restaurant features a wide and varied menu. For further details consult the Hotel Groups page.

Rooms 40 en suite **Conf** Thtr 30 Board 20

WROTHAM   MAP 06 TQ65

BUDGET HOTEL

Premier Travel Inn Sevenoaks/Maidstone

London Rd, Wrotham Heath TN15 7RX
☎ 08701 977227 📠 01732 870368
web: www.premiertravelinn.com

dir: *M20 junct 2, A20 to Wrotham Heath and West Malling. Inn past lights on right*

High quality, modern budget accommodation ideal for both families and business travellers. Spacious, en suite bedrooms feature bath and shower, satellite TV and many have telephones and modem points. The adjacent family restaurant features a wide and varied menu. For further details consult the Hotel Groups page.

Rooms 40 en suite **Conf** Thtr 18

LANCASHIRE

ACCRINGTON   MAP 18 SD72

★★★★ 74% HOTEL

Macdonald Dunkenhalgh Hotel & Spa

Blackburn Rd, Clayton-le-Moors BB5 5JP
☎ 0870 1942116 📠 01254 872230
e-mail: dunkenhalgh@macdonald-hotels.co.uk
web: www.macdonald-hotels.co.uk

dir: *adjacent to M65 junct 7*

Set in its own parkland just off the M65, this fine mansion has conference and banqueting facilities that attract the wedding and corporate markets. A new leisure complex offers guests a comprehensive range of fitness facilities and beauty treatments. Bedrooms come in a variety of styles, sizes and standards, some out with the main hotel building.

Rooms 78 en suite 97 annexe en suite (50 fmly) (12 GF) ⊛ in all bedrooms S £70-£120; D £70-£120 (incl. bkfst) **Facilities Spa** STV ℝ Sauna Solarium Gym Jacuzzi Wi-fi in bedrooms Thermal suite, Beauty spa, Dance studio Xmas **Conf** Thtr 400 Class 250 Board 100 Del from £115 **Services** Lift **Parking** 400 **Notes LB** ⊛ in restaurant Civ Wed 400

★★★ 75% HOTEL

Sparth House Hotel

Whalley Rd, Clayton Le Moors BB5 5RP
☎ 01254 872263 📠 01254 872263
e-mail: mail.sparth@btinternet.com
web: www.sparthhousehotel.co.uk

dir: *A6185 to Clitheroe along Dunkenhalgh Way, right at lights onto A678, left at next lights, A680 to Whalley. Hotel on left after 2 sets of lights*

This 18th-century listed building sits in three acres of well-tended gardens. Bedrooms offer a choice of styles from the cosy modern rooms ideal for business guests, to the spacious classical rooms - including one with furnishings from one of the great cruise liners. Public rooms feature a panelled restaurant and plush lounge bar.

Rooms 16 en suite (3 fmly) ⊛ in 2 bedrooms **Conf** Thtr 160 Class 50 Board 40 **Parking** 50 **Notes LB** ⊛ in restaurant Civ Wed 150

England

BARTON MAP 18 SD53

★★★★ 76% ⊛ HOTEL

Barton Grange

Garstang Rd PR3 5AA
☎ 01772 862551 📄 01772 861267
e-mail: stay@bartongrangehotel.com
web: www.bartongrange.co.uk

dir: *M6 junct 32, follow signs to Garstang (A6) for 2.5 miles. Hotel on right*

Situated close to the M6, this modern, stylish hotel benefits from extensive public areas that include an award-winning garden centre and leisure facilities. Comfortable, well-appointed bedrooms include four-poster and family rooms, as well as attractive rooms in an adjacent cottage. The unique Walled Garden restaurant offers all-day eating, whilst Healy's restaurant offers dishes prepared with flair and creativity.

Rooms 43 en suite 8 annexe en suite (4 fmly) (4 GF) ⊘ in 28 bedrooms S £55-£85; D £65-£120 **Facilities** STV ⬚ Sauna Gym Jacuzzi Wi-fi in bedrooms Garden Centre within the grounds, pool table, bar billiards Xmas **Conf** BC Thtr 300 Class 100 Board 80 Del from £100 **Services** Lift **Parking** 250 **Notes** LB ⊛ ⊘ in restaurant Civ Wed 120

BILSBORROW MAP 18 SD53

BUDGET HOTEL

Premier Travel Inn Preston North

premier travel inn

Garstang Rd PR3 0RN
☎ 0870 9906410 📄 0870 9906411
web: www.premiertravelinn.com

dir: *4m from M6 junct 32 on A6 towards Garstang. 7m from Preston*

High quality, modern budget accommodation ideal for both families and business travellers. Spacious, en suite bedrooms feature bath and shower, satellite TV and many have telephones and modem points. The adjacent family restaurant features a wide and varied menu. For further details consult the Hotel Groups page.

Rooms 40 en suite

BLACKBURN MAP 18 SD62

See also Langho

★★ 85% ⊛⊛ HOTEL

Millstone at Mellor

SHIRE HOTELS

Church Ln, Mellor BB2 7JR
☎ 01254 813333 📄 01254 812628
e-mail: info@millstonehotel.co.uk
web: www.shirehotels.com

dir: *3m NW off A59*

Once a coaching inn, the Millstone is situated in a village just outside the town. The hotel provides a very high standard of accommodation, professional and friendly service and good food. Bedrooms, some in an adjacent house, are comfortable and generally spacious, and all are very well equipped. A room for less able guests is also available.

Rooms 17 en suite 6 annexe en suite (5 fmly) (8 GF) ⊘ in 10 bedrooms S £74.50-£109; D £99-£129 (incl. bkfst) **Facilities** STV Wi-fi in bedrooms Xmas **Conf** Thtr 25 Class 15 Board 16 Del £115 **Parking** 40 **Notes** LB ⊛ ⊘ in restaurant Civ Wed 60

BUDGET HOTEL

Premier Travel Inn Blackburn North West

premier travel inn

Myerscough Rd, Balderstone BB2 7LE
☎ 0870 9906388 📄 0870 9906389
web: www.premiertravelinn.com

dir: *On A59 opp British Aerospace. Exit at M6 junct 3 take A59 to Clitheroe*

High quality, modern budget accommodation ideal for both families and business travellers. Spacious, en suite bedrooms feature bath and shower, satellite TV and many have telephones and modem points. The adjacent family restaurant features a wide and varied menu. For further details consult the Hotel Groups page.

Rooms 20 en suite **Conf** Board 12

BLACKPOOL MAP 18 SD33

★★★★ 79% HOTEL

De Vere Herons' Reach

DeVere HOTELS & RESORTS

East Park Dr FY3 8LL
☎ 01253 838866 📄 01253 798800
e-mail: reservations.herons@devere-hotels.com
web: www.devere.co.uk

dir: *M6 junct 32/M55 junct 4/A583. At 4th traffic lights turn right into South Park Dr for 0.25m, right at mini-rdbt onto East Park Drive, hotel 0.25m on right*

Set in over 200 acres of grounds, this hotel is popular with both business and leisure guests. The pleasure beach is a few minutes' walk from the hotel, and the Lake District and Trough of Bowland are an hour away. Extensive indoor and outdoor leisure facilities include an 18-hole championship golf course. Bedrooms include a number of suites and smart, well-appointed clubrooms.

Rooms 172 en suite (20 GF) ⊘ in all bedrooms S £79-£229; D £89-£249 (incl. bkfst) **Facilities** Spa STV ⬚ supervised ♨ 18 ⬚ Squash Sauna Solarium Gym Putt green Jacuzzi Wi-fi available Aerobic studio, Beauty room, Spinning Studio Xmas **Conf** BC Thtr 650 Class 250 Board 70 Del from £125 **Services** Lift **Parking** 500 **Notes** LB ⊛ ⊘ in restaurant Civ Wed 650

England

BLACKPOOL *continued*

★★★★ 74% HOTEL

Big Blue Hotel

Ocean Boulevard FY4 1ND
☎ 0845 367 3333 & 01253 400045 📠 01253 400046
e-mail: reservations@bpbltd.com

This stylish hotel is ideally located adjacent to the Pleasure Beach, boasting excellent family facilities. A large proportion of family suites offer separate children's rooms furnished with bunk beds, each with their own individual TV screens. Spacious executive rooms boast seating areas with flat screen TVs and DVD players. Public areas include a smart bar and brasserie, a range of meeting facilities and a residents' gym.

Rooms 157 en suite (84 fmly) (37 GF) ⊗ in 119 bedrooms S £65-£120; D £75-£120 (incl. bkfst) **Facilities** STV Gym Wi-fi available Xmas **Conf** BC Thtr 55 Class 25 Board 30 Del from £105 **Services** Lift air con **Parking** 250 **Notes** LB ⊗ ⊗ in restaurant Civ Wed 100

See advert on opposite page

★★★★ 74% HOTEL

Paramount Imperial

North Promenade FY1 2HB
☎ 01253 623971 📠 01253 751784
e-mail: imperialblackpool@paramount-hotels.co.uk
web: www.paramount-hotels.co.uk

dir: *M55 junct 2, take A583 North Shore, follow signs to North Promenade. Hotel on seafront, north of tower.*

Enjoying a prime seafront location, this grand Victorian hotel offers smartly appointed, well-equipped bedrooms and spacious, elegant public areas. Facilities include a smart leisure club; a comfortable lounge, the No.10 bar and an attractive split-level restaurant that overlooks the seafront. Conferences and functions are extremely well catered for.

Rooms 180 en suite (9 fmly) ⊗ in 156 bedrooms S £84-£134; D fr £168 (incl. bkfst) **Facilities** STV ➤ Sauna Solarium Gym Jacuzzi Wi-fi in bedrooms Xmas **Conf** Thtr 600 Class 240 Board 128 Del from £130 **Services** Lift **Parking** 150 **Notes** LB ⊗ in restaurant Civ Wed 200

★★★ 75% HOTEL

Carousel

663-671 New South Prom FY4 1RN
☎ 01253 402642 📠 01253 341100
e-mail: carousel@sleepwellhotels.com
web: www.sleepwellhotels.com

dir: *from M55 follow signs to airport, pass airport to lights. Turn right, hotel 100yds on right*

This friendly seafront hotel, close to the Pleasure Beach, offers smart, contemporary accommodation. Bedrooms are comfortably appointed and have a modern, stylish feel to them. An airy restaurant and a spacious bar/lounge both overlook the Promenade. The hotel has smart conference/meeting facilities and its own car park.

Rooms 92 en suite (7 fmly) ⊗ in 28 bedrooms S £45-£95; D £60-£120 (incl. bkfst) **Facilities** STV Wi-fi in bedrooms ♫ Xmas **Conf** Thtr 100 Class 30 Board 40 Del from £75 **Services** Lift **Parking** 46 **Notes** LB ⊗ ⊗ in restaurant Civ Wed 150

★★★ 74% HOTEL

Best Western Carlton

282-286 North Promenade FY1 2EZ
☎ 01253 628966 📠 01253 752587
e-mail: mail@carltonhotelblackpool.co.uk
web: www.carltonhotelblackpool.co.uk

dir: *M6 junct 32/M55 follow signs for North Shore. Between Blackpool Tower & Gynn Square*

Enjoying a prime seafront location, this hotel offers bedrooms that are brightly appointed and modern in style. Public areas include an open-plan dining room and lounge bar, and a spacious additional bar where lunches are served. Functions are well catered for and ample parking is available.

Rooms 58 en suite ⊗ in 20 bedrooms S £45-£75; D £65-£110 (incl. bkfst) **Facilities** STV Wi-fi in bedrooms Xmas **Conf** Thtr 90 Class 40 Board 40 Del from £90 **Services** Lift **Parking** 43 **Notes** LB ⊗ ⊗ in restaurant Civ Wed 80

See advert on this page

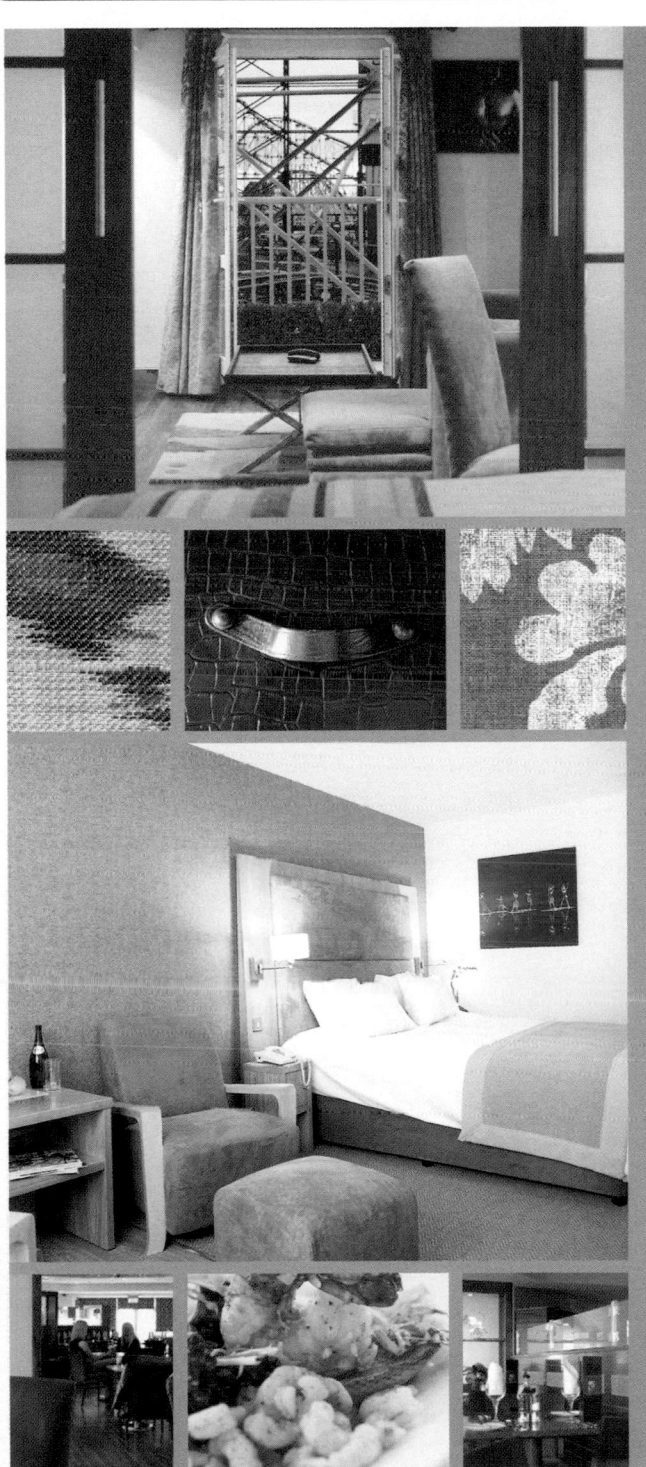

England

BLACKPOOL *continued*

★★ 69% **HOTEL**

Hotel Sheraton

54-62 Queens Promenade FY2 9RP

☎ 01253 352723 ▤ 01253 595499

e-mail: email@hotelsheraton.co.uk

web: www.hotelsheraton.co.uk

dir: *1m N from Blackpool Tower on promenade towards Fleetwood*

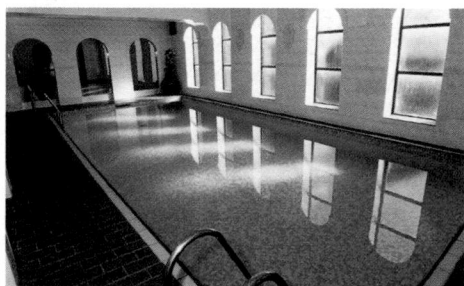

This family-owned and run hotel is situated at the quieter, northern end of the promenade. Public areas include a choice of spacious lounges with sea views, a large function suite where popular dancing and cabaret evenings are held, and a heated indoor swimming pool. The smartly appointed bedrooms come in a range of sizes and styles.

Rooms 104 en suite (45 fmly) **Facilities** ⚏ Sauna Table Tennis Darts ♫ Xmas **Conf** Thtr 200 Class 100 Board 150 **Services** Lift **Parking** 20 **Notes** ⊗ ⊘ in restaurant

★★ 67% **HOTEL**

Belgrave Madison

270-274 Queens Promenade FY2 9HD

☎ 01253 351570 ▤ 01253 500698

e-mail: info@belgravemadison.co.uk

dir: *From M55 follow signs for Tower/Promenade, turn right onto Promenade. Hotel is 2.5m N of tower.*

This family-run hotel, now under new ownership, enjoys a seafront location at the quieter end of town. Thoughtfully equipped bedrooms vary in size and include family and four-poster rooms. Spacious public areas include a choice of lounges with views over the promenade, a bar lounge where guests can enjoy live entertainment and a bright restaurant.

Rooms 43 en suite (10 fmly) (2 GF) S £28-£38; D £52-£72 (incl. bkfst) **Facilities** ♫ Xmas **Services** Lift **Parking** 28 **Notes LB** ⊗ ⊘ in restaurant

★★ 67% **HOTEL**

Headlands

611-613 South Promenade FY4 1NJ

☎ 01253 341179 ▤ 01253 342657

e-mail: headlands@blackpool.net

dir: *M55 & filter left, right at rdbt to Promenade, turn right & hotel 0.5m on right*

This friendly, family owned hotel stands on the South Promenade, close to the Pleasure Beach and many of the town's major attractions.

Bedrooms are traditionally furnished, many enjoying sea views. There is a choice of lounges and live entertainment is provided regularly. Home cooked food is served in the panelled dining room.

Rooms 41 en suite (10 fmly) S £38.50-£49.50; D £77-£99 (incl. bkfst) **Facilities** Snooker Solarium Darts Games Room Pool Snooker ♫ Xmas **Services** Lift **Parking** 46 **Notes LB** ⊘ in restaurant Closed 2-15 Jan

★★ 65% **HOTEL**

Warwick

603-609 New South Promenade FY4 1NG

☎ 01253 342192 ▤ 01253 405776

dir: *M55 junct 4/A5230 for South Shore then right on A584, Promenade South*

Located on the renovated South Promenade and close to pleasure beach, this friendly family hotel provides a range of thoughtfully furnished bedrooms with modern bathrooms. Spacious public areas include an attractive dining room, choice of bars and an indoor swimming pool.

Rooms 51 en suite (11 fmly) ⊘ in all bedrooms S £31-£45 (incl. bkfst) **Facilities** ⚐ Pool ♫ Xmas **Conf** Thtr 50 Class 24 Board 30 **Services** Lift **Parking** 24 **Notes LB** ⊗ ⊘ in restaurant Closed Jan RS Feb

BUDGET HOTEL

Premier Travel Inn Blackpool Airport

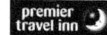

Squires Gare Ln FY4 2QS

☎ 08701 977034 ▤ 01253 362413

web: www.premiertravelinn.com

dir: *M55 junct 4/A5230 & turn left at 1st rdbt towards airport. Inn is just before Squires Gate railway station*

High quality, modern budget accommodation ideal for both families and business travellers. Spacious, en suite bedrooms feature bath and shower, satellite TV and many have telephones and modem points. The adjacent family restaurant features a wide and varied menu. For further details consult the Hotel Groups page.

Rooms 39 en suite **Conf** Thtr 15 Board 8

Premier Travel Inn Blackpool (Bispham)

Devonshire Rd, Bispham FY2 0AR

☎ 08701 977033 ▤ 01253 590498

dir: *M55 junct 4 right onto A583. At 5th set of lights turn right (Whitegate Drive) for approx. 4-5 miles onto Devonshire Rd (A587)*

Rooms 39 en suite **Conf** Thtr 50 Board 20

Premier Travel Inn Blackpool East

Whitehills Park, Preston New Rd FY4 5NZ

☎ 0870 9906608 ▤ 0870 9906609

dir: *Just off M55 junct 4. Take 1st left off rdbt. Inn on right*

Rooms 81 en suite

Premier Travel Inn Blackpool South

Yeadon Way, South Shore FY1 6BF

☎ 08701 977032 ▤ 01253 343805

dir: *M55, follow signs for central car park/coach area. Located next to Total garage*

Rooms 79 en suite **Conf** Thtr 40

continued

BURNLEY

MAP 18 SD83

★★★ 80% HOTEL

Oaks

Colne Rd, Reedley BB10 2LF
☎ 01282 414141 🖺 01282 433401
e-mail: oaks@shirehotels.com
web: www.shirehotels.com

dir: M65 junct 12. Follow signs to Burnley. At B&Q mini rdbt left, right at rdbt, right onto A682. Hotel 1m on left

The friendly team here provide super hospitality in this former Victorian coffee merchant's house. The hotel offers traditional public areas and modern, well-equipped bedrooms that come in a variety of styles and sizes. A well-equipped leisure club is available on site. The attractive, peaceful location and impressive function facilities makes this a popular wedding venue.

Rooms 50 en suite (10 fmly) ⊛ in 31 bedrooms S £80-£124; D £110-£124 (incl. bkfst) **Facilities** STV 🔄 Sauna Solarium Gym Jacuzzi Wi-fi in bedrooms Steam room Xmas **Conf** Thtr 120 Class 48 Board 60 Del £135 **Parking** 110 **Notes LB** ⊗ ⊛ in restaurant Civ Wed 100

★★★ 78% HOTEL

Best Western Higher Trapp Country House

Trapp Ln, Simonstone BB12 7QW
☎ 01202 227201 🖺 01202 227282
e-mail: reception@highertrapphotel.co.uk

Set in more than four acres of delightful terraced gardens, commanding magnificent countryside views from its hillside location, this Tudor-style hotel offers excellent accommodation. Three of the bedrooms have four-posters and there is also Parker Lodge which offers an extra ten rooms. Guests can dine in Fitzy's Bar which has a conservatory area.

Rooms 19 en suite 10 annexe en suite (4 GF) ⊛ in 10 bedrooms S £59-£69; D £78-£89 (incl. bkfst) **Facilities** STV Xmas **Conf** Thtr 100 Class 30 Board 30 Del from £89 **Parking** 100 **Notes** Civ Wed 100

★★★ 78% HOTEL

Rosehill House

Rosehill Av BB11 2PW
☎ 01282 453931 🖺 01282 455628
e-mail: rhhotel@provider.co.uk
dir: 0.5m S of Burnley town centre, off A682

This fine Grade II listed building stands its own leafy grounds in a quiet area of town. There are two restaurants (one a tapas bar) and stylish lounge bar. The hotel has been totally refurbished and features
continued

original beautifully ornate ceilings and mosaic flooring. The boutique-style bedrooms are tastefully finished and comfortably equipped; the two loft conversions and the former coach house offer spacious yet more traditional-style accommodation.

Rooms 34 en suite (3 fmly) (4 GF) ⊛ in 10 bedrooms **Facilities** STV Snooker **Conf** BC Thtr 50 Class 30 Board 30 **Parking** 52 **Notes LB** ⊗ ⊛ in restaurant Civ Wed 90

★★★ 67% HOTEL

Sparrow Hawk

Church St BB11 2DN
☎ 01282 421551 🖺 01282 456506
e-mail: enquiries@sparrowhawkhotel.co.uk
web: www.sparrowhawkhotel.co.uk

dir: M65 junct 10, 5th exit at traffic island (Cavalry Way). Left at next island, right lane along Westway, right at lights. Take 2nd exit from rdbt , 2nd exit at next rdbt. Hotel 300yds on right

A warm welcome awaits guests at this centrally located grand Victorian hotel, which is handy for key local attractions. Well-equipped bedrooms vary in size and style and include some very stylish rooms. Public areas include the Mediterranean-style Smithies Café Bar, Farriers Restaurant and a traditional bar serving speciality ales.

Rooms 35 en suite (1 fmly) ⊛ in 9 bedrooms S £47-£54; D £53-£62 (incl. bkfst) **Facilities** STV Wi-fi available 🎵 Xmas **Conf** Thtr 80 Class 50 Board 40 **Parking** 20 **Notes LB** ⊗ ⊛ in restaurant

BUDGET HOTEL

Premier Travel Inn Burnley

Queen Victoria Rd BB10 3EF
☎ 08701 977045 🖺 01282 448431
web: www.premiertravelinn.com

dir: M65 junct 12 take 5th exit at rdbt, 1st exit at rdbt, keep in right lane at lights, next rdbt, 2nd exit then 3rd at next rdbt, under bridge turn left before football ground

High quality, modern budget accommodation ideal for both families and business travellers. Spacious, en suite bedrooms feature bath and shower, satellite TV and many have telephones and modem points. The adjacent family restaurant features a wide and varied menu. For further details consult the Hotel Groups page.

Rooms 40 en suite

BUDGET HOTEL

Travelodge Burnley

Cavalry Barracks, Barracks Rd BB11 4AS
☎ 08700 850 950 🖺 01282 416039
web: www.travelodge.co.uk
dir: at junct of A671/A679

Travelodge offers good quality, good value, modern accommodation. Ideal for families, the spacious en suite bedrooms include remote-control TV, tea and coffee-making facilities and comfortable beds. Meals can be taken at the nearby family restaurant. See Hotel Groups pages for further details.

Rooms 32 en suite S fr £26; D fr £26

England

CARNFORTH
MAP 18 SD47

★★ 71% **HOTEL**

County
Lancaster Rd LA5 9LD
☎ 01524 732469 📠 01524 720142
e-mail: county@mitchellshotels.co.uk
dir: M6 junct 35 signed Carnforth, hotel on left by lights.

Located in the heart of the community, this very popular hotel provides a range of thoughtfully furnished bedrooms, within a separate accommodation block. Public areas include a spacious restaurant, with a wide range of dishes, a separate function suite and a well stocked bar featuring local ales.

Rooms 12 annexe en suite (3 fmly) (6 GF) ⊘ in 10 bedrooms S £49.50; D £49.50-£59 **Conf** Thtr 130 Class 50 Board 50 **Parking** 55 **Notes LB** ⊗ ⊘ in restaurant

★★ 65% **HOTEL**

Royal Station
Market St LA5 9BT
☎ 01524 732033 & 733636 📠 01524 720267
e-mail: royalstation@mitchellshotels.co.uk
dir: M6 junct 35 onto A6 signed Carnforth. After 1m at x-rds in town centre right into Market St. Hotel opposite railway station

This commercial hotel enjoys a town centre location close to the railway station. Bedrooms are well equipped and comfortably furnished. A good range of tasty good value meals can be taken in either the bright attractive lounge bar or the restaurant.

Rooms 13 en suite (1 fmly) **Conf** Thtr 130 Class 80 Board 80 **Parking** 4 **Notes LB** ⊘ in restaurant

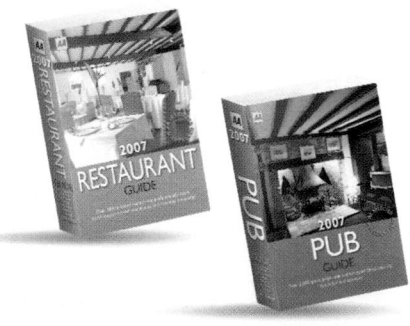

CHARNOCK RICHARD MOTORWAY SERVICE AREA (M6)
MAP 15 SD51

Welcome Lodge Charnock Richard

Welcome Break Service Area PR7 5LR
☎ 01257 791746 📠 01257 793596
e-mail: charnockhotel@welcomebreak.co.uk
web: www.welcomebreak.co.uk
dir: between junct 27 & 28 of M6 northbound. 500yds from Camelot Theme Park via Mill Lane

This modern building offers accommodation in smart, spacious and well-equipped bedrooms, suitable for families and business travellers, and all with en suite bathrooms. Refreshments may be taken at the nearby family restaurant. For further details consult the Hotel Groups page.

Rooms 100 en suite S £35-£50; D £35-£50 **Conf** Thtr 40 Class 16 Board 24 Del from £35

CHORLEY
MAP 15 SD51

★★★ 74% **HOTEL**

Best Western Park Hall

Park Hall Rd, Charnock Richard PR7 5LP
☎ 01257 455000 📠 01257 451838
e-mail: conference@parkhall-hotel.co.uk
web: www.parkhall-hotel.co.uk
dir: between Preston & Wigan, signed from M6 junct 27 N'bound & junct 28 S'bound, or from M61 junct 8

The popular Camelot Theme Park is just a short stroll across the grounds from this hotel, which focuses on the leisure and corporate/conference markets. Conveniently located for the motorway network, this idyllic country retreat is shared between the main hotel and The Village, a series of chalet/bungalows. The Cadbury and Bassett rooms with special themed furnishings will be a real hit with the kids.

Rooms 56 en suite 84 annexe en suite (52 fmly) (84 GF) ⊘ in 34 bedrooms **Facilities Spa** STV ⌕ supervised Sauna Solarium Gym Jacuzzi Steam room, air-conditioned Gymnasium **Conf** Thtr 700 Class 240 Board 40 **Services** Lift **Parking** 2600 **Notes LB** ⊗ ⊘ in restaurant Civ Wed 150

See advertisement under PRESTON

Premier Travel Inn Chorley

Malthouse Farm, Moss Ln, Whittle le Woods PR6 8AB
☎ 0870 9906376 📠 0870 9906377
e-mail: malthousefarm20@hotmail.com
web: www.premiertravelinn.com
dir: M61 junct 8 onto A674 (Wheelton), 400yds on left into Moss Lane

High quality, modern budget accommodation ideal for both families and business travellers. Spacious, en suite bedrooms feature bath and shower, satellite TV and many have telephones and modem points. The adjacent family restaurant features a wide and varied menu. For further details consult the Hotel Groups page.

Rooms 81 en suite **Conf** Board 15

Premier Travel Inn Chorley South

Bolton Rd PR7 4AB

☎ 0870 9906604 🖩 0870 9906605

dir: *From N, exit M61 junct 8 onto A6 to Chorley. From S, exit M6 junct 27 follow Standish signs. Left onto A5106 to Chorley then A6 towards Preston. Inn 0.5m on right*

Rooms 29 en suite **Conf** Board 12

BUDGET HOTEL

Travelodge Preston Chorley

Preston Rd, Clayton-le-Woods PR6 7JB

☎ 08700 850 950 🖩 01772 311963

web: www.travelodge.co.uk

dir: *from M6 junct 28 take B5256 for 2m, next to Halfway House pub*

Travelodge offers good quality, good value, modern accommodation. Ideal for families, the spacious en suite bedrooms include remote control TV, tea and coffee making facilities and comfortable beds. Meals can be taken at the nearby family restaurant. See Hotel Groups pages for further details.

Rooms 40 en suite S fr £26; D fr £26

CLITHEROE   MAP 18 SD74

★★★ 73% **HOTEL**

Eaves Hall Country Hotel

Eaves Hall Ln, West Bradford BB7 3JG

☎ 01200 425271 & 0845 345 3427 🖩 01200 425131

e-mail: eaves.hall@csma.uk.com

web: www.eaveshall.co.uk

dir: *Leave A59 onto Pimlico link take 3rd slip road on left towards Waddington at T-junct turn left, hotel first on right*

A Grade II listed Georgian-style house set in 13 acres of landscaped gardens and grounds with views to the Ribble Valley, this hotel has oak-panelled public areas that offer both space and tranquillity. Bedrooms vary in style and size, ranging from a standard room to a classic suite. Facilities also include bowling, pitch & putt and an indoor games room.

Rooms 34 en suite 2 annexe en suite ⊗ in all bedrooms S £60-£85; D £120-£170 (incl. bkfst) **Facilities** ⚓ Fishing Snooker Gym Putt green Bowling Green Pitch & putt Xmas **Conf** Thtr 80 Class 40 Board 30 Del from £106 **Services** Lift **Parking** 40 **Notes LB** ⊗ ⊗ in restaurant Civ Wed 80

★★★ 68% **HOTEL**

Shireburn Arms

Whalley Rd, Hurst Green BB7 9QJ

☎ 01254 826518 🖩 01254 826208

e-mail: sales@shireburnarmshotel.com

web: www.shireburnarmshotel.com

dir: *A59 to Clitheroe, left at lights to Ribchester, follow Hurst Green signs. Hotel on B6243 at entrance to Hurst Green village*

This long established, family-owned hotel dates back to the 17th century and enjoys panoramic views over the Ribble Valley. Rooms are individually designed and thoughtfully equipped. The lounge bar offers a selection of real ales, and the spacious restaurant, opening onto an attractive patio and garden, offers home-cooked food.

Rooms 18 en suite (3 fmly) ⊗ in 3 bedrooms S £45-£50; D £75-£100 (incl. bkfst) **Facilities** ch fac Xmas **Conf** Thtr 100 Class 50 Board 50 Del £80 **Parking** 71 **Notes LB** ⊗ in restaurant Civ Wed 100

DARWEN   MAP 15 SD62

BUDGET HOTEL

Premier Travel Inn Blackburn South

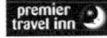

Oakenhurst Farm, Ecceslink Rd BB3 0SN

☎ 08701 977 187 🖩 08701 977701

web: www.premiertravelinn.com

dir: *off junction 4 of the M65, near Blackburn*

High quality, modern budget accommodation ideal for both families and business travellers. Spacious, en suite bedrooms feature bath and shower, satellite TV and many have telephones and modem points. The adjacent family restaurant features a wide and varied menu. For further details consult the Hotel Groups page.

Rooms 41 en suite

BUDGET HOTEL

Travelodge Blackburn (M65)

Darwen Motorway Services BB3 0AT

☎ 08700 850 950 🖩 01254 776058

web: www.travelodge.co.uk

Travelodge offers good quality, good value, modern accommodation. Ideal for families, the spacious en suite bedrooms include remote-control TV, tea and coffee-making facilities and comfortable beds. Meals can be taken at the nearby family restaurant. See Hotel Groups pages for further details.

Rooms S fr £26; D fr £26

FORTON MOTORWAY   MAP 18 SD55
SERVICE AREA (M6)

BUDGET HOTEL

Travelodge Lancaster (M6)

White Carr Ln, Bay Horse LA2 9DU

☎ 08700 850 950 🖩 01524 791703

web: www.travelodge.co.uk

dir: *between junct 32 & 33 of M6*

Travelodge offers good quality, good value, modern accommodation. Ideal for families, the spacious en suite bedrooms include remote-control TV, tea and coffee-making facilities and comfortable beds.

continued on page 380

FORTON MOTORWAY (M6) *continued*

Meals can be taken at the nearby family restaurant. See Hotel Groups pages for further details.

Rooms 53 en suite S fr £26; D fr £26

GARSTANG MAP 18 SD44

★★★ 75% HOTEL

Garstang Country Hotel & Golf Club

Garstang Rd, Bowgreave PR3 1YE
☎ 01995 600100 📠 01995 600950
e-mail: reception@ghgc.co.uk
web: www.garstanghotelandgolf.co.uk

dir: *M6 junct 32 take 1st right after Rogers Esso garage on A6 onto B6430. Continue for 1m and hotel on left*

This smart, purpose-built hotel enjoys a peaceful location alongside its own 18-hole golf course. Comfortable and spacious bedrooms are well equipped for both business and leisure guests, whilst inviting public areas include a choice of bars, one serving food, and a restaurant.

Rooms 32 en suite (16 GF) ⊘ in 20 bedrooms S £60-£95; D £85-£100 (incl. bkfst) **Facilities** STV ♨ 18 Golf driving range **Conf** Thtr 200 Class 100 Board 80 Del from £75 **Services** Lift **Parking** 172 **Notes LB** ⊗ ⊘ in restaurant Civ Wed 250

★★★ 68% HOTEL

Crofters

New Rd, A6 Cabus PR3 1PH
☎ 01995 604128 📠 01995 601646
e-mail: crofters@mitchellshotels.co.uk

dir: *on A6, midway between junc 32 & 33 of M6*

This is an attractive hotel close to the charming market town of Garstang. Bedrooms are spacious and well equipped, and meals are available either in the Crofters restaurant or the tavern bar. There are also extensive function facilities.

Rooms 21 en suite (4 fmly) **Facilities** STV ♫ Xmas **Conf** Thtr 200 Class 120 Board 50 Del £90 **Parking** 200 **Notes** Civ Wed 80

KIRKHAM MAP 18 SD43

BUDGET HOTEL

Premier Travel Inn Blackpool (Kirkham)

Fleetwood Rd, Greenhalgh PR4 3HE
☎ 0870 9906636 📠 0870 9906637
web: www.premiertravelinn.com

dir: *Exit M6 junct 32, take M55 to Blackpool. Inn just off junct 3 towards Kirkham, left of rdbt*

High quality, modern budget accommodation ideal for both families and business travellers. Spacious, en suite bedrooms feature bath and shower, satellite TV and many have telephones and modem points. The adjacent family restaurant features a wide and varied menu. For further details consult the Hotel Groups page.

Rooms 28 en suite

LANCASTER MAP 18 SD46

★★★★ 73% ⊛ HOTEL

Best Western Lancaster House

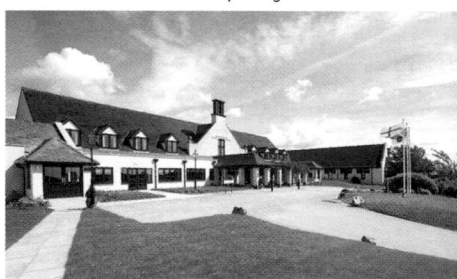

Green Ln, Ellel LA1 4GJ
☎ 01524 844822 📠 01524 844766
e-mail: lancaster@elhmail.co.uk
web: www.elh.co.uk/hotels/lancaster

dir: *M6 junct 33 N towards Lancaster. Through Galgate and into Green Ln. Hotel before university on right*

This modern hotel enjoys a rural setting south of the city and close to the university. The attractive open-plan reception and lounge boast a roaring log fire in colder months. Bedrooms are spacious, and the newer rooms are particularly well equipped for business guests. Public areas include extensive leisure facilities and a function suite.

Rooms 99 en suite (29 fmly) (44 GF) ⊘ in 79 bedrooms S £94-£146; D £94-£146 **Facilities** Spa STV ☒ supervised Sauna Solarium Gym Jacuzzi Wi-fi available Beauty salon, Outside Hot tub ♫ Xmas **Conf** BC Thtr 200 Class 60 Board 48 Del from £110 **Parking** 120 **Notes LB** ⊘ in restaurant Civ Wed 100

★★★ 61% HOTEL

The Mill Inn at Conder Green

Thurnham Mill Ln, Conder Green LA2 0BD
☎ 01524 752852 📠 01524 752477
e-mail: thurnham@mitchellshotels.co.uk

dir: *M6 junct 33 onto A6 towards Galgate, left at lights, 1st left, continue for 2m, hotel on left of bridge.*

This converted cloth mill dates from the 16th century and lies only a few miles from the M6 on the Lancaster Canal. Now refurbished with spacious

continued

bedrooms that include a number of family rooms. Dinner can be enjoyed overlooking the canal, or on sunny days on a popular terrace.

Rooms 15 en suite (1 fmly) S £50-£55; D £70-£75 (incl. bkfst)
Facilities STV FTV **Services** Lift **Parking** 50 **Notes** LB ⊘ in restaurant

★★ 65% **HOTEL**

The Greaves Hotel

Greaves Rd LA1 4UN
☎ 01524 63943 ▤ 01524 382679
e-mail: greaves@mitchellshotels.co.uk
dir: M6 junct 34 signed Lancaster, through town centre, signed M6 S, hotel on right after hospital.

Located to the south of the city centre, this popular hotel receives a good local following as the comfortable open-plan public areas are good places to enjoy a range of real ales and bar meals. Bedrooms are well equipped with both practical and homely extras.

Rooms 16 en suite (4 fmly) **Facilities** STV **Conf** Thtr 60 Class 40 Board 30 **Parking** 35 **Notes** ⊗ ⊘ in restaurant

Ⓤ

Swallow Royal Kings Arms

Market St LA1 1HP
☎ 01524 32451 ▤ 01524 841698
e-mail: generalmanager.lancaster@swallowhotels.com
web: www.swallowhotels.com
dir: M6 junct 33 towards centre near castle. Hotel at lights

At the time of going to press, the star classification for this hotel was not confirmed. Please refer to the AA internet site www.theAA.com for current information.

Rooms 55 en suite (15 fmly) ⊘ in 18 bedrooms S £68; D £85 (incl. bkfst) **Facilities** Xmas **Conf** Thtr 100 Class 50 Board 40 Del from £80 **Services** Lift **Parking** 26 **Notes** LB ⊘ in restaurant Civ Wed 100

BUDGET HOTEL

Premier Travel Inn Lancaster

Lancaster Business Park, Caton Rd LA1 3PE
☎ 0870 977 290 ▤ 01524 384801
web: www.premiertravelinn.com

High quality, modern budget accommodation ideal for both families and business travellers. Spacious, en suite bedrooms feature bath and shower, satellite TV and many have telephones and modem points. The adjacent family restaurant features a wide and varied menu. For further details consult the Hotel Groups page.

Rooms 60 en suite

LANGHO MAP 18 SD73

★★ 74% **HOTEL**

The Avenue

Brockhall Village BB6 8AY
☎ 01254 244811 ▤ 01254 244812
e-mail: bookingenquiries@theavenuehotel.co.uk
dir: exit A59 by Northcote Manor, follow for 1m. Right then 1st left into Brockhall Village

One of the Ribble Valley's newer hotels, The Avenue offers a modern and relaxed atmosphere throughout. The bedrooms are especially
continued

stylish being very well equipped and delightfully furnished. A wide range of dishes are available in the café bar/restaurant, and good conference facilities are on offer.

Rooms 21 en suite (9 fmly) (11 GF) ⊘ in 11 bedrooms S £55-£65; D £60-£70 (incl. bkfst) **Facilities** STV ♫ Xmas **Conf** Thtr 50 Class 30 Board 40 Del from £50 **Parking** 30 **Notes** LB ⊗ Closed 24-25 Dec Civ Wed 60

◉◉◉ **RESTAURANT WITH ROOMS**

Northcote Manor

Northcote Rd BB6 8BE
☎ 01254 240555 ▤ 01254 246568
e-mail: sales@northcotemanor.com
web: www.northcotemanor.com

Northcote Manor is a gastronomic haven where many guests return to sample the delights of its famous kitchen, which has twice in the past produced the Young Chef of the Year. Excellent cooking includes much of Lancashire's finest fare. Drinks can be enjoyed in the comfortable, elegantly furnished lounges and bar. Bedrooms have been individually furnished and thoughtfully equipped.

Rooms 14 en suite (4 GF) **Facilities** STV ⚜ Clay & game shooting **Conf** Thtr 40 Class 20 Board 26 **Parking** 50 **Notes** LB ⊗ Closed 25 Dec, 1 Jan & most BHs Civ Wed 40

See advert on this page

Northcote Road, Langho, Blackburn, Lancs. BB6 8BE

Tel: 01254 240555 Fax: 01254 246568
Web: www.northcotemanor.com

Northcote Manor is situated in the Ribble Valley, Lancashire. This fourteen bedroom country house hotel is a gourmet landmark that is internationally famous for its outstanding hospitality. Elegant wood panelling, warm welcoming lounges, beautiful gardens with organic vegetables, herbs and fruits.

Famous for its regional food and excellent wine, you can enjoy a Gourmet Overnight from £137.50 pp inc. overnight accommodation, English breakfast, champagne & canapés followed by a 5-course gourmet dinner.

LEYLAND
MAP 15 SD52

★★★ 81% HOTEL

Best Western Leyland
Leyland Way PR5 2JX
☎ 01772 422922 📠 01772 622282
e-mail: leylandhotel@feathers.uk.com
web: www.feathers.uk.com

dir: M6 junct 28, left at end of slip road, hotel 100mtrs on left

This purpose-built hotel enjoys a convenient location, just off the M6, within easy reach of Preston and Blackpool. Spacious public areas include J28 Meetings, lounge and café bar and the Four Seasons restaurant. Amenities include extensive conference and banqueting facilities as well as a smart leisure club.

Rooms 93 en suite (4 fmly) (31 GF) ⊛ in 62 bedrooms S £55-£99; D £65-£109 (incl. bkfst) **Facilities Spa** STV 🕏 supervised Sauna Solarium Gym Jacuzzi Wi-fi available Sculpture gardens Xmas **Conf** BC Thtr 500 Class 250 Board 250 Del from £95 **Parking** 150 **Notes LB** ⊛ in restaurant Civ Wed 200

LYTHAM ST ANNES
MAP 18 SD32

★★★★ 79% ⊛ HOTEL

Clifton Arms Hotel
West Beach, Lytham FY8 5QJ
☎ 01253 739898 📠 01253 730657
e-mail: welcome@cliftonarms-lytham.com
web: www.cliftonarms-lytham.com
dir: on A584 along seafront

This well established hotel occupies a prime position overlooking Lytham Green and the Ribble estuary beyond. Bedrooms vary in size and style but all are appointed to a high standard; front-facing rooms are particularly spacious and enjoy splendid views. There is an elegant restaurant, a stylish open-plan lounge and cocktail bar as well as function and conference facilities.

Rooms 48 en suite (2 fmly) ⊛ in 44 bedrooms S £100-£130; D £130-£160 (incl. bkfst) **Facilities** STV Wi-fi in bedrooms ch fac Xmas **Conf** Thtr 200 Class 100 Board 60 Del from £139 **Services** Lift **Parking** 50 **Notes LB** ⊛ ⊛ in restaurant Civ Wed 100

See advert on opposite page

★★★★ 76% HOTEL

Grand
South Promenade FY8 1NB
☎ 01253 721288 📠 01253 714459
e-mail: book@the-grand.co.uk
web: www.the-grand.co.uk

dir: M6 junct 32 take M55 to Blackpool then A5230 to South Shore. Follow signs for St Annes

This beautiful Victorian property stands in its own grounds with wonderful views of the coastline; Royal Lytham and other major golf courses are within easy reach. Elegant public areas include a contemporary restaurant and bar, an inviting lounge, extensive function facilities and an impressive leisure club. Stylish, well-equipped bedrooms include a number of stunning spacious executive rooms and suites.

Rooms 55 en suite (4 GF) ⊛ in all bedrooms **Facilities Spa** STV 🕏 supervised Sauna Solarium Gym 💆 Jacuzzi **Conf** Thtr 160 Class 80 Board 30 **Services** Lift **Parking** 75 **Notes LB** ⊛ ⊛ in restaurant Closed 24-26 Dec Civ Wed 150

★★★ 79% HOTEL

Bedford
307-311 Clifton Dr South FY8 1HN
☎ 01253 724636 📠 01253 729244
e-mail: reservations@bedford-hotel.com
web: www.bedford-hotel.com

dir: from M55 follow signs for airport to last lights. Left through 2 sets of lights. Hotel 300yds on left

This popular family-run hotel, close to the town centre and the seafront, has been stylishly extended. Bedrooms vary in size and style and include family and four-poster rooms. Newer bedrooms are particularly elegant and tastefully appointed. Spacious public areas include a choice of lounges, a coffee shop, fitness facilities and an impressive function suite.

Rooms 45 en suite (10 fmly) (6 GF) ⊛ in all bedrooms S £52-£60; D £82-£90 (incl. bkfst) **Facilities** STV Gym Wi-fi in bedrooms Xmas **Conf** Thtr 200 Class 140 Board 60 **Services** Lift **Parking** 25 **Notes LB** ⊛ ⊛ in restaurant Civ Wed 200

★★★ 75% HOTEL

Chadwick
THE INDEPENDENTS
South Promenade FY8 1NP
☎ 01253 720061 📠 01253 714455
e-mail: sales@thechadwickhotel.com
web: www.thechadwickhotel.com

dir: M6 junct 32 take M55 to Blackpool then A5230 to South Shore. Follow signs for St Annes

This popular, comfortable and traditional hotel enjoys a seafront location. Bedrooms vary in size and style, but all are very thoughtfully equipped; those at the front boast panoramic sea views. Public rooms are spacious and comfortably furnished and the smart bar is stocked with some 200 malt whiskies. The hotel has a well-equipped, air-conditioned gym and indoor pool.

Rooms 75 en suite (28 fmly) (13 GF) S £49-£52; D £68-£88 (incl. bkfst) **Facilities Spa** STV 🕏 Sauna Solarium Gym Jacuzzi Wi-fi in bedrooms Turkish bath Games room Soft play adventure area 🎵 ch fac Xmas **Conf** Thtr 72 Class 24 Board 28 Del from £65 **Services** Lift **Parking** 40 **Notes LB** ⊛ ⊛ in restaurant

See advert on opposite page

★★★ 75% HOTEL

Dalmeny House

19-33 South Promenade FY8 1LX
☎ 01253 712236 📠 01253 724447
e-mail: reservations@dalmeyhotel.co.uk
web: www.dalmenyhotel.co.uk

The Dalmeny is an established, friendly, family run hotel which offers spacious attractive accommodation. There is a choice of eating options including the Patio café bar, the Carvery and the more formal Atrium restaurant. There is also a well equipped leisure centre and a large indoor swimming pool.

Rooms 128 en suite (68 fmly) (11 GF) S £62.90-£105; D £85.80-£157 (incl. bkfst) **Facilities Spa** STV 🏊 Squash Sauna Solarium Gym Jacuzzi Beauty salon Aerobics centre. 🎵 Xmas **Conf** BC Thtr 150 Class 80 Board 50 Del from £112 **Services** Lift **Parking** 120 **Notes LB** ⊗ ⊜ in restaurant Closed 24-26 Dec

See advert on this page

★★★ 74% HOTEL

Best Western Glendower Hotel

North Promenade FY8 2NQ
☎ 01253 723241 📠 01253 640069
e-mail: recp@theglendowerhotel.co.uk
web: www.theglendowerhotel.com

dir: *M55 follow airport signs. Left at Promenade to St Annes. Hotel 500yds from pier*

Located on the seafront and with easy access to the town centre, this
continued on page 384

England

LYTHAM ST ANNES *continued*

popular, friendly hotel offers comfortably furnished, well-equipped accommodation. Bedrooms vary in size and style and include four-poster rooms and very popular family suites. Public areas feature a choice of smart, comfortable lounges, a bright and modern leisure club and function facilities.

Rooms 60 en suite (17 fmly) ⊛ in 12 bedrooms S £85-£130; D £110-£130 (incl. bkfst) **Facilities Spa** STV 🔄 supervised Snooker Sauna Solarium Gym Jacuzzi Wi-fi in bedrooms Childrens playroom, full size snooker table 🎵 Xmas **Conf** Thtr 150 Class 120 Board 50 Del from £90 **Services** Lift **Parking** 45 **Notes LB** ⊗ ⊛ in restaurant

★★ 72% **HOTEL**

Lindum

63-67 South Promenade FY8 1LZ
☎ 01253 721534 722516 ▤ 01253 721364
e-mail: info@lindumhotel.co.uk
web: www.lindumhotel.co.uk

dir: *from M55 follow A5230 & signs for Blackpool Airport. After airport, left at lights to St Annes, right at lights in town centre. 1st left onto seafront. Hotel 250yds on left*

The same family has run this friendly and popular seafront hotel for over 40 years. Well-equipped bedrooms are generally spacious and some enjoy superb coastal views. Extensive, stylish public areas include a choice of lounges and a popular health suite. The open-plan restaurant offers a good choice of well-cooked dishes at breakfast and dinner.

Rooms 76 en suite (25 fmly) ⊛ in all bedrooms **Facilities** Sauna Solarium Jacuzzi **Conf** Thtr 80 Class 30 Board 25 **Services** Lift air con **Parking** 20 **Notes LB** ⊛ in restaurant

BUDGET HOTEL

Premier Travel Inn Lytham St Annes

Church Rd FY8 5LH
☎ 0870 9906548 ▤ 0870 9906549
web: www.premiertravelinn.com

dir: *M55/A584 coast road. Follow station signs, Church Rd just behind Lytham Station*

High quality, modern budget accommodation ideal for both families and business travellers. Spacious, en suite bedrooms feature bath and shower, satellite TV and many have telephones and modem points. The adjacent family restaurant features a wide and varied menu. For further details consult the Hotel Groups page.

Rooms 22 en suite

MORECAMBE   MAP 18 SD46

★★★ 72% **HOTEL**

Elms

Bare Village LA4 6DD
☎ 01524 411501 ▤ 01524 831979
e-mail: elms@mitchellshotels.co.uk

dir: *M6 junct 34, follow Morecambe signs to large rdbt. Take 4th exit into Hall Drive which becomes Bare Lane. Over rail crossing. Hotel 200yds on right*

This long-established hotel lies just off the North Promenade and is popular with business and leisure guests. Public rooms include a

continued

spacious lounge bar, a classical style restaurant, function facilities and a pub in the grounds.

Rooms 39 en suite (3 fmly) ⊛ in 30 bedrooms S £45-£65; D £70-£90 (incl. bkfst) **Facilities** STV Wi-fi available Xmas **Conf** Thtr 200 Class 72 Board 60 Del from £65 **Services** Lift **Parking** 80 **Notes LB** ⊛ in restaurant Civ Wed 100

★★★ 68% **HOTEL**

Clarendon

76 Marine Rd West, West End Promenade LA4 4EP
☎ 01524 410180 ▤ 01524 421616
e-mail: clarendon@mitchellshotels.co.uk

dir: *M6 junct 34 follow Morecambe signs. At rdbt with 'The Shrimp' on corner 1st exit to Westgate, follow to seafront. Right at traffic lights, hotel 3rd block*

This traditional seafront hotel offers modern facilities, and several long serving key staff ensure guests a home-from-home atmosphere. Well maintained throughout, it offers bright, cheerful public areas and ample convenient parking.

Rooms 29 en suite (4 fmly) ⊛ in 10 bedrooms S £50-£60; D £70-£90 (incl. bkfst) **Facilities** STV Wi-fi in bedrooms Xmas **Conf** Thtr 90 Class 40 Board 40 Del from £75 **Services** Lift **Parking** 22 **Notes LB** ⊛ in restaurant Civ Wed 60

PRESTON   MAP 18 SD52

See also Garstang

★★★★ 76% ⊛ **HOTEL**

Barton Grange

Garstang Rd PR3 5AA
☎ 01772 862551 ▤ 01772 861267
e-mail: stay@bartongrangehotel.com
web: www.bartongrange.co.uk

CLASSIC
BRITISH HOTELS

(For full entry see Barton)

★★★★ 76% **HOTEL**

Preston Marriott Hotel

Garstang Rd, Broughton PR3 5JB
☎ 01772 864087 ▤ 01772 861728
e-mail: reservations.preston@marriotthotels.co.uk
web: www.prestonmarriott.co.uk

Marriott
HOTELS & RESORTS

dir: *M6 junct 32 onto M55 junct 1, follow A6 towards Garstang. Hotel 0.5m on right*

Exuding a country-club atmosphere this stylish hotel enjoys good links to both the city centre and motorway network. There are two dining

continued

options and the extensive leisure facilities ensure that there is plenty to do. The bedrooms are smartly decorated and equipped with a comprehensive range of extras.

Rooms 149 en suite (40 fmly) (63 GF) ⊘ in 93 bedrooms S £99-£112; D £99-£112 **Facilities Spa** STV ▸ supervised Sauna Solarium Gym Jacuzzi Wi-fi available Steam room, Beauty salon/hairdressing **Conf** BC Thtr 220 Class 100 Board 70 Del from £130 **Services** Lift air con **Parking** 250 **Notes LB** ⊗ ⊘ in restaurant Civ Wed 180

★★★ 78% ⊚ HOTEL

Pines

570 Preston Rd, Clayton-Le-Woods PR6 7ED
☎ 01772 338551 ▤ 01772 629002
e-mail: mail@thepineshotel.co.uk
dir: on A6, 1m S of M6 junct 29

This unique and stylish hotel sits in four acres of mature grounds just a short drive from the motorway network. Elegant bedrooms are individually designed and offer high levels of comfort and facilities. Day rooms include a smart bar and Haworths brasserie, while extensive function rooms make this hotel a popular venue for weddings.

Rooms 37 en suite (12 fmly) (14 GF) ⊘ in 21 bedrooms **Facilities** STV ♫ **Conf** BC Thtr 200 Class 150 Board 60 **Parking** 120 **Notes** ⊗ Closed 26 Dec Civ Wed 150

★★★ 73% HOTEL

Macdonald Tickled Trout

Preston New Rd, Samlesbury PR5 0UJ
☎ 0870 1942120 ▤ 01772 877463
e-mail: tickledtrout@macdonald-hotels.co.uk
web: www.macdonald-hotels.co.uk
dir: close to M6 junct 31

On the banks of the River Ribble, this hotel is conveniently located for the motorway, making it a popular venue for both business and leisure guests. Smartly appointed bedrooms are all tastefully decorated and equipped with a thoughtful range of extras. The hotel boasts a stylish wing of meeting rooms.

Rooms 102 en suite (6 fmly) ⊘ in all bedrooms S £65-£95; D £85-£115 (incl. bkfst) **Facilities** STV Fishing Wi-fi in bedrooms ♫ Xmas **Conf** BC Thtr 120 Class 60 Board 50 Del from £115 **Services** Lift **Parking** 240 **Notes LB** ⊘ in restaurant Civ Wed 100

★★★ 70% HOTEL

Novotel Preston

Reedfield Place, Walton Summit PR5 8AA
☎ 01772 313331 ▤ 01772 627868
e-mail: H0838@accor-hotels.com
web: www.novotel.com

dir: M6 junct 29, M61 junct 9, then A6 Chorley Road. Hotel next to Bamber Bridge rdbt

The hotel is ideally located just off main motorway networks. Bedrooms are spacious with additional bed space and an ample desk area and making them ideal for both families or business travellers. Flexible dining is a feature with the Garden Brassiere, open throughout the day until midnight. The hotel also boasts an outdoor pool and children's play area.

Rooms 95 en suite (17 fmly) (28 GF) ⊘ in 48 bedrooms S £50-£62; D £50-£62 **Facilities** STV ▸ Wi-fi in bedrooms **Conf** BC Thtr 180 Class 80 Board 52 Del from £95 **Services** Lift **Parking** 140 **Notes LB** ⊘ in restaurant RS 22 Dec-2 Jan

England

England

PRESTON *continued*

★★ 72% HOTEL

Haighton Manor Country House

Haighton Green Ln, Haighton PR2 5SQ
☎ 01772 663170 🖹 01772 663171
e-mail: info@haightonmanor.com
web: www.haightonmanor.com

dir: Off A6 onto Durton Rd, or from M6 junct 32 right at rdbt &
right onto Durton Rd. Right at end into Haighton Lane. Hotel 2m
on left

Located in sleepy, rolling countryside just ten minutes to the east of
city, this impressive hotel is ideally situated for both the business and
leisure guest. External appearances are deceptive, for once inside, this
17th-century manor house has ultra-modern bedrooms (including
modem points) and stylishly fashioned day rooms providing a
wonderful fusion of ancient and modern. Wide-ranging creative
menus can be sampled in the candlelit restaurant. This hotel is a
popular wedding venue.

Rooms 8 en suite (2 fmly) ⊛ in all bedrooms S £70-£110; D £90-£150
(incl. bkfst) **Facilities** STV Jacuzzi ♫ Xmas **Conf** BC Thtr 100 Class 80
Board 80 Del from £120 **Parking** 70 **Notes LB** ⊗ ⊛ in restaurant
Civ Wed 90

★ 67% HOTEL

Claremont

516 Blackpool Rd, Ashton-on-Ribble PR2 1HY
☎ 01772 729738 🖹 01772 726274

dir: M6 junct 31 onto A59 towards Preston. Right at hilltop rdbt
onto A583. Hotel on right past pub and over bridge

This family run hotel offers a relaxed and informal atmosphere for its
mainly business clientele. Bedrooms are comfortable and well
equipped, whilst public areas include a cosy bar lounge and adjacent
dining room offering a modest choice of good value home-cooked
dishes during the week.

Rooms 10 en suite **Conf** Thtr 85 Class 45 Board 50 **Parking** 27
Notes ⊗

Ⓤ

Swallow Preston

Preston New Rd, Samlesbury PR5 0UL   SWALLOW
☎ 01772 877351 & 872703 🖹 01772 877424
e-mail: reservation.preston@swallowhotels.com
web: www.swallowhotels.com

dir: M6 junct 31 signed for Clitheroe/Blackburn. Follow dual
carriageway up hill, hotel on left before lights

At the time of going to press, the star classification for this hotel was
not confirmed. Please refer to the AA internet site www.theAA.com for
current information.

Rooms 78 en suite (6 fmly) (26 GF) ⊛ in 52 bedrooms S £50-£85;
D £60-£95 (incl. bkfst) **Facilities** Spa STV ⛹ supervised Sauna
Solarium Gym Jacuzzi Health and beauty treatments Xmas **Conf** Thtr 250
Class 100 Board 60 Del from £95 **Services** Lift **Parking** 150 **Notes** ⊛ in
restaurant Civ Wed 250

BUDGET HOTEL

Hotel Ibis

Garstang Rd, Broughton PR3 5JE
☎ 01772 861800 🖹 01772 861900
e-mail: H3162@accor-hotels.com
web: www.ibishotel.com

dir: M6 junct 32, then M55 junct 1. Left lane onto A6. Left at slip
road, left again at mini-rdbt. 2nd turn, hotel on right past pub

Modern, budget hotel offering comfortable accommodation in bright
and practical bedrooms. Breakfast is self-service and dinner is available
in the restaurant. For further details, consult the Hotel Groups page.

Rooms 82 en suite S £41.95-£45.95; D £41.95-£45.95 **Conf** Thtr 30
Class 20 Board 20

BUDGET HOTEL

Premier Travel Inn Preston East

Bluebell Way, Preston East Link Rd, Fulwood PR2 5PZ
☎ 08701 977215 🖹 01772 651619
web: www.premiertravelinn.com

dir: M6 junct 31A left at rdbt, follow ring road under motorway &
Inn on left. No junction for southbound traffic so take junct 31 &
join motorway northbound, take exit off junct 31A

High quality, modern budget accommodation ideal for both families
and business travellers. Spacious, en suite bedrooms feature bath and
shower, satellite TV and many have telephones and modem points.
The adjacent family restaurant features a wide and varied menu. For
further details consult the Hotel Groups page.

Rooms 65 en suite **Conf** Thtr 20

Premier Travel Inn Preston South

Lostock Ln, Bamber Bridge PR5 6BA
☎ 0870 9906462 🖹 0870 9906463

dir: Off M65 junct 1 (0.5m from M6 junct 29) close to rdbt of
A582 & A6

Rooms 40 en suite **Conf** Thtr 30 Board 30

Premier Travel Inn Preston West

Blackpool Rd, Lea PR4 0XB
☎ 08701 977214 🖹 01772 729971
dir: off A583, opposite Texaco garage.
Rooms 38 en suite

BUDGET HOTEL

Travelodge Preston Central

Preston Farmers Office, New Hall Ln PR1 5JX
☎ 08700 850 950
web: www.travelodge.co.uk

dir: Exit M6 at junct 31. Follow signs for Preston. Travelodge on
right.

Travelodge offers good quality, good value, modern accommodation.
Ideal for families, the spacious en suite bedrooms include remote-
control TV, tea and coffee-making facilities and comfortable beds.
Meals can be taken at the nearby family restaurant. See Hotel Groups
pages for further details.

Rooms 72 en suite S fr £26; D fr £26

ST ANNES
See Lytham St Annes

WREA GREEN
MAP 18 SD33

★★★ 74% **HOTEL**

Villa Country House
Moss Side Ln PR4 2PE

☎ 01772 684347 ▤ 01772 687647

e-mail: info@villahotel-wreagreen.co.uk

dir: M55 junct 3 follow signs to Kirkham at Wrea Green follow signs to Hytham

This 19th-century residence stands in a peaceful location close to the village of Wrea Green. There are extensive bars and a good range of quality food is served either in the bar or the many-roomed restaurant. The modern, air-conditioned bedrooms are very well designed. The staff are friendly and helpful.

Rooms 25 en suite (1 fmly) (10 GF) ⊗ in all bedrooms S £90; D £105 (incl. bkfst) **Facilities** STV Xmas **Conf** Thtr 60 Class 15 Board 14 Del £150 **Services** Lift **Parking** 75 **Notes LB** ⊗ in restaurant Civ Wed 60

LEICESTERSHIRE

ASHBY-DE-LA-ZOUCH
MAP 11 SK31

★★★ Ⓐ

Royal
Station Raod LE65 2GP

☎ 01530 412833 ▤ 01530 564548

e-mail: theroyalhotel@email.com

web: www.royalhotelashby.com

dir: A42 junct 12, 3m hotel on right

Rooms 34 rms (33 en suite) (5 fmly) ⊗ in 23 bedrooms S £40-£70; D £70-£90 (incl. bkfst) **Facilities** STV Wi-fi available ♫ **Conf** Thtr 70 Class 26 Board 26 Del £105 **Parking** 100 **Notes** ⊗ in restaurant

BUDGET HOTEL

Premier Travel Inn Ashby de la Zouch
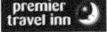

Flagstaff Island, Flagstaff Park LE65 1DS

☎ 08701 977281 ▤ 01530 561211

web: www.premiertravelinn.com

dir: Exit M1 junct 23a, follow signs for A42 (M42) to Tamworth and Birmingham. Inn just off rdbt at junct 13 of A42

High quality, modern budget accommodation ideal for both families and business travellers. Spacious, en suite bedrooms feature bath and
continued

---

shower, satellite TV and many have telephones and modem points. The adjacent family restaurant features a wide and varied menu. For further details consult the Hotel Groups page.

Rooms 40 en suite

CASTLE DONINGTON
See Nottingham East Midlands Airport

COALVILLE
MAP 11 SK41

★★ 67% **HOTEL**

Charnwood Arms Hotel
Beveridge Ln, Bardon Hill LE67 1TB

☎ 01530 813644 ▤ 01530 815425

e-mail: charnwoodarms.bardonhill@nhg.uk

dir: M1 junct 22, on A511 towards Coalville at 2nd rdbt. Stay left & hotel on right

This popular inn is conveniently located only a few minutes' drive from the M1. Public areas include a spacious open-plan lounge bar and restaurant offering a selection of cask ales and serving food throughout the day. The extremely well equipped bedrooms are situated around a courtyard.

Rooms 34 en suite ⊗ in 5 bedrooms **Conf** Thtr 200 Class 80 Board 80 **Parking** 200 **Notes** ⊗ Civ Wed 100

HINCKLEY
MAP 11 SP49

★★★★ 79% ⊛⊛ **HOTEL**

Best Western Sketchley Grange

Sketchley Ln, Burbage LE10 3HU

☎ 01455 251133 ▤ 01455 631384

e-mail: info@sketchleygrange.co.uk

web: www.bw-sketchleygrange.co.uk

dir: SE of town, off A5/M69 junct 1, take B4109 to Hinckley. Left at 2nd rdbt. 1st right onto Sketchley Lane

Close to motorway connections, this hotel is peacefully set in its own grounds, and enjoys open country views. Extensive leisure facilities include a stylish health and leisure spa with a crèche. Modern meeting facilities, a choice of bars, and two dining options, together with comfortable bedrooms furnished with many extras, make this a special hotel.

Rooms 52 en suite (9 fmly) (1 GF) ⊗ in 15 bedrooms S £50-£120; D £50-£140 **Facilities** Spa STV 🝙 supervised Sauna Solarium Gym Jacuzzi Wi-fi in bedrooms Steam room, Hairdressing, Creche, Beauty therapy ♫ ch fac **Conf** BC Thtr 300 Class 150 Board 30 Del from £125 **Services** Lift **Parking** 200 **Notes LB** ⊗ in restaurant Civ Wed 300

See advert on page 389

★★★★ 72% **HOTEL**

Paramount Hinckley Island Hotel
Watling St (A5) LE10 3JA

☎ 01455 631122 ▤ 01455 634536

e-mail: hinckleyisland@paramount-hotels.co.uk

web: www.paramount-hotels.co.uk

dir: on A5, S of junct 1 on M69

A large hotel offering good facilities for both conference and business guests. Bedrooms, many being refurbished, are spacious with the Club
continued on page 388

HINCKLEY *continued*

Floors providing high levels of comfort and workspace. A choice of dining styles is available in the Brasserie or Conservatory restaurants, and there is a pleasant leisure centre.

Hinckley Island Hotel

Rooms 350 en suite (156 fmly) (14 GF) ✪ in 200 bedrooms S £80-£160; D £80-£160 **Facilities Spa** 🔃 supervised Sauna Solarium Gym Putt green Jacuzzi Wi-fi available Steam room **Conf** BC Thtr 400 Class 180 Board 38 Del from £99 **Services** Lift air con **Parking** 600 **Notes LB** ⊗ ✪ in restaurant Civ Wed 350

★★ 78% HOTEL

Kings Hotel & Restaurant

13/19 Mount Rd LE10 1AD

☎ 01455 637193 📠 01455 636201

e-mail: info@kings-hotel.net

web: www.kings-hotel.net

dir: follow A447 signed to Hinckley. Under railway bridge, right at rdbt. 1st road left opposite railway station, then 3rd right

A friendly atmosphere exists at this privately owned and managed hotel, which is situated in a quiet road within easy walking distance of the town centre and station. Bedrooms are tastefully decorated and have attractive furnishings. The public rooms include a residents' lounge, a lounge-bar and a large restaurant.

Rooms 7 en suite ✪ in all bedrooms S £64.90-£74.90; D £74.90-£84.90 (incl. bkfst) **Facilities Spa** STV **Conf** Thtr 30 Class 40 Board 20 Del from £120 **Parking** 20 **Notes LB** ⊗ No children 10yrs ✪ in restaurant

KEGWORTH

See **Nottingham East Midlands Airport**

KIRBY MUXLOE   MAP 11 SK50

★★ 65% HOTEL

Castle Hotel & Restaurant

Main St LE9 2AP

☎ 0116 239 5337 📠 0116 238 7868

e-mail: thecastle.kirbymuxloe@snr.co.uk

dir: M1 junct 21a (N'bound), follow Kirby Muxloe signs into village. Hotel on main road

This attractive, creeper-clad former farmhouse dates back to the 16th century, when it was built using stone and timbers taken from the nearby castle. The property features inglenook fireplaces and exposed

continued

timbers and open-plan public rooms include a lounge bar and restaurant with a non-smoking area. Bedrooms vary in size and style, and all are pleasantly decorated.

Castle Hotel & Restaurant

Rooms 22 en suite (3 fmly) (4 GF) S £55; D £60 **Conf** Thtr 150 Class 100 Board 100 Del from £25 **Notes** ⊗ Civ Wed 100

LEICESTER   MAP 11 SK50

See also **Rothley**

★★★★ 77% HOTEL

Leicester Marriott   **Marriott**
HOTELS & RESORTS

Smith Way, Grove Park, Enderby LE19 1SW

☎ 0116 282 0100 📠 0116 282 0101

e-mail: eventsales.leicester@marriotthotels.co.uk

web: www.marriott.co.uk/emalm

dir: Exit M1 junct 21. Take slip road for A563 signed Leicester. At rdbt take 1st left A563. take right lane, at 2nd slip road turn right. At rdbt take last exit, hotel straight ahead

This new purpose-built hotel has a popular brasserie, cocktail bar, atrium lounge, indoor heated pool, gym, sauna and steam room. Some of bedrooms are executive rooms with access to the executive lounge. There are 18 meeting rooms that provide conference facilities for up to 400 delegates, and parking is extensive.

Rooms 227 en suite (91 fmly) ✪ in 30 bedrooms S £99-£125; D £99-£125 **Facilities** STV Wi-fi available 🔃 supervised Sauna Gym ⬥ **Conf** BC Thtr 400 Class 180 Board 52 Del from £130 **Services** Lift air con **Parking** 280 **Notes LB** ⊗ ✪ in restaurant

★★★ 85% ⊛ HOTEL

Best Western Belmont House

De Montfort St LE1 7GR

☎ 0116 254 4773 📠 0116 247 0804

e-mail: info@belmonthotel.co.uk

web: www.belmonthotel.co.uk

dir: from A6, take 1st right after rail station. Hotel 200yds on left

This well established hotel, under the same family ownership, has been welcoming guests for over 70 years. It is conveniently situated within easy walking distance of the railway station and city centre though it sits in a quiet leafy residential area. Extensive public rooms

continued

England

are smartly appointed and include the informal Bowie's Bistro, Jamie's Bar with its relaxed atmosphere, and formal dining in the Cherry Restaurant.

Best Western Belmont House

Rooms 77 en suite (7 fmly) ⊗ in 57 bedrooms S £110-£135; D £120-£140 **Facilities** STV Gym Wi-fi in bedrooms A Small Fibers Room **Conf** Thtr 175 Class 75 Board 65 Del from £140 **Services** Lift **Parking** 75 **Notes LB** ⊗ in restaurant Closed 25-26 Dec Civ Wed 120

★★★ 79% **HOTEL**

Ramada Leicester

® R A M A D A.

Granby St LE1 6ES

☎ 0116 255 5599 📠 0116 254 4736

e-mail: sales.leicester@ramadajarvis.co.uk

web: www.ramadajarvis.co.uk

dir: A5460 into city. Follow Leicester Central Station signs. Granby Street is left off St. Georges Way (A594)

This Grade II listed Victorian hotel is set in the heart of the commercial and shopping centre. Although bedrooms vary in size, all offer modern amenities and comfort; there is a popular restaurant and ample private parking.

Rooms 104 en suite (4 fmly) ⊗ in 80 bedrooms S £90-£116; D £90-£135 **Facilities** STV Wi-fi available Xmas **Conf** Thtr 450 Class 200 Board 35 Del £147 **Services** Lift **Parking** 120 **Notes LB** ⊗ ⊗ in restaurant Civ Wed 60

★★★ 75% **HOTEL**

Best Western Leicester Stage Hotel

Best Western

Leicester Rd, Wigston LE18 1JW

☎ 0116 288 6161 📠 0116 257 3900

e-mail: reservations@stagehotel.co.uk

web: www.stagehotel.co.uk

dir: M69/M1 junct 21 take ring road S to Leicester. Follow Oadby & Wigston signs, right onto A5199 towards Northampton. Hotel on left

This striking, purpose-built, glass-fronted building is situated to the south of the city centre. Bedrooms vary in style and include executive rooms and four-poster bridal suites. Open-plan public areas include a lounge bar, restaurant and a further seating area in the entrance hall. Staff are friendly and nothing is too much trouble. Ample parking is an added bonus.

Rooms 77 en suite (10 fmly) (39 GF) ⊗ in 30 bedrooms S £69-£79; D £79-£89 (incl. bkfst) **Facilities** STV 🏊 supervised Sauna Gym Jacuzzi Wi-fi in bedrooms Steam room sauna and fully equipped gym Xmas **Conf** Thtr 500 Class 320 Board 120 Del from £100 **Parking** 200 **Notes LB** ⊗ ⊗ in restaurant Civ Wed 200

★★★ 72% **HOTEL**

Regency

360 London Rd LE2 2PL

☎ 0116 270 9634 📠 0116 270 1375

e-mail: info@the-regency-hotel.com

web: www.the-regency-hotel.com

dir: on A6, 1.5m from city centre

This friendly hotel is located on the edge of town and provides smart accommodation, suitable for both business and leisure guests. Dining options include an airy conservatory brasserie and a formal restaurant. A relaxing lounge and bar are also available, along with good conference and banqueting facilities. Bedrooms vary in size and style and include some spacious and stylishly appointed rooms.

Rooms 32 en suite (4 fmly) S £48-£55; D £62-£70 (incl. bkfst) **Facilities** STV Xmas **Conf** Thtr 50 Class 50 Board 25 Del from £92 **Parking** 40 **Notes** ⊗ ⊗ in restaurant

---

England

LEICESTER *continued*

★★★ 68% **HOTEL**

Westfield House Hotel

Enderby Rd, Blaby LE8 4GD

☎ 0116 278 7898 & 0870 609 6106

📠 0116 278 1974

dir: *M1 junct 21, A5460 to Leicester. 4th exit at 1st rdbt, ahead at 2nd, left at 3rd. Follow signs to Blaby, over 4th rdbt. Hotel on left*

This establishment is situated in a quiet location on the outskirts of the city, yet is convenient for the adjacent link road. Public areas include a bar/ brasserie, Hunters Restaurant, various meeting rooms and an extensive gym and indoor pool. Bedrooms are comfortably appointed and generally quite spacious; many are decorated to a very high standard.

Rooms 48 en suite (5 fmly) ⊗ in 36 bedrooms S £45-£94; D £45-£94
Facilities Spa 🏊 Sauna Solarium Gym Wi-fi available Steam room Xmas **Conf** Thtr 70 Class 30 Board 36 **Parking** 110 **Notes LB** ⊗ in restaurant Civ Wed 60

BUDGET HOTEL

Campanile Leicester

St Matthew's Way, 1 Bedford St North LE1 3JE

☎ 0116 261 6600 📠 0116 261 6601

e-mail: leicester@campanile-hotels.com

web: www.envergure.fr

dir: *A5460. Right at end of road, left at rdbt on A594. Follow Vaughan Way, Burleys Way then St. Matthews Way. Hotel on left*

This modern building offers accommodation in smart, well-equipped bedrooms, all with en suite bathrooms. Refreshments may be taken at the informal Bistro. For further details consult the Hotel Groups page.

Rooms 93 en suite **Conf** Thtr 40 Class 30 Board 30 Del from £70

BUDGET HOTEL

Days Inn Leicester Central

14-17 Abbey St LE1 3TE

☎ 0116 251 0666 & 0870 033 9633

📠 0870 033 9634

e-mail: stephen.hughes@daysinn.co.uk

web: www.welcomebreak.co.uk

This modern building offers accommodation in smart, spacious and well-equipped bedrooms, suitable for families and business travellers, and all with en suite bathrooms. Continental breakfast is available and other refreshments may be taken at the nearby family restaurant. For further details see the Hotel Groups page.

Rooms 73 en suite **Conf** Thtr 150 Class 100 Board 40

BUDGET HOTEL

Hotel Ibis

St Georges Way, Constitution Hill LE1 1PL

☎ 0116 248 7200 📠 0116 262 0880

e-mail: H3061@accor-hotels.com

web: www.accorhotels.com

dir: *From M1/M69 junct 21, follow town centre signs, central ring road (A594)/railway station, hotel opposite the Leicester Mercury.*

Modern, budget hotel offering comfortable accommodation in bright and practical bedrooms. Breakfast is self-service and dinner is available in the restaurant. For further details, consult the Hotel Groups page.

Rooms 94 en suite

BUDGET HOTEL

Innkeeper's Lodge Leicester

Hinckley Rd LE3 3PG

☎ 0116 238 7878

web: www.innkeeperslodge.com

Smart, en suite accommodation ideal for both business & leisure guests. Bedrooms are very well equipped, including Sky TV, telephone, modem points, tea & coffee making facilities, (family rooms in most locations). Complimentary breakfast. The adjacent Pub Restaurant; a Harvester, Vintage Inn, Toby Carvery, Ember Inn, Sizzling Pubco or Pub & Carvery offers an all day menu. See Hotel Groups pages for further details.

Rooms 31 rms S £47.95-£55; D £47.95-£55

BUDGET HOTEL

Premier Travel Inn Leicester Central

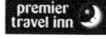

Heathley Park, Groby Rd LE3 9QF

☎ 0870 9906398 📠 0870 9906399

web: www.premiertravelinn.com

dir: *Off A50, city centre side of County Hall and Glenfield General Hospital*

High quality, modern budget accommodation ideal for both families and business travellers. Spacious, en suite bedrooms feature bath and shower, satellite TV and many have telephones and modem points. The adjacent family restaurant features a wide and varied menu. For further details consult the Hotel Groups page.

Rooms 72 en suite **Conf** Thtr 10 Class 10 Board 10

Premier Travel Inn Leicester (Forest East)

Hinckley Rd, Leicester Forest East LE3 3GD

☎ 08701 977155 ▤ 0116 239 3429

dir: M1 junct 21 onto A5460. At major junct (Holiday Inn on right), left into Braunstone Lane. After 2m , left onto A47 towards Hinkley. 400yds on left

Rooms 40 en suite **Conf** Thtr 50 Board 25

Premier Travel Inn Leicester North West

Leicester Rd, Glenfield LE3 8HB

☎ 0870 9906520 ▤ 0870 9906521

dir: Off A50, just before County Hall & Glenfield General Hospital. Into County Hall, Inn on left.

Rooms 43 en suite **Conf** Thtr 25 Class 20 Board 20

Premier Travel Inn Leicester South (Oadby)

Glen Rise, Oadby LE2 4RG

☎ 0870 9906452 ▤ 0870 9906453

dir: From M1 junct 21 A563 signed South. Right at Leicester racecourse. Follow Market Harborough signs. Dual carriageway, straight on at rdbt. Into single lane, hotel on right

Rooms 30 en suite **Conf** Thtr 10 Class 8 Board 10

Premier Travel Inn Leicester (Thorpe Astley)

Meridian Business Park, Meridian Way, Braunstone LE19 1LU

☎ 08701 977154 ▤ 0116 282 7486

dir: M1 junct 21 follow signs for A563 (outer ring road) W to Thorpe Astley. Slip road past Texaco garage, Inn on left.

Rooms 51 en suite **Conf** Class 20 Board 20

BUDGET HOTEL

Travelodge Leicester Central

Vaughan Way LE1 4NN

☎ 0870 1911755 ▤ 0116 251 0560

web: www.travelodge.co.uk

Travelodge offers good quality, good value, modern accommodation. Ideal for families, the spacious en suite bedrooms include remote control TV, tea and coffee-making facilities and comfortable beds. Meals can be taken at the nearby family restaurant. See Hotel Groups pages for further details.

Rooms 95 en suite S fr £26; D fr £26

LEICESTER FOREST **MAP 11 SK50**
MOTORWAY SERVICE AREA (M1)

BUDGET HOTEL

Days Inn Leicester Forest East

Leicester Forest East, Junction 21 M1 LE3 3GB

☎ 0116 239 0534 ▤ 0116 239 0546

e-mail: leicester.hotel@welcomebreak.co.uk

web: www.welcomebreak.co.uk

dir: on M1 northbound between junct 21 & 21A

This modern building offers accommodation in smart, spacious and well-equipped bedrooms, suitable for families and business travellers, and all with en suite bathrooms. Continental breakfast is available and other refreshments may be taken at the nearby family restaurant. For further details see the Hotel Groups page.

Rooms 92 en suite **Conf** Board 10

LOUGHBOROUGH **MAP 11 SK51**

★★★★ 74% ◉◉ **HOTEL**

Quorn Country Hotel

Charnwood House, 66 Leicester Rd LE12 8BB

☎ 01509 415050 ▤ 01509 415557

e-mail: reservations@quorncountryhotel.co.uk

web: www.quorncountryhotel.co.uk

(For full entry see Quorn)

See advert on this page

★★★ 71% **HOTEL**

The Quality Hotel & Suites Loughborough

New Ashby Rd LE11 4EX

☎ 01509 211800 ▤ 01509 211868

e-mail: enquiries@hotels-loughborough.com

web: www.choicehotelseurope.com

dir: M1 junct 23 take A512 towards Loughborough. Hotel 1m on left

Close to the motorway network, this popular, modern hotel offers comfortable, well-equipped accommodation. All of the bedrooms have a spacious work area, and some rooms have small lounges and kitchenettes. It is an ideal hotel for a long stay or for families. Open-plan public rooms include a lounge area, bar and carvery restaurant.

Rooms 94 en suite (12 fmly) (47 GF) ❷ in 71 bedrooms S £65 £115; D £75-£135 **Facilities** STV ⬚ Sauna Solarium Gym Jacuzzi Wi-fi available Xmas **Conf** Thtr 225 Class 120 Board 80 Del from £85 **Parking** 160 **Notes** LB ❷ in restaurant Civ Wed 150

England

England

LUTTERWORTH — MAP 11 SP58

BUDGET HOTEL

Travelodge Lutterworth
Mill Farm LE17 4BP
web: www.travelodge.co.uk

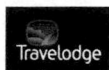

Travelodge offers good quality, good value, modern accommodation. Ideal for families, the spacious en suite bedrooms include remote-control TV, tea and coffee-making facilities and comfortable beds. Meals can be taken at the nearby family restaurant. See Hotel Groups pages for further details.

Rooms S fr £26; D fr £26

MARKET HARBOROUGH — MAP 11 SP78
See also Marston Trussell

★★★ 75% HOTEL

Best Western Three Swans
21 High St LE16 7NJ
☎ 01858 466644 📠 01858 433101
e-mail: sales@threeswans.co.uk
web: www.threeswans.co.uk

dir: M1 junct 20 take A4304 to Market Harborough. Through town centre on A6 from Leicester, hotel on right

Public areas in this former coaching inn include an elegant fine dining restaurant and cocktail bar, a smart foyer lounge and popular public bar areas. Bedroom styles and sizes vary, but are very well appointed and equipped. Those in the wing are particularly impressive, offering high quality and spacious accommodation.

Rooms 18 en suite 43 annexe en suite (8 fmly) (12 GF) ⊗ in 44 bedrooms S £55-£79; D £65-£89 (incl. bkfst) **Facilities** STV Wi-fi in bedrooms Xmas **Conf** Thtr 250 Class 180 Board 180 Del from £125 **Services** Lift **Parking** 100 **Notes LB** ⊗ in restaurant Civ Wed 140

MARKFIELD — MAP 11 SK40

Ⓤ

Field Head
Markfield Ln LE6 9PS
☎ 01530 245454 📠 01530 243740
e-mail: 9160@greeneking.co.uk
web: www.oldenglish.co.uk

OLD ENGLISH INNS

dir: M1 junct 22, towards Leicester. At rdbt left, then right

At the time of going to press, the star classification for this hotel was not confirmed. Please refer to the AA internet site www.theAA.com for
continued

current information.

Rooms 28 en suite (1 fmly) (13 GF) ⊗ in all bedrooms S £65-£75; D £75-£90 (incl. bkfst) **Facilities** 🎵 Xmas **Conf** Thtr 60 Board 36 Del from £110 **Parking** 65 **Notes** ⊗ in restaurant Civ Wed 50

BUDGET HOTEL

Travelodge Leicester Markfield
Littleshaw Ln LE6 0PP
☎ 08700 850 950 📠 01530 244580
web: www.travelodge.co.uk

Travelodge

dir: on A50 from M1 junct 22

Travelodge offers good quality, good value, modern accommodation. Ideal for families, the spacious en suite bedrooms include remote-control TV, tea and coffee-making facilities and comfortable beds. Meals can be taken at the nearby family restaurant. See Hotel Groups pages for further details.

Rooms 60 en suite S fr £26; D fr £26

MEDBOURNE — MAP 11 SP89

⊛⊛ RESTAURANT WITH ROOMS

The Horse & Trumpet
Old Green LE16 8DX
☎ 01858 565000 📠 01858 565551
e-mail: info@horseandtrumpet.com

dir: in village centre, opposite church

Tucked away behind the village bowling green, this carefully restored, thatched former farmhouse and pub now offers fine dining and quality accommodation. The golden stone building houses three intimate dining areas, where imaginative meals are offered. Smartly appointed and comfortably furnished bedrooms are located in a barn conversion to the rear of the main building.

Rooms 4 annexe en suite (2 GF) ⊗ in all bedrooms S £75; D £150 (incl. bkfst) **Facilities** FTV **Notes** ⊗ No children 5yrs Closed 1st wk Jan

---

MELTON MOWBRAY — MAP 11 SK71

INSPECTORS' CHOICE

★★★★ ⊛⊛ HOTEL

Stapleford Park
Stapleford LE14 2EF
☎ 01572 787522 📠 01572 787651
e-mail: reservations@stapleford.co.uk
web: www.staplefordpark.com

dir: 1m SW of B676, 4m E of Melton Mowbray and 9m W of Colsterworth

This stunning mansion, dating back to the 14th century, sits in over 500 acres of beautiful grounds. Spacious, sumptuous public rooms include a choice of lounges and an elegant restaurant; an additional brasserie-style restaurant is located in the golf complex. The hotel also boasts a spa with health and beauty treatments and gym, a golf course, horse-riding and many other country pursuits. Bedrooms are individually styled and furnished to a high standard. Attentive service is delivered with a relaxed yet
continued

professional style. Dinner, in the impressive dining room, is a highlight of any stay.

Stapleford Park

Rooms 48 en suite 7 annexe en suite (10 fmly) ⊗ in all bedrooms S tr £195; D £250-£560 (incl. bkfst) **Facilities Spa** STV 🔍 ♨ ⛳ ⚓ Fishing Riding Billiards Sauna Gym ⚓ Putt green Jacuzzi Archery, Croquet, Falconry, Horse Riding, Petanque, Shooting ♪ Xmas **Conf** BC Thtr 200 Class 140 Board 80 **Services** Lift **Parking** 120 **Notes LB** ⊗ in restaurant Civ Wed 200

★★★ 75% **HOTEL**

Sysonby Knoll

Asfordby Rd LE13 0HP
☎ 01664 563563 📠 01664 410364
e-mail: reception@sysonby.com
web: www.sysonby.com
dir: 0.5m from town centre beside A6006

This well-established hotel is on the edge of town and set in attractive gardens. A friendly and relaxed atmosphere prevails and the many returning guests have become friends. Bedrooms, including superior rooms in the annexe, are generally spacious and thoughtfully equipped. A choice of lounges, a cosy bar and a smart a restaurant offer carefully prepared meals.

Rooms 23 en suite 7 annexe en suite (1 fmly) (7 GF) ⊗ in 9 bedrooms S £62-£82; D £75-£105 (incl. bkfst) **Facilities** STV Fishing ⚓ Wi-fi in bedrooms **Conf** Thtr 50 Class 25 Board 34 **Parking** 48 **Notes LB** ⊗ in restaurant Closed 25 Dec-1 Jan

See advert on this page

Sysonby Knoll
Hotel & Restaurant

Asfordby Road, Melton Mowbray
Leicestershire, LE13 0HP
Tel: 01664 563563
Email: reception@sysonby.com
www.sysonby.com

AA

Privately owned Edwardian house set on the edge of the historic market town of Melton Mowbray. This friendly family-run hotel stands in 5 acres with river frontage and has 30 bedrooms ranging from well appointed standard rooms to superb executives & Four-Posters. Non-smoking executive bedrooms are available in an annexe.

The recently extended and refurbished conservatory style restaurant offers a light and airy dining environment. A wide choice of lunch and evening menus is available, and the emphasis is on quality and value throughout. This, coupled with exceptional hospitality, makes Sysonby Knoll one of the most popular restaurants in the area.

Melton Mowbray is perfectly placed for exploring the Heart of England and special Weekend break rates are available. Pets are very welcome at Sysonby Knoll and no extra charge is made.

Please see award winning website for more information.

England

MELTON MOWBRAY *continued*

★★★ 72% **HOTEL**

Quorn Lodge

46 Asfordby Rd LE13 0HR
☎ 01664 566660 📄 01664 480660
e-mail: quornlodge@aol.com
dir: *from town centre take A6006. Hotel 300yds from junct of A606/A607 on right*

Centrally located, this smart privately owned and managed hotel offers a comfortable and welcoming atmosphere. Bedrooms are individually decorated and thoughtfully designed. The public rooms consist of a bright restaurant overlooking the garden, a cosy lounge bar and a modern function suite. High standards are maintained throughout and extensive parking is a bonus.

Rooms 19 en suite (2 fmly) (3 GF) ⊘ in all bedrooms S £45-£65; D £70-£90 **Facilities** STV **Conf** BC Thtr 100 Class 70 Board 80 Del from £110 **Parking** 38 **Notes** LB ⊗ ⊘ in restaurant Closed 26 Dec-2 Jan

NORTH KILWORTH MAP 11 SP68

★★★★ 81% ◎◎ **HOTEL**

Kilworth House

Lutterworth Rd LE17 6JE
☎ 01858 880058 📄 01858 880349
e-mail: info@kilworthhouse.co.uk
web: www.kilworthhouse.co.uk
dir: *A4304 towards Market Harborough, after Walcote, hotel 1.5m on right*

A restored Victorian country house located in 38 acres of private grounds offering state-of-the-art conference rooms. The gracious public areas feature many period pieces and original art works. The bedrooms are very comfortable and well equipped, and the large Orangery is used for informal dining, while the opulent Wordsworth Restaurant has a more formal air.

Rooms 44 en suite (2 fmly) (13 GF) ⊘ in all bedrooms S £135-£180; D £135-£180 **Facilities** STV Fishing Gym ⌣ Wi-fi in bedrooms Beauty therapy rooms Xmas **Conf** Thtr 80 Class 30 Board 30 Del from £175 **Services** Lift **Parking** 140 **Notes** LB ⊗ ⊘ in restaurant Civ Wed 100

NOTTINGHAM EAST MIDLANDS AIRPORT MAP 11 SK42

★★★★ 78% ◎◎ **HOTEL**

The Priest House on the River Hand PICKED

Kings Mills, Castle Donington DE74 2RR
☎ 01332 810649 📄 01332 811141
web: www.handpicked.co.uk
dir: *M1 junct 24, onto A50, take 1st slip road signed Castle Donington. Right at lights, hotel in 2m*

A historic hotel peacefully situated in a picturesque riverside setting. Public areas include a fine-dining restaurant, a modern brasserie and conference rooms. Bedrooms are situated in both the main building and converted cottages, and the executive rooms feature state-of-the-art technology.

Rooms 24 en suite 18 annexe en suite (5 fmly) (16 GF) S £155-£225; D £155-£225 **Facilities Spa** STV Fishing Wi-fi in bedrooms Xmas **Conf** Thtr 120 Class 40 Board 40 Del from £130 **Parking** 200 **Notes** LB ⊗ ⊘ in restaurant Civ Wed 100

★★★ 76% ◎ **HOTEL**

BW Yew Lodge Hotel & Conference Centre

Packington Hill, Kegworth DE74 2DF
☎ 01509 672518 📄 01509 674730
e-mail: info@yewlodgehotel.co.uk
web: www.yewlodgehotel.co.uk
dir: *M1 junct 24. Follow signs to Loughborough & Kegworth on A6. At bottom of hill, 1st right, after 400yds lodge on right*

This smart, family-owned hotel is close to both the motorway and airport, yet is peacefully located. Modern bedrooms and public areas are thoughtfully appointed. The restaurant serves interesting dishes, while lounge service and extensive conference facilities are available. A very well equipped spa and leisure centre is also available.

Rooms 98 en suite (22 fmly) ⊘ in 74 bedrooms S £50-£85; D £60-£145 (incl. bkfst) **Facilities Spa** STV ⊠ supervised Sauna Solarium Gym Jacuzzi Wi-fi in bedrooms Beauty therapy suite, foot spas **Conf** Thtr 330 Class 150 Board 84 Del from £125 **Services** Lift **Parking** 180 **Notes** LB ⊘ in restaurant Civ Wed 130

★★★★ 75% **HOTEL**

Thistle Nottingham East Midlands Airport

THISTLE HOTELS

Castle Donington DE74 2SH
☎ 0870 333 9132 📠 0870 333 9232
e-mail: eastmidlandsairport@thistle.co.uk

dir: on A453

This large, well-presented hotel is conveniently located next to East Midlands Airport with easy access to the M1. Accommodation is generally spacious. Substantial public areas include the popular Lord Byron bar, a comprehensive range of meeting rooms and an Otium health and leisure club.

Rooms 164 en suite (10 fmly) (100 GF) ⊗ in 82 bedrooms **Facilities** ▣ supervised Sauna Solarium Gym Jacuzzi **Conf** BC Thtr 220 Class 140 Board 55 **Services** air con **Parking** 300 **Notes LB** ⊗ in restaurant Civ Wed 200

★★★ 73% **HOTEL**

Donington Manor

High St, Castle Donington DE74 2PP
☎ 01332 810253 📠 01332 850330
e-mail: enquiries@doningtonmanorhotel.co.uk
web: www.doningtonmanorhotel.co.uk

dir: 1m into village on B5430, left at traffic lights

Near the village centre, this refined Georgian building offers high standards of hospitality and a professional service. Many of the original architectural features have been preserved; the elegant dining room is particularly appealing. Bedrooms are individually designed, and the newer suites are especially comfortable and well equipped.

Rooms 26 en suite 6 annexe en suite (2 fmly) (4 GF) ⊗ in 16 bedrooms S £60-£75; D £75-£95 (incl. bkfst) **Facilities** STV Wi-fi in bedrooms **Conf** Thtr 120 Class 60 Board 40 Del from £125 **Parking** 40 **Notes LB** ⊗ in restaurant RS 25-26 Dec, 1 Jan Civ Wed 100

★★ 75% **HOTEL**

Tudor Hotel & Restaurant

Bond Gate, Castle Donington DE74 2NR
☎ 01332 810875 📠 01332 850883
e-mail: reservations@thetudorhotel.com
web: www.thetudorhotel.com

dir: M1 junct 24, A50 Castle Donington. 2m from Donington Park & Nottingham East Midlands Airport

This Tudor-style hotel is close to Donington racetrack and East Midlands Airport. The comfortable bedrooms have been tastefully furnished and are well equipped, and a suite is available too. Downstairs there is a large restaurant offering a wide range of traditional dishes, a character bar where meals can be ordered all day, and a beer garden. Free wireless broadband is available.

Rooms 10 en suite (2 fmly) ⊗ in 9 bedrooms S £49; D £65 (incl. bkfst) **Facilities** STV Xmas Wi-fi available **Conf** BC **Parking** 60 **Notes** ⊗ ⊗ in restaurant

Travelodge Nottingham EM Airport

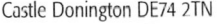

Castle Donington DE74 2TN
☎ 08700 850 950 📠 01509 673494
web: www.travelodge.co.uk

dir: M1 junct 23a follow signs for A453

Travelodge offers good quality, good value, modern accommodation. Ideal for families, the spacious en suite bedrooms include remote-control TV, tea and coffee-making facilities and comfortable beds. Meals can be taken at the nearby family restaurant. See Hotel Groups pages for further details.

Rooms 80 en suite S fr £26; D fr £26

QUORN   MAP 11 SK51

★★★★ 74% ◉◉ **HOTEL**

Quorn Country

Charnwood House, 66 Leicester Rd LE12 8BB
☎ 01509 415050 📠 01509 415557
e-mail: reservations@quorncountryhotel.co.uk
web: www.quorncountryhotel.co.uk

dir: M1 junct 23 onto A512 into Loughborough. Follow A6 signs. At 1st rdbt towards Quorn, through lights, hotel 500yds from 2nd rdbt

Professional service is one of the key strengths of this pleasing hotel, which sits beside the river in four acres of landscaped gardens and grounds. The smart modern conference centre and function suites have proved to be a great success for both corporate functions and weddings. Public rooms include a smart, comfortable lounge and bar, whilst guests have the choice from two dining options: the formal Shires restaurant and the informal conservatory-style Orangery.

Rooms 30 en suite (2 fmly) (9 GF) ⊗ in 19 bedrooms S £84-£110; D £95-£125 **Facilities** STV Fishing Wi-fi in bedrooms **Conf** BC Thtr 300 Class 162 Board 40 Del from £130 **Services** Lift **Parking** 100 **Notes LB** ⊗ Civ Wed 200

See advert on page 391

England

ROTHLEY
MAP 11 SK51

★★★ 68% **HOTEL**

Rothley Court
OLD ENGLISH INNS

Westfield Ln LE7 7LG
☎ 0116 237 4141 📄 0116 237 4483
e-mail: 6501@greeneking.co.uk
web: www.oldenglish.co.uk
dir: on B5328

Mentioned in the Domesday Book, and complete with its own chapel, this historic property sits in seven acres of well-tended grounds. Public areas retain much of their original character and include an oak-panelled restaurant and a choice of function and meeting rooms. Bedrooms, some located in an adjacent stable block, are individually styled.

Rooms 12 en suite 18 annexe en suite (3 fmly) (6 GF) ⊗ in all bedrooms **Facilities** STV **Conf** BC Thtr 100 Class 35 Board 35 **Parking** 100 **Notes LB** ⊗ ⊗ in restaurant Civ Wed 85

SIBSON
MAP 11 SK30

★★ 65% **HOTEL**

Millers
OLD ENGLISH INNS

Twycross Rd CV13 6LB
☎ 01827 880223 📄 01827 880990
e-mail: 6483@greeneking.co.uk
web: www.oldenglish.co.uk
dir: A5 onto A444 towards Burton. Hotel 3m on right.

This former bakery and water mill has been converted to create a small hotel. Several original features have been retained including the water wheel, which is a feature of the public bar. The well-equipped bedrooms have modern facilities, and the bar and restaurant are popular with the locals.

Rooms 35 en suite (3 fmly) (15 GF) ⊗ in 25 bedrooms S £55-£70; D £60-£75 (incl. bkfst) **Facilities** STV ♫ **Conf** Thtr 50 Class 24 Board 35 Del from £95 **Parking** 90 **Notes** ⊗ ⊗ in restaurant Civ Wed 80

SUTTON IN THE ELMS
MAP 11 SP59

★★ 64% **HOTEL**

Mill on the Soar
OLD ENGLISH INNS

Coventry Rd LE9 6QA
☎ 01455 282419 📄 01455 285937
e-mail: 1968@greeneking.co.uk
web: www.oldenglish.co.uk
dir: M1 junct 21, follow Narborough signs. 3m, hotel on left.

This is a popular inn that caters well for local family dining. The open-plan bar offers meals and snacks throughout the day, and is divided into non-smoking, family and adults-only areas. In the summer months there is also an attractive patio. Practical bedrooms are housed in a lodge-style annexe within the grounds.

Rooms 20 en suite 5 annexe en suite (19 fmly) (13 GF) ⊗ in 13 bedrooms S £43-£53; D £43-£53 **Facilities** Fishing Childrens outdoor play area Pool room **Conf** Thtr 50 Class 25 Board 25 **Parking** 80 **Notes** ⊗ ⊗ in restaurant

THRUSSINGTON
MAP 11 SK61

BUDGET HOTEL

Travelodge Leicester Thrussington
Travelodge

LE7 4TF
☎ 08700 850 950 📄 0870 1911584
web: www.travelodge.co.uk
dir: on A46, southbound

Travelodge offers good quality, good value, modern accommodation. Ideal for families, the spacious en suite bedrooms include remote-control TV, tea and coffee-making facilities and comfortable beds. Meals can be taken at the nearby family restaurant. See Hotel Groups pages for further details.

Rooms 32 en suite S fr £26; D fr £26

ULLESTHORPE
MAP 11 SP58

★★★ 77% **HOTEL**

BW Ullesthorpe Court Hotel & Golf Club
Best Western

Frolesworth Rd LE17 5BZ
☎ 01455 209023 📄 01455 202537
e-mail: bookings@ullesthorpecourt.co.uk
web: www.bw-ullesthorpecourt.co.uk
dir: M1junct 20 towards Lutterworth. Follow brown tourist signs

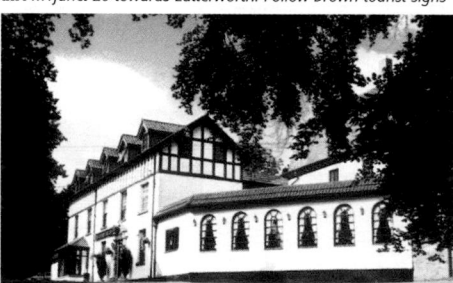

Complete with its own golf club, this impressively equipped hotel is within easy reach of the motorway network, NEC and Birmingham airport. Public areas include both formal and informal eating options, conference and extensive leisure facilities. Spacious bedrooms are thoughtfully equipped for both the corporate or leisure guests, and a four-poster room is available.

Rooms 72 en suite (3 fmly) (16 GF) ⊗ in 66 bedrooms S £70-£95; D £95-£120 (incl. bkfst) **Facilities** Spa STV ➰ supervised ↓ 18 ⚑ Snooker Sauna Solarium Gym Putt green Jacuzzi Wi-fi in bedrooms Beauty room, Steam Room **Conf** Thtr 80 Class 48 Board 30 Del from £120 **Parking** 500 **Notes LB** ⊗ in restaurant RS 25 & 26 Dec Civ Wed 120

LINCOLNSHIRE

BARTON-UPON-HUMBER   MAP 17 TA02

★★★ 74% HOTEL

Best Western Reeds

Westfield Lakes, Far Ings Rd DN18 5RG

☎ 01652 632313 ▤ 01652 636361

e-mail: info@bwreedshotel.co.uk

dir: A15 rdbt take 2nd exit (Humber Bridge) & exit at Barton-upon-Humber, left at rdbt. In 200yds right at hotel sign, down hill & hotel at junct

This hotel is situated in a quiet wildlife sanctuary, just upstream from the Humber Bridge. A very attractive lakeside restaurant commands tranquil views, and there is a new health spa offering various alternative therapies. Bedrooms are comfortable and well equipped, and service is both friendly and helpful.

Rooms 25 en suite (2 fmly) ⊗ in all bedrooms S £104; D £114 (incl. bkfst) **Facilities Spa** STV Xmas **Conf** Thtr 300 Class 200 Board 70 Del from £159 **Services** Lift **Parking** 100 **Notes LB** ⊛ ⊗ in restaurant Civ Wed 300

BELTON   MAP 11 SK93

★★★★ 77% HOTEL

De Vere Belton Woods

NG32 2LN

☎ 01476 593200 ▤ 01476 574547

e-mail: belton.woods@devere-hotels.com

web: www.devere.co.uk

dir: A1 to Gonerby Moor Services. B1174 towards Great Gonerby. At top of hill turn left towards Manthorpe/Belton. At T-junct turn left onto A607. Hotel 0.25m on left

Beautifully located amidst 475 acres of picturesque countryside, this is a destination venue for lovers of sport, especially golf, as well as a relaxing executive retreat for seminar delegates. Comfortable and well-equipped accommodation complements the elegant and spacious public areas, which provide a good choice of drinking and dining options.

Rooms 136 en suite (136 fmly) (68 GF) ⊗ in 117 bedrooms S £69-£135; D £79-£155 (incl. bkfst) **Facilities Spa** STV 🎾 ⚓ 45 🏊 Fishing Squash Sauna Gym 🏌 Putt green Jacuzzi Wi-fi available Outdoor activity centre - quad biking, laser shooting etc Xmas **Conf** Thtr 245 Class 180 Board 80 Del from £140 **Services** Lift **Parking** 350 **Notes LB** ⊛ ⊗ in restaurant Civ Wed 80

BOSTON   MAP 12 TF34

★★ 72% HOTEL

Poacher's Country Hotel

Swineshead Rd, Kirton Holme PE20 1SQ

☎ 01205 290310 ▤ 01205 290254

e-mail: poachers@kirtonholme.wandoo.co.uk

dir: A17 Bicker Bar, turn at rdbt onto A52, hotel 2m

A delightfully furnished and comfortable establishment offering a very wide range of well prepared dishes. The bedrooms are modern and have been delightfully furnished. Expect attentive and friendly service.

Rooms 16 en suite (2 fmly) (7 GF) ⊗ in 9 bedrooms S £35-£48; D £48-£180 (incl. bkfst) **Facilities** Xmas **Conf** Thtr 150 Class 100 Board 40 Del from £15 **Parking** 60 **Notes LB** ⊗ in restaurant Civ Wed 150

★★ 68% HOTEL

Comfort Inn

Donnington Rd, Bicker Bar Roundabout PE20 3AN

☎ 01205 820118 ▤ 01205 820228

e-mail: admin@gb607.u-net.com

dir: towards A16 Spalding, hotel on A17/A52 rdbt, 11m from Boston

Public areas within this purpose-built hotel include an open-plan lounge bar and adjacent restaurant. Reasonably priced meals are available all day. Bedrooms are well equipped, offering good levels of comfort and value for money. Several meeting rooms are also available.

Rooms 55 en suite (15 fmly) ⊗ in 25 bedrooms **Facilities** STV **Conf** Thtr 70 Class 30 Board 35 **Parking** 60 **Notes** ⊗ in restaurant

Ⓤ

Swallow New England

49 Wide Bargate PE21 6SH

☎ 01205 365255 ▤ 01205 310597

e-mail: swallow.boston@swallowhotels.com

web: www.swallowhotels.com

dir: A16, follow Skegness signs to end of dual carriageway, take 1st exit off rdbt, left at lights and then 1st left. Hotel on right

At the time of going to press, the star classification for this hotel was not confirmed. Please refer to the AA internet site www.theAA.com for current information.

Rooms 27 en suite (2 fmly) ⊗ in all bedrooms S £65-£75; D £80-£95 (incl. bkfst) **Facilities** STV **Conf** Thtr 30 Class 25 Board 25 Del from £75 **Parking** 25 **Notes LB** ⊛ ⊗ in restaurant

BUDGET HOTEL

Premier Travel Inn Boston

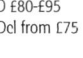

Wainfleet Rd PE21 9RW

☎ 08701 977035 ▤ 01205 310908

web: www.premiertravelinn.com

dir: A52, 300yds E of junct with A16 Boston/Grimsby road. (Nearest landmark is Pilgrim Hospital)

High quality, modern budget accommodation ideal for both families and business travellers. Spacious, en suite bedrooms feature bath and shower, satellite TV and many have telephones and modem points. The adjacent family restaurant features a wide and varied menu. For further details consult the Hotel Groups page.

Rooms 34 en suite **Conf** Thtr 12 Board 8

BRIGG
MAP 17 TA00

★★ 65% **HOTEL**

The Red Lion Inn at Redbourne
The Green, Redbourne DN21 4QR
☎ 01652 648302 ▤ 01652 648900
e-mail: enquiries@redlion.org

dir: *Off A15 to Redbourne, hotel 0.5m on left*

Dating back to the 17th century, this former coaching inn overlooks the village green, adjacent to the old fire station. The inn is comfortably furnished with modern bedrooms and a tempting range of food is available either in the popular bar, garden terrace or air-conditioned dining room. There is a warm and friendly atmosphere.

Rooms 12 rms (10 en suite) ⊗ in all bedrooms **Parking** 40 **Notes** ⊗ in restaurant

CLEETHORPES
MAP 17 TA30

★★★ 77% ⊛ **HOTEL**

Kingsway
Kingsway DN35 0AE
☎ 01472 601122 ▤ 0871 236 0671
e-mail: reception@kingsway-hotel.com
web: www.kingsway-hotel.com

dir: *leave A180 at Grimsby, to Cleethorpes seafront. Hotel at Kingsway and Queen Parade junct (A1098)*

This seafront hotel has been in the same family for four generations and continues to provide traditional comfort and friendly service. The lounges are comfortable and good food is served in the pleasant dining room. Most of the bedrooms are comfortably proportioned, and all are bright and nicely furnished.

Rooms 49 en suite ⊗ in 15 bedrooms S £55-£84; D £88-£99 (incl. bkfst) **Facilities** STV **Conf** Thtr 22 Board 18 Del from £110 **Services** Lift **Parking** 50 **Notes LB** ⊗ No children 5yrs ⊗ in restaurant Closed 25-26 Dec

★★ 72% **HOTEL**

Dovedale Hotel
14 Albert Rd DN35 8LX
☎ 01472 692988 ▤ 01472 313121
web: www.dovedalehotel.com

This newly refurbished hotel stands in a quite side road just off the seafront. The bedrooms offer good all-round comforts and there is a modern style bar and lounge. Cooking offers a wide choice of dishes served in delightful restaurant. Expect friendly and attentive service.

Rooms 26 en suite (10 fmly) (4GF)

★★ 68% **HOTEL**

Clee House Hotel & Bistro
31-33 Clee Rd DN35 8AD
☎ 01472 200850 & 07979 977696 ▤ 01472 200850
e-mail: david@cleehouse.com

dir: *A180 to Cleethorpes, right Isaac's Hill rdbt. 75yds on left*

Located close to the town centre, this detached Victorian house has been extended to provide modern spacious bedrooms. Imaginative evening meals are served in the modern brasserie, which features a

continued

well-stocked bar, and there is also a small lounge for residents. Bedrooms include several ground-floor rooms suitable for less mobile guests.

Rooms (2 fmly) (4 GF) ⊗ in 13 bedrooms S £50-£55; D £65 (incl. bkfst) **Facilities** FTV Wi-fi available **Conf** BC **Parking** 12 **Notes** ⊗ ⊗ in restaurant

COLSTERWORTH
MAP 11 SK92

BUDGET HOTEL

Travelodge Grantham Colsterworth
NG35 5JR
☎ 08700 850 950 ▤ 01476 860680
web: www.travelodge.co.uk

dir: *on A1/A151 s'bound at junct with A151/B676*

Travelodge offers good quality, good value, modern accommodation. Ideal for families, the spacious en suite bedrooms include remote-control TV, tea and coffee-making facilities and comfortable beds. Meals can be taken at the nearby family restaurant. See Hotel Groups pages for further details.

Rooms 31 en suite S fr £26; D fr £26

GRANTHAM
MAP 11 SK93

★★★★ 76% **HOTEL**

Grantham Marriott
Swingbridge Rd NG31 7XT
☎ 01476 593000 ▤ 01476 592592
e-mail: marriotthotels.co.uk
web: www.marriott.co.uk

dir: *exit A1 at Grantham/Melton Mowbray junct onto A607. From N: 1st exit at mini rdbt, hotel on right. From S: at rdbt 2nd exit. Next left at T-junct. At mini rdbt 2nd exit. Hotel on right*

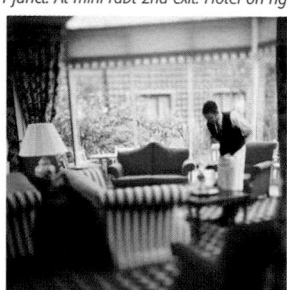

This smart, modern hotel is a convenient base from which to explore the countryside. Hotel bedrooms are spacious, tastefully decorated and have a wide range of extras. Public rooms, which extend into a pretty courtyard in the summer, include a serviced lounge, function rooms and a small leisure club with pool and fitness room.

Rooms 90 en suite (44 GF) ⊗ in 68 bedrooms S £65-£85; D £65-£85 **Facilities** Spa STV ▣ supervised Sauna Solarium Gym Wi-fi in bedrooms Steam room Xmas **Conf** Thtr 200 Class 90 Board 50 Del £155 **Parking** 150 **Notes LB** ⊗ ⊗ in restaurant Civ Wed 80

England

★★★ 77% ⊚ HOTEL

Angel & Royal

High St NG31 6PN

☎ 01476 565816 📠 01476 567149

e-mail: enquiries@angelandroyal.co.uk

web: www.angelandroyal.co.uk

dir: *Take Grantham exit off A1 & follow signs to town centre. Hotel on High Street*

This former coaching inn in the centre of town claims to be one of the oldest in the country and retains many original features. The accommodation is varied in size, but all rooms are stylish and comfortable. The bar offers over 200 whiskies and the brasserie provides a modern selection of dishes. Additionally, the historic King's Room restaurant is open at weekends.

Rooms 27 en suite 2 annexe en suite (4 fmly) (1 GF) ⊘ in 26 bedrooms S £65-£85; D £80-£130 (incl. bkfst) **Facilities** STV Xmas **Conf** Thtr 65 Class 30 Board 34 Del from £129 **Parking** 70 **Notes LB** ⊗ ⊘ in restaurant Civ Wed 65

★★★ 72% HOTEL

Best Western Kings

North Pde NG31 8AU

☎ 01476 590800 📠 01476 577072

e-mail: kings@bestwestern.co.uk

web: www.bwkh.co.uk

dir: *off A1 at rdbt N end of Grantham onto B1174, follow road for 2m. Hotel on left by bridge*

A friendly atmosphere exists within this extended Georgian house. Bedrooms are attractively decorated and furnished and modern. Dining options include the formal Victorian restaurant and the popular Orangery, which also operates as a coffee shop and breakfast room; a lounge bar and a comfortable open-plan foyer lounge are available.

Rooms 21 en suite (3 fmly) ⊘ in 14 bedrooms S £50-£69; D £60-£79 (incl. bkfst) **Facilities** STV **Conf** BC Thtr 100 Class 50 Board 40 Del £102 **Parking** 36 **Notes LB** ⊘ in restaurant Closed 25-26 Dec

BUDGET HOTEL

Premier Travel Inn Grantham

A1/A607 Junction, Harlaxton Rd NG31 7UA

☎ 0870 8500329 📠 0870 8500346

web: www.premiertravelinn.com

High quality, modern budget accommodation ideal for both families and business travellers. Spacious, en suite bedrooms feature bath and shower, satellite TV and many have telephones and modem points. The adjacent family restaurant features a wide and varied menu. For further details consult the Hotel Groups page.

Rooms 59 en suite

BUDGET HOTEL

Travelodge Grantham (A1)

Grantham Service Area, Grantham North, Gonerby Moor NG32 2AB

☎ 08700 850 950 📠 01476 577500

web: www.travelodge.co.uk

dir: *4m N on A1*

Travelodge offers good quality, good value, modern accommodation.

continued

Ideal for families, the spacious en suite bedrooms include remote-control TV, tea and coffee-making facilities and comfortable beds. Meals can be taken at the nearby family restaurant. See Hotel Groups pages for further details.

Rooms 39 en suite S fr £26; D fr £26

GRIMSBY   MAP 17 TA21

★★★ 73% ⊚ HOTEL

Beeches

42 Waltham Rd, Scartho DN33 2LX

☎ 01472 278830 📠 01472 752880

e-mail: themanager@thebeecheshotel.com

web: www.thebeecheshotel.com

In the suburb of Scartho, not far from the town centre, this contemporary hotel offers good modern accommodation and pleasing public rooms. Bedrooms are inviting and well equipped with a thoughtful range of facilities. There is a comfortable lounge bar and a popular brasserie where interesting, quality food is on offer.

Rooms 18 en suite (4 GF) ⊘ in all bedrooms S £54-£70; D £60-£85 (incl. bkfst) **Facilities** Wi-fi in bedrooms **Conf** Class 40 **Services** Lift **Parking** 70 **Notes** ⊗ ⊘ in restaurant Closed 25 Dec 1st wk Jan

★★★ 67% HOTEL

Hotel Elizabeth

Littlecoates Rd DN34 4LX

☎ 01472 240024 & 0870 1162716 📠 01472 241354

e-mail: elizabeth.grimsby@elizabethhotels.co.uk

web: www.elizabethhotels.co.uk

dir: *A1136 signed Greatcoates, 1st rdbt left, 2nd rdbt right. Hotel 200mtrs on right*

Bedrooms at this pleasantly situated hotel are equipped with modern comforts and many have large windows and balconies overlooking the adjoining golf course. The popular restaurant shares the same tranquil view. There is a large banqueting suite, smaller meeting and conference rooms, and extensive parking which makes this an ideal business centre.

Rooms 52 en suite (4 fmly) ⊘ in 27 bedrooms S £65-£75; D £75-£85 (incl. bkfst) **Facilities** STV Xmas **Conf** Thtr 300 Class 100 Board 60 **Services** Lift **Parking** 200 **Notes LB** ⊘ in restaurant Civ Wed 100

England

GRIMSBY *continued*

BUDGET HOTEL

Premier Travel Inn Grimsby

Europa Park, Appian Way, Off Gilbey Rd
DN31 2UT
☎ 08701 977121 📠 01472 241648
web: www.premiertravelinn.com

dir: *From M180 junct 5 take A180 towards Grimsby town centre. At 1st rbt take 2nd exit. Take 1st left, then left at mini rbt onto Appian Way*

High quality, modern budget accommodation ideal for both families and business travellers. Spacious, en suite bedrooms feature bath and shower, satellite TV and many have telephones and modem points. The adjacent family restaurant features a wide and varied menu. For further details consult the Hotel Groups page.

Rooms 40 en suite

HORNCASTLE

MAP 17 TF26

★★★ 70% **HOTEL**

Best Western Admiral Rodney

North St LN9 5DX
☎ 01507 523131 📠 01507 523104
e-mail: reception@admiralrodney.com
web: www.admiralrodney.com

dir: *off A153 - Louth to Horncastle*

Enjoying a prime location in the centre of town, this smart hotel offers a high standard of accommodation. Bedrooms are well appointed and thoughtfully equipped for both business and leisure guests. Public areas include the Rodney public bar, a selection of meeting and conference rooms and an open-plan restaurant and lounge bar.

Rooms 31 en suite (3 fmly) (7 GF) ⊘ in 18 bedrooms S £56-£64; D £76-£92 (incl. bkfst) **Facilities** STV Wi-fi in bedrooms Xmas **Conf** Thtr 140 Class 60 Board 50 Del from £89 **Services** Lift **Parking** 60 **Notes LB** ⊗ ⊘ in restaurant

---

LINCOLN

MAP 17 SK97

★★★ 85% **HOTEL**

Best Western Bentley Hotel & Leisure Club

Newark Rd, South Hykeham LN6 9NH
☎ 01522 878000 📠 01522 878001
e-mail: infothebentleyhotel@btconnect.com
web: www.thebentleyhotel.uk.com

dir: *from A1 take A46 E towards Lincoln for 10m. Over 1st rdbt on Lincoln Bypass to hotel 50yds on left*

This modern hotel is on a ring road, so conveniently located for all local attractions. Attractive bedrooms, most of which are air-conditioned, are well equipped and spacious. The hotel has a leisure suite with gym and large pool (with a hoist for the less able).

continued

Extensive conference facilities and licensed for civil partnerships and weddings.

Best Western Bentley Hotel & Leisure Club

Rooms 80 en suite (5 fmly) (26 GF) ⊘ in 50 bedrooms S £83-£93; D £98-£130 (incl. bkfst) **Facilities** STV ⅀ Sauna Gym Jacuzzi Wi-fi in bedrooms Beauty salon, Steam Room Xmas **Conf** Thtr 300 Class 150 Board 30 Del from £110 **Services** Lift **Parking** 170 **Notes LB** ⊗ ⊘ in restaurant Civ Wed 120

★★★ 73% ⊛ **HOTEL**

Branston Hall

Branston Park, Branston LN4 1PD
☎ 01522 793305 📠 01522 790734
e-mail: info@branstonhall.com
web: www.branstonhall.com

dir: *5 min drive from Lincoln on B1188*

Many original features have been retained in this country house, which sits in beautiful grounds complete with a lake. There is an elegant restaurant, a spacious bar and a beautiful lounge in addition to impressive conference and leisure facilities. Individually styled bedrooms vary in size and include several with four-poster beds.

Rooms 43 en suite 7 annexe en suite (3 fmly) (4 GF) ⊘ in 6 bedrooms S £70-£120; D £99-£164.50 (incl. bkfst) **Facilities Spa** STV ⅀ Sauna Gym Jacuzzi Jogging circuit Xmas **Conf** Thtr 200 Class 54 Board 40 Del £110 **Services** Lift **Parking** 100 **Notes LB** ⊗ ⊘ in restaurant Civ Wed 160

England

★★★ 72% HOTEL

The Lincoln

Eastgate LN2 1PN
☎ 01522 520348 📠 01522 510780
e-mail: sales@thelincolnhotel.com
web: www.thelincolnhotel.com
dir: *adjacent to cathedral*

This privately owned modern hotel enjoys superb uninterrupted views of Lincoln Cathedral. There are ruins of the Roman wall and Eastgate in the grounds. Bedrooms are in a contemporary style with up-to-the-minute facilities. An airy restaurant and bar, plus a comfortable lounge are provided, in addition to conference and meeting facilities.

Rooms 72 en suite (4 fmly) ⊗ in 46 bedrooms S £79-£109; D £109-£129 (incl. bkfst) **Facilities** FTV Wi-fi available **Conf** BC Thtr 100 Class 50 Board 40 Del from £119 **Services** Lift **Parking** 110 **Notes** LB ⊗ ⊗ in restaurant Civ Wed 100

★★★ 71% HOTEL

Courtyard by Marriott Lincoln

Brayford Wharf North LN1 1YW
☎ 01522 544244 📠 01522 560005
e-mail: res.lcncourtyard@kewgreen.co.uk
web: www.marriott.co.uk/LCNDT
dir: *A46 onto A57 to Lincoln. Left at lights, right, take next right onto Lucy Tower St right onto Brayford Wharf North*

A short walk away from the city centre, this smart hotel has an idyllic waterfront location overlooking Brayford Pool. Bedrooms are spacious and comfortably appointed, with many extra facilities. Public areas focus around a galleried restaurant that overlooks the lounge bar.

Rooms 97 en suite (44 fmly) (9 GF) ⊗ in 70 bedrooms S £79-£105; D £98-£116 (incl. bkfst) **Facilities** STV Wi-fi available Fitness Room Xmas **Conf** Thtr 30 Class 20 Board 20 Del from £105 **Services** Lift air con **Parking** 100 **Notes** LB ⊗ ⊗ in restaurant

★★★ 71% HOTEL

Washingborough Hall

Church Hill, Washingborough LN4 1BE
☎ 01522 790340 📠 01522 792936
e-mail: enquiries@washingboroughhall.com
web: www.washingboroughhall.com
dir: *B1190 into Washingborough. Right at rdbt, hotel 500yds*

This Georgian manor stands on the edge of the quiet village of Washingborough among attractive gardens, with an outdoor swimming pool available in the summer. Public rooms are pleasantly furnished and comfortable, whilst the restaurant offers interesting

continued

menus. Bedrooms are individually designed, and most have views out over the grounds and countryside.

Washingborough Hall

Rooms 12 en suite (3 fmly) ⊗ in all bedrooms S £70-£90; D £95-£140 (incl. bkfst) **Facilities** ⤷ Wi-fi in bedrooms Bicycles for hire Xmas **Conf** Thtr 50 Class 25 Board 25 Del from £115 **Parking** 50 **Notes** LB ⊗ ⊗ in restaurant Civ Wed 48

★★★ 68% HOTEL

The White Hart

Bailgate LN1 3AR
☎ 01522 526222 📠 01522 531798
e-mail: info@whitehart-lincoln.co.uk
web: www.whitehart-lincoln.co.uk
dir: *turn off A46 (right) at island onto B1226, through Newport Arch. Hotel 0.5m on left as road bends left*

Lying in the shadow of Lincoln's magnificent cathedral, this hotel is perfectly positioned for exploring the shops and the sights of this medieval city. The attractive bedrooms are furnished and decorated in a traditional style and many have views of the cathedral. Given the hotel's central location, parking is a real benefit.

Rooms 50 en suite (10 fmly) ⊗ in 23 bedrooms S £65-£85; D £90-£120 **Facilities** STV Wi-fi in bedrooms Xmas **Conf** Thtr 160 Board 103 Del from £115 **Services** Lift **Parking** 50 **Notes** LB ⊗ in restaurant Civ Wed 120

★★ 75% HOTEL

Castle

Westgate LN1 3AS
☎ 01522 538801 📠 01522 575457
e-mail: aa@castlehotel.net
web: www.castlehotel.net
dir: *follow signs for Historic Lincoln. Hotel at NE corner of castle*

Located in the heart of historic Lincoln, this privately owned and run hotel has been carefully restored to offer comfortable, attractive,

continued on page 402

England

LINCOLN *continued*

well-appointed accommodation. Bedrooms are thoughtfully equipped, particularly the deluxe rooms and the spacious Lincoln Suite. Specialising in traditional fayre, Knights Restaurant has an interesting medieval theme.

Castle

Rooms 16 en suite 3 annexe en suite (5 GF) ⊘ in 13 bedrooms S £70-£96; D £90-£175 (incl. bkfst) **Conf** Thtr 20 Class 40 Board 30 Del from £111 **Parking** 20 **Notes LB** ⊗ No children 8yrs ⊘ in restaurant RS Evening of Dec 25-26

★★ 74% HOTEL

Hillcrest

15 Lindum Ter LN2 5RT
☎ 01522 510182 ▤ 01522 538009
e-mail: reservations@hillcrest-hotel.com
web: www.hillcrest-hotel.com

dir: from A15 Wragby Rd and Lindum Rd, turn into Upper Lindum St at sign. Left at bottom for hotel 200mtrs on right

The hospitality offered by Jenny Bennett and her team is one of the strengths of the Hillcrest, which sits in a quiet residential location just a seven minute' walk from the cathedral and city shops. Well-equipped bedrooms come in a variety of sizes, and the pleasant conservatory/dining room, with views over the park, offers a good range of freshly prepared food. Free wireless internet access for residents.

Rooms 14 en suite (6 fmly) (6 GF) ⊘ in 6 bedrooms S £67-£78; D £87-£97 (incl. bkfst) **Facilities** Wi-fi available **Conf** Thtr 20 Class 16 Board 12 Del from £105 **Parking** 8 **Notes LB** ⊘ in restaurant Closed 23 Dec-3 Jan

★★ 67% HOTEL

Tower Hotel

38 Westgate LN1 3BD
☎ 01522 529999 ▤ 01522 560596
e-mail: tower.hotel@btclick.com

dir: from A46 follow signs to Lincoln N then to Bailgate area. Through arch and 2nd left

This hotel faces the Norman castle wall and is in a very convenient location for the city. The relaxed and friendly atmosphere is one of the strengths here. A modern conservatory bar, and a stylish restaurant where contemporary dishes are available throughout the day.

Rooms 14 en suite (1 fmly) ⊘ in 2 bedrooms S £55-£62; D £70-£90 (incl. dinner) **Conf** Thtr 24 Class 24 Board 16 Del from £67.50 **Parking** 4 **Notes LB** ⊘ in restaurant Closed 24 Dec-27 Dec & 1 Jan

BUDGET HOTEL

Hotel Ibis Lincoln

Runcorn Rd (A46), off Whisby Rd LN6 3QZ
☎ 01522 698333 ▤ 01522 698444
e-mail: H3161@accor-hotels.com
web: www.ibishotel.com

dir: off A46 ring road onto Whisby Rd. 1st turning on left

Modern, budget hotel offering comfortable accommodation in bright and practical bedrooms. Breakfast is self-service and dinner is available in the restaurant. For further details, consult the Hotel Groups page.

Rooms 86 en suite **Conf** Thtr 35 Class 12 Board 20

BUDGET HOTEL

Premier Travel Inn Lincoln

Lincoln Rd, Canwick Hill LN4 2RF
☎ 08701 977156 ▤ 01522 542521
web: www.premiertravelinn.com

dir: Approx 1 mile south of city centre at the junction of B1188 to Branston and B1131 to Brakebridge Heath

High quality, modern budget accommodation ideal for both families and business travellers. Spacious, en suite bedrooms feature bath and shower, satellite TV and many have telephones and modem points. The adjacent family restaurant features a wide and varied menu. For further details consult the Hotel Groups page.

Rooms 40 en suite

BUDGET HOTEL

Travelodge Lincoln Thorpe on the Hill

Thorpe on the Hill LN6 9AJ
☎ 08700 850 950 🖷 01522 697213
web: www.travelodge.co.uk
dir: on A46 Newark/Lincoln rdbt

Travelodge offers good quality, good value, modern accommodation. Ideal for families, the spacious en suite bedrooms include remote-control TV, tea and coffee-making facilities and comfortable beds. Meals can be taken at the nearby family restaurant. See Hotel Groups pages for further details.

Rooms 32 en suite S fr £26; D fr £26

LONG SUTTON   MAP 12 TF42

BUDGET HOTEL

Travelodge King's Lynn Long Sutton

Wisbech Rd PE12 9AG
☎ 08700 850 950 🖷 01406 362230
web: www.travelodge.co.uk
dir: on junct A17/A1101 rdbt

Travelodge offers good quality, good value, modern accommodation. Ideal for families, the spacious en suite bedrooms include remote-control TV, tea and coffee-making facilities and comfortable beds. Meals can be taken at the nearby family restaurant. See Hotel Groups pages for further details.

Rooms 40 en suite S fr £26; D fr £26

LOUTH   MAP 17 TF38

★★★ 75% **HOTEL**

Best Western Kenwick Park

Kenwick Park Estate LN11 8NR
☎ 01507 608806 🖷 01507 608027
e-mail: enquiries@kenwick-park.co.uk
web: www.kenwick-park.co.uk
dir: A16 from Grimsby, then A157 Mablethorpe/Manby Rd. Hotel 400mtrs down hill on right

This elegant Georgian house is situated on the 320-acre Kenwick Park estate, overlooking its own golf course. Bedrooms are spacious, comfortable and provide modern facilities. Public areas include a restaurant and a conservatory bar that overlook the grounds. There is also an extensive leisure centre and state-of-the-art conference and banqueting facilities.

Rooms 29 en suite 5 annexe en suite (10 fmly) ⊗ in 11 bedrooms **Facilities Spa** STV ⬆ supervised ♨ 18 ♨ Squash Sauna Solarium Gym Putt green Jacuzzi Health & Beauty Centre **Conf** Thtr 250 Class 40 Board 90 **Parking** 100 **Notes LB** ⊗ in restaurant Civ Wed 200

★★★ 72% **HOTEL**

Brackenborough Arms Hotel

Cordeaux Corner, Brackenborough LN11 0SZ
☎ 01507 609169 🖷 01507 609413
e-mail: arlidgard@oakridgehotels.co.uk
web: www.oakridgehotels.co.uk
dir: off A16 2m N of Louth

Set amid well-tended gardens and patios, this hotel offers attractive bedrooms, each individually decorated with co-ordinated furnishings and many extras. Tippler's Retreat lounge bar offers informal dining; the more formal Signature Restaurant provides dishes using the best of local produce including fish from Grimsby.

Rooms 24 en suite (1 fmly) (6 GF) ⊗ in 16 bedrooms S £65-£80; D £77-£99 (incl. bkfst) **Facilities** STV FTV Wi-fi in bedrooms Xmas **Conf** Thtr 34 Class 24 Board 30 Del £101.95 **Parking** 91 **Notes LB** ⊗ ⊗ in restaurant Closed 25-26 Dec Civ Wed 60

★★★ 70% **HOTEL**

Beaumont

66 Victoria Rd LN11 0BX
☎ 01507 605005 🖷 01507 607768
e-mail: beaumonthotel@aol.com

This smart, family-run hotel enjoys a quiet location, within easy reach of the town centre. Bedrooms are spacious and individually designed. Public areas include a smart restaurant with a strong Italian influence and an inviting lounge bar with comfortable deep sofas and open fires. Weddings and meetings are also catered for.

Rooms 16 en suite (2 fmly) (6 GF) S £55-£68; D £80-£130 (incl. bkfst) **Conf** Thtr 70 Class 50 Board 46 **Services** Lift **Parking** 70 **Notes** ⊗ in restaurant RS Sun

---

MARKET DEEPING   MAP 12 TF11

Swallow Towngate

SWALLOW

3 Towngate East PE6 8DP
☎ 01778 348000 🖷 01778 347947
web: www.swallowhotels.com

At the time of going to press, the star classification for this hotel was not confirmed. Please refer to the AA internet site www.theAA.com for current information.

Rooms 14 en suite

MARSTON

MAP 11 SK84

U

The Olde Barn

Toll Bar Rd NG32 2HT
☎ 01400 250909 📠 01400 250130
e-mail: reservations@theoldebarnhotel.co.uk

dir: *From A1 N to Marston next to the petrol station. From A2 S 1st right after Gonerby rdbt signed Marston*

At the time of going to press, the star classification for this hotel was not confirmed. Please refer to the AA internet site www.theAA.com for current information.

Rooms 103 en suite S £69-£109; D £79-£129 (incl. bkfst) **Facilities** Spa 🔾 Sauna Solarium Gym Jacuzzi Xmas **Conf** Del from £110 **Services** Lift **Notes** LB ⊘ in restaurant Civ Wed 250

SCUNTHORPE

MAP 17 SE81

★★★★ 77% ⊛ **HOTEL**

Forest Pines Hotel

QHOTELS

Ermine St, Broughton DN20 0AQ
☎ 01652 650770 📠 01652 650495
e-mail: enquiries@forestpines.co.uk
web: www.qhotels.co.uk

dir: *200yds from M180 junct 4, on Brigg-Scunthorpe rdbt*

This smart hotel provides a comprehensive range of leisure facilities. Extensive conference rooms, a modern health and beauty spa, and a championship golf course ensure that it is a popular choice with both corporate and leisure guests. Public areas include a choice of dining options - fine dining is available in the Beech Tree Restaurant and more informal eating in the Garden Room or Mulligan's Bar. Bedrooms are modern, spacious and very well equipped.

Rooms 114 en suite (66 fmly) (41 GF) ⊘ in 77 bedrooms **Facilities** Spa STV 🔾 supervised ♨ 27 Sauna Gym Putt green Jacuzzi Mountain bikes Jogging track 🎵 **Conf** Thtr 375 Class 142 Board 134 **Services** Lift **Parking** 300 **Notes** LB ⊗ ⊘ in restaurant Civ Wed 200

★★★ 73% **HOTEL**

Wortley House

Rowland Rd DN16 1SU
☎ 01724 842223 📠 01724 280646
e-mail: reception@wortleyhousehotel.co.uk
web: www.wortleyhousehotel.co.uk

dir: *M180 junct 3 take A18. Follow signs for Grimsby/Humberside airport, 2nd left into Brumby Wood Lane, over rdbt into Rowland Rd. Hotel 200yds on right*

A friendly hotel with good facilities for conferences, meetings, banquets and other functions. Bedrooms offer modern comfort and facilities. An extensive range of dishes is available in both the formal restaurant and the more relaxed bar.

Rooms 38 en suite 4 annexe en suite (5 fmly) (4 GF) ⊘ in 28 bedrooms S fr £85; D fr £95 (incl. bkfst) **Facilities** STV Xmas **Conf** Thtr 300 Class 250 Board 50 **Parking** 100 **Notes** ⊘ in restaurant Civ Wed 250

BUDGET HOTEL

Premier Travel Inn Scunthorpe

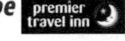

Lakeside Retail Park, Lakeside Parkway
DN16 3UA
☎ 08701 977226 📠 01724 278651
web: www.premiertravelinn.com

dir: *M180 junct 4, A18 towards Scunthorpe. At Morrisons rdbt left onto Lakeside Retail Park. Inn behind Morrisons petrol station*

High quality, modern budget accommodation ideal for both families and business travellers. Spacious, en suite bedrooms feature bath and shower, satellite TV and many have telephones and modem points. The adjacent family restaurant features a wide and varied menu. For further details consult the Hotel Groups page.

Rooms 40 en suite

BUDGET HOTEL

Travelodge Scunthorpe

Doncaster Rd, Gunness DN15 8TE
☎ 08700 850950 📠 01724 289 391
web: www.travelodge.co.uk

dir: *M18 junct 5, take M180 towards Scunthorpe. Take first exit signed Scunthorpe. After 1.5 m take 3rd exit at traffic island, Travelodge is on right.*

Travelodge offers good quality, good value, modern accommodation. Ideal for families, the spacious en suite bedrooms include remote-control TV, tea and coffee-making facilities and comfortable beds. Meals can be taken at the nearby family restaurant. See Hotel Groups pages for further details.

Rooms 40 en suite S fr £26; D fr £26

SKEGNESS

MAP 17 TF56

★★★ 68% **HOTEL**

Crown

Drummond Rd PE25 3AB
☎ 01754 610760 📠 01754 610847
e-mail: enquiries@crownhotel.biz

dir: *On entering town follow Gibraltor Point Nature Reserve signs*

The Crown is ideally situated just a short walk from the seafront and town centre, close to Seacroft Golf Course and bird sanctuary. Homely bedrooms are attractively decorated and thoughtfully equipped. Public areas include a spacious bar offering a wide selection of dishes, a formal restaurant, residents' TV lounge and indoor pool; ample parking is provided.

Rooms 29 en suite (4 fmly) ⊘ in 16 bedrooms S £50; D £80 (incl. bkfst) **Facilities** STV 🔾 **Conf** BC Thtr 100 Class 60 Board 60 **Services** Lift **Parking** 52 **Notes** LB ⊗ ⊘ in restaurant Civ Wed 120

See advert on opposite page

★★★ 66% **HOTEL**

Best Western Vine

Vine Rd, Seacroft PE25 3DB
☎ 01754 763018 & 610611 📠 01754 769845
e-mail: info@thevinehotel.com
dir: A52 to Skegness, S towards Gibraltar Point, turn right on to Drummond Rd, after 0.5m turn right into Vine Rd

Reputedly the second oldest building in Skegness, this traditional style hotel offers two character bars that serve excellent local beers. Freshly prepared dishes are served in both the bar and the restaurant; service is both friendly and helpful. The smartly decorated bedrooms are well equipped and comfortably appointed.

Rooms 24 en suite (3 fmly) ⊛ in 6 bedrooms S £59-£69; D £84-£110 (incl. bkfst) **Facilities** STV ⅃ 18 Putt green Wi-fi in bedrooms Xmas **Conf** Thtr 100 Class 25 Board 30 Del from £85 **Parking** 50 **Notes LB** ⊛ in restaurant Civ Wed 100

★★ 71% **HOTEL**

North Shore

North Shore Rd PE25 1DN
☎ 01754 763298 📠 01754 761902
e-mail: golf@north-shore.co.uk
web: www.north-shore.co.uk
dir: 1m N of town centre on A52, turn right into North Shore Road (opposite Fenland laundry)

This hotel enjoys an enviable position on the beachfront, adjacent to its own championship golf course and only ten minutes from the town centre. Spacious public areas include a terrace bar serving informal meals and real ales, a formal restaurant and impressive function rooms. Bedrooms are smartly decorated and thoughtfully equipped.

Rooms 33 en suite 3 annexe en suite (4 fmly) S £35-£59; D £53-£81 (incl. bkfst) **Facilities** ⅃ 18 Snooker Putt green Wi-fi in bedrooms Xmas **Conf** Thtr 220 Class 60 Board 60 Del from £85 **Parking** 200 **Notes LB** ⊛ ⊛ in restaurant Civ Wed 180

England

SLEAFORD
MAP 12 TF04

★★★ 67% **HOTEL**

Carre Arms Hotel & Conference Centre
1 Mareham Ln NG34 7JP
☎ 01529 303156 ▤ 01529 303139
e-mail: enquiries@carrearmshotel.co.uk
web: www.carrearmshotel.co.uk
dir: take A153 to Sleaford, hotel on right at level crossing

This friendly, family run hotel is located close to the station and offers suitably appointed non-smoking accommodation. Public areas include a smart brasserie and two spacious bars where a good selection of meals is offered. There is also a conservatory, and a former stable that houses the spacious function room.

Rooms 13 en suite (2 fmly) ⊗ in all bedrooms S fr £55; D fr £75 (incl. bkfst) **Conf** Thtr 120 Class 70 Board 40 Del from £52.00 **Parking** 100 **Notes** ⊗ ⊗ in restaurant

★★★ 67% **HOTEL**

The Lincolnshire Oak
THE INDEPENDENTS
East Rd NG34 7EH
☎ 01529 413807 ▤ 01529 413710
e-mail: reception@lincolnshire-oak.co.uk
web: www.lincolnshire-oak.co.uk
dir: From A17 onto A153 into Sleaford. Hotel 0.75m on left

Located on the edge of the town in well-tended grounds, this hotel has a relaxed and friendly atmosphere. A comfortable open-plan lounge bar is complemented by a cosy restaurant that looks out onto the rear garden. There are also several meeting rooms. Bedroom styles differ - all rooms are well furnished and suitably equipped; the superior rooms are more comfortably appointed.

Rooms 17 en suite ⊗ in 12 bedrooms S £59.50-£89.50; D £79.50-£95 (incl. bkfst) **Facilities** STV Wi-fi in bedrooms **Conf** Thtr 140 Class 70 Board 50 Del from £90 **Parking** 80 **Notes** LB ⊗ ⊗ in restaurant Civ Wed 90

See advert on opposite page

BUDGET HOTEL

Travelodge Sleaford

Holdingham NG34 8PN
☎ 08700 850 950 ▤ 01529 414752
web: www.travelodge.co.uk
dir: 1m N, at rdbt A17/A15

Travelodge offers good quality, good value, modern accommodation. Ideal for families, the spacious en suite bedrooms include remote-control TV, tea and coffee-making facilities and comfortable beds. Meals can be taken at the nearby family restaurant. See Hotel Groups pages for further details.

Rooms 40 en suite S fr £26; D fr £26

SOUTH WITHAM
MAP 11 SK91

BUDGET HOTEL

Travelodge Grantham South Witham
New Fox NG33 5LN
☎ 08700 850 950 ▤ 01572 767 586
web: www.travelodge.co.uk
dir: on A1, northbound

Travelodge offers good quality, good value, modern accommodation. Ideal for families, the spacious en suite bedrooms include remote-control TV, tea and coffee-making facilities and comfortable beds. Meals can be taken at the nearby family restaurant. See Hotel Groups pages for further details.

Rooms 32 en suite S fr £26; D fr £26

SPALDING
MAP 12 TF22

★★ 75% ❀ **HOTEL**

Cley Hall
22 High St PE11 1TX
☎ 01775 725157 ▤ 01775 710785
e-mail: cleyhall@kingscountryhotels.co.uk
dir: from A16/A151 rbt in Spalding direction, (with river on right) hotel 1.5m on left

This Georgian house overlooks the River Welland, with landscaped gardens to the rear. Most bedrooms are in an adjacent building; all are smart and include modern amenities. Public rooms include a choice of dining options that feature a brasserie restaurant and guests also have the use of a smart lounge bar.

Rooms 4 en suite 11 annexe en suite (2 GF) **Facilities** STV **Conf** Thtr 35 Class 20 Board 18 **Parking** 13 **Notes** LB Civ Wed 40

STALLINGBOROUGH
MAP 17 TA11

★★★ 72% **HOTEL**

Stallingborough Grange Hotel
Riby Rd DN41 8BU
☎ 01469 561302 ▤ 01469 561338
e-mail: grange.hot@virgin.net
web: www.stallingborough-grange.com
dir: from A180 follow Stallingborough Ind Est signs. Through village. From rdbt take A1173/Caistor. Hotel 1m on left just past windmill

This 18th-century country house has been tastefully extended to provide spacious and well-equipped bedrooms, particularly in the

continued

executive wing. A family-run hotel that is popular with locals who enjoy the wide range of food offered in either the Tavern or the restaurant.

Rooms 41 en suite (6 fmly) (9 GF) ⊗ in all bedrooms **Facilities** STV **Conf** Thtr 60 Class 40 Board 28 **Parking** 100 **Notes LB** ⊗ ⊘ in restaurant Civ Wed 65

STAMFORD   MAP 11 TF00

★★★ 85% ⊛ HOTEL

The George of Stamford

71 St Martins PE9 2LB

☎ 01780 750750 & 750700 (Res) 🖻 01780 750701

e-mail: reservations@georgehotelofstamford.com

web: www.georgehotelofstamford.com

dir: 15m N of Peterborough exit A1 onto B1081, 1m on left

Steeped in hundreds of years of history, this delightful coaching inn provides spacious public areas that include a choice of dining options, inviting lounges, a business centre and a range of quality shops. A highlight is afternoon tea, taken in the colourful courtyard when weather permits. Bedrooms are stylishly appointed and range from traditional to contemporary in design.

Rooms 47 en suite (2 fmly) ⊗ in all bedrooms S £78-£125; D £115-£225 (incl. bkfst) **Facilities** STV ⅃ Wi-fi in bedrooms Xmas **Conf** BC Thtr 50 Class 25 Board 25 Del from £145 **Parking** 120 **Notes LB** Civ Wed 50

★★★ 77% HOTEL

Crown

All Saints Place PE9 2AG

☎ 01780 763136 🖻 01780 756111

e-mail: reservations@thecrownhotelstamford.co.uk

web: www.thecrownhotelstamford.co.uk

dir: off A1 onto A43, straight through town until Red Lion Square, hotel is behind All Saints church in the square

This small, privately owned hotel is ideally situated in the town centre. Unpretentious British food is served in the modern dining areas and hospitality is spontaneous and sincere. The spacious bar is popular with locals. Bedrooms have been upgraded to a very high standard - quite contemporary in style and very well equipped, some have four-poster beds; additional 'superior' rooms are located in a renovated Georgian town house just a short walk up the street.

Rooms 17 en suite 7 annexe rms (6 en suite) (2 fmly) (1 GF) ⊗ in all bedrooms S £85-£110; D £100-£150 (incl. bkfst) **Facilities** STV Use of local health/gym club **Conf** BC Thtr 20 Class 12 Board 12 Del £140 **Parking** 21 **Notes LB** ⊗ ⊘ in restaurant

★★★ 72% HOTEL

Garden House

High St, St Martins PE9 2LP

☎ 01780 763359 🖻 01780 763339

e-mail: enquiries@gardenhousehotel.com

web: www.gardenhousehotel.com

dir: A1 to South Stamford, B1081, signed Stamford & Burghley House. Hotel on left on entering town

Situated within a few minutes' walk of the town centre, this transformed 18th-century town house provides pleasant accommodation. Bedroom styles vary; all are well equipped and comfortably furnished. Public rooms include a charming lounge bar, conservatory restaurant and a smart breakfast room. Service is attentive and friendly throughout.

Rooms 20 en suite (2 fmly) (4 GF) ⊗ in all bedrooms S £65-£90; D £90-£150 (incl. bkfst) **Facilities** STV Wi-fi in bedrooms Xmas **Conf** BC Thtr 40 Class 20 Board 20 Del from £110 **Parking** 22 **Notes LB** ⊘ in restaurant Closed 26-30 Dec RS 1-12 Jan Civ Wed 60

★★ Ⓐ

Lady Anne's

St Martins Without PE9 2LJ

☎ 01780 481184 🖻 01780 765422

e-mail: warrenatlah@yahoo.co.uk

Rooms 27 en suite (6 fmly) (4 GF) S £60-£75; D £80-£120 (incl. bkfst) **Conf** Thtr 150 Class 75 Board 40 **Parking** 100 **Notes** Closed 27-30 Dec RS Sun eve

England

SUTTON ON SEA
MAP 17 TF58

★★★ 71% ◉ **HOTEL**

The Grange & Links
Sea Ln, Sandilands LN12 2RA
☎ 01507 441334 📠 01507 443033
e-mail: grangeandlinkshotel@btconnect.com
web: www.grangeandlinkshotel.co.uk
dir: A1111 to Sutton-on-Sea, follow signs to Sandilands

This friendly, family-run hotel sits in five acres of grounds, close to both the beach and its own 18-hole links golf course. Bedrooms are pleasantly appointed and are well equipped for both business and leisure guests. Public rooms include ample lounge areas, a formal restaurant and a traditional bar, serving a wide range of meals and snacks.

Rooms 23 en suite (10 fmly) (3 GF) ⊗ in 3 bedrooms S fr £59.50; D fr £78 (incl. bkfst) **Facilities** ↓ 18 ⌇ Snooker Gym ⛳ Putt green Bowls ch fac **Conf** Thtr 200 Board 100 Del fr £87 **Parking** 60 **Notes LB** ⊗ Civ Wed 150

How do I find the perfect place?

WINTERINGHAM
MAP 17 SE92

★★★ ◉◉◉◉ **HOTEL**

Winteringham Fields
DN15 9PF
☎ 01724 733096 📠 01724 733898
e-mail: wintfields@aol.com
web: www.winteringhamfields.com
dir: in the centre of the village at the x-rds

This highly praised establishment, located deep in the north Lincolnshire countryside, has seen a change of ownership. But this 16th-century manor house definitely remains a destination to seek out for a relaxing and indulgent stay. There are luxury bedrooms, executive suites and the Dovecote and The Cottage that are just a couple of minutes' walk away. The young and talented chef, Robert Thompson uses vegetables and herbs from the hotel's own gardens, fish from Grimsby and game in season amongst the ingredients to create his own style of award-winning and inspiring cuisine.

Rooms 4 en suite 6 annexe en suite (3 GF) ⊗ in all bedrooms **Parking** 14 **Notes** ⊗ in restaurant Closed 25 Dec for 2 wks, last wk Oct, 2 wk Aug

WOODHALL SPA   MAP 17 TF16

★★★ 74% **HOTEL**

Petwood

Stixwould Rd LN10 6QF

☎ 01526 352411 📠 01526 353473

e-mail: reception@petwood.co.uk

web: www.petwood.co.uk

dir: *from Sleaford take A153 (signed Skegness). At Tattershall turn left on B1192. Hotel is signed from village*

This lovely Edwardian house, set in 30 acres of gardens and woodlands, is adjacent to Woodhall Golf Course. Built in 1905, the house was used by 617 Squadron, the famous Dambusters, as an officers' mess during World War II. Bedrooms and public areas are spacious and comfortable, and retain many original features. Weddings and conferences are well catered for in modern facilities.

Rooms 56 en suite (3 GF) ⊗ in 17 bedrooms S fr £92; D fr £136 (incl. bkfst) **Facilities** Snooker 🏌 Putt green Complimentary pass to leisure centre ♫ Xmas **Conf** Thtr 250 Class 100 Board 50 Del from £110 **Services** Lift **Parking** 140 **Notes LB** ⊗ in restaurant Civ Wed 200

★★★ 71% **HOTEL**

Woodhall Spa

The Broadway LN10 6ST

☎ 01526 353231 📠 01526 352797

e-mail: reception@woodhallspahotel.co.uk

dir: *In village centre, 500tmrs from golf course*

This family owned hotel is located in the centre of town, close to local shops and golf courses. Modern bedrooms are equipped for both business and leisure guests. Public areas include a bar and lounge in addition to a formal restaurant. A good range of local produce to suit all tastes is available.

Rooms 25 en suite (2 fmly) (2 GF) ⊗ in all bedrooms S £65-£105; D £84.50-£114.95 (incl. bkfst) **Facilities** STV FTV Wi-fi in bedrooms Xmas **Conf** Thtr 100 Class 40 Board 40 Del from £95 **Services** Lift **Parking** 30 **Notes LB** ⊛ ⊗ in restaurant Civ Wed 86

See advert on this page

★★★ 67% **HOTEL**

Golf Hotel

The Broadway LN10 6SG

☎ 01526 353535 📠 01526 353096

e-mail: reception@thegolf-hotel.com

web: www.thegolf-hotel.com

dir: *from Lincoln take B1189 to Metheringham onto B1191 towards Woodhall Spa. Hotel on left approx 500yds from rdbt*

Located near the centre of the village, this traditional hotel is ideally situated to explore the Lincolnshire countryside and coast. The adjacent golf course makes this a popular venue for golfers, and the hotels hydrotherapy suite uses the original spa water supplies. Bedrooms vary in size.

Rooms 50 en suite (4 fmly) (8 GF) ⊗ in 21 bedrooms S £65 £105; D £85-£125 (incl. bkfst) **Facilities Spa** STV Guests have use of private leisure centre 1m from hotel Xmas **Conf** Thtr 150 Class 50 Board 50 Del from £95 **Services** Lift **Parking** 100 **Notes LB** ⊗ in restaurant Civ Wed 150

Index of London Hotels

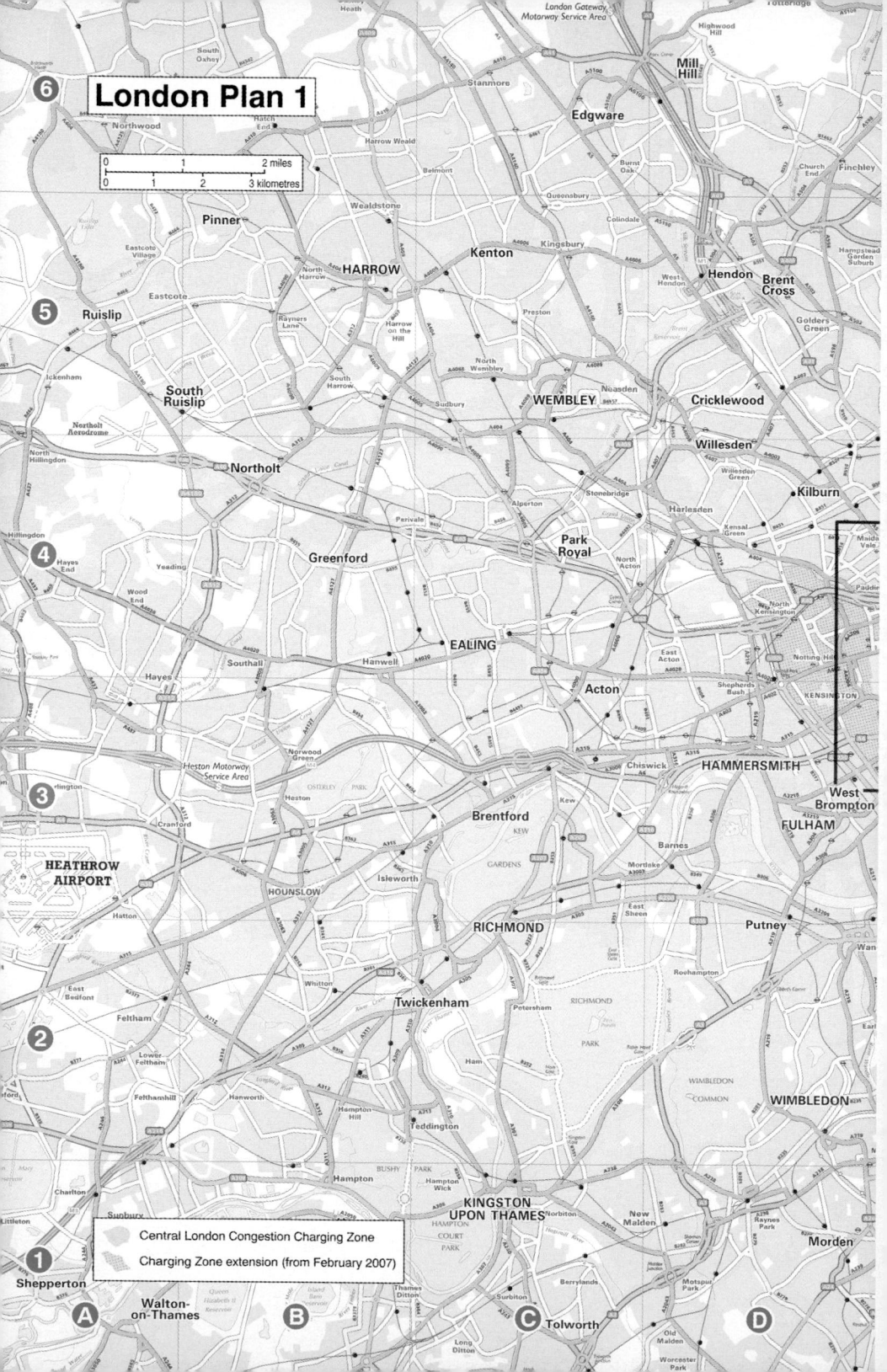

London Plan 1

0   1   2 miles
0   1   2   3 kilometres

Central London Congestion Charging Zone

Charging Zone extension (from February 2007)

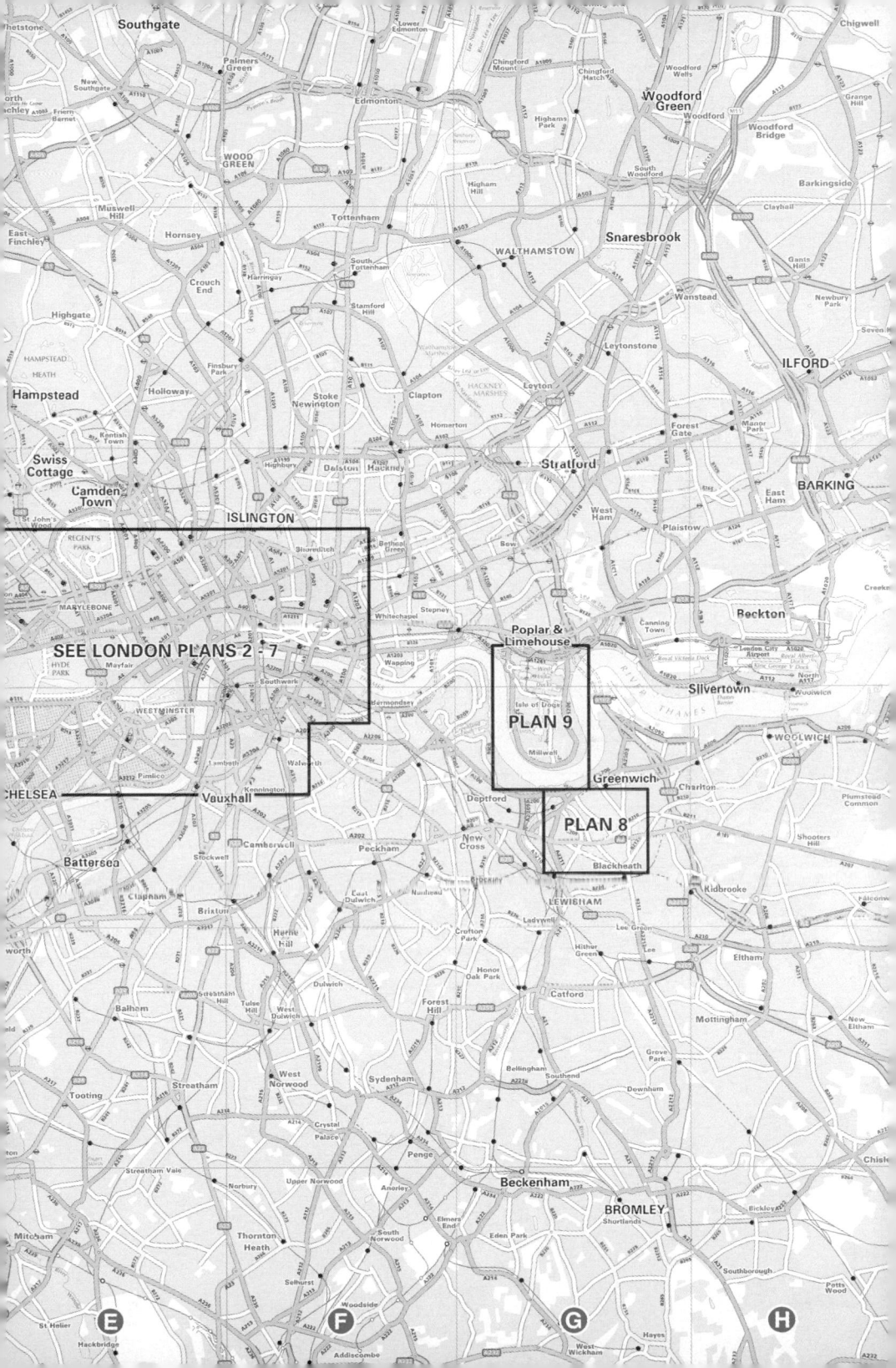

London Plan 2

Maida Vale

Paddington
Recreation
Ground

0   220   440 yards
0   100   200   300   400 metres

London
Marriott
Maida Vale

Westbourne
Green

Maida Vale
Station

Middlesex CCC
(Lord's Cricket
Ground)

Lord's Tour
& MCC
Museum

BBC
Studios

Warwick
Avenue Station

Warwick Avenue Station

Little
Venice

Paddington
Recreation
Ground

Park Station

PADDINGTON

Royal Oak
Station

Paddington
Station

St Marys
Hospital

Brunel
Estate

Delmere Hotel
Days Hotel
London Hyde Park

Best Western Paddington,
Court Hotel and Suites

Bayswater

Berjaya
Eden Park

Bayswater
Station

Royal
Lancaster Hotel

Thistle
Hyde Park

The Gresham
Hyde Park

Corus hotel
Hyde Park

Lancaster
Gate Station

Pembridge
Court
Hotel

Ramada
Hyde Park

Thistle
Kensington
Gardens

Queensway
Station

The Abbey
Court

Notting Hill Gate Stn

Kensington
Gardens

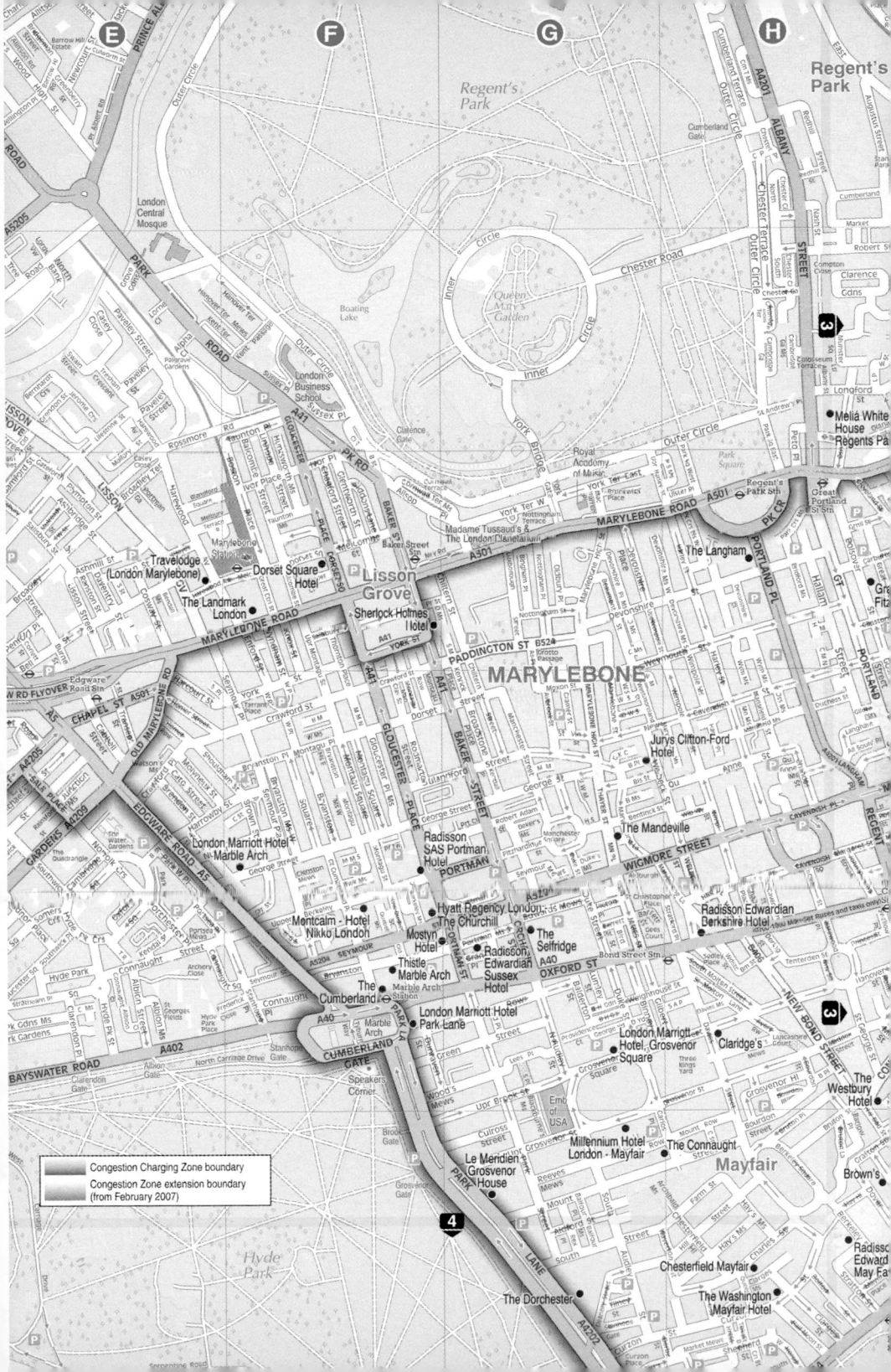

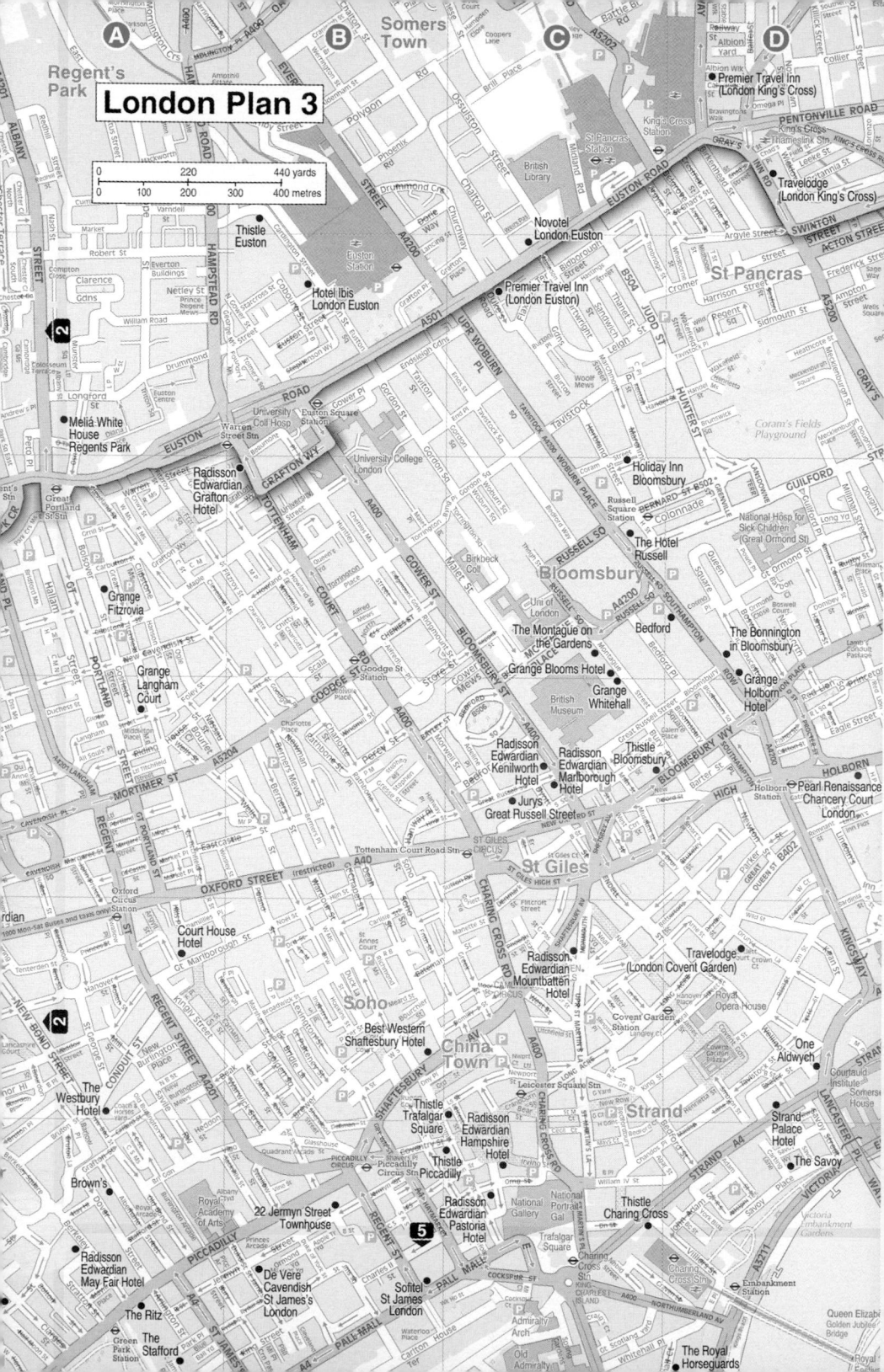

London Plan 4

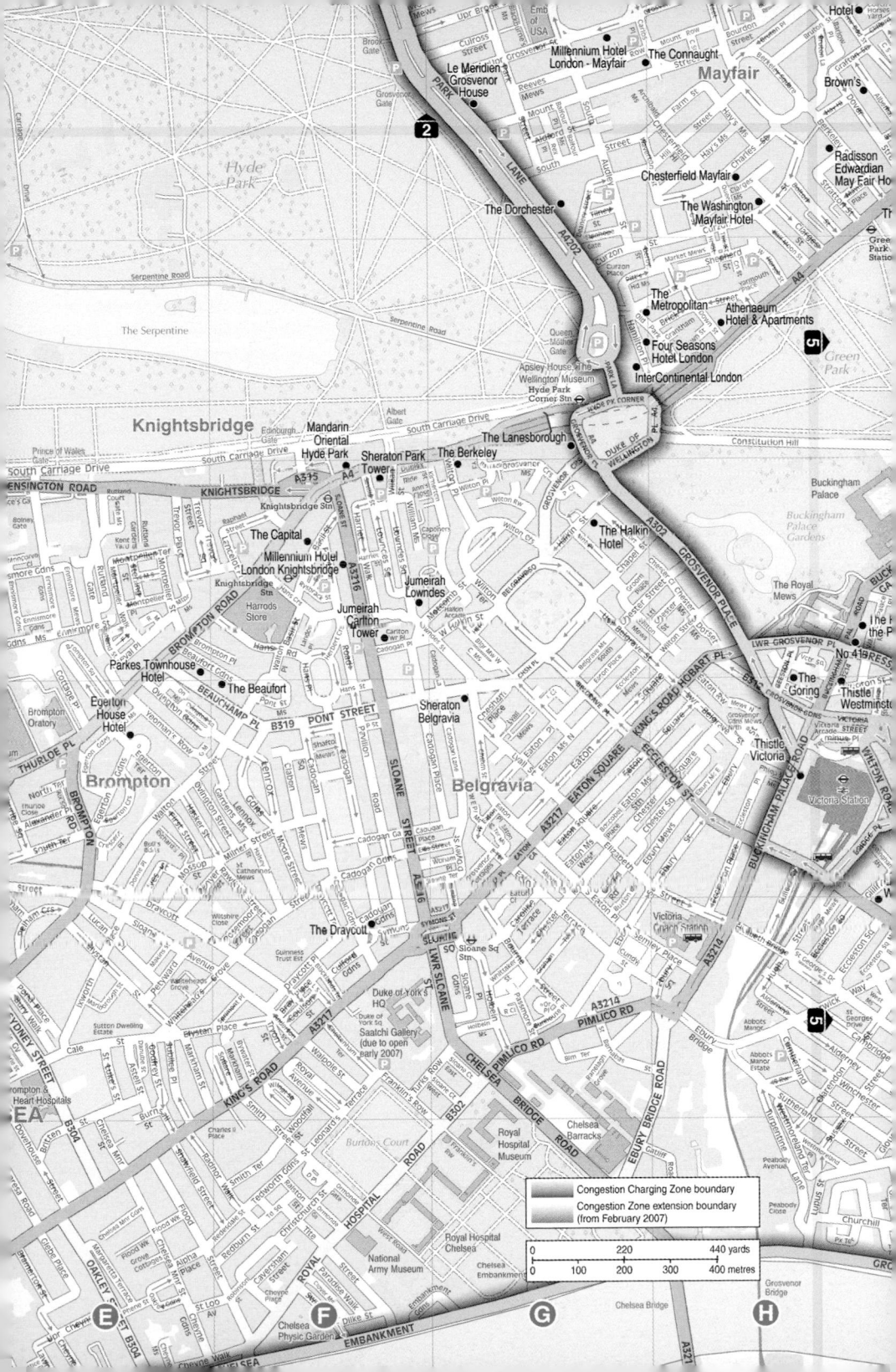

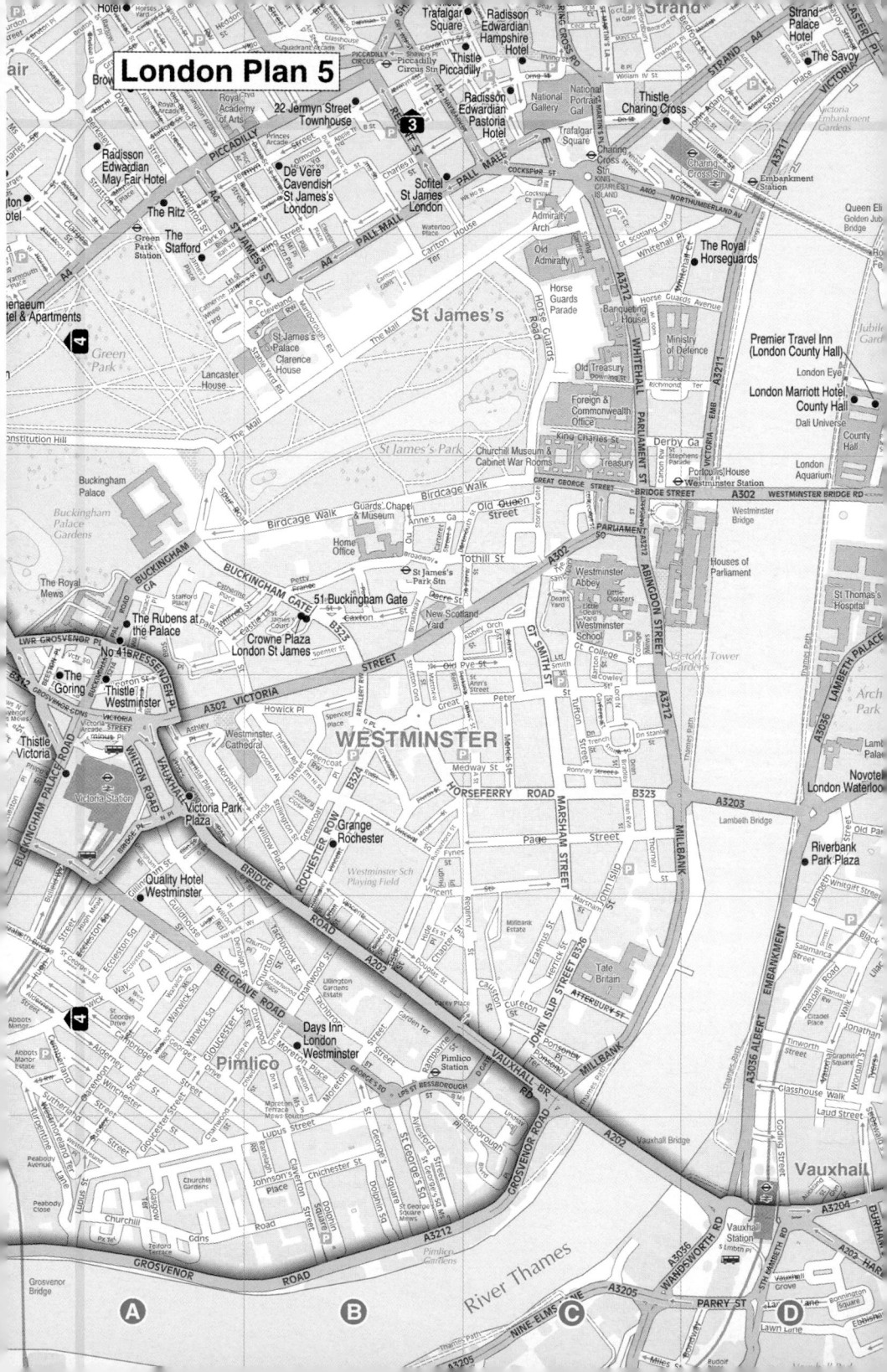

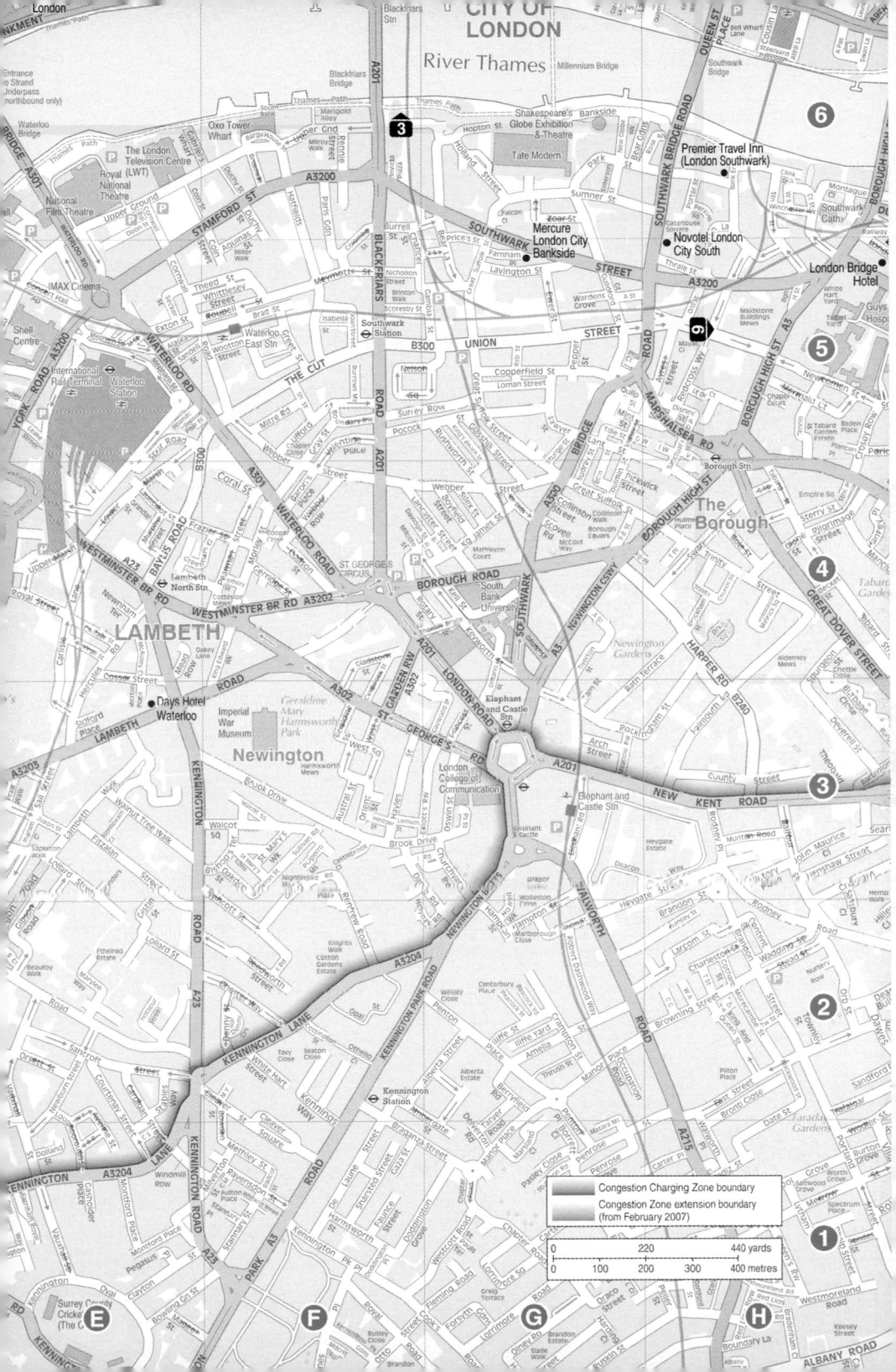

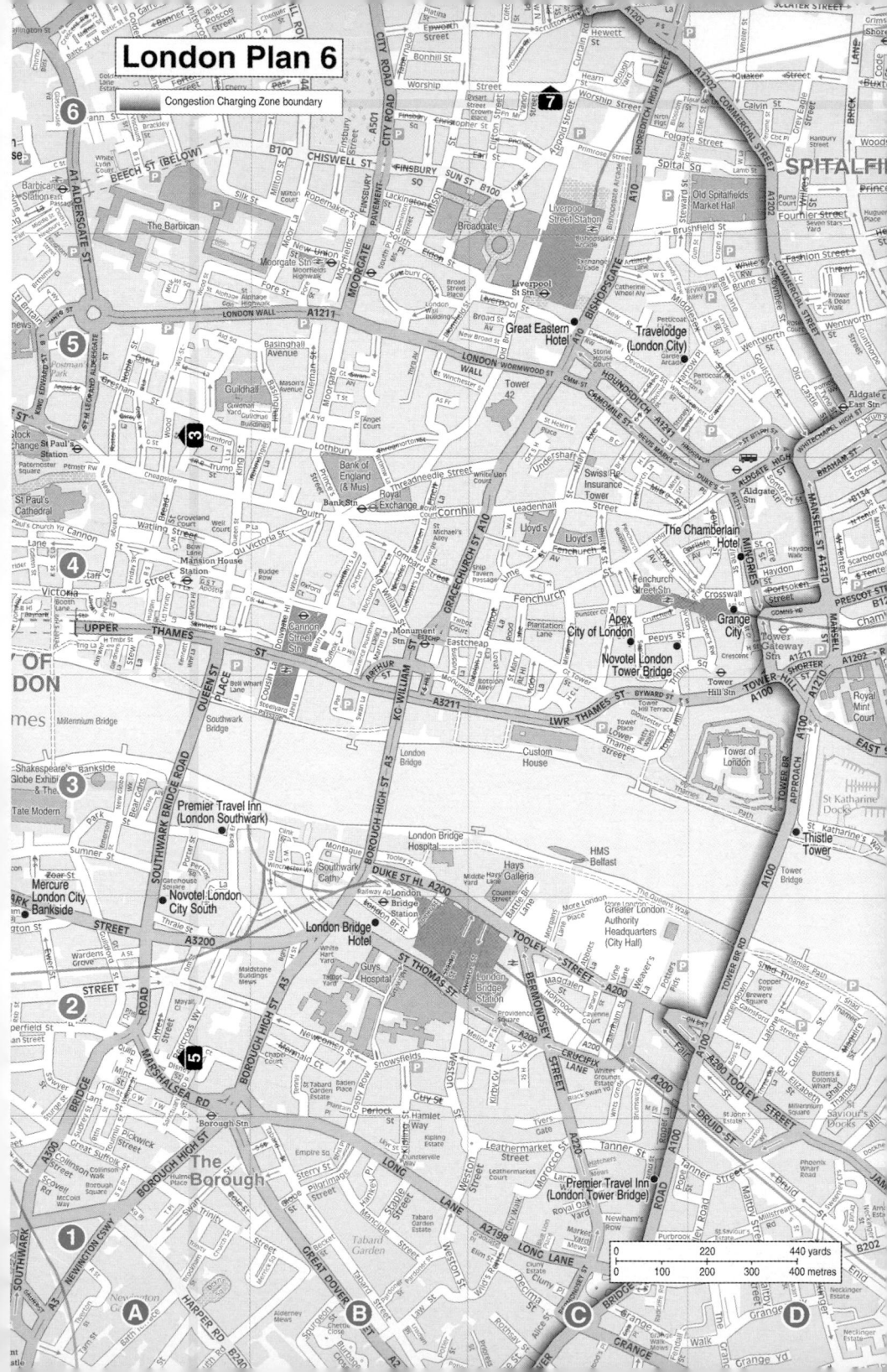

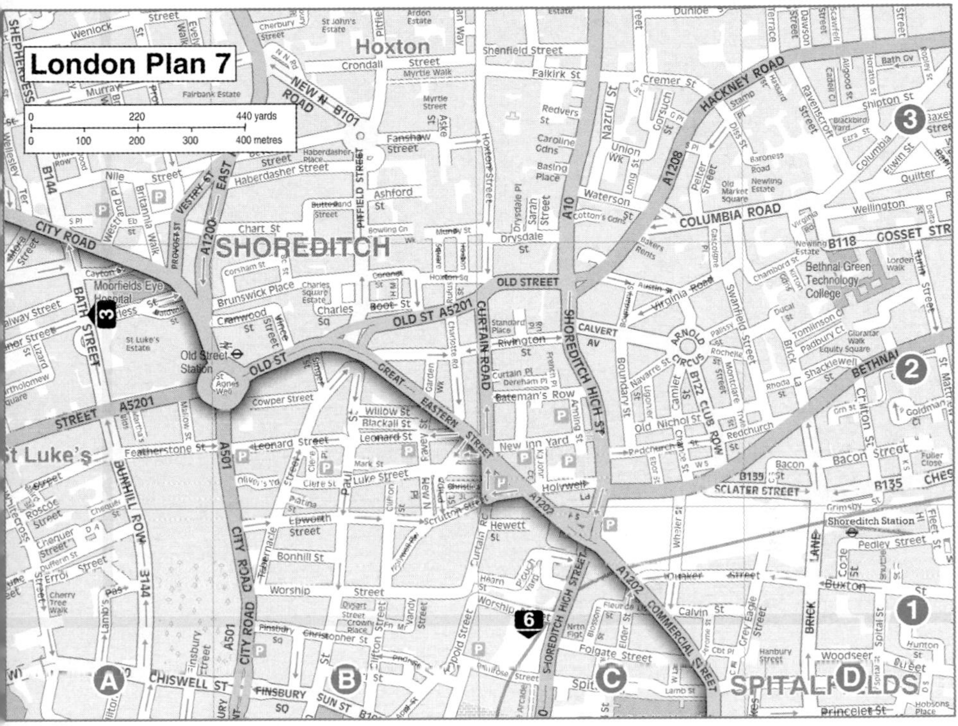

London Plan 7

Hoxton

SHOREDITCH

St Luke's

SPITALFIELDS

CITY ROAD

OLD STREET · OLD ST A5201

GREAT EASTERN STREET

SHOREDITCH HIGH ST

COLUMBIA ROAD

HACKNEY ROAD

GOSSET STR

BETHNAL

Bethnal Green Technology College

Moorfields Eye Hospital

Old Street Station

SLATER STREET

Shoreditch Station

COMMERCIAL STREET

CHISWELL ST · FINSBURY SQ · SUN ST

A B C D

220 440 yards
100 200 300 400 metres

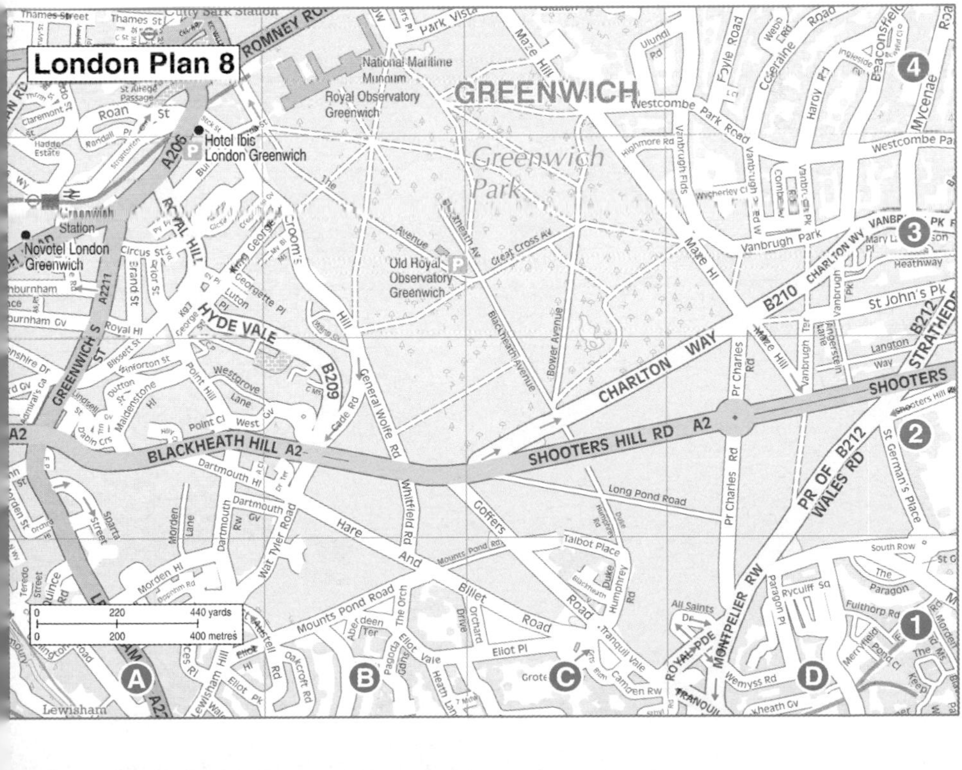

London Plan 8

GREENWICH

Greenwich Park

National Maritime Museum
Royal Observatory Greenwich

Hotel Ibis London Greenwich

Novotel London Greenwich

Greenwich Station

Old Royal Observatory Greenwich

CHARLTON WAY

SHOOTERS HILL RD A2

BLACKHEATH HILL A2

HYDE VALE

Mounts Pond Road

PR OF WALES RD

MONTPELIER RW

ROYAL PDE

A B C D

220 440 yards
200 400 metres

LONDON

Greater London Plans 1-9, pages 414-426. (Small scale maps 6 & 7 at back of book.) Hotels are listed below in postal district order, commencing East, then North, South and West, with a brief indication of the area covered. Detailed plans 2-9 show the locations of AA-appointed hotels within the Central London postal districts. If you do not know the postal district of the hotel you want, please refer to the index preceding the street plans for the entry and map pages.

E1 STEPNEY AND EAST OF THE TOWER OF LONDON

★★★★ 75% HOTEL  PLAN 6 D3

Thistle Tower

St Katherine's Way E1W 1LD

THISTLE HOTELS

☎ 0870 333 9106 📠 0870 333 9206

e-mail: tower@guoman.co.uk

dir: *Follow signs for Tower Bridge, turn left into St. Katherine's Way. Approach car park by barrier control.*

This extensive modern hotel enjoys superb views over the Thames, Tower Bridge and St Katherine's Docks. Public areas, which have been substantially refurbished, include several lounges, a modern, contemporary bar and a choice of restaurants. Bedrooms are traditionally furnished and include a selection of impressive suites.

Rooms 801 en suite ⊗ in 550 bedrooms **Facilities** STV Gym **Conf** BC Thtr 500 Class 350 Board 65 **Services** Lift air con **Parking** 120 **Notes** ⊛ Civ Wed 500

BUDGET HOTEL PLAN 6 C5

Travelodge London Liverpool Street

1 Harrow Place E1 7DB

Travelodge

☎ 08700 850 950 📠 020 7626 1105

web: www.travelodge.co.uk

Travelodge offers good quality, good value, modern accommodation. Ideal for families, the spacious en suite bedrooms include remote-control TV, tea and coffee-making facilities and comfortable beds. Meals can be taken at the nearby family restaurant. See Hotel Groups pages for further details.

Rooms 142 en suite S fr £26; D fr £26

E6 BECKTON

See **LONDON PLAN 1 H4**

BUDGET HOTEL

Premier Travel Inn London Beckton

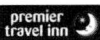

1 Woolwich Manor Way, Beckton E6 5NT

☎ 08701 977029 📠 020 7511 4214

web: www.premiertravelinn.com

dir: *from A13 take A117, Woolwich Manor Way, towards City Airport, on left after 1st rdbt*

High quality, modern budget accommodation ideal for both families and business travellers. Spacious, en suite bedrooms feature bath and shower, satellite TV and many have telephones and modem points. The adjacent family restaurant features a wide and varied menu. For further details consult the Hotel Groups page.

Rooms 90 en suite

E11 SNARESBROOK

See **LONDON PLAN 1 G5**

BUDGET HOTEL

Innkeeper's Lodge London Snaresbrook

Innkeeper's Lodge

73 Hollybush Hill, Snaresbrook E11 1PE

☎ 020 8989 7618

web: www.innkeeperslodge.com

Smart, en suite accommodation ideal for both business & leisure guests. Bedrooms are very well equipped, including Sky TV, telephone, modem points, tea & coffee making facilities, (family rooms in most locations). Complimentary breakfast. The adjacent Pub Restaurant; a Harvester, Vintage Inn, Toby Carvery, Ember Inn, Sizzling Pubco or Pub & Carvery offers an all day menu. See Hotel Groups pages for further details.

Rooms 24 rms S £59.95; D £59.95

E14 CANARY WHARF & LIMEHOUSE

See also **LONDON PLAN 1 G3**

INSPECTORS' CHOICE

★★★★★ ⊛ HOTEL PLAN 9 A6

Four Seasons Hotel Canary Wharf

Westferry Circus, Canary Wharf E14 8RS

☎ 020 7510 1999 📠 020 7510 1998

e-mail: res.canarywharf@fourseasons.com

web: www.fourseasons.com/canarywharf

dir: *From A13 follow signs to Canary Wharf, Isle of Dogs and Westferry Circus. Hotel off 3rd exit of Westferry Circus rdbt*

With superb views over the London skyline, this stylish modern hotel enjoys a delightful riverside location. Spacious contemporary bedrooms are particularly thoughtfully equipped. Public areas include the Italian Quadrato Bar and Restaurant, an impressive business centre and gym. Guests also have complimentary use of the impressive Holmes Place health club and spa. Welcoming staff provide exemplary levels of service and hospitality.

Rooms 142 en suite ⊗ in 120 bedrooms S £376-£2350; D £399.50-£2350 **Facilities Spa** STV FTV 🖭 supervised 🏊 Sauna Solarium Gym Jacuzzi Wi-fi available ♫ Xmas **Conf** BC Thtr 200 Class 120 Board 56 **Services** Lift air con **Parking** 54 **Notes** Civ Wed 200

England

E14 CANARY WHARF & LIMEHOUSE *continued*

★★★★★ 83% @ **HOTEL**   PLAN 9 B6

London Marriott West India Quay

Marriott
HOTELS & RESORTS

22 Hertsmere Rd, Canary Wharf E14 4ED
☎ 020 7093 1000 ▤ 020 7093 1001
web: www.marriott.co.uk

dir: *exit Aspen Way at Hertsmere Road. Hotel opposite, adjacent to Canary Wharf*

This spectacular skyscraper, with curved glass façade, is located at the Docklands' heart, adjacent to Canary Wharf and overlooking the water. The hotel is modern, but not pretentiously trendy, and eye-catching floral displays give warmth to the public areas. Bedrooms, many overlooking the quay, provide every modern convenience, including broadband access and air-conditioning. Curve Restaurant offers good quality cooking focusing on fresh fish.

Rooms 301 en suite (22 fmly) ⊗ in 232 bedrooms S £99-275; D £99-£275 **Facilities** STV Sauna Solarium Gym Wi-fi available **Conf** BC Thtr 290 Class 132 Board 27 **Services** Lift air con **Notes** ⊗ ⊗ in restaurant Civ Wed 290

BUDGET HOTEL   PLAN 9 D6

Hotel Ibis London Docklands

ibis
Accor
hotels

1 Baffin Way E14 9PE
☎ 020 7517 1100 ▤ 020 7987 5916
e-mail: H2177@accor.com
web: www.ibishotel.com

dir: *from Tower Bridge follow City Airport and Royal Docks signs, exit for 'Isle of Dogs'. Hotel 1st left opposite McDonalds*

Modern, budget hotel offering comfortable accommodation in bright and practical bedrooms. Breakfast is self-service and dinner is available in the restaurant. For further details, consult the Hotel Groups page.

Rooms 87 en suite S £58.95-£78.95; D £58.95-£78.95

BUDGET HOTEL

Travelodge London Docklands

Coriander Av, East India Dock Rd E14 2AA
☎ 08700 850 950 ▤ 020 7515 9178
web: www.travelodge.co.uk

Travelodge

dir: *on A13 at East India Dock Rd*

Travelodge offers good quality, good value, modern accommodation. Ideal for families, the spacious en suite bedrooms include remote-control TV, tea and coffee-making facilities and comfortable beds. Meals can be taken at the nearby family restaurant. See Hotel Groups pages for further details.

Rooms 232 en suite S fr £26; D fr £26

E15 STRATFORD
See LONDON PLAN 1 G4

BUDGET HOTEL

Hotel Ibis London Stratford

1A Romford Rd, Stratford E15 4LJ
☎ 020 8536 3700 ▤ 020 8519 5161
e-mail: h3099@accor.com
web: www.ibishotel.com

Modern, budget hotel offering comfortable accommodation in bright and practical bedrooms. Breakfast is self-service and dinner is available in the restaurant. For further details, consult the Hotel Groups page.

Rooms 108 en suite S £55.95-£67.95; D £55.95-£67.95

E16 SILVERTOWN
See LONDON PLAN 1 H3

★★★★ 74% **HOTEL**

Novotel London ExCel

NOVOTEL
Accor

7 Western Gateway, Royal Victoria Docks E16 1AA
☎ 020 7540 9700 ▤ 020 7540 9710
e-mail: H3656@accor.com
web: www.novotel.com

dir: *M25 junct 30. A13 towards 'City', exit at Canning Town. Follow signs to 'ExCel West'. Hotel adjacent*

This hotel is situated adjacent to the ExCel exhibition centre and overlooks the Royal Victoria Dock. Design throughout the hotel is contemporary and stylish. Public rooms include a range of meeting rooms, a modern coffee station, indoor leisure facilities and a smart bar and restaurant, both with a terrace overlooking the dock. Bedrooms feature modern decor, a bath and separate shower and an extensive range of extras.

Rooms 257 en suite (211 fmly) ⊗ in 183 bedrooms S £75-£175; D £85-£195 (incl. bkfst) **Facilities** STV Sauna Gym Wi-fi in bedrooms Steam room,relaxation room with massage bed Xmas **Conf** Thtr 70 Class 55 Board 30 Del from £165 **Services** Lift air con **Parking** 80 **Notes LB** No children Civ Wed 50

BUDGET HOTEL

Hotel Ibis London ExCel

ibis
Accor
hotels

9 Western Gateway, Royal Victoria Docks E16 1AB
☎ 020 7055 2300 ▤ 020 7055 2310
e-mail: H3655@accor-hotels.com
web: www.ibishotel.com

dir: *M25 then A13 to London, City Airport, ExCel East*

Modern, budget hotel offering comfortable accommodation in bright and practical bedrooms. Breakfast is self-service and dinner is available in the restaurant. For further details, consult the Hotel Groups page.

Rooms 278 en suite S fr £49.95; D fr £49.95

England

BUDGET HOTEL

Premier Travel Inn London Docklands (ExCeL)

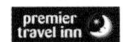

Royal Victoria Dock E16 1SL

☎ 0870 238 3322 🖷 020 7540 2250

web: www.premiertravelinn.com

dir: on ExCel East. A13 onto A1020. At Connaught rdbt take 2nd exit into Connaught Road. Inn on right

High quality, modern budget accommodation ideal for both families and business travellers. Spacious, en suite bedrooms feature bath and shower, satellite TV and many have telephones and modem points. The adjacent family restaurant features a wide and varied menu. For further details consult the Hotel Groups page.

Rooms 202 en suite

BUDGET HOTEL

Travelodge London City Airport

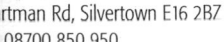

Hartman Rd, Silvertown E16 2BZ

☎ 08700 850 950

web: www.travelodge.co.uk

dir: Follow signs for London City Airport. Travelodge at entrance of Airport at junction between A1011 & A112.

Travelodge offers good quality, good value, modern accommodation. Ideal for families, the spacious en suite bedrooms include remote-control TV, tea and coffee-making facilities and comfortable beds. Meals can be taken at the nearby family restaurant. See Hotel Groups pages for further details.

Rooms 142 en suite S fr £26; D fr £26

EC1 CITY OF LONDON

★★★ 82% 🏵 HOTEL

PLAN 3 G4

Malmaison Charterhouse Square

Malmaison
hotels that dare to be different

18-21 Charterhouse Square, Clerkenwell EC1M 6AH

☎ 020 7012 3700 🖷 020 7012 3702

e-mail: london@malmaison.com

web: www.malmaison.com

dir: Exit Barbican Station turn left, take 1st left. Hotel on the far left corner of Charterhouse Square

Situated in a leafy and peaceful square Malmaison Charterhouse maintains the same focus on quality service and food as the other hotels in the group. The bedrooms, stylishly decorated in calming tones, have all the expected facilities including power showers, CD players and free internet access. The brasserie and bar at the hotel's centre has a buzzing atmosphere and traditional French cuisine. Malmaison - AA Hotel Group of the Year 2006-7.

Rooms 97 en suite (5 GF) ⊗ in 79 bedrooms S £205.63-£252.63; £229.13-£252.63 **Facilities** STV Gym Wi-fi available ch fac **Conf** Thtr 30 Board 16 Del £297 **Services** Lift air con **Notes** ⊗ in restaurant

★★★ 75% HOTEL

PLAN 3 G5

Thistle City Barbican

THISTLE HOTELS

Central St, Clerkenwell EC1V 8DS

☎ 0870 333 9101 🖷 0870 333 9201

e-mail: CityBarbican@Thistle.co.uk

dir: From Kings Cross E, follow Pentonville Rd, right into Goswell Rd. At lights left into Lever St. Hotel on x-rds with Lever St & Central St.

Situated on the edge of the City, this modern hotel offers a complimentary shuttle bus to Barbican, Liverpool Street and Moorgate tube stations at peak times. Bedrooms are well equipped and include some smart executive and superior rooms; public areas include a bar, a coffee shop and restaurant along with a smart Otium leisure club and spa.

Rooms 463 en suite ⊗ in 150 bedrooms **Facilities** 🏊 supervised Sauna Solarium Gym Jacuzzi **Conf** BC Thtr 80 Class 60 Board 40 **Services** Lift **Parking** 12 **Notes** ⊗ ⊗ in restaurant

EC2

★★★★★ 87% 🏵🏵🏵 HOTEL

PLAN 6 C5

Great Eastern Hotel

Liverpool St EC2M 7QN

☎ 020 7618 5000 🖷 020 7618 5001

e-mail: sales@great-eastern-hotel.co.uk

web: www.great-eastern-hotel.co.uk

The largest hotel in the city, the Great Eastern is adjacent to Liverpool Street station. Design-led bedrooms are stylish and come complete with all the extras you could need. The impressive array of restaurants includes the elegant Aurora offering fine dining, Fishmarket with its champagne bar, Terminus offering all-day meals and snacks and a Miyabi, a Japanese restaurant. The basement gym offers a range of treatments, and personal trainers are available.

Rooms 267 en suite ⊗ in 74 bedrooms S £245; D £295 **Facilities** STV Gym steam room **Conf** Thtr 200 Class 120 **Services** Lift air con **Notes** LB Civ Wed

EC3 CHEAPSIDE

★★★★★ 78% HOTEL

PLAN 6 D4

The Grange City

Coopers Row EC3 2BQ

☎ 020 7863 3700 🖷 020 7863 3701

e-mail: city@grangehotels.com

web: www.grangehotels.co.uk

dir: M4 E into A4 E, to Piccadilly, onto Trafalgar Sq, B308 to Victoria Embankment, follow river, just before Tower Hill. Coopers Row on left

Enjoying a prime location, this modern hotel has views over the Tower of London and Tower Bridge from many bedrooms. The bedrooms themselves tend to be spacious and equipped with a comprehensive range of extras; air-conditioning is standard throughout. Public areas include extensive conference facilities and a very impressive leisure club. Guests can also choose from a variety of eating options from the Forum Restaurant offering European cuisine, the informal brasserie and Koto II, a Japanese-style sushi and noodle bar.

Rooms 302 en suite ⊗ in 200 bedrooms S £215-£290; D £215-£290 **Facilities** Spa STV 🏊 Sauna Gym Jacuzzi Wi-fi available Virtual golf simulator Xmas **Conf** BC Thtr 800 Class 400 Board 200 Del £307 **Services** Lift air con **Notes** LB ⊗

EC3 CHEAPSIDE *continued*

★★★★ 82% @ @ HOTEL
PLAN 6 C4

Apex City of London
No 1 Seething Ln EC3N 4AX
☎ 0845 365 0000 🗎 0131 666 5128
e-mail: www.londonsales@apexhotels.co.uk
dir: 1 min walk from Tower Hill tube station.

Situated close to Tower Bridge, this is one of the city's newest luxury
hotels. Set at the heart of the business district, the Apex is also ideal
for leisure travellers. Bedrooms are of a high standard and include
walk-in power showers. The gym has all the most up-to-date
equipment, and there's a sauna room. The eating options are
Addendum Restaurant and the less formal brasserie.

Rooms 130 en suite ⊛ in 108 bedrooms S fr £269.08; D fr £269.08
Facilities STV Sauna Gym Wi-fi in bedrooms **Conf** Thtr 70 Class 36
Board 30 Del from £311 **Services** Lift air con **Notes LB** ⊗ ⊛ in restaurant

★★★★ 68% HOTEL
PLAN 6 D4

The Chamberlain
130-135 Minories EC3N 1NU
☎ 020 7680 1500 🗎 020 7702 2500
e-mail: thechamberlain@fullers.co.uk
web: www.thechamberlainhotel.com
dir: M25 junct 30, A13 W towards London. Follow into Aldgate,
left after bus station. Hotel halfway down Minories.

This smart hotel is ideally situated for the City, Tower Bridge, plus both
Aldgate and Tower Gateway tube stations. Impressive bedrooms are
stylish, well equipped and comfortable, and the modern bathrooms
are fitted with TVs to watch while you soak in the bath. Informal day
rooms include a popular pub, a lounge and an attractive split-level
dining room.

Rooms 64 en suite ⊛ in 49 bedrooms S £225; D £225 **Facilities** STV
Wi-fi available Discounted leisure facilities for hotel guests nearby
Conf Thtr 50 Class 20 Board 25 **Services** Lift air con **Notes LB** ⊗ ⊛ in
restaurant Closed 24 Dec-2 Jan (TBC)

★★★ 74% HOTEL
PLAN 6 C4

Novotel London Tower Bridge
10 Pepys St EC3N 2NR
☎ 020 7265 6000 🗎 020 7265 6060
e-mail: H3107@accor.com
web: www.novotel.com

Located near the Tower of London, this smart hotel is convenient for
Docklands, the City, Heathrow and London City airports.
continued

Air-conditioned bedrooms are spacious, modern, and offer a great
range of facilities. There is a smart bar and restaurant, a small gym,
children's play area and extensive meeting and conference facilities.

Rooms 203 en suite (54 fmly) ⊛ in 174 bedrooms S £175-£195;
D £195-£215 **Facilities** STV Sauna Gym Wi-fi in bedrooms Steam Room
Conf Thtr 100 Class 56 Board 18 Del from £230 **Services** Lift air con

N1 ISLINGTON

★★★ 73% HOTEL
PLAN 3 E6

Jurys Inn Islington
60 Pentonville Rd, Islington N1 9LA
☎ 020 7282 5500 🗎 020 7282 5511
e-mail: london_inn@jurysdoyle.com
web: www.jurysdoyle.com
dir: from A1 right onto A501, right again onto Pentonville Rd

This modern hotel offers spacious bedrooms with good facilities, and
provides guests with a choice of comfortable public areas. There is an
Irish pub serving snacks and a popular restaurant serving a daily
changing menu.

Rooms 229 en suite (116 fmly) ⊛ in 135 bedrooms **Facilities** STV
Conf Thtr 50 Class 24 Board 28 **Services** Lift air con **Notes** ⊗ Closed
24-27 Dec

BUDGET HOTEL
PLAN 3 D6

Premier Travel Inn London Kings Cross
York Way, Kings Cross N1 9AA
☎ 0870 9906414 🗎 0870 9906415
web: www.premiertravelinn.com
dir: Exit M25 junct 16 onto M40 (which becomes A40). Follow
City signs, exit at Euston Rd follow one-way system to York Way

High quality, modern budget accommodation ideal for both families
and business travellers. Spacious, en suite bedrooms feature bath and
shower, satellite TV and many have telephones and modem points.
The adjacent family restaurant features a wide and varied menu. For
further details consult the Hotel Groups page.

Rooms 278 en suite

N14 SOUTHGATE
See **LONDON SECTION PLAN 1 E6**

BUDGET HOTEL

Innkeeper's Lodge Southgate
22 The Green, Southgate N14 6EN
☎ 020 8447 8022 🗎 020 8447 8022
web: www.innkeeperslodge.com
dir: A111 junct 24, 3m to rdbt for A1004, turn right into High
Street, hotel at next rdbt

Smart, en suite accommodation ideal for both business & leisure
guests. Bedrooms are very well equipped, including Sky TV,
telephone, modem points, tea & coffee making facilities, (family
rooms in most locations). Complimentary breakfast. The adjacent Pub
Restaurant; a Harvester, Vintage Inn, Toby Carvery, Ember Inn, Sizzling
Pubco or Pub & Carvery offers an all day menu. See Hotel Groups
pages for further details.

Rooms 19 en suite S £59.95-£72.95; D £59.95-£72.95

England

NW1 REGENT'S PARK
see **LONDON SECTION PLAN 1 E4**

INSPECTORS' CHOICE

★★★★★ ◎◎ **HOTEL**   PLAN 2 F4

The Landmark London

222 Marylebone Rd NW1 6JQ
☎ 020 7631 8000 🖷 020 7631 8080
e-mail: reservations@thelandmark.co.uk
web: www.landmarklondon.co.uk
dir: *adjacent to Marylebone Station and near Paddington Station*

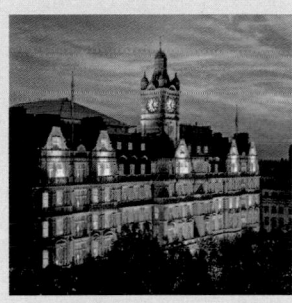

Once one of the last truly grand railway hotels, The Landmark boasts a number of stunning features, the most spectacular being the naturally lit central atrium which forms the focal point. When it comes to eating and drinking there are a number of choices, including the Cellars bar for cocktails and upmarket bar meals, or the newly created Mirror Bar. The Winter Garden restaurant has the centre stage in the atrium and is a great place to watch the world go by. The air-conditioned bedrooms are luxurious and have large, stylish bathrooms.

Rooms 299 en suite (60 fmly) ⊘ in 179 bedrooms S £260 £370; D £285-£395 **Facilities Spa** STV 🔲 Sauna Gym Jacuzzi Wi-fi available Beauty treatments and massages Xmas **Conf** BC Thtr 380 Class 224 Board 50 Del from £102 **Services** Lift air con **Parking** 80 **Notes LB** ⊗ Civ Wed 300

★★★★ 84% **HOTEL**   PLAN 3 A5

Meliá White House Regents Park

bany St, Regents Park NW1 3UP
☎ 020 7391 3000 🖷 020 7388 0091
-mail: melia.white.house@solmelia.com
r: *opposite Gt Portland St underground station*

wned by the Spanish Sol company, this impressive art deco property
continued

---

is located opposite Great Portland Street tube station. Spacious public areas offer a high degree of comfort and include an elegant cocktail bar, a fine dining restaurant and a more informal brasserie. Stylish bedrooms come in a variety of sizes, but all offer high levels of comfort and are thoughtfully equipped.

Rooms 582 en suite (7 fmly) ⊘ in 280 bedrooms S £130-£160; D £145-£180 **Facilities** STV 🔲 Sauna Gym Wi-fi available Xmas **Conf** BC Thtr 140 Class 80 Board 60 Del from £180 **Services** Lift air con **Parking** 7 **Notes LB** ⊗

★★★★ 78% ◎◎ **HOTEL**   PLAN 3 C5

Novotel London Euston

100-110 Euston Rd NW1 2AJ
☎ 020 7666 9000 🖷 020 7766 9100
e-mail: H5309@accor.com
web: www.novotel.com
dir: *between St Pancras & Euston stations*

This hotel enjoys a central location adjacent to the British Library and close to some of London's main transport hubs. The style is modern and contemporary throughout. Bedrooms are spacious, very well equipped and many have views over the city. Open-plan public areas include a leisure suite and extensive conference facilities including the Shaw Theatre.

Rooms 312 en suite (29 fmly) ⊘ in 268 bedrooms S £79-£550; D £79-£550 **Facilities** STV Sauna Gym Wi-fi in bedrooms Steam room Xmas **Conf** BC Thtr 446 Class 220 Board 80 Del from £192 **Services** Lift air con **Notes LB** ⊗ ⊘ in restaurant

★★★★ 76% ◎ **TOWN HOUSE HOTEL**   PLAN 2 F4

Dorset Square Hotel

39-40 Dorset Square NW1 6QN
☎ 020 7723 7874 🖷 020 7724 3328
e-mail: reservations@dorsetsquare.co.uk
dir: *M40 onto A40 (Euston Rd). Left lane off flyover. Turn left onto Gloucester Place. Hotel 1st left*

This delightfully restored Regency townhouse enjoys a prime location close to Hyde Park, Regents Park and all of central London's attractions. Stylish bedrooms are individually themed and extremely well equipped for both business and leisure guests. Elegant public areas include the popular Potting Shed Restaurant and Bar as well as an inviting sumptuous lounge. Service is personalised and attentive.

Rooms 37 en suite (2 fmly) (4 GF) S £220-£350; D £260-£350 **Facilities** STV FTV Wi-fi in bedrooms Xmas **Conf** Thtr 12 Class 20 Board 10 Del from £300 **Services** Lift air con **Notes** ⊗

NW1 REGENT'S PARK *continued*

★★★★ 73% **HOTEL**   PLAN 3 B6

Thistle Euston

Cardington St NW1 2LP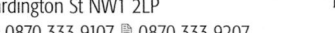
THISTLE HOTELS
☎ 0870 333 9107 🖹 0870 333 9207

e-mail: euston@thistle.co.uk

dir: From M40 continue to end of A40, follow Marylebone Rd, then take Euston Rd to Melton St & into Cardington St.

This smart, modern hotel is ideally located a short walk from Euston Station. Spacious public areas include a spacious bar/lounge, extensive meeting and function rooms and a bright basement restaurant. Bedrooms include a large number of deluxe and executive rooms that are spacious, comfortable and well equipped. The hotel also boasts limited on-site parking.

Rooms 362 en suite (15 fmly) (47 GF) ⊘ in 189 bedrooms D fr £93.60 (incl. bkfst) **Facilities** STV Xmas **Conf** Thtr 100 Class 45 Board 35 **Services** Lift air con **Parking** 21 **Notes** LB ⊗ ⊘ in restaurant

★★★★ 69% **HOTEL**

Holiday Inn Camden Lock

30 Jamestown Rd, Camden Lock NW1 7BY

☎ 020 7485 4343 🖹 020 7485 4344

e-mail: sales@holidayinncamden.co.uk

dir: from Camden tube station take left fork. Jamestown Rd 2nd on left

In the heart of Camden this smart modern hotel has rooms which overlook the Camden Lock. Bedrooms are spacious and well equipped, whilst the light and airy, first-floor restaurant offers delicious and innovative Mediterranean dishes. A small but well-equipped gym is located on the ground floor, as is a good selection of meeting rooms.

Rooms 130 en suite ⊘ in 65 bedrooms **Facilities** STV Gym **Conf** BC Thtr 200 Class 80 Board 40 **Services** Lift air con **Notes** LB ⊗ ⊘ in restaurant

BUDGET HOTEL   PLAN 3 B5

Hotel Ibis London Euston

3 Cardington St NW1 2LW

☎ 020 7388 7777 🖹 020 7388 0001

e-mail: H0921@accor-hotels.com

web: www.ibishotel.com

dir: from Euston Rd or station, right to Melton St leading to Cardington St

Modern, budget hotel offering comfortable accommodation in bright and practical bedrooms. Breakfast is self-service and dinner is available in the restaurant. For further details, consult the Hotel Groups page.

Rooms 380 en suite **Conf** BC Thtr 100 Class 40 Board 40

BUDGET HOTEL

Travelodge London Marylebone

Harewood Row NW1 6SE

☎ 020 7723 1735 🖹 020 7723 8569

web: www.travelodge.co.uk

dir: M40 onto A40 and over Paddington flyover onto Marylebone Rd, left into Lison Green, 1st left into Harewood Row.

Travelodge offers good quality, good value, modern accommodation. Ideal for families, the spacious en suite bedrooms include remote-control TV, tea and coffee-making facilities and comfortable beds. Meals can be taken at the nearby family restaurant. See Hotel Groups pages for further details.

Rooms 92 en suite S fr £26; D fr £26

NW2 BRENT CROSS & CRICKLEWOOD

See **LONDON PLAN 1 D5**

★★★★ 75% **HOTEL**

Crown Moran

142-152 Cricklewood Broadway, Cricklewood NW2 3ED

☎ 020 8452 4175 🖹 020 8452 0952

e-mail: crownres@moranhotels.com

web: www.crownmoranhotel.co.uk

dir: M1 junct 1 follow signs onto North Circular (W) A406. Junct with A5 (Staples Corner). At rdbt take 1st exit onto A5 to Cricklewood

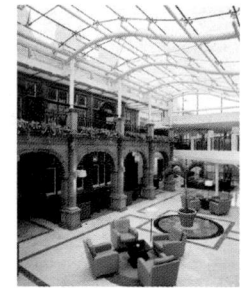

This striking hotel is connected by an impressive glass atrium to the popular Crown Pub. Features include excellent function and conference facilities, a leisure club, a choice of stylish lounges and bars and a contemporary restaurant. The air-conditioned bedrooms are appointed to a high standard and include a number of trendy suites.

Rooms 116 en suite (8 fmly) (20 GF) ⊘ in 60 bedrooms S £105-£145; D £125-£165 (incl. bkfst) **Facilities** STV 🔲 Sauna Gym Jacuzzi Wi-fi available 🎵 **Conf** Thtr 350 Class 120 Board 80 Del from £180 **Services** Lift air con **Parking** 41 **Notes** LB ⊗ Closed 25-26 Dec Civ Wed 100

NW3 HAMPSTEAD AND SWISS COTTAGE
See **LONDON PLAN 1 E4/E5**

★★★★ 78% HOTEL

London Marriott Hotel Regents Park

Marriott HOTELS & RESORTS

128 King Henry's Rd NW3 3ST
☎ 0870 400 7240 📠 0870 400 7340
e-mail: david.thomas@marriotthotels.com
web: www.marriott.co.uk
dir: 200yds off Finchley Rd on A41

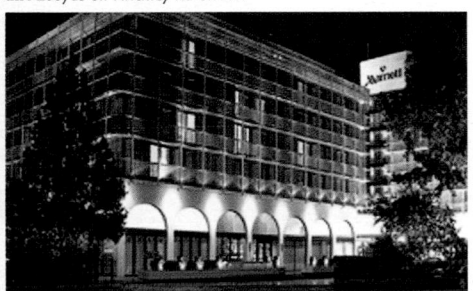

Situated in a quieter part of town and close to the tube station, this hotel offers guests comfortably appointed, air-conditioned accommodation; all rooms boast balconies and are particularly well equipped to meet the needs of today's business traveller. The open-plan ground floor is spacious and airy and includes a well-equipped leisure centre with indoor pool. Secure parking is a bonus.

Rooms 303 en suite ⊘ in 130 bedrooms S £99-£163; D £99-£163 **Facilities** STV ⊠ supervised Sauna Solarium Gym Wi-fi in bedrooms Hair & Beauty salon, Steam room **Conf** Thtr 440 Class 150 Board 175 Del from £195 **Services** Lift air con **Parking** 150 **Notes** ⊗ Civ Wed 300

★★ 72% METRO HOTEL

Best Western Swiss Cottage

Best Western

4 Adamson Rd, Swiss Cottage NW3 3HP
☎ 020 7722 2281

This smart Victorian property is in a peaceful residential location a short walk from Swiss Cottage tube station. Bedrooms are comfortable, smartly appointed and well equipped. There is a spacious lounge bar and room service refreshments and snacks are available. English breakfast is served in the basement dining room.

Rooms 59 en suite

NW4 HENDON
See **LONDON PLAN 1 D5**

Ⓤ

Hendon Hall

Ashley Ln, Hendon NW4 1HF
☎ 0870 333 9109 & 020 8457 2500 📠 0870 333 9209
e-mail: info@hendonhall.com
dir: M1 junct 2 follow A406 & City A1 signs. Right onto Parson St, right onto Ashley Ln. Hotel on right

At the time of going to press, the star classification for this hotel was

continued

not confirmed. Please refer to the AA internet site www.theAA.com for current information.

Rooms 57 en suite ⊘ in 48 bedrooms S £95-£215; D £95-£215 (incl. bkfst) **Facilities** STV Xmas **Conf** Thtr 350 Class 140 Board 76 Del from £160 **Services** Lift air con **Parking** 70 **Notes** ⊗ ⊘ in restaurant Civ Wed 130

NW6 MAIDA VALE

★★★★ 70% HOTEL   PLAN 2 B6

London Marriott Maida Vale

Marriott HOTELS & RESORTS

Plaza Pde, Maida Vale NW6 5RP
☎ 020 7543 6000 📠 020 7543 2100
e-mail: reservations.london.england.maidavale@marriotthotels.com
web: www.marriott.co.uk/LONWH
dir: From M1 take A5 southbound for 3m. Hotel on left. From Marble Arch take A5 northbound. Hotel on right

This smart, modern hotel is conveniently located just north of central London. Air-conditioned bedrooms are tastefully decorated and provide a range of extras. The hotel also boasts extensive function facilities as well as a smart indoor leisure centre, which has a swimming pool, gym and health and beauty salon.

Rooms 237 en suite (40 fmly) ⊘ in 110 bedrooms S £89-£149; D £89-£149 **Facilities** STV ⊠ Sauna Solarium Gym Wi-fi in bedrooms Hair & beauty salon including treatment rooms Exercise studio & classes. Xmas **Conf** BC Thtr 180 Class 70 Board 30 Del from £179 **Services** Lift air con **Parking** 39 **Notes** LB ⊗ ⊘ in restaurant Civ Wed 100

NW10 WILLESDEN
See **LONDON PLAN 1 D4**

BUDGET HOTEL

Travelodge Wembley

Travelodge

North Circular Rd NW10 7UG
☎ 0870 191 1966 📠 020 8963 1754
web: www.travelodge.co.uk
dir: A40, A406 N, keep left, 1st slip road on left

Travelodge offers good quality, good value, modern accommodation. Ideal for families, the spacious en suite bedrooms include remote-control TV, tea and coffee-making facilities and comfortable beds. Meals can be taken at the nearby family restaurant. See Hotel Groups pages for further details.

Rooms 168 en suite S fr £26; D fr £26 **Conf** BC Thtr 50 Class 20 Board 28

England

SE1 SOUTHWARK AND WATERLOO

★★★★★ 88% @ HOTEL   PLAN 5 D5

London Marriott Hotel County Hall

Marriott.
HOTELS & RESORTS

Westminster Bridge Rd, County Hall SE1 7PB
☎ 020 7928 5200 🖨 020 7928 5300
e-mail: mhrs.lonch.salesadmin@marriotthotels.com
web: www.marriott.co.uk
dir: on Thames South Bank, between Westminster Bridge & London Eye

This impressive building enjoys an enviable position on the south bank of the Thames, adjacent to the London Eye. Public areas have a traditional elegance and the crescent-shaped restaurant offers fine views of Westminster. All bedrooms are smartly laid out and thoughtfully equipped with the business traveller in mind.

Rooms 200 en suite (60 fmly) ⊗ in 147 bedrooms S £199-£259; D £199-£259 **Facilities Spa** STV 🔲 Sauna Solarium Gym Jacuzzi Wi-fi in bedrooms Health & beauty spa ♫ Xmas **Conf** BC Thtr 80 Class 40 Board 30 **Services** Lift air con **Parking** 70 **Notes** ⊗ Civ Wed 80

★★★★ 77% HOTEL   PLAN 5 D3

Riverbank Park Plaza

Park Plaza
Hotels & Resorts

Albert Embankment SE1 7SP
☎ 020 7958 8000 🖨 020 7769 2400
e-mail: rppres@parkplazahotels.co.uk
web: www.parkplaza.com
dir: From Houses of Parliament turn onto Millbank, at rdbt left onto Lambeth Bridge. At rdbt take third exit onto Albert Embankment.

Billed as the first new build hotel to be opened in central London for 30 years, the Park Plaza features eye catching, contemporary design coupled with a host of up-to-date facilities and a high level of comfort. Facilities include wireless connectivity, high tech conference rooms for up to 800 delegates, car parking and spa. The hotel also has its own pier and offers a river taxi service to the City and Canary Wharf.

Rooms 394 en suite ⊗ in 315 bedrooms **Facilities** STV Gym Wi-fi available Cardio machines, weights, exercise mats and stretch balls ♫ **Conf** Thtr 530 Class 405 Board 40 **Services** Lift air con **Parking** 120 **Notes** ⊗ ⊗ in restaurant Civ Wed 150

★★★★ 75% HOTEL   PLAN 6 B2

London Bridge Hotel

8-18 London Bridge St SE1 9SG
☎ 020 7855 2200 🖨 020 7855 2233
e-mail: sales@london-bridge-hotel.co.uk
web: www.londonbridgehotel.com
dir: Access through London Bridge Station (bus/taxi yard), into London Bridge St (one-way). Hotel on left, 50yds from station

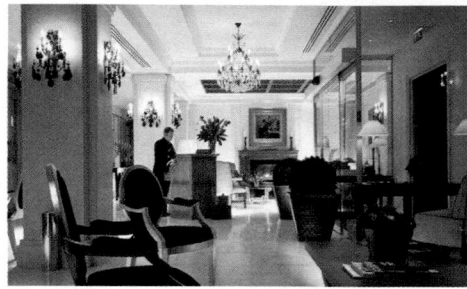

This elegant independently owned hotel enjoys a prime location on the edge of the City, adjacent to London Bridge station. Smartly appointed, well-equipped bedrooms include a number of spacious deluxe rooms and suites. Compact yet sophisticated public areas include a selection of meeting rooms and a well-equipped gym. The eating options are Georgetown for Asian cuisine, Londinium offering modern British food, and the Borough bar with an all-day menu.

Rooms 138 en suite (12 fmly) ⊗ in 108 bedrooms S £99-£199; D £99-£199 **Facilities** STV Sauna Solarium Gym Wi-fi available **Conf** Thtr 100 Class 40 Board 40 Del £266 **Services** Lift air con **Notes LB** ⊗

★★★★ 74% HOTEL   PLAN 5 H5

Novotel London City South

NOVOTEL
ACCOR
hotels

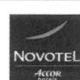

Southwark Bridge Rd SE1 9HH
☎ 020 7089 0400 🖨 020 7089 0410
e-mail: H3269@accor.com
web: www.novotel.com
dir: junct at Thrale St, off Southwark St

First of a new generation of Novotels, this hotel is contemporary in design with smart, modern bedrooms and spacious public rooms. There are a number of options for guests wanting to unwind, including treatments such as reflexology and immersion therapy, while a gym is available for the more energetic.

Rooms 182 en suite (139 fmly) ⊗ in 158 bedrooms S £79-£190; D £79-£210 **Facilities** STV Sauna Gym Wi-fi available Steam Room **Conf** Thtr 100 Class 40 Board 35 Del from £225 **Services** Lift air con **Parking** 80

★★★ 74% HOTEL — PLAN 5 G5

Mercure London City Bankside

71-79 Southwark St SE1 0JA
☎ 020 7902 0800 📠 020 7902 0810
e-mail: H2814@accor.com
web: www.mercure.com
dir: A200 to London Bridge. Left into Southwark St.

This smart, contemporary hotel forms part of the rejuvenation of the South Bank. With the City of London just over the river and a number of tourist attractions within easy reach, the hotel is well located for business and leisure visitors alike. Facilities include spacious air-cooled bedrooms, a modern bar and the stylish Loft Restaurant.

Rooms 144 en suite (24 fmly) (5 GF) ⊘ in 115 bedrooms S £79-£150; D £79-£170 **Facilities** STV Gym Wi-fi in bedrooms ♫ **Conf** Thtr 60 Class 40 Board 30 Del from £195 **Services** Lift air con **Parking** 6 **Notes LB** RS Xmas, Etr & BH's (restaurant closed)

★★★ 73% HOTEL — PLAN 5 D3

Novotel London Waterloo

113 Lambeth Rd SE1 7LS
☎ 020 7793 1010 📠 020 7793 0202
e-mail: h1785@accor.com
web: www.novotel.com
dir: opposite Houses of Parliament on S bank of River Thames, off Lambeth Bridge, opposite Lambeth Palace

This hotel has an excellent location with Lambeth Palace, the Houses of Parliament and Waterloo Station all within a short walk. Bedrooms are spacious and air conditioned, a number of rooms have been designed for less able guests. The open-plan public areas include the Garden Brasserie, the Flag and Whistle Pub and children's play area.

Rooms 187 en suite (80 fmly) ⊘ in 158 bedrooms S £150; D £170 **Facilities** Sauna Gym Wi-fi available Steam room Fitness room Pool Table **Conf** Thtr 40 Class 24 Board 24 Del from £211 **Services** Lift **Parking** 40

BUDGET HOTEL — PLAN 5 E3

Days Hotel London Waterloo

54 Kennington Rd SE1 7BJ
☎ 020 7922 1331 📠 020 7922 1441
e-mail: waterloores@khl.uk.com
web: www.welcomebreak.co.uk
dir: Corner of Kennington Rd and Lambeth Rd. Opposite the Imperial War Museum.

This modern building offers accommodation in smart, spacious and well-equipped bedrooms, suitable for families and business travellers,

continued

and all with en suite bathrooms. Continental breakfast is available and other refreshments may be taken at the nearby family restaurant. For further details see the Hotel Groups page.

Rooms 162 en suite

BUDGET HOTEL — PLAN 5 D5

Premier Travel Inn London County Hall

Belvedere Rd SE1 7PB
☎ 0870 238 3300 📠 020 7902 1619
web: www.premiertravelinn.com
dir: in County Hall building, next to London Eye

High quality, modern budget accommodation ideal for both families and business travellers. Spacious, en suite bedrooms feature bath and shower, satellite TV and many have telephones and modem points. The adjacent family restaurant features a wide and varied menu. For further details consult the Hotel Groups page.

Rooms 313 en suite

Premier Travel Inn London Southwark — PLAN 6 A3

Anchor, Bankside, 34 Park St SE1 9EF
☎ 0870 9906402 📠 0870 9906403
dir: From A3200 into Southwark Bridge Rd (A300), 1st left into Sumner St, right into Park St. From S, M3 (then A3) follow Central London signs
Rooms 56 en suite **Conf** Thtr 22 Board 22

Premier Travel Inn London Tower Bridge — PLAN 6 C1

Tower Bridge Rd SE1 3LP
☎ 0870 238 3303 📠 020 7940 3719
dir: South of Tower Bridge
Rooms 195 en suite

SE10 GREENWICH

★★★★ 72% HOTEL — PLAN 8 A3

Novotel London Greenwich

173-185 Greenwich High Rd SE10 8JA
☎ 020 8312 6800 📠 020 8312 6810
e-mail: H3476@accor.com
web: www.novotel.com
dir: next to Greenwich Station

This purpose-built hotel is conveniently located for rail and DLR stations, as well as major attractions such as the Royal Maritime Museum and the Royal Observatory. Air-conditioned bedrooms are spacious and equipped with a host of extras, and public areas include a small gym, contemporary lounge bar and restaurant.

Rooms 151 en suite (34 fmly) ⊘ in 115 bedrooms S fr £135; D fr £155 **Facilities** STV Gym Wi-fi available Steam room ♫ **Conf** Thtr 92 Class 40 Board 32 Del from £169 **Services** Lift air con **Parking** 30 **Notes LB** ⊘ in restaurant

England

SE10 GREENWICH *continued*

Hotel Ibis London Greenwich

30 Stockwell St, Greenwich SE10 9JN
☎ 020 8305 1177 🖷 020 8858 7139
e-mail: H0975@accor.com
web: www.ibishotel.com
dir: *from Waterloo Bridge, Elephant & Castle, A2 to Greenwich.*

Modern, budget hotel offering comfortable accommodation in bright and practical bedrooms. Breakfast is self-service and dinner is available in the restaurant. For further details, consult the Hotel Groups page.

Rooms 82 en suite   S £68.95-£78.95;   D £68.95-£78.95

SW1 WESTMINSTER

INSPECTORS' CHOICE

★★★★★ ❀❀❀❀❀ **HOTEL**   PLAN 4 G4

The Berkeley

MAYBOURNE
HOTEL
GROUP

Wilton Place, Knightsbridge SW1X 7RL
☎ 020 7235 6000 🖷 020 7235 4330
e-mail: info@the-berkeley.co.uk
dir: *300mtrs along Knightsbridge from Hyde Park Corner*

This stylish hotel, just off Knightsbridge, boasts an excellent range of bedrooms; each furnished with care and a host of thoughtful extras. Newer rooms feature trendy, spacious glass and marble bathrooms and some of the private suites have their own roof terrace. The striking Blue Bar enhances the reception rooms, all adorned with magnificent flower arrangements. The health spa offers a range of treatment rooms and includes a stunning open-air, roof-top pool. Two renowned, award-winning restaurants provide complete contrast in their culinary styles - the modern upscale New York style café, Boxwood, with 2 AA Rosettes, and the stunning cuisine of Marcus Wareing at Petrus, with 5 AA Rosettes.

Rooms 214 en suite ⊗ in 188 bedrooms **Facilities Spa** STV ⌨
supervised Sauna Solarium Gym Beauty/therapy treatments
Conf BC Thtr 250 Class 80 Board 52 **Services** Lift air con
Parking 50 **Notes** ⊗ Civ Wed 160

INSPECTORS' CHOICE

★★★★★ ❀❀❀❀❀ **HOTEL**   PLAN 4 F4

Mandarin Oriental Hyde Park

66 Knightsbridge SW1X 7LA
☎ 020 7235 2000 🖷 020 7235 2001
e-mail: molon-reservations@mohg.com
web: www.mandarinoriental.com/london
dir: *Harrods on right, hotel 0.5m on left opp Harvey Nichols*

Situated in fashionable Knightsbridge and overlooking Hyde Park, this landmark hotel is a popular venue for highfliers and the young and fashionable. Bedrooms, many of which have park views, are appointed to the highest standards with luxurious features such as the finest Irish linen and goose down pillows. Guests have a choice of dining options, from the brasserie-style, all-day dining Park Restaurant to the chic, award-winning Foliage Restaurant. The Mandarin Bar also serves light snacks and cocktails. The stylish spa is a destination in its own right and offers a range of innovative treatments.

Rooms 200 en suite ⊘ in 106 bedrooms D £488-£5552
Facilities Spa STV Sauna Gym Jacuzzi Wi-fi available Fitness
Centre, Steam Room, Sanarium, Vitality Pod, Zen Colour Therapy ♫
Xmas **Conf** BC Thtr 250 Class 120 Board 60 **Services** Lift air con
Parking 13 **Notes LB** ⊗ Civ Wed 220

INSPECTORS' CHOICE

★★★★★ ❀❀❀ **TOWN HOUSE HOTEL** PLAN 4 G4

The Halkin Hotel

Halkin St, Belgravia SW1X 7DJ
☎ 020 7333 1000 🖷 020 7333 1100
e-mail: res@halkin.como.bz
dir: *hotel between Belgrave Sq & Grosvenor Place. Via Chapel St into Headfort Place and left into Halkin St*

This smart, contemporary hotel celebrated its 15th birthday in 2006
continued

and has never looked better. It has an enviable and peaceful position just a short stroll from both Hyde Park and the designer shops of Knightsbridge. Service is attentive, friendly and very personalised. The stylish bedrooms and suites are equipped to the highest standard with smart, marble bathrooms and every conceivable extra. Each floor is discreetly designed following the themes of earth, wind, fire, water and the universe. Public areas include an airy bar lounge and the famous, award-winning Thai restaurant, Nahm.

Rooms 41 en suite ⊗ in 9 bedrooms S £239-£1200; D £239-£1200
Facilities STV Wi-fi in bedrooms **Conf** Thtr 40 Class 15 Board 22
Services Lift air con **Notes LB** ⊗ ⊗ in restaurant

INSPECTORS' CHOICE

★★★★★ ⊛ ⊛ **HOTEL**   PLAN 4 H3

The Goring

Beeston Place, Grosvenor Gardens SW1W 0JW
☎ 020 7396 9000 🖹 020 7834 4393

e-mail: reception@goringhotel.co.uk
web: www.goringhotel.co.uk

dir: off Lower Grosvenor Place, just prior to Royal Mews

Situated in central London, this icon of British hospitality is within walking distance of the Royal Parks and principal shopping areas. The well-equipped bedrooms are furnished in a traditional style and boast high levels of comfort and quality. Stylish reception rooms include the garden bar and the drawing room, both popular for afternoon tea and cocktails. The restaurant menu has a classic repertoire but also enjoys a well-deserved reputation for its contemporary British cuisine, all served in a light and airy, newly refurbished room.

Rooms 71 en suite (9 fmly) S £212-£323; D £258-£382
Facilities STV Wi-fi available Free membership of nearby Health Club ♫ Xmas **Conf** BC Thtr 50 Board 25 Del from £360 **Services** Lift air con **Parking** 16 **Notes LB** ⊗ Civ Wed 50

INSPECTORS' CHOICE

★★★★★ ⊛ ⊛ **HOTEL**   PLAN 4 F4

Jumeirah Carlton Tower

Cadogan Place SW1X 9PY
☎ 020 7235 1234 🖹 020 7235 9129

e-mail: contact@carltontower.com
web: www.carltontower.com

dir: A4 towards Knightsbridge, turn right onto Sloane St. Hotel on left before Cadogan Place

This impressive hotel enjoys an enviable position in the heart of *continued*

Knightsbridge, overlooking Cadogan Gardens. Bedrooms, including a number of suites, vary in size and style and many have wonderful city views. Leisure facilities include a glass-roofed swimming pool, a well-equipped gym and a number of treatment rooms. The renowned Rib Room & Oyster Bar provides an excellent dining option.

Jumeirah Carlton Tower

Rooms 220 en suite (60 fmly) ⊗ in 116 bedrooms **Facilities** Spa STV 🏊 supervised ♨ Sauna Gym Jacuzzi Massage and Spa treatments ♫ **Conf** BC Thtr 400 Class 250 Board 30 **Services** Lift air con **Parking** 50 **Notes** ⊗ Civ Wed 400

See advert on this page

England

SW1 WESTMINSTER *continued*

INSPECTORS' CHOICE

★★★★★ ◎◎ **HOTEL**   PLAN 4 G5

The Lanesborough

Hyde Park Corner SW1X 7TA
☎ 020 7259 5599 🖷 020 7259 5606
e-mail: info@lanesborough.co.uk
dir: *follow signs to central London and Hyde Park Corner*

Occupying an enviable position on Hyde Park Corner, this elegant hotel offers the highest international standards of comfort, quality and security, much appreciated by the loyal clientele. Stylish bedrooms reflect the historic nature of the property, offering high levels of comfort and a superb range of complimentary facilities including internet access, DVDs and CDs. Services are equally impressive with your own personal butler ensuring individual attention. The conservatory restaurant is in demand for meals, superb afternoon teas and Sunday Brunch. The Spa Studio has many original treatments to soothe and pamper.

Rooms 95 en suite (5 GF) ⊘ in 24 bedrooms S £370.13–£440.63; D £511.13–£7050 **Facilities Spa** STV Gym Wi-fi in bedrooms Fitness studio 🎵 ch fac Xmas **Conf** Thtr 85 Class 60 Board 48 **Services** Lift air con **Parking** 38 **Notes LB** Civ Wed 100

INSPECTORS' CHOICE

★★★★★ **TOWN HOUSE HOTEL**   PLAN 5 A4

No 41

41 Buckingham Palace Rd SW1W 0PS
☎ 020 7300 0041 🖷 020 7300 0141
e-mail: book41@rchmail.com
web: www.redcarnationhotels.com
dir: *opp Buckingham Palace Mews entrance.*

Red Carnation HOTELS

Small, intimate and very private, this stunning town house is located opposite the Royal Mews. Decorated in stylish black and white, bedrooms successfully combine comfort with state-of-the-art technology. The large lounge is the focal point food and drinks are available as is internet access and magazines and

continued

newspapers from around the world. Attentive personal service and a host of thoughtful extra touches make No 41 really special.

No 41

Rooms 24 en suite ⊘ in all bedrooms S £346; D £581 **Facilities** STV Wi-fi in bedrooms use of 2 health clubs ch fac **Conf** BC Board 10 **Services** Lift air con

★★★★★ 90% ◎◎◎ **HOTEL**   PLAN 4 F4

Sheraton Park Tower

101 Knightsbridge SW1X 7RN
☎ 020 7235 8050 🖷 020 7235 8231
e-mail: 00412.central.london.reservations@sheraton.com
web: www.starwood.com
dir: *next to Harvey Nichols*

THE LUXURY COLLECTION

Superbly located for some of London's most fashionable stores, the Park Tower offers stunning views over the city. Bedrooms combine a high degree of comfort with up-to-date decor and a super range of extras; the suites are particularly impressive. The hotel offers the intimate Knightsbridge lounge, the more formal Piano Bar and extensive conference and banqueting facilities. Restaurant One-O-One is renowned for its seafood.

Rooms 280 en suite (280 fmly) ⊘ in 116 bedrooms **Facilities** STV Gym Fitness room 🎵 **Conf** BC Thtr 120 Class 60 Board 26 **Services** Lift air con **Parking** 67 **Notes** ⊗

★★★★★ 89% **TOWN HOUSE HOTEL**   PLAN 5 B4

51 Buckingham Gate

SW1E 6AF
☎ 020 7769 7766 🖷 020 7828 3909
e-mail: info@51-buckinghamgate.co.uk

This all suites hotel is a favourite with those who desire a quiet sophisticated environment. Each of the suites has its own butler on hand, all have a kitchen and most have large lounge areas furnished in contemporary style with modern accessories. There are one, two, three and four bedroom suites to choose from. The spa specialises in Sodashi treatments and there is also has a well-equipped gym.

Rooms 84 en suite (84 fmly) (4 GF) S fr £393.63; D fr £393.63 **Facilities Spa** STV Sauna Solarium Gym Jacuzzi **Conf** BC Del from £245 **Services** Lift air con **Notes** ⊗

★★★★★ 82% **TOWN HOUSE HOTEL**   PLAN 3 B1

22 Jermyn Street

St James's SW1Y 6HL
☎ 020 7734 2353 📠 020 7734 0750
e-mail: office@22jermyn.com
web: www.22jermyn.com

dir: *A4 into Piccadilly, right into Duke St, left into King St. Through St James's Sq to Charles II St. Left into Regent St, left again*

This attractive townhouse enjoys an enviable location close to Piccadilly, Regent Street and the fashionable St James's area. Smartly appointed accommodation mainly consists of spacious suites with a few smaller studios. All are thoughtfully equipped with mini-bar, satellite TV, video recorder and fax/modem lines. 24-hour room service is available and breakfast is served in guest bedrooms.

Rooms 18 en suite (13 fmly) S fr £258.50; D fr £258.50 **Facilities** STV Wi-fi in bedrooms Membership of nearby Health Club ch fac **Conf** BC Thtr 15 Class 15 Board 10 **Services** Lift air con **Notes** ⊛ in restaurant

★★★★★ 71% ⊛⊛ **HOTEL**   PLAN 5 B6

Sofitel St James London

6 Waterloo Place SW1Y 4AN
☎ 020 7747 2222 📠 020 7747 2210
e-mail: H3144@accor.com

SOFITEL
ACCOR HOTELS & RESORTS

dir: *On corner of Pall Mall & Waterloo Place*

Located in the exclusive area of St James's, this Grade II listed, former bank is convenient for most of the city's attractions, theatres and the financial district. The modern bedrooms are equipped to a high standard and feature luxurious beds, whilst more traditional public areas, including the Brasserie Roux and the Rose Lounge, provide a taste of classical charm.

Rooms 186 en suite ⊛ in 97 bedrooms S £230-£305; D £230-£305 **Facilities** STV Gym Wi-fi available Steam room, Treatment rooms ♫ Xmas **Conf** BC Thtr 180 Class 110 Board 50 **Services** Lift air con **Notes** Civ Wed 140

INSPECTORS' CHOICE

★★★★ ⊛⊛ **HOTEL**   PLAN 5 A5

The Stafford

16-18 St James's Place SW1A 1NJ
☎ 020 7493 0111 📠 020 7493 7121
e-mail: information@thestafford.co.uk
web: www.shirehotels.com

dir: *off Pall Mall into St James's St. 2nd left into St James's Place*

Tucked away in a quiet corner of St James's, this lovely boutique hotel retains an air of understated luxury. The American Bar is a fabulous venue in its own right, festooned with an eccentric array of celebrity photos, caps and ties. Afternoon tea is a long established tradition here. From the pristine, tastefully decorated and air-conditioned bedrooms, to the highly professional, yet friendly service, this exclusive hotel is keeping the highest standards.

Rooms 81 en suite (6 GF) ⊛ in 79 bedrooms S £220-£270; D £250-£335 **Facilities** STV Wi-fi in bedrooms Use of nearby gym Xmas **Conf** Thtr 40 Board 24 **Services** Lift air con **Notes LB** ⊛ Civ Wed 44

★★★★ 85% ⊛ **HOTEL**   PLAN 5 A4

The Rubens at the Palace

39 Buckingham Palace Rd SW1W 0PS
☎ 020 7834 6600 📠 020 7233 6037
e-mail: bookrb@rchmail.com
web: www.redcarnationhotels.com

Red
Carnation

dir: *opposite Royal Mews*

This hotel enjoys an enviable location next to Buckingham Palace. Stylish, air-conditioned bedrooms include the pinstripe-walled Saville Row rooms, which follow a tailoring theme, and the opulent Royal rooms, named after different monarchs. Public rooms include the Library fine dining restaurant and a comfortable stylish cocktail bar and lounge. The team here pride themselves on their warmth and friendliness.

Rooms 168 en suite (13 fmly) ⊛ in 123 bedrooms S £229; D £265 **Facilities** STV Wi-fi available Health clubs locally ♫ **Conf** Thtr 90 Class 40 Board 30 Del £275 **Services** Lift air con **Notes LB** ⊛ in restaurant

England

SW1 WESTMINSTER *continued*

★★★★ 83% **HOTEL**   PLAN 4 G3

Sheraton Belgravia

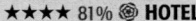

20 Chesham Place SW1X 8HQ

☎ 020 7235 6040 📠 020 7259 6243

e-mail: reservations.sheratonbelgravia@sheraton.com

web: www.starwood.com

dir: A4 Brompton Rd into Central London. After Brompton Oratory right into Beauchamp Pl. Follow into Pont St, cross Sloane St & hotel on corner

This smart, boutique-style hotel offers a real home-from-home experience with a friendly team on hand. Quiet and very well equipped bedrooms include a number of spacious executive rooms and suites. Bijou public areas include a stylish lounge where all-day snacks are available, and a restaurant offering a more formal eating option.

Rooms 89 en suite (16 fmly) ⊘ in 37 bedrooms S £149-£320; D £149-£320 **Facilities** STV Wi-fi in bedrooms Complimentary membership to local health spa, in-room spa ♬ **Conf** BC Thtr 35 Class 14 Board 20 **Services** Lift air con **Notes** ⊗

★★★★ 81% ⍟ **HOTEL**   PLAN 5 B4

Crowne Plaza London St James

Buckingham Gate SW1E 6AF

☎ 020 7834 6655 📠 020 7630 7587

e-mail: sales@cplonsj.co.uk

dir: facing Buckingham Palace, left to Buckingham Gate. After 100mtrs hotel on right

Enjoying a prestigious location in the heart of Westminster, this elegant Victorian hotel is just a few minutes' walk from Buckingham Place. Air-conditioned bedrooms are smartly appointed and superbly equipped. Public areas include a choice of three restaurants, two bars, conference and business facilities and a fitness club with Sodishi Spa. Service is attentive and friendly.

Rooms 342 en suite ⊘ in 181 bedrooms S £305.50; D £305.50 **Facilities Spa** STV Sauna Solarium Gym Jacuzzi ♬ Xmas **Conf** BC Thtr 180 Class 90 Board 4 Del from £245 **Services** Lift air con **Notes** ⊗ Civ Wed

★★★★ 78% **HOTEL**   PLAN 5 A3

Victoria Park Plaza

239 Vauxhall Bridge Rd SW1V 1EQ

☎ 020 7769 9999 & 020 7769 9800
📠 020 7769 9998

e-mail: info@victoriaparkplaza.com

web: www.parkplaza.com

dir: turn right out of Victoria Station.

This smart modern hotel close to Victoria station is well located for all of central London's major attractions. Air-conditioned bedrooms are tastefully appointed and thoughtfully equipped for both business and leisure guests. Airy, stylish public areas include an elegant bar and

continued

restaurant, a popular coffee bar and extensive conference facilities complete with a business centre.

Victoria Park Plaza

Rooms ⊘ in 116 bedrooms S £79-£245; D £79-£245 (incl. bkfst) **Facilities** STV FTV Gym Sauna ♬ **Conf** BC Thtr 550 Class 240 Board 45 Del £255 **Services** Lift air con **Notes LB** ⊘ in restaurant Civ Wed 500

★★★★ 77% ⍟⍟⍟ **HOTEL**   PLAN 4 F4

Millennium Hotel London Knightsbridge

17 Sloane St, Knightsbridge SW1X 9NU

☎ 020 7235 4377 📠 020 7235 3705

e-mail: knightsbridge.reservations@mill.cop.com

web: www.millenniumhotels.com

dir: from Knightsbridge tube station towards Sloane St. Hotel 70mtrs on right

This fashionable hotel boasts an enviable location in Knightsbridge's chic shopping district. Air-conditioned, thoughtfully equipped bedrooms are complemented by a popular lobby lounge and the much-acclaimed Mju Restaurant and Bar. Cuisine is French with Asian influences. Lighter meals may be taken in the Tangerine bar. Valet parking is available if pre-booked.

Rooms 222 en suite ⊘ in 150 bedrooms S £129.25-£258.50; D £152.75-£282 **Facilities** STV Wi-fi available **Conf** BC Thtr 120 Class 80 Board 50 Del from £272 **Services** Lift air con **Parking** 10 **Notes LB** ⊗ ⊘ in restaurant

★★★★ 75% **HOTEL**   PLAN 5 B6

De Vere Cavendish London

81 Jermyn St SW1Y 6JF

☎ 020 7930 2111 📠 020 7839 2125

e-mail: cavendish.reservations@devere-hotels.com

web: www.devere.co.uk

dir: from Marble Arch along Park Ln to Hyde Park Corner. Left to Piccadilly, past Ritz and right down Dukes St. Behind Fortnum and Mason

This smart, stylish hotel enjoys an enviable location in the prestigious St James's area, minutes' walk from Green Park and Piccadilly. Bedrooms have a fresh, contemporary feel and include a number of

continued

spacious executive rooms, studios and suites. Elegant public areas include a spacious first-floor lounge, the popular Aslan Restaurant and well-appointed conference and function facilities.

De Vere Cavendish London

Rooms 230 en suite ⊗ in 180 bedrooms S £163-£276; D £163-£276 **Facilities** STV Wi-fi available Xmas **Conf** BC Thtr 80 Class 50 Board 35 Del from £229 **Services** Lift air con **Parking** 60 **Notes LB** ⊗

★★★★ 75% **HOTEL**   PLAN 5 D5

The Royal Horseguards
2 Whitehall Court SW1A 2EJ   THISTLE HOTELS

☎ 0870 333 9122 ▤ 0870 333 9222

e-mail: RoyalHorseguards@Thistle.co.uk

dir: *2 mins walk from Embankment Station.*

This majestic looking hotel in the heart of Whitehall sits beside the Thames and enjoys unrivalled views of the London Eye and city skyline. Bedrooms are finished to a high standard, are well equipped whilst some of luxurious bathrooms are finished in marble. Impressive public areas and outstanding meeting rooms are also available.

Rooms 280 en suite (9 fmly) ⊗ in 188 bedrooms **Facilities** STV Gym **Conf** BC Thtr 240 Class 180 Board 80 **Services** Lift air con **Notes LB** ⊗ Civ Wed 200

★★★★ 72% **HOTEL**   PLAN 5 A3

Thistle Westminster
49 Buckingham Palace Rd SW1W 0QT   THISTLE HOTELS

☎ 0870 333 9121 ▤ 0870 333 9221

e-mail: westminster@thistle.co.uk

A purpose built hotel situated in the heart of London's political landmarks and close to Buckingham Palace. The spacious bedrooms come in a variety of styles; each one is smartly decorated and well equipped. Public rooms include a large lounge, a bar, a brasserie and a range of meeting rooms.

Rooms 134 en suite (20 fmly) ⊗ in 75 bedrooms S £200; D £231 **Facilities** STV **Conf** Thtr 364 Class 120 Board 136 Del from £165 **Services** Lift **Parking** 4 **Notes LB** ⊗ ⊗ in restaurant

---

★★★★ 64% **HOTEL**   PLAN 5 B3

Grange Rochester
69 Vincent Square SW1P 2PA

☎ 020 7828 6611 ▤ 020 7233 6724

e-mail: rochester@grangehotels.com

web: www.grangehotels.co.uk

dir: *From Hyde Park Cnr along Buckingham Palace Rd to Victoria & onto Vauxhall Bridge Rd, left into Rochester Row. Hotel on right*

Overlooking leafy Vincent Square, this boutique-style hotel is well
continued

---

located for access to London's finest shopping, theatres and tourist attractions. Stylish bedrooms are quiet and well equipped, but do vary in size. Some rooms have balconies with views over the square. The compact public rooms are elegant and offer all-day dining and drinking options.

Rooms 76 en suite (6 fmly) ⊗ in 30 bedrooms S £139-£175; D £149-£195 **Facilities** STV Xmas **Conf** Thtr 45 Class 35 Board 35 Del from £207 **Services** Lift **Notes LB** ⊗

★★★ 71% **HOTEL**   PLAN 5 A2

Quality Hotel Westminster
82-83 Eccleston Square SW1V 1PS

☎ 020 7834 8042 ▤ 020 7630 8942

e-mail: enquiries@hotels-westminster.com

web: www.choicehotelseurope.com

dir: *from Victoria Station, right into Wilton Rd, 3rd right into Gillingham St, hotel 150mtrs*

Situated close to Victoria, this hotel provides a good base for exploring London. Bedrooms vary in size and style and include a number of spacious premier rooms; the majority of bedrooms having been upgraded during 2006. Public areas include a bar/lounge, a range of conference rooms and a Brasserie, which provides a good range of meals.

Rooms 107 en suite (8 fmly) ⊗ in 80 bedrooms S £136-£156; D £155-£175 **Facilities** STV ☒ Wi-fi in bedrooms **Conf** Thtr 150 Class 60 Board 40 Del from £185 **Services** Lift air con **Notes LB** ⊗ ⊗ in restaurant

---

Ⓤ   PLAN 4 F4

Jumeriah Lowndes
21 Lowndes St SW1X 9ES

☎ 020 7823 1234 ▤ 020 7235 1154

e-mail: contact@lowndeshotel.com

dir: *M4 onto A4 into London. Left from Brompton Rd into Sloane St. Left into Pont St and Lowndes St next left. Hotel on right*

At the time of going to press, the hotel was due to re-open following a multi-million pound refurbishment. Bedrooms have been refurbished to a high standard decorated in seasonal themes and there is a new floor of nine suites. Public areas centre around the new Mimosa bar and restaurant offering Mediterranean cuisine. Please refer to the AA internet site www.theAA.com for current information.

Rooms 87 en suite (8 fmly) ⊗ in 31 bedrooms D fr £329 **Facilities** STV Wi-fi available Use of facilities at Jumeriah Carlton Tower Hotel ch fac **Conf** Thtr 25 Class 8 Board 18 **Services** Lift air con **Notes LB** ⊗

Ⓤ   PLAN 4 H3

Thistle Victoria
101 Buckingham Palace Rd SW1W 0SJ   THISTLE HOTELS

☎ 0870 333 9120 ▤ 0870 333 9220

e-mail: victoria@thistle.co.uk

dir: *adjacent to Victoria train, coach, tube & bus stations.*

At the time of going to press, the star classification for this hotel was not confirmed. Please refer to the AA internet site www.theAA.com for current information.

Rooms 357 en suite (8 fmly) ⊗ in 250 bedrooms S £92-£284; D £104-£302 **Facilities** STV **Conf** Thtr 90 Class 90 Board 70 Del from £140 **Services** Lift

England

SW1 WESTMINSTER *continued*

BUDGET HOTEL   PLAN 5 B2

Days Inn London Westminster

DAYS INN

80-86 Belgrave Rd SW1V 2BJ

☎ 020 7828 8661 & 020 7802 0507

🖷 020 7821 0525

e-mail: info@daysinn-westminster.co.uk

web: www.welcomebreak.co.uk

dir: *From Victoria Station take Vauxhall Bridge Rd. Turn right on Wilton Rd, after 2nd lights turn left. Hotel on right*

This modern building offers accommodation in smart, spacious and well-equipped bedrooms, suitable for families and business travellers, and all with en suite bathrooms. Continental breakfast is available and other refreshments may be taken at the nearby family restaurant. For further details see the Hotel Groups page.

Rooms 82 en suite

SW3 CHELSEA, BROMPTON

INSPECTORS' CHOICE

★★★★★ ◉◉◉◉ **TOWN HOUSE HOTEL** PLAN 4 F4

The Capital

Basil St, Knightsbridge SW3 1AT

☎ 020 7589 5171 🖷 020 7225 0011

e-mail: reservations@capitalhotel.co.uk

dir: *20yds from Harrods*

Personal service is assured at this small, family-owned hotel set in the heart of Knightsbridge. Beautifully designed bedrooms come in a number of styles; all rooms feature antique furniture, a marble bathroom and a thoughtful range of extras. Dinner is a highlight of any visit; Eric Chavot and his committed brigade continue to cook to a consistently superb standard. Cocktails are a speciality in the delightful, stylish bar, whilst afternoon tea in the elegant, bijou lounge is a must.

Rooms 49 en suite ◈ in 24 bedrooms S fr £246; D fr £335 **Facilities** STV Wi-fi in bedrooms **Conf** BC Thtr 30 Board 12 **Services** Lift air con **Parking** 15 **Notes LB** ◈ ◈ in restaurant

See advert on opposite page

★★★★★ 85% **TOWN HOUSE HOTEL**   PLAN 4 E3

Egerton House

Red Carnation HOTELS

17 Egerton Ter, Knightsbridge SW3 2BX

☎ 020 7589 2412 🖷 020 7584 6540

e-mail: bookings@rchmail.com

web: www.redcarnationhotels.com

dir: *Just off Brampton Rd, between Harrods and Victoria & Albert Museum, opposite Brompton Oratory.*

This delightful town house enjoys a prestigious Knightsbridge location, a short walk from Harrods and close to the Victoria & Albert Museum. The air-conditioned bedrooms and the public rooms are appointed to the highest standards, with luxurious furnishings and quality antique pieces. Bedrooms have an exceptional range of facilities that includes iPod docks and video iPods, safes, mini bars and flat screen TVs. Staff offer the highest levels of personalised, attentive service.

Rooms 29 en suite (4 fmly) (3 GF) S £188-£208; D £211.50-£330 **Facilities** STV Xmas **Conf** Thtr 12 Class 12 Board 12 **Services** Lift air con

★★★★★ 82% **TOWN HOUSE HOTEL**   PLAN 4 F2

The Draycott

26 Cadogan Gardens SW3 2RP

☎ 020 7730 6466 🖷 020 7730 0236

e-mail: reservations@draycotthotel.com

web: www.draycotthotel.com

dir: *From Sloane Sq station towards Peter Jones, keep to left. At Kings Rd take first right Cadogan Gdns, 2nd right, hotel on left.*

Enjoying a prime location just yards from Sloane Square, this town house provides an ideal base in one of the most fashionable areas of London. Many regular guests regard this as their London residence and staff pride themselves on their hospitality. Beautifully appointed bedrooms include a number of very spacious suites and all are equipped to a high standard. Attractive day rooms, furnished with antique and period pieces, include a choice of lounges, one with access to a lovely sheltered garden.

Rooms 35 en suite (9 fmly) (2 GF) ◈ in 30 bedrooms S £125-£135; D £180-£290 **Facilities** STV Wi-fi in bedrooms Beauty treatment, Massage ch fac **Conf** Thtr 20 Class 12 Board 12 **Services** Lift air con **Notes** ◈ in restaurant

★★★★ 79% **TOWN HOUSE HOTEL**   PLAN 4 F3

The Beaufort

33 Beaufort Gardens SW3 1PP

☎ 020 7584 5252 🖷 020 7589 2834

e-mail: reservations@thebeaufort.co.uk

web: www.thebeaufort.co.uk

dir: *100yds past Harrods on left of Brompton Rd*

This friendly, attractive town house enjoys a peaceful location in a tree-lined cul-de-sac just minutes' walk from Knightsbridge. Air-conditioned bedrooms are thoughtfully equipped with chocolates, fruit, fresh flowers, videos, CD players and free internet and movie channel access. Guests are offered complimentary drinks and

continued on page 444

The Capital

Voted "Best Hotel for Food" in the UK by Conde Nast Traveller Gold List 2006

&

The Capital, a unique townhouse hotel offers luxury accommodation and personal service in the heart of Knightsbridge.

Created by its Scottish proprietor, David Levin, 34 years ago, it is, to this day, a family-run hotel. With 49 suites and rooms, every piece of furniture and work of art is handpicked or commissioned by the Levin family. The renowned Capital Restaurant holds two Michelin stars.

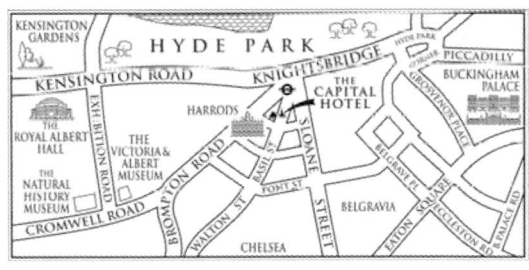

The Capital Hotel
22 Basil Street - Knightsbridge
London SW3 1AT
Tel. +44 (0)20 7589 5171
E-mail reservations@capitalhotel.co.uk
www.capitalhotel.co.uk

England

SW3 CHELSEA, BROMPTON *continued*

afternoon tea, served in the attractive drawing room. A good continental breakfast is served in guests' rooms.

The Beaufort

Rooms 29 en suite (3 GF) ⊘ in 12 bedrooms S £129.50-£182.13; D £164.50-£229.13 **Facilities** STV Wi-fi in bedrooms **Conf** BC Thtr 10 **Services** Lift air con **Notes** ⊗ ⊘ in restaurant

★★★★ 78% TOWN HOUSE HOTEL   PLAN 4 E4

Parkes

41 Beaufort Gardens, Knightsbridge SW3 1PW
☎ 020 7581 9944 ▤ 020 7581 1999
e-mail: reception@parkeshotel.com
web: www.parkeshotel.com
dir: off Brompton Rd, 100yds from Harrods

This sophisticated and friendly hotel is located in a tree-lined square in the heart of fashionable Knightsbridge. Stylish bedrooms and spacious suites with kitchens are beautifully appointed and equipped with every conceivable extra including UK/US modems and sockets, wireless ADSL and mini-bars. Whilst there is no hotel restaurant, a wide range of dishes from local eateries can be delivered to your room.

Rooms 33 en suite (16 fmly) (4 GF) S £234-£558; D £311-£558 **Facilities** STV Arrangement with nearby gym Wi-fi in bedrooms **Conf** Board 12 **Services** Lift air con **Notes** ⊗ ⊘ in restaurant

SW5 EARL'S COURT
See **LONDON SECTION PLAN 4 B2**

★★★★ 82% **HOTEL**   PLAN 4 B3

London Marriott Kensington   **Marriott**
                                  HOTELS & RESORTS

Cromwell Rd SW5 0TH
☎ 020 7973 1000 ▤ 020 7370 1685
e-mail: kensington.marriott@marriotthotels.com
web: www.marriott.com
dir: on A4, opposite Cromwell Rd Hospital

This stylish contemporary hotel features a stunning glass exterior and a seven-storey atrium lobby. Fully air conditioned throughout, the hotel has elegant design combined with a great range of facilities, including indoor leisure, a range of conference rooms and parking. Smart bedrooms offer a host of extras including the very latest communications technology.

Rooms 216 en suite (39 fmly) S £169; D £169 **Facilities** STV ⯑ Sauna Gym Jacuzzi Wi-fi in bedrooms **Conf** BC Thtr 200 Class 100 Board 60 Del from £195 **Services** Lift air con **Parking** 20 **Notes LB** ⊗ ⊘ in restaurant Civ Wed 60

★★★ 73% **HOTEL**   PLAN 4 A2

K + K Hotel George

1-15 Templeton Place, Earl's Court SW5 9NB
☎ 020 7598 8700 ▤ 020 7370 2285
e-mail: hotelgeorge@kkhotels.co.uk
web: www.kkhotels.com/george
dir: A3220 Earls Court Rd, right onto Trebovir Rd, right onto Templeton Place

This smart hotel enjoys a central location, just a few minutes' walk from Earls Court and with easy access to London's central attractions. Smart public areas include a bar/bistro, a stylish restaurant that overlooks the attractive rear garden, an executive lounge and meeting facilities. Bedrooms are particularly well equipped with a host of useful extras including free, high-speed internet access.

Rooms 154 en suite (38 fmly) (8 GF) ⊘ in 120 bedrooms S £182.12; D £217.27 (incl. bkfst) **Facilities** STV Wi-fi in bedrooms **Conf** BC Thtr 35 Class 14 Board 18 Del £175 **Services** Lift air con **Parking** 32 **Notes LB** ⊗ ⊘ in restaurant

England

★★ 68% METRO HOTEL
PLAN 4 A3

Comfort Inn Kensington

22-32 West Cromwell Rd, Kensington SW5 9QJ
☎ 020 7373 3300 ▤ 020 7835 2040
e-mail: enquiries@hotels-kensington.com
web: www.hotels-kensington.com

dir: on N side of West Cromwell Rd, between juncts of Cromwell Rd, Earls Court Rd & Warwick Rd

This cheerful, modern hotel is conveniently located for access to Earl's Court. Bedrooms vary in size but all are particularly well equipped and include rooms that are suitable for families. Bright public areas include a comfortable bar lounge and a bright dining room where cooked and continental breakfast is served.

Rooms 125 en suite (2 fmly) ⊗ in 48 bedrooms **Facilities** STV
Conf Thtr 80 Class 60 Board 30 **Services** Lift air con **Notes LB** ⊗ ⊗ in restaurant

---

U
PLAN 4 B2

Best Western Burns Hotel

18-26 Barkston Gardens, Kensington SW5 0EN
☎ 020 7373 3151 ▤ 020 7370 4090
e-mail: burnshotel@vienna-group.co.uk

dir: Off A4, right to Earls Court Rd (A3220), 2nd left. Hotel in Barkston Gardens, 2nd left past Earls Court underground station.

At the time of going to press, the star classification for this hotel was not confirmed. Please refer to the AA internet site www.theAA.com for current information.

Rooms 105 en suite (10 fmly) ⊗ in 38 bedrooms **Facilities** STV
Services Lift **Notes** ⊗ ⊗ in restaurant

U

The Rockwell

181-183 Cromwell Rd SW5 0SF
☎ 020 7244 2000 ▤ 020 7244 2001
e-mail: enquiries@therockwell.com

dir: From Central London proceed W down Cromwell Rd (A4), hotel on left shortly after Marloes Rd

At the time of going to press, the star classification for this hotel was not confirmed. Please refer to the AA internet site www.theAA.com for current information.

Rooms 40 en suite (4 fmly) (2 GF) ⊗ in all bedrooms S £100-£110; D £160-£200 **Facilities** STV **Conf** Board 10 **Services** Lift air con **Notes** ⊗

U
PLAN 4 B3

Shaftesbury Kensington

33 Hogarth Rd, Kensington SW5 0QQ
☎ 020 7370 6831 ▤ 020 7373 6179
e-mail: hogarth@marstonhotels.com

dir: Turn onto Earls Court Rd from Cromwell Rd on A4. 3rd left into Hogarth Rd, Hotel at end of road on left

At the time of going to press, the star classification for this hotel was not confirmed. Please refer to the AA internet site www.theAA.com for current information.

Rooms 85 en suite (2 fmly) ⊗ in 36 bedrooms **Facilities** STV
Conf Thtr 50 Class 20 Board 24 **Services** Lift **Parking** 18 **Notes** ⊗ ⊗ in restaurant

---

U
PLAN 4 A2

Twenty Nevern Square

20 Nevern Square, Earls Court SW5 9PD
☎ 020 7565 9555 & 7370 4934 ▤ 020 7565 9444
e-mail: hotel@twentynevernsquare.co.uk
web: www.twentynevernsquare.co.uk

dir: from station take Warwick Rd exit, right, 2nd right into Nevern Sq. Hotel 30yds on right

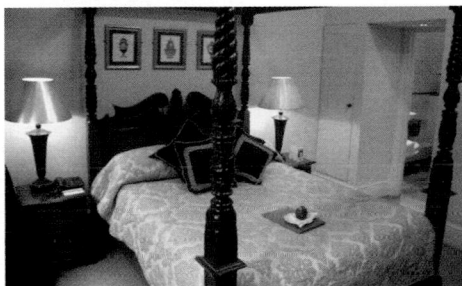

At the time of going to press, the star classification for this hotel was not confirmed. Please refer to the AA internet site www.theAA.com for current information.

Rooms 20 en suite (3 GF) ⊗ in 10 bedrooms **Facilities** STV
Arrangements for day membership at Cannons Leisure Centre **Conf** BC
Services Lift **Parking** 1 **Notes** ⊗ ⊗ in restaurant

BUDGET HOTEL
PLAN 4 B2

Premier Travel Inn London Kensington
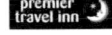

11 Knaresborough Place, Kensington SW5 0TJ
☎ 0870 238 3304 ▤ 020 7370 9292
web: www.premiertravelinn.com

dir: Just off A4 Cromwell Road, (2 minutes from Earls Court underground station)

High quality, modern budget accommodation ideal for both families and business travellers. Spacious, en suite bedrooms feature bath and shower, satellite TV and many have telephones and modem points. The adjacent family restaurant features a wide and varied menu. For further details consult the Hotel Groups page.

Rooms 183 en suite

SW6 FULHAM
See **LONDON PLAN 1 D2/3 & E3**

★★★★ 70% HOTEL

The Hotel at Chelsea

Stamford Bridge, Fulham Rd SW6 1HS
☎ 020 7565 1400 ▤ 020 7565 1450
e-mail: reservation@chelseafc.com

PREMIER

dir: 4 mins walk from Fulham Broadway tube station

This stylish, eye-catching hotel forms a part of the ambitious development of Chelsea Football Club and is situated adjacent to the ground. Public areas are extensive and feature a wide range of facilities including two restaurants and bars; the Chelsea Club is one of

continued on page 446

England

SW6 FULHAM *continued*

London's premier health and beauty spas. Air-conditioned bedrooms are spacious and well equipped.

Rooms 291 en suite (64 fmly) ⊗ in 138 bedrooms S £79-£160; D £79-£160 **Facilities Spa** STV ⬚ Gym Sauna Solarium Jacuzzi Wi-fi in bedrooms health club ♫ Xmas **Conf** BC Thtr 300 Class 250 Board 50 Del from £195 **Services** Lift air con **Parking** 290 **Notes** ⊗ ⊗ in restaurant Civ Wed 50

★★★ 74% HOTEL

Jurys Inn Chelsea

≋JURYS DOYLE
HOTELS

Imperial Rd, Imperial Wharf SW6 2GA

☎ 020 7411 2200 ▤ 020 7411 2444

e-mail: info@jurysdoyle.com

web: www.jurysdoyle.com

This modern hotel is located in Chelesa close to the Wharf. Bedrooms provide good guest comfort and in-room facilities are ideal for both leisure and business markets. There is even one floor designed by in Laura Ashley style. Public areas include a number of meeting rooms, a restaurant and a popular bar.

Rooms 172 en suite (172 fmly) ⊗ in 143 bedrooms S £65-£119; D £65-£119 **Facilities** STV Xmas **Conf** Thtr 15 Board 10 Del from £100 **Services** Lift air con **Notes LB** ⊗ ⊗ in restaurant Closed 24-26 Dec

★★★ 73% HOTEL   PLAN 4 A1

Hotel Ibis London Earls Court

ibis
ACCOR
hotels

47 Lillie Rd SW6 1UD

☎ 020 7610 0880 ▤ 020 7381 0215

e-mail: h5623@accor.com

web: www.ibishotels.com

dir: *From M4/A4 towards central London. Over Hammersmith flyover, keep in right lane, turn right at Kings pub on Talgarth Rd to join North End Road. To mini rdbt turn right. Hotel on left*

Situated opposite the Earls Court Exhibition Centre, this large, modern hotel is popular with business and leisure guests. Bedrooms are comfortable and well equipped. There is a café bar open all day and a restaurant that serves evening meals. There are also extensive conference facilities and an underground car park.

Rooms 504 en suite (20 fmly) ⊗ in 240 bedrooms S £62.95-£72.95; D £62.95-£72.95 **Facilities** STV Wi-fi available Health club and gym nearby **Conf** BC Thtr 1200 Class 750 Board 25 Del £150 **Services** Lift **Parking** 130 **Notes** ⊗ in restaurant

BUDGET HOTEL

Premier Travel Inn London Putney Bridge

3 Putney Bridge Approach SW6 3JD

☎ 0870 238 3302 ▤ 020 7471 8315

web: www.premiertravelinn.com

dir: *north bank of River Thames by Putney Bridge*

High quality, modern budget accommodation ideal for both families and business travellers. Spacious, en suite bedrooms feature bath and shower, satellite TV and many have telephones and modem points. The adjacent family restaurant features a wide and varied menu. For further details consult the Hotel Groups page.

Rooms 154 en suite

SW7 SOUTH KENSINGTON

HOTEL OF THE YEAR
INSPECTORS' CHOICE

★★★★★ ◉ ◉ HOTEL   PLAN 4 C4

Baglioni

60 Hyde Park Gate, Kensington Rd, Kensington SW7 5BB

☎ 020 7368 5700 ▤ 020 7368 5701

e-mail: info@baglionihotellondon.com

web: www.baglionihotellondon.com

dir: *on corner of Palace Gate Road*

Located in the heart of Kensington and overlooking Hyde Park, this small hotel buzzes with Italian style and chic. Bedrooms, predominantly suites, are generously sized, with bold dark colours and feature espresso machines, interactive plasma TV screens and a host of other excellent touches. Service is both professional and friendly, with personal butlers for the bedrooms. Public areas include the main open-plan space with bar, lounge and award-winning Brunello restaurant, all merging together with great elan; there is a small health club and a fashionable private club bar downstairs. AA Hotel of the Year for England 2006-7.

Rooms 68 en suite (16 fmly) ⊗ in all bedrooms S fr £352.50; D fr £352.50 **Facilities Spa** STV Sauna Gym Jacuzzi Wi-fi available Xmas **Conf** BC Thtr 60 **Services** Lift air con **Notes** ⊗

★★★★★ 88% ◉ ◉ ◉ HOTEL   PLAN 4 C2

The Bentley Kempinski

27-33 Harrington Gardens SW7 4JX

☎ 020 7244 5555 ▤ 020 7244 5566

e-mail: info@thebentley-hotel.com

web: www.thebentley-hotel.com

dir: *S of A4 into Knightsbridge at junct with Gloucester Rd, right, 2nd right turn, hotel on left just after mini-rdbt*

This hotel, discreetly located in the heart of Kensington, features lavish opulence throughout the public areas. Spacious air-conditioned bedrooms are equally luxurious, whilst marble clad bathrooms offer jacuzzi baths and walk-in showers. Public areas include the Peridot where breakfast and lunch are served, a cosy cigar den and the cocktail bar, Malachite. The fine dining restaurant, 1880, which is open for dinner, provides excellent contemporary cuisine and highly professional service.

continued

England

The Bentley Kempinski

Rooms 64 en suite ⊘ in 11 bedrooms S £450-£2500; D £450-£2500
Facilities Spa STV Sauna Gym Jacuzzi Wi-fi available Traditional Turkish
Hamam ♫ Xmas **Conf** Thtr 70 Class 60 Board 50 Del from £320
Services Lift air con **Notes** ⊘ in restaurant Civ Wed 80

★★★★ 75% **HOTEL**　　　　PLAN 4 C2

Millennium Gloucester Hotel London Kensington

4-18 Harrington Gardens SW7 4LH
☎ 020 7373 6030 🖷 020 7373 0409
e-mail: sales.gloucester@mill-cop.com
web: www.millenniumhotels.com
dir: opposite Gloucester Road underground station

This spacious, stylish hotel is centrally located, close to The Victoria &
Albert Museum and just minutes' walk from Gloucester Road tube
station. Air-conditioned bedrooms are furnished in a variety of
contemporary styles and Clubrooms benefit from a dedicated club
lounge with complimentary breakfast and snacks. A wide range of
eating options includes Singaporean and Mediterranean cuisine.

Rooms 610 en suite (6 fmly) ⊘ in 439 bedrooms **Facilities** STV Gym
Conf BC Thtr 500 Class 280 Board 40 **Services** Lift air con **Parking** 110
Notes LB ⊗

★★★★ 73% **HOTEL**　　　　PLAN 4 D2

Jurys Kensington Hotel

JURYS DOYLE
HOTELS

109-113 Queensgate, South Kensington SW7 5LR
☎ 020 7589 6300 🖷 020 7581 1492
e-mail: kensington@jurysdoyle.com
web: www.jurysdoyle.com
dir: From A4 take Cromwell Rd, turn right at V&A Museum onto
Queensgate, hotel at end on left

This beautiful building has been carefully refurbished and offers an
excellent location for visitors to London. Smartly appointed public
areas include an open-plan lobby/bar, Copplestones restaurant with
adjoining library lounge and the lively Kavanagh's bar. The upgraded
bedrooms vary in size but are well equipped and have duck down
duvets, crisp white linen and aromatherapy toiletries.

Rooms 174 annexe en suite (10 fmly) ⊘ in 142 bedrooms S £89-£190;
D £89-£190 (incl. bkfst) **Facilities** STV Wi-fi available Health Club facilities
available locally at discounted rate ♫ ch fac Xmas **Conf** Thtr 90 Class 45
Board 40 Del £225 **Services** Lift air con **Notes** ⊗ ⊘ in restaurant

---

★★★★ 72% **HOTEL**　　　　PLAN 4 C3

Millennium Baileys Hotel London Kensington

140 Gloucester Rd SW7 4QH
☎ 020 7373 6000 🖷 020 7370 3760
e-mail: reservations@mill-cop.com
web: www.millenniumhotels.com
dir: A4, turn right at Cromwell Hospital into Knaresborough
Place, follow to Courtfield Rd to corner of Gloucester Rd, hotel
opposite underground station

This elegant hotel has a townhouse feel to it and enjoys a prime
location opposite Gloucester Road tube station. Air-conditioned
bedrooms are smartly appointed and thoughtfully equipped,
particularly the club rooms which benefit from DVD players. Public
areas include a stylish contemporary restaurant and bar. Guests may
also use the facilities at the adjacent, larger sister hotel.

Rooms 212 en suite ⊘ in 120 bedrooms **Facilities** STV Gym
Conf Thtr 20 Class 18 Board 12 **Services** Lift air con **Parking** 70
Notes ⊗ ⊘ in restaurant

★★★★ 🅰　　　　PLAN 4 C3

Radisson Edwardian Vanderbilt

68-86 Cromwell Rd SW7 5BT
☎ 020 7761 9000 🖷 020 7761 9001
e-mail: resvand@radisson.com
web: www.radissonedwardian.com
dir: A4 into central London on Cromwell Rd. Hotel on left at
junct of Gloucester Rd & Cromwell Rd

Rooms 215 en suite (18 fmly) (28 GF) ⊘ in 115 bedrooms
Facilities Fitness room Business centre, Valet Laundry Service & Valet
Parking on request. **Conf** BC Thtr 100 Class 56 Board 40 **Services** Lift
air con **Notes** ⊗ No children

★★★ 74% **HOTEL**　　　　PLAN 4 C3

Grange Strathmore

41 Queens Gate Gardens SW7 5NB
☎ 020 7584 0512 🖷 020 7584 0246
e-mail: strathmore@grangehotels.com
web: www.grangehotels.co.uk
dir: M4 E into Kensington, left into Queens Gate Gardens

Formerly the residence of the Earl of Strathmore, this elegant property
retains many of its original features. Bedrooms, which vary in shape
and size, are appointed to a high standard. Public areas include a
selection of meeting rooms, the Glamis lounge bar and the
chandeliered Earls restaurant.

Rooms 77 en suite (10 fmly) ⊘ in 40 bedrooms S £109-£150;
D £119-£175 **Facilities** STV Xmas **Conf** Thtr 60 Class 25 Board 26 Del
£198 **Services** Lift **Notes** LB ⊗

England

SW10 WEST BROMPTON
See **LONDON PLAN 1 D/E3**

★★★★★ 87% HOTEL

Conrad London
Chelsea Harbour SW10 0XG
☎ 020 7823 3000 ▤ 020 7351 6525
e-mail: londoninfo@conradhotels.com
web: www.conradhotels.com

dir: *A4 to Earls Court Rd S towards river. Right into Kings Rd, left down Lots Rd*

Against the picturesque backdrop of Chelsea Harbour's small marina, this modern hotel offers spacious, comfortable accommodation. All rooms are suites, which are superbly equipped; many enjoy splendid views of the marina. In addition, there are also several luxurious penthouse suites. Public areas include a modern bar and restaurant, excellent leisure facilities and extensive meeting and function rooms.

Rooms 160 en suite (39 fmly) ⊗ in 110 bedrooms **Facilities** STV ▨ Sauna Solarium Gym Conrad Health Club with beauty treatments ♫ **Conf** Thtr 280 Class 120 Board 50 **Services** Lift air con **Parking** 17 **Notes** Civ Wed 200

SW11 BATTERSEA
See **LONDON PLAN 1 E3**

BUDGET HOTEL

Travelodge London Battersea
200 York Rd, Battersea SW11 3SA
☎ 08700 850 950 ▤ 020 7978 5898
web: www.travelodge.co.uk

dir: *from Wandsworth Bridge southern rdbt, take A3205 (York Rd) towards Battersea. 0.5m on left*

Travelodge offers good quality, good value, modern accommodation. Ideal for families, the spacious en suite bedrooms include remote-control TV, tea and coffee-making facilities and comfortable beds. Meals can be taken at the nearby family restaurant. See Hotel Groups pages for further details.

Rooms 87 en suite S fr £26; D fr £26

SW15 PUTNEY
See **LONDON PLAN 1 D2/3**

★★★ 64% METRO HOTEL

Best Western Lodge
52 -54 Upper Richmond Rd, Putney SW15 2RN
☎ 020 8874 1598 ▤ 020 8874 0910
e-mail: res@thelodgehotellondon.com

dir: *M25 junct 10/ A3 to Central London, then A219 to Putney, right to Upper Richmond, turn left at lights after 0.5m*

This friendly hotel is conveniently located for East Putney tube station. Public areas include a bar/lounge with satellite TV and conference and banqueting facilities. A buffet breakfast is served in the garden conservatory. Thoughtfully equipped, comfortable bedrooms include a selection of executive rooms and suites. Parking for residents is a definate asset.

Rooms 64 en suite (12 fmly) ⊗ in 37 bedrooms **Facilities** STV **Conf** Thtr 80 Class 40 Board 30 **Parking** 30 **Notes** Civ Wed

SW19 WIMBLEDON
See **LONDON PLAN 1 D2**

BUDGET HOTEL

Premier Travel Inn London Wimbledon South
Merantum Way, Merton SW19 2RD
☎ 0870 990 6342 ▤ 0870 9906343
web: www.premiertravelinn.com

High quality, modern budget accommodation ideal for both families and business travellers. Spacious, en suite bedrooms feature bath and shower, satellite TV and many have telephones and modem points. The adjacent family restaurant features a wide and varied menu. For further details consult the Hotel Groups page.

W1 WEST END

INSPECTORS' CHOICE

★★★★★ ◉◉◉ HOTEL   PLAN 2 H2

Claridge's
Brook St W1A 2JQ
☎ 020 7629 8860 ▤ 020 7499 2210
e-mail: info@claridges.co.uk

dir: *Take 1st turn after Green Park underground station to Berkeley Sq, 4th exit into Davies St. 3rd right into Brook St*

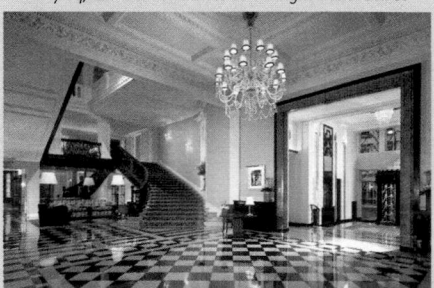

Once renowned as the resort of kings and princes, Claridge's today continues to set the standards by which other hotels are judged. The sumptuous, air-conditioned bedrooms are elegantly themed to reflect the Victorian or art deco architecture of the building. Gordon Ramsay at Claridge's has fast become one of London's most popular dining venues, while the stylish cocktail bar is proving to be equally well supported by residents and non-residents alike. Service throughout is punctilious and thoroughly professional.

Rooms 203 en suite (144 fmly) ⊗ in 34 bedrooms **Facilities** STV Gym Beauty & health treatments. Use of sister hotel swimming pool ♫ **Conf** Thtr 250 Class 130 Board 60 **Services** Lift air con **Notes LB** ⊗ Civ Wed 200

England

INSPECTORS' CHOICE

★★★★★ ◉◉◉ **HOTEL**   PLAN 2 G1

Connaught

Carlos Place W1K 2AL

☎ 020 7499 7070 🗊 020 7495 3262

e-mail: info@the-connaught.co.uk

dir: between Grosvenor Sq and Berkeley Sq in Mayfair

MAYBOURNE
HOTEL
GROUP

This hotel offers guests an intimate atmosphere, right in the heart of Mayfair. Couple this with exemplary standards of service and it is easy to see why people return time after time. To ensure that every guest is pampered, butlers and valets respond at the touch of a button and nothing is too much trouble. Dining in the very accomplished hands of Angela Hartnett and the menu has more than a hint of Italian about it.

Rooms 92 en suite S £169-£320; D £229-£429 **Facilities** STV Gym Fitness studio Health club facilities at sister hotels **Conf** Board 18 **Services** Lift air con **Notes** LB ⊗

INSPECTORS' CHOICE

★★★★★ ◉◉ **HOTEL**   PLAN 4 G6

The Dorchester

Park Ln W1A 2HJ

☎ 020 7629 8888 🗊 020 7409 0114

e-mail: reservations@dorchesterhotel.com

dir: between Hyde Park Corner & Marble Arch

One of London's finest, The Dorchester remains one of the best-loved hotels in the country and always delivers. Its sumptuous

continued

day rooms have now undergone a massive re-decoration program, which has resulted in them even more stunning than before. The spacious bedrooms and suites are beautifully appointed and feature fabulous marble bathrooms. Leading off from the foyer, The Promenade is the perfect setting for afternoon tea or drinks. In the evenings guests can relax to the sound of live jazz in the bar, and enjoy a cocktail or a meal in The Grill. Further dining options include the sophisticated new Chinese restaurant, China Tang, which has opened to rave reviews.

Rooms 250 en suite ⊗ in 34 bedrooms **Facilities Spa** STV Sauna Solarium Gym Jacuzzi The Dorchester Spa Health club 🎵 **Conf** BC Thtr 500 Class 300 Board 42 **Services** Lift air con **Parking** 21 **Notes** LB ⊗ Civ Wed 500

INSPECTORS' CHOICE

★★★★★ ◉◉ **HOTEL**   PLAN 5 A6

The Ritz

150 Piccadilly W1J 9BR

☎ 020 7493 8181 🗊 020 7493 2687

e-mail: enquire@theritzlondon.com

web: www.theritzlondon.com

dir: from Hyde Park Corner E on Piccadilly. Hotel on right after Green Park

This renowned, stylish hotel offers guests the ultimate in sophistication whilst still managing to retain all of its former historical glory. Bedrooms and suites are exquisitely furnished in Louis XVI style, with fine marble bathrooms and every imaginable comfort. Elegant reception rooms include the Palm Court with its legendary afternoon teas, the beautiful fashionable Rivoli Bar and the sumptuous Ritz Restaurant, complete with gold chandeliers and extraordinary trompe-l'oeil decoration.

Rooms 133 en suite ⊗ in 36 bedrooms S £230-£388; D £280-£470 **Facilities** STV Gym Treatment Room & hairdressing Room 🎵 Xmas **Conf** Thtr 180 Class 100 Board 43 Del from £200 **Services** Lift air con **Parking** 5 **Notes** LB ⊗ Civ Wed 70

England

W1 WEST END *continued*

★★★★★ ⊛ **HOTEL**   PLAN 4 H5

Athenaeum

116 Piccadilly W1J 7BJ
☎ 020 7499 3464 📠 020 7493 1860
e-mail: info@athenaeumhotel.com
web: www.athenaeumhotel.com

dir: on Piccadilly, overlooking Green Park

With a discreet address in Mayfair, this well-loved hotel has benefited from extensive refurbishment of public areas; a delightful bar that has retained its excellent stock of whiskies, complements the stunning Garden Lounge and stylish restaurant. Bedrooms are equipped to the highest standard and several have views over Green Park. A row of Edwardian townhouses adjacent to the hotel offers a range of spacious and well-appointed apartments. A delightful spa along with conference and meeting facilities complete the picture.

Rooms 157 en suite ⊘ in 58 bedrooms S £295; D £295
Facilities Spa STV Sauna Gym Jacuzzi Wi-fi available Steam rooms, spa treatments, hair dressing salon Xmas **Conf** BC Thtr 55 Class 35 Board 36 **Services** Lift air con **Notes LB** Civ Wed 80

★★★★★ ⊛ **HOTEL**   PLAN 4 G5

Four Seasons Hotel London

Hamilton Place, Park Ln W1A 1AZ
☎ 020 7499 0888 📠 020 7493 1895
e-mail: fsh.london@fourseasons.com

dir: from Piccadilly into Old Park Ln. Then Hamilton Place

This long-established, popular hotel is discreetly located near
continued

combines modern efficiency with traditional luxury. Guest care is Hyde Park Corner, in the heart of Mayfair. It successfully consistently of the highest order, even down to the smallest detail of a personalised wake-up call. The bedrooms are elegant and spacious, and the unique conservatory rooms are particularly special. Spacious public areas include extensive conference and banqueting facilities, Lane's bar and the fine-dining restaurant, together with an elegant lounge where wonderful afternoon teas are served.

Rooms 219 en suite ⊘ in 96 bedrooms S £394-£1998; D £459-£1998 **Facilities** STV Gym Wi-fi available 🎵 Xmas **Conf** BC Thtr 400 Class 180 Board 70 **Services** Lift air con **Parking** 72 **Notes LB** Civ Wed 180

★★★★★ 88% ⊛⊛⊛ **HOTEL**   PLAN 4 G5

The Metropolitan

Old Park Ln W1K 1LB
☎ 020 7447 1000 📠 020 7447 1100
e-mail: res.lon@metropolitan.como.bz

dir: on corner of Old Park Ln and Hertford St, within 200mtrs from Hyde Park corner

Overlooking Hyde Park on Park Lane, The Metropolitan is located within easy reach of the fashionable stores of Knightsbridge and Mayfair. The hotel's contemporary style allows freedom and space to relax. Understated luxury is the key here with bedrooms enjoying great natural light. There is the famous Met Bar and COMO Shambhala Urban Escape with steam room and fully equipped gym. For those seeking a culinary experience, Nobu offers innovative Japanese cuisine in an upbeat atmosphere.

Rooms 150 en suite (53 fmly) ⊘ in 127 bedrooms S £215-£3525; D £215-£3525 **Facilities Spa** STV Sauna Gym Treatments **Conf** BC Thtr 50 Board 30 **Services** Lift air con **Parking** 15 **Notes** ⊘ in restaurant

★★★★★ 86% ⊛⊛ **HOTEL**   PLAN 2 H4

Langham Hotel

1c Portland Place W1B 1JA
☎ 020 7636 1000 📠 020 7323 2340
e-mail: lon.info@langhamhotels.com

dir: N of Oxford Circus, left opposite All Souls Church

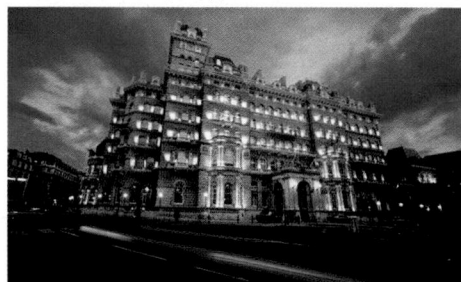

Originally opened in 1865, this elegant hotel enjoys a central location ideal for both theatreland and principal shopping areas. Bedrooms offer a choice of styles from traditional through to modern, all comfortably appointed with a full range of amenities. Public areas include the elegant Palm Court ideal for afternoon tea, Memories restaurant and an extensive health club complete with a 16-metre pool.

Rooms 427 en suite (5 fmly) D fr £300 **Facilities Spa** STV 🔍 Sauna Solarium Gym Jacuzzi Wi-fi available Heath club and spa facilities 🎵 Xmas **Conf** BC Thtr 584 Class 380 Board 260 **Services** Lift air con **Notes LB** Civ Wed 280

England

★★★★★ 84% ◎◎◎◎ **HOTEL**   PLAN 2 F2

Hyatt Regency London - The Churchill

30 Portman Square W1A 4ZX

☎ 020 7486 5800 🖹 020 7486 1255

e-mail: london.churchill@hyattintl.com

dir: from Marble Arch rdbt, follow signs for Oxford Circus onto Oxford St. Left turn after 2nd lights onto Portman St. Hotel on left

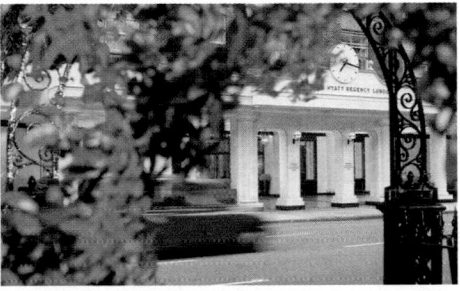

This smart hotel enjoys a central location overlooking Portman Square. Excellent conference, hairdressing and beauty facilities and a fitness room make this the ideal choice for both corporate and leisure guests. The Montagu restaurant offers contemporary dining within the hotel, while Locanda Locatelli showcases the enormous talents of Giorgio Locatelli in its fine Italian cuisine. The hotel is due to undergo a multi-million pound refurbishment.

Rooms 445 en suite ⊘ in 156 bedrooms S £176-£365; D £200-£388 **Facilities** STV FTV ⛱ Sauna Gym Wi-fi available Jogging track ♬ Xmas **Conf** BC Thtr 250 Class 160 Board 68 **Services** Lift air con **Parking** 48 **Notes** LB ⊛ Civ Wed 250

★★★★★ 82% **HOTEL**   PLAN 2 G1

Grosvenor House

Park Ln W1A 3AA

☎ 020 7499 6363 & 7399 8400 🖹 020 7493 3341

e-mail: grosvenor.house@marriotthotels.com

web: www.grosvenor-house.co.uk

dir: Marble Arch, halfway down Park Ln

This quintessentially British hotel, overlooking Hyde Park is currently enjoying an extensive restoration. Grosvenor House promises approachable luxury and epitomises the fine hotel culture and history of London. The property boasts the largest ballroom in Europe, and will feature a traditional brasserie and Champagne bar. The Park Room will also provide the perfect setting for afternoon tea. Please refer to the AA website www.theAA.com for further updates.

Rooms 446 en suite ⊘ in 236 bedrooms **Facilities Spa** STV ⌧ supervised Sauna Solarium Gym Jacuzzi Health & Fitness centre/Beauty salon ♬ Xmas **Conf** BC Thtr 1770 Class 800 Board 34 **Services** Lift air con **Parking** 80 **Notes** ⊛ Civ Wed 1500

★★★★★ 81% **HOTEL**   PLAN 2 F2

London Marriott Hotel Park Lane

Marriott HOTELS & RESORTS

140 Park Ln W1K 7AA

☎ 020 7493 7000 🖹 020 7493 8333

e-mail: mhrs.parklane@marriotthotels.com

web: www.marriott.co.uk

dir: From Hyde Park Corner left on Park Ln onto A4202, 0.8m. At Marble Arch onto Park Ln. 1st left onto North Row. Hotel on left

This modern and stylish hotel is situated in a prominent position in the heart of central London. Bedrooms are all superbly appointed and air conditioned. Public rooms include a popular lounge/bar, and there are excellent leisure facilities and an executive lounge.

Rooms 157 en suite ⊘ in 95 bedrooms **Facilities** STV ⌧ Gym Steam Room **Conf** BC Thtr 72 Class 33 Board 42 **Services** Lift air con **Notes** LB ⊛ ⊘ in restaurant

★★★★★ 75% ◎◎ **HOTEL**   PLAN 3 A1

Brown's

Albemarle St, Mayfair W1S 4BP

ℛℱ ROCCO FORTE HOTELS

☎ 020 7493 6020 🖹 020 7493 9381

e-mail: reservations.browns@roccofortehotels.com

web: www.roccofortehotels.com

dir: a short walk from Bond St & Piccadilly

Brown's is a London landmark and has now emerged from a complete refurbishment. Inside the hotel retains the charm in a successful balance of traditional and contemporary styles. Bedrooms are luxurious, furnished to a high standard and come with all the modern comforts you would expect of such a grand Mayfair hotel. The elegant restaurant (the oldest hotel restaurant in London) serves a traditional selection of excellent dishes; the lounges prove a popular venue for afternoon tea.

Rooms 117 en suite ⊘ in 93 bedrooms S £346 £3026; D £412 £3026 **Facilities Spa** STV FTV Wi-fi available Gym Spa Treatment Room ♬ **Conf** Thtr 70 Class 30 Board 30 **Services** Lift air con **Notes** ⊛ Civ Wed 70

★★★★★ 72% ◎◎ **HOTEL**   PLAN 4 G5

InterContinental London

INTER-CONTINENTAL HOTELS AND RESORTS

1 Hamilton Place, Hyde Park Corner W1J 7QY

☎ 020 7409 3131 🖹 020 7493 3476

e-mail: london@interconti.com

dir: at Hyde Park Corner, on corner of Park Lane and Piccadilly

A well-known and well-loved landmark on Hyde Park Corner, The InterContinental London is currently undergoing a multi-million pound restoration. The hotel is due to re-open in late 2006, revealing elegant guest rooms and designer suites, a new restaurant and bar, a contemporary event space and luxury spa.

Rooms 451 en suite ⊘ in 312 bedrooms **Facilities** STV Sauna Gym Jacuzzi Beauty treatments, Health Club, Horse riding, Crazy golf, Tennis courts nearby ♬ **Conf** BC Thtr 750 Class 340 Board 62 **Services** Lift air con **Parking** 100 **Notes** ⊛ Civ Wed 750

England

W1 WEST END *continued*

★★★★★ A PLAN 5 A6

Radisson Edwardian May Fair Hotel

Radisson EDWARDIAN

Stratton St W1J 8LL

☎ 020 7629 7777 📠 020 7629 1459

e-mail: mayfair@interconti.com

web: www.radissonedwardian.com

dir: *from Hyde Park Corner or Piccadilly left onto Stratton Street, hotel on left*

Rooms 289 en suite (14 fmly) ⊛ in 148 bedrooms **Facilities** STV Sauna Solarium Gym ♫ **Conf** Thtr 292 Class 108 Board 60 **Services** Lift air con **Notes LB** ⊗

★★★★ 87% ❀❀❀ HOTEL PLAN 2 G2

London Marriott Hotel Grosvenor Square

Marriott HOTELS & RESORTS

Grosvenor Square W1K 6JP

☎ 020 7493 1232 📠 020 7491 3201

e-mail: businesscentre@londonmarriott.co.uk

web: www.marriott.co.uk

dir: *M4 E to Cromwell Rd through Knightsbridge to Hyde Park Corner. Park Lane right at Brook Gate onto Upper Brook St to Grosvenor Sq*

Situated adjacent to Grosvenor Square in the heart of Mayfair, this hotel combines the best of a relatively peaceful setting with convenient access to the city, West End and some of the most exclusive shopping in London. Bedrooms and public areas are furnished and decorated to a high standard and retain the traditional elegance for which the area is known. An exciting addition to the hotel is Gordon Ramsay's latest restaurant, Maze.

Rooms 221 en suite (26 fmly) ⊛ in 120 bedrooms **Facilities** STV Gym Exercise & fitness centre **Conf** BC Thtr 900 Class 500 Board 120 **Services** Lift air con **Parking** 80 **Notes** ⊗ Civ Wed

★★★★ 85% HOTEL PLAN 2 F3

London Marriott Hotel Marble Arch

Marriott HOTELS & RESORTS

134 George St W1H 5DN

☎ 020 7723 1277 📠 020 7402 0666

e-mail: salesadmin.marblearch@marriotthotels.co.uk

web: www.marriott.co.uk

dir: *from Marble Arch turn into Edgware Rd, then 4th right into George St. Left into Dorset St for entrance*

Conveniently situated just off the Edgware Road and close to the Oxford Street shops, this friendly modern hotel offers smart, well-equipped, air-conditioned bedrooms. Public areas are stylish, and include a smart indoor leisure club, bar and Italian themed restaurant. Secure underground parking is available.

Rooms 240 en suite (100 fmly) ⊛ in 167 bedrooms S £199-£249; D £199-£249 **Facilities** STV Wi-fi in bedrooms ⊡ supervised Sauna Solarium Gym Jacuzzi Beauty parlour & Sun beds **Conf** Thtr 150 Class 75 Board 80 Del fr £260 **Services** Lift air con **Parking** 80 **Notes** ⊗ ⊛ in restaurant

★★★★ 83% ❀ HOTEL PLAN 4 H6

Chesterfield Mayfair

Red Carnation HOTELS

35 Charles St, Mayfair W1J 5EB

☎ 020 7491 2622 📠 020 7491 4793

e-mail: bookch@rchmail.com

web: www.redcarnationhotels.com

dir: *From Hyde Park Corner along Piccadilly, left into Half Moon St. At end left and 1st right into Queens St, then right into Charles St*

Quiet elegance and an atmosphere of exclusivity characterise this stylish Mayfair hotel where attentive, friendly service is a highlight. Bedrooms have been decorated in a variety of contemporary styles, some with fabric walls; all are extremely thoughtfully equipped and boast marble-clad bathrooms with heated floors and mirrors. Bedrooms and public areas are air conditioned.

Rooms 110 en suite (7 fmly) ⊛ in 52 bedrooms S £99-£225; D £119-£295 **Facilities** STV Wi-fi available ♫ Xmas **Conf** Thtr 100 Class 45 Board 45 Del from £195 **Services** Lift air con **Notes LB** Civ Wed 120

★★★★ 82% ❀ HOTEL PLAN 3 A2

The Westbury

Bond St W1S 2YF

☎ 020 7629 7755 📠 020 7495 1163

e-mail: reservations@westburymayfair.com

dir: *from Oxford Circus S down Regent St, right onto Conduit St, hotel at junct of Conduit St & Bond St*

A well-known favourite with an international clientele, The Westbury is located at the heart of London's finest shopping district and provides a calm atmosphere away from the hubbub. The standards of accommodation are high throughout. Reception rooms offer a good choice for both relaxing and eating and include the stylish Polo Bar and a smart, contemporary restaurant.

Rooms 247 en suite ⊛ in 150 bedrooms S £222-£387; D £222-£387 **Facilities** STV Gym Steam room Wi-fi in bedrooms Fitness centre, ♫ Xmas **Conf** BC Thtr 120 Class 55 Board 35 **Services** Lift air con **Parking** 8 **Notes LB** ⊛ in restaurant

See advert on opposite page

★★★★ 82% HOTEL PLAN 2 G3

The Mandeville

Mandeville Place W1U 2BE

☎ 020 7935 5599 📠 020 7935 9588

e-mail: info@mandeville.co.uk

web: www.mandeville.co.uk

dir: *off Oxford Street and Wigmore Street near Bond Street underground station*

This is a stylish and attractive boutique-style hotel with a very contemporary feel. The bedrooms, all with air conditioning, have state-of-the-art TVs and large very comfortable beds. One of the suites has a patio with views over London. The cocktail bar is a popular venue.

Rooms 142 en suite ⊛ in 30 bedrooms S £250; D £275 **Facilities** STV Wi-fi available Xmas **Conf** Thtr 35 Class 20 Board 20 Del £300 **Services** Lift air con **Notes LB** ⊗

★★★★ 80% **HOTEL** PLAN 4 H6

The Washington Mayfair Hotel

5-7 Curzon St, Mayfair W1J 5HE
☎ 020 7499 7000 📠 020 7495 6172
e-mail: sales@washington-mayfair.co.uk
web: www.washington-mayfair.co.uk

dir: from Green Park station take Piccadilly exit & turn right. 4th street on right into Curzon Street

Situated in the heart of Mayfair, this stylish independently owned hotel offers a very high standard of accommodation. Personalised, friendly service is noteworthy. Bedrooms are attractively furnished and provide high levels of comfort. The hotel is also a popular venue for afternoon tea and refreshments, served in the marbled and wood-panelled lounge.

Rooms 171 en suite ⊘ in 141 bedrooms **Facilities** STV Gym Wi-fi in bedrooms ♫ Xmas **Conf** BC Thtr 110 Class 40 Board 36 Del from £250 **Services** Lift air con **Notes** ⊗

★★★★ 79% ❀ **HOTEL** PLAN 2 G1

Millennium Hotel London Mayfair

Grosvenor Square W1K 2HP
☎ 020 7629 9400 📠 020 7629 7736
e-mail: sales.mayfair@mill-cop.com
web: www.millenniumhotels.com

dir: on S side of Grosvenor Square near Park Lane and Oxford St.

This hotel benefits from a prestigious location in the heart of Mayfair, close to Bond Street. Smart bedrooms are generally spacious and club-floor rooms have their own lounge with complimentary refreshments. A choice of bars and dining options include the stylish Brian Turner Restaurant offering classic British food, and also the Shogun Restaurant showcasing a range of Japanese eating options. Conference facilities along with a fitness room complete the picture.

Rooms 348 en suite ⊘ in 265 bedrooms **Facilities** STV Gym ♫ ch fac **Conf** BC Thtr 450 Class 250 Board 70 **Services** Lift air con **Notes LB** ⊗ Civ Wed 250

★★★★ 79% ❀ **HOTEL** PLAN 2 F2

The Montcalm Hotel Nikko London

Great Cumberland Place W1H 7TW
☎ 020 7402 4288 📠 020 7724 9180
e-mail: reservations@montcalm.co.uk
web: www.montcalm.co.uk

dir: 2 mins' walk N from Marble Arch station

Ideally located on a secluded crescent close to Marble Arch, this charming Georgian property is named after the Marquis de Montcalm.

continued

Japanese-owned, the hotel offers extremely comfortable accommodation, ranging from standard to duplex 'junior' and penthouse suites. The stylish restaurant has a reputation for creative, modern cooking. Restaurant prices include a half bottle of wine per person, and the weekly lunch is particularly good value. The staff are very thoughtful in their approach to customer care.

Rooms 120 en suite (4 fmly) ⊘ in 58 bedrooms S £130-£230; D £140-£250 **Facilities** STV **Conf** Thtr 80 Class 40 Board 36 **Services** Lift air con **Parking** 10 **Notes LB** ⊗

★★★★ 79% ❀ **HOTEL** PLAN 2 F4

Sherlock Holmes

108 Baker St W1U 6LJ
☎ 020 7486 6161 📠 020 7958 5211
e-mail: info@sherlockholmeshotel.com
web: www.parkplaza.com

dir: from Marylebone Flyover onto Marylebone Rd. At Baker Street turn right for hotel on left

Chic and modern, this boutique-style hotel is located near to a number of London underground lines and rail stations. Public rooms include a popular bar, sited just inside the main entrance, and Sherlock's Grill, where the mesquite-wood burning stove is a feature of the cooking. The hotel also features an indoor health suite and a relaxing lounge.

Rooms 119 en suite (20 fmly) ⊘ in 60 bedrooms S £133-£225; D £133-£225 **Facilities** Spa STV Sauna Gym Wi-fi in bedrooms Xmas **Conf** Thtr 80 Class 45 Board 40 Del from £189 **Services** Lift air con **Notes** ⊗ ⊘ in restaurant Civ Wed 50

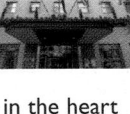
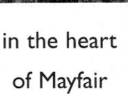

W1 WEST END *continued*

★★★★ 77% ⚜ **HOTEL**　　PLAN 2 F2

The Cumberland

Great Cumberland Place W1A 4RF　THISTLE HOTELS
☎ 0870 333 9280 📠 0870 333 9281
e-mail: enquiries@thecumberland.co.uk

This landmark hotel, occupying a prime position at Marble Arch, has undergone a complete transformation. A striking, airy lobby is the focal point, and a choice of bars, a Gary Rhodes' restaurant and extensive conference and meeting facilities are just some of what's on offer here. Bedrooms have a stylish contemporary feel and boast an excellent range of facilities.

Rooms 900 rms (886 en suite) 115 annexe en suite (29 fmly) (9 GF) ⊘ in 732 bedrooms **Facilities** STV Gym ♫ **Conf** BC Thtr 320 Class 180 Board 58 **Services** Lift air con **Notes LB** ⊗ Civ Wed 230

★★★★ 77% **HOTEL**　　PLAN 3 A4

Grange Fitzrovia

20-28 Bolsover St W1W 5NB
☎ 020 7467 7000 📠 020 7636 5085
e-mail: fitzrovia@grangehotels.com
web: www.grangehotels.co.uk

Situated in a quiet side street, this charming central London townhouse hotel is just minutes away from the theatres of the West End and the shops of Oxford Street and Bond Street. Guest bedrooms, accessed via panoramic glass lifts, are generally spacious and offer an excellent range of facilities. Public rooms feature a non-smoking lounge and an elegant lounge bar.

Rooms 88 en suite ⊘ in 40 bedrooms S £159-£200; D £159-£200 **Facilities** STV Wi-fi available Xmas **Conf** Thtr 100 Class 45 Board 40 Del £235 **Services** Lift **Notes LB** ⊗

★★★★ 76% **HOTEL**　　PLAN 2 F3

Radisson SAS Portman

22 Portman Square W1H 7BG
☎ 020 7208 6000 📠 020 7208 6001
e-mail: sales.london@radissonsas.com
web: www.radisson.com

dir: 100mtrs N of Oxford St and 500mtrs E of Edgware Rd

This smart, popular hotel enjoys a prime location, a short stroll from Oxford Street and close to all the city's major attractions. The spacious, well-equipped bedrooms are themed ranging from Oriental through to classical and contemporary Italian decor. Public areas include extensive conference facilities, a bar and the modern European Portman Restaurant.

Rooms 272 en suite (93 fmly) ⊘ in 129 bedrooms **Facilities** STV ☒ Sauna Solarium Gym ♫ **Conf** BC Thtr 600 Class 280 Board 70 **Services** Lift air con **Parking** 400 **Notes LB** ⊗ Civ Wed

★★★★ 74% **HOTEL**　　PLAN 2 G3

Jurys Clifton-Ford

47 Welbeck St W1M 8DN　JURYS DOYLE
☎ 020 7486 6600 📠 020 7486 7492
e-mail: cliftonford@jurysdoyle.com
web: www.jurysdoyle.com

dir: from Portland Place, turn into New Cavendish St. Welbeck St last turning on left

This well kept hotel enjoys a central location just 5 minutes' walk from Oxford Street and fashionable Bond Street. Bedrooms vary in space and style and include a number of penthouse apartments with balconies. Public areas include an excellent leisure club with a good size swimming pool, extensive conference facilities and a spacious lounge, bar and restaurant.

Rooms 256 en suite (7 fmly) ⊘ in 130 bedrooms S £95-£240; D £95-£240 **Facilities** STV ☒ Sauna Solarium Gym Jacuzzi Wi-fi available Leisure club Health/beauty treatments Dance studio ch fac **Conf** Thtr 120 Class 70 Board 40 Del from £209 **Services** Lift air con **Notes LB** ⊗ ⊘ in restaurant

★★★★ 73% **HOTEL**　　PLAN 2 F2

Thistle Marble Arch

Bryanston St W1A 4UR　THISTLE HOTELS
☎ 0870 333 9116 📠 0870 333 9216
e-mail: marblearch@thistle.co.uk

dir: From Marble Arch monument down Oxford St. 1st left onto Portman St, 1st left onto Bryanston St. Hotel on left.

This centrally located hotel, adjacent to a car park, is ideal for the attractions of Oxford Street and Knightsbridge. The spacious bedrooms come in a range of size and price options, but all are very well equipped and have air conditioning. The spacious public areas include a fast food service, Co-Motion, and a more leisurely carvery restaurant, which also offers a carte menu. There is also a gym, range of meeting rooms and an executive lounge.

Rooms 692 en suite (12 fmly) (22 GF) ⊘ in 218 bedrooms **Facilities** STV Gym **Services** Lift air con **Notes** ⊗

★★★★ 72% **HOTEL**　　PLAN 2 G2

Selfridge

Orchard St W1H 6JS　THISTLE HOTELS
☎ 0870 333 9117 📠 0870 333 9217
e-mail: selfridge@thistle.co.uk

dir: Behind Selfridge Hotel in Oxford St.

This traditional hotel enjoys an enviable location, just off Oxford Street; ideally located for all of central London's shops and attractions. Public rooms retain many original features and include a stylish restaurant and bar as well as a comfortable lounge and a selection of meeting rooms. Bedrooms are thoughtfully equipped and include a number of larger executive rooms and suites.

Rooms 294 en suite (3 fmly) ⊘ in 189 bedrooms D fr £117 (incl. bkfst) **Facilities** STV Xmas **Conf** BC Thtr 200 Class 110 Board 36 Del from £125 **Services** Lift **Notes** ⊗

England

England

★★★★ 🄰   PLAN 3 B4

Radisson Edwardian Grafton Hotel

Radisson
EDWARDIAN

130 Tottenham Court Rd W1T 5AY
☎ 020 7388 4131 📠 020 7387 7394
e-mail: resgraf@radisson.com
web: www.radissonedwardian.com

dir: *from Euston Rd onto Tottenham Court Rd. Past Warren Street underground station*

Rooms 330 en suite (23 fmly) ⊘ in 55 bedrooms **Facilities** STV Fitness room. Valet Laundry & Parking services on request. **Conf** BC Thtr 100 Class 50 Board 30 **Services** Lift air con **Notes** ⊗ No children 16yrs ⊘ in restaurant

★★★★ 🄰   PLAN 2 H2

Radisson Edwardian Berkshire

Radisson
EDWARDIAN

350 Oxford St W1N 0BY
☎ 020 7629 7474 📠 020 7629 8156
e-mail: resberk@radisson.com
web: www.radissonedwardian.com

dir: *opposite Bond Street underground. Entrance on Marylebone Lane.*

Rooms 147 en suite (10 fmly) ⊘ in 99 bedrooms **Facilities** STV Valet Laundry & Parking services on request **Conf** BC Thtr 40 Class 16 Board 16 **Services** Lift air con **Notes** ⊗ No children

★★★ 78% METRO HOTEL   PLAN 3 C1

Thistle Piccadilly

THISTLE HOTELS

39 Coventry St W1D 6BZ
☎ 0870 333 9118 📠 0870 333 9218
e-mail: Piccadilly@Thistle.co.uk

dir: *At Kings Cross follow signs for West End and Piccadilly.*

This popular hotel is centrally located between Leicester Square and Piccadilly Circus, ideal for all of the West End's attractions. Bedrooms vary in size and style but all are well equipped; deluxe and stylish executive rooms boast air-conditioning. Public areas include a cosy bar/lounge where snacks are available and a smart breakfast room. Numerous restaurants are located within walking distance.

Rooms 92 en suite (1 fmly) ⊘ in 52 bedrooms **Facilities** STV **Conf** Thtr 30 Class 16 Board 20 **Services** Lift air con **Notes** LB ⊗ ⊘ in restaurant

★★★ 75% ◉◉ HOTEL   PLAN 2 F2

Best Western Mostyn Hotel

Best Western

4 Bryanston St W1H 7BY
☎ 0871 437 0044 📠 0871 437 0280
e-mail: info@mostynhotel.co.uk
web: www.mostynhotel.co.uk

dir: *close to Marble Arch and Bond St underground*

The Mostyn enjoys an enviable location, just behind Oxford Street, in the heart of the West End. Originally built as a residence for Lady Back, a lady-in-waiting at the court of George II, the hotel retains many original features. Well-equipped, modern bedrooms have air conditioning, and public rooms include a stylish open-plan lounge and cocktail bar. Innovative Indian cooking is served in the restaurant.

continued

Rooms 121 en suite (15 fmly) ⊘ in 54 bedrooms **Facilities** STV **Conf** BC Thtr 130 Class 70 Board 50 **Services** Lift air con **Notes** ⊗

See advert on page 18

★★★ 72% HOTEL   PLAN 3 A3

Grange Langham Court

31-35 Langham St W1W 6BU
☎ 020 7436 6622 📠 020 7436 2303
e-mail: langhamcourt@grangehotels.com
web: www.grangehotels.co.uk

dir: *just off Regents Street*

Situated in a quiet, secluded street between Regents Park and Oxford Circus, this hotel has an elegant tiled façade. Formerly a nursing home, it now provides compact and well-equipped accommodation. Public areas include a wine bar serving snacks and light meals, a comfortable lounge and a basement dining room.

Rooms 56 en suite ⊘ in 20 bedrooms S £129-£154; D £139-£169 **Facilities** STV Wi-fi in bedrooms Xmas **Conf** Thtr 80 Class 35 Board 35 Del £198 **Services** Lift **Notes** LB ⊗

Ⓤ   PLAN 3 B2

Best Western Premier Shaftesbury

Best Western
PREMIER

65-73 Shaftesbury Av, Piccadilly W1V 6EX
☎ 020 7871 6000
e-mail: reservations@shaftesburyhotel.co.uk

dir: *At junct with Dean Street*

At the time of going to press, the star classification for this hotel was not confirmed. Please refer to the AA internet site www.theAA.com for current information.

Rooms 67 en suite (2 fmly) ⊘ in 28 bedrooms **Facilities** STV Gym **Conf** BC Board 12 **Services** Lift air con **Notes** ⊗ ⊘ in restaurant

Ⓤ   PLAN 3 A2

Courthouse Hotel Kempinski

Great Marlborough St W1F 7HL
☎ 020 7297 5555

At the time of going to press, the star classification for this hotel was not confirmed. Please refer to the AA internet site www.theAA.com for current information.

Rooms 116 en suite

Ⓤ   PLAN 2 G2

Radisson Edwardian Sussex

Radisson
EDWARDIAN

19-25 Granville Place W1H 6PA
☎ 020 7408 0130 📠 020 7493 2070
e-mail: ressuss@radisson.com
web: www.radissonedwardian.com

dir: *off Oxford St. Turn left to Portman St. Then right into Granville Place*

At the time of going to press, the star classification for this hotel was not confirmed. Please refer to the AA internet site www.theAA.com for current information.

Rooms 101 en suite (12 fmly) ⊘ in 70 bedrooms **Facilities** Gym **Conf** BC Board 10 **Services** Lift air con **Notes** LB ⊗

W2 BAYSWATER, PADDINGTON

★★★★ 81% @ HOTEL   PLAN 2 D2

Royal Lancaster

Lancaster Ter W2 2TY

☎ 020 7262 6737 ▤ 020 7724 3191

e-mail: book@royallancaster.com

web: www.royallancaster.com

dir: *adjacent to Lancaster Gate Underground Station*

This smart hotel has an excellent range of public facilities, including impressive conference rooms, 24-hour business centre and car park. The AA rosette-awarded Nipa Thai is among a choice of drinking and eating options that also includes the new Island Restaurant. Bedrooms are modern and well equipped, with upper floors enjoying stunning views across London.

Rooms 416 en suite (11 fmly) ⊕ in 200 bedrooms S £85-£247; D £85-£257 **Facilities** STV ♫ ch fac Xmas **Conf** BC Thtr 1400 Class 650 Board 40 Del from £200 **Services** Lift air con **Parking** 70 **Notes** ⊗

★★★★ 75% HOTEL   PLAN 2 B1

Ramada Hyde Park   ®RAMADA.

150 Bayswater Rd W2 4RT

☎ 020 7229 1212 ▤ 020 7229 2623

e-mail: sales.hydepark@ramadajarvis.co.uk

web: www.ramadajarvis.co.uk

dir: *From Hammersmith flyover left into Warwick Road. At Kensington High Street turn right, continue to Kensington Church Street, left to T-junct, right into Bayswater Road. Hotel 0.25m on left*

This large hotel overlooks Kensington Gardens and Hyde Park and is ideal for the West End, Oxford Street and Paddington. Modern styled air-conditioned bedrooms are comfortably appointed for both business and leisure guests. Public areas include the Arts restaurant and a range of refurbished meeting rooms. Limited parking is available.

Rooms 213 en suite (10 GF) ⊕ in 180 bedrooms S £65-£165; D £75-£235 **Facilities** STV Wi-fi available **Conf** Thtr 100 Class 50 Board 30 Del from £125 **Services** Lift **Parking** 39 **Notes LB** ⊗ ⊕ in restaurant

★★★★ 74% HOTEL   PLAN 2 C1

Thistle Hyde Park   THISTLE HOTELS

90-92 Lancaster Gate W2 3NR

☎ 0870 333 9110 ▤ 0870 333 9210

e-mail: hydepark@thistle.co.uk

dir: *At Marble Arch rdbt take 4th exit.*

Delightful building ideally situated overlooking Hyde Park and just a short walk from Kensington Gardens. The stylish public areas include a piano bar, a lounge and a smart restaurant. Bedrooms are tastefully appointed and equipped with many thoughtful touches; some rooms have views of the park.

Rooms 54 en suite (5 fmly) D fr £111.15 (incl. bkfst) **Facilities** Xmas **Conf** Thtr 30 Class 20 Board 22 **Services** Lift **Parking** 20 **Notes** ⊗ ⊕ in restaurant Civ Wed 50

★★★ 75% TOWN HOUSE HOTEL   PLAN 2 A1

The Abbey Court

20 Pembridge Gardens, Kensington W2 4DU

☎ 020 7221 7518 ▤ 020 7792 0858

e-mail: info@abbeycourthotel.co.uk

web: www.abbeycourthotel.co.uk

dir: *2 mins from Notting Hill Gate Underground station*

Situated in Notting Hill and close to Kensington, this five-storey Victorian town house stands in a quiet side road. Rooms are individually decorated and have marble bathrooms with jacuzzi baths. Room service is available for light snacks and full English breakfasts can be enjoyed in the conservatory.

Rooms 22 en suite (1 fmly) (3 GF) ⊕ in 10 bedrooms **Facilities Spa** STV **Conf** BC Board 10 **Notes** ⊗

★★★ 70% HOTEL   PLAN 2 D2

Corus hotel Hyde Park   cᴑrus hotels

1-7 Lancaster Gate W2 3LG

☎ 020 7262 5022 ▤ 020 7724 8666

e-mail: londonhydepark@corushotels.com

web: www.corushotels.com

dir: *200yds from Lancaster Gate underground. 0.25m from Paddington Station*

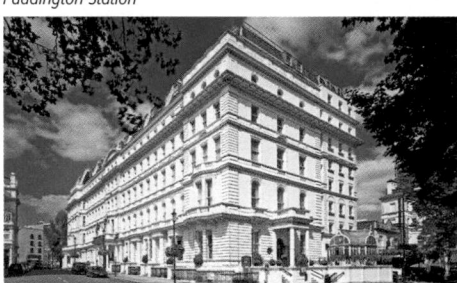

Centrally located adjacent to Hyde Park and a short walk from Marble Arch, this smart hotel is a great base to tour the city. Bedrooms, including a number of spacious executive rooms and suites, have been fitted out with modern colour schemes and a useful range of facilities; some have air conditioning. Open-plan public areas include a popular restaurant and bar.

Rooms 390 en suite (10 fmly) (12 GF) ⊕ in 285 bedrooms **Conf** BC Thtr 25 Class 16 Board 18 **Services** Lift **Notes** ⊗ ⊕ in restaurant

★★ 71% HOTEL   PLAN 2 D2

Best Western Delmere   Best Western

130 Sussex Gardens, Hyde Park W2 1UB

☎ 020 7706 3344 ▤ 020 7262 1863

e-mail: delmerehotel@compuserve.com

dir: *M25 take A40 to London, exit at Paddington. Along Westbourne Terrace and into Sussex Gardens*

This friendly, privately owned hotel is situated within walking distance of Paddington Station, Hyde Park and Marble Arch. The smartly presented bedrooms are extremely well equipped and include some ground floor rooms. A small bar, a comfortable, elegant lounge and an Italian style restaurant complete the picture.

Rooms 36 en suite (6 GF) ⊕ in 10 bedrooms **Facilities** STV **Services** Lift **Parking** 2 **Notes LB** ⊗

England

U   PLAN 2 C2

Best Western Paddington Court Hotel & Suites

27 Devonshire Ter W2 3DP

☎ 020 7745 1200 ▤ 020 7745 1221

e-mail: info@paddingtoncourt.com

web: www.paddingtoncourt.com

dir: *from A40 take exit before Paddington flyover, follow Paddington Station signs. Devonshire Terrace is off Craven Road*

At the time of going to press, the star classification for this hotel was not confirmed. Please refer to the AA internet site www.theAA.com for current information.

Rooms 165 en suite 35 annexe en suite (43 fmly) (33 GF) ⊗ in 106 bedrooms **Facilities** STV **Services** Lift **Notes** ⊗ ⊗ in restaurant

U   PLAN 2 C1

Thistle Kensington Gardens

THISTLE HOTELS

104 Bayswater Rd W2 3HL

☎ 0870 333 9102 ▤ 0870 333 9202

e-mail: kensingtongardens@thistle.co.uk

At the time of going to press, the star classification for this hotel was not confirmed. Please refer to the AA internet site www.theAA.com for current information.

Rooms 175 en suite (22 fmly) ⊗ in 131 bedrooms **Facilities** STV **Conf** BC Thtr 30 Class 40 Board 20 **Services** Lift air con **Parking** 69 **Notes** ⊗ ⊛ in restaurant

BUDGET HOTEL   PLAN 2 D2

Days Hotel London Hyde Park

DAYS INN

148/152 Sussex Gardens W2 1UD

☎ 020 7723 2939

web: www.welcomebreak.co.uk

This modern building offers accommodation in smart, spacious and well-equipped bedrooms, suitable for families and business travellers, and all with en suite bathrooms. Continental breakfast is available and other refreshments may be taken at the nearby family restaurant. For further details see the Hotel Groups page.

Rooms 50 en suite

W3 ACTON

See **LONDON PLAN 1 C3**

★★★ 75% HOTEL

Ramada Encore London West

4 Portal Way, Gypsy Corner, A40 Western Av W3 6RT

☎ 0870 0667 123 ▤ 0870 0667 144

e-mail: reservations@encorelondonwest.co.uk

Conveniently situated on the A40 this modern, purpose built, glass-fronted hotel is convenient for visitors to London. Air-conditioned bedrooms offer smartly appointed modern accommodation with en

continued

suite, power-shower rooms. Open-plan public areas include a popular Asian and European restaurant, and a 2go café serving Starbucks' coffee. Secure parking and a range of meeting rooms are available.

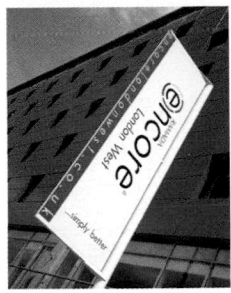

Ramada Encore London West

Rooms 150 en suite (35 fmly) ⊗ in 100 bedrooms **Facilities** STV **Conf** Thtr 50 Class 28 Board 26 **Services** Lift air con **Parking** 72 **Notes** ⊗

BUDGET HOTEL

Travelodge London Park Royal

Travelodge

A40 Western Ave, Acton W3 0TE

☎ 08700 850 950 ▤ 020 8752 1134

web: www.travelodge.co.uk

dir: *off A40 Western Ave eastbound*

Travelodge offers good quality, good value, modern accommodation. Ideal for families, the spacious en suite bedrooms include remote-control TV, tea and coffee-making facilities and comfortable beds. Meals can be taken at the nearby family restaurant. See Hotel Groups pages for further details.

Rooms 64 en suite S fr £26; D fr £26

W5 EALING

See **LONDON SECTION PLAN 1 C4**

★★★ 79% HOTEL

Ramada Ealing

RAMADA

Ealing Common W5 3HN

☎ 020 8896 8400 ▤ 020 8992 7082

e-mail: sales.ealing@ramadajarvis.co.uk

web: www.ramadajarvis.co.uk

dir: *at North Circular A406 & Uxbridge Road A4020 junction*

This large modern, comfortable hotel is conveniently located a few minutes' walk from Ealing Common underground and easy access to the M40. Bedrooms, which vary in size, are comfortably appointed for both business and leisure guests. There is substantial parking, the spacious Arts restaurant and a range of meeting rooms.

Rooms 189 en suite (3 fmly) ⊗ in 146 bedrooms S £140; D £165 **Facilities** STV Wi-fi available Xmas **Conf** Thtr 200 Class 110 Board 80 Del £165 **Services** Lift **Parking** 150 **Notes** LB ⊗ ⊗ in restaurant Civ Wed 200

England

W6 HAMMERSMITH
See **LONDON PLAN 1 D3**

★★★ 82% **HOTEL**

Novotel London West
1 Shortlands W6 8DR
☎ 020 8741 1555 📠 020 8741 2120
e-mail: H0737@accor-hotels.com
web: www.novotel.com

dir: M4 (A4) & A316 junct at Hogarth rdbt. Along Great West Rd, left for Hammersmith before flyover. On Hammersmith Bridge Rd to rdbt, take 5th exit. 1st left into Shortlands, 1st left to hotel main entrance

A Hammersmith landmark, this substantial hotel is a popular base for both business and leisure travellers. Spacious, air-conditioned bedrooms boast a good range of extras and many have additional beds, making them suitable for families. The hotel also has its own car park, business centre and shop, and boasts one of the largest convention centres in Europe.

Rooms 629 en suite (148 fmly) ⊗ in 473 bedrooms **Facilities** STV Snooker Gym **Conf** BC Thtr 1000 Class 525 Board 200 **Services** Lift air con **Parking** 240 **Notes** Civ Wed 1400

W8 KENSINGTON

INSPECTORS' CHOICE

★★★★★ ◉◉◉ **HOTEL**　　　PLAN 4 B5

Royal Garden Hotel
2-24 Kensington High St W8 4PT
☎ 020 7937 8000 📠 020 7361 1991
e-mail: sales@royalgardenhotel.co.uk
web: www.royalgardenhotel.co.uk
dir: next to Kensington Palace

Situated in fashionable Kensington, this well-known landmark hotel is just a short walk from the Albert Hall and London's smart shops. Bedrooms are of contemporary design, equipped with many up-to-date facilities. Many are large and have views over the park. The hotel's popular eating and drinking options are varied; among them is The Tenth, the hotel's showcase restaurant which has fantastic views.

Rooms 396 en suite (19 fmly) ⊗ in 300 bedrooms S £270-£317; D £330-£388 **Facilities** Spa STV Sauna Gym Health & fitness centre ♬ Xmas **Conf** BC Thtr 550 Class 260 Board 80 **Services** Lift air con **Parking** 160 **Notes** ⊛ Civ Wed 400

INSPECTORS' CHOICE

★★★★★ ◉ **HOTEL**　　　PLAN 4 B4

Milestone Hotel
1 Kensington Court W8 5DL
☎ 020 7917 1000 📠 020 7917 1010
e-mail: guestservicesms@rchmail.com
web: www.redcarnationhotels.com

Red Carnation HOTELS

dir: M4 into Central London. Into Warwick Rd, then right into Kensington High St. Hotel 400yds past Kensington underground

This delightful, stylish town house enjoys a wonderful location opposite Kensington Palace and is just a few minutes' walk from elegant shops. Individually themed bedrooms include a selection of stunning suites that are equipped with every conceivable extra. Public areas include the luxurious Park Lounge where afternoon tea is served, a delightful panelled bar, a sumptuous restaurant and a small gym and resistance pool.

Rooms 57 en suite (3 fmly) (2 GF) ⊗ in 22 bedrooms S £300; D £300 **Facilities** Spa STV 🄓 Sauna Gym Jacuzzi Wi-fi in bedrooms Health Club Resident Beauty ♬ ch fac Xmas **Conf** Thtr 50 Class 20 Board 20 Del from £295 **Services** Lift air con **Notes** LB ⊗ in restaurant Civ Wed 30

★★★★ 74% **HOTEL**　　　PLAN 4 B4

Copthorne Tara Hotel London Kensington
Scarsdale Place, Wrights Ln W8 5SR
☎ 020 7937 7211 📠 020 7937 7100
e-mail: sales.tara@mill-cop.com
web: www.millenniumhotels.com
dir: off Kensington High Street

MILLENNIUM
HOTELS AND RESORTS

This expansive hotel is ideally located for Kensington High Street's stylish shops and tube station. Smart public areas include a trendy coffee shop, a gym, a stylish brasserie and bar and extensive conference and meeting facilities. Bedrooms include several well-equipped rooms for less mobile guests in addition to a number of Connoisseur rooms that include use of a club lounge with many complimentary facilities.

Rooms 834 en suite (3 fmly) ⊗ in 424 bedrooms **Facilities** STV Gym Wi-fi available Xmas **Conf** BC Thtr 280 Class 160 Board 90 Del from £189 **Services** Lift air con **Parking** 101 **Notes** ⊛ Civ Wed 280

★★★★ 73% **TOWN HOUSE HOTEL**   PLAN 4 B4

Kensington House

15-16 Prince of Wales Ter W8 5PQ
☎ 020 7937 2345 ▤ 020 7368 6700
e-mail: sales@kenhouse.com
web: www.kenhouse.com
dir: off Kensington High St, opposite Kensington Palace

This beautiful and elegantly restored 19th-century property is located just off Kensington High Street and convenient for the park, The Royal Albert Hall and most of the major attractions. Bedrooms vary in size but all are stylish, comfortable and thoughtfully equipped - many have air conditioning. Tiger Bar provides an airy, informal setting for light snacks, meals and refreshments throughout the day.

Rooms 41 en suite (2 fmly) (3 GF) ⊗ in 30 bedrooms S £99-£150; D £125-£175 (incl. bkfst) **Facilities** STV Wi-fi in bedrooms Arrangement with local health club **Conf** BC **Services** Lift **Notes LB** ⊗

★★★ 79% **HOTEL**   PLAN 4 C4

Thistle Kensington Palace

De Vere Gardens, Kensington W8 5AF   THISTLE HOTELS
☎ 0870 333 9111 ▤ 0870 333 9211
e-mail: kensingtonpalace@thistle.co.uk
dir: Hotel is opposite Kensington Gardens.

This hotel is ideally located across from Kensington Palace and is convenient for The Royal Albert Hall and shopping in Kensington High Street. Bedrooms are generally spacious, are well appointed and some benefit from air-conditioning. Public areas include a popular bar and restaurant, a gift shop and a range of meeting and function rooms.

Rooms 205 en suite (6 fmly) (1 GF) ⊗ in 210 bedrooms **Facilities** STV **Conf** Thtr 180 Class 90 Board 60 **Services** Lift **Notes** ⊗

★★★ 78% **HOTEL**   PLAN 4 C4

Thistle Kensington Park

De Vere Gardens, Kensington W8 5AG   THISTLE HOTELS
☎ 0870 333 9112 ▤ 0870 333 9212
e-mail: KensingtonPark@Thistle.co.uk
dir: Hotel is opposite Kensington Gardens.

Large Victorian terrace ideally situated in a peaceful side road just a short walk from Knightsbridge. The spacious public areas include a smart cocktail bar, a lounge, coffee shop and brasserie restaurant. Bedrooms come in a variety of styles; each one is pleasantly decorated and equipped with modern facilities.

Rooms 353 en suite (9 fmly) (19 GF) ⊗ in 275 bedrooms **Facilities** STV **Conf** Thtr 100 Class 60 Board 35 **Services** Lift air con **Notes** ⊗

WC1 BLOOMSBURY, HOLBORN

★★★★★ 86% ⊛⊛ **HOTEL**   PLAN 3 D3

Pearl Renaissance Chancery Court London

RENAISSANCE HOTELS

252 High Holborn WC1V 7EN
☎ 020 7829 9888 ▤ 020 7829 9889
e-mail: sales.chancerycourt@renaissancehotels.com
web: www.renaissancechancerycourt.com
dir: A4 along Piccadilly onto Shaftesbury Av. Into High Holborn, hotel on right

This is a grand place with splendid public areas, decorated from top to bottom in rare marble. Craftsmen have meticulously restored the sweeping staircases, archways and stately rooms of the 1914 building. The result is a spacious, relaxed hotel offering everything from stylish, luxuriously appointed bedrooms to a health club and state-of-the-art meeting rooms. The sophisticated Pearl restaurant offers an impressive standard of cooking.

Rooms 356 en suite ⊗ in 280 bedrooms **Facilities Spa** STV Sauna Gym Jacuzzi Wi-fi available Spa treatments by ESPA Xmas ♫ **Conf** BC Thtr 435 Class 234 Board 40 **Services** Lift air con **Parking** 4 **Notes** ⊗ ⊗ in restaurant Civ Wed 260

★★★★ 79% ⊛ **HOTEL**   PLAN 3 C3

Jurys Great Russell Street

JURYS DOYLE HOTELS

16-22 Great Russell St WC1B 3NN
☎ 020 7347 1000 ▤ 020 7347 1001
e-mail: great_russell@jurysdoyle.com
web: www.jurysdoyle.com
dir: A40 onto A400, Gower St then south to Bedford Sq. Turn right, then first left to end of road

On the doorstep of Covent Garden, Oxford Street and the West End, this impressive building, designed by the renowned Sir Edwin Lutyens in the 1930s, retains many original features. Bedrooms are attractively appointed and benefit from an excellent range of facilities. Public areas include a grand reception lounge, an elegant bar and restaurant and extensive conference facilities.

Rooms 170 en suite (5 GF) ⊗ in 153 bedrooms S £95-£240; D £95-£240 **Facilities** STV Wi-fi available Xmas **Conf** BC Thtr 300 Class 180 Board 60 Del from £180 **Services** Lift air con **Notes LB** ⊗ ⊗ in restaurant

England

WC1 BLOOMSBURY, HOLBURN *continued*

★★★★ 79% HOTEL
PLAN 3 D4

Grange Holborn

50-60 Southampton Row WC1B 4AR
☎ 020 7242 1800 📠 020 7242 0057
e-mail: holborn@grangehotels.com
web: www.grangehotels.co.uk

This smart hotel is centrally located, close to Oxford Street and Covent Garden. The elegantly furnished, spacious bedrooms offer high levels of comfort and are equipped with every conceivable extra. Public areas include a smart leisure centre, a choice of restaurants and extensive meeting and function facilities.

Rooms 200 en suite (10 fmly) ❀ in 100 bedrooms S £215-£290; D £215-£290 **Facilities** STV 🏊 Sauna Gym Wi-fi available Xmas **Conf** Thtr 220 Class 120 Board 80 Del £275 **Services** Lift air con **Notes LB** ❂

★★★★ 74% HOTEL
PLAN 3 E5

Holiday Inn Kings Cross/ Bloomsbury
Holiday Inn
HOTELS · RESORTS
1 Kings Cross Rd WC1X 9HX
☎ 020 7833 3900 📠 020 7917 6163
e-mail: sales@holidayinnlondon.com

dir: 0.5m from Kings Cross Station on corner of King Cross Rd and Calthorpe St

Conveniently located for Kings Cross station and the City, this modern hotel offers smart, spacious air-conditioned accommodation with a wide range of facilities. The hotel offers a choice of restaurants including one serving Indian cuisine, versatile meeting rooms, a bar and a well-equipped fitness centre.

Rooms 405 en suite (163 fmly) ❀ in 160 bedrooms S £190-£210; D £210-£236 **Facilities** STV FTV 🏊 supervised Sauna Solarium Gym Jacuzzi Wi-fi in bedrooms **Conf** BC Thtr 220 Class 120 Board 30 Del from £170 **Services** Lift air con **Parking** 12 **Notes LB** ❂

★★★★ 73% ❀ HOTEL
PLAN 3 C4

The Montague on the Gardens
Red Carnation HOTELS
15 Montague St, Bloomsbury WC1B 5BJ
☎ 020 7637 1001 📠 020 7637 2516
e-mail: bookmt@rchmail.com
web: www.redcarnationhotels.com

dir: just off Russell Square

This stylish hotel is situated right next to the British Museum. A noteworthy feature is the alfresco terrace overlooking a delightful garden. Other public rooms include the Blue Door Bistro and Chef's Table, a bar, a lounge and a conservatory where traditional afternoon teas are served. The bedrooms are beautifully appointed and range from split-level suites to more compact rooms.

Rooms 99 en suite (19 GF) ❀ in 47 bedrooms S £159-£212; D £176-£245 **Facilities** STV Sauna Gym Wi-fi in bedrooms 🎵 ch fac Xmas **Conf** Thtr 120 Class 50 Board 50 Del from £215 **Services** Lift air con **Notes LB** ❀ in restaurant Civ Wed 90

★★★★ 73% TOWN HOUSE HOTEL
PLAN 3 C4

Grange Blooms

7 Montague St WC1B 5BP
☎ 020 7323 1717 📠 020 7636 6498
e-mail: blooms@grangehotels.com
web: www.grangehotels.co.uk

dir: off Russell Square, behind Brirish Museum

Conveniently located for London's theatre district and the British Museum, this elegant townhouse is part of an 18th-century terrace. The bedrooms feature Regency-style decor, and those at the rear of the hotel are quieter. Public rooms include a cosy lounge, garden terrace, breakfast room and small cocktail bar, all with antiques and paintings.

Rooms 26 en suite ❀ in 12 bedrooms S £159-£200; D £159-£200 **Facilities** STV Patio garde Xmas **Conf** Thtr 20 Class 10 Board 18 Del £235 **Services** Lift **Notes LB** ❂ Civ Wed 20

★★★★ 72% HOTEL
PLAN 3 C4

The Hotel Russell
PRINCIPAL HOTELS
Russell Square WC1B 5BE
☎ 020 7837 6470 📠 020 7837 2857
web: www.principal-hotels.com

dir: from A501 into Woburn Place. Hotel 500mtrs on left

This landmark Grade II, Victorian hotel is located on Russell Square, within walking distance of the West End and theatre district. Many bedrooms are stylish and state-of-the-art, and others are more traditional. Spacious public areas include the impressive foyer with a restored mosaic floor, a choice of lounges and an elegant restaurant.

Rooms 373 en suite ❀ in 192 bedrooms **Facilities** STV Wi-fi available **Conf** BC Thtr 450 Class 200 Board 75 **Services** Lift air con **Notes** ❂ ❀ in restaurant Civ Wed 300

★★★★ 71% HOTEL
PLAN 3 C3

Grange Whitehall

2-5 Montague St WC1B 5BP
☎ 020 7580 2224 📠 020 7580 5554
e-mail: whitehall@grangehotel.com
web: www.grangehotels.co.uk

dir: M40 to Euston Rd, right into Upper Woburn Place around Russell Sq, Montague St on Left

This elegant, small hotel is well located, close to the city's financial district and to the theatres of the West End. Smart bedrooms are decorated to a very high standard and many have views over the delightful landscaped rear gardens. Public areas include an elegant and cosy restaurant and a popular bar and lounge as well as conference facilities.

Rooms 58 en suite (2 fmly) (3 GF) ❀ in 20 bedrooms S £159-£200; D £159-£200 **Facilities** STV Wi-fi available Xmas **Conf** Thtr 90 Class 45 Board 45 Del £235 **Services** Lift air con **Notes LB** ❂

England

★★★★ Ⓐ — PLAN 3 C3

Radisson Edwardian Kenilworth
Radisson
EDWARDIAN

Great Russell St WC1B 3LB

☎ 020 7637 3477 📠 020 7631 3133

e-mail: reskeni@radisson.com

web: www.radissonedwardian.com

dir: *past Oxford St and down New Oxford St. Turn into Bloomsbury St then into Gr. Russell Street*

Rooms 186 en suite (15 fmly) ⊘ in 139 bedrooms **Facilities** STV Fitness room, Valet Laundry & Parking service on request. **Conf** BC Thtr 120 Class 50 Board 35 **Services** Lift air con **Notes** ⊗ No children

★★★★ Ⓐ — PLAN 3 C3

Radisson Edwardian Marlborough
Radisson
EDWARDIAN

Bloomsbury St WC1B 3QD

☎ 020 7636 5601 📠 020 7636 0532

e-mail: resmarl@radisson.com

web: www.radissonedwardian.com

dir: *past Oxford St, down New Oxford St and turn into Bloomsbury St*

Rooms 173 en suite (3 fmly) ⊘ in 82 bedrooms **Facilities** Valet Laundry & Parking Services on request. Fitness room at Kenilworth Hotel. **Conf** BC Thtr 300 Class 150 Board 70 **Services** Lift **Notes** ⊗ No children

★★★ 75% HOTEL — PLAN 3 D4

Bonnington Hotel, London

92 Southampton Row WC1B 4BH

☎ 020 7242 2828 📠 020 7831 9170

e-mail: reservations@bonnington.com

web: www.bonnington.com

dir: *M40 Euston Rd. Opposite station turn S into Upper Woburn Place past Russell Sq into Southampton Row. Hotel on left*

This smart hotel is centrally located close to the city, the British Museum and Covent Garden. Spacious public areas include the Malt Bar, an airy restaurant and a comfortable lobby lounge. Bedrooms are well equipped and include a number of superb executive rooms and suites. A good range of conference and meeting rooms is available.

Rooms 246 en suite (4 fmly) (6 GF) ⊕ in 170 bedrooms S £70-£150; D £90-£300 (incl. bkfst) **Facilities** STV Wi-fi in bedrooms Fitness room ♫ **Conf** BC Thtr 220 Class 80 Board 50 Del from £170 **Services** Lift air con **Notes** ⊗

★★★ 68% HOTEL — PLAN 3 D4

Bedford

83-93 Southampton Row WC1B 4HD

☎ 020 7636 7822 & 7692 3620 📠 020 7837 4653

e-mail: info@imperialhotels.co.uk

Just off Russell Square, this intimate hotel is ideal for visits to the British Museum and Covent Garden. The bedrooms are well equipped and all the expected facilities including modem points if requested. The newly refurbished ground floor has a lounge, bar and restaurant, and a delightful secret rear garden. An underground (pay) car park is a bonus.

Rooms 184 en suite (1 fmly) ⊘ in 90 bedrooms S £66; D £85 (incl. bkfst) **Facilities** STV Xmas **Conf** Board 12 Del from £30.50 **Services** Lift **Parking** 50 **Notes** LB ⊗

Ⓤ — PLAN 3 C3

Thistle Bloomsbury
THISTLE HOTELS

Bloomsbury Way WC1A 2SD

☎ 0870 333 9103 📠 0870 333 9203

e-mail: Bloomsbury@Thistle.co.uk

dir: *From A40(M) to A501 Marylebone Rd, take sliproad before underpass to Holburn. Travel down Gower St and Bloomsbury St A400. Turn left into Oxford St and onto Bloomsbury Way. Hotel left after St Georges Church.*

At the time of going to press, the star classification for this hotel was not confirmed. Please refer to the AA internet site www.theAA.com for current information.

Rooms 138 en suite (7 fmly) (6 GF) ⊘ in 52 bedrooms **Facilities** STV **Conf** BC Thtr 100 Class 55 Board 35 **Services** Lift **Notes** ⊗

BUDGET HOTEL — PLAN 3 C5

Premier Travel Inn London Euston
premier travel inn

1 Dukes Rd WC1H 9PJ

☎ 0870 238 3301 📠 020 7554 3419

web: www.premiertravelinn.com

dir: *On corner of Euston Road (south side) and Duke's Road, between Kings Cross/St Pancras and Euston stations. Inn is blue building*

High quality, modern budget accommodation ideal for both families and business travellers. Spacious, en suite bedrooms feature bath and shower, satellite TV and many have telephones and modem points. The adjacent family restaurant features a wide and varied menu. For further details consult the Hotel Groups page.

Rooms 220 en suite

BUDGET HOTEL — PLAN 3 E6

Travelodge London Farringdon

Travelodge

10-42 Kings Cross Rd WC1X 9QN

☎ 0870 191 1774 📠 020 7837 3776

web: www.travelodge.co.uk

Travelodge offers good quality, good value, modern accommodation. Ideal for families, the spacious en suite bedrooms include remote-control TV, tea and coffee-making facilities and comfortable beds. Meals can be taken at the nearby family restaurant. See Hotel Groups pages for further details.

Rooms 211 en suite S fr £26; D fr £26 **Conf** Thtr 50 Class 18 Board 30

Travelodge London Kings Cross — PLAN 3 D6

Willing House, Grays Inn Rd, Kings Cross WC1X 8BH

☎ 08700 850 950 📠 020 7278 7396

Rooms 140 en suite S fr £26; D fr £26

Travelodge London Kings Cross Royal Scot — PLAN 3 E5

100 Kings Cross Rd WC1X 9DT

☎ 0870 191 1773 📠 020 7833 0798

Rooms 351 en suite S £26-£102; D £26-£113 **Conf** Thtr 170 Class 60 Board 50

England

WC2 SOHO, STRAND

★★★★★ ◎◎ **HOTEL** PLAN 3 D2

One Aldwych

1 Aldwych WC2B 4RH

☎ 020 7300 1000 🖹 020 7300 1001

e-mail: reservations@onealdwych.com

web: www.onealdwych.com

dir: at Aldwych & The Strand junct near Waterloo Bridge

Regarded by many as the most contemporary address in the West End, One Aldwych is best known for its chic yet comfortable style and innovative, thought-provoking decor. There are a whole host of interesting features including a therapeutic pool with underwater music, the dramatic 'amber city' mural in the double height Axis restaurant and the contemporary lobby bar where the Martini cocktail is a speciality. Bedrooms are no less stylish and feature giant pillows, down duvets and TVs you can watch whilst relaxing in the bath.

Rooms 105 en suite ⊘ in 60 bedrooms S fr £325; D fr £345 **Facilities** STV 🔲 supervised Sauna Gym Wi-fi in bedrooms Steam room, 3 Treatment rooms 🎵 ch fac Xmas **Conf** BC Thtr 50 Board 50 **Services** Lift air con **Notes LB** ⊗ Civ Wed 50

★★★★★ ◎◎◎ 83% **HOTEL** PLAN 3 E2

Swissôtel The Howard, London

Temple Place WC2R 2PR

☎ 020 7836 3555 🖹 020 7379 4547

e-mail: ask-us-london@swissotel.com

web: www.swissotel-london.com

dir: From E turn off Aldwych, keep left of church (in centre of road). Turn left into Surrey St. Hotel at end

This smart hotel enjoys wonderful views across London's historic skyline from its riverside location, and the Eurostar terminal, Covent Garden and Theatreland are all within easy reach. The air-conditioned bedrooms offer a host of extra facilities. The restaurant, Jaan, is a blend of modern French cuisine with influences from Asia. The bar opens out onto a delightful garden offering alfresco dining whenever the weather permits.

Rooms 189 en suite ⊘ in 159 bedrooms **Facilities** STV Special rates for guests at health club 🎵 **Conf** BC Thtr 120 Class 60 Board 60 **Services** Lift air con **Parking** 30 **Notes LB** ⊗ Civ Wed 120

★★★★★ 🅰 PLAN 3 C1

Radisson Edwardian Hampshire Hotel

Radisson EDWARDIAN

31 Leicester Square WC2H 7LH

☎ 020 7839 9399 🖹 020 7930 8122

e-mail: reshamp@radisson.com

web: www.radissonedwardian.com

dir: from Charing Cross Rd turn into Cranbourn St at Leicester Sq. Left at end, hotel at bottom of square

Rooms 124 en suite (5 fmly) ⊘ in 93 bedrooms **Facilities** STV Gym Fitness room, Valet Laundry & Parking services on request. **Conf** Thtr 100 Class 48 Board 35 **Services** Lift air con **Notes** ⊗

★★★★ 75% **HOTEL** PLAN 3 C1

Thistle Charing Cross

THISTLE HOTELS

The Strand WC2N 5HX

☎ 0870 333 9105 🖹 020 7839 6685

e-mail: CharingCross@thistle.co.uk

dir: towards Trafalgar Square, E along The Strand, turn right into station forecourt.

This centrally located and historic landmark hotel provides a friendly welcome. Spacious in design, the original architecture blends nicely with the modern style of interior appointments, particularly in the bedrooms and bathrooms. There is a choice of dining options - for those in a hurry try Co-Motion which offers a range of snacks and speedy service. More leisurely dining can be enjoyed in The Strand Terrace, which has splendid views of London especially at night.

Rooms 239 en suite (16 fmly) ⊘ in 45 bedrooms **Facilities** STV **Conf** BC Thtr 65 Class 56 Board 50 **Services** Lift air con **Notes** ⊗ ⊘ in restaurant

★★★★ 🅰 PLAN 3 C2

Radisson Edwardian Mountbatten

Radisson EDWARDIAN

Monmouth St, Seven Dials, Covent Garden WC2H 9HD

☎ 020 7836 4300 🖹 020 7240 3540

e-mail: resmoun@radisson.com

web: www.radissonedwardian.com

dir: off Shaftesbury Av, on corner of Seven Dials rdbt

Rooms 151 en suite ⊘ in 104 bedrooms **Facilities** STV Fitness room, Valet Laundry & Parking services on request. **Conf** BC Thtr 90 Class 45 Board 32 **Services** Lift air con **Notes** ⊗

★★★ 74% **HOTEL** PLAN 3 D2

Strand Palace

372 The Strand WC2R 0JJ

☎ 020 7836 8080 & 0870 400 8702 🖹 020 7836 2077

e-mail: reservations@strandpalacehotel.co.uk

dir: From Trafalgar Square, on A4 to Charing Cross, 150mtrs, hotel on left.

At the heart of Theatreland, this vast hotel is proud of its friendly and efficient staff. The bedrooms vary in style and include bright Club

continued

rooms with enhanced facilities. The extensive public areas include shops, four eateries and a popular cocktail bar.

Strand Palace

Rooms 785 en suite ⊘ in 200 bedrooms S £80.50-£150; D £99-£180
Facilities STV Wi-fi available Xmas **Conf** BC Thtr 200 Class 90 Board 40
Del from £120 **Services** Lift **Notes LB** ⊗ ⊘ in restaurant

---

★★★ 68% **HOTEL**   PLAN 3 C2

Thistle Trafalgar Square
THISTLE HOTELS
Whitcomb St WC2H 7HG
☎ 0870 333 9110 📠 0870 333 9219
e-mail: trafalgarsquare@thistle.co.uk

dir: *100m from Trafalgar Sq adjacent to Sainsbury Wing of National Gallery*

Quietly located, this handily placed hotel is just a short walk from Trafalgar Square and theatre land. Bedrooms offer good levels of comfort with a variety of standards available. Dining options include the Savoria brasserie, or alternatively, light meals can be taken in the traditionally styled bar.

Rooms 116 en suite ⊘ in 62 bedrooms **Facilities** STV **Services** Lift air con **Notes LB** ⊗ ⊘ in restaurant

---

Ⓤ   PLAN 3 C1

Radisson Edwardian Pastoria Hotel
Radisson EDWARDIAN
3-6 Saint Martins St WC2H 7HL
☎ 020 7930 8641 & 020 7451 0227(res) 📠 020 7451 0191
e-mail: reshamp@radisson.com
web: www.radissonedwardian.com

dir: *Saint Martins Street off Leicester Square*

At the time of going to press, the star classification for this hotel was not confirmed. Please refer to the AA internet site www.theAA.com for current information.

Rooms 58 en suite ⊘ in 38 bedrooms **Facilities** STV Gym **Conf** BC **Services** Lift **Notes** ⊗

◎◎◎Ⓤ   PLAN 3 D1

The Savoy
Strand WC2R 0EU
☎ 020 7836 4343 📠 020 7240 6040
dir: *between Trafalgar Sq and Aldwych*

At the time of going to press, a multi-million pound refurbishment was scheduled to start at this landmark hotel. Please refer to the AA internet site www.theAA.com for current information.

continued

Rooms 263 en suite (6 fmly) ⊘ in 55 bedrooms **Facilities** STV 🏊
Sauna Gym Health & beauty treatments ♫ **Conf** Thtr 500 Class 200
Board 32 **Services** Lift air con **Parking** 65 **Notes LB** ⊗ Civ Wed 300

BUDGET HOTEL   PLAN 3 D2

Travelodge London Covent Garden

10 Drury Ln, High Holborn WC2B 5RE
☎ 08700 850 950 📠 01376 572 724
web: www.travelodge.co.uk

Travelodge offers good quality, good value, modern accommodation. Ideal for families, the spacious en suite bedrooms include remote-control TV, tea and coffee-making facilities and comfortable beds. Meals can be taken at the nearby family restaurant. See Hotel Groups pages for further details.

Rooms 163 en suite s fr £46; d fr £46 **Conf** Thtr 100 Class 40 Board 30

LONDON AIRPORTS
See under **Gatwick (Sussex, West) & Heathrow (London, Greater)**

LONDON GATEWAY MOTORWAY SERVICE AREA (M1)
See **LONDON PLAN1 C6**

★★★ 68% **HOTEL**

Days Hotel London North
DAYS INN
Welcome Break Service Area NW7 3HU
☎ 020 8906 7000 📠 020 8906 7011
e-mail: lgw.hotel@welcomebreak.co.uk
web: www.welcomebreak.co.uk

dir: *on M1 between junct 2/4 northbound & southbound*

This modern hotel is the flagship of the Days Inn brand and occupies a prime location on the outskirts of London at London Gateway Services. Bedrooms have a contemporary feel, are spacious and well equipped. Public rooms are airy and include an open plan restaurant and bar/lounge along with a range of meeting rooms. Ample parking is a bonus.

Rooms 200 en suite (190 fmly) (80 GF) ⊘ in 162 bedrooms
Facilities STV **Conf** Thtr 70 Class 30 Board 50 **Services** Lift air con
Parking 160 **Notes LB** ⊘ in restaurant

LONDON, GREATER

BARKING
See **LONDON SECTION PLAN 1 H4**

BUDGET HOTEL

Hotel Ibis
ibis
Highbridge Rd IG11 7BA
☎ 020 8477 4100 📠 020 8477 4101
e-mail: H2042@accor-hotels.com
web: www.ibishotel.com

dir: *exit Barking on A406*

Modern, budget hotel offering comfortable accommodation in bright and practical bedrooms. Breakfast is self-service and dinner is available in the restaurant. For further details, consult the Hotel Groups page.

Rooms 86 en suite S £51.95-£60.95; D £51.95-£60.95

England

BARKING *continued*

BUDGET HOTEL

Premier Travel Inn Barking

Highbridge Rd IG11 7BA
☎ 0870 9906318 🖹 0870 9906319
web: www.premiertravelinn.com

dir: 1.5m from Barking. Exit M25 after Dartford Tunnel at junct 30. Follow A13, signed to London City & Docklands, onto A406 North Circular

High quality, modern budget accommodation ideal for both families and business travellers. Spacious, en suite bedrooms feature bath and shower, satellite TV and many have telephones and modem points. The adjacent family restaurant features a wide and varied menu. For further details consult the Hotel Groups page.

Rooms 88 en suite

BECKENHAM
See **LONDON SECTION PLAN 1 G1**

BUDGET HOTEL

Innkeeper's Lodge London Beckenham
422 Upper Elmers End Rd BR3 3HQ
☎ 020 8650 2233
web: www.innkeeperslodge.com

dir: From M25 junct 6 Croydon, take A232 for Shirley. At West Wickham take A214 opposite Eden Park Station

Smart, en suite accommodation ideal for both business & leisure guests. Bedrooms are very well equipped, including Sky TV, telephone, modem points, tea & coffee making facilities, (family rooms in most locations). Complimentary breakfast. The adjacent Pub Restaurant; a Harvester, Vintage Inn, Toby Carvery, Ember Inn, Sizzling Pubco or Pub & Carvery offers an all day menu. See Hotel Groups pages for further details.

Rooms 24 en suite S £55-£65; D £55-£65

BEXLEY   MAP 06 TQ47

★★★★ 77% HOTEL

Bexleyheath Marriott Hotel   Marriott.
HOTELS & RESORTS
1 Broadway DA6 7JZ
☎ 020 8298 1000 🖹 020 8298 1234
e-mail: bexleyheath@marriotthotels.co.uk
web: www.marriott.co.uk

dir: M25 junct 2/A2 towards London. Exit at Black Prince junct onto A220, signed Bexleyheath. Left at 2nd set of lights into hotel

Well positioned for access to major road networks, this large, modern hotel offers spacious, air-conditioned bedrooms with a comprehensive range of extra facilities. Planters Bar is a popular venue for pre-dinner drinks and traditional English fare is served in the Copper Restaurant. The hotel also boasts a well-equipped leisure centre.

Rooms 142 en suite (16 fmly) (26 GF) ⊗ in 87 bedrooms S £114; D £114 **Facilities** Spa STV FTV 🏊 Solarium Gym Jacuzzi Wi-fi available Health & Beauty Treatment Steam Room Xmas **Conf** Thtr 250 Class 120 Board 34 **Services** Lift air con **Parking** 77 **Notes** LB ⊗ Civ Wed 40

BRENTFORD
See **LONDON PLAN 1 C3**

★★★★ 75% HOTEL

Holiday Inn London Brentford Lock
High St TW8 8JZ
☎ 020 8232 2000 🖹 020 8232 2001
e-mail: info@holidayinnbrentford.co.uk
web: www.holidayinnbrentford.co.uk

dir: Exit M4 junct 2 onto A4. At rdbt take 4th exit onto A315, hotel on right

This smart, modern hotel is located beside the Grand Union Canal in the heart of Brentford. Central London, the major motorway networks and Heathrow Airport are all within easy reach. Stylish bedrooms are thoughtfully equipped and contemporary public areas include a bar/lounge, restaurant, conference and function facilities and a spacious underground car park.

Rooms 134 en suite (30 fmly) ⊗ in 92 bedrooms S fr £129; D fr £129 **Facilities** STV Wi-fi in bedrooms **Conf** BC Thtr 700 Class 200 Board 120 **Services** Lift air con **Parking** 60 **Notes** ⊗ ⊗ in restaurant Civ Wed 150

BUDGET HOTEL

Premier Travel Inn London Kew
52 High St TW8 0BB
☎ 0870 9906304 🖹 0870 9906305
web: www.premiertravelinn.com

dir: At junct of A4 (M4), A205 & A406, Chiswick rdbt, take A205 towards Kew & Brentford. 200yds right fork onto A315 (High St), for 0.5m. Hotel on left

High quality, modern budget accommodation ideal for both families and business travellers. Spacious, en suite bedrooms feature bath and shower, satellite TV and many have telephones and modem points. The adjacent family restaurant features a wide and varied menu. For further details consult the Hotel Groups pages.

Rooms 141 en suite

BUDGET HOTEL

Travelodge London Kew Bridge
North Rd, High St TW8 0BD
☎ 08700 850 950 🖹 020 8758 1190
web: www.travelodge.co.uk

Travelodge offers good quality, good value, modern accommodation. Ideal for families, the spacious en suite bedrooms include remote-control TV, tea and coffee-making facilities and comfortable beds. Meals can be taken at the nearby family restaurant. See Hotel Groups pages for further details.

Rooms 111 en suite S fr £26; D fr £26

England

BROMLEY
See **LONDON SECTION PLAN 1 G1**

★★★ 77% HOTEL

Best Western Bromley Court
Bromley Hill BR1 4JD
☎ 020 8461 8600 ▤ 020 8460 0899
e-mail: info@bromleycourthotel.co.uk
web: www.bw-bromleycourthotel.co.uk

dir: N of Bromley town centre, off A21 London road. Private drive opposite Volkswagen garage on Bromley Hill

Set amid three acres of grounds in a peaceful residential area on the outskirts of town. The well maintained bedrooms are smartly appointed and thoughtfully equipped. The contemporary-style restaurant offers a good choice of meals in comfortable surroundings. Extensive facilities include a leisure club and a good range of meeting rooms.

Rooms 114 en suite (4 fmly) ⊗ in 50 bedrooms S £85-£109; D £95-£120 (incl. bkfst) **Facilities** Spa STV Sauna Gym Jacuzzi Wi-fi in bedrooms **Conf** Thtr 150 Class 80 Board 45 Del from £135 **Services** Lift **Parking** 100 **Notes** LB ⊗ in restaurant Civ Wed 55

CHESSINGTON   MAP 06 TQ16

BUDGET HOTEL

Premier Travel Inn Chessington
Leatherhead Rd KT9 2NE
☎ 08701 977057 ▤ 01372 720889
web: www.premiertravelinn.com

dir: From M25 junct 9, towards Kingston on A243, for approx 2 miles. The Inn is next to Chessington World of Adventures

High quality, modern budget accommodation ideal for both families and business travellers. Spacious, en suite bedrooms feature bath and shower, satellite TV and many have telephones and modem points. The adjacent family restaurant features a wide and varied menu. For further details consult the Hotel Groups page.

Rooms 42 en suite

CROYDON   MAP 06 TQ36

★★★★ 74% HOTEL

Selsdon Park Hotel & Golf Club
Addington Rd, Sanderstead CR2 8YA
PRINCIPAL HOTELS
☎ 020 8657 8811 ▤ 020 8651 6171
e-mail: sales.selsdonpark@principal-hotels.com
web: www.principal-hotels.com

dir: 3m SE of Croydon, off A2022

Surrounded by 200 acres of mature parkland with its own 18-hole golf course, this imposing Jacobean mansion is less than 20 minutes from central London. The hotel's impressive range of conference rooms, along with the spectacular views of the North Downs countryside, make this a popular venue for both weddings and meetings. Leisure facilities are impressive.

Rooms 204 en suite (12 fmly) (12 GF) S £69-£135; D £79-£165 **Facilities** Spa STV ⚑ ⚑ pool supervised ↓ 18 ⚐ Squash Sauna Solarium Gym ⚑ Putt green Jacuzzi Wi-fi available Boules, Jogging track, ♫ ch fac Xmas **Conf** BC Thtr 350 Class 220 Board 60 Del from £149 **Services** Lift **Parking** 300 **Notes** LB ⊗ ⊗ in restaurant Civ Wed 120

★★★ 75% HOTEL

Aerodrome
Purley Way CR9 4LT
CLASSIC BRITISH HOTELS
☎ 020 8710 9000 & 8680 1999 ▤ 020 8681 6458
e-mail: info@aerodrome-hotel.co.uk
web: www.aerodrome-hotel.co.uk

dir: Follow A23 Central London. Hotel on left

The Croydon Aerodrome was the world's first international airport and the starting point for Amy Johnson's record-breaking flight to Darwin. Bedrooms feature a smart, modern design and up-to-date facilities, including broadband internet access. Public areas include two restaurants, two bars and conference facilities.

Rooms 105 en suite ⊗ in 61 bedrooms S £55-£111; D £75-£141 (incl. bkfst) **Facilities** FTV Wi-fi available Complimentary pass to nearby health clubs Xmas **Conf** Thtr 100 Class 50 Board 40 Del from £125 **Parking** 200 **Notes** LB ⊗ ⊗ in restaurant Civ Wed 100

★★★ 75% HOTEL

Jurys Inn
Wellesley Rd CR0 9XY
JURYS DOYLE HOTELS
☎ 020 8448 6000 ▤ 020 8448 6111
e-mail: jurysinncroydon@jurysdoyle.com
web: www.jurysdoyle.com

dir: Off A212, in town centre adjacent to Whitgift Centre

This modern hotel, located in the town centre, has spacious bedrooms with air conditioning. The contemporary public areas include a choice of eating options and a busy state-of-the-art conference centre. Parking is available in a nearby multi-storey at reduced rates.

Rooms 240 en suite (168 fmly) ⊗ in 140 bedrooms S £59-£89; D £59-£89 **Facilities** STV Wi-fi available **Conf** BC Thtr 100 Class 50 Board 40 Del from £99 **Services** Lift air con **Notes** LB ⊗ Closed 24-28 Dec

★★ 71% HOTEL

South Park Hotel
3-5 South Park Hill Rd, South Croydon CR2 7DY
☎ 020 8688 5644 & 8688 0840/4385 ▤ 020 8760 0861
e-mail: reception@southparkhotel.co.uk
web: www.southparkhotel.co.uk

dir: follow A235 to town centre. At Coombe Rd lights turn right (A212) towards Addington 0.5m to rdbt take 3rd exit into South Park Hill Rd, hotel on left

This intimate hotel has easy access to rail and road networks with some off-street parking available. Attractively decorated bedrooms vary in size and offer a good range of in-room facilities. Public areas consist

continued on page 466

England

CROYDON *continued*

of a bar and lounge with large sofas and an informal dining area where meals are served.

Rooms 21 en suite (2 fmly) ⊘ in 8 bedrooms S £60-£70; D £65-£76 (incl. bkfst) **Parking** 15 **Notes** ⊗ ⊘ in restaurant

U

Swallow Coulsdon Manor Hotel & Golf Club

Coulsdon Court Rd, Coulsdon CR5 2LL
☎ 020 8668 0414 📠 020 8668 3118
e-mail: swallow.coulsdon@swallowhotels.com
web: www.swallowhotels.com

dir: From A23, take B2030 Stoats Nest Rd signed Old Coulsdon. After 1m turn left onto Coulsdon Court Rd

At the time of going to press, the star classification for this hotel was not confirmed. Please refer to the AA internet site www.theAA.com for current information.

Rooms 35 en suite (4 fmly) ⊘ in 22 bedrooms S £75-£129; D £95-£166 (incl. bkfst) **Facilities** STV ⅃ 18 ⅏ Squash Sauna Solarium Gym Putt green Aerobic studio Steam room ♬ Xmas **Conf** Thtr 180 Class 90 Board 70 Del from £150 **Services** Lift **Parking** 200 **Notes LB** ⊗ ⊘ in restaurant Civ Wed 60

BUDGET HOTEL

Innkeeper's Lodge Croydon South

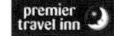

415 Brighton Rd CR2 6EJ
☎ 020 8680 4559 📠 020 8649 9802
web: www.innkeeperslodge.com

dir: M23 junct 7/ A23 or M25 junct 6/A22. At Purley take A235 Brighton Rd, N towards South Croydon, for 1m. Lodge on right.

Smart, en suite accommodation ideal for both business & leisure guests. Bedrooms are very well equipped, including Sky TV, telephone, modem points, tea & coffee making facilities, (family rooms in most locations). Complimentary breakfast. The adjacent Pub Restaurant; a Harvester, Vintage Inn, Toby Carvery, Ember Inn, Sizzling Pubco or Pub & Carvery offers an all day menu. See Hotel Groups pages for further details.

Rooms 30 en suite S £49.95-£62; D £49.95-£62

BUDGET HOTEL

Premier Travel Inn Croydon East

premier travel inn

104 Coombe Rd CR0 5RB
☎ 08701 977069 📠 020 8686 6439
web: www.premiertravelinn.com

dir: M25 junct 7, A23 to Purley, then follow A235 to Croydon. Pass Tree House pub on left. Turn right at lights, onto A212

High quality, modern budget accommodation ideal for both families and business travellers. Spacious, en suite bedrooms feature bath and shower, satellite TV and many have telephones and modem points. The adjacent family restaurant features a wide and varied menu. For further details consult the Hotel Groups page.

Rooms 39 en suite

Premier Travel Inn Croydon West

The Colonnades Leisure Park, 619 Purley Way CR0 4RQ
☎ 0870 990 6554 📠 0870 990 6555

dir: From N, exit M1, M25, then follow A23 towards Croydon. From S, hotel 8m from M25 junct 7 on A23 towards Purley Way, close to junct of Waddon Way

Rooms 82 en suite **Conf** Thtr 120

EDGWARE

See **LONDON SECTION PLAN 1 C6**

BUDGET HOTEL

Premier Travel Inn London Edgware

435 Burnt Oak Broadway HA8 5AQ
☎ 0870 9906522 📠 0870 9906523
web: www.premiertravelinn.com

dir: M1 junct 4 take A41 then A5 towards Edgware. 3m. Inn opp Peugeot dealership

High quality, modern budget accommodation ideal for both families and business travellers. Spacious, en suite bedrooms feature bath and shower, satellite TV and many have telephones and modem points. The adjacent family restaurant features a wide and varied menu. For further details consult the Hotel Groups page.

Rooms 111 en suite

ENFIELD   MAP 06 TQ39

★★★ 79% ֎ **HOTEL**

Royal Chace

The Ridgeway EN2 8AR
☎ 020 8884 8181 📠 020 8884 8150
e-mail: enquiries@royalchacehotel.co.uk

dir: M25 junct 24 take A1005 towards Enfield. Hotel 3m on right

This professionally run, privately owned hotel enjoys a peaceful location with open fields to the rear. Refurbished public rooms are smartly appointed; the first floor Chace Brasserie is particularly appealing with its warm colour schemes and friendly service. Bedrooms are well presented and thoughtfully equipped.

Rooms 92 en suite (2 fmly) (32 GF) ⊘ in 34 bedrooms **Facilities** STV ⅆ Free access to local leisure centre **Conf** Thtr 250 Class 100 Board 40 **Parking** 200 **Notes** ⊗ ⊘ in restaurant Closed 24-30 Dec RS Restaurant closed lunchtime/Sun eve Civ Wed 220

★★★ 71% **HOTEL**

Comfort Hotel Enfield

Comfort

52 Rowantree Rd EN2 8PW
☎ 020 8366 3511 📠 020 8366 2432
e-mail: admin@comfortenfield.co.uk

dir: M25 junct 24 follow signs for A1005 towards Enfield. Hospital on left, across mini-rdbt, 3rd left onto Bycullah Rd, 2nd left into Rowantree Rd.

This newly refurbished hotel is situated in a quiet residential area, close to the centre of Enfield. Comfortable accommodation is provided in the thoughtfully equipped bedrooms, which include ground floor and family rooms. Public areas include a cosy bar and

continued

lounge, conference and function rooms and the smart Etruscan restaurant.

Comfort Hotel Enfield

Rooms 34 annexe en suite (3 fmly) S £65-£75; D £75-£95 (incl. bkfst)
Facilities STV **Conf** Thtr 65 Class 25 Board 25 Del from £110
Parking 17 **Notes** ⊗ ⊛ in restaurant Civ Wed 65

BUDGET HOTEL

Premier Travel Inn Enfield

Innova Park, Mollison Av EN3 7XY
☎ 0870 238 3306 ▤ 01992 707070
web: www.premiertravelinn.com

dir: M25 junct 25, A10 to London, left onto Bullsmoor Lane/Mollison Avenue. Over rdbt, right at lights into Innova Science Park

High quality, modern budget accommodation ideal for both families and business travellers. Spacious, en suite bedrooms feature bath and shower, satellite TV and many have telephones and modem points. The adjacent family restaurant features a wide and varied menu. For further details consult the Hotel Groups page.

Rooms 159 en suite **Conf** Thtr 60 Board 26

GREENFORD
See **LONDON SECTION PLAN 1 B4**

BUDGET HOTEL

Premier Travel Inn Greenford, Middlesex

Western Av UB6 8TE
☎ 08701 977119 ▤ 020 8998 8823
web: www.premiertravelinn.com

dir: From Western Avenue (A40), Eastbound, exit Perivale. Turn right, then at 2nd lights turn left. Inn opposite Hoover Building

High quality, modern budget accommodation ideal for both families and business travellers. Spacious, en suite bedrooms feature bath and shower, satellite TV and many have telephones and modem points. The adjacent family restaurant features a wide and varied menu. For further details consult the Hotel Groups page.

Rooms 39 en suite

HADLEY WOOD　　　　　MAP 06 TQ29

★★★★ 77% ⊛⊛ HOTEL

West Lodge Park
Cockfosters Rd EN4 0PY
☎ 020 8216 3900 ▤ 020 8216 3937
e-mail: westlodgepark@bealeshotels.co.uk
dir: on A111, 1m S of M25 junct 24

Stylish country house set in stunning parkland and gardens, yet only 12 miles from central London and a few miles from the M25. The traditionally styled bedrooms are individually decorated and offer excellent in-room facilities. Annexe rooms feature air conditioning and have access to an outdoor patio area. Public rooms include the award-winning Cedar Restaurant, cosy bar area and separate lounge.

Rooms 46 en suite 13 annexe en suite (1 fmly) (11 GF) ⊛ in 53 bedrooms S £80-£110; D £105-£185 **Facilities** STV ⅃ Putt green Wi-fi in bedrooms Massage, Manicure, Free use of nearby leisure club ⽊ Xmas **Conf** Thtr 64 Class 30 Board 30 Del from £199 **Services** Lift **Parking** 200 **Notes LB** ⊗ ⊛ in restaurant RS Saturday Civ Wed 60

HAMPTON COURT
See **LONDON SECTION PLAN 1 B1**

★★★★ 73% HOTEL

The Carlton Mitre
Hampton Court Rd KT8 9BN
☎ 020 8979 9988 ▤ 020 8979 9777
e-mail: mitre@carltonhotels.co.uk
dir: M3 junct 1 follow signs to Sunbury & Hampton Court Palace. At Hampton Court Palace rdbt right and hotel on right

This hotel, dating back in parts to 1655, enjoys an enviable setting on the banks of the River Thames opposite Hampton Court Palace. The riverside restaurant and Edge bar/brasserie command wonderful views. Bedrooms are generally spacious with excellent facilities. Parking is limited.

Rooms 36 en suite (2 fmly) ⊛ in 20 bedrooms **Facilities** STV **Conf** BC Thtr 120 Class 60 Board 40 **Services** Lift **Parking** 13 **Notes LB** ⊗ ⊛ in restaurant Civ Wed 100

England

HAMPTON COURT *continued*

★★★ 68% **HOTEL**

Liongate

Hampton Court Rd KT8 9DD
☎ 020 8977 8121 📠 020 8943 4029
e-mail: lionres@dhillonhotels.co.uk

dir: M25 junct 12/M3 towards London. M3 junct 1 follow A308
at mini-rdbt turn left. Hotel opposite Hampton Court Palace
gates

Dating back to 1721 this hotel enjoys a wonderful location opposite
the Lion Gate entrance to Hampton Court and beside the gate into
Bushy Park. Despite its history it boasts rooms with plenty of
contemporary style. Public areas are all open-plan and includes a
modern European restaurant.

Rooms 14 en suite 18 annexe en suite (2 fmly) (12 GF) ⊗ in
5 bedrooms S £75-£165; D £90-£200 (incl. bkfst) **Facilities** Wi-fi in
bedrooms Xmas **Conf** Thtr 60 Class 50 Board 35 Del from £120
Parking 30 **Notes** ⊗ Civ Wed 50

HARROW

See **LONDON SECTION PLAN 1 B5**

★★★ 74% **HOTEL**

Quality Harrow Hotel

12-22 Pinner Rd HA1 4HZ
☎ 020 8427 3435 📠 020 8861 1370
e-mail: info@harrowhotel.co.uk
web: www.harrowhotel.co.uk

dir: off rdbt on A404 at junct with A312

This privately owned hotel offers a great variety of accommodation to
suit all needs. At the top of the range are the air-conditioned executive
rooms and suites. These have hi-tech facilities including MD/CD,
interactive TV and multiple phone lines. Public areas include a bar,
conservatory lounge, meeting rooms and a smart restaurant.

Rooms 79 en suite (4 fmly) (17 GF) ⊗ in 48 bedrooms S £70-£98;
D £80-£123 (incl. bkfst) **Facilities** STV Wi-fi in bedrooms **Conf** Thtr 160
Class 60 Board 60 Del from £140 **Services** Lift **Parking** 70 **Notes** ⊗ in
restaurant RS Xmas (limited service) Civ Wed 80

See advert on opposite page

★★★ 72% **HOTEL**

Best Western Cumberland

1 St Johns Rd HA1 2EF
☎ 020 8863 4111 📠 020 8861 5668
e-mail: reservations@cumberlandhotel.co.uk
web: www.cumberlandhotel.co.uk

dir: On reaching Harrow using Station or Sheepcote Rd, turn
onto Gayton Rd, then Lyon Rd which becomes St Johns Rd.

Situated within walking distance of the town centre, this hotel is ideally
located for all local attractions and amenities. Bedrooms provide good
levels of comfort and are practically equipped to meet the
requirements of all travellers. Impressive public areas include a
restaurant and bar, both serving a good variety of fresh food.

Rooms 31 en suite 53 annexe en suite (5 fmly) (15 GF) ⊗ in
51 bedrooms S £60-£98; D £75-£110 (incl. bkfst) **Facilities** STV FTV
Sauna Gym Wi-fi in bedrooms Xmas **Conf** Thtr 130 Class 70 Board 62
Del from £105 **Parking** 67 **Notes** ⊗ ⊗ in restaurant

HARROW WEALD

See **LONDON SECTION PLAN 1 B6**

★★★ 71% ⊛ **HOTEL**

Grim's Dyke Hotel

Old Redding HA3 6SH
☎ 020 8385 3100 📠 020 8954 4560
e-mail: enquiries@grimsdyke.com
web: www.grimsdyke.com

dir: Turn off A410 onto A409 North towards Bushey, at top of hill
at lights turn left into Old Redding

Once home to Sir William Gilbert, this Grade II mansion contains
many references to well-known Gilbert and Sullivan productions. The
house is set in over 40 acres of beautiful parkland and gardens.
Rooms in the main house are elegant and traditional, while those in
the adjacent lodge are aimed more at the business guest.

Rooms 10 en suite 39 annexe en suite (17 GF) ⊗ in 26 bedrooms
S £125-£230; D £125-£230 (incl. bkfst) **Facilities LB** STV ♬ Gilbert &
Sullivan opera dinner fortnightly ♬ **Conf** Thtr 100 Class 80 Board 32 Del
£160 **Parking** 97 **Notes** ⊗ in restaurant Closed 25-30 Dec RS 24 Dec

HEATHROW AIRPORT (LONDON)

See **LONDON SECTION PLAN 1 A3**

See also **Slough & Staines**

★★★★ 78% 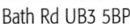 **HOTEL**

Crowne Plaza London - Heathrow

Stockley Rd UB7 9NA

☎ 0870 400 9140 📠 01895 445122

e-mail: reservations.cplhr@ichotelsgroup.com

web: www.london-heathrow.crowneplaza.com

dir: M4 junct 4 follow signs to Uxbridge on A408, hotel 400yds on left

This smart hotel is conveniently located for access to Heathrow Airport and the motorway network. Excellent facilities include versatile conference and meeting rooms, golfing and a spa and leisure complex. Guests have the choice of two bars, both serving food, and two restaurants. Air-conditioned bedrooms are furnished and decorated to a high standard and feature a comprehensive range of extra facilities.

Rooms 458 en suite (237 fmly) (35 GF) ⊗ in 370 bedrooms **Facilities** STV 🏊 supervised ♨ 9 Sauna Solarium Gym Jacuzzi Beauty room **Conf** BC Thtr 200 Class 120 Board 75 **Services** Lift air con **Parking** 410 **Notes** ⊗

★★★★ 78% 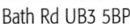 **HOTEL**

Sheraton Skyline

Bath Rd UB3 5BP

☎ 020 8759 2535 📠 020 8750 9150

e-mail: res260_skyline@sheraton.com

web: www.starwood.com

dir: M4 junct 4 for Heathrow, follow Terminal 1 ,2 & 3 signs. Before airport entrance take slip road to left for 0.25m signed A4 Central London

Within easy reach of all terminals this hotel offers well appointed bedrooms featuring air conditioning. Bedrooms provide excellent levels of quality and comfort. The extensive, contemporary public areas are light and spacious, and include a wide range of eating and drinking options, function rooms and a gym.

Rooms 350 en suite (10 fmly) ⊗ in 311 bedrooms S £79-£234; D £79-£234 **Facilities** STV 🏊 Gym Wi-fi available Pool table Kids indoor play area is supervised Monday to Sunday. 🎵 Xmas **Conf** BC Thtr 500 Class 325 Board 100 Del from £165 **Services** Lift air con **Parking** 320 **Notes LB** ⊗ in restaurant RS Xmas & New Year Civ Wed 200

★★★★ 75% **HOTEL**

Slough/Windsor Marriott Hotel **Marriott**
HOTELS & RESORTS

Ditton Rd, Langley SL3 8PT

☎ 0870 400 7244 📠 0870 400 7344

e-mail: conferenceandevents.sloughwindsor@marriotthotels.com

web: www.marriott.co.uk

dir: M4 junct 5, follow 'Langley' signs and left at lights into Ditton Rd

Ideally located for access to Heathrow and the M4, this smart hotel offers a wide range of facilities. The well-appointed leisure centre includes a spa, gym and pool. Extensive conference facilities, a bar offering 24hr snacks and light meals and a restaurant with a wide

continued

---

ranging cuisine are all available. Spacious bedrooms are well equipped for both leisure and business guests.

Rooms 382 en suite (120 fmly) (96 GF) ⊗ in 267 bedrooms S £75-£159; D £75-£159 **Facilities** STV 🏊 supervised ♨ Sauna Solarium Gym Wi-fi in bedrooms **Conf** Thtr 400 Class 220 Board 42 Del from £140 **Services** Lift air con **Parking** 550 **Notes** ⊗ ⊗ in restaurant Civ Wed 300

★★★★ 74% **HOTEL**

London Heathrow Marriott Hotel **Marriott**
HOTELS & RESORTS

Bath Rd UB3 5AN

☎ 0870 4007250 📠 0870 4007350

web: www.marriott.co.uk

dir: M4 junct 4, follow Terminal 1 2 & 3 signs via M4 and Heathrow Airport. Left at rdbt signed A4/London. Hotel 0.5m left through 2 sets of traffic lights

This smart, modern hotel, with its striking design, meets all the expectations of a successful airport hotel. The light and airy atrium offers several eating and drinking options, each with a different theme. Spacious bedrooms are appointed to a good standard with an excellent range of facilities, and there is a leisure club and business centre.

Rooms 393 en suite (143 fmly) ⊗ in 305 bedrooms S £82-£170.36; D £82-£170.36 **Facilities** STV 🏊 supervised Sauna Solarium Gym Jacuzzi Wi-fi available Steam Room Xmas **Conf** BC Thtr 550 Class 220 Board 65 Del from £175 **Services** Lift air con **Parking** 270 **Notes** ⊗ Civ Wed 112

HEATHROW AIRPORT *continued*

★★★★ 74% **HOTEL**

Park Inn Heathrow

Bath Rd, West Drayton UB7 0DU
☎ 020 8759 6611 ▯ 020 8759 3421
e-mail: info.heathrow@rezidorparkinn.com
web: www.heathrow.parkinn.co.uk

dir: *adjacent to M4 spur at junct with A4 exit 4*

Conveniently located for the airport, this busy, corporate hotel is one of the largest in the area. There is an extensive range of facilities including two bars, modern conference rooms, indoor leisure club and extensive parking. Bedrooms vary in size; the executive rooms are particularly impressive.

Rooms 880 en suite (43 fmly) (90 GF) ⊘ in 563 bedrooms S £119-£149; D £119-£149 **Facilities** STV ⬚ supervised Sauna Solarium Gym Jacuzzi Wi-fi in bedrooms Xmas **Conf** BC Thtr 220 Class 140 Board 60 Del from £205 **Services** Lift air con **Parking** 500 **Notes LB** ⊗ Civ Wed 200

★★★★ 73% **HOTEL**

The Renaissance London Heathrow Hotel

Bath Rd TW6 2AQ
☎ 020 8897 6363 ▯ 020 8897 1113
e-mail: lhrrenaissance@aol.com
web: www.renaissancehotels.com

dir: *M4 junct 4 follow spur road towards airport, then 2nd left. At rdbt take 2nd exit signed 'Renaissance Hotel'. Hotel next to Customs House*

Located right on the perimeter of the airport, this hotel commands superb views over the runways. The smart bedrooms are fully soundproofed and equipped with air conditioning - each is well suited to meet the needs of today's business travellers. The hotel boasts extensive conference facilities, and is a very popular venue for air travellers and conference organisers.

The Renaissance London Heathrow Hotel

Rooms 649 en suite (59 GF) ⊘ in 468 bedrooms S £82-£117; D £82-£117 **Facilities** STV Sauna Solarium Gym Steam Room Fitness Studio Massage treatment Personal trainer, studio classes Xmas **Conf** BC Thtr 400 Class 300 Board 60 Del from £140 **Services** Lift air con **Parking** 700 **Notes LB** ⊗ ⊘ in restaurant Civ Wed 150

★★★ 75% **HOTEL**

Jury's Inn Heathrow

Eastern Perimeter Rd, Hatton Cross TW6 2SR
☎ 020 8266 4664 ▯ 020 8266 4665
e-mail: jurysinnheathrow@jurysdoyle.com
web: www.jurysdoyle.com

dir: *200mtrs E of Hatton Cross station*

This modern hotel is located near Heathrow Airport and has good motorway access. Bedrooms provide good guest comfort and in room facilities are ideal for both leisure and business markets. Public areas include a number of meeting rooms, a small shop, a restaurant and popular bar.

Rooms 364 en suite (305 fmly) ⊘ in 260 bedrooms S £59-£119; D £59-£119 **Facilities** STV Wi-fi available **Conf** BC Thtr 45 Class 20 Board 24 Del from £90 **Services** Lift air con **Parking** 125 **Notes** ⊗

★★★ 73% **HOTEL**

Novotel London Heathrow

Cherry Ln UB7 9HB
☎ 01895 431431 ▯ 01895 431221
e-mail: H1551@accor-hotels.com
web: www.novotel.com

dir: *M4 junct 4, follow Uxbridge signs on A408. Keep left and take 2nd exit off traffic island into Cherry Ln signed West Drayton. Hotel on left*

Conveniently located for Heathrow and the motorway network, this modern hotel provides comfortable accommodation. The large, airy indoor atrium creates a sense of space to the public areas, which include an all-day restaurant and bar, meeting rooms, fitness centre and swimming pool. Ample secure parking is available.

Rooms 178 en suite (178 fmly) (10 GF) ⊘ in 140 bedrooms S £124-£135; D £124-£139 **Facilities** STV ⬚ Gym Wi-fi in bedrooms **Conf** BC Thtr 250 Class 100 Board 90 Del from £139 **Services** Lift air con **Parking** 100 **Notes LB** ⊘ in restaurant

★★★ 70% **HOTEL**

Comfort Hotel Heathrow

Shepiston Ln Hayes UB3 1LP
☎ 020 8573 6162 ▯ 020 8848 1057
e-mail: info@comfortheathrow.com

dir: *M4 junct 4, follow Hayes & Shepiston Lane signs, hotel approx 1m*

This hotel is located a short drive from the airport, and guests may prefer its quieter position. There is a frequent bus service, which runs to and from the hotel throughout the day. Bedrooms are particularly thoughtfully equipped and many benefit from air conditioning.

Rooms 184 en suite (7 fmly) (50 GF) ⊘ in 80 bedrooms S £45-£125; D £45-£125 **Facilities** STV Gym Wi-fi in bedrooms ch fac **Conf** Thtr 150 Class 72 Board 90 Del from £99 **Services** Lift **Parking** 120 **Notes LB** ⊗ ⊘ in restaurant Civ Wed 90

England

★★★ 68% HOTEL

Thistle London Heathrow

THISTLE HOTELS

Bath Rd, Longford UB7 0EQ

☎ 0870 333 9108 ▤ 0870 333 9208

e-mail: londonheathrow@thistle.co.uk

dir: Exit M25 junct 14 signed Terminal 4 & Cargo Area. Right at 1st rdbt signed Heathrow. Turn left at lights onto A0344 signed Colnbrook and Longford.

Located adjacent to airport and with the benefit of secure parking and regular coach transfers, this long-established hotel provides a range of well equipped bedrooms for both the business and leisure guest. Imaginative food is available in an attractive restaurant and comprehensive breakfasts are served in a separate first-floor dining room.

Rooms 314 en suite (55 fmly) (40 GF) ⊗ in 240 bedrooms **Facilities** STV 🎱 Snooker Sauna Gym Jacuzzi **Conf** Thtr 700 Class 400 Board 60 **Services** air con **Parking** 600 **Notes** Civ Wed 600

★★ 67% HOTEL

Best Western Master Robert

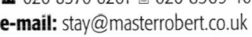

366 Great West Rd TW5 0BD

☎ 020 8570 6261 ▤ 020 8569 4016

e-mail: stay@masterrobert.co.uk

web: www.masterrobert.co.uk

dir: M4 junct 3 take A312 & follow airport signs. At 1st rdbt take 1st exit, 100yds straight onto 2nd rdbt, then turn left. Hotel on left by 2nd lights

A well-known landmark on the Great West Road, this hotel is conveniently located near to Heathrow and the area's business community. Bedrooms are set in motel-style buildings behind the main hotel; most are spacious with good facilities. There are residents' lounge bar, a restaurant and a popular pub.

Rooms 96 annexe en suite (22 fmly) (40 GF) ⊗ in 50 bedrooms S £40.50-£89.50; D £59.50-£99.50 **Facilities** STV Putt green Wi-fi in bedrooms Health club nearby **Conf** Thtr 150 Class 60 Board 40 Del from £125 **Parking** 200 **Notes LB** ⊗ ⊗ in restaurant Civ Wed 80

Ⓤ

Radisson Edwardian

Radisson
EDWARDIAN

Bath Rd UB3 5AW

☎ 020 8759 6311 ▤ 020 8759 4559

e-mail: resreh@radisson.com

web: www.radissonedwardian.com

At the time of going to press, the star classification for this hotel was not confirmed. Please refer to the AA internet site www.theAA.com for current information.

Rooms 459 en suite (83 GF) ⊗ in 132 bedrooms **Facilities** Spa STV Sauna Solarium Gym Jacuzzi Massage, Hairdressing **Conf** BC Thtr 700 Class 300 Board 60 **Services** Lift air con **Parking** 550 **Notes LB** ⊗ Civ Wed 368

BUDGET HOTEL

Hotel Ibis Heathrow

ibis

112/114 Bath Rd UB3 5AL

☎ 020 8759 4888 ▤ 020 8564 7894

e-mail: H0794@accor-hotels.com

web: www.ibishotel.com

dir: follow Heathrow Terminals 1,2 & 3 signs, then onto spur road, exit at sign for A4/ Central London. Hotel 0.5m on left

Modern, budget hotel offering comfortable accommodation in bright and practical bedrooms. Breakfast is self-service and dinner is available in the restaurant. For further details, consult the Hotel Groups page.

Rooms 347 en suite **Conf** BC

BUDGET HOTEL

Premier Travel Inn London Heathrow (M4/J4)

premier travel inn

Shepiston Ln, Heathrow Airport UB3 1RW

☎ 0870 9906612 ▤ 0870 9906613

web: www.premiertravelinn.com

dir: From M4 junct 4 take 3rd exit off rdbt. Hotel on right

High quality, modern budget accommodation ideal for both families and business travellers. Spacious, en suite bedrooms feature bath and shower, satellite TV and many have telephones and modem points. The adjacent family restaurant features a wide and varied menu. For further details consult the Hotel Groups page.

Rooms 133 en suite

Premier Travel Inn Hayes, Heathrow

362 Uxbridge Rd UB4 0HF

☎ 08701 977132 ▤ 020 8569 1204

dir: M4 junct 3 follow A312 north, straight across next rdbt onto dual carriageway, at A4020 junct left, Inn 100yds on right

Rooms 62 en suite

Premier Travel Inn London Heathrow

362 Uxbridge Rd UB4 0HF

☎ 08701 977 132 ▤ 020 8569 1204

Rooms 590 en suite

Premier Travel Inn London Heathrow (Bath Rd)

Bath Rd TW6 2AB

☎ 0870 6075 075 ▤ 0870 241 9000

dir: M4 junct 4 follow Heathrow Terminals 1, 2 & 3 signs. Left onto Bath Rd signed A4/London. Inn on right in 0.5m

Rooms 590 en suite

England

HESTON MOTORWAY SERVICE AREA (M4)
See **LONDON SECTION PLAN 1 B3**

BUDGET HOTEL

Travelodge Heathrow Heston (M4 Eastbound)

North Hyde Ln TW5 9NA
☎ 08700 850 950 📠 020 8580 2137
web: www.travelodge.co.uk

dir: M4 junct 2 & 3 eastbound

Travelodge offers good quality, good value, modern accommodation. Ideal for families, the spacious en suite bedrooms include remote-control TV, tea and coffee-making facilities and comfortable beds. Meals can be taken at the nearby family restaurant. See Hotel Groups pages for further details.

Rooms 66 en suite S fr £26; D fr £26

Travelodge Heathrow Heston (M4 Westbound)
Phoenix Way TW5 9NB
☎ 08700 850 950 📠 020 8580 2006
dir: M4 junct 2 & 3 westbound
Rooms 145 en suite S fr £26; D fr £26

ILFORD
See **LONDON SECTION PLAN 1 H5**

BUDGET HOTEL

Premier Travel Inn Ilford
Redbridge Ln East IG4 5BG
☎ 08701 977140 📠 020 8550 6214
web: www.premiertravelinn.com

dir: M11 (signed London East/A12 Chelmsford) follow A12 Chelmsford signs, Inn on left at bottom of slip road

High quality, modern budget accommodation ideal for both families and business travellers. Spacious, en suite bedrooms feature bath and shower, satellite TV and many have telephones and modem points. The adjacent family restaurant features a wide and varied menu. For further details consult the Hotel Groups page.

Rooms 44 en suite **Conf** Thtr 30

BUDGET HOTEL

Travelodge London Ilford
Clements Rd IG1 1BA
☎ 08700 850 950 📠 020 8553 2920
web: www.travelodge.co.uk

dir: M25 junct 28, A12 to Hackney, at A406, left A118 for Ilford/Romford, left before cinema complex

Travelodge offers good quality, good value, modern accommodation. Ideal for families, the spacious en suite bedrooms include remote-control TV, tea and coffee-making facilities and comfortable beds. Meals can be taken at the nearby family restaurant. See Hotel Groups pages for further details.

Rooms 91 en suite S fr £26; D fr £26

Travelodge London Ilford Gants Hill
Beehive Ln, Gants Hill IG4 5DR
☎ 08700 850 950 📠 020 8551 1712
dir: Off A12 on B192 adjacent Beehive Pub
Rooms 32 en suite S fr £26; D fr £26

KENTON
See **LONDON SECTION PLAN 1 C5**

BUDGET HOTEL

Premier Travel Inn Harrow
Kenton Rd HA3 8AT
☎ 08701 977146 📠 020 8909 1604
web: www.premiertravelinn.com

dir: M1 junct 5 follow signs to Harrow & Kenton. Between Harrow & Wembley on A4006 opposite Kenton Railway Station

High quality, modern budget accommodation ideal for both families and business travellers. Spacious, en suite bedrooms feature bath and shower, satellite TV and many have telephones and modem points. The adjacent family restaurant features a wide and varied menu. For further details consult the Hotel Groups page.

Rooms 70 en suite **Conf** Class 50

KINGSTON UPON THAMES
See **LONDON SECTION PLAN 1 C1**

★★★ 68% HOTEL

Swallow Kingston Lodge
Kingston Hill KT2 7NP
☎ 020 8541 4481 📠 020 8547 1013
e-mail: swallow.kingston@swallowhotels.com
web: www.swallowhotels.com

dir: From A3 Robin Hood rdbt turn left onto A308 to Kingston, Hotel 1.5m on left

At the time of going to press, the star classification for this hotel was not confirmed. Please refer to the AA internet site www.theAA.com for current information.

Rooms 63 en suite (4 fmly) (18 GF) ⊘ in 40 bedrooms S £85-£135; D £95-£145 (incl. bkfst) **Facilities** STV **Conf** Thtr 70 Class 30 Board 28 Del from £120 **Parking** 65 **Notes** LB ⊗ ⊘ in restaurant Civ Wed 60

BUDGET HOTEL

Travelodge London Kingston upon Thames
21-23 London Rd KT2 6ND
☎ 08700 850 950 📠 020 8546 5904
web: www.travelodge.co.uk

Travelodge offers good quality, good value, modern accommodation. Ideal for families, the spacious en suite bedrooms include remote-control TV, tea and coffee-making facilities and comfortable beds. Meals can be taken at the nearby family restaurant. See Hotel Groups pages for further details.

Rooms 72 en suite S fr £26; D fr £26

MORDEN
See **LONDON SECTION PLAN 1 D1**

Travelodge Wimbledon Morden
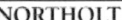
Epsom Rd SM4 5PH
☎ 08700 850 950 📠 020 8640 8227
web: www.travelodge.co.uk
dir: on A24

Travelodge offers good quality, good value, modern accommodation. Ideal for families, the spacious en suite bedrooms include remote-control TV, tea and coffee-making facilities and comfortable beds. Meals can be taken at the nearby family restaurant. See Hotel Groups pages for further details.

Rooms 32 en suite S fr £26; D fr £26

NORTHOLT
See **LONDON SECTION PLAN 1 B4**

Innkeeper's Lodge London Northolt
Mandeville Rd UB5 4LU
☎ 020 8422 2050
web: www.innkeeperslodge.com
dir: A40 at the Target roundabout

Smart, en suite accommodation ideal for both business & leisure guests. Bedrooms are very well equipped, including Sky TV, telephone, modem points, tea & coffee making facilities, (family rooms in most locations). Complimentary breakfast. The adjacent Pub Restaurant; a Harvester, Vintage Inn, Toby Carvery, Ember Inn, Sizzling Pubco or Pub & Carvery offers an all day menu. See Hotel Groups pages for further details.

Rooms 21 en suite S £59.95-£69; D £59.95-£69

PINNER
See **LONDON SECTION PLAN 1 A5**

★★ 64% **HOTEL**

Tudor Lodge
50 Field End Rd, Eastcote HA5 2QN
☎ 020 8429 0585 📠 020 8429 0117
e-mail: tudorlodge@meridianleisure.com
web: www.meridianleisure.com
dir: off A40 at Swakeleys rdbt to Ickenham, onto A312 to Harrow. Left at Northolt Station to Eastcote

This friendly hotel, set in its own grounds, is convenient for Heathrow Airport and many local golf courses. Bedrooms vary in style and size but all are well equipped, with some suitable for families. A good range of bar snacks is offered as an alternative to the main restaurant.

continued

Tudor Lodge

Rooms 24 en suite 22 annexe en suite (9 fmly) (17 GF) ⊛ in 6 bedrooms S £59-£89; D £69-£99 (incl. bkfst) **Facilities** STV FTV Wi-fi in bedrooms Xmas **Conf** Thtr 60 Class 20 Board 26 Del from £90 **Parking** 30 **Notes LB** ⊛ in restaurant Civ Wed 25

See advert on this page

England

RAINHAM
MAP 06 TQ58

BUDGET HOTEL

Premier Travel Inn Rainham
premier travel inn

New Rd, Wennington RM13 9ED

☎ 08701 977217 📄 01708 634821

web: www.premiertravelinn.com

dir: *M25 junct 30/31, A13 for Dagenham/Rainham, then A1306 for Wennington, Aveley, Rainham. Inn 0.5 mile on right.*

High quality, modern budget accommodation ideal for both families and business travellers. Spacious, en suite bedrooms feature bath and shower, satellite TV and many have telephones and modem points. The adjacent family restaurant features a wide and varied menu. For further details consult the Hotel Groups page.

Rooms 60 en suite

RICHMOND (UPON THAMES)
See **LONDON SECTION PLAN 1 C2**

★★★★ 76% ◉◉ HOTEL

Richmond Gate Hotel
152-158 Richmond Hill TW10 6RP

☎ 020 8940 0061 📄 020 8332 0354

e-mail: richmondgate@foliohotels.com

web: www.foliohotels.com/richmondgate

folio Hotels

dir: *from Richmond to top of Richmond Hill. Hotel on left opposite Star & Garter home at Richmond Gate exit*

This stylish Georgian hotel sits at the top of Richmond Hill, opposite the gates to Richmond Park and has a real country house feel to it. Bedrooms are equipped to a very high standard and include luxury doubles and spacious suites. Dinner in the Park Restaurant features bold, contemporary cooking and is the highlight of any visit. A smart leisure club and spa facilities complete the picture.

Rooms 68 en suite (12 fmly) (15 GF) ⊘ in 56 bedrooms S fr £180; D fr £190 (incl. bkfst) **Facilities Spa** STV 🔲 supervised Sauna Solarium Gym Jacuzzi Wi-fi in bedrooms Health & beauty suite Steam room ch fac **Conf** Thtr 50 Class 20 Board 30 Del £270 **Parking** 150 **Notes LB** ⊗ ⊘ in restaurant Civ Wed 70

★★★★ 67% ◉◉ HOTEL

The Petersham
Nightingale Ln TW10 6UZ

☎ 020 8940 7471 📄 020 8939 1098

e-mail: enq@petershamhotel.co.uk

web: www.petershamhotel.co.uk

dir: *From Richmond Bridge rdbt (A316) follow Ham & Petersham signs. Hotel in Nightingale Lane (small turning on left off Petersham Road)*

Managed by the same family for over 25 years, this attractive hotel is located on a hill overlooking water meadows and a sweep of the River Thames. Bedrooms and suites are comfortably furnished, whilst public areas combine elegance and some fine architectural features. High quality produce features in dishes offered in the restaurant that looks out over the Thames below.

continued

The Petersham

Rooms 61 en suite (4 fmly) (3 GF) S £135-£160; D £170-£275 (incl. bkfst) **Facilities** STV FTV Wi-fi in bedrooms Xmas **Conf** BC Thtr 35 Board 25 Del from £235 **Services** Lift **Parking** 50 **Notes LB** ⊗ ⊘ in restaurant Civ Wed 40

★★★ 81% HOTEL

Richmond Hill
Richmond Hill TW10 6RW

☎ 020 8940 2247 📄 020 8940 5424

e-mail: richmondhill@foliohotels.com

web: www.foliohotels.com/richmondhill

folio Hotels

dir: *top of Richmond Hill on B321*

This attractive Georgian Manor, currently undergoing a stylish refurbishment programme, is situated on Richmond Hill, enjoying elevated views of the Thames. The town and the park are within walking distance. Bedrooms vary in size and style, all are comfortable and of modern design. There is a stylish, well-designed health club which is shared with sister hotel, the Richmond Gate.

Rooms 138 en suite (2 fmly) (16 GF) ⊘ in 48 bedrooms S £90-£165; D £120-£175 **Facilities Spa** STV 🔲 supervised Sauna Solarium Gym Jacuzzi Wi-fi in bedrooms Steam room Health & beauty suite **Conf** Thtr 180 Class 100 Board 50 Del from £195 **Services** Lift **Parking** 150 **Notes LB** Civ Wed 182

★★★ 70% ◉ HOTEL

Bingham Hotel, Restaurant & Bar
61-63 Petersham Rd TW10 6UT

☎ 020 8940 0902 📄 020 8948 8737

e-mail: info@thebingham.co.uk

web: www.thebingham.co.uk

dir: *on A307*

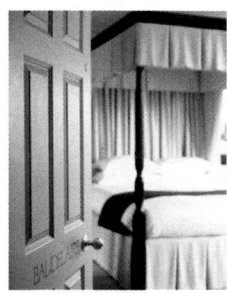

This Georgian building overlooks The Thames and is within walking distance of the town centre. Bedrooms vary in size and style and

continued

comfortable public rooms enjoy views of the pretty garden and river. Diners can choose from a selection of meals from light snacks to three-course dinners.

Rooms 15 en suite (2 fmly) S £160-£225; D £160-£225 (incl. bkfst) **Facilities** FTV Wi-fi in bedrooms ♫ Xmas Use of local gym **Conf** Thtr 60 Class 40 Board 25 Del from £195 **Services** air con **Parking** 12 **Notes LB** ® Civ Wed 40

ROMFORD   MAP 06 TQ58

BUDGET HOTEL

Premier Travel Inn Romford Central

Mercury Gardens RM1 3EN
☎ 08701 977220 📠 01708 760456
web: www.premiertravelinn.com

dir: off M25 junct 28, take A12 to Gallows Corner. Take A118 to next rdbt and turn left

High quality, modern budget accommodation ideal for both families and business travellers. Spacious, en suite bedrooms feature bath and shower, satellite TV and many have telephones and modem points. The adjacent family restaurant features a wide and varied menu. For further details consult the Hotel Groups page.

Rooms 64 en suite

Premier Travel Inn Romford West

Whalebone Ln North, Chadwell Heath RM6 6QU
☎ 0870 9906450 📠 0870 9906451
dir: 6m from M25 junct 28 on A12 at junct with A1112
Rooms 40 en suite **Conf** Thtr 50

RUISLIP

See **LONDON SECTION PLAN 1 A5**

★★★ 77% ®® **HOTEL**

Barn Hotel

West End Rd HA4 6JB
☎ 01895 636057 📠 01895 638379
e-mail: info@thebarnhotel.co.uk
web: www.thebarnhotel.co.uk

dir: take A4180 (Polish War Memorial) exit off A40 to Ruislip, 2m to hotel entrance off a mini-rdbt before Ruislip underground station

Once a farm, with parts dating back to the 17th century, this impressive property sits in three acres of gardens. Bedrooms vary in

continued

style, from contemporary to traditional, oak-beamed varieties - all are comfortable and well appointed. The refurbished public areas provide a high level of quality and luxury.

Rooms 59 en suite (3 fmly) (24 GF) ❷ in 10 bedrooms S £95-£130; D £125-£180 (incl. bkfst) **Facilities** STV Wi-fi available Xmas **Conf** Thtr 80 Class 50 Board 30 Del from £160 **Parking** 42 **Notes LB** ® ❷ in restaurant Civ Wed 74

See advertisement under UXBRIDGE

SOUTH RUISLIP

See **LONDON SECTION PLAN 1 B5**

BUDGET HOTEL

Days Hotel London South Ruislip

Long Dr, Station Approach HA4 0HG
☎ 020 8845 8400 📠 020 8845 5500
e-mail: info@dayshotelheathrow.com
web: www.welcomebreak.co.uk

dir: turn off A40 at Polish War Memorial, follow signs to Ruislip and South Ruislip

This modern building offers accommodation in smart, spacious and well-equipped bedrooms, suitable for families and business travellers, and all with en suite bathrooms. Continental breakfast is available and other refreshments may be taken at the nearby family restaurant. For further details see the Hotel Groups page.

Rooms 78 en suite **Conf** BC Thtr 60 Class 40 Board 30

SUTTON   MAP 06 TQ26

★★ 58% **HOTEL**

Thatched House

135 Cheam Rd SM1 2BN
☎ 020 8642 3131 📠 020 8770 0684
e-mail: thatchedhouse@btconnect.com

dir: M25 junct 8, A217 towards London right onto A232, hotel 0.25m on right

This family-run hotel is on a leafy road between Croydon and Epsom, within easy reach of the M25. Bedrooms are neatly presented with a good range of facilities, some of which overlook the attractive garden. Public areas include a cosy bar and a restaurant serving a good selection of dishes.

Rooms 32 rms (29 en suite) **Conf** Thtr 50 Class 30 Board 26 **Parking** 25 **Notes LB** ® ❷ in restaurant

BUDGET HOTEL

Innkeeper's Sutton

224 Sutton Common Rd SM3 9PW
☎ 020 8644 7577
web: www.innkeeperslodge.com

Smart, en suite accommodation ideal for both business & leisure guests. Bedrooms are very well equipped, including Sky TV, telephone, modem points, tea & coffee making facilities, (family rooms in most locations). Complimentary breakfast. The adjacent Pub Restaurant; a Harvester, Vintage Inn, Toby Carvery, Ember Inn, Sizzling Pubco or Pub & Carvery offers an all day menu. See Hotel Groups pages for further details.

Rooms 24 en suite S £49.95-£59.95; D £49.95-£59.95

TOLWORTH　　　　　　　MAP 06 TQ16

Travelodge Chessington Tolworth

Tolworth Tower KT6 7EL
☎ 08700 850950
web: www.travelodge.co.uk

dir: *Exit A3 at Tolworth junct. At rdbt, take 2nd exit signed London (A3), then immediate left onto Ewell Road. Travelodge is on the left.*

Travelodge offers good quality, good value, modern accommodation. Ideal for families, the spacious en suite bedrooms include remote-control TV, tea and coffee-making facilities and comfortable beds. Meals can be taken at the nearby family restaurant. See Hotel Groups pages for further details.

Rooms 120 en suite　S fr £26;　D fr £26

TWICKENHAM
See **LONDON SECTION PLAN 1 B2**

Premier Travel Inn Twickenham

Chertsey Rd, Whitton TW2 6LS
☎ 0870 9906416 ▤ 0870 9906417
web: www.premiertravelinn.com

dir: *M3 follow Central London signs. A316. In Richmond, over rdbt. Inn 500yds*

High quality, modern budget accommodation ideal for both families and business travellers. Spacious, en suite bedrooms feature bath and shower, satellite TV and many have telephones and modem points. The adjacent family restaurant features a wide and varied menu. For further details consult the Hotel Groups page.

Rooms 31 en suite

UXBRIDGE
See advert on this page

WEMBLEY
See **LONDON SECTION PLAN 1 C5**

Quality Hotel, Wembley

Empire Way HA9 0NN
☎ 020 8733 9000 ▤ 020 8733 9001
e-mail: gm@hotels-wembley.com

Conveniently situated within walking distance of both the Arena and conference centres this modern hotel offers smart, comfortable, spacious bedrooms; many are air conditioned. Some rooms offer wireless internet access. Air-conditioned public areas include a large restaurant serving a wide range of contemporary dishes.

Rooms 165 en suite　(10 fmly)　(3 GF) ✿ in 95 bedrooms　S £95;　D £105 (incl. dinner) **Facilities** STV Xmas **Conf** Thtr 150 Class 70 Board 70 **Services** Lift air con **Parking** 85 **Notes LB** ✖ Civ Wed 220

Hotel Ibis Wembley

Southway HA9 6BA
☎ 0870 220 6581 ▤ 020 8453 5110
e-mail: H3141@accor.com
web: www.ibishotel.com

dir: *on A40, A406 north, exit at Wembley. A404 to lights, right then 1st right into Southway*

Modern, budget hotel offering comfortable accommodation in bright and practical bedrooms. Breakfast is self-service and dinner is available in the restaurant. For further details, consult the Hotel Groups page.

Rooms 210 en suite　S £44.95-£54.95;　D £44.95-£54.95

Premier Travel Inn London Wembley

151 Wembley Park Dr HA9 8HQ
☎ 0870 9906484 ▤ 0870 9906485
web: www.premiertravelinn.com

dir: *From A406 take A404 towards Wembley. 2m right into Wembley Hill Rd, onto Empire Way (B4565) pass Wembley Arena. Inn 200yds on left*

High quality, modern budget accommodation ideal for both families and business travellers. Spacious, en suite bedrooms feature bath and shower, satellite TV and many have telephones and modem points.

continued

The adjacent family restaurant features a wide and varied menu. For further details consult the Hotel Groups page.

Rooms 154 en suite

WEST DRAYTON
Hotels are listed under **Heathrow Airport** page 469

WOODFORD GREEN
See **LONDON SECTION PLAN 1 G6**

BUDGET HOTEL

Innkeeper's Lodge Chigwell
735 Chigwell Rd IG8 8AS
☎ 020 8498 9401
web: www.innkeeperslodge.com

Smart, en suite accommodation ideal for both business & leisure guests. Bedrooms are very well equipped, including Sky TV, telephone, modem points, tea & coffee making facilities, (family rooms in most locations). Complimentary breakfast. The adjacent Pub Restaurant; a Harvester, Vintage Inn, Toby Carvery, Ember Inn, Sizzling Pubco or Pub & Carvery offers an all day menu. See Hotel Groups pages for further details.

Rooms 34 en suite S £45-£49; D £45-£49

MERSEYSIDE

BEBINGTON   MAP 15 SJ38

BUDGET HOTEL

Travelodge Wirral Eastham
New Chester Rd CH62 9AQ
☎ 08700 850 950 ▤ 0151 327 2489
web: www.travelodge.co.uk
dir: on A41, northbound off M53 junct 5

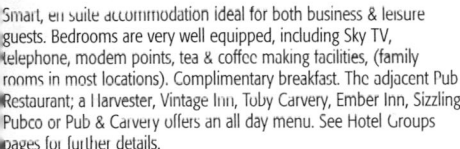

Travelodge offers good quality, good value, modern accommodation. Ideal for families, the spacious en suite bedrooms include remote-control TV, tea and coffee-making facilities and comfortable beds. Meals can be taken at the nearby family restaurant. See Hotel Groups pages for further details.

Rooms 31 en suite S fr £26; D fr £26

BIRKENHEAD   MAP 15 SJ38

★★★ 79% HOTEL

Riverhill
Talbot Rd, Prenton CH43 2HJ
☎ 0151 653 3773 ▤ 0151 653 7162
e-mail: reception@theriverhill.co.uk
dir: M53 junct 3, onto A552. Turn left onto B5151 at lights hotel 0.5m on right

Pretty lawns and gardens provide the setting for this friendly, privately owned hotel, which is conveniently situated about a mile from the M53. Attractively furnished, well-equipped bedrooms include ground floor, family, and four-poster rooms. Business meetings and weddings can be catered for. A wide choice of dishes is available in the restaurant, which overlooks the garden.

Rooms 15 en suite (1 fmly) S fr £69.75; D fr £79.75 **Facilities** STV Free use of local leisure facilities **Conf** Thtr 50 Class 30 Board 50 Del from £120.60 **Parking** 24 **Notes** LB ⊗ Civ Wed 40

See advert on page 484

BUDGET HOTEL

Premier Travel Inn Wirral (Greasby)
Greasby Rd CH49 2PP
☎ 0870 9906588 ▤ 0870 9906589
web: www.premiertravelinn.com
dir: 2m from M53 junct 2. Just off B5139

High quality, modern budget accommodation ideal for both families and business travellers. Spacious, en suite bedrooms feature bath and shower, satellite TV and many have telephones and modem points. The adjacent family restaurant features a wide and varied menu. For further details consult the Hotel Groups page.

Rooms 30 en suite

BOOTLE   MAP 15 SJ39

BUDGET HOTEL

Premier Travel Inn Liverpool North
Northern Perimiter Rd, Bootle L30 7PT
☎ 08701 977158 ▤ 0151 520 1842
web: www.premiertravelinn.com
dir: on A5207, off A5036, 0.25m from end of M58/M57

High quality, modern budget accommodation ideal for both families and business travellers. Spacious, en suite bedrooms feature bath and shower, satellite TV and many have telephones and modem points. The adjacent family restaurant features a wide and varied menu. For further details consult the Hotel Groups page.

Rooms 63 en suite **Conf** Thtr 50

BROMBOROUGH   MAP 15 SJ38

BUDGET HOTEL

Premier Travel Inn Wirral (Bromborough)
High St, Bromborough Cross CH62 7EZ
☎ 08701 977273 ▤ 0151 344 0443
web: www.premiertravelinn.com
dir: on A41 New Chester Road, 2m from M53 junct 5

High quality, modern budget accommodation ideal for both families and business travellers. Spacious, en suite bedrooms feature bath and shower, satellite TV and many have telephones and modem points. The adjacent family restaurant features a wide and varied menu. For further details consult the Hotel Groups page.

Rooms 32 en suite **Conf** Thtr 80 Board 35

FRANKBY   MAP 15 SJ28

★★★★ 85% HOTEL

Hillbark
Royden Park CH48 1NP
☎ 0151 625 2400 ▤ 0151 625 4040
e-mail: enquiries@hillbarkhotel.co.uk
web: www.hillbarkhotel.co.uk

Originally built in 1891 on Bidston Hill, this Elizabethan-style mansion was actually moved, brick by brick, to its current site in 1931. The house now sits in a 250-acre woodland estate and enjoys delightful

continued on page 478

England

FRANKBY *continued*

views towards the River Dee and to hills in north Wales. Bedrooms are luxuriously furnished and well equipped whilst elegant days rooms are richly styled. The lavish Yellow Room provides a delightful venue for enjoying skilfully prepared dishes.

Rooms 19 en suite (1 fmly) ⊗ in all bedrooms S £165-£445; D £165-£445 (incl. bkfst) **Facilities** STV ⚓ Putt green Jacuzzi Wi-fi in bedrooms ♫ Xmas **Conf** BC Thtr 750 Class 250 Board 100 Del from £220 **Services** Lift **Parking** 143 **Notes** ⊗ ⊗ in restaurant Civ Wed 160

HAYDOCK
MAP 15 SJ59

★★★★ 74% HOTEL

Thistle Haydock
Penny Ln WA11 9SG

THISTLE HOTELS

☎ 0870 333 9136 📄 0870 333 9236
e-mail: Haydock@Thistle.co.uk

dir: Exit M6 junct 23, follow Racecourse signs (A49) towards Ashton in Makerfield, take 1st left, after bridge take 1st turn

A smart, purpose built hotel which offers an excellent standard of thoughtfully equipped accommodation. It is conveniently situated between Liverpool and Manchester, just off the M6. The public areas, which include a wide range of leisure and meeting facilities, prove popular with guests.

Rooms 138 en suite (13 fmly) (78 GF) ⊗ in 72 bedrooms **Facilities Spa** STV 🖳 supervised Sauna Solarium Gym Jacuzzi **Conf** BC Thtr 300 Class 140 Board 80 **Parking** 200 **Notes** ⊗ in restaurant Civ Wed 110

BUDGET HOTEL

Premier Travel Inn Haydock
Yew Tree Way, Golborne WA3 3JD

premier travel inn 🌙

☎ 08701 977131 📄 01942 296100
web: www.premiertravelinn.com

dir: M6 junct 23, take A580 towards Manchester. Approx 2m straight on at major rdbt. Inn on left

High quality, modern budget accommodation ideal for both families and business travellers. Spacious, en suite bedrooms feature bath and shower, satellite TV and many have telephones and modem points. The adjacent family restaurant features a wide and varied menu. For further details consult the Hotel Groups page.

Rooms 60 en suite

BUDGET HOTEL

Travelodge Haydock St Helens
Piele Rd WA11 0JZ

Travelodge

☎ 08700 850 950 📄 01942 272067
web: www.travelodge.co.uk

dir: 1m W of junct 23 on M6, on A580 westbound

Travelodge offers good quality, good value, modern accommodation. Ideal for families, the spacious en suite bedrooms include remote-control TV, tea and coffee-making facilities and comfortable beds. Meals can be taken at the nearby family restaurant. See Hotel Groups pages for further details.

Rooms 62 en suite S fr £26; D fr £26

HESWALL
MAP 15 SJ28

BUDGET HOTEL

Premier Travel Inn Wirral (Heswall)
Chester Rd, Gayton CH60 3SD

☎ 08701 977274 📄 0151 342 8983
web: www.premiertravelinn.com

dir: M53 junct 4 follow A5137 signed Heswall for 3m & turn left at next rdbt, Inn on left

High quality, modern budget accommodation ideal for both families and business travellers. Spacious, en suite bedrooms feature bath and shower, satellite TV and many have telephones and modem points. The adjacent family restaurant features a wide and varied menu. For further details consult the Hotel Groups page.

Rooms 37 en suite

HOYLAKE
MAP 15 SJ28

★★★ 75% HOTEL

Kings Gap Court
CH47 1HE

☎ 0151 632 2073 📄 0151 632 0247
e-mail: kingsgapcourt@aol.com
web: www.kingsgapcourt.co.uk

In the reign of William III 'Hoyle Lake' was an army staging post from where the invasion of Ireland was launched in 1690, and the 'Kings Gap' area commemorates this time. The lake no longer exists but this hotel enjoys a peaceful residential location just a short walk from glorious sandy beaches. Modern bedrooms are stylish and comfortable whilst the bright and spacious day rooms include a popular bar and a conservatory restaurant.

Rooms 30 en suite (4 fmly) (7 GF) ⊗ in 15 bedrooms S £67-£69; D fr £84 (incl. bkfst) **Conf** Thtr 150 Class 100 Board 24 Del from £85 **Parking** 60 **Notes LB** ⊗ in restaurant Civ Wed 70

KNOWSLEY
MAP 15 SJ49

Ⓤ

Suites Hotel Knowsley
Ribblers Ln L34 9HA

☎ 0151 549 2222 📄 0151 549 1116
e-mail: enquiries@suiteshotelgroup.com

dir: M57 junct 4, at x-rds of A580 East Lancashire Rd.

At the time of going to press, the star classification for this hotel was not confirmed. Please refer to the AA internet site www.theAA.com for current information.

Rooms 80 en suite (19 fmly) (20 GF) ⊗ in 60 bedrooms S £67-£99; D £77-£109 (incl. bkfst) **Facilities** STV FTV 🖳 supervised Sauna Solarium Gym Jacuzzi Wi-fi in bedrooms Xmas **Conf** BC Thtr 240 Class 60 Board 50 Del from £90 **Services** Lift air con **Parking** 200 **Notes** ⊗ ⊗ in restaurant Civ Wed 140

LIVERPOOL

MAP 15 SJ39

★★★★ 81% @ HOTEL

Radisson SAS Hotel Liverpool

Radisson

107 Old Hall St L3 9BD

☎ 0151 966 1500 📠 0151 966 1501

e-mail: info.liverpool@radissonsas.com

web: www.radissonsas.com

dir: *Follow Liverpool City Centre & Albert Dock signs. Left onto Old Hall Street from main Leeds Street dual carriageway*

This smart, hotel enjoys an enviable location on the city's waterfront. The stylish bedrooms are designed in two eye-catching schemes, Ocean and Urban, and are particularly well equipped; junior suites and business rooms offer additional choices. Public areas include extensive conference and leisure facilities, the trendy White Bar and Filini Restaurant, serving imaginative, accomplished Italian cuisine.

Rooms 194 en suite ⊛ in 131 bedrooms S £110-£145; D £110-£145 **Facilities** STV ⬜ Sauna Solarium Gym Jacuzzi Wi-fi in bedrooms **Conf** BC Thtr 335 Class 108 Board 144 Del from £160 **Services** Lift air con **Parking** 25 **Notes LB** ⊛ ⊛ in restaurant Civ Wed 130

See advert on this page

★★★★ 79% HOTEL

Liverpool Marriott Hotel South

Marriott HOTELS & RESORTS

Speke Aerodrome L24 8QD

☎ 0870 4007269 📠 0151 494 5053

e-mail: liverpool.south@marriotthotels.co.uk

web: www.marriott.co.uk

dir: *M62 junct 6, take Knowsley Expressway towards Speke. At end of Expressway right onto A561 towards Liverpool. Approx 4m, hotel on left just after Estuary Commerce Park*

Previously Liverpool airport's building where fans gathered in the 1960s to see The Beatles, this hotel is now Grade II listed. It has a distinctive look, reflected by its art deco architecture and interior design. The spacious bedrooms are fully air-conditioned and feature a comprehensive range of facilities. Feature rooms include the Presidential Suite in the base of the old control tower.

Rooms 164 en suite (50 fmly) (46 GF) ⊛ in 100 bedrooms S £88-£129 **Facilities Spa** STV ⬜ ⬚ supervised ⬚ Squash Sauna Solarium Gym Jacuzzi Wi-fi available Selected use of David Lloyd Leisure Centre adjacent to hotel **Conf** Thtr 280 Class 120 Board 24 **Services** Lift air con **Parking** 200 **Notes LB** ⊛ ⊛ in restaurant Civ Wed 200

★★★★ 77% @ HOTEL

Thornton Hall Hotel and Health Club

CLASSIC BRITISH HOTELS

Neston Rd CH63 1JF

☎ 0151 336 3938 📠 0151 336 7864

e-mail: reservations@thorntonhallhotel.com

web: www.thorntonhallhotel.com

(For full entry see Thornton Hough)

★★★★ 75% HOTEL

Liverpool Marriott Hotel City Centre

Marriott HOTELS & RESORTS

1 Queen Square L1 1RH

☎ 0151 476 8000 📠 0151 474 5000

e-mail: liverpool.city@marriotthotels.com

web: www.marriott.co.uk

dir: *end of M62 follow City Centre signs, A5047, Edge Lane. From city centre follow orange signs for Queens Square parking*

An impressive modern hotel located in the heart of the city. The elegant public rooms include a ground-floor café bar, and a cocktail bar and stylish Oliver's Restaurant on the first floor. The hotel also boasts a well-equipped, indoor leisure health club with pool.

continued on page 480

A modern, contemporary design led hotel with waterfront views located in the heart of Liverpool's vibrant city centre. Offering stylishly themed bedrooms in Urban and Ocean along with 4 Junior suites and Liverpool's largest suite, the River Suite. A floor dedicated to meeting and events with spacious, well equipped, light and airy rooms, an award winning AA Rosette, Italian restaurant, Filini, the ultra cool White Bar and Ark Health & Fitness Club and spa.

Radisson SAS Hotel
107 Old Hall Street, Liverpool L3 9BD United Kingdom
Telephone 0151 966 1500
Facsimile 0151 966 1501
www.radissonsas.com

HOTEL LIVERPOOL

LIVERPOOL *continued*

Bedrooms are stylishly appointed and benefit from a host of extra facilities.

Rooms 146 en suite (29 fmly) ⊛ in 120 bedrooms S £80-£160; D £100-£180 (incl. bkfst) **Facilities** STV ⛌ Sauna Solarium Gym Jacuzzi Wi-fi available Xmas **Conf** Thtr 300 Class 90 Board 30 Del from £140 **Services** Lift air con **Parking** 158 **Notes LB** ⊛ in restaurant Civ Wed 150

★★★★ 74% HOTEL

Crowne Plaza Liverpool

St Nicholas Place, Princes Dock, Pier Head
L3 1QW
☎ 0151 243 8000 ▤ 0151 243 8008
web: www.crowneplaza.com/liverpooluk

Situated right on the waterfront, yet still within striking distance of the city centre this hotel offers comprehensive leisure and meeting facilities, whether taking a snack in the spacious lounge or using the business centre. Contemporary with superb quality this hotel offers a welcome to business or leisure guests alike.

Rooms 159 en suite **Facilities Spa** STV ⛌ Sauna Solarium Gym Jacuzzi **Services** Lift air con **Parking** 150 **Notes** ⊗ ⊛ in restaurant Civ Wed

★★★ 80% HOTEL

The Royal

THE INDEPENDENTS

Marine Ter, Waterloo L22 5PR
☎ 0151 928 2332 ▤ 0151 949 0320
e-mail: enquiries@liverpool-royalhotel.co.uk
web: www.liverpool-royalhotel.co.uk

dir: *6.5m NW of city centre, left off A565 Liverpool to Southport road at monument. Hotel at bottom of road*

Dating back to 1815, this Grade II listed hotel is situated on the outskirts of the city, beside the Marine Gardens. Bedrooms are smartly appointed and some feature four-poster beds and spa baths. Spacious public areas enjoy splendid views and include an elegant restaurant, an attractive bar lounge and a conservatory.

Rooms 25 en suite (5 fmly) ⊛ in 4 bedrooms S £55-£95; D £85-£160 (incl. bkfst) **Facilities** STV **Conf** Thtr 100 Class 70 Board 40 **Parking** 25 **Notes** ⊗ ⊛ in restaurant

★★★ 77% HOTEL

Best Western Alicia

Best Western

3 Aigburth Dr, Sefton Park L17 3AA
☎ 0151 727 4411 ▤ 0151 727 6752
e-mail: aliciahotel@feathers.uk.com
web: www.feathers.uk.com

dir: *From end of M62 take A5058 to Sefton Park, then left*

This stylish and friendly hotel overlooks Sefton Park and is just a few minutes' drive from both the city centre and John Lennon Airport. Bedrooms are well equipped and comfortable. Day rooms include a striking modern restaurant and bar. Extensive, stylish function facilities make this a popular wedding venue.

Rooms 41 en suite (8 fmly) ⊛ in 16 bedrooms S £55-£80; D £65-£120 (incl. bkfst) **Facilities** STV Wi-fi available Xmas **Conf** Thtr 120 Class 80 Board 40 Del from £110 **Services** Lift **Parking** 40 **Notes LB** ⊗ ⊛ in restaurant Civ Wed 120

Ⓤ

Thistle Liverpool

THISTLE HOTELS

Chapel St L3 9RE
☎ 0870 333 9137 ▤ 0870 333 9237
e-mail: liverpool@thistle.co.uk

dir: *Exit M6 signed for M62 Liverpool. At end of M62 follow signs for Albert Dock, turn right at Liver Building & stay in lane marked Chapel St, hotel on left.*

At the time of going to press, the star classification for this hotel was not confirmed. Please refer to the AA internet site www.theAA.com for current information.

Rooms 225 en suite ⊛ in 144 bedrooms **Facilities** STV **Conf** Thtr 120 Class 40 Board 30 **Services** Lift air con **Notes** ⊗ ⊛ in restaurant Civ Wed 80

BUDGET HOTEL

Campanile

Campanile

Chaloner St, Queens Dock L3 4AJ
☎ 0151 709 8104 ▤ 0151 709 8725
e-mail: liverpool@campanile-hotels.com
web: www.envergure.fr

dir: *follow tourist signs marked Albert Dock. Hotel on waterfront*

This modern building offers accommodation in smart, well-equipped bedrooms, all with en suite bathrooms. Refreshments may be taken at the informal Bistro. For further details consult the Hotel Groups page.

Rooms 100 en suite S £49.95-£65; D £49.95-£65 **Conf** Thtr 35 Class 18 Board 24 Del from £93.70

BUDGET HOTEL

Hotel Ibis Liverpool

ibis

27 Wapping L1 8LY
☎ 0151 706 9800 ▤ 0151 706 9810
e-mail: H3140@accor-hotels.com
web: www.ibishotel.com

dir: *from M62 follow Albert Dock signs. Hotel opposite Dock entrance*

Modern, budget hotel offering comfortable accommodation in bright and practical bedrooms. Breakfast is self-service and dinner is available in the restaurant. For further details, consult the Hotel Groups page.

Rooms 127 en suite S £51.95-£85; D £51.95-£85

BUDGET HOTEL

Innkeeper's Lodge Liverpool North

502 Queen's Dr, Stoneycroft L13 0AS

☎ 0151 254 2271 🖶 0151 254 2394

web: www.innkeeperslodge.com

dir: from M62 take A5080 N towards Bootle Docks. Continue at lights at junct with A57. Hotel on left in Queens Drive

Smart, en suite accommodation ideal for both business & leisure guests. Bedrooms are very well equipped, including Sky TV, telephone, modem points, tea & coffee making facilities, (family rooms in most locations). Complimentary breakfast. The adjacent Pub Restaurant; a Harvester, Vintage Inn, Toby Carvery, Ember Inn, Sizzling Pubco or Pub & Carvery offers an all day menu. See Hotel Groups pages for further details.

Rooms 21 annexe en suite S £49.95; D £49.95

Innkeeper's Lodge Liverpool South (Airport)

531 Aigburth Rd L19 9DN

☎ 0151 494 1032 🖶 0151 494 3345

dir: on A56, opposite Liverpool cricket ground

Rooms 32 en suite S £49.95; D £49.95 **Conf** Thtr 18 Class 20 Board 12

BUDGET HOTEL

Premier Travel Inn Liverpool (Aintree)

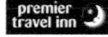

1 Ormskirk Rd, Aintree L9 5AS

☎ 08701 977157 🖶 0151 525 8696

web: www.premiertravelinn.com

dir: M58/57 then follow A59 to Liverpool. Past Aintree Retail Park, left at lights into Aintree Racecourse. Inn is on left

High quality, modern budget accommodation ideal for both families and business travellers. Spacious, en suite bedrooms feature bath and shower, satellite TV and many have telephones and modem points. The adjacent family restaurant features a wide and varied menu. For further details consult the Hotel Groups page.

Rooms 40 en suite **Conf** Thtr 40

Premier Travel Inn Liverpool Albert Dock

East Britannia Building, Albert Dock L3 4AD

☎ 0870 9906432 🖶 0870 9906433

dir: Inn just off A5036. In city centre, follow brown signs for Albert Dock & Beatles Story. Inn by Beatles Story

Rooms 130 en suite

Premier Travel Inn Liverpool City Centre

Vernon St L2 2AY

☎ 0870 238 3323 🖶 0870 241 9000

dir: from M62 follow Liverpool City Centre and Birkenhead Tunnel signs. At rbt take 3rd exit onto Dale St then right into Vernon St. Inn is on the left

Rooms 165 en suite

Premier Travel Inn Liverpool (Roby)

Roby Rd, Huyton L36 4HD

☎ 0870 9906596 🖶 0870 9906597

dir: Just off M62 junct 5 on A5080

Rooms 53 en suite **Conf** Thtr 25 Class 15 Board 22

Premier Travel Inn Liverpool (Tarbock)

Wilson Rd, Tarbock L36 6AD

☎ 08701 977159 🖶 0151 480 9361

dir: at junct M62/M57. M62 junct 6 take A5080 Huyton then 1st right into Wilson Rd

Rooms 40 en suite

Premier Travel Inn Liverpool (West Derby)

Queens Dr, West Derby L13 0DL

☎ 08701 977160 🖶 0151 220 7610

dir: At the end of M62 turn right under the flyover onto A5058 (following signs to the football stadium). Inn is 1.5 m on the left, just past the Esso garage

Rooms 84 en suite

BUDGET HOTEL

Travelodge Liverpool Central

25 Haymarket L1 6ER

☎ 08700 850 950 🖶 0151 227 5858

web: www.travelodge.co.uk

Travelodge offers good quality, good value, modern accommodation. Ideal for families, the spacious en suite bedrooms include remote-control TV, tea and coffee-making facilities and comfortable beds. Meals can be taken at the nearby family restaurant. See Hotel Groups pages for further details.

Rooms 105 en suite S fr £26; D fr £26

Travelodge Liverpool Docks

Brunswick Dock, Sefton St L3 4BH

☎ 08700 850 950 🖶 0151 707 7769

Rooms 31 en suite S fr £26; D fr £26

○ HOTEL

Liverpool Malmaison

William Jessop Way Princes Dock L3 1QW

e-mail: liverpool@malmaison.com

web: www.malmaison.com

Due to open November 2006.

Rooms 31 en suite

Malmaison - AA Hotel Group of the Year 2006-7.

England

MORETON
MAP 15 SJ28

★★★ 75% **HOTEL**

Leasowe Castle
Leasowe Rd CH46 3RF
☎ 0151 606 9191 🗎 0151 678 5551
e-mail: reservations@leasowecastle.com
web: www.leasowecastle.com
dir: M53 junct 1, 1st exit from rdbt, the take A551. Hotel 0.75m on right

Located adjacent to Leasowe Golf Course and within easy reach of Liverpool, Chester and all of the Wirral's attractions, this historic hotel dates back to 1592. Bedrooms are smartly appointed and well equipped, many enjoying ocean views. Public areas retain many original features. Weddings and functions are well catered for.

Rooms 47 en suite (3 fmly) ⊛ in 3 bedrooms S £72.50-£100; D £80-£175 **Facilities** STV FTV Sauna Gym Water sports, Sea Fishing, Sailing, Health club (mid Apr 2004) Xmas **Conf** Thtr 400 Class 200 Board 80 Del from £99 **Services** Lift **Parking** 200 **Notes LB** ⊛ ⊛ in restaurant Civ Wed 250

NEWTON-LE-WILLOWS
MAP 15 SJ59

★★ 65% **HOTEL**

Kirkfield Hotel
2/4 Church St WA12 9SU
☎ 01925 228196
e-mail: enquiries@kirkfieldhotel.co.uk
dir: on A49, opposite St Peter's Church

A conveniently located, family-run hotel that offers comfortable accommodation. Guests receive a friendly welcome and an informal atmosphere prevails throughout. A table d'hôte menu is available and there are options for lighter dining in the bar area. Parking is available.

Rooms 17 en suite (3 fmly) (1 GF) ⊛ in 8 bedrooms S £30-£40; D £52-£60 (incl. bkfst) **Conf** Thtr 70 Class 60 Board 20 Del from £50 **Parking** 50 **Notes** ⊛ in restaurant

RAINHILL
MAP 15 SJ49

BUDGET HOTEL

Premier Travel Inn Liverpool (Rainhill)
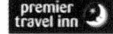
804 Warrington Rd, Rainhill L35 6PE
☎ 0870 9906446 🗎 0870 9906447
web: www.premiertravelinn.com
dir: Just off M62 junct 7, A57 towards Rainhill

High quality, modern budget accommodation ideal for both families and business travellers. Spacious, en suite bedrooms feature bath and shower, satellite TV and many have telephones and modem points. The adjacent family restaurant features a wide and varied menu. For further details consult the Hotel Groups page.

Rooms 34 en suite **Conf** Thtr 20

ST HELENS
MAP 15 SJ59
See also Rainhill

BUDGET HOTEL

Premier Travel Inn St Helens North
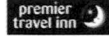
Garswood Old Rd, East Lancs Rd WA11 7LX
☎ 0870 9906374 🗎 0870 9906375
web: www.premiertravelinn.com
dir: 3m from M6 junct 23, on A580 towards Liverpool

High quality, modern budget accommodation ideal for both families and business travellers. Spacious, en suite bedrooms feature bath and shower, satellite TV and many have telephones and modem points. The adjacent family restaurant features a wide and varied menu. For further details consult the Hotel Groups page.

Rooms 43 en suite **Conf** Thtr 85 Class 30 Board 40

Premier Travel Inn St Helens South
Mickle Head Green, Eurolink, Lea Green WA9 4TT
☎ 08701 977237 🗎 01744 820531
dir: M62 junct 7, on A570 towards St Helens
Rooms 40 en suite

SOUTHPORT
MAP 15 SD31

★★★ 77% **HOTEL**

Scarisbrick
Lord St PR8 1NZ
☎ 01704 543000 🗎 01704 533335
e-mail: info@scarisbrickhotel.com
web: www.scarisbrickhotel.co.uk
dir: from S: M6 junct 26, M58 to Ormskirk then Southport. From N: A59 from Preston, well signed

Centrally located on Southport's famous Lord Street, this privately owned hotel offers a high standard of attractively furnished, thoughtfully equipped accommodation. A wide range of eating options is available, from the bistro style of Maloney's Kitchen to the more formal Knightsbridge restaurant. Extensive leisure and conference facilities are also available.

Rooms 88 en suite (5 fmly) ⊛ in 44 bedrooms S £50-£80; D £60-£120 (incl. bkfst) **Facilities Spa** STV ☒ Sauna Solarium Gym Jacuzzi Wi-fi available Use of private leisure centre, Beauty & aromatherapy studio ♫ ch fac Xmas **Conf** BC Thtr 200 Class 100 Board 80 Del from £70 **Services** Lift **Parking** 68 **Notes LB** ⊛ ⊛ in restaurant Civ Wed 170

★★★ 74% **HOTEL**

Best Western Stutelea Hotel & Leisure Club

Alexandra Rd PR9 0NB
☎ 01704 544220 🗎 01704 500232
e-mail: greg@warnerhotels.co.uk
dir: off promenade

This family owned and run hotel enjoys a quiet location in a residential area, a short walk from Lord Street and the Promenade. Bedrooms vary in size and style and include family suites and rooms with balconies overlooking the attractive gardens. The elegant

continued

restaurant has a cosmopolitan theme; alternatively the Garden Bar, in the leisure centre, offers light snacks throughout the day.

Rooms 22 en suite (4 fmly) (3 GF) ⊘ in 4 bedrooms **Facilities** STV ⊠ Sauna Solarium Gym Jacuzzi Games room Keep fit classes Steam room **Services** Lift **Parking** 15 **Notes** ⊗ ⊘ in restaurant

★★★ 73% HOTEL

Best Western Royal Clifton

Promenade PR8 1RB
☎ 01704 533771 ▤ 01704 500657
e-mail: sales@royalclifton.co.uk

dir: adjacent to Marine Lake

This grand, traditional hotel benefits from a prime location on the promenade. Bedrooms range in size and style, but all are comfortable and thoughtfully equipped. Public areas include the lively Bar C, the elegant Pavilion Restaurant and a modern, well-equipped leisure club. Extensive conference and banqueting facilities make this hotel a popular function venue.

Rooms 111 en suite (22 fmly) (6 GF) ⊘ in 30 bedrooms S £50-£85; D £80 £120 (incl. bkfst) **Facilities Spa** STV ⊠ Sauna Solarium Gym Jacuzzi Wi-fi available Hair & beauty Steam room, Aromatherapy Pool ♫ Xmas **Conf** Thtr 250 Class 100 Board 65 Del from £93.50 **Services** Lift **Parking** 60 **Notes LB** ⊗ ⊘ in restaurant Civ Wed 150

★★ 72% HOTEL

Bold

585 Lord St PR9 0BE
☎ 01704 532578 ▤ 01704 532528
e-mail: info@boldhotel.com
web: www.boldhotel.com

dir: M6 junct 26/M58/A570 towards Southport. In Southport follow signs to Lord St. Hotel on junct with Seabank Rd

Enjoying a central location, this family hotel is just a minute's walk from the promenade and local attractions. Thoughtfully equipped, spacious bedrooms are suitable for business or leisure guests as well as families. Public areas include a spacious bar, popular bistro, with an excellent range of dishes and a large carvery, available for parties.

Rooms 23 en suite (4 fmly) **Facilities** Special rates for local squash club **Conf** Thtr 40 Class 40 Board 11 **Services** air con **Parking** 15 **Notes LB** ⊛

★★ 69% HOTEL

Balmoral Lodge

41 Queens Rd PR9 9EX
☎ 01704 544298 & 530751 ▤ 01704 501224
e-mail: balmorallg@aol.com
web: www.balmorallodge.co.uk

dir: edge of town on A565 (Preston road). Turn E at rdbt at North Lord St, left at lights, hotel 200yds on left

Situated in a quiet residential area close to Lord Street, this friendly hotel is particularly popular with golfers. Smartly appointed bedrooms are well equipped for both business and leisure guests; some benefit from private patios overlooking the attractive gardens. Stylish public areas include Oscar's restaurant and an attractive bar lounge.

Rooms 15 en suite (1 fmly) (4 GF) ⊘ in 6 bedrooms S £35-£60; D £70-£90 (incl. bkfst) **Facilities** STV **Parking** 12 **Notes LB** ⊗ ⊘ in restaurant

★★ 65% HOTEL

Metropole

Portland St PR8 1LL
☎ 01704 556836 ▤ 01704 549041
e-mail: metropole.southport@btinternet.com
web: www.btinternet.com/~metropole.southport

dir: after Prince of Wales Hotel left off Lord St.

This family-run hotel of long standing, popular with golfers, is ideally situated just 50 yards from the famous Lord Street. Accommodation is comfortably equipped with family rooms available. In addition to the restaurant that offers a selection of freshly prepared dishes, there is a choice of lounges including a popular bar-lounge.

Rooms 23 en suite (4 fmly) ⊘ in 6 bedrooms S £30-£44; D £55-£78 (incl. bkfst) **Facilities** Snooker Golf can be arranged at 8 local courses Xmas **Parking** 12 **Notes LB** ⊘ in restaurant

U

Cambridge House

4 Cambridge Rd PR9 9NG
☎ 01704 538372
e-mail: info@cambridgehouschotel.co.uk
web: www.cambridgehousehotel.co.uk

dir: From Lord St towards Preston on A565. At rdbt follow A565, hotel on right after Hesketh Park

At the time of going to press, the star classification for this hotel was not confirmed. Please refer to the AA internet site www.theAA.com for current information.

Rooms 16 en suite (1 fmly) (2 GF) ⊘ in all bedrooms S £55-£110; D £69-£160 (incl. bkfst) **Parking** 20 **Notes** ⊘ in restaurant

BUDGET HOTEL

Premier Travel Inn Southport

Marine Dr PR8 1RY
☎ 08701 977071 ▤ 08701 977704
web: www.premiertravelinn.com

dir: from Southport follow signs for promenade and Marine Dr. Inn at junct of Marine Pde and Marine Dr

High quality, modern budget accommodation ideal for both families and business travellers. Spacious, en suite bedrooms feature bath and shower, satellite TV and many have telephones and modem points. The adjacent family restaurant features a wide and varied menu. For further details consult the Hotel Groups page.

Rooms 60 en suite

England

THORNTON HOUGH
MAP 15 SJ38

★★★★ 77% ⊛ **HOTEL**

Thornton Hall Hotel and Health Club

Neston Rd CH63 1JF

☎ 0151 336 3938 📠 0151 336 7864

e-mail: reservations@thorntonhallhotel.com

web: www.thorntonhallhotel.com

dir: M53 junct 4 take B5151 Neston onto B5136 to Thornton Hough

Dating back to the mid 1800s, this country-house hotel has been carefully extended and restored. Public areas include an impressive leisure spa boasting excellent facilities, a choice of restaurants and a spacious bar. Bedrooms vary in style and include feature rooms in the main house and more contemporary rooms in the garden wing. Delightful grounds and gardens and impressive function facilities make this a popular wedding venue.

Rooms 63 en suite (6 fmly) (28 GF) ⊘ in 36 bedrooms S £119; D £119 **Facilities Spa** STV ⬛ ⬛ Sauna Solarium Gym ⬛ Jacuzzi Wi-fi in bedrooms Hot tub Beauty Spa Hairdressing salon **Conf** BC Thtr 435 Class 225 Board 80 Del from £160 **Parking** 250 **Notes LB** ⊘ in restaurant Civ Wed 400

WALLASEY
MAP 15 SJ29

★★★ 78% **HOTEL**

Grove House

Grove Rd CH45 3HF

☎ 0151 639 3947 & 0151 630 4558 📠 0151 639 0028

e-mail: reception@thegrovehouse.co.uk

dir: M53 junct 1, A554 (Wallasey New Brighton), right after church onto Harrison Drive, left after Windsors Garage onto Grove Rd

Pretty lawns and gardens provide the setting for this friendly hotel, conveniently situated about a mile from the M53. Attractively furnished, well-equipped bedrooms include ground-floor, family, and four-poster rooms. Business meetings and weddings can be catered for. A wide choice of dishes is available in the restaurant, overlooking the garden.

Rooms 14 en suite (1 fmly) S fr £64.75; D £79.75-£89.75 **Facilities** STV **Conf** Thtr 50 Class 30 Board 50 Del from £107 **Parking** 24 **Notes LB** ⊛ RS Bank holidays Civ Wed 50

See advert on this page

NORFOLK

ACLE
MAP 13 TG41

BUDGET HOTEL

Travelodge Great Yarmouth Acle
NR13 3BE

☎ 08700 850 950 📠 01493 751970

web: www.travelodge.co.uk

dir: junct of A47 & Acle bypass

Travelodge offers good quality, good value, modern accommodation. Ideal for families, the spacious en suite bedrooms include remote-control TV, tea and coffee-making facilities and comfortable beds. Meals can be taken at the nearby family restaurant. See Hotel Groups pages for further details.

Rooms 40 en suite S fr £26; D fr £26

BARNHAM BROOM
MAP 13 TG00

★★★ 81% ⊛⊛ **HOTEL**

Barnham Broom Hotel, Golf & Restaurant
NR9 4DD

☎ 01603 759393 📠 01603 758224

e-mail: enquiry@barnhambroomhotel.co.uk

web: www.barnham-broom.co.uk

dir: From A11 onto A47 towards Swaffham, follow brown tourist signs

Situated in a peaceful rural location just a short drive from Norwich. The contemporary style bedrooms are tastefully furnished and thoughtfully equipped. The Sports bar serves a range of snacks and meals throughout the day, or guests may choose from the carte menu in Flints Restaurant. The hotel also has extensive leisure, conference and banqueting facilities.

Rooms 52 en suite (8 fmly) (6 GF) ⊛ in 37 bedrooms S £115-£170; D £140-£195 (incl. bkfst) **Facilities** STV ⊞ supervised ↓ 36 ♨ Squash Sauna Solarium Gym Putt green Jacuzzi Aerobics/yoga, pool table, Golf school **Conf** Thtr 180 Class 80 Board 70 Del from £125 **Parking** 200 **Notes LB** ⊗ ⊛ in restaurant Civ Wed 120

BLAKENEY
MAP 13 TG04

★★★ ⊛⊛⊛ **HOTEL**

Morston Hall
Morston, Holt NR25 7AA

☎ 01263 741041 📠 01263 740419

e-mail: reception@morstonhall.com

web: www.morstonhall.com

dir: 1m W of Blakeney on A149 Kings Lynn/Cromer Rd coastal road

This delightful 17th-century country-house hotel enjoys a tranquil setting amid well-tended gardens. The comfortable public rooms offer a choice of attractive lounges and a sunny conservatory, while the elegant dining room is a perfect setting to enjoy Galton Blackiston's award-winning cuisine. The spacious bedrooms are individually decorated and stylishly furnished with modern opulence.

Rooms 7 en suite (1 GF) **Parking** 40 **Notes** ⊛ in restaurant Closed 1 Jan-2 Feb & 2 days Xmas

---

★★★ 78% ⊛ **HOTEL**

The Blakeney
The Quay NR25 7NE

☎ 01263 740797 📠 01263 740795

e-mail: reception@blakeney-hotel.co.uk

web: www.blakeney-hotel.co.uk

dir: off A149 coast road, 8m W of Sheringham

A traditional, privately owned hotel situated on the quayside with superb views across the estuary and the salt marshes to Blakeney Point. Public rooms feature an elegant restaurant, ground-floor lounge, a bar and a first-floor sun lounge overlooking the harbour. Bedrooms are smartly decorated and equipped with modern facilities, some enjoy the lovely sea views.

Rooms 48 en suite 16 annexe en suite (20 fmly) (18 GF) ⊛ in all bedrooms S £84-£142; D £168-£284 (incl. bkfst & dinner) **Facilities** Spa ⊞ Snooker Sauna Gym Jacuzzi Table tennis Xmas **Conf** Thtr 200 Class 100 Board 100 Del from £116 **Services** Lift **Parking** 60 **Notes LB** ⊛ in restaurant

England

England

BLAKENEY *continued*

★★ 76% HOTEL

The Pheasant

Coast Rd, Kelling, Holt NR25 7EG

☎ 01263 588382 🖹 01263 588101

e-mail: enquiries@pheasanthotelnorfolk.co.uk

dir: *on A419 coast road, mid-way between Sheringham & Blakeney*

Popular hotel ideally situated on the main coast road just a short drive from the bustling town of Holt. Bedrooms are split between the main house and a modern wing of spacious rooms to the rear of the property. Public rooms include a busy lounge bar, a residents' lounge and a large restaurant.

Rooms 30 en suite (1 fmly) (24 GF) ⊗ in all bedrooms S £47.50-£57.50; D £95-£105 (incl. bkfst) **Facilities** Xmas **Conf** Thtr 80 Class 50 Board 50 **Parking** 80 **Notes LB** ⊗ in restaurant

★★ 75% HOTEL

Blakeney Manor

The Quay NR25 7ND

☎ 01263 740376 🖹 01263 741116

e-mail: reception@blakeneymanor.co.uk

dir: *exit A149 at Blakeney towards Blakeney Quay. Hotel at end of quay between Mariner's Hill & Friary Hills*

An attractive Norfolk flint building overlooking Blakeney Marshes close to the town centre and quayside. The bedrooms are located in flint-faced barns in a courtyard adjacent to the main building. The spacious public rooms include a choice of lounges, a conservatory, a popular bar and a large restaurant offering an interesting choice of dishes.

Rooms 7 en suite 28 annexe en suite (26 GF) **Parking** 40 **Notes LB** No children 14yrs ⊗ in restaurant

BRANCASTER STAITHE   MAP 13 TF74

★★ 82% ⊛ HOTEL

White Horse

PE31 8BY

☎ 01485 210262 🖹 01485 210930

e-mail: reception@whitehorsebrancaster.co.uk

web: www.whitehorsebrancaster.co.uk

dir: *on A149 coast road midway between Hunstanton & Wells-next-the-Sea*

A charming hotel situated on the north Norfolk coast with contemporary bedrooms in two wings, some featuring an interesting cobbled fascia. Each room is attractively decorated and thoughtfully equipped. There is a large bar and a lounge area leading through to the conservatory restaurant, with stunning tidal marshland views across to Scolt Head Island.

Rooms 7 en suite 8 annexe en suite (5 fmly) (8 GF) S £45-£70; D £90-£140 (incl. bkfst) **Facilities** Wi-fi in bedrooms Bar billiards Xmas **Parking** 60 **Notes LB** ⊗ in restaurant

BURNHAM MARKET   MAP 13 TF84

★★★ 80% ⊛⊛ HOTEL

Hoste Arms

The Green PE31 8HD

☎ 01328 738777 🖹 01328 730103

e-mail: reception@hostearms.co.uk

web: www.hostearms.co.uk

dir: *signed on B1155, 5m W of Wells-next-the-Sea*

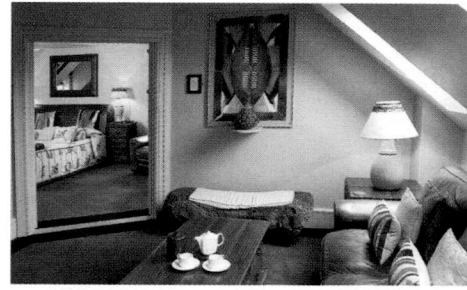

Stylish, privately owned inn situated in the heart of this bustling village close to the north Norfolk coast. The extensive public rooms feature a range of dining areas that include a conservatory with plush furniture, a sunny patio and a traditional pub. The tastefully furnished, thoughtfully equipped bedrooms are generally very spacious and offer a high degree of comfort.

Rooms 36 en suite (7 GF) ⊗ in all bedrooms S £88-£260; D £117-£260 (incl. bkfst) **Facilities** STV Wi-fi available Xmas **Conf** BC Thtr 25 Board 16 Del from £155 **Services** air con **Parking** 45

CROMER   MAP 13 TG24

★★★ 86% ⊛ HOTEL

Elderton Lodge Hotel & Langtry Restaurant

Gunton Park NR11 8TZ

☎ 01263 833547 🖹 01263 834673

e-mail: enquiries@eldertonlodge.co.uk

web: www.eldertonlodge.co.uk

dir: *at North Walsham take A149 towards Cromer, hotel 3m on left, just before Thorpe Market*

Ideally placed for touring the north Norfolk coastline, this delightful former shooting lodge is set amidst six acres of mature gardens

continued

adjacent to Gunton Hall estate. The individually decorated bedrooms are tastefully furnished and thoughtfully equipped. Public rooms include a smart lounge bar, an elegant restaurant and a sunny conservatory breakfast room.

Rooms 11 en suite (2 fmly) (2 GF) ⊗ in all bedrooms S £65, D £100-£120 (incl. bkfst) **Facilities** Xmas **Conf** BC **Parking** 50 **Notes** LB No children 6yrs ⊗ in restaurant Civ Wed 55

★★★ 85% ◉ HOTEL

Sea Marge

16 High St NR27 0AB
☎ 01263 579579 📠 01263 579524
e-mail: info@mackenziehotels.com

dir: A140 from Norwich until A149 to Cromer. Take B1159 to Overstrand. Hotel in village centre

An elegant Grade II listed Edwardian mansion perched on the cliff top amidst pretty landscaped gardens that lead down to the beach. Bedrooms are tastefully decorated and thoughtfully equipped, many have superb sea views. Public rooms offer a wide choice of areas in which to relax, including Frazer's restaurant and a smart lounge bar.

Rooms 18 en suite 5 annexe en suite (5 fmly) (2 GF) ⊗ in 17 bedrooms S fr £95; D fr £150 (incl. bkfst & dinner) **Facilities** ⋓ Xmas **Conf** Thtr 50 Class 40 Board 24 Del from £100 **Services** Lift **Parking** 50 **Notes** LB ⊛ ⊗ in restaurant

★★★ 75% HOTEL

Virginia Court Hotel

Cliff Av NR27 0AN
☎ 01263 512398 📠 01263 515529
e-mail: info@virginiacourt.co.uk
web: www.virginiacourt.co.uk

dir: A148 into town centre, pass church, left at lights, 1st right. A140 into Cromer over mini rdbt then 1st right.

Originally built in 1899 as a clubhouse for King Edward VII, this property is situated in a peaceful side road just a short walk from the town centre and seafront. The spacious bedrooms are smartly decorated and thoughtfully equipped. Public rooms include a smart restaurant, a cosy lounge bar and a further residents' lounge.

Rooms 25 en suite (2 fmly) (3 GF) ⊗ in all bedrooms S £45-£53; D £80-£96 (incl. bkfst) **Facilities** Xmas **Conf** Thtr 30 Class 30 Board 20 Del from £75 **Parking** 25 **Notes** LB ⊛ ⊗ in restaurant

★★★ 71% HOTEL

The Cliftonville

NR27 9AS
☎ 01263 512543 📠 01263 515700
e-mail: reservations@cliftonvillehotel.co.uk
web: www.cliftonvillehotel.co.uk

dir: From A149 (coastal road), 500yds from town centre, northbound

An imposing Edwardian hotel situated on the main coast road with stunning views of the sea. Public rooms feature a magnificent staircase, minstrels' gallery, coffee shop, lounge bar, a further residents' lounge, Boltons Bistro and an additional restaurant. The pleasantly decorated bedrooms are generally quite spacious and have lovely sea views.

Rooms 30 en suite (5 fmly) ⊕ in 21 bedrooms S £45-£62; D £90-£124 (incl. bkfst) **Facilities** Xmas **Conf** Thtr 150 Class 100 Board 60 Del from £75 **Services** Lift **Parking** 20 **Notes** LB ⊗ in restaurant

★★ 76% HOTEL

Red Lion

Brook St NR27 9HD
☎ 01263 514964 📠 01263 512834
e-mail: enquiries@yeolderedlionhotel.co.uk
web: www.yeolderedlionhotel.co.uk

dir: from town centre 1st left after church

Victorian property situated in an elevated position overlooking the beach and sea beyond. The smartly appointed public areas include a billiard room, lounge bar, a popular restaurant, a sunny conservatory and a first floor residents' lounge with superb sea views. The spacious bedrooms are tastefully decorated, with co-ordinated soft furnishings and many thoughtful touches.

Rooms 12 en suite (1 fmly) S £60; D £100 **Facilities** Snooker Sauna Discount for local leisure centre **Conf** Thtr 100 Class 50 Board 60 **Parking** 12 **Notes** LB ⊛ ⊗ in restaurant Closed Xmas Day

★★ 74% HOTEL

Green Farm Restaurant & Hotel

North Walsham Rd NR11 8TH
☎ 01263 833602 📠 01263 833163
e-mail: grfarmh@aol.com
web: www.greenfarmhotel.co.uk

dir: from A140 (Norwich to Cromer road) turn right at Roughton, (by fish & chip shop). 1.5m to 'Give Way' sign, turn right, hotel 200yds on left in village centre

A 16th-century flint faced inn situated a short drive from Cromer. Bedrooms are located in two courtyard-style wings and a converted

continued on page 488

CROMER *continued*

barn adjacent to the main building; each one is tastefully furnished and has co-ordinated fabrics. Public rooms include a restaurant, a comfortable lounge bar, a meeting room and a function suite.

Rooms 5 en suite 9 annexe en suite (1 fmly) **Conf** Thtr 50 Class 40 Board 100 **Parking** 50 **Notes LB** ⊗ in restaurant Civ Wed 50

★★ 69% HOTEL

Hotel de Paris

High St NR27 9HG

Leisureplex

☎ 01263 513141 🖹 01263 515217

e-mail: deparis.cromer@alfatravel.co.uk

web: www.alfatravel.co.uk

dir: enter Cromer on A140 Norwich Rd. Left at lights onto Mount St. 2nd traffic lights right into Prince of Wales Rd. 2nd right into New St leading into High St

An imposing, traditional-style resort hotel, situated in a prominent position overlooking the pier and beach. The bedrooms are pleasantly decorated and equipped with a good range of useful extras; many rooms have lovely sea views. The spacious public areas include a large lounge bar, restaurant, games room and a further lounge.

Rooms 56 en suite (5 fmly) ⊗ in all bedrooms S £27-£34; D £54-£68 (incl. bkfst) **Facilities** Games room ♫ Xmas **Services** Lift **Parking** 14 **Notes LB** ⊗ ⊗ in restaurant Closed Dec-Feb RS Mar & Nov

DEREHAM   MAP 13 TF91

★★★ 85% HOTEL

Hill House

26 Market Place NR19 2AP

☎ 01362 699857

e-mail: hillhouse@mjbhotels.com

dir: Follow main street through town. At mini rdbt turn right. Take right hand fork. Hotel car park entrance 1st left.

A delightful 16th-century Queen Anne property situated in the heart of this bustling town centre. The extensive public rooms include a smart lounge, an open-plan bar/carvery, a wine bar and a stylish restaurant. The tastefully furnished bedrooms offer a high degree of comfort and have many thoughtful touches.

Rooms 22 en suite (1 fmly) (6 GF) ⊗ in all bedrooms S £74-£89; D £95-£140 (incl. bkfst) **Parking** 12 **Notes** ⊗

★★ 74% HOTEL

George

Swaffham Rd NR19 2AZ

☎ 01362 696801 🖹 01362 695711

dir: From A47 follow signs for Dereham, on High St to the memorial, hotel on left

Delightful old Inn situated in the heart of this bustling market town and ideally placed for touring Norfolk. The spacious bedrooms are pleasantly decorated, furnished with pine pieces and have many thoughtful touches. Public rooms include a smart restaurant, a stylish lounge with leather sofas, a conservatory dining room and a large lounge bar.

Rooms 8 en suite (2 fmly) ⊗ in all bedrooms S fr £60; D fr £80 (incl. bkfst) **Parking** 50 **Notes LB** ⊗ ⊗ in restaurant Closed 26-Dec Civ Wed 50

DISS   MAP 13 TM18

🇺

Swallow Scole Inn

Ipswich Road Scole IP21 4DR

☎ 01379 740481 🖹 01379 740762

web: www.swallowhotels.com

At the time of going to press, the star classification for this hotel was not confirmed. Please refer to the AA internet site www.theAA.com for current information.

Rooms 22 en suite

DOWNHAM MARKET   MAP 12 TF60

★★ 78% HOTEL

Castle

High St PE38 9HF

☎ 01366 384311 🖹 01366 384311

e-mail: howards@castle-hotel.com

dir: M11 take A10 for Ely into Downham Market, hotel opposite traffic lights, on corner of High St

This popular coaching inn is situated close to the centre of town and has been welcoming guests for over 300 years. Well-maintained public areas include a cosy lounge bar and two smartly appointed restaurants. Inviting bedrooms, some with four-poster beds, are attractively decorated, thoughtfully equipped, and have bright, modern decor.

Rooms 12 en suite **Facilities** Xmas **Conf** Thtr 60 Class 30 Board 40 **Parking** 26 **Notes** ⊗ in restaurant

FRITTON   MAP 13 TG40

★★★ 77% HOTEL

Caldecott Hall Golf & Leisure

Caldecott Hall, Beccles Rd NR31 9EY

☎ 01493 488488 🖹 01493 488561

e-mail: hotel@caldecotthall.co.uk

web: www.caldecotthall.co.uk

dir: On A143 (Beccles to Great Yarmouth road), 4m from Great Yarmouth

Ideally situated in its own attractive landscaped grounds that include an 18-hole golf course, fishing lakes and the Redwings Horse sanctuary. The individually decorated bedrooms are spacious, and equipped with many thoughtful touches. Public rooms include a smart sitting room, a lounge bar, restaurant, clubhouse and smart leisure complex.

Rooms 8 en suite (3 fmly) ⊗ in all bedrooms S £75; D £85-£110 **Facilities Spa** 🏊 supervised ♨ 36 Gym Putt green Jacuzzi Driving range **Conf** Thtr 100 Class 80 Board 20 Del from £115 **Parking** 100 **Notes LB** ⊗ ⊗ in restaurant Civ Wed 150

England

GORLESTON ON SEA MAP 13 TG50
See also Great Yarmouth

★★ 71% HOTEL

The Pier
Harbourmouth, South Pier NR31 6PL
☎ 01493 662631 📠 01493 440263
e-mail: info@pierhotelgorleston.co.uk
dir: *from A143 left into Shrublands, into Church Lane, to Baker Street, right into Pier Plain, left into Pier Walk, right into Quay Road*

This small family run hotel sits adjacent to the harbour wall, with splendid views along the sandy beach. The smartly appointed public rooms include a popular bar and a pleasant restaurant where an interesting choice of home cooked food is available. Bedrooms are pleasantly decorated and equipped with modern facilities.

Rooms 19 en suite (1 fmly) ⊗ in 6 bedrooms S £40-£65; D £50-£125 (incl. bkfst) **Facilities** STV Wi-fi in bedrooms Xmas **Conf** Thtr 90 Class 120 Board 120 Del from £67 **Services** air con **Parking** 30 **Notes LB** ⊗ ⊛ in restaurant Civ Wed 140

GREAT BIRCHAM MAP 13 TF73

★★★ 85% ⊛ HOTEL

Kings Head
PE31 6RJ
☎ 01485 578265 📠 01485 578635
e-mail: welcome@the-kings-head-bircham.co.uk
web: www.the-kings-head-bircham.co.uk
dir: *From Kings Lynn take A149 towards Fakenham. After Hillington, turn left onto B1153 and continue to Great Bircham.*

New extended inn situated in a peaceful village location close to the north Norfolk coastline. The spacious, individually decorated bedrooms are tastefully appointed with superb co-ordinated furnishings and many thoughtful touches. The contemporary style public rooms include a brasserie restaurant, a relaxing lounge, a smart bar and a private dining room.

Rooms 9 en suite (8 fmly) ⊗ in all bedrooms S £69.50-£79.50; D £125-£175 (incl. bkfst) **Facilities** Xmas **Conf** Thtr 40 Class 14 Board 20 Del from £140 **Parking** 25 **Notes LB** ⊗ in restaurant Civ Wed 130

GREAT YARMOUTH MAP 13 TG50
See also Gorleston on Sea

★★★ 78% ⊛ HOTEL

Imperial
North Dr NR30 1EQ

THE INDEPENDENTS

☎ 01493 842000 📠 01493 852229
e-mail: imperial@scs-datacom.co.uk
web: www.imperialhotel.co.uk
dir: *follow seafront signs, turn left. Hotel opposite tennis courts*

This friendly, family-run hotel is situated at the quieter end of the seafront within easy walking distance of the town centre. Bedrooms are attractively decorated with co-ordinated soft furnishings and many thoughtful touches; most rooms have superb sea views. Public areas include the smart Savoie Lounge Bar and the Rambouillet Restaurant.

Rooms 39 en suite (4 fmly) ⊗ in 32 bedrooms S £60-£80; D £70-£100 (incl. bkfst) **Facilities** STV Wi-fi in bedrooms Xmas **Conf** Thtr 140 Class 40 Board 30 Del from £85 **Services** Lift **Parking** 50 **Notes LB** ⊛ in restaurant Civ Wed 140

★★★ 77% HOTEL

Best Western Cliff Hotel
Cliff Hill, Gorleston NR31 6DH

Best Western

☎ 01493 662179 📠 01493 653617
dir: *M11 onto A11 to Norwich then A47 to Gt Yarmouth. At N end of Gorleston's Upper Marine Parade*

Overlooking the harbour just a short walk from the beach, promenade and Gorleston town centre. Public rooms include a choice of bars, an attractive lounge and a stylish restaurant where an interesting choice of dishes is served. Bedrooms are smartly decorated, with co-ordinated soft furnishings and have many thoughtful touches; some rooms have lovely sea views.

Rooms 36 en suite (2 fmly) ⊗ in 2 bedrooms **Facilities** STV ♫ **Conf** Thtr 170 Class 130 Board 80 **Parking** 70 **Notes LB** ⊛ in restaurant Civ Wed 120

England

GREAT YARMOUTH *continued*

★★★ 73% HOTEL

Comfort Hotel Great Yarmouth

Albert Square NR30 3JH
☎ 01493 855070 📠 01493 853798
e-mail: info@regencydolphinhotel.co.uk
web: www.regencydolphinhotel.co.uk

dir: from seafront at Wellington Pier into Kimberley Terrace. Left into Albert Square, hotel on left

A large, well furnished hotel situated in the quieter end of town, just off the seafront and within easy walking distance of the town centre. The pleasantly decorated bedrooms are generally quite spacious and well equipped and include Wi-Fi connections. Public rooms include a comfortable lounge, a bar and intimate restaurant. The hotel also has an outdoor swimming pool.

Rooms 49 en suite (5 fmly) (2 GF) ⊗ in 12 bedrooms S £85-£105; D £95-£160 (incl. bkfst) **Facilities** STV ⊰ Wi-fi in bedrooms Xmas **Conf** Thtr 120 Class 50 Board 30 **Parking** 19 **Notes** LB ⊗ in restaurant Civ Wed 120

★★★ 68% HOTEL

Star

Hall Quay NR30 1HG
☎ 01493 842294 📠 01493 330215
e-mail: star.hotel@elizabethhotels.co.uk

dir: from Norwich on A47 over 1st rdbt. At 2nd rdbt 3rd exit. Hotel on left

The unusual façade of this 17th-century property makes it one of the town's most striking buildings. It overlooks the quay and is just a short walk from the town centre. The smartly appointed public rooms include a choice of bars, a restaurant and a tastefully furnished lounge. Bedrooms are pleasantly decorated and equipped with modern facilities.

Rooms 40 en suite (1 fmly) ⊗ in 13 bedrooms S £69-£122; D £90-£132 (incl. bkfst) **Facilities** STV Discount for the marina leisure centre pool, gym Xmas **Conf** Thtr 75 Class 30 Board 30 Del from £90 **Services** Lift **Parking** 20 **Notes** LB ⊗ ⊗ in restaurant Civ Wed 70

★★ 75% HOTEL

The Arden Court Hotel

93-94 North Denes Rd NR30 4LW
☎ 01493 855310 📠 01493 843413
e-mail: info@ardencourt-hotel.co.uk.
web: www.ardencourt-hotel.co.uk

dir: At seafront left onto North Drive. At boating lake left onto Beaconsfield Rd. At mini rdbt right into North Denes Rd

Friendly, family-run hotel situated in a residential area just a short walk from the seafront. The individually decorated bedrooms are smartly furnished and equipped with a good range of useful extras. Public rooms are attractively presented; they include a smart lounge bar and a restaurant serving an interesting choice of dishes.

Rooms 14 en suite (5 fmly) (2 GF) ⊗ in all bedrooms S £30-£45; D £60-£80 (incl. bkfst) **Facilities** ♫ Xmas **Conf** BC **Parking** 10 **Notes** LB ⊗ ⊗ in restaurant

★★ 74% HOTEL

Furzedown

19-20 North Dr NR30 4EW
☎ 01493 844138 📠 01493 844138
e-mail: paul@furzedownhotel.co.uk
web: www.furzedownhotel.co.uk

dir: at end of A47 or A12, towards seafront, left, hotel opposite Waterways

Expect a warm welcome at this family run hotel situated at the northern end of the seafront overlooking the Venetian Waterways. Bedrooms are pleasantly decorated and thoughtfully equipped; many rooms have superb sea views. The stylish public areas include a comfortable lounge bar, a smartly appointed restaurant and a cosy TV room.

Rooms 24 rms (20 en suite) (11 fmly) **Facilities** STV **Conf** Thtr 75 Class 80 Board 40 **Parking** 15 **Notes** ⊗ in restaurant

★★ 72% **HOTEL**

Burlington Palm Court Hotel

11 North Dr NR30 1EG
☎ 01493 844568 & 842095 📠 01493 331848
e-mail: enquiries@burlington-hotel.co.uk
web: www.burlington-hotel.co.uk
dir: A12 to seafront, left at Britannia Pier. Hotel near tennis courts

This privately owned hotel is situated at the quiet end of the resort, overlooking the sea. Bedrooms come in a variety of sizes and styles, they are pleasantly decorated and well equipped, and many have lovely sea views. The spacious public rooms include a range of seating areas, a choice of dining rooms and two bars.

Rooms 70 en suite (9 fmly) ⊗ in 14 bedrooms **Facilities Spa** STV 🏷
Jacuzzi Turkish steam room 🎵 **Conf** Thtr 120 Class 60 Board 30
Services Lift **Parking** 70 **Notes LB** ⊗ ⊘ in restaurant Closed Jan-Feb
RS Dec-Feb (group bookings only)

★★ 65% **HOTEL**

New Beach Hotel

67 Marine Pde NR30 2EJ   **Leisureplex**
☎ 01493 332300 📠 01493 331880
e-mail: newbeach.gtyarmouth@alfatravel.co.uk
web: www.alfatravel.co.uk
dir: Follow signs to seafront

This Victorian building is centrally located on the seafront, overlooking Britannia Pier and the sandy beach. Bedrooms are pleasantly decorated and equipped with modern facilities; many have lovely sea views. Dinner is taken in the restaurant which doubles as the ballroom, and guests can also relax in the bar or sunny lounge.

Rooms 75 en suite (3 fmly) ⊗ in all bedrooms S £31-£41; D £50-£70
(incl. bkfst) **Facilities** FTV 🎵 Xmas **Services** Lift **Notes LB** ⊗ ⊘ in
restaurant Closed Dec-Feb RS Nov & Mar

Swallow Horse & Groom

Main Rd, Rollesby NR29 5ER   SWALLOW
☎ 01493 740199 📠 01493 740022
web: www.swallowhotels.com

At the time of going to press, the star classification for this hotel was not confirmed. Please refer to the AA internet site www.theAA.com for current information.

Rooms 20 en suite

GRIMSTON   MAP 12 TF72

INSPECTORS' CHOICE

★★★ ◉◉ **HOTEL**

Congham Hall Country House Hotel

Lynn Rd PE32 1AH
☎ 01485 600250 📠 01485 601191
e-mail: info@conghamhallhotel.co.uk
web: www.vonessenhotels.co.uk
dir: at A149-A148 junct, NE of King's Lynn, take A148 towards Fakenham for 100yds. Right to Grimston, hotel 2.5m on left

An elegant 10th-century Georgian manor set amid 30 acres of mature landscaped grounds and surrounded by parkland. The inviting public rooms provide a range of tastefully furnished areas in which to sit and relax. The bedrooms are appointed with period pieces, have modern facilities and many thoughtful touches. Imaginative cuisine is served in the Orangery Restaurant, which has an intimate atmosphere and panoramic views of the gardens.

Rooms 14 en suite ⊗ in all bedrooms S £105-£295; D fr £185 (incl.
bkfst) **Facilities** 🏊 🎣 Putt green Xmas **Conf** Thtr 50 Class 20
Board 30 Del from £175 **Parking** 50 **Notes LB** ⊗ ⊘ in restaurant
Civ Wed 100

HETHERSETT   MAP 13 TG10

★★★ 80% ◉ **HOTEL**

Park Farm

NR9 3DL   CLASSIC
                                          BRITISH HOTELS
☎ 01603 810264 📠 01603 812104
e-mail: enq@parkfarm-hotel.co.uk
web: www.parkfarm-hotel.co.uk
dir: 5m S of Norwich, off A11 on B1172

Elegant Georgian farmhouse set in landscaped grounds surrounded by open countryside. The property has been owned and run by the Gowing family since 1958. Bedrooms are pleasantly decorated and tastefully furnished; some rooms have patio doors with a sun terrace.

continued on page 492

HETHERSETT *continued*

Public rooms include a stylish conservatory, a lounge bar, a smart restaurant and superb leisure facilities.

Park Farm

Rooms 3 en suite 39 annexe en suite (15 fmly) (22 GF) ⊘ in 15 bedrooms S £99-£135; D £128-£185 (incl. bkfst) **Facilities** ▣ supervised Sauna Solarium Gym Jacuzzi Wi-fi available Beauty salon, Hairdressing Xmas **Conf** Thtr 120 Class 50 Board 50 Del from £139 **Parking** 150 **Notes LB** ⊗ ⊘ in restaurant Civ Wed 100

See advert under NORWICH

HILLINGTON   MAP 12 TF72

★★ 71% **HOTEL**

Ffolkes Arms   THE INDEPENDENTS
Lynn Rd PE31 6BJ
☎ 01485 600210 📠 01485 601196
e-mail: ffolkespub@aol.com
dir: on A149 at Knights Hill rdbt, right onto A148 towards Cromer. Hotel in 6m

A popular 17th-century former coaching inn, situated close to the Norfolk coastline and within easy reach of King's Lynn. Facilities include a bar, restaurant and lounge area. Bedrooms are in an annexe adjacent to the main building; each one is pleasantly appointed and well equipped. The hotel also has a function suite and social club.

Rooms 20 annexe en suite (2 fmly) ⊘ in all bedrooms S fr £45; D fr £65 (incl. bkfst) **Facilities** Xmas **Conf** BC Thtr 200 Class 60 Board 50 Del from £72.50 **Parking** 200 **Notes** ⊗ ⊘ in restaurant Civ Wed 150

HOLKHAM   MAP 13 TF84

★★ 78% ◉◉ **HOTEL**

The Victoria at Holkham
Park Rd NR23 1RG
☎ 01328 711008 📠 01328 711009
e-mail: victoria@holkham.co.uk
web: www.victoriaatholkham.co.uk
dir: A149, 2m W of Wells-next-the-Sea

A Grade II listed property built from local flint ideally situated on the north Norfolk coast road and forming part of the Holkham Estate. Decor is very much influenced by the local landscape: the stylish bedrooms are individually decorated and tastefully furnished with

continued

---

pieces specially made for the hotel in India. The brasserie-style restaurant serves an interesting choice of dishes.

The Victoria at Holkham

Rooms 9 en suite 1 annexe en suite (2 fmly) (1 GF) ⊘ in all bedrooms S £95-£120; D £115-£210 (incl. bkfst) **Facilities** STV Fishing Shooting on Holkham Estate, Bird watching ch fac Xmas **Conf** Thtr 12 Class 40 Board 30 Del £200 **Parking** 30 **Notes LB** ⊗ ⊘ in restaurant Civ Wed 70

HUNSTANTON   MAP 12 TF64

★★★ 79% **HOTEL**

Best Western Le Strange Arms   Best Western
Golf Course Rd, Old Hunstanton PE36 6JJ
☎ 01485 534411 📠 01485 534724
e-mail: reception@lestrangearms.co.uk
dir: off A149 1m N of Hunstanton. Left at sharp right bend by pitch & putt course

Impressive hotel with superb views from the wide lawns down to the sandy beach and across The Wash. Bedrooms in the main house have period furnishings whereas the rooms in the wing are more contemporary in style. Public rooms include a comfortable lounge bar and an attractive restaurant, where an interesting choice of dishes is served.

Rooms 36 en suite (4 fmly) ⊘ in 6 bedrooms S £72-£77; D £115-£140 (incl. bkfst) **Facilities** STV Snooker Xmas **Conf** BC Thtr 180 Class 150 Board 50 Del from £125 **Parking** 80 **Notes LB** ⊘ in restaurant Civ Wed 70

★★ 76% **HOTEL**

Caley Hall

Old Hunstanton Rd PE36 6HH
☎ 01485 533486 🖷 01485 533348
e-mail: mail@caleyhallhotel.co.uk
web: www.caleyhallhotel.co.uk
dir: 1m from Hunstanton, on A149

Situated just off the A149 in Old Hunstanton and within easy walking distance of the seafront. The tastefully decorated bedrooms are in a series of converted outbuildings; each is smartly furnished and thoughtfully equipped. Public rooms feature a large open-plan lounge/bar with plush leather seating, and a restaurant offering an interesting choice of dishes.

Rooms 40 en suite (20 fmly) (30 GF) ⊛ in all bedrooms S £39-£89; D £70-£130 (incl. bkfst) **Facilities** STV **Parking** 80 **Notes LB** ⊛ in restaurant Closed 18 Dec-20 Jan

Ⓤ

Swallow Golden Lion

The Green PE36 6BQ
☎ 01485 532688
web: www.swallowhotels.com

SWALLOW
HOTELS

At the time of going to press, the star classification for this hotel was not confirmed. Please refer to the AA internet site www.theAA.com for current information.

Rooms 27 rms

Ⓤ

Swallow Lodge

Old Hunstanton Rd PE36 6HX
☎ 01485 532896 🖷 01485 535007
web: www.swallowhotels.com

SWALLOW
HOTELS

dir: A149 from King's Lynn to Hunstanton. Hotel on right

At the time of going to press, the star classification for this hotel was not confirmed. Please refer to the AA internet site www.theAA.com for current information.

Rooms 22 en suite

KING'S LYNN   MAP 12 TF62

★★★ ◉◉ **HOTEL**

Congham Hall
Country House Hotel

Lynn Rd PE32 1AH
☎ 01485 600250 🖷 01485 601191
e-mail: info@conghamhallhotel.co.uk
web: www.vonessenhotels.co.uk
(For full entry see Grimston)

★★★ 77% **HOTEL**

Best Western Knights Hill

Knights Hill Village, South Wootton PE30 3HQ
☎ 01553 675566 🖷 01553 675568
e-mail: reception@knightshill.co.uk
dir: junct A148/A149

Best
Western

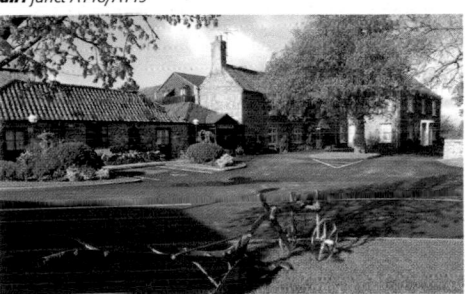

This hotel village complex is set on a 16th-century site on the outskirts of town. The smartly decorated, well-equipped bedrooms are situated in extensions of the original hunting lodge. Public areas have a wealth of historic charm; they include the Garden Restaurant and the Farmers Arms pub. The hotel also has conference, banqueting and leisure facilities.

Rooms 65 en suite 12 annexe en suite (38 GF) ⊛ in 52 bedrooms S £70-£115; D £85-£130 **Facilities** STV ⊠ ♨ Sauna Gym ♥ Jacuzzi Heli-pad Xmas **Conf** Thtr 200 Class 150 Board 30 **Parking** 350 **Notes LB** ⑪ ⊛ in restaurant Civ Wed 90

★★ 69% **HOTEL**

Stuart House

35 Goodwins Rd PE30 5QX
☎ 01553 772169 🖷 01553 774788
e-mail: reception@stuarthousehotel.co.uk
web: www.stuarthousehotel.co.uk

dir: at A47/A10/A149 rdbt take signs to King's Lynn town centre. Under Southgate Arch, right into Guanock Terrace and right Goodwins Rd

A small privately-owned hotel situated in a peaceful residential area just a short walk from the town centre. Bedrooms come in a variety of styles and sizes - all are pleasantly decorated and thoughtfully equipped. There is a choice of eating options with informal dining in the bar and a daily-changing menu offered in the elegant restaurant.

Rooms 18 en suite (2 fmly) ⊛ in 4 bedrooms S £68; D £89 (incl. bkfst) **Facilities** ♫ **Conf** BC Thtr 50 Class 30 Board 20 Del from £50 **Parking** 30 **Notes LB** ⑧ ⊛ in restaurant RS 25-26 Dec & 1 Jan Civ Wed

England

KING'S LYNN *continued*

★★ 65% **HOTEL**

Grange

Willow Park, South Wootton Ln PE30 3BP

☎ 01553 673777 & 671222 📠 01553 673777

e-mail: info@thegrangehotelkingslynn.co.uk

dir: *A148 towards King's Lynn for 1.5m. At traffic lights left into Wootton Rd, 400yds on right South Wootton Ln. Hotel 1st on left*

Expect a warm welcome at this Edwardian house, which is situated in a quiet residential area amid its own grounds. Public rooms include an entrance hall, smart lounge bar and a cosy restaurant. The spacious bedrooms are pleasantly decorated, with some located in an adjacent wing, and are equipped with many thoughtful touches.

Rooms 5 en suite 4 annexe en suite (2 fmly) (4 GF) ⊛ in 2 bedrooms **Facilities** Xmas **Conf** Thtr 20 Class 15 Board 12 **Parking** 15 **Notes** ⊛ in restaurant

BUDGET HOTEL

Premier Travel Inn King's Lynn

premier travel inn 🌙

Freebridge Farm PE34 3LJ

☎ 08701 977149 📠 01553 775827

web: www.premiertravelinn.com

dir: *junct of A47 & A17*

High quality, modern budget accommodation ideal for both families and business travellers. Spacious, en suite bedrooms feature bath and shower, satellite TV and many have telephones and modem points. The adjacent family restaurant features a wide and varied menu. For further details consult the Hotel Groups page.

Rooms 40 en suite

MUNDESLEY   MAP 13 TG33

★★ 74% **HOTEL**

Manor Hotel

Beach Rd NR11 8BG

☎ 01263 720309 📠 01263 721731

e-mail: manormundesley@aol.com

web: www.mundesleymanor.co.uk

dir: *B1150 Norwich-North Walsham, then follow coastal route & Mundesley signs*

An imposing Victorian property situated in an elevated position with superb views of the sea, that has been owned and run as a hotel by the same family for over 30 years. The spacious public rooms include a lounge bar, two further lounges, a conservatory, a traditional restaurant and the Bar Victoriana. Many of the smartly decorated bedrooms have lovely sea views.

Rooms 22 en suite 4 annexe en suite (3 fmly) (1 GF) ⊛ in 9 bedrooms S £50-£70; D £74-£90 (incl. bkfst) **Facilities** ⭥ Table Tennis, Pool table Xmas **Conf** Thtr 20 Class 20 Board 15 Del from £75 **Parking** 40 **Notes LB** ⊛ in restaurant Closed 2-18 Jan

NORTH WALSHAM   MAP 13 TG23

INSPECTORS' CHOICE

★★★ ⊛⊛ **HOTEL**

Beechwood Hotel

Cromer Rd NR28 0HD

☎ 01692 403231 📠 01692 407284

e-mail: enquiries@beechwood-hotel.co.uk

web: www.beechwood-hotel.co.uk

dir: *B1150 from Norwich. At North Walsham left at 1st lights, then right at next*

Expect a warm welcome at this elegant 18th-century house, situated just a short walk from the town centre. The individually styled bedrooms are tastefully furnished with well-chosen antique pieces, attractive co-ordinated soft fabrics and many thoughtful touches. The spacious public areas include a lounge bar with plush furnishings, a further lounge and a smartly appointed restaurant.

Rooms 17 en suite (4 GF) ⊛ in all bedrooms S £70; D £90-£160 (incl. bkfst) **Facilities** ⭲ **Conf** Thtr 20 Class 20 Board 20 **Parking** 20 **Notes LB** No children 10yrs ⊛ in restaurant

NORTHWOLD   MAP 13 TL79

★★ 71% **HOTEL**

Comfort Inn Thetford

Thetford Rd IP26 5LQ

☎ 01366 728888 📠 01366 727121

e-mail: enquiries@hotels-thetford.com

web: www.hotels-thetford.com

dir: *W of Mundford on A134*

A modern purpose-built hotel in a rural setting just off the main road. The generously proportioned bedrooms are situated in courtyard-style wings; each room is pleasantly decorated and well equipped. Dinner and breakfast are served in the beamed Woodland Inn, which combines the roles of country pub and hotel restaurant.

Rooms 34 en suite (12 fmly) (18 GF) ⊛ in 17 bedrooms **Facilities** STV **Conf** Thtr 150 Class 55 Board 60 **Parking** 250 **Notes LB** ⊛ in restaurant Civ Wed 95

NORWICH　　　　　　　MAP 13 TG20

★★★★ 78% ◉ HOTEL

Marriott Sprowston Manor Hotel & Country Club

Marriott HOTELS & RESORTS

Sprowston Park, Wroxham Rd, Sprowston NR7 8RP
☎ 01603 410871 🖹 01603 423911
e-mail: mhrs.nwigs.frontdesk@marriotthotels.com
web: www.marriott.co.uk/nwigs

dir: From A11/A47, 2m NE on A115 (Wroxham Rd). Follow signs to Sprowston Park

Surrounded by open parkland, this imposing property is set in attractively landscaped grounds and is just a short drive from the city centre. Bedrooms are spacious and feature a variety of decorative styles. The hotel also has extensive conference, banqueting and leisure facilities. Other public rooms include an array of seating areas and the elegant Manor Restaurant.

Rooms 94 en suite (3 fmly) (5 GF) ⊘ in 61 bedrooms S £115-£165; D £115-£230 **Facilities** Spa STV 🔲 supervised ♨ 18 Sauna Solarium Gym Putt green Jacuzzi Wi-fi in bedrooms Xmas **Conf** Thtr 500 Class 50 Board 50 Del from £160 **Services** Lift **Parking** 150 **Notes** ⊛ ⊘ in restaurant Civ Wed 300

★★★★ 77% ◉ HOTEL

De Vere Dunston Hall

De Vere HOTELS & RESORTS

Ipswich Rd NR14 8PQ
☎ 01508 470444 🖹 01508 471499
e-mail: dhreception@devere-hotels.com
web: www.devere.co.uk

dir: from A47, take A140 Ipswich road, hotel off road on left after 0.25m

Imposing Grade II listed building set amidst 170 acres of landscaped grounds just a short drive from the city centre. The spacious bedrooms are smartly decorated, tastefully furnished and equipped to a high standard. The attractively appointed public rooms offer a wide choice of areas in which to relax and the hotel also boasts a superb range of leisure facilities including an 18-hole PGA golf course, floodlit tennis courts and a football pitch.

Rooms 169 en suite (16 fmly) (16 GF) ⊘ in 151 bedrooms S £95-£135; D £125-£165 **Facilities** Spa STV 🔲 ♨ ♨ Snooker Sauna Solarium Gym Putt green Jacuzzi Wi-fi in bedrooms Floodlit driving range Xmas **Conf** Thtr 300 Class 140 Board 80 Del from £145 **Services** Lift **Parking** 500 **Notes LB** ⊛ ⊘ in restaurant Civ Wed 90

★★★ 83% ◉◉ HOTEL

Best Western Annesley House

Best Western

6 Newmarket Rd NR2 2LA
☎ 01603 624553 🖹 01603 621577
e-mail: annesleyhouse@bestwestern.co.uk

dir: on A11, 0.5m before city centre

Delightful Georgian property set in three acres of landscaped gardens close to the city centre. Bedrooms are split between three separate houses, two of which are linked by a glass walkway. Each one is attractively decorated, tastefully furnished and thoughtfully equipped. Public rooms include a comfortable lounge/bar and a smart conservatory restaurant, which overlooks the gardens.

Rooms 18 en suite 8 annexe en suite (3 fmly) (7 GF) ⊘ in 22 bedrooms S £60-£88; D £103-£118 (incl. bkfst) **Facilities** STV FTV Wi-fi in bedrooms **Conf** Thtr 16 Board 16 Del from £115 **Parking** 25 **Notes LB** ⊛ ⊘ in restaurant Closed 24-27 & 30-31 Dec

★★★ 81% ◉◉ HOTEL

Barnham Broom Hotel, Golf & Country Club

NR9 4DD
☎ 01603 759393 🖹 01603 758224
e-mail: enquiry@barnhambroomhotel.co.uk
web: www.barnham-broom.co.uk

(For full entry see Barnham Broom)

★★★ 75% ◉ HOTEL

Beeches Hotel & Victorian Gardens

THE INDEPENDENTS

2-6 Earlham Rd NR2 3DB
☎ 01603 621167 🖹 01603 620151
e-mail: reception@beeches.co.uk
web: www.mjbhotels.com

dir: W of city centre on B1108, next to St Johns Cathedral, off inner ring road

Ideally situated just a short walk from the city centre, and set amidst landscaped grounds that include a lovely sunken Victorian garden. The bedrooms are in three separate buildings; each one is tastefully decorated and equipped with many thoughtful touches. Public rooms include a smart lounge bar, a bistro-style restaurant and a residents' lounge.

Rooms 41 en suite (30 GF) ⊘ in all bedrooms S £74-£99; D £95-£140 (incl. bkfst) **Facilities** Xmas **Parking** 50 **Notes** ⊛ No children 12yrs ⊘ in restaurant

England

NORWICH *continued*

★★★ 73% HOTEL

Ramada Norwich
RAMADA
121-131 Boundary Rd NR3 2BA
☎ 01603 787260 🖨 01603 400466
e-mail: gm.norwich@ramadajarvis.co.uk
web: www.ramadajarvis.co.uk
dir: approx 2m from airport on A140 (Norwich ring road)

Purpose built hotel conveniently situated on the outer ring road close to the city centre. Bedrooms are pleasantly decorated and equipped with a good range of useful facilities. Public rooms include a large open-plan lounge bar and a smart restaurant. A range of meeting rooms as well as banqueting suites and leisure facilities are available.

Rooms 107 en suite (8 fmly) (22 GF) ⊗ in 75 bedrooms S £60-£109; D £70-£139 (incl. bkfst) **Facilities** STV 🏊 Sauna Gym Jacuzzi Xmas **Conf** Thtr 300 Class 150 Board 80 Del from £100 **Parking** 230 **Notes LB** ⊗ ⊘ in restaurant Civ Wed 400

★★★ 72% ◉ HOTEL

The Georgian House
THE INDEPENDENTS
32-34 Unthank Rd NR2 2RB
☎ 01603 615655 🖨 01603 765689
e-mail: reception@georgian-hotel.co.uk
dir: from city centre follow Roman Catholic Cathedral signs, hotel off inner ring road

Perfectly placed within easy walking distance of the historic city centre of Norwich. This independently owned hotel offers individually decorated bedrooms with many thoughtful touches. Public areas include a choice of lounges, a small bar and a smart restaurant serving an interesting choice of homemade dishes.

Rooms 27 en suite 1 annexe en suite (3 fmly) (10 GF) ⊗ in 23 bedrooms S £72.50-£105; D £91-£140 (incl. bkfst) **Facilities** FTV Wi-fi in bedrooms Xmas **Parking** 30 **Notes LB** ⊘ in restaurant

★★★ 70% ◉ HOTEL

Best Western George Hotel
Best Western
10 Arlington Ln, Newmarket Rd NR2 2DA
☎ 01603 617841 🖨 01603 663708
e-mail: reservations@georgehotel.co.uk
dir: on A11 follow city centre signs, Newmarket Rd towards centre. Hotel on left

Ideally situated just a few minutes' walk from the shops and well placed for guests wishing to explore the many sights of this historic city. The hotel occupies three adjacent buildings; the restaurant, bar

and most bedrooms are located in the main building, while the adjacent cottages have been converted into comfortable and modern guest bedrooms.

Rooms 38 en suite 5 annexe en suite (4 fmly) (19 GF) ⊗ in 12 bedrooms S £63-£77; D £87-£165 (incl. bkfst) **Facilities** Wi-fi in bedrooms Xmas **Conf** Thtr 70 Class 30 Board 30 Del from £99 **Parking** 40 **Notes LB** ⊗ ⊘ in restaurant

★★★ 70% HOTEL

Quality Hotel Norwich
QUALITY
2 Barnard Rd, Bowthorpe NR5 9JB
☎ 01603 741161 🖨 01603 741500
e-mail: enquiries@hotels-norwich.com
web: www.choicehotelseurope.com
dir: A1074 to Norwich & Cromer. Hotel off A47 southern bypass, 4m from city centre

Modern purpose built hotel situated on the west side of the city, four miles from the centre. The spacious bedrooms are pleasantly decorated and equipped with up-to-date facilities. Public areas include a carvery restaurant, bar and lounge. The hotel offers conference and banqueting facilities, as well as a leisure centre.

Rooms 80 en suite (13 fmly) (40 GF) ⊗ in 40 bedrooms S £60-£105; D £70-£115 **Facilities** STV 🏊 Sauna Solarium Gym Jacuzzi Wi-fi available Steamroom Xmas **Conf** Thtr 200 Class 80 Board 60 Del from £90 **Parking** 200 **Notes LB** ⊗ ⊘ in restaurant Civ Wed 75

★★★ 68% HOTEL

The Maids Head Hotel
folio Hotels
Tombland NR3 1LB
☎ 0870 609 6110 🖨 01603 613688
dir: follow city centre signs past Norwich Castle. 3rd turning after castle into Upper King St, hotel opposite Norman Cathedral

An imposing 13th-century building situated close to the impressive Norman cathedral, the Anglian TV studios and also within easy walking distance of the city centre. The bedrooms are pleasantly decorated and thoughtfully equipped; some rooms have original oak beams. The spacious public rooms include a Jacobean bar, a range of seating areas and the Courtyard restaurant.

Rooms 84 en suite (7 fmly) ⊗ in 52 bedrooms S £105-£110; D £105-£125 **Facilities** Wi-fi available Xmas **Conf** Thtr 150 Class 80 Board 40 **Services** Lift **Parking** 70 **Notes LB** ⊘ in restaurant Civ Wed 100

continued

★★ ◉◉ HOTEL

The Old Rectory

103 Yarmouth Rd, Thorpe St Andrew NR7 0HF

☎ 01603 700772 📠 01603 300772

e-mail: enquiries@oldrectorynorwich.com

web: www.oldrectorynorwich.com

dir: from A47 southern bypass onto A1042 towards Norwich N & E. Left at mini rdbt onto A1242. After 0.3m through lights. Hotel 100mtrs on right

This delightful Grade II listed Georgian property is ideally located in a peaceful area overlooking the River Yare, just a few minutes' drive from the city centre. Spacious bedrooms are individually designed with carefully chosen soft fabrics, plush furniture and many thoughtful touches; many of the rooms overlook the swimming pool and landscaped gardens. Accomplished cooking is offered via a interesting daily-changing menu, which features skilfully prepared local produce.

Rooms 5 en suite 3 annexe en suite ⊘ in all bedrooms S £78-£99; D £105-£135 (incl. bkfst) **Facilities** FTV ⛱ Wi-fi in bedrooms **Conf** Thtr 25 Class 18 Board 16 **Parking** 15 **Notes LB** ⊛ ⊘ in restaurant Closed 21 Dec-4 Jan

★★ 83% ◉ HOTEL

Stower Grange

School Rd, Drayton NR8 6EF

☎ 01603 860210 📠 01603 860464

e-mail: enquiries@stowergrange.co.uk

web: www.stowergrange.co.uk

dir: Norwich ring road N to Asda supermarket. Take A1067/ Fakenham Rd at Drayton village, right at traffic lights along School Rd. Hotel 150yds on right

Expect a warm welcome at this 17th-century, ivy-clad property situated
continued

in a peaceful residential area close to the city centre and airport. The individually decorated bedrooms are generally quite spacious; each one is tastefully furnished and equipped with many thoughtful touches. Public rooms include a smart open-plan lounge bar and an elegant restaurant.

Rooms 11 en suite (1 fmly) S £70-£90; D £90-£150 (incl. bkfst) **Facilities** ⛱ Wi-fi in bedrooms **Conf** Thtr 100 Class 45 Board 30 Del from £124.50 **Parking** 40 **Notes** ⊘ in restaurant Civ Wed 100

★★ 75% HOTEL

Wensum Valley Hotel Golf & Country Club

Beech Av, Taverham NR8 6HP

☎ 01603 261012 📠 01603 261664

e-mail: enqs@wensumvalley.co.uk

dir: Turn left off A1067 Norwich to Fakenham road at Taverham into Beech Avenue. Hotel entrance on right next to High School

Family-run hotel set amid 240 acres of lovely countryside just a short distance from the city centre and Norwich Airport. The modern, purpose-built bedrooms are generally spacious and thoughtfully equipped. Public rooms include a choice of bars, a lounge and a large restaurant overlooking the green. The hotel has superb golf and leisure facilities.

Rooms 84 en suite (12 fmly) (32 GF) ⊘ in all bedrooms **Facilities** ⛱ supervised ⌁ 36 Fishing Snooker Sauna Solarium Gym Putt green Jacuzzi Beauty therapy Golf driving range Hairdressing salon ♫ **Conf** Thtr 200 Board 30 **Parking** 250 **Notes LB** ⊛ ⊘ in restaurant Civ Wed 100

See advert on this page

England

NORWICH *continued*

★★ 74% HOTEL
The Old Rectory
North Walsham Rd, Crostwick NR12 7BG
☎ 01603 738513 📠 01603 738712
e-mail: Info@oldrectorycrostwick.com
web: www.oldrectorycrostwick.com
dir: left off Norwich ring road onto B1150. Hotel 4m on left

Attractive family-run hotel situated on the outskirts of Norwich city centre. Public rooms feature a superb hexagonal conservatory style dining room, which overlooks the pretty gardens, and guests have the use of a smart lounge as well as a cosy bar and private dining room. Bedrooms are attractively decorated and well equipped.

Rooms 13 en suite 4 annexe en suite (8 fmly) (17 GF) ❸ in 9 bedrooms S £50-£52; D £67.50-£70 (incl. bkfst) **Facilities** ᛘ Wi-fi in bedrooms **Conf** Thtr 110 Class 80 Board 50 **Parking** 100 **Notes** ❷ in restaurant Civ Wed 150

★★ 60% HOTEL
Cumberland
212-216 Thorpe Rd NR1 1TJ
☎ 01603 434550 📠 01603 433355
e-mail: cumberland@paston.co.uk
web: www.cumberlandhotel.com
dir: Hotel accessed from A47, then A1242 (past Norwich City FC)

This hotel is ideally situated just a short drive from the railway station and the historic city centre. Bedrooms styles vary, most are pleasantly decorated and thoughtfully equipped. Public areas include the Cape Dutch restaurant, a residents' lounge and a lounge bar.

Rooms 22 en suite 4 annexe en suite (3 fmly) (6 GF) ❸ in 10 bedrooms **Conf** Thtr 90 Class 30 Board 40 **Parking** 50 **Notes LB** ❽ ❷ in restaurant Closed 26-31 Dec

BUDGET HOTEL
Premier Travel Inn Norwich Airport
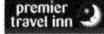
Holt Rd, Norwich Airport NR6 6JA
☎ 08701 977 291 📠 01603 428641
web: www.premiertravelinn.com
High quality, modern budget accommodation ideal for both families and business travellers. Spacious, en suite bedrooms feature bath and shower, satellite TV and many have telephones and modem points. The adjacent family restaurant features a wide and varied menu. For further details consult the Hotel Groups page.

Rooms 40 en suite

Premier Travel Inn Norwich City Centre
Duke St NR3 3AP
☎ 0870 9906632 📠 0870 9906633
dir: From A1047 right into St Benedicts Street. At lights into Duke Street. Inn on right
Rooms 117 en suite

Premier Travel Inn Norwich (Showground)
Longwater Interchange, Dereham Rd, New Costessey NR5 0TL
☎ 08701 977197 📠 01603 741219
dir: Follow brown tourist signs for Royal Norfolk Showground on A47 and A1074. Inn opposite showground and junctions A47 and A1074
Rooms 40 en suite

Premier Travel Inn Norwich South East
Broadland Business Park, Old Chapel Way NR7 0WG
☎ 08701 977198 📠 01603 307617
dir: A47 onto A1042, 3m E of city centre
Rooms 60 en suite **Conf** Thtr 20 Board 14

BUDGET HOTEL
Travelodge Norwich Central
Queens Rd NR1 2AA
web: www.travelodge.co.uk

Travelodge offers good quality, good value, modern accommodation. Ideal for families, the spacious en suite bedrooms include remote-control TV, tea and coffee-making facilities and comfortable beds. Meals can be taken at the nearby family restaurant. See Hotel Groups pages for further details.

Rooms S fr £26; D fr £26

Travelodge Norwich Cringleford
Thickthorn Service Area, Norwich Southern Bypass NR9 3AU
☎ 08700 850 950 📠 0870 191 1704
dir: at A11/A47 junct
Rooms 62 en suite S fr £26; D fr £26

REEPHAM   **MAP 13 TG12**

Ⓤ

Swallow Old Brewery
SWALLOW
Market Place NR10 4JJ
☎ 01603 870881 📠 01603 870969
web: www.swallowhotels.com
dir: off A1067 Norwich to Fakenham. Take B1145 signed Reepham

At the time of going to press, the star classification for this hotel was not confirmed. Please refer to the AA internet site www.theAA.com for current information.

Rooms 23 en suite

England

SHERINGHAM   MAP 13 TG14

★★★★ 77% ☺ HOTEL

Dales Country House Hotel

Lodge Hill, Upper Sheringham NR26 8TJ

☎ 01263 824555 📠 01263 822647

e-mail: dales@mackenziehotels.com

dir: on B1157 1m S of Sheringham, from A148 take turning at entrance to Sheringham Park continue for 0.5m hotel on left

Superb Grade II listed building situated in extensive landscaped grounds on the edge of Sheringham Park. The attractive public rooms are full of original character; they include a choice of lounges as well as an intimate restaurant and a cosy lounge bar. The spacious bedrooms are individually decorated, with co-ordinated soft furnishings and many thoughtful touches.

Rooms 17 en suite (2 GF) ❷ in all bedrooms S £82-£124; D fr £124 (incl. bkfst) **Facilities** ☕ ❤ Xmas **Conf** Thtr 40 Class 20 Board 27 **Services** Lift **Parking** 50 **Notes LB** ❷ No children 14yrs ❷ in restaurant

★★ 75% HOTEL

Beaumaris

South St NR26 8LL

☎ 01263 822370 📠 01263 821421

e-mail: beauhotel@aol.com

web: www.thebeaumarishotel.co.uk

dir: turn off A148, turn left at rdbt, 1st right over railway bridge, 1st left by church, 1st left into South St

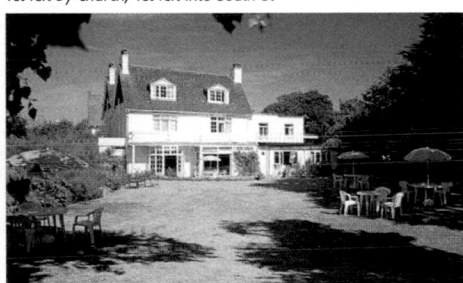

Situated in a peaceful side road a short walk from the beach, town centre and golf course. This friendly hotel has been owned and run by the same family for over 50 years and continues to provide comfortable, thoughtfully equipped accommodation throughout. Public rooms feature a smart dining room, a cosy bar and two quiet lounges.

Rooms 21 en suite (5 fmly) S £48-£55; D £96-£110 (incl. bkfst) **Facilities** ch fac **Parking** 25 **Notes LB** ❷ ❷ in restaurant Closed mid Dec-1 Mar

★★ 75% HOTEL

Roman Camp Inn

Holt Rd, Aylmerton NR11 8QD

☎ 01263 838291 📠 01263 837071

e-mail: romancampinn@lineone.net

web: www.romancampinn.co.uk

dir: on A148 between Sheringham and Cromer, approx 1.5m from Cromer

A smartly presented and well maintained hotel that is ideally placed for touring the north Norfolk coastline. The property provides

continued

spacious, pleasantly decorated bedrooms with a good range of useful facilities. Public rooms include a smart conservatory-style restaurant, a comfortable, open-plan lounge with an adjacent, smart bar and a dining area.

Rooms 15 en suite ❷ in 2 bedrooms S £54-£60; D £88-£100 (incl. bkfst) **Conf** Thtr 25 Class 6 Board 12 **Parking** 50 **Notes LB** ❷ ❷ in restaurant Closed 25-Dec

SNETTISHAM   MAP 12 TF63

★★ 76% ☺ HOTEL

Rose & Crown

Old Church Rd PE31 7LX

☎ 01485 541382 📠 01485 543172

e-mail: info@roseandcrownsnettisham.co.uk

web: www.roseandcrownsnettisham.co.uk

dir: A149 N from King's Lynn towards Hunstanton. Turn for Snettisham approx 10m. Into Old Church Rd. Hotel 100yds on left

This lovely village inn provides comfortable, well-equipped bedrooms. A range of quality meals is served in the many dining areas, complemented by a good variety of real ales and wines. Service is friendly and a delightful atmosphere prevails. A walled garden is available on sunny days, as is a children's play area.

Rooms 16 en suite (3 fmly) (2 GF) ❷ in all bedrooms S £60-£70; D £90-£100 (incl. bkfst) **Facilities** ☕ ❤ Wi-fi in bedrooms Xmas **Parking** 70 **Notes LB** ❷ in restaurant

SWAFFHAM   MAP 13 TF80

★★★ 72% HOTEL

Best Western George Hotel

Station Rd PE37 7LJ

☎ 01760 721238 📠 01760 725333

e-mail: georgehotel@bestwestern.co.uk

dir: exit A47 signed Swaffham. Hotel opposite St Peter & St Paul church

Georgian hotel situated in the heart of this bustling market town, which is ideally placed for touring north Norfolk. Bedrooms vary in size and style; each one is pleasantly decorated and well equipped. Public rooms include a cosy restaurant, a lounge and a busy bar where a range of drinks and snacks is available.

Rooms 29 en suite (1 fmly) ❷ in 20 bedrooms S fr £75; D fr £95 (incl. bkfst) **Facilities** STV **Conf** Thtr 150 Class 70 Board 70 Del from £95 **Parking** 100 **Notes LB** ❷ in restaurant

England

THETFORD

MAP 13 TL88

See also Brandon (Suffolk)

★★★ 66% **HOTEL**

Bell

OLD ENGLISH INNS

King St IP24 2AZ

☎ 01842 754455 ▤ 01842 755552

e-mail: bell.thetford@oldenglishinns.co.uk

web: www.oldenglish.co.uk

dir: From S exit A11 2m to 1st set of lights, turn right onto A134. 100yds turn left into Bridge St, 150yds & over bridge

Historic 15th-century coaching inn situated in the heart of the old part of town. The historic charm permeates through much of the building and the oak beamed bar is full of character. The accommodation is split between the main building and the more modern bedroom wings. Public areas include a restaurant and conference facilities.

Rooms 46 en suite (1 fmly) ⊗ in 24 bedrooms S £45-£75; D £65-£90 (incl. bkfst) **Facilities** Xmas **Conf** BC Thtr 70 Class 45 Board 40 Del from £100 **Parking** 55 **Notes LB** ⊗ in restaurant

★★ 69% **HOTEL**

The Thomas Paine Hotel

THE INDEPENDENTS

White Hart St IP24 1AA

☎ 01842 755631 ▤ 01842 766505

e-mail: bookings@thomaspainehotel.com

dir: N'bound on A11, at rdbt immediately before Thetford take A1075, hotel on right on approach to town

This Grade II listed building is situated close to the town centre and Thetford Forest Park is just a short drive away. Public rooms include a large lounge bar, a pleasantly appointed restaurant and a meeting room. Bedrooms vary in size and style; each one is attractively decorated and thoughtfully equipped.

Rooms 13 en suite (2 fmly) ⊗ in 5 bedrooms S £50-£55; D £66-£70 (incl. bkfst) **Facilities** Xmas **Conf** Thtr 70 Class 35 Board 30 **Parking** 30 **Notes LB** ⊗ in restaurant

THORNHAM

MAP 12 TF74

★★ 74% ⊛ **HOTEL**

Lifeboat Inn

Ship Ln PE36 6LT

☎ 01485 512236 ▤ 01485 512323

e-mail: reception@lifeboatinn.co.uk

web: www.lifeboatinn.co.uk

dir: follow coast road from Hunstanton A149 for approx 6m and take 1st left after Thornham sign

This popular 16th-century smugglers' alehouse enjoys superb views across open meadows to Thornham Harbour. The tastefully decorated bedrooms are furnished with pine pieces and have many thoughtful touches. The public rooms have a wealth of character and feature open fireplaces, exposed brickwork and oak beams.

Rooms 13 en suite (3 fmly) (1 GF) ⊗ in all bedrooms S £45-£68; D £96-£116 (incl. bkfst) **Facilities** Xmas **Conf** Thtr 50 Class 30 Board 30 **Parking** 120 **Notes LB** ⊗ in restaurant

TITCHWELL

MAP 13 TF74

★★ 80% ⊛⊛ **HOTEL**

Titchwell Manor

PE31 8BB

☎ 01485 210221 ▤ 01485 210104

e-mail: margaret@titchwellmanor.com

web: www.titchwellmanor.com

dir: on A149 coast road between Brancaster and Thornham

A friendly, family-run hotel ideally placed for touring the north Norfolk coastline. Bedrooms are comfortably appointed - some in the adjacent annexe have ground-floor access. Smart public rooms include a lounge area, a relaxed informal bar and a delightful conservatory restaurant overlooking the walled garden. Imaginative menus feature quality local produce and fresh fish.

Rooms 8 en suite 16 annexe en suite (4 fmly) (16 GF) ⊗ in all bedrooms S £65-£95; D £130-£160 (incl. bkfst) **Facilities** Wi-fi in bedrooms Xmas **Parking** 50 **Notes LB** ⊗ in restaurant

WATTON

MAP 13 TF90

★★★ Ⓐ

Broom Hall Country Hotel

Richmond Rd, Saham Toney IP25 7EX

☎ 01953 882125 ▤ 01953 885325

e-mail: enquiries@broomhallhotel.co.uk

web: www.broomhallhotel.co.uk

dir: exit A11 at Thetford onto A1075 to Watton (12m), B1108 towards Swaffham, in 0.5m at rdbt turn right to Saham Toney, hotel 0.5m on left

Rooms 10 en suite 5 annexe en suite (3 fmly) (5 GF) ⊗ in all bedrooms S £65-£80; D £85-£160 (incl. bkfst) **Facilities** Ⓣ **Conf** Thtr 50 Class 30 Board 22 Del from £80 **Parking** 30 **Notes LB** ⊗ in restaurant Closed 24 Dec-4 Jan

WROXHAM

MAP 13 TG31

★★ 69% **HOTEL**

Hotel Wroxham

The Bridge NR12 8AJ

☎ 01603 782061 ▤ 01603 784279

e-mail: reservations@hotelwroxham.co.uk

web: www.hotelwroxham.co.uk

dir: From Norwich, A1151 signed Wroxham & The Broads for approx 7m. Over bridge at Wroxham take 1st right, & sharp right again. Hotel car park on right

Perfectly placed for touring the Norfolk Broads in the heart of this

continued

bustling town centre. The bedrooms are pleasantly decorated and well equipped; some rooms have balconies with lovely views of the busy waterways. The open-plan public rooms include the lively riverside bar, a lounge, a large sun terrace and a smart restaurant.

Rooms 18 en suite **Facilities** Fishing Boating facilities (by arrangement) ♫ **Conf** Thtr 200 Class 50 Board 20 **Parking** 45 **Notes** ⊗ ⊘ in restaurant

★★ 67% HOTEL

Kings Head
Station Rd NR12 8UR
☎ 01603 782429 🖩 01603 784622
dir: in centre of village

Situated in the heart of a very busy town on the edge of the Norfolk Broads. This hotel has spacious public rooms leading out onto the river frontage and gardens. There is a popular carvery restaurant and a conservatory that overlooks the busy waterways. The well-equipped bedrooms are smartly furnished and pleasantly decorated.

Rooms 8 en suite (2 fmly) ⊘ in all bedrooms **Facilities** Fishing **Parking** 45 **Notes** ⊗ ⊘ in restaurant

WYMONDHAM   MAP 13 TG10

★★★ 72% HOTEL

Abbey
10 Church St NR18 0PH
☎ 01953 602148 🖩 01953 606247
e-mail: abbey@mjbhotels.com
web: www.mjbhotels.com

dir: from A11 follow Wymondham sign. At lights left and 1st left into one-way system. Left into Church Street

Charming 16th-century hotel situated close to the abbey just off the high street of this delightful market town. The spacious bedrooms are pleasantly decorated, tastefully furnished and thoughtfully equipped; five superior rooms are available. Public rooms include a cosy lounge bar, the Benims restaurant and a further sitting room.

Rooms 27 en suite 1 annexe en suite (3 fmly) (6 GF) ⊘ in all bedrooms S fr £55; D £75-£85 (incl. bkfst) **Facilities** STV Xmas **Services** Lift **Parking** 3 **Notes LB** ⊗ ⊘ in restaurant

★★ 79% HOTEL

Best Western Wymondham Consort
28 Market St NR18 0BB
☎ 01953 606721 🖩 01953 601361
e-mail: wymondham@bestwestern.co.uk
dir: off A11 (M11), left at lights and left again

Privately-owned hotel situated in the centre of this bustling market town. The individually decorated bedrooms come in a variety of sizes; each one is pleasantly decorated and thoughtfully equipped. Public rooms include a cosy bar, a separate lounge, the Rendezvous wine bar and an intimate restaurant, which overlooks the busy high street.

Rooms 20 en suite (1 fmly) (3 GF) ⊘ in all bedrooms S £60-£85; D £75-£90 (incl. bkfst) **Conf** Thtr 20 Board 20 **Parking** 16 **Notes LB** ⊘ in restaurant

NORTHAMPTONSHIRE

CASTLE ASHBY   MAP 11 SP85

★★ 69% ⊛ HOTEL

Falcon
OLD ENGLISH INNS
NN7 1LF
☎ 01604 696200 🖩 01604 696673
e-mail: falcon.castleashby@oldenglishinns.co.uk
web: www.oldenglish.co.uk
dir: off A428

Set in the heart of a peaceful village, this family-run hotel consists of a main house and two neighbouring cottages. Bedrooms are individually decorated and provide a wealth of thoughtful extras. Character public rooms, in the main house, include a first-floor sitting area, a choice of bars and a pretty restaurant serving good quality cuisine.

Rooms 5 en suite 11 annexe en suite (1 fmly) ⊘ in 3 bedrooms **Facilities** STV **Conf** Thtr 50 Class 30 Board 25 **Parking** 75 **Notes LB** Civ Wed 60

CRICK — MAP 11 SP57

BUDGET HOTEL

Hotel Ibis Rugby East

Parklands NN6 7EX
☎ 01788 824331 📠 01788 824332
e-mail: H3588@accor-hotels.com
web: www.ibishotel.com

dir: M1 junct 18 follow Daventry/Rugby A5 signs. At rdbt 3rd exit signed DIRFT East. Hotel on right

Modern, budget hotel offering comfortable accommodation in bright and practical bedrooms. Breakfast is self-service and dinner is available in the restaurant. For further details, consult the Hotel Groups page.

Rooms 111 en suite S £39.95-£48.95; D £39.95-£48.95 **Conf** BC Thtr 40 Class 25 Board 25 Del from £85

DAVENTRY — MAP 11 SP56

INSPECTORS' CHOICE

★★★★ ◉◉◉ **HOTEL**

Fawsley Hall

Fawsley NN11 3BA
☎ 01327 892000 📠 01327 892001
e-mail: reservations@fawsleyhall.com
web: www.fawsleyhall.com

dir: From A361 turn at 'Fawsley Hall' sign. Follow single track for 1.5m until reaching iron gates

Dating back to the 15th century, this delightful hotel is peacefully located in beautiful gardens designed by 'Capability' Brown. Spacious, individually designed bedrooms and stylish public areas are beautifully furnished with antique and period pieces. Afternoon tea is served in the impressive Great Hall with its sumptuous deep cushioned sofas and real fires. Dinner in Knightly Restaurant offers imaginative cuisine with Mediterranean influences.

Rooms 29 en suite 1 annexe en suite (6 GF) ⊗ in all bedrooms **Facilities Spa** STV FTV ♨ Sauna Gym ⛳ Putt green Jacuzzi Wi-fi in bedrooms Health & Beauty treatment rooms **Conf** Thtr 100 Class 45 Board 45 Del from £135 **Parking** 144 **Notes** ⊗ in restaurant Civ Wed 100

★★★★ 69% **HOTEL**

The Daventry Hotel

PARAMOUNT
GROUP OF HOTELS

Sedgemoor Way NN11 0SG
☎ 01327 307000 📠 01327 706313
e-mail: daventry@paramount-hotels.co.uk
web: www.paramount-hotels.co.uk

dir: M1 junct 16/A45 to Daventry at first rdbt turn right to Kilsby/M1(N). Hotel on right after 1m

This modern, striking hotel overlooking Drayton Water boasts spacious public areas that include a good range of banqueting, meeting and leisure facilities. It is a popular venue for conferences. Bedrooms all have double beds and excellent showers.

Rooms 138 en suite ⊗ in 100 bedrooms S £80-£130; D £110-£155 **Facilities Spa** STV 📶 supervised Sauna Solarium Gym Jacuzzi Wi-fi available Steam room Health & beauty salon Xmas **Conf** BC Thtr 600 Class 200 Board 30 Del from £140 **Services** Lift **Parking** 350 **Notes LB** ⊗ ⊗ in restaurant Civ Wed 250

ECTON — MAP 11 SP86

Ⓤ

The World's End

Main St NN6 0QN
☎ 01604 414521 📠 01604 400334
e-mail: info@theworldsend.org.uk

dir: on A4500 on outskirts of Ecton. Exit A45 for Cogenhoe/Gt Billing, follow signs for Ecton

At the time of going to press, the star classification for this hotel was not confirmed. Please refer to the AA internet site www.theAA.com for current information.

Rooms 20 en suite (9 GF) ⊗ in all bedrooms S £40-£95; D £40-£95 (incl. bkfst) **Facilities** Xmas **Conf** Thtr 35 Class 16 Board 16 Del £119.95 **Services** Lift **Parking** 50 **Notes** ⊗ ⊗ in restaurant

FINEDON — MAP 11 SP97

Ⓤ

Swallow Tudor Gate

SWALLOW
HOTELS

35 High St NN9 5JN
☎ 01933 680408 📠 01933 680754
e-mail: tudorgate@swallowinns.co.uk
web: www.swallowhotels.com

At the time of going to press, the star classification for this hotel was not confirmed. Please refer to the AA internet site www.theAA.com for current information.

Rooms 26 en suite (2 fmly) (5 GF) ⊗ in 7 bedrooms S £45-£55; D £55-£75 (incl. bkfst) **Facilities** ♫ Xmas **Conf** Thtr 60 Class 50 Board 40 Del from £110 **Parking** 50 **Notes LB** ⊗ in restaurant

FLORE
MAP 11 SP66

★★★ 75% **HOTEL**

Courtyard by Marriott Daventry

High St NN7 4LP

☎ 01327 349022 🖹 01327 349017

e-mail: res.ntwcourtyard@kewgreen.co.uk

web: www.kewgreen.co.uk

dir: M1 junct 16 onto A45 towards Daventry. Hotel 1m on right between Upper Heyford and Flore

Just off the M1 in rural surroundings, this modern hotel is particularly suited to the business guest. Professional staff offer a warm welcome and provide helpful service throughout. The public areas comprise a lounge bar and restaurant, and the bedrooms have smart decor, plenty of workspace and a good range of facilities.

Rooms 53 en suite (7 fmly) ⊗ in 34 bedrooms S £42-£85; D £42-£85 **Facilities** STV Gym Beauty treatments Xmas **Conf** Thtr 80 Class 40 Board 40 **Parking** 120 **Notes LB** ⊗ ⊗ in restaurant Civ Wed 100

HELLIDON
MAP 11 SP55

★★★★ 78% ⊛ **HOTEL**

Hellidon Lakes

NN11 6GG

☎ 01327 262550 🖹 01327 262559

e-mail: hellidon@marstonhotels.com

web: www.marstonhotels.com

dir: off A361 between Daventry and Banbury, signed

Some 220 acres of beautiful countryside, which include 27 holes of golf and 12 lakes, combine to form a rather spectacular backdrop to this impressive hotel. Bedroom styles vary, from ultra smart, modern rooms through to those in the original wing that offer superb views. There is an extensive range of facilities available from meeting rooms

continued

---

to swimming pool, gym and ten-pin bowling - golfers of all levels can try some of the world's most challenging courses on the indoor golf simulator.

Rooms 110 en suite ⊗ in 72 bedrooms S fr £132.50; D fr £171 (incl. bkfst) **Facilities Spa** STV ⊗ ♨ 27 ♨ Solarium Gym Putt green Wi-fi available Beauty therapist, Indoor smartgolf, 10 pin bowling, Steam room Xmas **Conf** Thtr 300 Class 150 Board 80 Del from £210 **Services** Lift **Parking** 150 **Notes LB** ⊗ ⊗ in restaurant Civ Wed 220

See advert on this page & page 525

HORTON
MAP 11 SP85

★★ 85% ⊛⊛ **HOTEL**

The New French Partridge

Newport Pagnell Rd NN7 2AP

☎ 01604 870033 🖹 01604 870032

e-mail: info@newfrenchpartridge.co.uk

web: www.newfrenchpartridge.co.uk

dir: On B526 Newport Pagnell road, 0.5m from Northampton & Milton Keynes

Set in private grounds within the rural village of Horton, a short drive from Northampton, this unique and historic manor house offers superb accommodation and good food. Individually appointed bedrooms are attractively presented and extremely well equipped, well suited to both corporate and leisure guests. Accomplished cooking is served in the restaurant, whilst the friendly team provide

continued on page 504

England

HORTON *continued*

attentive service. The day rooms which include small lounge areas and a character cellar bar.

The New French Partridge

Rooms 10 en suite ⊘ in all bedrooms S £140-£250; D £140-£250 (incl. bkfst) **Facilities** Xmas **Conf** Thtr 50 Class 40 Board 25 **Parking** 30 **Notes LB** ⊘ in restaurant Civ Wed 70

KETTERING   MAP 11 SP87

★★★★ 79% ⊛ **HOTEL**

Kettering Park

Kettering Parkway NN15 6XT

SHIRE HOTELS

☎ 01536 416666 📠 01536 416171

e-mail: kpark@shirehotels.com

web: www.shirehotels.com

dir: *off A14 junct 9 (M1 to A1 link road), hotel on Kettering Venture Park*

Expect a warm welcome at this stylish hotel situated just off the A14. The spacious, smartly decorated bedrooms are well equipped and meticulously maintained. Guests can choose from classical or contemporary dishes in the restaurant and lighter meals are served in the bar. The extensive leisure facilities are impressive and the Conference Café is a useful addition.

Rooms 119 en suite (29 fmly) (35 GF) ⊘ in 101 bedrooms S £93-£154; D £136-£179 (incl. bkfst) **Facilities** STV 🔖 Sauna Solarium Gym Jacuzzi Wi-fi in bedrooms Steam rooms, Childrens splash pool, Activity studio Xmas **Conf** BC Thtr 260 Class 120 Board 40 Del £189 **Services** Lift air con **Parking** 200 **Notes LB** ⊗ ⊘ in restaurant Civ Wed 120

Rushton Hall

Rushton Hall, Rushton NN14 1RR

☎ 01536 713001 📠 01536 713010

e-mail: enquiries@rushtonhall.com

dir: *Exit A14 junct 7. A43 to Corby then A6003 until Rushton turn off after bridge*

At the time of going to press, the star classification for this hotel was not confirmed. Please refer to the AA internet site www.theAA.com for current information.

continued

Rushton Hall

Rooms 30 en suite (4 fmly) (3 GF) ⊘ in all bedrooms S £100-£180; D £120-£250 (incl. bkfst) **Facilities Spa** STV 🔖 ⊰ supervised ⊰ Fishing Snooker Sauna Solarium Gym ⊰ Jacuzzi Xmas **Conf** Thtr 675 Class 500 Board 320 Del from £160 **Services** Lift **Parking** 140 **Notes LB** ⊗ ⊘ in restaurant Civ Wed 300

See advert on opposite page

BUDGET HOTEL

Premier Travel Inn Kettering

premier travel inn 🌙

Rothwell Rd NN16 8XF

☎ 08701 977147 📠 01536 415020

web: www.premiertravelinn.com

dir: *on A14, off junct 7*

High quality, modern budget accommodation ideal for both families and business travellers. Spacious, en suite bedrooms feature bath and shower, satellite TV and many have telephones and modem points. The adjacent family restaurant features a wide and varied menu. For further details consult the Hotel Groups page.

Rooms 39 en suite **Conf** Thtr 15

BUDGET HOTEL

Travelodge Kettering

Travelodge

On the A14 (Westbound) NN14 1RW

☎ 08700 850 950

web: www.travelodge.co.uk

dir: *M6 junct 1 or M1 junct 19, take A14, 0.5m past A43 junct*

Travelodge offers good quality, good value, modern accommodation. Ideal for families, the spacious en suite bedrooms include remote-control TV, tea and coffee-making facilities and comfortable beds. Meals can be taken at the nearby family restaurant. See Hotel Groups pages for further details.

Rooms 40 en suite S fr £26; D fr £26

MARSTON TRUSSELL   MAP 11 SP68

★★ 74% **HOTEL**

The Sun Inn

Main St LE16 9TY

☎ 01858 465531 📠 01858 433155

e-mail: manager@suninn.com

dir: *M1 junct 20 take A4304, right into Marston Trussell*

This pleasant inn successfully combines a mixture of modern facilities and accommodation with the classical traditions of the rural English inn. Bedrooms are comfortably furnished and tastefully appointed and offer a host of thoughtful facilities. Public areas consist of two elegant

continued

dining areas and a bar with open log fires. Service is both friendly and attentive.

The Sun Inn

Rooms 20 en suite (1 fmly) (10 GF) ⊛ in 10 bedrooms **Facilities** Rambling trails **Conf** BC Thtr 60 Class 40 Board 28 **Parking** 60 **Notes LB** ⋒

NORTHAMPTON   MAP 11 SP76
See also Flore

★★★★ 73% **HOTEL**

Northampton Marriott Hotel   **Marriott.**
HOTELS & RESORTS

Eagle Dr NN4 7HW
☎ 01604 768700 🗎 01604 769011
e-mail: northampton@marriotthotels.com
web: www.marriott.co.uk

dir: M1 junct 15, follow signs to Delapre Golf Course, hotel on right

Located on the outskirts of town, close to major road networks, this modern hotel caters to a cross section of guests. A self-contained management centre makes this a popular conference venue, and its spacious and well-designed bedrooms cater for business travellers particularly well. The hotel's proximity to a number of attractions makes this a good base to explore the area.

Rooms 120 en suite (10 fmly) (52 GF) ⊛ in 82 bedrooms S £69-£135; D £78-£145 (incl. bkfst) **Facilities Spa** STV ⬜ supervised Sauna Solarium Gym Jacuzzi Wi-fi available Steam room, beauty treatment room Xmas **Conf** BC Thtr 250 Class 72 Board 30 Del from £140 **Services** air con **Parking** 200 **Notes LB** ⊗ ⊛ in restaurant Civ Wed 180

★★★ 71% **HOTEL**

Best Western Lime Trees
Best Western

8 Langham Place, Barrack Rd NN2 6AA
☎ 01604 632188 🗎 01604 233012
e-mail: info@limetreeshotel.co.uk
web: www.limetreeshotel.co.uk

dir: from city centre 0.5m N on A508 towards Market Harborough, near racecourse park and cathedral

This well-presented hotel is popular with business travellers during the week and leisure guests at the weekend. Service is both efficient and friendly. Bedrooms are comfortable and in addition to all the usual facilities, many offer air conditioning. Notable features include an internal courtyard, and a row of charming mews houses that have been converted into bedrooms.

Rooms 20 en suite 8 annexe en suite (4 fmly) (5 GF) ⊛ in 19 bedrooms S £42-£105; D £50-£160 (incl. bkfst) **Facilities** Wi-fi in bedrooms Xmas **Conf** Thtr 110 Class 80 Board 86 Del from £89 **Parking** 25 **Notes LB** ⊛ in restaurant Civ Wed 100

★★★ 71% **HOTEL**

Courtyard by Marriott Northampton

COURTYARD
Marriott

Bedford Rd NN4 7YF
☎ 0870 400 7214 🗎 0870 400 7314
e-mail: res.ntncourtyard@kewgreen.co.uk
web: www.kewgreen.co.uk

dir: M1 junct 15 onto A508 towards Northampton. Follow A45 towards Wellingborough for 2m then A428 towards Bedford, hotel on left

With its convenient location on the eastern edge of town and easy access to transport links, this modern hotel is particularly popular with business travellers. Accommodation is spacious, smartly refurbished, and a good range of accessories is provided. The re-styled

continued on page 506

England

NORTHAMPTON *continued*

contemporary, open-plan public areas help to create an informal atmosphere, and the staff are genuinely friendly.

Rooms 104 en suite (50 fmly) (27 GF) ⊘ in 91 bedrooms S £65–£120; D £75–£120 (incl. bkfst) **Facilities** STV Gym Wi-fi available Xmas **Conf** Thtr 60 Class 40 Board 40 Del from £120 **Services** Lift air con **Parking** 156 **Notes LB** ⊛ ⊘ in restaurant

★★★ 66% HOTEL

Quality Hotel Northampton

Ashley Way, Weston Favell NN3 3EA
☎ 01604 739955 🗎 01604 415023
e-mail: enquiries@hotels-northampton.com
web: www.choicehotelseurope.com

dir: leave A45 at junct with A43 towards Weston Favell. Take 3rd exit, signed A4500. then 1st right

On the edge of town, this hotel offers well-equipped accommodation in an older-style building and a more modern block. Public rooms are attractive and include an air-conditioned lounge area, an attractively furnished flag-stoned conservatory restaurant and a number of versatile meeting rooms.

Rooms 33 en suite 38 annexe en suite (5 fmly) (19 GF) ⊘ in 45 bedrooms **Facilities** STV Wi-fi available Xmas **Conf** Thtr 140 Class 40 Board 50 Del from £115 **Notes** ⊘ in restaurant Civ Wed 140

BUDGET HOTEL

Hotel Ibis Northampton

Sol Central, Marefair NN1 1SR
☎ 01604 608900 🗎 01604 608910
e-mail: H3657@accor-hotels.com
web: www.ibishotel.com

dir: M1 junct 15/15a & city centre towards railway station

Modern, budget hotel offering comfortable accommodation in bright and practical bedrooms. Breakfast is self-service and dinner is available in the restaurant. For further details, consult the Hotel Groups page.

Rooms 151 en suite

BUDGET HOTEL

Innkeeper's Lodge Northampton East

Talavera Way, Round Spinney NN3 8RN
☎ 01604 494241 🗎 01604 673701
web: www.innkeeperslodge.com

dir: M1 junct 15a, N on A43. Right at rdbt, pass 2 further rdbts. At 3rd rdbt, A45 N until exit for A43, continue to Round Spinney rdbt and Talavera Way

Smart, en suite accommodation ideal for both business & leisure guests. Bedrooms are very well equipped, including Sky TV, telephone, modem points, tea & coffee making facilities, (family rooms in most locations). Complimentary breakfast. The adjacent Pub Restaurant; a Harvester, Vintage Inn, Toby Carvery, Ember Inn, Sizzling Pubco or Pub & Carvery offers an all day menu. See Hotel Groups pages for further details.

Rooms 31 en suite **Conf** Thtr 36 Class 24 Board 28

Innkeeper's Lodge Northampton M1 Jct 15

London Rd, Wootton NN4 0TG
☎ 01604 769676 🗎 01604 677981

dir: M1 junct 15 take A508, towards Northampton. Pass under flyover, exit left immediately & turn right at rdbt into London Rd. Lodge on right.

Rooms 51 en suite **Conf** Thtr 100 Board 40

BUDGET HOTEL

Premier Travel Inn Northampton East (Great Billing/A45)

Crow Ln, Great Billing NN3 9DA
☎ 0870 9906510 🗎 0870 9906511
web: www.premiertravelinn.com

dir: 5m from M1 junct 15. A508 to A45 then follow Billing Aquadrom signs

High quality, modern budget accommodation ideal for both families and business travellers. Spacious, en suite bedrooms feature bath and shower, satellite TV and many have telephones and modem points. The adjacent family restaurant features a wide and varied menu. For further details consult the Hotel Groups page.

Rooms 60 en suite **Conf** Thtr 10 Board 10

Premier Travel Inn Northampton East (Haughton/A428)

The Lakes, Bedford Rd NN4 7YD
☎ 08701 977196 🗎 01604 621935

dir: M1 junct 15 follow A508 (A45) to Northampton. Take A428 exit at rdbt take 4th exit (signed Bedford). Left at next rdbt for Inn on right

Rooms 44 en suite

Premier Travel Inn Northampton South

Newport Pagnell Rd West, Wootton NN4 7JJ
☎ 0870 9906426 🗎 0870 9906427

dir: Exit M1 junct 15 onto A508 towards Northampton. Exit at junct with A45. At rdbt take B526. Inn on B526 on right

Rooms 39 en suite **Conf** Thtr 75 Class 48 Board 30

Premier Travel Inn Northampton West (Harpole)

Harpole Turn, Weedon Rd, Harpole NN7 4DD
☎ 08701 977195 🗎 01604 831807

dir: From M1 junct 16, take A45 to Northampton. After 1 mile turn left into Harpole Turn. Inn is on the left

Rooms 51 en suite **Conf** Thtr 40 Board 30

BUDGET HOTEL

Travelodge Northampton Upton Way

Upton Way NN5 6EG
☎ 08700 850 950 🗎 01604 758395
web: www.travelodge.co.uk

dir: A45, towards M1 junct 16

Travelodge offers good quality, good value, modern accommodation. Ideal for families, the spacious en suite bedrooms include remote-

continued

control TV, tea and coffee-making facilities and comfortable beds. Meals can be taken at the nearby family restaurant. See Hotel Groups pages for further details.

Rooms 62 en suite S fr £26; D fr £26

OUNDLE — MAP 11 TL08

★★ 67% HOTEL

Talbot

New St PE8 4EA

☎ 01832 273621 ▤ 01832 274545

e-mail: talbot.oundle@oldenglishinns.co.uk

web: www.oldenglish.co.uk

dir: A1(M) junct 17 take A605. At 3rd rdbt turn right signed Oundle A427. Hotel in town centre

This historic hotel, situated in the centre of the town, dates back to the 16th century. Bedrooms, some of which surround a secluded garden, are soundly furnished and well equipped. Public areas, with beams and open fires, portray the character of the Elizabethan period.

Rooms 35 en suite (3 fmly) (11 GF) ✆ in 12 bedrooms S £75-£125; D £95 £145 (incl. bkfst) **Facilities** Xmas **Conf** Thtr 200 Class 70 Board 100 Del from £115 **Parking** 25 **Notes LB** ❀ ✆ in restaurant Civ Wed 60

RUSHDEN — MAP 11 SP96

BUDGET HOTEL

Travelodge Wellingborough Rushden

Saunders Lodge NN10 6AP

☎ 08700 850 950 ▤ 01933 57008

web: www.travelodge.co.uk

dir: on A45, eastbound

Travelodge offers good quality, good value, modern accommodation. Ideal for families, the spacious en suite bedrooms include remote control TV, tea and coffee-making facilities and comfortable beds. Meals can be taken at the nearby family restaurant. See Hotel Groups pages for further details.

Rooms 40 en suite S fr £26; D fr £26

SILVERSTONE — MAP 11 SP64

BUDGET HOTEL

Premier Travel Inn Silverstone

Brackley Hatch, Syresham NN13 5TX

☎ 0870 9906382 ▤ 0870 9906383

web: www.premiertravelinn.com

dir: On A43 near Silverstone.

High quality, modern budget accommodation ideal for both families and business travellers. Spacious, en suite bedrooms feature bath and shower, satellite TV and many have telephones and modem points. The adjacent family restaurant features a wide and varied menu. For further details consult the Hotel Groups page.

Rooms 41 en suite

THRAPSTON — MAP 11 SP97

BUDGET HOTEL

Travelodge Kettering Thrapston

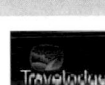

Thrapston Bypass NN14 4UR

☎ 08700 850 950 ▤ 01832 735199

web: www.travelodge.co.uk

dir: on A14 link road A1/M1

Travelodge offers good quality, good value, modern accommodation. Ideal for families, the spacious en suite bedrooms include remote-control TV, tea and coffee-making facilities and comfortable beds. Meals can be taken at the nearby family restaurant. See Hotel Groups pages for further details.

Rooms 40 en suite S fr £26; D fr £26

TOWCESTER — MAP 11 SP64

★★ 68% HOTEL

Saracens Head

219 Watling St NN12 7BX

☎ 01327 350414 ▤ 01327 359879

e-mail: saracenshead.towcester@greeneking.co.uk

web: www.oldenglish.co.uk

dir: A5 to Towcester. Follow signs into town centre

This historic coaching inn, rumoured to be the inspiration for *Pickwick Papers* by Charles Dickens, has been extensively modernised throughout with smart bedrooms, a convivial bar and restaurant. Staff are young and friendly, and the hotel provides an excellent base for horse-racing enthusiasts visiting the Towcester course and for motor racing fans heading for Silverstone.

Rooms 21 en suite (3 fmly) ✆ in all bedrooms S £70-£80; D £80-£95 (incl. bkfst) **Facilities** ♬ Xmas **Conf** Thtr 80 Class 50 Board 50 Del £95 **Parking** 20 **Notes LB** ❀ ✆ in restaurant RS 25 Dec Civ Wed 90

BUDGET HOTEL

Travelodge Towcester Silverstone

NN12 6TQ

☎ 08700 850 950 ▤ 01327 359105

web: www.travelodge.co.uk

dir: A43 East Towcester by-pass

Travelodge offers good quality, good value, modern accommodation. Ideal for families, the spacious en suite bedrooms include remote-control TV, tea and coffee-making facilities and comfortable beds. Meals can be taken at the nearby family restaurant. See Hotel Groups pages for further details.

Rooms 55 en suite S fr £26; D fr £26

England

England

WATFORD GAP MOTORWAY SERVICE AREA (M1)
MAP 11 SP66

BUDGET HOTEL

Premier Travel Inn Daventry (Watford Gap)

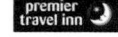

NN6 7UZ

☎ 08701 977301 🖨 01327 871333

web: www.premiertravelinn.com

dir: M1 southbound between junct 16/17. (Access from northbound via barrier access)

High quality, modern budget accommodation ideal for both families and business travellers. Spacious, en suite bedrooms feature bath and shower, satellite TV and many have telephones and modem points. The adjacent family restaurant features a wide and varied menu. For further details consult the Hotel Groups page.

Rooms 36 en suite

WEEDON
MAP 11 SP64

BUDGET HOTEL

Premier Travel Inn Daventry

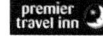

High St NN7 4PX

☎ 0870 9906364 🖨 0870 9906365

web: www.premiertravelinn.com

dir: Exit M1 junct 16 onto A45 towards Daventry. Through Upper Heyford & Flore. Inn on left before Weedon & A5 junct

High quality, modern budget accommodation ideal for both families and business travellers. Spacious, en suite bedrooms feature bath and shower, satellite TV and many have telephones and modem points. The adjacent family restaurant features a wide and varied menu. For further details consult the Hotel Groups page.

Rooms 46 en suite **Conf** Thtr 70 Class 25 Board 24

WELLINGBOROUGH
MAP 11 SP86

★★★ 66% HOTEL

The Hind

Sheep St NN8 1BY

☎ 01933 222827 🖨 01933 441921

e-mail: enquiries@thehind.co.uk

dir: on A509 in town centre

Dating back to Jacobean times, this centrally located hotel provides a good base for business and leisure guests visiting the town. A good choice of dishes is available in the restaurant; alternatively the all-day coffee shop offers light snacks. Bedrooms come in a variety of styles, mostly of spacious dimensions.

Rooms 34 en suite (2 fmly) (5 GF) ⊗ in 20 bedrooms S £62.50-£67.50; D £70-£75 (incl. bkfst) **Facilities** Wi-fi available Pool table in public bar **Conf** Thtr 70 Class 40 Board 40 **Parking** 17 **Notes LB** ⊗ in restaurant RS 24 Dec-2 Jan Civ Wed 70

BUDGET HOTEL

Hotel Ibis Wellingborough

Enstone Court NN8 2DR

☎ 01933 228333 🖨 01933 228444

e-mail: H3164@accor-hotels.com

web: www.ibishotel.com

dir: at junct of A45 & A509 towards Kettering, SW outskirts of Wellingborough

Modern, budget hotel offering comfortable accommodation in bright and practical bedrooms. Breakfast is self-service and dinner is available in the restaurant. For further details, consult the Hotel Groups page.

Rooms 78 en suite

BUDGET HOTEL

Premier Travel Inn Wellingborough

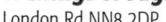

London Rd NN8 2DP

☎ 08701 977262 🖨 01933 275947

web: www.premiertravelinn.com

dir: 0.5m from Wellingborough town centre on A5193 near Dennington Industrial Estate

High quality, modern budget accommodation ideal for both families and business travellers. Spacious, en suite bedrooms feature bath and shower, satellite TV and many have telephones and modem points. The adjacent family restaurant features a wide and varied menu. For further details consult the Hotel Groups page.

Rooms 40 en suite

WHITTLEBURY
MAP 11 SP64

★★★★ 80% ◉◉ HOTEL

Whittlebury Hall

NN12 8QH

☎ 01327 857857 🖨 01237 857867

e-mail: sales@whittleburyhall.co.uk

web: www.whittleburyhall.co.uk

dir: A43/A413 towards Buckingham, through Whittlebury, turn for hotel on right (signed)

A purpose-built, Georgian-style country house hotel with excellent spa and leisure facilities and pedestrian access to the Silverstone circuit. Grand public areas include F1 car racing memorabilia, and the accommodation includes some lavishly appointed suites. Food is a strength, with a choice of various dining options. Particularly noteworthy are the afternoon teas in the spacious, comfortable lounge and the fine dining in Murray's Restaurant.

Rooms 211 en suite (3 fmly) ⊗ in 160 bedrooms S £100-£130; D £125-£155 (incl. bkfst) **Facilities Spa** STV ⬚ Sauna Solarium Gym Jacuzzi Beauty treatments Relaxation room Hair studio Heat and Ice experience Wi-fi available Ch fac **Conf** Thtr 500 Class 175 Board 40 Del fr £145 **Services** Lift **Parking** 450 **Notes LB** ⊗ ⊗ in restaurant

NORTHUMBERLAND

ALNWICK
MAP 21 NU11

See also Embleton

★★★ 67% HOTEL

White Swan

Bondgate Within NE66 1TD

☎ 01665 602109 ⧉ 01665 510400

e-mail: info.whiteswan@classiclodges.co.uk

dir: *from A1 follow town centre signs. Hotel in town centre near Bondgate Tower*

This former coaching inn is situated in the centre of the town. Bedrooms are modern, while public areas include the Atlantic Suite, which features original wooden panelling and fittings from the sister ship of the SS Titanic.

Rooms 56 en suite (5 fmly) (11 GF) ⊘ in 35 bedrooms **Conf** Thtr 150 Class 50 Board 40 **Parking** 25 **Notes LB** ⊘ in restaurant Civ Wed 150

BAMBURGH
MAP 21 NU13

★★★ 78% COUNTRY HOUSE HOTEL

Waren House

Waren Mill NE70 7EE

☎ 01668 214581 ⧉ 01668 214484

e-mail: enquiries@warenhousehotel.co.uk

web: www.warenhousehotel.co.uk

dir: *2m E of A1 turn onto B1342 to Waren Mill, at T-junct turn right, hotel 100yds on right*

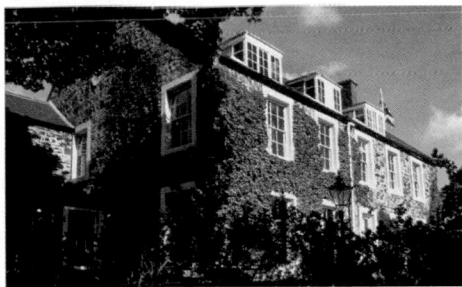

This delightful Georgian mansion is set in six acres of woodland and offers a welcoming atmosphere and views of the coastline. The individually themed bedrooms and suites include many with large

continued

bathrooms. Good, home-cooked food is served in the elegant dining room. A comfortable lounge and library are also available.

Rooms 13 en suite (1 GF) ⊘ in all bedrooms S £83-£100; D £103-£137 (incl. bkfst) **Facilities** Xmas **Conf** Class 24 Board 24 Del from £125 **Parking** 20 **Notes LB** No children 14yrs ⊘ in restaurant

★★ 80% HOTEL

Victoria

Front St NE69 7BP

☎ 01668 214431 ⧉ 01668 214404

e-mail: enquiries@victoriahotel.net

web: www.victoriahotel.net

dir: *off A1, N of Alnwick onto B1342, near Belford & follow signs to Bamburgh. Hotel in town centre*

Overlooking the village green, this hotel offers an interesting blend of traditional and modern. Both the pub bar and a residents'/diners' bar lounge are relaxing venues throughout the day and evening, while the brasserie, with its conservatory roof, provides a contemporary dinner menu. Bedrooms come in a variety of styles and sizes.

Rooms 29 en suite (2 fmly) (2 GF) ⊘ in 18 bedrooms S £55-£60; D £105-£120 (incl. bkfst) **Facilities** Wi-fi available Xmas **Conf** Thtr 50 Class 30 Board 20 Del from £92 **Notes LB** ⊘ in restaurant Closed 8-23 Jan Civ Wed 50

★★ 72% HOTEL

The Lord Crewe

Front St NE69 7BL

☎ 01668 214243 ⧉ 01668 214273

e-mail: lordcrewebamburgh@tiscali.co.uk

dir: *just below the castle*

Located in the heart of the village in the shadow of impressive Bamburgh Castle, this hotel has been developed from an old inn. Public areas include a choice of lounges, a cosy bar and a smart modern restaurant. Bedrooms vary in size, all offer good levels of comfort and are well equipped.

Rooms 18 rms (17 en suite) S £47-£52; D £88-£98 (incl. bkfst) **Parking** 20 **Notes** ⊗ No children 5yrs ⊘ in restaurant Closed Dec/Jan

England

BELFORD

MAP 21 NU13

★★ 71% **HOTEL**

Blue Bell

Market Place NE70 7NE
☎ 01668 213543 📠 01668 213787
e-mail: bluebel@globalnet.co.uk
web: www.bluebellhotel.com

dir: centre of village on left of St Mary's Church

Formerly a coaching inn, this popular and long established hotel is located in the village square. It offers a choice of superior and standard bedrooms all in classical style. Well-prepared meals can be enjoyed in the restaurant and in addition to the bar there is a comfortable lounge in which to relax.

Rooms 17 en suite (1 fmly) (1 GF) **Facilities** Riding 🏌 Putt green **Parking** 16 **Notes LB** ⊗ in restaurant

★★ 69% **HOTEL**

Purdy Lodge

Adderstone Services NE70 7JU
☎ 01668 213000 📠 01668 213131
e-mail: stay@purdylodge.co.uk
web: www.purdylodge.co.uk

dir: turn off A1 onto B1341 then immediately left

Situated near the A1, this family-owned lodge provides quiet bedrooms that look out over fields towards Bamburgh Castle. Food is readily available in the attractive restaurant, the smart 24-hour café, or the cosy lounge bar.

Rooms 20 en suite (4 fmly) (10 GF) ⊗ in 8 bedrooms S £52.95-£62.95; D £52.95-£62.95 **Facilities** STV Xmas **Parking** 60 **Notes LB** Closed 39076

BERWICK-UPON-TWEED

MAP 21 NT95

★★★ 72% **HOTEL**

Marshall Meadows Country House

TD15 1UT
☎ 01289 331133 📠 01289 331438
e-mail: stay@marshallmeadows.co.uk
web: www.marshallmeadows.co.uk

dir: signed directly off A1, 300yds from Scottish border

This stylish Georgian mansion is set in wooded grounds flanked by farmland and has convenient access from the A1. A popular venue for weddings and conferences, it offers comfortable and well-equipped
continued

bedrooms. Public rooms include a cosy bar, a relaxing lounge and a two-tier restaurant, which serves imaginative dishes.

Rooms 19 en suite (1 fmly) ⊗ in 14 bedrooms S £85-£95; D £120-£150 (incl. bkfst) **Facilities** 🏌 **Conf** Thtr 200 Class 120 Board 40 Del from £105 **Parking** 87 **Notes LB** ⊗ in restaurant Closed 15-27 Dec Civ Wed 200

★★ 71% **HOTEL**

Queens Head

Sandgate TD15 1EP
☎ 01289 307852 📠 01289 307858
e-mail: info@queensheadberwick.co.uk

dir: A1 towards centre & Town Hall, along High St. Turn right at bottom to Hide Hill. Hotel next to cinema

This small hotel is situated in the town centre, close to the old walls of this former garrison town. The bright stylish bedrooms are furnished in pine and are well equipped. For eating the focus is on a daily-changing blackboard menu that offers an impressive choice of tasty, freshly prepared dishes served in the reception lounge or dining room.

Rooms 6 en suite (2 fmly) ⊗ in all bedrooms S £55; D £80 (incl. bkfst) **Notes** ⊗ ⊗ in restaurant

BUDGET HOTEL

Travelodge Berwick-upon-Tweed

Loaning Meadow, North Rd TD15 1UQ
☎ 08700 850 950 📠 01289 306555
web: www.travelodge.co.uk

dir: From A1 to rdbt with A1167, Safeway ahead.

Travelodge offers good quality, good value, modern accommodation. Ideal for families, the spacious en suite bedrooms include remote-control TV, tea and coffee-making facilities and comfortable beds. Meals can be taken at the nearby family restaurant. See Hotel Groups pages for further details.

Rooms 40 en suite S fr £26; D fr £26

CHOLLERFORD

MAP 21 NY97

U

Swallow George

NE46 4EW
☎ 01434 681611 📠 01434 681727
e-mail: generalmanager.chollerford@swallowhotels.com
web: www.swallowhotels.com

SWALLOW HOTELS

dir: Turn off A68 onto B6318. Hotel near Chesters Bridge and Humshaugh

At the time of going to press, the star classification for this hotel was not confirmed. Please refer to the AA internet site www.theAA.com for current information.

Rooms 47 en suite (2 fmly) (5 GF) ⊗ in 38 bedrooms S £60-£85; D £80-£150 (incl. bkfst) **Facilities** 🏊 supervised Fishing Sauna Gym Jacuzzi Xmas **Conf** Thtr 60 Class 32 Board 32 Del from £99 **Parking** 60 **Notes** ⊗ in restaurant Civ Wed 40

CORNHILL-ON-TWEED   MAP 21 NT83

★★★ 83% ◉◉ **HOTEL**

Tillmouth Park Country House

TD12 4UU

☎ 01890 882255 📄 01890 882540

e-mail: reception@tillmouthpark.force9.co.uk

web: www.tillmouthpark.com

dir: off A1(M) at East Ord rdbt at Berwick-upon-Tweed. Take
A698 to Cornhill and Coldstream. Hotel 9m on left

An imposing mansion set in landscaped grounds by the River Till.
Gracious public rooms include a stunning galleried lounge with a
drawing room adjacent. The quietly elegant dining room overlooks the
gardens, whilst lunches and early dinners are available in the bistro.
Bedrooms retain traditional character and include several magnificent
master rooms.

Rooms 12 en suite 2 annexe en suite (1 fmly) S £50-£140; D £90-£180
(incl. bkfst) **Facilities** FTV ⤴ 3/4 snooker table, Game shooting, fishing
Xmas **Conf** Thtr 50 Class 20 Board 20 Del from £125 **Parking** 50
Notes LB ◎ in restaurant Civ Wed 50

CRAMLINGTON   MAP 21 NZ27

BUDGET HOTEL

Innkeeper's Lodge Cramlington

Blagdon Ln NE23 8AU

☎ 01670 736111 📄 01670 715709

web: www.innkeeperslodge.com

dir: from A1, exit for A19. At rdbt, left onto A1068, lodge at junct
of Blagdon Lane and Fisher Lane

Smart, en suite accommodation ideal for both business & leisure
guests. Bedrooms are very well equipped, including Sky TV,
telephone, modem points, tea & coffee making facilities, (family
rooms in most locations). Complimentary breakfast. The adjacent Pub
Restaurant; a Harvester, Vintage Inn, Toby Carvery, Ember Inn, Sizzling
Pubco or Pub & Carvery offers an all day menu. See Hotel Groups
pages for further details.

Rooms 18 en suite **Conf** Board 24

BUDGET HOTEL

Premier Travel Inn Newcastle (Cramlington)

Moor Farm Roundabout, off Front St NE23 7QA

☎ 08701 977188 📄 0191 250 2216

web: www.premiertravelinn.com

dir: at rdbt on junction of A19/A189 S of Cramlington

High quality, modern budget accommodation ideal for both families
and business travellers. Spacious, en suite bedrooms feature bath and
shower, satellite TV and many have telephones and modem points.
The adjacent family restaurant features a wide and varied menu. For
further details consult the Hotel Groups page.

Rooms 40 en suite

EMBLETON   MAP 21 NU22

★★ 74% **HOTEL**

Dunstanburgh Castle Hotel

NE66 3UN

☎ 01665 576111 📄 01665 576203

e-mail: stay@dunstanburghcastlehotel.co.uk

web: www.dunstanburghcastlehotel.co.uk

dir: from A1, take B1340 to Denwick past Rennington & Masons
Arms. Take next right signed Embleton, and into village

The focal point of the village, this friendly family-run hotel has a dining
room and grill room offering different menus, plus a cosy bar and two
lounges. In addition to the main bedrooms, a small courtyard
conversion houses three stunning suites, each with a lounge and
gallery bedroom above.

Rooms 20 en suite (4 fmly) ◎ in all bedrooms S £35.50-£53.50; D £71-£107
(incl. bkfst) **Parking** 16 **Notes LB** ◎ in restaurant Closed Dec-Jan

HEXHAM   MAP 21 NY96

★★★★ 80% **HOTEL**

Langley Castle

Langley on Tyne NE47 5LU

☎ 01434 688888 📄 01434 684019

e-mail: manager@langleycastle.com

web: www.langleycastle.com

dir: from A69 5 on A688 for 2m. Castle on right

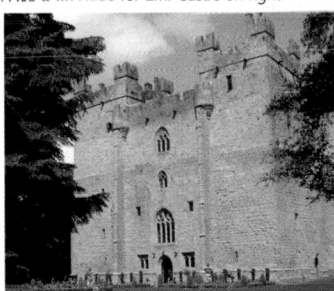

Langley is a magnificent 14th-century fortified castle, set in ten acres of
parkland. There is a restaurant, a comfortable drawing room and a
cosy bar. Bedrooms are furnished with period pieces and most feature
window seats, and restored buildings in the grounds have been
converted into very comfortable 'Castle View' bedrooms.

Rooms 9 en suite 10 annexe en suite (4 fmly) (5 GF) S £99.50-£184.50;
D £119-£239 (incl. bkfst) **Facilities** STV Xmas **Conf** Thtr 120 Class 60
Board 40 Del from £150 **Parking** 70 **Notes LB** ◎ ◎ in restaurant
Civ Wed 120

England

HEXHAM *continued*

★★★★ 78% ⓦ HOTEL

De Vere Slaley Hall
Slaley NE47 0BX
☎ 01434 673350 📠 01434 673962
e-mail: slaley.hall@devere-hotels.com
web: www.devere.co.uk

dir: A1 from S to A68 link road follow signs for Slaley Hall

One thousand acres of Northumbrian forest and parkland, two championship golf courses and indoor leisure facilities can all be found here. Spacious bedrooms are fully air-conditioned and equipped with a range of extras. Public rooms include a number of lounges, conference and banqueting rooms, the informal Golf Clubhouse restaurant and the impressive main restaurant.

Rooms 139 en suite (22 fmly) ⊘ in 101 bedrooms **Facilities Spa** STV ◨ supervised ⌿ 18 Sauna Solarium Gym Jacuzzi Quad bikes, Archery, Clay pigeon shoot, 4x4 driving, Creche **Conf** Thtr 300 Class 220 Board 150 **Services** Lift air con **Parking** 500 **Notes LB** ⊘ in restaurant Civ Wed 250

★★★ 75% HOTEL

Best Western Beaumont
Beaumont St NE46 3LT
☎ 01434 602331 📠 01434 606184
e-mail: reservations@beaumonthotel.eclipse.co.uk

dir: A69 towards Hexham town centre

In a region steeped in history, this hotel is located in the centre of the popular county town, overlooking the park and 6th-century abbey. The hotel has two bars, a comfortable reception lounge and a first-floor restaurant; bedrooms are stylish and comfortably equipped.

Rooms 25 en suite (3 fmly) ⊘ in all bedrooms S £80-£90; D £110 (incl. bkfst) **Facilities** STV Snooker Solarium Wi-fi in bedrooms **Conf** Thtr 100 Class 60 Board 40 Del from £85 **Services** Lift **Parking** 16 **Notes LB** ⊗ ⊘ in restaurant Closed 25-26 Dec

★★ 68% HOTEL

The County Hotel & Restaurant
Priestpopple NE46 1PS
☎ 01434 603601
e-mail: reception@thecountyhexham.co.uk

dir: off A69 at Hexham, follow signs for General Hospital. Hotel at top of hill

Centrally located in the popular market town. The resident owners provide caring and personal service. Bedrooms are comfortably

continued

equipped. Dining options are the County Restaurant and Bottles bistro - both offer an interesting selection of freshly prepared dishes that utilise local produce.

Rooms 7 en suite (1 fmly) ⊘ in 2 bedrooms S £45-£47.50; D £67.50-£75 (incl. bkfst) **Notes** ⊗ ⊘ in restaurant

LONGHORSLEY   MAP 21 NZ19

★★★★ 75% ⓦⓦ HOTEL

Macdonald Linden Hall, Golf & Country Club
NE65 8XF
☎ 01670 500 000 📠 01670 500 001
e-mail: lindenhall@macdonaid-hotels.co.uk
web: www.macdonald-hotels.co.uk

dir: northbound on A1 take A697 towards Coldstream. Hotel 1m N of Longhorsley

This impressive Georgian mansion lies in 400 acres of parkland and offers extensive indoor and outdoor leisure facilities including a golf course. Elegant public rooms include an imposing entrance hall, drawing room and cocktail bar. The Dobson restaurant provides a fine dining experience, or guests can eat in the more informal Linden Tree pub which is located in the grounds.

Rooms 50 en suite (4 fmly) (20 GF) ⊘ in 40 bedrooms S £77-£220; D £112-£270 (incl. bkfst) **Facilities Spa** STV ◨ supervised ⌿ 18 ⌘ Snooker Sauna Solarium Gym ↳ Putt green Jacuzzi Wi-fi in bedrooms Clay pigeon Driving range Chipping green Xmas **Conf** Thtr 300 Class 100 Board 30 Del from £115 **Services** Lift **Parking** 260 **Notes LB** ⊘ in restaurant Civ Wed 120

See advert on opposite page

MATFEN   MAP 21 NZ07

★★★★ 80% ⓦⓦ HOTEL

Matfen Hall
NE20 0RH
☎ 01661 886500 & 855708 📠 01661 886055
e-mail: info@matfenhall.com
web: www.matfenhall.com

dir: off A69 to B6318. Hotel just before village

This fine mansion lies in landscaped parkland overlooking its own golf course. Bedrooms are a blend of contemporary and traditional, but all are very comfortable and well equipped. Impressive public rooms include a splendid drawing room and the elegant Library and Print Room Restaurant, as well as a conservatory bar and very stylish spa, leisure and conference facilities.

continued

Rooms 53 en suite (11 fmly) ⊛ in all bedrooms S £105-£160; D £160-£255 (incl. bkfst) **Facilities Spa** STV ❑ supervised ♨ 18 Sauna Solarium Gym Putt green Jacuzzi Wi-fi in bedrooms Xmas **Conf** Thtr 120 Class 46 Board 40 Del from £150 **Services** Lift **Parking** 150 **Notes LB** ⊛ in restaurant Civ Wed 120

See advertisement under NEWCASTLE UPON TYNE, Tyne & Wear

OTTERBURN
MAP 21 NY89

★★★ 72% **HOTEL**

The Otterburn Tower Hotel
NE19 1NS
☎ 01830 520620 ▤ 01830 521504
e-mail: info@otterburntower.com
web: www.otterburntower.com
dir: in village, on A696 (Newcastle to Edinburgh road)

Built by the cousin of William the Conqueror, this mansion is set in its own grounds. The hotel is steeped in history - Sir Walter Scott stayed here in 1812. Bedrooms come in a variety of sizes and some have huge ornamental fireplaces. Though furnished in period style, they are equipped with all modern amenities. The restaurant features 16th-century oak panelling.

Rooms 18 en suite (2 fmly) (2 GF) ⊛ in all bedrooms S fr £180; D fr £130 (incl. bkfst) **Facilities** STV Fishing ☝ Wi-fi available Xmas **Conf** Thtr 120 Class 40 Board 40 Del from £140 **Parking** 70 **Notes LB** ⊛ in restaurant Civ Wed 250

★★ 69% **HOTEL**

Percy Arms
NE19 1NR
☎ 01830 520261 ▤ 01830 520567
e-mail: percyarmshotel@yahoo.co.uk
dir: centre of Otterburn on A696

This former coaching inn lies in the centre of the village, with good access to the Northumberland countryside. The welcoming public areas boast real fires in the cooler months. A very good range of dishes are offered in either the restaurant or cosy bar/bistro. Bedrooms are cheerfully decorated and thoughtfully equipped.

Rooms 27 en suite (2 fmly) (3 GF) ⊛ in 2 bedrooms S £57.50-£70; D £80-£100 (incl. bkfst) **Facilities** STV Fishing ☝ Xmas **Conf** Thtr 70 Class 40 Board 50 Del from £85 **Parking** 74 **Notes LB** ⊛ in restaurant Civ Wed 80

SEAHOUSES
MAP 21 NU23

★★★ 72% **HOTEL**

Bamburgh Castle
NE68 7SQ
☎ 01665 720283 ▤ 01665 720848
e-mail: bamburghcastlehotel@btinternet.com
web: www.bamburghcastlehotel.co.uk
dir: A1 to Seahouses, car park opposite Barclays Bank

This family-run hotel enjoys a seafront location overlooking the harbour. There is a relaxed and friendly atmosphere with professional, friendly staff providing attentive service. The attractively appointed bedrooms vary in size and style, with superior rooms being more spacious. Many rooms take advantage of the panoramic sea views.

Rooms 20 en suite (3 fmly) (3 GF) ⊛ in 16 bedrooms S £48.95-£56.95; D £87.90-£105 (incl. bkfst) **Conf** Thtr 40 Class 20 Board 25 **Parking** 30 **Notes LB** ⊛ in restaurant Closed 24-26 Dec & 2wks mid Jan

SEAHOUSES *continued*

★★ 75% HOTEL

Olde Ship
NE68 7RD
☎ 01665 720200 📄 01665 721383
e-mail: theoldeship@seahouses.co.uk
dir: *lower end of main street above harbour*

Under the same ownership since 1910, this friendly hotel overlooks the harbour. Lovingly maintained, its sense of history is evident by the amount of nautical memorabilia on display. Public areas include a character bar, cosy snug, restaurant and guests' lounge with snooker area. The individual bedrooms are smartly presented. Two separate building contain executive apartments, all with sea views.

Rooms 12 en suite 6 annexe en suite (3 GF) ⊘ in all bedrooms
S £48-£55; D £96-£110 (incl. bkfst) **Parking** 18 **Notes LB** ⊗
No children 10yrs ⊘ in restaurant Closed Dec-Jan

★★ 71% HOTEL

Beach House
Sea Front NE68 7SR
☎ 01665 720337 📄 01665 720921
e-mail: enquiries@Beachhousehotel.co.uk
web: www.beachhousehotel.co.uk
dir: *follow signs from A1 between Alnwick & Berwick*

Enjoying a seafront location and views of the Farne Islands, this family-run hotel offers a relaxed and friendly atmosphere. Bedrooms come in a variety of sizes, but all are bright and airy. Dinner makes use of fresh produce and breakfast features local specialities. There is a well-stocked bar and comfortable lounge.

Rooms 14 en suite (5 fmly) ⊘ in all bedrooms S £36.75-£48;
D £73.50-£119.50 (incl. bkfst) **Conf** Thtr 50 Del from £135 **Parking** 16
Notes ⊗ No children 5yrs ⊘ in restaurant Closed Jan

WARKWORTH MAP 21 NU20

★★★ 72% HOTEL

Warkworth House Hotel
16 Bridge St NE65 0XB
☎ 01665 711276 📄 01665 713323
e-mail: welcome@warkworthhousehotel.co.uk
web: www.warkworthhousehotel.co.uk
dir: *A1 onto B6345 for Amble & Felton. Follow Warkworth Castle signs. Hotel down hill from castle before bridge*

Located in the centre of the village, this small friendly hotel offers a range of bedrooms that are classically styled and well equipped. Well-prepared meals can be enjoyed in both the restaurant and the lounge bar. A separate lounge is available to relax in.

Rooms 14 en suite (2 GF) ⊘ in 8 bedrooms S £49-£58; D £79-£99 (incl. bkfst) **Facilities** Xmas **Conf** Thtr 32 Class 14 Del from £92 **Parking** 14
Notes LB ⊘ in restaurant

WOOLER MAP 21 NT92

★★ 72% HOTEL

Tankerville Arms
Cottage Rd NE71 6AD
☎ 01668 281581 📄 01668 281387
e-mail: enquiries@tankervillehotel.co.uk
web: www.tankervillehotel.co.uk
dir: *on A697*

Dating from the 17th century, this popular inn is ideally placed for the many local attractions. The comfortable and thoughtfully equipped bedrooms come in a variety of styles and sizes. The traditional bar has an adjacent brasserie and there is a spacious restaurant. Wide-ranging menus provide a choice to suit all.

Rooms 16 en suite (2 fmly) S fr £55; D fr £52 (incl. bkfst) **Conf** Thtr 60
Class 60 Board 30 Del from £90 **Parking** 100 **Notes LB** ⊘ in restaurant
Closed 22-28 Dec Civ Wed 70

NOTTINGHAMSHIRE

BARNBY MOOR MAP 16 SK68

★★★ 67% HOTEL

Swallow Ye Olde Bell SWALLOW
DN22 8QS
☎ 01777 705121 📄 01777 860424
e-mail: swallow.retford@swallowhotels.com
web: www.swallowhotels.com
dir: *On A638 between Retford & Bawtry*

Formerly a posting house on the London to York mail coach route, this charming inn has been welcoming guests for more than three centuries. Public rooms include the very smart, oak-panelled 1650 restaurant, a choice of lounges and an informal bar. The well-

continued

Some hotels, although accepting children, may not have any special facilities for them so it is well worth checking before booking

England

equipped bedrooms vary in size and style and an excellent range of conference facilities is available.

Swallow Ye Olde Bell

Rooms 48 en suite (5 fmly) ⊘ in 26 bedrooms S £49-£80; D £79-£125 (incl. bkfst) **Facilities** ⅃ Wi-fi in bedrooms Xmas **Conf** Thtr 250 Class 150 Board 60 Del from £75 **Parking** 150 **Notes LB** ⊘ in restaurant Civ Wed 250

BLYTH   MAP 16 SK68

★★★ 85% **HOTEL**

Best Western Charnwood
Sheffield Rd S81 8HF
☎ 01909 591610 ▤ 01909 591429
e-mail: charnwood@bestwestern.co.uk
web: www.bw-charnwoodhotel.com

dir: *A614 into Blyth village, right past church onto A634 Sheffield road. Hotel 0.5m on right past humpback bridge*

A peaceful rural setting, surrounded by attractive views and gardens, this hotel offers a range of carefully prepared meals and snacks in either the formal restaurant, or the comfortable lounge bar. Bedrooms are comfortably furnished and attractively decorated. Service is friendly and attentive.

Rooms 47 en suite (1 fmly) ⊘ in 16 bedrooms S £70-£100; D £80-£120 (incl. bkfst & dinner) **Facilities** STV Mini-gym **Conf** Thtr 135 Class 60 Board 45 Del from £102 **Parking** 120 **Notes LB** ⊗ ⊘ in restaurant Civ Wed 110

BUDGET HOTEL

Travelodge Blyth (A1(M))
Hilltop Roundabout S81 8HG
☎ 08700 850 950 ▤ 01909 591831
web: www.travelodge.co.uk

dir: *at junct of A1(M)/A614*

Travelodge offers good quality, good value, modern accommodation. Ideal for families, the spacious en suite bedrooms include remote-

continued

control TV, tea and coffee-making facilities and comfortable beds. Meals can be taken at the nearby family restaurant. See Hotel Groups pages for further details.

Rooms 38 en suite S fr £26; D fr £26

HUCKNALL   MAP 16 SK54

BUDGET HOTEL

Premier Travel Inn Nottingham North West
Nottingham Rd NG15 7PY
☎ 0870 9906518 ▤ 0870 9906519
web: www.premiertravelinn.com

dir: *A611/A6002 straight over 2 rdbts. Inn 500yds on right.*

High quality, modern budget accommodation ideal for both families and business travellers. Spacious, en suite bedrooms feature bath and shower, satellite TV and many have telephones and modem points. The adjacent family restaurant features a wide and varied menu. For further details consult the Hotel Groups page.

Rooms 35 en suite **Conf** Thtr 80

LANGAR   MAP 11 SK73

★★★ 79% ⊛ ⊛ **HOTEL**

Langar Hall
NG13 9HG
☎ 01949 860559 ▤ 01949 861045
e-mail: info@langarhall.co.uk
web: www.langarhall.com

dir: *via Bingham from A52 or Cropwell Bishop from A46, both signed. Hotel behind church.*

This delightful hotel enjoys a picturesque rural location, yet is only a short drive from Nottingham. Individually styled bedrooms are furnished with fine period pieces and benefit from some thoughtful extras. There is a choice of lounges, warmed by real fires, and a snug little bar. Imaginative food is served in a pillared dining room and the garden conservatory provides a lighter menu.

Rooms 12 en suite (1 fmly) ⊘ in all bedrooms S £75-£110; D £90-£210 (incl. bkfst) **Facilities** FTV Fishing ⅃ Wi-fi in bedrooms ch fac **Conf** BC Thtr 16 Class 16 Board 12 Del £175 **Parking** 20 **Notes LB** ⊘ in restaurant Civ Wed 40

England

MANSFIELD   MAP 16 SK56

★★ 69% HOTEL

Pine Lodge
281-283 Nottingham Rd NG18 4SE
☎ 01623 622308 ▤ 01623 656819
e-mail: enquiries@pinelodge-hotel.co.uk
web: www.pinelodge-hotel.co.uk
dir: on A60 Nottingham to Mansfield road, hotel is 1m S of Mansfield

Located on the edge of Mansfield, this hotel offers welcoming and personal service to its guests - many return time and again. The public rooms include a comfortable lounge bar, a cosy restaurant and a choice of meeting and function rooms. Bedrooms are thoughtfully equipped, and are carefully maintained; a suite is also available.

Rooms 20 en suite (2 fmly) ⊛ in all bedrooms S £45-£70; D £65-£80 (incl. bkfst) **Facilities** STV Sauna **Conf** Thtr 50 Class 30 Board 35 **Parking** 40 **Notes** LB ⊗ ⊛ in restaurant Closed 25-26 Dec

★★ 67% HOTEL

Portland Hall
THE INDEPENDENTS

Carr Bank Park, Windmill Ln NG18 2AL
☎ 01623 452525 ▤ 01623 452550
e-mail: enquiries@portlandhallhotel.co.uk
web: www.portlandhallhotel.co.uk
dir: from town centre take A60 to Worksop for 100yds then right at pelican crossing into Nursery St, Carr Bank Park 50yds on right

A former Georgian mansion, overlooking 15 acres of renovated parklands, the house retains some fine features, with original plasterwork and friezes in the cosy lounge bar and around the domed skylight over the spiral stairs. The attractive restaurant proves popular, offering a flexible choice of carvery or menu options; service is skilled and attentive.

Rooms 10 en suite (1 fmly) ⊛ in 5 bedrooms **Facilities** ⌣ Bowls Green **Conf** Thtr 60 Class 30 Board 20 **Parking** 80 **Notes** ⊛ in restaurant Civ Wed 66

BUDGET HOTEL

Travelodge Mansfield
Lakeside Point, Mansfield Rd,
Sutton in Ashfield NG17 4NU
web: www.travelodge.co.uk

Travelodge

Travelodge offers good quality, good value, modern accommodation. Ideal for families, the spacious en suite bedrooms include remote-control TV, tea and coffee-making facilities and comfortable beds. Meals can be taken at the nearby family restaurant. See Hotel Groups pages for further details.

Rooms S fr £26; D fr £26

MARKHAM MOOR   MAP 17 SK77

BUDGET HOTEL

Travelodge Retford Markham Moor
DN22 0QU
☎ 08700 850 950 ▤ 01777 838091
web: www.travelodge.co.uk
dir: on A1 at junct with A57 northbound

Travelodge

Travelodge offers good quality, good value, modern accommodation. Ideal for families, the spacious en suite bedrooms include remote-control TV, tea and coffee-making facilities and comfortable beds. Meals can be taken at the nearby family restaurant. See Hotel Groups pages for further details.

Rooms 40 en suite S fr £26; D fr £26

NEWARK-ON-TRENT   MAP 17 SK75

★★★ 80% HOTEL

The Grange Hotel
73 London Rd NG24 1RZ
☎ 01636 703399 ▤ 01636 702328
e-mail: info@grangenewark.co.uk
web: www.grangenewark.co.uk
dir: from A1 follow signs to town centre. At castle rdbt follow signs to Balderton. Over 2 sets of lights. Hotel 0.25m on left

Expect a warm welcome at this family-run hotel, situated just a short walk from the town. Bedrooms are attractively decorated with co-ordinated soft furnishings and equipped with many thoughtful extras. Public rooms include the Potters Bar, Cutlers Restaurant and a residents' lounge. In the summer guests can enjoy the delightful terrace gardens.

Rooms 10 en suite 9 annexe en suite (1 fmly) ⊛ in 15 bedrooms S £72-£100; D £96-£150 (incl. bkfst) **Parking** 17 **Notes** LB ⊗ ⊛ in restaurant

BUDGET HOTEL

Premier Travel Inn Newark
premier travel inn

Lincoln Rd NG24 2DB
☎ 08701 977186 ▤ 01636 605135
web: www.premiertravelinn.com
dir: at intersection of A1/A46/A17, follow signs B6166

High quality, modern budget accommodation ideal for both families and business travellers. Spacious, en suite bedrooms feature bath and shower, satellite TV and many have telephones and modem points. The adjacent family restaurant features a wide and varied menu. For further details consult the Hotel Groups page.

Rooms 40 en suite

England

NORTH MUSKHAM   MAP 17 SK75

BUDGET HOTEL

Travelodge Newark North Muskham

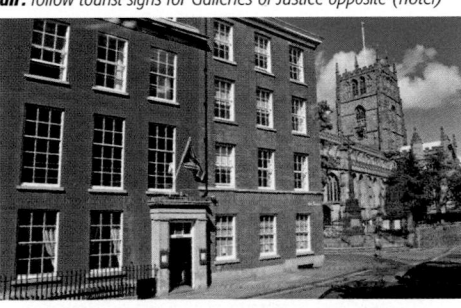

NG23 6HT

☎ 08700 850 950 📠 01636 703635

web: www.travelodge.co.uk

dir: 4m N, on A1 southbound

Travelodge offers good quality, good value, modern accommodation. Ideal for families, the spacious en suite bedrooms include remote-control TV, tea and coffee-making facilities and comfortable beds. Meals can be taken at the nearby family restaurant. See Hotel Groups pages for further details.

Rooms 30 en suite S fr £26; D fr £26

NOTTINGHAM   MAP 11 SK53

See also Langar

★★★★ 82% ◉◉ **HOTEL**

Hart's

Standard Hill, Park Row NG1 6FN

☎ 0115 988 1900 📠 0115 947 7600

e-mail: ask@hartshotel.co.uk

web: www.hartsnottingham.co.uk

dir: at junct of Park Row & Rope Walk, close to city centre

This outstanding modern building stands on the site of the ramparts of the medieval castle, overlooking the city. Many of the bedrooms enjoy splendid views. Rooms are well appointed and stylish, while the Park Bar is the focal point of the public areas; service is professional and caring. Fine dining is offered at nearby Hart's Restaurant. Secure parking and private gardens are an added bonus

Rooms 32 en suite (1 fmly) (5 GF) ⊗ in all bedrooms D £120-£255
Facilities STV Gym Wi-fi in bedrooms Small, unsupervised exercise room Xmas **Conf** Thtr 80 Class 75 Board 33 Del from £190 **Services** Lift **Parking** 19 **Notes** LB ⊗ in restaurant Civ Wed 80

★★★★ 75% ◉ **TOWN HOUSE HOTEL**

Lace Market

29-31 High Pavement NG1 1HE

☎ 0115 852 3232 📠 0115 852 3223

e-mail: stay@lacemarkethotel.co.uk

web: www.lacemarkethotel.co.uk

dir: follow tourist signs for Galleries of Justice opposite (hotel)

This smart town house, a conversion of two Georgian houses, is located in the trendy Lace Market area of the city. Smart public areas, including the stylish and very popular Merchants Restaurant and Saints Bar, are complemented by the 'Cock and Hoop', a traditional pub offering real ales and fine wines. Accommodation is stylish and contemporary and includes spacious superior rooms and split-level suites; are all thoughtfully equipped with a host of extras including CD players and mini bars.

Rooms 42 en suite ⊗ in all bedrooms S £75-£119; D £99-£239
Facilities STV Wi-fi in bedrooms Complimentary use of nearby health club, including indoor pool. **Conf** Thtr 35 Class 35 Board 20 Del from £130 **Services** Lift **Notes** LB ⊗ in restaurant Civ Wed 60

★★★★ 74% **HOTEL**

Park Plaza Nottingham

41 Maid Marian Way NG1 6GD

☎ 0115 947 7200 📠 0115 947 7300

e-mail: info@parkplazanottingham.com

web: www.parkplaza.com

dir: A6200 Derby Road onto Wollaton St. 2nd exit onto Maid Marian Way. Hotel on left

This ultra modern hotel is located in the centre of the city within walking distance of retail, commercial and tourist attractions. Bedrooms are spacious and comfortable, with many extras, including laptop safes, high-speed telephone lines and air-conditioning. Service is discreetly attentive in the Foyer lounge and the Chino Latino restaurant, where Pan Asian cooking is a feature.

Rooms 178 en suite (10 fmly) ⊗ in 126 bedrooms S £90-£145; D £90-£145 **Facilities** STV Gym Wi-fi in bedrooms Complimentary fitness suite **Conf** BC Thtr 200 Class 100 Board 54 Del from £135 **Services** Lift air con **Notes** ⊗ ⊗ in restaurant

England

NOTTINGHAM *continued*

★★★★ 81% ⊛ HOTEL

Nottingham Belfry

 MarstonHotels

Mellor's Way, Off Woodhouse Way NG8 6PY

☎ 0115 973 9393 📄 0115 973 9494

e-mail: nottingham@marstonhotels.com

web: www.marstonhotels.com

dir: A610 towards Nottingham. A6002 to Stapleford/Strelley. 0.75m, last exit of rdbt, hotel on right.

Set conveniently close to the motorway links, yet not far from the city centre attractions, this newly built hotel has a stylish and impressive interior. Bedrooms and bathrooms are spaciously appointed and very comfortable. There are two restaurants and two bars, both offer interesting and satisfying cuisine. Staff are friendly and helpful.

Rooms 120 en suite (20 fmly) (36 GF) ⊘ in all bedrooms S £85-£134.50; D £120-£219 (incl. bkfst) **Facilities Spa** STV ⊠ supervised Sauna Gym Jacuzzi Steam room Treatment rooms Aerobic studio Xmas **Conf** Thtr 320 Class 150 Board 90 Del from £140 **Services** Lift **Parking** 250 **Notes LB** ⊗ ⊘ in restaurant Civ Wed 150

★★★★ 72% HOTEL

Crowne Plaza Nottingham

Wollaton St NG1 5RH

☎ 0115 936 9988 & 0870 787 5161 📄 0115 947 5667

e-mail: cpnottingham@qmh-hotels.com

dir: Follow city centre signs on A6200 to Canning Circus. Down hill & straight ahead at bottom lights.

Located in the heart of the city centre this large purpose built hotel has undergone a multi million pound refurbishment. Spacious public areas uniquely centre on a tree-lined avenue and include a popular bar and extensive meeting rooms. Air-conditioned bedrooms, which

continued

vary in size, have all been refurbished and include flat screen televisions. The hotel also has a leisure club and extensive parking.

Rooms 210 en suite ⊘ in 161 bedrooms S £94-£158; D £94-£158 **Facilities** STV ⊠ supervised Sauna Solarium Gym Jacuzzi Beautician Hairdresser Florist Dance studio **Conf** BC Thtr 400 Class 300 Board 40 Del from £130 **Services** Lift air con **Parking** 600 **Notes** ⊗ ⊘ in restaurant Civ Wed 400

★★★ ⊛⊛⊛⊛ HOTEL

Restaurant Sat Bains with Rooms

Trentside, Lenton Ln NG7 2SA

☎ 0115 986 6566 📄 0115 986 0343

e-mail: info@restaurantsatbains.net

web: www.restaurantsatbains.com

dir: M1 junct 24 take A453 Nottingham S. Over River Trent in central lane to rdbt. Left then left again towards river. Hotel on left after bend

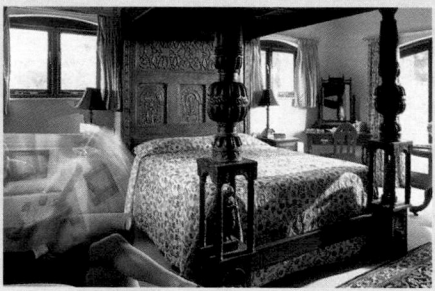

This petite restaurant with rooms, a sympathetic conversion of Victorian farm buildings, is situated on the river, and close to the industrial area of Nottingham. The bedrooms create a warmth and magic using quality soft furnishings and antique and period furniture; suites and four-poster bedrooms are available. Public rooms are chic and cosy, and the delightful restaurant complements the outstanding cuisine on offer. AA Restaurant of the Year for England 2006-7.

Rooms 8 en suite (7 GF) ⊘ in all bedrooms S £90-£100; D £100-£150 (incl. bkfst) **Facilities** STV Xmas **Parking** 22 **Notes LB** ⊗ ⊘ in restaurant Closed 1st 2 wks Jan & 2 wks mid Aug RS Sun & Mon

★★★ 77% METRO HOTEL

Citilodge

Wollaton St NG1 5FW

☎ 0115 912 8000 📄 0115 912 8080

e-mail: mail@citilodge.co.uk

web: www.citilodge.co.uk

dir: From M1 junct 26, follow A610 into city centre. Hotel opposite Royal Centre on Wollaton Street

This city centre hotel offers superior accommodation along with a good range of bar and food in the adjacent Vision café/bar and restaurant. Conferencing is a strength, with a range of quality meeting rooms and an impressive 100-seater tiered lecture theatre. Bedrooms

continued

are spacious and light with an excellent range of facilities including air conditioning, broadband access and a separate Citinet internet room is available. Discounted parking nearby.

Rooms 90 en suite (5 fmly) ⊘ in 72 bedrooms S fr £60; D fr £60 **Facilities** STV Wi fi available Discount at local Leisure Centre 5 mins' walk. **Conf** Thtr 100 Class 30 Board 30 Del from £115 **Services** Lift air con **Notes** ⊗ Closed 25-26 Dec

---

★★★ 74% **HOTEL**

Best Western Westminster

312 Mansfield Rd, Carrington NG5 2EF
☎ 0115 955 5000 🖺 0115 955 5005
e-mail: mail@westminster-hotel.co.uk
web: www.westminster-hotel.co.uk
dir: on A60 1m N of town centre

This smart hotel is conveniently located close to the city centre, and offers well-appointed accommodation, suitably equipped for both business and leisure guests. Spacious superior rooms are particularly impressive. Public areas include a lounge bar, restaurant and range of meeting and function rooms. There is a complimentary internet booth in reception and Wi-Fi access in all ground floor areas and most bedrooms.

Best Western Westminister

Rooms 73 en suite (9 GF) ⊘ in 40 bedrooms **Facilities** STV Wi-fi available **Conf** Thtr 60 Class 30 Board 30 **Services** Lift **Parking** 66 **Notes LB** ⊗ ⊘ in restaurant Closed 25 Dec 2 Jan

---

★★★ 74% **HOTEL**

Jury's Inn Nottingham

🔷JURYS DOYLE
HOTELS

46 London Rd NG2 3BJ
☎ 0115 901 6700 & 0115 901 6800 🖺 0115 901 6777
e-mail: john-murphy@jurysdoyle.com
web: www.jurysdoyle.com

This new hotel is modern, stylish, opposite the railway station, and easily accessible from all road networks. Bedrooms provide good guest comfort and in-room facilities are suited to both leisure and business markets. Public areas include a number of meeting rooms, a popular bar and restaurant. Parking is across the road.

Rooms 264 en suite (264 fmly) ⊘ in 203 bedrooms S £59-£99; D £59-£99 **Facilities** Wi-fi available **Conf** BC Thtr 100 Class 30 Board 36 Del from £115 **Notes LB** ⊗ Closed Xmas

---

★★★ 70% **HOTEL**

Best Western Bestwood Lodge

Bestwood Country Park, Arnold NG5 8NE
☎ 0115 920 3011 🖺 0115 964 9678
e-mail: bestwoodlodge@btconnect.com
web: www.bw-bestwoodlodge.co.uk

dir: *3m N off A60. Left at lights into Oxclose Ln, right at next lights into Queens Bower Rd. 1st right keep right at fork in road*

A hunting lodge in 700 acres of parkland, the stunning architecture includes Gothic features and high vaulted ceilings. Bedrooms include all modern comforts, suitable for both business and leisure guests, and a popular restaurant serves an extensive menu.

Rooms 39 en suite (5 fmly) ⊘ in 5 bedrooms **Facilities** ⊱ Riding Guided walks ch fac **Conf** Thtr 200 Class 85 Board 50 **Parking** 120 **Notes LB** ⊘ in restaurant RS 25 Dec & 1 Jan

See advert on this page

England

NOTTINGHAM *continued*

★★★ 70% **HOTEL**

Rutland Square Hotel

St James St NG1 6FJ

☎ 0115 941 1114 📠 0115 941 0014

e-mail: rutland.square@forestdale.com

web: www.forestdale.com

dir: *follow signs to castle. Hotel on right 50yds beyond castle*

In an enviable location in the heart of the city adjacent to the castle makes this hotel a popular choice with both leisure and business travellers. Behind its mock Regency façade the hotel is modern and comfortable with good business facilities. Bedrooms come in a variety of styles with the Premier rooms offering a host of thoughtful extras. Public rooms include Woods Restaurant.

Rooms 87 en suite (3 fmly) ✆ in 38 bedrooms S £85; D £140 (incl. bkfst) **Facilities** STV Wi-fi in bedrooms Discounted day passes to nearby gym Xmas **Conf** Thtr 200 Class 70 Board 45 Del from £99 **Services** Lift **Parking** 30 **Notes LB** ✆ in restaurant

★★★ 68% **HOTEL**

Swans Hotel & Restaurant

84-90 Radcliffe Rd, West Bridgford NG2 5HH

☎ 0115 981 4042 📠 0115 945 5745

e-mail: enquiries@swanshotel.co.uk

web: www.swanshotel.co.uk

dir: *from A60 or A52, Hotel on A6011 close to Trent Bridge*

This privately owned hotel is located on the outskirts of the city, conveniently placed for the various sports stadia. Bedrooms vary in size, but are all equipped to meet the needs of both business and leisure visitors. An interesting range of dishes is served in either the cosy bar or, more formally, in the restaurant.

Rooms 30 en suite (3 fmly) (1 GF) ✆ in all bedrooms S £45-£60; D £60-£75 (incl. bkfst) **Facilities** STV Wi-fi available **Conf** Thtr 50 Class 10 Board 24 Del from £100 **Services** Lift **Parking** 31 **Notes LB** ✉ ✆ in restaurant Closed 24-28 Dec

★★★ 67% **HOTEL**

Comfort Hotel Nottingham

George St NG1 3BP

☎ 0115 947 5641 📠 0115 948 3292

e-mail: enquiries@comfort-hotels-nottingham.com

web: www.comfort-hotels-nottingham.com

dir: *M1 junct 24, follow City Centre signs. Left into George Street, hotel at end on left*

Situated in heart of the city, this hotel dates back to the late 17th century. Smartly appointed, compact public areas include a bar lounge, where all-day snacks are served, and a brightly decorated restaurant. The bedrooms are very comfortable and thoughtfully equipped, well suited for both business and leisure guests. Parking is available at a multi-storey, a short walk from the hotel.

Rooms 70 en suite (7 fmly) ✆ in 45 bedrooms **Facilities** STV **Conf** Thtr 150 Class 100 Board 60 **Services** Lift **Notes** ✆ in restaurant

★★ 65% **HOTEL**

The Strathdon

PEEL HOTELS

Derby Rd, City Centre NG1 5FT

☎ 0115 941 8501 📠 0115 948 3725

e-mail: info@strathdon-hotel-nottingham.com

web: www.peelhotel.com

dir: *follow city centre signs. Enter one-way system into Wollaton St, keep right and next right to hotel*

This city-centre hotel has modern facilities and is very convenient for all city attractions. A popular themed bar includes large-screen TV and serves an extensive range of popular fresh food, while more formal dining is available in Bobbins Restaurant on certain evenings.

Rooms 68 en suite (4 fmly) ✆ in 46 bedrooms S £50-£85; D £69-£105 **Facilities** STV **Conf** Thtr 150 Class 60 Board 40 Del from £95 **Services** Lift

🅄

Nottingham Gateway

Nuthall Rd, Cinderhill NG8 6AZ

☎ 0115 979 4949 📠 0115 979 4744

e-mail: sales@nottinghamgatewayhotel.co.uk

web: www.nottinghamgatewayhotel.co.uk

dir: *M1 junct 26, A610, hotel on 3rd rdbt on left*

At the time of going to press, the star classification for this hotel was not confirmed. Please refer to the AA internet site www.theAA.com for current information.

Rooms 108 en suite (18 fmly) ✆ in 30 bedrooms S £45-£80; D £50-£90 (incl. bkfst) **Facilities** Xmas **Conf** Thtr 250 Class 150 Board 60 Del from £110 **Services** Lift **Parking** 250 **Notes** ✆ in restaurant Civ Wed 250

BUDGET HOTEL

Innkeeper's Lodge Nottingham

Derby Rd, Wollaton Vale NG8 2NR

☎ 0115 922 1691

web: www.innkeeperslodge.com

dir: *M1 junct 25, take A52 to Nottingham. At 3rd rdbt, left into Wollaton Vale, right across central reservation into car park*

Smart, en suite accommodation ideal for both business & leisure guests. Bedrooms are very well equipped, including Sky TV, telephone, modem points, tea & coffee making facilities, (family rooms in most locations). Complimentary breakfast. The adjacent Pub Restaurant; a Harvester, Vintage Inn, Toby Carvery, Ember Inn, Sizzling Pubco or Pub & Carvery offers an all day menu. See Hotel Groups pages for further details.

Rooms 34 en suite **Conf** Thtr 105 Class 62 Board 70

England

Premier Travel Inn Nottingham City Centre (London Road)

Island Site, London Rd NG2 4UU
☎ 0870 9906574 ▤ 0870 9906575
web: www.premiertravelinn.com

dir: *Exit M1 junct 25, A52 into city centre. Then follow signs for A60 to Loughborough. Inn next to BBC building*

High quality, modern budget accommodation ideal for both families and business travellers. Spacious, en suite bedrooms feature bath and shower, satellite TV and many have telephones and modem points. The adjacent family restaurant features a wide and varied menu. For further details consult the Hotel Groups page.

Rooms 8/ en suite

Premier Travel Inn Nottingham City Centre (Goldsmith Street)

Goldsmith St NG1 5LT
☎ 0870 238 3314 ▤ 0115 908 1388

dir: *A610 to City Centre. Follow signs for Nottingham Trent University into Talbot Street. Take 1st left into Clarendon Street and at lights turn right. Inn on right.*

Rooms 161 en suite

Premier Travel Inn Nottingham City South

Castle Marina Park, Castle Bridge Rd NG7 1GX
☎ 08701 977199 ▤ 0115 958 2362

dir: *0.5m from Nottingham city centre, follow signs for Castle Marina*

Rooms 38 en suite

Premier Travel Inn Nottingham North

101 Mansfield Rd, Daybrook NG5 6BH
☎ 0870 9906328 ▤ 0870 9906329

dir: *Exit M1 junct 26, A610 towards Nottingham. Left onto A6514. Left onto A60 towards Mansfield. Inn 0.25m on left*

Rooms 64 en suite **Conf** Thtr 50 Class 50

Premier Travel Inn Nottingham South

Loughborough Rd, Ruddington NG11 6LS
☎ 0870 9906422 ▤ 0870 9906423

dir: *Exit M1 junct 24, follow signs for A453 to Nottingham, then A52 to Grantham. Inn at 1st rdbt on left*

Rooms 42 en suite

Premier Travel Inn Nottingham West

The Phoenix Centre, Millennium Way West NG8 6AS
☎ 08701 977200 ▤ 0115 977 0113

dir: *M1 junct 26, 1m on A610 towards Nottingham*

Rooms 86 en suite

Travelodge Nottingham Central

New City House, Maid Marion Way NG1 6DD
web: www.travelodge.co.uk

Travelodge offers good quality, good value, modern accommodation. Ideal for families, the spacious en suite bedrooms include remote-control TV, tea and coffee-making facilities and comfortable beds. Meals can be taken at the nearby family restaurant. See Hotel Groups pages for further details.

Rooms S fr £26; D fr £26

Travelodge Nottingham Riverside

Riverside Retail Park NG2 1RT
☎ 08700 850 950 ▤ 0115 986 0467

dir: *M1 junct 21, follow signs for A453, on Riverside Retail Park*
Rooms 61 en suite S fr £26; D fr £26

RETFORD (EAST)　　　　　MAP 17 SK78

★★★ 67% **HOTEL**

Best Western West Retford

24 North Rd DN22 7XG
☎ 01777 706333 & 0870 609 6162
▤ 01777 709951

e-mail: reservations@westretfordhotel.co.uk

dir: *From A1 take A620 to Ranby/Retford. Left at rdbt into North Rd (A638). Hotel on right*

Stylishly refurbished throughout, and set in attractive grounds close to the town centre, this 18th-century manor house offers a good range of well-equipped meeting facilities. The spacious, well-laid out bedrooms and suites are located in separate buildings and all offer modern facilities and comforts.

Rooms 63 en suite (32 GF) ⊛ in 37 bedrooms S fr £74; D fr £74
Facilities FTV Wi-fi in bedrooms Xmas **Conf** Thtr 150 Class 45 Board 40 Del from £99 **Parking** 100 **Notes LB** ⊛ in restaurant Civ Wed 100

SOUTHWELL　　　　　MAP 17 SK65

★★★ 71% **HOTEL**

Saracens Head

Market Place NG25 0HE
☎ 01636 812701 ▤ 01636 815408
e-mail: cc@saracensheadhotel.co.uk
web: www.saracensheadhotel.net

dir: *from A1 to Newark turn off & follow B6386 for approx 7m*

This half-timbered inn, rich in history, is set in the centre of town and close to the Minster. There is a relaxing atmosphere within the sumptuous public areas, which include a small bar, a comfortable

continued on page 522

SOUTHWELL *continued*

lounge and a fine dining restaurant. Bedroom styles vary - all are appealing, comfortable and well equipped.

Saracens Head

Rooms 27 en suite (2 fmly) ⊗ in all bedrooms **Facilities** STV **Conf** BC Thtr 80 Class 60 Board 40 **Parking** 102 **Notes LB** ⊗ ⊗ in restaurant

TROWELL MOTORWAY	MAP 11 SK43
SERVICE AREA (M1)	

BUDGET HOTEL

Travelodge Nottingham Trowell (M1)

NG9 3PL

☎ 08700 850 950 📠 0115 944 7815

web: www.travelodge.co.uk

dir: *M1 junct 25/26 northbound*

Travelodge offers good quality, good value, modern accommodation. Ideal for families, the spacious en suite bedrooms include remote-control TV, tea and coffee-making facilities and comfortable beds. Meals can be taken at the nearby family restaurant. See Hotel Groups pages for further details.

Rooms 35 en suite S fr £26; D fr £26

WORKSOP	MAP 16 SK57

★★★ 78% HOTEL

Best Western Lion

112 Bridge St S80 1HT

☎ 01909 477925 📠 01909 479038

e-mail: reception@thelionworksop.co.uk

dir: *A57 to town centre, turn at Walkers Garage on right and follow road to Norfolk Arms and turn left*

This former coaching inn lies on the edge of the main shopping

precinct, with a car park to the rear. It has been extended to offer modern accommodation, and the excellent executive rooms are worth asking for. A wide range of interesting dishes is offered in both the restaurant and bar.

Rooms 45 en suite (3 fmly) (7 GF) ⊗ in 32 bedrooms S £65-£85; D £75-£95 (incl. bkfst) **Facilities** FTV Wi-fi in bedrooms Xmas **Conf** Thtr 160 Class 80 Board 70 Del from £95 **Services** Lift **Parking** 50 **Notes LB** ⊗ in restaurant Civ Wed 150

★★★ 70% HOTEL

Clumber Park

Clumber Park S80 3PA

☎ 0870 609 6158 📠 01623 835525

e-mail: clumberpark@corushotels.com

web: www.corushotels.com

dir: *M1 junct 30/31 follow signs to A57 and A1. A1 take A614 towards Nottingham. Hotel is 2m on the left*

Beside the A614, this hotel is situated in open countryside, edging on to Sherwood Forest and Clumber Park. Bedrooms are comfortably furnished and well equipped, and public areas include a choice of formal and informal eating options. Dukes Tavern is a lively and casual venue, while the restaurant offers a more traditional style of service.

Rooms 48 en suite (7 fmly) (16 GF) ⊗ in 31 bedrooms S £79; D £79 **Facilities** STV Xmas **Conf** Thtr 250 Class 150 Board 90 Del from £125 **Parking** 200 **Notes LB** ⊗ in restaurant Civ Wed 100

BUDGET HOTEL

Travelodge Worksop

St Anne's Dr, Dukeries Dr S80 3QD

☎ 08700 850 950 📠 0870 191 1684

web: www.travelodge.co.uk

dir: *on rdbt junct of A619/A57*

Travelodge offers good quality, good value, modern accommodation. Ideal for families, the spacious en suite bedrooms include remote-control TV, tea and coffee-making facilities and comfortable beds. Meals can be taken at the nearby family restaurant. See Hotel Groups pages for further details.

Rooms 40 en suite S fr £26; D fr £26

continued

OXFORDSHIRE

ABINGDON
MAP 05 SU49

★★★ 75% **HOTEL**

Abingdon Four Pillars Hotel
Marcham Rd OX14 1TZ

☎ 0800 374 692 & 01235 553456 📠 01235 554117

e-mail: abingdon@four-pillars.co.uk

web: www.four-pillars.co.uk

dir: A34 at junct with A415, in Abingdon, turn right at rdbt, hotel on right

On the outskirts of Abingdon, this busy commercial hotel is well located for access to major roads. Bedrooms are comfortable and well equipped with extras such as satellite TV and trouser presses. All day refreshments are offered in the lounge and conservatory.

Rooms 63 en suite (7 fmly) (31 GF) ⊛ in 40 bedrooms S £58-£108; D £76-£134 (incl. bkfst) **Facilities** STV FTV ♬ Xmas **Conf** Thtr 140 Class 80 Board 48 Del £159 **Parking** 85 **Notes** LB ⊗ ⊛ in restaurant Civ Wed 100

★★ 72% **HOTEL**

Crown & Thistle
18 Bridge St OX14 3HS

☎ 01235 522556 📠 01235 553281

e-mail: reception@crownandthistle.com

dir: follow A415 towards Dorchester into town centre

A cosy hotel situated at edge of this historical market town and a just stone's throw from the Thames. There is a variety of bar and lounge areas and a maze of bright, airy corridors linking individually styled bedrooms. The spacious reception leads to an outdoor courtyard for drinks and snacks. The Gallery restaurant and bar provides a pleasant atmosphere with friendly, efficient staff and satisfying cuisine.

Rooms 19 en suite (3 fmly) S £72.50; D £80 **Facilities** STV Pool table **Conf** Thtr 12 Class 8 Board 12 Del £100 **Parking** 35 **Notes** LB ⊗ ⊛ in restaurant

★★ 71% **HOTEL**

Dog House
Old English Inns

Faringdon Rd, Frilford Heath OX13 6QJ

☎ 01865 390830 📠 01865 390860

e-mail: doghouse.frilford@oldenglishinns.co.uk

web: www.oldenglish.co.uk

As its name suggests, The Dog House was once the kennels (and the stables) for a local manor house. Situated in the heart of the Oxfordshire countryside, this is a popular small hotel with a spacious bar and restaurant that offers a wide variety of meals and lighter options with carvery available on Sundays. Conference facilities and weddings are also catered for.

Rooms 20 en suite (2 fmly) (4 GF) ⊛ in all bedrooms S £49-£73; D £55-£95 (incl. bkfst) **Facilities** Xmas **Conf** Thtr 30 Class 15 Board 12 **Parking** 40 **Notes** ⊛ in restaurant

BUDGET HOTEL

Premier Travel Inn Abingdon
premier travel inn

Marcham Rd OX14 1AD

☎ 08701 977014 📠 01235 554149

web: www.premiertravelinn.com

dir: On A415 0.5 m from Abingdon town centre. Approx. 0.5m from the A34 at the Abingdon South junct

High quality, modern budget accommodation ideal for both families and business travellers. Spacious, en suite bedrooms feature bath and shower, satellite TV and many have telephones and modem points. The adjacent family restaurant features a wide and varied menu. For further details consult the Hotel Groups page.

Rooms 25 en suite

ADDERBURY
MAP 11 SP43

★★ 75% **HOTEL**

Red Lion
Old English Inns

The Green, Oxford Rd OX17 3LU

☎ 01295 810269 📠 01295 811906

e-mail: 6496@greeneking.co.uk

web: www.oldenglish.co.uk

dir: M40 junct 11 into Banbury, take A4260 towards Bodicote and into Adderbury, hotel on left.

This charming, former coaching inn was once an important stop-over on the old Banbury to Oxford road. The atmosphere typifies an English inn, and dedicated staff offer a warm welcome. The comfortable and spacious bedrooms are attractively decorated - some are split-level and one has a four-poster. Honest, fresh food is served in the restaurant and the bar.

Rooms 12 en suite (1 GF) ⊛ in all bedrooms S £65-£75; D £85-£90 (incl. bkfst) **Facilities** Xmas **Conf** Thtr 20 Class 16 Board 15 Del £105 **Parking** 20 **Notes** ⊗ ⊛ in restaurant

BANBURY
MAP 11 SP44

★★★ 79% **HOTEL**

Macdonald Whately Hall
MACDONALD HOTELS & RESORTS

Banbury Cross OX16 0AN

☎ 0870 400 8104 📠 01295 271736

e-mail: whatelyhall@macdonald-hotels.co.uk

web: www.macdonald-hotels.co.uk

dir: M40 junct 11, straight over 2 rdbts, left at 3rd, 0.25m to Banbury Cross, hotel on right

Dating back to 1677, this historic inn boasts many original features such as stone passages, priests' holes and a fine wooden staircase. Spacious public areas include the oak-panelled restaurant, which overlooks the attractive well-tended gardens, a choice of lounges and a traditional bar. Smartly appointed bedrooms vary in size and style but all are thoughtfully equipped.

Rooms 69 en suite (3 fmly) (2 GF) ⊛ in all bedrooms D £130-£170 (incl. bkfst) **Facilities** STV ♨ Wi-fi in bedrooms Xmas **Conf** Thtr 150 Class 80 Board 40 Del £165 **Services** Lift **Parking** 80 **Notes** LB ⊛ in restaurant Civ Wed 100

England

BANBURY *continued*

★★★ 77% HOTEL

Best Western Banbury House

Oxford Rd OX16 9AH

☎ 01295 259361 🖹 01295 270954

e-mail: sales@banburyhouse.co.uk

web: www.banburyhouse.co.uk

dir: *approx 200yds from Banbury Cross on A423 towards Oxford*

Within easy reach of the Banbury Cross, this attractive Georgian property offers smart, comfortable accommodation in individually decorated and furnished bedrooms. The contemporary rooms and a spacious suite are particularly stylish. The public areas include a spacious foyer lounge and a contemporary bar and restaurant, both offering a good choice of menus. Staff are particularly friendly and helpful.

Rooms 64 en suite (4 fmly) (8 GF) ⊗ in 24 bedrooms S £48-£120; D £96-£150 **Facilities** STV Wi-fi available **Conf** Thtr 70 Class 35 Board 28 Del from £110 **Parking** 60 **Notes LB** ⊗ ⊘ in restaurant Closed 24 Dec-2 Jan

★★★ 70% HOTEL

Best Western Wroxton House

Wroxton St Mary OX15 6QB

☎ 01295 730777 🖹 01295 730800

e-mail: reservations@wroxtonhousehotel.com

dir: *A422 from Banbury, 2.5m to Wroxton, hotel on right entering village*

Dating in parts from 1647, this partially thatched hotel is set just off the main road. Bedrooms, which have either been created out of converted cottages or are situated in a more modern wing, are comfortable and well equipped. The public areas are open plan and consist of a reception lounge and a bar, and the low-beamed Inglenook Restaurant has a peaceful atmosphere for dining.

Rooms 32 en suite (1 fmly) (7 GF) ⊗ in 15 bedrooms S £75-£99; D £85-£150 (incl. bkfst) **Facilities** STV Xmas **Conf** Thtr 45 Class 20 Board 25 Del from £99 **Parking** 50 **Notes LB** ⊘ in restaurant Civ Wed 60

★★ 71% HOTEL

Cromwell Lodge Hotel

OLD ENGLISH INNS

9-11 North Bar OX16 0TB

☎ 01295 259781 🖹 01295 276619

e-mail: 6434@greeneking.co.uk

web: www.oldenglish.co.uk

dir: *M40 junct 11 towards Banbury, through 3 sets of lights, hotel on left just before Banbury Cross.*

Enjoying a central location, this stylishly refurbished 17th-century property has loads of character. The comfortable bedrooms are furnished and equipped to a high standard, and include a number of spacious suites. Diners can choose between the smart, modern restaurant or the contemporary lounge bar that leads onto the patio and delightful walled garden.

Rooms 23 en suite (1 fmly) (3 GF) ⊗ in all bedrooms S £50-£80; D £65-£95 (incl. bkfst) **Facilities** STV Xmas **Conf** Thtr 30 Class 30 Board 20 Del from £95 **Parking** 20 **Notes** ⊘ in restaurant

BUDGET HOTEL

Premier Travel Inn Banbury

premier travel inn

Warwick Rd, Warmington OX17 1JJ

☎ 0870 9906512 🖹 0870 9906513

web: www.premiertravelinn.com

dir: *5m from Banbury. From N, M40 junct 12 onto B4100 towards Warmington. From S, exit M40 junct 11 onto A423. Take A442, right at B4100*

High quality, modern budget accommodation ideal for both families and business travellers. Spacious, en suite bedrooms feature bath and shower, satellite TV and many have telephones and modem points. The adjacent family restaurant features a wide and varied menu. For further details consult the Hotel Groups page.

Rooms 39 en suite

| BICESTER | MAP 11 SP52 |

★★★ 74% ⊛ HOTEL

Bignell Park Hotel & Restaurant

THE INDEPENDENTS

Chesterton OX26 1UE

☎ 01869 326550 🖹 01869 322729

e-mail: enq@bignellparkhotel.co.uk

dir: *M40 junct 9/A41 to Bicester, over 1st & 2nd rdbts, left at mini-rdbt, follow signs to Witney A4095. Hotel 0.5m*

Charming 16th-century property situated in the peaceful village of Chesterton, just a short drive from Bicester Village Retail Outlet, the M40 and Oxford. Public rooms feature a superb oak beamed restaurant, a smart bar and a comfortable lounge with plush sofas. Bedrooms are smartly decorated, well maintained and equipped with modern facilities.

Rooms 23 en suite (1 fmly) (5 GF) S £90-£145; D £100-£155 (incl. bkfst) **Facilities** STV FTV Xmas **Conf** Thtr 40 Class 16 Board 22 Del from £135 **Parking** 40 **Notes** ⊗ ⊘ in restaurant Civ Wed 40

BUDGET HOTEL

Travelodge Bicester Cherwell Valley (M40)

Travelodge

Moto Service Area, Northampton Rd, Ardley OX27 7RD

☎ 08700 850 950 🖹 01869 346390

web: www.travelodge.co.uk

dir: *M40 junct 10*

Travelodge offers good quality, good value, modern accommodation. Ideal for families, the spacious en suite bedrooms include remote-control TV, tea and coffee-making facilities and comfortable beds. Meals can be taken at the nearby family restaurant. See Hotel Groups pages for further details.

Rooms 98 en suite S fr £26; D fr £26 **Conf** Thtr 40 Class 20 Board 20

England

BLETCHINGDON — MAP 11 SP51

★★★ 68% **HOTEL**

The Oxfordshire Inn

Heathfield Village OX5 3DX

☎ 01869 351444 🖹 01869 351555

e-mail: staff@oxfordshireinn.co.uk

web: www.oxfordshireinn.co.uk

dir: From M40 junct 9 take A34 towards Oxford, and A4027 towards Bletchingdon. Hotel signed 0.7m on right

Located a short drive from major road networks this property sits in a tranquil rural location. The accommodation varies in size but all is finished to a good decorative standard. Home-cooked meals are available either in the bar or extensive restaurant.

Rooms 28 en suite (1 fmly) (15 GF) ⊘ in all bedrooms S £49-£69; D £59-£89 (incl. bkfst) **Facilities** Wi-fi available Xmas **Conf** BC Thtr 140 Class 80 Board 30 **Parking** 50 **Notes LB** ⊘ in restaurant

BURFORD — MAP 05 SP21

★★★ 78% ◉◉ **HOTEL**

The Lamb Inn

Sheep St OX18 4LR

☎ 01993 823155 🖹 01993 822228

e-mail: info@lambinn-burford.co.uk

web: www.cotswold-inns-hotels.co.uk

dir: Turn off A40 into Burford, downhill, take 1st left into Sheep St, hotel last on right

This enchanting old inn is just a short walk from the centre of a delightful Cotswold village. An abundance of character and charm is found inside with a cosy lounge and log fire, and in intimate bar with flagged floors. An elegant restaurant is on offer where locally sourced produce is carefully prepared. Bedrooms, some with original features are comfortable and well appointed.

Rooms 15 en suite (1 fmly) (3 GF) ⊘ in all bedrooms **Parking** 15 **Notes LB** ⊘ in restaurant

★★★ 77% ◉ **HOTEL**

The Bay Tree Hotel

CLASSIC
BRITISH HOTELS

12-14 Sheep St OX18 4LW

☎ 01993 822791 🖹 01993 823008

e-mail: info@baytreehotel.info

web: www.cotswold-inns-hotels.co.uk/index.aspx

dir: M40 junct 8 or M5 junct 11, then follow A40 to Burford. Or M4 junct 15, then A419 then A361 to Burford. From High St turn into Sheep St, next to the old market square. Hotel is on right

History and modern flair sit happily side by side at this delightful old inn, situated near the town centre. Bedrooms are tastefully furnished using the original features to good effect and some have four-poster or half-tester beds. Public areas consist of a character bar, a sophisticated airy restaurant, a selection of meeting rooms and an attractive walled garden.

Rooms 8 en suite 13 annexe en suite (2 fmly) ⊘ in all bedrooms S £60-£119; D £81-£175 (incl. bkfst) **Facilities** ⇜ Xmas **Conf** Thtr 40 Class 12 Board 25 Del £155 **Parking** 50 **Notes LB** ⊘ in restaurant Civ Wed 60

BURFORD *continued*

★★★ 73% HOTEL

Cotswold Gateway

Cheltenham Rd OX18 4HX
☎ 01993 822695 📄 01993 823600
e-mail: cotswold.gateway@dial.pipex.com
web: www.cotswold-gateway.co.uk
dir: *Hotel on rdbt at A40 Oxford/Cheltenham at junct with A361*

Ideally suited for both business and pleasure guests, this hotel is prominently situated on the A40 and yet only a short walk away from Burford. The tastefully decorated bedrooms include two four-poster rooms. Diners have an extensive choice of popular dishes and the option of eating in the character bar, the coffee shop or in the more formal restaurant.

Rooms 13 en suite 8 annexe en suite (2 fmly) ⊛ in all bedrooms
Facilities Xmas **Conf** Thtr 40 Class 20 Board 24 **Parking** 60 **Notes** ⊗
⊗ in restaurant

★★ 75% HOTEL

The Inn For All Seasons

THE INDEPENDENTS

The Barringtons OX18 4TN
☎ 01451 844324 📄 01451 844375
e-mail: sharp@innforallseasons.com
web: www.innforallseasons.com
dir: *3m W of Burford on A40 towards Cheltenham*

This 16th-century coaching inn is conveniently near to Burford. Bedrooms are comfortable and steadily being upgraded, and public areas retain a feeling of period charm with original fireplaces and oak beams. A good selection of bar meals is available at lunchtime, while the evening menu includes an appetising selection of fresh fish.

Rooms 9 en suite 1 annexe en suite (2 fmly) (1 GF) ⊛ in 5 bedrooms
S £51.50-£59; D £87-£102 **Facilities** STV Clay pigeon shooting Local. Riding
Stables Xmas **Conf** Thtr 25 Class 30 Board 30 Del from £110 **Parking** 62

BUDGET HOTEL

Travelodge Burford Cotswolds

Bury Barn OX18 4JF
☎ 08700 850 950 📄 01993 822699
web: www.travelodge.co.uk
dir: *A40/A361*

Travelodge offers good quality, good value, modern accommodation. Ideal for families, the spacious en suite bedrooms include remote-control TV, tea and coffee-making facilities and comfortable beds. Meals can be taken at the nearby family restaurant. See Hotel Groups pages for further details.

Rooms 40 en suite S fr £26; D fr £26

CHARLBURY   MAP 11 SP31

★★ 67% ⊛ HOTEL

The Bell

Church St OX7 3PP
☎ 01608 810278 📄 01608 811447
e-mail: bellhotel.charlbury@hotmail.co.uk
web: www.bellhotel-charlbury.co.uk

dir: *from Oxford take A34 towards Woodstock, then B4437 towards Charlbury. In village, 2nd on left, hotel opposite St Mary's Church*

Now under new ownership this mellow Cotswold-stone inn dates back to the 16th century, when it was home to Customs & Excise, and sits close to the town centre. Popular with locals, the bar has an enjoyable and relaxed atmosphere and comes complete with flagstone floors and log fires. The well-equipped bedrooms are situated in the main building and the adjacent converted barn.

Rooms 7 en suite 4 annexe en suite (2 fmly) ⊛ in all bedrooms S £69;
D £85 (incl. bkfst) **Facilities** FTV Wi-fi in bedrooms Xmas **Conf** Thtr 60
Class 60 Board 30 Del from £90 **Parking** 40 **Notes LB** ⊗ in restaurant

If the freedom to smoke or be in a
non-smoking atmosphere is important to you,
check the rules when you book

CHIPPING NORTON   MAP 10 SP32

★★★ 68% HOTEL

Best Western Crown & Cushion

23 High St OX7 5AD

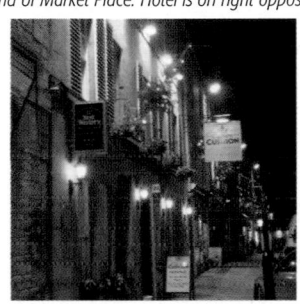

☎ 01608 642533 📠 01608 642926

e-mail: alan@thecrownandcushion.com

web: www.thecrownandcushion.com

dir: *west end of Market Place. Hotel is on right opposite TIC*

A former coaching inn with the ambience of a past age but with the comforts of today. Guests can enjoy the popular and welcoming bar, the more formal restaurant and the indoor leisure facilities. Bedrooms, a variety of sizes and styles, are situated in the main building and in the courtyard.

Rooms 40 en suite (5 fmly) (5 GF) ⊛ in 10 bedrooms S £64; D £75-£85 (incl. bkfst) **Facilities** 🏋 supervised Squash Gym Wi-fi available Xmas **Conf** BC Thtr 180 Class 120 Board 80 Del £125 **Parking** 45 **Notes LB** ⊛ in restaurant

DEDDINGTON   MAP 11 SP43

★★★ 73% ⊛ HOTEL

Deddington Arms

Horsefair OX15 0SH

☎ 0800 3287031 01869 338364 📠 01869 337010

e-mail: deddarms@oxfordshire-hotels.co.uk

web: www.oxfordshire-hotels.co.uk

dir: *From S: M40 junct 10 signed Northampton onto A43. 1st dbt left to Aynho and left to Deddington. From N: M40 junct 11 to Banbury. Through Banbury to hospital & Adderbury on A4260, then to Deddington*

This charming and friendly old inn is conveniently located off the Market Square. The well-equipped bedrooms are comfortably appointed and either situated in the main building or a purpose built

continued

courtyard wing. The bar is full of character and the delightful restaurant enjoys a well-deserved, local following.

Rooms 27 en suite (4 fmly) (9 GF) ⊛ in 7 bedrooms S fr £90; D fr £99 (incl. bkfst) **Facilities** STV Wi-fi in bedrooms Many facilities avaliable locally Xmas **Conf** Thtr 40 Class 20 Board 25 Del £135 **Parking** 56 **Notes LB** ⊛ ⊛ in restaurant

★★★ 72% HOTEL

Holcombe Hotel & Restaurant

High St OX15 0SL

☎ 01869 338274 📠 01869 337010

e-mail: holcombe@oxfordshire-hotels.co.uk

web: www.holcombe-hotel.co.uk

dir: *on A4260 (Banbury to Oxford road). From M40 junct 11 follow Adderbury signs, then Deddington. From M40 junct 10 take B4100 to Aynho, then B4031 to Deddington*

This hotel enjoys a convenient roadside location, within easy reach of the village centre. Public areas include the stylish Peppers bar and an eye-catching restaurant serving pasta, pizzas and other specialities; in the warmer months the gardens offer a peaceful place in which to relax. Bedrooms are traditional in design with many thoughtful touches.

Rooms 15 en suite (2 fmly) ⊛ in 14 bedrooms S £90-£99; D £99-£110 (incl. bkfst) **Facilities** Wi-fi in bedrooms Xmas **Conf** Thtr 25 Class 15 Board 18 **Parking** 40 **Notes LB** ⊛ ⊛ in restaurant

DIDCOT   MAP 05 SU59

BUDGET HOTEL

Premier Travel Inn Didcot

Milton Interchange, Milton OX14 4DP

☎ 08701 977073 📠 01235 820465

web: www.premiertravelinn.com

dir: *on A4130 at junct with A34*

High quality, modern budget accommodation ideal for both families and business travellers. Spacious, en suite bedrooms feature bath and shower, satellite TV and many have telephones and modem points. The adjacent family restaurant features a wide and varied menu. For further details consult the Hotel Groups page.

Rooms 60 en suite

England

DORCHESTER (ON THAMES) MAP 05 SU59

★★★ 73% ◉◉ **HOTEL**

White Hart

High St OX10 7HN

☎ 01865 340074 📠 01865 341082

e-mail: whitehart@oxfordshire-hotels.co.uk

web: www.oxfordshire-hotels.co.uk

dir: *M40 junct 6, take B4009 through Watlington & Benson to A4074. Follow signs to Dorchester. Hotel on right*

Period charm and character are plentiful throughout this 17th-century coaching inn, which is situated in the heart of a picturesque village. The spacious bedrooms are individually decorated and thoughtfully equipped. Public rooms include a cosy bar, a choice of lounges and an atmospheric restaurant, complete with vaulted timber ceiling.

Rooms 22 en suite 4 annexe en suite (2 fmly) (9 GF) ⊗ in 6 bedrooms **Facilities** STV Xmas **Conf** BC Thtr 30 Class 20 Board 18 **Parking** 36 **Notes** ⊗

★★★ 67% ◉ **HOTEL**

George

25 High St OX10 7HH

☎ 01865 340404 📠 01865 341620

e-mail: thegeorgehotel@fsmail.net

dir: *M40 junct 6 onto B4009 through Watlington & Benson. Take A4074 at BP petrol station, follow Dorchester signs. Hotel on left*

Full of character and charm, this quintessential coaching inn stands beside Dorchester Abbey and dates back to the 15th century. The bedrooms are decorated in keeping with the style of the building, and are divided between the main house and the courtyard. Meals can be taken either in the lively, atmospheric bar or in the intimate restaurant.

Rooms 9 en suite 8 annexe en suite (1 fmly) ⊗ in 4 bedrooms **Conf** Thtr 40 Class 36 Board 24 Del from £120 **Parking** 75 **Notes** ⊗ in restaurant

FARINGDON MAP 05 SU29

★★★ 75% **HOTEL**

BW Sudbury House Hotel & Conference Centre

London St SN7 8AA

☎ 01367 241272 📠 01367 242346

e-mail: stay@sudburyhouse.co.uk

web: www.sudburyhouse.co.uk

dir: *off A420, signed Folly Hill*

Set in pleasant grounds this hotel offers bedrooms that are attractive, decorated in warm colour schemes, spacious and well equipped. Dining options include the restaurant, bar and a comprehensive room service menu.

Rooms 49 en suite (2 fmly) (10 GF) ⊗ in 28 bedrooms S £85-£95; D £95-£105 (incl. bkfst) **Facilities** STV Gym 🏌 Putt green Wi-fi in bedrooms Pitch & Putt, Badminton, Boules Xmas **Conf** Thtr 100 Class 30 Board 34 Del from £135 **Services** Lift **Parking** 100 **Notes LB** ⊗ in restaurant Civ Wed 160 *See advert on this page*

GREAT MILTON   MAP 05 SP60

INSPECTORS' CHOICE

★★★★★ ◉ ◉ ◉ ◉ ◉ **HOTEL**

Le Manoir Aux Quat' Saisons

Church Rd OX44 7PD

☎ 01844 278881 📠 01844 278847

e-mail: lemanoir@blanc.co.uk

web: www.manoir.com

dir: from A329 2nd right to Great Milton Manor, hotel 200yds on right

Le Manoir may have celebrated its 21st birthday in 2005, but its iconic chef patron, Raymond Blanc, still fizzes with new ideas and projects. His first loves are his kitchen and his garden and the vital link between them. The fascinating grounds now feature a Malaysian theme alongside the Japanese garden and extensive vegetable cultivation. Even the car park has a stunning artichoke sculpture. The kitchen is the epicentre, with outstanding cooking highlighting freshness and seasonality. Bedrooms in this idyllic 'grand house on a small scale' are either in the main house or around an outside courtyard. All offer the highest levels of comfort and quality, have magnificent marble bathrooms and are equipped with a host of thoughtful extra touches.

Rooms 9 en suite 23 annexe en suite S £360-£895; D £360-£895 (incl. bkfst) **Facilities** STV 🏊 Cookery School, Water Gardens Xmas **Conf** Thtr 24 Board 20 **Parking** 60 **Notes LB** ⊗ ⊘ in restaurant Civ Wed 50

HENLEY-ON-THAMES   MAP 05 SU78

★★★★ 75% ◉ **TOWN HOUSE HOTEL**

Hotel du Vin and Bistro

New St RG9 2BP

☎ 01491 848400 📠 01491 848401

e-mail: info@henley.hotelduvin.com

web: www.hotelduvin.com

dir: M4 junct 8/9 signed High Wycombe, A404, A4130 to Henley. Over bridge, up Hart St, right onto Bell St, right onto New St

This hotel retains much of the architecture of the former Breakspears brewery, and sits only 50 yards from the water. Food, and naturally wine take high priority here; alfresco dining is possible too. Bedrooms provide comfort, style and a good range of facilities.

Rooms 43 en suite (4 fmly) (4 GF) ⊘ in all bedrooms S £115-£395; D £115-£395 **Facilities** STV **Conf** Thtr 30 Class 20 Board 36 Del £205 **Services** air con **Parking** 36 **Notes** ⊘ in restaurant Civ Wed 60

★★★ 72% ◉ ◉ **HOTEL**

The White Hart Nettlebed

High St, Nettlebed RG9 5DD

☎ 01491 641245 📠 01491 649018

e-mail: info@whitehartnettlebed.com

web: www.whitehartnettlebed.com

dir: on A4130 3.5m from Henley-on-Thames towards Oxford

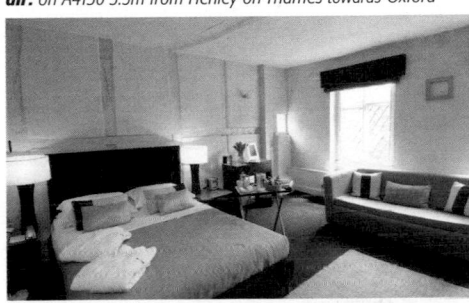

The combination of traditional and contemporary within the relaxed atmosphere of this pleasant hotel creates unique surroundings in which to enjoy the attentive service. Bedrooms are located in the main building and the courtyard, and are equipped with a host of modern comforts and thoughtful extras. A wide selection of dishes, featuring carefully sourced, organic ingredients can be enjoyed in either the bar or the restaurant where cooking could be described as delightfully straightforward.

Rooms 6 en suite 6 annexe en suite (3 fmly) (3 GF) ⊘ in all bedrooms S £85-£125; D £95-£125 (incl. bkfst) **Facilities** Wi-fi in bedrooms 🎵 Xmas **Conf** BC Thtr 60 Class 30 Board 20 Del from £145 **Parking** 50 **Notes LB** ⊗ ⊘ in restaurant

England

KINGHAM   MAP 10 SP22

★★★ 79% ◉◉ **HOTEL**

Mill House Hotel & Restaurant

OX7 6UH

☎ 01608 658188 🖷 01608 658492

e-mail: stay@millhousehotel.co.uk

web: www.millhousehotel.co.uk

dir: off A44 onto B4450. Hotel indicated by tourist sign

This Cotswold-stone, former mill house has been carefully converted into a comfortable and attractive hotel. It is set in well-kept grounds bordered by its own trout stream. Bedrooms are comfortable and provide thoughtfully equipped accommodation. There is a peaceful lounge and bar, plus an atmospheric restaurant where the imaginative, skilfully cooked dishes are a highlight of any stay.

Rooms 21 en suite 2 annexe en suite (1 fmly) (7 GF) S £115-£125; D £180-£200 (incl. bkfst & dinner) **Facilities** STV Fishing ❧ Wi-fi available Xmas **Conf** BC Thtr 70 Class 24 Board 20 Del from £135 **Parking** 62 **Notes LB** ❷ in restaurant Civ Wed 150

KIRTLINGTON   MAP 11 SP41

★★★ 75% **HOTEL**

Dashwood Hotel and Restaurant

South Green, Heyford Rd OX5 3HJ

☎ 01869 352707 🖷 01869 351432

e-mail: info@thedashwood.co.uk

web: www.thedashwood.co.uk

dir: M40 junct 10, S on B430 signed Middleton Stoney. After lights in Middleton Stoney right onto A4095 signed Kirtlington. In village hotel approx 800mtrs on right just before sharp bend

This village centre, former inn has been lovingly and completely refurbished to provide smart modern bedrooms, some of which are situated in a nearby annexe. A sophisticated bar and restaurant comes complete with a wealth of period features and an open plan kitchen.

Rooms 5 en suite 7 annexe en suite (1 fmly) (3 GF) ❷ in all bedrooms S fr £85; D £110-£150 (incl. bkfst) **Facilities** FTV Xmas **Parking** 27 **Notes** ❽ ❷ in restaurant

MIDDLETON STONEY   MAP 11 SP52

★★ 75% **HOTEL**

Best Western Jersey Arms

OX25 4AD

☎ 01869 343234 🖷 01869 343565

e-mail: jerseyarms@bestwestern.co.uk

web: www.jerseyarms.co.uk

Best Western

dir: on B430, 10m N of Oxford, between junct 9 & 10 of M40

With a history dating back to the 13th century, the Jersey Arms combines old-fashioned charm with contemporary style and elegance. The individually designed bedrooms are well equipped and comfortable. The lounge has an open fire, and the smartly refurbished spacious restaurant provides a calm atmosphere in which to enjoy the hotel's popular cuisine.

Rooms 6 en suite 14 annexe en suite (3 fmly) (9 GF) ❷ in 6 bedrooms S £85-£100; D £99-£158 (incl. bkfst) **Facilities** Wi-fi in bedrooms Xmas **Conf** Board 20 Del from £135 **Parking** 55 **Notes LB** ❽ ❷ in restaurant

MILTON COMMON   MAP 05 SP60

★★★★ 78% **HOTEL**

The Oxford Belfry

OX9 2JW

MarstonHotels

☎ 01844 279381 🖷 01844 279624

e-mail: oxfordbelfry@marstonhotels.com

web: www.marstonhotels.com

dir: M40 junct 7 onto A329 to Thame. Left onto A40 by Three Pigeons pub. Hotel 300yds on right

This modern hotel has a relatively rural location and enjoys lovely views of the countryside to the rear. The hotel is built around two very attractive courtyards and has a number of lounges and conference rooms, as well as indoor leisure facilities and outdoor tennis courts. Bedrooms are large and feature a range of extras.

Rooms 130 en suite (10 fmly) ❷ in 72 bedrooms S fr £132; D fr £171 (incl. bkfst) **Facilities** STV ☒ ♨ Sauna Solarium Gym ❧ Wi-fi available **Conf** Thtr 300 Class 180 Board 100 Del from £210 **Services** Lift **Parking** 250 **Notes LB** ❽ ❷ in restaurant Civ Wed 110

See advert on opposite page

OXFORD
See also Milton Common

MAP 05 SP50

★★★★★ ◎◎◎◎◎ **HOTEL**

Le Manoir Aux Quat' Saisons

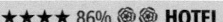

Church Rd OX44 7PD
☎ 01844 278881 📠 01844 278847
e-mail: lemanoir@blanc.co.uk
web: www.manoir.com

RELAIS &
CHATEAUX.

(For full entry see Great Milton)

★★★★ 86% ◎◎ **HOTEL**

Macdonald Randolph

🏰 MACDONALD
HOTELS & RESORTS

Beaumont St OX1 2LN
☎ 0870 400 8200 📠 01865 791678
e-mail: randolph@macdonald-hotels.co.uk
web: www.macdonald-hotels.co.uk

dir: M40 junct 8, A40 towards Oxford. Follow City Centre signs, leading to St Giles, hotel on right

Superbly located near the town centre, The Randolph boasts impressive neo-Gothic architecture and tasteful decor. The spacious and traditional restaurant, complete with picture windows, is an ideal place to watch the world go by and enjoy freshly prepared, modern dishes. Bedrooms include a mix of classical and contemporary rooms, which have been appointed to a high standard. Parking is a real bonus.

Rooms 150 en suite ⊘ in 121 bedrooms S £140-£180; D £150-£450 **Facilities Spa** STV Sauna Gym Wi-fi in bedrooms Treatment rooms Xmas **Conf** Thtr 300 Class 130 Board 60 Del from £150 **Services** Lift **Parking** 50 **Notes LB** ⊘ in restaurant Civ Wed 120

★★★★ 78% ◎ **HOTEL**

The Old Bank Hotel

92-94 High St OX1 4BN
☎ 01865 799599 📠 01865 799598
e-mail: info@oldbank-hotel.co.uk
web: www.oldbank-hotel.co.uk

dir: from Magdalen Bridge into High St, hotel 50yds on left

Located close to the city centre and colleges this former bank benefits from an excellent location. An eclectic collection of modern pictures and photographs, many by well-known artists, can be seen here. Bedrooms are small with excellent business facilities plus the benefit of air conditioning. Public areas include the vibrant all-day Quod Bar and Restaurant. The hotel also has a residents' lounge and its own car park.

Rooms 42 en suite (10 fmly) (1 GF) ⊘ in all bedrooms S £150-£305; D £165-£325 **Facilities** STV Discounts with various leisure facilities **Conf** Thtr 30 Board 18 **Services** Lift air con **Parking** 40 **Notes** ⊗ Closed 25-27 Dec

★★★★ 76% **HOTEL**

The Paramount Oxford Hotel

Godstow Rd, Wolvercote Roundabout OX2 8AL
☎ 01865 489988 📠 01865 489952
e-mail: oxford@paramount-hotels.co.uk
web: www.paramount-hotels.co.uk

PARAMOUNT
GROUP OF HOTELS

dir: adjacent to A34/A40, 2m from city centre

Conveniently located on the northern edge of the city centre, this purpose-built hotel offers bedrooms that are bright, modern and well equipped. Guests can eat in the 'Medio' restaurant or try the Cappuccino bar menu. The hotel offers impressive conference, business and leisure facilities.

Rooms 168 en suite (13 fmly) (89 GF) ⊘ in 140 bedrooms S £69-£160; D £79-£160 **Facilities** STV 🏊 supervised Squash Sauna Solarium Gym Wi-fi in bedrooms Steam room **Conf** BC Thtr 300 Class 150 Board 60 Del from £139 **Parking** 250 **Notes LB** ⊘ in restaurant Civ Wed 250

OXFORD *continued*

★★★★ 73% TOWN HOUSE HOTEL

Old Parsonage

1 Banbury Rd OX2 6NN
☎ 01865 310210 📠 01865 311262
e-mail: info@oldparsonage-hotel.co.uk
web: www.oldparsonage-hotel.co.uk

dir: from Oxford ring road to city centre via Summertown. Hotel last building on right next to St Giles Church before city centre

Dating back in parts to the 16th century, this stylish hotel offers great character and charm and is conveniently located at the northern edge of the city centre. Refurbished bedrooms are attractively furnished and particularly well appointed. The focal point of the operation is the busy all-day bar restaurant, whilst the small garden areas and terraces are popular in summer months.

Rooms 30 en suite (4 fmly) (10 GF) ⊘ in all bedrooms S £135-£225; D £155-£225 **Facilities** STV Wi-fi available Complimentary use of punt and house bikes ♫ Xmas **Conf** Board 20 Del from £210 **Services** air con **Parking** 16 **Notes** ⊘ in restaurant Civ Wed 20

★★★★ 73% HOTEL

Oxford Thames Four Pillars Hotel

Henley Rd, Sandford-on-Thames OX4 4GX
☎ 0800 374 692 & 01865 334444 📠 01865 334400
e-mail: thames@four-pillars.co.uk
web: www.four-pillars.co.uk

dir: M40 junct 8 towards Oxford, follow ring road. Left at rdbt towards Cowley. At rdbt with lights turn left to Littlemore, hotel approx 1m on right

The main house of this hotel is built from local, yellow stone. The spacious and traditional River Restaurant has superb views over the hotel's own boat, moored on the river. The gardens can be enjoyed

continued

from the patios or balconies in the bedroom wings. Public rooms include a beamed bar and lounge area with minstrels' gallery.

Rooms 60 en suite (4 fmly) (24 GF) ⊘ in 35 bedrooms S £79-£162; D £92-£209 (incl. bkfst) **Facilities** FTV 🎾 ♨ Sauna Gym Jacuzzi Wi-fi in bedrooms Steam room Xmas **Conf** BC Thtr 160 Class 80 Board 60 Del £189 **Parking** 120 **Notes** LB ⊗ ⊘ in restaurant Civ Wed 120

★★★★ 71% ❀ HOTEL

Cotswold Lodge

66a Banbury Rd OX2 6JP
☎ 01865 512121 📠 01865 512490
e-mail: info@cotswoldlodgehotel.co.uk
web: www.cotswoldlodgehotel.co.uk

dir: off A40 Oxford ring road onto A4165 Banbury Rd. Signed city centre and Summertown. Hotel 2m on left

This family-run Victorian property is located close to the centre of Oxford and offers smart, comfortable accommodation. Stylish bedrooms and suites are attractively presented and some have balconies. The public areas have an elegant country-house feel. The hotel is popular with business guests and caters for conferences and banquets.

Rooms 49 en suite (8 GF) ⊘ in all bedrooms **Facilities** STV Wi-fi in bedrooms Discount at local gym **Conf** Thtr 100 Class 60 Board 60 Del from £120 **Parking** 40 **Notes** ⊗ ⊘ in restaurant

★★★★ 67% HOTEL

Oxford Spires Four Pillars Hotel

Abingdon Rd OX1 4PS
☎ 0800 374 692 & 01865 324324 📠 01865 324325
e-mail: spires@four-pillars.co.uk
web: www.four-pillars.co.uk

dir: M40 junct 8 towards Oxford. Left towards Cowley. At 3rd rdbt follow City Centre signs. Hotel 1m

This purpose-built hotel is surrounded by extensive parkland, yet is only a short walk from the city centre. Bedrooms are attractively furnished, well equipped and include several apartments. Smartly appointed public areas include a spacious restaurant, open plan bar/lounge, leisure club and extensive conference facilities.

Rooms 123 en suite (54 GF) ⊘ in 44 bedrooms S £79-£162; D £92-£209 (incl. bkfst) **Facilities** FTV 🎾 Sauna Gym Jacuzzi Wi-fi in bedrooms Beauty, steam rooms ♫ Xmas **Conf** BC Thtr 266 Class 96 Board 76 Del £189 **Services** Lift **Parking** 95 **Notes** LB ⊗ ⊘ in restaurant Civ Wed 140

★★★ 85% ❀ HOTEL

Malmaison Oxford

3 Oxford Castle, New Rd OX1 1AY
☎ 01865 268400 📠 01865 268402
web: www.malmaison.com

This one time prison is now Oxford's latest destination hotel with many of the guest rooms transformed from the old cells. Be reassured though, there have been significant improvements since the previous occupants left - exceedingly comfortable beds and luxury bathrooms to name a couple. There is a popular brasserie, run on the same lines as the other Malmaisons, providing both quality and value. Limited parking space is available.
Malmaison - AA Hotel Group of the Year 2006-7.

Rooms 94 en suite (5 GF) S £140-£350; D £140-£350 **Facilities** STV Snooker Gym Xmas **Services** Lift **Parking** 20 **Notes** LB ⊘ in restaurant

★★★ 78% **METRO HOTEL**

Macdonald Eastgate Townhouse

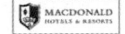

73 High St OX1 4BE

☎ 0870 400 8201 & 01865 248332 📠 01865 791681

e-mail: sales.eastgate@macdonald-hotels.co.uk

web: www.macdonald-hotels.co.uk

dir: A40 follow signs to Headington & Oxford city centre, over Magdalen Bridge, stay in left lane, left into Merton St, entrance to car park on left

Just a short stroll from the city centre, this hotel, as its name suggests, occupies the site of the city's medieval East Gate and boasts its own car park. Bedrooms are appointed and equipped to a high standard. Stylish public areas include the all-day Town House Brasserie and Bar.

Rooms 63 en suite (3 fmly) ⊘ in 30 bedrooms **Facilities** STV **Conf** Board 16 **Services** Lift **Parking** 40 **Notes LB** ⊗ ⊘ in restaurant

★★★ 78% ◉ **HOTEL**

Weston Manor Hotel

OX25 3QL

☎ 01869 350621 📠 01869 350901

e-mail: reception@westonmanor.co.uk

web: www.westonmanor.co.uk

(For full entry see Weston-on-the-Green)

★★★ 77% **HOTEL**

Westwood Country

Hinksey Hill, Boars Hill OX1 5BG

☎ 01865 735408 📠 01865 736536

e-mail: reservations@westwoodhotel.co.uk

web: www.westwoodhotel.co.uk

dir: off Oxford ring road at Hinksey Hill junct towards Boars Hill & Wootton. At top of hill road bends to left. Hotel on right

This Edwardian country-house hotel is prominently set in terraced landscaped grounds and is within easy reach of the city centre by car. The hotel is modern in style with very comfortable, well-equipped and tastefully decorated bedrooms. Public areas include a contemporary bar, a cosy lounge and a restaurant overlooking the pretty garden.

Rooms 23 en suite (4 fmly) (6 GF) S £65-£85; D £99-£125 (incl. bkfst) **Facilities** ⊌ Wi-fi in bedrooms Arrangement with local health club ch fac **Conf** Thtr 60 Class 36 Board 35 Del from £135 **Parking** 60 **Notes** ⊗ ⊘ in restaurant Civ Wed 200

★★★ 71% **HOTEL**

Hawkwell House

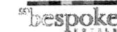

Church Way, Iffley Village OX4 4DZ

☎ 01865 749988 📠 01865 748525

e-mail: reservations@hawkwellhouse.co.uk

web: www.bespokehotels.com

dir: A34 follow signs to Cowley. At Littlemore rdbt take A4158 exit onto Iffley Rd. After traffic lights left to Iffley

Set in a peaceful residential location, Hawkwell House is just a few minutes' drive from the Oxford ring road. The spacious rooms are modern, attractively decorated and well equipped. Public areas are tastefully appointed and the conservatory-style restaurant offers an interesting choice of dishes. The hotel also has a range of conference and function facilities.

Rooms 66 en suite (10 fmly) (4 GF) ⊘ in 55 bedrooms S £105-£115; D £140-£150 (incl. bkfst) **Facilities** STV Gym ⊌ Wi-fi available ch fac Xmas **Conf** Thtr 200 Class 100 Board 80 Del from £155 **Services** Lift **Parking** 120 **Notes LB** ⊗ ⊘ in restaurant Civ Wed 150

★★★ 67% **HOTEL**

Best Western Linton Lodge

11-13 Linton Rd OX2 6UJ

☎ 01865 553461 📠 01865 553691

e-mail: sales@lintonlodge.com

web: www.lintonlodge.com

dir: to Oxford city centre, along Banbury Rd. After 0.5m right into Linton Rd. Hotel opposite St Andrews Church

Located in a residential area, this hotel is within walking distance of the town centre. Bedrooms are modern, well equipped and comfortable. The restaurant has a library theme, and the bar overlooks extensive lawned gardens to the rear of the hotel.

Rooms 71 en suite (2 fmly) (14 GF) ⊘ in 40 bedrooms S £75-£95; D £85-£135 (incl. bkfst) **Facilities** STV ⊌ Putt green Wi-fi in bedrooms **Conf** Thtr 120 Class 50 Board 40 Del from £100 **Services** Lift **Parking** 40 **Notes LB** ⊗ ⊘ in restaurant Civ Wed 120

★★ 74% **HOTEL**

The Balkan Lodge Hotel

315 Iffley Rd OX4 4AG

☎ 01865 244524 📠 01865 251090

e-mail: balkanlodge@aol.co.uk

dir: from M40/A40 take eastern bypass, into city on A4158

Conveniently located for the city centre and the ring road, this family operated hotel offers a comfortable stay. Bedrooms are attractive and well equipped; one has a four-poster bed and jacuzzi bath. Public

continued on page 534

England

OXFORD *continued*

areas include a lounge, bar and restaurant. A large, secure, private car park is located to the rear.

Rooms 13 en suite ⊗ in all bedrooms S £55.50-£68.50; D £68.50-£82.50 (incl. bkfst) **Facilities** STV **Notes LB** ⊗ in restaurant

★★ 71% HOTEL

Victoria
180 Abingdon Rd OX1 4RA
☎ 01865 724536 📠 01865 794909
e-mail: victoriahotel@aol.com
dir: from M40/A40 take Eastern bypass and A4144 into city

Located within easy reach of Oxford city centre and the motorway networks, this hotel offers a warm welcome. Bedrooms are comfortable, well maintained and furnished to a high standard. A conservatory bar and large dining room are ideal places to relax.

Rooms 15 en suite 5 annexe en suite (2 fmly) (6 GF) ⊗ in 15 bedrooms S £62.50-£68.50; D £78.50-£85.50 (incl. bkfst) **Conf** Board 20 **Parking** 20 **Notes LB** ⊗ in restaurant

★★ 68% METRO HOTEL

Manor House
250 Iffley Rd OX4 1SE
☎ 01865 727627 📠 01865 200478
dir: on A4158 1m from city centre

This family-run establishment is easily accessible from the city centre and all major road links. It provides informal, friendly yet attentive service. and a bar is also available. The comfortably furnished bedrooms are well equipped and have en suite facilities. The hotel has its own bar but various restaurants and popular pubs are within easy walking distance. Private parking is available.

Rooms 8 en suite (2 fmly) ⊗ in all bedrooms S £69-£79; D £79-£99 (incl. bkfst) **Facilities** Garden available for families **Parking** 6 **Notes LB** ⊗ Closed 20 Dec-20 Jan

BUDGET HOTEL

Express by Holiday Inn Oxford-Kassam Stadium
Grenoble Rd OX4 4XP
☎ 01865 780888 📠 01865 780999
e-mail: reservations@expressoxford.com
dir: M40 junct 8 onto A40 for 4m. Left at McDonalds onto A4142. After 3.5m left onto A4074, take 1st exit signed Science Park & Kassam Stadium

A modern hotel ideal for families and business travellers. Fresh and uncomplicated, the spacious bedrooms include Sky TV, power shower and tea and coffee-making facilities. Continental buffet breakfast is included in the room rate; other meals may be taken at the nearby family pub or restaurant. For further details consult the Hotel Groups page.

Rooms 162 en suite

BUDGET HOTEL

Premier Travel Inn Oxford

Oxford Business Park, Garsington Rd OX4 2JZ
☎ 08701 977204 📠 01865 775887
web: www.premiertravelinn.com
dir: on Oxford Business Park, just off A4142 & B480 junct

High quality, modern budget accommodation ideal for both families and business travellers. Spacious, en suite bedrooms feature bath and shower, satellite TV and many have telephones and modem points. The adjacent family restaurant features a wide and varied menu. For further details consult the Hotel Groups page.

Rooms 120 en suite

BUDGET HOTEL

Travelodge Oxford Peartree
Peartree Roundabout, Woodstock Rd OX2 8JZ
☎ 08700 850 950 📠 01865 513474
web: www.travelodge.co.uk
dir: at junct of A34/A44

Travelodge offers good quality, good value, modern accommodation. Ideal for families, the spacious en suite bedrooms include remote-control TV, tea and coffee-making facilities and comfortable beds. Meals can be taken at the nearby family restaurant. See Hotel Groups pages for further details.

Rooms 150 en suite S fr £26; D fr £26 **Conf** Thtr 300 Class 150 Board 60

Travelodge Oxford Wheatley
London Rd, Wheatley OX33 1JH
☎ 08700 850 950 📠 01865 875905
dir: off A40 next to The Harvester on outskirts of Wheatley
Rooms 36 en suite S fr £26; D fr £26

OXFORD MOTORWAY SERVICE AREA (M40)
MAP 05 SP60

BUDGET HOTEL

Days Inn Oxford
M40 junction 8A, Waterstock OX33 1LJ
☎ 01865 877000 📠 01865 877016
e-mail: oxford.hotel@welcomebreak.co.uk
web: www.welcomebreak.co.uk
dir: M40 junct 8a, Welcome Break service area.

This modern building offers accommodation in smart, spacious and well-equipped bedrooms, suitable for families and business travellers, and all with en suite bathrooms. Continental breakfast is available and other refreshments may be taken at the nearby family restaurant. For further details see the Hotel Groups page.

Rooms 59 en suite

STADHAMPTON   MAP 05 SU69

◉ ◉ **RESTAURANT WITH ROOMS**

The Crazy Bear Hotel

Bear Lane OX44 7UR

☎ 01865 890714 🖨 01865 400481

e-mail: sales@crazybearhotel.co.uk

dir: M40 junct 7 left at end of slip road, into Stadhampton. Over mini-rdbt at petrol station. Hotel 2nd left

This popular and attractive restaurant with rooms successfully combines modern chic with old world character. Cuisine is extensive and varied with award-winning Thai and English restaurants under the same roof (both awarded two AA rosettes). Those choosing to make a night of it can enjoy the concept bedrooms, all presented and equipped to a very high standard; the 'infinity suites' have state-of-the-art facilities.

Rooms 5 en suite 12 annexe en suite (3 fmly) (2 GF) S £80-£140 D £120-£375 **Facilities** STV Wi-fi available Beauty salon Treatments **Conf** Max 40 Thr 30 Class 30 Board 30 Del from £185 **Parking** 50 **Notes** Civ Wed 50 ⊗

STEEPLE ASTON   MAP 11 SP42

★★★ 68% **HOTEL**

The Holt Hotel

Oxford Rd OX25 5QQ

☎ 01869 340259 🖨 01869 340865

e-mail: info@holthotel.co.uk

web: www.holthotel.co.uk

dir: junct of B4030/A4260

This attractive former coaching inn has given hospitality to many over the centuries, not least to Claude Duval, a notorious 17th-century highwayman. Today guests are offered well-equipped modern bedrooms and attractive public areas, which include a relaxing bar, restaurant and a well-appointed lounge. A selection of meeting rooms is available.

Rooms 86 en suite (19 fmly) ⊛ in 16 bedrooms S £75-£85; D £85-£95 (incl. bkfst) **Facilities** STV Wi-fi in bedrooms Xmas **Conf** BC Thtr 140 Class 70 Board 44 Del from £110 **Parking** 200 **Notes** LB ⊛ in restaurant Civ Wed 100

THAME   MAP 05 SP70

★★★ 82% ◉ **HOTEL**

Spread Eagle

Cornmarket OX9 2BW

☎ 01844 213661 🖨 01844 261380

e-mail: enquiries@spreadeaglethame.co.uk

web: www.spreadeaglethame.co.uk

dir: town centre on A418 Oxford to Aylesbury Road, M40 junct 6 S, junct 8 N

This former coaching inn, which is privately owned, is set on the main thoroughfare of this delightful market town. Well-equipped bedrooms vary in size and style, with some located in a sympathetically constructed extension. Public areas include a comfortable bar and the

continued

informal Fothergills Brasserie, named after the diarist and raconteur who owned the hotel in the 1920s.

Spread Eagle

Rooms 33 en suite (1 fmly) S £99.95-£114.95; D £114.95-£134.95 (incl. bkfst) **Facilities** Xmas **Conf** Thtr 250 Class 100 Board 50 Del from £125 **Parking** 80 **Notes** LB ⊗ ⊛ in restaurant Civ Wed 200

BUDGET HOTEL

Travelodge Thame

OX9 3AX

☎ 08700 850 950 🖨 01844 218740

web: www.travelodge.co.uk

dir: A418/B4011

Travelodge offers good quality, good value, modern accommodation. Ideal for families, the spacious en suite bedrooms include remote-control TV, tea and coffee-making facilities and comfortable beds. Meals can be taken at the nearby family restaurant. See Hotel Groups pages for further details.

Rooms 31 en suite S fr £26; D fr £26

WALLINGFORD   MAP 05 SU68

★★★ 78% ◉ **HOTEL**

The Springs Hotel & Golf Club

Wallingford Rd, North Stoke OX10 6BE

☎ 01491 836687 🖨 01491 836877

e-mail: info@thespringshotel.com

web: www.thespringshotel.com

dir: off A4074 (Oxford-Reading road) onto B4009 (Goring). Hotel approx 1m on right

Set on its own golf course, this Victorian mansion has a timeless and peaceful atmosphere. The generously equipped bedrooms vary in size but many are spacious. The elegant restaurant enjoys splendid views over the spring-fed lake where a variety of wildfowl enjoy the natural

continued on page 536

England

WALLINGFORD *continued*

surroundings. There is also a comfortable lounge with original features, and a cosy bar to relax in.

Rooms 32 en suite (4 fmly) (8 GF) ⊗ in 20 bedrooms S £95-£140; D £110-£155 (incl. bkfst) **Facilities** STV FTV ⁇ ⅃ 18 Fishing Sauna ⅗ Putt green Wi-fi available Golf course on sight, putting green, clay pigeon shooting nearby ♫ Xmas **Conf** BC Thtr 60 Class 16 Board 26 Del from £155 **Parking** 150 **Notes LB** ⊗ in restaurant Civ Wed 90

★★★ 74% HOTEL

Shillingford Bridge

Shillingford OX10 8LZ

☎ 01865 858567 📄 01865 858636

e-mail: shillingford.bridge@forestdale.com

web: www.forestdale.com

dir: M4 junct 10, A329 through Wallingford towards Thame, then B4009 through Watlington. Right on A4074 at Benson, then left at Shillingford rdbt (unclass road) Wallingford road

This hotel enjoys a superb position right on the banks of the River Thames, and benefits from private moorings and a waterside open-air swimming pool. The public areas, appointed to a high standard, have large picture windows making the best use of the view. Bedrooms are well equipped and furnished with guest comfort in mind.

Rooms 32 en suite 8 annexe en suite (6 fmly) (9 GF) ⊗ in 23 bedrooms S £90; D £125 (incl. bkfst) **Facilities** STV FTV ⁇ supervised Fishing Wi-fi in bedrooms Table tennis ♫ Xmas **Conf** Thtr 80 Class 36 Board 36 Del £125 **Parking** 100 **Notes LB** ⊗ in restaurant Civ Wed 150

★★★ 71% HOTEL

The George

High St OX10 0BS

☎ 01491 836665 📄 01491 825359

e-mail: info@george-hotel-wallingford.com

web: www.peelhotel.com

dir: E side of A329 on N entry to town

Old world charm and modern facilities merge seamlessly in this former coaching inn. Bedrooms in the main house have charm and character in abundance. Those in the wing have a more contemporary style, but all are well equipped and attractively decorated. Diners can choose between the restaurant and bistro, or relax in the cosy bar.

Rooms 39 en suite (1 fmly) (9 GF) ⊗ in 21 bedrooms S £115-£135; D £130-£145 **Facilities** STV Wi-fi in bedrooms Xmas **Conf** Thtr 120 Class 60 Board 40 Del £139 **Parking** 60 **Notes LB** ⊗ ⊗ in restaurant Civ Wed 100

WESTON-ON-THE-GREEN   MAP 11 SP51

★★★ 78% ⊛ HOTEL

Weston Manor

OX25 3QL

☎ 01869 350621 📄 01869 350901

e-mail: reception@westonmanor.co.uk

web: www.westonmanor.co.uk

dir: M40 junct 9, A34 towards Oxford. Turn right at rdbt (B4030), hotel 100yds on left

Character, charm and sophistication blend effortlessly in this friendly hotel that is set in well-tended grounds. Bedrooms are well equipped and are located in the main house, coach house or a cottage annexe. Award-winning food can be enjoyed in the impressive vaulted restaurant, complete with original oak panelling and minstrels' gallery; other public areas include an atmospheric foyer lounge, a bar and meeting facilities.

Rooms 15 en suite 20 annexe en suite (5 fmly) (6 GF) ⊗ in all bedrooms S £99-£115; D £121-£154 (incl. bkfst) **Facilities** ⁇ ⅗ Wi-fi available **Conf** Thtr 60 Class 20 Board 32 Del from £140 **Parking** 100 **Notes LB** ⊛ ⊗ in restaurant Civ Wed 100

WITNEY   MAP 05 SP31

★★★ 75% HOTEL

Witney Four Pillars Hotel

Ducklington Ln OX28 4TJ

☎ 0800 374 692 & 01993 779777 📄 01993 703467

e-mail: witney@four-pillars.co.uk

web: www.four-pillars.co.uk

dir: M40 junct 9, A34 to A40, exit A415 Witney/Abingdon. Hotel on left, 2nd exit for Witney

This attractive modern hotel is close to Oxford and Burford and offers spacious, well-equipped bedrooms. The cosy Spinners Bar has comfortable seating areas and the popular Weavers Restaurant offers a

continued

good range of dishes. Other amenities include extensive function and leisure facilities, complete with indoor swimming pool.

Rooms 86 en suite (16 fmly) (20 GF) ⊘ in all bedrooms S £69-£108; D £79-£134 (incl. bkfst) **Facilities** Spa FTV 🔍 Sauna Gym Wi-fi in bedrooms Steam room ♫ Xmas **Conf** Thtr 160 Class 80 Board 46 Del £159 **Services** air con **Parking** 170 **Notes** LB ⊗ ⊘ in restaurant Civ Wed 120

WOODSTOCK   MAP 11 SP41

★★★ 81% ⦾⦿ **HOTEL**

Feathers   bespoke

Market St OX20 1SX

☎ 01993 812291 📠 01993 813158

e-mail: enquiries@feathers.co.uk

web: www.bespokehotels.com

dir: from Oxford take A44 to Woodstock, 1st left after lights. Hotel on left

This intimate, individual hotel enjoys a town centre location with easy access to nearby Blenheim Palace. Public areas are elegant and full of traditional character from the cosy drawing room to the atmospheric restaurant. Individually styled bedrooms are appointed to a high standard and are furnished with attractive period and reproduction furniture.

Rooms 20 en suite (4 fmly) (2 GF) D £145-£275 (incl. bkfst) **Facilities** 1 suite has steam room ch fac Xmas **Conf** Thtr 25 Class 20 Board 16 Del from £150 **Notes** LB ⊘ in restaurant

★★★ 81% ⦾⦿ **HOTEL**

Macdonald Bear   MACDONALD
                               HOTELS & RESORTS

Park St OX20 1SZ

☎ 0870 400 8202 & 01993 811124 📠 01993 813380

e-mail: bear@macdonald-hotels.co.uk

web: www.macdonald-hotels.co.uk

dir: M40 junct 8 onto A40 to Oxford/M40 junct 9 onto A34 S to Oxford. Take A44 into Woodstock. Left to town centre hotel on left opp town hall

With its ivy-clad facade, oak beams and open fireplaces, this 13th-century coaching inn exudes charm and cosiness. The hotel boasts bedrooms decorated in a modern style that is sympathetic to their original character. Public rooms include a variety of function rooms, an intimate bar area and an attractive restaurant where attentive service and good food are offered.

Rooms 36 en suite 18 annexe en suite (1 fmly) (9 GF) ⊘ in all bedrooms S £122-£132; D £144-£164 (incl. bkfst) **Facilities** STV Wi-fi in bedrooms Xmas **Conf** Thtr 60 Class 14 Board 24 Del from £135 **Parking** 40 **Notes** LB ⊘ in restaurant RS 01-Jan

★★★ 71% **HOTEL**

Kings Arms

19 Market St OX20 1SU

☎ 01993 813636 📠 01993 813737

e-mail: stay@kingshotelwoodstock.co.uk

web: www.kings-hotel-woodstock.co.uk

dir: on corner of Market St and A44 Oxford Rd in town centre

This appealing and contemporary hotel is situated in the centre of town just a short walk from Blenheim Palace. Public areas include an attractive bistro-style restaurant and a smart bar. Bedrooms and bathrooms are comfortably furnished and equipped, having been totally refurbished to a high standard.

Rooms 15 en suite ⊘ in 14 bedrooms S £70-£100; D £130-£150 (incl. bkfst) **Facilities** Wi-fi in bedrooms **Notes** LB ⊗ No children 12yrs ⊘ in restaurant

★★ 🅰

Marlborough Arms

26 Oxford St OX20 1TS

☎ 01993 811227 📠 01993 811657

e-mail: themarlborough@ic24.net

dir: 200mtrs from Blenheim Palace

Rooms 10 en suite (2 fmly) **Conf** Board 14 **Parking** 11 **Notes** ⊘ in restaurant

RUTLAND

EMPINGHAM   MAP 11 SK90

★★ 74% **HOTEL**

The White Horse Inn

Main St LE15 8PS

☎ 01780 460221 📠 01780 460521

e-mail: info@whitehorserutland.co.uk

web: www.whitehorserutland.co.uk

dir: on A606, Oakham to Stamford road

This attractive stone-built inn, offering bright, comfortable accommodation, is conveniently located just minutes from the A1. Bedrooms in the main building are spacious and include a number of family rooms. Public areas include a well-stocked bar, a bistro and restaurant where a wide range of meals is served.

Rooms 4 en suite 9 annexe en suite (3 fmly) (5 GF) ⊘ in 4 bedrooms S £50; D £65-£80 (incl. bkfst) **Conf** Thtr 50 Class 40 Board 30 Del from £60 **Parking** 60 **Notes** LB ⊘ in restaurant Closed 25th Dec

GREETHAM   MAP 11 SK91

★★★ 74% **HOTEL**

Greetham Valley

Wood Ln LE15 7NP

☎ 01780 460444 📠 01780 460623

e-mail: info@gvgc.co.uk

web: www.greethamvalley.co.uk

Spacious bedrooms with storage facilities designed for golfers, offer high levels of comfort and many with superb views over the two 18-hole golf courses. Meals are taken in the clubhouse restaurants

continued on page 538

GREETHAM *continued*

with a choice of informal or formal styles. A beauty suite and extensive conference facilities are ideal for both large or small groups.

Rooms 35 en suite (17 GF) ⊘ in all bedrooms S £52.50-£70; D £52.50-£70 **Facilities** Spa STV FTV ♪ 36 Fishing Solarium Putt green 4x4 course Off road training course Archery centre ch fac Xmas **Conf** Thtr 200 Class 150 Board 80 Del from £95 **Services** Lift **Parking** 300 **Notes LB** ⊗ ⊘ in restaurant Civ Wed 200

MORCOTT   MAP 11 SK90

BUDGET HOTEL

Travelodge Uppingham Morcott

Uppingham LE15 8SA

☎ 08700 850 950 🖺 01572 747719

web: www.travelodge.co.uk

dir: on A47, eastbound

Travelodge offers good quality, good value, modern accommodation. Ideal for families, the spacious en suite bedrooms include remote-control TV, tea and coffee-making facilities and comfortable beds. Meals can be t1aken at the nearby family restaurant. See Hotel Groups pages for further details.

Rooms 40 en suite S fr £26; D fr £26

NORMANTON   MAP 11 SK90

★★★ 74% HOTEL

Normanton Park Hotel

Oakham LE15 8RP

☎ 01780 720315 🖺 01780 721086

e-mail: info@normantonpark.co.uk

web: www.normantonpark.com

dir: From A1 follow A606 towards Oakham, Normanton sign in 1m. Turn left, 1.5m. Hotel on right

This delightful hotel, set in its own grounds on the shore of Rutland Water, has now been refurbished to high standard and there are two dining styles available including an extensive Chinese menu. Bedrooms are well furnished and there are ample public rooms for guest use.

Rooms 23 en suite (7 fmly) (8 GF) ⊘ in all bedrooms S £70-£90; D £90-£140 (incl. bkfst) **Facilities** STV Xmas **Conf** Thtr 100 Class 25 Board 30 Del from £145 **Parking** 70 **Notes LB** ⊗ ⊘ in restaurant Civ Wed 100

Some hotels have restricted service during quieter months, and at this time some of the facilities will not be available

OAKHAM   MAP 11 SK80

INSPECTORS' CHOICE

★★★★ ◎◎◎◎ COUNTRY HOUSE HOTEL

Hambleton Hall

Hambleton LE15 8TH

☎ 01572 756991 🖺 01572 724721

e-mail: hotel@hambletonhall.com

web: www.hambletonhall.com

dir: 3m E off A606

Established over 25 years ago by Tim and Stefa Hart this delightful country house enjoys tranquil and spectacular views over Rutland Water. The beautifully manicured grounds are a delight to walk in. The bedrooms in the main house are stylish, individually decorated and equipped with a range of thoughtful extras. A two-bedroom folly, with its own sitting and breakfast room, is only a short walk away. Day rooms include a cosy bar and a sumptuous drawing room, both featuring open fires. The elegant restaurant serves skilfully prepared, award-winning cuisine with menus highlighting locally sourced, seasonal produce - some grown in the hotel's own grounds.

Rooms 15 en suite 2 annexe en suite ⊘ in 3 bedrooms S £165-£195; D £195-£360 **Facilities** STV ⇲ supervised ⛳ ♨ Private access to lake Xmas **Conf** Thtr 40 Board 24 Del from £260 **Services** Lift **Parking** 40 **Notes LB** ⊘ in restaurant Civ Wed 64

★★★ 74% ◎ HOTEL

Barnsdale Lodge

The Avenue, Rutland Water, North Shore LE15 8AH

☎ 01572 724678 🖺 01572 724961

e-mail: enquiries@barnsdalelodge.co.uk

web: www.barnsdalelodge.co.uk

dir: off A1 onto A606. Hotel 5m on right, 2m E of Oakham

A popular and interesting hotel converted from a farmstead and

continued

England

overlooking Rutland Water. The public areas are dominated by a successful food operation with a good range of appealing meals on offer. Bedrooms are comfortably appointed with excellent beds and period furnishings, enhanced by contemporary soft furnishings and thoughtful extras.

Rooms 44 en suite (2 fmly) (15 GF) ⊗ in 45 bedrooms S £75-£80; D £99-£110 (incl. bkfst) **Facilities Spa** STV Fishing ⚓ Shooting Archery Golf Riding arranged Beauty treatments Xmas **Conf** BC Thtr 330 Class 120 Board 76 Del from £132.19 **Parking** 200 **Notes LB** ⊗ in restaurant Civ Wed 200

UPPINGHAM   MAP 11 SP89

★★★ 66% **HOTEL**

Falcon

The Market Place LE15 9PY
☎ 01572 823535 🖹 01572 821620
e-mail: sales@thefalconhotel.com
web: www.thefalconhotel.com

dir: A47 onto A6003, left at lights, hotel on right

An attractive, 16th-century coaching inn situated in the heart of this bustling market town. Public areas feature an open-plan lounge bar, with a relaxing atmosphere and comfortable sofas. The brasserie area offers a cosmopolitan-style snack menu, while more formal meals are provided in the Garden Terrace Restaurant.

Rooms 25 en suite (4 fmly) (3 GF) S £60; D £95-£130 (incl. bkfst) **Facilities** FTV Snooker Wi-fi in bedrooms 🎵 ch fac Xmas **Conf** Thtr 60 Class 40 Board 34 Del from £98 **Parking** 33 **Notes LB** ⊗ in restaurant Civ Wed 150

★★ 76% ◉◉ **HOTEL**

The Lake Isle Restaurant & Town House Hotel

16 High St East LE15 9PZ
☎ 01572 822951 🖹 01572 824400
e-mail: info@lakeislehotel.com
web: www.lakeislehotel.com

dir: in the centre of Uppingham via Queen Street

This attractive, townhouse hotel centres round a delightful restaurant and small elegant bar. There is also an inviting first-floor guest lounge. Bedrooms are extremely well appointed and thoughtfully equipped and include spacious split-level cottage suites situated in a quiet courtyard. Imaginative cooking and an extremely impressive list of wines are highlights.

Rooms 9 en suite 3 annexe en suite (1 fmly) (1 GF) ⊗ in all bedrooms **Facilities** ch fac **Conf** Board 10 **Parking** 7 **Notes LB** ⊗ in restaurant

---

SHROPSHIRE

ALVELEY   MAP 10 SO78

★★★★ 68% **HOTEL**

Mill Hotel & Restaurant

WV15 6HL
☎ 01746 780437 🖹 01746 780850
e-mail: info@themill-hotel.co.uk
web: www.themill-hotel.co.uk

dir: midway between Kidderminster & Bridgnorth, turn off A442 signed Enville & Turley Green

Built around a 17th-century water mill, with the original water wheel still on display, this extended and renovated hotel is set in eight acres of landscaped grounds. Bedrooms are pleasant, well equipped and include some superior rooms, which have sitting areas. There are also some rooms with four-poster beds. The restaurant provides carefully prepared dishes and there are extensive wedding and function facilities.

Rooms 41 en suite (3 fmly) ⊗ in 25 bedrooms S £80-£125; D £90-£150 **Facilities** STV FTV Gym Wi-fi in bedrooms **Conf** Thtr 220 Class 150 Board 80 Del from £135 **Services** Lift **Parking** 200 **Notes LB** ⊗ ⊗ in restaurant Civ Wed 200

BRIDGNORTH   MAP 10 SO79

★★★ ◉◉◉ **HOTEL**

Old Vicarage Hotel and Restaurant

Worfield WV15 5JZ
☎ 01746 716497 🖹 01746 716552
e-mail: admin@the-old-vicarage.demon.co.uk
web: www.oldvicarageworfield.com

(For full entry see Worfield)

CHURCH STRETTON   MAP 15 SO49

★★★ 70% ◉ **HOTEL**

Stretton Hall Hotel

All Stretton SY6 6HG   THE INDEPENDENTS
☎ 01694 723224 & 0845 1668404 🖹 01694 724365
e-mail: aa@strettonhall.co.uk

dir: from Shrewsbury, on A49, right onto B4370 signed All Stretton. Hotel 1m on left opposite The Yew Tree pub

This fine 18th-century country house stands in spacious gardens. Original oak panelling features throughout the lounge bar, lounge and halls. Bedrooms are traditionally furnished and have modern facilities. Family and four-poster rooms are available and the restaurant is tastefully appointed.

Rooms 12 en suite (1 fmly) S £50-£115; D £85-£130 (incl. bkfst) **Facilities** Wi-fi in bedrooms ch fac Xmas **Conf** BC Thtr 70 Class 24 Board 18 Del from £100 **Parking** 70 **Notes LB** ⊗ in restaurant Civ Wed 60

England

CHURCH STRETTON *continued*

★★ 68% HOTEL

Longmynd Hotel
Cunnery Rd SY6 6AG
☎ 01694 722244 ▤ 01694 722718
e-mail: info@longmynd.co.uk

dir: *A49 into town centre on Sandford Ave, left at Lloyds TSB, over mini-rdbt, 1st right into Cunnery Rd, hotel at hill top on left*

This family-run hotel, set in attractive gardens, overlooks this country town and the views from many of the rooms are breathtaking. Bedrooms are generally spacious, comfortable and well equipped. Facilities include a range of comfortable lounges.

Rooms 50 en suite (8 fmly) ⊘ in all bedrooms S £55-£80; D £110-£160 (incl. bkfst) **Facilities** ★ Sauna Wi-fi available Putt green Pitch and putt course **Conf** Thtr 100 Class 50 Board 40 Del £105 **Services** Lift **Parking** 100 **Notes** LB ⊘ in restaurant Civ Wed 100

HODNET   MAP 15 SJ62

★★ 65% HOTEL

Bear
TF9 3NH   THE INDEPENDENTS
☎ 01630 685214 & 685788 ▤ 01630 685787
e-mail: info@bearhotel.org.uk
web: www.bearhotel.org.uk

dir: *junct of A53 & A442 in village*

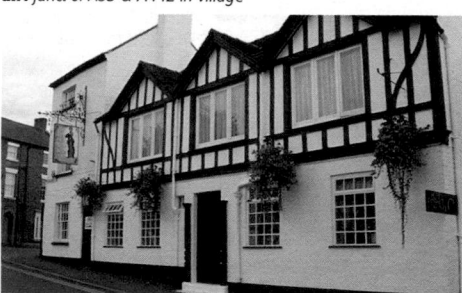

This 16th-century former coaching inn provides bedrooms equipped with all modern comforts. The public areas have a wealth of charm and character, enhanced by features such as exposed beams. There is a large baronial-style function room and medieval banquets are something of a speciality here.

Rooms 6 en suite 2 annexe en suite (2 fmly) S £50-£55; D £65-£75 (incl. bkfst) **Conf** Thtr 60 Class 40 Board 30 **Parking** 70 **Notes** ⊗ ⊘ in restaurant Civ Wed 100

LUDLOW   MAP 10 SO57

★★★ 83% ֎ ֎ ֎ HOTEL

Overton Grange Country House
Old Hereford Rd SY8 4AD
☎ 01584 873500 ▤ 01584 873524
e-mail: info@overtongrangehotel.com
web: www.overtongrangehotel.com

dir: *off A49 at B4361 to Ludlow. Hotel 200yds on left*

Overton Grange is a traditional country-house hotel with stylish, comfortable bedrooms, and high standards of guest care. Food is an important part of what the hotel has to offer, so the restaurant serves classically based, French-style cuisine, using locally sourced produce where possible. Meeting and conference rooms are available.

Rooms 14 en suite ⊘ in all bedrooms S £95-£160; D £140-£240 (incl. bkfst) **Facilities Spa** ֎ supervised Sauna ⅏ Jacuzzi Wi-fi available Xmas **Conf** BC Thtr 100 Class 40 Board 20 Del from £135 **Parking** 50 **Notes** LB ⊘ in restaurant Civ Wed 60 Closed 29 Dec-7 Jan

★★★ 78% ֎ ֎ HOTEL

Dinham Hall
By the Castle SY8 1EJ
☎ 01584 876464 ▤ 01584 876019
e-mail: info@dinhamhall.co.uk
web: www.dinhamhall.co.uk

dir: *opposite the castle*

Built in 1792, this lovely old house stands in attractive gardens immediately opposite Ludlow Castle. It has a well-deserved reputation for warm hospitality and fine cuisine. Well-equipped bedrooms include two in a converted cottage and some with four-poster beds. The comfortable public rooms are elegantly appointed.

Rooms 11 en suite 2 annexe en suite (3 fmly) (1 GF) S £110-£210; D £140-£240 (incl. bkfst) **Facilities** Xmas **Conf** Thtr 80 Class 50 Board 26 Del from £135 **Parking** 16 **Notes** LB ⊘ in restaurant Civ Wed 150

★★★ 67% ֎ HOTEL

Feathers
The Bull Ring SY8 1AA
☎ 01584 875261 ▤ 01584 876030
e-mail: feathers.ludlow@btconnect.com
web: www.feathersatludlow.co.uk

dir: *from A49 and follow town centre signs to centre of Ludlow. Hotel on left*

Famous for the carved woodwork outside and in, this picturesque 17th-century hotel is one of the town's best-known landmarks and is

continued

in an excellent location. Bedrooms are traditional in style and décor. Public areas have retained much of the traditional charm; the first-floor lounge is particularly stunning.

Rooms 40 en suite (3 fmly) ⊗ in 19 bedrooms S £75-£85; D £90-£180 (incl. bkfst) **Facilities** Xmas **Conf** Thtr 80 Class 40 Board 40 Del from £120 **Services** Lift **Parking** 33 **Notes LB** ⊗ in restaurant Civ Wed 25

★★ 68% HOTEL

Cliffe
Dinham SY8 2JE
☎ 01584 872063 🖹 01584 873991
e-mail: thecliffehotel@hotmail.com
dir: in town centre turn left at castle gates to Dinham, follow over bridge. Take right fork, hotel 200yds on left

Built in the 19th century and standing in extensive grounds and gardens, this privately owned and personally run hotel is quietly located close to the castle and the river. It provides well-equipped accommodation, and facilities include a lounge bar, a pleasant restaurant and a patio overlooking the garden.

Rooms 9 en suite (2 fmly) ⊗ in all bedrooms S £50-£60; D £80-£100 (incl. bkfst) **Parking** 22 **Notes LB** ⊗ in restaurant

BUDGET HOTEL

Travelodge Ludlow Woofferton
Woofferton SY8 4AL
☎ 08700 850 950 🖹 01584 711695
web: www.travelodge.co.uk
dir: on A49 at junct A456/B4362

Travelodge offers good quality, good value, modern accommodation. Ideal for families, the spacious en suite bedrooms include remote-control TV, tea and coffee-making facilities and comfortable beds. Meals can be taken at the nearby family restaurant. See Hotel Groups pages for further details.

Rooms 32 en suite S fr £26; D fr £26

MARKET DRAYTON   MAP 15 SJ63

★★★ 78% ⊛ HOTEL

Goldstone Hall
Goldstone TF9 2NA
☎ 01630 661202 🖹 01630 661585
e-mail: enquiries@goldstonehall.com
web: www.goldstonehall.com
dir: 4m S of Market Drayton off A529 signed Goldstone Hall Hotel. 4m N of Newport signed from A41

Situated in extensive grounds, this charming period property is a family-run hotel. It provides traditionally furnished, well-equipped accommodation, with some more contemporary artistic touches. Public rooms are extensive and include a choice of lounges, a snooker room and a conservatory. The hotel has a well-deserved reputation for good food.

Rooms 11 en suite (2 GF) S £80-£98; D £120-£150 (incl. bkfst) **Facilities** STV Snooker **Conf** BC Thtr 50 Class 30 Board 30 Del from £115 **Parking** 60 **Notes LB** ⊗ ⊗ in restaurant Civ Wed 70

★★ 76% ⊛ HOTEL

Rosehill Manor
Rosehill, Ternhill TF9 2JF
☎ 01630 638532 🖹 01630 637008
dir: from rdbt at Ternhill A53 S towards Newport. Hotel 2m on right

Parts of this charming old house, which stands in mature gardens, date back to the 16th century. Privately owned and personally run, it provides well-equipped accommodation including family rooms. Public areas comprise a pleasant restaurant serving award-winning cuisine, a bar and a comfortable lounge. There is also a conservatory, which is available for functions.

Rooms 8 en suite (2 fmly) S fr £57.50; D fr £85 (incl. bkfst) **Facilities** ⊰ **Conf** Thtr 100 Class 60 Board 40 **Parking** 80 **Notes** ⊗ in restaurant Civ Wed 100

MUCH WENLOCK   MAP 10 SO69

★★★ 75% ⊛ HOTEL

Raven
Barrow St TF13 6EN
☎ 01952 727251 🖹 01952 728416
e-mail: enquiry@ravenhotel.com
web: www.ravenhotel.com
dir: M54 junct 4 or 5, take A442 S, then A4169 to Much Wenlock

This town centre hotel is spread across several historic buildings with a 17th-century coaching inn at its centre. Accommodation is well furnished and equipped to offer modern comfort, with some ground floor rooms. Public areas feature an interesting collection of prints and memorabilia connected with the modern-day Olympic Games - an idea which was, interestingly, born in Much Wenlock.

Rooms 8 en suite 7 annexe en suite **Facilities** STV Beauty salon **Conf** Thtr 16 Board 16 **Parking** 30 **Notes LB** ⊗ ⊗ in restaurant

★★ 79% HOTEL

Gaskell Arms
Bourton Rd TF13 6AQ
☎ 01952 727212 🖹 01952 728505
e-mail: maxine@gaskellarms.co.uk
web: www.gaskellarms.co.uk
dir: from M6 turn off at junct 10A onto M54. Take junct 4 off M54 follow signs for Ironbridge/Much Wenlock

This 17th-century former coaching inn has exposed beams and log fires in the public areas. In addition to the lounge bar and restaurant, offering a wide range of meals and snacks, there is a small bar which

continued on page 542

England

MUCH WENLOCK *continued*

is popular with locals. Well-maintained bedrooms, some located within sympathetically renovated stables, have good standards of comfort and facilities.

Rooms 16 rms (14 en suite) (3 fmly) (5 GF) ✆ in 5 bedrooms S £60-£75; D £80-£100 (incl. bkfst) **Facilities** Walking, horse riding **Parking** 40 **Notes LB** ✆ ✆ in restaurant

---

NORTON
MAP 10 SJ70

★★ 76% ◉◉ HOTEL

Hundred House Hotel
Bridgnorth Rd TF11 9EE
☎ 01952 730353 🗎 01952 730355
e-mail: reservations@hundredhouse.co.uk
web: www.hundredhouse.co.uk
dir: *midway between Telford and Bridgnorth on A442. In centre of Norton*

Primarily Georgian, but with parts dating back to the 14th century, this friendly family owned and run hotel offers individually styled, well-equipped bedrooms which have period furniture and attractive soft furnishings. Public areas include cosy bars and intimate dining areas where memorable meals are served. There is an attractive conference centre in the old barn.

Rooms 10 en suite (4 fmly) **Conf** Thtr 80 Class 30 Board 32 **Parking** 45 **Notes LB** Closed 25 & 26 Dec nights RS Sun evenings

---

OSWESTRY
MAP 15 SJ22

★★★ 85% ◉◉ HOTEL

Best Western Wynnstay
Church St SY11 2SZ
☎ 01691 655261 🗎 01691 670606
e-mail: info@wynnstayhotel.com
web: www.wynnstayhotel.com

dir: *B4083 to town, fork left at Honda Garage and right at traffic lights. Hotel opposite church*

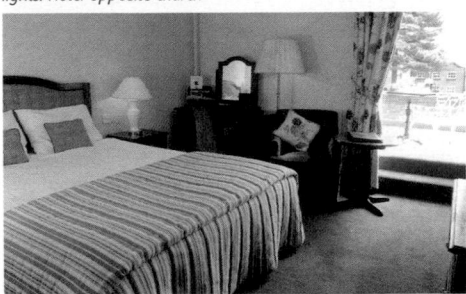

This Georgian property was once a coaching inn and posting house and surrounds a unique 200-year-old Crown Bowling Green. Elegant public areas include a health, leisure and beauty centre, which is housed in a former coach house. Well-equipped bedrooms are individually styled and decorated and include several suites, four-poster rooms and a self-catering apartment. The Four Seasons

continued

Restaurant has a well deserved reputation for its food, and the bar meal operation provides a less formal alternative.

Rooms 29 en suite (4 fmly) ✆ in 14 bedrooms S £85-£90; D £100-£135 **Facilities Spa** STV 🏊 Sauna Solarium Gym Jacuzzi Wi-fi in bedrooms Crown green bowling Beauty suite **Conf** Thtr 290 Class 150 Board 50 Del from £85 **Parking** 70 **Notes LB** ✆ in restaurant Civ Wed 90

See advert on opposite page

★★★ 77% ◉◉ HOTEL

Pen-y-Dyffryn Hall Country Hotel
Rhydycroesau SY10 7JD
☎ 01691 653700 🗎 01978 211004
e-mail: stay@peny.co.uk
web: www.peny.co.uk

dir: *from A5 into Oswestry town centre. Follow signs to Llansilin on B4580, hotel 3m W of Oswestry before Rhydycroesau village*

Peacefully situated in five acres of grounds, this charming old house dates back to around 1840, when it was built as a rectory. The tastefully appointed public rooms have real fires during cold weather, and the accommodation includes several mini-cottages, each with its own patio. This hotel attracts many guests for its food and the attentive, friendly service.

Rooms 8 en suite 4 annexe en suite (1 fmly) (1 GF) ✆ in all bedrooms S £84; D £114-£152 (incl. bkfst) **Facilities** STV FTV Riding Jacuzzi Wi-fi in bedrooms Guided walks Xmas **Parking** 18 **Notes LB** No children 3yrs ✆ in restaurant Closed 18 Dec-19 Jan

★★ 85% SMALL HOTEL

Sebastian's Hotel & Restaurant
45 Willow St SY11 1AQ
☎ 01691 655444 🗎 01691 653452
e-mail: sebastians.rest@virgin.net
web: www.sebastians-hotel.co.uk

dir: *Follow town centre signs. Take road towards Selattyn and Llansilin for 300yds into Willow St, hotel on left*

Parts of this privately owned and personally run small hotel and restaurant date back to 1640. It has a wealth of charm and character, enhanced by original features such as exposed beams and oak panelling in the cosy lounge, bar and popular bistro-style restaurant, where skilfully prepared dishes are served. The well-equipped bedrooms including four in a separate building at the rear, are tastefully appointed in a style befitting the age and character of the property.

Rooms 3 en suite 4 annexe en suite (7 fmly) (2 GF) ✆ in all bedrooms S £60; D £70 **Parking** 7 **Notes LB** ✆ ✆ in restaurant

BUDGET HOTEL

Travelodge Oswestry
Mile End Service Area SY11 4JA
☎ 08700 850 950 🗎 0870 191 1596
web: www.travelodge.co.uk

dir: *at junct of A5/A483*

Travelodge offers good quality, good value, modern accommodation. Ideal for families, the spacious en suite bedrooms include remote-control TV, tea and coffee-making facilities and comfortable beds. Meals can be taken at the nearby family restaurant. See Hotel Groups pages for further details.

Rooms 40 en suite S fr £26; D fr £26

SHIFNAL

MAP 10 SJ70

★★★★ 75% **HOTEL**

Park House

Park St TF11 9BA

☎ 01952 460128 📠 01952 461658

e-mail: reception@parkhousehotel.net

dir: M54 junct 4 follow A464 Wolverhampton Rd for approx 2m, under railway bridge and hotel is 100yds on left

This hotel was created from what were originally two country houses of very different architectural styles. Located on the edge of the

continued

historic market town, it offers guests easy access to motorway networks, a choice of banqueting and meeting rooms, and leisure facilities.

Rooms 38 en suite 16 annexe en suite (4 fmly) (8 GF) ⊗ in 16 bedrooms S £105, D £115 (incl. bkfst) **Facilities Spa** STV 🏊 Sauna Solarium Gym Jacuzzi Wi-fi available Xmas **Conf** Thtr 160 Class 80 Board 40 Del from £132.50 **Services** Lift **Parking** 90 **Notes LB** ⊗ in restaurant Civ Wed 200

★★ 66% **HOTEL**

Haughton Hall

Haughton Ln TF11 8HG

☎ 01952 468300 📠 01952 468313

e-mail: hotel@hostcomputers.co.uk

dir: M54 junct 4 take A464 into Shifnal. Turn left into Haughton Lane, hotel 600yds on left

This listed building dates back to 1718 and stands in open parkland close to the town. It is well geared for the conference trade and also has a 9 hole/par 4 golf course, fishing lake and fine leisure club attached. Comfortable public rooms are available and the dinner menu is extensive. Bedrooms are comfortable and well equipped.

continued on page 544

★★★ ◎◎ 88%

BEST WESTERN

WYNNSTAY HOTEL

Church Street, Oswestry SY11 2SZ

Tel: 01691 655261 Fax: 01691 670606 Email: info@wynnstayhotel.com

The Wynnstay was a well-known posting house on the Liverpool to Cardiff route. The Georgian style building has been preserved through the years with subtle refurbishment in keeping with modern comforts.

Two unique features of the hotel are the 200 year old walled Crown Bowling Green

and the Health, Fitness and Beauty suite, converted in 1995 from the original Coach house and stables. The award winning restaurant is renowned for its relaxing ambience and imaginative food; the Pavilion Lounge Bar, town's best known meeting place offers a choice of lighter meals and a selection of local beers. Executive bedrooms feature sofas and coffee tables; suites have whirlpool baths and many other extras.

SHIFNAL *continued*

Haughton Hall

Rooms 26 en suite 6 annexe en suite (5 fmly) (3 GF) ⊗ in 26 bedrooms
S £70–£100; D £100–£120 (incl. bkfst) **Facilities Spa** ☒ supervised ⚓ 9
⚓ Fishing Sauna Solarium Gym Wi-fi in bedrooms Steam Room,
Therapy Room **Conf** BC Thtr 80 Board 16 **Parking** 60 **Notes** ⊗ in
restaurant Closed 25 & 31 Dec (evening) RS 1 Jan Civ Wed 70

SHREWSBURY
See also Church Stretton

MAP 15 SJ41

★★★★ 75% HOTEL

Macdonald Albrighton Hall

MACDONALD
HOTELS & RESORTS

Albrighton SY4 3AG
☎ 0870 1942129 🖷 01939 291123
e-mail: albrighton@macdonald-hotels.co.uk
web: www.macdonald-hotels.co.uk
dir: *from S M6 junct 10a to M54 to end. From N M6 junct 12 to
M5 then M54. Follow signs Harlescott & Ellesmere to A528*

Dating back to 1630, this former ancestral home is set within 15 acres
of attractive gardens. Rooms are generally spacious and the attic
rooms are particularly popular. Elegant public rooms have rich oak
panelling and there is a modern, well-equipped health and fitness
centre.

Rooms 29 en suite 42 annexe en suite (18 fmly) (11 GF) ⊗ in
49 bedrooms **Facilities Spa** STV ☒ Squash Sauna Solarium Gym
Jacuzzi Beauty treatment rooms **Conf** Thtr 400 Class 120 Board 60
Services Lift **Parking** 200 **Notes LB** ⊗ in restaurant Civ Wed 350

★★★★ 71% ⊛ HOTEL

Albright Hussey Manor
Hotel & Restaurant

Ellesmere Rd SY4 3AF
☎ 01939 290571 & 290523 🖷 01939 291143
e-mail: info@albrighthussey.co.uk
web: www.albrighthussey.co.uk

dir: *2.5m N of Shrewsbury on A528, follow signs for Ellesmere*

First mentioned in the Domesday Book, this enchanting medieval
manor house comes complete with a moat. Bedrooms are situated in
either the sumptuously appointed main house or in the more modern
wing. The intimate restaurant displays an abundance of original
features and there is also a comfortable cocktail bar and lounge.

Rooms 26 en suite (4 fmly) (8 GF) ⊗ in 16 bedrooms S £79–£110;
D £95–£190 **Facilities** ⚓ Jacuzzi Wi-fi in bedrooms ch fac Xmas
Conf BC Thtr 250 Class 180 Board 80 **Parking** 101 **Notes LB** ⊗ in
restaurant Civ Wed 180

★★★ 88% ⊛ HOTEL

Rowton Castle Hotel

Halfway House SY5 9EP
☎ 01743 884044 🖷 01743 884949
e-mail: post@rowtoncastle.com
web: www.rowtoncastle.com
dir: *from A5 near Shrewsbury take A458 to Welshpool. Hotel 4m
on right*

Standing in 17 acres of grounds where a castle has stood for nearly
800 years, this Grade II listed building dates in parts back to 1696.
Many original features remain, including the oak panelling in the
restaurant and a magnificent carved oak fireplace. Most bedrooms are
spacious and all have modern facilities; some have four-poster beds.
The hotel is popular for the quality of its food and is understandably a
popular venue for weddings.

Rooms 19 en suite (3 fmly) **Facilities** ⚓ **Conf** Thtr 80 Class 30
Board 30 **Parking** 100 **Notes LB** ⊛ ⊗ in restaurant Civ Wed 110

★★★ 79% HOTEL

Prince Rupert

Butcher Row SY1 1UQ
☎ 01743 499955 🖷 01743 357306
e-mail: post@prince-rupert-hotel.co.uk
web: www.prince-rupert-hotel.co.uk

dir: *follow town centre signs, over English Bridge & Wyle Cop
Hill. Right into Fish St, 200yds*

Parts of this popular town centre hotel date back to medieval times
and many bedrooms have exposed beams and other original features.
continued

Luxury suites, family rooms and rooms with four-poster beds are all available. As an alternative to the main Royalist Restaurant, diners have two less formal options including an Italian restaurant and a popular bar-bistro. The hotel's car parking service comes recommended.

Prince Rupert

Rooms 70 en suite (4 fmly) S fr £85; D £105-£175 **Facilities** Snooker Sauna Gym Jacuzzi Weight training room Beauty Salon Xmas
Conf Thtr 120 Class 80 Board 40 Del from £110 **Services** Lift
Parking 70 **Notes LB** ⊗ ⊗ in restaurant

See advert on this page

★★★ 74% ⊛⊛ **HOTEL**

Mytton & Mermaid
Atcham SY5 6QG
☎ 01743 761220 ▤ 01743 761292
e-mail: admin@myttonandmermaid.co.uk
web: www.myttonandmermaid.co.uk
dir: *from Shrewsbury over old bridge in Atcham. Hotel opposite main entrance to Attingham Park*

Convenient for Shrewsbury, this ivy-clad former coaching inn enjoys a pleasant location beside the River Severn. Some bedrooms, including family suites, are in a converted stable block adjacent to the hotel. There is a large lounge bar, a comfortable lounge, and a brasserie that is gaining a well-deserved local reputation for its food.

Rooms 11 en suite 7 annexe en suite (1 fmly) ⊛ In all bedrooms S fr £80; D £100-£160 (incl. bkfst) **Facilities** Fishing ♫ Xmas **Conf** BC Thtr 70 Class 24 Board 28 Del £122.50 **Parking** 50 **Notes** ⊗ in restaurant Civ Wed 80

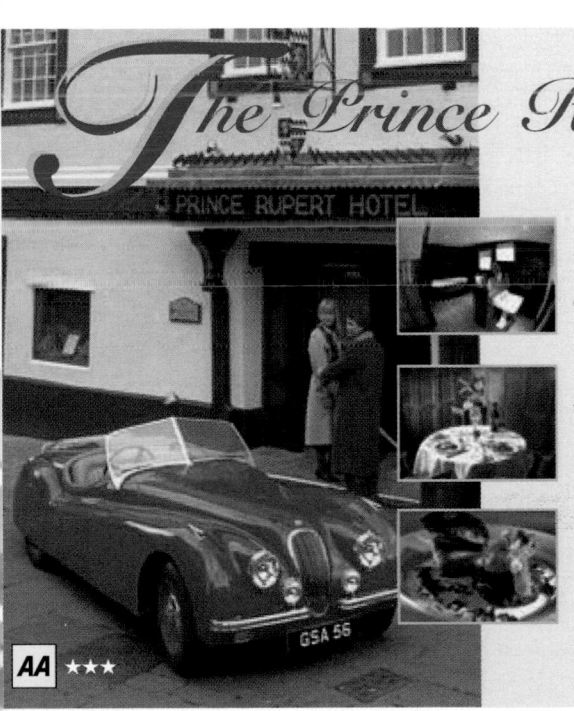

England

SHREWSBURY *continued*

★★★ 72% HOTEL

Lord Hill
Abbey Foregate SY2 6AX
☎ 01743 232601 🖨 01743 369734
e-mail: reservations@lordhill.u-net.com
web: www.lordhill.u-net.com

dir: *from M54 take A5, at 1st rdbt left then 2nd rdbt take 4th exit into London Rd. At next rdbt (Lord Hill Column) take 3rd exit, hotel 300yds on left*

This pleasant, attractively appointed hotel is located close to the town centre. Most of the modern bedrooms are set in a separate purpose-built property, but those in the main building include one with a four-poster, as well as full suites. There is also a conservatory restaurant and a large function suite.

Rooms 12 en suite 24 annexe en suite (2 fmly) (8 GF) ⊘ in 12 bedrooms S £63-£73; D £83-£92 (incl. bkfst) **Facilities** Wi-fi in bedrooms **Conf** Thtr 250 Class 180 Board 180 Del from £90 **Parking** 110 **Notes** ⊘ in restaurant Civ Wed 70

★★★ 66% HOTEL

The Lion
Wyle Cop SY1 1UY
☎ 0870 609 6167 🖨 01743 352744
e-mail: thelion@corushotels.com
web: www.corushotels.com

dir: *from S cross English Bridge, take right fork, hotel at top of hill on left. From N to town centre, follow Castle St into Dogpole, hotel is ahead*

This 14th-century coaching inn, located in the town centre, boasts Charles Dickens amongst its previous guests. Bedrooms come in a variety of sizes, those at the rear being quieter. Public areas include the magnificent ballroom and a bar and restaurant with oak beams and a large original fireplace.

Rooms 59 en suite ⊘ in 30 bedrooms S £79; D £79 **Facilities** use of local gym Xmas **Conf** Thtr 200 Class 80 Board 60 Del from £90 **Services** Lift **Parking** 70 **Notes LB** ⊘ in restaurant Civ Wed 200

Sleep Inn Shrewsbury
Shrewsbury Business Park, Sitra Dr SY2 6LG
☎ 01743 276020 🖨 01743 276039
e-mail: enquiries@hotels-shrewsbury.com

dir: *From A5 junct & B4380, SE of town follow B4380 500yds to rdbt, right into business park*

This modern, purpose built accommodation offers smartly appointed, well-equipped bedrooms, with good power showers. There is a choice of adjacent food outlets where guests may enjoy breakfast, snacks and meals.

Rooms 75 en suite S £50-£62.50; D £62.50-£69.50 **Conf** Thtr 30 Class 22 Board 18 Del from £70

Travelodge Shrewsbury Battlefield
A49/A53 Roundabout, Battlefield SY4 3EQ
☎ 08700 850 950
web: www.travelodge.co.uk

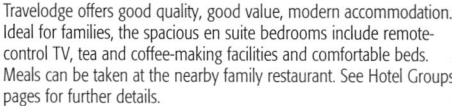

Travelodge offers good quality, good value, modern accommodation. Ideal for families, the spacious en suite bedrooms include remote-control TV, tea and coffee-making facilities and comfortable beds. Meals can be taken at the nearby family restaurant. See Hotel Groups pages for further details.

Rooms 41 en suite S fr £26; D fr £26

Travelodge Shrewsbury Bayston Hill
Bayston Hill Services SY3 0DA
☎ 08700 850 950 🖨 01743 874256
dir: *A5/A49 junct*
Rooms 40 en suite S fr £26; D fr £26

TELFORD
See also Worfield

MAP 10 SJ60

★★★ 80% ⍟⍟ HOTEL

Best Western Valley
TF8 7DW
☎ 01952 432247 🖨 01952 432308
e-mail: info@thevalleyhotel.co.uk
dir: *M6, M54 junct 6 onto A5223 to Ironbridge*

This privately owned hotel is situated in attractive gardens, close to the famous Iron Bridge. It was once the home of the Maws family who manufactured ceramic tiles, and fine examples of their craft are found throughout the house. Bedrooms vary in size and are split between the main house and a mews development; imaginative meals are served in the attractive Chez Maws restaurant

Rooms 35 en suite (2 fmly) (9 GF) ⊘ in 18 bedrooms S £65-£110; D £80-£140 (incl. bkfst) **Facilities** STV Wi-fi in bedrooms **Conf** BC Thtr 150 Class 80 Board 60 Del from £110 **Parking** 100 **Notes LB** ⊗ ⊘ in restaurant RS 24 Dec-2 Jan Civ Wed 150

★★★ 77% ⊛ HOTEL

Hadley Park House

Hadley Park TF1 6QJ
☎ 01952 677269 🖷 01952 676938
e-mail: info@hadleypark.co.uk

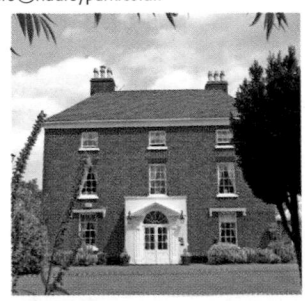

Located in Telford, but close to Ironbridge this elegant Georgian mansion is situated within three acres of its own grounds. Bedrooms are spacious and well equipped. There is a comfortable bar and lounge and meals are served in the attractive conservatory-style restaurant.

Rooms 12 en suite (3 fmly) ⊛ in 10 bedrooms S £65-£85; D £80-£95 (incl. bkfst) **Facilities** STV **Conf** Thtr 80 Class 40 Board 30 Del from £115 **Parking** 40 **Notes LB** ⊗ ⊛ in restaurant Closed 24-26 Dec & 1-7 Jan Civ Wed 80

★★★ 75% HOTEL

Clarion Hotel Madeley Court, Telford

Clarion

Castlefields Way, Madeley TF7 5DW
☎ 01952 680068 🖷 01952 684275
e-mail: enquiries@hotels-telford.com
web: www.hotels-telford.com

dir: M54 junct 4, A464 onto A442 then A4169 (do not turn off Madeley/Kidderminster A442). 1st left at rdbt onto B4373

This beautifully restored 16th-century manor house is set in extensive grounds and gardens. Bedrooms vary between character rooms and the newer annexe rooms. There are two wood-panelled lounges and the restaurant features a mix of old stone walls and modern colour themes. Facilities include a large self-contained banqueting suite and a lakeside bar.

Rooms 29 en suite 18 annexe en suite (1 fmly) (21 GF) ⊛ in 16 bedrooms S £40-£111; D £49-£126 **Facilities** Wi-fi available Archery, Horse riding arranged Xmas **Conf** Thtr 175 Class 100 Board 45 Del from £115 **Parking** 180 **Notes LB** ⊛ in restaurant Civ Wed 175

Ⓤ

Swallow Buckatree Hall

SWALLOW

The Wrekin, Wellington TF6 5AL
☎ 01952 641821 🖷 01952 247540
web: www.swallowhotels.com

dir: M54 junct 7, turn left, at T-junct turn left, hotel 0.25mile on left

At the time of going to press, the star classification for this hotel was not confirmed. Please refer to the AA internet site www.theAA.com for current information.

Rooms 62 en suite

Ⓤ

Swallow Telford Hotel & Golf Club

SWALLOW

Great Hay Dr, Sutton Heights TF7 4DT
☎ 01952 429977 🖷 01952 586602
e-mail: reservations.telfordgolf@swallowhotels.com
web: www.swallowhotels.com

dir: M54 junct 4, A442. Follow signs for Telford Golf Club

At the time of going to press, the star classification for this hotel was not confirmed. Please refer to the AA internet site www.theAA.com for current information.

Rooms 96 en suite (3 fmly) (55 GF) ⊛ in 48 bedrooms S £55-£85; D £70-£85 (incl. bkfst & dinner) **Facilities Spa** STV supervised ⌀ 18 Squash Snooker Sauna Solarium Putt green Jacuzzi Steam room Xmas **Conf** BC Thtr 490 Class 288 Board 206 Del from £115 **Services** Lift **Parking** 200 **Notes** ⊛ in restaurant Civ Wed 100

The vast majority of establishments in this guide accept credit and debit cards. We indicate only those that don't take any

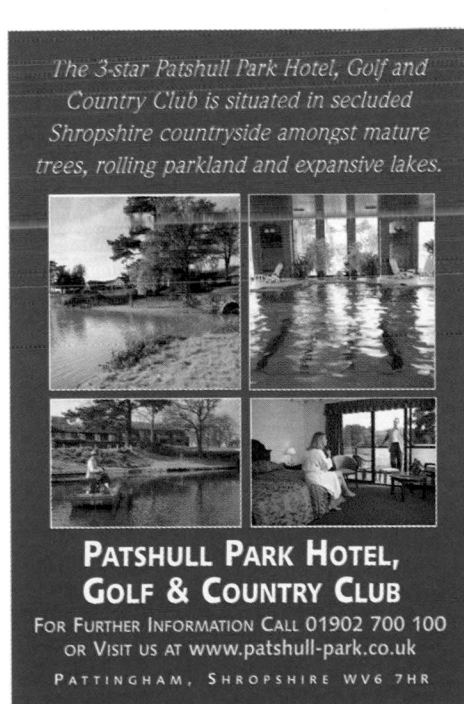

England

TELFORD *continued*

BUDGET HOTEL

Premier Travel Inn Telford

Euston Way TF3 4LY

☎ 08701 977251 📠 01952 290742

web: www.premiertravelinn.com

dir: M54 junct 5 follow signs for Central Railway Station. Inn on 2nd exit off rdbt

High quality, modern budget accommodation ideal for both families and business travellers. Spacious, en suite bedrooms feature bath and shower, satellite TV and many have telephones and modem points. The adjacent family restaurant features a wide and varied menu. For further details consult the Hotel Groups page.

Rooms 60 en suite **Conf** Thtr 30 Board 20

BUDGET HOTEL

Travelodge Telford Shawbirch

Whitchurch Dr, Shawbirch TF1 3QA

☎ 08700 850 950 📠 01952 246534

web: www.travelodge.co.uk

dir: 1m NW, on A5223 at junct of A442 & B5063

Travelodge offers good quality, good value, modern accommodation. Ideal for families, the spacious en suite bedrooms include remote-control TV, tea and coffee-making facilities and comfortable beds. Meals can be taken at the nearby family restaurant. See Hotel Groups pages for further details.

Rooms 40 en suite S fr £26; D fr £26

TELFORD SERVICE AREA (M54)

MAP 10 SJ70

BUDGET HOTEL

Days Inn Telford

Telford Services, Priorslee Rd TF11 8TG

☎ 01952 238400 📠 01952 238410

e-mail: telford.hotel@welcomebreak.co.uk

web: www.welcomebreak.co.uk

dir: M54 junct 4

This modern building offers accommodation in smart, spacious and well-equipped bedrooms, suitable for families and business travellers, and all with en suite bathrooms. Continental breakfast is available, and other refreshments may be taken at the nearby family restaurant. For further details see the Hotel Groups page.

Rooms 48 en suite

WHITCHURCH

MAP 15 SJ54

★★★ 71% **HOTEL**

Dodington Lodge

Dodington SY13 1EN

☎ 01948 662539 📠 01948 667992

e-mail: info@dodingtonlodge.co.uk

web: www.dodingtonlodge.co.uk

dir: from S approach Whitchurch via A41/A49, hotel on left of mini rdbt on outskirts of town

This privately owned hotel is conveniently situated close to the centre of the town, within easy reach of Chester and North Wales. Bedrooms are tastefully decorated and well equipped while a welcoming atmosphere prevails in the lounge bar. A choice of eating options is offered, from a light snack to a full meal. The function suite is a popular choice for weddings and meetings.

Rooms 10 en suite (2 fmly) S £59.50-£61.50; D £69.50-£71.50 (incl. bkfst) **Conf** Thtr 60 Class 40 Board 25 **Parking** 45 **Notes** ⊗ ⊗ in restaurant

WORFIELD

MAP 10 SO79

INSPECTORS' CHOICE

★★★ ⊚⊚⊚ **HOTEL**

Old Vicarage Hotel and Restaurant

Worfield WV15 5JZ

☎ 01746 716497 📠 01746 716552

e-mail: admin@the-old-vicarage.demon.co.uk

web: www.oldvicarageworfield.com

dir: off A454 between Bridgnorth & Wolverhampton, 5m S of Telford's southern business area

This delightful property is set in acres of farm and woodland in a quiet and peaceful area of Shropshire, and was originally an elegant Edwardian vicarage. Service is friendly and helpful, and customer care is one the many strengths of this charming small hotel. The restaurant is a joy, serving award-winning modern British cuisine in elegant surroundings. The lounge and conservatory are the perfect places to enjoy a pre-dinner drink or the complimentary afternoon tea. The well-equipped bedrooms are individually appointed, and thoughtfully and luxuriously furnished.

Rooms 10 en suite 4 annexe en suite (1 fmly) (2 GF) ⊗ in all bedrooms S £60-£110; D £80-£175 (incl. bkfst) **Facilities** ⑨ Wi-fi in bedrooms **Conf** BC Thtr 45 Class 30 Board 20 Del from £125 **Parking** 30 **Notes LB** ⊗ in restaurant

SOMERSET

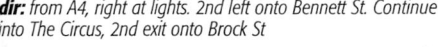

BATH   **MAP 04 ST76**

See also Colerne, Wiltshire & Hinton Charterhouse, Somerset

★★★★★ 83% ◎◎◎ **HOTEL**

The Royal Crescent

16 Royal Crescent BA1 2LS
☎ 01225 823333 📠 01225 339401
e-mail: info@royalcrescent.co.uk
web: www.vonessenhotels.co.uk

dir: from A4, right at lights. 2nd left onto Bennett St. Continue into The Circus, 2nd exit onto Brock St

John Wood's masterpiece of fine Georgian architecture provides the setting for this elegant hotel in the centre of the world famous Royal Crescent. Spacious, air-conditioned bedrooms are individually designed and furnished with antiques. Delightful central grounds lead to a second house, which is home to further rooms, the award-winning Pimpernel's restaurant and the Bath House which offers therapies and treatments.

Rooms 45 en suite (8 fmly) ⊛ in 8 bedrooms D £235-£850 (incl. bkfst)
Facilities STV 🏊 Sauna Gym ♨ Wi-fi available 1920s river launch
Xmas **Conf** Thtr 50 Class 25 Board 24 Del from £210 **Services** Lift
air con **Parking** 27 **Notes LB** ⊛ in restaurant Civ Wed 50

★★★★★ 82% ◎◎ **HOTEL**

Macdonald Bath Spa

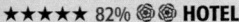

Sydney Rd BA2 6JF
☎ 0870 400 8222 📠 01225 444006
e-mail: sales.bathspa@macdonald-hotels.co.uk
web: www.macdonald hotels.co.uk

dir: M4 junct 18/A46 for Bath/A4 city centre. Left onto A36 at 1st lights. Right at lights after pedestrian crossing then left into Sydney Place. Hotel 200yds on right

A delightful Georgian mansion set amidst seven acres of pretty landscaped grounds, just a short walk from the many and varied delights of the city centre. A timeless elegance pervades the gracious public areas and bedrooms. Facilities include a popular leisure club, a choice of dining options and a number of meeting rooms.

Rooms 129 en suite (3 fmly) (17 GF) ⊛ in all bedrooms S £170-£215;
D £280-£370 (incl. bkfst) **Facilities** STV 🏊 supervised Sauna Gym ♨
Jacuzzi Wi-fi in bedrooms Beauty treatment, Hair salon Thermal suite
Outdoor hydro pool ♫ Xmas **Conf** Thtr 120 Class 100 Board 50 Del
from £199 **Services** Lift **Parking** 156 **Notes LB** ⊛ in restaurant
Civ Wed 120

★★★★ ◎◎◎ **HOTEL**

The Bath Priory Hotel and Restaurant

Weston Rd BA1 2XT
☎ 01225 331922 📠 01225 448276
e-mail: mail@thebathpriory.co.uk
web: www.thebathpriory.co.uk
dir: adjacent to Victoria Park

Set in delightful walled gardens, this attractive Georgian house provides peace and tranquillity and yet is near to the historic city centre. An extensive display of paintings and fine art creates an impression of opulence and the sumptuously furnished public rooms offer great comfort. Cuisine is accomplished with excellently sourced ingredients and flavours, complemented by an impressive wine list. Bedrooms, including some suites in an adjacent building, are well proportioned and offer the many thoughtful touches expected in an establishment of this quality.

Rooms 27 en suite 4 annexe en suite (6 fmly) (5 GF) ⊛ in all
bedrooms S £200-£300; D £245-£425 (incl. bkfst) **Facilities** STV 🏊
♨ Sauna Solarium Gym ♨ Jacuzzi Wi-fi available Holistic beauty
therapy and treatments, steam room ♫ Xmas **Conf** BC Thtr 60
Board 30 Del £250 **Parking** 40 **Notes LB** ⊛ ⊛ in restaurant
Civ Wed 64

★★★★ 73% ◎ **HOTEL**

Combe Grove Manor Hotel & Country Club

PARAMOUNT
GROUP OF HOTELS

Brassknocker Hill, Monkton Combe BA2 7HS
☎ 01225 834644 📠 01225 834961
e-mail: info@combegrovemanor.com
web: www.combegrovemanor.com

dir: M4 junct 18/A46 to city centre, then signs for University & American Museum. Hotel 2m past University on left

Set in over 80 acres of gardens, this Georgian mansion commands stunning views over Limpley Stoke Valley. Most bedrooms are in the Garden Lodge, a short walk from the main house. The superb range

continued on page 550

England

England

BATH *continued*

of indoor and outdoor leisure facilities includes a beauty clinic with holistic therapies, golf, tennis and two pools.

Combe Grove Manor Hotel & Country Club

Rooms 9 en suite 33 annexe en suite (11 fmly) (11 GF) D £138-£158 (incl. bkfst) **Facilities Spa** STV ⚐ ⚐ supervised ⚐ 5 ⚐ Squash Sauna Solarium Gym ⚐ Putt green Jacuzzi Wi-fi available Aerobics, Beauty salon, Jogging trail, Indoor tennis **Conf** Thtr 120 Class 50 Board 40 Del from £149 **Parking** 150 **Notes LB** ⚐ ⚐ in restaurant Civ Wed 50

INSPECTORS' CHOICE

★★★ ◎◎ **HOTEL**

The Queensberry

Russel St BA1 2QF

☎ 01225 447928 ▤ 01225 446065

e-mail: reservations@thequeensberry.co.uk

web: www.thequeensberry.co.uk

dir: 100mtrs from the Assembly Rooms

This charming family-run hotel, situated in a quiet residential street near the city centre, consists of four delightful townhouses. The spacious bedrooms offer deep armchairs, marble bathrooms and a range of modern comforts. Sumptuously furnished sitting rooms add to The Queensberry's appeal and allow access to the very attractive and peaceful walled gardens. The Olive Tree is a stylish restaurant that combines Georgian opulence with contemporary simplicity. Innovative menus are based on best quality ingredients and competent cooking. Valet parking proves a useful service.

Rooms 29 en suite S £110-£300; D £110-£300 **Conf** Thtr 35 Board 25 Del from £175 **Services** Lift **Parking** 9 **Notes LB** ⚐ ⚐ in restaurant

---

★★★ 85% ◉ **HOTEL**

Best Western Cliffe

Cliffe Dr, Crowe Hill, Limpley Stoke BA2 7FY

☎ 01225 723226 ▤ 01225 723871

e-mail: cliffe@bestwestern.co.uk

dir: A36 S from Bath. At A36/B3108 lights left towards Bradford-on-Avon, 0.5m. Right before bridge through village, hotel on right

With stunning countryside views, this attractive country house is just a short drive from the City of Bath. Bedrooms vary in size and style but are well equipped; several are particularly spacious and a number of rooms are on the ground floor. The restaurant overlooks the well-tended garden and offers a tempting selection of carefully prepared dishes. Wi-fi is available throughout.

Rooms 8 en suite 3 annexe en suite (2 fmly) (4 GF) ⚐ in 5 bedrooms S £97-£126; D £124-£166 (incl. bkfst) **Facilities** STV ⚐ Wi-fi available peaceful gardens Xmas **Conf** Thtr 20 Class 15 Board 10 Del from £150 **Parking** 20 **Notes LB** ⚐ in restaurant

See advert on opposite page

★★★ 82% ◎◎ **SMALL HOTEL**

Dukes

Great Pulteney St BA2 4DN

☎ 01225 787960 ▤ 01225 787961

e-mail: info@dukesbath.co.uk

web: www.dukesbath.co.uk

dir: Exit M4 junct 18 onto A46. At Bath turn left towards A36, right at next lights and right again onto Great Pulteney St.

A fine elegant, Grade I listed Georgian building, just a few minutes' walk from Pulteney Brige. Staff are particularly friendly and attentive, the atmosphere is relaxed. Bedrooms, which differ in size and style, are well equipped and have comfortable beds and flat-screen TVs; some suites are available. There is a courtyard terrace, leading from the garden room lounge/bar, where guests enjoy lunch or an aperitif during the summer months. The Cavendish restaurant offers a creative and interesting menu.

Rooms 17 en suite (1 fmly) (2 GF) ⚐ in all bedrooms S £95-£115; D £125-£215 (incl. bkfst) **Facilities** Xmas **Notes** ⚐ in restaurant

England

★★★ 74% ⍟ TOWN HOUSE HOTEL

The Windsor Hotel

69 Great Pulteney St BA2 4DL
☎ 01225 422100 📠 01225 422550
e-mail: sales@bathwindsorhotel.com
web: www.bathwindsorhotel.com

dir: *M4 junct 18/A4. Turn left onto A36, after 500yds turn right at mini rdbt. 2nd left into Great Pulteney Street*

This delightful Grade I listed, terraced Georgian town house is a short walk from the town centre. It has been refurbished to the highest standard and sumptuously furnished with antique pieces. The restaurant has Japanese decor and offers a choice of either sukiyaki or shabu shabu; fresh ingredients are cooked at the table. The Windsor is a non-smoking establishment.

Rooms 14 en suite (3 fmly) ⊘ in all bedrooms S £85-£115; D £145-£250 (incl. bkfst) **Facilities** STV **Conf** Thtr 16 Class 14 Board 12 Del from £165 **Parking** 15 **Notes LB** ⊛ No children 12yrs ⊘ in restaurant Closed Xmas wk

★★★ 73% HOTEL

Pratt's

South Pde BA2 4AB
☎ 01225 460441 📠 01225 448807
e-mail: pratts@forestdale.com
web: www.forestdale.com

dir: *A46 into city centre. Left at 1st lights ('Curfew Pub), right at next lights. 2nd exit at next rdbt, right at lights, left at next lights, 1st left into South Parade*

Part of a Georgian terrace, this long-established and popular hotel is situated close to the city centre. Public rooms and bedrooms have decor that has been chosen to complement the Georgian surroundings. The ground-floor day rooms include two lounges, a writing room and a very comfortable restaurant.

Rooms 46 en suite (2 fmly) ⊘ in 15 bedrooms S £90-£125; D £135-£145 (incl. bkfst) **Facilities** STV Wi-fi available Xmas **Conf** Thtr 50 Class 12 Board 20 Del from £125 **Services** Lift **Notes LB** ⊘ in restaurant

★★★ 72% HOTEL

Best Western Abbey Hotel

North Pde BA1 1LF
☎ 0845 130 2556 01225 461603
📠 0870 950 2443
e-mail: ahres@compasshotels.co.uk

dir: *close to the Abbey in city centre*

Originally built for a wealthy merchant in the 1740s and forming part of a handsome Georgian terrace, this welcoming hotel is situated in the heart of the city. The thoughtfully equipped bedrooms vary in size and style. Public areas include a smart lounge bar and although the restaurant is available, many guests have dinner in the lounge or choose from extensive room service menu.

Rooms 60 en suite (4 fmly) (2 GF) ⊘ in 55 bedrooms S £65-£149; D £75-£149 (incl. bkfst) **Facilities** FTV Wi-fi in bedrooms Bath Leisure Centre 200m **Services** Lift **Notes LB** ⊛ ⊘ in restaurant Closed 23-27 Dec

England

BATH *continued*

★★★ 70% HOTEL

Macdonald Francis

MACDONALD
HOTELS & RESORTS

Queen Square BA1 2HH
☎ 0870 400 8223 📠 01225 319715
e-mail: francis@macdonald-hotels.co.uk
web: www.macdonald-hotels.co.uk

dir: *M4 junct 18/A46 to Bath junct. Take 3rd exit onto A4. Right fork into George St, sharp left into Gay St onto Queen Sq, hotel on left*

Overlooking Queen Square in the centre of the city, this elegant Georgian hotel is situated within walking distance of Bath's many attractions. Public rooms provide a variety of environments where guests can eat, drink and relax - from the informal café-bar to the traditional lounge and more formal restaurant. Bedrooms have air conditioning.

Rooms 95 en suite (16 fmly) ⊘ in all bedrooms S £100-£120; D £140-£170 (incl. bkfst) **Facilities** STV Wi-fi in bedrooms Xmas **Conf** Thtr 80 Class 40 Board 30 Del from £140 **Services** Lift **Parking** 42 **Notes LB** ⊘ in restaurant Civ Wed 100

★★ 79% SMALL HOTEL

Haringtons

8-10 Queen St BA1 1HE
☎ 01225 461728 & 445883 📠 01225 444804
e-mail: post@haringtonshotel.co.uk
web: www.haringtonshotel.co.uk

dir: *A4 to George St & turn into Milsom St. 1st right into Quiet St & 1st left into Queen St*

Dating back to the 18th century this hotel, set in the heart of the city, provides its guests with all modern facilities and comforts. The café-bistro is light & airy & is open throughout the day for light meals and refreshments. A warm welcome is assured from the proprietors and staff - a delightful place to stay.

Rooms 13 en suite (3 fmly) ⊘ in all bedrooms S £68-£138; D £88-£138 (incl. bkfst) **Facilities** STV Xmas **Parking** 11 **Notes LB** ⊗ ⊘ in restaurant

Some hotels, although accepting children, may not have any special facilities for them so it is well worth checking before booking

★★ 72% HOTEL

Old Malt House

Radford, Timsbury BA2 0QF
☎ 01761 470106 📠 01761 472726
e-mail: hotel@oldmalthouse.co.uk
web: www.oldmalthouse.co.uk

dir: *A367 towards Radstock for 1m pass Park & Ride, right onto B3115 towards Tunley/Timsbury. At sharp bend straight ahead & hotel 2nd left*

This friendly, privately owned and personally run hotel provides an ideal base for exploring the many attractions the area has to offer. Formerly a brewery malt house, it is peacefully located within easy reach of Bath. Bedrooms, including two on the ground floor, are well equipped and include some thoughtful touches. A varied choice of home-cooked meals is served in the pleasant restaurant.

Rooms 11 en suite (1 fmly) (2 GF) ⊘ in all bedrooms S £60; D £79 (incl. bkfst) **Parking** 25 **Notes LB** ⊗ ⊘ in restaurant Closed Xmas/New Year

★★ 69% HOTEL

Wentworth House Hotel

106 Bloomfield Rd BA2 2AP
☎ 01225 339193 📠 01225 310460
e-mail: stay@wentworthhouse.co.uk

dir: *From M4 take A4 into Bath. Follow signs for 'through traffic', A39/Wells. Take 2nd right*

This small personally managed hotel on the outskirts of Bath offers a homely atmosphere, comfortable accommodation and delicious home-cooked dishes from a varied menu. Many bedrooms have four-poster beds and two have conservatory lounges. There is an outdoor swimming pool and a hot tub in the garden from where stunning views across the city can be enjoyed.

Rooms 19 en suite (2 fmly) ⊘ in 16 bedrooms S £60-£75; D £85-£115 (incl. bkfst) **Facilities** ⌇ Xmas **Parking** 19 **Notes LB** ⊗ No children 7yrs ⊘ in restaurant

Ⓤ

Swallow Lansdown Grove

SWALLOW
HOTELS

Lansdown Rd BA1 5EH
☎ 01225 483888 📠 01225 483838
e-mail: swallow.bath@swallowhotels.com
web: www.swallowhotels.com

dir: *From A4 into Lansdown Rd. Hotel approx 1m up hill on right*

At the time of going to press, the star classification for this hotel was not confirmed. Please refer to the AA internet site www.theAA.com for current information.

Rooms 60 en suite (4 fmly) ⊘ in 25 bedrooms S £75-£90; D £102-£155 (incl. bkfst) **Facilities** Xmas **Conf** Thtr 100 Class 25 Board 50 Del from £130 **Services** Lift **Parking** 40 **Notes** ⊗ ⊘ in restaurant Civ Wed

BUDGET HOTEL

Travelodge Bath Central

York Buildings, George St BA1 2EB
☎ 08700 850 950 📠 01225 442061
web: www.travelodge.co.uk

Travelodge

dir: *at corner of George St (A4) & Broad St*

Travelodge offers good quality, good value, modern accommodation. Ideal for families, the spacious en suite bedrooms include remote-

continued

control TV, tea and coffee-making facilities and comfortable beds. Meals can be taken at the nearby family restaurant. See Hotel Groups pages for further details.

Rooms 66 en suite S fr £26; D fr £26

BECKINGTON   MAP 04 ST85

★★ 69% HOTEL

Woolpack Inn

OLD ENGLISH INNS

BA12 6SP

☎ 01373 831244 📠 01373 831223

web: www.oldenglish.co.uk

dir: on A36

This charming coaching inn dates back to the 16th century and retains many original features including flagstone floors, open fireplaces and exposed beams. The bar is popular with visitors and locals alike. There is a garden room lounge and a choice of places to eat: the bar for light snacks, the Oak Room for more substantial meals or the Garden Room, which leads onto a pleasant courtyard.

Rooms 12 en suite ⊘ in 1 bedroom **Facilities** S TV **Conf** Thtr 30 Class 20 Board 20 **Parking** 16 **Notes LB** No children 5yrs

BUDGET HOTEL

Travelodge Beckington

Travelodge

BA11 6SF

☎ 08700 850 950 📠 01373 830251

web: www.travelodge.co.uk

dir: at junct of A36/A361

Travelodge offers good quality, good value, modern accommodation. Ideal for families, the spacious en suite bedrooms include remote-control TV, tea and coffee-making facilities and comfortable beds. Meals can be taken at the nearby family restaurant. See Hotel Groups pages for further details.

Rooms 40 en suite S fr £26; D fr £26

BRENT KNOLL   MAP 04 ST35

★★ 74% HOTEL

Woodlands Country House

Hill Ln TA9 4DF

☎ 01278 760232 📠 01278 769090

e-mail: info@woodlands-hotel.co.uk

web: www.woodlands-hotel.co.uk

dir: A38 take 1st left into village, then 5th right & 1st left, follow brown tourist signs

With glorious countryside views, this family-run hotel is set in four

continued

acres of wooded parkland and offers a relaxed and peaceful environment. The attractively co-ordinated bedrooms are comfortable and very well equipped. Guests are welcome to use the outdoor pool and enjoy the terrace seating. Imaginative dishes make up the daily-changing dinner menu.

Rooms 9 en suite (1 fmly) (1 GF) ⊘ in all bedrooms S £69-£95; D £99-£135 (incl. bkfst) **Facilities** ↘ Xmas **Conf** Thtr 30 Class 20 Board 30 Del from £99 **Parking** 16 **Notes LB** ⊗ ⊘ in restaurant RS Sun Civ Wed 65

See advertisement under WESTON-SUPER-MARE

★★ 69% HOTEL

Battleborough Grange Country Hotel

Bristol Rd TA9 4HJ

☎ 01278 760208 📠 01278 761950

e-mail: info@battleboroughgrangehotel.co.uk

dir: M5 junct 22, right at rdbt onto A38 past garden centre on right, hotel 500yds on left

Conveniently located, this popular hotel is surrounded by mellow Somerset countryside. Bedrooms are well equipped and some have superb views of the Iron Age fort of Brent Knoll. In the conservatory restaurant, both fixed-price and carte menus are offered. Relax in the convivial bar after a busy day either working or exploring the area's many attractions. Extensive function facilities are also provided.

Rooms 21 en suite (3 fmly) (1 GF) ⊘ in 3 bedrooms S £58-£65; D £80-£139 (incl. bkfst) **Facilities** HV **Conf** Thtr 85 Class 40 Board 40 Del from £80 **Parking** 60 **Notes LB** ⊗ ⊘ in restaurant Closed 26 Dec-1 Jan Civ Wed 90

★★ 75% HOTEL

Brent Knoll Lodge & Fox & Goose Inn

Bristol Rd TA9 4HH

☎ 01278 760008 📠 01278 769236

e-mail: reception@brentknolllodge.com

web: www.brentknolllodge.com

dir: On A38 approx 500mtrs N of M5 junct 22

This accommodation is conveniently located just a few minutes' drive from the M5. It is situated adjacent to the Fox and Goose Inn which offers a wide range of beverages and freshly prepared dishes. Bedrooms, some located at ground-floor level, are quite spacious and well equipped.

Rooms 14 en suite (3 fmly) ⊘ in all bedrooms S £49; D £59 **Facilities** Xmas **Conf** Thtr 32 Class 32 Board 20 Del from £56 **Services** Lift air con **Parking** 60 **Notes LB** ⊘ in restaurant

England

BRIDGWATER
MAP 04 ST23

See also Holford

★★★ 68% HOTEL

Best Western Walnut Tree
North Petherton TA6 6QA
☎ 01278 662255 0845 360 7000
🖷 01278 663946
e-mail: sales@walnuttreehotel.com
web: www.walnuttreehotel.com

dir: A38, 1m S of M5 junct 24 in the centre of North Petherton.

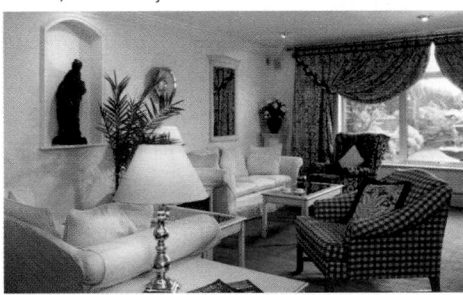

Popular with business and leisure guests, this 18th-century former coaching inn, now under new ownership, is located within easy reach of the M5. Smartly decorated bedrooms are well furnished and equipped with a range of facilities. An extensive selection of dishes is offered and guests can dine in either the restaurant, bistro area or bar.

Rooms 33 en suite (5 fmly) (13 GF) ⊛ in 26 bedrooms S £65-£110; D £90-£140 (incl. bkfst) **Facilities** STV Xmas **Conf** Thtr 120 Class 60 Board 68 Del from £125 **Parking** 70 **Notes LB** ⊗ ⊛ in restaurant Civ Wed 80

★★ 72% **HOTEL**

Apple Tree
Keenthorne TA5 1HZ
☎ 01278 733238 🖷 01278 732693
e-mail: reservations@appletreehotel.com
web: www.appletreehotel.com

(For full entry see Nether Stowey)

Premier Travel Inn Bridgwater
Express Park, Bristol Rd TA6 4RR
☎ 0870 242 3344 🖷 0870 241 9000
web: www.premiertravelinn.com

High quality, modern budget accommodation ideal for both families and business travellers. Spacious, en suite bedrooms feature bath and shower, satellite TV and many have telephones and modem points. The adjacent family restaurant features a wide and varied menu. For further details consult the Hotel Groups page.

Rooms 40 en suite

Travelodge Bridgwater (M5)
Huntsworth Business Park TA6 6TS
☎ 08700 850950 🖷 01278 450 432
web: www.travelodge.co.uk

dir: Exit M5 at junct 24 towards Bridgwater A38. Follow signs for Services. Travelodge within Service Area.

Travelodge offers good quality, good value, modern accommodation. Ideal for families, the spacious en suite bedrooms include remote-control TV, tea and coffee-making facilities and comfortable beds. Meals can be taken at the nearby family restaurant. See Hotel Groups pages for further details.

Rooms 29 en suite S fr £26; D fr £26

CASTLE CARY
MAP 04 ST63

★★ 64% **HOTEL**

The George
Market Place BA7 7AH
☎ 01963 350761 🖷 01963 350035
e-mail: thegeorgehotel@castlecary.co.uk
web: www.georgehotel-castlecary.co.uk

dir: Turn off A303 onto A371. Signed Castle Cary, 2m on left

This 15th-century coaching inn provides well equipped bedrooms that are generally spacious. Most rooms are at the back of the house, enjoying a quiet aspect, but some are on the ground floor. One of these is suitable for disabled guests. Diners can choose to eat in the more formal dining room, or in one of the two cosy bars.

Rooms 12 en suite 5 annexe en suite (1 fmly) (5 GF) S £55-£59.50; D £75-£79.50 (incl. bkfst) **Facilities** Xmas **Conf** Thtr 50 Class 40 Board 20 Del from £90 **Parking** 7 **Notes LB** ⊛ in restaurant

CHARD
MAP 04 ST30

★★★ 74% **HOTEL**

Lordleaze
Henderson Dr, Forton Rd TA20 2HW
☎ 01460 61066 🖷 01460 66468
e-mail: info@lordleazehotel.co.uk
web: www.lordleazehotel.co.uk

dir: from Chard take A358, at St Mary's Church turn left to Forton & Winsham on B3162. Follow signs to hotel

The hotel is quietly located close to the Devon, Dorset and Somerset borders. All bedrooms are well equipped and comfortable. The friendly lounge bar has a wood-burning stove and a tempting bar

continued

England

meal selection. The conservatory restaurant offers more formal carte dining.

Rooms 25 en suite (2 fmly) (7 GF) ❷ in 21 bedrooms S £65-£70; D £95-£100 (incl. bkfst) **Facilities** FTV ch fac Xmas **Conf** Thtr 180 Class 60 Board 40 Del from £92.50 **Parking** 55 **Notes LB** ❷ in restaurant Civ Wed 100

CLEVEDON   MAP 04 ST47

★★★ 70% HOTEL

Best Western Walton Park

Wellington Ter BS21 7BL

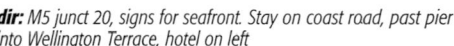

☎ 01275 874253 📇 01275 343577

e-mail: waltonpark@aol.com

dir: M5 junct 20, signs for seafront. Stay on coast road, past pier into Wellington Terrace, hotel on left

Quietly located with spectacular views across the Bristol Channel to Wales, this popular Victorian hotel offers a relaxed atmosphere. Bedrooms are well decorated and equipped to meet the demands of both business and leisure guests. In the comfortable restaurant, a high standard of home-cooked food is served and lighter meals are available in the convivial bar at lunchtime.

Rooms 40 en suite (4 fmly) ❷ in 23 bedrooms S £52-£87; D £87-£110 (incl. bkfst) **Facilities** STV Wi-fi in bedrooms **Conf** Thtr 120 Class 80 Board 80 Del from £115 **Services** Lift **Parking** 50 **Notes LB** Civ Wed 150

DULVERTON   MAP 03 SS92

★★ 83% HOTEL

Ashwick House

TA22 9QD

☎ 01398 323868

e-mail: reservations@ashwickhouse.com

web: www.ashwickhouse.co.uk

dir: In Dulverton left at post office, 3m NW on B3223, over 2 cattlegrids, signed on left

A small yet inviting Edwardian hotel (now under new ownership) set on the edge of Exmoor in six beautiful acres above the breathtaking valley of the River Barle. Exuding a quintessential country-house atmosphere, the public areas include a galleried hall with a welcoming log fire, and stylish lounges, which boast deep sofas. Bedrooms are spacious, comfortable and are equipped with a host of thoughtful touches.

Rooms 6 en suite ❷ in all bedrooms S £95-£102; D £150-£184 (incl. bkfst & dinner) **Facilities** Gym ❧ Wi-fi in bedrooms Xmas **Parking** 6 **Notes LB** ❽ No children 10yrs ❷ in restaurant

Some hotels have restricted service during quieter months, and at this time some of the facilities will not be available

★★ 64% HOTEL

Lion

Bank Square TA22 9BU

☎ 01398 323444 📇 01398 323980

e-mail: jeffeveritt@tiscali.co.uk

dir: from A361 at Tiverton rdbt onto A396. Left at Exbridge onto B3223. Over bridge in Dulverton, hotel in Bank Square

Old-fashioned hospitality is always evident at this charming, traditional inn in the centre of Dulverton, an ideal base from which to explore Exmoor National Park. The bar is popular with locals and visitors alike, offering a variety of local real ales and quality meals. A pleasant dining room provides a quieter, non-smoking option.

Rooms 13 en suite (2 fmly) ❷ in 2 bedrooms S £45-£55; D £74-£78 (incl. bkfst) **Facilities** Xmas **Parking** 6 **Notes LB** ❷ in restaurant

DUNSTER   MAP 03 SS94

★★★ 74% ❀ HOTEL

The Luttrell Arms Hotel

High St TA24 6SG

☎ 01643 821555 📇 01643 821567

e-mail: info@luttrellarms.fsnet.co.uk

web: www.luttrellarms.co.uk/main.htm

dir: A39/A396 S toward Tiverton. Hotel on left opposite Yarn Market

Occupying an enviable position on the high street, this 15th-century hotel looks up to the town's famous castle. Beautifully renovated and decorated, high levels of comfort can be found throughout. Some bedrooms have four-poster beds and are spacious. The warm and friendly staff provide attentive service within a relaxed atmosphere.

Rooms 28 en suite (3 fmly) ❷ in all bedrooms S £65-£95; D £96-£110 (incl. bkfst) **Facilities** Exmoor safaris, Historic tours, Walking tours Xmas **Conf** Thtr 35 Class 20 Board 20 **Notes LB** ❷ in restaurant

★★★ 🅰

Yarn Market Hotel

25-33 High St TA24 6SF

☎ 01643 821425 📇 01643 821475

e-mail: yarnmarket.hotel@virgin.net

web: www.yarnmarkethotel.co.uk

dir: M5 junct 23, follow A39. Hotel in centre of village

Rooms 15 en suite 5 annexe en suite (3 fmly) ❷ in all bedrooms S £40-£60; D £30-£40 (incl. bkfst) **Facilities** Xmas **Conf** Thtr 60 Class 30 Board 25 **Parking** 4 **Notes LB** ❷ in restaurant

England

EXFORD   MAP 03 SS83

★★★ 74% ◉◉ **HOTEL**

Crown
TA24 7PP
☎ 01643 831554 📠 01643 831665
e-mail: info@crownhotelexmoor.co.uk
web: www.crownhotelexmoor.co.uk

dir: M5 junct 25, follow Taunton signs. Take A358 out of
Taunton, then B3224 via Wheddon Cross into Exford

Guest comfort is certainly the hallmark here. Afternoon tea is served
in the lounge beside a roaring fire and tempting menus in the bar and
restaurant are all part of the charm of this delightful old coaching inn
that specialises in breaks for shooting and other country sports.
Bedrooms retain a traditional style yet offer a range of modern
comforts and facilities, many with views of this pretty moorland village.

Rooms 17 en suite (3 fmly) ⊘ in 6 bedrooms S £65-£85; D £99-£130
(incl. bkfst) **Facilities** Riding Xmas **Conf** Del from £125 **Parking** 30
Notes LB ⊘ in restaurant

FROME   MAP 04 ST74

★★★ 75% **HOTEL**

Best Western Mendip House
Bath Rd BA11 2HP
☎ 01373 463223 📠 01373 463990
e-mail: latonamlh@aol.com

dir: on Bath side of Frome, on B3090, opp Frome College

Located on the edge of town, this welcoming hotel is set in attractive
grounds. Bedrooms, some on the ground floor, enjoy glorious country
views over the Mendip Hills. Relaxed and friendly service can be
enjoyed in the bar, on the outdoor terrace and in the comfortable
restaurant.

Rooms 40 en suite (3 fmly) (20 GF) S £59.95-£69.95; D £79.95-£99.95
(incl. bkfst) **Facilities** STV Wi-fi in bedrooms Xmas **Conf** Thtr 80
Class 40 Board 40 Del from £105 **Parking** 80 **Notes LB** ⊘ in restaurant
Civ Wed 85

★★ 67% **HOTEL**

The George at Nunney
11 Church St BA11 4LW
☎ 01373 836458 📠 01373 836565
e-mail: georgenunneyhotel@barbox.net

(For full entry see Nunney)

GORDANO SERVICE AREA   MAP 04 ST57
(M5)

BUDGET HOTEL

Days Inn Bristol West
BS20 7XJ
☎ 01275 373709 & 373624 📠 01275 374104
e-mail: gordano.hotel@welcomebreak.co.uk
web: www.welcomebreak.co.uk

dir: M5 junct 19, follow signs for Gordano services

This modern building offers accommodation in smart, spacious and
well-equipped bedrooms, suitable for families and business travellers,
and all with en suite bathrooms. Continental breakfast is available and
other refreshments may be taken at the nearby family restaurant. For
further details see the Hotel Groups page.

Rooms 60 en suite **Conf** Board 10

HIGHBRIDGE   MAP 04 ST34

★★ 68% **HOTEL**

Sundowner
74 Main Rd, West Huntspill TA9 3QU
☎ 01278 784766 📠 01278 794133
e-mail: runnalls@msn.com

dir: from M5 junct 23, 3m N on A38

Friendly service and an informal atmosphere are just two of the
highlights of this small hotel. The open-plan lounge/bar is a
comfortable, homely area in which to relax after a busy day exploring
the area or working in the locality. An extensive menu, featuring
freshly cooked, imaginative dishes, is offered in the popular restaurant.

Rooms 8 en suite (1 fmly) S £50; D £65 (incl. bkfst) **Conf** Thtr 40
Board 24 **Parking** 18 **Notes** ⊘ in restaurant Closed 26-31 Dec & 1 Jan
RS 25-Dec

★★ 🅰

Laburnum House Lodge
Sloway Ln, West Huntspill TA9 3RJ
☎ 01278 781830 📠 01278 781612
e-mail: laburnumhh@aol.com
web: www.laburnumhh.co.uk

dir: M5 junct 22. W on A38 approx 5m, right at Crossways Inn.
300yds & left into Sloway Ln, 300yds to hotel

Rooms 60 annexe en suite (10 fmly) (60 GF) ⊘ in 30 bedrooms
S £48-£64; D £68-£84 (incl. bkfst) **Facilities** 🎾 ♨ Fishing Sauna
Solarium Gym Jacuzzi Wi-fi available Clay pigeon shooting, Water-ski
park, Go-karting 🎵 Xmas **Conf** BC Thtr 140 Class 60 Board 40 Del from
£84 **Parking** 100 **Notes LB** ⊘ in restaurant

HINTON CHARTERHOUSE   MAP 04 ST75

★★★ 82% ◉ ◉ **HOTEL**

Homewood Park

BA2 7TB

☎ 01225 723731 🗏 01225 723820

e-mail: info@homewoodpark.co.uk

web: www.vonessenhotels.co.uk

dir: 6m SE of Bath on A36, turn left at 2nd sign for Freshford

Homewood Park, an unassuming yet stylish Georgian house set in delightful grounds, offers relaxed surroundings and maintains high standards of quality and comfort throughout. Bedrooms, all individually decorated, include thoughtful extras to ensure a comfortable stay. The hotel has a reputation for excellent cuisine - offering an imaginative interpretation of classical dishes.

Rooms 19 en suite (3 fmly) (2 GF) ⊘ in all bedrooms S £130-£145; D £170-£310 (incl. bkfst) **Facilities** STV ➴ supervised ☺ ⤙ Putt green Xmas **Conf** Thtr 40 Class 30 Board 25 Del from £180 **Parking** 30 **Notes LB** ⊘ in restaurant Civ Wed 50

HOLCOMBE   MAP 04 ST64

★★ 74% **HOTEL**

The Ring O' Roses

Stratton Rd BA3 5EB

☎ 01761 232478 🗏 01761 233737

e-mail: ringorosesholcombe@tesco.net

dir: A367 to Stratton on The Fosse, take hidden left turn opposite Downside Abbey, signed Holcombe. Next right, hotel 1.5m on left

With views of Downside Abbey in the distance, this inn dates back to the 16th century. The attentive owners and pleasant staff create a friendly and relaxed atmosphere. Bedrooms are individually furnished and very comfortable. Real ales are served in the bar, which is open-plan with the attractive split-level restaurant.

Rooms 8 en suite ⊘ in all bedrooms **Conf** Thtr 40 Class 40 Board 14 **Parking** 35 **Notes LB** ⊘ in restaurant

HOLFORD   MAP 04 ST14

★★ 79% ◉ **HOTEL**

Combe House

TA5 1RZ

☎ 01278 741382 🗏 01278 741322

e-mail: enquiries@combehouse.co.uk

web: www.combehouse.co.uk

dir: from A39 W left in Holford then left at T-junct. Left at fork, 0.25m to Holford Combe

Once a tannery, this 17th-century longhouse is peacefully situated in lovely grounds, and provides an ideal retreat for walking in the Quantock Hills. Bedrooms are traditional in style and the public rooms include a choice of sitting areas. There is a focus on home cooking in the dining room.

Rooms 17 en suite 1 annexe en suite (3 fmly) (1 GF) ⊘ in all bedrooms S £65-£75; D £115-£125 (incl. bkfst) **Facilities** STV ▣ ☺ Sauna Gym ⤙ Xmas **Parking** 43 **Notes LB** ⊘ in restaurant

HUNSTRETE   MAP 04 ST66

★★★ 82% ◉ ◉ **COUNTRY HOUSE HOTEL**

Hunstrete House

BS39 4NS

☎ 01761 490490 🗏 01761 490732

e-mail: reception@hunstretehouse.co.uk

web: www.hunstretehouse.co.uk

dir: from Bath take A4 to Bristol. At Globe Inn rdbt 2nd left onto A368 to Wells. 1m after Marksbury turn right for Hunstrete village. Hotel next left

This delightful Georgian house enjoys a stunning setting in 92 acres of deer park and woodland on the edge of the Mendip Hills. Elegant bedrooms in the main building and coach house are both spacious and comfortable. Public areas feature antiques, paintings and fine china. The restaurant enjoys a well-deserved reputation for fine food and utilises much home-grown produce.

Rooms 25 en suite (2 fmly) (8 GF) ⊘ in 14 bedrooms S £135-£145; D £185-£180 (incl. bkfst) **Facilities** STV ➴ ☺ ⤙ Xmas **Conf** Thtr 50 Class 40 Board 30 Del from £175 **Parking** 50 **Notes LB** ⊘ in restaurant Civ Wed 50

England

ILMINSTER   MAP 04 ST31

★★★ 77% HOTEL

Best Western Shrubbery
TA19 9AR

☎ 01460 52108 ▤ 01460 53660
e-mail: stuart@shrubberyhotel.com
web: www.shrubberyhotel.com

dir: 0.5m from A303 towards Ilminster town centre

Set in attractive terraced gardens, the Shrubbery is a well established hotel in this small town. Bedrooms are well equipped and bright, they include three ground-floor rooms. Bar meals or full meals are available in the bar, lounges and restaurant. Additional facilities include a range of function rooms.

Rooms 21 en suite (3 fmly) S £90-£120; D £120-£130 (incl. bkfst)
Facilities STV FTV ⌇ Wi-fi in bedrooms Xmas **Conf** BC Thtr 250 Class 120 Board 80 Del from £120 **Parking** 100 **Notes LB** ⊛ in restaurant Civ Wed 200

BUDGET HOTEL

Travelodge Ilminster
Southfields Roundabout, Horton Cross
TA19 9PT

☎ 08700 850 950 ▤ 01460 53748
web: www.travelodge.co.uk

dir: on A303/A358 atjunct with Ilminster bypass

Travelodge offers good quality, good value, modern accommodation. Ideal for families, the spacious en suite bedrooms include remote-control TV, tea and coffee-making facilities and comfortable beds. Meals can be taken at the nearby family restaurant. See Hotel Groups pages for further details.

Rooms 32 en suite S fr £26; D fr £26

LOXTON   MAP 04 ST35

★★★ 67% HOTEL

Best Western Webbington
BS26 2XA

☎ 01934 750100 ▤ 01934 750020
e-mail: webbington@latonahotels.co.uk

Despite being clearly visible from the M5 motorway, this popular hotel is situated in the countryside and has splendid views from many bedrooms and public areas. The hotel is well suited for a wide range of guests, from business to leisure to families, and offers a warm welcome to all. Facilities include an indoor swimming pool, tennis courts, cardio-gym and varied conference rooms.

Rooms 59 en suite (2 fmly) ⊛ in 10 bedrooms **Facilities** ⚑ ⌇ Sauna Solarium Gym Beauty treatments Cardiovascular suite Steam Room Xmas **Conf** Thtr 1000 Class 600 Del from £108 **Parking** 450 **Notes** ⊗ ⊛ in restaurant Civ Wed 500

LYMPSHAM   MAP 04 ST35

★★ 72% HOTEL

Batch Country Hotel
Batch Ln BS24 0EX

THE CIRCLE
Selected Individual Hotels
GREAT BRITAIN

☎ 01934 750371 ▤ 01934 750501
web: www.batchcountryhotel.co.uk

dir: M5 junct 22, take last exit on rdbt signed A370 to Weston-Super-Mare. 3.5m, left into Lympsham. 1m, sign at end of road

Rurally situated between Weston-Super-Mare and Burnham-on-Sea, this former farmhouse offers a relaxed, friendly and peaceful environment. The comfortable bedrooms have views to the Mendip and Quantock Hills. Spacious lounges overlook the extensive, well-tended gardens and the comfortably furnished function room and restaurant ensure this is a popular location for wedding ceremonies.

Rooms 10 en suite (6 fmly) (1 GF) ⊛ in 2 bedrooms **Facilities** Fishing **Conf** Thtr 80 Class 60 Board 100 **Parking** 80 **Notes LB** ⊗ ⊛ in restaurant Closed 25-26 Dec Civ Wed 120

See advert under WESTON-SUPER-MARE

MARTOCK   MAP 04 ST41

★★★ 77% ⊛ COUNTRY HOUSE HOTEL

Ash House Country Hotel
41 Main St, Ash TA12 6PB

☎ 01935 822036 & 823126 ▤ 01935 822992
e-mail: reception@ashhousecountryhotel.co.uk

dir: Off A303 at Tintinhull Forts junct and left at top of slip road. 0.5m into Ash, on right opposite Ash recreation ground

Set in its own grounds, the host and hostess personally make guests feel welcome at this Georgian hotel. Bedrooms are equipped with considerate extras. There is a choice of two lounge areas and dinner, featuring fresh local produce, is served in either the traditionally styled, formal restaurant or the relaxed environment of the conservatory which overlooks the gardens.

Rooms 9 en suite (2 fmly) ⊛ in all bedrooms S £60-£85; D £95-£105 (incl. bkfst) **Facilities** STV **Conf** Thtr 50 Class 30 Board 20 Del from £96.50 **Parking** 35 **Notes LB** ⊗ ⊛ in restaurant Civ Wed 60

★★★ 74% HOTEL

The Hollies

Bower Hinton TA12 6LG

☎ 01935 822232 🖨 01935 822249

e-mail: info@thehollieshotel.com

web: www.thehollieshotel.com

dir: *on B3165 S of town centre off A303, take Bower Hinton slip road & follow hotel signs*

Within easy access of the A303, this popular establishment offers spacious, well-equipped bedrooms that are located to the rear of the property in a purpose-built wing and include both suites and mini-suites. The bar and restaurant are housed in an attractive 17th-century farmhouse; bar meals are available in addition to the interesting main menu.

Rooms 42 annexe en suite (2 fmly) (30 GF) ⊘ in 30 bedrooms S £75-£115; D £90-£130 (incl. bkfst) **Facilities** STV Wi-fi in bedrooms **Conf** BC Thtr 150 Class 80 Board 60 **Parking** 80 **Notes LB** ⊗ ⊘ in restaurant RS Xmas & New Year

---

MIDSOMER NORTON   MAP 04 ST65

★★★ 78% HOTEL

Centurion

Charlton Ln BA3 4BD

☎ 01761 417711 🖨 01761 418357

e-mail: enquiries@centurionhotel.co.uk

web: www.centurionhotel.com

dir: *off A367, 10m S of Bath*

This privately owned, purpose built hotel incorporates the adjacent Fosse Way Country Club with its 9-hole golf course and extensive leisure amenities. Bedrooms, some at ground-floor level, are well equipped. Public areas include a choice of bars, a comfortable lounge and a range of meeting/function rooms. The restaurant is stylish, light and airy with large windows overlooking the grounds.

Rooms 44 en suite (4 fmly) (18 GF) ⊘ in all bedrooms S £75-£105; D £100-£130 (incl. bkfst) **Facilities Spa** STV ⌨ ♪9 Sauna Gym Jacuzzi Bowling green Sports field **Conf** Thtr 180 Class 70 Board 50 Del from £110 **Parking** 100 **Notes LB** ⊗ ⊘ in restaurant Closed 24 Dec-1 Jan Civ Wed 100

★★★ 77% ◉◉ SMALL HOTEL

The Moody Goose At The Old Priory

Church Square BA3 2HX

☎ 01761 416784 & 410846 🖨 01761 417851

e-mail: info@theoldpriory.co.uk

dir: *A362 for 1m left to High St to lights, turn right to small rdbt by St John's Church turn right. Hotel ahead*

Dating back to the 12th century, this establishment has been sensitively restored, maintaining some original features and plenty of historic charm and character. Bedrooms, one with a four-poster, are individually sized and styled but all are equipped with useful extras. The intimate restaurant serves innovative, carefully prepared dishes and there are two cosy lounges, where log fires burn in cooler months.

Rooms 7 en suite (2 fmly) ⊘ in all bedrooms S £80-£95; D £100-£135 (incl. bkfst) **Conf** Thtr 16 Class 6 Board 12 **Parking** 14 **Notes** ⊗ ⊘ in restaurant RS Sun

---

MINEHEAD   MAP 03 SS94

★★★ 74% HOTEL

Best Western Northfield

Northfield Rd TA24 5PU

☎ 01643 705155 0845 1302678 🖨 01643 707715

e-mail: reservations@northfield-hotel.co.uk

web: www.northfield-hotel.co.uk

dir: *M5 junct 25, follow A38 to Bridgwater then A39 to Minehead*

Located conveniently close to the town centre and the seafront, this hotel is set in delightfully maintained gardens and has a loyal following. A range of comfortable sitting rooms and leisure facilities, including an indoor, heated pool is provided. A fixed-price menu is served every evening in the oak-panelled dining room. The attractively co-ordinated bedrooms vary in size and are equipped to a good standard.

Rooms 28 en suite (7 fmly) S £57-£82; D £114-£142 (incl. bkfst & dinner) **Facilities** STV ⌨ Gym Putt green Jacuzzi Steam room Xmas **Conf** BC Thtr 70 Class 45 Board 30 Del from £55 **Services** Lift **Parking** 44 **Notes LB** ⊘ in restaurant

England

MINEHEAD *continued*

★★ 85% HOTEL

Alcombe House
Bircham Rd, Alcombe TA24 6BG
☎ 01643 705130 ▤ 01643 705130
e-mail: alcombe.house@virgin.net
web: www.alcombehouse.co.uk

Located midway between Minehead and Dunster on the coastal fringe of Exmoor National Park, this Grade II listed, Georgian hotel offers a delightful combination of efficient service and genuine hospitality delivered by the very welcoming resident proprietors. Public areas include a comfortable lounge and a candlelit dining room where a range of carefully prepared dishes is offered from a daily-changing menu.

Rooms 7 en suite ⊘ in all bedrooms S fr £40; D fr £60 (incl. bkfst)
Facilities Xmas **Parking** 9 **Notes LB** No children 15yrs ⊘ in restaurant Closed 8 Nov-18 Mar

★★ 78% SMALL HOTEL

Channel House
Church Path TA24 5QG
☎ 01643 703229 ▤ 01643 708925
e-mail: channel.house@virgin.net
dir: *from A39 right at rdbt to seafront, then left onto promenade. 1st right, 1st left to Blenheim Gdns and 1st right into Northfield Rd*

This family-run hotel offers relaxing surroundings, yet is only a short walk from the town centre. The South West coastal path starts from the hotel's two-acre gardens. Many of the exceptionally well-equipped bedrooms benefit from wonderful views. Imaginative menus are created from the best local produce. The hotel is totally non-smoking.

Rooms 8 en suite (1 fmly) ⊘ in all bedrooms S £83-£97; D £136-£164 (incl. bkfst & dinner) **Services** air con **Parking** 10 **Notes LB** ⊗ No children 15yrs ⊘ in restaurant Closed 29 Dec-15 Feb

See advert on opposite page

NETHER STOWEY   MAP 04 ST13

★★ 72% HOTEL

Apple Tree
Keenthorne TA5 1HZ
☎ 01278 733238 ▤ 01278 732693
e-mail: reservations@appletreehotel.com
web: www.appletreehotel.com
dir: *from Bridgwater follow A39 towards Minehead. Hotel on left 2m past Cannington*

Parts of this cottage-style property, convenient for the coast and the M5, date back some 340 years. Bedrooms, which vary in character and style, are suited to both leisure and corporate guests; some are in a single storey annexe adjacent to the main hotel. The friendly owners and their staff make every effort to guarantee an enjoyable stay. Public areas include an attractive conservatory restaurant, a bar and a library lounge.

Rooms 15 en suite (2 fmly) (5 GF) ⊘ in 7 bedrooms S £60-£68; D £78-£88 (incl. bkfst) **Facilities** FTV Wi-fi available **Conf** BC Thtr 25 Class 12 Board 14 **Parking** 30 **Notes LB** ⊗ ⊘ in restaurant

NUNNEY   MAP 04 ST74

★★ 67% HOTEL

The George at Nunney
11 Church St BA11 4LW
☎ 01373 836458 ▤ 01373 836565
e-mail: georgenunneyhotel@barbox.net
dir: *0.5m N off A361 Frome to Shepton Mallet road*

Situated in the centre of Nunney, opposite the castle, The George dates back to the 17th century. Bedrooms although varying in size have plenty of character and offer a very good selection of extras. Guests may choose from an extensive range of bar meals or a selection of dishes offered in the more intimate restaurant.

Rooms 9 rms (8 en suite) (2 fmly) ⊘ in 2 bedrooms **Parking** 30 **Notes LB** ⊗

PODIMORE   MAP 04 ST52

BUDGET HOTEL

Travelodge Yeovil Podimore
BA22 8JG
☎ 08700 850 950 ▤ 01935 840074
web: www.travelodge.co.uk

dir: *on A303, near junct with A37*

Travelodge offers good quality, good value, modern accommodation. Ideal for families, the spacious en suite bedrooms include remote-control TV, tea and coffee-making facilities and comfortable beds. Meals can be taken at the nearby family restaurant. See Hotel Groups pages for further details.

Rooms 41 en suite S fr £26; D fr £26

PORLOCK   MAP 03 SS84

★★★ ◉ HOTEL

The Oaks

TA24 8ES

☎ 01643 862265 📠 01643 863131

e-mail: info@oakshotel.co.uk

A relaxing atmosphere is found at this charming Edwardian house, located near to the setting of R D Blackmore's novel *Lorna Doone*. Quietly located and set in attractive grounds, the hotel enjoys elevated views across the village towards the sea. Bedrooms are thoughtfully furnished and comfortable, and the public rooms include a charming bar and a peaceful drawing room. In the dining room, guests can choose from the daily-changing menu, which features fresh, quality local produce.

Rooms 8 en suite ⊘ in all bedrooms S £85; D £120 (incl. bkfst)
Facilities FTV Xmas **Parking** 12 **Notes LB** ⊛ No children 8yrs ⊘ in restaurant Closed Nov-Mar (excl. Xmas & New Year)

◉◉◉ RESTAURANT WITH ROOMS

Andrews on the Weir

Porlock Weir TA24 8PB

☎ 01643 863300 📠 01643 863311

e-mail: information@andrewsontheweir.co.uk

web: www.andrewsontheweir.co.uk

dir. A39 from Minehead to Porlock, through village, 1st right signed Harbour (Porlock Weir) 1.5m

Enjoying a delightful elevated position overlooking Porlock Bay, Andrews on the Weir is furnished and decorated in country house style. Bedrooms are spacious and comfortable; one room boasts a four-poster bed. The sitting room/bar is elegant and a log fire creates a cosy atmosphere. One of the highlights of a stay here is the choice of imaginative and innovative dishes available in the restaurant.

Rooms 5 en suite ⊘ in all bedrooms **Parking** 6 **Notes LB** No children 12yrs ⊘ in restaurant Closed Jan & Mon, Tue

PORTISHEAD   MAP 04 ST47

Premier Travel Inn Portishead

Wyndham Way BS20 7GA

☎ 08701 977212 📠 01275 846534

web: www.premiertravelinn.com

dir: *From M5 junct 19 follow A369 towards Portishead. Over 1st rdbt, Inn on next rdbt*

High quality, modern budget accommodation ideal for both families and business travellers. Spacious, en suite bedrooms feature bath and shower, satellite TV and many have telephones and modem points. The adjacent family restaurant features a wide and varied menu. For further details consult the Hotel Groups page.

Rooms 40 en suite

> If the freedom to smoke or be in a
> non-smoking atmosphere is important to you,
> check the rules when you book

England

SEDGEMOOR MOTORWAY SERVICE AREA (M5)

MAP 04 ST35

BUDGET HOTEL

Days Inn Sedgemoor

M5 Northbound J22-21, Sedgemoor BS24 0JL
☎ 01934 750831 📄 01934 750808
e-mail: sedgemoor.hotel@welcomebreak.co.uk
web: www.welcomebreak.co.uk

dir: M5 junct 21/22

This modern building offers accommodation in smart, spacious and well-equipped bedrooms, suitable for families and business travellers, and all with en suite bathrooms. Continental breakfast is available and other refreshments may be taken at the nearby family restaurant. For further details see the Hotel Groups page.

Rooms 40 en suite **Conf** BC

SHEPTON MALLET

MAP 04 ST64

INSPECTORS' CHOICE

★★★★ HOTEL

Charlton House

Charlton Rd BA4 4PR
☎ 01749 342008 📄 01749 346362
e-mail: enquiry@charltonhouse.com
web: www.charltonhouse.com

dir: on A361 towards Frome, 1m from town centre

Attention to detail is paramount at this wonderful hotel where the design throughout is modelled on Mulberry fabrics and furnishings. The bedrooms are decorated in individual style and all are supremely comfortable. Monty's Spa has hydrotherapy pools and spa treatment rooms for the ultimate pampering experience. At the time of going to press a new chef was in the process of being appointed therefore the rosette award has not been confirmed.

Rooms 22 en suite 4 annexe en suite (1 fmly) ⊗ in 20 bedrooms
S £135-£220; D £170-£445 (incl. bkfst) **Facilities Spa** STV 🏊
Fishing Sauna Gym 🏊 Jacuzzi Wi-fi in bedrooms Archery Clay
pigeon shooting Ballooning, Spa retreat programmes Xmas
Conf Thtr 100 Class 60 Board 40 Del from £220 **Parking** 72
Notes LB ⊗ in restaurant Civ Wed 100

★★ 74% HOTEL

Shrubbery

17 Commercial Rd BA4 5BU
☎ 01749 346671 📄 01749 346581
e-mail: reservations@shrubberyhotel17.fsnet.co.uk

dir: off A37 at Shepton Mallet onto A371 Wells Rd, hotel 50mtrs past lights in town centre

This small hotel is located in the town centre and offers comfortable, well-equipped bedrooms, several of which are on the ground floor of a separate building. The atmosphere here is relaxed and informal, and the intimate restaurant, which overlooks a delightful garden, offers a varied choice of enjoyable and well-presented dishes.

Rooms 6 en suite 4 annexe en suite (3 fmly) (4 GF) ⊗ in 4 bedrooms
S fr £65; D fr £90 (incl. bkfst) **Parking** 30 **Notes** ⊗ ⊗ in restaurant

SIMONSBATH

MAP 03 SS73

★★ 75% HOTEL

Simonsbath House

TA24 7SH
☎ 01643 831259 & 831382 📄 01643 831557
e-mail: hotel@simonsbathhouse.co.uk
web: www.simonsbathhouse.co.uk

dir: from Exford to Lynton, hotel on right of B3223

This 17th-century house boasts a stunning moorland setting and its relaxed and friendly atmosphere ensures a memorable stay. Bedrooms have plenty of character, are equipped with modern facilities and offer good levels of comfort. Delightful public rooms include a choice of lounges with original features such as wood panelling and ornate fireplaces.

Rooms 8 en suite (1 GF) ⊗ in all bedrooms S £44.50-£60; D £89 (incl.
bkfst) **Facilities** Fishing Mountain biking, Archery, Orienteering trails,
Nature walks Xmas **Conf** BC Thtr 50 Class 35 Board 20 **Parking** 25
Notes LB No children 12yrs ⊗ in restaurant Closed 25-26 Dec

STON EASTON

MAP 04 ST65

@@@ U

Ston Easton Park

BA3 4DF
☎ 01761 241631 📄 01761 241377
e-mail: info@stoneaston.co.uk
web: www.vonessenhotels.co.uk

dir: on A37

At the time of going to press, the star classification for this hotel was not confirmed. Please refer to the AA internet site www.theAA.com for current information.

Rooms 19 en suite 3 annexe en suite (2 fmly) (2 GF) ⊗ in all bedrooms
Facilities 🏊 Fishing Snooker 🏊 By prior arrangement Archery Clay
pigeon shooting Quad bikes Hot air balloon Xmas **Conf** Thtr 100 Board 30
Del from £210 **Parking** 120 **Notes** ⊗ in restaurant Civ Wed

STREET
MAP 04 ST43

★★ 65% HOTEL

Wessex
High St BA16 0EF
☎ 01458 443383 📠 01458 446589
e-mail: info@wessexhotel.com

dir: *from A303, onto B3151 to Somerton. Then 7m, pass lights by Millfield School. Left at mini-rdbt*

This centrally situated hotel has plenty of parking and is but a short walk from Clarks Village Retail Outlet Centre. Spacious bedrooms are equipped with modern facilities. Public areas include a range of function rooms and a spacious restaurant.

Rooms 49 en suite (4 fmly) ⊗ in 24 bedrooms S £65; D £89 (incl. bkfst) **Facilities** STV FTV Xmas **Conf** BC Thtr 400 Class 120 Board 80 **Services** Lift **Parking** 70 **Notes LB** ⊗ ⊗ in restaurant Closed 27-29 Dec 2 31 Jan

TAUNTON
MAP 04 ST22

★★★ 78% ⑧⑧ HOTEL

The Mount Somerset
Lower Henlade TA3 5NB
☎ 01823 442500 📠 01823 442900
e-mail: info@mountsomersethotel.co.uk
web: www.vonessenhotels.co.uk

dir: *M5 junct 25, A358 towards Chard/Ilminster, at Henlade right into Stoke Road, left at T-junct at end, then right into drive*

From its elevated and rural position, this impressive Regency house has wonderful views over Taunton Vale. Some of the well appointed bedrooms have feature bathrooms, and the elegant public rooms are stylish with an intimate atmosphere. In addition to the daily-changing, fixed-price menu, a carefully selected seasonal carte is available.

Rooms 11 en suite (1 fmly) ⊗ in all bedrooms S £105-£140; D £140 £255 (incl. bkfst) **Facilities** ᐟ Xmas **Conf** Thtr 60 Class 30 Board 20 Del £175 **Services** Lift **Parking** 100 **Notes LB** ⊗ in restaurant Civ Wed 60

★★★ 77% HOTEL

Best Western Rumwell Manor
Rumwell TA4 1EL
☎ 01823 461902 📠 01823 254861
e-mail: reception@rumwellmanor.co.uk

dir: *M5 junct 26 follow signs to Wellington, turn right onto A38 to Taunton, hotel is 3m on right*

A countryside location, surrounded by lovingly tended gardens, Rumwell Manor provides easy access to Taunton and the M5.

continued

Bedrooms vary in style, with those in the main house offering greater space and character. A selection of freshly prepared dishes is served in the restaurant. In addition to the cosy bar and adjacent lounge, several meeting/conference rooms are available.

Rooms 10 en suite 10 annexe en suite (3 fmly) (6 GF) ⊗ in 6 bedrooms S £69-£94; D £89-£156 (incl. bkfst) **Facilities** Wi-fi in bedrooms Xmas **Conf** BC Thtr 40 Class 24 Board 26 Del from £119 **Parking** 40 **Notes LB** ⊗ ⊗ in restaurant Civ Wed 50

★★★ 72% ⑧ HOTEL

Corner House Hotel
Park St TA1 4DQ
☎ 01823 284683 📠 01823 323464
e-mail: res@corner-house.co.uk
web: www.corner-house.co.uk

dir: *0.3m from town centre. Hotel on junct of Park Street & A38 Wellington Road*

The unusual Victorian façade of the Corner House, with its turrets and stained glass windows, belies a wealth of innovation, quality and style. The contemporary bedrooms are equipped with state-of-the-art facilities but also offer traditional comforts. Informality and exceptional value for money are the hallmark of the smart public areas, which include Bistro 4DQ - a relaxed place to eat good food.

Rooms 28 en suite (12 fmly) (1 GF) ⊗ in 20 bedrooms **Facilities** Wi-fi in bedrooms **Conf** Thtr 50 Class 30 Board 28 Del from £115 **Parking** 40 **Notes** ⊗

★★ 79% ⑧ SMALL HOTEL

Farthings Hotel & Restaurant
Village Rd, Hatch Beauchamp TA3 6SG
☎ 01823 480664 📠 01823 481118
e-mail: info@farthingshotel.com
web: www.farthingshotel.com

dir: *from A358, between Taunton and Ilminster turn into Hatch Beauchamp for hotel in village centre*

This delightful hotel, set in its own extensive gardens in a peaceful village location, offers comfortable accommodation, combined with all the character and charm of a building dating back over 200 years. The atmosphere is traditionally classic and calm. Dinner service is attentive and menus feature best quality local ingredients prepared and presented with care.

Rooms 9 en suite (1 fmly) ⊗ in all bedrooms S £80-£90; D £110-£130 (incl. bkfst) **Conf** Thtr 20 Class 20 Board 20 Del from £136 **Parking** 20 **Notes LB** ⊗ in restaurant Civ Wed 50

England

TAUNTON continued

BUDGET HOTEL

Premier Travel Inn Taunton Central (North)

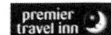

Massingham Park TA2 7RX
☎ 08701 977 293 📠 01823 422350
web: www.premiertravelinn.com

High quality, modern budget accommodation ideal for both families and business travellers. Spacious, en suite bedrooms feature bath and shower, satellite TV and many have telephones and modem points. The adjacent family restaurant features a wide and varied menu. For further details consult the Hotel Groups page.

Rooms 40 en suite

Premier Travel Inn Taunton East

81 Bridgwater Rd TA1 2DU
☎ 08701 977249 📠 01823 322054
dir: M5 junct 25 follow signs to Taunton over 1st rdbt & keep left at Creech Castle traffic lights, Inn 200yds on right
Rooms 40 en suite

Premier Travel Inn Taunton (Ruishton)

Ilminster Rd, Ruishton TA3 5LU
☎ 0870 9906534 📠 0870 9906535
dir: Just off M5 junct 25 on A38
Rooms 38 en suite

BUDGET HOTEL

Travelodge Taunton

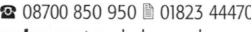

Riverside Retail Park, Hankridge Farm TA1 2LR
☎ 08700 850 950 📠 01823 444704
web: www.travelodge.co.uk
dir: M5 junct 25

Travelodge offers good quality, good value, modern accommodation. Ideal for families, the spacious en suite bedrooms include remote-control TV, tea and coffee-making facilities and comfortable beds. Meals can be taken at the nearby family restaurant. See Hotel Groups pages for further details.

Rooms 48 en suite S fr £26; D fr £26

TAUNTON DEANE MOTORWAY SERVICE AREA (M5)

MAP 04 ST12

BUDGET HOTEL

Premier Travel Inn Taunton Deane

Trull TA3 7PF
☎ 08701 977250 📠 01823 338131
web: www.premiertravelinn.com
dir: M5 southbound between junct 25 & 26

High quality, modern budget accommodation ideal for both families and business travellers. Spacious, en suite bedrooms feature bath and shower, satellite TV and many have telephones and modem points. The adjacent family restaurant features a wide and varied menu. For further details consult the Hotel Groups page.

Rooms 39 en suite

WELLINGTON

MAP 03 ST12

★★★ ◉◉ COUNTRY HOUSE HOTEL

Bindon Country House Hotel & Restaurant

Langford Budville TA21 0RU
☎ 01823 400070 📠 01823 400071
e-mail: stay@bindon.com
web: www.bindon.com

dir: from Wellington B3187 to Langford Budville, through village, right towards Wiveliscombe, right at junct, pass Bindon Farm, right after 450yds

This delightful country-house hotel is set in seven acres of formal woodland gardens. Mentioned in the Domesday Book, this tranquil retreat is the perfect antidote to stress. Bedrooms are named after battles fought by the Duke of Wellington and each is individually decorated with sumptuous fabrics and equipped with useful extras. Public rooms are elegant and stylish, and the dining room is the venue for impressive and accomplished cuisine.

Rooms 12 en suite (2 fmly) (1 GF) ⊘ in all bedrooms S £95-£115; D £115-£215 (incl. bkfst) **Facilities** FTV ⚘ ⚿ ⚽ Wi-fi in bedrooms ♫ Xmas **Conf** Thtr 50 Class 25 Board 25 Del from £135 **Parking** 30 **Notes** ⊘ in restaurant Civ Wed 50

★★★ 66% HOTEL

The Cleve Hotel & Country Club

Mantle St TA21 8SN
☎ 01823 662033 📠 01823 660874
e-mail: reception@clevehotel.com
web: www.clevehotel.com
dir: M5 junct 26 follow signs to Wellington. Left before Total petrol station

Offering comfortable bedrooms and public areas, this hotel is quietly located in an elevated position above the town. The atmosphere is relaxed and guests can enjoy Mediterranean-influenced cuisine in the stylish restaurant. Extensive leisure facilities are available including a heated indoor pool, well-equipped gym, sauna, and snooker table.

Rooms 20 en suite (5 fmly) (3 GF) ⊘ in all bedrooms S £55-£79.50; D £70-£95.50 (incl. bkfst) **Facilities Spa** ⚑ supervised Snooker Sauna Solarium Gym Xmas **Conf** Thtr 300 Class 130 Board 70 Del from £75.50 **Parking** 100 **Notes LB** ⊘ in restaurant Civ Wed 150

WELLS
MAP 04 ST54

★★★ 85% ⊛ **HOTEL**

Best Western Swan

Sadler St BA5 2RX

☎ 01749 836300 🖷 01749 836301

e-mail: swan@bhere.co.uk

web: www.swanhotelwells.co.uk

dir: A39, A371, on entering Wells follow signs for Hotels & Deliveries. Hotel on right opposite cathedral

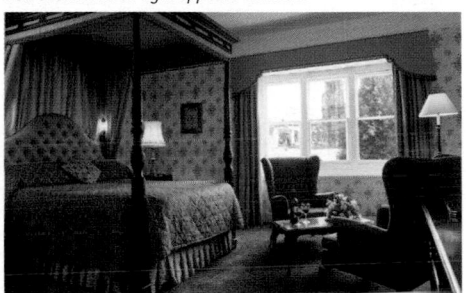

Once a coaching inn, The Swan commands a wonderful view of the west front of the cathedral. The individually decorated bedrooms vary in size and style from the newer ones in an adjacent wing to the more traditionally furnished rooms, many with four-poster beds. Dinner includes a varied selection of carefully prepared dishes.

Rooms 49 en suite (4 fmly) (4 GF) ⊛ in all bedrooms S £90-£98; D £130-£165 (incl. bkfst) **Facilities** Wi-fi in bedrooms Xmas **Conf** Thtr 120 Class 45 Board 40 Del from £132 **Parking** 30 **Notes LB** ⊛ ⊛ in restaurant Civ Wed 90

★★ 76% **HOTEL**

White Hart

Sadler St BA5 2EH

☎ 01749 672056 🖷 01749 671074

e-mail: info@whitehart-wells.co.uk

web: www.whitehart-wells.co.uk

dir: Sadler St at start of one-way system. Hotel opposite cathedral

A former coaching inn dating back to the 15th century, this hotel offers comfortable, modern accommodation. Some bedrooms are in an adjoining former stable block and some are at ground-floor level. Public areas include a guest lounge, a popular restaurant and bar.

continued

The restaurant serves a good choice of fish, meat and vegetarian dishes plus daily specials.

Rooms 15 en suite (3 fmly) (2 GF) ⊛ in 5 bedrooms S £78-£83; D £99-£110 (incl. bkfst) **Facilities** Wi-fi in bedrooms Xmas **Conf** Thtr 150 Class 50 Board 35 Del from £99 **Parking** 17 **Notes LB** ⊛ in restaurant Civ Wed 100

★★ 75% **HOTEL**

Crown at Wells

Market Place BA5 2RP

☎ 01749 673457 🖷 01749 679792

e-mail: stay@crownatwells.co.uk

web: www.crownatwells.co.uk

dir: on entering Wells follow signs for Hotels/Deliveries. Hotel in Market Place

Retaining its original period charm, this historic inn is situated in the heart of the city, just a short stroll from the cathedral. The building's frontage has even been used for film sets. Bedrooms, all with modern facilities, vary in size and style. Public areas focus around Anton's, the popular bistro, is a light and airy environment with a relaxed atmosphere. The Penn Bar is an alternative eating option that also serves real ales.

Rooms 15 en suite (2 fmly) ⊛ in all bedrooms S £60-£90; D £70-£110 (incl. bkfst) **Conf** BC **Parking** 15 **Notes LB** ⊛ in restaurant RS 25 Dec food not available in evening

★★ 72% **HOTEL**

Coxley Vineyard

Coxley BA5 1RQ

☎ 01749 670285 🖷 01749 679708

e-mail: max@orofino.freeserve.co.uk

dir: A39 from Wells signed Coxley. Village halfway between Wells & Glastonbury. Hotel off main road at end of village.

This privately owned and personally run hotel was built on the site of an old cider farm. It was later part of a commercial vineyard and some

continued on page 566

England

WELLS continued

of the vines are still in evidence. It provides well equipped, modern bedrooms; most are situated on the ground floor. There is a comfortable bar and a spacious restaurant with an impressive lantern ceiling. The hotel is a popular venue for conferences and other functions.

Rooms 9 en suite (5 fmly) (8 GF) ⊘ in all bedrooms S £65-£72.50; D £75-£89.50 (incl. bkfst) **Facilities** ⊀ Xmas **Conf** Thtr 90 Class 50 Board 40 Del from £99 **Parking** 50 **Notes LB** ⊘ in restaurant

★★ 67% **HOTEL**

Ancient Gate House
20 Sadler St BA5 2SE
☎ 01749 672029 📄 01749 670319
e-mail: info@ancientgatehouse.co.uk
dir: 1st hotel on left on Cathedral Green

Guests are treated to good old-fashioned hospitality in a friendly informal atmosphere at this charming hotel. Bedrooms, many of which boast unrivalled cathedral views and four-poster beds, are well equipped and furnished in keeping with the age and character of the building. The hotel's Rugantino Restaurant remains popular, offering typically Italian specialities and traditional English dishes.

Rooms 8 en suite ⊘ in 2 bedrooms S fr £76; D fr £91 (incl. bkfst) **Facilities** Xmas **Notes LB** ⊘ in restaurant Closed 27-29 Dec

WEST CAMEL   MAP 04 ST52

★★ 79% ⊛ **HOTEL**

Walnut Tree
Fore St BA22 7QW
☎ 01935 851292 📄 01935 852119
e-mail: info@thewalnuttreehotel.com
web: www.thewalnuttreehotel.com
dir: From Yeovil take A303, pass Fleet Air Arm Museum turn right to West Camel Hotel on this road.

This small hotel has the character and atmosphere of a village inn, with friendliness and personal service high on the agenda. The accommodation is of a good standard, with well-maintained modern bedrooms. The focus of the Walnut Tree is its restaurants; one being more family orientated and the other fine dining. Both offer a wealth

continued

of fresh produce imaginatively served. The bar is traditional with oak beams and exposed brickwork.

Walnut Tree

Rooms 13 en suite (6 GF) ⊘ in all bedrooms S £68; D £98 (incl. bkfst) **Parking** 40 **Notes** ⊗ No children 5yrs ⊘ in restaurant Closed 25-26 Dec & 1 Jan

See advertisement under BATH

WESTON-SUPER-MARE   MAP 04 ST36

★★★ 70% **HOTEL**

Beachlands
17 Uphill Rd North BS23 4NG
☎ 01934 621401 📄 01934 621966
e-mail: info@beachlandshotel.com
web: www.beachlandshotel.com
dir: M5 junct 21, follow signs for Hospital. At Hospital rdbt follow signs for beach, hotel 300yds before beach

This popular hotel has the bonus of a 10-metre indoor pool and sauna. It is very close to the 18-hole links course and a short walk from the seafront. Elegant public areas include a bar, a choice of lounges and a bright dining room. Bedrooms vary slightly in size, but all are well equipped for both the business and leisure guest.

Rooms 23 en suite (6 fmly) (11 GF) ⊘ in all bedrooms S £60-£80; D £89-£109 (incl. bkfst) **Facilities** 🏊 Sauna Wi-fi in bedrooms ch fac **Conf** Thtr 60 Class 20 Board 30 Del from £90 **Parking** 28 **Notes LB** ⊗ ⊘ in restaurant Closed 23 Dec-2 Jan Civ Wed 110

★★★ 68% **HOTEL**

The Royal Hotel

1 South Pde BS23 1JP
☎ 01934 423100 📠 01934 415135
e-mail: royalwsm@btopenworld.com

The Royal, which opened in 1810, was the first hotel in Weston and occupies a prime seafront position. It is a grand building and many of the bedrooms, including some with sea views, are spacious and comfortable. Public areas include a choice of bars and the restaurant offers a range of dishes to meet all tastes. Entertainment is provided during the season with a regular jazz slot on Sundays.

Rooms 37 en suite (5 fmly) ⊘ in 27 bedrooms S £66-£85; D £83-£110 (incl. bkfst) **Facilities** STV Wi-fi in bedrooms Beauty room ♪ ch fac
Conf Thtr 200 Class 100 Board 60 Del from £105 **Services** Lift
Parking 152 **Notes** ⊗ ⊘ in restaurant Civ Wed 200

★★★ 64% **HOTEL**

Commodore

Beach Rd, Sand Bay, Kewstoke BS22 9UZ
☎ 01934 415778 📠 01934 750020
e-mail: latonacom@aol.com

dir: *From Weston-Super-Mare take Kewstoke road through Weston Woods*

Located in the pleasant village of Kewstoke by unspoilt Sand Bay, this popular hotel has direct access to the beach. There is a range of dining options, from the relaxed carvery and two-for-one specials in the beamed bar, to the more formal menu of Alice's Restaurant. Bedrooms vary in size and are split between the main hotel and two adjacent buildings.

Rooms 19 en suite (2 fmly) (4 GF) ⊘ in 6 bedrooms S £65-£75; D £85-£95 (incl. bkfst) **Facilities** Wi-fi in bedrooms Putt green Xmas
Conf Thtr 120 Class 50 Board 40 Del from £85 **Parking** 70 **Notes LB** ⊘ in restaurant Civ Wed 100

★★ 74% **HOTEL**

Woodlands Country House

Hill Ln TA9 4DF
☎ 01278 760232 📠 01278 769090
e-mail: info@woodlands-hotel.co.uk
web: www.woodlands-hotel.co.uk
(For full entry see Brent Knoll)

See advert on this page

England

WESTON-SUPER-MARE *continued*

★★ 69% **HOTEL**

Battleborough Grange Country Hotel

Bristol Rd - A38 TA9 4HJ
☎ 01278 760208 🖹 01278 761950
e-mail: info@battleboroughgrangehotel.co.uk

(For full entry see Brent Knoll)

★★ 69% **HOTEL**

Madeira Cove Hotel

32-34 Birnbeck Rd BS23 2BX
☎ 01934 626707 🖹 01934 624882
e-mail: madeiracove@telco4u.net

dir: follow Western Seafront signs, then Madeira Cove sign,
north towards Kewstoke & Sand Bay, pass Grand Pier, hotel on
right

Within easy walking distance of the town centre, this popular and
friendly hotel, now under new ownership, enjoys an ideal location
overlooking the sea. It provides comfortable and well-equipped
accommodation. A good range of food is offered in the spacious
restaurant and in addition to the bar, a separate upper floor lounge is
available to guests.

Rooms 22 rms (21 en suite) 4 annexe en suite (2 fmly) ⊗ in
22 bedrooms **Facilities** Xmas **Conf** Thtr 20 **Services** Lift **Notes** ⊗ in
restaurant

★★ 69% **HOTEL**

New Birchfield

8-9 Manilla Crescent BS23 2BS
☎ 01934 621839 🖹 01934 626474
e-mail: newbirchfieldhotel@aol.com

dir: Exit M5 junct 21/22. Hotel on seafront at N end

This establishment, popular with coach parties, is located just across
the road from the beach. Bedrooms are individually sized and styled,
some have sea views and some are on the ground floor. There is a
first-floor lounge and the dining room has large picture windows to
make the most of the views. There is daily entertainment after dinner.

Rooms 30 en suite S £30-£45; D £60-£90 (incl. bkfst) **Facilities** ♫ Xmas
Services Lift **Parking** 10 **Notes LB** ⊗ ⊗ in restaurant Closed Jan

★★ 65% **HOTEL**

Anchor Head

19 Claremont Crescent, Birnbeck Rd
BS23 2EE

Leisureplex

☎ 01934 620880 🖹 01934 621767
e-mail: anchor.weston@alfatravel.co.uk
web: www.alfatravel.co.uk

dir: M5 junct 21/A370 to Weston Seafront, right towards north
end of resort past Grand Pier towards Brimbeck Pier. Hotel at
end of terrace on left

Enjoying a very pleasant location with views across the bay, the
Anchor Head offers a varied choice of comfortable lounges and a
relaxing outdoor patio area. Bedrooms and bathrooms are traditionally
furnished and include several ground-floor rooms. Dinner and
breakfast are served in the spacious dining room that also benefits
from sea views.

Rooms 52 en suite (1 fmly) (5 GF) ⊗ in all bedrooms S £31-£41;
D £50-£70 (incl. bkfst) **Facilities** ♫ Xmas **Services** Lift **Notes LB** ⊗
⊗ in restaurant Closed Dec-Feb RS Mar & Nov

★★ 65% **HOTEL**

New Ocean

Madeira Cove BS23 2BS
☎ 01934 621839 🖹 01934 626474
e-mail: newoceanhotel@aol.com
web: www.newoceanhotel.co.uk

dir: on seafront

Ideally positioned on the seafront, opposite the Marine Lake, several
bedrooms at this family-run hotel enjoy pleasant views over Weston
Bay. In the downstairs restaurant, dinner offers traditional home
cooking using fresh ingredients. The smart public areas include a well-
furnished bar and lounge, where entertainment is regularly provided.

Rooms 53 en suite (2 fmly) **Facilities** ♫ Xmas **Services** Lift **Parking** 6
Notes ⊗ ⊗ in restaurant RS Jan

★ 68% **HOTEL**

Timbertop Aparthotel

8 Victoria Park BS23 2HZ
☎ 01934 631178 & 01934 424348 🖹 01934 414716
e-mail: stay@aparthoteltimbertop.com
web: www.aparthoteltimbertop.com

dir: follow signs to pier, then 1st right after Winter Gardens, 1st
left (Lower Church Rd). Left, then right to hotel

Located in a leafy cul-de-sac, close to the seafront and Winter
Gardens, this homely hotel offers a warm and personal welcome.
Bedrooms are bright and fresh with pine furnishings and in addition
to a small bar there is a relaxing lounge. Substantial home-cooked
breakfasts are provided with the emphasis on fresh ingredients.

Rooms 8 en suite 5 annexe en suite (2 fmly) **Conf** BC Thtr 10 Class 10
Board 10 **Parking** 15 **Notes LB** ⊗ ⊗ in restaurant

continued

BUDGET HOTEL

Premier Travel Inn Weston-Super-Mare

Hutton Moor Rd BS22 8IY

☎ 08701 977266 🖹 01934 627401

web: www.premiertravelinn.com

dir: M5 junct 21, A370 to Weston-Super-Ware. After 3rd rdbt right at lights into Hutton Moor Leisure Centre. Turn left

High quality, modern budget accommodation ideal for both families and business travellers. Spacious, en suite bedrooms feature bath and shower, satellite TV and many have telephones and modem points. The adjacent family restaurant features a wide and varied menu. For further details consult the Hotel Groups page.

Rooms 60 en suite

Rooms 16 en suite 5 annexe en suite (2 fmly) S £95-£250; D £140-£250 (incl. bkfst) **Facilities** STV 🗔 ☒ Sauna Solarium Gym 😘 Jacuzzi Wi-fi in bedrooms Beauty treatment, exercise classes in dance studio 🎵 ch fac Xmas **Conf** Thtr 200 Class 50 Board 55 Del from £110 **Parking** 100
Notes LB ⊘ in restaurant Civ Wed 90

WINSCOMBE   MAP 04 ST45

BUDGET HOTEL

Premier Travel Inn Bristol Airport

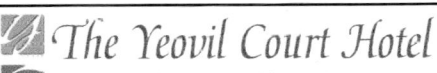

Bridgwater Rd BS25 1NN

☎ 0870 9906302 🖹 0870 9906303

web: www.premiertravelinn.com

dir: Between M5 junct 21 & 22 (9m from Bristol Airport). Exit onto A371 towards Banwell, Winscombe to A38. Right at lights, Hotel 300yds on left

High quality, modern budget accommodation ideal for both families and business travellers. Spacious, en suite bedrooms feature bath and shower, satellite TV and many have telephones and modem points. The adjacent family restaurant features a wide and varied menu. For further details consult the Hotel Groups page.

Rooms 31 en suite

WILLITON   MAP 03 ST04

★★ 73% ◉◉ HOTEL

White House

Long St TA4 4QW

☎ 01984 632306 & 632777

dir: on A39 in village centre

A relaxed and easy-going atmosphere is the hallmark of this charming little Georgian hotel. Bedrooms in the main building are more spacious, and all well-equipped with extra touches that make the White House a home-from-home. Delicious award winning cooking and an impressive wine list can be found in the dining room.

Rooms 6 rms (5 en suite) 4 annexe en suite (1 fmly) (4 GF) **Parking** 12
Notes LB No credit cards accepted ⊘ in restaurant Closed 28 Oct -mid May

WINCANTON   MAP 04 ST72

★★★ 78% ◉◉ COUNTRY HOUSE HOTEL

Holbrook House

Holbrook BA9 8BS

☎ 01963 824466 🖹 01963 32681

e-mail: enquiries@holbrookhouse.co.uk

dir: from A303 at Wincanton, turn left on A371 towards Castle Cary and Shepton Mallet

This handsome country house offers a unique blend of quality and comfort combined with a friendly atmosphere. Set in peaceful gardens and a wooded ground, Holbrook House is the perfect retreat. The restaurant provides a selection of innovative dishes prepared with enthusiasm and served by a team of caring staff.

continued

WITHYPOOL
MAP 03 SS83

★★ 69% **HOTEL**

Royal Oak Inn
TA24 7QP

☎ 01643 831506 📠 01643 831659

e-mail: manage.roy@ccinns.com

dir: 7m N of Dulverton, off B3223

For centuries this old inn has provided travellers with food, drink and shelter. Lovers of the great outdoors will find this an ideal base for exploration. Bedrooms are comfortable and each displays individuality and charm. Public areas include a choice of bars, complete with beams and crackling log fires, and the Acorn Restaurant serves cuisine with an emphasis on local produce.

Rooms 8 rms (7 en suite) **Facilities** Riding Shooting Safaris arranged **Parking** 20 **Notes** ⊘ in restaurant

---

WIVELISCOMBE
MAP 03 ST02

★★ 74% **HOTEL**

White Hart
West St TA4 2JP

☎ 01984 623344 📠 01984 624748

e-mail: reservations@whitehartwiveliscombe.co.uk

web: www.whitehartwiveliscombe.co.uk

dir: M5 junct 25 then A38 to Taunton. Follow signs for A358 to Minehead then B3227 to Wiveliscombe

This establishment is the focal point of this delightful town situated near the foot of the Quantock Hills. Exmoor is on the doorstep and the coast is just a few miles' drive. Bedrooms have been refurbished and offer contemporary accommodation with a good range of facilities. Innovative dishes are offered in the restaurant and the bar has good range of locally produced beers.

Rooms 16 en suite (2 fmly) ⊘ in all bedrooms S fr £45; D fr £70 (incl. bkfst) **Facilities** STV **Conf** BC Thtr 40 Class 12 Board 26 Del £99 **Parking** 12 **Notes** ⊗ ⊘ in restaurant

---

YATTON
MAP 04 ST46

★★ 65% **HOTEL**

Bridge Inn
OLD ENGLISH INNS

North End Rd BS49 4AU

☎ 01934 839100 & 839101 📠 01934 839149

e-mail: bridge.yatton@newbridgeinns.co.uk

web: www.oldenglish.co.uk

dir: Exit M5 junct 20, take B3133 to Yatton. Take 1st left at rdbt and 1st left at 2nd rdbt. Hotel 2.5m on right

This hotel offers spacious well-equipped bedrooms. The bar/restaurant offers a variety of dishes on the menu throughout the day in a relaxed and informal environment. There is a playzone for children. Breakfast is a choice of a self-service buffet or a full English breakfast served at the table.

Rooms 41 en suite (4 fmly) (20 GF) ⊘ in 34 bedrooms S £35-£85; D £85 **Facilities** STV ♫ Xmas **Conf** BC Thtr 100 Class 30 Board 50 Del from £99 **Parking** 150

YEOVIL
MAP 04 ST51

See also Martock

★★★ 79% ⊛ **HOTEL**

Lanes
West Coker BA22 9AJ

☎ 01935 862555 📠 01935 864260

e-mail: stay@laneshotel.net

web: www.laneshotel.net.

dir: 2m W of Yeovil on A30 in centre of West Coker

This splendid traditional building, once a rectory, has been cleverly fused with an internal contemporary style. Guests are assured of a relaxed and friendly stay within a light and airy atmosphere. Bedrooms are stylish and equipped with many considerate extras. The brasserie-style restaurant offers an imaginative range of dishes, using local produce whenever possible.

Rooms 10 en suite 17 annexe en suite (3 fmly) (8 GF) ⊘ in 10 bedrooms S fr £80; D fr £100 (incl. bkfst) **Facilities** Spa FTV Sauna Gym 🧖 Jacuzzi Wi-fi available Xmas **Conf** BC Thtr 60 Class 40 Board 20 Del from £120 **Services** Lift **Parking** 40 **Notes LB** ⊗ ⊘ in restaurant

---

★★★ 75% ⊛⊛ **HOTEL**

The Yeovil Court Hotel & Restaurant
West Coker Rd BA20 2HE

☎ 01935 863746 📠 01935 863990

e-mail: unwind@yeovilhotel.com

web: www.yeovilhotel.com

dir: 2.5m W of town centre on A30

This comfortable, family-run hotel benefits from a very relaxed and caring atmosphere. Bedrooms are well equipped and neatly presented; some are located in an adjacent building. Public areas consist of a smart lounge, a popular bar and an attractive restaurant.

continued

Menus combine an interesting selection including lighter options and dishes suited to special occasion dining.

Rooms 18 en suite 12 annexe en suite (3 fmly) (11 GF) ⊘ in 16 bedrooms S £60-£67; D £80-£150 (incl. bkfst) **Facilities** FTV Wi-fi in bedrooms ch fac **Conf** Thtr 50 Class 18 Board 22 Del from £100 **Parking** 65 **Notes LB** ⊘ in restaurant RS Sat lunch, 25 Dec eve

See advert on page 569

★★★ 71% HOTEL

Manor
OLD ENGLISH INNS

Hendford BA20 1TG

☎ 01935 423116 ▤ 01935 706607

e-mail: manor.yeovil@oldenglishinns.co.uk

web: www.oldenglish.co.uk

dir: *A303 onto A3088 to Yeovil. Once over River Yeo take 2nd exit at rdbt and turn immediately left into Hendford.*

This manor house, dating from 1735, stands in the centre of Yeovil and has the benefit of its own spacious car park. There is a bar and an open-plan lounge area where afternoon tea may be enjoyed. Breakfast and dinner is served in the light and airy conservatory dining area.

Rooms 41 en suite (1 fmly) (10 GF) ⊘ in 21 bedrooms S £55-£75; D £70-£100 (incl. bkfst) **Facilities** STV **Conf** Thtr 150 Class 50 Board 45 Del £105 **Parking** 60 **Notes LB** ⊗ ⊘ in restaurant Civ Wed 60

★★ 62% HOTEL

Preston

64 Preston Rd BA20 2DL

☎ 01935 474400 ▤ 01935 410142

e-mail: prestonhotelyeo@aol.co.uk

web: www.preston-hotel.net

dir: *A303 onto A3088, left at 1st rdbt, over 2nd rdbt & turn right at 3rd rdbt*

A relaxed and friendly atmosphere has been maintained at this popular hotel. Suited to both business and leisure guests, a number of well-equipped rooms are located in an annexe at ground floor level. There are two bars (one with a pool table) and a cosy dining room, where an extensive menu is available.

Rooms 6 en suite 7 annexe en suite (1 fmly) (7 GF) ⊘ in 7 bedrooms **Conf** BC Class 40 Board 15 **Parking** 32 **Notes** ⊘ in restaurant

◉◉◉ RESTAURANT WITH ROOMS

Little Barwick House

Barwick Village BA22 9TD

☎ 01935 423902 ▤ 01935 420908

e-mail: littlebarwick@hotmail.com

dir: *From Yeovil on A37 towards Dorchester, left at 1st rdbt. 1st left, Hotel 0.25m on left*

Situated in a quiet hamlet in 3.5 acres of gardens and grounds, this delightful listed Georgian dower house is an ideal retreat for those seeking peaceful surroundings and good food. Tim Ford cooks from the heart making best use of local ingredients. Each of the bedrooms has its own character, charm and a range of thoughtful extras such as fresh flowers, bottled water and magazines. The informal atmosphere of a private home, coupled with the facilities and comforts of a modern hotel, result in a very special combination.

Rooms 6 en suite S £75-£110; D £126-£140 **Parking** 30 **Notes LB** No children 5yrs ⊘ in restaurant

---

STAFFORDSHIRE

BARTON-UNDER-NEEDWOOD MAP 10 SK11

BUDGET HOTEL

Travelodge Burton (A38 Northbound)

DE13 8EG

☎ 08700 850 950 ▤ 01283 716343

web: www.travelodge.co.uk

dir: *on A38, northbound*

Travelodge offers good quality, good value, modern accommodation. Ideal for families, the spacious en suite bedrooms include remote-control TV, tea and coffee-making facilities and comfortable beds. Meals can be taken at the nearby family restaurant. See Hotel Groups pages for further details.

Rooms 20 en suite S fr £26; D fr £26

Travelodge Burton (A38 Southbound)

Rykneld St DE13 8EH

☎ 08700 850 950 ▤ 01283 716784

dir: *on A38, southbound*

Rooms 40 en suite S fr £26; D fr £26

Boars Head Hotel

**Lichfield Road
Sudbury
Derbyshire
DE6 5GX**

AA ★★★

73%

Tel: **(01283) 820344**
Fax: **(01283) 820075**

A country hotel of warmth and character dating back to the 17th century. The family run hotel has 22 en suite bedrooms all tastefully decorated and well equipped. The elegant à la carte restaurant – The Royal Boar and the less formal Hunter's Table Carvery and Bistro both provide a good selection of dishes along with an extensive bar snack menu available in the public bar. The hotel is the perfect setting for weddings, family parties or a weekend break. Ideally situated for visiting the numerous local and sporting attractions and many places of interest.

England

England

BURTON UPON TRENT   MAP 10 SK22

★★★ 80% **HOTEL**

Three Queens
One Bridge St DE14 1SY
☎ 01283 523800 ▤ 01283 523823
e-mail: hotel@threequeenshotel.co.uk
web: www.threequeenshotel.co.uk

dir: on A511 in Burton upon Trent at the junct of Bridge St & High St. Town side of Old River Bridge.

Located in the centre of the town close to the river, this smartly presented hotel provides an appealing, high quality base from which to tour the local area. Bedrooms come in a mix of styles that include spacious duplex suites and executive rooms located in the original Jacobean heart of the building. Smart day rooms include the medieval styled Grill Restaurant, a modern bar and a contemporary breakfast room. A warm welcome is assured from the professional team of staff.

Rooms 38 en suite S £54.50-£69.50; D £64.50-£79.50 (incl. bkfst) **Facilities** STV Wi-fi in bedrooms Xmas **Conf** Thtr 60 Class 40 Board 30 Del from £104 **Services** Lift air con **Parking** 40 **Notes LB** ⊗ ⊘ in restaurant

★★★ 77% **HOTEL**

Ramada Newton Park   ⓦRAMADA.
DE15 0SS
☎ 01283 703568 ▤ 01283 709235
e-mail: sales.newtonpark@ramadajarvis.co.uk
web: www.ramadajarvis.co.uk

Set in well tended gardens, this country-house hotel is a popular venue for conferences and meetings. Bedrooms are comfortably appointed for both business and leisure guests.

Rooms 50 en suite (5 fmly) (7 GF) ⊘ in 40 bedrooms S fr £120; D fr £120 **Facilities** STV FTV Wi-fi available Xmas **Conf** Thtr 260 Class 155 Board 143 Del from £135 **Services** Lift **Parking** 120 **Notes LB** ⊘ in restaurant Civ Wed 100

★★ 72% **HOTEL**

Riverside   OLD ENGLISH INNS
Riverside Dr, Branston DE14 3EP
☎ 01283 511234 ▤ 01283 511441
e-mail: riverside.branston@oldenglishinns.co.uk
web: www.oldenglish.co.uk

dir: on A5121 follow signs for Branston until small humped-back bridge, over bridge and right into Warren Lane. 2nd left

With its quiet residential location and well-kept terraced garden stretching down to the River Trent, this hotel has all the ingredients for a relaxing stay. Many of the tables in the Garden Room restaurant have views over the garden. Bedrooms are tastefully furnished and decorated and provide a good range of extras.

Rooms 22 en suite (10 GF) ⊘ in all bedrooms **Facilities** STV Fishing **Conf** Thtr 120 Class 60 Board 30 **Parking** 200 **Notes LB** ⊘ in restaurant Civ Wed 120

CANNOCK   MAP 10 SJ91

Ⓤ

Swallow Roman Way   SWALLOW
Watling St WS11 1SH
☎ 01543 572121 ▤ 01543 502749
e-mail: reservations.cannock@swallowhotels.com
web: www.swallowhotels.com

dir: Exit M6 junct 11 and follow A460 to Cannock, at first island turn left, hotel 200yds on left

At the time of going to press, the star classification for this hotel was not confirmed. Please refer to the AA internet site www.theAA.com for current information.

Rooms 56 annexe en suite (21 fmly) (23 GF) ⊘ in 44 bedrooms S £49-£83; D £59-£93 **Facilities** Snooker **Conf** Thtr 150 Class 100 Board 45 Del from £90 **Parking** 300 **Notes LB** ⊘ in restaurant Civ Wed 140

BUDGET HOTEL

Premier Travel Inn Cannock   premier travel inn
Watling St WS11 1SJ
☎ 08701 977048 ▤ 01543 466130
web: www.premiertravelinn.com

dir: on at junct of A5/A460, 2m from M6 junct 11/12

High quality, modern budget accommodation ideal for both families and business travellers. Spacious, en suite bedrooms feature bath and shower, satellite TV and many have telephones and modem points. The adjacent family restaurant features a wide and varied menu. For further details consult the Hotel Groups page.

Rooms 60 en suite **Conf** Thtr 80 Board 40

HIMLEY   MAP 10 SO89

★★★ 63% **HOTEL**

The Himley Country Hotel
School Rd DY3 4LG
☎ 0870 609 6112 ▤ 01902 896668
e-mail: reservations@himleycountryhotel.com

dir: leave A449 into School Rd at lights by Dudley Arms

This modern hotel, now under new ownership, has been tastefully built around a 19th-century village schoolhouse. Bedrooms are well equipped and many are quite spacious. Day rooms include a stylish conservatory restaurant where wide-ranging menus and traditional buffet roasts are offered.

Rooms 73 en suite (1 fmly) ⊘ in 38 bedrooms **Facilities** STV **Conf** Thtr 150 Class 80 Board 50 **Parking** 100 **Notes LB** ⊘ in restaurant Civ Wed 100

★★ 72% **HOTEL**

Himley House Hotel
Stourbridge Rd DY3 4LD
☎ 01902 892468 ▤ 01902 892604
e-mail: himleyhouse@hotmail.com
web: www.himleyhousehotel.com

dir: on A449 N of Stourbridge

Dating back to the 17th century, and formerly the lodge for nearby Himley Hall, this hotel offers well-equipped and comfortable

continued

accommodation. The comfortable bedrooms of varying sizes are located both in the main house and separate buildings nearby, and the busy restaurant offers a wide selection of dishes.

Rooms 24 en suite (2 fmly) **Facilities** ch fac **Conf** Thtr 50 Class 30 Board 22 **Parking** 162 **Notes LB** ⊗

LEEK　　　　　　　　　MAP 16 SJ95

★★★ 62% HOTEL

Hotel Rudyard

Lake Rd, Rudyard ST13 8RN
☎ 01538 306208 ▤ 01538 306208

This large stone-built Victorian property is set in extensive wooded grounds in the centre of Rudyard village. It provides modern and well-equipped accommodation and a room with a four-poster bed is also available. There is a function room, a large carvery restaurant and a traditionally furnished bar.

Rooms 15 en suite (2 fmly) ⊗ in 2 bedrooms **Conf** Thtr 80 Class 60 Board 40 **Parking** 100 **Notes LB** ⊗ in restaurant

★★ 79% ֎ HOTEL

Three Horseshoes Inn & Restaurant

Buxton Rd, Blackshaw Moor ST13 8TW
☎ 01538 300296 ▤ 01538 300320
e-mail: enquires@threeshoesinn.co.uk
web: www.threeshoesinn.co.uk
dir: 2m N of Leek on A53

A family owned hostelry in spacious grounds that include a beer garden and children's play area. The non smoking bedrooms are tastefully appointed and furnished in keeping with the character of the hotel. Public areas include a choice of bars and eating options. New for 2007 - an additional 20 bedrooms and a new brasserie

Rooms 26 en suite (2 fmly) (10 GF) ⊗ in all bedrooms S £68-£90; D £76-£120 (incl. bkfst) **Facilities** Putt green **Conf** Thtr 60 Class 50 Board 25 **Services** Lift **Parking** 80 **Notes LB** ⊗ ⊗ in restaurant Closed 24 Dec-1 Jan Civ Wed 120

֎ RESTAURANT WITH ROOMS

Number 64

64 Saint Edwards St ST13 5DL
☎ 01538 381900 ▤ 01538 370918
e-mail: enquiries@number64.com
web: www.number64.com
dir: In town centre near junct A520 & A53

This Grade II listed Georgian house in the centre of the town offers very well-furnished bedrooms, one with a four poster. A wide range of

continued

eating options is available, including a speciality food shop, a patisserie, and a restaurant for well presented dishes.

Rooms 3 en suite ⊗ in all bedrooms S £65-£85; D £75-95 **Conf** Board 14 **Notes** ⊗ ⊗ in restaurant Civ Wed 50

LICHFIELD　　　　　　　MAP 10 SK10

INSPECTORS' CHOICE

★★★★ ֎֎ HOTEL

Swinfen Hall

Swinfen WS14 9RE
☎ 01543 481494 ▤ 01543 480341
e-mail: info@swinfenhallhotel.co.uk
web: www.swinfenhallhotel.co.uk
dir: set back from A38 2.5m outside Lichfield, towards Birmingham

Dating from 1757, this lavishly decorated mansion has been painstakingly restored by the present owners. Public rooms are particularly stylish, with intricately carved ceilings and impressive oil portraits. Rooms on the first floor boast period features and tall sash windows; those on the second floor (the former servants' quarters) are smaller and more contemporary by comparison. Service within the award-winning restaurant is both professional and attentive.

Rooms 19 en suite S £125-£225; D £135-£250 **Facilities** STV ⌣ Fishing ⌣ Wi-fi in bedrooms 100 acres of parkland with 45 acres private deer park **Conf** Thtr 96 Class 50 Board 120 Del from £180 **Parking** 80 **Notes** ⊗ ⊗ in restaurant Civ Wed 120

★★★ 78% HOTEL

Best Western George

12-14 Bird St WS13 6PR
☎ 01543 414822 ▤ 01543 415817
e-mail: mail@thegeorgelichfield.co.uk
web: www.thegeorgelichfield.co.uk

Best Western

dir: from Bowling Green Island on A461 take Lichfield exit. Left at next island into Swan Road, as road bears left, turn right for hotel straight ahead

Situated in the city centre, this privately owned hotel provides good quality, well-equipped accommodation, which includes a room with a

continued on page 574

LICHFIELD *continued*

four-poster bed. Facilities here include a large ballroom, plus several other rooms for meetings and functions.

Best Western George

Rooms 45 en suite (5 fmly) ⊘ in 28 bedrooms S £58-£124; D £68-£134 (incl. bkfst) **Facilities** Wi-fi in bedrooms **Conf** Thtr 110 Class 60 Board 40 Del from £100 **Services** Lift **Parking** 45 **Notes LB** ⊘ in restaurant Civ Wed 110

See also advert on page 651

★★★ 74% HOTEL

Little Barrow

62 Beacon St WS13 7AR
☎ 01543 414500 🗎 01543 415734
e-mail: reservations@tlbh.co.uk
web: www.tlbh.co.uk

Conveniently situated for the cathedral and the city, this friendly hotel provides well-equipped accommodation. The cosy lounge bar, popular with locals and visitors alike, has a good range of drinks and a choice of bar meals. More formal dining is offered in the attractive restaurant. Service is hospitable and attentive.

Rooms 32 en suite (2 fmly) ⊘ in 8 bedrooms S £70-£79; D £85-£100 (incl. bkfst) **Facilities** STV Wi-fi available Xmas **Conf** BC Thtr 150 Class 100 Board 80 Del from £100 **Parking** 60 **Notes LB** ⊗ ⊘ in restaurant Civ Wed 120

★★ 65% HOTEL

Olde Corner House

Walsall Rd, Muckley Corner WS14 0BG
☎ 01543 372182 🗎 01543 372211
e-mail: philip@emerton.fsbusiness.co.uk
dir: *at junct of A5 & A461*

Well located on the A5 this family owned and run hotel offers modern bedrooms and friendly and attentive service. A good range of good value food is available either in the bar or tastefully furnished restaurant.

Rooms 23 en suite (1 fmly) (5 GF) ⊘ in 12 bedrooms **Parking** 60

★★ 61% HOTEL

Angel Croft

Beacon St WS13 7AA
☎ 01543 258737 🗎 01543 415605
dir: *opposite west gate entrance to Lichfield Cathedral*

This traditional, family-run, Georgian hotel is close to the cathedral and city centre. A comfortable lounge leads into a pleasantly

continued

appointed dining room; there is also a cosy bar on the lower ground floor. Bedrooms vary and most are spacious, particularly those in the adjacent Westgate House.

Rooms 10 rms (8 en suite) 8 annexe en suite (1 fmly) **Conf** Thtr 30 Board 20 **Parking** 60 **Notes** ⊗ ⊘ in restaurant Closed 25 & 26 Dec RS Sun evenings

BUDGET HOTEL

Innkeeper's Lodge Lichfield

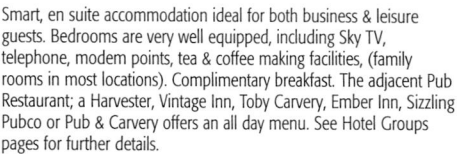

Stafford Rd WS13 8JB
☎ 01543 415789 🗎 01543 420752
web: www.innkeeperslodge.com
dir: *on A51, 0.75m outside city centre*

Smart, en suite accommodation ideal for both business & leisure guests. Bedrooms are very well equipped, including Sky TV, telephone, modem points, tea & coffee making facilities, (family rooms in most locations). Complimentary breakfast. The adjacent Pub Restaurant; a Harvester, Vintage Inn, Toby Carvery, Ember Inn, Sizzling Pubco or Pub & Carvery offers an all day menu. See Hotel Groups pages for further details.

Rooms 10 en suite

BUDGET HOTEL

Premier Travel Inn Lichfield

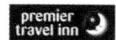

Rykneld St, Fradley WS13 8RD
☎ 0870 9906438 🗎 0870 9906439
web: www.premiertravelinn.com
dir: *From N, M6 junct 15, A500/A50 to Uttoxeter. A50 onto A38 to Lichfield. Hotel on left past petrol station. From S, M42 junct 9, A446, A38 to Lichfield, then Fradley signs. Do not exit at Fradley Park*

High quality, modern budget accommodation ideal for both families and business travellers. Spacious, en suite bedrooms feature bath and shower, satellite TV and many have telephones and modem points. The adjacent family restaurant features a wide and varied menu. For further details consult the Hotel Groups page.

Rooms 30 en suite **Conf** Thtr 40

LONGNOR
MAP 16 SK06

RESTAURANT WITH ROOMS

The Crewe and Harpur Arms

Market Square SK17 0NS
☎ 01298 83205 🗎 01298 83689
e-mail: enquiries@creweandharpur.co.uk
dir: *S from Buxton on A515, after 3m, right onto B5053. Hotel in Market Square*

Located in the heart of the Staffordshire moors this Georgian pub has been refurbished with care. Bedrooms are stylish, fully equipped and each has a modern ensuite. Public areas include the oak panelled bar (featuring real ales) and separate dining room - both offering a tempting range of bar meals and a frequently changing carte menu.

Rooms 8 en suite 3 annexe rms (3 fmly) ⊘ in all bedrooms S £35-£65; D £70-£130 **Facilities** STV **Conf** Board 25 **Parking** 100 **Notes LB** ⊗ ⊘ in restaurant

England

NEWCASTLE-UNDER-LYME   MAP 10 SJ84

★★ 62% HOTEL

Stop Inn Newcastle-under-Lyme

Liverpool Rd, Cross Heath ST5 9DX

☎ 01782 717000 📠 01782 713669

e-mail: enquiries@hotels-newcastle-under-lyme.com

web: www.hotels-newcastle-under-lyme.com

dir: M6 junct 16 onto A500 to Stoke-on-Trent. Take A34 to Newcastle-under-Lyme, hotel on right after 1.5m

Some of the well-equipped bedrooms at this purpose-built hotel are in a separate block at the rear. There is a large lounge bar with a pool table and the restaurant offers a good range of food.

Rooms 43 rms (42 en suite) 24 annexe en suite (13 fmly) (23 GF) ⊗ in 31 bedrooms **Facilities** STV Xmas **Conf** Thtr 150 Class 80 Board 80 **Parking** 160 **Notes** ⊗ in restaurant

BUDGET HOTEL

Premier Travel Inn Newcastle-under-Lyme

Talke Rd, Chesterton ST5 7AH

☎ 08701 977191 📠 01782 578901

web: www.premiertravelinn.com

dir: Exit M6 junct 16 - follow A500 for approx. 3.5 miles. Take A34 towards Newcastle-under-Lyme. Inn 0.5m on the right

High quality, modern budget accommodation ideal for both families and business travellers. Spacious, en suite bedrooms feature bath and shower, satellite TV and many have telephones and modem points. The adjacent family restaurant features a wide and varied menu. For further details consult the Hotel Groups page.

Rooms 58 en suite

NORTON CANES   MAP 10 SK00
MOTORWAY SERVICE AREA (M6 TOLL)

BUDGET HOTEL

Premier Travel Inn Birmingham North (M6 Toll)

Norton Canes MSA, M6 Toll Rd, North Canes WS11 9UX

☎ 08701 977070 📠 08701 977 700

web: www.premiertravelinn.com

dir: on motorway service area between junct 6 & / on M6. Access from both sides via barrier and from A5

High quality, modern budget accommodation ideal for both families and business travellers. Spacious, en suite bedrooms feature bath and shower, satellite TV and many have telephones and modem points. The adjacent family restaurant features a wide and varied menu. For further details consult the Hotel Groups page.

Rooms 40 en suite

PATTINGHAM   MAP 10 SO89

★★★ 77% HOTEL

Patshull Park Hotel Golf & Country Club

Patshull Park WV6 7HR

☎ 01902 700100 📠 01902 700874

e-mail: sales@patshull-park.co.uk

web: www.patshull-park.co.uk

dir: 1.5m W of Pattingham, at church take Patshull Rd, hotel 1.5m on right

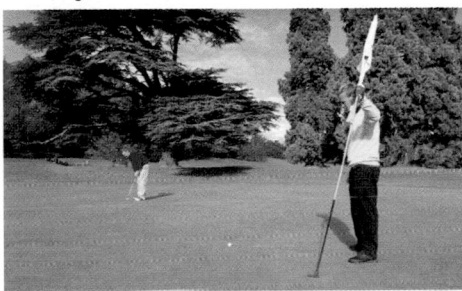

There has been a manor house here since before the Norman Conquest - the present house dates back to the 1730s. Sitting within 280 acres of parkland (with good golf and fishing) this comfortably appointed hotel has a range of modern leisure and conference facilities. Public rooms include a lounge bar, coffee shop and restaurant with delightful views over the lake. Bedrooms are well appointed and thoughtfully equipped; most have good views.

Rooms 49 en suite (15 fmly) (16 GF) ⊗ in all bedrooms S £99-£119; D £119-£159 (incl. bkst) **Facilities Spa** STV 🏊 supervised ⌃ 18 Fishing Sauna Solarium Gym Putt green Jacuzzi Beauty therapist Pool table Cardio suite ♫ Xmas **Conf** BC Thtr 160 Class 75 Board 44 Del from £110 **Parking** 200 **Notes LB** ⊗ ⊗ in restaurant RS 24-26 Dec Civ Wed 100

See advertisement under TELFORD, Shropshire

PENKRIDGE   MAP 10 SJ91

★★★ 71% HOTEL

Quality Hotel Stafford

Pinfold Ln ST19 5QP

☎ 01785 712459 📠 01785 715532

e-mail: enquiries@hotels-stafford.com

web: www.choicehotelseurope.com

dir: M6 junct 12 onto A5 towards Telford. Right at 1st rdbt onto A449, 2m into Penkridge, left just beyond Ford Garage, opposite White Hart

Just a few minutes' drive from the M6, this hotel is pleasantly located down a country lane. Bedrooms are comfortable with a good range of facilities. Public areas are neatly appointed with conference rooms and a leisure club. The Choices Restaurant makes a good dining option.

Rooms 47 en suite (2 fmly) (6 GF) ⊗ in 25 bedrooms S £50-£94; D £70-£103 (incl. bkfst) **Facilities** STV 🏊 supervised ⌃ Squash Sauna Solarium Gym Wi-fi available Xmas **Conf** Thtr 300 Class 120 Board 60 Del from £90 **Parking** 175 **Notes LB** ⊗ in restaurant Civ Wed 200

England

RUGELEY   MAP 10 SK01

BUDGET HOTEL

Travelodge Rugeley
Western Springs Rd WS15 2AS
☎ 08700 850 950 📠 01889 570096
web: www.travelodge.co.uk
dir: on A51/B5013

Travelodge offers good quality, good value, modern accommodation. Ideal for families, the spacious en suite bedrooms include remote-control TV, tea and coffee-making facilities and comfortable beds. Meals can be taken at the nearby family restaurant. See Hotel Groups pages for further details.

Rooms 32 en suite S fr £26; D fr £26

STAFFORD   MAP 10 SJ92

★★★★ 82% ◉◉ **HOTEL**

The Moat House
Lower Penkridge Rd, Acton Trussell ST17 0RJ
☎ 01785 712217 📠 01785 715344
e-mail: info@moathouse.co.uk
web: www.moathouse.co.uk
dir: M6 junct 13 onto A449 through Acton Trussell. Hotel on right on the way out of village

This 17th-century timbered building, with an idyllic canal-side setting, has been skilfully extended. Bedrooms are stylishly furnished, well equipped and comfortable. The bar offers a range of snacks and the restaurant boasts a popular fine dining option where the head chef displays his skills using top quality produce.

Rooms 41 en suite (4 fmly) (12 GF) ⊗ in 40 bedrooms S fr £125; D fr £140 (incl. bkfst) **Facilities** STV Wi-fi in bedrooms **Conf** Thtr 200 Class 60 Board 50 Del £160 **Services** Lift **Parking** 200 **Notes LB** ⊗ ⊘ in restaurant Closed 25 Dec & 1 Jan Civ Wed 150

★★★ 81% ◉ **HOTEL**

The Swan
46 Greengate St ST16 2JA
☎ 01785 258142 📠 01785 223372
e-mail: info@theswanstafford.co.uk
dir: from north on A34, access via Mill Street in town centre. From south on A449

This former coaching inn located in the town centre offers spacious, modern public areas that include a popular brasserie, a choice of elegant bars, a coffee shop and conference facilities. Individually styled bedrooms, many with original period features, are tastefully appointed

continued

and include two four-poster suites. Executive rooms are air conditioned.

Rooms 31 en suite (2 fmly) ⊗ in 29 bedrooms S £70-£80; D £98-£130 (incl. bkfst) **Facilities** STV Wi-fi available **Services** Lift **Parking** 40 **Notes** ⊗ ⊘ in restaurant Closed 25-26 Dec, 1 Jan

★★ 72% **HOTEL**

Abbey
65-68 Lichfield Rd ST17 4LW
☎ 01785 258531 📠 01785 246875
dir: M6 junct 13 towards Stafford. Right at Esso garage, to mini-rdbt, follow Silkmore Lane to 2nd rdbt. Hotel 0.25m on right

This friendly privately owned and personally run hotel provides well-equipped accommodation and is particularly popular with commercial visitors. Family and ground floor rooms are both available. Facilities here include a choice of lounges and the spacious car park, close to centre is a real benefit.

Rooms 17 en suite (3 fmly) S £45-£58; D £60-£75 (incl. bkfst) **Parking** 25 **Notes LB** ⊗ ⊘ in restaurant Closed 22 Dec-7 Jan

BUDGET HOTEL

Premier Travel Inn Stafford North (Hurricane)
1 Hurricane Close ST16 1GZ
☎ 0870 9906478 📠 0870 9906479
web: www.premiertravelinn.com
dir: Exit M6 junct 14, A34 towards Stafford. Inn approx 2m NW of town centre

High quality, modern budget accommodation ideal for both families and business travellers. Spacious, en suite bedrooms feature bath and shower, satellite TV and many have telephones and modem points. The adjacent family restaurant features a wide and varied menu. For further details consult the Hotel Groups page.

Rooms 96 en suite **Conf** Thtr 30

Premier Travel Inn Stafford North (Spitfire)
1 Spitfire Close ST16 1GX
☎ 08708 500689 📠 08701 977 706
dir: Exit M6 junct 14 and take A34 north. Inn approx. 1m on left
Rooms 60 en suite

STAFFORD MOTORWAY SERVICE AREA (M6)   MAP 10 SJ82

BUDGET HOTEL

Premier Travel Inn Stafford (M6 Southbound)
Stafford Motorway Service Area ST15 0EU
☎ 08701 977239 📠 01785 826303
web: www.premiertravelinn.com
dir: M6 junct 15 southbound, 8m

High quality, modern budget accommodation ideal for both families and business travellers. Spacious, en suite bedrooms feature bath and shower, satellite TV and many have telephones and modem points. The adjacent family restaurant features a wide and varied menu. For further details consult the Hotel Groups page.

Rooms 40 en suite **Conf** Thtr 25 Board 15

BUDGET HOTEL

Travelodge Stafford (M6)

Moto Service Area, Eccleshall Rd ST15 0EU
☎ 08700 850 950 ▤ 01785 816107
web: www.travelodge.co.uk

dir: *between M6 juncts 14 & 15 northbound only*

Travelodge offers good quality, good value, modern accommodation. Ideal for families, the spacious en suite bedrooms include remote-control TV, tea and coffee-making facilities and comfortable beds. Meals can be taken at the nearby family restaurant. See Hotel Groups pages for further details.

Rooms 49 en suite S fr £26; D fr £26

STOKE-ON-TRENT   MAP 10 SJ84
See also Newcastle-under-Lyme

★★★★ 76% HOTEL

Best Western Stoke-on-Trent Moat House

Etruria Hall, Festival Way, Etruria ST1 5BQ
☎ 01782 609988 ▤ 01782 206101
e-mail: reservations.stoke@moathousehotels.com

dir: *from M6 take A500. Turn off at A53 Leek. Keep in left lane and take first slip road on left. Left at island, hotel opposite at next island*

A large modern hotel located in Stoke's Festival Park, that adjoins Etruria Hall, the former home of Josiah Wedgwood. The bedrooms are all spacious and well equipped and include family rooms, suites and executive rooms. Public areas include a spacious lounge bar and restaurant as well as a business centre, extensive conference facilities and a leisure club and spa.

Rooms 143 en suite (50 fmly) ⊘ in 107 bedrooms S £64-£94; D £64-£94 **Facilities** STV ⊠ supervised Sauna Solarium Gym Jacuzzi Beauty treatments **Conf** Thtr 550 Class 400 Board 40 **Services** Lift air con **Parking** 350 **Notes LB** ⊘ in restaurant Civ Wed 80

★★★ 82% ⊛ HOTEL

Best Western Manor House

Audley Rd ST7 2QQ
☎ 01270 884000 ▤ 01270 882483
e-mail: mhres@compasshotels.co.uk
web: www.compasshotels.co.uk
(For full entry see Alsager, Cheshire)

★★★ 70% ⊛ HOTEL

Haydon House

Haydon St, Basford ST4 6JD
☎ 01782 711311 ▤ 01782 717470
e-mail: enquiries@haydon-house-hotel.co.uk

dir: *M6 junct 15, A500 to Stoke-on-Trent, then A53 Hanley/Newcastle. At rdbt take 1st exit, up hill, 2nd left at top of hill before lights*

A Victorian property, within easy reach of Newcastle-under-Lyme. The public rooms are furnished in a style befitting the age and character of the house and bedrooms have modern furnishings; several rooms are located in a separate house across the road. The hotel has a good reputation for its food and is popular with locals.

Rooms 17 en suite 6 annexe en suite (4 fmly) S £40-£65; D £60-£85 (incl. bkfst) **Conf** Thtr 80 Class 30 Board 30 **Parking** 52 **Notes LB** ⊘ in restaurant Civ Wed 80

★★★ 67% HOTEL

Quality Hotel

66 Trinity St, Hanley ST1 5NB
☎ 01782 202361 ▤ 01782 286464
e-mail: enquiries@hotels-stoke.com

dir: *M6 junct 15(S)/16(N) then A500 to city centre & Festival Park. A53 to Leek, keep in left lane, 3rd exit at rdbt for Hanley/City Centre/Cultural Quarter. Hotel on left at top of hill*

This large city centre hotel provides a range of bedrooms and extensive public areas including a choice of popular bars. A well lit spacious car park and modern leisure facilities are additional benefits

Rooms 128 en suite 8 annexe en suite (54 fmly) (5 GF) ⊘ in 85 bedrooms S £33-£110; D £36-£120 **Facilities Spa** STV ⊠ supervised Sauna Solarium Gym Jacuzzi Wi-fi available **Conf** Thtr 300 Class 125 Board 60 Del from £85 **Services** Lift **Parking** 150 **Notes LB** ⊘ in restaurant Civ Wed 250

★★ 63% HOTEL

Weathervane

Lysander Rd ST3 7WA
☎ 01782 388799 ▤ 01782 900004
e-mail: 5305@greenking.co.uk
web: www.oldenglish.co.uk

A few minutes from A50 and convenient for both city and industrial areas, this popular, modern pub & restaurant, under the 'Hungry Horse' brand, provides hearty well-cooked food at reasonable prices. Adjacent bedrooms are furnished for both commercial and leisure customers; all have the benefit of smart, modern en suite bathrooms.

Rooms 39 en suite (8 fmly) (18 GF) ⊘ in 32 bedrooms S £30-£50; D £40-£60 **Conf** Thtr 20 Class 20 Board 20 Del from £120 **Parking** 90 **Notes** ⊘ in restaurant

We have indicated only the hotels that do not
accept credit or debit cards

England

STOKE-ON-TRENT *continued*

Swallow George

Swan Square, Burslem ST6 2AE

☎ 01782 577544 ▤ 01782 837496

e-mail: swallow.stoke@swallowhotels.com

web: www.swallowhotels.com

dir: Take A527 towards Tunstall/Burslem, follow sign at rdbt for Burslem. After Ceramica in town centre, at main lights turn right 200mtrs. Hotel on right

At the time of going to press, the star classification for this hotel was not confirmed. Please refer to the AA internet site www.theAA.com for current information.

Rooms 40 en suite (5 fmly) ⊗ in 15 bedrooms S £35-£65; D £50-£85 (incl. bkfst) **Facilities** STV Wi-fi in bedrooms Xmas **Conf** Thtr 140 Class 120 Board 80 Del from £69 **Services** Lift **Parking** 15 **Notes** ⊘ in restaurant Civ Wed 140

BUDGET HOTEL

Innkeeper's Lodge Stoke-on-Trent

Longton Rd ST4 8BU

☎ 01782 644448 ▤ 01782 644163

web: www.innkeeperslodge.com

dir: M6 junct 15, follow A500 until slip road for A34 towards Stone. At rdbt take left onto A5035, lodge 0.5m on right

Smart, en suite accommodation ideal for both business & leisure guests. Bedrooms are very well equipped, including Sky TV, telephone, modem points, tea & coffee making facilities, (family rooms in most locations). Complimentary breakfast. The adjacent Pub Restaurant; a Harvester, Vintage Inn, Toby Carvery, Ember Inn, Sizzling Pubco or Pub & Carvery offers an all day menu. See Hotel Groups pages for further details.

Rooms 30 en suite

STONE   MAP 10 SJ93

★★★ 73% HOTEL

Crown

38 High St ST15 8AS

☎ 01785 813535 ▤ 01785 815942

e-mail: info@stonehotels.co.uk

dir: M6 junct 14, A34 N to Stone. M6 junct 15, A34 S to Stone

A former coaching inn within the town centre where staff are helpful and friendly. The hotel has a glass domed restaurant that offers a choice of menus, and the front lounge is delightfully furnished. Bedrooms, some of which are located in a separate building, are well equipped and comfortable.

Rooms 9 en suite 16 annexe en suite (2 fmly) (8 GF) ⊗ in 12 bedrooms S £59-£75; D £59-£95 **Facilities** STV **Conf** Thtr 150 Class 80 Board 60 **Parking** 40 **Notes** ⊗ ⊘ in restaurant Civ Wed 100

Swallow Stone House

Stafford Rd ST15 0BQ

☎ 01785 815531 ▤ 01785 814764

web: www.swallowhotels.com

dir: M6, junct 14 northbound or junct 15 southbound. Hotel on A34

At the time of going to press, the star classification for this hotel was not confirmed. Please refer to the AA internet site www.theAA.com for current information.

Rooms 50 en suite (1 fmly) (15 GF) ⊗ in 37 bedrooms S £79-£83; D £79-£88 **Facilities** ⬚ supervised Sauna Gym **Conf** Thtr 190 Class 80 Board 60 Del from £110 **Parking** 200 **Notes LB** ⊘ in restaurant Civ Wed 60

TALKE   MAP 15 SJ85

BUDGET HOTEL

Travelodge Stoke Talke

Newcastle Rd ST7 1UP

☎ 08700 850 950 ▤ 01782 777000

web: www.travelodge.co.uk

dir: at junct of A34/A500

Travelodge offers good quality, good value, modern accommodation. Ideal for families, the spacious en suite bedrooms include remote-control TV, tea and coffee-making facilities and comfortable beds. Meals can be taken at the nearby family restaurant. See Hotel Groups pages for further details.

Rooms 62 en suite S fr £26; D fr £26 **Conf** Thtr 50 Class 25 Board 32

TAMWORTH   MAP 10 SK20

★★ 80% HOTEL

Drayton Court Hotel

65 Coleshill St, Fazeley B78 3RG

☎ 01827 285805 ▤ 01827 284842

e-mail: draytoncthotel@yahoo.co.uk

web: www.draytoncourthotel.co.uk

dir: M42 junct 9, A446 to Litchfield, at next rdbt right onto A4091. 2m & Drayton Manor Park on left. Hotel on right

Conveniently located close to the M42, this lovingly restored hotel offers bedrooms that are elegant and have been thoughtfully equipped to suit both business and leisure guests. Beds are particularly comfortable, and one room has a four poster. Public areas include a panelled bar, a relaxing lounge and an attractive restaurant.

Rooms 19 en suite (3 fmly) S £55-£72.50; D £79.50-£125 (incl. bkfst) **Conf** Thtr 8 Board 14 **Parking** 23 **Notes LB** ⊗ ⊘ in restaurant Closed 24-27 Dec

BUDGET HOTEL

Premier Travel Inn Tamworth

Bonehill Rd, Bitterscote B78 3HQ

☎ 08701 977248 ▤ 01827 310420

web: www.premiertravelinn.com

dir: M42 junct 10 follow A5 towards Tamworth. After 3m turn left onto A51. Straight over 1st rdbt, 3rd exit off next rdbt

High quality, modern budget accommodation ideal for both families and business travellers. Spacious, en suite bedrooms feature bath and shower, satellite TV and many have telephones and modem points. The adjacent family restaurant features a wide and varied menu. For further details consult the Hotel Groups page.

Rooms 58 en suite **Conf** Thtr 50 Board 20

BUDGET HOTEL

Travelodge Tamworth (M42)

Green Ln B77 5PS

☎ 08700 850 950 & 0800 850950

▤ 01827 260145

web: www.travelodge.co.uk

dir: A5/M42 junct 10

Travelodge offers good quality, good value, modern accommodation. Ideal for families, the spacious en suite bedrooms include remote-control TV, tea and coffee-making facilities and comfortable beds. Meals can be taken at the nearby family restaurant. See Hotel Groups pages for further details.

Rooms 62 en suite S fr £26; D fr £26

UTTOXETER   MAP 10 SK03

BUDGET HOTEL

Premier Travel Inn Uttoxeter

Derby Rd, (A518/A50) ST14 5AA

☎ 08701 977256 ▤ 01889 561801

web: www.premiertravelinn.com

dir: at junction of A50/A518, 1m north of town centre

High quality, modern budget accommodation ideal for both families and business travellers. Spacious, en suite bedrooms feature bath and shower, satellite TV and many have telephones and modem points. The adjacent family restaurant features a wide and varied menu. For further details consult the Hotel Groups page.

Rooms 41 en suite

BUDGET HOTEL

Travelodge Uttoxeter

Ashbourne Rd ST14 5AA

☎ 08700 850 950 ▤ 01889 562043

web: www.travelodge.co.uk

dir: on A50/B5030

Travelodge offers good quality, good value, modern accommodation. Ideal for families, the spacious en suite bedrooms include remote-control TV, tea and coffee-making facilities and comfortable beds. Meals can be taken at the nearby family restaurant. See Hotel Groups pages for further details.

Rooms 32 en suite S fr £26; D fr £26

SUFFOLK

ALDEBURGH   MAP 13 TM45

★★★ 85% ❀❀ **HOTEL**

Wentworth

Wentworth Rd IP15 5BD

☎ 01728 452312 ▤ 01728 454343

e-mail: stay@wentworth-aldeburgh.co.uk

web: www.wentworth-aldeburgh.com

dir: off A12 onto A1094, 6m to Aldeburgh, with church on left & left at bottom of hill

A delightful privately owned hotel overlooking the beach and sea beyond. The attractive, well-maintained public rooms include three stylish lounges as well as a bar and elegant restaurant. Bedrooms are

continued on page 580

WENTWORTH

HOTEL AND RESTAURANT

Aldeburgh

Telephone +44 (0)1728 452312

Email: stay@wentworth-aldeburgh.co.uk

www.wentworth-aldeburgh.com

EVERYTHING A SEASIDE
HOTEL SHOULD BE

England

England

ALDEBURGH *continued*

smartly decorated with co-ordinated fabrics and have many thoughtful touches; some rooms have superb sea views. Several very spacious Mediterranean-style rooms are located across the road.

Rooms 28 en suite 7 annexe en suite (5 GF) ⊗ in all bedrooms
S £61-£94; D £105-£211 (incl. bkfst) **Facilities** FTV Xmas **Conf** Thtr 15
Class 12 Board 12 Del from £120 **Parking** 30 **Notes LB** ⊗ in restaurant

See advert on page 579

★★★ 85% ⊚ ⊚ **HOTEL**

The Brudenell
The Parade IP15 5BU
☎ 01728 452071 ⓘ 01728 454082
e-mail: info@brudenellhotel.co.uk

dir: *A12/A1094, on reaching town, turn right at junct into High St. Hotel on seafront adjoining Fort Green car park*

Situated at the far end of the town centre just a step away from the beach, this hotel has a contemporary appearance, enhanced by subtle lighting and quality soft furnishings. Many of the bedrooms have superb sea views; they include deluxe rooms with king-sized beds and superior rooms suitable for families.

Rooms 42 en suite (15 fmly) ⊗ in all bedrooms S £83-£107;
D £106-£154 (incl. bkfst) **Facilities** STV Xmas **Services** Lift **Parking** 20
Notes LB ⊗ in restaurant

★★★ 80% ⊚ **HOTEL**

Best Western White Lion
Market Cross Place IP15 5BJ
☎ 01728 452720 ⓘ 01728 452986
e-mail: whitelionaldeburgh@btinternet.com
web: www.whitelion.co.uk

dir: *exit A12 onto A1094, follow signs to Aldeburgh at junct on left. Hotel on right*

A popular 15th-century hotel situated at the quiet end of town overlooking the sea. Bedrooms are pleasantly decorated and thoughtfully equipped, many rooms have lovely sea views. Public

continued

areas include two lounges and an elegant restaurant, where locally-caught fish and seafood are served. There is also a modern brasserie.

Best Western White Lion

Rooms 38 en suite (1 fmly) ⊗ in all bedrooms S £63.50-£106.50;
D £103-£220 (incl. bkfst & dinner) **Facilities** STV Xmas **Conf** Thtr 120
Class 50 Board 50 **Parking** 15 **Notes LB** ⊗ in restaurant Civ Wed 100

BARTON MILLS   MAP 12 TL77

BUDGET HOTEL

Travelodge Barton Mills
Fiveways IP28 6AE
☎ 08700 850 950 ⓘ 01638 717675
web: www.travelodge.co.uk

dir: *on A11 at Fiveways rdbt*

Travelodge offers good quality, good value, modern accommodation. Ideal for families, the spacious en suite bedrooms include remote-control TV, tea and coffee-making facilities and comfortable beds. Meals can be taken at the nearby family restaurant. See Hotel Groups pages for further details.

Rooms 40 en suite S fr £26; D fr £26

BECCLES   MAP 13 TM48

★★★ 61% **HOTEL**

Waveney House
Puddingmoor NR34 9PL
☎ 01502 712270 ⓘ 01502 470370
e-mail: enquiries@waveneyhousehotel.co.uk
web: www.waveneyhousehotel.co.uk

dir: *From A146 turn right onto Common Lane North, left into Pound Rd, bear left into Ravensmere, right onto Smallgate, right onto Old Market & continue onto Puddingmoor.*

An exceptionally well presented, privately owned hotel situated by the River Waveney on the edge of this busy little market town. The stylish

continued

public rooms include a smart lounge bar and a contemporary-style restaurant with views over the river. The spacious bedrooms are attractively decorated with co-ordinated fabrics and have many thoughtful touches.

Rooms 12 en suite (3 fmly) ⊗ in all bedrooms **Conf** Thtr 160 Class 100 Board 50 **Parking** 45 **Notes LB** ⊗ ⊗ in restaurant Civ Wed

BILDESTON MAP 13 TL94

★★★ 85% ⑩ ⑩ **HOTEL**

Bildeston Crown
104 High St IP7 7EB
☎ 01449 740510 📄 01449 741843
e-mail: hayley@thebildestoncrown.co.uk
web: www.thebildestoncrown.co.uk

Charming inn situated in a peaceful village close to the historic town of Lavenham. Public areas feature beams, exposed brickwork and oak floors, with contemporary style decor; they include a choice of bars, a lounge and a restaurant. The tastefully decorated bedrooms have lovely co-ordinated fabrics and modern facilities that include a Yamaha music system and LCD TVs.

Rooms 10 en suite ⊗ in all bedrooms **Facilities** STV **Services** Lift **Parking** 30 **Notes** ⊗ in restaurant

BRANDON MAP 13 TL78

★★ 66% **HOTEL**

Brandon House
High St IP27 0AX
☎ 01842 810171 📄 01842 814859
dir: In town centre left at traffic lights into High St. Hotel 400yds on right after small bridge over River Ouse

An 18th-century, red brick manor house set in landscaped gardens a short walk from the town centre. The pleasantly decorated, well-maintained bedrooms are thoughtfully equipped and come in a

continued

variety of styles. Public rooms include a comfortable lounge bar, the Conifers English Restaurant and a more relaxed bistro.

Rooms 21 en suite (3 fmly) S fr £50; D £60-£80 (incl. bkfst) **Facilities** STV Wi-fi in bedrooms ♪ ch fac Xmas **Conf** Thtr 70 Class 25 Board 20 Del from £60 **Parking** 40 **Notes LB** ⊗ in restaurant

BROME MAP 13 TM17

★★★ 74% ⑩ **HOTEL**

Brome Grange
IP23 8AP
☎ 01379 870456 📄 01379 870921
e-mail: bromegrange@fastnet.co.uk
web: www.bromegrange.co.uk
dir: A12 take A140 turn off towards Norwich, hotel on right

Expect a warm welcome at this charming inn situated on the A140 between Diss and Ipswich. Bedrooms are located around a large courtyard to the rear of the property; each one is pleasantly decorated and thoughtfully equipped. Public rooms include a smartly appointed restaurant, a lounge bar and banqueting suite.

Rooms 21 annexe rms (19 en suite) (4 fmly) (21 GF) ⊗ in all bedrooms S £60-£75; D £75-£95 (incl. bkfst) **Facilities** FTV Jacuzzi Wi-fi available Xmas **Conf** Thtr 80 Class 30 Board 30 **Parking** 70 **Notes** ⊗ ⊗ in restaurant Civ Wed 75

BUNGAY MAP 13 TM38

★★ 65% **HOTEL**

Kings Head
2 Market Place NR35 1AW
☎ 01986 893583
e-mail: info@kingsheadhotel.biz
web: www.kingsheadhotel.biz
dir: Off A143 to town centre.

An 18th-century coaching inn situated in the heart of town, amid a range of antique shops. The spacious bedrooms are furnished with pine pieces and have a good range of useful extras; one room has a superb four-poster bed. Public rooms include a restaurant, the Duke of Wellington lounge bar and Oddfellows bar.

Rooms 13 en suite (1 fmly) ⊗ in 4 bedrooms S £40-£45; D £55-£65 (incl. bkfst) **Facilities** ♪ **Conf** Thtr 100 Class 50 Board 50 **Parking** 29 **Notes LB** ⊗ ⊗ in restaurant

England

BURY ST EDMUNDS
MAP 13 TL86

★★★ 87% ◉ ◉ **HOTEL**

Angel
Angel Hill IP33 1LT
☎ 01284 714000 📠 01284 714001
e-mail: staying@theangel.co.uk
web: www.theangel.co.uk
dir: from A134, left at rdbt into Northgate St. Continue to lights, right into Mustow St, left into Angel Hill, hotel on right

An impressive building situated just a short walk from the town centre. One of the Angel's more notable guests in the last 400 years was Charles Dickens who is reputed to have written part of the *Pickwick Papers* whilst in residence. The hotel offers a range of individually designed bedrooms that include several four-poster rooms and a suite.

Rooms 76 en suite (7 fmly) (7 GF) ⊗ in 64 bedrooms S fr £125; D £135-£195 (incl. bkfst) **Facilities** STV Wi-fi in bedrooms Xmas **Conf** BC Thtr 90 Class 20 Board 30 Del from £135 **Services** Lift **Parking** 20 **Notes LB** ⊗ in restaurant Civ Wed 80

★★★ 86% ◉ ◉ **HOTEL**

Ravenwood Hall
Rougham IP30 9JA
☎ 01359 270345 📠 01359 270788
e-mail: enquiries@ravenwoodhall.co.uk
web: www.ravenwoodhall.co.uk
dir: 3m E off A14 junct 45. Hotel on left

Delightful 15th-century property set in seven acres of woodland and landscaped gardens. The building has many original features including carved timbers and inglenook fireplaces. The spacious bedrooms are attractively decorated, tastefully furnished with well-chosen pieces and equipped with many thoughtful touches. Public rooms include an elegant restaurant and a smart lounge bar with an open fire.

Rooms 7 en suite 7 annexe en suite (5 GF) ⊗ in all bedrooms S £85-£115; D £110-£165 (incl. bkfst) **Facilities** ⚒ supervised Riding ⛵ Shooting & fishing Hunting can be arranged ch fac Xmas **Conf** Thtr 150 Class 80 Board 40 Del from £150.35 **Parking** 150 **Notes LB** ⊗ in restaurant Civ Wed 130

★★★ 79% ◉ ◉ **HOTEL**

The Priory
Milden Hall Rd IP32 6EH
☎ 01284 766181 📠 01284 767604
e-mail: reservations@prioryhotel.co.uk
web: www.prioryhotel.co.uk
dir: from A14 take Bury St Edmunds W slip road. Follow signs to Brandon. At mini-rdbt turn right. Hotel 0.5m on left

An 18th-century Grade II listed building set in landscaped grounds on the outskirts of town. The attractively decorated, tastefully furnished and thoughtfully equipped bedrooms are split between the main house and garden wings, and have their own patios. Public rooms feature a smart restaurant, a conservatory dining room and a lounge bar.

Rooms 9 en suite 30 annexe en suite (1 fmly) (30 GF) ⊗ in 15 bedrooms S £91-£95; D £123 (incl. bkfst) **Facilities** STV Wi-fi in bedrooms Xmas **Conf** Thtr 40 Class 20 Board 20 Del from £139 **Parking** 60 **Notes LB** ⊗ in restaurant

Ⓤ

Swallow Suffolk
Fornham St Genevieve IP28 6JQ
☎ 01284 706777 📠 01284 706721
web: www.swallowhotels.com

At the time of going to press, the star classification for this hotel was not confirmed. Please refer to the AA internet site www.theAA.com for current information.

Rooms 40 en suite

DEBENHAM
MAP 13 TM16

◉ **RESTAURANT WITH ROOMS**

The Angel Inn
5 High St IP14 6QL
☎ 01728 860954 📠 01728 861854
e-mail: d.given@btconnect.com
dir: A14 junct 51, 2m A140 right for Stonhams, follow Debenhams signs, approx 3m

Expect a warm welcome at this charming inn, set in the heart of this peaceful village. Public rooms include a cosy lounge bar and a comfortable restaurant with pine furniture. Bedrooms are generally quite spacious; each one is simply decorated, tastefully furnished and equipped with modern facilities.

Rooms 3 en suite (1 fmly) ⊗ in all bedrooms S fr £50; D fr £70 **Conf** Thtr 30 Class 30 Board 30 **Parking** 14 **Notes** ⊗ ⊗ in restaurant

EYE
MAP 13 TM17

Ⓤ

Swallow Cornwallis
Rectory Rd, Brome IP23 8AS
☎ 01379 870326 📠 01379 870051
web: www.swallowhotels.com

At the time of going to press, the star classification for this hotel was not confirmed. Please refer to the AA internet site www.theAA.com for current information.

Rooms 16 en suite

FELIXSTOWE
MAP 13 TM33

★★★ 78% **HOTEL**

Elizabeth Orwell
Hamilton Rd IP11 7DX
☎ 01394 285511 📠 01394 670687
e-mail: elizabeth.orwell@elizabethhotels.co.uk
dir: from A14 over Dock rdbt and next rdbt. At 3rd rdbt 4th exit to Beatrice Ave. At end of road hotel over rdbt

Imposing Victorian building situated just a short walk from the town centre. The pleasantly decorated, well-equipped bedrooms come in a variety of styles and feature several large, superior rooms. Public areas
continued

are superbly appointed and offer a wealth of charm and character; they include two bars, a choice of lounges, an informal buttery and the Westerfield's restaurant.

Elizabeth Orwell

Rooms 60 en suite (8 fmly) ⊘ in 15 bedrooms **Facilities** STV ♫ **Conf** Thtr 200 Class 100 Board 60 **Services** Lift **Parking** 70 **Notes LB** ⊘ in restaurant Civ Wed 200

★★ 69% **HOTEL**

Marlborough

Sea Front IP11 2BJ

☎ 01394 285621 📠 01394 670724

e-mail: hsm@marlborough-hotel-felix.com

web: www.marlborough-hotel-felix.com

dir: from A14 follow Docks signs. Over Dock rdbt, railway crossing and lights. Left at T-junct, hotel 400mtrs on left

Situated on the seafront, overlooking the beach and just a short stroll from the pier and town centre. This traditional resort hotel offers a good range of facilities including the smart Rattan Restaurant, Flying Boat Bar and L'Aperitif lounge. The pleasantly decorated bedrooms come in a variety of styles; some have lovely sea views.

Rooms 48 en suite (1 fmly) ⊘ in 9 bedrooms S £52-£70; D £67-£90 (incl. bkfst) **Facilities** STV Wi-fi available Pool table Xmas **Conf** Thtr 80 Class 60 Board 40 Del £75 **Services** Lift **Parking** 16 **Notes LB** ⊗ ⊘ in restaurant

HINTLESHAM   MAP 13 TM04

INSPECTORS' CHOICE

★★★★ ◉◉◉ **HOTEL**

Hintlesham Hall

George St IP8 3NS

☎ 01473 652334 📠 01473 652463

e-mail: reservations@hintleshamhall.com

web: www.hintleshamhall.com

dir: 4m W of Ipswich on A1071 to Hadleigh & Sudbury

Hospitality and service are key features at this imposing Grade I listed country-house hotel, situated in 175 acres of grounds and landscaped gardens. Individually decorated bedrooms offer a high degree of comfort; each one is tastefully furnished and equipped with many thoughtful touches. The spacious public rooms include
continued

a series of comfortable lounges and an elegant restaurant, which serves fine classical cuisine.

Hintlesham Hall

Rooms 33 en suite (10 GF) S £120-£165; D £150-£450 **Facilities** ⌇ ⌇ 18 ⌇ Gym ⌇ Putt green Wi-fi in bedrooms Health & Beauty services Clay pigeon shooting ♫ Xmas **Conf** BC Thtr 80 Class 50 Board 32 Del from £205 **Parking** 60 **Notes LB** ⊘ in restaurant Civ Wed 110

HORRINGER   MAP 13 TL86

★★★★ 81% ◉◉ **HOTEL**

The Ickworth

IP29 5QE

☎ 01284 735350 📠 01284 736300

e-mail: ickworth@ickworthhotel.com

dir: from A14 take 1st exit for Bury St Edmunds, follow brown signs for Ickworth House, 4th exit at rdbt, to staggered x-rds. Then on to T-junct, left into village, almost immediately right into Ickworth Estate

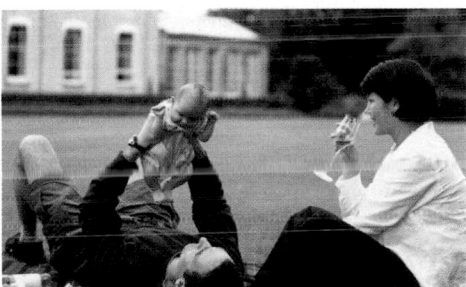

Gifted to the National Trust in 1956 this stunning property is in part a luxurious hotel that combines the glorious design and atmosphere of the past with a reputation for making children very welcome. The staff are friendly and easy going, there is a children's play area, crèche, horses and bikes to ride, and wonderful 'Capability' Brown gardens to roam in. Plus tennis, beauty treatments and two dining rooms.

Rooms 27 en suite 11 annexe en suite (35 fmly) (4 GF) ⊘ in all bedrooms S £185-£330 (incl. bkfst & dinner) **Facilities** STV ⌇ ⌇ Riding ⌇ Wi-fi in bedrooms Childrens creche, massage, manicures, aromatherapy ch fac Xmas **Conf** Thtr 35 Class 30 Board 20 Del from £175 **Services** Lift **Parking** 40 **Notes LB** ⊘ in restaurant Civ Wed 40

England

IPSWICH
MAP 13 TM14

★★★★ @ @ @ **HOTEL**

Hintlesham Hall
George St IP8 3NS
☎ 01473 652334 ▤ 01473 652463
e-mail: reservations@hintleshamhall.com
web: www.hintleshamhall.com

(For full entry see Hintlesham)

★★★★ 80% @ @ **TOWN HOUSE HOTEL**

Salthouse Harbour
No 1 Neptune Quay IP4 1AS
☎ 01473 226789 ▤ 01473 226927
e-mail: staying@salthouseharbour.co.uk

Situated just a short walk from the town centre, overlooking Neptune Marina, this hotel offers accommodation that is a clever mix of contemporary style and original features. Spacious bedrooms provide luxurious comfort with good facilities; two air-conditioned suites with stunning views are available. Award-winning food is served in the busy ground-floor brasserie.

Rooms 43 en suite (4 fmly) ⊘ in 35 bedrooms S £100-£130;
D £130-£140 (incl. bkfst) **Facilities** STV Wi-fi in bedrooms **Conf** Board 24
Del from £170 **Services** Lift **Parking** 30 **Notes LB** ⊘ in restaurant
Civ Wed 70

★★★ 74% **HOTEL**

Best Western Claydon Country House
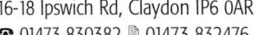
16-18 Ipswich Rd, Claydon IP6 0AR
☎ 01473 830382 ▤ 01473 832476
e-mail: reception@hotelsipswich.com
dir: from A14, NW of Ipswich. After 4m take Great Blakenham
Rd, B1113 to Claydon, hotel on left

Delightful hotel situated just off the A14 within easy driving distance of the town centre. The pleasantly decorated bedrooms are thoughtfully equipped and one room has a lovely four-poster bed. An interesting choice of freshly prepared dishes is available in the smart restaurant, and guests have the use of a relaxing lounge bar.

Rooms 36 en suite (5 fmly) (13 GF) ⊘ in 28 bedrooms S £59-£79;
D £69-£99 (incl. bkfst) **Facilities** STV Wi-fi in bedrooms Xmas
Conf Thtr 120 Class 60 Board 55 Del from £99 **Parking** 60 **Notes LB**
⊗ ⊘ in restaurant Civ Wed 150

★★★ 74% **HOTEL**

Hotel Elizabeth
Old London Rd, Copdock IP8 3JD
☎ 01473 209988 ▤ 01473 730801
e-mail: pauline.dable@elizabethhotels.co.uk
dir: near A12/A14 junct, S of Ipswich. Exit A12 at Washbrook & Copdock sign. Hotel 1m on left

A purpose-built hotel situated on the outskirts of the town centre, and close to the major road networks. The spacious bedrooms are pleasantly decorated and equipped with all the usual facilities.

continued

The open-plan public areas include a smart restaurant, a bar and a comfortable lounge, as well as leisure facilities.

Hotel Elizabeth

Rooms 76 en suite (51 fmly) (23 GF) ⊘ in 60 bedrooms **Facilities** 🎾
Sauna Gym Jacuzzi **Conf** BC Thtr 400 Class 200 Board 40 **Services** Lift
Parking 280 **Notes LB** ⊗ ⊘ in restaurant Civ Wed 90

★★★ 72% **HOTEL**

Courtyard by Marriott Ipswich
The Havens, Ransomes Europark IP3 9SJ
☎ 01473 272244 ▤ 01473 272484
e-mail: res.ipscourtyard@kewgreen.co.uk
web: www.kewgreen.co.uk
dir: off A14 Ipswich bypass at 1st junct after Orwell Bridge signed Ransomes Europark. Hotel faces slip road

Conveniently situated within easy striking distance of the town centre and major road networks, this modern and well-maintained hotel offers stylish accommodation with attractive, spacious bedrooms. The open-plan public rooms include a restaurant, a bar and a suite of conference rooms. Guests also have the use of a small fitness studio.

Rooms 60 en suite (14 fmly) (30 GF) ⊘ in 44 bedrooms **Facilities** STV
Gym **Conf** Thtr 160 Class 70 Board 55 **Services** Lift **Parking** 150
Notes LB ⊗ Civ Wed 100

★★★ 72% **HOTEL**

Novotel Ipswich
Greyfriars Rd IP1 1UP
☎ 01473 232400 ▤ 01473 232414
e-mail: h0995@accor.com
web: www.novotel.com

dir: from A14 towards Felixstowe. Left onto A137, follow for 2m into town centre. Hotel on double rdbt by Stoke Bridge

Modern, red-brick hotel perfectly placed in the centre of town close to shops, bars and restaurants. The open-plan public areas include a

continued

Mediterranean-style restaurant and a bar with a small games area. The newly refurbished bedrooms are smartly appointed and have many thoughtful touches; three rooms are suitable for less mobile guests.

Rooms 101 en suite (8 fmly) ⊗ in 88 bedrooms S £55-£105; D £55-£105 **Facilities** STV Wi fi in bedrooms Pool table, Complimentary use of gym, sauna, jacuzzi Xmas **Conf** BC Thtr 180 Class 75 Board 45 Del from £138 **Services** Lift air con **Parking** 53 **Notes LB** ⊗ in restaurant Civ Wed 70

[U]

Swallow Belstead Brook

SWALLOW

Belstead Rd IP2 9HB
☎ 01473 684241 🖷 01473 681249
web: www.swallowhotels.com

dir: from junct of A12 & A14 take A1214, follow hotel signs

At the time of going to press, the star classification for this hotel was not confirmed. Please refer to the AA internet site www.theAA.com for current information.

Rooms 88 en suite

BUDGET HOTEL

Premier Travel Inn Ipswich North

premier travel inn

Paper Mill Ln, Claydon IP6 0BE
☎ 0870 238 3311 🖷 01473 833127
e-mail: ipswich.mti@whitbread.com
web: www.premiertravelinn.com

dir: on A14 NW of Ipswich at Great Blakenham/Claydon/RAF Wattisham junct, at rdbt take exit into Papermill Ln, Inn on left

High quality, modern budget accommodation ideal for both families and business travellers. Spacious, en suite bedrooms feature bath and shower, satellite TV and many have telephones and modem points. The adjacent family restaurant features a wide and varied menu. For further details consult the Hotel Groups page.

Rooms 59 en suite

Premier Travel Inn Ipswich South

Bourne Hill, Wherstead IP2 8ND
☎ 08701 977143 🖷 01473 692283

dir: From A14 follow signs for Ipswich Central A137 and then Ipswich Central & Docks. At bottom of hill take 2nd exit off rdbt. Inn on right

Rooms 40 en suite **Conf** Thtr 30 Board 20

BUDGET HOTEL

Travelodge Ipswich Capel St Mary

Travelodge

Capel St Mary IP9 2JP
☎ 08700 850 950 🖷 0870 1911542
web: www.travelodge.co.uk

dir: 5m S on A12

Travelodge offers good quality, good value, modern accommodation. Ideal for families, the spacious en suite bedrooms include remote-control TV, tea and coffee-making facilities and comfortable beds. Meals can be taken at the nearby family restaurant. See Hotel Groups pages for further details.

Rooms 32 en suite S fr £26; D fr £26

LAVENHAM   MAP 13 TL94

★★★★ 79% ⊛⊛ **HOTEL**

The Swan

"bespoke"

High St CO10 9QA
☎ 01787 247477 🖷 01787 248286
e-mail: info@theswanatlavenham.co.uk
web: www.bespokehotels.com

dir: from A12 or A14 onto A134, then B1071 to Lavenham

Expect a warm welcome from the caring staff at this delightful hotel, a collection of listed buildings, which dates back to the 14th century. The extensive public areas are full of original charm; they include a range of comfortable lounge areas, a charming rustic bar, an informal brasserie and a fine-dining restaurant. Bedrooms are tastefully furnished and equipped with many thoughtful touches. The hotel is under new ownership.

Rooms 51 en suite (4 fmly) (12 GF) ⊗ in all bedrooms S £62.50-£97.50; D £125-£195 (incl. bkfst & dinner) **Facilities** STV Xmas **Conf** Thtr 50 Board 30 Del from £135 **Parking** 62 **Notes** ⊗ in restaurant Civ Wed 90

★★ 75% ⊛ **HOTEL**

Angel

Market Place CO10 9QZ
☎ 01787 247388 🖷 01787 248344
e-mail: angellav@aol.com
web: www.theangelhotel.com

dir: from A14 take Bury East and Sudbury turn off onto A143. After 4m take A1141 to Lavenham. Hotel off high street

A charming 15th-century inn situated in this historic, medieval town overlooking the market place. The Angel is well known for its cuisine and offers an imaginative menu based on fresh ingredients. Public rooms include a spacious first-floor lounge and an open plan bar/dining area. Bedrooms are tastefully furnished, attractively decorated and thoughtfully equipped. Guests are assured of a hospitable welcome.

Rooms 8 en suite (1 fmly) (1 GF) ⊗ in all bedrooms S fr £55; D fr £80 (incl. bkfst) **Facilities** Wi-fi in bedrooms Use of Lavenham Tennis Club facilities ♫ ch fac **Parking** 5 **Notes LB** ⊛ ⊗ in restaurant Closed 25-26 Dec

Packed in a hurry?
Ironing facilities should be available at all star
levels, either in the rooms or on request

England

LONG MELFORD   MAP 13 TL84

★★★ 80% ⊛ **HOTEL**

The Black Lion

Church Walk, The Green CO10 9DN

☎ 01787 312356 ▤ 01787 374557

e-mail: enquiries@blacklionhotel.net

web: www.blacklionhotel.net

dir: *at junct of A134 & A1092*

This welcoming 15th-century hotel is situated on the edge of this
bustling town overlooking the green. Bedrooms are generally spacious
and each is attractively decorated, tastefully furnished and equipped
with useful extras. An interesting range of dishes is served in the
lounge bar or guests may choose options from the same innovative
menu in the more formal restaurant.

Rooms 10 en suite (1 fmly) ⊛ in all bedrooms S £87.50-£110;
D £120-£165 (incl. bkfst) **Facilities** Board games ch fac Xmas
Conf Thtr 50 Class 28 Board 28 Del from £115 **Parking** 10 **Notes LB**
⊛ in restaurant Civ Wed 50

★★★ 75% **HOTEL**

The Bull

OLD ENGLISH INNS

Hall St CO10 9JG

☎ 01787 378494 ▤ 01787 880307

e-mail: bull.longmelford@greeneking.co.uk

web: www.oldenglish.co.uk

dir: *3m N of Sudbury on A134*

The public areas of this 14th-century property feature a wealth of
charm and character, including exposed beams, carvings, heraldic
markings and huge open fireplaces. Bedrooms are smartly decorated,
thoughtfully equipped and retain many original features. Snacks and
light lunches are served in the bar, or guests can choose to dine in the
more formal restaurant.

Rooms 25 en suite (4 fmly) ⊛ in 20 bedrooms S £75-£85; D £110-£120
(incl. bkfst) **Facilities** Xmas **Conf** Thtr 100 Class 40 Board 30 Del from
£130 **Parking** 35 **Notes LB** ⊗ ⊛ in restaurant Civ Wed 100

LOWESTOFT   MAP 13 TM59

★★★ 82% ⊛⊛ **HOTEL**

Ivy House Country Hotel

Ivy Ln, Beccles Rd, Oulton Broad NR33 8HY

☎ 01502 501353 & 588144 ▤ 01502 501539

e-mail: aa@ivyhousecountryhotel.co.uk

web: www.ivyhousecountryhotel.co.uk

dir: *on A146 SW of Oulton Broad turn into Ivy Ln beside Esso
petrol station. Over railway bridge and follow private driveway*

Peacefully located, family-run hotel set in three acres of mature
landscaped grounds just a short walk from Oulton Broad. Public
rooms include an 18th-century thatched barn restaurant where an
interesting choice of dishes is served. The attractively decorated

continued

Some hotels have restricted service during
quieter months, and at this time some of the
facilities will not be available

bedrooms are housed in garden wings, and many have lovely views of
the grounds to the countryside beyond.

Ivy House Country Hotel

Rooms 20 annexe en suite (1 fmly) (17 GF) ⊛ in all bedrooms
S £92.50-£129; D £122.50-£225 (incl. bkfst) **Facilities** FTV Reduced rates
at neighbouring leisure club **Conf** Thtr 55 Board 22 Del from £135
Parking 50 **Notes LB** ⊛ in restaurant Closed 23 Dec-6 Jan Civ Wed 200

★★★ 74% **HOTEL**

Hotel Victoria

Kirkley Cliff NR33 0BZ

☎ 01502 574433 ▤ 01502 501529

e-mail: info@thehotelvictoria.co.uk

dir: *A12 to seafront on one-way system signed A12 Ipswich.
Hotel on seafront just beyond the Thatched Cottage*

Attractive Victorian building situated on the esplanade overlooking the
sea and has direct access to the beach. Bedrooms are pleasantly
decorated and thoughtfully equipped; many rooms have sea views.
Public rooms include modern conference and banqueting facilities, a
choice of lounges, a comfortable bar and a restaurant, which
overlooks the pretty garden.

Rooms 24 en suite (4 fmly) S £85-£100; D £115-£150 (incl. bkfst)
Facilities STV FTV ⸚ ♫ Xmas **Conf** Thtr 200 Class 150 Board 50 Del
from £115 **Services** Lift **Parking** 45 **Notes LB** ⊗ ⊛ in restaurant
Civ Wed 200

★★★ 72% **HOTEL**

Best Western Hotel Hatfield

The Esplanade NR33 0QP

☎ 01502 565337 ▤ 01502 511885

e-mail: hotelhatfield@elizabethhotels.co.uk

dir: *from town centre follow 'South Beach' signs on A12 Ipswich
road. Hotel 200yds on left*

Ideally situated overlooking the sea, this hotel is in a prominent
position on the esplanade. Bedrooms are pleasantly decorated and

continued

thoughtfully equipped and some have superb sea views. The spacious public rooms include a popular lounge bar, a cocktail bar and the Shoreline restaurant where an interesting choice of dishes is served.

Rooms 33 en suite (1 fmly) ⊘ in 7 bedrooms **Facilities** STV
Conf Thtr 100 Class 50 Board 40 **Services** Lift **Parking** 26 **Notes LB** Civ Wed 200

BUDGET HOTEL

Premier Travel Inn Lowestoft

249 Yarmouth Rd NR32 4AA
☎ 08701 977165 ▤ 01502 581223
web: www.premiertravelinn.com

dir: on A12, 2m N of Lowestoft

High quality, modern budget accommodation ideal for both families and business travellers. Spacious, en suite bedrooms feature bath and shower, satellite TV and many have telephones and modem points. The adjacent family restaurant features a wide and varied menu. For further details consult the Hotel Groups page.

Rooms 40 en suite

MILDENHALL   MAP 12 TL77

★★★ 70% HOTEL

Best Western Smoke House

Beck Row IP28 8DH
☎ 01638 713223 ▤ 01638 712202
e-mail: enquiries@smoke-house.co.uk
web: www.smoke-house.co.uk

dir: A1101 into Mildenhall, follow Beck Row signs. Hotel after mini rdbt through Beck Row on right

An extended 16th-century inn situated just a short drive from the town centre and ideally placed for touring the Suffolk countryside. Public areas have been sympathetically restored and retain much of their original character. The spacious bedrooms are attractively decorated and well equipped. Facilities include a shopping mall.

Rooms 94 en suite 2 annexe en suite (96 GF) ⊘ in 20 bedrooms
S £60-£97.50; D £85-£140 (incl. bkfst) **Facilities** Wi-fi in bedrooms ♫
Xmas **Conf** Thtr 120 Class 80 Board 50 Del from £90 **Parking** 100
Notes LB ⊗ ⊘ in restaurant Civ Wed 100

Swallow Riverside

Mill St IP28 7DP
☎ 01638 717274 ▤ 01638 715997
web: www.swallowhotels.com

dir: A11 at Fiveways rdbt take A1101 in Mildenhall. Left at mini rdbt along High St. Hotel last building on left before bridge

At the time of going to press, the star classification for this hotel was not confirmed. Please refer to the AA internet site www.theAA.com for current information.

Rooms 22 rms

NEEDHAM MARKET   MAP 13 TM05

BUDGET HOTEL

Travelodge Ipswich Beacon Hill

Beacon Hill IP6 8LP
☎ 08700 850 950 ▤ 01449 721640
web: www.travelodge.co.uk

dir: A14/A140

Travelodge offers good quality, good value, modern accommodation. Ideal for families, the spacious en suite bedrooms include remote-control TV, tea and coffee-making facilities and comfortable beds. Meals can be taken in the nearby family restaurant. See Hotel Groups pages for further details.

Rooms 40 en suite S fr £26; D fr £26

England

NEWMARKET　　　　　　　MAP 12 TL66

★★★★ 78% ⑱ **HOTEL**

Bedford Lodge
Bury Rd CB8 7BX

CLASSIC
BRITISH HOTELS

☎ 01638 663175 📠 01638 667391
e-mail: info@bedfordlodgehotel.co.uk
web: www.classicbritishhotels.com
dir: *from town centre take Bury St Edmunds road, hotel 0.5m on left*

Imposing 18th-century Georgian hunting lodge set in three acres of secluded landscaped gardens. Public rooms feature the elegant Orangery restaurant, a smart lounge bar and a small lounge. The hotel also features superb leisure facilities and self-contained conference and banqueting suites. Contemporary bedrooms have a light, airy feel, and each is tastefully furnished and well equipped.

Rooms 55 en suite (3 fmly) (16 GF) ⊘ in 39 bedrooms S £100-£160; D £140-£300 (incl. bkfst) **Facilities** STV ⌇ Sauna Solarium Gym Jacuzzi Wi-fi in bedrooms Steam room & beauty salon Xmas **Conf** Thtr 200 Class 80 Board 60 Del from £145 **Services** Lift **Parking** 120 **Notes LB** ⊗ ⊘ in restaurant Civ Wed 150

★★★ 80% ⑱ **HOTEL**

Swynford Paddocks Hotel
CB8 0UE

☎ 01638 570234 📠 01638 570283
e-mail: info@swynfordpaddocks.com
web: www.swynfordpaddocks.com

(For full entry see Six Mile Bottom, Cambridgeshire)

★★★ 75% **HOTEL**

Best Western Heath Court
Moulton Rd CB8 8DY

Best
Western

☎ 01638 667171 📠 01638 666533
e-mail: quality@heathcourthotel.com
dir: *leave A14 at Newmarket and Ely exit on A142. Follow town centre signs over mini rdbt. At clocktower left into Moulton Rd*

Modern red-brick hotel situated close to Newmarket Heath and perfectly placed for the town centre. Public rooms include a choice of dining options - informal meals can be taken in the lounge bar or a modern carte menu is offered in the restaurant. The smartly presented bedrooms are mostly spacious and some have air conditioning.

Rooms 41 en suite (2 fmly) ⊘ in 19 bedrooms S £75-£100; D £110-£130 (incl. bkfst) **Facilities** STV Wi-fi in bedrooms Health & beauty salon **Conf** Thtr 130 Class 50 Board 40 Del from £90 **Services** Lift **Parking** 60 **Notes LB** ⊘ in restaurant Civ Wed 80

Ⓤ

Swallow Rutland Arms

SWALLOW
HOTELS

High St CB8 8NB
☎ 01638 664251 📠 01638 666298
e-mail: newmarket.reservations@swallowhotels.com
web: www.swallowhotels.com

At the time of going to press, the star classification for this hotel was not confirmed. Please refer to the AA internet site www.theAA.com for current information.

Rooms 46 en suite (1 fmly) ⊘ in 27 bedrooms S £50-£110; D £70-£145 (incl. bkfst) **Facilities** STV **Conf** Thtr 70 Class 40 Board 35 Del from £100 **Parking** 35 **Notes** ⊗ ⊘ in restaurant

ORFORD　　　　　　　　MAP 13 TM45

★★ 85% ⑱⑱ **HOTEL**

The Crown & Castle
IP12 2LJ
☎ 01394 450205
e-mail: info@crownandcastle.co.uk
web: www.crownandcastle.co.uk
dir: *turn right from B1084 on entering village, towards castle*

Delightful inn situated adjacent to the Norman castle keep. Contemporary style bedrooms are spilt between the main house and the garden wing; the latter are more spacious and have patios with access to the garden. The restaurant has an informal atmosphere with polished tables and local artwork; the menu features quality locally sourced produce.

Rooms 7 en suite 11 annexe en suite (1 fmly) (11 GF) ⊘ in all bedrooms S £72-£145; D £90-£145 (incl. bkfst) **Facilities** Wi-fi available **Conf** Board 10 Del from £95 **Parking** 20 **Notes LB** ⊘ in restaurant Closed 19-22 Dec & 3-4 Jan

SOUTHWOLD　　　　　　MAP 13 TM57

★★★ 80% ⑱⑱ **HOTEL**

Swan
Market Place IP18 6EG
☎ 01502 722186 📠 01502 724800
e-mail: swan.hotel@adnams.co.uk
dir: *A1095 to Southwold. Hotel in town centre. Parking via archway to left of building*

A charming 17th-century coaching inn situated in the heart of this bustling town centre overlooking the market place. Public rooms feature an elegant restaurant, a comfortable drawing room, a cosy bar and a lounge where guests can enjoy afternoon tea. The spacious

continued

bedrooms are attractively decorated, tastefully furnished and thoughtfully equipped. This hotel is now totally non-smoking.

Swan

Rooms 25 en suite 17 annexe en suite (17 GF) ⊛ in all bedrooms S £80-£90; D £140-£220 (incl. bkfst) **Facilities** Xmas **Conf** Thtr 40 Class 24 Board 12 **Services** Lift **Parking** 35 **Notes** LB ⊛ in restaurant Civ Wed 40

★★ 85% ◉ ◉ **HOTEL**

The Crown
90 High St IP18 6DP
☎ 01502 722275 🖹 01502 727263
e-mail: crown.hotel@adnams.co.uk
dir: *A12 onto A1095 to Southwold. Hotel on left in High Street*

Delightful old posting inn situated in the heart of this bustling town. The property combines a pub, wine bar and restaurant with superb accommodation. The tastefully decorated bedrooms have attractive co-ordinated soft furnishings and many thoughtful touches. Public rooms feature an elegant lounge and a back room bar serving traditional Adnams ales.

Rooms 14 rms (13 en suite) (2 fmly) ⊛ in all bedrooms S £80-£85; D £120-£130 (incl. bkfst) **Facilities** Xmas **Parking** 23 **Notes** LB ⊗ ⊛ in restaurant

STOWMARKET   MAP 13 TM05

★★ 75% **HOTEL**

Cedars
THE INDEPENDENTS

Needham Rd IP14 2AJ
☎ 01449 612668 🖹 01449 674704
e-mail: info@cedarshotel.co.uk
dir: *A14 junct 15, A1120 towards Stowmarket At junct with A1113 turn right. Hotel on right*

Expect a friendly welcome at this privately owned hotel, which is situated just off the A14 within easy reach of the town centre. Public rooms are full of charm and character with features such as exposed beams and open fireplaces. Bedrooms are pleasantly decorated and thoughtfully equipped with modern facilities.

Rooms 25 en suite (3 fmly) (9 GF) **Conf** Thtr 150 Class 60 Board 40 **Parking** 75 **Notes** LB ⊛ in restaurant Closed 25 Dec-1 Jan Civ Wed 50

BUDGET HOTEL

Travelodge Ipswich Stowmarket
Travelodge

IP14 3PY
☎ 08700 850 950 🖹 01449 615347
web: www.travelodge.co.uk
dir: *on A14 westbound*

Travelodge offers good quality, good value, modern accommodation. Ideal for families, the spacious en suite bedrooms include remote-control TV, tea and coffee-making facilities and comfortable beds. Meals can be taken at the nearby family restaurant. See Hotel Groups pages for further details.

Rooms 40 en suite S fr £26; D fr £26

SUDBURY   MAP 13 TL84

★★★ 69% **HOTEL**

Mill
The Mill, Walnut Tree Ln CO10 1BD
☎ 01787 375544 🖹 01787 373027
e-mail: elizabeth.mill@elizabethhotels.co.uk
dir: *from Colchester take A134 to Sudbury, follow signs for Chelmsford after town square take 2nd right*

Impressive building situated on the banks of the River Stour, overlooking open pastures on the edge of town. The hotel has its own millpond and retains many charming features such as open fires, exposed beams and a working waterwheel. Bedrooms vary in size and style; each one is thoughtfully equipped and pleasantly furnished.

Rooms (2 fmly) (9 GF) ⊛ in 45 bedrooms **Conf** Thtr 70 Class 35 Board 35 **Parking** 60 **Notes** LB ⊛ in restaurant

THORPENESS   MAP 13 TM45

★★★ 74% **HOTEL**

Thorpeness Hotel
Lakeside Av IP16 4NH
☎ 01728 452176 🖹 01728 453868
e-mail: info@thorpeness.co.uk
web: www.thorpeness.co.uk
dir: *A1094 towards Aldeburgh, then coast road north for 2m*

Ideally situated in an unspoilt, tranquil setting close to Aldeburgh and Snape Maltings. The extensive public rooms include a choice of lounges, a restaurant, a smart bar, a snooker room and clubhouse. The spacious bedrooms are pleasantly decorated, tastefully furnished

continued on page 590

THORPENESS *continued*

and equipped with modern facilities. An 18-hole golf course and tennis courts are also available.

Rooms 30 annexe en suite (10 fmly) (10 GF) @ in all bedrooms S £75-£102; D £96-£146 (incl. bkfst) **Facilities** ↕ 18 ☺ Fishing Snooker Putt green Cycle hire. Indoor golf school Xmas **Conf** Thtr 130 Class 30 Board 24 Del from £110 **Parking** 60 **Notes** LB @ in restaurant Civ Wed 130

WESTLETON   MAP 13 TM46

★★★ 79% @ @ **HOTEL**

Westleton Crown

The Street IP17 3AD

☎ 01728 648777 📠 01728 648239

e-mail: reception@westletoncrown.co.uk

web: www.westletoncrown.co.uk

dir: A12 N turn right for Westleton just after Yoxford. Hotel opposite on entering Westleton

A charming coaching inn, now under new ownership, that is situated in a peaceful village location just a few minutes from the A12. Public rooms include a smart, award-winning restaurant, comfortable lounge, and a busy bar with exposed beams and open fireplaces. The bedrooms are individually decorated and equipped with many thoughtful little extras.

Rooms 22 en suite 3 annexe en suite (2 fmly) (8 GF) @ in all bedrooms S £80-£85; D £95-£160 (incl. bkfst) **Facilities** Xmas **Conf** Thtr 60 Class 40 Board 30 **Parking** 40 **Notes** LB @ in restaurant Closed 25-26 Dec

WOODBRIDGE   MAP 13 TM24

★★★ 78% @ @ **COUNTRY HOUSE HOTEL**

Seckford Hall

IP13 6NU

☎ 01394 385678 📠 01394 380610

e-mail: reception@seckford.co.uk

web: www.seckford.co.uk

dir: signed on A12. (Do not follow signs for town centre)

An elegant Tudor manor house set amid landscaped grounds just off the A12. It is reputed that Queen Elizabeth I visited this property, and it retains much of its original character. Public rooms include a superb panelled lounge, a cosy bar and an intimate restaurant. The spacious bedrooms are attractively decorated, tastefully furnished and thoughtfully equipped.

Rooms 22 en suite 10 annexe en suite (4 fmly) @ in all bedrooms S £85; D £135-£210 (incl. bkfst) **Facilities** Spa FTV ⬚ ↕ 18 Fishing Gym Putt green Wi-fi available Beauty Salon **Conf** Thtr 100 Class 46 Board 40 **Parking** 100 **Notes** LB @ in restaurant Closed 25-Dec Civ Wed 120

★★★ 77% **HOTEL**

Best Western Ufford Park Hotel Golf & Leisure

Yarmouth Rd, Ufford IP12 1QW

☎ 0844 4773737 📠 0844 4773727

e-mail: mail@uffordpark.co.uk

web: www.bw-uffordparkhotel.co.uk

dir: A12 N to A1152, in Melton turn left at lights, premises 1m on right

A modern hotel set in open countryside boasting superb leisure facilities that include a challenging golf course. The spacious public rooms provide a wide choice of areas in which to relax and include a busy lounge bar, a carvery restaurant and the Vista restaurant. Bedrooms are smartly appointed and pleasantly decorated, each thoughtfully equipped; many rooms overlook the golf course.

Rooms 87 en suite (26 fmly) (32 GF) @ in 63 bedrooms S £80-£120; D £110-£150 (incl. bkfst) **Facilities Spa** STV ⬚ supervised ↕ 18 Fishing Sauna Solarium Gym Putt green Jacuzzi Wi-fi in bedrooms Steam room, Golf with PGA tuition, Beauty salon, 32 Bay Driving range Pool table Xmas **Conf** Thtr 200 Class 80 Board 80 Del from £110 **Services** Lift **Parking** 250 **Notes** LB ⊗ @ in restaurant Civ Wed 120

YOXFORD   MAP 13 TM36

★★ 81% @ @ **HOTEL**

Satis House

IP17 3EX

☎ 01728 668418 📠 01728 668640

e-mail: yblackmore@aol.com

dir: off A12 between Ipswich & Lowestoft. 9m E Aldeburgh & Snape

Delightful hotel set in landscaped grounds just off the A12. The property was once frequented by Charles Dickens, and the name Satis House features in '*Great Expectations*'. The spacious, individually

continued

decorated bedrooms are tastefully furnished and equipped with many thoughtful touches. Public areas include an elegant lounge, smart bar and a choice of dining rooms.

Rooms 8 en suite (1 GF) ⊘ in 1 bedroom **Facilities** ♨ Sauna Jacuzzi **Conf** Thtr 22 Class 20 Board 14 **Parking** 30 **Notes** ⊗ No children 7yrs ⊘ in restaurant Closed 26-27 Dec, 2 wks Jan RS 25-Dec

SURREY

BAGSHOT   MAP 06 SU96

INSPECTORS' CHOICE

★★★★★ ◉◉◉ **HOTEL**

Pennyhill Park Hotel & The Spa

London Rd GU19 5EU

☎ 01276 471774 🖷 01276 473217

e-mail: enquiries@pennyhillpark.co.uk

web: www.exclusivehotels.co.uk

dir: on A30 between Bagshot & Camberley

This delightful country-house hotel, set in 120-acre grounds, provides every modern comfort. The stylish bedrooms are individually designed and have impressive bathrooms. The award-winning Latymer Restaurant is among the range of dining options and there is a choice of lounges and bars. Leisure facilities include a jogging trail, a golf course and a state-of-the-art spa with a thermal sequencing experience, ozone treated swimming and hydrotherapy pools along with a comprehensive range of therapies and treatments.

Rooms 26 en suite 97 annexe en suite (6 fmly) (26 GF) ⊘ in 20 bedrooms S £185-£550; D £225-£650 (incl. bkfst) **Facilities Spa** STV ⊠ ⊰ ⅃9 ♨ Fishing Sauna Gym ↳ Jacuzzi Wi-fi available Archery, Clay shooting, Plunge pool, Turkish Steam Room, Volleyball, ♫ Xmas **Conf** BC Thtr 160 Class 80 Board 60 Del from £340 **Services** Lift **Parking** 500 **Notes LB** ⊘ in restaurant Civ Wed 160

BUDGET HOTEL

Premier Travel Inn Bagshot

premier travel inn ☾

1 London Rd GU19 5HR

☎ 08701 977021 🖷 01276 451357

web: www.premiertravelinn.com

dir: on A30, 0.25m from Bagshot

High quality, modern budget accommodation ideal for both families and business travellers. Spacious, en suite bedrooms feature bath and shower, satellite TV and many have telephones and modem points.

continued

The adjacent family restaurant features a wide and varied menu. For further details consult the Hotel Groups page.

Rooms 40 en suite

CAMBERLEY   MAP 06 SU86

See also Yateley, Hampshire

★★★★ 80% ◉ **HOTEL**

Macdonald Frimley Hall Hotel & Spa

MACDONALD HOTELS & RESORTS

Lime Av GU15 2BG

☎ 0870 400 8224 🖷 01276 670362

e-mail: sales.frimleyhall@macdonald-hotels.co.uk

web: www.macdonald-hotels.co.uk

dir: M3 junct 3, A321 follow Bagshot signs. Through lights, left onto A30 signed Camberley/Basingstoke. To rdbt, 2nd exit onto A325, take 5th right

The epitome of classic English elegance, this ivy-clad Victorian manor house is set in two acres of immaculate grounds in the heart of Surrey. The bedrooms and public areas are smart and feature a modern decorative theme. The hotel boasts an impressive health club and spa with treatment rooms, a fully equipped gym and indoor swimming pool.

Rooms 98 en suite (15 fmly) ⊘ in all bedrooms D fr £120 (incl bkfst) **Facilities Spa** STV ⊠ supervised Sauna Gym ↳ Putt green Wi-fi available Beauty treatment rooms ♫ Xmas **Conf** Thtr 250 Class 100 Board 60 Del from £240 **Services** air con **Parking** 100 **Notes LB** ⊘ in restaurant Civ Wed 220

★★★ 70% **HOTEL**

Lakeside International

Wharf Rd, Frimley Green GU16 6JR

☎ 01252 838000 🖷 01252 837857

dir: off A321 at mini-rdbt turn into Wharf Rd, Lakeside complex on right

This hotel, geared towards the business market, enjoys a lakeside location with noteworthy views. Bedrooms are modern, comfortable and with a range of facilities. Public areas are spacious and include a residents' lounge, bar and games room, a smart restaurant and an established health and leisure club. Bedrooms are modern, comfortable with a range of facilities.

Rooms 98 en suite (1 fmly) ⊘ in 18 bedrooms **Facilities** STV ⊠ Squash Snooker Sauna Solarium Gym Jacuzzi **Conf** Thtr 120 Class 100 Board 40 **Services** Lift **Parking** 250 **Notes** ⊗ ⊘ in restaurant Civ Wed 100

England

England

CAMBERLEY *continued*

BUDGET HOTEL

Premier Travel Inn Camberley

221 Yorktown Rd, College Town GU47 0RT
☎ 08701 977047 ▤ 01582 842811
web: www.premiertravelinn.com

dir: M3 junct 4 follow A331 to Camberley. At large rdbt, exit to A321 towards Bracknell. At 3rd set of traffic lights, Inn on left

High quality, modern budget accommodation ideal for both families and business travellers. Spacious, en suite bedrooms feature bath and shower, satellite TV and many have telephones and modem points. The adjacent family restaurant features a wide and varied menu. For further details consult the Hotel Groups page.

Rooms 40 en suite

CHIDDINGFOLD   MAP 06 SU93

RESTAURANT WITH ROOMS

The Swan Inn
Petworth Rd GU8 4TY
☎ 01428 682073 ▤ 01428 683259
e-mail: the-swan-inn@btconnect.com

This lovely 14th-century village inn, where a sympathetic refurbishment has resulted in a surprisingly airy and modern interior, offers home-cooked food, real ales and a good choice of wines. The smart dining area has a relaxed atmosphere. There are extensive terrace gardens to enjoy when the weather allows. The air conditioned bedrooms are very smartly appointed and have flat screen TVs and DVDs.

Rooms 11 rms (10 en suite) (1 fmly) ⊗ in 9 bedrooms **Parking** 40 **Notes** ⊗ No children

---

CHURT   MAP 05 SU83

★★★ 75% HOTEL

Best Western Frensham Pond Hotel
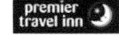
Bacon Ln GU10 2QB
☎ 01252 795161 ▤ 01252 792631
e-mail: info@frenshampondhotel.co.uk
web: www.frenshampondhotel.co.uk

dir: A3 onto A287. 4m left at 'Beware Horses' sign. Hotel 0.25m

This 15th-century house occupies a superb location on the edge of Frensham Pond. Bedrooms are mostly spacious, but the superior

continued

garden rooms have their own patio and flat screen TVs. The contemporary bar and lounge offer a wide range of snacks, and the leisure club has extensive facilities.

Best Western Frensham Pond Hotel

Rooms 39 en suite 12 annexe en suite ⊗ in 21 bedrooms **Facilities** STV ⊡ supervised Squash Sauna Solarium Gym Jacuzzi Steam room Xmas **Conf** Thtr 120 Class 45 Board 40 Del from £125 **Parking** 120 **Notes** ⊗ ⊗ in restaurant Civ Wed 130

See advert on under FARNHAM

CLACKET LANE MOTORWAY   MAP 06 TQ45 SERVICE AREA (M25)

BUDGET HOTEL

Premier Travel Inn Westerham (Clacket Lane)
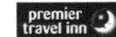
TN16 2ER
☎ 08701 977265 ▤ 01959 561311
web: www.premiertravelinn.com

dir: M25 between junct 5 & 6

High quality, modern budget accommodation ideal for both families and business travellers. Spacious, en suite bedrooms feature bath and shower, satellite TV and many have telephones and modem points. The adjacent family restaurant features a wide and varied menu. For further details consult the Hotel Groups page.

Rooms 58 en suite **Conf** Thtr 50 Board 30

COBHAM   MAP 06 TQ16

BUDGET HOTEL

Premier Travel Inn Cobham
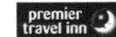
Portsmouth Rd, Fairmile KT11 1BW
☎ 0870 9906358 ▤ 0870 9906359
web: www.premiertravelinn.com

dir: M25 junct 10, A3 towards London, onto A245 towards Cobham. In town centre left onto A307. Hotel on left

High quality, modern budget accommodation ideal for both families and business travellers. Spacious, en suite bedrooms feature bath and shower, satellite TV and many have telephones and modem points. The adjacent family restaurant features a wide and varied menu. For further details consult the Hotel Groups page.

Rooms 48 en suite **Conf** Board 12

DORKING   MAP 06 TQ14

★★★★ 81% ◉◉ **HOTEL**

Macdonald Burford Bridge

MACDONALD
HOTELS & RESORTS

Burford Bridge, Box Hill RH5 6BX
☎ 0870 400 8283 📠 01306 880386
e-mail: burfordbridge@macdonald-hotels.co.uk
web: www.macdonald-hotels.co.uk
dir: M25 junct 9 follow Dorking signs on A24. Hotel on left

Steeped in history, this hotel was reputedly where Lord Nelson and
Lady Hamilton met for the last time, and it is said that the landscape
around the hotel has inspired many poets. The hotel has a
contemporary feel throughout. The grounds, running down to the
River Mole, are extensive, and there are good transport links to major
centres, including London.

Rooms 57 en suite (14 fmly) (8 GF) ⊗ in all bedrooms S £124–£139;
D £138–£168 (incl. bkfst) **Facilities** STV ₹ ✈ Putt green Wi-fi available
♫ Xmas **Conf** Thtr 200 Class 100 Board 60 Del from £150 **Parking** 140
Notes LB ⊗ in restaurant Civ Wed 200

★★★ 73% **HOTEL**

Gatton Manor Hotel Golf & Country Club

Standon Ln RH5 5PQ
☎ 01306 627555 📠 01306 627713
e-mail: info@gattonmanor.co.uk
web: www.gattonmanor.co.uk
(For full entry see Ockley)

★★★ 68% **HOTEL**

Macdonald White Horse

MACDONALD
HOTELS & RESORTS

High St RH4 1BE
☎ 0870 400 8282 📠 01306 887241
e-mail: whitehorsedorking@macdonald-hotels.co.uk
web: www.macdonald-hotels.co.uk
dir: M25 junct 9, A24 S towards Dorking. Hotel in town centre

The hotel was first established as an inn in 1750, although parts of the
building date back as far as the 15th century. Its town centre location
and Dickensian charm have long made this a popular destination for
travellers. Character features include beamed ceilings, open fires and
four-poster beds although more contemporary rooms can be found in
the garden wing.

Rooms 37 en suite 41 annexe en suite (2 fmly) (5 GF) ⊗ in
59 bedrooms S £60–£145; D £80–£160 (incl. bkfst) **Facilities** STV Xmas
Conf Thtr 50 Class 30 Board 30 Del from £135 **Parking** 73 **Notes LB**
⊗ in restaurant

BUDGET HOTEL

Travelodge Dorking

Travelodge

Reigate Rd RH4 1QB
☎ 08700 850 950 📠 01306 741673
web: www.travelodge.co.uk
dir: 0.5m E of Dorking, on A25

Travelodge offers good quality, good value, modern accommodation.
Ideal for families, the spacious en suite bedrooms include remote-
control TV, tea and coffee-making facilities and comfortable beds.
Meals can be taken at the nearby family restaurant. See Hotel Groups
pages for further details.

Rooms 55 en suite S fr £26; D fr £26

EAST HORSLEY   MAP 06 TQ05

★★★ 79% **HOTEL**

Ramada Guildford/ Leatherhead

◉RAMADA

Guildford Rd KT24 6TB
☎ 01483 280500 📠 01483 284222
e-mail: sales.guildford@ramadajarvis.co.uk
web: www.ramadajarvis.co.uk
dir: A25 towards Leatherhead/Dorking. Pass West Horsley, hotel
0.5m on left

With easy access to the M25 the hotel's 19th-century oak beamed
exterior conceals a wide range of modern facilities. Bedrooms are
comfortably appointed for both business and leisure guests.

Rooms 87 en suite (11 fmly) (20 GF) ⊗ in 46 bedrooms S £79–£169;
D £92–£169 **Facilities** STV Wi-fi in bedrooms Xmas **Conf** Thtr 500
Class 250 Board 202 Del from £110 **Services** Lift **Parking** 110 **Notes LB**
⊗ in restaurant Civ Wed 120

EGHAM   MAP 06 TQ07

★★★★ 77% **HOTEL**

Runnymede Hotel & Spa

Windsor Rd TW20 0AG
☎ 01784 436171 📠 01784 436340
e-mail: info@runnymedehotel.com
web: www.runnymedehotel.com
dir: M25 junct 13, onto A308 towards Windsor

Enjoying a peaceful location beside the River Thames, this large
modern hotel attracts a largely business clientele during the week.
Extensive function suites are available, together with spacious lounges
and practically laid out bedrooms. At weekends, leisure visitors come
to enjoy impressive spa facilities and regular dinner dances in the airy
restaurant overlooking the river.

Rooms 180 en suite (19 fmly) ⊗ in 116 bedrooms S £211–£234;
D £253–£287 **Facilities** STV ₹ ♨ Sauna Gym ✈ Putt green Jacuzzi
Wi-fi available Beauty Salon Dance studio ♫ ch fac **Conf** BC Thtr 300
Class 250 Board 76 Del from £255 **Services** Lift air con **Parking** 280
Notes LB ⊗ RS Restaurant closed Sat lunch/Sun dinner Civ Wed 140

See advertisement under WINDSOR, Berkshire

EPSOM
MAP 06 TQ26

★★★ 77% ◎◎ **HOTEL**

Chalk Lane Hotel
Chalk Ln, Woodcote End KT18 7BB
☎ 01372 721179 ▤ 01372 727878
e-mail: smcgregor@chalklanehotel.com
web: www.chalklanehotel.com

dir: from M25 junct 9 onto A24 to Epsom. Right at lights by BP
garage. Left into Avenue Rd, right into Worple Rd. Left at T-junct
& hotel on right

This delightful privately owned hotel enjoys a peaceful location just
ten minutes' walk from Epsom racecourse. Stylish bedrooms are
generally spacious and all are appointed to a high standard. Public
areas are attractively furnished and include a choice of lounges, an
excellent range of function and meeting facilities. A smartly appointed
restaurant offers imaginative, accomplished cuisine.

Rooms 22 en suite (1 fmly) ⊗ in all bedrooms S £95; D £130-£150
(incl. bkfst) **Facilities** STV Wi-fi available Complimentary membership at
local health club **Conf** Thtr 140 Class 40 Board 30 Del from £175
Parking 60 **Notes** ⊗ in restaurant

BUDGET HOTEL

Premier Travel Inn Epsom Central
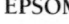
2-4 St Margarets Dr, Off Dorking Rd KT18 7LB
☎ 08701 977096 ▤ 01372 739761
web: www.premiertravelinn.com

dir: M25 junct 9, A24 towards Epsom, Inn on left, just before
town centre

High quality, modern budget accommodation ideal for both families
and business travellers. Spacious, en suite bedrooms feature bath and
shower, satellite TV and many have telephones and modem points.
The adjacent family restaurant features a wide and varied menu. For
further details consult the Hotel Groups page.

Rooms 40 en suite **Conf** Thtr 40

Premier Travel Inn Epsom North
272 Kingston Rd, Ewell KT19 0SH
☎ 0870 9906466 ▤ 0870 9906467
dir: Exit M25 junct 8 onto A217 towards Sutton. Take A240
towards Ewell. At Beggars Hill rdbt take 2nd exit into Kingston Rd
Rooms 29 en suite

FARNHAM
MAP 05 SU84

★★★ 75% ◎◎ **HOTEL**

Best Western Bishop's Table
27 West St GU9 7DR
☎ 01252 710222 ▤ 01252 733494
e-mail: welcome@bishopstable.com
web: www.bishopstable.com

dir: from M3 junct 4 take A331 or from A3 take A31 and follow
town centre signs. Hotel next to library

This family-run Georgian townhouse hotel is in the centre of Farnham
and offers comfortable accommodation and friendly, attentive service.
Each bedroom is individual in style and some are situated in a restored
coach house. Public areas include a cosy bar and an elegant restaurant

Rooms 9 en suite 8 annexe en suite (6 GF) ⊗ in 5 bedrooms
S £107-£120; D £120-£165 **Facilities** Wi-fi in bedrooms **Conf** BC Thtr 26
Class 10 Board 20 Del from £172 **Notes LB** ⊗ No children 16yrs ⊗ in
restaurant Closed 25 Dec-3 Jan RS Closed for lunch Mon

★★★ 75% **HOTEL**

Best Western Frensham Pond Hotel
Bacon Ln GU10 2QB
☎ 01252 795161 ▤ 01252 792631
e-mail: info@frenshampondhotel.co.uk
web: www.frenshampondhotel.co.uk
(For full entry see Churt)

See advert on opposite page

★★★ 73% **HOTEL**

Macdonald Bush
The Borough GU9 7NN
☎ 0870 400 8225 & 01252 715237 ▤ 01252 733530
e-mail: gm.bush@macdonald-hotels.co.uk
web: www.macdonald-hotels.co.uk

dir: M3 junct 4 onto A31, follow town centre signs. At East Street
traffic lights turn left, hotel on right

Dating back to the 17th century, this extended coaching inn is
attractively presented and has a courtyard and a lawned garden. The
bedrooms are well appointed, with quality fabrics and good facilities.
The public areas include the panelled Oak Lounge, a smart cocktail
bar and a conference facility in an adjoining building.

Rooms 83 en suite (3 fmly) (22 GF) ⊗ in 60 bedrooms S £95-£185;
D £125-£210 **Facilities** Wi-fi in bedrooms **Conf** Thtr 140 Class 80
Board 30 Del from £140 **Parking** 70 **Notes LB** ⊗ in restaurant
Civ Wed 90

★★★ 67% HOTEL

Farnham House

Alton Rd GU10 5ER
☎ 01252 716908 ▤ 01252 722583
e-mail: mail@farnhamhousehotel.com
web: www.farnhamhousehotel.com

dir: 1m from town, off A31 Alton road

Popular for conferences and weddings, Farnham House is surrounded by five acres of grounds. The architecture is part Tudor, part baronial in style, and features an oak-panelled bar with an inglenook fireplace. Most bedrooms enjoy countryside views, and a tennis court and swimming pool are peacefully set in the tranquil gardens.

Rooms 25 en suite (1 fmly) (5 GF) ⊗ in 8 bedrooms S £84-£98; D £92-£108 (incl. bkfst) **Facilities** STV ⚒ ♨ **Conf** Thtr 55 Class 14 Board 25 Del from £140 **Parking** 75 **Notes LB** ⊗ RS 25 & 26 Dec Civ Wed 74

FRIMLEY
MAP 05 SU85

BUDGET HOTEL

Innkeeper's Lodge Camberley Frimley

114 Portsmouth Rd GU15 1HS
☎ 01276 691939 ▤ 01276 605900
web: www.innkeeperslodge.com

dir: M3 junct 4/A321 for Frimley take A325 (towards A30 Bagshot), over 1st rdbt past Frimley Park Hospital, straight over 2nd rdbt into Portsmouth Rd. Lodge 500mtrs on left.

Smart, en suite accommodation ideal for both business & leisure guests. Bedrooms are very well equipped, including Sky TV, telephone, modem points, tea & coffee making facilities, (family rooms in most locations). Complimentary breakfast. The adjacent Pub Restaurant; a Harvester, Vintage Inn, Toby Carvery, Ember Inn, Sizzling Pubco or Pub & Carvery offers an all day menu. See Hotel Groups pages for further details.

Rooms 45 en suite **Conf** Thtr 40 Class 20 Board 20

GODALMING
MAP 06 SU94

BUDGET HOTEL

Innkeeper's Lodge Godalming

Ockford Rd GU7 1RH
☎ 01483 419997 ▤ 01483 410852
web: www.innkeeperslodge.com

dir: Turn off A3/Milford at petrol station turn left onto A3100 through Milford under railway bridge. Lodge on rdbt on right

Smart, en suite accommodation ideal for both business & leisure guests. Bedrooms are very well equipped, including Sky TV, telephone, modem points, tea & coffee making facilities, (family rooms in most locations). Complimentary breakfast. The adjacent Pub restaurant; a Harvester, Vintage Inn, Toby Carvery, Ember Inn, Sizzling Pubco or Pub & Carvery offers an all day menu. See Hotel Groups pages for further details.

Rooms 19 rms

GUILDFORD
MAP 06 SU94

★★★ 70% HOTEL

Manor House

Newlands Corner GU4 8SE
☎ 01483 222624 ▤ 01483 211389
e-mail: mail@manorhouse-hotel.com
web: www.manorhouse-hotel.com

dir: 3.5m on A25 to Dorking

Set peacefully in its own grounds, this conveniently located hotel is a popular choice for weddings and conferences. The well-appointed public areas include a selection of meeting rooms, a choice of bars and a spa and leisure facility. Bedrooms, which are mostly modern, are tastefully furnished and have a good range of facilities.

Rooms 50 en suite (4 fmly) ⊗ in 4 bedrooms S fr £79; D fr £82 **Facilities** STV ▨ Sauna Solarium Gym ♨ Jacuzzi Steam room, dance studio **Conf** Thtr 150 Class 50 Board 50 **Parking** 100 **Notes LB** ⊗ in restaurant Civ Wed 120

England

GUILDFORD *continued*

BUDGET HOTEL

Premier Travel Inn Guildford
Parkway GU1 1UP
☎ 08701 977122 📠 01483 450678
web: www.premiertravelinn.com

dir: From M25 junct 10 follow signs to Portsmouth (A3). Turn off at Guildford centre/Leisure Centre (A322/A320/A25) sign. Turn left and Inn is on the left

High quality, modern budget accommodation ideal for both families and business travellers. Spacious, en suite bedrooms feature bath and shower, satellite TV and many have telephones and modem points. The adjacent family restaurant features a wide and varied menu. For further details consult the Hotel Groups page.

Rooms 87 en suite **Conf** Thtr 45 Board 25

BUDGET HOTEL

Travelodge Guildford
Woodbridge Rd, Woodbridge Meadows GU1 1BD
☎ 08700 850 890
web: www.travelodge.co.uk

dir: M3 junct 3, A322 onto Guildford road, then A25. Left onto Woodbridge Meadows, then right.

Travelodge offers good quality, good value, modern accommodation. Ideal for families, the spacious en suite bedrooms include remote-control TV, tea and coffee-making facilities and comfortable beds. Meals can be taken at the nearby family restaurant. See Hotel Groups pages for further details.

Rooms 152 en suite S fr £26; D fr £26

HASLEMERE   MAP 06 SU93

★★★★ 77% ◉◉ HOTEL

Lythe Hill Hotel and Spa
Petworth Rd GU27 3BQ
☎ 01428 651251 📠 01428 644131
e-mail: lythe@lythehill.co.uk
web: www.lythehill.co.uk

dir: left from High St onto B2131. Hotel 1.25m on right

This privately owned hotel sits in 30 acres of attractive parkland with lakes, complete with roaming geese. The hotel has been described as a hamlet of character buildings, each furnished in a style that complements the age of the property; the oldest one dating back to 1475. Cuisine in the adjacent 'Auberge de France' offers interesting,
continued

quality dishes, whilst breakfast is served in the hotel dining room. The bedrooms are split between a number of 15th-century buildings and vary in size. The stylish spa includes a 16-metre swimming pool.

Rooms 41 en suite (8 fmly) (18 GF) ⊛ in all bedrooms S £140-£275; D £140-£275 (incl. bkfst) **Facilities Spa** STV 📶 ⌁ Fishing Sauna Solarium Gym 🌳 Jacuzzi Wi-fi in bedrooms Boules Games Room, Giant Draughts ch fac Xmas **Conf** Thtr 128 Class 40 Board 30 Del from £150 **Parking** 200 **Notes LB** ⊛ in restaurant Civ Wed 128

★★★ 68% HOTEL

Georgian House Hotel
High St GU27 2JY
☎ 01428 656644 📠 01428 645600
e-mail: mail@georgianhousehotel.com
web: www.georgianhousehotel.com

dir: A3 onto A287, then A286. Past station, hotel on left

An attractive and imposing Georgian building, situated on the High Street. Bedrooms in the old wing offer the most character with oak beams and four-poster beds, but all rooms are spacious and well furnished. Public areas include a bar and brasserie, while the leisure centre boasts an indoor pool and jacuzzi.

Rooms 51 en suite (7 GF) ⊛ in 15 bedrooms S £80-£109; D £85-£109 (incl. bkfst) **Facilities** STV 📶 supervised Sauna Solarium Gym Jacuzzi Wi-fi in bedrooms Beauty treatments **Conf** Thtr 150 Class 50 Board 30 Del from £110 **Services** Lift **Parking** 50 **Notes LB** ⊛ Civ Wed 100

HORLEY   MAP 06 TQ24
Hotels are listed under **Gatwick Airport, Sussex, West**

LEATHERHEAD   MAP 06 TQ15

★★ 67% HOTEL

Bookham Grange
Little Bookham Common, Bookham KT23 3HS
☎ 01372 452742 📠 01372 450080
e-mail: bookhamgrange@easynet.co.uk
web: www.bookham-grange.co.uk

dir: off A246 at Bookham High Street onto Church Rd, 1st right after Bookham railway station

This attractive family-run hotel is situated in over two acres of landscaped grounds with extensive parking. Spacious bedrooms are individually decorated and well equipped. Public areas include extensive banqueting facilities and a beamed bar. This is a popular wedding venue.

Rooms 27 en suite (3 fmly) **Conf** Thtr 80 Class 24 Board 24 **Parking** 60 **Notes LB** ⊛ in restaurant Civ Wed 90

England

BUDGET HOTEL

Travelodge Leatherhead

The Swan Centre, High St KT22 8AA
☎ 0870 191 1748 📠 01372 386577
web: www.travelodge.co.uk

Travelodge offers good quality, good value, modern accommodation. Ideal for families, the spacious en suite bedrooms include remote-control TV, tea and coffee-making facilities and comfortable beds. Meals can be taken at the nearby family restaurant. See Hotel Groups pages for further details.

Rooms 91 en suite S fr £26; D fr £26

OCKLEY   MAP 06 TQ14

★★★ 73% HOTEL

Gatton Manor Hotel Golf & Country Club

Standon Ln RH5 5PQ
☎ 01306 627555 📠 01306 627713
e-mail: info@gattonmanor.co.uk
web: www.gattonmanor.co.uk
dir: off A29 at Ockley turn into Cat Hill Lane. Hotel signed 2m on right

This establishment enjoys a peaceful setting in private grounds. It is a popular golf and country club, with an 18-hole professional course and offers a range of comfortable, modern bedrooms. The public areas include the refurbished main club bar and restaurant. Conference facilities are available.

Rooms 18 en suite (2 fmly) ⊗ in 12 bedrooms S fr £65; D fr £75 (incl. bkfst) **Facilities** STV ⌀ 18 Fishing Sauna Gym Putt green Wi-fi in bedrooms ch fac **Conf** Thtr 50 Class 40 Board 30 Del from £105 **Parking** 250 **Notes LB** ⊛ ⊗ in restaurant Civ Wed 50

OTTERSHAW   MAP 06 TQ06

★★★★ 79% HOTEL

Foxhills Club & Resort

Stonehill Rd KT16 0EL
☎ 01932 872050 📠 01932 874762
e-mail: reservations@foxhills.co.uk
dir: M25, A320 to Woking. 2nd rdbt last exit into Chobham Road. Right into Foxhills Road, left into Stonehill Road

This hotel enjoys a peaceful setting in extensive grounds, not far from the M25 and Heathrow. Spacious well-appointed bedrooms are provided in a choice of annexes, a short walk from the main house. Golf, tennis, three pools and impressive indoor leisure facilities are on offer. Two styles of restaurant are available.

continued

Rooms 70 en suite (7 fmly) (39 GF) S £170-£300; D £170-£300
Facilities STV FTV ⌀ ⌀ ⌀ 45 ⌀ Squash Sauna Solarium Gym ⌀ Putt green Wi-fi in bedrooms Childrens adventure playground, country pursuits, off-road course, ch fac Xmas **Conf** Thtr 100 Class 52 Board 56 Del from £220 **Services** Lift **Parking** 500 **Notes LB** ⊗ Civ Wed 75

PEASLAKE   MAP 06 TQ04

★★★ 73% ⊛ HOTEL

Hurtwood Inn Hotel

Walking Bottom GU5 9RR
☎ 01306 730851 📠 01306 731390
e-mail: sales@hurtwoodinnhotel.com
web: www.hurtwoodinnhotel.com
dir: off A25 at Gomshall opposite Jet Filling Station towards Peaslake. After 2.5m turn right at village shop, hotel in village centre

With its tranquil location this hotel makes an ideal base for exploring the attractions of the area. The brightly decorated bedrooms are well appointed, and some have views over the gardens. Public areas include the restaurant, a private dining room and a bar/bistro where drinks by the open fire can be enjoyed. 'Oscars' is the setting to enjoy award-winning meals.

Rooms 15 en suite 6 annexe en suite (6 fmly) (6 GF) ⊗ in 5 bedrooms S £45-£65; D £50-£100 **Facilities** Wi-fi in bedrooms **Conf** Thtr 40 Class 25 Board 20 Del from £126.95 **Parking** 22 **Notes LB** ⊗ in restaurant

---

REDHILL   MAP 06 TQ25

★★★★ 81% ⊛⊛ HOTEL

Nutfield Priory   Hand PICKED

Nutfield RH1 4EL
☎ 01737 824400 📠 01737 824410
e-mail: nutfieldpriory@handpicked.co.uk
web: www.handpicked.co.uk
dir: M25 junct 6, follow Redhill signs via Godstone on A25. Hotel 1m on left after Nutfield Village. Or M25 junct 8 follow A25 through Reigate, Redhill & Godstone. Hotel on right 1.5m after railway bridge

This Victorian country house dates back to 1872 and is set in 40 acres of grounds with stunning views over the Surrey countryside. Bedrooms are individually decorated and equipped with an excellent range of facilities. Public areas include the impressive grand hall, Cloisters restaurant, the library, and a cosy lounge bar area.

Rooms 60 en suite (4 fmly) ⊗ in 24 bedrooms S £180; D £195-£265
Facilities Spa STV ⌀ Squash Sauna Solarium Gym Jacuzzi Wi-fi available Steam room Beauty therapy Aerobic & Step classes Xmas
Conf Thtr 80 Class 45 Board 40 Del from £235 **Services** Lift air con
Parking 130 **Notes LB** ⊗ in restaurant Civ Wed 80

REDHILL *continued*

BUDGET HOTEL

Innkeeper's Lodge Redhill (Gatwick)

2 Redstone Hill RH1 4BL
☎ 01737 768434 📄 01737 770742
web: www.innkeeperslodge.com

dir: M25 junct 8, follow signs for Redhill (A25). At railway station, left towards Godstone. Inn on right

Smart, en suite accommodation ideal for both business & leisure guests. Bedrooms are very well equipped, including Sky TV, telephone, modem points, tea & coffee making facilities, (family rooms in most locations). Complimentary breakfast. The adjacent Pub Restaurant; a Harvester, Vintage Inn, Toby Carvery, Ember Inn, Sizzling Pubco or Pub & Carvery offers an all day menu. See Hotel Groups pages for further details.

Rooms 37 en suite **Conf** Thtr 50 Class 20 Board 24

BUDGET HOTEL

Premier Travel Inn Redhill

premier travel inn

Brighton Rd, Salfords RH1 5BT
☎ 08701 977218 📄 01737 778099
web: www.premiertravelinn.com

dir: on A23, 2m south of Redhill, 3m north of Gatwick Airport

High quality, modern budget accommodation ideal for both families and business travellers. Spacious, en suite bedrooms feature bath and shower, satellite TV and many have telephones and modem points. The adjacent family restaurant features a wide and varied menu. For further details consult the Hotel Groups page.

Rooms 48 en suite **Conf** Thtr 35

REIGATE   MAP 06 TQ25

★★★ 72% HOTEL

Best Western Reigate Manor

Best Western

Reigate Hill RH2 9PF
☎ 01737 240125 📄 01737 223883
e-mail: hotel@reigatemanor.co.uk
web: www.reigatemanor.co.uk

dir: on A217, 1m S of junct 8 on M25

On the slopes of Reigate Hill, the hotel is ideally located for access to the town and for motorway links. A range of public rooms is provided along with a variety of function rooms. Bedrooms are either traditional in style in the old house or of contemporary design in the wing.

Rooms 50 en suite (1 fmly) ⊗ in all bedrooms S £89-£105; D £99-£120 (incl. bkfst) **Facilities** STV Wi-fi in bedrooms **Conf** Thtr 200 Class 80 Board 50 Del from £130 **Parking** 130 **Notes** ⊗ ⊘ in restaurant Civ Wed 200

Ⓤ

Swallow Reigate

SWALLOW HOTELS

Reigate Hill RH2 9RP
☎ 01737 246801 📄 01737 223756
e-mail: reservations.reigate@swallowhotels.com
web: www.swallowhotels.com

dir: Exit M25 junct 8, A217. Hotel on right just after High Foot bridge

At the time of going to press, the star classification for this hotel was not confirmed. Please refer to the AA internet site www.theAA.com for current information.

Rooms 39 en suite (2 fmly) (12 GF) ⊗ in 23 bedrooms S £95; D £110 (incl. bkfst) **Facilities** STV ♫ Xmas **Conf** Thtr 60 Class 60 Board 35 Del £140 **Parking** 100 **Notes LB** ⊗ ⊘ in restaurant Civ Wed 70

SEALE   MAP 06 SU84

★★★ 75% HOTEL

Ramada Farnham

Ⓡ RAMADA.

Hog's Back GU10 1EX
☎ 01252 782345 📄 01252 783113
e-mail: sales.farnham@ramadajarvis.co.uk
web: www.ramadajarvis.co.uk

dir: on A31

Set high on the Hog's Back Ridge in well-presented grounds, this large hotel is a popular venue for both conferences and meetings. Bedrooms are comfortably appointed for both business and leisure guests. Public areas include a range of meeting rooms and the Sebastian Coe health club.

Rooms 96 en suite (6 fmly) (27 GF) ⊗ in 71 bedrooms S £149-£174; D £169-£194 **Facilities** STV ⊡ Sauna Solarium Gym Jacuzzi Wi-fi in bedrooms Xmas **Conf** Thtr 420 Class 188 Board 160 Del from £140 **Parking** 150 **Notes LB** ⊗ ⊘ in restaurant Civ Wed 140

SHEPPERTON   MAP 06 TQ06

★★★★ 70% HOTEL

Holiday Inn London - Shepperton

Holiday Inn HOTELS · RESORTS

Felix Ln TW17 8NP
☎ 0870 2258 701 & 01932 899900 📄 01932 245231
e-mail: hishepperton@qmh-hotels.com

dir: M3 junct 1, 6th exit Green Ln, right at T-junct. Felix Lane 1.5m on left

This hotel has a range of modern, well-equipped leisure and conference facilities. It's hidden, tranquil location also makes it ideal

continued

for a family break. The spacious bedrooms are pleasantly appointed and have air conditioning. The restaurant offers a carte menu and the bar also provides an alternative dining venue.

Rooms 185 en suite (9 fmly) (37 GF) ⊛ in 154 bedrooms S £51-£139; D £51-£139 **Facilities** STV ⬚ supervised Sauna Solarium Gym Jacuzzi Wi-fi in bedrooms Steam room Beauty therapy **Conf** Thtr 120 Class 60 Board 40 Del from £125 **Services** Lift air con **Parking** 160 **Notes LB** ⊛ in restaurant Civ Wed 80

STAINES   MAP 06 TQ07

★★★ 74% **HOTEL**

Macdonald Thames Lodge

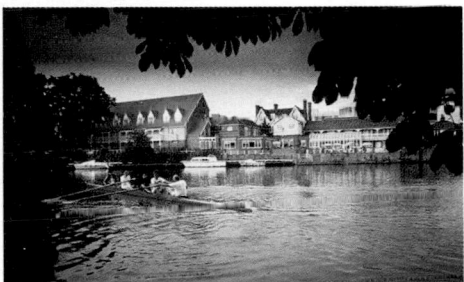

Thames St TW18 4SF

☎ 0870 400 8121 & 01784 464433 ▤ 01784 454858

e-mail: sales.thameslodge@macdonald-hotels.co.uk

web: www.macdonald-hotels.co.uk

dir: M25 junct 13. Follow A30/Town Centre signs (bus station on right). Hotel straight ahead

Dating back to the 19th-century, this popular hotel enjoys an idyllic riverside setting. Bedrooms, many with river views, are smartly decorated and equipped with a host of extras. Public rooms include a no-smoking lounge, a lounge/bar with outside terrace, a smart, modern brasserie and a range of function rooms.

Rooms 78 en suite (17 fmly) (22 GF) ⊛ in 64 bedrooms S £100-£160; D £120-£180 (incl. bkfst) **Facilities** STV FTV Wi-fi available Riverside tea garden with mooring, Use of facilities at local leisure centre Xmas **Conf** Thtr 50 Class 40 Board 40 Del from £130 **Parking** 40 **Notes LB** ⊛ in restaurant

BUDGET HOTEL

Travelodge Staines

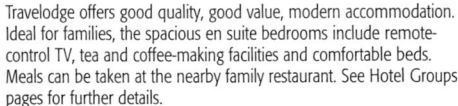

Hale St, Two Rivers Retail Park TW18 4UW

☎ 08700 850 950 ▤ 01784 491 026

web: www.travelodge.co.uk

Travelodge offers good quality, good value, modern accommodation. Ideal for families, the spacious en suite bedrooms include remote-control TV, tea and coffee-making facilities and comfortable beds. Meals can be taken at the nearby family restaurant. See Hotel Groups pages for further details.

Rooms 65 en suite S fr £26; D fr £26

STOKE D'ABERNON   MAP 06 TQ15

★★★★ 84% ⊛⊛ **HOTEL**

Woodlands Park

Hand PICKED

Woodlands Ln KT11 3QB

☎ 01372 843933 ▤ 01372 842704

e-mail: woodlandspark@handpicked.co.uk

web: www.handpicked.co.uk

dir: from A3 towards London, exit at Cobham. Through town centre & Stoke D'Abernon, left at garden centre into Woodlands Lane, hotel 0.5m on right

Originally built for the Bryant family, the matchmakers, this lovely Victorian mansion enjoys an attractive parkland setting in ten and a half acres of Surrey countryside. Bedrooms in the wing are contemporary in style while those in the main house are more traditionally decorated. The hotel boasts two dining options, Quotes Bar & Brasserie and the Oak Room Restaurant.

Rooms 57 en suite (4 fmly) ⊛ in 47 bedrooms S £125-£170; D £135-£190 **Facilities** STV ⬚ ⬚ Wi-fi available Xmas **Conf** Thtr 150 Class 20 Board 50 Del from £220 **Services** Lift **Parking** 150 **Notes LB** Civ Wed 200

TADWORTH   MAP 06 TQ25

BUDGET HOTEL

Premier Travel Inn Epsom South

premier travel inn

Brighton Rd, Burgh Heath KT20 6BW

☎ 0870 9906442 ▤ 0870 9906443

web: www.premiertravelinn.com

dir: Just off M25 junct 8 on A217 towards Sutton

High quality, modern budget accommodation ideal for both families and business travellers. Spacious, en suite bedrooms feature bath and shower, satellite TV and many have telephones and modem points. The adjacent family restaurant features a wide and varied menu. For further details consult the Hotel Groups page.

Rooms 78 en suite

VIRGINIA WATER   MAP 06 TQ06

★★ 79% **HOTEL**

The Wheatsheaf

London Rd GU25 4QF

☎ 01344 842057 ▤ 01344 842932

e-mail: sales@wheatsheafhotel.com

web: www.wheatsheafhotel.com

dir: off A30, N of Sunningdale, pass Wentworth Golf Course. Hotel on left at lights

This 19th-century inn is in a prime location overlooking the lake in Great Windsor Park. Bedrooms are well proportioned and comfortable, with stylish decor and a good range of facilities. The

continued on page 600

England

VIRGINIA WATER *continued*

public rooms consist of a country-style bar and restaurant which offers a substantial lunch and dinner menu. Secure parking is provided.

The Wheatsheaf

Rooms 17 en suite (2 fmly) ⊘ in 10 bedrooms **Facilities** STV
Conf Thtr 50 Class 30 Board 25 **Services** air con **Parking** 100
Notes LB ⊗ Civ Wed 60

WALTON-ON-THAMES
See **LONDON SECTION plan 1 A1**

BUDGET HOTEL

Innkeeper's Lodge Walton-on-Thames
Ashley Park Rd KT12 1JP
☎ 01932 220196 🗋 01932 220660
web: www.innkeeperslodge.com

dir: M25 junct 11 east towards A317 towards Weybridge, at B365 roundabout for Ashley Park, turn left then right into Station Avenue, left opposite station

Smart, en suite accommodation ideal for both business & leisure guests. Bedrooms are very well equipped, including Sky TV, telephone, modem points, tea & coffee making facilities, (family rooms in most locations). Complimentary breakfast. The adjacent Pub Restaurant; a Harvester, Vintage Inn, Toby Carvery, Ember Inn, Sizzling Pubco or Pub & Carvery offers an all day menu. See Hotel Groups pages for further details.

Rooms 32 en suite **Conf** Thtr 60 Class 24 Board 24

WEYBRIDGE   MAP 06 TQ06
See **LONDON SECTION plan 1 A1**

★★★★ 72% **HOTEL**

Oatlands Park
146 Oatlands Dr KT13 9HB
☎ 01932 847242 🗋 01932 842252
e-mail: info@oatlandsparkhotel.com
web: www.oatlandsparkhotel.com

dir: through Weybridge High Street to top of Monument Hill. Hotel on left

Once a palace for Henry VIII, this impressive building sits in extensive grounds encompassing tennis courts, a gym and a 9-hole golf course. The spacious lounge and bar create a wonderful first impression with

continued

tall marble pillars and plush comfortable seating. Most of the bedrooms are very spacious, and all are well equipped.

Oatlands Park

Rooms 144 en suite (5 fmly) (31 GF) ⊘ in 68 bedrooms **Facilities** STV
⅃ 9 ⍟ Gym ⍤ Putt green Jogging course Fitness suite, board games ♫
Conf BC Thtr 300 Class 150 Board 80 **Services** Lift **Parking** 140
Notes Civ Wed 220

★★★ 71% **HOTEL**

The Ship
Monument Green KT13 8BQ
☎ 01932 848364 🗋 01932 857153
e-mail: reservations@desboroughhotels.com
dir: M25 junct 11, at 3rd rdbt left into High St. Hotel 300yds on left

A former coaching inn, The Ship retains its period charm and is now a spacious and comfortable hotel. Bedrooms, some of which overlook a delightful courtyard, are spacious and cheerfully decorated. Public areas include a lounge and cocktail bar, restaurant and a popular pub. The high street location and private parking are a bonus.

Rooms 77 en suite (2 fmly) ⊘ in 52 bedrooms S £55-£175; D £70-£195
(incl. bkfst) **Facilities** STV **Conf** Thtr 180 Class 70 Board 60 **Del** from
£150 **Services** Lift **Parking** 65 **Notes LB** ⊘ in restaurant

BUDGET HOTEL

Innkeeper's Lodge Weybridge
25 Oatlands Chase KT13 9RW
☎ 01932 253277 🗋 01932 252412
e-mail: badgers.rest@bass.com
web: www.innkeeperslodge.com

dir: M25 junct 11, A317 towards Weybridge, at 3rd rdbt take A3050, left 1m. Turn into Oatlands Chase, lodge on right

Smart, en suite accommodation ideal for both business & leisure guests. Bedrooms are very well equipped, including Sky TV, telephone, modem points, tea & coffee making facilities, (family rooms in most locations). Complimentary breakfast. The adjacent Pub Restaurant; a Harvester, Vintage Inn, Toby Carvery, Ember Inn, Sizzling Pubco or Pub & Carvery offers an all day menu. See Hotel Groups pages for further details.

Rooms 18 en suite

England

WOKING
MAP 06 TQ05

BUDGET HOTEL

Innkeeper's Lodge Woking

Chobham Rd, Horsell GU21 4AL

☎ 01483 733047

web: www.innkeeperslodge.com

Smart, en suite accommodation ideal for both business & leisure guests. Bedrooms are very well equipped, including Sky TV, telephone, modem points, tea & coffee making facilities, (family rooms in most locations). Complimentary breakfast. The adjacent Pub Restaurant; a Harvester, Vintage Inn, Toby Carvery, Ember Inn, Sizzling Pubco or Pub & Carvery offers an all day menu. See Hotel Groups pages for further details.

Rooms 33 en suite

BUDGET HOTEL

Premier Travel Inn Woking

Bridge Barn Ln GU21 6NL

☎ 00701 977276 ▤ 01483 771755

web: www.premiertravelinn.com

dir: *M25 junct 11 follow A320. Turn right at traffic lights by Toys r Us. Take 3rd mini rbt 0.75m down Goldsworth Rd. Turn right into Bridge Barn Ln. Inn on left*

High quality, modern budget accommodation ideal for both families and business travellers. Spacious, en suite bedrooms feature bath and shower, satellite TV and many have telephones and modem points. The adjacent family restaurant features a wide and varied menu. For further details consult the Hotel Groups page.

Rooms 34 en suite

SUSSEX, EAST

ALFRISTON
MAP 06 TQ50

★★★ 80% **HOTEL**

Best Western Deans Place

Seaford Rd BN26 5TW

☎ 01323 870248 ▤ 01323 870918

e-mail: mail@deansplacehotel.co.uk

web: www.bw-deansplacehotel.co.uk

dir: *off A27 signed Alfriston & Drusillas Zoo Park. Continue south through village*

Situated on the southern fringe of the village, this friendly hotel is set in attractive gardens. Bedrooms vary in size and are well appointed with good facilities. A wide range of food is offered including an extensive bar menu and a fine dining option in Harcourt's Restaurant.

Rooms 36 en suite (4 fmly) (8 GF) ⊗ in 17 bedrooms S £71-£88; D £88-£136 (incl. bkfst) **Facilities** STV ⊰ ⊌ Putt green Boules ♫ Xmas **Conf** Thtr 200 Class 100 Board 60 Del from £125 **Parking** 100 **Notes LB** ⊗ in restaurant Civ Wed 150

★★★ 70% **HOTEL**

The Star Inn

BN26 5TA

☎ 01323 870495 ▤ 01323 870922

e-mail: bookings@star-inn-alfriston.com

web: www.star-inn-alfriston.com

dir: *2m off A27 at Drusillas rdbt follow Alfriston signs, hotel on right in centre of High Street*

Located in a sleepy town on the edge of the South Downs this 14th-century inn provides smart accommodation. Whilst some rooms retain original features, the majority are contemporary in style and design. Public areas maintain the original charm and character of the house including open fires and flagstones.

Rooms 37 en suite (12 GF) ⊗ in all bedrooms S £49-£69; D £98-£138 (incl. bkfst) **Facilities** Xmas **Conf** Thtr 30 Class 15 Del £140 **Parking** 40 **Notes LB** ⊗ in restaurant

BATTLE
MAP 07 TQ71

★★★ 75% **HOTEL**

Brickwall Hotel

The Green, Sedlescombe TN33 0QA

☎ 01424 870253 & 870339 ▤ 01424 870785

e-mail: info@brickwallhotel.com

web: www.brickwallhotel.com

dir: *off A21 on B2244 at top of Sedlescombe Green*

This is a well-maintained Tudor house, which is situated in the heart of this pretty village and overlooks the green. The spacious public rooms feature a lovely wood-panelled restaurant with a wealth of oak beams, a choice of lounges and a smart bar. Bedrooms are pleasantly decorated and some have garden views.

Rooms 25 en suite (2 fmly) (17 GF) ⊗ in 1 bedroom S £60-75; D £92-£110 (incl. bkfst) **Facilities** STV ⊰ Xmas **Conf** Thtr 30 Class 40 Board 30 **Parking** 50 **Notes LB** ⊗ in restaurant

★★★ 75% ⊛ **HOTEL**

Powder Mills

Powdermill Ln TN33 0SP

☎ 01424 775511 ▤ 01424 774540

e-mail: powdc@aol.com

web: www.powdermillshotel.com

dir: *pass Abbey on A2100. 1st right, hotel 1m on right*

A delightful 18th-century country house hotel set amidst 150 acres of landscaped grounds with lakes and woodland. The individually decorated bedrooms are tastefully furnished and thoughtfully

continued on page 602

BATTLE *continued*

equipped, some rooms have sun terraces with lovely views over the lake. Public rooms include a cosy lounge bar, music room, drawing room, library, restaurant and conservatory.

Rooms 30 en suite 10 annexe en suite (3 GF) S £99–£120; D £130–£160 (incl. bkfst) **Facilities** STV ⚓ ⚒ Fishing Wi-fi in bedrooms Jogging trails & woodland walks ♫ Xmas **Conf** Thtr 250 Class 50 Board 16 Del from £130 **Parking** 101 **Notes LB** ⊗ in restaurant Civ Wed 100

BRIGHTON & HOVE
MAP 06 TQ30

★★★★★ 78% **HOTEL**

De Vere Grand Brighton
King's Rd BN1 2FW
☎ 01273 224300 ▨ 01273 224321
e-mail: reservations@grandbrighton.co.uk
web: www.devere.co.uk

dir: on seafront between piers, next to Brighton Centre

Dating back to the mid 19th century, this landmark seafront hotel, with its eye-catching white façade and intricate balconies, is as grand as the name suggests. Bedrooms include a number of deluxe sea-view rooms, some with balconies, and suites that also have panoramic views. The hotel is perhaps best known for its extensive conference and banqueting facilities; there is also a well-equipped leisure centre and an impressive conservatory adjoining the bar.

Rooms 200 en suite (60 fmly) ⊗ in all bedrooms S £115–£395; D £115–£395 (incl. bkfst) **Facilities Spa** STV 🄫 supervised Sauna Solarium Gym Jacuzzi Wi-fi available Hairdresser, Tropicarium, Beauty salon & treatment rooms ♫ Xmas **Conf** Thtr 800 Class 420 Board 50 Del from £160 **Services** Lift **Parking** 70 **Notes LB** ⊗ in restaurant Civ Wed 800

★★★★ 76% ❀ **TOWN HOUSE HOTEL**

Hotel du Vin Brighton
2-6 Ship St BN1 1AD
☎ 01273 718588 ▨ 01273 718599
e-mail: info@brighton.hotelduvin.com
web: www.hotelduvin.com

dir: A23 from London, signs to seafront/city centre. Right at seafront, into Middle St follow road in U shape to Ship St

This tastefully converted mock-Tudor building occupies a convenient location in a quiet side street close to the seafront. The individually designed bedrooms have a wine theme, and all are comprehensively equipped. Public areas offer a spacious split-level bar, an atmospheric and locally popular restaurant, plus useful private dining and meeting facilities.

Rooms 37 en suite (4 GF) ⊗ in all bedrooms S £135–£145; D £135–£145 **Facilities** STV Snooker Wi-fi in bedrooms Xmas **Conf** Thtr 30 Board 22 Del from £210 **Services** air con **Parking** 9 **Notes** ⊗ in restaurant

★★★★ 72% **HOTEL**

Old Ship
King's Rd BN1 1NR
☎ 01273 329001 ▨ 01273 820718
e-mail: oldship@paramount-hotels.co.uk
web: www.paramount-hotels.co.uk

PARAMOUNT
GROUP OF HOTELS

dir: A23 to seafront, right at rdbt along Kings Rd. Hotel 200yds on right

The Old Ship enjoys a stunning seafront location and offers guests elegant surroundings to relax in. Bedrooms are well designed, with modern facilities ensuring comfort. Many original features have been retained, including the oak-panelled bar. Facilities include a variety of conference rooms and a car park.

Rooms 152 en suite (10 fmly) ⊗ in 15 bedrooms D £220–£450 (incl. bkfst) **Facilities** Wi-fi in bedrooms Xmas **Conf** Thtr 300 Class 100 Board 60 Del from £140 **Services** Lift **Parking** 40 **Notes LB** Civ Wed 150

★★★★ 71% **HOTEL**

Alias Hotel Seattle
The Strand, Brighton Marina BN2 5WA
☎ 01273 679799 ▨ 01273 679899
e-mail: seattle@aliashotels.com
web: www.aliashotels.com

dir: Follow signs to seafront. Hotel in Marina 1m E of Brighton Pier

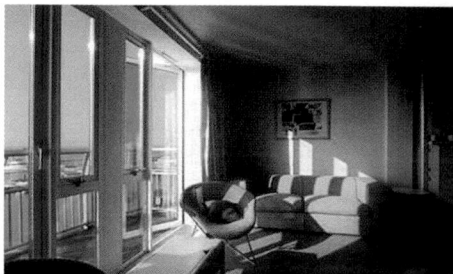

This chic hotel enjoys a prime position overlooking Brighton Marina and has much to offer guests. The majority of public rooms have fabulous sea views, as do many of the bedrooms. The spacious, atmospheric Café Paradiso offers cuisine with a Mediterranean theme. Parking is just a short walk away.

Rooms 71 en suite **Facilities** STV Special rates for hotel guests at nearby David Lloyd Leisure Centre **Conf** Thtr 120 Class 50 Board 70 **Services** Lift **Notes LB** ⊗ in restaurant Civ Wed 100

See advert on opposite page

★★★★ 72% **HOTEL**

Thistle Brighton
King's Rd BN1 2GS
☎ 0870 333 9129 ▨ 0870 333 9229
e-mail: Brighton@Thistle.co.uk

THISTLE HOTELS

dir: A23 to seafront. At rdbt turn right, hotel is 200yds on right.

Situated overlooking the sea and within easy reach of the town's many attractions this hotel is built around an atrium and offers air-conditioned rooms including suites. There is a restaurant, lounge and

continued

bar offering drinks, light refreshments and meals, and the Otium Health & fitness club with pool, sauna, and gym facilities plus health and beauty treatment rooms.

Rooms 208 en suite ⊘ in 100 bedrooms **Facilities** STV 🖳 supervised **Conf** BC Thtr 300 Class 180 Board 120 **Services** Lift air con **Notes LB** ⊘ in restaurant Civ Wed 150

★★★ 72% HOTEL

The Granville

124 King's Rd BN1 2FA
☎ 01273 326302 🖷 01273 728294
e-mail: granville@brighton.co.uk
web: www.granvillehotel.co.uk
dir: opposite West Pier

This stylish hotel is located on Brighton's busy seafront. Bedrooms are carefully furnished and decorated with great style. A trendy cocktail bar and restaurant is located in the cellar with street access and a cosy terrace for warmer months. Tasty traditional breakfasts are also available.

Rooms 24 en suite (2 fmly) (1 GF) ⊘ in all bedrooms **Facilities** Jacuzzi **Conf** BC Thtr 50 Class 30 Board 30 **Services** Lift **Parking** 3

★★★ 71% HOTEL

Imperial

First Av BN3 2GU
☎ 01273 777320 🖷 01273 777310
e-mail: info@imperial-hove.com
web: www.imperial-hove.com
dir: M23 to Brighton seafront, right at rdbt to Hove, 1.5m to First Avenue turn right

Located within minutes of the seafront, this Regency property offers a good range of conference suites that complement the comfortable public rooms, which include a lounge, a smart bar area and an attractive restaurant. Bedrooms are generally of comfortable proportions, well appointed and with a good range of facilities.

Rooms 76 en suite (4 fmly) ⊘ in 10 bedrooms S £45-£75; D£80-£125 (incl. bkfst) **Facilities** Wi-fi in bedrooms **Conf** BC Thtr 110 Class 30 Board 34 Del fr £85 **Services** Lift **Notes LB** ⊗ ⊘ in restaurant

★★★ 70% HOTEL

Best Western Princes Marine

153 Kingsway BN3 4GR
☎ 01273 207660 🖷 012/3 325913
e-mail: princesmarine@bestwestern.co.uk

dir: right at Brighton Pier, follow seafront for 2m. Hotel 200yds from King Alfred leisure centre

This friendly hotel enjoys a seafront location and offers spacious, comfortable bedrooms equipped with a good range of facilities. There is a cosy restaurant, a bar and a useful meeting room plus limited parking at the rear.

Rooms 48 en suite (4 fmly) ⊘ in 36 bedrooms S £50-£70; D £80-£160 (incl. bkfst) **Facilities** Wi-fi in bedrooms Xmas **Conf** BC Thtr 80 Class 40 Board 40 Del from £95 **Services** Lift **Parking** 30 **Notes LB** ⊘ in restaurant

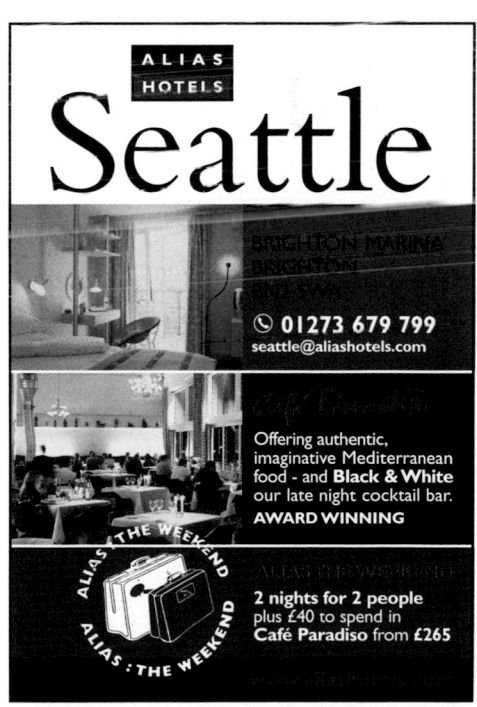

England

BRIGHTON & HOVE *continued*

★★★ 70% HOTEL

Ramada Brighton
R A M A D A

149 Kings Rd BN1 2PP
☎ 01273 738201 📠 01273 821752
e-mail: sales.brighton@ramadajarvis.co.uk
web: www.ramadajarvis.co.uk

dir: *Take A23, follow signs for seafront, turn right at Brighton Pier rdbt. Hotel on right, just after West Pier*

This Regency-style hotel enjoys a prime seafront location on the Kings Road. Bedrooms, many of which have undergone a significant refurbishment, are comfortably appointed for both business and leisure guests. Public areas include the Arts bar and restaurant and a range of meeting rooms. Limited parking is available.

Rooms 123 rms (82 en suite) (2 fmly) ⊘ in 80 bedrooms S £49-£99; D £59-£129 **Facilities** STV Wi-fi available Xmas **Conf** Thtr 455 Class 160 Board 185 Del from £102 **Services** Lift **Parking** 41 **Notes** ⊗ ⊘ in restaurant Civ Wed 60

★★★ 68% HOTEL

The Courtlands

15-27 The Drive BN3 3JE
☎ 01273 731055 📠 01273 328295
e-mail: info@courtlandshotel.com

dir: *At A23/A27 junct. 1st exit to Hove, 2nd exit at rdbt, right at 1st junct and left at shops. Straight on at junct. Hotel on left*

THE COURTLANDS
HOTEL AND CONFERENCE CENTRE

This hotel is located on a tree-lined avenue within walking distance of the seafront and has its own small car park. The bedrooms come in a variety of styles and include Executive rooms and Suites. Guests have the use of a comfortable lounge, a light and spacious restaurant; service is both friendly and attentive.

Rooms 60 en suite 7 annexe en suite (8 fmly) ⊘ in 20 bedrooms S £46-£98; D £68-£125 **Facilities** FTV 🏊 Wi-fi in bedrooms Xmas **Conf** Thtr 60 Class 20 Board 30 Del from £80 **Services** Lift **Parking** 24 **Notes LB** ⊗ ⊘ in restaurant

★★★ 68% HOTEL

Best Western Brighton Hotel

143/145 King's Rd BN1 2PQ
☎ 01273 820555 📠 01273 821555
e-mail: info@thebrightonhotel.com
web: www.bw-brightonhotel.co.uk

dir: *M23 S, join A23 to pier. Turn right at rdbt, hotel is just past West Pier.*

This friendly, family-run hotel is well placed in a prime seafront

continued

location that is close to the historic West Pier. All of the bedrooms are bright, comfortably appointed and well equipped. The parking facilities, though limited, are a real bonus in this area of town.

Best Western Brighton Hotel

Rooms 52 en suite (6 fmly) ⊘ in 38 bedrooms S £39-£95; D £59-£185 (incl. bkfst) **Facilities** STV Wi-fi in bedrooms **Conf** Thtr 95 Class 25 Board 35 Del from £130 **Services** Lift **Parking** 10 **Notes LB** ⊗ ⊘ in restaurant Civ Wed 60

★★★ 67% HOTEL

Quality Hotel Brighton
QUALITY

West St BN1 2RQ
☎ 01273 220033 📠 01273 778000
e-mail: enquiries@hotels-brighton.com
web: www.choicehotelseurope.com

dir: *A23 into Brighton, then town centre/seafront signs. A259 to Hove & Worthing. Hotel next to Brighton Centre*

Conveniently located for the seafront and close to the town centre, this purpose-built hotel offers newly refurbished, modern and well-equipped bedrooms. Public areas include a spacious, open-plan lounge bar area with a feature staircase. A choice of restaurants serves a wide selection of dishes.

Rooms 140 en suite ⊘ in 60 bedrooms S £40-£105; D £40-£121 **Facilities** Wi-fi available Xmas **Conf** Thtr 200 Class 80 Board 60 Del from £85 **Services** Lift **Notes LB** ⊗ ⊘ in restaurant

★★★ Ⓐ

The Kings Hotel

139-141 Kings Rd BN1 2NA
☎ 01273 820854 📠 01273 828309
e-mail: info@kingshotelbrighton.co.uk

dir: *Follow signs to seafront. At Brighton Pier rdbt take 3rd exit & drive west (seafront on left). Hotel adjacent to West Pier.*

Rooms 90 en suite (3 fmly) (6 GF) ⊘ in 30 bedrooms **Facilities** STV **Conf** Thtr 50 Class 40 Board 40 **Services** Lift **Parking** 12 **Notes** ⊗

★★ 65% HOTEL

Preston Park Hotel

216 Preston Rd BN1 6UU
☎ 01273 507853 📠 01273 540039
e-mail: manager@prestonparkhotel.co.uk

This hotel enjoys a convenient roadside location on the outskirts of Brighton. Bedrooms are modern and are well provisioned for both the leisure and business guest. Freshly prepared meals are offered in the spacious bar or the more intimate and relaxing restaurant.

Rooms 33 en suite (4 fmly) ⊘ in 20 bedrooms S £50-£92; D £60-£110 (incl. bkfst) **Facilities** 🏊 supervised Sauna Gym Xmas **Conf** Thtr 100 Class 60 Board 60 Del from £115 **Parking** 60 **Notes LB** ⊘ in restaurant Civ Wed 80

England

[U]

Lansdowne Place

Lansdowne Place BN3 1HQ

☎ 01273 736266 🖹 01273 729802

e-mail: bookings@lansdowneplace.co.uk

web: www.lansdowneplace.co.uk

dir: *A23 to seafront. Right at Brighton Pier, along seafront, right at Lansdowne Place*

At the time of going to press, the star classification for this hotel was not confirmed. Please refer to the AA internet site www.theAA.com for current information.

Rooms 84 en suite (3 fmly) ⊘ in all bedrooms **Facilities** Spa STV Sauna Gym **Conf** BC Thtr 200 Class 60 Board 30 **Services** Lift **Parking** 16 **Notes** ⊗ ⊘ in restaurant Civ Wed

BUDGET HOTEL

Innkeeper's Lodge Brighton

London Rd, Patcham BN1 8YQ

☎ 01273 552886

web: www.innkeeperslodge.com

Smart, en suite accommodation ideal for both business & leisure guests. Bedrooms are very well equipped, including Sky TV, telephone, modem points, tea & coffee making facilities, (family rooms in most locations). Complimentary breakfast. The adjacent Pub Restaurant; a Harvester, Vintage Inn, Toby Carvery, Ember Inn, Sizzling Pub co or Pub & Carvery offers an all day menu. See Hotel Groups pages for further details.

Rooms 18 rms

BUDGET HOTEL

Premier Travel Inn Brighton City Centre

144 North St BN1 1RE

☎ 0870 9906340 🖹 0870 9906341

web: www.premiertravelinn.com

dir: *From A23 follow signs for city centre. Right at lights nr Royal Pavilion, then take road ahead on left (runs adjacent to Pavilion) onto Church St, 1st left onto New Rd leading into North Street*

High quality, modern budget accommodation ideal for both families and business travellers. Spacious, en suite bedrooms feature bath and shower, satellite TV and many have telephones and modem points. The adjacent family restaurant features a wide and varied menu. For further details consult the Hotel Groups page.

Rooms 160 en suite

BUDGET HOTEL

Travelodge Brighton

Preston Rd BN1 6AU

☎ 08700 850 950 🖹 01273 554917

web: www.travelodge.co.uk

dir: *on A23 follow signs for town centre. Lodge on right*

Travelodge offers good quality, good value, modern accommodation. Ideal for families, the spacious en suite bedrooms include remote-control TV, tea and coffee-making facilities and comfortable beds. Meals can be taken at the nearby family restaurant. See Hotel Groups pages for further details.

Rooms 94 en suite S fr £26; D fr £26

EASTBOURNE

See also Wilmington

MAP 06 TV69

★★★★★ 85% ◎ ◎ **HOTEL**

Grand

King Edward's Pde BN21 4EQ

☎ 01323 412345 🖹 01323 412233

e-mail: reservations@grandeastbourne.com

dir: *on seafront W of Eastbourne, 1m from railway station*

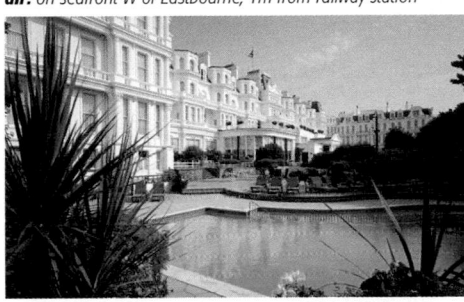

This famous Victorian hotel offers high standards of service and hospitality. The extensive public rooms feature a magnificent Great Hall, with marble columns and high ceilings, where guests can relax and enjoy afternoon tea. The spacious bedrooms provide high levels of comfort and some rooms have balconies with stunning sea views. There is a choice of restaurants and bars as well as superb leisure facilities.

Rooms 152 en suite (20 fmly) S £140-£145; D £170-£175 (incl. bkfst) **Facilities** Spa STV 🏊 ⛹ supervised Snooker Sauna Solarium Gym Putt green Jacuzzi Hairdressing, Beauty therapy 🎵 ch fac Xmas **Conf** BC Thtr 350 Class 200 Board 40 Del from £245 **Services** Lift **Parking** 60 **Notes** LB ⊘ in restaurant Civ Wed 300

★★★ 77% **HOTEL**

Hydro

Mount Rd BN20 7HZ

☎ 01323 720643 🖹 01323 641167

e-mail: sales@hydrohotel.com

dir: *from pier/seafront, right along Grand Parade. At Grand Hotel follow Hydro Hotel sign. Up South Cliff 200yds*

This well-managed and popular hotel enjoys an elevated position with views of attractive gardens and the sea beyond. The spacious bedrooms are attractive and well-equipped. In addition to the comfortable lounges, guests also have access to fitness facilities and a

continued on page 606

England

EASTBOURNE *continued*

hairdressing salon. Service is both professional and efficient throughout.

Rooms 84 rms (83 en suite) (3 fmly) (3 GF) ⊛ in 36 bedrooms S £48-£186; D £96-£186 (incl. bkfst) **Facilities** STV ⊀ ⚐ Putt green Wi-fi in bedrooms Beauty room, Hairdressing salon 3/4 Size snooter table Xmas **Conf** Thtr 140 Class 90 Board 40 **Services** Lift **Parking** 40 **Notes LB** ⊛ in restaurant RS 24-28 & 30-31 Dec Civ Wed 120

★★★ 74% HOTEL

Best Western Lansdowne

King Edward's Pde BN21 4EE
☎ 01323 725174 ▤ 01323 739721
e-mail: reception@lansdowne-hotel.co.uk
web: www.bw-lansdownehotel.co.uk
dir: hotel at W end of seafront (B2103)

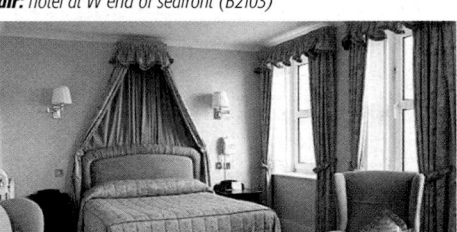

Enjoying an enviable position at the quieter end of the parade, this hotel overlooks the Western Lawns and Wish Tower and is just a few minutes' walk from many of the town's attractions. Public rooms include a variety of lounges, a range of meeting rooms and games rooms. Bedrooms are attractively decorated and many offer sea views.

Rooms 101 en suite (10 fmly) ⊛ in 25 bedrooms S £47-£75; D £94-£170 (incl. bkfst) **Facilities** STV Snooker Wi-fi in bedrooms Table tennis, Pool table Xmas **Conf** Thtr 80 Class 40 Board 40 Del from £100 **Services** Lift **Parking** 22 **Notes LB** ⊛ in restaurant Closed 2-11 Jan Civ Wed 80
See advert on opposite page

★★★ 72% HOTEL

Devonshire Park

27-29 Carlisle Rd BN21 4JR
☎ 01323 728144 ▤ 01323 419734
e-mail: info@devonshire-park-hotel.co.uk
dir: Follow signs to seafront, turn off at Wish Tower. Hotel opposite Congress Theatre

A family owned and run hotel that has seen much investment over recent times. Rooms are comfortable and well equipped, public areas are pleasing to use and it enjoys a handy location for the seafront with good parking.

Rooms 35 en suite (8 GF) ⊛ in all bedrooms S £35-£60; D £70-£120 (incl. bkfst) **Facilities** STV Xmas **Services** Lift **Parking** 25 **Notes LB** ⊗ No children 12yrs ⊛ in restaurant

★★★ 71% HOTEL

Albany Lions Hotel

Grand Pde BN21 4DJ
☎ 01323 722788 ▤ 01323 419373
e-mail: reception@albanylionshotel.com
dir: From town centre, follow signs to Seafront/Pier.

The hotel is situated close to the bandstand and holds a seafront location within walking distance of the main town shopping. A carvery dinner is served in the restaurant, which has great sea views from most tables, and a relaxing drink or afternoon tea can be enjoyed in the sun lounge.

Rooms 57 en suite (5 fmly) ⊛ in 30 bedrooms S £50-£60; D £75-£115 (incl. bkfst) **Facilities** STV ♫ ch fac Xmas **Conf** Thtr 120 Class 60 Board 40 Del from £90 **Services** Lift **Notes LB** ⊗ ⊛ in restaurant

★★★ 70% HOTEL

Best Western York House

14-22 Royal Pde BN22 7AP
☎ 01323 412918 ▤ 01323 646238
e-mail: frontdesk@yorkhousehotel.co.uk
web: www.yorkhousehotel.co.uk
dir: A27 to Eastbourne. On seafront 0.25m E of pier

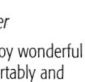

With a prime location on the seafront many rooms enjoy wonderful panoramic views. Bedrooms vary in size but are comfortably and practically fitted. Public areas include a spacious lobby, cosy bar, games room and indoor swimming pool. The only parking available is on the street in front of the hotel.

Rooms 87 en suite (15 fmly) (5 GF) ⊛ in 30 bedrooms S £55-£75; D £75-£120 (incl. bkfst) **Facilities** STV ⌨ Wi-fi in bedrooms ♫ Xmas **Conf** Thtr 100 Class 40 Board 24 Del from £100 **Services** Lift **Notes** ⊛ in restaurant Civ Wed 50

★★★ 67% HOTEL

Langham

Royal Pde BN22 7AH
☎ 01323 731451 ▤ 01323 646623
e-mail: info@langhamhotel.co.uk
web: www.langhamhotel.co.uk
dir: In Eastbourne, follow seafront signs. Hotel 0.5m E of pier

This popular hotel is situated in a prominent position with superb views of the sea and pier. Bedrooms, most of which have been refurbished, are pleasantly decorated and equipped with modern facilities. The spacious public rooms include a terrace restaurant, business lounge area and Grand Parade bar.

Rooms 85 en suite (4 fmly) (2 GF) ⊛ in 17 bedrooms S £75; D £70-£122 (incl. bkfst) **Facilities** Wi-fi in bedrooms ♫ Xmas **Conf** Thtr 80 Class 40 Board 30 Del from £95 **Services** Lift **Parking** 6 **Notes LB** ⊛ in restaurant

★★★ 64% **HOTEL**

Chatsworth

Grand Pde BN21 3YR
☎ 01323 411016 📠 01323 643270
e-mail: stay@chatsworth-hotel.com
web: www.chatsworth-hotel.com

dir: *M23 then A27 to Polegate. A2270 into Eastbourne, follow seafront & signs. Hotel near pier*

Within minutes of the town centre and pier, this attractive Edwardian hotel is located on the seafront. Service is friendly and helpful throughout the public areas, which consist of the new Chatsworth Bar, a cosy lounge and the Devonshire Restaurant. Bedrooms, many with sea views, are traditional in style and have a range of facilities.

Rooms 47 en suite (2 fmly) ⊗ in 10 bedrooms S £55-£65; D £95-£125 (incl. bkfst) **Facilities** STV ♫ Xmas **Conf** Thtr 100 Class 60 Board 40 Del from £102.50 **Services** Lift **Notes LB** ⊗ in restaurant Civ Wed 140

See advert on this page

★★★ 62% **HOTEL**

Mansion Lions Hotel

Grand Pde BN21 3YS
☎ 01323 727411 📠 01323 720665
e-mail: reception@mansionlionshotel.com

dir: *In town centre follow signs to the Seafront/Pier. Hotel on seafront*

Directly overlooking the beach, this Victorian hotel is only two minutes' walk from the magnificent pier, the shopping centre and bandstand. The well equipped bedrooms are comfortably furnished and some have sea views. An enjoyable four-course evening meal, and a filling breakfast is served in the Hartington Restaurant. A pretty garden can be found at the back of the hotel.

Rooms 95 en suite (6 fmly) (4 GF) ⊗ in 60 bedrooms S £45-£55; D £65-£105 (incl. bkfst) **Facilities** STV ♫ ch fac Xmas **Conf** Thtr 150 Class 80 Board 40 Del from £90 **Services** Lift **Notes LB** ⊗ ⊗ in restaurant Civ Wed 150

★★ 74% **HOTEL**

New Wilmington

25 Compton St BN21 4DU
☎ 01323 721219 📠 01323 746255
e-mail: info@new-wilmington-hotel.co.uk
web: www.new-wilmington-hotel.co.uk

dir: *A22 to Eastbourne seafront. Right along promenade to Wish Tower. Right, then left at end of road, hotel 2nd on left*

This friendly, family-run hotel is conveniently located close to the seafront, the Congress Theatre and Winter Gardens. Public rooms are

continued on page 808

England

EASTBOURNE *continued*

well presented and include a cosy bar, small comfortable non-smoking lounge and a spacious restaurant. Bedrooms are comfortably appointed and tastefully decorated; family and superior bedrooms are available.

Rooms 40 en suite (14 fmly) (3 GF) ⊛ in 12 bedrooms S £39.25-£76.75; D £68.50-£89.50 (incl. bkfst) **Facilities** FTV Wi-fi available ♫ ch fac Xmas **Conf** Thtr 40 Class 20 Board 20 **Services** Lift **Parking** 2 **Notes LB** ⊗ ⊛ in restaurant Closed 3 Jan - mid-Feb

★★ 71% HOTEL

Oban
King Edwards Pde BN21 4DS
☎ 01323 731581 📄 01323 721994
e-mail: info@oban-hotel.co.uk
web: www.oban-hotel.co.uk
dir: opposite Wish Tower on seafront

Situated on the seafront overlooking the Wishing Tower this privately owned hotel provides a friendly welcome. Bedrooms vary in size and are pleasantly decorated; some of bedrooms and bathrooms have now been upgraded to a good modern standard. Public areas include a smartly decorated large open-plan lounge bar area with a small terrace. Enjoyable meals are served in the lower ground-floor dining room.

Rooms 31 en suite (2 fmly) (4 GF) D £60-£120 (incl. bkfst & dinner) **Facilities** ♫ Xmas **Services** Lift **Notes LB** ⊛ in restaurant

★★ 68% HOTEL

Courtlands
3-5 Wilmington Gardens BN21 4JN
☎ 01323 723737 📄 01323 732902
e-mail: bookings@courtlandseastbourne.com
dir: Turn off Grand Parade at Carlisle Rd, hotel is opposite Congress Theatre

Situated opposite the Congress Theatre, this hotel, now under new ownership, is just a short walk from both the seafront and Devonshire Park. Bedrooms are comfortably furnished and pleasantly decorated. Public areas are smartly appointed and include a cosy bar, a separate lounge and an attractive downstairs dining room.

Rooms 46 en suite (4 fmly) (3 GF) ⊛ in all bedrooms S £36-£48; D £72-£100 (incl. bkfst) **Facilities** STV ⤓ Wi-fi in bedrooms ♫ Xmas **Conf** BC Thtr 60 Class 60 Board 60 **Services** Lift **Parking** 36 **Notes LB** ⊛ in restaurant

★★ 67% HOTEL

Afton
2-8 Cavendish Place BN21 3EJ
☎ 01323 733162 📄 01323 645720
e-mail: info@aftonhotel.com
dir: from A22, A27 or A259 follow directions to seafront. Hotel by pier

This is a friendly family run hotel that has now changed hands. Ideally located in the centre of this town, opposite the pier and close to the shopping centre. Bedrooms vary in size but are all comfortable and well co-ordinated.

Rooms 56 en suite (4 fmly) (4 GF) ⊛ in all bedrooms S £40-£55; D £65-£105 (incl. bkfst) **Facilities** ♫ Xmas **Services** Lift **Notes LB** ⊛ in restaurant

★★ 67% HOTEL

Queens Hotel
Marine Pde BN21 3DY
☎ 01323 722822 📄 01323 731056
e-mail: queens.eastbourne@alfatravel.co.uk
web: www.alfatravel.co.uk
dir: proceed to seafront, hotel opposite pier on left

Leisureplex

Popular with tour groups, this long-established hotel enjoys a central, prominent seafront location overlooking the pier. Spacious public areas include a choice of lounges, and regular entertainment is also provided. Bedrooms are suitably appointed and equipped.

Rooms 122 en suite (1 fmly) ⊛ in all bedrooms S £34-£46; D £56-£80 (incl. bkfst) **Facilities** FTV Snooker ♫ Xmas **Services** Lift **Parking** 50 **Notes LB** ⊗ ⊛ in restaurant Closed Jan RS Nov, Feb-Mar

★★ 66% HOTEL

Alexandra
King Edwards Pde BN21 4DR
☎ 01323 720131 📄 01323 417769
e-mail: alexandrahotel@mistral.co.uk
web: http://alexandrahotel.eastbourne.biz
dir: at junct of Carlisle Rd & King Edward Parade

Located at the west end of the town, opposite the Wishing Tower, this hotel boasts panoramic views of the sea from many rooms. Bedrooms vary in size but are comfortable with good facilities for guests. A warm welcome is guaranteed at this long-standing, family run establishment.

Rooms 38 en suite (2 fmly) (3 GF) ⊛ in all bedrooms S £30-£45; D £60-£90 (incl. bkfst) **Facilities** ♫ Xmas **Services** Lift **Notes LB** ⊛ in restaurant Closed Jan & Feb RS Mar

★★ 64% HOTEL

West Rocks
Grand Pde BN21 4DL
☎ 01323 725217 📄 01323 720421
e-mail: westrockshotel@btinternet.com
dir: western end of seafront

Ideally located near to the pier and bandstand, this hotel is only a short walk from the town centre. Bedrooms vary in size, with many offering a stunning sea views. Guests have the choice of two comfortable lounges and a bar.

Rooms 47 rms (45 en suite) (8 fmly) (6 GF) **Facilities** ♫ **Conf** BC Thtr 20 Class 12 Board 12 **Services** Lift **Notes** ⊗ ⊛ in restaurant Closed 3 Jan -20 Feb

BUDGET HOTEL

Premier Travel Inn Eastbourne North

Polegate Roundabout, Polegate BN26 6QL

☎ 0870 850 0950

web: www.premiertravelinn.com

At the time of going to press, the star classification for this hotel was not confirmed. Please refer to the AA internet site www.theAA.com for current information.

Rooms 40 en suite

BUDGET HOTEL

Innkeeper's Lodge Eastbourne

Highfield Park, Willingdon Drove BN23 8AL

☎ 01323 507222

web: www.innkeeperslodge.com

Smart, en suite accommodation ideal for both business & leisure guests. Bedrooms are very well equipped, including Sky TV, telephone, modem points, tea & coffee making facilities, (family rooms in most locations). Complimentary breakfast. The adjacent Pub Restaurant; a Harvester, Vintage Inn, Toby Carvery, Ember Inn, Sizzling Pubco or Pub & Carvery offers an all day menu. See Hotel Groups pages for further details.

Rooms 42 en suite

BUDGET HOTEL

Premier Travel Inn Eastbourne

Willingdon Dr BN23 8AL

☎ 08701 977089 ▤ 01323 767379

web: www.premiertravelinn.com

dir: A22, towards Eastbourne. At next rdbt left. Inn on the left

High quality, modern budget accommodation ideal for both families and business travellers. Spacious, en suite bedrooms feature bath and shower, satellite TV and many have telephones and modem points. The adjacent family restaurant features a wide and varied menu. For further details consult the Hotel Groups page

Rooms 47 en suite

FOREST ROW   MAP 06 TQ43

INSPECTORS' CHOICE

★★★★ @@ @ HOTEL

Ashdown Park Hotel and Country Club

Wych Cross RH18 5JR

☎ 01342 824988 ▤ 01342 826206

e-mail: reservations@ashdownpark.com

web: www.ashdownpark.com

dir: A264 to East Grinstead, then A22 to Eastbourne, 2m S of Forest Row at Wych Cross traffic lights. Left to Hartfield, hotel on right 0.75m

Situated in 186 acres of landscaped gardens and parkland, this impressive country house enjoys a peaceful countryside setting in the heart of the Ashdown Forest. Bedrooms are individually styled and decorated. Public rooms include a chapel, now converted to

continued

a conference room, extensive indoor and outdoor leisure facilities, including three drawing rooms, a cocktail bar and restaurant plus an 18-hole, par 3 golf course.

Ashdown Park Hotel and Country Club

Rooms 106 en suite (16 GF) ◈ in 49 bedrooms S £140-£345; D £170-£375 (incl. bkfst) **Facilities** Spa STV ☜ ↨ 18 ◢ Snooker Sauna Solarium Gym ⇘ Putt green Jacuzzi Wi-fi available Beauty/Hair salon, Aerobics, Treatment room, Mountain bike hire, Steam room ♫ ch fac Xmas **Conf** BC Thtr 170 Class 80 Board 40 Del from £235 **Services** Lift **Parking** 200 **Notes** LB ⊗ ◈ in restaurant Civ Wed 150

★★ 72% HOTEL

Roebuck

OLD ENGLISH INNS

Wych Cross RH18 5JL

☎ 01342 823811 ▤ 01342 824790

e-mail: 6499@greeneking.co.uk

web: www.oldenglish.co.uk

dir: M25 junct 6, follow A22 towards E Grinstead or Eastbourne, pass E Grinstead, hotel is on A22.

The well-equipped bedrooms of this skilfully extended 17th-century house have undergone a complete refurbishment, which has resulted in good standards of comfort and décor; some ground floor rooms are available. Staff throughout the hotel are friendly and welcoming, creating a relaxed atmosphere. Meals are provided in both the restaurant and more informally in the bar.

Rooms 30 en suite (0 GF) ◈ in 29 bedrooms S £70; D £100 (incl. bkfst) **Facilities** STV Xmas **Conf** Thtr 80 Class 50 Board 50 Del £125 **Parking** 80 **Notes** ◈ in restaurant Civ Wed 100

HAILSHAM   MAP 06 TQ50

★★★ 71% HOTEL

Boship Farm

Lower Dicker BN27 4AT

☎ 01323 844826 ▤ 01323 843945

e-mail: info@boshipfarmhotel.co.uk

dir: on A22 at Boship rdbt, junct of A22, A267 and A271

Dating back to 1652, a lovely old farmhouse forms the hub of this hotel, which is set in 17 acres of well-tended grounds. Guests have the use of an all-weather tennis court, an outdoor pool and a croquet lawn. Bedrooms are smartly appointed and well-equipped; most have views across open fields and countryside. The hotel is under new ownership.

Rooms 47 annexe en suite (5 fmly) (21 GF) ◈ in 26 bedrooms S £70-£95; D £90-£135 (incl. bkfst) **Facilities** ⊰ ◢ Sauna ⇘ Jacuzzi ch fac Xmas **Conf** Thtr 175 Class 40 Board 46 Del from £100 **Parking** 100 **Notes** LB ◈ in restaurant Civ Wed 100

HAILSHAM *continued*

★★ 75% HOTEL

The Olde Forge Hotel & Restaurant

Magham Down BN27 1PN

☎ 01323 842893 🖹 01323 842893

e-mail: theoldeforgehotel@tesco.net

web: www.theoldeforgehotel.co.uk

dir: *off Boship rdbt on A271 to Bexhill & Herstmonceux. 3m on left*

In the heart of the countryside, this family-run hotel offers a friendly welcome and an informal atmosphere. The bedrooms are attractively decorated with thoughtful extras. The restaurant, with its timbered beams and log fires, was a forge in the 16th century; today it has a good local reputation for its cuisine and service.

Rooms 7 en suite ⊗ in all bedrooms S fr £48; D fr £75 (incl. bkfst) **Parking** 11 **Notes LB** ⊗ in restaurant

BUDGET HOTEL

Travelodge Hellingly Eastbourne

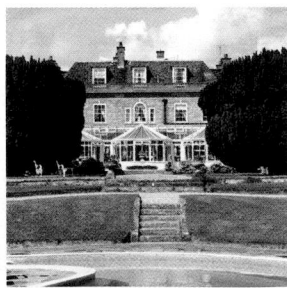

Boship Roundabout, Hellingly BN27 4DT

☎ 08700 850 950 🖹 01323 844556

web: www.travelodge.co.uk

dir: *on A22 at Boship rdbt*

Travelodge offers good quality, good value, modern accommodation. Ideal for families, the spacious en suite bedrooms include remote-control TV, tea and coffee-making facilities and comfortable beds. Meals can be taken at the nearby family restaurant. See Hotel Groups pages for further details.

Rooms 58 en suite S fr £26; D fr £26

HASTINGS & ST LEONARDS   MAP 07 TQ80

★★★ 72% HOTEL

Beauport Park

Battle Rd TN38 8EA

☎ 01424 851222 🖹 01424 852465

e-mail: reservations@beauportparkhotel.co.uk

web: www.beauportparkhotel.co.uk

dir: *3m N off A2100*

Elegant Georgian manor house set in 40 acres of mature gardens on the outskirts of Hastings. The individually decorated bedrooms are tastefully furnished and thoughtfully equipped with modern facilities. Public rooms convey much original character and feature a large

continued

conservatory, a lounge bar, a restaurant and a further lounge, as well as conference and banqueting rooms.

Rooms 25 en suite (2 fmly) ⊗ in 11 bedrooms S fr £95; D fr £130 (incl. bkfst) **Facilities** STV 🏖 supervised 🎾 ⌀ 18 🏊 Riding Sauna Gym 🏌 Putt green Jacuzzi Country walks around estate 🎵 Xmas **Conf** Thtr 70 Class 25 Board 30 Del from £140 **Parking** 60 **Notes LB** ⊗ in restaurant Civ Wed 70

See advert on opposite page

★★★ 70% HOTEL

Best Western Royal Victoria

Marina, St Leonards-on-Sea TN38 0BD

☎ 01424 445544 🖹 01424 721995

e-mail: reception@royalvichotel.co.uk

web: www.royalvichotel.co.uk

dir: *on A259 seafront road 1m W of Hastings pier*

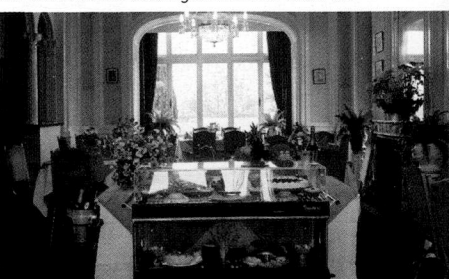

This imposing 18th-century property is situated in a prominent position overlooking the sea. A superb marble staircase leads up from the lobby to the main public areas on the first floor, which has panoramic views of the sea. The spacious bedrooms are pleasantly decorated and well equipped, and include duplex and family suites.

Rooms 50 en suite (15 fmly) S £60-£120; D £70-£160 (incl. bkfst) **Facilities** Xmas **Conf** Thtr 100 Class 40 Board 40 Del from £100 **Services** Lift **Parking** 6 **Notes LB** ⊗ in restaurant Civ Wed 50

★★★ 68% HOTEL

High Beech

Eisenhower Dr, Battle Rd, St Leonards on Sea TN37 7BS

☎ 01424 851383 🖹 01424 854265

e-mail: highbeech@barbox.net

dir: *Off A2100 into Washington Ave from Battle Rd.*

Now in new hands this privately owned hotel is situated between the historic towns of Hastings and Battle in a woodland setting. The generously proportioned bedrooms are pleasantly decorated and

continued

thoughtfully equipped. Public rooms include St. Patricks Bar, which also doubles as the lounge area, and the elegant Wedgwood Restaurant where an interesting and varied menu is served.

Rooms 17 en suite (4 fmly) ⊘ in 14 bedrooms S £65; D £95-£125 (incl. bkfst) **Facilities** STV Wi-fi in bedrooms **Conf** BC Thtr 200 Class 100 Board 50 Del from £90 **Parking** 70 **Notes LB** ⊗ ⊘ in restaurant Civ Wed 55

See advert on this page

★★ 71% ◎ **HOTEL**

Chatsworth

Carlisle Pde TN34 1JG

☎ 01424 720188 📠 01424 445865

e-mail: info@chatsworthhotel.com

dir: *A21 to town centre. At seafront turn right before lights.*

Enjoying a central position on the seafront, close to the pier, this much-improved hotel is a short walk from the old town and within easy reach of the county's many attractions. Bedrooms are smartly decorated, equipped with a range of extras and many rooms enjoy

continued on page 612

The Beauport Park Hotel

Hastings, Sussex TN38 8EA ★ ★ ★

Tel: 01424 851222 Fax: 01424 852465

www.beauportparkhotel.co.uk

A Georgian country house hotel set in 38 acres of parkland with indoor swimming pool, gym, sauna, steam room, tennis court, putting green, badminton lawn, French boules, outdoor chess, croquet lawn and country walks. Candle-lit restaurant and brasserie and open log fires. Adjacent to 18 hole and 9 hole golf courses and riding stables.

Resident Directors:
Kenneth Melsom and Stephen Bayes

Special country house bargain breaks available all year. Please send for our colour brochure and tariff. Inclusive Golfing Breaks also available.

AA ★ ★ ◎ **The**
Chatsworth Hotel

Carlisle Parade, Hastings TN34 1JG
Tel: 01424 720188 Fax: 01424 445865
Email: info@chatsworthhotel.com
Web: www.chatsworthhotel.com

The Chatsworth Hotel is one of Hasting's premier hotels.
Ideally situated on the seafront and only minutes from
the town centre. Whether staying on business or pleasure
the Chatsworth is the place to stay. Easy walking to all
local attractions, the castle, Hastings Caves, Old Town
and local shops. Stay at the Chatsworth and explore the
South East and all it has to offer. The Jali Bar &
Restaurant is a reputed feature of the hotel offering
superb Indian & European delicacies. Please call today
to learn of our latest offers.

HIGH BEECH HOTEL

EISENHOWER DRIVE, BATTLE ROAD,
ST LEONARDS ON SEA, HASTINGS,
EAST SUSSEX TN37 7BS

Tel: 01424 851383   Fax: 01424 854265
Email: highbeech@barbox.net
www.highbeechhotel.com

Privately Owned hotel, situated between two historic towns of Hastings & Battle — Heart of 1066 Countryside.

Ideal location for both
seaside and touring.
Luxury accommodation,
all rooms en-suite, some
executive suites with king
size beds and jacuzzi baths.
Colour television with free
satellite stations. Superb
French/English cuisine,
served in elegant Edwardian
restaurant. Special breaks
available throughout the
year. Conference & function
facilities for up to 250.

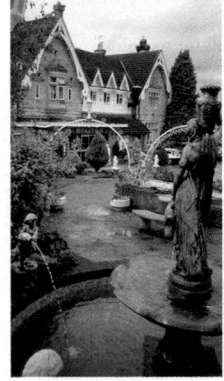

Choose the
High Beech Hotel
for a Professional
and Caring Service   AA ★ ★ ★

HASTINGS & ST LEONARDS *continued*

splendid sea views. Guests can also enjoy an exciting Indian meal in the contemporary restaurant.

Chatsworth

Rooms 52 en suite (5 fmly) ⊛ in 37 bedrooms S £45-£65; D £50-£90 (incl. bkfst) **Facilities** STV Xmas **Conf** Thtr 40 Class 20 Board 20 Del from £75 **Services** Lift **Parking** 8 **Notes LB** ⊛ ⊛ in restaurant

See advert on page 611

BUDGET HOTEL

Premier Travel Inn Hastings

premier travel inn ●

1 John Macadam Way, St Leonards-on-Sea TN37 7DB

☎ 08701 977128 📄 01424 756911

web: www.premiertravelinn.com

dir: into Hastings on A21. Inn on right after junct with A2100

High quality, modern budget accommodation ideal for both families and business travellers. Spacious, en suite bedrooms feature bath and shower, satellite TV and many have telephones and modem points. The adjacent family restaurant features a wide and varied menu. For further details consult the Hotel Groups page.

Rooms 44 en suite

BUDGET HOTEL

Travelodge Hastings

Travelodge

Bohemia Rd TN34 1ET

☎ 01424 439222 📄 01424 437277

web: www.travelodge.co.uk

dir: A21 into Hastings. Police HQ and courts on left, hotel next left before ambulance HQ

Travelodge offers good quality, good value, modern accommodation. Ideal for families, the spacious en suite bedrooms include remote-control TV, tea and coffee-making facilities and comfortable beds. Meals can be taken at the nearby family restaurant. See Hotel Groups pages for further details.

Rooms 40 en suite S fr £26; D fr £26 **Conf** Thtr 250 Class 150 Board 120

HOVE
See **Brighton & Hove**

LEWES MAP 06 TQ41

★★★ 79% ◉◉ **HOTEL**

Shelleys Hotel

High St BN7 1XS

☎ 01273 472361 📄 01273 483152

e-mail: info@shelleys-hotel-lewes.com

web: www.shelleys-hotel.com

dir: A23 to Brighton onto A27 to Lewes. At 1st rdbt left for town centre, after x-rds hotel on left

This elegant hotel enjoys a central location and is steeped in history, with previous owners including the Earl of Dorset. Nowadays Shelleys boasts beautifully appointed bedrooms, furnished and decorated in a traditional style. The elegant restaurant overlooks the enclosed garden and serves good food using local produce.

Rooms 19 en suite (2 fmly) ⊛ in 4 bedrooms **Facilities** STV ⬥ **Conf** Thtr 50 Class 24 Board 28 **Parking** 25 **Notes LB** ⊛ in restaurant Civ Wed 50

NEWHAVEN MAP 06 TQ40

BUDGET HOTEL

Premier Travel Inn Newhaven

premier travel inn ●

The Drove, Avis Rd BN9 0AG

☎ 08701 977192 📄 01273 612359

web: www.premiertravelinn.com

dir: from A26 (New Rd) through Drove Industrial Estate, left turn after underpass. On same complex as Sainsburys, A259

High quality, modern budget accommodation ideal for both families and business travellers. Spacious, en suite bedrooms feature bath and shower, satellite TV and many have telephones and modem points. The adjacent family restaurant features a wide and varied menu. For further details consult the Hotel Groups page.

Rooms 40 en suite

The vast majority of establishments in this guide accept credit and debit cards. We indicate only those that don't take any

Some hotels have restricted service during quieter months, and at this time some of the facilities will not be available

NEWICK   MAP 06 TQ42

INSPECTORS' CHOICE

★★★ ◎◎ HOTEL

Newick Park Hotel & Country Estate

BN8 4SB

☎ 01825 723633 🖹 01825 723969

e-mail: bookings@newickpark.co.uk

web: www.newickpark.co.uk

dir: *S off A272 in Newick between Haywards Heath and Uckfield. Pass church, left at junct and hotel 0.25m on right*

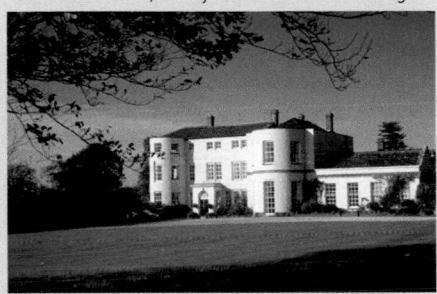

Delightful Grade II listed Georgian country house set amid 250 acres of Sussex parkland and landscaped gardens. The spacious, individually decorated bedrooms are tastefully furnished, thoughtfully equipped and have superb views of the grounds; many rooms have huge American king-size beds. The comfortable public rooms include a study, a sitting room, lounge bar and an elegant restaurant.

Rooms 13 en suite 3 annexe en suite (5 fmly) (1 GF) ⊗ in all bedrooms S £125; D £165-£285 (incl. bkfst) **Facilities** STV ↖ ॐ Fishing ♨ Wi-fi available Badminton, Tank driving, Quad biking, Clay pigeon shooting Xmas **Conf** Thtr 80 Class 40 Board 40 Del £205 **Parking** 52 **Notes LB** ⊗ in restaurant Civ Wed 100

See advert on this page

PEASMARSH   MAP 07 TQ82

★★★ 78% HOTEL

Best Western Flackley Ash

TN31 6YH

Best Western

☎ 01797 230651 🖹 01797 230510

e-mail: enquiries@flackleyashhotel.co.uk

web: www.flackleyashhotel.co.uk

dir: *exit A21 onto A268 to Newenden, next left A268 to Rye. Hotel on left on entering Peasmarsh*

Five acres of beautifully kept grounds are the lovely backdrop to this elegant Georgian country house. The hotel is superbly situated for exploring the many local attractions, including the ancient Cinque Port of Rye, just a short drive away. The pleasantly decorated bedrooms have co-ordinated fabrics and many thoughtful touches.

Rooms 45 en suite (5 fmly) S £87-£127; D £144-£194 (incl. bkfst) **Facilities** Spa STV 🔲 supervised Sauna Gym ♨ Putt green Jacuzzi Wi-fi in bedrooms Beauty salon ch fac Xmas **Conf** BC Thtr 100 Class 60 Board 40 Del from £125 **Parking** 80 **Notes LB** ⊗ in restaurant Civ Wed 100

ROTTINGDEAN   MAP 06 TQ30

★★ 69% HOTEL

White Horse

OLD ENGLISH INNS

Marine Dr BN2 7HB

☎ 01273 300301 & 0800 917 3085 🖹 01273 308716

e-mail: 5308@greeneking.co.uk

web: www.oldenglish.co.uk

dir: *A27, at Falmer take B2123 to Rottingdean. Hotel on seafront*

In a prime seaside location with extensive views, this hotel offers well equipped modern accommodation and lively lounge bar and restaurant serving food throughout the day. It has good off-road parking too, and quick and easy access to Brighton.

Rooms 18 en suite ⊗ in 15 bedrooms S £65-£75; D £85-£130 (incl. bkfst) **Facilities** STV Xmas **Conf** Thtr 50 Board 25 Del from £93 **Parking** 45 **Notes LB** ⊗ ⊗ in restaurant

England

RYE   MAP 07 TQ92

★★★ 75% ✹ HOTEL

Mermaid Inn
Mermaid St TN31 7EY
☎ 01797 223065 & 223788 📠 01797 225069
e-mail: mermaidinnrye@btclick.com
web: www.mermaidinn.com
dir: A259, follow signs to town centre then into Mermaid Street

Situated near the top of a cobbled side street, this famous smugglers' inn is steeped in history. The charming interior has many architectural features such as attractive stone work. The bedrooms vary in size and style but all are tastefully furnished. Delightful public rooms include a choice of lounges, cosy bar and smart restaurant.

Rooms 31 en suite (5 fmly) S £85-£90; D £160-£220 (incl. bkfst)
Facilities Xmas **Conf** Thtr 50 Class 40 Board 30 Del from £160
Parking 25 **Notes LB** ⊗ ⊘ in restaurant

★★★ 75% HOTEL

Rye Lodge
Hilders Cliff TN31 7LD
☎ 01797 223838 📠 01797 223585
e-mail: info@ryelodge.co.uk
web: www.ryelodge.co.uk
dir: one-way system in Rye, follow signs for town centre, through Landgate arch, hotel 100yds on right

Standing in an elevated position, Rye Lodge has panoramic views across Romney Marshes and the Rother Estuary. Bedrooms come in a variety of sizes and styles; they are attractively decorated, tastefully furnished and thoughtfully equipped. Public rooms feature indoor leisure facilities, and The Terrace Room Restaurant where an interesting choice of home-made dishes is offered.

Rooms 18 en suite (5 GF) ⊘ in 4 bedrooms S £75-£120; D £100-£200 (incl. bkfst) **Facilities Spa** STV 🔲 Sauna Aromatherapy Steam cabinet Xmas **Parking** 20 **Notes LB** ⊘ in restaurant

See advert on opposite page

★★★ 74% **HOTEL**

The Hope Anchor
Watchbell St TN31 7HA
☎ 01797 222216 📠 01797 223796
e-mail: info@thehopeanchor.co.uk
web: www.thehopeanchor.co.uk
dir: from A268, Quayside, turn right into Wish Ward, up Mermaid Street, right into West Street, right into Watchbell Street, hotel at end

This historic inn sits high above the town with enviable views out over the harbour and Romney Marsh, and is accessible via delightful cobbled streets. A relaxed and friendly atmosphere prevails within the cosy public rooms, while the attractively furnished bedrooms are well equipped and many enjoy good views over the marshes.

Rooms 15 en suite (1 fmly) ⊘ in all bedrooms S £65-£85; D £110-£210 (incl. bkfst) **Facilities** Xmas **Notes LB** ⊗ ⊘ in restaurant Closed 9 Jan-16 Jan

ST LEONARDS-ON-SEA
See **Hastings & St Leonards**

TICEHURST   MAP 06 TQ63

★★★★ 80% ✹ HOTEL

Dale Hill Hotel & Golf Club
TN5 7DQ
☎ 01580 200112 📠 01580 201249
e-mail: info@dalehill.co.uk
web: www.dalehill.co.uk
dir: M25 junct 5/A21. 5m after Lamberhurst turn right at traffic lights onto B2087 to Flimwell. Hotel 1m on the left

This modern hotel is situated just a short drive from the village. Extensive public rooms include a lounge bar, a conservatory brasserie, a formal restaurant and the Spike Bar, which is mainly frequented by

continued

golf club members and has a lively atmosphere. The hotel also has two superb 18-hole golf courses, swimming pool and gym.

Rooms 35 en suite (8 fmly) (23 GF) ❷ in all bedrooms S £110-£130; D £120-£250 (incl. bkfst) **Facilities** STV ⬆ Sauna Gym Putt green Covered driving range, putting green, Pool table and golf course on site. Xmas **Conf** Thtr 120 Class 50 Board 50 Del from £150 **Services** Lift **Parking** 220 **Notes LB** ❽ ❷ in restaurant Civ Wed 150

UCKFIELD   MAP 06 TQ42

★★★★ 87% ⚫⚫ HOTEL

Buxted Park
Country House Hotel

Hand PICKED
HOTELS

Buxted TN22 4AY

☎ 01825 733333 📠 01825 732 990

e-mail: buxtedpark@handpicked.co.uk

web: www.handpicked.co.uk

dir: From A26 (Uckfield bypass) take A272 signed Buxted. Through lights, hotel 1m on right

An attractive Grade II listed Georgian mansion dating back to the 17th century. The property is set amidst 300 acres of beautiful countryside and landscaped gardens. The stylish, thoughtfully equipped bedrooms are split between the main house and the modern garden wing. An interesting choice of dishes is served in the restaurant.

Rooms 44 en suite (6 fmly) (16 GF) ❷ in 22 bedrooms S £150; D £190 (incl. bkfst) **Facilities** STV Fishing Snooker Sauna Gym ⬆ Putt green Wi-fi available Clay pigeon shoot, Archery, fishing, Mountain biking, Orienteering Xmas **Conf** Thtr 130 Class 70 Board 60 **Services** Lift **Parking** 150 **Notes LB** ❷ in restaurant Civ Wed 130

INSPECTORS' CHOICE

★★★ ⚫⚫ HOTEL

Horsted Place

Little Horsted TN22 5TS

☎ 01825 750581 📠 01825 750459

e-mail: hotel@horstedplace.co.uk

dir: 2m S on A26 towards Lewes

Dating from 1850, Horsted Place is one of Britain's finest examples of Gothic revivalist architecture. It is situated in extensive landscaped grounds, with a tennis court and croquet lawn, and is adjacent to the East Sussex National Golf Club. The spacious bedrooms are attractively decorated, tastefully furnished

continued

and equipped with many thoughtful touches such as flowers and books. Most rooms also have a separate sitting area.

Rooms 17 en suite 3 annexe en suite (5 fmly) (2 GF) S £130-£350; D £130-£350 (incl. bkfst) **Facilities** STV ⬇ 36 ☺ ⬆ Wi-fi in bedrooms ♫ Xmas **Conf** Thtr 80 Class 50 Board 40 Del from £160 **Services** Lift **Parking** 32 **Notes LB** ❽ No children 7yrs ❷ in restaurant Civ Wed 100

WILMINGTON   MAP 06 TQ50

⚫⚫ RESTAURANT WITH ROOMS

Crossways

Lewes Rd BN26 5SG

☎ 01323 482455 📠 01323 487811

e-mail: stay@crosswayshotel.co.uk

web: www.crosswayshotel.co.uk

dir: On A27 between Lewes and Polegate, 2m E of Alfriston rdbt

A well-established restaurant with a good local reputation is the focus of this attractive property. Bedrooms are also provided, and all are individually decorated with taste and style and superior rooms are available. Guest comfort is paramount and there are excellent facilities and the kind of hospitality that ensures guests return often.

Rooms 7 en suite S £62; D £85-£110 **Parking** 30 **Notes LB** ❽ No children 12yrs ❷ in restaurant Closed 24 Dec-23 Jan

England

SUSSEX, WEST

ARUNDEL
MAP 06 TQ00

★★★ 71% HOTEL

Norfolk Arms

Forestdale Hotels

High St BN18 9AB
☎ 01903 882101 📠 01903 884275
e-mail: norfolk.arms@forestdale.com
web: www.forestdale.com

Built by the 10th Duke of Norfolk, this Georgian coaching inn enjoys a superb setting beneath the battlements of Arundel Castle. Bedrooms come in a variety of sizes and styles, all are well equipped. Public areas include two bars, a comfortable lounge, a traditional English restaurant and a range of meeting rooms.

Rooms 21 en suite 13 annexe en suite (4 fmly) (8 GF) ⊛ in 11 bedrooms S £75; D £125 (incl. bkfst) **Facilities** Xmas **Conf** Thtr 100 Class 40 Board 40 Del from £95 **Parking** 34 **Notes LB** ⊛ in restaurant Civ Wed 60

★★ 69% HOTEL

Comfort Inn

Comfort

Crossbush BN17 7QQ
☎ 01903 840840 📠 01903 849849
e-mail: reservations@comfortinnarundel.co.uk
dir: A27/A284, 1st right into services

This modern, purpose-built hotel provides a good base for exploring the nearby historic town. Good access to local road networks and a range of meeting rooms, all air-conditioned, also make this an ideal venue for business guests. Bedrooms are spacious, smartly decorated and well equipped.

Rooms 53 en suite (25 GF) ⊛ in 39 bedrooms D £55-£120 (incl. bkfst) **Facilities** STV Wi-fi in bedrooms Xmas **Conf** BC Thtr 30 Class 30 Board 30 **Parking** 53 **Notes LB** ⊛ in restaurant

BUDGET HOTEL

Innkeeper's Arundel

Innkeeper's Lodge

Fontwell Park Racecourse, Fontwell BN18 0SY
☎ 0870 2430500
web: www.innkeeperslodge.com

Smart, en suite accommodation ideal for both business & leisure guests. Bedrooms are very well equipped, including Sky TV, telephone, modem points, tea & coffee making facilities, (family rooms in most locations). Complimentary breakfast. The adjacent Pub Restaurant; a Harvester, Vintage Inn, Toby Carvery, Ember Inn, Sizzling Pubco or Pub & Carvery offers an all day menu. See Hotel Groups pages for further details.

Rooms 40 en suite

BUDGET HOTEL

Premier Travel Inn Arundel

premier travel inn

Crossbush Ln BN18 9PQ
☎ 08701 977016 📠 01903 884381
web: www.premiertravelinn.com
dir: 1m E of Arundel at junct of A27/A284

High quality, modern budget accommodation ideal for both families and business travellers. Spacious, en suite bedrooms feature bath and shower, satellite TV and many have telephones and modem points. The adjacent family restaurant features a wide and varied menu. For further details consult the Hotel Groups page.

Rooms 30 en suite **Conf** Thtr 50 Board 26

BOGNOR REGIS
MAP 06 SZ99

★★★ 73% HOTEL

Royal Norfolk

The Esplanade PO21 2LH
☎ 01243 826222 📠 01243 826325
e-mail: accommodation@royalnorfolkhotel.com
web: www.royalnorfolkhotel.com
dir: from A259 follow Longford Rd, through lights to Canada Grove to T-junct. Turn right and take 2nd exit at roundabout. Hotel on right

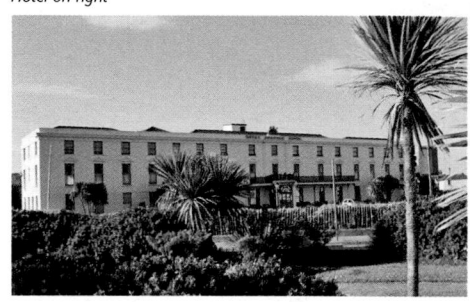

On the Esplanade, but set back behind its own lawns and gardens, this fine-looking hotel has been welcoming guests since Regency times. Today the traditionally furnished bedrooms, four with four-poster beds, are well provided with all the modern comforts. Public areas offer sea views from the elegant restaurant and comfortable lobby lounge.

Rooms 41 en suite (6 fmly) ⊛ in all bedrooms S £55-£80; D £110-£150 (incl. bkfst) **Facilities** ♫ Xmas **Conf** BC Thtr 140 Class 140 Board 140 Del from £85 **Services** Lift **Parking** 60 **Notes LB** ⊛ in restaurant Civ Wed 100

★★★ 70% HOTEL

The Inglenook

255 Pagham Rd, Nyetimber PO21 3QB
☎ 01243 262495 & 265411 📠 01243 262668
e-mail: reception@the-inglenook.com
dir: A27 to Vinnetrow Rd, left at Walnut Tree, 2.5m on right

This 16th-century inn retains much of its original character, including exposed beams throughout. Bedrooms are individually decorated and vary in size. There is a cosy lounge, a well-kept garden and a bar that offers a popular evening menu and convivial atmosphere. The restaurant, overlooking the garden, also serves enjoyable cuisine.

Rooms 18 en suite (1 fmly) (2 GF) ⊛ in all bedrooms S £50-£60; D £90-£200 (incl. bkfst) **Facilities** STV Xmas **Conf** BC Thtr 100 Class 50 Board 50 Del from £95 **Parking** 35 **Notes LB** ⊛ in restaurant Civ Wed 80

continued

★★ 71% HOTEL

Beachcroft

Clyde Rd, Felpham Village PO22 7AH
☎ 01243 827142 ▤ 01243 863500
e-mail: reservations@beachcroft-hotel.co.uk
web: www.beachcroft-hotel.co.uk

dir: From A259 between Chichester and Littlehampton at
Felpham, follow signs for the village, hotel signed.

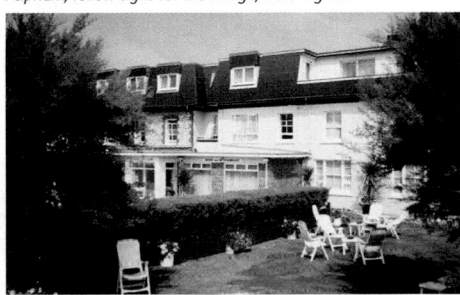

This popular family-run hotel, now under new ownership, overlooks a
secluded part of the seafront. Bedrooms are bright and spacious with
a good range of facilities, and leisure facilities include a heated indoor
swimming pool. Diners may choose from the varied choice of the
traditional restaurant menus or the more informal cosy bar.

Rooms 35 en suite (4 fmly) (6 GF) S £55-£65; D £65-£85 (incl. bkfst)
Facilities 🖥 Wi fi available Xmas **Conf** BC Thtr 60 Class 30 Board 30
Del from £80 **Parking** 27 **Notes** LB ⊗ ⊘ in restaurant

★★ 🅰

The Royal

The Esplanade PO21 1SZ
☎ 01243 864665 ▤ 863175
e-mail: david@royalhotelbognor.co.uk

dir: opposite Bognor Pier, 300yds from town centre

Rooms 22 en suite (3 fmly) S £35-£50; D £65-£80 (incl. bkfst)
Facilities Xmas **Conf** Thtr 60 Class 30 Board 30 Del from £45
Services Lift

BUDGET HOTEL

Premier Travel Inn
Bognor Regis

premier
travel inn

Shripney Rd PO22 9PA
☎ 0870 9906434 ▤ 0870 9906435
web: www.premiertravelinn.com

dir: From A27 take Bognor Regis exit at rdbt junct of A29.
Continue approx 4m. Inn on left.

High quality, modern budget accommodation ideal for both families
and business travellers. Spacious, en suite bedrooms feature bath and
shower, satellite TV and many have telephones and modem points.
The adjacent family restaurant features a wide and varied menu. For
further details consult the Hotel Groups page.

Rooms 24 en suite **Conf** Thtr 80 Class 40 Board 30

BOSHAM   MAP 05 SU80

★★★ 76% ⑳ HOTEL

The Millstream

Bosham Ln PO18 8HL
☎ 01243 573234 ▤ 01243 573459
e-mail: info@millstream-hotel.co.uk
web: www.millstream-hotel.co.uk

dir: 4m W of Chichester on A259, left at Bosham rdbt. After 1m
right at T-junct signed to church & quay. Hotel 0.5m on right

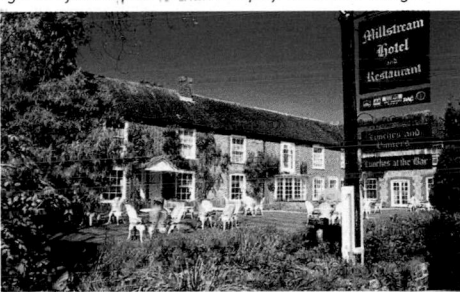

Lving in the idyllic village of Bosham, this attractive hotel provides
comfortable, well-equipped and tastefully decorated bedrooms. Many
guests regularly return here for the relaxed atmosphere created by the
notably efficient and friendly staff. Public rooms include a cocktail bar,
that opens onto the garden, and a pleasant restaurant where
varied and freshly prepared cuisine can be enjoyed.

Rooms 33 en suite 2 annexe en suite (2 fmly) (9 GF) ⊘ in all bedrooms
S £79-£89; D £138-£158 (incl. bkfst) **Facilities** Wi-fi in bedrooms Bridge
breaks ♫ Xmas **Conf** Thtr 45 Class 20 Board 20 Del from £115
Parking 44 **Notes** LB ⊗ ⊘ in restaurant Civ Wed 92

See advertisement on page 619

CHICHESTER
MAP 05 SU80

★★★★ 76% ◎◎ **HOTEL**

Marriott Goodwood Park Hotel & Country Club

Marriott.
HOTELS & RESORTS

PO18 0QB

☎ 0870 400 7225 🖷 0870 400 7325

e-mail: reservations.goodwood@marriotthotels.co.uk

web: www.marriott.co.uk

(For full entry see Goodwood)

★★★ 77% ◎ **HOTEL**

Crouchers Country Hotel & Restaurant

Birdham Rd PO20 7EH

☎ 01243 784995 🖷 01243 539797

e-mail: crouchers@btconnect.com

dir: off A27 to A286, 1.5m from Chichester centre opposite Black Horse pub

This friendly, family-run hotel is situated in open countryside and just a short drive from the harbour. The comfortable and well-equipped rooms include some in a separate barn and coach house and the open-plan public areas have pleasant views.

Rooms 18 en suite (1 fmly) (12 GF) ⊗ in 9 bedrooms S £65-£105; D £105-£130 (incl. bkfst) **Facilities** STV Wi-fi in bedrooms Xmas **Conf** BC Thtr 80 Class 80 Board 50 **Parking** 80 **Notes LB** ⊗ in restaurant

See advert on opposite page

★★★ 76% ◎ **HOTEL**

The Millstream

Bosham Ln PO18 8HL

☎ 01243 573234 🖷 01243 573459

e-mail: info@millstream-hotel.co.uk

web: www.millstream-hotel.co.uk

(For full entry see Bosham)

See advert on opposite page

★★★ 70% **HOTEL**

The Ship Hotel

North St PO19 1NH

☎ 01243 778000 🖷 01243 788000

e-mail: booking.shiphotel@eldridge-pope.co.uk

dir: from A27, onto inner ring road to Northgate. At large Northgate rdbt left into North St, hotel on left

Now in new hands this well-presented Georgian hotel has a prime position at the top of North Street. The bar and brasserie offer a contemporary lively venue for refreshments and meals, with cocktails and a wine list that might prove tempting. The hotel is in a good location for the Festival Theatre, so pre- and post-performance dinner offers are popular.

Rooms 36 en suite (2 fmly) ⊗ in all bedrooms S £79; D £99 (incl. bkfst) **Facilities** STV Xmas **Conf** Thtr 70 Class 35 Board 40 Del from £95 **Services** Lift **Parking** 35

◎◎ **RESTAURANT WITH ROOMS**

West Stoke House

Downs Rd, West Stoke PO18 9BN

☎ 01243 575226 🖷 01243 574655

e-mail: info@weststokehouse.co.uk

dir: Turn off B286 1.5m just beyond West Stoke village

The large 18th-century house lies on the edge of the South Downs. The large bedrooms have contemporary bathrooms and great country views, and a terrace leads onto over five acres of lawns and gardens. The restaurant, also open to non-residents, offers a relaxed atmosphere.

Rooms 6 en suite (1 fmly) ⊗ in all bedrooms S £85-£150; D £130-£150 **Facilities** 🍴 **Parking** 20 **Notes LB** ⊗ in restaurant Closed 24-28 Dec Civ Wed 140

BUDGET HOTEL

Premier Travel Inn Chichester

premier
travel inn

Chichester Gate Leisure Park, Terminus Rd PO19 8EL

☎ 0870 9906578 🖷 0870 9906579

web: www.premiertravelinn.com

dir: Exit A27 at Stockbridge rdbt towards city centre. Follow Terminus Road Industrial Estate signs. Left at 1st lights, left at next lights into Chichester Gate Leisure Park. Inn on right

High quality, modern budget accommodation ideal for both families and business travellers. Spacious, en suite bedrooms feature bath and shower, satellite TV and many have telephones and modem points. The adjacent family restaurant features a wide and varied menu. For further details consult the Hotel Groups page.

Rooms 83 en suite

CLIMPING
MAP 06 SU90

★★★ 82% ◎◎ **HOTEL**

Bailiffscourt Hotel & Health Spa

Climping St BN17 5RW

☎ 01903 723511 🖷 01903 718987

e-mail: bailiffscourt@hshotels.co.uk

web: www.hshotels.co.uk

dir: exit A259 at Climping, follow Climping Beach signs. Hotel 0.5m on right

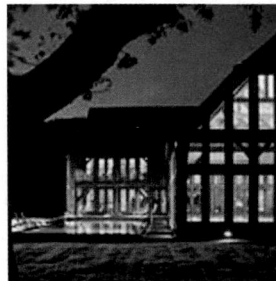

This delightful 'medieval manor' dating back only to the 1920s has the appearance of having been in existence for centuries. Bedrooms vary

continued

from atmospheric feature rooms with log fires, oak beams and four-poster beds to spacious, stylish, and contemporary rooms located in the grounds. Classic European cooking is a highlight, while a stylish spa and choice of cosy lounges completes the package.

Rooms 9 en suite 30 annexe en suite (25 fmly) (16 GF) S £175-£430; D £195-£480 (incl. bkfst) **Facilities Spa** STV 🏊 ⚗ supervised 🎾 Sauna Gym ⚓ Jacuzzi Wi-fi available Xmas **Conf** Thtr 40 Class 20 Board 26 Del from £165 **Parking** 100 **Notes LB** ⊗ in restaurant Civ Wed 60

COPTHORNE
See **Gatwick Airport**

CRAWLEY
See **Gatwick Airport**

CUCKFIELD   MAP 06 TQ32

INSPECTORS' CHOICE

★★★ @@@ HOTEL

Ockenden Manor
Ockenden Ln RH17 5LD
☎ 01444 416111 🖷 01444 415549
e-mail: reservations@ockenden-manor.com
web: www.hshotels.co.uk
dir: from N, at end of M23 onto A23 towards Brighton. 4.5m left onto B2115 towards Haywards Heath. Cuckfield 3m. Ockenden Lane off High St. Hotel at end

This charming 16th century hotel enjoys fine views of the South Downs. Bedrooms offer high standards of accommodation, some with historic features. Public rooms, retaining much of the original character, include an elegant sitting room with all the elements for a relaxing afternoon in front of the fire. Imaginative, noteworthy cuisine is a highlight to any stay.

Rooms 22 en suite (4 fmly) (4 GF) S £108-£175; D £160-£330 (incl. bkfst) **Facilities** STV Wi-fi available Xmas **Conf** Thtr 50 Class 20 Board 26 Del £205 **Parking** 43 **Notes LB** ⊗ in restaurant Civ Wed 75

We have indicated only the hotels that do not accept credit or debit cards

England

CUCKFIELD *continued*

★★ 72% **HOTEL**

Hilton Park Hotel

Tylers Green RH17 5EG

☎ 01444 454555 ▤ 01444 457222

e-mail: hiltonpark@janus-systems.com

web: www.janus-systems.com/hiltonpark.htm

dir: *on A272*

Situated between the delightful villages of Cuckfield and Haywards Heath, this charming Victorian country house is set in three acres of grounds. The comfortable bedrooms are tastefully decorated and equipped with an excellent range of facilities. In addition to an elegant drawing room, the public rooms include a contemporary bar and restaurant and two conference rooms.

Rooms 11 en suite (2 fmly) S £75-£80; D £105-£115 (incl. bkfst)
Facilities STV Wi-fi in bedrooms **Conf** Thtr 30 Board 20 Del from £130
Parking 50 **Notes LB** ⊗ ⊘ in restaurant

EAST GRINSTEAD   MAP 06 TQ33

INSPECTORS' CHOICE

★★★ ◉◉◉ **HOTEL**

Gravetye Manor

RH19 4LJ

☎ 01342 810567 ▤ 01342 810080

e-mail: info@gravetyemanor.co.uk

web: www.gravetyemanor.co.uk

dir: *B2028 to Haywards Heath. 1m after Turners Hill fork left towards Sharpthorne, immediate 1st left into Vowels Lane*

This beautiful Elizabethan mansion was built in 1598 and enjoys a tranquil setting. It was one of the first country-house hotels and remains a shining example in its class. There are several day rooms, each with oak panelling, fresh flowers and open fires that offer guests a relaxing atmosphere. Bedrooms are decorated in traditional English style, furnished with antiques and with many thoughtful extras. The cuisine is excellent and makes full use of home grown fruit and vegetables. Guests should make a point of exploring the outstanding gardens.

Rooms 18 en suite S £100-£170; D £155-£330 **Facilities** Fishing ⬥
Wi-fi in bedrooms **Conf** Del from £235 **Parking** 35 **Notes** ⊗
No children 7yrs ⊘ in restaurant RS 25-Dec Civ Wed 45

BUDGET HOTEL

Premier Travel Inn East Grinstead

London Rd, Felbridge RH19 2QR

☎ 08701 977088 ▤ 01342 326187

web: www.premiertravelinn.com

dir: *at junction of A22 & A264 south from M25 junct 6*

High quality, modern budget accommodation ideal for both families and business travellers. Spacious, en suite bedrooms feature bath and shower, satellite TV and many have telephones and modem points. The adjacent family restaurant features a wide and varied menu. For further details consult the Hotel Groups page.

Rooms 41 en suite

FIVE OAKS   MAP 06 TQ02

BUDGET HOTEL

Travelodge Billingshurst Five Oaks

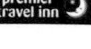

Staines St RH14 9AE

☎ 08700 850 950 ▤ 01403 782711

web: www.travelodge.co.uk

dir: *on A29, northbound, 1m N of Billingshurst*

Travelodge offers good quality, good value, modern accommodation. Ideal for families, the spacious en suite bedrooms include remote-control TV, tea and coffee-making facilities and comfortable beds. Meals can be taken at the nearby family restaurant. See Hotel Groups pages for further details.

Rooms 26 en suite S fr £26; D fr £26

FONTWELL   MAP 06 SU90

BUDGET HOTEL

Travelodge Arundel Fontwell

BN18 0SB

☎ 08700 850 950 ▤ 01243 543973

web: www.travelodge.co.uk

dir: *on A27/A29 rdbt*

Travelodge offers good quality, good value, modern accommodation. Ideal for families, the spacious en suite bedrooms include remote-control TV, tea and coffee-making facilities and comfortable beds. Meals can be taken at the nearby family restaurant. See Hotel Groups pages for further details.

Rooms 63 en suite S fr £26; D fr £26

Some hotels, although accepting children, may not have any special facilities for them so it is well worth checking before booking

GATWICK AIRPORT (LONDON)

MAP 06 TQ24

See also Dorking (Surrey), East Grinstead & Reigate (Surrey)

★★★★ 74% **HOTEL**

Copthorne Hotel and Resort Effingham Park Gatwick

COPTHORNE

West Park Rd RH10 3EU

☎ 01342 714994 🖹 01342 716039

e-mail: sales.effingham@mill-cop.com

web: www.copthorneeffingham.com

dir: M23 junct 10, take A264 towards East Grinstead. Over rdbt and at 2nd rdbt left onto B2028. Effingham Park on right

A former stately home, set in 40 acres of grounds, this hotel is popular for conference and weekend functions. The main restaurant is an open-plan brasserie serving modern continental cuisine, and snacks are also available in the bar. Bedrooms are spacious and well equipped. Facilities include an 18-hole golf course and a leisure club.

Rooms 122 en suite (6 fmly) (20 GF) ⊛ in 74 bedrooms S £69-£175; D £77-£175 (incl. bkfst) **Facilities** STV FTV 🏊 ♪ 9 ⊰ Sauna Solarium Gym ⛳ Putt green Jacuzzi Wi-fi available Aerobic studio Bowls Xmas **Conf** Thtr 600 Class 250 Board 30 Del from £145 **Services** Lift **Parking** 500 **Notes LB** ⊛ ⊛ in restaurant Civ Wed 150

★★★★ 72% **HOTEL**

Ramada Plaza Gatwick

RAMADA PLAZA

Tinsley Ln South, Three Bridges RH10 8XH

☎ 01293 561186 🖹 01293 561169

e-mail: sales.plazagatwick@ramadajarvis.co.uk

web: www.ramadajarvis.co.uk

dir: From M23 junct 10, follow A2011 to Crawley. Hotel is at 1st rdbt on left.

This modern, purpose built hotel is just four miles from the airport with easy access to the M23. Spacious bedrooms are comfortably appointed and well equipped including some family rooms. Air-conditioned public areas include a brightly appointed Arts restaurant, first-floor conference centre and Sebastian Coe Health Club.

Rooms 151 en suite (31 fmly) ⊛ in all bedrooms S £99-£130; D £99-£130 **Facilities** Spa STV 🏊 supervised Sauna Solarium Gym Jacuzzi Wi-fi available Beauty salon hairdresser **Conf** Thtr 210 Class 80 Board 40 Del from £120 **Services** Lift air con **Parking** 150 **Notes** ⊛ ⊛ in restaurant Closed Xmas Civ Wed 100

★★★★ 71% **HOTEL**

Copthorne Hotel London Gatwick

COPTHORNE

Copthorne Way RH10 3PG

☎ 01342 348800 & 348888 🖹 01342 348833

e-mail: coplgw@mill-cop.com

web: www.copthorne.com

dir: on A264, 2m E of A264/B2036 rdbt

Situated in a tranquil position, the Copthorne is set in 100 acres of wooded, landscaped gardens containing jogging tracks, a putting green and a petanque pit. The sprawling building is built around a 16th-century farmhouse and has comfortable bedrooms, many of

continued

which are air conditioned. There are three dining options, ranging from the informal bar and carvery to the more formal Lion d'Or.

Rooms 227 en suite (10 fmly) ⊛ in 136 bedrooms **Facilities Spa** STV 🏊 ⊰ Squash Sauna Solarium Gym Jacuzzi Wi-fi available Petanque pit, Aerobic studio **Conf** BC Thtr 135 Class 60 Board 40 Del from £145 **Services** Lift **Parking** 300 **Notes** Civ Wed 100

★★★★ 70% **HOTEL**

Sofitel London Gatwick

SOFITEL
ACCOR HOTELS & RESORTS

North Terminal RH6 0PH

☎ 01293 567070 🖹 01293 567739

e-mail: h6204-re@accor.com

dir: M23 junct 9, follow to 2nd rdbt. Hotel large white building straight ahead

One of the closest hotels to the airport, this modern, purpose-built hotel is located only minutes from the terminals. Bedrooms are contemporary and all are air-conditioned. Guests have a choice of eating options including a French-style café, brasserie and oriental restaurant.

Rooms 500 en suite (18 fmly) ⊛ in 283 bedrooms S £95-£220; D £95-£220 **Facilities** STV Sauna Solarium Gym **Conf** BC Thtr 300 Class 150 Board 90 Del from £143 **Services** Lift air con **Parking** 120 **Notes** ⊛

GATWICK AIRPORT (LONDON) *continued*

★★★ ◉◉ **HOTEL**

Langshott Manor

Langshott Ln, Horley RH6 9LN
☎ 01293 786680 🖹 01293 783905
e-mail: admin@langshottmanor.com

dir: from A23 take Ladbroke Rd, off Chequers rdbt to
Langshott, after 0.75m hotel on right

Charming timber-framed Tudor house set amidst beautifully
landscaped grounds on the outskirts of town. The stylish public
areas feature a choice of inviting lounges with polished oak
panelling, exposed beams and log fires. The individually
decorated bedrooms combine the most up-to-date modern
comforts with flair, individuality and traditional elegance. The
Mulberry restaurant overlooks a picturesque pond and offers an
imaginative menu.

Rooms 14 en suite 8 annexe en suite ⊗ in all bedrooms
S £150-£220; D £190-£320 (incl. bkfst) **Facilities** STV ⊌ Wi-fi in
bedrooms Xmas **Conf** Thtr 40 Class 20 Board 22 Del from £252.63
Parking 25 **Notes LB** ⊗ ⊗ in restaurant Civ Wed 60

★★★ 79% ◉ **HOTEL**

Stanhill Court

Stanhill Rd, Charlwood RH6 0EP
☎ 01293 862166- 🖹 01293 862773
e-mail: enquiries@stanhillcourthotel.co.uk
web: www.stanhillcourthotel.co.uk

dir: N of Charlwood towards Newdigate

This hotel dates back to 1881 and enjoys a secluded location in 35
acres of well-tended grounds with views over the Downs. Bedrooms
are individually furnished and decorated, and many have four-poster
continued

beds. Public areas include a library, a bright Spanish-style bar and a
traditional wood-panelled restaurant. Extensive and varied function
facilities make this a popular wedding venue.

Rooms 34 en suite (3 fmly) (1 GF) ⊗ in all bedrooms **Facilities** STV
Fishing Putt green Wi-fi in bedrooms **Conf** Thtr 250 Class 100 Board 60
Del from £139 **Parking** 110 **Notes** ⊗ in restaurant Civ Wed 220

See advert on opposite page

★★★ 78% **HOTEL**

Best Western Gatwick
Moat House

Longbridge Roundabout, Horley RH6 0AB
☎ 01293 899988 🖹 01293 899904
e-mail: conferences.gatwick@moathousehotels.com

dir: M23 junct 9, follow signs for North Terminal, take 4th exit at
rdbt signed A23 Redhill. At 1st rdbt take 1st exit then 1st left.

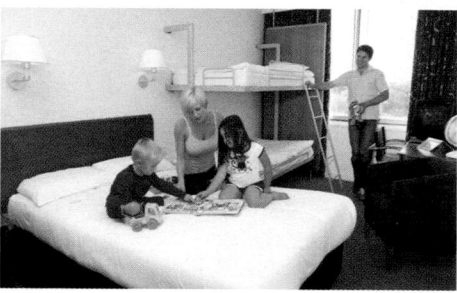

Ideally situated for both terminals, this hotel provides a shuttle service
to the airport and boasts secure undercover parking. Modern
conference facilities and a café break out area are provided. The smart
bedrooms all have air conditioning and a contemporary feel; some
family suites can sleep up to seven guests.

Rooms 125 en suite (20 fmly) ⊗ in all bedrooms S £59-£99; D £59-£99
Facilities STV **Conf** Thtr 40 Class 20 Board 18 Del from £109
Services Lift air con **Parking** 138 **Notes** ⊗ ⊗ in restaurant

★★★ 74% **HOTEL**

Gatwick Worth Hotel

Crabbet Park, Turners Hill Rd, Crawley Worth RH10 4ST
☎ 01293 884806 🖹 01293 882444
e-mail: management@gatwickworthhotel.com
web: www.gatwickworthhotel.co.uk

dir: M23 junct 10, left to A264. At 1st rdbt take last exit. Take 1st
left and 1st right at T-junct, hotel next right.

This purpose-built hotel is ideally placed for access to Gatwick Airport.
The bedrooms are spacious and suitably appointed with good
facilities. Public areas consist of a light and airy bar area and a
brasserie-style restaurant offering good value meals. Guests have use
of the superb leisure club next door.

Rooms 118 en suite (24 fmly) (56 GF) ⊗ in 90 bedrooms S £45-£80;
D £50-£100 **Conf** BC Thtr 300 Class 150 Board 150 Del from £110
Parking 150 **Notes** ⊗ Civ Wed 250

★★★ 72% HOTEL

Thistle London Gatwick

THISTLE HOTELS

Brighton Rd, Horley RH6 8PH
☎ 0870 333 9134 🖷 0870 333 9234
e-mail: londongatwick@thistle.co.uk

dir: M23 junct 9, A23 towards Redhill. At 'Longbridge' rdbt take 3rd exit signed Horley/A23. 1m to Sainsbury/Shell rdbt. Take 1st exit, hotel on right.

This hotel, once a Tudor coaching inn, offers a shuttle bus service to and from the airport, just two miles away, for guests making flight connections. It offers 104 bedrooms, including executive rooms. There is an air-conditioned restaurant and several bars, plus meeting rooms are available.

Rooms 104 en suite (17 fmly) (47 GF) ⊘ in 80 bedrooms **Facilities** STV 🎵 **Conf** Thtr 70 Class 25 Board 32 **Services** Lift air con **Parking** 120 **Notes LB** ⊗ ⊘ in restaurant

BUDGET HOTEL

Hotel Ibis London Gatwick

ibis
Accor
hotels

London Rd, County Oak, Crawley RH11 0PF
☎ 01293 590300 🖷 01293 590310
e-mail: H1889@accor.com
web: www.ibishotel.com

dir: M23 junct 10, A2011 towards Crawley. At rdbt 3rd exit, at next rdbt (Hazelwick) take 4th exit signed Manor Royal Industrial Estate. After 2 rdbts, follow A23/Gatwick Airport signs. On A23 left towards Crawley/Brighton. Hotel on left

Modern, budget hotel offering comfortable accommodation in bright and practical bedrooms. Breakfast is self-service and dinner is available in the restaurant. For further details, consult the Hotel Groups page.

Rooms 141 en suite S £49.95-£54.95; D £49.95-£54.95

BUDGET HOTEL

Premier Travel Inn Crawley (Pound Hill)

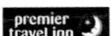
premier travel inn

Balcombe Rd, Crawley RH10 3NL
☎ 08701 977067 🖷 01293 873034
web: www.premiertravelinn.com

dir: On B2036 south towards Crawley from M23 junct 10

High quality, modern budget accommodation ideal for both families and business travellers. Spacious, en suite bedrooms feature bath and shower, satellite TV and many have telephones and modem points. The adjacent family restaurant features a wide and varied menu. For further details consult the Hotel Groups page.

Rooms 41 en suite

Premier Travel Inn Gatwick Airport South

London Rd, Lowfield Heath, Crawley RH10 9ST
☎ 0870 9906354 🖷 0870 9906355

dir: Near airport on A23. From M23 junct 9a towards North Terminal rdbt then follow A23/Crawley signs. 2m

Rooms 102 en suite **Conf** Thtr 200 Class 100 Board 80

Premier Travel Inn Gatwick/Crawley East

Crawley Av, Gossops Green, Crawley RH10 8BA
☎ 0870 9906546 🖷 0870 9906547

dir: 2m from M23/5m from Gatwick Airport. Exit M23 junct 11 onto A23 towards Crawley & Gatwick Airport

Rooms 83 en suite

Premier Travel Inn Gatwick/Crawley South

Goffs Park Rd, Crawley RH11 8AX
☎ 0870 9906390 🖷 0870 9906391

dir: Exit M23 junct 11onto A23 towards Crawley. At 2nd rdbt take 3rd exit for town centre, then 2nd right into Goffs Park Rd

Rooms 57 en suite **Conf** Thtr 120 Class 70 Board 40

Premier Travel Inn London Gatwick Airport

North Terminal, Longbridge Way, Crawley RH6 0NX
☎ 0870 238 3305 🖷 01293 568278

dir: M23 junct 9/9A towards North Terminal, at rdbt take 3rd exit. Inn on right

Rooms 219 en suite

GATWICK AIRPORT (LONDON) *continued*

BUDGET HOTEL

Travelodge Gatwick Airport

Church Rd, Lowfield Heath RH11 0PQ
☎ 08700 850 950 ▤ 01293 535369
web: www.travelodge.co.uk

dir: M23 junct 10, follow signs for Crawley, take A23 to Gatwick

Travelodge offers good quality, good value, modern accommodation. Ideal for families, the spacious en suite bedrooms include remote-control TV, tea and coffee-making facilities and comfortable beds. Meals can be taken at the nearby family restaurant. See Hotel Groups pages for further details.

Rooms 186 en suite S fr £26; D fr £26 **Conf** Thtr 60 Class 25 Board 25

GOODWOOD   MAP 06 SU81

★★★★ 76% ◎◎ HOTEL

Marriott Goodwood Park Hotel & Country Club

Marriott
HOTELS & RESORTS

PO18 0QB
☎ 0870 400 7225 ▤ 0870 400 7325
e-mail: reservations.goodwood@marriotthotels.co.uk
web: www.marriott.co.uk

dir: off A285, 3m NE of Chichester

Set in the middle of the 12,000-acre Goodwood Estate, this attractive hotel boasts extensive indoor and outdoor leisure facilities, along with a range of meeting rooms and conference and banqueting facilities. Bedrooms are furnished to a consistently high standard. Public rooms include the Richmond Restaurant and a smart cocktail bar, which reflects motor-racing heritage at Goodwood.

Rooms 94 en suite ⊗ in 54 bedrooms S £119-£169; D £129-£169 (incl. bkfst) **Facilities** STV ⬚ supervised ♨ 18 ♨ Sauna Solarium Gym Putt green Jacuzzi Wi-fi in bedrooms Beauty salon Xmas **Conf** BC Thtr 150 Class 60 Board 50 **Parking** 350 **Notes** LB ⊗ in restaurant Civ Wed 120

HAYWARDS HEATH   MAP 06 TQ32

★★★ 74% HOTEL

Best Western Birch

Best Western

Lewes Rd RH17 7SF
☎ 01444 451565 ▤ 01444 440109
e-mail: info@birchhotel.co.uk

dir: on A272 opposite Princess Royal Hospital and behind Shell Garage

Originally the home of an eminent Harley Street surgeon, this attractive Victorian property has been extended to combine modern facilities with the charm of its original period. Public rooms include the conservatory-style Pavilion Restaurant, along with an open-plan lounge and brasserie-style bar serving a range of light meals.

Rooms 51 en suite (3 fmly) (12 GF) ⊗ in 29 bedrooms S £70-£90; D £90-£105 (incl. bkfst) **Facilities** STV Wi-fi available **Conf** Thtr 60 Class 30 Board 26 Del £130 **Parking** 60 **Notes** ⊗ ⊗ in restaurant Civ Wed 60

HICKSTEAD   MAP 06 TQ22

BUDGET HOTEL

Travelodge Hickstead

Jobs Ln RH17 5NX
☎ 08700 850 950 ▤ 01444 881377
web: www.travelodge.co.uk

dir: A23 southbound

Travelodge offers good quality, good value, modern accommodation. Ideal for families, the spacious en suite bedrooms include remote-control TV, tea and coffee-making facilities and comfortable beds. Meals can be taken at the nearby family restaurant. See Hotel Groups pages for further details.

Rooms 55 en suite S fr £26; D fr £26

HORSHAM   MAP 06 TQ13

BUDGET HOTEL

Premier Travel Inn Horsham

premier
travel inn

57 North St RH12 1RB
☎ 08701 977136 ▤ 01403 270797
web: www.premiertravelinn.com

dir: opposite railway station, 5m from M23 junct 11

High quality, modern budget accommodation ideal for both families and business travellers. Spacious, en suite bedrooms feature bath and shower, satellite TV and many have telephones and modem points. The adjacent family restaurant features a wide and varied menu. For further details consult the Hotel Groups page.

Rooms 40 en suite

LOWER BEEDING   MAP 06 TQ22

INSPECTORS' CHOICE

★★★★ ◎◎◎ COUNTRY HOUSE HOTEL

South Lodge

Brighton Rd RH13 6PS
☎ 01403 891711 ▤ 01403 891766
e-mail: enquiries@southlodgehotel.co.uk
web: www.exclusivehotels.co.uk

dir: on A23 left onto B2110. Turn right through Handcross to A281 junct. Turn left and hotel on right

This impeccably presented 19th-century lodge with stunning views of the rolling South Downs is an ideal retreat. The

continued

traditional, award-winning restaurant offers memorable, seasonal dishes, and the elegant lounge is popular for afternoon teas. Bedrooms are individually designed with character and quality throughout. Leisure and conference facilities are impressive.
Rooms 45 en suite (4 fmly) (7 GF) **Facilities** STV ↓ 18 ⌣ Gym ⌣ Putt green Can organise riding, shooting, fishing & quad biking ♫ **Conf** BC Thtr 160 Class 60 Board 50 **Services** Lift **Parking** 100 **Notes LB** ⊗ ⊘ in restaurant Civ Wed 120

⊍

Swallow Cisswood House

SWALLOW HOTELS

Sandygate Ln RH13 6NF
☎ 01403 891216 ▤ 01403 891621
e-mail: reservations.cisswood@swallowhotels.com
web: www.swallowhotels.com
dir: M23 onto A23. Exit junct 11 and follow signs for Lower Beeding

At the time of going to press, the star classification for this hotel was not confirmed. Please refer to the AA internet site www.theAA.com for current information.

Rooms 51 en suite (25 GF) ⊗ in 25 bedrooms S £108; D £148 (incl. bkfst) **Facilities** FTV ☐ supervised Sauna Solarium Gym Jacuzzi Health & beauty salon Xmas **Conf** Thtr 150 Class 80 Board 60 Del £150 **Parking** 60 **Notes LB** ⊗ ⊘ in restaurant Civ Wed 150

MIDHURST   MAP 06 SU82

★★★ 80% ◉◉ HOTEL

Spread Eagle Hotel and Health Spa

South St GU29 9NH
☎ 01730 816911 ▤ 01730 815668
e-mail: spreadeagle@hshotels.co.uk
web: www.hshotels.co.uk/spread/spreadeagle-main.htm
dir: from M25 junct 10 follow A3 S, exit A3 at Milford and follow A286 to Midhurst. Hotel adjacent to Market Square on South Street

Offering accommodation since 1430, this historic property is full of character, evident in its sloping floors and inglenook fireplaces. Individually styled bedrooms provide modern comforts; those in the main house have oak panelling and include some spacious feature rooms. The hotel also boasts a well-equipped spa and offers noteworthy food in the oak beamed restaurant.

Rooms 35 en suite 4 annexe en suite (8 GF) ⊗ in 6 bedrooms S £80-£180; D £99-£240 (incl. bkfst) **Facilities** Spa STV ☐ Sauna Gym Jacuzzi Wi-fi in bedrooms Health & beauty treatment rooms Steam room Fitness trainer Xmas **Conf** Thtr 80 Class 40 Board 34 Del from £135 **Parking** 75 **Notes LB** ⊘ in restaurant Civ Wed 80

★★★ 66% HOTEL

Southdowns Country

Dumpford Ln, Trotton GU31 5JN
☎ 01730 821521 ▤ 01730 821790
e-mail: reception@southdownshotel.com
web: www.southdownshotel.com
dir: on A272, after town turn left at Keepers Arms

Ideal for a relaxing break, this private hotel enjoys a secluded location with views over the Sussex countryside. It is a popular choice for weddings, due to its beautiful setting and spacious public areas. Some of the comfortable bedrooms overlook the grounds. Meals are available in the bar and in the more formal restaurant that offers dishes based on local produce.

Rooms 22 en suite (2 fmly) (2 GF) ⊗ in 12 bedrooms S £50-£180; D £60-£180 (incl. bkfst) **Facilities** ☐ Sauna Xmas **Conf** Thtr 100 Class 50 Board 30 Del from £100 **Parking** 70 **Notes LB** ⊘ in restaurant Civ Wed 100

See advert under PETERSFIELD, Hampshire

RUSPER   MAP 06 TQ23

★★★ 85% ◉◉ COUNTRY HOUSE HOTEL

Ghyll Manor

High St RH12 4PX
☎ 0845 345 3426 ▤ 01293 871419
e-mail: ghyllmanor@csma.uk.com
dir: turn off A24 onto A264. Turn off at Faygate, follows signs for Rusper. 2m to village

Located in the quiet village of Rusper, this traditional mansion house is set in 45 acres of idyllic, peaceful grounds. Accommodation is in either the main house or a range of courtyard-style cottages. A pre-dinner drink can be taken by the fire, followed by an imaginatively created meal in the charming restaurant.

Rooms 8 en suite 21 annexe en suite (1 fmly) (19 GF) ⊗ in all bedrooms **Facilities** STV Gym ⌣ **Conf** Thtr 120 Class 50 Board 45 **Parking** 100 **Notes LB** ⊗ ⊘ in restaurant Civ Wed 80

If the freedom to smoke or be in a non-smoking atmosphere is important to you, check the rules when you book

RUSTINGTON   MAP 06 TQ00

BUDGET HOTEL

Travelodge Littlehampton Rustington

Worthing Rd BN17 6LZ

☎ 08700 850 950 📠 01903 733150

web: www.travelodge.co.uk

dir: *on A259, 1m E of Littlehampton*

Travelodge offers good quality, good value, modern accommodation. Ideal for families, the spacious en suite bedrooms include remote-control TV, tea and coffee-making facilities and comfortable beds. Meals can be taken at the nearby family restaurant. See Hotel Groups pages for further details.

Rooms 36 en suite S fr £26; D fr £26

STEYNING   MAP 06 TQ11

★★★ 72% HOTEL

Best Western The Old Tollgate

The Street BN44 3WE

☎ 01903 879494 📠 01903 813399

e-mail: info@oldtollgatehotel.com

web: www.bw-oldtollgatehotel.com

dir: *from A283 at Steyning rdbt, turn to Bramber. Hotel 200yds on right*

As its name suggests, this well-presented hotel is built on the site of the old toll house. The spacious bedrooms are smartly designed and are furnished to a high standard. Open for both lunch and dinner, the popular carvery-style restaurant offers an extensive choice of dishes. The hotel also has adaptable function rooms for weddings and conferences.

Rooms 11 en suite 28 annexe en suite (5 fmly) (14 GF) ⊛ in all bedrooms D £82-£135 **Facilities** STV Wi-fi available **Conf** Thtr 50 Class 32 Board 26 **Services** Lift **Parking** 60 **Notes** LB ⊛ ⊛ in restaurant Civ Wed 70

TURNERS HILL   MAP 06 TQ33

INSPECTORS' CHOICE

★★★★ ⊛⊛ HOTEL

Alexander House Hotel & Utopia Spa

East St RH10 4QD

☎ 01342 714914 📠 01342 717328

e-mail: info@alexanderhouse.co.uk

web: www.alexanderhouse.co.uk

dir: *6m from M23 junct 10, on B2110 between Turners Hill & East Grinstead*

Set in 175 acres of parklands and landscaped gardens, this delightful country house hotel dates back to the 17th century. The latest addition is the stunning spa wing with a state-of-the-art pool and gym, as well as specialised treatments. All bedrooms are very spacious with luxurious bathrooms. The new Brasserie

continued

complements Alexander's restaurant for those who prefer a more casual eating style.

Alexander House Hotel & Utopia Spa

Rooms 32 en suite (12 fmly) (1 GF) ⊛ in all bedrooms S £125-£145; D £155-£370 **Facilities Spa** STV FTV 🎾 🧖 💆 Sauna Solarium Gym 💆 Jacuzzi Wi-fi in bedrooms Clay Shooting Archery (by arrangement), Mountain bikes, Jogging Pony trekking Xmas **Conf** BC Thtr 150 Del from £250 **Services** Lift **Parking** 100 **Notes** LB ⊛ No children 7yrs ⊛ in restaurant Civ Wed 100

See advert under GATWICK AIRPORT

WEST CHILTINGTON   MAP 06 TQ01

★★★ 75% HOTEL

Best Western Roundabout

Monkmead Ln RH20 2PF

☎ 01798 813838 📠 01798 812962

e-mail: roundabouthotelltd@btinternet.com

web: www.bw-roundabouthotel.co.uk

dir: *A24 onto A283, right at mini rdbt in Storrington, left at hill top. Left after 1m*

Enjoying a most peaceful setting, surrounded by gardens, this well-established hotel is located deep in the Sussex countryside. Mock Tudor in style, the hotel has plenty of character. The comfortably furnished bedrooms are well equipped, and public areas offer a spacious lounge, bar and terrace. A variety of dishes to suit all tastes can be enjoyed in the restaurant.

Rooms 23 en suite (4 fmly) (5 GF) ⊛ in 5 bedrooms S £62-£67; D £110-£128 **Facilities** STV Xmas **Conf** Thtr 60 Class 20 Board 26 Del from £94 **Parking** 46 **Notes** LB ⊛ No children 3yrs ⊛ in restaurant Civ Wed 49

See advert on opposite page

WORTHING

MAP 06 TQ10

★★★ 77% ⊛ **HOTEL**

Ardington

Steyne Gardens BN11 3DZ

☎ 01903 230451 ▯ 01903 526526

e-mail: reservations@ardingtohotal.co.uk

dir: *A27 to Lancing, then to seafront. Follow signs for Worthing. Left at 1st church into Steyne Gardens*

Overlooking the Steyne Gardens next to the seafront, this popular hotel offers well-appointed bedrooms with a good range of facilities. An elegant lounge/bar area caters for guests throughout the day and has ample seating. The restaurant has been designed in a contemporary style, and offers good standards of cuisine.

Rooms 45 en suite (4 fmly) ⊛ in 10 bedrooms S £60-£95, D £90-£120 (incl. bkfst) **Facilities** STV Wi-fi in bedrooms Xmas **Conf** Thtr 140 Class 60 Board 35 **Notes LB** ⊛ in restaurant Closed 25 Dec-4 Jan

★★★ 74% **HOTEL**

Windsor

14/20 Windsor Rd BN11 2LX

☎ 01903 239655 & 0800 9804442 ▯ 01903 210703

e-mail: reception@thewindsor.co.uk

web: www.thewindsor.co.uk

dir: *From A27, A259. Follow hotel signs through town centre to seafront towards Brighton*

Located on a quiet road near to the seafront, this well-established hotel is popular with both business and leisure guests. Public areas include a smart lounge bar, an appealing conservatory reception and lounge area, and a popular restaurant. A choice of tastefully furnished bedrooms is available, each with a good range of facilities.

Rooms 30 en suite (4 fmly) (5 GF) ⊛ in 15 bedrooms S £84-£99; D £99-£130 (incl. bkfst) **Facilities** STV FTV Wi-fi in bedrooms **Conf** Thtr 120 Class 48 Board 40 Del from £95 **Services** air con **Parking** 28 **Notes LB** ⊛ ⊛ in restaurant Closed 23-31 Dec Civ Wed 100

★★★ 72% **HOTEL**

Beach

Marine Pde BN11 3QJ

☎ 01903 234001 ▯ 01903 234567

e-mail: info@thebeachhotel.co.uk

web: www.thebeachhotel.co.uk

dir: *W of town centre, approx 0.3m from pier*

With an impressive 1930's façade this well-established hotel is extremely popular with both leisure and business guests. Bedrooms, some with sea views and balconies, are comfortable and well

equipped. Spacious public areas incorporate a busy restaurant serving a range of popular dishes. Secure parking is available.

Rooms 79 en suite (8 fmly) ⊛ in all bedrooms S £62-£95; D £106-£144 (incl. bkfst & dinner) **Facilities** STV **Conf** Thtr 250 Class 60 Board 60 Del from £70 **Services** Lift **Parking** 55 **Notes LB** ⊛ ⊛ in restaurant

★★★ 72% **HOTEL**

Best Western Berkeley

86-95 Marine Pde BN11 3QD

☎ 01903 820000 ▯ 01903 821333 & 01903 821234

e-mail: reservations@berkeleyhotel.worthing.co.uk

dir: *follow signs to seafront; hotel 0.5m W of pier*

This hotel occupies a prime location on the seafront just a short walk from the high street. Bedrooms are modern in style and equipped with a good range of facilities; many have superb sea views. The public areas are tastefully decorated, and include a comfortable cocktail bar and a spacious restaurant.

Rooms 80 en suite (3 fmly) ⊛ in 29 bedrooms S £60-£85; D £70-£135 (incl. bkfst) **Facilities** STV Wi-fi in bedrooms Xmas **Conf** Thtr 100 Class 50 Board 50 Del from £95 **Services** Lift **Parking** 35 **Notes LB** ⊛ ⊛ in restaurant Civ Wed 50

continued

England

WORTHING *continued*

★★★ 68% HOTEL

Findon Manor

High St, Findon BN14 0TA

☎ 01903 872733 📠 01903 877473

e-mail: hotel@findonmanor.com

web: www.findonmanor.com

dir: 500yds off A24 between Worthing & Horsham, at the sign for Findon follow signs to Findon Manor into village

Located in the centre of the village, Findon Manor was built as a rectory and has a beamed lounge, which doubles as the reception area. Bedrooms, several with four-poster beds, are attractively decorated in a traditional style. The cosy bar offers a very good range of bar food, and is popular with locals, while the restaurant overlooks a garden and offers modern and traditional dishes.

Rooms 11 en suite (2 GF) ⊗ in 5 bedrooms S £65-£75; D £100-£150 (incl. bkfst) **Facilities** 😉 Wi-fi in bedrooms Boule Xmas **Conf** Thtr 50 Class 18 Board 25 Del from £90 **Parking** 25 **Notes LB** ⊗ No children 12yrs ⊗ in restaurant RS 24-30 Dec Civ Wed 60

★★★ 67% HOTEL

Kingsway

Marine Pde BN11 3QQ

☎ 01903 237542 📠 01903 204173

e-mail: kingsway-hotel@btconnect.com

THE CIRCLE
Selected Individual Hotels

dir: A27 follow signs to Worthing, then at seafront follow signs 'Hotel West'. Hotel 0.75m west of pier

Ideally located on the seafront and close to the town centre, the Kingsway continues to provide warm hospitality. Bedrooms are comfortably furnished and equipped with modern facilities. Day rooms include two comfortable lounge areas, a bar serving snacks and a well-appointed restaurant.

Rooms 29 en suite 7 annexe en suite (2 fmly) (3 GF) ⊗ in 21 bedrooms **Facilities** STV **Conf** Thtr 40 Class 20 Board 30 **Services** Lift **Parking** 9 **Notes LB** ⊗ in restaurant

★★ 62% HOTEL

Cavendish

THE INDEPENDENTS

115 Marine Pde BN11 3QG

☎ 01903 236767 📠 01903 823840

e-mail: reservations@cavendishworthing.co.uk

web: www.cavendishworthing.co.uk

dir: on seafront, 600yds W of pier

This popular, family-run hotel enjoys a prominent seafront location. Bedrooms are well equipped and soundly decorated. Guests have an
continued

extensive choice of meal options, with a varied bar menu, and carte and daily menus offered in the restaurant. Limited parking is available at the rear of the hotel.

Rooms 17 en suite (4 fmly) ⊗ in 3 bedrooms S £45-£50; D £69-£85 (incl. bkfst) **Facilities** STV Wi-fi available **Services** air con **Parking** 5 **Notes LB** ⊗ in restaurant

TYNE & WEAR

GATESHEAD   MAP 21 NZ26

See also Beamish (County Durham) & Whickham

★★★★ 75% HOTEL

Newcastle Marriott Hotel
MetroCentre

Marriott
HOTELS & RESORTS

MetroCentre NE11 9XF

☎ 0191 493 2233 📠 0191 493 2030

e-mail: reservations.newcastle@marriotthotels.co.uk

web: www.marriott.co.uk

dir: from N leave A1 at MetroCentre exit, take 'Other Routes'. From S leave A1 at MetroCentre exit and turn right.

Set in acres of woodland, this hotel was originally built in the 18th century. The public rooms have been sympathetically restored in keeping with the age of the building, yet with a contemporary twist. Four bedrooms are in the main house with others in an adjacent well-designed block, accessed by a glazed link.

Rooms 150 en suite (145 fmly) ⊗ in 90 bedrooms **Facilities** STV 🏊 supervised Sauna Solarium Gym Jacuzzi Health & beauty clinic Dance studio Hairdressers **Conf** BC Thtr 400 Class 147 Board 12 **Services** Lift air con **Parking** 300 **Notes LB** ⊗ ⊗ in restaurant Civ Wed 100

★★★ 78% HOTEL

Tulip Inn Newcastle/Gateshead

TULIP INN

Maingate, Kingsway North, Team Valley NE11 0BE

☎ 0191 491 3131 & 497 3380 📠 0191 491 3132

e-mail: info@tulipinnnewcastlegateshead.co.uk

dir: Exit A1 onto B1426 signed Teams

Located just off the A1, and convenient for the city centre, this newly opened hotel provides stylish, modern accommodation for business or leisure guests. Attentive staff provide friendly service in the 'Bibo Bar and Bistro', which offers full English breakfast and evening meals.

Rooms 115 en suite (59 fmly) ⊗ in 98 bedrooms S £59-£85; D £59-£90 **Facilities** STV **Conf** Thtr 30 Class 16 Board 20 Del from £120 **Services** Lift **Parking** 300 **Notes LB** ⊗ ⊗ in restaurant

★★★ 77% ⊛⊛ HOTEL

Eslington Villa

8 Station Rd, Low Fell NE9 6DR

☎ 0191 487 6017 & 420 0666 📠 0191 420 0667

e-mail: home@eslingtonvilla.co.uk

dir: off A1 onto Team Valley Trading Est. Right at 2nd rdbt along Eastern Av then left past Belle Vue Motors, hotel on left

Set in a residential area, this smart hotel combines a bright, contemporary atmosphere with the period style of a fine Victorian villa. The overall ambience is relaxed and inviting. Chunky sofas grace the cocktail lounge, while tempting dishes can be enjoyed in either the classical dining room or modern conservatory overlooking the Team Valley.
continued

England

Rooms 17 en suite (2 fmly) (3 GF) S £69.50–£74.50; D £84.50–£89.50 (incl. bkfst) **Facilities** Wi-fi in bedrooms **Conf** Thtr 36 Class 30 Board 25 Del from £92.50 **Parking** 28 **Notes** ⊗ ⊛ in restaurant Closed 25-26 Dec RS Sun/BHs (restricted restaurant service)

Swallow Gateshead

SWALLOW

High West St NE8 1PE

☎ 0191 477 1105 🗎 0191 478 7214

web: www.swallowhotels.com

dir: From A1 take A184 to Gateshead town centre. Straight over rdbt, right at lights, past bus station. Continue over next rdbt and through lights, 1st left after car wash centre

At the time of going to press, the star classification for this hotel was not confirmed. Please refer to the AA internet site www.theAA.com for current information.

Rooms 103 en suite (3 fmly) ⊛ in 59 bedrooms S £50-£65; D £85-£95 (incl. bkfst) **Facilities** Spa STV 🔄 supervised Sauna Solarium Gym Jacuzzi Beauty Therapist Xmas **Conf** Thtr 350 Class 150 Board 100 Del from £99 **Services** Lift **Parking** 100 **Notes** ⊛ in restaurant Civ Wed 80

Swallow Springfield Gateshead

SWALLOW

Durham Rd NE9 5BT

☎ 0191 477 4121 & 499 8508 🗎 0191 477 7213

e-mail: reservations.springfield@swallowhotels.com

web: www.swallowhotels.com

dir: From A1 take junct 65 signed Gateshead A167. Hotel on right 4m from motorway

At the time of going to press, the star classification for this hotel was not confirmed. Please refer to the AA internet site www.theAA.com for current information

Rooms 61 en suite (5 fmly) (2 GF) ⊛ in 21 bedrooms S £45-£71; D £65-£93 (incl. bkfst) **Facilities** STV Xmas **Conf** Thtr 140 Class 60 Board 60 Del from £99 **Services** Lift **Parking** 80 **Notes** LB ⊛ in restaurant

BUDGET HOTEL

Premier Travel Inn Gateshead

premier travel inn

Derwent Haugh Rd, Swalwell NE16 3BL

☎ 08701 977283 🗎 0191 414 5032

web: www.premiertravelinn.com

dir: From A1/A694 junct into Derwent Haugh Rd. 1m from Metro Centre

High quality, modern budget accommodation ideal for both families and business travellers. Spacious, en suite bedrooms feature bath and shower, satellite TV and many may have telephones and modem points. The adjacent family restaurant features a wide and varied menu. For further details consult the Hotel Groups page.

Rooms 40 en suite

Premier Travel Inn Newcastle South

Lobley Hill Rd NE11 9NA

☎ 0870 9906590 🗎 0870 9906591

dir: Just off A1, on A692, 2m from Angel of the North. 3m from Metro Centre

Rooms 40 en suite

BUDGET HOTEL

Travelodge Gateshead

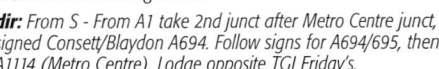

Clasper Way, Swalwell NE16 3BE

☎ 08700 850 950

web: www.travelodge.co.uk

dir: From S - From A1 take 2nd junct after Metro Centre junct, signed Consett/Blaydon A694. Follow signs for A694/695, then A1114 (Metro Centre). Lodge opposite TGI Friday's.

Travelodge offers good quality, good value, modern accommodation. Ideal for families, the spacious en suite bedrooms include remote-control TV, tea and coffee-making facilities and comfortable beds. Meals can be taken at the nearby family restaurant. See Hotel Groups pages for further details.

Rooms 60 en suite S fr £26; D fr £26

HOUGHTON-LE-SPRING   MAP 19 NZ34

★★ 68% **HOTEL**

Chilton Lodge

Black Boy Rd, Chilton Moor, Fencehouses DH4 6LX

☎ 0191 385 2694 🗎 0191 385 6762

dir: A1(M) junct 62, onto A690 to Sunderland. Left at Rainton Bridge and Fencehouses sign, cross rdbt and 1st left

This country pub and hotel has been extended from the original farm cottages. Bedrooms are modern and comfortable and some rooms are particularly spacious. This hotel is popular for weddings and functions; there is also a well stocked bar, and a wide range of dishes is served in the Orangery and restaurant.

Rooms 25 en suite (7 fmly) ⊛ in 7 bedrooms **Facilities** STV Horse riding 🎵 **Conf** Thtr 60 Class 50 Board 30 **Parking** 100 **Notes** LB ⊗

NEWCASTLE UPON TYNE   MAP 21 NZ26

See also Seaton Burn & Whickham

★★★★ 83% ⊛⊛ **HOTEL**

Jesmond Dene House

Jesmond Dene Rd NE2 2EY

☎ 0191 212 3000 🗎 0191 212 3001

e-mail: info@jesmonddenehouse.co.uk

web: www.jesmonddenehouse.co.uk

dir: A167 N to A184. Right, then right again along Jesmond Dene Rd, hotel on left

This Arts and Crafts house, overlooking the wooded valley of Jesmond Dene yet just five minutes from the centre of town, has been sympathetically and successfully converted into a contemporary hotel.

continued on page 630

England

NEWCASTLE UPON TYNE *continued*

Bedrooms, varying in size, are split between the main house and adjacent New House, all offering quality and comfort. Public areas retain many of the original features and the restaurant provides the setting for carefully prepared meals.

Rooms 32 en suite 8 annexe en suite (1 fmly) (4 GF) ⊛ in all bedrooms **Facilities** STV **Conf** Thtr 125 Class 80 Board 44 **Services** Lift **Parking** 64 **Notes** ⊗ ⊛ in restaurant

★★★★ 79% ⊛ **HOTEL**

Vermont

Castle Garth NE1 1RQ

☎ 0191 233 1010 ▤ 0191 233 1234

e-mail: info@vermont-hotel.co.uk

web: www.vermont-hotel.com

dir: *city centre by high level bridge and Castle Keep*

Adjacent to the castle and close to the buzzing quayside area, this imposing hotel enjoys fine views of the Tyne Bridge. Thoughtfully equipped bedrooms offer a variety of styles, including grand suites. The elegant reception lounge and adjoining bar invite relaxation, while the Bridge restaurant is the focus for dining.

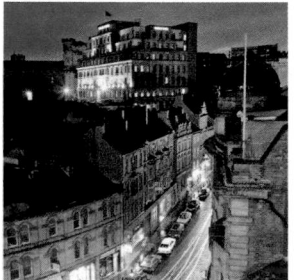

Vermont

Rooms 101 en suite (12 fmly) ⊛ in 79 bedrooms S £120-£185; D £120-£185 **Facilities** STV Solarium Gym Wi-fi in bedrooms Xmas **Conf** BC Thtr 200 Class 60 Board 30 Del from £165 **Services** Lift **Parking** 100 **Notes LB** Civ Wed 120

★★★★ 77% ⊛⊛ **HOTEL**

Newcastle Marriott Hotel Gosforth Park

Marriott.
HOTELS & RESORTS

High Gosforth Park, Gosforth NE3 5HN

☎ 0191 236 4111 ▤ 0191 236 8192

web: www.marriott.co.uk

dir: *onto A1056 to Killingworth and Wideopen. 3rd exit to Gosforth Park, hotel ahead*

Set within its own grounds, this modern hotel offers extensive conference and banqueting facilities, along with indoor and outdoor leisure and a choice of formal and informal dining. Many of the air-conditioned bedrooms have views over the park; executive rooms feature extras such as CD players. The hotel is conveniently located for the by-pass, airport and racecourse.

Rooms 178 en suite (30 fmly) ⊛ in 145 bedrooms S £89-£119; D £89-£119 (incl. bkfst) **Facilities Spa** STV ⊠ supervised ⌣ Squash Sauna Solarium Gym Jacuzzi Wi-fi available Trim & jogging trail in hotel grounds 𝄐 **Conf** BC Thtr 750 Class 280 Board 50 Del from £125 **Services** Lift air con **Parking** 340 **Notes LB** RS Xmas & New Year Civ Wed 300

★★★★ 75% **HOTEL**

Copthorne Hotel Newcastle

▥
COPTHORNE

The Close, Quayside NE1 3RT

☎ 0191 222 0333 ▤ 0191 230 1111

e-mail: sales@newcastle.mill-cop.com

web: www.copthorne.com

dir: *follow signs to Newcastle city centre. Take B1600 Quayside exit, hotel on right*

Set on the banks of the River Tyne close to the city centre, this stylish purpose-built hotel provides modern amenities including a leisure centre, conference facilities and a choice of restaurants for dinner. Bedrooms overlook the river, and there is a floor of 'Connoisseur' rooms that have their own dedicated exclusive lounge and business support services.

Rooms 156 en suite ⊛ in 85 bedrooms S £99-£190; D £105-£190 **Facilities Spa** STV ⊠ Sauna Solarium Gym Jacuzzi Wi-fi available Steam room, Beauty treatment room, fitness studio Xmas **Conf** Thtr 200 Class 85 Board 50 Del £185 **Services** Lift air con **Parking** 200 **Notes** ⊛ in restaurant Civ Wed 150

★★★★ 75% **HOTEL**

Newcastle Marriott Hotel MetroCentre

Marriott.
HOTELS & RESORTS

MetroCentre NE11 9XF

☎ 0191 493 2233 ▤ 0191 493 2030

e-mail: reservations.newcastle@marriotthotels.co.uk

web: www.marriott.co.uk

(For full entry see Gateshead)

★★★ 85% ⊛ **HOTEL**

Malmaison

Malmaison
hotels that dare to be different

Quayside NE1 3DX

☎ 0191 245 5000 ▤ 0191 245 4545

e-mail: newcastle@malmaison.com

web: www.malmaison.com

dir: *follow signs for Newcastle City Centre, then for Quayside/Law Courts. Hotel 100yds past Law Courts*

Overlooking the river and the Millennium Bridge, the hotel has a prime position in the very popular re-developed quayside district. Bedrooms have striking decor, CD/DVD players, mini-bars and a number of individual touches. Food and drink are an integral part of the operation here, with a stylish brasserie-style restaurant and café bar, plus the new Café Mal, a deli-style café next door to the main entrance. Bookings are recommended for Le Petit Spa. Malmaison - AA Hotel Group of the Year 2006-7.

Rooms 120 en suite (10 fmly) ⊛ in 22 bedrooms S £75-£350; D £75-£350 **Facilities Spa** STV Wi-fi available **Conf** Thtr 30 Board 18 Del from £165 **Services** Lift air con **Parking** 50

England

★★★ 80% **HOTEL**

Holiday Inn Newcastle

Great North Rd, Seaton Burn NE13 6BP

☎ 0191 201 9988 & 0870 787 3291 📠 0191 236 8091

e-mail: res.hinewcastle@qmh-hotels.com

dir: *A1/A19 6m N of Newcastle. A190/Tyne Tunnel turn off A1. Follow brown Holiday Inn signs.*

This modern hotel is set in 16 acres and is convenient for Newcastle International Airport, Tyne Tunnel and the North Sea Ferry Terminal. Each bedroom is fully equipped with all necessary facilities, and Executive rooms are available. The Convivium Restaurant serves breakfast and dinner, and the Mercury Bar offers a snack menu from 11 to 11. A leisure club is available, and there are plenty of activities for children.

Rooms 154 en suite (56 fmly) (72 GF) ⚫ in 146 bedrooms S £80-£150; D £80-£150 (incl. bkfst) **Facilities** STV ⚐ supervised Sauna Solarium Gym Jacuzzi Cardiovascular and weights room ♫ Xmas **Conf** BC Thtr 400 Class 150 Board 60 Del from £119 **Services** air con **Parking** 550 **Notes** ⊗ ⚫ in restaurant Civ Wed 300

★★★ 77% ⍟ ⍟ **HOTEL**

Eslington Villa

8 Station Rd, Low Fell NE9 6DR

☎ 0191 487 6017 & 420 0666 📠 0191 420 0667

e-mail: home@eslingtonvilla.co.uk

(For full entry see Gateshead)

★★★ 75% **HOTEL**

Thistle Newcastle

THISTLE HOTELS

Neville St NE1 5DF

☎ 0191 232 2471 & 0870 333 9142 📠 0870 333 9242

e-mail: Newcastle@Thistle.co.uk

dir: *Off A1 onto A184 cross Redheugh Bridge turn right at 2nd lights, turn right after Cathedral.*

A 19th-century listed building, the hotel enjoys a central location opposite the city's Central Station, which also has links to the Metro system. Bedrooms are comfortably appointed for both business and leisure guests. Limited free parking is available.

Rooms 114 en suite (1 fmly) ⚫ in 87 bedrooms **Conf** Thtr 200 Class 100 Board 60 **Services** Lift **Parking** 20 **Notes** LB ⊗ ⚫ in restaurant Civ Wed 180

★★★ 73% **HOTEL**

George Washington County Hotel

Stone Cellar Rd, High Usworth NE37 1PH

☎ 0191 402 9988 📠 0191 415 1166

e-mail: reservations@georgewashington.co.uk

web: www.georgewashington.co.uk

(For full entry see Washington)

★★★ 73% **HOTEL**

Jurys Inn Newcastle

🖤JURYS DOYLE
HOTELS

St James Gate, Scotswood Rd NE4 7JH

☎ 0191 201 4400 📠 0191 201 4411

e-mail: jurysinnnewcastle@jurysdoyle.com

web: www.jurysdoyle.com

Lying west of the city centre, this modern, stylish hotel is easily accessible from major road networks. Bedrooms provide good guest comfort and in-room facilities are suited for both leisure and business markets. Public areas include a number of meeting rooms and a popular bar and restaurant.

Rooms 274 en suite ⊗ in 215 bedrooms **Conf** BC Thtr 90 Class 50 Board 45 **Services** Lift **Notes** ⊗ Closed 24-26 Dec

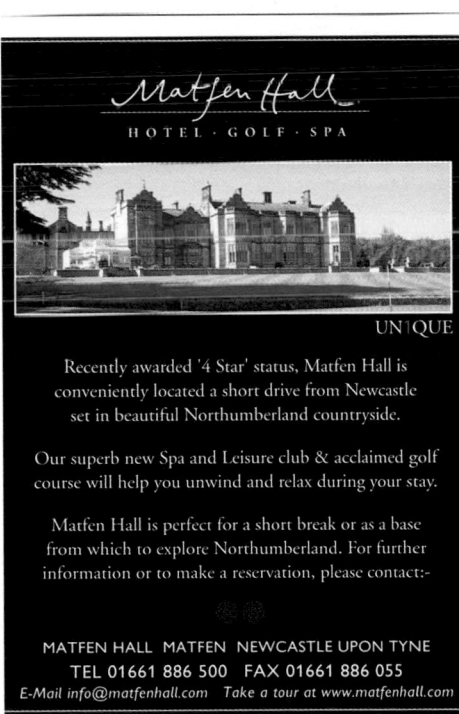

NEWCASTLE UPON TYNE *continued*

★★★ 72% HOTEL

The Caledonian Hotel, Newcastle

PEEL HOTELS

64 Osborne Rd, Jesmond NE2 2AT
☎ 0191 281 7881 🖷 0191 281 6241
e-mail: info@caledonian-hotel-newcastle.com
web: www.peelhotel.com
dir: from A1 follow signs to Newcastle City, cross Tyne Bridge to Tynemouth. Left at traffic lights at Osborne Rd, hotel on right

This hotel is located in the Jesmond area of the city, popular for its vibrant nightlife. Bedrooms are comfortable and well equipped for business guests. Public area include the trendy Billabong Bar and Bistro, which serves food all day, and also on the terrace where a cosmopolitan atmosphere prevails.

Rooms 89 en suite (6 fmly) (7 GF) ⊘ in 32 bedrooms S £99; D £110
Facilities STV Wi-fi available Xmas **Conf** Thtr 100 Class 50 Board 50 Del from £115 **Services** Lift **Parking** 35 **Notes LB** ⊛ Civ Wed 70

★★★ 72% HOTEL

Novotel Newcastle

NOVOTEL

Ponteland Rd, Kenton NE3 3HZ
☎ 0191 214 0303 🖷 0191 214 0633
e-mail: H1118@accor-hotels.com
web: www.novotel.com
dir: off A1(M) airport junct onto A696, take Kingston Park exit

This modern well-proportioned hotel lies just off the bypass and is within easy reach of the airport and city centre. Bedrooms are spacious with a range of extras. The Garden Brasserie offers a flexible dining option and is open until late. There is also a small leisure centre for the more energetic.

Rooms 126 en suite (56 fmly) ⊘ in 82 bedrooms **Facilities** STV 🏊
Sauna Gym **Conf** Thtr 200 Class 90 Board 40 **Services** Lift **Parking** 260
Notes LB Civ Wed 200

★★★ 71% HOTEL

Best Western New Kent Hotel

Best Western

127 Osborne Rd NE2 2TB
☎ 0191 281 7711 🖷 0191 281 3369
e-mail: newkenthotel@hotmail.com
dir: beside B1600, opposite St Georges Church

This popular business hotel offers relaxed service and typical Geordie hospitality. The bright modern bedrooms are well equipped and the modern bar is an ideal meeting place. A range of generous good value dishes is served in the restaurant, which doubles as a wedding venue.
continued

Rooms 32 en suite (4 fmly) S £52.50-£69.50; D £89.50 (incl. bkfst)
Facilities STV Wi-fi available Xmas **Conf** Thtr 60 Class 30 Board 40 Del £99.50 **Parking** 22 **Notes LB** ⊘ in restaurant Civ Wed 90

★★★ 68% HOTEL

Quality Hotel Newcastle upon Tyne

QUALITY

Newgate St NE1 5SX
☎ 0191 232 5025 🖷 0191 232 8428
e-mail: enquiries@hotels-newcastle-upon-tyne.com
web: www.choicehotelseurope.com
dir: A1(M) take A184, follow A6082. Cross Redheugh Bridge into right lane, right at 3rd lights, immediate right onto Fenkle Street. Car park behind Old Assembly Rooms

Benefiting from a city centre location and a secure rooftop car park, this hotel is popular with business travellers. Accommodation is provided in compact yet thoughtfully equipped bedrooms. The rooftop restaurant and lounge give fine views over the city.

Rooms 93 en suite (4 fmly) ⊘ in 42 bedrooms S £70-£104; D £80-£120
Facilities STV Wi-fi available Xmas **Conf** Thtr 100 Class 40 Board 40 Del from £105 **Services** Lift **Parking** 120 **Notes LB** ⊘ in restaurant

★★ 67% HOTEL

Cairn

THE INDEPENDENTS

97/103 Osborne Rd, Jesmond NE2 2TJ
☎ 0191 281 1358 🖷 0191 281 9031
e-mail: info@cairnnewcastle.com

A smart modern reception hall welcomes guests to this commercial hotel in the village suburb of Jesmond. Bedrooms are well equipped. There is a lively bar and a bright colourful restaurant. The hotel benefits from limited parking to the rear of the property.

Rooms 50 en suite (2 fmly) S £59-£69; D £85-£95 **Facilities** STV **Conf** Thtr 150 Class 110 Board 100 **Parking** 22 **Notes LB** Civ Wed 150

🇺 U

Swallow Imperial

SWALLOW HOTELS

Jesmond Rd NE2 1PR
☎ 0191 281 5511 🖷 0191 281 8472
e-mail: generalmanager.newcastle@swallowhotels.com
web: www.swallowhotels.com
dir: just off A167 on main road to coast

At the time of going to press, the star classification for this hotel was not confirmed. Please refer to the AA internet site www.theAA.com for current information.
continued

England

Rooms 122 en suite (3 fmly) (5 GF) ⊛ in 109 bedrooms S £75-£110; D £75-£135 (incl. bkfst) **Facilities Spa** STV ⬚ Sauna Solarium Gym Jacuzzi Xmas **Conf** Thtr 150 Class 60 Board 48 Del from £99 **Services** Lift **Parking** 84 **Notes LB** ⊛ in restaurant Civ Wed 120

Rooms 30 en suite **Conf** Thtr 40 Class 25 Board 20

Innkeeper's Newcastle/Gosforth

Vintage Inns, Falcons Nest, Rotary Way NE3 5EH
☎ 0191 236 7078

Rooms 53 en suite

BUDGET HOTEL

Premier Travel Inn Newcastle City Centre

City Rd, Quayside NE1 2AN
☎ 0870 238 3318 🖹 0191 232 6557
web: www.premiertravelinn.com

dir: at corner of City Rd (A186) & Crawhall Rd

High quality, modern budget accommodation ideal for both families and business travellers. Spacious, en suite bedrooms feature bath and shower, satellite TV and many have telephones and modem points. The adjacent family restaurant features a wide and varied menu. For further details consult the Hotel Groups page.

Rooms 81 en suite **Conf** Thtr 15 Board 12

Premier Travel Inn Newcastle (Holystone)

Holystone Roundabout NE27 0DA
☎ 08701 977189 🖹 0191 259 9509

dir: 3m N of Tyne Tunnel, adjacent to A19. Take A191 signed Gosforth/Whitley Bay

Rooms 40 en suite

Premier Travel Inn Newcastle (Quayside)

The Quayside NE1 3DW
☎ 0870 9906530 🖹 0870 9906531

dir: From N, follow A1, A167, A186 Walker & Wallsend. From S, follow A1, A184, A189 to city centre onto B1600 Quayside. Hotel by Tyne Bridge

Rooms 150 en suite **Conf** Thtr 30 Class 30 Board 30

BUDGET HOTEL

Travelodge Newcastle Central

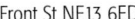

Forster St NE1 2NH
☎ 08700 850 950 🖹 0191 261 7105
web: www.travelodge.co.uk

dir: from A1 or A194 (M) to city centre, over Tyne Bridge, right into Melbourne St, right into Forster St

Travelodge offers good quality, good value, modern accommodation. Ideal for families, the spacious en suite bedrooms include remote-control TV, tea and coffee-making facilities and comfortable beds. Meals can be taken at the nearby family restaurant. See Hotel Groups pages for further details.

Rooms 120 en suite S fr £26; D fr £26

NEWCASTLE UPON TYNE AIRPORT

MAP 21 NZ17

BUDGET HOTEL

Innkeeper's Lodge Newcastle (Airport)

Kenton Bank NE3 3TY
☎ 0191 214 0877 🖹 0191 214 1922
web: www.innkeeperslodge.com

dir: from A1(M), exit A696/B6918. At 1st rdbt, take B6918 (Kingston Park), 2nd rdbt turn right. Lodge located on left

Smart, en suite accommodation ideal for both business & leisure guests. Bedrooms are very well equipped, including Sky TV, telephone, modem points, tea & coffee making facilities, (family rooms in most locations). Complimentary breakfast. The adjacent Pub Restaurant; a Harvester, Vintage Inn, Toby Carvery, Ember Inn, Sizzling Pubco or Pub & Carvery offers an all day menu. See Hotel Groups pages for further details.

BUDGET HOTEL

Premier Travel Inn Newcastle Airport

Newcastle International Airport, Ponteland Rd, Prestwick NE20 9DB
☎ 08701 977190 🖹 01661 824940
web: www.premiertravelinn.com

dir: adjacent to main entrance

High quality, modern budget accommodation ideal for both families and business travellers. Spacious, en suite bedrooms feature bath and shower, satellite TV and many have telephones and modem points. The adjacent family restaurant features a wide and varied menu. For further details consult the Hotel Groups page.

Rooms 86 en suite **Conf** Thtr 20

Premier Travel Inn Newcastle Airport (South)

Callerton Ln Ends, Woolsington NE13 8DF
☎ 0870 9906338 🖹 0870 9906339

dir: Just off A696 on B6910, 0.3m from airport. 4m from city centre

Rooms 42 en suite 10 annexe en suite **Conf** Thtr 60 Class 20 Board 20

SEATON BURN

MAP 21 NZ27

BUDGET HOTEL

Travelodge Newcastle Seaton Burn

Front St NE13 6ED
☎ 08700 850 950 🖹 0191 217 0107
web: www.travelodge.co.uk

dir: A1 northbound, exit for Tyne Tunnel (A19). Lodge at 1st rdbt

Travelodge offers good quality, good value, modern accommodation. Ideal for families, the spacious en suite bedrooms include remote-control TV, tea and coffee-making facilities and comfortable beds. Meals can be taken at the nearby family restaurant. See Hotel Groups pages for further details.

Rooms 40 en suite S fr £26; D fr £26

England

SOUTH SHIELDS   MAP 21 NZ36

★★★ 66% **HOTEL**

Best Western Sea

Sea Rd NE33 2LD

☎ 0191 427 0999 📠 0191 454 0500

e-mail: sea@bestwestern.co.uk

dir: A1(M) past Washington Services onto A194. Take A183 through South Shields town centre along Ocean Rd. Hotel on seafront

Dating from the 1930s this long-established business hotel overlooks the boating lake and the Tyne estuary. Bedrooms are generally spacious and well equipped and include five new annexe rooms with wheelchair access. A range of generously portioned meals are served in both the bar and restaurant.

Rooms 32 en suite 5 annexe en suite (5 fmly) ⊗ in 8 bedrooms S fr £63; D fr £75 (incl. bkfst) **Facilities** STV Wi-fi in bedrooms **Conf** Thtr 200 Class 100 Board 50 Del from £80 **Parking** 70 **Notes** ⊗ in restaurant RS 26-Dec

SUNDERLAND   MAP 19 NZ35

★★★★ 75% **HOTEL**

Sunderland Marriott

Marriott
HOTELS & RESORTS

Queen's Pde, Seaburn SR6 8DB

☎ 0191 529 2041 📠 0191 529 4227

e-mail: sunderland.marriott@whitbread.com

web: www.marriott.co.uk

dir: A19, A184 (Boldon/Sunderland North), then 3m. At rdbt turn left, then right. At rdbt turn left, follow to coast. Turn right, hotel on right

Comfortable and spacious accommodation, some with fabulous views of the North Sea and vast expanses of sandy beach, is provided in this seafront hotel. Public rooms are bright and modern and a number of meeting rooms are available. The hotel is conveniently located for access to the local visitor attractions.

Rooms 82 en suite (16 fmly) (4 GF) ⊗ in 55 bedrooms **Facilities** STV ⚡ supervised Sauna Solarium Gym Jacuzzi **Conf** Thtr 300 Class 100 Board 70 **Services** Lift **Parking** 120 **Notes LB** ⊗ in restaurant Civ Wed 80

★★★ 74% **HOTEL**

Quality Hotel Sunderland

Witney Way, Boldon NE35 9PE

☎ 0191 519 1999 📠 0191 519 0655

e-mail: enquiries@hotels-sunderland.com

web: www.choicehotelseurope.com

QUALITY

dir: From Tyne Tunnel (A19), 2.5m S take 1st exit to rdbt with A184

This modern, purpose-built hotel is within easy reach of major business and tourism amenities and is well suited to the needs of both business and leisure travellers. The bedrooms are spacious and well equipped. Public areas include a leisure centre, a variety of meeting rooms and a spacious bar and restaurant.

Rooms 82 en suite (10 fmly) (41 GF) ⊗ in 42 bedrooms S £50-£98; D £60-£120 **Facilities** ⚡ supervised Sauna Gym Jacuzzi Wi-fi available Xmas **Conf** Thtr 230 Class 100 Board 100 Del from £80 **Parking** 150 **Notes LB** ⊗ in restaurant Civ Wed 200

BUDGET HOTEL

Premier Travel Inn Sunderland North West

premier travel inn

Timber Beach Rd, Off Wessington Way, Castletown SR5 3XG

☎ 0870 9906514 📠 0870 9906515

web: www.premiertravelinn.com

dir: Just off A1(M) junct 65. Follow A1231 towards Sunderland

High quality, modern budget accommodation ideal for both families and business travellers. Spacious, en suite bedrooms feature bath and shower, satellite TV and many have telephones and modem points. The adjacent family restaurant features a wide and varied menu. For further details consult the Hotel Groups page.

Rooms 63 en suite **Conf** Thtr 12 Class 12 Board 12

Premier Travel Inn Sunderland West

Wessington Way, Castletown SR5 3HR

☎ 08701 977245 📠 0191 548 4044

dir: from A19 take A1231 towards Sunderland, Inn 100yds

Rooms 41 en suite **Conf** Thtr 15 Board 10

BUDGET HOTEL

Travelodge Sunderland Central

Low Row SR1 3PT

☎ 08700 850 950 📠 0191 514 3453

web: www.travelodge.co.uk

Travelodge offers good quality, good value, modern accommodation. Ideal for families, the spacious en suite bedrooms include remote-control TV, tea and coffee-making facilities and comfortable beds. Meals can be taken at the nearby family restaurant. See Hotel Groups pages for further details.

Rooms 60 en suite S fr £26; D fr £26

TYNEMOUTH
MAP 21 NZ36

★★★ 75% **HOTEL**

Grand
Grand Pde NE30 4ER
☎ 0191 293 6666 ▤ 0191 293 6665
e-mail: info@grandhotel-uk.com
web: www.grandhotel-uk.com

dir: A1058 for Tynemouth. At coast rdbt turn right. Hotel on right approx 0.5m

This grand Victorian building offers stunning views of the coastline. In addition to the restaurant there are two bars and an elegant and imposing staircase is the focal point. Bedrooms come in a variety of styles and are well equipped, tastefully decorated and have impressive bathrooms.

Rooms 40 en suite 4 annexe en suite (12 fmly) S £70-£160; D £80-£160 (incl. bkfst) **Facilities** STV Wi-fi available ♬ Xmas **Conf** Thtr 130 Class 40 Board 40 **Services** Lift **Parking** 16 **Notes** ⊗ ⊛ in restaurant RS Sun evening Civ Wed 120

WARDLEY
MAP 21 NZ36

BUDGET HOTEL

Travelodge Newcastle Whitemare Pool
Wardley, Whitemare Pool NE10 8YB
☎ 08700 850 950 ▤ 0191 469 5718
web: www.travelodge.co.uk

dir: From N and W follow A1 S, take A184 through Gateshead to Sunderland and South Shields. 4 miles E of Gateshead take A194 to South Shields.

Travelodge offers good quality, good value, modern accommodation. Ideal for families, the spacious en suite bedrooms include remote-control TV, tea and coffee-making facilities and comfortable beds. Meals can be taken at the nearby family restaurant. See Hotel Groups pages for further details.

Rooms 71 en suite S fr £26; D fr £26

WASHINGTON
MAP 19 NZ35

★★★ 73% **HOTEL**

George Washington Golf & Country Club
Stone Cellar Rd, High Usworth NE37 1PH
☎ 0191 402 9988 ▤ 0191 415 1166
e-mail: reservations@georgewashington.co.uk
web: www.georgewashington.co.uk

dir: Exit A1(M) junct 65 onto A194(M). Take A195 signed Washington North. Take last exit from rdbt for Washington then right at mini-rdbt. Hotel 0.5m on right

Popular with business and leisure guests, this purpose-built hotel boasts two golf courses and a driving range. Bedrooms, many now refurbished, are stylish and modern, generally spacious and comfortably equipped. Public areas include extensive conference facilities, a business centre and fitness club.

Rooms 103 en suite (9 fmly) (41 GF) ⊛ in 44 bedrooms S £89; D £99 **Facilities** Spa ⌨ supervised ♨ 18 Squash Sauna Solarium Gym Putt green Jacuzzi Wi-fi in bedrooms Golf driving range, Pitch & Putt, Pool table, Beauty salon Xmas **Conf** BC Thtr 200 Class 80 Board 80 Del £125 **Parking** 180 **Notes** LB ⊗ ⊛ in restaurant Civ Wed 180

BUDGET HOTEL

Campanile
Emerson Rd, District 5 NE37 1LE
☎ 0191 416 5010 ▤ 0191 416 5023
e-mail: washington@campanile-hotels.com
web: www.envergure.fr

Campanile

dir: A1(M) junct 64, A195 to Washington, 1st left at rdbt into Emerson Road. Hotel 800yds on left

This modern building offers accommodation in smart, well-equipped bedrooms, all with en suite bathrooms. Refreshments may be taken at the informal Bistro. For further details consult the Hotel Groups page.

Rooms 79 annexe en suite **Conf** Thtr 25 Class 15 Board 15 Del from £70

WASHINGTON SERVICE AREA (A1(M))
MAP 19 NZ23

BUDGET HOTEL

Travelodge Washington A1 Northbound
Motorway Service Area, Portobello DH3 2SJ
☎ 08700 850 950
web: www.travelodge.co.uk

dir: on northbound carriageway of A1(M)

Travelodge offers good quality, good value, modern accommodation. Ideal for families, the spacious en suite bedrooms include remote-control TV, tea and coffee making facilities and comfortable beds. Meals can be taken at the nearby family restaurant. See Hotel Groups pages for further details.

Rooms 31 en suite S fr £26; D fr £26

Travelodge Washington A1 Southbound
Portobello DH3 2SJ
☎ 08700 850 950
dir: on southbound carriageway of A1(M)
Rooms 36 en suite S fr £26; D fr £26

England

WHICKHAM   MAP 21 NZ26

★★★ 74% **HOTEL**

Gibside

Front St NE16 4JG

☎ 0191 488 9292 🖺 0191 488 8000

e-mail: reception@gibside-hotel.co.uk

web: www.gibside-hotel.co.uk

dir: *off A1(M) towards Whickham on B6317, onto Front St, 2m on right*

Conveniently located in the village centre, this hotel is close to the Newcastle by-pass and its elevated position affords views over the Tyne Valley. Bedrooms come in two styles, classical and contemporary. Public rooms include the Egyptian-themed Sphinx bar and a more formal restaurant. Secure garage parking is available.

Rooms 45 en suite (2 fmly) (13 GF) ⊛ in 10 bedrooms **Facilities** STV Golf Academy at The Beamish Park ♫ Xmas **Conf** Thtr 100 Class 50 Board 50 **Services** Lift **Parking** 28

WHITLEY BAY   MAP 21 NZ37

★★★ 71% **HOTEL**

Windsor

South Pde NE26 2RF

☎ 0191 251 8888 0191 232 3158 🖺 0191 297 0272

e-mail: info@windsorhotel-uk.com

dir: *from A19/Tyne Tunnel follow for A1058 to Tynemouth. At coast rdbt left to Whitley Bay. After 2m left at Rex Hotel. Hotel on left*

This tastefully modernised hotel is conveniently located between the town centre and the seafront, and has lively bars that transform Thursday to Sunday nights with a carnival atmosphere. Bedrooms are very comfortably equipped and most boast superior bathrooms with bath and separate shower cubicle. Public areas are smartly presented and include the smart and stylish Bazil Brasserie.

Rooms 69 en suite (24 fmly) (4 GF) ⊛ in 49 bedrooms S £59-£69; D £65-£75 **Facilities** STV Wi-fi available **Conf** Thtr 80 Class 40 Board 40 Del fr £69 **Services** Lift **Parking** 46 **Notes LB** ⊛ ⊛ in restaurant

WARWICKSHIRE

ABBOT'S SALFORD   MAP 10 SP05

★★★ 80% ⊛ **HOTEL**

Best Western Salford Hall

WR11 5UT

☎ 01386 871300 & 0800 212671 🖺 01386 871301

e-mail: reception@salfordhall.co.uk

web: www.salfordhall.co.uk

dir: *from A46 take road signed Salford Priors, Abbot's Salford & Harvington. Hotel 1.5m on left*

Built in 1470 as a retreat for the Abbot of Evesham, this impressive building retains many original features. Bedrooms have their own individual character and most offer a view of the attractive gardens. Oak-panelling, period tapestries, open fires and fresh flowers grace the public areas, while leisure facilities include a snooker room, tennis court, solarium and sauna.

Rooms 14 en suite 19 annexe en suite (4 GF) ⊛ in 4 bedrooms S £75-£100; D £115-£150 (incl. bkfst) **Facilities** STV ⌖ Snooker Sauna Solarium Wi-fi available Xmas **Conf** Thtr 50 Class 35 Board 25 Del from £110 **Parking** 51 **Notes LB** ⊛ ⊛ in restaurant Closed 24-30 Dec Civ Wed 80

See advertisement under STRATFORD-UPON-AVON

ALCESTER   MAP 10 SP05

★★★ 74% ⊛ **HOTEL**

Kings Court

Kings Coughton B49 5QQ

☎ 01789 763111 🖺 01789 400242

e-mail: info@kingscourthotel.co.uk

dir: *1m N on A435*

This privately-owned hotel dates back to Tudor times and the bedrooms in the original house have oak beams. Most guests are accommodated in the well-appointed modern wings. The bar and restaurant offer very good cooking from interesting menus. The hotel is licensed to hold civil ceremonies and the pretty garden is ideal for summer weddings.

Rooms 4 en suite 37 annexe en suite (3 fmly) (22 GF) ⊛ in 15 bedrooms S £42-£68; D £76-£90 (incl. bkfst) **Facilities** STV Riding **Conf** Thtr 100 Class 60 Board 40 Del from £104 **Parking** 120 **Notes LB** Closed 24-30 Dec Civ Wed 100

BUDGET HOTEL

Travelodge Stratford Alcester

Oversley Mill Roundabout B49 6AA
☎ 08700 850 950 📠 01789 766987
web: www.travelodge.co.uk
dir: *at junct A46/A435*

Travelodge offers good quality, good value, modern accommodation. Ideal for families, the spacious en suite bedrooms include remote-control TV, tea and coffee-making facilities and comfortable beds. Meals can be taken at the nearby family restaurant. See Hotel Groups pages for further details.

Rooms 66 en suite S fr £26; D fr £26

ALDERMINSTER   MAP 10 SP24

INSPECTORS' CHOICE

★★★★ ◉◉ HOTEL

Ettington Park

HANDPICKED
HOTELS

CV37 8BU
☎ 01789 450123 📠 01789 450472
e-mail: ettingtonpark@handpicked.co.uk
web: www.handpicked.co.uk
dir: *off A3400, 5m S of Stratford, just outside Alderminster*

Set in 40-acre grounds in the picturesque Stour Valley, Ettington Park offers the best of both worlds - the peace of the countryside and easy access to main roads and motorway networks. Bedrooms are spacious and individually decorated; views include the formal gardens, or the chapel. Public rooms include the period drawing room, the oak-panelled dining room with inlay of family crests, a range of contemporary meeting rooms and indoor leisure centre.

Rooms 28 en suite 20 annexe en suite (5 fmly) (10 GF) ⊘ in 25 bedrooms S £110-£200; D £150-£330 (incl. bkfst) **Facilities** STV FTV 🅡 ♨ Fishing Sauna ♨ Jacuzzi Wi-fi available Clay pigeon shooting, Archery, Health & Beauty treatments Xmas **Conf** Thtr 90 Class 48 Board 48 Del from £180 **Services** Lift **Parking** 150 **Notes** ⊘ in restaurant Civ Wed 96

ANSTY   MAP 11 SP48

★★★★ 73% HOTEL

Macdonald Ansty Hall

MACDONALD
HOTELS & RESORTS

Main Rd CV7 9HZ
☎ 0870 1942125 📠 024 7660 2155
e-mail: ansty@macdonald-hotels.co.uk
web: www.macdonald-hotels.co.uk
dir: *M6 junct 2 onto B4065 signed 'Ansty'. Hotel 1.5m on left*

Dating back to 1678, this Grade II listed Georgian house is set within eight acres of attractive grounds and woodland. The hotel enjoys the best of both worlds as it has a central yet tranquil location. Spacious bedrooms feature a traditional decorative style and a range of extras. Rooms are divided between the main house and the more recently built annexe.

Rooms 23 en suite 39 annexe en suite (4 fmly) (22 GF) ⊘ in 55 bedrooms **Facilities** STV Xmas **Conf** Thtr 200 Class 60 Board 60 Del from £155 **Services** Lift **Parking** 150 **Notes** ⊘ in restaurant Civ Wed 100

ATHERSTONE   MAP 10 SP39

★★ 76% ◉ HOTEL

Chapel House

Friar's Gate CV9 1EY
☎ 01827 718949 📠 01827 717702
e-mail: info@chapelhousehotel.co.uk
dir: *turn off A5, follow signs to town centre, half way up Long St turn right into Church St.*

Sitting next to the church this 18th-century establishment offers excellent hospitality and service while the cooking, using much local produce, is very notable. Bedrooms are well equipped and lounges are extensive; there is also a delightful walled garden for guests to use.

Rooms 12 en suite ⊘ in all bedrooms S £70-£75; D fr £100 (incl. bkfst) **Facilities** Wi-fi in bedrooms **Conf** Board 20 **Notes LB** ⊗ ⊘ in restaurant Closed 24 Dec-1 Jan, 6-14 Apr

---

BARFORD   MAP 10 SP26

★★★ 75% HOTEL

The Glebe at Barford

Church St CV35 8BS
☎ 01926 624218 📠 01926 624625
e-mail: sales@glebehotel.co.uk
dir: *M40 junct 15/A429 (Stow). At mini island turn left, hotel 500mtrs on right*

The giant Lebanese cedar tree in front of this hotel was ancient even in 1820, when the original rectory was built. Public rooms within the house include a lounge bar and the aptly named Cedars Conservatory Restaurant which offers interesting cuisine. Individually appointed bedrooms are tastefully decorated in soft pastel fabrics, with coronet, tented ceiling or four-poster style beds.

Rooms 39 en suite (3 fmly) (4 GF) ⊘ in 2 bedrooms S £105; D £125 (incl. bkfst) **Facilities** STV 🅡 Sauna Solarium Gym Jacuzzi Beauty salon Xmas **Services** Lift **Parking** 60 **Notes LB** ⊘ in restaurant Civ Wed 70

England

BRANDON

MAP 11 SP47

★★★★ 72%  **HOTEL**

Macdonald Brandon Hall Hotel & Spa

MACDONALD HOTELS & RESORTS

Main St CV8 3FW

☎ 0870 400 8105 📠 024 7654 4909

e-mail: general.brandonhall@macdonald-hotels.co.uk

web: www.macdonald-hotels.co.uk

dir: *A45 towards Coventry S. After Peugeot-Citroen garage on left, at island take 5th exit to M1 South/London (back onto A45). After 200yds, immediately after Texaco garage, left into Brandon Ln, hotel after 2.5m*

Set within 17 acres of well-tended lawns and woodland, this former shooting lodge is located within easy reach of both Coventry and Rugby. Public rooms are stylishly decorated and fairly modern in style, bedrooms are more traditional. Excellent leisure and spa facilities are provided.

Rooms 60 en suite 60 annexe en suite (12 fmly) (50 GF) ⊘ in all bedrooms **Facilities Spa** STV 🏊 supervised Sauna Solarium Gym ⛳ Steam room. Xmas **Conf** Thtr 280 Class 120 Board 80 Del from £145 **Services** Lift **Parking** 200 **Notes** ⊘ in restaurant Civ Wed 80

CLAVERDON

MAP 10 SP16

★★★★ 79%   **HOTEL**

Ardencote Manor Hotel, Country Club & Spa

Lye Green Rd CV35 8LT

☎ 01926 843111 📠 01926 842646

e-mail: hotel@ardencote.com

web: www.ardencote.com

dir: *in Claverdon centre follow Shrewley signs off A4189. Hotel 0.5m on right*

Originally built as a gentleman's residence around 1860, this hotel is set in 45 acres of landscaped grounds. Public rooms include a choice of lounge areas, a cocktail bar and conservatory breakfast room. Main meals are served in the Lodge, a separate building that has been strikingly appointed in a light contemporary style, which sits on the shoreline of a small lake. An extensive range of leisure and conference facilities is provided and bedrooms are smartly decorated and tastefully furnished.

Rooms 75 en suite (5 fmly) (11 GF) ⊘ in all bedrooms S £90-£105; D £120-£160 (incl. bkfst) **Facilities Spa** STV 🏊 ♪ 9 ⛳ Squash Sauna Solarium Gym ⛳ Putt green Jacuzzi Wi-fi available Xmas **Conf** Thtr 200 Class 100 Board 50 Del from £110 **Services** Lift air con **Parking** 150 **Notes LB** ⊗ ⊘ in restaurant Civ Wed 150

See advertisement under WARWICK

COLESHILL

MAP 10 SP28

★★★ 71% **HOTEL**

Grimstock Country House

Gilson Rd, Gilson B46 1LJ

☎ 01675 462121 & 462161 📠 01675 467646

e-mail: enquiries@grimstockhotel.co.uk

dir: *off A446 at rdbt onto B4117 to Gilson, hotel 100yds on right*

This privately owned hotel is convenient for Birmingham International Airport and the NEC, and benefits from a peaceful rural setting. Bedrooms are spacious and comfortable. Public rooms include two restaurants, a wood-panelled bar, good conference facilities and a gym featuring the latest cardiovascular equipment.

Rooms 44 en suite (1 fmly) (13 GF) S £70-£95; D £75-£109 (incl. bkfst) **Facilities** STV Solarium Gym Wi-fi available Xmas **Conf** Thtr 100 Class 60 Board 50 Del from £130 **Parking** 100 **Notes LB** ⊘ in restaurant Civ Wed 90

★★ 68% **HOTEL**

Coleshill Hotel

OLD ENGLISH INNS

152 High St B46 3BG

☎ 01675 465527 📠 01675 464013

e-mail: 9130@greeneking.co.uk

web: www.oldenglish.co.uk

dir: *M6 junct 4. After 2nd island slip off right onto Coventry road. Hotel on left approximately 100yds after mini rdbt*

This friendly hotel is convenient for both the NEC and Birmingham International Airport. Bedrooms, some of which are in a separate house opposite, provide comfortable and well-equipped facilities. The bar and bistro are attractively appointed. Additional features include a car park and self-contained function suite.

Rooms 15 en suite 8 annexe en suite (3 fmly) (3 GF) ⊘ in 16 bedrooms S £75-£79.50; D £85-£89.50 (incl. bkfst) **Facilities** ♪ Xmas **Conf** Thtr 100 Class 50 Board 40 Del from £75 **Parking** 30

BUDGET HOTEL

Innkeeper's Lodge Birmingham Coleshill (NEC)

High St B46 3BL

☎ 01675 462212

web: www.innkeeperslodge.com

Smart, en suite accommodation ideal for both business & leisure guests. Bedrooms are very well equipped, including Sky TV, telephone, modem points, tea & coffee making facilities, (family rooms in most locations). Complimentary breakfast. The adjacent Pub Restaurant; a Harvester, Vintage Inn, Toby Carvery, Ember Inn, Sizzling Pubco or Pub & Carvery offers an all day menu. See Hotel Groups pages for further details.

Rooms 32 en suite

Some hotels have restricted service during quieter months, and at this time some of the facilities will not be available

DUNCHURCH
MAP 11 SP47

BUDGET HOTEL

Travelodge Rugby Dunchurch
London Rd, Thurlaston CV23 9LG
☎ 08700 850 950 ▤ 01788 521538
web: www.travelodge.co.uk
dir: *4m S of Rugby, on A45, westbound*

Travelodge offers good quality, good value, modern accommodation. Ideal for families, the spacious en suite bedrooms include remote-control TV, tea and coffee-making facilities and comfortable beds. Meals can be taken at the nearby family restaurant. See Hotel Groups pages for further details.

Rooms 40 en suite S fr £26; D fr £26

HONILEY
MAP 10 SP27

★★★ 75% HOTEL

Honiley Court Hotel & Conference Centre
Meer End Rd CV8 1NP
☎ 01926 484234 ▤ 01926 484474
dir: *M40 junct 15, A46 then A4177 to Solihull. Right at 1st main rdbt, hotel 2m on left*

Incorporating an inn with 16th-century origins, this busy hotel provides brightly decorated and open plan public areas. The spacious bedrooms are comfortably appointed and well equipped for both business and leisure guests. A good choice of meals and snacks is readily available in the contemporary Boot Inn and Bistro.

Rooms 62 en suite (2 fmly) (14 GF) ⊘ in 44 bedrooms D £99-£115 **Facilities** STV Wi-fi available Xmas **Conf** Thtr 200 Class 80 Board 40 Del from £130 **Services** Lift **Parking** 250 **Notes LB** ⊘ in restaurant Civ Wed 160

If the freedom to smoke or be in a non-smoking atmosphere is important to you, check the rules when you book

KENILWORTH
MAP 10 SP27

★★★★ 71% HOTEL

Chesford Grange
Chesford Bridge CV8 2LD
☎ 01926 859331 ▤ 01926 859272
e-mail: chesfordgrangereservations@qhotels.co.uk
web: www.qhotels.co.uk
dir: *0.5m SE of junct A46/A452. At rdbt turn right signed Leamington Spa. After 250yds at x-rds turn right and hotel on left*

This much-extended hotel set in 17 acres of private grounds is well situated for Birmingham International Airport, the NEC and major routes. Bedrooms range from traditional style to contemporary Art + Tech rooms featuring state-of-the-art technology. Public areas include a leisure club and extensive conference and banqueting facilities.

Rooms 209 en suite (20 fmly) (43 GF) ⊘ in 146 bedrooms **Facilities** Spa ▣ supervised Solarium Gym Jacuzzi Wi-fi in bedrooms Xmas **Conf** BC Thtr 710 Class 350 Board 50 Del £199 **Services** Lift **Parking** 500 **Notes** ⊘ in restaurant Civ Wed 700

★★★ 80% HOTEL

Best Western Peacock
149 Warwick Rd CV8 1HY
☎ 01926 851156 & 864500 ▤ 01926 864644
e-mail: reservations@peacockhotel.com
dir: *A46/A452 signed Kenilworth. Hotel 0.25m on right after St John's Church*

Conveniently located for the town centre, the Peacock offers a peaceful retreat and service is delivered in a most professional manner by friendly staff. Vibrant colour schemes run through pleasing public rooms and the attractive accommodation is complemented by two dining options: the Malabar room, offering modern European dining, and the Coconut Lagoon serving southern Indian dishes.

Rooms 23 en suite 6 annexe en suite (5 fmly) (10 GF) ⊘ in 18 bedrooms S £52-£80, D £65-£100 (incl. bkfst) **Facilities** STV Wi-fi in bedrooms Xmas **Conf** BC Thtr 90 Class 50 Board 50 Del from £85 **Parking** 50 **Notes** ⊗ Civ Wed 90

★★★ 74% HOTEL

Macdonald De Montfort
Abbey End CV8 1ED
☎ 0870 1942127 ▤ 01926 857830
e-mail: demontfort@macdonald-hotels.co.uk
web: www.macdonald-hotels.co.uk
dir: *from A46 take A452 towards Leamington. At rdbt left to town centre, along high street. Hotel at top*

Situated in the centre of town, in the heart of Shakespeare country, this popular business hotel is well located for access to the major commercial centres of the Midlands. Public areas include a range of meeting and function rooms, a comfortable lounge/bar area and a traditional restaurant.

Rooms 108 en suite (15 fmly) ⊘ in all bedrooms S £48-£118; D £95-£155 (incl. bkfst) **Facilities** STV Xmas **Conf** Thtr 300 Class 100 Board 40 Del from £125 **Services** Lift **Parking** 65 **Notes LB** ⊘ in restaurant Civ Wed 116

England

KENILWORTH *continued*

★★ 65% HOTEL

Clarendon House

OLD ENGLISH INNS

6 High St CV8 1LZ
☎ 01926 857668 📠 01926 850669
e-mail: 1963@greeneking.co.uk
web: www.oldenglish.co.uk

dir: *M40 junct 15 then A46 towards Coventry. Take 3rd exit into Kenilworth & follow signs for town centre. Follow Warwick road to clock tower island and take 2nd exit. Follow road to lights, hotel on left.*

Incorporating the original 15th-century Castle Tavern, this hotel has plenty of old-world charm, including a wealth of beams and an indoor well. Bedrooms have character and are thoughtfully equipped with useful extras. Meals can be taken in the spacious brasserie or alternatively an extensive menu is available in the bar.

Rooms 20 en suite (2 GF) ⊗ in 9 bedrooms S £60-£70; D £80-£90 (incl. bkfst) **Facilities** Xmas **Conf** Thtr 40 Class 30 Board 30 Del from £99 **Parking** 20 **Notes** LB ⊗ ⊗ in restaurant Civ Wed 50

LEA MARSTON   MAP 10 SP29

★★★★ 75% HOTEL

BW Lea Marston Hotel & Leisure Complex

Best Western

Haunch Ln B76 0BY
☎ 01675 470468 📠 01675 470871
e-mail: info@leamarstonhotel.co.uk

dir: *M42 junct 9, A4097 to Kingsbury. Hotel signed 1.5m on right*

Excellent access to the motorway network and a good range of sports facilities make this hotel a popular choice for conferences and leisure breaks. Bedrooms are mostly set around an attractive quadrangle and are generously equipped. Diners can choose between the popular Sportsman's Lounge Bar and the elegant Adderley Restaurant.

Rooms 80 en suite (4 fmly) (46 GF) ⊗ in 74 bedrooms S £75-£125; D £95-£145 (incl. bkfst) **Facilities Spa** STV ⓡ ♨ 9 ♨ Sauna Solarium Gym Putt green Jacuzzi Wi-fi available Golf driving range, Beauty Salon, Children's play area, Golf simulator Xmas **Conf** Thtr 140 Class 50 Board 30 Del from £135 **Services** Lift **Parking** 220 **Notes** LB ⊗ ⊗ in restaurant Civ Wed 100

See also advert on page 651

LEAMINGTON SPA (ROYAL)   MAP 10 SP36

★★★ ◉◉◉ HOTEL

Mallory Court

Harbury Ln, Bishop's Tachbrook CV33 9QB
☎ 01926 330214 📠 01926 451714
e-mail: reception@mallory.co.uk
web: www.mallory.co.uk

dir: *2m S off B4087 towards Harbury*

RELAIS & CHATEAUX

With its tranquil rural setting, this elegant Lutyens-style country house is an idyllic retreat. Set in ten acres of landscaped gardens with immaculate lawns and orchard. Relaxation is easy in the two sumptuous lounges, drawing room or conservatory. Dining is a treat in either the elegant restaurant or the newly opened Brasserie. Simon Haigh heads up a team of expert chefs producing dishes that continue to delight. Bedrooms in the main house are luxurious, each individual in style, beautifully decorated and most with wonderful views. Those in the Knights Suite are more contemporary and have their own access via a smart conference and banqueting facility.

Rooms 19 en suite 11 annexe en suite (2 fmly) (4 GF) S £125-£270; D £135-£340 (incl. bkfst) **Facilities** STV ⓣ ♨ ♨ Wi-fi in bedrooms Use of nearby club facilities Xmas **Conf** Thtr 200 Class 160 Board 50 Del from £195 **Services** Lift **Parking** 80 **Notes** LB ⊗ ⊗ in restaurant Civ Wed 160

★★★ 74% HOTEL

Angel

143 Regent St CV32 4NZ
☎ 01926 881296 📠 01926 313853
e-mail: angelhotel143@hotmail.com
web: www.angelhotelleamington.co.uk

dir: *in town centre at junct of Regent St and Holly Walk*

This centrally located hotel is divided in two parts - the original inn and a more modern extension. Public rooms include a comfortable foyer lounge area, a smart restaurant and an informal bar. Bedrooms are individual in style, and, whether modern or traditional, all have the expected facilities.

Rooms 48 en suite (3 fmly) S £55-£75; D £75-£85 (incl. bkfst) **Facilities** STV Xmas **Conf** Thtr 70 Class 40 Board 40 Del from £90 **Services** Lift **Parking** 38 **Notes** LB ⊗ in restaurant

★★★ 70% **HOTEL**

Best Western Falstaff

16-20 Warwick New Rd CV32 5JQ
☎ 01926 312044 📠 01926 450574
e-mail: falstaff@meridianleisure.com
web: www.meridianleisure.com

dir: M40 junct 13 or 14 follow signs for Leamington Spa. Over 4 rdbts under bridge. Left into Princes Drive, right at mini rdbt

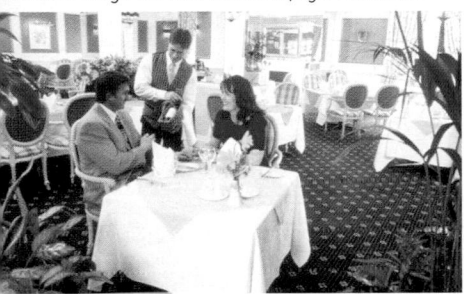

Bedrooms at this hotel come in a variety of sizes and styles and are well equipped, with many thoughtful extras. Snacks can be taken in the relaxing lounge bar, and an interesting selection of English and continental dishes is offered in the restaurant; 24-hour room service is also available. Conference and banqueting facilities are extensive.

Rooms 63 en suite (2 fmly) (16 GF) ⊗ in 28 bedrooms S £65-£85; D £75-£95 (Incl. bkfst) **Facilities** FTV Wi-fi in bedrooms Arrangement with local Health Club Xmas **Conf** Thtr 70 Class 30 Board 30 Del from £105 **Parking** 50 **Notes LB** ⊗ in restaurant Civ Wed 50

See advert on this page

★★★ 70% **HOTEL**

Courtyard by Marriott Leamington Spa

Olympus Av, Tachbrook Park CV34 6RJ
☎ 01926 425522 📠 01926 881322
e-mail: res.lspcourtyard@kewgreen.co.uk
web: www.kewgreen.co.uk

dir: M40 junct 13 (northbound exit) or M40 junct 14 (southbound exit) follow signs for Leamington Spa/A452

Just a short distance from both Warwick and Leamington Spa, this modern hotel is conveniently situated for local businesses and tourist attractions. Bedrooms are furnished and decorated to a high standard providing a comprehensive range of extras. A friendly and helpful team efficiently delivers a professional service.

Rooms 91 en suite (14 fmly) (13 GF) ⊗ in 48 bedrooms **Facilities** STV Gym **Conf** Thtr 70 Class 30 Board 40 **Services** Lift **Parking** 150 **Notes** ⊗ in restaurant

LEAMINGTON SPA (ROYAL) *continued*

★★★ 65% **HOTEL**

Episode Leamington

64 Upper Holly Walk CV32 4JL
☎ 01926 883777 📠 01926 330467
e-mail: leamington@episodehotels.com
dir: M40 junct 13, follow A452 signed Leamington Spa

This Victorian town house is situated near the thriving shopping centre of Leamington Spa, yet retains the relaxed and peaceful feel of yesteryear. Bedrooms are individually appointed and well equipped; public areas are full of character and include a traditional residents' lounge. Guests can dine in the atmospheric brasserie, or choose from the room service menu.

Rooms 32 en suite (3 GF) ⊗ in 20 bedrooms S £65-£85; D £75-£95 (incl. bkfst) **Facilities** Spa STV Wi-fi available Xmas **Conf** BC Thtr 40 Class 26 Board 20 Del from £120 **Parking** 20 **Notes** ⊗ in restaurant Civ Wed 60

See advert on page 641

BUDGET HOTEL

Travelodge Leamington Spa

The Parade CV32 4AT
☎ 08700 850950 📠 01926 432 473
web: www.travelodge.co.uk
dir: A425 follow town centre signs. Lodge off B4087

Travelodge offers good quality, good value, modern accommodation. Ideal for families, the spacious en suite bedrooms include remote-control TV, tea and coffee-making facilities and comfortable beds. Meals can be taken at the nearby family restaurant. See Hotel Groups pages for further details.

Rooms 54 en suite S fr £26; D fr £26

NUNEATON   **MAP 11 SP39**

★★★ 72% **HOTEL**

Best Western Weston Hall

Weston Ln, Bulkington CV12 9RU
☎ 024 7631 2989 📠 024 7664 0846
e-mail: info@westonhallhotel.co.uk
dir: M6 junct 2 follow B4065 through Ansty. Left in Shilton, follow Nuneaton signs out of Bulkington, turn into Weston Ln at 30mph sign

This Grade II listed hotel, whose origins date back to the reign of Elizabeth I, sits within seven acres of peaceful grounds. The original three-gabled building retains many original features, such as the
continued

---

carved wooden fireplace situated in the library. Friendly service is provided; and bedrooms, that vary in size, are thoughtfully equipped

Rooms 40 en suite (1 fmly) (14 GF) ⊗ in 26 bedrooms S £79-£105; D £100-£131 (incl. bkfst) **Facilities** Spa FTV 🏊 Wi-fi in bedrooms Steam room **Conf** BC Thtr 200 Class 100 Board 60 Del £145 **Parking** 300 **Notes LB** ⊗ in restaurant Civ Wed 200

See advert under COVENTRY, West Midland

BUDGET HOTEL

Days Inn Nuneaton

St David's Way, Bermuda Park CV10 7SD
☎ 024 7635 7370 & 0870 428 0928
📠 0870 428 0929
e-mail: reservations@daysinnnuneaton.co.uk
web: www.welcomebreak.co.uk
dir: M6 junct 3 onto A444 Nuneaton. Continue for 1m, left onto Bermuda Park. At rdbt right onto St David's Way, hotel on right.

This modern building offers accommodation in smart, spacious and well-equipped bedrooms, suitable for families and business travellers and all with en suite bathrooms. Continental breakfast is available and other refreshments may be taken at the nearby family restaurant. For further details see the Hotel Groups page.

Rooms 101 en suite **Conf** Thtr 30 Class 20 Board 24

BUDGET HOTEL

Premier Travel Inn Nuneaton/Coventry

Coventry Rd CV10 7PJ
☎ 08701 977201 📠 024 7632 7156
web: www.premiertravelinn.com
dir: M6 junct 3 follow A444 towards Nuneaton. Inn on the right just off Griff rdbt towards Bedworth on the B4113

High quality, modern budget accommodation ideal for both families and business travellers. Spacious, en suite bedrooms feature bath and shower, satellite TV and many have telephones and modem points. The adjacent family restaurant features a wide and varied menu. For further details consult the Hotel Groups page.

Rooms 48 en suite **Conf** Thtr 25

BUDGET HOTEL

Travelodge Nuneaton

St Nicholas Park Dr CV11 6EN
☎ 08700 850 950 📠 0870 1911594
web: www.travelodge.co.uk
dir: on A47

Travelodge offers good quality, good value, modern accommodation. Ideal for families, the spacious en suite bedrooms include remote-control TV, tea and coffee-making facilities and comfortable beds. Meals can be taken at the nearby family restaurant. See Hotel Groups pages for further details.

Rooms 28 en suite S fr £26; D fr £26

Travelodge Nuneaton Bedworth

Bedworth CV10 7TF
☎ 08700 850 950 📠 024 7638 2541
dir: on A444
Rooms 40 en suite S fr £26; D fr £26

RUGBY   MAP 11 SP57

★★★ 74% **HOTEL**

Golden Lion Hotel

Easenhall CV23 0JA

☎ 01788 833577 & 832265 📠 01788 832878

e-mail: reception@goldenlioninn.co.uk

web: www.goldenlioninn.co.uk

dir: A426 Avon Mill rdbt turn to Newbold-upon-Avon B4112, approx 2m left at Harborough Parva sign, opposite agricultural showroom, then 1m to Easenhall

This friendly, family run 16th-century inn is situated between Rugby and Coventry, convenient for access to the M6. Bedrooms, some of which are within a smart extension, are equipped with both practical and homely items and one features a stunning Chinese bed. The beamed bar and restaurant retain many original features and a warm welcome is assured.

Rooms 21 en suite (2 fmly) (6 GF) ⊗ in all bedrooms S £54-£84; D £64-£89 (incl. bkfst) **Facilities** FTV Wi-fi in bedrooms Xmas **Conf** Thtr 60 Class 30 Board 30 Del from £130 **Parking** 80 **Notes** ⊗ ⊛ in restaurant Civ Wed 100

★★★ 72% **HOTEL**

Grosvenor Hotel Rugby

81-87 Clifton Rd CV21 3QQ

☎ 01788 535686 📠 01788 541297

e-mail: reception@grosvenorhotelrugby.co.uk

dir: M6 junct 1, turn right onto A426 towards Rugby centre, at 1st rdbt turn left, on to T-junct and turn right onto B5414, hotel 1m on right

Close to the town centre, this family-owned hotel is popular with both business and leisure guests. The public rooms are cosy, inviting and pleasantly furnished, and service is both friendly and attentive.

continued

Bedrooms come in a variety of styles and sizes and include several newer rooms.

Rooms 26 en suite ⊗ in 9 bedrooms S £35-£70; D £50-£82.50 (incl. bkfst) **Facilities** Wi-fi available **Conf** Thtr 100 Class 50 Board 60 Del from £120 **Parking** 50 **Notes** LB ⊗ ⊛ in restaurant Civ Wed 100

★★★ 68% **HOTEL**

Brownsover Hall Hotel

Brownsover Ln, Old Brownsover CV21 1HU

☎ 0870 609 6104 & 01788 546100

📠 01788 579241

folio Hotels

dir: M6 junct 1, signs to Rugby A426. Dual-carriageway for 0.5m at rdbt signed "Ambulance & Brownsover Hall Hotel" turn right. Hotel 400mtrs on right

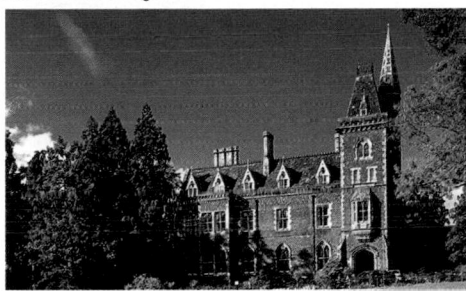

A mock-Gothic hall designed by Sir Gilbert Scott, set in seven acres of wooded parkland. Bedrooms vary in size and style, including spacious and contemporary rooms in the converted stable block. The former chapel makes a stylish restaurant, and for a less formal meal or a relaxing drink, the rugby themed bar is popular.

Rooms 27 en suite 20 annexe en suite (4 fmly) (12 GF) ⊗ in 38 bedrooms S £110; D £110 **Facilities** STV Free use of Virgin Active gym (0.5m away) Xmas **Conf** Thtr 70 Class 36 Board 35 Del £148 **Parking** 100 **Notes** LB ⊗ ⊛ in restaurant Civ Wed 56

BUDGET HOTEL

Hotel Ibis Rugby East

Parklands NN6 7EX

☎ 01788 824331 📠 01788 824332

e-mail: H3588@accor-hotels.com

web: www.ibishotel.com

(For full entry see Crick, Northamptonshire)

BUDGET HOTEL

Innkeeper's Lodge Rugby

The Green, Dunchurch CV22 6NJ

☎ 01788 810305 📠 01788 810931

web: www.innkeeperslodge.com

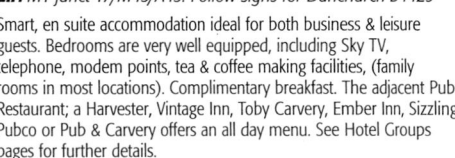

dir: M1 junct 17/M45/A45. Follow signs for Dunchurch B4429

Smart, en suite accommodation ideal for both business & leisure guests. Bedrooms are very well equipped, including Sky TV, telephone, modem points, tea & coffee making facilities, (family rooms in most locations). Complimentary breakfast. The adjacent Pub Restaurant; a Harvester, Vintage Inn, Toby Carvery, Ember Inn, Sizzling Pubco or Pub & Carvery offers an all day menu. See Hotel Groups pages for further details.

Rooms 16 en suite

England

RUGBY *continued*

BUDGET HOTEL

Premier Travel Inn Rugby

Central Park Dr, Central Park CV23 0WE

☎ 08701 977 223 🗎 01788 565949

web: www.premiertravelinn.com

High quality, modern budget accommodation ideal for both families and business travellers. Spacious, en suite bedrooms feature bath and shower, satellite TV and many have telephones and modem points. The adjacent family restaurant features a wide and varied menu. For further details consult the Hotel Groups page.

Rooms 60 en suite

STRATFORD-UPON-AVON   MAP 10 SP25

★★★★ @ @ HOTEL

Ettington Park

CV37 8BU

Hand PICKED

☎ 01789 450123 🗎 01789 450472

e-mail: ettingtonpark@handpicked.co.uk

web: www.handpicked.co.uk

(For full entry see Alderminster)

★★★★ 80% @ HOTEL

Macdonald Alveston Manor

Clopton Bridge CV37 7HP

MACDONALD
HOTELS & RESORTS

☎ 0870 400 8181 🗎 01789 414095

e-mail: sales.alvestonmanor@macdonald-hotels.co.uk

web: www.macdonald-hotels.co.uk

dir: S of Clopton Bridge

A striking red-brick and timbered façade, well-tended grounds, and a giant cedar tree all contribute to the charm of this well-established hotel, just five minutes from Stratford. The bedrooms vary in size and character - the coach house conversion offers an impressive mix of full and junior suites. The superb leisure complex offers a 20-metre swimming pool and steam room and sauna, a high-tech gym and a host of beauty treatments.

Rooms 113 en suite (8 fmly) (45 GF) ⊛ in 46 bedrooms S £75-£185; D £150-£185 **Facilities** STV ⊠ supervised Sauna Solarium Gym Wi-fi available Techno-gym, Beauty treatments Xmas **Conf** Thtr 140 Class 80 Board 40 Del from £150 **Services** air con **Parking** 150 **Notes LB** ⊛ in restaurant Civ Wed 110

Some hotels, although accepting children, may not have any special facilities for them so it is well worth checking before booking

---

★★★★ 80% @ HOTEL

Stratford Manor

MarstonHotels

Warwick Rd CV37 0PY

☎ 01789 731173 🗎 01789 731131

e-mail: stratfordmanor@marstonhotels.com

web: www.marstonhotels.com

dir: M40 junct 15, take A439, hotel 2m on left

Just outside Stratford, this hotel is set against a rural backdrop with lovely gardens and ample parking. Public areas include a lounge bar and a contemporary restaurant. Service is both professional and helpful. Bedrooms are smartly appointed, spacious and have generously sized beds, and a range of useful facilities. The leisure centre boasts a large indoor pool.

Rooms 104 en suite (8 fmly) ⊛ in all bedrooms S fr £32.50; D fr £171 (incl. bkfst) **Facilities Spa** STV ⊠ ☃ Sauna Solarium Gym Xmas **Conf** Thtr 350 Class 200 Board 100 Del from £210 **Services** Lift **Parking** 250 **Notes LB** ⊛ ⊛ in restaurant Civ Wed 250

★★★★ 77% @ @ HOTEL

Billesley Manor

Billesley, Alcester B49 6NF

PARAMOUNT
GROUP OF HOTELS

☎ 01789 279955 🗎 01789 764145

e-mail: enquiries@billesleymanor.co.uk

web: www.billesleymanor.co.uk

dir: A46 towards Evesham. Over 3 rdbts, right for Billesley after 2m

This 16th-century manor is set in peaceful grounds and parkland with a delightful yew topiary garden and fountain. The spacious bedrooms and suites, most in traditional country-house style, are thoughtfully designed and well equipped. Conference facilities and some of the bedrooms are found in the cedar barns. Public areas retain many original features, such as oak panelling, fireplaces and exposed stone.

continue

Rooms 43 en suite 29 annexe en suite (8 fmly) (5 GF) **Facilities** Spa TV 🗟 ♨ Sauna Solarium Gym 🏊 Wi-fi available Steam room, Beauty treatments, Yoga studio **Conf** Thtr 100 Class 60 Board 50 **Parking** 100 **Notes** ⊗ in restaurant Civ Wed 75

★★★★ 76% ⧆ **HOTEL**

Stratford Victoria

Arden St CV37 6QQ

☎ 01789 271000 📠 01789 271001

e-mail: stratfordvictoria@marstonhotels.com

web: www.marstonhotels.com

dir: A439 into Stratford. In town follow A3400/Birmingham, at lights left into Arden Street, hotel 150yds on right

Situated adjacent to the hospital, this eye-catching, modern hotel with its red-brick façade is within walking distance of the town centre. Bedrooms come in family, standard and executive styles, and also there is a luxury suite. The open-plan public areas include a comfortable lounge, a small atmospheric bar and spacious restaurant with exposed beams and ornately carved furniture.

Rooms 102 en suite (35 fmly) ⊗ in 40 bedrooms S fr £103; D fr £171 (incl. bkfst) **Facilities** Spa STV Gym Wi-fi available Xmas **Conf** Thtr 140 Class 66 Board 54 Del from £185 **Services** Lift **Parking** 100 **Notes LB** ⊗ in restaurant Civ Wed 160

★★★★ 71% ⧆ **HOTEL**

Macdonald Shakespeare

MACDONALD
HOTELS & RESORTS

Chapel St CV37 6ER

☎ 0870 400 8182 📠 01789 415411

e-mail: shakespeare@macdonald-hotels.co.uk

web: www.macdonald-hotels.co.uk

dir: M40 junct 15, A46 then A439 into one-way system, left at tbt opposite HSBC bank, hotel on left

Dating back to the early 17th century, The Shakespeare is one of the oldest hotels in this historic town. The hotel name also represents one of the earliest exploitations of Stratford as the birthplace of one of the world's leading poets and playwrights. With exposed beams and open fires, the public rooms retain an ambience reminiscent of this era. Bedrooms are appointed to a good standard and remain in keeping with the style of the property.

Rooms 63 en suite 11 annexe en suite (3 GF) ⊗ in 18 bedrooms **Facilities** STV Use of swimming pool at sister hotel **Conf** Thtr 80 Class 60 Board 40 **Services** Lift **Parking** 34 **Notes LB** ⊗ in restaurant Civ Wed 50

★★★★ 71% **HOTEL**

Holiday Inn Stratford-upon-Avon

Holiday Inn
HOTELS · RESORTS

Bridgefoot CV37 6YR

☎ 0870 225 4701 & 01789 279988 📠 01789 298589

e-mail: histratford@qmh-hotels.com

dir: A439 to Stratford-upon-Avon. Upon entering town road bears to left, hotel 200mtrs on left.

This large, modern hotel sits beside the River Avon within landscaped grounds which provides ample parking. Bedrooms have a light contemporary feel and are equipped with a good range of facilities that include air conditioning and Wi-Fi access. There is a terrace

continued on page 646

STRATFORD-UPON-AVON *continued*

lounge and bar, carvery restaurant and the Club Moativation health and fitness club.

Rooms 259 en suite (8 fmly) ⊗ in 201 bedrooms S £67-£155; D £67-£155 (incl. bkfst) **Facilities** ⌐ supervised Sauna Solarium Gym Jacuzzi **Conf** BC Thtr 550 Class 340 Board 42 Del from £120 **Services** Lift air con **Parking** 350 **Notes LB** ⊗ ⊗ in restaurant

★★★ 80% ⊛ HOTEL

Best Western Salford Hall
WR11 5UT

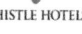

☎ 01386 871300 & 0800 212671 ▤ 01386 871301
e-mail: reception@salfordhall.co.uk
web: www.salfordhall.co.uk

(For full entry see Abbot's Salford)

See advert on page 645

★★★ 79% HOTEL

Best Western Grosvenor House
Warwick Rd CV37 6YT

☎ 01789 269213 ▤ 01789 266087
e-mail: info@groshotelstratford.co.uk

dir: *M40 junct 15, follow Stratford signs to A439 Warwick Rd. Hotel 7m, on one-way system*

This hotel is a short distance from the town centre and many of the historic attractions. Bedroom styles and sizes vary and the friendly staff offer an efficient service. Refreshments are served in the lounge all day, plus room service is available. The Garden Room restaurant offers a choice of dishes from set priced and carte menus.

Rooms 73 en suite (16 fmly) (25 GF) ⊗ in 25 bedrooms **Facilities** STV Wi-fi available Xmas **Conf** Thtr 100 Class 45 Board 50 Del from £145 **Parking** 55 **Notes** ⊗ ⊗ in restaurant Civ Wed 70

★★★ 78% HOTEL

Thistle Stratford-upon-Avon
Waterside CV37 6BA

THISTLE HOTELS

☎ 0870 333 9146 ▤ 0870 333 9246
e-mail: stratforduponavon@thistle.co.uk

dir: *M40 junct 15, A46 to Stratford-upon-Avon, take 1st exit at rdbt towards town centre, A439.*

The hotel is located just a very short walk from the town centre, sitting directly opposite the world famous Shakespeare and Swan theatres and is fronted by award-winning gardens. Service throughout the day rooms is both friendly and professional, offering separate bar and lounge areas, with the dining room providing interesting menu selections. Bedrooms are well equipped and comfortably appointed.

Rooms 63 en suite (4 fmly) ⊗ in 30 bedrooms **Facilities** STV **Conf** Thtr 50 Class 20 Board 20 **Parking** 55 **Notes LB** ⊗ in restaurant Civ Wed 50

★★ 72% HOTEL

The New Inn Hotel & Restaurant
Clifford Chambers CV37 8HR

☎ 01789 293402 ▤ 01789 292716
e-mail: thenewinn65@aol.com
web: www.thenewinnhotel.co.uk

dir: *A3400 onto B4632, 500yds on left*

This welcoming, family-run hotel is located in the pretty village of Clifford Chambers. The bar has an open log fire and, together with the restaurant, offers a choice of dining options. Bedrooms are attractive and some rooms have four-poster beds; rooms suitable for disabled guests are available.

Rooms 13 en suite (2 fmly) (3 GF) ⊗ in all bedrooms S £49.50-£73; D £73-£120 (incl. bkfst) **Facilities** ♫ Ch fac **Conf** Del from £77.50 **Parking** 40 **Notes LB** ⊗ ⊗ in restaurant Closed 23-28 Dec

★★ 62% HOTEL

Charlecote Pheasant Hotel
Charlecote CV35 9EW

*f*olio
Hotels

☎ 01789 279954 ▤ 01789 470222

dir: *M40 junct 15, take A429 towards Cirencester through Barford village after 2m turn right into Charlecote, hotel opposite Charlecote Manor Park*

Located just outside Stratford, this hotel is set in extensive grounds and is a popular conference venue. Various bedroom styles are available within the annexe wings, ranging from standard rooms to executive suites. The main building houses the restaurant and a lounge bar area.

Rooms 70 en suite (38 fmly) (20 GF) ⊗ in 26 bedrooms S £45-£98; D £90-£196 **Facilities** STV ⌐ ⌐ Childrens Play area Xmas **Conf** Thtr 160 Class 90 Board 50 Del from £105 **Parking** 100 **Notes LB** ⊗ in restaurant Civ Wed 176

Packed in a hurry?
Ironing facilities should be available at all star levels, either in the rooms or on request

[U]

Macdonald Swan's Nest

Bridgefoot CV37 7LT

☎ 0870 400 8183 📠 01789 414547

e-mail: sales.swansnest@macdonld-hotels.co.uk

web: www.macdonald-hotels.co.uk

dir: M40 junct 15, A46 for 2m, at 1st island turn left onto A439 towards Stratford. Follow one-way system, left over river bridge, hotel on right by river

At the time of going to press, the star classification for this hotel was not confirmed. Please refer to the AA internet site www.theAA.com for current information.

Rooms 67 en suite (2 fmly) (25 GF) ⊘ in 45 bedrooms **Facilities** Use of facilities at sister hotel **Conf** Thtr 150 Class 80 Board 40 **Parking** 80 **Notes** ⊘ in restaurant Civ Wed 110

WARWICK   MAP 10 SP26
See also Honiley & Leamington Spa (Royal)

★★★★ 79% ❀❀ **HOTEL**

Ardencote Manor Hotel, Country Club & Spa
Lye Green Rd CV35 8LS

☎ 01926 843111 📠 01926 842646

e-mail: hotel@ardencote.com

web: www.ardencote.com

(For full entry see Claverdon)

See advert on this page

★★★★ 64% **HOTEL**

Chesford Grange
Chesford Bridge CV8 2LD

☎ 01926 859331 📠 01926 859272

e-mail: chesfordgrangereservations@qhotels.co.uk

web: www.qhotels.co.uk

(For full entry see Kenilworth)

★★★ 66% **HOTEL**

Lord Leycester
Jury St CV34 4EJ

☎ 01926 491481 📠 01926 491561

e-mail: reception@lord-leycester.co.uk

web: www.lord-leycester.co.uk

dir: M40 junct 15/A429 into town centre, past West Gate onto High St & Jury St

This historic Grade II listed property is just a short walk from the famous castle. Attractive bedrooms and public rooms provide comfortable accommodation. A choice of eating options is available in either the informal Squires Buttery or the Knights Restaurant.

Rooms 48 en suite (3 fmly) ⊘ in 25 bedrooms S fr £57; D £75-£90 (incl. bkfst) **Facilities** STV Wi-fi in bedrooms Xmas **Conf** Thtr 120 Class 50 Board 40 Del from £105 **Services** Lift **Parking** 40 **Notes LB** ✗ ⊘ in restaurant Civ Wed 200

See advert on this page

England

WARWICK MOTORWAY SERVICE AREA (M40)
MAP 10 SP35

BUDGET HOTEL

Days Inn Stratford-upon-Avon

Warwick Services, M40 Northbound junction
12-13, Banbury Rd CV35 0AA
☎ 01926 651681 📠 01926 651634
e-mail: warwick.north.hotel@welcomebreak.co.uk
web: www.welcomebreak.co.uk
dir: M40 northbound between junct 12 & 13

This modern building offers accommodation in smart, spacious and well-equipped bedrooms, suitable for families and business travellers, and all with en suite bathrooms. Continental breakfast is available and other refreshments may be taken at the nearby family restaurant. For further details see the Hotel Groups page.

Rooms 54 en suite **Conf** Board 10

BUDGET HOTEL

Days Inn Warwick South
Warwick Services, M40 Southbound, Banbury Rd CV35 0AA
☎ 01926 650168 📠 01926 651601
dir: M40 southbound between junct 14 & 12

This modern building offers accommodation in smart, spacious and well-equipped bedrooms, suitable for families and business travellers, and all with en suite bathrooms. Continental breakfast is available and other refreshments may be taken at the nearby family restaurant. For further details see the Hotel Groups page.

Rooms 40 en suite

WELLESBOURNE
MAP 10 SP25

BUDGET HOTEL

Innkeeper's Lodge Stratford-upon-Avon East

Warwick Rd CV35 9LX
☎ 01789 840206 📠 01789 472902
web: www.innkeeperslodge.com
dir: M40 junct 15 S onto A429 towards Wellesbourne. Turn left at rdbt onto B4086 & lodge 300yds on right.

Smart, en suite accommodation ideal for both business & leisure guests. Bedrooms are very well equipped, including Sky TV, telephone, modem points, tea & coffee making facilities, (family rooms in most locations). Complimentary breakfast. The adjacent Pub Restaurant; a Harvester, Vintage Inn, Toby Carvery, Ember Inn, Sizzling Pubco or Pub & Carvery offers an all day menu. See Hotel Groups pages for further details.

Rooms 9 en suite

The vast majority of establishments in this guide accept credit and debit cards. We indicate only those that don't take any

WISHAW
MAP 10 SP1⁹

★★★★ 80% 🏵 **HOTEL**

The De Vere Belfry
B76 9PR
☎ 0870 900 0066 📠 01675 470256
e-mail: enquiries@thebelfry.com
web: www.thebelfry.com
dir: M42 junct 9, A446 towards Lichfield, hotel 1m on right

Well known as a venue for the Ryder Cup, The Belfry has three championship golf courses along with many other leisure facilities. There is a sophisticated French restaurant and cocktail bar, and the spa centre boasts an impressive range of health and beauty treatments. Bedrooms vary in size, style and location; many have spectacular views.

Rooms 324 en suite (134 fmly) (50 GF) ⊘ in all bedrooms
Facilities Spa STV 🔍 supervised 🏌 18 🏊 Squash Snooker Sauna Solarium Gym Putt green Jacuzzi Wi-fi available Hair & day spa, night club 🎵 Xmas **Conf** Thtr 400 Class 260 Board 42 **Services** Lift **Parking** 1000 **Notes** ❉ ⊘ in restaurant Civ Wed 400

WROXALL
MAP 10 SP2⁷

🇺

Wroxall Abbey Estate
Birmingham Rd CV35 7NB
☎ 01926 484470 📠 01926 485206
e-mail: info@wroxall.com
dir: between Solihull and Warwick on A4141

At the time of going to press, the star classification for this hotel was not confirmed. Please refer to the AA internet site www.theAA.com for current information.

Rooms 48 en suite 22 annexe en suite (10 GF) ⊘ in 2 bedrooms
S £79-£99; D £79-£99 **Facilities** Spa STV 🔍 🏊 Fishing Sauna Gym Jacuzzi 🎵 Xmas **Conf** Thtr 160 Class 80 Board 60 Del from £159
Services Lift **Parking** 200 **Notes** LB ❉ No children 12yrs ⊘ in restaurant Civ Wed 200

WEST MIDLANDS

BALSALL COMMON
MAP 10 SP2⁷

★★★★ 76% 🏵🏵 **HOTEL**

Nailcote Hall
Nailcote Ln, Berkswell CV7 7DE
☎ 024 7646 6174 📠 024 7647 0720
e-mail: info@nailcotehall.co.uk
web: www.nailcotehall.co.uk
dir: on B4101

This 17th-century house, set in 15 acres of grounds, boasts a 9-hole championship golf course and Roman bath-style swimming pool amongst its many facilities. Rooms are spacious and elegantly furnished. Dinner may be taken in the fine dining restaurant where smart casual dress is required, or informal meals in The Piano Bar.

Rooms 21 en suite 19 annexe en suite (2 fmly) (15 GF) ⊘ in 30 bedrooms S £100-£185; D £110-£195 (incl. bkfst) **Facilities** Spa STV 🔍 supervised 🏌 9 🏊 Snooker Solarium Gym 🏌 Putt green Jacuzzi W fi in bedrooms 🎵 Xmas **Conf** Thtr 140 Class 80 Board 44 Del from £14⁵ **Services** Lift **Parking** 200 **Notes** LB ❉ ⊘ in restaurant Civ Wed 120

★★★ 74% ◎ HOTEL

Haigs

Kenilworth Rd CV7 7EL

☎ 01676 533004 ▤ 01676 535132

e-mail: info@haigsemail.co.uk

dir: on A452 4m N of Kenilworth & 6m S of M6 junct 4. 5m S of M42 junct 6. 8m N of M40 junct 15

This hotel, set in residential surroundings, offers a warm welcome, highly attentive service and good food. The comfortable bedrooms are decorated in an attractive, homely style, and facilities include a lounge bar and a meeting room. It is well positioned for Birmingham NEC and just 5 miles from the M6.

Rooms 23 en suite (5 GF) ⊗ in 8 bedrooms S £60-£75; D £85-£107 (incl. bkfst) **Conf** Thtr 25 Board 16 Del £140 **Parking** 23 **Notes LB** ⊛ ⊗ in restaurant Closed 26 Dec-3 Jan & Etr RS Mon-Sat & Sun Lunch

BUDGET HOTEL

Premier Travel Inn Balsall Common (Near NEC)

Kenilworth Rd CV7 7EX

☎ 08701 977022 ▤ 01676 535929

web: www.premiertravelinn.com

dir: M42 junct 6, A45 towards Coventry for 0.5m, then A452 towards Leamington, Inn 3m on right

High quality, modern budget accommodation ideal for both families and business travellers. Spacious, en suite bedrooms feature bath and shower, satellite TV and many have telephones and modem points. The adjacent family restaurant features a wide and varied menu. For further details consult the Hotel Groups page.

Rooms 42 en suite

BIRMINGHAM   MAP 10 SP08

See also Bromsgrove (Worcestershire), Lea Marston (Warwickshire), Oldbury & Sutton Coldfield

★★★★ 80% ◎ HOTEL

Birmingham Marriott Hotel

Marriott
HOTELS & RESORTS

12 Hagley Rd, Five Ways B16 8SJ

☎ 0121 452 1144 ▤ 0121 456 3442

e-mail: pascal.demarchi@whitbread.com

web: www.marriott.co.uk

Situated in the suburb of Edgbaston, this Edwardian hotel is a prominent landmark on the outskirts of the city centre. Air-conditioned bedrooms are decorated in a comfortable, modern style and provide a

continued

comprehensive range of extra facilities. Public rooms include the contemporary, brasserie-style West 12 Bar and Restaurant.

Rooms 104 en suite ⊗ in 80 bedrooms S £135 D £135 **Facilities Spa** STV ⊠ Solarium Gym Jacuzzi Wi-fi available Beauty salon, Steam room Xmas **Conf** Thtr 80 Board 35 Del from £140 **Services** Lift air con **Parking** 50 **Notes LB** ⊛ ⊗ in restaurant Civ Wed 60

★★★★ 77% HOTEL

Macdonald Burlington

MACDONALD
HOTELS & RESORTS

Burlington Arcade, 126 New St B2 4JQ

☎ 0870 1942124 ▤ 0121 628 5005

e-mail: mail@burlingtonhotel.com

web: www.macdonald-hotels.co.uk

dir: M6 junct 6, follow signs for city centre, then onto A38

The Burlington's original Victorian grandeur - marble and iron staircases, high ceilings - has been blended together with modern facilities. Bedrooms are equipped to a good standard and public areas include a stylish bar and coffee lounge. The Berlioz Restaurant specialises in innovative dishes using fresh produce.

Rooms 112 en suite (6 fmly) ⊗ in 49 bedrooms S£149-£159; D £159-£180 **Facilities Spa** STV Sauna Gym Jacuzzi Wi-fi available **Conf** Thtr 400 Class 175 Del £150 **Services** Lift air con **Notes LB** Closed 25-26 Dec Civ Wed 320

★★★★ 76% ◎ TOWN HOUSE HOTEL

Hotel du Vin & Bistro

Hotel du Vin
&
Bistro

25 Church St B3 2NR

☎ 0121 200 0600 ▤ 0121 236 0889

e-mail: info@birmingham.hotelduvin.com

web: www.hotelduvin.com

dir: M6 junct 6/A38(M) to city centre, over flyover. Keep left & exit at St Chads Circus signed Jewellery Quarter. At traffic lights & rdbt take 1st exit, follow signs for Colmore Row, opposite Cathedral. Right into Church St, across Berwick St. Hotel on right

The former Birmingham Eye Hospital has certainly been dramatically transformed, with the Victorian structure becoming a chic, sophisticated hotel. Stylish, high-ceilinged rooms, all with a wine theme, are luxuriously appointed and feature stunning bathrooms, sumptuous duvets and Egyptian cotton sheets. The Bistro offers relaxed dining and a top-notch wine list, while other attractions include a champagne bar, a cigar and wine boutique and a health club.

Rooms 66 en suite S fr £135; D fr £135 **Facilities** STV Snooker Sauna Solarium Gym Wi-fi in bedrooms Treatment rooms Xmas **Conf** Thtr 80 Class 40 Board 40 Del £205 **Services** Lift air con **Notes** ⊗ in restaurant Civ Wed 60

★★★★ 73% ◎ HOTEL

Copthorne Hotel Birmingham

COPTHORNE

Paradise Circus B3 3HJ

☎ 0121 200 2727 ▤ 0121 200 1197

e-mail: reservations.birmingham@mill-cop.com

web: www.copthornebirmingham.co.uk

dir: M6 junct 6, city centre A38(M). After Queensway Tunnel emerge left, follow International Convention Centre signs . Paradise Circus island - follow right lane - hotel in centre.

This hotel is one of the few establishments in the city that benefits from its own car park. Bedrooms are spacious and come in a choice

continued on page 650

England

BIRMINGHAM *continued*

of styles, all with excellent facilities. Guests can enjoy a variety of dining options, including the contemporary menu in Goldies Brasserie.

Rooms 212 en suite ⊘ in 108 bedrooms S £165-£195; D £185-£215 **Facilities** STV Gym Wi-fi available Xmas **Conf** BC Thtr 200 Class 120 Board 30 Del £185 **Services** Lift **Parking** 88 **Notes LB** ⊗

★★★ 80% ⊛ **HOTEL**

Malmaison Birmingham

1 Wharfside St, The Mailbox B1 1RD
☎ 0121 246 5000 📠 0121 246 5002
e-mail: birmingham@malmaison.com
web: www.malmaison.com

Malmaison
hotels that dare to be different

dir: M6 junct 6, follow A38 towards B'ham, hotel signed

The 'Mailbox' development, of which this stylish and contemporary hotel is a part, incorporates the very best in fashionable shopping, an array of restaurants and ample parking. Air-conditioned bedrooms are stylishly decorated and feature comprehensive facilities. Public rooms include a contemporary bar and brasserie which are proving a hit with guests and locals alike. Gymtonic and a Petit Spa are also available, offering rejuvenating treatments.
Malmaison - AA Hotel Group of the Year 2006-7.

Rooms 189 en suite ⊘ in 132 bedrooms S £99-£140; D £99-£140 **Facilities Spa** STV Sauna Gym Jacuzzi Wi-fi available **Conf** Thtr 40 Class 24 Board 24 Del from £175 **Services** Lift air con **Notes** ⊘ in restaurant

★★★ 78% **HOTEL**

Best Western Westley

80-90 Westley Rd, Acocks Green B27 7UJ
☎ 0121 706 4312 📠 0121 706 2824
e-mail: reservations@westley-hotel.co.uk
web: www.westley-hotel.co.uk

Best Western

dir: A41 signed Birmingham on Solihull by-pass, continue to Acocks Green. At rdbt, 2nd exit B4146 Westley Rd. Hotel 200yds on left

Situated in the city suburbs and conveniently located for the N.E.C. and the airport, this friendly hotel provides well-equipped, smartly presented bedrooms. In addition to the main restaurant, there is also a lively bar and brasserie together with a large function room.

Rooms 26 en suite 11 annexe en suite (1 fmly) ⊘ in 15 bedrooms **Facilities** STV ♫ **Conf** Thtr 200 Class 80 Board 50 **Parking** 150 **Notes LB** ⊘ in restaurant Civ Wed 200

See also advert on page 651

★★★ 74% **HOTEL**

Thistle Birmingham City

St Chads, Queensway B4 6HY
☎ 0870 333 9126 📠 0870 333 9226
e-mail: reservations.birmingham@thistle.co.uk

THISTLE HOTELS

dir: M6 junct 6 onto Aston Expressway towards city centre, after 1m exit A38 signed Jewellery Quarter. Hotel to left of exit.

This hotel benefits from a central location and is convenient for both the motorway network and extensive parking facilities. Bedrooms range in size and style with executive rooms providing air conditioning and a host of thoughtful extras. A modern comfortable lounge bar links to an alfresco terrace whilst a Mediterranean restaurant specialises in imaginative theme nights.

Rooms 133 en suite (3 fmly) ⊘ in 69 bedrooms **Facilities** STV **Conf** Thtr 180 Class 80 Board 30 **Services** Lift **Notes LB** ⊗ ⊘ in restaurant Civ Wed 140

★★★ 73% **HOTEL**

Thistle Birmingham Edgbaston

225 Hagley Rd, Edgbaston B16 9RY
☎ 0870 333 9127 📠 0870 333 9227
e-mail: reservations.birminghamedgebaston@thistle.co.uk

THISTLE HOTELS

dir: From A38 follow signs for ICC onto Broad St. Towards Five Ways island take underpass to Hagley Rd. Hotel 1m on right.

Located a few minutes from central attractions and with the benefit of excellent parking, this hotel provides a range of bedrooms (with exterior rooms being of a superior standard) but all offer good business communications and in-room entertainment. The public bar features a large screen with sports television channels.

Rooms 151 en suite ⊘ in 69 bedrooms **Facilities** Pool table **Conf** Thtr 170 Class 90 Board 50 **Services** Lift **Parking** 120 **Notes LB** ⊗ ⊘ in restaurant Civ Wed 40

★★★ 72% **HOTEL**

Novotel Birmingham Centre

70 Broad St B1 2HT
☎ 0121 643 2000 📠 0121 643 9796
e-mail: h1077@accor.com
web: www.novotel.com

NOVOTEL
Accor

This large, modern, purpose-built hotel benefits from an excellent city centre location, with the bonus of secure parking. Bedrooms are spacious, modern and well equipped especially for business users; four rooms have facilities for less mobile guests. Public areas include the Garden Brasserie, function rooms and a fitness room.

Rooms 148 en suite (148 fmly) ⊘ in 112 bedrooms S £85-£155; D £95-£165 (incl. bkfst) **Facilities** STV Sauna Gym Jacuzzi Wi-fi in bedrooms **Conf** Thtr 300 Class 120 Board 90 Del from £130 **Services** Lift air con **Parking** 53 **Notes LB** ⊘ in restaurant

★★★ 68% **HOTEL**

Great Barr Hotel & Conference Centre

Pear Tree Dr, Newton Rd, Great Barr B43 6HS

☎ 0121 357 1141 📠 0121 357 7557

e-mail: sales@thegreatbarrhotel.com

web: www.thegreatbarrhotel.com

dir: M6 junct 7, at Scott Arms x-rds turn right towards West Bromwich (A4010) Newton Rd. Hotel 1m from Scotts Arms, on right

This busy hotel, situated in a residential area, is particularly popular with business people. Bedrooms are well equipped and modern in style. There is a wide range of meeting rooms, a traditional oak-panelled bar and formal restaurant.

Rooms 105 en suite (6 fmly) ⊗ in 50 bedrooms **Facilities** STV Xmas **Conf** Thtr 200 Class 90 Board 60 **Parking** 200 **Notes** ⊗ RS BH (Restaurant may be closed) Civ Wed 200

★★★ 68% **HOTEL**

Jurys Inn Birmingham

JURYS DOYLE HOTELS

245 Broad St B1 2HQ

☎ 0121 626 0626 & 606 9000 📠 0121 626 0627

e-mail: jurysinn_birmingham@jurysdoyle.com

web: www.jurysdoyle.com

dir: on A456 in city centre

This large hotel is ideally located in the centre of the city and offers extensive conference facilities. Bedrooms are spacious and modern in design and the restaurant is designed for efficiency, offering a buffet-style operation.

Rooms 445 en suite (336 fmly) ⊗ in 325 bedrooms S £49-£175; D £49-£175 **Facilities** STV Wi-fi available **Conf** Thtr 280 Class 144 Board 44 Del from £145 **Services** Lift air con **Parking** 230 **Notes** ⊗ ⊗ in restaurant Closed 24-26 Dec

★★★ 67% **HOTEL**

The Westmead Hotel

folio Hotels

Redditch Rd, Hopwood B48 7AL

☎ 0870 609 6119 📠 0121 445 6163

dir: M42 junct 2 towards Birmingham on A441. At rdbt turn right and follow A441 for 1m. Hotel on right

In a quiet location on the outskirts of the city, yet close to the M42, this hotel offers a number of meeting and conference rooms. The bedrooms are generally spacious, well equipped and comfortable.

continued on page 652

BIRMINGHAM *continued*

A spacious bar offers carvery lunches and dinner is served in the adjacent restaurant.

The Westmead Hotel

Rooms 58 en suite (2 fmly) ⊛ in 31 bedrooms S £93; D £93 **Facilities** STV **Conf** Thtr 220 Class 120 Board 80 Del from £130 **Parking** 200 **Notes LB** ⊛ in restaurant Civ Wed 120

★★★ 66% HOTEL

Quality Hotel Birmingham

166 Hagley Rd B66 9NZ
☎ 0121 454 6621 ▤ 0121 456 2935
e-mail: gm@quality-hotel-birmingham.com
web: www.choicehotelseurope.com

dir: on A456, accessible from M5 junct 3 or M6 junct 6

Located a few minutes' drive from central attractions, this popular hotel provides a range of bedrooms that have undergone refurbished throughout 2006. Public areas include a terrace bar offering a happy hour, and a spacious restaurant serving specialities on some evenings. A leisure club is available for guest use.

Rooms 177 en suite (29 GF) ⊛ in 91 bedrooms S £25-£85; D £41-£140 **Facilities** Spa STV ⬚ supervised Solarium Gym Jacuzzi Xmas **Conf** Thtr 100 Class 50 Board 40 Del from £85 **Services** Lift **Parking** 120 **Notes LB** ⊛ in restaurant Civ Wed 50

★★ 76% HOTEL

Copperfield House

60 Upland Rd, Selly Park B29 7JS
☎ 0121 472 8344 ▤ 0121 415 5655
e-mail: info@copperfieldhousehotel.fsnet.co.uk

dir: M6 junct 6/A38 through city centre. After tunnels, right at lights into Belgrave Middleway. Right at rdbt onto A441. At Selly Park Tavern, right into Upland Rd

A delightful Victorian hotel, situated in a leafy suburb, close to the BBC's Pebble Mill Studios and within easy reach of the centre. Accommodation is smartly presented and well equipped, and the executive rooms are particularly spacious. There is a lounge with an honesty bar and the restaurant offers carefully prepared, seasonally-inspired food accompanied by a well-chosen wine list.

Rooms 17 en suite (1 fmly) (2 GF) S £45-£69.50; D £65-£85 (incl. bkfst) **Facilities** FTV **Conf** BC **Parking** 11 **Notes LB** ⊛ in restaurant Closed 24 Dec-2 Jan

★★ 68% HOTEL

Fountain Court

339-343 Hagley Rd, B17 8NH
☎ 0121 429 1754 ▤ 0121 429 1209
e-mail: info@fountain-court.co.uk

THE INDEPENDENTS

dir: on A456, towards Birmingham, 3m from M5 junct 3

This family-owned hotel is on the A456, near to the M5 and a short drive from the city centre. A warm welcome is assured and day rooms include comfortable lounges and a cottage-style dining room, the setting for home-cooked dinners and comprehensive breakfasts.

Rooms 23 en suite (4 fmly) (3 GF) S £39.50-£48.50; D £60-£70 (incl. bkfst) **Parking** 20 **Notes** ⊛ in restaurant

★★ Ⓐ

Woodlands

379-381 Hagley Rd, Edgbaston B17 8DL
☎ 0121 420 2341
e-mail: hotel@woodlands2000.freeserve.co.uk
web: www.thewoodlandshotel.co.uk

Rooms 20 en suite (2 fmly) ⊛ in 4 bedrooms S £45-£50; D £56-£64 (incl. bkfst) **Facilities** Snooker Xmas **Parking** 25 **Notes LB** ⊗ ⊛ in restaurant

Ⓤ

Swallow Plough & Harrow

135 Hagley Rd B16 8LS
☎ 0121 454 4111 ▤ 0121 454 1868
e-mail: swallow.birmingham@swallowhotels.com
web: www.swallowhotels.com

SWALLOW
HOTELS

dir: M5 junct 3, A456 towards Birmingham. Hotel approx 4.5m on left

At the time of going to press, the star classification for this hotel was not confirmed. Please refer to the AA internet site www.theAA.com for current information.

Rooms 44 en suite (6 fmly) (11 GF) ⊛ in 33 bedrooms S £50-£106; D £70-£113 (incl. bkfst) **Facilities** STV **Conf** Thtr 80 Class 40 Board 20 Del from £105 **Parking** 90 **Notes** ⊛ in restaurant Civ Wed 100

BUDGET HOTEL

Campanile

Aston Locks, Chester St B6 4BE
☎ 0121 359 3330 ▤ 0121 359 1223
e-mail: birmingham@envergure.co.uk
web: www.envergure.fr

Campanile

dir: next to rdbt at junct of A4540/A38

This modern building offers accommodation in smart, well-equipped bedrooms, all with en suite bathrooms. Refreshments may be taken

continued

at the informal Bistro. For further details consult the Hotel Groups page.

Campanile

Rooms 109 en suite **Conf** Del from £75

Comfort Inn Birmingham City Centre

Station St B5 4DY

☎ 0121 643 1134

e-mail: comfort.inn2talk.com

dir: M6 junct 6. A38 city centre, Queensway ring road to Holloway Head/Smallbridge Queensway, left into hill street and 1st right.

This modern building offers accommodation in smart, spacious and well equipped bedrooms, all with en suite bathrooms. Refreshments may be taken at the nearby family restaurant. For further details and the Comfort Inn phone number, consult the Hotel Groups page under 'Choice'.

Rooms 40 en suite **Conf** Thtr 50 Class 25 Board 30

Days Inn Birmingham

Poet's Corner, Golden Hillcock Rd B11 2PN **DAYSINN**

This modern building offers accommodation in smart, spacious and well-equipped bedrooms, suitable for families and business travellers, and all with en suite bathrooms. Continental breakfast is available and other refreshments may be taken at the nearby family restaurant. For further details see the Hotel Groups page.

Rooms 52 en suite

Hotel Ibis Birmingham Holloway

ibis

55 Irving St B1 1DH

☎ 0121 622 4925 ▤ 0121 622 4195

e-mail: H2092@accor.com

web: www.ibishotel.com

dir: from M6 take A38/City Centre, left after 2nd tunnel. Right at rdbt, 4th left (Sutton St) into Irving St. Hotel on left

Modern, budget hotel offering comfortable accommodation in bright and practical bedrooms. Breakfast is self-service and dinner is available in the restaurant. For further details, consult the Hotel Groups page.

Rooms 51 en suite

Hotel Ibis Birmingham Bordesley

1 Bordesley Park Rd, Bordesley B10 0PD

☎ 0121 506 2600 ▤ 0121 506 2610

e-mail: H2178@accor-hotels.com

Rooms 87 en suite

Hotel Ibis Birmingham Centre

Arcadian Centre, Ladywell Walk B5 4ST

☎ 0121 622 6010 ▤ 0121 622 6020

e-mail: h1459@accor-hotels.com

dir: Follow signs to city centre from all motorways. Then follow Bullring or Indoor Market signs. Hotel next to market.

Rooms 159 en suite S £57-£72; D £57-£72 **Conf** BC Thtr 100 Class 60 Board 40

Innkeeper's Lodge Birmingham West (Quinton)

Innkeeper's Lodge

563 Hagley Rd West, Quinton B32 1HP

☎ 0121 423 3895

web: www.innkeeperslodge.com

dir: M5 junct 3/A456 westbound. On opposite side of dual carriageway, accessed a short distance from rdbt

Smart, en suite accommodation ideal for both business & leisure guests. Bedrooms are very well equipped, including Sky TV, telephone, modem points, tea & coffee making facilities, (family rooms in most locations). Complimentary breakfast. The adjacent Pub Restaurant; a Harvester, Vintage Inn, Toby Carvery, Ember Inn, Sizzling Pubco or Pub & Carvery offers an all day menu. See Hotel Groups pages for further details.

Rooms 24 en suite

Premier Travel Inn Birmingham Broad Street

premier travel inn

20 Bridge St B1 2JH

☎ 08701 977031 ▤ 0121 633 4779

web: www.premiertravelinn.com

dir: From M6/M5/M42 follow signs for city centre. Bridge St off A456 (Broad Street). Turn left in front of Hyatt Hotel, Inn on right

High quality, modern budget accommodation ideal for both families and business travellers. Spacious, en suite bedrooms feature bath and shower, satellite TV and many have telephones and modem points. The adjacent family restaurant features a wide and varied menu. For further details consult the Hotel Groups page.

Rooms 53 en suite

Premier Travel Inn Birmingham Central East

Richard St, Aston, Waterlinks B7 4AA

☎ 0870 238 3312 ▤ 0121 333 6490

dir: On ring road A4540 at junct with A38(M). From M6 junct 6 take 2nd exit off A38(M), ring road, left at island, 1st left

Rooms 60 en suite **Conf** Thtr 14

England

BIRMINGHAM *continued*

Premier Travel Inn Birmingham South

Birmingham Great Park, Ashbrook Drive, Parkway, Rubery B45 9FP

☎ 0870 9906538 📠 0870 9906539

dir: *M5 junct 4 onto A38 towards Birmingham. Left into Birmingham Great Park. Hotel behind superstore*

Rooms 62 en suite **Conf** Board 12

Premier Travel Inn Broad Street (Fiveways)

80 Broad St B15 1AU

☎ 0870 9906404 📠 0870 9906405

dir: *Exit M6 junct 6 onto A38 Aston Expressway. Follow city centre, ICC & NIA signs, onto Broad St. Right at lights, 2nd left at rdbt. Hotel on left*

Rooms 60 en suite **Conf** Thtr 60

BUDGET HOTEL

Ramada Hotel Birmingham City Centre

160 Wharfside St, The Mailbox B1 1RL

☎ 0121 643 9344 📠 0121 643 2044

e-mail: reservations.mailbox@dayshotel.co.uk

Rooms 90 en suite **Conf** Thtr 90 Board 52

BUDGET HOTEL

Sleep Inn

Heartlands Park Way, Star City

☎ 0500 616263 📠 0500 005000

dir: *Exit M6 junct 6, follow directions to Star City. Hotel opposite road to Star City*

This modern, purpose built accommodation offers smartly appointed, well-equipped bedrooms, with good power showers. There is a choice of adjacent food outlets where guests may enjoy breakfast, snacks and meals.

Rooms 90 en suite S £62.50-£69.50; D £62.50-£69.50 **Conf** Thtr 35 Class 25 Board 18 Del from £75

BUDGET HOTEL

Travelodge Birmingham Central

230 Broad St B15 1AY

☎ 08700 850 950 📠 0121 644 5251

web: www.travelodge.co.uk

dir: *lodge on left corner of Broad St/Granville St*

Travelodge offers good quality, good value, modern accommodation. Ideal for families, the spacious en suite bedrooms include remote-control TV, tea and coffee-making facilities and comfortable beds. Meals can be taken at the nearby family restaurant. See Hotel Groups pages for further details.

Rooms 136 en suite S fr £26; D fr £26

Travelodge Birmingham Fort Dunlop

Fort Parkway, Erdington B24 9FD

☎ 0870 191 1812 📠 0121 747 9958

Rooms 100 en suite S fr £26; D fr £26

Travelodge Birmingham Yardley

A45 Coventry Rd, Acocks Green, Yardley B26 1DS

☎ 08700 850 950 📠 0121 764 5882

dir: *on A45 approx 5m from M42 junct 6*

Rooms 40 en suite S fr £26; D fr £26

BIRMINGHAM AIRPORT   **MAP 10 SP08**

★★★ 73% **HOTEL**

Novotel Birmingham Airport

B26 3QL

☎ 0121 782 7000 & 782 4111 📠 0121 782 0445

e-mail: H1158@accor.com

web: www.novotel.com

dir: *M42 junct 6/A45 to Birmingham, signed to airport. Hotel opposite main terminal*

This large, purpose-built hotel is located opposite the main passenger terminal. Bedrooms are spacious, modern in style and well equipped, including Playstations to keep the children busy. Several rooms have facilities for less able guests. The Garden Brasserie is open from noon until midnight, the bar is open 24 hours and a full room service is available. Overall facilities have been further upgraded in 2006.

Rooms 195 en suite (31 fmly) ⊛ in 159 bedrooms S £85-£150; D £85-£150 **Facilities** STV Wi-fi in bedrooms **Conf** BC Thtr 35 Class 20 Board 22 Del from £159 **Services** Lift

---

BIRMINGHAM   **MAP 10 SP18**
(NATIONAL EXHIBITION CENTRE)

★★★★ 76% ❀ **HOTEL**

Nailcote Hall

Nailcote Ln, Berkswell CV7 7DE

☎ 024 7646 6174 📠 024 7647 0720

e-mail: info@nailcotehall.co.uk

web: www.nailcotehall.co.uk

(For full entry see Balsall Common)

★★★★ 71% **HOTEL**

Best Western Premier Moor Hall Hotel & Spa

Moor Hall Dr, Four Oaks B75 6LN

☎ 0121 308 3751 📠 0121 308 8974

e-mail: mail@moorhallhotel.co.uk

web: www.moorhallhotel.co.uk

(For full entry see Sutton Coldfield)

★★★ 74% ❀ **HOTEL**

Haigs

Kenilworth Rd CV7 7EL

☎ 01676 533004 📠 01676 535132

e-mail: info@haigsemail.co.uk

(For full entry see Balsall Common)

★★★ 71% HOTEL

Arden Hotel & Leisure Club

Coventry Rd, Bickenhill B92 0EH

☎ 01675 443221 ▤ 01675 445604

e-mail: enquiries@ardenhotel.co.uk

dir: *M42 junct 6/A45 towards Birmingham. Hotel 0.25m on right, just off Birmingham International railway island*

This smart hotel neighbouring the NEC offers modern rooms and well-equipped leisure facilities. After dinner in the formal restaurant, the place to relax is the spacious lounge area. A buffet breakfast is served in the bright and airy Meeting Place.

Rooms 216 en suite (6 fmly) (6 GF) ⊛ in 121 bedrooms S £75-£119.75; D £89-£159.50 **Facilities** STV ❊ supervised Snooker Jacuzzi Sauna Solarium Gym Wi-fi in bedrooms Steamroom ♫ Xmas **Conf** Thtr 200 Class 40 Board 60 Del from £150 **Services** Lift **Parking** 300 **Notes** ⊛ in restaurant RS 25 20 Dec Civ Wed 100

See advert on this page

★★ 68% HOTEL

Heath Lodge

117 Coleshill Rd, Marston Green B37 7HT

☎ 0121 779 2218 ▤ 0121 770 5648

e-mail: reception@heathlodgehotel.freeserve.co.uk

dir: *1m N of NEC, Birmingham International Airport and station. From M6 take A446, A452, junct 4.*

This privately owned and personally run hotel is ideally located for visitors to the NEC and Birmingham Airport. Hospitality and service standards are high and while some bedrooms are compact, all are well equipped and comfortable. Public areas include a bar, a lounge and dining room which overlooks the pretty garden.

Rooms 17 rms (16 en suite) (1 fmly) (1 GF) ⊛ in 6 bedrooms S £49-£59; D £69-£77 (incl. bkfst) **Facilities** Wi-fi available ch fac **Conf** BC Thtr 20 Class 16 Board 14 **Parking** 24 **Notes** LB ⊛ in restaurant Closed 25-26 Dec, 1 Jan

BUDGET HOTEL

Premier Travel Inn Birmingham NEC/Airport

Bickenhill Parkway, Northway, National Exhibition Centre B40 1QA

☎ 0870 9906326 ▤ 0870 9906327

web: www.premiertravelinn.com

dir: *From M6 junct 4 onto A446 towards Warwick, left in 0.5m signed NEC. 2nd exit at rdbt. At next rdbt take 2nd exit onto Bickenhill Parkway, follow Birmingham Airport signs. At next rdbt take 1st exit to hotel*

High quality, modern budget accommodation ideal for both families and business travellers. Spacious, en suite bedrooms feature bath and shower, satellite TV and many have telephones and modem points. The adjacent family restaurant features a wide and varied menu. For further details consult the Hotel Groups page.

Rooms 199 en suite **Conf** Class 12

COVENTRY

MAP 10 SP37

See also Brandon (Warwickshire), Meriden & Nuneaton (Warwickshire)

★★★ 73% HOTEL

Courtyard by Marriott Coventry

London Rd, Ryton on Dunsmore CV8 3DY

☎ 0870 400 7216 ▤ 0870 400 7316

e-mail: res.cvcourtyard@kewgreen.co.uk

web: www.kewgreen.co.uk

dir: *M6 junct 2, take A46 towards Warwick, then A45 London at Coventry Airport*

Located on the outskirts of the city, this modern hotel appeals to both business and leisure guests. A range of meeting rooms along with convenient access to the road networks makes this an ideal business venue, while the hotel's proximity to a number of attractions also makes it an excellent base for a weekend of sightseeing. The public areas and accommodation are smartly presented and the spacious bedrooms are particularly well equipped for corporate guests.

Rooms 51 en suite (2 fmly) (22 GF) ⊛ in 25 bedrooms S £50-£115; D £60-£125 (incl. bkfst) **Facilities** STV Gym Wi-fi available Small fitness centre Xmas **Conf** Thtr 300 Class 100 Board 24 Del from £140 **Parking** 120 **Notes** LB ⊛ in restaurant Civ Wed 116

England

England

COVENTRY *continued*

★★★ 72% [●] HOTEL

Brooklands Grange Hotel & Restaurant

Holyhead Rd CV5 8HX
☎ 024 7660 1601 📠 024 7660 1277
e-mail: info@brooklands-grange.co.uk
web: www.brooklands-grange.co.uk

dir: exit A45 at city centre rdbt. At next rdbt take A4114. Hotel 100yds on left

Behind the Jacobean façade of Brooklands Grange is a well run modern and comfortable business hotel. Well-appointed bedrooms are thoughtfully equipped and a smartly appointed four-poster bedroom has been created. The food continues to be worthy of note, with the emphasis on contemporary, well-flavoured dishes.

Rooms 31 en suite (3 fmly) (11 GF) ⊗ in 25 bedrooms S £75-£105; D £85-£120 (incl. bkfst) **Facilities** Wi-fi in bedrooms **Conf** BC Thtr 20 Class 10 Board 14 Del £130 **Parking** 52 **Notes LB** ⊗ in restaurant Closed 26-28 Dec & 1-2 Jan RS 24 Dec-2 Jan

★★★ 72% HOTEL

The Chace

London Rd, Toll Bar End CV3 4EQ
☎ 0870 609 6130 📠 024 7630 1816
e-mail: chacehotel@corushotels.com
web: www.corushotels.com

dir: A45 or A46 follow to Toll Bar Roundabout/Coventry Airport, take B4116 to Willenhall, over mini-rdbt, hotel on left

A former doctor's mansion, the main building retains many of its original Victorian features, including public rooms with high ceilings, stained glass windows, oak panelling and an impressive staircase; there is also a patio and well-kept gardens. Bedroom styles and sizes vary somewhat; most are attractively appointed, bright and modern.

Rooms 66 en suite (23 fmly) (24 GF) ⊗ in 34 bedrooms **Facilities** STV ⊱ nearby leisure centre Xmas **Conf** Thtr 100 Class 60 Board 45 Del from £100 **Parking** 120 **Notes** ⊗ ⊗ in restaurant Civ Wed 150

★★★ 72% HOTEL

Novotel Coventry

Wilsons Ln CV6 6HL
☎ 024 7636 5000 📠 024 7636 2422
e-mail: h0506@accor-hotels.com
web: www.novotel.com

dir: M6 junct 3. Follow signs for B4113 towards Longford and Bedworth. 3rd exit on large rdbt

A modern hotel convenient for Birmingham, Coventry and the motorway network, offering spacious, well-equipped accommodation. The bright brasserie offers extended dining hours, or alternatively there is an extensive room-service menu. Family rooms and a play area make this a child-friendly hotel; there is also a selection of meeting rooms.

Rooms 98 en suite (15 fmly) ⊗ in 70 bedrooms S £55-£105; D £55-£105 **Facilities** STV ⊱ Wi-fi in bedrooms Petanque, Pool table **Conf** Thtr 200 Class 100 Board 40 Del from £105 **Services** Lift **Parking** 120 **Notes LB** ⊗ in restaurant

★★★ 63% HOTEL

Allesley

Birmingham Rd, Allesley Village CV5 9GP
☎ 024 7640 3272 📠 024 7640 5190
e-mail: info@allesleyhotel.com

dir: from A45 take A4114 towards Coventry city, take 1st left onto Birmingham Rd, hotel on left

This purpose built hotel provides well-equipped bedrooms suited to the corporate guest. Public rooms are split over two levels and include a spacious reception foyer, a large restaurant and a lounge bar. Extensive conference and function facilities are available and prove popular.

Rooms 75 en suite 15 annexe en suite (2 fmly) ⊗ in 45 bedrooms **Conf** BC Thtr 450 Class 150 Board 80 **Services** Lift **Parking** 500 **Notes LB** ⊗ in restaurant Civ Wed 300

★★★ 63% HOTEL

Best Western Hylands

Warwick Rd CV3 6AU
☎ 024 7650 1600 📠 024 7650 1027
e-mail: hylands@bestwestern.co.uk

dir: Take A46 towards Coventry, onto A45 (W) for 200yds. At rdbt take 3rd exit (B4113). Right at end of road. Hotel 50yds on right

This hotel is convenient for the station and the city centre and overlooks an attractive park. Bedroom styles vary, yet each room is well equipped; the most recent additions are smartly decorated and
continued

modern, with bold colour schemes. Public rooms offer an open-plan lounge bar and Restaurant 153.

Rooms 61 en suite **Facilities** STV **Conf** Thtr 50 Class 20 Board 30 **Notes LB** ⊗ ⊘ in restaurant

[U]

Swallow Hotel Coventry

SWALLOW

80-90 Holyhead Rd CV1 3AS
☎ 024 7625 8585 📠 024 7622 5547
e-mail: reservations.coventry@swallowhotels.com
web: www.swallowhotels.com

dir: From junct 8 on ring road turn into Barras Ln then 1st left onto Meriden St. Hotel at end of street

At the time of going to press, the star classification for this hotel was not confirmed. Please refer to the AA internet site www.theAA.com for current information.

Rooms 81 en suite (10 fmly) (5 GF) ⊗ in 43 bedrooms S £70-£120; D £80-£130 (incl. bkfst) **Facilities** Xmas **Conf** Thtr 300 Class 140 Board 100 Del from £95 **Services** Lift **Parking** 60 **Notes** ⊘ in restaurant Civ Wed 300

BUDGET HOTEL

Hotel Campanile

Campanile

4 Wigston Rd, Walsgrave CV2 2SD
☎ 024 7662 2311 📠 024 7660 2362
e-mail: coventry@campanile-hotels.com
web: www.envergure.fr
dir: M6 exit 2, 2nd rdbt turn right

This modern building offers accommodation in smart, well-equipped bedrooms, all with en suite bathrooms. Refreshments may be taken at the informal Bistro. For further details consult the Hotel Groups page.

Rooms 47 en suite S £37.50-£60; D £37.50-£60 **Conf** Thtr 35 Class 18 Board 24 Del from £70

BUDGET HOTEL

Hotel Ibis Coventry Centre

ibis

Mile Ln, St John's Ringway CV1 2LN
☎ 024 7625 0500 📠 024 7655 3548
e-mail: H2793@accor.com
web: www.ibishotel.com

dir: A45 to Coventry, then A4114 signed to Jaguar Assembly Plant. At inner ring road towards ring road S. Off exit 5 for Mile Lane

Modern, budget hotel offering comfortable accommodation in bright and practical bedrooms. Breakfast is self-service and dinner is

continued

available in the restaurant. For further details, consult the Hotel Groups page.

Rooms 89 en suite S £44.95-£68.95; D £44.95-£68.95

Hotel Ibis Coventry South

Abbey Rd, Whitley CV3 4BJ
☎ 024 7663 9922 📠 024 7630 6898
e-mail: H2094@accor-hotels.com

dir: signed from A46/A423 rdbt. Take A423 towards A45. Follow signs for Esporta Health Club and Jaguar Engineering Plant

Rooms 51 en suite **Conf** BC Thtr 20 Class 20

BUDGET HOTEL

Innkeeper's Lodge Coventry

Brinklow Rd, Binley CV3 2DS
☎ 024 76458456
web: www.innkeeperslodge.com

Smart, en suite accommodation ideal for both business & leisure guests. Bedrooms are very well equipped, including Sky TV, telephone, modem points, tea & coffee making facilities, (family rooms in most locations). Complimentary breakfast. The adjacent Pub Restaurant; a Harvester, Vintage Inn, Toby Carvery, Ember Inn, Sizzling Pubco or Pub & Carvery offers an all day menu. See Hotel Groups pages for further details.

Rooms 40 rms

England

COVENTRY *continued*

Innkeeper's Lodge Meriden/Solihull (NEC)

Main Rd, Meriden CV7 7NN

☎ 01676 523798 📠 01676 531922

dir: in village of Meriden, just off main A45 between Coventry & Birmingham on B4102. Lodge on left down the hill from Meriden Village Green

Rooms 13 en suite

BUDGET HOTEL

Premier Travel Inn Coventry

Rugby Rd, Binley Woods CV3 2TA

☎ 08701 977066 📠 024 7643 1178

web: www.premiertravelinn.com

dir: from M6 junct 12 follow signs Warwick (A46 & M40). Follow "All traffic" signs, under bridge onto A46. Left at 1st rdbt to Binley. Inn is on the right at next rdbt

High quality, modern budget accommodation ideal for both families and business travellers. Spacious, en suite bedrooms feature bath and shower, satellite TV and many have telephones and modem points. The adjacent family restaurant features a wide and varied menu. For further details consult the Hotel Groups page.

Rooms 75 en suite **Conf** Thtr 25 Board 18

Premier Travel Inn Coventry East

Combe Fields Rd, Ansty CV7 9JP

☎ 0870 9906472 📠 0870 9906473

dir: Exit M6 junct 2 onto B4065 towards Ansty. After village right onto B4029 signed Brinklow. Right into Coombe Fields Rd, Inn on right.

Rooms 28 en suite **Conf** Thtr 12 Class 14 Board 14

DORRIDGE   MAP 10 SP17

◎◎ RESTAURANT WITH ROOMS

The Forest

25 Station Rd B93 8JA

☎ 01564 772120 📠 01564 732680

e-mail: info@forest-hotel.com

web: www.forest-hotel.com

dir: In town centre near station

The well-established and very individual establishment is well placed for routes to Birmingham, Stratford-upon-Avon and Warwick. Rooms are very well equipped with modern facilities, and imaginative food is served in the bars and intimate restaurant. A warm welcome is assured.

Rooms 12 en suite ⊘ in all bedrooms S £92.50; D £92.50-£110 **Conf** Thtr 100 Class 60 Board 40 **Parking** 50 **Notes** ⊗ RS Sun eve Civ Wed 75

DUDLEY   MAP 10 SO99
See also Himley, Staffordshire

★★★★ 79% HOTEL

Copthorne Hotel Merry Hill-Dudley

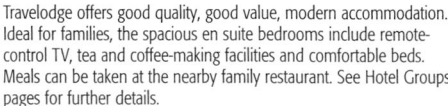

The Waterfront, Level St, Brierley Hill DY5 1UR

☎ 01384 482882 📠 01384 482773

e-mail: apearson@mill-cop.com

web: www.copthorne.com

dir: follow signs for Merry Hill Centre

The hotel enjoys a waterfront aspect and is close to the Merry Hill shopping mall. Polished marble floors, rich fabrics and striking interior design are features of the stylish public areas. Bedrooms are spacious and some have Connoisseur status, which includes the use of a private lounge. A modern leisure centre with pool occupies the lower level.

Rooms 138 en suite (14 fmly) ⊘ in 90 bedrooms **Facilities** STV 🔍 supervised Sauna Solarium Gym Jacuzzi Aerobics Beauty/massage therapists **Conf** BC Thtr 570 Class 240 Board 60 **Services** Lift **Parking** 100 **Notes LB** ⊗ Civ Wed 400

BUDGET HOTEL

Travelodge Birmingham Dudley

Dudley Rd, Brierley Hill DY5 1LQ

☎ 08700 850 950 📠 0870 1911563

web: www.travelodge.co.uk

dir: 3m W of Dudley, on A461

Travelodge offers good quality, good value, modern accommodation. Ideal for families, the spacious en suite bedrooms include remote-control TV, tea and coffee-making facilities and comfortable beds. Meals can be taken at the nearby family restaurant. See Hotel Groups pages for further details.

Rooms 32 en suite S fr £26; D fr £26

FRANKLEY MOTORWAY SERVICE AREA (M5)   MAP 10 SO98

BUDGET HOTEL

Travelodge Birmingham Frankley

Illey Ln, Frankley Motorway Service Area, Frankley B32 4AR

☎ 08700 850 950 📠 0121 501 2880

web: www.travelodge.co.uk

dir: between juncts 3 and 4 on s'bound carriageway of M5

Travelodge offers good quality, good value, modern accommodation. Ideal for families, the spacious en suite bedrooms include remote-control TV, tea and coffee-making facilities and comfortable beds. Meals can be taken at the nearby family restaurant. See Hotel Groups pages for further details.

Rooms 62 en suite S fr £26; D fr £26

HILTON PARK MOTORWAY SERVICE AREA (M6)

MAP 10 SJ90

BUDGET HOTEL

Travelodge Birmingham Hilton Park

Hilton Park Services (M6), Essington
WV11 2AT

☎ 08700 850 950 ▤ 01922 701967

web: www.travelodge.co.uk

dir: M6 between junct 10a & 11 southbound

Travelodge offers good quality, good value, modern accommodation. Ideal for families, the spacious en suite bedrooms include remote-control TV, tea and coffee-making facilities and comfortable beds. Meals can be taken at the nearby family restaurant. See Hotel Groups pages for further details.

Rooms 63 en suite S fr £26; D fr £26

HOCKLEY HEATH

MAP 10 SP17

★★★ 84% ❀ **HOTEL**

Nuthurst Grange Country House & Restaurant

Nuthurst Grange l n B94 5NL

☎ 01564 783972 ▤ 01564 783919

e-mail: info@nuthurst-grange.com

web: www.nuthurst-grange.com

dir: off A3400, 0.5m south of Hockley Heath. Turn at sign into Nuthurst Grange Lane

A stunning avenue drive is the approach to this country-house hotel, set amid several acres of well-tended gardens and mature grounds with views over rolling countryside. The spacious bedrooms and bathrooms offer considerable luxury and comfort, and public areas include restful lounges, meeting rooms and a sunny restaurant. The kitchen brigade produces highly imaginative British and French cuisine, complemented by very attentive, professional restaurant service.

Rooms 15 en suite (15 fmly) (2 GF) **Facilities** STV ⬥ Helipad **Conf** BC Thtr 100 Class 50 Board 45 **Parking** 80 **Notes LB** ❀ ⊘ in restaurant Closed 1 wk Xmas Civ Wed 70

BUDGET HOTEL

Premier Travel Inn Solihull (Hockley Heath)

Stratford Rd, Hockley Heath B94 6NX

☎ 08701 977230 ▤ 01564 783197

web: www.premiertravelinn.com

dir: on A3400, 2m S of M42 junct 4

High quality, modern budget accommodation ideal for both families and business travellers. Spacious, en suite bedrooms feature bath and shower, satellite TV and many have telephones and modem points. The adjacent family restaurant features a wide and varied menu. For further details consult the Hotel Groups page.

Rooms 55 en suite **Conf** Thtr 25

KINGSWINFORD

MAP 10 SO88

BUDGET HOTEL

Innkeeper's Lodge Dudley Kingswinford

Swindon Rd DY6 9XA

☎ 01384 295254 & 270066 ▤ 01384 287959

web: www.innkeeperslodge.com

dir: A491 into Kingswinford, at x-rds lights, turn onto A4101 towards Kidderminster along 'Summerhill'. At 1st set of lights, hotel on right

Smart, en suite accommodation ideal for both business & leisure guests. Bedrooms are very well equipped, including Sky TV, telephone, modem points, tea & coffee making facilities, (family rooms in most locations). Complimentary breakfast. The adjacent Pub Restaurant; a Harvester, Vintage Inn, Toby Carvery, Ember Inn, Sizzling Pubco or Pub & Carvery offers an all day menu. See Hotel Groups pages for further details.

Rooms 22 en suite

BUDGET HOTEL

Premier Travel Inn Dudley (Kingswinford)

Dudley Rd DY6 8WT

☎ 08701 977303 ▤ 01384 402736

web: www.premiertravelinn.com

dir: A4123 to Dudley, A461 following signs for Russell's Hall Hospital. On A4101 to Kingswinford, the Inn is opposite Pensnett Trading Estate

High quality, modern budget accommodation ideal for both families and business travellers. Spacious, en suite bedrooms feature bath and shower, satellite TV and many have telephones and modem points. The adjacent family restaurant features a wide and varied menu. For further details consult the Hotel Groups page.

Rooms 43 en suite **Conf** Thtr 30 Board 20

KNOWLE

MAP 10 SP17

BUDGET HOTEL

Innkeeper's Lodge Knowle/Solihull

Warwick Rd, Knowle B93 0EE

☎ 01564 771177 ▤ 01564 730862

web: www.innkeeperslodge.com

dir: on A41

Smart, en suite accommodation ideal for both business & leisure guests. Bedrooms are very well equipped, including Sky TV, telephone, modem points, tea & coffee making facilities, (family rooms in most locations). Complimentary breakfast. The adjacent Pub Restaurant; a Harvester, Vintage Inn, Toby Carvery, Ember Inn, Sizzling Pubco or Pub & Carvery offers an all day menu. See Hotel Groups pages for further details.

Rooms 13 en suite

England

MERIDEN
MAP 10 SP28

★★★★ 81% HOTEL

Marriott Forest of Arden Hotel & Country Club

Marriott
HOTELS & RESORTS

Maxstoke Ln CV7 7HR
☎ 0870 400 7272 🖷 0870 400 7372
web: www.marriott.co.uk

dir: *M42 junct 6 onto A45 towards Coventry, over Stonebridge flyover. After 0.75m left into Shepherds Ln. Hotel 1.5m on left*

The ancient oaks, rolling hills and natural lakes of the 10,000 acre Forest of Arden estate provide an idyllic backdrop for this modern hotel and country club. The hotel boasts an excellent range of leisure facilities and is regarded as one of the finest golfing destinations in the UK. Bedrooms provide every modern convenience and a full range of facilities.

Rooms 214 en suite (4 fmly) (65 GF) ⊛ in 135 bedrooms S fr £155; D fr £155 **Facilities Spa** STV 🔃 supervised ♨ 18 ⌘ Fishing Sauna Gym ♨ Putt green Jacuzzi Wi-fi available Health & Beauty salon, Floodlit golf academy Xmas **Conf** Thtr 300 Class 180 Board 40 Del from £185 **Services** Lift air con **Parking** 300 **Notes LB** ⊛ in restaurant Civ Wed 160

★★★ 74% ⚜ HOTEL

Manor

Main Rd CV7 7NH
☎ 01676 522735 🖷 01676 522186
e-mail: reservations@manorhotelmeriden.co.uk
web: www.manorhotelmeriden.co.uk

dir: *M42 junct 6, A45 towards Coventry then A452 signed Leamington. At rdbt take B4102 signed Meriden, hotel on left*

A sympathetically extended Georgian manor, in the heart of a sleepy village, that is just a few minutes away from the M6, M42 and National Exhibition Centre. The Regency Restaurant offers modern dishes, while the Triumph Buttery serves lighter meals and snacks. Following a refurbishment the accommodation offers smart well-equipped bedrooms.

Rooms 110 en suite (20 GF) ⊛ in 54 bedrooms S £75-£135; D £85-£145 (incl. bkfst) **Facilities** Wi-fi in bedrooms **Conf** Thtr 250 Class 150 Board 60 Del from £85 **Services** Lift **Parking** 200 **Notes LB** ⊛ in restaurant RS 24 Dec-2 Jan Civ Wed 150

OLDBURY
MAP 10 SO98

BUDGET HOTEL

Premier Travel Inn Oldbury

Wolverhampton Rd B69 2BH
☎ 08701 977202 🖷 0121 552 1012
web: www.premiertravelinn.com

dir: *M5 junct 2, take A4123 towards Wolverhampton. Inn 0.75m on left*

High quality, modern budget accommodation ideal for both families and business travellers. Spacious, en suite bedrooms feature bath and shower, satellite TV and many have telephones and modem points. The adjacent family restaurant features a wide and varied menu. For further details consult the Hotel Groups page.

Rooms 40 en suite

BUDGET HOTEL

Travelodge Birmingham Oldbury

Travelodge

Wolverhampton Rd B69 2BH
☎ 08700 850 950 🖷 0121 552 2967
web: www.travelodge.co.uk

dir: *on A4123, northbound off M5 junct 2*

Travelodge offers good quality, good value, modern accommodation. Ideal for families, the spacious en suite bedrooms include remote-control TV, tea and coffee-making facilities and comfortable beds. Meals can be taken at the nearby family restaurant. See Hotel Groups pages for further details.

Rooms 33 en suite S fr £26; D fr £26

SOLIHULL
MAP 10 SP17
See also Dorridge

★★★★ 77% HOTEL

Renaissance Solihull

RENAISSANCE
HOTELS

651 Warwick Rd B91 1AT
☎ 0121 711 3000 🖷 0121 705 6629
e-mail: ed.schofield@whitbread.com
web: www.marriott.co.uk/bhxsl

dir: *M42 junct 5, follow Solihull centre signs. 2nd left at rdbt (Warwick Rd). Straight over 3rd sets of lights. (Barley Mow pub on left on approaching large rdbt). Straight ahead, hotel on right.*

With its town centre location, this modern hotel is conveniently situated for the NEC, Birmingham and many local attractions. Bedrooms are air conditioned, attractively decorated and equipped with a comprehensive range of extras. The hotel provides extensive conference facilities, an indoor leisure facility and extensive parking.

Rooms 179 en suite (6 fmly) ⊛ in 87 bedrooms **Facilities** STV 🔃 Sauna Solarium Gym Jacuzzi Beauty therapist Large screen TV ♫ **Conf** Thtr 700 Class 350 Board 60 **Services** Lift **Parking** 300 **Notes LB** Civ Wed 70

★★★ 77% HOTEL

Ramada Solihull/Birmingham

⊛ RAMADA.

The Square B91 3RF
☎ 0121 711 2121 🖷 0121 711 3374
e-mail: sales.solihull@ramadajarvis.co.uk
web: www.ramadajarvis.co.uk

dir: *M42 junct 5, A41 towards Solihull. 1st left on slip road. Right at island, left at 2 set of lights. Hotel 600yds on right*

Within a few minutes' walk of the central attractions, this modern hotel provides a range of well-equipped bedrooms, with Studio rooms being particularly attractive. Extensive conference facilities are available. Public areas include Arts Restaurant, overlooking one of the world's oldest bowling greens, and cosy bars, dating from the 16th century, that retain many original features.

Rooms 145 en suite (14 fmly) (36 GF) ⊛ in 95 bedrooms S £50-£205; D £50-£205 **Facilities** STV Wi-fi available Crown Green bowling Green Xmas **Conf** Thtr 568 Class 186 Board 289 Del from £129.25 **Services** Lift **Parking** 180 **Notes LB** ⊛ in restaurant Civ Wed 120

★★★ 71% **HOTEL**

Corus hotel Solihull

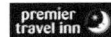

Stratford Rd, Shirley B90 4EB
☎ 0870 609 6133 📇 0121 733 3801
e-mail: solihull@corushotels.com
web: www.corushotels.com

dir: *M42 junct 4 onto A34 for Shirley, cross 1st 3 rdbts, then double back along dual carriageway, hotel on left*

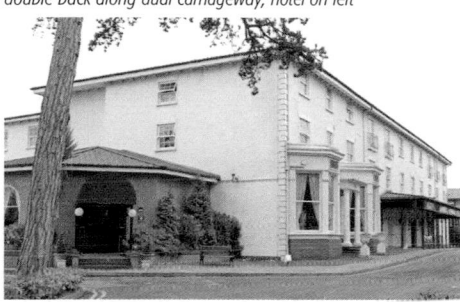

A large friendly hotel attracting both the corporate and leisure markets. Ideally located within minutes of all major transportation links and benefiting from its own leisure centre that includes, amongst its many facilities, a lagoon pool, sauna and gym.

Rooms 111 en suite (11 fmly) (13 GF) ⊘ in 64 bedrooms S £45-£130;
D £45-£130 **Facilities** Spa STV 🔅 Sauna Solarium Gym Jacuzzi WI-fi available Steam room **Conf** Thtr 180 Class 80 Board 60 Del from £110
Services Lift **Parking** 275 **Notes LB** ⊘ in restaurant

Ⓤ

Holiday Inn Solihull

Holiday Inn
HOTELS · RESORTS

61 Homer Rd B91 3QD
☎ 0870 2255 401 📇 0121 711 2696
e-mail: gm.hisolihull@qmh hotels.com

dir: *M42 junct 5 follow signs to town centre, left at St Alphege Church into Church Hill Rd, continue to rdbt & hotel on right.*

At the time of going to press, the star classification for this hotel was not confirmed. Please refer to the AA internet site www.theAA.com for current information.

Rooms 115 en suite (8 fmly) ⊘ in 100 bedrooms S £109-£175;
D £109-£175 (incl. bkfst) **Facilities** STV 🔅 supervised Sauna Solarium Gym Jacuzzi Beauty therapist Xmas **Conf** BC Thtr 250 Class 180
Board 100 Del from £135 **Services** Lift air con **Parking** 162 **Notes LB**
Civ Wed 60

BUDGET HOTEL

Premier Travel Inn Solihull North

premier
travel inn

Stratford Rd, Shirley B90 3AG
☎ 08701 977231 📇 0121 733 2762
web: www.premiertravelinn.com

dir: *M42 junct 4 follow signs for Birmingham. Inn in Shirley town centre, on A34*

High quality, modern budget accommodation ideal for both families and business travellers. Spacious, en suite bedrooms feature bath and shower, satellite TV and many have telephones and modem points. The adjacent family restaurant features a wide and varied menu. For further details consult the Hotel Groups page.

Rooms 44 en suite

Premier Travel Inn Solihull (Shirley)

Stratford Rd, Shirley B90 4EP
☎ 08701 977232 📇 0121 733 7075
dir: *1m from M42 junct 4 on A34, north*
Rooms 51 en suite

STOURBRIDGE   MAP 10 SO88

★★ 61% **HOTEL**

The Mount Hotel

Mount Ln, Clent DY9 9PR
☎ 01562 885904 📇 01562 885022
e-mail: edward@gibbsprivate.fsnet.co.uk
dir: *off A491 Stourbridge Road*

Located within a residential area close to major road networks, this period hotel, formally a private school, is being totally renovated to provide a range of well-equipped bedrooms and attractive public areas, which include a conservatory dining room.

Rooms 15 en suite (4 fmly) (1 GF) ⊘ in 12 bedrooms **Facilities** STV ch
fac **Conf** Thtr 60 Class 100 Board 40 **Parking** 30 **Notes LB** ⊗ ⊘ in restaurant

---

SUTTON COLDFIELD   MAP 10 SP19

★★★★ 80% ⑧ **HOTEL**

De Vere Belfry

B76 9PR
☎ 0870 900 0066 📇 01675 470256
e-mail: enquiries@thebelfry.com
web: www.devere.co.uk

(For full entry see Wishaw, Warwickshire)

England

SUTTON COLDFIELD *continued*

★★★★ 77% ◉◉ **HOTEL**

New Hall
Walmley Rd B76 1QX
☎ 0121 378 2442 & 0870 333 9147 📠 0870 333 9247
e-mail: info@newhalluk.com

dir: *Follow Walmley Rd through Walmley Village northbound. At signal Heyes Rd turn left. At rdbt take 2nd exit. Hotel on left.*

Lying within 26 acres of mature, elegant grounds this hotel is widely reputed to be the oldest inhabited, moated house in the country. Sympathetic renovation has provided up-to-the-minute facilities whilst retaining most of its medieval charm and character. Public areas with their fine panelling and mullioned stained-glass windows, create a unique historical ambience; the magnificent Great Chamber is particularly impressive.

Rooms 60 en suite (14 fmly) (25 GF) ⌖ in 54 bedrooms S £120-£170; D £125-£270 (incl. bkfst) **Facilities Spa** STV 🏊 supervised ♨9 ⚓ Fishing Sauna Gym ⚴ Jacuzzi Xmas **Conf** BC Thtr 150 Board 35 Del £170 **Parking** 80 **Notes LB** ⌖ in restaurant Civ Wed 60

★★★★ 71% **HOTEL**

Best Western Premier Moor Hall Hotel & Spa
Moor Hall Dr, Four Oaks B75 6LN
☎ 0121 308 3751 📠 0121 308 8974
e-mail: mail@moorhallhotel.co.uk
web: www.moorhallhotel.co.uk

dir: *at junct of A38/A453 take A453 towards Sutton Coldfield, at traffic lights turn right into Weeford Rd, Moor Hall drive is 150yds on left*

Although only a short distance from the city centre this hotel enjoys a peaceful setting, overlooking extensive grounds and an adjacent golf course. Bedrooms are well equipped and executive rooms are particularly spacious. Public rooms include the formal Oak Room Restaurant, and the informal Country Kitchen, which offers carvery and blackboard specials.

Rooms 82 en suite (5 fmly) (33 GF) ⌖ in 53 bedrooms S £64-£168; D £82-£168 (incl. bkfst) **Facilities Spa** STV 🏊 Sauna Gym Jacuzzi Wi-fi in bedrooms Steam room, 3 Spa treatment rooms **Conf** BC Thtr 250 Class 120 Board 45 Del from £153 **Services** Lift **Parking** 170 **Notes LB** 🚭 ⌖ in restaurant Civ Wed 180

See advertisement under BIRMINGHAM

★★★ 72% **HOTEL**

Ramada Hotel & Resort Birmingham

Penns Ln, Walmley B76 1LH
☎ 0121 351 3111 📠 0121 313 1297
e-mail: sales.birmingham@ramadajarvis.co.uk
web: www.ramadajarvis.co.uk

dir: *A5127 towards Sutton Coldfield for 2m, through lights, 4th right into Penns Lane. Hotel 1m on right*

Conveniently located for both M42 and M6 this large hotel is set in private grounds overlooking a lake. Bedrooms are comfortably appointed for both business and leisure guests. Public areas include the Club restaurant and bar, a leisure club and extensive conference facilities.

Rooms 170 en suite (1 fmly) ⌖ in 123 bedrooms S £89-£155; D £99-£165 (incl. bkfst) **Facilities Spa** 🏊 supervised Fishing Squash Sauna Solarium Gym Xmas **Conf** Thtr 500 Class 200 Board 40 **Services** Lift **Parking** 500 **Notes** ⌖ in restaurant Civ Wed 150

BUDGET HOTEL

Innkeeper's Lodge Birmingham Sheldon (NEC)

2225 Coventry Rd, Sheldon B26 3EH
☎ 0121 742 6201 📠 0121 722 2703
web: www.innkeeperslodge.com

dir: *M42 junct 6/A45 towards Birmingham for 2m. Lodge on left approaching overhead traffic lights*

Smart, en suite accommodation ideal for both business & leisure guests. Bedrooms are very well equipped, including Sky TV, telephone, modem points, tea & coffee making facilities, (family rooms in most locations). Complimentary breakfast. The adjacent Pub Restaurant; a Harvester, Vintage Inn, Toby Carvery, Ember Inn, Sizzling Pubco or Pub & Carvery offers an all day menu. See Hotel Groups pages for further details.

Rooms 85 en suite

Innkeeper's Lodge Birmingham Sutton Coldfield
Chester Rd, Streetley B73 6SP
☎ 0121 353 7785 📠 0121 352 1443

dir: *M6 junct 7 to A34 S'bound, left onto A4041. At 4th rdbt right onto A452-Chester road, lodge less 1m on right*

Rooms 7 en suite 59 annexe en suite **Conf** Thtr 40 Board 20

BUDGET HOTEL

Premier Travel Inn Birmingham North
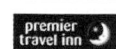
Whitehouse Common Rd B75 6HD
☎ 0870 9906320 📠 0870 9906321
web: www.premiertravelinn.com

dir: *Approx 6m from M42 junct 9. Follow A446 towards Lichfield, then A453 to Sutton Coldfield. Left into Whitehouse Common Rd, Inn on left*

High quality, modern budget accommodation ideal for both families and business travellers. Spacious, en suite bedrooms feature bath and shower, satellite TV and many have telephones and modem points. The adjacent family restaurant features a wide and varied menu. For further details consult the Hotel Groups page.

Rooms 42 en suite **Conf** Board 10

BUDGET HOTEL

Travelodge Birmingham Sutton Coldfield

Boldmere Rd B73 5UP

☎ 08700 850 950 📠 0121 355 0017

web: www.travelodge.co.uk

dir: 2m S, on B4142

Travelodge offers good quality, good value, modern accommodation. Ideal for families, the spacious en suite bedrooms include remote-control TV, tea and coffee-making facilities and comfortable beds. Meals can be taken at the nearby family restaurant. See Hotel Groups pages for further details.

Rooms 32 en suite S fr £26; D fr £26

WALSALL   **MAP 10 SP09**

★★★ 85% ⬤⬤ **HOTEL**

Best Western Fairlawns at Aldridge

178 Little Aston Rd, Aldridge WS9 0NU

☎ 01922 455122 📠 01922 743210

e-mail: welcome@fairlawns.co.uk

web: www.fairlawns.co.uk

dir: off A452 towards Aldridge at x-roads with A454. Hotel 600yds on right

In a rural location with immaculate landscaped grounds, this constantly improving hotel offers a wide range of facilities and modern, comfortable bedrooms. Family rooms, one with a four-poster bed and suites are also available. The Fairlawns Restaurant serves a wide range of award-winning seasonal dishes. The extensive comprehensively equipped leisure complex is predominantly for adult use as there is restricted availability to young people.

Rooms 59 en suite (8 fmly) (1 GF) ⊗ in 55 bedrooms S £65-£165; D £89.50-£225 (incl. bkfst) **Facilities Spa** STV FTV 🏊 supervised 🎾 Sauna Solarium Gym 🏌 Wi-fi in bedrooms Dance studio Beauty Salon, Bathing suite, Foot spa, Rasul **Conf** BC Thtr 80 Class 40 Board 30 Del from £127.50 **Services** Lift **Parking** 150 **Notes LB** ⊗ in restaurant Civ Wed 100

See also advert on page 651

★★★ 74% **HOTEL**

Quality Hotel & Suites Walsall

20 Wolverhampton Rd West, Bentley WS2 0BS

☎ 01922 724444 📠 01922 723148

e-mail: enquiries@hotels-walsall.com

web: www.choicehotelseurope.com

dir: on rdbt at M6 junct 10

All the accommodation at this conveniently located hotel is well equipped. It includes air-conditioned suites, which have a fax machine and a kitchen with a microwave and fridge. There is an extensive all day menu, plus room service. Guests can also choose to dine in the carvery restaurant.

Rooms 154 en suite (120 fmly) (78 GF) ⊗ in 64 bedrooms S £20-£150; D £25-£150 **Facilities Spa** STV 🏊 supervised Sauna Solarium Gym Jacuzzi Wi-fi available Xmas **Conf** Thtr 180 Class 70 Board 80 Del from £75 **Parking** 160 **Notes LB** ⊗ ⊗ in restaurant Civ Wed 150

★★★ 73% **HOTEL**

Beverley

58 Lichfield Rd WS4 2DJ

☎ 01922 614967 & 622999 📠 01922 724187

e-mail: beverleyhotel@aol.com

dir: 1m N of Walsall town centre on A461 to Lichfield

This privately owned hotel dates back to 1880. Bedrooms are comfortably appointed and equipped with thoughtful extras. The tastefully decorated public areas include a relaxing guest lounge and a spacious bar combined with a conservatory. The Gallery Restaurant offers guests a choice of carefully prepared, appetising dishes.

Rooms 40 en suite (2 fmly) (4 GF) ⊗ in 6 bedrooms S £60-£70; D £70-£100 (incl. bkfst) **Facilities** Games room with pool table **Conf** BC Thtr 60 Class 30 Board 30 Del from £100 **Parking** 68 **Notes LB** ⊗ ⊗ in restaurant RS 24 Dec-2 Jan Civ Wed 58

BUDGET HOTEL

Travelodge Birmingham Walsall

Birmingham Rd WS5 3AB

☎ 0870 191 1023 📠 01922 631 734

web: www.travelodge.co.uk

dir: M6 junct 7, A34 N to Walsall. Hotel 2m on left

Travelodge offers good quality, good value, modern accommodation. Ideal for families, the spacious en suite bedrooms include remote-control TV, tea and coffee-making facilities and comfortable beds. Meals can be taken at the nearby family restaurant. See Hotel Groups pages for further details.

Rooms 96 en suite S fr £26 **Conf** Thtr 60 Class 30 Board 30 Del from £99

England

WALSALL *continued*

BUDGET HOTEL

Premier Travel Inn Walsall

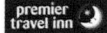

Bentley Green, Bentley Rd North WS2 0WB
☎ 08701 977258 🖷 01922 724098
web: www.premiertravelinn.com

dir: M6 junct 10, A454 signed Wolverhampton & then 2nd exit
(Ansons junct). Left at rdbt, 1st left at next rdbt, Inn on right

High quality, modern budget accommodation ideal for both families
and business travellers. Spacious, en suite bedrooms feature bath and
shower, satellite TV and many have telephones and modem points.
The adjacent family restaurant features a wide and varied menu. For
further details consult the Hotel Groups page.

Rooms 40 en suite

WEST BROMWICH   MAP 10 SP09

★★★ 68% HOTEL

Park Inn

Birmingham Rd B70 6RS
☎ 0121 609 9988 🖷 0121 525 7403
e-mail: reservations.birminghamwestbromwich@
moathousehotels.com

dir: take Birmingham Rd to West Bromich town centre, turn 1st
*right into Beeches Rd, take 2nd right into Europa Ave. Hotel is on
the right*

Convenient for the M5, M42 and M6, this large, purpose-built hotel
provides versatile and well-equipped accommodation. Facilities
include a spacious restaurant, bright lounges, a comfortable bar and a
secure car park, as well as meeting rooms and function suites. There is
a modern leisure complex.

Rooms 168 en suite (20 fmly) ⊗ in 106 bedrooms **Facilities** STV ⬚
supervised Sauna Solarium Gym Jacuzzi Beauty treatments **Conf** BC
Thtr 475 Class 237 Board 289 **Services** Lift **Parking** 250 **Notes LB**
Civ Wed 60

BUDGET HOTEL

Premier Travel Inn
West Bromwich

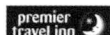

New Gas St B70 0NP
☎ 08701 977264 🖷 0121 500 5670
web: www.premiertravelinn.com

dir: From M5 junct 1 take A41 Expressway towards
Wolverhampton. At 3rd rdbt. Inn on right

High quality, modern budget accommodation ideal for both families
and business travellers. Spacious, en suite bedrooms feature bath and
shower, satellite TV and many have telephones and modem points.
The adjacent family restaurant features a wide and varied menu. For
further details consult the Hotel Groups page.

Rooms 40 en suite

WOLVERHAMPTON   MAP 10 SO99
See also Himley (Staffordshire) & Worfield (Shropshire)

★★★ 75% HOTEL

The Mount Hotel and Conference Centre

Mount Rd, Tettenhall Wood WV6 8HL
☎ 01902 752055 🖷 01902 745263
e-mail: nmines@dunchurch.co.uk

dir: Off A454 signed Wighthaven onto Wightwick Bank, take 3rd
right, hotel is 500yds on right

Built in the 1870s as the private home of a paint magnate, The Mount
is set in 4.5 acres of gardens and woods, yet is just 10 minutes' drive
from the centre of Wolverhampton. Public areas retain many original
features, including intricate ceiling designs, wood panelling and a
ballroom with minstrels' gallery and balcony. Bedrooms are well
equipped and extensive conference facilities feature the latest
innovations.

Rooms 68 en suite (4 fmly) (23 GF) ⊗ in all bedrooms S fr £95;
D fr £105 (incl. bkfst) **Facilities** STV FTV Gym ⛳ Wi-fi available Xmas
Conf BC Thtr 200 Class 150 Board 60 Del from £165 **Parking** 200
Notes ⊗ in restaurant Civ Wed 150

★★★ 74% HOTEL

Novotel Wolverhampton

Union St WV1 3JN
☎ 01902 871100 🖷 01902 870054
e-mail: H1188@accor.com
web: www.novotel.com

dir: 6m from M6 junct 10. A454 to Wolverhampton. Hotel on
main ring road

This large, modern, purpose-built hotel stands close to the town
centre and ring road. It provides spacious, smartly presented and well-
equipped bedrooms, all of which contain convertible bed settees for
family occupancy. In addition to the open-plan lounge and bar area,
there is an attractive brasserie-style restaurant, which overlooks the
small outdoor swimming pool.

Rooms 132 en suite (9 fmly) ⊗ in 14 bedrooms S £49-£131; D £49-£142
(incl. bkfst) **Facilities** STV ⬚ Wi-fi in bedrooms Pool table in bar area
Conf Thtr 200 Class 100 Board 80 Del from £120 **Services** Lift
Parking 120 **Notes LB** ⊗ in restaurant Civ Wed 200

★★★ 74% HOTEL

Park Hall Hotel

Park Dr, Goldthorn Park WV4 5AJ
☎ 01902 349500 🖷 01902 344760
e-mail: enquiries@parkhallhotel.co.uk

dir: off A4039 towards Penn and Wombourne, 2nd left (Ednam
Rd), hotel at end of road

This 18th-century house stands in extensive grounds and gardens, a
short drive from the town centre. Bedrooms vary in style, but all are
well equipped. Meals can be taken in the Terrace restaurant, which
offers a carvery buffet. Conference and wedding facilities are available.

Rooms 75 en suite (17 GF) ⊗ in 37 bedrooms **Facilities** STV Leisure
facilities planned for 2006 **Conf** Thtr 700 Class 350 Board 100
Parking 250 **Notes LB** ⊗ in restaurant Civ Wed 700

★★★ 72% **HOTEL**

Quality Hotel Wolverhampton

Penn Rd WV3 0ER

☎ 01902 429216 ▤ 01902 710419

e-mail: enquiries@hotels-wolverhampton.com

web: www.choicehotelseurope.com

dir: on A449, Wolverhampton to Kidderminster, 0.25m from ring road on right, turn onto Oaklands Rd at 1st lights

The original Victorian house here has been considerably extended to create a large, busy and popular hotel. Ornately carved woodwork and ceilings still remain in the original building. All the bedrooms are well equipped. The pleasant public areas have a lot of character and offer a choice of bars.

Rooms 66 en suite 26 annexe en suite (6 fmly) (21 GF) ⊛ in 32 bedrooms S £55-£102; D £65-£119 **Facilities Spa** STV ☜ Sauna Gym Wi-fi available Steam room, Playstation, Pay movies, Big screen TV Pool table Xmas **Conf** BC Thtr 140 Class 60 Board 40 Del from £95 **Parking** 124 **Notes LB** ⊛ in restaurant Civ Wed 100

BUDGET HOTEL

Premier Travel Inn Wolverhampton

premier travel inn

Wolverhampton Business Park, Stafford Rd WV10 6TA

☎ 08701 977277 ▤ 01902 785260

web: www.premiertravelinn.com

dir: Inn 100 yds off M54 junct 2

High quality, modern budget accommodation ideal for both families and business travellers. Spacious, en suite bedrooms feature bath and shower, satellite TV and many have telephones and modem points. The adjacent family restaurant features a wide and varied menu. For further details consult the Hotel Groups section.

Rooms 54 en suite **Conf** Thtr 20 Board 10

WIGHT, ISLE OF

BEMBRIDGE

MAP 05 SZ68

★★★ 70% **HOTEL**

Windmill Inn Hotel & Restaurant

1 Steyne Rd PO35 5UH

☎ 01983 872875 ▤ 01983 874760

e-mail: info@thewindmillhotel.co.uk

web: www.windmill-inn.com

dir: 0.5m from town centre, towards lifeboat station

This hotel offers a range of comfortably furnished public rooms where an excellent choice of freshly prepared food is available to suit virtually all tastes. Bedrooms are well presented and thoughtfully equipped, while service is both attentive and friendly. There is an attractive garden to the rear.

Rooms 14 en suite (2 fmly) ⊛ in 3 bedrooms **Conf** Thtr 100 Class 100 Board 100 **Parking** 50 **Notes LB** ⊛ ⊛ in restaurant Civ Wed 100

COWES

MAP 05 SZ49

★★★ 73% **HOTEL**

Best Western New Holmwood

Queens Rd, Egypt Point PO31 8BW

Best Western

☎ 01983 292508 ▤ 01983 295020

e-mail: nholmwdh@aol.com

dir: from A3020 at Northwood Garage lights, left & follow road to rdbt. 1st left then sharp right into Baring Rd, 4th left into Egypt Hill. At bottom turn right, hotel on right

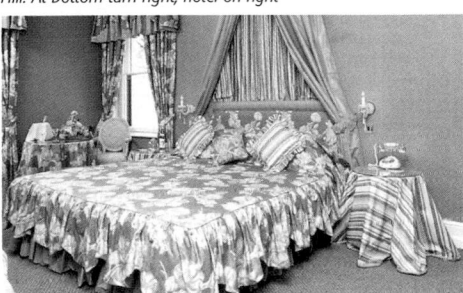

Just by the Esplanade, this hotel has an enviable outlook. Bedrooms are comfortable and very well equipped, and the light and airy, glass-fronted restaurant looks out to sea and serves a range of interesting meals. The sun terrace is delightful in the summer and there is a small pool area.

Rooms 26 en suite (1 fmly) (9 GF) ⊛ in all bedrooms S £80-£125; D £96-£125 (incl. bkfst) **Facilities Spa** STV ☜ Wi-fi in bedrooms Xmas **Conf** Thtr 130 Class 60 Board 50 Del from £105 **Parking** 20 **Notes LB** ⊛ in restaurant

See advert on page 667

★ 70% **HOTEL**

Duke of York

Mill Hill Rd PO31 7BT

☎ 01983 295171 ▤ 01983 295047

This family-run inn is quietly situated close to the town centre. Bedrooms are divided between the main building and a nearby annexe and are neatly appointed. There is a well-stocked bar and a pleasant restaurant offering a good range of popular dishes, many featuring fish and seafood. The inn has a nautical theme enhanced by an abundance of maritime memorabilia.

Rooms 8 en suite 5 annexe en suite (2 fmly) (1 GF) ⊛ in 4 bedrooms **Parking** 12

FRESHWATER

MAP 05 SZ38

★★★ 75% ⊛ **HOTEL**

Farringford

Bedbury Ln PO40 9PE

☎ 01983 752500 ▤ 01983 756515

e-mail: enquiries@farringford.co.uk

web: www.farringford.co.uk

dir: A3054, left to Norton Green down Pixlie Hill. Left to Freshwater Bay. At bay turn right into Bedbury Ln, hotel on left

Upon seeing Farringford, Alfred Lord Tennyson is said to have remarked "we will go no further, this must be our home" and so it

continued on page 666

England

FRESHWATER *continued*

was for some forty years. One hundred and fifty years later, the hotel provides bedrooms ranging in style and size, from large rooms in the main house to adjoining chalet-style rooms. The atmosphere is relaxed and dinner features fresh local produce.

Rooms 14 en suite 4 annexe en suite (5 fmly) (4 GF) S £40-£62; D £80-£170 **Facilities** ⚒ ↧ 9 ♨ ⚘ Putt green Bowling green Beauty treatment room ♫ Xmas **Conf** BC Thtr 120 Class 50 Board 50 Del from £70 **Parking** 55 **Notes LB** ⊘ in restaurant Civ Wed 130

NEWPORT   MAP 05 SZ58

BUDGET HOTEL

Premier Travel Inn
Isle of Wight (Newport)

premier travel inn

Seaclose, Fairlee Rd PO30 2DN
☎ 08701 977144 📠 0870 241 9000
web: www.premiertravelinn.com
dir: *From Newport town centre take A3054 signed Ryde. After 0.75m at Seaclose lights, turn left. Inn adjacent to council offices*

High quality, modern budget accommodation ideal for both families and business travellers. Spacious, en suite bedrooms feature bath and shower, satellite TV and many have telephones and modem points. The adjacent family restaurant features a wide and varied menu. For further details consult the Hotel Groups page.

Rooms 42 en suite

RYDE   MAP 05 SZ59

★★★ 70% HOTEL

Yelf's

Union St PO33 2LG
☎ 01983 564062 📠 01983 563937
e-mail: manager@yelfshotel.com
web: www.yelfshotel.com
dir: *from Ryde Esplanade, turn into Union St. Hotel on right*

This former coaching inn has smart public areas including a busy bar, a separate lounge and an attractive dining room. Bedrooms are comfortably furnished and well equipped and some are located in an adjoining wing. A conservatory lounge bar and stylish terrace are ideal for relaxing.

Rooms 31 en suite 9 annexe en suite (5 fmly) (3 GF) ⊘ in 5 bedrooms S £61-£75; D £75-£89 (incl. bkfst) **Facilities** STV **Conf** Thtr 100 Class 30 Board 50 **Services** Lift **Parking** 23 **Notes LB** ⊘ in restaurant Civ Wed 100

★★ 68% HOTEL

Appley Manor

Appley Rd PO33 1PH
☎ 01983 564777 📠 01983 564704
e-mail: appleymanor@lineone.net
dir: *A3055 onto B3330. Hotel 0.25m on left*

Located only five minutes from the town centre this property, which sits in peaceful surroundings, was once a Victorian manor house. The spacious bedrooms are well furnished and decorated. Dinner can be taken in the popular adjoining Manor Inn.

Rooms 12 en suite (2 fmly) ⊘ in 3 bedrooms S £38; D £48 **Facilities** Wi-fi in bedrooms **Conf** Thtr 40 Class 40 Board 30 **Parking** 60 **Notes** ⊗

Ⓤ

Hotel Ryde Castle

OLD ENGLISH INNS

The Esplanade PO33 1JA
☎ 01983 563755 📠 01983 566906
e-mail: 6506@greeneking.co.uk
web: www.oldenglish.co.uk

At the time of going to press, the star classification for this hotel was not confirmed. Please refer to the AA internet site www.theAA.com for current information.

Rooms 18 en suite (2 fmly) ⊘ in all bedrooms S £70-£95; D £100-£150 (incl. bkfst) **Facilities** STV ♫ Xmas **Conf** Thtr 200 Class 80 Board 50 Del £175 **Parking** 40 **Notes LB** ⊗ ⊘ in restaurant

SANDOWN   MAP 05 SZ58

★★ 68% HOTEL

Bayshore

Leisureplex

12-16 Pier St PO36 8JX
☎ 01983 403154 📠 01983 406574
e-mail: bayshore.sandown@alfatravel.co.uk
web: www.alfatravel.co.uk
dir: *from the Broadway into Melville St, signed to Tourist Information Office. Across High St and bear right opposite pier. Hotel on right*

This large hotel is located on the seafront opposite the pier and offers extensive public rooms where live entertainment is provided in season. The bedrooms are well equipped and staff very friendly and helpful.

Rooms 78 en suite (19 fmly) ⊘ in all bedrooms S £31-£41; D £50-£78 (incl. bkfst) **Facilities** FTV Sauna ♫ Xmas **Services** Lift **Notes LB** ⊗ ⊘ in restaurant Closed Dec-Feb RS Mar & Nov

★★ 68% HOTEL

Cygnet Hotel

58 Carter St PO36 8DQ
☎ 01983 402930 📠 01983 405112
e-mail: info@cygnethotel.com
dir: *on corner of Broadway and Carter St*

Popular with tour groups, this family-run hotel offers bedrooms that are generally spacious, comfortably furnished and well equipped. Extensive public areas include an indoor swimming pool, two lounge areas and a bar where live entertainment is regularly staged.

Rooms 45 en suite (14 fmly) (21 GF) ⊘ in all bedrooms **Facilities** Spa ⚒ ⚒ Sauna Pool table ♫ Xmas **Services** Lift **Parking** 18 **Notes** ⊗ ⊘ in restaurant Closed Jan

★★ 68% **HOTEL**

Riviera

2 Royal St PO36 8LP

☎ 01983 402518 ▤ 01983 402518

e-mail: enquiries@rivierahotel.org.uk

web: www.rivierahotel.org.uk

dir: Top of Sandown High St, turning past main Post Office.

Regular guests return year after year to this friendly and welcoming family-run hotel, now under new ownership. It is located near the High Street and just a short stroll from the beach, pier and shops. Bedrooms, including several at ground floor level, are very well furnished and comfortably equipped. Enjoyable home-cooked meals are served in the spacious dining room.

Rooms 43 en suite (6 fmly) (11 GF) ⊘ in 25 bedrooms **Facilities** ♫ Xmas **Parking** 30 **Notes** ⊘ in restaurant

★★ 67% **HOTEL**

Sandringham

Esplanade PO36 8AH

☎ 01983 406655 ▤ 01983 404395

e-mail: info@sandringhamhotel.co.uk

With a prime seafront location and splendid views, this is one of the largest hotels on the island. Comfortable public areas include a spacious lounge and a heated indoor swimming pool and jacuzzi. Bedrooms vary in size and many sea-facing rooms have a balcony. Regular entertainment is provided in the ballroom.

Rooms 110 en suite (39 fmly) (6 GF) ⊘ in 3 bedrooms **Facilities** 🏇 Snooker Sauna Jacuzzi ♫ **Services** Lift **Parking** 82 **Notes LB** ⊛ ⊘ in restaurant

Ⓤ

Corner House

1-5 Fitzroy St PO36 8HY

☎ 01983 403176 & 07977 918177 ▤ 01983 403176

e-mail: j.blow@btconnect.com

At the time of going to press, the star classification for this hotel was not confirmed. Please refer to the AA internet site www.theAA.com for current information.

Rooms 24 en suite (3 GF) S £22-£30; D £44-£60 (incl. bkfst) **Facilities** Xmas **Notes LB** ⊛ ⊘ in restaurant RS Nov-Feb

England

SANDOWN *continued*

U

Melville Hall Hotel & Utopia Spa

Melville St PO36 9DH

☎ 01983 400500 & 406526 🖹 01983 407093

e-mail: enquiries@melvillehall.co.uk

dir: *Exit A3055, hotel 30yds on left. (5min walk from train station)*

At the time of going to press, the star classification for this hotel was not confirmed. Please refer to the AA internet site www.theAA.com for current information.

Rooms 30 en suite (3 fmly) (4 GF) ⊗ in 18 bedrooms S £89-£119; D £118-£158 (incl. bkfst & dinner) **Facilities Spa** STV ⬚ ⬚ Sauna Solarium Putt green Jacuzzi Xmas **Parking** 20 **Notes LB** ⊗ ⊗ in restaurant

U

Montrene

11 Avenue Rd PO36 8BN

☎ 01983 403722 🖹 01983 405553

e-mail: enquiries@montrene.co.uk

web: www.montrene.co.uk

dir: *100yds after mini-rdbt between High St and Avenue Rd*

At the time of going to press, the star classification for this hotel was not confirmed. Please refer to the AA internet site www.theAA.com for current information.

Rooms 41 en suite (19 fmly) (19 GF) S £38-£47; D £76-£94 (incl. bkfst) **Facilities** ⬚ supervised Snooker Gym Jacuzzi Table tennis Pool table ch fac Xmas **Parking** 40 **Notes LB** ⊗ in restaurant Closed 4 Jan-8 Feb

---

SEAVIEW   MAP 05 SZ69

★★★ 79% ⊛ **HOTEL**

Priory Bay

Priory Dr PO34 5BU

☎ 01983 613146 🖹 01983 616539

e-mail: enquiries@priorybay.co.uk

web: www.priorybay.co.uk

dir: *B3330 towards Seaview, through Nettlestone. Do not take Seaview turn, but continue 0.5m until hotel sign*

This peacefully located hotel has much to offer and comes complete with its own stretch of private beach, 9-hole golf course and an outdoor swimming pool. Bedrooms are a wonderful mix of styles, but

continued

---

all provide ample comfort and much character. Public areas are equally impressive with a choice of enticing lounges to relax and unwind in. The kitchen creates interesting and imaginative dishes, using the excellent island produce whenever possible.

Rooms 19 en suite 12 annexe en suite (13 fmly) (2 GF) S £45-£80; D £90-£190 (incl. bkfst) **Facilities** STV FTV ⬚ ⬚ 6 ⬚ ⬚ Wi-fi in bedrooms Private beach, 70 acres of woodland lawns and formal gardens. ch fac Xmas **Conf** Thtr 80 Class 60 Board 40 Del from £75 **Parking** 100 **Notes LB** ⊗ in restaurant Civ Wed 100

★★★ 77% ⊛⊛ **HOTEL**

Seaview Hotel & Restaurant

High St PO34 5EX

☎ 01983 612711 🖹 01983 613729

e-mail: reception@seaviewhotel.co.uk

dir: *from B3330 (Ryde-Seaview road), turn left via Puckpool along seafront*

This charming hotel enjoys a quiet location just a short stroll from the seafront. Guests are offered a choice of tastefully and nautically themed dining and bar venues, and can relax in the homely lounge and well-appointed bedrooms. Parking is available at the rear of the property.

Rooms 17 en suite (3 fmly) (3 GF) ⊗ in 13 bedrooms S £58-£149; D £74-£177 (incl. bkfst) **Facilities** Wi-fi available Arrangement with nearby sports club **Parking** 10 **Notes LB** ⊗ ⊗ in restaurant Closed 24-26 Dec

---

★★ 67% **HOTEL**

Springvale Hotel & Restaurant

Springvale PO34 5AN

☎ 01983 612533 🖹 01983 812905

e-mail: reception@springvalehotel.com

web: www.springvalehotel.com

dir: *towards Ryde, follow A3055 onto A3330 towards Bembridge. Left at signs to Seaview, follow brown tourist signs for hotel*

A friendly hotel in a quiet beachfront location with views across the Solent. Bedrooms, which differ in shape and size, are attractive and well equipped. Public areas are traditionally furnished and include a cosy bar, dining room and small separate lounge.

Rooms 13 en suite (2 fmly) **Facilities** ⬚ Jacuzzi Sailing dinghy hire & tuition, Cruiser Charter ⬚ ch fac **Conf** Class 30 Board 20 **Parking** 1 **Notes LB** ⊗ in restaurant

---

SHANKLIN   MAP 05 SZ58

★★★ 74% **HOTEL**

Luccombe Hall

8 Luccombe Rd PO37 6RL

☎ 01983 869000 🖹 01983 863082

e-mail: enquiries@luccombehall.co.uk

dir: *take A3055 to Shanklin, through old village then 1st left into Priory Rd, left into Popham Rd, 1st right into Luccombe Rd. Hotel on left*

Appropriately described as 'the view with the hotel', this property was originally built in 1870 as a summer home for the Bishop of Portsmouth. Enjoying an impressive cliff-top location, the hotel benefits from wonderful sea views, delightful gardens and direct

continued

ccess to the beach. Well-equipped bedrooms are comfortably urnished and there is a range of leisure facilities.

Luccombe Hall

Rooms 30 en suite (15 fmly) (7 GF) ⊗ in 11 bedrooms S £35-£112.50,) £70-£150 **Facilities** 🏊 🎾 Squash Sauna Solarium Gym Putt green acuzzi Games room, Treatment room ♫ Ch fac **Parking** 20 **Notes** ⊛ ⊗ in restaurant

★★★ 73% HOTEL

Keats Green

Queens Rd PO37 6AN

☎ 01983 862742 📠 01983 868572

e-mail: enquiries@keatsgreenhotel.co.uk

dir: on A3055 follow Old Village/Ventnor signs, avoiding town centre, hotel on left past St Saviours Church

This well-established hotel enjoys a super location overlooking Keats Green and Sandown Bay. Bedrooms are attractively decorated in a variety of styles and many have lovely sea views. Public rooms offer a comfortable bar/lounge and a smartly appointed dining room.

Rooms 33 en suite (6 fmly) (3 GF) ⊗ in 1 bedroom S £39-£55;) £70 £110 (incl. bkfst) **Facilities** 🎾 Xmas **Services** Lift **Parking** 26 **Notes LB** ⊗ in restaurant Closed Jan-Mar

★★ 76% HOTEL

Channel View

Hope Rd PO37 6FH

☎ 01983 862309 📠 01983 868400

e-mail: enquiries@channelviewhotel.co.uk

dir: Exit A3055 at Esplanade/Beach sign. Hotel 250mtrs on left

With an elevated cliff-top location overlooking Shanklin Bay, several rooms at this hotel enjoy pleasant views and all are very well decorated and furnished. The hotel is family run, and guests can enjoy

continued

efficient service, regular evening entertainment, a heated indoor swimming pool and holistic therapy.

Rooms 56 en suite (15 fmly) S £28-£37; D £56-£74 (incl. bkfst) **Facilities Spa** 🏊 Sauna Solarium ♫ **Services** Lift **Parking** 22 **Notes LB** ⊗ in restaurant Closed Jan-Feb

★★ 76% HOTEL

Melbourne Ardenlea

4-6 Queens Rd PO37 6AP

☎ 01983 862283 📠 01983 862865

e-mail: reservations@melbourneardenlea.co.uk

dir: from ferry take A3055 to Shanklin. Then follow signs to Ventnor via B3328 (Queens Rd). Hotel just before end of road on right

This quietly located hotel is within easy walking distance of the town centre and the lift down to the promenade. It successfully caters for the needs of holidaymakers. Bedrooms are traditionally furnished and guests can enjoy the various spacious public areas including a welcoming bar and a large heated indoor swimming pool.

Rooms 54 en suite (5 fmly) (6 GF) **Facilities** 🏊 Snooker Sauna Jacuzzi ♫ **Services** Lift **Parking** 26 **Notes LB** ⊗ in restaurant Closed 27 Dec-3 Jan

★★ 74% HOTEL

Cliff Hall

16 Crescent Rd PO37 6DJ

☎ 01983 862828

e-mail: cliffhallhotel@btconnect.com

web: www.cliffhallhotel.co.uk

dir: A3055/A3056 to Shanklin. Right at lake, down Lake Hill, left at Clarendon Rd, hotel at top of hill

A privately owned hotel situated close to the beach lift and town centre. The pleasantly decorated bedrooms are generally quite spacious and have all the usual facilities; many rooms also have stunning sea views. Public areas include a lounge, bar, restaurant, coffee shop and a superb terrace with an outdoor swimming pool.

Rooms 26 en suite (16 fmly) (9 GF) ⊗ in all bedrooms S £32-£49; D £64-£98 (incl. bkfst & dinner) **Facilities** 🎾 Snooker 2 pool tables, table tennis ♫ Xmas **Parking** 30 **Notes LB** ⊛ ⊗ in restaurant Closed Jan/Feb

★★ 69% HOTEL

Curraghmore

22 Hope Rd PO37 6EA

☎ 01983 862605 📠 01983 863342

e-mail: curraghmorehotel@aol.com

dir: Turn off A3055 signed Esplande, hotel is 100mtrs left.

This hotel has a pleasant location, close to the beach and just a short stroll from the shops and Shanklin village. Bedrooms include several with sea views. Entertainment is provided three or four nights of the week with dancing in the lounge and a separate adjoining bar.

Rooms 23 en suite (7 fmly) (6 GF) ⊗ in 15 bedrooms S £33-£38 (incl. bkfst & dinner) **Facilities** ♫ Xmas **Parking** 20 **Notes** ⊗ in restaurant

England

SHANKLIN *continued*

★★ 69% **HOTEL**

Somerton Lodge
43 Victoria Av PO37 6LT
☎ 01983 862710 ▤ 01983 863841
e-mail: somerton@wightbiz.com
web: www.somertonlodgehotel.co.uk
dir: *on A3020 into town*

The hotel is walking distance from the town, old village, Shanklin Chine and the sea. It is situated in a peaceful tree-lined avenue within easy reach of the railway station and main bus routes. Guests can make use of the leisure facilities of the hotel next door, for a small additional charge.

Rooms 16 rms (13 en suite) 5 annexe en suite (2 fmly) (5 GF) **Parking** 15 **Notes** ⊗ No children ⊘ in restaurant

★★ 69% **HOTEL**

Villa Mentone
11 Park Rd PO37 6AY
☎ 01983 862346 ▤ 01983 862130
e-mail: enquiry@villa-mentone.co.uk

Built in 1860, Villa Mentone enjoys an excellent cliff-top position close to the town centre. Bedrooms vary in size but are all well equipped, and a smart conservatory extension offers views over Shanklin Bay. Enjoyable home cooking is served in the pleasant dining room, and entertainment is regularly provided in the bar.

Rooms 30 en suite (3 fmly) (7 GF) S £30-£40; D £45-£70 (incl. bkfst) **Facilities** STV ♫ Xmas **Conf** Thtr 45 Class 25 Board 10 **Parking** 10 **Notes LB** ⊗ ⊘ in restaurant

★★ 64% **HOTEL**

Malton House
8 Park Rd PO37 6AY
☎ 01983 865007 ▤ 01983 865576
e-mail: couvoussis@maltonhouse.freeserve.co.uk
web: www.maltonhouse.co.uk
dir: *up hill from Hope Road lights then 3rd left*

A well-kept Victorian hotel set in its own gardens in a quiet area, conveniently located for cliff-top walks and the public lift down to the promenade. The bedrooms are comfortable and public rooms include a small lounge, a separate bar and a dining room where traditional homemade meals are served.

Rooms 15 en suite (3 fmly) S £30-£34; D £50-£58 (incl. bkfst) **Parking** 12 **Notes** ⊗ ⊘ in restaurant Closed Apr-Oct

TOTLAND BAY   MAP 05 SZ38

★★★ 72% **HOTEL**

Sentry Mead
Madeira Rd PO39 0BJ
☎ 01983 753212 ▤ 01983 754710
e-mail: info@sentrymead.co.uk
web: www.sentrymead.co.uk
dir: *off A3054 onto B3322. At 1st roundabout turn right into Madeira Rd. Hotel is 250mtrs on right*

Just two minutes' walk from the sea at Totland Bay, this well-kept Victorian villa has a comfortable lounge and separate bar, as well as a conservatory that looks out over the delightful garden. Bedrooms feature co-ordinated soft furnishings and welcome extras such as mineral water and biscuits.

Rooms 14 en suite (2 fmly) ⊛ in all bedrooms S £45-£60; D £90-£120 (incl. bkfst) **Parking** 12 **Notes LB** ⊘ in restaurant

VENTNOR   MAP 05 SZ57

★★★★ 76% ⍟⍟ **HOTEL**

The Royal Hotel
Belgrave Rd PO38 1JJ
☎ 01983 852186 ▤ 01983 855395
e-mail: enquiries@royalhoteliow.co.uk
web: www.royalhoteliow.co.uk
dir: *A3055 into Ventnor follow one-way system, after lights left into Belgrave Road. Hotel on right*

The Royal continues with improvements each year, with most of the bedrooms having been refurbished to a high standard. Staff deliver friendly professional service in a relaxed manner. Public areas include a sunny conservatory and bar and lounges. The restaurant provides traditional surroundings in which to enjoy modern British cuisine.

Rooms 55 en suite (7 fmly) ⊛ in all bedrooms S £75-£150; D £130-£200 (incl. bkfst) **Facilities** FTV ♦ ♨ Xmas **Conf** Thtr 100 Class 40 Board 24 Del from £100 **Services** Lift **Parking** 56 **Notes LB** ⊗ ⊘ in restaurant Closed 1st 2 wks Jan Civ Wed 150

See advert on opposite page

★★★ 75% **HOTEL**

Best Western Ventnor Towers
Madeira Rd PO38 1QT
☎ 01983 852277 ▤ 01983 855536
e-mail: reservations@ventnortowers.com
web: www.ventnortowers.com
dir: *1st left after Trinity church, follow Madeira Rd for 0.25m*

This mid-Victorian hotel set in spacious grounds - from which a path leads down to the shore - is high above the bay and enjoys splendid sea views. Many potted plants and fresh flowers grace the day rooms, which include two lounges and a spacious bar. Bedrooms include two four-poster rooms and some that have their own balconies.

Rooms 25 en suite (4 fmly) (6 GF) ⊛ in 14 bedrooms S £30-£80; D £60-£110 (incl. bkfst) **Facilities** ♦ ♨ Putt green Wi-fi available ♫ **Conf** Thtr 80 Class 50 Board 35 **Parking** 25 **Notes LB** ⊘ in restaurant Closed 21-27 Dec

★★★ 73% **HOTEL**

Burlington

Bellevue Rd PO38 1DB

☎ 01983 852113 📠 01983 853862

e-mail: patmctoldrige@burlingtonhotel.uk.com

Eight of the attractively decorated bedrooms at this establishment benefit from balconies, and the three ground floor rooms have French doors that lead onto the garden. There is a cosy bar, a comfortable lounge and a dining room where home-made bread rolls accompany the five-course dinners. Service is friendly and attentive.

Rooms 24 en suite (8 fmly) (3 GF) ⊗ in all bedrooms S £40-£55; D £80-£110 (incl. bkfst & dinner) **Facilities** ⊰ **Parking** 20 **Notes LB** ⊗ No children 3yrs ⊗ in restaurant Closed Nov-Etr

★★★ 71% **HOTEL**

Eversley

Park Av PO38 1LB

☎ 01983 852244 & 852462 📠 01983 856534

e-mail: eversleyhotel@yahoo.co.uk

web: www.eversleyhotel.com

dir: on A3055 W of Ventnor, next to Ventnor Park

Located west of Ventnor, this hotel enjoys a quiet location and has some rooms offering garden and pool views. The spacious restaurant is sometimes used for local functions, and there is a bar, television room, lounge area and a card room as well as a jacuzzi and gym. Bedrooms are generally a good size.

Rooms 30 en suite (8 fmly) (2 GF) S £40-£70; D £60-£110 (incl. bkfst) **Facilities Spa** ⊰ Gym Pool table Xmas **Conf** Class 40 Board 20 Del from £60 **Parking** 23 **Notes LB** ⊗ in restaurant Closed 30 Nov-22 Dec & 2 Jan 8 Feb

★★ 85% ◉◉ **HOTEL**

Hambrough

Hambrough Rd PO38 1SQ

☎ 01983 856333 📠 01983 857260

e-mail: info@thehambrough.com

A former Victorian villa set on the hillside above Ventnor and with memorable views out to sea. Extensive refurbishment has resulted in a modern stylish interior with well equipped and comfortable bedrooms. The team's passion for food is clearly evident in the award-winning cuisine served in the minimalist themed restaurant.

Rooms 7 en suite

★★ 63% **HOTEL**

Hillside Hotel

Mitchell Av PO38 1DR

☎ 01983 852271 📠 01983 852271

e-mail: aa@hillside-hotel.co.uk

dir: off A3055 onto B3327. Hotel 0.5m on right behind tennis courts

Hillside Hotel dates back to the 19th century and enjoys a superb location overlooking Ventnor and the sea beyond. Public areas consist of a traditional lounge, a cosy bar area with an adjoining conservatory and a light, airy dining room. A welcoming and homely atmosphere is assured.

Rooms 12 en suite (1 fmly) (1 GF) ⊗ in all bedrooms **Facilities**
Parking 12 **Notes LB** No children 5yrs ⊗ in restaurant Closed Xmas

England

YARMOUTH
MAP 05 SZ38

INSPECTORS' CHOICE

★★★ ◉◉◉ **HOTEL**

George Hotel
Quay St PO41 0PE
☎ 01983 760331 ◻ 01983 760425
e-mail: res@thegeorge.co.uk
dir: between the castle and the pier

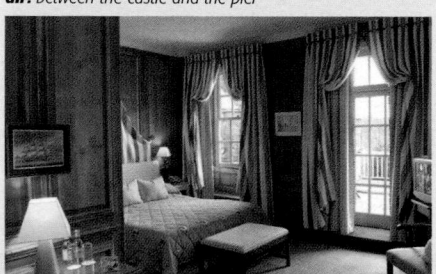

This delightful 17th-century hotel enjoys a wonderful location at the water's edge, adjacent to the castle and the quay. Public areas include an elegant fine dining restaurant, and a bright brasserie for more informal eating. In addition, guests can also relax in either the cosy bar or an inviting lounge. Individually styled bedrooms, with many thoughtful extras, are beautifully appointed; some benefit from spacious balconies. The hotel's motor yacht is available for hire by guests.

Rooms 17 en suite ⊗ in 4 bedrooms S fr £130; D fr £180 (incl. bkfst) **Facilities** STV Sailing from Yarmouth, Mountain Biking Xmas **Conf** Thtr 30 Class 10 Board 18 Del from £200 **Notes** No children 10yrs ⊗ in restaurant Civ Wed 60

[U]

Bugle Coaching Inn
The Square PO41 0NS
☎ 01983 760272 ◻ 01983 760883
dir: 200yds from Yarmouth Wightlink Ferry Terminal, in town square

At the time of going to press, the star classification for this hotel was not confirmed. Please refer to the AA internet site www.theAA.com for current information.

Rooms 7 en suite (1 fmly) ⊗ in all bedrooms S £45-£55; D £90-£110 (incl. bkfst) **Facilities** ♫ **Parking** 15 **Notes** ⊗ ⊗ in restaurant

---

WILTSHIRE

AMESBURY
MAP 05 SU14

BUDGET HOTEL

Travelodge Amesbury Stonehenge
Countess Services SP4 7AS
☎ 08700 850 950 ◻ 01980 625273
web: www.travelodge.co.uk
dir: at junct A345 & A303 eastbound

Travelodge offers good quality, good value, modern accommodation. Ideal for families, the spacious en suite bedrooms include remote-control TV, tea and coffee-making facilities and comfortable beds. Meals can be taken at the nearby family restaurant. See Hotel Groups pages for further details.

Rooms 48 en suite S fr £26; D fr £26

BRADFORD-ON-AVON
MAP 04 ST86

★★★ 82% ◉◉ **HOTEL**

Woolley Grange
Woolley Green BA15 1TX
☎ 01225 864705 ◻ 01225 864059
e-mail: info@woolleygrangehotel.co.uk
web: www.vonessenhotels.co.uk
dir: Turn off A4 onto B3109. Bradford Leigh, left at crossroads, hotel 0.5m on right at Woolley Green

This splendid Cotswold manor house is set in beautiful countryside. Children are made especially welcome; there is a trained nanny on duty in the nursery. Bedrooms and public areas are charmingly furnished and decorated in true country-house style, with many thoughtful touches and luxurious extras. The hotel offers a varied and well-balanced menu selection, including ingredients from the hotel's own garden.

Rooms 14 en suite 12 annexe en suite (8 fmly) S £120-£355; D £200-£425 (incl. bkfst & dinner) **Facilities** FTV ♋ ⛳ Putt green Wi-fi available Badminton, Beauty treatments, Football, Games room Table Tennis ch fac Xmas **Conf** Thtr 35 Class 12 Board 22 Del £175 **Parking** 40 **Notes** LB ⊗ in restaurant Civ Wed 40

★★★ 78% COUNTRY HOUSE HOTEL

Best Western Leigh Park Hotel

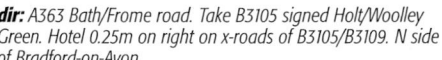

Leigh Park West BA15 2RA

☎ 01225 864885 ▤ 01225 862315

e-mail: inof@leighparkhotel.eclipse.co.uk

dir: A363 Bath/Frome road. Take B3105 signed Holt/Woolley Green. Hotel 0.25m on right on x-roads of B3105/B3109. N side of Bradford-on-Avon

Enjoying splendid countryside views, this relaxing Georgian hotel is set in five acres of well-tended grounds, complete with a vineyard. Combining charm and character with modern facilities, the hotel is equally well suited to business and leisure travellers. The restaurant serves dishes cooked to order, using home-grown fruit and vegetables, and wine from the vineyard.

Rooms 22 en suite (4 fmly) (7 GF) ⊗ in 14 bedrooms
Facilities Vineyard **Conf** Thtr 120 Class 60 Board 60 **Parking** 80
Notes LB ⊗ in restaurant Civ Wed 120

Ⓤ

Widbrook Grange

Trowbridge Rd, Widbrook BA15 1UH

☎ 01225 864750 & 863173 ▤ 01225 862890

e-mail: stay@widbrookgrange.com

dir: 1m SE from Bradford on A363, diagonally opposite Bradford Marina & Arabian Stud

At the time of going to press, the star classification for this hotel was not confirmed. Please refer to the AA internet site www.theAA.com for current information.

Rooms 5 en suite 15 annexe en suite (4 fmly) (13 GF) **Facilities** 🔾
Gym children's weekend play room **Parking** 50 **Notes** ⊗ RS Sun
Civ Wed 48

CALNE   MAP 04 ST97

★★★ 67% HOTEL

Best Western Lansdowne Strand

The Strand SN11 0EH

☎ 01249 812488 ▤ 01249 815323

e-mail: reservations@lansdownestrand.co.uk

dir: off A4, in town centre

In the centre of the market town, this 16th-century, former coaching inn (now under new ownership) still retains many period features. Individually decorated bedrooms vary in size. There are two friendly bars; one offers a wide selection of ales and a cosy fire. An interesting menu is available in the brasserie-style restaurant.

Rooms 21 en suite 5 annexe en suite (3 fmly) ⊗ in 19 bedrooms S £89;
D £102 (incl. bkfst) **Facilities** STV Complimentary use of nearby leisure centre Xmas **Conf** Thtr 90 Class 28 Board 30 Del £98.95 **Parking** 21

CASTLE COMBE   MAP 04 ST87

INSPECTORS' CHOICE

★★★★ ◉◉◉ COUNTRY HOUSE HOTEL

Manor House

SN14 7HR

☎ 01249 782206 ▤ 01249 782159

e-mail: enquiries@manor-housecc.co.uk

web: www.exclusivehotels.co.uk

dir: M4 junct 17 follow Chippenham signs onto A420 Bristol, then right onto B4039. Through village, right after bridge

This delightful hotel is situated in a secluded valley adjacent to a picturesque village, where there have been no new buildings for 300 years. There are 365 acres of grounds to enjoy, complete with an Italian garden and an 18-hole golf course. Bedrooms, some in the main house and some in a row of stone cottages, have been superbly furnished, and public rooms include a number of cosy lounges with roaring fires. Service is a pleasing blend of professionalism and friendliness. The food offered utilises top quality local produce.

Rooms 22 en suite 26 annexe en suite (8 fmly) (12 GF) ⊗ in all
bedrooms S £150-£600; D £180-£600 (incl. bkfst) **Facilities** STV
↕ 18 ⚲ Fishing Sauna 😊 Putt green Wi-fi available Jogging track
Xmas **Conf** BC Thtr 70 Class 70 Board 30 Del from £200
Parking 100 **Notes LB** ⊗ in restaurant Civ Wed 110

CHIPPENHAM   MAP 04 ST97

★★★ 79% HOTEL

Best Western Angel Hotel

Market Place SN15 3HD

☎ 01249 652615 ▤ 01249 443210

e-mail: reception@angelhotelchippenham.co.uk

web: www.angelhotelchippenham.co.uk

dir: follow tourist signs for Bowood House. Under railway arch, follow 'Borough Parade Parking' signs. Hotel next to car park

These impressive buildings make up a smart, comfortable hotel. The well-equipped bedrooms vary, from those in the main house where character is the key, to the smart executive-style, courtyard rooms. The lounge and restaurant are bright and modern where in addition to the imaginative carte, an all-day menu is served.

Rooms 15 en suite 35 annexe en suite (3 fmly) (12 GF) ⊗ in
29 bedrooms S £75.50-£131.25; D £95.50-£155.50 (incl. bkfst)
Facilities STV 🔾 Gym Wi-fi in bedrooms **Conf** Thtr 100 Class 50
Board 50 **Parking** 50

England

CHIPPENHAM *continued*

★★★ 77% **HOTEL**

Stanton Manor Country House

SN14 6DQ

☎ 01666 837552 & 0870 890 02880 📠 01666 837022

e-mail: reception@stantonmanor.co.uk

web: www.stantonmanor.co.uk

(For full entry see Stanton St Quintin)

BUDGET HOTEL

Premier Travel Inn Chippenham

premier travel inn

Cepen Park, West Cepen Way SN14 6UZ

☎ 08701 977061 📠 01249 461359

web: www.premiertravelinn.com

dir: *M4 junct 17, take A350 towards Chippenham. Inn is at 1st main rdbt at gateway to Chippenham*

High quality, modern budget accommodation ideal for both families and business travellers. Spacious, en suite bedrooms feature bath and shower, satellite TV and many have telephones and modem points. The adjacent family restaurant features a wide and varied menu. For further details consult the Hotel Groups page.

Rooms 79 en suite

COLERNE   MAP 04 ST87

INSPECTORS' CHOICE

★★★★★ ◉◉◉ **HOTEL**

Lucknam Park

SN14 8AZ

☎ 01225 742777 📠 01225 743536

e-mail: reservations@lucknampark.co.uk

web: www.lucknampark.co.uk

dir: *M4 junct 17, A350 to Chippenham, then A420 to Bristol for 3m. At Ford village, left to Colerne, 3m right at x-rds. Entrance on right*

RELAIS & CHATEAUX

Guests on arrival at this Palladian mansion may well experience a sense of the theatrical as they drive along a magnificent mile-long avenue of beech and lime trees. Surrounded by 500 acres of parkland and beautiful gardens, this fine hotel offers a wealth of choices ranging from enjoying pampering treatments to taking vigorous exercise. Elegant bedrooms and suites are split between the main building and adjacent courtyard. Dining options range

continued

from the informal Pavilion Restaurant, to the formal, and very accomplished, main restaurant.

Rooms 23 en suite 18 annexe en suite (16 GF) S £245-840; D £245-£840 **Facilities** Spa STV ⚒ 🏊 Riding Snooker Sauna Gym ⚒ Jacuzzi Wi-fi in bedrooms Whirlpool, Beauty & hair salon, Steam room, Cross country course, Mountain bikes ♫ Xmas **Conf** BC Thtr 60 Class 24 Board 24 Del from £260 **Parking** 70 **Notes LB** ⊗ ⊛ in restaurant Civ Wed 80

CRICKLADE   MAP 05 SU09

★★★ 77% **HOTEL**

Cricklade Hotel

Common Hill SN6 6HA

☎ 01793 750751 📠 01793 751767

e-mail: reception@crickladehotel.co.uk

web: www.crickladehotel.co.uk

dir: *off A419 onto B4040. Turn left at clock tower. Right at rdbt. Hotel 0.5m up hill on left*

A haven of peace and tranquillity with spectacular views, this hotel is surrounded by over 30 acres of beautiful countryside. Bedrooms vary in size and style with a choice of rooms in the main building or courtyard, all of which offer high levels of comfort and quality. Public areas include an elegant lounge, dining room and a Victorian-style conservatory that runs the full length of the building. Extensive leisure facilities include a 9-hole golf course, indoor pool and gym.

Rooms 25 en suite 21 annexe en suite (1 fmly) ⊛ in all bedrooms S £115-£120; D £155-£158 (incl. bkfst) **Facilities** STV ⚒ ⚒9 🏊 Snooker Solarium Gym ⚒ Jacuzzi Wi-fi available Aromatherapy, Beautician, Golf professional ♫ Xmas **Conf** Thtr 80 Class 60 Board 30 Del from £160 **Parking** 100 **Notes LB** ⊗ No children 14yrs ⊛ in restaurant Closed 25-26 Dec Civ Wed 120

See advert under SWINDON

DEVIZES   MAP 04 SU06

★★★ 72% **HOTEL**

Bear

Market Place SN10 1HS

☎ 01380 722444 📠 01380 722450

e-mail: info@thebearhotel.net

web: www.thebearhotel.net

dir: *in town centre*

Set in the market place of this small Wiltshire town, this attractive hotel has a strong local following. Newly refurbished bedrooms and bathrooms offer a range of shapes and sizes. The attractive lounge

continued

includes a quiet area for residents to enjoy afternoon tea. Homemade cakes are available throughout the day and dinner includes a new and very popular homemade pizza parlour in addition to the main restaurant.

Rooms 24 en suite (5 fmly) ⊘ in all bedrooms S £70-£75, D £95-£115 (incl. bkfst) **Facilities** Solarium Wi-fi in bedrooms **Conf** Thtr 100 Class 60 Board 60 Del from £115 **Services** Lift **Parking** 14 **Notes** ⊗ ⊘ in restaurant Closed 25-26 Dec Civ Wed 100

LEIGH DELAMERE MAP 04 ST87
MOTORWAY SERVICE AREA (M4)

BUDGET HOTEL

Travelodge Chippenham Leigh Delamere M4 Eastbound

SN14 6LB

☎ 08700 850 950 🗎 01666 837112

web: www.travelodge.co.uk

dir: between juncts 17 & 18 on M4

Travelodge offers good quality, good value, modern accommodation. Ideal for families, the spacious en suite bedrooms include remote-control TV, tea and coffee-making facilities and comfortable beds. Meals can be taken at the nearby family restaurant. See Hotel Groups pages for further details.

Rooms 69 en suite S fr £26; D fr £26

Travelodge Chippenham Leigh Delamere M4 Westbound

Service Area SN14 6LB

☎ 08700 850 950 🗎 01666 838529

dir: between juncts 17 & 18 on M4

Rooms 31 en suite S fr £26; D fr £26

LIMPLEY STOKE MAP 04 ST76

★★★ 74% HOTEL

Best Western Limpley Stoke

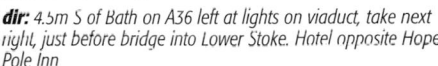

BA2 7FZ

☎ 01225 723333 🗎 01225 722406

e-mail: latonalsh@aol.com

dir: 4.5m S of Bath on A36 left at lights on viaduct, take next right, just before bridge into Lower Stoke. Hotel opposite Hope Pole Inn

This quietly located former Georgian mansion is on the outskirts of Bath in a peaceful village setting; easily accessible from the M4. Attentive levels of service and friendly hospitality are to be found throughout the hotel. Bedrooms come in various shapes and sizes and some enjoy memorable views over the valley below.

Rooms 60 en suite (8 fmly) ⊘ in 10 bedrooms S £75-£95; D £75-£115 **Facilities** ♫ Xmas Wi-fi in bedrooms **Conf** Thtr 120 Class 40 Board 30 Del from £115 **Services** Lift **Parking** 90 **Notes** ⊘ in restaurant Civ Wed 120

MALMESBURY MAP 04 ST98

INSPECTORS' CHOICE

★★★★★ ❀❀❀ HOTEL

Whatley Manor

Easton Grey SN16 0RB

☎ 01666 822888 🗎 01666 826120

e-mail: reservations@whatleymanor.com

web: www.whatleymanor.com

dir: M4 junct 17 to Malmesbury, left at T-junct, left at next T-junct onto B4040, hotel 2m on left

Nestling in 12 acres of beautiful Wiltshire countryside, this impressive country house has been lovingly renovated to provide the most luxurious surroundings. Spacious bedrooms, most with views over the attractive gardens, are individually decorated with splendid features. Two restaurants are available: Le Mazot, a Swiss-style brasserie and The Dining Room that serves classical French cuisine with a contemporary twist. The magnificent Aquarius Spa is a must on any visit, offering an unforgettable experience.

Rooms 23 en suite (4 GF) ⊘ in 6 bedrooms D £280-£850 (incl. bkfst) **Facilities** Spa STV Fishing Sauna Solarium Gym Putt green Wi-fi available Cinema, Hydro pool Xmas **Conf** BC Thtr 40 Class 20 Board 25 Del from £265 **Services** Lift **Parking** 100 **Notes** LB No children 12yrs ⊘ in restaurant Civ Wed 120

See advert on page 677

★★★ 81% ❀❀ HOTEL

Old Bell

Abbey Row SN16 0AG

☎ 01666 822344 🗎 01666 825145

e-mail: info@oldbellhotel.com

web: www.oldbellhotel.com

dir: M4 junct 11, follow A429 north. Left at first rdbt. Left at T-junct. Hotel next to Abbey

Dating back to 1220, the Old Bell is reputed to be the oldest purpose-built hotel in England. Bedrooms vary in size and style; those in the main house are traditionally furnished with antiques, while the newer bedrooms have a contemporary feel. Guests have a choice of comfortable sitting areas and dining options.

Rooms 15 en suite 15 annexe en suite (7 GF) ⊘ in all bedrooms S fr £95; D fr £125 (incl. bkfst) **Facilities** STV Wi-fi available Aromatherapy massages Xmas **Conf** Thtr 60 Class 32 Board 32 Del from £150 **Parking** 31 **Notes** LB ⊘ in restaurant Civ Wed 80

England

MALMESBURY *continued*

★★★ 75% ◉ ◉ **HOTEL**

The Rectory Hotel
SN16 9EP
☎ 01666 577194 📠 01666 577853
e-mail: info@therectoryhotel.com
web: www.therectoryhotel.com
dir: M4 junct 17. Follow A429 to Cirencester, right opposite
Plough pub in Crudwell. Hotel next to church

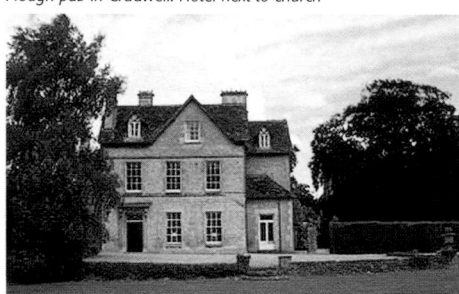

A former rectory, this beautiful house, with its Victorian walled garden,
offers a feeling of peace and seclusion. Individually decorated
bedrooms offer comfort coupled with a host of thoughtful touches for
guests' enjoyment. The highlight is the wood-panelled restaurant
where local produce forms the basis of well-prepared dishes.
Rooms 12 en suite (1 fmly) ⊛ in all bedrooms S £85-£105; D £95-£155
(incl. bkfst) **Facilities** ⬩ ⬩ Wi-fi in bedrooms Xmas **Conf** BC Thtr 50
Class 30 Board 30 Del from £130 **Parking** 40 **Notes LB** ⊛ in restaurant
Civ Wed 60

★★★ 73% ◉ **HOTEL**

Best Western Mayfield House
Crudwell SN16 9EW
☎ 01666 577409 📠 01666 577977
e-mail: reception@mayfieldhousehotel.co.uk
web: www.mayfieldhousehotel.co.uk
dir: 3m N on A429 from Malmesbury

This cared for popular hotel, on the edge of the Cotswolds is
impeccably presented. The bedrooms are equipped with modern
facilities; some ground-floor rooms are available and others are
situated in adjacent cottages. A variety of freshly prepared dinners are
served in the smart restaurant, which has a relaxed environment.
There is a foyer lounge and a bar. The well-tended garden is equipped
with seating, on the patio and dotted around the lawn, for summer
leisure.
Rooms 21 en suite 5 annexe en suite (2 fmly) ⊛ in all bedrooms
S £70-£75; D £90-£98 (incl. bkfst) **Facilities** Wi-fi in bedrooms Xmas
Conf Thtr 40 Class 30 Board 25 Del from £118 **Parking** 50 **Notes LB**
⊛ in restaurant

See advert on opposite page

MARLBOROUGH   MAP 05 SU16

★★★ 70% **HOTEL**

Ivy House
43 High St SN8 1HJ
☎ 01672 515333 📠 01672 515338
e-mail: enquiries@ivyhousemarlborough.co.uk
web: www.ivyhousemarlborough.co.uk
dir: in town centre

Set in the delightful high street of this attractive and historic town, The
Ivy House has friendly and attentive staff. The bedrooms are spacious
and comfortable and very well equipped. Cuisine is enjoyable here
and features fresh local produce. The hotel has a pleasant terrace
where in warmer months guests can dine alfresco.
Rooms 28 en suite (3 fmly) (8 GF) ⊛ in 22 bedrooms S £80-£95;
D £90-£125 (incl. bkfst) **Facilities** STV **Conf** Thtr 60 Class 30 Board 30
Del from £125 **Parking** 35 **Notes** ⊛ ⊛ in restaurant

★★★ 66% **HOTEL**

The Castle & Ball   OLD ENGLISH INNS
High St SN8 1LZ
☎ 01672 515201 📠 01672 515895
web: www.oldenglish.co.uk
dir: A338 and A4 to Marlborough

This traditional coaching inn in the town centre has now been
upgraded. Bedrooms have been refurbished in a contemporary style
and are very well equipped. Open-plan public areas include a
comfortable bar/lounge area and a smartly appointed restaurant,
which serves food all day. Meeting rooms are also available.
Rooms 34 en suite (1 fmly) ⊛ in 13 bedrooms **Facilities** STV
Conf Thtr 45 Class 20 Board 30 **Parking** 48 **Notes LB** ⊛ in restaurant

MELKSHAM   MAP 04 ST96

★★ 74% **HOTEL**

Shaw Country
Bath Rd, Shaw SN12 8EF
☎ 01225 702836 & 790321 📠 01225 790275
e-mail: info@shawcountryhotel.co.uk
web: www.shawcountryhotel.co.uk
dir: 1m from Melksham, 9m from Bath on A365

Located within easy reach of both Bath and the M4, this relaxed and
friendly hotel sits in its own gardens, that has a patio area ideal for
enjoying a cool drink during warm summer months. The house boasts
some very well-appointed bedrooms, a comfortable lounge and bar
continued

and the Mulberry Restaurant, where a wide selection of innovative dishes make up both carte and set menus. A spacious function room is a useful addition.

Rooms 13 en suite (2 fmly) ⊘ in all bedrooms **Conf** Thtr 60 Class 40 Board 20 **Parking** 30 **Notes** ⊘ in restaurant RS 26 27 Dec & 1 Jan Civ Wed 90

PURTON   MAP 05 SU08

★★★ 80% ◉◉ **HOTEL**

The Pear Tree at Purton
Church End SN5 4ED

☎ 01793 772100 📠 01793 772369

e-mail: stay@peartreepurton.co.uk

dir: M4 junct 16 follow signs to Purton, at Spar shop turn right. Hotel 0.25m on left

Charming 15th-century, former vicarage set amidst fully landscaped gardens in a peaceful location. The resident proprietors and staff provide efficient, dedicated service and friendly hospitality. The spacious bedrooms are individually decorated and have a good range of thoughtful extras such as fresh flowers and sherry. Fresh ingredients feature on the menus at both lunch and dinner.

Rooms 17 en suite (2 fmly) (6 GF) S £110-£140; D £110-£170 (incl. bkfst) **Facilities Spa** STV ⚓ Wi-fi in bedrooms Outdoor giant chess, Vineyard **Conf** Thtr 70 Class 30 Board 30 Del £170 **Parking** 60 **Notes LB** ⊘ in restaurant Closed 26-30 Dec Civ Wed 50

SALISBURY
See also Landford

MAP 05 SU12

★★★ 75% **HOTEL**

Milford Hall

CLASSIC
BRITISH HOTELS

206 Castle St SP1 3TE
☎ 01722 417411 & 424116 📠 01722 419444
e-mail: reception@milfordhallhotel.com
web: www.milfordhallhotel.com

dir: near junct of Castle St, A36 (ring road) & A345 (Amesbury road)

This hotel offers high standards of accommodation within easy walking distance of the city centre. There are two categories of bedroom; traditional rooms in the original Georgian house and spacious, modern rooms in a purpose built extension - all are extremely well equipped. Meals are served in the smart brasserie where a varied choice of dishes is provided.

Rooms 35 en suite (1 fmly) (20 GF) ⊘ in 15 bedrooms S £108-£130; D £118-£150 **Facilities** STV Wi-fi in bedrooms Free facilities at local leisure centre ch fac **Conf** Thtr 90 Class 70 Board 40 Del £155 **Parking** 60 **Notes LB** ⊘ in restaurant Civ Wed 80

★★★ 74% 🏵 **HOTEL**

Best Western Red Lion

Milford St SP1 2AN
☎ 01722 323334 📠 01722 325756
e-mail: reception@the-redlion.co.uk
web: www.the-redlion.co.uk

dir: in city centre close to Guildhall Square

This 750-year-old hotel is full of character. The individual bedrooms combine contemporary comforts with historic features, including one room with a medieval fireplace, dating back to 1220. Public areas are also distinctive with a bar, lounge and the elegant Vine Restaurant, serving an interesting mix of modern and traditional dishes.

Rooms 51 en suite (2 fmly) ⊘ in 40 bedrooms S £91-£100; D £116-£130 (incl. bkfst) **Facilities** STV Wi-fi in bedrooms Xmas **Conf** Thtr 100 Class 50 Board 40 Del from £110 **Services** Lift **Notes LB** ⊗ ⊘ in restaurant Civ Wed 80

See advert on opposite page

★★★ 74% **HOTEL**

Macdonald White Hart

MACDONALD
HOTELS & RESORTS

St John St SP1 2SD
☎ 0870 400 8125 & 01722 327476 📠 01722 412761
e-mail: whitehartsalisbury@macdonald-hotels.co.uk
web: www.macdonald-hotels.co.uk

dir: M3 junct 7/8, A303 to A343 for Salisbury then A30. Follow city centre signs on ring road, into Exeter Street, leading into St. John Street. Car park at rear

There has been a hotel on this site since the 16th century. Bedrooms vary between the contemporary-style rooms and those decorated in more traditional style, all of which boast a comprehensive range of facilities. The bar and lounge areas are popular with guests and locals for morning coffees and afternoon teas.

Rooms 68 en suite (6 fmly) ⊘ in 62 bedrooms S £92-£136; D £107-£146 (incl. bkfst) **Facilities** STV Xmas **Conf** Thtr 100 Class 40 Board 40 Del from £140 **Parking** 60 **Notes LB** ⊘ in restaurant Civ Wed 100

★★★ 68% **HOTEL**

Grasmere House Hotel

Harnham Rd SP2 8JN
☎ 01722 338388 📠 01722 333710
e-mail: grasmerehotel@mistral.co.uk
web: www.grasmerehotel.com

dir: on A3094 on S side of Salisbury next to All Saints Church in Harnham

This popular hotel dates from 1896 and has gardens overlooking the water meadows and the cathedral. The attractive bedrooms vary in size, some offer excellent quality and comfort, and some rooms are specially equipped for less mobile guests. In summer, guests have the option of dining on the pleasant outdoor terrace.

Rooms 7 en suite 31 annexe en suite (16 fmly) (9 GF) ⊘ in 30 bedrooms S £82.50-£95.50; D £125.50-£135.50 (incl. bkfst) **Facilities** STV Fishing 🛁 Jacuzzi Wi-fi in bedrooms Xmas **Conf** Thtr 110 Class 45 Board 45 Del from £135.50 **Parking** 64 **Notes LB** Civ Wed 120

See advert on opposite page

ⓊSwallow Rose & Crown

SWALLOW HOTELS

Harnham Rd, Harnham SP2 8JQ

☎ 01722 399955 📠 01722 339816

web: www.swallowhotels.com

dir: *M3 junct 8, A303. Remain on Salisbury Ring Road towards Harnham*

At the time of going to press, the star classification for this hotel was not confirmed. Please refer to the AA internet site www.theAA.com for current information.

Rooms 28 en suite

BUDGET HOTEL

Kings Head Inn

1 Bridge St SP1 2ND

☎ 01722 342050 438400 📠 01722 326743

e-mail: salisburylodge@jdwetherspoon.co.uk

dir: *in town centre*

Very centrally located, with some rooms overlooking the high street, this lodge offers a lively atmosphere with its popular Lloyds No 1 bar and extensive menus. The well-equipped bedrooms have a number of welcome extras. Some outdoor seating is available in summer.

Rooms 32 en suite

BUDGET HOTEL

Premier Travel Inn Salisbury

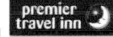 premier travel inn

Bishopdown Retail Park, Pearce Way SP1 3YU

☎ 08701 977225 📠 01722 337889

web: www.premiertravelinn.com

dir: *From Salisbury centre, follow A30 towards Marlborough for 1m. Inn is located off Hampton Park at rdbt*

High quality, modern budget accommodation ideal for both families and business travellers. Spacious, en suite bedrooms feature bath and shower, satellite TV and many have telephones and modem points. The adjacent family restaurant features a wide and varied menu. For further details consult the Hotel Groups page.

Rooms 60 en suite

STANTON ST QUINTIN　　MAP 04 ST97

★★★ 77% **HOTEL**

Stanton Manor Country House Hotel

SN14 6DQ

☎ 01666 837552 & 0870 890 02880 📠 01666 837022

e-mail: reception@stantonmanor.co.uk

web: www.stantonmanor.co.uk

dir: M4 junct 17 onto A429 Malmesbury/Cirencester, within 200yds turn 1st left signed Stanton St Quintin, entrance to hotel on left just after church

Set in five acres of lovely gardens that includes a short golf course, this charming manor house (mentioned in the Domesday Book) has easy access to the M4. Public areas are a delight offering both character and comfort. The restaurant offers a short carte of imaginative dishes and an interesting wine selection.

Rooms 23 en suite (3 fmly) (7 GF) ✖ in 18 bedrooms S £115; D £135-£210 (incl. bkfst) **Facilities** STV FTV ⬆9 ⬆ Putt green Wi-fi in bedrooms ch fac Xmas **Conf** BC Thtr 120 Class 80 Board 40 Del from £176.25 **Parking** 60 **Notes LB** ✖ in restaurant Civ Wed 120

SWINDON　　MAP 05 SU18

See also Wootton Bassett

★★★★ 77% ⊛ **HOTEL**

Blunsdon House Hotel & Leisure Club

Blunsdon SN26 7AS

Best Western PREMIER

☎ 01793 721701 📠 01793 721056

e-mail: info@blunsdonhouse.co.uk

web: www.blunsdonhouse.co.uk

dir: 200yds off A419 at Swindon

Located just to the north of Swindon, Blunsdon House is set in 30 acres of well-kept grounds and offers extensive leisure facilities and spacious day rooms. The hotel has a choice of eating and drinking options; there are three bars and two restaurants. Bedrooms are comfortably furnished, and the contemporary Pavilion rooms are especially spacious.

Rooms 117 en suite (15 fmly) (27 GF) ✖ in 75 bedrooms S £96-£125; D £75-£135 (incl. bkfst) **Facilities** STV 🕸 ⬆9 ⬆ Squash Sauna Solarium Gym Putt green Jacuzzi Wi-fi available Beauty therapy, Woodland walk, 9 hole par 3 golf course ch fac Xmas **Conf** Thtr 300 Class 200 Board 40 Del from £130 **Services** Lift **Parking** 300 **Notes LB** ✖ ✖ in restaurant Civ Wed 200

★★★★ 74% **HOTEL**

Swindon Marriott Hotel

Marriott HOTELS & RESORTS

Pipers Way SN3 1SH

☎ 0870 400 7281 📠 0870 400 7381

web: www.swindonmarriott.co.uk

dir: M4 junct 15, follow A419, then A4259 to Coate rdbt and B4006 signed 'Old Town'

With convenient access to the motorway, this hotel is an easily accessible venue for meetings, and an ideal base from which to explore Wiltshire and the Cotswolds. The hotel offers a good range of public rooms, including a well-equipped leisure centre, Chats café bar and the informal, brasserie-style Mediterrano restaurant.

Rooms 156 en suite (42 fmly) ✖ in 137 bedrooms S £49-£119; D £49-£119 **Facilities** Spa STV 🕸 ⬆ Sauna Solarium Gym Jacuzzi Wi-fi in bedrooms Steam Room, Health & Beauty, Hair salon, Sports massage therapy **Conf** Thtr 280 Class 100 Board 40 **Services** Lift air con **Parking** 185 **Notes LB** ✖ ✖ in restaurant Civ Wed 280

★★★★ 70% **HOTEL**

De Vere Shaw Ridge, Swindon

DeVere HOTELS & RESORTS

Shaw Ridge Leisure Park, Whitehill Way SN5 7DW

☎ 01793 878785 📠 01793 877822

e-mail: dvs.sales@devere-hotels.com

web: www.devere.co.uk

dir: M4 junct 16, signs for Swindon off 1st rdbt, 2nd rdbt follow signs for Link Centre over next 2 rdbts, 2nd left at 3rd rdbt, left onto slip road

This stylish, modern hotel is located close to the motorway network and the local business district. Day rooms are extensive and include a smart fitness centre, conference facilities and a popular restaurant.

continued

Bedrooms are very well equipped and come in a variety of sizes and styles. The staff deliver efficient service in a friendly manner.

Rooms 152 en suite (12 fmly) ⊛ in 127 bedrooms S £65-£125; D £65-£125 (incl. bkfst) **Facilities** STV 🏓 Sauna Solarium Gym Jacuzzi Wi-fi in bedrooms Health & beauty treatment rooms Aerobic studio Xmas **Conf** BC 1htr 300 Class 160 Board 80 Del from £120 **Services** Lift **Parking** 170 **Notes LB** ⊛ in restaurant Civ Wed 300

★★★ 80% ⊛⊛ **HOTEL**

The Pear Tree at Purton

Church End SN5 4ED

☎ 01793 772100 📠 01793 772369

e-mail: stay@peartreepurton.co.uk

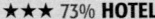

(For full entry see Purton)

★★★ 73% **HOTEL**

Best Western Chiseldon House

New Rd, Chiseldon SN4 0NE

☎ 01793 741010 📠 01793 741059

e-mail: info@chiseldonhousehotel.co.uk

web: www.chiseldonhousehotel.co.uk

dir: M4 junct 15, A346 signed Marlborough, at brow of hill turn right by Esso garage onto B4005 into New Rd, hotel 200yds on right

Chiseldon is a traditional country house near Swindon that provides a peaceful location, yet is within minutes of the M4. Quiet and spacious bedrooms are tastefully decorated and include a number of thoughtful extras. Guests can relax in the comfortable lounge and enjoy the well-kept gardens.

Rooms 21 en suite (4 fmly) ⊛ in 15 bedrooms **Facilities** STV 🏓 **Conf** Thtr 50 Class 30 Board 20 **Parking** 40 **Notes** Civ Wed 85

★★★ 73% **HOTEL**

Stanton House

The Avenue, Stanton Fitzwarren SN6 7SD

☎ 0870 084 1388 📠 01793 861857

e-mail: info@stantonhouse.co.uk

dir: off A419 onto A361 towards Highworth, pass Honda factory and turn left towards Stanton Fitzwarren about 600yds past business park, hotel on left

Extensive grounds and superb gardens surround this Cotswold-stone manor house. Smart, well-maintained bedrooms have been equipped

continued

with modern comforts. Public areas include a games room, a lounge, a bar, conference facilities and an informal restaurant specialising in English and Japanese cuisine; the Mt Fuji Restaurant serves authentic Japanese food in Japanese surroundings. Multi-lingual staff are friendly and a relaxed atmosphere prevails.

Stanton House

Rooms 82 en suite (31 GF) ⊛ in 35 bedrooms S £94 £148; D £109-£163 (incl. bkfst) **Facilities** STV 🏊 Wi-fi in bedrooms Xmas **Conf** Thtr 110 Class 70 Board 40 Del from £123.50 **Services** Lift **Parking** 110 **Notes LB** ⊛ ⊛ in restaurant Civ Wed 110

England

SWINDON *continued*

★★★ 72% HOTEL

Marsh Farm
Coped Hall SN4 8ER
☎ 01793 848044 🖹 01793 851528
e-mail: marshfarmhotel@btconnect.com
dir: *M4 junct 16, A3102, straight on at 1st rdbt, at next rdbt (with garage on left) turn right. Hotel 200yds on left*

The stylish, well appointed bedrooms at this hotel are situated in converted barns and extensions around the original farmhouse, which is set in its own grounds less than a mile from the M4. An extensive range of dishes makes up the menu offered in Reids, the smart conservatory restaurant.

Rooms 11 en suite 39 annexe en suite (1 fmly) ⊘ in 23 bedrooms S £40-£110; D £70-£135 (incl. bkfst) **Facilities** STV Putt green Wi-fi in bedrooms Clay pigeon shooting nearby Gym facilities available at local gym **Conf** Thtr 120 Class 60 Board 50 Del from £115 **Parking** 150 **Notes LB** ⊗ ⊘ in restaurant RS 26-30 Dec Civ Wed 100

See advert on opposite page

★★★ 71% HOTEL

The Madison Hotel
Oxford Rd, Stratton St Margaret SN3 4TL
☎ 0870 609 6150 🖹 01793 831401

folio Hotels

dir: *M4 junct 15, A419 to Cirencester. Over rdbt, then exit left (signed Oxford A420). Right at next 2 rdbts, hotel on left*

Conveniently located just off the M4, the hotel is ideal for touring the area. The Great Western Designer Outlet and Steam Museum are just 10 minutes' drive away. Bedrooms are large and well appointed, rooms to the rear being quieter. Facilities include four versatile conference rooms and the Olio bar and restaurant.

Rooms 94 en suite (3 fmly) (45 GF) ⊘ in 73 bedrooms **Facilities** STV Free use of nearby gym, pool and beauty parlour **Conf** Thtr 100 Class 50 Board 40 **Parking** 150 **Notes LB** ⊗ ⊘ in restaurant Civ Wed 70

★★★ 70% HOTEL

Goddard Arms
High St, Old Town SN1 3EG
☎ 01793 692313 🖹 01793 512984
e-mail: goddard.arms@forestdale.com
web: www.forestdale.com

Forestdale Hotels

dir: *M4 junct 15, A4259 towards Swindon, onto B4006 to Old Town follow signs for PM Hospital. Hotel in High St opp Wood St next to Lloyds Bank*

Situated in the attractive Old Town area, this ivy-clad coaching inn offers bedrooms in either the main building or in a modern annexe to the rear of the property. Public areas are tastefully decorated in a traditional style; there is a lounge, Vaults bar and the popular Buccleuch Grill, with its modern approach to food. The conference rooms are extensive and the car park secure.

Rooms 18 en suite 47 annexe en suite (3 fmly) (24 GF) ⊘ in 33 bedrooms S £55; D £110 **Facilities** STV ch fac **Conf** Thtr 180 Class 100 Board 40 Del £99 **Parking** 90 **Notes LB** ⊗ ⊘ in restaurant Civ Wed 180

★★★ 68% HOTEL

Thistle Swindon
Fleming Way SN1 1TN
☎ 0870 333 9148 🖹 0870 333 9248
e-mail: Reservations.Swindon@Thistle.co.uk

THISTLE HOTELS

dir: *Exit M4 junct 15/16 and follow signs for Town Centre*

This modern hotel is conveniently located in the centre of Swindon with the added advantage of nearby parking. Bedrooms and bathrooms are well equipped with plenty of useful extras. Guests can enjoy a range of dining options whether by way of room service, the popular bar or more formal Shelley's restaurant.

Rooms 94 en suite (2 fmly) ⊘ in 45 bedrooms **Facilities** STV **Conf** Thtr 200 Class 80 Board 60 **Services** Lift **Notes** ⊗ ⊘ in restaurant Civ Wed 200

🅄

Swallow Swindon
South Marston SN3 4SH
☎ 01793 833700 🖹 01793 833775
e-mail: reservations.swindon@swallowhotels.com
web: www.swallowhotels.com

SWALLOW HOTELS

dir: *Exit M4 junct 15, take A419 N to Cirencester. Exit off 2nd junct signed A420 Oxford, turn left to South Marston. Hotel past the pub on the left*

At the time of going to press, the star classification for this hotel was not confirmed. Please refer to the AA internet site www.theAA.com for current information.

Rooms 60 en suite (14 fmly) (30 GF) ⊘ in 43 bedrooms S £60-£85; D £70-£95 (incl. bkfst) **Facilities Spa** 🏊 supervised Squash Sauna Solarium Gym Jacuzzi Health & Beauty salon Xmas **Conf** Thtr 150 Class 75 Board 60 Del from £99 **Parking** 200 **Notes** ⊗ ⊘ in restaurant Civ Wed 100

BUDGET HOTEL

Hotel Ibis Swindon

Delta Business Park, Great Western Way SN5 7XG
☎ 01793 514777 🗋 01793 514570
e-mail: h1041@accor.com
web: www.ibishotel.com

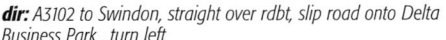

dir: *A3102 to Swindon, straight over rdbt, slip road onto Delta Business Park , turn left*

Modern, budget hotel offering comfortable accommodation in bright and practical bedrooms. Breakfast is self-service and dinner is available in the restaurant. For further details, consult the Hotel Groups page.

Rooms 120 en suite S £47; D £47 **Conf** Thtr 70 Class 40 Board 40

BUDGET HOTEL

Premier Travel Inn Swindon Central

Kembrey Business Park, Cirencester Way, Cricklade Rd SN2 8YS
☎ 08701 977310 🗋 08701 977707
web: www.premiertravelinn.com

High quality, modern budget accommodation ideal for both families and business travellers. Spacious, en suite bedrooms feature bath and shower, satellite TV and many have telephones and modem points. The adjacent family restaurant features a wide and varied menu. For further details consult the Hotel Groups page.

Rooms 50 en suite

Premier Travel Inn Swindon North

Ermin St, Blunsdon SN26 8DJ
☎ 0870 9906356 🗋 0870 9906357
dir: *N of Swindon. 5m from M4 junct 15. At junct of A419 & B4019*
Rooms 60 en suite

Premier Travel Inn Swindon West

Lydiard Way, Great Western Way SN5 8UY
☎ 08701 977247 🗋 01793 886890
dir: *M4 junct 16, take left lane towards Swindon, A3102*
Rooms 63 en suite

TROWBRIDGE — MAP 04 ST85

★★ 69% HOTEL

Fieldways Hotel & Health Club

Hilperton Rd BA14 7JP
☎ 01225 768336 🗋 01225 753649
e-mail: fieldwayshotel@yahoo.co.uk

dir: *Leave Trowbridge on A361 towards Melksham/Chippenham/Devizes - last property on left*

Originally part of a Victorian mansion this hotel is quietly set in well-kept grounds and provides a pleasant combination of spacious, comfortably furnished bedrooms. There are two splendid wood-panelled dining rooms, one of which is impressively finished in oak, pine, rosewood and mahogany. The indoor leisure facilities include a gym, a pool and treatment rooms. 'Top to Toe' days are especially popular.

Rooms 8 en suite 5 annexe en suite (2 fmly) (2 GF) S £60; D £80-£90 (incl. bkfst) **Facilities Spa** 🏊 Sauna Solarium Gym Jacuzzi Range of beauty treatments/massage Specialists in pampering days **Conf** Thtr 40 Class 40 Board 20 **Parking** 70 **Notes LB** ⊗ ⊘ in restaurant

---

This beautiful and prestigious grade 2 listed Victorian farmhouse has been tastefully restored and converted into a 50 bedroom country hotel.

Standing in its own three acres of garden and surrounded by open countryside, the hotel offers an oasis of tranquillity to business and leisure travellers.

Conference and banqueting facilities and licensed for weddings.

MARSH FARM HOTEL

Wootton Bassett Swindon Wiltshire SN4 8ER
(01793) 842800

WARMINSTER — MAP 04 ST84

★★★★ 79% ⚜⚜ HOTEL

Bishopstrow House

BA12 9HH
☎ 01985 212312 🗋 01985 216769
e-mail: info@bishopstrow.co.uk
web: www.vonessenhotels.co.uk

dir: *A303, A36, B3414, hotel 2m on right*

This is a fine example of a Georgian country home, situated in 27 acres of grounds. Public areas are traditional in style and feature antiques and open fires. Most bedrooms offer DVD players. A spa, a tennis court and several country walks ensure there is something for all guests. The restaurant serves quality contemporary cuisine.

Rooms 32 en suite (3 fmly) (4 GF) ⊘ in 1 bedroom S fr £99; D £199-£360 (incl. bkfst) **Facilities Spa** STV 🏊 ⌁ ♨ Fishing Sauna Gym 🏋 Clay pigeon shooting Archery Cycling Xmas **Conf** Thtr 65 Class 32 Board 36 Del from £175 **Parking** 100 **Notes LB** ⊘ in restaurant Civ Wed 90

BUDGET HOTEL

Travelodge Warminster

A36 Bath Rd BA12 7RU
☎ 08700 850 950 🗋 01985 214380
web: www.travelodge.co.uk

dir: *at junct of A350/A36*

Travelodge offers good quality, good value, modern accommodation. Ideal for families, the spacious en suite bedrooms include remote-

continued on page 684

England

WARMINSTER *continued*

control TV, tea and coffee-making facilities and comfortable beds. Meals can be taken at the nearby family restaurant. See Hotel Groups pages for further details.

Rooms 31 en suite S fr £26; D fr £26

WESTBURY MAP 04 ST85

★★ 72% HOTEL

The Cedar

THE INDEPENDENTS

Warminster Rd BA13 3PR

☎ 01373 822753 📠 01373 858423

e-mail: cedarwestbury@aol.com

dir: *on A350, 0.5m S of town towards Warminster*

This 18th-century hotel is an ideal base for exploring Bath and the surrounding area and is popular with both leisure and corporate guests. The bedrooms are attractive and well equipped - some are located at ground-floor level in an annexe. An interesting selection of meals is available in both the bar lounge and conservatory; the Regency restaurant is popular for more formal dining.

Rooms 8 en suite 12 annexe en suite (5 fmly) (10 GF) ⊘ in all bedrooms **Facilities** ch fac **Conf** Thtr 35 Class 20 Board 20 **Parking** 30 **Notes** ⊘ in restaurant

WHITLEY MAP 04 ST86

◉◉ RESTAURANT WITH ROOMS

The Pear Tree Inn

Top Ln SN12 8QX

☎ 01225 709131 📠 01225 702276

e-mail: enquiries@peartreeinn.co.uk

This inn provides luxurious bedrooms, some in an adjoining annexe at ground floor level, some in the main building. The restaurant draws visitors from a wide area to experience the interesting menu, the rustic atmosphere and the friendliness of the hosts.

Rooms 4 en suite 4 annexe en suite S £75; D £105

WOOTTON BASSETT MAP 05 SU08

★★★ 75% HOTEL

The Wiltshire Hotel & Country Club

SN4 7PB

☎ 01793 849999 📠 01793 849988

e-mail: reception@the-wiltshire.co.uk

dir: *M4 junct 16 follow signs for Wootton Bassett. Entrance 1m S of Wootton Bassett on the left on A3102 to Lyneham*

Overlooking rolling Wiltshire countryside and set on a parkland golf course, this hotel offers contemporary bedrooms that include purpose-designed disabled access rooms. The air-conditioned restaurant and bar open onto a large patio which overlooks the 18th

continued

green, and there are splendid leisure facilities including a techno gym and 18-meter swimming pool; beauty treatments are also on offer.

The Wiltshire Hotel & Country Club

Rooms 58 rms (56 en suite) (3 fmly) (29 GF) ⊘ in 27 bedrooms S £75-£115; D £80-£115 (incl. bkfst) **Facilities Spa** STV ⊞ ♨ ♨ 27 Sauna Solarium Gym Putt green Jacuzzi Wi-fi in bedrooms Beauty Salon Steam Room Covered driving range **Conf** Thtr 250 Class 120 Board 30 Del from £120 **Services** Lift **Parking** 200 **Notes LB** ⊗ ⊘ in restaurant Closed 24 & 25 Dec Civ Wed

WORCESTERSHIRE

ABBERLEY MAP 10 SO76

★★★ 85% ◉◉ HOTEL

The Elms Hotel & Restaurant

Stockton Rd WR6 6AT

☎ 01299 896666 📠 01299 896804

e-mail: info@theelmshotel.co.uk

web: www.vonessenhotels.co.uk

dir: *on A443 2m beyond Great Witley*

Surrounded by its own well manicured grounds, this imposing Queen Anne mansion dates back to 1710 and offers a sophisticated and relaxed ambience throughout. The spacious public rooms and generously proportioned bedrooms have much elegance and charm. The restaurant overlooks the gardens and serves imaginative and memorable dishes.

Rooms 16 en suite 5 annexe en suite (1 fmly) (3 GF) **Facilities** ♨ ♨ **Conf** Thtr 70 Class 30 Board 30 **Parking** 50 **Notes** ⊗ ⊘ in restaurant Civ Wed 70

BEWDLEY

MAP 10 SO77

★★★ 77% **HOTEL**

Ramada Hotel & Resort Kidderminster

Habberley Rd DY12 1LJ

☎ 01299 406400 🖷 01299 400921

e-mail: sales.kidderminster@ramadajarvis.co.uk

dir: *A456 towards Kidderminster to ring road, follow signs to Bewdley. Pass Safari Park then exit A456 Town Centre, take sharp right after 200yds onto B4190, hotel 400yds on right.*

Located within 16 acres of landscaped grounds, this Victorian house has been sympathetically renovated and extended to provide good standards of comfort and facilities. A wide range of well-equipped bedrooms includes both family and executive rooms and the hotel benefits from an on-site Sebastian Coe Health Club, available to resident guests.

Rooms 44 en suite (3 fmly) (18 GF) ⊗ in 38 bedrooms S £109; D £109 **Facilities Spa** STV 🖳 ⬇ 18 ♨ Sauna Solarium Gym Jacuzzi Beauty & Hair salon Dance studio Steam room **Conf** Thtr 350 Class 120 Board 60 Del from £112 **Parking** 150 **Notes LB** ⊗ in restaurant Civ Wed 250

★★ 65% **HOTEL**

Black Boy

Kidderminster Rd DY12 1AG

☎ 01299 402119 🖷 01299 405761

e-mail: info@blackboyhotel.co.uk

dir: *follow town centre signs*

This privately-owned and personally-run 18th-century inn (now under new ownership) stands close to both the River Severn and the centre of this lovely old town. A good range of food is served in both the cosy restaurant and bar. The accommodation, which has private, rather than en suite bathrooms, includes a two-bedroom unit that is located in a separate house, making it ideal for families. The Severn Valley Steam Railway is nearby.

Rooms 8 en suite (2 fmly) **Conf** Thtr 20 Class 20 Board 20 **Parking** 28 **Notes** ⊛ ⊗ in restaurant

BROADWAY

MAP 10 SP03

See also Buckland (Gloucestershire)

★★★★ 85% ⑱⑱ **HOTEL**

Lygon Arms

High St WR12 7DU

☎ 01386 852255 🖷 01386 854470

e-mail: info@thelygonarms.co.uk

web: www.the-lygon-arms.com

PARAMOUNT GROUP OF HOTELS

dir: *From Evesham take A44 signed for Oxford 5m. Follow signs for Broadway, hotel on left*

A hotel with a wealth of historic charm and character, the Lygon Arms dates back to the 16th century. There is a choice of restaurants, a stylish cosy bar, an array of lounges and a smart spa and leisure club. Bedrooms vary in size and style, but all are thoughtfully equipped and include a number of stylish contemporary rooms as well as a cottage in the grounds.

Rooms 66 en suite (8 fmly) (9 GF) S £129-£290; D £164-£315 (incl. bkfst) **Facilities Spa** STV 🖳 supervised ♨ Snooker Sauna Solarium Gym ♨ Jacuzzi Xmas **Conf** Thtr 80 Class 46 Board 30 **Parking** 200 **Notes LB** ⊗ in restaurant Civ Wed 80

★★★ 83% ⑱⑱ **HOTEL**

Dormy House

Willersey Hill WR12 7LF

☎ 01386 852711 🖷 01386 858636

e-mail: reservations@dormyhouse.co.uk.

web: www.dormyhouse.co.uk

dir: *2m E off A44, top of Fish Hill, turn for Saintbury/Picnic area. After 0.5m fork left and hotel on left*

A converted 17th-century farmhouse set in extensive grounds and with stunning views over Broadway. Some rooms are in an annexe at ground-floor level, some have a contemporary style. The best traditions are retained - customer care, real fires, comfortable sofas and afternoon teas. Dinner features an interesting choice of dishes, created by a skilled kitchen brigade.

Rooms 25 en suite 20 annexe en suite (8 fmly) (21 GF) ⊗ in all bedrooms S £120-£160; D £160-£210 (incl. bkfst) **Facilities** STV Sauna Gym ♨ Putt green Wi-fi available Games room, nature & jogging trail **Conf** Thtr 170 Class 100 Board 25 Del from £185 **Parking** 80 **Notes LB** ⊗ in restaurant Closed 25-26 Dec Civ Wed 170

See advert on page 687

★★★ 79% **HOTEL**

Broadway

The Green, High St WR12 7AA

☎ 01386 852401 🖷 01386 853879

e-mail: info@broadwayhotel.info

web: www.cotswolds-inns-hotels.co.uk

dir: *From A44 follow signs to Evesham, then Broadway*

This half-timbered, Cotswold-stone property was built in the 15th century as a retreat for the Abbots of Pershore. The hotel now combines modern, attractive decor with original charm and character. Bedrooms are tastefully furnished and well equipped while public rooms include a relaxing lounge, cosy bar and charming restaurant; alfresco all day dining in summer months proves popular.

Rooms 20 en suite (1 fmly) ⊗ in all bedrooms S £95-£135; D £135-£175 (incl. bkfst) **Facilities** Xmas **Conf** Thtr 20 Board 12 Del from £130 **Parking** 20 **Notes LB** ⊗ in restaurant Civ Wed 50

England

BROADWAY continued

Russell's

20 High St WR12 7DT

☎ 01386 853555 🖺 01386 853964

e-mail: info@russellsofbroadway.com

dir: on high street opposite village green

Situated in the centre of a picturesque Cotswold village this restaurant with rooms is a great base for exploring local attractions. Bedrooms, each with their own character, boast superb quality, air conditioning and a wide range of extras for guests. Cuisine is a real draw with freshly prepared local produce used with skill.

Rooms 7 en suite (3 fmly) (2 GF) ⊗ in all bedrooms S £85-£295; D £105-£295 (incl. bkfst) **Facilities** FTV **Services** air con **Parking** 16 **Notes** ⊗ in restaurant

BROMSGROVE   MAP 10 SO97

★★★★ 66% @ **HOTEL**

The Bromsgrove Hotel

Kidderminster Rd B61 9AB

☎ 01527 576600 🖺 01527 878981

e-mail: info@thebromsgrovehotel.co.uk

Public areas in this striking building have a Mediterranean theme with white-washed walls, a courtyard garden and plenty of natural light. Bedrooms are in a variety of styles; some are more compact than others but all offer an excellent working environment for the business guest. Leisure facilities include a steam room, sauna, pool and gym.

Rooms 109 en suite (17 fmly) (34 GF) ⊗ in 77 bedrooms S £135; D £150 **Facilities Spa** STV 🔄 supervised Snooker Sauna Gym Jacuzzi Wi-fi available Beauty Salon **Conf** BC Thtr 250 Class 120 Board 50 Del £165 **Services** Lift **Parking** 250 **Notes LB** ⊗ in restaurant Civ Wed 180

Innkeeper's Lodge Bromsgrove

462 Birmingham Rd, Marlbrook B61 0HR

☎ 01527 878060

web: www.innkeeperslodge.com

dir: on the A38 0.5m between M5 & M42

Smart, en suite accommodation ideal for both business & leisure guests. Bedrooms are very well equipped, including Sky TV, telephone, modem points, tea & coffee making facilities, (family rooms in most locations). Complimentary breakfast. The adjacent Pub Restaurant; a Harvester, Vintage Inn, Toby Carvery, Ember Inn, Sizzling Pubco or Pub & Carvery offers an all day menu. See Hotel Groups pages for further details.

Rooms 29 en suite S £45-£49.95; D £45-£49.95

Premier Travel Inn Bromsgrove Central

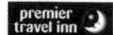

Birmingham Rd B61 0BA

☎ 08701 977 044 🖺 01527 834719

web: www.premiertravelinn.com

High quality, modern budget accommodation ideal for both families and business travellers. Spacious, en suite bedrooms feature bath and shower, satellite TV and many have telephones and modem points. The adjacent family restaurant features a wide and varied menu. For further details consult the Hotel Groups page.

Rooms 74 en suite

Premier Travel Inn Bromsgrove South

Worcester Rd, Upton Warren B61 7ET

☎ 0870 9906408 🖺 0870 9906409

dir: 1.2m from M5 junct 5 towards Bromsgrove on A38. From M42 junct 1 follow A38 south, crossing over A448

Rooms 27 en suite **Conf** Board 10

CHADDESLEY CORBETT   MAP 10 SO87

INSPECTORS' CHOICE

★★★ @@ **HOTEL**

Brockencote Hall Country House

DY10 4PY

☎ 01562 777876 🖺 01562 777872

e-mail: info@brockencotehall.com

web: www.brockencotehall.com

dir: 0.5m W, off A448, opposite St Cassian's Church

Glorious countryside extends all around this magnificent mansion, and grazing sheep can be seen from the conservatory. Not surprisingly, relaxation comes high on the list of priorities here. Despite its very English location the hotel's owner actually hails from Alsace and the atmosphere is very much that of a provincial French château. The chef too is French (from Brittany) and the chandeliered dining room is a popular venue for the accomplished modern French cuisine.

Rooms 17 en suite (2 fmly) (5 GF) S £93-£140; D £116-£180 (incl. bkfst) **Facilities** FTV ♨ Fishing ⚑ Wi-fi in bedrooms Reflexology/ aromatherapy Xmas **Conf** Thtr 30 Class 20 Board 20 Del from £160 **Services** Lift **Parking** 45 **Notes LB** ⊗ ⊗ in restaurant Civ Wed 60

DROITWICH MAP 10 SO86

★★★★ 72% **HOTEL**

Raven

Victoria Square WR9 8DQ
☎ 01905 772224 🖹 01905 797100
e-mail: sales@impney.demon.co.uk

dir: in town centre on A38, 1.5m from M5 junct 5 towards Droitwich/Worcester

Situated in the heart of the spa town, close to the Brine Baths, this timber-framed property dates back to the early 16th century. Considerably extended over the years, it provides comfortable, well-equipped accommodation. Public areas have a gentlemen's club feel with leather sofas in the lounge and a relaxing bar.

Rooms 72 en suite (1 fmly) S £69.90-£129.90; D £79.90-£149.90 (incl. bkfst) **Conf** Thtr 150 Class 70 Board 40 Del from £159.85 **Services** Lift **Parking** 250 **Notes** ⊗ ⊘ in restaurant Closed Xmas

BUDGET HOTEL

Travelodge Droitwich

Rashwood Hill WR9 0BJ
☎ 08700 850 950 🖹 01527 861807
web: www.travelodge.co.uk

dir: 0.5m W of M5 junct 5

Travelodge offers good quality, good value, modern accommodation. Ideal for families, the spacious en suite bedrooms include remote-control TV, tea and coffee-making facilities and comfortable beds. Meals can be taken at the nearby family restaurant. See Hotel Groups pages for further details.

Rooms 32 en suite S fr £26; D £26

EVESHAM MAP 10 SP04

★★★ 79% ⊛ **HOTEL**

The Evesham

Coopers Ln, Off Waterside WR11 1DA
☎ 01386 765566 & 0800 716969 (Res) 🖹 01386 765443
e-mail: reception@eveshamhotel.com
web: www.eveshamhotel.com

dir: Coopers Lane is off road by River Avon

Dating from 1540 and set in extensive grounds, this delightful hotel has well-equipped accommodation that includes a selection of quirkily themed rooms - Alice in Wonderland, Egyptian, and Aquarium (which has a tropical fish tank in the bathroom). A reputation for food is well deserved, with a particularly strong choice for vegetarians. Children are welcome and toys are always available.

Rooms 39 en suite 1 annexe en suite (3 fmly) (11 GF) ⊘ in 28 bedrooms S £78-£92; D fr £128 (incl. bkfst) **Facilities** 🐟 💲 Putt green Wi-fi in bedrooms **Conf** Thtr 12 Class 12 Board 12 Del £134 **Parking** 50 **Notes** LB ⊘ in restaurant Closed 25-26 Dec

★★★ 74% **HOTEL**

Best Western Northwick Hotel

Waterside WR11 1BT
☎ 01386 40322 🖹 01386 41070
e-mail: enquiries@northwickhotel.co.uk

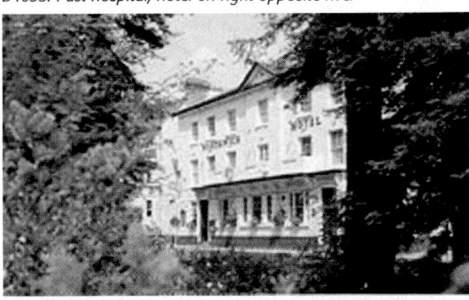

dir: off A46 onto A44 over traffic lights and right at next set onto B4035. Past hospital, hotel on right opposite river

Located close to the centre of the town, the hotel benefits from its position overlooking the River Avon and its adjacent park. Bedrooms are traditional in style and feature broadband internet access; one room has been adapted for disabled access. Public areas offer a choice of drinking options, meeting rooms and a restaurant

Rooms 29 en suite (4 fmly) (1 GF) ⊘ in all bedrooms S £71-£81; D fr £107.50 (incl. bkfst) **Facilities** STV **Conf** Thtr 240 Class 150 Board 80 **Parking** 85 **Notes** LB ⊘ in restaurant Civ Wed 60

England

EVESHAM *continued*

★★★ 73% HOTEL

Dumbleton Hall

WR11 7TS

☎ 01386 881240 🖺 01386 882142

e-mail: dh@pofr.co.uk

(For full entry see Dumbleton)

★★ 74% ◉◉ HOTEL

Riverside

The Parks, Offenham Rd WR11 8JP

☎ 01386 446200 🖺 01386 49755

e-mail: info@theparksoffenham.freeserve.co.uk

web: www.river-side-hotel.co.uk

dir: *from A46 follow signs for Offenham, right onto B4510. Hotel 0.5m on left on private drive*

Riverside
Hotel and Restaurant

A secluded hotel offering personal attention and service that stands in three acres of gardens sloping down to the River Avon. The lounge, restaurant and many of the comfortable bedrooms overlook the river. Cooking remains one of the hotel's strong points, with a menu of imaginative dishes created from high-quality produce.

Rooms 10 rms (7 en suite) (5 GF) **Facilities** Fishing Wi-fi in bedrooms **Conf** BC **Parking** 30 **Notes** ⊛ in restaurant

BUDGET HOTEL

Premier Travel Inn Evesham

Evesham Country Park, A46 Trunk Rd
WR11 4TP

☎ 08701 977 288 🖺 01386 444301

web: www.premiertravelinn.com

High quality, modern budget accommodation ideal for both families and business travellers. Spacious, en suite bedrooms feature bath and shower, satellite TV and many have telephones and modem points. The adjacent family restaurant features a wide and varied menu. For further details consult the Hotel Groups page.

Rooms 40 en suite

HAGLEY   MAP 10 SO98

BUDGET HOTEL

Premier Travel Inn Hagley

Birmingham Rd DY9 9JS

☎ 08701 977123 🖺 01562 884416

web: www.premiertravelinn.com

dir: *5m off M5 junct 3 on opposite side of the A456 dual carriageway towards Kidderminster*

High quality, modern budget accommodation ideal for both families and business travellers. Spacious, en suite bedrooms feature bath and shower, satellite TV and many have telephones and modem points. The adjacent family restaurant features a wide and varied menu. For further details consult the Hotel Groups page.

Rooms 40 en suite **Conf** Thtr 20 Board 18

HARTLEBURY   MAP 10 SO87

BUDGET HOTEL

Travelodge Hartlebury

Shorthill Nurseries DY13 9SH

☎ 08700 850 950 🖺 01299 251774

web: www.travelodge.co.uk

dir: *A449 southbound*

Travelodge offers good quality, good value, modern accommodation. Ideal for families, the spacious en suite bedrooms include remote-control TV, tea and coffee-making facilities and comfortable beds. Meals can be taken at the nearby family restaurant. See Hotel Groups pages for further details.

Rooms 32 en suite S fr £26; D fr £26

KIDDERMINSTER   MAP 10 SO87

★★★★ 78% HOTEL

Stone Manor

Stone DY10 4PJ

☎ 01562 777555 🖺 01562 777834

e-mail: enquiries@stonemanorhotel.co.uk

dir: *2.5m from Kidderminster on A448, on right*

This converted, much extended former manor house stands in 25 acres of impressive grounds and gardens. The well-equipped accommodation includes rooms with four-poster beds and luxuriously appointed annexe bedrooms. Quality furnishing and decor styles throughout the public areas highlight the intrinsic charm of the interior. The hotel is a popular venue for wedding receptions.

Rooms 52 en suite 5 annexe en suite (7 GF) ⊛ in 46 bedrooms S £110-£160; D £110-£160 **Facilities** STV ✦ ⚲ ⚲ Wi-fi in bedrooms Pool Table ch fac **Conf** Thtr 150 Class 48 Board 60 Del from £160 **Parking** 400 **Notes** ⊛ ⊛ in restaurant Civ Wed 150

★★★ 75% ◉ **HOTEL**

The Granary Hotel & Restaurant

Heath Ln, Shenstone DY10 4BS
☎ 01562 777535 ▣ 01562 777722
e-mail: info@granary-hotel.co.uk
web: www.granary-hotel.co.uk
dir: on A450, 0.5m from junct with A448

This modern hotel offers spacious, well-equipped accommodation with many rooms enjoying views towards Great Witley and the Amberley Hills. There is an attractive modern restaurant and a carvery is available at weekends. There are also extensive conference facilities and the hotel is popular as a wedding venue.

Rooms 18 en suite (1 fmly) (18 GF) ⊗ in all bedrooms S £65-£90; D £85-£140 (incl. bkfst) **Conf** Thtr 200 Class 80 Board 70 Del from £120 **Parking** 96 **Notes LB** ⊗ in restaurant Closed 24-26 Dec Civ Wed 120

★★★ 72% **HOTEL**

Gainsborough House

Bewdley Hill DY11 6BS
☎ 01562 820041 ▣ 01562 66179
e-mail: reservations@gainsboroughhotel.co.uk
web: www.gainsborough-hotel.co.uk
dir: on A456. At hospital, over lights, hotel 200yds on right

This listed Georgian property is situated on the edge of the town. The no smoking bedrooms are well equipped and comfortable. Additional features include a bar lounge, the attractive restaurant and a selection of function rooms.

Rooms 42 en suite (32 fmly) ⊗ in 12 bedrooms S £50-£75; D £60-£95 (incl. bkfst) **Facilities** Solarium & beauty salon Xmas **Conf** Thtr 250 Class 80 Board 60 Del from £100 **Parking** 130 **Notes LB** ⊗ in restaurant Civ Wed 200

MALVERN   MAP 10 SO74

★★★ 80% ◉◉ **HOTEL**

Colwall Park

Walwyn Rd, Colwall WR13 6QG
☎ 01684 540000 ▣ 01684 540847
e-mail: hotel@colwall.com
web: www.colwall.com
dir: Between Malvern & Ledbury in centre of Colwall on B4218

Standing in extensive gardens, this hotel was purpose built in the early 20th century to serve the local racetrack. Today the proprietors and loyal staff provide high levels of hospitality and service. The Seasons

continued

restaurant has a well-deserved reputation for its cuisine. Bedrooms are tastefully appointed and public areas help to create a fine country-house atmosphere.

Colwall Park

Rooms 22 en suite (1 fmly) ⊗ in all bedrooms S £79-£89; D £120-£140 (incl. bkfst) **Facilities** STV ≋ Wi-fi in bedrooms Boules Xmas **Conf** Thtr 150 Class 80 Board 50 Del from £140 **Parking** 40 **Notes LB** ⊗ in restaurant

See advert on this page

England

MALVERN *continued*

★★★ 74% ⊛ ⊛ HOTEL

The Cottage in the Wood Hotel and Restaurant

Holywell Rd, Malvern Wells WR14 4LG

☎ 01684 575859 📠 01684 560662

e-mail: reception@cottageinthewood.co.uk

web: www.cottageinthewood.co.uk

dir: *3m S of Great Malvern off A449, 500yds N of B4209, on opposite side of road*

Sitting high up on a wooded hillside, this delightful, family-run hotel boasts lovely views over the Severn Valley. The bedrooms are divided between the main house, Beech Cottage and the Pinnacles. Quality decor and furnishing styles highlight the charm of public areas. Imaginative food is served in the elegant dining room that overlooks the immaculate grounds.

Rooms 8 en suite 23 annexe en suite (9 GF) ⊗ in 14 bedrooms S £68.50-£99.50; D £78-£164 **Facilities** STV Direct access to Malvern Hills Xmas **Conf** Thtr 20 Board 14 Del from £145 **Parking** 40 **Notes LB** ⊗ in restaurant

See advert on opposite page

★★★ 71% ⊛ HOTEL

Foley Arms

14 Worcester Rd WR14 4QS

☎ 01684 573397 📠 01684 569665

e-mail: reservations@foleyarmshotel.com

web: www.foleyarmshotel.co.uk

dir: *M5 junct 8 N or junct 7 S or M50 junct 1 to Great Malvern on A449*

Situated in the centre of town and with spectacular views of the Severn Valley, this hotel is reputed to be the oldest hotel in Malvern. The bedrooms are comfortable and tastefully decorated with period furnishings and modern facilities. Public areas include the Terrace restaurant, a popular bar and a choice of comfortable lounges. Service throughout is attentive.

Rooms 28 en suite (2 fmly) ⊗ in 8 bedrooms S £74-£89; D £105-£140 **Facilities** STV Wi-fi in bedrooms Free use leisure centre pool, gym, solarium & sauna (5 mins' walk) Xmas **Conf** Thtr 150 Class 40 Board 45 Del from £140 **Parking** 60 **Notes LB** ⊗ in restaurant Civ Wed 100

★★ 79% HOTEL

The Malvern Hills Hotel

Wynds Point WR13 6DW

☎ 01684 540690 📠 01684 540327

e-mail: malhilhotl@aol.com

web: www.malvernhillshotel.co.uk

dir: *4m S, at junct of A449 with B4232*

This 19th-century hostelry is situated to the west of Malvern, opposite the British Camp, a fortified Iron Age hill fort. Bedrooms are well equipped and benefit from smart modern bathrooms. Public areas include a choice of bars, retaining original features, modern conference facilities and an attractive restaurant.

Rooms 14 en suite (1 fmly) (2 GF) ⊗ in all bedrooms S £50-£60; D £95-£110 (incl. bkfst) **Facilities** FTV Wi-fi in bedrooms Xmas **Conf** Thtr 40 Class 24 Board 30 **Parking** 30 **Notes LB** ⊗ in restaurant

★★ 75% ⊛ HOTEL

Holdfast Cottage

Marlbank Rd, Welland WR13 6NA

☎ 01684 310288 📠 01684 311117

e-mail: enquiries@holdfast-cottage.co.uk

web: www.holdfast-cottage.co.uk

dir: *A438 to Tewkesbury, at War Memorial rdbt turn right signed A438, at mini rdbt left for Ledbury*

At the base of the Malvern Hills this delightful wisteria-covered hotel sits in attractive manicured grounds. Charming public areas include an intimate bar, lounge with log fire and an elegant dining room. Bedrooms vary in size but all are comfortable and well appointed. Fresh local and seasonal produce are the basis for award-winning cuisine.

Rooms 8 en suite (3 fmly) ⊗ in all bedrooms **Facilities** ⅃ **Conf** Class 30 Board 30 **Parking** 15 **Notes LB** ⊗ in restaurant Civ Wed 25

★★ 74% HOTEL

Cotford

51 Graham Rd WR14 2HU

☎ 01684 572427 📠 01684 572952

e-mail: reservations@cotfordhotel.co.uk

web: www.cotfordhotel.co.uk

dir: *from Worcester follow signs to Malvern on A449. Left into Graham Rd signed town centre, hotel on right*

This delightful house, built in 1851, reputedly for the Bishop of Worcester, stands in attractive gardens with stunning views of the Malverns. Rooms have been authentically renovated, retaining many

continued

original features, and include all the expected comforts. Food, service and hospitality are major strengths.

Rooms 15 en suite (4 fmly) (1 GF) ⊗ in all bedrooms S £55-£69; D £89-£109 (incl. bkfst) **Facilities** STV Wi-fi available complimentary use of local leisure centre **Conf** Thtr 26 Class 26 Del from £70 **Parking** 18 **Notes LB** ⊗ in restaurant

★★ 68% HOTEL

Great Malvern

Graham Rd WR14 2HN

☎ 01684 563411 📠 01684 560514

e-mail: sutton@great-malvern-hotel.co.uk

web: www.great-malvern-hotel.co.uk

dir: from Worcester on A449, left beyond fire station into Graham Rd. Hotel at end of road on right

Close to the town centre this privately owned and managed hotel is ideally situated for the numerous cultural and scenic attractions. Bedrooms are mostly spacious and well equipped. Public areas include a popular and busy bar, lounge and a function room.

Rooms 15 rms (14 en suite) S £59.50-£67.50; D £80-£88 (incl. bkfst) **Facilities** FTV Full membership for all guests to nearest 'splash' & gym. **Conf** Thtr 60 Class 20 Board 30 **Services** Lift **Parking** 9 **Notes LB** ⊗ Closed 25 Dec-1 Jan

★★ 68% HOTEL

Mount Pleasant

Belle Vue Ter WR14 4PZ

☎ 01684 561837 📠 01684 569968

e-mail: reception@mountpleasanthotel.co.uk

web: www.mountpleasanthotel.co.uk

dir: on A449, in central Malvern by crossroads opposite Priory Church

This is an attractive Georgian house in the town centre that, from its elevated position, overlooks the picturesque Severn Valley and Priory

continued

Church. Bedrooms are spacious, and there is a smart and light bar and brasserie, where guests can enjoy a drink, snack or full meal. In warmer months a small terrace on the lawn is delightful for relaxation.

Rooms 14 en suite (1 fmly) **Conf** Thtr 90 Class 40 Board 50 **Parking** 20 **Notes LB** ⊗

REDDITCH — MAP 10 SP06

★★★★ 80% HOTEL

Best Western Abbey Hotel Golf & Country Club

Hither Green Ln, Dagnell End Rd, Bordesley B98 9BE

☎ 01527 406600 📠 01527 406514

e-mail: info@theabbeyhotel.co.uk

dir: M42 junct 2 take A441 to Redditch. End of carriageway turn left (A441), Dagnell End Rd on left. Hotel 600yds on right

With its convenient access to the motorway and its proximity to local attractions, this modern hotel is popular with both business and leisure travellers. Bedrooms are well-equipped and attractively decorated; the executive corner rooms are especially spacious. Hotel

continued on page 692

England

REDDITCH *continued*

facilities include an 18-hole golf course, pro shop, large indoor pool and extensive conference facilities.

BW Abbey Hotel Golf & Country Club

Rooms 100 en suite (2 fmly) (30 GF) ⊘ in 80 bedrooms S £75-£165; D £95-£185 (incl. bkfst) **Facilities** STV FTV 🏊 ♪ 18 Fishing Sauna Solarium Gym Putt green Jacuzzi Wi-fi in bedrooms Beauty Salon,Golf driving range Xmas **Conf** Thtr 150 Class 60 Board 30 Del from £115 **Services** Lift **Parking** 200 **Notes LB** ⊗ ⊘ in restaurant Civ Wed 100

See also advert on page 651

★★★ 66% HOTEL

Quality Hotel Redditch

Pool Bank, Southcrest B97 4JS
☎ 01527 541511 📠 01527 402600
e-mail: enquiries@hotels-redditch.com
web: www.choicehotelseurope.com

dir: *A441 into Redditch follow signs for all other Redditch Districts until Southcrest signed, then follow hotel signs*

Originally a manor house, this hotel enjoys a peaceful location in extensive wooded grounds. Bedrooms vary in size and style, but all are well appointed and equipped. Both the restaurant and bar/conservatory overlook the attractive, sloping gardens, with views stretching across to the Vale of Evesham.

Rooms 73 en suite (20 fmly) (22 GF) ⊘ in 60 bedrooms S £50-£95; D £60-£105 **Facilities** STV Wi-fi available Xmas **Conf** Thtr 100 Class 45 Board 50 Del from £99 **Parking** 100 **Notes LB** ⊘ in restaurant Civ Wed 70

★★ 64% HOTEL

Montville

101 Mount Pleasant, Southcrest B97 4JE
☎ 01527 544411 📠 01527 544341
e-mail: sales@montvillehotel.co.uk

dir: *M42 junct 2 then A441 Alvechurch. Redditch Ringway onto Mount Pleasant, hotel on left*

Situated less than half a mile from the town centre, this is a small, friendly, privately owned hotel, suitable for both business and leisure guests. Rooms vary in size and style, and all have the necessary comforts. Cooking is Indian fusion in style and is served in the modern restaurant with its attached bar.

Rooms 14 en suite (1 fmly) (1 GF) **Parking** 8 **Notes LB** ⊗

BUDGET HOTEL

Campanile

Far Moor Ln, Winyates Green B98 0SD
☎ 01527 510710 📠 01527 517269
e-mail: redditch@campanile-hotels.com
web: www.envergure.fr

dir: *A435 towards Redditch, then A4023 to Redditch and Bromsgrove*

This modern building offers accommodation in smart, well-equipped bedrooms, all with en suite bathrooms. Refreshments may be taken at the informal Bistro. For further details consult the Hotel Groups page.

Rooms 46 annexe en suite **Conf** Thtr 25 Class 15 Board 15 Del from £70

BUDGET HOTEL

Premier Travel Inn Redditch

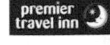

Birchfield Rd B97 6PX
☎ 0870 9906392 📠 0870 9906393
web: www.premiertravelinn.com

dir: *Exit M5 junct 4, A38 towards Bromsgrove. At rdbt take A448 to Redditch. 1st exit for Webheath. At next rdbt take 3rd exit then 1st right into Birchfield Rd*

High quality, modern budget accommodation ideal for both families and business travellers. Spacious, en suite bedrooms feature bath and shower, satellite TV and many have telephones and modem points. The adjacent family restaurant features a wide and varied menu. For further details consult the Hotel Groups page.

Rooms 33 en suite **Conf** Thtr 150

STRENSHAM MOTORWAY SERVICE AREA (M5)4   MAP 10 SO8

BUDGET HOTEL

Premier Travel Inn Tewkesbury (Strensham)

WR8 0BZ
☎ 08701 977252 📠 01684 273606
web: www.premiertravelinn.com

dir: *M5 junct 8 Northbound M5/M50 Interchange (access available to southbound)*

High quality, modern budget accommodation ideal for both families and business travellers. Spacious, en suite bedrooms feature bath and shower, satellite TV and many have telephones and modem points. The adjacent family restaurant features a wide and varied menu. For further details consult the Hotel Groups page.

Rooms 49 en suite **Conf** Thtr 22 Class 18 Board 24

TENBURY WELLS   MAP 10 SO56

★★ 75% ⊛ **HOTEL**

Cadmore Lodge

Berrington Green, St Michaels WR15 8TQ
☎ 01584 810044 🖺 01584 810044
e-mail: info@cadmorelodge.co.uk
web: www.cadmorelodge.co.uk
dir: Off A4112 Leominster-Tenbury Wells road, follow sign on left for Berrington

Cadmore Lodge is situated in an idyllic rural location overlooking a private lake. On a 70-acre private estate that features a 9-hole golf course, two fishing lakes and with indoor leisure facilities, the hotel is also earning itself a well-deserved reputation for its food. The traditionally styled bedrooms have modern amenities, and a large function room with lake views is popular for weddings and special occasions.

Rooms 15 rms (14 en suite) (1 fmly) ⊛ in all bedrooms S £56-£70; D £85-£125 (incl. bkfst) **Facilities** ⬚ ♨ 9 Fishing Gym Jacuzzi Bowling green Steam room Nature reserve Xmas **Conf** BC Thtr 100 Class 40 Board 20 Del from £96.50 **Parking** 100 **Notes LB** ⊛ ⊛ in restaurant Civ Wed 160

RESTAURANT WITH ROOMS

The Peacock Inn

Worcester Rd WR15 8LL
☎ 01584 810506 🖺 01584 811236
e-mail: peacockinn001@aol.com
dir: A456 from Worcester take A443 to Tenbury Wells. Inn 1.25m E of Tenbury Wells

A warm welcome can be expected from resident proprietors at this 14th-century roadside inn, which has a wealth of original features such as wood panelling, beams and low ceilings. The atmospheric bar and restaurant are popular locally, and bedrooms are not only spacious and comfortable but are also usefully and thoughtfully equipped.

Rooms 6 en suite (1 fmly) (1 GF) ⊛ in all bedrooms S £55; D £75-£85 **Conf** Thtr 20 Class 30 Board 20 **Parking** 30 **Notes LB** ⊛

UPTON UPON SEVERN   MAP 10 SO84

★★★ 74% ⊛ **HOTEL**

White Lion

21 High St WR8 0HJ
☎ 01684 592551 🖺 01684 593333
e-mail: reservations@whitelionhotel.biz
dir: A422, A38 towards Tewkesbury. In 8m take B4104, after 1m cross bridge, turn left to hotel, past bend on left

Famed for being the inn depicted in Henry Fielding's novel *Tom Jones*, this 16th-century hotel is a reminder of old England with its exposed beams, wall timbers etc. The quality furnishing and decor schemes throughout the public areas all enhance its character. The hotel has a well-deserved reputation for its food, which is complemented by friendly, attentive service.

Rooms 11 en suite 2 annexe en suite (2 fmly) (2 GF) S fr £70; D £99-£125 (incl. bkfst) **Facilities** FTV **Conf** Thtr 24 Class 12 Board 12 **Parking** 18 **Notes LB** ⊛ in restaurant Closed 1 Jan RS 25 Dec

---

WORCESTER   MAP 10 SO85

★★★ 81% **HOTEL**

Pear Tree Inn & Country Hotel

Smite WR3 8SY
☎ 01905 756565 🖺 01905 756777
e-mail: thepeartreeuk@aol.com
dir: M5 junct 6 take Droitwich road. In 300yds take 1st right into small country lane over canal bridge, up hill, hotel on left

Located close to M5 within pretty landscaped grounds, this traditional English inn and country hotel has spacious bedrooms, which include four suites and air conditioning, with attractive colour schemes and good facilities. Guests can enjoy good food and a drink in warm and

continued on page 694

England

WORCESTER *continued*

relaxed surroundings; there is also an excellent range of conference/function rooms.

Rooms 24 en suite (2 fmly) (12 GF) ☻ in 18 bedrooms S £70-£89.95; D £92-£109.95 (incl. bkfst) **Facilities** STV Fishing Wi-fi in bedrooms **Conf** Thtr 250 Class 150 Board 40 Del £155 **Services** Lift air con **Parking** 200 **Notes** ☻ in restaurant Closed 25-26 Dec Civ Wed 120

★★★ 70% **HOTEL**

Fownes
City Walls Rd WR1 2AP
☎ 01905 613151 ▤ 01905 23742
e-mail: reservations@fowneshotel.co.uk
web: www.fownesgroup.co.uk/fownes
dir: M5 junct 7 take A44 for Worcester city centre. Turn right at 4th set of traffic lights into City Walls Rd

On the Birmingham Canal and located close to the city centre this former Victorian glove factory has been converted into an interesting-looking, modern hotel with well proportioned bedrooms. Snacks are available in the lounge bar and the King's restaurant offers an interesting carte menu. Conference and meeting facilities are available.

Rooms 61 en suite (10 GF) ☻ in 28 bedrooms S £65-£98; D £89-£115 (incl. bkfst) **Facilities** Wi-fi in bedrooms Xmas **Conf** Thtr 100 Class 35 Board 25 Del from £135 **Services** Lift **Parking** 82 **Notes LB** ☻ in restaurant Civ Wed 80

★★ 67% **HOTEL**

Ye Olde Talbot
Friar St WR1 2NA
☎ 01905 23573 ▤ 01905 612760
e-mail: 9250@greeneking.co.uk
web: www.oldenglish.co.uk

Located within the heart of thr city, close to the cathedral, this period inn has been sympathetically renovated to provide attractive and cosy public areas in which to enjoy a wide range of imaginative food, wine and real ales. Bedrooms are throughtfully furnished and concessionary parking is available at the adjacent NCP Cathedral car park.

Rooms 29 en suite (6 fmly) (6 GF) ☻ in 21 bedrooms S £55-£65; D £65-£85 (incl. bkfst) **Facilities** Xmas **Notes LB** ☻ in restaurant

Swallow Bank House Hotel & Golf Club
Bransford WR6 5JD
☎ 01886 833551 ▤ 01886 832641
e-mail: reservations.worcester@swallowhotels.com
web: www.swallowhotels.com
dir: M5 junct 7 follow signs to Worcester West, then Hereford on A4440, & A4103. Turn left, hotel approx 2m on left

At the time of going to press, the star classification for this hotel was not confirmed. Please refer to the AA internet site www.theAA.com for current information.

Rooms 68 en suite (2 fmly) (12 GF) ☻ in 28 bedrooms S £74-£92; D £94-£120 (incl. bkfst) **Facilities** Spa ⚜ ♨ 18 Sauna Solarium Gym Putt green Xmas **Conf** Thtr 400 Class 150 Board 70 Del from £120 **Parking** 300 **Notes** ☻ ☻ in restaurant Civ Wed 250

BUDGET HOTEL

Premier Travel Inn Worcester
Wainwright Way, Warndon WR4 9FA
☎ 08701 977278 ▤ 01905 756601
web: www.premiertravelinn.com
dir: M5 junct 6, at entrance of Warndon commercial development area

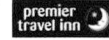

High quality, modern budget accommodation ideal for both families and business travellers. Spacious, en suite bedrooms feature bath and shower, satellite TV and many have telephones and modem points. The adjacent family restaurant features a wide and varied menu. For further details consult the Hotel Groups page.

Rooms 60 en suite **Conf** Thtr 8

BUDGET HOTEL

Travelodge Worcester
Cathedral Plaza, 3 High St WR1 2QS
☎ 08700 850950
web: www.travelodge.co.uk
dir: Exit M5 Junct 7 (A44). Follow signs to Worcester City Centre. Lodge opposite cathedral. The entrance to Lodge in Cathedral Plaza Shopping Mall.

Travelodge offers good quality, good value, modern accommodation. Ideal for families, the spacious en suite bedrooms include remote-control TV, tea and coffee-making facilities and comfortable beds. Meals can be taken at the nearby family restaurant. See Hotel Groups pages for further details.

Rooms 92 rms S fr £26; D fr £26

YORKSHIRE, EAST RIDING OF

BEVERLEY
MAP 17 TA03

★★★ 73% ◉◉ **HOTEL**

Tickton Grange
Tickton HU17 9SH
☎ 01964 543666 🖹 01964 542556
e-mail: info@ticktongrange.co.uk
dir: 3m NE on A1035

A charming Georgian country house situated in four acres of private grounds and attractive gardens. Bedrooms are individual, and redecorated to a high specification. Pre-dinner drinks may be enjoyed in the comfortable library lounge, prior to enjoying fine, modern British cooking in the restaurant. There are excellent facilities for both weddings and business conferences.

Rooms 17 en suite (2 fmly) (4 GF) ⊘ in all bedrooms S £90; D £120 (incl. bkfst) **Conf** Thtr 200 Class 100 Board 80 Del from £141 **Parking** 90 **Notes LB** ⊛ ⊘ in restaurant RS 25-29 Dec Civ Wed 200

★★★ 71% **HOTEL**

Lairgate Hotel
30/32 Lairgate HU17 8EP
☎ 01482 882141 🖹 01482 861067
dir: A63 towards town centre. Hotel 220yds on left (follow one-way system)

Located just off the Market Square, this pleasing Georgian hotel has been appointed to offer stylish accommodation. Bedrooms are elegant and well equipped, and public rooms include a comfortable lounge, a lounge bar, and restaurant with a popular sun terrace.

Rooms 16 en suite (1 fmly) (2 GF) ⊘ in 13 bedrooms **Conf** Thtr 50 Board 20 **Parking** 16 **Notes LB** ⊛ ⊘ in restaurant Civ Wed 80

★★ 76% ◉◉ **HOTEL**

Manor House
Northlands, Walkington HU17 8RT
☎ 01482 881645 🖹 01482 866501
e-mail: info@walkingtonmanorhouse.co.uk
web: www.walkingtonmanorhouse.co.uk
dir: from M62 junct 38 follow 'Walkington' signs. 4m SW off B1230 Through Walkington, left at lights. Left at 1st x-roads. Approx 400yds hotel on left

This delightful country-house hotel is set in open country amid well-tended gardens. The spacious bedrooms have been attractively decorated and thoughtfully equipped. Public rooms include a conservatory restaurant and a very inviting lounge. A good range of dishes is available from two menus, with an emphasis on fresh local produce.

Rooms 6 en suite 1 annexe en suite (1 fmly) (1 GF) S £75-£85; D £120-£140 (incl. bkfst) **Conf** Thtr 24 Class 16 Board 16 Del from £120 **Parking** 40 **Notes** ⊘ in restaurant Closed 26 Dec-4 Jan RS Sun Civ Wed 40

Ⓤ

Swallow Beverley Arms
North Bar Within HU17 8DD
SWALLOW HOTELS
☎ 01482 869241 🖹 01482 870907
web: www.swallowhotels.com
dir: opp St Marys Church. Left lane at lights just before North Bar. Hotel 100yds on left. Car park at rear

At the time of going to press, the star classification for this hotel was not confirmed. Please refer to the AA internet site www.theAA.com for current information.

Rooms 56 en suite

BRANDESBURTON
MAP 17 TA14

★★ 69% **HOTEL**

Burton Lodge
YO25 8RU
☎ 01964 542847 🖹 01964 544771
e-mail: enquires@burton-lodge.co.uk
dir: 7m from Beverley off A165, at Hainsworth Park Golf Club

A tennis court, sports play area and extensive lawn are features of this friendly hotel, which is situated on a golf course. Rooms are modern and there is a comfortable lounge, while the spacious restaurant serves tasty home cooking.

Rooms 7 en suite 2 annexe en suite (3 fmly) (2 GF) ⊘ in 5 bedrooms S £37-£40; D £59-£62 (incl. bkfst) **Facilities** ↧ 18 ⚑ Putt green Pitch and putt **Conf** Class 20 **Parking** 15 **Notes LB** ⊘ in restaurant

BRIDLINGTON
MAP 17 TA16

★★★ 74% **HOTEL**

Expanse
North Marine Dr YO15 2LS
☎ 01262 675347 🖹 01262 604928
e-mail: expanse@brid.demon.co.uk
web: www.expanse.co.uk
dir: follow North Beach signs, pass under railway arch for North Marine Drive. Hotel at bottom of hill

This traditional seaside hotel overlooks the bay and has been in the same family's ownership for many years. Service is relaxed and friendly and the modern bedrooms are well equipped. Comfortable

continued on page 696

England

BRIDLINGTON *continued*

public areas include a conference suite, a choice of bars and an inviting lounge.

Rooms 48 en suite (4 fmly) ⊗ in 12 bedrooms **Facilities** STV ♫ **Conf** Thtr 180 Class 50 Board 50 **Services** Lift **Parking** 23 **Notes LB** ⊗ ⊗ in restaurant Civ Wed

See advert on opposite page

★★★ 73% **HOTEL**

Revelstoke

1-3 Flamborough Rd YO15 2HU
☎ 01262 672362 📠 01262 672362
e-mail: info@revelstokehotel.co.uk
web: www.revelstokehotel.co.uk
dir: B1255 Flamborough Head Rd, 0.5m right at mini rdbt to junct of Promenade & Flamborough Rd. Hotel opp Holy Trinity Church

Family owned and run, this friendly hotel is close to both the town centre and the North Bay seafront and is a popular choice. Bedrooms are well equipped and very comfortable. Public areas include the well-furnished lounge bar where informal bar meals can be taken, and the attractive dining room for a more formal dining atmosphere.

Rooms 26 en suite (6 fmly) **Facilities** STV ♫ **Conf** BC Thtr 250 Class 200 Board 100 **Parking** 14 **Notes LB** ⊗ ⊗ in restaurant RS 25-28 Dec Civ Wed 200

See advert on this page

DRIFFIELD (GREAT)   MAP 17 TA05

★★★ 77% **HOTEL**

Best Western Bell

46 Market Place YO25 6AN
☎ 01377 256661 📠 01377 253228
e-mail: bell@bestwestern.co.uk
web: www.bw-bellhotel.co.uk
dir: from A164, right at lights. Car park 50yds on left behind black railings

This 250-year-old hotel incorporates the old corn exchange and the old town hall. It is furnished with antique and period pieces, and contains many items of local historical interest. The bedrooms vary in size, but all offer modern facilities and some have their own sitting rooms. The hotel has a relaxed and very friendly atmosphere. The spa provides a superb range of facilities and treatments.

continued

Best Western Bell

Rooms 16 en suite (3 GF) ⊗ in 11 bedrooms **Facilities Spa** ⊗ Squash Snooker Sauna Solarium Gym Jacuzzi Masseur, Hairdressing, Chiropody ♫ **Conf** Thtr 150 Class 100 Board 40 **Services** Lift **Parking** 18 **Notes LB** ⊗ No children 16yrs ⊗ in restaurant

FLAMBOROUGH   MAP 17 TA27

★★ 74% **HOTEL**

North Star

North Marine Dr YO15 1BL
☎ 01262 850379 📠 01262 850379
web: www.puffinsatflamborough.co.uk
dir: follow signs for North Landing. Hotel 100yds from sea

Standing close to the North Landing of Flamborough Head, this family-run hotel overlooks delightful countryside. It provides excellent accommodation and caring hospitality. A good range of fresh local food, especially fish, is available in both the bar and the dining room.

Rooms 7 en suite **Parking** 30 **Notes** ⊗ ⊗ in restaurant Closed Xmas & 2wks Nov & Jan

England

GOOLE
MAP 17 SE72

BUDGET HOTEL

Premier Travel Inn Goole

Rawcliffe Rd, Airmyn DN14 8JS
☎ 08701 977 031 🗎 0121 633 4779
web: www.premiertravelinn.com

dir: Leave M62 at junct 36, onto A614 signed Rawcliffe. Inn immediately on left.

High quality, modern budget accommodation ideal for both families and business travellers. Spacious, en suite bedrooms feature bath and shower, satellite TV and many have telephones and modem points. The adjacent family restaurant features a wide and varied menu. For further details consult the Hotel Groups page.

Rooms 79 en suite **Conf** Board 12

KINGSTON UPON HULL
MAP 17 TA02
See also Little Weighton

★★★ 79% @@ HOTEL

Best Western Willerby Manor

Well Ln HU10 6ER
☎ 01482 652616 🗎 01482 653901
e-mail: willerbymanor@bestwestern.co.uk
web: www.willerbymanor.co.uk
(For full entry see Willerby)

★★★ 75% HOTEL

Portland
Paragon St HU1 3JP
☎ 01482 326462 🗎 01482 213460
e-mail: info@portland-hotel.co.uk
web: www.portland-hull.com

dir: M62 onto A63, to 1st main rdbt. Left at 2nd lights and over x-rds. Right at next junct onto Carr Ln, follow one-way system

A modern hotel situated next to the City Hall providing a good range of accommodation. Most of the public rooms are on the first floor and all offer wireless internet facilities. In addition, the street-level Bay Tree Café is open during the day and evening. The staff are friendly and helpful, and will take care of parking cars for hotel guests.

Rooms 126 en suite (4 fmly) ⊗ in 70 bedrooms S £58-£85; D £58-£85 **Facilities** STV Wi-fi in bedrooms Complimentary use of nearby health & fitness centre Xmas **Conf** BC Thtr 220 Class 100 Board 50 Del from £115 **Services** Lift **Parking** 12 **Notes** ⊗ in restaurant

★★★ 72% HOTEL

Quality Hotel Royal Hull

170 Ferensway HU1 3UF
☎ 01482 325087 🗎 01482 323172
e-mail: enquiries@hotel-hull.com
web: www.choicehotelseurope.com

dir: From M62 take A63 to Hull. Over flyover, left at 2nd lights signed Railway Station. Hotel on left at 2nd lights

A former Victorian railway hotel modernised in recent years. Bedrooms are well equipped, most with air conditioning, and a number of premier rooms. A spacious lounge provides an ideal setting for light meals, drinks and relaxation. There are extensive banqueting and conference facilities, as well as an adjacent leisure club.

Rooms 155 en suite (6 fmly) ⊗ in 85 bedrooms S £40-£107; D £48-£114 **Facilities** Spa ⬚ Sauna Solarium Gym Jacuzzi Steamroom Xmas **Conf** Thtr 450 Class 150 Board 105 Del from £80 **Services** Lift **Parking** 130 **Notes LB** Civ Wed 450

★★★ 68% HOTEL

Elizabeth Hotel Hull
THE INDEPENDENTS

Ferriby High Rd HU14 3LG
☎ 01482 645212 🗎 01482 643332
e-mail: elizabeth.hull@elizabethhotels.co.uk
web: www.elizabethhotels.co.uk
(For full entry see North Ferriby)

★★ 69% HOTEL

The Rowley Manor
Rowley Rd HU20 3XR
☎ 01482 848248 🗎 01482 849900
e-mail: info@rowleymanor.com
(For full entry see Little Weighton)

★★ 65% HOTEL

Stop Inn Hull
StopInn

11 Anlaby Rd HU1 2PJ
☎ 01482 323299 🗎 01482 214730
e-mail: hull@stop-inns.com
web: www.stop-inns.com/hull

dir: M62 to A63, over flyover, left at lights, hotel 500yds on left

An unpretentious hotel situated in the centre of the city with well-equipped and generally spacious bedrooms. Staff are friendly, and whilst there is no formal restaurant a limited range of dishes is served in the lounge bar during the evening. Free parking is available and guests have complimentary use of an adjacent leisure centre.

Rooms 59 en suite (5 fmly) ⊗ in 29 bedrooms S £46; D £52 (incl. bkfst) **Facilities** leisure facilities at sister hotel Xmas **Services** Lift **Parking** 15 **Notes LB** ⊗ in restaurant

U

Swallow Dorchester

SWALLOW
HOTELS

273-277 Beverley Rd HU5 2TH
☎ 01482 343276 🖹 01482 444924
e-mail: dorchester@swallowinns.co.uk
web: www.swallowhotels.com

dir: M62 E junct 38 onto A63 turning onto Hessle Rd. Left at rdbt, straight on at lights onto A1079, straight on through 2nd & 3rd lights. After 2nd pedestrian crossing, hotel on left

At the time of going to press, the star classification for this hotel was not confirmed. Please refer to the AA internet site www.theAA.com for current information.

Rooms 25 en suite (2 fmly) (25 GF) ⊘ in 11 bedrooms S £35-£45; D £39-£50 **Facilities** ♫ Xmas **Conf** Thtr 100 Class 60 Board 30 Del from £60 **Parking** 40 **Notes LB** ⊗ Civ Wed 120

BUDGET HOTEL

Campanile

Campanile

Beverley Rd, Freetown Way HU2 9AN
☎ 01482 325550 🖹 01482 587538
e-mail: hull@campanile-hotels.com.
web: www.envergure.fr

dir: From M62 join A63 to Hull, pass Humber Bridge on right. Over flyover, follow railway station signs onto A1079. Hotel at bottom of Ferensway

This modern building offers accommodation in smart, well-equipped bedrooms, all with en suite bathrooms. Refreshments may be taken at the informal Bistro. For further details consult the Hotel Groups page.

Rooms 47 annexe en suite **Conf** Thtr 25 Class 15 Board 15 Del from £70

BUDGET HOTEL

Hotel Ibis Hull

ibis
Accor
hotels

Osborne St HU1 2NL
☎ 01482 387500 🖹 01482 385510
e-mail: h3479-gm@accor-hotels.com
web: www.ibishotel.com

dir: M62/A63 straight across at rdbt, follow signs for Princes Quay onto Myton St. Hotel on corner of Osborne St & Ferensway

Modern, budget hotel offering comfortable accommodation in bright and practical bedrooms. Breakfast is self-service and dinner is available in the restaurant. For further details, consult the Hotel Groups page.

Rooms 106 en suite S £43.95-£45.95; D £43.95-£45.95

BUDGET HOTEL

Premier Travel Inn Hull North

premier
travel inn

Kingswood Park, Ennerdale HU7 4HS
☎ 08701 977137 🖹 01482 820300
web: www.premiertravelinn.com

dir: N of Hull, Ennerdale link road in Kingswood Park. A63 to city centre, then A1079 north, right onto A1033, hotel on 2nd rdbt

High quality, modern budget accommodation ideal for both families and business travellers. Spacious, en suite bedrooms feature bath and shower, satellite TV and many have telephones and modem points. The adjacent family restaurant features a wide and varied menu. For further details consult the Hotel Groups page.

Rooms 42 en suite

Premier Travel Inn Hull West

Ferriby Rd, Hessle HU13 0JA
☎ 08701 977138 🖹 01482 645285
dir: From A63 take exit for A164/A15 to Humber Bridge, Beverley & Hessle Viewpoint. Inn on 1st rdbt
Rooms 40 en suite

BUDGET HOTEL

Travelodge Hull South Cave

Travelodge

Beacon Service Area HU15 1RZ
☎ 08700 850 950 🖹 01430 424455
web: www.travelodge.co.uk
(For full entry see South Cave)

LANGTOFT   MAP 17 TA06

★★ 74% **HOTEL**

Old Mill Hotel & Restaurant

Mill Ln YO25 3BQ
☎ 01377 267284 & 07910 071641 🖹 01377 267383
e-mail: enquiries@oldbiggesmill.co.uk

dir: A64 eastbound, right at Staxton Hill traffic lights, through Foxholes village. Straight across at rdbt then 1st right

Standing in the open countryside of the Wolds, this modern hotel has been very well furnished throughout. Bedrooms are thoughtfully equipped, and there is a popular bar/lounge where a good range of well produced food is available. There is also a charming restaurant that is popular with locals.

Rooms 9 en suite ⊘ in 6 bedrooms S £35-£42.50; D £70-£85 (incl. bkfst) **Conf** BC Thtr 50 Class 30 Board 30 **Parking** 25 **Notes LB** ⊗ in restaurant Civ Wed 65

England

LITTLE WEIGHTON
MAP 17 SE93

★★ 69% **HOTEL**

The Rowley Manor
Rowley Rd HU20 3XR
☎ 01482 848248 📠 01482 849900
e-mail: info@rowleymanor.com

dir: leave A63 at South Cave/Market Weighton exit. Into South Cave, right into Beverley Rd at clock tower, and follow signs

A Georgian country house and former vicarage set in rural gardens and parkland. Bedrooms are traditionally decorated and furnished with period pieces; many rooms have panoramic views, and some are particularly spacious. The public rooms include a magnificent pine-panelled study, and the gardens feature croquet lawns.

Rooms 16 en suite (2 fmly) ⊗ in 5 bedrooms D £80-£100 (incl. bkfst)
Facilities ⊌ Xmas **Conf** Thtr 110 Class 48 Board 50 Del from £110
Parking 100 **Notes LB** ⊗ in restaurant Civ Wed 110

NORTH FERRIBY
MAP 17 SE92

★★★ 68% **HOTEL**

Elizabeth Hotel Hull
THE INDEPENDENTS
Ferriby High Rd HU14 3LG
☎ 01482 645212 📠 01482 643332
e-mail: elizabeth.hull@elizabethhotels.co.uk
web: www.elizabethhotels.co.uk

dir: M62, A63 to Hull. Exit for Humber Bridge. At rdbt follow Leeds signs then signs for North Ferriby. Hotel 0.5m on left

A modern, purpose built hotel that enjoys spectacular views of the Humber Bridge. Bedrooms are comfortable and well equipped. Public areas are spacious and both the restaurant and lounge bar look out over the river. There is ample parking and also a children's play area at the rear.

Rooms 95 en suite (6 fmly) (17 GF) ⊗ in 77 bedrooms S £50-£75; D £60-£85 (incl. bkfst) **Facilities** STV Xmas **Conf** Thtr 200 Class 85 Board 86 Del from £95 **Parking** 140 **Notes LB** Civ Wed 70

POCKLINGTON
MAP 17 SE84

★★ 65% **HOTEL**

Feathers
56 Market Place YO42 2AH
☎ 01759 303155 📠 01759 304382
e-mail: info@thefeathers-hotel.co.uk

dir: from York, B1246 signed Pocklington. Hotel just off A1079

This busy, traditional inn has been sympathetically furnished to provide comfortable, well-equipped and spacious accommodation. Public areas are smartly presented and enjoyable meals are served in the bar and the conservatory restaurant. A wide choice of dishes makes excellent use of local and seasonal produce.

Rooms 10 en suite 6 annexe en suite (1 fmly) (10 GF) ⊗ in 4 bedrooms S fr £47; D fr £52 (incl. bkfst) **Facilities** ♫ **Conf** Thtr 80 Class 40 Board 30 **Parking** 51 **Notes LB** ⊗

SOUTH CAVE
MAP 17 SE93

BUDGET HOTEL

Travelodge Hull South Cave

Beacon Service Area HU15 1RZ
☎ 08700 850 950 📠 01430 424455
web: www.travelodge.co.uk

dir: A63 eastbound, 0.5m from M62 junct 38

Travelodge offers good quality, good value, modern accommodation. Ideal for families, the spacious en suite bedrooms include remote-control TV, tea and coffee-making facilities and comfortable beds. Meals can be taken at the nearby family restaurant. See Hotel Groups pages for further details.

Rooms 40 en suite S fr £26; D fr £26

SUTTON UPON DERWENT
MAP 17 SE74

★★ 67% **HOTEL**

Old Rectory
Sandhill Ln YO41 4BX
☎ 01904 608548 📠 01904 608548
web: www.oldrectoryhotel.freeserve.co.uk

dir: off A1079 at Grimston Bar rdbt onto B1228 for Howden, through Elvington to Sutton-upon-Derwent, hotel on left opposite tennis courts

Dating from 1854, this large country rectory on the outskirts of York stands in the village centre, overlooking the Derwent Valley and offers a very friendly welcome. The hotel is handy for the Retail Outlet, the Yorkshire Air Museum and the city. Bedrooms and public areas are spacious and comfortable, and home cooking is a speciality in the dining room.

Rooms 6 rms (5 en suite) (2 fmly) S £35-£45; D £58-£62 (incl. bkfst)
Parking 30 **Notes LB** ⊗ in restaurant Closed 2wks Xmas

WILLERBY
MAP 17 TA03

★★★ 79% ⊛⊛ **HOTEL**

Best Western Willerby Manor
Best Western
Well Ln HU10 6ER
☎ 01482 652616 📠 01482 653901
e-mail: willerbymanor@bestwestern.co.uk
web: www.willerbymanor.co.uk

dir: off A63, signed Humber Bridge. Follow road, right at rdbt by Waitrose. At next rdbt hotel signed

Set in a quiet residential area, amid well-tended gardens, this hotel was originally a private mansion; it has now been thoughtfully extended to provide very comfortable bedrooms, equipped with many useful extras. There are extensive leisure facilities and a choice of eating options in various styles, including the smart Icon Restaurant.

Rooms 51 en suite (6 fmly) (16 GF) ⊗ in 47 bedrooms S £52-£94; D £82-£123 (incl. bkfst) **Facilities** Spa STV ⊠ supervised Sauna Gym ⊌ Wi-fi available Steam room Beauty therapist Aerobic classes **Conf** Thtr 500 Class 200 Board 100 Del £115 **Parking** 300 **Notes LB** ⊗ ⊗ in restaurant Closed 24-26 Dec RS 24-26 Dec Civ Wed 150

★★★ 75% HOTEL

Ramada Hull

®RAMADA

Main St HU10 6EA

☎ 01482 656488 🖶 01482 655048

e-mail: sales.hull@ramadajarvis.co.uk

web: www.ramadajarvis.co.uk

dir: *A164 to Beverley signed Willerby Shopping Park. Left at rdbt into Grange Park Lane, hotel at end*

Situated between Hull and Beverley, this large hotel is set in 12 acres of landscaped gardens. Bedrooms are comfortably appointed for both business and leisure guests, and there are extensive conference facilities, The Seb Coe Leisure Club and a hair and beauty spa.

Rooms 100 en suite (8 fmly) (15 GF) ⊗ in 88 bedrooms S £50-£120; D £60-£130 **Facilities Spa** STV 🔁 Sauna Gym Jacuzzi Xmas **Conf** Thtr 550 Class 250 Board 80 Del from £106 **Services** Lift **Parking** 600 **Notes LB** ⊗ in restaurant Civ Wed 120

BUDGET HOTEL

Innkeeper's Lodge Hull

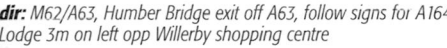

Beverley Rd HU10 6NI

☎ 01482 651518 🖶 01482 658380

web: www.innkeeperslodge.com

dir: *M62/A63, Humber Bridge exit off A63, follow signs for A164. Lodge 3m on left opp Willerby shopping centre*

Smart, en suite accommodation ideal for both business & leisure guests. Bedrooms are very well equipped, including Sky TV, telephone, modem points, tea & coffee making facilities, (family rooms in most locations). Complimentary breakfast. The adjacent Pub Restaurant; a Harvester, Vintage Inn, Toby Carvery, Ember Inn, Sizzling Pubco or Pub & Carvery offers an all day menu. See Hotel Groups pages for further details.

Rooms 32 en suite S £52; D £52

YORKSHIRE, NORTH

ALDWARK
MAP 19 SE46

★★★★ 85% ®® HOTEL

Aldwark Manor

Marston Hotels

YO61 1UF

☎ 01347 838146 🖶 01347 838867

e-mail: aldwark@marstonhotels.com

web: www.marstonhotels.com

dir: *A1/A59 towards Green Hammerton, then B6265 Little Ouseburn. Follow signs for Aldwark Bridge/Manor. A19 through Linton-on-Ouse*

Mature parkland forms the impressive backdrop for this rambling 19th-century mansion, with the River Ure flowing gently through the hotel's own 18-hole golf course. Bedrooms vary - the main-house rooms are traditional and those in the extension are modern in

continued

design. Impressive conference and banqueting facilities and a stylish, very well-equipped leisure club are available.

Aldwark Manor

Rooms 55 en suite (6 fmly) ⊗ in 37 bedrooms S fr £132.50; D fr £171 (incl. bkfst) **Facilities Spa** STV 🔁 ♪ 18 Sauna Solarium Gym Putt green Jacuzzi Health & beauty Xmas **Conf** Thtr 240 Class 100 Board 80 Del from £85 **Services** Lift **Parking** 150 **Notes LB** ⊛ ⊗ in restaurant Civ Wed 140

See advert under HARROGATE & YORK

ARNCLIFFE
MAP 18 SD97

★★ 78% ®® HOTEL

Amerdale House

BD23 5QE

☎ 01756 770250 🖶 01756 770266

dir: *left at Threshfield-Kettlewell road 0.5m past Kilnsey Crag*

This former manor house enjoys a peaceful, idyllic location with wonderful views of the dale and fells from every room. Spacious, inviting public areas are tastefully furnished and have real fires in winter. A daily-changing imaginative menu and impressive wine list are offered in the elegant dining room. Bedrooms are beautifully decorated and elegantly furnished.

Rooms 10 en suite 1 annexe en suite (3 fmly) **Parking** 30 **Notes LB** ⊛ ⊗ in restaurant Closed mid Nov-mid Mar

AUSTWICK
MAP 18 SD76

★★ 79% ® SMALL HOTEL

The Austwick Traddock

LA2 8BY

☎ 015242 51224 🖶 015242 51796

e-mail: info@austwicktraddock.co.uk

dir: *Off A65 into village centre*

Privately owned this country house is surrounded by Yorkshire Dales National Park's breathtaking scenery so it is a good base for walkers, climbers and those touring the area. The bedrooms are stylishly and individually appointed, and guests can relax on sofas by log fires in the winter or enjoy a drink on the garden deck in summer. The award-winning restaurant uses local, organic and seasonal ingredients on its modern British menus.

Rooms 10 en suite (1 fmly) **Conf** Board 16 **Services** Lift **Parking** 20

England

AYSGARTH   MAP 19 SE08

★★ 71% **HOTEL**

The George & Dragon Inn
DL8 3AD
☎ 01969 663358 🗎 01969 663773
e-mail: info@georgeanddragonaysgarth.co.uk

This 17th-century coaching inn offers spacious, comfortably appointed rooms. Popular with walkers, the cosy bar has a real fire and a good selection of local beers. The beamed restaurant serves hearty breakfasts and interesting meals using fresh local produce. Service is very friendly and attentive.

Rooms 7 en suite (2 fmly) S £41-£55; D £72-£84 (incl. bkfst)
Facilities Xmas **Parking** 35 **Notes LB** ⊘ in restaurant

BAINBRIDGE   MAP 18 SD99

★★ 67% **HOTEL**

Rose & Crown
DL8 3EE
☎ 01969 650225 🗎 01969 650735
e-mail: info@theprideofwensleydale.com
dir: on A684 between Hawes & Leyburn

This traditional coaching inn, overlooking the village green, is full of character. Bedrooms are appropriately furnished and comfortably equipped. There are two well-stocked bars, one very popular with locals, both offering an interesting range of dishes. Finer dining is served in the restaurant and a cosy residents' lounge is also provided.

Rooms 12 rms (11 en suite) (1 fmly) ⊘ in 2 bedrooms **Conf** Class 30 Board 30 **Parking** 65 **Notes LB** ⊘ in restaurant

BILBROUGH   MAP 16 SE54

BUDGET HOTEL

Premier Travel Inn York South West

Bilborough Top, Colton YO23 3PP
☎ 0870 238 3317 🗎 01937 835934
web: www.premiertravelinn.com
dir: on A64 between Tadcaster & York

High quality, modern budget accommodation ideal for both families and business travellers. Spacious, en suite bedrooms feature bath and shower, satellite TV and many have telephones and modem points. The adjacent family restaurant features a wide and varied menu. For further details consult the Hotel Groups page.

Rooms 59 en suite **Conf** Thtr 20 Board 12

BUDGET HOTEL

Travelodge York Tadcaster
Tadcaster LS24 8EG
☎ 08700 850 950 🗎 0870 1911685
web: www.travelodge.co.uk
dir: on A64 eastbound

Travelodge offers good quality, good value, modern accommodation. Ideal for families, the spacious en suite bedrooms include remote-control TV, tea and coffee-making facilities and comfortable beds. Meals can be taken at the nearby family restaurant. See Hotel Groups pages for further details.

Rooms 62 en suite S fr £26; D fr £26

BOLTON ABBEY   MAP 19 SE05

INSPECTORS' CHOICE

★★★★ ⊛⊛⊛⊛ **HOTEL**

The Devonshire Arms Country House Hotel & Spa
BD23 6AJ
☎ 01756 710441 & 718111 🗎 01756 710564
e-mail: reservations@thedevonshirearms.co.uk
web: www.devonshirehotels.co.uk
dir: on B6160, 250yds N of junct with A59

With stunning views of the Wharfedale countryside, this beautiful hotel, owned by the Duke and Duchess of Devonshire, dates back to the 17th century. Bedrooms are elegantly furnished; those in the old part of the house are particularly spacious, complete with four-posters and fine antiques. The sitting rooms are delightfully cosy with log fires, and the dedicated staff deliver service with a blend of friendliness and professionalism. The Burlington Restaurant offers award-winning, highly accomplished cuisine, while the brasserie provides a lighter alternative. AA Wine Award winner for England and Overall AA Wine Award winner 2006-7.

Rooms 40 en suite (1 fmly) (17 GF) ⊘ in 30 bedrooms S £160-£380; D £195-£380 **Facilities Spa** STV ⬛ supervised ⋚ Fishing Sauna Solarium Gym ⬥ Putt green Jacuzzi Wi-fi in bedrooms Classic cars, Falconry, Laser pigeon shooting. Flyfishing, walking, Cricket Xmas **Conf** BC Thtr 90 Class 80 Board 30 Del from £185 **Parking** 150 **Notes LB** ⊘ in restaurant Civ Wed 90

See advertisement under HARROGATE & SKIPTON

BOROUGHBRIDGE   MAP 19 SE36

★★★ 77% **HOTEL**

Best Western Crown
Horsefair YO51 9LB
☎ 01423 322328 🗎 01423 324512
e-mail: sales@crownboroughbridge.co.uk
web: www.crownboroughbridge.co.uk
dir: A1(M) junct 48. Hotel 1m towards town centre at T-junct

Situated in the centre of town but convenient for the A1, The Crown provides a full leisure complex, conference rooms and a secure car park. Bedrooms are well appointed. A wide range of well-prepared dishes can be taken in both the restaurant and bar.

Rooms 37 en suite (3 fmly) (2 GF) ⊘ in all bedrooms **Facilities** STV ⬛ supervised Sauna Solarium Gym Jacuzzi **Conf** Thtr 150 Class 80 Board 80 **Services** Lift **Parking** 60 **Notes LB** ⊗ ⊘ in restaurant Civ Wed 120

BURNSALL
MAP 19 SE06

★★ 72% ◉ **HOTEL**

Red Lion Hotel
By the Bridge BD23 6BU
☎ 01756 720204 📠 01756 720292
e-mail: redlion@daelnet.co.uk
web: www.redlion.co.uk
dir: on B6160 between Grassington and Bolton Abbey

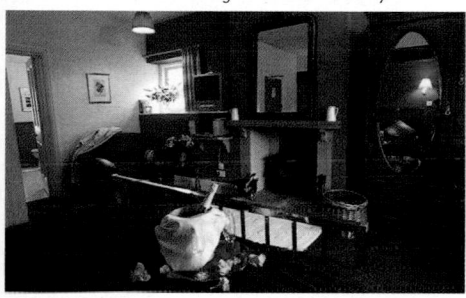

This delightful 16th-century Dales inn stands adjacent to a five-arch bridge over the scenic River Wharfe. Stylish, comfortable bedrooms are all individually decorated and well equipped. Public areas include a tasteful lounge and a traditional oak-panelled bar. The elegant restaurant makes good use of fresh local ingredients, and breakfasts are memorable. Guests are free to fish in the hotel's own stretch of water.

Rooms 11 en suite 4 annexe en suite (2 fmly) (2 GF) S £60-£85;
D £120-£150 (incl. bkfst) **Facilities** Fishing Xmas **Conf** Thtr 60 Class 10
Board 40 Del from £100 **Parking** 80 **Notes LB** ⊘ in restaurant
Civ Wed 100

CRATHORNE
MAP 19 NZ40

INSPECTORS' CHOICE

★★★★ ◉◉ **HOTEL**

Crathorne Hall
TS15 0AR

HAND PICKED

☎ 01642 700398 📠 01642 700814
e-mail: crathorne-cro@handpicked.co.uk
web: www.handpicked.co.uk
dir: off A19, take slip road signed Teesside Airport and Kirklevington, then right signed Crathorne to hotel

This splendid Edwardian hall sits in its own landscaped grounds and enjoys fine views of the Leven Valley and rolling Cleveland
continued

Hills. Both the impressively equipped bedrooms and the delightful public areas offer sumptuous levels of comfort, with elegant antique furnishings that complement the hotel's architectural style. Conference and banqueting facilities are available

Rooms 37 en suite (4 fmly) ⊘ in 15 bedrooms S £90-£160;
D £120-£200 (incl. bkfst) **Facilities** STV FTV ⤸ Wi-fi in bedrooms
Jogging track, Clay pigeon shooting ch fac Xmas **Conf** Thtr 120
Class 80 Board 60 Del from £120 **Parking** 88 **Notes LB** ⊘ in
restaurant Civ Wed 120

EASINGWOLD
MAP 19 SE56

★★ 75% **HOTEL**

George

THE CIRCLE
Selected Individual Hotels
GREAT BRITAIN

Market Place YO61 3AD
☎ 01347 821698 📠 01347 823448
e-mail: info@the-george-hotel.co.uk
web: www.the-george-hotel.co.uk
dir: off A19 midway between York & Thirsk, in Market Place

A friendly welcome awaits at this former coaching inn that faces the Georgian market square. Bedrooms are very comfortably furnished and well equipped, and the mews rooms have their own external access. An extensive range of well-produced food is available both in the bar and restaurant. There are two comfortable lounges and complimentary use of a local fitness centre.

Rooms 15 en suite (2 fmly) (6 GF) ⊘ in all bedrooms S fr £70;
D £90-£95 (incl. bkfst) **Facilities** Complimentry use of local fitness centre
Xmas **Conf** Board 12 **Parking** 10 **Notes LB** ⊛ ⊘ in restaurant

ESCRICK
MAP 16 SE64

★★★ 70% ◉ **HOTEL**

Parsonage Country House
York Rd YO19 6LF
☎ 01904 728111 📠 01904 728151
e-mail: reservations@parsonagehotel.co.uk
web: www.parsonagehotel.co.uk
dir: From A64 take A19 Selby. Follow to Escrick . Hotel on right of St Helens Church

This 19th-century former parsonage, has been carefully restored and extended to provide delightful accommodation, set in well-tended gardens. Bedrooms are smartly appointed and well equipped both for business and leisure guests. Spacious public areas include an elegant

continued on page 704

England

ESCRICK *continued*

restaurant, excellent meeting and conference facilities and a choice of attractive lounges.

Rooms 12 en suite 36 annexe en suite (4 fmly) (6 GF) ⊗ in 30 bedrooms **Facilities** STV Able to book tee times al local courses. Xmas **Conf** Thtr 160 Class 80 Board 50 **Services** Lift **Parking** 100 **Notes** ⊗ ⊗ in restaurant Civ Wed 160

See advertisement under YORK

FILEY   MAP 17 TA18

★★ 76% **HOTEL**

Downcliffe House

6 The Beach YO14 9LA

☎ 01723 513310 📠 01723 512659

e-mail: info@downcliffehouse.co.uk

web: www.downcliffehouse.co.uk

dir: *A165/A1039 into Filey, through town centre along Cargate Hill & turn right. Hotel 200yds along seafront*

This very friendly hotel is set right on the seafront and the inviting public areas include a cosy bar and an attractive restaurant serving an excellent range of freshly prepared meals. Furnished throughout to a high standard, the bedrooms are smart and well equipped; some are very spacious and enjoy panoramic sea views.

Rooms 12 en suite (5 fmly) ⊗ in all bedrooms S £48-£65; D £96-£130 (incl. bkfst) **Facilities** Xmas **Parking** 4 **Notes LB** ⊗ in restaurant Closed Jan-1 Feb

GRASSINGTON   MAP 19 SE06

★★ 67% **HOTEL**

Grassington House

5 The Square BD23 5AQ

☎ 01756 752406 📠 01756 752135

e-mail: info@grassingtonhousehotel.co.uk

dir: *B6265 from Skipton towards Grassington*

Looking over the cobbled square of a quaint village, this historic hotel skilfully combines the smart provision of spacious, stylish bedrooms with the flair, character, great beer and food of one of the region's finest inns. Imaginative food is served in either the elegant renovated dining room or attractive conservatory and a warm welcome is assured.

Rooms 9 en suite (2 fmly) ⊗ in all bedrooms **Parking** 20 **Notes LB** ⊗ in restaurant Closed 24-25 Dec

GUISBOROUGH   MAP 19 NZ61

★★★★ 80% ◉ **HOTEL**

Macdonald Gisborough Hall

Whitby Ln TS14 6PT

🏛 MACDONALD
HOTELS & RESORTS

☎ 0870 400 8191 📠 01287 610844

e-mail: general.gisboroughhall@macdonald-hotels.co.uk

web: www.macdonald-hotels.co.uk

dir: *A171, follow signs for Whitby until Waterfall rdbt then into Whitby Lane, hotel 500yds on right*

Dating back to the mid-19th century, this elegant establishment provides a pleasing combination of original features and modern facilities. Bedrooms, including four-poster and family rooms, are richly

continued

furnished, while there is a choice of welcoming lounges with log fires. Imaginative fare is served in Tockett's restaurant.

Rooms 71 en suite (2 fmly) (12 GF) ⊗ in 37 bedrooms S £160; D £160 **Facilities** STV ♨ Sauna ♋ Wi-fi in bedrooms Revival zone-2 beauty treatment zones Xmas **Conf** BC Thtr 400 Class 150 Board 32 Del from £125 **Services** Lift **Parking** 180 **Notes LB** ⊗ in restaurant Closed 2-6 Jan Civ Wed 250

◉ **RESTAURANT WITH ROOMS**

Pinchinthorpe Hall

Pinchinthorpe TS14 8HG

☎ 01287 630200 📠 01287 632000

e-mail: nybrewery@pinchinthorpe.wanadoo.co.uk

dir: *Between Guisborough & Great Ayton on A173*

An elegant 17th-century country manor house that has stylish bedrooms, each very individually and tastefully decorated and with many thoughtful extras. The Brewhouse Bistro serves interesting dishes using home grown and local produce, and offers caring and attentive service.

Rooms 6 en suite ⊗ in all bedrooms **Conf** Thtr 50 Class 20 Board 24 **Parking** 110 **Notes LB** ⊗ ⊗ in restaurant Civ Wed 80

BUDGET HOTEL

Premier Travel Inn Middlesbrough South

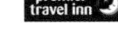

Middlesbrough Rd, Upsall TS14 6RW

☎ 0870 9906540 📠 0870 9906541

web: www.premiertravelinn.com

dir: *Off A171 towards Whitby.*

High quality, modern budget accommodation ideal for both families and business travellers. Spacious, en suite bedrooms feature bath and shower, satellite TV and many have telephones and modem points. The adjacent family restaurant features a wide and varied menu. For further details consult the Hotel Groups page.

Rooms 20 en suite

HACKNESS   MAP 17 SE99

★★★ 73% **HOTEL**

Hackness Grange Country House

North York National Park YO13 0JW

☎ 01723 882345 📠 01723 882391

e-mail: admin@englishrosehotels.co.uk

dir: *A64 to Scarborough, then A171 to Whitby and Scalby. Follow Hackness and Forge Valley National Park signs, through village, hotel on left*

Close to Scarborough, and set in the North Yorkshire Moors National Park, Hackness Grange is surrounded by well-tended gardens. Comfortable bedrooms have views of the open countryside; those in the cottages are ideally suited to families, and the courtyard rooms include facilities for the less mobile. Lounges and the restaurant are spacious and relaxing.

Rooms 33 en suite (5 fmly) (8 GF) **Facilities** 🎣 ♨ 9 hole pitch & putt **Conf** Thtr 20 Board 14 **Parking** 60 **Notes LB** ⊗ ⊗ in restaurant

HAROME

See **Helmsley**

HARROGATE

See also Knaresborough

MAP 19 SE35

INSPECTORS' CHOICE

★★★★ ◉◉ **HOTEL**

Rudding Park Hotel & Golf

Rudding Park, Follifoot HG3 1JH

☎ 01423 871350 📠 01423 872286

e-mail: reservations@ruddingpark.com

web: www.ruddingpark.com

dir: from A61 at rdbt with A658 take York exit and follow signs to Rudding Park

In the heart of 200-year-old landscaped parkland, this modern hotel is elegant and stylish. Bedrooms, including two luxurious

continued

suites, are smartly presented and thoughtfully equipped. Carefully prepared meals are served in the Clocktower, with its striking, contemporary decor. A spacious bar and comfortable lounges are also available. There is an adjoining 18-hole, par 72 golf course and an 18-bay floodlit, covered driving range.

Rooms 49 en suite (19 GF) ⊘ in 39 bedrooms S £145-£330; D £175-£330 (incl. bkfst) **Facilities** STV ♨ 18 ♣ Putt green Wi-fi in bedrooms Driving range Jogging trail Membership of local gym Xmas **Conf** BC Thtr 300 Class 150 Board 36 Del from £155 **Services** Lift **Parking** 150 **Notes** LB ⊘ in restaurant Civ Wed 300

★★★★ 81% ◉ **TOWN HOUSE HOTEL**

Hotel du Vin & Bistro

Prospect Place HG1 1LB

☎ 01423 856800 📠 01423 856801

e-mail: info@harrogate.hotelduvin.com

web: www.hotelduvin.com

dir: Enter town centre & stay in right lane, pass West Park Church on right. Hotel on right

This town house hotel was created from eight Georgian-style properties and overlooks the Stray. The spacious, open-plan lobby has seating, a bar and the reception desk. Hidden downstairs is a cosy snug cellar. The French-influenced Bistro offers high quality cooking and a great choice of wines. Bedrooms face front and back, are smart and modern, and have excellent 'deluge' showers.

Rooms 43 en suite (2 GF) ⊘ in all bedrooms S £95; D £105-£120 **Facilities** STV Snooker Gym Wi-fi in bedrooms Xmas **Conf** Thtr 50 Board 20 Del from £160 **Services** Lift **Parking** 30 **Notes** ⊘ in restaurant Civ Wed 90

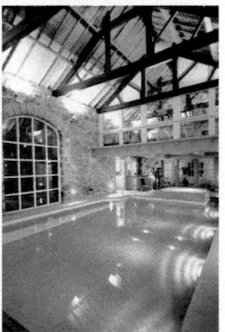

England

HARROGATE *continued*

★★★★ 75% **HOTEL**

Paramount Majestic

Ripon Rd HG1 2HU

☎ 01423 700300 📄 01423 521332

e-mail: majestic@paramount-hotels.co.uk

web: www.paramount-hotels.co.uk

PARAMOUNT
GROUP OF HOTELS

dir: *from M1 onto A1(M) at Wetherby. Take A661 to Harrogate. Hotel in town centre adjacent to Royal Hall*

Popular for conferences and functions, this grand Victorian hotel is set in 12 acres of landscaped grounds and is centrally located within walking distance of the town centre and benefits from spacious public areas. The bedrooms are comfortably equipped; these come in a variety of sizes and include several spacious suites.

Rooms 156 en suite (9 fmly) ⊗ in 86 bedrooms **Facilities** STV 📺 supervised ♨ Snooker Sauna Solarium Gym Jacuzzi Golf practice net **Conf** BC Thtr 500 Class 250 Board 70 **Services** Lift **Parking** 250 **Notes LB** ⊗ in restaurant Civ Wed 200

★★★★ 72% **HOTEL**

Holiday Inn Harrogate

Kings Rd HG1 1XX

☎ 0870 4431 761 📄 01423 524435

e-mail: gm.hiharrogate@qmh-hotels.com

Holiday Inn
HOTELS · RESORTS

dir: *Hotel adjoins International Conference Centre.*

Situated just a short walk from the town centre, this impressive hotel lies adjacent to the International Conference Centre. Fully refurbished bedrooms are stylishly furnished. Extensive conference facilities and a business centre are provided. Public areas include the upgraded first floor restaurant and ground-floor lounge bar, currently being upgraded. Nearby private parking is a bonus.

Rooms 214 en suite (7 fmly) ⊗ in 107 bedrooms S £54-£174; D £54-£174 **Facilities** Gym **Conf** BC Thtr 300 Class 150 Board 100 Del from £108 **Services** Lift **Parking** 160 **Notes LB** ⊗ in restaurant

★★★ 83% ❀❀ **HOTEL**

The Boar's Head Hotel

Ripley Castle Estate HG3 3AY

☎ 01423 771888 📄 01423 771509

e-mail: reservations@boarsheadripley.co.uk

dir: *on A61 Harrogate to Ripon road. Hotel in centre of Ripley*

Part of the Ripley Castle estate, this delightful and popular hotel is renowned for its warm hospitality and as a dining destination. Bedrooms offer many comforts, and the luxurious day rooms feature

continued

works of art from the nearby castle. The banqueting suites in the castle are very impressive.

The Boar's Head Hotel

Rooms 19 en suite 6 annexe en suite (2 fmly) ⊗ in all bedrooms S £105-£125; D £125-£150 (incl. bkfst) **Facilities** ♨ Fishing Clay pigeon shooting, Tennis, Fishing ♪ Xmas **Conf** BC Thtr 150 Class 80 Board 150 Del from £155 **Parking** 50 **Notes LB** ⊗ in restaurant Civ Wed 120

★★★ 78% **HOTEL**

Grants

3-13 Swan Rd HG1 2SS

☎ 01423 560666 📄 01423 502550

e-mail: enquiries@grantshotel-harrogate.com

web: www.grantshotel-harrogate.com

dir: *off A61*

A long established, family-run hotel with an attractive flower bedecked patio. The smartly presented, well-equipped bedrooms include some with four-poster beds. A comfortable lounge bar with plenty of interesting old photographs, and imaginative food in the colourful Chimney Pots Bistro, are just some of the features of this friendly hotel.

Rooms 42 en suite (2 fmly) **Facilities** STV Use of local Health & Leisure Club Xmas **Conf** Thtr 70 Class 20 Board 30 **Services** Lift **Parking** 26 **Notes** ⊗ in restaurant

★★★ 74% **HOTEL**

Studley

Swan Rd HG1 2SE

☎ 01423 560425 📄 01423 530967

e-mail: info@studleyhotel.co.uk

web: www.studleyhotel.co.uk

dir: *Swan Rd adjacent to Valley Gardens and opposite Mercer Gallery*

This friendly, well-established hotel, close to the town centre and Valley Gardens, is renowned for its Orchid Restaurant, which provides

continued

a dynamic and authentic approach to Pacific Rim and Asian cuisine. Bedrooms are modern and come in a variety of styles and sizes, whilst the stylish bar lounge provides guests with an excellent place for relaxing.

Rooms 36 en suite (1 fmly) ⊘ in 6 bedrooms S fr £70; D £94-£104 (incl. bkfst) **Facilities** STV FTV Wi-fi in bedrooms Free use of local Health & Spa Club **Conf** Thtr 15 Class 15 Board 12 **Services** Lift **Parking** 15 **Notes LB** ⊘ in restaurant

---

★★★ 72% **HOTEL**

Best Western Cedar Court

Queens Buildings, Park Pde HG1 5AH
☎ 01423 858585 & 858595(res) 🖷 01423 504950
e-mail: cedarcourt@bestwestern.co.uk
web: www.cedarcourthotels.co.uk
dir: *from A1(M) follow signs to Harrogate on A661 past Sainsburys. At rdbt left onto A6040. Hotel right after church*

This Grade II listed building was Harrogate's first hotel and enjoys a peaceful location in landscaped grounds, close to the town centre. It provides spacious, well-equipped accommodation. Public areas include a brasserie-style restaurant, a small gym and an open-plan lounge and bar. Functions and conferences are particularly well catered for.

Rooms 100 en suite (8 fmly) (7 GF) ⊘ in 75 bedrooms S £85-£144; D £110-£160 (incl. bkfst) **Facilities** STV Gym Wi-fi in bedrooms Xmas **Conf** BC Thtr 650 Class 300 Board 240 **Services** Lift air con **Parking** 150 **Notes LB** ⊗ ⊘ in restaurant Civ Wed 150

★★ 74% **HOTEL**

Ascot House

53 Kings Rd HG1 5IIJ
☎ 01423 531005 🖷 01423 503523
e-mail: admin@ascothouse.com
web: www.ascothouse.com
dir: *follow signs for Town Centre/Conference & Exhibition Centre into Kings Rd, hotel on left after park*

This late-Victorian house is situated a short distance from the International Conference Centre and provides comfortable, well equipped bedrooms and smartly presented bathrooms. The attractive public areas include an inviting lounge, bar, elegant dining room and beautiful stained glass window on the main staircase.

Rooms 19 en suite (2 fmly) (5 GF) ⊘ in all bedrooms S £63-£99; D £93-£117 (incl. bkfst) **Facilities** Wi-fi in bedrooms Xmas **Conf** Thtr 80 Class 36 Board 36 Del from £130 **Parking** 14 **Notes LB** ⊘ in restaurant Closed New Year & 28 Jan-11 Feb 2007 Civ Wed 80

HARROGATE *continued*

⊛ RESTAURANT WITH ROOMS

Harrogate Brasserie with Rooms

28-30 Cheltenham Pde HG1 1DB
☎ 01423 505041 📠 01423 722300
e-mail: info@brasserie.co.uk
web: www.brasserie.co.uk

dir: *On A61 town centre behind theatre*

This town-centre establishment has a distinctly continental style. The brasserie covers three cosy and richly decorated dining areas, and live jazz features on Wednesday, Friday and Sunday nights. The individual bedrooms have period collectibles, lots to read, and many rooms have DVD players.

Rooms 17 en suite (3 fmly) S fr £55; D fr £85 **Facilities** ch fac **Parking** 12 **Notes LB** Closed 26 Dec-2 Jan

---

Ⓤ

Kimberley

11-19 Kings Rd HG1 5JY
☎ 01423 505613 0800 7837642 📠 01423 530276
e-mail: info@thekimberley.co.uk

dir: *Follow signs for Harrogate International Conference Centre or Kings Rd, 150yds N of centre*

At the time of going to press, the star classification for this hotel was not confirmed. Please refer to the AA internet site www.theAA.com for current information.

Rooms 48 en suite (3 fmly) (15 GF) ⊘ in 36 bedrooms **Services** Lift **Parking** 50

Ⓤ

Old Swan

Swan Rd HG1 2SR
☎ 01423 500055 📠 01423 501154
e-mail: gm.oldswan@macdonald-hotels.co.uk
web: www.macdonald-hotels.co.uk

dir: *from A1, A59 Ripon, left Empress rdbt, stay on left, right Princess rdbt. Continue to x-rds, straight across & turn left into Swan Rd*

At the time of going to press, the star classification for this hotel was not confirmed. Please refer to the AA internet site www.theAA.com for current information.

Rooms 136 en suite ⊘ in all bedrooms **Facilities** STV ♨ **Conf** Thtr 300 Class 130 Board 100 Del from £130 **Services** Lift **Parking** 200 **Notes LB** ⊘ in restaurant Civ Wed 300

Ⓤ

Swallow St George

1 Ripon Rd HG1 2SY
☎ 01423 561431 📠 01423 530037
e-mail: reservations.harrogate@swallowhotels.com
web: www.swallowhotels.com

dir: *On A61 adjacent to the Harrogate International Conference Centre and opposite Tourist Information Office*

At the time of going to press, the star classification for this hotel was
continued

not confirmed. Please refer to the AA internet site www.theAA.com for current information.

Rooms 90 en suite (7 fmly) (1 GF) ⊘ in 50 bedrooms **Facilities Spa** 🏊 supervised Sauna Solarium Gym Jacuzzi **Services** Lift **Parking** 60

Ⓤ

Swallow Yorkshire

Prospect Place HG1 1LA
☎ 01423 565071 📠 01423 500082
e-mail: generalmanager.yorkshirehotel@swallowhotels.com
web: www.swallowhotels.com

dir: *Exit A1 junct 24 & take A59 to Harrogate town centre, right at Betty's Tea Rooms*

At the time of going to press, the star classification for this hotel was not confirmed. Please refer to the AA internet site www.theAA.com for current information.

Rooms 80 en suite (1 fmly) ⊘ in 50 bedrooms S £45-£75; D £75-£195 (incl. bkfst) **Facilities** Xmas **Conf** Thtr 130 Class 72 Board 45 Del from £92 **Services** Lift **Parking** 38 **Notes LB** ⊘ in restaurant Civ Wed 100

BUDGET HOTEL

Innkeeper's Lodge Harrogate West

Otley Rd, Beckwith Knowle HG3 1PR
☎ 01423 533091 📠 01423 533092
web: www.innkeeperslodge.com

dir: *from A1(M) junct 47, take A59 for Harrogate. Over 2 rdbts, at 3rd rdbt straight over onto B6162. Hotel on left opp church*

Smart, en suite accommodation ideal for both business & leisure guests. Bedrooms are very well equipped, including Sky TV, telephone, modem points, tea & coffee making facilities, (family rooms in most locations). Complimentary breakfast. The adjacent Pub Restaurant; a Harvester, Vintage Inn, Toby Carvery, Ember Inn, Sizzling Pubco or Pub & Carvery offers an all day menu. See Hotel Groups pages for further details.

Rooms 11 en suite S £65-£95; D £65-£95 **Conf** Thtr 30 Class 30 Board 30

BUDGET HOTEL

Premier Travel Inn Harrogate

premier travel inn 🌙

Hornbeam Park Ave, Hornbeam Park HG2 8RA
☎ 08701 977 126 📠 01423 878581
web: www.premiertravelinn.com

dir: *A1(M) junct 46 west then A661 to Harrogate. After 2m left at The Woodlands lights. Hornbeam Park Avenue 1.5m on left*

High quality, modern budget accommodation ideal for both families and business travellers. Spacious, en suite bedrooms feature bath and shower, satellite TV and many have telephones and modem points. The adjacent family restaurant features a wide and varied menu. For further details consult the Hotel Groups page.

Rooms 50 en suite

Travelodge Harrogate

The Gubbel HG1 2RR

☎ 0870 1911737 📠 01423 562734

web: www.travelodge.co.uk

Travelodge offers good quality, good value, modern accommodation. Ideal for families, the spacious en suite bedrooms include remote-control TV, tea and coffee-making facilities and comfortable beds. Meals can be taken at the nearby family restaurant. See Hotel Groups pages for further details.

Rooms 46 en suite S fr £26; D fr £26

HAWES   **MAP 18 SD88**

★★ 76% **HOTEL**

Simonstone Hall

Simonstone DL8 3LY

☎ 01969 667255 📠 01969 667741

e-mail: hotel@simonstonehall.demon.co.uk

web: www.simonstonehall.co.uk

dir: 1.5m N on road signed to Muker and Buttertubs

This former hunting lodge provides professional, friendly service and a relaxed atmosphere. There is an inviting drawing room, stylish fine dining restaurant, a bar and conservatory. The generally spacious bedrooms are elegantly finished to reflect the style of the house, and many offer spectacular views of the countryside.

Rooms 18 en suite (10 fmly) (2 GF) ❀ in all bedrooms **Facilities** Xmas **Conf** Thtr 50 Class 20 Board 20 Del £165 **Parking** 40 **Notes** ❀ in restaurant Civ Wed 72

HELMSLEY   **MAP 19 SE68**

★★★ 78% **HOTEL**

Pheasant

Harome YO62 5JG

☎ 01439 771241 📠 01439 771744

dir: 2.5m SE, leave A170 after 0.25m. Right signed Harome for further 2m

Guests can expect a family welcome at this hotel, which has spacious, comfortable bedrooms and enjoys a delightful setting next to the village pond. The beamed, flagstoned bar leads into the charming lounge and conservatory dining room, where very enjoyable English food is served. A separate building contains the swimming pool. The hotel offers dinner-inclusive tariffs, and has many regulars.

Rooms 12 en suite 2 annexe en suite (1 GF) ❀ in all bedrooms S £75.50-£82; D £151-£165 (incl. bkfst & dinner) **Facilities** STV FTV 🏊 **Parking** 20 **Notes LB** No children 12yrs ❀ in restaurant Closed Xmas & Jan-Feb

---

★★★ 77% **HOTEL**

Macdonald Black Swan

Market Place YO62 5BJ

☎ 0870 400 8112 📠 01439 770174

e-mail: blackswan@macdonald-hotels.co.uk

web: www.macdonald-hotels.co.uk

dir: A170 towards Scarborough into Helmsley. Hotel at top of Market Place

The façade of this former coaching inn is a blend of Elizabethan, Georgian and Tudor, and inside there are warm, welcoming interiors with candlelight, oak beams and open fireplaces. There are six guest lounges and plenty of cosy nooks for quiet conversation plus a popular restaurant. The comfortable bedrooms are individually decorated.

Rooms 45 en suite (4 fmly) ❀ in all bedrooms S £100-£130; D £160-£220 (incl. bkfst) **Facilities** 🍴 Wi-fi in bedrooms Xmas **Conf** Thtr 50 Class 18 Board 24 Del from £145 **Parking** 60 **Notes LB** ❀ in restaurant

---

HOVINGHAM   **MAP 19 SE67**

★★★ 71% ❀ **HOTEL**

Worsley Arms

High St YO62 4LA

☎ 01653 628234 📠 01653 628130

e-mail: worsleyarms@aol.com

dir: from S take A64, signed York, towards Malton. At dual carriageway left to Hovingham. At Slingsby left, then 2m. Hotel on main street

Overlooking the village green, this hotel has relaxing and attractive lounges with welcoming open fires. Bedrooms are also comfortable and several are contained in cottages across the green. The restaurant provides interesting quality cooking, with less formal dining in the Cricketers' Bar and Bistro to the rear.

Rooms 12 en suite 8 annexe en suite (2 fmly) (4 GF) ❀ in all bedrooms S £85-£95; D £105-£210 (incl. bkfst) **Facilities** 🎾 Squash Shooting Xmas **Conf** BC Thtr 40 Class 40 Board 20 Del from £95 **Parking** 25 **Notes LB** ❀ in restaurant Civ Wed 75

See advertisement under YORK

HUNMANBY   MAP 17 TA07

★★ 71% HOTEL

Wrangham House Hotel

10 Stonegate YO14 0NS

☎ 01723 891333 📄 01723 892973

e-mail: staciedevos@aol.com

dir: *A64 onto A1039 to Filey. Right onto Hunmanby Rd, hotel behind All Saints Church*

This former Georgian vicarage is only a few minutes' drive from lovely sandy beaches, and stands in beautiful wooded gardens next to the village church. This well-furnished hotel has individually styled bedrooms, a comfortable sitting room and cosy bar. The spacious dining room offers a good selection of well produced dishes.

Rooms 8 en suite 4 annexe en suite (1 fmly) (2 GF) ⊗ in all bedrooms **Conf** Thtr 50 Class 20 Board 20 **Parking** 20 **Notes LB** ⊗ in restaurant Civ Wed 46

KIRKBYMOORSIDE   MAP 19 SE68

★★ 69% HOTEL

George & Dragon Hotel

17 Market Place YO62 6AA

☎ 01751 433334 📄 01751 432933

e-mail: reception@georgeanddragon.net

dir: *off A170 between Thirsk and Scarborough, in town centre*

Set in the market square, this coaching inn dates from the 17th century. With its blazing fire in season and its sporting theme the pub offers a cosy and welcoming atmosphere. A wide range of hearty dishes is offered from both the menu and a specials board. Spacious bedrooms are individually furnished and housed in the quiet courtyard buildings.

Rooms 12 en suite 7 annexe en suite (2 fmly) (3 GF) S £54-£64; D £89-£109 (incl. bkfst) **Facilities** Xmas **Parking** 20 **Notes LB** ⊗ in restaurant

KNARESBOROUGH   MAP 19 SE35

★★★ 78% ⊛ HOTEL

Best Western Dower House

Bond End HG5 9AL

☎ 01423 863302 📄 01423 867665

e-mail: enquiries@bwdowerhouse.co.uk

dir: *A1(M) onto A59 Harrogate Rd. Through Knaresborough, hotel on right after lights at end of high street*

This attractive 15th-century house, now under new ownership, stands in pleasant gardens on the edge of the town. Features such as welcoming real fires enhance its charm and character. Restaurant 48 has a relaxed and comfortable atmosphere and overlooks the garden. There is a cosy bar and comfortable non-smoking lounge. Other facilities include two function rooms and a popular health and leisure club, which has its own lounge bar.

Rooms 28 en suite 3 annexe en suite (2 fmly) (3 GF) ⊗ in 27 bedrooms S £59-£95; D £80-£130 (incl. bkfst) **Facilities** STV 🔲 supervised Sauna Gym Jacuzzi ch fac Xmas **Conf** BC Thtr 65 Class 35 Board 36 Del from £95 **Parking** 100 **Notes LB** ⊛ ⊗ in restaurant Civ Wed 70

★★★ 77% ⊛ ⊛ HOTEL

General Tarleton Inn

Boroughbridge Rd, Ferrensby HG5 0PZ

☎ 01423 340284 📄 01423 340288

e-mail: gti@generaltarleton.co.uk

web: www.generaltarleton.co.uk

dir: *A1(M) junct 48 at Boroughbridge, take A6055 to Knaresborough. Inn 4m on right*

Food is a real feature here with skilfully prepared meals served in the restaurant, traditional bar and modern conservatory. Accommodation is provided in brightly decorated and airy rooms, and the bathrooms are thoughtfully equipped. Enjoying a country location, yet close to the A1(M), ensures the hotel remains popular with both business and leisure guests.

Rooms 14 en suite (7 GF) ⊗ in all bedrooms S £85-£108; D £97-£120 (incl. bkfst) **Conf** Thtr 40 Class 35 Board 20 Del from £140 **Parking** 40 **Notes LB** ⊗ in restaurant

BUDGET HOTEL

Innkeeper's Lodge Harrogate East

Wetherby Rd, Plompton HG5 8LY

☎ 01423 797979 📄 01423 887276

web: www.innkeeperslodge.com

dir: *turn off A658 onto A661 towards Harrogate, lodge on left*

Smart, en suite accommodation ideal for both business & leisure guests. Bedrooms are very well equipped, including Sky TV, telephone, modem points, tea & coffee making facilities, (family rooms in most locations). Complimentary breakfast. The adjacent Pub Restaurant; a Harvester, Vintage Inn, Toby Carvery, Ember Inn, Sizzling Pubco or Pub & Carvery offers an all day menu. See Hotel Groups pages for further details.

Rooms 11 en suite S £55-£57.95; D £55-£57.95

LASTINGHAM   MAP 19 SE79

★★★ 80% HOTEL

Lastingham Grange

YO62 6TH

☎ 01751 417345 & 417402 📄 01751 417358

e-mail: lastinghamgrange@aol.com

dir: *A170 follow signs for Appleton-le-Moors, continue into Lastingham, pass church on left & turn right then left up hill. Hotel on right*

A warm welcome and sincere hospitality have been the hallmarks of this hotel for over 50 years. Antique furniture is plentiful, and the

continued

England

lounge and the dining room both look out onto the terrace and sunken rose garden below. There is a large play area for older children and the moorland views are breathtaking.

Rooms 12 en suite (2 fmly) S £60-£105; D £100-£195 (incl. bkfst) **Facilities** 🍴 Large adventure playground **Parking** 30 **Notes** LB ⊘ in restaurant Closed Dec-Feb

LEEMING BAR MAP 19 SE28

★★ 64% **HOTEL**

The White Rose
Bedale Rd DL7 9AY
☎ 01677 422707 📠 01677 425123
e-mail: john@whiterosehotel.co.uk

dir: turn off A1 onto A684 and turn left towards Northallerton. Hotel 0.25m on left

Conveniently situated just minutes from the A1, this commercial hotel boasts pleasant, well-equipped bedrooms contained in a modern block to the rear. Good-value meals are offered in either the traditional bar or attractive dining room.

Rooms 18 en suite (2 fmly) (1 GF) S £49; D £63 (incl. bkfst) **Facilities** FTV ♫ **Conf** BC **Parking** 50 **Notes** LB ⊘ in restaurant

★★ 🅰

Lodge at Leeming Bar
The Great North Rd DL8 1DT
☎ 01677 422122 📠 01677 424507
e-mail: thelodgeatleemingbar@btinternet.com

dir: Just off A1/A684 junct

Rooms 39 en suite (incl. bkfst) S £45-£80; D £60-£95 **Conf** Thtr 120 Class 50 Board 50 Del from £90

LEYBURN MAP 19 SE19

★ 65% **HOTEL**

Golden Lion
Market Place DL8 5AS
☎ 01969 622161 📠 01969 623836
e-mail: annegoldenlion@aol.com
web: www.thegoldenlion.co.uk

dir: on A684 in market square

Dating back to 1765, this traditional inn overlooks the cobbled market square where weekly markets still take place. Bedrooms, including some family rooms, offer appropriate levels of comfort. The restaurant, with murals depicting scenes of the Dales, offers a good range of meals. Food can also be enjoyed in the cosy bar which is a popular meeting place for local people.

Rooms 15 rms (14 en suite) (5 fmly) S £28-£36; D £56-£72 (incl. bkfst) **Facilities** Wi-fi in bedrooms **Conf** Del from £56 **Services** Lift **Notes** LB ⊘ in restaurant Closed 25 & 26 Dec

LUMBY MAP 16 SE43

★★★ 72% **HOTEL**

Quality Hotel Leeds Selby Fork
LS25 5LF
☎ 01977 682761 📠 01977 685462
e-mail: info@qualityhotelleeds.co.uk

dir: A1M junct 42/A63 signposted Selby, hotel on A63 on left

A modern hotel situated in extensive grounds near the A1/A63 junction. Attractive day rooms include the Seasons Restaurant and the Spa Leisure Club is a popular feature. Service, provided by friendly staff, includes an all-day lounge menu and 24-hour room service.

Rooms 97 en suite (18 fmly) (56 GF) ⊘ in 57 bedrooms S fr £85; D fr £95 **Facilities** 🖥 🏊 Sauna Gym Xmas **Conf** Thtr 160 Class 60 Board 70 Del from £99 **Parking** 230 **Notes** Civ Wed 100

MALHAM MAP 18 SD96

★★ 68% **HOTEL**

The Buck Inn
BD23 4DA
☎ 01729 830317 📠 01729 830670
e-mail: thebuckinn@ukonline.co.uk

dir: A65 to Gargrave, follow Malham signs. 7m to Malham. Hotel in village centre

Situated in the centre of a popular village, this attractive inn is full of character and offers a very friendly welcome. Bedrooms are individual, some with four-poster beds; all are comfortable and well equipped. Imaginative menus offer a good choice of homemade dishes. A wide range of real ales and malt whiskies are served in the two cosy bars.

Rooms 10 en suite (3 fmly) S £40-£50; D £65-£90 (incl. bkfst) **Facilities** Riding **Conf** Del fr £85 **Parking** 25 **Notes** LB ⊛ ⊘ in restaurant Civ Wed 150

MALTON MAP 19 SE77

★★★ 79% ⊛ **COUNTRY HOUSE HOTEL**

Burythorpe House
Burythorpe YO17 9LB
☎ 01653 658200 📠 01653 658204
e-mail: reception@burythorpehousehotel.com
web: www.burythorpehousehotel.com

dir: 4m S of Malton, outside Burythorpe and 4m from A64 (York to Scarborough)

This charming house offers spacious and individually furnished bedrooms. Five rooms are situated in a rear courtyard, two of which are equipped for less able guests, and all benefit from small kitchen areas. Comfortable, spacious lounge areas are provided along with an impressive oak-panelled dining room where interesting, freshly prepared meals are served; meals are also available in the conservatory.

Rooms 11 en suite 5 annexe en suite (2 fmly) (5 GF) ⊘ in all bedrooms S £56; D £78-£120 (incl. bkfst) **Facilities** 🖥 🏊 Snooker Sauna Solarium Gym Xmas **Parking** 40 **Notes** LB ⊘ in restaurant

England

MALTON continued

★★ 64% **HOTEL**

Talbot

Yorkersgate YO17 7AJ

☎ 01653 694031 ▤ 01653 693355

e-mail: sales@englishrosehotels.co.uk

dir: off A64 towards Malton. Hotel on right

Situated close to the centre of town this long-established, creeper-covered hotel looks out towards the River Derwent and open countryside. Bedroom sizes vary, but all are comfortable. The public rooms are traditional and elegantly furnished and include a bar plus a separate lounge.

Rooms 31 en suite (3 fmly) S £55; D £90 (incl. bkfst) **Facilities** Xmas **Conf** Thtr 50 Board 20 Del from £89.50 **Parking** 30 **Notes LB** ⊗ ⊘ in restaurant

★★ 63% **HOTEL**

Green Man

15 Market St YO17 7LY

☎ 01653 600370 ▤ 01653 696006

e-mail: greenman@englishrosehotels.co.uk

dir: from A64 follow signs to Malton town centre. Left into Market St, hotel on left

This friendly hotel set in the centre of town includes an inviting reception lounge where a log fire burns in winter. There is also a cosy bar, and dining takes place in the traditional restaurant at the rear. Bedrooms vary in size and are thoughtfully equipped.

Rooms 24 en suite (4 fmly) S fr £65; D fr £100 (incl. bkfst) **Facilities** Xmas **Conf** Thtr 100 Class 20 Board 40 Del from £85 **Parking** 40 **Notes LB** ⊗ ⊘ in restaurant

MARKINGTON   MAP 19 SE26

★★★ 80% **HOTEL**

Hob Green

HG3 3PJ

☎ 01423 770031 ▤ 01423 771589

e-mail: info@hobgreen.com

web: www.hobgreen.com

dir: from A61, 4m N of Harrogate, left at Wormald Green, follow hotel signs

This hospitable country house is set in delightful gardens amidst rolling countryside midway between Harrogate and Ripon. The inviting lounges boast open fires in season and there is an elegant restaurant

continued

with a small private dining room. The individual bedrooms are very comfortable and come with a host of thoughtful extras.

Rooms 12 en suite (1 fmly) ⊘ in all bedrooms S £90-£95; D £115-£125 **Facilities** FTV ⅏ Wi-fi in bedrooms ch fac Xmas **Conf** Thtr 15 Class 10 Board 10 Del from £145 **Parking** 40 **Notes LB** ⊘ in restaurant Civ Wed 35

See advert under HARROGATE

MASHAM   MAP 19 SE28

INSPECTORS' CHOICE

★★★★ 🏵🏵🏵 **HOTEL**

Swinton Park

HG4 4JH

☎ 01765 680900 ▤ 01765 680901

e-mail: enquiries@swintonpark.com

web: www.swintonpark.com

dir: A1 onto B6267/8 to Masham. Follow signs through town centre & turn right onto Swinton Terrace. 1m past golf course over bridge, up hill. Hotel is on right

Extended during the Victorian and Edwardian eras, the original part of this welcoming castle dates from the 17th century. Bedrooms are luxuriously furnished and come with a host of thoughtful extras. Samuel's restaurant (built by the current owner's great-great-great grandfather) is very elegant and serves imaginative dishes using local produce, much being sourced from the Swinton estate itself.

Rooms 30 en suite (4 fmly) ⊘ in all bedrooms S £150-£350; D £150-£350 (incl. bkfst) **Facilities** Spa STV ♨9 Fishing Riding Snooker Sauna Gym ⅏ Putt green Jacuzzi Wi-fi in bedrooms Shooting, Falconry, Pony Trekking, Cookery school Off-road driving Xmas **Conf** Thtr 120 Class 60 Board 40 Del from £185 **Services** Lift **Parking** 50 **Notes LB** ⊘ in restaurant Civ Wed 120

★★ 68% **HOTEL**

The Kings Head

Market Place HG4 4EF

☎ 01765 689295 ▤ 01765 689070

e-mail: kings.head.6395@thespiritgroup.com

dir: from A1 take the B6267/8 to Masham - follow the Market Place signs

This historic hotel, with its uneven floors, beamed bars and attractive window boxes, looks out over the large market square. Guests have the option of choosing either the elegant bedrooms in the main building or the more contemporary ones at the rear of the property; all rooms are thoughtfully equipped. Public areas are traditional and include a popular bar and smartly appointed restaurant.

continued

Rooms 13 en suite 11 annexe en suite (3 fmly) (9 GF) ⊗ in all bedrooms **Conf** Thtr 40 Class 24 Board 30 **Parking** 3 **Notes** ⊗ in restaurant Civ Wed 40

MIDDLESBROUGH — MAP 19 NZ41

★★★★ 82% **HOTEL**

Thistle Middlesbrough

Fry St TS1 1JH

THISTLE HOTELS

☎ 0870 333 9141 ▤ 0870 333 9241

e-mail: Middlesbrough@Thistle.co.uk

dir: Exit A19 onto A66 signed Middlesbrough. Exit A66 after Zetland car park. 3rd exit at 1st rdbt, 2nd exit at 2nd rdbt.

Here you find that the staff are committed to guest care and nothing is too much trouble. Located close to the town centre and football ground this establishment offers bedrooms, of varying sizes, that are well furnished and comfortably equipped. The contemporary first-floor CoMotion café bar leads into the open plan Gengis restaurant featuring an interesting range of global dishes. Guests have full use of the hotel's Otium health club.

Rooms 132 en suite (12 fmly) ⊗ in 95 bedrooms **Facilities** STV [image] supervised Sauna Solarium Gym Jacuzzi Beautician **Conf** BC Thtr 400 Class 250 Board 50 **Services** Lift air con **Parking** 64 **Notes** ⊗ in restaurant Civ Wed 200

★★★ 73% ⊛ **HOTEL**

Best Western Highfield Hotel

335 Marton Rd TS4 2PA

☎ 01642 817638 ▤ 01642 821219

e-mail: info@thehighfieldhotel.co.uk

web: www.thehighfieldhotel.co.uk

dir: From A66 onto A172 to Stokesley, right at rdbt, straight on at mini rdbt. Left at next mini rdbt, hotel 150yds on right

A newly moderised, small hotel in the residential suburbs offering comfortable and practical bedrooms. Both informal and more formal dining is available in the Terrasse Restaurant and Brasserie. The staff are helpful and friendly.

Rooms 23 en suite (2 fmly) ⊗ in 12 bedrooms S £50-£83; D £60-£100 **Facilities** STV Wi-fi in bedrooms Xmas **Conf** Thtr 170 Class 100 Board 65 Del from £110 **Parking** 100 **Notes LB** ⊛ ⊗ in restaurant Civ Wed 100

MONK FRYSTON — MAP 16 SE52

★★★ 80% **HOTEL**

Monk Fryston Hall

LS25 5DU

☎ 01977 682369 ▤ 01977 683544

e-mail: reception@monkfryston-hotel.co.uk

web: www.monkfrystonhotel.co.uk

dir: A1M junct 42/A63 towards Selby. Monk Fryston village in 2m, hotel on left

This delightful 16th-century mansion house enjoys a peaceful location in 30 acres of grounds, yet is only minutes' drive from the A1. Many original features have been retained and the public rooms are furnished with antique and period pieces. Bedrooms are individually styled and thoughtfully equipped for both business and leisure guests.

Rooms 29 en suite (2 fmly) (5 GF) ⊗ in 20 bedrooms S £95-£105; D £120-£175 (incl. bkfst) **Facilities** STV ⚲ Wi-fi available Xmas **Conf** Thtr 50 Class 20 Board 20 Del from £140 **Parking** 80 **Notes LB** ⊗ in restaurant Civ Wed 72

NORTHALLERTON — MAP 19 SE39

★★★ 68% **HOTEL**

Solberge Hall

Newby Wiske DL7 9ER

☎ 01609 779191 ▤ 01609 780472

e-mail: sales@solbergehall.co.uk

dir: Turn off A1 at Leeming Bar, follow A684, turn right at x-rds, follow road for 2m, hotel on right.

This Grade II listed Georgian country house, now under new ownership, is set in 16 acres of parkland and commands panoramic views over open countryside. Spacious bedrooms, some with four-poster beds, vary in style. Public areas include a comfortable lounge bar and an elegant drawing room. The restaurant offers an interesting range of carefully prepared dishes.

Rooms 24 en suite (2 fmly) (5 GF) ⊗ in 20 bedrooms S £80-£100; D £120-£160 (incl. bkfst) **Facilities** STV ⚲ Xmas **Conf** Thtr 100 Class 20 Board 40 Del from £119.50 **Parking** 100 **Notes LB** ⊗ in restaurant Civ Wed 100

RESTAURANT WITH ROOMS

Three Tuns

9 South End, Osmotherley DL6 3BN

☎ 01609 883301 ▤ 01609 883988

e-mail: enquiries@threetunsrestaurant.co.uk

dir: Turn of A19 signed Northallerton/Osmotherley. Turn at junct signed Osmotherley at Kings Head Hotel. Into village, inn straight ahead.

Situated in the popular village of Osmotherley, this restaurant-with-rooms is full of character. Bedrooms, set above the bar and also in an adjoining building, vary in size but are stylishly furnished in pine and equipped to meet the needs of tourists and business travellers alike. The restaurant offers an imaginative menu of wholesome, modern British dishes.

Rooms 3 en suite 4 annexe en suite (1 fmly) (1 GF) ⊗ in all bedrooms S fr £55; D fr £75 **Parking** 2 **Notes** ⊛

England

PICKERING

MAP 19 SE78

★★★ 81% **HOTEL**

Best Western Forest & Vale

Malton Rd YO18 7DL

☎ 01751 472722 📠 01751 472972

e-mail: forestvale@bestwestern.co.uk

web: www.bw-forestandvalehotel.co.uk

dir: on A169 between York and Pickering at rdbt on outskirts of Pickering

This lovely 18th-century hotel is an excellent base from which to explore the North Yorkshire Moors, one of England's most beautiful retreats. A robust maintenance programme means that the hotel is particularly well kept, inside and out. Bedrooms vary in size and include some spacious 'superior' rooms, including one with a four-poster bed.

Rooms 18 en suite 5 annexe en suite (7 fmly) (5 GF) ❀ in 10 bedrooms S £69-£94; D £99-£160 (incl. bkfst) **Facilities** FTV Wi-fi in bedrooms **Conf** Thtr 120 Class 50 Board 30 Del from £125 **Parking** 70 **Notes LB** ❀ ❀ in restaurant Civ Wed 90

★★ 78% ❀ **HOTEL**

The White Swan Inn

Market Place YO18 7AA

☎ 01751 472288 📠 01751 475554

e-mail: welcome@white-swan.co.uk

web: www.white-swan.co.uk

dir: in town, between church & steam railway station

This 16th-century coaching inn offers well-equipped, comfortable bedrooms, including suites, either of a more traditional style in the main building or modern rooms in the newly refurbished annexe. Service is friendly and attentive and the standard of cuisine high, in both the attractive restaurant and the cosy bar and lounge where log fires burn in the cooler months. A comprehensive wine list specialises in many fine vintages. A private dining room is also available.

continued

Rooms 12 en suite 9 annexe en suite (3 fmly) (8 GF) ❀ in all bedrooms S £89-£129; D £129-£229 (incl. bkfst) **Facilities** FTV Wi-fi in bedrooms Xmas **Conf** Thtr 35 Class 18 Board 25 Del from £135 **Parking** 35 **Notes LB** ❀ in restaurant Civ Wed 40

★★ 74% ❀ **HOTEL**

Fox & Hounds Country Inn

Main St, Sinnington YO62 6SQ

☎ 01751 431577 📠 01751 432791

e-mail: foxhoundsinn@easynet.co.uk

web: www.thefoxandhoundsinn.co.uk

dir: 3m W of Pickering, off A170

This attractive inn lies in the quiet village of Sinnington just off the main road. The smartly maintained, yet traditional public areas are cosy and inviting. The elegant restaurant offers good selections of freshly cooked, modern British dishes and bar meals are also available. Bedrooms and bathrooms are well equipped and offer a good standard of quality and comfort. Service throughout is friendly and attentive.

Rooms 10 en suite (4 GF) ❀ in all bedrooms S £49-£69; D £80-£120 (incl. bkfst) **Parking** 40 **Notes LB** ❀ in restaurant

★★ 72% **HOTEL**

Old Manse

19 Middleton Rd YO18 8AL

☎ 01751 476484 📠 01751 477124

e-mail: the_old_manse@btopenworld.com

dir: A169, left at rdbt, through lights, 1st right into Potter Hill. Follow road to left. From A170 left at 'local traffic only' sign

A peacefully located house standing in mature grounds close to the town centre. It offers a combined dining room and lounge area and comfortable bedrooms that are also well equipped. Expect good hospitality from the resident owners.

Rooms 10 en suite (2 fmly) (2 GF) ❀ in all bedrooms **Facilities** Xmas **Conf** Thtr 20 Class 12 Board 10 **Parking** 12 **Notes** ❀ in restaurant

PICKHILL
MAP 19 SE38

★★ 72% **HOTEL**

Nags Head Country Inn

YO7 4JG

☎ 01845 567391 & 567570 📠 01845 567212

e-mail: reservations@nagsheadpickhill.freeserve.co.uk

web: www.nagsheadpickhill.co.uk

dir: 4m SE of Leeming Bar, 1.25m E of A1

Convenient for the A1, this 200-year-old country inn offers superb hospitality and an extensive range of food either in the bar or the attractive Library Restaurant. The bars, offering a wide range of handpicked wines, are full of character and feature country sports memorabilia. Bedrooms are well equipped and several have been refurbished to a high standard.

Rooms 8 en suite 7 annexe en suite (1 fmly) S £55-£65; D £75-£90 (incl. bkfst) **Facilities** ⚑ Putt green Quoits pitch, Petanque **Conf** BC Thtr 36 Class 18 Board 18 Del from £68.50 **Parking** 50 **Notes LB** ⊗ in restaurant Closed 25 Dec

RAMSGILL
MAP 19 SE17

◉◉◉ **RESTAURANT WITH ROOMS**

Yorke Arms

HG3 5RL

☎ 01423 755243 📠 01423 755330

e-mail: enquiries@yorke-arms.co.uk

web: www.yorke-arms.co.uk

dir: Off B6265 at Pateley at Nidderdale filling station onto Low Wath Rd, signed to Ramsgill 4.5m

A welcoming atmosphere pervades this ivy-clad former hunting lodge overlooking the village green in picturesque Nidderdale. Flagstone floors lead to the cosy bar, and beams and open fires grace the delightful dining rooms where excellent cuisine is matched by caring service. The bedrooms have been refurbished to a high standard.

Rooms 14 en suite (2 fmly) (5 GF) ⊗ in all bedrooms S £100-£150; D £150-£340 **Facilities** Shooting Mountain biking **Conf** Class 20 Board 10 **Parking** 20 **Notes LB** ⊛ RS Sun

RAVENSCAR
MAP 19 NZ90

★★★ 70% **HOTEL**

Raven Hall Country House

YO13 0ET

☎ 01723 870353 📠 01723 870072

e-mail: enquiries@ravenhall.co.uk

web: www.ravenhall.co.uk

dir: from Scarborough take A171 towards Whitby. At Cloughton turn right onto unclassified road to Ravenscar

This impressive cliff top mansion enjoys breathtaking views over Robin Hood's Bay. Extensive well-kept grounds include tennis courts, putting green, swimming pools and historic battlements. The bedrooms vary in size but all are comfortably equipped, many offer panoramic views. The extensive public rooms include the restaurant that enjoys fine views over the bay.

Rooms 52 en suite (20 fmly) (5 GF) ⊗ in 2 bedrooms S £41.50-£75.50; D £83-£151 **Facilities** ⚑ supervised ⚑♪ ⚑ Riding Sauna Gym ⚑ Putt green Bowls, Table tennis Xmas **Conf** Thtr 100 Class 80 Board 40 Del from £71.50 **Services** Lift **Parking** 200 **Notes LB** ⊗ in restaurant Civ Wed 100

REETH
MAP 19 SE09

★★ 71% **SMALL HOTEL**

The Arkleside Hotel

DL11 6SG

☎ 01748 884200 📠 01748 884200

e-mail: info@arklesidehotel.co.uk

dir: Off B6270 on NE corner of village green

Located in Swaledale, midway along Wainwright's Coast to Coast walk, the hotel is popular with walkers and those wishing to explore the beautiful Yorkshire Dales. Converted from three minor's cottages, accommodation includes charming bedrooms, a comfortable lounge, well stocked bar and elegant dining room. The daily changing dinner menu and breakfast make good use of fresh, local ingredients and a warm welcome is assured.

Rooms 8 en suite 1 annexe en suite (2 GF) ⊗ in all bedrooms S £55-£62; D £82-£92 (incl. bkfst) **Facilities** Xmas **Parking** 6 **Notes LB** No children 11yrs ⊗ in restaurant Closed Jan

RICHMOND
MAP 19 NZ10

★★★ 66% **HOTEL**

King's Head

Market Place DL10 4HS

☎ 01748 850220 📠 01748 850635

e-mail: res@kingsheadrichmond.co.uk

dir: exit A1 or A66 at Scotch Corner & take A6108 to Richmond. Follow signs to town centre

Centrally located in the historic market square, this hotel, now under new ownership, is a converted coaching inn. Bedrooms are comfortably furnished. Guests can relax in the elegant lounge, furnished with deep sofas. Afternoon tea is served in the lounge/bar along with good selection of light meals, and the first-floor restaurant offers a varied choice of more formal yet relaxed dining together with views over the square.

Rooms 26 en suite 4 annexe en suite S £65-£85; D £80-£120 (incl. bkfst) **Facilities** Riding Walking Cycling Xmas **Conf** BC Thtr 250 Class 150 Board 100 Del from £90 **Parking** 25 **Notes LB** ⊗ in restaurant Civ Wed 150

England

RICHMOND *continued*

★★ 72% ● **HOTEL**

Frenchgate

59-61 Frenchgate DL10 7AE

☎ 01748 822087 ▤ 01748 823596

e-mail: info@thefrenchgate.co.uk

web: www.thefrenchgate.co.uk

dir: *A1 into Richmond, on A6108 past war memorial on left at lights. 1st left into Lile Close for hotel car park*

A friendly welcome is offered at this elegant Georgian townhouse that sits on a quiet cobbled street. Bedrooms are comfortably equipped. Public areas offer an interesting blend of traditional and modern and include an upstairs lounge with a feature fireplace crafted by the famous 'Mouseman'. Carefully cooked, contemporary dishes are served in the stylish restaurant that features local artwork.

Rooms 8 en suite (1 fmly) (1 GF) ⊗ in all bedrooms S £58-£88; D £98-£108 (incl. bkfst) **Facilities** Xmas **Conf** Thtr 20 Class 20 Board 20 Del from £150 **Parking** 12 **Notes LB** ⊗ ⊗ in restaurant

See advert on opposite page

RIPON   MAP 19 SE37

★★★ 79% **HOTEL**

Best Western Ripon Spa

Park St HG4 2BU

☎ 01765 602172 ▤ 01765 690770

e-mail: spahotel@bronco.co.uk

web: www.bw-riponspa.com

dir: *From A61 follow signs for B6265 towards Fountains Abbey. Hotel on left after hospital*

This privately owned hotel is set in extensive and attractive gardens just a short walk from the city centre. The bedrooms are well equipped to meet the needs of leisure and business travellers alike, while the comfortable lounges are complemented by the convivial atmosphere of the Turf Bar.

Rooms 40 en suite (5 fmly) (4 GF) ⊗ in 8 bedrooms S £98-£123; D £108-£123 (incl. bkfst) **Facilities** STV ⚒ Wi-fi available Free use of local gym - approx 1m away Xmas **Conf** Thtr 150 Class 35 Board 40 Del from £110 **Services** Lift **Parking** 60 **Notes LB** ⊗ in restaurant Civ Wed 150

★★★ 77% ● **HOTEL**

The Old Deanery

Minster Rd HG4 1QS

☎ 01765 600003 ▤ 01765 600027

e-mail: reception@theolddeanery.co.uk

web: www.theolddeanery.co.uk

dir: *A168 onto B6265 to Ripon for 5m. Straight over rdbt, over bridge, right at rdbt, hotel on left*

In the shadow of the cathedral, and close to the Market Square, this sensitive restoration of one of the town's oldest buildings offers modern comfortable facilities and carefully prepared cuisine. Many original features are still evident among the minimalist décor schemes and staff are helpful and friendly.

Rooms 11 en suite ⊗ in all bedrooms S £95; D £110 (incl. bkfst) **Facilities** FTV **Conf** BC Thtr 40 Class 12 Board 22 Del £130 **Parking** 20 **Notes** ⊗ in restaurant RS 25 Dec Civ Wed 50

★★ 62% **HOTEL**

Unicorn

Market Place HG4 1BP

☎ 01765 602202 ▤ 01765 690734

e-mail: info@unicorn-hotel.co.uk

web: www.unicorn-hotel.co.uk

dir: *on SE corner of Market Place, 4m from A1 on A61*

Centrally located in Ripon's ancient market place, this traditional inn dates back 500 years to when it was a coaching house. The busy pub and attractive restaurant feature a wide selection of good-value dishes. Bedrooms are comfortable of mixed styles and all offer the expected amenities.

Rooms 33 en suite (4 fmly) **Facilities** ♫ **Conf** Thtr 60 Class 10 Board 26 **Parking** 20 **Notes LB** ⊗ in restaurant Closed 24-25 Dec

ROSEDALE ABBEY   MAP 19 SE79

★★★ 69% **HOTEL**

Blacksmith's Country Inn

Hartoft End YO18 8EN

☎ 01751 417331 ▤ 01751 417167

e-mail: office@blacksmithsinn.co.uk

web: www.hartoft-bci.co.uk

dir: *off A170 in village of Wrelton, N to Hartoft*

Set amongst the wooded valleys and hillsides of the Yorkshire Moors, this charming hotel offers a choice of popular bars and intimate, cosy lounges, and retains the friendly atmosphere of a country inn. Food is available either in the bars or the spacious restaurant, while bedrooms vary in size all equipped to comfortable modern standards.

Rooms 19 en suite (2 fmly) (4 GF) ⊗ in all bedrooms **Facilities** Fishing **Parking** 100 **Notes LB** ⊗ in restaurant RS Oct-Mar

★★ 72% **HOTEL**

Milburn Arms

YO18 8RA

☎ 01751 417312 ▤ 01751 417541

e-mail: info@milburnarms.co.uk

This attractive inn dates back to the 16th century and enjoys an idyllic, peaceful location in this scenic village. Bedrooms, some of which are located in an adjacent stone block, are spacious, comfortable and

continued

smartly appointed. Guests can enjoy carefully prepared food either in the traditional bar or in the elegant restaurant.

Milburn Arms

Rooms 5 en suite 8 annexe en suite (3 fmly) (4 GF) ⊛ in all bedrooms S £47.50-£62.50; D £80-£120 (incl. bkfst) **Facilities** Xmas **Conf** Thtr 50 Class 20 Board 20 **Parking** 10 **Notes LB** ⊛ in restaurant Civ Wed 100

SALTBURN-BY-THE-SEA   MAP 19 NZ62

★★★ 73% **HOTEL**

Rushpool Hall Hotel

Saltburn Ln TS12 1HD

☎ 01287 624111 ▤ 01287 625255

A grand Victorian mansion nestling in its own grounds and woodlands. Stylish, elegant bedrooms are well equipped and spacious; many enjoy excellent sea views. The interesting public rooms are filled with charm and character, and roaring fires welcome guests in cooler months. The hotel boasts an excellent reputation as a wedding venue thanks to its superb location and experienced event management

Rooms 21 en suite S £75-£85; D £150-£160 (incl. bkfst) **Facilities** STV Fishing ❧ Bird watching, Walking, Jogging Track ch fac Xmas **Conf** Thtr 100 Class 75 Board 60 Del from £115 **Parking** 120 **Notes LB** ⊛ ⊛ in restaurant Civ Wed 110

★★ 69% **HOTEL**

Hunley Hall Golf Club & Hotel

Ings Ln, Brotton TS12 2QQ

☎ 01287 676216 ▤ 01287 678250

e-mail: enquiries@hunleyhall.co.uk

web: www.hunleyhall.co.uk

dir: A174 bypass take left at rdbt with monument, at T-junct turn left, pass church, turn right. 50yds turn right through housing estate, approx 0.5m

Spectacularly situated, this hotel overlooks a 27-hole golf course and beyond to the coastline. The members' bar is licensed and serves

continued

snacks all day, and the restaurant offers a wide choice of food. Bedrooms are comfortable and well equipped.

Rooms 28 en suite (2 fmly) (18 GF) ⊛ in all bedrooms S £47.50-£70; D £75-£105 (incl. bkfst) **Facilities** FTV ♨ 27 Snooker Putt green **Conf** Thtr 20 Class 12 Board 10 Del from £75 **Parking** 100 **Notes LB** ⊛ ⊛ in restaurant RS 24-26 Dec

SCARBOROUGH   MAP 17 TA08

★★★ 75% **HOTEL**

Royal

St Nicholas St YO11 2HE

CLASSIC
BRITISH HOTELS

☎ 01723 364333 & 374374 ▤ 01723 371780

e-mail: royalhotel@englishrosehotels.co.uk

web: www.englishrosehotels.co.uk

dir: A64 into town. Follow town centre/South Bay signs. Hotel opposite town hall

This smart hotel enjoys a central location. Bedrooms are neatly appointed and offer a variety of styles from contemporary to traditional and include some suites. Public areas are elegant and include well-equipped conference and banqueting facilities, a leisure suite and the popular and modern Café Bliss where light snacks are served all day.

Rooms 118 en suite (14 fmly) ⊛ in 16 bedrooms S £49.50-£80; D £130-£250 (incl. bkfst) **Facilities** STV ॼ supervised Sauna Solarium Gym Jacuzzi Wi-fi in bedrooms Steam room, massage available ♬ Xmas **Conf** BC Thtr 300 Class 125 Board 75 Del from £95 **Services** Lift **Notes LB** ⊛ ⊌ in restaurant Civ Wed 150

England

SCARBOROUGH *continued*

★★★ 74% **HOTEL**

The Crescent

2 Belvoir Ter YO11 2PP
☎ 01723 360929 ▤ 01723 354126
e-mail: reception@thecrescenthotel.com
web: www.thecrescenthotel.com

dir: *From A64 towards railway station, follow signs to Brunswick Pavilion. At lights turn into hotel entrance*

This smart Grade II listed hotel is a short distance from the town centre. The comfortable accommodation is comprehensively equipped, and there are spacious bars and lounges. There is a choice of dining areas and bars: Reflections, an elegant restaurant, serves a set-price menu and a carte. A separate carvery, Cooney's, offers a less formal option. Service is caring and attentive.

Rooms 22 en suite ⊛ in 12 bedrooms S £52.50; D £98 (incl. bkfst) **Facilities** Wi-fi available **Conf** Thtr 30 Class 25 Board 25 Del from £95 **Services** Lift **Notes LB** ⊗ No children 6yrs ⊛ in restaurant Closed 25-26 Dec

★★★ 73% ֎ **HOTEL**

Beiderbecke's Hotel

1-3 The Crescent YO11 2PW
☎ 01723 365766 ▤ 01723 367433
e-mail: info@beiderbeckes.com

dir: *in town centre, 200mtrs from railway station*

Situated in a Georgian crescent this hotel is close to all the main attractions. Bedrooms are very smart, well equipped and offer plenty of space and comfort. Some rooms have views over the town to the sea. Marmalade's, the hotel restaurant, offers international cuisine with a modern twist, and hosts live music acts at weekends, including the resident jazz band.

Rooms 27 en suite (1 fmly) ⊛ in 10 bedrooms **Facilities** Snooker ♬ **Conf** Thtr 35 Class 35 Board 28 **Services** Lift **Parking** 18 **Notes LB** ⊗

★★★ 73% **HOTEL**

Ox Pasture Hall

Lady Edith's Dr, Raincliffe Woods YO12 5TD
☎ 01723 365295 ▤ 01723 355156
e-mail: oxpasturehall@btconnect.com
web: www.oxpasturehall.com

dir: *from A171 (Scarborough to Scalby road) turn into Lady Edith's Drive*

This delightful family-run, country hotel is set in the quiet North Riding Forest Park and has a very friendly atmosphere. Bedrooms, split

between the main house, town house and the delightful courtyard, are individual, stylish and comfortably equipped. Public areas include a split-level bar, quiet lounge, and attractive restaurant. There is also an extensive banqueting area licensed for civil weddings.

Ox Pasture Hall

Rooms 17 en suite 6 annexe en suite (1 fmly) (14 GF) ⊛ in all bedrooms S £37.50-£80; D £75-£140 (incl. bkfst) **Facilities** Fishing ♨ Xmas **Conf** Thtr 150 Class 100 Board 80 Del from £80 **Parking** 50 **Notes LB** ⊛ in restaurant Civ Wed 150

★★★ 73% **HOTEL**

Wrea Head Country Hotel

Barmoor Ln, Scalby YO13 0PB
☎ 01723 378211 ▤ 01723 371780
e-mail: wreahead@englishrosehotels.co.uk
web: www.englishrosehotels.co.uk

dir: *from Scarborough follow A171 to hotel sign on left, turn into Barmoor Lane, follow road through ford & hotel entrance is immediately on left*

This elegant country house is situated in 14 acres of grounds and gardens near the Scarborough to Whitby road. Bedrooms are individually furnished and decorated - many have fine views. Public rooms include the oak-panelled lounge with inglenook fireplace and a beautiful library lounge, full of books and games. A conservatory has now been added.

Rooms 20 en suite (2 fmly) (1 GF) **Facilities** STV ♨ Putt green **Conf** Thtr 30 Class 16 Board 20 **Parking** 50 **Notes LB** ⊗ ⊛ in restaurant Civ Wed 50

★★★ 72% **HOTEL**

Palm Court

St Nicholas Cliff YO11 2ES
☎ 01723 368161 ▤ 01723 371547
e-mail: palmcourt@scarborough.co.uk

dir: *follow signs for Town Centre & Town Hall, hotel before Town Hall on right*

The public rooms are spacious and comfortable at this modern, town centre hotel. Traditional cooking is provided in the attractive restaurant and staff are friendly and helpful. Bedrooms are quite delightfully furnished and are also well equipped. Extra facilities include a swimming pool and free, covered parking.

Rooms 40 en suite (7 fmly) **Facilities** 🏊 ♬ Xmas **Conf** Thtr 200 Class 100 Board 60 Del from £75 **Services** Lift **Parking** 80 **Notes** ⊗ ⊛ in restaurant

continued

★★★ 70% **HOTEL**

The Crown Spa

Esplanade YO11 2AG
☎ 01723 357400 📠 01723 357404
e-mail: info@crownspahotel.com
web: www.crownspahotel.com

dir: *on A64 follow town centre signs to lights opp railway station, turn right across Valley Bridge, then 1st left, right up Belmont Rd to cliff top*

This well known hotel offers a superb leisure and spa facility. The hotel's enviable position overlooking the harbour and South Bay means that most of the front facing bedrooms have superb views. The hotel has two restaurants and significant conference facilities.

Rooms 86 en suite (7 fmly) ⊗ in 20 bedrooms S £40-£85; D £59-£130 (incl. bkfst) **Facilities Spa** ✒ supervised Sauna Solarium Gym Jacuzzi Health spa 🎵 Wi-fi in bedrooms **Conf** BC Thtr 200 Class 110 Board 100 Del fr £55 **Services** Lift **Parking** 25 **Notes LB** ⊗ in restaurant Civ Wed 160

★★★ 70% **HOTEL**

Esplanade

Belmont Rd YO11 2AA
☎ 01723 360382 📠 01723 376137
e-mail: enquiries@theesplanade.co.uk

dir: *from town centre over Valley Bridge, left then immediately right onto Belmont Rd, hotel 100mtrs on right*

This large hotel enjoys a superb position overlooking South Bay and the harbour. Both the terrace, leading from the lounge bar, and the restaurant, with its striking oriel window, benefit from magnificent views. Touring groups are also well catered for.

Rooms 73 en suite (9 fmly) S £53; D £100 (incl. bkfst) **Facilities** Table tennis Xmas **Conf** Thtr 140 Class 100 Board 40 Del £70 **Services** Lift **Parking** 15 **Notes LB** ⊗ in restaurant Closed 2 Jan-9 Feb RS 9 Feb-1 March

★★★ 68% **HOTEL**

Ambassador

Centre of the Esplanade YO11 2AY
☎ 01723 362841 📠 01723 366166
e-mail: ask@ambassadorhotelscarborough.co.uk
web: www.ambassadorhotelscarborough.co.uk

dir: *A64, right at 1st small rdbt opposite B&Q, right at next small rdbt, immediate left down Avenue Victoria to Cliff Top*

Standing on the South Cliff with excellent views over the bay, this friendly hotel offers well-equipped bedrooms, some of which are executive rooms. An indoor swimming pool, sauna and solarium are
continued

also available. Entertainment is provided during the summer season.

Ambassador

Rooms 59 en suite (10 fmly) ⊗ in 10 bedrooms S £25-£72; D £50-£144 (incl. bkfst) **Facilities Spa** STV ✒ Sauna Solarium Steam room 🎵 Xmas **Conf** BC Thtr 140 Class 90 Board 60 Del from £55 **Services** Lift air con **Notes** ⊗ in restaurant

See advert on this page

★★★ 68% **HOTEL**

East Ayton Lodge Country House

Moor Ln, Forge Valley YO13 9EW
☎ 01723 864227 📠 01723 862680
e-mail: ealodgehtl@cix.co.uk

dir: *400yds off A170*

Set in three acres of grounds close to the River Derwent and discreetly situated in a quiet lane on the edge of the forest, this hotel is
continued on page 720

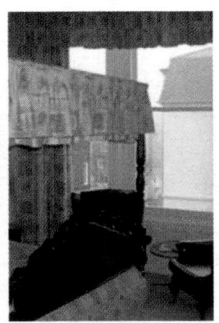

SCARBOROUGH *continued*

constructed around two cottages, the original buildings on the site. Bedrooms are well equipped and those on the courtyard are particularly spacious; public rooms include a large conservatory. A good range of food is available.

East Ayton Lodge Country House

Rooms 12 en suite 14 annexe en suite (5 fmly) (7 GF) ⊗ in 12 bedrooms S £49-£65; D £95-£110 (incl. bkfst) **Facilities** STV Wi-fi available ch fac Xmas **Conf** Thtr 50 Board 30 **Parking** 70 **Notes** ⊗ in restaurant

★★ 74% HOTEL

The Mount

Cliff Bridge Ter, Saint Nicholas Cliff YO11 2HA
☎ 01723 360961 📠 01723 360961

Standing in a superb, elevated position and enjoying magnificent views of the South Bay, this elegant Regency hotel is owned and operated to the highest standard. The richly furnished and comfortable public rooms are inviting, and the well-equipped bedrooms have been attractively decorated. The deluxe rooms are mini-suites that are very spacious and comfortable.

Rooms 50 en suite (5 fmly) ⊗ in 2 bedrooms **Services** Lift **Notes** Closed Jan-mid Mar

See advert on opposite page

★★ 72% HOTEL

Red Lea

Prince of Wales Ter YO11 2AJ
☎ 01723 362431 📠 01723 371230
e-mail: redlea@globalnet.co.uk
web: www.redleahotel.co.uk
dir: *follow South Cliff signs. Prince of Wales Terrace is off Esplanade opposite cliff lift*

This friendly, family-run hotel is situated close to the cliff lift.

continued

Bedrooms are well equipped and comfortably furnished, and many at the front have picturesque views of the coast. There are two large lounges and a spacious dining room in which good-value, traditional food is served.

Rooms 67 en suite (7 fmly) (2 GF) S £52.50-£54.50; D £105-£109 (incl. bkfst & dinner) **Facilities** 🔍 Sauna Solarium Gym Xmas **Conf** Thtr 40 Class 25 Board 25 **Services** Lift **Notes LB** ⊗ ⊗ in restaurant

★★ 69% HOTEL

Park Manor

Northstead Manor Dr YO12 6BB
☎ 01723 372090 📠 01723 500480
e-mail: info@parkmanor.co.uk
web: www.parkmanor.co.uk
dir: *off A165, next to Peasholm Park*

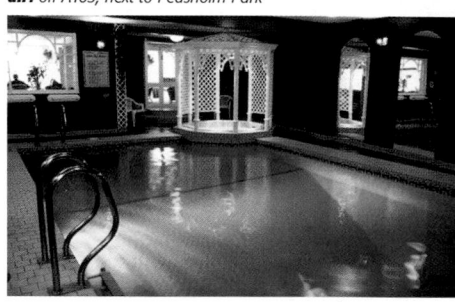

Enjoying a peaceful residential setting with some sea views, this smartly presented, friendly hotel provides the seaside tourist with a wide range of facilities. Bedrooms vary in size and style but all are smartly furnished and well equipped. There is a spacious lounge, smart restaurant, games room and indoor pool and steam room for relaxation.

Rooms 42 en suite (6 fmly) ⊗ in all bedrooms S £36-£42; D £72-£84 (incl. bkfst) **Facilities** Spa 🔍 Pool table Steam room Table tennis Xmas **Conf** Thtr 25 Class 20 Board 20 Del from £55 **Services** Lift **Parking** 20 **Notes LB** ⊗ No children 3yrs ⊗ in restaurant

★★ 68% HOTEL

Bradley Court Hotel

Filey Rd, South Cliff YO11 2SE
☎ 01723 360476 📠 01723 376661
e-mail: info@bradleycourthotel.co.uk
dir: *from A64 into Scarborough, at 1st rdbt right signed Filey & South Cliff, left at next rdbt, hotel 50yds on left*

This popular hotel is only a short walk from both the town centre and the South Cliff promenade. Bedrooms are well equipped and there are spacious public rooms which include a bar lounge and a large, modern function room suitable for weddings and conferences.

Rooms 40 en suite (4 fmly) (8 GF) ⊗ in 30 bedrooms S £30-£60; D £55-£120 (incl. bkfst) **Facilities** Wi-fi available Xmas **Conf** Thtr 100 Class 70 Board 60 Del from £55 **Services** Lift **Parking** 20 **Notes LB** ⊗ ⊗ in restaurant

★★ 68% HOTEL

Clifton

Queens Pde, North Cliff YO12 7HX

☎ 01723 375691 🖹 01723 364203

e-mail: clifton@englishrosehotels.co.uk

dir: on entering town centre, follow signs for North Bay

Standing in an impressive position commanding fine views over the bay, this large holiday hotel is convenient for Peasholm Park and other local leisure attractions; tour groups are especially well catered for. Bedrooms are pleasant and entertainment is provided in the spacious public rooms during high season.

Rooms 71 en suite (11 fmly) **Facilities** Sauna Solarium **Conf** Thtr 120 Class 50 Board 50 **Services** Lift **Parking** 45 **Notes LB** ⊗ ⊘ in restaurant

★★ 65% HOTEL

The Cumberland

Leisureplex

Belmont Rd YO11 2AB

☎ 01723 361826 🖹 01723 500081

e-mail: cumberland.scarborough@alfatravel.co.uk

web: www.alfatravel.co.uk

dir: From A64, turn right on B1437, turn left at A165 towards town centre. Right into Ramshill Road and right into Belmont Rd

On the South Cliff, convenient for the Spa Complex, beach and town centre shops, no smoking bedrooms are comfortably appointed and accessed by lift. Entertainment is provided most evenings and attractive meals are carefully cooked and served in the restaurant.

Rooms 117 en suite (4 fmly) ⊗ in all bedrooms S £34-£40; D £56-£68 (incl. bkfst) **Facilities** FTV ♫ Xmas **Services** Lift **Notes LB** ⊗ ⊘ in restaurant Closed Jan RS Nov, Dec Feb

★★ 65% HOTEL

Manor Heath Hotel

67 Northstead Manor Dr YO12 6AF

☎ 01723 365720 🖹 01723 365720

e-mail: info@manorheath.co.uk

dir: follow signs for North Bay & Peasholm Park, at rdbt for Whitby turn left up hill

A warm welcome is offered at this pleasant, non-smoking, private hotel. Public areas include a comfortable lounge and a relaxing dining room. The bedrooms vary in size and style but all are bright and offer all the expected comforts. Private parking is available.

Rooms 14 en suite (6 fmly) ⊗ in all bedrooms S £24-£34; D £48-£56 (incl. bkfst) **Parking** 11 **Notes** ⊗ ⊘ in restaurant Closed Nov-Jan

★★ 65% HOTEL

Victoria

79 Westborough YO11 1TP

☎ 01723 355495 🖹 01723 378028

e-mail: info@thevictoriahotel.biz

web: www.thevictoriahotel.biz

dir: opposite railway station

Directly opposite the railway station in the centre of town, and handy for The Stephen Joseph Theatre, shops and cricket ground, the hotel has been refurbished to offer comfortable modern bedrooms and

continued

SCARBOROUGH *continued*

public rooms include golf simulators, a pleasant restaurant, and busy locals' bar.

Rooms 16 en suite (3 fmly) ⊛ in all bedrooms S fr £45; D fr £60 (incl. bkfst) **Facilities** 2 Golf simulators ♫ Xmas **Services** Lift **Notes** ⊛ ⊛ in restaurant

See advert on page 721

★★ 63% HOTEL

Delmont

18/19 Blenheim Ter YO12 7HE

☎ 01723 364500 ▤ 01723 363554

e-mail: enquiries@delmonthotel.co.uk

dir: Follow signs to North Bay. At seafront to top of cliff. Hotel near castle

Popular with groups, a friendly welcome is found at this hotel on the North Bay. Bedrooms are comfortable, and many have sea views. There are two lounges, a bar and a spacious dining room in which good-value, traditional food is served along with entertainment on most evenings.

Rooms 51 en suite (18 fmly) (5 GF) S £21-£38; D £42-£76 (incl. bkfst) **Facilities** Games Room with Pool Table, Table Tennis, Dart Board ♫ Xmas **Services** Lift **Parking** 2 **Notes LB** ⊛ in restaurant

★★ 60% HOTEL

Brooklands

Esplanade Gardens, South Cliff YO11 2AW

☎ 01723 376576 ▤ 01723 341093

dir: from A64 York, left at B&Q rdbt, right at next mini-rdbt, 1st left onto Victoria Ave, at end turn left then 2nd left

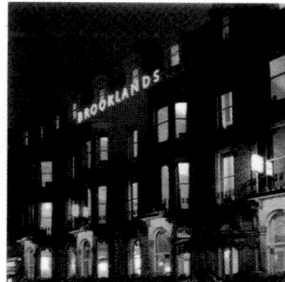

Brooklands is a traditional seaside hotel that also caters for coach tours, and offers good value for money. The hotel stands on the South Cliff overlooking Esplanade Gardens, and has easy access of the sea. There are ample lounges to relax in and entertainment is provided every night.

Rooms 61 en suite (9 fmly) ⊛ in 20 bedrooms **Facilities** Snooker ♫ Xmas **Conf** Thtr 100 Class 40 Board 40 **Services** Lift **Notes** ⊛ in restaurant Closed Jan

---

Ⓤ

Swallow St Nicholas

St Nicholas Cliff YO11 2EU

SWALLOW
HOTELS

☎ 01723 364101 ▤ 01723 500538

e-mail: reservations.scarborough@swallowhotels.com
web: www.swallowhotels.com

dir: In town centre, railway station on right, right at lights, left at next lights, across rdbt, 2nd right, opposite Grand Hotel

At the time of going to press, the star classification for this hotel was not confirmed. Please refer to the AA internet site www.theAA.com for current information.

Rooms 138 en suite (17 fmly) ⊛ in 58 bedrooms S £35-£79; D £60-£135 (incl. bkfst) **Facilities** STV ⦖ supervised Sauna Gym Hair & beauty salon ♫ Xmas **Conf** Thtr 400 Class 150 Board 50 Del from £95 **Services** Lift **Parking** 15 **Notes** ⊛ ⊛ in restaurant Civ Wed 250

SCOTCH CORNER
(NEAR RICHMOND)

MAP 19 NZ20

BUDGET HOTEL

Travelodge Scotch Corner (A1)

Skeeby DL10 5EQ

Travelodge

☎ 08700 850 950 ▤ 0870 1911675

web: www.travelodge.co.uk

dir: off rdbt at junct of A1/A66 southbound

Travelodge offers good quality, good value, modern accommodation. Ideal for families, the spacious en suite bedrooms include remote-control TV, tea and coffee-making facilities and comfortable beds. Meals can be taken at the nearby family restaurant. See Hotel Groups pages for further details.

Rooms 40 en suite S fr £26; D fr £26

Travelodge Scotch Corner Skeeby

Middleton Tyas Ln DL10 6PQ

☎ 08700 850 950 ▤ 01325 377616

dir: On A1 northbound 0.5m S of Scotch Corner

Rooms 50 en suite S fr £26; D fr £26

SKIPTON

MAP 18 SD95

★★★ 79% HOTEL

The Coniston

Coniston Cold BD23 4EB

☎ 01756 748080 ▤ 01756 749487

e-mail: info@theconistonhotel.com

dir: on A65, 6m NW of Skipton

Privately owned and situated on a 1,400 acre estate centred around a
continued

England

beautiful 24-acre lake this hotel offers guests many exciting outdoor activities. The modern bedrooms are comfortable and most have king-size beds. Macleod's Bar and the main restaurant offer all-day meals and fine dining is available in the evening on both carte and fixed-price menus. Staff are very friendly and nothing is too much trouble.

Rooms 50 en suite (13 fmly) (25 GF) ⊛ in 42 bedrooms S £75-£125; D £75-£125 **Facilities** STV Fishing Wi-fi available Clay pigeon shooting, Falconry, fishing Off road Land Rover driving, Xmas **Conf** Thtr 200 Class 80 Board 50 Del from £145 **Parking** 120 **Notes LB** ⊛ in restaurant Civ Wed 100

★★★ 77% HOTEL

Rendezvous

Keighley Rd BD23 2TA
☎ 01756 700100 ≣ 01756 700107
e-mail: admin@rendezvous-skipton.com

Located beside the canal just outside the town, the hotel has the advantage of plenty of parking and good amenities for the leisure guest. Bedrooms are well equipped and spacious, and have delightful views over the rolling countryside. Added attractions include the indoor pool and gym. There are extensive conference facilities.

Rooms 75 en suite (13 fmly) (12 GF) ⊛ in 63 bedrooms S £60-£115; D £60-£115 **Facilities** STV 🏊 supervised Sauna Solarium Gym Jacuzzi Xmas **Conf** Thtr 500 Class 200 Board 120 Del from £105 **Services** Lift **Parking** 120 **Notes LB** ⊗ ⊛ in restaurant Civ Wed 400

★★★ 74% HOTEL

Herriots Hotel

Broughton Rd BD23 1RT
☎ 01756 792781 ≣ 01756 793967
e-mail: info@herriotsforleisure.co.uk
web: www.herriotsforleisure.co.uk
dir: *off A59, opposite railway station*

Close to the centre of the market town, this friendly hotel offers tastefully decorated bedrooms that are well equipped. The open-plan brasserie is a relaxing place in which to dine, and has a varied and interesting menu. Meals and snacks are also available in the bar. The extension includes modern well-equipped bedrooms and a stylish conservatory lounge.

Rooms 23 rms (13 en suite) (3 fmly) S £70; D £95-£135 (incl. bkfst) ⊛ in 18 bedrooms **Conf** BC Thtr 100 Class 50 Board 52 **Services** Lift **Parking** 26 **Notes LB** ⊛ in restaurant Civ Wed 80

England

SKIPTON *continued*

BUDGET HOTEL

Travelodge Skipton

Gargrave Rd BD23 1UD
☎ 08700 850 950 📄 0870 1911676
web: www.travelodge.co.uk

dir: A65/A59 rdbt

Travelodge offers good quality, good value, modern accommodation. Ideal for families, the spacious en suite bedrooms include remote-control TV, tea and coffee-making facilities and comfortable beds. Meals can be taken at the nearby family restaurant. See Hotel Groups pages for further details.

Rooms 32 en suite S fr £26; D fr £26

TADCASTER   MAP 16 SE44

★★★ 77% ◉◉ HOTEL

Hazlewood Castle

Paradise Ln, Hazlewood LS24 9NJ
☎ 01937 535353 📄 01937 530630
e-mail: info@hazlewood-castle.co.uk
web: www.hazlewood-castle.co.uk

dir: signed off A64, W of Tadcaster & before A1/M1 link road

Mentioned in the Domesday Book, this castle is set in 77 acres of parkland. Hospitality and service are keenly delivered and staff are only too happy to assist. Bedrooms, many with private sitting rooms, are split between the main house and other buildings in the courtyard. Dinner provides the highlight of any stay with eclectic, creative dishes.

Rooms 9 en suite 12 annexe en suite (6 fmly) (6 GF) ⊗ in all bedrooms S £140-£280; D £155-£295 (incl. bkfst) **Facilities** STV ✦ Wi-fi in bedrooms Clay pigeon shooting Jogging Walking trails Falconry Archery Castle tour Xmas **Conf** Thtr 160 Class 60 Board 36 Del from £165 **Parking** 150 **Notes LB** ⊗ ⊗ in restaurant Civ Wed 120

THIRSK   MAP 19 SE48

★★ 76% HOTEL

Golden Fleece

42 Market Place YO7 1LL
☎ 01845 523108 📄 01845 523996
e-mail: reservations@goldenfleecehotel.com

dir: off A19 to Thirsk

This delightful hotel began life as a coaching inn, and enjoys a central location in the market square. Bedrooms are comfortably furnished, extremely well equipped and individually styled with beautiful soft furnishings. Guests can eat in the attractive bar, or choose more formal dining in the smart restaurant where there is guaranteed friendly, attentive service.

Rooms 23 en suite (3 fmly) ⊗ in 4 bedrooms S £55-£75; D £70-£90 (incl. bkfst) **Facilities** STV Xmas **Conf** Thtr 75 Class 20 Board 30 Del from £105 **Parking** 35 **Notes LB** ⊗ in restaurant Civ Wed 70

THORNTON WATLASS   MAP 19 SE28

★ 69% HOTEL

Buck Inn

HG4 4AH
☎ 01677 422461 📄 01677 422447
e-mail: innwatlass1@btconnect.com

dir: A684 towards Bedale, B6268 towards Masham, after 2m turn right at x-roads to Thornton Watlass

This traditional country inn is situated on the edge of the village green overlooking the cricket pitch. Cricket prints and old photographs are found throughout and an open fire in the bar adds to the warm and intimate atmosphere. Wholesome lunches and dinners, from an extensive menu, are served in the bar or dining room. Bedrooms are brightly decorated and well equipped.

Rooms 7 rms (5 en suite) (1 fmly) (1 GF) **Facilities** Fishing Quoits Childrens play area ♫ **Conf** Thtr 70 Class 40 Board 30 **Parking** 10 **Notes LB** ⊗ in restaurant Closed 24 & 25 Dec for accommodation

---

TOPCLIFFE   MAP 19 SE37

★★ 71% HOTEL

The Angel Inn

Long St YO7 3RW
☎ 01845 577237 📄 01845 578000
e-mail: info@angelinn.co.uk

dir: turn off A168 (between A1(M) & A19)

Located in the heart of Topcliffe, this attractive inn, with its friendly staff, is popular for its country-style cooking using high quality local produce. There are pleasant bars plus a fine pub water garden. The very comfortable bedrooms are well equipped. A function suite is available for wedding ceremonies, meetings and functions.

Rooms 15 en suite (1 fmly) S £55-£60; D £75 (incl. bkfst) **Facilities** STV **Conf** BC Thtr 150 Class 60 Board 50 Del from £105 **Parking** 150 **Notes LB** ⊗ ⊗ in restaurant Civ Wed 130

WEST WITTON   MAP 19 SE08

★★ 79% ® **HOTEL**

Wensleydale Heifer

Main St DL8 4LS

☎ 01969 622322 01969 622725 📠 01969 624183

e-mail: info@wensleydaleheifer.co.uk

web: www.wensleydaleheifer.co.uk

dir: A1 to Leeming Bar junct, A684 towards Bedale for approx 10m to Leyburn, then towards Hawes, 3.5m to West Witton

New owners have transformed the ground floor of this 17th-century coaching inn, and introducing a light and modern fish restaurant and bistro. A good selection of real ales is offered in the popular and a roaring log fire warms the inviting lounge. Spacious bedrooms are comfortably furnished.

Rooms 9 en suite (3 fmly) ⊗ in all bedrooms S £80; D £98-£120 (incl. bkfst) **Facilities** Xmas **Parking** 40 **Notes LB** ⊗ in restaurant

WHITBY   MAP 19 NZ81

★★★ 80% ® **COUNTRY HOUSE HOTEL**

Dunsley Hall

Dunsley YO21 3TL

☎ 01947 893437 📠 01947 893505

e-mail: reception@dunsleyhall.com

web: www.dunsleyhall.com

dir: 3m N of Whitby, signed off A171

Friendly service is found at this fine country mansion set in a quiet hamlet with coastal views north of Whitby. The house has Gothic overtones and boasts fine woodwork and panelling, no more so than in the magnificent lounge. Two lovely dining rooms offer imaginative dishes and there is also a cosy bar.

Rooms 18 en suite (2 fmly) (2 GF) ⊗ in all bedrooms S fr £87.50; D fr £140 (incl. bkfst) **Facilities** 🎱 ♨ Sauna Solarium Gym ⛳ Putt green Wi-fi available Xmas **Conf** Thtr 95 Class 50 Board 40 Del from £110 **Parking** 30 **Notes LB** ⊗ in restaurant Civ Wed 60

★★★ 75% **HOTEL**

Saxonville

Ladysmith Av, Argyle Rd YO21 3HX

☎ 01947 602631 📠 01947 820523

e-mail: newtons@saxonville.co.uk

web: www.saxonville.co.uk

dir: A174 on to North Promenade. Turn inland at large four towered building visible on West Cliff, turn into Argyle Road, then 1st right

Friendly service is a feature of this long-established holiday hotel. Well maintained throughout it offers comfortable bedrooms and inviting public areas that include a well-proportioned restaurant where quality dinners are served.

Rooms 23 en suite (2 fmly) (1 GF) ⊗ in all bedrooms S £60-£85; D £120-£150 (incl. bkfst) **Conf** Thtr 100 Class 40 Board 40 Del from £90 **Parking** 20 **Notes LB** ⊛ ⊗ in restaurant Closed Dec Jan RS Feb Mar & Nov

★★ 70% **HOTEL**

White House

Upgang Ln, West Cliff YO21 3JJ

☎ 01947 600469 📠 01947 821600

e-mail: enquiries@whitehouse-whitby.co.uk

dir: turn off A171 onto High Stakesby road, follow signs for West Cliff and Sandsend. Hotel adjacent to golf course

Set on the cliff top overlooking the golf course and Sandsend Bay, this hotel has attractive and stylish public rooms. There are two bar areas and a dining room between, with an extensive menu available in all. Bedrooms are smartly presented and include two with balconies and four contained in a converted stone building.

Rooms 11 en suite 5 annexe en suite (5 fmly) (5 GF) S fr £40, D fr £80 (incl. bkfst) **Parking** 30 **Notes LB** ⊛ ⊗ in restaurant

★★ 68% **HOTEL**

Cliffemount

Bank Top Ln, Runswick Bay TS13 5HU

☎ 01947 840103 📠 01947 841025

e-mail: info@cliffemounthotel.co.uk

dir: turn off A174 8m N of Whitby, follow road 1m to end

Enjoying an elevated position above the cliff-side village and with splendid views across the bay, this hotel offers a warm welcome. The cosy bar leads to the restaurant where locally caught fish features on the extensive menus. The bedrooms, many with sea-view balconies, are well equipped with both practical and homely extras.

Rooms 20 en suite (4 fmly) (5 GF) S £35-£65; D £79-£123 (incl. bkfst) **Facilities** FTV Wi-fi in bedrooms Xmas **Parking** 25 **Notes LB** ⊗ in restaurant

England

WHITBY *continued*

★★ 64% HOTEL

Old West Cliff Hotel

42 Crescent Av YO21 3EQ

☎ 01947 603292

e-mail: oldwestcliff@telinco.co.uk

web: www.oldwestcliff.telinco.co.uk

dir: from A171 follow signs for West Cliff, approach spa complex. Hotel 100yds from centre, off Crescent Gardens

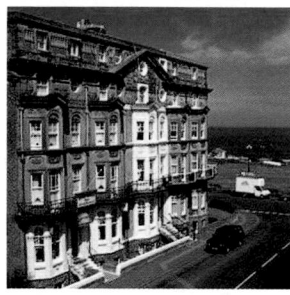

This family owned and run hotel is close to the sea and convenient for the town centre. It provides well-equipped bedrooms, a cosy lounge and separate bar. A wide range of food is served in the cosy basement restaurant.

Rooms 12 en suite (6 fmly) S £52; D £64 (incl. bkfst) **Notes** ⊗ ⊘ in restaurant Closed 24 Dec-31 Jan

⊛ RESTAURANT WITH ROOMS

Estbek House

East Row, Sandsend YO21 3SU

☎ 01947 893424 🖹 01947 893625

e-mail: reservations@estbekhouse.co.uk

dir: On Cleveland Way, within Sandsend, next to East Beck

A speciality seafood restaurant on the first floor is the focus of this listed building in a small coastal village north west of Whitby. Below is a small bar and breakfast room, while up above are four individually presented en suite bedrooms offering luxury and comfort, that vary in size.

Rooms 4 rms (3 en suite) ⊘ in all bedrooms S £50; D £80-£100 **Facilities** Jacuzzi **Parking** 6 **Notes LB** No children 14yrs

See advert on opposite page

YARM

MAP 19 NZ41

INSPECTORS' CHOICE

★★★ ⊛⊛ HOTEL

Judges Country House Hotel

Kirklevington Hall TS15 9LW

☎ 01642 789000 🖹 01642 782878

e-mail: enquiries@judgeshotel.co.uk

web: www.judgeshotel.co.uk

dir: 1.5m from A19. At A67 junct, follow Yarm road, hotel on left

Formerly a lodging for local circuit judges, this gracious mansion lies in landscaped grounds through which a stream runs. Stylish bedrooms are individually decorated and come with 101 extras, including a pet goldfish! The Conservatory restaurant serves award-winning cuisine, and the genuinely caring and attentive service is equally memorable.

Rooms 21 en suite (3 fmly) (5 GF) ⊘ in 10 bedrooms S £137-£150; D £165-£175 **Facilities** STV FTV ⬳ Gym ⬳ Wi-fi in bedrooms Boating, 4x4 hire, mountain bikes, nature trails Xmas **Conf** BC Thtr 200 Class 120 Board 80 Del £225 **Parking** 102 **Notes LB** ⊗ ⊘ in restaurant Civ Wed 200

YORK

MAP 16 SE65

See also Aldwark, Escrick (North Yorkshire), Pocklington & Sutton upon Derwent (East Riding of Yorkshire)

★★★★ 75% HOTEL

York Marriott

Marriott
HOTELS & RESORTS

Tadcaster Rd YO24 1QQ

☎ 01904 701000 🖹 01904 702308

e-mail: mhrs.qqyyk.guestrelationsofficer@marriotthotels.com

web: www.marriott.co.uk

dir: from A64 at York 'West' onto A1036, follow signs to city centre. Approx 1.5m, hotel on right after church and lights

Overlooking the racecourse and Knavesmire Parkland, the hotel offers modern accommodation, including family rooms, all with comfort cooling. Within the hotel, guests enjoy the use of extensive leisure facilities including indoor pool, putting green and tennis court. For those wishing to explore the historic and cultural attractions, the city is less than a mile away.

Rooms 151 en suite (14 fmly) (27 GF) ⊘ in 60 bedrooms S £99-£250 **Facilities** Spa STV ⬚ ⬳ Sauna Solarium Gym Putt green Jacuzzi Wi-fi in bedrooms Beauty treatment ♫ Xmas **Conf** BC Thtr 190 Class 90 Board 40 Del £165 **Services** Lift air con **Parking** 160 **Notes LB** ⊗ ⊘ in restaurant Civ Wed 140

See advert on opposite page

★★★★ 73% **HOTEL**

The Royal York Hotel & Events Centre

Station Rd YO24 2AA

☎ 01904 653681 📠 01904 623503

e-mail: sales.york@principal-hotels.com

web: www.principal-hotels.com

PRINCIPAL
H O T E L S

dir: adjacent to railway station

Situated in three acres of landscaped grounds in the very heart of the city, this Victorian railway hotel has views over the city and York Minster. Contemporary bedrooms are divided between those in the main hotel and the air-conditioned garden mews. There is also a leisure complex and state-of-the-art conference centre.

Rooms 167 en suite (8 fmly) ⊘ in 123 bedrooms S £154; D £169
Facilities STV ⌨ supervised Sauna Solarium Gym Jacuzzi Wi-fi available Steam room Xmas **Conf** BC Thtr 410 Class 250 Board 80 Del from £139
Services Lift **Parking** 80 **Notes LB** ⊘ in restaurant Civ Wed 160

★★★★ 69% **COUNTRY HOUSE HOTEL**

Ramada York

®RAMADA

Shipton Rd, Skelton YO30 1XW

☎ 01904 670222 📠 01904 670311

e-mail: sales.york@ramadajarvis.co.uk

web: www.ramadajarvis.co.uk

dir: Turn off A1237 onto A19, hotel 1m on left

This stylish country-house hotel stands in six acres of private grounds on the outskirts of the city. Bedrooms are comfortably appointed for

continued on page 728

This Charming William IV listed building is situated just minutes away from the hustle and bustle of the town centre.
Twenty four very individual bedrooms
A cosy bar and restaurant overlooking the old English gardens serving the best in Mediterranean / British cuisine.
Open air heated swimming pool
(open May to September)
Hot tub , Sauna and Steam room
(Open all year round)
Beauty treatment Centre
The Mount Royale Hotel ,The Mount ,York ,Yo24 1GU
Tel 01904 628856 Fax 01904 611171
Reservations@mountroyale.co.uk
www.mountroyale.co.uk

York where the Streets are Gates ,The Gates are Bars , And the Bars are Pubs

Built in 1876, with ample free car parking, this 151 four star deluxe bedroom hotel includes 16 Grandstands and two Grandstand Penthouse suites. Relax and unwind in our swimming pool, sauna or steam jacuzzi, or even work up an appetite in our gymnasium and outdoor tennis court.

Tadcaster Road, Dringhouses
York YO24 1QQ
Direct dial: 01904 770611
Email: york@marriotthotels.co.uk

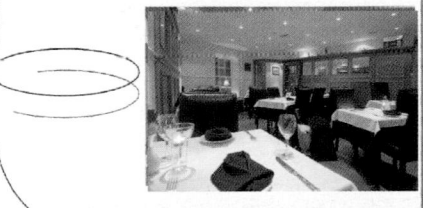

www.estbekhouse.co.uk

Restaurant with Rooms

Rosette awarded restaurant, situated in the beautiful village of Sandsend, 2 miles north of Whitby.

Fresh Wild Fish Policy...

To ensure all fish served at Estbek is of the finest quality we only serve fresh wild fish.

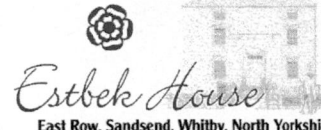

Estbek House

East Row, Sandsend, Whitby, North Yorkshire
Tel: 01947 893424 Fax: 01947 893625

YORK *continued*

both business and leisure guests. There are good conference facilities, a restaurant and ample parking.

Rooms 89 en suite (20 fmly) (24 GF) ⊗ in 65 bedrooms S £69-£119; D £69-£119 **Facilities** STV Wi-fi available Xmas **Conf** Thtr 180 Class 72 Board 60 Del from £125 **Services** Lift **Parking** 130 **Notes LB** ⊗ in restaurant Civ Wed 150

INSPECTORS' CHOICE

★★★ ◉◉◉ **HOTEL**

Middlethorpe Hall & Spa

Bishopthorpe Rd, Middlethorpe YO23 2GB
☎ 01904 641241 ▤ 01904 620176
e-mail: info@middlethorpe.com

dir: A1/A64 follow York West (A1036) signs, then Bishopthorpe/Middlethorpe/racecourse signs

This fine house, dating from the reign of William and Mary, sits in acres of beautifully landscaped gardens. The bedrooms vary in size but all comfortably furnished; some in the main house, some in converted courtyard stables and some in a cottage. Public areas include a stately drawing room, where afternoon tea is quite an event, and an oak-panelled dining room offering inventive food. There is also a small spa.

Rooms 29 en suite (10 GF) ⊗ in 10 bedrooms S £115-£150; D £180-£315 **Facilities** Spa STV ⬚ Sauna Gym ⬚ Jacuzzi Wi-fi in bedrooms Health & Beauty Spa Xmas **Conf** Thtr 56 Class 30 Board 25 Del from £130 **Services** Lift **Parking** 71 **Notes LB** ⊗ No children 6yrs ⊗ in restaurant RS 25 & 31 Dec Civ Wed 56

INSPECTORS' CHOICE

★★★ ◉◉ **HOTEL**

The Grange

1 Clifton YO30 6AA
☎ 01904 644744 ▤ 01904 612453
e-mail: info@grangehotel.co.uk
web: www.grangehotel.co.uk

dir: on A19 York/Thirsk road, approx 500yds from city centre

This bustling Regency town house is just a few minutes' walk from the centre of York. A professional service is efficiently delivered by caring staff in a very friendly and helpful manner. Public rooms are comfortable and have been stylishly furnished; these include three dining options, the popular and informal cellar brasserie, seafood bar and The Ivy, which offers fine dining

continued

---

in a lavishly decorated environment. The individually designed bedrooms are comfortably appointed and have been thoughtfully equipped.

The Grange

Rooms 30 en suite (6 GF) S £115-£260; D £125-£260 (incl. bkfst) **Facilities** STV Wi-fi in bedrooms Discount at local health spa Xmas **Conf** Thtr 60 Class 45 Board 30 Del from £150 **Parking** 26 **Notes LB** ⊗ in restaurant Civ Wed 90

★★★ 85% ◉◉ **HOTEL**

Best Western Dean Court

Duncombe Place YO1 7EF
☎ 01904 625082 ▤ 01904 620305
e-mail: info@deancourt-york.co.uk
web: www.deancourt-york.co.uk

dir: city centre opposite York Minster

This smart hotel enjoys a central location overlooking the Minster. Public areas have been re-furbished in an elegant, contemporary style and include the popular D.C.H. restaurant which enjoys wonderful views of the cathedral. Bedrooms are stylishly appointed. Service is particularly friendly and efficient and light snacks are served all day in Terry's conservatory café. Valet parking is offered.

Rooms 37 en suite (4 fmly) ⊗ in 31 bedrooms S £80-£120; D £125-£205 (incl. bkfst) **Facilities** FTV Wi-fi in bedrooms Xmas **Conf** Thtr 50 Class 10 Board 32 Del from £140 **Services** Lift **Parking** 30 **Notes LB** ⊗ ⊗ in restaurant Civ Wed 60

England

★★★ 79% ◉◉ **HOTEL**

Best Western York Pavilion

45 Main St, Fulford YO10 4PJ

☎ 01904 622099 📄 01904 626939

e-mail: reservations@yorkpavilionhotel.com

web: www.yorkpavilionhotel.com

dir: off A64 York ringroad at A19 junct towards York. Hotel 0.5m on right opposite Pavilion Court

An attractive Georgian hotel situated in its own grounds. All the bedrooms are individually designed to a high specification; some are in the old house and some in the converted stables set around a garden terrace. There is a comfortable lounge, a conference centre and an inviting brasserie-style restaurant with a regularly changing menu.

Rooms 57 en suite (4 fmly) (11 GF) ⊛ in 23 bedrooms S £80-£100; D £110-£150 (incl. bkfst) **Facilities** STV Wi-fi in bedrooms Xmas **Conf** Thtr 150 Class 60 Board 45 **Parking** 40 **Notes LB** ⊗ ⊛ in restaurant Civ Wed 80

See advert on this page

★★★ 78% **HOTEL**

Best Western Kilima Hotel

129 Holgate Rd YO24 4AZ

☎ 01904 625787 📄 01904 612083

e-mail: sales@kilima.co.uk

web: www.kilima.co.uk

dir: on A59, on W outskirts

The Kilima is conveniently situated within easy walking distance of the city centre. There is a relaxed and friendly atmosphere in the hotel, with professional, friendly staff providing attentive service. Bedrooms are comfortable and well equipped. The hotel benefits from private parking and leisure facilities.

Rooms 26 en suite (2 fmly) (10 GF) ⊛ in all bedrooms S £78-£103; D £116-£146 (incl. bkfst) **Facilities** ⊠ Gym Wi-fi in bedrooms Leisure complex, Steam room, Fitness Suite Xmas **Conf** Board 14 Del from £118 **Parking** 26 **Notes LB** ⊗ ⊛ in restaurant

★★★ 78% ◉ **HOTEL**

Parsonage Country House

York Rd YO19 6LF

☎ 01904 728111 📄 01904 728151

e-mail: reservations@parsonagehotel.co.uk

web: www.parsonagehotel.co.uk

(For full entry see Escrick)

See advert on this page

England

YORK *continued*

★★★ 77% **HOTEL**

Best Western Monkbar

Monkbar YO31 7JA
☎ 01904 638086 📠 01904 629195
e-mail: june@monkbarhotel.co.uk

dir: A64 onto A1079 to city, turn right at city wall, take middle lane at lights. Hotel on right

This smart hotel enjoys a prominent position adjacent to the city walls, and just a few minutes' walk from the cathedral. Individually styled bedrooms are well equipped for both business and leisure guests. Spacious public areas include comfortable lounges, an American-style bar, an airy restaurant and impressive meeting and training facilities.

Rooms 99 en suite (3 fmly) ⊛ in 45 bedrooms S £110-£125; D £145-£190 (incl. bkfst) **Facilities** STV FTV Wi-fi in bedrooms Xmas **Conf** Thtr 140 Class 80 Board 50 Del from £110 **Services** Lift **Parking** 70 **Notes LB** ⊛ in restaurant Civ Wed 80

★★★ 74% ⊛ **HOTEL**

Mount Royale

The Mount YO24 1GU
☎ 01904 628856 📠 01904 611171
e-mail: reservations@mountroyale.co.uk
web: www.mountroyale.co.uk

dir: W on A1036, 0.5 mile after racecourse. Hotel on right

This friendly hotel offers comfortable bedrooms in a variety of styles, several leading onto the delightful gardens. Public rooms include a lounge, a meeting room and a cosy bar. There is an outdoor pool, a sauna and a hot tub plus a beauty therapist. There is a separate

continued

restaurant called One 19 The Mount and a cocktail lounge overlooking the gardens (all meals and drinks can be charged to room accounts).

Rooms 24 en suite (3 fmly) (6 GF) ⊛ in all bedrooms S £85-£120; D £97.50-£180 (incl. bkfst) **Facilities** STV FTV ⅄ supervised Sauna Solarium Jacuzzi Wi-fi available Beauty treatment centre, Outdoor Hot-tub ♫ Xmas **Conf** Thtr 35 Board 25 Del from £145 **Parking** 27 **Notes LB** ⊛ in restaurant

See advert on page 727

★★★ 73% **HOTEL**

The Gateway to York

Hull Rd, Kexby YO4 5LD
☎ 01759 388223 📠 01759 388822
e-mail: gatetoyork@aol.com

dir: off A64 onto A1079, 3m from York, hotel on left

Close to York's Park & Ride and the retail shopping outlet, this hotel is set in eight acres of gardens where private fishing is available for residents. Its spacious bedrooms are very comfortable and well equipped including free Wi-fi access. There is a pleasant bar/lounge and a restaurant serving interesting and enjoyable dishes.

Rooms 30 en suite (17 fmly) (14 GF) ⊛ in 22 bedrooms S £40-£55; D £60-£80 (incl. bkfst) **Facilities** STV Wi-fi in bedrooms Riding ch fac Xmas **Conf** Thtr 60 Class 40 Board 40 Del from £79 **Parking** 60 **Notes LB** ⊗ ⊛ in restaurant Closed Jan Civ Wed 70

★★★ 72% **HOTEL**

Novotel York

Fishergate YO10 4FD
☎ 01904 611660 📠 01904 610925
e-mail: H0949@accor-hotels.com
web: www.novotel.com

dir: A19 north to city centre, hotel set back on left

Set just outside the ancient city walls, this modern, family-friendly hotel is conveniently located for visitors to the city. Bedrooms feature bathrooms with separate toilet room, plus excellent desk space and sofa beds. Four rooms are equipped for less able guests. The hotel's facilities include indoor and outdoor children's play areas and an indoor pool.

Rooms 124 en suite (124 fmly) ⊛ in 91 bedrooms **Facilities** STV ⅄ Wi-fi in bedrooms **Conf** BC Thtr 220 Class 100 Board 120 **Services** Lift **Parking** 150

★★★ 70% **HOTEL**

Minster Hotel

60 Bootham YO30 7BZ
☎ 01904 621267 📠 01904 654719
e-mail: info@yorkminsterhotel.co.uk

dir: from A1237 (York outer ringroad) exit A19 N into city centre. Hotel on right 150yds from Bootham Bar

Within easy walking distance of the Minster and the city centre, this careful conversion of two large Victorian houses provides stylish, comfortable and well-equipped bedrooms. There is a cosy bar and a bistro serving imaginative dishes, and conference facilities are also available along with secure parking.

Rooms 31 en suite 3 annexe en suite (10 fmly) (7 GF) ⊛ in all bedrooms S £55-£85; D £69-£150 (incl. bkfst) **Facilities** STV Jacuzzi Wi-fi available **Conf** Thtr 65 Class 45 Board 30 Del fr £79 **Services** Lift **Parking** 35 **Notes LB** ⊗ ⊛ in restaurant

★★ 74% **HOTEL**

Beechwood Close

19 Shipton Rd, Clifton YO30 5RE

☎ 01904 658378 & 627093 📠 01904 647124

e-mail: bch@selcom.co.uk

web: www.beechwood-close.co.uk

dir: on A19 (Thirsk Road, between ring road and city centre) on right entering 30mph zone

This long-established, comfortable hotel, personally managed by the owners, is situated just a mile north of the city centre. It offers spacious, well-equipped and well-maintained bedrooms. There is a cosy bar-lounge, and wide-ranging menus in the dining room.

Rooms 14 en suite (2 fmly) S £49-£52; D £72-£80 (incl. bkfst) **Facilities** STV Wi-fi in bedrooms **Conf** Thtr 50 Class 40 Board 30 Del from £75.60 **Parking** 36 **Notes** LB ⊗ ⊜ in restaurant Closed 25-Dec

★★ 72% **HOTEL**

Alhambra Court

31 St Mary's, Bootham YO30 7DD

☎ 01904 628474 📠 01904 610690

e-mail: enq@alhambracourthotel.co.uk

web: www.alhambracourthotel.co.uk

dir: off A19

In a quiet side road within easy walking distance of the Minster, this attractive Georgian building is pleasantly furnished and the bedrooms are well equipped. Service is careful, friendly and attentive, and the good home cooking and a car park for residents are added bonuses.

Rooms 24 en suite (4 fmly) (4 GF) ⊜ in all bedrooms S £37.50-£62.50; D £55-£105 (incl. bkfst) **Services** Lift **Parking** 25 **Notes** LB ⊗ ⊜ in restaurant Closed 24-31 Dec & 1-7 Jan

★★ 72% **HOTEL**

Clifton Bridge

Water End YO30 6LL

☎ 01904 610510 📠 01904 640208

e-mail: enq@cliftonbridgehotel.co.uk

dir: turn off A1237 onto A19 towards city centre. Right at lights by church, hotel 50yds on left

Standing between Clifton Green and the River Ouse, and within walking distance of the city, this hotel offers good hospitality and attentive service. The house is well furnished and features oak panelling in the public rooms. Bedrooms are attractively decorated and thoughtfully equipped. Good home cooking is served in the cosy dining room.

Rooms 15 en suite (1 fmly) (3 GF) ⊜ in all bedrooms **Conf** Board 12 **Parking** 10 **Notes** ⊜ in restaurant

YORK *continued*

★★ 72% HOTEL

Knavesmire Manor

302 Tadcaster Rd YO24 1HE

☎ 01904 702941 🖹 01904 709274

e-mail: enquire@knavesmire.co.uk

web: www.knavesmiremanorhotel.co.uk

dir: A1036 into city centre. Hotel on right, overlooking racecourse

THE CIRCLE
Selected Individual Hotels

Commanding superb views across York's famous racecourse, this former manor house offers comfortable, well-equipped bedrooms, either in the main house or the garden rooms to the rear. Comfortable day rooms are stylishly furnished, whilst the heated indoor pool provides a popular addition.

Rooms 11 en suite 9 annexe en suite (3 fmly) S £55-£79; D £79-£89 (incl. bkfst) **Facilities** 🏊 Sauna Xmas **Conf** Thtr 40 Class 36 Board 30 Del £99 **Services** Lift **Parking** 28 **Notes LB** ⊘ in restaurant Closed 23-27 Dec Civ Wed 60

★★ 68% HOTEL

Jacobean Lodge

Plainville Ln, Wigginton YO32 2RG

☎ 01904 762749 🖹 01904 768403

e-mail: anthony.heath5@btinternet.com

dir: A64/A1237/B1363 signed to Wigginton. Past Wigginton & Haxby sign. Next left at major junct into Corban Ln. 0.5m right at x-rds into Plainville Ln. Hotel 0.5m on right

This comfortable inn stands in extensive lawned gardens amid open farmland along a quiet lane. The hotel provides comfortable well-equipped bedrooms. Home-cooked meals are available in the pleasant bars or the restaurant, which are well patronised by locals. Small conferences are also catered for.

Rooms 8 en suite **Conf** Thtr 35 Class 20 Board 35 **Parking** 40 **Notes** ⊗ ⊘ in restaurant

★★ 67% HOTEL

Blue Bridge

Fishergate YO10 4AP

☎ 01904 621193 🖹 01904 671571

e-mail: book@bluebridgehotel.co.uk

dir: from A64 (outer ring road) take A19 (York/Selby) S exit into York. Approx 2m, hotel on right

Convenient for the Barbican Centre and within walking distance of the city centre, this hotel provides pine-furnished bedrooms, which include three spacious apartment rooms across the courtyard. Good value breakfast and dinner will satisfy the heartiest of appetites. Residents and diners have their own bar. Private parking is available.

Rooms 19 en suite (4 fmly) (1 GF) ⊘ in 19 bedrooms S £40-£60; D £49-£95 (incl. bkfst) **Facilities** STV Wi-fi available **Parking** 15 **Notes LB** ⊗ ⊘ in restaurant

★★ 67% HOTEL

Lady Anne Middletons Hotel

Skeldergate YO1 6DS

☎ 01904 611570 🖹 01904 613043

e-mail: bookings@ladyannes.co.uk

web: www.ladyannes.co.uk

dir: A1036 towards city centre. Right at City Walls lights, keep left, 1st left before bridge, then 1st left into Cromwell Rd. Hotel on right

This hotel has been created from several listed buildings and is very well located in the centre of York. Bedrooms are comfortably equipped. Among its amenities is a bar-lounge and a dining room where a satisfying range of food is served. An extensive fitness club is also available along with private parking.

Rooms 37 en suite 15 annexe en suite (3 fmly) (12 GF) ⊘ in 54 bedrooms S £65-£85; D £95-£135 (incl. bkfst) **Facilities** 🏊 supervised Sauna Solarium Gym Wi-fi available **Conf** Thtr 100 Class 30 Board 30 Del from £100 **Parking** 40 **Notes LB** ⊗ ⊘ in restaurant Closed 24-29 Dec

BUDGET HOTEL

Innkeeper's Lodge York

Hull Rd YO10 3LF

☎ 01904 411856

web: www.innkeeperslodge.com

Smart, en suite accommodation ideal for both business & leisure guests. Bedrooms are very well equipped, including Sky TV, telephone, modem points, tea & coffee making facilities, (family rooms in most locations). Complimentary breakfast. The adjacent Pub Restaurant; a Harvester, Vintage Inn, Toby Carvery, Ember Inn, Sizzling Pubco or Pub & Carvery offers an all day menu. See Hotel Groups pages for further details.

Rooms 40 en suite S £59; D £59

England

BUDGET HOTEL

Premier Travel Inn York City Centre

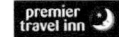

20 Blossom St YO24 1AJ

☎ 0870 9906594 ▤ 0870 9906595

web: www.premiertravelinn.com

dir: *12m from A1 junct 47, off A59. Close to city centre*

High quality, modern budget accommodation ideal for both families and business travellers. Spacious, en suite bedrooms feature bath and shower, satellite TV and many have telephones and modem points. The adjacent family restaurant features a wide and varied menu. For further details consult the Hotel Groups page.

Rooms 86 en suite

Premier Travel Inn York North West

White Rose Close, York Business Park, Nether Poppleton YO26 6RL

☎ 08701 977280 ▤ 01904 787633

dir: *on A1237 between A19 Thirsk road & A59 Harrogate road*

Rooms 44 en suite

BUDGET HOTEL

Travelodge York Central

90 Piccadilly YO1 9NX

☎ 08700 850 950 ▤ 01904 652171

web: www.travelodge.co.uk

dir: *Exit A1(M) follow A64, 3rd turn for A19, York*

Travelodge offers good quality, good value, modern accommodation. Ideal for families, the spacious en suite bedrooms include remote-control TV, tea and coffee-making facilities and comfortable beds. Meals can be taken at the nearby family restaurant. See Hotel Groups pages for further details.

Rooms 90 en suite S fr £26; D fr £26

YORKSHIRE, SOUTH

BARNSLEY   **MAP 16 SE30**

See also Tankersley

★★★★ 75% HOTEL

Tankersley Manor

Church Ln S75 3DQ

☎ 01226 744700 ▤ 01226 745405

e-mail: tankersley@marstonhotels.com

web: www.marstonhotels.com

(For full entry see Tankersley, South Yorkshire)

See advert on this page

★★★ 78% HOTEL

Ardsley House

Doncaster Rd, Ardsley S71 5EH

☎ 01226 309955 ▤ 01226 205374

e-mail: ardsley.house@forestdale.com

web: www.forestdale.com

dir: *on A635, 0.75m from Stairfoot rdbt*

Quietly situated on the Barnsley to Doncaster road, this hotel has

continued

many regular customers. Comfortable and well-equipped bedrooms, excellent leisure facilities including a gym and pool, and good conference facilities are just some of the attractions here. Public rooms include a choice of bars and a busy restaurant.

Rooms 75 en suite (12 fmly) (14 GF) ⊘ in 50 bedrooms **Facilities** STV ▣ supervised Sauna Solarium Gym Jacuzzi Wi-fi in bedrooms Beauty Spa ♫ Xmas **Conf** Thtr 350 Class 250 Board 40 Del £135 **Parking** 200 **Notes** Civ Wed 250

BUDGET HOTEL

Premier Travel Inn Barnsley

Meadow Gate, Dearne Valley, Wombwell S73 0UN

☎ 08701 977024 ▤ 01226 273810

web: www.premiertravelinn.com

dir: *M1 junct 36, eastbound. Take A6195 (A635) to Doncaster for 5 miles. Inn is adjacent to rdbt*

High quality, modern budget accommodation ideal for both families and business travellers. Spacious, en suite bedrooms feature bath and shower, satellite TV and many have telephones and modem points. The adjacent family restaurant features a wide and varied menu. For further details consult the Hotel Groups page.

Rooms 41 en suite

England

BARNSLEY *continued*

BUDGET HOTEL

Travelodge Barnsley

School St S70 3PE

☎ 08700 850 950 📠 01226 298799

web: www.travelodge.co.uk

dir: at Stairfoot rdbt A633/A635

Travelodge offers good quality, good value, modern accommodation. Ideal for families, the spacious en suite bedrooms include remote-control TV, tea and coffee-making facilities and comfortable beds. Meals can be taken at the nearby family restaurant. See Hotel Groups pages for further details.

Rooms 32 en suite S fr £26; D fr £26

CARCROFT   MAP 16 SE50

BUDGET HOTEL

Travelodge Doncaster

Great North Rd DN6 9LF

☎ 08700 850 950 📠 0870 1911631

web: www.travelodge.co.uk

dir: on A1 northbound

Travelodge offers good quality, good value, modern accommodation. Ideal for families, the spacious en suite bedrooms include remote-control TV, tea and coffee-making facilities and comfortable beds. Meals can be taken at the nearby family restaurant. See Hotel Groups pages for further details.

Rooms 40 en suite S fr £26; D fr £26

DONCASTER   MAP 16 SE50

★★★ 77% HOTEL

Holiday Inn Doncaster A1(M) Jct 36

High Rd, Warmsworth DN4 9UX

☎ 0870 442 8761 & 01302 799988 📠 01302 310197

e-mail: hidoncaster@qmh-hotels.com

dir: 200mtrs W off A1(M) junct 36

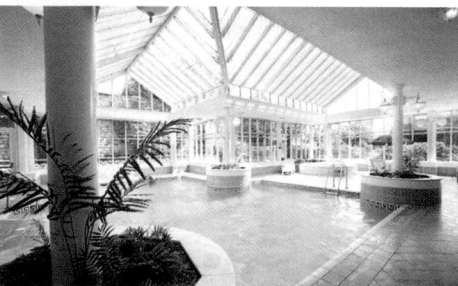

This hotel is situated in the grounds of the 17th-century Warmsworth Hall, which has been splendidly restored and is used as the meetings centre. All of the bedrooms have been refurbished and are very well appointed and have air conditioning; there are also rooms designed for disabled guests. The restaurant provides a wide range of dishes

continued

and the informal atmosphere makes a comfortable and relaxing environment.

Rooms 102 en suite (6 fmly) (22 GF) ⊗ in 90 bedrooms S £65-£150; D £65-£150 **Facilities** STV 🏊 supervised Sauna Gym Jacuzzi Beautician Steam room ch fac **Conf** Thtr 300 Class 250 Board 100 **Services** Lift Parking 250 **Notes** LB ⊗ ⊗ in restaurant Civ Wed 250

★★★ 74% HOTEL

Regent

Regent Square DN1 2DS

☎ 01302 364180 📠 01302 322331

e-mail: reservations@theregenthotel.co.uk

web: www.theregenthotel.co.uk

dir: on corner of A630 & A638, 1m from racecourse

This town centre hotel overlooks a delightful small square. Public rooms include the modern style bar and delightful restaurant, where an interesting range of dishes is offered. Service is friendly and attentive. Modern bedrooms have been furnished in a contemporary style and offer high levels of comfort.

Rooms 52 en suite (6 fmly) (8 GF) S £65-£95; D £75-£110 (incl. bkfst) **Facilities** STV Wi-fi available 🎵 **Conf** Thtr 150 Class 50 Board 40 Del from £125 **Services** Lift **Parking** 20 **Notes** LB ⊗ in restaurant Closed 25 Dec & 1 Jan RS Bank Hols Civ Wed 100

★★★ 70% HOTEL

Danum

High St DN1 1DN

☎ 01302 342261 📠 01302 329034

e-mail: info@danumhotel.com

web: www.danumhotel.co.uk

dir: M18 junct 3, A6182 to Doncaster. Over rdbt, right at next. Right at 'give way' sign, left at mini rdbt, hotel ahead

Situated in the centre of the town, this Edwardian hotel offers spacious public rooms together with soundly equipped accommodation. A pleasant restaurant on the first floor serves quality dinners, and especially negotiated rates at a local leisure centre are offered.

Rooms 64 en suite (5 fmly) ⊗ in 12 bedrooms S £65-£85; D £80-£105 (incl. bkfst) **Facilities** STV Jacuzzi Wi-fi in bedrooms Special rates with Cannons health club 🎵 Xmas **Conf** Thtr 350 Class 160 Board 100 Del from £80 **Services** Lift **Parking** 36 **Notes** LB RS 26 Dec-30 Dec (B&B only) Civ Wed 250

★★★ 66% HOTEL

Grand St Leger

Bennetthorpe DN2 6AX

☎ 01302 364111 📠 01302 329865

e-mail: sales@grandstleger.com

web: www.grandstleger.com

dir: follow Doncaster Racecourse signs, at Racecourse rdbt hotel on corner

This friendly hotel is located next to the racecourse and is only ten minutes' walk from the town centre. There is a cheerful bar-lounge and an elegant restaurant offering an extensive choice of dishes. The bedrooms are comfortable and thoughtfully equipped.

Rooms 20 en suite ⊗ in all bedrooms S £55-£65; D £60-£135 (incl. bkfst) **Facilities** ch fac **Conf** Thtr 80 Class 50 Board 50 Del from £90 **Parking** 28 **Notes** LB ⊗ ⊗ in restaurant RS Xmas Day (open for lunch only) Civ Wed 60

BUDGET HOTEL

Campanile

Doncaster Leisure Park, Bawtry Rd DN4 7PD
☎ 01302 370770 ◫ 01302 370813
e-mail: doncaster@campanile-hotels.com
web: www.campanile.com

dir: follow signs to Doncaster Leisure Centre, left at rdbt before Dome complex

This modern building offers accommodation in smart, well-equipped bedrooms, all with en suite bathrooms. Refreshments may be taken at the informal Bistro. For further details consult the Hotel Groups page.

Rooms 50 en suite **Conf** Thtr 20 Class 18 Board 10 Del from £55

BUDGET HOTEL

Innkeeper's Lodge Doncaster

Bawtry Rd, Bessacarr DN4 7BS
☎ 01302 370037
web: www.innkeeperslodge.com

Smart, en suite accommodation ideal for both business & leisure guests. Bedrooms are very well equipped, including Sky TV, telephone, modem points, tea & coffee making facilities, (family rooms in most locations). Complimentary breakfast. The adjacent Pub Restaurant; a Harvester, Vintage Inn, Toby Carvery, Ember Inn, Sizzling Pubco or Pub & Carvery offers an all day menu. See Hotel Groups pages for further details.

Rooms 24 rms S £45-£52.95; D £45-£52.95 **Conf** Thtr 40 Class 30 Board 20

BUDGET HOTEL

Premier Travel Inn Doncaster

Wilmington Dr, Doncaster Carr DN4 5PJ
☎ 08701 977074 ◫ 01302 364811
web: www.premiertravelinn.com

dir: off A6182 near junct with access road to M18 junct 3

High quality, modern budget accommodation ideal for both families and business travellers. Spacious, en suite bedrooms feature bath and shower, satellite TV and many have telephones and modem points. The adjacent family restaurant features a wide and varied menu. For further details consult the Hotel Groups page.

Rooms 42 en suite **Conf** Class 32

BUDGET HOTEL

Travelodge Doncaster (M18/M180)

DN8 5GS
☎ 08700 850 950 ◫ 01302 845469
web: www.travelodge.co.uk

dir: M18 junct 5/M180

Travelodge offers good quality, good value, modern accommodation. Ideal for families, the spacious en suite bedrooms include remote-control TV, tea and coffee-making facilities and comfortable beds. Meals can be taken at the nearby family restaurant. See Hotel Groups pages for further details.

Rooms 39 en suite S fr £26; D fr £26

MEXBOROUGH
MAP 16 SE40

★★ 65% HOTEL

Pastures

Pastures Rd S64 0JJ
☎ 01709 577707 ◫ 01709 577795
e-mail: info@pastureshotel.co.uk
web: www.pastureshotel.co.uk

dir: 0.5m from town centre on A6023, left by ATS Tyres, signed Denaby Ings & Cadeby. Hotel on right

This private hotel has a modern, purpose-built block of bedrooms and a separate lodge where food is served. It is in a rural setting beside a working canal and convenient for Doncaster or the Dearne Valley with its nature reserves and leisure centre. Compact bedrooms are quiet, comfortable and equipped with many modern facilities.

Rooms 29 en suite (6 fmly) (14 GF) ⊗ in 21 bedrooms S fr £47.50; D fr £47.50 **Facilities** STV **Conf** Thtr 250 Class 170 Board 100 Del from £79 **Services** Lift **Parking** 155 **Notes** ⊗ Civ Wed 200

ROSSINGTON
MAP 16 SK69

★★★★ 77% ⊛ HOTEL

Best Western Mount Pleasant

Great North Rd DN11 0HW
☎ 01302 868696 & 868219 ◫ 01302 865130
e-mail: reception@mountpleasant.co.uk
web: www.mountpleasant.co.uk

dir: on A638 Great North Rd between Bawtry and Doncaster

This charming 18th-century house stands in 100 acres of wooded parkland. The spacious bedrooms have been thoughtfully equipped and pleasantly furnished; the premier bedrooms being particularly comfortable. Public rooms include an elegant restaurant and a very comfortable bar lounge. The hotel has extensive conference facilities and a licence for civil weddings.

Rooms 57 en suite (12 fmly) (28 GF) ⊗ in 56 bedrooms S £79-£125; D £99-£150 (incl. bkfst) **Facilities** STV FTV Wi-fi available Beauty Therapy Full range of Treatments **Conf** BC Thtr 200 Class 70 Board 70 Del from £145 **Services** Lift **Parking** 100 **Notes** LB ⊗ ⊗ in restaurant Closed 25-Dec RS 24-Dec Civ Wed 150

ROTHERHAM   MAP 16 SK49

★★★★ 71% **HOTEL**

Hellaby Hall

Old Hellaby Ln, Hellaby S66 8SN

☎ 01709 702701 📠 01709 700979

e-mail: reservations@hellabyhallhotel.co.uk

web: www.hellabyhallhotel.co.uk

dir: 1m off M18 junct 1, onto A631 towards Maltby, in Hellaby

This 17th-century house was built to a Flemish design with high, beamed ceilings, and staircases which lead off to private meeting rooms and a series of oak-panelled lounges. Bedrooms are elegant and well equipped and guests can dine in the formal Attic Restaurant. There are extensive leisure facilities and conference areas, and the hotel holds a licence for civil weddings.

Rooms 90 en suite (2 fmly) (17 GF) ⊘ in 71 bedrooms S £45-£99; D £79-£115 (incl. bkfst) **Facilities** Spa STV 🏊 supervised Sauna Solarium Gym Beauty room Xmas **Conf** Thtr 500 Class 300 Board 150 Del from £130 **Services** Lift **Parking** 250 **Notes** LB ⊗ ⊘ in restaurant Civ Wed 200

See advert on opposite page

★★★ 79% **HOTEL**

Best Western Consort Hotel

Brampton Rd, Thurcroft S66 9JA

☎ 01709 530022 📠 01709 531529

e-mail: info@consorthotel.com

web: www.consorthotel.com

dir: M18 junct 1, right towards Bawtry on A631. 250yds to rdbt in 200yds turn left then 1.5m to x-rds, hotel opposite

Bedrooms at this modern, friendly hotel are comfortable, attractive and air-conditioned, and include ten superior rooms. A wide range of dishes is served in the open-plan bar and restaurant, and there is a comfortable foyer lounge. There are good conference and function facilities, and entertainment evenings are often hosted here.

Rooms 27 en suite (2 fmly) (9 GF) ⊘ in 15 bedrooms S £54-£80; D £75-£89 (incl. bkfst) **Facilities** FTV Wi-fi in bedrooms ♫ **Conf** Thtr 300 Class 120 Board 50 Del from £85 **Services** air con **Parking** 90 **Notes** LB ⊗ ⊘ in restaurant Civ Wed 300

See advert on opposite page

★★★ 77% **HOTEL**

Best Western Elton

Main St, Bramley S66 2SF

☎ 01709 545681 📠 01709 549100

e-mail: bestwestern.eltonhotel@btinternet.com

web: www.bw-eltonhotel.co.uk

dir: M18 junct 1 follow A631 Rotherham, turn right to Ravenfield, hotel at end of Bramley village, follow brown signs

Within easy reach of the M18, this welcoming, stone-built hotel is set in well-tended gardens. The Elton offers good modern accommodation, with larger rooms in the extension that are particularly comfortable and well equipped. A civil licence is held for wedding ceremonies and conference rooms are available.

Rooms 13 en suite 16 annexe en suite (4 fmly) (11 GF) ⊘ in 11 bedrooms S £55-£90; D £76-£96 (incl. bkfst) **Facilities** STV Wi-fi in bedrooms **Conf** Thtr 55 Class 24 Board 26 Del from £105 **Parking** 48 **Notes** LB ⊘ in restaurant Civ Wed 48

★★★ 74% **HOTEL**

Carlton Park

102/104 Moorgate Rd S60 2BG

☎ 01709 849955 📠 01709 368960

e-mail: reservations@carltonparkhotel.com

dir: M1 junct 33, onto A631, then A618. Hotel 800yds past hospital

This modern hotel is situated in a pleasant residential area of the town, close to the District General Hospital, yet within minutes of the M1. Bedrooms and bathrooms offer very modern comfort and facilities. Three have separate sitting rooms. The restaurant and bar provide a lively atmosphere, and are popular with locals.

Rooms 80 en suite (14 fmly) (16 GF) ⊘ in 64 bedrooms S £82; D £92 (incl. bkfst) **Facilities** STV 🏊 Sauna Solarium Gym Jacuzzi ♫ Xmas **Conf** Thtr 250 Class 160 Board 60 Del from £99 **Services** Lift **Parking** 120 **Notes** LB ⊗ ⊘ in restaurant Civ Wed 100

★★★ 73% **HOTEL**

Courtyard by Marriott, Rotherham

West Bawtry Rd S60 4NA

☎ 0870 400 7235 📠 0870 400 7335

web: www.kewgreen.co.uk

dir: M1 junct 33, A630 towards Rotherham, hotel 0.5m on right

Stylish and contemporary, this modern hotel is well located just five minutes from the motorway. Bedrooms are spacious and boast an excellent range of facilities. Guests have the use of the leisure club with its large swimming pool, spa bath and steam room.

Rooms 104 en suite (10 fmly) (22 GF) ⊘ in 76 bedrooms **Facilities** Spa STV 🏊 supervised Solarium Gym Steam room Children's pool **Conf** BC Thtr 300 Class 120 Board 40 **Services** Lift **Parking** 222 **Notes** LB ⊗ Civ Wed 70

★★ 67% **HOTEL**

Restover Lodge

Hellaby Industrial Estate, Lowton Way, off Denby Way
S66 8RY

☎ 01709 700255 🖷 01709 545169

e-mail: rotherham@envergure.co.uk

dir: *M18 junct 1. Follow signs for Maltby. Left at lights, 2nd on left*

This modern building offers accommodation in smart, well equipped bedrooms, all with en suite bathrooms. Refreshments may be taken at the informal restaurant or bar.

Rooms 50 en suite (12 fmly) ⊘ in 35 bedrooms S fr £45; D fr £45
Facilities STV FTV Wi-fi available Xmas **Conf** Thtr 40 Class 35 Board 30
Parking 40

BUDGET HOTEL

Hotel Ibis Rotherham

Moorhead Way, Bramley S66 1YY

☎ 01709 730333 🖷 01709 730444

e-mail: H3163@accor-hotels.com

web: www.ibishotel.com

dir: *M18 junct 1, left at rdbt & left at 1st lights*

Modern, budget hotel offering comfortable accommodation in bright and practical bedrooms. Breakfast is self-service and dinner is available in the restaurant. For further details, consult the Hotel Groups page.

Rooms 86 en suite **Conf** Thtr 40 Class 30 Board 30

BUDGET HOTEL

Premier Travel Inn Rotherham premier travel inn

Bawtry Rd S65 3JB

☎ 08701 977222 🖷 01709 531546

web: www.premiertravelinn.com

dir: *on A631 towards Wickersley, between M18 junct 1 & M1 junct 33*

High quality, modern budget accommodation ideal for both families and business travellers. Spacious, en suite bedrooms feature bath and shower, satellite TV and many have telephones and modem points. The adjacent family restaurant features a wide and varied menu. For further details consult the Hotel Groups page.

Rooms 37 en suite

SHEFFIELD   MAP 16 SK49

★★★★ 76% **HOTEL**

Sheffield Marriott Hotel   **Marriott.**
                                    HOTELS & RESORTS
Kenwood Rd S7 1NQ

☎ 0870 400 7261 🖷 0870 400 7361

e-mail: mhrs.szdfs.eventsorganiser@marriotthotels.com

web: www.marriott.co.uk

dir: *follow A61 S past station, ring road Barnsley into St Marys Rd. At rdbt straight across, left into London Rd, right at lights, at hill top straight on 1st & 2nd rdbt*

A smart, modern hotel peacefully located in a residential suburb a few miles from the city centre. Stylishly decorated bedrooms are spacious, quiet and are all very well equipped. The hotel also has an extensive

continued on page 738

England

SHEFFIELD *continued*

range of leisure and meeting facilities, and secure parking is located in extensive landscaped gardens.

Rooms 114 en suite (14 fmly) (27 GF) ✆ in 90 bedrooms S £70-£129; D £90-£139 **Facilities** Spa STV ⬡ Fishing Sauna Solarium Gym ⚄ Jacuzzi Wi-fi available Steam room, Health & beauty treatments ♫ **Conf** Thtr 250 Class 100 Board 60 Del from £135 **Services** Lift **Parking** 200 **Notes** LB ⊘ in restaurant Civ Wed 200

★★★★ 75% HOTEL

Macdonald St. Paul's Hotel

MACDONALD HOTELS & RESORTS

119 Norfolk St S1 2JE

☎ 0870 122 6585 & 0114 278 2000 📄 0870 122 6586

e-mail: general.stpauls@macdonald-hotels.co.uk

web: www.macdonald-hotels.co.uk

Located right next to the city's Winter Garden and Millennium Galleries, this brand new hotel offers luxurious rooms with contemporary decor and state-of-the-art facilities that include broadband access and plasma screen TVs. The hotel has two restaurants: Zucca, offering Italian food, and The Yard which is a seafood and steak restaurant. Guests can also unwind in The Champagne Bar or coffee bar.

Rooms 161 en suite (33 fmly) ✆ in all bedrooms S £104-£185; D £104-£185 (incl. bkfst) **Facilities** Spa STV ⬡ Sauna Gym Xmas **Conf** BC Thtr 600 Class 450 Board 30 **Services** Lift air con **Notes** ⊘ in restaurant Civ Wed 400

★★★★ Ⓐ

Holiday Inn Royal Victoria

Holiday Inn
HOTELS · RESORTS

Victoria Station Rd S4 7YE

☎ 0114 276 8822 📄 0114 2724519

e-mail: stay@holidayinnsheffield.co.uk

dir: M1 junct 33, take A57 to city centre. At rdbt follow signs to hotel

Rooms 83 en suite 24 annexe en suite (43 fmly) ✆ in 87 bedrooms S £78-£145; D £78-£145 (incl. bkfst) **Facilities** STV Sauna Gym Wi-fi in bedrooms Beauty salon Xmas **Conf** Thtr 400 Class 200 Board 45 Del from £138 **Services** Lift **Parking** 240 **Notes** ⊗ ⊘ in restaurant

★★★ 79% ⊛ HOTEL

Staindrop Lodge

Ln End, Chapeltown S35 3UH

☎ 0114 284 3111 📄 0114 284 3110

e-mail: info@staindroplodge.co.uk

dir: M1 junct 35, take A629 for 1m, straight over 1st rdbt, right at 2nd rdbt, hotel approx 0.5m on right

This bar, brasserie and hotel offers smart modern public areas and accommodation. An art deco theme continues throughout the open-plan public rooms and the comfortably appointed, spacious bedrooms. Service is relaxed and friendly, and all-day menus are available.

Rooms 32 en suite (6 fmly) (3 GF) ✆ in 26 bedrooms **Facilities** STV **Conf** Thtr 80 Class 60 Board 40 **Services** Lift air con **Parking** 80 **Notes** LB ⊗ ⊘ in restaurant Civ Wed 80

★★★ 77% HOTEL

Best Western Mosborough Hall

Best Western

High St, Mosborough S20 5EA

☎ 0114 248 4353 📄 0114 247 9759

e-mail: hotel@mosboroughhall.co.uk

web: www.mosboroughhall.co.uk

dir: M1 junct 30, take A6135 towards Sheffield. Follow Eckrington/Mosborough signs. Sharp bend at top of hill, hotel set back on right

This 16th-century, Grade II listed manor house is set in gardens not far from the M1 and is convenient for the city centre. Most bedrooms are newly appointed and offer very high quality and amenities; some are very spacious. There is a galleried bar and conservatory lounge, and freshly prepared dishes are served in the traditional style dining room.

Rooms 47 en suite (1 fmly) (16 GF) ✆ in 41 bedrooms S £75-£120; D £75-£120 **Facilities** Wi-fi in bedrooms Xmas **Conf** Thtr 300 Class 125 Board 70 Del from £95 **Parking** 100 **Notes** LB ⊘ in restaurant Civ Wed 250

★★★ 74% HOTEL

Whitley Hall

Elliott Ln, Grenoside S35 8NR

☎ 0114 245 4444 📄 0114 245 5414

e-mail: reservations@whitleyhall.com

web: www.whitleyhall.com

dir: A61 past football ground, then 2m, right just before Norfolk Arms, left at bottom of hill. Hotel on left

This 16th-century house stands in 20 acres of landscaped grounds and gardens. Public rooms are full of character and interesting architectural features, and command the best views of the gardens. Bedrooms are individually styled and furnished in keeping with this country house setting, as are the oak-panelled restaurant and bar.

Rooms 20 en suite (2 fmly) (1 GF) S £70-£89; D £92-£140 (incl. bkfst) **Facilities** STV FTV ⚄ Wi-fi available ♫ **Conf** Thtr 70 Class 50 Board 34 Del from £145 **Parking** 100 **Notes** LB ⊗ ⊘ in restaurant Civ Wed 90

★★★ 73% **HOTEL**

The Beauchief Hotel

161 Abbeydale Rd South S7 2QW
☎ 0114 262 0500 📠 0114 235 0197
e-mail: beauchief@corushotels.com
web: www.corushotels.com
dir: from city centre 2m on A621 signed Bakewell

On the southern outskirts of the city, this busy property attracts both resident and local business. The popular restaurant and Merchant's bar have an excellent reputation in the area for good food and hospitality. The well-equipped bedrooms come in various styles and sizes. Ample parking is also a bonus.

Rooms 50 en suite (2 fmly) (19 GF) ⊘ in 39 bedrooms S £65-£79; D fr £79 **Facilities** STV **Conf** Thtr 100 Class 50 Board 50 Del from £95 **Parking** 200 **Notes LB** ⊘ in restaurant Civ Wed 95

England

SHEFFIELD *continued*

★★★ 71% **HOTEL**

Novotel Sheffield

50 Arundel Gate S1 2PR

☎ 0114 278 1781 🖷 0114 278 7744

e-mail: h1348-re@accor.com

web: www.novotel.com

dir: *between Registry Office and Crucible/Lyceum Theatres, follow signs to Town Hall/Theatres & Hallam University*

In the heart of the city centre, this "new generation" Novotel has stylish public areas including a very modern restaurant, indoor swimming pool and a range of meeting rooms. Spacious bedrooms are suitable for family occupation and "Novation" rooms are ideal for business users.

Rooms 144 en suite (40 fmly) ⊗ in 108 bedrooms **Facilities** STV 🔀 Wi-fi in bedrooms Local gym facilities free for residents use Xmas **Conf** BC Thtr 220 Class 180 Board 100 Del from £110 **Services** Lift air con **Parking** 60 **Notes** Civ Wed 180

★★★ 70% **HOTEL**

The Garrison

Hillsborough Barracks, Penistone Rd S6 2GB

☎ 0114 249 9555 🖷 0114 249 1900

e-mail: garrisonhotel@btconnect.com

web: www.garrisonhotel.com

This unique hotel as been created from the former Hillsborough barracks and retains some of the original features. Bedrooms are modern and well equipped and a wide range of food is available in the main building. The adjacent Supertram provides easy access to the city.

Rooms 43 en suite (2 fmly) ⊗ in 34 bedrooms S £53.50-£63.50; D £53.50-£63.50 **Facilities** STV Wi-fi in bedrooms **Conf** Thtr 30 Class 30 Board 30 Del from £84 **Parking** 60 **Notes** ⊗ ⊗ in restaurant Closed 24 Dec-28 Dec Civ Wed 120

★★ 66% **HOTEL**

Cutlers Hotel

Theatreland George St S1 2PF

☎ 0114 273 9939 🖷 0114 276 8332

e-mail: enquiries@cutlershotel.co.uk

web: www.cutlershotel.co.uk

dir: *In retail, commerce & academic centre, 50mtrs from Crucible Theatre. Follow theatre signs*

Situated close to the Crucible Theatre in the city centre, this small hotel offers accommodation in well-equipped bedrooms with extras including hairdryers, trouser presses and business facilities. Public areas include a lower ground floor bistro, and room service is an option. Small meeting rooms are also available. Discounted overnight parking is provided in the nearby public car park.

Rooms 45 en suite (4 fmly) ⊗ in 18 bedrooms S £80; D £90 (incl. bkfst) **Facilities** STV **Conf** BC Thtr 90 Class 40 Board 30 **Services** Lift **Notes** LB ⊗ in restaurant Closed 24-26 Dec Civ Wed 50

Hotel Ibis Sheffield City

Shude Hill S1 2AR

☎ 0114 241 9600 🖷 0114 241 9610

e-mail: H2891@accor-hotels.com

web: www.ibishotel.com

dir: *M1 junct 33, follow signs to Sheffield City Centre(A630/A57), at rdbt take 5th exit, signed Ponds Forge, for hotel*

Modern, budget hotel offering comfortable accommodation in bright and practical bedrooms. Breakfast is self-service and dinner is available in the restaurant. For further details, consult the Hotel Groups page.

Rooms 95 en suite S £47.95-£50.95; D £47.95-£50.95

Innkeeper's Lodge Sheffield South

Hathersage Rd, Longshaw S11 7TY

☎ 01433 630374 🖷 01433 637102

web: www.innkeeperslodge.com

dir: *8m from Sheffield city centre on A625 Sheffield Castleton Road at junction of A625 & B6051.*

Smart, modern en suite accommodation ideal for both business & leisure guests. Bedrooms are very well equipped, including Sky TV, telephone, modem points, tea & coffee making facilities, (family rooms in most locations). Complimentary breakfast. The adjacent Pub Restaurant; a Harvester, Vintage Inn, Toby Carvery, Ember Inn, Sizzling Pubco or Pub & Carvery offers an all day menu. See Hotel Groups pages for further details.

Rooms 10 annexe en suite S £49.95; D £49.95

Premier Travel Inn Sheffield (Arena)

Attercliffe Common Rd S9 2LU

☎ 0870 238 3316 🖷 0114 242 3703

web: www.premiertravelinn.com

dir: *M1 junct 34, follow signs to city centre. Inn is opposite the Arena*

High quality, modern budget accommodation ideal for both families and business travellers. Spacious, en suite bedrooms feature bath and shower, satellite TV and many have telephones and modem points. The adjacent family restaurant features a wide and varied menu. For further details consult the Hotel Groups page.

Rooms 61 en suite

Premier Travel Inn Sheffield (City Centre)

Angel St/Bank St Corner S3 8LN

☎ 0870 238 3324 🖷 0870 241 9000

dir: *M1 junct 33, follow signs for city centre A630/A57. At Park Square rdbt 4th exit (A61 Barnsley). Left at 4th set of lights into Snig Hill then right at lights into Bank St*

Rooms 160 en suite

Premier Travel Inn Sheffield (Meadowhall)

Sheffield Rd, Meadowhall S9 2YL
☎ 0870 9906440 📠 0870 9906441
dir: On A6178 approx 6m from city centre
Rooms 103 en suite

Travelodge Sheffield Richmond

340 Prince of Wales Rd S2 1FF
☎ 08700 850 950 📠 0114 253 0935
web: www.travelodge.co.uk
dir: follow A630, take exit for ring road & services

Travelodge offers good quality, good value, modern accommodation. Ideal for families, the spacious en suite bedrooms include remote-control TV, tea and coffee-making facilities and comfortable beds. Meals can be taken at the nearby family restaurant. See Hotel Groups pages for further details.

Rooms 67 en suite S fr £26; D fr £26 **Conf** Thtr 30 Board 20

TANKERSLEY   MAP 16 SK39

★★★★ 75% **HOTEL**

Tankersley Manor

MarstonHotels

Church Ln S75 3DQ
☎ 01226 744700 📠 01226 745405
e-mail: tankersley@marstonhotels.com
web: www.marstonhotels.com
dir: M1 junct 36 take A61 Sheffield road. Hotel 0.5m on left

High on the moors with views over the countryside, this 17th-century residence is well located for major cities, tourist attractions and motorway links. Where appropriate, bedrooms retain original features such as exposed beams or Yorkshire-stone window sills. The hotel has its own traditional country pub, complete with old beams and open fires, alongside the more formal restaurant and bar. A well-equipped leisure centre is the latest addition.

Rooms 99 en suite (2 fmly) ⊗ in 79 bedrooms S fr £132; D fr £171 (incl. bkfst) **Facilities** Spa STV ⬚ Sauna Gym Wi-fi available Swimming lessons, beauty treatments Xmas **Conf** Thtr 400 Class 200 Board 100 Del from £185 **Parking** 200 **Notes LB** ⊗ ⊗ in restaurant Civ Wed 95

See advert under BARNSLEY & SHEFFIELD

Premier Travel Inn Sheffield/Barnsley

premier travel inn

Maple Rd S75 3DL
☎ 08701 977228 📠 01226 741524
web: www.premiertravelinn.com
dir: M1 junct 35A (northbound exit only) follow A616 for 2m. From junct 36 take A61 towards Sheffield

High quality, modern budget accommodation ideal for both families and business travellers. Spacious, en suite bedrooms feature bath and shower, satellite TV and many have telephones and modem points. The adjacent family restaurant features a wide and varied menu. For further details consult the Hotel Groups page.

Rooms 42 en suite

THORNE   MAP 17 SE61

★★★ 70% **HOTEL**

Belmont

Horsefair Green DN8 5EE
☎ 01405 812320 📠 01405 740508
e-mail: belmonthotel@aol.com
dir: M18 junct 6, A614 signed Thorne. Hotel on right of Market Place

This privately owned, smartly appointed hotel enjoys a prime location in the centre of town. Bedrooms vary in size and style and are all extremely well equipped for both business and leisure guests. Public areas include the popular Belmont Bar offering a good range of meals and snacks at both lunch and dinner, along with the more formal restaurant and cocktail bar.

Rooms 23 en suite (3 fmly) (5 GF) ⊗ in 10 bedrooms S £82-£85; D £94-£118 (incl. bkfst) **Facilities** STV Putt green **Conf** Thtr 60 Class 20 Board 25 Del from £85.50 **Parking** 30 **Notes LB** ⊗ in restaurant Closed 24-28 Dec, 1 Jan

---

TODWICK   MAP 16 SK48

★★★ 64% **HOTEL**

Red Lion

Old English Inns

Worksop Rd S26 1DJ
☎ 01909 771654 📠 01909 773704
e-mail: 7933@greeneking.co.uk
web: www.oldenglish.co.uk
dir: on A57, 1m from M1 junct 31 towards Worksop

Originally a roadside public house, the Red Lion is now a popular bar and restaurant offering a wide range of drinks and food. Bedrooms are well equipped, modern and comfortable, and there is a small meeting room and ample parking facilities.

Rooms 27 en suite (1 fmly) (14 GF) ⊗ in all bedrooms S fr £58; D fr £75 (incl. bkfst) **Facilities** STV Xmas **Conf** Thtr 25 Class 30 Board 25 **Parking** 80 **Notes LB** ⊗ ⊗ in restaurant

England

WOODALL MOTORWAY SERVICE AREA (M1)
MAP 16 SK48

BUDGET HOTEL

Days Inn Sheffield

DAYS INN

Woodall Service Area S26 7XR
☎ 0114 248 7992 📠 0114 248 5634
e-mail: woodall.hotel@welcomebreak.co.uk
web: www.welcomebreak.co.uk

dir: M1 southbound, at Woodall Services, between juncts 30/31

This modern building offers accommodation in smart, spacious and well-equipped bedrooms, suitable for families and business travellers, and all with en suite bathrooms. Continental breakfast is available and other refreshments may be taken at the nearby family restaurant. For further details see the Hotel Groups page.

Rooms 38 en suite **Conf** Board 10

WORTLEY
MAP 16 SK39

★★ 65% **HOTEL**

Wortley Hall

Wortley Village S35 7DB
☎ 0114 288 2100 📠 0114 283 0695
e-mail: info@wortleyhall.org.uk
web: www.wortleyhall.org.uk

dir: Leave M1 junct 35a, straight over 2nd rdbt signed A616 Manchester. 3m take left to Wortley.

Standing in 26 acres of parkland, this listed country house has been in the custody of the Trades Union Movement for the last 50 years and displays much of their history. Bedrooms are mixed in size and quality, but are comfortable and there are spacious day rooms reminiscent of the hall's original grandeur.

Rooms 49 rms (10 en suite) (7 fmly) (4 GF) ⊗ in 42 bedrooms
S £46-£90; D £70-£130 (incl. bkfst) **Facilities** Snooker **Conf** Thtr 150
Class 70 Board 30 Del fr £74 **Services** Lift **Parking** 60 **Notes LB** ⊗
⊗ in restaurant Civ Wed 100

YORKSHIRE, WEST

BATLEY
MAP 19 SE22

★★ 71% **HOTEL**

Alder House

Towngate Rd, Healey Ln WF17 7HR
☎ 01924 444777 📠 01924 442644
e-mail: info@alderhousehotel.co.uk

dir: M62 junct 27/A62. After 2m turn left into Whitelee Rd, left at next junct. Left into Healey Ln & after 0.25m hotel on left

An attractive Georgian house tucked away in leafy grounds that is now under new ownership. Bedrooms are pleasantly furnished and contain many comfortable extras. There is an intimate dining room offering a selection of interesting dishes, as well as a bar with a separate lounge area. The service and hospitality are both caring and friendly.

Rooms 20 en suite (1 fmly) (2 GF) ⊗ in 3 bedrooms **Facilities** STV
Conf BC Thtr 80 Class 40 Board 35 **Parking** 52 **Notes LB** ⊗ in
restaurant Civ Wed 80

BINGLEY
MAP 19 SE13

★★★ 68% **HOTEL**

Ramada Bradford/Bingley

®RAMADA.

Bradford Rd BD16 1TU
☎ 01274 567123 📠 01274 551331
e-mail: sales.bradford@ramadajarvis.co.uk
web: www.ramadajarvis.co.uk

dir: From M62 junct 26 onto M606, at rdbt follow signs for A650 Skipton/Keighley, hotel is 2m out of Shipley.

This large hotel is set in private landscaped grounds with views over the Aire Valley. Bedrooms split between various wings are neatly appointed for both business and leisure guests. Public areas include the Club House restaurant, a substantial conference centre and extensive parking.

Rooms 103 en suite (5 fmly) (2 GF) ⊗ in 66 bedrooms S £36-£92;
D £50-£92 **Facilities** STV Fishing Putt green Wi-fi available Xmas
Conf Thtr 560 Class 328 Board 246 Del from £95 **Services** Lift
Parking 300 **Notes LB** ⊗ in restaurant Civ Wed 300

BUDGET HOTEL

Premier Travel Inn Bradford North (Bingley)

premier travel inn ☾

Off Bradford Rd BD20 5NH
☎ 08701 977038 📠 01274 551692
web: www.premiertravelinn.com

dir: M62 junct 27 follow signs for A650, then to Bingley Main Street. At next rdbt straight on, inn 50mtrs on left

High quality, modern budget accommodation ideal for both families and business travellers. Spacious, en suite bedrooms feature bath and shower, satellite TV and many have telephones and modem points. The adjacent family restaurant features a wide and varied menu. For further details consult the Hotel Groups page.

Rooms 40 en suite

England

BRADFORD
See also Gomersal & Shipley

MAP 19 SE13

★★★ 79% HOTEL

Midland Hotel

PEEL HOTELS

Forster Square BD1 4HU
☎ 01274 735735 📠 01274 720003
e-mail: info@midland-hotel-bradford.com
web: www.peelhotel.com

dir: A6177/A641/A6181. Past St Georges Hall to Eastbrook Well rdbt. Take 1st exit along Petergate to Forster Sq, left to Cheapside. Hotel on right

Ideally situated in the heart of the city, this grand Victorian hotel provides modern, very well equipped accommodation and comfortable, spacious day rooms. Ample parking is available in what used to be the city's railway station, and a preserved walkway dating from Victorian times linking the hotel to the old platform can still be used today.

Rooms 90 en suite (4 fmly) ⊛ in 40 bedrooms S £88-£118; D £98-£128 **Facilities** STV Wi-fi available Free use of local health club ♬ Xmas **Conf** BC Thtr 450 Class 150 Board 100 Del from £115 **Services** Lift **Parking** 50 **Notes** Civ Wed 100

★★★ 74% HOTEL

Courtyard by Marriott Leeds/Bradford

COURTYARD Marriott

The Pastures, Tong Ln BD4 0RP
☎ 0113 285 4646 📠 0113 285 3661
e-mail: res.lbrcourtyard@kewgreen.co.uk
web: www.kewgreen.co.uk

dir: M62 junct 27/A650 towards Bradford. 3rd rdbt, take 3rd exit to Tong Village & Pudsey. Left into Tong Lane. Hotel 0.5m on right

Built onto an elegant, 19th-century former vicarage, this modern, stylish hotel has been sympathetically designed to complement its Victorian heritage. The hotel is particularly well located for both Leeds and Bradford and the local motorway networks. The well-equipped bedrooms are furnished and decorated to a high standard.

Rooms 53 en suite (8 fmly) (11 GF) ⊛ in 31 bedrooms S £52-£85; D £64-£95 (incl. bkfst) **Facilities** STV Gym Wi-fi available **Conf** Thtr 200 Class 150 Board 100 **Services** Lift **Parking** 230 **Notes** ⊗ Civ Wed 100

★★★ 73% HOTEL

Best Western Guide Post Hotel

Best Western

Common Rd, Low Moor BD12 0ST
☎ 01274 607866 📠 01274 671085
e-mail: sales@guideposthotel.net
web: www.guideposthotel.net

dir: take M606, then signed

Situated south of the city, this hotel offers attractively styled, modern, comfortable bedrooms. The restaurant offers an extensive range of food using fresh, local produce; lighter snack meals are served in the bar. There is also a choice of well-equipped meeting and function rooms.

Rooms 43 en suite (3 fmly) (14 GF) ⊛ in 8 bedrooms S £29.50-£80; D £29.50-£90 (incl. bkfst) **Facilities** STV Wi-fi in bedrooms **Conf** BC Thtr 120 Class 80 Board 60 Del from £105.50 **Parking** 100 **Notes** ⊗ in restaurant Civ Wed 100

★★★ 70% HOTEL

Cedar Court Hotel

Mayo Av, Off Rooley Ln BD5 8HZ
☎ 01274 406606 📠 01274 406600
e-mail: sales@cedarcourtbradford.co.uk

dir: M62 junct 26/M606. At end take 3rd exit off rdbt onto A6177 towards Bradford. Take 1st sharp right at lights

This purpose built, modern hotel is conveniently located just off the motorway and close to the city centre and the airport. The hotel boasts extensive function and conference facilities, a well-equipped leisure club and an elegant restaurant. Bedrooms are comfortably appointed for both business and leisure guests.

Rooms 131 en suite (7 fmly) (25 GF) ⊛ in 75 bedrooms S £55-£125; D £55-£125 **Facilities** STV 🏊 supervised Sauna Solarium Gym Jacuzzi Wi-fi in bedrooms Pool table Xmas **Conf** BC Thtr 800 Class 300 Board 150 Del from £99 **Services** Lift **Parking** 300 **Notes** LB Civ Wed 800

★★★ 68% HOTEL

Novotel Bradford

NOVOTEL
ACCOR

6 Roydsdale Way BD4 6SA
☎ 01274 683683 📠 01274 651342
e-mail: h0510@accor.com
web: www.novotel.com

dir: M606 junct 2, exit to Euroway Trading Estate turn right at traffic lights at bottom of slip road, take 2nd right onto Roydsdale Way

This purpose-built hotel stands in a handy location for access to the motorway. It provides spacious bedrooms that are comfortably

continued on page 744

England

BRADFORD *continued*

equipped. Open-plan day rooms include a stylish bar, and a lounge that leads into the Garden Brasserie. Several function rooms are also available.

Rooms 119 en suite (37 fmly) (9 GF) ⊛ in 69 bedrooms S £45-£69; D £45-£69 **Facilities** STV Wi-fi available Xmas **Conf** Thtr 300 Class 100 Board 100 Del from £105 **Services** Lift **Parking** 200 **Notes LB** ⊛ in restaurant Civ Wed 200

BUDGET HOTEL

Premier Travel Inn Leeds/Bradford (South)

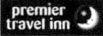

Wakefield Rd, Drighlington BD11 1EA

☎ 08701 977152 📄 0113 287 9115

web: www.premiertravelinn.com

dir: on Drighlington bypass, adjacent to M62 junct 27. A650 to Bradford then right to Drighlington, right, Inn on left

High quality, modern budget accommodation ideal for both families and business travellers. Spacious, en suite bedrooms feature bath and shower, satellite TV and many have telephones and modem points. The adjacent family restaurant features a wide and varied menu. For further details consult the Hotel Groups page.

Rooms 42 en suite

BRIGHOUSE   MAP 16 SE12

BUDGET HOTEL

Premier Travel Inn Huddersfield North

Wakefield Rd HD6 4HA

☎ 0870 9906360 📄 0870 9906361

web: www.premiertravelinn.com

dir: Exit M62 junct 25, follow A644 Huddersfield, Dewsbury & Wakefield signs. Inn 500mtrs up hill on right

High quality, modern budget accommodation ideal for both families and business travellers. Spacious, en suite bedrooms feature bath and shower, satellite TV and many have telephones and modem points. The adjacent family restaurant features a wide and varied menu. For further details consult the Hotel Groups page.

Rooms 71 en suite

CASTLEFORD   MAP 16 SE42

★★★ 77% HOTEL

Tulip Inn Leeds/Castleford

TULIP INN

Colorado Way WF10 4TA

☎ 01977 667700 📄 01977 667711

e-mail: info@tulipinnleedscastleford.co.uk

dir: Turn off M62 junct 32, follow signs for Xscape. Hotel next to Xscape complex

Conveniently located south of Leeds City Centre, just off the M62, this newly opened hotel provides stylish, modern accommodation for business or leisure guests. Attentive staff provide friendly service in the 'Bibo Bar and Bistro', which offers full English breakfast and evening meals.

Rooms 119 en suite (24 fmly) (7 GF) ⊛ in 91 bedrooms S £50-£80; D £50-£80 **Conf** Thtr 45 Class 24 Board 24 **Services** Lift **Parking** 119

BUDGET HOTEL

Premier Travel Inn Castleford

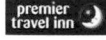

Pioneer Way WF10 5TG

☎ 0870 9906592 📄 0870 9906593

web: www.premiertravelinn.com

dir: Just off A655. From M62 junct 31 take A655 towards Castleford, right at 1st lights, then left

High quality, modern budget accommodation ideal for both families and business travellers. Spacious, en suite bedrooms feature bath and shower, satellite TV and many have telephones and modem points. The adjacent family restaurant features a wide and varied menu. For further details consult the Hotel Groups page.

Rooms 62 en suite **Conf** Thtr 20 Class 8 Board 10

CLECKHEATON   MAP 19 SE12

★★★ 67% HOTEL

The Whitcliffe

Prospect Rd BD19 3HD

☎ 01274 873022 📄 01274 870376

e-mail: info@thewhitcliffehotel.co.uk

dir: M62 junct 26, follow A638 to Dewsbury, over 1st lights, right into Mount St, to T-junct, right then 1st left

This popular and conveniently located commercial hotel offers comfortably equipped bedrooms, many of which have been refurbished. Spacious public areas provide a variety of amenities, including several meeting rooms, two attractive bars, and Flickers Brasserie.

Rooms 35 en suite 6 annexe rms (5 en suite) (3 fmly) (7 GF) ⊛ in 17 bedrooms S £59.50; D £75 **Facilities** FTV ♫ **Conf** Thtr 120 Class 60 Board 40 **Parking** 150 **Notes LB** ⊛ ⊛ in restaurant Civ Wed 80

BUDGET HOTEL

Premier Travel Inn Bradford South

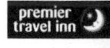

Whitehall Rd BD19 6HG

☎ 08701 977037 📄 01274 855901

web: www.premiertravelinn.com

dir: on A58 at intersection with M62 & M606

High quality, modern budget accommodation ideal for both families and business travellers. Spacious, en suite bedrooms feature bath and shower, satellite TV and many have telephones and modem points. The adjacent family restaurant features a wide and varied menu. For further details consult the Hotel Groups page.

Rooms 40 en suite

DARRINGTON   MAP 16 SE42

BUDGET HOTEL

Premier Travel Inn Pontefract South

premier travel inn

Great North Rd WF8 3BL

☎ 0870 9906386 📄 0870 9906387

web: www.premiertravelinn.com

dir: Just off A1, 2m south of A1/M62 junct

High quality, modern budget accommodation ideal for both families and business travellers. Spacious, en suite bedrooms feature bath and

continued

shower, satellite TV and many have telephones and modem points. The adjacent family restaurant features a wide and varied menu. For further details consult the Hotel Groups page.

Rooms 28 en suite **Conf** Thtr 10 Class 10 Board 10

DEWSBURY   MAP 16 SE22

★★★ 73% **HOTEL**

Heath Cottage Hotel & Restaurant
Wakefield Rd WF12 8ET
☎ 01924 465399 📠 01924 459405
e-mail: bookings@heathcottage.co.uk
web: www.heathcottage.co.uk
dir: M1 junct 40/A638 for 2.5m towards Dewsbury. Hotel before traffic lights, opposite Earlsheaton Cemetery

Standing in an acre of grounds, Heath Cottage is just two and a half miles from the M1, and offers friendly and professional service. All the bedrooms are modern and well appointed, and some are in a converted stable building. The lounge bar and restaurant are air conditioned. Extensive parking is provided.

Rooms 22 en suite 6 annexe en suite (3 fmly) (2 GF) ⊗ in 18 bedrooms S £39-£54; D £54-£68 (incl. bkfst) **Facilities** Xmas **Conf** Thtr 80 Class 40 Board 50 Del from £89 **Parking** 80 **Notes LB** ⊗ ⊘ in restaurant Civ Wed 90

★★★ 71% ⊛ **HOTEL**

Healds Hall
Leeds Rd, Liversedge WF15 6JA   THE INDEPENDENTS
☎ 01924 409112 📠 01924 401895
e-mail: enquire@healdshall.co.uk
web: www.healdshall.co.uk
dir: on A62 between Leeds and Huddersfield. 50yds on left after Swan Pub traffic lights

This 18th-century house in the heart of West Yorkshire offers comfortable and well-equipped accommodation and excellent
continued

hospitality. The hotel has earned a good local reputation for the quality of its food and offers a choice of casual or more formal dining styles, with a wide range of dishes on the various menus.

Rooms 24 en suite (3 fmly) (3 GF) ⊘ in 4 bedrooms S £40-£63; D £60-£75 (incl. bkfst) **Conf** Thtr 100 Class 60 Board 80 Del from £90 **Parking** 90 **Notes LB** ⊗ ⊘ in restaurant Closed New Years Day and BH Mondays Civ Wed 100

FERRYBRIDGE SERVICE   MAP 16 SE42
AREA (M62/A1)

BUDGET HOTEL

Travelodge Pontefract Ferrybridge (M62/A1)
WF11 0AF
☎ 08700 850 950 📠 01977 622509
web: www.travelodge.co.uk
dir: M62 junct 33

Travelodge

Travelodge offers good quality, good value, modern accommodation. Ideal for families, the spacious en suite bedrooms include remote-control TV, tea and coffee-making facilities and comfortable beds. Meals can be taken at the nearby family restaurant. See Hotel Groups pages for further details.

Rooms 36 en suite S fr £26; D fr £26

GARFORTH   MAP 16 SE43

★★★ 78% **HOTEL**

Best Western Milford Hotel
A1 Great North Rd, Peckfield LS25 5LQ   *Best Western*
☎ 01977 681800 📠 01977 681245
e-mail: enquiries@mlh.co.uk
web: www.mlh.co.uk
dir: On A63, 1.5m W of A1(M) junct 42 & 4.5m E of M1 junct 46

This friendly, family owned and run hotel conveniently situated on the A1, provides comfortable modern accommodation. The comfortable, air conditioned bedrooms are particularly spacious and have been well insulated against traffic noise. Public areas include a stylish lounge area and the contemporary Watermill Restaurant and Bar which features a working waterwheel.

Rooms 46 en suite (10 fmly) (14 GF) ⊘ in 19 bedrooms S £68-£75; D £68-£75 **Facilities** STV Wi-fi available Xmas **Conf** Thtr 70 Class 35 Board 30 Del from £125 **Services** air con **Parking** 80

See advert under LEEDS

GOMERSAL · MAP 19 SE22

★★★ 77% HOTEL

Gomersal Park

CLASSIC
BRITISH HOTELS

Moor Ln BD19 4LJ
☎ 01274 869386 📠 01274 861042
e-mail: enquiries@gomersalparkhotel.com
web: www.gomersalparkhotel.com
dir: A62 to Huddersfield. At junct with A65, by Greyhound Pub
right, after 1m take 1st right after Oakwell Hall

Constructed around a 19th-century house, this stylish, modern hotel
enjoys a peaceful location and pleasant grounds. Deep sofas ensure
comfort in the open-plan lounge and imaginative meals are served in
the popular Brasserie 101. The well-equipped bedrooms provide high
quality and comfort. Extensive public areas include a well-equipped
leisure complex and pool, and a wide variety of air-conditioned
conference rooms.

Rooms 100 en suite (3 fmly) (32 GF) ⊗ in 80 bedrooms S £105; D £105
(incl. bkfst) **Facilities** STV 🏊 supervised Sauna Solarium Gym Jacuzzi
Conf Thtr 250 Class 130 Board 60 Del £140 **Services** Lift **Parking** 150
Notes LB ⊗ in restaurant Civ Wed 200

★★ 65% HOTEL

Gomersal Lodge

Spen Ln BD19 4PJ
☎ 01274 861111 📠 01274 861111
e-mail: enquiries@gomersallodge.co.uk
dir: M62 junct 27, A62 towards Huddersfield. Right at
Greyhound Pub, hotel 1m on right

This 19th-century house sits in five acres of landscaped grounds and
attractive gardens, and offers well-furnished bedrooms together with a
cosy bar. The elegant restaurant is noted for its flexible, contemporary
menu, and is popular as a venue for weddings.

Rooms 9 en suite (1 fmly) ⊗ in 4 bedrooms S fr £55; D fr £62 (incl.
bkfst) **Conf** Thtr 20 Class 12 Board 12 Del from £70 **Parking** 70
Notes ⊗ ⊗ in restaurant

HALIFAX · MAP 19 SE02

★★★ 83% ◉◉ HOTEL

Holdsworth House

Holdsworth HX2 9TG
☎ 01422 240024 📠 01422 245174
e-mail: info@holdsworthhouse.co.uk
web: www.holdsworthhouse.co.uk
dir: from town centre take A629 Keighley Road. Right at garage
up Shay Ln after 1.5m. Hotel on right after 1m

This delightful 17th-century Jacobean manor house, set in well tended
gardens, offers individually decorated, thoughtfully equipped
bedrooms. Public rooms, adorned with beautiful paintings and antique
pieces, include a choice of inviting lounges and superb conference
and function facilities. Dinner provides the highlight of any stay and is
served in the elegant restaurant, by friendly, attentive staff.

continued

Holdsworth House

Rooms 40 en suite (2 fmly) (15 GF) ⊗ in all bedrooms S fr £105;
D £120-£175 (incl. bkfst) **Facilities** STV Wi-fi in bedrooms **Conf** Thtr 150
Class 75 Board 50 Del from £145 **Parking** 60 **Notes LB** ⊗ in restaurant
Civ Wed 120

★★★ 64% HOTEL

Imperial Crown Hotel

corus
hotels

42/46 Horton St HX1 1QE
☎ 0870 609 6114 📠 01422 349866
e-mail: imperialcrown@corushotels.com
web: www.corushotels.com
dir: opposite railway station & Eureka Children's Museum

This friendly hotel enjoys a central location and, in addition to the
main accommodation, there are ten contemporary rooms in a
building opposite. The Wallis Simpson Restaurant and Bar feature
interesting memorabilia and extensive conference and banqueting
facilities are available.

Rooms 41 en suite 15 annexe en suite (3 fmly) ⊗ in 22 bedrooms
Facilities Complimentary use of Workout Warehouse gym, opposite the
hotel **Conf** Thtr 150 Class 120 Board 70 **Parking** 63 **Notes** ⊗ ⊗ in
restaurant Civ Wed 150

BUDGET HOTEL

Premier Travel Inn Halifax

premier
travel inn

Salterhebble Hill, Huddersfield Rd HX3 0QT
☎ 0870 9906308 📠 0870 9906309
web: www.premiertravelinn.com
dir: Just off M62 junct 24 on A629 towards Halifax

High quality, modern budget accommodation ideal for both families
and business travellers. Spacious, en suite bedrooms feature bath and
shower, satellite TV and many have telephones and modem points.
The adjacent family restaurant features a wide and varied menu. For
further details consult the Hotel Groups page.

Rooms 31 en suite **Conf** Thtr 30

BUDGET HOTEL

Travelodge Halifax

Dean Clough Park HX3 5AY

☎ 08700 850 950 ▤ 01422 362669

web: www.travelodge.co.uk

dir: M62 junct 24, take A629, follow signs for town centre, then brown tourist signs for Dean Clough Mills

Travelodge offers good quality, good value, modern accommodation. Ideal for families, the spacious en suite bedrooms include remote-control TV, tea and coffee-making facilities and comfortable beds. Meals can be taken at the nearby family restaurant. See Hotel Groups pages for further details.

Rooms 52 en suite S fr £26; D fr £26

HARTSHEAD MOOR MOTORWAY SERVICE AREA (M62)
MAP 19 SE12

BUDGET HOTEL

Days Inn Bradford

Hartshead Moor Service Area, Clifton HD6 4JX

☎ 01274 851706 ▤ 01274 855169

e-mail: hartsheadmoor.hotel@welcomebreak.co.uk

web: www.welcomebreak.co.uk

dir: M62 between junct 25 and 26

This modern building offers accommodation in smart, spacious and well-equipped bedrooms, suitable for families and business travellers, and all with en suite bathrooms. Continental breakfast is available and other refreshments may be taken at the nearby family restaurant. For further details see the Hotel Groups page.

Rooms 38 en suite **Conf** Board 10

HAWORTH
MAP 19 SE03

★★ 69% HOTEL

Old White Lion

Main St BD22 8DU

☎ 01535 642313 ▤ 01535 646222

e-mail: enquiries@oldwhitelionhotel.com

web: www.oldwhitelionhotel.com

dir: from A629 onto B6142, hotel 0.5m past Haworth Station, at top of cobbled main street leading to Tourist Information Centre

Prominently situated at the top of the old cobbled street in this popular village, this hotel is steeped in history. There is a small oak-panelled residents' lounge and a choice of cosy bars, serving a range of meals. More formal style dining is available in the popular restaurant. Comfortably furnished bedrooms are well equipped and vary in size and style.

Rooms 15 en suite (3 fmly) S £54.50-£64.50; D £76-£86 (incl. bkfst) **Facilities** STV Wi-fi in bedrooms Xmas **Conf** Thtr 90 Class 20 Board 38 **Parking** 10 **Notes LB** ⊗

RESTAURANT WITH ROOMS

Weavers Restaurant with Rooms

13/17 West Ln BD22 8DU

☎ 01535 643822 ▤ 01535 644832

e-mail: weaversinnhaworth@aol.com

dir: A629/B6142 towards Haworth/Stanbury & Colne. At top of village pass Brontë Weaving Shed on right. Left after 100yds to Parsonage car park

Centrally located on the cobbled main street, this family-owned restaurant provides well-equipped, stylish and comfortable accommodation. Each of the thoughtfully equipped rooms is en suite. The kitchen serves both modern and traditional dishes with flair and creativity.

Rooms 3 en suite S £55; D £90 **Notes** ⊗ ⊚ in restaurant RS Mon & Sun

---

HOLMFIRTH
MAP 16 SE10

★★ 72% HOTEL

Old Bridge

HD9 7DA

☎ 01404 601212 ▤ 01484 687978

e-mail: oldbridgehotel@enterprise.net

web: www.oldbridgehotel.com

dir: at traffic lights on A6024/A635 in centre of Holmfirth, turn into Victoria St, left after bank and shops to hotel

Located centrally in the town that became famous for the BBC's *The Last of the Summer Wine*. With ample and convenient parking, this stone-built hotel offers well-equipped, stylishly bedrooms and a variety of spacious public rooms. There is a wide range of food available in both the attractive restaurant and the cosy bars.

Rooms 20 en suite S £50; D £65-£75 (incl. bkfst) **Facilities** STV **Conf** Thtr 80 Class 50 Board 40 Del from £64.50 **Parking** 30 **Notes** ⊗

HUDDERSFIELD
MAP 16 SE11

★★★★ 68% HOTEL

Cedar Court

Ainley Top HD3 3RH

☎ 01422 375431 ▤ 01422 314050

e-mail: huddersfield@cedarcourthotels.co.uk

web: www.cedarcourthotels.co.uk

dir: 500yds from M62 junct 24

Sitting adjacent to the M62, this hotel is an ideal location for business travellers or for those touring West Yorkshire. Bedrooms are spacious and comfortable and there is a busy lounge with snacks available all day, as well as a modern restaurant and a fully equipped leisure centre. There are extensive meeting and banqueting facilities.

Rooms 114 en suite (6 fmly) (10 GF) ⊗ in 70 bedrooms S £65-£144.50; D £75-£159 (incl. bkfst) **Facilities** STV ▨ supervised Sauna Solarium Gym Jacuzzi Wi-fi in bedrooms Steam room **Conf** BC Thtr 500 Class 150 Board 100 Del from £110 **Services** Lift **Parking** 250 **Notes LB** ⊗ in restaurant Civ Wed 400

HUDDERSFIELD *continued*

★★★ 74% **HOTEL**

Bagden Hall

Wakefield Rd, Scissett HD8 9LE
☎ 01484 865330 📱 01484 861001
e-mail: info@bagdenhallhotel.co.uk
web: www.bagdenhallhotel.co.uk
dir: on A636, between Scissett and Denby Dale

This elegant mansion house with wonderful views over the valley boasts its own nine-hole golf course. Comfortable bedrooms include classical feature rooms in the main house and newer contemporary rooms in a separate building. Guests can dine in the all day Mediterranean bistro or the more formal elegant restaurant. An airy, stylish conference suite and beautiful grounds make this a popular wedding destination.

Rooms 16 en suite (3 fmly) (10 GF) S fr £70; D £100-£135 (incl. bkfst) **Facilities** STV ♪ 9 Putt green **Conf** Thtr 180 Class 120 Board 50 Del from £110 **Parking** 96 **Notes** ⊗ ⊘ in restaurant RS 25 Dec Civ Wed 150

★★★ 74% **HOTEL**

Best Western Pennine Manor

Nettleton Hill Rd, Scapegoat Hill HD7 4NH
☎ 01484 642368 📱 01484 642866
e-mail: penninemanor@bestwestern.co.uk
web: www.bw-penninemanor.co.uk
dir: M62 junct 24, signed Rochdale (A640)/Outlane Village, left after Highlander pub, hotel signed

Set high in The Pennines, this attractive stone-built hotel enjoys magnificent panoramic views. Bedrooms are thoughtfully equipped.

continued

There is a popular bar with log burning stove and a cosy atmosphere, offering a good selection of snacks and meals. The restaurant enjoys views over the valley as does the modern function facilities, which is a popular venue for both weddings and business meetings.

Rooms 30 en suite (4 fmly) (15 GF) ⊘ in 24 bedrooms S £52-£79; D £64-£83 (incl. bkfst) **Facilities** STV **Conf** BC Thtr 132 Class 56 Board 40 Del from £100 **Parking** 115 **Notes LB** ⊗ ⊘ in restaurant Civ Wed 100

★★★ 68% **HOTEL**

The Old Golf House Hotel

New Hey Rd, Outlane HD3 3YP
☎ 0870 609 6128 📱 01422 372694
e-mail: oldgolfhouse@corushotels.com
web: www.corushotels.com
dir: M62 junct 23 (eastbound only), or junct 24. Follow A640 to Rochdale. Hotel on A640

corus
hotels

Situated close to the M62, this traditionally styled hotel offers well-equipped bedrooms. A wide choice of dishes is offered in the restaurant, and lighter meals are available in the lounge bar. The hotel, with lovely grounds, is a popular venue for weddings.

Rooms 52 en suite (4 fmly) (19 GF) ⊘ in 30 bedrooms S £40-£65; D £45-£65 **Facilities** STV Putt green Xmas **Conf** Thtr 70 Class 35 Board 30 Del from £90 **Parking** 100 **Notes LB** ⊘ in restaurant Civ Wed 90

Ⓤ

Swallow Huddersfield

33-47 Kirkgate HD1 1QT
☎ 01484 512111 📱 01484 435262
web: www.swallowhotels.com
dir: on A62 ring road, below parish church, opposite sports centre

SWALLOW
HOTELS

At the time of going to press, the star classification for this hotel was not confirmed. Please refer to the AA internet site www.theAA.com for current information.

Rooms 39 en suite

England

BUDGET HOTEL

Premier Travel Inn Huddersfield West

premier travel inn

New Hey Rd, Ainley Top HD2 2EA
☎ 0870 9906488 ▤ 0870 9906489
web: www.premiertravelinn.com

dir: Just off M62 junct 24. From M62 take Brighouse exit from rdbt (A643). 1st left into Grimescar Rd, right into New Hey Rd

High quality, modern budget accommodation ideal for both families and business travellers. Spacious, en suite bedrooms feature bath and shower, satellite TV and many have telephones and modem points. The adjacent family restaurant features a wide and varied menu. For further details consult the Hotel Groups page.

Rooms 40 en suite

BUDGET HOTEL

Travelodge Huddersfield Mirfield

Travelodge

Leeds Rd, Mirfield WF14 0BY
☎ 08700 850 950 ▤ 01924 489921
web: www.travelodge.co.uk

dir: M62 junct 25, follow A62 across 2 rdbts. Lodge on right

Travelodge offers good quality, good value, modern accommodation. Ideal for families, the spacious en suite bedrooms include remote-control TV, tea and coffee-making facilities and comfortable beds. Meals can be taken at the nearby family restaurant. See Hotel Groups pages for further details.

Rooms 27 en suite S fr £26; D fr £26

ILKLEY   MAP 19 SE14

★★★ 82% ◎◎ HOTEL

Best Western Rombalds Hotel & Restaurant

Best Western

11 West View, Wells Rd LS29 9JG
☎ 01943 603201 ▤ 01943 816586
e-mail: reception@rombalds.demon.co.uk
web: www.rombalds.co.uk

dir: A65 from Leeds. Left at 3rd main lights, follow Ilkley Moor signs. Right at HSBC Bank onto Wells Rd. Hotel 600yds on left

This elegantly furnished Georgian townhouse is located in a peaceful terrace between the town and the moors. Delightful day rooms include a choice of comfortable lounges and an attractive restaurant which provides a relaxed venue in which to sample the skilfully

continued

---

prepared, imaginative meals. The bedrooms are tastefully furnished, well-equipped and include several spacious suites.

Rooms 15 en suite (4 fmly) ⊗ in 9 bedrooms **Facilities** STV
Conf Thtr 70 Class 40 Board 25 **Parking** 28 **Notes LB** ⊗ in restaurant Closed 28 Dec-2 Jan Civ Wed 70

★★★ 70% HOTEL

The Craiglands

Cowpasture Rd LS29 8RQ
☎ 01943 430001 ▤ 01943 430002
e-mail: reservations@craiglands.co.uk
web: www.craiglands.co.uk

dir: off A65 into Ilkley centre. Right at rail station onto Cowpasture Rd, hotel at top

This grand Victorian hotel is ideally situated close to the town centre. Spacious public areas and a good range of services are ideal for business or leisure. Extensive conference facilities are available along with an elegant restaurant and traditionally styled bar and lounge. Bedrooms, varying in size and style, are comfortably furnished and well equipped.

Rooms 60 en suite (6 fmly) ⊗ in 19 bedrooms S £53-£85; D £63-£195 (incl. bkfst) **Facilities** Wi-fi in bedrooms Complimentary use of local fitness centre **Conf** Thtr 1000 Class 400 Board 200 Del fr £120
Services Lift **Parking** 200 **Notes** ⊗ Civ Wed 500

BUDGET HOTEL

Innkeeper's Lodge Ilkley

Innkeeper's Lodge

Hangingstone Rd LS29 8BT
☎ 01943 607335 ▤ 01943 604712
web: www.innkeeperslodge.com

dir: from A65 turn towards town centre, at station turn right into Cowpasture Rd. Lodge 0.75m on left

Smart, en suite accommodation ideal for both business & leisure guests. Bedrooms are very well equipped, including Sky TV, telephone, modem points, tea & coffee making facilities, (family rooms in most locations). Complimentary breakfast. The adjacent Pub Restaurant; a Harvester, Vintage Inn, Toby Carvery, Ember Inn, Sizzling Pubco or Pub & Carvery offers an all day menu. See Hotel Groups pages for further details.

Rooms 16 en suite S £52-£55; D £52-£55

KEIGHLEY   MAP 19 SE04

★★ 67% HOTEL

Dalesgate

406 Skipton Rd, Utley BD20 6HP
☎ 01535 664930 ▤ 01535 611253
e-mail: stephen.e.atha@btinternet.com

dir: In town centre follow A629 over rdbt. Right after 0.75m into St. John's Rd. 1st right into hotel car park

Originally the residence of a local chapel minister, this modern, well-established hotel provides well-equipped, comfortable bedrooms. It also boasts a cosy bar and pleasant restaurant, serving an imaginative range of dishes. A large car park is provided to the rear.

Rooms 20 en suite (2 fmly) (3 GF) **Parking** 25 **Notes LB** ⊗ in restaurant RS 22 Dec-4 Jan

KEIGHLEY *continued*

BUDGET HOTEL

Innkeeper's Lodge Keighley

Bradford Rd BD21 4BB
☎ 01535 610611
web: www.innkeeperslodge.com

dir: From M606 rdbt take A6177, at next rdbt A641 & A650 towards Keighley. Lodge on 2nd rdbt

Smart, en suite accommodation ideal for both business & leisure guests. Bedrooms are very well equipped, including Sky TV, telephone, modem points, tea & coffee making facilities, (family rooms in most locations). Complimentary breakfast. The adjacent Pub Restaurant; a Harvester, Vintage Inn, Toby Carvery, Ember Inn, Sizzling Pubco or Pub & Carvery offers an all day menu. See Hotel Groups pages for further details.

Rooms 43 en suite S £45; D £45

KIRKBURTON   MAP 16 SE11

BUDGET HOTEL

Innkeeper's Lodge Huddersfield

36a Penistone Rd HD8 0PQ
☎ 01484 602101 ■ 01484 603938
web: www.innkeeperslodge.com

dir: from A62 Huddersfield ring road onto A629 towards Wakefield

Smart, en suite accommodation ideal for both business & leisure guests. Bedrooms are very well equipped, including Sky TV, telephone, modem points, tea & coffee making facilities, (family rooms in most locations). Complimentary breakfast. The adjacent Pub Restaurant; a Harvester, Vintage Inn, Toby Carvery, Ember Inn, Sizzling Pubco or Pub & Carvery offers an all day menu. See Hotel Groups pages for further details.

Rooms 20 en suite 3 annexe en suite S £45-£48; D £45-£48
Conf Thtr 30 Board 20

LEEDS   MAP 19 SE23
See also Gomersal & Shipley

★★★★★ 81% ⊛⊛ HOTEL

De Vere Oulton Hall

Rothwell Ln, Oulton LS26 8HN
☎ 0113 282 1000 ■ 0113 282 8066
e-mail: oulton.hall@devere-hotels.com
web: www.devere.co.uk

dir: 2m from M62 junct 30 on left, or 1m from M1 junct 44. Follow Castleford and Pontefract signs on A639

Surrounded by the beautiful Yorkshire Dales, yet within 15 minutes of the city centre, this elegant 19th-century house really does offer the best of both worlds. Impressive features of the hotel include the formal gardens, which have been faithfully restored to their original design, and the galleried Great Hall. The hotel also offers a choice of dining options and golfers can book preferential tee times at the adjacent golf club.

Rooms 152 en suite ⊘ in 144 bedrooms S £80-£170; D £90-£180 (incl. bkfst) **Facilities** Spa STV ⌖ ↧ 27 Sauna Solarium Gym ⌣ Jacuzzi Wi-fi available Beauty therapy Aerobics, spa treatments Xmas **Conf** Thtr 350 Class 150 Board 40 Del from £145 **Services** Lift **Parking** 260 **Notes LB** ⊗ ⊘ in restaurant Civ Wed 100

★★★★ 83% ⊛ HOTEL

The Thorpe Park Hotel

SHIRE
HOTELS

Century Way, Thorpe Park LS15 8ZB
☎ 0113 264 1000 ■ 0113 264 1010
e-mail: thorpepark@shirehotels.com
web: www.shirehotels.com

dir: M1 junct 46 left at top of slip road, then right at rdbt into Thorpe Park

Conveniently close to the M1, this hotel offers bedrooms that are modern in both style and facilities. The terrace and courtyard offer all-day casual dining and refreshments, and the restaurant features a Mediterranean-themed menu. There is also a state-of-the-art spa and leisure facility.

Rooms 123 en suite (31 GF) ⊘ in 80 bedrooms S £93-£155; D £136-£175 (incl. bkfst) **Facilities** Spa STV ⌖ Sauna Solarium Gym Jacuzzi Wi-fi in bedrooms Steam room, Activity studio, 7 spa treatment rooms Xmas **Conf** BC Thtr 200 Class 100 Board 50 Del £185 **Services** Lift air con **Parking** 200 **Notes LB** ⊗ ⊘ in restaurant Civ Wed 150

★★★★ 77% HOTEL

Queens

QHOTELS

City Square LS1 1PL
☎ 0113 243 1323 ■ 0113 242 5154
e-mail: queensreservations@qhotels.co.uk
web: www.qhotels.co.uk

dir: M621 junct 3. Follow signs for City Centre, under railway bridge. Left at 2nd lights, hotel on left.

This grand Victorian hotel has now undergone an impressive refurbished, but still retains much of its original splendour. A legacy from the golden age of railways it is located in the heart of the city, overlooking city square. Public rooms include the spacious lounge bar, a range of conference and function rooms along with the grand ballroom. Bedrooms vary in size but all are very well equipped, and there is a choice of suites available.

Rooms 217 en suite (25 fmly) ⊘ in 157 bedrooms S £139-£250; D £139-£250 **Facilities** STV Wi-fi in bedrooms Free access to fitness centre **Conf** BC Thtr 600 Class 255 Board 80 Del £169 **Services** Lift **Parking** 70 **Notes** Civ Wed 600

★★★★ 76% HOTEL

Leeds Marriott Hotel

Marriott
HOTELS & RESORTS

4 Trevelyan Square, Boar Ln LS1 6ET
☎ 0113 236 6366 ■ 0113 236 6367
web: www.marriott.co.uk

dir: M621/M1 junct 3. Follow signs for city centre on A653. Stay in right lane. Energis building on left, right and follow signs to hotel

With a charming courtyard setting in the heart of the city, this modern, elegant hotel provides the perfect base for shopping and sightseeing. Air-conditioned bedrooms are tastefully decorated and offer good workspace. Public areas include a leisure club, an informal bar, lobby lounge area and Georgetown, which offers Colonial Malaysian cuisine.

Rooms 244 en suite ⊘ in 194 bedrooms S £120-£150; D £130-£160 **Facilities** STV ⌖ supervised Sauna Solarium Gym Jacuzzi Wi-fi in bedrooms Subsidised use of NCP car park **Conf** BC Thtr 280 Class 120 Board 80 Del from £135 **Services** Lift air con **Notes LB** ⊗ Civ Wed 300

England

★★★★ 74% HOTEL

Park Plaza Leeds

Boar Ln LS1 5NS

Park Plaza
Hotels & Resorts

☎ 0113 380 4000 🖨 0113 380 4100

e-mail: pplinfo@parkplazahotels.co.uk

web: www.parkplaza.com

dir: Follow signs for Leeds city centre

Chic, stylish, ultra modern, city-centre hotel located just opposite City Square. Chino Latino, located on the first floor, is a fusion Far East and modern Japanese restaurant with a Latino bar. Stylish, air conditioned bedrooms are spacious and have a range of modern facilities, including high-speed internet connection.

Rooms 186 en suite ⌘ in 96 bedrooms **Facilities** STV Gym **Conf** BC Thtr 160 Class 70 Board 40 **Services** Lift air con **Notes** ⌘ Closed 24 Dec-27 Dec Civ Wed 120

★★★★ 74% HOTEL

Radisson SAS Leeds

No 1 The Light, The Headrow LS1 8TL

Radisson
HOTELS & RESORTS

☎ 0113 236 6000 🖨 0113 236 6100

e-mail: annettejung@radissonsas.com

web: www.radisson.com

dir: follow city centre 'loop' up Park Row, straight at lights onto Cockeridge St, hotel on left

Situated in the shopping complex known as 'The Light', the hotel occupies a converted building that was formerly the headquarters of the Leeds Permanent Building Society. Three styles of decor have been used in the bedrooms: Art Deco, Hi Tech and Italian. All rooms are air conditioned and have excellent business facilities. The lobby bar area serves substantial meals and is ideal for relaxation. Public parking is available, contact the hotel for details

Rooms 147 en suite ⌘ in 130 bedrooms S £135-£165; D £135-£175 **Facilities** STV Wi-fi in bedrooms Access to Esporta Health Club Xmas **Conf** BC Thtr 60 Class 28 Board 24 Del from £185 **Services** Lift air con **Notes LB** ⌘ Civ Wed 60

★★★★ 73% HOTEL

The Metropole Leeds

King St LS1 2HQ

PRINCIPAL
HOTELS

☎ 0113 245 0841 🖨 0113 242 5156

e-mail: metropole.sales@principal-hotels.com

web: www.principal-hotels.com

dir: from M1, M62 and M621 follow city centre signs. Take A65 into Wellington St. At 1st traffic island right into King St, hotel on right

Said to be the best example of this type of building in the city, this splendid terracotta-fronted, Grade II listed hotel is centrally located and convenient for the railway station. All the bedrooms are appointed to suit the business traveller with hi-speed internet access and a working area. The Tempus Bar & Restaurant makes a convenient dining option. There are impressive conference and banqueting facilities. Some parking space is available.

Rooms 120 en suite ⌘ in 77 bedrooms S £135-£145; D £145-£155 **Facilities** STV FTV Wi-fi available **Conf** BC Thtr 250 Class 100 Board 80 Del from £139 **Services** Lift **Parking** 40 **Notes LB** ⌘ ⌘ in restaurant RS 24 Dec-1 Jan Civ Wed 200

★★★ 81% ⊛ HOTEL

Malmaison Hotel

1 Swinegate LS1 4AG

Malmaison
hotels that dare to be different

☎ 0113 398 1000 🖨 0113 398 1002

e-mail: leeds@malmaison.com

web: www.malmaison.com

dir: M621/M1 junct 3, follow city centre signs. At KPMG building, right into Sovereign Street. Hotel at end on right

Close to the waterfront, this stylish property offers striking bedrooms with CD players and air conditioning. The popular bar and brasserie feature vaulted ceilings, intimate lighting and offer a choice of a full three-course meal or a substantial snack. Service is both willing and friendly. A small fitness centre and impressive meeting rooms complete the package.
Malmaison - AA Hotel Group of the Year 2006-7.

Rooms 100 en suite ⌘ in 70 bedrooms S £99; D £99-£140 **Facilities** STV Gym Wi-fi available Xmas **Conf** Thtr 45 Class 20 Board 24 Del £175 **Services** Lift air con **Notes LB** ⌘ in restaurant

★★★ 80% HOTEL

Novotel Leeds Centre

4 Whitehall, Whitehall Quay LS1 4HR

NOVOTEL
ACCOR hotels

☎ 0113 242 6446 🖨 0113 242 6445

e-mail: H3270@accor.com

web: www.novotel.com

dir: M621 junct 3, follow signs to train station. Turn into Aire St and left at lights

With a minimalist style, this contemporary hotel provides a quality, value-for-money experience close to the city centre. Spacious, air conditioned bedrooms are provided, whilst public areas offer deep leather sofas and an eye catching water feature in reception. Light snacks are provided in the airy bar and the restaurant doubles as a bistro. Staff are committed to guest care and nothing is too much trouble.

Rooms 195 en suite (50 fmly) ⌘ in 159 bedrooms S £55-£139; D £55-£139 **Facilities** STV Sauna Gym Wi-fi in bedrooms Play station computers in rooms & play area Steam room Xmas **Conf** Thtr 100 Class 50 Board 50 Del from £99 **Services** Lift air con **Parking** 90 **Notes LB** Civ Wed 70

★★★ 79% ⊛⊛ HOTEL

Haley's Hotel & Restaurant

Shire Oak Rd, Headingley LS6 2DE

☎ 0113 278 4446 🖨 0113 275 3342

e-mail: info@haleys.co.uk

dir: Exit A660. Shire Oak Rd between HSBC & Starbucks.

Only ten minutes from the city centre yet this hotel has a real country house feel to it. The bedrooms offer tasteful decor, some with interesting period furnishings. The modern restaurant is decorated with contemporary works of art (all for sale) and is the setting for imaginative meals. There is also a choice of comfortable lounges.

Rooms 22 en suite 6 annexe en suite (5 fmly) (2 GF) ⌘ in 11 bedrooms S £85-£125; D £120-£160 (incl. bkfst) **Facilities** STV **Conf** Thtr 45 Class 25 Board 30 Del from £140 **Parking** 26 **Notes LB** ⌘ ⌘ in restaurant Closed 25-30 Dec Civ Wed 100

See advert on page 753

England

LEEDS *continued*

★★★ 78% HOTEL

Best Western Milford Hotel

A1 Great North Rd, Peckfield LS25 5LQ
☎ 01977 681800 🖺 01977 681245
e-mail: enquiries@mlh.co.uk
web: www.mlh.co.uk

(For full entry see Garforth)

See advert on opposite page

★★★ 77% ⊛ ⊛ HOTEL

Hazlewood Castle

Paradise Ln, Hazlewood LS24 9NJ
☎ 01937 535353 🖺 01937 530630
e-mail: info@hazlewood-castle.co.uk
web: www.hazlewood-castle.co.uk

(For full entry see Tadcaster, North Yorkshire)

★★★ 75% HOTEL

Bewleys Hotel Leeds

Bewleys Hotels.com

City Walk, Sweet St LS11 9AT
☎ 0113 234 2340 🖺 0113 234 2349
e-mail: leeds@bewleyshotels.com
web: www.bewleyshotels.com

dir: M621 junct 3, at 2nd lights turn left onto Sweet Street then right & right again

Located on the edge of the city centre, this hotel has the added advantage of secure underground parking. Bedrooms are spacious and comfortable. Downstairs, the light and airy bar lounge leads into a brasserie where a wide selection of popular dishes is offered. High quality meeting rooms are also available.

Rooms 334 en suite (99 fmly) ⊗ in 246 bedrooms S £69; D £69
Facilities STV Wi-fi available **Conf** BC Board 16 Del £129 **Services** Lift
Parking 160 **Notes** ⊗ ⊗ in restaurant Closed 24-26 Dec

★★★ 75% HOTEL

Ramada Leeds Parkway

⊛ RAMADA

Otley Rd LS16 8AG
☎ 0113 269 9000 🖺 0113 267 4410
e-mail: sales.leeds@ramadajarvis.co.uk
web: www.ramadajarvis.co.uk

dir: A1 take A58 towards Leeds, then right onto A6120. At A660 turn right towards Airport/Skipton. Hotel 2m on right

This large hotel is situated next to Golden Acre Park and Nature Reserve. Bedrooms are comfortably appointed for both business and leisure guests.

Rooms 118 en suite (2 fmly) (2 GF) ⊗ in 69 bedrooms S £60-£115;
D £60-£125 **Facilities Spa** STV ⊠ supervised ⊆ Sauna Solarium Gym
Wi-fi available Xmas **Conf** Thtr 300 Class 120 Board 40 Del from £85
Services Lift **Parking** 250 **Notes LB** ⊗ in restaurant Civ Wed 200

★★★ 73% ⊛ HOTEL

Best Western Chevin Country Park Hotel

Yorkgate LS21 3NU
☎ 01943 467818 🖺 01943 850335
e-mail: reception@chevinhotel.com

(For full entry see Otley)

★★★ 72% HOTEL

Golden Lion

PEEL HOTELS

2 Lower Briggate LS1 4AE
☎ 0113 243 6454 🖺 0113 243 4241
e-mail: info@goldenlion-hotel-leeds.com
web: www.peelhotel.com

dir: M621 junct 3. Keep in right lane. Follow until road splits into 4 lanes. Keep right. Right at lights. (Asda House on left). Left at lights. Over bridge, turn left, hotel opposite. Parking in 150mtrs

This smartly presented hotel is set in a Victorian building on the south side of the city. The well-equipped bedrooms offer a choice of standard or executive grades. Staff are friendly and helpful, ensuring a warm and welcoming atmosphere. Free overnight parking is provided in a 24-hour car park close to the hotel.

Rooms 89 en suite (5 fmly) ⊗ in 46 bedrooms S £102-£114;
D £112-£120 **Facilities** STV Wi-fi in bedrooms Xmas **Conf** Thtr 120
Class 45 Board 40 Del from £120 **Services** Lift **Notes** ⊗ in restaurant

★★★ 72% **HOTEL**

Jurys Inn Leeds

JURYS DOYLE
HOTELS

Kendell St, Brewery Place, Brewery Wharf LS10 1NE
☎ 0113 283 8800 ▤ 0113 283 8888
e-mail: info@jurysdoyle.com
web: www.jurysdoyle.com

This modern hotel is located near the Tetley Brewery, close to the centre of Leeds. Bedrooms provide good levels of comfort and in-room facilities are spot on for both the leisure and the business markets. Public areas include a number of meeting rooms, a restaurant and a popular bar.

Rooms 248 en suite ⊘ in 200 bedrooms **Facilities** STV **Conf** Thtr 60 Class 50 Board 25 **Services** Lift air con **Notes** ⊗ ⊘ in restaurant

★★★ 72% **HOTEL**

The Merrion

Merrion Centre LS2 8NH
☎ 0113 243 9191 ▤ 0113 242 3527
e-mail: themerrion@brook-hotels.co.uk
dir: from M1, M62 and A61 onto city loop road to junct 7

This smart, modern hotel benefits from a city centre location. Bedrooms are smartly appointed and thoughtfully equipped for both business and leisure guests. Public areas include a comfortable lounge and a pleasing restaurant with an adjacent bar. There is direct access to a car park via a walkway

Rooms 109 en suite ⊘ in 48 bedrooms **Facilities** STV Discount at local leisure centre **Conf** Thtr 80 Class 25 Board 25 **Services** Lift **Notes LB** ⊘ in restaurant

★★★ 66% **HOTEL**

Ramada Leeds North

Ⓡ RAMADA.

Ring Rd, Seacroft LS14 5QF
☎ 0113 273 2323 ▤ 0113 232 3018
e-mail: sales.leedsnorth@ramadajarvis.co.uk
web: www.ramadajarvis.co.uk

dir: M1 junct 46 towards Leeds/Airport. Follow A6120 over several rdbts to Crossgates. Hotel 1m on right - double back at next rdbt

Located on the outskirts of the city, this modern hotel is within easy reach of the city centre, A1/M1 and M62. Bedrooms vary in size and style but are all comfortably appointed for both business and leisure guests. Events and meeting facilities are available with ample parking proving a bonus.

Rooms 105 en suite (12 fmly) (21 GF) ⊘ in 73 bedrooms S £60-£99; D £70-£99 (incl. bkfst) **Facilities** STV Wi-fi available Xmas **Conf** Thtr 340 Class 200 Board 40 **Services** Lift **Parking** 150 **Notes LB** ⊘ in restaurant Civ Wed 250

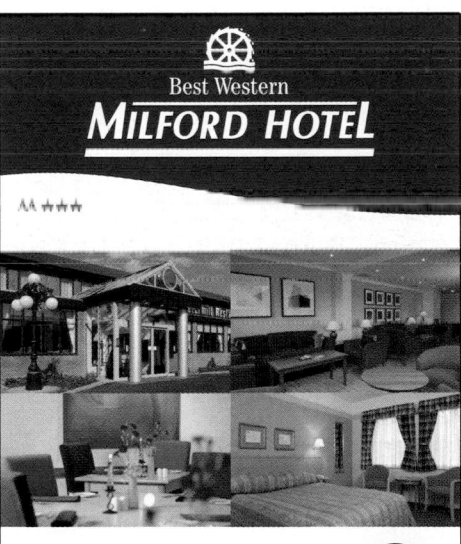

England

LEEDS *continued*

BUDGET HOTEL

Hotel Ibis Leeds

Marlborough St LS1 4PB

☎ 0113 220 4100 📠 0113 220 4110

e-mail: H3652@accor.com

web: www.ibishotel.com

dir: *From M1 junct 43 or M62 junct 2 take A643 & follow city centre signs. Turn left on slip road opposite Yorkshire Post. Hotel opposite*

Modern, budget hotel offering comfortable accommodation in bright and practical bedrooms. Breakfast is self-service and dinner is available in the restaurant. For further details, consult the Hotel Groups page.

Rooms 168 en suite S £49.95-£59.95; D £49.95-£59.95

BUDGET HOTEL

Innkeeper's Lodge Leeds South

Bruntcliffe Rd, Morley LS27 0LY

☎ 0113 253 3115 📠 0113 253 9365

web: www.innkeeperslodge.com

dir: *M62 junct 27 take A650 towards Morley. On junct of A650 and A643*

Smart, en suite accommodation ideal for both business & leisure guests. Bedrooms are very well equipped, including Sky TV, telephone, modem points, tea & coffee making facilities, (family rooms in most locations). Complimentary breakfast. The adjacent Pub Restaurant; a Harvester, Vintage Inn, Toby Carvery, Ember Inn, Sizzling Pubco or Pub & Carvery offers an all day menu. See Hotel Groups pages for further details.

Rooms 32 en suite S £45-£57; D £45-£57

BUDGET HOTEL

Premier Travel Inn Leeds City Centre

Citygate, Wellington St LS3 1LW

☎ 08701 977150 📠 0113 242 8105

web: www.premiertravelinn.com

dir: *on junct of A65 & A58*

High quality, modern budget accommodation ideal for both families and business travellers. Spacious, en suite bedrooms feature bath and shower, satellite TV and many have telephones and modem points. The adjacent family restaurant features a wide and varied menu. For further details consult the Hotel Groups page.

Rooms 139 en suite **Conf** Class 16 Board 16

Premier Travel Inn Leeds City West

City West One Office Park, Gelderd Rd LS12 6LX

☎ 0870 9906448 📠 0870 9906449

dir: *Exit M621 junct 1 take ring road towards Leeds. At 1st lights right into Gelderd Rd, right at rdbt*

Rooms 126 en suite **Conf** Thtr 12 Class 12 Board 12

Premier Travel Inn Leeds East

Selby Rd, Whitkirk LS15 7AY

☎ 08701 977151 📠 0113 232 6195

dir: *M1 junct 46 towards Leeds. At 2nd rdbt follow Temple Newsam signs. Inn 500mtrs on right.*

Rooms 87 en suite

BUDGET HOTEL

Travelodge Leeds Central

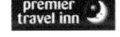

Blaydes Court, Blaydes Yard, off Swinegate LS1 4AD

☎ 08700 850 950 📠 0113 246 0076

web: www.travelodge.co.uk

dir: *Exit M62 at M621 to city centre, right before Hilton Hotel into Sovereign St*

Travelodge offers good quality, good value, modern accommodation. Ideal for families, the spacious en suite bedrooms include remote-control TV, tea and coffee-making facilities and comfortable beds. Meals can be taken at the nearby family restaurant. See Hotel Groups pages for further details.

Rooms 100 en suite S fr £26; D fr £26

Travelodge Leeds Colton

Stile Hill Way, Colton LS15 9JA

☎ 08700 850 950 📠 0113 264 8839

dir: *M1 junct 46*

Rooms 60 en suite S fr £26; D fr £26

LEEDS/BRADFORD AIRPORT   MAP 19 SE23

BUDGET HOTEL

Premier Travel Inn Leeds/Bradford Airport

Victoria Av, Yeadon LS19 7AW

☎ 08701 977153 📠 0113 202 9383

web: www.premiertravelinn.com

dir: *on A658, near Leeds/Bradford Airport*

High quality, modern budget accommodation ideal for both families and business travellers. Spacious, en suite bedrooms feature bath and shower, satellite TV and many have telephones and modem points. The adjacent family restaurant features a wide and varied menu. For further details consult the Hotel Groups page.

Rooms 40 en suite **Conf** Thtr 12

BUDGET HOTEL

Travelodge Leeds Bradford Airport

White House Ln LS19 7TZ

☎ 0113 250 3996 📠 0113 250 6842

web: www.travelodge.co.uk

Travelodge offers good quality, good value, modern accommodation. Ideal for families, the spacious en suite bedrooms include remote-control TV, tea and coffee-making facilities and comfortable beds. Meals can be taken at the nearby family restaurant. See Hotel Groups pages for further details.

Rooms 48 en suite S fr £26; D fr £26

MARSDEN
MAP 16 SE01

★★ 78% ⊛ ⊛ **HOTEL**

Hey Green Country House
Waters Rd HD7 6NG
☎ 01484 848000 📠 01484 847605
e-mail: info@heygreen.com
web: www.heygreen.com
dir: off A62 1m outside village, towards Manchester.

This delightful Victorian property is set in extensive landscaped gardens, close to the restored Huddersfield Canal and The Standedge Visitor Centre. Spacious bedrooms are stylishly designed, thoughtfully equipped and boast smart, modern en suite bathrooms. A contemporary brasserie offers imaginative dishes and excellent value. The beautiful conservatory and function suite make this a popular venue for weddings.

Rooms 12 en suite ⊗ in 10 bedrooms S £79-£149; D £109-£179 (incl. bkfst) **Facilities** FTV Wi-fi available Xmas **Conf** Thtr 50 Class 50 Board 30 Del £120 **Parking** 70 **Notes LB** ⊗ in restaurant RS 2-3 Jan Civ Wed 120

MORLEY
MAP 19 SE22

★★ 69% **HOTEL**

The Old Vicarage
THE INDEPENDENTS
Bruntcliffe Rd LS27 0JZ
☎ 0113 253 2174 📠 0113 253 3549
e-mail: sales@oldvicaragehotel.co.uk
web: www.oldvicaragehotel.co.uk
dir: M62 junct 27, A650 towards Wakefield. Hotel on left adjacent to St Andrews Church

A warm welcome awaits guests at this extended Victorian vicarage. The bedrooms are split between the main house and the modern

continued

extension - all offer a range of extra facilities. There is a cosy lounge with honesty bar and hearty meals are served in the pleasant dining room. Private parking is provided.

Rooms 22 en suite (1 fmly) (2 GF) ⊗ in 15 bedrooms S £36-£52; D £47-£65 (incl. bkfst) **Facilities** Wi-fi available **Parking** 22 **Notes** ⊗ in restaurant

OTLEY
MAP 19 SE24

★★★ 73% ⊛ **HOTEL**

Best Western Chevin Country Park Hotel
Best Western
Yorkgate LS21 3NU
☎ 01943 467818 📠 01943 850335
e-mail: reception@chevinhotel.com
dir: From Leeds/Bradford Airport rdbt take A658 N, towards Harrogate, for 0.75m to 1st traffic lights. Turn left, then 2nd left onto 'Yorkgate'. Hotel 0.5m on left

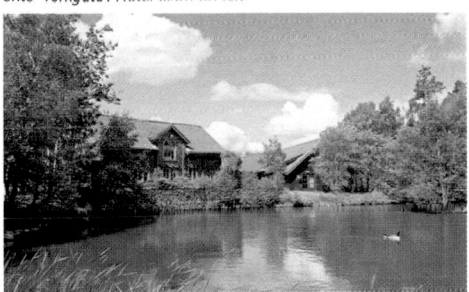

This hotel, peacefully situated in its own woodland yet conveniently located for major road links and the airport, offers comfortable accommodation. Rooms are split between the original main log building and chalet-style accommodation, situated in the extensive grounds. Public areas are spacious and well equipped. The Lakeside restaurant provides views over the small lake and good leisure facilities are also available.

Rooms 19 en suite 30 annexe en suite (7 fmly) (45 GF) ⊗ in 30 bedrooms S £104-£142, D £115-£220 (incl. bkfst) **Facilities** STV ⬚ ♨ Fishing Sauna Solarium Gym Jacuzzi Mountain bikes Jogging trails Xmas **Conf** BC Thtr 120 Class 90 Board 50 Del from £142 **Parking** 100 **Notes LB** ⊗ in restaurant Civ Wed 120

PONTEFRACT
MAP 16 SE42

★★★ 79% ⊛ **HOTEL**

Wentbridge House
Wentbridge WF8 3JJ
☎ 01977 620444 📠 01977 620148
e-mail: info@wentbridgehouse.co.uk
web: www.wentbridgehouse.co.uk
dir: 0.5m off A1 & 4m S of M62 junct 33 onto A1 south

This well-established hotel sits in 20 acres of landscaped gardens, offering spacious, well-equipped bedrooms and a choice of dining styles. Service in the Fleur de Lys restaurant is polished and friendly,

continued on page 756

England

PONTEFRACT continued

and a varied menu offers a good choice of interesting dishes. The Brasserie offers a more relaxed style of modern dining.

Wentbridge House

Rooms 14 en suite 4 annexe en suite (4 GF) S £80–£120; D £105–£150 (incl. bkfst) **Facilities** Wi-fi in bedrooms **Conf** Thtr 130 Class 100 Board 60 Del from £100 **Parking** 100 **Notes LB** ⊗ Closed 25 Dec-evening only Civ Wed 130

★★★ 74% HOTEL

Best Western Rogerthorpe Manor

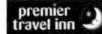

Thorpe Ln, Badsworth WF9 1AB
☎ 01977 643839 📠 01977 641571
e-mail: ops@rogerthorpemanor.co.uk
dir: A639 from Pontefract to Badsworth. Follow B6474. Hotel on left at end of Thorpe Audlin village

This Jacobean manor house is situated in extensive grounds and lovely gardens, within easy access of road networks. Bedrooms vary between those in the old house with their inherent charm, and the more modern rooms in the extensions. A choice of dining styles, real ales, civil weddings, modern conference facilities and ample parking are all offered. Complimentary Wi-fi access is also available.

Rooms 23 en suite (4 fmly) ⊗ in 16 bedrooms S £75–£85; D £85–£100 (incl. bkfst) **Facilities** STV Wi-fi in bedrooms Xmas **Conf** Thtr 250 Class 80 Board 50 Del from £100 **Services** air con **Parking** 150 **Notes** ⊗ ⊗ in restaurant Civ Wed 200

BUDGET HOTEL

Days Inn Ferrybridge

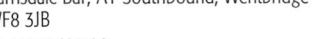

Barnsdale Bar, A1 Southbound, Wentbridge WF8 3JB
☎ 01977 621129
web: www.welcomebreak.co.uk

This modern building offers accommodation in smart, spacious and well-equipped bedrooms, suitable for families and business travellers, and all with en suite bathrooms. Continental breakfast is available and other refreshments may be taken at the nearby family restaurant. For further details see the Hotel Groups page.

Rooms 56 en suite

BUDGET HOTEL

Premier Travel Inn Pontefract North

Pontefract Rd, Knottingley WF11 0BU
☎ 08701 977209 📠 01977 607954
web: www.premiertravelinn.com
dir: From M62 junct 33 onto A1 North. Take next junction (A645) Pontefract. Follow road to T-junct, right towards Pontefract. Inn on right

High quality, modern budget accommodation ideal for both families and business travellers. Spacious, en suite bedrooms feature bath and shower, satellite TV and many have telephones and modem points. The adjacent family restaurant features a wide and varied menu. For further details consult the Hotel Groups page.

Rooms 40 en suite

PUDSEY   MAP 19 SE23

BUDGET HOTEL

Travelodge Bradford

1 Mid Point, Dick Ln BD3 8QD
☎ 08700 850 950 📠 01274 665436
web: www.travelodge.co.uk
dir: M62 junct 26 (M606), take A6177 towards Leeds, A647, lodge 2m on left

Travelodge offers good quality, good value, modern accommodation. Ideal for families, the spacious en suite bedrooms include remote-control TV, tea and coffee-making facilities and comfortable beds. Meals can be taken at the nearby family restaurant. See Hotel Groups pages for further details.

Rooms 48 en suite S fr £26; D fr £26

SHIPLEY   MAP 19 SE13

★★★★ 78% ❀ HOTEL

Marriott Hollins Hall Hotel & Country Club

Hollins Hill, Baildon BD17 7QW
☎ 0870 400 7227 📠 0870 400 7327
e-mail: mhrs.16ags.eventorganiser@marriotthotels.com
web: www.marriott.co.uk
dir: from A650 follow signs to Salt Mill. At lights in Shipley take A6038. Hotel is 3m on left

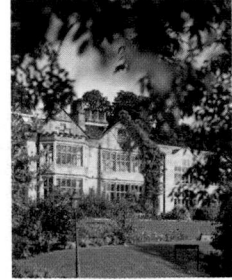

The hotel is located just to the north of Bradford and is easily accessible from motorway networks. Built in the 19th-century this Elizabethan-style building is set within 200 acres of grounds and offers

continued

extensive leisure facilities, including a golf course and gym. Bedrooms are attractively decorated and have a range of additional facilities.

Rooms 122 en suite (50 fmly) (25 GF) ⊘ in 75 bedrooms S £75-£165; D £80-£175 (incl. bkfst) **Facilities Spa** STV 🔁 supervised ♨ 18 Sauna Solarium Gym 🐾 Putt green Jacuzzi Wi-fi available Creche, Health Spa, Dance studio, Swimming lessons Xmas **Conf** BC Thtr 175 Class 90 Board 80 Del from £135 **Services** Lift **Parking** 260 **Notes LB** ⊗ ⊘ in restaurant Civ Wed 70

BUDGET HOTEL

Hotel Ibis Bradford

Quayside, Salts Mill Rd BD18 3ST
☎ 01274 589333 📠 01274 589444
e-mail: H3158@accor.com
web: www.ibishotel.com

dir: follow tourist signs for Salts Mill. Follow A650 signs through Bradford for approx 5m to Shipley. Hotel on Salts Mill Rd

Modern, budget hotel offering comfortable accommodation in bright and practical bedrooms. Breakfast is self-service and dinner is available in the restaurant. For further details, consult the Hotel Groups page.

Rooms 78 en suite S £42.95-£49.95; D £42.95-£49.95 **Conf** Thtr 20 Class 16 Board 18

WAKEFIELD   MAP 16 SE32

★★★★ 71% HOTEL

Cedar Court

Denby Dale Rd WF4 3QZ
☎ 01924 276310 📠 01924 280221
e-mail: sales@cedarcourthotels.co.uk
web: www.cedarcourthotels.co.uk

dir: adjacent to M1 junct 39

This hotel enjoys a convenient location just off the M1. Traditionally styled bedrooms offer a good range of facilities while open-plan public areas include a busy bar and restaurant operation. Conferences and functions are extremely well catered for and a modern leisure club completes the picture.

Rooms 150 en suite (2 fmly) (74 GF) ⊘ in 100 bedrooms **Facilities Spa** STV 🔁 supervised Sauna Solarium Gym Jacuzzi Xmas **Conf** BC Thtr 400 Class 140 Board 80 **Services** Lift air con **Parking** 350 **Notes** ⊘ in restaurant Civ Wed 250

★★★ 81% ⑧ HOTEL

Best Western Waterton Park

Walton Hall, The Balk, Walton WF2 6PW
☎ 01924 257911 & 249800 📠 01924 259686
e-mail: watertonpark@bestwestern.co.uk
web: www.watertonparkhotel.co.uk

dir: 3m SE off B6378. Exit M1 junct 39 towards Wakefield. At 3rd rdbt take right for Crofton. At 2nd lights right & follow signs

A stately private house, built on an island in a lake makes an ideal setting. The main house contains many feature bedrooms, and the annexe has more spacious rooms - all are equally well equipped with
continued

---

modern facilities. The delightful beamed restaurant, two bars and leisure centre are located in the old hall. Hotel has a licence for civil weddings.

Best Western Waterton Park

Rooms 25 en suite 43 annexe en suite (23 GF) ⊘ in 34 bedrooms S £75-£99; D £100-£140 (incl. bkfst) **Facilities Spa** STV 🔁 supervised Fishing Sauna Solarium Gym Jacuzzi Wi-fi in bedrooms Steam room **Conf** Thtr 150 Class 80 Board 80 **Services** Lift **Parking** 200 **Notes LB** ⊗ ⊘ in restaurant Civ Wed 130

★★★ 74% HOTEL

Best Western Stoneleigh

Doncaster Rd WF1 5HA
☎ 01924 369461 📠 01924 201041
e-mail: stoneleigh@bestwestern.co.uk

dir: A636 Wakefield, follow Asdale Rd then Agbrigg Rd. Hotel 1m from M1 junct 39

This hotel is a conversion of a Victorian stone terrace dating back to 1870. The modern bedrooms are located on two floors and a lift is available. The well-decorated restaurants include both traditional and Chinese cuisine. Guests have complimentary use of a nearby health club and gym.

Rooms 28 en suite **Conf** Thtr 200 Class 80 Board 60 **Services** Lift **Parking** 70 **Notes** ⊘ in restaurant Civ Wed 250

★★★ 69% HOTEL

Hotel St Pierre

THE INDEPENDENTS

Barnsley Rd, Newmillerdam WF2 6QG
☎ 01924 255596 📠 01924 252746
e-mail: enq@hotelstpierre.co.uk

dir: M1 junct 39 take A636 to Wakefield, turn right at rdbt, on to Asdale Road to traffic lights. Turn right onto A61 towards Barnsley. Hotel just after lake

This well-furnished hotel lies south of Wakefield, close to Newmiller Dam and is now under new ownership. The interior of the modern building has comfortable and thoughtfully equipped bedrooms and smart public rooms. There is a good selection of conference rooms, a small gym and an intimate restaurant.

Rooms 54 en suite (3 fmly) (4 GF) ⊘ in 33 bedrooms S £49-£69; D £55-£75 (incl. bkfst) **Facilities** STV Wi-fi in bedrooms Xmas **Conf** Thtr 120 Class 60 Board 60 Del from £80 **Services** Lift **Parking** 70 **Notes LB** Civ Wed 130

England

WAKEFIELD *continued*

[U]

Chasley

Queen St WF1 1JU

☎ 01924 372111 📠 01924 383648

e-mail: admin@chasleywakefield.supanet.com

dir: *M1 junct 39, follow town centre signs. Queen Street on left*

At the time of going to press, the star classification for this hotel was not confirmed. Please refer to the AA internet site www.theAA.com for current information.

Rooms 64 en suite (8 fmly) ⊘ in 18 bedrooms **Conf** Thtr 250 Class 110 Board 88 **Services** Lift **Parking** 40 **Notes** ⊗ ⊘ in restaurant Civ Wed 250

BUDGET HOTEL

Campanile

Monckton Rd WF2 7AL

☎ 01924 201054 📠 01924 290976

e-mail: wakefield@campanile-hotels.com

web: www.campanile.com

dir: *M1 junct 39, A636 1m towards Wakefield, left onto Monckton Rd, hotel on left*

This modern building offers accommodation in smart, well-equipped bedrooms, all with en suite bathrooms. Refreshments may be taken at the informal Bistro. For further details consult the Hotel Groups page.

Rooms 77 annexe en suite **Conf** Thtr 30 Class 18 Board 20 Del from £70

BUDGET HOTEL

Days Hotel Leeds/Wakefield

Fryers Way, Silkwood Park, Ossett WF5 9TJ

☎ 01924 274200 & 0800 0280 400

📠 01924 274246

e-mail: wakefield@dayshotel.co.uk

web: www.welcomebreak.co.uk

dir: *Exit M1 junct 40, follow signs to Wakefield, hotel is 400yds on left*

This modern building offers accommodation in smart, spacious and well-equipped bedrooms, suitable for families and business travellers, and all with en suite bathrooms. Continental breakfast is available and other refreshments may be taken at the nearby family restaurant. For further details see the Hotel Groups page.

Rooms 100 en suite **Conf** BC Thtr 40 Class 18 Board 22

BUDGET HOTEL

Premier Travel Inn Wakefield

Thornes Park, Denby Dale Rd WF2 8DY

☎ 08701 977257 📠 01924 373620

web: www.premiertravelinn.com

dir: *M1 junct 39 take A636 towards Wakefield town centre. Inn is on left at 3rd rdbt*

High quality, modern budget accommodation ideal for both families and business travellers. Spacious, en suite bedrooms feature bath and shower, satellite TV and many have telephones and modem points. The adjacent family restaurant features a wide and varied menu. For further details consult the Hotel Groups page.

Rooms 42 en suite **Conf** Thtr 54 Board 24

WETHERBY

MAP 16 SE44

INSPECTORS' CHOICE

★★★★ ◎◎ COUNTRY HOUSE HOTEL

Wood Hall

Trip Ln, Linton LS22 4JA

☎ 01937 587271 📠 01937 584353

e-mail: woodhall@handpicked.co.uk

web: www.handpicked.co.uk

dir: *from Wetherby take Harrogate Rd N (A661) for 0.5m, left to Sicklinghall & Linton. Cross bridge, left to Linton & Wood Hall. Turn right opposite Windmill Inn, 1.25m to hotel*

A striking Georgian building sitting in 100 acres of woods and parkland, this hotel has been restored to its former glory. Spacious bedrooms are appointed to an impressive standard and feature comprehensive facilities, including large plasma screen TVs and DVDs. Public rooms reflect the same elegance and include a smart drawing room and dining room, both with fantastic sweeping views. Guests can dine in the sophisticated Georgian Restaurant that offers a menu of both classic and modern British dishes. A state-of-the-art Technogym is available.

Rooms 14 en suite 30 annexe en suite (5 fmly) ⊘ in 18 bedrooms S £190-£310; D £240-£360 (incl. bkfst) **Facilities Spa** STV ⊠ supervised Fishing Gym Jacuzzi Wi-fi available Beauty spa Treatment rooms ch fac Xmas **Conf** Thtr 140 Class 70 Board 40 **Services** Lift **Parking** 200 **Notes LB** ⊗ ⊘ in restaurant Civ Wed 110

★★★ 81% **HOTEL**

The Bridge Hotel

THE INDEPENDENTS

Walshford LS22 5HS
☎ 01937 580115 📠 01937 580556
e-mail: info@bridgeinn-bridgehotel.co.uk
web: www.walshford.co.uk

dir: S'bound - A1(M) junct 47, 1st left, Walshford, follow brown signs. N'bound - A1(M) junct 46, B1224, Wetherby

A very conveniently located hotel close to the A1 with spacious public areas and a good range of services make this an ideal venue for business or leisure. Stylish bedrooms are comfortable and well equipped. The Bridge offers a choice of bars and a large open-plan restaurant.

Rooms 30 en suite (1 fmly) S £67-£77; D £87-£127 (incl. bkfst)
Facilities FTV Gym Wi-fi in bedrooms Xmas **Conf** BC Thtr 150 Class 50 Board 50 Del from £120 **Parking** 150 **Notes LB** Civ Wed

★★★ 70% **HOTEL**

Ramada Wetherby

⊛ RAMADA.

Leeds Rd LS22 5HE
☎ 01937 583881 📠 01937 580062
e-mail: sales.wetherby@ramadajarvis.o.uk
web: www.ramadajarvis.co.uk

dir: junct A1/A58

Set in the countryside, just a few minutes from the town centre and conveniently located close to the A58 and A1, this large hotel is particularly popular with business guests and features extensive conference facilities. Bedrooms are modern, well equipped and comfortable. Public areas include a spacious bar area/coffee lounge and large restaurant

Rooms 103 en suite (2 fmly) (51 GF) ⊛ in 87 bedrooms S £69-£105; D £69-£105 **Facilities** STV Wi-fi available Xmas **Conf** Thtr 150 Class 50 Board 50 Del from £95 **Services** Lift **Parking** 170 **Notes LB** ⊛ in restaurant Civ Wed 150

WOOLLEY EDGE   MAP 16 SE31
MOTORWAY SERVICE AREA (M1)

BUDGET HOTEL

Travelodge Wakefield Woolley Edge (M1 North)

M1 Service Area, West Bretton WF4 4LQ
☎ 08700 850 950 📠 01924 830609
web: www.travelodge.co.uk

dir: between juncts 38 & 39 on M1, adjacent to service area

Travelodge offers good quality, good value, modern accommodation. Ideal for families, the spacious en suite bedrooms include remote-control TV, tea and coffee-making facilities and comfortable beds. Meals can be taken at the nearby family restaurant. See Hotel Groups pages for further details.

Rooms 32 en suite S fr £26; D fr £26

Travelodge Wakefield Woolley Edge (M1 South)

M1 Service Area Southbound, West Bretton WF4 4LQ
☎ 08700 850 950 📠 01924 830174
Rooms 41 en suite S fr £26; D fr £26

CHANNEL ISLANDS

Guernsey

CASTEL   MAP 24

★★★★ 71% **HOTEL**

La Grande Mare Hotel Golf & Country Club

The Coast Rd, Vazon Bay GY5 7LL
☎ 01481 256576 📠 01481 256532
e-mail: reservations@lagrandemare.com
web: www.lgm.guernsey.net

dir: Exit airport and turn right. Proceed to Coast Rd. Turn right again.

Set in 110 acres of private grounds, this hotel is located next to a sandy bay, incorporates an 18-hole golf course and has a health suite. Bedrooms range from spacious studios to deluxe suites, and feature handcrafted furniture and impressive decor. The health suite features a 40ft swimming pool that has dedicated children's swimming times.

Rooms 24 en suite (13 fmly) (5 GF) **Facilities** STV ⬚ supervised ⬚ ⬚ 18 ⬚ Fishing Sauna Gym Putt green Jacuzzi ⬚ **Services** Lift **Parking** 200 **Notes LB** ⊛

England

CASTEL *continued*

★★★ 67% ⊛ **HOTEL**

Hotel Hougue du Pommier

Hougue du Pommier Rd GY5 7FQ

☎ 01481 256531 📠 01481 256260

e-mail: hotel@houguedupommier.guernsey.net

web: www.hotelhouguedupommier.com

dir: *turn inland from Cobo Village (coast road). Turn left at first junct. Hotel 50yds on right*

Retaining much of its 18th-century character and charm, this hotel combines modern comforts with friendly yet efficient service. Bedrooms vary in size and standard, and include exceptionally well-appointed and spacious deluxe rooms. In addition to the restaurant an informal eating option is available in the beamed bar featuring an open fire, spit-roast menu.

Rooms 37 en suite 6 annexe en suite (5 fmly) ⊘ in all bedrooms **Facilities** STV ⊀ ♨ 6 Sauna ♨ Xmas **Parking** 50 **Notes** ⊘ in restaurant

See advert on page 759

COBO   MAP 24

★★★ 75% ⊛⊛ **HOTEL**

Cobo Bay

Coast Rd GY5 7HB

☎ 01481 257102 📠 01481 254542

e-mail: reservations@cobobayhotel.com

web: www.cobobayhotel.com

dir: *from airport turn right, follow road to W coast at L'Eree. Turn right onto coast road for 3m to Cobo Bay. Hotel on right*

Popular hotel situated on the seafront overlooking Cobo Bay. The well-equipped bedrooms are pleasantly decorated; many of the front rooms have balconies and there is a secluded sun terrace to the rear. Public rooms include a candlelit restaurant with stunning views of the Bay and the Chesterfield bar with its leather sofas and armchairs.

Rooms 36 en suite (4 fmly) S £34-£89; D £68-£118 (incl. bkfst) **Facilities** STV Snooker Sauna Jacuzzi **Conf** Thtr 50 Class 30 Board 20 Del from £75 **Services** Lift **Parking** 60 **Notes** LB ⊗ ⊘ in restaurant Closed Jan

FERMAIN BAY   MAP 24

★★★ 74% **HOTEL**

Le Chalet

GY4 6SD

☎ 01481 235716 📠 01481 235718

e-mail: chalet@sarniahotels.com

dir: *from airport left towards St Martins village. Right at filter to Sausmarez Rd, follow sign for Fermain Bay & Le Chalet Hotel*

A popular family run hotel nestling in a wooded valley above Fermain Bay. Bedrooms vary in size and style; each one is pleasantly decorated and equipped with many thoughtful touches. Public areas include a panelled lounge, a bar area, a restaurant and a stunning sun terrace adjoining the small indoor leisure facility.

Rooms 40 en suite (5 fmly) S £42-£80; D £70-£110 (incl. bkfst) **Facilities** STV Sauna Solarium Jacuzzi Spa pool **Parking** 35 **Notes LB** ⊗ ⊘ in restaurant Closed mid Oct-mid Apr

FOREST   MAP 24

★★ 69% **HOTEL**

Le Chene

Forest Rd GY8 0AH

☎ 01481 235566 📠 01481 239456

e-mail: info@lechene.co.uk

web: www.lechene.co.uk

dir: *Between airport & St Peter Port*

This Victorian manor house is well located for guests wishing to explore Guernsey's spectacular south coast. The building has been skilfully extended to house a range of well-equipped, modern bedrooms. There is a swimming pool, a cosy cellar bar and a varied range of enjoyable freshly cooked dishes at dinner.

Rooms 26 en suite (2 fmly) (1 GF) **Facilities** ⊀ Library **Parking** 20 **Notes LB** ⊗ No children 10yrs ⊘ in restaurant

PERELLE   MAP 24

★★★ 74% ⊛⊛ **HOTEL**

Atlantique

Perelle Bay GY7 9NA

☎ 01481 264056 📠 01481 263800

e-mail: enquiries@perellebay.com

web: www.perellebay.com

dir: *from airport, turn right & continue to sea. Turn right & follow coast road for 1.5m*

This modern seaside hotel offers spectacular views of the sea and often, memorable sunsets. Bedrooms vary, those with sea views have balconies, and there are suites suitable for families. Restaurant L'Atlantique has an enviable reputation on the island, and the Victorian bar offers a less formal dining option.

Rooms 23 rms (21 en suite) (4 fmly) ⊘ in 12 bedrooms S £50-£90; D £100-£140 (incl. bkfst) **Facilities** ⊀ **Conf** Thtr 40 Class 20 Board 14 Del from £100 **Parking** 80 **Notes LB** ⊗ ⊘ in restaurant Closed Nov-Mar

ST MARTIN MAP 24

★★★ 77% ◉ HOTEL

La Barbarie

Saints Rd, Saints Bay GY4 6ES

☎ 01481 235217 ▧ 01481 235208

e-mail: reservations@labarbariehotel.com

web: www.labarbariehotel.com

This former priory dates back to the 17th century and retains much charm and style. Staff provide a very friendly and attentive environment, and the modern facilities offer guests a relaxing stay. Excellent choices and fresh local ingredients form the basis of the interesting menus in the attractive restaurant and bar.

Rooms 22 en suite (4 fmly) (8 GF) ❷ in all bedrooms S £50-£68; D £60-£96 (incl. bkfst) **Facilities** ⌇ **Parking** 50 **Notes LB** ❷ ❷ in restaurant Closed 29 Oct -9 Mar

★★★ 77% ◉ HOTEL

Hotel Jerbourg

Jerbourg Point GY4 6BJ

☎ 01481 238826 ▧ 01481 238238

e-mail: stay@hoteljerbourg.com

dir: from airport turn left and follow road to St Martin village, right onto filter road, straight on at lights, hotel at end of road

This hotel boasts excellent sea views from its cliff-top location. Public areas are smartly appointed and include a bar/lounge and bright conservatory-style restaurant. In addition to the fairly extensive carte, a daily-changing menu is available. Bedrooms are well presented and comfortable, and the luxury Bay rooms are generally more spacious.

Rooms 32 en suite (4 fmly) (5 GF) ❷ in all bedrooms S £50-£80; D £75-£110 (incl. bkfst) **Facilities** STV ⌇ **Parking** 50 **Notes** ❷ ❷ in restaurant Closed 31 Oct-18 Mar

★★★ 77% COUNTRY HOUSE HOTEL

La Trelade

Forest Rd GY4 6UB

☎ 01481 235454 ▧ 01481 237855

e-mail: latrelade@guernsey.net

web: www.latrelade.co.uk

dir: 3m from St Peter Port, 1m from airport

This hotel offers a stylish and versatile range of public areas and an impressive leisure suite. Located close to the airport, La Trelade is an ideal base from which to explore the island, and is equally suitable for business guests. Bedrooms and bathrooms are tastefully decorated and equipped to high standards with modern comforts.

Rooms 45 en suite (3 fmly) S £66-£78; D £92-£108 (incl. bkfst) **Facilities** STV ⌇ Sauna Gym Wi-fi in bedrooms Xmas **Conf** Thtr 120 Class 48 Board 40 **Services** Lift **Parking** 80 **Notes LB** ❷ in restaurant

★★★ 73% HOTEL

Saints Bay Hotel

Icart Rd GY4 6JG

☎ 01481 238888 ▧ 01481 235558

e-mail: info@saintsbayhotel.com

dir: from St Martin village take Saints Rd and turn onto Icart Rd

Ideally situated in an elevated position near Icart Point headland and above the harbour at Saints Bay, the hotel enjoys superb views. The spacious public rooms include a smart lounge bar, a first-floor lounge and a smart conservatory restaurant that overlooks the heated swimming pool. Bedrooms are pleasantly decorated and thoughtfully equipped.

Rooms 35 en suite (3 fmly) (13 GF) ❷ in all bedrooms **Facilities** ⌇ **Parking** 15 **Notes** ❷ ❷ in restaurant

★★★ 73% HOTEL

La Villette Hotel & Leisure Suite

GY4 6QG

☎ 01481 235292 ▧ 01481 237699

e-mail: reservations@lavillettehotel.co.uk

dir: turn left out of airport. Follow road past La Trelade Hotel. Take next right, hotel on left

Set in spacious grounds, this peacefully located, family run hotel has a friendly atmosphere. The well equipped bedrooms are spacious and comfortable. Live music is a regular feature in the large bar, while in the separate restaurant a fixed-price menu is provided. Residents have use of the excellent indoor leisure facilities.

Rooms 37 en suite (7 fmly) (14 GF) ❷ in all bedrooms S £41-£57; D £70-£96.50 (incl. bkfst) **Facilities** ⌇ supervised ⌇ Solarium Gym Jacuzzi Steam room Petanque Leisure suite Beauty salon hairdressers Xmas **Conf** Thtr 80 Board 40 **Parking** 50 **Notes** ❷ ❷ in restaurant

England

ST MARTIN *continued*

★★ 76% **HOTEL**

Hotel La Michele

Les Hubits GY4 6NB

☎ 01481 238065 ▤ 01481 239492

e-mail: info@lamichelehotel.com

dir: approx 1.5m from St Peter Port

Expect a warm welcome from the caring hosts at this friendly family run hotel, which is situated in a peaceful location. Bedrooms are particularly well equipped; each one is pleasantly decorated with co-ordinated fabrics. Public areas include a conservatory and a cosy bar, and guests can relax in the well-tended gardens or around the pool.

Rooms 16 en suite (3 fmly) (6 GF) ⊗ in all bedrooms S £39-£56; D £78-£112 (incl. bkfst & dinner) **Facilities** ₹ **Parking** 16 **Notes LB** ⊗ No children 10yrs ⊗ in restaurant Closed Nov-Mar

ST PETER PORT   MAP 24

★★★★ 78% ⊛ ⊛ **HOTEL**

Old Government House Hotel & Spa

St Ann's Place GY1 2NU

☎ 01481 724921 ▤ 01481 724429

e-mail: ogh@theoghhotel.com

web: www.theoghhotel.com

dir: at junct of St. Julians Ave & College St.

The affectionately known OGH is one of the island's leading hotels. Bedrooms vary in size but are comfortable and offer high-quality accommodation. The restaurant overlooks the town and neighbouring islands, and offers fine dining, while snacks are available in the Centenary Bar. The varied leisure facilities, including 'Beauty and The East', are well worth a visit.

Rooms 63 en suite (3 fmly) (1 GF) ⊗ in all bedrooms S £125-£245; D £160-£245 (incl. bkfst) **Facilities** Spa STV ₹ Sauna Solarium Gym Jacuzzi Wi-fi available Steam room, Eastern treatments, Aerobics studio Whirlpool ♫ Xmas **Conf** Thtr 300 Class 180 Board 90 Del from £175 **Services** Lift **Parking** 28 **Notes LB** ⊗ ⊗ in restaurant

★★★★ 77% ⊛ ⊛ **HOTEL**

St Pierre Park

Rohais GY1 1FD

☎ 01481 728282 ▤ 01481 712041

e-mail: info@stpierreparkhotel.com

dir: 10 mins from airport. From harbour straight over rdbt, up hill through 3 sets of lights. Right at filter and continue to lights. Straight ahead, hotel 100mtrs on left

Peacefully located on the outskirts of town amidst 45 acres of grounds featuring a 9-hole golf course. Most of the bedrooms overlook the pleasant gardens and have either a balcony or a terrace. Public areas

continued

include a choice of restaurants and a lounge bar that opens onto a spacious terrace with an elegant water feature.

St Pierre Park

Rooms 131 en suite (4 fmly) (20 GF) ⊗ in 17 bedrooms S £100-£315; D £110-£355 (incl. bkfst) **Facilities** STV ₹ ♪ 9 ⌘ Snooker Sauna Solarium Gym ⚘ Putt green Jacuzzi Wi-fi available Bird watching, Children's playground, Crazy golf ♫ Xmas **Conf** BC Thtr 300 Class 120 Board 30 Del from £199 **Services** Lift **Parking** 150 **Notes LB** ⊗

★★★ 79% ⊛ ⊛ **HOTEL**

La Fregate

Les Cotils GY1 1UT

☎ 01481 724624 ▤ 01481 720443

e-mail: c.sharp@lafregatehotel.com

web: www.lafregatehotel.com

dir: next to Candie Gardens & Museum

Ask for directions to this charming small hotel, which enjoys splendid views over the town and harbour from its elevated position. Bedrooms are comfortably furnished and well-equipped; many have private balconies. The restaurant is popular with both residents and locals for its carefully cooked meals and formal yet efficient service.

Rooms 13 en suite S £85-£170; D £145-£185 (incl. bkfst) **Facilities** Wi-fi in bedrooms **Conf** BC Thtr 40 Class 24 Board 22 **Parking** 25 **Notes LB** ⊗

★★★ 77% **HOTEL**

Best Western Hotel de Havelet

Havelet GY1 1BA

☎ 01481 722199 ▤ 01481 714057

e-mail: havelet@sarniahotels.com

web: www.havelet.sarniahotels.com

dir: from airport follow signs for St Peter Port through St. Martins. At bottom of 'Val de Terres' hill turn left into Havelet

This extended Georgian hotel looks over the harbour to Castle Cornet. Many of the well-equipped bedrooms are set around a pretty colonial-style courtyard. Day rooms in the original building have period elegance; the restaurant and bar are on the other side of the car park in converted stables.

Rooms 34 en suite (4 fmly) (8 GF) ⊗ in 8 bedrooms S £48-£105; D £82-£132 (incl. bkfst) **Facilities** STV ₹ Sauna Jacuzzi Wi-fi in bedrooms Xmas **Conf** Thtr 40 Class 24 Board 26 Del £125 **Parking** 40 **Notes LB** ⊗ ⊗ in restaurant

★★★ 74% **HOTEL**

Best Western Moore's

Pollet GY1 1WH

☎ 01481 724452 📠 01481 714037

e-mail: moores@sarniahotels.com

dir: left at airport, follow signs to St Peter Port, Fort Road to seafront, straight on, turn right before rdbt, continue to hotel

Elegant granite town house situated in the heart of St Peter Port amidst the shops and amenities. Public rooms feature a smart conservatory restaurant, which leads out onto a first floor terrace for alfresco dining; there is also a choice of lounges and bars as well as a patisserie. Bedrooms are pleasantly decorated and thoughtfully equipped.

Rooms 46 en suite 3 annexe en suite (8 fmly) ⊗ in 12 bedrooms S £48-£95; D £83.50-£198 (incl. bkfst) **Facilities** STV Sauna Solarium Gym Jacuzzi Wi-fi available Xmas **Conf** Thtr 40 Class 20 Board 18 Del from £100 **Services** Lift **Notes LB** ⊗ ⊗ in restaurant

★★★ 74% **HOTEL**

The Duke of Richmond

Cambridge Park GY1 1UY

☎ 01481 726221 📠 01481 728945

e-mail: duke@guernsey.net

web: www.dukeofrichmond.com

dir: hotel on corner of Cambridge Park Rd and L'Hyvreuse Ave, opposite leisure centre

Peacefully located in a predominantly residential area overlooking Cambridge Park, this hotel has comfortable, well-appointed bedrooms that vary in size. Public areas include a spacious lounge, a terrace and the unique Sausmarez Bar, with its nautical theme. The smartly uniformed team of staff provide professional standards of service.

Rooms 75 en suite (16 fmly) ⊗ in 61 bedrooms S £50-£130; D fr £75 (incl. bkfst) **Facilities** STV ⊰ Wi-fi available Leisure centre close to hotel Xmas **Conf** BC Thtr 150 Class 50 Board 36 Del from £110 **Services** Lift Parking 6 **Notes LB** ⊗ in restaurant

★★★ 73% **HOTEL**

Les Rocquettes

Les Gravees GY1 1RN

☎ 01481 722146 📠 01481 714543

e-mail: rocquettes@sarniahotels.com

dir: From ferry terminal take 2nd exit at rdbt, continue through 5 sets of lights. After 5th lights continue straight into Les Gravees. Hotel on right opposite church.

This late 18th-century country mansion is in a good location close to St Peter Port and Beau Sejour. Guests can eat in the dining room or the Tartan Bar. Bedrooms come in three grades, Deluxe, Superior and Standard, but all have plenty of useful facilities. The hotel's new wing provides attractive lounge areas on three levels. The health suite has a gym and swimming pool with integrated children's pool.

Rooms 51 en suite (5 fmly) **Facilities** ⊠ Sauna Gym Jacuzzi **Conf** Thtr 100 Class 60 Board 60 **Services** Lift **Parking** 60 **Notes LB** ⊗ ⊗ in restaurant

England

ST PETER PORT *continued*

★★ 72% **HOTEL**

Duke of Normandie

Lefebvre St GY1 2JP

☎ 01481 721431 📠 01481 711763

e-mail: dukeofnormandie@cwgsy.net

web: www.dukeofnormandie.com

dir: from harbour rdbt St Julians Ave, 3rd left into Anns Place, continue to right, up hill, then left into Lefebvre St, archway entrance on right

An 18th-century hotel situated close to the high street and just a short stroll from the harbour. Bedrooms vary; some have been completely refurbished in modern styles and some are situated with their own access from the courtyard. Public areas feature a smart brasserie, a contemporary style lounge/lobby area and a busy bar with beams and an open fireplace.

Rooms 20 en suite 17 annexe en suite (1 fmly) ⊗ in 13 bedrooms S £38.50-£46; D £77-£92 (incl. bkfst) **Facilities** STV Wi-fi in bedrooms Xmas **Conf** BC Thtr 40 Class 30 Board 20 Del from £48.50 **Parking** 15 **Notes LB** ⊗ ⊗ in restaurant

See advert on page 763

VALE   MAP 24

★★★ 68% **HOTEL**

Peninsula

Les Dicqs GY6 8JP

☎ 01481 248400 📠 01481 248706

e-mail: peninsula@guernsey.net

dir: Coast Rd, Grand Havre Bay

Adjacent to the sandy beach and set in five acres of grounds, this modern hotel provides comfortable accommodation. Bedrooms have an additional sofa bed to suit families and good workspace for the business traveller. Both fixed-price and carte menus are served in the restaurant, or guests can eat informally in the bar.

Rooms 99 en suite (99 fmly) (25 GF) ⊗ in 38 bedrooms S £51-£63; D £78-£102 (incl. bkfst) **Facilities** STV ⚲ Putt green Petanque Playground ♫ Xmas **Conf** Thtr 250 Class 140 Board 105 **Services** Lift **Parking** 120 **Notes LB** ⊗ ⊗ in restaurant

Herm

HERM   MAP 24

★★★ 75% ⊛ **HOTEL**

White House

GY1 3HR

☎ 01481 722159 📠 01481 710066

e-mail: hotel@herm-island.com

web: www.herm-island.com

dir: close to harbour

Enjoying a unique island setting, this attractive hotel is just 20 minutes from Guernsey by sea. Set in well-tended gardens, the hotel offers neatly decorated bedrooms, located in either the main house or

continued

adjacent cottages; the majority of rooms have sea views. Guests can relax in one of several lounges, enjoy a drink in one of two bars and choose from two dining options.

White House

Rooms 17 en suite 23 annexe en suite (23 fmly) (7 GF) S £73-£126; D £146-£210 (incl. bkfst & dinner) **Facilities** no TV in bdrms ⚲ ⚓ ⛵ Fishing trips, Yacht & Motor boat charters **Conf** Board 10 **Notes LB** ⊗ ⊗ in restaurant Closed 8 Oct-29 Mar

Jersey

GOREY   MAP 24

★★★ 72% **HOTEL**

The Moorings

Gorey Pier JE3 6EW

☎ 01534 853633 📠 01534 857618

e-mail: reservations@themooringshotel.com

web: www.themooringshotel.com

dir: at foot of Mont Orgueil Castle

Enjoying an enviable position by the harbour, the heart of this hotel is the restaurant where a selection of menus offers an extensive choice of dishes. Other public areas include a bar, coffee shop and a comfortable first-floor residents' lounge. Bedrooms at the front have a fine view of the harbour; three have access to a balcony. A small sun terrace at the back of the hotel is available to guests.

Rooms 15 en suite S £67.50-£82.50; D £95-£125 (incl. bkfst) **Facilities** STV **Conf** Thtr 20 Class 20 Board 20 **Notes LB** ⊗

★★★ 72% **HOTEL**

Old Court House

JE3 9FS

☎ 01534 854444 📠 01534 853587

e-mail: ochhotel@itl.net

web: www.ochhotel.co.uk

Situated on the east of the island, a short walk from the beach, this long established hotel continues to have a loyal following for its relaxed atmosphere and friendly staff. Bedrooms are of similar standard throughout and some have balconies overlooking the gardens. Spacious public areas include a restaurant, a large bar with a dance floor and a comfortable, quiet lounge.

Rooms 58 en suite (4 fmly) (9 GF) S £58-£74.50; D £116-£161 (incl. bkfst & dinner) **Facilities** STV ⚲ Sauna Wi-fi available ♫ **Services** Lift **Parking** 40 **Notes** ⊗ in restaurant Closed Nov-Mar

GROUVILLE
MAP 24

★★★ 71% **HOTEL**

Beausite

Les Rue des Pres, Grouville Bay JE3 9DJ

☎ 01534 857577 📠 01534 857211

e-mail: beausite@jerseymail.co.uk

web: www.southernhotels.com

Within 300 metres of the Royal Jersey Golf Club, this hotel is situated on the south-east side of the island; a short distance from the picturesque harbour at Gorey. With parts dating back to 1636, the public rooms retain original character and charm; bedrooms are generally spacious and modern in design. The indoor swimming pool, fitness room, saunas and spa bath are an added bonus.

Rooms 75 en suite (5 fmly) (18 GF) S £42.25-£82; D £70-£108.50 (incl. bkfst) **Facilities Spa** STV 🔲 Snooker Sauna Gym **Parking** 60 **Notes LB** ⊘ in restaurant Closed Nov-Mar

ROZEL
MAP 24

INSPECTORS' CHOICE

★★★ ◉◉ **HOTEL**

Château la Chaire

Rozel Bay JE3 6AJ

☎ 01534 863354 📠 01534 865137

e-mail: res@chateau-la-chaire.co.uk

web: www.chateau-la-chaire.co.uk

dir: from St Helier on B38 turn left in village by the Rozel Bay Inn, hotel 100yds on right

Built as a gentleman's residence in 1843, Château la Chaire is a haven of peace and tranquillity, set within a secluded wooded valley. Picturesque Rozel Harbour is within easy walking distance and the house is surrounded by terraced gardens. There is a wonderful atmosphere here and the helpful staff deliver high standards of guest care. Imaginative menus, making best use of local produce, are served in the oak-panelled dining room. Bedrooms are intentionally varied, with a range of different sizes and styles available.

Rooms 14 en suite (2 fmly) (1 GF) ⊘ in 4 bedrooms S £87.50-£99; D £114-£192 (incl. bkfst) **Facilities** STV Wi-fi in bedrooms Xmas **Conf** Thtr 20 Class 20 Board 20 Del from £195 **Parking** 30 **Notes LB** ⊗ No children 7yrs ⊘ in restaurant Civ Wed 60

ST AUBIN
MAP 24

★★★ 83% ◉◉ **HOTEL**

Somerville

Mont du Boulevard JE3 8AD

☎ 01534 741226 📠 01534 746621

e-mail: somerville@dolanhotels.com

web: www.dolanhotels.com

dir: from village, follow harbour then take Mont du Boulevard and 2nd right bend

Enjoying spectacular views of St Aubin's Bay, this friendly hotel is very popular. Bedrooms vary in style and a number of superior rooms offer higher levels of luxury. Public areas are smartly presented and include a spacious bar-lounge and elegant dining room, both of which take full advantage of the hotel's enviable views.

Rooms 58 en suite (7 fmly) (4 GF) S £32-£67; D £64-£134 (incl. bkfst) **Facilities** STV 🔲 Wi-fi in bedrooms 🎵 Xmas **Conf** Thtr 18 Class 12 Board 12 Del £124 **Services** Lift **Parking** 26 **Notes** ⊗ No children 11yrs ⊘ in restaurant Civ Wed 40

See advert on page 767

★★★ 73% ◉◉ **HOTEL**

Hotel La Tour

La Rue du Crocquet JE3 8BZ

☎ 01534 743770 📠 01534 747143

e-mail: enquiries@hotellatour.com

web: www.hotellatour.com

dir: on High St behind church, one street parallel to seafront.

This elevated hotel has been carefully refurbished to exhibit contemporary style yet retain historic character. Public rooms are light and airy. The restaurant has large picture windows and is set on two tiers to enable all diners to enjoy the superb views whilst enjoying freshly prepared dishes, featuring local produce and fresh fish. Bedrooms are individually designed. The hosts make guests feel welcome and provide a shuttle service to and from the airport.

Rooms 26 en suite (2 fmly) ⊘ in all bedrooms S £45-£57; D £90-£154 (incl. bkfst) **Facilities** Personal trainer on request Xmas **Parking** 15 **Notes LB** ⊘ in restaurant Closed 2 Jan-28 Feb

England

ST BRELADE
MAP 24

INSPECTORS' CHOICE

★★★★ ◉◉◉ **HOTEL**

The Atlantic

Le Mont de la Pulente JE3 8HE

☎ 01534 744101 📠 01534 744102

e-mail: info@theatlantichotel.com

dir: from Petit Port turn right into Rue de la Sergente & right again, hotel signed

Adjoining the manicured fairways of La Moye championship golf course, this hotel enjoys a peaceful setting with breathtaking views over St Ouen's Bay. Stylish bedrooms look out over the course or the sea and offer a blend of high quality and reassuring comfort. An air of understated luxury is apparent throughout, and the attentive service achieves the perfect balance of friendliness and professionalism. The Ocean restaurant offers sophisticated, modern surroundings in which to enjoy some highly accomplished cooking.

Rooms 50 en suite (8 GF) **Facilities** STV ⬚ supervised ⬚ ⬚ Sauna Solarium Gym Jacuzzi ♫ Xmas **Conf** Thtr 60 Class 40 Board 20 **Services** Lift **Parking** 60 **Notes** ⊗ ⊘ in restaurant Closed 8 Jan-5 Feb

---

★★★★ 80% ◉◉ **HOTEL**

L'Horizon Hotel & Spa

HandPICKED

St Brelade's Bay JE3 8EF

☎ 01534 743101 📠 01534 746269

e-mail: lhorizon@handpicked.co.uk

web: www.handpicked.co.uk/lhorizon

dir: 3m from airport. From airport right at rdbt towards St Brelades & Red Houses. Through Red Houses, hotel 300mtrs on right

A combination of a truly wonderful setting on the golden sands of St Brelade's Bay, a relaxed atmosphere and excellent facilities prove a winning formula here. Bedrooms are stylish and have a real contemporary feel to them; all have a plasma TV and a host of extras, and many have balconies or terraces commanding superb sea views. Spacious public areas include a spa and leisure club, a choice of dining options and relaxing lounges.

Rooms 106 en suite (2 fmly) (15 GF) ⊘ in 32 bedrooms S £115-£350; D £380-£490 (incl. bkfst) **Facilities** STV ⬚ supervised Sauna Gym Jacuzzi Wi-fi in bedrooms Windsurfing Water skiing Treatment rooms ♫ Xmas **Conf** Thtr 250 Class 100 Board 50 Del from £120 **Services** Lift **Parking** 125 **Notes** LB Civ Wed 250

★★★★ 78% **HOTEL**

St Brelade's Bay Hotel

JE3 8EF

☎ 01534 746141 📠 01534 747278

e-mail: info@stbreladesbayhotel.com

web: www.stbreladesbayhotel.com

dir: SW corner of the island

This family hotel overlooking the bay has many loyal guests and members of staff. The attractive tiered grounds, with easy access to the beach, are ablaze with colour in summer. There is an extensive range of indoor and outdoor recreational facilities including a choice of pools. Most bedrooms have king-size beds, many have inter-connecting children's rooms; there are stunning penthouse suites too. The tariff includes morning and afternoon tea.

Rooms 72 en suite (50 fmly) S £75-£114; D £110-£288 (incl. bkfst) **Facilities** STV ⬚ supervised ⬚ Snooker Sauna Gym ⬚ Putt green Petanque, Mini-gym, Games room, Table tennis ♫ **Conf** Thtr 20 Board 12 Del from £125 **Services** Lift **Parking** 60 **Notes** LB ⊗ ⊘ in restaurant Closed 3 Oct-21 Apr

---

★★★★ 77% ◉ **HOTEL**

Hotel La Place

Route du Coin, La Haule JE3 8BT

☎ 01534 744261 📠 01534 745164

e-mail: reservations@hotellaplacejersey.com

dir: off main St Helier/St Aubin coast road at La Haule Manor (B25). Up hill, 2nd left (to Red Houses), 1st right. Hotel is 100mtrs on right

Developed around a 17th-century farmhouse and well placed for exploration of the island this hotel is now under new ownership. Attentive, friendly service is the ethos here. A range of bedroom types is provided, some having private patios and direct access to the pool

continued

area. The cocktail bar is popular for pre-dinner drinks and a traditional lounge has a log fire in colder months. An interesting menu is offered.

Rooms 42 en suite (1 fmly) (10 GF) ⊗ in 25 bedrooms S £90-£170; D £70-£150 (incl. bkfst) **Facilities** STV ⚡ Wi-fi available Discount at Les Ormes Country Club, including golf, gym & indoor tennis Xmas **Conf** Thtr 100 Class 40 Board 40 Del from £145 **Parking** 100 **Notes LB** ⊗ in restaurant Civ Wed 100

See advert on this page

★★★ 73% **HOTEL**

Golden Sands

St Brelade's Bay JE3 8EF

☎ 01534 741241 📠 01534 499366

e-mail: goldensands@dolanhotels.com

web: www.dolanhotels.com

dir: follow St Brelade's Bay signs. Hotel on coastal side of road

With direct access to the beach, this popular hotel overlooks the wonderful sandy expanse of St Brelade's Bay. Many of the comfortable bedrooms are sea-facing with balconies where guests can relax and breathe in the fresh air. Public areas include a lounge, bar and restaurant, all of which have bay views.

Rooms 62 en suite (5 fmly) S £40-£75; D £60-£130 (incl. bkfst) **Facilities** STV Wi-fi available Children's play room 🎵 **Services** Lift **Notes** ⊗ ⊗ in restaurant Closed Nov-mid Apr

See advert on this page

AA ★★★★ ✿

ST BRELADE, JERSEY

★ Rural location close to St Aubin's Bay
★ Superb cuisine, service and hospitality
★ Swimming pool, sauna, gardens
★ Short Breaks, holidays and special rates
  available year round

Telephone: 01534 744261
Email: reservations@hotellaplacejersey.com
www.hotellaplacejersey.com

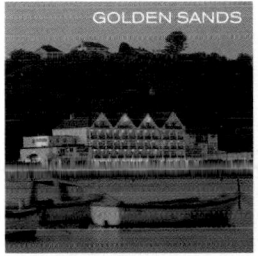

THREE HOTELS, THREE WONDERFUL LOCATIONS, ONE STANDARD

Dolan Hotels offer some of the finest 3-star accommodation in Jersey. Each of our hotels is in a beautiful location and most of the bedrooms have excellent ocean or countryside views. The Somerville overlooks picturesque St. Aubin's Harbour, The Cristina has a peaceful countryside location but is only five minutes from the sea and The Golden Sands is situated on one of the Island's best beaches.

To request a brochure or find out more about our rates, room availability and current special offers please telephone:

Golden Sands +44 (0) 1534 741241
Cristina   +44 (0) 1534 758024
Somerville   +44 (0) 1534 741226

www.dolanhotels.com

England

ST BRELADE *continued*

★★ 74% **HOTEL**

Beau Rivage

St Brelade's Bay JE3 8EF
☎ 01534 745983 🖹 01534 747127
e-mail: beau@jerseyweb.demon.co.uk
web: www.jersey.co.uk/hotels/beau

dir: *sea side of coast road in centre of St Brelade's Bay, 1.5m S of airport*

With direct access to one of Jersey's most popular beaches, residents and non-residents alike are welcome to this hotel's bar and terrace. Most of the well-equipped bedrooms have wonderful sea views, and some have the bonus of balconies. Residents have a choice of lounges, plus a sun deck exclusively for their use. A range of dishes featuring English and Continental cuisine is available on the carte menu.

Rooms 27 en suite (9 fmly) ⊗ in 1 bedroom **Facilities** STV Sunbathing terrace, Games Room 🎵 **Services** Lift **Parking** 16 **Notes LB** ⊗ ⊗ in restaurant RS Nov-Mar Civ Wed 80

🇺

Hotel Miramar

Mont Gras d'Eau JE3 8ED
☎ 01534 743831 🖹 01534 745009
e-mail: miramarjsy@localdial.com

dir: *From airport take B36 at lights, turn left onto A13, take 1st turning on right down Mont Gras D'Eau*

At the time of going to press, the star classification for this hotel was not confirmed. Please refer to the AA internet site www.theAA.com for current information.

Rooms 38 en suite (2 fmly) (14 GF) S £28-£38; D £56-£76 (incl. bkfst) **Facilities** ⚓ Jacuzzi **Parking** 30 **Notes** ⊗ in restaurant Closed Oct-mid Apr

Some hotels, although accepting children, may not have any special facilities for them so it is well worth checking before booking

ST HELIER
MAP 24

INSPECTORS' CHOICE

★★★★ ⚜⚜⚜⚜ **TOWN HOUSE HOTEL**

The Club Hotel & Spa

CLASSIC
BRITISH HOTELS

Green St JE2 4UH
☎ 01534 876500 🖹 01534 720371
e-mail: reservations@theclubjersey.com
web: www.huggler.com/index.cfm

dir: *5 mins walk from main shopping centre*

This swish, town-house hotel is conveniently located close to the centre of town and features stylish, contemporary decor throughout. All the guest rooms and suites include power showers and state-of-the-art technology including wide-screen LCD TV, DVD and CD systems. The choice of restaurants includes Bohemia; a sophisticated eating option that continues to offer highly accomplished cooking. For relaxing there is an elegant spa offering a luxurious range of treatments.

Rooms 46 en suite (4 fmly) (4 GF) ⊗ in 39 bedrooms **Facilities Spa** STV ⊡ ⚓ supervised Sauna **Conf** BC Thtr 30 Class 20 Board 14 **Services** Lift air con **Parking** 30 **Notes LB** ⊗ ⊗ in restaurant

★★★★ 77% ⚜⚜ **HOTEL**

Pomme d'Or

Liberation Square JE1 3UF
☎ 01534 880110 🖹 01534 737781
e-mail: enquiries@pommedorhotel.com

dir: *opposite harbour*

This historic hotel overlooks Liberation Square and the marina and offers comfortably furnished, well-equipped bedrooms. Popular with

continued

business fraternity for its range of conference facilities. Dining options include the traditional fine dining of the 'Petite Pomme', the smart carvery restaurant or the informal coffee shop.

Rooms 143 en suite (3 fmly) ⊘ in 105 bedrooms S £75-£110; D £104-£180 (incl bkfst) **Facilities** STV Use of Aquadome at Merton Hotel Wi-fi available Xmas **Conf** Thtr 220 Class 100 Board 50 Del from £142 **Services** Lift air con **Notes LB** ⊗

★★★★ 71% HOTEL

The Grand, Jersey

The Esplanade JE4 8WD

☎ 01534 722301 🖹 01534 737815

e-mail: grand.jersey@devere-hotels.com

Now under new ownership this local landmark is located on The Esplanade with pleasant views across St Aubin's Bay to the front. Bedrooms have a variety of styles, some with their own balcony. Guests can also enjoy spacious public areas, many of which look onto the bay. A full range of indoor leisure is available including pool, sauna, steam room, gym and many health and beauty treatments.

Rooms 118 en suite (7 GF) ⊘ in 22 bedrooms **Facilities Spa** STV 🏊 supervised Snooker Sauna Solarium Gym Jacuzzi Beauty therapy, Hairdressing ♫ **Conf** Thtr 200 Class 100 Board 80 **Services** Lift **Parking** 27 **Notes** ⊗ ⊘ in restaurant Civ Wed

---

★★★ 75% HOTEL

Best Western Royal

David Place JE2 4TD

☎ 01534 726521 🖹 01534 811046

e-mail: enquiries@royalhoteljersey.com

web: www.royalhoteljersey.com

dir: follow signs for Ring Rd, pass Queen Victoria rdbt keep left, left at lights, left into Piersons Rd. Follow one-way system to Cheapside. At A14 into Midvale Rd, hotel on left

This long established hotel is located in the centre of town and is within easy walking distance of the business district and shops. Seasons offers a modern approach to dining and with its adjoining bar provides a relaxed venue for hotel residents and locals alike. It provides individual bedrooms and a range of public areas.

Rooms 88 en suite (39 fmly) ⊘ in 16 bedrooms S £85-£100; D £100-£115 (incl. bkfst) **Facilities** STV Xmas **Conf** BC Thtr 300 Class 120 Board 80 Del £110 **Services** Lift **Parking** 15 **Notes LB** ⊗ ⊘ in restaurant Civ Wed 30

★★★ 74% HOTEL

Apollo

St Saviours Rd JE2 4GJ

☎ 01534 725441 🖹 01534 722120

e-mail: reservations@huggler.com

web: www.huggler.com

dir: on St Saviours Road at its junct with La Motte Street

Centrally located, this popular hotel has a relaxed, informal atmosphere. Bedrooms are comfortably furnished and include useful extras. Many guests return regularly to enjoy the variety of leisure facilities including an outdoor pool with water slide and indoor pool

continued

with separate jacuzzi. The elegant cocktail bar is an ideal place for a pre-dinner drink.

Apollo

Rooms 85 en suite (5 fmly) ⊘ in 20 bedrooms S £39-£112; D £78-£140 (incl. bkfst) **Facilities** 🏊 ⃗ supervised Sauna Solarium Gym Wi-fi available Jacuzzi Xmas **Conf** Thtr 150 Class 100 Board 80 **Services** Lift **Parking** 50 **Notes LB** ⊗ ⊘ in restaurant

---

★★★ 64% HOTEL

Royal Yacht

The Weighbridge JE2 3NF

☎ 01534 720511 🖹 01534 767729

e-mail: theroyalyacht@mail.com

dir: *in town centre, opp Marina and harbour*

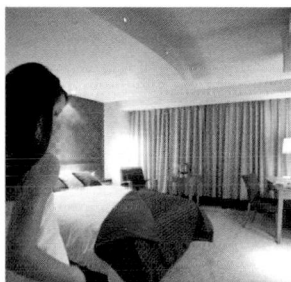

Overlooking the marina and steam clock, the Royal Yacht is thought to be the oldest established hotel on the island. However, it is undergoing a renovation and as part of this, there will be a contemporary-style building, due for completion in early 2007. Bedrooms are generally spacious, soundproofed and thoughtfully equipped. There is something for everyone here, including a choice of dining options.

Rooms 45 en suite **Facilities** STV ♫ **Conf** Thtr 80 Class 20 Board 20 **Services** Lift **Notes** ⊗ Civ Wed 100

★★★ 🅰

Hotel Revere

Kensington Place JE2 3PA

☎ 01534 611111 🖹 01534 611116

e-mail: reservations@revere.co.uk

web: www.revere.co.uk

dir: *From airport towards St Helier along the Esplanade. After The Grand Jersey turn left into Kensington Place.*

Rooms 58 rms (32 en suite) (2 fmly) (3 GF) ⊘ in 47 bedrooms S £40-£68; D £80-£136 (incl. bkfst) **Facilities** STV FTV ⃗ Wi-fi in bedrooms ♫ Xmas **Notes** ⊗

England

ST LAWRENCE _____ MAP 24

★★★ 74% **HOTEL**

Hotel Cristina
Mont Feland JE3 1JA
☎ 01534 758024 📠 01534 758028
e-mail: cristina@dolanhotels.com
web: www.dolanhotels.com
dir: turn off A10 onto Mont Felard, hotel on left

This hotel offers smartly styled and comfortable accommodation. Public areas reflect a contemporary style that makes this a refreshingly different hotel, with the modern restaurant serving a range of fresh produce in a bistro-like atmosphere. The terrace is adorned with flowers and is a popular place for soaking up the sun.

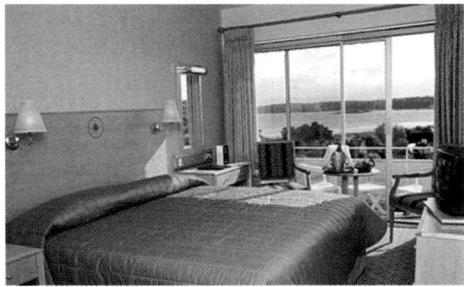

Hotel Cristina

Rooms 63 en suite (3 fmly) S £54-£135; D £60-£150 (incl. bkfst)
Facilities STV ⚡ Off peak membership to Les Ormes Golf/Leisure Club
🎵 **Conf** Thtr 100 Class 70 **Parking** 60 **Notes LB** ⊗ ⊘ in restaurant
Closed Nov-Mar Civ Wed 30

See advert on page 767

ST MARY _____ MAP 24

★★ 68% **HOTEL**

West View
La Grande Rue JE3 3BD
☎ 01534 481643 📠 01534 483283
e-mail: westview@jerseymail.co.uk
web: www.westviewhoteljersey.com
dir: N of island, at junct of B33 & C103, rear of St Mary's village

Located in the quiet parish of St. Mary and close to the delightful walks and cycle routes of the north coast. Bedrooms here are well equipped especially the larger, superior rooms. Entertainment is provided in the lounge bar during the summer months when guests can also enjoy a swim in the heated outdoor pool.

Rooms 42 en suite (3 fmly) (18 GF) S £27-£42; D £48-£78 (incl. bkfst)
Facilities ⚡ Wi-fi available **Parking** 38 **Notes** ⊗ ⊘ in restaurant
Closed 4 Nov-10 Mar

ST PETER _____ MAP 24

[U]

Greenhills
Mont De L'ecole JE3 7EL
☎ 01534 481042 📠 01534 485322
e-mail: greenhills@messages.co.uk

At the time of going to press, the star classification for this hotel was not confirmed. Please refer to the AA internet site www.theAA.com for current information.

Rooms 31 en suite (2 fmly) (9 GF) S £50-£71; D £100-£182 (incl. bkfst)
Facilities STV ⚡ **Conf** BC Thtr 20 Class 12 Board 16 Del from £100
Parking 40 **Notes LB** ⊘ in restaurant Closed mid Dec-mid Feb Civ Wed 40

ST SAVIOUR _____ MAP 24

INSPECTORS' CHOICE

★★★★ ◉◉◉ **HOTEL**

Longueville Manor
JE2 7WF
☎ 01534 725501 📠 01534 731613
e-mail: info@longuevillemanor.com
web: www.longuevillemanor.com
dir: A3 E from St Helier towards Gorey. Hotel 1m on left

RELAIS & CHATEAUX

Dating back to the 13th century, there is something very special about Longueville, which is why so many guests return. It is set in 17 acres of grounds including woodland walks, a spectacular rose garden and a lake. Bedrooms have great style and individuality boasting fresh flowers, fine embroidered bed linen and a host of extras. The committed team of staff create a welcoming atmosphere and every effort is made to ensure a memorable stay. The accomplished cuisine is a highlight.

Rooms 29 en suite 1 annexe en suite (7 GF) S £175-£225;
D £200-£300 (incl. bkfst) **Facilities** STV ⚡ 🏊 ⛳ Wi-fi in bedrooms
Xmas **Conf** Thtr 45 Class 30 Board 30 Del £245 **Services** Lift
Parking 40 **Notes LB** Civ Wed 40

TRINITY   MAP 24

★★★ 77% **HOTEL**

Best Western Highfield Country

Route d'Ebenezer JE3 5DT

☎ 01534 862194 ▤ 01534 865342

e-mail: reservations@highfieldjersey.com

web: www.highfieldjersey.com

dir: on A8 next to Ebenezer Chapel

Rurally located, this family-friendly hotel offers spacious, comfortable bedrooms, some with a kitchenette. Public areas are light and attractively styled, with the conservatory a popular venue for pre-dinner drinks. Leisure facilities include indoor and outdoor pools, and a sauna. A varied menu is provided at dinner, and breakfast is a self-service buffet.

Rooms 38 en suite (32 fmly) (1 GF) ⊛ in all bedrooms S £65-£75; D £100-£120 (incl. bkfst) **Facilities Spa** ⧖ ⧖ Sauna Gym Wi-fi in bedrooms Petanque ch fac **Services** Lift **Parking** 41 **Notes LB** ⊛ ⊛ in restaurant Closed Nov-Mar

★★★ 77% ⊛⊛ **HOTEL**

Water's Edge

Bouley Bay JE3 5AS

☎ 01534 862777 ▤ 01534 863645

e-mail: mail@watersedgehotel.co.je

web: www.watersedgehotel.co.je

Set in the tranquil surroundings of Bouley Bay on Jersey's north coast, this hotel is exactly as its name conveys and offers breathtaking views. The bedrooms offer high standards of quality and comfort. Dining options include the relaxed atmosphere of the adjoining Black Dog bar or the more formal award-winning restaurant.

Rooms 50 en suite (3 fmly) S £40-£90; D £80-£130 (incl. bkfst) **Facilities** ⧖ ♬ **Conf** Thtr 30 Class 25 Board 20 Del from £95 **Services** Lift **Parking** 20 **Notes LB** ⊛ ⊛ in restaurant Closed 16 Oct-17 Apr Civ Wed 80

MAN, ISLE OF

DOUGLAS   MAP 24 SC37

★★★★ 77% ⊛ **HOTEL**

Sefton

Harris Promenade IM1 2RW

☎ 01624 645500 ▤ 01624 676004

e-mail: info@seftonhotel.co.im

web: www.seftonhotel.co.im

dir: 500yds from Ferry Dock on Douglas promenade

This Victorian hotel has been sympathetically extended and upgraded over the years. Many of the spacious and comfortably furnished bedrooms have balconies overlooking the atrium water garden, while others enjoy sweeping views across the bay. A choice of comfortable lounges is available and freshly prepared dishes are served in the informal Gallery restaurant.

Sefton

Rooms 96 en suite ⊛ in 36 bedrooms S £80-£160; D £90-£160 **Facilities Spa** STV ⧖ Sauna Solarium Gym Jacuzzi Wi-fi in bedrooms Cycle hire, Steam room, Atrium water garden, Library **Conf** BC Thtr 150 Class 30 Board 50 Del from £130 **Services** Lift **Parking** 44 **Notes LB** ⊛ ⊛ in restaurant

★★★★ 74% **HOTEL**

Mount Murray

Santon IM4 2HT

☎ 01624 661111 ▤ 01624 611116

e-mail: manager@mountmurray.com

web: www.mountmurray.com

dir: 4m from Douglas towards airport. Hotel signed at Santon

This large, modern hotel and country club offers a wide range of sporting and leisure facilities, and a superb health and beauty salon. The attractively appointed public areas give a choice of bars and eating options. The spacious bedrooms are well equipped and many

continued on page 772

England

DOUGLAS *continued*

enjoy fine views over the 200-acre grounds and golf course. There is a very large conference suite.

Rooms 90 en suite (4 fmly) (28 GF) ⊗ in 12 bedrooms S £63.50-£98; D £69-£121 (incl. bkfst) **Facilities** Spa STV ⊠ ♨ 18 ♨ Squash Sauna Solarium Gym Putt green Jacuzzi Wi-fi in bedrooms Bowling green, Driving range, Sports hall Xmas **Conf** Thtr 300 Class 200 Board 100 Del from £135 **Services** Lift **Parking** 400 **Notes** LB ⊛ ⊘ in restaurant

★★★ 75% HOTEL

Empress

Central Promenade IM2 4RA
☎ 01624 661155 ◳ 01624 673554
e-mail: reservations@theempresshotel.net
web: www.theempresshotel.net

This hotel is a large Victorian building on the central promenade overlooking Douglas Bay. Well-equipped, modern bedrooms include suites and rooms with sea views. A pianist entertains in the lounge bar most evenings. Other facilities include a lounge, a sun lounge and a brasserie-style restaurant.

Rooms 102 en suite ⊗ in 73 bedrooms S £59.50-£75; D £75-£95 (incl. bkfst) **Facilities** Spa STV ⊠ Sauna Gym Jacuzzi Wi-fi available ♪ Xmas **Conf** BC Thtr 200 Class 150 Board 50 Del £108 **Services** Lift **Notes** LB ⊛

★★★ 74% HOTEL

Welbeck Hotel

13/15 Mona Dr IM2 4LF
☎ 01624 675663 ◳ 01624 661545
e-mail: mail@welbeckhotel.com
dir: at crossroads of Mona & Empress Drive off Central Promenade

The Welbeck is a privately owned and personally run hotel situated within easy reach of the seafront. It offers guests a friendly welcome and a choice of attractive accommodation, ranging from well-equipped bedrooms to six luxury apartments, each with its own lounge and small kitchen. Other facilities include two rooms for meetings and functions, plus a mini-gym and steam room.

Rooms 27 en suite (7 fmly) ⊗ in all bedrooms **Facilities** STV Gym Wi-fi in bedrooms Steam room Gym **Conf** BC **Services** Lift **Notes** ⊛ ⊘ in restaurant Closed 19 Dec-5 Jan

PEEL   MAP 24 SC28

★★ 74% HOTEL

Ballacallin House

Dalby Village, Patrick IM5 3BT
☎ 01624 841100 ◳ 01624 845055
e-mail: ballacallin@advsys.co.uk
web: www.ballacallin.com

THE INDEPENDENTS

dir: A27 Peel to Port Erin Rd at S end of Dalby Village

This small, privately owned hotel situated in Dalby village is personally run and offers well-equipped, modern accommodation of a very good standard. Bedrooms with four-posters and a two-bedroom suite are available. Sea views can be enjoyed from some of the bedrooms, the bright restaurant and the spacious lounge bar.

Rooms 10 en suite (1 fmly) ⊗ in all bedrooms **Conf** Thtr 30 Class 24 Board 24 **Parking** 70 **Notes** LB ⊘ in restaurant Closed 5-25 Jan

PORT ERIN   MAP 24 SC16

★★ 69% HOTEL

Falcon's Nest

The Promenade IM9 6AF
☎ 01624 834077 ◳ 01624 835370
e-mail: falconsnest@enterprise.net
web: www.falconsnesthotel.co.uk

dir: follow coastal road, S from airport or ferry. Hotel on seafront, immediately after steam railway station

Situated overlooking the bay and harbour, this Victorian hotel offers generally spacious bedrooms. There is a choice of bars, one of which is very popular with the locals. Meals can be taken in the lounge bar, the conservatory or in the attractively decorated main restaurant.

Rooms 35 en suite (9 fmly) ⊗ in 3 bedrooms S £35-£42.50; D £70-£85 (incl. bkfst) **Facilities** STV Wi-fi in bedrooms Xmas **Conf** Thtr 50 Class 50 Board 50 Del from £150 **Parking** 40 **Notes** LB ⊘ in restaurant

Find it with theAA.com

Click on to the AA website, **theAA.com**, to find AA listed guest houses, hotels, pubs and restaurants – some 12,000 establishments – the **AA Route Planner and Map Finder will help you find the way**.

Search for a Hotel/B&B or a Pub/Restaurant by location or establishment name and then scroll down the list of establishments for the interactive map and local routes.

To use the **Route Planner** on the Home page, simply enter your postcode and the establishment postcode given in this guide and click **Get route**. Check your details and then you are on your way.

Discover new horizons with Britain's largest travel publisher

Scotland

Stromness,
Orkney

Scotland

ABERDEEN CITY

ABERDEEN

See also Aberdeen Airport

MAP 23 NJ90

HOTEL OF THE YEAR

★★★★ 86% @ **HOTEL**

Marcliffe Hotel and Spa

North Deeside Rd AB15 9YA

☎ 01224 861000 📠 01224 868860

e-mail: enquiries@marcliffe.com

web: www.marcliffe.com

dir: A90 onto A93 signed Braemar. 1m on right after turn at lights

Set in attractive landscaped grounds west of the city, this impressive hotel presents a blend of styles backed by caring and attentive service. A split-level conservatory restaurant, terraces and courtyards all give a sense of the Mediterranean, whilst the elegant and sophisticated cocktail lounge is classical in style. Bedrooms are well-proportioned and thoughtfully equipped. AA Hotel of the Year for Scotland 2006-7.

Rooms 42 en suite (4 fmly) (12 GF) ⊘ in all bedrooms S £140-£295; D £140-£295 (incl. bkfst) **Facilities Spa** STV Snooker Gym Putt green Wi-fi in bedrooms ch fac Xmas **Conf** BC Thtr 500 Class 300 Board 84 Del from £225 **Services** Lift **Parking** 222 **Notes LB** ⊘ in restaurant Civ Wed 450

See advert on opposite page

★★★★ 79% @ **HOTEL**

Norwood Hall

Garthdee Rd, Cults AB15 9FX

☎ 01224 868951 📠 01224 869868

e-mail: info@norwood-hall.co.uk

web: www.norwood-hall.co.uk

dir: off A90, at 1st rdbt cross Bridge of Dee, left at rdbt onto Garthdee Rd (B&Q and Sainsbury on left) continue to hotel sign

This imposing Victorian mansion has retained many of its features, most notably the fine oak staircase, stained glass and ornately decorated walls and ceilings. Accommodation comes in three different styles - individual bedrooms in the main house, a wing of spacious superior rooms and an older wing of modern but less spacious rooms. The extensive grounds ensure the hotel is a popular wedding venue.

Rooms 37 en suite (3 fmly) ⊘ in 15 bedrooms **Facilities** STV **Conf** Thtr 200 Class 100 Board 70 **Services** Lift **Parking** 100 **Notes LB** ⊗ ⊘ in restaurant Civ Wed 150

★★★★ 77% **HOTEL**

Aberdeen Patio

Beach Boulevard AB24 5EF

☎ 01224 633339 & 380000 📠 01224 638833

e-mail: info@patiohotels.com

web: www.patiohotels.com

dir: from A90 follow signs for city centre, then for sea. On Beach Blvd, turn left at lights, hotel on right

This modern, purpose-built hotel lies close to the seafront. Bedrooms come in two different styles - the retro-style Classics and spacious Premiers. The Platinum Club offers a unique experience of 44 superb high spec bedrooms that have their own reception and bar/lounge/dinner/breakfast room. The restaurant and striking Atrium bar is housed in the main building.

Rooms 124 en suite 44 annexe en suite (8 fmly) (22 GF) ⊘ in 127 bedrooms S £60-£165; D £70-£175 **Facilities** STV ⚒ supervised Sauna Solarium Gym Jacuzzi Wi-fi in bedrooms Steam room, Treatment Room Xmas **Conf** Thtr 150 Class 80 Board 50 Del from £110 **Services** Lift **Parking** 172 **Notes LB** ⊘ in restaurant

★★★★ 77% **HOTEL**

Macdonald Ardoe House

South Deeside Rd, Blairs AB12 5YP

☎ 0870 194 2104 📠 01224 861283

e-mail: ardoe@macdonald-hotels.co.uk

web: www.macdonald-hotels.co.uk

dir: 4m W of city off B9077

From its elevated position on the banks of the River Dee, this baronial-style mansion commands excellent countryside views. Tastefully decorated, thoughtfully equipped bedrooms are located in the main house, or more modern extension. Public rooms include a spa and leisure club, a cosy lounge and cocktail bar and impressive function facilities.

continued

Rooms 109 en suite (4 fmly) ⊘ in all bedrooms S £180-£220; D £180-£235 **Facilities Spa** STV ☒ supervised ⌣ Sauna Solarium Gym Jacuzzi Wi-fi in bedrooms Xmas **Conf** Thtr 500 Class 200 Board 150 Del from £170 **Services** Lift **Parking** 250 **Notes LB** ⊘ in restaurant Civ Wed 70

★★★★ 74% ◉◉ **HOTEL**

Copthorne Hotel Aberdeen

122 Huntly St AB10 1SU

COPTHORNE

☎ 01224 630404 📠 01224 640573

e-mail: reservations.aberdeen@mill-cop.com

web: www.copthorne.com

dir: W of city centre, off Union Street, up Rose Street, hotel 0.25m on right on corner with Huntly Street

Situated just out of the city centre, this hotel offers friendly, attentive service. The smart bedrooms are well proportioned and guests will appreciate the added quality of the Connoisseur rooms. Mac's bar provides a relaxed atmosphere in which to enjoy a drink or to dine informally, whilst Poachers Restaurant offers a slightly more formal dining experience.

Rooms 89 en suite (15 fmly) ⊘ in 69 bedrooms S £69-£205; D £69-£205 **Facilities** STV Wi-fi available **Conf** Thtr 200 Class 100 Board 70 Del from £130 **Services** Lift **Parking** 15 **Notes LB** RS 25-26 Dec Civ Wed 150

★★★★ 72% **HOTEL**

Thistle Aberdeen Caledonian

10-14 Union Ter AB10 1WE

THISTLE HOTELS

☎ 0870 333 9151 📠 0870 333 9251

e-mail: aberdeencaledonian@thistle.co.uk

dir: Follow signs to city centre and Union St. Turn onto Union Terrace, hotel on left.

Centrally located just off Union Street & overlooking Union Terrace Gardens this traditional hotel offers comfortable & well-appointed bedrooms & public areas in keeping with the age & style of the building. The upbeat Café Bar Caley also serves informal food with a more formal dining experience available in the 'Restaurant on the Terrace'. A small car park is available to the rear of the hotel.

Rooms 77 en suite (2 fmly) ⊘ in 65 bedrooms **Facilities** STV **Conf** BC Thtr 75 Class 48 Board 40 **Services** Lift **Parking** 18 **Notes** ⊗ ⊘ in restaurant

★★★ 79% **HOTEL**

Atholl

54 Kings Gate AB15 4YN

☎ 01224 323505 📠 01224 321555

e-mail: info@atholl-aberdeen.co.uk

web: www.atholl-aberdeen.com

dir: in West End 400yds from Anderson Drive, on A90

A high level of hospitality and guest care feature at this hotel, set in the suburbs within easy reach of central amenities and the ring road. The modern bedrooms include free broadband internet access. Guests

continued on page 778

Scotland

ABERDEEN *continued*

can choose between the restaurant and bar to enjoy the great value menu.

Atholl

Rooms 34 en suite (1 fmly) ⊘ in all bedrooms S £75-£105; D £120-£130 (incl. bkfst) **Facilities** STV **Conf** Thtr 60 Class 25 Board 25 Del from £125 **Parking** 60 **Notes** LB ⊗ ⊘ in restaurant Closed 1 Jan

★★★ 79% ⊛ HOTEL

The Mariner Hotel

349 Great Western Rd AB10 6NW

☎ 01224 588901 🖷 01224 571621

e-mail: info@themarinerhotel.co.uk

dir: E off Anderson Drive (A90) at Great Western Rd. Hotel on right on corner of Gray St

This well maintained family operated hotel is located west of the city centre. The smart, spacious bedrooms are well equipped and particularly comfortable, with executive suites available. The public rooms are restricted to the lounge bar, which is food driven, and the Atlantis restaurant that showcases the region's wide choice of excellent seafood and meats.

Rooms 17 en suite 8 annexe en suite (4 GF) ⊘ in 19 bedrooms S £80-£115; D £95-£130 (incl. bkfst) **Facilities** STV Wi-fi in bedrooms Xmas **Parking** 51 **Notes** ⊗ ⊘ in restaurant

★★★ 77% HOTEL

Queens Hotel

49-53 Queens Rd AB15 4YP

☎ 01224 209999 🖷 01224 209009

e-mail: enquiries@the-queens-hotel.com

web: www.the-queens-hotel.com

dir: Turn off A90 from Anderson Drive at Queens Rd, hotel is 400yds on right. From city centre take West End exit

Popular with business travellers and as a function venue, this well-

continued

established hotel lies east of the city centre. Public areas include a reception lounge and an intimate restaurant; however the extensive bar menu remains a preferred choice for many regulars. There are two styles of accommodation, with the superior rooms being particularly comfortable and well equipped.

Rooms 32 en suite 2 annexe en suite (6 fmly) (10 GF) ⊘ in 12 bedrooms S £50-£110; D £65-£125 (incl. bkfst) **Facilities** STV Wi-fi in bedrooms **Conf** Thtr 400 Class 150 Board 60 Del from £132.50 **Parking** 80 **Notes** ⊗ ⊘ in restaurant Closed 25-26 Dec & 1-2 Jan Civ Wed 120

★★★ 74% HOTEL

The Craighaar

Waterton Rd, Bucksburn AB21 9HS

☎ 01224 712275 🖷 01224 716362

e-mail: info@craighaar.co.uk

dir: turn off A96 (Airport/Inverness) onto A947, hotel signed

Conveniently located for the airport, this welcoming hotel is a popular base for business people and tourists alike. Guests can make use of a quiet library lounge, and enjoy meals in the bar or restaurant. All bedrooms are well equipped, plus there is a wing of duplex suites that provide additional comfort.

Rooms 55 en suite (6 fmly) (18 GF) ⊘ in 12 bedrooms S £89-£119; D £99-£129 (incl. bkfst) **Facilities** FTV Wi-fi in bedrooms Library **Conf** BC Thtr 90 Class 33 Board 30 Del from £120 **Parking** 80 **Notes** LB ⊗ ⊘ in restaurant Civ Wed 40

★★★ 74% ⊛ HOTEL

Maryculter House Hotel

South Deeside Rd, Maryculter AB12 5GB

☎ 01224 732124 🖷 01224 733510

e-mail: info@maryculterhousehotel.com

web: www.maryculterhousehotel.com

dir: off A90 on S side of Aberdeen, onto B9077. Hotel 8m on right, 0.5m beyond Lower Deeside Caravan Park

Set in grounds on the banks of the River Dee, this charming Scottish mansion dates back to medieval times and is a popular wedding and conference venue. Exposed stonework and open fires feature in the oldest parts, which house the cocktail bar and Priory Restaurant. Lunch and breakfast are taken overlooking the river and bedrooms are equipped with business travellers in mind.

Rooms 40 en suite (4 fmly) (16 GF) ⊘ in 34 bedrooms S £65-£110; D £75-£130 (incl. bkfst) **Facilities** STV FTV Fishing Wi-fi available Clay pigeon shooting, Archery Xmas **Conf** BC Thtr 220 Class 100 Board 50 Del from £125 **Parking** 150 **Notes** LB ⊘ in restaurant Civ Wed 150

★★★ 74% HOTEL

Thistle Aberdeen Altens

THISTLE HOTELS

Souter Head Rd, Altens AB12 3LF
☎ 0870 333 9150 🖷 0870 333 9250
e-mail: aberdeenaltens@thistle.co.uk

dir: A90 onto A956 signed Aberdeen Harbour. Hotel just off rdbt.

Popular with oil industry personnel, this large purpose-built hotel lies in the Altens area south east of the city. It's worth asking for one of the huge executive bedrooms that provide excellent space. Guests have a choice of eating in either the restaurant, brasserie or the bar.

Rooms 206 en suite (3 fmly) (39 GF) ⊘ in 124 bedrooms **Facilities** STV ⯑ Sauna Solarium Gym Jacuzzi **Conf** Thtr 400 Class 150 Board 100 **Services** Lift **Parking** 300 **Notes LB** Civ Wed 200

★★ 59% HOTEL

Dunavon House

THE INDEPENDENTS

60 Victoria St, Dyce AB21 7EE
☎ 01224 722483 🖷 01224 772721
e-mail: info@dunavonhousehotel.co.uk

dir: from A96 north to Inverness follow A947 into Victoria St. Hotel 500yds on right

In Dyce, north of the city and convenient for the airport, this hotel is housed in a sympathetically converted Victorian villa. Bedrooms are well equipped and come in a variety of sizes. An extensive range of meals is served in both the lounge bar and the restaurant.

Rooms 18 en suite (5 GF) ⊘ in 7 bedrooms S £67-£120; D £89-£150 (incl. bkfst) **Facilities** Free access to local leisure facilities **Conf** BC **Parking** 26 **Notes LB** ⊗ ⊘ in restaurant

🅰

Swallow Waterwheel Inn

SWALLOW

203 North Deeside Rd, Bieldside AB15 9EN
☎ 01224 860100 🖷 01224 860102
web: www.swallowhotels.com
Rooms 21 en suite **Notes** ★★

BUDGET HOTEL

Premier Travel Inn Aberdeen Central West

premier travel inn

North Anderson Dr AB15 6DW
☎ 0870 9906430 🖷 0870 9906431
web: www.premiertravelinn.com

dir: 3m from city centre, 5m from Aberdeen Airport. Follow A90 towards city centre. From S, follow airport signs. Inn 1st left after fire station

High quality, modern budget accommodation ideal for both families and business travellers. Spacious, en suite bedrooms feature bath and shower, satellite TV and many have telephones and modem points. The adjacent family restaurant features a wide and varied menu. For further details consult the Hotel Groups page.

Rooms 60 en suite

Premier Travel Inn Aberdeen City Centre

Inverlair House, West North St AB24 5AR
☎ 0870 9906300 🖷 0870 9906301

dir: From A90, follow A9013 into city centre. Turn onto A966 towards King St, then 1st left

Rooms 162 en suite **Conf** Thtr 80

Premier Travel Inn Aberdeen North

Ellon Rd, Murcar, Bridge of Don AB23 8BP
☎ 08701 977012 🖷 01224 706869

dir: From City Centre take A90 north. At rdbt, 1m past Exhibition Centre, turn left onto B999. Inn is on right

Rooms 40 en suite

Premier Travel Inn Aberdeen South

Mains of Balquharn, Portlethen AB12 4QS
☎ 08701 977013 🖷 01224 783836

dir: on A90, exit signed Portlethen Shopping Centre & Badentoy Industrial Estate

Rooms 40 en suite

Premier Travel Inn Aberdeen (Westhill)

Straik Rd, Westhill AB32 6HF
☎ 0870 9906348 🖷 0870 9906349

dir: 6m from city centre on A944

Rooms 61 en suite

Scotland

Scotland

ABERDEEN *continued*

BUDGET HOTEL

Travelodge Aberdeen Bucksburn

Inverurie Rd, Bucksburn AB21 9BB

☎ 08700 850 950 🖨 01224 715609

web: www.travelodge.co.uk

dir: west of A96 & A947 junct, towards Inverurie

Travelodge offers good quality, good value, modern accommodation. Ideal for families, the spacious en suite bedrooms include remote-control TV, tea and coffee-making facilities and comfortable beds. Meals can be taken at the nearby family restaurant. See Hotel Groups pages for further details.

Rooms 48 en suite S fr £26; D fr £26

Travelodge Aberdeen Central

9 Bridge St AB11 6JL

☎ 08700 850 950 🖨 01224 584587

dir: into city on A90, lodge at junct of Union St & Bridge St

Rooms 97 en suite S fr £26; D fr £26

ABERDEEN AIRPORT   MAP 23 NJ81

★★★★ 77% HOTEL

Aberdeen Marriott Hotel

Marriott HOTELS & RESORTS

Overton Circle, Dyce AB21 7AZ

☎ 01224 770011 🖨 01224 722347

e-mail: reservations.scotland@marriotthotels.com

web: www.marriott.com

dir: follow A96 to Bucksburn, right at rdbt onto A947. Hotel in 2m at 2nd rdbt

Close to the airport and conveniently located for the business district, this purpose-built hotel is a popular conference venue. The well-proportioned bedrooms come with many thoughtful extras. Public areas include an informal bar and lounge, a split-level restaurant and a leisure centre that can be accessed directly from a number of bedrooms.

Rooms 155 en suite (68 fmly) (61 GF) ⊗ in 124 bedrooms S £124-£164; D £124-£164 **Facilities Spa** STV ⊡ supervised Sauna Solarium Gym Jacuzzi Wi-fi available Xmas **Conf** BC Thtr 400 Class 200 Board 60 Del from £140 **Services** air con **Parking** 180 **Notes LB** ⊗ ⊗ in restaurant

★★★★ 77% HOTEL

Thistle Aberdeen Airport

THISTLE HOTELS

Aberdeen Airport, Argyll Rd AB21 0AF

☎ 0870 333 9149 🖨 0870 333 9249

e-mail: aberdeenairport@thistle.co.uk

dir: adjacent to Aberdeen Airport

Ideally located at the entrance to the airport whilst offering ample parking & a courtesy bus service to the terminal. A well presented hotel that benefits from good-sized bedrooms & comfortable public areas. 'Just Gym' offers a good selection of equipment.

Rooms 147 en suite (40 fmly) (77 GF) ⊗ in 113 bedrooms **Facilities** STV Gym **Conf** Thtr 600 Class 250 Board 80 **Parking** 400 **Notes** ⊗ ⊗ in restaurant Civ Wed 400

U

Dyce Skean Dhu

THISTLE HOTELS

Farburn Ter, Dyce AB21 7DW

☎ 0870 333 9152 🖨 0870 333 9252

e-mail: dyceskeandhu@thistle.co.uk

dir: 1m from airport, next to Dyce railway station

At the time of going to press, the star classification for this hotel was not confirmed. Please refer to the AA internet site www.theAA.com for current information.

Rooms 78 en suite 141 annexe en suite (78 fmly) ⊗ in 94 bedrooms **Facilities** Snooker **Conf** Thtr 400 Class 160 Board 120 **Parking** 250 **Notes** ⊗ in restaurant

BUDGET HOTEL

Travelodge Aberdeen Airport

Burnside Dr, off Riverside Dr, Dyce AB21 0HW

☎ 08700 850950 🖨 01224 772968

web: www.travelodge.co.uk

dir: from Aberdeen A96 towards Inverness, turn right at rdbt onto A947, at 2nd rdbt turn right then 2nd right

Travelodge offers good quality, good value, modern accommodation. Ideal for families, the spacious en suite bedrooms include remote-control TV, tea and coffee-making facilities and comfortable beds. Meals can be taken at the nearby family restaurant. See Hotel Groups pages for further details.

Rooms 40 en suite S fr £26; D fr £26

ABERDEENSHIRE

BALLATER   MAP 23 NO39

INSPECTORS' CHOICE

★★★ ⊛⊛⊛ SMALL HOTEL

Darroch Learg

Braemar Rd AB35 5UX

☎ 013397 55443 🖨 013397 55252

e-mail: nigel@darrochlearg.co.uk

web: www.darrochlearg.co.uk

dir: on A93, at western side of Ballater

Set high above the road in extensive wooded grounds, this renowned hotel offers fine views over the spectacular countryside of Royal Deeside. Bedrooms, some with four-poster beds, are

continued

individually styled, bright and spacious. Food is a highlight of any visit, whether it is a freshly prepared breakfast, a light lunch or the award-winning Scottish cuisine served in the delightful conservatory restaurant.

Rooms 12 en suite 5 annexe en suite (1 GF) ⊘ in all bedrooms **Conf** Thtr 25 Board 12 **Parking** 25 **Notes LB** ⊘ in restaurant Closed Xmas & Jan (ex New Year)

★★★ 80% HOTEL

Loch Kinord
Ballater Rd, Dinnet AB34 5JY
☎ 013398 85229 📄 013398 87007
e-mail: stay@kinord.com
dir: on A93 in village of Dinnet

Family-run, this roadside hotel lies between Aboyne and Ballater and is well located for leisure and sporting pursuits. It has lots of character and a friendly atmosphere. There are two bars, one outside and a cosy one inside, plus a dining room in bold, tasteful colour schemes. The stylish bedrooms boast smart bathrooms.

Rooms 20 en suite (3 fmly) (4 GF) ⊘ in 5 bedrooms S £65-£90; D £85 £99 (incl. bkfst) **Facilities** Sauna Jacuzzi Wi fi available Pool table ch fac Xmas **Conf** Thtr 40 Class 30 Board 30 **Parking** 20 **Notes LB** ⊘ in restaurant Civ Wed 50

A

Cambus O'May
AB35 5SE
☎ 013397 55428 📄 013397 55428
e-mail: mckechnie@cambusomay.freeserve.co.uk
web: www.cambusomayhotel.co.uk
dir: A93 from Ballater for 4m towards Aberdeen, hotel on left
Rooms 12 en suite (1 fmly) **Parking** 12 **Notes** ★★★ **LB** ⊘ in restaurant No credit cards accepted

A

Swallow Loirston
Victoria Rd AB35 5RA   SWALLOW
☎ 01339 755413 📄 01339 755027
web: www.swallowhotels.com
Rooms 58 en suite **Notes** ★★

BANCHORY   MAP 23 NO69

★★★ 86% ◉◉ COUNTRY HOUSE HOTEL

Raemoir House
Raemoir AB31 4ED
☎ 01330 824884 📄 01330 822171
e-mail: hotel@raemoir.com
dir: A93 to Banchory, then onto A980 to Torphins, 2m at T-junct

Set in extensive grounds, this country mansion dates from the mid-18th century and retains many period features. Gracious public rooms have tapestry-covered walls, open fires in massive fireplaces and fine antiques. Bedrooms offer individual styles and come in various sizes; most are well proportioned and reflect the character of the house. Service is very attentive.

Rooms 14 en suite 6 annexe en suite (1 fmly) (3 GF) ⊘ in 2 bedrooms S £70-£90; D £110-£160 (incl. bkfst) **Facilities** ⥮ ⥮ Putt green Wi-fi in bedrooms Shooting Stalking ♫ Xmas **Conf** Thtr 45 Class 25 Board 30 Del £125 **Parking** 60 **Notes LB** ⊘ in restaurant Civ Wed 40

★★★ 81% COUNTRY HOUSE HOTEL

Banchory Lodge
AB31 5HS
☎ 01330 822625 📄 01330 825019
e-mail: enquiries@banchorylodge.co.uk
dir: off A93, 13m W of Aberdeen, hotel off Dee Street

This hotel enjoys a scenic setting in grounds by the River Dee. Inviting public areas include a choice of lounges, a cosy bar and a restaurant with views of the river. Bedrooms come in two distinct styles; those in the original part of the house contrasting with the newer wing rooms, which are particularly spacious.

Rooms 22 en suite (11 fmly) ⊘ in 10 bedrooms S £70-£85; D £130-£150 (incl. bkfst) **Facilities** Fishing Pool room Xmas **Conf** Thtr 90 Class 30 Board 28 Del from £120 **Parking** 50 **Notes LB** ⊘ in restaurant Civ Wed 150

Scotland

BANCHORY *continued*

★★ 72% **HOTEL**

Best Western Burnett Arms

25 High St AB31 5TD
☎ 01330 824944 ▤ 01330 825553
e-mail: theburnett@btconnect.com
dir: *town centre on N side of A93, 18m from centre of Aberdeen*

This popular hotel is located in the heart of the town centre and gives easy access to the many attractions of Royal Deeside. Public areas include a choice of eating and drinking options, with food served in the restaurant, bar and foyer lounge. Bedrooms are thoughtfully equipped and comfortably modern.

Rooms 17 en suite (1 fmly) ⊛ in 7 bedrooms S £46-£71; D £69-£99 (incl. bkfst) **Facilities** STV Xmas **Conf** Thtr 100 Class 50 Board 50 Del from £781.50 **Parking** 40 **Notes LB** ⊛ in restaurant Civ Wed 100

See advertisement under ABERDEEN

BANFF   MAP 23 NJ66

★★★ 75% **HOTEL**

Banff Springs

Golden Knowes Rd AB45 2JE
☎ 01261 812881 ▤ 01261 815546
e-mail: info@banffspringshotel.co.uk
dir: *western outskirts of town on A98, Banff to Inverness road*

Attentive service by friendly staff is a feature of this comfortable business and tourist hotel overlooking the Moray Firth. Public areas include a smart foyer lounge and a popular bar/bistro, which provides an informal dining alternative to the restaurant. Bedrooms are smartly furnished, with the front facing ones enjoying greater space as well as splendid coastal views.

Rooms 35 en suite (4 GF) ⊛ in all bedrooms S £39-55; D £68-£97 (incl. bkfst) **Facilities** STV Gym Wi-fi in bedrooms Air con **Conf** Thtr 400 Class 100 Board 40 Del from £72.50 **Parking** 200 **Notes LB** ⊛ in restaurant Closed 25-26 Dec Civ Wed 200

CRUDEN BAY   MAP 23 NK03

★★ 69% **HOTEL**

Kilmarnock Arms

Bridge St AB42 0HD
☎ 01779 812213 ▤ 01779 812153
e-mail: reception@kilmarnockarms.com
web: www.kilmarnockarms.com
dir: *off A90 onto A975 N of Ellon (8m S of Peterhead)*

Lying by the riverside at the northern end of the village close to the golf course and beach, this family-run hotel offers smart, attractive modern accommodation. There is also an inviting reception lounge, plus a bar and restaurant offering a good range of popular dishes.

Rooms 14 en suite (1 fmly) **Facilities** STV **Parking** 10 **Notes LB** ⊛ in restaurant

★★ 69% **HOTEL**

Red House

Aulton Rd AB42 0NJ
☎ 01779 812215 ▤ 01779 812246
dir: *off A952 Aberdeen/Peterhead road onto A975 (Cruden Bay), hotel opposite golf course*

Naturally popular with golfers, this welcoming small hotel overlooks the famous golf course and the sea beyond. Bedrooms are spacious and well furnished, and several provide superb coastal views. Guests can eat in the attractive dining room or in a choice of bars, from an extensive menu selection.

Rooms 6 rms (5 en suite) (1 fmly) ⊛ in all bedrooms **Facilities** STV Pool tables ♪ Xmas **Parking** 40 **Notes** ⊛ in restaurant

HUNTLY   MAP 23 NJ53

★★ 65% **HOTEL**

Gordon Arms Hotel

The Square AB54 8AF
☎ 01466 792288 ▤ 01466 794556
e-mail: reception@gordonarms.demon.co.uk
dir: *off A96 Aberdeen to Inverness road at Huntly*

This friendly family-run hotel is located in the town square and offers a good selection of tasty, well-portioned dishes served in the bar (or in the restaurant at weekends and midweek by appointment). Bedrooms come in a variety of sizes, and all come with a good range of accessories.

Rooms 13 en suite (3 fmly) ⊛ in 12 bedrooms S £37.50; D £48.50-£62.50 (incl. bkfst) **Facilities** ♪ **Conf** Thtr 160 Class 80 Board 60 Del from £52 **Notes LB** ⊛ in restaurant

INVERURIE   MAP 23 NJ72

★★★ 74% HOTEL

Macdonald Pittodrie House

Chapel of Garioch, Pitcaple AB51 5HS
☎ 0870 1942111 ▤ 01467 681648
e-mail: pittodrie@macdonald-hotels.co.uk
web: www.macdonald-hotels.co.uk
dir: from A96 take exit for Chapel of Garioch

Set in extensive grounds this house dates from the 15th century and retains many of its original features. Public rooms include a gracious drawing room, restaurant and a cosy bar boasting an impressive selection of whiskies. The well-proportioned bedrooms are contained in both the original house and a sympathetically designed extension that retains the character of the house.

Rooms 27 en suite (6 fmly) ⊛ in 13 bedrooms S £55-£164; D £70-£171 (incl. bkfst) **Facilities** STV Squash Snooker ⤷ Clay pigeon shooting Quad biking Archery etc on estate Xmas **Conf** Thtr 100 Class 70 Board 40 Del from £140 **Parking** 150 **Notes LB** ⊛ in restaurant Civ Wed 120

A

Swallow Kintore Arms

SWALLOW
HOTELS

83 High St AB51 3QJ
☎ 01467 621367 ▤ 01467 625620
web: www.swallowhotels.com
Rooms 21 en suite **Notes** ★★★

A

Swallow Thainstone House

SWALLOW
HOTELS

AB51 5NT
☎ 01467 621643 ▤ 01467 625084
web: www.swallowhotels.com
dir: A96 from Aberdeen. Entrance to hotel at Thainstone Rdbt. Take 1st left then sharp right
Rooms 48 en suite **Notes** ★★★★

NEWBURGH   MAP 23 NJ92

A

Swallow Udny Arms

SWALLOW
HOTELS

Main St AB41 6BL
☎ 01358 789444 ▤ 01358 789012
web: www.swallowhotels.com
dir: off A92 at signed Newburgh, hotel 2m, in centre of village
Rooms 25 en suite **Notes** ★★★

OLDMELDRUM   MAP 23 NJ82

★★★ 78% ⊚ COUNTRY HOUSE HOTEL

Meldrum House Hotel Golf & Country Club

AB51 0AE
☎ 01651 872294 ▤ 01651 872464
e-mail: enquiries@meldrumhouse.com
dir: 11m from Aberdeen on A947 (Aberdeen to Banff road)

Set in 350 acres of wooded parkland this imposing baronial country mansion has a golf course as its centrepiece. Tastefully restored to highlight its original character it provides a peaceful retreat. Bedrooms are massive, and like the public rooms, transport guests back to a bygone era, but at the same time providing all modern amenities including smart bathrooms.

Rooms 9 en suite (1 fmly) (1 GF) ⊛ in all bedrooms S £100-£130; D £120-£150 (incl. bkfst) **Facilities** ↕ 18 ⤷ Putt green Xmas **Conf** Thtr 80 Class 20 Board 30 Del from £130 **Parking** 45 **Notes** ⊛ in restaurant Civ Wed 70

PETERHEAD   MAP 23 NK14

★★★ 70% HOTEL

Palace

Prince St AB42 1PL
☎ 01779 474821 ▤ 01779 476119
e-mail: info@palacehotel.co.uk
web: www.palacehotel.co.uk
dir: A90 from Aberdeen, follow signs to Peterhead, on entering town turn into Prince St, then right into main car park

This town centre hotel is popular with business travellers and for social events. Bedrooms come in two styles, with the executive rooms being particularly smart and spacious. Public areas include a themed bar, an informal diner reached via a spiral staircase, and a brasserie restaurant and cocktail bar.

Rooms 64 en suite (2 fmly) (14 GF) ⊛ in 44 bedrooms S £50-£65; D £60-£80 (incl. bkfst) **Facilities** STV Snooker Pool table Gym rates reduced for guests ♫ Xmas **Conf** Thtr 250 Class 120 Board 50 **Services** Lift **Parking** 90 **Notes LB** Civ Wed 280

Scotland

PETERHEAD *continued*

A

Swallow Waterside Inn

Fraserburgh Rd AB42 3BN

SWALLOW HOTELS

☎ 01779 471121 ▤ 01779 470670

web: www.swallowhotels.com

dir: from Aberdeen A90, 1st rdbt turn left signed Fraserburgh, cross small rdbt, hotel at end of road

Rooms 69 en suite **Facilities** Snooker Sauna Solarium Gym Jacuzzi Beauty treatment rooms, Pool table, Bouncy castle, Swimming pool supervised ♫ **Notes** ★★★

ANGUS

BRIDGEND OF LINTRATHEN MAP 23 NO25

◉◉ RESTAURANT WITH ROOMS

Lochside Lodge & Roundhouse Restaurant

DD8 5JJ

☎ 01575 560340 ▤ 01575 560251

e-mail: enquiries@lochsidelodge.com

dir: B951 from Kirriemuir towards Glenisla for 7m left to Lintrathen. Hotel on left in village

This converted farmstead enjoys a rural location in the heart of Angus. The comfortable bedrooms that offer private facilities are in a former hayloft and the original windows have been retained. Accomplished modern cuisine is served in the Roundhouse Restaurant. A spacious bar featuring agricultural implements and church pews, has a wide range of drinks including local beers.

Rooms 6 en suite (1 fmly) (2 GF) ⊗ in all bedrooms S £77-£115; D £135-£175 (incl. bkfst & dinner) **Facilities** STV **Conf** Class 20 Board 25 **Parking** 40 **Notes LB** ⊗ in restaurant Closed 25-26 Dec & 1-24 Jan RS Sun & Mon

CARNOUSTIE MAP 21 NO53

A

Swallow Carnoustie

The Links DD7 7JE

SWALLOW HOTELS

☎ 01241 411999 ▤ 01241 411998

web: www.swallowhotels.com

dir: right turn into Carnoustie from A92, follow golf course signs

Rooms 85 en suite **Notes** ★★★★

EDZELL MAP 23 NO66

★★★ 66% HOTEL

Glenesk

High St DD9 7TF

☎ 01356 648319 ▤ 01356 647333

e-mail: gleneskhotel@btconnect.com

web: www.gleneskhotel.co.uk

dir: off A90 just after Brechin Bypass

Set in gardens by the golf course, this long established hotel is popular with both leisure and business guests. Public areas are comfortable and include a leisure club with a swimming pool.

Rooms 24 en suite (5 fmly) S £60-£80; D £95-£110 (incl. bkfst) **Facilities** ⬚ Snooker Sauna Gym ⬩ Jacuzzi Wi-fi available Xmas **Conf** Thtr 120 Class 60 Board 30 Del from £110 **Parking** 80 **Notes LB** ⊛ ⊗ in restaurant Civ Wed 100

FORFAR MAP 23 NO45

A

Swallow Royal

33 Castle St DD8 3AE

SWALLOW HOTELS

☎ 01307 462691 ▤ 01307 462691

web: www.swallowhotels.com

Rooms 21 en suite **Notes** ★★★

GLAMIS MAP 21 NO34

INSPECTORS' CHOICE

★★★ ◉◉◉ COUNTRY HOUSE HOTEL

Castleton House

Castleton of Eassie DD8 1SJ

☎ 01307 840340 ▤ 01307 840506

e-mail: hotel@castletonglamis.co.uk

web: www.castletonglamis.co.uk

dir: on A94 between Forfar/Cupar Angus, 3m W of Glamis

Set in its own grounds and with a moat, this impressive Victorian house has a relaxed and friendly atmosphere. Accommodation is provided in individually designed, spacious bedrooms. Personal service from the enthusiastic proprietors is a real feature and many guests return time and again. Accomplished cooking, utilising the best local produce, is served in the conservatory restaurant.

Rooms 6 en suite (2 fmly) ⊗ in 1 bedroom **Facilities** ⬩ Putt green ch fac **Conf** Thtr 30 Class 20 Board 20 **Parking** 50 **Notes LB** Civ Wed 50

KIRRIEMUIR   MAP 23 NO35

A

Airlie Arms
4 St Malcolms Wynd DD8 4IIB
☎ 01575 572847 📠 01575 573055
e-mail: info@airliearms-hotel.co.uk
web: www.airliearms-hotel.co.uk
dir: From Dundee on A90 take A926 to Kirriemuir
Rooms 10 en suite (2 fmly) (5 GF) ⊘ in 2 bedrooms S £40-£50;
D £65-£75 (incl. bkfst) **Facilities** STV ♬ Xmas **Conf** Thtr 80 Class 70
Board 50 **Parking** 5 **Notes** ★★★ **LB** ⊘ in restaurant

MONIFIETH   MAP 21 NO43

A

Swallow Panmure
Tay St DD5 4AX
☎ 01382 532911 📠 01382 535859
web: www.swallowhotels.com
Rooms 13 en suite **Notes** ★★★

SWALLOW

MONTROSE   MAP 23 NO75

★★★ 78% ⊛ **HOTEL**

Best Western Links Hotel
Mid Links DD10 8RL
☎ 01674 671000 📠 01674 672698
e-mail: reception@linkshotel.com
web: www.bw-linkshotelmusic.com
dir: A935 to Montrose then right at Lochside junct, left at swimming pool and right by tennis courts for hotel 200yds

This former Edwardian town house is a popular venue for touring jazz and folk musicians. Bedrooms offer a choice of attractive modern styles and are extremely well equipped to cater for business guests. Public areas include a bar, a restaurant, and a popular coffee shop where food is available all day.

Rooms 25 en suite (1 GF) ⊘ in 24 bedrooms S £65-£88; D £74-£98 (incl. bkfst) **Facilities** FTV Wi-fi in bedrooms ♬ Xmas **Conf** Thtr 220 Class 70 Board 70 Del from £110 **Parking** 45 **Notes** **LB** ⊘ in restaurant Civ Wed 120

A

Swallow Park
51 John St DD10 8RJ
☎ 01674 663400 📠 01674 677091
web: www.swallowhotels.com
dir: from A90 off at A935 to A92, from A92 turn off Montrose High St into John St
Rooms 57 en suite **Notes** ★★★

SWALLOW

ARDUAINE   MAP 20 NM71

★★★ 82% ⊛⊛ **HOTEL**

Loch Melfort
PA34 4XG
☎ 01852 200233 📠 01852 200214
e-mail: reception@lochmelfort.co.uk
web: www.lochmelfort.co.uk
dir: on A816, midway between Oban and Lochgilphead

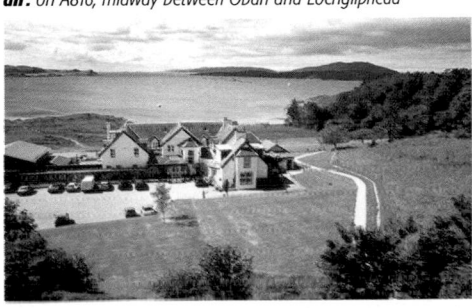

Enjoying one of the finest locations on the West Coast, this popular, family-run hotel has outstanding views across Asknish Bay towards the Islands of Jura, Scarba and Shuna. Accommodation is provided in either the balconied rooms of the Cedar wing or the more traditional rooms in the main hotel. Skilfully cooked dinners remain the highlight of any visit.

Rooms 6 en suite 20 annexe en suite (2 fmly) (10 GF) ⊘ in all bedrooms S £54-£89; D £85-£178 (incl. bkfst) **Facilities** FTV Xmas **Conf** Thtr 50 Class 35 Board 24 Del from £80 **Parking** 65 **Notes** **LB** ⊘ in restaurant Closed 3 Jan-15 Feb

ARROCHAR   MAP 20 NN20

A

Swallow Arrochar
G83 7AU
☎ 01301 702484 📠 01301 702599
web: www.swallowhotels.com
Rooms 70 en suite **Notes** ★★

SWALLOW

CAIRNDOW   MAP 20 NN11

★★ 66% **HOTEL**

Cairndow Stagecoach Inn
PA26 8BN
☎ 01499 600286 & 600252 📠 01499 600220
e-mail: cairndowinn@aol.com

THE CIRCLE
Selected Individual Hotels

dir: either A82 to Tarbet, then A83 to Cairndown or A85 to Palmally, A819 to Inveraray and A83 to Cairndown.

A relaxed, friendly atmosphere prevails at this 18th-century inn, overlooking the beautiful Loch Fyne. Bedrooms offer individual décor and thoughtful extras. Traditional public areas include a comfortable

continued on page 786

Scotland

Scotland

CAIRNDOW *continued*

beamed lounge, a well-stocked bar where food is served throughout the day, and a spacious restaurant with conservatory extension.

Cairndow Stagecoach Inn

Rooms 13 en suite (2 fmly) ⊘ in 3 bedrooms **Facilities** Sauna Solarium Gym **Parking** 32 **Notes LB** ⊘ in restaurant

CAMPBELTOWN   MAP 20 NR72

🅐

Swallow White Hart

Main St PA28 6AN

☎ 01586 552440 ▤ 01586 554972

web: www.swallowhotels.com

SWALLOW

dir: Exit M8 junct 30, after bridge W onto A82. Follow Loch Lomond to Tarbet junct and take A83. In Campbeltown town centre turn right at T-junct, hotel 300yds on left.

Rooms 19 en suite (2 fmly) ⊘ in 5 bedrooms S £35-£49.50; D £50-£75 (incl. bkfst) **Facilities** ♫ Xmas **Conf** Thtr 60 **Notes** ★★ **LB** ⊘ in restaurant

CARRADALE   MAP 20 NR83

🅐 **SMALL HOTEL**

Dunvalanree

Port Righ Bay PA28 6SE

☎ 01583 431226 ▤ 01583 431339

e-mail: stay@dunvalanree.com

dir: From centre of Carradale, turn right at x-rds and continue to end of the road

Rooms 7 rms (5 en suite) (1 GF) ⊘ in all bedrooms D £120-£132 (incl. bkfst & dinner) **Facilities** ♨ Fishing Riding Putt green **Parking** 8 **Notes** ★★★★ **LB** ⊗ Closed Nov-Feb

CLACHAN   MAP 20 NR75

★★ 76% ⊚ **COUNTRY HOUSE HOTEL**

Balinakill Country House

PA29 6XL

☎ 01880 740206 ▤ 01880 740298

e-mail: info@balinakill.com

dir: access from A83, 50mtrs beyond Thames Garage

This imposing B-listed country mansion is set in grounds on the Kintyre peninsula. Graced with antiques and period pieces it boasts beautiful wood panelling and plasterwork. Many bedrooms reflect the Victorian era, with the larger ones featuring real fires. Service by

continued

hands-on owners is friendly and attentive. Meals focus on interesting menus and well-sourced produce.

Rooms 10 en suite (1 GF) ⊘ in all bedrooms S £50-£100; D £90-£110 (incl. bkfst) **Facilities** Fishing Aromatherapy Reflexology Relaxing health treatments Xmas **Parking** 20 **Notes LB** ⊘ in restaurant

See advert on opposite pag

CLACHAN-SEIL   MAP 20 NM7?

★★ 85% ⊚ ⊚ **SMALL HOTEL**

Willowburn

PA34 4TJ

☎ 01852 300276

e-mail: willowburn.hotel@virgin.net

web: www.willowburn.co.uk

dir: 0.5m from Atlantic Bridge, on left

This welcoming small hotel enjoys a peaceful setting, with grounds stretching down to the shores of Clachan Sound. Friendly unassuming service, a relaxed atmosphere and fine food are keys to its success. Bedrooms are bright, cheerful and thoughtfully equipped. Guests can watch the wildlife from the dining room, lounge or cosy bar.

Rooms 7 en suite (1 GF) ⊘ in all bedrooms S £80; D £160 (incl. bkfst & dinner) **Parking** 20 **Notes LB** No children 8yrs ⊘ in restaurant Closed Dec-Feb

CONNEL   MAP 20 NM9?

★★★ 75% **HOTEL**

Falls of Lora

PA37 1PB

☎ 01631 710483 ▤ 01631 710694

e-mail: enquiries@fallsoflora.com

web: www.fallsoflora.com

dir: A85 from Glasgow, 0.5m past Connel sign

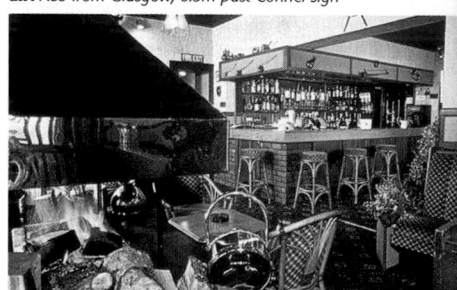

Personally run and welcoming, this long-established and thriving holiday hotel enjoys inspiring views over Loch Etive. The spacious ground floor takes in a comfortable, traditional lounge and a well-stocked bar. Guests can eat in the popular, informal bistro that caters specifically for families from 5pm onwards. Bedrooms come in a variety of styles, ranging from the cosy standard rooms to high quality luxury rooms.

Rooms 30 en suite (4 fmly) (4 GF) S £41-£69; D £49-£119 (incl. bkfst) **Conf** Thtr 45 Class 20 Board 15 **Parking** 40 **Notes LB** ⊘ in restaurant Closed mid Dec & Jan

See advertisement under OBA?

COVE

MAP 20 NS28

U

Knockderry House

Shore Rd G84 0NX

☎ 01436 842283

e-mail: info@knockderryhouse.co.uk

web: www.knockderryhouse.co.uk

dir: *A82 to Lochlomondside, turn W on A817 Garelochhead, follow signs to Coulport, turn S to hotel 2.5m*

At the time of going to press, the star classification for this hotel was not confirmed. Please refer to the AA internet site www.theAA.com for current information.

Rooms 9 en suite ⊗ in all bedrooms S £60-£95; D £110-£160 (incl. bkfst)
Facilities Xmas **Conf** BC **Parking** 30 **Notes** LB ⊗ in restaurant

DUNOON

MAP 20 NS17

★★ 79% **HOTEL**

Royal Marine

Hunters Quay PA23 8HJ

☎ 01369 705810 ▤ 01369 702329

e-mail: rmhotel@sol.co.uk

web: www.rmhotel.co.uk

dir: *on A815 opposite Western Ferries terminal*

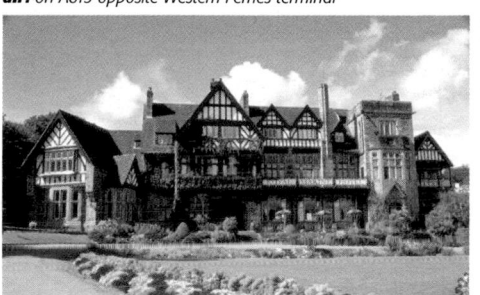

This welcoming privately owned hotel commands impressive views over the Firth of Clyde. The bedrooms vary in size and are modern in appointment, offering a good range of amenities. Public areas include a formal dining room where a fixed-price menu is available, a well-stocked bar and the popular Ghillies café-bar with its attractive garden area.

Rooms 31 en suite 10 annexe en suite (3 fmly) (5 GF) S £54-£67; D £75-£86 (incl. bkfst) **Facilities** ♫ Xmas **Conf** Thtr 90 Class 40 Board 30 **Parking** 40 **Notes** LB ⊛ ⊗ in restaurant Civ Wed

Scotland

DUNOON *continued*

★★ 69% HOTEL

Selborne

Clyde St, West Bay PA23 7HU

Leisureplex

☎ 01369 702761 📠 01369 704032

e-mail: selborne.dunoon@alfatravel.co.uk

web: www.alfatravel.co.uk

dir: from Caledonian Macbrayne pier. Follow road past castle, left into Jane St and then right into Clyde St

This holiday hotel is situated overlooking the West Bay and provides unrestricted views of the Clyde Estuary towards the Isles of Cumbrae. Tour groups are especially well catered for in this good-value establishment, which offers entertainment most nights. Bedrooms are comfortable with many having sea views.

Rooms 98 en suite (14 GF) ❷ in all bedrooms S £29-£34; D £48-£58 (incl. bkfst) **Facilities** Pool table, Table tennis ♫ Xmas **Services** Lift **Parking** 30 **Notes LB** ❸ ❷ in restaurant Closed Dec-Feb ex Xmas RS Nov & Mar

★★ 68% HOTEL

Esplanade Hotel

West Bay PA23 7HU

☎ 01369 704070 📠 01369 702129

e-mail: relax@ehd.co.uk

dir: 100mtrs from Dunoon pier, 1st left after Castle House Museum

This well presented hotel enjoys a prime location and views over the Firth of Clyde. Public areas include relaxing lounges on both the first and ground floors and a large dining room. Thoughtfully equipped bedrooms, many of which are spacious, come in a variety of styles.

Rooms 60 en suite 5 annexe en suite (5 fmly) (17 GF) ❷ in 30 bedrooms **Facilities** STV ♥ Putt green ♫ **Conf** Thtr 50 Class 50 Board 40 **Services** Lift **Parking** 23 **Notes LB** ❸ ❷ in restaurant Closed 2 Jan-9 Apr, 17 Oct-23 Dec

ERISKA   **MAP 20 NM94**

INSPECTORS' CHOICE

★★★★★ ◉◉◉ COUNTRY HOUSE HOTEL

Isle of Eriska

Eriska, Ledaig PA37 1SD

☎ 01631 720371 📠 01631 720531

e-mail: office@eriska-hotel.co.uk

dir: leave A85 at Connel, onto A828, follow for 4m, then follow signs from N of Benderloch

Situated on its own private island with delightful beaches and walking trails, this hotel offers a tranquil setting for total relaxation. Spacious bedrooms are comfortable and boast some fine antique pieces. Local seafood, meats and game feature prominently on the award-winning menu, as do vegetables and herbs grown in the hotel's kitchen garden. Leisure facilities include an indoor swimming pool, gym, spa treatment rooms and a small golf course.

continued

Isle of Eriska

Rooms 22 en suite 5 annexe en suite (2 GF) ❷ in 3 bedrooms S £210; D £275-£350 (incl. bkfst) **Facilities** Spa ⚐ supervised ⚓ 6 ⚑ Fishing Sauna Gym ♥ Putt green Jacuzzi Wi-fi in bedrooms Steam room, Skeet shooting, Nature trails Xmas **Conf** Thtr 30 Class 30 Board 30 Del from £145 **Parking** 40 **Notes LB** ❷ in restaurant Closed Jan Civ Wed 44

HELENSBURGH   **MAP 20 NS28**

BUDGET HOTEL

Innkeeper's Lodge Helensburgh

112-17 West Clyde St G84 8ES

☎ 01436 676924 📠 01436 676233

web: www.innkeeperslodge.com

dir: on A814 seafront, 400m W of Pier

Smart, en suite accommodation ideal for both business & leisure guests. Bedrooms are very well equipped, including Sky TV, telephone, modem points, tea & coffee making facilities, (family rooms in most locations). Complimentary breakfast. The adjacent Pub Restaurant; a Harvester, Vintage Inn, Toby Carvery, Ember Inn, Sizzling Pubco or Pub & Carvery offers an all day menu. See Hotel Groups pages for further details.

Rooms 44 en suite S £49.95-£54.95; D £49.95-£54.95 **Conf** Thtr 200 Class 100 Board 80

INVERARAY   **MAP 20 NN00**

★★★ 81% HOTEL

Loch Fyne Hotel & Leisure Club

CRERAR
HOTELS

PA32 8XT

☎ 0870 950 6270 📠 01499 302348

e-mail: lochfyne@crerarhotels.com

web: www.crerarhotels.com

dir: from A83 Loch Lomond, through town centre on A80 to Lochgilphead. Hotel in 0.5m

This popular holiday hotel overlooks Loch Fyne. Bedrooms are mainly spacious and offer comfortable modern appointments. Guests can relax in the well-stocked bar and enjoy views over the Loch, or enjoy a meal in the delightful restaurant. There is also a well-equipped leisure centre.

continued

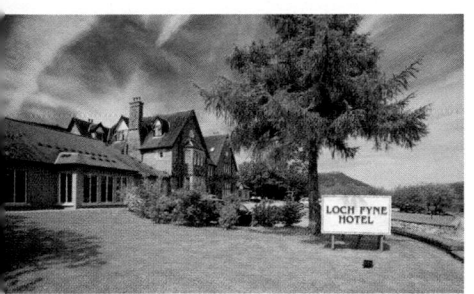

Loch Fyne Hotel & Leisure Club

Rooms 74 en suite ⊘ in all bedrooms S £55-£75; D £110-£160 (incl. bkfst) **Facilities Spa** ⌧ supervised Sauna Jacuzzi Wi-fi in bedrooms Steam Room Hot tub (outdoor), Massage Aromatherapy Relaxation suite ♫ Xmas **Conf** Thtr 50 Class 30 Board 20 Del from £99 **Services** Lift **Parking** 50 **Notes LB** ⊘ in restaurant

A

Swallow Argyll

Front St PA32 8XB

SWALLOW

☎ 01499 302466 🖷 01499 302389

web: www.swallowhotels.com

dir: *A83 (Tarbet to Inveraray). Hotel 1st building facing loch*

Rooms 36 en suite **Notes** ★★★

KILCHRENAN   MAP 20 NN02

★★★ 81% ◉◉ COUNTRY HOUSE HOTEL

Taychreggan

PA35 1HQ

☎ 01866 833211 & 833366 🖷 01866 833244

e-mail: info@taychregganhotel.co.uk

dir: *W from Crianlarich on A85 to Taynuilt, S for /m on B845 to Kilchrenan and Taychreggan*

Surrounded by stunning Highland scenery this stylish and superbly presented hotel enjoys an idyllic setting, in 40 acres of grounds, on the shores of Loch Awe. Ground floor areas include a smart bar with adjacent Orangery and a choice of quiet lounges with deep, luxurious sofas. The kitchen has earned a well deserved reputation for the skilfully prepared dinners that showcase the local and seasonal Scottish larder.

Rooms 20 en suite ⊘ in 9 bedrooms S £99-£117; D £100-£127 (incl. bkfst) **Facilities** no TV in bdrms Fishing Snooker ⤢ Jacuzzi **Conf** Class 35 Board 20 **Parking** 40 **Notes LB** No children 14yrs ⊘ in restaurant Civ Wed 70

★★★ 76% ◉◉ HOTEL

The Ardanaiseig

by Loch Awe PA35 1HE

☎ 01866 833333 🖷 01866 833222

e-mail: ardanaiseig@clara.net

dir: *turn S off A85 at Taynuilt onto B845 to Kilchrenan. Left in front of pub (road very narrow) signed 'Ardanaiseig Hotel' & 'No Through Road'*

Set amid lovely gardens and breathtaking scenery beside the shore of Loch Awe, this peaceful country-house hotel was built in a Scottish baronial style in 1834. Many fine pieces of furniture are evident in the bedrooms and charming day rooms, which include a drawing room, a library bar, and an elegant dining room. Dinner provides the highlight

continued on page 790

KILCHRENAN *continued*

of any visit with skilfully cooked dishes making excellent use of local, seasonal produce.

Rooms 16 en suite (4 fmly) **Facilities** STV 🏊 Fishing Snooker ⛳ Boating, Clay pigeon shooting, Bikes for hire **Parking** 20 **Notes LB** ⊘ in restaurant Closed 2 Jan-14 Feb Civ Wed 50

See advert on page 789

LOCHGILPHEAD   MAP 20 NR88

★★★ 80% ◉ **HOTEL**

Cairnbaan

Crinan Canal, Cairnbaan PA31 8SJ
☎ 01546 603668 📄 01546 606045
e-mail: info@cairnbaan.com
web: www.cairnbaan.com

dir: 2m N, A816 from Lochgilphead, hotel off B841

Located on the Crinan Canal, this small hotel offers relaxed hospitality in a delightful setting. Bedrooms are thoughtfully equipped, generally spacious and benefit from stylish decor. Fresh seafood is a real feature in both the formal restaurant and the comfortable bar area. Alfresco dining is popular in the warmer months.

Rooms 12 en suite ⊘ in all bedrooms **Conf** Thtr 160 Class 100 Board 80 **Parking** 53 **Notes LB** ⊘ in restaurant Civ Wed 120

LUSS   MAP 20 NS39

★★★ 79% ◉◉ **HOTEL**

The Lodge on Loch Lomond

G83 8PA
☎ 01436 860201 📄 01436 860203
e-mail: res@loch-lomond.co.uk
web: www.loch-lomond.co.uk
dir: off A82, follow sign for hotel

This hotel is idyllically set on the shores of Loch Lomond. Public areas consist of an open-plan, split-level bar and fine dining restaurant overlooking the loch. The pine-finished bedrooms also enjoy the views and are comfortable, spacious and well equipped. All have saunas and some have DVDs/internet access. There is a stunning state-of-the-art leisure suite.

Rooms 29 en suite 17 annexe en suite (20 fmly) (13 GF) ⊘ in all bedrooms S £67-£349; D £87-£369 (incl. bkfst) **Facilities Spa** STV 🖵 Sauna Jacuzzi Fishing Boating Residents only health suite & spa Xmas **Conf** Thtr 150 Class 80 Board 60 Del from £150 **Parking** 120 **Notes LB** ⊘ in restaurant Civ Wed 100

OBAN   MAP 20 NM93

★★★ 80% ◉ **HOTEL**

Manor House

Gallanach Rd PA34 4LS
☎ 01631 562087 📄 01631 563053
e-mail: info@manorhouseoban.com
web: www.manorhouseoban.com

dir: follow signs MacBrayne Ferries and pass ferry entrance for hotel on right

Handy for the ferry terminal and with views of the bay and harbour, this elegant Georgian residence was built for the Duke of Argyll. Comfortable and attractive public rooms invite relaxation, whilst most of the well-equipped bedrooms are graced by period pieces.

Rooms 11 en suite ⊘ in all bedrooms **Facilities** STV **Parking** 20 **Notes** No children 12yrs ⊘ in restaurant Closed 25-26 Dec

★★★ 75% **HOTEL**

Falls of Lora

PA37 1PB
☎ 01631 710483 📄 01631 710694
e-mail: enquiries@fallsoflora.com
web: www.fallsoflora.com

(For full entry see Connel)

See advert on opposite page

★★★ 72% **HOTEL**

Oban Bay Hotel and Spa   CRERAR

The Esplanade PA34 5AG
☎ 0870 950 6273 📄 01631 564006
e-mail: obanbay@crerarhotels.com
web: www.crerarhotels.com

dir: Follow A85 into Oban. Straight at 1st rdbt & right at 2nd, hotel 200yds on right.

Situated on the esplanade, this completely refurbished hotel enjoys splendid views across the bay to nearby islands. Smart and comfortable lounges set the scene, along with the stylish bedrooms. There are also two very impressive suites. A small spa includes an outside hot tub.

continued

Oban Bay Hotel and Spa

Rooms 80 en suite (3 GF) ⊗ in all bedrooms S £55-£110; D £65-£200 (incl. bkfst) **Facilities Spa** Sauna Steam room Hot tub ♫ Xmas **Conf** Thtr 10 Class 10 Board 10 Del from £69 **Services** Lift **Parking** 20 **Notes LB** ⊗ in restaurant

★★★ 64% **HOTEL**

Columba

North Pier PA34 5QD
☎ 01631 562183 🖹 01631 564683
e-mail: columbahotel@freeuk.com

dir: A85 to Oban, 1st set of lights in town and turn right

This popular tourist hotel is located on the North Pier and many of the bedrooms overlook the bay. Public areas include a restaurant, breakfast room and a choice of contrasting bars. Guests are welcome to use the leisure facilities at the sister hotel, The Alexandra.

Rooms 48 en suite (6 fmly) **Facilities** ♫ **Conf** Class 40 Board 30 **Services** Lift **Parking** 10 **Notes LB** ⊗ in restaurant

★★ 85% ⊛⊛ **SMALL HOTEL**

Willowburn

PA34 4TJ
☎ 01852 300276
e-mail: willowburn.hotel@virgin.net
web: www.willowburn.co.uk

(For full entry see Clachan-Seil)

★★ 78% ⊛ **HOTEL**

The Kimberley Hotel

13 Dalriach Rd PA34 5EQ
☎ 01631 571115 🖹 01631 571120
e-mail: info@kimberley-hotel.com
web: www.kimberley-hotel.com

dir: exit A85 onto Dalriach Rd (signed Swimming Pool & Sports Facilities). Continue to end of road

Set in an elevated location the Kimberley enjoys panoramic views of Oban harbour and the islands beyond. Bedrooms are spacious and well equipped. There is a guest lounge with internet facilities and

continued

Bachler's Conservatory, where delicious meals are served, has now been added.

The Kimberley Hotel

Rooms (4 GF) ⊗ in 12 bedrooms S fr £80; D £104-£122 (incl. bkfst) **Facilities** ⌣ Fishing **Parking** 9 **Notes LB** ⊗ in restaurant Closed Nov-1wk before Etr

Ⓐ

Swallow Caledonian Oban

SWALLOW HOTELS

Station Square PA34 5RT
☎ 01631 563133 🖹 01631 562998
web: www.swallowhotels.com

dir: at head of main pier, close to rail terminal

Rooms 59 en suite **Notes** ★★★★

Scotland

OBAN *continued*

A

Swallow Queens

SWALLOW HOTELS

Esplanade PA34 5AG
☎ 01631 562505 🖷 01631 566217
web: www.swallowhotels.com
Rooms 43 en suite **Notes** ★★★

A

Swallow Regent

SWALLOW HOTELS

The Esplanade PA34 5PZ
☎ 01631 562341 🖷 01631 565816
web: www.swallowhotels.com
Rooms 82 en suite **Notes** ★★

PORT APPIN MAP 20 NM94

INSPECTORS' CHOICE

★★★★ 🏵🏵🏵 **HOTEL**

Airds

PA38 4DF
☎ 01631 730236 🖷 01631 730535
e-mail: airds@airds-hotel.com
web: www.airds-hotel.com
dir: *from A828 (Oban to Fort William road), turn at Appin signed Port Appin. Hotel 2.5m on left.*

The views are stunning from this small, luxury hotel on the shores of Loch Linnhe where the staff are delightful and nothing is too much trouble. The well-equipped bedrooms provide style and luxury whilst many bathrooms are furnished in marble and have power showers. Expertly prepared dishes utilising the finest of ingredients are served in the elegant dining room. Comfortable lounges with deep sofas and roaring fires provide the ideal retreat for relaxation. A real get-away-from-it-all experience.

Rooms 12 en suite (2 fmly) (2 GF) ⊗ in all bedrooms S £175-£265; D £285-£395 (incl. bkfst & dinner) **Facilities** STV Xmas **Conf** Thtr 16 Class 16 Board 16 **Parking** 21 **Notes LB** ⊗ in restaurant Closed 8-30 Jan RS Nov-Feb Civ Wed 40

STRACHUR MAP 20 NN00

★★★ 72% 🏵 **HOTEL**

Creggans Inn

PA27 8BX
☎ 01369 860279 🖷 01369 860637
e-mail: info@creggans-inn.co.uk
web: www.creggans-inn.co.uk

dir: *follow A82/A83 Loch Lomond road to Arrochar. Continue on A83 then take A815 Strachur*

Benefiting from a super location on the shores of Loch Fyne, this well-established hotel is well placed for both tourists and business travellers. Many of the bedrooms have fine views and a number have high quality bathrooms. There is a choice of spacious lounges and freshly prepared meals can be enjoyed in either the popular bar or stylish restaurant.

Rooms 14 en suite S £55-£105; D £110-£170 (incl. bkfst) **Facilities** Fishing Wi-fi available Xmas **Conf** Thtr 25 Class 25 Board 25 Del from £100 **Parking** 50 **Notes LB** ⊗ ⊗ in restaurant

TARBERT LOCH FYNE MAP 20 NN30

★★★ 78% 🏵 **HOTEL**

Stonefield Castle

PA29 6YJ
☎ 01880 820836 🖷 01880 820929
e-mail: enquiries@stonefieldcastle.co.uk

dir: *off A83, 2m N of Tarbert, hotel approx 0.25m down driveway*

This fine baronial castle commands a superb lochside setting amidst beautiful woodland gardens renowned for their rhododendrons - visit in late spring to see them at their best. Elegant public rooms are a feature, and the picture-window restaurant offers unrivalled views across Loch Fyne. Bedrooms are split between the main house and a purpose-built wing.

Rooms 33 rms (32 en suite) (10 GF) **Facilities** Fishing Snooker **Conf** Thtr 180 Class 140 Board 40 **Services** Lift **Parking** 50 **Notes LB** ⊗ in restaurant Civ Wed 120

TIGHNABRUAICH MAP 20 NR97

★★★ 85% 🏵🏵 **SMALL HOTEL**

The Royal at Tighnabruaich

Shore Rd PA21 2BE
☎ 01700 811239 🖷 01700 811300
e-mail: info@royalhotel.org.uk
web: www.royalhotel.org.uk

dir: *from Strachur on A886 right onto A8003 to Tighnabruaich. Hotel on right at bottom of hill*

This outstanding family-run hotel provides high levels of personal care from the proprietors and their local staff. Set just yards from the loch shore, stunning views are guaranteed from many rooms, including the elegant Crustacean restaurant and the more informal Deck restaurant where fresh seafood and game are served. The comfortable bedrooms vary in size and style.

Rooms 11 en suite ⊗ in all bedrooms S £100-£180; D £100-£180 (incl. bkfst) **Facilities Spa** sailing, fishing, windsurfing, riding, walking, bird watching Xmas **Conf** Class 20 Board 10 **Parking** 20 **Notes LB** ⊗ in restaurant Closed 4 days Xmas

CITY OF EDINBURGH

EDINBURGH   **MAP 21 NT27**

INSPECTORS' CHOICE

★★★★★ ◉◉ **TOWN HOUSE HOTEL**

Prestonfield

Priestfield Rd EH16 5UT
☎ 0131 225 7800 🖷 0131 220 4392
e-mail: reservations@prestonfield.com
web: www.prestonfield.com

dir: A7 towards Cameron Toll. 200mtrs beyond Royal Commonwealth Pool, into Priestfield Rd

This centuries-old landmark has been lovingly restored and enhanced to provide deeply comfortable and dramatically furnished bedrooms. The building demands to be explored: from the tapestry lounge to the whisky room and the restaurant, where the walls are adorned with pictures of former owners. Facilities and services are up to the minute, and carefully prepared meals are served in the Rhubarb restaurant.

Rooms 24 en suite (6 GF) ⊗ in 3 bedrooms **Facilities** STV ♨ 18 ⚑
Xmas **Conf** BC Thtr 700 Class 500 Board 40 **Services** Lift
Parking 250 **Notes** Civ Wed 350

★★★★★ 86% ◉◉◉ **HOTEL**

Balmoral

1 Princes St EH2 2EQ
☎ 0131 556 2414 🖷 0131 557 3747
e-mail: reservations@thebalmoralhotel.com
web: www.roccofortehotels.com

ROCCO FORTE
HOTELS

dir: follow city centre signs. Adjacent to Waverley Station

This elegant hotel enjoys a prestigious address at the top of Princes Street, with fine views over the city and the castle. Bedrooms and suites are stylishly furnished and decorated, all boasting a thoughtful range of extras and impressive marble bathrooms. Hotel amenities include a Roman-style health spa, extensive function facilities, a choice of bars and two very different dining options; Number One offers inspired fine dining whilst Hadrians is a bustling, informal brasserie.

Rooms 188 en suite ⊗ in 173 bedrooms S £270-£1500; D £320-£1500
Facilities Spa STV FTV ⬚ supervised Sauna Solarium Gym Steam
room Exercise Studio Wi-fi available ♬ Xmas **Conf** BC Thtr 350
Class 180 Board 60 Del from £255 **Services** Lift air con **Parking** 100
Notes LB ⊗ Civ Wed 60

★★★★★ 85% ◉◉ **HOTEL**

Sheraton Grand Hotel & Spa

Ⓢ

Sheraton
HOTELS & RESORTS

1 Festival Square EH3 9SR
☎ 0131 229 9131 🖷 0131 228 4510
e-mail: grandedinburgh.sheraton@sheraton.com
web: www.starwood.com

dir: follow City Centre signs (A8). Through Shandwick, right at lights into Lothian Rd. Right at next lights. Hotel on left at next lights

This modern hotel boasts one of the best spas in Scotland - the external top floor hydro pool is definitely worth a look whilst the thermal suite provides a unique venue for serious relaxation. The spacious bedrooms are available in a variety of styles, and the suites prove very popular. There is a wide range of eating options - The Terrace, Santini's and the Grill Room that all have a loyal local following.

Rooms 260 en suite (21 fmly) ⊗ in all bedrooms S £105-£260;
D £105-£300 **Facilities** Spa STV ⬚ ♨ Sauna Gym Jacuzzi Wi-fi in
bedrooms Indoor/Outdoor hydropool, Thermal suite, Spa treatment rooms
♬ Xmas **Conf** BC Thtr 485 Class 350 Board 120 **Services** Lift air con
Parking 121 **Notes LB** ⊗ in restaurant Civ Wed 485

★★★★★ 84% ◉◉ **HOTEL**

The Scotsman

20 North Bridge EH1 1YT
☎ 0131 556 5565 🖷 0131 652 3652
e-mail: reservations@thescotsmanhotelgroup.co.uk
web: www.thescotsmanhotel.co.uk

dir: A8 to city centre, left onto Charlotte St. Right into Queen St, right at rdbt onto Leith Street. Left onto North Bridge, hotel on right

This stunning conversion was formerly the headquarters of The Scotsman newspaper. The classical elegance of the public areas, complete with a marble staircase, blends seamlessly with the contemporary bedrooms and their state-of-the-art technology. The superbly equipped leisure club includes a stainless steel swimming pool and large gym. Eat in either the funky North Bridge Brasserie, or the opulent, award-winning Vermilion restaurant.

Rooms 69 en suite (4 GF) ⊗ in 60 bedrooms D £270-£350
Facilities Spa STV ⬚ supervised Sauna Solarium Gym Jacuzzi Wi-fi in
bedrooms Beauty treatments **Conf** Thtr 100 Class 50 Board 40
Services Lift **Notes** ⊗ in restaurant Civ Wed 70

Scotland

EDINBURGH *continued*

INSPECTORS' CHOICE

★★★★ ◉◉ **TOWN HOUSE HOTEL**

Channings

15 South Learmonth Gardens EH4 1EZ
☎ 0131 332 3232 & 315 2226 ▤ 0131 332 9631
e-mail: reserve@channings.co.uk
web: www.channings.co.uk

dir: *from A90 & Forth Road Bridge, follow city centre signs*

Just minutes from the city centre, this elegant town house occupies five Edwardian terraced houses. The public areas include sumptuous, inviting lounges and a choice of dining options. The Ochre Vita wine bar and Mediterranean restaurant offer the popular choice, but for a special occasion dinner try the seven-course tasting menu with wines, in the intimate Channings Restaurant. The attractive and individually designed bedrooms have a hi-tech spec for business guests.

Rooms 41 en suite (4 GF) ⊗ in 39 bedrooms S £85-£140; D £120-£185 (incl. bkfst) **Facilities** STV FTV Wi-fi available Xmas **Conf** Thtr 35 Board 28 Del from £185 **Services** Lift **Notes LB** ⊗ ⊗ in restaurant

INSPECTORS' CHOICE

★★★★ ◉ **TOWN HOUSE HOTEL**

The Howard

34 Great King St EH3 6QH
☎ 0131 274 7402 ▤ 0131 274 7405
e-mail: reserve@thehoward.com
web: www.thehoward.com

dir: *E on Queen St, 2nd left, Dundas St. Through 3 lights, right, hotel on left*

Quietly elegant and splendidly luxurious The Howard provides an intimate and high quality experience for the discerning traveller. It comprises three linked Georgian houses and is situated just a short walk from Princes Street. The sumptuous bedrooms, in a variety of styles, include spacious suites, well-equipped bathrooms and a host of thoughtful touches. Ornate chandeliers and lavish drapes adorn the drawing room, while the Atholl
continued

Dining Room contains unique, hand-painted murals dating from the 1800s.

The Howard

Rooms 18 en suite ⊗ in all bedrooms **Facilities** STV FTV Xmas **Conf** Thtr 30 Board 20 Del £210 **Services** Lift **Parking** 10 **Notes** ⊗ ⊗ in restaurant Civ Wed 36

★★★★ 85% ◉◉◉ **HOTEL**

Norton House

Ingliston EH28 8LX

Han*d*PICKED HOTELS

☎ 0131 333 1275 ▤ 0131 333 5305
e-mail: nortonhouse-cro@handpicked.co.uk
web: www.handpicked.co.uk

dir: *off A8, 5m W of city centre*

This extended Victorian mansion, set in 55 acres of parkland, is peacefully situated just outside the city and convenient for the airport. Both contemporary and more traditional bedrooms are offered - some are very spacious. Each room provides an impressive range of accessories including plasma screen TVs with DVDs. Public areas take in a choice of lounges as well as dining options, with a popular brasserie and Ushers, the intimate award-winning restaurant.

Rooms 47 en suite (2 fmly) (10 GF) ⊗ in 27 bedrooms **Facilities** STV Archery, Laser, Clay pigeon shooting, Quad biking **Conf** Thtr 300 Class 100 Board 60 **Parking** 200 **Notes LB** ⊗ in restaurant Civ Wed 150

★★★★ 80% ◉◉ **TOWN HOUSE HOTEL**

The Bonham

35 Drumsheugh Gardens EH3 7RN
☎ 0131 274 7400 ▤ 0131 2747405
e-mail: reserve@thebonham.com
web: www.thebonham.com

dir: *close to West End & Princes St*

Overlooking tree-lined gardens, this Victorian town house combines classical elegance with a contemporary style. Inviting day rooms include a reception lounge and smart restaurant. Bedrooms, in a variety of sizes, focus on contemporary design and include good internet access and an interactive TV system.

Rooms 48 en suite (1 GF) ⊗ in 44 bedrooms S £108-£145; D £146-£195 **Facilities** STV FTV Wi-fi available Xmas **Conf** Thtr 50 Board 26 Del from £185 **Services** Lift **Parking** 20 **Notes LB** ⊗ ⊗ in restaurant

★★★★ 80% ◉◉ HOTEL

Marriott Dalmahoy Hotel & Country Club

Marriott.
HOTELS & RESORTS

Kirknewton EH27 8EB

☎ 0131 333 1845 📠 0131 333 1433

e-mail: dalmahoy@marriotthotels.com

web: www.marriott.co.uk

dir: *Edinburgh City Bypass (A720) turn onto A71, on left*

The rolling Pentland Hills and beautifully kept parkland provide a stunning backdrop for this imposing Georgian mansion. With two championship golf courses and a health and beauty club, there is plenty here to occupy guests. Bedrooms are spacious and most have fine views, while public rooms offer a choice of formal and informal drinking and dining options.

Rooms 43 en suite 172 annexe en suite (59 fmly) ⊘ in 136 bedrooms S £115-£185; D £115-£185 **Facilities** STV 🏹 ♨ 36 ♨ Sauna Solarium Gym Putt green Jacuzzi Wi-fi in bedrooms Health & beauty treatments, Steam room, Dance studio, Driving range Xmas **Conf** Thtr 500 Class 200 Board 120 Del from £145 **Services** Lift **Parking** 350 **Notes LB** ⊗ ⊘ in restaurant Civ Wed 250

★★★★ 78% HOTEL

The Roxburghe Hotel

MACDONALD
HOTELS & RESORTS

38 Charlotte Square EH2 4HQ

☎ 0870 1942108 📠 0131 240 5555

e-mail: roxburghe@macdonald-hotels.co.uk

web: www.macdonald-hotels.co.uk

dir: *on corner of Charlotte St & George St*

This long-established hotel lies in the heart of the city overlooking Charlotte Square Gardens. Public areas are inviting and include relaxing lounges, a choice of bars (in the evening) and an inner concourse that looks onto a small lawn area. Smart bedrooms come

continued

in classic or contemporary style. There is a secure underground car park.

Rooms 197 en suite (4 fmly) ⊘ in 167 bedrooms **Facilities Spa** STV 🏹 Sauna Solarium Gym Dance studio, Spa treatment rooms, steam room ♫ **Conf** Thtr 300 Class 120 Board 80 **Services** Lift **Parking** 20 **Notes LB** ⊗ ⊘ in restaurant Civ Wed 280

★★★★ 76% HOTEL

Apex International

APEX
HOTELS

31/35 Grassmarket EH1 2HS

☎ 0131 300 3456 & 0845 365 0000

📠 0131 220 5345

e-mail: reservations@apexhotels.co.uk

web: www.apexhotels.co.uk

dir: *into Lothian Rd at west end of Princes Street, then 1st left into King Stables Rd, leads into Grassmarket*

A sister to the Apex City Hotel close by, the International lies in a historic yet trendy square in the shadow of Edinburgh Castle. It has a versatile business and conference centre and residents' spa. Bedrooms are contemporary in style and very well equipped. The fifth floor restaurant boasts stunning views of the castle.

Rooms 171 en suite (99 fmly) ⊘ in 119 bedrooms S £89 £230; D £99-£240 (incl. bkfst) **Facilities** STV 🏹 supervised Gym Wi-fi in bedrooms Tropicarium Xmas **Conf** Thtr 200 Class 80 Board 40 Del from £125 **Services** Lift **Parking** 60 **Notes LB** ⊗ ⊘ in restaurant Civ Wed 200

★★★★ 76% HOTEL

Carlton

⚜
PARAMOUNT
GROUP OF HOTELS

North Bridge EH1 1SD

☎ 0131 472 3000 📠 0131 556 2691

e-mail: carlton@paramount-hotels.co.uk

web: www.paramount-hotels.co.uk

dir: *on North Bridge which links Princes St to the Royal Mile*

The Carlton occupies a city centre location just off the Royal Mile. Inside, it is modern and stylish in design, with an impressive open-plan reception/lobby, spacious first-floor lounge, bar and restaurant, plus a basement leisure club. Bedrooms, many air-conditioned, are generally spacious, with an excellent range of accessories.

Rooms 189 en suite (20 fmly) ⊘ in 140 bedrooms **Facilities Spa** STV 🏹 Squash Sauna Solarium Gym Jacuzzi Table tennis, Dance studio, Creche, Exercise classes ♫ **Conf** BC Thtr 240 Class 100 Board 60 **Services** Lift **Notes LB** ⊘ in restaurant Civ Wed 160

★★★★ 75% HOTEL

Edinburgh Marriott Hotel

Marriott.
HOTELS & RESORTS

111 Glasgow Rd EH12 8NF

☎ 0131 334 9191 📠 0131 316 4507

e-mail: edinburgh@marriotthotels.com

web: www.marriott.co.uk

dir: *M8 junct 1 for Gogar, at rdbt turn right for city centre, hotel on right*

Located on the city's western edge, this purpose built hotel is convenient for the bypass, airport, showground and business park. Public areas include an attractive marbled foyer, extensive conference facilities and a restaurant serving a range of international dishes

continued on page 796

EDINBURGH *continued*

alongside an attractive carvery. Air-conditioned bedrooms are spacious and equipped with a range of extras.

Edinburgh Marriott Hotel

Rooms 245 en suite (76 fmly) (64 GF) ⊘ in 189 bedrooms S £115-£185; D £115-£185 **Facilities** STV ⊠ Sauna Solarium Gym Jacuzzi Wi-fi in bedrooms Steam room, Massage and beauty treatment room, Hairdresser **Conf** BC Thtr 250 Class 120 Board 45 Del from £140 **Services** Lift air con **Parking** 300 **Notes LB** ⊗ ⊘ in restaurant Civ Wed 80

★★★★ 75% ❀ HOTEL

Macdonald Holyrood

Holyrood Rd EH8 8AU
☎ 0870 1942106 📄 0131 550 4545
e-mail: holyrood@macdonald-hotels.co.uk
web: www.macdonald-hotels.co.uk
dir: parallel to Royal Mile

MACDONALD
HOTELS & RESORTS

Situated just a short walk from Holyrood Palace, this impressive hotel lies next to the Scottish Parliament building. Air-conditioned bedrooms are comfortably furnished, whilst the Club floor boasts a private lounge. Full business services complement the extensive conference suites and the spa provides an opportunity for relaxation.

Rooms 156 en suite ⊘ in all bedrooms S £135-£240; D £170-£280 (incl. bkfst) **Facilities** STV ⊠ Sauna Solarium Gym Wi-fi in bedrooms Beauty treatment rooms ♫ Xmas **Conf** BC Thtr 200 Class 100 Board 80 Del from £150 **Services** Lift air con **Parking** 70 **Notes LB** ⊗ ⊘ in restaurant Civ Wed 100

★★★★ 74% HOTEL

Apex City

61 Grassmarket EH1 2JF
☎ 0131 243 3456 & 0845 365 0000
📄 0131 225 6346
e-mail: reservations@apexhotels.co.uk

APEX
HOTELS

dir: into Lothian Rd at the west end of Princes Street, 1st left into King Stables Rd. Leads into Grassmarket

This modern, stylish hotel lies in the historic and fashionable Grassmarket dominated by Edinburgh Castle above. The design-led bedrooms are fresh and contemporary and each has artwork by Richard Demarco. Agua Bar and Restaurant is a smart open-plan area in dark wood and chrome that serves a range of meals and cocktails. Residents can use the spa at sister hotel, the International, which is nearby.

Rooms 119 en suite ⊘ in 84 bedrooms S £89-£229; D £89-£229 **Facilities** STV Wi-fi in bedrooms Complimentary use of facilities at neighbouring hotel Xmas **Conf** Thtr 70 Class 24 Board 34 Del from £125 **Services** Lift **Parking** 10 **Notes LB** ⊗ ⊘ in restaurant Civ Wed 60

★★★★ 71% HOTEL

The Royal Terrace

18 Royal Ter EH7 5AQ
☎ 0131 557 3222 & 524 5000 📄 0131 557 5334
e-mail: sales@royalterracehotel.co.uk
web: www.royalterracehotel.co.uk

dir: A71 to city centre, follow one-way system, left into Charlotte Sq. At end right into Queens St. Left at rdbt. At next island right into London Rd, right into Royal Terrace

Forming part of a quiet Georgian terrace close to the city centre, this hotel has been undergoing a total makeover. Many of the bedrooms have now been refurbished in a style that successfully blends the historic architecture of the building with state-of-the-art facilities. Top floor rooms provide excellent rooftop views of the city.

Rooms 108 en suite (6 fmly) (5 GF) ⊘ in 83 bedrooms S £75-£115; D £135-£175 **Facilities** STV ⊠ supervised Sauna Gym Jacuzzi Wi-fi in bedrooms Steam room Xmas **Conf** BC Thtr 90 Class 60 Board 40 Del from £135 **Services** Lift **Notes LB** ⊗ ⊘ in restaurant Civ Wed 80

See advert on opposite page

Scotland

★★★★ 70% **HOTEL**

Novotel Edinburgh Centre

Lauriston Place, Lady Lawson St EH3 9DE
☎ 0131 656 3500 📠 0131 656 3510
e-mail: H3271@accor.com
web: www.novotel.com

dir: *from Edinburgh Castle right onto George IV Bridge from Royal Mile. Follow to junct, then right onto Lauriston Place for hotel 700mtrs on right.*

One of the new generations of Novotels, this modern hotel is located in the centre of the city, close to Edinburgh Castle. Smart and stylish public areas include a cosmopolitan bar, brasserie-style restaurant and indoor leisure facilities. The air-conditioned bedrooms feature a comprehensive range of extras and bathrooms with baths and separate shower cabinets.

Rooms 180 en suite (146 fmly) ⊗ in 135 bedrooms S £99-£209; D £90-£209 **Facilities** STV FTV 🏊 Sauna Gym Jacuzzi Wi-fi in bedrooms Xmas **Conf** BC Thtr 80 Class 50 Board 32 Del from £135 **Services** Lift air con **Parking** 15 **Notes LB** ⊗ in restaurant

★★★ 83% ❀❀ **HOTEL**

Dalhousie Castle & Aqueous Spa

Bonnyrigg EH19 3JB
☎ 01875 820153 📠 01875 821936
e-mail: info@dalhousiecastle.co.uk
web: www.vonessenhotels.co.uk

dir: *A7 S from Edinburgh through Lasswade/Newtongrange, right at Shell Garage (B704), hotel 0.5m from junct*

A popular wedding venue, this imposing medieval castle sits amid lawns and parkland and even has a falconry that guests can visit. Bedrooms offer a mix of styles and sizes, including richly decorated themed rooms named after various historical figures. The Dungeon restaurant provides an atmospheric setting for dinner, and the less formal Orangery serves food all day.

Rooms 29 en suite 7 annexe en suite (3 fmly) ⊗ in all bedrooms S £150-£160; D £195-£220 **Facilities Spa** STV Fishing Sauna Solarium Jacuzzi Wi-fi in bedrooms Falconry, Clay pigeon shooting, Archery, Loch fishing Xmas **Conf** Thtr 120 Class 60 Board 45 Del from £200 **Parking** 110 **Notes LB** ⊗ in restaurant Civ Wed 100

★★★ 81% ❀ **HOTEL**

Best Western Bruntsfield

69/74 Bruntsfield Place EH10 4HH
☎ 0131 229 1393 📠 0131 229 5634
e-mail: sales@thebruntsfield.co.uk
web: www.bw-bruntsfieldhotel.co.uk

dir: *from S into Edinburgh on A702. Hotel 1m S of west end of Princes Street*

Overlooking Bruntsfield Links, this smart hotel has stylish public rooms including relaxing lounge areas and a lively pub. Bedrooms come in a variety of sizes and styles but all are well equipped. Imaginative dinner menus and hearty Scottish breakfasts are served in the bright, modern Cardoon conservatory restaurant. Smart staff provide good levels of service and attention.

continued

Best Western Bruntsfield

Rooms 71 en suite (5 fmly) ⊗ in all bedrooms S £95-£140; D £180-£250 (incl. bkfst) **Facilities** STV FTV Wi-fi in bedrooms Xmas **Conf** Thtr 75 Class 30 Board 30 Del from £145 **Services** Lift **Parking** 25 **Notes LB** ⊗ ⊗ in restaurant Closed 25-Dec Civ Wed 85

★★★ 81% ❀ **HOTEL**

Malmaison

One Tower Place EH6 7DB
☎ 0131 468 5000 📠 0131 468 5002
e-mail: edinburgh@malmaison.com
web: www.malmaison.com

dir: *A900 from city centre towards Leith, at end of Leith Walk , & through 3 lights, left into Tower St. Hotel on right at end of road*

The trendy Port of Leith is home to this stylish Malmaison. Inside, bold contemporary designs make for a striking effect. Bedrooms are

continued on page 798

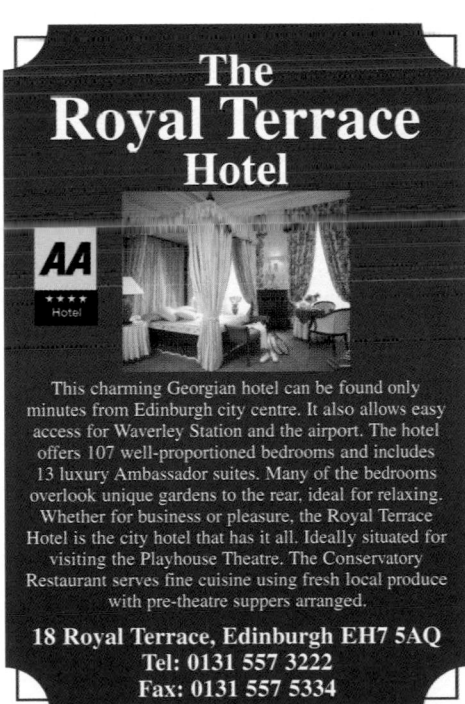

EDINBURGH continued

comprehensively equipped with CD players, mini-bars and loads of individual touches. Go for a stunning superior room for really memorable stay. The smart brasserie and a café bar are popular with the local clientele.
Malmaison - AA Hotel Group of the Year 2006-7.

Rooms 100 en suite (18 fmly) ⊗ in all bedrooms S £140-£245; D £140-£245 **Facilities** STV Gym Wi-fi available Xmas **Conf** Thtr 55 Class 30 Board 40 Del £160 **Services** Lift **Parking** 50 **Notes LB** ⊗ in restaurant

★★★ 81% **HOTEL**

Thistle Edinburgh

107 Leith St EH1 3SW
☎ 0870 333 9153 📄 0870 333 9253
e-mail: Edinburgh@Thistle.co.uk

THISTLE HOTELS

dir: Exit M8/M9 onto A8 signed City Centre. Hotel located at the end of Princes St next to St James shopping centre.

This purpose-built hotel adjoins one of Edinburgh's premier shopping malls at the east end of Princes Street in the heart of the city. A friendly team of staff are keen to please whilst stylish, well-equipped bedrooms provide excellent levels of comfort and facilities. Public areas include a spacious restaurant, popular bar, and an elegant lobby lounge.

Rooms 143 en suite ⊗ in 100 bedrooms **Facilities** STV **Conf** Thtr 250 Class 150 **Services** Lift air con **Parking** 18 **Notes** ⊗ ⊗ in restaurant

★★★ 80% **HOTEL**

Best Western Braid Hills

134 Braid Rd EH10 6JD
☎ 0131 447 8888 📄 0131 452 8477
e-mail: bookings@braidhillshotel.co.uk
web: www.braidhillshotel.co.uk
dir: 2.5m S A702, opposite Braid Burn Park

From its elevated position on the south side, this long-established hotel enjoys splendid panoramic views of the city and castle. Bedrooms are smart, stylish and well equipped. The public areas are comfortable and inviting, and guests can dine in either the restaurant or popular bistro/bar.

Rooms 67 en suite (6 fmly) ⊗ in 8 bedrooms **Facilities** STV **Conf** Thtr 100 Class 50 Board 30 **Parking** 38 **Notes LB** ⊗ ⊗ in restaurant Civ Wed 100

See advert on opposite page

★★★ 79% ⊛ **HOTEL**

Melville Castle

Melville Gate, Gilmerton Rd EH18 1AP
☎ 0131 654 0088 📄 0131 654 4666
e-mail: reception@melvillecastle.com
web: www.melvillecastle.com

dir: Leave city bypass at Sheriffhall rdbt and take the A68. Take 1st right on to Melville Gate Rd, castle gates at end of road

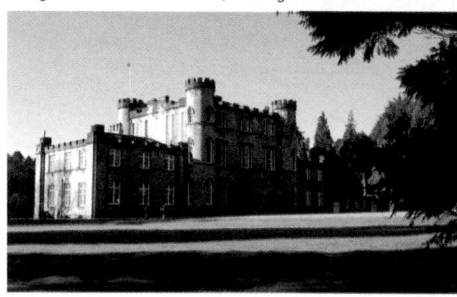

A castellated mansion set in wooded grounds close to the bypass near the city's southern boundary. It focuses on wedding receptions, small conferences and corporate events. The business and leisure guest will appreciate the lovely bedrooms, including superb galleried suites. Meals are served in the historic vaulted cellar bar and brasserie.

Rooms 32 en suite (2 fmly) (10 GF) ⊗ in all bedrooms S £80-£130; D £120-£175 (incl. bkfst) **Facilities** STV Fishing ⤙ Wi-fi in bedrooms Cycling Xmas **Conf** BC Thtr 90 Class 45 Board 45 **Services** Lift **Parking** 100 **Notes LB** ⊗ ⊗ in restaurant Civ Wed 80

★★★ 78% **HOTEL**

Best Western Kings Manor

100 Milton Rd East EH15 2NP
☎ 0131 669 0444 & 468 8003 📄 0131 669 6650
e-mail: reservations@kingsmanor.com
web: www.kingsmanor.com

dir: A720 E to Old Craighall junct, left into city, right att A1/A199 junct, hotel 200mtrs on right

Lying on the eastern side of the city and convenient for the by-pass, this hotel is popular with business guests, tour groups and for conferences. It boasts a fine leisure complex and a bright modern

continued

bistro, which complements the quality, creative cooking in the main restaurant.

Rooms 95 en suite (8 fmly) (13 GF) ⊛ in all bedrooms S £65-£100; D £96-£160 (incl. bkfst) **Facilities** STV ⬚ ⬚ Sauna Solarium Gym Jacuzzi Wi-fi in bedrooms Health & beauty salon ,Steam room Xmas **Conf** BC Thtr 140 Class 70 Board 50 Del from £120 **Services** Lift **Parking** 100 **Notes LB** ⊛ in restaurant Civ Wed 100

★★★ 77% HOTEL

Apex European

90 Haymarket Ter EH12 5LQ
☎ 0131 474 3456 & 0845 365 0000
🖷 0131 474 3400

e-mail: reservations@apexhotels.co.uk
web: www.apexhotels.co.uk

dir: A8 to city centre, hotel at Haymarket just after Donaldsons School for Deaf.

Lying just west of the city centre, close to Haymarket Station and handy for the Conference Centre, this modern hotel is popular with business travellers. Smart, stylish bedrooms offer an excellent range of facilities and have been designed with work requirements in mind. Public areas include Metro, an informal bistro. Service is friendly and pro-active.

Rooms 66 en suite (3 GF) ⊛ in 51 bedrooms **Facilities** STV **Conf** Thtr 80 Class 30 Board 36 **Services** Lift **Parking** 17 **Notes LB** ⊗ ⊛ in restaurant Closed 24-27 Dec

★★★ 77% HOTEL

Best Western Edinburgh City

79 Lauriston Place EH3 9HZ
☎ 0131 622 7979 🖷 0131 622 7900

e-mail: reservations@bestwesternedinburghcity.co.uk

dir: follow signs for city centre A8. Onto A702, 3rd exit on left, hotel on right

Occupying a site that was once a maternity hospital, this tasteful conversion is located close to the city centre. Spacious bedrooms are smartly modern and well equipped to include fridges. Meals can be enjoyed in the bright contemporary restaurant and guests can relax in the cosy but stylish bar and reception lounge. Staff are friendly and obliging.

Rooms 52 en suite (12 fmly) (5 GF) ⊛ in 37 bedrooms **Facilities** STV **Services** Lift **Notes LB** ⊗ ⊛ in restaurant

★★★ 75% HOTEL

Best Western Edinburgh Capital

187 Clermiston Rd EH12 6UG
☎ 0131 535 9988 🖷 0131 334 9712

e-mail: manager@edinburghcapitalhotel.co.uk

dir: from A8 turn left into Clermiston Rd at the National Tyre Garage. Hotel is at the top of the hill.

Attracting business, conference and leisure guests alike, this purpose-built hotel lies on the west side of the city and is convenient for the airport and the north. The conservatory restaurant provides friendly service and good value meals combined with fine views.

Rooms 111 en suite (6 fmly) (14 GF) ⊛ in 68 bedrooms S £65-£134; D £89-£159 **Facilities** Spa STV FTV ⬚ supervised Sauna Solarium Gym Wi-fi in bedrooms Beautician and sunbeds Hotel has sunbed room. Xmas **Conf** BC Thtr 320 Class 130 Board 80 Del from £110 **Services** Lift **Parking** 106 **Notes LB** ⊛ in restaurant Civ Wed 200

★★★ 74% HOTEL

Old Waverley

43 Princes St EH2 2BY
☎ 0131 556 4648 🖷 0131 557 6516
e-mail: reservations@oldwaverley.co.uk
web: www.oldwaverley.co.uk

dir: in city centre, opposite Waverley Station & Jenners

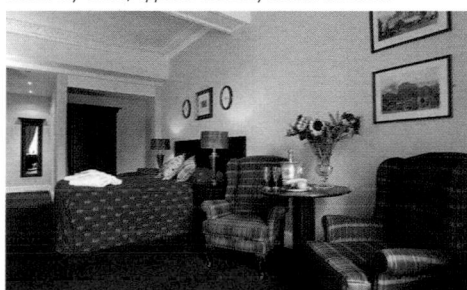

Occupying a commanding position opposite Sir Walter Scott's famous monument on Princes Street, this hotel lies right in the heart of the city close to the station. The comfortable public rooms are all on first floor level and along with front-facing bedrooms enjoy the fine views.

Rooms 80 en suite (3 fmly) ⊛ in 53 bedrooms S £129; D £169 **Facilities** STV Wi-fi in bedrooms leisure facilities at sister hotel Xmas **Services** Lift **Notes LD** ⊛ ⊛ in restaurant

EDINBURGH *continued*

★★★ 73% HOTEL

Quality Hotel

Edinburgh Airport, Ingliston EH28 8AU
☎ 0131 333 4331 📠 0131 333 4124
e-mail: info@qualityhoteledinburgh.com

dir: from M8, M9 & Forth Road Bridge follow signs for airport

Just twenty minutes from the city centre, this modern hotel is
convenient for Edinburgh International Airport, only two minutes away
by courtesy minibus. The spacious executive bedrooms are the pick of
the accommodation, and there is a bright restaurant offering a range
of contemporary dishes.

Rooms ⊘ in 64 bedrooms S £65-£185; D £65-£185 **Facilities** STV
Conf Thtr 70 Class 24 Board 24 Del from £90 **Services** Lift **Parking** 100
Notes ⊘ in restaurant Civ Wed 80

★★★ 72% HOTEL

Jurys Inn Edinburgh

43 Jeffrey St EH1 1DH
☎ 0131 200 3300 📠 0131 200 0400
e-mail: jurysinnedinburgh@jurysdoyle.com
web: www.jurysdoyle.com

dir: A8/M8 to City Centre, follow one-way system, across
Waverley Bridge, 1st left, hotel on right.

A smart, elegant reception lounge greets guests at this modern hotel set
in the heart of the city close to Waverley Station and the Royal Mile.
There is a pub and an informal restaurant serving a wide range of dishes,
including a canteen-style breakfast. Bedrooms are bright and spacious.

Rooms 186 en suite (150 fmly) ⊘ in 170 bedrooms S £55-£167;
D £55-£167 **Facilities** STV Wi-fi available Discounted leisure facilities at
nearby hotel. ♬ ch fac **Conf** Thtr 50 Class 35 Board 30 Del from £138
Services Lift **Notes** ⊗ ⊘ in restaurant Closed 24-25 Dec

◉ RESTAURANT WITH ROOMS

The Witchery by the Castle

352 Castlehill, The Royal Mile EH1 2NF
☎ 0131 225 5613 📠 0131 220 4392
e-mail: mail@thewitchery.com
web: www.thewitchery.com

dir: At top of Royal Mile

Originally built in 1595, the Witchery by the Castle is situated in a
historic building at the gates of Edinburgh Castle. The two luxurious

and theatrically decorated suites, known as the Inner Sanctum and the
Old Rectory are located above the restaurant and are reached via a
winding stone staircase. Filled with antiques, opulently draped beds,
large roll-top baths and a plethora of memorabilia, this ancient and
exciting establishment is often described as one of the world's most
romantic destinations.

Rooms 2 en suite 5 annexe en suite (1 GF) ⊘ in all bedrooms S £295;
D £295 **Facilities** STV **Notes** ⊗ No children 12yrs ⊘ in restaurant
Closed 25-26 Dec

Ⓐ

Ramada Mount Royal   ® R A M A D A.

Princes St EH2 2DG
☎ 0131 225 7161 📠 0131 220 4671
e-mail: sales.mountroyal@ramadajarvis.co.uk
web: www.ramadajarvis.co.uk

dir: opposite Scott Monument & Waverley Station

Rooms 158 en suite ⊘ in 100 bedrooms S £79-£195; D £79-£195
Facilities STV Wi-fi available Xmas **Conf** Thtr 70 Class 40 Board 27 Del
from £95 **Services** Lift **Notes** ★★★ LB ⊗ ⊘ in restaurant

Ⓐ

Swallow Albany   SWALLOW

39 Albany St EH1 3QY
☎ 0131 556 0397 📠 0131 557 6633
web: www.swallowhotels.com
Rooms 22 en suite **Notes** ★★★

Ⓐ

Swallow Greens   SWALLOW

24 Eglinton Crescent, Haymarket EH12 5BY
☎ 0131 337 1565 📠 0131 337 9405
web: www.swallowhotels.com

dir: close to Haymarket Station

Rooms 55 en suite **Notes** ★★★

Ⓐ

Swallow Learmonth   SWALLOW

18-20 Learmonth Ter EH4 1PW
☎ 0131 343 2671 📠 0131 315 2232
web: www.swallowhotels.com
Rooms 62 en suite **Notes** ★★

Ⓐ

Swallow Thistle Court   SWALLOW

5 Hampton Ter EH12 5JD
☎ 0131 313 5500 📠 0131 313 5511
web: www.swallowhotels.com
Rooms 15 en suite **Notes** ★★★

continued

Scotland

BUDGET HOTEL

Hotel Ibis

6 Hunter Square, (off The Royal Mile) EH1 1QW
☎ 0131 240 7000 ⓘ 0131 240 7007
e-mail: H2039@accor-hotels.com
web: www.ibishotel.com

dir: from Queen St (M8/M9) or Waterloo Pl (A1) over North Bridge (A7) & High St, take 1st right off South Bridge

Modern, budget hotel offering comfortable accommodation in bright and practical bedrooms. Breakfast is self-service and dinner is available in the restaurant. For further details, consult the Hotel Groups page.

Rooms 99 en suite

BUDGET HOTEL

Innkeeper's Lodge Edinburgh West (Airport)

114-116 St John's Rd, Corstophine EH12 8AX
☎ 0131 334 8235 ⓘ 0131 316 5012
web: www.innkeeperslodge.com

dir: M8 junct 1, N on A720. At Gogar rdbt, right onto A8, straight over next rdbt, hotel on left just past church at St John's Rd

Smart, en suite accommodation ideal for both business & leisure guests. Bedrooms are very well equipped, including Sky TV, telephone, modem points, tea & coffee making facilities, (family rooms in most locations). Complimentary breakfast. The adjacent Pub Restaurant; a Harvester, Vintage Inn, Toby Carvery, Ember Inn, Sizzling Pubco or Pub & Carvery offers an all day menu. See Hotel Groups pages for further details.

Rooms 28 en suite S £64.95; D £64.95

BUDGET HOTEL

Premier Travel Inn Edinburgh City Centre

1 Morrison Link EH3 8DN
☎ 0870 238 3319 ⓘ 0131 228 9836
web: www.premiertravelinn.com

dir: next to Edinburgh International Conference Centre

High quality, modern budget accommodation ideal for both families and business travellers. Spacious, en suite bedrooms feature bath and shower, satellite TV and many have telephones and modem points. The adjacent family restaurant features a wide and varied menu. For further details consult the Hotel Groups page.

Rooms 281 en suite

Premier Travel Inn Edinburgh East

228 Willowbrae Rd EH8 7NG
☎ 08701 977091 ⓘ 0131 652 2789

dir: M8 junct 1/A720 S for 12m, turn off for A1. At Asda rdbt turn left. Follow road for 2m, Inn on left before Esso garage

Rooms 39 en suite

Premier Travel Inn Edinburgh (Inveresk)

Carberry Rd, Inveresk, Musselburgh EH21 8PT
☎ 08701 977092 ⓘ 0131 653 2270

dir: from A1, take exit signed Dalkeith (A6094). Follow signs until rdbt, turn right, Inn 300yds on right

Rooms 40 en suite **Conf** Thtr 80

Premier Travel Inn Edinburgh (Lauriston Place)

Lauriston Place, Lady Lawson St EH3 9HZ
☎ 0870 9906610 ⓘ 0870 9906611

dir: From A8 right onto A702 (Lothian Rd) to Tollcross. Left into Lauriston Place, Inn at junct with Lauriston St on left

Rooms 112 en suite

Premier Travel Inn Edinburgh (Leith)

Pier Place, Newhaven Dicks EH6 4TX
☎ 08701 977093 ⓘ 0131 554 5994

dir: From A1 follow coast road through Leith. Pass Ocean Terminal, straight ahead at mini-rdbt, take 2nd exit signed Harry Ramsden's car park

Rooms 60 en suite **Conf** Thtr 35 Board 25

Premier Travel Inn Edinburgh (Newcraighall)

91 Newcraighall Rd, Newcraighall EH21 8RX
☎ 0870 9906336 ⓘ 0870 9906337

dir: on junct of A1 & A6095 towards Musselburgh

Rooms 42 en suite

BUDGET HOTEL

Travelodge Edinburgh Central

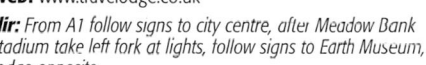

33 Saint Marys St EH1 1TA
☎ 08700 850 950 ⓘ 0131 557 3681
web: www.travelodge.co.uk

dir: From A1 follow signs to city centre, after Meadow Bank stadium take left fork at lights, follow signs to Earth Museum, lodge opposite

Travelodge offers good quality, good value, modern accommodation. Ideal for families, the spacious en suite bedrooms include remote control TV, tea and coffee-making facilities and comfortable beds. Meals can be taken at the nearby family restaurant. See Hotel Groups pages for further details.

Rooms 193 en suite S fr £26; D fr £26

Travelodge Edinburgh Dreghorn

46 Dreghorn Link EH13 9QR
☎ 08700 850 950 ⓘ 0131 441 4296

dir: E'bound carriageway of A720, Edinburgh City bypass at Dreghorn/Colinton exit

Rooms 72 en suite S fr £26; D fr £26

Travelodge Edinburgh Mussleburgh

Old Craighall EH21 8RE
☎ 08700 850 950 ⓘ 0131 653 6106

dir: off A1/A720, 2m from Edinburgh outskirts

Rooms 45 en suite S fr £26; D fr £26

Scotland

CITY OF GLASGOW

GLASGOW　　　　　　**MAP 20 NS66**

INSPECTORS' CHOICE

★★★★ ◉◉ **TOWN HOUSE HOTEL**

One Devonshire Gardens

1 Devonshire Gardens G12 0UX
☎ 0141 339 2001 📠 0141 337 1663
e-mail: reservations@onedevonshiregardens.com
web: www.onedevonshiregardens.com

dir: *M8 junct 17, follow signs for A82, after 1.5m turn left into Hyndland Rd, 1st right, right at mini rdbt, right at end, continue to end*

This renowned townhouse occupies four houses of a Victorian terrace in a residential area. Bedrooms, including a number of suites and four-poster rooms, are stylish, individually designed and thoughtfully equipped to a high standard. Public rooms include a choice of inviting drawing rooms, meeting and conference facilities and a smart restaurant offering imaginative cooking. Personal, attentive service is a highlight.

Rooms 35 en suite (4 GF) ⊘ in all bedrooms S £135-£295; D fr £135 **Facilities** STV ⌇ Squash Gym Wi-fi in bedrooms Tennis facilities at nearby club in-room spa treatments **Conf** BC Thtr 40 Class 30 Board 30 Del from £250 **Notes** ⊘ in restaurant Civ Wed 48

★★★★ 83% **HOTEL**

Radisson SAS Glasgow

Radisson HOTELS & RESORTS

301 Argyle St G2 8DL
☎ 0141 204 3333 📠 0141 204 3344
e-mail: reservations.glasgow@radissonsas.com
web: www.radisson.com

dir: *M8 junct 19. Hotel opp Glasgow Central Station*

Located within the heart of the city centre this modern, stylish international hotel provides a high quality destination. The huge glass atrium forms the central core of the hotel, leading to the lobby, bar, restaurants and the leisure centre. Spacious bedrooms feature good design with the focus on comfort, facilities and quality.

Rooms 247 en suite ⊘ in 200 bedrooms S fr £145; D fr £145 **Facilities** STV 🏊 supervised Sauna Solarium Gym Jacuzzi Wi-fi in bedrooms Aerobics & Spinning Studio, Beauty Treatment Rooms ♫ **Conf** BC Thtr 800 Class 360 Board 40 Del from £175 **Services** Lift air con **Notes LB** ⊗ ⊘ in restaurant Civ Wed 240

★★★★ 78% ◉◉ **HOTEL**

Beardmore

Beardmore St G81 4SA
☎ 0141 951 6000 📠 0141 951 6018
e-mail: info@beardmore.scot.nhs.uk

(For full entry see Clydebank, West Dunbartonshire)

★★★★ 77% ◉◉ **HOTEL**

Langs Hotel

2 Port Dundas Place G2 3LD
☎ 0141 333 1500 & 352 2452 📠 0141 333 5700
e-mail: reservations@langshotels.co.uk
web: www.langshotels.co.uk

dir: *M8 junct 16, follow signs for George Square. Hotel immediately left after Concert Square car park*

A sharply styled, modern city centre hotel offering a choice of restaurants for dinner. Oshi has a spacious split-level Euro fusion style, whilst Aurora has award-winning food in a more formal dining environment. Bedrooms, all with good facilities, offer various designs and some feature interesting duplex suites. State-of-the-art spa facilities ensure guests can relax and unwind.

Rooms 100 en suite (4 fmly) ⊘ in all bedrooms S fr £90; D fr £100 (incl. bkfst) **Facilities Spa** STV Gym Wi-fi in bedrooms **Conf** Thtr 60 Class 10 Board 12 Del from £145 **Services** Lift **Notes** ⊘ in restaurant

---

★★★★ 77% ◉ **HOTEL**

Millennium Hotel Glasgow

MILLENNIUM HOTELS AND RESORTS

George Square G2 1DS
☎ 0141 332 6711 📠 0141 332 4264
e-mail: reservations.glasgow@mill-cop.com
web: www.millenniumhotels.com

dir: *M8 junct 15, through 4 sets of lights, at 5th set turn left into Hanover Street. George Square directly ahead, hotel on right*

Right in the heart of the city, the Millennium has pride of place overlooking George Square. Inside, the property has a contemporary air, with a spacious reception concourse and a glass veranda overlooking the square. There is a stylish brasserie and separate lounge bar, and bedrooms come in a variety of sizes.

Rooms 117 en suite ⊘ in 37 bedrooms S £75-£185; D £75-£185 **Facilities Spa** STV Wi-fi available Soul Therapies Health & Beauty Spa Xmas **Conf** Thtr 40 Class 24 Board 32 Del from £155 **Services** Lift air con **Notes** ⊗ ⊘ in restaurant

★★★★ 76% ⑳⑳ **HOTEL**

Abode Hotel Glasgow ₡Bode

129 Bath St G2 2SZ
☎ 0141 221 6789 & 572 6000 ⬛ 0141 221 6777
e-mail: info@arthousehotel.com

Set in the heart of the city, this concept hotel offers super rooms in a choice of sizes; all are contemporary and well appointed, including internet access and CD players. Formerly the Department of Education offices, the hotel has been transformed, yet keeps most of the grander features. The public areas are now rather 'funky' with a stylish café bar, and the more formal, fine-dining Michael Caines restaurant which is particularly popular.

Rooms 63 en suite (18 fmly) (10 GF) ⊘ in 39 bedrooms **Conf** BC Thtr 70 Class 40 Board 35 **Services** Lift air con **Notes** Civ Wed 100

★★★★ 76% **HOTEL**

Glasgow Marriott Hotel .Marriott.

HOTELS & RESORTS

500 Argyle St, Anderston G3 8RR
☎ 0870 400 7230 ⬛ 0870 400 7330
web: www.marriott.co.uk

dir: M8 junct 19, turn left at lights, then left into hotel

Conveniently located for all major transport links and the city centre, this hotel benefits from extensive conference and banqueting facilities and a spacious car park. Public areas include an open-plan lounge/bar and a Mediterranean styled restaurant. High quality, well-equipped bedrooms benefit from air conditioning and generously sized beds; the suites are particularly comfortable.

Rooms 300 en suite (89 fmly) ⊘ in 212 bedrooms **Facilities** STV 🖭 Sauna Solarium Gym Beautician, poolside steam room **Conf** BC Thtr 800 Class 500 Board 50 **Services** Lift air con **Parking** 180 **Notes** ⊗

★★★★ 75% **HOTEL**

Thistle Glasgow 🍷

THISTLE HOTELS

36 Cambridge St G2 3HN
☎ 0870 333 9154 ⬛ 0870 333 9254
e-mail: glasgow@thistle.co.uk

dir: In heart of city centre, just off Sauchiehall St.

Ideally located within the centre of Glasgow and with ample parking. On going investment ensures the hotel is well presented with the lobby area offering a great first impression on arrival. The hotel also benefits from having a well-presented leisure club along with the largest ballroom in Glasgow. Service is friendly & attentive.

Rooms 300 en suite ⊘ in 160 bedrooms **Facilities** Spa STV 🖭 Sauna Solarium Gym Jacuzzi **Conf** Thtr 1500 Class 800 Board 30 **Services** Lift air con **Parking** 250 **Notes LB** ⊘ in restaurant Civ Wed 1000

★★★ 81% ⑳ **HOTEL**

Malmaison *Malmaison*

hotels that dare to be different

278 West George St G2 4LL
☎ 0141 572 1000 ⬛ 0141 572 1002
e-mail: glasgow@malmaison.com
web: www.malmaison.com

dir: from S & E - M8 junct 18 (Charing Cross), from W & N - M8 (City Centre Glasgow)

Built around a former church in the historic Charing Cross area, this hotel is a smart, contemporary establishment offering impressive levels of service and hospitality. Bedrooms are spacious and feature a host of modern facilities, such as CD players and mini bars. Dining is a treat, with French brasserie-style cuisine served in the original crypt. Malmaison - AA Hotel Group of the Year 2006-7.

Rooms 72 en suite (4 fmly) (19 GF) S fr £140; D fr £140 **Facilities** STV Gym Wi-fi in bedrooms Cardiovascular gym **Conf** Thtr 30 Board 22 Del from £150 **Services** Lift **Notes LB** ⊘ in restaurant

★★★ 75% **HOTEL**

Novotel Glasgow Centre NOVOTEL

ACCOR

181 Pitt St G2 4DT
☎ 0141 222 2775 ⬛ 0141 204 5438
e-mail: H3136@accor.com
web: www.novotel.com

dir: next to Strathclyde Police HQ. Just off Sauchiehall Street

Enjoying a convenient city centre location and with limited parking spaces, this hotel is ideal for both business and leisure travellers. Well-equipped bedrooms are brightly decorated and offer functional design. Modern public areas include a brasserie serving a range of meals all day and a small fitness club.

Rooms 139 en suite (139 fmly) ⊘ in 90 bedrooms **Facilities** STV Sauna Gym Pool table, play station **Conf** Thtr 40 Class 20 Board 20 **Services** Lift air con **Parking** 19

★★★ 75% **HOTEL**

Tulip Inn Glasgow 🟡

TULIP INN

80 Ballater St G5 0TW
☎ 0141 429 4233 ⬛ 0141 429 4244
e-mail: info@tulipinnglasgow.co.uk
web: www.tulipinnglasgow.co.uk

dir: M8 junct 21 follow East Kilbride signs, right onto A8 into Kingston St. Right into South Portland St, left into Norfolk St, through Gorbals St & into Ballater St

Centrally located just minutes from the heart of the main retail district of Glasgow. This modern budget hotel is suitable for business travellers, families and tourists. Bedrooms are bright, well-proportioned and comprehensively equipped. There is a bistro, bar & ample parking.

Rooms 114 en suite (40 fmly) ⊘ in 76 bedrooms **Facilities** STV Gym **Conf** BC Thtr 180 Class 100 Board 60 **Services** Lift **Parking** 120 **Notes LB** ⊘ in restaurant

Scotland

GLASGOW *continued*

★★★ 74% HOTEL

Jurys Inn Glasgow

JURYS DOYLE HOTELS

80 Jamaica St G1 4QE

☎ 0141 314 4800 🖨 0141 314 4888

e-mail: bookings@jurysdoyle.com

web: www.jurysdoyle.com

dir: *M8 junct 19 westbound. Left onto A814 Stobcross St, then left onto Oswald St, right into Midland St, right into Jamaica St. Hotel 200yds on right*

This modern, stylish hotel is easily accessible from major road networks and occupies a prominent location in the city, close to the river. Bedrooms provide good guest comfort and in-room facilities are suited to both leisure and business markets. Public areas include a number of meeting rooms, a popular bar and restaurant.

Rooms 321 en suite (321 fmly) ⊘ in 249 bedrooms S £76-£140; D £76-£140 **Facilities** STV Wi-fi in bedrooms Xmas **Conf** BC Thtr 100 Class 35 Board 40 Del from £90 **Services** Lift air con **Notes** ⊗ ⊘ in restaurant Closed 25-26 Dec

★★★ 72% HOTEL

Bewleys Hotel Glasgow

Bewleys Hotels.com

110 Bath St G2 2EN

☎ 0141 353 0800 & 0845 234 5959 🖨 0141 353 0900

e-mail: gla@bewleyshotels.com

web: www.bewleyshotels.com

dir: *M8 junct 18, left to Sauchiehall St & right to Birthwood St then left to West Regent St & left into Bath St.*

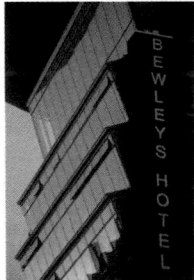

Enjoying a prominent position in the heart of the city, this modern, stylish hotel is ideally suited for business and for leisure breaks. Bedrooms are comfortable and well equipped, with several enjoying impressive views over the Glasgow skyline. Loop café and bar serves good value, modern cooking all day in a relaxed informal setting. Free wireless broadband is provided throughout.

Rooms 103 en suite (47 fmly) ⊘ in 77 bedrooms S £69; D £69 **Facilities** STV Wi-fi available **Services** Lift **Notes** ⊗ ⊘ in restaurant Closed 24-28 Dec

★★★ 68% HOTEL

Quality Hotel Glasgow

QUALITY

99 Gordon St G1 3SF

☎ 0141 221 9680 🖨 0141 226 3948

e-mail: enquiries@quality-hotels-glasgow.com

web: www.choicehotelseurope.com

dir: *M8 junct 19, left into Argyle St and left into Hope St*

A splendid Victorian railway hotel, forming part of Central Station. It retains much original charm combined with modern facilities. Public rooms are impressive and include a bar area. Bedrooms continue to be upgraded and are generally spacious and well-laid out.

Rooms 222 en suite (8 fmly) ⊘ in 70 bedrooms S £110-£135; D £115-£135 **Facilities Spa** STV 🔍 supervised Sauna Solarium Gym Jacuzzi Hair & beauty salon, Sports therapist Xmas **Conf** BC Thtr 600 Class 160 Board 40 Del from £85 **Services** Lift **Notes LB** ⊘ in restaurant Civ Wed 250

★★★ 60% HOTEL

Hotel 377

folio Hotels

377 Argyle St G2 8LL

☎ 0870 609 6166 🖨 0141 221 1014

dir: *from S, M8 junct 19, at pedestrian lights turn left onto Argyle St. Hotel 200yds on right*

Handy for the city centre, this hotel has been designed in a contemporary style. The bright modern bedrooms are well equipped and practically laid out to appeal to both business and leisure guests. The restaurant and bar provide a wide choice of generously portioned dishes. There is also a stylish coffee bar.

Rooms 121 en suite ⊘ in 79 bedrooms S £89-£109; D £89-£109 **Facilities** STV **Conf** Thtr 70 Class 25 Board 30 Del from £85 **Services** Lift **Notes LB** ⊗ ⊘ in restaurant

★★ 76% ◉◉ HOTEL

Uplawmoor

THE CIRCLE
Selected Individual Hotels
GREAT BRITAIN

Neilston Rd G78 4AF

☎ 01505 850565 🖨 01505 850689

e-mail: info@uplawmoor.co.uk

web: www.uplawmoor.co.uk

(For full entry see Uplawmoor, East Renfrewshire)

See advert on opposite page

Scotland

A

Crowne Plaza Glasgow

Congress Rd G3 8QT
☎ 0870 443 1691 📠 0141 221 2022
e-mail: cpglasgow@qmh-hotels.com
dir: M8 junct 19, follow signs for SECC, hotel adjacent to centre

Rooms 283 en suite (15 fmly) ⊗ in 245 bedrooms S £79-£170,
D £79-£170 (incl. bkfst) **Facilities** STV ☒ supervised Gym Wi-fi in
bedrooms Xmas **Conf** Thtr 800 Class 482 Board 68 Del from £150
Services Lift air con **Parking** 300 **Notes** ★★★★ **LB** ⊗ ⊗ in restaurant

A

Ramada Glasgow City

® RAMADA

Ingram St G1 1DQ
☎ 0141 248 4401 📠 0141 226 5149
e-mail: sales.glasgow@ramadajarvis.co.uk
web: www.ramadajarvis.co.uk
dir: M8 junct 15, straight through 4 lights, left at 5th into
Hanover St, left into George Sq, right into Frederick St. Right at
2nd lights into Ingram St
Rooms 91 en suite (2 fmly) ⊗ in 61 bedrooms **Facilities** STV
Conf Thtr 200 Class 80 Board 60 **Services** Lift **Parking** 30
Notes ★★★ **LB** ⊗ ⊗ in restaurant

A

Swallow Glasgow

SWALLOW
HOTELS

517 Paisley Rd West G51 1RW
☎ 0141 427 3146 📠 0141 427 4059
web: www.swallowhotels.com
dir: M8 junct 24, into Helen St at lights. At rdbt turn left, on to
next lights. Hotel 0.25m on left
Rooms 117 rms **Notes** ★★★

U

City Aparthotel Glasgow

27 Elmbank St G2 4PB
☎ 0141 227 2772 & 419 1915 📠 0141 227 2774
e-mail: sales@cityaparthotels.co.uk
dir: Adjacent to Kings Theatre
At the time of going to press, the star classification for this hotel was
not confirmed. Please refer to the AA internet site www.theAA.com for
current information.
Rooms 53 en suite 30 annexe en suite (18 fmly) (12 GF) ⊗ in all
bedrooms S £59-£99; D £69-£149 **Facilities** STV Xmas **Services** Lift
Notes **LB** ⊗ ⊗ in restaurant

BUDGET HOTEL

Campanile Glasgow

Campanile

10 Tunnel St G3 8HL
☎ 0141 287 7700 📠 0141 287 7701
e-mail: glasgow@campanile.com
web: www.envergure.fr
dir: M8 junct 19, follow signs to SECC. Hotel located next to
SECC and Rotunda Casino

This modern building offers accommodation in smart, well-equipped
bedrooms, all with en suite bathrooms. Refreshments may be taken at
the informal Bistro. For further details consult the Hotel Groups page.
Rooms 106 en suite S £54.95-£85; D £54.95-£85 **Conf** Thtr 150 Class 60
Board 90

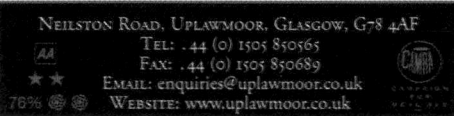
Scotland

GLASGOW *continued*

BUDGET HOTEL

Hotel Ibis Glasgow City Centre

220 West Regent St G2 4DQ
☎ 0141 225 6000 📠 0141 225 6010
e-mail: H3139@accor-hotels.com
web: www.ibishotel.com

Modern, budget hotel offering comfortable accommodation in bright and practical bedrooms. Breakfast is self-service and dinner is available in the restaurant. For further details, consult the Hotel Groups page.

Rooms 141 en suite

BUDGET HOTEL

Innkeeper's Lodge Glasgow/Cumbernauld

1 Auchenkilns Park, Cumbernauld G68 9AT
☎ 01236 795861
web: www.innkeeperslodge.com

Smart, en suite accommodation ideal for both business & leisure guests. Bedrooms are very well equipped, including Sky TV, telephone, modem points, tea & coffee making facilities, (family rooms in most locations). Complimentary breakfast. The adjacent Pub Restaurant; a Harvester, Vintage Inn, Toby Carvery, Ember Inn, Sizzling Pubco or Pub & Carvery offers an all day menu. See Hotel Groups pages for further details.

Rooms 57 en suite S £45-£49.95; D £45-£49.95

BUDGET HOTEL

Premier Travel Inn Glasgow (Cambuslang)

Cambuslang G32 8EY
☎ 08701 977306 📠 0141 778 1703
web: www.premiertravelinn.com

dir: on rdbt at end of M74, turn right at rdbt, at lights turn right & Inn on right

High quality, modern budget accommodation ideal for both families and business travellers. Spacious, en suite bedrooms feature bath and shower, satellite TV and many have telephones and modem points. The adjacent family restaurant features a wide and varied menu. For further details consult the Hotel Groups page.

Rooms 40 en suite S fr £26; D fr £26

Premier Travel Inn Glasgow (Charing Cross)

10 Elmbank Gardens G2 4PP
☎ 0870 9906312 📠 0870 9906313
e-mail: glasgow@premierlodge.co.uk

dir: From S, exit M8 junct 18, through 2 sets of lights, left into Elmbank Cres. From N, exit M8 junct 18 follow city centre signs. Left at lights, left again at next. Down hill, right at lights into Elmbank St, left at BP station

Rooms 278 en suite **Conf** Thtr 50 Class 25 Board 20

Premier Travel Inn Glasgow City Centre

Montrose House, 187 George St G1 1YU
☎ 0870 238 3320 📠 0141 553 2719
dir: off M8 junct 15
Rooms 254 en suite **Conf** Thtr 20 Board 10

Premier Travel Inn Glasgow East

601 Hamilton Rd G71 7SA
☎ 08701 977109 📠 0141 773 8554

dir: From M73/M74 junct 4 follow signs to Uddingston Mt. Vernon and then Zoo Park. At entrance to Glasgow Zoo
Rooms 66 en suite

BUDGET HOTEL

Travelodge Glasgow Central

9 Hill St G3 6PR
☎ 08700 850 950 📠 0141 333 1221
web: www.travelodge.co.uk

dir: M8 junct 17, at lights left into West Graham St. Right into Cowcaddens Rd. Right into Cambridge St. Right into Hill Street

Travelodge offers good quality, good value, modern accommodation. Ideal for families, the spacious en suite bedrooms include remote-control TV, tea and coffee-making facilities and comfortable beds. Meals can be taken at the nearby family restaurant. See Hotel Groups pages for further details.

Rooms 95 en suite S fr £26; D fr £26

Travelodge Glasgow Paisley Road

251 Paisley Rd G5 8RA
☎ 08700 850 950 📠 0141 420 3884

dir: 0.5m from city centre just off M8 junct 20 from S, M8 junct 21 from N. Behind Harry Ramsden's
Rooms 75 en suite S fr £26; D fr £26

SOUTH QUEENSFERRY   MAP 21 NT17

BUDGET HOTEL

Innkeeper's Lodge South Queensferry (Airport)

7 Newhalls Rd EH30 9TA
☎ 0131 331 1990 📠 0131 331 3168
web: www.innkeeperslodge.com

dir: M8 junct 2 follow signs for Forth Road Bridge onto M9/A8000. At rdbt take B907 to junction with B249. Turn right and lodge close to Forth Railway Bridge

Smart, en suite accommodation ideal for both business & leisure guests. Bedrooms are very well equipped, including Sky TV, telephone, modem points, tea & coffee making facilities, (family rooms in most locations). Complimentary breakfast. The adjacent Pub Restaurant; a Harvester, Vintage Inn, Toby Carvery, Ember Inn, Sizzling Pubco or Pub & Carvery offers an all day menu. See Hotel Groups pages for further details.

Rooms 16 en suite S £62.95; D £62.95 **Conf** Class 18 Board 18

Scotland

BUDGET HOTEL

Premier Travel Inn (South Queensferry)

Builyeon Rd EH30 9YJ

☎ 08701 977094 ▤ 0131 319 1156

web: www.premiertravelinn.com

dir: *M8 junct 2 follow signs M9 Stirling, leave at junct 1A take A8000 towards Forth Road Bridge, at 3rd rdbt take 2nd exit into Builyeon Road (do not go onto Forth Road Bridge)*

High quality, modern budget accommodation ideal for both families and business travellers. Spacious, en suite bedrooms feature bath and shower, satellite TV and many have telephones and modem points. The adjacent family restaurant features a wide and varied menu. For further details consult the Hotel Groups page.

Rooms 46 en suite

CLACKMANNANSHIRE

DOLLAR
MAP 21 NS99

★★ 75% SMALL HOTEL

Castle Campbell Hotel

11 Bridge St FK14 7DE

☎ 01259 742519 ▤ 01259 743742

e-mail: bookings@castle-campbell.co.uk

web: www.castle-campbell.co.uk

dir: *on A91 Stirling to St Andrews Rd, in the centre of Dollar*

Set in the centre of a delightful country town, this hotel is popular with both local people and tourists. Accommodation ranges in size, though all rooms are thoughtfully equipped. Inviting public rooms feature a delightful lounge with real fire, a well-stocked whisky bar and a stylish restaurant.

Rooms 9 en suite (2 fmly) ⊘ in all bedrooms S £62.50; D £95 (incl. bkfst) **Facilities** Xmas **Conf** Thtr 80 Class 60 Board 40 **Parking** 8 **Notes LB** ⊘ in restaurant Civ Wed 30

DUMFRIES & GALLOWAY

ANNANDALE WATER MOTORWAY SERVICE AREA (M74)
MAP 21 NY19

BUDGET HOTEL

Premier Travel Inn Lockerbie (Annandale Water)

Johnstonbridge DG11 1HD

☎ 08701 977163 ▤ 01576 470644

web: www.premiertravelinn.com

dir: *A74(M) junct 16. Accessible north and southbound*

High quality, modern budget accommodation ideal for both families and business travellers. Spacious, en suite bedrooms feature bath and shower, satellite TV and many have telephones and modem points. The adjacent family restaurant features a wide and varied menu. For further details consult the Hotel Groups page.

Rooms 42 en suite

AUCHENCAIRN
MAP 21 NX75

★★★ 85% ◉◉ HOTEL

Balcary Bay

DG7 1QZ

☎ 01556 640217 & 640311 ▤ 01556 640272

e-mail: reservations@balcary-bay-hotel.co.uk

web: www.balcary-bay-hotel.co.uk

dir: *on the A711 between Dalbeattie and Kirkcudbright, hotel on Shore road, 2m from village*

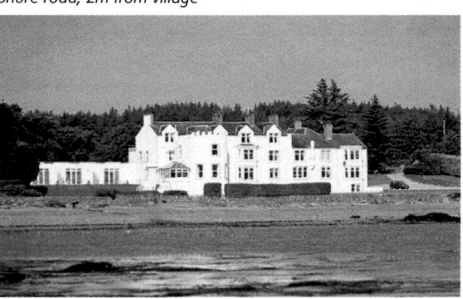

Taking its name from the bay on which it lies, this hotel has lawns running down to the shore. The larger bedrooms enjoy stunning views over the bay, whilst others overlook the gardens. Comfortable public areas invite relaxation. Imaginative dishes feature at dinner, accompanied by a good wine list.

Rooms 20 en suite (1 fmly) (3 GF) S £67; D £120-£150 (incl. bkfst) **Parking** 50 **Notes LB** ⊘ in restaurant Closed Dec-Jan Civ Wed 40

CANONBIE
MAP 21 NY37

★★ 69% HOTEL

Cross Keys

DG14 0SY

☎ 01387 371205 & 371382 ▤ 01387 371878

e-mail: enquiries@crosskeys.biz

web: www.crosskeys.biz

A 17th-century former coaching inn, this friendly hotel boasts a tastefully modern split-level lounge bar offering a good selection of dishes supplemented by a carvery at weekends. Bedrooms are cheerfully decorated and are furnished with either fine traditional pieces or stylish pine.

Rooms 10 rms (9 en suite) (1 fmly) S £30-£48; D £60-£68 (incl. bkfst) **Parking** 30 **Notes** ⊘ in restaurant

CARRUTHERSTOWN
MAP 21 NY17

★★★ 73% HOTEL

Best Western Hetland Hall

DG1 4JX

☎ 01387 840201 ▤ 01387 840211

e-mail: info@hetlandhallhotel.co.uk

web: www.hetlandhallhotel.co.uk

dir: *midway between Annan & Dumfries on A75*

An imposing mansion, Hetland Hall lies in attractive parkland just off the A75. It is popular for weddings and conferences, and its menus,

continued on page 808

Scotland

CARRUTHERSTOWN *continued*

available in both bar and restaurant, also draw praise. Bedrooms come in contrasting styles and sizes.

Best Western Hetland Hall

Rooms 14 en suite 15 annexe en suite (5 fmly) (1 GF) ⊘ in 5 bedrooms **Facilities** STV ⊠ Sauna Gym Putt green Mini Pitch & putt, Toning tables ch fac **Conf** Thtr 200 Class 100 Board 100 **Parking** 60 **Notes LB** ⊘ in restaurant Civ Wed 150

CASTLE DOUGLAS   MAP 21 NX76

★★ 68% **HOTEL**

Imperial

35 King St DG7 1AA
☎ 01556 502086 🖷 01556 503009
e-mail: david@thegolfhotel.co.uk
web: www.thegolfhotel.co.uk

dir: exit A75 at sign for Castle Douglas, hotel opposite library

Situated in the main street, this former coaching inn, popular with golfers, offers guests well-equipped and cheerfully decorated bedrooms. There is a choice of bars and good-value meals are served either in the foyer bar or the upstairs dining room.

Rooms 12 en suite (1 fmly) ⊘ in all bedrooms S £44-£55; D £70 (incl. bkfst) **Conf** Thtr 40 Class 20 Board 20 **Parking** 29 **Notes LB** ⊘ in restaurant Closed 23-26 Dec & 1-3 Jan

DUMFRIES   MAP 21 NX97

★★★ 79% **HOTEL**

Best Western Station

49 Lovers Walk DG1 1LT
☎ 01387 254316 🖷 01387 250388
e-mail: info@stationhotel.co.uk
web: www.stationhotel.co.uk

dir: A75, follow signs to Dumfries town centre, hotel opp railway station

This hotel, sympathetically modernised in harmony with its fine Victorian features, offers well-equipped bedrooms. The Courtyard Bistro has undergone a major refurbishment and offers a popular menu in an informal atmosphere during the evening. In addition good

continued

value meals are also served in the lounge bar and conservatory during the day.

Best Western Station

Rooms 32 en suite (2 fmly) ⊘ in 25 bedrooms S £50-£75; D £80-£120 (incl. bkfst) **Facilities** STV Jacuzzi Wi-fi in bedrooms Use of local gym Xmas **Conf** Thtr 60 Class 35 Board 30 **Services** Lift **Parking** 34 **Notes LB** ⊘ in restaurant Civ Wed 60

★★★ 75% ⊛ **HOTEL**

Cairndale Hotel & Leisure Club

English St DG1 2DF
☎ 01387 240289 🖷 01387 250555
e-mail: sales@cairndale.fsnet.co.uk
web: www.cairndalehotel.co.uk

dir: from S turn off M6 onto A75 to Dumfries, left at 1st rdbt, cross railway bridge, continue to traffic lights, hotel 1st building on left

Within walking distance of the town centre, this hotel provides a wide range of amenities, including leisure facilities and an impressive conference and entertainment centre. Bedrooms range from stylish suites to cosy singles. There's a choice of eating options in the evening; the Reivers Restaurant is smartly modern with food to match.

Rooms 91 en suite (22 fmly) (5 GF) ⊘ in 45 bedrooms S £59-£89; D £79-£149 (incl. bkfst) **Facilities Spa** STV ⊠ supervised Sauna Solarium Gym Jacuzzi Wi-fi in bedrooms Steam room ♫ Xmas **Conf** BC Thtr 300 Class 150 Board 50 Del from £79 **Services** Lift **Parking** 100 **Notes LB** ⊘ in restaurant Civ Wed 200

BUDGET HOTEL

Premier Travel Inn Dumfries

Annan Rd, Collin DG1 3JX
☎ 08701 977078 🖷 01387 266475
web: www.premiertravelinn.com

dir: on main central rdbt junct of the Euroroute bypass (A75)

High quality, modern budget accommodation ideal for both families and business travellers. Spacious, en suite bedrooms feature bath and

continued

shower, satellite TV and many have telephones and modem points. The adjacent family restaurant features a wide and varied menu. For further details consult the Hotel Groups page.

Rooms 40 en suite

BUDGET HOTEL

Travelodge Dumfries
Annan Rd, Collin DG1 3SE
☎ 08700 850 950 ▤ 01387 750658
web: www.travelodge.co.uk
dir: 2m E of Dumfries, on A75

Travelodge offers good quality, good value, modern accommodation. Ideal for families, the spacious en suite bedrooms include remote-control TV, tea and coffee-making facilities and comfortable beds. Meals can be taken at the nearby family restaurant. See Hotel Groups pages for further details.

Rooms 40 en suite S fr £26; D fr £26

ECCLEFECHAN   MAP 21 NY17

Swallow Kirkconnel Hall
DG11 3JH
☎ 01576 300277 ▤ 01576 300402
web: www.swallowhotels.com
Rooms 11 en suite **Notes** ★★★

GATEHOUSE OF FLEET   MAP 20 NX55
★★★★ 79% ◎ **HOTEL**

Cally Palace
DG7 2DL
☎ 01557 814341 ▤ 01557 814522
e-mail: info@callypalace.co.uk
web: www.callypalace.co.uk
dir: M6 & A74, signed A75 Dumfries then Stranraer. At Gatehouse-of-Fleet turn right onto B727, left at Cally

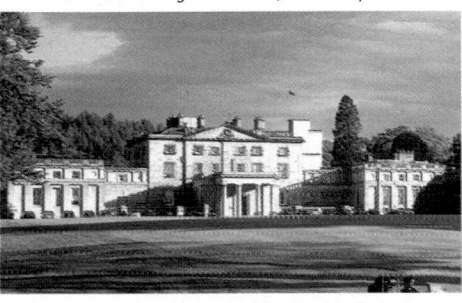

A resort hotel with extensive leisure facilities, this grand 18th-century building is set in 500 acres of forest and parkland that incorporates its own golf course. Bedrooms are spacious and well equipped, whilst public rooms retain a quiet elegance. The short dinner menu focuses

continued on page 810

GATEHOUSE OF FLEET *continued*

on freshly prepared dishes. A pianist plays most nights, and jackets and ties are obligatory.

Rooms 55 en suite (7 fmly) ⊗ in all bedrooms S £94-£138; D £178-£202 (incl. bkfst & dinner) **Facilities** STV ⊠ ♨ 18 ♨ Fishing Snooker Sauna Gym ♨ Putt green Jacuzzi Wi-fi in bedrooms Table tennis Practice fairway Xmas **Conf** Thtr 40 Class 40 Board 25 **Services** Lift **Parking** 100 **Notes LB** ⊗ ⊗ in restaurant Closed Jan-early Feb

See advert on page 809

★★★ 73% HOTEL

Murray Arms

DG7 2HY

☎ 01557 814207 🖹 01557 814370

e-mail: murrayarmshotel@ukonline.co.uk

web: www.murrayarms.com

dir: off A75, hotel at edge of town, near clock tower

A relaxed and welcoming atmosphere prevails at this historic coaching inn that has associations with Robert Burns. Public areas retain a comfortable, traditional feel and include a choice of sitting areas, a snug bar and an all-day restaurant serving honest and popular dishes. Bedrooms are comfortable and well presented.

Rooms 12 en suite (3 fmly) ⊗ in 8 bedrooms S £48; D £96 (incl. bkfst) **Facilities** ♨ Fishing ♨ Xmas **Conf** Thtr 120 Class 50 Board 30 **Parking** 50 **Notes LB** ⊗ in restaurant Civ Wed 120

GRETNA (WITH GRETNA GREEN)

MAP 21 NY36

★★★ 74% HOTEL

Garden House

Sarkfoot Rd DG16 5EP

☎ 01461 337621 🖹 01461 337692

e-mail: info@gardenhouse.co.uk

web: www.gardenhouse.co.uk

dir: just off M6 junct 45 at Gretna

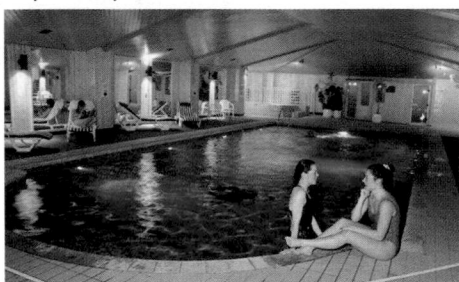

This purpose-built modern hotel lies on the edge of the village. With a focus on weddings its landscaped gardens provide an ideal setting, while inside corridor walls are adorned with photographs portraying that 'special day'. Accommodation is well presented and there is a wing of spacious and comfortable bedrooms, many overlooking the Japanese water gardens.

Rooms 38 en suite (11 fmly) (14 GF) **Facilities** Spa STV ⊠ supervised Sauna Jacuzzi ♬ **Conf** BC Thtr 150 Class 80 Board 40 **Services** Lift **Parking** 105 **Notes** ⊗ ⊗ in restaurant Civ Wed 150

See advert on opposite page

★★★ 74% HOTEL

Gretna Chase

THE INDEPENDENTS

DG16 5JB

☎ 01461 337517 🖹 01461 337766

e-mail: enquiries@gretnachase.co.uk

dir: off M74 onto B7076, left at top of slip road, hotel 400yds on right

With its colourful landscaped gardens, this hotel is a favourite venue for wedding parties. Bedrooms range from the comfortable, traditional, standard rooms to the impressively spacious superior and honeymoon rooms; all are well equipped. There is a foyer lounge, a spacious dining room that can accommodate functions, and a popular lounge bar serving food.

Rooms 19 en suite (9 fmly) ⊗ in 6 bedrooms S £70-£100; D £89-£185 (incl. bkfst) **Facilities** Jacuzzi **Conf** Thtr 50 Class 30 Board 20 **Del** from £79.95 **Parking** 40 **Notes LB** ⊗

A

Swallow Gretna Hall

SWALLOW
HOTELS

Gretna Green DG16 5DY

☎ 01461 338257 🖹 01461 338911

web: www.swallowhotels.com

dir: 8m N of Carlisle, in centre of village opposite church

Rooms 100 en suite **Notes** ★★★

U

Smiths at Gretna Green

Gretna Green DG16 5EA

☎ 01461 337007 🖹 01461 336000

e-mail: info@smithsgretnagreen.com

web: www.smithsgretnagreen.com

dir: Follow signs off motorway for 'Old Blacksmith's Shop'

At the time of going to press, the star classification for this hotel was not confirmed. Please refer to the AA internet site www.theAA.com for current information.

Rooms 50 en suite (8 fmly) ⊗ in all bedrooms S £75-£115; D £85-£125 (incl. bkfst) **Facilities** Spa STV **Conf** Thtr 250 Class 100 Board 40 **Del** from £135 **Services** Lift air con **Parking** 75 **Notes** ⊗ ⊗ in restaurant Civ Wed 150

GRETNA SERVICE AREA (A74(M))

MAP 21 NY36

BUDGET HOTEL

Days Inn Gretna Green

Welcome Break Service Area DG16 5HQ

☎ 01461 337566 🖹 01461 337823

e-mail: gretna.hotel@welcomebreak.co.uk

web: www.welcomebreak.co.uk

dir: between junct 21/22 on M74 - accessible from both N'bound & S'bound carriageway

This modern building offers accommodation in smart, spacious and well-equipped bedrooms, suitable for families and business travellers, and all with en suite bathrooms. Continental breakfast is available and other refreshments may be taken at the nearby family restaurant. For further details see the Hotel Groups page.

Rooms 64 en suite **Conf** Thtr 40 Board 20

KIRKBEAN   MAP 21 NX95

★★ 87% ◉ HOTEL

Cavens

DG2 8AA

☎ 01387 880234 📠 01387 880467

e-mail: enquiries@cavens.com

web: www.cavens.com

dir: *on entering Kirkbean on A710, hotel signed*

Set in parkland gardens, Cavens encapsulates all the virtues of an intimate country-house hotel. Quality is the keynote, and the proprietors have spared no effort in completing a fine renovation of the house. Bedrooms are delightfully individual and very comfortably equipped, and a choice of lounges invites peaceful relaxation. A set dinner offers the best of local and home-made produce.

Rooms 6 en suite ⊘ in all bedrooms S £70-£120; D £80-£150 (incl. bkfst) **Facilities** ⅏ Shooting, Fishing, Horse Riding Xmas **Conf** Thtr 20 Class 20 Board 20 **Parking** 12 **Notes LB** No children 12yrs ⊘ in restaurant Civ Wed 100

KIRKCUDBRIGHT   MAP 20 NX65

★★ 67% HOTEL

Arden House Hotel

Tongland Rd DG6 4UU

☎ 01557 330544 📠 01557 330742

dir: *4m W of Castle Douglas onto A711. Follow Kirkcudbright signs, cross Telford Bridge. Hotel 400m on left*

Set well back from the main road in extensive grounds on the northeast side of town, this spotlessly maintained hotel offers attractive bedrooms, a lounge bar and adjoining conservatory serving a range of popular dishes, which are also available in the dining room. It boasts an impressive function suite in its grounds.

Rooms 9 rms (8 en suite) (7 fmly) S £45; D £65 (incl. bkfst) **Conf** Thtr 175 Class 175 **Parking** 70 **Notes** No credit cards accepted

LOCKERBIE   MAP 21 NY18

★★★ 79% ◉ HOTEL

Dryfesdale

Dryfebridge DG11 2SF

☎ 01576 202427 📠 01576 204187

e-mail: reception@dryfesdalehotel.co.uk

web: www.dryfesdalehotel.co.uk

dir: *from M74 junct 17 take 'Lockerbie North', 3rd left at 1st rdbt, 1st exit left at 2nd rdbt, hotel is 200yds on left*

Conveniently situated for the M74, yet discreetly screened from it, this friendly hotel provides attentive service. Bedrooms, some with access to patio areas, vary in size and style, offer good levels of comfort and are well equipped. Creative, good value dinners make use of local produce and are served in the airy restaurant overlooking the manicured gardens and rolling countryside.

Rooms 16 en suite (4 fmly) (6 GF) ⊘ in 8 bedrooms **Facilities** STV ⅏ Putt green Clay pigeon shooting, Fishing ♫ Xmas **Conf** Thtr 150 Class 100 Board 100 Del from £115 **Parking** 60 **Notes** ⊘ in restaurant Civ Wed 150

★★ 75% HOTEL

Somerton House

35 Carlisle Rd DG11 2DR

☎ 01576 202583 & 202384 📠 01576 204218

e-mail: somerton@somertonhotel.co.uk

dir: *off A74*

This long established Victorian mansion has been sympathetically upgraded in recent years so that original features blend seamlessly with the latest styles in eye-catching interior design. Bedrooms are well equipped and comfortable whilst day rooms include several venues for dining, the best being the conservatory restaurant. Friendly proprietors and a team of long standing staff ensure the warmest of welcomes plus attentive service.

Rooms 7 en suite 4 annexe en suite (1 fmly) ⊘ in 7 bedrooms **Conf** Thtr 60 Class 25 Board 25 **Parking** 100 **Notes LB** ⊘ in restaurant

★★ 72% HOTEL

Kings Arms Hotel

High St DG11 2JL

☎ 01576 202410 📠 01576 202410

e-mail: reception@kingsarmshotel.co.uk

web: www.kingsarmshotel.co.uk

dir: *A74(M), 0.5m into town centre, hotel opposite town hall*

Dating from the 17th century this former inn lies right in the town centre. Now a family-run hotel, it provides attractive well-equipped

continued on page 812

Scotland

Scotland

LOCKERBIE *continued*

bedrooms. At lunch and dinner a menu ranging from snacks to full meals is served in the two cosy bars; one is non-smoking.

Rooms 13 en suite (2 fmly) ⊗ in all bedrooms S £45; D £75 (incl. bkfst) **Facilities** FTV Wi-fi in bedrooms Xmas **Conf** Thtr 80 Class 40 Board 30 **Parking** 8 **Notes** ⊗ in restaurant

★★ 67% **HOTEL**

Ravenshill House

12 Dumfries Rd DG11 2EF
☎ 01576 202882 📠 01576 202882
e-mail: aaenquiries@ravenshillhotellockerbie.co.uk
web: www.ravenshillhotellockerbie.co.uk
dir: from A74(M) Lockerbie junct onto A709. Hotel 0.5m on right

Set in spacious gardens on the fringe of the town, this friendly, family-run hotel offers cheerful service and good value, home-cooked meals. Bedrooms are generally spacious and comfortably equipped, including an ideal two-room family unit.

Rooms 8 rms (7 en suite) (2 fmly) ⊗ in all bedrooms S £45-£65; D £70-£80 (incl. bkfst) **Conf** Thtr 30 Class 20 Board 12 **Parking** 35 **Notes LB** ⊗ in restaurant

MOFFAT   MAP 21 NT00

★★★ 71% **HOTEL**

Best Western Moffat House

High St DG10 9HL
☎ 01683 220039 📠 01683 221288
e-mail: moffat@talk21.com
web: www.moffathouse.co.uk
dir: M74 junct 15, Beattock, take A701. Hotel in 1m

This fine Adam mansion, in its own neatly tended gardens, is set back from the main road in the centre of this popular country town. Inviting public areas include a quiet sun lounge to the rear, a comfortable lounge bar serving tasty meals and an attractive restaurant for the more formal occasion. Bedrooms present a mix of classical and modern styles.

Rooms 20 en suite (2 fmly) (5 GF) ⊗ in all bedrooms **Facilities** Xmas **Conf** BC Thtr 100 Class 80 Board 60 Del from £109 **Parking** 30 **Notes** ⊗ in restaurant Civ Wed 110

★★ 68% **HOTEL**

The Star

44 High St DG10 9EF
☎ 01683 220156 📠 01683 221524
e-mail: tim@famousstarhotel.com
dir: M74 junct 15 signed Moffat, hotel in 2m

This establishment claims to be the world's narrowest hotel, which makes a novel talking point. Well-equipped bedrooms plus a good range of food, served either in the bar or the restaurant, are two features of this friendly hotel.

Rooms 8 en suite (1 fmly) **Facilities** STV Large screen in bar for sport **Notes** ⊗ ⊗ in restaurant

NEWTON STEWART   MAP 20 NX46

INSPECTORS' CHOICE

★★★ ❀❀ **HOTEL**

Kirroughtree House

Minnigaff DG8 6AN
☎ 01671 402141 📠 01671 402425
e-mail: info@kirroughtreehouse.co.uk
web: www.kirroughtreehouse.co.uk
dir: from A75 take A712, New Galloway road, entrance to hotel 300yds on left

This imposing mansion enjoys a peaceful location in eight acres of landscaped gardens near Galloway Forest Park. The inviting day rooms comprise a choice of lounges and two elegant dining rooms. Well-proportioned, individually styled bedrooms include some suites and mini-suites and many rooms enjoy fine views. Service is very friendly and attentive.

Rooms 17 en suite ⊗ in all bedrooms S £85-£120; D £150-£210 (incl. bkfst) **Facilities** STV ⌣ ⌣ 9 hole pitch and putt Xmas **Conf** Thtr 30 Class 20 Board 20 Del from £125 **Services** Lift **Parking** 50 **Notes LB** No children 10yrs ⊗ in restaurant Closed 4 Jan-16 Feb

See also advert on page 809

PORTPATRICK   MAP 20 NW95

INSPECTORS' CHOICE

★★★ ◉◉◉ **HOTEL**

Knockinaam Lodge

DG9 9AD

☎ 01776 810471 📠 01776 810435

e-mail: reservations@knockinaamlodge.com

web: www.knockinaamlodge.com

dir: from A77 or A75 follow signs to Portpatrick. Through
Lochans. After 2m left at signs for hotel

Any tour of Dumfries & Galloway would not be complete without
a night or two at this gastronomic haven of tranquillity and
relaxation. An extended Victorian house that is set back from its
own pebble beach but is sheltered by majestic cliffs and
woodlands. A warm welcome is assured from the proprietors and
their committed team, and much emphasis is placed on providing
a sophisticated but intimate home-from-home experience. The
cooking here is a real treat and showcases superb local produce.

Rooms 9 en suite ⊘ in all bedrooms S £165-£290; D £260-£390
(incl. bkfst & dinner) **Facilities** Fishing ⌘ Shooting, Walking, Sea
fishing, Clay pigeon shooting Xmas **Conf** Thtr 30 Class 10 Board 16
Del from £150 **Parking** 20 **Notes LB** ⊘ in restaurant Civ Wed 40

★★★ 80% ◉ **HOTEL**

Fernhill

Heugh Rd DG9 8TD

☎ 01776 810220 📠 01776 810596

e-mail: info@fernhillhotel.co.uk

web: www.fernhillhotel.co.uk

dir: from Stranraer A77 to Portpatrick, 100yds past Portpatrick
village sign, turn right before war memorial. Hotel is 1st on left

Set high above the village, this hotel looks out over the harbour and
Irish Sea. Many of the bedrooms take advantage of the views. A
modern wing offers particularly spacious and well-appointed rooms -
some have balconies. The smart conservatory restaurant offers
interesting freshly prepared dishes.

continued

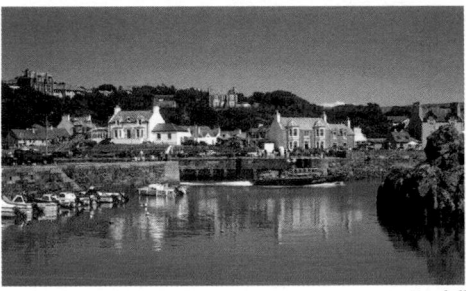

Fernhill

Rooms 27 en suite 9 annexe en suite (3 fmly) (8 GF) ⊘ in all bedrooms
S fr £83; D fr £116 (incl. bkfst) **Facilities** STV Wi-fi in bedrooms Leisure
facilities available at sister hotel in Stranraer Xmas **Conf** Thtr 24 Class 12
Board 12 **Parking** 45 **Notes LB** ⊘ in restaurant Closed mid-Jan - mid-
Feb Civ Wed 40

See also advert on page 809

POWFOOT   MAP 21 NY16

🅰

Powfoot Golf Hotel

Links Av DG12 5PN

☎ 01461 700254 📠 01461 700288

e-mail: rooms@powfootgolfhotel.co.uk

web: www.powfootgolfhotel.co.uk

dir: A75 onto B721, through Annan. B724, approx 3m, left onto
unclassified road

Rooms 15 en suite (4 fmly) **Conf** Thtr 120 Class 60 Board 40
Parking 40 **Notes** ★★ **LB** ⊘ in restaurant Closed 25-26 Dec

---

STRANRAER   MAP 20 NX06

★★★★ 76% ◉ **HOTEL**

North West Castle

DG9 8EH

☎ 01776 704413 📠 01776 702646

e-mail: info@northwestcastle.co.uk

web: www.northwestcastle.co.uk

dir: on seafront, close to Stena ferry terminal

This long-established hotel overlooks the bay and the ferry terminal.
The public areas include a classical dining room where a pianist plays
during dinner and an adjoining lounge with large leather armchairs and

continued on page 814

Scotland

STRANRAER *continued*

blazing fire in season. There is a shop, leisure centre, and a curling rink that is the focus in winter. Bedrooms are comfortable and spacious.

Rooms 70 en suite 2 annexe en suite (22 fmly) ⊛ in all bedrooms S £75-£85; D £118-£158 (incl. bkfst & dinner) **Facilities** STV ⛱ supervised Snooker Sauna Gym Jacuzzi Wi-fi in bedrooms Curling (Oct-Apr) Games room Xmas **Conf** Thtr 150 Class 60 Board 40 **Services** Lift **Parking** 100 **Notes LB** ⊛ in restaurant Civ Wed 130

See also advert on page 809

★★★ 75% ◉ **HOTEL**

Corsewall Lighthouse Hotel

Corsewall Point, Kirkcolm DG9 0QG
☎ 01776 853220 ▤ 01776 854231
e-mail: lighthousehotel@btinternet.com
web: www.lighthousehotel.co.uk
dir: A718 from Stranraer to Kirkcolm then follow hotel signs

Looking for something completely different? A unique hotel converted from buildings that adjoin a listed 19th-century lighthouse set on a rocky coastline. Bedrooms come in a variety of sizes, some reached by a spiral staircase, and as with the public areas, are cosy and atmospheric. Three cottage suites in the grounds offer greater space.

Rooms 6 en suite 3 annexe en suite (2 fmly) (5 GF) ⊛ in 6 bedrooms S £110-£250; D £130-£280 **Conf** Thtr 20 **Parking** 20 **Notes LB** ⊛ in restaurant Civ Wed 28

DUNDEE CITY

BROUGHTY FERRY   MAP 21 NO43

BUDGET HOTEL

Premier Travel Inn Dundee East

premier travel inn

115-117 Lawers Dr, Panmurefield Village DD5 3UP
☎ 0870 9906324 ▤ 0870 9906325
web: www.premiertravelinn.com
dir: From N, take A92 Dundee to Arbroath. Hotel 1.5m after Sainsbury's. From S, follow A90 Perth to Dundee signs. At end of dual carriageway follow Dundee to Arbroath signs

High quality, modern budget accommodation ideal for both families and business travellers. Spacious, en suite bedrooms feature bath and shower, satellite TV and many have telephones and modem points. The adjacent family restaurant features a wide and varied menu. For further details consult the Hotel Groups page.

Rooms 60 en suite

DUNDEE   MAP 21 NO43

★★★★ 81% ◉◉ **HOTEL**

Apex City Quay Hotel & Spa

APEX HOTELS

1 West Victoria Dock Rd DD1 3JP
☎ 01382 202404 & 0845 365 0000 ▤ 01382 201401
e-mail: reservations@apexhotels.co.uk
dir: A85 Riverside Drive to Discovery Quay. Exit rdbt for City Quay.

This stylish, purpose-built, modern hotel occupies an enviable position at the heart of Dundee's regenerated quayside. Bedrooms, including a number of smart suites, feature the very latest in design. Warm hospitality and professional service are an integral part of the appeal. Open-plan public areas with panoramic windows and contemporary food options complete the package.

Rooms 153 en suite (16 fmly) ⊛ in 122 bedrooms S £69-£200; D £79-£200 (incl. bkfst) **Facilities** Spa STV ⛱ supervised Sauna Gym Jacuzzi Wi-fi in bedrooms Elemis treatment rooms, steam room Xmas **Conf** BC Thtr 400 Class 180 Board 120 Del from £120 **Services** Lift **Parking** 150 **Notes LB** ⊛ ⊛ in restaurant Civ Wed 300

★★ 68% **HOTEL**

Sandford Country House Hotel

Newton Hill, Wormit DD6 8RG
☎ 01382 541802 ▤ 01382 542136
e-mail: sandford.hotel@btinternet.com
web: www.sandfordhotelfife.com
dir: off A92 at B946, hotel 100yds on left

Built around the turn of the last century, this hotel lies in wooded grounds well off the main road outside the village of Wormit. Set around a small terraced courtyard, it is a popular venue for meals, which are served in the bar or restaurant. Bedrooms come in a variety of sizes and are modern in style.

Rooms 16 en suite (2 fmly) ⊛ in 15 bedrooms **Facilities** STV Cycle hire **Conf** Thtr 45 Class 25 Board 25 **Parking** 30 **Notes LB** ⊛ in restaurant Civ Wed 40

A

Swallow Dundee

SWALLOW HOTELS

Kingsway West, Invergowrie DD2 5JT
☎ 01382 641122 ▤ 01382 631201
web: www.swallowhotels.com
dir: off A90/A929 rdbt follow Denhead of Gray sign, hotel on left
Rooms 103 en suite **Notes** ★★★

BUDGET HOTEL

Premier Travel Inn Dundee Centre

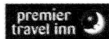

Discovery Quay, Riverside Dr DD1 4XA
☎ 08701 977079 📠 01382 203237
web: www.premiertravelinn.com

dir: follow signs for Discovery Quay, situated on waterfront

High quality, modern budget accommodation ideal for both families and business travellers. Spacious, en suite bedrooms feature bath and shower, satellite TV and many have telephones and modem points. The adjacent family restaurant features a wide and varied menu. For further details consult the Hotel Groups page.

Rooms 40 en suite

Premier Travel Inn Dundee (Monifieth)

Ethiebeaton Park, Arbroath Rd, Monifieth DD5 4HB
☎ 08701 977080 📠 01382 530468

dir: From A90 Kingsway Road follow signs for Carnoustie/Arbroath (A92)
Rooms 40 en suite **Conf** Board 8

Premier Travel Inn Dundee North

Dayton Dr, Camperdown Leisure Park, Kingsway DD2 3SQ
☎ 0870 990 6420 📠 0870 990 6421

dir: 2m N of city centre on A90 at junct with A923, next to cinema & entrance to Camperdown Leisure Park
Rooms 78 en suite

Premier Travel Inn Dundee West

Kingsway West, Invergowrie DD2 5JU
☎ 08701 977081 📠 01382 568431

dir: approaching Swallow rdbt next to Technology Park rdbt take A90 towards Aberdeen, Inn on left after 250yds
Rooms 64 en suite

BUDGET HOTEL

Travelodge Dundee

A90 Kingsway DD2 4TD
☎ 08700 850 950 📠 01382 610488
web: www.travelodge.co.uk

dir: on A90

Travelodge offers good quality, good value, modern accommodation. Ideal for families, the spacious en suite bedrooms include remote-control TV, tea and coffee-making facilities and comfortable beds. Meals can be taken at the nearby family restaurant. See Hotel Groups pages for further details.

Rooms 32 en suite S fr £26; D fr £26

Travelodge Dundee Central

152-158 West Marketgait DD1 1NL
☎ 08700 850 950

dir: From Airport turn right towards city centre. At 3rd rdbt take 1st exit. At next rdbt take 2nd exit.
Rooms 48 en suite S fr £26; D fr £26

KILMARNOCK   **MAP 20 NS43**

★★★ 73% **HOTEL**

Best Western Fenwick

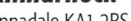

Fenwick KA3 6AU
☎ 01560 600478 📠 01560 600334
e-mail: fenwick@bestwestern.co.uk
web: www.fenwickhotel.com

dir: M77 junct 8 southbound. 3m N of Kilmarnock

Conveniently located between Glasgow and the Ayrshire coast on the A77, this modern hotel provides good facilities for both the business and leisure guest. Bedrooms are well equipped and comfortable whilst stylish public rooms include a cosy fireside lounge, a brasserie-style restaurant and informal bar.

Rooms 31 en suite (2 fmly) (10 GF) ⊗ in 25 bedrooms S £55-£85; D £65-£115 (incl. bkfst) **Facilities** STV Putt green Wi-fi in bedrooms Clay pigeon Quad bike ch fac Xmas **Conf** BC Thtr 160 Class 60 Board 50 Del from £92.50 **Parking** 80 **Notes LB** ⊗ in restaurant Civ Wed 140

BUDGET HOTEL

Premier Travel Inn Kilmarnock

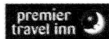

Annadale KA1 2RS
☎ 08701 977148 📠 01563 570536
web: www.premiertravelinn.com

dir: M74 junct 8 signed Kilmarnock (A71). From M77 join A71 to Irvine. At next rdbt turn right onto B7064 signed Crosshouse Hospital. Inn is on right

High quality, modern budget accommodation ideal for both families and business travellers. Spacious, en suite bedrooms feature bath and shower, satellite TV and many have telephones and modem points. The adjacent family restaurant features a wide and varied menu. For further details consult the Hotel Groups page.

Rooms 40 en suite

BUDGET HOTEL

Travelodge Kilmarnock

Kilmarnock By Pass KA1 5LQ
☎ 08700 850 950 📠 01563 573810
web: www.travelodge.co.uk

dir: at Bellfield junct just off A77

Travelodge offers good quality, good value, modern accommodation. Ideal for families, the spacious en suite bedrooms include remote-control TV, tea and coffee-making facilities and comfortable beds. Meals can be taken at the nearby family restaurant. See Hotel Groups pages for further details.

Rooms 40 en suite S fr £26; D fr £26

Scotland

Scotland

SORN
MAP 20 NS52

◉◉ RESTAURANT WITH ROOMS

The Sorn Inn
35 Main St KA5 6HU
☎ 01290 551305 🖶 01290 553470
e-mail: craig@sorninn.com
dir: A70 from S or A76 from N onto B743 to Sorn

Centrally situated in this rural village, which is convenient for many of Ayrshire's attractions, this renovated inn is a fine dining restaurant with a cosy lounge area. There is also a popular chop house with a pub-like environment. The freshly decorated bedrooms have comfortable beds and good facilities.

Rooms 4 en suite (1 fmly) ⊗ in all bedrooms S £35-£50; D £70-£90
Facilities Fishing **Parking** 9 **Notes LB** ⊗ Closed 2wks Jan

EAST DUNBARTONSHIRE

BEARSDEN
MAP 20 NS57

BUDGET HOTEL

Premier Travel Inn Glasgow (Bearsden)
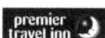
Milngavie Rd G61 3EA
☎ 0870 9906532 🖶 0870 9906533
web: www.premiertravelinn.com
dir: From E, exit M8 junct 16. From W, exit M8 junct 17. Follow A81 signed Milngavie. Hotel on left

High quality, modern budget accommodation ideal for both families and business travellers. Spacious, en suite bedrooms feature bath and shower, satellite TV and many have telephones and modem points. The adjacent family restaurant features a wide and varied menu. For further details consult the Hotel Groups page.

Rooms 61 en suite

MILNGAVIE
MAP 20 NS57

BUDGET HOTEL

Premier Travel Inn Glasgow (Milngavie)
premier travel inn
103 Main St G62 6JQ
☎ 08701 977112 🖶 0141 956 7839
web: www.premiertravelinn.com
dir: From M8 junct 16 follow signs A879 to Milngavie

High quality, modern budget accommodation ideal for both families and business travellers. Spacious, en suite bedrooms feature bath and shower, satellite TV and many have telephones and modem points. The adjacent family restaurant features a wide and varied menu. For further details consult the Hotel Groups page.

Rooms 60 en suite **Conf** Class 16 Board 16

EAST LOTHIAN

DIRLETON
MAP 21 NT58

★★★ 78% ◉ **SMALL HOTEL**

The Open Arms
EH39 5EG
☎ 01620 850241 🖶 01620 850570
e-mail: openarms@clara.co.uk
web: www.openarmshotel.com
dir: from A1, follow signs for North Berwick, through Gullane, 2m on left

Long-established, this hotel lies across from the picturesque village green and Dirleton Castle. Inviting public areas include a choice of lounges and a cosy bar. Four new garden bedrooms (and a new lounge) provide particularly high standards. A variety of carefully prepared meals can be enjoyed in both the informal setting of Deveau's brasserie or the more intimate Library restaurant.

Rooms 10 en suite (1 fmly) **Conf** Thtr 200 Class 150 Board 100
Parking 30 **Notes LB** ⊗ in restaurant Closed 4-15 Jan

GULLANE
MAP 21 NT48

INSPECTORS' CHOICE

★★★ ◉◉◉ **HOTEL**

Greywalls
Muirfield EH31 2EG
☎ 01620 842144 🖶 01620 842241
e-mail: hotel@greywalls.co.uk
web: www.greywalls.co.uk
dir: A198, hotel signed at E end of village

A dignified and relaxing Edwardian country house designed by Sir Edwin Lutyens; Greywalls overlooks the famous Muirfield Golf Course and is ideally placed just a half hour's drive from Edinburgh. Delightful public rooms look onto beautiful gardens and freshly prepared cuisine may be enjoyed in the restaurant. Stylish bedrooms, whether cosy singles or spacious master rooms, are thoughtfully equipped and many command views of the course. A gatehouse lodge is ideal for golfing parties.

Rooms 17 en suite 6 annexe en suite (9 GF) S £135-£270; D £240-£285 (incl. bkfst) **Facilities** STV 🌺 🍃 Putt green Wi-fi available **Conf** Thtr 30 Class 20 Board 20 Del from £180
Parking 40 **Notes LB** ⊗ in restaurant Closed Nov-Mar

NORTH BERWICK MAP 21 NT58

★★★★ 80% ® HOTEL

Macdonald Marine

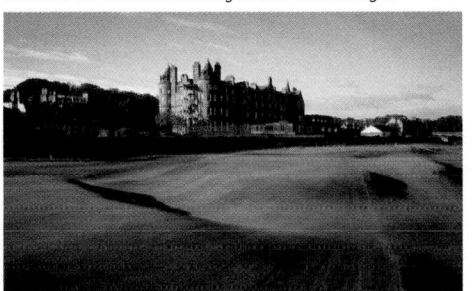

Cromwell Rd EH39 4LZ
☎ 0870 400 8129 📠 01620 894480
e-mail: sales.marine@macdonald-hotels.co.uk
web: www.macdonald-hotels.co.uk
dir: A198 into Hamilton Rd at lights then take 2nd right

This imposing leisure, conference and golfing hotel commands stunning views across the golf course to the Firth of Forth. A good range of leisure facilities accompanies well-proportioned public areas. Bedrooms come in a variety of sizes, some being impressively large.

Rooms 83 en suite (4 fmly) (4 GF) ⊗ in 20 bedrooms **Facilities Spa** STV 🏊 supervised 🏊 Sauna Solarium Gym Putt green Wi-fi available Indoor & outdoor salt water hydro pool Xmas **Conf** Thtr 395 Class 120 Board 120 Del from £140 **Services** Lift **Parking** 50 **Notes** ⊗ ⊘ in restaurant Civ Wed 150

★★ 69% HOTEL

Nether Abbey

20 Dirleton Av EH39 4BQ
☎ 01620 892802 📠 01620 895298
e-mail: bookings@netherabbey.co.uk
web: www.netherabbey.co.uk
dir: exit A1 at junct with A198, S to rdbt, take B6371 to N Berwick, hotel 2nd on left on entering town

Popular with golfers, this hotel boasts stunningly contemporary public areas that include open-plan reception, dining areas and bar. Equally contemporary menus offer a good range of dishes. Upstairs, modern well-equipped bedrooms include two junior suites with CD/video players.

Rooms 13 en suite (4 fmly) ⊗ in all bedrooms S fr £70; D fr £100 (incl. bkfst) **Facilities** Xmas **Conf** Thtr 30 Class 20 Board 20 **Parking** 20 **Notes LB** ⊘ in restaurant Civ Wed 60

EAST RENFREWSHIRE

UPLAWMOOR MAP 20 NS45

★★ 76% ®® HOTEL

Uplawmoor Hotel

THE CIRCLE
Selected Individual Hotels
GREAT BRITAIN

Neilston Rd G78 4AF
☎ 01505 850565 📠 01505 850689
e-mail: info@uplawmoor.co.uk
web: www.uplawmoor.co.uk
dir: M77 junct 2, A736 signed Barrhead & Irvine. Hotel 4m beyond Barrhead

Originally an old coaching inn, this friendly hotel is set in a village off the Glasgow to Irvine road. The comfortable restaurant (with cocktail lounge adjacent) features imaginative dishes, whilst the separate lounge bar is popular for freshly prepared bar meals. The modern bedrooms are both comfortable and well equipped.

Rooms 14 en suite (1 fmly) ⊗ in 9 bedrooms S £52-£59; D £59-£79 (incl. bkfst) **Facilities** STV Wi-fi in bedrooms **Conf** BC Thtr 40 Class 12 Board 10 Del from £69 **Parking** 40 **Notes LB** ⊗ ⊘ in restaurant

See advertisement under GLASGOW

FALKIRK

CASTLECARY MAP 21 NS77

★★ 84% HOTEL

Castlecary House

Castlecary Rd G68 0HD
☎ 01324 840233 📠 01324 841608
e-mail: enquiries@castlecaryhotel.com
web: www.castlecaryhotel.com
dir: off A80 onto B816 between Glasgow and Stirling - hotel by Castlecary Arches

Close to the Forth Clyde Canal and convenient for the M80, this popular hotel provides a versatile range of accommodation, within purpose-built units in the grounds and also in an extension to the original house. The attractive and spacious restaurant serves a short carte menu and enjoyable meals are also served in the busy bars.

Rooms 60 rms (55 en suite) (2 fmly) S £65-£85; D £65-£85 (incl. bkfst) **Facilities** Wi-fi available **Conf** BC Thtr 140 Class 120 Board 60 Del from £130 **Services** Lift **Parking** 100 **Notes** ⊘ in restaurant RS 1 Jan Civ Wed 90

Scotland

Scotland

FALKIRK   MAP 21 NS88

★★★ 72% **HOTEL**

Best Western Park

Camelon Rd FK1 5RY

☎ 01324 628331 🖹 01324 611593

e-mail: reservations@parkhotelfalkirk.co.uk

web: www.parkhotelfalkirk.co.uk

dir: from M8 take A803 into Falkirk, hotel 1m beyond Mariner Leisure Centre, opposite Dollar Park. From M9, A803 through Falkirk, follow signs for Dollar Park

This purpose-built, well-established hotel is popular with business travellers and easily accessible from all major transport routes. Smart contemporary public areas feature a spacious and inviting lounge and restaurant with a bar. Well-equipped bedrooms come in a variety of sizes.

Rooms 55 en suite (3 fmly) ⊛ in 32 bedrooms S £70-£83; D £70-£83 (incl. bkfst) **Facilities** STV Wi-fi in bedrooms **Conf** BC Thtr 300 Class 140 Board 50 Del from £95 **Services** Lift **Parking** 160 **Notes LB** ⊛ in restaurant Civ Wed 120

BUDGET HOTEL

Premier Travel Inn Falkirk West

Glenbervie Business Park, Bellsdyke Rd, Larbert FK5 4EG

☎ 0870 9906550 🖹 0870 9906551

web: www.premiertravelinn.com

dir: Just off A88. Approx 1m from M876 junct 2

High quality, modern budget accommodation ideal for both families and business travellers. Spacious, en suite bedrooms feature bath and shower, satellite TV and many have telephones and modem points. The adjacent family restaurant features a wide and varied menu. For further details consult the Hotel Groups page.

Rooms 60 en suite

GRANGEMOUTH   MAP 21 NS98

★★★ 85% ◉◉ **HOTEL**

The Grange Manor

Glensburgh FK3 8XJ

☎ 01324 474836 🖹 01324 665861

e-mail: info@grangemanor.co.uk

web: www.grangemanor.co.uk

dir: E: off M9 junct 6, hotel 200mtrs to right. W: off M9 junct 5, A905 for 2m

Located south of town close to the M9, this stylish hotel, popular with business and corporate clientele, benefits from hands-on family ownership. It offers spacious, high quality accommodation with superb bathrooms. Public areas include a comfortable foyer area, lounge bar and smart restaurant. There is also a smart modern brasserie in the grounds. Staff throughout the manor are very friendly.

Rooms 6 en suite 30 annexe en suite (6 fmly) (15 GF) ⊛ in 22 bedrooms S £140; D £140 (incl. bkfst) **Facilities** STV Wi-fi available Xmas **Conf** Thtr 190 Class 68 Board 40 Del from £155 **Services** Lift **Parking** 154 **Notes LB** ⊗ ⊛ in restaurant Civ Wed 160

POLMONT   MAP 21 NS97

★★★★ 75% **HOTEL**

Macdonald Inchyra Grange

Grange Rd FK2 0YB

☎ 01324 711911 🖹 01324 716134

e-mail: inchyra@macdonald-hotels.co.uk

web: www.macdonald-hotels.co.uk

dir: just beyond BP Social Club on Grange Rd

Ideally placed for the M9 and Grangemouth terminal, this former manor house has been tastefully extended. It provides extensive conference facilities and a choice of eating options: the relaxed atmosphere of the Steakhouse or the Priory Restaurant, which provides a more formal dining experience. Bedrooms are mostly spacious and comfortable.

Rooms 101 en suite (5 fmly) (34 GF) ⊛ in all bedrooms S £95-£145; D £120-£170 (incl. bkfst) **Facilities** Spa STV ℞ supervised ⧖ Sauna Solarium Gym Jacuzzi Steam room, Beauty therapy, Aromatherapist ♫ Xmas **Conf** BC Thtr 700 Class 250 Board 80 Del from £130 **Services** Lift **Parking** 400 **Notes LB** ⊛ in restaurant Civ Wed 500

BUDGET HOTEL

Premier Travel Inn Falkirk East

Beancross Rd FK2 0YS

☎ 08701 977098 🖹 01324 720777

web: www.premiertravelinn.com

dir: M9 junct 5 at rdbt take exit signed Polmont A9. Inn is on left

High quality, modern budget accommodation ideal for both families and business travellers. Spacious, en suite bedrooms feature bath and shower, satellite TV and many have telephones and modem points. The adjacent family restaurant features a wide and varied menu. For further details consult the Hotel Groups page.

Rooms 40 en suite

FIFE

ABERDOUR
MAP 21 NT18

★★ 65% **HOTEL**

The Aberdour Hotel

THE CIRCLE
Selected Individual Hotels

38 High St KY3 0SW
☎ 01383 860325 ▤ 01383 860808
e-mail: reception@aberdourhotel.co.uk
web: www.aberdourhotel.co.uk

dir: M90 junct 1, E on A921 for 5m. Hotel in centre of village

This small hotel has a relaxed and welcoming atmosphere. Real ale is featured in the cosy bar where good-value, home-cooked meals are available, as they are in the cosy dining room with its nautical theme. Bedrooms vary in size and style but all are well equipped, and those in the stable block are particularly comfortable.

Rooms 12 en suite 4 annexe en suite (4 fmly) (2 GF) ⊗ in 12 bedrooms S £40 £50; D £60 £70 (incl. bkfst) **Facilities** STV Wi-fi in bedrooms **Parking** 8 **Notes LB** ⊗ in restaurant

★ 64% **SMALL HOTEL**

The Cedar Inn

20 Shore Rd KY3 0TR
☎ 01383 860310 ▤ 01383 860004
e-mail: enquiries@cedarinn.co.uk

dir: in Aberdour turn right off A921 into Main St then right into Shore Rd. Hotel 100yds on left

Lying between the village centre and the beach, this small hotel has three character bars, one dedicated to malt whiskies, and impressive bar and dinner menus. Bedrooms offer a mix of standards but all are well equipped.

Rooms 9 en suite (2 fmly) ⊗ in 5 bedrooms S £39-£80; D £60-£70 (incl. bkfst) **Facilities** ♫ Xmas **Conf** Del from £40 **Parking** 12 **Notes LB** ⊗ in restaurant

BURNTISLAND
MAP 21 NT28

★★★ 70% **HOTEL**

Kingswood

Kinghorn Rd KY3 9LL
☎ 01592 872329 ▤ 01592 873123
e-mail: rankin@kingswoodhotel.co.uk
web: www.kingswoodhotel.co.uk

dir: A921 coastal road at Burntisland, right at rdbt, left at T-junct, at bottom of hill to Kingshorn road, hotel 0.5m on left

Lying east of the town, this hotel has views across the Firth of Forth to Edinburgh. Public rooms feature a range of cosy sitting areas, a spacious and attractive restaurant serving good value meals. There is also a good-size function room and multi-purpose conservatory. Bedrooms include two family suites and front-facing rooms with balconies.

Rooms 13 en suite (3 fmly) (1 GF) ⊗ in all bedrooms S £47-£66; D £76-£105 (incl. bkfst) **Conf** Thtr 150 Class 20 Board 40 Del from £80 **Parking** 50 **Notes LB** ⊛ ⊗ in restaurant Closed 26 Dec & 1 Jan Civ Wed 120

★★ 79% **HOTEL**

Inchview Hotel

65-69 Kinghorn Rd KY3 9EB
☎ 01592 872239 ▤ 01592 872888
e-mail: reception@inchview.co.uk

dir: M90 junct 1, follow Fife Coastal Route signed Burntisland

Looking out across the links to the Firth of Forth, this friendly hotel is undergoing a complete refurbishment. Bedrooms provide a variety of styles, with the superior rooms reflecting the Georgian character of the house. Both the restaurant and bar menus offer a wide and interesting choice.

Rooms 16 en suite (1 fmly) (2 GF) ⊗ in all bedrooms S £60-£80; D £80-£125 (incl. bkfst) **Facilities** ♨ **Conf** Thtr 64 Class 64 Board 16 Del from £99.95 **Parking** 16 **Notes LB** No children 12yrs ⊗ in restaurant

CRAIL

MAP 21 NO60

★★ 68% SMALL HOTEL

Balcomie Links

Balcomie Rd KY10 3TN

☎ 01333 450237 📠 01333 450540

e-mail: mikekadir@balcomie.fsnet.co.uk

web: www.balcomie.co.uk

dir: *follow road to village shops, at junct of High St & Market Gate turn right. This road becomes Balcomie Rd, hotel on left*

Especially popular with visiting golfers, this family-run hotel on the east side of the village represents good value for money and has a relaxing atmosphere. Bedrooms come in a variety of sizes and styles and offer all the expected amenities. Food is served from midday in the attractive lounge bar and in the evening also in the bright cheerful dining room.

Rooms 15 rms (13 en suite) (2 fmly) ⊗ in all bedrooms S fr £55; D fr £73 (incl. bkfst) **Facilities** STV Games room 🎵 ch fac Xmas **Parking** 20 **Notes LB** ⊗ in restaurant Civ Wed 45

DUNFERMLINE

MAP 21 NT08

★★★ 85% HOTEL

Garvock House Hotel

St John's Dr, Transy KY12 7TU

☎ 01383 621067 📠 01383 621168

e-mail: sales@garvock.co.uk

dir: *M90 junct 3/A907 (Dunfermline). Left after football stadium (Garvock Hill), 1st right (St John's Drive), hotel on right*

A warm welcome is assured at this impeccably presented Georgian house, which stands in its own beautifully landscaped gardens. Modern stylish bedrooms set high standards of quality and comfort and include DVD players. A spacious modern function suite makes this a popular venue for weddings and conferences, whilst the restaurant attracts a loyal clientele.

Rooms 26 en suite (1 fmly) (10 GF) ⊗ in all bedrooms S £85-£90; D £95-£135 (incl. bkfst) **Facilities** FTV 🌊 Wi-fi in bedrooms Xmas **Conf** Thtr 70 Class 50 Board 30 Del from £118.50 **Parking** 70 **Notes LB** ⊗ in restaurant Civ Wed 120

★★★ 79% ⚘ HOTEL

Best Western Keavil House Hotel

Crossford KY12 8QW

☎ 01383 736258 📠 01383 621600

e-mail: reservations@keavilhouse.co.uk

web: www.keavilhouse.co.uk

dir: *2m W of Dunfermline on A994*

Dating from the 16th century, this former manor house is set in gardens and parkland. With a modern leisure centre and conference rooms it is suited to both business and leisure guests. Bedrooms come in a variety of sizes and occupy the original house and a modern wing. Cardoons, a contemporary conservatory restaurant, is the focal point of public rooms.

Rooms 47 en suite (6 fmly) (17 GF) ⊗ in all bedrooms **Facilities Spa** STV FTV 🏊 supervised Sauna Solarium Gym Jacuzzi Wi-fi in bedrooms Aerobics studio, Steam room, Beautician ch fac Xmas **Conf** Thtr 200 Class 60 Board 50 Del from £120 **Parking** 150 **Notes** ⊗ ⊗ in restaurant Civ Wed 200

★★★ 75% HOTEL

Pitbauchlie House

Aberdour Rd KY11 4PB

☎ 01383 722282 📠 01383 620738

e-mail: info@pitbauchlie.com

web: www.pitbauchlie.com

dir: *M90 junct 2, onto A823, then B916. Hotel 0.5m on right*

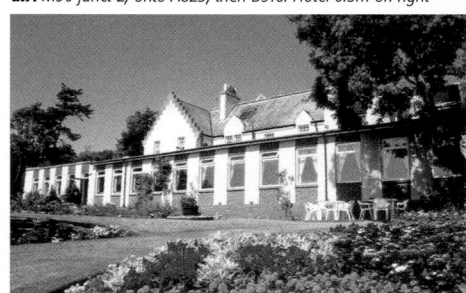

This hotel is set in landscaped gardens a mile south of the town centre. A stylish foyer and cocktail lounge catch the eye; the latter overlooking the garden, as does the restaurant and separate bar/bistro. The modern bedrooms are well equipped, the deluxe rooms having CD players and videos.

Rooms 50 en suite (3 fmly) (19 GF) ⊗ in 31 bedrooms S £90-£100; D £108-£118 (incl. bkfst) **Facilities** STV Gym Wi-fi available **Conf** BC Thtr 150 Class 80 Board 60 Del from £140 **Parking** 80 **Notes LB** ⊗ in restaurant Civ Wed 150

★★★ 70% **HOTEL**

King Malcolm

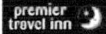

Queensferry Rd KY11 8DS
☎ 01383 722611 ▤ 01383 730865
e-mail: info@kingmalcoim-hotel-dunfermilne.com
web: www.peelhotel.com
dir: on A823, S of town

Located to the south of the city, this purpose-built hotel remains popular with business clientele and is convenient for access to both Edinburgh and Fife. Public rooms include a small foyer lounge and a conservatory bar, as well as a restaurant. Bedrooms, although not large, are well laid out and well equipped.

Rooms 48 en suite (2 fmly) (24 GF) ⊗ in 36 bedrooms S fr £95; D fr £125 **Facilities** STV FTV N ♫ Xmas **Conf** Thtr 150 Class 60 Board 50 Del from £95 **Services** Lift **Parking** 60 **Notes LB** ⊗ in restaurant Civ Wed 120

BUDGET HOTEL

Premier Travel Inn Dunfermline

premier
travel inn

Fife Leisure Park, 4-12 Wimbrel Place KY11 8EX
☎ 0870 6001486 ▤ 0870 600 1487
web: www.premiertravelinn.com

High quality, modern budget accommodation ideal for both families and business travellers. Spacious, en suite bedrooms feature bath and shower, satellite TV and many have telephones and modern points. The adjacent family restaurant features a wide and varied menu. For further details consult the Hotel Groups page

Rooms 40 en suite

BUDGET HOTEL

Travelodge Dunfermline

Halbeath Junction KY11 8PG
☎ 08700 850950
web: www.travelodge.co.uk
dir: M90 junct 3 north

Travelodge offers good quality, good value, modern accommodation. Ideal for families, the spacious en suite bedrooms include remote-control TV, tea and coffee-making facilities and comfortable beds. Meals can be taken at the nearby family restaurant. See Hotel Groups pages for further details.

Rooms 50 en suite S fr £26; D fr £26

GLENROTHES   **MAP 21 NO20**

★★ 75% ◉ **SMALL HOTEL**

Rescobie House Hotel & Restaurant

6 Valley Dr, Leslie KY6 3BQ
☎ 01592 749555 ▤ 01592 620231
e-mail: rescobiehotel@compuserve.com
web: www.rescobie-hotel.co.uk

dir: off A92 at Glenrothes onto A911, through Leslie. End of High St follow straight ahead. Take 1st left, hotel entrance 2nd left

Hospitality and guest care are second to none at this relaxing country house, which lies secluded in gardens on the fringe of Leslie. Period architecture is enhanced by a combination of contemporary and art deco styling, a theme carried through to the bright airy bedrooms. There is an inviting lounge and an intimate restaurant serving memorable meals.

Rooms 10 en suite ⊗ in all bedrooms S £49.95-£69.95; D £79.95-£99.95 (incl. bkfst) **Parking** 12 **Notes** ⊗ in restaurant Closed 26 Dec-8 Jan Civ Wed 24

BUDGET HOTEL

Premier Travel Inn Glenrothes

premier
travel inn

Beaufort Dr KY7 4UJ
☎ 08701 977114 ▤ 01592 773453
web: www.premiertravelinn.com

dir: M90 junct 2a, northbound, take A92 to Glenrothes. At 2nd rbt (Bankhead), take 3rd exit. Inn is on left (Beaufort Drive)

High quality, modern budget accommodation ideal for both families and business travellers. Spacious, en suite bedrooms feature bath and shower, satellite TV and many have telephones and modern points. The adjacent family restaurant features a wide and varied menu. For further details consult the Hotel Groups page.

Rooms 40 en suite

BUDGET HOTEL

Travelodge Glenrothes

Travelodge

Bankhead Park KY7 6GH
☎ 0070 050 950 ▤ 01470 577500
web: www.travelodge.co.uk

dir: From M90 follow the A92 to the junct with A910/B981 (signed Glenrothes), follow to Redhouse rdbt take 2nd exit (signed Glenrothes, Tay bridge) follow to Bankhead rdbt - junct with B921.

Travelodge offers good quality, good value, modern accommodation. Ideal for families, the spacious en suite bedrooms include remote-control TV, tea and coffee-making facilities and comfortable beds. Meals can be taken at the nearby family restaurant. See Hotel Groups pages for further details.

Rooms 50 en suite S fr £26; D fr £26

Scotland

INVERKEITHING MAP 21 NT18

★★★ 71% **HOTEL**

The Queensferry Hotel

St Margaret's Head, North Queensferry
KY11 1HP

☎ 0870 6096160 ▤ 01383 419708

dir: *from N take exit after M90 junct 1 signed Park & Ride, follow signs for Deep Sea World, hotel on left. From S over Forth Road Bridge, then 1st exit then 1st left, hotel 0.5m on left*

From its position on the north side of the Firth of Forth, this modern hotel enjoys splendid views of the road bridge and across the river. Public areas include a restaurant, which along with the main banqueting complex, command the very best of the views. Bedrooms are extremely spacious and offer a good range of amenities.

Rooms 77 en suite (4 fmly) (15 GF) ⊘ in 38 bedrooms S £50-£95; D £60-£105 **Facilities** STV Wi-fi available **Conf** Thtr 150 Class 70 Board 30 Del £89 **Services** Lift **Parking** 200 **Notes LB** ⊘ in restaurant Civ Wed 200

KINCARDINE MAP 21 NS98

BUDGET HOTEL

Premier Travel Inn Falkirk North

Bowtrees Farm FK2 8PJ

☎ 08701 977099 ▤ 01324 831934

web: www.premiertravelinn.com

dir: *From north M9 junct 7 towards Kincardine Bridge, from south M876 for Kincardine Bridge. On rdbt at end of slip road*

High quality, modern budget accommodation ideal for both families and business travellers. Spacious, en suite bedrooms feature bath and shower, satellite TV and many have telephones and modem points. The adjacent family restaurant features a wide and varied menu. For further details consult the Hotel Groups page.

Rooms 40 en suite

KIRKCALDY MAP 21 NT29

★★★ 75% ◉ **HOTEL**

Dunnikier House Hotel

Dunnikier Park KY1 3LP

☎ 01592 268393 ▤ 01592 642340

e-mail: recp@dunnikier-house-hotel.co.uk
web: www.dunnikier-house-hotel.co.uk

dir: *off A92 at Kirkcaldy West, then 3rd exit on rdbt signed 'Hospital/Crematorium'. 1st left past school*

This imposing 18th-century manor house is set in parkland adjacent to Dunnikier Golf Course. Public areas contain many original features. Views over the park can be enjoyed from the lounge, and the bar offers a wide selection of whiskies as well as a comprehensive food menu. The Oswald restaurant provides fine meals featuring fresh, carefully prepared local produce.

Rooms 15 en suite (1 fmly) **Conf** Thtr 60 Class 20 Board 30 **Parking** 100 **Notes** ⊘ in restaurant

★★★ 71% **HOTEL**

Dean Park

Chapel Level KY2 6QW

☎ 01592 261635 ▤ 01592 261371

e-mail: reception@deanparkhotel.co.uk

dir: *signed from A92, Kirkcaldy West junct*

Popular with both business and leisure guests, this hotel has extensive conference and meeting facilities. Executive bedrooms are spacious and comfortable; all are well equipped with modern decor and amenities. Twelve direct-access, chalet-style rooms are set in the grounds and are appointed to the same specification as main bedrooms. Public areas include a choice of bars and a restaurant.

Rooms 34 en suite 12 annexe en suite (2 fmly) (5 GF) ⊘ in 10 bedrooms **Facilities** STV ch fac **Conf** Thtr 250 Class 125 Board 54 **Services** Lift **Parking** 250 **Notes** ⊗ ⊘ in restaurant

A

Swallow Parkway

6 Abbotshall Rd KY2 5PQ

☎ 01592 262143 ▤ 01592 200433

web: www.swallowhotels.com
Rooms 31 en suite **Notes** ★★

LADYBANK MAP 21 NO30

★★★ 66% **HOTEL**

Fernie Castle

Letham KY15 7RU

☎ 01337 810381 ▤ 01337 810422

e-mail: mail@ferniecastle.demon.co.uk

dir: *M90 junct 8 take A91 E (Tay Bridge/St Andrews) to Melville Lodges rdbt. Left onto A92 signed Tay Bridge. Hotel 1.2m*

An historic, turretted castle set in 17 acres of wooded grounds in the heart of Fife, which proves an extremely popular venue for weddings. Bedrooms range from King and Queen rooms, to the more standard-sized Squire and Lady rooms. The elegant Auld Alliance Restaurant

continued

provides a formal setting for dining, but guests can also eat in the bistro or bar with its impressive vaulted stone walls and ceiling.

Fernie Castle

Rooms 20 en suite (2 fmly) ⊛ in 15 bedrooms S £65-£105; D £130-£198 (incl. bkfst) **Facilities** ❧ Xmas **Conf** Thtr 180 Class 120 Board 25 Del from £130 **Parking** 80 **Notes LB** ⊛ in restaurant Civ Wed 200

LUNDIN LINKS · MAP 21 NO40

A

Swallow Old Manor

SWALLOW

Leven Rd KY8 6AJ
☎ 01333 320368 📠 01333 320911
web: www.swallowhotels.com
dir: 1m E of Leven on A915 (Kirkcaldy St Andrews road) for hotel on right

Rooms 26 en suite **Notes** ★★★★

MARKINCH · MAP 21 NO20

INSPECTORS' CHOICE

★★★★ ⊛⊛ HOTEL

Balbirnie House

Balbirnie Park KY7 6NE
☎ 01592 610066 📠 01592 610529
e-mail: reservations@balbirnie.co.uk
web: www.balbirnie.co.uk
dir: off A92 onto B9130, entrance 0.5m on left

The perfect venue for a business trip, wedding or romantic break, this imposing Georgian mansion lies in formal gardens and grounds amidst scenic Balbirnie Park. Delightful public rooms include a choice of inviting lounges. Accommodation features some splendid well-proportioned bedrooms with the best overlooking the gardens. But even the smaller standard rooms include little touches such as
continued

sherry, shortbread/fudge and mineral water. There is a choice of restaurant, the Orangery or the more informal bistro.

Rooms 30 en suite (9 fmly) (7 GF) ⊛ in all bedrooms S £135-£165; D £195-£250 (incl. bkfst) **Facilities** STV FTV ⭣ 18 ❧ Putt green Wi-fi available Woodland walks Jogging trails Xmas **Conf** Thtr 220 Class 100 Board 60 Del from £165 **Parking** 120 **Notes LB** ⊛ in restaurant Civ Wed 150

PEAT INN · MAP 21 NO40

★★ 80% HOTEL

Peat Inn

KY15 5LH
☎ 01334 840206 📠 01334 840530
e-mail: reception@thepeatinn.co.uk
dir: 6m SW of St Andrews at junct B940/B941

This 300-year-old former coaching inn enjoys a rural location yet is close to St Andrews. Accommodation, luxuriously appointed, is provided in an adjacent building and comprises split-level suites with a comfortable lounge upstairs.

Rooms 8 en suite (2 fmly) **Parking** 24 **Notes LB** ⊛ in restaurant Closed Sun, Mon, 25 Dec & 1 Jan

ST ANDREWS · MAP 21 NO51

INSPECTORS' CHOICE

★★★★★ ⊛⊛⊛ HOTEL

The Old Course Hotel, Golf Resort & Spa

KY16 9SP
☎ 01334 474371 📠 01334 477668
e-mail: reservations@oldcoursehotel.co.uk
dir: M90 junct 8 then A91 to St Andrews

A haven for golfers, this internationally renowned hotel sits adjacent to the 17th hole of the championship course. Bedrooms vary in size and style but all have now refurbished to provide decadent levels of luxury. Day rooms include intimate lounges, a bright conservatory, a brand new spa and a range of pro golf shops. The fine dining 'Grill', the seafood bar 'Sands' and the informal Jigger pub are all popular eating venues. Staff throughout are friendly whilst services are impeccably delivered.

Rooms 146 en suite (3 fmly) ⊛ in all bedrooms S £155-£665; D £171-£681 (incl. bkfst) **Facilities Spa** STV 📶 ⭣ 18 Sauna Gym Putt green Jacuzzi Wi-fi in bedrooms Xmas **Conf** Thtr 500 Class 300 Board 108 Del from £219 **Services** Lift **Parking** 125 **Notes LB** ⊛ in restaurant Civ Wed 130

ST ANDREWS continued

★★★★★ 83% ◉◉ HOTEL

St Andrews Bay Golf Resort & Spa
KY16 8PN
☎ 01334 837000 ◨ 01334 471115
e-mail: info@standrewsbay.com

Enjoying breathtaking coastal views, this modern hotel is flanked by its two golf courses. Spacious public areas centre round a stunning two-storey atrium. The lower floor contains an open-plan lounge and restaurant, whilst the upper floor features a plush bar and the delightful Esperante fine dining restaurant and cocktail bar. A stylish spa with full-length pool complements the extensive conference and golfing facilities. The hotel provides excellent value.

Rooms 209 en suite 8 annexe en suite (86 fmly) (57 GF) ⊘ in 195 bedrooms **Facilities Spa** STV ⬚ ♨ 36 Sauna Gym Putt green Jacuzzi Clay pigeon shooting etc can be organised **Conf** BC Thtr 500 Class 450 Board 168 **Services** Lift air con **Notes** ⊘ in restaurant Civ Wed 600

INSPECTORS' CHOICE

★★★★ ◉◉◉ HOTEL

Rufflets Country House
Strathkinness Low Rd KY16 9TX
☎ 01334 472594 ◨ 01334 478703
e-mail: reservations@rufflets.co.uk
web: www.rufflets.co.uk
dir: 1.5m W on B939

This charming property is set in extensive award-winning gardens, a few minutes' drive from the town centre. Stylish, spacious

continued

bedrooms are individually decorated and most benefit from impressive bathrooms. Public rooms include a well-stocked bar, a choice of inviting lounges and the delightful Garden Room restaurant; imaginative, carefully prepared cooking utilises produce from the hotel's own gardens whenever possible.

Rooms 19 en suite 5 annexe en suite (2 fmly) ⊘ in 13 bedrooms S £100-£199; D £160-£210 (incl. bkfst) **Facilities** STV Putt green Wi-fi in bedrooms Golf driving net Xmas **Conf** Thtr 50 Class 30 Board 25 **Parking** 52 **Notes LB** ⊗ ⊘ in restaurant Civ Wed 60

★★★ 72% ◉◉ HOTEL

Macdonald Rusacks
 MACDONALD
HOTELS & RESORTS

Pilmour Links KY16 9JQ
☎ 0870 400 8128 ◨ 01334 477896
e-mail: general.rusacks@macdonald-hotels.co.uk
web: www.macdonald-hotels.co.uk
dir: from W on A91 past golf course, through an old viaduct, hotel 200mtrs on left before rdbt

This long-established hotel enjoys an almost unrivalled location with superb views across the famous golf course. Bedrooms, though varying in size, are comfortably appointed and well equipped. Classical public rooms include an elegant reception lounge and a smart restaurant.

Rooms 68 en suite S £95-£155; D £190-£340 (incl. bkfst) **Facilities** STV Wi-fi in bedrooms Golf Xmas **Conf** Thtr 90 Class 40 Board 20 Del from £125 **Services** Lift **Parking** 21 **Notes LB** ⊘ in restaurant Civ Wed 60

INSPECTORS' CHOICE

★★★ ◉◉ HOTEL

St Andrews Golf
40 The Scores KY16 9AS
☎ 01334 472611 ◨ 01334 472188
e-mail: reception@standrews-golf.co.uk
web: www.standrews-golf.co.uk
dir: follow signs 'Golf Course' into Golf Place and in 200yds turn right into The Scores

A genuinely warm approach to guest care is found at this delightful, family-run hotel. In a stunning location the views of the beach, golf links and coastline can be enjoyed from the inviting day rooms. There is a choice of bars and an informal atmosphere in Ma Bell's. Bedrooms come in two distinct styles with those on the higher floors offering stylish, modern design and comfort.

continued

St Andrews Golf

Rooms 21 en suite ⊘ in all bedrooms S £100-£130; D £200-£240 (incl. bkfst) **Facilities** STV Wi-fi available Xmas **Conf** Thtr 200 Class 80 Board 20 Del from £100 **Services** Lift **Parking** 6 **Notes LB** ⊘ in restaurant Closed 26-28 Dec Civ Wed 180

★★★ 78% **HOTEL**

Best Western Scores

76 The Scores KY16 9BB
☎ 01334 472451 🗎 01334 473947
e-mail: reception@scoreshotel.co.uk
web: www.scoreshotel.co.uk

dir: on entering St Andrews follow West Sands & Sea Life Centre signs, hotel diagonally opposite Royal & Ancient Clubhouse

Enjoying views over St Andrews Bay, this well presented hotel is situated only a short pitch from the first tee of the famous Old Course. Bedrooms are impressively furnished and come in various sizes, many quite spacious. Smart public areas include a restaurant offering food all day in addition to dinner. Alexander's Restaurant & Cocktail Bar opens during summer months and on Friday and Saturday nights in winter.

Rooms 30 en suite (1 fmly) ⊘ in all bedrooms S £88-£134; D £118-£177 (incl. bkfst) **Facilities** STV Wi-fi in bedrooms Xmas **Conf** Thtr 180 Class 60 Board 40 **Services** Lift **Parking** 10 **Notes LB** ⊗ ⊘ in restaurant Civ Wed 80

★★ 72% ◎ **HOTEL**

Russell Hotel

26 The Scores KY16 9AS
☎ 01334 473447 🗎 01334 478279
e-mail: russellhotel@talk21.com

dir: A91-St Andrews turn left at 2nd rdbt into Golf Place, turn right after 200yds into The Scores, hotel in 300yds on the left

Lying on the east bay, this friendly, family-run hotel provides well appointed bedrooms in varying sizes, some of which enjoy fine sea

continued

views. Cosy public areas include a popular bar and an intimate restaurant, both offering a good range of freshly prepared dishes.

Russell Hotel

Rooms 10 en suite (3 fmly) **Facilities** STV **Notes LB** ⊗ ⊘ in restaurant Civ Wed 40

HIGHLAND

ALNESS   MAP 23 NH66

★★ 71% ◎ **HOTEL**

Teaninich Castle

IV17 0XB
☎ 01349 883231 🗎 01349 880940
e-mail: info@teaninichcastle.com
web: www.teaninichcastle.com

dir: A9 N from Inverness over Cromarty Bridge, left to Alness. 600mtrs. Hotel 2nd right

Overlooking the Cromarty Firth with breathtaking views to the Black Isle beyond, Teaninich Castle sits on the outskirts of the pretty town of Alness, famous as a winner in both 'Scotland in Bloom' and 'Britain in Bloom'. Bedrooms are spacious and well appointed, with either sea or woodland views. There is a choice of lounges in which to relax with a coffee or a dram after enjoying the delicious meals served in the dining room.

Rooms 6 en suite (1 GF) ⊘ in all bedrooms S £65-£100; D £130-£140 (incl. bkfst) **Facilities** Gym ⅃ Jacuzzi **Conf** Thtr 30 Class 15 Board 10 **Parking** 20 **Notes LB** ⊗ ⊘ in restaurant Civ Wed 40

BEAULY
MAP 23 NH54

★★★ 74% **HOTEL**

Priory
The Square IV4 7BX
☎ 01463 782309 📠 01463 782531
e-mail: reservations@priory-hotel.com
web: www.priory-hotel.com

dir: *signed from A832, into Beauly, hotel in square on left*

This popular hotel occupies a central location in the town square. Standard and executive rooms are on offer, both providing a good level of comfort and range of facilities. Food is served throughout the day in the open-plan public areas, with menus offering a first rate choice.

Rooms 34 en suite (3 fmly) ⊛ in 9 bedrooms S £42.50-£52.50; D £55-£95 (incl. bkfst) **Facilities** STV Snooker Xmas **Conf** BC Thtr 40 Class 40 Board 30 Del from £65 **Services** Lift **Parking** 20 **Notes LB** ⊛ ⊛ in restaurant

BOAT OF GARTEN
MAP 23 NH91

★★★ 85% ⊛⊛ **HOTEL**

Boat
PH24 3BH

☎ 01479 831258 & 831696 📠 01479 831414
e-mail: info@boathotel.co.uk
web: www.boathotel.co.uk

dir: *off A9 N of Aviemore onto A95, follow signs to Boat of Garten*

In the heart of the Spey Valley, this delightful Victorian station hotel sits adjacent to the Strathspey Steam Railway. Bedrooms, all individually decorated, have been stylishly appointed and many boast DVD players and modern, eye-catching bathrooms. The Capercaille Restaurant offers classic cuisine with a Scottish twist, whilst the cocktail bar has a selection of meals and specialises in a wide range of malt whiskies.

Rooms 22 en suite (2 fmly) ⊛ in all bedrooms S £89.50-£109.50; D £139-£159 (incl. bkfst) **Facilities** Wi-fi in bedrooms Golf course adjacent Xmas **Conf** Thtr 40 Class 30 Board 25 Del from £110.50 **Parking** 36 **Notes LB** ⊛ in restaurant RS 2 wks Jan

BRORA
MAP 23 NC90

★★★ 78% ⊛ **HOTEL**

Royal Marine
Golf Rd KW9 6QS

☎ 01408 621252 📠 01408 621181
e-mail: info@highlandescape.com
web: www.highlandescapehotels.com

dir: *off A9 in village toward beach and golf course*

A distinctive Edwardian residence sympathetically extended, the Royal Marine attracts a mixed market. Its leisure centre is popular, and the restaurant, Hunters Lounge and café bar offer three contrasting eating options. In addition to the original bedrooms there is a modern wing, and luxury apartments a short walk away.

Rooms 22 en suite (1 fmly) (2 GF) ⊛ in all bedrooms S £79-£99; D £120-£160 (incl. bkfst) **Facilities** FTV 🏊 ♨ 18 ⛳ Fishing Snooker Sauna Solarium Gym 🏋 Putt green Jacuzzi ch fac Xmas **Conf** Thtr 70 Class 40 Board 40 Del from £125 **Parking** 40 **Notes LB** ⊛ in restaurant Civ Wed 60

CARRBRIDGE
MAP 23 NH92

★★★ 73% **HOTEL**

Dalrachney Lodge
PH23 3AT

☎ 01479 841252 📠 01479 841383
e-mail: dalrachney@aol.com
web: www.dalrachney.co.uk

dir: *follow Carrbridge signs off A9. In village on A938*

A traditional Highland lodge, Dalrachney lies in grounds by the River Dulnain on the edge of the village. Spotlessly maintained public areas include a comfortable and relaxing sitting room and a cosy well-stocked bar, which has a popular menu providing an alternative to the dining room. Bedrooms are generally spacious.

Rooms 11 en suite (3 fmly) ⊛ in all bedrooms S £78-£120; D £95-£140 (incl. bkfst) **Facilities** STV Fishing Wi-fi in bedrooms Xmas **Parking** 40 **Notes LB** ⊛ in restaurant

CLUANIE INN
MAP 22 NH01

★★ 71% **HOTEL**

Cluanie Inn
Glenmoriston IV63 7YW
☎ 01320 340238 📠 01320 340293
e-mail: enquiries@cluanieinn.com
web: www.cluanieinn.com

dir: *On A87*

This delightful inn lies at the western end of Loch Cluanie and is surrounded by breathtaking Highland scenery. It's a popular base for

continued

climbers and walkers and provides the perfect stepping-stone to the Isle of Skye. Cosy bars offer roaring fires in cooler months while bedrooms are spacious and smartly furnished. Lunches are excellent value and there's an extensive and creative dinner menu.

Rooms 10 en suite (2 fmly) (10 GF) ✆ in all bedrooms S £45; D £99-£120 (incl. bkfst) **Facilities** Fishing Xmas **Parking** 20 **Notes LB** ✆ ✆ in restaurant RS Xmas

CONTIN   MAP 23 NH45

★★★ 75% ◎ **COUNTRY HOUSE HOTEL**

Coul House
IV14 9ES
☎ 01997 421487 🖹 01997 421945
e-mail: stay@coulhousehotel.com
dir: Exit A9 north onto A835. Hotel on right

This imposing mansion house is set back from the road in extensive grounds. A number of the generally spacious bedrooms have superb views of the distant mountains and all are thoughtfully equipped. The Octagonal Restaurant offers guestscontemporary Scottish cuisine.

Rooms 20 en suite (3 fmly) (4 GF) ✆ in all bedrooms S £59-£89.50; D £98-£140 (incl. bkfst) **Facilities** STV Putt green 9 hole pitch & putt ch fac Xmas **Conf** Thtr 80 Class 30 Board 30 Del from £81.50 **Parking** 60 **Notes LB** ✆ in restaurant Civ Wed 70

★★★ 72% **HOTEL**

Achilty
IV14 9EG
☎ 01997 421355 🖹 01997 421923
e-mail: info@achiltyhotel.co.uk
web: www.achiltyhotel.co.uk
dir: A9 onto A835, hotel on right

Friendly owners contribute to great hospitality and a relaxed atmosphere at this roadside hotel. Public areas are full of interest; the lounges have books and games and the dining room has a musical

continued

theme. The Steading bar features exposed stone walls and offers a good selection of tasty home-cooked meals. Bedrooms are smartly furnished and cheerfully decorated.

Rooms 9 en suite 2 annexe en suite (3 GF) ✆ in 9 bedrooms **Conf** Thtr 50 Class 50 Board 20 **Parking** 100 **Notes LB** ✆ ✆ in restaurant

DALWHINNIE   MAP 23 NN68

Ⓐ

The Inn at Loch Ericht
PH19 1AG
☎ 01528 522257 🖹 01528 522270
e-mail: reservations@priory-hotel.com
dir: off A9 onto A886. 1m on right opposite filling station
Rooms 27 en suite (2 fmly) (14 GF) ✆ in 4 bedrooms **Facilities** Fishing **Conf** Thtr 50 Class 30 Board 30 **Parking** 60 **Notes** ★ **LB** ✆
See advert on this page

DINGWALL   MAP 23 NH55

Ⓐ

Swallow Tulloch Castle
Tulloch Castle Dr IV15 9ND
☎ 01349 861325 🖹 01349 863993
web: www.swallowhotels.com
Rooms 19 en suite **Notes** ★★★★

Scotland

Scotland

DORNOCH
MAP 23 NH78

★★★ 72% ◉ **HOTEL**

Dornoch Castle Hotel
Castle St IV25 3SD
☎ 01862 810216 📠 01862 810981
e-mail: enquiries@dornochcastlehotel.com
web: www.dornochcastlehotel.com

dir: 2m N of Dornoch Bridge on A9, turn right to Dornoch. Hotel in village centre

Set opposite the cathedral, this fully restored ancient castle has become a popular wedding venue. Within the original castle are some splendid themed bedrooms, and elsewhere the more modern bedrooms have all the expected facilities. There is a character bar and a delightful conservatory restaurant overlooking the garden, where seating is also provided.

Rooms 21 en suite (3 fmly) (4 GF) ⊗ in all bedrooms S £50-£140; D £97-£220 (incl. bkfst) **Conf** Thtr 60 Class 30 Board 30 **Parking** 16 **Notes LB** ⊗ in restaurant Civ Wed 95

★★ 67% **HOTEL**

Burghfield House
IV25 3HN
☎ 01862 810212 📠 01862 810404
e-mail: burghfield@cali.co.uk
web: www.burghfieldhouse.co.uk

dir: off A9 at Evelix junct, 1m into Dornoch. Just before War Memorial turn left and follow road up hill to tower in the trees

Set in gardens above the town this extended Victorian mansion provides a friendly and relaxing atmosphere. Public areas, including a delightful lounge, are enhanced with antiques, fresh flowers and real fires. Bedrooms are generally well proportioned and split between the main house and the adjacent garden wing.

Rooms 14 rms (13 en suite) 15 annexe en suite (1 fmly) (10 GF) **Facilities** Putt green **Conf** Thtr 100 Board 80 **Parking** 62 **Notes LB** ⊗ in restaurant Closed Jan - Feb RS Nov-Dec Civ Wed 50

A

Swallow Royal Golf
The 1st Tee IV25 3LG   SWALLOW
☎ 01862 810283 📠 01862 810923
web: www.swallowhotels.com

dir: from A9, right to Dornoch and continue through main street. Straight ahead at x-roads, hotel 200yds on right

Rooms 25 en suite **Notes** ★★★★

DRUMNADROCHIT
MAP 23 NH53

A

Loch Ness Lodge
IV63 6TU
☎ 01456 450342 📠 01456 450429
e-mail: info@lochness-hotel.com

dir: off A82 onto A831 Cannich R

Rooms 50 en suite (4 fmly) (10 GF) ⊗ in 10 bedrooms **Facilities** Visitors Centre, Shops, Cinema ♫ **Conf** Thtr 50 Class 40 Board 40 Del from £78 **Parking** 80 **Notes** ★★★ **LB** ⊗ Closed 5 Jan-Feb RS Mid-Jan to Mid-Feb

DUNDONNELL
MAP 22 NH08

★★★ 70% **HOTEL**

Dundonnell
IV23 2QR
☎ 01854 633204 📠 01854 633366
e-mail: enquiries@dundonnellhotel.co.uk
web: www.dundonnellhotel.com

dir: A835 onto A832. Hotel in 14m

A beautiful, isolated location at the head of Little Loch Broom is perhaps an unlikely spot for such a smart and extensively developed hotel as this. A haven of relaxation and good food, it offers a range of attractive and comfortable public areas and a choice of eating options and bars. Many of the bedrooms enjoy fine views.

Rooms 29 en suite 3 annexe en suite (2 fmly) (3 GF) S £30-£45; D £60-£90 (incl. bkfst) **Facilities** Xmas **Conf** Thtr 70 Class 50 Board 40 Del from £30 **Parking** 60 **Notes LB** ⊗ in restaurant

FORT WILLIAM
MAP 22 NN17

INSPECTORS' CHOICE

★★★★★ ◉◉◉ **COUNTRY HOUSE HOTEL**

Inverlochy Castle
Torlundy PH33 6SN
☎ 01397 702177 📠 01397 702953
e-mail: info@inverlochy.co.uk
web: www.inverlochycastlehotel.com

RELAIS & CHATEAUX

dir: accessible from either A82 Glasgow-Fort William or A9 Edinburgh-Dalwhinnie. Hotel 3m N of Fort William on A82, in Torlundy

With a backdrop of Ben Nevis, this imposing and gracious castle sits amidst extensive gardens and grounds overlooking the hotel's own loch. Lavishly appointed in classic country-house style, spacious bedrooms are extremely comfortable and boast flat screen TVs and laptops with internet access. The sumptuous main hall and lounge provide the perfect setting for afternoon tea or a pre-dinner cocktail, whilst imaginative cuisine is served in one of three dining rooms. A snooker room and a DVD library are also available.

Rooms 17 en suite (6 fmly) ⊗ in all bedrooms S £250-£350; D £390-£490 (incl. bkfst) **Facilities** STV ⌔ Fishing Snooker ↝ Wi-fi in bedrooms Fishing on loch Massage Riding Hunting Stalking Clay pigeon shooting ♫ Xmas **Conf** BC Thtr 50 Class 20 Board 20 Del from £250 **Parking** 17 **Notes LB** ⊗ in restaurant Civ Wed 80

See advert on opposite page

Inverlochy Castle Hotel

Torlundy, Fort William PH33 6SN
Tel: 01397 702177 Fax: 01397 702953
www.inverlochycastlehotel.com Email: info@inverlochy.co.uk

Steeped in history Inverlochy was built in 1863 as a private residence and in 1969 was converted into a country house hotel. Nestling in the foothills of the mighty Ben Nevis and sits amidst some of Scotland's finest scenery. Visitors can reflect in the relaxed and tranquil atmosphere of a bygone era, wonderfully crafted and richly decorated, beautiful Venetian crystal chandeliers, frescoed ceiling and a handsome staircase. Each of the 17 bedrooms, all with private bathroom, have their own individual design and character, along with splendid views of the grounds and surrounding mountains. Dinner at Inverlochy is an experience to savour in any of our three dining rooms, each decorated with period and elaborate furniture presented as gifts to Inverlochy Castle from the King of Norway.

Inverlochy Castle is also the perfect location for a Highland wedding. Hotel staff can arrange everything to suit your requirements for your special day.

A wealth of sporting activities can be enjoyed in the surrounding grounds and mountains.

Four miles north of Fort William, on the A82 north towards Inverness.

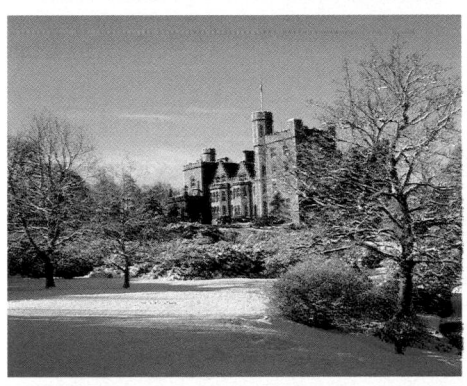

FORT WILLIAM *continued*

★★★ 79% ◉ HOTEL

Moorings

Banavie PH33 7LY

☎ 01397 772797 📠 01397 772441

e-mail: reservations@moorings-fortwilliam.co.uk

web: www.moorings-fortwilliam.co.uk

dir: take A380 (N from Fort William), cross Caledonian Canal, 1st right

Located on the Caledonian Canal next to a series of locks known as Neptune's Staircase, and close to Thomas Telford's house, this hotel with its dedicated, young staff offers friendly service. Accommodation comes in two distinct styles and the newer rooms are particularly appealing. Meals can be taken in the bars or the spacious dining room.

Rooms 27 en suite (1 fmly) (1 GF) ⊗ in 24 bedrooms S £39-£94; D £78-£118 (incl. bkfst) **Facilities** STV **Conf** Thtr 120 Class 40 Board 40 Del £125 **Parking** 60 **Notes LB** ⊗ in restaurant Closed 22-27 Dec Civ Wed 120

★★★ 75% HOTEL

Grand

Gordon Square PH33 6DX

☎ 01397 702928 📠 01397 702928

e-mail: grandhotel.scotland@virgin.net

web: www.grandhotel-scotland.co.uk

dir: on A82 at W end of High St

A relaxed and welcoming atmosphere is provided at this long-established, family-run hotel, at the south end of the high street. Bedrooms are well appointed and there is a choice of lounges. A good range of innovative dishes is served in both the restaurant and bar.

Rooms 30 en suite (4 fmly) ⊗ in 15 bedrooms S £39.40-£49.50; D £59-£79 (incl. bkfst) **Conf** Thtr 110 Class 60 Board 20 **Parking** 20 **Notes LB** ⊗ ⊗ in restaurant Closed 24 Dec-8 Feb Civ Wed

★★ 81% HOTEL

Best Western Imperial

Fraser's Square PH33 6DW

☎ 01397 702040 & 703921 📠 01397 706277

e-mail: imperial@bestwestern.co.uk

dir: from town centre, along Middle St, approx 400mtrs from junct with A82

Benefiting from a town centre location this hotel is popular with both business and leisure guests, and is ideally placed for many of the area's attractions. Stylish public areas include a cosy lounge bar,

continued

---

attractive restaurant and reception lounge. The smart modern bedrooms are comfortable and well equipped.

Rooms 34 en suite (2 fmly) ⊗ in 6 bedrooms **Conf** Thtr 60 Class 12 Board 16 **Parking** 15 **Notes LB** ⊗ in restaurant

★★ 72% HOTEL

Nevis Bank

Belford Rd PH33 6BY

☎ 01397 705721 📠 01397 706275

e-mail: info@nevisbankhotel.co.uk

web: www.nevisbankhotel.co.uk

dir: on A82, at junct to Glen Nevis

A warm welcome is assured at this long-established hotel. It enjoys a fine location on the outskirts of the town close to the access road for the West Highland Way and Glen Nevis. Accommodation is provided

continued

Scotland

in thoughtfully equipped bedrooms of different sizes. There is a choice of bars and dining options.

Rooms 31 en suite (3 fmly) (2 GF) S £30-£59; D £50-£80 (incl. bkfst) **Facilities** Xmas **Conf** BC Thtr 50 Class 30 Board 25 Del from £45 **Parking** 50 **Notes LB** ⊗ ⊘ in restaurant

See advert on this page

★★ 64% HOTEL

Croit Anna

Achintore Rd, Drimarben PH33 6RR
☎ 01397 702268 ▤ 01397 704099
e-mail: croitanna.fortwilliam@alfatravel.co.uk
web: www.alfatravel.co.uk

dir: *from Glencoe on A82 into Fort William, hotel 1st on right*

Located on the edge of Loch Linnhe, just two miles out of town, this hotel offers some spacious bedrooms, many with fine views over the loch. There is a choice of two comfortable lounges and a large airy restaurant. The hotel appeals to coach parties and individual visitors alike.

Rooms 93 en suite (5 fmly) (13 GF) ⊘ in all bedrooms S £32-£39; D £54-£74 (incl. bkfst) **Facilities** ♫ ch fac Xmas **Parking** 25 **Notes LB** ⊗ ⊘ in restaurant Closed Dec-Jan RS Nov, Feb, Mar

Ⓐ

Swallow Highland

Union Rd PH33 6QY
☎ 01397 702291 ▤ 01397 700133
web: www.swallowhotels.com
Rooms 105 en suite **Notes** ★★

BUDGET HOTEL

Premier Travel Inn Fort William

Loch Iall, An Aird PH33 6AN
☎ 08701 977104 ▤ 01397 703618
web: www.premiertravelinn.com

dir: *N end of Fort William Shopping Centre, just off A82*

High quality, modern budget accommodation ideal for both families and business travellers. Spacious, en suite bedrooms feature bath and shower, satellite TV and many have telephones and modem points. The adjacent family restaurant features a wide and varied menu. For further details consult the Hotel Groups page.

Rooms 40 en suite

GLENFINNAN   MAP 22 NM98

★★ 75% ◉◉ HOTEL

The Prince's House

PH37 4LT
☎ 01397 722246 ▤ 01397 722323
e-mail: princeshouse@glenfinnan.co.uk
web: www.glenfinnan.co.uk

dir: *on A830, 0.5m on right past Glenfinnan Monument. 200mtrs from railway station*

This delightful hotel enjoys a well deserved reputation for fine food and excellent hospitality. The hotel sits close to where 'Bonnie' Prince Charlie raised the Jacobite standard and enjoys inspiring views. Comfortably appointed bedrooms offer pleasing decor and

continued

---

bathrooms. Excellent local game and seafood can be enjoyed in the restaurant and the bar.

Rooms 9 en suite (1 fmly) ⊘ in all bedrooms S £50-£60 (incl. bkfst) **Facilities** Fishing Xmas **Conf** Thtr 40 Class 20 **Parking** 18 **Notes LB** ⊘ in restaurant Closed Xmas & Jan-Feb

GRANTOWN-ON-SPEY   MAP 23 NJ03

★★★ 75% ◉◉ HOTEL

Muckrach Lodge

Dulnain Bridge PH26 3LY
☎ 01479 851257 ▤ 01479 851325
e-mail: info@muckrach.co.uk

dir: *from A95 Dulnain Bridge exit follow A938 towards Carrbridge. Hotel 500mtrs on right*

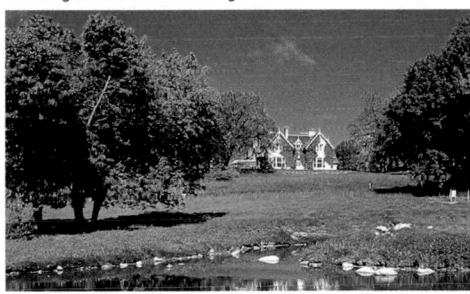

This former sporting lodge is set in ten acres of landscaped grounds, at the foot of the Cairngorm Mountains. Bedrooms come in a variety

continued on page 832

Scotland

GRANTOWN-ON-SPEY *continued*

of sizes and styles; the larger ones are particularly well appointed. The cosy bar is popular with the sporting clientele and features a roaring log fire. Dinner can be taken in either the bistro or award-winning Finlarig restaurant.

Rooms 10 en suite 4 annexe en suite (3 fmly) ⊗ in all bedrooms **Facilities** Fishing ⅃ Beauty & aroma therapy **Conf** Thtr 30 Class 20 Board 16 **Parking** 53 **Notes LB** ⊗ in restaurant Closed 5-20 Jan RS Nov-Mar Civ Wed 50

★★ 85% ◎ **SMALL HOTEL**

Culdearn House

Woodlands Ter PH26 3JU
☎ 01479 872106 ▤ 01479 873641
e-mail: enquiries@culdearn.com
web: www.culdearn.com
dir: *from SW into Grantown on A95, left at 30mph sign, hotel opposite*

This immaculately maintained small hotel sits in well-tended gardens on the edge of town and has a country-house atmosphere. The renovation of the bedrooms has taken the quality and comfort to new heights. Hospitality is excellent and every effort is made to make guests feel at home.

Rooms 7 en suite (1 GF) ⊗ in all bedrooms S £88; D £176 (incl. bkfst & dinner) **Parking** 12 **Notes LB** ⊗ No children 12yrs ⊗ in restaurant Closed Feb

A

Swallow Craiglynne

Woodlands Ter PH26 3JX
☎ 01479 872597 ▤ 01479 873675
web: www.swallowhotels.com
Rooms 83 en suite **Notes** ★★★

SWALLOW

INVERGARRY   MAP 22 NH30

★★★ 80% ◎ **COUNTRY HOUSE HOTEL**

Glengarry Castle

PH35 4HW
☎ 01809 501254 ▤ 01809 501207
e-mail: castle@glengarry.net
web: www.glengarry.net
dir: *on A82 beside Loch Oich, 0.5m from A82/A87 junct*

This charming country-house hotel is set in 50 acres of grounds on the shores of Loch Oich. The spacious day rooms include comfortable sitting rooms with lots to read and board games to play. The classical dining room boasts an innovative menu that showcases local Scottish produce. The smart bedrooms vary in size and style but all boast magnificent loch or woodland views.

Rooms 26 en suite (2 fmly) ⊗ in 18 bedrooms S £61-£93; D £86-£160 (incl. bkfst) **Facilities** FTV ⅃ Fishing Wi-fi in bedrooms **Parking** 32 **Notes** ⊗ in restaurant Closed mid Nov-mid Mar

See advert on opposite page

INVERGORDON   MAP 23 NH76

★★★ 83% **HOTEL**

Kincraig House

IV18 0LF
☎ 01349 852587 ▤ 01349 852193
e-mail: info@kincraig-house-hotel.co.uk
dir: *off A9 past Alness towards Tain. Hotel entrance on left 0.25m past Rosskeen Church*

This mansion house is set in well-tended grounds in an elevated position with views over the Cromarty Firth. It offers smart well-equipped bedrooms and inviting public areas that retain the

continued

original features of the house. However it is the friendly service and commitment to guest care that will leave the lasting impression.

Rooms 15 en suite (1 fmly) (1 GF) ⊛ in all bedrooms S £65-£75; D £110-£130 (incl. bkfst) **Facilities** Wi-fi in bedrooms Xmas **Conf** Thtr 50 Class 30 Board 24 Del from £90 **Parking** 30 **Notes LB** ⊗ ⊘ in restaurant Civ Wed 50

See advert on this page

INVERMORISTON
MAP 23 NH41

★★★ 68% ⊚⊚ **SMALL HOTEL**

Glenmoriston Arms Hotel & Restaurant
IV63 7YA

☎ 01320 351206 ▤ 01320 351308

e-mail: reception@glenmoristonarms.co.uk

web: www.glenmoristonarms.co.uk

dir: on junct of A82 & A887 (road to Isle of Skye)

This charming, well-maintained, small hotel, which is steeped in history, offers a warm welcome. Inviting public areas include a cosy bar and attractive formal restaurant where fine dinners, prepared and cooked with care and dedication, are served. An alternative is offered by the Tavern bar/bistro in the grounds. The well-equipped bedrooms reflect the individuality of the house.

Rooms 8 en suite (1 fmly) ⊛ in 2 bedrooms S £47.50-£75; D £37.50-£100 (incl. bkfst) **Facilities** Fishing Wi-fi in bedrooms ♫ Xmas **Conf** BC Board 8 **Parking** 24 **Notes LB** ⊗ ⊘ in restaurant Closed 5 Jan-end Feb

INVERNESS
MAP 23 NH64

★★★★ 80% ⊚⊚ **HOTEL**

The Drumossie
Old Perth Rd IV2 5BE

☎ 01463 236451 & 0870 1942110 ▤ 01463 712858

e-mail: stay@drumossiehotel.co.uk

dir: from A9 follow signs for Culloden Battlefield, hotel on left after 1m

Set in nine acres of landscaped hillside grounds south of Inverness, this hotel has fine views of the Moray Firth towards Ben Wyvis. A full refurbishment program has resulted in art deco style decoration together with a country-house atmosphere. Service is friendly and attentive, food imaginative and enjoyable and bedrooms spacious and well presented. The main function room is probably the largest in this area.

Rooms 44 en suite (10 fmly) (6 GF) ⊛ in all bedrooms S £95-£180; D £150-£200 (incl. bkfst) **Facilities** STV Fishing Other activities by arrangement Xmas **Conf** Thtr 500 Class 200 Board 40 Del from £145 **Services** Lift **Parking** 200 **Notes LB** ⊗ ⊘ in restaurant Civ Wed 400

INVERNESS *continued*

★★★★ 75% ⚜⚜ HOTEL

Culloden House

Culloden IV2 7BZ

☎ 01463 790461 📄 01463 792181

e-mail: reserv@cullodenhouse.co.uk

web: www.cullodenhouse.co.uk

dir: *from Inverness take A96, turn right for Culloden. After 1m after 2nd lights left at White Church*

Dating from the late 1700s this impressive mansion is set in extensive grounds close to the famous Culloden battlefield. High ceilings and intricate cornices are particular features of the public rooms, including the elegant Adam dining room. Bedrooms come in a range of sizes and styles, with a number situated in a separate house.

Rooms 23 en suite 5 annexe en suite (1 fmly) ⊘ in all bedrooms S £170; D £310 (incl. bkfst) **Facilities** STV ⚲ Sauna ⚲ Boules Badminton Golf driving net Putting green ♫ **Conf** Thtr 60 Class 40 Board 30 **Parking** 50 **Notes LB** No children 10yrs ⊘ in restaurant Closed 24-28 Dec Civ Wed 65

★★★★ 73% HOTEL

Inverness Marriott Hotel

Marriott.
HOTELS & RESORTS

Culcabock Rd IV2 3LP

☎ 01463 237166 📄 01463 225208

e-mail: events@marriotthotels.co.uk

web: www.marriott.co.uk

dir: *from A9 S, exit Culduthel/Kingsmills 5th exit at rdbt, 0.5m, over mini-rdbt past golf club. Hotel on left after lights*

Located just one mile from the city and set in four acres, this smart, 18th-century manor hotel is easily accessed by road and rail, and only minutes away from the airport. Accommodation is provided in spacious, thoughtfully equipped rooms, and those in the newer wing are particularly impressive. There is a choice of restaurants, a cocktail lounge bar, a leisure club and conference facilities.

Rooms 76 en suite 6 annexe en suite (11 fmly) (26 GF) ⊘ in 29 bedrooms S £115-£172; D £135-£214 (incl. bkfst) **Facilities** Spa STV 🄑 supervised Sauna Solarium Gym Putt green Wi-fi available Hair & beauty salon Steam room Xmas **Conf** Thtr 100 Class 35 Board 36 Del from £145 **Services** Lift **Parking** 120 **Notes LB** ⊘ in restaurant

★★★ 85% ⚜⚜⚜ HOTEL

Glenmoriston Town House Hotel

20 Ness Bank IV2 4SF

☎ 01463 223777 📄 01463 712378

e-mail: reservations@glenmoristontownhouse.com

web: www.glenmoristontownhouse.com

dir: *on riverside opposite theatre*

Bold contemporary designs blend seamlessly with the classical architecture of this stylish hotel, situated on the banks of the River Ness. Delightful day rooms include a cosy cocktail bar and a sophisticated restaurant where outstanding authentic French cuisine can be sampled. The smart, modern bedrooms have many facilities, including CD players, DVD players and flat screen TVs.

continued

Glenmoriston Town House Hotel

Rooms 30 en suite (1 fmly) (6 GF) ⊘ in all bedrooms S £95-£115; D £130-£170 (incl. bkfst) **Facilities** STV Wi-fi in bedrooms ch fac Xmas **Conf** Thtr 15 Class 10 Board 10 Del from £150 **Parking** 40 **Notes LB** ⊘ ⊘ in restaurant RS Mon (restaurant closed)

★★★ 81% HOTEL

Best Western Lochardil House

Best Western

Stratherrick Rd IV2 4LF

☎ 01463 235995 📄 01463 713394

e-mail: reservations@lochardil.co.uk

dir: *A9 Police HQ, take Sir Walter Scott Drive through rdbts, turn right onto Stratherrick Rd*

This hotel enjoys a peaceful location in a residential area just a mile from the town centre. Smart, comfortable bedrooms ensure a relaxed stay whilst spacious day rooms include an eye-catching conservatory restaurant, a stylish lounge bar, and a popular function suite. Staff throughout are friendly and provide a warm Highland welcome.

Rooms 12 en suite 16 annexe en suite (6 GF) ⊘ in 20 bedrooms S £75-£168; D £88-£179 (incl. bkfst) **Facilities** FTV Wi-fi in bedrooms **Conf** Thtr 200 Class 100 Board 60 Del from £130 **Parking** 123 **Notes LB** ⊗ ⊘ in restaurant Civ Wed 150

★★★ 78% ⚜⚜ HOTEL

Bunchrew House

Bunchrew IV3 8TA

☎ 01463 234917 📄 01463 710620

e-mail: welcome@bunchrew-inverness.co.uk

web: www.bunchrew-inverness.co.uk

dir: *W on A862, on shore of Beauly Firth. Hotel 2m after canal on right*

Overlooking the Beauly Firth this impressive mansion house dates from the 17th century and retains much original character. Individually styled bedrooms are spacious and tastefully furnished. A wood-

continue

...anelled restaurant is the setting for artfully constructed cooking and ...here is a choice of comfortable lounges complete with real fires.

Rooms 16 en suite (4 fmly) (1 GF) S £97-£137; D £145-£240 (incl. bkfst) **Facilities** Fishing **Conf** Thtr 80 Class 30 Board 30 Del from £138.50 **Parking** 40 **Notes LB** ⊘ in restaurant Closed 24-27 Dec Civ Wed 92

★★★ 73% **HOTEL**

Best Western Palace Hotel & Spa

Ness Walk IV3 5NG
☎ 01463 223243 ≣ 01463 236865
e-mail: palace@miltonhotels.com
web: www.bw-invernesspalace.co.uk
dir: A82 Glenurquhart Rd onto Ness Walk. Hotel 300yds on right opposite Inverness Castle

...et on the north side of the River Ness close to the Eden Court theatre ...nd a short walk from the town, this hotel has seen a significant ...efurbishment resulting in a contemporary look. Bedrooms offer good ...evels of comfort and equipment, and a smart re-styled leisure centre ...ttracts a mixed market.

Rooms 40 en suite 48 annexe en suite (4 fmly) ⊘ in 51 bedrooms ... £69.90-£169.90; D £69.90-£169.90 **Facilities Spa** STV ☐ supervised ...auna Gym Jacuzzi Wi-fi in bedrooms Beautician, steam room, classes ...mas **Conf** Thtr 80 Class 40 Board 30 Del from £99.90 **Services** Lift **Parking** 18 **Notes** ⊘ in restaurant

★★★ 73% **HOTEL**

Thistle Inverness

Millburn Rd IV2 3TR
☎ 0870 333 9155 ≣ 0870 333 9255
e-mail: inverness@thistle.co.uk
dir: From A9 take Raigmore Interchange exit (towards ...berdeen) then 3rd left towards centre. Hotel opposite

...Vell located within easy distance of Inverness town centre. A well ...resented hotel currently benefiting from a programme of bedroom ...efurbishment. A well equipped leisure centre along with an informal ...rasserie & open plan bar/lounge. Ample parking is an added benefit ...t this hotel.

Rooms 118 en suite ⊘ in 60 bedrooms **Facilities Spa** STV ☐ ...upervised Sauna Solarium Gym Jacuzzi **Conf** Thtr 240 Class 120 ...oard 30 **Services** Lift **Parking** 150 **Notes** ⊘ in restaurant Civ Wed 240

★★★ 70% **HOTEL**

Royal Highland

Station Square, Academy St IV1 1LG
☎ 01463 231926 ≣ 01463 710705
e-mail: info@royalhighlandhotel.co.uk
web: www.royalhighlandhotel.co.uk
dir: from A9 into town centre. Hotel next to rail station & ...astgate Retail Centre

...uilt in 1858 adjacent to the railway station, this hotel has the typically ...rand foyer of the Victorian era with comfortable seating. The ...ontemporary ASH Brasserie and bar offers a refreshing style for both ...ating and drinking throughout the day. The generally spacious ...edrooms are comfortably equipped for the business traveller.

Rooms 70 en suite (12 fmly) ⊘ in 40 bedrooms S £94.95-£104.95; ...) £134.95-£154.95 (incl. bkfst) **Facilities** STV FTV Putt green Jacuzzi Wi-...in bedrooms Xmas **Conf** Thtr 200 Class 80 Board 80 Del from £35 **Services** Lift **Parking** 8 **Notes LB** ⊘ in restaurant Civ Wed 200

★★★ 66% **HOTEL**

Loch Ness House

THE INDEPENDENTS

Glenurquhart Rd IV3 8JL
☎ 01463 231248 ≣ 01463 239327
e-mail: lnhhchris@aol.com
dir: From A9, left at Longman rdbt, follow signs for A82 for 2.5m

This is a family-run hotel, lying close to the canal, that offers friendly and attentive service. Tasty meals can be chosen from a good range of dishes, available in the restaurant or the bar.

Rooms 21 en suite (3 fmly) ⊘ in 6 bedrooms S £50-£110; D £50-£120 (incl. bkfst) **Facilities** STV Xmas **Conf** Thtr 150 Class 60 Board 40 Del from £60 **Parking** 60 **Notes LB** ⊘ in restaurant Civ Wed 75

A

Ramada Inverness

RAMADA

Church St IV1 1DX
☎ 01463 235181 ≣ 01463 711206
e-mail: sales.inverness@ramadajarvis.co.uk
web: www.ramadajarvis.co.uk
dir: exit A9 at Kessock Bridge, take 1st exit at rdbt, 2nd exit at next rdbt past Inverness College. 1st exit at 2nd rdbt, right at lights, hotel on left

Rooms 106 en suite (12 fmly) ⊘ in 95 bedrooms S £49-£125; D £79-£135 (incl. bkfst) **Facilities** STV ☐ Sauna Gym Jacuzzi Wi-fi in bedrooms Xmas **Conf** Thtr 200 Class 100 Board 100 Del from £79 **Services** Lift **Parking** 80 **Notes** ★★★ **LB** ⊗ ⊘ in restaurant

A

Swallow Columba

SWALLOW

Ness Walk IV3 5NF
☎ 01463 231391 ≣ 01463 715526
web: www.swallowhotels.com
dir: from city centre towards River Ness. Hotel opposite castle

Rooms 76 en suite **Notes** ★★★

A

Swallow Craigmonie

SWALLOW

9 Anfield Rd IV2 3HX
☎ 01463 231649 ≣ 01463 233720
web: www.swallowhotels.com
dir: off A9/A96 follow signs to Hilton & Culcabock. Pass golf course to traffic lights, 1st right after lights

Rooms 35 en suite **Notes** ★★★

A

Swallow Crown Court

SWALLOW

25 Southside Rd IV2 3BG
☎ 01463 234816 ≣ 01463 714900
web: www.swallowhotels.com
dir: A96 into Milburn Rd. At next rdbt 1st left for Raigmore Hospital. At mini-rdbt turn right. Turn right by Marriott Hotel

Rooms 9 en suite **Notes** ★★★

Scotland

INVERNESS *continued*

BUDGET HOTEL

Premier Travel Inn Inverness Centre

Millburn Rd IV2 3QX

☎ 08701 977141 ▤ 01463 717826

web: www.premiertravelinn.com

dir: on A9 junct with A96 (Raigmore Interchange, signed Airport/Aberdeen), follow B865 towards town centre, hotel 100yds past next rdbt

High quality, modern budget accommodation ideal for both families and business travellers. Spacious, en suite bedrooms feature bath and shower, satellite TV and many have telephones and modem points. The adjacent family restaurant features a wide and varied menu. For further details consult the Hotel Groups page.

Rooms 39 en suite

Premier Travel Inn Inverness East

Beechwood Business Park IV2 3BW

☎ 08701 977142 ▤ 01463 225233

dir: on A9, turn left signed Raigmore Hospital, Police HQ & Inshes Retail Park

Rooms 60 en suite

BUDGET HOTEL

Travelodge Inverness

Stoneyfield, A96 Inverness Rd IV2 7PA

☎ 08700 850 950 ▤ 01463 718152

web: www.travelodge.co.uk

dir: at junct of A9/A96

Travelodge offers good quality, good value, modern accommodation. Ideal for families, the spacious en suite bedrooms include remote-control TV, tea and coffee-making facilities and comfortable beds. Meals can be taken at the nearby family restaurant. See Hotel Groups pages for further details.

Rooms S fr £26; D fr £26

Travelodge Inverness Fairways

Castle Heather IV2 6AA

☎ 08700 880950 ▤ 01463 250 703

dir: From A9 follow signs for Raigmore Hospital. At 1st rdbt take 3rd exit, follow B8082 toward Hilton/Culduthel. Approx 1.5 m, pass 2 more rdbts (2nd exit/3rd exit respectively). At the 4th rdbt take 1st exit, Travelodge is on left.

Rooms 80 en suite S fr £26; D fr £26

| KINGUSSIE | MAP 23 NH70 |

★★ 71% HOTEL

The Scot House

Newtonmore Rd PH21 1HE

☎ 01540 661351 ▤ 01540 661111

e-mail: enquiries@scothouse.com

dir: A9, take Kingussie exit, hotel approx 0.5m

Lying peacefully at the edge of the village this long established hotel offers comfortable accommodation in thoughtfully equipped, generally

continued

spacious rooms. Bar meals and snacks are served in the well stocked bar with more formal dining available in the restaurant.

Rooms 9 en suite (1 fmly) ⊗ in all bedrooms S £39-£60; D £48-£90 (incl. bkfst) **Facilities** Wi-fi in bedrooms Xmas **Conf** Thtr 25 Class 25 Board 16 **Parking** 35 **Notes LB** ⊗ in restaurant

⊛⊛⊛ RESTAURANT WITH ROOMS

The Cross at Kingussie

Tweed Mill Brae, Ardbroilach Rd PH21 1LB

☎ 01540 661166 ▤ 01540 661080

e-mail: relax@thecross.co.uk

dir: From lights in Kingussie centre, along Ardbroilach Rd for 300mtrs, left into Tweed Mill Brae

Situated in the valley above the town of Kingussie, the Old Tweed Mill sits next to a river, with wild flower gardens and a sunny terrace. Hospitality and food are clearly the strengths here in this special restaurant with rooms. Bedrooms are spacious and airy, whilst fluffy towels and handmade toiletries provide extra luxury.

Rooms 8 en suite (1 fmly) ⊗ in all bedrooms S £120-£210; D £180-£250 (incl. dinner) **Facilities** Petanque **Conf** Thtr 20 Class 20 Board 20 Del from £105 **Parking** 12 **Notes LB** ⊗ No children 8yrs ⊗ in restaurant Closed Xmas & Jan (ex New Year) RS Sun & Mon

| KYLE OF LOCHALSH | MAP 22 NG72 |

Ⓐ

Swallow Kyle

Main St IV40 8AB

☎ 01599 534204 ▤ 01599 534932

web: www.swallowhotels.com

dir: A87 just before Skye bridge, turn right into main street

Rooms 30 en suite **Notes** ★★★

| LAIRG | MAP 23 NC50 |

★★ 72% SMALL HOTEL

Overscaig House Hotel

Loch Shin IV27 4NY

☎ 01549 431203

e-mail: enquiries@overscaig.com

dir: N from Lairg on A836 for 3m. Turn left onto A838 towards Durness. Follow for 14m

Popular with fishermen and birdwatchers, this friendly family-run hotel enjoys a lochside location amid unspoilt scenery. Hearty meals are served in the conservatory dining room that overlooks the loch. There is a cosy bar and a comfortable lounge with lots to read. The well-equipped bedrooms include two ideal family units, but for a special occasion it's worth asking for one of the stylish executive rooms.

Rooms 8 en suite (2 fmly) ⊗ in all bedrooms S £40-£55; D £68-£80 (incl. bkfst) **Facilities** Fishing Wi-fi available Fishing boats Pool table **Parking** 10 **Notes LB** ⊗ in restaurant Closed Nov - Mar

LETTERFINLAY — MAP 22 NN29

★★ 69% **HOTEL**

Letterfinlay Lodge
PH34 4DZ
☎ 01397 712622
e-mail: info@letterfinlaylodgehotel.com
web: www.letterfinlaylodgehotel.com
dir: 7m N of Spean Bridge, on A82 beside Loch Lochy

Boasting one of the most enviable locations in the Highlands, this long established hotel enjoys stunning views overlooking Loch Lochy. Bedrooms provide a mix of styles with loch view rooms proving popular with guests. Wide-ranging menus are available in the bar and restaurant, and hearty breakfasts set guests up for the day.

Rooms 13 rms (11 en suite) (5 fmly) S £35-£45; D £70-£90 (incl. bkfst) **Facilities** Fishing **Parking** 100 **Notes LB** ⊗ in restaurant Closed Nov-Feb

LOCHINVER — MAP 22 NC02

INSPECTORS' CHOICE

★★★★ ❀ **HOTEL**

Inver Lodge
IV27 4LU
☎ 01571 844496 📠 01571 844395
e-mail: stay@inverlodge.com
web: www.inverlodge.com
dir: A835 to Lochinver, through village, left after village hall, follow private road for 0.5m

CLASSIC
BRITISH HOTELS

Genuine hospitality is noteworthy at this delightful, purpose-built hotel. Set high on the hillside above the village, all bedrooms and public rooms enjoy stunning views. There is a choice of lounges and a restaurant where chefs make use of the abundant local produce. Bedrooms are spacious, stylish and come with an impressive range of accessories. There is no night service between 11pm and 7am.

Rooms 20 en suite (11 GF) ⊗ in 15 bedrooms S fr £100; D fr £160 (incl. bkfst) **Facilities** STV Fishing Snooker Sauna Solarium Wi-fi available **Conf** Thtr 30 Board 20 Del from £100 **Parking** 30 **Notes LB** ⊗ in restaurant Closed Nov-Etr Civ Wed 50

❀❀ **RESTAURANT WITH ROOMS**

The Albannach
Badidarrach IV27 4LP
☎ 01571 844407 📠 01571 844285
e-mail: info@thealbannach.co.uk
web: www.thealbannach.co.uk
dir: From Ullapool turn right over old stone bridge at foot of hill, signed Baddidarrach & Highland Stoneware Potter. After 0.5m cross cattle grid, turn left

Enjoying a fine reputation for its cooking and stylish accommodation, The Albannach has established itself as one of the 'must visit' destinations of any gastronomic tour of Scotland. The set menu at dinner is a theatrical indulgence of fresh produce, and outstanding breakfasts showcase the local, seasonal larder. The bedrooms are furnished with flair and enjoy stunning loch and mountain views. Guests are greeted like old friends by the professional and caring staff.

Rooms 5 en suite 1 annexe en suite (1 GF) ⊗ in all bedrooms S £125-£145; D £220-£290 (incl. bkfst & dinner) **Facilities** STV **Parking** 8 **Notes** No children 12yrs ⊗ in restaurant Closed mid Nov-mid Mar RS mid Mar-mid Nov, excl Mon

LYBSTER — MAP 23 ND23

Ⓐ

Swallow Portland Arms
KW3 6BS
☎ 01593 721721 📠 01593 721722
web: www.swallowhotels.com
dir: from Inverness on A9. Hotel on left
Rooms 22 en suite **Conf** Class 280 Board 100 **Notes** ★★★

SWALLOW
HOTELS

MALLAIG — MAP 22 NM69

★★ 70% **HOTEL**

West Highland
PH41 4QZ
☎ 01687 462210 📠 01687 462130
e-mail: westhighland.hotel@virgin.net
dir: from Fort William turn right at rdbt then 1st right up hill, from ferry left at rdbt then 1st right uphill

Built in the early 20th century, this is a family-run hotel in the lovely fishing port of Mallaig. Public rooms, including the bright conservatory enjoy wonderful views over to the Isle of Skye. The attractive bedrooms, most with the sea views, are thoughtfully equipped and are generally spacious.

Rooms 34 en suite (6 fmly) ⊗ in 6 bedrooms S £40-£45; D £70-£78 (incl. bkfst) **Facilities** FTV ♫ **Conf** Thtr 100 Class 80 Board 100 **Parking** 40 **Notes LB** ⊗ in restaurant Closed 16 Oct-15 Mar RS 16 Mar-1 Apr

Ⓐ

Swallow Marine
Station Rd PH41 4PY
☎ 01687 462217 📠 01687 462821
web: www.swallowhotels.com
dir: 1st Hotel on right on entering Mallaig off A830
Rooms 19 rms **Notes** ★★

SWALLOW
HOTELS

Scotland

Scotland

MUIR OF ORD   MAP 23 NH55

★★ 71% ◉ **HOTEL**

Ord House

IV6 7UH

THE CIRCLE
Selected Individual Hotels
GREAT BRITAIN

☎ 01463 870492 🖹 01463 870297

e-mail: admin@ord-house.co.uk

dir: off A9 at Tore rdbt onto A832. 5m, through Muir of Ord. Left towards Ullapool (still A832). Hotel 0.5m on left

Dating back to 1637, this country-house hotel is situated peacefully in wooded grounds and offers brightly furnished and well-proportioned accommodation. Comfortable day rooms reflect the character and charm of the house, with inviting lounges, a cosy snug bar and an elegant dining room where wide-ranging, creative menus are offered.

Rooms 12 en suite (3 GF) S £40-£75; D £80-£120 (incl. bkfst) **Facilities** no TV in bdrms 🏌 Putt green Wi-fi in bedrooms Clay pigeon shooting **Parking** 30 **Notes** ⊘ in restaurant Closed Nov-Apr

NAIRN   MAP 23 NH85

INSPECTORS' CHOICE

★★★ ◉◉◉◉ **HOTEL**

Boath House

Auldearn IV12 5TE

☎ 01667 454896 🖹 01667 455469

e-mail: wendy@boath-house.com

web: www.boath-house.com

dir: 2m past Nairn on A96, E towards Forres, signed on main road

Standing in its own grounds, this splendid Georgian mansion has been lovingly restored. Hospitality is first class; owners, Don and Wendy Matheson, are passionate about what they do and have an ability to establish a special relationship with their guests. The food is memorable - the five-course dinners are a culinary adventure, matched only by the excellence of breakfasts. The house itself is delightful, with inviting lounges and a dining room overlooking a trout loch. Bedrooms are striking, comfortable, and include many fine antique pieces. The small spa offers a number of treatments.

Rooms 6 en suite (1 fmly) (1 GF) ⊘ in all bedrooms S £120-£180; D £190-£280 (incl. bkfst) **Facilities** Spa Fishing Sauna Gym 🏌 Jacuzzi Wi-fi available Beauty salon **Conf** Board 10 **Parking** 20 **Notes LB** ⊘ in restaurant Closed Xmas Civ Wed 30

★★ 65% **HOTEL**

Alton Burn

Alton Burn Rd IV12 5ND

☎ 01667 452051 & 453325 🖹 01667 456697

e-mail: enquiries@altonburn.co.uk

dir: follow signs from A96 at western boundary of Nairn

This long-established, family-run hotel is located on the western edge of town and enjoys delightful views over the Moray Firth and adjacent golf course. Bedrooms, originally furnished in the 1950s, have been thoughtfully maintained to provide a reminder of that era whilst spacious day rooms include a well-stocked bar, several comfortable lounges and a popular restaurant.

Rooms 23 en suite (7 GF) **Facilities** 🏌 ⚓ Putt green Table tennis, pool table, croquet **Conf** Thtr 100 Class 50 Board 40 **Parking** 40 **Notes LB** ⊘ in restaurant Closed Nov-Mar

🅰

Swallow Golf View

SWALLOW
HOTELS

The Seafront IV12 4HD

☎ 01667 458800 🖹 01667 455267

web: www.swallowhotels.com

dir: off A96 into Seabank Rd, follow road to end, hotel on right

Rooms 42 en suite **Notes** ★★★★

🅰

Swallow Newton

SWALLOW
HOTELS

Inverness Rd IV12 4RX

☎ 01667 453144 🖹 01667 454026

web: www.swallowhotels.com

dir: 15m from Inverness on A96, turn left into tree lined driveway

Rooms 56 en suite **Notes** ★★★★

NETHY BRIDGE   MAP 23 NJ02

★★★ 68% **HOTEL**

Nethybridge

PH25 3DP

☎ 01479 821203 🖹 01479 821686

e-mail: salesnethybridge@strathmorehotels.com

dir: A9 onto A95, then onto B970 to Nethy Bridge

This popular tourist and coaching hotel enjoys a central location amidst the majestic Cairngorm Mountains. Bedrooms are stylishly furnished in bold tartans whilst traditionally styled day rooms include two bars and a popular snooker room. Staff are friendly and keen to please.

Rooms 69 en suite (3 fmly) (7 GF) ⊘ in 50 bedrooms **Facilities** Snooker Putt green Bowling green ♫ Xmas **Services** Lift **Parking** 80 **Notes** ⊘ in restaurant

★★ 74% ®® HOTEL

The Mountview Hotel

Grantown Rd PH25 3EB
☎ 01479 821248 🗎 01479 821515
e-mail: mviewhotel@aol.com

dir: from Aviemore follow signs through Boat of Garten to Nethy Bridge. On main road through village, hotel on right, 100mtrs beyond Nethybridge Hotel

Aptly named, this country-house hotel enjoys stunning panoramic views from its elevated position on the edge of the village. It specialises in guided holidays and is a favoured base for birdwatching and for walking groups. Public rooms include inviting lounges, while imaginative, well-prepared dinners are served in a bright and modern restaurant extension.

Rooms 12 rms (11 en suite) (1 GF) S £37.50-£45; D £70-90 (incl. bkfst) ⊘ in 12 bedrooms **Parking** 20 **Notes** ⊗ ⊘ in restaurant

NEWTONMORE   MAP 23 NN79

A

Swallow Highlander

PH20 1AY
☎ 01540 673341 🗎 01540 673708
web: www.swallowhotels.com
Rooms 85 en suite **Notes** ★★

ONICH   MAP 22 NN06

★★★ 81% ® HOTEL

Onich

PH33 6RY
☎ 01855 821214 🗎 01855 821484
e-mail: enquiries@onich-fortwilliam.co.uk
web: www.onich-fortwilliam.co.uk

dir: beside A82, 2m N of Ballachulish Bridge

Genuine hospitality is part of the appeal of this hotel, which lies right beside Loch Linnhe with gardens extending to shores. Nicely presented public areas include a choice of inviting lounges and contrasting bars, and views of the loch can be enjoyed from the attractive restaurant. Bedrooms, with pleasing colour schemes, are comfortably modern in appointment.

Rooms 26 en suite (6 fmly) ⊘ in 21 bedrooms S £39 £90; D £70-£118 (incl. bkfst) **Facilities** STV Jacuzzi Games room Xmas **Conf** Thtr 30 Class 20 Board 20 Del £125 **Parking** 50 **Notes LB** ⊘ in restaurant Closed 22-27 Dec

★★★ 73% ® HOTEL

Lodge on the Loch

PH33 6RY
☎ 01855 821237 & 821238 🗎 01855 821190
e-mail: reservation@lodgeontheloch.com
web: www.lodgeontheloch.com

dir: beside A82 in village of Onich - 5m N of Glencoe, 10m S of Fort William

First class Highland hospitality is a real feature of this idyllically located, holiday hotel. Fine views over Loch Linnhe can be enjoyed from the public areas and many of the individually styled bedrooms. A real fire

continued

warms the cosy lounge in the cooler months and accomplished cooking features on the dinner menus.

Rooms 15 en suite (1 GF) ⊘ in all bedrooms **Facilities** Free use of leisure facilities at sister hotel Xmas **Parking** 20 **Notes** No children 16yrs ⊘ in restaurant Civ Wed 80

PLOCKTON   MAP 22 NG83

★★ 76% HOTEL

The Plockton

41 Harbour St IV52 8TN
☎ 01599 544274 🗎 01599 544475
e-mail: info@plocktonhotel.co.uk

dir: 6m from Kyle of Lochalsh. 6m from Balmacara

This very popular hotel occupies an idyllic position on the waterfront of Loch Carron. Stylish bedrooms offer individual, pleasing decor and many have spacious balconies or panoramic views. There is a choice of three dining areas and seafood is very much a speciality. The staff and owners provide a relaxed and informal style of attentive service. In addition to the hotel a self-contained cottage is available for group bookings.

Rooms 11 en suite 4 annexe en suite (1 fmly) (1 GF) ⊘ in all bedrooms S £55-£60, D £90-£100 (incl. bkfst) **Facilities** STV Wi-fi in bedrooms Pool table 🎵 ch fac New Year **Notes LB** ⊗ ⊘ in restaurant Civ Wed 45

★★ 75% HOTEL

Haven

3 Innes St IV52 8TW
☎ 01599 544223 & 544334 🗎 01599 544467
e-mail: reception@havenhotelplockton.co.uk

dir: off A87 just before Kyle of Lochalsh, after Balmacara signed to Plockton, hotel on main road just before lochside

A delightful hotel situated in the picturesque west Highland village of Plockton and only a short walk from the seashore. A choice of eating

continued on page 840

Scotland

PLOCKTON *continued*

options includes an attractive restaurant offering an imaginative dinner menu, or Motley's the popular bistro. Smart modern bedrooms include two delightful and very spacious suites.

Rooms 15 en suite (1 fmly) ❀ in all bedrooms S £62-£103; D £94-£136 (incl. bkfst) **Facilities** Xmas **Conf** Thtr 20 Class 20 Board 12 Del from £95 **Parking** 5 **Notes LB** ❀ in restaurant

---

POOLEWE
MAP 22 NG88

INSPECTORS' CHOICE

★★★ ◉◉ SMALL HOTEL

Pool House Hotel

IV22 2LD

☎ 01445 781272 📠 01445 781403

e-mail: enquiries@poolhousehotel.com

dir: *6m N of Gairloch on A832. Village centre*

Set on the shores of Loch Ewe where the river meets the bay, this hotel's understated roadside facade gives little hint of its splendid interior, nor of the views out to the bay. Memorable features are its delightful public rooms, a six-course dinner and stunningly romantic suites all individual in style and with lovely bathrooms. The hotel is run very much as a country house. Hospitality and guest care by the Harrison Family are second to none and will leave a lasting impression.

Rooms 6 en suite 1 annexe en suite (3 GF) ❀ in all bedrooms D £285-£450 (incl. bkfst) **Facilities** Snooker Wi-fi available Sea fishing from jetty by hotel Xmas **Parking** 12 **Notes LB** ❀ No children 18yrs ❀ in restaurant Closed Jan-mid Feb RS Nov & Dec

---

ROY BRIDGE
MAP 22 NN28

★★★ 81% ◉ HOTEL

Best Western Glenspean Lodge Hotel

Best Western

PH31 4AW

☎ 01397 712223 📠 01397 712660

e-mail: reservations@glenspeanlodge.com

web: www.glenspeanlodge.com

dir: *2m E of Roy Bridge, right off A82 at Spean Bridge onto A86*

Originally a Victorian hunting lodge, this hotel has been impressively extended and sits in gardens in an elevated position in the Spean Valley. Accommodation is provided in well laid out bedrooms, some

continued

suitable for families. Inviting public areas include a comfortable lounge bar and a restaurant that enjoys stunning views of the valley.

Rooms 17 en suite (1 fmly) ❀ in all bedrooms S £45-£75; D £110-£200 (incl. bkfst) **Facilities** STV Sauna Gym Jacuzzi snooker room, library Xmas **Conf** Thtr 50 Class 25 Board 25 Del from £80 **Parking** 50 **Notes LB** ❀ in restaurant Civ Wed 50

★★ 76% HOTEL

The Stronlossit Inn

PH31 4AG

☎ 01397 712253 & 0800 015 5321 📠 01397 712641

e-mail: stay@stronlossit.co.uk

web: www.stronlossit.co.uk

dir: *off A82 at Spean Bridge onto A86, signed Roy Bridge. Hotel on left*

Appointed to modern standards with the character and hospitality of a traditional hostelry, The Stronlossit Inn is proving quite a draw for the discerning Highland tourist. The spacious bar is the focal point, with a peat burning fire providing a warm welcome in cooler months; guests can eat in the attractive restaurant. Bedrooms come in a mix of sizes and styles, most being smartly modern and well equipped.

Rooms 10 en suite (5 GF) ❀ in all bedrooms S £40-£50; D £70-£86 (incl. bkfst) **Facilities** Free internet access Xmas **Conf** Thtr 30 Class 18 Board 12 **Parking** 30 **Notes LB** ❀ No children 12yrs ❀ in restaurant Closed 25 Nov-10 Dec Civ Wed 30

SCOURIE
MAP 22 NC14

★★ 78% HOTEL

Scourie

IV27 4SX

☎ 01971 502396 📠 01971 502423

e-mail: patrick@scourie-hotel.co.uk

dir: *N'bound on A894. Hotel in village on left*

This well-established hotel is an angler's paradise with extensive fishing rights available on a 25,000-acre estate. Public areas include a choice of comfortable lounges, a cosy bar and a smart dining room offering wholesome fare. The bedrooms are comfortable and generally spacious. The resident proprietors and their staff create a relaxed and friendly atmosphere.

Rooms 18 rms (17 en suite) 2 annexe en suite (2 fmly) (5 GF) ❀ in all bedrooms S £55-£66; D £100-£120 (incl. bkfst & dinner) **Facilities** no TV in bdrms Fishing Sea,Trout & Salmon fishing **Parking** 30 **Notes LB** ❀ in restaurant Closed mid Oct-end Mar Civ Wed 40

★★ 72% COUNTRY HOUSE HOTEL

Eddrachilles

Badcall Bay IV27 4TH

☎ 01971 502080 & 502211 📠 01971 502477

e-mail: enq@eddrachilles.com

web: www.eddrachilles.com

dir: *2m S of Scourie on A894. 7m N of Kylesku Bridge*

Enjoying a peaceful location in a secluded setting above Badcall Bay, this hotel enjoys stunning sea and island views. There is a choice of lounges as well as a conservatory. The dining room with its natural stone walls and floor is a feature, as is the focus on fresh local produce from the daily-changing dinner menu. Bedrooms offer a host of accessories.

continued

Eddrachilles

Rooms 11 en suite (1 fmly) (4 GF) ⊘ in all bedrooms S £63.90-£66.95; D £87.80-£93.90 (incl. bkfst) **Facilities** Fishing **Parking** 16 **Notes** ⊗ ⊘ in restaurant Closed mid Oct-mid Mar

SHIELDAIG   MAP 22 NG85

★★ 76% ◉◉ **SMALL HOTEL**

Tigh an Eilean

IV54 8XN

☎ 01520 755251 📠 01520 755321

e-mail: tighaneileanhotel@shieldaig.fsnet.co.uk

dir: off A896 onto village road signed Shieldaig, hotel in centre of village on loch front

A splendid location by the sea, with views over the bay, is the icing on the cake for this delightful small hotel. It can be a long drive to reach Shieldaig but guests remark that the journey is more than worth the effort. The brightly decorated bedrooms are comfortable though don't expect television, except in one of the lounges. For many, it's the food that attracts, with fish and seafood featuring strongly.

Rooms 11 en suite (1 fmly) S fr £68; D fr £144 (incl. bkfst) **Facilities** no TV in bdrms Wi-fi available Bird watching, Boat available, Kayaks, Astronomy **Parking** 15 **Notes LB** ⊘ in restaurant Closed late Oct-mid Mar Civ Wed 40

SOUTH BALLACHULISH   MAP 22 NN05

Ⓐ

Swallow Ballachulish   SWALLOW

PH49 4JY

☎ 01855 811606 📠 01855 811629

web: www.swallowhotels.com

dir: on A828, Fort William-Oban road, 3m N of Glencoe

Rooms 53 en suite **Conf** Thtr 100 Class 50 Board 30 **Notes** ★★★★

Ⓐ

Swallow Isles of Glencoe   SWALLOW

PH49 4HL

☎ 01855 811602 📠 01855 811770

web: www.swallowhotels.com

Rooms 59 en suite **Notes** ★★★★

SPEAN BRIDGE   MAP 22 NN28

★★ 75% ◉ **SMALL HOTEL**

Old Pines

PH34 4EG

☎ 01397 712324

e-mail: enquiries@oldpines.co.uk

dir: 1m N of Spean Bridge on A82 next to Commando Memorial take B8004 towards Gairlochy. Hotel 300mtrs on right

Enjoying a peaceful location just on the fringes of the village, the Old Pines offers comfortable accommodation in a woodland setting. Bedrooms are well appointed and well equipped. There is a comfortable lounge and airy dining room where delicious meals are served.

Rooms 8 en suite (1 fmly) (8 GF) ⊘ in all bedrooms S £40-£52; D £80-£105 (incl. bkfst) **Facilities** ch fac Xmas **Parking** 12 **Notes LB** ⊘ in restaurant Civ Wed 30

Ⓐ

Corriegour Lodge

Loch Lochy PH34 4EB

☎ 01397 712685 📠 01397 712696

e-mail: info@corriegour-lodge-hotel.com

web: www.corriegour-lodge-hotel.com

dir: N of Fort William on A82 (south of Loch Lochy). Between Spean Bridge & Invergarry

Rooms 9 en suite (3 fmly) (1 GF) ⊘ in all bedrooms S £79.50-£99.50; D £159-£199 (incl. bkfst & dinner) **Facilities** Xmas **Parking** 20 **Notes** ★★★★ **LB** ⊗ No children 8yrs ⊘ in restaurant Closed Dec-Jan ex New Year RS Nov-Feb wknds only

See advertisement under FORT WILLIAM

STRATHPEFFER   MAP 23 NH45

★★★ 75% **HOTEL**

Ben Wyvis Hotel   CRERAR
                                        HOTELS

IV14 9DN

☎ 0870 950 6264 📠 01997 421228

e-mail: benwyvis@crerarhotels.com

web: www.crerarhotels.com

dir: From S A862 to Dingwall, then A834 to Strathpeffer. Hotel 3rd exit on left.

This imposing hotel, built in 1877, lies in its own extensive, landscaped grounds in the centre of the Victorian spa town of Strathpeffer. It has now been tastefully fully refurbished to provide spacious lounges with open log fires, sparkling chandeliers and even has its own 32-seat

continued on page 842

Scotland

Scotland

STRATHPEFFER *continued*

cinema. The hotel is popular for meetings and conferences as it has several private function rooms.

Rooms 92 en suite (5 fmly) (8 GF) ⊘ in all bedrooms S £75-£80; D £100-£150 (incl. bkfst) **Facilities** STV FTV Putt green Wi-fi in bedrooms Cinema Putting green ♫ Xmas **Conf** Thtr 200 Class 180 Board 120 Del from £75 **Services** Lift **Parking** 40 **Notes LB** ⊘ in restaurant Civ Wed 100

STRONTIAN   MAP 22 NM86

INSPECTORS' CHOICE

★★★ ◉◉ COUNTRY HOUSE HOTEL

Kilcamb Lodge

PH36 4HY

☎ 01967 402257 ▤ 01967 402041

e-mail: enquiries@kilcamblodge.co.uk

dir: *off A861, via Corran Ferry*

This historic house on the shores of Loch Sunart was one of the first stone buildings in the area and was used as military barracks around the time of the Jacobite uprising. Accommodation is provided in tastefully decorated rooms with high quality fabrics. Accomplished cooking, utilising much local produce, can be enjoyed in the stylish dining room. Warm hospitality is assured.

Rooms 12 en suite ⊘ in all bedrooms **Facilities** Fishing Boating **Parking** 18 **Notes LB** No children 12yrs ⊘ in restaurant Closed 2 Jan-11 Feb Civ Wed 60

TAIN   MAP 23 NH88

INSPECTORS' CHOICE

★★ ◉◉ COUNTRY HOUSE HOTEL

Glenmorangie Highland Home at Cadboll

Cadboll, Fearn IV20 1XP

☎ 01862 871671 ▤ 01862 871625

e-mail: relax@glenmorangieplc.co.uk

dir: *from A9 onto B9175 towards Nigg. Follow tourist signs*

This historic Highland home superbly balances top class service and superb customer care. Evenings are focussed around the highly successful 'house party' where guests are introduced to each other in the drawing room, sample whiskies then take dinner (a set, six-course meal) seated at one long table. Conversation can extend well into the evening. Stylish bedrooms

continued

are divided between the traditional main house and some cosy cottages in the grounds. This is an ideal base for the world famous whisky tours.

Glenmorangie Highland Home at Cadboll

Rooms 6 en suite 3 annexe en suite (4 fmly) (3 GF) ⊘ in all bedrooms S £100-£180; D £320-£390 (incl. bkfst & dinner) **Facilities** Fishing ⌣ Putt green Falconry, Clay pigeon shooting, Beauty treatments, Husky Sledding, Archery ♫ Xmas **Conf** Thtr 12 Class 12 Board 12 Del from £110 **Parking** 60 **Notes LB** No children 14yrs ⊘ in restaurant Closed 3-31 Jan Civ Wed 70

A

Swallow Mansfield Castle

SWALLOW

Scotsburn Rd IV19 1PR

☎ 01862 892052 ▤ 01862 892260

web: www.swallowhotels.com

dir: *A9 from S, (ignore 1st exit signed Tain) take 2nd exit signed 'Police Station'*

Rooms 19 en suite **Notes** ★★★★

A

Swallow Morangie House

SWALLOW

Morangie Rd IV19 1PY

☎ 01862 892281 ▤ 01862 892872

web: www.swallowhotels.com

dir: *turn right off A9 northbound*

Rooms 26 en suite **Notes** ★★★

THURSO   MAP 23 ND16

A

Station Hotel & Apartments

54-58 Princes St KW14 7DH

☎ 01847 892003 ▤ 01847 891820

e-mail: stationhotel@lineone.net

web: www.stationthurso.co.uk

dir: *from A9, in Thurso turn left at 2nd lights. Hotel at end of Sinclair St next to library. 2m from ferry terminal for Orkney*

Rooms 21 en suite 9 annexe en suite (8 fmly) (8 GF) ⊘ in 5 bedrooms S £45-£60; D £60-£80 (incl. bkfst) **Facilities** STV Xmas **Parking** 35 **Notes** ★★★ **LB** ⊘ in restaurant

A

Swallow Royal

SWALLOW
HOTELS

Traill St KW14 8EH
☎ 01847 893191 ☐ 01847 895338
web: www.swallowhotels.com
dir: *A9 to Thurso, cross Thurso Bridge, at 1st lights turn right. Hotel on right*
Rooms 103 en suite **Notes** ★★★

TONGUE   MAP 23 NC55

★★ 76% ◉ HOTEL

Borgie Lodge Hotel

Skerray KW14 7TH
☎ 01641 521332 ☐ 01641 521889
e-mail: info@borgielodgehotel.co.uk
dir: *A836 between Tongue & Bettyhill. 0.5m from Skerray Junct*

This small outdoor-sport orientated hotel lies in a glen close to the Borgie River. Whilst fishing parties predominate, those who are not anglers are made equally welcome, and indeed the friendliness and commitment to guest care is paramount. Cosy public rooms offer a choice of lounges and an anglers' bar - they all boast welcoming log fires. The dinner menu is short but well chosen.
Rooms 8 rms (7 en suite) (1 GF) ⊗ in all bedrooms S fr £97; D fr £159 (incl. bkfst & dinner) **Facilities** Fishing ◡ Mountain bikes, Shooting, Stalking, Boating **Parking** 20 **Notes LB** No children 12yrs ⊗ in restaurant RS 25 Dec

★★ 74% ◉ HOTEL

Ben Loyal

Main St IV27 4XE
☎ 01847 611216 ☐ 01847 611212
e-mail: benloyalhotel@btinternet.com
web: www.benloyal.co.uk
dir: *at junct of A838/A836. Hotel by Royal Bank of Scotland*

Enjoying a super location close to Ben Loyal and with views of the Kyle of Tongue, this hotel more often that not marks the welcome completion of a stunning highland and coastal drive. Bedrooms are thoughtfully equipped and brightly decorated whilst day rooms extend to a traditionally styled dining room and a cosy bar. Expertly cooked meals showcase quality local ingredients and the extensive menus ensure there's something for everyone. Staff are especially friendly.
Rooms 11 en suite ⊗ in all bedrooms S £35-£40; D £70-£80 (incl. bkfst) **Facilities** Fishing Fly fishing tuition and equipment **Parking** 20 **Notes** ⊗ in restaurant Closed 24 Dec-1 Mar RS Nov-Mar

TORRIDON   MAP 22 NG95

INSPECTORS' CHOICE

★★★ ◉◉ COUNTRY HOUSE HOTEL

Loch Torridon Country House Hotel

By Achnasheen, Wester Ross IV22 2EY
☎ 01445 791242 ☐ 01445 712253
e-mail: stay@lochtorridonhotel.com
web: www.lochtorridonhotel.com
dir: *from A832 at Kinlochewe, take A896 towards Torridon. (Do not turn into village) continue 1m, hotel on right*

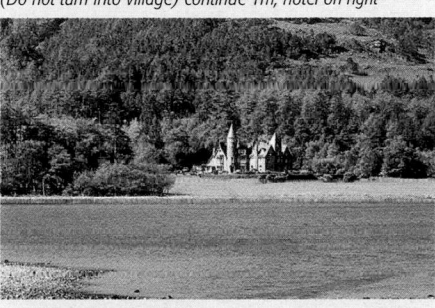

Delightfully set amidst inspiring loch and mountain scenery, this elegant Victorian shooting lodge has been beautifully restored to make the most of its many original features. The attractive bedrooms are all individually furnished and most enjoy stunning Highland views. Comfortable day rooms feature fine wood panelling and roaring fires in cooler months. The whisky bar is aptly named, boasting over 300 malts and in-depth tasting notes. Outdoor activities include shooting, cycling and walking.
Rooms 19 en suite (7 GF) ⊗ in all bedrooms S £115-£160; D £175-£440 (incl. bkfst & dinner) **Facilities** STV Fishing ◡ Wi-fi in bedrooms Mountain biking, Archery, Clay pigeon shooting, Falconry, Climbing ch fac Xmas **Conf** Board 16 Del from £225 **Services** Lift **Parking** 20 **Notes LB** ⊗ in restaurant Closed 3-27 Jan RS 1 Nov-14 Mar Civ Wed 42

ULLAPOOL   MAP 22 NH19

A

Swallow Royal Golf

SWALLOW
HOTELS

Quay St IV26 2UG
☎ 01854 612306 ☐ 01854 612679
web: www.swallowhotels.com
Rooms 83 en suite **Notes** ★★

A

Swallow Royal Golf

SWALLOW
HOTELS

North Rd IV26 2TG
☎ 01854 612314 ☐ 01854 612158
web: www.swallowhotels.com
Rooms 60 en suite **Notes** ★★★

Scotland

WHITEBRIDGE   MAP 23 NH41

★★ 68% HOTEL

Whitebridge
IV2 6UN

☎ 01456 486226 🖺 01456 486413

e-mail: info@whitebridgehotel.co.uk

dir: off A9 onto B851, follow signs to Fort Augustus. Off A82 onto B862 at Fort Augustus

Close to Loch Ness and set amid rugged mountain and moorland scenery this hotel is popular with tourists, fishermen and deer stalkers. Guests have a choice of more formal dining in the restaurant or lighter meals in the popular cosy bar. Bedrooms are thoughtfully equipped and brightly furnished.

Rooms 12 en suite (3 fmly) S £35-£40; D £55-£60 (incl. bkfst) **Facilities** Fishing Wi-fi in bedrooms **Parking** 32 **Notes** ⊗ in restaurant Closed 11 Dec-9 Jan

WICK   MAP 23 ND35

★★ 75% HOTEL

Mackay's
Union St KW1 5ED

☎ 01955 602323 🖺 01955 605930

e-mail: res@mackayshotel.co.uk

dir: opposite Caithness General Hospital

This well-established hotel is situated just outside the town centre overlooking the River Wick. MacKay's provides well-equipped and attractive accommodation, suited to both the business and leisure traveller. There is a stylish bistro that serves food throughout the day and a choice of bars that also offer food.

Rooms 30 en suite (19 en suite) (4 fmly) S fr £65; D fr £90 (incl. bkfst) **Facilities** STV Wi-fi available ♫ **Conf** Thtr 100 Class 100 Board 60 **Services** Lift **Notes LB** ⊗ in restaurant Closed 1-2 Jan

A

Swallow Norseman
Riverside KW1 4NL   SWALLOW

☎ 01955 603344 🖺 01955 605456

web: www.swallowhotels.com

Rooms 48 en suite **Notes** ★★

INVERCLYDE

GOUROCK   MAP 20 NS27

A

Ramada Gourock   ®RAMADA
Cloch Rd PA19 1AR

☎ 01475 634671 🖺 01475 632490

e-mail: sales.gourock@ramadajarvis.co.uk

web: www.ramadajarvis.co.uk

dir: A770 into Gourock, pass railway station, 2m on coast road. Hotel on left

Rooms 98 en suite (3 fmly) (30 GF) ⊗ in 75 bedrooms S £50-£145; D £50-£145 (incl. bkfst) **Facilities** STV ▣ supervised ॐ Sauna Gym Jacuzzi Beauty therapist ♫ Xmas **Conf** Thtr 365 Class 124 Board 146 Del from £78 **Services** Lift **Parking** 200 **Notes** ★★★ **LB** ⊗ ⊘ in restaurant

GREENOCK   MAP 20 NS27

BUDGET HOTEL

Premier Travel Inn Greenock   premier travel inn
1-3 James Watt Way PA15 2AJ

☎ 08701 977120 🖺 01475 730890

web: www.premiertravelinn.com

dir: Follow M8 until it becomes A8 at Langbank, straight ahead through rdbt to Greenock, turn right off A8 at 3rd rdbt, next to McDonalds

High quality, modern budget accommodation ideal for both families and business travellers. Spacious, en suite bedrooms feature bath and shower, satellite TV and many have telephones and modem points. The adjacent family restaurant features a wide and varied menu. For further details consult the Hotel Groups page.

Rooms 40 en suite

PENICUIK   MAP 21 NT25

A

Swallow Craigiebield House   SWALLOW
50 Bog Rd EH26 9BZ

☎ 01968 672557 🖺 01968 671610

web: www.swallowhotels.com

Rooms 18 en suite **Notes** ★★★

MORAY

ARCHIESTOWN   MAP 23 NJ24

★★ 82% ⊛ SMALL HOTEL

Archiestown
AB38 7QL

☎ 01340 810218 🖺 01340 810239

e-mail: jah@archiestownhotel.co.uk

web: www.archiestownhotel.co.uk

dir: A95 Craigellachie, follow B9102 to Archiestown 4m

Set in the heart of a Speyside village this small hotel is proves popular with locals and anglers. It is rightly noteable for its great hospitality, attentive service and good food. Cosy and comfortable public rooms include a choice of lounges (there is no bar as such) and a bistro offering an inviting choice of dishes at both lunch and dinner.

Rooms 11 en suite (1 fmly) ⊗ in all bedrooms S £55-£70; D £110-£110 (incl. bkfst) **Facilities** ⌄ Xmas **Conf** Thtr 20 Board 12 Del from £95 **Parking** 20 **Notes LB** ⊗ in restaurant Closed 24-27 Dec & 3 Jan-9 Feb Civ Wed 25

CRAIGELLACHIE

MAP 23 NJ24

★★★ 85% ◉◉ **HOTEL**

Craigellachie

AB38 9SR

☎ 01340 881204 📠 01340 881253

e-mail: info@craigellachie.com

web: www.craigellachie.com

dir: on A95 in Craigellachie, 300yds from A95/A941 junct

This impressive and popular hotel is located in the heart of Speyside, so it is no surprise that malt whisky takes centre stage in the Quaich bar with over 600 featured. Bedrooms come in various sizes, all are

continued

tastefully decorated and bathrooms are of a high specification. Creative dinners showcase local ingredients in the traditionally styled dining room.

Rooms 26 en suite (5 GF) ⊗ in all bedrooms S £110-£150; D £135-£175 (incl. bkfst) **Facilities** STV Gym ch fac Xmas **Conf** Thtr 60 Class 36 Board 26 Del from £125 **Parking** 50 **Notes LB** ⊗ in restaurant Civ Wed 50

CULLEN

MAP 23 NJ56

★★★ 72% **HOTEL**

Cullen Bay Hotel

A98 AB56 4XA

☎ 01542 840432 📠 01542 840900

e-mail: stay@cullenbayhotel.com

web: www.cullenbayhotel.com

dir: on A98, 1m west of Cullen

This family-run hotel sits on the hillside west of the town and gives lovely views of the golf course, beach and Moray Firth. The spacious restaurant, which offers a selection of fine dishes, makes the most of the view, as do many of the bedrooms. There is a comfortable modern bar, a quiet lounge and a second dining room where breakfasts are served.

Rooms 14 en suite (3 fmly) ⊗ in all bedrooms S £48-£60; D £78-£100 (incl. bkfst) **Facilities** Wi-fi available Xmas **Conf** Thtr 200 Class 80 Board 80 **Parking** 100 **Notes LB** ⊗ in restaurant Civ Wed 200

Scotland

Mansion House Hotel

A baronial-style mansion close to the River Lossie.

Bedrooms are individual in size and style with a wide range of amenities and many have four poster beds. Attractive public areas include a lounge, bar, snooker table and a leisure club.

The popular Bistro is an informal alternative to the elegant restaurant where fine cooking is offered.

The Haugh, Elgin, Moray IV30 1AW

Tel: 01343 548811   Fax: 01343 547916   Email: reception@mhelgin.co.uk

CULLEN *continued*

★★★ 67% ⊛ **HOTEL**

The Seafield Hotel

Seafield St AB56 4SG
☎ 01542 840791 🖺 01542 840736
e-mail: accom@theseafieldhotel.com
dir: in centre of town on A950

Originally built by the Earl of Seafield as a coaching inn, this hotel was modernised in the early 1970s to provide individually designed, comfortable bedrooms and is now gradually being refurbished. One of the features here is a lovely, carved wooden fireplace in the spacious lounge bar. Service is friendly and attentive with good-value and enjoyable meals served in the restaurant.

Rooms 19 en suite (2 fmly) **Facilities** STV ⬚ Snooker Clay pigeon shooting, Cycling, Quads, 4x4 driving, Archery Xmas **Conf** BC Thtr 140 Class 90 Board 30 **Parking** 28 **Notes** ⊘ in restaurant Civ Wed 90

ELGIN
MAP 23 NJ26

★★★ 79% ⊛ **HOTEL**

Mansion House

The Haugh IV30 1AW
☎ 01343 548811 🖺 01343 547916
e-mail: reception@mhelgin.co.uk
web: www.mansionhousehotel.co.uk

dir: turn off A96 into Haugh Rd, then 1st left

Set in grounds by the River Lossie, this baronial mansion is popular with leisure and business guests as well as being a wedding venue. Bedrooms are spacious, many having views of the river. Extensive public areas include a choice of restaurants, with the bistro contrasting with the classical main restaurant. There is an indoor pool and a beauty and hair salon.

Rooms 23 en suite (5 GF) ⊘ in 5 bedrooms **Facilities Spa** STV ⬚ supervised Fishing Snooker Sauna Solarium Gym Jacuzzi Xmas **Conf** BC Thtr 200 Class 1 Board 1 **Parking** 50 **Notes** ⊛ ⊘ in restaurant Civ Wed 160

See advert on page 845

BUDGET HOTEL

Premier Travel Inn Elgin

1 Linkwood Way IV30 1HY
☎ 08701 977095 🖺 01343 540635
web: www.premiertravelinn.com
dir: on A96, 1.5m E of city centre

High quality, modern budget accommodation ideal for both families and business travellers. Spacious, en suite bedrooms feature bath and shower, satellite TV and many have telephones and modem points. The adjacent family restaurant features a wide and varied menu. For further details consult the Hotel Groups page.

Rooms 40 en suite **Conf** Thtr 24

FORRES
MAP 23 NJ05

★★★ 73% **HOTEL**

Ramnee

Victoria Rd IV36 3BN
☎ 01309 672410 🖺 01309 673392
e-mail: info@ramneehotel.com
dir: off A96 at rdbt on E side of Forres, hotel 200yds on right

Genuinely friendly staff ensure this well-established hotel remains popular with business travellers. Accommodation, including a family suite, varies in size, although all rooms are well-presented. Hearty bar food provides a less formal dining option to the imaginative restaurant menu. Current refurbishment of bedrooms is showing good results.

Rooms 20 en suite (4 fmly) ⊘ in 10 bedrooms S £70-£120; D £90-£155 (incl. bkfst) **Facilities** STV Wi-fi in bedrooms use of leisure facilities at sister hotel **Conf** Thtr 100 Class 30 Board 45 Del from £115 **Parking** 50 **Notes LB** ⊘ in restaurant Closed 25 Dec & 1-3 Jan Civ Wed 100

LOSSIEMOUTH
MAP 23 NJ27

Ⓐ

Swallow Stotfield

Stotfield Rd IV31 6QS
☎ 01343 812011 🖺 01343 814820
web: www.swallowhotels.com
dir: A96 to Elgin then A941 to Lossiemouth, follow sign showing West Beach, Golf Club
Rooms 47 en suite **Notes** ★★★

NORTH AYRSHIRE

IRVINE
MAP 20 NS33

★★★★ 75% **HOTEL**

Thistle Irvine
THISTLE HOTELS

46 Annick Rd KA11 4LD
☎ 0870 333 9156 📠 0870 333 9256
e-mail: irvine@thistle.co.uk

dir: *Follow A71 bypass round Kilmarnock then follow signs to Irvine/Irvine Central until Warrix Interchange, take 2nd exit Irvine Central. At rdbt take 2nd exit Town Centre. At next rdbt right onto A71 Kilmarnock. Hotel 100mtrs on left.*

Situated on the edge of Irvine with good transportation links, this is a well-presented hotel that has benefited from some refurbishment, and has an extremely friendly team with good customer care awareness. Lobby and bar décor are reminiscent of Tangier. For the family there is a large tropical lagoon swimming pool along with a 9 hole, par 3 golf course.

Rooms 128 en suite (7 fmly) (64 GF) ⊗ in 64 bedrooms **Facilities** STV ▣ ♨ 9 Fishing Putt green Jacuzzi **Conf** Thtr 280 Class 140 Board 100 **Services** air con **Parking** 250 **Notes** LB ⊗ in restaurant Civ Wed 200

★★★ 73% **HOTEL**

Gailes Lodge Restaurant and Hotel
Marine Dr, Gailes KA11 5AE
☎ 01294 204040 📠 01294 204047
e-mail: info@gaileshotel.com
web: www.gaileshotel.com

With several golf courses on its doorstep and within easy reach of Prestwick Airport, this smart modern hotel offers spacious bedrooms furnished in contemporary style. A spacious three-bedroom penthouse suite offers something really special. A bright attractive café bar/restaurant provides food throughout the day until late. There is also an impressive conference centre.

Rooms 41 en suite (10 fmly) (20 GF) ⊗ in 31 bedrooms S £105; D £125 (incl. bkfst) **Facilities Spa** STV Sauna Gym Jacuzzi Wi fi in bedrooms Complimentary leisure facilities adjacent to hotel Xmas **Conf** BC Thtr 500 Class 200 Board 80 Del from £105 **Services** Lift **Parking** 130 **Notes** LB ⊗ Civ Wed 180

KILWINNING
MAP 20 NS34

★★★ 75% **HOTEL**

Montgreenan Mansion House
Montgreenan Estate KA13 7QZ
☎ 01294 850005 📠 01294 850397
e-mail: reservations@montgreenhotel.com
web: www.montgreenanhotel.com

dir: *hotel signs 4m N of Irvine on A736 & from A737*

In a peaceful setting of 48 acres of parkland and woods, this 19th-century mansion retains many of its original features. Public areas include a splendid drawing room, a library, a club-style bar and a restaurant. Accommodation ranges from compact modern rooms to the well-proportioned classical rooms of the original house.

Rooms 21 en suite (1 fmly) ⊗ in 16 bedrooms **Facilities** STV ♨ 5 ᛘ Snooker ⬥ Putt green ch fac **Conf** Thtr 100 Class 60 Board 40 **Parking** 50 **Notes** LB ⊗ in restaurant Civ Wed 140

LARGS
MAP 20 NS25

★★ 81% **HOTEL**

Willowbank
96 Greenock Rd KA30 8PG
☎ 01475 672311 & 675435 📠 01475 689027
e-mail: iaincsmith@btconnect.com

dir: *on A78*

A relaxed, friendly atmosphere prevails at this well-maintained hotel where hanging baskets are a feature in summer months. The nicely decorated bedrooms are, in general, spacious and offer comfortable modern appointments. The public areas include a large, well-stocked bar, a lounge and a dining room.

Rooms 30 en suite (4 fmly) S £60-£80; D £90-£120 (incl. bkfst) **Facilities** ᛘ Xmas **Conf** Thtr 200 Class 100 Board 40 **Parking** 40 **Notes** LB ⊗ in restaurant

NORTH LANARKSHIRE

COATBRIDGE
MAP 20 NS76

Ⓐ

Georgian Hotel
26 Lefroy St ML5 1LZ
☎ 01236 421888 📠 01236 421173
e-mail: thegeorgian@btconnect.com

dir: *Follow tourist signs for Time Capsule, hotel signed on A89*

Rooms 8 rms (6 en suite) (1 GF) ⊗ in all bedrooms S £25-£45; D £45-£65 (incl. bkfst) **Conf** BC Thtr 120 Class 70 Board 60 Del from £65 **Parking** 16 **Notes** ★★ ⊛ ⊗ in restaurant

CUMBERNAULD
MAP 21 NS77

★★★★ 74% **HOTEL**

Westerwood
QHOTELS

1 St Andrews Dr, Westerwood G68 0EW
☎ 01236 457171 📠 01236 738478
e-mail: westerwood@qhotels.co.uk
web: www.qhotels.co.uk

This stylish, contemporary hotel enjoys an elevated position within 400 acres at the foot of the Camspie Hills. Accommodation is provided in spacious, bright bedrooms, many with super bathrooms,

continued on page 848

Scotland

CUMBERNAULD *continued*

and day rooms include sumptuous lounges, an airy restaurant and extensive golf, fitness and conference facilities.

Rooms 100 en suite (14 fmly) (35 GF) ⊗ in all bedrooms S £75-£120; D £85-£180 (incl. bkfst) **Facilities Spa** STV ⅀ ♨ 18 ☼ Sauna Solarium Gym Putt green Jacuzzi Wi-fi in bedrooms Beauty salon Hairdresser Xmas **Conf** Thtr 200 Class 120 Board 60 Del from £110 **Services** Lift air con **Parking** 200 **Notes LB** ⊗ in restaurant Civ Wed 166

BUDGET HOTEL

Premier Travel Inn Glasgow (Cumbernauld)

4 South Muirhead Rd G67 1AX
☎ 08701 977108 ▤ 01236 736380
web: www.premiertravelinn.com

dir: *From A80, A8011 following signs to Cumbernauld and town centre. Inn opposite Asda/McDonalds. Turn at rdbt towards Esso garage. Turn right at mini-rdbt*

High quality, modern budget accommodation ideal for both families and business travellers. Spacious, en suite bedrooms feature bath and shower, satellite TV and many have telephones and modem points. The adjacent family restaurant features a wide and varied menu. For further details consult the Hotel Groups page.

Rooms 37 en suite

MOTHERWELL   MAP 21 NS75

BUDGET HOTEL

Innkeeper's Lodge Glasgow/Strathclyde Park

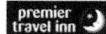

Hamilton Rd ML1 3RB
☎ 01698 854715
web: www.innkeeperslodge.com

Smart, en suite accommodation ideal for both business & leisure guests. Bedrooms are very well equipped, including Sky TV, telephone, modem points, tea & coffee making facilities, (family rooms in most locations). Complimentary breakfast. The adjacent Pub Restaurant; a Harvester, Vintage Inn, Toby Carvery, Ember Inn, Sizzling Pubco or Pub & Carvery offers an all day menu. See Hotel Groups pages for further details.

Rooms 28 rms S £45-£55; D £45-£55

BUDGET HOTEL

Premier Travel Inn Glasgow (Bellshill)

Belziehill Farm, New Edinburgh Rd ML4 3HH
☎ 08701 977106 ▤ 01698 845969
web: www.premiertravelinn.com

dir: *M74 junct 5 follow signs towards Coatbridge & Bellshill on the A725. At the 2nd exit. Inn on left of rdbt*

High quality, modern budget accommodation ideal for both families and business travellers. Spacious, en suite bedrooms feature bath and shower, satellite TV and many have telephones and modem points. The adjacent family restaurant features a wide and varied menu. For further details consult the Hotel Groups page.

Rooms 40 en suite

Premier Travel Inn Glasgow (Motherwell)

Edinburgh Rd, Newhouse ML1 5SY
☎ 08701 977164 ▤ 01698 861353

dir: *From south M74 junct 5 onto A725 towards Coatbridge. Take A8 towards Edinburgh & leave at junct 6, follow signs for Lanark. Inn 400yds on right*

Rooms 40 en suite **Conf** Thtr 40

STEPPS   MAP 20 NS66

★★★ 73% HOTEL

Best Western Garfield House Hotel

Cumbernauld Rd G33 6HW
☎ 0141 779 2111 ▤ 0141 779 9799
e-mail: rooms@garfieldhotel.co.uk

dir: *M8 junct 11 exit at Stepps/Queenslie, follow Stepps/A80 signs*

Situated close to the A80, this considerably extended business hotel is a popular venue for local conferences and functions. Public areas include a welcoming reception lounge and the popular Distillery Bar/Restaurant, an all-day eatery providing good value meals in an informal setting. Smart, well-presented bedrooms come in a range of sizes and styles. Staff are friendly and keen to please.

Rooms 45 en suite (10 fmly) (13 GF) ⊗ in all bedrooms S £55-£100; D £70-£117 (incl. bkfst) **Facilities** STV Wi-fi in bedrooms **Conf** Thtr 100 Class 40 Board 36 Del from £125 **Parking** 90 **Notes LB** ⊗ in restaurant Closed 1-2 Jan Civ Wed 80

BUDGET HOTEL

Premier Travel Inn Glasgow (Stepps)

Crowood Roundabout, Cumbernauld Rd G33 6LE
☎ 08701 977111 ▤ 0141 779 8060
web: www.premiertravelinn.com

dir: *M8 junct 13 signed M80. Exit M80 at Crowwood rdbt, take 3rd exit signed A80 west. Inn is 1st left*

High quality, modern budget accommodation ideal for both families and business travellers. Spacious, en suite bedrooms feature bath and shower, satellite TV and many have telephones and modem points. The adjacent family restaurant features a wide and varied menu. For further details consult the Hotel Groups page.

Rooms 80 en suite

PERTH & KINROSS

AUCHTERARDER   MAP 21 NN91

INSPECTORS' CHOICE

★★★★★ ◉◉◉◉ **HOTEL**

The Gleneagles Hotel

PH3 1NF

☎ 01764 662231 📠 01764 662134

e-mail: resort.sales@gleneagles.com

dir: off A9 at exit for A823 follow signs for Gleneagles Hotel

With its international reputation for high standards, this grand hotel provides something for everyone. Set in a delightful location, Gleneagles offers a peaceful retreat, as well as many sporting activities, including the famous championship golf courses. All bedrooms are appointed to a high standard and offer both traditional and modern contemporary styles. Stylish public areas include various dining options, which include the Strathearn, with two AA rosettes, as well as some inspired cooking at Andrew Fairlie at Gleneagles, a restaurant with four rosettes. Service is always professional, staff are friendly and nothing is too much trouble.

Rooms 266 en suite (115 fmly) (11 GF) ☻ in all bedrooms D £285-£500 (incl. bkfst) **Facilities Spa** STV ▣ supervised ↖ ♨ 54 ⚓ Fishing Squash Riding Snooker Sauna Gym ⚓ Putt green Jacuzzi Wi-fi in bedrooms Falconry, Off road driving, Golf range, Archery, Clay target shooting ♫ Xmas **Conf** BC Thtr 360 Class 240 Board 60 Del from £260 **Services** Lift **Parking** 277 **Notes LB** ☻ in restaurant Civ Wed 360

★★ 85% ◉ **HOTEL**

Cairn Lodge

Orchil Rd PH3 1LX

☎ 01764 662634 📠 01764 662866

e-mail: info@cairnlodge.co.uk

web: www.cairnlodge.co.uk

dir: leave A9 at Gleneagles exit. Turn left on A823, pass entrance to Gleneagles Hotel and take 2nd turning towards Auchterarder on Orchil Rd

This twin turreted hotel stands in large grounds on the edge of the town. Bedrooms differ in style and size, with the newer rooms offering superb levels of quality and comfort. Public areas are smartly appointed and food can be enjoyed in either the informal atmosphere of the bar or the Capercaillie restaurant.

Rooms 10 en suite (6 fmly) (2 GF) **Parking** 30 **Notes LB** ☻ Civ Wed 30

BLAIR ATHOLL   MAP 23 NN86

★★ 76% **HOTEL**

Atholl Arms

Old North Rd PH18 5SG

☎ 01796 481205 📠 01796 481550

e-mail: hotel@athollarms.co.uk

web: www.athollarmshotel.co.uk

dir: off A9 to B8079, 1m into Blair Atholl, hotel near entrance to Blair Castle

Situated close to Blair Castle and conveniently adjacent to the railway station, this stylish hotel has historically styled public rooms that include a choice of bars, and a splendid baronial-style dining room. Bedrooms vary in size and style. Staff throughout are friendly and very caring.

Rooms 30 en suite (3 fmly) S £35-£65; D £50-£65 (incl. bkfst) **Facilities** Fishing Rough shooting ♫ Xmas **Conf** BC Thtr 120 Class 80 Board 60 Del from £55 **Parking** 103 **Notes LB** ☻ in restaurant Civ Wed 120

Scotland

BLAIRGOWRIE   MAP 21 NO14

★★★ 67% **HOTEL**

Angus

Wellmeadow PH10 6NH

☎ 01250 872455 ▤ 01250 875615

e-mail: reservations@theangushotel.com

dir: 20 mins north of Perth. On A93 Perth/Blairgowrie Rd overlooking gardens in town centre

Inside this traditional town centre building is an attractive modern hotel which is popular with visiting tour groups. Bedrooms are smartly furnished and come in a variety of sizes. There is a spacious bar lounge and a restaurant offering good value meals.

Rooms 81 en suite (4 fmly) ⊛ in all bedrooms S £35-£45; D £47-£55 (incl. bkfst) **Facilities Spa** FTV ▣ Sauna Solarium Wi-fi in bedrooms ♫ Xmas **Conf** Thtr 200 Class 100 Board 50 Del from £69 **Services** Lift **Parking** 62 **Notes LB** ⊛ in restaurant Civ Wed 180

COMRIE   MAP 21 NN72

★★★ 80% ⊛ **HOTEL**

Royal

Melville Square PH6 2DN

☎ 01764 679200 ▤ 01764 679219

e-mail: reception@royalhotel.co.uk

web: www.royalhotel.co.uk

dir: off A9 on A822 to Crieff, then B827 to Comrie. Hotel in main square on A85

A traditional façade gives little indication of the style and elegance inside this long-established hotel located in the village centre. Public areas include a bar and library, a bright modern restaurant and a conservatory-style brasserie. Bedrooms are tastefully appointed and furnished with smart reproduction antiques.

Rooms 11 en suite S fr £80; D fr £130 (incl. bkfst) **Facilities** STV Fishing Pool table, Fishing/shooting arranged Xmas **Conf** Thtr 20 Class 10 Board 20 Del from £120 **Parking** 22 **Notes LB** ⊛ in restaurant

COUPAR ANGUS   MAP 21 NO23

Ⓤ

Enverdale House

6 Pleasure Rd PH13 9JB

☎ 01828 627606 ▤ 01828 627239

e-mail: yvonne@yhb-54.wanadoo.co.uk

dir: on A94 northbound. Turn right onto A923 50yds, turn right, hotel 50yds

At the time of going to press, the star classification for this hotel was not confirmed. Please refer to the AA internet site www.theAA.com for current information.

Rooms 5 en suite (1 fmly) ⊛ in all bedrooms S fr £45; D fr £65 (incl. bkfst) **Facilities** Xmas **Conf** Del from £80 **Parking** 51 **Notes** ⊛ ⊛ in restaurant Civ Wed 200

CRIEFF   MAP 21 NN82

Ⓐ

Swallow Drummond Arms   SWALLOW

James Square PH7 3HZ

☎ 01764 652151 ▤ 01764 655222

web: www.swallowhotels.com

Rooms 36 en suite **Notes** ★★

DUNKELD   MAP 21 NO04

INSPECTORS' CHOICE

★★★★ ⊛⊛⊛ **HOTEL**

Kinnaird

Kinnaird Estate PH8 0LB

☎ 01796 482440 ▤ 01796 482289

e-mail: enquiry@kinnairdestate.com

dir: from Perth, A9 towards Inverness towards Dunkeld but do not enter town, continue N for 2m then B898 on left

RELAIS & CHATEAUX

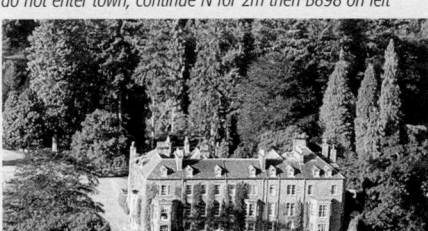

An imposing Edwardian mansion set in 9,000 acres of beautiful countryside on the west bank of the River Tay. Sitting rooms are warm and inviting with deep-cushioned sofas and open fires. Bedrooms are furnished with rich, soft, luxurious fabrics, and have marble bathrooms. Food is creative and imaginative, with abundant local produce featuring on all menus. While jacket and tie are required at dinner, the atmosphere overall is tranquil and relaxed.

Rooms 9 en suite (1 GF) **Facilities Spa** STV ⊛ Fishing Snooker ⊛ Shooting **Conf** Thtr 25 Class 10 Board 15 **Services** Lift **Parking** 22 **Notes LB** ⊛ No children 12yrs ⊛ in restaurant Civ Wed 36

GLENEAGLES
See **Auchterarder**

GLENSHEE (SPITTAL OF)   MAP 21 NO17

★★ 81% ◉ ◉ **COUNTRY HOUSE HOTEL**

Dalmunzie House
PH10 7QG
☎ 01250 885224 🗎 01250 885225
e-mail: reservations@dalmunzie.com
web: www.dalmunzie.com
dir: on A93 at Spittal of Glenshee, follow signs to hotel

This turreted mansion house enjoys a remote setting in the heart of a 6,500-acre estate, yet is within easy reach of the ski slopes of Glenshee. Accommodation ranges in style from large rooms with period furnishings to more compact rooms with modern decor. Public areas include a traditional bar, a spacious restaurant and a choice of lounges.

Rooms 17 en suite (2 fmly) ❀ in 16 bedrooms S £85-£135; D £140-£230 (incl. bkfst & dinner) **Facilities** ♨ 9 ♨ Fishing ↝ Clay pigeon shooting, Mountain bikes, Estate tours, Grouse shooting, Stalking Xmas **Conf** Thtr 20 Class 20 Board 20 **Services** Lift **Parking** 33 **Notes LB** ❀ Closed 1-28 Dec Civ Wed

---

KENMORE   MAP 21 NN74

★★★ 72% **HOTEL**

Kenmore Hotel
The Square PH15 2NU
☎ 01007 830205 🗎 01887 830269
e-mail: reception@kenmorehotel.co.uk
web: www.kenmorehotel.com
dir: off A9 at Ballinluig onto A827, through Aberfeldy to Kenmore for hotel in village centre

Dating back to 1572, this riverside hotel is Scotland's oldest inn and has a rich and interesting history. Bedrooms offer tasteful decor and
continued

---

meals can be enjoyed in the restaurant with its panoramic views of the River Tay. The choice of bars includes one with real fires.

Rooms 27 en suite 13 annexe en suite (4 fmly) (7 GF) ❀ in 29 bedrooms S £50-£67; D £70-£104 (incl. bkfst) **Facilities** STV ♨ Fishing Jacuzzi Salmon fishing on River Tay for residents Xmas **Conf** Thtr 80 Class 60 Board 50 Del from £82 **Services** Lift **Parking** 30 **Notes LB** ❀ in restaurant Civ Wed 40

KINCLAVEN   MAP 21 NO13

★★★ ◉ ◉ **COUNTRY HOUSE HOTEL**

Ballathie House
PH1 4QN
☎ 01250 883268 🗎 01250 883396
e-mail: email@ballathiehousehotel.com
web: www.ballathiehousehotel.com
dir: from A9 2m N of Perth, B9099 through Stanley & signed, or off A93 at Beech Hedge follow signs for Ballathie 2.5m

Set in delightful grounds, this splendid Scottish mansion house combines classical grandeur with modern comfort. Bedrooms range from well-proportioned master rooms to modern standard rooms and many boast antique furniture and art deco bathrooms. For the ultimate in quality, request one of the Riverside Rooms, a purpose-built development right on the banks of the river, complete with balconies and terraces. The elegant restaurant has views over the River Tay.

Rooms 25 en suite 16 annexe en suite (2 fmly) (10 GF) ❀ in all bedrooms S £82.50-£102.50; D £165-£205 (incl. bkfst) **Facilities** FTV Fishing ↝ Putt green Xmas **Conf** BC Thtr 50 Class 20 Board 30 Del from £150 **Services** Lift **Parking** 50 **Notes LB** ❀ in restaurant Civ Wed 90

KINLOCH RANNOCH   MAP 23 NN65

★★★ 75% **HOTEL**

Macdonald Loch Rannoch Hotel & Resort

PH16 5PS
☎ 0870 1942112 🗎 01882 632203
web: www.macdonald-hotels.co.uk
dir: off A9 onto B847 Calvine. Follow signs to Kinloch Rannoch, hotel 1m from village

Set in the Perthshire countryside and looking out across Loch Rannoch, this hotel, built around a 19th-century hunting lodge, is geared to the leisure market. The smart and spacious bedrooms in the

continued on page 852

KINLOCH RANNOCH continued

newer wing are worth asking for. It provides a range of indoor and outdoor pursuits.

Macdonald Loch Rannoch Hotel & Resort

Rooms 52 en suite (25 fmly) ⊗ in all bedrooms **Facilities** ⤵ Fishing Squash Snooker Sauna Solarium Gym Quad biking Archery Clay pigeon shooting Off road driving Bike hire **Conf** Thtr 160 Class 80 Board 50 **Services** Lift **Parking** 52 **Notes LB** ⊗ in restaurant Civ Wed 160

★★★ 73% ⊛ **HOTEL**

Dunalastair

PH16 5PW
☎ 01882 632323 632218 ⧉ 01882 632371
e-mail: robert@dunalastair.co.uk
web: www.dunalastair.co.uk
dir: A9 to Pitlochry, at northern end take B8019 to Tummel Bridge then A846 to Kinloch Rannoch

A traditional Highland hotel that is being steadily transformed. Inviting public rooms are full of character - log fires, stags heads, wood panelling and an extensive selection of malt whiskies. Standard and superior bedrooms are on offer. However, it is the friendly attentive service by delightful staff, as well as first class dinners that will leave lasting impressions.

Rooms 28 en suite (4 fmly) (9 GF) ⊗ in 15 bedrooms S £40-£65; D £65-£130 (incl. bkfst) **Facilities** STV Fishing Riding Wi-fi in bedrooms Fishing, 4x4 & adventure safaris, Rafting, Clay Pigeon shooting Abseiling Pony trekking Sailing Bike hire Quad bikes Xmas **Conf** BC Thtr 60 Class 40 Board 40 Del from £80 **Parking** 33 **Notes LB** No children 8yrs ⊗ in restaurant Civ Wed 70

See advert on opposite page

KINROSS

MAP 21 NO10

★★★ 80% **HOTEL**

Green

2 The Muirs KY13 8AS
☎ 01577 863467 ⧉ 01577 863180
e-mail: reservations@green-hotel.com
web: www.green-hotel.com
dir: M90 junct 6 follow Kinross signs, onto A922, hotel on this road

A long-established hotel offering a wide range of indoor and outdoor activities. Public areas include a classical restaurant, a choice of bars and a well-stocked gift shop. The comfortable, well-equipped bedrooms, most of which are generously proportioned, boast attractive colour schemes and smart modern furnishings.

Rooms 46 en suite (4 fmly) (14 GF) ⊗ in all bedrooms S £90-£110; D £150-£165 (incl. bkfst) **Facilities** STV ⤵ supervised ♨ 36 ♒ Fishing Squash Sauna Solarium Gym ⛳ Putt green Wi-fi in bedrooms Curling in season, Petanque ch fac Xmas **Conf** BC Thtr 130 Class 75 Board 60 Del from £150 **Parking** 60 **Notes LB** ⊗ in restaurant Closed 23-28 Dec excluding Xmas day RS 25-Dec Civ Wed 100

★★★ 70% **HOTEL**

The Windlestrae Hotel & Leisure Centre

The Muirs KY13 8AS
☎ 0870 609 6153 ⧉ 01577 864733
e-mail: windlestrae@corushotels.com
web: www.corushotels.com
dir: M90 junct 6 into Kinross, left at 2nd mini rdbt. Hotel 400yds on right

Set in landscaped gardens back from the main road, this hotel is just a short walk from the town centre. Bedrooms and public areas are

continued

comfortable and well proportioned; there is also a leisure centre. Staff are friendly and obliging.

Rooms 45 en suite (13 GF) ⊘ in 34 bedrooms S fr £75; D fr £75
Facilities STV [🎱] Snooker Sauna Solarium Gym Jacuzzi Beautician, Steam room, Toning tables Xmas **Conf** Thtr 250 Class 100 Board 80 Del from £95 **Parking** 80 **Notes LB** ⊘ in restaurant Civ Wed 100

BUDGET HOTEL

Travelodge Kinross (M90)

Kincardine Rd, Moto Service Area, Turfhill Tourist Area KY13 0NQ
☎ 08700 850 950 📠 01577 861641
web: www.travelodge.co.uk

dir: on A977, M90 junct 6, Turfhills Tourist Centre

Travelodge offers good quality, good value, modern accommodation. Ideal for families, the spacious en suite bedrooms include remote-control TV, tea and coffee-making facilities and comfortable beds. Meals can be taken at the nearby family restaurant. See Hotel Groups pages for further details.

Rooms 35 en suite S fr £26; D fr £26

PERTH   MAP 21 NO12

★★★ 85% ◉◉ **HOTEL**

Murrayshall Country House Hotel & Golf Course

New Scone PH2 7PH
☎ 01738 551171 📠 01738 552595
e-mail: lin.murrayshall@virgin.net

dir: from Perth take A94 (Coupar Angus), 1m from Perth, right to Murrayshall just before New Scone

This imposing country house is set in 350 acres of grounds, including two golf courses, one of which is of championship standard. Bedrooms come in two distinct styles: modern suites in a purpose-built building contrast with more classic rooms in the main building. The Clubhouse bar serves a range of meals all day, whilst more accomplished cooking can be enjoyed in the Old Masters Restaurant.

Rooms 27 en suite 14 annexe en suite (17 fmly) (4 GF) ⊘ in 1 bedroom **Facilities** STV ✦ 3G 🌳 Sauna Gym Putt green Driving range **Conf** Thtr 180 Class 60 Board 30 **Parking** 80 **Notes LB** ⊘ in restaurant Civ Wed 130

★★★ 81% ◉ **HOTEL**

Parklands Hotel

2 St Leonards Bank PH2 8EB
☎ 01738 622451 📠 01738 622046
e-mail: info@theparklandshotel.com
web: www.theparklandshotel.com

dir: M90 junct 10, in 1m left at lights at end of park area, hotel on left

Ideally located close to the centre of town, with open views over the South Inch the enthusiastic proprietors continue to invest heavily in the business and have given bedrooms a smart contemporary feel. Public areas include a choice of restaurants with a fine dining experience offered in Acanthus.

Rooms 14 en suite (3 fmly) (4 GF) ⊘ in 4 bedrooms **Facilities** STV **Conf** BC Thtr 24 Class 18 Board 20 **Parking** 30 **Notes LB** ⊘ in restaurant RS 25-26 Dec & 31 Dec-3 Jan Civ Wed 40

★★★ 78% ◉◉ **HOTEL**

Best Western Huntingtower

Crieff Rd PH1 3JT
☎ 01738 583771 📠 01738 583777
e-mail: reservations@huntingtowerhotel.co.uk
web: www.huntingtowerhotel.co.uk

dir: 3m W off A85

Set in landscaped grounds in a rural setting, this Edwardian house has been extended to offer smart, comfortable public areas and a series of high quality bedrooms. It's worth asking for one of the executive bedrooms. Comfortable lounges lead to a conservatory popular at lunchtime, whilst the elegant panelled Oak Room restaurant offers skilfully prepared dinners.

Rooms 31 en suite 3 annexe en suite (2 fmly) (8 GF) **Facilities** STV **Conf** BC Thtr 200 Class 140 Board 30 Del from £125 **Services** Lift **Parking** 150 **Notes LB** ⊘ in restaurant Civ Wed 200

Scotland

Scotland

PERTH *continued*

★★★ 72% **HOTEL**

Best Western Queens Hotel

Leonard St PH2 8HB

☎ 01738 442222 ◫ 01738 638496

e-mail: email@queensperth.co.uk

dir: from M90 follow to 2nd lights, turn left. Hotel on right, opposite railway station

This popular hotel benefits from a central location close to both the bus and rail stations. Bedrooms vary in size and style with top floor rooms offering extra space and excellent views of the town. Public rooms include a smart leisure centre and versatile conference space. A range of meals is served in both the bar and restaurant.

Rooms 50 en suite (4 fmly) ⊛ in all bedrooms S £63-£109; D £93-£129 (incl. bkfst) **Facilities Spa** STV 🏊 Sauna Gym Jacuzzi Wi-fi in bedrooms Steam room Xmas **Conf** Thtr 200 Class 70 Board 50 Del from £105 **Services** Lift **Parking** 50 **Notes LB** ⊗ ⊛ in restaurant Closed 3-7 Jan Civ Wed 220

★★★ 72% **HOTEL**

Lovat

90 Glasgow Rd PH2 0LT

☎ 01738 636555 ◫ 01738 643123

e-mail: e-mail@lovat.co.uk

dir: from M90 follow Stirling signs to rdbt. Right into Glasgow Rd, hotel 1.5m on right

This popular, long established hotel on the Glasgow road offers good function facilities and largely attracts a business clientele. There is a bright contemporary brasserie serving a good range of meals throughout the day until late.

Rooms 30 en suite (1 fmly) (9 GF) ⊛ in all bedrooms S £35-£93; D £70-£118 (incl. bkfst) **Facilities** STV Wi-fi in bedrooms Use of facilities at nearby sister hotel (indoor pool, gym, steam room, jacuzzi) Xmas **Conf** Thtr 200 Class 60 Board 50 Del £120 **Parking** 40 **Notes LB** ⊗ ⊛ in restaurant Civ Wed 180

★★★ 71% **HOTEL**

Quality Hotel

Leonard St PH2 8HE

☎ 01738 624141 ◫ 01738 639912

e-mail: reservations@hotels-perth.com

web: www.choicehotelseurope.com

dir: Follow signs for Railway station. Hotel adjacent

Situated beside the railway station this substantial Victorian hotel has undergone a full refurbishment. Public rooms are well proportioned; whilst the well-equipped accommodation includes some massive bedrooms.

Rooms 71 en suite (4 fmly) ⊛ in 57 bedrooms S £79-£89; D £94-£129 (incl. bkfst & dinner) **Facilities** STV Xmas **Conf** Thtr 300 Class 150 Board 80 Del from £98 **Services** Lift **Parking** 100 **Notes LB** Civ Wed 70

A

Ramada Perth

West Mill St PH1 5QP

☎ 01738 628281 ◫ 01738 643423

e-mail: sales.perth@ramadajarvis.co.uk

web: www.ramadajarvis.co.uk

dir: From A9 follow signs for Perth City Centre. At 2nd set of lights turn left into Marshall Place, then 4th right into King St, straight through 2 sets of lights and then left into West Mill St, hotel on the right.

Rooms 76 en suite (2 fmly) ⊛ in 57 bedrooms S £50-£99; D £50-£99 **Facilities** STV FTV Xmas **Conf** Thtr 120 Board 40 Del from £100 **Parking** 50 **Notes** ★★★ ⊛ in restaurant

BUDGET HOTEL

Innkeeper's Perth

Crieff Rd (A85), Huntingtower

☎ 0870 243500

web: www.innkeeperslodge.com

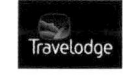

Smart, en suite accommodation ideal for both business & leisure guests. Bedrooms are very well equipped, including Sky TV, telephone, modem points, tea & coffee making facilities, (family rooms in most locations). Complimentary breakfast. The adjacent Pub Restaurant; a Harvester, Vintage Inn, Toby Carvery, Ember Inn, Sizzling Pubco or Pub & Carvery offers an all day menu. See Hotel Groups pages for further details.

Rooms 53 en suite S £49.95-£52.95; D £49.95-£52.95

Innkeeper's Lodge Perth

18 Dundee Rd PH2 7AB

☎ 01738 624471

Rooms 41 rms S £49.95-£52.95; D £49.95-£52.95 **Conf** Thtr 200 Class 120 Board 120

BUDGET HOTEL

Travelodge Perth Broxden Junction

PH2 0PL

☎ 08700 850 950 ◫ 01738 444783

web: www.travelodge.co.uk

Travelodge offers good quality, good value, modern accommodation. Ideal for families, the spacious en suite bedrooms include remote-control TV, tea and coffee-making facilities and comfortable beds. Meals can be taken at the nearby family restaurant. See Hotel Groups pages for further details.

Rooms S fr £26; D fr £26

PITLOCHRY   MAP 23 NN95
See also Kinloch Rannoch

★★★ 85% ⊛ **COUNTRY HOUSE HOTEL**

Pine Trees

Strathview Ter PH16 5QR
☎ 01796 472121 📠 01796 472460
e-mail: info@pinetreeshotel.co.uk
web: www.pinetreeshotel.co.uk
dir: *along main street (Atholl Rd), into Larchwood Rd, follow hotel signs*

Set in ten acres of tree-studded grounds high above the town, this fine Victorian mansion retains many fine features including wood panelling, ornate ceilings and a wonderful marble staircase. The atmosphere is refined and relaxing, with public rooms looking onto the lawns. Bedrooms come in a variety of sizes and many are well proportioned. Staff are friendly and keen to please.

Rooms 20 en suite (3 fmly) ⊗ in all bedrooms S £56-£84; D £112-£168 (incl. bkfst & dinner) **Facilities** Xmas **Parking** 20 **Notes LB** ⊗ in restaurant Civ Wed 70

★★★ 85% ⊛ **COUNTRY HOUSE HOTEL**

Green Park

Clunie Bridge Rd PH16 5JY
☎ 01796 473248 📠 01796 473520
e-mail: bookings@thegreenpark.co.uk
web: www.thegreenpark.co.uk
dir: *turn off A9 at Pitlochry, follow signs 0.25m through town*

Guests return year after year to this lovely hotel that is situated in a stunning setting on the shores of Loch Faskally. Most of the thoughtfully designed bedrooms, including a splendid new wing, the restaurant and the comfortable lounges enjoy these views. Dinner utilises fresh produce, much of it grown in the kitchen garden.

Rooms 51 en suite (16 GF) ⊗ in all bedrooms S £62-£87; D £124-£174 (incl. bkfst & dinner) **Facilities** Putt green Xmas **Parking** 51 **Notes LB** ⊗ in restaurant

See advert on this page

★★★ 79% **HOTEL**

Dundarach

Perth Rd PH16 5DJ
☎ 01796 472862 📠 01796 473024
e-mail: aa@pitlochryhotel.co.uk
web: www.dundarach.co.uk
dir: *S of town centre on main route*

This welcoming, family-run hotel stands in mature grounds at the south end of town. Bedrooms offer a variety of styles, including a block of large purpose-built rooms that will appeal to business guests. Well-proportioned public areas feature inviting lounges and a conservatory restaurant giving fine views of the Tummel Valley.

Rooms 20 en suite 19 annexe en suite (7 fmly) ⊗ in 11 bedrooms S £68; D £92 (incl. bkfst) **Facilities** STV Sauna Wi-fi in bedrooms **Conf** Thtr 60 Class 40 Board 40 **Parking** 39 **Notes LB** ⊗ ⊗ in restaurant Closed Jan RS Dec-early Feb

---

PITLOCHRY *continued*

★★★ 74% HOTEL

BW Scotland's Hotel and Leisure Club

CRERAR
HOTELS

40 Bonnethill Rd PH16 5BT

☎ 0870 9506276 📠 01796 473284

e-mail: stay@scotlandshotel.co.uk

web: www.crerarhotels.com

dir: *follow A924 Perth road into town until War Memorial then take next right for hotel 200mtrs on right*

Enjoying a convenient town centre location, this long-established hotel is a popular base for tourists. Bedrooms, including family rooms and some with four-poster beds, vary in size and style. A choice of restaurants and bars is offered in the summer.

Rooms 57 en suite 15 annexe en suite (21 fmly) (8 GF) ⊗ in all bedrooms S £60-£100; D £80-£150 (incl. bkfst) **Facilities Spa** 🔄 Sauna Solarium Gym Jacuzzi Wi-fi in bedrooms Therapy treatments, Aromatherapy, Reflexology, Beauty Treatments, Sports Massage Xmas **Conf** Thtr 200 Class 75 Board 30 Del from £99 **Services** Lift **Parking** 100 **Notes LB** ⊗ in restaurant

★★★ 73% HOTEL

Knockendarroch House

Higher Oakfield PH16 5HT

☎ 01796 473473 📠 01796 474068

e-mail: bookings@knockendarroch.co.uk

dir: *N'bound on A9, turn off at Pitlochry sign. After rail bridge take 1st right, then 2nd left.*

This establishment has now changed hands and is owned by Allan and Alison Inglis. An immaculate Victorian mansion overlooking the

continued

town and Tummel Valley. There is no bar, but guests can enjoy a drink in the delightful lounge while studying the daily menu of freshly prepared and enjoyable dishes. Bedrooms are tastefully furnished, comfortable and well equipped. Those on the top floor are smaller but are not without character and appeal.

Rooms 12 en suite ⊗ in all bedrooms S £73-£99; D £100-£156 (incl. bkfst & dinner) **Facilities** Leisure facilities at nearby hotel **Parking** 30 **Notes LB** ⊛ No children 10yrs ⊗ in restaurant Closed 2nd wk Nov-mid Feb

★★ 76% HOTEL

Moulin Hotel

11-13 Kirkmichael Rd, Moulin PH16 5EW

☎ 01796 472196 📠 01796 474098

e-mail: sales@moulinhotel.co.uk

web: www.moulinhotel.co.uk

dir: *off A9 into town centre take A924 signed Braemar. Moulin village 0.75m outside Pitlochry*

Steeped in history, original parts of this friendly hotel date back to 1695. The Moulin bar serves an excellent choice of bar meals as well as real ales from the hotel's own microbrewery. Alternatively, the comfortable restaurant overlooks the Moulin Burn. Bedrooms are well equipped. AA Pub of the Year for Scotland 2006-7.

Rooms 15 en suite (3 fmly) S £40-£70; D £55-£85 (incl. bkfst) **Facilities** Xmas **Conf** Thtr 15 Class 12 Board 10 **Parking** 30 **Notes LB** ⊗ in restaurant

★★ 75% HOTEL

Balrobin

Higher Oakfield PH16 5HT

THE CIRCLE
Selected Individual Hotels
GREAT BRITAIN

☎ 01796 472901 📠 01796 474200

e-mail: info@balrobin.co.uk

web: www.balrobin.co.uk

dir: *leave A9 at Pitlochry junct, continue to town centre and follow brown tourists signs to hotel*

A welcoming atmosphere prevails at this family-run hotel, which, from its position above the town, enjoys delightful countryside views. Public rooms include a relaxing lounge, a well-stocked bar and an attractive restaurant offering traditional home-cooked fare. The bedrooms are comfortable and many enjoy the fine views.

Rooms 14 en suite (2 fmly) (4 GF) ⊗ in all bedrooms S £41-£49.50; D £68-£84 (incl. bkfst) **Parking** 15 **Notes LB** No children 5yrs ⊗ in restaurant Closed Nov-Feb

Scotland

A

Swallow Fishers

Atholl Rd PH16 5BN

☎ 01796 472000 🖷 01796 473949

web: www.swallowhotels.com

SWALLOW

dir: N'bound on A9 to Pitlochry, 3m after Ballinluig. S'bound on A9 turn left to Pitlochry, 10m after Bruar

Rooms 138 en suite **Notes** ★★★

POWMILL   MAP 21 NT09

A

Swallow Perth & Kinross

FK14 7NW

☎ 01577 840595 🖷 01577 840779

web: www.swallowhotels.com

SWALLOW

Rooms 21 en suite **Notes** ★★★

ST FILLANS   MAP 20 NN62

★★★ 82% ◉◉ **HOTEL**

The Four Seasons Hotel

Loch Earn PH6 2NF

☎ 01764 685333 🖷 01764 685444

e-mail: info@thefourseasonshotel.co.uk

web: www.thefourseasonshotel.co.uk

dir: on A85, towards W of village facing Loch

Set on the edge of Loch Earn, this welcoming hotel and many of its bedrooms benefit from the excellent views. There is a choice of lounges, including a library warmed by log fires during winter. Local produce is used to good effect in both the Meall Reamhar restaurant and the more informal Tarken Room.

Rooms 12 en suite 6 annexe en suite (7 fmly) ⊘ in 3 bedrooms S £53-£78; D £106-£126 (incl. bkfst) **Facilities** Xmas **Conf** Thtr 95 Class 45 Board 38 **Parking** 40 **Notes LB** ⊘ in restaurant Closed 2 Jan-15 Feb RS Nov, Dec, Mar Civ Wed 80

★★ 76% **HOTEL**

Achray House

PH6 2NF

☎ 01764 685231 🖷 01764 685320

e-mail: info@achray-house.co.uk

dir: follow A85 towards Crainlarich, from Stirling follow A9 then B822 at Braco, B827 to Comrie. Turn left onto A85 to St Fillans

A friendly holiday hotel set in gardens overlooking picturesque Loch Earn, Achray House offers smart, attractive and well-equipped bedrooms. An interesting range of freshly prepared dishes is served both in the conservatory and in the adjoining dining rooms.

Rooms 8 en suite 2 annexe en suite (2 fmly) (3 GF) ⊘ in all bedrooms S £50-£75; D £100-£150 (incl. bkfst & dinner) **Facilities** ch fac Xmas **Conf** Class 20 Board 20 Del from £70 **Parking** 30 **Notes LB** ⊘ in restaurant

---

TUMMEL BRIDGE   MAP 23 NN75

U

Loch Tummel Inn

Queens View PH16 5RP

☎ 01882 634272 & 632323 🖷 01882 634272

e-mail: info@lochtummelinn.co.uk

web: www.lochtummelinn.co.uk

dir: From Perth A9 N, turn off N of Pitlochry for Killiecrankie. Left onto B8019 for Tummel Bridge. Hotel 8m on right

At the time of going to press, the star classification for this hotel was not confirmed. Please refer to the AA internet site www.theAA.com for current information.

Rooms 7 en suite (1 fmly) (1 GF) ⊘ in all bedrooms S £45-£50; D £75-£85 (incl. bkfst) **Facilities Spa** Fishing Riding Jacuzzi Outdoor activity & adventure centre Xmas **Conf** BC Thtr 20 Class 12 Board 10 Del from £70 **Parking** 21 **Notes LB** ⊘ in restaurant

Scotland

RENFREWSHIRE

GLASGOW AIRPORT   MAP 20 NS46

★★★ 79% HOTEL

Glynhill Hotel & Leisure Club
Paisley Rd PA4 8XB

☎ 0141 886 5555 🖨 0141 885 2838

e-mail: glynhillleisurehotel@msn.com

dir: *M8 junct 27, A741 towards Renfrew. 300yds cross small rdbt, hotel on right*

A smart and welcoming hotel with bedrooms ranging from spacious executive rooms to smaller standard rooms. All are tastefully appointed and have a good range of amenities. The hotel boasts a luxurious leisure complex and extensive conference facilities. The choice of contrasting bars and restaurants should suit most tastes and budgets.

Rooms 145 en suite (25 fmly) ⊘ in 72 bedrooms **Facilities** STV 🔲 supervised Sauna Solarium Gym Jacuzzi 🎵 **Conf** Thtr 450 Class 240 **Parking** 230 **Notes** ⊗ Civ Wed 450

A

Ramada Glasgow Airport   ®RAMADA.
Marchburn Dr, Glasgow Airport Business Park PA3 2SJ

☎ 0141 840 2200 🖨 0141 889 6830

e-mail: sales.glasgowairport@ramadajarvis.co.uk

web: www.ramadajarvis.co.uk

dir: *From Glasgow & east exit M8 junct 28. From west exit M8 junct 29*

Rooms 108 en suite (108 fmly) (12 GF) ⊘ in 80 bedrooms S £50-£89; D £50-£89 **Facilities** STV Wi-fi available **Conf** Thtr 40 Class 16 Board 20 Del from £100 **Services** Lift **Parking** 170 **Notes** ★★★ ⊗ ⊘ in restaurant

BUDGET HOTEL

Premier Travel Inn Glasgow Airport
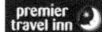
Whitecart Rd PA3 2TH

☎ 0870 238 3321 🖨 0141 842 1570

web: www.premiertravelinn.com

dir: *close to airport terminal, follow signs*

High quality, modern budget accommodation ideal for both families and business travellers. Spacious, en suite bedrooms feature bath and shower, satellite TV and many have telephones and modem points. The adjacent family restaurant features a wide and varied menu. For further details consult the Hotel Groups page.

Rooms 104 en suite **Conf** Thtr 30

Premier Travel Inn Glasgow (Paisley)
Phoenix Retail Park PA1 2BH

☎ 08701 977113 🖨 0141 887 2799

dir: *M8 junct 28a St James Interchange follow A737 signed Irvine, take 1st exit signed Linwood & turn left at 1st rdbt to Phoenix Park*

Rooms 40 en suite **Conf** Thtr 20 Board 15

BUDGET HOTEL

Travelodge Glasgow Airport

Marchburn Dr, Glasgow Airport Business Park, Paisley PA3 2AR

☎ 08700 850 950 🖨 0141 889 0583

web: www.travelodge.co.uk

dir: *M8 junct 28, 0.5m from Glasgow Airport*

Travelodge offers good quality, good value, modern accommodation. Ideal for families, the spacious en suite bedrooms include remote-control TV, tea and coffee-making facilities and comfortable beds. Meals can be taken at the nearby family restaurant. See Hotel Groups pages for further details.

Rooms 98 en suite S fr £26; D fr £26

HOWWOOD   MAP 20 NS36

★★★ 75% ◉◉ HOTEL

Bowfield Hotel & Country Club
PA9 1DB

☎ 01505 705225 🖨 01505 705230

e-mail: enquiries@bowfieldcountryclub.co.uk

web: www.bowfieldcountryclub.co.uk

dir: *M8 junct 28a/29, onto A737 for 6m, left onto B787, right after 2m, follow for 1m to hotel*

This former textile mill is now a popular hotel which has become a convenient stopover for travellers using Glasgow Airport. The leisure club has been considerably expanded and offers very good facilities. Public areas have beamed ceilings, brick and white painted walls, and welcoming open fires. Bedrooms are housed in a separate wing and offer good modern comforts and facilities.

Rooms 23 en suite (3 fmly) (7 GF) ⊘ in all bedrooms S fr £85; D fr £130 (incl. bkfst) **Facilities Spa** 🔲 supervised ⌀ 18 Squash Snooker Sauna Solarium Gym Jacuzzi Wi-fi in bedrooms Childrens soft play Aerobics studio Heath & beauty Xmas **Conf** Thtr 100 Class 60 Board 40 Del from £85 **Parking** 120 **Notes LB** ⊘ in restaurant Civ Wed 80

LANGBANK   MAP 20 NS37

A

Swallow Gleddoch House   SWALLOW
Old Greenock Rd PA14 6YE

☎ 01475 540711 🖨 01475 540201

web: www.swallowhotels.com

Rooms 75 en suite **Notes** ★★★★

Scotland

SCOTTISH BORDERS

CHIRNSIDE   MAP 21 NT85

★★★ 78% **HOTEL**

Chirnside Hall

TD11 3LD

☎ 01890 818219 📠 01890 818231

e-mail: chirnsidehall@globalnet.co.uk

dir: on A6105 (Berwick-on-Tweed/Duns road), approx 3m after Foulden, hotel sign on right

At the end of a tree-lined drive this hotel is ideal for guests wishing to get away from the hustle and bustle of city life and where genuine hospitality is found. Bedrooms are spacious, many with views of the rolling Borders countryside. Real fires warm the elegant lounges, and fresh local produce features on the restaurant menus.

Rooms 10 en suite (2 fmly) S £85-£150; D £150-£165 (incl. bkfst)
Facilities Fishing Snooker Gym ⛳ Shooting Xmas **Conf** Board 16
Parking 20 **Notes** LB ⊗ in restaurant Civ Wed 40

GALASHIELS   MAP 21 NT43

★★★ 73% **HOTEL**

Kingsknowes

Selkirk Rd TD1 3HY

☎ 01896 758375 📠 01896 750377

e-mail: enq@kingsknowes.co.uk

web: www.kingsknowes.co.uk

dir: off A7 at Galashiels/Selkirk rdbt

An imposing turreted mansion, this hotel lies in attractive gardens on the outskirts of town close to the River Tweed. It boasts elegant public areas and many spacious bedrooms, some with excellent views. There is a choice of bars, one with a popular menu to supplement the restaurant.

Rooms 12 en suite (2 fmly) S £65-£80; D £90-£110 (incl. bkfst)
Facilities STV **Conf** Thtr 60 Class 40 Board 30 **Parking** 50 **Notes** LB
⊗ in restaurant Civ Wed 75

JEDBURGH   MAP 21 NT62

★★★ 81% ⚜ **HOTEL**

Jedforest Hotel

Camptown TD8 6PJ

☎ 01835 840222 📠 01835 840226

e-mail: info@jedforesthotel.com

web: www.jedforesthotel.com

dir: 4m S of Jedburgh on A68

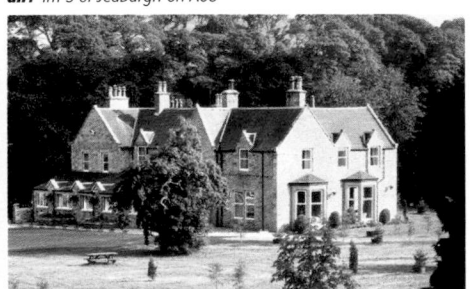

The phrase 'small is beautiful' aptly applies to this friendly and very

continued

well maintained country hotel set in extensive grounds by the River Jed with private fishing. Bedrooms are extremely smart, and the larger ones are particularly impressive - one has a four-poster bed. Inviting public rooms include two lounges and an attractive restaurant offering interesting, freshly based dishes.

Rooms 8 en suite 4 annexe en suite (1 fmly) (4 GF) ⊗ in all bedrooms S £65-£115; D £100-£210 (incl. bkfst) **Facilities** FTV Fishing ⛳ Wi-fi in bedrooms Xmas **Conf** Thtr 35 Class 18 Board 12 Del from £130
Parking 25 **Notes** No children 12yrs ⊗ in restaurant Civ Wed 150

KELSO   MAP 21 NT73

★★★ 83% ⚜⚜ **HOTEL**

The Roxburghe Hotel & Golf Course

Heiton TD5 8JZ

☎ 01573 450331 📠 01573 450611

e-mail: hotel@roxburghe.net

web: www.roxburghe.net

dir: from A68 Jedburgh take A698 to Heiton, 3m SW of Kelso

Outdoor sporting pursuits are popular at this impressive Jacobean mansion owned by the Duke of Roxburghe and set in 500 acres of woods and parkland. Gracious public areas are the perfect settings for afternoon teas and carefully prepared meals. Bedrooms are individually designed, with some of the superior rooms having their own fires.

Rooms 16 en suite 6 annexe en suite (3 fmly) (3 GF) S £134-£200;
D £170-£280 (incl. bkfst) **Facilities** STV ♨ 18 ☺ Fishing ⛳ Putt green Clay shooting Health & beauty saloon Mountain bike hire Xmas **Conf** BC Thtr 50 Class 20 Board 20 Del from £115 **Parking** 150 **Notes** LB ⊗ in restaurant Civ Wed 60

★★★ 77% **HOTEL**

Ednam House

Bridge St TD5 7HT

☎ 01573 224168 📠 01573 226319

e-mail: contact@ednamhouse.com

web: www.ednamhouse.com

dir: 50mtrs from town square

Overlooking a wide expanse of the River Tweed, this fine Georgian mansion has been under the Brooks family ownership for over 75 years. Accommodation styles range from standard to grand, plus a house in the grounds converted into a gracious two-bedroom apartment. Public areas include a choice of lounges and an elegant dining room that has views of the gardens.

Rooms 30 en suite 2 annexe en suite (4 fmly) ⊗ in 3 bedrooms S £68-£76; D £100-£139 (incl. bkfst) **Facilities** ⛳ Free access to Abbey Fitness Centre **Conf** Thtr 250 Board 200 **Parking** 60 **Notes** LB ⊗ in restaurant Closed 24 Dec-6 Jan Civ Wed 100

Scotland

KELSO *continued*

★★★ 73% **HOTEL**

Cross Keys

36-37 The Square TD5 7HL
☎ 01573 223303 📠 01573 225792
e-mail: reception@cross-key-hotel.co.uk
web: www.cross-keys-hotel.co.uk

dir: follow signs for town centre. Hotel in main square

Originally a coaching inn, but now stylishy modernised, this family-run hotel overlooks the cobbled square identified by the colourful window boxes. Bedrooms offer either superior or standard, the former ones being very well proportioned. The spacious lounge bar and restaurant are supplemented by the Oak Room bar/bistro.

Rooms 27 en suite (5 fmly) ⊘ in 15 bedrooms **Facilities** STV Wi-fi in bedrooms Xmas **Conf** BC Thtr 220 Class 160 Board 60 **Services** Lift **Notes** ⊘ in restaurant Closed 25-28 Dec & 1-15 Jan Civ Wed 150

LAUDER

★★ 68% **HOTEL**

Lauderdale

1 Edinburgh Rd TD2 6TW
☎ 01578 722231 📠 01578 718642
e-mail: enquiries@lauderdalehotel.co.uk
web: www.lauderdalehotel.co.uk

dir: on A68 from S, through Lauder centre, hotel on right. From Edinburgh, hotel on left at 1st bend after passing Lauder sign

Lying on the north side of the village with spacious gardens to the side and rear, this friendly hotel is ideally placed for those who don't want to stay in Edinburgh itself. The well-equipped bedrooms come in a variety of sizes, and a good range of meals is served in both the bar and the restaurant.

Rooms 10 en suite (1 fmly) ⊘ in all bedrooms **Facilities** STV **Parking** 200 **Notes** ⊗ ⊘ in restaurant

MELROSE   MAP 21 NT53

★★★ 75% ⊛⊛ **HOTEL**

Burt's

Market Square TD6 9PL
☎ 01896 822285 📠 01896 822870
e-mail: burtshotel@aol.com
web: www.burtshotel.co.uk

dir: A6091, 2m from A68 3m S of Earlston

Recognised by its whitewashed façade and colourful window boxes in

continued

the heart of this small market town, this hotel has been under the same family ownership for over 30 years and the genuine warmth of hospitality is notable. Food is important at Burt's and the elegant restaurant is well complemented by the range of tasty meals in the bar.

Rooms 20 en suite ⊘ in all bedrooms S fr £56; D fr £106 (incl. bkfst) **Facilities** STV Shooting Salmon fishing **Conf** Thtr 38 Class 20 Board 20 Del from £92 **Parking** 40 **Notes** LB ⊘ in restaurant Closed 24-26 Dec

★★★ 73% **HOTEL**

The Townhouse Hotel

3 Market Square TD6 9PQ
☎ 01896 822645 📠 01896 823474
e-mail: info@thetownhousemelrose.co.uk
web: www.thetownhousemelrose.co.uk

dir: from A68 into Melrose

Situated on the square this smart hotel, as the name suggests, has the typical style of a Scottish town house. Bedrooms vary in size and some have views of the hills but all are well equipped and beautifully decorated - it's worth requesting one of two superior rooms. Guests can eat in either the brasserie or more traditional restaurant - both offer the same menu.

Rooms 11 en suite (1 fmly) (1 GF) ⊘ in all bedrooms S £65-£96; D £96-£116 (incl. bkfst) **Facilities** FTV Xmas **Conf** Thtr 60 Class 30 Board 40 Del from £100 **Notes** LB ⊗ ⊘ in restaurant Closed 26-27 Dec

PEEBLES   MAP 21 NT24

★★★★ ⊛⊛ **HOTEL**

Cringletie House

Edinburgh Rd EH45 8PL
☎ 01721 725750 📠 01721 725751
e-mail: enquiries@cringletie.com
web: www.cringletie.com

dir: 2m N on A703

This long-established hotel is a romantic baronial mansion set in 28 acres of gardens and woodland with stunning views from all rooms. Delightful public rooms include a cocktail lounge with adjoining conservatory, whilst the first-floor restaurant is graced

continued

by a magnificent hand-painted ceiling. Bedrooms, many of them particularly spacious, are most attractively furnished.

Cringletie House

Rooms 13 en suite (2 GF) ⊗ in all bedrooms S £110-£130; D £170-£200 (incl. bkfst) **Facilities** STV 🏌 Putt green Wi-fi in bedrooms Petanque, Giant chess & draughts Xmas **Conf** BC Thtr 45 Class 20 Board 24 Del from £170 **Services** Lift **Parking** 30 **Notes LB** ⊗ in restaurant Closed early Jan-early Feb Civ Wed 45

★★★★ 79% **HOTEL**

Macdonald Cardrona Hotel Golf & Country Club

MACDONALD
HOTELS & RESORTS

Cardrona Mains EH45 6LZ
☎ 0070 1942114 📠 01096 031166
e-mail: general.cardrona@macdonald-hotels.co.uk
web: www.macdonald-hotels.co.uk
dir: 20m S of Edinburgh on A72, 3m S of Peebles.

The rolling hills of the Scottish Borders are a stunning backdrop for this modern, purpose-built hotel. Spacious bedrooms are traditional in style, equipped with a range of extras, and most enjoy fantastic countryside. The hotel features some impressive leisure facilities, including an 18-hole golf course, 18-metre indoor pool and state-of-the-art gym.

Rooms 99 en suite (23 fmly) (17 GF) ⊗ in all bedrooms **Facilities Spa** STV 🔧 ⚓ 18 Fishing Sauna Solarium Gym Putt green Wi-fi in bedrooms Quad biking, Kayaking, Shooting, Archery, Horse riding, Bike Trail. **Conf** Thtr 250 Class 120 Board 90 **Services** Lift **Parking** 200 **Notes** ⊗ in restaurant Civ Wed 250

★★★★ 75% **HOTEL**

Peebles Hotel Hydro

EH45 8LX
☎ 01721 720602 📠 01721 722999
e-mail: info@peebleshotelhydro.co.uk
dir: on A702, 0.3m from town

A majestic building, this resort hotel sits in grounds on the edge of the town, its elevated position giving striking views across the valley. Its range of indoor and outdoor leisure activities is second to none and makes the hotel a favourite with both families and conference delegates. Accommodation comes in a range of styles and includes a number of family rooms.

Rooms 128 en suite (24 fmly) (15 GF) S £119-£128; D £204-£232 (incl. bkfst & dinner) **Facilities Spa** STV 🔧 ⚓ Riding Snooker Sauna Gym Putt green Wi-fi in bedrooms Badminton, Beautician, Hairdressing, Giant Chess & Draughts, Pitch & Putt 🎵 Xmas **Conf** Thtr 450 Class 200 Board 74 Del from £106 **Services** Lift **Parking** 200 **Notes LB** ⊗ ⊗ in restaurant Civ Wed 200

★★★ 83% ◉◉ **COUNTRY HOUSE HOTEL**

Castle Venlaw

Edinburgh Rd EH45 8QG
☎ 01721 720384 📠 01721 724066
e-mail: stay@venlaw.co.uk
web: www.venlaw.co.uk
dir: off A703 Peebles/Edinburgh road, 0.75m from Peebles

This 18th-century castle is set in four acres of landscaped gardens, set high above the town. Most bedrooms are spacious and all have smart modern bathrooms, but those in the Romantic and Four-poster rooms are stunning and worth asking for. There is a cosy library bar and classically elegant restaurant. Service is friendly and obliging.

Rooms 12 en suite (3 fmly) ⊗ in all bedrooms D £120-£230 (incl. bkfst) **Facilities** STV Wi-fi in bedrooms Xmas **Conf** BC Thtr 30 Class 20 Board 20 Del from £120 **Parking** 30 **Notes LB** ⊗ in restaurant Civ Wed 35

Scotland

PEEBLES *continued*

★★★ 74% HOTEL

Park

Innerleithen Rd EH45 8BA
☎ 01721 720451 ▯ 01721 723510
e-mail: reserve@parkpeebles.co.uk
dir: in town centre opposite filling station

This hotel offers pleasant, well-equipped bedrooms of various sizes - those in the original house are particularly spacious. Public areas enjoy views of the gardens and include a tartan-clad bar, a relaxing lounge and a spacious wood-panelled restaurant. Guests can use the extensive leisure facilities on offer at the sister hotel, The Hydro.

Rooms 24 en suite ⊘ in 6 bedrooms S £87.50-£112.50; D £161-£201 (incl. bkfst & dinner) **Facilities** STV Putt green Wi-fi in bedrooms Use of facilities of Peebles Hotel Hydro Xmas **Services** Lift **Parking** 50 **Notes LB** ⊘ in restaurant

★★★ 74% HOTEL

Tontine

High St EH45 8AJ
☎ 01721 720892 ▯ 01721 729732
e-mail: info@tontinehotel.com
web: www.tontinehotel.com
dir: in town centre, on High St

Conveniently situated in the main street, this long-established hotel offers comfortable public rooms including an elegant Adam restaurant, inviting lounge and 'clubby' bar. Bedrooms - contained in the original house and the river-facing wing - offer a smart, classical style of accommodation. However the lasting impression is the excellent level of hospitality and guest care.

Rooms 36 en suite (3 fmly) ⊘ in 20 bedrooms S £45-£55; D £80-£110 (incl. bkfst) **Facilities** FTV Wi-fi in bedrooms Xmas **Conf** Thtr 40 Class 24 Board 24 Del from £75 **Parking** 24 **Notes LB** ⊘ in restaurant

ST BOSWELLS   MAP 21 NT53

★★★ 77% ⚜ HOTEL

Dryburgh Abbey

TD6 0RQ
☎ 01835 822261 ▯ 01835 823945
e-mail: enquiries@dryburgh.co.uk
web: www.dryburgh.co.uk

dir: from A68 at St Boswells turn onto B6404, through village. Continue 2m, turn left B6356 Scott's View. Through Clintmains village, hotel 1.8m

A long established hotel, this red-stone baronial mansion enjoys a wonderful setting next to the Dryburgh Abbey and commands fine views of the River Tweed. Comfortable and well-proportioned public areas include a choice of lounges and an elegant restaurant. Bedrooms are generally spacious and include a number of suites.

Rooms 38 en suite (5 fmly) (8 GF) ⊘ in all bedrooms S £69-£159; D £138-£218 (incl. bkfst) **Facilities** FTV 🎣 Fishing Sauna 🏌 Putt green Wi-fi available Falconry centre Xmas **Conf** Thtr 150 Class 90 Board 70 Del from £110 **Services** Lift **Parking** 103 **Notes LB** ⊘ in restaurant Civ Wed 110

★★ 72% HOTEL

Buccleuch Arms

The Green TD6 0EW
☎ 01835 822243 ▯ 01835 823965
e-mail: info@buccleucharmshotel.co.uk
web: www.buccleucharmshotel.co.uk
dir: on A68, 8m N of Jedburgh

Formerly a coaching inn, this long-established hotel stands opposite the village green. The lounge bar is a popular eating venue and complements the attractive restaurant. Morning coffees and afternoon teas are served in the comfortable lounge with its open fire. The well-equipped bedrooms come in a variety of sizes.

Rooms 19 en suite (2 fmly) ⊘ in all bedrooms **Facilities** 🏃 **Conf** Thtr 100 Class 40 Board 30 **Parking** 50 **Notes LB** ⊘ in restaurant Closed 25 Dec Civ Wed 100

SWINTON   MAP 21 NT84

◉⚜ RESTAURANT WITH ROOMS

Wheatsheaf at Swinton

TD11 3JJ
☎ 01890 860257 ▯ 01890 860688
e-mail: reception@wheatsheaf-swinton.co.uk
dir: From Edinburgh turn off A697 onto B6461. From East Lothian, turn off A1 onto B6461

Overlooking the village green, this restaurant with rooms could equally be considered an inn, as it has built its reputation on food. Bedrooms are stylishly furnished, all having smart en suite facilities, the largest ones featuring a bath and separate shower cubicle. Newly added executive bedrooms are of a very high standard.

Rooms 10 en suite (2 fmly) (1 GF) ⊘ in all bedrooms S £67-£94; D £102-£132 **Facilities** STV **Conf** Thtr 18 Class 18 Board 12 **Parking** 7 **Notes LB** ⊛ ⊘ in restaurant Closed 25-27 Dec RS 1 Dec-31 Jan Civ Wed 50

SOUTH AYRSHIRE

ALLOWAY
MAP 20 NS31

A

Swallow Ivy House
SWALLOW HOTELS

2 Alloway KA7 4NL
☎ 01292 442336 📠 01292 445572
web: www.swallowhotels.com

dir: M74 junct 8, A71/A77 S, for approx 2m & follow signs for Burns National Heritage Park. Right along Doonholm Rd to T-junct. Right past Burns Cottage, hotel 300mtrs on left

Rooms 5 en suite **Notes** ★★★

AYR
MAP 20 NS32

★★★★ 87% ◎ **HOTEL**

The Western House Hotel
2 Whitletts Rd KA8 0JE
☎ 01292 619357 & 0870 850 5666 📠 01292 262340
e-mail: cbrownlie@ayr-racecourse.co.uk

This impressive hotel, with attentive and welcoming staff, is located in its own attractive gardens on the edge of Ayr racecourse. Bedrooms in the main house are superbly appointed, whilst guests occupying the courtyard rooms will certainly not be disappointed. Comfortable day rooms include the light and airy restaurant, with views across the course.

Rooms 10 en suite 39 annexe en suite (39 fmly) **Facilities** STV **Conf** Thtr 1200 Class 300 Board 36 **Services** Lift **Notes LB** ⊘ in restaurant Civ Wed 180

★★★★ 80% ◎◎ **HOTEL**

Fairfield House
12 Fairfield Rd KA7 2AR
☎ 01292 267461 📠 01292 261456
e-mail: reservations@fairfieldhotel.co.uk

dir: from A77 towards Ayr South (A30). Follow signs for town centre, down Miller Road and turn left then right into Fairfield Road

Situated in a leafy cul-de-sac close to the esplanade, this hotel enjoys stunning seascapes towards to the Isle of Arran. Bedrooms offer either modern or classical styles, the latter featuring impressive bathrooms. Public areas have been refurbished to provide stylish, modern rooms in which to relax. Skillfully prepared meals are served in the casual brasserie or elegant restaurant.

Rooms 40 en suite 4 annexe en suite (3 fmly) (9 GF) ⊘ in 14 bedrooms S £89-£149; D £99-£169 (incl. bkfst) **Facilities** STV ⊠ supervised Sauna Solarium Gym Jacuzzi Xmas **Conf** BC Thtr 80 Class 50 Board 40 Del from £130 **Services** Lift **Parking** 50 **Notes LB** ⊗ ⊘ in restaurant Civ Wed 150

See advert on this page

★★★ 77% **HOTEL**

Savoy Park
THE INDEPENDENTS

16 Racecourse Rd KA7 2UT
☎ 01292 266112 📠 01292 611488
e-mail: mail@savoypark.com

dir: from A77 follow A70 for 2m, Parkhouse Street, left into Beresford Terrace, 1st right into Bellevue Rd

This well-established hotel retains many of its traditional values including friendly, attentive service. Public rooms feature impressive panelled walls, ornate ceilings and open fires. The restaurant is reminiscent of a Highland shooting lodge and offers a wide ranging, good value menu to suit all tastes. The large superior bedrooms retain a classical elegance while others are smart and modern; all have well equipped modern bathrooms.

Rooms 15 en suite (3 fmly) ⊘ in all bedrooms S £70-£85; D £95-£115 (incl. bkfst) **Facilities** STV Xmas **Conf** Thtr 50 Class 40 Board 30 Del from £100 **Parking** 60 **Notes LB** ⊘ in restaurant Civ Wed 100

See advert on page 864

Scotland

AYR *continued*

ⒶRamada Ayr
®RAMADA.

Dalblair Rd KA7 1UG
☎ 01292 269331 📠 01292 610722
e-mail: sales.ayr@ramadajarvis.co.uk
web: www.ramadajarvis.co.uk

dir: M27 towards Prestwick Airport, then A77 Ayr, 1st rdbt 3rd exit, 2nd rdbt straight over, left at lights, then 2nd set of lights turn left, bottom of road turn right, hotel on left

Rooms 118 en suite (8 fmly) ⊘ in 87 bedrooms S £39.50-£85; D £79-£115 (incl. bkfst) **Facilities Spa** STV 🔲 supervised Sauna Gym Jacuzzi Xmas **Conf** Thtr 460 Class 160 Board 200 Del from £105 **Services** Lift **Parking** 70 **Notes** ★★★ **LB** ⊘ in restaurant

ⒶSwallow Station
SWALLOW
HOTELS

Burns Statue Square KA7 3AT
☎ 01292 263268 📠 01292 262293
web: www.swallowhotels.com
Notes ★★★

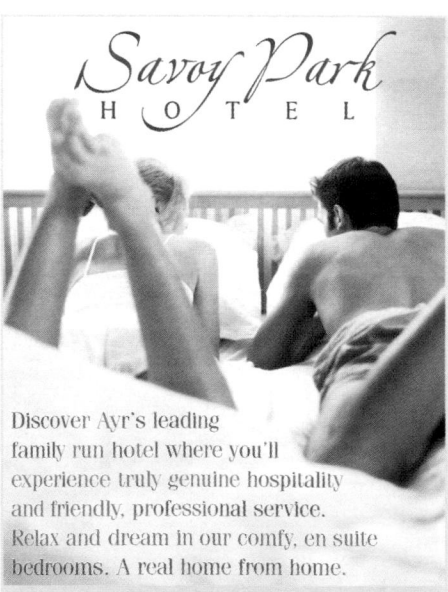

BUDGET HOTEL

Premier Travel Inn Ayr
premier travel inn ☽

Kilmarnock Rd, Monkton KA9 2RJ
☎ 08701 977020 📠 01292 678248
web: www.premiertravelinn.com

dir: on A77/A78 rdbt approx 2m from Prestwick Airport

High quality, modern budget accommodation ideal for both families and business travellers. Spacious, en suite bedrooms feature bath and shower, satellite TV and many have telephones and modem points. The adjacent family restaurant features a wide and varied menu. For further details consult the Hotel Groups page.

Rooms 40 en suite **Conf** Thtr 50 Board 20

BALLANTRAE
MAP 20 NX08

INSPECTORS' CHOICE

★★★★ ⑧⑧⑧ HOTEL

Glenapp Castle
RELAIS & CHATEAUX.

KA26 0NZ
☎ 01465 831212 📠 01465 831000
e-mail: enquiries@glenappcastle.com
web: www.glenappcastle.com
dir: 1m from A77 near Ballantrae

Friendly hospitality and attentive service prevail at this stunning Victorian castle, set in extensive private grounds to the south of the village. Impeccably furnished bedrooms are graced with antiques and period pieces and there are a number of spacious, luxurious suites. Breathtaking views of Arran and Ailsa Craig can be enjoyed from the delightful, sumptuous day rooms and from many of the bedrooms. Accomplished, imaginative cuisine using quality local ingredients is a highlight of any stay.

Rooms 17 en suite (2 fmly) (7 GF) ⊘ in all bedrooms S £255-£455; D £375-£575 (incl. bkfst & dinner) **Facilities** STV FTV 🛁 🏌 Wi-fi in bedrooms 30 acres of beautifully tended gardens Xmas **Conf** Thtr 17 Class 12 Board 17 Del from £280 **Services** Lift **Parking** 20 **Notes LB** ⊘ in restaurant Closed Dec Civ Wed 34

MAYBOLE   MAP 20 NS20

INSPECTORS' CHOICE

★★ ◉ **HOTEL**

Ladyburn
KA19 7SG

☎ 01655 740585 📱 01655 740580

e-mail: jh@ladyburn.co.uk

dir: A77 (Glasgow/Stranraer) at Maybole turn to B7023 to Crosshill and right at War Memorial. In 2m turn left for hotel approx 1m on right

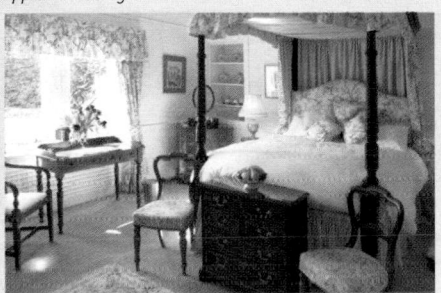

This charming country house is the home of the Hepburn family, who take great pride in the warmth of their welcome. Sitting in open countryside with attractive gardens, it's a great place to come to relax. Classically styled bedrooms, two with four-poster beds, offer every comfort and are complemented by the library and the drawing room. Dinner comprises a carefully cooked three course set menu, and is served in a gracious candlelit setting.
Rooms 5 en suite ❷ in all bedrooms **Facilities** ❤ Boules
Parking 12 **Notes LB** ❽ No children 16yrs ❷ in restaurant RS 2 wks Nov-Dec, 4 wks Jan/Mar Civ Wed 50

PRESTWICK   MAP 20 NS32

★★★ 75% ◉ **HOTEL**

Parkstone
Esplanade KA9 1QN

☎ 01292 477286 📱 01292 477671

e-mail: info@parkstonehotel.co.uk

web: www.parkstonehotel.co.uk

dir: from Prestwick Main St (A79) turn W to seafront - hotel 600yds

Situated on the seafront in a quiet residential area only one mile from Prestwick Airport, this family-run hotel caters for business visitors as

well as golfers. Bedrooms come in a variety of sizes; all being furnished in a smart, contemporary style. The attractive, modern look of the bar and restaurant is matched by an equally up-to-date menu.
Rooms 30 en suite (2 fmly) ❷ in all bedrooms S £49-£66; D £82-£98 (incl. bkfst) **Facilities** Xmas **Conf** Thtr 100 **Parking** 34 **Notes LB** ❽ ❷ in restaurant Civ Wed 100

TROON   MAP 20 NS33

INSPECTORS' CHOICE

★★★★ ◉◉◉ **COUNTRY HOUSE HOTEL**

Lochgreen House Hotel
Monktonhill Rd, Southwood KA10 7EN

☎ 01292 313343 📱 01292 318661

e-mail: lochgreen@costley-hotels.co.uk

web: www.lochgreenhouse.co.uk

dir: from A77 follow Prestwick Airport signs. 0.5m before airport take B749 to Troon. Hotel 1m on left

Set in immaculately maintained grounds, Lochgreen House is graced by tasteful extensions which have created stunning public rooms and spacious, comfortable and elegantly furnished bedrooms. Extra facilities include a coffee shop, gift shop and beauty treatments in The Retreat. The magnificent Tapestry Restaurant provides the ideal setting for dinners that are immaculately presented.
Rooms 31 en suite 7 annexe en suite (17 GF) ❷ in all bedrooms S £99-£125; D £150-£170 (incl. bkfst) **Facilities** STV ❄ Beauty treatments Xmas **Conf** BC Thtr 70 Class 50 Board 50 Del from £150 **Services** Lift **Parking** 50 **Notes** ❽ ❷ in restaurant Civ Wed 100

Some hotels, although accepting children, may not have any special facilities for them so it is well worth checking before booking

Scotland

TROON *continued*

★★★★ 75% HOTEL

Marine

PARAMOUNT
GROUP OF HOTELS

Crosbie Rd KA10 6HE
☎ 01292 314444 📠 01292 316922
e-mail: marine@paramount-hotels.co.uk
web: www.paramount-hotels.co.uk

dir: A77 to A78, then A79 onto B749. Hotel on left after golf course

A favourite with conference and leisure guests, this hotel overlooks Royal Troon's 18th fairway. The cocktail lounge and split-level restaurant enjoy panoramic views of the Firth of Clyde across to the Isle of Arran. Bedrooms and public areas have now all been attractively refurbished.

Rooms 89 en suite (6 fmly) ⊘ in all bedrooms S £70-£190; D £80-£190 (incl. bkfst) **Facilities** STV 🏊 supervised Squash Sauna Solarium Gym Jacuzzi Wi-fi in bedrooms Steam room, Beauty room Xmas **Conf** BC Thtr 220 Class 120 Board 60 Del from £130 **Services** Lift **Parking** 200 **Notes** LB ⊘ in restaurant Civ Wed 100

★★★ 83% HOTEL

Piersland House

Craigend Rd KA10 6HD
☎ 01292 314747 📠 01292 315613
e-mail: reservations@piersland.co.uk
web: www.piersland.co.uk

dir: just off A77 on B749 opposite Royal Troon Golf Club

A Grade I listed building, this well presented hotel is located opposite to the famous championship golf course. Public areas retain delightful oak panelling. Bedrooms are thoughtfully equipped and include a row of 15 'cottages' each with a lounge and its own entrance, ideal for golfers. The hotel is popular both for its bar and for the good food in the restaurant.

Rooms 15 en suite 15 annexe en suite (15 fmly) (15 GF) **Facilities** STV **Conf** Thtr 100 Class 60 Board 30 **Parking** 150 **Notes** LB ⊘ in restaurant Civ Wed 85

TURNBERRY

MAP 20 NS20

INSPECTORS' CHOICE

★★★★★ ◉◉ HOTEL

Westin Turnberry Resort

WESTIN
HOTELS & RESORTS

KA26 9LT
☎ 01655 331000 📠 01655 331706
e-mail: turnberry@westin.com
web: www.westin.com/turnberry

dir: from Glasgow take A77/M77 S towards Stranraer, 2m past Kirkoswald, follow signs for A719/Turnberry. Hotel 500mtrs on right

This famous hotel enjoys magnificent views over to Arran, Ailsa Craig and the Mull of Kintyre. Facilities include a world-renowned golf course, the excellent Colin Montgomerie Golf Academy, a luxurious spa and a host of outdoor and country pursuits. Elegant bedrooms and suites are located in the main hotel, while adjacent lodges provide spacious, well-equipped accommodation. The Ailsa lounge is very welcoming, and in addition to the elegant main restaurant for dining, there is a Mediterranean Terrace Brasserie and the relaxed Clubhouse.

Rooms 131 en suite 89 annexe en suite (9 fmly) (16 GF) ⊘ in 219 bedrooms S fr £340; D fr £395 (incl. bkfst) **Facilities** Spa STV 🏊 supervised ⛳36 ⚓ Fishing Riding Snooker Sauna Gym Putt green Jacuzzi Wi-fi available Leisure Club, Outdoor activity centre, Colin Montgomerie Golf Academy ♫ Xmas **Conf** BC Thtr 300 Class 145 Board 80 Del from £195 **Services** Lift **Parking** 200 **Notes** LB ⊘ in restaurant Closed 12-27 Dec Civ Wed 220

★★★ 81% ◉ HOTEL

Malin Court

KA26 9PB

☎ 01655 331457 🗎 01655 331072

e-mail: info@malincourt.co.uk

web: www.malincourt.co.uk

dir: on A74 to Ayr then A719 to Turnberry & Maidens

Forming part of the Malin Court Residential and Nursing Home Complex, this friendly and comfortable hotel enjoys delightful views over the Firth of Clyde and Turnberry golf courses. Standard and executive rooms are available; all are well equipped. Public areas are plentiful, with the restaurant serving high teas, dinners and light lunches.

Rooms 18 en suite (9 fmly) ⊘ in 9 bedrooms S £72-£82; D £104-£124 (incl. bkfst) **Facilities** STV ⌣ Putt green Xmas **Conf** Thtr 200 Class 60 Board 30 Del from £65.50 **Services** Lift **Parking** 110 **Notes LB** ⊗ ⊘ in restaurant RS Oct-Mar Civ Wed 80

SOUTH LANARKSHIRE

ABINGTON MOTORWAY SERVICE AREA (M74)   MAP 21 NS92

BUDGET HOTEL

Days Inn Abington

ML12 6RG

☎ 01864 502782 🗎 01864 502759

e-mail: abington.hotel@welcomebreak.co.uk

web: www.welcomebreak.co.uk

dir: M74 junct 13, accessible from N'bound and S'bound carriageways

This modern building offers accommodation in smart, spacious and well-equipped bedrooms, suitable for families and business travellers, and all with en suite bathrooms. Continental breakfast is available and other refreshments may be taken at the nearby family restaurant. For further details see the Hotel Groups page.

Rooms 52 en suite **Conf** Board 10

BIGGAR   MAP 21 NT03

★★★ 80% ◉◉ COUNTRY HOUSE HOTEL

Shieldhill Castle

Quothquan ML12 6NA

☎ 01899 220035 🗎 01899 221092

e-mail: enquiries@shieldhill.co.uk

web: www.shieldhill.co.uk

dir: A702 onto B7016 (Biggar to Carnwath road), after 2m left into Shieldhill Rd. Hotel 1.5m on right

Shieldhill Castle

Food and wine are an important focus at this imposing fortified country mansion dating back almost 800 years. Public room are atmospheric and include the classical Chancellor's restaurant, oak-panelled lounge and the Gun Room bar that offers its own menu. Bedrooms, many with feature baths, are spacious and comfortable. A friendly welcome is assured, even from the estate's dog!

Rooms 16 en suite ⊘ in all bedrooms S £85-£248; D £100-£248 (incl. bkfst) **Facilities** ⦿ Jacuzzi Cycling Clay shoot Hot air balooning Falconry Laser & game bird shooting Xmas **Conf** Thtr 500 Class 200 Board 250 **Parking** 50 **Notes LB** ⊘ in restaurant Civ Wed 200

Ⓐ

Swallow Tinto

 SWALLOW HOTELS

Symington ML12 6FT

☎ 01899 308454 🗎 01899 308520

web: www.swallowhotels.com

dir: SW on A72

Rooms 37 en suite **Notes** ★★★

BOTHWELL   MAP 20 NS75

★★★ 74% HOTEL

Bothwell Bridge

89 Main St G71 8EU

☎ 01698 852246 🗎 01698 854686

e-mail: enquiries@bothwellbridge-hotel.com

web: www.bothwellbridge-hotel.com

dir: M74 junct 5 & follow signs to Uddingston, right at mini-rdbt. Hotel just past shops on left

This red-sandstone mansion house is a popular business, function and conference hotel conveniently placed for the motorway. Most bedrooms are spacious and all are well equipped. The conservatory is a bright and comfortable restaurant serving Italian dishes. The lounge bar offers a comfortable seating area.

Rooms 90 en suite (14 fmly) (26 GF) ⊘ in 53 bedrooms **Facilities** STV ♫ **Conf** BC Thtr 200 Class 80 Board 50 **Services** Lift **Parking** 125 **Notes LB** ⊗ Civ Wed 180

Scotland

Scotland

EAST KILBRIDE · MAP 20 NS65

★★★★ 74% ⊛ **HOTEL**

Macdonald Crutherland House · MACDONALD HOTELS & RESORTS

Strathaven Rd G75 0QZ
☎ 0870 1942109 🖹 01355 220855
e-mail: crutherland@macdonald-hotels.co.uk
web: www.macdonald-hotels.co.uk

dir: Follow A726 signed Strathaven, straight over Torrance rdbt, hotel on left after 250yds

Extensively renovated, this mansion is set in 37 acres of landscaped grounds two miles from the town centre. Behind its Georgian façade is a very relaxing hotel with elegant public areas plus extensive banqueting and leisure facilities. The bedrooms are spacious and comfortable. Staff provide good levels of attention and enjoyable meals are served in the restaurant.

Rooms 75 en suite (16 fmly) (16 GF) ⊛ in all bedrooms S £75-£145; D £110-£205 **Facilities** STV 🏊 Sauna Solarium Gym Wi-fi in bedrooms Xmas **Conf** Thtr 500 Class 100 Board 50 Del from £125 **Services** Lift **Parking** 200 **Notes** ⊗ ⊛ in restaurant Civ Wed 300

BUDGET HOTEL

Premier Travel Inn Glasgow East Kilbride · premier travel inn

Brunel Way, The Murray G75 0LD
☎ 08701 977110 🖹 01355 230517
web: www.premiertravelinn.com

dir: M74 junct 5, follow signs for East Kilbride A725, then signs Paisley A726, turn left at Murray rdbt and left into Brunel Way

High quality, modern budget accommodation ideal for both families and business travellers. Spacious, en suite bedrooms feature bath and shower, satellite TV and many have telephones and modem points. The adjacent family restaurant features a wide and varied menu. For further details consult the Hotel Groups page.

Rooms 40 en suite

Premier Travel Inn Glasgow East Kilbride West

Eaglesham Rd G75 8LW
☎ 0870 9906542 🖹 0870 9906543
dir: 8m from M74 junct 5 on A726 at rdbt of B764
Rooms 40 en suite

HAMILTON MOTORWAY SERVICE AREA (M74) · MAP 20 NS75

BUDGET HOTEL

Premier Travel Inn Glasgow (Hamilton) · premier travel inn

Hamilton Motorway Service Area ML3 6JW
☎ 08701 977124 🖹 01698 891682
web: www.premiertravelinn.com

dir: M74 northbound, 1m N of junct 6. For southbound access exit junct 6 onto A723, double back at rdbt & join M74 Glasgow exit

High quality, modern budget accommodation ideal for both families and business travellers. Spacious, en suite bedrooms feature bath and

continued

shower, satellite TV and many have telephones and modem points. The adjacent family restaurant features a wide and varied menu. For further details consult the Hotel Groups page.

Rooms 36 en suite **Conf** Thtr 30 Board 20

LANARK · MAP 21 NS84
See also Biggar

★★★ 73% **HOTEL**

Cartland Bridge

Glasgow Rd ML11 9UF
☎ 01555 664426 🖹 01555 663773
e-mail: sales@cartlandbridge.co.uk

dir: follow A73 through Lanark towards Carluke. Hotel in 1.25m

Nestling in wooded grounds on the edge of the town, this Grade I listed mansion continues to be popular with both business and leisure guests. Public areas feature wood panelling, a gallery staircase and a magnificent dining room. Well-equipped bedrooms vary in size and are being refurbished.

Rooms 20 rms (18 en suite) (2 fmly) ⊛ in 9 bedrooms S £55-£75; D £69-£109 (incl. bkfst) **Facilities** STV Wi-fi in bedrooms Xmas **Conf** Thtr 250 Class 180 Board 30 Del from £129 **Parking** 120 **Notes** ⊗ ⊛ in restaurant Civ Wed 200

NEW LANARK · MAP 21 NS84

★★★ 80% **HOTEL**

New Lanark Mill Hotel

Mill One, New Lanark Mills ML11 9DB
☎ 01555 667200 🖹 01555 667222
e-mail: hotel@newlanark.org
web: www.newlanark.org

dir: signed from all major roads, M74 junct 7 & M8

Originally built as a cotton mill in the 18th-century, this hotel forms part of a fully restored village, now a World Heritage Site. There's a bright modern style throughout which contrasts nicely with features from the original mill. There is a comfortable foyer-lounge with a galleried restaurant above. The hotel enjoys stunning views.

Rooms 38 en suite (2 fmly) ⊛ in 28 bedrooms S £69.50-£94.50; D £109-£134 (incl. bkfst) **Facilities** Fishing about 1m away Xmas **Conf** Thtr 200 Class 60 Board 40 Del from £115 **Services** Lift **Parking** 75 **Notes** LB ⊛ in restaurant Civ Wed 110

ROSEBANK · MAP 21 NS84

★★★ 79% **HOTEL**

Best Western Popinjay Hotel & Leisure Club · Best Western

Lanark Rd ML8 5QB
☎ 01555 860441 🖹 01555 860204
e-mail: popinjayhotel@attglobal.net
web: www.popinjayhotel.co.uk

dir: on A72 between Hamilton & Lanark

This attractive Tudor-style hotel is set in landscaped grounds leading down to the River Clyde. There is a comfortable oak-panelled bar and a light and airy restaurant; meals are served in both areas. Well-

continued

equipped bedrooms come in a variety of sizes, whilst the function suites ensure the hotel's popularity for weddings and conferences.

Rooms 34 en suite (4 fmly) (2 GF) ⊘ in 19 bedrooms S £62.50; D £80-£170 (incl. bkfst) **Facilities Spa** STV ₹ Fishing Snooker Solarium Gym Jacuzzi Wi-fi in bedrooms **Conf** Thtr 250 Class 120 Board 60 Del from £95 **Parking** 300 **Notes LB** ⊘ in restaurant Civ Wed 200

See advert on this page

STRATHAVEN   MAP 20 NS74

★★★ 79% **HOTEL**

Best Western Strathaven

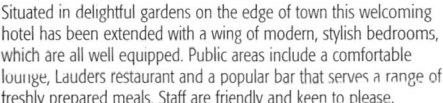

Hamilton Rd ML10 6SZ
☎ 01357 521778 🖶 01357 520789
e-mail: info@strathavenhotel.com
web: www.strathavenhotel.com

Situated in delightful gardens on the edge of town this welcoming hotel has been extended with a wing of modern, stylish bedrooms, which are all well equipped. Public areas include a comfortable lounge, Lauders restaurant and a popular bar that serves a range of freshly prepared meals. Staff are friendly and keen to please.

Rooms 22 en suite ⊘ in 12 bedrooms S £59-£80; D £85-£120 (incl. bkfst) **Facilities** STV Wi-fi in bedrooms **Conf** Thtr 180 Class 120 Board 40 Del from £80 **Parking** 80 **Notes LB** ⊗ ⊘ in restaurant Closed 1 Jan Civ Wed 120

ABERFOYLE   MAP 20 NN50

★★★★ 75% **HOTEL**

Macdonald Forest Hills Hotel & Resort

Kinlochard FK8 3TL
☎ 0870 1942105 🖶 01877 387307
e-mail: forest_hills@macdonald-hotels.co.uk
web: www.macdonald-hotels.co.uk
dir: 3m W on B829

Situated in the heart of The Trossachs with wonderful views of Loch Ard, this popular hotel forms part of a resort complex offering a range

continued on page 870

Scotland

ABERFOYLE *continued*

of indoor and outdoor facilities. The main hotel has relaxing lounges and a restaurant which overlook landscaped gardens. A separate building houses the leisure centre, lounge bar and bistro.

Rooms 54 en suite (16 fmly) (12 GF) ⊗ in 26 bedrooms **Facilities** ⚑ supervised ⌇ Fishing Snooker Sauna Solarium Gym Putt green Jacuzzi Quad biking, Sailing, Canoeing, Abseiling, Archery, Mountain bikes, Guided walks ch fac **Conf** Thtr 150 Class 60 Board 45 **Services** Lift **Parking** 80 **Notes LB** ⊗ ⊗ in restaurant Civ Wed 80

BRIDGE OF ALLAN   MAP 21 NS79

★★★ 75% **HOTEL**

Best Western Royal

Henderson St FK9 4HG
☎ 01786 832284 ▤ 01786 834377
e-mail: stay@royal-stirling.co.uk
web: www.royal-stirling.co.uk

Best Western

dir: *M9 junct 11, turn right at rdbt for Bridge of Allan. Hotel in centre on left*

This impressive Victorian building enjoys a central location in the town yet has quick access to the motorway network. The bedrooms vary in size and offer a good range of amenities; some are located in a smart lodge situated just five minutes from the main hotel. Public areas include an elegant restaurant serving innovative dishes and a bar providing a good range of bar meals.

Rooms 32 en suite (4 fmly) ⊗ in all bedrooms S £70-£110; D £110-£168 (incl. bkfst) **Facilities** STV Xmas **Conf** Thtr 150 Class 60 Board 50 Del from £120 **Services** Lift **Parking** 40 **Notes LB** ⊗ in restaurant Civ Wed 100

CALLANDER   MAP 20 NN60

★★★ 83% ◉◉◉ **HOTEL**

Roman Camp Country House

FK17 8BG
☎ 01877 330003 ▤ 01877 331533
e-mail: mail@romancamphotel.co.uk

dir: *N on A84, left at east end of High Street. 300yds to hotel*

Originally a shooting lodge, this charming country house has a rich history. 20 acres of gardens and grounds lead down to the River Teith, and the town centre and its attractions are only a short walk away. Food is a highlight of any stay and menus are dominated by high-quality Scottish produce that is sympathetically treated by the talented

continued

kitchen team. Real fires warm the atmospheric public areas and service is friendly yet professional.

Roman Camp Country House

Rooms 14 en suite (3 fmly) (7 GF) ⊗ in all bedrooms S £75-£125; D £125-£185 (incl. bkfst) **Facilities** STV Fishing Wi-fi available All ensuite baths are spa baths Xmas **Conf** Thtr 100 Class 40 Board 30 Del from £159 **Parking** 80 **Notes LB** ⊗ in restaurant Civ Wed 100

🅰

Swallow Dreadnought

Station Rd FK17 8AN
☎ 01877 330184 ▤ 01877 330228
web: www.swallowhotels.com
Rooms 63 en suite **Notes** ★★

SWALLOW
HOTELS

DRYMEN   MAP 20 NS48

★★★ 79% **HOTEL**

Buchanan Arms Hotel and Leisure Club

23 Main St G63 0BQ
☎ 01360 660588 ▤ 01360 660943
e-mail: enquiries@buchananarms.co.uk
web: www.innscotland.com

dir: *N from Glasgow on A81 then take A811, hotel at S end of Main Street*

This former coaching inn offers comfortable bedrooms in a variety of styles, with spacious public areas that include an intimate bar, a formal dining room and good function and meeting facilities as well as a fully equipped leisure centre. Teas and light meals can be served in the conservatory lounge which looks over the gardens towards Campsie Fells.

Rooms 52 en suite (3 GF) ⊗ in all bedrooms S £95-£115; D £190 (incl. bkfst & dinner) **Facilities Spa** ⚑ supervised Squash Sauna Solarium Gym Jacuzzi Wi-fi in bedrooms Bowling Green ♫ Xmas **Conf** Thtr 180 Class 140 Board 60 Del from £120 **Parking** 100 **Notes LB** ⊗ in restaurant Civ Wed 100

★★★ 77% **HOTEL**

Best Western Winnock

The Square G63 0BL
☎ 01360 660245 ▤ 01360 660267
e-mail: info@winnockhotel.com

Best Western

dir: *from S follow M74 onto M8 through Glasgow. Exit junct 16b, follow A809 to Aberfoyle*

Occupying a prominent position overlooking the village green, this popular hotel offers well-equipped bedrooms of various sizes and

continued

Scotland

styles. The public rooms include a bar, a lounge and an attractive formal dining room that serves good, locally produced food.

style public rooms include a bar, serving light meals, a wood-panelled dining room and an elegant lounge.

Best Western Winnock

Rooms 48 en suite (12 fmly) (7 GF) ⊗ in 17 bedrooms S £49-£79; D fr £98 (incl. bkfst) **Facilities** STV Wi-fi in bedrooms ♫ Xmas **Conf** Thtr 140 Class 60 Board 70 Del from £69 **Parking** 60 **Notes** LB ⊗ ⊗ in restaurant Civ Wed 100

Culcreuch Castle

Rooms 10 en suite 4 annexe en suite (3 fmly) (4 GF) S £95-£115; D £140-£180 (incl. bkfst) **Facilities** Fishing Xmas **Conf** BC Thtr 140 Class 70 Del from £97.50 **Parking** 100 **Notes** LB ⊗ in restaurant Civ Wed 110

DUNBLANE MAP 21 NN70

★★★ 84% ⊛ HOTEL

Cromlix House

Kinbuck FK15 9JT

☎ 01786 822125 🖷 01786 825450

e-mail: reservations@cromlixhouse.com

dir: off A9 N of Dunblane. Exit B8033 to Kinbuck Village, after village cross narrow bridge, hotel 200yds on left

Situated in sweeping gardens and surrounded by a 2000 acre estate, Cromlix House is an imposing Victorian mansion, boasting gracious and inviting public areas. Well-appointed bedrooms, some of which are suites, are spacious and elegant. The two dining rooms offer contrasting decor but both are ideal for enjoying the skilfully prepared food. Guest care is refreshingly sincere and nothing is too much trouble.

Rooms 14 en suite (8 fmly) ⊗ in 5 bedrooms **Facilities** Fishing ⬥ **Conf** BC Thtr 40 Class 24 Board 24 **Parking** 51 **Notes** LB ⊗ in restaurant Civ Wed 50

FINTRY MAP 20 NS68

★★★ 71% HOTEL

Culcreuch Castle

Kippen Rd G63 0LW

☎ 01360 860555 & 860228 🖷 01360 860556

e-mail: info@culcreuch.com

web: www.culcreuch.com

dir: on B822, 17m W of Stirling. 20m N of Glasgow

Peacefully located in 1600 acres of parkland, this ancient castle dates back to 1296. Tastefully restored accommodation is in a mixture of individually themed castle rooms, some with four-poster beds and more modern courtyard rooms, which are suitable for families. Period

continued

KILLEARN MAP 20 NS58

★★★ 72% SMALL HOTEL

Black Bull

2 The Square G63 9NG

☎ 01360 550215 🖷 01360 550143

e-mail: sales@blackbullhotel.com

web: www.blackbullhotel.com

dir: N from Glasgow on A81, through Blanefield just past Glengoyne Distillery, take A875 to Killearn

This long established village inn is an ideal destination for those travelling on business to Glasgow as well as tourists wishing to enjoy the scenic splendour of the nearby Trossachs. The public areas boast a large public bar, a popular bistro, and an elegant and spacious conservatory restaurant overlooking the attractive gardens. Accommodation is comfortable and well equipped.

Rooms 12 en suite (2 fmly) ⊗ in all bedrooms **Facilities** STV ⬥ ♫ ch fac **Conf** Thtr 80 Class 32 Board 24 **Parking** 100 **Notes** LB ⊗ in restaurant Civ Wed 150

KILLIN MAP 20 NN53

Ⓐ

Swallow Killin

Main St FK21 8TP

☎ 01567 820296 🖷 01567 820647

web: www.swallowhotels.com

Rooms 32 en suite **Parking** 5 **Notes** ★★

SWALLOW HOTELS

STIRLING　　　　　　　MAP 21 NS79

★★★★ 74% HOTEL

Paramount Stirling Highland
Spittal St FK8 1DU
☎ 01786 272727 🖷 01786 272829
e-mail: stirling@paramount-hotels.co.uk
web: www.paramount-hotels.co.uk

dir: take A84 into Stirling. Follow Stirling Castle signs as far as Albert Hall. Left and left again, following Castle signs

Enjoying a location close to the castle and historic old town, this atmospheric hotel was previously the High School. Public rooms have been converted from the original classrooms and retain many interesting features. Bedrooms are more modern in style and comfortably equipped.

Rooms 96 en suite (4 fmly) ⊘ in 67 bedrooms S £89-£138; D £118-£158 (incl. bkfst) **Facilities** STV 🖳 Squash Sauna Solarium Gym Jacuzzi Wi-fi in bedrooms Steam room Dance studio Beauty therapist Xmas **Conf** Thtr 100 Class 80 Board 45 Del from £150 **Services** Lift **Parking** 96 **Notes LB** ⊘ in restaurant Civ Wed 100

BUDGET HOTEL

Premier Travel Inn Stirling
Whins of Milton, Glasgow Rd FK7 8EX
☎ 08701 977241 🖷 01786 816415
web: www.premiertravelinn.com

dir: on A872, 0.25m from M9/M80 junct 9 intersection

High quality, modern budget accommodation ideal for both families and business travellers. Spacious, en suite bedrooms feature bath and shower, satellite TV and many have telephones and modem points. The adjacent family restaurant features a wide and varied menu. For further details consult the Hotel Groups page.

Rooms 60 en suite

BUDGET HOTEL

Travelodge Stirling (M80)
Pirnhall Roundabout, Snabhead FK7 8EU
☎ 08700 850 950 🖷 01786 817646
web: www.travelodge.co.uk

dir: junct 9, M9/M80

Travelodge offers good quality, good value, modern accommodation. Ideal for families, the spacious en suite bedrooms include remote-control TV, tea and coffee-making facilities and comfortable beds. Meals can be taken at the nearby family restaurant. See Hotel Groups pages for further details.

Rooms 37 en suite S fr £26; D fr £26

STRATHYRE　　　　　　MAP 20 NN51

◎◎ RESTAURANT WITH ROOMS

Creagan House
FK18 8ND
☎ 01877 384638 🖷 01877 384319
e-mail: eatndstay@creaganhouse.co.uk
web: www.creaganhouse.co.uk

dir: 0.25m N of Strathyre on A84

Originally a farmhouse dating from the 17th century, this restored little gem has operated as a restaurant with rooms for many years. The baronial-style dining room provides a wonderful setting for sympathetic cooking providing superbly flavoursome dishes. Warm hospitality and attentive service are the highlight of any stay.

Rooms 5 en suite (1 fmly) (1 GF) ⊘ in all bedrooms S £65; D £110 **Conf** Thtr 35 Class 12 Board 35 **Parking** 26 **Notes LB** Closed 21 Jan-9 Mar & 4-23 Nov RS 24 Nov-20 Dec

WEST DUNBARTONSHIRE

BALLOCH　　　　　　　MAP 20 NS38

★★★★★ 81% ◎◎◎ HOTEL

De Vere Cameron House
G83 8QZ
☎ 01389 755565 🖷 01389 759522
e-mail: reservations@cameronhouse.co.uk
web: www.devere.co.uk

dir: M8 (W) junct 30 for Erskine Bridge. Then A82 for Crainlarich. After 14m, at rdbt signed Luss straight on towards Luss, hotel on right

Enjoying an idyllic location on the banks of Loch Lomond, this leisure orientated hotel offers spacious, well-equipped accommodation. Bedrooms vary in size and style and many boast wonderful views of the loch. A choice of restaurants, bars and lounges, a host of indoor and outdoor sporting activities and a smart spa are just some of the facilities available. Dinner in the Georgian Room is a highlight of any stay.

Rooms 96 en suite (9 fmly) ⊘ in all bedrooms S £120-£208; D £150-£248 (incl. bkfst) **Facilities Spa** STV 🖳 ⌣9 🏊 Fishing Squash Snooker Sauna Solarium Gym ⌣ Jacuzzi Wi-fi in bedrooms Range of outdoor sports, Motor boat on Loch Lomond, Hairdresser Xmas **Conf** Thtr 300 Class 80 Board 80 Del from £150 **Services** Lift **Parking** 200 **Notes LB** ⊗ ⊘ in restaurant Civ Wed 200

See advert on opposite page

BUDGET HOTEL

Innkeeper's Lodge Loch Lomond
Balloch Rd G83 8LQ
☎ 01389 752579
web: www.innkeeperslodge.com

dir: M8 junct 30 onto M898. Left at Duntocher rdbt onto A82, right at rdbt (A811), left into Daluart Rd, lodge opposite

Smart, en suite accommodation ideal for both business & leisure guests. Bedrooms are very well equipped, including Sky TV, telephone, modem points, tea & coffee making facilities, (family rooms in most locations). Complimentary breakfast. The adjacent Pub Restaurant; a Harvester, Vintage Inn, Toby Carvery, Ember Inn, Sizzling

continued

Pubco or Pub & Carvery offers an all day menu. See Hotel Groups pages for further details.

Rooms 14 en suite S £62.95; D £62.95

CLYDEBANK MAP 20 NS47

★★★★ 78% ◎ ◎ **HOTEL**

Beardmore

Beardmore St G81 4SA

☎ 0141 951 6000 ▤ 0141 951 6018

e-mail: info@beardmore.scot.nhs.uk

dir: M8 junct 19/A814 towards Dumbarton then follow tourist signs. Turn left onto Beardmore St & follow signs

Attracting much business and conference custom, this stylish modern hotel lies beside the River Clyde and shares an impressive site with a

continued

hospital (although the latter does not intrude). Spacious and imposing public areas include the stylish Arcoona Restaurant providing innovative contemporary cooking. The café bar offers a more extensive choice of informal lighter dishes.

Rooms 166 en suite ⊘ in all bedrooms S fr £99; D fr £99 **Facilities Spa** STV ⬚ supervised Sauna Solarium Gym Wi-fi in bedrooms Complimentary therapies Xmas **Conf** BC Thtr 170 Class 24 Board 26 Del from £120 **Services** Lift air con **Parking** 400 **Notes** ⊗ ⊘ in restaurant Civ Wed 170

DUMBARTON MAP 20 NS37

BUDGET HOTEL

Travelodge Dumbarton

Milton G82 2TZ

☎ 08700 850 950 ▤ 01389 765202

web: www.travelodge.co.uk

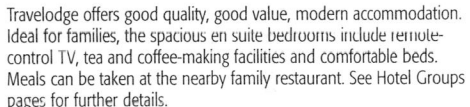

dir: 2m E of Dumbarton, on A82 westbound

Travelodge offers good quality, good value, modern accommodation. Ideal for families, the spacious en suite bedrooms include remote-control TV, tea and coffee-making facilities and comfortable beds. Meals can be taken at the nearby family restaurant. See Hotel Groups pages for further details.

Rooms 32 en suite S fr £26; D fr £26

Cameron House stands on the peaceful southern shores of Loch Lomond looking across its shimmering waters to the majestic hills beyond. Occupying over 100 acres of magnificent woodland, it provides an inspirational setting, yet is conveniently located just 20 minutes from Glasgow Intenational Airport. This exclusive 5 star 96-bedroom resort provides an inspirational setting offering deluxe accommodation, award winning cuisine and superb sporting and leisure facilities. The addition of a world class golf course "The Carrick" and exclusive spa will complete this premier location in early 2007.

Hotels of Character, run with pride
Loch Lomond, Dunbartonshire, G83 8QZ. Tel: 01389 755565 Fax: 01389 759522
Email: reservations@cameronhouse.co.uk Web: www.devere.co.uk

Scotland

WEST LOTHIAN

BATHGATE
MAP 21 NS96

A

Swallow Kaim Park
SWALLOW HOTELS

Edinburgh Rd EH48 1EP
☎ 01506 653399 📠 01506 633358
web: www.swallowhotels.com
Rooms 25 en suite **Notes** ★★★

LIVINGSTON
MAP 21 NT06

A

Ramada Livingston
RAMADA.

Almondview EH54 6QB
☎ 01506 431222 📠 01506 434666
e-mail: sales.livingston@ramadajarvis.co.uk
web: www.ramadajarvis.co.uk

dir: From M8 junct 3 take A899 towards Livingston, leave at
Centre Interchange, left at next rdbt, hotel on left

Rooms 120 en suite (13 fmly) (54 GF) ⊘ in 80 bedrooms S £55-£95;
D £80-£120 **Facilities** STV ⬚ Sauna Gym Steam room Xmas
Conf Thtr 100 Class 55 Board 60 Del from £100 **Parking** 130
Notes ★★★ ⊘ in restaurant

BUDGET HOTEL

Premier Travel Inn Livingston (Nr Edinburgh)

Deer Park Av, Knightsridge EH54 8AD
☎ 08701 977161 📠 01506 438912
web: www.premiertravelinn.com

dir: At M8 junct 3. Follow road to rdbt. Inn opposite

High quality, modern budget accommodation ideal for both families
and business travellers. Spacious, en suite bedrooms feature bath and
shower, satellite TV and many have telephones and modem points.
The adjacent family restaurant features a wide and varied menu. For
further details consult the Hotel Groups page.

Rooms 83 en suite

BUDGET HOTEL

Travelodge Livingston
Travelodge

Almondvale Cresent EH54 6QX
☎ 08700 850 950 📠 0121 521 6026
web: www.travelodge.co.uk

dir: M8 junct 3 onto A899 towards Livingston. At 2nd rdbt turn
right onto A779. At 2nd rdbt turn left. Lodge is on left

Travelodge offers good quality, good value, modern accommodation.
Ideal for families, the spacious en suite bedrooms include remote-
control TV, tea and coffee-making facilities and comfortable beds.
Meals can be taken at the nearby family restaurant. See Hotel Groups
pages for further details.

Rooms 60 en suite S fr £26; D fr £26

UPHALL
MAP 21 NT07

★★★★ 77% ◉ **HOTEL**

Macdonald Houstoun House
MACDONALD HOTELS & RESORTS

EH52 6JS
☎ 0870 1942107 📠 01506 854220
e-mail: houstoun@macdonald-hotels.co.uk
web: www.macdonald-hotels.co.uk

dir: M8 junct 3 follow Broxburn signs, straight over rdbt then at
mini-rdbt turn right towards Uphall, hotel 1m on right

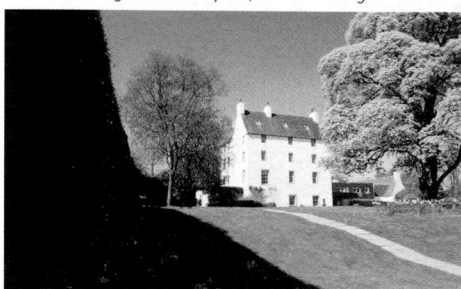

This historic 17th-century tower house lies in beautifully landscaped
grounds and gardens and features a modern leisure club and spa, a
choice of dining options, a vaulted cocktail bar and extensive
conference and meeting facilities. Stylish bedrooms, some located
around a courtyard, are comfortably furnished and well equipped.

Rooms 24 en suite 47 annexe en suite (10 GF) ⊘ in all bedrooms S fr £85;
D fr £85 **Facilities Spa** STV ⬚ ⬚ Sauna Solarium Gym Wi-fi in
bedrooms Health and beauty salon Xmas **Conf** Thtr 400 Class 80 Board 80
Del from £135 **Parking** 250 **Notes LB** ⊗ ⊘ in restaurant Civ Wed 200

WHITBURN
MAP 21 NS96

★★★ 77% **HOTEL**

Best Western Hilcroft
Best Western

East Main St EH47 0JU
☎ 01501 740818 📠 01501 744013
e-mail: hilcroft@bestwestern.co.uk

dir: M8 junct 4 follow signs for Whitburn, hotel 0.5m on left

This purpose-built, well-established hotel is popular with business
travellers and easily accessible from all major transport routes. Smart
contemporary public areas feature a spacious and inviting lounge bar
and restaurant. Well-equipped bedrooms come in a variety of sizes.

Rooms 32 en suite (7 fmly) (5 GF) ⊘ in 23 bedrooms S £80-£95; D £95
(incl. bkfst) **Facilities** STV Wi-fi in bedrooms Xmas **Conf** Thtr 200
Class 50 Board 30 Del £95 **Parking** 80 **Notes LB** ⊗ ⊘ in restaurant
Civ Wed 180

SCOTTISH ISLANDS

Isle of Arran

BLACKWATERFOOT
MAP 20 NR92

★★★ 77% **HOTEL**

Best Western Kinloch
KA27 8ET

☎ 01770 860444 🖷 01770 860447

e-mail: reservations@kinlochhotel.eclipse.co.uk

dir: Ferry from Ardrossan to Brodick, follow signs for Blackwaterfoot, hotel in centre of village

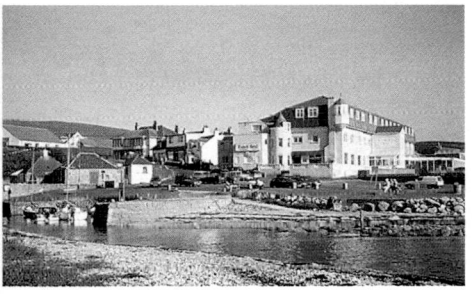

Well known for providing an authentic island experience, this long established stylish hotel offers an idyllic venue for exploring the beauty of Arran. Smart public areas include a choice of lounges, popular bars and well-presented leisure facilities. Bedrooms vary in size and style but most enjoy panoramic seaviews and several family suites offer excellent value. The spacious restaurant provides a wealth of choice though it closes during winter; however a creative menu is offered in the comfortable bar.

Rooms 43 en suite (7 fmly) (7 GF) ⊘ in all bedrooms S £45-£110; D £60-£110 (incl. bkfst) **Facilities** STV ⅜ Squash Snooker Sauna Gym Beauty therapy ♫ Xmas **Conf** Thtr 120 Class 20 Board 40 Del from £75 **Services** Lift **Parking** 2 **Notes LB** ⊘ in restaurant Civ Wed 60

BRODICK
MAP 20 NS03

★★★★ 79% ◉◉ **HOTEL**

Auchrannie House
KA27 8BZ

☎ 01770 302234 🖷 01770 302812

e-mail: info@auchrannie.co.uk

dir: right from Brodick Ferry terminal, through Brodick, 2nd left after Brodick Golf Course clubhouse, hotel 300yds

This Victorian mansion lies in landscaped grounds and provides well-equipped bedrooms. Guests can dine in the Garden Restaurant, the bistro, or in the brasserie which is situated in the extensive spa centre, which also offers excellent family accommodation. Residents have their own leisure facilities.

Rooms 28 en suite (3 fmly) (4 GF) ⊘ in all bedrooms S £49.50-£124.50; D £99-£189 (incl. bkfst) **Facilities Spa** STV ⅜ supervised ⌀ Snooker Sauna Solarium Gym Hair & Beauty salons, Aromatherapy, Shiatsu, Hockey, Badminton ch fac Xmas **Conf** BC Thtr 120 Class 80 Board 50 **Parking** 50 **Notes LB** ⊛ ⊘ in restaurant Civ Wed 120

★★★ ◉◉ **HOTEL**

Kilmichael Country House
Glen Cloy KA27 8BY

☎ 01770 302219 🖷 01770 302068

e-mail: enquiries@kilmichael.com

web: www.kilmichael.com

dir: from Brodick ferry terminal follow Lochranza road for 1m. Left at golf course, inland between sports field & church, follow signs

Reputed to be the oldest on the island, this lovely house lies in attractive gardens in a quiet glen less than five minutes' drive from the ferry terminal. It has been lovingly restored to create a stylish, elegant country house, adorned with ornaments from around the world. There are two inviting drawing rooms and a bright dining room, serving award-winning contemporary cuisine. The delightful bedrooms are furnished in classical style; some are contained in a pretty courtyard conversion.

Rooms 4 en suite 3 annexe en suite (6 GF) ⊘ in all bedrooms S £95; D £120-£190 (incl. bkfst) **Facilities** STV Jacuzzi **Parking** 12 **Notes LB** No children 12yrs ⊘ in restaurant Closed Nov-Feb (ex for prior bookings)

Isle of Barra

TANGUSDALE
MAP 22 NF60

★★ 69% **HOTEL**

Isle of Barra
Tangasdale Beach HS9 5XW

☎ 01871 810383 🖷 01871 810385

e-mail: barrahotel@aol.com

dir: left from ferry terminal onto A888, hotel 2m on left

It may well take the better part of a day to reach the most westerly hotel in Britain, but few journeys could be better rewarded. Overlooking the white sands of Halaman Bay and the crystal clear shallows of the Atlantic, the hotel's situation is quite breathtaking. It is comfortably furnished and most of the bedrooms enjoy the stunning views. At dinner guests can experience the finest shellfish in British waters. Staff provide warm hospitality and have a wealth of knowledge about the island.

Rooms 30 en suite (2 fmly) (7 GF) ⊘ in 26 bedrooms S £52; D £90 (incl. bkfst) **Facilities** STV Beach **Conf** BC Thtr 70 Class 70 Board 60 Del from £60 **Parking** 50 **Notes LB** ⊘ in restaurant Closed Oct-Etr

Scotland

Isle of Harris

SCARISTA
MAP 22 NG09

◉ ◉ **RESTAURANT WITH ROOMS**

Scarista House
HS3 3HX
☎ 01859 550238 ▤ 01859 550277
e-mail: timandpatricia@scaristahouse.com
dir: On A859, 15m S of Tarbert

A former manse, this establishment is now a haven for food lovers who seek to explore the magnificent Island of Harris. The house enjoys breathtaking views of the Atlantic and is just a short stroll from miles of golden sandy beaches. The house is run in a relaxed country-house manner by the friendly hosts. Expect wellies in the hall and masses of books and CDs in one of two lounges. Bedrooms are cosy, and delicious set dinners and memorable breakfasts are provided.

Rooms 3 en suite 2 annexe en suite (2 GF) ⊗ in all bedrooms S £120-£140; D £165-£190 **Parking** 12 **Notes LB** Closed Xmas RS Nov-Mar Civ Wed 40

Isle of Islay

PORT ASKAIG
MAP 20 NR46

★★ 64% **HOTEL**

Port Askaig
PA46 7RD
☎ 01496 840245 ▤ 01496 840295
e-mail: hotel@portaskaig.co.uk
web: www.portaskaig.co.uk
dir: at Ferry Terminal

This endearing family-run hotel, set in an 18th-century building, offers comfortable bedrooms. The lounge provides fine views over the Sound of Islay to the island of Jura, and there is a choice of bars that are popular with locals. Traditional dinners are served in the bright restaurant and a full range of bar snacks and meals is also available.

Rooms 8 rms (6 en suite) (1 fmly) **Parking** 21 **Notes** No children 5yrs ⊗ in restaurant

Isle of Mull

CRAIGNURE
MAP 20 NM73

★★★ 71% **HOTEL**

Isle of Mull Hotel
PA65 6BB
☎ 0870 950 6267 ▤ 01680 812462
e-mail: isleofmull@british-trust-hotels.com
web: www.crerarhotels.com

CRERAR
HOTELS

dir: ferry from Oban. Turn right onto main road. In 0.5m turn right at hotel sign

Just half a mile from the ferry terminal, this spacious hotel looks out over the tranquil Craignure Bay and has gardens stretching down to the shore. There are comfortable panoramic lounges and two bars, including Muileach Bar with a vast choice of malt whiskies. The bedrooms have bay views and include satellite TVs. New for 2007 - a 17-metre swimming pool with spa rooms.

Rooms 85 en suite (6 fmly) ⊗ in all bedrooms S £75-£110; D £140-£200 (incl. bkfst) **Facilities Spa** STV ⧉ FTV Solarium ♫ Xmas **Conf** Thtr 150 Class 85 Board 60 Del from £90 **Parking** 36 **Notes LB** ⊗ ⊗ in restaurant

TOBERMORY
MAP 22 NM55

INSPECTORS' CHOICE

★★★ ◉ ◉ **SMALL HOTEL**

Highland Cottage
Breadalbane St PA75 6PD
☎ 01688 302030
e-mail: davidandjo@highlandcottage.co.uk
web: www.highlandcottage.co.uk
dir: A848 Craignure/Fishnish ferry terminal, pass Tobermory signs, straight on at mini-rdbt across narrow bridge, turn right. Hotel on right opposite fire station

Providing the highest level of natural, unassuming hospitality, this delightful little gem lies high above the island's capital. Don't be fooled by its side street location, a stunning view over the bay is just a few meters away. A 'country house hotel in town' it is an Aladdin's cave of collectibles and treasures, as well as masses of books and magazines. There are two inviting lounges, one with
continued

an honesty bar. The cosy dining room offers memorable dinners and splendid breakfasts. Bedrooms are individual; some have four-posters and all are comprehensively equipped and include video TVs and music centres.

Highland Cottage

Rooms 6 en suite (1 GF) ⊗ in all bedrooms S fr £100; D £130-£165 (incl. bkfst) **Facilities** STV FTV Wi-fi available ch fac **Parking** 6 **Notes LB** No children 10yrs ⊗ in restaurant RS Nov-Feb

★★★ 73% HOTEL

Western Isles

PA75 6PR
☎ 01688 302012 🖹 01688 302297
e-mail: wihotel@aol.com

dir: from ferry follow signs to Tobermory. Over 1st mini-rdbt in Tobermory then over small bridge and immediate right & follow road to T-junct. Right again then keep left and take 1st left for hotel at top of hill on right

Please note that this establishment has recently changed hands. Built in 1883 and standing high above the village, this hotel enjoys spectacular views over Tobermory harbour and the Sound of Mull. Public rooms range from the classical drawing room and restaurant to the bright modern conservatory bar/bistro. Bedrooms come in a variety of styles; the impressive superior rooms include a suite complete with its own piano.

Rooms 28 en suite **Conf** Thtr 35 Class 20 Board 20 **Parking** 28 **Notes LB** ⊗ in restaurant Closed 17-27 Dec Civ Wed 70

★★ 74% ⊛ HOTEL

Tobermory

53 Main St PA75 6NT
☎ 01688 302091 🖹 01688 302254
e-mail: tobhotel@tinyworld.co.uk
web: www.thetobermoryhotel.com

dir: on waterfront, overlooking Tobermory Bay

This friendly hotel, with its pretty pink frontage, sits on the seafront amid other brightly coloured, picture-postcard buildings. There is a comfortable and relaxing lounge where drinks are served (there is no bar) prior to dining in the stylish restaurant. Bedrooms come in a variety of sizes; all are bright and vibrant with the superior rooms having video TVs.

Rooms 16 rms (15 en suite) (3 fmly) (2 GF) ⊗ in all bedrooms S £38-£57; D £76-£114 (incl. bkfst) **Facilities** Xmas **Notes LB** ⊗ in restaurant Closed Xmas

Shetland

LERWICK   **MAP 24 HU44**

★★★ 73% HOTEL

Lerwick

15 South Rd ZE1 0RB
☎ 01595 692166 🖹 01595 694419
e-mail: reception@lerwickhotel.co.uk
web: www.shetlandhotels.com

dir: near town centre. On main road from airport. (25m)

Enjoying fine views across Breiwick Bay from the restaurant and some of the bedrooms, this purpose-built hotel appeals to tourists and business guests alike. Bedrooms, which vary in size and aspect, are attractively furnished and family accommodation is available. The Breiwick restaurant has fine sea views, and there is also a more informal brasserie.

Rooms 34 en suite (3 fmly) S £79.95; D £98 (incl. bkfst) **Facilities** STV Wi-fi in bedrooms **Conf** BC Thtr 100 Class 40 Board 26 **Parking** 50 **Notes LB** ⊗ Civ Wed 100

★★★ 71% HOTEL

Shetland

Holmsgarth Rd ZE1 0PW
☎ 01595 695515 🖹 01595 695828
e-mail: reception@shetlandhotel.co.uk

dir: opposite ferry terminal, on main route N from town centre

This purpose-built hotel, situated opposite the main ferry terminal, offers spacious and comfortable bedrooms on three floors. Two dining options are available, including the informal Oasis bistro and Ninians Restaurant. Service is prompt and friendly.

Rooms 64 en suite (4 fmly) ⊗ in 14 bedrooms S £79; D £97.50 (incl. bkfst) **Facilities** STV Wi-fi in bedrooms **Conf** Thtr 300 Class 75 Board 50 Del from £128.95 **Services** Lift **Parking** 150 **Notes LB** ⊗ ⊗ in restaurant Civ Wed 200

Scotland

Isle of Skye

ARDVASAR
MAP 22 NG60

★★ 70% **HOTEL**

Ardvasar Hotel
Sleat IV45 8RS
☎ 01471 844223 📠 01471 844495
e-mail: richard@ardvasar-hotel.demon.co.uk
web: www.ardvasarhotel.com
dir: from ferry, 500mtrs & turn left

The Isle of Skye is dotted with cosy, welcoming hotels that make touring the island easy and convenient. This hotel ranks highly amongst its peers thanks to great hospitality and a preservation of community spirit. The hotel sits less than five minutes' drive from the Mallaig ferry and provides comfortable bedrooms and a cosy bar lounge for residents. Seafood is prominent on menus, and meals can be enjoyed in either the popular bar or the attractive dining room.

Rooms 10 en suite (4 fmly) ⊘ in all bedrooms S £65-£95; D £80-£110 (incl. bkfst) **Facilities** ♪ Xmas **Conf** Thtr 50 Board 24 **Parking** 30 **Notes LB** ⊘ in restaurant

See advert on opposite page

BROADFORD
MAP 22 NG62

A

Swallow Dunollie
IV49 9AE
SWALLOW ✔
☎ 01471 822253 📠 01471 822060
web: www.swallowhotels.com
Rooms 80 en suite **Notes** ★★★

U

Broadford
IV49 9AB
☎ 01471 822204 📠 01471 822414
dir: Cross over bridge to Skye and take A87 towards Portree. Hotel at end of village on left.

At the time of going to press, the star classification for this hotel was not confirmed. Please refer to the AA internet site www.theAA.com for current information.

continued

Rooms 17 en suite S £30-£50; D £56-£90 (incl. bkfst) **Facilities** Fishing Xmas **Conf** BC Thtr 150 Class 80 Board 50 **Parking** 20 **Notes LB** ⊘ in restaurant Civ Wed

COLBOST
MAP 22 NG24

◎ ◎ ◎ **RESTAURANT WITH ROOMS**

The Three Chimneys & The House Over-By
IV55 8ZT
☎ 01470 511258 📠 01470 511358
e-mail: eatandstay@threechimneys.co.uk
web: www.threechimneys.co.uk
dir: 4m W of Dunvegan village on B884 signed Glendale

A visit to this delightful property and restaurant will make a trip to Skye memorable. Shirley Spear's stunning food is the result a deft approach using quality local ingredients. Breakfast is an impressive array of local fish, meats and cheeses, served with fresh home baking and home-made preserves. The stylish, thoughtfully equipped bedrooms in the House Over-By have spacious en suites and wonderful views across Loch Dunvegan.

Rooms 6 en suite (1 fmly) ⊘ in all bedrooms D £250 **Facilities** STV **Notes** ⊗

Scotland

ISLEORNSAY — MAP 22 NG71

★★ 80% ◉◉ **HOTEL**

Hotel Eilean Iarmain

IV43 8QR ☎ 01471 833332 🖶 01471 833275

THE CIRCLE
Selected Individual Hotels
GREAT BRITAIN

e-mail: hotel@eileaniarmain.co.uk
web: www.eileaniarmain.co.uk
dir: A851, A852, right to Isle Ornsay Harbour front

A hotel of charm and character, this 19th-century former inn lies by the pier and enjoys fine views across the sea lochs. Bedrooms are individual and retain a traditional style, and a stable block has been converted into four delightful suites. Public rooms are cosy and inviting, and the dining room has an attractive extension.

Rooms 6 en suite 10 annexe en suite (6 fmly) (4 GF) ⊘ in all bedrooms S £45-£95; D £90-£150 (incl. bkfst) **Facilities** Fishing Shooting Exhibitions Whisky tasting ♫ Xmas **Conf** Thtr 50 Class 30 Board 25 **Parking** 35
Notes LB ⊘ in restaurant Civ Wed 27 *See advert on this page*

Scotland

ISLEORNSAY continued

★★ 78% ⊚ **HOTEL**

Toravaig House Hotel
Knock Bay IV44 8RE
☎ 01471 820200 & 833231 📠 01471 833231
e-mail: info@skyehotel.co.uk

dir: cross Skye Bridge, turn left at Broadford onto A851, hotel 11m on left. Ferry to Armadale, take A851, hotel 4m on right

Set in two acres and enjoying panoramic views to the Knoydart Hills, this hotel is a haven of peace. The bedrooms are stylish, well-equipped and beautifully decorated. There is an inviting lounge complete with deep sofas and an elegant dining room where delicious meals are the order of the day.

Rooms 9 en suite ⊘ in all bedrooms S £65-£85; D £130-£150 (incl. bkfst) **Facilities** STV Daily excursions for residents on hotel yacht Xmas **Parking** 20 **Notes LB** ⊗ ⊘ in restaurant

See advert on this page

KYLEAKIN
MAP 22 NG72

A

Swallow Kings Arms
SWALLOW HOTELS

Kyleakin IV41 8PH
☎ 01599 534109 📠 01599 534190
web: www.swallowhotels.com
Rooms 81 en suite **Notes** ★★

PORTREE
MAP 22 NG44

★★★ 81% ⊚⊚ **HOTEL**

Cuillin Hills
IV51 9QU
☎ 01478 612003 📠 01478 613092
e-mail: info@cuillinhills-hotel-skye.co.uk
web: www.cuillinhills-hotel-skye.co.uk

dir: turn right 0.25m N of Portree off A855. Follow hotel signs

This imposing building enjoys a superb location overlooking Portree Bay and the Cuillin Hills. Accommodation is provided in smart, well-equipped rooms that are generally spacious. Some bedrooms are found in an adjacent building. Public areas include a restaurant with fine views. Service is particularly attentive.

Rooms 20 en suite 7 annexe en suite (4 fmly) (8 GF) ⊘ in all bedrooms S £60-£80; D £120-£250 (incl. bkfst) **Facilities** STV Xmas **Conf** Thtr 160 Class 70 Board 40 **Parking** 56 **Notes LB** ⊗ ⊘ in restaurant Civ Wed 70

See advert on opposite page

★★★ 78% ⊚⊚ **HOTEL**

Bosville
Bosville Ter IV51 9DG
☎ 01478 612846 📠 01478 613434
e-mail: bosville@macleodhotels.co.uk
web: www.macleodhotels.com

dir: A87 signed Portree, then A855 into town

This stylish, popular hotel enjoys fine views over the harbour. Bedrooms are furnished to a high specification and have a fresh, contemporary feel. Public areas include a smart bar, bistro and the Chandlery restaurant where fantastic local produce is treated with respect and refreshing restraint.

Rooms 19 en suite (2 fmly) ⊘ in all bedrooms S £59-£135; D £78-£250 (incl. bkfst) **Facilities** FTV Wi-fi in bedrooms Use of nearby leisure club payable ch fac Xmas **Conf** Thtr 20 Class 20 Board 20 **Parking** 10 **Notes LB** ⊘ in restaurant Civ Wed 80

See advert on opposite page

Scotland

Scotland

PORTREE *continued*

★★ 75% ◉ **HOTEL**

Rosedale
Beaumont Crescent IV51 9DB
☎ 01478 613131 ▤ 01478 612531
e-mail: rosedalehotelsky@aol.com
web: www.rosedalehotelskye.co.uk
dir: *follow directions to village centre & harbour*

The atmosphere is wonderfully warm at this delightful family-run waterfront hotel. A labyrinth of stairs and corridors connects the comfortable lounges, bar and charming restaurant, which are set on different levels. The restaurant offers fine views of the bay. Modern bedrooms offer a good range of amenities.

Rooms 18 en suite (1 fmly) (3 GF) ◈ in all bedrooms S £30-£130; D £60-£130 **Parking** 2 **Notes LB** ◈ in restaurant Closed Nov-mid Mar

SKEABOST BRIDGE   MAP 22 NG44

A

Swallow Skeabost House
IV51 9NP
☎ 01470 532202 ▤ 01470 532454
web: www.swallowhotels.com
dir: *on A87 north of Portree, left onto A850. Hotel 1.5m on right, just beyond Snizort river bridge*
Rooms 20 en suite **Notes** ★★★

STRUAN   MAP 22 NG3

★★ 85% ◉◉ **HOTEL**

Ullinish Country Lodge
IV56 8FD
☎ 01470 572214 ▤ 01470 572341
e-mail: ullinish@theisleofskye.co.uk
web: www.theisleofskye.co.uk
dir: *N on A863*

Ullinish Country Lodge, which has been sympathetically and tastefully refurbished, enjoys breathtaking views of the Black Cuillins and MacLeods Tables. Set at the end of a narrow lane and surrounded by lochs on three sides, this historic building offers a haven of peace. Bedrooms are attractively furnished and there is a welcoming lounge with log fires. Carefully prepared evening meals combine good quality local produce with a sense of fun.

Rooms 6 en suite ◈ in all bedrooms S £90-£120; D £120-£160 (incl. bkfst) **Facilities** Xmas **Parking** 8 **Notes LB** ⊗ No children 16yrs ◈ in restaurant Closed 4-31 Jan

How do I find the perfect place?

Discover new horizons with
Britain's largest travel publisher **AA**

Wales

Tenby Seafront,
Pembrokeshire

ANGLESEY, ISLE OF

AMLWCH
MAP 14 SH49

★★ 76% **HOTEL**

Lastra Farm
Penrhyd LL68 9TF
☎ 01407 830906 ▤ 01407 832522
e-mail: booking@lastra-hotel.com
web: www.lastra-hotel.com

dir: *after 'Welcome to Amlwch' sign turn left. Straight across main road, left at T-junct on to Rhosgoch Rd*

This 17th-century farmhouse offers pine-furnished, colourfully decorated bedrooms. There is also a comfortable lounge and a cosy bar. A wide range of good-value food is available either in the restaurant or Granary's Bistro. The hotel can cater for functions in a separate, purpose built suite.

Rooms 5 en suite 3 annexe en suite (1 fmly) (3 GF) ⊛ in all bedrooms S £45-£49.50; D £65-£73 (incl. bkfst) **Conf** Thtr 100 Class 80 Board 30 **Parking** 40 **Notes LB** ⊛ in restaurant Civ Wed 100

BEAUMARIS
MAP 14 SH67

★★★ 74% **HOTEL**

Best Western Bulkeley Hotel
Castle St LL58 8AW
☎ 01248 810415 ▤ 01248 810146
e-mail: bulkeley@bestwestern.co.uk

dir: *from M56 & M6 take A5 or A55 coast road*

A Grade I listed hotel built in 1831, the Bulkeley has fine views from many rooms. Well-equipped bedrooms are generally spacious, with pretty fabrics and wallpapers. There is a choice of bars, an all-day coffee lounge and a health club. Regular jazz evenings, a resident pianist and friendly staff create a relaxed atmosphere.

Rooms 43 en suite (6 fmly) ⊛ in 10 bedrooms **Facilities Spa** Sauna Solarium Gym Jacuzzi Hair & Beauty Salon **Conf** Thtr 180 Class 120 Board 36 **Services** Lift **Parking** 30 **Notes LB** ⊛ in restaurant Civ Wed 140

★★ 83% ◉◉ **HOTEL**

Ye Olde Bulls Head Inn
Castle St LL58 8AP
☎ 01248 810329 ▤ 01248 811294
e-mail: info@bullsheadinn.co.uk

dir: *from Britannia road bridge follow A545, inn in town centre*

Charles Dickens and Samuel Johnson were regular visitors to this inn which features exposed beams and antique weaponry. Richly decorated bedrooms are well equipped and there is a spacious lounge. Meetings and small functions are catered for, and food continues to attract praise in both The Loft restaurant and the less formal brasserie.

Rooms 12 en suite 1 annexe en suite (2 GF) ⊛ in all bedrooms S £75-£77; D £98-£100 (incl. bkfst) **Facilities** FTV Leisure centre nearby **Conf** Thtr 25 Board 16 **Parking** 10 **Notes LB** ⊗ ⊛ in restaurant Closed 25-26 Dec & 1 Jan

★★ 76% ◉ **HOTEL**

Bishopsgate House
54 Castle St LL58 8BB
☎ 01248 810302 ▤ 01248 810166
e-mail: hazel@johnson-ollier.freeserve.co.uk

dir: *from Menai Bridge onto A545 to Beaumaris. Hotel on left in main street*

This immaculately maintained, privately owned and personally run small hotel dates back to 1760. It features fine examples of wood panelling and a Chinese Chippendale staircase. Thoughtfully furnished bedrooms are attractively decorated and two have four-poster beds. Quality cooking is served in the elegant restaurant and guests have a comfortable lounge and cosy bar to relax in.

Rooms 9 en suite S £52-£63; D £83-£97 (incl. bkfst) **Parking** 8 **Notes LB** ⊛ in restaurant

CEMAES BAY
MAP 14 SH39

★★ 64% **HOTEL**

Harbour Hotel
Harbour View LL67 0NN
☎ 01407 710273 & 710977 ▤ 01407 710956
e-mail: enquiries@angleseyharbour.co.uk

dir: *take A5025 from Britannia Bridge (A55) through Benlech & Amlwch*

This hotel has a wonderful location close to the village and overlooking Cemaes Bay. Bedrooms are comfortable and well equipped - seven have balconies with fine views. A choice of meals is served in both the bar or the restaurant.

Rooms 17 en suite (4 fmly) S £45; D £60 (incl. bkfst) **Facilities** STV Wi-fi in bedrooms **Parking** 12 **Notes LB** ⊛ in restaurant

HOLYHEAD
MAP 14 SH28

★★ 68% **HOTEL**

Boathouse
Newry Promenade, Newry Beach LL65 1YF
☎ 01407 762094 ▤ 01407 764898
e-mail: boathousehotel@supanet.com

dir: *follow expressway into Holyhead, through yellow box, follow Marina signs. From ferry terminal right at 1st lights, (cross rail bridge) right at 2nd lights. Hotel at bottom of hill on seafront*

Situated in a prominent position overlooking the harbour, this hotel makes an ideal stop for ferry travellers. Bedrooms are attractively decorated to a high standard and are well equipped. The attractive lounge bar offers a wide range of home-cooked food; there is also a separate dining room.

Rooms 17 en suite (1 fmly) (5 GF) ⊛ in 15 bedrooms S £45-£55; D £75-£85 (incl. bkfst) **Facilities** Painting & sketching workshops **Conf** BC Thtr 40 Class 30 Board 30 **Parking** 40 **Notes LB** ⊛ in restaurant

LLANFAIRPWLLGWYNGYLL MAP 14 SH57

★★ 74% **HOTEL**

Carreg Bran Country Hotel

Church Ln LL61 5YH

☎ 01248 714224 🗈 01248 716516

e-mail: info@carregbran.uk.com

dir: from Holyhead 1st junct for Llanfairpwll. Through village then 1st right before dual carriageway and bridge

This privately owned and personally run hotel is situated close to the banks of the Menai Strait. Rooms are spacious and well equipped. The restaurant is attractive and the food is locally inspired. There is a choice of bars and a large function room, popular for weddings and business meetings.

Rooms 20 en suite (2 fmly) ⊘ in 5 bedrooms S £45-£49; D £60-£69 (incl. bkfst) **Conf** Thtr 120 Class 60 Board 30 **Parking** 150 **Notes** ⊘ in restaurant Civ Wed 100

LLANGEFNI MAP 14 SH47

★★★ 78% **HOTEL**

Tre-Ysgawen Hall Country House Hotel & Spa

Capel Coch LL77 7UR

☎ 01248 750750 🗈 01248 750035

e-mail: enquiries@treysgawen-hall.co.uk

web: www.treysgawen-hall.co.uk

dir: From North Wales Expressway junct 6, take B5111 from Llangefni for Amlwch/Llanerchymedd. After Rhosmeich right to Capel Coch. Hotel 1m on left at end of long drive

Quietly located in extensive wooded grounds, this charming mansion was built in 1882 and has been extended over time. It offers a range of delightful bedrooms, with many personal touches. Public areas are elegant, spacious and comfortable. The restaurant offers an interesting choice of dishes. There is a bar/bistro, a coffee shop and extensive leisure facilities.

Rooms 19 en suite 10 annexe en suite (2 fmly) (9 GF) ⊘ in 15 bedrooms S £80-£105; D £130-£166 (incl. bkfst) **Facilities Spa** STV 🏊 Sauna Gym ⚓ Jacuzzi Steam Room, Beauty Therapy Suite, Treatment Rooms **Conf** Thtr 200 Class 75 Board 50 Del from £132.50 **Parking** 140 **Notes LB** ⊗ ⊘ in restaurant Closed 25 Dec-2 Jan Civ Wed 200

See advert on this page

★★★ 72% **HOTEL**

Bull Hotel

Bulkley Square LL77 7LR

☎ 01248 722119 🗈 01248 750488

e-mail: bull@welsh-historic-inns.com

web: www.welsh-historic-inns.com

dir: exit A55 at Llangefni, follow town centre signs, hotel on right through one-way system

This town centre hostelry was built in 1817, and provides well-equipped, tastefully furnished accommodation both in the main building and the annexe, including a room with a four-poster bed and a family room. Public areas offer a choice of bars, a spacious and traditional restaurant together with a comfortable, relaxing lounge.

continued

Bull Hotel

Rooms 20 en suite (2 fmly) ⊘ in all bedrooms S £65-£70; D £75-£90 (incl. bkfst) **Facilities** STV Xmas **Conf** Thtr 60 Class 40 Board 30 **Parking** 18 **Notes LB** ⊗ ⊘ in restaurant

MENAI BRIDGE MAP 14 SH57

★★ 71% **HOTEL**

Victoria Hotel

Telford Rd LL59 5DR

☎ 01248 712309 🗈 01248 716774

e-mail: vicmenai@barbox.net

dir: over Menai Bridge, take 2nd exit from rdbt continue 100yds, hotel on right

This family-run hotel is situated in Menai Bridge and has panoramic views of the Menai Straits and Britannia Bridge. Many bedrooms have

continued on page 888

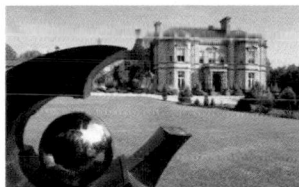
Wales

MENAI BRIDGE *continued*

their own balconies. There are two character bars where meals are available, and also a more formal conservatory dining room. The hotel holds a civil wedding licence.

Rooms 14 en suite 3 annexe en suite (4 fmly) (1 GF)
Facilities Childrens playground **Conf** Thtr 80 Class 80 Board 50
Parking 40 **Notes** ⊗ in restaurant RS 25-Dec Civ Wed 85

TREARDDUR BAY   MAP 14 SH27

★★★ 77% **HOTEL**

Trearddur Bay

LL65 2UN

☎ 01407 860301 📠 01407 861181

e-mail: enquiries@trearddurbayhotel.co.uk

dir: *from A5 towards Holyhead left at lights in Valley onto B4545 towards Trearddur Bay, (Power garage on right), left opp garage, hotel on right*

Facilities at this fine modern hotel include extensive function and conference rooms, an indoor swimming pool and a games room. Bedrooms are well equipped, many have sea views, and suites are available. An all-day bar serves a wide range of snacks and lighter meals, supplemented by a cocktail bar and the more formal hotel restaurant.

Rooms 34 en suite 6 annexe en suite (7 fmly) ⊗ in all bedrooms S £90; D £135-£168 (incl. bkfst) **Facilities** STV 🏊 Wi-fi in bedrooms Sailing, Shooting, Horse riding, Fishing, Diving, Golf packages 🎵 Xmas **Conf** Thtr 190 Class 100 Board 78 Del from £115 **Parking** 200 **Notes LB** ⊗ ⊗ in restaurant Civ Wed 150

BRIDGEND

BRIDGEND   MAP 09 SS97

★★★★ 74% **COUNTRY HOUSE HOTEL**

Coed-Y-Mwstwr

Coychurch CF35 6AF

☎ 01656 860621 📠 01656 863122

e-mail: hotel@coed-y-mwstwr.com

web: www.coed-y-mwstwr.com

dir: *exit A473 at Coychurch, right at petrol station. Follow signs at top of hill*

This former Victorian mansion, set in 17 acres of grounds, is an inviting retreat. Public areas are full of character featuring an impressive contemporary restaurant. Bedrooms have individual styles with a good range of extras, and include two full suites. Facilities include a large and attractive function suite with syndicate rooms, gym and outdoor swimming pool.

Rooms 28 en suite (2 fmly) ⊗ in 20 bedrooms S £98-£110; D £113-£150 (incl. bkfst) **Facilities** STV 🏊 🏌 Putt green Sauna Gym Wi-fi available Xmas **Conf** Thtr 180 Class 120 Board 50 Del from £146.80 **Services** Lift **Parking** 100 **Notes LB** ⊗ Civ Wed 150

★★★ 80% ◉◉ **SMALL HOTEL**

The Great House Restaurant & Hotel

Laleston CF32 0HP

☎ 01656 657644 📠 01656 668892

e-mail: enquiries@great-house-laleston.co.uk

web: www.great-house-laleston.co.uk

dir: *on A473, 400yds from junct with A48*

A delightful Grade II listed building, dating back to 1550. Traditional features throughout the house add plenty of character. Leicester's restaurant offers a wide range of freshly prepared dishes; lighter snacks can be taken in the more informal bistro. The stylish, well-equipped bedrooms are located in the original building and a separate wing.

Rooms 8 en suite 8 annexe en suite (8 GF) ⊗ in 4 bedrooms S £70-£90; D £100-£130 (incl. bkfst) **Facilities** STV Sauna Gym 🛁 Jacuzzi Health suite with sauna **Conf** Thtr 40 Class 25 Board 20 Del £110 **Parking** 40 **Notes LB** ⊗ ⊗ in restaurant Closed 25 Dec-2 Jan Civ Wed 50

★★★ 72% **HOTEL**

Best Western Heronston

Ewenny Rd CF35 5AW

☎ 01656 668811 & 666084 📠 01656 767391

e-mail: reservations@heronston-hotel.demon.co.uk

dir: *M4 junct 35, follow signs for Porthcawl, at 4th rdbt turn left towards Ogmore-by-Sea (B4265) hotel 200yds on left*

Best Western

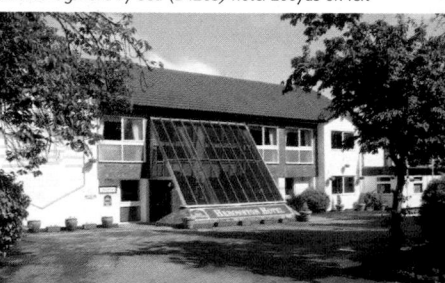

Situated within easy reach of the town centre and the M4, this large modern hotel offers spacious well-equipped accommodation, including no-smoking bedrooms and ground floor rooms. Public areas include an open plan lounge/bar, attractive restaurant and a smart leisure & fitness club. The hotel also has a choice of function/conference rooms.

Rooms 69 en suite 6 annexe en suite (4 fmly) (37 GF) ⊗ in 21 bedrooms S £55-£105; D £79-£125 (incl. bkfst) **Facilities** STV 🏊 🏌 supervised Sauna Solarium Gym Jacuzzi Wi-fi in bedrooms Steamroom Xmas **Conf** Thtr 250 Class 80 Board 60 Del from £99.50 **Services** Lift **Parking** 160 **Notes LB** ⊗ in restaurant Civ Wed 150

PENCOED   MAP 09 SS98

★★★ 74% **HOTEL**

St Mary's Hotel & Country Club

St Marys Golf Club CF35 5EA

☎ 01656 861100 📠 01656 863400

e-mail: stmarysgolfhotel@btinternet.com

dir: *M4 junct 35, on A473*

This charming 16th-century farmhouse has been converted and extended into a modern and restful hotel, surrounded by its own two

continued

Wales

olf courses. Bedrooms are generously appointed, well-equipped and
most feature whirlpool baths. Guests are offered a choice of bars,
which are popular with club members, and a good range of dining
options is also available.

Rooms 24 en suite (19 fmly) (10 GF) ⊗ in 12 bedrooms S £70–£79;
D £84–£109 (incl. bkfst) **Facilities** STV ♨ 30 Putt green Wi-fi in bedrooms
Floodlit driving range Xmas **Conf** Thtr 120 Class 60 Board 40 Del from
105 **Parking** 140 **Notes LB** ⊗ ⊘ in restaurant Civ Wed 120

BUDGET HOTEL

Premier Travel Inn Bridgend

Pantruthyn Farm, Pencoed CF35 5HY
☎ 08701 977041 ▤ 01656 864792
web: www.premiertravelinn.com

dir: off rdbt at M4 junct 35, behind petrol station and
McDonalds

High quality, modern budget accommodation ideal for both families
and business travellers. Spacious, en suite bedrooms feature bath and
shower, satellite TV and many have telephones and modem points.
The adjacent family restaurant features a wide and varied menu. For
further details consult the Hotel Groups page.

Rooms 40 en suite

BUDGET HOTEL

Travelodge Bridgend Pencoed

Old Mill, Felindre Rd CF3 5HU
☎ 08700 850 950 ▤ 01656 864404
web: www.travelodge.co.uk

dir: on A473

Travelodge offers good quality, good value, modern accommodation.
Ideal for families, the spacious en suite bedrooms include remote-
control TV, tea and coffee-making facilities and comfortable beds.
Meals can be taken at the nearby family restaurant. See Hotel Groups
pages for further details.

Rooms 39 en suite S fr £26; D fr £26

PORTHCAWL   MAP 09 SS87

★★★ 71% HOTEL

Atlantic

West Dr CF36 3LT
☎ 01656 785011 ▤ 01656 771877
e-mail: enquiries@atlantichotelporthcawl.co.uk

dir: M4 junct 35/37, follow signs to Porthcawl. Then follow
seafront/Promenade signs

This hotel is located on the seafront, a short walk from the town
centre. Guests can enjoy sea views from the sun terrace, bright
conservatory and some of the bedrooms, which are well equipped
and tastefully decorated. A welcoming atmosphere is created here,
especially in the restaurant where a good selection of tempting dishes
is available.

Rooms 18 en suite (2 fmly) S £64–£74; D £85–£95 (incl. bkfst)
Facilities STV Wi-fi in bedrooms Xmas **Conf** Thtr 50 Class 50 Board 25
Services Lift **Parking** 20 **Notes** ⊗

★★★ 67% HOTEL

Seabank

The Promenade CF36 3LU
☎ 01656 782261 ▤ 01656 785363
e-mail: info@seabankhotel.co.uk

dir: M4 junct 37, follow A4229 to seafront

This large, privately owned hotel stands on the promenade. The
majority of the well-equipped bedrooms enjoy panoramic sea views
and several have four-poster beds. There is a spacious restaurant, a
lounge bar and a choice of lounges. The hotel is a popular venue for
coach-tour parties, as well as weddings and conferences.

Rooms 67 en suite (2 fmly) ⊗ in 14 bedrooms **Facilities** STV Sauna
Gym Jacuzzi ♬ **Conf** Thtr 250 Class 150 Board 70 **Services** Lift
Parking 140 **Notes LB** ⊗ Civ Wed 100

SARN PARK MOTORWAY   MAP 09 SS98
SERVICE AREA (M4)

BUDGET HOTEL

Days Inn Cardiff West

Sarn Park Services CF32 9RW
☎ 01656 659218 ▤ 01656 768665
e-mail: sarnpark.hotel@welcomebreak.co.uk
web: www.welcomebreak.co.uk

dir: M4 junct 36

This modern building offers accommodation in smart, spacious and well
equipped bedrooms, suitable for families and business travellers, and all
with en suite bathrooms. Refreshments may be taken at the nearby
family restaurant. For further details consult the Hotel Groups page.

Rooms 40 en suite S £35–£55; D £35–£55

CAERPHILLY

BLACKWOOD   MAP 09 ST19

★★★ 70% HOTEL

Maes Manor

NP12 0AG
☎ 01495 220011 ▤ 01495 228217
e-mail: info@maesmanor.com

dir: A4048 to Tredega. At Pontllanfraith left at rdbt, through
Blackwood High St. After 1.25m left at Rack Inn. Hotel 400yds on
left

Standing high above the town, this 19th-century manor house is set in
nine acres of gardens and woodland. Bedrooms are located either in
the main house or an adjacent coach house and are attractively

continued on page 890

Wales

BLACKWOOD *continued*

decorated with co-ordinated furnishings. As well as the popular restaurant, public rooms include a choice of bars, a lounge/lobby area and a large function room.

Rooms 13 en suite 14 annexe en suite (6 fmly) (8 GF) S £68-£100; D £80-£120 (incl. bkfst) **Conf** Thtr 200 Class 200 Board 50 **Parking** 100 **Notes** ⊗ ⊘ in restaurant Closed 24-25 Dec Civ Wed 200

See advert on opposite page

CAERPHILLY   MAP 09 ST18

BUDGET HOTEL

Premier Travel Inn Caerphilly North

Corbetts Ln CF83 3HX
☎ 0870 9906368 📠 0870 9906369
web: www.premiertravelinn.com

dir: *4m from M4 junct 32. Follow A470, take 2nd left signed Caerphilly. At rdbt take 4th exit, at next rdbt take 2nd exit. Straight over next, and at Pwllypant rdbt, Inn on left*

High quality, modern budget accommodation ideal for both families and business travellers. Spacious, en suite bedrooms feature bath and shower, satellite TV and many have telephones and modem points. The adjacent family restaurant features a wide and varied menu. For further details consult the Hotel Groups page.

Rooms 40 en suite

Premier Travel Inn Caerphilly North East

Crossways Business Park, Pontypandy CF83 3NL
☎ 08701 977046 📠 029 2086 5546

dir: *M4 junct 32/A470 towards Merthyr Tydfil, junct 4 take A458 to Caerphilly. Stay on ring road until Crossways Business Park (5th rdbt). Inn on right of McDonald's rdbt.*

Rooms 40 en suite **Conf** Class 30

HENGOED   MAP 09 ST19

★★★★ 79% **HOTEL**

Bryn Meadows Golf & Country Club

Maesycwmmer, Ystrad Mynach CF82 7SN
☎ 01495 225590 📠 01495 228272
e-mail: reception@brynmeadow.co.uk

dir: *Exit M4 junct 28, 10m to Newbridge follow A472 signed Ystrad Mynach. 1m before Ystrad Mynach off Crown rdbt signed for golf course*

Surrounded by mature parkland and an 18-hole golf course, this impressive hotel, golf, leisure and function complex provides a range of high quality, well equipped bedrooms (several have their own balconies or patio areas). The attractive public areas include a pleasant restaurant that, like many of the bedrooms, enjoys impressive views of the golf course. This is a popular venue for weddings.

Rooms 42 en suite 1 annexe en suite (4 fmly) (21 GF) ⊘ in all bedrooms S £85-£110; D £98-£125 (incl. bkfst) **Facilities Spa** 🏊 supervised ♨ 18 Sauna Solarium Gym Putt green Jacuzzi **Conf** Thtr 120 Class 70 Board 60 **Services** air con **Parking** 120 **Notes LB** ⊗ ⊘ in restaurant Closed 25 Dec Civ Wed

CARDIFF

CARDIFF   MAP 09 ST17
See also Barry (Vale of Glamorgan)

★★★★★ 84% ⊕⊛ **HOTEL**

St David's Hotel & Spa

ℛℱ
ROCCO FORTE
HOTELS

Havannah St CF10 5SD
☎ 029 2045 4045 📠 029 2048 7056
e-mail: reservations@thestdavidshotel.com
web: www.roccofortehotels.com

dir: *M4 junct 33/A4232 for 9m, for Techniquest, at top exit slip road, 1st left at rdbt, 1st right*

This imposing contemporary building sits in a prime position on Cardiff Bay and has a seven-storey atrium which certainly creates a dramatic impression. Leading from this are the practically designed and comfortable bedrooms. Tides restaurant, adjacent to the stylish cocktail bar, has views across the water to Penarth, and there is a quiet first-floor lounge for guests seeking a peaceful environment. A well-equipped spa and extensive business areas complete the package.

Rooms 132 en suite (6 fmly) ⊘ in 108 bedrooms **Facilities Spa** STV 🏊 supervised Sauna Gym Jacuzzi Fitness studio, 14 treatment rooms 🎵 Xmas **Conf** BC Thtr 270 Class 110 Board 60 **Services** Lift air con **Parking** 80 **Notes** ⊗ ⊘ in restaurant Civ Wed

---

HOTEL OF THE YEAR

★★★★ 80% ⊛ **HOTEL**

Park Plaza Cardiff

Park Plaza
Hotels & Resorts

Greyfriars Rd CF10 3AL
☎ 029 2011 1111 📠 029 2011 1112
e-mail: ppcres@parkplazahotels.co.uk
web: www.parkplaza.com

A smart, new-build hotel located in the city centre. The hotel features eye-catching, contemporary decor, a state-of-the-art indoor leisure facility, extensive conference and banqueting facilities and the spacious Laguna kitchen and bar. Bedrooms are also contemporary in style and feature a host of extras including private bar, safe and modem points. AA Hotel of the Year for Wales 2006-7.

Rooms 129 en suite ⊘ in 96 bedrooms S £95-£200; D £110-£320 (incl. bkfst) **Facilities Spa** STV 🏊 Gym Jacuzzi Wi-fi in bedrooms Dance studio Xmas **Conf** Thtr 150 Class 80 Board 60 Del from £160 **Services** Lift air con **Notes LB** ⊘ in restaurant Civ Wed 120

★★★★ 77% ◉◉ **HOTEL**

Macdonald Holland House

24/26 Newport Rd CF24 0DD

☎ 0870 122 0020 🖷 029 2048 8894

e-mail: revenue.holland@macdonald-hotels.co.uk

web: www.macdonald-hotels.co.uk

Conveniently located just a few minutes' walk from the centre, this exciting hotel combines contemporary styling with a genuinely friendly welcome. Bedrooms, including five luxurious suites, are spacious and include many welcome extras. A state-of-the-art leisure club and spa is available in addition to a large function room. An eclectic menu provides a varied range of freshly prepared, quality dishes.

Rooms 165 en suite (80 fmly) ⊘ in all bedrooms **Facilities Spa** STV 🔄 Sauna Gym Jacuzzi full leisure facilities & 14 treatment rooms 🎵 **Conf** BC Thtr 710 Class 400 Board 50 **Services** Lift air con **Parking** 80 **Notes LB** 🐾 ⊘ in restaurant Civ Wed 500

★★★★ 75% **HOTEL**

Cardiff Marriott Hotel

Marriott
HOTELS & RESORTS

Mill Ln CF10 1EZ

☎ 029 2039 9944 🖷 029 2039 5578

e-mail: sara.nurse@marriotthotels.co.uk

web: www.marriott.co.uk

dir: M4 junct 29 follow signs city centre. Turn left into High Street opposite Castle, then 2nd left, at bottom of High St into Mill Lane

A centrally located modern hotel, with spacious public areas and a good range of services, is ideal for business or leisure. Eating options

continued on page 892

Wales

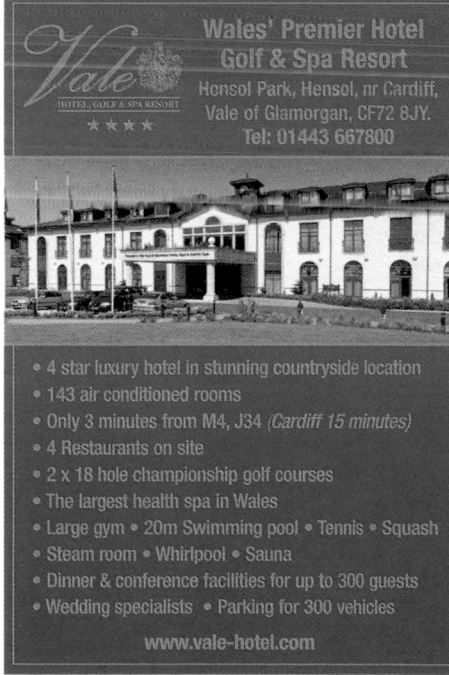

CARDIFF *continued*

include the informal Chats café bar and the contemporary Mediterrano restaurant. The well-equipped bedrooms are comfortable and air conditioned. The leisure suite includes a gym and good sized pool.

Cardiff Marriott Hotel

Rooms 184 en suite (68 fmly) ⊘ in 146 bedrooms **Facilities** STV 🖾 Sauna Solarium Gym Jacuzzi Steam room **Conf** Thtr 400 Class 200 Board 100 **Services** Lift air con **Parking** 110 **Notes LB** ⊗ ⊘ in restaurant Civ Wed 100

★★★★ 73% **HOTEL**

Jurys Cardiff

JURYS DOYLE
HOTELS

Mary Ann St CF10 2JH

☎ 029 2034 1441 📄 029 2022 3742

e-mail: info@jurysdoyle.com

web: www.jurysdoyle.com

dir: next to Ice Rink

A modern city centre hotel, located opposite the Cardiff International Arena. The hotel is built around a central atrium in which the reception, Dylan's Restaurant and Kavanagh's Irish Bar are all located. Some bedrooms overlook the atrium, while others have external views. Rooms are generally spacious, have modern decor and are equipped with a range of extras including safes.

Rooms 146 en suite (6 fmly) ⊘ in 109 bedrooms S £65-£265; D £65-£275 **Facilities** STV Wi-fi available **Conf** Thtr 300 Class 120 Board 50 Del from £115 **Services** Lift **Parking** 40 **Notes LB** ⊗ ⊘ in restaurant Civ Wed 150

★★★★ 71% **HOTEL**

Novotel Cardiff Central

NOVOTEL
ACCOR hotels

Schooner Way, Atlantic Wharf CF10 4RT

☎ 029 2047 5000 📄 029 2048 1491

e-mail: h5982@accor.com

web: www.novotel.com

dir: M4 junct 33/A4232 follow Cardiff Bay signs, to Atlantic Wharf & Novotel Hotel

Situated in the heart of the city's new development area, this hotel is equally convenient for the centre and Cardiff Bay. Bedrooms vary between standard rooms in the modern extention and executive rooms in the original wing. The hotel offers good seating space in public rooms, a popular leisure club and the innovative 'Elements' dining concept.

Rooms 138 en suite (100 fmly) ⊘ in 114 bedrooms S £55-£155; D £55-£155 **Facilities Spa** STV 🖾 supervised Sauna Solarium Gym Jacuzzi Wi-fi in bedrooms **Conf** BC Thtr 250 Class 90 Board 65 Del from £99 **Services** Lift air con **Parking** 120 **Notes LB** ⊗ ⊘ in restaurant Civ Wed 250

★★★★ 70% **HOTEL**

Angel Hotel

PARAMOUNT
GROUP OF HOTELS

Castle St CF10 1SZ

☎ 029 2064 9200 📄 029 2039 6212

e-mail: angelreservations@paramount-hotels.co.uk

web: www.paramount-hotels.co.uk

dir: opposite Cardiff Castle

This well-established hotel is in the heart of the city overlooking the castle. All bedrooms offer air conditioning and are decorated and furnished to a high standard. Public areas include an impressive lobby, a modern restaurant and a selection of conference rooms. There is limited parking at the rear of the hotel.

Rooms 102 en suite (3 fmly) ⊘ in 62 bedrooms S £70-£150; D £90-£210 (incl. bkfst) **Facilities** STV Wi-fi in bedrooms Xmas **Conf** Thtr 300 Class 180 Board 80 Del from £125 **Services** Lift air con **Parking** 60 **Notes LB** ⊘ in restaurant Civ Wed 200

★★★★ 68% ⊛ **HOTEL**

Copthorne Hotel Cardiff-Caerdydd

COPTHORNE

Copthorne Way, Culverhouse Cross CF5 6DA

☎ 029 2059 9100 📄 029 20599080

e-mail: reservations.cardiff@mill-cop.com

web: www.copthone.com

dir: M4 junct 33, A4232 for 2.5m towards Cardiff West. Then A48 W to Cowbridge

A comfortable, popular and modern hotel, conveniently located for the airport and city. Bedrooms are a good size and some have a private lounge. Public areas are smartly presented with features including a gym, pool, meeting rooms and a comfortable restaurant with views of the adjacent lake.

Rooms 135 en suite (14 fmly) (27 GF) ⊘ in 114 bedrooms S £59-£247.50; D £59-£247.50 **Facilities** STV 🖾 Sauna Gym Jacuzzi Wi-fi available Steam room **Conf** Class 300 Board 140 Del from £99 **Services** Lift **Parking** 225 **Notes LB** ⊘ in restaurant Civ Wed 200

★★★ 81% ⊛ **HOTEL**

Best Western New House Country Hotel

Best Western

Thornhill CF14 9UA

☎ 029 2052 0280 📄 029 2052 0324

e-mail: enquiries@newhousehotel.com

web: www.newhousehotel.com

dir: M4 junct 32, A470 towards Cardiff, then A469 to Caerphilly. Pass Thornhill Crematorium, 1m on left

Enjoying an elevated, hilltop position, the New House enjoys unrivalled views of the city and, on clear days, across the channel to the coast of Somerset. The public areas comprise a lounge and bar, an elegant restaurant and various function suites. Accommodation is spacious and comfortable, in attractive, well-equipped rooms, many having their own balcony or terrace.

Rooms 36 en suite (5 fmly) (10 GF) ⊘ in 18 bedrooms S £50-£98; D £70-£140 (incl. bkfst) **Facilities Spa** STV Sauna Gym Jacuzzi Wi-fi in bedrooms Xmas **Conf** Thtr 200 Class 150 Board 200 **Parking** 100 **Notes LB** ⊗ ⊘ in restaurant Civ Wed

★★★ 72% HOTEL

Swallow St Mellons Hotel & Country Club

SWALLOW

Castleton CF3 2XR

☎ 01633 680355 📠 01633 680399

e-mail: reception@stmellonshotel.co.uk

web: www.swallowhotels.com

dir: M4 junct 28 follow A48 Castleton/ST Mellons. Hotel on left past garage

This former Regency mansion has been tastefully converted into an elegant hotel and has an adjoining leisure complex with a strong local following. Bedrooms are spacious and smart; some are in purpose-built wings. The public areas retain their pleasing former proportions and include relaxing lounges and a restaurant serving a varied range of carefully prepared and enjoyable dishes.

Rooms 21 en suite 20 annexe en suite (9 fmly) (5 GF) ⊘ in 34 bedrooms S £115-£145; D £125-£155 (incl. bkfst) **Facilities** STV ⊠ Squash Sauna Solarium Gym Jacuzzi Beauty salon Xmas **Conf** Thtr 220 Class 100 Board 40 Del from £110 **Parking** 100 **Notes** ⊘ in restaurant Civ Wed 160

★★★ 72% ❀ HOTEL

Manor Parc Country Hotel & Restaurant

Thornhill Rd, Thornhill CF14 9UA

☎ 029 2069 3723 📠 029 2061 4624

e-mail: enquiry@manorparc.com

dir: M4 junct 32. Turn left at lights, pass Den Inn. Take next left, left at lights on A469

Set in open countryside on the outskirts of Cardiff, this delightful hotel retains traditional values of hospitality and service. Bedrooms, including a suite, are spacious and attractive, whilst public areas comprise a comfortable lounge and a restaurant with a magnificent lantern ceiling overlooking the well-tended grounds.

Rooms 21 en suite (4 fmly) (1 GF) ⊘ in all bedrooms S £65-£72; D £95-£130 (incl. bkfst) **Facilities** STV ⊰ **Conf** Thtr 120 Class 80 Board 50 Del from £115 **Parking** 100 **Notes** LB ⊗ ⊘ in restaurant Closed 26 Dec-1Jan Civ Wed 100

★★★ 71% HOTEL

Quality Hotel & Suites Cardiff

QUALITY

Merthyr Rd, Tongwynlais CF15 7LD

☎ 029 2052 9988 📠 029 2052 9977

e-mail: enquiries@quality-hotels-cardiff.com

web: www.choicehotelseurope.com

dir: M4 junct 32, take exit for Tongwynlais A4054 off large rdbt, hotel on right

This modern hotel is conveniently located off the M4 with easy access to Cardiff. Guests can enjoy the spacious open-plan public areas and impressive leisure facilities and relax in the well-proportioned and equipped bedrooms, which include some suites. A good range of meeting rooms make this hotel a popular conference venue.

Rooms 95 en suite (12 fmly) (19 GF) ⊘ in 64 bedrooms S £45-£120; D £60-£145 (incl. bkfst) **Facilities** ⊠ supervised Sauna Solarium Gym Jacuzzi Wi-fi in bedrooms **Conf** Thtr 200 Class 140 Board 60 Del from £75 **Services** Lift air con **Parking** 130 **Notes** LB ⊗ ⊘ in restaurant Civ Wed 180

★★★ 71% HOTEL

Thistle Cardiff

THISTLE HOTELS

Park Place CF10 3UD

☎ 0870 333 9157 📠 0870 333 9257

e-mail: cardiff@thistle.co.uk

dir: M4 junct 29, A48, take 4th exit signed City Centre/A470. At rdbt take 2nd exit signed City Centre/A470

Ideally located in the very centre of Cardiff, this bustling hotel is well suited for either the business or leisure guest. Bedrooms are spacious and well equipped and a very good range of dining options is available from the bar, lounge and restaurant areas. An adjacent car park is another bonus.

Rooms 136 en suite (4 fmly) ⊘ in 68 bedrooms **Facilities** STV **Conf** Thtr 300 Class 170 Board 100 **Services** Lift **Parking** 65 **Notes** LB ⊗ ⊘ in restaurant Civ Wed 250

★★ 68% HOTEL

Sandringham

21 St Mary St CF10 1PL

☎ 029 2023 2161 📠 029 2038 3998

e-mail: mm@sandringham-hotel.com

dir: M4 junct 29 follow 'City Centre' signs. Opposite castle turn left into High Street; leads to Saint Mary Street. Hotel on left

This friendly, privately owned and personally run hotel is near to the Millennium Stadium and offers a convenient base for access to the city centre. Bedrooms are well equipped, and diners can relax in Café Jazz, the hotel's adjoining restaurant, where live music is provided most week nights. There is also a separate lounge/bar for residents, and an airy breakfast room.

Rooms 28 en suite (1 fmly) ⊘ in 21 bedrooms S £35-£100, D £45-£130 (incl. bkfst) **Facilities** ♬ **Conf** Thtr 100 Class 70 Board 60 Del from £65 **Parking** 10 **Notes** LB ⊗ ⊘ in restaurant

❀❀ RESTAURANT WITH ROOMS

The Old Post Office

Greenwood Ln, St Fagans CF5 6EL

☎ 029 2056 5400 📠 029 2056 3400

e-mail: heidi@theoldpost@aol.com

dir: M4 junct 33 onto A4323. Take Culverhouse Cross exit then 1st exit then left onto Michaelston Rd. Over rdbt and level crossing, left at Castle Hill, right past church.

Located just five miles from Cardiff in the historic village of St Fagans, this establishment offers contemporary style based on New England design. Bedrooms, like the dining room, feature striking white walls with spotlights that create a fresh, clean feel. Delicious meals include a carefully prepared selection of local produce.

Rooms 6 en suite (2 fmly) (6 GF) ⊘ in all bedrooms S £70; D £100 **Parking** 40 **Notes** LB ⊗

Wales

Wales

CARDIFF *continued*

BUDGET HOTEL

Campanile
Caxton Place, Pentwyn CF23 8HA
☎ 029 2054 9044 ▤ 029 2054 9900
e-mail: cardiff@campanile-hotles.com
web: www.envergure.fr

dir: take Pentwyn exit from A48M, follow hotel signs

This modern building offers accommodation in smart, well-equipped bedrooms, all with en suite bathrooms. Refreshments may be taken at the informal Bistro. For further details consult the Hotel Groups page.

Campanile

Rooms 47 annexe en suite S £46.50–£65; D £46.50–£65 **Conf** Thtr 35 Class 18 Board 16 Del from £90.25

Rooms 36 en suite

BUDGET HOTEL

Days Inn Cardiff
Port Rd, Rhoose, Nr. Barry CF62 3BT
☎ 01466 710787
web: www.welcomebreak.co.uk

This modern building offers accommodation in smart, spacious and well-equipped bedrooms, suitable for families and business travellers, and all with en suite bathrooms. Continental breakfast is available and other refreshments may be taken at the nearby family restaurant. For further details see the Hotel Groups page.

Rooms 36 en suite

BUDGET HOTEL

Hotel Ibis Cardiff
Churchill Way CF10 2HA
☎ 029 2064 9250 ▤ 029 2920 9260
e-mail: H2969@accor.com
web: www.ibishotel.com

dir: M4, then A48 2nd exit A4232. Follow signs to City Centre on Newport Rd, left after railway bridge, left after Queen St station.

Modern, budget hotel offering comfortable accommodation in bright and practical bedrooms. Breakfast is self-service and dinner is available in the restaurant. For further details, consult the Hotel Groups page.

Rooms 102 en suite S £52.95–£59.95; D £52.95–£59.95

Hotel Ibis Cardiff Gate
Malthouse Av, Cardiff Gate Business Park, Pontprennau CF23 8RA
☎ 029 2073 3222 ▤ 029 2073 4222
e-mail: H3159@accor.com

dir: M4 junct 30, take slip rd signed Cardiff Service Station. Hotel on left.

Rooms 78 en suite S £41.95–£48.95; D £41.95–£48.95 **Conf** Thtr 9 Class 24

BUDGET HOTEL

Innkeeper's Lodge Cardiff
Tyn-y-Parc Rd, Whitchurch CF14 6BG
☎ 029 2069 2554 ▤ 029 2052 7052
web: www.innkeeperslodge.com

dir: M4 junct 32, southbound on A470. At 3rd set of T-lights, turn left. Inn opposite Safeway

Smart, en suite accommodation ideal for both business & leisure guests. Bedrooms are very well equipped, including Sky TV, telephone, modem points, tea & coffee making facilities, (family rooms in most locations). Complimentary breakfast. The adjacent Pub Restaurant; a Harvester, Vintage Inn, Toby Carvery, Ember Inn, Sizzling Pubco or Pub & Carvery offers an all day menu. See Hotel Groups pages for further details.

Rooms 52 en suite S £49.95; D £49.95 **Conf** Thtr 40 Class 40 Board 20

BUDGET HOTEL

Premier Travel Inn Cardiff Ocean Park
Keen Rd CF24 5JT
☎ 08701 977050 ▤ 029 2049 0403
web: www.premiertravelinn.com

dir: Cardiff Docks & Bay signs from A48(M), over flyover & next 4 rdbts. At 5th rdbt, take 3rd exit. Inn 1st right & 1st right again

High quality, modern budget accommodation ideal for both families and business travellers. Spacious, en suite bedrooms feature bath and shower, satellite TV and many have telephones and modem points. The adjacent family restaurant features a wide and varied menu. For further details consult the Hotel Groups page.

Rooms 73 en suite **Conf** Thtr 15

Premier Travel Inn Cardiff (Roath)
David Lloyd Leisure Club, Ipswich Rd, Roath CF23 9AQ
☎ 08701 977049 ▤ 029 2046 2482

dir: M4 junct 30 take A4232 to A48. 2nd exit off A48 to Cardiff East and Docks, (A4161). Follow signs for David Lloyd Leisure Club.

Rooms 70 en suite **Conf** Thtr 300

Premier Travel Inn Cardiff West
The Walston Castle, Port Road, Nantisaf, Wenvoe CF5 6DD
☎ 08701 977052 ▤ 029 2059 1436

dir: From M4 junct 33 S on A4232. Take 2nd exit (signed Airport), then 3rd exit at Culverhouse Cross rddt. Inn 0.5m on Barry Rd (A4050)

Rooms 39 en suite **Conf** Thtr 12

BUDGET HOTEL

Travelodge Cardiff Central

Imperial Gate, Saint Marys St CF10 1FA
☎ 08700 850 950 🖷 029 2039 8737
web: www.travelodge.co.uk

dir: M4 junct 32, A470 to city centre

Travelodge offers good quality, good value, modern accommodation. Ideal for families, the spacious en suite bedrooms include remote-control TV, tea and coffee-making facilities and comfortable beds. Meals can be taken at the nearby family restaurant. See Hotel Groups pages for further details.

Rooms 100 en suite S fr £26; D fr £26

Travelodge Cardiff Llanedeyrn

Circle Way East, Llanedeyrn CF23 9PD
☎ 08700 850 950 🖷 029 2054 9564

dir: M4 junct 30, A4232 to North Pentwyn junct. A48 & follow Cardiff East & Docks signs. 3rd exit at Llanedeyrn junct, follow Circle Way East signs

Rooms 32 en suite S fr £26; D fr £26

Travelodge Cardiff (M4)

Granada Service Area M4, Pontyclun CF72 8SA
☎ 08700 850 950 🖷 029 2089 9412

dir: M4, junct 33/A4232

Rooms 50 en suite S fr £26; D fr £26 **Conf** Thtr 45 Board 34

CARMARTHENSHIRE

AMMANFORD   MAP 08 SN61

★★ 63% HOTEL

Mill at Glynhir

Glynhir Rd, Llandybie SA18 2TE
☎ 01269 850672 🖷 01269 850672
e-mail: millatglynhir@aol.com
web: www.glynhir.co.uk

dir: exit A483 at Llandybie signed 'Golf Course'

This former flour mill is set peacefully on a hillside with a river at the end of the garden. There is an indoor swimming pool and a golf driving range in the extensive grounds. The bedrooms are all a good size, well equipped and most have private balconies. Public areas consist of a comfortable lounge bar and a cheerful dining room.

Rooms 7 en suite 3 annexe en suite S £38-£60; D £58-£76 (incl. bkfst) **Facilities Spa** 🎱 supervised ♨ 18 Fishing Putt green **Parking** 15 **Notes LB** No children 11yrs ⊗ in restaurant Closed 24-29 Dec

CARMARTHEN   MAP 08 SN42

★★★ 75% HOTEL

Ivy Bush Royal

Spilman St SA31 1LG
☎ 01267 235111 🖷 01267 234914
e-mail: reception@ivybushroyal.co.uk
web: www.ivybushroyal.co.uk

dir: M4 onto A48 W, over 1st rdbt, 2nd rdbt turn right. Straight over next 2 rdbts. Left at lights. Hotel on right at top of hill

This hotel has been tastefully refurbished over recent years to offer
continued

guests spacious, well equipped bedrooms and bathrooms, a relaxing lounge with outdoor patio seating and a comfortable restaurant serving a varied selection of carefully prepared meals. Weddings, meetings and conferences are all well catered for at this friendly, family run establishment.

Rooms 70 en suite (4 fmly) ⊛ in 60 bedrooms S £55-£75; D £75-£99 (incl. bkfst) **Facilities** STV Sauna Gym Wi-fi available Xmas **Conf** BC Thtr 200 Class 50 Board 40 Del from £95 **Services** Lift **Parking** 83 **Notes LB** ⊗ ⊛ in restaurant Civ Wed 150

★★ 71% ⊛ HOTEL

Falcon

Lammas St SA31 3AP
☎ 01267 234959 & 237152 🖷 01267 221277
e-mail: reception@falconcarmarthen.co.uk
web: www.falconcarmarthen.co.uk

dir: in town centre pass bus station turn left, hotel 200yds on left

This friendly hotel has been owned by the Exton family for over 45 years. Personally run, it is well placed in the centre of the town. Bedrooms, some with four-poster beds, are tastefully decorated with good facilities. There is a comfortable lounge with adjacent bar, and the restaurant, open for lunch and dinner, has a varied selection of enjoyable dishes.

Rooms 16 en suite (1 fmly) **Conf** Thtr 80 Class 50 Board 40 **Parking** 36 **Notes LB** ⊛ in restaurant Closed 26 Dec RS Sun

CROSS HANDS   MAP 08 SN51

BUDGET HOTEL

Travelodge Llanelli Cross Hands

SA14 6NW
☎ 08700 850 950 🖷 0870 191 1729
web: www.travelodge.co.uk

dir: on A48, westbound

Travelodge offers good quality, good value, modern accommodation. Ideal for families, the spacious en suite bedrooms include remote-control TV, tea and coffee-making facilities and comfortable beds. Meals can be taken at the nearby family restaurant. See Hotel Groups pages for further details.

Rooms 32 en suite S fr £26; D fr £26

CRUGYBAR   MAP 09 SN63

🇺

Glanrannell Park Country House

SA19 8SA
☎ 01558 685230
e-mail: enquiry@glanrannellpark.co.uk

dir: from A40 take A482 to Lampeter after 5.5m follow signs to hotel. From Llandeilo take B4302 for 10.5m, hotel signed

At the time of going to press, the star classification for this hotel was not confirmed. Please refer to the AA internet site www.theAA.com for current information.

Rooms 8 en suite (2 fmly) **Facilities** Fishing **Parking** 33 **Notes LB** ⊛ in restaurant Closed Nov-Mar

Wales

LLANDEILO
MAP 08 SN62

★★★ 73% HOTEL

The Plough Inn
Rhosmaen SA19 6NP
☎ 01558 823431 📠 01558 823969
e-mail: info@ploughrhosmaendemon.co.uk
web: www.ploughrhosmaen.com
dir: 0.5m N of Llandeilo on A40

This privately owned hotel has memorable views over the Towy Valley and the Black Mountains. Bedrooms, situated in a separate wing, are tastefully furnished, spacious and comfortable. The public lounge bar is popular with locals, as is the spacious restaurant where freshly prepared food can be enjoyed. Additional facilities include a sauna, gym and conference facilities.

Rooms 14 en suite (10 fmly) (5 GF) ⊘ in all bedrooms S fr £60; D £80-£80 (incl. bkfst) **Facilities** STV Sauna Gym Wi-fi in bedrooms Xmas **Conf** Thtr 100 Class 60 Board 30 Del from £75 **Parking** 70 **Notes** ⊗ ⊘ in restaurant Civ Wed 100

★★ 69% HOTEL

White Hart Inn
36 Carmarthen Rd SA19 6RS
☎ 01558 823419 📠 01558 823089
e-mail: therese@thewhitehartinn.fsnet.co.uk
web: www.whitehartinnwales.co.uk
dir: off A40 onto A483, hotel 200yds on left

This privately owned, 19th-century roadside hostelry is on the outskirts of town. The modern bedrooms are well-equipped and tastefully furnished, family rooms are available. Public areas include a choice of bars and both smoking and non-smoking dining areas, where a wide range of grill type dishes is available. There are several function rooms, including a large self-contained suite.

Rooms 11 en suite (3 fmly) ⊘ in 4 bedrooms S £36-£40; D £54-£60 (incl. bkfst) **Facilities** STV **Parking** 50 **Notes** ⊗ Civ Wed 70

LLANELLI
MAP 08 SN50

★★★ 70% HOTEL

Best Western Diplomat Hotel
Felinfoel SA15 3PJ
☎ 01554 756156 📠 01554 751649
e-mail: reservations@diplomat-hotel-wales.com
web: www.diplomat-hotel-wales.com
dir: M4 junct 48 onto A4138 then B4303, hotel in 0.75m on right

This Victorian mansion, set in mature grounds, has been extended over the years to provide a comfortable and relaxing hotel. The well-appointed bedrooms are located in the main house and there is a new wing of bedrooms. Public areas include Trubshaw's restaurant, a large function suite and a modern leisure centre.

Rooms 23 en suite 8 annexe en suite (2 fmly) (4 GF) ⊘ in 37 bedrooms S £65-£70; D £85-£90 (incl. bkfst) **Facilities Spa** ⬚ supervised Sauna Solarium Gym Jacuzzi ♫ Xmas **Conf** Thtr 450 Class 150 Board 100 Del from £78 **Services** Lift **Parking** 250 **Notes LB** Civ Wed 300

★★★ 70% HOTEL

Stradey Park
Furnace SA15 4HA
☎ 01554 758171 📠 01554 777974
e-mail: reservations@stradeyparkhotel.com
web: www.stradeyparkhotel.com
dir: M4 junct 48/A484 to B4309

This modern complex continues to offer a good range of comfortable accommodation including family suites, no-smoking bedrooms and bedrooms at ground-floor level. The Rooftop Lounge offers guests a place to relax whilst taking afternoon tea and enjoying the far reaching views. Other public areas are spacious and include a choice of lounges, a pleasant bar and the brasserie-style restaurant.

Rooms 84 en suite (3 fmly) (19 GF) ⊘ in 70 bedrooms S £85-£110; D £110-£125 (incl. bkfst) **Facilities** Wi-fi in bedrooms Xmas **Conf** BC Thtr 300 Class 300 Board 240 Del from £95.40 **Services** Lift **Parking** 100 **Notes LB** ⊗ ⊘ in restaurant Civ Wed 200

★★ 72% HOTEL

Ashburnham
Ashburnham Rd, Pembrey SA16 0TH
☎ 01554 834343 & 834455 📠 01554 834483
e-mail: info@ashburnham-hotel.co.uk
dir: M4 junct 48, A4138 to Llanelli, A484 West to Pembrey. Follow sign as entering village

Amelia Earhart stayed at this friendly hotel after finishing her historic trans-Atlantic flight in 1928. Public areas include a bright bar and

continued

restaurant offering a good choice of menus, extensive function facilities and a children's outdoor play area. Bedrooms have modern furnishings and facilities. The hotel is licensed for civil wedding ceremonies and proves a popular venue.

Rooms 13 en suite (2 fmly) ⊗ in 3 bedrooms S £60-£80; D £80-£100 (incl. bkfst) **Facilities** Wi-fi in bedrooms ch fac **Conf** Thtr 150 Class 150 Board 80 Del £90 **Parking** 100 **Notes LB** ⊗ ⊗ in restaurant RS 24-26 Dec Civ Wed 130

Hotel Miramar

158 Station Rd SA15 1YU
☎ 01554 754726 ▤ 01554 772454
e-mail: miramar2002d@aol.com
dir: M4 junct 48. In Llanelli follow rail station signs

This privately owned hotel is conveniently located near to the railway station and is within walking distance of the town centre. Bedrooms are well maintained and generously equipped, whilst public areas include a cheerful bar providing a good range of bar meals and a pleasantly appointed restaurant where a good choice is also available.

Rooms 12 en suite (2 fmly) (2 GF) S £40; D £60 (incl. bkfst)
Facilities ch fac **Parking** 10 **Notes** ⊗ ⊗ in restaurant RS 25-26 Dec

ST CLEARS   MAP 08 SN21

Travelodge St Clears Carmarthen

Tenby Rd SA33 4JN
☎ 08700 850 950 ▤ 01994 231227
web: www.travelodge.co.uk
dir: A40 westbound, before rdbt junct of A477 & A4066

Travelodge offers good quality, good value, modern accommodation. Ideal for families, the spacious en suite bedrooms include remote-control TV, tea and coffee-making facilities and comfortable beds. Meals can be taken at the nearby family restaurant. See Hotel Groups pages for further details.

Rooms 32 en suite S fr £26; D fr £26

CEREDIGION

ABERPORTH   MAP 08 SN25

Hotel Penrallt

SA43 2BS
☎ 01239 810227 & 810927 ▤ 01239 811375
e-mail: info@hotelpenrallt.co.uk
dir: take B4333 signed Aberporth. Hotel 1m on right

This magnificent Edwardian mansion is peacefully located in extensive grounds and offers spacious accommodation. The well-maintained public areas feature original carved ceiling beams, an impressive staircase and an eye-catching stained glass window. Guests can enjoy a relaxing atmosphere in the comfortable lounge, the popular bar and

continued

elegant restaurant. The leisure and fitness centre has a choice of swimming pools.

Rooms 15 en suite (2 fmly) S £75; D £110-£120 (incl. bkfst) **Facilities** ⊠ ⊱ supervised ⅃9 ⌣ Sauna Gym ⍾ Putt green Jacuzzi Wi-fi available Pool table,Golf Driving net, Table Tennis, Childrens Play Area Xmas **Conf** Class 24 Board 20 **Parking** 100 **Notes LB** ⊗ ⊗ in restaurant Civ Wed 40

ABERYSTWYTH   MAP 08 SN58

Conrah

Ffosrhydygaled, Chancery SY23 4DF
☎ 01970 617941 ▤ 01970 624546
e-mail: enquiries@conrah.co.uk
web: www.conrah.co.uk
dir: on A487, 3.5m S of Aberystwyth

This privately owned and personally run country-house hotel stands in 22 acres of mature grounds. The elegant public rooms include a choice of comfortable lounges with welcoming open fires. Bedrooms are located in the main house, a wing and converted outbuildings. The modern cuisine, with international influences, achieves very high standards. Conference facilities are available.

Rooms 11 en suite 6 annexe en suite (1 fmly) (3 GF) S £85-£100; D £130-£160 (incl. bkfst) **Facilities** ⍾ Wi-fi in bedrooms Table tennis **Conf** Thtr 40 Class 20 Board 20 Del £130 **Services** Lift **Parking** 50 **Notes LB** ⊗ No children 5yrs ⊗ in restaurant Closed 22-30 Dec

Belle Vue Royal

Marine Ter SY23 2BA
☎ 01970 617558 ▤ 01970 612190
e-mail: reception@bellevueroyalhotel.co.uk
dir: on promenade, 200yds from pier

This large privately owned hotel dates back more than 170 years, stands on the promenade and is a short walk from the shops. All bedrooms are well equipped and include both family and sea-view rooms. Public areas include extensive function rooms and a choice of bars. Dining choices include bar meals or a more formal restaurant.

Rooms 37 rms (34 en suite) (6 fmly) (1 GF) ⊗ in 12 bedrooms S £63; D £95-£105 (incl. bkfst) **Facilities** STV ch fac Xmas **Conf** Thtr 100 Class 30 Board 30 Del from £95 **Parking** 14 **Notes** ⊗ ⊗ in restaurant Civ Wed 100

Wales

ABERYSTWYTH *continued*

★★ 79% **HOTEL**

Marine Hotel

The Promenade SY23 2BX

☎ 01970 612444 📠 01970 617435

e-mail: marinehotel1@btconnect.com

web: www.marinehotelaberystwyth.co.uk

dir: *from W on A44. From N or S Wales on A487. On seafront, west of pier*

The Marine is a privately owned hotel situated on the promenade overlooking Cardigan Bay. Bedrooms have been tastefully decorated, some have four-poster beds and many have sea views. The reception rooms are comfortable and relaxing, and meals are served in the elegant dining room or the bar.

Rooms 44 rms (43 en suite) (7 fmly) ⊘ in 1 bedroom S £45-£70; D £50-£95 (incl. bkfst) **Facilities Spa** Sauna Solarium Gym Jacuzzi Xmas **Conf** BC Thtr 220 Class 150 Board 60 Del from £99 **Services** Lift **Parking** 22 **Notes LB** Civ Wed 200

★★ 75% **SMALL HOTEL**

Richmond

44-45 Marine Ter SY23 2BX

☎ 01970 612201 📠 01970 626706

e-mail: reservations@richmondhotel.uk.com

web: www.richmondhotel.uk.com

dir: *on entering town follow signs for Promenade*

This privately owned and personally run, friendly hotel has good sea views from its day rooms and many of the bedrooms. The public areas and bedrooms are comfortably furnished. An attractive dining room and a comfortable lounge and bar are provided.

Rooms 15 en suite (6 fmly) ⊘ in all bedrooms **Facilities** STV **Conf** Thtr 60 Class 22 Board 28 **Parking** 22 **Notes LB** ⊗ ⊘ in restaurant Closed 20 Dec-3 Jan

★★ 69% **HOTEL**

Four Seasons Hotel

50-54 Portland St SY23 2DX

☎ 01970 612120 📠 01970 627458

e-mail: reservations@fourseasonshotel.demon.co.uk

dir: *From rail station left onto Terrace Rd by lights, into North Pde & left into Queens Rd, then 2nd left into Portland St. Hotel on right*

This privately owned hotel is soundly maintained and friendly. Bedrooms are well equipped. A pleasant lounge bar is provided, plus an attractive restaurant where a good choice of food is available.

Rooms 16 rms (15 en suite) (1 fmly) ⊘ in 14 bedrooms S £50-£65; D £75-£80 (incl. bkfst) **Parking** 16 **Notes LB** ⊗ ⊘ in restaurant

★★ 68% ⊛ **HOTEL**

Harry's

40-46 North Pde SY23 2NF

☎ 01970 612647 📠 01970 627068

e-mail: info@harrysaberystwyth.com

dir: *N on A487, in town centre*

Conveniently located for the shopping area and seafront, this is a friendly and popular hotel. The main attraction is the popular Harry's Restaurant, with its wide selection of dishes and specialising in local produce. Bedrooms are well equipped with modern facilities.

Rooms 24 en suite (2 fmly) ⊘ in 6 bedrooms **Conf** Thtr 24 Class 24 Board 40 **Parking** 6 **Notes** Closed 25-26 Dec

DEVIL'S BRIDGE   MAP 09 SN77

★★ 74% **HOTEL**

Hafod Arms

SY23 3JL

☎ 01970 890232 📠 01970 890394

e-mail: enquiries@hafodarms.co.uk

dir: *leave A44 at Ponterwyd. Hotel 5m along A4120, 11m E of Aberystwyth*

This former hunting lodge dates back to the 17th century and is situated in six acres of grounds. Now a family-owned and run hotel, it provides accommodation suitable for both business people and tourists. Family rooms and a four-poster room are available. In addition to the dining area and lounge, the hotel has tea rooms.

Rooms 15 rms (12 en suite) **Parking** 30 **Notes LB** ⊗ No children 12yrs ⊘ in restaurant Closed 15 Dec-Jan RS Mid Oct-14 Dec & Feb-mid March

EGLWYSFACH
MAP 14 SN69

INSPECTORS' CHOICE

★★★ ◉◉◉◉ HOTEL

Ynyshir Hall
SY20 8TA

☎ 01654 781209 & 781268 ▤ 01654 781366

e-mail: ynyshir@relaischateaux.com

web: www.ynyshir-hall.co.uk

dir: off A487, 5.5m S of Machynlleth, signed from main road

Set in beautifully landscaped grounds and surrounded by an RSBP reserve, Ynyshir Hall is a haven of calm. Lavishly styled bedrooms provide high standards of luxury and comfort - each is individually designed by taking inspiration from a great painter. The lounge and bar have different moods, but both feature an abundance of fresh flowers. The dining room offers outstanding modern cooking using the best ingredients.

Rooms 7 en suite 2 annexe en suite ⊗ in all bedrooms S £110-£270; D £210-£375 (incl. bkfst) **Facilities** ↘ Xmas **Conf** Thtr 25 Class 20 Board 18 Del from £175 **Parking** 20 **Notes LB** No children 9yrs ⊗ in restaurant Closed 5-29 Jan Civ Wed 40

GWBERT-ON-SEA
MAP 14 SN69

★★★ 68% HOTEL

The Cliff
SA43 1PP

☎ 01239 613241 ▤ 01239 615391

e-mail: reservations@cliffhotel.com

dir: off A487 into Cardigan, follow signs to Gwbert, 3m to hotel

Set in 30 acres of grounds that include a 9-hole golf course, and enjoying a cliff-top location overlooking Cardigan Bay, this hotel offers superb sea views. Bedrooms come in a variety of sizes, with some

continued

overlooking the bay. Public areas are spacious and offer a choice of bars and lounges.

Rooms 47 en suite 22 annexe en suite (5 fmly) (6 GF) ⊗ in 10 bedrooms S £50-£80; D £80-£110 (incl. bkfst) **Facilities Spa** STV ⚐ ⚐ ↓9 Fishing Sauna Gym Jacuzzi Xmas **Conf** Thtr 250 Class 150 Board 140 Del from £99 **Services** Lift **Parking** 150 **Notes LB** ⊗ in restaurant Civ Wed 200

LAMPETER
MAP 08 SN54

★★★ 80% ◉ HOTEL

Best Western Falcondale Mansion
SA48 7RX

☎ 01570 422910 ▤ 01570 423559

e-mail: info@falcondalehotel.com

web: www.falcondalehotel.com

dir: 800yds W of High St A475 or 1.5m NW of Lampeter A482

Built in the Italianate style, this charming Victorian property is set in extensive grounds and beautiful parkland. Bedrooms are generally spacious, well equipped and tastefully decorated. Bars and lounges are similarly well appointed with additional facilities including a conservatory and function room. Diners have a choice of either the restaurant or the less formal brasserie.

Rooms 20 en suite (2 fmly) ⊗ in 12 bedrooms S £95-£168; D £130-£168 (incl. bkfst) **Facilities** ↘ Wi-fi in bedrooms Xmas **Conf** Thtr 60 Class 30 Board 25 Del from £129 **Services** Lift **Parking** 60 **Notes LB** ⊗ in restaurant Civ Wed 60

PONTERWYD
MAP 09 SN78

★★ 71% HOTEL

The George Borrow Hotel
SY23 3AD

THE CIRCLE
Selected Individual Hotels
GREAT BRITAIN

☎ 01970 890230 ▤ 01970 890587

e-mail: georgeborrow@lycos.co.uk

dir: on A44 (Aberystwyth-Llangurig road). On Aberystwyth side of village

This family owned and personally run, friendly hotel sits in the foothills of the Cambrian Mountains, about 12 miles from the university town of Aberystwyth. The hotel provides an ideal base for walking, fishing and bird watching (look out for the red kites). Bedrooms, including family rooms, are comfortable and well equipped. There are two character bars and a restaurant where an extensive choice of food is available.

Rooms 9 en suite (2 fmly) ⊗ in all bedrooms S £45-£75; D £75-£80 (incl. bkfst) **Facilities** Wi-fi available **Parking** 30 **Notes LB** ⊗ ⊗ in restaurant Closed 25-26 Dec

Wales

CONWY

ABERGELE — MAP 14 SH97

★★★ 71% HOTEL

Kinmel Manor

St George's Rd LL22 9AS

☎ 01745 832014 📠 01745 832014

e-mail: kinmelmanor@virgin.net

dir: exit A55 at junct 24, hotel entrance on rdbt

Parts of this predominantly modern hotel complex date back to the 16th century and some original features are still in evidence. Set in spacious grounds, it provides well-equipped rooms and extensive leisure facilities.

Rooms 51 en suite (3 fmly) ⊛ in 12 bedrooms S £59.50-£62.50; D £79.50-£85 (incl. bkfst) **Facilities Spa** STV 🔁 Sauna Solarium Gym Wi-fi in bedrooms Steam room Xmas **Conf** Thtr 250 Class 100 Board 100 Del from £85 **Parking** 120 **Notes LB** ⊛ in restaurant Civ Wed 250

BETWS-Y-COED — MAP 14 SH75

See also Llanrwst

★★★ 81% ⊛ HOTEL

Royal Oak

Holyhead Rd LL24 0AY

☎ 01690 710219 📠 01690 710603

e-mail: royaloakmail@btopenworld.com

web: www.royaloakhotel.net

dir: on A5 in town centre, next to St Mary's church

Centrally situated in the village, this fine, privately owned hotel started life as a coaching inn and now provides smart bedrooms and a wide range of public areas. The choice of eating options includes the Grill Bistro, the Stables Bar which is much frequented by locals and the more formal Llugwy Restaurant.

Rooms 27 en suite (3 fmly) ⊛ in 6 bedrooms S £65-£85; D £80-£135 (incl. bkfst) **Facilities** STV Wi-fi in bedrooms 🎵 **Conf** BC Thtr 20 Class 20 Board 20 Del from £80 **Parking** 90 **Notes LB** ⊗ ⊛ in restaurant Closed 25-26 Dec Civ Wed 35

See advert on opposite page

★★★ 77% COUNTRY HOUSE HOTEL

Craig-y-Dderwen Riverside Hotel

LL24 0AS

☎ 01690 710293 📠 01690 710362

e-mail: craig-y-dderwen@betws-y-coed.co.uk

web: www.snowdonia-hotel.com

dir: A5 to town, cross Waterloo Bridge and take 1st left

This Victorian country-house hotel is set in well-maintained grounds alongside the River Conwy, at the end of a tree-lined drive. Very pleasant views can be enjoyed from many rooms, and two of the bedrooms have four-poster beds. There are comfortable lounges and the atmosphere is tranquil and relaxing.

Rooms 16 en suite (2 fmly) (1 GF) ⊛ in 3 bedrooms S £70-£130; D £80-£140 (incl. bkfst) **Facilities** STV FTV 🛶 Jacuzzi Badminton, Volleyball Xmas **Conf** Thtr 50 Class 25 Board 20 Del from £116.50 **Parking** 50 **Notes LB** ⊛ in restaurant Closed 23-26 Dec & 2 Jan-1 Feb

★★★ 75% HOTEL

Best Western Waterloo

LL24 0AR

☎ 01690 710411 📠 01690 710666

e-mail: reservations@waterloo-hotel.info

web: www.waterloo-hotel.info

dir: A5, near Waterloo Bridge

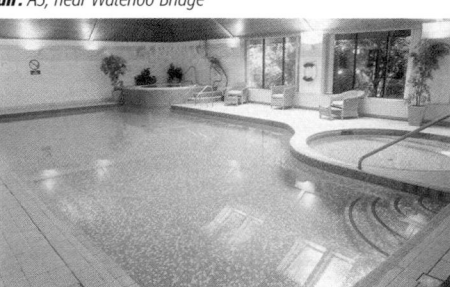

This long-established hotel, named after the nearby Waterloo Bridge, is ideally located for Snowdonia. Accommodation is split between rooms in the main hotel and modern, cottage-style rooms located in buildings to the rear. The attractive Garden Room Restaurant serves traditional Welsh specialities, and the Wellington Bar offers light meals and snacks.

Rooms 10 en suite 30 annexe en suite (2 fmly) (30 GF) ⊛ in 20 bedrooms **Facilities** 🔁 supervised Sauna Solarium Gym Jacuzzi Steam room **Conf** Thtr 50 Class 18 Board 18 **Parking** 100 **Notes LB** ⊛ in restaurant Closed 25-26 Dec

★★ 74% HOTEL

Fairy Glen

LL24 0SH

☎ 01690 710269

e-mail: fairyglen@youe.fsworld.co.uk

web: www.fairyglenhotel.co.uk

dir: A5 onto A470 S'bound (Dolwyddelan road). Hotel 0.5m on left by Beaver Bridge

This privately owned and personally run former coaching inn is over 300 years old. It is located near the Fairy Glen beauty spot, south of

continued

Betws-y-Coed. The modern accommodation is well equipped and service is willing, friendly and attentive. Facilities include a cosy bar and a separate comfortable lounge.

Rooms 8 en suite (1 fmly) ⊛ in all bedrooms S £26-£40; D £52-£56 (incl. bkfst) **Parking** 10 **Notes LB** ⊛ ⊛ in restaurant Closed Nov-Jan RS Feb

CAPEL CURIG   MAP 14 SH75

★★ 71% SMALL HOTEL

Cobdens

LL24 0EE

☎ 01690 720243 ▤ 01690 720354

e-mail: info@cobdens.co.uk

dir: on A5, 4m N of Betws-y-Coed

Situated in the heart of Snowdonia, this hotel has been a centre for mountaineering and other outdoor pursuits for many years. The bedrooms are modern and well equipped, and many enjoy lovely views. A wide range of meals using local produce is served in the restaurant or bar. A sauna room is also available.

Rooms 17 en suite (4 fmly) S £29.50-£35.50; D £59-£71 (incl. bkfst) **Facilities** Fishing Sauna Pool table ch fac **Conf** Thtr 50 Class 25 Board 30 Del from £70 **Parking** 40 **Notes** ⊛ in restaurant Closed Jan RS 24-25 & 31 Dec

COLWYN BAY   MAP 14 SH87

★★★ 68% HOTEL

Hopeside

63-67 Princes Dr, West End LL29 8PW

☎ 01492 533244 ▤ 01492 532850

e-mail: hopesidehotel@aol.com

dir: exit A55 at Rhos-on-Sea, exit B5155 towards Colwyn Bay town centre. Left at next lights into Princes Drive

Both the promenade and town centre are within easy walking distance of this friendly, privately owned and personally run hotel. The attractively decorated bedrooms are mostly pine-furnished. Facilities include a small conference room, a mini gym and a sauna.

Rooms 16 en suite (1 fmly) ⊛ in 8 bedrooms S fr £49; D £69-£99 (incl. bkfst) **Facilities** Sauna Gym Xmas **Conf** Thtr 40 Class 40 Board 26 Del from £80 **Parking** 15 **Notes LB** ⊛ in restaurant Civ Wed 50

★★ 69% HOTEL

Lyndale

THE INDEPENDENTS

410 Abergele Rd, Old Colwyn LL29 9AB

☎ 01492 515429 ▤ 01492 518805

e-mail: lyndale@tinyworld.co.uk

dir: A55 junct 22 Old Colwyn, turn left. At rdbt through village, then 1m on A547

A range of accommodation is available at this friendly, family-run hotel, including suites that are suitable for family use and a four-poster bedroom. There is a cosy bar and a comfortable foyer lounge, and weddings and other functions can be catered for.

Rooms 14 en suite (3 fmly) ⊛ in 4 bedrooms S £39-£49; D £59-£69 (incl. bkfst) **Conf** Thtr 40 Class 20 Board 20 Del from £59 **Parking** 20 **Notes LB** ⊛ in restaurant

CONWY   MAP 14 SH77

★★★ 78% ◉◉ HOTEL

Castle Hotel Conwy

High St LL32 8DB

☎ 01492 582800 ▤ 01492 582300

e-mail: mail@castlewales.co.uk

web: www.castlewales.co.uk

dir: A55 junct 18, follow town centre signs, cross estuary (castle on left). Right then left at mini-rdbts onto one-way system. Right at Town Wall Gate, right onto Berry St then along High St on left

This family-run, 16th-century hotel is one of Conwy's most distinguished buildings and offers a relaxed and friendly atmosphere.

continued on page 902

Wales

CONWY *continued*

Bedrooms are appointed to an impressive standard and include a stunning suite. Public areas include a popular modern bar and the award-winning Shakespeare's restaurant.

Rooms 28 en suite (2 fmly) ⊛ in 20 bedrooms S £75-£85; D £110-£135 (incl. bkfst) **Facilities** STV Wi-fi available ch fac **Conf** Thtr 30 Class 20 Board 20 Del from £95 **Parking** 34 **Notes** LB ⊛ in restaurant

★★★ 78% ◉ HOTEL

Groes Inn

Tyn-y-Groes LL32 8TN
☎ 01492 650545 ▤ 01492 650855
e-mail: enquries@thegroes.com
web: www.groesinn.com
dir: A55, over Old Conwy Bridge, 1st left through Castle Walls on B5106 (Trefriw road), hotel 2m on right.

This inn dates back in part to the 16th century and has charming features. It offers a choice of bars and has a beautifully appointed restaurant, with a conservatory extension opening on to the lovely rear garden. The comfortable, well-equipped bedrooms are contained in a separate building; some have balconies or private terraces. The inn has a deservedly high reputation for its food.

Rooms 14 en suite (1 fmly) (4 GF) ⊛ in 6 bedrooms S £79-£120; D £95-£175 (incl. bkfst) **Facilities** FTV **Conf** Thtr 22 Class 20 Board 20 **Parking** 100 **Notes** LB ⊛ in restaurant

DEGANWY   MAP 14 SH77

A

Deganwy Castle

Station Rd LL31 9DA
☎ 01492 583555 ▤ 01492 583555
e-mail: deganwycastlehtl@yahoo.co.uk
dir: A55 junct 18 signed Deganwy. Hotel on left through village.
Rooms 30 en suite (4 fmly) ⊛ in 2 bedrooms S £43; D £78 (incl. bkfst) **Facilities** Spa ⊞ supervised Sauna Solarium Gym ♫ **Conf** Thtr 120 Class 80 Board 60 Del fr £60 **Parking** 70 **Notes** ★★

DOLWYDDELAN   MAP 14 SH75

★★ 71% HOTEL

Elen's Castle

LL25 0EJ
☎ 01690 750207
e-mail: reception@elanscastlehotel.co.uk
dir: From N on A470, 5m S of Betws-y-Coed

This small, friendly hotel operated as a beer house in the 18th century. The original bar remains, complete with a slab floor and potbelly stove, and there are two cosy sitting rooms with open fires and exposed timbers. Two of the bedrooms have four-poster beds and families can be accommodated. A good range of bar and restaurant food is provided.

Rooms 10 rms (8 en suite) (2 fmly) ⊛ in all bedrooms S £25-£50; D £50-£90 (incl. bkfst) **Parking** 15 **Notes** LB ⊛ in restaurant

LLANDUDNO   MAP 14 SH78

INSPECTORS' CHOICE

★★★★ ◉◉◉ HOTEL

Bodysgallen Hall and Spa

LL30 1RS
☎ 01492 584466 ▤ 01492 582519
e-mail: info@bodysgallen.com
web: www.bodysgallen.com
dir: A55 junct 19, A470 towards Llandudno. Hotel 2m on right

Situated in idyllic surroundings of its own parkland and formal gardens, this 17th-century house is in an elevated position, with views towards Snowdonia and across to Conwy Castle. The lounges and dining room have fine antiques and great character. Accommodation is provided in the house, but also in delightfully converted cottages, together with a superb spa. Friendly and attentive service is discreetly offered, whilst the restaurant features fine local produce prepared with great skill.

Rooms 18 en suite 16 annexe en suite (3 fmly) (4 GF) ⊛ in 18 bedrooms S £125-£180; D £165-£375 **Facilities** Spa STV ⊞ Sauna Solarium Gym ⛲ Jacuzzi Wi-fi available Beauty treatment room, Steam room, Club room, Relaxation Room Xmas **Conf** BC Thtr 50 Class 30 Board 24 Del from £145 **Parking** 50 **Notes** LB ⊗ No children 6yrs ⊛ in restaurant Civ Wed 50

Wales

Osborne House

17 North Parade, Llandudno LL30 2LP
Tel: 01492 860330
www.osbornehouse.co.uk
sales@osbornehouse.co.uk

WTB ★★★★★
AA ★★★★

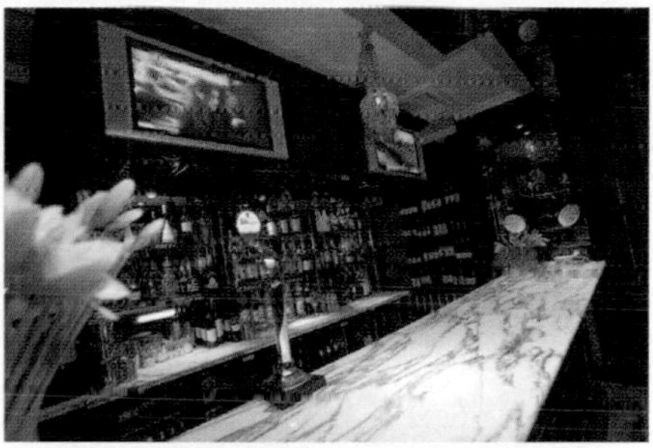

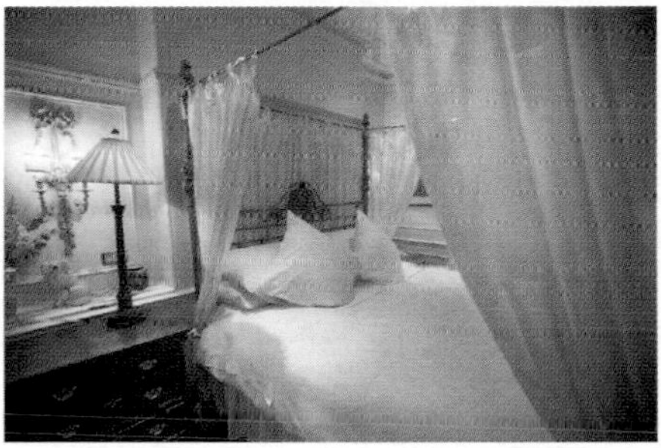

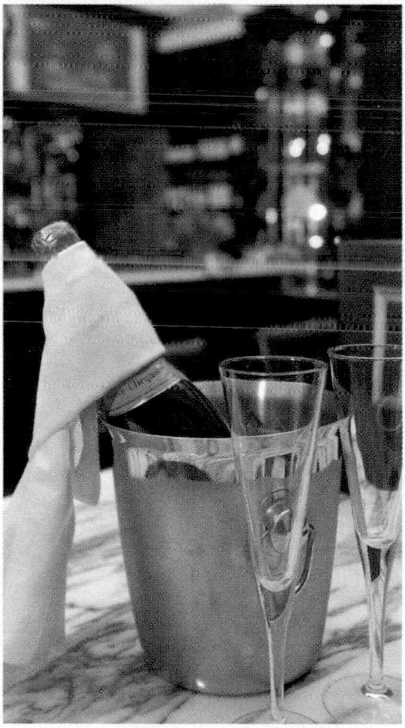

Intimate luxury Townhouse hotel. Six suites all with stunning sea views, King-size beds (one has twin beds), sitting area with Sony wide screen TV and DVD player and working gas fire. Bathrooms are Italian marble with double ended cast iron bath and walk-in marble shower. All suites have their own car space at rear of the hotel. There is free wireless broadband in suites and Cafe area.

Osborne's Cafe & Grill on the ground floor serves drinks, light bites and main meals all day till late and in an elegant yet informal atmosphere.

Wales

LLANDUDNO *continued*

INSPECTORS' CHOICE

★★★★ @ **TOWN HOUSE HOTEL**

Osborne House

17 North House LL30 2LP

☎ 01492 860330 📄 01492 860791

e-mail: sales@osbornehouse.com

web: www.osbornehouse.com

dir: exit A55 junct 19. Follow signs for Llandudno then
Promenade. Continue to junct, turn right. hotel on left
opposite pier entrance

Built in 1832, this Victorian house has been restored and
converted into a luxurious townhouse by the Maddocks family.
Spacious suites offer unrivalled comfort and luxury, combining
antique furnishings with state-of-the-art technology and facilities.
Each suite provides super views over the pier and bay. Osborne's
café grill is open throughout the day and offers high quality food,
whilst the bar blends elegance with plasma screens, dazzling
chandeliers and guilt-edged mirrors.

Rooms 6 en suite S £145-£200; D £145-£200 (incl. bkfst)
Facilities STV FTV Wi-fi in bedrooms use of swimming
pool/sauna/jacuzzi at Empire Hotel (100 yds) Xmas **Services** air con
Parking 6 **Notes** ⊗ No children 11yrs ⊘ in restaurant Closed
16-28 Dec

See advert on page 903

★★★★ 77% @ **HOTEL**

St George's

The Promenade LL30 2LG

☎ 01492 877544 📄 01492 877788

e-mail: stgeorges@countrytown-hotels.co.uk

web: www.macdonald-hotels.co.uk

dir: A55-A470, follow to promenade, 0.25m, hotel on corner

This large and impressive seafront property was the first hotel to be
built in the town. Extensive refurbishment work has now restored it to
its former glory and the accommodation is of very high quality. Its
many Victorian features include the splendid, ornate Wedgwood
Room restaurant. The terrace Restaurant and main lounges overlook
the bay. Hot and cold snacks are available all day.

Rooms 75 en suite ⊘ in all bedrooms **Facilities** Sauna Solarium Jacuzzi
Wi-fi in bedrooms Hairdressing Health & beauty salon Xmas
Conf Thtr 250 Class 200 Board 45 Del from £135 **Notes** ⊗

See advert on opposite page

★★★ 81% @ **HOTEL**

Empire

Church Walks LL30 2HE

☎ 01492 860555 📄 01492 860791

e-mail: reservations@empirehotel.co.uk

web: www.empirehotel.co.uk

dir: from Chester, A55 junct 19 for Llandudno. Follow town
centre signs. Hotel at end facing main street

Run by the same family for over almost 60 years, the Empire offers
luxuriously appointed bedrooms with every modern facility. The
'Number 72' rooms in an adjacent house are particularly sumptuous.
The indoor pool is overlooked by a lounge area where snacks are
served all day, and in summer an outdoor pool and roof garden are
available. The Watkins restaurant offers an interesting fixed-price
menu.

Rooms 49 en suite 8 annexe en suite (3 fmly) (2 GF) S £70-£100;
D £100-£130 (incl. bkfst) **Facilities Spa** STV FTV ⃞ ⃗ Sauna Wi-fi in
bedrooms Full range of beauty treatments Xmas **Conf** Thtr 24 Class 20
Board 20 Del from £97.50 **Services** Lift air con **Parking** 40 **Notes** LB
⊗ ⊘ in restaurant Closed 16-28 Dec

See advert on opposite page

★★★ 81% @ **HOTEL**

Imperial

The Promenade LL30 1AP

CLASSIC
BRITISH HOTELS

☎ 01492 877466 📄 01492 878043

e-mail: imphotel@btinternet.com

web: www.theimperial.co.uk

dir: A470 to Llandudno

The Imperial is a large and impressive hotel, situated on the
promenade, within easy reach of the town centre and other amenities.
Many of the bedrooms have views over the bay and there are also
several suites available. The elegant Chantrey restaurant offers a fixed-
price menu which changes monthly and dishes take full advantage of
local produce.

continued

Wales

Rooms 100 en suite (10 fmly) ⊗ in 60 bedrooms S £110; D fr £140 (incl. bkfst) **Facilities** STV 🎣 Sauna Solarium Gym Jacuzzi Beauty therapist Hairdressing ♫ Xmas **Conf** Thtr 150 Class 50 Board 50 **Services** Lift **Parking** 25 **Notes LB** ⊗ ⊗ in restaurant Civ Wed 150

See advert on this page

★★★ 78% **HOTEL**

Dunoon

Gloddaeth St LL30 2DW

☎ 01492 860787 📠 01492 860031

e-mail: reservations@dunoonhotel.co.uk

web: www.dunoonhotel.co.uk

dir: exit Promenade at war memorial by pier onto wide avenue. 200yds on right

This smart, privately owned hotel is centrally located and offers a

continued on page 906

Wales

LLANDUDNO *continued*

variety of styles and sizes of attractive, well-equipped bedrooms. The elegant public areas include a tastefully appointed restaurant, where competently prepared dishes are served and are complemented by a very good choice of carefully selected, good value wines. Caring, attentive service is also a strength here.

Rooms 49 en suite (7 fmly) S £55-£85; D £96 (incl. bkfst) **Facilities** STV ♫ **Conf** BC **Services** Lift **Parking** 24 **Notes LB** ⊗ in restaurant Closed 22 Dec-mid Mar

INSPECTORS' CHOICE

★★ ◉◉ **HOTEL**

St Tudno Hotel and Restaurant

The Promenade LL30 2LP

☎ 01492 874411 🖹 01492 860407

e-mail: sttudnohotel@btinternet.com

web: www.st-tudno.co.uk

dir: *on Promenade towards pier, hotel opposite pier entrance*

A high quality family-owned hotel with friendly, attentive staff, and enjoying fine sea views. The stylish bedrooms are well equipped with mini-bars, robes, satellite TVs with videos and many other thoughtful extras. Public rooms include a lounge, a welcoming bar and a small indoor pool. The Terrace Restaurant, where seasonal and daily-changing menus are offered, has a delightful Mediterranean atmosphere. Afternoon tea is a real highlight.

Rooms 18 en suite (4 fmly) ⊗ in all bedrooms S £75-£85; D £94-£220 (incl. bkfst) **Facilities** STV ⌧ supervised ♫ ch fac Xmas **Conf** Thtr 40 Class 25 Board 20 Del from £145 **Services** Lift **Parking** 12 **Notes LB** ⊗ in restaurant

★★ 81% **SMALL HOTEL**

Tan Lan

Great Orme's Rd, West Shore LL30 2AR

☎ 01492 860221 🖹 01492 870219

e-mail: info@tanlanhotel.co.uk

dir: *off A55 junct 18 onto A546 signed Deganwy. Approx 3m, straight over mini-rdbt, hotel 50mtrs on left*

Warm and friendly hospitality is one of the many strengths at this small, well-maintained, privately owned and personally run hotel. It is located on Llandudno's West Shore, close to the Great Orme. The bedrooms, some on the ground floor, are modern and well equipped. Facilities include a pleasant dining room, lounge and bar. This is a totally non-smoking establishment.

continued

Rooms 17 en suite (1 fmly) (6 GF) ⊗ in all bedrooms S £35-£40; D £50-£56 (incl. bkfst) **Parking** 12 **Notes LB** ⊗ No children 6yrs ⊗ in restaurant Closed Nov-mid Mar

★★ 80% **HOTEL**

Tynedale

Central Promenade LL30 2XS

☎ 01492 877426 🖹 01492 871213

e-mail: enquiries@tynedalehotel.co.uk

web: www.tynedalehotel.co.uk

dir: *on promenade opposite bandstand*

Tour groups are well catered for at this privately owned and personally run hotel, where regular live entertainment is a feature. Public areas include good lounge facilities and an attractive patio overlooking the bay. The well maintained, no-smoking bedrooms are fresh and well equipped. Many have good views over the seafront and the Great Orme.

Rooms 54 en suite (1 fmly) ⊗ in all bedrooms S £32-£50; D £64-£106 (incl. bkfst) **Facilities** ♫ Xmas **Services** Lift **Parking** 30 **Notes LB** ⊗ ⊗ in restaurant

★★ 79% **SMALL HOTEL**

Epperstone

15 Abbey Rd LL30 2EE

☎ 01492 878746 🖹 01492 871223

e-mail: epperstonehotel@btconnect.com

dir: *A55-A470 to Mostyn Street. Left at rdbt, 4th right into York Rd. Hotel on junct of York Rd & Abbey Rd*

This delightful hotel is located in wonderful gardens in a residential part of town, within easy walking distance of the seafront and shopping area. Bedrooms are attractively decorated and thoughtfully equipped. Two lounges, a comfortable non-smoking room and a Victorian-style conservatory are available. A daily changing menu is offered in the bright dining room.

Rooms 8 en suite (5 fmly) (1 GF) ⊗ in all bedrooms S £27-£39.50; D £54-£79 (incl. bkfst) **Facilities** STV Xmas **Parking** 8 **Notes LB** No children 5yrs ⊗ in restaurant

★★ 75% **HOTEL**

Ambassador Hotel

THE INDEPENDENTS

Grand Promenade LL30 2NR

☎ 01492 876886 🖹 01492 876347

e-mail: reception@ambasshotel.demon.co.uk

dir: *off A55 onto A470. Take turn to Promenade, then left towards pier*

This friendly, family-run hotel is located on the seafront, close to the town centre. Bedrooms are tastefully appointed and many have sea

continued

views. There is a choice of lounges, a patisserie, bar and restaurant.

Rooms 57 en suite (8 fmly) S £36-£56; D £62-£104 (incl. bkfst) **Facilities** ♫ Xmas **Conf** Thtr 45 Class 14 Board 20 Del from £68 **Services** Lift **Parking** 11 **Notes LB** ⊗ ⊘ in restaurant

★★ 74% HOTEL

Sandringham

West Pde LL30 2BD

☎ 01492 876513 ▣ 01492 877916

e-mail: enquiries@thesandringhamhotel.co.uk

web: www.thesandringhamhotel.co.uk

dir: enter Llandudno on A470 & follow signs for West Shore

This pleasant and friendly hotel is privately owned and personally run. It is located at the West Shore area of Llandudno. The accommodation is well equipped and there are popular bar and restaurant operations which provide an extensive choice of wholesome food.

Rooms 18 en suite (3 fmly) (2 GF) ⊘ in all bedrooms S £35-£37.50; D £70-£75 (incl. bkfst) **Facilities** STV **Notes LB** ⊗ ⊘ in restaurant RS 1-14 Jan

★★ 74% HOTEL

Sunnymede

West Pde LL30 2BD

☎ 01492 877130 ▣ 01492 871824

e-mail: sunnymedehotel@yahoo.co.uk

dir: from A55 follow Llandudno & Deganwy signs. At 1st rdbt after Deganwy take 1st exit towards sea. Left at corner, then 400yds

Sunnymede is a friendly family-run hotel located on town's West Shore. Many rooms have views over the Conwy Estuary and Snowdonia. The modern bedrooms are attractively decorated and well equipped. Bar and lounge areas are particularly comfortable and attractive.

Rooms 15 en suite (3 fmly) (4 GF) ⊘ in all bedrooms S £49-£112; D £94-£117 (incl. bkfst & dinner) **Facilities** Xmas **Parking** 18 **Notes LB** No children 3yrs ⊘ in restaurant Closed Jan-Feb & Nov RS Xmas period

★★ 72% HOTEL

Chatsworth House

Central Promenade LL30 2XS

☎ 01492 860788 ▣ 01492 871417

e-mail: manager@chatsworth-hotel.co.uk

web: www.chatsworth-hotel.co.uk

This traditional family-run Victorian hotel occupies a central position on the promenade and caters for many families and groups. There is

continued

---

an indoor swimming pool, a sauna and a solarium. Public areas are well maintained, and bedrooms are modern, some of them quite spacious.

Rooms 72 en suite (19 fmly) **Facilities** ⊠ Sauna Jacuzzi **Services** Lift **Parking** 9

★★ 69% HOTEL

Min-y-Don

North Pde LL30 2LP

☎ 01492 876511 ▣ 01492 878169

e-mail: minydonhotelllan@btconnect.com

dir: exit A55 junct 19 onto A470. Through Mostyn St, turn right at rdbt then left into North Parade

This cheerful family-run hotel is located under the Great Orme, opposite the pier. Bedrooms include several suitable for families and many have lovely views over the bay. Regular entertainment is held and there are comfortable lounge and bar areas.

Rooms 28 rms (19 en suite) (12 fmly) S £35-£39; D £60-£70 (incl. bkfst) **Facilities** Xmas **Services** air con **Parking** 7 **Notes LB** ⊗ ⊘ in restaurant Closed Jan-Feb

★★ 68% HOTEL

Somerset

St Georges Crescent, Promenade LL30 2LF

☎ 01492 876540 & 860615 ▣ 01492 863700

e-mail: somerset@favroy.freeserve.co.uk

dir: on the Promenade

This friendly and cheerful holiday hotel occupies an ideal location on the central promenade and affords superb views over the bay from many rooms. Regular entertainment is provided as well as a range of bar and lounge areas. Bedrooms are well decorated and modern facilities are provided.

Rooms 78 en suite (4 fmly) **Facilities** STV Games room ♫ Xmas **Conf** Thtr 70 Class 70 Board 30 **Services** Lift **Parking** 20 **Notes** ⊘ in restaurant Closed Jan-Feb

★★ 67% HOTEL

Esplanade

Glan-y-Mor Pde, Promenade LL30 2LL

☎ 0800 318688 (freephone) & 01492 860300

▣ 01492 860418

e-mail: info@esplanadehotel.co.uk

web: www.esplanadehotel.co.uk

dir: exit A55 at junct 19 onto A470, follow signs to promenade. Left towards Great Orme. Hotel 500yds left

This family owned and run hotel stands on the promenade, conveniently close to the town centre and with views of the bay. Bedrooms vary in size and style, but all have modern equipment and facilities. Public areas are bright and attractively appointed, and include a room for functions and conferences. The hotel is popular with golfers.

Rooms 59 en suite (17 fmly) ⊘ in 36 bedrooms S £15-£48; D £30-£96 (incl. bkfst) **Facilities** ♫ Xmas **Conf** Thtr 80 Class 40 Board 40 Del from £62.50 **Services** Lift **Parking** 30 **Notes LB** ⊗ ⊘ in restaurant Closed 3-24 Jan

LLANDUDNO *continued*

★★ 67% **HOTEL**

Hydro Hotel
Leisureplex

Neville Crescent LL30 1AT
☎ 01492 870101 ▤ 01492 870992
e-mail: hydro.llandudno@alfatravel.co.uk
web: www.alfatravel.co.uk

dir: *follow signs for theatre to seafront, towards pier. Hotel near theatre on left*

This large hotel is situated on the promenade overlooking the sea, and offers good, value-for-money, modern accommodation. Public areas are quite extensive and include a choice of lounges, a games/snooker room and a ballroom, where entertainment is provided every night. The hotel is a popular venue for coach tour parties.

Rooms 118 en suite (4 fmly) (8 GF) ⊛ in all bedrooms S £31-£41; D £50-£70 (incl. bkfst) **Facilities** FTV Snooker Table tennis ♫ Xmas **Services** Lift **Parking** 10 **Notes LB** ⊛ ⊘ in restaurant Closed Jan-mid Feb RS Nov -Dec & mid Feb-Mar

★★ 65% **HOTEL**

Royal
Church Walks LL30 2HW
☎ 01492 876476 ▤ 01492 870210
e-mail: royalllandudno@aol.com

dir: *exit A55/A470 to Llandudno. Follow through town to T-junct, then left into Church Walks. Hotel 200yds on left, almost opposite Great Orme tram station*

Reputed to be the first hotel in Llandudno, the Royal is located on the eastern side of the Great Orme, close to the town centre and sea front. The well-equipped accommodation is particularly popular with golfers and coach tour groups

Rooms 38 rms (36 en suite) (7 fmly) **Facilities** Putt green **Services** Lift **Parking** 20 **Notes LB** ⊛ ⊘ in restaurant

LLANDUDNO JUNCTION MAP 14 SH77

BUDGET HOTEL

Premier Travel Inn Llandudno
premier travel inn

Afon Conway, Llandudno Junction LL28 5LB
☎ 08701 977162 ▤ 01492 583614
web: www.premiertravelinn.com

dir: *off A55 at junct 19. Exit rdbt at A470 Betws-y-Coed. Inn is immediately on left, opposite petrol station*

High quality, modern budget accommodation ideal for both families and business travellers. Spacious, en suite bedrooms feature bath and shower, satellite TV and many have telephones and modem points. The adjacent family restaurant features a wide and varied menu. For further details consult the Hotel Groups page.

Rooms 40 en suite

LLANRWST MAP 14 SH86
See also Betws-y-Coed

★★★ 73% **HOTEL**

Maenan Abbey
Maenan LL26 0UL
☎ 01492 660247 ▤ 01492 660734
e-mail: reservations@manab.co.uk
dir: *3m N on A470*

Set in its own spacious grounds, this privately owned hotel was built as an abbey in 1850 on the site of a 13th-century monastery. It is now a popular venue for weddings as the grounds and magnificent galleried staircase make an ideal backdrop for photographs. Bedrooms include a large suite and are equipped with modern facilities. Meals are served in the bar and newly refurbished restaurant.

Rooms 14 en suite (2 fmly) **Facilities** Fishing guided mountain walks **Conf** BC Thtr 50 Class 30 Board 30 **Parking** 60 **Notes LB** ⊘ in restaurant Civ Wed 55

TREFRIW MAP 14 SH76

★★ 73% **HOTEL**

Hafod Country House
LL27 0RQ
☎ 01492 640029 ▤ 01492 641351
e-mail: hafod@breathemail.net
web: www.hafodhouse.co.uk

dir: *on B5106 between A5 at Betws-y-Coed & A55 at Conwy. 2nd entrance on right on entering Trefriw from south*

This former farmhouse is a personally run and friendly hotel with a wealth of charm and character. The tasteful bedrooms feature period furnishings and thoughtful extras such as fresh fruit. There is a comfortable sitting room and a cosy bar. The fixed-price menu is imaginative and makes good use of fresh, local produce while the breakfast menu offers a wide choice.

Rooms 6 en suite ⊛ in all bedrooms **Parking** 14 **Notes LB** No children 11yrs ⊘ in restaurant Closed early Jan-mid Feb

DENBIGHSHIRE

LLANDRILLO
MAP 15 SJ03

◉ ◉ RESTAURANT WITH ROOMS

Tyddyn Llan
LL21 0ST
☎ 01490 440264 🖺 01490 440414
e-mail: tyddynllan@compuserve.com
web: www.tyddynllan.co.uk
dir: *Take B4401 from Corwen to Llandrillo. Tyddyn Llan on the right leaving the village.*

An elegant Georgian House set within its own grounds in a peaceful and relaxing location. Bedrooms vary for size but all are comfortably furnished and include some welcome extras. The restaurant and lounges are quite delightful and offer pleasant views over the surrounding gardens. Emphasis is on local produce, carefully prepared by the chef/proprietor and his team.

Rooms 13 en suite (1 GF) ⊗ in all bedrooms S £65-£95; D £110-£180
Facilities ❧ ch fac **Conf** Thtr 30 Class 10 Board 20 **Parking** 20
Notes LB Closed 2 wks Jan RS Nov-Mar Civ Wed 40

LLANGOLLEN
MAP 15 SJ24
See also Glyn Ceiriog (Wrexham)

★★★ 80% ◉ HOTEL

The Wild Pheasant Hotel & Restaurant
Berwyn Rd LL20 8AD
☎ 01978 860629 🖺 01978 861837
e-mail: wild.pheasant@talk21.com
web: www.wildpheasanthotel.co.uk
dir: *hotel 0.5m from town centre on left of A5 towards Betws-y-Coed/Holyhead*

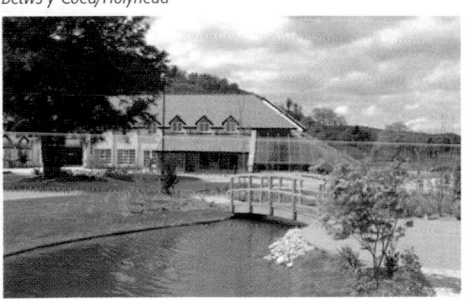

This professionally run, privately owned hotel provides friendly hospitality and smart accommodation, including ground-floor, four-poster and no-smoking rooms. There is also an extension with a range of superior rooms and suites, as well as a hydro therapy pool and beauty facilities. There's a choice of eating options, either in the Cinnamon Restaurant or in the Chef's Bar for snacks. The hotel is a popular venue for weddings and conferences.

Rooms 46 en suite (4 fmly) (12 GF) ⊗ in 9 bedrooms S £42.95-£230; D £65.90-£230 **Facilities Spa** Sauna Jacuzzi Wi-fi available Hydro pool Steam room & Beauty treatment rooms Xmas **Conf** BC Thtr 200 Class 70 Board 50 Del from £100 **Services** Lift **Parking** 100 **Notes LB** ⊛ ⊗ in restaurant Civ Wed 80

RUTHIN
MAP 15 SJ15

★★★ 75% ◉ HOTEL

Ruthin Castle
LL15 2NU
☎ 01824 702664 🖺 01824 705978
e-mail: reservations@ruthincastle.co.uk
web: www.ruthincastle.co.uk
dir: *A550 to Mold, A494 to Ruthin, hotel at end of Castle St*

The main part of this impressive castle was built in the early 19th century, but the many ruins in the impressive grounds date back much further. The elegantly panelled public areas include a restaurant and bar along with a medieval banqueting hall. Many of the bedrooms are spacious and furnished with fine period pieces.

Rooms 58 en suite (6 fmly) ⊗ in 10 bedrooms **Facilities** Fishing Snooker Gym Beauty suites ♫ **Conf** BC Thtr 130 Class 108 Board 48 **Services** Lift **Parking** 200 **Notes LB** ⊛ Civ Wed 130

★★ 71% ◉ HOTEL

Woodlands Hall
Llanfwrog LL15 2AN
☎ 01824 705107 🖺 01824 704817
e-mail: info@woodlandshallhotel.co.uk
dir: *B5105 from Ruthin (Cerrig-y-Drudion road). Right at Cross Keys Inn. 0.75m to hotel*

This attractive, timber-framed house is set in 30-acre grounds (including a caravan park). The interior abounds with ornate and intricately carved woodwork, which greatly enhances the character. Privately owned and run, it provides comfortable, well-equipped accommodation and very pleasant public areas. Skilfully prepared food is a highlight here and can be enjoyed in either the restaurant or less formal conservatory.

Rooms 6 en suite (1 fmly) ⊗ in all bedrooms S £43.50-£48.50; D £60-£67.50 (incl. bkfst) **Facilities** Use of sauna and gym nearby **Conf** Thtr 30 Class 12 Board 18 Del from £80 **Parking** 30 **Notes LB** ⊗ in restaurant Closed 15 Feb-1Mar

Wales

ST ASAPH
MAP 15 SJ07

★★★ 79% ❀ **HOTEL**

Oriel House
Upper Denbigh Rd LL17 0LW
☎ 01745 582716 ▤ 01745 585208
e-mail: mail@orielhousehotel.com
web: www.orielhousehotel.com

dir: A55 onto A525, left at cathedral, 1m on right

Set in several acres of mature grounds south of St Asaph, Oriel House offers generally spacious, well-equipped bedrooms and has a friendly and hospitable staff. The Terrace restaurant serves imaginative food with an emphasis on local produce. Extensive function facilities cater for business meetings and weddings, and the leisure club is available to guests.

Rooms 39 en suite (3 fmly) (13 GF) ⊗ in 26 bedrooms S £56-£115; D £79-£115 (incl. bkfst) **Facilities** Spa STV ▣ Fishing Sauna Solarium Gym Wi-fi in bedrooms Xmas **Conf** Thtr 220 Class 100 Board 50 Del from £115 **Parking** 200 **Notes LB** ⊗ ⊘ in restaurant Civ Wed 200

★★ 74% **SMALL HOTEL**

Plas Elwy Hotel & Restaurant
The Roe LL17 0LT
☎ 01745 582263 & 582089 ▤ 01745 583864
e-mail: plaselwy@gtleisure.co.uk

dir: off A55 junct 27, A525 signed Rhyl/St Asaph. On left opposite Total petrol station

This hotel, which dates back to 1850, has retained much of its original character. Bedrooms in the purpose-built extension are spacious, and one has a four-poster bed; those in the main building are equally well equipped. Public rooms are smart and comfortably furnished and a range of food options is provided in the attractive restaurant.

Rooms 7 en suite 6 annexe en suite (3 fmly) (2 GF) ⊗ in 7 bedrooms S £46-£52; D £62-£72 (incl. bkfst) **Facilities** ch fac **Parking** 25 **Notes** ⊗ ⊘ in restaurant Closed 25 Dec-1 Jan

FLINTSHIRE

EWLOE
MAP 15 SJ36

★★★★ 76% ❀ **HOTEL**

De Vere St David's Park
St Davids Park CH5 3YB
☎ 01244 520800 ▤ 01244 520930
e-mail: reservations.stdavids@devere-hotels.com
web: www.devere.co.uk

dir: A494 Queensferry to Mold for 4m, then left slip road B5127 signed Buckley, hotel visible at rdbt

This modern purpose built hotel is conveniently situated and offers a range of rooms, including four-poster suites and family rooms. Public areas include leisure and spa facilities, an all-day café, and, nearby, the hotel's own golf course. The hotel is a popular venue for conferences and other functions. Younger guests are not forgotten either and can have fun in the Dai the Dove Club.

Rooms 147 en suite (24 fmly) (45 GF) ⊗ in 54 bedrooms S £79-£119; D £85-£125 (incl. bkfst) **Facilities** Spa STV ▣ supervised ⌇ Sauna Solarium Gym Putt green Jacuzzi Wi-fi available Steam bath, Beauty Therapist, Playroom Xmas **Conf** BC Thtr 300 Class 150 Board 40 Del from £130 **Services** Lift **Parking** 240 **Notes LB** ⊗ ⊘ in restaurant Civ Wed 60

FLINT
MAP 15 SJ27

★★★ 73% **HOTEL**

Mountain Park Hotel
Northop Rd, Flint Mountain CH6 5QG
☎ 01352 736000 & 730972 ▤ 01352 736010
e-mail: reception@mountain.co.uk

dir: exit A55 onto A5119 for Flint, hotel 1m on left

This former farmhouse has modern, well-equipped bedrooms, many at ground-floor level with direct access to the car park. It is conveniently situated close to the A55. Facilities include the Sevens Brasserie Restaurant serving modern cuisine, a comfortable lounge bar offering a range of bar meals, and an attractively designed function/conference room. There is also a 9-hole golf course.

Rooms 21 annexe en suite (3 fmly) (11 GF) **Facilities** STV ⌁ 9 Jacuzzi Xmas **Conf** Thtr 150 Class 80 Board 60 **Services** air con **Parking** 94 **Notes** ⊗ ⊘ in restaurant

HALKYN
MAP 15 SJ27

BUDGET HOTEL

Travelodge Halkyn
CH8 8RF
☎ 08700 850 950 ▤ 01352 781966
web: www.travelodge.co.uk

dir: on A55, westbound

Travelodge offers good quality, good value, modern accommodation. Ideal for families, the spacious en suite bedrooms include remote-control TV, tea and coffee-making facilities and comfortable beds. Meals can be taken at the nearby family restaurant. See Hotel Groups pages for further details.

Rooms 31 en suite S fr £26; D fr £26

HOLYWELL
MAP 15 SJ17

★★ 71% **HOTEL**

Stamford Gate
Halkyn Rd CH8 7SJ
☎ 01352 712942 ▤ 01352 713309
e-mail: hotel@stamfordgate.freeserve.co.uk

dir: take Holywell turn off A55 onto A5026, hotel 1m on right

This popular, friendly hotel enjoys impressive views across the Dee Estuary from its elevated position. It provides well-equipped accommodation, including a number of ground floor bedrooms. Public areas include a smart nautical themed restaurant, a stylish, spacious bar and there are meeting and function facilities.

Rooms 12 en suite (6 GF) **Facilities** STV ⌁ **Conf** Thtr 100 Class 50 Board 30 **Parking** 100 **Notes** ⊗

Wales

MOLD
MAP 15 SJ26

★★★ 73% **HOTEL**

Beaufort Park Hotel
Alltami Rd, New Brighton CH/ 6RQ
☎ 01352 758646 📠 01352 757132
e-mail: info@beaufortparkhotel.co.uk
web: www.beaufortparkhotel.co.uk

dir: *A55/A494. Through Alltami lights, over mini rdbt by petrol station towards Mold, A5119. Hotel 100yds on right*

This large, modern hotel is conveniently located a short drive from the North Wales Expressway and offers various styles of spacious accommodation. There are extensive public areas, and several meeting and function rooms are available. There is a wide choice of meals in the formal restaurant and in the popular Arches bar.

Rooms 106 en suite (4 fmly) (33 GF) ⊘ in 41 bedrooms S fr £95; D fr £110 (incl. bkfst) **Facilities** STV Squash ♫ Xmas **Conf** Thtr 250 Class 120 Board 120 Del from £120 **Parking** 200 **Notes LB** ⊘ in restaurant Civ Wed 250

See advertisement under CHESTER, Cheshire

NORTHOP
MAP 15 SJ26

★★★ 79% **COUNTRY HOUSE HOTEL**

Soughton Hall
CH7 6AB
☎ 01352 840811 📠 01352 840382
e-mail: info@soughtonhall.co.uk

dir: *A55/B5126, after 500mtrs turn left for Northop, left at lights (A5119-Mold). After 0.5m follow signs*

Built as a bishop's palace in 1714, this elegant country house has magnificent grounds. Bedrooms are individually decorated and furnished with fine antiques and rich fabrics. There are several spacious day rooms furnished in keeping with the style of the house. The trendy Stables Bar and restaurant offer a good range of dishes at both lunch and dinner. Understandably, the hotel is a very popular venue for weddings.

Rooms 15 en suite (2 fmly) (2 GF) ⊘ in all bedrooms S £99; D £130-£180 (incl. bkfst) **Facilities Spa** ☺ Riding ❧ Jacuzzi Riding stables nearby Xmas **Conf** BC Thtr 40 Class 40 Board 20 Del £158.63 **Parking** 100 **Notes LB** ⊛ ⊘ in restaurant Civ Wed 100

NORTHOP HALL
MAP 15 SJ26

★★★ 75% **HOTEL**

Northop Hall Country House
THE INDEPENDENTS
Chester Rd CH7 6HJ
☎ 01244 816181 📠 01244 814661
e-mail: northop@hotel-chester.com
web: www.hotel-chester.com

dir: *From Buckley/St David's Park 3rd exit at rdbt, 1st right to Northop Hall 2m. Left at mini-rdbt, 200yds on left*

Located within large grounds and woodland, this sympathetically renovated and extended period house retains many original features within public areas and is a popular conference and wedding venue. Bedrooms provide both practical and thoughtful extras and a warm welcome is assured.

Rooms 39 en suite (15 fmly) ⊘ in all bedrooms S £58-£68; D £60-£78 **Facilities** ch fac **Conf** Thtr 80 Class 40 Board 50 Del £105 **Parking** 70 **Notes LB** ⊘ in restaurant Civ Wed 50

BUDGET HOTEL

Travelodge Chester Northop Hall
Travelodge
CH7 6IIB
☎ 08700 850 950 📠 01244 816473
web: www.travelodge.co.uk

dir: *on A55, eastbound*

Travelodge offers good quality, good value, modern accommodation. Ideal for families, the spacious en suite bedrooms include remote-control TV, tea and coffee making facilities and comfortable beds. Meals can be taken at the nearby family restaurant. See Hotel Groups pages for further details.

Rooms 40 en suite S fr £26; D fr £26

GWYNEDD

ABERDYFI
MAP 14 SN69

★★★ 81% HOTEL

Trefeddian
LL35 0SB
☎ 01654 767213 ▤ 01654 767777
e-mail: info@trefwales.com
web: www.trefwales.com
dir: 0.5m N of Aberdyfi off A493

This large privately owned hotel in its own grounds overlooks Cardigan Bay and offers well-equipped bedrooms and bathrooms, plus some luxury rooms with balconies and sea views. Public areas include elegantly furnished lounges, a beauty salon and indoor pool. Children are welcome and recreation areas are provided. The hotel is 102-years-old, and 2007 sees the Cave family celebrating the centenary of their ownership.

Rooms 59 en suite (13 fmly) ✆ in all bedrooms S £45-£55; D £90-£110 (incl. bkfst) **Facilities** ⚐ ♨ Snooker Solarium Putt green Wi-fi available Table tennis Play area Beauty salon Xmas **Services** Lift **Parking** 68 **Notes LB** ✆ in restaurant

★★ 82% ⚜ SMALL HOTEL

Penhelig Arms Hotel & Restaurant
LL35 0LT
☎ 01654 767215 ▤ 01654 767690
e-mail: info@penheligarms.com
web: www.penheligarms.com
dir: take A493 coastal road, hotel faces Penhelig harbour

Situated opposite the old harbour, this delightful 18th-century hotel overlooks the Dyfi Estuary. The well-maintained bedrooms have good quality furnishings and modern facilities. Some are situated in a purpose-built cliff top annexe, and a self-contained family suite is located in an adjacent cottage. The public bar is much loved by locals who enjoy the real ale and excellent food.

Rooms 10 en suite 5 annexe en suite (5 fmly) ✆ in all bedrooms S fr £55; D £79-£130 (incl. bkfst) **Parking** 14 **Notes LB** ✆ in restaurant Closed 25 & 26 Dec

★★ 75% SMALL HOTEL

Dovey Inn
Seaview Ter LL35 0EF
☎ 01654 767332 ▤ 01654 767996
e-mail: info@doveyinn.com
web: www.doveyinn.com
dir: in village centre on A493, 9m from Machynlleth

Situated in the heart of Aberdyfi, this inn offers attractive rooms which are comfortable and very well equipped; most have sea views. Downstairs there are four bars where a wide range of dishes, using local produce, is available. Breakfast is served in a separate upstairs dining room. Residents have free use of nearby leisure facilities.

Rooms 11 en suite (2 fmly) ✆ in all bedrooms S £49-£80; D £80 (incl. bkfst) **Facilities** STV Guest may use facilities at Plas Talgarth Country Club **Notes** ⊗ ✆ in restaurant

ABERSOCH
MAP 14 SH32

★★★ 78% ⚜⚜ COUNTRY HOUSE HOTEL

Porth Tocyn
Bwlch Tocyn LL53 7BU
☎ 01758 713303 ▤ 01758 713538
e-mail: bookings@porthtocyn.fsnet.co.uk
web: www.porth-tocyn-hotel.co.uk
dir: 2.5m S follow signs 'Porth Tocyn', after passing through hamlet of Sarnbach

Located above Cardigan Bay with fine views over the area, Porth Tocyn is set in attractive gardens. Several elegantly furnished sitting rooms are provided and bedrooms are comfortably furnished. Children are especially welcome and have a playroom. Award-winning food is served in the restaurant.

Rooms 17 en suite (1 fmly) (3 GF) ✆ in all bedrooms S £65-£85; D £87-£162 (incl. bkfst) **Facilities** ⚐ ♨ Wi-fi available Table Tennis **Parking** 50 **Notes LB** ✆ in restaurant Closed mid Nov-wk before Etr

See advert on opposite page

★★ 79% ⚜ HOTEL

Neigwl
Lon Sarn Bach LL53 7DY
☎ 01758 712363 ▤ 01758 712544
e-mail: relax@neigwl.com
web: www.neigwl.com
dir: on A499, through Abersoch, hotel on left

This delightful, small hotel is privately owned and personally run. It is conveniently located for access to the town, harbour and beach. It has a deservedly high reputation for its food and warm hospitality. Both the attractive restaurant and the pleasant lounge bar overlook the sea, as do several of the tastefully appointed bedrooms.

Rooms 9 en suite (3 fmly) (2 GF) S £95; D £165 (incl. bkfst & dinner) **Parking** 20 **Notes LB** ⊗ Closed Jan

★★ 71% HOTEL

Deucoch
LL53 7LD
☎ 01758 712680 ▤ 01758 712670
e-mail: deucoch@supanet.com
dir: through Abersoch follow Sarn Bach signs. At x-roads in Sarn Bach (approx 1m from village centre) turn right, hotel on hill top

This hotel sits in an elevated position above the village and enjoys lovely views. There is a choice of bars and food options; the regular
continued

carvery is excellent value and has a loyal following, so booking is essential. Pretty bedrooms are equipped with modern amenities and the hotel specialises in golfing packages.

Rooms 10 rms (9 en suite) (2 fmly) ❷ in all bedrooms S £38-£48 (incl. bkfst) **Facilities** Xmas **Parking** 30 **Notes LB** ❷ in restaurant Closed Nov-Feb

---

BALA   MAP 14 SH93

★★★ 85% ⚫ COUNTRY HOUSE HOTEL

Palé Hall Country House

Palé Estate, Llandderfel LL23 7PS
☎ 01678 530285 📠 01678 530220
e-mail: enquiries@palehall.co.uk
web: www.palehall.co.uk
dir: off B4401 (Corwen/Bala road) 4m from Llandrillo

This enchanting mansion was built in 1870 and overlooks extensive grounds and beautiful woodland scenery. The fine entrance hall, with its stained glass lantern ceiling and galleried oak staircase, leads off to the library bar, two elegant lounges and the smart dining room. The standard of cooking remains high and is complemented by fine wines. The spacious bedrooms are furnished to the highest standards with many thoughtful extras.

Rooms 17 en suite (1 fmly) ❷ in all bedrooms S £85-£150; D £115-£200 (incl. bkfst) **Facilities** Fishing ⚓ Clay pigeon/Game shooting Xmas **Conf** Board 22 Del from £145 **Parking** 40 **Notes LB** ❌ No children ❷ in restaurant Civ Wed 40

See advert on this page

★★ 69% SMALL HOTEL

Plas Coch

High St LL23 7AB
☎ 01678 520309 📠 01678 521135
e-mail: plascoch@tiscali.co.uk
dir: on A494, in town centre

A focal point in a bustling town, this 18th-century former coaching inn is popular with locals and resident guests alike. The public areas are very attractive and bedrooms are spacious.

Rooms 10 en suite (4 fmly) ❷ in all bedrooms S £42-£49; D £69 (incl bkfst) **Facilities** Windsurfing, Canoeing, Sailing, Whitewater Rafting **Conf** Thtr 30 Class 20 Board 20 **Parking** 12 **Notes LB** ❌ ❷ in restaurant

---

BANGOR   MAP 14 SH57

BUDGET HOTEL

Premier Travel Inn Bangor

Menai Business Park LL57 4FA
☎ 08701 977023 📠 01248 679214
web: www.premiertravelinn.com
dir: From A55 take 3rd Bangor exit signed Caernarfon A487, Bangor & Hospital. Take 3rd exit at 1st rdbt

High quality, modern budget accommodation ideal for both families and business travellers. Spacious, en suite bedrooms feature bath and shower, satellite TV and many have telephones and modem points. The adjacent family restaurant features a wide and varied menu. For further details consult the Hotel Groups page.

Rooms 40 en suite

Wales

BANGOR *continued*

BUDGET HOTEL

Travelodge Bangor

Llys-y-Gwynt LL57 4BG
☎ 08700 850 950 🗐 0870 1911561
web: www.travelodge.co.uk

dir: at junct of A5/A55

Travelodge offers good quality, good value, modern accommodation. Ideal for families, the spacious en suite bedrooms include remote-control TV, tea and coffee-making facilities and comfortable beds. Meals can be taken at the nearby family restaurant. See Hotel Groups pages for further details.

Rooms 62 en suite S fr £26; D fr £26

BARMOUTH   MAP 14 SH61

★★★ 78% ⚜ HOTEL

Bae Abermaw

Panorama Hill LL42 1DQ
☎ 01341 280550 🗐 01341 280346
e-mail: enquiries@baeabermaw.com
web: www.baeabermaw.com

Located in an idyllic spot on a hillside, with striking panoramic views of the Mawddach Estuary this Victorian house has been lovingly restored and transformed into a stylish contemporary hotel. Bedrooms and bathrooms are modern, spacious and well equipped. Popular, award-winning cuisine, utilising local produce, is served in the attractive dining room and should not be missed.

Rooms 14 en suite (4 fmly) ⊗ in all bedrooms S £77-£100; D £110-£150 (incl. bkfst) **Facilities** Xmas **Conf** Thtr 100 Class 40 Board 40 Del from £146 **Parking** 40 **Notes LB** ⊗ ⊘ in restaurant RS Mon Civ Wed 100

BEDDGELERT   MAP 14 SH54

★★★ 75% HOTEL

The Royal Goat

LL55 4YE
☎ 01766 890224 🗐 01766 890422
e-mail: info@royalgoathotel.co.uk
web: www.royalgoathotel.co.uk

THE CIRCLE
Selected Individual Hotels

dir: On A498 at Beddgelert

An impressive building steeped in history, the Royal Goat provides well-equipped accommodation. Attractively appointed, comfortable

continued

public areas include a choice of bars and restaurants, a residents' lounge and function rooms.

Rooms 32 en suite (4 fmly) ⊘ in 20 bedrooms S £53-£70; D £90-£120 (incl. bkfst) **Facilities** Fishing Xmas **Conf** Thtr 70 Class 70 Board 30 **Services** Lift **Parking** 100 **Notes LB** ⊘ in restaurant Closed Jan-1 Mar RS Nov-1 Jan

★★ 79% HOTEL

Tanronnen Inn

LL55 4YB
☎ 01766 890347 🗐 01766 890606

dir: in village centre

This delightful small hotel offers comfortable, well equipped and attractively appointed accommodation, including a family room. There is also a selection of pleasant and relaxing public areas. The wide range of bar food is popular with tourists, and more formal meals are served in the restaurant.

Rooms 7 en suite (3 fmly) ⊘ in all bedrooms S £55; D £100 (incl. bkfst) **Facilities** Xmas **Parking** 15 **Notes LB** ⊗ ⊘ in restaurant

CAERNARFON   MAP 14 SH46

INSPECTORS' CHOICE

★★★ ⚜⚜ COUNTRY HOUSE HOTEL

Seiont Manor

Llanrug LL55 2AQ
☎ 01286 673366 🗐 01286 672840
e-mail: seiontmanor-cro@handpicked.co.uk
web: www.handpicked.co.uk

HANDPICKED HOTELS

dir: E on A4086, 2.5m from Caernarfon

A splendid hotel created from authentic rural buildings, set in the tranquil countryside near Snowdonia. Bedrooms are individually decorated and well equipped, with luxurious extra touches. Public rooms are cosy and comfortable and furnished in country-house style. The kitchen team use the best of local produce to provide exciting takes on traditional dishes.

Rooms 28 en suite (2 fmly) (14 GF) ⊘ in 15 bedrooms S £124-£155; D £152-£190 (incl. bkfst) **Facilities** Spa STV 🏊 Fishing Sauna Gym Wi-fi available Xmas **Conf** Thtr 100 Class 40 Board 40 Del from £125 **Parking** 60 **Notes LB** ⊘ in restaurant Civ Wed 90

★★★ 75% **HOTEL**

Celtic Royal Hotel

Bangor St LL55 1AY
☎ 01286 674477 📄 01286 674139
e-mail: admin@celtic-royal.co.uk
web: www.celtic-royal.co.uk
dir: Exit A55 at Bangor. Follow A487 towards Caernarfon

This large, impressive, privately owned hotel is situated in the town centre. It provides attractively appointed accommodation, which includes non-smoking rooms, bedrooms for less able guests and family rooms. The spacious public areas include a bar, a choice of lounges and a pleasant split-level restaurant. Guests also have the use of the impressive health club.

Rooms 110 en suite (12 fmly) ⊛ in 73 bedrooms S fr £77, D fr £110 (incl. bkfst) **Facilities** STV 🏊 Sauna Solarium Gym Jacuzzi Sun shower, Steam room 🎵 Xmas **Conf** BC Thtr 300 Class 120 Board 120 Del from £99 **Services** Lift **Parking** 180 **Notes LB** ⊗ ⊛ in restaurant Civ Wed 200

★★ 67% **HOTEL**

Stables

Llanwnda LL54 5SD
☎ 01286 830711 📄 01286 830413
dir: 3m S of Caernarfon, on A499

This privately owned and personally run hotel is set in 15 acres of its own land, south of Caernarfon. The bar and restaurant are located in converted stables. The bedrooms are all situated in two purpose-built, motel style wings.

Rooms 22 annexe en suite (8 fmly) **Facilities** Guests may bring own horse to stables **Conf** Thtr 50 Class 30 Board 30 **Parking** 40

CRICCIETH   MAP 14 SH43

★★★ 83% ⊛ **COUNTRY HOUSE HOTEL**

Bron Eifion Country House

LL52 0SA
☎ 01766 522385 📄 01766 522003
e-mail: stay@broneifion.co.uk
dir: A497 between Porthmadog & Pwllheli, 0.5m from Criccieth village, on right towards Pwhelli.

This delightful country house built in 1883, is set in extensive grounds to the west of Criccieth. Now a privately owned and personally run

continued

hotel, it provides warm and very friendly hospitality as well as attentive service. Most of the tasteful bedrooms have period and antique furniture. The very impressive central hall features a minstrels' gallery, and there is a choice of comfortable lounges. The restaurant overlooks the gardens.

Rooms 19 en suite (1 fmly) (1 GF) ⊛ in 4 bedrooms S fr £80; D fr £120 (incl. bkfst) **Facilities** Xmas **Conf** Thtr 30 Class 25 Board 25 **Parking** 50 **Notes LB** ⊗ ⊛ in restaurant

★★ 72% **HOTEL**

Caerwylan

LL52 0HW
☎ 01766 522547
e-mail: caerwylan_hotel@plevy.fsbusiness.co.uk
dir: near lifeboat station

Privately owned and personally run, this long established holiday hotel commands panoramic sea views of Cardigan Bay and the castle. Comfortably furnished lounges are available for residents and the five-course menu changes daily. Bedrooms, including family rooms, are smart and modern, and several have their own private sitting areas. The friendly atmosphere ensures that many guests return.

Rooms 25 en suite (3 fmly) S £50-£52; D £60-£68 (incl. bkfst) **Services** Lift **Parking** 9 **Notes LB** ⊛ in restaurant Closed Nov-Etr

DOLGELLAU   MAP 14 SH71

★★★ 80% ⊛⊛ **HOTEL**

Penmaenuchaf Hall

Penmaenpool LL40 1YB
☎ 01341 422129 📄 01341 422787
e-mail: relax@penhall.co.uk
web: www.penhall.co.uk
dir: off A470 onto A493 to Tywyn. Hotel approx 1m on left

Built in 1860, this impressive hall stands in 20 acres of formal gardens, grounds and woodland and enjoys magnificent views across the River Mawddach. Careful restoration has created a comfortable and welcoming hotel. Fresh produce cooked in modern British style is served in the panelled restaurant.

Rooms 14 en suite (2 fmly) ⊛ in all bedrooms S £75-£135; D £130-£200 (incl. bkfst) **Facilities** Fishing Snooker 🏌 Complimentary salmon & trout fishing Xmas **Conf** BC Thtr 50 Class 30 Board 22 Del from £155 **Parking** 30 **Notes LB** No children 6yrs ⊛ in restaurant Civ Wed 50

Wales

DOLGELLAU *continued*

★★★ 77% ® **HOTEL**

Dolserau Hall

LL40 2AG

☎ 01341 422522 📠 01341 422400

e-mail: welcome@dolserau.co.uk

web: www.dolserau.co.uk

dir: *1.5m outside Dolgellau between A494 to Bala and A470 to Dinas Mawddy*

This privately owned, friendly hotel lies in attractive grounds extending to the river and is surrounded by green fields. Several comfortable lounges are provided and welcoming log fires are lit during cold weather. The smart bedrooms are spacious, well equipped and comfortable. A varied menu offers very competently prepared dishes.

Rooms 15 en suite 5 annexe en suite (1 fmly) (3 GF) ⊛ in all bedrooms S £66-£80; D £132-£160 (incl. bkfst & dinner) **Facilities** STV Fishing Xmas **Services** Lift **Parking** 40 **Notes LB** No children 12yrs ⊛ in restaurant Closed Dec-Jan (ex Xmas & New Year)

★★ 72% **HOTEL**

Royal Ship

Queens Square LL40 1AR

☎ 01341 422209 📠 01341 424693

dir: *in town centre*

The Royal Ship dates from 1813 when it was a coaching inn. There are three bars and several lounges, all comfortably furnished and attractively appointed. It is very much the centre of local activities and a wide range of food is available. Bedrooms are tastefully decorated.

Rooms 24 en suite (4 fmly) S £47.50-£50; D £70-£87.50 (incl. bkfst) **Facilities** Fishing arrangements available Xmas **Conf** Thtr 80 Class 60 Board 60 **Parking** 12 **Notes LB** ⊗ ⊛ in restaurant

See advert on opposite page

★★ 67% **HOTEL**

Fronoleu Country Hotel

Tabor LL40 2PS

☎ 01341 422361 & 422197 📠 01341 422023

e-mail: fronoleu@fronoleu.co.uk

web: www.fronoleu.co.uk

dir: *A487/A470 junct, towards Tabor opposite Cross Foxes & continue for 1.25m. From Dolgellau take road for hospital & continue 1.25m up the hill*

This 16th-century farmhouse lies in the shadow of Cader Idris. Carefully extended, it retains many original features. The bar and lounge are located in the old building where there are exposed timbers and open fires, and the restaurant attracts a large local following. Most of the bedrooms are in a modern extension.

Rooms 11 en suite (3 fmly) ⊛ in 6 bedrooms **Facilities** Fishing Pool table, Childrens play area **Conf** BC Thtr 150 Class 100 Board 50 **Parking** 60 **Notes LB** ⊛ in restaurant Civ Wed 150

★★ 67% **HOTEL**

George III Hotel

Penmaenpool LL40 1YD

☎ 01341 422525 📠 01341 423565

e-mail: reception@george-3rd.co.uk

dir: *2m from Dolgellau on A493*

On the banks of the Mawddach Estuary, this delightful small hotel, now under new ownership, started life as an inn and chandlers to the local boatyard. A nearby building, now housing several bedrooms, was the local railway station. Bedrooms are well equipped and many enjoy river views. There is a choice of bars and a formal restaurant, all provide a wide range of food.

Rooms 6 en suite 5 annexe en suite **Facilities** Fishing **Conf** Class 32 **Parking** 30 **Notes** ⊛ in restaurant Closed 25 Dec

HARLECH   MAP 14 SH53

★★★ 78% ®® **HOTEL**

Maes y Neuadd Country House

LL47 6YA

☎ 01766 780200 📠 01766 780211

e-mail: maes@neuadd.com

web: www.neuadd.com

dir: *3m NE of Harlech, signed on unclassified road, off B4573*

This 14th-century hotel enjoys fine views over the mountains and across the bay to the Lleyn Peninsula. The team here is committed to restoring some of the hidden features of the house. Bedrooms, some in an adjacent coach house, are individually furnished and many boast fine antique pieces. Public areas display a similar welcoming charm, including the restaurant, which serves many locally-sourced and home-grown ingredients.

Rooms 15 en suite (5 fmly) (3 GF) ⊛ in all bedrooms S £160-£245 D £185-£270 (incl. bkfst & dinner) **Facilities** ↳ clay pigeon, cooking tuition ch fac Xmas **Conf** Thtr 15 Class 10 Board 12 Del from £185 **Parking** 50 **Notes LB** ⊛ in restaurant Civ Wed 65

Ⓐ

The Castle

Castle Square LL46 2YH

☎ 01766 780529 📠 01766 780499

dir: *directly opposite the entrance to Harlech Castle*

Rooms 7 en suite (1 fmly) S £35-£50; D £60-£80 (incl. bkfst) **Parking** 30 **Notes** ★★ ⊗ ⊛ in restaurant

continued

Wales

LLANBEDR

MAP 14 SH52

★★ 68% SMALL HOTEL

Ty Mawr

LL45 2NH

☎ 01341 241440 🖹 01341 241440

e-mail: tymawrhotel@onetel.com

web: www.tymawrhotel.org.uk

dir: from Barmouth A496 (Harlech road). In Llanbedr turn right after bridge, hotel 50yds on left, brown tourist signs on junct

Located in a picturesque village, this family-run hotel has a relaxed, friendly atmosphere. Bedrooms are smart and brightly decorated. The pleasant grounds become popular in fine weather as a beer garden. The attractive, cane-furnished bar offers a blackboard selection of food and a good choice of real ales. A more formal menu is available in the restaurant.

Rooms 10 en suite (2 fmly) ⊘ in all bedrooms S £45-£55; D £70 (incl. bkfst) **Facilities** STV **Conf** Class 25 **Parking** 30 **Notes LB** ⊘ in restaurant Closed 24-26 Dec

LLANBERIS

MAP 14 SH56

★★★ 72% HOTEL

Quality Hotel Snowdonia (Royal Victoria)

LL55 4TY

☎ 01286 870253 🖹 01286 870149

e-mail: enquiries@hotels-snowdonia.com

web: www.choicehotelseurope.com

dir: on A4086 (Caernarfon to Llanberis road), directly opposite Snowdon Mountain Railway

This well-established hotel sits near the foot of Snowdon, between the Peris and Padarn lakes. Pretty gardens and grounds make an attractive backdrop for the many weddings held here. Bedrooms have been refurbished and are well equipped. There are spacious lounges and

continued

---

bars, and a large dining room with conservatory overlooks the lakes.

Rooms 106 en suite (7 fmly) ⊘ in 40 bedrooms S £30-£65; D £50-£110 (incl. bkfst) **Facilities** STV Mountaineering, Cycling, Walking ♫ Xmas **Conf** Thtr 100 Class 60 Board 50 Del from £70 **Services** Lift **Parking** 300 **Notes LB** ⊘ in restaurant Civ Wed 100

A

Lake View Hotel & Restaurant

Tan-y-Pant LL55 4EL

☎ 01286 870422 🖹 01286 872591

e-mail: reception@lakeviewhotel.co.uk

web: www.lakeviewhotel.co.uk

dir: 0.5m from Llanberis on A4086 towards Caernarfon

Rooms 10 rms (9 en suite) (1 fmly) ⊘ in all bedrooms S £30-£50; D £50-£68 (incl. bkfst) **Parking** 20 **Notes ★★ LB** No children ⊘ in restaurant RS Jan-Feb

PORTHMADOG

MAP 14 SH53

★★★ 70% HOTEL

Royal Sportsman

131 High St LL49 9HB

☎ 01766 512015 🖹 01766 512490

e-mail: enquiries@royalsportsman.co.uk

dir: by rdbt, at A497 & A487 junct

Ideally located in the centre of Porthmadog, this former coaching inn dates from the Victorian era and has been restored into a friendly,

continued on page 918

Wales

PORTHMADOG *continued*

privately owned and personally run hotel. Rooms are tastefully decorated and well equipped, and some are in an annexe close to the hotel. There is a large comfortable lounge and a wide range of meals is served in the bar or restaurant.

Rooms 19 en suite 9 annexe en suite (7 fmly) (9 GF) ⊗ in all bedrooms
S £48-£70; D £74-£86 (incl. bkfst) **Facilities** Wi-fi available Xmas
Conf BC Thtr 50 Class 50 Board 30 **Parking** 18 **Notes LB** ⊘ in restaurant

PORTMEIRION   MAP 14 SH53

★★★★ 75% ⊛ **HOTEL**

Castell Deudraeth

LL48 6EN
☎ 01766 770000 📄 01766 771771
e-mail: castell@portmeirion-village.com
web: www.portmeirion-village.com

dir: A4212 for Trawsfynydd/Porthmadog. 1.5m beyond Penrhyndeudraeth, hotel on right

A refurbished castellated mansion that overlooks Snowdonia and the famous Italianate village featured in the 1960s cult series *The Prisoner*. An original concept, Castell Deudraeth combines traditional materials, such as oak and slate, with state-of-the-art technology and design. Dynamically styled bedrooms boast underfloor heating, real-flame gas fires and wide-screen TVs with DVDs and cinema surround-sound. The brasserie-themed dining room provides an informal option at dinner.

Rooms 11 en suite (5 fmly) D £209-£225 (incl. bkfst) **Facilities Spa** STV
⚘ 🏊 ♫ Xmas **Conf** Thtr 30 Class 18 Board 25 **Services** Lift air con
Parking 30 **Notes LB** ⊗ ⊘ in restaurant Civ Wed 30

★★★★ 75% ⊛ **HOTEL**

The Hotel Portmeirion

LL48 6ET
☎ 01766 770000 📄 01766 771331
e-mail: hotel@portmeirion-village.com
web: www.portmeirion-village.com

dir: 2m W, Portmeirion village is S off A487

Saved from dereliction in the 1920s by Clough Williams-Ellis, the elegant Hotel Portmeirion enjoys one of the finest settings in Wales,

continued

located beneath the wooded slopes of the village, and overlooking the sandy estuary towards Snowdonia. Many rooms have private sitting rooms and balconies with spectacular views. The mostly Welsh-speaking staff provide a good mix of warm hospitality and efficient service.

The Hotel Portmeirion

Rooms 25 en suite 26 annexe en suite (4 fmly) D £167-£209 (incl. bkfst)
Facilities STV ⚘ 🏊 Beauty Salon Xmas **Conf** Thtr 100 **Parking** 40
Notes LB ⊗ ⊘ in restaurant Civ Wed 100

MERTHYR TYDFIL

MERTHYR TYDFIL   MAP 09 SO00
See also Nant-Ddu (Powys)

★★★ 72% **HOTEL**

Bessemer

Hermon Close, Dowlais CF48 3DP
☎ 01685 350780 📄 01685 352874
e-mail: sales@bessemerhotel.co.uk

A modern hotel, with a friendly and relaxed atmosphere, that has high quality bedrooms and bathrooms. Business guests will appreciate the spacious work desks and modem points. Dinner includes the popular option of a self-service carvery, and there are three bars including one in a large function room catering for up to 160 guests.

Rooms 17 en suite ⊗ in 12 bedrooms **Facilities** STV Jacuzzi
Services Lift **Parking** 30 **Notes LB** ⊗

A

Tregenna

Park Ter CF47 8RF

☎ 01685 723627 382055 🖹 01685 721951

e-mail: reception@tregennahotel.co.uk

dir: *M4 junct 32, onto A465 follow signs for Merthyr Tydfil signed from town centre*

Rooms 21 en suite (6 fmly) (7 GF) ❸ in 7 bedrooms S £50-£55; D £65-£75 (incl. bkfst) **Facilities** STV **Parking** 12 **Notes** ★★★ **LB** ❸ in restaurant

---

BUDGET HOTEL

Premier Travel Inn Merthyr Tydfil

premier travel inn

Pentrebach CF48 4BD

☎ 08701 977183 🖹 01443 699171

web: www.premiertravelinn.com

dir: *M4 junct 32 follow A470 to Merthyr Tydfil. At 2nd rdbt turn right to Pentrebach, follow signs to Industrial Estate*

High quality, modern budget accommodation ideal for both families and business travellers. Spacious, en suite bedrooms feature bath and shower, satellite TV and many have telephones and modem points. The adjacent family restaurant features a wide and varied menu. For further details consult the Hotel Groups page.

Rooms 40 en suite **Conf** Thtr 65 Board 30

MONMOUTHSHIRE

ABERGAVENNY   MAP 09 SO21

★★★ 77% ◉◉ COUNTRY HOUSE HOTEL

Llansantffraed Court

Llanvihangel Gobion NP7 9BA

☎ 01873 840678 🖹 01873 840674

e-mail: reception@llch.co.uk

web: www.llch.co.uk

dir: *at A465/A40 Abergavenny junct take B4598 signed Usk (do not join A40). Continue towards Raglan, hotel on left in 4.5m*

In a commanding position and in its own extensive grounds, this very impressive property, now a privately owned country house hotel, has

continued

---

enviable views of the Brecon Beacons. Extensive public areas include a relaxing lounge and a spacious restaurant offering imaginative and enjoyable dishes. Bedrooms are comfortably furnished and have modern facilities.

Llansantffraed Court

Rooms 21 en suite (1 fmly) ❸ in 7 bedrooms S £86-£115; D £115-£175 (incl. bkfst) **Facilities** STV FTV ⚓ Fishing ⛳ Putt green Wi-fi available Ornamental trout lake, Salmon fishing on River Usk ch fac **Conf** BC Thtr 220 Class 120 Board 100 Del from £150 **Services** Lift **Parking** 250 **Notes LB** ❸ in restaurant Civ Wed 150

★★★ 74% ◉ HOTEL

Angel

15 Cross St NP7 5EN

☎ 01873 857121 🖹 01873 858059

e-mail: mail@angelhotelabergavenny.com

web: www.angelhotelabergavenny.com

dir: *follow town centre signs from rdbt, S of Abergavenny, past rail and bus stations. Turn left by hotel*

This has long been a popular venue for both local people and visitors; the two traditional function rooms and ballroom are in regular use. In addition there is a comfortable lounge, a relaxed bar and an award-winning restaurant.

Rooms 29 en suite ❸ in 14 bedrooms S £60-£100; D fr £85 (incl. bkfst) **Facilities** STV FTV Wi-fi in bedrooms ♫ Xmas **Conf** Thtr 200 Class 120 Board 60 Del fr £146.88 **Parking** 30 **Notes LB** ❸ in restaurant Closed 25-Dec RS 24-26 Dec Civ Wed 200

★★★ 72% COUNTRY HOUSE HOTEL

Allt-yr-Ynys Country House Hotel

HR2 0DU

☎ 01873 890307 🖹 01873 890539

e-mail: allthotel@compuserve.com

dir: *take A465 N of Abergavenny. After 5m turn left at Old Pandy Inn in Pandy. After 300yds turn right, hotel on right*

Set in rolling countryside, the main house of this charming hotel dates back to 1550 and Queen Elizabeth I is reputed to have stayed here. Most of the comfortable bedrooms are contained in separate, purpose-built buildings, located within the extensive grounds. Homely

continued on page 920

Wales

ABERGAVENNY *continued*

lounges, a bar with a cider mill, and an adjoining swimming pool complete the experience, together with the charming restaurant.

Allt-yr-Ynys Country House Hotel

Rooms 3 en suite 18 annexe en suite (2 fmly) (18 GF) ⊘ in 6 bedrooms
Facilities Spa 🎣 Fishing Sauna Clay pigeon range **Conf** BC Thtr 100
Class 30 Board 40 **Parking** 100 **Notes LB** ⊗ ⊘ in restaurant Civ Wed 80

★★ 78% ⊛ **HOTEL**

Llanwenarth

Brecon Rd NP8 1EP
☎ 01873 810550 📄 01873 811880
e-mail: info@llanwenarthhotel.com
web: www.llanwenarthhotel.com
dir: *A40 from Abergavenny towards Brecon. Hotel 3m past hospital on left*

Dating from the 16th century and set in magnificent scenery, this delightful hotel offers guests the chance to relax and unwind in style. Bedrooms, in a detached wing, offer plenty of quality and comfort plus pleasant river views; many have a private balcony. The airy conservatory lounge and restaurant offer a varied selection of carefully prepared dishes.

Rooms 17 en suite (3 fmly) (7 GF) ⊘ in all bedrooms S £63; D £85
(incl. bkfst) **Facilities** Fishing & Riding Stables nearby **Parking** 30
Notes ⊗ ⊘ in restaurant

CHEPSTOW   MAP 04 ST59

★★★★ 75% **HOTEL**

Marriott St Pierre Hotel & Country Club

Marriott
HOTELS & RESORTS

St Pierre Park NP16 6YA
☎ 01291 625261 📄 01291 629975
web: www.marriott.co.uk
dir: *M48 junct 2. At rdbt on slip road take A466 Chepstow. At next rdbt take 1st exit Caerwent A48. Hotel approx 2m on left*

This 14th-century property offers an extensive range of leisure and conference facilities. Bedrooms are well equipped, comfortable and located in adjacent wings or in a lakeside cottage complex. The main bar, popular with golfers, overlooks the 18th green, whilst diners can choose between a traditional elegant restaurant and modern brasserie.

continued

Marriott St Pierre Hotel & Country Club

Rooms 148 en suite (16 fmly) (75 GF) ⊘ in 74 bedrooms S £99-£119;
D £99-£119 **Facilities Spa** STV 🎾 ♨ 36 ⚒ Fishing Sauna Solarium
Gym 🏌 Putt green Jacuzzi Wi-fi in bedrooms Health spa, Floodlit driving
range, Chipping green Xmas **Conf** Thtr 240 Class 120 Board 90 Del from
£150 **Parking** 430 **Notes LB** ⊗ ⊘ in restaurant Civ Wed 200

★★★ 66% **HOTEL**

Chepstow

THE INDEPENDENTS

Newport Rd NP16 5PR
☎ 01291 626261 & 0845 6588700 📄 01291 626263
e-mail: info@chepstowhotel.com
web: www.chepstowhotel.com
dir: *M48 junct 2, follow Chepstow signs, A466 & A48 into town*

This privately owned hotel has easy access to the M4 and M48. Bedrooms vary in size and style, but all have modern equipment and facilities. The attractively appointed public areas include an air-conditioned conference room and a large ballroom.

Rooms 31 en suite (4 fmly) ⊘ in 20 bedrooms S £57; D £69
Facilities FTV Wi-fi in bedrooms Xmas **Conf** Thtr 200 Class 70 Board 50
Del from £92.50 **Services** Lift **Parking** 100 **Notes LB** ⊘ in restaurant
Civ Wed 150 *See advert on opposite page*

★★ 68% **HOTEL**

Castle View

16 Bridge St NP6 5EZ ☎ 01291 620349 📄 01291 627397
e-mail: dave@castview.demon.co.uk
dir: *M48 junct 2, A466 for Wye Valley, A48 towards Gloucester. Follow 2nd sign to town centre*

This privately owned inn is situated opposite the Norman castle. Bedrooms vary in size, and all are similarly furnished and well equipped, with some rooms situated in separate buildings. Several family rooms are available. Public areas include a comfortable lounge, a pleasant lounge bar and a cosy restaurant.

Rooms 9 en suite 4 annexe en suite (7 fmly) **Notes** ⊘ in restaurant
See advert on opposite page

LLANTRISANT   MAP 09 ST39

🅰

Greyhound Inn

NP15 1LE ☎ 01291 673447 672505 📄 01291 673255
e-mail: enquiry@greyhound-inn.com
web: www.greyhound-inn.com
dir: *M4 junct 24, A449, exit for Usk, follow Llantrisant signs*
Rooms 10 en suite (2 fmly) (5 GF) ⊘ in all bedrooms S £49-£52;

continued

Wales

D £64-£74 (incl. bkfst) **Parking** 60 **Notes** ★★★ **LB** ⊗ ⊘ in restaurant
Closed 25-26 Dec RS Sunday eve no food

MAGOR SERVICE AREA (M4) MAP 09 ST48

BUDGET HOTEL

Travelodge Magor Newport

Magor Service Area NP26 3YL
☎ 08700 850 950 📠 01633 881896
web: www.travelodge.co.uk

dir: M4 junct 23a

Travelodge offers good quality, good value, modern accommodation.
Ideal for families, the spacious en suite bedrooms include remote-
control TV, tea and coffee-making facilities and comfortable beds.
Meals can be taken at the nearby family restaurant. See Hotel Groups
pages for further details.

Rooms 43 en suite S fr £26; D fr £26

RAGLAN   MAP 09 SO40

★★ 75% HOTEL

The Beaufort Arms Coaching Inn & Restaurant

High St NP15 2DY
☎ 01291 690412 📠 01291 690935
e-mail: thebeauforthotel@hotmail.com
web: www.beaufortraglan.co.uk

dir: M4 junct 24 (Newport/Abergavenny) A449 then A40 to
Raglan. Opposite church in Raglan

This friendly, family-run village inn dating back to the 15th century has
historic links with nearby Raglan Castle. The bright, stylish and
beautifully refurbished bedrooms in the main house are suitably
equipped for both tourists and for business guests. Food is served in
either the restaurant or traditional lounge and both offer relaxed
service and an enjoyable selection of carefully prepared dishes.

Rooms 10 en suite 5 annexe en suite (5 GF) ⊘ in all bedrooms
S £55-£75; D £65-£95 (incl. bkfst) **Facilities** Wi-fi available **Conf** Thtr 120
Class 60 Board 30 Del from £100 **Parking** 30 **Notes LB** ⊗ ⊘ in
restaurant

Wales

Wales

RAGLAN *continued*

BUDGET HOTEL

Travelodge Monmouth
Granada Services A40, Nr Monmouth
NP5 4BG
☎ 08700 850 950 📠 01600 740329
web: www.travelodge.co.uk
dir: *on A40 near junct with A449*

Travelodge offers good quality, good value, modern accommodation. Ideal for families, the spacious en suite bedrooms include remote-control TV, tea and coffee-making facilities and comfortable beds. Meals can be taken at the nearby family restaurant. See Hotel Groups pages for further details.

Rooms 43 en suite S fr £26; D fr £26

SKENFRITH   MAP 09 SO42

◉◉ RESTAURANT WITH ROOMS

The Bell at Skenfrith
NP7 8UH
☎ 01600 750235 📠 01600 750525
e-mail: enquiries@skenfrith.co.uk
web: www.skenfrith.co.uk
dir: *A40/A466 N towards Hereford 4m, turn left onto B4521 signed Abergavenny. Hotel 2m on left*

The Bell is a beautifully restored, 17th-century former coaching inn which still retains much of its original charm and character. It is peacefully situated on the banks of The Monnow, a tributary of the River Wye, and is ideally placed for exploring the numerous delights of the counties of Herefordshire and Monmouthshire. Natural materials have been used to create a relaxing atmosphere, while the bedrooms, which include full suites and rooms with four-poster beds, are stylish, luxurious and equipped with DVD players.

Rooms 8 en suite ⊘ in all bedrooms S £75-£120; D £100-£180 (incl. bkfst) **Facilities** Wi-fi in bedrooms Xmas **Conf** Thtr 20 Board 16 Del £185 **Parking** 36 **Notes** ⊘ in restaurant Closed Last wk Jan-1st wk Feb RS Oct-Mar

---

TINTERN PARVA   MAP 04 SO50

★★★ 72% HOTEL

Best Western Royal George
NP16 6SF
☎ 01291 689205 📠 01291 689448
e-mail: royalgeorgetintern@hotmail.com
dir: *off M48/A466, 4m to Tintern, 2nd on left*

This privately owned and personally run hotel provides comfortable, spacious accommodation, including bedrooms with balconies overlooking the well-tended garden. There are a number of ground floor rooms. The public areas include a choice of bars, and a large function room. A varied and popular menu choice is available in either the bar or restaurant.

Rooms 2 en suite 14 annexe en suite (13 fmly) (10 GF) ⊘ in 11 bedrooms **Facilities** ♪ **Conf** Thtr 120 Class 40 Board 50 **Parking** 50 **Notes LB** ⊗ ⊘ in restaurant Civ Wed 120

★★★ 70% HOTEL

The Abbey Hotel
NP16 6SF
☎ 01291 689777 📠 01291 689727
e-mail: info@theabbey-hotel.co.uk
web: www.theabbey-hotel.co.uk
dir: *M48 junct 2/A466, hotel opposite the abbey ruins*

Appointed to a high standard and commanding stunning views of nearby Tintern Abbey, this friendly hotel provides modern bedrooms, including a family suite. Diners are spoilt for choice between the brasserie with its daytime carvery, the more formal carte service for dinner, and the pleasant hotel bar where lighter meal options are on offer.

Rooms 23 en suite ⊘ in 7 bedrooms S £45-£65; D £75-£125 (incl. bkfst) **Facilities** STV Fishing Wi-fi in bedrooms Xmas **Conf** Thtr 150 Class 60 Board 30 Del from £99 **Parking** 60 **Notes LB** ⊘ in restaurant Civ Wed 140

★★ 65% HOTEL

Parva Farmhouse
Monmouth Rd NP16 6SQ
☎ 01291 689411 📠 01291 689941
e-mail: parvahoteltintern@fsmail.net
dir: *1m from Tintern Abbey on A466 Monmouth Road. Last hotel in village on right*

This relaxed and friendly hotel, now under new ownership, is situated on a sweep of the River Wye with far reaching views of the valley. Originally a farmhouse dating from the 17th century, many of the original features have been retained to provide a lounge full of character, which has a fire in colder months, and an atmospheric restaurant. Bedrooms are tastefully decorated and enjoy pleasant views.

Rooms 8 en suite (2 fmly) ⊘ in all bedrooms S £55; D £67-£85 (incl. bkfst) **Parking** 8 **Notes LB** No children 12yrs ⊘ in restaurant

continued

USK
MAP 09 SO30

★★★ 75% **HOTEL**

Glen-yr-Afon House
Pontypool Rd NP15 1SY
☎ 01291 672302 & 673202 📠 01291 672597
e-mail: enquiries@glen-yr-afon.co.uk
web: www.glen-yr-afon.co.uk
dir: *A472 through High St, over river bridge, follow road to right. Hotel 200yds on left*

On the edge of this delightful old market town, Glen yr Afon, a unique Victorian villa, offers all the facilities expected of a modern hotel combined with the warm atmosphere of a family home. Bedrooms are furnished to a high standard and several overlook the hotel's well-tended gardens. There is a choice of comfortable sitting areas and a stylish and spacious banqueting suite.

Rooms 28 en suite (2 fmly) ⊘ in 14 bedrooms S £85.78-£109.28; D £117.50-£141 (incl. bkfst) **Facilities** STV ☞ Wi-fi in bedrooms Xmas **Conf** Thtr 100 Class 200 Board 30 Del from £130 **Services** Lift **Parking** 101 **Notes** LB ⊘ in restaurant Civ Wed 200

★★★ 68% ⚜ **HOTEL**

Three Salmons
Porthycarne St NP15 1RY
☎ 01291 672133 📠 01291 673979
e-mail: threesalmons.hotel@talk21.com
web: www.3-salmons.usk.co.uk
dir: *off A449, 1m into Usk, hotel on corner of Porthycarne St, B4598*

This 17th-century coaching inn in the heart of Usk offers spacious bedrooms that are comfortably furnished and well maintained. Both the restaurant and bar offer a wide range of carefully prepared dishes. The function room and meeting room overlook the pretty garden and courtyard to the rear.

Rooms 10 en suite 14 annexe en suite (2 fmly) **Facilities** STV **Conf** Thtr 100 Class 40 Board 50 **Parking** 38 **Notes** ⊗ ⊘ in restaurant Civ Wed 100

◎◎ **RESTAURANT WITH ROOMS**

The Newbridge
Tredunnock NP15 1LY
☎ 01633 451000 📠 01633 451001
e-mail: thenewbridge@tinyonline.co.uk
web: www.thenewbridge.co.uk

This 200-year-old inn stands alongside the River Usk at Tredunnock, just four miles south of Usk. It has been renovated and converted

continued

into a spacious, traditionally furnished restaurant occupying the ground and first-floor levels. Six smart, modern and well-equipped bedrooms are located in a stone-clad, purpose-built unit adjacent to the restaurant.

Rooms 6 en suite ⊘ in all bedrooms S £95-£105; D £140-£160 **Facilities** STV Fishing **Conf** Thtr 20 **Parking** 60 **Notes** ⊘ in restaurant Closed 1 wk Jan Civ Wed 80

WHITEBROOK

◎◎ **RESTAURANT WITH ROOMS**

The Crown at Whitebrook
NP25 4TX
☎ 01600 860254 📠 01600 860607
e-mail: crown@whitebrook.demon.co.uk
dir: *0.5m W of village, off A449*

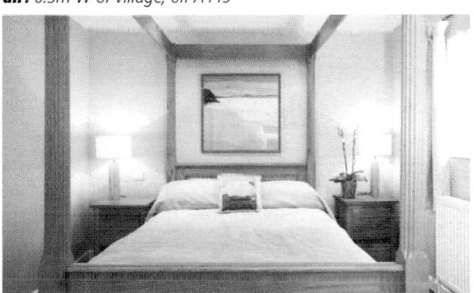

The 17th-century former drover's cottage lies in a secluded wooded valley that falls to the River Wye. Its refurbished bedrooms have a contemporary feel with modern facilities, and the restaurant and lounge combine original features with a bright fresh look that creates a very comfortable and appealing environment. The memorable cuisine features local ingredients, skilfully prepared.

Rooms 8 en suite ⊘ in all bedrooms S £70-£85; D £85-£120 **Facilities** STV Fishing Shooting **Conf** Thtr 16 Board 10 Del from £105 **Parking** 20 **Notes** LB ⊗ No children 12yrs Closed 26 Dec-12 Jan RS Sun-Mon

NEATH PORT TALBOT

NEATH
MAP 09 SS79

★★★ 70% **HOTEL**

Castle Hotel
The Parade SA11 1RB
☎ 01639 641119 📠 01639 641624
e-mail: info@castlehotelneath.co.uk
web: www.castlehotelneath.co.uk
dir: *M4 junct 43, follow signs for Neath, 500yds past rail station, hotel on right. Car park on left 50yds further*

Situated in the town centre, this Georgian property, once a coaching inn, has a wealth of history and character. Lord Nelson and Lady Hamilton are reputed to have stayed here and the Welsh Rugby Union was founded here in 1881. The hotel provides well-equipped accommodation and pleasant public areas. Bedrooms include one with a four-poster bed, non-smoking rooms and family bedded rooms. Facilities include functions and meeting rooms.

Rooms 29 en suite (3 fmly) ⊘ in 4 bedrooms S £45-£60; D £60-£80 (incl. bkfst) **Facilities** STV **Conf** Thtr 160 Class 75 Board 50 **Parking** 26 **Notes** LB ⊗ Civ Wed 100

PORT TALBOT
MAP 09 SS78

★★★ 70% HOTEL

Best Western Aberavon Beach
SA12 6QP
☎ 01639 884949 📠 01639 897885
e-mail: sales@aberavonbeach.com
web: www.aberavonbeach.com

dir: *M4 junct 41/A48 & follow signs for Aberavon Beach & Hollywood Park*

This friendly, purpose-built hotel enjoys a prominent position on the seafront overlooking Swansea Bay. Bedrooms, many of which have sea views, are comfortably appointed and thoughtfully equipped. Public areas include a leisure suite with swimming pool, open-plan bar and restaurant and a selection of function rooms.

Rooms 52 en suite (6 fmly) ⊗ in 40 bedrooms S £95-£105; D £105-£115 (incl. bkfst) **Facilities** FTV 🏊 Sauna Jacuzzi Wi-fi in bedrooms All weather leisure centre ♫ Xmas **Conf** Thtr 300 Class 200 Board 100 Del from £110 **Services** Lift **Parking** 150 **Notes** LB ⊗ in restaurant Civ Wed 300

See advertisement under SWANSEA, page 939

BUDGET HOTEL

Premier Travel Inn Port Talbot
Baglan Rd, Baglan SA12 8ES
☎ 08701 977211 📠 01639 823096
web: www.premiertravelinn.com

dir: *Exit M4 junct 41 westbound. Follow road to rdbt. Inn just off 4th exit, junct 42 eastbound, left turn for Port Talbot. 2nd exit off 2nd rdbt*

High quality, modern budget accommodation ideal for both families and business travellers. Spacious, en suite bedrooms feature bath and shower, satellite TV and many have telephones and modem points. The adjacent family restaurant features a wide and varied menu. For further details consult the Hotel Groups page.

Rooms 42 en suite

NEWPORT

CASTLETON
MAP 09 ST28

BUDGET HOTEL

Premier Travel Inn Cardiff East
Newport Rd CF3 2UQ
☎ 08701 977051 📠 01633 681143
web: www.premiertravelinn.com

dir: *M4 junct 8, at rdbt take 2nd exit A48 Castleton and follow for 3m, Inn on right*

High quality, modern budget accommodation ideal for both families and business travellers. Spacious, en suite bedrooms feature bath and shower, satellite TV and many have telephones and modem points. The adjacent family restaurant features a wide and varied menu. For further details consult the Hotel Groups page.

Rooms 49 en suite

NEWPORT
MAP 09 ST38
See also Cwmbran (Torfaen)

★★★★★ 85% ◎◎ HOTEL

The Celtic Manor Resort
Coldra Woods NP18 1HQ
☎ 01633 413000 📠 01633 412910
e-mail: postbox@celtic-manor.com

dir: *M4 junct 24, take B4237 towards Newport. Hotel 1st on right*

This luxurious resort offers a whole host of facilities to suit any guest, whether they are conference delegates, business users or leisure guests. Three challenging golf courses are complemented by superb leisure facilities, whilst the convention centre can accommodate 1500 delegates. There is also a wide choice of dining options to tempt guests out of the deeply comfortable bedrooms and suites.

Rooms 330 en suite (7 fmly) ⊗ in all bedrooms S fr £225; D fr £225 **Facilities Spa** STV 🏊 supervised ♨ 18 ⌖ Fishing Snooker Sauna Solarium Gym Putt green Jacuzzi Wi-fi available Golf Academy ,Clay pigeon shooting, Mountain bike trail ♫ ch fac Xmas **Conf** BC Thtr 1500 Class 300 Board 50 Del from £190 **Services** Lift air con **Parking** 1300 **Notes** LB ⊗ ⊗ in restaurant Civ Wed 100

★★★ 68% HOTEL

Kings
High St NP20 1QU
☎ 01633 842020 📠 01633 244667
e-mail: info@kingshotelsnewport.co.uk

dir: *from town centre take left road (not flyover) into right lane to next rdbt, take 3rd exit, pass front of hotel then left for car park*

This large, imposing property is situated right in the town centre and helpfully has its own car park. Privately owned, it offers comfortable bedrooms including non-smoking and family rooms, and bright spacious public areas. Facilities include a choice of function rooms and a large ballroom.

Rooms 61 en suite (15 fmly) ⊗ in 20 bedrooms S £72-£90; D £90-£150 **Facilities** STV ♫ Xmas **Conf** Thtr 150 Class 70 Board 50 Del from £110 **Services** Lift **Parking** 50 **Notes** LB ⊗ ⊗ in restaurant Closed 26 Dec-4 Jan Civ Wed 100

See advert on opposite page

Wales

★★★ 68% **HOTEL**

Newport Lodge

Bryn Bevan, Brynglas Rd NP20 5QN
☎ 01633 821818 ▤ 01633 856360
e-mail: info@newportlodgehotel.co.uk
web: www.newportlodgehotel.co.uk

dir: M4 junct 26 follow signs Newport. Turn left after 0.5m onto
Malpas Rd, up hill for 0.5m to hotel

On the edge of the town centre and convenient for the M4, this
purpose-built, friendly hotel provides comfortable and well-maintained
bedrooms, with modern facilities. A room with a four-poster bed is
available, as are ground floor bedrooms and no-smoking rooms. The
bistro-style restaurant offers a wide range of freshly prepared dishes,
often using local ingredients.

Rooms 27 en suite (11 GF) ⊗ in 8 bedrooms S £73-£79.50;
D £91.50-£125 (incl. bkfst) **Facilities** Wi-fi available **Conf** Thtr 25 Class 20
Del fr £110 Board 20 **Parking** 63 **Notes LB** No children 14yrs ⊗ in
restaurant

BUDGET HOTEL

Premier Travel Inn Newport, South Wales

Coldra Junction, Chepstow Rd NP18 2NX
☎ 08701 977193 ▤ 01633 411376
web. www.premiertravelinn.com

dir: M4 junct 24. Take A48 to Langstone, at next rdbt return
towards junct 24. Inn is 50 metres on left

High quality, modern budget accommodation ideal for both families
and business travellers. Spacious, en suite bedrooms feature bath and
shower, satellite TV and many have telephones and modem points.
The adjacent family restaurant features a wide and varied menu. For
further details consult the Hotel Groups page.

Rooms 63 en suite

PEMBROKESHIRE

FISHGUARD   MAP 08 SM93

★★ 63% **HOTEL**

Cartref

15-19 High St SA65 9AW
☎ 01348 872430 ▤ 01348 873664
e-mail: cartrefhotel@btconnect.com
web: www.cartrefhotel.co.uk

dir: on A40 in town centre

Personally run by the proprietor, this friendly hotel offers convenient
access to the town centre and ferry terminal. Bedrooms are well
maintained and include some family bedded rooms. There is also a
cosy lounge bar and a welcoming restaurant that looks out onto the
high street.

Rooms 10 en suite (2 fmly) S £35-£39; D £60-£63 (incl. bkfst)
Parking 4 **Notes LB** ⊗ in restaurant

HAVERFORDWEST — MAP 08 SM91

★★ 67% HOTEL

Hotel Mariners

THE INDEPENDENTS

Mariners Square SA61 2DU

☎ 01437 763353 📄 01437 764258

dir: follow town centre signs, over bridge, up High St, 1st turning on right, hotel at the end

Located a few minutes walk from the town centre, this privately owned and friendly hotel is reputed to date back to 1625. The bedrooms are equipped with modern facilities and are soundly maintained. A good range of food is offered in the popular bar, which is a focus for the town. The restaurant offers a more formal dining option. Facilities include a choice of meeting rooms.

Rooms 28 en suite (5 fmly) ⊘ in 16 bedrooms S £59.50-£69; D £79-£87.50 (incl. bkfst) **Facilities** STV **Conf** Thtr 50 Class 20 Board 20 **Parking** 50 **Notes LB** ⊘ in restaurant Closed 25-Dec-2 Jan

★★ 61% HOTEL

Castle Hotel

Castle Square SA61 2AA

☎ 01437 769322 📄 01437 768806

dir: from the main rdbt into Haverfordwest follow town centre signs, follow the road for approx 200yds, hotel on right

At the centre of the bustling town, this former coaching inn is very much at the heart of local activities and is a favourite with locals. A

continued

good range of wholesome food is available in both the restaurant and bar. Bedrooms have modern furnishings and facilities.

Rooms 9 en suite (1 fmly) **Notes** ⊗ No children 14yrs ⊘ in restaurant Closed 24-25 & 31 Dec

MANORBIER — MAP 08 SS09

★★ 69% HOTEL

Castle Mead

SA70 7TA

THE CIRCLE
Selected Individual Hotels
GREAT BRITAIN

☎ 01834 871358 📄 01834 871358

e-mail: castlemeadhotel@aol.com

web: www.castlemeadhotel.com

dir: A4139 towards Pembroke, turn onto B4585 into village & follow signs to beach & castle. Hotel on left above beach

Benefiting from a superb location with spectacular views of the bay, the Norman church and Manorbier Castle, this family-run hotel is friendly and welcoming. Bedrooms which include some in a converted former coach house, are generally quite spacious and have modern facilities. Public areas include a sea view restaurant, bar and residents' lounge, as well as an extensive garden.

Rooms 5 en suite 3 annexe en suite (2 fmly) (3 GF) ⊘ in all bedrooms S fr £45; D fr £82 (incl. bkfst) **Parking** 20 **Notes LB** ⊘ in restaurant Closed Dec-Feb RS Nov

MILFORD HAVEN

See advert below

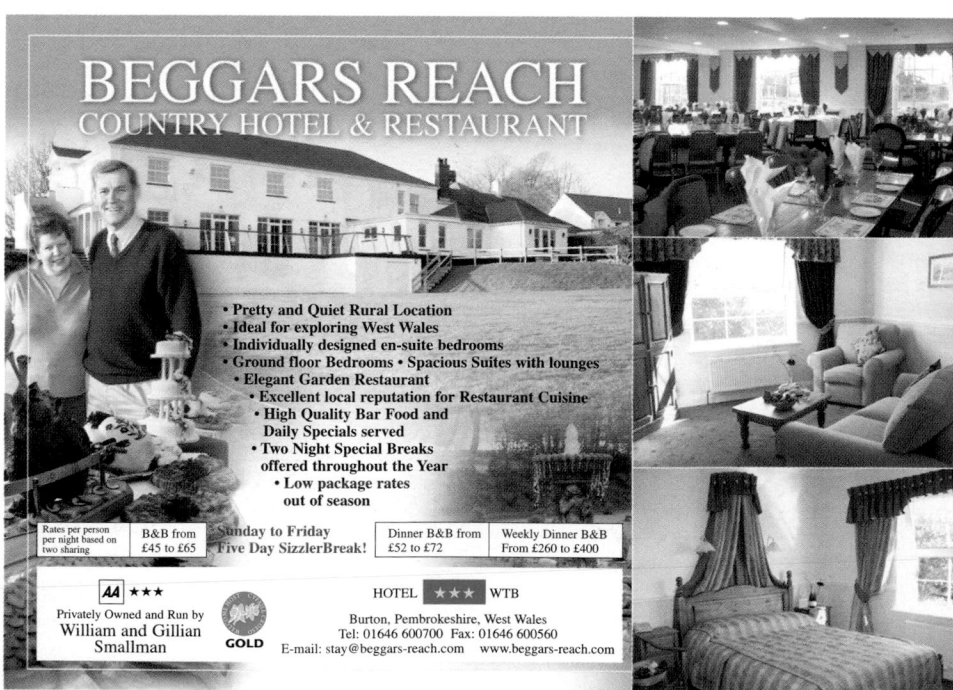

NEVERN
MAP 08 SN04

★★ 71% HOTEL

Trewern Arms
SA42 0NB
☎ 01239 820395 📠 01239 820173
e-mail: trewern.arms@virgin.net

dir: off A487, midway between Cardigan and Fishguard

Set in a peaceful and picturesque village, this charming 16th-century inn is well positioned to offer a relaxing stay. There are many original features to be seen in the two character bars and attractive restaurant, and the spacious bedrooms are appointed to a high standard and include some family rooms.

Rooms 10 en suite (4 fmly) S £50; D fr £75 (incl. bkfst)
Facilities Fishing Riding Xmas **Parking** 100 **Notes** ⊗ ⊘ in restaurant

NEWPORT
MAP 08 SN03

A

Salutation Inn
Felindre Farchog SA41 3UY
☎ 01239 820564 📠 01239 820355
e-mail: johndenley@aol.com
web: www.salutationcountryhotel.co.uk

dir: on A487 between Cardigan & Fishguard. 3m N of Newport

Rooms 8 en suite (2 fmly) (8 GF) ⊗ in all bedrooms S £32-£38; D £48-£60 (incl. bkfst) **Parking** 60 **Notes** ★★★ LB ⊘ in restaurant

PEMBROKE
MAP 08 SM90

★★★ 79% HOTEL

Beggars Reach
SA73 1PD
☎ 01646 600700 📠 01646 600560
e-mail: stay@beggars-reach.com
web: www.beggars-reach.com

dir: 8m S of Haverfordwest, 6m N of Pembroke, off A477

This privately owned and personally run hotel was once a Georgian rectory. It stands in four acres of grounds peacefully located close to the village of Burton. It provides modern, well-equipped

continued

accommodation and two of the bedrooms are located in former stables, which date back to the 14th century. Milford Haven and the ferry terminal at Pembroke Dock are both within easy reach.

Rooms 14 en suite 16 annexe en suite (4 fmly) (8 GF) ⊗ in 26 bedrooms S £69.50-£89.50; D £100-£130 (incl. bkfst) **Facilities** STV FTV Wi-fi available **Conf** Thtr 100 Class 60 Board 60 Del from £100 **Parking** 80 **Notes LB** ⊗ ⊘ in restaurant

See advertisement on opposite page

★★★ 73% HOTEL

Best Western Lamphey Court
Lamphey SA71 5NT
☎ 01646 672273 📠 01646 672480
e-mail: info@lampheycourt.co.uk
web: www.lampheycourt.co.uk

dir: A477 to Pembroke. Turn left at Milton village for Lamphey, hotel on right

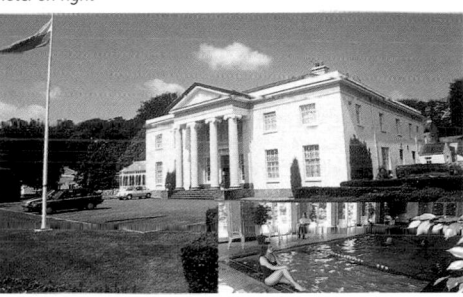

This former Georgian mansion is set in attractive countryside and well situated for exploring the stunning Pembrokeshire coast and beaches. Well-appointed bedrooms and family suites are situated in a converted coach house in the grounds. The elegant public areas include a leisure spa with treatment rooms, and formal and informal dining rooms that both feature dishes inspired by the local produce.

Rooms 26 en suite 12 annexe en suite (7 fmly) (6 GF) ⊗ in 18 bedrooms D £105-£160 (incl. bkfst) **Facilities** ⊠ ⤴ Sauna Solarium Gym Jacuzzi Wi-fi in bedrooms Yacht charter Xmas **Conf** Thtr 60 Class 40 Board 30 Del from £135 **Parking** 50 **Notes LB** ⊗ ⊘ in restaurant Civ Wed 60

See advertisement under TENBY

★★ 83% HOTEL

Lamphey Hall
Lamphey SA71 5NR
☎ 01646 672394 📠 01646 672369
e-mail: andrewjones1990@aol.com

dir: From M4 follow signs for A48 towards Carmarthen, then A40 to St Clears. Follow signs for A477, left at Milton Village

Now under new ownership and set in a delightful village, this very friendly hotel offers an ideal base from which to explore the surrounding countryside. Bedrooms are well equipped, comfortably

continued on page 928

Wales

PEMBROKE continued

furnished and includes a family room as well as rooms on the ground floor. Diners have an extensive choice of dishes and a choice of restaurants. There is also a lounge, a bar and attractive gardens.

Lamphey Hall

Rooms 10 en suite (1 fmly) (2 GF) ⊘ in all bedrooms S £60-£65; D £75-£85 (incl. bkfst) **Parking** 32 **Notes** ⊗ ⊘ in restaurant

★★ 65% **HOTEL**

Old Kings Arms

Main St SA71 4JS

☎ 01646 683611 ▤ 01646 682335

e-mail: info@oldkingsarmshotel.co.uk

dir: *M4/A477 to Pembroke. Turn left for Pembroke, at rdbt follow town centre sign. Turn right onto the parade, car park is signed*

At the centre of the bustling town, this former coaching inn is very much at the heart of local activities and is a favourite with locals. The restaurant and bar have traditional stone walls, flagstone floors and roaring log fires. Both areas offer good, wholesome food.

Rooms 18 en suite S £40-£60; D £70 (incl. bkfst) **Facilities** STV **Parking** 21 **Notes** ⊘ in restaurant Closed 25-26 Dec & 1 Jan

PEMBROKE DOCK   MAP 08 SM90

★★★ 64% **HOTEL**

Cleddau Bridge

Essex Rd SA72 6EG

☎ 01646 685961 ▤ 01646 685746

e-mail: information@cleddaubridgehotel.co.uk

dir: *M4/A40 to St Clears. A477 to Pembroke Dock. At rdbt 2nd exit for Haverfordwest via toll bridge, left before toll bridge*

This modern, purpose-built hotel is sited adjacent to the Cleddau Bridge and affords excellent views overlooking the river. The well-equipped bedrooms are all on the ground floor, while the comfortable public areas comprise an attractive bar and restaurant, both taking advantage of the impressive views.

Rooms 24 en suite (2 fmly) ⊘ in 12 bedrooms **Facilities** STV **Conf** Thtr 160 Class 60 Board 60 **Parking** 140 **Notes LB** ⊗ ⊘ in restaurant Civ Wed 150

ST DAVID'S   MAP 08 SM72

★★★ 79% ⍟ ⍟ **COUNTRY HOUSE HOTEL**

Warpool Court

SA62 6BN

☎ 01437 720300 ▤ 01437 720676

e-mail: info@warpoolcourthotel.com

web: www.warpoolcourthotel.com

dir: *At Cross Square left by Cartref Restaurant (Goat St). Pass Farmers Arms pub, after 400mtrs left, follow hotel signs, entrance on right*

Originally the cathedral choir school, Warpool Court Hotel is set in landscaped gardens looking out to sea and is within easy walking distance of the Pembrokeshire coastal path. The lounges are spacious and comfortable and bedrooms are well furnished and equipped with modern facilities. The restaurant offers delightful cuisine.

Rooms 25 en suite (3 fmly) ⊘ in all bedrooms S £95-£110; D £160-£220 (incl. bkfst) **Facilities** ⍰ ⍰ ⍰ Xmas **Conf** Thtr 40 Class 25 Board 25 Del from £140 **Parking** 100 **Notes LB** ⊘ in restaurant Closed Jan Civ Wed 100

★★ 69% **HOTEL**

Old Cross

Cross Square SA62 6SP

☎ 01437 720387 ▤ 01437 720394

e-mail: enquiries@oldcrosshotel.co.uk

web: www.oldcrosshotel.co.uk

dir: *in town centre*

This friendly and comfortable hotel is situated in the centre of the town, just a short walk from the famous cathedral. Bedrooms are generally spacious and have a good range of facilities with some being suitable for families. Public areas include comfortable lounges, a popular bar and an airy restaurant where good wholesome food is offered.

Rooms 16 en suite 1 annexe en suite (2 fmly) ⊘ in 11 bedrooms S £38-£62; D £68-£105 (incl. bkfst) **Parking** 17 **Notes LB** ⊘ in restaurant Closed end Dec-last week Jan

★ 73% **HOTEL**

Y Glennydd

51 Nun St SA62 6NU

☎ 01437 720576 ▤ 01437 720184

dir: *On one-way system next to fire station*

Dating back to the 18th century this hotel is situated within a few minutes' walk of the centre of St David's and the cathedral. The differently styled bedrooms vary in size, and include a ground-floor

continued

room and family bedded rooms. There is a lounge, a cottage-style restaurant and a small bar.

Rooms 10 rms (8 en suite) (3 fmly) S £30-£40; D £50-£60 **Parking** 5 **Notes** ⊗ Closed Nov-Feb

SAUNDERSFOOT   MAP 08 SN10

★★ 68% HOTEL

Merlewood

St Brides Hill SA69 9NP

☎ 01834 812421 📠 01834 814886

e-mail: merlehotels@aol.com

dir: A477/A4316, hotel on other side of village on St Brides Hill

Offering delightful views over the village and bay, and providing regular live entertainment, this hotel is a popular destination for coach parties. Bedrooms include ground floor and family rooms and there is a comfortable dining room and a large lounge bar. A pleasant outdoor swimming pool is also available for guests' use.

Rooms 29 en suite (8 fmly) (11 GF) ⊗ in 28 bedrooms **Facilities** ⌇ Putt green Children's swings, Table tennis ♫ ch fac **Conf** Thtr 60 Class 100 Board 40 **Parking** 34 **Notes LB** ⊗ ⊘ in restaurant Closed Nov-Mar RS Xmas & New Year

TENBY   MAP 08 SN10

★★★ 77% HOTEL

Heywood Mount Hotel & Spa Leisure Suite

Heywood Ln SA70 8DA

☎ 01834 842087 📠 01834 842113

e-mail: reception@heywoodmount.co.uk

web: www.heywoodmount.co.uk

dir: A478 into Tenby, follow Heywood Mount signs, right into Serpentine Rd, right at T-junct into Heywood Lane, 3rd hotel on left

This privately owned hotel is situated in a peaceful residential area, close to Tenby's beaches and town centre. The well-maintained house is surrounded by extensive gardens, and public areas include a comfortable lounge, bar, restaurant and health & fitness spa. Several of the well-appointed bedrooms are on the ground floor and the executive style rooms are particularly well equipped.

Rooms 28 en suite (6 fmly) (10 GF) ⊗ in all bedrooms S £45 £65, D £90-£170 (incl. bkfst) **Facilities Spa** ⌇ supervised Sauna Solarium Gym Jacuzzi Beauty therapist ♫ Xmas **Conf** BC Thtr 80 Class 50 Board 25 Del from £90 **Parking** 28 **Notes LB** ⊗ ⊘ in restaurant Civ Wed 90

★★★ 75% HOTEL

Atlantic

The Esplanade SA70 7DU

☎ 01834 842881 📠 01834 840911

e-mail: enquiries@atlantic-hotel.uk.com

web: www.atlantic-hotel.uk.com

dir: A478 into Tenby & follow town centre signs, keep town walls on left then turn right at Esplanade, hotel half way along on right

This privately owned and personally run, friendly hotel has an enviable position looking out over South Beach towards Caldy Island. Bedrooms vary in size and style, and are well equipped and tastefully appointed. The comfortable public areas include a choice of restaurants and, in

continued

---

fine weather guests can also enjoy the cliff-top gardens.

Rooms 42 en suite (11 fmly) (4 GF) ⊗ in 8 bedrooms S £72-£83; D £96-£174 (incl. bkfst) **Facilities Spa** STV ⌇ Solarium Steam room **Conf** Board 8 **Services** Lift **Parking** 25 **Notes** Closed Approx mid Dec-mid Jan

★★★ 74% ⊛ COUNTRY HOUSE HOTEL

Penally Abbey Country House

Penally SA70 7PY

☎ 01834 843033 📠 01834 844714

e-mail: penally.abbey@btinternet.com

web: www.penally-abbey.com

dir: 1.5m from Tenby, off A4139, near village green

With monastic origins, this delightful country house stands in five acres of grounds with views over Carmarthen Bay. The drawing room, bar

continued on page 930

TENBY *continued*

and restaurant are tastefully decorated and attractively furnished and set the scene for a relaxing stay. An impressive range of comfortable accommodation is offered. In the main hotel there are country-house style rooms or cottage-style rooms with four posters, and the lodge has rooms that combine classic and contemporary style.

Rooms 8 en suite 4 annexe en suite (3 fmly) **Facilities** Snooker **Conf** Board 14 **Parking** 17 **Notes** ⊗ ⊘ in restaurant Civ Wed 45

★★★ 72% **HOTEL**

Fourcroft

North Beach SA70 8AP
☎ 01834 842886 🖺 01834 842888
e-mail: staying@fourcroft-hotel.co.uk
web: www.fourcroft-hotel.co.uk

dir: A478, after 'Welcome to Tenby' sign left towards North Beach & Walled Town. At seafront turn sharp left. Hotel on left

This friendly hotel has been owned and run by the same family since 1946. It offers a beach-front location, together with a number of extra facilities that make it particularly suitable for families with children. Guests have direct access to Tenby's North Beach through the hotel's cliff top gardens. Bedrooms are of a good size and have modern facilities.

Rooms 40 en suite (12 fmly) ⊘ in 25 bedrooms S £40-£65; D £80-£130 (incl. bkfst) **Facilities Spa** FTV ⤳ Sauna Jacuzzi Wi-fi available Table tennis Giant chess Human Gyroscope Snooker Pool ch fac Xmas **Conf** BC Thtr 90 Class 40 Board 50 Del from £100 **Services** Lift **Parking** 12 **Notes LB** ⊘ in restaurant Civ Wed 90

★★ 74% @ **HOTEL**

Panorama Hotel & Restaurant

The Esplanade SA70 7DU
☎ 01834 844976 🖺 01834 844976
e-mail: mail@panoramahotel.f9.co.uk
web: www.panoramahotel.force9.co.uk

dir: A478 follow 'South Beach' & 'Town Centre' signs. Sharp left under railway arches, up Greenhill Rd, onto South Pde then Esplanade

This charming little hotel is part of a Victorian terrace, overlooking the South Beach and Caldy Island. It provides a variety of non-smoking bedrooms, all of which are well-equipped. Facilities include a cosy bar and an elegant restaurant, where a good choice of skilfully prepared dishes is available.

Rooms 7 en suite (1 fmly) ⊘ in all bedrooms S £42.50-£55; D £70-£110 (incl. bkfst) **Notes LB** ⊗ No children 5yrs ⊘ in restaurant

WOLF'S CASTLE   MAP 08 SM92

★★ 76% @ **COUNTRY HOUSE HOTEL**

Wolfscastle Country Hotel

SA62 5LZ
☎ 01437 741688 & 741225 🖺 01437 741383
e-mail: enquiries@wolfscastle.com
web: www.wolfscastle.com

dir: on A40 in village at top of hill. 6m N of Haverfordwest

This large stone house dates back to the mid-19th century and commands a regal position in the village. Now a friendly, privately

owned and personally run hotel, it provides modern, well-maintained and equipped bedrooms. There is a pleasant bar and an attractive restaurant, which has a well-deserved reputation for its food.

Wolfscastle Country Ho...

Rooms 20 en suite 4 annexe en suite (2 fmly) ⊘ in 21 bedrooms S £60-£80; D £85-£115 (incl. bkfst) **Facilities** STV Wi-fi available **Conf** Thtr 100 Class 100 Board 30 Del from £119 **Parking** 60 **Notes LB** ⊘ in restaurant Closed 24-26 Dec Civ Wed 70

POWYS

BRECON   MAP 09 SO0..

★★★ 79% @@ **COUNTRY HOUSE HOTEL**

Peterstone Court

Llanhamlach LD3 7YB
☎ 01874 665387 🖺 01874 665376
e-mail: info@peterstone-court.com
web: www.peterstone-court.com

dir: from Brecon take A40 towards Abergavenny, hotel approx 4m on right

This establishment provides stunning views, standing on the edge of the Brecon Beacons and overlooking the River Usk. The style is friendly and informal, without any unnecessary fuss. No two bedrooms are alike, but all share comparable levels of comfort, quali.. and elegance. Public areas reflect similar standards, eclectically styled with a blend of contemporary and traditional. Quality produce is cooked with care in a range of enjoyable dishes.

Rooms 8 en suite 4 annexe en suite (4 fmly) ⊘ in 4 bedrooms S £90-£130; D £110-£170 (incl. bkfst) **Facilities** ⤳ Sauna Gym Jacuzzi **Conf** Thtr 150 Class 150 Board 100 Del from £140 **Parking** 50 **Notes LB** ⊘ in restaurant Civ Wed 100

continued

Wales

★★★ 77% ⊛ HOTEL

ant Ddu Lodge, Bistro & Spa

vm Taf, Nant Ddu CF48 2HY

☎ 01685 379111 🖹 01685 377088

mail: enquiries@nant-ddu-lodge.co.uk

eb: www.nant-ddu-lodge.co.uk

or full entry see Nant-Ddu)

★★ 68% HOTEL

he Castle of Brecon

stle Square LD3 9DB

☎ 01874 624611 🖹 01874 623737

mail: hotel@breconcastle.co.uk

eb: www.breconcastle.co.uk

r: A40 to Brecon, follow town centre signs for 2kms, left at
ema, straight over at lights, right into Castle Square

is former coaching inn occupies an elevated position overlooking
e town and River Usk. This view is shared by the restaurant and
ne of the bedrooms, whilst the remaining public areas are roomy
d relaxed. Function and meeting rooms are available and
orporate one of the castle walls.

oms 30 en suite 12 annexe en suite (8 fmly) (2 GF) ⊛ in
bedrooms S £50-£64; D £60-£85 (incl. bkfst) **Facilities** STV Xmas
nf Thtr 160 Class 60 Board 80 Del from £90 **Parking** 30 **Notes LB**
in restaurant Civ Wed 120

★★ 67% HOTEL

ansdowne Hotel & Restaurant

e Watton LD3 7EG

☎ 01874 623321 🖹 01874 610438

mail: reception@lansdownehotel.co.uk

: A40/A470 onto B4601

w a privately owned and personally run hotel, this Georgian house
conveniently located close to the town centre. The accommodation
vell equipped and includes family rooms and a bedroom on
und floor level. There is a comfortable lounge and an attractive
t level dining room containing a bar.

oms 9 en suite (2 fmly) (1 GF) **Notes** No children 5yrs ⊛ in
taurant

UILTH WELLS   MAP 09 SO05

★★★ 75% HOTEL

aer Beris Manor   THE INDEPENDENTS

2 3NP

☎ 01982 552601 🖹 01982 552586

mail: caerberismanor@btinternet.com

eb: www.caerberis.co.uk

r: from town centre follow A483/Llandovery signs. Hotel on left

th extensive landscaped grounds, guests can expect a relaxing stay
his friendly and privately owned hotel. Bedrooms are individually
corated and furnished to retain an atmosphere of a bygone era.
olic areas include a spacious and comfortable lounge, a lounge bar,
d an elegant restaurant complete with 16th-century panelling.

oms 23 en suite (1 fmly) (3 GF) **Facilities** STV Fishing Riding Sauna
m Clay pigeon shooting ch fac **Conf** BC Thtr 100 Class 75 Board 50
rking 32 **Notes LB** ⊛ in restaurant Civ Wed 100

⊛ ⊛ RESTAURANT WITH ROOMS

The Drawing Room

Cwmbach, Newbridge-on-Wye LD2 3RT

☎ 01982 552493

e-mail: post@the-drawing-room.co.uk

dir: A470 towards Rhayader, approx 3m on left

This delightful Georgian country house has been extensively and
tastefully renovated by the present owners, to provide three
comfortable and very well equipped bedrooms, all with luxurious
en suite facilities. Public rooms include two comfortable lounges with
welcoming log fires, a room for private dining and a very elegant and
intimate dining room, which provides the ideal setting to appreciate
the excellent cooking skills of Colin Dawson.

Rooms 3 en suite ⊗ in all bedrooms S £120; D £190-£220 (incl.
bkfst & dinner) **Parking** 14 **Notes** ⊗ No children 12yrs Closed
Sun & Mon, 2wks Jan & end of summer

A

Pencerrig Gardens

Llandrindod Wells Rd LD2 3TF

☎ 01982 553226 🖹 01982 552347

e-mail: invoices@pencerrig.co.uk

web: www.pencerrig.co.uk

dir: 2m N on A483 towards Llandrindod Wells

Rooms 10 en suite 10 annexe en suite (4 fmly) (5 GF) S £48; D £70
(incl. bkfst) **Facilities** ➣ **Conf** Thtr 135 Class 90 Board 80 Del £69.95
Parking 50 **Notes** ★★ **LB** ⊛ in restaurant

CAERSWS   MAP 15 SO09

★★★ 74% HOTEL

Maesmawr Hall

SY17 5SF

☎ 01686 688255 🖹 01686 688410

e-mail: reception@maesmawr.co.uk

dir: 6m from Newtown on A489 on right. 7m from Llanidloes
A470/A489 on left

This 16th-century timbered framed manor house, now under new
ownership, is set in several acres of lawns, gardens and woodland.
Many bedrooms have beamed ceilings, whilst the lounges have oak-
panelled walls and carved fireplaces with cheerful log fires. It is a
popular venue for weddings and meetings.

Rooms 17 en suite (2 fmly) (5 GF) ⊛ in 11 bedrooms **Conf** Thtr 120
Class 60 Board 36 **Parking** 60 **Notes LB** ⊛ in restaurant Closed
Xmas & New Year Civ Wed 120

Wales

CRICKHOWELL   MAP 09 SO21

★★★ 80% ◉ HOTEL

Gliffaes Country House Hotel

NP8 1RH

☎ 01874 730371 📠 01874 730463

e-mail: calls@gliffaeshotel.com

web: www.gliffaeshotel.com

dir: 1m off A40, 2.5m W of Crickhowell

This impressive Victorian mansion, standing in 33 acres of its own gardens and wooded grounds by the River Usk, is a privately owned and personally run hotel. Public rooms retain elegance and generous proportions and include a balcony and conservatory from which to enjoy the views. Bedrooms are very well decorated and furnished and offer high levels of comfort.

Rooms 19 en suite 3 annexe en suite ⊗ in all bedrooms S fr £75; D £85-£200 (incl. bkfst) **Facilities** ⌘ Fishing Snooker ⛳ Putt green Wi-fi available Cycling Birdwatching Walking Fishing Falconry Xmas **Conf** Thtr 40 Class 16 Board 16 Del from £150 **Parking** 34 **Notes** LB ⊗ ⊗ in restaurant Closed 2-26 Jan Civ Wed 50

★★★ 78% ◉◉ HOTEL

Bear

NP8 1BW

☎ 01873 810408 📠 01873 811696

e-mail: bearhotel@aol.com

dir: on A40 between Abergavenny and Brecon

A favourite with locals as well as visitors, the character and friendliness of this 15th-century coaching inn are renowned. The bar and restaurant are furnished in keeping with the style of the building and provide comfortable areas in which to enjoy some of the very popular dishes that use the finest locally-sourced ingredients.

Rooms 21 en suite 13 annexe en suite (6 fmly) ⊗ in 29 bedrooms S £65-£115; D £80-£150 (incl. bkfst) **Conf** Thtr 40 Class 20 Board 20 **Parking** 45 **Notes** RS 25 Dec

★★★ 72% ◉ HOTEL

Manor

Brecon Rd NP8 1SE

☎ 01873 810212 📠 01873 811938

e-mail: info@manorhotel.co.uk

web: www.manorhotel.co.uk

dir: on A40, Crickhowell/Brecon, 0.5m from Crickhowell

This impressive manor house set in a stunning location was the birthplace of Sir George Everest. The bedrooms and public areas are

continued

elegant, and there are extensive leisure facilities. The restaurant, with panoramic views, is the setting for exciting modern cooking. Guests can also dine informally at the nearby Nantyffin Cider Mill, a sister operation of the hotel.

Man

Rooms 22 en suite (1 fmly) ⊗ in 8 bedrooms S £65-£75; D £75-£105 (incl. bkfst) **Facilities** STV ⊡ Sauna Solarium Gym Jacuzzi Fitness assessment Sunbed Xmas **Conf** Thtr 400 Class 300 Board 300 Del from £110 **Parking** 200 **Notes** LB ⊗ in restaurant Civ Wed 100

★★ 74% ◉ HOTEL

Ty Croeso

The Dardy, Llangattock NP8 1PU

☎ 01873 810573 📠 01873 810573

e-mail: info@ty-croeso.co.uk

dir: A40 at Shell garage take road opposite, down hill over bridge. Right, after 0.5m left, up hill over canal, hotel signed

Ty Croeso, meaning 'House of Welcome' certainly lives up to its nam under the careful guidance of the owners. The restaurant offers carefully prepared dishes with a real emphasis on Welsh produce, a theme that continues at breakfast when Glamorgan sausages and laverbread are available. A comfortable lounge features a log fire. Bedrooms are decorated with pretty fabrics and equipped with good facilities.

Rooms 8 en suite (1 fmly) ⊗ in all bedrooms S £50-£65; D £68-£85 (incl. bkfst) **Facilities** Wi-fi available Xmas **Parking** 16 **Notes** LB ⊗ ⊗ in restaurant

HAY-ON-WYE   MAP 09 SO2

★★★ 71% HOTEL

The Swan-at-Hay

Church St HR3 5DQ

☎ 01497 821188 📠 01497 821424

e-mail: info@swanathay.co.uk

dir: From Brecon on B4350, hotel on left. From any other route follow signs for Brecon & just before leaving town, hotel on righ

This former coaching inn dates back to the 1800s and is only a short walk from the town centre. Bedrooms are well equipped and some are located in either the main hotel or in converted cottages across the courtyard. Spacious, relaxing public areas include a comfortable lounge, a choice of bars and a more formal restaurant. There is also large function room and a smaller meeting room.

Rooms 15 en suite 4 annexe en suite (1 fmly) (2 GF) ⊗ in 16 bedroom S £67.50-£105; D £95-£140 (incl. bkfst) **Facilities** Fishing Xmas **Conf** Thtr 140 Class 60 Board 50 Del from £110 **Parking** 18 **Notes** LB ⊗ in restaurant Civ Wed 50

Wales

★★ 71% **HOTEL**

Kilverts Hotel

he Bull Ring HR3 5AG

☎ 01497 821042 📠 01497 821580

e-mail: info@kilverts.co.uk

dir: from Brecon on B4350, on entering Hay-on-Wye take 1st
right after Cinema Bookshop. Then 1st left hotel on right

Situated in the centre of this fascinating town, Kilverts is a genuinely
friendly and welcoming hotel. The committed staff provide attentive
hospitality within a convivial atmosphere. Well-equipped bedrooms
are cosy, with plenty of character. Food has an international influence,
available in either the bar or stylish restaurant. The extensive gardens
are ideal in the summer months.

Rooms 12 en suite (2 fmly) (1 GF) ❷ in 1 bedroom **Conf** Thtr 30
Class 10 Board 16 **Parking** 13 **Notes LB** ❷ in restaurant Closed 25-Dec

★★ 71% ❀ **HOTEL**

Old Black Lion

6 Lion St HR3 5AD

☎ 01497 820841 📠 01497 822960

e-mail: info@oldblacklion.co.uk

dir: Take B4351 into Hay. Left at junct, then 1st right. Hotel
300yds on left.

This fine old coaching inn, with a history stretching back several
centuries, has a wealth of charm and character. It was occupied by
Oliver Cromwell during the siege of Hay Castle. Privately owned and
personally run, it provides cosy and well-equipped bedrooms, some
located in an adjacent building. A wide range of well-prepared food is
provided, and the service is relaxed and friendly.

Rooms 6 en suite 4 annexe en suite (2 GF) ❷ in all bedrooms
Parking 14 **Notes LB** ❌ No children 5yrs Closed 24-26 Dec

★★ 69% **HOTEL**

Baskerville Arms

Clyro HR3 5RZ

☎ 01497 820670 📠 01497 821609

e-mail: info@baskervillearms.co.uk

dir: from Hereford follow Brecon A438 into Clyro. Hotel signed

Situated near Hay-on-Wye in the peaceful village of Clyro, this former
Georgian coaching inn is personally run by its friendly and enthusiastic
owners. Bedrooms offer a range of styles while public areas include a
bar with a village inn atmosphere, a separate restaurant and a
comfortable residents' lounge. There is also a large function room,
plus a meeting room.

Rooms 13 en suite (1 fmly) ❷ in 6 bedrooms S £40-£44.50; D £78-£85
(incl. bkfst) **Facilities** Wi-fi in bedrooms Xmas **Parking** 12 **Notes LB**
❷ in restaurant

KNIGHTON   MAP 09 SO27

★★ 82% ❀❀ **HOTEL**

Milebrook House

Milebrook LD7 1LT

☎ 01547 528632 📠 01547 520509

e-mail: hotel@milebrook.kc3ltd.co.uk

web: www.milebrookhouse.co.uk

dir: 2m E of Knighton, on A4113

Set in three acres of grounds and gardens in the Teme Valley, this
charming house dates back to 1760. Over the years since its
conversion into a hotel, it has acquired a well-deserved reputation for
its warm hospitality, comfortable accommodation and the quality of its
cuisine, that uses local produce and home-grown vegetables.

Rooms 10 en suite (2 fmly) (2 GF) ❷ in all bedrooms S £62-£66;
D £95-£101 (incl. bkfst) **Facilities** Fishing 🏸 Badminton, Trout Fly Fishing
Xmas **Conf** Class 30 **Parking** 21 **Notes LB** ❌ No children 8yrs ❷ in
restaurant RS Mon

LLANDRINDOD WELLS   MAP 09 SO06

★★★ 78% ❀ **HOTEL**

The Metropole

Temple St LD1 5DY

☎ 01597 823700 📠 01597 824828

e-mail: info@metropole.co.uk

web: www.metropole.co.uk

dir: on A483 in town centre

CLASSIC

The centre of this famous spa town is dominated by this large
Victorian hotel, which has been personally run by the same family for

continued on page 934

LLANDRINDOD WELLS *continued*

well over 100 years. The lobby leads to a choice of bars and an elegant lounge. Bedrooms, many of which are non-smoking, vary in style and all are quite spacious and well equipped. Facilities here include an extensive selection conference and function rooms, as well as a leisure centre.

Rooms 120 en suite (7 fmly) ⊗ in 57 bedrooms S £81-£96; D £106-£126 (incl. bkfst) **Facilities** ⬚ Sauna Solarium Gym Jacuzzi Wi-fi in bedrooms Mini-gym, Beauty and holistic treatments Xmas **Conf** Thtr 300 Class 200 Board 80 Del from £112 **Services** Lift **Parking** 150 **Notes LB** ⊗ in restaurant Civ Wed 300

See advert on opposite page

LLANFYLLIN   MAP 15 SJ11

★★ 75% **HOTEL**

Cain Valley
High St SY22 5AQ
☎ 01691 648366 📄 01691 648307
e-mail: info@cainvalleyhotel.co.uk

dir: *at end of A490. Hotel in town centre, car park at rear*

This Grade II listed coaching inn has a lot of charm and character including features such as exposed beams and a Jacobean staircase. The comfortable accommodation includes family rooms and a wide range of food is available in a choice of bars, or in the restaurant, which has a well-deserved reputation for its locally sourced steaks.

Rooms 13 en suite (2 fmly) S £42-£47; D £69-£75 (incl. bkfst) **Parking** 10 **Notes LB** ⊗ in restaurant

LLANGAMMARCH WELLS   MAP 09 SN94

INSPECTORS' CHOICE

★★★ ⑧⑧ **COUNTRY HOUSE HOTEL**

Lake Country House Hotel & Spa
LD4 4BS
☎ 01591 620202 & 620474 📄 01591 620457
e-mail: info@lakecountryhouse.co.uk
web: www.lakecountryhouse.co.uk

dir: *W from Builth Wells on A483 to Garth (approx 6m). Left for Llangammarch Wells, follow hotel signs*

Expect good old-fashioned values and hospitality at this Victorian country house hotel. In fact, the service is so traditionally English, guests may believe they have a butler! The establishment offers a 9-hole, par 3 golf course, 50 acres of wooded grounds and a

continued

newly developed spa where the hot tub overlooks the lake. Bedrooms, some located in an annexe, and some at ground-floor level, are individually styled and have many extra comforts. Traditional afternoon teas are served in the lounge and award-winning cuisine is provided in the spacious and elegant restaurant.

Lake Country House Hotel & Spa

Rooms 30 en suite (7 GF) ⊗ in all bedrooms S £110-£175; D £160-£240 (incl. bkfst) **Facilities** STV ⚓9 ⤴ Fishing Snooker ⤴ Putt green Clay pigeon shooting, horse riding, mountain biking, quad biking, archery Xmas **Conf** BC Thtr 80 Class 30 Board 25 Del from £142 **Parking** 72 **Notes LB** ⊗ in restaurant Civ Wed 100

LLANWDDYN   MAP 15 SJ01

★★★ 75% ⑧ **COUNTRY HOUSE HOTEL**

Lake Vyrnwy

CLASSIC
BRITISH HOTELS

Lake Vyrnwy SY10 0LY
☎ 01691 870692 📄 01691 870259
e-mail: res@lakevyrnwy.com
web: www.lakevyrnwy.com

dir: *on A4393, 200yds past dam turn sharp right into drive*

This fine country-house hotel lies in 26,000 acres of woodland above Lake Vyrnwy. It provides a wide range of bedrooms, most with superb views and many with four-poster beds and balconies. The extensive public rooms are elegantly furnished and include a terrace, a choice of bars serving meals and the more formal restaurant.

Rooms 38 en suite (4 fmly) S £75-£170; D £100-£210 (incl. bkfst) **Facilities** STV ⤴ Fishing Wi-fi available Clay shooting, Sailing, Archery, bird watching, canoeing/kayaking Xmas **Conf** Thtr 120 Class 50 Board 45 Del from £135 **Parking** 70 **Notes LB** ⊗ in restaurant Civ Wed 120

LLANWRTYD WELLS   MAP 09 SN84

★★ 79% ⑧ **SMALL HOTEL**

Lasswade Country House Hotel
Station Rd LD5 4RW
☎ 01591 610515 📄 01591 610611
e-mail: info@lasswadehotel.co.uk
web: www.lasswadehotel.co.uk

dir: *off A483 into Ifron Terrace, right into Station Rd, hotel 350yds on right*

This friendly hotel on the edge of the town has impressive views over the countryside. Bedrooms are comfortably furnished and well equipped, while the public areas consist of a tastefully decorated lounge, an elegant restaurant and an airy conservatory which looks out on to the neighbouring hills. The hotel is non-smoking throughout

continued

and utilises fresh, local produce to provide an enjoyable dining experience.

Rooms 8 en suite ⊘ in all bedrooms S £49-£55; D £80-£95 (incl. bkfst)
Facilities Fishing Riding Sauna Mountain biking, Trekking **Conf** Thtr 20 Class 20 Board 16 Del from £110 **Parking** 8 **Notes LB** ⊛ ⊘ in restaurant

◎◎◎ RESTAURANT WITH ROOMS

Carlton House
Dolycoed Rd LD5 4RA
☎ 01591 610248
e-mail: info@carltonrestaurant.co.uk

dir: in town centre

Guests are made to feel like one of the family at this character property, set amidst stunning countryside in what is reputedly the smallest rural town in Britain. Carlton House offers award-winning cuisine for which Mary Ann Gilchrist relies on the very best of local ingredients. The menu is complemented by a well-chosen wine list and dinner is served in an atmospheric restaurant. The themed bedrooms, like the public areas, have period furniture and are decorated in warm colours.

Rooms 6 rms (5 en suite) (2 fmly) S £40-£45; D £60-£90 **Notes LB** ⊘ in restaurant Closed 15-30 Dec

---

LLYSWEN
MAP 09 SO13

★★★★ 86% ◎◎ HOTEL

Llangoed Hall
LD3 0YP
☎ 01874 754525 🖹 01874 754545
e-mail: enquiries@llangoedhall.com
web: www.llangoedhall.com

dir: A470 through village for 2m. Hotel drive on right

Set against the stunning backdrop of the Black Mountains and the Wye Valley, this imposing country house is a haven of peace and quiet. The interior is no less impressive, with a noteworthy art collection complementing the many antiques in the day rooms and bedrooms. Comfortable, spacious bedrooms and suites are matched by equally inviting lounges.

Rooms 23 en suite S £150-£345; D £195-£385 (incl. bkfst) **Facilities** STV ⊗ Fishing Snooker ⊛ Wi-fi in bedrooms Maze Clay pigeon shooting ♫ Xmas **Conf** Thtr 00 Class 30 Board 30 Del £187 **Parking** 80 **Notes LB** ⊛ No children 8yrs ⊘ in restaurant Civ Wed 80

See advert on this page

MACHYNLLETH
MAP 14 SH70
See also Eglwysfach (Ceredigion)

★★★ 70% ◎ HOTEL

Wynnstay
Maengwyn St SY20 8AE
☎ 01654 702941 🖹 01654 703884
e-mail: info@wynnstay-hotel.com
web: www.wynnstay-hotel.com

dir: at junct of A487/A489, in the town centre

Long established, this former posting house lies in the centre of this historic town. Bedrooms, some with four-poster beds, have modern facilities and include family rooms. There is a comfortable lounge bar area and a good range of food and wines is available. Guests can also

continued on page 936

Wales

MACHYNLLETH *continued*

dine in the Wynnstay Pizzeria or the restaurant, which offers more formal dining.

Rooms 23 en suite (3 fmly) ⊘ in all bedrooms S £55-£95; D £80-£110 (incl. bkfst) **Facilities** STV Wi-fi available Clay shooting Game shooting, Mountain biking Golf Xmas **Conf** Thtr 25 Class 12 Board 16 **Parking** 40 **Notes LB** ⊘ in restaurant

MONTGOMERY   MAP 15 SO29

★★ 79% ◉ **HOTEL**

Dragon

SY15 6PA

☎ 01686 668359 ▤ 0870 011 8227

e-mail: reception@dragonhotel.com

web: www.dragonhotel.com

dir: *behind the Town Hall*

This fine 17th-century coaching inn stands in the centre of Montgomery. Beams and timbers from the nearby castle, which was destroyed by Cromwell, are visible in the lounge and bar. A wide choice of soundly prepared, wholesome food is available in both the restaurant and bar. Bedrooms are well equipped and family rooms are available.

Rooms 20 en suite (6 fmly) ⊘ in 16 bedrooms S £51-£61; D £87.50-£97.50 (incl. bkfst) **Facilities** ⓡ Sauna ♫ Xmas **Conf** Thtr 40 Class 30 Board 25 Del from £79 **Parking** 21 **Notes LB** ⊘ in restaurant

NANT-DDU   MAP 09 SO01
(NEAR MERTHYR TYDFIL)

★★★ 77% ◉ **HOTEL**

Nant Ddu Lodge

Cwm Taf, Nant-Ddu CF48 2HY

☎ 01685 379111 ▤ 01685 377088

e-mail: enquiries@nant-ddu-lodge.co.uk

web: www.nant-ddu-lodge.co.uk

dir: *6m N of Merthyr Tydfil, 12m S of Brecon on A470*

Close to the Brecon Beacons and with a history stretching back 200 years, this delightful hotel has seen many improvements in the hands of the present owners. Decor throughout is contemporary and the bedrooms are thoughtfully furnished and well equipped. Meals can be taken in the modern bistro and there is a bar with a more traditional 'village inn' atmosphere. There is also a well-equipped health, beauty, leisure and fitness centre and spa.

Rooms 27 en suite 4 annexe en suite (5 fmly) (12 GF) S £69.50-£95; D £89.50-£125 (incl. bkfst) **Facilities Spa** STV ⓡ supervised Sauna Solarium Gym Jacuzzi **Conf** BC Thtr 20 Class 20 Board 20 Del from £115 **Parking** 60 **Notes** ⊘ in restaurant RS 24-26 Dec

RHAYADER   MAP 09 SN9

🅰

Elan

West St LD6 5AF

☎ 01597 810109 ▤ 01597 810524

e-mail: davemackie@elanhotel.fsnet.co.uk

web: www.elanhotel.co.uk

dir: *600mtrs from junct of A44/A470 Rhayader*

Rooms 10 en suite (1 fmly) ⊘ in all bedrooms **Parking** 16 **Notes** ★★ **LB** ⊘ in restaurant

WELSHPOOL   MAP 15 SJ2

★★★ 73% **HOTEL**

Royal Oak

The Cross SY21 7DG

☎ 01938 552217 ▤ 01938 556652

e-mail: relax@royaloakhotel.info

web: www.royaloakhotel.info

dir: *by traffic lights at junct of A483/A458*

This traditional market town hotel dates back over 350 years. It provides well-equipped bedrooms, a choice of bars and extensive function and conference facilities. The attractively appointed restauran is a popular venue for dining out and there is also a busy coffee shop open throughout the day. At the time of our last inspection, considerable upgrading work was in progress.

Rooms 25 en suite (3 fmly) ⊘ in all bedrooms S £64-£84; D £94-£150 **Facilities** STV Wi-fi in bedrooms ♫ Xmas **Conf** Thtr 150 Class 60 Board 60 Del from £85 **Parking** 30 **Notes LB** ⊘ in restaurant

RHONDDA CYNON TAFF

MISKIN   MAP 09 ST08

★★★★ 74% ◉ **COUNTRY HOUSE HOTEL**

Miskin Manor Country Hotel

Pendoylan Rd CF72 8ND

☎ 01443 224204 ▤ 01443 237606

e-mail: info@miskin-manor.co.uk

web: www.miskin-manor.co.uk

dir: *M4 junct 34, exit onto A4119, signed Llantrisant, hotel is 300yds on left*

This historic manor house is peacefully located in 20-acre grounds yet only minutes away from the M4. Bedrooms are furnished to a high standard and include some located in converted stables and cottages.

continue

ublic areas are spacious and comfortable and include a variety of
unction rooms. The relaxed atmosphere and the surroundings ensure
is hotel remains popular for wedding functions as well as with
usiness guests.

ooms 34 en suite 9 annexe en suite (2 fmly) (7 GF) ⊗ in 18 bedrooms
£85–£105; D £110–£130 (incl. bkfst) **Facilities** STV ⬜ supervised
quash Sauna Solarium Gym ⛲ Jacuzzi Wi-fi available Xmas
onf Thtr 160 Class 80 Board 65 Del from £145 **Parking** 200 **Notes LB**
in restaurant Civ Wed 120

See advert under CARDIFF, page 891

PONTYPRIDD   MAP 09 ST08

★★★ 77% **HOTEL**

Heritage Park

oed Cae Rd, Trehafod CF37 2NP
☎ 01443 687057 🖹 01443 687060
-mail: reservations@heritageparkhotel.co.uk
web: www.heritageparkhotel.co.uk
ir: M4 junct 32 follow brown signs to Rhondda Heritage Park
otel adjacent.

his modern hotel is under new ownership. The spacious bedrooms
clude ground floor and interconnecting rooms, and a room
quipped for less mobile guests. Meals can be taken in the attractive,
ood-beamed Loft Restaurant. Set in the beautiful Rhondda Valley,
e hotel is an ideal base from which to explore South Wales.

ooms 44 en suite (1 fmly) (19 GF) ⊗ in 34 bedrooms S £84–£94;
£107–£112 (incl. bkfst) **Facilities** STV ⬜ Sauna Solarium Gym Jacuzzi
i-fi available **Conf** Thtr 200 Class 70 Board 40 Del from £82.50
arking 150 **Notes LB** ⊗ in restaurant Civ Wed 90

★★★ 73% **HOTEL**

Ilechwen Hall

anfabon CF37 4HP
☎ 01443 742050 & 743020 🖹 01443 742189
-mail: llechwen@aol.com
web: www.llechwen.com
ir: A470 N towards Merthyr Tydfil, then A472, then onto A4054
r Cilfynydd. After 0.25m, turn left at hotel sign

et on top of a hill with a stunning approach, this establishment has
erved many purposes in its 200-year-old history, which includes a
rivate school and a magistrates' court. Bedrooms are individually
ecorated and well equipped, and some are situated in the
omfortable coach house nearby. The Victorian-style public areas are
tractively appointed and the hotel is a popular venue for weddings.

ooms 12 en suite 8 annexe en suite (11 fmly) (4 GF) ⊗ in 8 bedrooms
£59.50–£64.50; D £75 **Facilities** ch fac Xmas **Conf** Thtr 80 Class 30
oard 30 Del from £80 **Parking** 100 **Notes** ⊗ in restaurant Closed
–28 Dec Civ Wed 60

SWANSEA

LLANRHIDIAN   MAP 08 SS49

★★ 61% **HOTEL**

North Gower

SA3 1EE
☎ 01792 390042 🖹 01792 391401
e-mail: enquiries@northgowerhotel.co.uk
web: www.northgowerhotel.co.uk
dir: on B4295, turn left at Llanrhidian Esso Service Station

Situated on the Gower Peninsula with delightful views over the sea,
this family-owned hotel offers guests a relaxing and comfortable stay.
Bedrooms are spacious and airy, whilst public areas consist of a bar

continued on page 938

Wales

LLANRHIDIAN *continued*

full of character, a pleasant restaurant and a choice of meeting and function rooms.

Rooms 18 en suite (10 fmly) (7 GF) ⊗ in 8 bedrooms S £45-£55; D £60-£75 (incl. bkfst) **Facilities** FTV Wi-fi in bedrooms ch fac Xmas **Conf** BC Thtr 250 Class 170 Board 60 Del £72 **Parking** 100 **Notes** LB ⊗ in restaurant Civ Wed 100

See advert on page 937

| REYNOLDSTON | MAP 08 SS48 |

INSPECTORS' CHOICE

★★★ ◉◉ **COUNTRY HOUSE HOTEL**

Fairyhill

SA3 1BS

☎ 01792 390139 📠 01792 391358

e-mail: postbox@fairyhill.net

web: www.fairyhill.net

dir: just outside Reynoldston off A4118

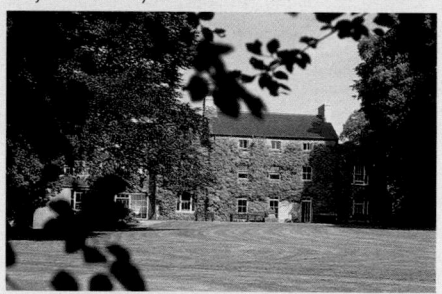

Peace and tranquillity are never far away at this charming Georgian mansion set in the heart of the beautiful Gower peninsula. Bedrooms are furnished with care individually and are filled with many thoughtful extras. There is also a range of comfortable seating areas with crackling log fires to choose from and a smartly appointed restaurant offering menus, based on local produce, and an excellent wine list. The hotel sometimes has special wine events so do ask when you book.

Rooms 8 en suite S £130-£230; D £150-£250 (incl. bkfst) **Facilities** FTV ♨ Wi-fi available mountain bikes available **Conf** Thtr 40 Class 20 Board 16 **Parking** 50 **Notes** LB ⊗ No children 8yrs ⊗ in restaurant Closed 24-26 Dec & 3-21 Jan

---

| SWANSEA | MAP 09 SS69 |

See also Port Talbot (Neath Port Talbot)

★★★★ 76% ◉◉ **HOTEL**

The Grand

Ivey Place, High St SA1 1NE

☎ 01792 645898

e-mail: info@thegrandhotelswansea.co.uk

dir: M4 junct 42, follow rail station signs

The Grand stands next to the railway station, offering spacious, contemporary accommodation in superbly equipped bedrooms. Choose between the informal bistro bar or the more exciting cuisine

continued

---

offered in the Beach Restaurant. Any excess calories can be burnt up in the small but well equipped gym and leisure area.

Rooms 31 en suite (4 fmly) ⊗ in 19 bedrooms **Facilities** Spa STV Sauna Solarium Gym Jacuzzi ♫ **Services** Lift air con **Notes** LB ⊗ ⊗ in restaurant

---

★★★★ 75% **HOTEL**

Swansea Marriott Hotel

Marriott
HOTELS & RESORTS

The Maritime Quarter SA1 3SS

☎ 0870 400 7282 📠 0870 400 7382

web: www.marriott.co.uk

dir: M4 junct 42, A483 to city centre past Leisure Centre, then follow signs to Maritime Quarter

Just opposite City Hall, this busy hotel enjoys fantastic views over the bay and marina. Bedrooms are spacious and equipped with a range of extras. Public rooms include a popular leisure club and Abernethy's restaurant, which overlooks the marina. It is worth noting, however, that lounge seating is limited.

Rooms 122 en suite (50 fmly) (11 GF) ⊗ in 90 bedrooms S £80-£120; D £110-£139 (incl. bkfst) **Facilities** STV ⊇ Sauna Gym Jacuzzi Wi-fi in bedrooms **Conf** Thtr 250 Class 120 Board 30 Del from £135 **Services** Lift air con **Parking** 122 **Notes** LB ⊗ ⊗ in restaurant Civ Wed 200

★★★ 74% **HOTEL**

Ramada Swansea

◉ RAMADA

Phoenix Way, Swansea Enterprise Park SA7 9EG

☎ 01792 310330 📠 01792 787535

e-mail: sales.swansea@ramadajarvis.co.uk

web: www.ramadajarvis.co.uk

dir: M4 junct 44, A48 (Llansamlet), left at 3rd lights, right at 1st mini rdbt, left into Phoenix Way at 2nd mini rdbt. Hotel 400yds on right

This large, modern hotel is conveniently situated on the outskirts of the city with easy access to the M4. Bedrooms are comfortably appointed for both business and leisure guests.

Rooms 119 en suite (12 fmly) (50 GF) ⊗ in 100 bedrooms S £39.50-£139; D fr £79 (incl. bkfst) **Facilities** STV ⊇ supervised Sauna Wi-fi available Xmas **Conf** Thtr 200 Class 80 Board 60 Del from £79 **Parking** 180 **Notes** LB ⊗ in restaurant Civ Wed 120

★★ 68% HOTEL

Beaumont

72-73 Walter Rd SA1 4QA

☎ 01792 643956 🖷 01792 643044

e-mail: info@beaumonthotel.co.uk

dir: M4, towards city centre. Follow Uplands & Sketty signs. 0.5m from centre along Walter Rd, hotel on left

Situated within walking distance of the city centre, this hotel, now under new ownership, offers a high level of comfort and stylish decor. Bedrooms are well equipped and thoughtfully furnished. There is a relaxing lounge bar where guests can enjoy a drink before sampling good home cooking in the Conservatory Restaurant. There is a secure car park, which is locked each evening.

Rooms 16 en suite (3 fmly) **Conf** BC Class 50 Board 30 **Parking** 12
Notes LB ⊗ in restaurant Closed 25-26 Dec & 31 Dec-1 Jan

★★ 68% ⦿ HOTEL

Windsor Lodge Hotel & Restaurant

Mount Pleasant SA1 6EG

☎ 01792 642158 🖷 01792 648996

e-mail: reservations@windsor-lodge.co.uk

web: www.windsor-lodge.co.uk

dir: M4 junct 42, A483, right at lights past Sainsbury's, left at station, right immediately after 2nd set of lights

This privately owned and personally run, smart and stylish hotel is just a short walk from the city centre. Bedrooms vary in size, but all are similarly well equipped. There is a choice of lounge areas and a deservedly popular restaurant.

Rooms 19 en suite (2 fmly) S £50-£65; D £65-£75 (incl. bkfst)
Conf Thtr 30 Class 15 Board 24 **Parking** 20 **Notes LB** ⊗ in restaurant
Closed 23 Dec-2 Jan RS Sun & BH's

Ⓤ

Dragon

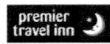

The Kingsway Circle SA1 5LS

☎ 01792 657100 & 0870 4299 848 🖷 01792 456044

e-mail: info@dragon-hotel.co.uk

web: www.dragon-hotel.co.uk

dir: A483 follow signs for city centre. After lights at Sainsbury's right onto Strand then left. Hotel straight ahead

At the time of going to press, the star classification for this hotel was not confirmed. Please refer to the AA internet site www.theAA.com for current information.

continued

Rooms 106 en suite (5 fmly) ⊘ in 88 bedrooms S £65-£110; D £65-£175 **Facilities** STV ⬚ supervised Sauna Solarium Gym Beauty therapist 🎵 Xmas **Conf** Thtr 230 Class 120 Board 60 Del from £125 **Services** Lift air con **Parking** 40 **Notes LB** ⊗ ⊘ in restaurant

Wales

SWANSEA *continued*

Travelodge Swansea (M4)

Penllergaer SA4 9GT

☎ 08700 850 950 📄 01792 898972

web: www.travelodge.co.uk

dir: M4 junct 47

Travelodge offers good quality, good value, modern accommodation. Ideal for families, the spacious en suite bedrooms include remote-control TV, tea and coffee-making facilities and comfortable beds. Meals can be taken at the nearby family restaurant. See Hotel Groups pages for further details.

Rooms 50 en suite S fr £26; D fr £26 **Conf** Thtr 25 Class 32 Board 20

TORFAEN

CWMBRAN   MAP 09 ST29

★★★★ 72% **HOTEL**

Best Western Parkway

Cwmbran Dr NP44 3UW

☎ 01633 871199 📄 01633 869160

e-mail: enquiries@parkwayhotel.co.uk

web: www.bw-parkwayhotel.co.uk

dir: M4 junct 25A/26/A4051 follow signs Cwmbran-Llantarnam Park. Turn right at rdbt then right for hotel

This hotel is purpose-built and offers comfortable bedrooms and public areas suitable for a wide range of guests. There is a sports centre and a range of conference and meeting facilities. The coffee shop offers an informal eating option during the day and there is fine dining in Ravello's Restaurant.

Rooms 70 en suite (4 fmly) (34 GF) ⊘ in 46 bedrooms S £85-£110; D £95-£125 **Facilities** STV ⬚ Sauna Solarium Gym Jacuzzi Wi-fi available Steam room, Private sun bathing terrace, Sports shop, Solaria ♫ Xmas **Conf** Thtr 500 Class 240 Board 100 Del from £91.50 **Parking** 300 **Notes LB** ⊘ in restaurant Civ Wed 200

See advertisement under NEWPORT, page 925

VALE OF GLAMORGAN

BARRY   MAP 09 ST16

★★★ 79% ⊛ **COUNTRY HOUSE HOTEL**

Egerton Grey Country House

Porthkerry CF62 3BZ

☎ 01446 711666 📄 01446 711690

e-mail: info@egertongrey.co.uk

web: www.egertongrey.co.uk

dir: M4 junct 33 follow signs for airport, left at rdbt for Porthkerry, after 500yds turn left down lane between thatched cottages

This former rectory enjoys a peaceful setting and views over delightful countryside with distant glimpses of the sea. The non-smoking bedrooms are spacious and individually furnished. Public areas offer charm and elegance, and include an airy lounge and restaurant, which has been sympathetically converted from the billiards room.

Rooms 10 en suite (4 fmly) ⊘ in all bedrooms S £90-£120; D £120-£160 (incl. bkfst) **Facilities** ⚑ Putt green Wi-fi in bedrooms 9 hole golf course 200 yds away. Xmas **Conf** BC Thtr 30 Class 30 Board 22 Del from £145 **Parking** 40 **Notes LB** ⊘ in restaurant Civ Wed 40

★★★ 70% **HOTEL**

Best Western Mount Sorrel

Porthkerry Rd CF62 7XY

☎ 01446 740069 📄 01446 746600

e-mail: reservations@mountsorrel.co.uk

dir: M4 junct 33 onto A4232. Follow signs for A4050 through Barry. At mini -rdbt (with church opposite) turn left, hotel 300mtrs on left

Situated in an elevated position above the town centre, this extended Victorian property is ideally placed for exploring the nearby coast and Cardiff, and offers comfortable accommodation. The public areas include a choice of conference rooms, a new restaurant and bar, and leisure facilities that includes an indoor swimming pool.

Rooms 42 en suite (3 fmly) (5 GF) ⊘ in 8 bedrooms S £60-£90; D £90-£140 (incl. bkfst) **Facilities** STV ⬚ supervised Sauna Gym Xmas **Conf** Thtr 150 Class 100 Board 50 Del from £100 **Parking** 17 **Notes LB** ⊛ ⊘ in restaurant Civ Wed 150

Innkeeper's Lodge Cardiff Airport

Port Rd West CF62 3BA

☎ 01446 700075

web: www.innkeeperslodge.com

dir: from M4 junct 33 follow signs from airport

Smart, en suite accommodation ideal for both business & leisure guests. Bedrooms are very well equipped, including Sky TV, telephone, modem points, tea & coffee making facilities, (family rooms in most locations). Complimentary breakfast. The adjacent Pub Restaurant; a Harvester, Vintage Inn, Toby Carvery, Ember Inn, Sizzling Pubco or Pub & Carvery offers an all day menu. See Hotel Groups pages for further details.

Rooms 30 rms S fr £49.95; D fr £49.95

Wales

COWBRIDGE

MAP 09 SS97

★★★ 68% HOTEL

The Bear Hotel

63 High St CF71 7AF

☎ 01446 774814 📠 01446 775425

e-mail: enquiries@bearhotel.com

web: www.bearhotel.com

dir: *in town centre*

Guests receive a genuinely friendly welcome at this famous coaching inn. It is infused with character throughout and features oak beams, real fires and a vaulted bear pit where Napoleon's troops were apparently held. Guests have the choice of dining in the hotel restaurant or at the modern style Oscars Bar & Grill next door. Rooms vary in size and style and are individually decorated. The hotel is a popular wedding venue.

Rooms 19 en suite 14 annexe en suite (2 fmly) (4 GF) ⊗ in 28 bedrooms S £60-£80; D £95-£130 (incl. bkfst) **Facilities** STV Wi-fi available Pool table Xmas **Conf** Thtr 150 Class 80 Board 80 Del from £107.50 **Parking** 70 **Notes LB** ⊗ ⊘ in restaurant Civ Wed 100

HENSOL

MAP 09 ST07

★★★★ 79% HOTEL

Vale Hotel Golf & Spa Resort

Hensol Park CF72 8JY

☎ 01443 667000 📠 01443 665050

e-mail: reservations@vale-hotel.com

web: www.vale-hotel.com

dir: *M4 junct 34 towards Pendoylan, hotel signed approx 3 mins' drive from junct*

A wealth of leisure facilities are offered at this large and modern, purpose-built complex, including two golf courses and a driving range, extensive health spa, gym, swimming pool, squash courts and an orthopaedic clinic. Public areas are spacious and attractive, whilst bedrooms, many with balconies, are well appointed. Meeting and conference facilities are available. Guests can dine either in La Cucina which boasts a wood fired oven, or the more traditional Lakes restaurant.

Rooms 29 en suite 114 annexe en suite (17 fmly) (46 GF) ⊗ in 71 bedrooms S £80-£350; D £90-£370 (incl. bkfst) **Facilities** Spa STV ॐ ♨ 36 ♨ Fishing Squash Riding Sauna Solarium Gym Putt green Jacuzzi Wi-fi in bedrooms Childrens club, Indoor training arena, 18 Room day & residential spa Xmas **Conf** Thtr 300 Class 180 Board 60 Del from £135 **Services** Lift air con **Parking** 300 **Notes LB** ⊗ ⊘ in restaurant Civ Wed 200

See advertisement under CARDIFF, page 891

Some hotels, although accepting children, may not have any special facilities for them so it is well worth checking before booking

WREXHAM

GLYN CEIRIOG

MAP 15 SJ23

★★★ 72% COUNTRY HOUSE HOTEL

Golden Pheasant

Llwynmawr LL20 7BB

☎ 01691 718281 📠 01691 718479

e-mail: goldenpheasant@micro-plus-web.net

web: www.goldenpheasanthotel.co.uk

dir: *A5/B4500 at Chirk, then 5m to Pontfadog, follow hotel signs, 1st left after Cheshire Home. Hotel at top of small hill*

This 18th-century hostelry is quietly situated on the edge of the village and is surrounded by rolling hills. The bedrooms include four-poster and family rooms and there is a choice of bars, as well as a lounge and a restaurant. To the rear is an attractive courtyard with shrubs and flowerbeds.

Rooms 19 en suite (5 fmly) S £45-£98; D £88-£115 (incl. bkfst) **Conf** Thtr 60 Board 20 **Parking** 45 **Notes LB** ⊘ in restaurant RS 25-Dec

LLANARMON DYFFRYN CEIRIOG

MAP 15 SJ13

★★★ 83% ◉◉ HOTEL

West Arms

LL20 7LD

☎ 01691 600665 & 600612 📠 01691 600622

e-mail: gowestarms@aol.com

dir: *Off A483/A5 at Chirk, take B4500 to Ceiriog Valley. Llanarmon 11m at end of B4500*

Set in the beautiful Ceiriog Valley, this delightful hotel has a wealth of charm and character. There is a comfortable lounge, a room for private dining and two bars, as well as a pleasant, award-winning

continued on page 942

Wales

LLANARMON DYFFRYN CEIRIOG *continued*

restaurant offering a set-price menu of freshly cooked dishes. The attractive bedrooms have a mixture of modern and period furnishings.

Rooms 15 en suite (2 fmly) (3 GF) **Facilities** Fishing ch fac Xmas **Conf** Thtr 60 Class 50 Board 50 **Parking** 22 **Notes** ⊘ in restaurant Civ Wed 50

★★ 76% SMALL HOTEL

The Hand at Llanarmon

LL20 7LD
☎ 01691 600666 📠 01691 600262
e-mail: reception@thehandhotel.co.uk
web: www.thehandhotel.co.uk

dir: Turn off A5 at Chirk and follow B4500 signed Ceiriog Valley, continue for 11m.

This small, pleasant, privately owned and run hotel is located in the village centre and has a wealth of charm and character. Apart from warm and friendly hospitality, it provides a variety of bedroom styles, including rooms on ground floor level and two in a separate annexe building. A very good choice of competently prepared food is provided.

Rooms 13 en suite (4 GF) ⊘ in all bedrooms S £45-£60; D £70-£100 (incl. bkfst) **Conf** BC **Parking** 18 **Notes** LB ⊘ in restaurant RS 24-26 Dec Civ Wed 60

ROSSETT　　　　　　　　　MAP 15 SJ35

★★★ 79% HOTEL

Best Western Rossett Hall

Chester Rd LL12 0DE
☎ 01244 571000 📠 01244 571505
e-mail: reservations@rossetthallhotel.co.uk
web: www.rossetthallhotel.co.uk

dir: M56/M53/A55. Take Wrexham/Chester exit towards Wrexham. Onto B5445, hotel entrance in Rossett village

This privately owned and personally run hotel lies in several acres of mature gardens in the lovely Welsh border country. Pretty bedrooms are generally spacious and well equipped, and include ground-floor rooms and a full suite. A comfortable foyer lounge is provided and Oscar's bistro serves a wide range of skilfully prepared dishes.

Rooms 30 en suite (2 fmly) (10 GF) ⊘ in 24 bedrooms S fr £68; D fr £92 (incl. bkfst) **Facilities** STV Wi-fi in bedrooms ch fac Xmas **Conf** Thtr 120 Class 50 Board 50 Del from £82 **Parking** 120 **Notes** LB ⊛ ⊘ in restaurant Civ Wed 150

★★★ 71% HOTEL

Best Western Llyndir Hall

Llyndir Ln LL12 0AY
☎ 01244 571648 📠 01244 571258
e-mail: llyndirhallhotel@feathers.uk.com

dir: 5m S of Chester on B5445 follow Pulford signs

Located on the English/Welsh border within easy reach of Chester and Wrexham, this charming manor house lies in several acres of mature grounds. The well-equipped accommodation is popular with leisure and business guests. Facilities include conference rooms, the Business Training Centre, an impressive leisure centre, a choice of comfortable lounges and a brasserie-style restaurant.

Rooms 48 en suite (3 fmly) (20 GF) ⊘ in 2 bedrooms S £65-£95; D £85-£135 (incl. bkfst) **Facilities** Spa STV FTV 🐾 supervised Sauna Solarium Gym Jacuzzi Wi-fi in bedrooms Steam room, Beauty salon. Xmas **Conf** BC Thtr 120 Class 60 Board 40 Del from £115 **Parking** 80 **Notes** LB ⊛ ⊘ in restaurant Civ Wed 120

WREXHAM　　　　　　　　MAP 15 SJ35

★★★ 74% ⚜ HOTEL

Best Western Cross Lanes Hotel & Restaurant

Cross Lanes, Bangor Rd, Marchwiel LL13 0TF
☎ 01978 780555 📠 01978 780568
e-mail: guestservices@crosslanes.co.uk

dir: 3m SE of Wrexham, on A525, between Marchwiel & Bangor-on-Dee

This hotel was built as a private house in 1890 and stands in over six acres of beautiful grounds. Bedrooms are well equipped and meet the needs of today's traveller, and include two with four-poster beds. A fine selection of well prepared food is available in Kagan's Brasserie.

Rooms 16 en suite (1 fmly) ⊘ in 6 bedrooms S £70-£85; D £90-£130 (incl. bkfst) **Facilities** ⛳ Putt green Xmas **Conf** Thtr 120 Class 60 Board 40 Del from £135 **Parking** 80 **Notes** LB ⊛ ⊘ in restaurant Closed 25 Dec (night) & 26 Dec Civ Wed 120

★★★ 72% **HOTEL**

Llwyn Onn Hall

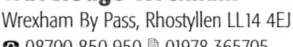

Cefn Rd LL13 0NY

☎ 01978 261225 🗎 01978 363233

e-mail: reception@llwynonnhallhotel.co.uk

dir: between A525 (Wrexham-Whitchurch) & A534 (Wrexham-Nantwich). Easy access Wrexham Ind Estate, 2m off A483

Surrounded by open countryside, this fine 17th-century manor house is set in several acres of mature grounds. Exposed timbers remain and the original oak staircase is still in use. Bedrooms are equipped with modern facilities and one room has a four-poster bed which 'Bonnie' Prince Charlie is reputed to have slept in.

Rooms 13 en suite (1 fmly) ⊗ in 7 bedrooms S £74-£82; D £94-£104 (incl. bkfst) **Conf** Thtr 60 Class 40 Board 12 Del from £90 **Parking** 40 **Notes LB** ⊛ ⊗ in restaurant Closed 26 Dec-2 Jan Civ Wed 60

BUDGET HOTEL

Premier Travel Inn Wrexham

Chester Rd, Gresford LL12 8PW

☎ 08701 977279 🗎 01978 856838

web: www.premiertravelinn.com

dir: on B5445 just off A483 dual carriageway near Gresford

High quality, modern budget accommodation ideal for both families and business travellers. Spacious, en suite bedrooms feature bath and shower, satellite TV and many have telephones and modem points. The adjacent family restaurant features a wide and varied menu. For further details consult the Hotel Groups page.

Rooms 36 en suite

BUDGET HOTEL

Travelodge Wrexham

Wrexham By Pass, Rhostyllen LL14 4EJ

☎ 08700 850 950 🗎 01978 365705

web: www.travelodge.co.uk

dir: 2m S, A483/A5152 rdbt

Travelodge offers good quality, good value, modern accommodation. Ideal for families, the spacious en suite bedrooms include remote control TV, tea and coffee-making facilities and comfortable beds. Meals can be taken at the nearby family restaurant. See Hotel Groups pages for further details.

Rooms 32 en suite S fr £26; D fr £26

Wales

How do I find the perfect place?

Ireland

Roundstone Harbour,
Co.Galway

Additional Information for Northern Ireland & the Republic of Ireland

Licensing Regulations

Northern Ireland: Public houses open Mon-Sat 11.30-23.00. Sun 12.30-22.00. Hotels can serve residents without restriction. Non-residents can be served 12.30-22.00 on Christmas Day. Children under 18 are not allowed in the bar area and may neither buy nor consume liquor in hotels.

Republic of Ireland: General licensing hours are Mon-Thu 10.30-23.30, Fri & Sat 10.30-00.30. Sun 12.30-23.00 (or 00.30 if the following day is a Bank Holiday). There is no service (except for hotel residents) on Christmas Day or Good Friday.

The Fire Services (NI) Order 1984

This covers establishments accommodating more than six people, which must have a certificate from the Northern Ireland Fire Authority. Places accommodating fewer than six people need adequate exits. AA inspectors check emergency notices, fire fighting equipment and fire exits here.

The Republic of Ireland safety regulations are a matter for local authority regulations. For your own and others' safety, read the emergency notices and be sure you understand them.

Telephone numbers

Area codes for numbers in the Republic of Ireland apply only within the Republic. If dialling from outside check the telephone directory (from the UK the international dialling code is 00 353). Area codes for numbers in Britain and Northern Ireland cannot be used directly from the Republic.

For the latest information on the Republic of Ireland visit the AA Ireland's website: www.aaireland.ie

Ireland

NORTHERN IRELAND

CO ANTRIM

BALLYMENA MAP 01 D5

★★★★ 59% **HOTEL**

Galgorm Manor

BT42 1EA

☎ 028 2588 1001 📠 028 2588 0080

e-mail: mail@galgorm.com

dir: *1m outside Ballymena on A42, between Galgorm & Cullybackey*

Standing in 85 acres of private woodland and sweeping lawns beside the River Maine, this 19th-century mansion offers spacious comfortable bedrooms. Public areas include a welcoming cocktail bar and elegant restaurant, as well as Gillies, a lively and atmospheric locals' bar. Also on the estate is an equestrian centre and a conference hall. A new spa and leisure facility is due to open early in 2007.

Rooms 24 en suite (6 fmly) **Facilities** STV Fishing Riding Clay pigeon shooting,Archery,Waterskiing ♫ **Conf** Thtr 500 Class 200 Board 12 **Parking** 170 **Notes LB** ⊗ RS 25-26 Dec Civ Wed 250

CARNLOUGH MAP 01 D6

★★★ 72% ⊛ **HOTEL**

Londonderry Arms

IRISH COUNTRY HOTELS

20 Harbour Rd BT44 0EU

☎ 028 2888 5255 📠 028 2888 5263

e-mail: lda@glensofantrim.com

dir: *14m N from Larne on coast road, A2*

This delightful hotel was built in the mid-19th century by Lady Londonderry, whose grandson, Winston Churchill, also owned it at one time. Today the hotel's Georgian architecture and rooms are still evident, and spacious bedrooms can be found in the modern extension. The hotel enjoys a prime location in this pretty fishing village overlooking the Antrim coast.

Rooms 35 en suite (5 fmly) S £59; D £90 (incl. bkfst) **Facilities** Fishing Wi-fi available ♫ Xmas **Conf** Thtr 120 Class 60 Board 40 Del from £90 **Services** Lift **Parking** 50 **Notes LB** ⊗ Closed Xmas

CARRICKFERGUS MAP 01 D5

★★ 68% **HOTEL**

Dobbins Inn

6-8 High St BT38 7AP

☎ 028 9335 1905 📠 028 9335 1905

e-mail: info@dobbinsinnhotel.co.uk

dir: *M2 from Belfast, right at rdbt onto A2 to Carrickfergus. Left opposite castle*

Colourful window boxes adorn the front of this popular inn near the ancient castle and seafront. Public areas are furnished to a modern standard without compromising the inn's interesting, historical character. Bedrooms vary in size and style, all provide modern comforts. Staff throughout are very friendly and attentive to guests needs.

Rooms 15 en suite (2 fmly) S £40-£50; D £60-£70 (incl. bkfst) **Facilities** ♫ **Notes LB** Closed 25-26 Dec & 1 Jan RS Good Fri

PORTBALLINTRAE MAP 01 C6

★★★ 70% **HOTEL**

Bayview

2 Bayhead Rd BT57 8RZ

☎ 028 2073 4100 📠 028 2073 4330

e-mail: info@bayviewhotelni.com

dir: *M2 (Belfast to Ballymena) then A26 to Ballymena, onto B62 to Portrush, approx 7m right onto B17 to Bushmills. Left then immediate right to Portballintrae in 1m*

This stylish hotel commands excellent views of the ocean, beach and harbour. Bedrooms are bright, modern and well equipped and include rooms for less mobile guests, rooms for families, interconnecting

continued

rooms and non-smoking rooms. Public areas are airy and comfortable with a relaxing conservatory lounge at the front. Conference and meeting rooms are available.

Rooms 25 en suite (12 fmly) ⊛ in 2 bedrooms **Facilities** ♫
Conf Thtr 40 Class 30 Board 20 **Services** Lift **Parking** 25 **Notes LB** ⊗

CO ARMAGH

ARMAGH   MAP 01 C5

★★★ 64% HOTEL

Charlemont Arms Hotel
57/65 English St BT61 7LB
☎ 028 3752 2028 📠 028 3752 6979
e-mail: info@charlemontarmshotel.com
web: www.charlemontarmshotel.com

dir: A3 from Portadown or A28 from Newry, into Armagh. Follow signs to Tourist Information. Hotel 100yds on right

Centrally located for all of this historic city's principal attractions, this hotel has been under the same family ownership for almost 70 years and offers a choice of dining styles and bars. The mostly spacious bedrooms have all been appointed in a contemporary style and provide all the expected facilities.

Rooms 30 en suite (2 fmly) ⊛ in all bedrooms S £50-£60; D £75-£85 (incl. bkfst) **Facilities** ♫ Xmas **Conf** Thtr 150 Class 100 Board 80 Del from £80 **Services** Lift **Parking** 30 **Notes LB** ⊗ Closed 25-26 Dec

---

BELFAST

BELFAST   MAP 01 D5

★★★ 77% HOTEL

Malmaison Belfast
34-38 Victoria St BT1 3GH
☎ 028 9022 0200 📠 028 9022 0220
e-mail: mdavies@malmaison.com
web: www.malmaison.com

dir: M1 along Westlink to Grosvenor Rd. Follow City Centre signs. Pass City Hall on right, left onto Victoria St. Hotel on right

Situated in a former seed warehouse, this smart, contemporary hotel is ideally located for the city centre. Comfortable bedrooms offer a host of modern facilities, whilst the stylish public areas include a popular bar and a brasserie producing carefully prepared meals. The warm hospitality is notable.
Malmaison - AA Hotel Group of the Year 2006-7.

Rooms 64 en suite ⊛ in 50 bedrooms S fr £135; D fr £135
Facilities STV Gym Wi-fi available **Conf** Board 16 Del from £165
Services Lift **Notes** ⊛ in restaurant

★★★ 75% HOTEL

Malone Lodge
60 Eglantine Av BT9 6DY
☎ 028 9038 8000 📠 028 9038 8088
e-mail: info@malonelodgehotel.com
web: www.malonelodgehotel.com

dir: at hospital rdbt exit towards Bouchar Rd, left at 1st rdbt, right at lights at top, then 1st left

Situated in the leafy suburbs of the university area of south Belfast, this stylish hotel forms the centrepiece of an attractive row of Victorian
continued

terraced properties. The unassuming exterior belies an attractive and spacious interior with a smart lounge, popular bar and stylish Green Door restaurant. The hotel also has a small, well-equipped fitness room.

Rooms 51 en suite (5 fmly) (1 GF) S £89-£129; D £89-£129 (incl. bkfst) **Facilities** STV Sauna Gym Wi-fi in bedrooms **Conf** Thtr 150 Class 90 Board 40 Del from £75 **Services** Lift **Parking** 35 **Notes LB** ⊗ ⊛ in restaurant Civ Wed 120

★★★ 73% ⊛ HOTEL

The Crescent Townhouse
13 Lower Crescent BT7 1NR
☎ 028 9032 3349 📠 028 9032 0646
e-mail: info@crescenttownhouse.com

dir: S towards Queens University, hotel opposite Botanic Train Station

This stylish, smartly presented Regency town house enjoys a central location close to the botanic gardens and railway station. The popular Bar Twelve and Metro Brasserie are found on the ground floor whilst a clubby lounge and well-equipped bedrooms are situated on the upper floors.

Rooms 17 en suite (1 fmly) ⊛ in 4 bedrooms S £85-£120; D £85-£145 (incl. bkfst) **Facilities** STV ♫ **Conf** Thtr 40 Class 20 Board 20 **Notes** ⊗ Closed 25-27 Dec, 1 Jan & part of Jul

★★★ 71% HOTEL

Jurys Inn Belfast   ⊛JURYS DOYLE
Fisherwick Place, Great Victoria St BT2 7AP   HOTELS
☎ 028 9053 3500 📠 028 9053 3511
e-mail: info@jurys.com
web: www.jurysdoyle.com

dir: at junct of Grosvenor Rd & Great Victoria St, beside Opera House

Enjoying a central location, this modern hotel is well equipped for business guests. Public areas are contemporary in style and include a foyer lounge, a bar and a smart restaurant. Spacious bedrooms provide modern facilities.

Rooms 190 en suite ⊛ in 140 bedrooms S £65-£120; D £65-£120 **Facilities** STV Wi-fi available ♫ **Conf** Thtr 30 Class 16 Board 16 Del from £120 **Services** Lift **Notes** ⊗ Closed 24-26 Dec

Ⓤ

Days Hotel Belfast   DAYS INN
40 Hope St BT12 5EE
☎ 028 9024 2494 📠 028 9024 2495
e-mail: reservations@dayshotelbelfast.co.uk
web: www.welcomebreak.co.uk

dir: From end of M1 take exit off Grosvenor rdbt, at 1st traffic lights turn right. Over bridge and 1st left.

At the time of going to press, the star classification for this hotel was not confirmed. Please refer to the AA internet site www.theAA.com for current information.

Rooms 250 en suite ⊛ in 180 bedrooms S £65-£95; D £65-£95 (incl. bkfst) **Facilities** STV **Services** Lift **Parking** 300 **Notes** ⊗

Ireland

BELFAST *continued*

Travelodge Belfast Central
15 Brunswick St BT2 7GE
☎ 08700 850 950 ▤ 028 9023 2999
web: www.travelodge.co.uk

dir: from M2 follow city centre signs to Oxford St. Turn right to May St, Brunswick St is 4th on left

Travelodge offers good quality, good value, modern accommodation. Ideal for families, the spacious en suite bedrooms include remote-control TV, tea and coffee-making facilities and comfortable beds. Meals can be taken at the nearby family restaurant. See Hotel Groups pages for further details.

Rooms 90 en suite S fr £26; D fr £26 **Conf** Thtr 65 Class 50 Board 34

CO DOWN

BANGOR   **MAP 01 D5**

★★★★ 74% ● HOTEL

Clandeboye Lodge
10 Estate Rd, Clandeboye BT19 1UR
☎ 028 9185 2500 ▤ 028 9185 2772
e-mail: info@clandeboyelodge.co.uk
web: www.clandeboyelodge.com

dir: A2 from Belfast turn right at Blackwood Golf Centre & Hotel sign. 500yds down Ballysallagh Rd turn left into Crawfordsburn Road. Hotel 200yds on left

The hotel is located west of Bangor and sits in delightful landscaped grounds adjacent to the Clandeboye Estate. The newly upgraded bedrooms are contemporary in design and all have wireless internet access and satellite, flat-screen TVs. Extensive conference, banqueting and wedding facilities are detached from the main hotel. Public areas also include a bright open-plan foyer bar and attractive lounge area.

Rooms 43 en suite (2 fmly) (13 GF) ⊘ in 36 bedrooms S £85-£105; D £95-£115 (incl. bkfst) **Facilities** STV Wi-fi in bedrooms ch fac Xmas **Conf** Thtr 450 Class 150 Board 50 Del from £101.50 **Services** Lift **Parking** 250 **Notes LB** ⊗ ⊘ in restaurant Closed 24-26 Dec Civ Wed 400

If the freedom to smoke or be in a non-smoking atmosphere is important to you, check the rules when you book

★★★ 82% ●● HOTEL

The Old Inn
15 Main St, Crawfordsburn, BT19 1JH
☎ 028 9185 3255 ▤ 028 9185 2775
e-mail: info@theoldinn.com

dir: A2, pass Belfast Airport & Holywood. 3m past sign for The Old Inn, 100yds turn left at lights, into Crawfordsburn and hotel on left

This delightful hotel enjoys a peaceful rural setting just a short drive from Belfast. Dating from 1614, many of the day rooms exude charm and character. Individually styled bedrooms, some with feature beds, offer comfort and modern facilities. The popular bar and intimate restaurant both offer a variety of creative menus, and staff throughout are keen to please.

Rooms 29 en suite 1 annexe en suite (7 fmly) (6 GF) ⊘ in all bedrooms **Facilities** STV ♪ **Conf** Thtr 120 Class 27 Board 40 Del £135 **Parking** 105 **Notes LB** ⊗ ⊘ in restaurant Civ Wed

★★★ 75% HOTEL

Marine Court
The Marina BT20 5ED
☎ 028 9145 1100 ▤ 028 9145 1200
e-mail: marinecourt@btconnect.com
web: www.marinecourthotel.net

dir: pass Belfast city airport, follow A2 through Holywood to Bangor, down main street follow road to left for seafront

Enjoying a delightful location overlooking the marina, this hotel offers a good range of conference and leisure facilities suited to both the business and leisure guest. Extensive public areas include the first-floor restaurant and cocktail bar. Alternatively, the popular Lord Nelson's Bistro/Bar is more relaxed and there is also the lively Bar Mocha.

Rooms 52 en suite (11 fmly) ⊘ in 16 bedrooms S £80-£90; D £90-£100 (incl. bkfst) **Facilities** Spa STV ▣ supervised Sauna Solarium Gym Wi-fi in bedrooms Steam room ♪ Xmas **Conf** Thtr 350 Class 150 Board 60 Del from £110 **Services** Lift **Parking** 30 **Notes LB** ⊗ ⊘ in restaurant Closed 25 Dec Civ Wed 250

★★★ 68% **HOTEL**

Royal

Seafront BT20 5ED

☎ 028 9127 1866 ▪ 028 9146 7810

e-mail: royalhotelbangor@aol.com

web: www.royalhotelbangor.com

dir: *A2 from Belfast. Through town centre to seafront. Turn right, hotel 300yds*

This substantial Victorian hotel enjoys a prime seafront location and overlooks the marina. Bedrooms are comfortable and practical in style. Public areas are traditional and include a choice of contrasting bars whilst traditional Irish cooking can be sampled in the popular brasserie.

Rooms 50 en suite (5 fmly) ⊗ in 10 bedrooms S £58-£68; D £70 (incl. bkfst) **Facilities** ♫ **Conf** Thtr 120 Class 90 Board 80 Del from £75 **Services** Lift **Notes LB** ⊗ Closed 25 Dec

---

NEWCASTLE   MAP 01 D5

★★ 69% **HOTEL**

Enniskeen House

98 Bryansford Rd BT33 0LF

☎ 028 4372 2392 ▪ 028 4372 4084

e-mail: info@enniskeen-hotel.demon.co.uk

dir: *from Newcastle town centre follow signs for Tollymore Forest Park, hotel 1m on left*

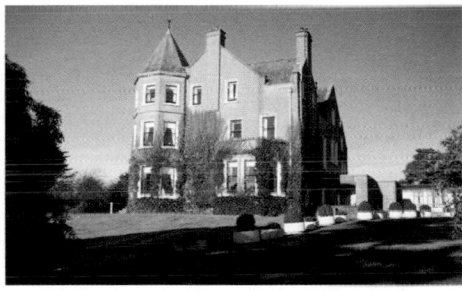

Set in ten acres of grounds and in the same family ownership for over 40 years, this hotel is a real home-from-home. Bedrooms vary but all are well equipped and many enjoy super mountain and countryside views. The formal dining room serves traditional cuisine and the first-floor lounge makes the most of the coastal views.

Rooms 12 en suite (1 fmly) ⊗ in 3 bedrooms **Conf** Thtr 60 Class 24 **Services** Lift **Parking** 45 **Notes LB** ⊗ ⊗ in restaurant Closed 12 Nov-14 Mar

---

ENNISKILLEN   MAP 01 C5

★★★★ 80% **HOTEL**

Killyhevlin

BT74 6RW

IRISH COUNTRY HOTELS

☎ 028 6632 3481 ▪ 028 6632 4726

e-mail: info@killyhevlin.com

web: www.killyhevlin.com

dir: *2m S, off A4*

This modern, stylish hotel is situated on the shores of Lough Erne, south of the town. The well-equipped bedrooms are particularly spacious and enjoy fine views of the gardens and lake. The restaurant, informal bar and comfortable lounges all share the views. Staff are friendly and helpful. There are extensive leisure facilities and spa.

Rooms 70 en suite (42 fmly) (22 GF) ⊗ in 49 bedrooms S £89.50-£98.50; D £119-£137 (incl. bkfst) **Facilities** Spa STV ⊠ supervised Fishing Sauna Gym Jacuzzi Wi-fi available Leisure club ♫ **Conf** Thtr 500 Class 160 Board 100 Del from £95 **Parking** 500 **Notes LB** ⊗ ⊗ in restaurant Closed 24-25 Dec

---

IRVINESTOWN   MAP 01 C5

★★ 64% **HOTEL**

Mahons

Mill St BT94 1GS

☎ 028 6862 1656 & 6862 1657 ▪ 028 6862 8344

e-mail: info@mahonshotel.co.uk

dir: *on A32 midway between Enniskillen & Omagh*

This lively hotel has been in the same family for over 137 years and continues to undergo refurbishment. The bar retains a wealth of charm and character, whilst other public rooms reflect a more modern style. In the spacious restaurant the menu offers a wide range of popular dishes. The newer wing of bedrooms offers very good standards, and the older rooms come in a variety of sizes and styles.

Rooms 24 en suite (10 fmly) (1 GF) ⊗ in 2 bedrooms **Facilities** STV ⊗ Riding Solarium ♫ **Conf** Thtr 400 Class 250 Board 100 **Services** air con **Parking** 40 **Notes LB** Closed 25 Dec

---

AGHADOWEY   MAP 01 C6

★★ 71% **HOTEL**

Brown Trout Golf & Country Inn

209 Agivey Rd BT51 4AD

IRISH COUNTRY HOTELS

☎ 028 7086 8209 ▪ 028 7086 8878

e-mail: bill@browntroutinn.com

dir: *at junct of A54 & B66 junct on road to Coleraine*

Set alongside the Agivey River and featuring its own 9-hole golf course, this welcoming inn offers a choice of spacious accommodation. Comfortably furnished bedrooms are situated around a courtyard area whilst the cottage suites also have lounge areas. Home-cooked meals are served in the restaurant and lighter fare is available in the charming lounge bar which has entertainment at weekends.

Rooms 15 en suite (11 fmly) S £55-£65; D £70-£90 (incl. bkfst) **Facilities** ⌁ 9 Fishing Gym Putt green Game fishing ♫ Xmas **Conf** Thtr 40 Class 24 Board 28 Del from £75 **Parking** 80 **Notes LB** ⊗ in restaurant

Ireland

LIMAVADY   MAP 01 C6

★★★★ 74% ⊛ HOTEL

Radisson SAS Roe Park Resort *Radisson*

BT49 9LB

☎ 028 7772 2222 ▤ 028 7772 2313

e-mail: reservations@radissonroepark.com

web: www.radisson.com

dir: on A2 (Londonderry - Limavady road), 1m from Limavady

This impressive, popular hotel is part of its own modern golf resort. The spacious, contemporary bedrooms are well equipped and many have excellent views of the fairways and surrounding estate. The Greens Restaurant provides a refreshing dining experience and the Coach House brasserie offers a lighter menu. The leisure options are extensive.

Rooms 118 en suite (15 fmly) (37 GF) ⊛ in 113 bedrooms S £100-£110; D £146-£156 (incl. bkfst) **Facilities** Spa STV ⬚ supervised ♨ 18 Fishing Sauna Solarium Gym 🏌 Putt green Jacuzzi Wi-fi available Driving range Outside tees Golf training Bicycle hire ♫ Xmas **Conf** Thtr 450 Class 190 Board 140 Del from £110 **Services** Lift **Parking** 350 **Notes LB** ⊗ Civ Wed 300

★★★ 70% HOTEL

Gorteen House

Deerpark, Roemill Rd BT49 9EX

☎ 028 7772 2333 ▤ 028 7772 2333

e-mail: info@gorteen.com

dir: A2 Londonderry/Coleraine. 12m from Coleraine. 0.5m from town centre on Ballyquinn road

Situated on the outskirts of the town and popular as a function venue, this 18th-century country house has been converted and extended to provide pleasant public areas and a modern wing of bedrooms. The spacious restaurant enjoys a good local reputation for its portion sizes and value for money.

Rooms 26 en suite (2 fmly) (5 GF) S £35-£48; D £60-£65 (incl. bkfst) **Facilities** Snooker ♫ **Conf** Thtr 350 Class 250 Board 100 Del from £60.10 **Parking** 250 **Notes LB** ⊗ Closed 25 Dec Civ Wed

LONDONDERRY   MAP 01 C5

★★★★ 71% HOTEL

City Hotel

Queens Quay BT48 7AS

☎ 028 7136 5800 ▤ 028 7136 5801

e-mail: res@derry-gsh.com

dir: Follow city centre signs. Hotel on waterfront

In a central position overlooking the River Foyle, this stylish, contemporary hotel will appeal to business and leisure guests alike. All bedrooms have excellent facilities including internet access; executive rooms make a particularly good working environment. Meeting and function facilities are extensive and there are good leisure facilities.

Rooms 145 en suite (16 fmly) ⊛ in 112 bedrooms S fr £75; D fr £95 (incl. bkfst) **Facilities** ⬚ supervised Gym Jacuzzi Steam Room, Massage and Beauty Treatments ♫ Xmas **Conf** BC Thtr 350 Class 150 Board 80 Del from £135 **Services** Lift air con **Parking** 48 **Notes LB** ⊗ Closed 25 Dec Civ Wed 350

★★★★ 70% ⊛ HOTEL

Tower Hotel Derry

Off The Diamond
Butcher St BT48 6HL

☎ 028 7137 1000 ▤ 028 7137 1234

e-mail: info@thg.ie

web: www.towerhotelderry.com

dir: from Craigavon Bridge into city centre. Take 2nd exit at end of bridge into Carlisle Rd then Ferryquay St. Hotel straight ahead

This stylish hotel is popular with tourists and corporate guests alike. Modern bedrooms are furnished with flair and style and those on the upper floors enjoy superb views of the city. Minimalist day rooms include a bistro, and staff in the contemporary bar provide true Irish hospitality.

Rooms 93 en suite (26 fmly) ⊛ in 12 bedrooms **Facilities** STV Sauna Gym ♫ **Conf** Thtr 250 Class 150 Board 50 Del from £90 **Services** Lift **Parking** 25 **Notes** ⊗ Closed 24-27 Dec Civ Wed 300

★★★ 75% ⊛ HOTEL

Beech Hill Country House Hotel

32 Ardmore Rd BT47 3QP

☎ 028 7134 9279 ▤ 028 7134 5366

e-mail: info@beech-hill.com

web: www.beech-hill.com

dir: from A6 take Faughan Bridge turn, 1m to hotel opposite Ardmore Chapel

Dating back to 1729, Beech Hill is an impressive mansion, standing in 32 acres of glorious woodlands and gardens. Traditionally styled day rooms provide deep comfort, and ambitious cooking is served in the attractively extended dining room. The splendid bedroom wing provides spacious, well-equipped rooms in addition to the more classically designed bedrooms in the main house.

Rooms 17 en suite 10 annexe en suite (4 fmly) ⊛ in 20 bedrooms S £70-£80; D £100-£130 (incl. bkfst) **Facilities** ♨ Sauna Gym Jacuzzi Wi-fi in bedrooms **Conf** Thtr 100 Class 50 Board 30 Del from £115 **Services** Lift **Parking** 75 **Notes LB** ⊗ ⊛ in restaurant Closed 24-25 Dec Civ Wed 80

BUDGET HOTEL

Travelodge Derry

22-24 Strand Rd BT47 2AB

☎ 08700 850 950 ▤ 01287 127 1277

web: www.travelodge.co.uk

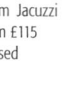

Travelodge offers good quality, good value, modern accommodation. Ideal for families, the spacious en suite bedrooms include remote-control TV, tea and coffee-making facilities and comfortable beds. Meals can be taken at the nearby family restaurant. See Hotel Groups pages for further details.

Rooms 39 en suite S fr £26; D fr £26 **Conf** Thtr 70 Class 30 Board 25

Ireland

MAGHERA   MAP 01 C5

★★ 85% 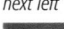 HOTEL

Ardtara Country House
8 Gorteade Rd, Upperlands BT46 5SA
☎ 028 7964 4490 📠 028 7964 5080
e-mail: valerie@ardtara.fsbusiness.co.uk
web: www.ardtara.com
dir: *from Maghera take A29 towards Coleraine, in 2m take B75 for Kilrea through Upperlands, pass sign Wm Clark & Sons then next left*

Ardtara is a delightful, high quality Victorian country house set in eight acres of mature gardens and woodland. The stylish public rooms include a choice of lounges and a sunroom, whilst the elegant period dining room is the perfect venue for enjoying the skilfully prepared cuisine. Bedrooms vary in style and size; all are richly furnished with fine antiques, have open fires and well equipped bathrooms.

Rooms 9 en suite (1 fmly) (1 GF) S £85-£100; D £130-£150 (incl. bkfst) **Facilities** ⚓ Wi-fi in bedrooms ♬ Xmas **Conf** Thtr 45 Board 20 **Parking** 40 **Notes LB** ⊘ in restaurant Civ Wed 150

CO TYRONE

DUNGANNON   MAP 01 C5

★★ 68% HOTEL

Cohannon Inn
212 Ballynakilly Rd BT71 6HJ
☎ 028 8772 4488 📠 028 8775 2217
e-mail: enquiries@cohannon-inn.com
dir: *400yds from M1 junct 14*

Handy for the M1 and the nearby towns of Dungannon and Portadown, this establishment offers competitive prices and well-maintained bedrooms, located behind the inn complex in a smart purpose-built wing. Public areas are smartly furnished and wide-ranging menus are offered throughout the day.

Rooms 42 en suite (20 fmly) (21 GF) ⊘ in 20 bedrooms S £50; D £50 **Conf** Thtr 160 Class 100 Board 40 Del from £48 **Parking** 160 **Notes LB** ⊗ RS 25 Dec

REPUBLIC OF IRELAND
CO CARLOW

CARLOW   MAP 01 C3

★★★ 75% HOTEL

Seven Oaks
Athy Rd
☎ 059 913 1308 📠 059 913 2155
e-mail: info@sevenoakshotel.com

IRISH COUNTRY HOTELS

This smart hotel is conveniently situated within walking distance of Carlow town centre. Public areas include comfortable lounges, a traditional style bar and restaurant. Bedrooms are spacious and very well appointed. There are extensive leisure and banqueting facilities and a secure car park.

Rooms 59 en suite (5 fmly) S €70-€115, D €130-€210 (incl. bkfst) **Facilities** STV ⬚ supervised Sauna Gym Jacuzzi Wi-fi in bedrooms Aerobic studio, Steam room ♬ **Conf** Thtr 400 Class 150 Board 80 Del from €120 **Services** Lift air con **Parking** 200 **Notes LB** ⊗ ⊘ in restaurant Closed 25-26 Dec RS Good Fri

TULLOW   MAP 01 D3

★★★★ 78% HOTEL

The Mount Wolseley Hilton
☎ 059 915 1674 📠 059 915 2123
e-mail: info@mountwolseley.ie

Located on a vast estate associated with the Wolseley family of motoring fame, this newly expanded hotel has much to offer. Public areas are very spacious and there are a range of comfortable bedrooms and suites. Leisure pursuits include golf, together with a health centre and spa facilities. The hotel offers a number of dining options.

Rooms 142 en suite ⊘ in 128 bedrooms **Facilities** Spa STV ⬚ supervised ♨ 18 ⚓ Snooker Sauna Gym Putt green Jacuzzi ♬ ch fac **Conf** BC Thtr 750 Class 288 Board 70 **Services** Lift air con **Parking** 160 **Notes** ⊗ ⊘ in restaurant Closed 25-26 Dec

CO CAVAN

BALLYCONNELL   MAP 01 C4

★★★★ 76% 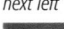 HOTEL

Slieve Russell Hotel Golf & Country Club
☎ 049 9526444 📠 049 9526046
e-mail: slieve-russell@quinn-hotels.com
dir: *N3 towards Cavan. At rdbt before Cavan follow signs for Enniskillen to Belturbe, then towards Ballyconnell, hotel approx 6m on left*

This imposing hotel stands on 300 acres, encompassing a championship golf course and a nine-hole par three course. The spacious public areas include relaxing lounges, three restaurants and extensive leisure and banqueting facilities. Bedrooms are comfortable and tastefully furnished.

Rooms 219 en suite (87 fmly) ⊘ in 189 bedrooms S €84-€140; D €168-€250 (incl. bkfst) **Facilities** Spa STV ⬚ ♨ 9&18 ⚓ Sauna Solarium Gym Putt green Jacuzzi Wi-fi available Floodlit driving range, Wellness centre ♬ Xmas **Conf** BC Thtr 1200 Class 600 Board 40 Del from €145 **Services** Lift **Parking** 600 **Notes LB** ⊗ ⊘ in restaurant

CAVAN
MAP 01 C4

★★★★ 78% ◎ **HOTEL**

Cavan Crystal
Dublin Rd
☎ 049 4360600 ▤ 049 4360699
e-mail: info@cavancrystalhotel.com
dir: *N3 towards Cavan, at 1st rdbt take N55 signed Athlone*

Contemporary design, matched with the use of native timber, handcrafted brick and crystal chandeliers, make this a particularly distinctive hotel. This is complemented by excellent hospitality from all of the highly trained staff. Located on the southern edge of the town, the hotel also features a well-equipped health and beauty clinic, and extensive banquet and conference facilities.

Rooms 85 en suite (2 fmly) (9 GF) S €110-€160; D €170-€350 (incl. bkfst) **Facilities** STV ﹖ supervised Sauna Gym Jacuzzi Wi-fi in bedrooms ♫ Xmas **Conf** Thtr 500 Class 300 Board 100 Del from €150 **Services** Lift **Parking** 216 **Notes LB** ⊛ ⊘ in restaurant Closed 24 & 25 Dec

★★★ 70% **HOTEL**

Kilmore
Dublin Rd
☎ 049 4332288 ▤ 049 4332458
e-mail: kilmore@quinn-hotels.com
dir: *approx 3km from Cavan on N3*

Located on the outskirts of Cavan, easily accessible from the N3, this comfortable hotel features spacious and welcoming public areas. Good food is served in the Annalee Restaurant, which is always appreciated by guests returning from nearby fishing or golf.

Rooms 39 en suite (17 fmly) (19 GF) **Facilities** STV Free use of facilities at Slieve Russell Golf & Country Club ♫ **Conf** Thtr 500 Class 200 Board 60 **Services** air con **Parking** 450 **Notes LB** ⊛ ⊘ in restaurant Closed 25 Dec

U

Radisson SAS Farnham Estate
Farnham Estate
☎ 049 4377700 ▤ 049 4377701
e-mail: info.farnham@radissonsas.com
dir: *From N3 continue to Cavan then take Killeshandra road, hotel in 4km*

At the time of going to press, the star classification for this hotel was not confirmed. Please refer to the AA internet site www.theAA.com for current information.

Rooms 158 en suite ⊘ in 128 bedrooms S €105-€165; D €130-€190 (incl. bkfst) **Facilities** Spa ﹖ ﹖ Fishing Sauna Solarium Gym Jacuzzi Health spa Xmas **Conf** BC Thtr 440 Class 172 Board 54 Del from €195 **Services** Lift **Parking** 250 **Notes** ⊛ ⊘ in restaurant

KINGSCOURT
MAP 01 C4

★★★ 73% **HOTEL**

Cabra Castle Hotel

☎ 042 9667030 ▤ 042 9667039
e-mail: sales@cabracastle.com

Rebuilt in 1808 the castle stands on 100 acres of parkland with a 9-hole golf course and is surrounded by Dun a Ri Forest Park. In addition to the bedrooms in 'The Old House' there are spacious

continued

courtyard rooms in what was formerly a granary. The main reception rooms are inviting and there is a relaxing lounge bar, sun terrace, restaurant and extensive banqueting facilities.

Rooms 20 en suite 46 annexe en suite (5 fmly) **Facilities** ♨ 9 Riding ♫ **Conf** Thtr 300 Class 100 Board 50 Del from €155 **Parking** 200 **Notes** ⊘ in restaurant Closed 25-27 Dec

VIRGINIA
MAP 01 C4

★★ 67% ◎ **HOTEL**

The Park
Virginia Park
☎ 049 8546100 ▤ 049 8547203
e-mail: virginiapark@eircom.net
dir: *turn off N3 in Virginia onto R194. Hotel 500yds on left*

A charming hotel, built in 1750 as the summer retreat of the Marquis of Headford. Situated overlooking Lake Ramor on a 100-acre estate, it has a 9-hole golf course, lovely mature gardens and woodland. This hotel brings together generous hospitality and a relaxed leisurely way of life.

Rooms 26 en suite (1 fmly) (8 GF) **Facilities** ♨ 9 Fishing Sauna ch fac **Conf** Thtr 70 Class 40 Board 40 **Parking** 50 **Notes** ⊛ ⊘ in restaurant Closed 25 Dec

CO CLARE

BALLYVAUGHAN
MAP 01 B3

COURTESY & CARE AWARD
INSPECTORS' CHOICE

★★★ ◎◎ **COUNTRY HOUSE HOTEL**

Gregans Castle
☎ 065 7077005 ▤ 065 7077111
e-mail: stay@gregans.ie
dir: *3.5m S of Ballyvaughan on N67*

The Hayden family, together with their welcoming staff, offer a high level of personal service; hospitality, good food and relaxation are all notable here. Situated in the heart of The Burren and the hotel enjoys splendid views towards Galway Bay. The area is rich in archaeological, geological and botanical interest. Bedrooms are individually decorated; superior rooms and suites are particularly comfortable, and some of these are on the ground floor. AA Ireland has awarded this hotel their Courtesy & Care Award for the Republic of Ireland 2006-7.

Rooms 21 en suite (3 fmly) (7 GF) ⊘ in all bedrooms S €120-€180; D €180-€225 (incl. bkfst) **Facilities** no TV in bdrms ﹗ Wi-fi in bedrooms ♫ ch fac **Conf** Thtr 25 Class 25 Board 14 **Parking** 25 **Notes LB** ⊛ ⊘ in restaurant Closed Jan-5 Apr & 15 Oct-Dec

Ireland

★★★ 70% **HOTEL**

Hylands Burren

IRISH COUNTRY HOTELS

☎ 065 707 7037 ▤ 065 707 7131
e-mail: hylandsburren@eircom.net

This charming village hotel, dating from the 18th century, is set in the picturesque village of Ballyvaughan. In the heart of the unique Burren landscape it is ideally located for touring County Clare. Open fires burn in the traditional bar and lounges and local seafood is a speciality in the restaurant. Bedrooms are comfortable and well appointed.

Rooms 29 en suite (2 fmly) ⊘ in 6 bedrooms **Facilities** STV ♫
Parking 30 **Notes LB** ⊛ ⊘ in restaurant Closed 22-25 Dec

BUNRATTY   MAP 01 B3

★★★ 70% **HOTEL**

Bunratty Shannon Shamrock

☎ 061 361177 ▤ 061 471252
e-mail: reservations@dunnehotels.com

dir: take Bunratty by-pass, exit off Limerick/Shannon dual carriageway

Situated in the shadow of Bunratty's famous medieval castle in a pretty village, this hotel is surrounded by well-maintained lawns and mature trees. Bedrooms and public areas are spacious and comfortable. There is a leisure centre plus impressive conference and banqueting facilities.

Rooms 115 en suite (12 fmly) (91 GF) ⊘ in 10 bedrooms **Facilities** Spa STV ⬚ Sauna Solarium Gym Jacuzzi Hair & beauty salon ♫ **Conf** BC Thtr 1200 Class 650 Board 300 **Parking** 300 **Notes LB** ⊛ ⊘ in restaurant Closed 24-26 Dec

---

DOOLIN   MAP 01 B3

★★★ 67% **HOTEL**

Aran View House

Coast Rd
☎ 065 7074061 & 7074420 ▤ 065 7074540
e-mail: bookings@aranview.com

Situated in 100 acres of rolling farmland and commanding panoramic views of the Cliffs of Moher and the Aran Islands, this family-run hotel offers comfortable accommodation. With welcoming staff and a convivial atmosphere, guests are assured of a relaxing stay. Seafood is a feature of the menu served in the attractive restaurant.

Rooms 13 en suite 6 annexe en suite (1 fmly) **Facilities** ♫ **Parking** 40
Notes Closed Nov-1 Apr

ENNIS   MAP 01 B3

★★★ 70% ⊛ **HOTEL**

Temple Gate

The Square
☎ 065 6823300 ▤ 065 6823322
e-mail: info@templegatehotel.com

dir: turn off N18 onto Tulla Rd for 0.25m, hotel on left

This smart hotel is located in the very centre of the town, accessed from the public car park at the rear. Incorporating a 19th-century Gothic-style building, the public areas are well planned and include a comfortable lounge, popular pub and JM's Bistro restaurant. Bedrooms are attractive and well equipped.

Rooms 70 en suite (3 fmly) (14 GF) ⊘ in 36 bedrooms
S €102.50-€170; D €145-€270 (incl. bkfst) **Facilities** STV Wi-fi in bedrooms ♫ **Conf** Thtr 220 Class 100 Board 80 Del from €164
Services Lift **Parking** 52 **Notes LB** ⊛ ⊘ in restaurant Closed 25-26 Dec RS 24-Dec Civ Wed 150

Ⓤ

Woodstock

Shanaway Rd

MANOR HOUSE

☎ 065 6846600 ▤ 065 6846611
e-mail: info@woodstockhotel.com

dir: From Ennis continue on N18 until rdbt, take N85 to Lahinch, after 1km turn left for Woodstock & continue for 1km

At the time of going to press, the star classification for this hotel was not confirmed. Please refer to the AA internet site www.theAA.com for current information.

Rooms 67 en suite (20 GF) ⊘ in 47 bedrooms **Facilities** STV ⬚ supervised ⌁ 18 Sauna Gym Jacuzzi Steam room ♫ **Conf** BC Thtr 200 Class 160 Board 50 **Services** Lift air con **Notes LB** ⊛ Closed 25-26 Dec

---

KILKEE   MAP 01 B3

★★ 64% **HOTEL**

Halpin's

Erin St
☎ 065 9056032 ▤ 065 9056317
e-mail: halpinshotel@iol.ie

dir: in centre of town

The finest tradition of hotel service is offered at this family-run hotel which has a commanding view over the old Victorian town. The attractive bedrooms are comfortable.

Rooms 12 en suite (6 fmly) ⊘ in 4 bedrooms S €70-€90; D €90-€130 (incl. bkfst) **Facilities** STV **Conf** Thtr 60 Class 36 Board 30 Del from €149 **Services** air con **Parking** 3 **Notes LB** ⊛ ⊘ in restaurant Closed 16 Nov-14 Mar

Ireland

LISDOONVARNA
MAP 01 B3

★★★ 70% ◎◎ **HOTEL**

Sheedys Country House
☎ 065 7074026 📠 065 7074555
e-mail: info@sheedys.com

dir: *200mtrs from The Square in town centre*

Dating in part from the 17th century and set in an unrivalled location on the edge of the Burren, this house is full of character and has an intimate atmosphere. Fine cuisine can be enjoyed in the contemporary restaurant. Bedrooms are spacious and well appointed. An ideal base for touring; close to Lahinch golf course, Doolin and the Cliffs of Moher.

Rooms 11 en suite (1 fmly) (5 GF) ⊘ in all bedrooms **Parking** 40 **Notes** ⊗ ⊘ in restaurant Closed mid Oct-mid Mar

NEWMARKET-ON-FERGUS
MAP 01 B3

INSPECTORS' CHOICE

★★★★★ ◎◎ **HOTEL**

Dromoland Castle
☎ 061 368144 📠 061 363355
e-mail: sales@dromoland.ie

dir: *N18 from Shannon, left signed 'Dromoland Interchange'*

Dromoland Castle, dating from the early 18th century, stands on a 375-acre estate and offers extensive indoor leisure activities and outdoor pursuits. The team are wholly committed to caring for guests. The thoughtfully equipped bedrooms and suites vary in style but all provide excellent levels of comfort. The hotel has two restaurants, the elegant fine-dining Earl of Thomond, and less formal Fig Tree in the golf clubhouse.

Rooms 100 en suite (20 fmly) **Facilities** STV 🔖 supervised ♨ 18 ♨ Fishing Snooker Sauna Solarium Gym Putt green Jacuzzi Beauty clinic, Archery, Clay shooting, Mountain bikes 🎵 **Conf** BC Thtr 450 Class 220 Board 80 **Parking** 120 **Notes LB** ⊗ ⊘ in restaurant

SPANISH POINT
MAP 01 B3

★★★ 72% **HOTEL**

Burkes Armada
☎ 065 7084110 📠 065 7084632
e-mail: info@burkesarmadahotel.com

IRISH COUNTRY HOTELS

dir: *N18 from Ennis take N85 Inagh, then R460 to Miltown Malbay. Follow signs for Spanish Point*

Situated on the coastline, overlooking breaking waves and golden sands, this friendly, family run hotel is located in a natural, unspoiled environment. The public areas benefit from views of this stunning location, especially the contemporary restaurant and the recently opened Lower Bar. Bedrooms, many with sea views, are well equipped and brightly decorated. Good bar food menu served throughout the day.

Rooms 61 en suite (53 fmly) S €80-€100; D €150-€180 (incl. bkfst) **Facilities** STV Gym 🎵 Xmas **Conf** Thtr 600 Class 400 Board 60 **Services** Lift **Parking** 175 **Notes LB** ⊗

CO CORK

BALLINCOLLIG
MAP 01 B2

Ⓤ

Oriel House Hotel & Leisure Centre
☎ 021 4870888

At the time of going to press, the star classification for this hotel was not confirmed. Please refer to the AA internet site www.theAA.com for current information. **Rooms** 80 en suite

BALLYCOTTON
MAP 01 C2

INSPECTORS' CHOICE

★★★ ◎◎ **HOTEL**

Bay View
☎ 021 4646746 📠 021 4646075
e-mail: res@thebayviewhotel.com

dir: *N25 Castlemartyr, right through Ladysbridge onto Ballycotton.*

Situated in a fishing village overlooking Ballycotton Bay, the Bay View has a very pleasant atmosphere and a stunning outlook. The public rooms and the bedrooms are very comfortable and make the most of the views, but it is the warm and friendly team that impresses most. Dinner in the Capricho Room is a delight.

Rooms 35 en suite (5 GF) ⊘ in 25 bedrooms S €118-€137; D €172-€210 (incl. bkfst) **Facilities** STV ♨ Fishing Riding Pitch and putt, Sea angling **Conf** Thtr 60 Class 30 Board 24 Del from €150 **Services** Lift air con **Parking** 40 **Notes LB** ⊘ in restaurant Closed Nov-Apr

BALLYLICKEY
MAP 01 B2

INSPECTORS' CHOICE

★★★ ◉◉ **COUNTRY HOUSE HOTEL**

Sea View House Hotel
☎ 027 50073 & 50462 ▤ 027 51555
e-mail: info@seaviewhousehotel.com
dir: 5km from Bantry, 11km from Glengarriff on N71

Colourful gardens and glimpses of Bantry Bay through the mature trees frame this delightful country house. Owner Kathleen O'Sullivan's team of staff are exceptionally pleasant. Guest comfort and good cuisine are the top priorities. Bedrooms are spacious and individually styled; some on the ground floor are appointed to facilitate less able guests.

Rooms 25 en suite (3 fmly) (5 GF) **Facilities** STV **Parking** 32 **Notes LB** ⊘ in restaurant Closed mid Nov-mid Mar

BALTIMORE
MAP 01 B1

★★★ 70% ◉ **HOTEL**

Baltimore Harbour Resort Hotel & Leisure Centre
☎ 028 20361 ▤ 028 20466
e-mail: info@bhrhotel.ie
dir: N71 to Skibbereen, then R595, 13km to Baltimore

Overlooking the natural harbour of Baltimore, this family orientated leisure hotel is perfect for a relaxing break. Bedrooms are well appointed and most have a sea view. The popular bar and sun room open out onto the patio and gardens.

Rooms 64 en suite (30 fmly) **Facilities** ⬚ supervised Sauna Gym ⬚ Jacuzzi Table Tennis, In-house video channel, Indoor bowls ♫ **Conf** Thtr 120 Class 100 Board 30 **Services** Lift **Parking** 80 **Notes LB** ⊗ ⊘ in restaurant Closed Jan RS Nov-Dec & Feb-mid Mar

We have indicated only the hotels that do not accept credit or debit cards

★★★ 70% ◉ **HOTEL**

Casey's of Baltimore
☎ 028 20197 ▤ 028 20509
e-mail: info@caseysofbaltimore.com
dir: from Cork take N71 to Skibbereen, then take R595

IRISH COUNTRY HOTELS

This relaxed family run hotel is situated in the sailing and fishing village of Baltimore. There are comfortable bedrooms, cosy lounge and bar with open fires and traditional music at weekends. The Casey's ensure that a variety of the freshest seafood, from the owner's fishing trawler, is served in the restaurant. They also organise trips to the Islands.

Rooms 14 en suite (1 fmly) (4 GF) ⊘ in all bedrooms S €89-€110; D €146-€174 (incl. bkfst) **Facilities** STV ♫ **Conf** Thtr 45 Class 30 Board 25 Del from €115 **Parking** 50 **Notes LB** ⊗ ⊘ in restaurant Closed 21-27 Dec

BANTRY
MAP 01 B2

★★★ 67% **HOTEL**

Westlodge
☎ 027 50360 ▤ 027 50438
e-mail: reservations@westlodgehotel.ie
web: www.westlodgehotel.ie
dir: N71 to West Cork

A superb leisure centre and good children's facilities makes this hotel very popular with families. Its situation on the outskirts of the town also makes it an ideal base for touring west Cork and south Kerry. All the staff are friendly and hospitable. There are extensive banqueting facilities and lovely walks in the grounds.

Rooms 90 en suite (20 fmly) (20 GF) ⊘ in 15 bedrooms S €80-€95; D €130-€150 (incl. bkfst) **Facilities** STV ⬚ ⬚ Squash Snooker Sauna Solarium Gym Putt green Jacuzzi Wi-fi available ♫ **Conf** BC Thtr 400 Class 200 Board 24 Del from €99 **Services** Lift air con **Parking** 400 **Notes LB** ⊗ ⊘ in restaurant Closed 23-27 Dec

Ireland

BLARNEY
MAP 01 B2

★★★ 70% **HOTEL**

Blarney Castle
The Village Green
☎ 021 4385116 📠 021 4385542
e-mail: info@blarneycastlehotel.com

dir: *N20 (Cork to Limerick road) onto R617 for Blarney*

Situated in the centre of the town within walking distance of the renowned Blarney Stone, this friendly hotel has been in the same family since 1873. Many of the bedrooms are spacious but all are appointed to a very comfortable standard. The popular bar serves good food throughout most of the day.

Rooms 13 en suite ⊘ in all bedrooms S €55-€80; D €110-€130 (incl. bkfst) **Facilities** STV **Conf** Thtr 120 **Services** air con **Parking** 5 **Notes** LB ⊗ ⊘ in restaurant Closed 24-25 Dec

U

Ramada Hotel & Suites at Blarney Golf Resort
Tower
☎ 021 438 4477 📠 021 451 6453
e-mail: info.blarney@ramadaireland.com

At the time of going to press, the star classification for this hotel was not confirmed. Please refer to the AA internet site www.theAA.com for current information.

Rooms 118 rms

CARRIGALINE
MAP 01 B2

★★★★ 73% **HOTEL**

Carrigaline Court Hotel & Leisure Centre
☎ 021 4852100 📠 021 4371103
e-mail: reception@carrigcourt.com
web: www.carrigcourt.com

dir: *From South Link road (E from airport or W from Dublin/Lee Tunnel) take exit for Carrigaline. Stay in right lane*

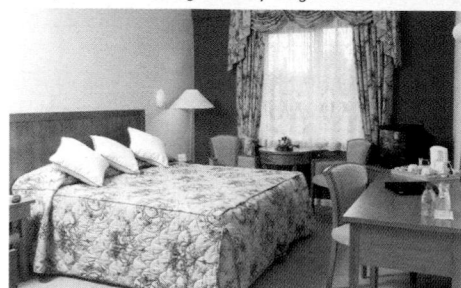

This smart, modern hotel is situated only minutes' drive from Cork City Airport and the Ringaskiddy Port. Bedrooms are spacious and very well appointed. Public areas include Collins, the traditional, themed Irish pub, The Bistro and extensive conference, leisure and beauty facilities. Golf, sailing, angling and horse riding are available locally.

Rooms 91 en suite (3 fmly) ⊘ in 39 bedrooms **Facilities** STV ☒ supervised Sauna Solarium Gym Jacuzzi Beauty salon, Massage treatment rooms ♫ **Conf** Thtr 400 Class 200 Board 150 **Services** Lift **Parking** 220 **Notes** LB ⊗ ⊘ in restaurant Closed 25 Dec

CLONAKILTY
MAP 01 B2

★★★★ 81% ◉◉ **HOTEL**

Inchydoney Island Lodge & Spa
☎ 023 33143 📠 023 35229
e-mail: reservations@inchydoneyisland.com

dir: *follow N71 (West Cork road) to Clonakilty. At entry rdbt in Clonakilty take 2nd exit, follow signs to hotel*

This modern hotel is stunningly located on the coastline with steps down to two long sandy beaches. Bedrooms are decorated in warm colours and are well appointed. Diners have a choice of the third floor Gulfstream restaurant or the more casual Dunes bar and bistro.

Rooms 67 en suite (24 fmly) (18 GF) ⊘ in 17 bedrooms S €209-€214; D €319-€341 (incl. bkfst) **Facilities** Spa STV ☒ supervised Fishing Riding Snooker Sauna Gym Jacuzzi Wi-fi available Thalassotherapy Spa ♫ **Conf** Thtr 300 Board 50 **Services** Lift **Parking** 200 **Notes** LB ⊗ ⊘ in restaurant Closed 24-26 Dec

CORK

MAP 01 B2

INSPECTORS' CHOICE

★★★★ ◎◎ **HOTEL**

Hayfield Manor

Perrott Av, College Rd
☎ 021 4845900 ▤ 021 4316839
e-mail: enquiries@hayfieldmanor.ie

dir: 1m W of city centre on N22 towards Killarney, turn left at University Gates off Western Rd. Turn right into College Rd, left into Perrott Ave

As part of a grand two-acre estate with lovely walled gardens, Hayfield Manor offers luxury and seclusion, just a short distance from UCC. This fine hotel has every modern comfort and maintains an atmosphere of tranquillity, with real fires in the public areas where elegant architecture and fine furnishings create a beautiful setting. Bedrooms offer very high levels of comfort with many thoughtful extras. There are beauty treatments and leisure facilities available for resident guests.

Rooms 88 en suite ⊘ in 25 bedrooms S €380; D €380 **Facilities Spa** STV ⬚ Gym ⬚ Jacuzzi Wi-fi in bedrooms Steam room ♬ Xmas **Conf** Thtr 100 Class 60 Board 40 **Services** Lift air con **Parking** 100 **Notes LB** ⊗ ⊘ in restaurant

★★★★ 79% ◎ **HOTEL**

Maryborough Hotel & Spa

Maryborough Hill
☎ 021 4365555 ▤ 021 4365662
e-mail: info@maryborough.com

dir: from Jack Lynch Tunnel take 2nd exit signed Douglas. Right at 1st rdbt, follow Rochestown road to fingerpost rdbt. Left, hotel on left 0.5m up hill

Dating from 1715, Maryborough House has been renovated and extended to become a fine hotel set in beautifully landscaped grounds. The suites in the main house and the bedrooms in the wing are well appointed and comfortable. The extensive lounge is very popular for the range of food served throughout the day.

Rooms 94 en suite (6 fmly) ⊘ in 37 bedrooms S €145-€250; D €198-€500 (incl. bkfst) **Facilities Spa** STV ⬚ supervised Snooker Sauna Gym ⬚ Jacuzzi Wi-fi in bedrooms **Conf** BC Thtr 500 Class 250 Board 60 Del from €230 **Services** Lift **Parking** 300 **Notes LB** ⊗ ⊘ in restaurant

★★★★ 78% **HOTEL**

Rochestown Park Hotel

Rochestown Rd, Douglas
☎ 021 4890800 ▤ 021 4892178
e-mail: info@rochestownpark.com

dir: from Lee Tunnel, 2nd exit left off dual carriageway. 400mtrs then 1st left and right at small rdbt. Hotel 600mtrs on right

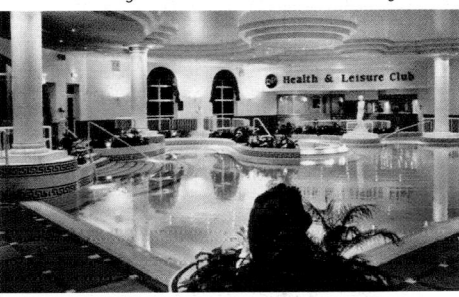

This modern hotel is situated in mature gardens on the south side of Cork city. Various bedroom styles, including suites, are available, most rooms are air-conditioned and overlook Mahon Golf Club. Public areas include a traditional bar and Gallery Restaurant. There are extensive leisure, conference and exhibition facilities. Convenient for both the airport and the ferries.

Rooms 160 en suite (17 fmly) (23 GF) ⊘ in 120 bedrooms S €80 €120; D €100-€160 (incl. bkfst) **Facilities Spa** STV ⬚ supervised Sauna Solarium Gym Jacuzzi Wi-fi in bedrooms Thalassotherapy & beauty centre Xmas **Conf** BC Thtr 800 Class 360 Board 100 **Services** Lift **Parking** 300 **Notes LB** ⊗ ⊘ in restaurant Closed 25-26 Dec Civ Wed 20

★★★★ 77% **HOTEL**

Silver Springs Moran

Tivoli

MORAN HOTELS

☎ 021 450 7533 ▤ 021 450 7641
e-mail: silverspringsres@moranhotels.com
web: www.moranhotels.com

dir: N8 south Silver Springs exit and right across overpass then right for hotel on left

The public areas of this hotel create a smart, contemporary atmosphere. Bedrooms are comfortable, many offering good views

continued on page 958

CORK *continued*

over the River Lee. Guests have use of a nearby leisure centre. Excellent conference facilities are available in a separate building.

Rooms 109 en suite (29 fmly) ⊘ in 30 bedrooms S €115-€185; D €140-€250 (incl. bkfst) **Facilities Spa** STV ⌇ supervised ⌇ Squash Snooker Sauna Solarium Gym Jacuzzi Wi-fi in bedrooms Aerobics classes ♫ ch fac Xmas **Conf** BC Thtr 800 Class 400 Board 30 Del from €146 **Services** Lift **Parking** 325 **Notes LB** ⊗ ⊘ in restaurant Closed 24-26 Dec

★★★★ 74% **HOTEL**

The Clarion Hotel

Lapps Quay

☎ 021 422 4900 ⬚ 021 422 4901

e-mail: info@clarionhotelcorkcity.com

This new hotel has commanding views of the River Lee and City Hall. Rooms are particularly comfortable, with stylish décor and air conditioning. Excellent leisure and meeting facilities are available together with secure underground parking. Dining options include Synergie Restaurant and a popular bar menu with oriental influences.

Rooms 191 rms

★★★★ 72% **HOTEL**

The Kingsley Hotel

Victoria Cross

☎ 021 4800500 ⬚ 021 4800527

e-mail: resv@kingsleyhotel.com

dir: off N22 opposite County Hall

Situated on the banks of the River Lee, this luxurious hotel has excellent facilities. The bedrooms are spacious and feature thoughtful additional touches. The contemporary bar and restaurant have an informal atmosphere, and both the lounge and library are elegant and relaxing.

Rooms 69 en suite (4 fmly) ⊘ in 36 bedrooms **Facilities** STV ⌇ supervised Fishing Sauna Solarium Gym Jacuzzi Treatment rooms **Conf** Thtr 95 Class 50 Board 32 **Services** Lift air con **Parking** 150 **Notes LB** ⊗

See advert on opposite page

★★★ 75% **HOTEL**

Ambassador

Military Hill, St Lukes

☎ 021 4551996 ⬚ 021 4551997

e-mail: reservations@ambassadorhotel.ie

dir: city centre, just off Wellington Rd

Many pleasing features distinguish this 19th-century sandstone and granite building that has commanding views over the city. There is a feeling of space throughout the public areas which include a cocktail lounge, bar and restaurant. All bedrooms are well equipped and some have balconies. A fitness suite is available.

Rooms 58 en suite (8 fmly) ⊘ in 12 bedrooms **Facilities** STV Sauna Gym Jacuzzi ♫ **Conf** BC Thtr 220 Class 100 Board 50 **Services** Lift **Parking** 60 **Notes LB** ⊗ ⊘ in restaurant Closed 24-26 Dec

★★★ 73% **HOTEL**

Gresham Metropole

GRESHAM HOTELS

MacCurtain St

☎ 021 4643700 ⬚ 021 4506450

e-mail: info@gresham-metropolehotel.com

dir: in city centre, opposite Merchant Quay Shopping Centre

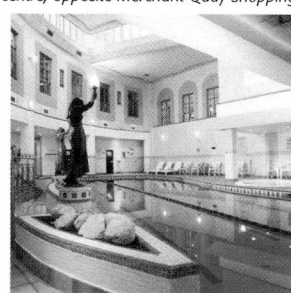

This long-established property is now a very comfortable city centre hotel. Bedrooms vary in size and are well equipped. Public areas include the popular Met bar, spacious lounge areas and a good leisure centre. Enquire on reservation about undercover parking arrangements.

Rooms 113 en suite (3 fmly) ⊘ in 90 bedrooms S €90-€200; D €90-€260 (incl. bkfst) **Facilities** STV ⌇ supervised Sauna Solarium Gym Jacuzzi Wi-fi available Aerobic studio Steam room ♫ Xmas **Conf** Thtr 500 Class 180 Board 60 **Services** Lift **Parking** 240 **Notes LB** ⊗ ⊘ in restaurant

★★★ 73% **HOTEL**

Imperial Hotel, Escape Salon & Spa

South Mall

☎ 021 4274040 ⬚ 021 4275375

e-mail: info@imperialhotelcork.ie

dir: in city centre business area

This fine, long established hotel has a hospitable and welcoming atmosphere. The reception rooms are on a grand scale, especially the foyer and coffee shop. Bedrooms are appointed to a high standard. Parking, about five minutes' away, is available by prior arrangement.

continued

Imperial Hotel, Escape Salon & Spa

Rooms 130 en suite (4 fmly) ⊗ in 116 bedrooms S €125-€175; D €150-€950 **Facilities Spa** STV FTV Gym Jacuzzi Wi-fi available ♪ **Conf** BC Thtr 280 Class 150 Board 80 Del from €160 **Services** Lift **Notes** LB ⊕ ⊗ in restaurant Closed 24-27 Dec

★★★ 68% HOTEL

Jurys Inn

⅃JURYSDOYLE
HOTELS

Anderson's Quay

☎ 021 4943000 📠 021 4276144

e-mail: enquiry@jurys.com

web: www.jurysdoyle.com

dir: in city centre

This hotel overlooks the River Lee and is just a short walk from the main street and shopping area. Attractively decorated in a modern style. Rooms are spacious and can accommodate families. The restaurant is informal and there is also a lively pub.

Rooms 133 en suite ⊗ in 32 bedrooms S €65 €155; D €65-€155 **Facilities** STV Wi-fi in bedrooms **Conf** Thtr 35 Class 20 Board 20 **Services** Lift **Parking** 22 **Notes** ⊕ Closed 24-26 Dec

★★ 59% HOTEL

Ashley

Coburg St

☎ 021 4501518 📠 021 4501178

e-mail: info@ashleyhotel.com

dir: From N8 to 4th bridge (do not cross any bridges). Right then right at next junct

This hotel is centrally located near the railway station and much of Cork's nightlife, with a nightclub next door at weekends. Bedrooms vary in size, but are warm and comfortable. The bar is welcoming and serves food at lunch and dinner. Secure parking is available to the rear of the hotel.

Rooms 27 en suite (1 fmly) ⊗ in 15 bedrooms **Facilities** STV **Parking** 8 **Notes** ⊕ ⊗ in restaurant Closed 22 Dec-5 Jan

---

BUDGET HOTEL

Travelodge Cork Airport

Blackash

☎ 08700 850 950 📠 021 4310723

web: www.travelodge.co.uk

dir: at rdbt junct of South Ring Road/Kinsale Rd, R600

Travelodge offers good quality, good value, modern accommodation. Ideal for families, the spacious en suite bedrooms include remote-control TV, tea and coffee-making facilities and comfortable beds. Meals can be taken at the nearby family restaurant. See Hotel Groups pages for further details.

Rooms 60 en suite S fr £26; D fr £26

GARRYVOE   **MAP 01 C2**

★★★ 70% ⊛ HOTEL

Garryvoe

☎ 021 4646718 📠 021 4646824

e-mail: res@garryvoehotel.com

IRISH COUNTRY
HOTELS

dir: off N25 onto L72 at Castlemartyr (between Midleton & Youghal) then 6km

A comfortable, family-run hotel with caring staff, the Garryvoe offers bedrooms that are appointed to a very high standard following a major refurbishment programme. It stands in a delightful position facing a sandy beach and Ballycotton Bay. A popular bar serves light

continued on page 960

Ireland

GARRYVOE *continued*

meals throughout the day, with a more formal dinner menu offered in the spacious dining room.

Garryvoe

Rooms 48 en suite (6 fmly) ⊗ in 15 bedrooms S €85-€150; D €99-€149 **Facilities** STV ☙ Putt green **Conf** BC Thtr 300 Class 150 Board 12 Del from €120 **Services** Lift **Parking** 100 **Notes LB** ⊗ ⊘ in restaurant Closed 24-25 Dec

GOUGANE BARRA · · · · · · · · · · · · · MAP 01 B2

★★ 70% HOTEL

Gougane Barra

☎ 026 47069 📱 026 47226

e-mail: gouganbarrahotel@tinet.ie

IRISH COUNTRY HOTELS

dir: off N22

Picturesquely situated on the shore of Gougane Barra Lake and at the entrance to the National Park this family run hotel offers tranquillity and very good cooking. Bedrooms and public areas are comfortable and enjoy lovely views. Guests can be met from their train, boat or plane by prior arrangement.

Rooms 25 en suite (12 GF) ⊗ in all bedrooms **Facilities** STV Fishing Boating Cycling **Parking** 25 **Notes** ⊗ ⊘ in restaurant Closed 10 Oct-18 Apr

INNISHANNON · · · · · · · · · · · · · · · MAP 01 B2

★★★ 66% HOTEL

Innishannon House

☎ 021 4775121 📱 021 4775609

e-mail: info@innishannon-hotel.ie

dir: off N71 at east end of village, left onto Kinsale road, hotel right approx 1m

This charming country house was built in 1720 in a beautiful location in lovely gardens that run down to the banks of the River Bandon, close to Kinsale. Public areas are comfortable and there is a relaxed atmosphere. Bedrooms range from cosy and charming to large and gracious.

Rooms 12 en suite (4 fmly) **Facilities** STV Fishing **Conf** BC Thtr 200 Class 80 Board 50 **Parking** 100 **Notes LB** ⊗ ⊘ in restaurant Closed 22-26 Dec

KINSALE · · · · · · · · · · · · · · · · · · · MAP 01 B2

★★★ 77% ⊛ HOTEL

Actons

Pier Rd

☎ 021 4772135 📱 021 4772231

e-mail: information@actonshotelkinsale.com

dir: in town centre, 500yds from Yacht Club Marina

Located on a site overlooking the harbour, Actons is a well established hotel with a good reputation for its friendly and courteous staff. Bedrooms are well appointed and many of them enjoy sea views, as does the restaurant where enjoyable dinners are served. The adjoining leisure centre is well equipped.

Rooms 76 en suite (20 fmly) **Facilities Spa** STV ⚲ supervised Sauna Solarium Gym Jacuzzi Aerobics studio, Outdoor hot tub, Steam room ♫ **Conf** Thtr 300 Class 200 Board 100 **Services** Lift **Parking** 70 **Notes** ⊗ ⊘ in restaurant Closed 24-27 Dec & early-mid Jan

★★★ 75% ⊛ HOTEL

Trident

Worlds End

☎ 021 4779300 📱 021 4774173

e-mail: info@tridenthotel.com

dir: R600 from Cork to Kinsale, along Kinsale waterfront, hotel beyond pier

Located at the harbour's edge, the Trident Hotel has its own marina with boats for hire. Many of the bedrooms have superb views and two have balconies. The restaurant and lounge both overlook the harbour and pleasant staff provide hospitable service.

Rooms 75 en suite (2 fmly) ⊗ in 48 bedrooms **Facilities** Sauna Gym Jacuzzi Steam room, Deep sea angling, Yacht charter **Conf** Thtr 220 Class 130 Board 40 **Services** Lift **Parking** 60 **Notes** ⊗ ⊘ in restaurant Closed 24-26 Dec

★★★ 70% HOTEL

Blue Haven Hotel & Restaurant

3 Pearse St

☎ 021 4772209 📱 021 4774268

e-mail: info@bluehavenkinsale.com

dir: in town centre

In the heart of this historic town, the Blue Haven offers a welcoming lobby lounge, an elegant restaurant, a lively and atmospheric bar with

continued

an open deck area and the trendy Café Blue coffee/wine bar. Bedrooms vary in size and are furnished to a high standard.

Blue Haven Hotel & Restaurant

Rooms 17 en suite ⊗ in all bedrooms **Facilities** STV Wi-fi available ♫ **Conf** Thtr 70 Class 35 Board 25 **Notes LB** ⊗ ⊗ in restaurant Closed 25 Dec

MACROOM   MAP 01 B2

★★★ 78% ⊛ HOTEL

Castle
Main St

IRISH COUNTRY HOTELS

☎ 026 41074 📠 026 41505

e-mail: castlehotel@eircom.net

dir: on N22 midway between Cork & Killarney

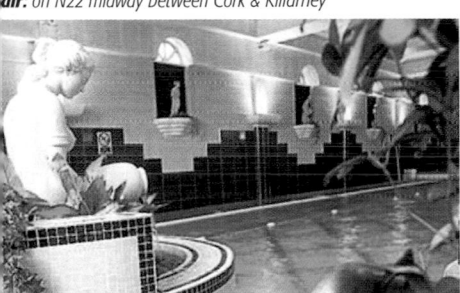

This town centre property is a fine hotel with excellent service provided by the Buckley Family and their team. Bedrooms are very comfortable, as are the extensive public areas. Secure parking is available to the rear.

Rooms 60 en suite (6 fmly) ⊗ in 30 bedrooms S €98-€110; D €145-€175 (incl. bkfst) **Facilities Spa** STV 🎿 supervised Gym Jacuzzi Wi-fi in bedrooms Steam Room ♫ ch fac **Conf** Thtr 200 Class 80 Board 60 Del from €145 **Services** Lift air con **Parking** 30 **Notes LB** ⊗ ⊗ in restaurant Closed 24-28 Dec

MALLOW   MAP 01 B2

INSPECTORS' CHOICE

★★★ ⊚ ⊚ ⊚ COUNTRY HOUSE HOTEL

Longueville House
☎ 022 47156 & 47306 📠 022 47459

e-mail: info@longuevillehouse.ie

RELAIS & CHATEAUX

dir: 3m W of Mallow via N72 road to Killarney, right turn at Ballyclough junct, hotel entrance 200yds left

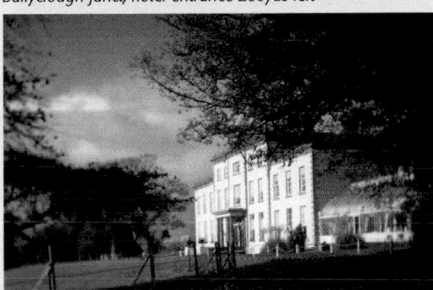

This 18th-century Georgian mansion is set in a wooded estate on a 500-acre farm. The beautifully appointed bedrooms overlook the Backwater Valley. Two elegantly furnished sitting rooms feature fine examples of Italian plasterwork. William O'Callaghan's cuisine is served in the Presidents' Restaurant and the Victorian Turner conservatory. Most ingredients are grown or raised on the farm including fish from the river that runs through the estate.

Rooms 20 en suite (5 fmly) ⊗ in all bedrooms **Facilities** STV Fishing 🛥 **Conf** Thtr 50 Class 30 Board 30 **Parking** 30 **Notes LB** ⊗ ⊗ in restaurant Closed Feb 14-23 Mar RS Nov-mid-end Mar

★★★ 68% HOTEL

Springfort Hall Country House Hotel
☎ 022 21278 📠 022 21557

e-mail: stay@springfort-hall.com

web: www.springfort-hall.com

dir: on Mallow/Limerick road N20, right turn off at new Two Pot House R581, hotel 500mtrs on right sign over gate

This 18th-century country manor is tucked away amid tranquil woodlands located just 6km from Mallow off the N20. There is an attractive oval dining room, drawing room and lounge bar. The comfortable bedrooms are in a wing and are spacious, well appointed and command superb country views. There are extensive banqueting and conference facilities.

Rooms 49 en suite (4 fmly) **Facilities** STV ♫ **Conf** BC Thtr 300 Class 200 Board 50 **Parking** 200 **Notes LB** ⊗ ⊗ in restaurant Closed 23 Dec-2 Jan

Ireland

MIDLETON   MAP 01 C2

★★★ 79% **HOTEL**

Midleton Park Hotel & Spa

☎ 021 4631767 🖹 021 4631605

e-mail: info@midletonparkhotel.ie

dir: *from Cork, turn off N25 hotel on right. From Waterford, turn off N25, over bridge to T-junct, right, hotel on right*

This hotel is located just off the N25. The comfortable public areas include a relaxing lobby lounge and bedrooms are spacious and attractively decorated. An interesting menu is available in the popular Park Café Bar while The Park Restaurant offers fine dining. There are extensive banqueting, private dining rooms and leisure facilities.

Rooms 40 en suite (12 fmly) ⊗ in 6 bedrooms **Facilities** STV
Conf Thtr 400 Class 200 Board 40 **Services** air con **Parking** 500
Notes ⊗ Closed 25 Dec

ROSSCARBERY   MAP 01 B2

★★★ 73% **HOTEL**

Celtic Ross

☎ 023 48722 🖹 023 48723

e-mail: info@celticrosshotel.com

dir: *take N71 from Cork city, through Bandon towards Clonakilty. Follow signs for Skibbereen*

This hotel is situated on the edge of the village overlooking Rosscarbery Bay. Richly textured fabrics add warmth to the polished wood public areas that includes a 5000-year-old Bog Yew Tree sculpture. There is a library and a newly refurbished bar and bistro that provides a second dining option. The spacious bedrooms are comfortable and well appointed.

Rooms 66 en suite (30 fmly) ⊗ in 10 bedrooms **Facilities** STV 🔁
supervised Sauna Gym Steam room, Bubble pool, Video rentals ♫
Conf BC Thtr 300 Class 150 Board 60 **Services** Lift air con **Parking** 200
Notes LB ⊗ ⊗ in restaurant Closed mid Jan–mid Feb

CO DONEGAL

DONEGAL   MAP 01 B5

★★★★ 82% ⊛⊛ **HOTEL**

Harvey's Point Country

Lough Eske

☎ 074 972 2208 🖹 074 972 2352

e-mail: reservations@harveyspoint.com

dir: *N56 from Donegal, then 1st right (Loch Eske/Harvey's Point). Hotel approx 10 mins' drive*

Situated by the lake's shore, this hotel is an oasis for relaxation - comfort and attentive guest care are the norm here. A range of particularly spacious suites has now been added that take advantage of the lovely views. The kitchen brigade maintains consistently high standards in the dining room, with a very popular Sunday buffet lunch served weekly.

Rooms 20 en suite **Facilities** STV ♫ **Conf** Thtr 200 Class 200 Board 50
Parking 300 **Notes LB** No children 10yrs ⊗ in restaurant

★★★ 74% **HOTEL**

Mill Park

The Mullins

☎ 074 972 2880 🖹 074 972 2640

e-mail: info@millparkhotel.com

IRISH COUNTRY HOTELS

The gentle flow of the millstream and open fires create a welcoming atmosphere at this hotel that is within walking distance of the town centre. Wood and stone are incorporated with flair in the design of the public areas, as in the first-floor, fine-dining Granary restaurant and the less formal Café bar that serves food all day. Bedrooms are spacious and well appointed. There are extensive leisure and banqueting facilities.

Rooms 114 en suite (15 fmly) (44 GF) ⊗ in 35 bedrooms **Facilities** 🔁
supervised 🔁 Solarium Gym Jacuzzi Wellness Centre ♫ **Conf** Thtr 500
Class 250 Board 80 **Services** Lift **Parking** 250 **Notes** ⊗ ⊗ in restaurant
Closed 24-26 Dec

DUNFANAGHY   MAP 01 C6

★★★ 72% **HOTEL**

Arnold's

☎ 074 913 6208 🖹 074 913 6352

e-mail: arnoldshotel@eircom.net

IRISH COUNTRY HOTELS

dir: *on N56 from Letterkenny, hotel on left entering the village*

This family run hotel is noted for its warm welcome and good food. Situated in a coastal village with sandy beaches, links golf courses and beautiful scenery. Public areas and bedrooms are comfortable, there is

continued

a traditional bar, choice of two restaurants, delightful garden and riding stables available.

Rooms 30 en suite (10 fmly) S €95-€125; D €130-€190 (incl. bkfst) **Facilities** STV Fishing Riding Putt green ♬ **Parking** 60 **Notes LB** ⊗ ⊘ in restaurant Closed Nov-mid March

DUNGLOW (AN CLOCHÁN LIATH)   MAP 01 B5

★★★ 65% **HOTEL**

Ostan Na Rosann

Mill Rd

☎ 074 9522444 📄 074 9522400

e-mail: info@ostannarosann.com

Overlooking the spectacular bay and within walking distance of the town, this warm, family-run hotel is known for its informal and friendly atmosphere. Bedrooms are comfortable. Local ingredients are prepared with care and served in the restaurant, which makes the most of the great views. At the time of inspection the popular leisure centre was being refurbished.

Rooms 48 en suite (6 fmly) (24 GF) ⊘ in 12 bedrooms S €67-€79; D €114-€138 (incl. bkfst) **Facilities** STV ⧉ supervised Sauna Solarium Gym Jacuzzi Steam room beautician ♬ Xmas **Conf** Thtr 300 Class 200 Board 50 Del from €55 **Parking** 100 **Notes** ⊗ ⊘ in restaurant

MALIN   MAP 01 C6

★★ 65% **HOTEL**

Malin

Malin Town

☎ 074 937 0606 📄 074 937 0770

e-mail: info@malinhotel.ie

dir: From Derry on Molville Rd, turn left at Quigleys Point to Cardonagh, then follow to Malin

Overlooking the village green in the most northerly village in Ireland, the hotel has a friendly, welcoming atmosphere and is an ideal centre for exploring the rugged coastline and sandy beaches. Public areas include an attractive restaurant where dinner is served Wed/Sun and food is available daily in the cosy bar.

Rooms 18 en suite (1 fmly) tⱽ in all bedrooms S €65-€90; D €110-€150 (incl. bkfst) **Facilities** ⧉ Fishing Riding Gym ♬ Xmas **Conf** Thtr 200 Class 100 Board 60 **Services** lift **Parking** 40 **Notes LB** ⊗ ⊘ in restaurant

RATHMULLAN   MAP 01 C6

★★★ 79% ⚜ **HOTEL**

Fort Royal Hotel

Fort Royal

☎ 074 9158100 📄 074 9158103

e-mail: fortroyal@eircom.net

dir: take R245 from Letterkenny, through Rathmullan, hotel signed

On the western shores of Lough Swilly, this family-run period house stands in 18 acres of well-maintained grounds that include a 9-hole

continued

golf and tennis court. Private access is available to the secluded sandy beach. The restful lounges and inviting bar have open log fires, the fine dine restaurant overlooks the gardens and bedrooms enjoy the spectacular views.

Rooms 11 en suite 4 annexe en suite (1 fmly) **Facilities** ⌇9 ⧉ ⤸ **Parking** 30 **Notes LB** ⊘ in restaurant Closed Nov-Mar

ROSSNOWLAGH   MAP 01 B5

★★★ 83% **HOTEL**

Sandhouse

☎ 071 985 1777 📄 071 985 2100

e-mail: info@sandhouse.ie

dir: from Donegal on coast road to Ballyshannon. In centre of Donegal Bay

Located on Rossnowlagh sandy beach, which is a haven for surfers. This hotel offers very comfortable lounges and restaurant, cocktail bar and Surfers bar. Bedrooms are spacious and well appointed, most enjoy the splendid sea views. Known for its hospitality, good food and service, this is an ideal base for touring the north west of Ireland.

Rooms 55 en suite (6 fmly) ⊘ in 30 bedrooms S €90-€110; D €180-€280 (incl. bkfst) **Facilities Spa** STV ⧉ Sauna Solarium Jacuzzi Wi-fi in bedrooms Mini-golf Surfing Canoeing Sailing **Conf** Thtr 60 Class 40 Board 50 **Services** Lift **Parking** 42 **Notes LB** ⊘ in restaurant Closed Dec & Jan

CO DUBLIN

DONABATE   MAP 01 D4

★★★ 68% **HOTEL**

Waterside House

☎ 01 8436153 📄 01 8436111

e-mail: info@watersidehousehotel.ie

This family owned hotel is situated in an unenviable position overlooking the beach at Donnabate and close to Dublin Airport. The public areas and the bedrooms have now been refurbished in a contemporary style, with the comfortable lounge bar and restaurant taking advantage of the breathtaking views.

Rooms 20 en suite

Ireland

Ireland

DUBLIN
See also Portmarnock

MAP 01 D4

★★★★★ ◉◉◉◉ HOTEL

The Merrion Hotel
Upper Merrion St
☎ 01 6030600 🖨 01 6030700
e-mail: info@merrionhotel.com
dir: at top of Upper Merrion St on left, beyond Government buildings on right

This terrace of gracious Georgian buildings, reputed to have been the birthplace of the Duke of Wellington, embraces the character of many changes of use through over 200 years. Bedrooms and suites are spacious, offering comfort and a wide range of extra facilities. The lounges retain the charm and opulence of days gone by while the Cellar bar area is ideal for a relaxing drink. There is also a choice of dining options. Irish favourites utilise fresh and simply prepared ingredients in the Cellar Restaurant and, for that very special occasion, award-winning Restaurant Patrick Guilbaud is Dublin's finest.

Rooms 143 en suite ⊘ in 65 bedrooms S €410-€2450; D €430-€2450 **Facilities** STV 🖾 supervised Gym Wi-fi in bedrooms Steam room, 2 treatment rooms **Conf** BC Thtr 60 Class 25 Board 25 Del from €385 **Services** Lift air con **Parking** 60 **Notes LB** ⊗ ⊘ in restaurant

★★★★★ 72% HOTEL

Berkeley Court
Lansdowne Rd
☎ 01 665 3200 🖨 01 6617238
e-mail: berkeley_court@jurysdoyle.com
web: www.jurysdoyle.com
dir: from N11 turn right at Donnybrook Church, 1st left to bridge, right immediately then 1st left, hotel 1st on left

JURYS DOYLE
HOTELS

Located in the leafy suburb of Ballsbridge, near the rugby stadium, this modern hotel is well positioned for business and leisure visitors alike. A choice of two pleasant restaurants is available, together with lounge food in an elegant area off the spacious lobby. The hotel offers a range of well-appointed bedrooms and suites.

Rooms 186 en suite ⊘ in 155 bedrooms S €215-€338; D €215-€338 **Facilities** STV Wi-fi available Hair & Beauty salon, ♫ Xmas **Conf** BC Thtr 450 Class 210 Board 110 Del from €269 **Services** Lift air con **Parking** 130 **Notes LB** ⊗ ⊘ in restaurant

★★★★ HOTEL

The Clarence
6-8 Wellington Quay
☎ 01 4070800 🖨 01 4070820
e-mail: reservations@theclarence.ie
dir: from O'Connell Bridge, W along Quays, through 1st lights (at Ha'penny Bridge) hotel 500mtrs

Located on the banks of the River Liffey in the city centre, The Clarence is within walking distance of the shops and visitor attractions. This is a very distinctive property, where the character of the 1850 building has been successfully combined with contemporary design of the bedrooms and suites. The friendly staff provides unobtrusive professional service.

Rooms 49 en suite ⊘ in 4 bedrooms **Facilities** STV Gym Treatment and massage room **Conf** Thtr 50 Class 24 Board 35 **Services** Lift **Parking** 15 **Notes LB** ⊗ ⊘ in restaurant Closed 24-27 Dec
See advert on opposite page

★★★★ 87% ◉◉ HOTEL

The Herbert Park Hotel
Ballsbridge
☎ 01 6672200 🖨 01 6672595
e-mail: reservations@herbertparkhotel.ie
dir: 2m from city centre along Nassau St, Mount St over canal bridge along Northumberland Rd. Cross bridge in Ballsbridge, 1st right

In an enviable location adjoining the lovely park of the same name and close to the US Embassy, RDS and convenient to the city centre, Herbert Park Hotel has spacious, light-filled and very comfortable public areas. Staff are professional and very friendly. Views of the park from the Pavilion Restaurant and many of the contemporary style bedrooms are delightful in any season. Secure underground parking is available.

Rooms 153 en suite (4 fmly) ⊘ in 60 bedrooms S €119-€230; D €119-€275 **Facilities** STV 🖾 Gym 🏊 Wi-fi available ♫ **Conf** Thtr 120 Class 70 Board 50 Del from €216 **Services** Lift air con **Parking** 80 **Notes** ⊗ ⊘ in restaurant

THE CLARENCE

6-8 WELLINGTON QUAY

DUBLIN 2

IRELAND

TEL 353 (0)1 407 0800

FAX 353 (0)1 407 0820

reservations@theclarence.ie

www.theclarence.ie

AWARD-WINNING FOOD

& COCKTAILS

THE TEA ROOM

AND

THE OCTAGON BAR

Ireland

DUBLIN *continued*

★★★★ 85% ⊛⊛ **HOTEL**

The Fitzwilliam

St Stephen's Green
☎ 01 4787000 🖨 01 4787878
e-mail: enq@fitzwilliamhotel.com
dir: *in city centre, adjacent to top of Grafton Street*

In a central position on St Stephen's Green, this friendly hotel is a pleasant blend of contemporary style with all the traditions of good hotel keeping. Bedrooms, many overlooking an internal rooftop garden, have been equipped with a wide range of thoughtful extras. There is plenty to tempt the palate - Citron offers an informal eating option while Thornton's provides a fine dining alternative.

Rooms 140 en suite ⊘ in 90 bedrooms **Facilities** STV Gym **Conf** BC Thtr 80 Class 50 Board 35 **Services** Lift air con **Parking** 85 **Notes LB** ⊗ ⊘ in restaurant

★★★★ 79% ⊛ **HOTEL**

Clarion Hotel Dublin IFSC

☎ 01 4338800 🖨 01 4338801
e-mail: info@clarionhotelifsc.com
dir: *N1 to city centre, at Dorset St turn left onto North Circular Rd, then to 5 Lamps-Portland Row. Right into Amiens St, left after IFSC Building/Custom House, onto North Wall Quay. Through 2 sets of lights, hotel on left*

Located at the heart of the International Financial Services Centre, this well designed hotel has stylish decor, comfortable bedrooms, and staff that are both pleasant and attentive. Whether staying here for business or leisure, or eating in the restaurant, this hotel is totally focused on providing a professional service to its guests.

Rooms 147 en suite (5 fmly) ⊘ in 87 bedrooms **Facilities** STV 🖳 supervised Sauna Solarium Gym Jacuzzi Spinning room, treatment room, aerobics area **Conf** Thtr 110 Class 42 Board 34 **Services** Lift air con **Parking** 55 **Notes** ⊗ ⊘ in restaurant RS 24-26 Dec

★★★★ 79% ⊛ **HOTEL**

Crowne Plaza Dublin Airport

Northwood Park, Santry Demesne, Santry
☎ 01 8628888 🖨 01 8628800
e-mail: info@crowneplazadublin.ie

This smart, contemporary hotel is situated in 160 acres of parkland; it is a peaceful, country setting yet is very close to Dublin Airport. The air-conditioned bedrooms are furnished to a high standard and the clubrooms benefit from having their own lounge. Public areas are stylish with dining options and comfortable lounges. There are extensive conference facilities and a courtesy airport coach. AA Ireland has awarded this hotel the Business Hotel of the Year for the Republic of Ireland 2006-7.

Rooms 204 en suite (17 fmly) ⊘ in 158 bedrooms **Facilities** STV Gym **Conf** BC Thtr 240 Class 110 Board 45 **Services** Lift air con **Parking** 240 **Notes** ⊗ ⊘ in restaurant RS 25 Dec

★★★★ 77% **HOTEL**

Clarion Hotel Dublin Liffey Valley

Liffey Valley
☎ 01 6258000 🖨 01 6258001
e-mail: info@clarionhotelliffeyvalley.com
dir: *M50 exit 7 for N4 Sligo/The West. Follow signs for Liffey Valley Shopping Centre, hotel on left.*

This recently opened hotel is well positioned near the orbital M50 motorway, not far from the city centre. Stylish décor and comfortable, well-equipped bedrooms and suites are matched with a wide range of dining options. Service is very guest focussed. Excellent leisure and meeting facilities are available, together with secure underground and surface car parking.

Rooms 284 en suite (130 fmly) (55 GF) ⊘ in 197 bedrooms **Facilities** STV 🖳 Sauna Gym Jacuzzi Aerobics studio **Conf** Thtr 390 Class 170 Board 105 **Services** Lift **Parking** 300 **Notes LB** ⊗ ⊘ in restaurant Closed 24-25 Dec RS 23 & 26-31 Dec

★★★★ 77% **HOTEL**

Gresham

GRESHAM HOTELS

O'Connell St
☎ 01 8746881 🖨 01 8787175
e-mail: info@thegresham.com
dir: *just off M1, near GPO*

This elegant hotel enjoys a prime centre city location close to theatres, shops and museums. Excellent conference, the choice of restaurants and bars make this an ideal choice for both corporate and leisure guests. A range of bedroom options is available and the staff are very friendly. The hotel has a multi-storey car park.

Rooms 287 en suite (4 fmly) ⊘ in 200 bedrooms S €140-€393.75; D €140-€393.75 **Facilities** STV Gym Wi-fi in bedrooms Xmas **Conf** BC Thtr 350 Class 150 Board 80 Del from €265 **Services** Lift air con **Parking** 150 **Notes LB** ⊗ ⊘ in restaurant

★★★★ 76% **HOTEL**

The Morrison

Lower Ormond Quay
☎ 01 8872400 🖨 01 8783185
e-mail: info@morrisonhotel.ie

This hotel was designed in association with the renowned John Rocha. Inside, wood, stone and natural fabrics are combined with vibrant

continued

colours to create a relaxing environment. There is a lobby lounge, café bar and the Halo Restaurant. Bedrooms and suites have a contemporary style, air conditioned and appointed to a high standard. Spa facilities are currently being developed. A dedicated and hospitable team ensures a pleasant stay.

Rooms 138 en suite ⊗ in 69 bedrooms **Facilities** STV **Conf** BC Thtr 230 Class 92 Board 42 **Services** Lift air con **Notes** ⊗ ⊗ in restaurant Closed 24-27 Dec

★★★★ 76% ® **HOTEL**

Stillorgan Park

Stillorgan Rd

☎ 01 2881621 ▤ 01 2831610

e-mail: sales@stillorganpark.com

web: www.stillorganpark.com

dir: *on N11 follow signs for Wexford, pass RTE studios on left, through next 5 sets of lights. Hotel on left*

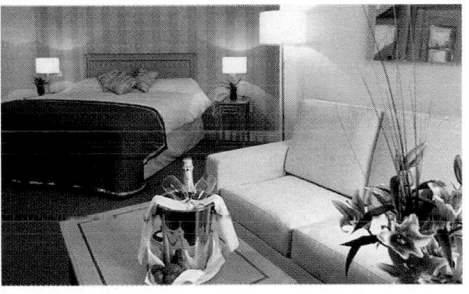

This modern hotel is attractively decorated and is situated on the southern outskirts of the city. Comfortable public areas include a spacious lobby, contemporary restaurant and inviting bar and air-conditioned banqueting and conference centre. There is a gym, a spa and treatment rooms.

Rooms 165 en suite (12 fmly) ⊗ in 25 bedrooms **Facilities Spa** STV Sauna Gym Jacuzzi Beauty treatment room ♫ **Conf** BC Thtr 500 Class 220 Board 130 **Services** Lift air con **Parking** 350 **Notes** LB ⊗ ⊗ in restaurant RS 25 Dec Civ Wed 300

★★★★ 74% **HOTEL**

Burlington

Upper Leeson St   ⌥JURYS DOYLE
                                    HOTELS

☎ 01 660 5222 ▤ 01 660 8496

web: www.jurysdoyle.com

dir: *From airport take M1 into city centre, follow signs for St. Stephen's Green. From Leeson St into Upper Leeson St*

Close to the city, this bustling hotel, one of Ireland's largest, features comfortable bedrooms that are well appointed. An executive floor offers additional services and a lounge area serving continental breakfast. Smart public areas include the popular Buck Mulligan pub, spacious lounges, the Sussex Room and Diplomat restaurants.

Rooms 500 en suite ⊗ in 245 bedrooms S €140-€284; D €140-€314 **Facilities** STV Gym Wi-fi in bedrooms Night club, use of fitness club, (small gym for executive floor guests) ♫ Xmas **Conf** BC Thtr 1200 Class 600 Board 40 Del from €249 **Services** Lift **Parking** 400 **Notes** LB ⊗ ⊗ in restaurant

★★★★ 74% **HOTEL**

Castleknock Hotel & Country Club

Porterstown Rd, Castleknock

☎ 01 640 6300 ▤ 01 640 6303

e-mail: info@chcc.ie

This newly built hotel has been finished to a very high standard. It has an airy feel to the open-plan public areas, with excellent conference and banqueting facilities. Bedrooms are particularly comfortable and well appointed. There is a choice of two bars, together with a brasserie and the more formal Park Restaurant.

Rooms 143 en suite ⊗ in 106 bedrooms S €99-€190; D €99-€240 (incl. bkfst) **Facilities** STV ◲ supervised ♨ 18 Sauna Solarium Gym Jacuzzi Wi-fi available **Conf** BC Thtr 500 Class 200 Board 80 Del from €215 **Services** Lift **Notes** LB ⊗ ⊗ in restaurant Closed 24-25 Dec

★★★★ 70% **HOTEL**

Red Cow Morans

Red Cow Complex, Naas Rd   ♔
                                    MORAN
                                    HOTELS

☎ 01 4593650 ▤ 01 4591588

e-mail: redcowres@moranhotels.com

web: www.redcowhotel.com

dir: *at junct of M50 & N7 Naas road on city side of motorway*

Located just off the M50, this hotel is 20 minutes from the airport and only minutes away from the city centre via the Luas light rail system. Classical elegance and modern design are combined throughout and the staff shows a genuine willingness to make your stay memorable. Bedrooms are well equipped and comfortable, and the public areas and conference rooms are spacious. Ample free parking is available.

Rooms 123 en suite (21 fmly) ⊗ in 84 bedrooms S €110-€190; D €120-€380 (incl. bkfst) **Facilities** FTV Wi-fi in bedrooms Night club on complex ♫ Xmas **Conf** Thtr 700 Class 350 Board 150 Del from €185 **Services** Lift air con **Parking** 700 **Notes** LB ⊗ ⊗ in restaurant Closed 24-26 Dec

Ireland

Ireland

DUBLIN *continued*

★★★★ 69% **HOTEL**

The Plaza Hotel

Belgard Rd, Tallaght
☎ 01 4624200 📋 01 4624600
e-mail: reservations@plazahotel.ie
web: www.plazahotel.ie
dir: from Dublin Airport take M50 to Tallaght sign. Turn right
onto Tallaght by-pass. 1m, hotel on right

A contemporary hotel conveniently situated just off the M50 and beside
The Square Shopping Centre. Public areas are spacious and there are
good corporate facilities and secure underground parking. Bedrooms are
comfortable and well equipped. The Vista Café and Olive Restaurant are
on the first-floor mezzanine and enjoy views of the Dublin Mountains.

Rooms 122 en suite (2 fmly) ⊘ in 61 bedrooms **Facilities** STV Wi-fi in
bedrooms **Conf** BC Thtr 200 Class 150 Board 50 **Services** Lift air con
Parking 520 **Notes** ⊗ ⊘ in restaurant Closed 24-30 Dec

★★★ 75% **HOTEL**

Buswells

23-25 Molesworth St
☎ 01 614 6500 📋 01 676 2090
e-mail: buswells@quinn-hotels.com
dir: on corner of Molesworth St & Kildare St opposite Dail
Eireann (Government Buildings)

Originally a number of Georgian townhouses, Buswells is a popular
meeting place in the city centre for the parliamentarians from the Dail
opposite. Bedrooms are comfortable and attractively decorated. The
renovated public areas are particularly attractive. Buswells is renowned
for the friendliness of the staff.

Rooms 67 en suite (17 fmly) ⊘ in 33 bedrooms S €120-€195;
D €145-€240 (incl. bkfst) **Facilities** Gym Wi-fi in bedrooms Leisure
suite **Conf** BC Thtr 70 Class 30 Board 25 **Services** Lift **Notes LB** ⊗
⊘ in restaurant Closed 25-26 Dec RS 24 Dec

★★★ 74% ⊛ **HOTEL**

Finnstown Country House Hotel & Golf Course

Newcastle Rd, Lucan
☎ 01 601 0700 📋 01 628 1088
e-mail: manager@finnstown-hotel.ie
dir: from M1 take 1st exit onto M50 S/bound. 1st exit after Toll
Bridge. At rdbt take 3rd left (N4 W). Left at lights. Over next 2
rdbts. Hotel on right

Set in 45 acres of wooded grounds, Finnstown is a calm and peaceful
country house. There is a wide choice of bedroom style available, with
the garden suites being particularly comfortable. Long stay apartments

continued

are being developed. Lounge areas are numerous with games facilities
provided. Staff members are very guest-focussed.

Finnstown Country House Hotel & Golf Course

Rooms 25 en suite 28 annexe en suite (6 fmly) (9 GF) ⊘ in
27 bedrooms **Facilities** STV 🎾 ♨ Solarium Gym ⛳ Putt green Wi-fi in
bedrooms Turkish bath Table tennis Massage Xmas **Conf** Thtr 300
Class 60 Board 40 Del from €199 **Parking** 90 **Notes** ⊘ in restaurant
Closed 23-27 December

★★★ 74% **HOTEL**

Jurys Montrose

Stillorgan Rd
☎ 01 2693311 📋 01 2691164
e-mail: montrose@jurysdoyle.com
web: www.jurysdoyle.com
dir: From city centre follow signs for N11

Opposite the university campus at Belfield, this hotel offers
comfortable bedrooms and smart lounges with a choice of bars and
dedicated meeting rooms. Casual dining is available throughout the
day, with a more formal service in the restaurant at both lunch and
dinner.

Rooms 178 en suite ⊘ in 30 bedrooms **Facilities** STV **Conf** BC Thtr 80
Class 30 Board 30 **Services** Lift **Parking** 100 **Notes LB** ⊗

★★★ 74% **HOTEL**

Lynch Green Isle

Naas Rd, Newlands Cross, Naas Rd
☎ 01 4593406 📋 01 4592178
e-mail: sales@lynchotels.com
dir: on N7, 10km SW of the city centre

This hotel lies on the southern outskirts of Dublin just off the M50. All
rooms are generously proportioned and there is an Escape Spa with
an indoor pool and gym. Public areas include spacious conference
facilities, Sorrels restaurant and Rosie O'Grady's pub, which offers a
popular carvery at lunchtime.

Rooms 240 en suite (10 fmly) ⊘ in 144 bedrooms **Facilities** Spa STV
🎾 supervised Gym Jacuzzi Treatment rooms, Steam room ♫
Conf Thtr 300 Class 100 Board 100 **Services** Lift **Parking** 350 **Notes LB**
⊗ ⊘ in restaurant

★★★ 72% HOTEL

Bewleys Hotel Leopardstown

Central Park, Leopardstown Rd

☎ 01 2935 000 ▤ 021 2935 099

e-mail: leop@bewleyshotel.com

dir: M50 junct 18, follow signs for Leopardstown, at rdbt take 2nd exit. Hotel on right.

This hotel is conveniently situated close to the Central Business Park and Leopardstown racecourse, and serviced by the Luas light rail system and Aircoach. Contemporary in style, the open plan public areas include a spacious lounge bar, brasserie and a selection of conference rooms. Bedrooms are well appointed. There is free underground parking.

Rooms 352 rms (70 fmly) ⊛ in 304 bedrooms S €89; D €89 **Facilities** STV Wi-fi available Day membership at local club 10-15mins drive **Conf** Board 14 **Services** Lift **Parking** 228 **Notes** ⊛ ⊘ in restaurant Closed 24-25 Dec

★★★ 72% HOTEL

Camden Court

Camden St

☎ 01 4759666 ▤ 01 4759677

e-mail: reservations@camdencourthotel.ie

dir: off Camden St close to St Stephen's Green & Grafton St

This hotel has a number of fine features in addition to its convenient location. These include spacious public areas, a leisure centre, well equipped bedrooms, and the bonus of having a car park in the city centre. Conference facilities are also available

Rooms 246 en suite (33 fmly) ⊛ in 13 bedrooms S €99-€230; D €99-€290 (incl. bkfst) **Facilities** ℞ supervised Sauna Solarium Gym Jacuzzi Wi-fi in bedrooms **Conf** Thtr 115 Class 75 Board 30 **Services** Lift **Parking** 125 **Notes** ⊛ ⊘ in restaurant RS 23-28 Dec

★★★ 72% HOTEL

The Carnegie Court

North St, Swords

☎ 01 840 4384 ▤ 01 840 4505

e-mail: info@carnegiecourt.com

dir: from Dublin Airport take N1 towards Belfast. At 5th rdbt take 1st exit for Swords, then sharp left for hotel

This modern hotel has been tastefully built and is conveniently located close to Dublin Airport just off the N1 in Swords village. The air-conditioned bedrooms are well appointed, and many are particularly spacious. Public areas include a residents' lounge, contemporary Courtyard Restaurant, a dramatically designed Harp Bar and modern

conference and banqueting facilities. Extensive underground parking is available.

Rooms 36 en suite (4 fmly) (1 GF) ⊛ in 7 bedrooms S €135; D €240 (incl. bkfst) **Facilities** STV Wi-fi available ♫ **Conf** Thtr 280 Class 50 Board 40 **Services** Lift air con **Parking** 150 **Notes** LB ⊛ ⊘ in restaurant Closed 25-26 Dec

★★★ 72% HOTEL

Grand Canal Hotel

Grand Canal St

☎ 01 646 1000 ▤ 01 645 1001

e-mail: reservations@grandcanalhotel.com

This hotel is situated on the banks of the Grand Canal in Ballsbridge, close to Lansdowne Road Stadium, RDS and the city centre. Bedrooms are well appointed. The contemporary public areas are spacious and include a comfortable lounge, restaurant, Kitty O'Shea's pub and extensive conference rooms. Secure underground parking is available.

Rooms 142 en suite (20 fmly) ⊛ in 105 bedrooms S €99 €225; D €99-€225 **Facilities** STV Wi-fi in bedrooms ♫ **Conf** Thtr 140 Class 64 Board 60 **Services** Lift **Parking** 66 **Notes** LB ⊛ ⊘ in restaurant Closed 23-28 Dec

★★★ 70% HOTEL

Bewleys Hotel Ballsbridge

Merrion Rd, Ballsbridge

☎ 01 6681111 ▤ 01 6681999

e-mail: bb@bewleyshotels.com

This stylish hotel is conveniently situated near the RDS Showgrounds and is close to city centre. It offers comfortable, good value accommodation O'Connell's Restaurant and café provides food throughout the day on interesting menus. The spacious lounge is a popular meeting place. There is secure underground parking.

Rooms 304 en suite (64 fmly) (50 GF) ⊛ in 254 bedrooms S €99; D €99 **Facilities** Wi-fi in bedrooms **Conf** BC Class 30 Board 14 **Services** Lift **Parking** 240 **Notes** ⊛ ⊘ in restaurant Closed 24-26 Dec

★★★ 70% HOTEL

Jurys Inn Parnell Street

Parnell St

☎ 01 8784900 ▤ 01 8784999

e-mail: jurysinnparnellst.@jurysdoyle.com

web: www.jurysdoyle.com

dir: Left off O'Connell St onto Parnell St, hotel 50yds on left

This modern, stylish hotel is prominently located in the city, close to the shopping and theatre area. Bedrooms provide good guest comfort and facilities suited to both leisure and business markets. Public areas

continued on page 970

Ireland

DUBLIN *continued*

include dedicated meeting rooms, a popular bar and restaurant on the first floor.

Rooms 253 en suite (116 fmly) ⊗ in 186 bedrooms S €95-€250; D €95-€250 **Facilities** STV Wi-fi in bedrooms **Conf** BC Thtr 50 Class 24 Board 20 Del from €200 **Services** Lift air con **Notes LB** ⊛ ⊗ in restaurant

---

★★★ **69% HOTEL**

Bewleys Hotel Newlands Cross

Newlands Cross, Naas Rd
☎ 01 4640140 🗎 01 4640900
e-mail: res@bewleyshotels.com

dir: M50 junct 9 take N7 Naas road, hotel near N7- Belgard Rd junct

This modern hotel is situated on the outskirts of Dublin off the N7 and close to M50. Bedrooms are well furnished and prices are competitive. The restaurant is open for casual dining all day and serves more formal meals in the evening. There is a comfortable lounge and bar and ample parking is available.

Rooms 258 en suite (123 fmly) (63 GF) ⊗ in 183 bedrooms S €89; D €89 **Facilities** STV Wi-fi in bedrooms **Conf** Board 12 **Services** Lift **Parking** 200 **Notes** ⊛ ⊗ in restaurant Closed 24-26 Dec

---

★★★ **69% HOTEL**

Tara Towers

Merrion Rd
☎ 01 2694666 🗎 01 2691027
e-mail: tara@jurysdoyle.com

dir: N11/University College follow towards Montrose Hotel. 1st left before hotel into Woodbine Rd. Left at traffic lights

There are spectacular views over Dublin Bay from this modern hotel situated on the coast close to the city. Bedrooms are spacious and well equipped. Attractively decorated public areas include a comfortable and relaxing foyer lounge, PJ Branagans Pub and a split-level conservatory restaurant. There are extensive banqueting facilities and ample parking is available.

Rooms 113 en suite (2 fmly) ⊗ in 20 bedrooms **Facilities** STV **Conf** Thtr 300 Class 100 Board 40 **Services** Lift **Parking** 100 **Notes** ⊛

★★★ **68% HOTEL**

Cassidys

Cavendish Row, Upper O'Connell St
☎ 01 8780555 🗎 01 8780687
e-mail: stay@cassidyshotel.com

dir: in city centre at north end of O'Connell St. Opposite Gate Theatre

This family-run hotel is located at the top of O'Connell Street, on a terrace of red-brick Georgian townhouses. The warm and welcoming atmosphere of Grooms Bar lends a traditional air to Cassidy's Hotel, and Restaurant 6 is contemporary and stylish. The modern bedrooms are well appointed. Limited guest parking and conference facilities are available.

Rooms 88 en suite (3 fmly) (12 GF) ⊗ in 23 bedrooms **Facilities** STV ♬ **Conf** Thtr 80 Class 45 Board 45 **Services** Lift **Parking** 15 **Notes LB** ⊛ ⊗ in restaurant Closed 24-26 Dec

---

★★★ **68% HOTEL**

Jurys Christchurch Inn

Christchurch Place
☎ 01 4540000 🗎 01 4540012
e-mail: info@jurysdoyle.com
web: www.jurysdoyle.com

dir: N7 onto Naas Rd, follow city centre signs to O'Connell St, continue past Trinity College. Right onto Dame St to Lord Edward St, hotel on left

Centrally located opposite the 12th-century Christchurch Cathedral, this hotel is close to the Temple Bar and all the city amenities. The foyer lounge and pub are popular meeting places and there is also an informal restaurant. The bedrooms are well appointed and can accommodate families. The adjoining car park is a bonus.

Rooms 182 en suite ⊗ in 114 bedrooms **Services** Lift **Notes** ⊛ ⊗ in restaurant Closed 24-26 Dec

---

★★★ **68% HOTEL**

Jurys Custom House Inn

Custom House Quay
☎ 01 6075000 🗎 01 8290400
e-mail: jurysinncustomhouse@jurysdoyle.com
web: www.jurysdoyle.com

Overlooking the River Liffey, close to the International Financial Services Centre and less than ten minutes' walk away from the city's main shopping and tourist areas. Bedrooms are spacious and well equipped. Public area and contemporary in style and include facilities for business guests.

Rooms 239 en suite ⊗ in 145 bedrooms S €93-€130; D €93-€140 **Facilities** STV Wi-fi in bedrooms **Conf** Thtr 60 Class 30 Board 30 **Services** Lift **Notes** ⊛ ⊗ in restaurant Closed 25-26 Dec

★★★ 68% **HOTEL**

Mount Herbert Hotel

Herbert Rd, Lansdowne Rd
☎ 01 6684321 🖷 01 6607077
e-mail: info@mountherberthotel.ie

dir: *close to Lansdowne Road Rugby Stadium, 200mtrs from Dart Rail Station*

Located in the leafy suburb of Ballsbridge, this family-run hotel is an oasis of calm, offering true hospitality. Bedrooms are comfortable, as are the lounge areas. Good value cuisine is served in the restaurant at weekends overlooking the floodlit gardens, but food is available in the bar every night.

Rooms 173 en suite (15 fmly) (56 GF) ⊗ in 110 bedrooms
Facilities STV Childrens playground Free use of local gym **Conf** BC Thtr 88 Class 45 Board 38 **Services** Lift **Parking** 90 **Notes** ⊗ ⊗ in restaurant Closed 22-30 Dec

★★★ 66% **HOTEL**

The Mercer Hotel

Mercer St Lower
☎ 01 4782179 & 4744120 🖷 01 4780328
e-mail: stay@mercerhotel.ie

dir: *St Stephen's Green before shopping centre turn left down York St, then right at end of road, hotel on right*

This modern hotel is situated in the city centre close to Grafton Street. Bedrooms are attractively decorated and well equipped with fridges and CD players, as well as the usual facilities. Public areas include an open-plan lounge with cocktail bar and a restaurant. Parking is available next door.

Rooms 41 en suite ⊗ in 4 bedrooms **Facilities** STV **Conf** Thtr 100 Class 80 Board 60 **Services** air con **Parking** 41 **Notes LB** ⊗ ⊗ in restaurant Closed 24-26 Dec

★★★ 66% **HOTEL**

Temple Bar

Fleet St, Temple Bar
☎ 01 6773333 🖷 01 6773088
e-mail: reservations@tbh.ie

dir: *from Trinity College towards O'Connell Bridge. 1st left onto Fleet St. Hotel on right*

This hotel is situated in the heart of Dublin's Temple Bar, and in close to the shops, restaurants and cultural life of the city. Bedrooms are comfortable and well equipped. Food is served throughout the day in Buskers theme bar. There is a multi-storey car park nearby.

Rooms 129 en suite (6 fmly) ⊗ in 92 bedrooms S €90-€180; D €120-€275 (incl. bkfst) **Facilities** STV Wi-fi in bedrooms **Conf** Thtr 60 Class 40 Board 40 Del €150 **Services** Lift **Notes LB** ⊗ ⊗ in restaurant Closed 23-25 Dec RS Good Friday

★★★ 63% **HOTEL**

Abberley Court

Belgard Rd, Tallaght
☎ 01 4596000 🖷 01 4621000
e-mail: abberley@iol.ie

dir: *opposite The Square town centre at the junct of Belgard Rd and Tallaght by-pass (N81)*

Located beside an excellent complex of shops, restaurants and cinema, this hotel offers comfortable well-appointed bedrooms, the choice of two bars, a carvery and a Chinese restaurant. There are sports facilities available nearby.

Rooms 40 en suite (34 fmly) ⊗ in 8 bedrooms **Conf** Thtr 40 Class 25 Board 20 **Services** Lift **Parking** 450 **Notes** ⊗ Closed 25 Dec

★★★ 60% **HOTEL**

The Parliament Hotel

Lord Edward St
☎ 01 6708777 🖷 01 6708787
e-mail: parl@regencyhotels.com

dir: *adjacent to Dublin Castle*

An attractive hotel, near to the Temple Bar area and Dublin Castle, offering a friendly welcome to all its guests. It provides well-furnished bedrooms, decorated in a modern style. There is also a popular bar and a separate restaurant.

Rooms 63 en suite (0 fmly) ⊗ in 22 bedrooms **Facilities** STV **Conf** Thtr 20 Board 10 **Services** Lift **Notes LB** ⊗ ⊗ in restaurant

★★ 69% **HOTEL**

West Country Hotel

Chapelizod
☎ 01 6264011 🖷 01 6231378
e-mail: info@westcountyhotel.ie

dir: *From city centre follow signs for N4(W), 4m from city centre between Palmerstown and Ballyfermot on N4*

This family run hotel is situated just off the N4 and within walking distance of Chapelizod village. Bedrooms are well appointed. Public areas include a comfortable lobby lounge and bar where a carvery lunch is served daily and dinner in the Pine restaurant. There are conference facilities and a large car park available.

Rooms 48 en suite (10 fmly) ⊗ in 25 bedrooms S €60-€80; D €120-€140 (incl. bkfst) **Facilities** STV ♫ Xmas **Conf** Thtr 200 Class 100 Board 60 **Services** Lift **Parking** 200 **Notes LB** ⊗ ⊗ in restaurant Closed 24-25 Dec

Ⓤ

The Beacon

Beacon Court, Sandyford Business Region
☎ 01 291 5000 🖷 01 2912005
e-mail: sales@thebeacon.com

dir: *exit M50 & follow signs for Sandyford. Hotel on right after approx 2m*

At the time of going to press, the star classification for this hotel was not confirmed. Please refer to the AA internet site www.theAA.com for current information.

Rooms 82 en suite ⊗ in 69 bedrooms **Facilities** ♫ **Conf** BC Thtr 40 Class 30 Board 25 **Services** Lift **Parking** 90 **Notes LB** ⊗ ⊗ in restaurant

Ireland

DUBLIN *continued*

Bewleys Hotel Dublin Airport

Malahide Rd (N32)

☎ 01 871 1000 📄 01 871 1001

e-mail: dublinairport@bewleyshotel.com

At the time of going to press, the star classification for this hotel was not confirmed. Please refer to the AA internet site www.theAA.com for current information.

Rooms 450 en suite

Longfield's Hotel

Fitzwilliam St Lower

☎ 01 6761367 📄 01 6761542

e-mail: info@longfields.ie

dir: *take Shelbourne Hotel exit from St Stephen's Green, continue down Baggot St for 400mtrs, turn left at Fitzwilliam St junct, hotel on left*

At the time of going to press, the star classification for this hotel was not confirmed. Please refer to the AA internet site www.theAA.com for current information.

Rooms 26 en suite **Facilities** STV **Conf** Thtr 20 Board 20 **Services** Lift **Notes LB** ⊗ ⊘ in restaurant RS 23-27 Dec

Radisson SAS St Helen's Hotel

Stillorgan Rd

☎ 01 218 6000 📄 01 218 6010

e-mail: info.dublin@radissonsas.com

web: www.radisson.com

dir: *from centre take N11 S, hotel 4km on left*

At the time of going to press, the star classification for this hotel was not confirmed. Please refer to the AA internet site www.theAA.com for current information.

Rooms 151 en suite (102 fmly) (39 GF) ⊘ in 100 bedrooms **Facilities** STV Snooker Gym Beauty salon 🎵 ch fac **Services** Lift air con **Parking** 220 **Notes LB** ⊗ ⊘ in restaurant

The Shelbourne

27 St Stephen's Green

☎ 01 6634500 📄 01 6616006

e-mail: shelbourneinfo@lemeridien.com

web: www.shelbourne.ie

dir: *M1 to city centre, along Parnell St to O'Connell St towards Trinity College, take 3rd right along Kildare St, hotel on left*

At the time of going to press, the star classification for this hotel was not confirmed. Please refer to the AA internet site www.theAA.com for current information.

Rooms 168 en suite

BUDGET HOTEL

Days Hotel Dublin Rathmines

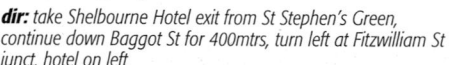

121 Lower Rathmines Rd

☎ 01 4066100 📄 01 4066200

e-mail: info@dayshotelrathmines.com

web: www.welcomebreak.co.uk

dir: *Take M1 for City Centre, onto M50 Southbound through toll bridge. Take N81 exit through Templeoglee, Tenanure, Rathgor. Hotel on left next to Renault Garage.*

This modern building offers accommodation in smart, spacious and well-equipped bedrooms, suitable for families and business travellers, and all with en suite bathrooms. Continental breakfast is available and other refreshments may be taken at the nearby family restaurant. For further details see the Hotel Groups page.

Rooms 66 en suite S €79-€220; D €79-€220

Days Inn Dublin Talbot Street

95-98 Talbot St

☎ 01 8749202 📄 01 8749672

e-mail: info@daysinntalbot.com

dir: *Take M1 to City Centre turn left of Dorset St onto Upper Gardiner St. Turn right off Lower Gardiner St onto Talbot St. Hotel 100mtrs on left past Leish Life Mall.*

Rooms 60 en suite

BUDGET HOTEL

Travelodge City Rathmines

Rathmines Rd

☎ 01 4911402 📄 01 4967688

web: www.travelodge.co.uk

Travelodge offers good quality, good value, modern accommodation. Ideal for families, the spacious en suite bedrooms include remote-control TV, tea and coffee-making facilities and comfortable beds. Meals can be taken at the nearby family restaurant. See Hotel Groups pages for further details.

Rooms S fr £26; D fr £26

Travelodge Dublin Airport

Swords By Pass

☎ 08700 850 950 📄 01 8409235

dir: *on N1 (Dublin/Belfast road) on s'bound carriageway of Swords Rdbt*

Rooms 100 en suite S fr £26; D fr £26

Travelodge Dublin Castleknock

Auburn Av Roundabout, Navan Rd

☎ 08700 850 950

dir: *just off M50 (Dublin ring road) at junct with Navan Rd, N3 junct 6*

Rooms 100 en suite S fr £26; D fr £26

HOWTH
MAP 01 D4

★★★ 72% **HOTEL**

Deer Park Hotel, Golf & Spa

☎ 01 8322624 📄 01 8392405

IRISH COUNTRY HOTELS

e-mail: sales@deerpark.iol.ie

dir: follow coast road from Dublin via Clontarf. Through Sutton Cross pass Offington Park. Hotel 0.5m after lights on right

This modern hotel is situated on its own parkland golf courses and overlooking Dublin Bay and Ireland's Eye. The spacious well equipped bedrooms have spectacular views. Four Earls Restaurant is famous for fresh fish from Howth Harbour, and there is a lively bar and bistro, a leisure centre, tennis courts and a choice of four golf courses. Convenient to Dublin Airport, ferry port and the DART service to the city centre.

Rooms 80 en suite (4 fmly) (36 GF) **Facilities Spa** ⬛ supervised ⬛ 36 ⬛ Sauna Putt green **Conf** Thtr 95 Class 60 Board 25 **Parking** 200 **Notes LB** ⊗ ⊜ in restaurant Closed 23-26 Dec

KILLINEY
MAP 01 D4

★★★★ 72% **HOTEL**

Fitzpatrick Castle

☎ 01 2305400 📄 01 2305430

e-mail: reservations@fitzpatricks.com

dir: from Dun Laoghaire port turn left, on coast road right at lights, left at next lights. Follow to Dalkey, right at McDonaghs pub, Immediate left, up hill, hotel at top

This family owned 18th-century castle has comfortable bedrooms in the modern wing, and many enjoying stunning views over Dublin Bay. Facilities include a large lounge, excellent leisure centre and a choice of restaurants. A range of conference and banqueting rooms is also available.

Rooms 113 en suite (36 fmly) ⊜ in 87 bedrooms S €190-€220; D €245-€275 **Facilities** STV ⬛ supervised Sauna Solarium Gym Jacuzzi Wi-fi in bedrooms Beauty/hairdressing salon, Steam room ♫ Xmas **Conf** BC Thtr 500 Class 250 Board 80 Del from €216 **Services** Lift **Parking** 300 **Notes LB** ⊗ ⊜ in restaurant RS 25-Dec

LUCAN
See also Dublin
MAP 01 D4

★★★ 67% **HOTEL**

Lucan Spa

☎ 01 6280494 📄 01 6280841

e-mail: info@lucanspahotel.ie

dir: on N4, approx 11km from city centre, (20mins from Dublin airport)

Set in its own grounds off the N4 and close to the M50, the Lucan Spa is a fine Georgian house with modern extension. Bedrooms vary in size and are well equipped. There are two dining options; dinner is served in Honora D Restaurant and The Earl Bistro for more casual dining. A conference centre is also available.

Rooms 71 rms (61 en suite) (15 fmly) (9 GF) ⊜ in 50 bedrooms S €60-€95; D €120-€190 (incl. bkfst) **Facilities** STV Wi-fi available ♫ **Conf** Thtr 600 Class 250 Board 80 **Services** Lift air con **Parking** 200 **Notes LB** ⊗ ⊜ in restaurant Closed 25-Dec

Ireland

PORTMARNOCK   MAP 01 D4

INSPECTORS' CHOICE

★★★★ ◎◎ **HOTEL**

Portmarnock Hotel & Golf Links
Strand Rd
☎ 01 8460611 🖹 01 8462442
e-mail: sales@portmarnock.com

dir: *Dublin Airport, N1, rdbt 1st exit, 2nd rdbt 2nd exit, next rdbt 3rd exit, T-junct turn left, over x-rds. Hotel on left past the Strand*

This 19th-century former home of the Jameson whiskey family is now a well run and smartly presented hotel, enjoys a superb location overlooking the sea and the PGA Championship Golf Links. Bedrooms are modern and equipped to high standard, public areas are spacious and very comfortable. The Osborne Restaurant comes highly recommended and a team of friendly staff goes out of their way to welcome guests.

Rooms 98 en suite (32 GF) ⊘ in 33 bedrooms **Facilities Spa** STV
↨ 18 Sauna Gym Putt green Beauty therapist Balinotherapy
Bath & treatments. **Conf** BC Thtr 300 Class 110 Board 80
Services Lift **Parking** 200 **Notes LB** ⊗ ⊘ in restaurant RS
Christmas Eve/Day

See advert on page 973

SKERRIES   MAP 01 D4

◎ **RESTAURANT WITH ROOMS**

Redbank House & Restaurant   THE INDEPENDENTS
5-7 Church St
☎ 01 8491005 & 8490439 🖹 01 8491598
e-mail: redbank@eircom.net

dir: *N1 north past the airport & bypass Swords. 3m N at the end of dual carriageway at Esso station right towards Rush, Lusk & Skerries*

Adjacent to the well-known restaurant of the same name, this comfortable double fronted period town house has two reception rooms, en suite bedrooms and a secluded garden. The restaurant is the setting for quality local produce used with an emphasis on fresh fish in imaginative cooking, served by friendly and attentive staff.

Rooms 7 en suite 5 annexe en suite (12 fmly) **Facilities** STV **Parking** 4
Notes LB ⊗ Closed 24-28 Dec

CO GALWAY

CARNA (CARNA)   MAP 01 A4

★★★ 66% **HOTEL**

Carna Bay Hotel
☎ 095 32255 🖹 095 32530

IRISH COUNTRY
HOTELS

dir: *from Galway take N59 to Recess, then left onto R340 for 8-10m*

This family owned and run hotel is in the little village of Carna on the Connemara coastline and has a very friendly and relaxed atmosphere. Public areas are bright and spacious with casual meals served in the bar at lunch and in the evenings. More formal dinner is available in the restaurant where there is an emphasis on good quality local ingredients.

Rooms 26 en suite (1 fmly) (11 GF) ⊘ in 10 bedrooms **Parking** 60
Notes LB ⊘ in restaurant Closed 23-26 Dec

CASHEL   MAP 01 A4

INSPECTORS' CHOICE

★★★ ◎◎ **COUNTRY HOUSE HOTEL**

Cashel House
☎ 095 31001 🖹 095 31077
e-mail: info@cashel-house-hotel.com
web: www.cashel-house-hotel.com

RELAIS &
CHATEAUX

dir: *S off N59, 1.5km W of Recess, well signed*

Cashel House is a mid-19th century property, standing at the head of Cashel Bay, in the heart of Connemara. Quietly secluded in award-winning gardens and woodland walks. Attentive service comes with the perfect balance of friendliness and professionalism from McEvilly family and their staff. The comfortable lounges have turf fires and antique furnishings. The restaurant offers local produce such as the famous Connemara Lamb, and fish from the nearby coast.

Rooms 32 en suite (4 fmly) (6 GF) ⊘ in 20 bedrooms
S €95.63-€270; D €191.26-€281.25 (incl. bkfst) **Facilities** ♨ ch
fac Xmas **Parking** 40 **Notes LB** No children 5yrs ⊘ in restaurant
Closed 4 Jan-4 Feb

Ireland

★★★ 80% ⚜⚜ HOTEL

Zetland Country House

Cashel Bay

☎ 095 31111 ▤ 095 31117

e-mail: zetland@iol.ie

web: www.zetland.com

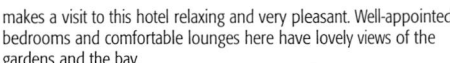

dir: N59 from Galway towards Clifden, right after Recess onto R340, left after 4m (R341), hotel 1m on right

Standing on the edge of Cashel Bay, this former sporting lodge is a cosy and relaxing family run hotel that exudes charm. Many of the comfortable rooms have sea views, as has the restaurant where very good cuisine is served. Lounge areas feature turf fires.

Rooms 19 en suite (10 fmly) **Facilities** STV ⚓ Snooker ⚽ Xmas **Conf** Board 20 **Parking** 32 **Notes** ⊘ in restaurant Closed Nov-9 Apr

---

CLIFDEN   MAP 01 A4

★★★★ 77% ⚜ HOTEL

Abbeyglen Castle

Sky Rd

☎ 095 21201 ▤ 095 21797

e-mail: info@abbeyglen.ie

dir: N59 from Galway towards Clifden. Hotel 1km from Clifden

The tranquil setting overlooking Clifden, matched with the dedication of the Hughes's father and son team and their attentive staff, combine to create a magical atmosphere. Well-appointed rooms and very comfortable suites are available, together with a range of relaxing lounge areas.

Rooms 45 en suite (9 GF) ⊘ in all bedrooms S €125-€207; D €185-€301 (incl. bkfst) **Facilities** STV ⚓ ⚓ Snooker Sauna Putt green Jacuzzi ♫ Xmas **Conf** Thtr 100 Class 50 Board 40 Del from €213 **Services** Lift **Parking** 50 **Notes LB** ⊗ No children ⊘ in restaurant Closed 7 Jan-2 Feb

★★★ 77% ⚜⚜ HOTEL

Ardagh

Ballyconneely Rd

☎ 095 21384 ▤ 095 21314

e-mail: ardaghhotel@eircom.net

dir: N59 (Galway to Clifden), signed to Ballyconneely

Situated at the head of Ardbear Bay, this family-run hotel makes full use of the spectacular scenery in the area. The restaurant is renowned for its cuisine, which is complemented by friendly and knowledgeable service. Many of the spacious and well appointed bedrooms have large picture windows and plenty of comfort.

Rooms 19 en suite (2 fmly) ⊘ in all bedrooms S €105-€117.50; D €150-€175 (incl. bkfst) **Facilities** Pool room ♫ **Parking** 35 **Notes LB** ⊘ in restaurant Closed Nov-Mar

★★★ 75% HOTEL

Rock Glen Country House Hotel

☎ 095 21035 ▤ 095 21737

e-mail: rockglen@iol.ie

dir: N6 from Dublin to Galway. N57 from Galway to Clifden. Hotel 1.5m from Clifden

The attractive clematis and creeper-framed façade of this house is an introduction to the comfort found inside. The hospitality of the staff

continued

---

makes a visit to this hotel relaxing and very pleasant. Well-appointed bedrooms and comfortable lounges here have lovely views of the gardens and the bay.

Rooms 26 en suite (2 fmly) (18 GF) **Facilities** ⚓ Snooker ⚽ Putt green ♫ **Parking** 50 **Notes LB** ⊘ in restaurant Closed mid Nov-mid Feb (ex New Year)

★★★ 70% ⚜ HOTEL

Alcock & Brown Hotel

☎ 095 21206 & 21086 ▤ 095 21842

e-mail: alcockandbrown@eircom.net

dir: take N59 from Galway via Oughterard, hotel in town centre

This comfortable family owned hotel is situated on the town square. There is a cosy bar and lounge with open fire. Brown's the restaurant is attractively decorated where the dinner menu offers a wide menu with good food with many fresh, local fish specialities. Bedrooms are well appointed. The friendly and attentive staff offer good service.

Rooms 19 en suite ⊘ in 9 bedrooms **Facilities** STV ♫ **Notes LB** ⊘ in restaurant Closed 19-26 Dec

---

GALWAY   MAP 01 B3

★★★★ 85% ⚜ COUNTRY HOUSE HOTEL

Glenlo Abbey

Bushypark

☎ 091 526666 ▤ 091 527800

e-mail: info@glenloabbey.ie

dir: 4km from city centre on N59

This cut-stone Abbey was built in 1740 and has been lovingly restored to its original glory and features sculpted cornices and fine antique furniture. There is an elegant drawing room, a cocktail bar, a library, the delightful River Room restaurant and a cellar bar. The unique Orient Express Pullman Restaurant provides a second dining option. Bedrooms in the modern wing are spacious and well appointed.

Rooms 46 en suite ⊘ in all bedrooms S €155-€220, D €210-€315 **Facilities** STV FTV ⚓ 18 Fishing Putt green Wi-fi available Boating, Clay pigeon shooting, Archery ♫ Xmas **Conf** BC Thtr 180 Class 100 Board 50 **Services** Lift **Parking** 150 **Notes LB** ⊗ ⊘ in restaurant Closed 24-28 Dec

★★★★ 79% ⚜ HOTEL

Radisson SAS Hotel & Spa

Lough Atalia Rd

☎ 091 538300 ▤ 091 538380

e-mail: sales.galway@radissonsas.com

web: www.radisson.com

dir: take N6 into Galway City. At Hunstman Inn rdbt turn 1st left. At next lights take left fork. 0.5m, hotel at next right junct

In a prime position on the waterfront at Lough Atalia, striking interior design and good levels of comfort and quality are the keynotes of this hotel. Bedrooms are well equipped and there is an executive floor. The corporate and leisure facilities are very good.

Rooms 217 en suite (7 fmly) ⊘ in 177 bedrooms **Facilities** Spa STV ⚑ supervised Sauna Solarium Gym Putt green Jacuzzi Outdoor Canadian Hot-tub **Conf** BC Thtr 750 Class 540 Board 70 **Services** Lift air con **Parking** 260 **Notes** ⊗ ⊘ in restaurant

GALWAY *continued*

★★★★ 77% ® **HOTEL**

Park House Hotel & Park Room Restaurant

Forster St, Eyre Square
☎ 091 564924 🖃 091 569219
e-mail: parkhousehotel@eircom.net

dir: city centre

This centre city property offers well decorated and comfortable bedrooms that vary in size. The public areas have now been enlarged and refurbished. The spacious restaurant has been a popular spot for the people of Galway for many years; a range of bar food is also available in Boss Doyle's bar throughout the day.

Rooms 84 en suite ⊗ in 66 bedrooms S fr €75; D fr €90 (incl. bkfst & dinner) **Facilities** STV Jacuzzi Wi-fi in bedrooms ♫ **Conf** Thtr 50 Class 30 Board 30 **Services** Lift air con **Parking** 48 **Notes LB** ® ⊗ in restaurant Closed 24-26 Dec

See advert on opposite page

★★★★ 76% ® **HOTEL**

Ardilaun Conference & Leisure Centre

Taylor's Hill
☎ 091 521433 🖃 091 521546
e-mail: info@ardilaunhousehotel.ie
web: www.ardilaunhousehotel.ie

dir: N6 to Galway City West, then follow signs for N59 Clifden, then N6 towards Salthill, hotel on this road

Located on five acres of private grounds and landscaped gardens, the original Ardilaun House was built in 1840 and converted to a hotel over 40 years ago. The bedrooms have been thoughtfully equipped and pleasantly furnished. Public areas include an elegant restaurant overlooking the garden, comfortable lounges and a bar, and there are extensive banqueting and leisure facilities.

Rooms 125 en suite (7 fmly) (8 GF) ⊗ in 69 bedrooms S €95-€180; D €110-€320 (incl. bkfst) **Facilities Spa** STV ⬚ supervised Snooker Sauna Solarium Gym Jacuzzi Wi-fi in bedrooms Treatment & analysis rooms, Beauty salon, Spinning room ♫ Xmas **Conf** Thtr 650 Class 300 Board 100 Del from €180 **Services** Lift **Parking** 320 **Notes LB** ⊗ in restaurant

★★★★ 76% ® **HOTEL**

Galway Bay Hotel Conference & Leisure Centre

The Promenade, Salthill
☎ 091 520520 🖃 091 520530
e-mail: info@galwaybayhotel.net

dir: follow signs to Salthill from all major roads. On promenade on coast road to Connemara.

This smart modern hotel enjoys a most spectacular location overlooking Galway Bay and most bedrooms, lounges and the restaurant enjoy these views. There are two dining options, fine dining

continued

in the Lobster Pot and the less formal Café Lido. Conference and banqueting facilities are impressive.

Galway Bay Hotel Conference & Leisure Centre

Rooms 153 en suite (10 fmly) (8 GF) ⊗ in 24 bedrooms S €90-€180; D €120-€280 (incl. bkfst) **Facilities** STV ⬚ supervised Sauna Gym Wi-fi in bedrooms Steam room, beauty salon ♫ Xmas **Conf** BC Thtr 1100 Class 325 Del from €134 **Services** Lift air con **Parking** 300 **Notes LB** ® ⊗ in restaurant

See advert on opposite page

★★★★ 68% **HOTEL**

Galway Great Southern Hotel

Eyre Square
☎ 091 564041 🖃 091 566704
e-mail: res@galway-gsh.com

Built in 1875, the Galway Great Southern Hotel has benefited from extensive refurbishment, which skilfully combines elegance with contemporary facilities. Amenities include comfortable lounges, two bars, a fully equipped business and conference centre and a health club. The well-appointed bedrooms vary in size; those to the front offer a greater degree of luxury.

Rooms 54 en suite 45 annexe en suite ⊗ in 46 bedrooms **Facilities Spa** STV Sauna Gym Jacuzzi ♫ **Conf** BC Thtr 350 Class 150 Board 60 **Services** Lift **Parking** 26 **Notes LB** ® ⊗ in restaurant Closed 24-26 Dec

★★★★ 62% **HOTEL**

Westwood House Hotel

Dangan, Upper Newcastle
☎ 091 521442 🖃 091 521400
e-mail: resmanager@westwoodhousehotel.com

dir: from N6 into Galway, then follow signs for Clifden (N59). House on left

Close to the university and on the main road to Connemara, this modern hotel is well appointed with spacious public areas, and a very popular bar that serves food throughout the day. Bedrooms are comfortably equipped, as are the conference facilities.

Rooms 58 en suite (44 fmly) ⊗ in 17 bedrooms S €99-€300; D €120-€300 (incl. bkfst) **Facilities** STV Wi-fi available Arrangement with local health and leisure club ♫ **Conf** Thtr 350 Class 200 Board 70 Del from €42.50 **Services** Lift air con **Parking** 130 **Notes LB** ® ⊗ in restaurant Closed 24-25 Dec **Civ Wed** 275

★★★ 70% HOTEL

The Harbour

The Harbour
☎ 091 569466 📠 091 569455
e-mail: stay@harbour.ie
dir: follow signs for Galway City East, at rdbt take 1st exit to Galway City, follow signs to docks, hotel approx 1m

This hotel is situated on the Galway harbour development in the heart of the city. Contemporary in style, the ground floor includes a large lobby lounge with open fires. Krusoes café bar and restaurant offers modern cuisine. Bedrooms are smartly furnished, comfortable and well equipped. Guests have the benefit of complimentary secure parking and there is a leisure suite with treatment rooms.

Rooms 96 en suite ⊗ in 34 bedrooms **Facilities Spa** STV Gym Jacuzzi ♬ **Conf** Thtr 100 Class 80 Board 40 **Services** Lift **Parking** 64 **Notes LB** ❀ ⊗ in restaurant Closed 23-27 Dec

★★★ 69% HOTEL

Menlo Park Hotel

Terryland
☎ 091 761122 📠 091 761222
e-mail: menlopkh@iol.ie
web: www.menloparkhotel.com
dir: at Terryland rdbt off N6 & N84 (Castlebar Rd)

This hotel's location on the outskirts of the city makes it equally well suited to both tourists and business guests. Bedrooms are spacious, well appointed and offer a choice of standard and executive rooms. The restaurant, bar and lounge are comfortably furnished. Conference facilities and ample parking is available.

Rooms 64 en suite (6 fmly) ⊗ in 10 bedrooms S €69-€150; D €110-€200 (incl. bkfst) **Facilities** STV Wi-fi available ♬ **Conf** Thtr 350 Class 190 Board 40 **Services** Lift air con **Parking** 100 **Notes LB** ❀ ⊗ in restaurant Closed 24-25 Dec

★★★ 67% HOTEL

Jurys Galway Inn

Quay St   ☷JURYS DOYLE
                              HOTELS
☎ 091 566444 📠 091 568415
e-mail: enquiry@jurys.com
web: www.jurysdoyle.com
dir: N6 follow signs for Docks. At Docks take Salthill Rd

This modern hotel stands in the heart of the city, opposite the famous Spanish Arch. The hotel has an attractive patio by the river and a popular contemporary bar and restaurant. The room-only rate is ideal for families and budget travellers. There is a public indoor car park adjacent to the hotel.

Rooms 132 en suite (6 fmly) (12 GF) ⊗ in 111 bedrooms **Facilities** STV **Services** Lift **Notes** ❀ ⊗ in restaurant

Ireland

GALWAY *continued*

U

The House
Lower Merchants Rd
☎ 091 568166 ▤ 091 568262
e-mail: info@thehousehotel.ie

At the time of going to press, the star classification for this hotel was not confirmed. Please refer to the AA internet site www.theAA.com for current information.

Rooms 45 en suite **Facilities** STV ♫ **Services** Lift **Notes LB** ⊗ ⊘ in restaurant Closed 21-28 Dec

BUDGET HOTEL

Days Hotel Galway
Dublin Rd, Galway City East
☎ 091 381200 ▤ 091 753187
e-mail: res@dayshotelgalway.com
web: www.welcomebreak.co.uk

dir: Off N6 between Wellpark Retail Park and hospital

This modern building offers accommodation in smart, spacious and well-equipped bedrooms, suitable for families and business travellers, and all with en suite bathrooms. Continental breakfast is available and other refreshments may be taken at the nearby family restaurant. For further details see the Hotel Groups page.

Rooms 311 en suite

BUDGET HOTEL

Travelodge Galway City
Tuam Rd
☎ 08700 850 950
web: www.travelodge.co.uk

Travelodge offers good quality, good value, modern accommodation. Ideal for families, the spacious en suite bedrooms include remote-control TV, tea and coffee-making facilities and comfortable beds. Meals can be taken at the nearby family restaurant. See Hotel Groups pages for further details.

Rooms S fr £26; D fr £26

PORTUMNA
MAP 01 B

★★★ 70% **HOTEL**

Shannon Oaks Hotel & Country Club
St Joseph Rd
☎ 090 974 1777 ▤ 090 974 1357
e-mail: sales@shannonoaks.ie
dir: exiting Portumna, on left of St Joseph Rd

Located in eight acres of parkland by Portumna National Park, this modern hotel offers very comfortable and spacious bedrooms and suites. The popular bar has food available most of the day, with more formal dining available in the Castle Gates Restaurant. Extensive conference and leisure facilities are also on site.

Rooms 63 en suite **Facilities** STV ⊠ ♨ Sauna Solarium Gym Jacuzzi ♫ **Conf** Thtr 600 Class 320 Board 280 **Services** Lift air con **Parking** 360 **Notes LB** ⊗

RECESS (SRAITH SALACH)
MAP 01 A

★★★★ 82% ⚜ ⚜ **COUNTRY HOUSE HOTEL**

Ballynahinch Castle
☎ 095 31006 ▤ 095 31085
e-mail: bhinch@iol.ie

dir: W from Galway on N59 towards Clifden. After Recess take Roundstone turn on left

Open log fires and friendly professional service are just some of the delights of staying at this castle originating from the 16th century. Set in 350 acres of woodland, rivers and lakes, this hotel has many suites and rooms with stunning views, as does the award-winning Owenmore restaurant where the linen is crisp and the silver gleams.

Rooms 40 en suite ⊘ in 4 bedrooms S €138-€171; D €209-€275 (incl. bkfst) **Facilities** STV ♨ Fishing ⛵ River & Lakeside walks; tennis Xmas **Conf** Thtr 30 Class 20 Board 20 **Parking** 55 **Notes LB** ⊗ ⊘ in restaurant Closed 28 Jan-22 Feb & 14-27 Dec RS Good Friday

INSPECTORS' CHOICE

★★★ ◉ COUNTRY HOUSE HOTEL

Lough Inagh Lodge

Inagh Valley

☎ 095 34706 & 34694 🖹 095 34708

e-mail: inagh@iol.ie

dir: *after Recess R344 towards Kylemore*

This 19th-century, former fishing lodge is a relaxing, comfortable hotel in a setting is superb. Situated in the middle of Connemara it is fronted by a good fishing lake and enjoys beautiful mountain views. Bedrooms are smartly decorated and spacious, and there is a choice of lounges and a cosy traditional bar. The delightful restaurant offers an extensive range of seafood.

Rooms 12 en suite (4 GF) **Facilities** STV Fishing Hill walking, Fly fishing, Cycling **Conf** Thtr 20 Class 20 Board 20 **Services** air con **Parking** 16 **Notes LB** ⊘ in restaurant Closed mid Dec-mid Mar

---

RENVYLE   MAP 01 A4

★★★ 74% ◉ HOTEL

Renvyle House Hotel

☎ 095 43511 🖹 095 43515

e-mail: info@renvyle.com

web: www.renvyle.com

dir: *Hotel signed from Recess*

This comfortable house has been operating as a hotel for over 120 years. Located on the unspoilt coast of Connemara it provides a range of outdoor leisure pursuits. The spacious lounges are comfortable with turf fires and the bedrooms are well equipped. The relaxed, friendly staff will make any visit here memorable.

Rooms 68 en suite (8 fmly) ⊘ in 5 bedrooms **Facilities** STV ⚑ ⚐9 ⚑ Fishing Riding Snooker ⚑ Putt green Clay pigeon shooting ♫ ch fac **Conf** Thtr 200 Class 80 Board 80 **Parking** 60 **Notes LB** ⊘ in restaurant Closed 6 Jan-14 Feb

---

ROUNDSTONE   MAP 01 A4

★★ 70% ◉ HOTEL

Roundstone House Hotel

☎ 095 35864 🖹 095 35944

e-mail: vaughanhotel@eircom.net

IRISH COUNTRY HOTELS

dir: *From Galway take N59. After Recess take 2nd left, 9km.*

This delightful hotel has been in operation since 1894 and owned by the Vaughan family for many years. The comfortable bedrooms enjoy

continued

---

the magnificent sea views and the rugged Connemara landscape. Vaughan's Restaurant is renowned for its seafood.

Rooms 12 en suite (1 fmly) **Notes** ⊗ ⊘ in restaurant Closed Oct-Etr Civ Wed

SALTHILL
See **Galway**

CO KERRY

BALLYHEIGE   MAP 01 A2

★★★ 72% HOTEL

The White Sands

☎ 066 7133102 🖹 066 7133357

e-mail: whitesands@eircom.net

IRISH COUNTRY HOTELS

dir: *18km from Tralee on coast road. Hotel in main street*

Friendly staff welcomes guests to this family run hotel, situated beside the sandy beach and close to golf clubs. Attractively decorated throughout, facilities include lounge bar, traditional pub where there is entertainment most nights and a good restaurant.

Rooms 81 en suite (2 fmly) **Facilities** STV ♫ ch fac **Conf** Class 40 Board 40 **Services** Lift air con **Parking** 40 **Notes LB** ⊗ ⊘ in restaurant Closed Nov-Feb RS Mar-Apr & Oct

---

CAHERDANIEL   MAP 01 A2
(CATHAIR DÓNALL)

★★★ 69% ◉ HOTEL

Derrynane

☎ 066 947 5136 🖹 066 947 5160

e-mail: info@derrynane.com

dir: *just off main road, half way round Ring of Kerry on N70*

Super clifftop location overlooking Derrynane Bay with spectacular views adding a stunning dimension to this well run hotel where pleasant, efficient staff contribute to the very relaxed atmosphere. Public areas include spacious lounges, a bar and restaurant. Bedrooms are well appointed and most enjoy the views.

Rooms 70 en suite (30 fmly) (32 GF) ⊘ in 40 bedrooms S €75-€120; D €150-€190 (incl. bkfst) **Facilities** STV ⚑ supervised ⚑ Sauna Solarium Gym Steam room, seaweed therapy room ♫ Xmas **Parking** 60 **Notes LB** ⊗ ⊘ in restaurant Closed 4 Oct-15 Apr

continued on page 980

Ireland

CAHERSIVEEN   MAP 01 A2

★★★ 69% **HOTEL**

Ring of Kerry Hotel
Valentia Rd
☎ 066 9472543 🖨 066 9472893
e-mail: ringhotel@eircom.net
dir: on Ring of Kerry road

This hotel is situated in the town of Cahersiveen and ideal for touring the Ring of Kerry and nearby islands. Bedrooms are spacious and attractively decorated. There are two dining options, dinner is served nightly in the cosy restaurant and less formal fare is available in the inviting John D's bar.

Rooms 24 en suite (2 fmly) ⊗ in 20 bedrooms **Facilities** STV ♫ **Parking** 24 **Notes LB** ⊛ ⊗ in restaurant

KENMARE   MAP 01 B2

INSPECTORS' CHOICE

★★★★ ◉◉◉ **COUNTRY HOUSE HOTEL**

Sheen Falls Lodge
☎ 064 41600 🖨 064 41386
e-mail: info@sheenfallslodge.ie
dir: N71 to Glengarriff over bridge, 1st left

This former fishing lodge has been developed into a beautiful hotel run by a friendly team of expertly managed staff. The cascading Sheen Falls are floodlit at night, forming a romantic backdrop to the enjoyment of award-winning cuisine in La Cascade restaurant. Bedrooms are very comfortably appointed; many of the suites are particularly spacious.

continued

Rooms 66 en suite (14 fmly) (14 GF) ⊗ in 10 bedrooms
S €230-€445; D €290-€445 **Facilities** STV ⛳ supervised ⑆
Fishing Riding Snooker Sauna Gym ⑆ Jacuzzi Wi-fi in bedrooms
Table tennis,steam room,clay pigeon shooting,cycling,vintage car
rides,library ♫ **Xmas** **Conf** BC Thtr 120 Class 65 Board 50
Services Lift **Parking** 76 **Notes LB** ⊛ ⊗ in restaurant Closed
2 Jan-1 Feb RS Dec

★★★ 69% **HOTEL**

The Lansdowne Arms Hotel
Main St
☎ 064 41368 🖨 064 41114
e-mail: info@lansdownearms.com
dir: From N22 through Kilgarvan to Kenmare.

This was Kenmare's first hotel, dating back to the 1760s, and now owned by the Quill family. It has been extensively renovated to a high standard. Dinner is served in the Quill room and more casual dining is available in the Poets Bar; traditional music is played in the Bold Thady Quill bar at weekends.

Rooms 26 en suite (9 GF) ⊗ in 20 bedrooms S €70-€90; D €90-€160 (incl. bkfst) **Facilities** ♫ ch fac **Parking** 20 **Notes LB** ⊛ ⊗ in restaurant Closed 25 Dec

KILLARNEY   MAP 01 B2

INSPECTORS' CHOICE

★★★★★ ◉ **HOTEL**

Aghadoe Heights
☎ 064 31766 🖨 064 31345
e-mail: info@aghadoeheights.com
dir: 16km S of Kerry Airport. 5km N of Killarney. Signed off N22

The exterior of this superbly positioned hotel belies the opulence within. Overlooking Loch Lein with spectacular views of Killarney's lakes and mountains, Aghadoe Heights is appointed to the very highest standard. Friendly staff display a genuine willingness to make everyone's stay special so that happy memories are assured. Many of the bedrooms have sun decks that make the most of the panoramic scenery, and the Penthouse Suite is truly stunning.

Rooms 74 en suite (6 fmly) ⊗ in all bedrooms S €180-€300; D €250-€450 (incl. bkfst) **Facilities Spa** STV ⛳ ⑆ Fishing Sauna Solarium Gym Jacuzzi Wi-fi available The Heights spa, treatment rooms, thermal suites ♫ **Xmas** **Conf** BC Thtr 120 Class 60 Board 40 Del from €240 **Services** Lift **Parking** 120 **Notes LB** ⊛ ⊗ in restaurant Closed Jan-1 Mar

See advert on opposite page

Paradise found

From the moment you arrive, you'll welcome the difference at the Aghadoe Heights Hotel. From our attentive service to awe inspiring views of the world famous Killarney lakes to the tranquil elegance of our luxury suites, the sumptuous cuisine of our AA-acclaimed restaurant, and, of course, our rejuvenating and relaxing health spa.

The Aghadoe Heights Hotel. Welcome to your personal paradise.

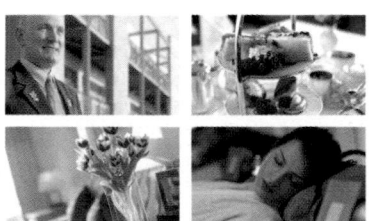

Aghadoe Heights
HOTEL AND SPA
★★★★★

FOR FURTHER INFORMATION PLEASE CONTACT RESERVATIONS AT +353 (0) 64 31766
OR VISIT OUR WEBSITE: WWW.AGHADOEHEIGHTS.COM
AGHADOE HEIGHTS HOTEL, LAKES OF KILLARNEY, CO KERRY, IRELAND.

KILLARNEY continued

INSPECTORS' CHOICE

★★★★ ◉◉ HOTEL

Killarney Park

☎ 064 35555 📄 064 35266

e-mail: info@killarneyparkhotel.ie

dir: N22. At 1st rdbt to town centre. At 2nd rdbt take 2nd exit, 3rd rdbt take 1st exit. Hotel on left

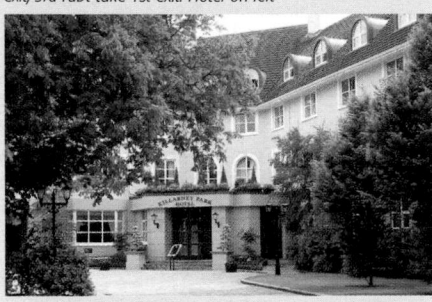

This charming hotel on the edge of the town combines elegance with comfort. It has a warm atmosphere with open fires, restful colours and friendly caring staff who ensure your stay is an enjoyable one. Bedrooms and suites are spacious and many have air conditioning and open fires. A health spa is included in the leisure facilities.

Rooms (4 fmly) ⊘ in 68 bedrooms **Facilities Spa** STV 📶 supervised Snooker Sauna Gym Jacuzzi Wi-fi available Outdoor Canadian hot-tub Plunge pool, Caldarium, Relaxation room, Bubble pool Xmas **Conf** BC Thtr 150 Class 70 Board 35 **Services** Lift air con **Parking** 70 **Notes** ⊗ ⊘ in restaurant Closed 24-26 Dec

---

★★★★ 80% HOTEL

Great Southern

☎ 064 38000 📄 064 35300

e-mail: res@killarney-gsh.com

dir: From Limerick take N21 to Killarney. From Cork take N22

Dating from 1854 as a railway hotel, this fine property offers bedrooms that vary in style but all are well equipped and comfortable. Public areas are elegant, particularly the Garden room where breakfast is served. There is a choice of two restaurants for dinner, with more casual dining in the lounge and bar.

Rooms 171 en suite (35 fmly) S €265; D €280 (incl. bkfst) **Facilities Spa** STV 📶 supervised 🏊 Gym Wi-fi available Jacuzzi, Plunge pool, Steam room, Hydrotherary bath 🎵 Xmas **Conf** Thtr 1000 Class 700 Board 40 Del from €180 **Services** Lift **Parking** 200 **Notes LB** ⊘ in restaurant RS Closed Mon-Wed in Feb

---

★★★★ 78% ◉◉ HOTEL

Cahernane House

Muckross Rd

☎ 064 31895 📄 064 34340

e-mail: cahernane@eircom.net

web: www.cahernane.com

dir: On N22 to Killarney, take 1st exit off rdbt then left at church and 1st exit at next rdbt leading to Muckross Road

This fine country mansion, former home of the Earls of Pembroke, has a magnificent mountain backdrop and panoramic views from its lakeside setting. Elegant period furniture is complemented by more modern pieces to create a comfortable hotel offering a warm atmosphere with a particularly friendly team dedicated to guest care.

Rooms 12 en suite 26 annexe en suite S €220-€275; D €264-€420 (incl. bkfst) **Facilities** 🎣 Fishing 🏌 ch fac **Conf** Thtr 15 Class 10 Board 10 **Services** Lift air con **Parking** 50 **Notes LB** ⊗ ⊘ in restaurant Closed 21 Dec-31 Jan

---

★★★★ 78% HOTEL

Randles Court

Muckross Rd

☎ 064 35333 📄 064 35206

e-mail: info@randlescourt.com

dir: N22 towards Muckross, turn tight at T-junct on right. From N72 take 3rd exit on 1st rdbt into town & follow signs for Muckross, hotel on left

Close to all the town's attractions, this is a friendly family-run hotel with an emphasis on customer care. Bedrooms are particularly comfortable. Checkers is the chic bistro restaurant where good food is served in the evenings, perhaps following a relaxing drink in the cosy bar. A swimming pool and other leisure facilities are also available.

Rooms 52 en suite **Facilities** STV 📶 Sauna Gym Putt green **Conf** Thtr 80 Class 60 Board 40 **Services** Lift **Parking** 39 **Notes** Closed 23-27 Dec

---

★★★★ 75% HOTEL

Muckross Park Hotel

Muckross Village

☎ 064 31938 📄 064 31965

e-mail: info@muckrosspark.com

dir: from Killarney to Kenmare, hotel 4km on left, adjacent to Muckross House & Gardens

Offering hospitality since 1795, this comfortable hotel is located a few kilometres from the centre of the town amid well-tended gardens. Spacious bedrooms are individually designed. Informal dining is

continued

available in the popular Molly Darcy's pub throughout the day, with dinner served in GB Shaw's Restaurant.

Rooms 108 en suite (40 fmly) (12 GF) ⊘ in 23 bedrooms **Facilities Spa** STV Sauna Solarium Gym Jacuzzi Treatment rooms ♫ **Conf** BC Thtr 450 Class 250 Board 200 **Services** Lift **Parking** 250 **Notes LB** ⊗ ⊘ in restaurant Mar-Nov Civ Wed 300

★★★★ 74% HOTEL

The Brehon

Muckross Rd

☎ 064 30700 ▤ 064 30701

e-mail: info@thebrehon.com

dir: 1m outside Killarney on N71

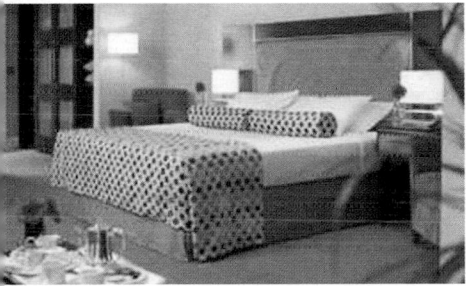

The Brehon is a spectacular hotel close to Killarney National Park and town. Public areas are particularly spacious, with comfortable lounges, bars and a restaurant. Bedrooms are well equipped and there is a range of suites. The hotel offers a specialised Thai spa, and extensive conference facilities. Other leisure facilities are available nearby.

Rooms 125 en suite (3 fmly) ⊘ in all bedrooms **Facilities Spa** STV supervised Sauna Gym Putt green Jacuzzi Thai Spa inc treatments and massages. **Conf** BC Thtr 250 Class 120 Board 60 **Services** Lift air con **Parking** 126 **Notes LB** ⊗ ⊘ in restaurant

★★★ 76% HOTEL

Lake

Muckross Rd

☎ 064 31035 ▤ 064 31902

e-mail: info@lakehotel.com

dir: N22 to Killarney. Hotel 2km from town on Muckross road

This family operated hotel is located on the shores of Killarney's lakes and offers a relaxed and friendly atmosphere with views of the mountains. Bedrooms are well appointed some with balconies, four-poster beds and jacuzzis. The comfortable lounges and bar have open log fires and guests can enjoy the stunning views from the attractive restaurant.

Rooms 125 en suite (6 fmly) (23 GF) ⊘ in all bedrooms S €45-€200; D €90-€300 (incl. bkfst) **Facilities Spa** STV Fishing Sauna Gym Wi-fi available Jacuzzi Hot tub Library ♫ Xmas **Conf** BC Thtr 80 Class 60 Board 40 **Services** Lift air con **Parking** 140 **Notes LB** ⊗ ⊘ in restaurant Closed 3-28 Dec Civ Wed 50

See advert on this page

★★★ 74% HOTEL

Gleneagle

Muckross Rd

☎ 064 36000 ▤ 064 32646

e-mail: info@gleneaglehotel.com

dir: 1m outside Killarney town on N71 Kenmare road

The facilities at this large hotel are excellent and numerous. Family entertainment is a strong element of the Gleneagle experience, popular with the Irish market for almost 50 years. Comfortable rooms are matched with a range lounges, restaurants a leisure centre and INEC, one of Ireland's largest events centres.

Rooms 250 en suite (57 fmly) ⊘ in 20 bedrooms **Facilities** STV supervised Squash Snooker Sauna Gym Jacuzzi Pitch & Putt Steam room Games room ♫ **Conf** Thtr 2500 Class 1000 Board 50 **Services** Lift **Parking** 500 **Notes LB** ⊗ ⊘ in restaurant

Ireland

KILLARNEY *continued*

★★★ 73% HOTEL

Castlerosse

TOWER HOTEL GROUP

☎ 064 31144 ▤ 064 31031

e-mail: res@castlerosse.ie

web: www.castlerossehotel.com

dir: *from Killarney take R562 for Killorglin and The Ring of Kerry, hotel 1.5km on left*

A lovely location on 6,000 acres of land overlooking Lough Leane. Bedrooms are well appointed and comfortable. The restaurant enjoys panoramic views from its elevated position. Golf is available on site, together with a leisure centre.

Rooms 121 en suite (27 fmly) ⊛ in 4 bedrooms S €95-€110; D €128-€170 (incl. bkfst) **Facilities** 🔧 supervised ♨ 9 ⌇ Sauna Gym Jacuzzi Wi-fi available Golfing & riding arranged ♫ **Conf** Thtr 200 Class 100 Board 40 Del from €150 **Services** Lift **Parking** 100 **Notes LB** ⊗ ⊛ in restaurant Closed Dec-Feb

★★★ 73% HOTEL

International

East Avenue Rd

Best Western

☎ 064 31816 ▤ 064 31837

e-mail: inter@iol.ie

dir: *N21 from Limerick to Farranfore, then N22 to Killarney, right at 1st rdbt into Killarney follow bypass to hotel*

Quality bedrooms with modern comforts are on offer at this warm and friendly hotel in the heart of the town. Hannigan's bar and brasserie serves food throughout the day, with an inviting mahogany-panelled room open in the evenings. Relaxing lounge areas include a snooker room and a library.

Rooms 90 en suite (6 fmly) ⊛ in 70 bedrooms S €85-€135; D €100-€160 (incl. bkfst) **Facilities** STV Wi-fi available Billiards, 3 Dimensional Golf Simulator/Leisure Suite Hot Tub & Jacuzzis ♫ **Conf** Thtr 150 Class 100 Board 25 **Services** Lift **Notes LB** ⊗ ⊛ in restaurant Closed 23-27 Dec

★★★ 72% ⊛ HOTEL

Arbutus

College St

☎ 064 31037 ▤ 064 34033

e-mail: stay@arbutuskillarney.com

web: www.arbutuskillarney.com

Situated in the town centre this smart hotel has been run by the Buckley family since 1926. Many of the comfortable bedrooms are air-conditioned. Public areas include a comfortable foyer lounge, a sitting room and restaurant. Guests can enjoy traditional Irish music in the bar on selected nights. Staff are friendly and helpful.

Rooms 35 en suite (4 fmly) ⊛ in 25 bedrooms **Facilities** STV ♫ **Services** Lift **Notes LB** ⊗ ⊛ in restaurant Closed 12 Dec-30 Jan

★★★ 70% HOTEL

Killarney Valley Hotel & Suites

Fossa

☎ 064 23600 ▤ 064 23601

e-mail: killarneyvalley@eircom.net

dir: *from N72 3m town on right*

Located in Fossa Village, just 6km from Killarney, this newly built hotel offers spacious bedrooms; many are interconnecting with kitchenettes and sitting areas. Smart public areas include a popular bar and a first-floor restaurant, and a penthouse lounge making the most of the views.

Rooms 63 en suite (20 GF) ⊛ in all bedrooms S €95-€190; D €110-€195 (incl. bkfst) **Facilities** STV ♫ **Services** Lift **Parking** 74 **Notes LB** ⊗ ⊛ in restaurant Closed Nov-Jan

★★★ 67% HOTEL

White Gates

Muckross Rd

IRISH COUNTRY HOTELS

☎ 064 31164 ▤ 064 34850

e-mail: whitegates@iol.ie

dir: *1km from Killarney town on Muckross road on left*

The eye is definitely drawn to this hotel with its ochre and blue painted frontage. The same flair for colour is in evidence throughout the interior where bedrooms of mixed sizes are well decorated and very comfortable. There is also a light-filled restaurant, with casual dining in the bar, which has a popular local trade.

Rooms 27 en suite (4 fmly) (4 GF) **Facilities** STV ♫ **Conf** Class 50 **Parking** 50 **Notes LB** ⊗ Closed 25-26 Dec

★★★ 66% HOTEL

Victoria House Hotel

Muckross Rd

☎ 064 35430 ▤ 064 35439

e-mail: info@victoriahousehotel.com

dir: *On N71, 1.5km from Killarney*

This family managed hotel is just one kilometre from the town, and overlooks the National Park. Friendliness is the key word to the style of service, with good food served in both the restaurant and throughout the day in the bar. Bedrooms are well equipped and undergo constant renovation, further increasing guest comfort.

Rooms 35 rms S €59-€99; D €98-€178 (incl. bkfst) **Facilities** STV Putt green Wi-fi available ♫ **Parking** 60 **Notes LB** ⊗ ⊛ in restaurant Closed 4 Dec-2 Feb

⊔

Scotts Garden Hotel

College St

☎ 064 31060 ▤ 064 36656

e-mail: scottskill@eircom.net

dir: *N20, N22 to town, at Friary turn left. 500mtrs on East Avenue Rd to car park entrance*

At the time of going to press, the star classification for this hotel was not confirmed. Please refer to the AA internet site www.theAA.com for current information.

Rooms 52 en suite (4 fmly) **Facilities** ♫ **Services** Lift **Parking** 60 **Notes** ⊗ ⊛ in restaurant Closed 24-25 Dec

Ireland

PARKNASILLA   MAP 01 A2

★★★★ 81% ❀ **HOTEL**

Great Southern

☎ 064 45122 📠 064 45323
e-mail: res@parknasilla-gsh.com
dir: *on Kenmare road 3km from Sneem village*

This delightful hotel which has been in business for over a hundred years, is a popular haven of relaxation and rejuvenation for generations of Irish families. There are many spacious lounges, that together with the restaurant and many of the bedrooms, have wonderful sea views. Service is warm and friendly, underpinned by smooth professionalism.

Rooms 24 en suite 59 annexe en suite (6 fmly) ❷ in 11 bedrooms **Facilities Spa** STV 🎾 supervised ♨ 12 ⛳ Fishing Riding Snooker Sauna ⛳ Putt green Jacuzzi Bike hire, Windsurfing, Clay pigeon shooting, Archery 🎵 **Conf** BC Thtr 80 Class 60 Board 20 **Services** Lift **Parking** 60 **Notes LB** ⊗ ❷ in restaurant

See advert on this page

TRALEE   MAP 01 A2

★★★★ 77% **HOTEL**

Manor West

Killarney Rd
☎ 066 7194500 📠 066 7194545
e-mail: res@manorwesthotel.ie
web: www.manorwesthotel.ie

Just five minutes from the centre of town, this hotel is part of a large retail park with many shopping opportunities. Spacious well-equipped bedrooms are matched by smart public areas, including a very well finished leisure facility. The Mercantile is a popular bar serving food throughout the day, with fine dining available in The Walnut Room for dinner.

Rooms 77 en suite ❷ in 68 bedrooms S €85-€100; D €140-€180 (incl. bkfst) **Facilities** STV 🎾 supervised Sauna Gym Jacuzzi 🎵 Xmas **Conf** Thtr 250 Class 200 Board 60 **Services** Lift air con **Parking** 200 **Notes** ⊗ ❷ in restaurant

★★★★ 76% **HOTEL**

Ballygarry House

Killarney Rd
☎ 066 7123322 📠 066 7127630
e-mail: info@ballygarryhouse.com
dir: *1.5km from Tralee, on N22*

Set in six acres of well-tended gardens, this fine hotel has been family run for the last 50 years and totally renovated in recent years to a very high standard. The elegant and stylishly decorated bedrooms are spacious and relaxing. Good cuisine is served in the split-level restaurant. The staff are friendly and professional. A spa has now been added to the leisure facilities.

Rooms 46 en suite (10 fmly) (6 GF) ❷ in all bedrooms **Facilities Spa** STV 🎵 **Conf** BC **Services** lift **Parking** 105 **Notes** ⊗ ❷ in restaurant Closed 20-26 Dec Civ Wed 350

Ireland

TRALEE *continued*

★★★★ 76% **HOTEL**

Meadowlands Hotel

Oakpark

☎ 066 7180444 📄 066 7180964

e-mail: info@meadowlands-hotel.com

dir: *1km from Tralee town centre on N69*

This smart hotel has been extended and is within walking distance of the town centre. Bedrooms are tastefully decorated and comfortable. Johnny Frank's is the very popular pub where a wide range of food is offered throughout the day, with more formal dining in An Pota Stor, specialising in seafood.

Rooms 57 en suite (1 fmly) (4 GF) ⊛ in 17 bedrooms S €70-€150; D €150-€250 (incl. bkfst) **Facilities** STV ♫ **Conf** Thtr 250 Class 110 Board 30 **Services** Lift air con **Parking** 200 **Notes LB** ⊗ ⊛ in restaurant Closed 24-26 Dec

★★★ 72% **HOTEL**

Abbey Gate

Maine St

☎ 066 7129888 📄 066 7129821

e-mail: info@abbeygate-hotel.com

dir: *take N21 or N22 to town centre*

The Abbey Gate is a smart town centre hotel. The comfortable well-equipped bedrooms include some suitable for those with mobility difficulties. The bar is popular with local business people and features music at weekends. Food is served daily in the bar, or in the bistro or the Italian restaurant.

Rooms 100 en suite (4 fmly) **Facilities** STV ♫ **Conf** BC Thtr 450 Class 250 Board 40 **Services** Lift **Parking** 40 **Notes LB** ⊗ ⊛ in restaurant RS 24-26 Dec

WATERVILLE (AN COIREÁN)   MAP 01 A2

★★★ 79% **HOTEL**

Butler Arms

☎ 066 947 4144 📄 066 947 4520

e-mail: butarms@iol.ie

dir: *village centre on seafront. N70 Ring of Kerry*

This smartly presented hotel on the Ring of Kerry, has been in the Huggard family for four generations. A range of comfortable lounges creates a relaxing atmosphere, and excellent bar food is served in the Fisherman's bar through the day. More formal dining is available in the restaurant, which has commanding views of the sea and town.

Rooms 40 en suite (1 fmly) ⊛ in 12 bedrooms **Facilities** STV ⛵ Fishing Snooker Billiards room **Services** Lift **Parking** 50 **Notes LB** ⊗ ⊛ in restaurant Closed Nov-Apr

CO KILDARE

ATHY   MAP 01 C3

[U]

Clanard Court

Dublin Rd

☎ 059 864 0666 📄 059 864 0888

e-mail: sales@clanardcourt.ie

dir: *Take N7 at Red Cow rdbt, M7 signed Limerick & Cork. At junct 9 onto M9. Exit M9 signed for Athy, right onto N78.*

At the time of going to press, the star classification for this hotel was not confirmed. Please refer to the AA internet site www.theAA.com for current information.

Rooms 38 en suite (2 fmly) (17 GF) ⊛ in 33 bedrooms S €69-€150; D €69-€230 (incl. bkfst) **Facilities** STV Xmas **Conf** BC Thtr 400 Class 300 Board 20 Del from €149 **Services** Lift **Parking** 250 **Notes LB** ⊗ ⊛ in restaurant

CASTLEDERMOT   MAP 01 C3

★★★★ 67% **HOTEL**

Kilkea Castle Hotel

☎ 059 914 5156 & 914 5100 📄 059 914 5187

e-mail: kilkea@iol.ie

dir: *From Dublin take M9 S, take exit for High Cross Inn. Left after pub, hotel 3m on right*

Dating from 1180, this is reputed to be Ireland's oldest inhabited castle. Surrounded by an 18-hole golf course, the castle offers a number of comfortable bars and lounges, and D'Lacy's, a fine dining restaurant. Bedrooms vary in style but are all well equipped. Banqueting and conference facilities are in the converted stables.

Rooms 11 en suite 25 annexe en suite (2 fmly) (5 GF) S €140-€210; D €240-€360 (incl. bkfst) **Facilities** STV ⛳ supervised ♨ 18 ⛵ Fishing Sauna Gym Putt green Jacuzzi **Conf** BC Thtr 300 Board 50 Del from €250 **Services** Lift **Parking** 100 **Notes LB** ⊗ ⊛ in restaurant Closed 23-26 Dec

Ireland

LEIXLIP   MAP 01 D4

★★★ 79% ◉ **HOTEL**

Leixlip House
Captains Hill
☎ 01 6242268 ▤ 01 6244177
e-mail: info@leixliphouse.com
dir: from Leixlip motorway junct continue into village. Turn right at lights and continue up hill

This Georgian house dates back to 1772 and retains many of its original features. Overlooking Leixlip, the hotel is just eight miles from Dublin city centre. Bedrooms and public areas are furnished and decorated to a high standard. The Bradaun Restaurant offers a wide range of interesting dishes at dinner, with a popular bar menu served throughout the day.

Rooms 19 en suite (2 fmly) **Facilities** STV **Conf** Thtr 130 Class 60 Board 40 **Parking** 64 **Notes** LB ⊗ ⊘ in restaurant

U

Courtyard
Main St
☎ 01 629 5100 ▤ 01 629 5111
e-mail: info@courtyard.ie
At the time of going to press, the star classification for this hotel was not confirmed. Please refer to the AA internet site www.theAA.com for current information.

Rooms 40 en suite

NAAS   MAP 01 D3

★★★★ 76% ◉ **HOTEL**

Killashee House Hotel & Villa Spa
☎ 045 879277 ▤ 045 879266
e-mail: reservations@killasheehouse.com
dir: N7, then straight through town on Old Kilcullen Rd (R448), hotel on left, 1.5m from centre of Naas

This Victorian manor house, set in magnificent parkland and landscaped gardens, has been successfully converted to a large hotel with spacious public areas, very comfortable bedrooms and two dining options; fine dining in Turners, and the Nun's Kitchen and bar that caters for casual dining. There are extensive banqueting and leisure facilities.

Rooms 142 en suite (10 fmly) (48 GF) ⊘ in 61 bedrooms S €155-€495; D €220-€495 (incl. bkfst) **Facilities** Spa STV ⊞ supervised Sauna Solarium Gym ⊗ Jacuzzi Archery, Biking, Clay pigeon shooting ♫ **Conf** Thtr 1600 Class 144 Board 84 Del from €205 **Services** Lift **Parking** 600 **Notes** LB ⊗ ⊘ in restaurant Closed 25-26 Dec

See advert on this page

NEWBRIDGE   MAP 01 C3

★★★★ 78% ◉◉ **HOTEL**

Keadeen
☎ 045 431666 ▤ 045 434402
e-mail: info@keendeanhotel.ie
dir: M7 junct 10, (Newbridge, Curragh) at rdbt follow signs to Newbridge, hotel on left in 1km

This family operated hotel is set in eight acres of award-winning gardens on the outskirts of the town and just off the N7. Comfortable public areas include spacious drawing rooms, an excellent leisure centre, fine dining in the Derby Restaurant and more casual fare in the bar. Ideally located for the Curragh racecourse which is nearby.

Rooms 75 en suite (4 fmly) (58 GF) ⊘ in 25 bedrooms S €125-€140; D €175-€225 (incl. bkfst) **Facilities** STV ⊞ supervised Sauna Solarium Gym Wi-fi in bedrooms Jacuzzi Aerobics studio Treatment room Massage ♫ **Conf** Thtr 800 Class 300 Board 40 **Services** Lift **Parking** 200 **Notes** LB ⊗ ⊘ in restaurant Closed 24 Dec-2 Jan

STRAFFAN   MAP 01 D4

INSPECTORS' CHOICE

★★★★★ ◎◎◎ **COUNTRY HOUSE HOTEL**

The K Club

☎ 01 6017200 📄 01 6017298

e-mail: resortsales@kclub.ie

dir: *from Dublin take N4, exit for R406, hotel on right in Straffan*

The K Club, set in 700 acres of rolling woodland has two magnificent championship golf courses and a spa facility that complements the truly luxurious hotel that is the centrepiece of the resort. Public areas and bedrooms are opulently furnished, and have views of the formal gardens. Fine dining is served in the elegant Byerly Turk restaurant, with more informal dining offered in Legends and Monza restaurants in the golf pavilions.

Rooms 69 en suite 10 annexe en suite (10 fmly) **Facilities** Spa STV ⚡ supervised ⚓ 36 Fishing Snooker Sauna Solarium Gym ☜ Putt green Jacuzzi Beauty salon Driving range Golf tuition Fishing tuition Horse riding nearby ♫ **Conf** Thtr 300 Class 300 Board 160 **Services** Lift **Parking** 205 **Notes** LB ⊗ ⊘ in restaurant

Ⓤ

Barberstown Castle

☎ 01 6288157 📄 01 6277027

e-mail: barberstowncastle@ireland.com

web: www.barberstowncastle.ie

At the time of going to press, the star classification for this hotel was not confirmed. Please refer to the AA internet site www.theAA.com for current information.

Rooms 59 en suite S €150-€200; D €230-€280 (incl. bkfst) **Facilities** STV ♫ Xmas **Conf** Thtr 150 Class 120 Board 30 Del from €209 **Services** Lift **Parking** 200 **Notes** LB ⊗ ⊘ in restaurant Closed Dec 24-26 & Jan

CO KILKENNY

KILKENNY   MAP 01 C3

★★★★ 75% ◎ **HOTEL**

Kilkenny River Court Hotel

The Bridge, John St

☎ 056 772 3388 📄 056 772 3389

e-mail: reservations@kilrivercourt.com

dir: *at bridge in town centre, opposite castle*

Hidden behind archways on John Street, this is a very comfortable and welcoming establishment. The restaurant, bar and many of the well-equipped bedrooms command great views of Kilkenny Castle and the River Nore. Attentive, friendly staff ensure good service in all areas. Excellent corporate and leisure facilities are provided.

Rooms 90 en suite (4 fmly) ⊘ in 20 bedrooms S €55-€155; D €90-€260 (incl. bkfst) **Facilities** STV ⚡ supervised Sauna Gym Jacuzzi Beauty Salon ♫ Xmas **Conf** Thtr 260 Class 110 Board 45 Del from €150 **Services** Lift **Parking** 84 **Notes** LB ⊗ ⊘ in restaurant Closed 24-26 Dec

★★★ 79% **HOTEL**

Newpark

☎ 056 776 0500 📄 056 776 0555

e-mail: info@newparkhotel.com

dir: *on N77, Castlecomer-Durrow road*

This hotel offers a range of well-appointed rooms, to match the impressive foyer lounge, leisure club and other public areas. Renowned for the friendliness of the staff, there is also a choice of two dining rooms, The Bistro and Gulliver's, the more formal option.

Rooms 129 en suite (20 fmly) (52 GF) ⊘ in 86 bedrooms S €125-€165; D €180-€500 (incl. bkfst) **Facilities** STV ⚡ supervised Sauna Solarium Gym Jacuzzi Wi-fi available Plunge pool ♫ ch fac Xmas **Conf** Thtr 600 Class 250 Board 50 **Services** Lift **Parking** 350 **Notes** LB ⊗ ⊘ in restaurant

★★★ 70% **HOTEL**

Langtons

69 John St

☎ 056 776 5133 552 1728 📄 056 776 3693

e-mail: reservations@langtons.ie

dir: *take N9 & N10 from Dublin follow signs for city centre at outskirts of Kilkenny turn to left Langtons. 500mtrs on left after 1st set of lights*

Langton's has a long and well-founded reputation as an entertainment venue, nightclub and bar. A range of bedroom accommodation, many of which are in the garden annexe, complements these facilities. All are very comfortable tastefully decorated and well appointed. The busy restaurant is popular with visitors and locals alike.

Rooms 14 en suite 16 annexe en suite (4 fmly) (8 GF) **Facilities** STV ♫ **Conf** Thtr 600 Class 250 Board 50 **Parking** 60 **Notes** LB ⊗ ⊘ in restaurant Closed Good Fri, 25 Dec

★★★ 69% **HOTEL**

The Kilkenny Inn Hotel

15/15 Vicar St

☎ 056 7772828 📠 056 7761902

e-mail: info@kilkennyinn.com

dir: *take the N7/N9 from Dublin. From Rosslare take N25 to Waterford and N9 to Kilkenny*

Within walking distance of the heart of Kilkenny medieval city this hotel occupies a quite location with the added advantage of complimentary parking. Newly built and designed to incorporate traditional features with modern comforts the public areas include JB's bar and Grill Room Restaurant. Bedrooms are comfortable and stylishly appointed.

Rooms 30 en suite (7 fmly) ☺ in all bedrooms S €60-€100, D €100-€200 (incl. bkfst) **Facilities** STV Jacuzzi Xmas **Conf** Thtr 45 Class 18 Board 25 Del from €70 **Services** Lift **Parking** 25 **Notes LB** ⊛ ⊘ in restaurant

⊛ **RESTAURANT WITH ROOMS**

Lacken House & Restaurant

Dublin Rd

☎ 056 7761085 📠 056 7762435

e-mail: info@lackenhouse.ie

dir: *in city at start of N10 (Dublin-Carlow road)*

Located just five minutes' walk from Kilkenny City, this fine Victorian house offers comfortable accommodation in a friendly and relaxing atmosphere. The restaurant, open from Tuesday to Saturday, has an interesting menu using carefully chosen local produce. An ideal base to explore the historic sites of Kilkenny.

Rooms 10 en suite (2 fmly) (4 GF) ☺ in all bedrooms **Facilities** Spa STV **Conf** Thtr 25 Class 20 Board 12 **Parking** 25 **Notes LB** ⊛ ⊘ in restaurant Closed 24-26 Dec Civ Wed 40

THOMASTOWN   MAP 01 C3

INSPECTORS' CHOICE

★★★★ ⊛⊛ **COUNTRY HOUSE HOTEL**

Mount Juliet Conrad

☎ 056 777 3000 📠 056 777 3019

e-mail: info@mountjuliet.ie

dir: *M7 from Dublin, N9 towards Waterford then to Mount Juliet via Carlow and Gowran*

Mount Juliet Conrad is set in 1,500 acres of parkland with a Jack Nicklaus designed golf course and an equestrian centre. The elegant and spacious public areas retain much of the original architectural features including ornate plasterwork and Adam fireplaces. Bedrooms, in both the main house the Hunters Yard annexe, are comfortable and well appointed. Fine dining is on offer at Lady Helen, overlooking the river, and more casual dining is available in Kendels in the Hunters Yard, which also has a spa and health club.

Rooms 32 en suite 27 annexe en suite ☺ in 1 bedroom **Facilities** Spa STV ⊡ ⌿ 18 ⊰ Fishing Riding Snooker Sauna Gym ⊰ Putt green Spa Archery Cycling Clay pigeon shooting Golf tuition **Conf** Thtr 75 Class 40 Board 20 **Parking** 200 **Notes LB** ⊛ ⊘ in restaurant

CO LAOIS

PORTLAOISE   MAP 01 C3

★★★★ 73% **HOTEL**

The Heritage Hotel

Jessop St

☎ 057 8678588

The Heritage is situated in the town just off the N7. Public areas include a spacious lobby lounge, two bars and dining options, The Fitzmaurice where breakfast and dinner are served and Spago an Italian Bistro. Bedrooms are well appointed and there are extensive leisure and conference facilities, and an indoor secure car park.

Rooms 110 en suite (6 fmly) ☺ in 90 bedrooms **Facilities** Spa STV ⊡ supervised Sauna Gym Putt green Jacuzzi Wi-fi in bedrooms Health & fitness club, Beauty spa ♫ **Conf** BC Thtr 500 Class 300 Board 50 Del from €170 **Notes** ⊛ RS Good Friday

Ireland

CO LEITRIM

CARRICK-ON-SHANNON   MAP 01 C4

★★★★ 66% **HOTEL**

The Landmark

☎ 071 962 2222 📠 071 962 2233
e-mail: landmarkhotel@eircom.net
dir: from Dublin on N4 approaching Carrick-on-Shannon, take
1st exit at rdbt, hotel on right

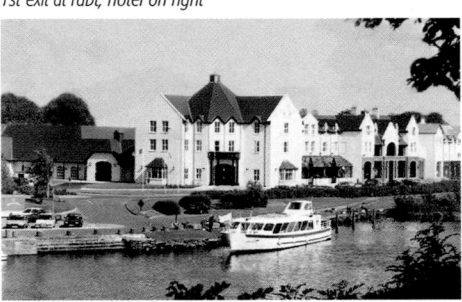

Overlooking the River Shannon, close to the Marina, this hotel offers
comfortable public areas and well-equipped bedrooms and suites.
Ferrari's Restaurant serves imaginative cusine, the Boardwalk café
serves food and drinks and there's the new Aroma Café for a variety
of coffees, teas and pastries. Pleasant staff will be pleased to arrange a
cruise, horse riding, golf and angling.

Rooms 50 en suite (4 fmly) ⊘ in 26 bedrooms S €119-€144;
D €190-€228 (incl. bkfst) **Facilities** STV Wi-fi available ♫ Xmas
Conf Thtr 550 Class 210 **Services** Lift **Parking** 100 **Notes LB** ⊗ ⊘ in
restaurant Closed 24-25 Dec RS 26-Dec

DRUMSHANBO   MAP 01 C4

Ⓤ

Ramada Hotel & Suites at Lough Allen

☎ 071 9640100 📠 071 9640101
e-mail: info@loughallenhotel.com
web: www.loughallenhotel.com

At the time of going to press, the star classification for this hotel was
not confirmed. Please refer to the AA internet site www.theAA.com for
current information.

Rooms 88 rms

CO LIMERICK

ADARE   MAP 01 B3

★★★★ 78% ⊛⊛ **HOTEL**

Dunraven Arms

☎ 061 396633 📠 061 396541
e-mail: reservations@dunravenhotel.com

This charming hotel was established in 1792 in the heart of one of
Ireland's prettiest villages. It is a traditional country inn both in style
and atmosphere. Comfortable lounges, spacious bedrooms, attractive
gardens, leisure and beauty facilities and good cuisine all add up to an
enjoyable visit at the hotel. Golf and equestrian activities are
specialities in Adare.

continued

Rooms 86 en suite (2 fmly) (40 GF) ⊘ in all bedrooms **Facilities** STV
🎾 supervised Fishing Riding Sauna Gym Jacuzzi Wi-fi in bedrooms
Beauty salon ♫ Xmas **Conf** Thtr 180 Class 60 Board 12 **Services** Lift
Parking 90 **Notes** ⊘ in restaurant

★★★ 68% **HOTEL**

Fitzgeralds Woodlands House Hotel

Knockanes

IRISH COUNTRY HOTELS

☎ 061 605100 📠 061 396073
e-mail: reception@woodlands-hotel.ie
dir: left at Lantern Lodge rdbt on N21 S of Limerick. Hotel 0.5m
on right

Located close to Adare, this family-run hotel is friendly and
welcoming. Bedrooms are well appointed. The comfortable public
areas include, Woodcock bar, Timmy Mac's traditional bar and bistro
and the Brennan Restaurant. There are extensive leisure and beauty
facilities. Close to Limerick Racecourse, Adare and many other golf
courses.

Rooms 92 en suite (36 fmly) **Facilities** STV 🎾 Sauna Solarium Gym
Jacuzzi Health & beauty salon Thermal spa ♫ ch fac **Conf** Thtr 400
Class 200 Board 50 **Services** air con **Parking** 290 **Notes LB** ⊗ Closed
24-25 Dec

LIMERICK   MAP 01 B3

★★★★ 78% ⊛ **HOTEL**

Castletroy Park

Dublin Rd

☎ 061 335566 📠 061 331117
e-mail: sales@castletroy-park.ie
dir: on N7 (Dublin road), 3m from Limerick city, 25mins from
Shannon Airport

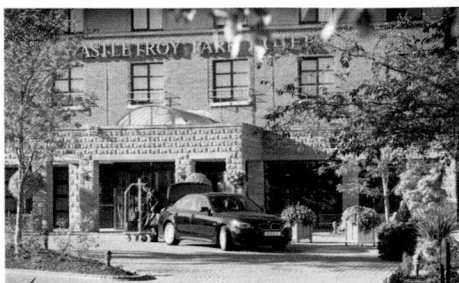

This fine modern hotel is close to the University of Limerick. Public
areas combine modern comforts with very attractive decor and

continued

Ireland

clude the Merry Pedler pub and the fine dining McLaughlins restaurant, which has a splendid view of the gardens and Clare Hills. edrooms are very well equipped to suit both leisure and business uests. There are extensive leisure and banqueting facilities.

ooms 107 en suite (78 fmly) ⊗ in 79 bedrooms S fr €180; D fr €205 ncl. bkfst) **Facilities** STV ⬚ supervised Sauna Gym Jacuzzi Wi-fi in edrooms Running track, Steam & Beauty Treatments Room/Massage herapy/Tanning Facility ♫ **Conf** BC Thtr 1000 Class 490 Board 192 Del om €180 **Services** Lift **Parking** 160 **Notes LB** ⊗ ⊗ in restaurant S 24-26 Dec

★★★★ 76% **HOTEL**

Radisson SAS

nnis Rd

☎ 061 456200 ▤ 061 327418

-mail: reservations.limerick@radissonsas.com

ir: on N18 (Ennis Road)

ituated between Limerick and Shannon International Airport this mart hotel has comfortable lounge areas and a choice of dining ptions; the contemporary styled Porters Restaurant offers fine dining, while more casual eating can be enjoyed in Heron's Irish Pub. edrooms are spacious and very well appointed. There is extensive eisure and corporate facilities.

ooms 154 en suite (7 fmly) ⊗ in 70 bedrooms S €99-€125; ▪ €115-€145 (incl. bkfst) **Facilities Spa** STV ⬚ supervised ♨ Sauna olarium Gym Wi-fi in bedrooms ♫ Xmas **Conf** BC Thtr 500 Class 250 oard 50 Del from €170 **Services** Lift air con **Parking** 300 **Notes** ⊗ ⊛ in restaurant

★★★★ 73% **HOTEL**

Clarion Hotel Limerick

teamboat Quay

☎ 061 444100 ▤ 061 444101

-mail: info@clarionhotellimerick.com

ir: From Shannon Airport take N18 W to city, follow Cork/Kerry xit on 1st rdbt. Over Shannon Bridge then 3rd exit onto Dock 'd. Hotel 1st right

he Clarion makes an imposing silhouette on Limerick's skyline, and as a spectacular location on the banks of the River Shannon. The ame sleek design is to be found throughout this 17 storey hotel, with ontemporary styling combining architectural mastery in the edrooms and public areas alike. Rooms vary in size and are all well ppointed. Some two-bedded apartments are available for those taying longer than a few nights.

ooms 123 en suite (14 fmly) ⊗ in 110 bedrooms S €120 €230; ▪ €140-€260 **Facilities** STV ⬚ supervised Sauna Gym Jacuzzi Wi-fi vailable Steam room, fully equipped leisure centre **Conf** Thtr 120 lass 70 Board 45 Del from €210 **Services** Lift air con **Notes LB** ⊗ ⊛ in restaurant Closed 24-25 Dec RS 26 Dec

★★★ 70% **HOTEL**

Hotel Greenhills

Caherdavin

☎ 061 453033 ▤ 061 453307

-mail: info@greenhillgroup.com

ir: on N18, approx 2m from city centre

ituated on the outskirts of Limerick, and set amongst its own andscaped grounds, the hotel is only a short drive from Shannon

continued

International Airport. Bedrooms are attractively decorated and well appointed. There is a traditional-style bar and comfortable lounge, a restaurant and impressive leisure and conference facilities.

Rooms 18 rms (13 en suite) (4 fmly) **Facilities** STV ⬚ ♨ Sauna Solarium Gym Jacuzzi Beauty parlour Massage ♫ **Conf** Thtr 500 Class 200 Board 50 **Parking** 150 **Notes LB** ⊗

★★★ 66% **HOTEL**

Jurys Inn Limerick

☷JURYS DOYLE
HOTELS

Lower Mallow St

☎ 061 207000 ▤ 061 400966

e-mail: info@jurysdoyle.com

web: www.jurysdoyle.com

dir: from N7 follow signs for City Centre into O'Connell St, turn off at N18 (Shannon/Galway), hotel is off O'Connell St

Conveniently situated in the shopping and business area overlooking the River Shannon this modern hotel has a spacious lobby, cosy bar, restaurant and boardroom for meetings. The 'one price' room rate and comfortable bedrooms ensure its popularity.

Rooms 151 en suite (108 fmly) (10 GF) ⊗ in 123 bedrooms **Facilities** STV **Conf** Thtr 50 Class 25 Board 18 **Services** Lift **Notes** ⊗ ⊛ in restaurant Closed 24-26 Dec

★★★ 66% **HOTEL**

Woodfield House

Ennis Rd

☎ 061 453022 ▤ 061 326755

e-mail: woodfieldhousehotel@eircom.net

dir: on outskirts of city on main Shannon road

This family-run hotel is situated on the N18 a short distance from the city centre and within easy reach of Shannon Airport. There is a relaxing atmosphere in the cosy traditional bar and patio beer garden. Bedrooms are comfortable and well appointed. Food is available in the bar all day, and dinner is served in the restaurant.

Rooms 26 en suite (3 fmly) (5 GF) **Facilities** STV ♨ **Conf** BC Thtr 130 Class 60 Board 60 **Services** air con **Parking** 80 **Notes** ⊗ Closed 24-25 Dec Civ Wed

BUDGET HOTEL

Travelodge Limerick

Ennis Rd, Clondrinagh

☎ 08700 850 950

Travelodge

web: www.travelodge.co.uk

Travelodge offers good quality, good value, modern accommodation. Ideal for families, the spacious en suite bedrooms include remote-control TV, tea and coffee-making facilities and comfortable beds. Meals can be taken at the nearby family restaurant. See Hotel Groups pages for further details.

Rooms 40 en suite S fr £26; D fr £26

Ireland

CO LOUTH

DROGHEDA
MAP 01 D4

★★★ 70% **HOTEL**

Boyne Valley Hotel & Country Club
Stameen, Dublin Rd
☎ 041 983 7737 ▤ 041 983 9188
e-mail: admin@boyne-valley-hotel.ie
dir: M1 towards Belfast, N of Dublin Airport on right

This historic mansion stands in 16 acres of mature gardens and woodlands on the outskirts of Drogheda. The new bedrooms are very smart and provide high standards of comfort. Public areas include relaxing lounges, Terrace bar, Cellar Bistro, extensive conference and banqueting facilities, a leisure centre and hard tennis courts.

Rooms 73 en suite (4 fmly) (26 GF) ✆ in 35 bedrooms **Facilities** Spa STV ▣ supervised ♨ Sauna Solarium Gym Jacuzzi Hot stone therapy ♫ **Conf** BC Thtr 500 Class 350 Board 25 **Services** Lift **Parking** 200 **Notes** LB ⊗ ✆ in restaurant Civ Wed 300

DUNDALK
MAP 01 D4

★★★★ 77% **HOTEL**

Ballymascanlon House
☎ 042 9358200 ▤ 042 9371598
e-mail: info@ballymascanlon.com

Best Western

dir: N of Dundalk take T62 to Carlingford. Hotel is approx 1km

This Victorian mansion is set in 130 acres of woodland at the foot of the Cooley Mountains. The original house, elegantly in design, and the modern extension make this a very comfortable hotel with some really stylish bedrooms. Public areas include a restaurant and spacious lounge and bar, and a well equipped leisure centre.

Rooms 90 en suite (11 fmly) (5 GF) ✆ in 28 bedrooms **Facilities** STV ▣ supervised ♨ 18 ♨ Sauna Gym Putt green Jacuzzi Steam room, Plunge pool, Massage ♫ **Conf** BC Thtr 300 Class 160 Board 75 **Services** Lift **Parking** 250 **Notes** LB ⊗ ✆ in restaurant

★★★ 69% **HOTEL**

Fairways Hotel
Dublin Rd
☎ 042 9321500 ▤ 042 9321511
e-mail: info@fairways.ie
dir: on N1 3km S of Dundalk

Situated south of Dundalk on the Castlebellingham road, this modern hotel is appointed to a high standard. A wide range of food is available all day in the carvery/grill, with a more formal dinner served in Modi's restaurant. Golf can be arranged by the hotel on a choice of nearby courses.

Rooms 101 en suite (2 fmly) (30 GF) ✆ in 30 bedrooms **Facilities** Spa STV ▣ supervised Sauna Gym Jacuzzi ♫ **Conf** BC Thtr 1000 Class 500 **Services** Lift **Parking** 700 **Notes** ⊗ ✆ in restaurant Closed 25 Dec

CO MAYO

ACHILL ISLAND
MAP 01 A4

★★★ 64% **HOTEL**

Achill Cliff House
Keel
☎ 098 43400 ▤ 098 43007
e-mail: info@achillcliff.com
web: www.achillcliff.com
dir: From Castlebar take Newport Rd, then onto Mulranny and R319 to Achill Sound. Hotel on right, in the village of Keel.

This family run hotel is situated on Achill Island, an unspoilt place made famous by painter Paul Henry and has a lot to offer those seeking relaxation, dramatic scenery, hill walking and historic interest. Bedrooms are comfortable and the popular restaurant serves local fish and lamb dishes.

Rooms 10 en suite (4 fmly) (2 GF) ✆ in all bedrooms S €40-€100; D €70-€120 (incl. bkfst) **Facilities** Sauna **Parking** 20 **Notes** LB ⊗ ✆ in restaurant Closed 23-26 Dec

BALLINA
MAP 01 B4

★★★ 74% ❀ **HOTEL**

Teach Iorrais
Geesala
☎ 097 86888 ▤ 097 86855
e-mail: teachior@iol.ie

Located in the heart of the Erris peninsula this is a warm friendly hotel offering spacious well appointed bedrooms. The public areas include a relaxing bar and a restaurant on the first floor where quality cuisine is served. A good base for golfers and anglers.

Rooms 31 en suite (2 fmly) (15 GF) **Facilities** STV ♫ **Conf** BC Thtr 300 Class 150 Board 80 **Services** air con **Parking** 85 **Notes** LB ⊗ ✆ in restaurant

CASTLEBAR
MAP 01 B4

★★ 64% **HOTEL**

Welcome Inn
☎ 094 902 2288 & 902 2054 ▤ 094 902 1766
e-mail: welcomeinn@eircom.net
dir: take N5 to Castlebar. Hotel near town centre, via ring road & rdbts past Church of the Holy Rosary

This town centre hotel offers a range of modern facilities behind its Tudor frontage, including a banqueting/conference centre. Bedrooms are comfortable and well equipped. Enjoyable food is served in
continued

Reynards Restaurant and there is a traditional style bar and a nightclub with disco at weekends.

Rooms 40 en suite (5 fmly) **Facilities** STV ♫ **Conf** Thtr 500 Class 350 **Services** Lift **Parking** 100 **Notes** LB ⊗ Closed 23-25 Dec

CONG
MAP 01 B4

★★★★★ 85% HOTEL

Ashford Castle

☎ 094 954 6003 📠 094 954 6260

e-mail: ashford@ashford.ie

dir: In village of Cross turn left at church signed for Cong and continue onto R345. Turn left at Ashford Castle sign through castle entrance gates.

Set in over 300 acres of beautifully grounds, this magnificent castle, dating from 1228, occupies a stunning position on the edge of Lough Corrib. Bedrooms vary in style but all benefit from a pleasing combination of character and charm and modern comforts. The hotel offers an extensive range of both indoor and outdoor leisure pursuits including falconry, golf, shooting, fishing and an equestrian centre.

Rooms 83 en suite (5 fmly) (22 GF) S €225-€1095; D €225-€1095 **Facilities** STV ♨9 ♥ Fishing Riding Sauna Gym Putt green Jacuzzi Archery Clay pigeon shooting Falconry Lake cruises Treatment rooms ♫ Xmas **Conf** Thtr 110 Class 65 Del from €260 **Services** Lift **Parking** 200 **Notes** LB ⊗ ⊘ in restaurant

FOXFORD
MAP 01 B4

★★ 88% ⊛ HOTEL

Healys Restaurant & Country House Hotel

Pontoon

☎ 094 9256443 📠 094 9256572

e-mail: info@healyspontoon.com

web: www.healyspontoon.com

This attractive creeper clad former shooting lodge is now a comfortable

continued

and friendly hotel with a great view of Lough Cullen. Both the bar and restaurant serve enjoyable meals. Bedrooms are cosy and comfortable.

Rooms 14 en suite (1 fmly) S €65; D €90 (incl. bkfst) **Facilities** Fishing ♫ Xmas **Parking** 300 **Notes** ⊗ ⊘ in restaurant Closed 25 Dec

KILTIMAGH
MAP 01 B4

★★★ 67% HOTEL

Cill Aodain

Main St

☎ 094 9381761 📠 094 9381838

e-mail: cillaodain@eircom.net

IRISH COUNTRY HOTELS

dir: in town centre

Situated in the heart of historic Kiltimagh, this hotel has been appointed in a smart, contemporary style and offers comfortable well-appointed bedrooms. Public areas include The Gallery Restaurant, Court Bar & Bistro. Easy on and off-street parking is available opposite the hotel. Close to Knock Shrine and the airport.

Rooms 17 en suite (4 fmly) ⊘ in 4 bedrooms S fr €58; D fr €79 (incl. bkfst) **Facilities** STV FTV Riding Xmas **Conf** 1hr 25 Class 24 Board 25 Del from €28 **Notes** LB ⊗ ⊘ in restaurant

KNOCK
MAP 01 B4

★★★ 69% HOTEL

Knock House

Ballyhaunis Rd

☎ 094 938 8088 📠 094 938 8044

e-mail: info@knockhousehotel.ie

dir: 0.5km from Knock village

Adjacent to the Marian Shrine and Basilica, this creatively designed limestone clad building is surrounded by landscaped gardens. Facilities include comfortable lounges and bedrooms, a dispense bar, conference rooms and an attractive restaurant where lunch and dinner is served. There are six rooms adapted to facilitate wheelchair users.

Rooms 68 en suite (12 fmly) (40 GF) **Conf** 1hr 150 Class 90 Board 45 **Services** Lift **Parking** 150 **Notes** LB ⊗ ⊘ in restaurant

★★★ 67% HOTEL

Belmont

☎ 094 938 8122 📠 094 938 8532

e-mail: reception@belmonthotel.ie

dir: on N17, Galway side of Knock. Turn right at Burke's supermarket & pub. Hotel 150yds on right

This hotel has an Old World charm and offers lounges, a traditional

continued on page 994

Ireland

KNOCK continued

bar, and the An Bialann Restaurant. Bedroom standards vary, all are well appointed and comfortable and there are specially adapted room for the less able. A natural health and fitness club offers a range of therapies. The hotel is close to the Marian Shrine and the Basilica.

Rooms 63 en suite (6 fmly) (12 GF) ⊘ in 13 bedrooms
Facilities Solarium Gym Jacuzzi Steamroom Natural health therapies, hydrotherapic bath ♫ **Conf** Thtr 500 Class 100 Board 20 **Services** Lift
Parking 110 **Notes LB** ⊗ ⊘ in restaurant

MULRANY   MAP 01 B4

[U]

Park Inn
☎ 098 36000 🖹 098 36899

e-mail: info.mulranny@rezidorparkinn.com

dir: R311 from Castlebar to Newport, onto N59. Hotel on right.

At the time of going to press, the star classification for this hotel was not confirmed. Please refer to the AA internet site www.theAA.com for current information.

Rooms 61 en suite (22 fmly) (36 GF) ⊘ in 58 bedrooms **Facilities** STV
🔲 supervised Snooker Sauna Solarium Gym Jacuzzi Canadian hot tub
♫ **Conf** Thtr 400 Class 140 Board 50 **Services** Lift **Notes LB** ⊗ ⊘ in restaurant Closed 24-26 Dec

NEWPORT   MAP 01 B4

★★★ 68% **HOTEL**

Hotel Newport
Main St
☎ 098 41155 🖹 098 42548

e-mail: info@hotelnewportmayo.com

At the time of going to press, the star classification for this hotel was not confirmed. Please refer to the AA internet site www.theAA.com for current information.

Rooms 30 en suite

WESTPORT   MAP 01 B3

★★★★ 78% ◉ **HOTEL**

Knockranny House Hotel
☎ 098 28600 🖹 098 28611

e-mail: info@khh.ie

dir: on N5 (Westport-Castlebar road)

Overlooking Westport with Clew Bay and Croagh Patrick in the distance, the reception rooms of this family-run hotel take full

continued

---

advantage of the lovely views. The luxurious furnishings create an inviting and relaxing atmosphere throughout the lounge, bar and restaurant. The spacious bedrooms are well appointed. There is a helicopter-landing pad in the well-maintained grounds, and a luxury SpaSalveo is a new addition.

Rooms 97 en suite (4 fmly) ⊘ in all bedrooms S €125-€175; D fr €200
(incl. bkfst) **Facilities Spa** STV Sauna Gym Jacuzzi Wi-fi in bedrooms ♫
Xmas Local leisure centre free to guests **Conf** Thtr 700 Class 400
Board 40 **Services** Lift **Parking** 120 **Notes LB** ⊗ ⊘ in restaurant
Closed 24-26 Dec

★★★ 82% **HOTEL**

Hotel Westport Leisure, Spa & Conference
Newport Rd
☎ 098 25122 🖹 098 26739

e-mail: reservations@hotelwestport.ie

dir: N5 to Westport, right at end of Castlebar St turn, 1st right, 1st left, follow to end

Located in private woodlands and just a short river walk to the town, this hotel offers welcoming public areas, a spacious restaurant and comfortable bedrooms. Both leisure and business guests are well catered for by the enthusiastic and friendly team.

Rooms 129 en suite (67 fmly) (42 GF) ⊘ in 86 bedrooms S fr €85;
D fr €130 (incl. bkfst) **Facilities Spa** STV 🔲 supervised Sauna Solarium
Gym Jacuzzi Wi-fi in bedrooms Children's pool Jet stream Lounger pool
Steam room ♫ ch fac Xmas **Conf** Thtr 500 Class 150 Board 60 Del from
€179 **Services** Lift **Parking** 220 **Notes LB** ⊗ ⊘ in restaurant

★★★ 75% ◉ **HOTEL**

Carlton Atlantic Coast
The Quay
☎ 098 29000 🖹 098 29111

e-mail: info@carltonatlanticcoasthotel.com

dir: from N5 follow signs into Westport then Louisburgh on R335. 1m from Westport

This distinctive hotel is in a former mill and has been renovated to a good contemporary standard with modern facilities. Many of the rooms have sea views, as has the award-winning restaurant on the fourth floor. The ground floor has comfortable lounge areas and a lively bar. Spa and treatment rooms have been added to the leisure centre. Parking available to the rear.

Rooms 85 en suite (6 fmly) ⊘ in 58 bedrooms S €70-€160;
D €110-€270 (incl. bkfst) **Facilities Spa** STV 🔲 supervised Sauna
Solarium Gym Treatment rooms, Health & beauty spa ♫ ch fac Xmas
Conf BC Thtr 180 Class 100 Board 70 **Services** Lift **Parking** 60
Notes ⊗ ⊘ in restaurant Closed 23-27 Dec

continued

Ireland

★★★ 68% HOTEL

Clew Bay Hotel
☎ 098 28088

IRISH COUNTRY HOTELS

dir: at bottom of James St (parallel to main street)

Newly extended and renovated, this long established, family-run hotel offers a range of comfortable well-appointed bedrooms together with some very smart public areas. Guest can dine in the Riverside Restaurant or in the very popular Madden's Bistro. Arrangements can be made for residents to use the nearby leisure centre.

Rooms 35 en suite (3 fmly) ⊛ in 5 bedrooms **Facilities** STV ♫ **Notes** Closed Xmas & New Year

★★★ 68% HOTEL

The Wyatt
The Octagon
☎ 098 25027 📠 098 26316
e-mail: info@wyatthotel.com

dir: Follow one-way system in town. Hotel by tall monument

This stylish, welcoming hotel is situated in the famous town centre Octagon. Bedrooms are attractively decorated and well equipped. Public areas are very comfortable with open fires and include a lively contemporary bar. There are two dining options, JW for bar food and The Wyatt Restaurant offering a more formal option.

Rooms 52 en suite (2 GF) ⊛ in 42 bedrooms S €55-€140; D €70-€220 (incl. bkfst) **Facilities** STV Complimentary use of nearby leisure park ♫ **Conf** BC Thtr 300 Class 200 Board 80 Del from €155 **Services** Lift air con **Parking** 20 **Notes** LB ⊗ ⊘ in restaurant Closed 25-26 Dec

★★ 67% HOTEL

The Westport Inn
Mill St
☎ 098 29200 📠 098 29250
e-mail: info@westportinn.ie

dir: In town centre

Situated in the centre of Westport town close to the shops and many pubs, and ideal for visiting Westport leisure centre, beaches and many golf courses near by. Bedrooms are traditional in style and public areas are comfortable. There is a lively bar with entertainment at weekends.

Rooms 34 en suite ⊛ in 4 bedrooms **Facilities** ♫ **Conf** Thtr 100 Class 50 Board 40 **Services** Lift **Parking** 19 **Notes** ⊗ ⊘ in restaurant Closed 24-26 Dec

CO MEATH

KELLS
MAP 01 C4

★★★ 72% HOTEL

Headfort Arms
Headfort Place
☎ 0818 222800 & 046 924 0063 📠 046 924 0587
e-mail: info@headfortarms.ie

IRISH COUNTRY HOTELS

dir: on N3 between Dublin and Donegal

Situated in the famous heritage town of Kells, the Duff family run a very smart hotel. Now refurbished to a high standard, there are comfortable lounges with open log fires, a café carvery, Vanilla Pod

continued

Brassiere, traditional pub, banqueting facilities and treatment rooms. The bedrooms are impressively appointed.

Headfort Arms

Rooms 45 en suite (5 fmly) ⊛ in 32 bedrooms S €60-€105; D €100-€220 (incl. bkfst) **Facilities Spa** STV ♫ Xmas **Conf** Thtr 400 Class 200 Board 30 Del from €75 **Services** Lift **Parking** 45 **Notes LB** ⊗ ⊘ in restaurant

DUNBOYNE
MAP 01 D4

★★★★ 78% HOTEL

Dunboyne Castle Hotel & Spa
☎ 01 801 3500 📠 01 436 6801
e-mail: info@dunboynecastlehotel.com

dir: In Dunboyne take R157 towards Maynooth. Hotel on left.

With a history dating back as far as the 13th century, this mid-Georgian house has been renovated and expanded into a fine hotel, with a number of bars and dining options. Bedrooms and suites are contemporary in style, with a choice of lounges including a formal drawing room and an atmospheric bar in the original cellar.

Rooms 145 en suite (36 GF) ⊛ in 100 bedrooms S €115-€180; D €145-€240 (incl. bkfst) **Facilities Spa** STV Sauna Gym Jacuzzi ♫ Xmas **Conf** BC Thtr 600 Class 300 Board 40 Del from €170 **Services** Lift air con **Parking** 300 **Notes LB** ⊗ ⊘ in restaurant

ENFIELD
MAP 01 C4

★★★★ 77% HOTEL

Marriott Johnstown House Hotel & Spa
☎ 046 9540000 📠 046 9540001
e-mail: info@johnstownhouse.com
web: www.marriott.johnstownhouse.com

Marriott HOTELS & RESORTS

This hotel is developed around a Georgian listed mansion situated in 120 acres of parkland and landscaped gardens. The reception hall and

continued on page 996

Ireland

ENFIELD *continued*

library reflect the elegance of the 18th-century design. There are hi-tech conference facilities, comfortable bedrooms and suites, two restaurants and bars plus an extensive spa with treatment facilities and boutiques.

Rooms 126 en suite (8 fmly) (41 GF) ⊘ in 83 bedrooms S €145-€365; D €200-€380 (incl. bkfst) **Facilities** Spa STV FTV ⏏ supervised Fishing Sauna Gym Jacuzzi Golf simulator Wi-fi available ♫ Xmas **Conf** BC Thtr 900 Class 400 Board 50 Del from €223 **Services** Lift air con **Parking** 350 **Notes** LB ⊗ ⊘ in restaurant

★★★ 70% **HOTEL**

The Hamlet Court Hotel

Johnstownbridge
☎ 046 954 1200 ▤ 046 954 1704
e-mail: info@thehamlet.ie

dir: After toll bridge take first exit at Kilcock on M4. Left then right at rdbt, hotel in 0.5km on left

This newly built hotel has been developed to the rear of the long established Hamlet bar and lounge. It features very comfortable bedrooms, relaxing lounge and the Sabayon Restaurant where food standards are very good. This is an ideal location for those with an interest in horseracing and golf. It is also a popular wedding venue.

Rooms 30 en suite (2 fmly) (19 GF) ⊘ in 20 bedrooms S €60-€100; D €120-€180 (incl. bkfst) **Facilities** STV Fishing Riding ♫ Xmas **Conf** Thtr 350 Class 240 Board 80 Del from €90 **Services** Lift **Parking** 320 **Notes** LB ⊗ ⊘ in restaurant

---

KILMESSAN   MAP 01 C/D4

★★★ 72% ⊛ **HOTEL**

The Station House Hotel

☎ 046 9025239 ▤ 046 9025588
e-mail: info@thestationhousehotel.com

dir: M50, N3 towards Navan. At Dunshaughlin turn left at end of village, follow signs

The Station House saw its last train in 1963, and is now a comfortable, family-run hotel with a popular restaurant. The Carriage House was refurbished and bedrooms added; the Signal Box houses a suite. There is a sun terrace and conference/banqueting suite.

Rooms 6 en suite 14 annexe en suite (3 fmly) (5 GF) ⊘ in 15 bedrooms S €85-€130; D €130-€240 (incl. bkfst) **Facilities** ♫ ch fac Xmas **Conf** BC Thtr 400 Class 300 Board 100 Del from €165 **Parking** 200 **Notes** LB ⊗ ⊘ in restaurant

---

CO MONAGHAN

CARRICKMACROSS   MAP 01 C4

★★★★ 79% ⊛⊛⊛ **HOTEL**

Nuremore

☎ 042 9661438 ▤ 042 9661853
e-mail: info@nuremore.com

dir: 3km S of Carrickmacross, on N2 (Dublin to Derry road)

Overlooking its own golf course and lakes, the Nuremore is a quiet retreat with excellent facilities. Public areas are spacious and include an indoor pool and gym. Ray McArdle's food in the restaurant continues to impress, with an imaginative range of dishes on offer.

Rooms 72 en suite (4 fmly) ⊘ in 30 bedrooms S €150-€230; D €250-€310 (incl. bkfst) **Facilities** Spa STV FTV ⏏ ♨ 18 ♨ Fishing Snooker Sauna Solarium Gym Putt green Wi-fi in bedrooms Beauty treatments, Aromatherapy, Massage ♫ Xmas **Conf** BC Thtr 250 Class 100 Board 30 Del from €200 **Services** Lift **Parking** 200 **Notes** LB ⊗ ⊘ in restaurant

---

MONAGHAN   MAP 01 C5

Ⓤ

Hillgrove

Old Armagh Rd
☎ 047 4781288 ▤ 047 4784951
e-mail: info@hillgrovehotel.com

dir: turn off N2 at Cathedral, 400mtrs, hotel on left

At the time of going to press, the star classification for this hotel was not confirmed. Please refer to the AA internet site www.theAA.com for current information.

Rooms 44 en suite (3 fmly) (9 GF) ⊘ in 7 bedrooms **Facilities** STV ⏏ supervised Jacuzzi ♫ **Conf** BC Thtr 1800 Class 900 Board 400 **Services** Lift air con **Parking** 430 **Notes** LB ⊗ ⊘ in restaurant Closed 25 Dec

---

CO OFFALY

TULLAMORE   MAP 01 C4

BUDGET HOTEL

Days Hotel Tullamore

Main St
☎ 0163 91136 ▤ 057 9320350
e-mail: info@dayshoteltullamore.com
web: www.welcomebreak.co.uk

DAYS INN

dir: Take N6 to Kilbeggon, then N52 to Tullamore town centre. Take right at 2nd set of lights after canal. Turn left after Ganda Station & into Main St.

This modern building offers accommodation in smart, spacious and well-equipped bedrooms, suitable for families and business travellers, and all with en suite bathrooms. Continental breakfast is available and other refreshments may be taken at the nearby family restaurant. For further details see the Hotel Groups page.

Rooms 62 en suite

Ireland

CO ROSCOMMON

ROSCOMMON
MAP 01 B4

★★★ 75% **HOTEL**

Abbey
Galway Rd

☎ 090 662 6240 🖷 090 662 6021

e-mail: info@abbeyhotel.ie

IRISH COUNTRY HOTELS

dir: on main Galway Rd

The Grealy family has restored this fine manor house with great care and attention to detail. The spacious bedrooms are tastefully furnished, individually designed and overlook the magnificent gardens. The smart bar and Terrace Restaurant have views of the 12th-century Dominican abbey, and the carvery is very popular at lunchtime. There are extensive leisure and conference facilities.

Rooms 50 en suite (5 fmly) (10 GF) ⊘ in 35 bedrooms S €70-€125, D €120-€130 (incl. bkfst) **Facilities** ℝ supervised Sauna Solarium Gym Jacuzzi Xmas **Conf** 1hr 250 Class 140 Board 50 **Services** Lift **Parking** 100 **Notes LB** ⊗ Closed 25-26 Dec

RESTAURANT WITH ROOMS

Gleesons Townhouse & Restaurant
Market Square

☎ 090 662 6954 🖷 090 662 7425

e-mail: info@gleesonstownhouse.com

This 19th-century cut-limestone town house has been very tastefully restored. The bedrooms are decorated and furnished to a high standard. Dinner is served nightly in the Manse Restaurant and there is an extensive lunch and afternoon tea menu in the café or in the beautifully landscaped front courtyard. Conference facilities and secure parking are both available.

Rooms 19 en suite (1 fmly) ⊘ in 6 bedrooms **Facilities** STV Jacuzzi **Conf** BC Thtr 80 Class 30 Board 34 **Parking** 25 **Notes** ⊘ in restaurant Closed 25 Dec RS Good Fri

CO SLIGO

SLIGO
MAP 01 B5

★★★ 76% **HOTEL**

Sligo Park
Pearse Rd

☎ 071 9190400 🖷 071 916 9556

e-mail: sligo@leehotels.com

dir: On N4 to Sligo take 1st exit Carrowroe/R287 and follow signs for Sligo. Hotel 1m ahead on right

Set on seven acres on the southern side of town, off the Carrowroe interchange, this hotel is well positioned for touring the many attractions of the northwest and Yeats' Country. Bedrooms are spacious and appointed to a high standard. There are two dining options, good leisure and banqueting facilities.

Rooms 137 en suite (10 fmly) (45 GF) ⊘ in 60 bedrooms S €79-€100; D €98-€234 (incl. bkfst) **Facilities** STV FTV ℝ supervised ⊰ Sauna Gym Jacuzzi Wi-fi in bedrooms Steam room, Holistic treatment centre, Plunge pool ♫ Xmas **Conf** Thtr 520 Class 290 Board 80 **Del** from €100 **Services** Lift **Parking** 200 **Notes LB** ⊗ ⊘ in restaurant RS 24-26 Dec

Ⓤ

The Clarion Hotel Sligo
Ballinode

☎ 071 911 9000 & 911 9006 🖷 071 911 9001

e-mail: info@clarionhotelsligo.com

dir: On N side of Sligo off Enniskillen Rd (N16). Hotel opposite Sligo Institute of Technology

At the time of going to press, the star classification for this hotel was not confirmed. Please refer to the AA internet site www.theAA.com for current information.

Rooms 167 en suite (91 fmly) (47 GF) ⊘ in 115 bedrooms **Facilities Spa** STV ℝ supervised Sauna Gym Jacuzzi Gym classes ♫ ch fac **Conf** BC Thtr 500 Class 300 Board 80 **Services** Lift **Parking** 250 **Notes LB** ⊘ in restaurant Civ Wed 250

CO TIPPERARY

CASHEL
MAP 01 C3

★★★★ 80% ⑧ **HOTEL**

Cashel Palace Hotel
☎ 062 62707 🖷 062 61521

e-mail: reception@cashel-palace.ie

dir: On N8 through town centre, hotel on main street near lights

The Rock of Cashel, floodlit at night, forms a dramatic backdrop to this fine 18th-century house. Once an archbishop's palace, it is elegantly furnished with antiques and fine art. The drawing room has garden access and luxurious bedrooms in the main house are very comfortable; those in the adjacent mews are ideal for families.

Rooms 13 en suite 10 annexe en suite (8 fmly) ⊘ in 5 bedrooms **Facilities** STV Fishing Private path walk to the Rock of Cashel ♫ **Conf** Thtr 80 Class 45 Board 40 **Services** Lift **Parking** 35 **Notes LB** ⊗ Closed 2 weeks in Xmas - Jan

CLONMEL
MAP 01 C2

★★★ 79% **HOTEL**

Hotel Minella
☎ 052 22388 🖷 052 24381

e-mail: hotelminella@eircom.net

IRISH COUNTRY HOTELS

dir: Hotel S of River Suir

This family-run hotel is set on 9 acres of well-tended gardens on the banks of the Suir River. Originating from the 1860s, the public areas include a cocktail bar and a range of lounges; some of the bedrooms are particularly spacious. The leisure centre in the grounds is noteworthy. Two-bedroom holiday homes are also available.

Rooms 70 en suite (8 fmly) (14 GF) ⊘ in 16 bedrooms **Facilities** STV ℝ ⊰ Fishing Sauna Gym ⊰ Jacuzzi Aerobics room **Conf** Thtr 500 Class 300 Board 20 **Services** Lift **Parking** 100 **Notes LB** ⊗ ⊘ in restaurant Closed 24-28 Dec

Ireland

DUNDRUM
MAP 01 C3

★★★ 76% **HOTEL**

Dundrum House
☎ 062 71116 📠 062 71366

This Georgian mansion dates from 1730 and was tastefully restored by the Crowe family. Bedrooms vary in style and are comfortably furnished, rooms in the original house with antique pieces and the newer rooms feature a modern theme. There are relaxing lounges with open fires and a fine dining room, with more informal food available in the golf club. The extensive facilities include a leisure centre and an 18-hole championship golf course.

Rooms 55 en suite (6 fmly) **Facilities** no TV in bdrms 🎣 Fishing Snooker ch fac **Services** Lift **Parking** 300 **Notes** ⊗

ROSCREA
MAP 01 C3

★★★ 70% **HOTEL**

Racket Hall Country Golf & Conference Hotel
Dublin Rd
☎ 0505 21748 📠 0505 23701
e-mail: racketh@iol.ie

Ideally situated on the N7 just outside the heritage town of Roscrea, this long established house has been a popular stopping point for travellers for many years. It has well-equipped bedrooms. Lilly Bridges' bar offers food from early morning till late in the evening, with more formal fare in the restaurant.

Rooms 40 en suite

CO WATERFORD

DUNGARVAN
MAP 01 C2

★★★ 63% **HOTEL**

Lawlors
☎ 058 41122 & 41056 📠 058 41000
e-mail: info@lawlorshotel.com
dir: off N25

This town centre hotel enjoys a busy local trade especially in the bar where food is served throughout the day. The restaurant offers a wide choice of menu. Many of the bedrooms are spacious. Conference and meeting rooms are available. Public parking is near by.

Rooms 89 en suite (8 fmly) **Facilities** ♫ Xmas **Conf** Thtr 420 Class 215 Board 420 **Services** Lift **Notes** ⊘ in restaurant Closed 25 Dec

TRAMORE
MAP 01 C2

★★★ 68% **HOTEL**

Majestic
☎ 051 381761 📠 051 381766
e-mail: info@majestic-hotel.ie
dir: turn off N25 through Waterford onto R675 to Tramore. Hotel is on right, opposite lake

A warm welcome awaits visitors to this long established family friendly hotel in the holiday resort of Tramore. Many of the comfortable and well-equipped bedrooms have sea views.

Rooms 60 en suite (4 fmly) ⊗ in all bedrooms **Facilities** STV Free access to Splashworld swimming pool & leisure club ♫ ch fac **Services** Lift **Parking** 10 **Notes LB** ⊗ ⊘ in restaurant Civ Wed 250

WATERFORD
MAP 01 C2

INSPECTORS' CHOICE

★★★★ ⍟⍟ **HOTEL**

Waterford Castle
The Island
☎ 051 878203 📠 051 879316
e-mail: info@waterfordcastle.com
dir: from city centre, turn onto Dunmore East Rd, 1.5m, pass hospital, 0.5m left after lights, ferry at bottom of road

This enchanting and picturesque castle dates back to Norman times and is located on a 320-acre island just a five minute journey from the mainland by chain-link ferry. Bedrooms vary in style and size, but all are individually decorated and offer high standards of comfort. Dinner is served in the oak-panelled Munster Room, with breakfast taken in the conservatory. The 18-hole golf course is set in beautiful parkland where deer can be seen.

Rooms 19 en suite (2 fmly) ⊗ in all bedrooms S €160-€245; D €195-€380 **Facilities** STV ⌀ 18 🎣 ⛳ Putt green Clay pigeon shooting, archery ♫ Xmas **Conf** BC Thtr 30 Board 15 **Services** Lift **Parking** 50 **Notes LB** ⊗ ⊘ in restaurant RS 1st wk Jan-Feb

★★★★ 74% **HOTEL**

Faithlegg House
Faithlegg
☎ 051 382000 📠 051 382010
e-mail: reservations@fhh.ie

Faithlegg House is surrounded by a championship golf course, overlooking the estuary of the River Suir. The restored house has 14 original bedrooms, with the balance in a modern block to the side.
continued

Ireland

Comprehensive meeting facilities are provided together with a range of comfortable lounges. The leisure and treatment rooms are the perfect way to work off the excesses of the food offered in the Roseville Restaurant.

Rooms 82 rms **Facilities** STV 🔲 supervised ♨ 18 ☯ Sauna Gym Putt green Jacuzzi 🎵 **Conf** BC **Services** Lift **Parking** 100 **Notes LB** ⊗ ⊘ in restaurant Civ Wed 130

★★★ 79% ◉ HOTEL

Athenaeum House

Christendon, Ferrybank
☎ 051 833 999 📠 051 833 977
e-mail: info@athenaeumhousehotel.com

dir: N25 to Wexford, through 1st traffic lights, turn right and continue turning right into Abbey Rd. Take 1st right after bridge, hotel on right.

Set in 10 acres of parkland, this new hotel was originally built in the 18th century. The public rooms have been sympathetically restored in keeping with the age of the building, yet with a contemporary twist. Four bedrooms are in the main house with the others in a well-designed block on the side, accessed by a glazed link. Zak's is the bright airy restaurant where innovative food is served.

Rooms 29 en suite (5 GF) ⊘ in all bedrooms S €99-€170; D €100-€283 **Facilities** STV Wi fi in bedrooms 🎵 Xmas **Conf** Thtr 40 Class 35 Board 45 Del from €150 **Services** Lift **Parking** 35 **Notes LB** ⊗ ⊘ in restaurant Closed 24-26 Dec

★★★ 78% HOTEL

Granville

The Quay
☎ 051 305555 📠 051 305566
e-mail: stay@granville-hotel.ie

dir: take N25 to waterfront, city centre, opp Clock Tower

Centrally located on the quayside, this long established hotel has been extensively refurbished to a very high standard, while still keeping its true character. The bedrooms come in a choice of standard or executive, and are all well equipped and very comfortable. Friendliness and hospitality are hallmark of a stay here.

continued

Rooms 100 en suite (5 fmly) ⊘ in 20 bedrooms S €77.50-€150; D €140-€220 (incl. bkfst) **Facilities** STV 🎵 Xmas **Conf** Thtr 200 Class 150 Board 30 Del from €135 **Services** Lift **Parking** 300 **Notes LB** ⊗ ⊘ in restaurant Closed 25-26 Dec

★★★ 75% HOTEL

Tower

TOWER HOTEL GROUP

The Mall
☎ 051 875801 & 862300 📠 051 870129
e-mail: info@thw.ie

dir: opp Reginald's Tower in town centre. Hotel at end of quay on N25

An extensive refurbishment programme has given this long established hotel a new look that includes two smart restaurants, a riverside bar and upgraded bedrooms together with three river view suites. At the time of inspection the leisure centre was about to undergo further development. Good parking is provided at the rear.

Rooms 139 en suite (20 fmly) ⊘ in 85 bedrooms **Facilities** 🔲 supervised Sauna Solarium Gym Jacuzzi 🎵 **Conf** BC **Thtr** 500 Class 250 Board 80 **Services** Lift **Parking** 100 **Notes LB** ⊗ ⊘ in restaurant Closed 24-28 Dec

★★★ 73% HOTEL

Dooley's

30 The Quay
☎ 051 873531 📠 051 870262
e-mail: hotel@dooleys-hotel.ie

dir: on N25

Situated on the Quay in Waterford overlooking the River Suir and facing a convenient public car park. This family run hotel offers friendly and relaxed atmosphere the contemporary public areas include the New Ship Restaurant, more casual dining is available in the Dry Dock Bar. Bedrooms are comfortable and well appointed.

Rooms 113 en suite (3 fmly) ⊘ in 75 bedrooms S €70-€130; D €60-€99 (incl. bkfst) **Facilities** STV Wi-fi available Land & water based activities 🎵 **Conf** Thtr 240 Class 150 Board 100 **Services** Lift **Notes LB** ⊗ ⊘ in restaurant Closed 25-27 Dec

★★★ 70% HOTEL

Waterford Manor

Killotteran, Butlerstown
☎ 051 377814 📠 051 354545
e-mail: sales@waterfordmanorhotel.ie

dir: N25 from Waterford to Cork, right 2m after Waterford Crystal, left at end of road, hotel on right

Dating back to 1730 this manor house is set in delightful landscaped

continued on page 1000

Ireland

WATERFORD *continued*

and wooded grounds. The hotel provides high quality accommodation as well as extensive conference and banqueting facilities. Public areas include a charming drawing room and restaurant for intimate dining, plus a brasserie with its own bar that serves a carvery lunch daily.

Rooms 21 en suite (3 fmly) ⊘ in all bedrooms **Facilities** STV ♨
Conf BC Thtr 600 Class 300 Board 40 **Parking** 400 **Notes** ⊗ ⊘ in restaurant RS 25 Dec

BUDGET HOTEL

Travelodge Waterford

Cork Rd

☎ 08700 850 950 📄 051 358890
web: www.travelodge.co.uk

dir: on N25, 1km from Waterford Glass Visitors Centre

Travelodge offers good quality, good value, modern accommodation. Ideal for families, the spacious en suite bedrooms include remote-control TV, tea and coffee-making facilities and comfortable beds. Meals can be taken at the nearby family restaurant. See Hotel Groups pages for further details.

Rooms 32 en suite S fr £26; D fr £26

CO WESTMEATH

ATHLONE   MAP 01 C4

★★★★ 74% ❀ HOTEL

Hodson Bay

Hodson Bay

☎ 090 6442000 📄 090 6442020
e-mail: info@hodsonbayhotel.com

dir: from N6 take N61 to Roscommon. Turn right. Hotel 1km on Lough Rea

On the shores of Lough Ree, just 4km from Athlone, this hotel has its own marina and is surrounded by the golf course. Spacious public areas are comfortable, with a carvery bar, an attractive restaurant and excellent conference and banqueting facilities. The spacious bedrooms have been designed to take in the magnificent lake views. New developments include upgraded bedrooms, leisure centre and spa treatment rooms.

Rooms 133 en suite (23 fmly) (12 GF) ⊘ in 3 bedrooms **Facilities** STV 🔄 supervised ♪ 18 Fishing Sauna Gym Steam room, play room, beauty salon ♫ **Conf** Thtr 700 Class 250 Board 200 **Services** Lift **Parking** 300
Notes LB ⊗ ⊘ in restaurant

See advert on opposite page

★★★ 74% HOTEL

Glasson Golf Hotel & Country Club

Glasson

☎ 090 6485120 📄 090 6485444
e-mail: info@glassongolf.ie

dir: 6m N of Athlone on N55

Superb new bedrooms have been developed here, many of them making the most of the lake views. Set in the heart of a golf course, the overall feeling at the hotel is of a comfortable and welcoming club. Work is being planned to further develop the restaurant and other public areas.

Rooms 29 en suite (13 fmly) **Facilities** STV ♪ 21 Putt green
Conf Thtr 120 Class 50 Board 30 **Services** Lift **Parking** 150 **Notes** ⊗

❀ RESTAURANT WITH ROOMS

Wineport Lodge

Glasson

☎ 090 643 9010 📄 090 648 5471
e-mail: lodge@wineport.ie

dir: from N6 (Dublin/Galway road) take N55 north (Longford/Cavan exit) at Athlone. Left at Dog & Duck pub. Lodge 1m on left

In an enviable location, three miles north of Athlone on the shores of the inner lakes of Lough Rea on the Shannon. Guests can arrive by road or water, and dine on the deck or in the attractive dining room. The cuisine is both wholesome and innovative, using the best of local produce. There are ten luxurious lakeshore bedrooms with balconies - the perfect setting for breakfast.

Rooms 10 en suite ⊘ in all bedrooms **Facilities** STV Massage, boat hire ch fac **Conf** Thtr 50 Class 30 Board 20 **Services** air con **Parking** 60
Notes LB ⊗ ⊘ in restaurant Closed 24-26 Dec

MULLINGAR   MAP 01 C4

★★★★ 73% HOTEL

Mullingar Park

Dublin Rd

☎ 044 44446 & 37500 📄 044 35937
e-mail: info@mullingarparkhotel.com

Just 2km from Mullingar towards Dublin, this hotel has much to offer. Spacious public areas, flexible banqueting suites and a well-equipped leisure centre are complemented by comfortably appointed bedrooms. The friendly staff are very guest focussed. The Terrace Restaurant is particularly popular for its lunch buffet.

Rooms 95 en suite (12 fmly) ⊘ in 28 bedrooms S €85-€105; D €130-€190 (incl. bkfst) **Facilities** Spa STV 🔄 supervised Sauna Solarium Gym Jacuzzi Wi-fi in bedrooms Aerobic studio, children's pool, hydrotherapy pool **Conf** Thtr 1000 Class 750 Board 40 Del from €160
Services Lift **Parking** 500 **Notes LB** ⊗ ⊘ in restaurant Closed 24-25 Dec RS 26-Dec Civ Wed 500

★★★ 73% HOTEL

Bloomfield House

Belvedere

☎ 044 40894 📄 044 43767
e-mail: info@bloomfieldhouse.com

Located in lovely parkland overlooking Lough Ennell on the southern outskirts of Mullingar town. Bedrooms vary in style with the wing and

continued

suites enjoying the spectacular views. Public areas include comfortable relaxing lounges with open fires, informal food is available from the bar/carvery, while the smart restaurant serves dinner nightly. There are extensive leisure/spa and banqueting facilities.

Rooms 111 en suite (8 fmly) ⊗ in 24 bedrooms **Facilities Spa** STV 🔄 supervised Sauna Solarium Gym Jacuzzi ch fac **Conf** BC Thtr 500 Class 350 Board 12 **Services** Lift **Parking** 500 **Notes LB** ⊗ ⊘ in restaurant Closed 24-26 Dec

CO WEXFORD

BUNCLODY
MAP 01 D3

★★★★ 76% **HOTEL**

Carlton Millrace
☎ 054 75100 📠 054 75124
e-mail: info@millrace.ie

Located on the edge of the picturesque town of Bunclody, this hotel offers well-appointed bedrooms and smartly presented public areas, not least of which is the rooftop Lady Lucy restaurant. Separate spa and leisure centres are also a feature. Some self-catering family suites are available.

Rooms 72 en suite (12 fmly) ⊗ in 38 bedrooms **Facilities Spa** STV 🔄 supervised Fishing Sauna Solarium Gym Jacuzzi ♫ ch fac **Conf** Thtr 250 Class 100 Board 50 **Services** Lift air con **Notes** ⊗ ⊘ in restaurant Closed 23-26 Dec

COURTOWN HARBOUR
MAP 01 D3

★★★ 63% **HOTEL**

Courtown
☎ 055 25210 & 25108 📠 055 25304
e-mail: info@courtownhotel.com
dir: Turn left on approach to Gorey, 5km on left

Situated in the town centre, near to the beach and an 18 hole golf course, this family run hotel offers relaxing public areas. There is a comfortable lounge, spacious bar and an attractive restaurant and the leisure centre includes a swimming pool, gym and solarium.

Rooms 21 en suite (4 fmly) **Facilities** 🔄 supervised ♨ Squash Sauna Solarium Gym Jacuzzi Steam room, Massage, Crazy golf ♫ **Parking** 10 **Notes LB** ⊗ Closed mid Nov - early Mar

ENNISCORTHY
MAP 01 D3

★★★ 67% **HOTEL**

Treacy's
Templeshannon
☎ 054 37798 📠 054 37733
e-mail: info@treacyshotel.com
dir: N11 into Enniscorthy, over bridge in left lane. Hotel on right

This modern hotel is family run and conveniently located near the town centre. There is a choice of dining options in the Chang Thai and Begenal Harvey restaurants, with Benedict's super-pub open at weekends. Guests have complimentary use of the nearby car park and Waterfront Leisure centre.

Rooms 59 en suite (3 fmly) ⊗ in 11 bedrooms S €50-€90; D €90-€160 (incl. bkfst) **Facilities** STV 🔄 supervised Sauna Gym Discount at adjacent leisure complex Steam Room, Kids' Club (certain weeks in the year) ♫ ch fac **Services** Lift **Parking** 70 **Notes LB** ⊗ ⊘ in restaurant Closed 23-25 Dec

GOREY
MAP 01 D3

★★★★ 73% ❀ **HOTEL**

Ashdown Park Hotel
The Coach Rd
☎ 053 9480500 📠 053 94777
e-mail: info@ashdownparkhotel.com
dir: from N11, on approaching Gorey, 1st left before railway bridge, hotel on left

Situated on an elevated position overlooking the town, this modern hotel has excellent health, leisure and banqueting facilities. There are comfortable lounges and two dining options - the popular carvery bar and first-floor fine dining restaurant. Bedrooms are spacious and well equipped. Close to golf, beaches and hill walking.

Rooms 79 en suite (12 fmly) (20 GF) S €110-€150; D €170-€210 (incl. bkfst) **Facilities** 🔄 supervised Sauna Gym Jacuzzi Wi-fi available Steam & Therapy rooms, Beauty salon ♫ **Conf** Thtr 800 Class 315 Board 100 Del €160 **Services** Lift **Parking** 150 **Notes LB** ⊗ ⊘ in restaurant

Ireland

GOREY *continued*

★★★ ◉◉ **COUNTRY HOUSE HOTEL**

Marlfield House

☎ 055 21124 ▤ 055 21572

e-mail: info@marlfieldhouse.ie

dir: *1.5 hrs S of Dublin off N11, 1m outside Gorey on Courtown Road*

RELAIS & CHATEAUX

This Regency-style building has been sympathetically extended and developed into an excellent hotel. An atmosphere of elegance and luxury permeates every corner of the house, underpinned by truly friendly yet professional service led by the Bowe family who are always in evidence. The bedrooms are decorated in keeping with the style of the house, with some really spacious rooms and suites on the ground floor. Dinner in the restaurant is always a highlight of a stay at Marlfield.

Rooms 20 en suite (3 fmly) (6 GF) ⊘ in all bedrooms
Facilities STV ⊰ Sauna ⊌ **Conf** Thtr 60 Board 20 **Parking** 50
Notes LB ⊘ in restaurant Closed 15 Dec-30 Jan

NEW ROSS   MAP 01 C3

★★★ 70% **HOTEL**

Cedar Lodge

Carrigbyrne, Newbawn

☎ 051 428386 ▤ 051 428222

e-mail: cedarlodge@eircom.net

web: www.cedarlodgewexford.com

IRISH COUNTRY HOTELS

dir: *On N25 between Wexford and New Ross*

Cedar sits in a tranquil setting beneath the slopes of Carrigbyrne Forest, just a 30-minute drive from Rosslare Port. The Martin family extend warm hospitality and provide good food in the charming conservatory restaurant with its central log fire. There are comfortable lounges, and the bedrooms, which overlook the attractive landscape gardens, are spacious and thoughtfully appointed.

Rooms 28 en suite (2 fmly) (10 GF) **Conf** Thtr 100 Class 60 Board 60
Parking 60 **Notes** LB ⊗ ⊘ in restaurant Closed 21 Dec-31 Jan

ROSSLARE   MAP 01 D2

★★★★ ◉◉ **HOTEL**

Kelly's Resort

☎ 053 32114 ▤ 053 32222

e-mail: kellyhot@iol.ie

dir: *10m from Wexford town, turn off N25 onto Rosslare/Wexford road*

Since 1895, the Kelly Family has been running this excellent hotel, where together with a dedicated team, they provide very professional and friendly service. The resort is adjacent to both the beach and Rosslare Strand. Bedrooms are thoughtfully equipped and comfortably furnished. The extensive facilities include a smart leisure club, health treatments, a children's creche and spacious gardens. La Marine Bistro offers modern cuisine and the Beaches restaurant serves award-winning food. AA Hotel of the Year for the Republic of Ireland 2006-7.

Rooms 118 annexe en suite (15 fmly) (20 GF) ⊘ in 110 bedrooms
Facilities Spa STV ⏺ supervised ⊰ Snooker Sauna Gym ⊌
Jacuzzi Bowls Plunge pool Badminton Crazy golf Outdoor Canadian
hot tub New Sea Spa ⋔ ch fac **Conf** Thtr 30 Class 30 Board 20
Services Lift **Parking** 120 **Notes LB** ⊗ ⊘ in restaurant
Closed mid Dec-late Feb

WEXFORD   MAP 01 D3

★★★★ 78% ◉◉ **HOTEL**

Ferrycarrig

Ferrycarrig Bridge

☎ 053 9120999 ▤ 053 9120982

e-mail: reservations@ferrycarrighotel.com

dir: *on N11 by Slaney Estuary, beside Ferrycarrig Castle*

This fine property has sweeping views of the Slaney Estuary from nearly every angle. Bedrooms are comfortable and well appointed, many of them having access to balconies. The leisure centre is

continued

particularly well equipped. The staff offer professional and friendly service.

Ferrycarrig

Rooms 102 en suite (10 fmly) ⊗ in all bedrooms **Facilities** STV 🔾 supervised Sauna Solarium Gym Jacuzzi Aerobics beauty treatments on request Hairdresser 🎵 **Conf** Thtr 400 Class 250 Board 60 **Services** Lift **Parking** 235 **Notes LB** ⊗ ⊗ in restaurant

★★★ 78% HOTEL

Talbot

The Quay
☎ 053 22566 & 55559 ▤ 053 23377
e-mail: sales@talbothotel.ie

dir: *N11 from Rosslare, follow Wexford signs, 12m, hotel on right*

Centrally situated on the quayside, this hotel has been extensively refurbished. The well-equipped bedrooms have custom-made oak furniture and attractive décor; many have sea views. Public areas include a spacious foyer, comfortable lounges and the Ballast Quay bar, serving food all day. The attractive restaurant serves interesting food, and there are good leisure facilities.

Rooms 109 en suite (12 fmly) ⊗ in 87 bedrooms **Facilities Spa** STV 🔾 supervised Sauna Solarium Gym Jacuzzi Childrens room Beauty Salon 🎵 **Conf** BC Thtr 450 Class 250 Board 110 **Services** Lift air con **Parking** 160 **Notes** ⊗ ⊗ in restaurant Closed 24-25 Dec

★★★ 74% HOTEL

Stanville Lodge

☎ 053 34300 ▤ 053 34989
e-mail: scarroll@stanville.ie

Located just off the N25 to the west of the town, this new hotel is well positioned for visitors using Rosslare Ferryport. Bedrooms are spacious and comfortably appointed with a number of dining options available throughout the day. There are two bright conference rooms on the first floor.

Rooms 32 en suite

★★★ 74% ◉ HOTEL

Whitford House Hotel Health & Leisure Club

New Line Rd
☎ 053 914 3444 ▤ 053 914 6399
e-mail: info@whitford.ie
web: www.whitford.ie

dir: *Just off N25 (Duncannon rdbt), take exit for R733 (Wexford), hotel immediately left*

This is a friendly family-run hotel just 2km from the town centre within easy reach of the Rosslare ferry. Comfortable rooms range from standard to deluxe; they are spacious and luxuriously decorated and furnished. Public areas include a choice of lounges and a popular bar where food is also served. More formal dinner is on offer in Footprints Restaurant.

Rooms 36 en suite (28 fmly) (18 GF) ⊗ in 26 bedrooms S €67-€155; D €96-€234 (incl. bkfst) **Facilities Spa** STV 🔾 supervised Sauna Solarium Gym Jacuzzi Childrens playground Beer garden/Adult reading room, 🎵 Xmas **Conf** Thtr 50 Class 45 Board 25 **Parking** 200 **Notes LB** ⊗ ⊗ in restaurant RS 23-27 Dec

★★★ 69% HOTEL

Riverbank House Hotel

☎ 053 23611 ▤ 053 23342
e-mail: river@indigo.ie

dir: *beside Wexford Bridge on R741*

Overlooking the estuary of the Slaney River, this hotel is at the foot of the Wexford Bridge, a short distance from the town centre. Both the bar and restaurant have views of the harbour. Bedrooms are well equipped and comfortable. Impressive banqueting facilities have also been added.

Rooms 23 en suite (6 fmly) (7 GF) ⊗ in 8 bedrooms S €55-€110; D €80-€170 (incl. bkfst) **Facilities** STV Wi-fi in bedrooms 🎵 ch fac **Conf** Thtr 350 Class 180 Board 48 Del from €92.30 **Services** Lift **Parking** 25 **Notes LB** ⊗ ⊗ in restaurant Closed 24-25 Dec

◉ RESTAURANT WITH ROOMS

Newbay Country House & Restaurant

Newbay, Carrick
☎ 053 42779 ▤ 053 46318
e-mail: newbay@newbayhouse.com

Built in the 1840s, Newbay offers a choice of two dining areas, the casual Cellar Bistro on the lower floor, or the more formal restaurant in the original house. Seafood is a passion here, indeed they have their own trawler. The very comfortable bedrooms are situated in both the house and a wing.

Rooms 12 en suite

Ireland

CO WICKLOW

ARKLOW — MAP 01 D3

★★★ 73% **HOTEL**

Arklow Bay Conference, Leisure & Spa Hotel

Ferrybank
☎ 0402 32309 📠 0402 32300
e-mail: sales@arklowbay.com
dir: off N11. 1m turn left, hotel 200yds on left

This hotel enjoys panoramic views of Arklow Bay and many of the well-appointed bedrooms take full advantage of this. The public areas are decorated in a contemporary style, and include a spacious lobby lounge and a comfortable bar where casual dining is available. For more formal dining, Howard's restaurant opens for dinner. Extensive leisure and spa treatment facilities are available.

Rooms 92 en suite (3 fmly) (27 GF) ⊘ in 30 bedrooms **Facilities** Spa STV ❓ supervised Sauna Solarium Gym Jacuzzi Wi-fi available ♬ ch fac Xmas **Conf** Thtr 500 Class 200 Board 60 **Services** Lift **Parking** 100 **Notes** ⊗ ⊘ in restaurant

AUGHRIM — MAP 01 D3

★★★ 68% **HOTEL**

Lawless

☎ 0402 36146 📠 0402 36384
e-mail: info@lawlesshotel.com

IRISH COUNTRY HOTELS

dir: N11 to Rathnew, R752 to Rathdrum, R753 to Aughrim. Hotel between bridges on outskirts of village

Established in 1787, this family-run hotel is located in the pretty village of Aughrim. Bedrooms, some with river views, are individually decorated and well appointed, and inviting public areas include a comfortable lounge, smart restaurant and the Thirsty Trout Bar and conservatory, which offers an imaginative menu. Golf courses and an angling park nearby.

Rooms 14 en suite (2 fmly) ⊘ in 5 bedrooms **Facilities** STV ⛲ **Conf** BC Thtr 100 Class 60 Board 40 **Parking** 40 **Notes** ⊗ ⊘ in restaurant Closed 23-26 Dec

BRAY — MAP 01 D4

★★★ 68% **HOTEL**

Royal

Main St
☎ 01 2862935 📠 01 2867373
e-mail: royal@regencyhotels.com
dir: from N11, 1st exit for Bray, 2nd exit from rdbt, through 2 sets of lights, across bridge, hotel on left

The Royal Hotel stands on the main street, close to the seafront, and within easy reach of the Dun Laoighaire ferry port. Public areas offer comfortable lounges, traditional bar and The Heritage Restaurant. Bedrooms vary in size and are well appointed. There is a well-equipped leisure centre and a supervised car park is available.

Rooms 98 en suite (9 fmly) ⊘ in 51 bedrooms **Facilities** ❓ supervised Sauna Solarium Gym Jacuzzi Massage & beauty clinic Therapy room Whirlpool spa Madhatters creche ♬ **Conf** BC Thtr 400 Class 300 Board 200 **Services** Lift **Parking** 60 **Notes** LB ⊗ ⊘ in restaurant Civ Wed 225

DELGANY — MAP 01 D3

★★★★ 69% **HOTEL**

Glenview

Glen O' the Downs
☎ 01 2873399 📠 01 2877511
e-mail: glenview@iol.ie
dir: from Dublin city centre follow signs for N11, past Bray on southbound N11

Set in a lovely hillside location, overlooking terraced gardens, this hotel boasts an excellent range of leisure and conference facilities. Impressive public areas include a conservatory bar, lounge and choice of dining options. Bedrooms are spacious, many enjoying great views over the valley. Championship golf, horse riding and many tourist amenities are available nearby.

Rooms 70 en suite (11 fmly) (16 GF) ⊘ in 11 bedrooms **Facilities** Spa STV ❓ supervised Snooker Sauna Solarium Gym ⛱ Jacuzzi Aerobics studio, Massage, Beauty treatment room ♬ ch fac **Conf** Thtr 220 Class 120 Board 50 **Services** Lift **Parking** 200 **Notes** ⊗ ⊘ in restaurant

GLENDALOUGH — MAP 01 D3

★★★ 68% **HOTEL**

The Glendalough

☎ 0404 45135 📠 0404 45142
e-mail: info@glendaloughhotel.ie
dir: N11 to Kilmacongue, right onto R755, straight on at Caragh then right onto R756

Mountains and forest provide the setting for this long-established hotel at the edge of the famed monastic site. Many of the well-appointed bedrooms have superb views. Food is served daily in the very popular bar while relaxing dinners are served in the charming restaurant that overlooks the river and forest.

Rooms 44 en suite (3 fmly) **Facilities** STV Fishing ♬ **Conf** Thtr 200 Class 150 Board 50 **Services** Lift **Parking** 100 **Notes** LB ⊗ Closed Dec-Jan

MACREDDIN   MAP 01 D3

★★★★ 82% ◉ ◉ **HOTEL**

The Brooklodge Hotel & Wells Spa

☎ 0402 36444 ▤ 0402 36580

e-mail: brooklodge@macreddin.ie

dir: N11 to Rathnew, R752 to Rathdrum, R753 to Aughrim follow signs to Macreddin Village

The Brooklodge is a luxurious country house hotel situated in Macreddin Village near Aughrim, comprising of a pub, café, organic bakery and smokehouse and equestrian centre. Comfort predominates among restful lounges, well-appointed bedrooms and mezzanine suites. Award-winning Strawberry Tree Restaurant is a truly romantic setting, specialising in organic and wild food. The Wells spa centre offers extensive treatments and leisure facilities.

Rooms 66 en suite (27 fmly) (4 GF) ⊗ in 28 bedrooms S €135–€170; D €190–€260 (incl. bkfst) **Facilities Spa** STV ⬚ ⬚ ⬚ Riding Snooker Sauna Gym Jacuzzi Archery Clay pigeon shooting Falconry Shiatsu massage Off-road driving ♫ Xmas **Conf** Thtr 300 Class 120 Board 40 Del from €145 **Services** Lift **Parking** 200 **Notes LB** ⊗ in restaurant

NEWTOWNMOUNTKENNEDY   MAP 01 D3

★★★★★ 81% **HOTEL**

Marriott Druids Glen Hotel & Country Club

Marriott HOTELS & RESORTS

☎ 01 287 0800 ▤ 01 287 0801

e-mail: mhrs.dubgs.reservations@marriothotels.com.

web: www.marriott.co.uk

dir: N11 s'bound, off at Newtownmountkennedy. Follow signs for hotel

This fine hotel, situated between the Wicklow Mountains and the coast, has two fabulous golf courses and a range of smart indoor

continued

leisure facilities. Bedrooms have been equipped to the highest standard and service is delivered in a most professional manner and always with a smile.

Rooms 145 en suite ⊗ in 103 bedrooms S €105–€185; D €130–€210 (incl. bkfst) **Facilities Spa** STV ⬚ ⬚ 36 Sauna Gym Putt green Jacuzzi 4 Treatment Rooms, Plunge Pool, 18 metre swimming room ♫ Xmas **Conf** BC Thtr 400 Class 180 Board 30 Del from €220 **Services** Lift air con **Parking** 350 **Notes** ⊗ ⊗ in restaurant

RATHNEW   MAP 01 D3

★★★ 72% ◉ **HOTEL**

Hunter's

☎ 0404 40106 ▤ 0404 40338

e-mail: reception@hunters.ie

dir: 1.5km from village off N11

A charming country house built in 1720, which is one of Ireland's oldest coaching inns. It is full of character and atmosphere stemming from five generations. The comfortable bedrooms have wonderful views over prize-winning gardens bordering the River Vartry. The restaurant has a good reputation for carefully prepared dishes, which make the best use of high quality local produce including fruit and vegetables from their own garden.

Rooms 16 en suite (2 fmly) (2 GF) **Conf** Thtr 40 Class 40 Board 16 **Parking** 50 **Notes LB** ⊗ ⊗ in restaurant Closed 24-26 Dec

WOODENBRIDGE   MAP 01 D3

★★★ 70% ◉ **HOTEL**

Woodenbridge

☎ 0402 35146 ▤ 0402 35573

e-mail: reservations@woodenbridgehotel.com

dir: between Avoca & Arklow, off N11.

Situated in the beautiful Vale of Avoca and owner-managed by the hospitable O'Brien family this smart hotel is beside the Woodenbridge Golf Club. Public areas are comfortable with open fires and good food is assured in the newly-built Italian restaurant. The new lodge bedrooms are well equipped, spacious and enjoy a peaceful riverside setting.

Rooms 23 en suite (13 fmly) **Facilities** STV Pool table ♫ **Conf** Thtr 200 Class 200 Board 200 **Parking** 100 **Notes LB** ⊗ ⊗ in restaurant

Some hotels have restricted service during quieter months, and at this time some of the facilities will not be available

Ireland

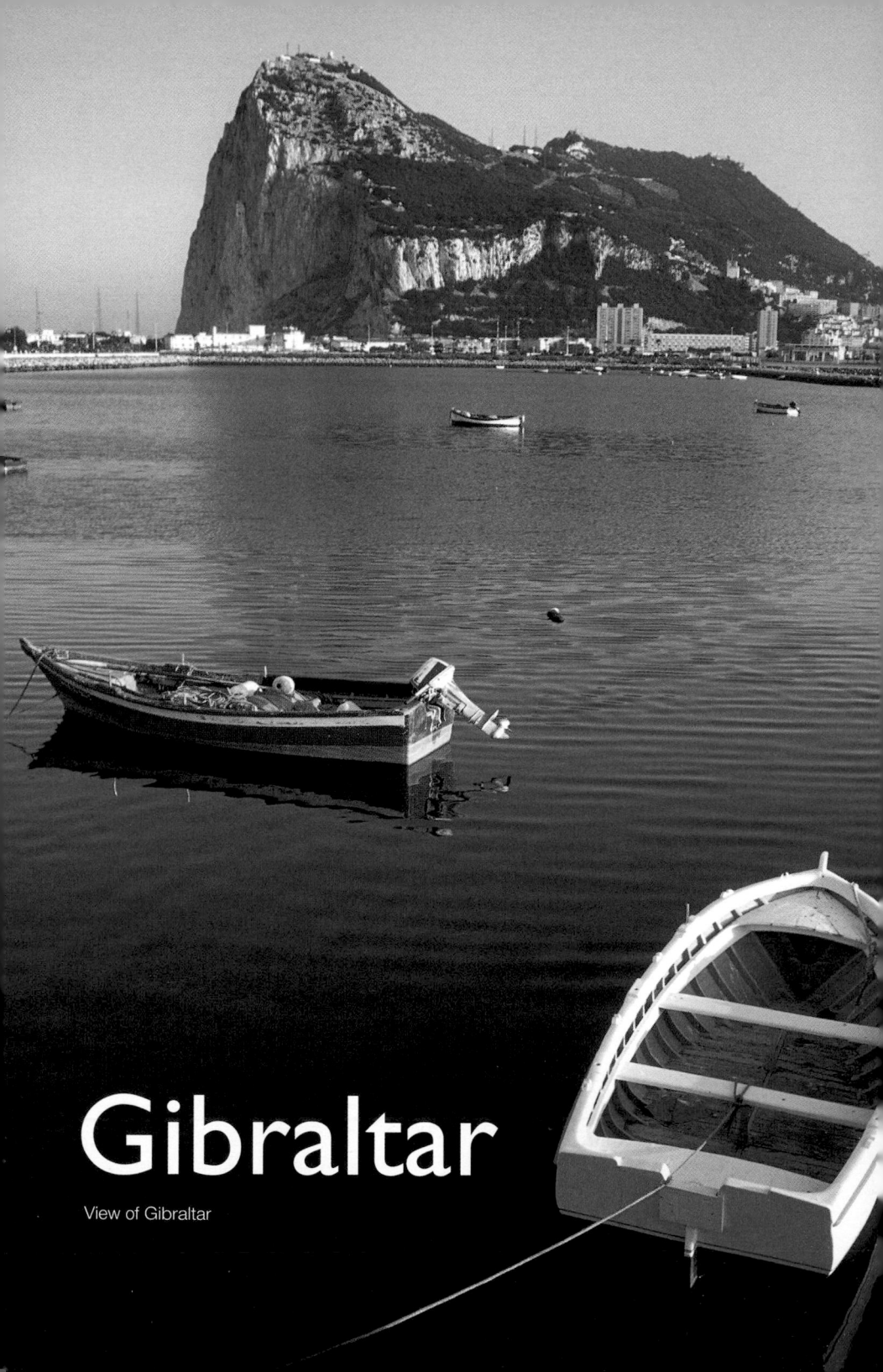

Gibraltar

View of Gibraltar

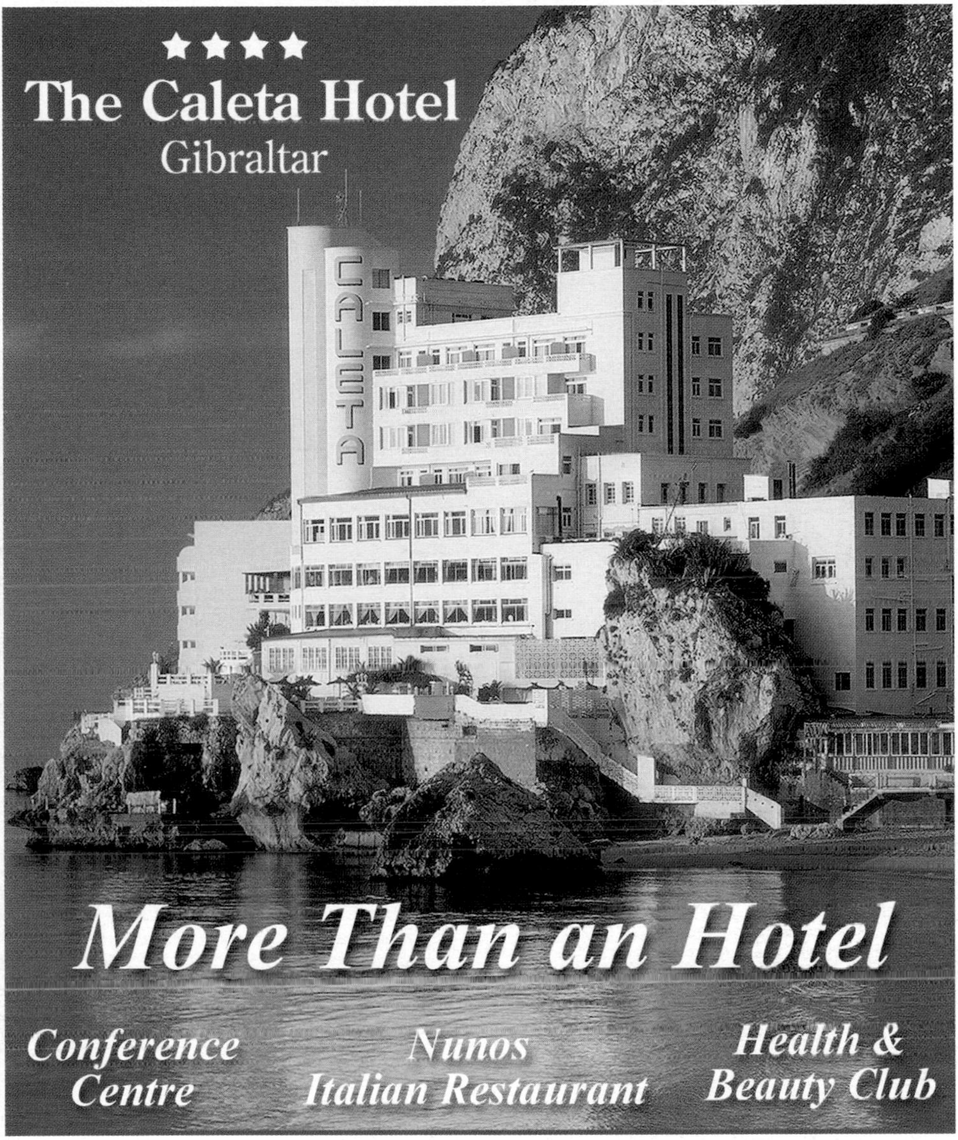
★★★★
The Caleta Hotel
Gibraltar
CALETA
More Than an Hotel
Conference Centre
Nunos Italian Restaurant
Health & Beauty Club

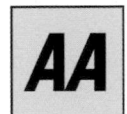

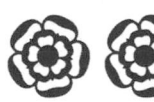

GIBRALTAR

★★★★ 78% ◎ **HOTEL**

Rock

Europa Rd
☎ 00 350 73000 📠 00 350 73513
e-mail: rockhotel@gibtelecom.net
web: www.rockhotelgibraltar.com

dir: *From airport follow tourist board signs. Situated on left halfway up Europa Rd*

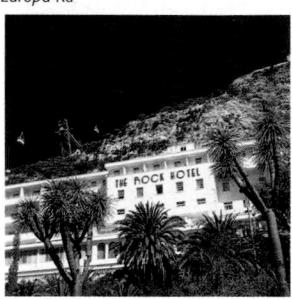

Enjoying a prime elevated location directly below the Rock, this long established art deco styled hotel has been the destination of celebrities and royalty since it was built in 1932. Bedrooms are spacious and well equipped and many boast stunning views across the Mediterranean to Morocco. Staff are friendly, and service is delivered with flair and enthusiasm. Creative dinners and hearty breakfasts are offered.

Rooms 104 en suite ⊗ in 60 bedrooms **Facilities** STV ⚡ supervised ♬ **Conf** Thtr 70 Class 24 Board 30 Del from £135 **Services** Lift air con **Parking** 40 **Notes** ⊗ in restaurant RS 5 Oct-1 Apr Civ Wed 40

See advert on page 1009

★★★★ 76% **HOTEL**

O'Callaghan Eliott

2 Governor's Pde
☎ 00 350 70500 75905 📠 00 350 70243
e-mail: eliott@ocallaghanhotels.com

Located in the heart of the old town, this hotel provides a convenient central base for exploring the duty-free shopping district and other key

continued

attractions on foot. Having just completed a major refurbishment, the bedrooms are stylish, spacious and well equipped. The roof-top restaurant provides stunning bay views, and guests can also take a swim in the roof-top pool.

Rooms 120 en suite ⊗ in 36 bedrooms S £110-£430; D £110-£430 **Facilities** STV ⚡ Sauna Gym ♬ Xmas **Conf** Thtr 180 Class 80 Board 70 Del from £140 **Services** Lift air con **Parking** 17 **Notes** LB ⊗ ⊗ in restaurant Civ Wed 120

★★★★ 74% ◎◎ **HOTEL**

Caleta

Sir Herbert Miles Rd, PO Box 73
☎ 00 350 76501 📠 00 350 42143
e-mail: sales@caletahotel.gi

dir: *Enter Gibraltar via Spanish border & cross runway. At 1st rdbt turn left, hotel in 2kms*

For travellers arriving by air the Caleta is an eye-catching coastal landmark. This imposing and stylish hotel sits on a cliff top, and all sea-facing rooms enjoy panoramic views across the straights to Morocco. Bedrooms vary in size and style - some have spacious balconies, flat screen TVs and mini bars. Several dining venues are available but Nunos provides a fine-dining Italian experience. Staff are friendly; service is professional.

Rooms 72 en suite 89 annexe en suite (13 fmly) ⊗ in 32 bedrooms S £70-£180; D £70-£180 **Facilities** STV ⚡ supervised Gym Health & beauty club Xmas **Conf** Thtr 140 Class 85 Board 85 **Services** Lift **Parking** 32 **Notes** LB ⊗ Civ Wed 300

See advert on opposite page

★★ 64% **HOTEL**

Continental

1 Engineers Ln
☎ 00 350 76900 📠 00 350 41702
e-mail: contihotel@gibtelecom.net

dir: *2 min walk from Casemate's Sq, off Main St*

Conveniently situated in the town centre this traditionally styled hotel provides good value, comfortable accommodation within easy reach of the resorts' key attractions. Bedrooms are spacious and well equipped and bathrooms provide modern facilities. A popular ground-floor café provides an informal venue for dining.

Rooms 18 en suite (3 fmly) S £46.80-£52; D £63-£70 **Facilities** STV **Services** Lift

An oasis...

...in a busy world!

Bedrooms
104 bedrooms and suites in a colonial style all with a sea view

Conference facilities
Full upgraded conference facilities available for board meetings, training courses and presentations

Internet Facilities
Wireless broadband available throughout the hotel

Weddings
The Rock is an ideal wedding venue whether it be a small intimate wedding or large family gathering. We are also a recognised venue for civil marriages and ceremonies can now be conducted in various parts of the hotel

Banqueting
Weddings, banqueting, private dining or office parties catered for

Swimming pool
Outdoor swimming pool with pool side bar and pool side menu. We welcome private pool membership, our Lido Club, with private pool hire for parties and barbecues and children's parties

Restaurant
The restaurant has stunning views over the bay. Our "house" menu is excellent value for three courses including an aperitif Manzanilla, olives and coffee. A full à la carte menu along with a superb eclectic wine list is also available

Wisteria Terrace
The Wisteria Terrace for lunches, dinner, barbecues, afternoon teas, evening drinks and informal dining

Barbary Bar
Barbary Bar and terrace for a relaxing drink and, for the wine buff, a choice of nine wines by the glass

Lounges
Take a good old fashioned English tea in one of the spacious lounges

Europa Road, Gibraltar
Tel: (+350) 73000 Fax: (+350) 73513
E-mail: info@rockhotel.gi
Web site: www.rockhotelgibraltar.com

78%

County Maps

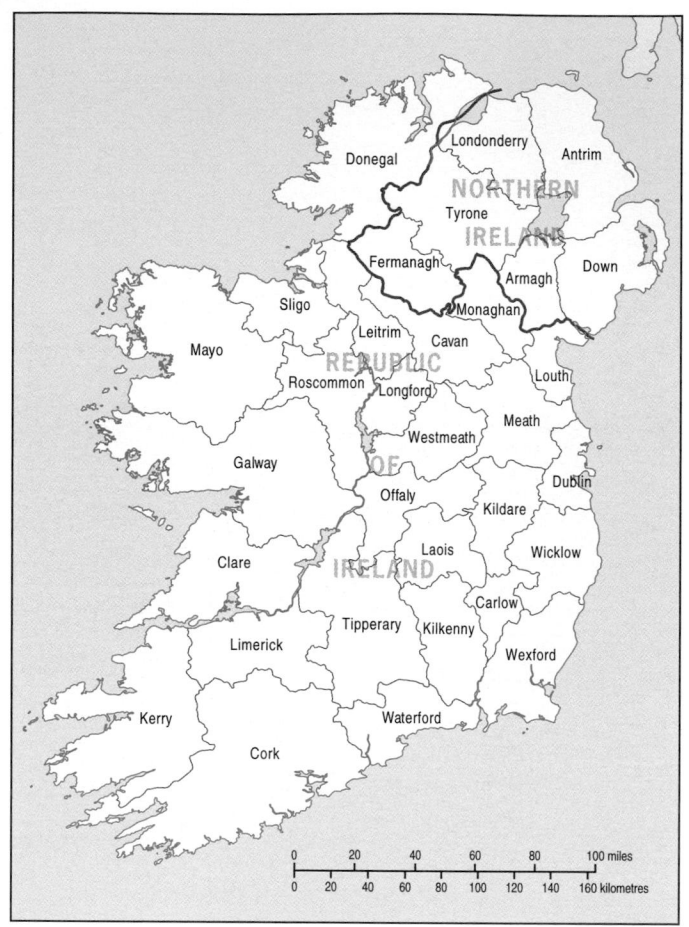

England

1 Bedfordshire
2 Berkshire
3 Bristol
4 Buckinghamshire
5 Cambridgeshire
6 Greater Manchester
7 Herefordshire
8 Hertfordshire
9 Leicestershire
10 Northamptonshire
11 Nottinghamshire
12 Rutland
13 Staffordshire
14 Warwickshire
15 West Midlands
16 Worcestershire

Scotland

17 City of Glasgow
18 Clackmannanshire
19 East Ayrshire
20 East Dunbartonshire
21 East Renfrewshire
22 Perth & Kinross
23 Renfrewshire
24 South Lanarkshire
25 West Dunbartonshire

Wales

26 Blaenau Gwent
27 Bridgend
28 Caerphilly
29 Denbighshire
30 Flintshire
31 Merthyr Tydfil
32 Monmouthshire
33 Neath Port Talbot
34 Newport
35 Rhondda Cynon Taff
36 Torfaen
37 Vale of Glamorgan
38 Wrexham

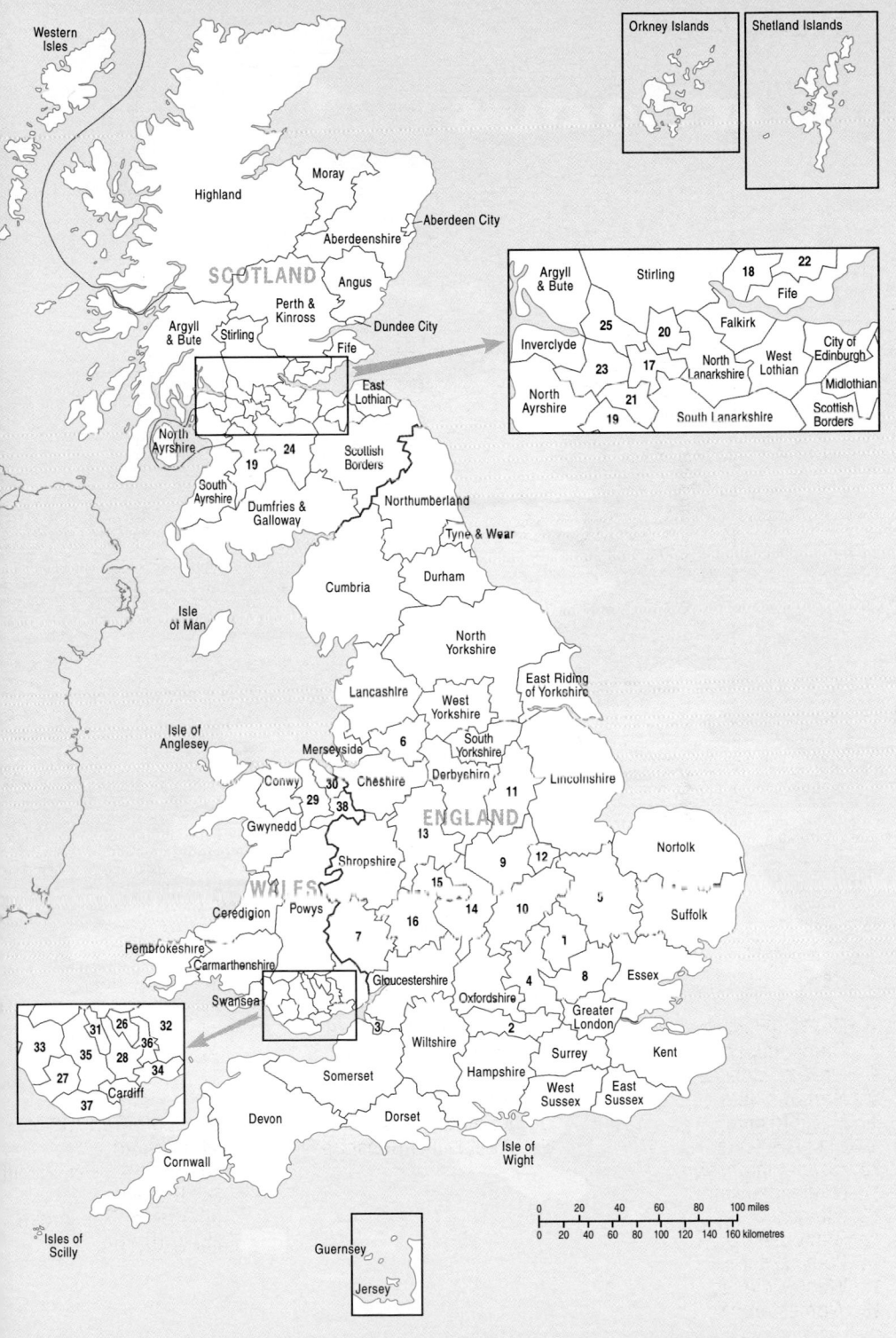

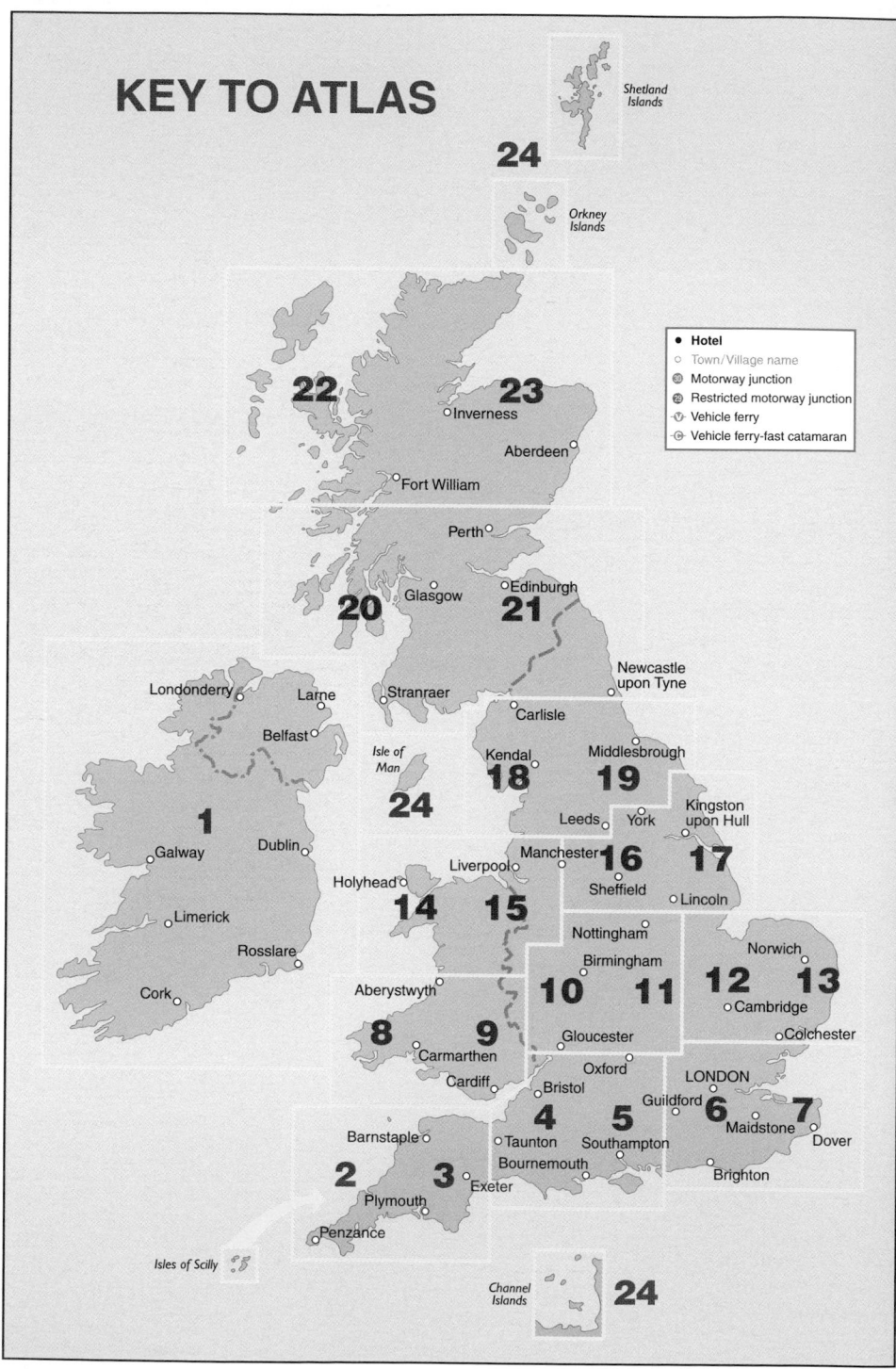

KEY TO ATLAS

Shetland Islands

24

Orkney Islands

Hotel
○ Town/Village name
⊗ Motorway junction
⊗ Restricted motorway junction
⌄ Vehicle ferry
⌁ Vehicle ferry-fast catamaran

22   **23**

○ Inverness

Aberdeen ○

○ Fort William

Perth ○

20   ○ Glasgow   ○ Edinburgh   **21**

Newcastle upon Tyne

Londonderry ○   Larne ○   ○ Stranraer   ○ Carlisle

Belfast ○

Isle of Man   Kendal ○   Middlesbrough

18   **19**

24

Leeds ○   ○ York   Kingston upon Hull

1   Liverpool ○   Manchester ○   **16**   **17**

Galway ○   Dublin ○

Holyhead ○   Sheffield ○   ○ Lincoln

14   **15**

Limerick ○

Nottingham ○

Rosslare ○   Birmingham ○

Cork ○   Aberystwyth ○   **10**   **11**   **12**   **13**

Norwich ○

○ Cambridge

8   **9**   Gloucester ○   ○ Colchester

Carmarthen ○   Oxford ○   LONDON

Cardiff ○   ○ Bristol   Guildford ○   **6**   **7**

Barnstaple ○   **4**   **5**   Maidstone ○

○ Taunton   Southampton ○   Dover ○

Bournemouth ○   Brighton ○

2   **3**   ○ Exeter

Plymouth ○

Penzance ○

Isles of Scilly

Channel Islands   **24**

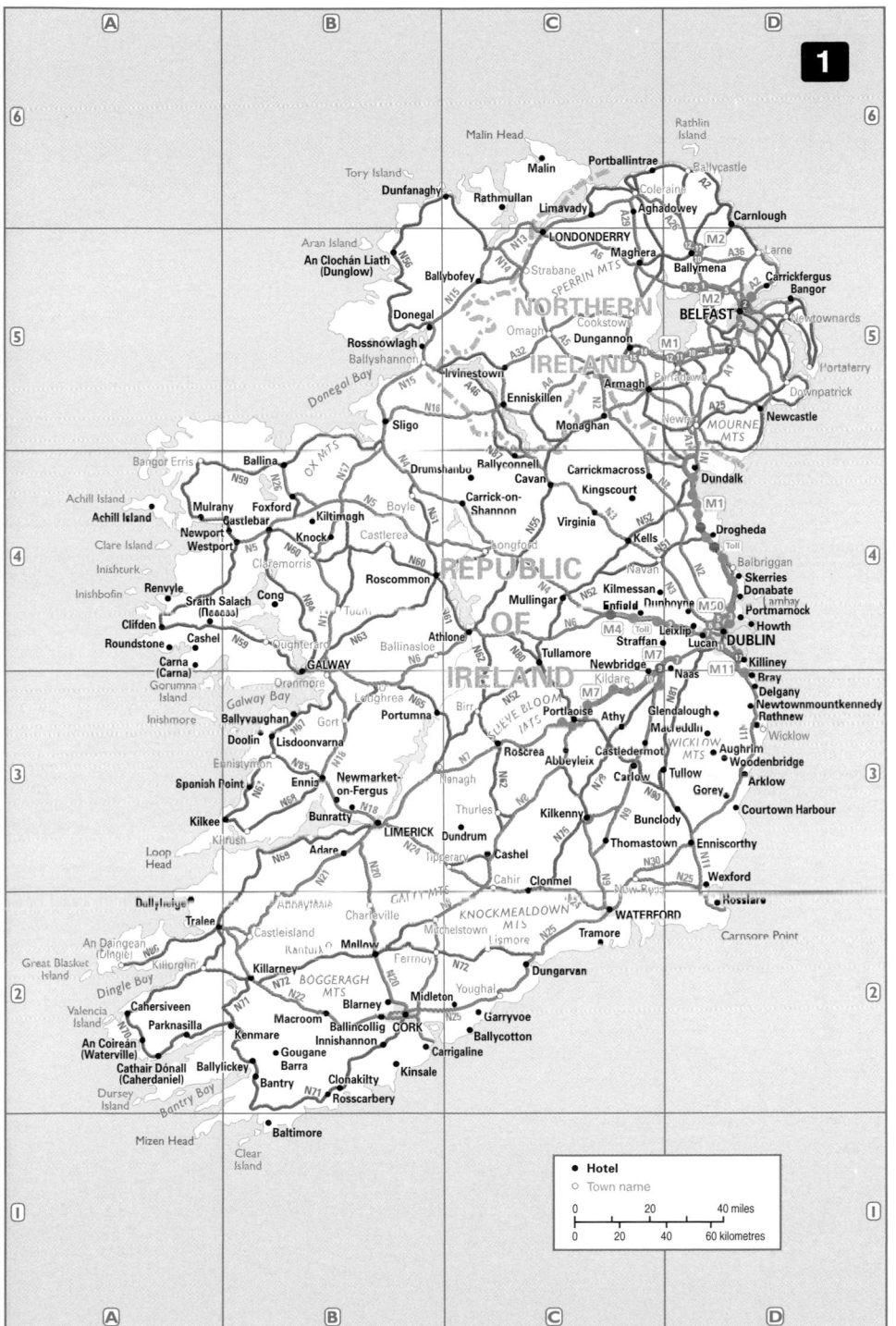

1

For continuation pages refer to numbered arrows

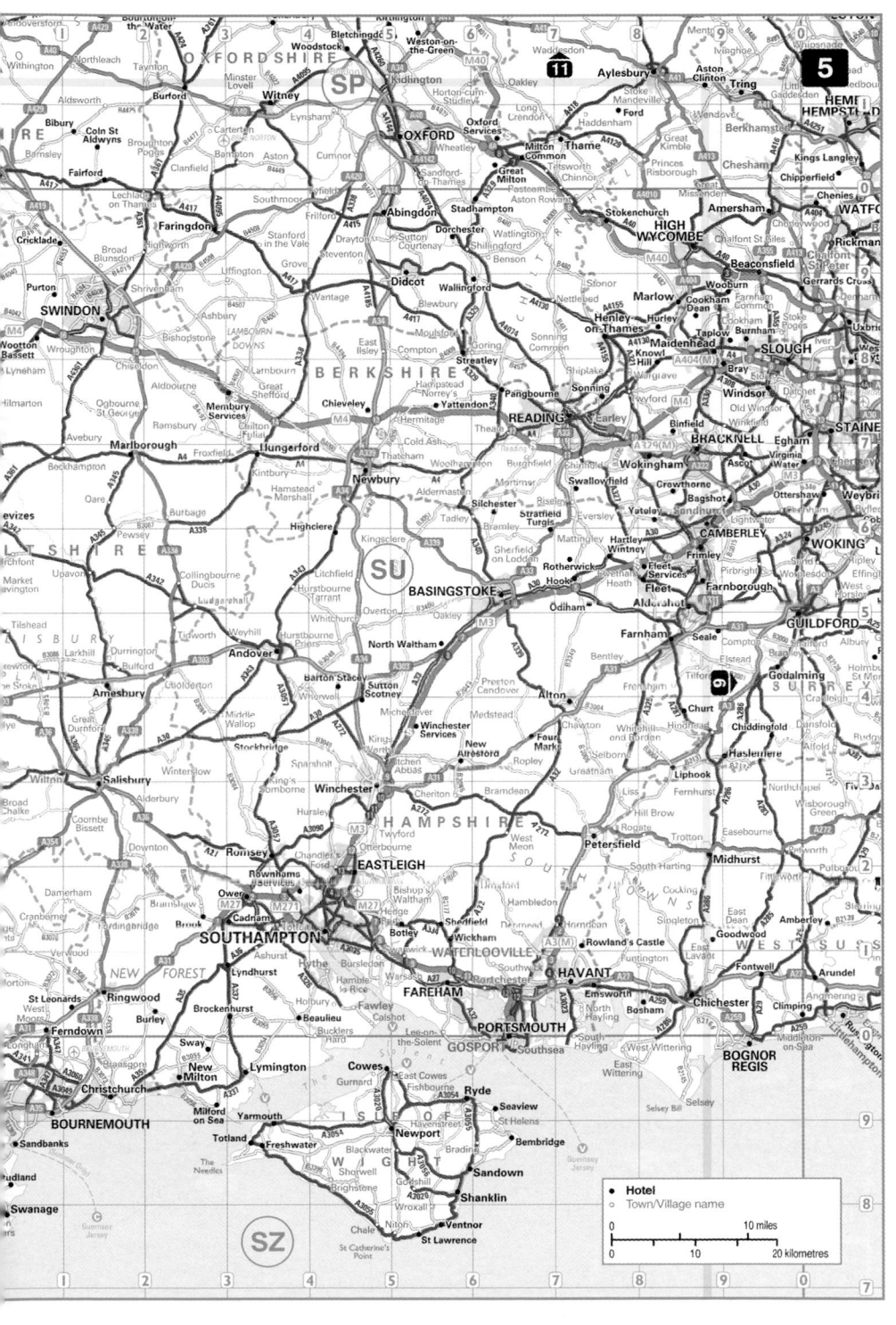

TM

TR

KENT

Hotel
Town/Village name

0   10 miles
0   10   20 kilometres

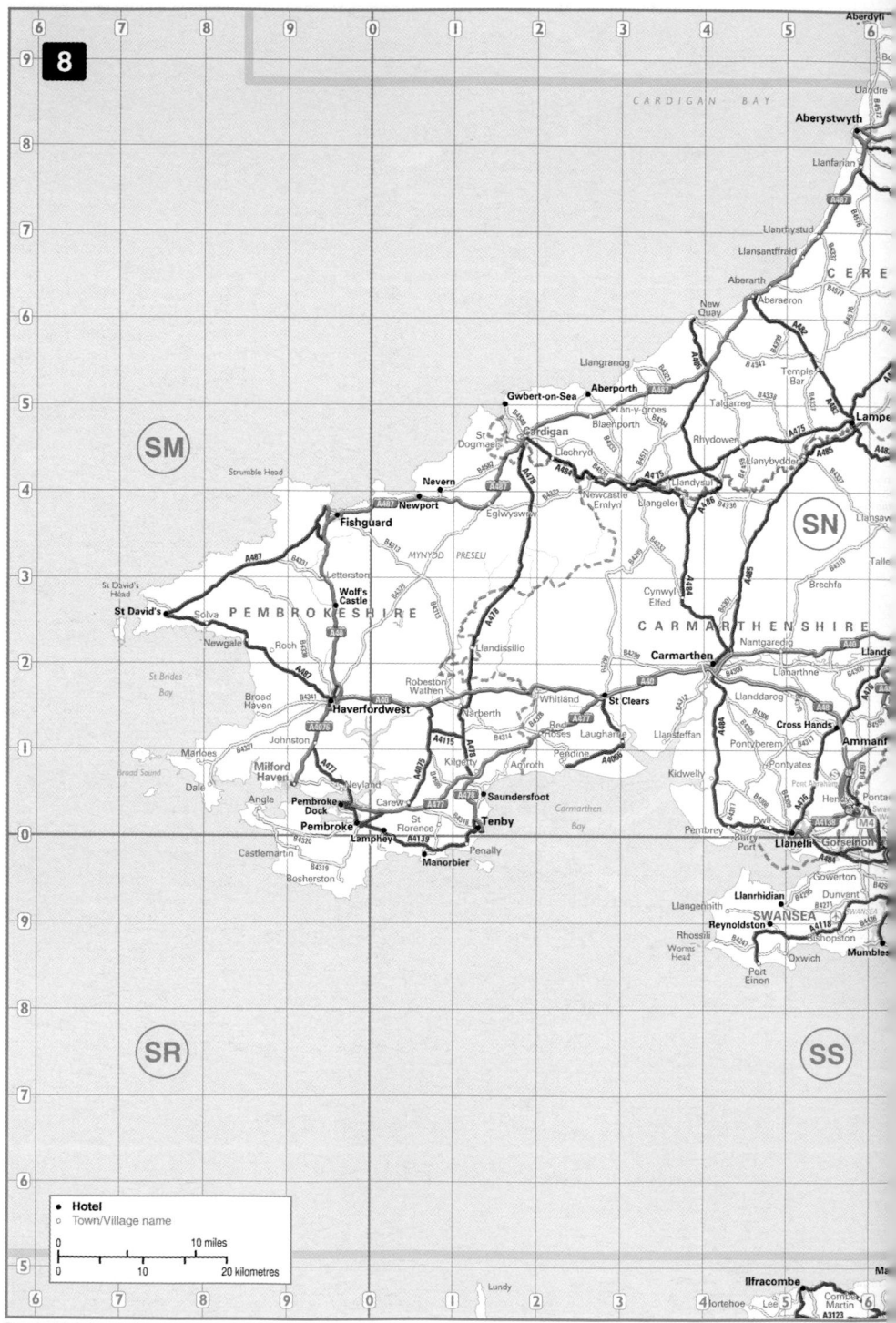

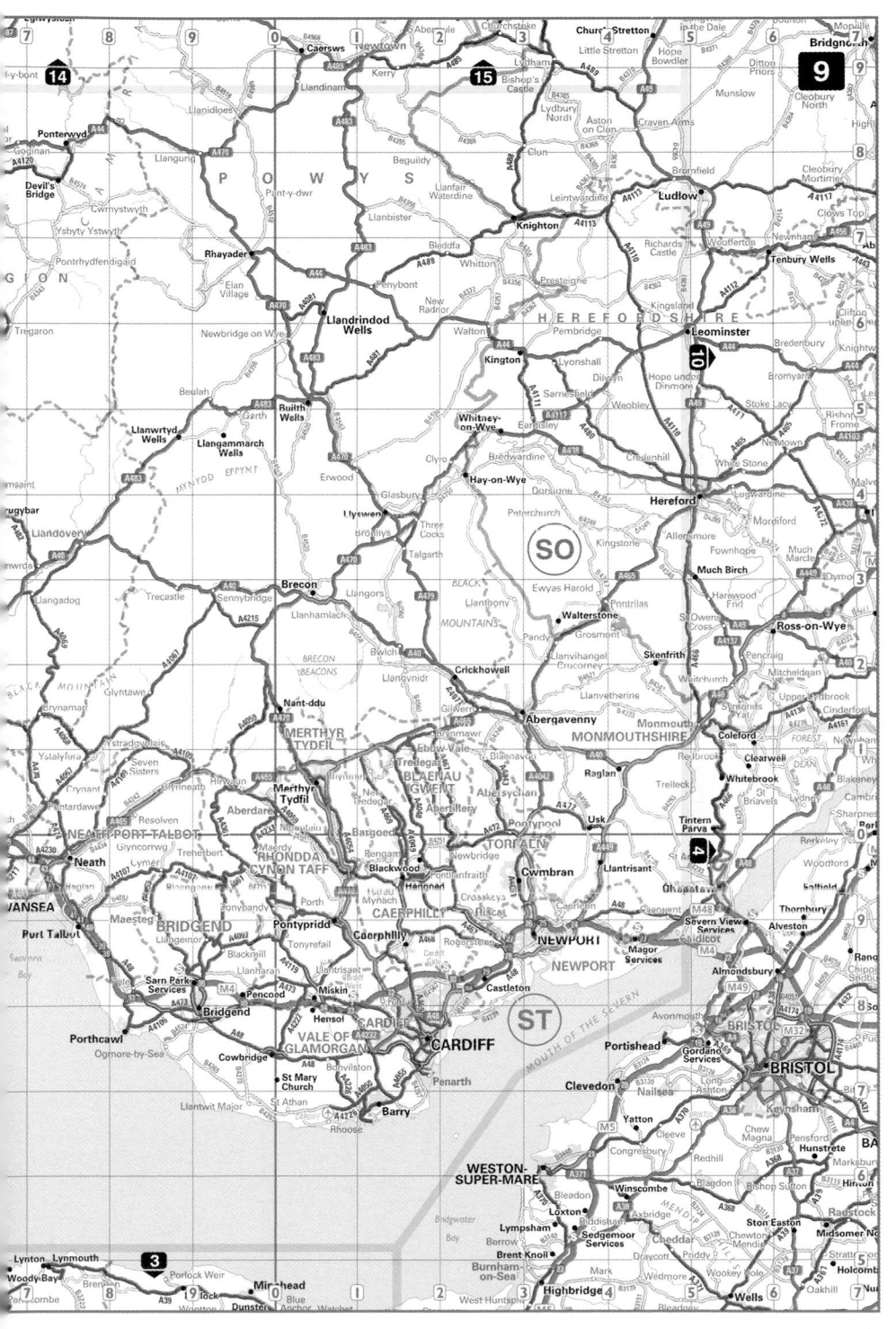

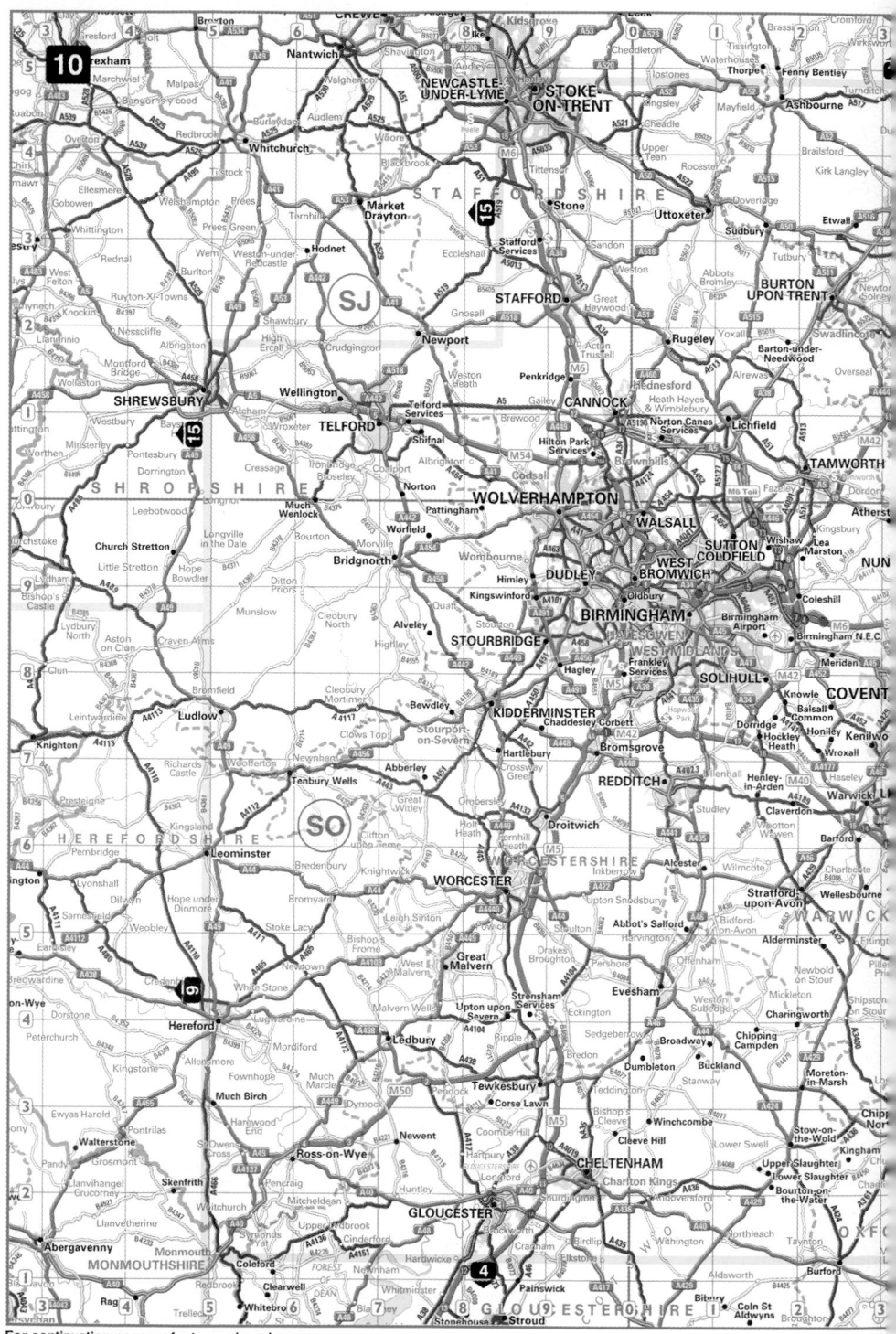

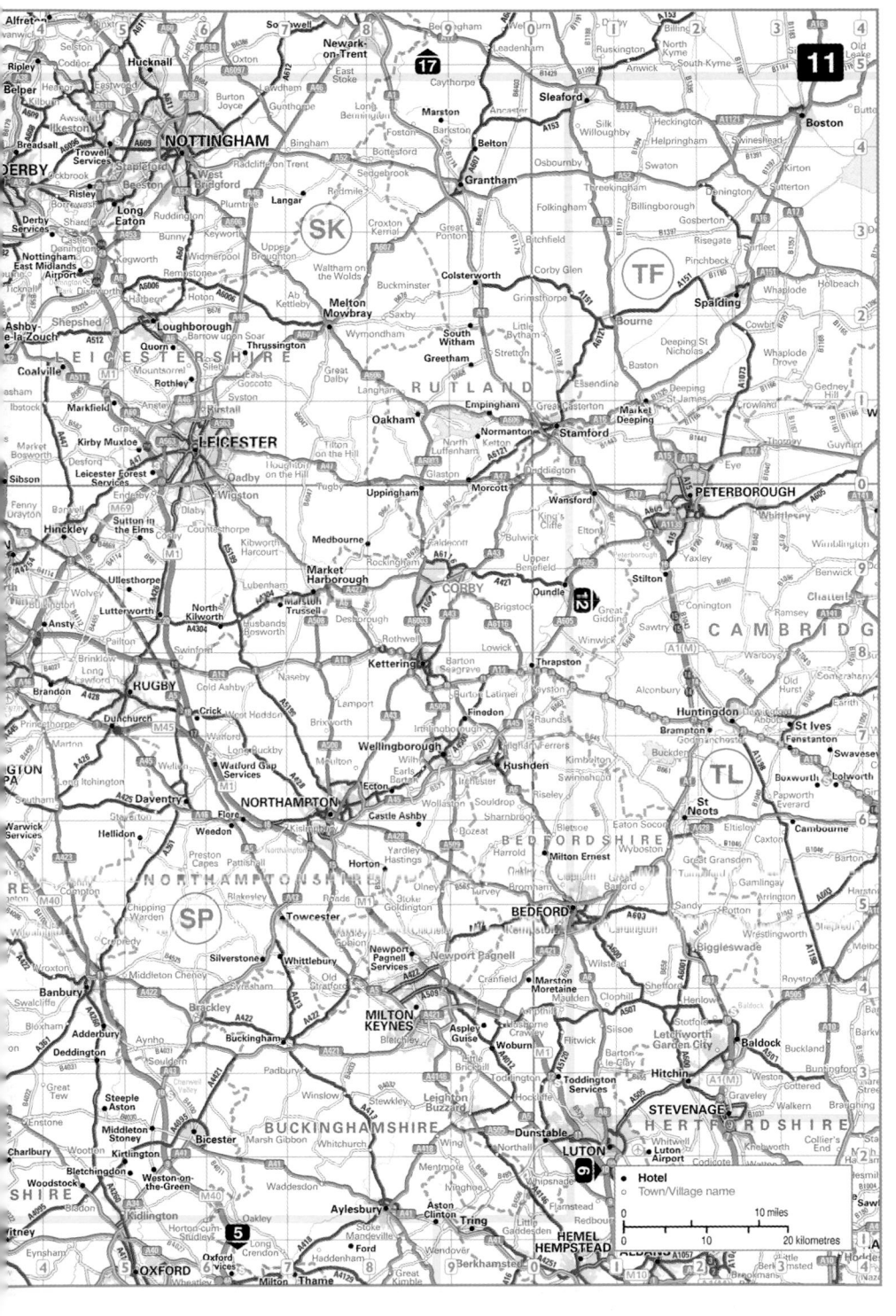

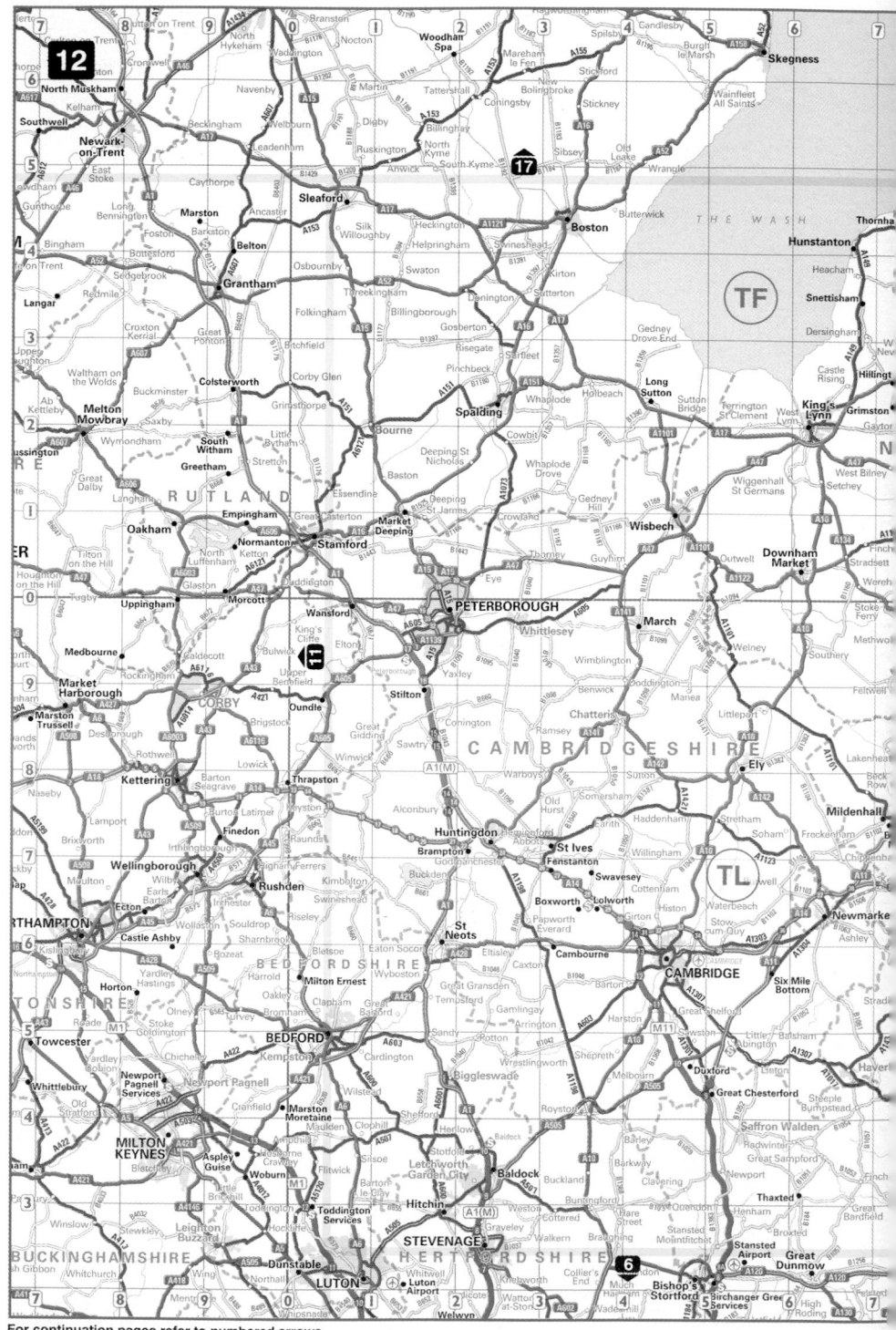

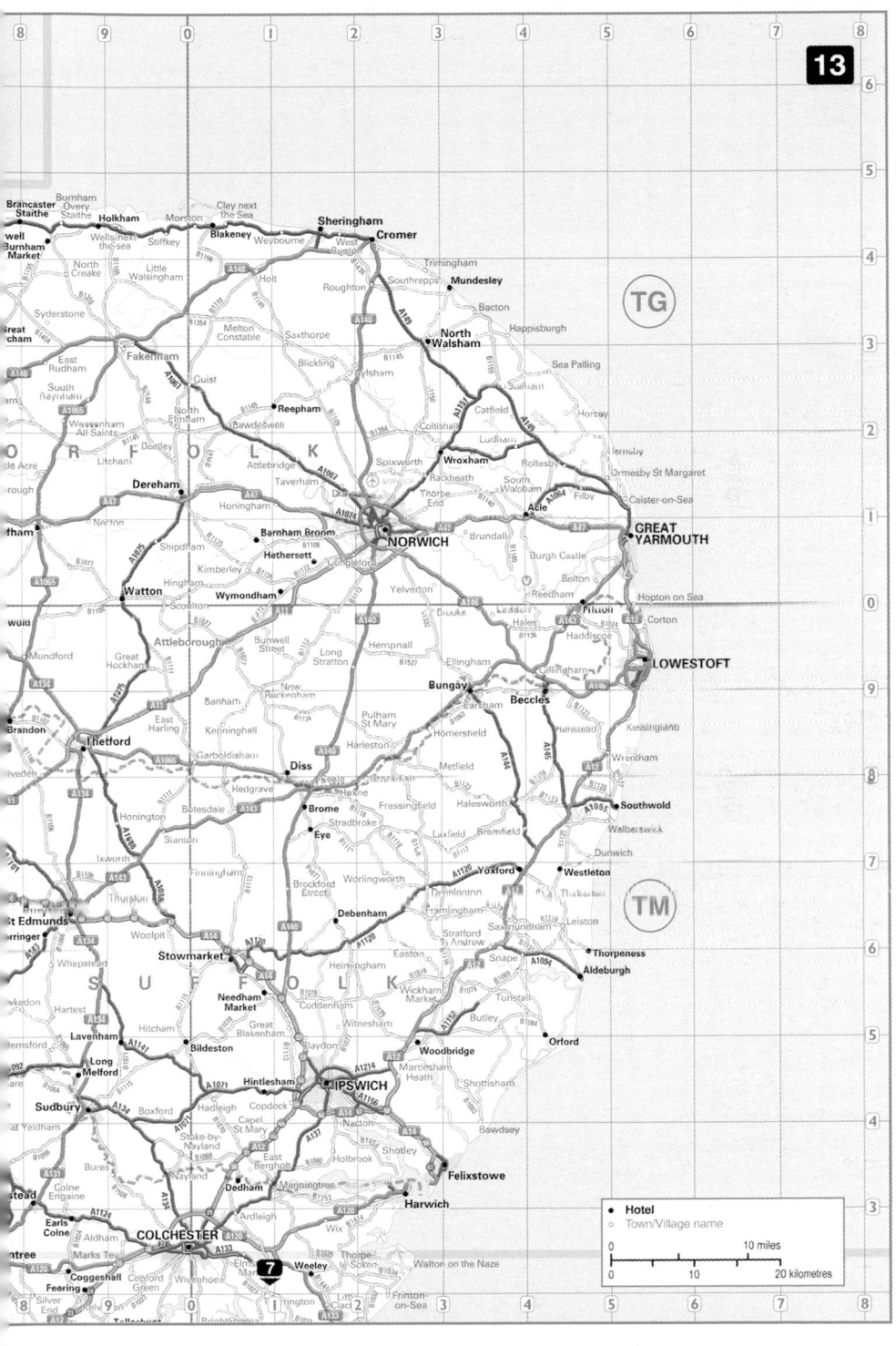

13

Brancaster Staithe · Burnham Overy Staithe · Holkham · Morston · Cley next the Sea · Sheringham · Cromer

Burnham Market · North Creake · Wells-next-the-sea · Stiffkey · Weybourne · West Runton · Trimingham

Syderstone · Little Walsingham · Holt · Southrepps · Mundesley · Bacton · Happisburgh

Great ·cham · East Rudham · Fakenham · Melton Constable · Saxthorpe · Roughton · North Walsham · Sea Palling

South Raynham · Guist · Blickling · Aylsham · Catfield · Horsey

Weasenham All-Saints · North Elmham · Reepham · Coltishall · Ludham · ·emsby

·le Acre · Litcham · Deopham · Bawdeswell · Spixworth · Wroxham · Rollesby · Ormesby St Margaret

·rough · Dereham · Attlebridge · Taverham · Rackheath · South Walsham · Caister-on-Sea

Honingham · Thorpe End · Acle · Filby

Barnham Broom · Hethersett · NORWICH · Brundall · Burgh Castle · GREAT YARMOUTH

tham · Narford · Shipdham · Kimberley · Longstratton · Belton · Hopton on Sea

Watton · Hingham · Wymondham · Yelverton · Reedham · Friton · Corton

·wold · Scoulton · Brooke · Ledaln · Hales · Haddiscoe · LOWESTOFT

Mundford · Attleborough · Bunwell Street · Long Stratton · Hempnall · Ellingham · Gillingham

Great Hockham · New Buckenham · Pulham St Mary · Earsham · Beccles

Brandon · Thetford · Banham · Kenninghall · Homersfield · Hunstead · Kessingland · Wrentham

Garboldisham · Diss · Harleston · Metfield · Wrentham

Iveden · Honington · Hedgrave · Botesdale · Brome · Fressingfield · Halesworth · A1095 · Southwold

·18 · Stanton · Eye · Stradbroke · Laxfield · Bromfield · Walberswick · Dunwich

Ixworth · Finningham · Brockford Street · Worlingworth · Yoxford · Westleton

·t Edmunds · Thurston · Debenham · Dennington · Framlingham · Thaberton · Leiston

·rringer · Woolpit · Stowmarket · Easton · Saxmundham · Snape · Thorpeness

Whepstead · Heiningham · Wickham Market · Tunstall · Aldeburgh

·vkedon · Hartest · Needham Market · Coddenham · Witnesham · Butley

·lemsford · Hitcham · Great Blakenham · Orford

Laveham · Bildeston · Sladyon · Woodbridge

Long Melford · Hintlesham · IPSWICH · Martlesham Heath · Shottisham

Sudbury · Boxford · Hadleigh · Copdock · Nacton · Bawdsey

·at Yeldham · Bures · Stoke-by-Nayland · Capel St Mary · East Bergholt · Shotley · Holbrook · Felixstowe

Colne Engaine · Nayland · Dedham · Manningtree · Harwich

Earls Colne · Ardleigh · Wix

·ntree · Marks Tey · COLCHESTER · Thorpe le Soken · Walton on the Naze

A125 · Coggeshall · Copford · Wivenhoe · Weeley · Frinton-on-Sea

Silver End · Feering · Green · ·rrington

TG

TM

Hotel
Town/Village name

0 ———— 10 miles

0 ———— 10 ———— 20 kilometres

7

14

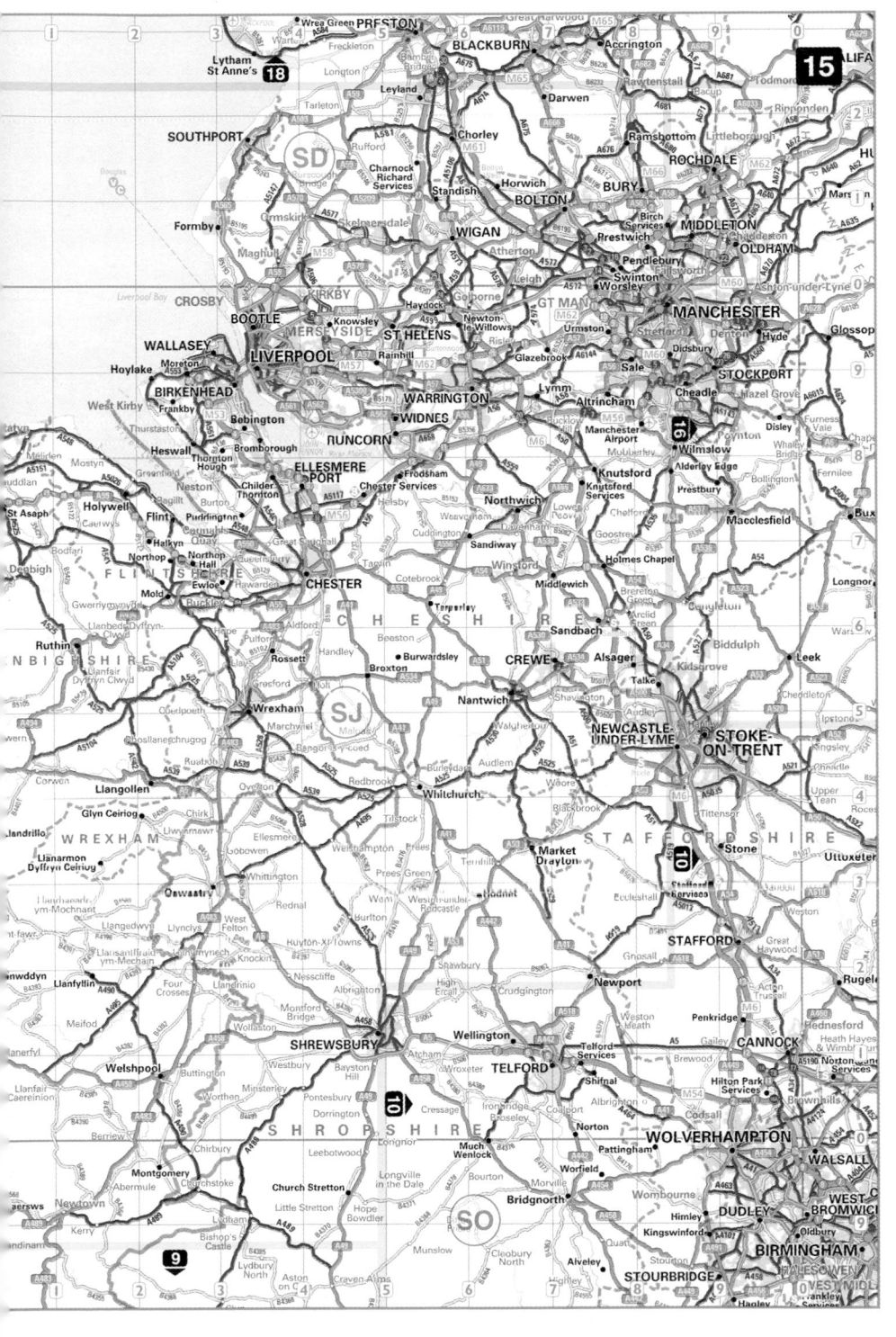

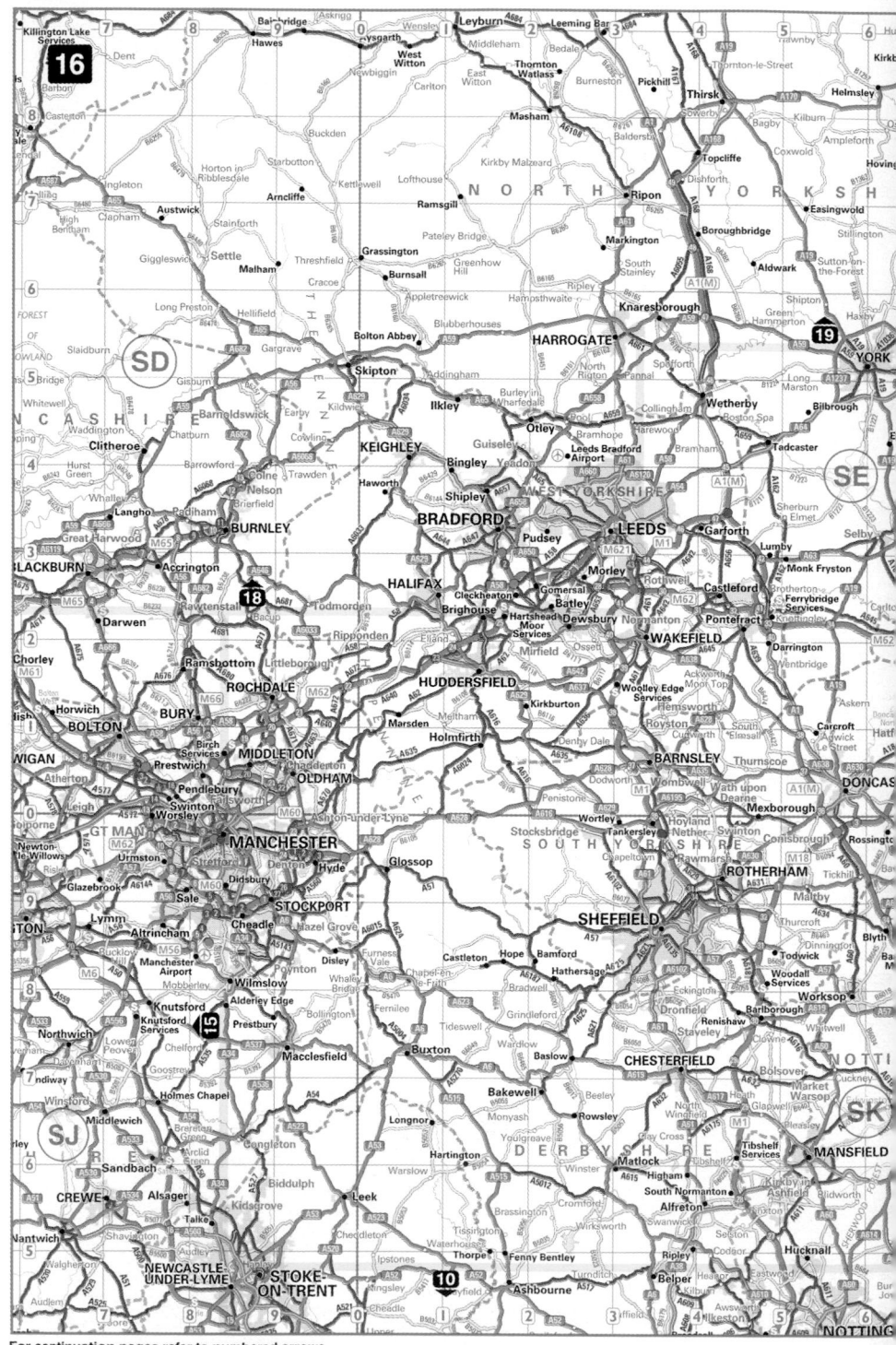

Lastingham
Cropton
Wrelton
Lockton
Hackness
Scarborough
Pickering
East Ayton
Thornton
le Dale
Spainton
Brompton
Seamer
Cayton
Kirby
Misperton
Sherburn
Staxton
Filey
Flixton
A1039
Hunmanby
Malton
Norton
Rillington
Reighton
Bempton
North Grimston
Sledmere
Burton
Fleming
Flamborough Head
Rudston
Carnaby
Flamborough
Fridaythorpe
Wetwang
Langtoft
Kilham
Bridlington
Burton
Agnes
Driffield
Barmston
North
Dalton
Bainton
Skipsea
Wilberfoss
Stamford Bridge
Middleton
on the Wolds
North
Frodingham
Beeford
Atwick
Sutton upon
Derwent
Pocklington
EAST RIDING
Brandesburton
Hornsea
OF YORKSHIRE
Leven
Barmby
Moor
Shiptonthorpe
Market
Weighton
TA
Holme upon
Spalding Moor
Walkington
Beverley
Aldbrough
North
Cave
Little
Weighton
Sproatley
South
Cave
Cottingham
Willerby
Goole
Elloughton
KINGSTON
UPON HULL
Hedon
Withernsea
Melton
North
Ferriby
New
Holland
Winteringham
Barton-
upon-Humber
Goxhill
Patrington
Easington
Burton upon
Stather
Winterton
Wootton
Immingham
Dock
Ulceby
SCUNTHORPE
Broughton
Keelby
Stallingborough
GRIMSBY
Spurn Head
M181
Wrawby
Barnetby
le Wold
Cleethorpes
M180
Brigg
Scawby
Humberston
Belton
Messingham
Scotter
Hibaldstow
Caistor
Swallow
Humber le Clay
North Cotes
Epworth
Haxey
Kirton in
Lindsey
Ludborough
North Somercotes
Misterton
Blyton
Binbrook
Saltfleet
Gringley
on the Hill
Gainsborough
Middle
Rasen
Market
Rasen
Louth
Mablethorpe
Saundby
Ingham
Faldingworth
Lissington
Legbourne
Sutton
on Sea
Retford
Sturton
by Stow
Wragby
East
Barkwith
Withern
Markham Moor
Saxilby
Langworth
Scamblesby
Alford
Huttoft
Tuxford
Skellingthorpe
LINCOLN
LINCOLNSHIRE
Baumber
Tetford
Bilsby
Chapel St
Leonards
Sutton on Trent
North
Hykeham
Washingborough
Bardney
Edlington
Horncastle
Hagworthingham
Spilsby
Candleby
Hogsthorpe
Ingoldmells
Carlton-on-Trent
Waddington
Nocton
Woodhall
Spa
Mareham
le Fen
Stickford
Burgh
le Marsh
Skegness
North Muskham
Navenby
Martin
Tattershall
New
Bolingbroke
Stickney
Wainfleet
All Saints
Kelham
Beckingham
Welbourn
Digby
Coningsby
TF
Newark-
on-Trent
Leadenham
Ruskington
North
Kyme
Sibsey
Old
Leake
Wrangle
East
Stoke
Caythorpe
Anwick
South Kyme
Long
Bennington
Marston
Ancaster
Sleaford
Butterwick
THE WASH
Thornham
Foston
Helpringham
Swineshead
Boston
Hunstanton

A170 A169 A64 A1039 A165 A614 A166 A163 A1079 A1034 M62 M181 M180 A18 A159 A156 A1500 A46 A631 A157 A153 A155 A52 A17 A1

Hotel
Town/Village name
0   10 miles
0   10   20 kilometres

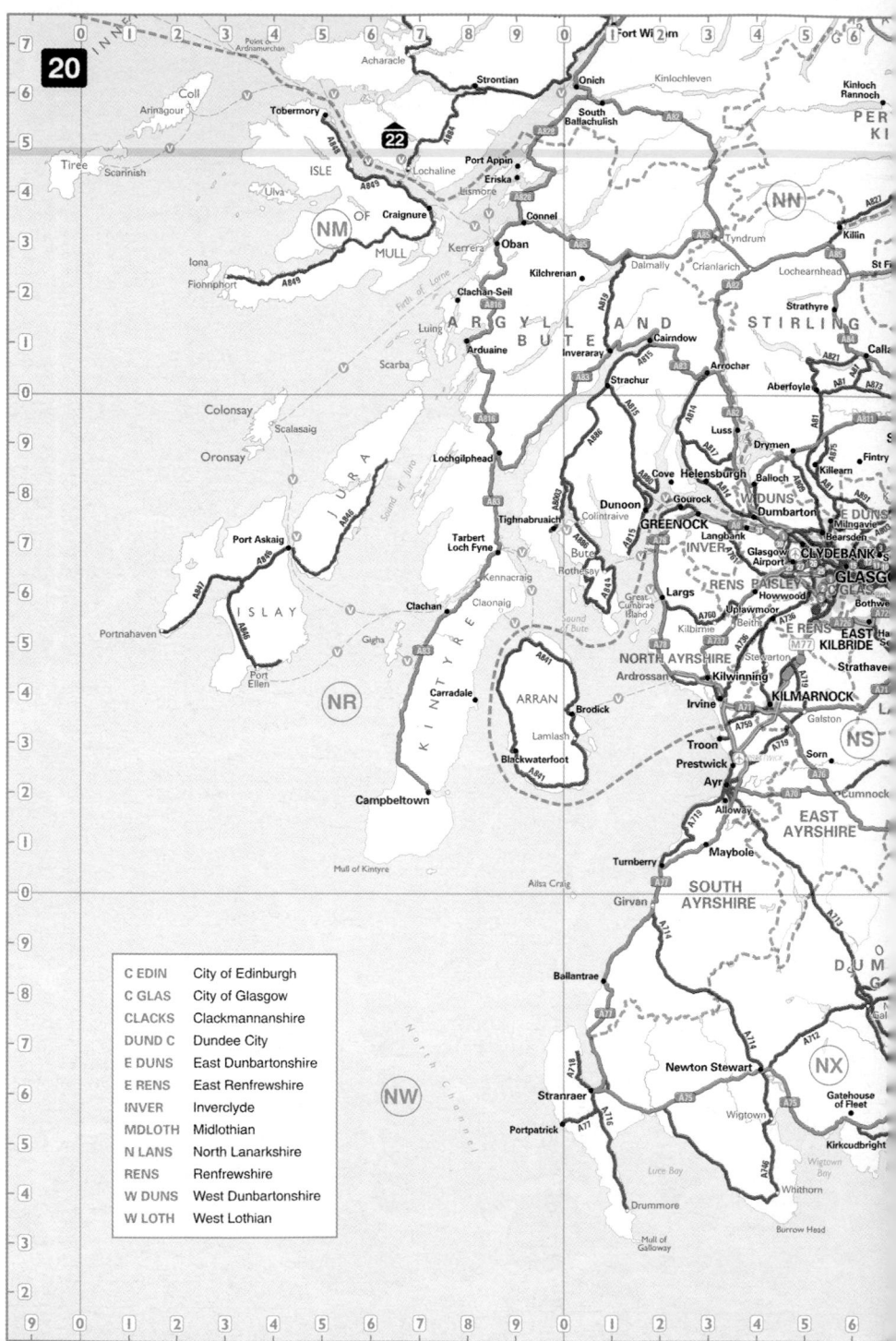

C EDIN   City of Edinburgh
C GLAS   City of Glasgow
CLACKS   Clackmannanshire
DUND C   Dundee City
E DUNS   East Dunbartonshire
E RENS   East Renfrewshire
INVER   Inverclyde
MDLOTH   Midlothian
N LANS   North Lanarkshire
RENS   Renfrewshire
W DUNS   West Dunbartonshire
W LOTH   West Lothian

For continuation pages refer to numbered arrows

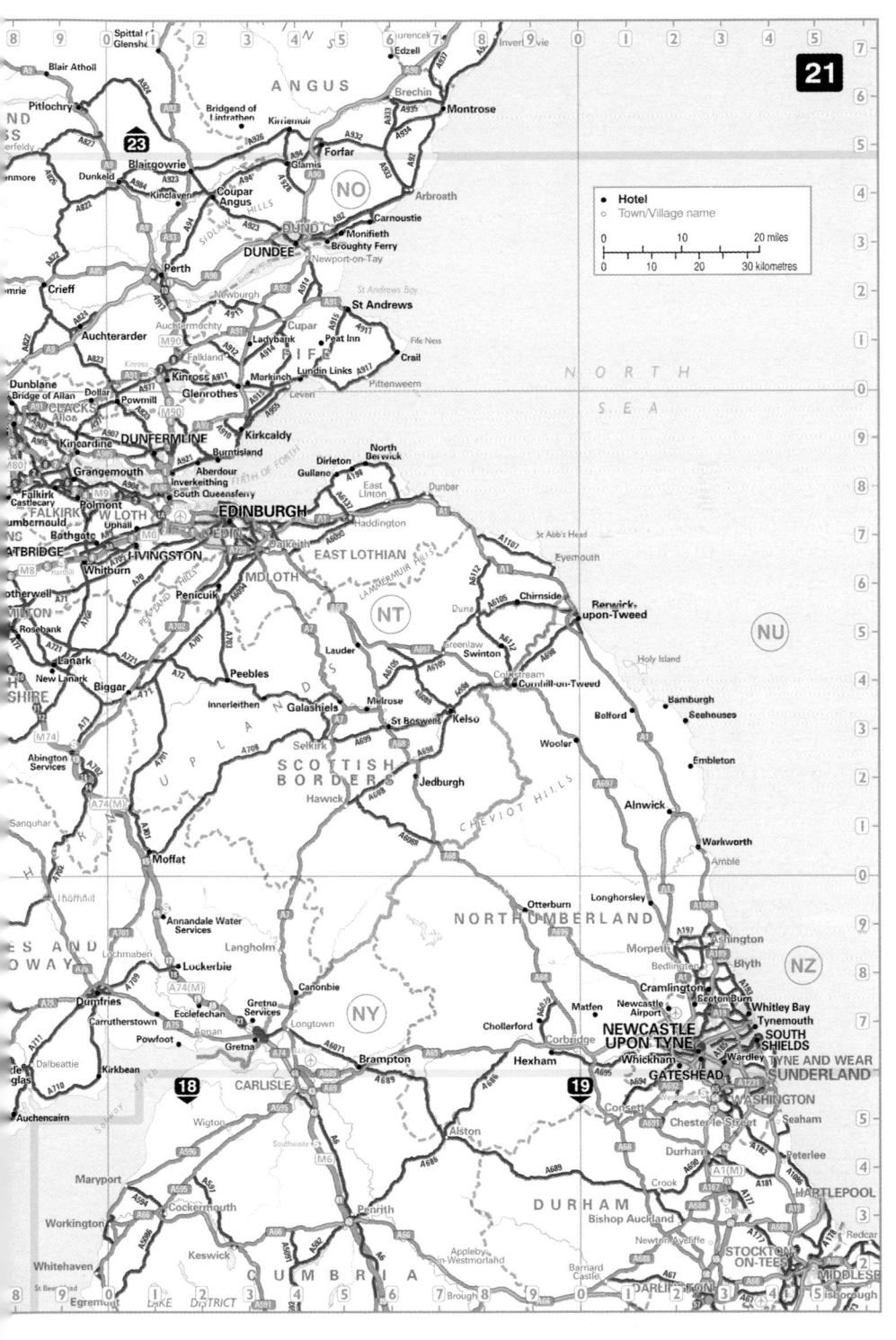

21

Hotel
Town/Village name

0   10   20 miles

0   10   20   30 kilometres

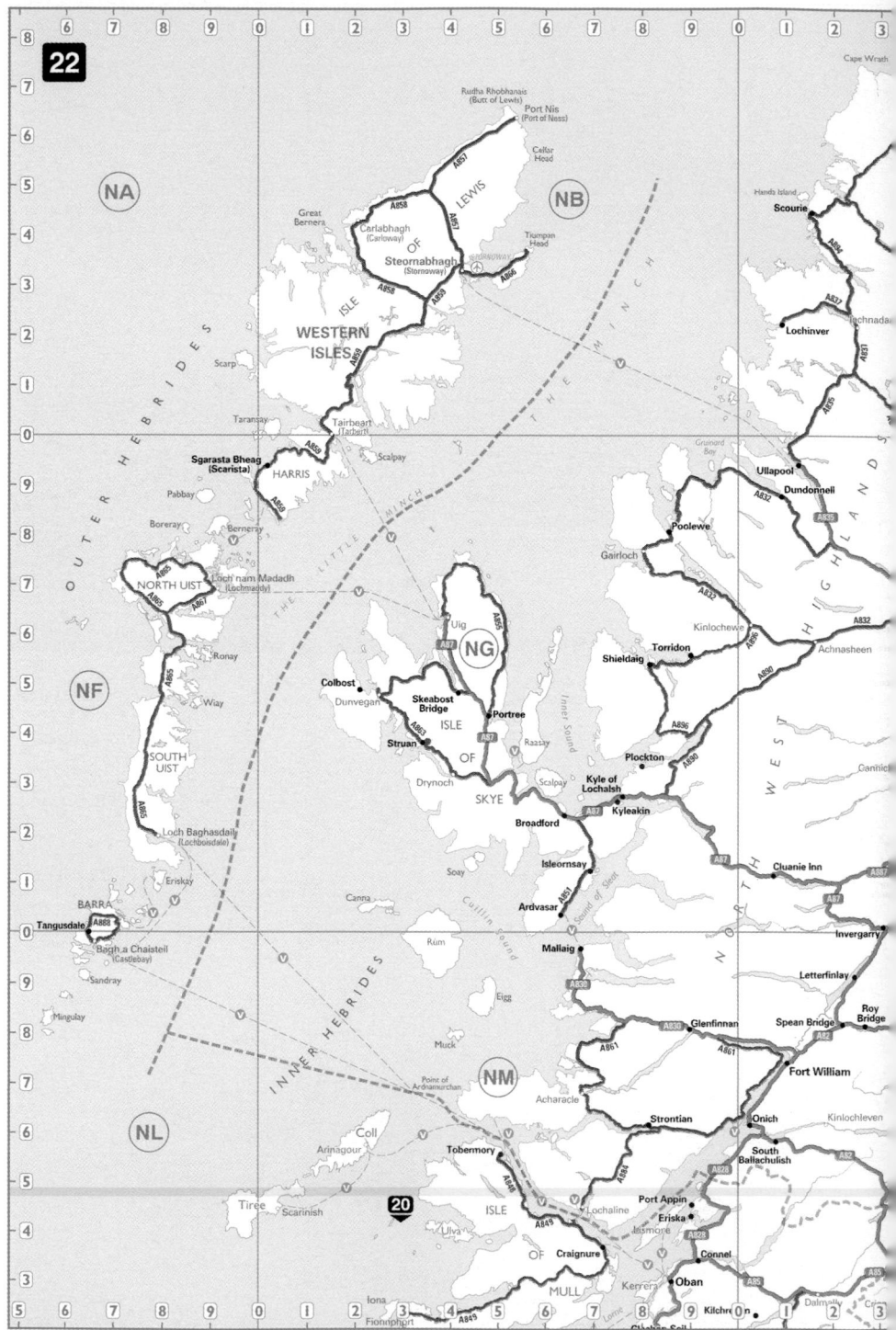

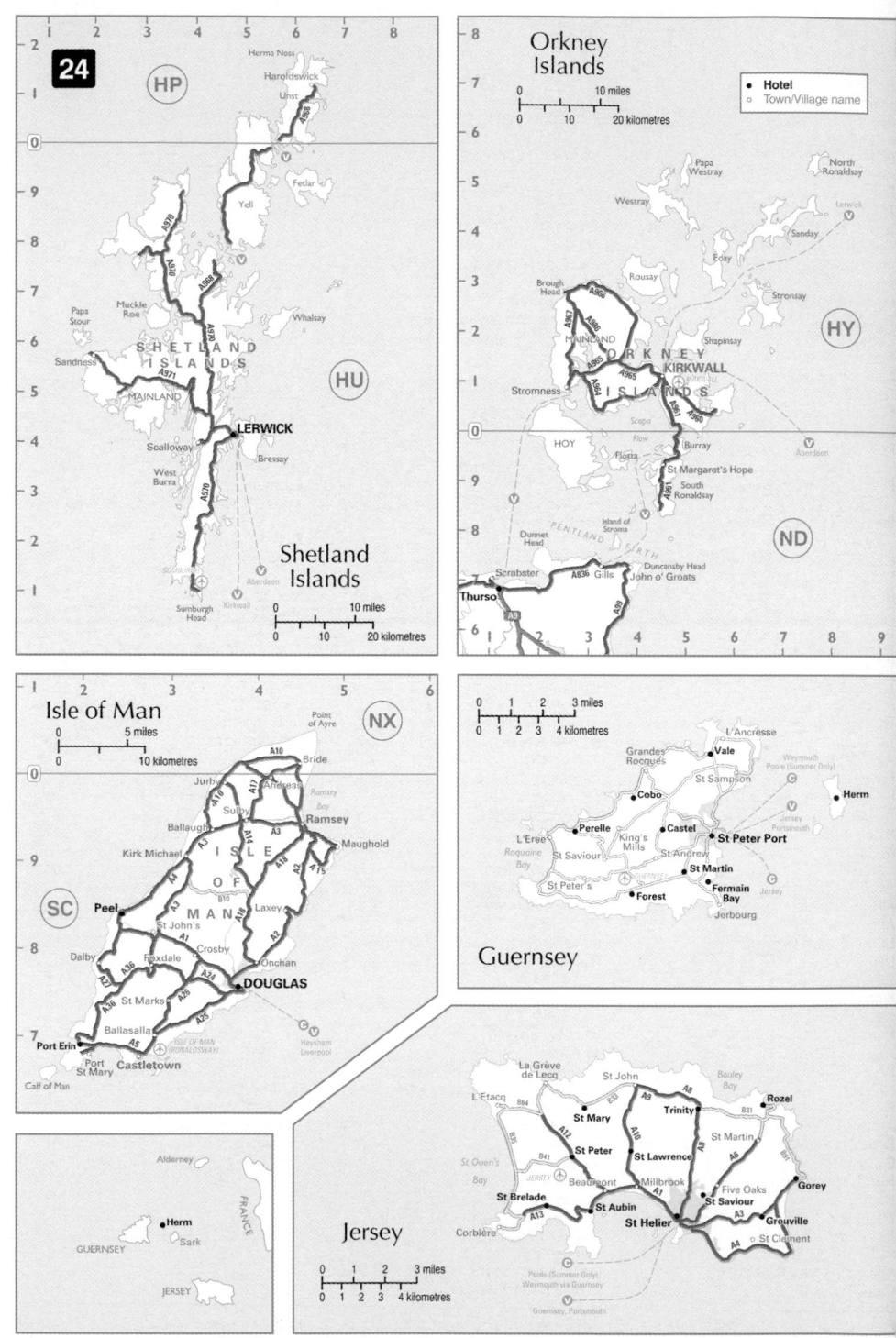

Index of Hotels

Index

Index

Index

Index

Index

Index

Index

Index

Index

Index

Index

Index

Index

The Automobile Association wishes to thank the following picture library for their assistance:

Stockbyte 13tl

The remaining photographs are held in the Association's own photo library (AA World Travel Library) and were taken by the following photographers:

1 AA/J Smith; 3t AA/A Mockford & N Bonetti; 3bl AA/J Smith; 3br AA/C Sawyer; 4tl AA S McBride; 4tr AA/J Smith; 5l AA/J Smith; 5tr AA/A Mockford & N Bonetti; 6tl AA/S McBride; 6tr AA/C Sawyer; 7tl AA/C Sawyer; 7tr AA/A Mockford & N Bonetti; 7br AA/J Smith; 8tl AA/S McBride; 8tr AA/C Sawyer; 9tr AA/A Mockford & N Bonetti; 9br AA/J Smith; 10tl AA/S McBride; 10/11t AA/J Smith; 11tr, 11b AA/A Mockford & N Bonetti; 12tl AA/S McBride; 12ct AA/J Smith; 12tr AA/C Sawyer; 13ct AA/C Sawyer; 13tr AA/A Mockford & N Bonetti; 14tl AA/S McBride; 15tr AA/A Mockford & N Bonetti; 16tl AA/S McBride; 17tr AA/A Mockford & N Bonetti; 19 Four Seasons Hotel, Canary Wharf; 20tl AA/S McBride; 20/21ct AA/L Dunmore; 21tr AA/A Mockford & N Bonetti; 22tl AA/S McBride; 23tl AA/C Sawyer; 23tr AA/A Mockford & N Bonetti; 24tl AA/S McBride; 24tr / 37tr AA/A Mockford & N Bonetti.

Every effort has been made to trace the copyright holders, and we apologise in advance for any accidental errors. We would be happy to apply the corrections in the following edition of this publication

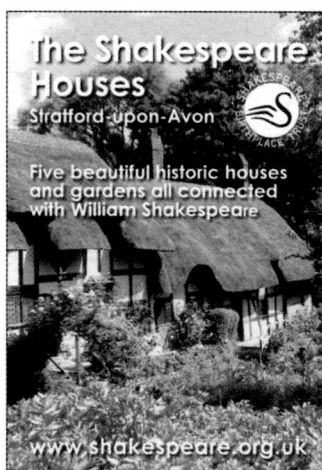

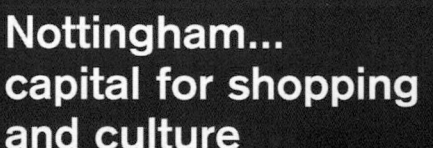

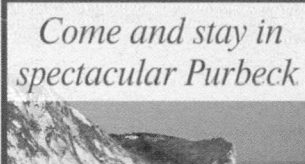

  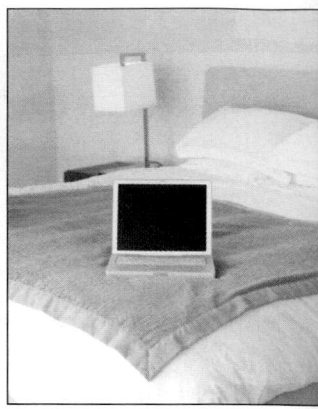

NEW!

Real-time, online booking at

www.theAA.com

Take the hassle out of booking accommodation online

We are delighted to announce that it is now possible
to book many AA establishments on the website

Visit www.theAA.com to search and book
AA inspected and rated hotels and B&Bs online.

Hotel
Service

Please send this form to:
  Editor, The Hotel Guide
  AA Lifestyle Guides,
  Fanum House,
  Basingstoke RG21 4EA

  or fax 01256 491647
  or email lifestyleguides@theAA.com

Please use this form to recommend any hotel where you have stayed, whether it is included in the guide or not. You can also help us to improve the guide by completing the short questionnaire on the reverse.

The AA does not undertake to arbitrate between guide readers and hotels, or to obtain compensation or engage in correspondence.

Date:

Your name (block capitals)

Your address (block capitals)

....

....

....

....

email address:

Name of hotel:

Comments

....

....

....

....

....

....

....

(please attach a separate sheet if necessary)

Please tick here if you DO NOT wish to receive details of AA offers or products ☐

Reader's Report Form

Have you bought this guide before?   YES   NO

Have you bought any other accommodation, restaurant, pub or food guides recently? If yes, which ones?

....

....

Why did you buy this guide? (circle all that apply)

holiday   short break   business travel   special occasion

overnight stop   find a venue for an event e.g. conference

other ....

How often do you stay in hotels? (circle one choice)

more than once a month   once a month   once in 2-3 months

once in six months   once a year   less than once a year

Please answer these questions to help us make improvements to the guide:

Which of these factors are most important when choosing a hotel?

Price   Location   Awards/ratings   Service

Decor/Surroundings   Previous experience   Recommendation

Other (please state) ....

Do you read the editorial features in the guide?

Do you use the location atlas?

Which elements of the guide do you find the most useful when choosing somewhere to stay?

Description   Photo   Advertisement   Star rating

Can you suggest any improvements to the guide?

....

....

....